AMERICAN
REFERENCE
BOOKS
ANNUAL
1994 VOLUME 25

AMERICAN REFERENCE BOOKS ANNUAL

1994 VOLUME 25

Bohdan S. Wynar EDITOR IN CHIEF
Anna Grace Patterson EDITOR

ASSISTANT EDITOR
D. A. Rothschild

Comprehensive annual reviewing service for
reference books published in the United States and Canada

1994

LIBRARIES UNLIMITED
ENGLEWOOD, COLORADO

Copyright © 1994 Libraries Unlimited, Inc.
All Rights Reserved
Printed in the United States of America

No part of this publication may be reproduced, stored in a retrieval system, or transmitted, in any form or by any means, electronic, mechanical, photocopying, recording, or otherwise, without the prior written permission of the publisher.

LIBRARIES UNLIMITED, INC.
P.O. Box 6633
Englewood, CO 80155-6633
1-800-237-6124

Library of Congress Cataloging-in-Publication Data

American reference books annual. 1970-
  Englewood, Colo., Libraries Unlimited.

  v. 19x26 cm.

Indexes:
  1970-74. 1v.
  1975-79. 1v.
  1980-84. 1v.
  1985-89. 1v.
  1990-94. 1v.

  1. Reference books--Bibliography--Periodicals.
I. Wynar, Bohdan S. II. Patterson, Anna Grace.
Z1035.1.A55   011'.02   75-120328
ISBN 1-56308-177-6(1994 edition)
ISSN 0065-9959

Contents

Introduction xiii
Contributors xv
Journals Cited xxvii

Part I
GENERAL REFERENCE WORKS

1—General Reference Works

Almanacs 3
Bibliography 4
  Bibliographic Guides 4
  National and Trade Bibliography 4
    International 4
    United States 5
Biography 6
  International 6
  United States 11
Catalogs and Collections 13
Dictionaries and Encyclopedias 14
Directories 19
Government Publications 23
Handbooks and Yearbooks 24
Indexes 25
Museums 25
Periodicals and Serials 25
Quotation Books 28

Part II
SOCIAL SCIENCES

2—Social Sciences in General

Social Sciences in General 33

3—Area Studies

General Works 37
United States 37
Africa 39
  General Works 39
  Angola 41
  Central African Republic 41
  Gabon and Botswana 42
  Malawi 42
  Mauritania 43
  Sierra Leone 43
  South Africa 43
  Sudan 44
Asia 44
  General Works 44
  China 46
  Hong Kong and Macau 46
  Indonesia 47
  Japan 48
  Korea 49
  Malaysia 50
  Maldives 50
  Polynesia 50
  Taiwan 51
  Vietnam 51
Australia 52
Canada 53
Europe 54
  General Works 54
  Armenia 54
  Eastern Europe 55
  Great Britain 56
  Poland 57
  Portugal 57
  Russia 57
  Ukraine 58
  Yugoslavia 59
Indian Ocean Area 60
  Seychelles 60
Latin America and the Caribbean 60
  General Works 60
  Paraguay 63
  St. Vincent and Grenadine Islands 63
  Suriname and the Netherlands Antilles . . . 64
Middle East 64
  General Works 64
  Israel 65

4—Economics and Business

General Works 67
  Bio-bibliography 67
  Catalogs and Collections 68
  Dictionaries and Encyclopedias 68
  Directories 70
  Handbooks and Yearbooks 73
Accounting 76

4—Economics and Business (continued)

Business Services and Investment Guides . . . 77
   Dictionaries and Encyclopedias 77
   Directories 77
   Handbooks and Yearbooks 80
Consumer Education 85
Finance and Banking 87
Industry and Manufacturing 89
Insurance 92
International Business 93
   General Works 93
      Bibliography 93
      Biography 93
      Directories 94
      Handbooks and Yearbooks 95
   Asia 100
   Canada 102
   Europe 104
      General Works 104
      Eastern Europe 107
      Great Britain 108
      Italy 110
Labor 110
   Bibliography 110
   Dictionaries and Encyclopedias 111
   Directories 111
   Handbooks and Yearbooks 113
   Indexes 116
Management 117
Marketing and Trade 117
Office Practices 122
Taxation 123

5—Education

General Works 125
   Bibliography 125
   Catalogs and Collections 125
   Dictionaries and Encyclopedias 126
   Handbooks and Yearbooks 126
Canada 127
Early Childhood Education 128
Elementary and Secondary Education . . 130
Higher Education 131
   Atlases 131
   Bibliography 132
   Directories 133
   Handbooks and Yearbooks 141
   Indexes 147
International Exchange Programs
   and Opportunities 147
Learning Disabilities and Disabled 149
Nonprint Materials and Resources 150

Reading 153
Vocational and Continuing Education . . . 154

6—Ethnic Studies and Anthropology

Anthropology and Ethnology 159
Ethnic Studies 161
   General Works 161
   Asian-Americans 162
   Blacks 162
   Canadians 165
   German-Americans 166
   Hispanic-Americans 167
   Indians of North America 167
   Japanese-Americans 172
   Jews 173

7—Genealogy and Heraldry

Genealogy 175
   Atlases 175
   Bibliography 175
   Chronology 176
   Directories 176
   Handbooks and Yearbooks 177
   Indexes 178
Heraldry 179
Personal Names 180

8—Geography and Travel Guides

Geography 183
   General Works 183
   Atlases 183
      United States, 183; International,
      184; Australia, 187; Canada, 187;
      Developing Countries, 188; Middle
      East, 188
   Bibliography 189
   Biography 190
   Dictionaries and Encyclopedias 191
   Handbooks and Yearbooks 191
Place Names 192
Travel Guides 193
   General Works 193
   United States 194
   Europe 196
   Great Britain 196
   Latin America and the Caribbean 197
   New Zealand 197
   Ukraine 198

9—History

Archaeology 199
American History 201
   Atlases 201
   Bibliography 202
   Biography 205
   Chronology 206
   Dictionaries and Encyclopedias 207
   Handbooks and Yearbooks 211
   Indexes 212
Asian History 212
Australian History 213
Canadian History 213
European History 214
   British 214
   Eastern European 214
   French 215
   German 215
   Russian 216
   Scandinavian 217
   Spanish 217
World History 218
   Atlases 218
   Bibliography 219
   Chronology 220
   Dictionaries and Encyclopedias 221
   Handbooks and Yearbooks 222
   Periodicals and Serials 224

10—Law

General Works 225
   Acronyms and Abbreviations 225
   Bibliography 225
   Biography 228
   Dictionaries and Encyclopedias 228
   Directories 230
   Handbooks and Yearbooks 233
   Indexes 238
   Quotation Books 239
Criminology 240
Human Rights 242
Victims of Abuse 244

11—Library and Information Science and Publishing and Bookselling

Library and Information Science 245
   General Works 245
      Acronyms and Abbreviations 245
      Catalogs and Collections 245
      Dictionaries and Encyclopedias 246
      Directories 248
      Handbooks and Yearbooks 249
      Indexes 252
      Periodicals and Serials 253
   Bibliometrics 253
   Careers and Education 253
   Cataloging and Classification 254
   Comparative and International
      Librarianship 257
   Copyright 258
   Indexing 259
   Information Technology 259
   Intellectual Freedom and Censorship ... 260
   Inter-Library Loans 260
   Library Automation 261
   Public Libraries 262
   School Libraries 263
   Special Libraries and Collections 263
   University and College Libraries 267
Publishing and Bookselling 267
   General Works 267
      Bibliography 267
      Catalogs and Collections 268
      Directories 268
      Handbooks and Yearbooks 273

12—Military Studies

General Works 275
   Acronyms and Abbreviations 275
   Atlases 275
   Bibliography 276
   Biography 278
   Dictionaries and Encyclopedias 279
   Handbooks and Yearbooks 280
   Quotation Books 283
Air Force 283
Army 284
Navy 285
Uniforms 287
Weapons 288

13—Political Science

General Works 289
   Atlases 289
   Bibliography 289
   Biography 290
   Dictionaries and Encyclopedias 291
   Directories 292
   Handbooks and Yearbooks 292
   Quotation Books 294

13—Political Science (continued)

Politics and Government 294
    United States 294
        Atlases 294
        Bibliography 295
        Biography 295
        Dictionaries and Encyclopedias 296
        Directories 298
        Handbooks and Yearbooks 302
        Indexes 307
        Periodicals and Serials 308
    African 308
    Asian 309
    European 310
        General Works 310
        German 313
        Great Britain 313
        Russian 314
        Ukrainian 316
    Latin American and Caribbean ... 316
    Middle Eastern 317
Ideologies 317
International Organizations 318
International Relations 321
Peace Movement 322
Public Policy and Administration 323

14—Psychology

General Works 327
    Bibliography 327
    Dictionaries and Encyclopedias 328
    Handbooks and Yearbooks 329
Parapsychology 330

15—Recreation and Sports

General Works 333
    Acronyms and Abbreviations 333
    Almanacs 333
    Atlases 334
    Bibliography 334
    Dictionaries and Encyclopedias 335
    Handbooks and Yearbooks 335
Baseball 338
Basketball 341
Card Games 342
Chess 342
Fitness 342
Football 343
Golf 344
Hockey 346
Martial Arts 346

Olympic Games 347
Pool 348
Sailing 349
Swimming 349
Wrestling 350

16—Sociology

General Works 351
Aging 352
Community Life 356
Death 357
Disabled 357
Family, Marriage, and Divorce 359
Philanthropy 359
    Bibliography 359
    Directories 360
    Handbooks and Yearbooks 362
Poverty 366
Sex Studies 367
Social Welfare and Social Work 368
Substance Abuse 370
Youth and Child Development 371

17—Statistics, Demography, and Urban Studies

Demography 375
Statistics 378
Urban Studies 380

18—Women's Studies

Almanacs 383
Bibliography 383
Biography 387
Catalogs and Collections 390
Dictionaries and Encyclopedias 390
Directories 391
Handbooks and Yearbooks 393
Indexes 393
Quotation Books 394

Part III
HUMANITIES

19—Humanities in General

General Works 397
    Bibliography 397
    Biography 398
    Catalogs and Collections 398

Dictionaries and Encyclopedias 399
Directories 401
Handbooks and Yearbooks 401
Periodicals and Serials 402

20—Communication and Mass Media

General Works 403
Authorship 404
   General Works 404
   Style Manuals 407
Newspapers and Magazines 408
Radio, Television, Audio, and Videos . . . 411
   Bibliography 411
   Directories 413
   Handbooks and Yearbooks 413
   Indexes 415

21—Decorative Arts

General Works 417
Collecting 417
   Antiques 417
   Books 418
   Coins 419
Crafts 420
Photography 422

22—Fine Arts

General Works 423
   Bibliography 423
   Biography 423
   Dictionaries and Encyclopedias 424
   Handbooks and Yearbooks 425
   Indexes 427
Architecture 427
Drawing 429
Graphic Arts 430
Painting 431
Sculpture 433

23—Language and Linguistics

General Works 435
English-Language Dictionaries 438
   Abridged 438
   Etymology 440
   General Usage 442
   Homonyms and Homographs 443
   Idioms, Colloquialisms, and
      Special Usage 443

   Juvenile 445
   New Words 446
   Other English-Speaking Countries 447
   Slang 449
   Spelling 449
   Synonyms and Antonyms 450
   Terms and Phrases 451
   Thesauri 451
Non-English-Language Dictionaries . . . 452
   General Works 452
   Albanian 452
   Chinese 453
   Dakota 453
   French 454
   German 454
   Hebrew 455
   Indonesian 456
   Japanese 456
   Korean 458
   Latvian 458
   Ojibway 458
   Persian 459
   Portuguese 459
   Russian 460
   Spanish 461
   Tongan 462
   Turkish 463
   Welsh 463
   Yiddish 464

24—Literature

General Works 465
   Bibliography 465
   Biography 467
   Dictionaries and Encyclopedias 470
   Handbooks and Yearbooks 471
   Indexes 475
   Periodicals and Serials 476
Children's Literature 476
   Bibliography 476
   Biography 486
   Dictionaries and Encyclopedias 487
   Handbooks and Yearbooks 488
   Indexes 490
Classical Literature 491
Drama 492
Fiction 493
   General Works 493
   Crime and Mystery 494
   Science Fiction, Fantasy, and Horror . . . 496
   Short Stories 497

24—Literature (continued)

National Literature 499
  American Literature 499
    General Works 499
    Drama 502
    Fiction 503
    Individual Authors 504
      S. N. Behrman, 504; *Emily Dickinson*, 505; *Hilda Doolittle (H. D.)*, 505; *Chester Himes*, 506; *Dorothy Parker*, 506; *Ann Petry*, 507; *Robert Reginald*, 507; *Lionel Trilling*, 507; *Mark Twain*, 508; *Walt Whitman*, 508; *Thornton Wilder*, 509
  British Literature 509
    General Works 509
    Individual Authors 511
      Patrick Branwell Bronte, 511; *Elizabeth Barrett Browning*, 511; *Leslie Charteris*, 512; *Geoffrey Chaucer*, 512; *Charles Dickens*, 513; *Richard Jefferies*, 513; *William Langland*, 514; *C. S. Lewis*, 514; *Christopher Marlowe*, 514; *William Shakespeare*, 515; *Leslie Stephen*, 516; *Oscar Wilde*, 517
    Poetry 517
  African Literature 519
  Australian Literature 519
  Canadian Literature 520
  Chinese Literature 522
  European Literature 523
  French Literature 523
  German Literature 525
  Iberian Literature 526
  Indic Literature 526
  Irish Literature 527
  Japanese Literature 528
  Latin American and Caribbean Literature .. 529
Poetry 532
Wit and Humor 533

25—Music

General Works 535
  Bibliography 535
  Catalogs and Collections 537
  Chronology 538
  Dictionaries and Encyclopedias 538
  Discography 539
  Handbooks and Yearbooks 540
  Indexes 541
Composers 541

Instruments 547
Musical Forms 549
  Church 549
  Classical 550
  Operatic 552
  Popular 556
    General Works 556
    Jazz and Blues 561
    Rap 563
    Rock 563
    Salsa 565
    Steel Band 566

26—Mythology, Folklore, and Popular Culture

Folklore 567
Mythology 570
Popular Culture 573

27—Performing Arts

General Works 577
  Bio-bibliography 577
  Dictionaries and Encyclopedias 581
  Directories 582
  Handbooks and Yearbooks 582
Dance 582
Film 584
  Bibliography 584
  Biography 586
  Dictionaries and Encyclopedias 587
  Directories 588
  Filmography 589
  Handbooks and Yearbooks 595
  Indexes 598
Theater 599
  Bibliography 599
  Biography 600
  Chronology 601
  Dictionaries and Encyclopedias 602
  Directories 604
  Handbooks and Yearbooks 605
  Indexes 606

28—Philosophy and Religion

Philosophy 607
  Bibliography 607
  Dictionaries and Encyclopedias 611
  Directories 613
  Quotation Books 613

Religion 614	**31—Biological Sciences**
General Works 614	
Bibliography 614	**Biology** 671
Biography 617	**Botany** 672
Dictionaries and Encyclopedias 618	General Works 672
Directories 620	Bibliography 672
Handbooks and Yearbooks 621	Dictionaries and Encyclopedias 673
Buddhism 622	Handbooks and Yearbooks 674
Christianity 623	Indexes 676
General Works 623	Flowering Plants 677
Bibliography, 623; *Biography*, 624;	Fungi 681
Dictionaries and Encyclopedias,	Grasses and Weeds 682
625; *Directories*, 627; *Handbooks*	Medicinal and Edible Plants 683
and Yearbooks, 627	Mosses and Lichens 684
Bible Studies 628	Trees and Shrubs 684
Bibliography, 628; *Biography*, 629;	**Natural History** 687
Catalogs and Collections, 630;	**Zoology** 691
Dictionaries and Encyclopedias,	General Works 691
631; *Handbooks and Yearbooks*,	Birds 693
632; *Indexes*, 633; *Periodicals and*	Butterflies 697
Serials, 634	Domestic Animals 698
Quotation Books 635	Fishes 700
Islam 636	Insects 704
Judaism 637	Mammals 707
	Marine Animals 713
	Reptiles and Amphibians 714

Part IV
SCIENCE AND TECHNOLOGY

29—Science and Technology in General

Bibliography 641	**32—Engineering**
Biography 642	General Works 717
Dictionaries and Encyclopedias 643	Agricultural Engineering 717
Directories 647	Astronautical Engineering 718
Handbooks and Yearbooks 649	Chemical Engineering 719
	Civil Engineering 722
	Computing Engineering 723
30—Agricultural Sciences	Electric Engineering and Electronics . . . 724
	Environmental Engineering 728
General Works 653	Genetic Engineering 728
Bibliography 653	Human Engineering 729
Handbooks and Yearbooks 654	Materials Science 729
Food Sciences and Technology 657	Mechanical Engineering 731
Bibliography 657	Mining Engineering 732
Dictionaries and Encyclopedias 657	Nuclear Engineering 732
Directories 659	
Handbooks and Yearbooks 659	**33—Health Sciences**
Forestry 662	
Horticulture 663	**General Works** 733
Dictionaries and Encyclopedias 663	Atlases 733
Handbooks and Yearbooks 666	Dictionaries and Encyclopedias 733
Veterinary Science 669	Directories 735
	Handbooks and Yearbooks 736

33—Health Sciences (continued)

Medicine 738
  General Works 738
    Acronyms and Abbreviations 738
    Atlases 739
    Bibliography 739
    Catalogs and Collections 741
    Dictionaries and Encyclopedias ... 741
    Directories 744
    Handbooks and Yearbooks 745
  Psychiatry 748
  Specific Diseases 750
    AIDS 750
    Birth Related Conditions 753
    Cancer 753
    Chemically Related Conditions 754
    Neurological Disorders 754
    Rare Diseases 755
Nursing 755
Optometry 756
Pharmacy and Pharmaceutical Sciences .. 757
  Dictionaries and Encyclopedias 757
  Directories 759
  Handbooks and Yearbooks 759

34—High Technology

General Works 763
Artificial Intelligence 763
Computing 764
  General Works 764
    Acronyms and Abbreviations 764
    Bibliography 765
    Dictionaries and Encyclopedias ... 766
    Directories 769
    Handbooks and Yearbooks 770
  Computer Graphics 771
  Software 772
Optical Storage Devices 773
  CAD/CAM 773
  CD-ROM 774
  Microforms 776
Telecommunication 776

35—Physical Sciences and Mathematics

General Works 777
Astronomy 777
Chemistry 780
  Bibliography 780
  Dictionaries and Encyclopedias 780

  Directories 782
  Handbooks and Yearbooks 782
  Indexes 782
  Thesauri 783
Earth and Planetary Sciences 783
  General Works 783
  Climatology 785
  Geology 786
  Hydrology 786
  Mineralogy 787
  Paleontology 789
Physics 791
Mathematics 791

36—Resource Sciences

Energy Resources 793
  Bibliography 793
  Biography 793
  Directories 794
  Handbooks and Yearbooks 795
Environmental Science 798
  Almanacs 798
  Atlases 799
  Bibliography 799
  Biography 801
  Dictionaries and Encyclopedias 801
  Directories 804
  Handbooks and Yearbooks 807

37—Transportation

Air 811
Ground 811
  Dictionaries and Encyclopedias 811
  Directories 812
  Handbooks and Yearbooks 812
Water 814

Author/Title Index 817

Subject Index 851

Introduction

PURPOSE AND SCOPE

American Reference Books Annual, a far-reaching reviewing service for reference books, is now in its 25th volume. The 2,031 books reviewed in this volume cover imprints from 1993 and some from 1992 that were received too late to be reviewed in the previous volume. In the 25 volumes of ARBA published since 1970, a total of 43,404 titles have been reviewed. Four cumulative indexes for ARBA cover the years 1970-1974, 1975-1979, 1980-1984, and 1985-1989. The 1990-1994 cumulative index is currently in production. These indexes facilitate the use of the annual volumes.

ARBA differs significantly from other reviewing media in its basic purpose, which is to provide comprehensive coverage of English-language reference books published in the United States and Canada during a single year. The categories of reference books reviewed in ARBA and the policy regarding them can be summarized as follows: (1) Dictionaries, encyclopedias, indexes, directories, bibliographies, guides, concordances, atlases, gazetteers, and other types of ready-reference tools are routinely reviewed in each volume of ARBA; coverage of this category of reference materials is nearly complete. (2) General encyclopedias that are updated annually, yearbooks, almanacs, indexing and abstracting services, and other annuals or serials are usually reviewed at intervals of three, four, or five years. The first review of such works generally provides an appropriate historical background. Subsequent reviews of these publications attempt to point out changes in scope, editorial policy, and similar matters. (3) New editions of reference books are ordinarily reviewed with appropriate comparisons to the older editions. (4) Traditionally, foreign reference titles have been reviewed only if they had an exclusive distributor in the United States. In 1987 coverage was expanded to include Canadian publications that do not have U.S. distributors. Prices for such titles are in Canadian dollars unless otherwise indicated. Substantial coverage of Canadian reference publications has been achieved and will continue until it is as complete for Canada as it is for the United States. Other foreign title coverage is restricted to English-language publications from Great Britain, Australia, and India. (5) Government publications are reviewed on a highly selective basis because other Libraries Unlimited works, *Government Reference Books* and *Government Reference Serials*, provide the library profession with comprehensive coverage of government reference publications. In ARBA 94 only Library of Congress publications and international publications, such as those of the United Nations, are covered. (6) Reprints are reviewed in ARBA on a selective basis as they often are produced in limited quantities. (7) Titles produced for the mass market in the areas of collectibles, travel guides, and genealogy receive selective coverage.

Certain categories of reference books are usually not reviewed in ARBA: those of fewer than 48 pages, those produced by vanity presses or by the author as publisher, and those generated by library staffs for internal use. Highly specialized reference works printed in a limited number of copies and that do not appeal to the general library audience ARBA serves may also be omitted.

Because there has been a significant increase and interest in electronic publishing, ARBA has begun reviewing this medium. Ten CD-ROMs receive comprehensive and lengthy evaluations in this volume. Future volumes will continue to include reviews of these state-of-the-art information storage devices in a variety of subject areas.

REVIEWING POLICY

To ensure well-written and erudite reviews, the ARBA staff maintains a roster of more than 425 scholars, practitioners, and library educators in all subject specialties at libraries and universities throughout the United States and Canada. Because ARBA is not a selective reviewing source, such as *Choice* or *Library Journal*, the reviews are generally longer and more critical and detail the strengths and weaknesses of important reference works. Reviewers are asked to examine a book and provide well-documented critical comments, both positive and negative. Coverage usually includes the usefulness of a given work; organization, execution, and pertinence of contents; prose style; format; availability of supplementary materials (e.g., indexes, appendixes); and similarity to other works and previous editions. Reviewers are encouraged to address the intended audience but not necessarily to give specific recommendations for purchase. An adequate description and evaluation of the reference book are sufficient. All reviews in ARBA are signed.

ARRANGEMENT

ARBA 94 consists of 37 chapters, an author/title index and a subject index. It is divided into four alphabetically arranged parts: "General Reference Works," "Social Sciences," "Humanities," and "Science and Technology." "General Reference Works" is subdivided by form: bibliography, biography, catalogs and collections, dictionaries and encyclopedias, handbooks and yearbooks, indexes, and so on. Within the remaining three parts, chapters are organized by topic. Thus, under "Social Sciences" the reader will find chapters titled "Economics and Business," "Education," "History," "Law," and "Sociology."

Each chapter is subdivided to reflect the arrangement strategy of the entire volume. There is a section on general works followed by a topical breakdown. For example, in the chapter titled "Performing Arts," "General Works" is followed by "Dance" and "Film." The latter is divided into sections by format, which include "Biography" and "Filmography." Subdivisions are based on the amount of material available on a given topic and vary from year to year.

ACKNOWLEDGMENTS

In closing, we wish to express our gratitude to the many talented contributors without whose support this volume of ARBA could not have been compiled. We would also like to thank the members of our staff who were instrumental in the preparation: Pamela Getchell, Stephen Haenel, David V. Loertscher, Beth Partin, Jo Anne H. Ricca, and D. A. Rothschild.

Bohdan S. Wynar, Editor in Chief
Anna Grace Patterson, Editor

Editorial Staff

Bohdan S. Wynar, Editor in Chief
Anna Grace Patterson, Editor
D. A. Rothschild, Assistant Editor

Contributors

Ben Abel, Cornell Univ. Library, Ithaca, N.Y.

Stephen H. Aby, Education Bibliographer, Bierce Library, Univ. of Akron, Ohio.

Diana Accurso, Bibliographic Instruction Coordinator/Reference Librarian, Denison Univ. Libraries, Granville, Ohio.

Walter C. Allen, Assoc. Professor Emeritus, Graduate School of Library and Information Science, Univ. of Illinois, Urbana.

Donald Altschiller, Reference Librarian, Harvard Univ. Library, Cambridge, Mass.

Byron P. Anderson, Coordinator, Computer Reference Services, Northern Illinois Univ., De Kalb.

Frank J. Anderson, Librarian Emeritus, Sandor Teszler Library, Wofford College, Spartanburg, S.C.

James D. Anderson, Assoc. Dean and Professor, School of Communication, Information, and Library Studies, Rutgers Univ., New Brunswick, N.J.

Robert T. Anderson, Professor, Religious Studies, Michigan State Univ., East Lansing.

Charles R. Andrews, Dean of Library Services, Hofstra Univ., Hempstead, N.Y.

Susan B. Ardis, Head, McKinney Engineering Library, Univ. of Texas, Austin.

Henry T. Armistead, Head, Collection Development, Scott Memorial Library, Thomas Jefferson Univ., Philadelphia.

Roslyn Attinson, Professor Emerita, College of Staten Island, N.Y.

Lawrence W. S. Auld, Chairman, Dept. of Library and Information Studies, East Carolina Univ., Greenville, N.C.

Susan C. Awe, Arvada Branch Manager, Jefferson County Public Library, Arvada, Colo.

Bill Bailey, Head of Reference, Newton Gresham Library, Sam Houston State Univ., Huntsville, Tex.

Susan D. Baird-Joshi, Database Programmer/Analyst, Rho, Redmond, Wash.

Jack Bales, Reference Librarian, Mary Washington College Library, Fredericksburg, Va.

Betty Bankhead, Library Media Coordinator, Cherry Creek High School Library, Englewood, Colo.

Gary D. Barber, Head of Reference, Daniel A. Reed Library, State Univ. of New York, Fredonia.

Helen M. Barber, Reference Librarian, New Mexico State Univ., Las Cruces.

Suzanne I. Barchers, Deputy Director, Exhibits and Programs, Children's Museum of Denver, Colo.

Donald A. Barclay, Reference Librarian, New Mexico State Univ., Las Cruces.

David Bardack, Professor, Dept. of Biological Sciences, Univ. of Illinois, Chicago.

Pam M. Baxter, Psychological Sciences Librarian, Psychological Sciences Library, Purdue Univ., West Lafayette, Ind.

Craig W. Beard, Head of Reference Services, Mervyn H. Sterne Library, Univ. of Alabama, Birmingham.

Sandra E. Belanger, Reference Librarian, San Jose State Univ. Library, Calif.

Carol Willsey Bell, Head, Local History and Genealogy Dept., Warren-Trumbull County Public Library, Warren, Ohio.

George H. Bell, Assoc. Librarian, Daniel E. Noble Science & Engineering Library, Arizona State Univ., Tempe.

Bernice Bergup, Humanities Reference Librarian, Davis Library, Univ. of North Carolina, Chapel Hill.

Carl T. Berkhout, Assoc. Professor, Department of English, Univeristy of Arizona, Tucson.

Karen Berland, Psychologist, Denver Public Schools and Aurora Mental Health Center, Colo.

John B. Beston, Professor of English, Nazareth College of Rochester, N.Y.

Barbara M. Bibel, Reference Librarian Science Business/Sociology Dept., Main Library, Oakland Public Library, Oakland, Calif.

David Bickford, Information Specialist, Univ. of Phoenix, Ariz.

Kerranne G. Biley, Reference Librarian, Univ. of Colorado, Denver.

Terry D. Bilhartz, Assoc. Professor of History, Sam Houston State Univ., Huntsville, Tex.

Ron Blazek, Professor, School of Library Science, Florida State Univ., Tallahassee.

Daniel K. Blewett, Reference Librarian, Cudahy Library, Loyola Univ., Chicago.

Marjorie E. Bloss, Director, Technical Services Division, Center for Research Libraries, Chicago.

George S. Bobinski, Dean and Professor, School of Information and Library Studies, State Univ. of New York, Buffalo.

Bobray Bordelon, Social Science Reference Center, Firestone Library, Princeton Univ Libraries.

Melvin M. Bowie, Assoc. Professor, Dept. of Instructional Technology, Univ. of Georgia, Athens.

Kathleen Nelson Boyle, formerly Staff, Libraries Unlimited, Inc.

James K. Bracken, Head, Second Floor Main Library Information Services, Ohio State Univ., Columbus.

William Bright, Research Associate in Linguistics, Univ. of Colorado, Boulder.

Robert N. Broadus, formerly Professor, School of Library Science, Univ. of North Carolina, Chapel Hill.

Simon J. Bronner, Distinguished Professor of Folklore and American Studies, Capitol College, Pennsylvania State Univ., Middletown.

Barbara E. Brown, formerly Head, General Cataloguing Section, Library of Parliament, Ottawa.

Melvin Marlo Brown, Reference Librarian/Information Technology Specialist, Branson Library, New Mexico State Univ., Las Cruces.

Judith M. Brugger, Catalog Management and Authorities Librarian, Cornell Univ., Ithaca, N.Y.

Betty Jo Buckingham, Consultant, Iowa Dept. of Education, Des Moines.

Lois J. Buttlar, Assoc. Professor, School of Library and Information Science, Kent State Univ., Ohio.

Hans E. Bynagle, Library Director and Professor of Philosophy, Whitworth College, Spokane, Wash.

Diane M. Calabrese, Research Associate for Planning and Eisenhower Grant Programs, Coordinating Board for Higher Education, Jefferson City, Mo.

John Lewis Campbell, Online Services Coordinator, Univ. of Georgia Libraries, Athens.

Esther Jane Carrier, Reference Librarian, Lock Haven Univ. of Pennsylvania, Lock Haven.

James A. Casada, Professor of History, Winthrop College, Rock Hill, S.C.

Joseph Cataio, Manager, Booklegger's Bookstore, Chicago.

Jo A. Cates, Head, Transportation Library, Northwestern Univ. Library, Chicago.

G. A. Cevasco, Assoc. Professor of English, St. John's Univ., Jamaica, N.Y.

Bert Chapman, Reference/Documents Librarian, Mary and John Gray Library, Lamar Univ., Beaumont, Tex.

John Y. Cheung, Assoc. Professor, Univ. of Oklahoma, Norman.

Boyd Childress, Reference Librarian, Ralph B. Draughon Library, Auburn Univ., Ala.

Dene L. Clark, Reference Librarian, Auraria Library, Denver, Colo.

Paul F. Clark, Assoc. Professor, Pennsylvania State Univ., University Park.

Beth Clewis, Collection Specialist, Prince William Public Library, Va.

Harriette M. Cluxton, formerly Director of Medical Library Services, Illinois Masonic Medical Center, Chicago.

Gary R. Cocozzoli, Director of the Library, Lawrence Technological Univ., Southfield, Mich.

Donald E. Collins, Assoc. Professor, Dept. of Library and Information Studies, East Carolina Univ., Greenville, N.C.

Barbara Conroy, Career Connections, Santa Fe, N.Mex.

Kay O. Cornelius, formerly Teacher and Magnet School Lead Teacher, Huntsville City Schools, Ala.

Paul B. Cors, Catalog Librarian, Univ. of Wyoming, Laramie.

Brian E. Coutts, Head, Dept. of Library Public Services, Helm-Cravens Library, Western Kentucky Univ., Bowling Green.

Kathleen W. Craver, Head Librarian, National Cathedral School, Washington, D.C.

Milton H. Crouch, Asst. Director for Reader Services, Bailey/Howe Library, Univ. of Vermont, Burlington.

Linda Cullum, Asst. Public Services Librarian, Kenneth J. Shouldice Library, Lake Superior State Univ., Sault Sainte Marie, Mich.

Gregory Curtis, Reference Librarian, Univ. of Maine, Presque Isle.

William J. Dane, Supervising Librarian, Special Libraries, Newark Public Library, N.J.

C. B. (Bob) Darrell, Professor of English and Dept. Chair, Kentucky Wesleyan College, Owensboro.

Joseph W. Dauben, Professor of History and History of Science, City Univ. of New York.

Estelle A. Davis, Reference Librarian and Assistant Professor, Science/Engineering Library, City College of the City Univ. of New York.

Donald G. Davis, Jr., Professor, Graduate School of Library and Information Science, Univ. of Texas, Austin.

Dominique-Rene de Lerma, Professor, Conservatory of Music, Lawrence Univ., Appleton, Wis.

Bonnie A. Dede, Head, Special Formats Cataloging, Univ. of Michigan Library, Ann Arbor.

Elie M. Dick, Director of Business Development, ISCO, Inc., Lincoln, Neb.

Donald C. Dickinson, Professor, Graduate Library School, Univ. of Arizona, Tucson.

John B. Dillon, European Humanities Bibliographer, Memorial Library, Univ of Wisconsin, Madison.

Carol A. Doll, Asst. Professor, Graduate School of Library and Information Science, Univ. of Washington, Seattle.

Margaret F. Dominy, Head, Mathematics-Physics-Astronomy Library, Univ. of Pennsylvania, Philadelphia.

Edith M. Dorenfeld, School Psychologist, Denver Public Schools, Colo.

G. Kim Dority, Editorial Director, Jones 21st Century, Englewood, Colo.

Karen Markey Drabenstott, Asst. Professor, School of Information and Library Studies, Univ. of Michigan, Ann Arbor.

John E. Druesedow, Jr., Director of the Music Library/Adjunct Asst. Professor of Music, Duke Univ., Durham, N.C.

Gordon H. Dunkin, Education Librarian, Univ. of Alabama, Birmingham.

Joe P. Dunn, Charles A. Dana Professor of History and Politics, Converse College, Spartanburg, S.C.

Susan Ebershoff-Coles, Supervisor, Technical Services, Indianapolis-Marion County Public Library, Ind.

David Eggenberger, Freelance Writer and Editor, Vienna, Va.

Marie Ellis, English and American Literature Bibliographer, Univ. of Georgia Libraries, Athens.

Edward Erazo, Reference/Outreach Librarian, New Mexico State Univ., Las Cruces.

Jonathon Erlen, Curator, History of Medicine, Univ. of Pittsburgh, Pa.

G. Edward Evans, Univ. Librarian, Charles Von der Ahe Library, Loyola Marymount Univ., Los Angeles, Calif.

Andrew Ezergailis, Professor of History, Ithaca College, N.Y.

Ian Fairclough, Head of Cataloging, Noel Memorial Library, Louisiana State Univ., Shreveport, La.

Kathleen Farago, Reference Librarian, Lakewood Public Library, Ohio.

Evan Ira Farber, Librarian, Lilly Library, Earlham College, Richmond, Ind.

Megan S. Farrell, Collection Development Librarian and Asst. Professor, Dupre Library, Univ. of Southwestern Louisiana, Lafayette.

Lorene S. Farris, Seminole Health Clinic, Hollywood, Fla.

Adele M. Fasick, Dean and Professor, School of Library and Information Science, Univ. of Toronto.

Robin Riley Fast, Assoc. Professor, Division of Writing, Literature, and Publishing, Emerson College, Boston.

Eleanor Ferrall, Librarian Emerita, Arizona State Univ., Tempe.

Joan B. Fiscella, Bibliographer for Professional Studies, Library, Univ. of Illinois, Chicago.

Virginia S. Fischer, Reference/Documents Librarian, Univ. of Maine, Presque Isle.

Jerry D. Flack, Assoc. Professor of Education, Univ. of Colorado, Colorado Springs.

Patricia Fleming, Professor, Faculty of Library and Information Science, Univ. of Toronto.

Michael A. Foley, Honors Director, Marywood College, Scranton, Pa.

Harold O. Forshey, Assoc. Dean, Miami University, Oxford, Ohio.

A. David Franklin, Professor of Music, Winthrop Univ., Rock Hill, S.C.

Darlene H. Franklin, Staff, Libraries Unlimited, Inc.

David K. Frasier, Asst. Librarian, Reference Dept., Indiana Univ., Bloomington.

Suzanne G. Frayser, Social Science Research Consultant and Faculty, Univ. College, Univ. of Denver, Colo.

Susan J. Freiband, Assoc. Professor, Graduate School of Librarianship, Univ. of Puerto Rico, San Juan.

David O. Friedrichs, Professor, Univ. of Scranton, Pa.

Jeanne Friedrichs, Asst. Professor of Occupational Therapy, College Misericordia, Dallas, Pa.

Ronald H. Fritze, Assoc. Professor, Dept. of History, Lamar Univ., Beaumont, Tex.

Ahmad Gamaluddin, Professor, School of Library Science, Clarion State College, Pa.

Joan Garner, Staff, Libraries Unlimited, Inc.

Gregg S. Geary, Music Librarian, Sinclair Library, Univ. of Hawaii, Honolulu.

Carol R. Glatt, Chief, Library Service, VA Medical Center, Philadelphia.

Edwin S. Gleaves, State Librarian and Archivist, Tennessee State Library and Archives, Nashville.

Lisha E. Goldberg, Technical Writer, Safety Insurance Co., Boston.

Harold Goldwhite, Professor of Chemistry, California State Univ., Los Angeles.

Kevin L. Gomez, Program Specialist, Head Start—HHS/Administration for Children and Families, Denver, Colo.

Helen M. Gothberg, Assoc. Professor, Graduate Library School, Univ. of Arizona, Tucson.

Allie Wise Goudy, Professor, Western Illinois Univ., Macomb.

M. Patrick Graham, Director, Pitts Theology Library, Emory Univ., Atlanta, Ga.

Marilynn Green, Sciences Reference Librarian, Information Service Dept., Univ. of Houston Libraries, Tex.

Leonard J. Greenspoon, Professor of Religion, Clemson Univ., S.C.

Richard W. Grefrath, Reference Librarian, Univ. of Nevada, Reno.

Arthur Gribben, Professor, Union Institute, Los Angeles, Calif.

Janice M. Griggs, Mathematics Librarian, Univ. of Minnesota, Minneapolis.

Laurel Grotzinger, Professor, University Libraries, Western Michigan Univ., Kalamazoo.

Leonard Grundt, Professor, A. Holly Patterson Library, Nassau Community College, Garden City, N.Y.

Stephen Haenel, Staff, Libraries Unlimited, Inc.

Blaine H. Hall, English Language & Literature Librarian, Harold B. Lee Library, Brigham Young Univ., Provo, Utah.

Deborah Hammer, Head, History, Travel and Biography Division, Queens Borough Public Library, Jamaica, N.Y.

Joseph Hannibal, Curator of Invertebrate Paleontology, Cleveland Museum of Natural History, Ohio.

Roberto P. Haro, Director and Professor, Monterey County Campus, San Jose State Univ., Salinas, Calif.

Chauncy D. Harris, Samuel N. Harper Distinguished Service Professor Emeritus of Geography, Univ. of Chicago.

Linda Suttle Harris, Business Librarian, Univ. of Alabama, Birmingham.

Marvin K. Harris, Professor of Entomology, Texas A & M Univ., College Station.

Ann Hartness, Asst. Head Librarian, Benson Latin American Collection, Univ. of Texas, Austin.

Joy Hastings, Manager, Technical Library, Hunt-Wesson, Inc., Fullerton, Calif.

Robert J. Havlik, Librarian Emeritus and Exhibit Coordinator, Univ. of Notre Dame, Ind.

Fred J. Hay, Reference and Acquisition Librarian, Tozzer Library, Harvard Univ., Cambridge, Mass.

James S. Heller, Director of the Law Library and Assoc. Professor of Law, Marshall-Wythe Law Library, College of William and Mary, Williamsburg, Va.

Mary Hemmings, Technical Services Librarian, Law Library, Univ. of Calgary, Alta.

David Henige, African Studies Bibliographer, Memorial Library, Univ. of Wisconsin, Madison.

Mark Y. Herring, Dean of Libraries, Oklahoma Baptist Univ., Shawnee.

Susan Davis Herring, Reference Librarian, Univ. of Alabama Library, Huntsville.

Janet Swan Hill, Assoc. Director for Technical Services, Univ. Libraries, Univ. of Colorado, Boulder.

Louise E. Hoffman, Assoc. Professor of Humanities and History, Pennsylvania State Univ., Middletown.

Richard E. Holl, Asst. Professor, History Dept., Lees College, Jackson, Ky.

Susan Tower Hollis, Dean, Sierra Nevada College, Incline Village.

Paul L. Holmer, Reference Librarian, Buley Library, Southern Connecticut State Univ., New Haven.

Curtis D. Holmes, Managing Editor, *University of Denver Journal*, Univ. of Denver, Colo.

Shirley L. Hopkinson, Professor, Division of Library and Information Science, San Jose State Univ., Calif.

Renee B. Horowitz, Professor, Dept. of Technology, College of Engineering, Arizona State Univ., Tempe.

Valerie R. Hotchkiss, Director, Bridwell Library, Perkins School of Theology, Southern Methodist Univ., Dallas, Tex.

William E. Hug, Professor, University of Georgia, Athens.

John H. Hunter, Reference/Collection Development Librarian, Fondren Library, Rice Univ., Houston, Tex.

C. D. Hurt, Director, Graduate Library School, Univ. of Arizona, Tucson.

Jonathan F. Husband, Program Chair of the Library/Reader Services Librarian, Henry Whittemore Library, Framingham State College, Mass.

Ludmila N. Ilyina, Professor, Natural Resources Institute, Univ. of Manitoba, Winnipeg.

David Isaacson, Asst. Head of Reference and Humanities Librarian, Waldo Library, Western Michigan Univ., Kalamazoo.

Barbara Ittner, Staff, Libraries Unlimited, Inc.

Eugene B. Jackson, Professor Emeritus, Graduate School of Library and Information Science, Univ. of Texas, Austin.

D. Barton Johnson, Professor Emeritus of Russian, Univ. of California, Santa Barbara.

Jennie S. Johnson, formerly Reference Librarian, Univ. of Toledo, Ohio.

Richard D. Johnson, Director of Libraries, James M. Milne Library, State Univ. College, Oneonta, N.Y.

Raymond E. Jones, Assoc. Professor of English, Univ. of Alberta, Edmonton.

Robert L. Jones, Assoc. Professor, Dept. of Family and Community Medicine, Pennsylvania State College of Medicine, Hershey.

Rebecca Jordan, Director of Composition, Division of English, Emporia State Univ., Kans.

Jane Jurgens, Reference Librarian, St. Cloud State Univ., Minn.

Thomas A. Karel, Assoc. Director for Public Services, Shadek-Fackenthal Library, Franklin and Marshall College, Lancaster, Pa.

Edmund D. Keiser, Jr., Professor of Biology, Univ. of Mississippi, University.

John Laurence Kelland, Reference Bibliographer for Life Sciences, Univ. of Rhode Island Library, Kingston.

Dean H. Keller, Assoc. Dean of Libraries, Kent State Univ., Ohio.

Joanne Kelly, Champaign, Ill.

Barbara E. Kemp, Library Applications Specialist, PSS Tapestry, Reston, Va.

Vicki J. Killion, Asst. Professor of Library Science and Pharmacy, Nursing and Health Sciences Librarian, Purdue Univ., West Lafayette, Ind.

Sung Ok Kim, Senior Asst. Librarian/Social Sciences Cataloging Librarian, Cornell Univ., Ithaca, N.Y.

Norman L. Kincaide, Citation Editor, Shepard's/McGraw-Hill, Inc., Colorado Springs, Colo.

Christine E. King, Reference Librarian, State Univ. of New York, Stony Brook.

Zsuzsa Koltay, Mann Library, Cornell Univ., Ithaca, N.Y.

Johan Koren, Lecturer, Library Science Program, Wayne State Univ., Detroit.

Betsy J. Kraus, Librarian/Technical Editor, Environmental Evaluation Group, Albuquerque.

Linda A. Krikos, Head, Women's Studies Library, Ohio State Univ., Columbus.

Colby H. Kullman, Assoc. Professor and Editor, *Studies in American Drama*, Univ. of Mississippi, University.

R. Errol Lam, Reference Librarian, Bowling Green State Univ., Ohio.

Sharon Langworthy, Production Supervisor/Supplement Editor, Wiley Law Publications, Colorado Springs, Colo.

Mary Larsgaard, Asst. Head, Map and Imagery Laboratory Library, Univ. of California, Santa Barbara.

John R. M. Lawrence, Reference and Interlibrary Loan Librarian, College of William and Mary, Williamsburg, Va.

Binh P. Le, Reference Librarian, Pennsylvania State Univ./Ogontz, Abington.

Patricia M. Leach, Editorial Technician Training Leader, Group Publishing, Loveland, Colo.

Charles Leck, Professor of Biological Sciences, Rutgers Univ., New Brunswick, N.J.

Mary Lou LeCompte, Asst. Professor, Kinesiology and Health Education, Univ. of Texas at Austin.

Hwa-Wei Lee, Dean of Libraries, Ohio Univ., Athens.

Joann H. Lee, formerly Head of Reader Services, Lake Forest College, Ill.

R. S. Lehmann, Rocky Mountain BankCard System, Colorado National Bank, Denver.

Richard A. Leiter, Director and Assoc. Professor of Law, Regent Univ., Virginia Beach, Va.

Tze-chung Li, Professor, Graduate School of Library and Information Science, Rosary College, River Forest, Ill.

Charlotte Lindgren, Professor Emerita of English, Emerson College, Boston.

Koraljka Lockhart, Publications Editor, San Francisco Opera, Calif.

David V. Loertscher, Staff, Libraries Unlimited, Inc.

Elisabeth Logan, Assoc. Professor, School of Library and Information Studies, Florida State Univ., Tallahassee.

Jeffrey R. Luttrell, Leader, Humanities Cataloging Team, Princeton Univ. Library, N.J.

Marit S. MacArthur, Reference Librarian, Auraria Libraries, Univ. of Colorado, Denver.

Sara R. Mack, Professor Emerita, Dept. of Library Science, Kutztown Univ., Pa.

Linda Main, Assoc. Professor, San Jose State Univ., Calif.

Cheryl Knott Malone, History, Government, American Studies, and Australian Studies Bibliographer, General Libraries, Univ. of Texas, Austin.

Judy Gay Matthews, Staff, Libraries Unlimited, Inc.

George Louis Mayer, formerly Senior Principal Librarian, New York Public Library and Part-Time Librarian, Adelphi, Manhattan Center and Brooklyn College, N.Y.

James P. McCabe, Univ. Librarian, Fordham Univ., Bronx, N.Y.

James R. McDonald, Professor of Geography, Eastern Michigan Univ., Ypsilanti.

Robert B. McKee, Professor, Mechanical Engineering, Univ. of Nevada, Reno.

Susan V. McKimm, Business Reference Specialist, Cuyahoga County Library System, Maple Heights, Ohio.

T. McKimmie, Reference Librarian, New Mexico State Univ., Las Cruces.

Marian B. McLeod, Professor of Speech Communication and Theater, Trenton State College, N.J.

Maria O'Neil McMahon, Professor, School of Social Work, East Carolina Univ., Greenville, N.C.

Margo B. Mead, Asst. Professor, Library, Univ. of Alabama, Huntsville.

Lillian R. Mesner, Technical Services Librarian, Agricultural Library, Univ. of Kentucky, Lexington.

Michael G. Messina, Assoc. Professor, Dept. of Forest Science, Texas A&M Univ., College Station.

Bogdan Mieczkowski, Professor of Economics, Ithaca College, N.Y.

Seiko Mieczkowski, Hobart & William Smith Colleges, Geneva, N.Y.

Edward P. Miller, Payson Public Library, Ariz.

Jerome K. Miller, (deceased), formerly President, Copyright Information Services, Friday Harbor, Wash.

Richard A. Miller, Professor of Economics, Wesleyan Univ., Middletown, Conn.

James Moffet, Head, Reference Dept, Baldwin Public Library, Birmingham, Mich.

Janet Mongan, Research Officer, Cleveland State Univ. Library, Ohio.

Terry Ann Mood, Humanities Bibliographer, Univ. of Colorado, Denver.

Gerald D. Moran, Librarian, Geneva College, Beaver Falls, Pa.

P. Grady Morein, Director of Libraries, Univ. of West Florida, Pensacola.

K. Mulliner, Asst. to the Director of Libraries, Ohio Univ. Library, Athens.

James M. Murray, Director, East Bonner County Library, Sandpoint, Idaho.

Linda A. Naru, Planning and Development Officer, Center for Research Libraries, Chicago.

Charles Neuringer, Professor of Psychology and Theatre and Film, Univ. of Kansas, Lawrence.

Danuta A. Nitecki, Assoc. Director for Public Services, Univ. of Maryland Libraries, College Park.

Joseph Z. Nitecki, Professor Emeritus, School of Information Science and Policy, State Univ. of New York, Albany.

Eric R. Nitschke, Reference Librarian, Robert W. Woodruff Library, Emory Univ., Atlanta, Ga.

Christopher W. Nolan, Head, Reference Services, Maddux Library, Trinity Univ., San Antonio, Tex.

Carol L. Noll, Treasurer and Board Member, Tinton Falls Public Library, N.J.

Margaret Norden, Head of Public Services, Library, Marymount Univ., Arlington.

O. Gene Norman, Head, Reference Dept., Indiana State Univ. Libraries, Terre Haute.

Marilyn Strong Noronha, Reference Librarian, Harleigh B. Trecker Library, Univ. of Connecticut, West Hartford.

Marshall E. Nunn, Professor, Dept. of History, Glendale Community College, Calif.

Herbert W. Ockerman, Professor, Ohio State Univ., Columbus.

Lori L. Oling, Reference Librarian, Auraria Library, Denver, CO.

Berniece M. Owen, Coordinator, Library Technical Services, Portland Community College, Oreg.

John Howard Oxley, Halifax, N.S.

Mark Padnos, Humanities Reference Librarian, Mina Rees Library, Graduate School and Univ. Center, City Univ. of New York.

Joseph W. Palmer, Assoc. Professor, School of Information and Library Studies, State Univ. of New York, Buffalo.

Robert Palmieri, Professor Emeritus, School of Music, Kent State Univ., Ohio.

Maureen Pastine, Director, Central Libraries, Southern Methodist Univ., Dallas, Tex.

Anna Grace Patterson, Staff, Libraries Unlimited, Inc.

Elizabeth Patterson, Head, Reference and Computer Reference Services, Robert W. Woodruff Library, Emory Univ., Atlanta, Ga.

Gari-Anne Patzwald, Freelance Editor and Indexer, Lexington, Ky.

Harry E. Pence, Professor of Chemistry, State Univ. of New York, Oneonta.

Karin Pendle, Professor of Musicology, Univ. of Cincinnati, Ohio.

Kevin W. Perizzolo, Staff, Libraries Unlimited, Inc..

C. Michael Phillips, Asst. Reference Librarian, Robert Scott Small Library, College of Charleston, S.C.

Edwin D. Posey, Engineering Librarian, Purdue Univ. Libraries, West Lafayette, Ind.

Daphne Fallieros Potter, Database Specialist, American Mathematical Society, Providence, R.I.

Phillip P. Powell, Asst. Reference Librarian, Robert Scott Small Library, College of Charleston, S.C.

Carl Pracht, Reference Librarian, Southeast Missouri State Univ., Cape Girardeau.

Ann E. Prentice, Dean, College of Library and Information Services, Univ. of Maryland, College Park.

William S. Proudfoot, Asst. Librarian, Science Library, Univ. of California, Santa Cruz.

Randall Rafferty, Reference Librarian, Mississippi State Univ. Library, Mississippi State.

Kristin Ramsdell, Assoc. Librarian, California State Univ., Hayward.

Lise Rasmussen, Reference Librarian, Dowling College, Oakdale, N.Y.

Jack Ray, Asst. Director, Loyola/Notre Dame Library, Baltimore, Md.

Lorna K. Rees-Potter, Asst. Professor, Graduate School of Library and Information Studies, McGill Univ., Montreal.

James Rettig, Asst. Univ. Librarian for Reference and Information Services, Swem Library, College of William and Mary, Williamsburg, Va.

Diane B. Rhodes, Life Sciences and Agriculture Librarian, Arizona State Univ., Tempe.

Henry J. Ricardo, Assoc. Professor of Mathematics, Medgar Evers College, City University of New York.

Jo Anne H. Ricca, Staff, Libraries Unlimited, Inc.

Anne F. Roberts, Adjunct Professor, School of Education, State Univ. of New York, Albany.

William B. Robison, Asst. Professor, History, Southeastern Louisiana Univ., Hammond.

Ilene F. Rockman, Interim Assoc. Dean of Library Services, California Polytechnic State Univ., San Luis Obispo.

Anne C. Roess, Librarian, Peoples Gas, Light & Coke Co., Chicago.

JoAnn V. Rogers, Professor, College of Library and Information Science, Univ. of Kentucky, Lexington.

Deborah V. Rollins, Reference Librarian, Univ. of Maine, Orono.

Bertram H. Rothschild, Asst. Chief of Psychology, V.A. Medical Center, Denver, Colo.

D. A. Rothschild, Staff, Libraries Unlimited, Inc.

Marilyn Rothschild, formerly School Psychologist, Denver Public Schools, Colo.

Samuel Rothstein, Professor Emeritus, School of Librarianship, Univ. of British Columbia, Vancouver.

Edmund F. SantaVicca, Head, Reference Services, Hayden Library, Arizona State Univ., Tempe.

Patricia A. Sarles, Librarian, Kensington Branch, Brooklyn Public Library, N.Y.

Jay Schafer, Coordinator of Collections, Auraria Library, Denver, Colo.

Frederick A. Schlipf, Executive Director, Urbana Free Library and Adjunct Professor, Graduate School of Library and Information Science, Univ. of Illinois.

Diane Schmidt, Asst. Biology Librarian, Univ. of Illinois, Urbana.

Steven J. Schmidt, Assoc. Librarian, Indiana Univ.-Purdue Univ. at Indianapolis Libraries.

Willa Schmidt, Reference Librarian, Univ. of Wisconsin, Madison.

John P. Schmitt, Head of Reference, Univ. of Wyoming Libraries, Laramie.

Isabel Schon, Director, Center for the Study of Books in Spanish, California State Univ., San Marcos.

Deborah K. Scott, Asst. Librarian, Employer's Reinsurance Corporation, Overland Park, Kans.

Ralph Lee Scott, Assoc. Professor, East Carolina Univ. Library, Greenville, N.C.

Robert A. Seal, Director of Libraries, Univ. of Texas, El Paso.

Margretta Reed Seashore, Professor of Genetics and Pediatrics, Yale Univ. School of Medicine, New Haven, Conn.

Tama J. Serfoss, Staff, Libraries Unlimited, Inc,.

Ravindra Nath Sharma, Library Director, Univ. of Evansville, Ind.

Patricia Tipton Sharp, Professor of Curriculum and Instruction, Baylor Univ., Waco, Tex.

Christine M. Sheetz, Librarian, Univ. of Rochester, N.Y.

Bruce A. Shuman, Adjunct Professor, Univ. of South Florida, Tampa.

Stephanie C. Sigala, Head Librarian, Richardson Memorial Library, St. Louis Art Museum, Mo.

Robert Skinner, Technology Development Librarian, Central Univ. Libraries, Southern Methodist Univ., Dallas, Tex.

Jeanette C. Smith, Head, Government Documents, New Mexico State Univ. Library, Las Cruces.

Linda Sue Smith, Staff, Libraries Unlimited, Inc.

Nathan M. Smith, Director, School of Library and Information Sciences, Brigham Young Univ., Provo, Utah.

Mary Ellen Snodgrass, Freelance Writer and Columnist, Charlotte Observer, Charlotte, NC.

Natalia Sonevytsky, Head, Reference Dept., Barnard College Library, New York.

Lev I. Soudek, Professor of English Linguistics and Coordinator, Programs in Linguistics and TESOL, Northern Illinois Univ., De Kalb.

Karen Y. Stabler, Head of Information Services, New Mexico State Univ. Library, Las Cruces.

Mary J. Stanley, Acting Head of Periodicals/Liaison to the School of Social Work, Indiana Univ.- Purdue Univ. at Indianapolis.

Allen E. Staver, Assoc. Professor, Dept. of Geography, Northern Illinois Univ., De Kalb.

Roger Steeb, Science Librarian, Univ. Library, New Mexico State Univ., Las Cruces.

Norman D. Stevens, Director, Univ. of Connecticut Libraries, Storrs.

John P. Stierman, Reference Librarian, Western Illinois Univ., Macomb.

John W. Storey, Professor of History, Lamar Univ., Beaumont, Tex.

William C. Struning, Professor, Seton Hall Univ., South Orange, N.J.

Bruce Stuart, Assoc. Professor of Health Administration, Pennsylvania State Univ., University Park.

Timothy E. Sullivan, Asst. Professor of Economics, Towson State Univ., Md.

Richard H. Swain, Head of Reference, Fogler Library, Univ. of Maine, Orono.

James H. Sweetland, Assoc. Professor, School of Library and Information Science, Univ. of Wisconsin, Milwaukee.

Nigel Tappin, General Librarian, North York Public Library, Ont.

Deborah A. Taylor, Staff, Libraries Unlimited, Inc.

Glynys R. Thomas, Reference Assistant, Wheelock College, Boston.

Katherine Margaret Thomas, formerly Biologist, Long Point Bird Observatory, Toronto.

Christine E. Thompson, Head, Catalog Department and Assoc. Professor, Univ. of Alabama Libraries, Tuscaloosa.

Mary Ann Thompson, Asst. Professor of Nursing, Saint Joseph College, West Hartford, Conn.

Angela Marie Thor, Information Consultant, Syracuse, N.Y.

Bruce H. Tiffney, Assoc. Professor of Geology and Biological Sciences, Univ. of California, Santa Barbara.

Andrew G. Torok, Assoc. Professor, Northern Illinois Univ., De Kalb.

Gregory M. Toth, Reference Librarian, State Univ. of New York, Brockport.

John U. Trefny, Head and Professor, Dept. of Physics, Colorado School of Mines, Golden.

Carol Truett, Assoc. Professor, Appalachian State Univ., Boone, N.C.

John Mark Tucker, Senior Reference Librarian, Humanities, Social Science and Education Library, Purdue Univ., West Lafayette, Ind.

Dean Tudor, Professor, School of Journalism, Ryerson Polytechnical Institute, Toronto.

Elias H. Tuma, Professor of Economics, Univ. of California, Davis.

Diane J. Turner, Science/Engineering Liaison, Auraria Library, University of Colorado, Denver.

Robert L. Turner, Jr., Librarian and Asst. Professor, Radford Univ., Va.

Arthur R. Upgren, Professor of Astronomy and Director, Van Vleck Observatory, Wesleyan Univ., Middletown, Conn.

Vandelia L. VanMeter, Assoc. Professor and Chair, Department of Library and Information Science, Spalding Univ., Louisville, Ky.

Dario J. Villa, Reference Librarian/Bibliographer, Ronald Williams Library, Northeastern Illinois Univ., Chicago.

Kathleen J. Voigt, Head, Reference Dept., Carlson Library, Univ. of Toledo, Ohio.

Mary Jo Walker, Special Collections Librarian, Eastern New Mexico Univ., Portales.

Lydia W. Wasylenko, Assoc. Librarian, Syracuse Univ. Library, N.Y.

Jean Weihs, Principal Consultant, Technical Services Group, Toronto.

Bella Hass Weinberg, Assoc. Professor, Division of Library and Information Science, St. John's Univ., Jamaica, N.Y.

Emily L. Werrell, Reference/Instructional Services Librarian, Northern Kentucky Univ., Highland Heights.

Lucille Whalen, Dean of Graduate Programs, Immaculate Heart College Center, Los Angeles, Calif.

Carol Wheeler, Government Documents Reference Librarian, Univ. of Georgia Libraries, Athens.

Cathy Seitz Whitaker, formerly Social Work Librarian, Hillman Library, Univ. of Pittsburgh, Pa.

David L. White, Professor, History Dept., Appalachian State Univ., Boone, N.C.

George M. White, Assoc. Professor, Univ. of Ottawa.

Marilyn Domas White, Assoc. Professor, College of Library and Information Services, Univ. of Maryland, College Park.

Robert L. Wick, Asst. Professor and Fine Arts Bibliographer, Auraria Library, Univ. of Colorado, Denver.

William H. Wiese, Science and Reference Librarian, Parks Library, Iowa State Univ., Ames.

Dorothy M. Williams, Instructor, English/Communications, Front Range Community College, Westminster, Colo.

Lynn F. Williams, Professor, Division of Writing, Literature, and Publishing, Emerson College, Boston.

Robert V. Williams, Assoc. Professor, College of Library and Information Science, Univ. of South Carolina, Columbia.

Wiley J. Williams, Professor Emeritus, School of Library Science, Kent State Univ., Ohio.

Liz Willis, Reference Librarian, Auraria Library, Denver, Colo.

Frank L. Wilson, Professor and Head, Dept. of Political Science, Purdue Univ., West Lafayette, Ind.

Patricia S. Wilson, Public Services Librarian, Agriculture Library, Univ. of Kentucky, Lexington.

Wayne Wilson, Director, Research and Library Services, Amateur Athlete Foundation, Los Angeles, Calif.

Glenn R. Wittig, Director of Library Services, Criswell College, Dallas, Tex.

Randy M. Wood, Assoc. Professor, Baylor Univ., Waco, Tex.

Raymund F. Wood, Editor, *The Westerners*, Encino, Calif.

Hensley C. Woodbridge, Professor of Spanish, Dept. of Foreign Languages, Southern Illinois Univ., Carbondale.

Dorothy C. Woodson, Social Sciences Bibliographer, State Univ. of New York at Buffalo.

Bohdan S. Wynar, Staff, Libraries Unlimited, Inc.

Lubomyr R. Wynar, Professor, School of Library Science and Director, Center for Ethnic Studies, Kent State Univ., Ohio.

Martha Miller Yazhari, Belle Mead, N.J.

A. Neil Yerkey, Assoc. Professor, School of Information and Library Studies, State Univ. of New York, Buffalo.

Henry E. York, Head, Collection Management, Cleveland State Univ., Ohio.

Arthur P. Young, Director, Northern Illinois Libraries, Northern Illinois Univ., De Kalb.

Louis G. Zelenka, Public Services Librarian, Southwest Georgia Regional Library, Bainbridge.

L. Zgusta, Professor of Linguistics and the Classics and Member of the Center for Advanced Study, Univ. of Illinois, Urbana.

Oleg Zinam, Professor of Economics, Univ. of Cincinnati, Ohio.

Anita Zutis, Adjunct Librarian, Queensborough Community College, Bayside, N.Y.

Journals Cited

FORM OF CITATION	JOURNAL TITLE
BL	Booklist
BR	Book Report
Choice	Choice
C&RL	College & Research Libraries
EL	Emergency Librarian
JAL	Journal of Academic Librarianship
JOYS	Journal of Youth Services in Libraries
LAR	Library Association Record
LJ	Library Journal
RBB	Reference Books Bulletin
RQ	RQ
SBF	Science Books & Films
SLJ	School Library Journal
SLMQ	School Library Media Quarterly
VOYA	Voice of Youth Advocates
WLB	Wilson Library Bulletin

Part I
GENERAL REFERENCE WORKS

1 General Reference Works

ALMANACS

1. **The Canadian Global Almanac 1993: A Book of Facts.** John Robert Colombo, ed. Toronto, Macmillan Canada, 1992. 728p. maps. index. $14.95pa. 031.02. ISBN 0-7715-9185-3. ISSN 1187-4570.

Originally published in 1987 under the title *Canadian World Almanac and Book of Facts*, this almanac is in its second year under the new title. Under the editorship of Colombo it offers value at an affordable price.

Compared with the *Canadian Almanac & Directory* (see ARBA 92, entry 98) and *Corpus Almanac & Canadian Sourcebook* (Southam Information & Technology Group, 1992), the *Global Almanac* provides more almanac and less directory. Organized in three sections, it covers information about Canada; international information; and facts about arts, entertainment, sports, and news events. The Canadian section features current facts on the land, people, economy, and government organization. International information includes former Soviet jurisdictions and provides geographical, demographic, and political summaries. The science and nature section is a new addition and includes space, environmental, earth, physical sciences, and scientific achievements. The arts and entertainment section contains popular media facts. The sports section covers the Olympics as well as professional competitive sports. The quick reference section offers useful lists and charts for first aid, weights and measures, and travel. The previous year's obituaries and news events are summarized in the final section.

The indexing is simple, clear, and concise. Easy to use, it complements this well-designed paperback. Finally, although the Canadian content of this volume is emphasized, the global nature of the coverage is a deliberate attempt to offer a competitive alternative to such titles as *The World Almanac and Book of Facts* (see ARBA 90, entry 3) and *Information Please Almanac* (see ARBA 90, entry 2). Future plans include the release of a CD-ROM version in 1994.—**Mary Hemmings**

2. **The Information Please Kids' Almanac.** By Alice Siegel and Margo McLoone Basta. Boston, Houghton Mifflin, 1992. 363p. illus. maps. index. $16.95; $7.95pa. ISBN 0-395-64737-1; 0-395-58801-4pa.

Kids of all ages will enjoy browsing through this almanac, although grades 4-8 are its intended audience. Fifteen chapters cover such broad categories as animals, the environment, sports, and "People Pamphlet." Definitions and lists of facts are served up in a fun and easily digestible format. Most of the illustrations serve a design rather than informational role, but dozens of timelines, tables, maps, and sidebars for such things as modes of transportation, currency equivalents, cloud types, greetings around the world, and star sizes are useful and attractively presented.

The index is inadequate for identifying specific facts or sections of text. For example, the entry for "mountains" refers the reader to the section on biomes but not to the page that lists the tallest mountain; and an eight-page section on the meaning of colors is indexed under "Language and color" but not under "Colors." While this title does not obviate the need for a standard almanac, it is recommended for those libraries that serve children. [R: SLJ, Feb 93, p. 124]—**Deborah V. Rollins**

BIBLIOGRAPHY

Bibliographic Guides

3. **Reference Books Bulletin 1991-1992: A Compilation of Evaluations September 1, 1991 through August 1992.** By the American Library Association Reference Books Bulletin Editorial Board. Sandy Whiteley, ed., and Denise Blank, comp. Chicago, American Library Association, 1992. 184p. index. $25.00pa. LC 73-159565. ISBN 0-8389-3417-X. ISSN 8755-0962.

This annual compilation of reviews from "Reference Books Bulletin" (RBB) in *Booklist* is always a useful addition to the reference reviewing shelf. This year the volume contains 500 reviews of individual titles plus 6 omnibus reviews, including the annual encyclopedia update, "Law Books for Laypeople," and reference materials on animals.

This collection will be useful to small and medium-sized public and academic libraries for identification and evaluation of important titles issued over the past year. For those who follow the regular RBB section in *Booklist*, there is nothing new in this volume. It is convenient, however, to have all the reviews in one place.—**Donald C. Dickinson**

4. Wynar, Bohdan S., and Anna Grace Patterson, eds. **Recommended Reference Books for Small and Medium-sized Libraries and Media Centers 1993.** Englewood, Colo., Libraries Unlimited, 1993. 281p. index. $39.50. Z1035.1.R435. 011'.02. LC 81-12394. ISBN 1-56308-155-5. ISSN 0277-5948.

This work reprints 540 of the 1,792 citations from the larger *American Reference Books Annual* (ARBA) 1993, those most appropriate for smaller libraries. Entries are divided into 36 chapters under 4 major subdivisions: general reference works, social sciences, humanities, and science and technology. Each source is designated as recommended for college, public, or media center collections. As usual the reviews are generally of high quality, and published reviews in other library journals are listed at the end of the entries.

Small institutions may rely upon entries in this source as confirmation of purchases most appropriate for their limited budgets. However, the comprehensive ARBA is a more valuable tool whose price is not significantly greater. Most institutions would be better served to purchase it rather than this source.

—**Joe P. Dunn**

National and Trade Bibliography

International

5. **New Zealand Books in Print 1993: Including Books Published in the Pacific Islands.** 21st ed. Port Melbourne, Austral., D. W. Thorpe; distr., New Providence, N. J., Reed Reference Publishing, 1993. 373p. $64.00. ISBN 1-875589-21-X. ISSN 0157-7662.

This is the standard reference work of its kind. It includes in its scope Pacific islands as well as New Zealand. For instance, Western Samoa, which was under a New Zealand trusteeship until 1962, has recently developed a flourishing literature of its own and has become a center for the encouragement of writing in other Pacific island groups, such as Fiji, Tonga, Vanuatu, and the Solomons.

As the books listed are those still in print, this reference work is designed primarily for booksellers and librarians. The date of publication of the books listed is inexplicably omitted, and so the work is less useful for scholars. But it contains much useful information on sources of assistance for New Zealand writers (an important issue in this thinly populated land), and on New Zealand literary awards and their past winners. From these listings one can derive culturally significant information, such as the emergence of Cilla McQueen as a leading younger poet and the abiding deep interest of New Zealanders in the flora of their beautiful country.

The book has been carefully proofread but has an odd error in a bad place—the paradigmatic key to book entries that precedes the lists of books in print. It punctuates the ISBN with a comma before as well as after the parentheses in which the ISBN is recorded—and the error is repeated from the standard title entry to the standard author entry. However, the error does not appear in the actual list of books in print.—**John B. Beston**

6. **Whitaker's Books in Print 1993: The Reference Catalogue of Current Literature.** London, J. Whitaker; distr., New Providence, N.J., Reed Reference Publishing, 1993. 4v. index. $426.00/set. ISBN 0-85021-230-8. ISSN 0953-0398.

As every reference librarian knows, *Whitaker's Books in Print* (WBIP) lists titles published in the United Kingdom available to the general public through the book trade. However, not all may know that this bibliography is unique, being the only exhaustive list of British books in print; that since 1971 it has been computer-produced; that in 1988 its title was changed from *British Books in Print*; and that it now inventories both books and microfiche editions. Because of Whitaker's continuous updating procedures, this latest edition contains some 380,000 amendments—additions, deletions, price changes, corrections, and more.

An informative prefatory section notes, among other tidbits of information, that 60,000 new titles and editions are published in the United Kingdom each year; it also contains a valuable guide to publishers. An index appended to the fourth volume alphabetizes the publishers and supplies their complete addresses, along with an identifying code used in conjunction with a standard book number to distinguish titles issued by that publisher or group.

To claim that this book-trade bibliography is a must for all large academic libraries is bromidic. Because WBIP has been published annually since 1967, whether or not this 1993 edition should supplant the 1992 edition, or even the 1991 edition, is best left to individual acquisition librarians.

—**G. A. Cevasco**

United States

7. **Books in Print 1993-94.** New Providence, N.J., R. R. Bowker/Reed Reference Publishing, 1993. 10v. index. $425.00/set. LC 4-12648. ISBN 0-8352-3354-5.

8. **Books in Print Plus.** [CD-ROM]. New Providence, N.J., R. R. Bowker/Reed Reference Publishing, 1993. Hardware requirements: IBM PC, XT, XT-286, AT, PS/2 Model 25, 30 or full compatible; 640K memory with 535K free; MS-DOS Extensions. $1,095.00/yr.

Reliance on *Books in Print* (BIP) by libraries and booksellers is as strong as ever, with the exception of smaller libraries that rely on the databases of jobbers to handle their in-print queries. (In recent years, the merger of publishing houses and high finance/bottom-line syndrome have created such havoc in the industry that the concept of "in-print" is cloudy at best; many consider it total chaos.) R. R. Bowker, now part of Reed Reference Publishing, first produced BIP in 1948. Since that time, their database has grown to some 1.5 million titles published by more than 41,000 publishers. BIP can no longer be considered a single entity; it is now a family of products available in printed or electronic form. The database containing the book titles is as current and accurate as regular publishers' reports and database entry can make it. In 1993, Bowker announced BowkerPower, which allows publishers to submit data electronically and as often as needed rather than on paper in quarterly reports. Theoretically, the accuracy of the entire database will improve when publishers have more control.

BIP and its various spin-offs and related products (e.g., *Children's Books in Print* [Reed Reference Publishing, annual], *Scientific and Technical Books and Serials in Print* [see ARBA 92, entry 1453]) have individual selection criteria but essentially the same access points in the print versions: by author, title, and subject. Information provided about individual publications has remained fairly constant in the last 10 years, as have arrangement and alphabetical sequences. All the books have such microscopic print that prolonged usage may be harmful to eyesight. Recently, Bowker has been encouraging publishers to buy advertising space in the printed volumes, which they tout as major book publicity. But if users have the same tastes as this reviewer, they will find the three column-inch advertisements bothersome and counterproductive.

Librarians and booksellers can contribute substantially to the forests and eyes of the world by replacing the printed volumes with the CD-ROM versions, which not only will save paper but also have infinitely superior searching capabilities. The CD-ROM versions of BIP must also be considered as a family of products, each with a hefty price and features designed for various functions. (The user should test the different databases before purchase.) A look at the engine that drives these products shows that minor improvements have been made, but *BIP Plus* has the same look and feel of earlier versions. All the products have the same manual, which can be confusing to the novice.

The CD-ROM versions are not only easier and faster to search, but the expanded capability of reading professional reviews of individual titles and linking the computer and database directly to jobbers for acquisition makes the product much more valuable. One small point: Installation of the product requires both a CD-ROM disc and a floppy disk. Bowker should eliminate the latter, as others have done, so the entire product is contained on a single disc.—**David V. Loertscher**

9. **Children's Books in Print 1993: An Author, Title, and Illustrator Index to Books for Children and Young Adults.** New Providence, N.J., R. R. Bowker/Reed Reference Publishing, 1993. 2v. index. $139.00/set. LC 70-101705. ISBN 0-8352-3229-8. ISSN 0069-3480.

This edition of *Children's Books in Print* (see ARBA 92, entry 16 for a previous review) has a new look for 1993: It has been split into two volumes. Volume 1 includes awards, authors, and illustrators and volume 2 contains titles and publishers. This useful arrangement has resulted in less unwieldy volumes. Another new feature is that publishers may now purchase space to include annotations with book entries; this occurs infrequently. More than 81,000 books published in the United States are listed in the volumes. The indexes are preceded by a foreword, a "How to Use" section, and a key to abbreviations. Information has been provided by the publishers of the books, which may lead to some variations in spellings throughout the listings. This set remains an invaluable reference for anyone working with children's books.—**Suzanne I. Barchers**

10. Rinderknecht, Carol, and Scott Bruntjen, comps. **Checklist of American Imprints for 1843: Items 43-1 - 43-5445.** Metuchen, N.J., Scarecrow, 1993. 424p. $52.50. LC 64-11784. ISBN 0-8108-2653-4.

The appearance of the volume for 1843 marks another step in the publication of this series that, when complete, will cover American publishing from 1820 to 1875. Books, state and local documents, pamphlets, broadsides, and other printed material issued in the United States in 1843 are listed in alphabetical order by personal or corporate author. Entries include the title of the work, place of publication, publisher, date, number of pages, location symbols for institutions holding copies, and item number. The easier-to-read format and improved numbering system, which were established with the publication of the 1840 volume, are continued in this volume.—**Dean H. Keller**

BIOGRAPHY

International

11. **Biography Today: Profiles of People of Interest to Young Readers. 1992 Annual Cumulation.** Laurie Lanzen Harris, ed. Detroit, Omnigraphics, 1993. 498p. illus. index. $38.50. ISBN 1-55888-139-5.

Biography Today is designed for young people ages nine and up as a quarterly magazine. Each issue contains 15 biographical sketches of entertainers, athletes, writers, illustrators, cartoonists, and political leaders. The issues cumulate into this annual volume. Individual sketches contain a picture and information on the person's birth, youth, early memories, education, first jobs, marriage and family, career highlights, memorable experiences, hobbies, and honors and awards. At the end of the sketch, writings by and about the person are listed with an address (usually a publisher or organization address). The writing style is casual, designed to engage upper elementary readers, with enough information to write the ubiquitous "report on your favorite person." The 1992 annual covers such notables as Larry Bird, Judy Blume, Bill Clinton, Spike Lee, and Jay Leno. Late-breaking news that was not included in the quarterly sketches, such as Clinton's election to the presidency and Larry Bird's retirement (although his Boston Celtics address is still given), has been added at the end of the sketch (but it is not integrated).

This tool has been designed as a junior *Current Biography* (see ARBA 93, entry 37), and as such competes well with its big brother. Selections of biographees are done by an advisory board of school and public librarians, and there is a wide mix of people of interest to the younger crowd. The format and covers are attractive, and the print is easy to read for the young person, but the reading level presumes approximately fourth grade.

Recommended instead of *Current Biography* for elementary and junior high schools and children's rooms of public libraries. High schools that desire an easier and more popularized source will want to consider this set as well.—**David V. Loertscher**

12. Camp, Roderic Ai. **Who's Who in Mexico Today.** 2d ed. Boulder, Colo., Westview Press, 1993. 197p. $65.00. CT552.C36. 920.072. LC 92-35773. ISBN 0-8133-8452-4.

The first edition of this work, published in 1988, contained 391 entries; this new edition is only 12 pages longer. The biographies are usefully arranged in 12 categories: date of birth, birthplace, education, elected office, political party offices, governmental appointments, leadership in national organizations, private-sector positions, family information, military activities, national awards, and sources of information. The word *letter* at the end of an entry indicates that Camp either interviewed the biographee or received information in writing. Although Camp does not explain why a few entries from the first edition are omitted, it is assumed that these persons are no longer living. It is stated that more than half of the entries have been updated, but most appear to be the same, with additional information for occurrences after 1988. Thirteen additional sources for background information were used in this 2d edition. Camp notes that the book is not comprehensive because viable information is not always available. All sectors of society, especially decisionmakers, are included, as well as people usually omitted from this type of work, such as clergy and women (whom the author categorizes as pioneers).

This volume fills a gap with current Mexican biographies in English. It is essential for those libraries with emphasis on Latin American Studies. Recommended for public and academic libraries.
—**Karen Y. Stabler**

13. **The Concise Dictionary of National Bibliography: From Earliest Times to 1985.** New York, Oxford University Press, 1992. 3v. $195.00/set. ISBN 0-19-865305-0.

The Dictionary of National Bibliography (DNB) is a major set of volumes containing biographical sketches of notable persons from Great Britain and the Commonwealth from the beginning of time until 1985. The main set consists of a basic group of volumes first published in 1908 and supplemented at 10-year (now 5-year) intervals, the latest supplement being issued in 1990 (see ARBA 91, entry 13). From the entire main set, including the supplements, the concise DNB has been created. Twice before, concise versions have appeared, so this current work might be thought of as a 3d edition of the *Concise*, although it is not labeled as such.

The work contains every name listed in the entire set, but biographical material has been condensed anywhere from a few lines to a few column inches. The *Concise* is uneven in its treatment of individuals. The longest sketches are for those people who appeared in the DNB supplements, and brief sketches are used for persons in the main volumes. Very important people, such as kings and William Shakespeare, are treated extensively no matter when they appeared in the original volumes. One can understand the differences in editorial practices over the decades, but the result is inconsistency.

The advantage to a smaller library of the *Concise* is the extensive coverage for a reasonable cost. If a person is found in the *Concise*, the user knows that the main volumes can be consulted at another library with the major set for more complete information. No cross-references to the main set are provided, however, so one is uncertain whether to begin looking in the main volumes or one of the supplements.

The *Concise* is a first source to consult if the person sought is British and died before 1985. Because the DNB is biased toward men in politics and the humanities, other sources will be needed to help with women and people in the sciences if a first search is unsuccessful. If an individual is located, users can be certain that they have the most authoritative information.

Recommended for libraries needing British biographical information that cannot afford the main volumes or branch libraries that want some coverage but have access to the whole set at a central location. It is also great for telephone reference centers. [R: Choice, May 93, p. 1436; RBB, 1 Mar 93, p. 1251; WLB, May 93, p. 114]—**David V. Loertscher**

14. **Index to Who's Who Books 1992.** New Providence, N.J., Marquis Who's Who/Reed Reference Publishing, 1992. 467p. $79.50.LC 74-17540. ISBN 0-8379-1429-9.

Anyone who wants to locate biographical material on important recent individuals will find this index to be of value. It contains approximately 379,000 entries for biographical sketches published in 14 Marquis Who's Who publications, including *Who's Who in America* (Reed Reference Publishing, 1992), *Who's Who in the World* (see ARBA 88, entry 36), and *Who's Who of American Women* (see ARBA 93, entry 56). Entries are arranged alphabetically by last name, followed by a reference (or references, if an individual appeared in more than one *Who's Who* volume) to the volume in which complete biographical information is found. This easy-to-use work is a valuable and time-saving reference tool for every library.—**Binh P. Le**

15. Nicholls, C. S., ed. **The Dictionary of National Biography: Missing Persons.** New York, Oxford University Press, 1993. 768p. index. $115.00. DA28.D525. 920.041. LC 92-9744. ISBN 0-19-865211-9.

For biographical sources of persons of the British Isles (and some Commonwealth individuals) from the beginning until 1985, no source has equaled the Dictionary of National Biography (DNB) (see ARBA 91, entry 13). The main set of 63 volumes covered 29,120 persons, and supplements (first 10-year, now 5-year) keep the set up-to-date. Now, because of changing times and differing societal values on what constitutes importance, the publishers of DNB have added 1,086 biographical sketches of people who, for one reason or another, did not get into the original set. These missing persons span the entire time period from the beginning of recorded history to 1985 and include many women, businesspersons, engineers, and scientists. As in the other volumes, each biographical sketch is carefully researched and approximately half a page in length (unless the person is of particular importance). A must purchase for libraries owning the set. [R: Choice, Oct 93, p. 265; RBB, 1 Sept 93, p. 82; WLB, Sept 93, p. 116]

—**David V. Loertscher**

16. Rollyson, Carl. **Biography: An Annotated Bibliography.** Pasadena, Calif., Salem Press, 1992. 215p. index. (Magill Bibliographies). $40.00. Z5301.R57. 016.808'066. LC 92-574. ISBN 0-89356-678-0.

This book surveys and annotates the substantial (and growing) literature on biography in English, including a few book reviews that raise important questions about biography. Chapter 1 covers biographers' comments on biography, including their brief statements made at the beginning of biographies. Chapter 2 annotates historical and critical studies of biography in the tradition of John Dryden, Samuel Johnson, and James Boswell, although the emphasis here is on scholars since the nineteenth century. Chapter 3 focuses on the extensive literature devoted specifically to Johnson and Boswell, and chapter 4 to works by and about Leon Edel, a particularly influential theorist of biography whose use of psychoanalytic principles in writing about Henry James proved especially interesting.

Chapter 5, in turn, is devoted to the "burgeoning" field of psychobiography, including the pioneering works of Sigmund Freud and Erik Erikson. Subsequent chapters take up feminist biography and various innovations in writing biographies, with an entire chapter devoted to Virginia Woolf's fictional biography *Orlando*, along with a small group of other fictional works that focus on biography and the biographer, usually in terms of the relationship between biographer and subject. The book includes a list of biographical subjects and a general index that lists all of the authors annotated in the bibliography. [R: Choice, July/Aug 93, p. 1754]—**Joseph W. Dauben**

17. Snodgrass, Mary Ellen. **Crossing Barriers: People Who Overcame.** Englewood, Colo., Libraries Unlimited, 1993. 248p. index. $32.50. CT120.S588. 920'.009'04. LC 92-39789. ISBN 0-87287-992-5.

This eclectic mix of 38 biographical sketches will appeal to secondary school students for its "examples of admirable courage and determination" in many different people. Individuals span several centuries and reflect a multitude of occupations and ethnicities. Some surprises pop up, such as the inclusion of Nelson Rockefeller (for having dyslexia), the late actor Herve Villechaize (for overcoming height discrimination), and author Gary Paulsen (for battling poverty, alcoholism, and low self-esteem).

All entrants were selected by the author, but each seems to reflect the fact that no obstacle can prevent success. Yet, the title would not lead one to expect biographical sketches of the likes of Marian Anderson, Corazon Aquino, Joan Baez, Johnny Cash, Jack London, Claude Pepper, Renee Richards, Gloria Steinem, and Elie Wiesel in the same source. Each descriptive, in-depth sketch is approximately six to seven pages in length, and an appended bibliography lists sources for further information. No photographs are included. The price of this source, coupled with its unusual mix of popular and lesser-known individuals, will cause librarians to carefully consider its purchase. [R: RBB, 1 Nov 93, p. 561; VOYA, Dec 93, p. 326]—**Ilene F. Rockman**

18. Stamp, Robert M. **The Canadian Obituary Record 1991: A Biographical Dictionary of Canadians....** Toronto, Dundurn Press, 1992. 256p. index. $39.99.

Canada lacks an encyclopedia yearbook, and obituaries are not included in that country's almanacs and current biographical sources. Now in its fourth year, *The Canadian Obituary Record* (COR) offers interpretive biographies, ranging in length from 100 to 800 words, of 500 Canadians "prominent in all fields of endeavor and all parts of the country" who died in 1991. In this volume the short subjects include local politicians, community volunteers, and a small-town doctor who made house calls for 50 years. More widely familiar are Northrop Frye, two church leaders, a provincial premier, a governor general, and the last Father of Confederation. The style is crisp and uncompromising, providing such details as the discovery of marijuana in a politician's suitcase during a royal visit. Each biography concludes with citations to one or more of 70 sources, most newspapers or reference books.

The geographical index, arranged by province and then city (with a second section for other countries), includes places of birth, death, and major work activity. The identification index uses 19 categories, many subdivided (e.g., "Academia" is broken into 26 disciplines). A cumulative nominal index for 1988-1991 concludes the volume. Printed in two-column format with pleasant type and a clearly lettered binding, *The Canadian Obituary Record* fills a need admirably.—**Patricia Fleming**

19. **Who's Who in Canada, 1992: An Illustrated Biographical Record....** 83d ed. Catherine Brown and Kimberley Lund, eds. Agincourt, Ont., Global Press; distr., Bristol, Pa., Taylor & Francis, 1992. 899p. illus. $125.00. ISBN 0-7715-3972-X.

In this biographical dictionary of notable Canadian business, government, professional, and academic individuals, the emphasis is on businesspeople. Each entry contains the standard features for such a dictionary: brief information on education, career history, memberships, honors, publications, and residence. Photographs accompany most entries. The dictionary is organized in alphabetical order, and it also contains an index of entries, a list of abbreviations, and a cross-reference listing by corporation or professional body.

There is some inconsistency in the language of presentation. Some entries are in one language (English or French); some are in both. The language used does not appear to depend on the linguistic background of the individual. This publication is not the best biographical dictionary of Canadians available, but it is useful for the information that it provides on the business community.

—**Lorna K. Rees-Potter**

20. **Who's Who in Italy 1992: A Biographical Encyclopaedia....** 1992 ed. John C. Dove, ed. Bresso/Milano, Italy, Who's Who in Italy; distr., Hauppauge, N.Y., Ballen Booksellers International, 1992. 2v. index. (Sutter's International Red Series). $260.00/set. ISBN 88-85246-16-8.

"Biographical encyclopaedia" describes the 3,293 pages of this set fairly well. Still, there is much more in this publication than is generally included in books of the genre. First of all, there are 11,000 biographical sketches of all manner of prominent living Italians, with all entries attractively laid out and written in a little more lively fashion than one generally encounters in similar volumes. Where the sketches stop, midway through volume 2, a fascinating section begins: 842 pages of Italy-related information that starts with a historical survey (from prehistory to today) and a breakdown of the government structure with the names of all currently relevant politicians and addresses for their offices. The economic section is broken down into several parts, ranging from the aerospace industry to transportation. Cultural life covers institutions of learning, miscellaneous awards, broadcasting, publishing, and more. Social life includes information on associations and trade unions, social security, and sports organizations. The section on religious life provides an overview of the Vatican state and other Italian religious organizations. The entire nonbiographical section is generously interlaced with advertisements, most of them from industrial establishments. The set is handsomely printed and bound in red cloth with gold lettering. Any business organization that frequently deals with Italian clients or organizations will find this work an indispensable aid in day-to-day dealings with their transatlantic counterparts.—**Koraljka Lockhart**

21. **Who's Who in Spain 1992: A Biographical Encyclopedia of Sutter's International Red Series....** 1992 ed. John C. Dove, ed. Barcelona, Who's Who in Spain; distr., Hauppauge, N.Y., Ballen Booksellers International, 1992. 1927p. index. (Who's Who the International Red Series). $230.00. ISBN 88-85246-14-1.

This welcome contribution provides key biographical facts for 7,500 prominent personalities currently residing in Spain and also includes selected foreign nationals who are actively contributing to Spanish life. Alphabetically arranged by last name, the clear and easy-to-read entries generally include title, field, pseudonym (if any), place and date of birth, family details, home and business address, education, career, publications and awards, professional memberships, and recreation. Some entries refer the user to the excellent survey section, which provides background information, including some statistical data, on the economic, cultural, social, and political aspects of Spain. This section, divided into four chapters, includes a sketchy but useful index and provides directory information on major companies by type, museums, libraries, universities, all levels of government, diplomatic representation, chambers of commerce, and much more. The few advertisements found in this latter section are somewhat distracting but do not take away from the outstanding value of this reference work. As Spain continues to enjoy international prominence, purchase of this work is a must for any large public and academic library.

—**Isabel Schon**

22. **Who's Who in the World 1993-1994.** 11th ed. New Providence, N.J., Marquis Who's Who/Reed Reference Publishing, 1992. 1299p. $319.00. LC 79-139215. ISBN 0-8379-1111-7.

In an age of electronic access and budgetary restraint, standing orders to costly yearly editions of biographical dictionaries should be questioned by all acquisitions librarians. Patrons seldom browse these sources. Mainly they are used to build a library's biographical arsenal to satisfy reference inquiries. The information yielded by the "who's who" variety of biographical sources is cursory at best. Unfortunately, the 11th edition of *Who's Who in the World* is no exception. Each biographical sketch simply lists profession, place of birth, parents, marital status, names of children, education, professional qualifications, career highlights, publications, awards and fellowships, religious preference, memberships, avocations, and home and work addresses.

As always, the criteria for inclusion pose a problem. It is stated that an individual's reference value is determined by the level of position or of achievement. Admission to this edition based upon position level is supposed to encompass, for example, heads of state and other key government officials. But just a brief search for biographees within these two categories yields startling inconsistencies. Why, for example, is Senator Edward Kennedy included and not Senator Daniel Patrick Moynihan? Why is Bill Clinton, in an edition called "1993-1994," still described as governor of Arkansas? The second standard for admission, individual achievement, is also inconsistently applied. John McEnroe, who has not won a major tennis title in several years, is included while Pete Sampras, recent winner of the U.S. Open and ranked number one in the world, has been omitted. Boris Becker, multiple winner at Wimbledon, is also absent. The lack of quality review as a requirement for each biographee's inclusion in forthcoming editions substantially weakens the value of this type of reference. So does capriciousness in selecting entrants. Libraries would be more likely to purchase these biographical sources if they could rely, for example, upon the inclusion of all heads of state or all high-ranking military officers rather than the often puzzling selections that are represented.

The availability of online bibliographical databases, Internet, and multitype library networks, coupled with the frequency of biographical reference questions by patrons, should be the determining factors in acquiring this expensive resource. If the former are easily attainable and the need for biographical information is infrequent, purchase this edition as a supplementary item. Only large public and academic libraries should give it further consideration.—**Kathleen W. Craver**

United States

23. Who Was Who in America with World Notables. Index 1993: Volumes I-X and Historical Volume. New Providence, N.J., Marquis Who's Who/Reed Reference Publishing, 1993. 283p. $42.50. LC 81-84493. ISBN 0-8379-0221-5.

Indexing 122,000 deceased biographees, this new cumulative index to *Who Was Who in America* (Reed Reference Publishing, 1993) contains 10,000 more names than the one published in 1985 (see ARBA 87, entry 35). This book continues to index deceased persons who formerly appeared in *Who's Who in America* (Reed Reference Publishing, 1993) as well as the regional works. In addition, deceased biographees in the subject who's whos, such as *Who's Who in Finance and Industry* (see ARBA 93, entry 179), are also included. The introduction states that the death date and burial site have been added to the biographical sketch in *Who Was Who in America*, but the place of interment is often missing.

Each biographee is listed in the index by surname, followed by the volume number of *Who Was Who in America* in which the person's biography can be found. An asterisk indicates that more than one person with that name can be found in the volume. When the historical volume (1607-1896) contains the biography, the letter *H* follows the name. Parentheses around a portion of a name identifies the part of the name that tends to be omitted in regular usage. For example, "Taylor, C(larence) J(ohn)" indicates that the full names "Clarence John" generally are not used. Libraries that own the complete set of *Who Was Who in America* will find this useful new cumulative index worth the price.—**O. Gene Norman**

24. Who's Who in America 1992-1993. 47th ed. New Providence, N.J., Marquis Who's Who/Reed Reference Publishing, 1992. 2v. $399.00/set. LC 4-16934. ISBN 0-8379-0147-2.

Within six years of its 100th anniversary, *Who's Who in America* remains the standard biographical directory. Its two volumes contain 80,500 biographees; the first edition contained 8,602. As is stated in the preface and in the invitation packet, neither the desire to appear nor wealth nor social position is the criterion for inclusion. The vast majority of biographies were submitted by the individuals themselves; a few (often those on celebrities) were compiled by Marquis staff members, as denoted by asterisks. Typical information consists of the person's name, occupation, place and date of birth, parents, spouse and children, education, accomplishments, memberships, and address (usually office). Other information may include religion and political affiliation. Some entries also have a few lines that "reflect those principles, goals, ideals, and values" that have led to the person's success. A few cross-references in the text (e.g., from Randall James Hamilton Zwinge to James Randi) lead users to biographees' preferred names, and there are indexes to retirees, to deceased individuals, and to individuals in the regional and topical spin-off *Who's Who* directories.

Who's Who in America is a classic reference to current, prominent individuals. All academic and large public libraries should have it. Smaller and specialized libraries may prefer the regional or topical volumes.—**D. A. Rothschild**

25. Who's Who in the East 1993-1994. 24th ed. New Providence, N.J., Marquis Who's Who/Reed Reference Publishing, 1993. 1040p. $259.00. LC 43-18522. ISBN 0-8379-0624-5.

This directory offers biographical sketches of distinguished people whose influence is concentrated in the eastern United States (Maine to Washington, D.C.) and eastern Canada. This edition contains approximately 26,750 names of persons in a wide range of fields. Admission to the volume is based on the extent of the person's reference interest, judged on either the position of responsibility held or the level of achievement attained by the individual. For most sketches, information is provided by the biographees; for some, the publisher's staff compiled the data. Entries are short but highlight 19 data points, including information on personal, education, and professional factors. A random check of a few persons fitting the admission criteria confirmed the work's broad coverage of positions, except for the omission of the president of the flagship public university in one of the states covered.

Each edition of this regional directory expands the coverage of the previous year; this edition contains 1,250 more names than its immediate predecessor. The entry format and the alphabetical arrangement have remained constant since the first edition; the present layout has been retained since the early 1970s. There is some overlap between this volume and *Who's Who in America* (Reed Reference Publishing, 1993).

The key advantage of using this directory is the convenience of a single-volume list of notable people in one geographical region across disciplines. Other sources offer access to persons from a geographical region by special index listings, but no other print directory makes geographical orientation integral to the volume and has coverage across disciplines. Access to this biographical data can also be achieved through searching the Dialog file of *Who's Who in America*; the electronic alternative may be of greater value than the print to libraries where there is infrequent need for this data. However, in most eastern larger academic and public libraries, the print format could be used more often.—**Danuta A. Nitecki**

26. **Who's Who in the South and Southwest.** 23d ed. New Providence, N.J., Marquis Who's Who/Reed Reference Publishing, 1993. 920p. $210.00. LC 50-58231. ISBN 0-8379-0823-X.

Some 23,500 persons from virtually every important field of endeavor are represented in this work. Geographic coverage is no less broad, comprising southern states from the East Coast to Texas. Unexpectedly, people from Puerto Rico, the Virgin Islands, and Mexico are also included.

Checking the entry for H. Ross Perot to determine currency, one finds the added line "Independent candidate for President of the U.S., 1992." However, the ex-mayor of Houston, Kathryn Jean Whitmire, who appeared in the 22d edition, is not listed in this one. She is still a notable person; her accomplishments and awards have been many, and when she lost the election, she became a professor of political science at Rice University. The same thing happened to Henry G. Cisneros, former mayor of San Antonio—he was in the 22d edition but has been omitted from this one. His situation is different from Whitmire's in that he is now Secretary of Housing and Urban Development in the Clinton cabinet. Reference librarians are familiar with this problem and know to look in other editions for information. Still, there should be some continuity as long as the person is alive. Such omissions are glaring and should be rectified by the editorial staff. Recommended with these caveats.—**Bill Bailey**

27. **Who's Who of Emerging Leaders in America 1993-1994.** 4th ed. New Providence, N.J., Marquis Who's Who/Reed Reference Publishing, 1993. 758p. $229.00. LC 86-63225. ISBN 0-8379-7203-5.

Marquis Who's Who has produced some excellent reference volumes that are worthy of shelf space in both municipal and research libraries. Unfortunately, this work is not among those volumes. This edition of *Who's Who of Emerging Leaders in America* provides up to 19 pieces of information on approximately 20,500 individuals who, according to the editors, "warrant entry into this valuable reference source" (p. vi). The biographical data provided on each listee is similar to the information supplied in other Marquis Who's Who directories. Each entry, for instance, includes vital statistics, education, career history, awards and publications, and address. The information was obtained from the biographees.

The limitation of this particular volume is in the selections of the listees. Although the editors insist individuals "became eligible for listing because their positions and/or noteworthy accomplishments proved to be of significant value to society, and, thus, rendered them reference-worthy" (p. vi), an inspection of the selectees arouses suspicion. Nearly 90 percent of those included have surnames beginning with the first 13 letters of the alphabet, while the N-Z listees warranted only about 10 percent of the space in the volume. No explanation is given for this apparent discrepancy in coverage. Unless a library wishes to specialize in reference materials that cover only the first half of the alphabet, it would be prudent to save the cost of this volume and wait for the next edition, which one hopes will be more complete in its coverage.—**Terry D. Bilhartz**

CATALOGS AND COLLECTIONS

28. **A Guide to the Manuscript Collections in the Rare Book and Manuscript Library of Columbia University.** New York, G. K. Hall, 1992. 512p. index. $150.00. ISBN 0-8161-0516-2.

The Rare Book and Manuscript Library of Columbia University, located in the Butler Library, contains more than 25 million items in approximately 2,200 separate and distinct collections. Except for the 900 collections in the Bakhmeteff Archive, which were described in a separate catalog in 1987, this guide includes entries for all the manuscript and archival holdings of this major research repository. The strengths of the collections are in literature, history, economics, publishing, journalism, performing arts, politics and diplomacy, applied science and mathematics, social work, library science, and other subjects in the humanities and social sciences.

A valuable feature of the guide is Kenneth A. Lohf's introduction, which provides a history of the manuscript collection and a summary of its contents. The main entries are usually personal or corporate names arranged alphabetically. Each entry includes collection name; birth and death dates (when the main entry is an individual); size of the collection and dates covered; arrangement of the collection; restrictions on access, if any; a biographical or historical note on the primary individual or institution; a summary of the contents of the collection; and a provenance note. The summary section provides a detailed description of the collection, including the type of documents in the collection, subjects covered, and selected names of correspondents or authors found in the file. From the information included in this summary, an index of names and subjects has been created that gives access to the entire contents of the guide.

—**Dean H. Keller**

29. Randall, Lilian M. C., with Christopher Clarkson and Jeanne Krochalis. **Medieval and Renaissance Manuscripts in the Walters Art Gallery. Volume II: France, 1420-1540.** Baltimore, Md., Johns Hopkins University Press, 1992. 2pts. illus. index. $135.95/set. ND2920.W36. 745.6'7'0940747526. LC 88-45410. ISBN 0-8018-2870-8.

This is the second of four projected volumes to cover the medieval and renaissance manuscript collection of the Walters Art Gallery in Baltimore, Maryland. Volume 1 covers manuscripts from 875 to 1420, and this second volume brings the survey through 1540. Volume 3 will cover manuscripts from the rest of Northern Europe, and volume 4 will deal with manuscripts from Spain and Italy.

Volume 2 contains descriptions of 213 French manuscripts in the Gallery. The work includes a list of manuscripts and illustrations, two concordances relating the numbers of this catalog to standard manuscript catalogs, and a brief description of the format of the catalog entries. An appendix provides a survey of French manuscripts from 1540 to 1910. There are a complete list of bibliographical abbreviations and three indexes: a general index, an iconographic index, and an index of incipits.

The catalog describes 113 manuscripts in chronological order. Each entry is divided into six parts: text, decoration, textblock, binding, history, and bibliography. There are clearly marked and excellent editorial comments throughout, numerous color plates, and at least one black-and-white illustration for each manuscript. Unfortunately, the illustrations are not printed with the descriptions. Except for the frontispiece, all the illustrations follow the text of the catalog in part 2.

This specialized, scholarly catalog is a model of the bibliographer-scholar's craft. It is hard to imagine a clearer or more thorough description of both illustration and text. Scholars will be well served by the library that purchases these volumes.—**Richard H. Swain**

30. Shailor, Barbara A. **Catalogue of Medieval and Renaissance Manuscripts in the Beinecke Rare Book and Manuscript Library, Yale University. Volume III: Marston Manuscripts.** Binghamton, N.Y., Medieval & Renaissance Texts & Studies, State University of New York, 1992. 643p. illus. index. (Medieval & Renaissance Texts & Studies, v.100). $50.00. Z6621.B4213. 011'.31. LC 84-667. ISBN 0-86698-115-2.

This is the third and final volume of a catalog of early manuscripts in the general and Marston collections of the Beinecke Library. Yale alumnus Thomas E. Marston (1904-1984) had amassed a collection of nearly 300 early manuscripts (as well as many early printed books and other items). He dispersed some of his manuscripts by sale and donation in his later years, but in 1962, shortly before the opening of the Beinecke, he sold 230 of them to Yale. These 230 manuscripts, preserved as a separate deposit in the Beinecke, are thoroughly described in this volume. Their contents and European provenances range widely, but they are especially rich in texts by or of interest to Italian humanists in the fourteenth and fifteenth centuries.

As did the first two volumes (see ARBA 86, entry 503 and ARBA 89, entry 483), this one meets the highest standards of bibliographical, paleographic, and codicological analysis and presentation. The entire catalog is a splendid complement to the sumptuous collections it describes. Its breadth and generous indexing make it a valuable reference tool even for medieval and Renaissance scholars who have little interest in the particular manuscripts in the Beinecke. It is also a convenient model of the superior modern standards that, from now on, catalogers of early manuscripts must either meet or conspicuously fall short of. Editor/publisher Mario DiCesare and his staff at Medieval & Renaissance Texts & Studies deserve praise for their service to learning. All good libraries serving scholars in the humanities should have this catalog.—**Carl T. Berkhout**

31. Walsh, James E. **A Catalogue of the Fifteenth-Century Printed Books in the Harvard University Library. Volume II: Books Printed in Rome and Venice.** Binghamton, N.Y., Medieval & Renaissance Texts & Studies, State University of New York, 1993. 672p. index. (Medieval & Renaissance Texts & Studies, v.97). $50.00. Z240.H37. 015.744'4042. LC 90-6658. ISBN 0-86698-111-X.

This volume describes 1,479 books printed in Rome and Venice during the incunabula period. The first volume of the work (see ARBA 92, entry 36) described books printed in Germany, German-speaking Switzerland, and Austria-Hungary; the format and features established in that book are maintained in this one. The books printed in Rome are described first and listed chronologically under the name of each printer. Entries include author, title, date, size (number of leaves and measurement of the leaf), information about editorial matters, illustrations, binding, citations to appropriate bibliographies and catalogs, and provenance. Transcriptions of the incipit and explicit are provided only if no satisfactory description of the book is found in a standard catalog of incunabula.

References—additional to those given in volume 1—are given at the beginning of the book, and there are indexes by author and title; editors, translators and secondary works, printers, and places; provenance; incunabula containing manuscripts; and incunabula with identified bindings. There are also concordances to various related catalogs. The volume ends with 16 plates illustrative of books described in the catalog.—**Dean H. Keller**

DICTIONARIES AND ENCYCLOPEDIAS

32. **Barron's New Student's Concise Encyclopedia.** 2d ed. Compiled by the editors of Barron's Educational Series, Inc. Hauppauge, N.Y., Barron's Educational Series, 1993. 1v. (various paging). illus. maps. index. $29.95. AG6.B37. 031. LC 93-1066. ISBN 0-8120-6329-5.

This encyclopedia is arranged in 24 subject areas beginning with art and ending with a country-by-country survey of the world with detailed black-and-white and color maps. The book contains short definitions, tables, charts, and many illustrations. The most comprehensive sections are those on the history of the United States and the history of the world. Each section comprises about 135 pages. The topics of chemistry and mathematics are two of the longer sections; the shortest sections are on mythology and religion. The language arts chapter is especially useful, with its four pages on making a speech and seven pages on writing with clarity. The same chapter included helpful sections on words and phrases frequently misused and commonly misspelled words. The currency of this encyclopedia is demonstrated by several references to events in 1993. A 50-page index provides sections and page numbers for the references. This excellent, reasonably priced work is recommended for school, public, and undergraduate libraries as well as for seekers of general information.—**Karen Y. Stabler**

33. **The Cambridge Encyclopedia.** David Crystal, ed. New York, Cambridge University Press, c1990, 1992. 1334p. illus. maps. index. $49.95. AG5.C26. 031. ISBN 0-521-39528-3.

If one cannot afford the *New Encyclopaedia Britannica* (see ARBA 92, entry 41) and would like more material than can be found in a compact desk encyclopedia, this volume would be a good substitute. First published in 1990, it is now in its second update. Entries number 25,000, with an additional 7,000 crammed into a wonderful section in the back of the book called "Ready Reference." In its 128 bright yellow pages, one can find such items as automobile country codes for the whole world, solar and lunar eclipses for 1991-2000, conversion tables from Fahrenheit to Celsius and vice versa, international clothing care symbols, the table of elements, international direct dialing codes, aircraft and airline codes, and maps of the near and far side of the moon. The main body of the book is extremely well researched, and it is hard to find omissions. There are, of course, a few: Soprano Elisabeth Schwarzkopf is listed, but general Norman Schwarzkopf is not; one can find a megabyte, but not a gigabyte; and Gaetano Donizetti appears but not Vincenzo Bellini. Between the main body of the book and the back section is a segment devoted to glossy four-color plates that depict such items as the ozone hole over Antarctica, various crystals, principles of color reproduction, and fractal geometry.

Due to the volume's British provenance, United Kingdom entries are prevalent, in spite of the editor's aim to be truly international. Recent political and geographic changes in the world's map have been dealt with as well as can be expected, and—as of right now—the encyclopedia is up-to-date. This book would be perfect for a student or scholar in need of quick reference; it is irresistible for a trivia buff.—**Koraljka Lockhart**

34. **Compton's Encyclopedia & Fact-Index.** Chicago, Compton's Learning Company/Encyclopaedia Britannica, 1993. 26v. illus. maps. index. $699.00/set (individuals); $499.00/set (schools and institutions). LC 91-75908. ISBN 0-85229-572-3.

The ongoing purpose of *Compton's*, first published as an eight-volume work in 1922, is to serve as a family reference for students ranging from elementary to high school. To that end, articles are written in pyramid style (with easier or more essential information at the beginning) and are generally clear. Most articles are unsigned, although credit is given in certain cases. The list of contributors is impressive, but one is unsure of the contributors' actual input.

Previous editions of *Compton's* have been reviewed in ARBA several times (see ARBA 90, entry 53; ARBA 87, entry 53; and ARBA 82, entry 49). These reviews have described the various features of *Compton's*, including a major revision of the set that began in the early 1980s. This edition contains 34,278 articles in the main text and 28,996 concise articles in the *Fact-Index*. New biographies in *Compton's* include new U.S. governors, Nobel prize winners, and members of the football and baseball halls of fame. Articles on Ukraine and other former Soviet Union republics have been revised and retitled with the country name. Peking, China, has been updated and retitled Beijing, China. The *Fact-Index* contains approximately 68,250 entries and 209 tables. There are more than 16,200 cross-references in the main text and more than 114,000 references in the *Fact-Index*. About 536 articles in the encyclopedia have been rewritten or revised, and some 320 articles in the *Fact-Index* have been updated or expanded.

Among new or expanded features are more than 140 new photographs and drawings. *Compton's* was the first major encyclopedia to use photographs and illustrations integrated with their intended subjects. Its use of a high-quality layout, good typography, and clear black-and-white and color illustrations continue to be major assets of the set. The illustrations occupy approximately 30 percent of the space. Although *World Book Encyclopedia* (see ARBA 93, entry 64) contains more illustrations, *Compton's* are of better quality. The new and revised four-color maps are excellent and easy to use. The international boundaries through December 1992 are accurate on all maps. (This includes new countries of the former Soviet Union.)

One of the major criticisms of *Compton's* has been its coverage of controversial or sensitive subjects. This edition is no different. In the entries on AIDS and abortion, both are a little more informative than the ones previously included, but the language and information are somewhat controlled (the article on abortion still maintains a matter-of-fact, neutral tone). Articles on certain topics, such as Croatia, follow the same format: A sanitized history is given, but the horrors of the war taking place there are not elucidated.

Although there is constant change in the area of high technology and it would be impossible to be totally current, the article on computers is dated—one area where constant revision is essential. Although there are bibliographies after many articles, the list is usually short, and titles are mostly from the 1980s, with only one or two from the 1990s. Generally, bibliographies are only included for subjects of a historical nature.

In the past, *Compton's* has been favorably compared with *World Book Encyclopedia* and *Merit Students Encyclopedia* (no longer published). Its competition remains *World Book*. Each encyclopedia has outstanding features and would be good as a home set, and both are necessary for elementary and middle school classroom and libraries. *Compton's Encyclopedia and Fact-Index* is also available in nine different electronic versions under various titles. [Editor's note: Since the publication of this edition, *Compton's* has been sold to the Chicago Tribune.] [R: RBB, 15 Sept 93, pp. 176-78]—**Anna Grace Patterson**

35. Dilbert, Sheila, ed. **Subject Index to Feature Articles and Special Reports in Encyclopedia Yearbooks 1975-1991.** Hewlett, N.Y., Infodatafacts, 1992. 83p. $15.00pa. ISBN 0-9625739-0-6.

At first glance this subject index appears to fill a void in reference collections. The annual yearbooks issued by an encyclopedia are not cumulatively indexed, and Dilbert's work, covering 12 separate titles published from 1975 to 1991, provides bibliographical control over material that would otherwise remain difficult to find. Her subject headings are based on those suggested in the 14th edition of *Sears List of Subject Headings*.

A reading of the entries in the index, however, shows that students and researchers would have little use for much of this information, even if a library has most of the yearbooks covered. A student looking for articles on computer crime would most certainly prefer searching through a current issue of the *Readers' Guide to Periodical Literature* (see ARBA 92, entry 60) rather than consult the 1975 *Encyclopedia Science Supplement*. It is hard to imagine that anyone interested in the laws and legislation of firearms would rely on the 1982 *Collier's Year Book*. Kenneth F. Kister succinctly sums up the problem of encyclopedia yearbooks on page 8 of his *Best Encyclopedias*, 4th ed. (see ARBA 87, entry 54): "Although some are excellent, yearbooks (or annual supplements) are usually expensive, only indirectly relate to the encyclopedia, and are often never used."

Although Dilbert's index represents a reference work that heretofore has never been published, it is probably safe to assume that there is little need for such a book. Moreover, the stapled, paper binding would not hold up to even a modicum of handling.—**Jack Bales**

36. Kiger, Joseph C., ed. **International Encyclopedia of Learned Societies and Academies.** Westport, Conn., Greenwood Press, 1993. 377p. index. $95.00. AS8.I637. 060'.3. LC 92-35598. ISBN 0-313-27646-3.

One expects a book with the words "International Encyclopedia of" in its title to treat its subject matter comprehensively, or at least approach comprehensiveness. This volume, however, covers only the most significant national learned societies and academies currently in operation worldwide and located outside the United States. The criteria for "most significant" are many, including honorific membership, significant research and publications, adequate budget, and renown of officers and members. Some 103 organizations in 50 countries met those criteria. A supplementary chapter briefly deals with three international societies and five regional associations. Three appendixes provide a chronological list of the organizations, their genealogies, and a listing by general areas of interest. A selective index and a list of the 58 contributors conclude the volume.

As one might expect, individual treatments vary widely—not in style (for which Kiger should be commended) but in thoroughness and details. Some of that variation derives from the disparity in the organizations' importances and ages (e.g., the Royal Society of London and the Afghanistan Academy of Sciences), but much of it seems idiosyncratic. Some profiles, for example, contain extensive listings of societies' publications; others contain none. Some have lengthy bibliographies of secondary works; others, none. One could also question the omission of a few important organizations (e.g., the Schweizerische Naturforschende Gesellschaft). But the fundamental question is: Who needs the work? *The World of Learning* (Gale, 1993) contains the basic information about such organizations (and many more, of course) that most library patrons would want. And for historians, there is not enough detail here for most of their needs. [R: Choice, Dec 93, pp. 586-87]—**Evan Ira Farber**

37. **The Kingfisher Children's Encyclopedia.** John Paton, ed. New York, Chambers Kingfisher Graham, 1992. 780p. illus. maps. index. $29.95. AG5.D74. 031. LC 92-4785. ISBN 1-85697-800-1.

This attractively designed encyclopedia contains 50,000 words and 2,000 color illustrations (photographs, drawings, charts, and maps). It is geared toward elementary- and intermediate-age children. Some 16 subject symbols (e.g., history, science) help youngsters see relationships between the 1,300 entries. In addition, generous sidebars (e.g., using red cabbage to conduct an acid rain experiment) help to illuminate the text and make learning relevant and fun. Most entries are two to three inches in length; some are given more space. Such contemporary topics as AIDS, telecommunications, and women's rights are included. Terms are arranged in one alphabetical sequence; general words are integrated with biographical and geographical names. *See* references are provided in both the text and the index. There is also a subject index. However, unlike a dictionary, there is no phonetic pronunciation key.

Because the work was completed in late 1992, the entry on Yugoslavia is not current. In addition, there are no entries for such contemporary phenomena as credit cards and recycling. Yet, given the scope and price, this work is useful for both home and school libraries. It should appeal to children, parents, and teachers for its solid content and ease of use. [R: SLJ, Feb 93, p. 123]—**Ilene F. Rockman**

38. **Purchasing an Encyclopedia: 12 Points to Consider.** 4th ed. Chicago, American Library Association, 1992. 45p. $7.00pa. AE1.A48. 031. ISBN 0-8389-5754-4.

This guide describes criteria to use when deciding on the purchase of a multivolume, general encyclopedia. It presents 12 points to consider, such as how easy it is to locate information, how well subjects relate to the intended audience, and whether articles contain racial and sexual biases. In addition, there are practical tips one can use when applying the criteria, such as checking for accuracy by looking up a familiar subject and checking for currency by looking at the year on which statistics are based or if newly formed countries are included. There are reviews for nine multivolume encyclopedias; they were reprinted from the September 15, 1992, issue of *Booklist/Reference Books Bulletin*. The guide also lists toll-free customer service numbers for the four main encyclopedia companies.

Considering that encyclopedias are available in print, online, and on CD-ROM through a variety of outlets—mail order, supermarkets, direct sales, and the like—this information should make for a better-informed buying public. While other, more comprehensive guides are available, the brevity and ease of use of this guide will appeal to many. Highly recommended for all public libraries. [R: SLMQ, Summer 93, p. 264]—**Byron P. Anderson**

39. Rowland-Entwistle, Theodore, and Jean Cooke, comps. **Factfinder.** New York, Chambers Kingfisher Graham, 1992. 278p. illus. maps. index. $12.95pa. AG5.F29. 031. LC 92-53118. ISBN 1-85697-803-6.

Similar to an almanac or one-volume encyclopedia, but not as accessible or well organized for information retrieval, this work appears to be aimed at grades three through five. However, older students reading at a lower grade level might also find it of interest. It is more of a browsing book than it is a tool for finding specific facts because the table of contents and the index lack detail and specificity.

Information is arranged into 13 broad areas of knowledge such as the universe, a world atlas, countries of the world, animals, science, and sports. Most articles lack depth as they are overviews of the topics covered. Some sections, such as that on countries of the world, could be called superficial because their detail is so sparse. The maps are too small to provide useful detail; for example, the U.S. map lacks boundaries for the 50 states.

The work's greatest strength lies in its numerous colorful pictures, charts, and diagrams, many of which are not normally found in an almanac. For example, there are a chronology of the history of printing, a table listing animal speed records, and an illustrated chart of the various types of clouds. The only drawback is that most of these wonderful charts and diagrams cannot be precisely identified or easily found through the index. One country, Russia, was not listed in the index at all, not even as a cross-reference to "U.S.S.R., former," where it was actually found, and this might prove problematic for youngsters who are struggling to learn the use of reference tools.

Given the strengths and weaknesses discussed, this work should be considered as a recommended supplementary purchase for schools and public library children's collections that already have the basic almanacs and one-volume encyclopedias. The educational enjoyment that students could get out of leafing through this colorful, attractive book is well worth its reasonable price. [R: RBB, Aug 93, p. 2088; SLJ, May 93, p. 139]—**Carol Truett**

40. **Running Press Cyclopedia: The Portable, Visual Encyclopedia.** Philadelphia, Running Press, 1993. 638p. illus. maps. index. $8.95pa. LC 93-085694. ISBN 1-56138-343-0.

This pocket-sized volume claims to contain more than 20,000 facts and 800 illustrations within its 6 major sections: the world, countries of the world, history, science, the arts, and the United States. Many of its simplified tables, charts, diagrams, and maps are well done and cover a truly broad spectrum of topics, from anatomy to world history. The outline-form table of contents is quite good and detailed enough to provide access to the work's major information. Thus, for tabular or diagrammatic types of quick information, especially for individuals, the book appears to be useful.

However, the work is not without drawbacks. The index has major shortcomings because it lacks specific entries. Another concern is accuracy of data; no sources are given for any of the information. The inclusion of Washington, D.C., as the smallest state is surprising, given that it is not a state. The illustrations would have been greatly enhanced with a few more colors, being limited to black, white, red, pink, and gray. This results in the U.S. flag being shown as red, white, and black (although mention is made that the black is supposed to be blue). Coverage of some areas, such as computers, is superficial. Also, the accuracy of some facts is questionable. For example, the storage capacity of hard disks today greatly exceeds the 80-megabyte maximum given in the computer section. Terminology occasionally seems dated; few young people would use *spectacles* for the more contemporary *eyeglasses* or *glasses*.

If one wants this work mainly for its broad scope, illustrations, and size, it is recommended. However, if one needs a greater depth of indexing and information, consider the standard almanacs first.—**Carol Truett**

41. Watson, Carol. **My First Encyclopedia.** New York, Dorling Kindersley, 1993. 77p. illus. maps. index. $16.95. AG5.W337. 031. LC 92-53477. ISBN 1-56458-214-0. [Also available in Canada as *My First Book of Facts: A Picture Book of Discovery for the Very Young*. Richmond Hill, Ont., Scholastic Canada, 1993. $18.95. ISBN 0-590-74341-4.]

Designed for preschools and beginning readers, this British import seeks to bridge the gap from simple word-picture identification books, such as those done by Richard Scarry, to a more encyclopedia-like format. Divided into 32 double-page, highly illustrated topics, the pages are similar to other Dorling Kindersley publications, containing excellent full-color photographs interspersed with bits of text. For a double-page spread on the human body, a parent can read to the child a sentence about skin, skeleton, speech, hearing, sight, or other aspect of the body in addition to showing a nice diagram of internal organs.

The publishers have stressed a multicultural frame of reference, which is a strength, but the British emphasis shows up in pictures that will be unfamiliar to U.S. children, such as European models of town halls or city centers. This shows through even more in some definitions. For example, the book says, "Librarians buy and sort the books in a library. They make sure that all the books are in the right place so that we can find them easily"—exactly the stereotype U.S. librarians want to avoid. Until the publisher becomes more adept at adapting its works to the U.S. market, this book, while fun to look at, is not recommended for library purchase. [R: RBB, July 93, pp. 2003-04; SLJ, July 93, p. 83]

—**David V. Loertscher**

42. **Webster's New World Encyclopedia.** college ed. Stephen P. Elliott, Martha Goldstein, and Michael Upshall, eds. New York, Prentice Hall General Reference, 1993. 1156p. illus. maps. $35.00. AG5.W386. 031. LC 93-387. ISBN 0-671-85016-4.

43. **Webster's New World Encyclopedia.** pocket ed. New York, Prentice Hall General Reference, 1993. 913p. $14.00pa. AG5.W388. 031. LC 93-388. ISBN 0-671-85035-0.

The college edition of *Webster's New World Encyclopedia* is a wonderful addition to the category of single-volume encyclopedias. Containing more than 20,000 entries and 500 black-and-white illustrations, it provides concise and up-to-date coverage at a reasonable price. Arranged alphabetically with exceptional cross-referencing, this book is straightforward and easy to use. It makes excellent use of tables to provide information on countries and the order of historical events. Unfortunately, there is a lack of suitable maps, and no color maps are found. In comparing this encyclopedia to other one-volume selections, the *Concise Columbia Encyclopedia* (see ARBA 90, entry 49) was found to most closely approximate it. *Columbia* is much more extensive, with 50,000 entries, but in terms of value, *Webster's* is a great bargain. Every library should be able to afford a copy.

The pocket edition is a good addition to a personal library but not to a collection in an academic or public library. The number of entries is reduced to 15,000, and no illustrations or maps appear. The articles, most of which are less than 50 words, only skim the essentials on a subject. [R: JAL, Nov 93, p. 347; SLJ, Nov 93, p. 147; WLB, Nov 93, p. 106]—**Carl Pracht**

DIRECTORIES

44. **Books & Periodicals Online.** Nuchine Nobari, ed. New York, Library Alliance, 1992. 1619p. index. $249.00pa. ISBN 0-9630277-1-9. ISSN 0951-838X.

This is a greatly expanded and improved international directory of computerized databases and publications available from producers, networks, or other online services. Expanded by incorporating earlier editions of the *Directory of Periodicals Online*, this catalog has doubled in size and now lists more than 43,000 publications in 1,800 databases, or 84,640 entries. It has been improved by an easier-to-use arrangement of titles and an updated listing of coverage and publishers' names and addresses. The coverage of databases is very comprehensive and has been further enhanced by the inclusion of several nonbibliographical databases, such as reference books and news wires.

The names of databases are listed alphabetically and can be grouped into four categories: bibliographical, fulltext, numeric, and referral. Each entry lists the title of publication, country of origin, former or continuing names, publisher, reference numbers, databases in which the publication is included and which of those are available in CD-ROM, a list of vendors for each database, and the scope of editorial coverage. Because the directory is indexed by titles of publications, publishers' names, vendors' names, databases, and titles available on CD-ROM, it can be accessed by a variety of users.

The obvious advantage of having a comprehensive guide to electronic information lies with reducing search time, storage, and other costs. By making such a vast and expanding body of information more accessible, this directory will benefit researchers and libraries alike. Users can learn which databases offer what information before retrieving it, and libraries can more efficiently allocate scarce physical and financial resources. [R: JAL, Sept 93, p. 274]—**Timothy E. Sullivan**

45. Coleman, Edwin J., and Ronald A. Morse. **Data: Where It Is and How to Get It. The 1993 Directory of Business, Environment, and Energy Data Sources.** Arnold, Md., Coleman/Morse Associates; distr., Upland, Pa., DIANE Publishing, 1992. 257p. index. $24.95pa. ISBN 0-941375-56-0.

This directory is a guide to agencies, sources, and people that can be used as resources when searching for information in such areas as business and industry, land or water use, employment figures, foreign trade, and fossil fuels. The first part of the directory introduces the user to government agencies responsible for producing data, commercial data services, data publications, and economic and statistical jargon. The second part, which is the strength of the book, identifies more than 2,500 experts in 64 specific agencies or organizations and their telephone numbers. These people can be called for answers to specific questions on, for example, ethnic population data, emissions and compliance data, state sales of gasoline, and crop commodity programs and policies. (The directory optimistically suggests that if the experts identified cannot help, "they can surely direct you to someone who can.") Additionally, state and regional data centers are listed, and there is a subject index. Overall, this work is potentially useful to economists, businesspeople, reference librarians, information consultants, and other interested parties. Recommended for larger libraries. [R: Choice, Nov 93, p. 426; RBB, 15 Dec 93, p. 775]—**Byron P. Anderson**

46. **Directories in Print 1993: An Annotated Guide to Over 14,000 Directories Published Worldwide....** 10th ed. Charles B. Montney and Pamela Dundas, eds. Detroit, Gale, 1992. 2v. index. $270.00/set. LC 90-32021. ISBN 0-8103-7627-X. ISSN 0899-353X.

Directories in Print provides access to more than 14,000 directories worldwide in all subject areas. This edition adds some 970 new entries, including directories related to the former Soviet republics and many previously unavailable from Soviet bloc countries in Eastern Europe. Current issues in health, ecology, and international trade have also expanded the work. The two volumes provide a complete descriptive listing of each entry and indexes to this primary file by alternative formats (those other than print), subjects, and titles and keywords. To be included, a directory must contain a list of names and addresses, cover a wide geographical area, and have directory listings as its primary contents. Special issues of nondirectory publications that contain directory listings or have as their main purpose such listings are included as well. Both volumes have user's guides and lists of abbreviations and symbols.

Each annotated entry gives up to 27 pieces of information about the directory. The entries are arranged in 26 subject categories, ranging from general business, manufacturing industries, and commercial services through library and information sciences, telecommunications and computer science, and medicine. Each entry provides title, publisher, address, and telephone number. The annotations give information about the directory's size and scope, language, entries, arrangement, indexes, frequency, price, and availability in the United States. The subject index in volume 2 includes parenthetical information on the directory's subject where necessary, such as *Deutsche Telegramm-Addressbuch* (Cable addresses of West German companies). This work is highly recommended for academic and large public libraries as well as special libraries in marketing and business.—**Edward P. Miller**

47. **Directory of National Helplines: A Guide to Toll-Free Public Service Numbers, 1993.** Ann Arbor, Mich., Pierian Press, 1993. 96p. $8.00pa. ISBN 0-87650-326-1.

This small publication has a large and varied amount of useful information. Its purpose is to provide assistance to persons in need of support and advice. One of its strengths is that it is well organized and easy to read. It is cross-referenced with descriptions at the beginning and indexed by name at the end. The description of each helpline includes hours of availability, information offered, and presence of bilingual operators.

Although small, this publication is well worth its cost. It covers a wide array of interest areas and would be useful to libraries, counselors, advisers, researchers, and administrators.—**Lorene S. Farris**

48. **Encyclopedia of Associations International Organizations 1993: A Guide to Over 2,000 International Nonprofit Membership Organizations....** 27th ed. Linda Irvin and Jacqueline K. Barrett, eds. Detroit, Gale, 1993. 2pts. index. $455.00/set. LC 76-46129. ISBN 0-8103-7673-3.

This title originally appeared as volume 4 of the highly regarded *Encyclopedia of Associations* (see ARBA 91, entries 37-38) series. In 1989 it began appearing separately without significantly changing its name or purpose. *International Organizations* supplements the parent volumes by providing information on more than 12,000 primarily nonprofit organizations that are international in scope, membership, or interest. Also included are multinational and binational groups and national organizations headquartered outside the United States. This edition adds 900 organizations, with more than 45 percent located in Asian and Pacific countries, and provides increased coverage of European business associations.

User appeal is broad, with coverage of international organizations, agencies, and groups in such far-ranging fields as business, government, law, education, technology, culture, health, medicine, hereditary interests, patriotic, hobby, sports, and labor. Format and kinds of data remain the same as in other volumes in the series. The contents are grouped into 15 broad subject categories. Data is well organized and easy to find through the table of contents and the name, keyword, executive, and geographic indexes. Highly recommended for college, university, public, and other libraries and institutions with a need for information about international organizations.—**Donald E. Collins**

49. **Encyclopedia of Associations 1994: A Guide to Nearly 23,000 National and International Organizations.... Volume 1: National Organizations of the U.S.** 28th ed. Peggy Kneffel Daniels and Carol A. Schwartz, eds. Detroit, Gale, 1993. 3pts. index. $375.00/set. LC 76-46129. ISBN 0-8103-8314-4. ISSN 0071-0202.

50. **Encyclopedia of Associations 1994: A Guide to Nearly 23,000 National and International Organizations.... Volume 2: Geographic and Executive Indexes.** Peggy Kneffel Daniels and Carol A. Schwartz, eds. Detroit, Gale, 1993. 950p. $295.00. LC 76-46129. ISBN 0-8103-8318-7. ISSN 0071-0202.

51. **Encyclopedia of Associations CD-ROM. June 1993.** [CD-ROM]. Detroit, Gale and Norwood, Mass., SilverPlatter Information, 1993. Hardware requirements: DOS-compatible personal computer; 640K of RAM, including 500K of conventional RAM free; hard disk drive with at least 3.5MB free; MS-DOS or PC-DOS 3.1 or higher; MS-DOS CD-ROM Extensions 2.0 or higher; ISO 9660-compatible CD-ROM drive; floppy disk drive. $995.00.

The 1994 print edition of *Encyclopedia of Associations* (EA) continues the format and coverage of previous editions, listing nearly 23,000 national and international nonprofit organizations. Coverage includes trade and professional associations; social welfare and public affairs groups; labor unions; fraternal and patriotic organizations; and religious, sports, and hobby groups. There are 600 new entries for this edition and, according to the publisher, more than 100,000 revisions and updates since the 1993 edition.

Volume 1, on national organizations of the United States, consists of 3 parts containing 23,000 entries organized into 18 subject-oriented chapters and a name and keyword index. Volume 2 has the geographic and executive indexes. Both index volumes provide addresses with each association's index listing. In what must be acknowledged as an excellent marketing technique, the publisher has also included in both indexes the names of "selected organizations listed in six other Gale directories if their names suggest that they might qualify for a full listing in volume 1 of the *Encyclopedia*."

The user can also turn to the mother of all Gale directories, the Encyclopedia of Associations on CD-ROM, which provides the equivalent of 13 print volumes and 87,000 descriptive entries. DOS-based, the database uses the SilverPlatter Information Retrieval System (SPIRS) search software, which comes with a separate installation disk. Since the SilverPlatter platform is in use with so many library CD products, its approach will be familiar for those who have learned to use it; however, there is a learning curve involved (as evidenced by a hefty user's manual for SPIRS). Documentation for Encyclopedia of Associations on CD-ROM consists of a 13-page searching overview and a couple of "quick reference guides," but those who have used the work in either its print or online versions will quickly grasp the techniques necessary for tracking down the associations sought. Online help is also available.

The searchable fields include name and acronym, key words, subject category, address, city, state, zip code, country, area code, officer name, budget size, and publications. A mailing label option lets users display, print, or download the information in label format; a citation option displays, prints, or downloads just the association name, address, officer, staff, membership, budget, and keyword fields. Search options include Boolean operators, limit fields, and truncation.

The benefits of being able to cross-search 87,000 entries without flipping back and forth from page to page, taking copious notes, and cross-referencing them for hours on end are obvious. In a situation where one is looking for groups or associations that meet specific criteria, therefore, this CD is beneficial. For an inexperienced searcher, this CD offers a chance to take the time necessary to do a thorough, methodical search. However, this is not an inexpensive product, and libraries do not have the option of purchasing a less-expensive CD that might cover, say, just the national organizations, as they do with the print version. Probably the best determinant for choosing the appropriate EA format is to examine how EA is currently used in the library. If it is just for a quick look-up of national organizations' names, addresses, and telephone numbers, the print version is probably the best choice. However, for libraries that already purchase all three of the directories included in the CD format, the added convenience of speed, multiple search avenues, and downloading and printing options make this a dream resource.

—**G. Kim Dority**

52. **Encyclopedia of Associations: Regional, State, and Local Organizations 1992-93: A Guide to More Than 53,000 United States Nonprofit Membership Organizations....** 3d ed. Grant J. Eldridge, ed. Detroit, Gale, 1992. 5v. index. $469.00/set. LC 76-46129. ISBN 0-8103-7696-2. ISSN 0894-2846.

The scope of this work is nonprofit organizations concerned with all subjects or areas of activity. Each volume covers a region of the United States. Arrangement is by state, then by city or town, based upon the organization's mailing address. Thus, a user knowing the name of a town can find organizations there, including those of state and regional significance. Sixteen other categories of data are given if available (e.g., acronym, telephone number, affiliations, publications, name changes, meetings), along with a brief description. Interpretation of the entries is greatly facilitated by the sample entry provided.

The degree of coverage varies. The publishers relied principally on a questionnaire sent to associations. Chambers of commerce and parent-teacher associations are well represented, as are professional bodies and trade councils, health support groups, and YMCAs. Chess and bicycling clubs, on the other hand, are rather thinly represented, and although local churches or other religious groups are within scope, very few are present.

For best use of the name and keyword index presented in each volume, one should scan the six-column keyword list to find suitable terms with which to search the index. In addition to those in the list, other key words are generated through permutation of terms in the name and are presented as keywords-in-context. For example, the term *abortion* is not given in the list of key words, but the index has a dozen entries so generated that begin with that word. No cross-references are provided in either index or key word list. Arrangement by subject, with access to states, towns, and the like through the indexes, would provide greater accessibility. Users would also benefit from an index of acronyms.

Notwithstanding these criticisms, the work gives access to a wealth of organizations throughout the United States. Most libraries, however, will want only the volume covering their own region. A companion set for organizations at the subnational level in other countries would go well in Gale's fine series.

—Ian Fairclough

53. Levine, Michael. **The Kid's Address Book: Over 1,500 Addresses of Celebrities....** New York, Perigee Books/Putnam, 1992. 190p. $8.95pa. CT107.L52. 920'.0025'73. LC 92-6815. ISBN 0-399-51783-9.

This book not only provides entertainment but also empowers children by giving them access to people and organizations who influence them. Levine's introductory notes emphasize the how's and why's of writing celebrities and the power of the pen as a means of expressing opinions. The major categories are listed in the table of contents. The people-oriented categories include general fan mail, music makers, sports fans, and "On the Tube and On the Screen." Entries are listed alphabetically within each major category and contain complete addresses with brief explanatory notes.

This work's great strength lies in the categories that focus on organizations, businesses, and agencies. Included are "Get Busy" (clubs and organizations), "It's Your Business" (businesses that cater to kids), "Let's Read and Explore" (publishers, magazines, and museums), "Need a Helping Hand or a Sympathetic Ear?" (hot line telephone numbers), and "Who's in Charge Here and in the Rest of the World." These listings give one-stop general information just for kids, which is sometimes difficult to find.

The lack of an index makes searching for movie and television characters, actors, and shows difficult. Another drawback to this directory is its currency (e.g., George Bush is president).

Although the work is aimed toward children ages 6 through 15, teachers will be able to use it as a catalyst for teaching communication through letter writing. The modest cost of this paperback makes it worthwhile for school and public libraries. [R: VOYA, April 93, p. 65]—**Jennie S. Johnson**

54. **National Trade and Professional Associations of the United States 1993.** 28th ed. Buck J. Downs, Amy J. Misner, and Melissa L. Georgopolis, eds. Washington, D.C., Columbia Books, 1993. 637p. index. $65.00pa. ISBN 1-880873-00-1. ISSN 0734-354X.

The 28th annual edition of this work has been updated to include about 7,300 national associations that serve organizations for business, labor, and the professions. The directory includes trade associations; scientific, technical, and learned societies; and political action committees. Professional science societies, foundations of various trade associations, and about 175 national labor unions of the United States also appear. Excluded are fraternal, sporting, patriotic, and hobby organizations. Each association entry includes information on size and budget, a historical sketch, membership fees, acronyms, serial publications, and schedules of meetings and conventions. Each entry is concise, and all entries checked were accurate. The associations are listed in alphabetical order by official title in an association index. There are also a geographic index, a budget index, an executive index, an acronym index, and an index of U.S. association management companies that serve about 500 national and 1,000 local and regional organizations. Additionally, there is an extensive subject and keyword index. Cross-references help to track associations through name changes and significant evolutions.

The directory is reasonably priced; however, it is mistaken in its assertion that it is the only place to find this kind of information. The multivolume *Encyclopedia of Associations* (Gale, 1992) is a much more comprehensive directory with a broader scope. For libraries that have the *Encyclopedia of Associations*, the work under review is not essential, but for small libraries it would be helpful and very cost effective. [R: RBB, June 93, pp. 1900-02]—**Gerald D. Moran**

GOVERNMENT PUBLICATIONS

55. Andriot, Donna, ed. **Guide to U.S. Government Publications.** 1993 ed. McLean, Va., Documents Index, 1993. 1588p. index. $305.00.

The purpose of this guide is to provide "an annotated guide to the important series and periodicals currently being published by the various U.S. Government agencies ... and ... a complete listing of Superintendent of Documents [SuDocs] classification numbers issued since the turn of the century ... to ... December 31, 1992." As can be expected, the guide is an enormous work and one that would be invaluable to those working with government documents.

The guide begins with "A Practical Guide to the Superintendent of Documents Classification System," a detailed, cogent explanation of the SuDocs classification. Most of the work (907 pages) consists of listings of all publications with SuDocs numbers. The listings are organized by SuDocs number—that is, by issuing agency (e.g., department, bureau, commission). Each agency listing has its active dates, a statement of creation and authority, an address for further information, and publications. Most of the publications are annotated and include a brief publication history as appropriate. Because the work is comprehensive, it has value for its historical information on various defunct bureaus, commissions, and committees. The work has three indexes: agency, title, and key word in title. The keyword index is more than 400 pages long and can be used in lieu of a subject index.

The guide notes the problem of frequent reorganizations of government agencies, resulting in changes in SuDocs numbers. To tame this beast, the guide includes an agency class chronology that helps users trace the varied classifications of issuing agencies. For instance, the Peace Corps was originally a component of ACTION and became an independent agency in 1981. The SuDocs classes changed from SE 19 (1961-1971) to AA 4 (1971-1982) to PE 1 (from 1981 to present). All these classes are cross-referenced in the agency chronology.

It is hard to imagine anyone working in government documents without this guide. It is highly recommended for any library with a significant collection of U.S. government documents and any library that wants to assist patrons in locating such documents.—**Stephen Haenel**

56. Robinson, Judith Schiek. **Tapping the Government Grapevine: The User-Friendly Guide to U.S. Government Information Sources.** 2d ed. Phoenix, Ariz., Oryx Press, 1993. 227p. illus. index. $34.50pa. Z1223.Z7R633. 025.17'34. LC 92-40201. ISBN 0-89774-712-7.

Robinson's new edition improves and updates an already outstanding work. She provides a witty and comprehensive overview of government information sources in all formats. While the book's focus is on U.S. publications, it also covers local, state, foreign, and international sources, including a new section on the European Community. Organized in chapters according to type of information (e.g., scientific information, legislative information sources), the work contains pertinent quotations and anecdotes about government resources and the personalities behind them. It also has practical tips on how to use specific publications. Two new appendixes contain suggestions for an inexpensive bare-bones documents reference collection (Documents Toolkit) and detailed exercises and solutions. Highly recommended as a text for library school students and as a resource for librarians and patrons who use government information. [R: RBB, June 93, pp. 1904-06]—**Jeanette C. Smith**

HANDBOOKS AND YEARBOOKS

57. Croteau, Maureen, and Wayne Worcester. **The Essential Researcher.** New York, HarperPerennial/HarperCollins, 1993. 608p. index. $35.00; $17.00pa. AG105.C86. 031.02. LC 91-58264. ISBN 0-06-271514-3; 0-06-273040-1pa.

The goal for this work is "to be the reference book that is turned to first, that is used most, that becomes tattered and dog-eared while others remain pristine." The book does contain data on a wide range of topics. Information is organized into 15 chapters covering such subjects as politics, law, mathematics, journalism, religion, and sports. The contents pages give chapter subdivisions: For example, under popular culture the section on award winners lists Grammy awards, Nobel prizes, and Miss America winners. The work also has an index listing people, places, and topics, with subdivisions and cross-references. Some of the chapters contain annals of facts presented in a chronological narrative. Elsewhere, such as in the section on common illegal drugs, a dictionary arrangement is used (with *see* references). Data can also be presented in tabular form. In some cases contact addresses and telephone numbers are provided.

From the contents pages, users will quickly learn whether this work is likely to contain the type of information needed. Because of the wide scope, information is understandably sketchy. Less understandable is the inconsistency in the level of accuracy and detail. For example, a list of nations of the world (containing political states) has a reference from Vatican City to Holy See, giving a misleading impression that the latter term is authoritative and that the Vatican is a "nation." The United Kingdom of Great Britain and Northern Ireland (so listed in the index) is given as United Kingdom, and the index listing for England refers only to the section on world history; no cross-reference is given in the list of nations. These and other inconsistencies call into question how authoritative this work is supposed to be. No sources are given for information in the work as a whole, although some sections provide a few bibliographical references.

A good idea, the book might have been more carefully prepared. Its usefulness depends largely on the user's expectations. The cover says it is for "journalists, writers, students, and everyone who needs facts fast." However, the book's hurried tone communicates itself readily and detracts from the work's potential worth. [R: Choice, Nov 93, p. 426; LJ, 15 April 93, p. 82; RBB, 1 Sept 93, p.66]—**Ian Fairclough**

58. Novallo, Annette, Joyce Jakubiak, and Joseph M. Palmisano, eds. **Student Contact Book: How to Find Low-Cost, Expert Information on Today's Issues....** Detroit, Gale, 1993. 657p. index. $29.95pa. ISBN 0-8103-8876-6. ISSN 1066-2413.

Student Contact Book is a tool of first recourse for the novice researcher seeking readily accessible primary source material on contemporary issues. Its organization is by chapter, with three modes of access: the table of contents, the list of topics covered, and the index. (The list of topics is hard to find without first consulting the contents page, which also lists topics.) Other preliminaries are sections on how to use the book and how to contact organizations and people. The combined alphabetical and subject index includes organizations, agencies, and publications.

Among the 10 chapters are ones on government and public affairs; social issues; and beliefs, cults, and sects. Under chapter headings, topics are listed again, followed by ideas for research subjects. In the chapter on arts and entertainment, topics include advertising, magazines, television, television violence, and the depiction of women and minorities in the media. Organizations and publications are presented alphabetically within each chapter. Entries contain the organization's name, such phrases as "provides information on," keywords, a paragraph of description, contact addresses, and telephone numbers. Any publications such as books or serials are briefly annotated.

The editors have produced a commendable compendium of information, often on controversial subjects and from a variety of positions. The topic of suicide, for example, is represented by several groups that advocate prevention as well as the Hemlock Society. The work does not cover the whole range of knowledge uniformly, but low-cost, expert information is more readily available for some topics than others.

High school and public libraries will welcome the *Student Contact Book*, which fulfills its goal of providing information to students on low-cost sources outside the library. College students will also welcome it, as will collection development officers. It could also be useful to help develop and maintain a vertical file. [R: Choice, June 93, p. 1611; RBB, 15 May 93, pp. 1724-25; SLJ, May 93, p. 138; VOYA, Oct 93, p. 261]—**Ian Fairclough**

INDEXES

59. **Book Review Index: A Cumulated Index to More Than 148,000 Reviews of Approximately 75,000 Titles. 1991 Cumulation.** Neil E. Walker and Beverly Baer, eds. Detroit, Gale, 1992. 1512p. index. $202.00. LC 65-9908. ISBN 0-8103-0585-2. ISSN 0524-0581.

Providing access to reviews of thousands of books, periodicals, and books on tape, *Book Review Index* (BRI) indexes standard reviewing journals, such as *Library Journal* and *Choice*; general interest indexed journals, such as *Newsweek* and *Southern Living*; and literary journals, such as *Sewanee Review* and *Shakespeare Quarterly*. The work is published in six paperbound issues a year: The second issue cumulates the first, the fourth cumulates the third, and so on, with a cumulated hardbound volume (such as the one under review) appearing at the end of the year. BRI contains indexes to reviews of current books, periodicals, and reference books of at least 50 pages. Entries provide author or editor, title of work, illustrator (if applicable), code type or age of user, and abbreviation of reviewing source (with volume number, dates, and page numbers). A major source for those who need reviews of various titles, BRI remains an integral tool.—**Anna Grace Patterson**

MUSEUMS

60. **Museums of the World.** 4th ed. New Providence, N.J., K. G. Saur/Reed Reference Publishing, 1992. 642p. index. $325.00. ISBN 3-598-20533-3.

The *International Directory of Arts* (see ARBA 92, entry 64) is familiar to many art librarians as the most current and comprehensive source of foreign art museum address and contact information. Because of its annual updates, it has long been the directory of choice for contact information over dated competitors. It is hampered, however, by a hard-to-read typeface and an obscure coding system for museum type and museum collections.

Museums of the World is a newly reactivated international museum directory in its first revision since 1981. It lists the information that art professionals want—museum director names, addresses, and telephone and fax numbers—in clear English-language entries that also contain brief collection information that students and travelers can use. The scope and currency of information also give the new source a temporary edge over the *International Directory*. Among the 23,997 entries are 5,000 new museums of all types in 182 countries, which are listed in a scheme that makes museums in the unified Germany and former Soviet countries easy to find.

The last edition of this work was published more than a decade ago. No directory, not even one as good as this, can maintain its usefulness on a 12-year update schedule. For now, this title is worth purchasing for its currency, scope, and clarity, but time and current affairs will date the information and diminish its value dramatically in a few years.—**Stephanie C. Sigala**

PERIODICALS AND SERIALS

61. Dameron, J. Lasley, and Pamela Palmer. **An Index to the Critical Vocabulary of *Blackwood's Edinburgh Magazine*, 1830-1840.** West Cornwall, Conn., Locust Hill Press, 1993. 277p. index. $40.00. AP4.B6. 051. LC 93-5478. ISBN 0-933951-52-3.

Dameron and Palmer, both associated with Memphis State University, have created a compilation of literary terms and phrases that appeared in *Blackwood's Edinburgh Magazine* during the 1830s. Introductory essays by Dameron and Kenneth Curry (University of Tennessee) discuss the background and significance of *Blackwood's* (nicknamed "Maga"). Each term or phrase is followed by its verbal context, volume number, date, and page number. Included in the book are an index to annotated critical articles by volume and an index of contributors to *Blackwood's* during the period. The book provides extremely useful insights to any student of *Blackwood's*, permitting cross-referencing of terms by volume, date, page, and contributor. The index can serve as an adjunct to understanding the concepts and ideas that prevailed in Great Britain during the fourth decade of the 1800s.—**William C. Struning**

62. **The National Directory of Magazines 1994: The Most Comprehensive Guide to U.S. & Canadian Magazines.** New York, Oxbridge Communications, 1993. 1790p. index. $395.00pa. ISBN 0-917460-47-2. ISSN 1063-7010.

This directory purports to offer comprehensive coverage of magazines published in the United States and Canada, and although it has more than 20,000 title entries in approximately 250 subject areas, the coverage does not compare with such sources as the *Standard Periodical Directory* (75,000 titles, also produced by Oxbridge [see ARBA 91, entry 65]) or *Ulrich's International Periodicals Directory* (international coverage, 126,000 titles [see ARBA 93, entry 88]). In addition, the directory lacks a preface or any sort of explanatory user information (other than an annotated sample entry), so the criteria for inclusion are unclear. For example, various types of publications, such as consumer magazines and scholarly journals, are listed; however, the selection of individual titles within a discipline or subject area appears to be erratic. Academic Press journals in the biological and medical sciences are included, yet not one of its 25 mathematics titles is listed in the mathematics subject section. In addition, the last time this work was reviewed (see ARBA 91, entry 62), three titles were identified as having been excluded: *Armchair Detective, Library Management Quarterly,* and *International Organizations.* They are still missing.

Entries are organized alphabetically by subject and include, when available, magazine title and publisher, type of readership (e.g., consumer, association, business), advertising costs, contact names, printing method and binding type, circulation figures, list company, and printing company. Indexes include an alphabetical list of subjects, a detailed cross-index of subjects, a multipublisher index, an index to publishers by state, a telephone contact listing, and a title/ISSN index. Such thorough indexing makes this directory particularly easy to use, especially for advertisers, who appear to be its primary audience. In fact, the detailed information on advertising costs, circulation, and personnel contacts is what originally separated this source from the *Serials Directory* (see ARBA 91, entry 64) and *Ulrich's*, although *Ulrich's 1992-1993* now includes full-page advertising rates and a contact name. The titles of entries that include advertising information are apparently set in boldface type for easy identifiability. However, without information on it in a preface or user's guide, this distinction could well go unnoticed.

Although this directory has more finely defined its subject areas since it was last reviewed, increasing from 190 to 250 subject headings, the number of titles covered does not appear to have increased significantly. The work would be strengthened by more comprehensive coverage, stated criteria for inclusion, a preface, and indexing and abstracting information. As it stands, this directory should be useful to public libraries and those libraries serving a business and marketing clientele.—**Janice M. Griggs**

63. **The Serials Directory: An International Reference Book.** 7th ed. Birmingham, Ala., EBSCO Publishing, 1993. 3v. index. price not reported/set. ISBN 0-913956-68-6. ISSN 0886-4179.

64. **The Serials Directory: EBSCO CD-ROM.** Summer 1993. [CD-ROM]. Peabody, Mass., EBSCO Publishing, 1993. Hardware requirements: IBM PC or compatible; hard disk with 4MB free; 640K RAM; MS-DOS 3.1 or higher; Microsoft Extensions 2.1 or higher. $525.00.

65. **Ulrich's International Periodicals Directory 1993-94: Including Irregular Serials & Annuals.** 32d ed. New Providence, N.J., R. R. Bowker, 1993. 5v. index. $395.00/set. LC 32-16320. ISBN 0-8352-3368-5. ISSN 0000-0175.

66. **Ulrich's Plus.** [CD-ROM]. New Providence, N.J., R. R. Bowker/Reed Reference Publishing, 1993. Hardware requirements: IBM PC, XT, XT-286, AT, PS/2 Model 25, 30 or full compatible; 640K memory with 535K free; MS-DOS Extensions. $465.00/yr.

Having both the printed and CD-ROM versions of these two competing and long-standing products available together provides a good opportunity to analyze and compare both tools. *Ulrich's* has undergone the more drastic change in the last year. Now in its 61st year, this tool has always been a trusted source for information on periodicals and monographic serials. This edition expands coverage to include more than 7,000 daily and weekly newspapers published in the United States. These newspapers are listed in a new fifth volume, complete with its own index. Topical and subject-oriented newspapers from around the world continue to be listed as before in the main volumes. Thus, total newspaper coverage is in two main sections. The editors plan to increase international newspaper coverage in subsequent editions.

Users of *Ulrich's* should study the preface and the introduction carefully to note new features and changes to entry information. These changes reflect the expansion of the concept of serials into the high-tech world of CD-ROM, online access, copyright considerations, and electronic format. For example, newly added features include flags for titles registered with the Copyright Clearance Center (CCC); document type descriptions; and availability of titles on services such as ADONIS, Bowker A&I Publishing, the British Library Document Supply Centre, Engineering Information, Faxon, and UnCover. The method of finding the main entry for a serial has not changed, but new subject classifications, such as alternative medicine, robotics, and physical medicine, have been added. Also new are a title change index and page references to full listings in the ISSN index. This edition includes 3,838 serials available exclusively online and 880 serials available on CD-ROM. Newer titles begun in the last three years are identified by a symbol in the title index for easier spotting. Other detail changes need careful analysis by those who use this tool on a regular basis.

The Serials Directory began as a listing of periodicals available from the EBSCO subscription service and then became a sister division. The 1993 edition has more than 145,000 international serial titles, of which 11,000 are new active titles (these are noted with a bullet before the entry). Also included are 4,500 ISI Impact Factors (a gauge of how often articles from a journal are cited in citation indexes) and more than 7,000 peer-reviewed titles. Some 50 new subject classifications have been added or modified, with major changes in medicine completed. The alphabetical title index has been improved, and ceased titles have been deleted from the print edition (but they are still included on the CD-ROM version). Updating of the databases is from three sources: through the EBSCO Subscription Service database, from the Library of Congress's CONSER file, and from detailed questionnaires sent to thousands of publishers worldwide.

Examining the CD-ROM versions of these two important tools exposes the strengths and weaknesses of each in ways hard to discern in the printed works. Both have adequate search engines that allow a minimal access time to titles in ways difficult to duplicate in the print versions. Variations in the search engines can be learned quickly by regular users, and both titles should be available on a single search station so that switching back and forth between the two can provide maximum information in a minimum of time. For both, the CD-ROM product is to be preferred over the hefty print volumes.

Comparing the same titles in both products, serious defects of currency in *The Serials Directory* become immediately apparent and currency is still a major problem for *Ulrich's* even though the publishers claim to contact 70,000 publishers every year. While in every comparison *Ulrich's* had more up-to-date data than *The Serials Directory*, neither work can be considered really current. Users, of course, understand that the massive task of controlling serials is almost an impossible one, so both products, while imperfect, are essential. However, *The Serials Directory* should be consulted largely when *Ulrich's* does not suffice. Large libraries will want both tools. *Ulrich's* is a first purchase for smaller libraries, particularly now that it includes expanded newspaper coverage. For both, the addition of computerized work stations increases productivity in searching so much that the monetary investment can be recovered quickly.—**G. Kim Dority and David V. Loertscher**

67. **The Standard Periodical Directory 1993: The Largest Authoritative Guide to United States and Canadian Periodicals....** 16th ed. Deborah Waithe and others, eds. New York, Oxbridge Communications; distr., Detroit, Gale, 1993. 1831p. index. $495.00. LC 64-7598. ISBN 0-917460-44-8. ISSN 0895-4321.

Since its start in 1964, *The Standard Periodical Directory* has established itself as a useful reference tool for most libraries. The directory clearly presents information on more than 75,000 periodicals, defined as those issued at least once every 2 years. The introductory material claims that the directory has the most comprehensive coverage of United States and Canadian periodicals, although one suspects that either *Ulrich's International Periodicals Directory* (see ARBA 93, entry 88) or *The Serials Directory* (see ARBA 91, entry 64) has similar coverage of North American periodicals. What *The Standard Periodical Directory* offers is more information in each entry. Entries vary in length, but all offer basic directory information, such as address, telephone number, and frequency; many provide complementary information, such as circulation, subscription costs, advertising information, color capability, and availability on microforms or online. Coverage includes magazines and journals of all kinds as well as newsletters, newspapers, house organs, yearbooks, and transactions and proceedings of scientific societies. The directory information was provided by the publishers and is arranged under 265 subject headings. There is a title/ISSN index with cross-references, although many ISSN numbers are missing. In addition, there is a separate cross-index to subjects and an online index that lists vendor availability to periodicals online. While expensive, this work is essential for most larger libraries and for consideration in other libraries.

—**Byron P. Anderson**

QUOTATION BOOKS

68. **The Harper Book of Quotations.** 3d ed. Robert I. Fitzhenry, ed. New York, HarperPerennial/HarperCollins, 1993. 528p. index. $25.00; $10.00pa. LC 92-54681. ISBN 0-06-271566-6; 0-06-273213-7pa.

This book is a compilation of 6,500 quotations drawn from sources ranging from ancient to contemporary. These quotations cover the whole range of attitudes and conditions, such as anger, profundity, humor, sarcasm, and whimsy. In addition to the observations of both wise and witty (although not necessarily famous) writers, the editor has included many proverbs, quotations from religious writings, and even graffiti. Access is primarily by broad topics, which are listed in the table of contents. There is also an author index.

As interesting as this book is, its usefulness depends upon the user. Patrons will likely enjoy it because it encourages browsing and serendipity. For librarians, however, it might not be particularly helpful. As mentioned before, access points are limited. There is no permuted index, and quotation entries do not cite the sources from which they are derived. Thus, the primary purposes for which a librarian uses a book of quotations are not well served. The book should be in public and academic library collections as a source of quotations, but not as a verification tool. [R: RBB, 15 Dec 93, p. 777]—**Phillip P. Powell**

69. **Ireland's Index to Inspiration: A Thesaurus of Sources for Speakers and Writers. Continued into 1990.** Joseph W. Sprug, comp. Metuchen, N.J., Scarecrow, 1993. 553p. $67.50. PN198.I7. 082. LC 93-3245. ISBN 0-8108-2566-X.

This work is intended for clergy, lecturers, speakers, students, writers, businesspeople, or anyone wanting to communicate with others. Some 396 books of short material are indexed. Sources of caricatures, proverbs, quotations, and thought-starters range from Miss Piggy to Mother Teresa. Unlike the 1976 edition (see ARBA 77, entry 94), this book does include personal names of presidents, authors, celebrities, sports figures, and other such individuals, both living and deceased. Most of the books indexed were published between 1980 and 1987. Selection was based on research and recommendations.

Entries are arranged alphabetically, word by word, with articles ignored as introductory words and major headings printed in boldface type capitals. *See* and *see also* references are used generously. Headings are specific and particular; if too little is listed, one can go to a more general term. To further help the user, a short list of collections analyzed is given prior to the index, and a complete list of collections analyzed with annotations and review citations follows it.

This continuation of the first *Index to Inspiration* will be useful to all libraries and librarians needing quotations or inspiration. In addition, the list of collections is a helpful collection development tool. [R: RBB, 1 Nov 93, p. 567]—**Susan C. Awe**

70. Mason, Eileen. **Witty Words: A Hilarious Collection of Outrageous Quotations for Every Day of the Year.** New York, Sterling Publishing, 1992. 256p. illus. index. $18.95. PN6081.M45. 082. LC 92-25145. ISBN 0-8069-8604-2.

"I never read a book before reviewing it. It prejudices one so." This quotation from Sydney Smith, who wrote almost two centuries ago, may be found in this treasury of clever and acid bons mots. Mason's book is arranged chronologically, from January 1 through December 31, with each day of the year bearing at least one person, place, or thing associated with that date. The relationship is often tenuous; for instance, a reference to the birthday of inventor Louis Braille is celebrated with a seminaughty limerick ending with the word "Braille." The work is, however, at once reminiscent of both *Chase's Annual Events* (see ARBA 91, entry 2) and Bartlett's *Familiar Quotations* (see ARBA 93, entry 89). The table of contents lists 12 chapters named for the months of the calendar, and there are indexes of people, holidays, and subjects.

Any book that refers to itself on the cover as "hilarious" had better have the goods, and this one frequently does, despite an uneven and spotty assortment of quotables. Mason states that she assembled this book because a daily laugh is therapeutic. So what is a typical day like? January 1 explains the meaning of the "toast" in New Year's toasts and then supplies two quotations from E. M. Forster and J. D. Salinger, both born on January 1. But some days are better than others. The only valid criticism is that Mason's word has to be taken for a quotation's provenance and authenticity, because citation, location information, and context are nowhere to be found.

This book draws together some wonderfully good quotations, whether the rigors of scholarship are observed or not. It is fun to browse through, and anyone with a rudimentary funny bone will find something to chortle over. It is not really a reference book, though; it is more appropriate for the circulating collection.—**Bruce A. Shuman**

71. **The New York Public Library Book of 20th-Century American Quotations.** Stephen Donadio and others, eds. New York, Warner Books, 1992. 622p. index. $24.95. PN6081.N53. 081. LC 91-50395. ISBN 0-446-51639-2.

This compilation focuses on the words of twentieth-century Americans. Quotations are arranged in such broad subject areas as age, American mosaic, children and youth, economics, education, tradition, the human condition, religion and spirituality, states and regions, time, and work. Many of these topics are further subdivided; for example, adversity, creativity, humor, talent and 30 other specific attributes are subheadings under the human condition. The 9,000 quotations, which can be brief or extensive, have been taken from political slogans, advertisements, posters, speeches, and newspaper articles. Famous and lesser-known political figures, authors, commentators, radio announcers, reporters, and clergy are included. The volume is indexed by author and subject and is adequately cross-referenced. One minor cause of confusion is the use of boldface type for chapter headings in the subject index. [R: RBB, 15 Jan 93, pp. 946-47]—**Margaret Norden**

72. Riley, Dorothy Winbush, ed. **My Soul Looks Back, 'Less I Forget: A Collection of Quotations by People of Color.** New York, HarperCollins, 1993. 498p. index. $27.50. PN6081.3.R5M9. 081'.08996073. LC 92-25754. ISBN 0-06-270086-3.

Books of quotations abound. And while many of them include sayings by Afro-Americans, Native Americans, Latin Americans, and Asian Americans, it is difficult to find these utterances in most quotation books. Now, finding quotations from people of color will be much easier. While this work includes significant words of people of color from antiquity to the present, including such individuals as Mahatma Gandhi, Alexandre Dumas pere, and Aleksandr Pushkin (who has Abyssinian ancestry); from Native Americans and Latin Americans; and from Egypt, Somalia, and other African sources, most of the quotations are from Afro-Americans. The more than 7,000 items are arranged chronologically under 453 topical headings from ability to youth. Taken from books, magazines, historical documents, speeches, and radio and television programs, this compilation of "inspiring quotes of pride and heritage about people of color" were selected and arranged to create a sense of history. The selections were chosen for their lyricism, the points they make, their uniqueness and ingenuity of expression, or their presentation of memorable images. Riley includes many controversial ones reflecting the conflict, suppression, and prejudice that people of color have endured.

Many of the quotations bear the marks of their origins, but numerous others derive from universal human concerns and experiences. The ideas expressed here touch life from all perspectives, from the intimately personal to the profoundly universal, from the exalted to the self-serving. Booker T. Washington reminds us that "Great men cultivate love ... only little men cherish a spirit of hatred," while Mike Tyson insists that "To be the best you have to be cocky, arrogant and conceited. Conceited is just loving yourself. If you don't love yourself, you can never achieve anything. And I love myself." Without question, this book fills an important gap in the genre and should be acquired by all types of libraries. [R: Choice, Dec 93, p. 588; LJ, Aug 93, p. 96; RBB, 15 Nov 93, pp. 651-52]—**Blaine H. Hall**

Part II
SOCIAL SCIENCES

2 Social Sciences in General

73. **The Blackwell Dictionary of Twentieth-Century Social Thought.** William Outhwaite and Tom Bottomore, eds. Cambridge, Mass., Basil Blackwell, 1993. 864p. index. $49.95. H41.B53. 300'.3. LC 92-20837. ISBN 0-631-15262-8.

This dictionary provides a comprehensive overview of the main themes of twentieth-century social thought. Many bodies of thought have remained influential for the entire period: individual social sciences, philosophical schools, political doctrines, and distinctive styles of art and literature. Continuing issues include the nature of work, the role of the nation-state, the relation between the individual and society, the impact of money on social relations, stratification and equality, and the complexity of achieving objective social science. A sampling of the entries reveals the encompassing nature of the coverage: artificial intelligence, colonialism, Durkheim School, leisure, materialism, pluralism, race, social democracy, trade unions, urbanism, and welfare state.

The alphabetically arranged entries range from one to four pages in length and have been written by more than 200 scholars from many countries. Entries furnish current definitions together with the appropriate historical context. Cross-references appear generously throughout the volume. The entries are concise, informative, and smoothly written. A brief bibliography follows each, and a collective bibliography of all works cited may be found at the end of the volume. Individual thinkers are covered in a biographical appendix to avoid repetitive mention in the main text. Finally, a general index facilitates access to concepts, schools, and individual thinkers. Recommended as an essential purchase for libraries that need an authoritative one-volume compendium of the great social themes of this century. [R: Choice, July/Aug 93, p. 1744; RBB, June 93, pp. 1890-92]—**Arthur P. Young**

74. Brockway, Sandi, ed. **Macrocosm USA: Possibilities for a New Progressive Era....** Cambria, Calif., Macrocosm USA, 1992. 421p. illus. index. $24.95pa. LC 92-080678. ISBN 0-9632315-5-3.

The stated purpose of this handbook is to serve as an interdisciplinary presentation of and guide to progressive issues and grassroots activism while revolutionizing journalism, education, and politics. The book is composed of two sections of roughly equal length. One is a collection of more than 200 mostly reprinted articles, and the other is a directory of more than 5,000 entries. The articles—grouped in 14 chapters—are short (usually a page or less) reprints from a handful of progressive periodicals. Topics covered include peace, the Third World, the environment, energy, economics, education, health, politics, the media, feminism, spirituality, and urban life. It is an odd assortment of articles and lacks a unifying theme.

The directory section is divided into six cross-referenced categories: organizations, periodicals, media, publishing, business, and reference books. It begins with an index, using 236 subject headings, that lists the directory's entries for each of the 6 categories. Full information (address, telephone number, brief description, officers or editors, and price) is contained in the alphabetical listings for each category. Entries are coded with one of 24 letters or images that further define their subject. The work has an extensive general index and a personal name index.

Directory entries are drawn primarily from other published reference works and are far from comprehensive or consistently progressive. For example, the mainstream publications *Newsweek*, the *Atlantic*, and *Harper's Magazine* are listed, but the progressive publications *Lies of Our Times* and *Progressive Librarian* are omitted. In spite of its drawbacks, and because of its broad coverage and low price, this guide will be a useful addition to many smaller libraries.—**Fred J. Hay**

75. **Index to International Public Opinion, 1991-1992.** By Survey Research Consultants International. Elizabeth Hann Hastings and Philip K. Hastings, eds. Westport, Conn., Greenwood Press, 1993. 702p. index. $199.50. LC 80-643917. ISBN 0-313-28670-1. ISSN 0193-905X.

This index is the single best source of polling data available on international public opinion. Published annually since 1978, the index includes data from 127 reputable polling organizations in 71 countries. The polls refer to more than 130 countries and include such perennial topics as Middle East issues or problems of minorities, and such transitory topics as attitudes toward specific political parties or leaders. Included are a number of time series tables covering a decade or longer. New to this volume is "Changing Opinions: A 50-Year Retrospective," which relates to issues still current today.

Arrangement is in 23 major topic categories, each subdivided into specific subject groups. Multinational surveys are listed separately. Entries under each topic vary in number; for example, "surrogate mothers" has a single entry, and "standard of living" has 23. Each entry identifies the survey organization and sample size. Indexes include subject, geographical location of the poll, and geographical subject of the poll. Indexes list page number only, requiring additional effort to locate the proper poll. Individually numbered entries would enhance future editions. This work complements *American Public Opinion Index* (see ARBA 92, entry 72). Recommended for larger academic and research libraries.—**Byron P. Anderson**

76. Kadrey, Richard. **Covert Culture Sourcebook.** New York, St. Martin's Press, 1993. 216p. illus. index. $12.95pa. HN17.5.K33. 306. LC 93-2563. ISBN 0-312-09776-X.

"Nothing interesting happens in the center," so this sourcebook surfs to the edges of cyberspace and introduces readers to a 1990s high-tech counterculture. Covert culture includes a whole range of twisted ideas and personal obsessions, including body piercing, "smart" drugs, computer hacking, new music, and visual entertainment. This is an annotated guide to books, catalogs, magazines, music, videos, technology, software, networked special interest groups, and fashion associated with the culture. Many individuals probably do not even know that this fringe culture exists to the extent that it does, but this book will bring it to light in a big way. This is a unique source, although it overlaps or complements the organizations, groups, and presses listed in Richard Gardner's *Alternative America* (Gardner, 1992). The sourcebook will allow users to track down diverse fringe-culture items, and it can be safely added to most larger public library and popular culture collections. Recommended. [R: LJ, Aug 93, p. 94]—**Byron P. Anderson**

77. Mayne, Alan J. **Resources for the Future: An International Annotated Bibliography for the 21st Century.** Westport, Conn., Greenwood Press, 1993. 351p. index. (Bibliographies and Indexes in Economics and Economic History, no.13). $69.95. Z5990.M39. 016.30349. LC 92-35820. ISBN 0-313-28911-5.

Designed to serve the needs of those attempting to anticipate economic, environmental, political, social, scientific, technological, and conceptual developments in the twenty-first century, this selective bibliography briefly describes 1,651 sources of information. Included are more than 1,000 English-language monographs and scores of journals, newsletters, CD-ROMs, online databases, computer software products, organizations, foundations, and twenty-first-century projects. Excluded are films, radio and television programs, and audio and video recordings. Most of the items cited are British, as is Mayne. The vast majority of publications listed are current and still in print. A list of book publishers, a subject index, and an index by publisher complete this useful volume. It should be helpful to researchers engaged in forecasting future trends.—**Leonard Grundt**

78. McGuire, William, and Leslie Wheeler. **American Social Leaders.** Santa Barbara, Calif., ABC-Clio, 1993. 500p. illus. (Biographies of American Leaders). $65.00. HN65.M38. 303.48'4'092273. LC 93-3991. ISBN 0-87436-633-X.

This biographical work, the second in the series, profiles 350 U.S. men and women who have had an influence on the social movements that have shaped this country since the seventeenth century. The book's strength lies in the broad definition of *social leader* used. Major names and well-known movements are included, of course, but so are lesser-known, important leaders, such as Mother Cabrini, Philip Murray, and Rabbi Isaac Mayer Wise. Also included are figures who became leaders through their ideas, scientific achievements, or philanthropy rather than their leadership of reform movements: Hannah Arendt, Alfred Kinsey, and Andrew Carnegie fall into this category. Finally, the coverage of current figures is excellent. There are entries for Faye Wattleton, Gary Wills, William F. Buckley, Jr., and Ralph Nader among others.

The 700- to 1000-word entries (many with accompanying black-and-white portrait) are arranged alphabetically by last name. The first paragraph of these engaging profiles summarizes the subject's accomplishments; following paragraphs provide more detailed information on the subject's life, emphasizing the contribution as a social leader. Cross-references guide the reader to related entries, and a brief bibliography at the end of each essay suggests items for further research.

This volume complements *American Reformers* (see ARBA 86, entry 788), which covers 500 figures in slightly longer profiles and has more extensive bibliographies. Although the two volumes treat many of the same figures, *American Social Leaders* contains enough significant information on more recent and nontraditional reformers to make it a worthwhile purchase. Recommended for all libraries including secondary, academic, and public. [R: Choice, Dec 93, p. 588; LJ, 1 June 93, p. 106; RBB, 15 Sept 93, p. 183; WLB, Oct 93, p. 85]—**Diana Accurso**

79. Vogt, W. Paul. **Dictionary of Statistics and Methodology: A Nontechnical Guide for the Social Sciences.** Newbury Park, Calif., Sage, 1993. 253p. $38.95; $18.95pa. HA17.V64. 300'.1'5195. LC 93-728. ISBN 0-8039-5276-7; 0-8039-5277-5pa.

Written for those who are more comfortable with verbal expressions than with algebraic formulas, this dictionary provides nontechnical definitions of more than 1,000 statistical and methodological terms used by researchers in the social and behavioral sciences. Vogt, who teaches at the State University of New York at Albany, emphasizes concepts rather than calculations in his brief definitions. He uses letter-by-letter alphabetization and supplies cross-references liberally. Whenever a definition makes use of a related term that is defined in another entry, that term is preceded by an asterisk. While most entries include examples of usage as well as definitions, only 35 contain illustrative diagrams or charts. The volume concludes with some suggestions for further reading. Although *A Dictionary of Statistical Terms* (see ARBA 92, entry 847) is far more comprehensive, containing 3,400 items, Vogt's work will be appreciated by students and general readers lacking a solid background in mathematics. [R: Choice, Nov 93, p. 440]—**Leonard Grundt**

80. Wynar, Bohdan S. **The International Writings of Bohdan S. Wynar, 1949-1992: A Chronological Bibliography.** Englewood, Colo., Ukrainian Academic Press/Libraries Unlimited, 1993. 265p. index. $55.00. Z8989.63.W96. 016.02. LC 93-8710. ISBN 1-56308-158-X.

This volume represents a comprehensive and detailed summation of the professional career of distinguished library educator and publisher Bohdan S. Wynar. A short introductory biography by Yaroslav Isajevych gives the setting for Wynar's career: his youth and education through his doctorate in Eastern Europe and Germany; his career as library educator and dean in New York and Colorado; and his major achievement, as publisher (Libraries Unlimited). The bibliography of 2,025 entries is arranged chronologically, with items for each year divided in two sections: books and articles and reviews. Through 1961, most items listed are works on economics in Ukrainian. English-language works, emphasizing librarianship, take over in the years following. Full bibliographical information is given for each item, and reviews of Wynar's books are also listed. An index of books and articles included completes the volume. This very specialized work will find its home in research libraries and in large collections on library and information science.—**Richard D. Johnson**

81. Suttles, Steven A., and Sharon F. Suttles, eds. **Educators Guide to Free Social Studies Materials.** 33d ed. Randolph, Wis., Educators Progress Service, 1993. 476p. index. $28.95pa. LC 61-65910. ISBN 0-87708-257-X.

Anyone who has ever taught a class has yearned for that perfect resource to draw together the hour's ruminations. And teachers who found it soon discovered that for a mere $295, it could be theirs. The disappointment is profound, the agony of defeat unnerving. This volume, however, promises, at least in the area of social studies, to uplift teachers while calming their jangled nerves. This edition includes everything from films and filmstrips to videotapes and printed materials. As the title indicates, the materials are free.

More than 2,200 tapes, slides, transparencies, videotapes, and printed materials are described and sourced. Some 20 percent of all the materials in this edition are new, while more than half of the charts, posters, exhibits, and other printed materials appear for the first time. Included are maps; country studies;

works on history, geography, and social problems; and more for countries throughout the world, as well as professional growth materials for teachers. The Canadian index lists the availability of materials in that country. Also included are tips on securing the items, how soon something should be requested before it is needed, and sample documents. Annotations to the materials are expansive, informative, and well executed.

The volume comes in familiar rainbow colors, an occupational hazard, apparently, for anyone teaching in elementary or secondary schools. The volume needs proofreading, but it has been produced so inexpensively that errors must be accepted as a necessary evil. Other guides in this educators' series cover films; filmstrips and slides; teaching aids; videotapes; science, guidance, health, and home economics materials; computer items; and curriculum sources. Considerable overlap will occur among these volumes, but all remain useful aids for teachers.—**Mark Y. Herring**

3 Area Studies

GENERAL WORKS

82. **The Europa World Year Book 1992.** 33d ed. London, Europa; distr., Detroit, Gale, 1992. 2v. index. $530.00/set. LC 59-2942. ISBN 0-946653-76-3. ISSN 0956-2273.

This edition of a standard reference work (see ARBA 90, entry 91 for a review of the 1989 edition) follows its traditional format. The beginning of the first volume contains extensive information on approximately 90 international organizations and brief information on nearly 1,200 others. An unfortunate omission from this part of the set is the table called "International Comparisons." It was a handy source of information on land area, population, population density, average population increase, life expectancy, GNP (gross national product), and per capita GNP for the countries of the world. The rest of the work contains an introductory survey, statistics, and directory information for each country in the world. The topics covered remain the same as in previous editions. Political changes in the world are reflected as allowed by the work's publication schedule: The Baltic republics of Estonia, Latvia, and Lithuania appear in the alphabetical sequence of countries under their individual names, while Georgia and members of the Commonwealth of Independent States appear under "USSR—Former Territories." Similarly, the states that have declared their independence from Yugoslavia are included under "Yugoslavia and Its Successor States."

It should be noted that there are seven regional volumes by the same publisher. They contain the same statistical tables and directory information for each country as appear in *Europa*, and they also have bibliographies for additional reading and longer narrative essays covering geography, history, and economy in great depth.

The Europa World Year Book remains an outstanding reference work, pulling together current information that cannot be found in any other single source. Unfortunately, the price, which has increased more than 30 percent since the 1989 edition, may be beyond the means of many libraries needing an authoritative source of information on international organizations and the countries of the world.—**Carol Wheeler**

UNITED STATES

83. Benson, Margie, and Nancy Jacobson. **Awesome Almanac—Wisconsin.** Fontana, Wis., B & B Publishing, 1993. 159p. illus. maps. index. $12.95pa. F579.B53. 977.5'003. LC 92-074706. ISBN 1-880190-02-8.

84. Blashfield, Jean F. **Awesome Almanac—Illinois.** Fontana, Wis., B & B Publishing, 1993. 199p. illus. maps. index. $12.95pa. F539.B53. 977.3'003. LC 92-074707. ISBN 1-880190-04-4.

85. Blashfield, Jean F. **Awesome Almanac—Minnesota.** Fontana, Wis., B & B Publishing, 1993. 175p. illus. maps. index. $12.95pa. F604.B53. 977.6'003. LC 92-074710. ISBN 1-880190-07-9.

86. Jacobson, Nancy. **Awesome Almanac—Indiana.** Fontana, Wis., B & B Publishing, 1993. 151p. illus. maps. index. $12.95pa. F524.B53. 977.2'003. LC 92-074708. ISBN 1-880190-04-4.

87. Newcomb, Annette. **Awesome Almanac—Michigan.** Fontana, Wis., B & B Publishing, 1993. 167p. illus. maps. index. $12.95pa. F564.B53. 977.4'003. LC 92-074709. ISBN 1-880190-06-0.

These are the first 5 titles of what appears to be a series that will cover at least the 50 states. While the specifics of arrangement vary a bit, each title includes sections on government origin and organization, history, major cities and towns, the arts, sports, popular entertainment, business and industry, natural features, and miscellany. In addition, each volume includes a chronology of events (primarily birthdays). Access is through a proper name index; there is no subject index.

The typical entry is a breezy short paragraph set off with a marginal caption (the margins are especially wide for an "almanac"); many have a black-and-white photograph. It is clear from the captions, the general tone of the books, and the advertising blurbs included that the intended market is trivia buffs. Certainly the books provide some interesting reading. Just as certainly, they are nearly useless as reference sources. The lack of subject access makes reference use difficult; the lack of any documentation or bibliographical references makes the reliability and authority of the data suspect. While there is a map of counties in each volume, there is no general map, gazetteer, or other way of locating any of the places mentioned. And, adding to the frustration, there are neither cross-references in the text nor in the index to the volume, nor among volumes.

As there appears to be an insatiable popular demand for trivia, and because these works do include considerable recent material not readily available in one source, there is some justification for producing them. The resulting product, however, is of little value to the library, unless as part of a general popular culture collection. [R: RBB, Aug 93, p. 2085]—**James H. Sweetland**

88. Browning, James A. **The Western Reader's Guide: A Selected Bibliography of Nonfiction Magazines 1953-91.** Stillwater, Okla., Barbed Wire Press, 1992. 344p. $29.95. Z1251.W5B87. 016.978. LC 92-35419. ISBN 0-935269-09-6.

Despite the rather misleading (or perhaps too-embrasive) title, this work covers an impressive number of names of obscure (as well as well-known) men who lived during the period called "the opening of the West." From 1953 to 1991 as many as two dozen nonfiction magazines were published, all purporting to tell true tales of Western characters. Today only three survive: *True West, Old West,* and *Wild West*. The book under review consists of a listing, by last name, of all the Western characters about whom an article was written in any of the two dozen publications during the time period. There are cross-references from nicknames, and if a person had more than one alias, all are given in the main entry. Billy the Kid, Kid Antrim, and Billy Bonney are all listed under the real name: McCarty, Patrick Henry. Each entry gives the name of the writer, title of article, title of magazine, date, and beginning page. Length of article is not given, nor any annotation.

One of the important uses of the book will be to find information, even though it may be one short article, about obscure names that are not found in Dan Thrapp's *Encyclopedia of Frontier Biography* (see ARBA 89, entry 446). A check of the entries under the letter A, for example, turned up 24 names of people not listed in Thrapp. Based on a random page count of entries, the book contains about 2,400 names (although a few entries are multiple, such as "Apache Scouts" or "Lincoln County Gang"). The number of articles listed for each entry varies greatly, from a single article to as many as 60 for Billy the Kid.

Libraries with a clientele interested in the West will find this work a blessing, even though it may result in an increased volume of interlibrary loans. Unfortunately, as the author bemoans in his introduction, copies of these "pulps" are hard to find. But they do exist somewhere, and this book is their well-conceived and well-edited index. [R: RBB, 15 Mar 93, p. 1379]—**Raymund F. Wood**

89. Marten, James, comp. **Texas.** Santa Barbara, Calif., ABC-Clio, 1992. 229p. maps. index. (World Bibliographical Series, v.144). $80.00. 016.9764. ISBN 1-85109-184-X.

The World Bibliographical Series is a set of books that will eventually cover every country (and many of the world's principal regions), with annotated entries to works that deal with the area's history, geography, economy, politics, and people. *Texas* covers the largest of the contiguous United States. This invaluable research tool includes current scholarship and classic studies, business analyses, social commentary, biographies, and monographs. Along with the aforementioned subsections are interesting ones on women, religion, folklore and linguistics, media, performing arts, fine arts, and medicine. The annotations describe the contents of each book and their possible practical value to a wide variety of readers, including students, librarians, businesspeople, and tourists. The journals and periodicals section and the index of authors, titles, and subjects are particularly helpful for the researcher. The sports section is also helpful but could be more complete. In some areas Marten seems to have selected the best books rather than to have been exhaustive.—**Randy M. Wood**

90. Morris, Nancy J., and Love Dean, comps. **Hawai'i.** Santa Barbara, Calif., ABC-Clio, 1992. 324p. maps. index. (World Bibliographical Series, v.146). $75.00. 016.9969. ISBN 1-85109-175-0.

The 812 entries in this bibliography cover a wide range of topics, from Hawaii's history, geography, climate, politics, culture, social organization, and religion to current political and social issues and problems. Especially thorough coverage has been given to works on Hawaii's natural environment, including that of the uninhabited northwestern archipelago. In choosing works for inclusion, the compilers have emphasized recent books, both scholarly and popular, although some basic older works and reprints of classic publications have been included. Some periodical articles that cover material not otherwise available and a few important government publications, dissertations, and theses are listed. All works cited are in English.

Clear, concise, descriptive annotations accompany each entry. They describe not only the subject contents and scope but also the authors' tone and style. In the entries, diacritical marks are used whenever they appeared in the original titles. A short introduction summarizes the history of Hawaii and social, cultural, and economic aspects of Hawaiian life. A chronology lists important events from 300 to 1992. A detailed set of author, title, and subject indexes provides quick access to specific subjects and names. The compilers are well qualified, and the bibliography meets the standards of the World Bibliographical Series. [R: Choice, Nov 93, p. 437]—**Shirley L. Hopkinson**

AFRICA

General Works

91. **Africa South of the Sahara 1993.** 22d ed. London, Europa; distr., Detroit, Gale, 1992. 986p. $295.00. LC 78-112271. ISBN 0-946653-81-X. ISSN 0065-3896.

This is the latest edition of what is probably the first-call resource for current information on Africa for most librarians. The organization remains as in the past: Background essays are followed by a section on regional organizations (probably the single most useful feature) and 49 country-by-country surveys. The recent history sections on about 20 countries have been revised this year, and most others have at least been updated, so that coverage reaches mid-1992 in most cases (but only May 1991 for Liberia). The statistical tables, largely drawn from United Nations publications, have almost all been updated by a year or more. Regrettably, the practice of providing no index continues.

Despite these continuities, however, there are drastic changes between this year's edition and previous ones. In particular, there is rather less of most things, as the total number of pages has decreased from 1,147 to 986. Hardest hit are the introductory essays, which have declined from 18 essays that covered 146 pages to 8 that cover only 64 pages. The individual recent history sections have also been reduced, often by as much as half. The reductions are not evenly spread; the entry for Ghana is 26 percent shorter than last year, whereas that for Zaire remains virtually the same. Oddly, the material on South Africa, the country likely to be of most interest, is 10 pages shorter than last year.

This marked attrition is not noted in the book; nor are the book's premises at all evident, as is clear from these examples. All this blunts the value of the latest edition in that users must now consult several editions to ensure the best results. Nonetheless, this work remains the single most useful reference source for providing users with at least the broader contours of contemporary Africa.—**David Henige**

92. **African Socio-Economic Indicators 1989. Indicateurs Socio-economiques Africains.** New York, United Nations, 1992. 69p. $25.00pa. ISBN 92-1-025033-8. S/N E/F.92.II.K.7.

Any reference sources for Third World countries, which are not covered as well as other nations, are welcome. This series was begun in 1986 and comes with graphs, charts, and some limited source notes. The table headings and the introduction that defines the sections are in both French and English. Nine sections cover demographic and social indicators (e.g., education, population), while the remaining 25 sections provide statistical data on exports, energy, and government finances, among other economic topics. Unfortunately, this book does not provide as much data as it could, so, depending on the research need, one must be prepared to consult several different sources to find statistics on Africa. The time lag between data collection and date of publication can also sometimes be lengthy. Many of the same figures are included in the UN's *Statistical Yearbook* (see ARBA 92, entry 849) and the *Demographic Yearbook* (see ARBA 87, entry 824). Sometimes these two volumes are more up-to-date, while in other subjects the title under review has the more recent statistics. This booklet is recommended for larger academic and public libraries and those institutions collecting United Nations documents or materials on Africa.

—**Daniel K. Blewett**

93. **Directory of Development Research and Training Institutes in Africa. Inventaire des Instituts de Recherche et de Formation en Matiere de Developpement en Afrique.** Washington, D.C., OECD Publications & Information Center, 1992. 248p. index. $40.00pa. ISBN 92-64-03539-7.

This publication expands and updates the 1986 edition; it covers 641 institutions as opposed to 497 in the older edition. The data in the numbered entries includes address; parent organization; fax, telephone number, telex, and cable numbers; educational courses offered by the institution; number of staff; founding date; director's name; library and conference space; computers in use; names of publications; and a description of other activities. The entries are arranged by country. There are descriptor indexes for research, graduate education courses, and other activities. A companion OECD (Organization for Economic Cooperation and Development) volume, prepared in collaboration with the Council for the Development of Economic and Social Research in Africa, is *Register of Development Research Projects in Africa* (1992).

One can, of course, look for these institutions in *International Research Centers Directory 1992-93* (see ARBA 93, entry 68), but this is a more focused volume. It is suitable for academic and larger public libraries and those special collections interested in Africa.—**Daniel K. Blewett**

94. McIlwaine, John. **Africa: A Guide to Reference Material.** New York, Hans Zell/Reed Reference Publishing, 1993. 507p. index. (Regional Reference Guides, no.1). $95.00. Z3501.M3. 016.96. LC 92-38578. ISBN 0-905450-43-4.

African studies have not lacked good reference materials from their inception. This work aims to continue, and to some extent to encapsulate, that tradition. On its own terms it succeeds well. These terms, however, belie and somewhat delimit the title. Handbooks, yearbooks, statistical compendia, biographical sources, atlases, and gazetteers are included, but bibliographies, dictionaries, and comparative and narrowly specialized materials are deliberately eschewed on the grounds that they have been covered adequately elsewhere. This is substantially true, but a brief list of the best bibliographies of bibliographies, for instance, would have reaped great benefits at small cost.

As with most such works, this one is divided geographically. Of the 1,766 entries, roughly a quarter deal with Africa as a whole, another half with western and southern Africa, and the remainder with eastern and central Africa. Northern Africa is excluded. Within these areas and their constituents, entries are arranged chronologically to illustrate the march of these materials over time. A substantial appendix indexes the annual reports of the various British possessions in Africa, a useful enterprise because most of these works have recently been published in microform. A valuable aspect of this book, although one likely to be overlooked by those using it as a reference work, is McIlwaine's introduction, in which he discusses the nature of both earlier and more recent reference publishing and its critical reception.

There is an author-title index but none devoted to subjects—a pity, as the arrangement of entries hardly precludes its need. On balance, though, this is certain to become a most useful tool, not least because of its emphasis on that most elusive of categories—governmental and parastatal publications. [R: Choice, Oct 93, pp. 268-70; LAR, Oct 93, p. 574; LJ, 15 Nov 93, p. 68]—**David Henige**

95. Westfall, Gloria D. **French Colonial Africa: A Guide to Official Sources.** New Providence, N.J., Hans Zell/Reed Reference Publishing, 1992. 226p. index. $85.00. DT532.W47. 016.966'0917521. LC 92-11731. ISBN 1-873836-60-0.

This bibliographical guide seeks to aid access to the publications of governmental and semiofficial sources on the French colonial experience in Africa. Westfall, the foreign documents librarian at the Indiana University Libraries, indicates that there are only a few articles published on this aspect of French government; she hopes to facilitate access to these underused sources.

The first chapter gives an overview of general guides to publications, research guides, and bibliographies that cover several or all French African colonies as well as manuals on the organization of the colonial governments and their personnel and sources of biographical information on colonial administrators. Next the author deals with archives and access aids to them, both in France and in Africa, including a discussion of classification systems. The remaining three chapters provide information on the publications of the metropolitan government, semiofficial organizations, and the colonial governments. Within each chapter, information is divided into sections, and the same pattern is followed where subject matter permits. For example, there are sections on political, legal, or administrative items; on economic and financial information; and on social and cultural affairs. All of these sections are subdivided further. A large amount of fascinating contextual information is supplied, and access to it is facilitated by a 28-page, double-columned index and a detailed table of contents. This excellent bibliographical tool should be acquired by all research institutions with the relevant clientele interests.—**Nigel Tappin**

Angola

96. Black, Richard, comp. **Angola.** Santa Barbara, Calif., ABC-Clio, 1992. 176p. maps. index. (World Bibliographical Series, v.151). $75.00. 016.9673. ISBN 1-85109-143-2.

This is a well-constructed, selective, general bibliography on a poor, war-torn country that is usually ignored by the West. It has complete bibliographic citations for 565 items, most in English. The annotations provide a good description of the contents and purposes of the cited materials. The broad scope of this book's arrangement and coverage is similar to the other volumes in this well-known series, with chapters on literature, the economy, demographics, and the like. The sections on statistics, the mass media, reference books, and libraries and archives will be particularly useful to researchers. The 12-page introduction provides an overview of the country's history and economy and turbulent recent events. At the end of the introduction are names of archives and their addresses. Ten theses and dissertations done in the United Kingdom and the United States are listed at the beginning of the bibliography, along with a 28-item glossary. There are separate author, title, and subject indexes, and a general map of the country rounds out the book. The quality of the printing is good.

Because of its high price, this book is only recommended for larger public and academic libraries and those institutions that have a lot of demand for information on Africa. All others will be able to get by using cheaper materials and online services. [R: Choice, Oct 93, p. 262]—**Daniel K. Blewett**

Central African Republic

97. Kalck, Pierre, comp. **Central African Republic.** Santa Barbara, Calif., ABC-Clio, 1993. 153p. maps. index. (World Bibliographical Series, v.152). $75.00. 016.96741. ISBN 1-85109-172-6.

This volume deals with one of the least-known African nations, about which there are few relevant works in English. During the period 1883-1984, the exploration and study of Ubangi-Shari (which became independent in 1958 and changed its name to the Central African Republic [CAR] in 1960) was done almost exclusively by French writers. Thus, most of the 538 entries in the topical arrangement are for French works. The CAR is probably, unfortunately, best known for the 1966-1979 rule of Jean-Bedel Bokassa, known as the "mad Emperor." His downfall was brought about by Amnesty International's 1979 denunciation of his massacre of children.

Kalck is also author of two editions of the *Historical Dictionary of the Central African Republic* (see ARBA 93, entry 113). He is clearly critical of Bokassa; for example, item 156 terms him a "megalomaniac tyrant," and item 347 refers to his "monstrous and farcical image." The 25-page introduction is a useful but somewhat complex historical summary. The most serious shortcoming in the book is the inadequate map at the end of the volume. The maps should devote at least two pages to the CAR, with another page showing its location within Africa. Recommended for libraries with African studies programs.—**Karen Y. Stabler**

Gabon and Botswana

98. Gardinier, David E., comp. **Gabon.** Santa Barbara, Calif., ABC-Clio, 1992. 178p. maps. index. (World Bibliographical Series, v.149). $72.50. 016.96721. ISBN 1-85109-174-2.

99. Wiseman, John A., comp. **Botswana.** Santa Barbara, Calif., ABC-Clio, 1992. 187p. maps. index. (World Bibliographical Series, v.150). $72.50. 016.96883. ISBN 1-85109-171-8.

These two similarly arranged volumes are part of the well-known and long-running bibliographical series from ABC-Clio that is represented in many libraries. Selected books, journal articles, and publications from governments and international organizations are all included and have at least one line of annotation. There are 549 numbered bibliographical citations in *Gabon* and 723 in *Botswana*. The majority of items were published after 1970, and non-English titles are translated. The introductions provide background information regarding the varied makeup of the countries. There are chapters on history, demographics, languages, foreign relations, the economy, and more in each. Each sturdily constructed book has indexes of authors, titles, and subjects, along with a single map of the country. The printing is clear and easy to read, with the titles in boldface type. While one can, of course, find these citations scattered about in other subject and general bibliographies and indexes, it is nice to have them all collected and described in one place. Both compilers have conducted extensive research in African affairs; Gardinier had earlier written the *Historical Dictionary of Gabon* (see ARBA 82, entry 329), while Wiseman put together *Political Leaders in Black Africa* (see ARBA 93, entry 761).

The main problem with these books is their high prices when compared to the extent of their contents; the costs might inhibit some libraries from purchasing them. Overall, the two titles are suitable for inclusion in either the reference or circulating collections of all academic and large public libraries, especially those with an interest in Africa or those that need bibliographies on these two small African nations. [R: Choice, Oct 93, p. 274]—**Daniel K. Blewett**

Malawi

100. Crosby, Cynthia A. **Historical Dictionary of Malawi.** 2d ed. Metuchen, N.J., Scarecrow, 1993. 202p. (African Historical Dictionaries, no.54). $30.00. DT3169.C76. 968.97'003. LC 93-15740. ISBN 0-8108-2628-3.

Malawi is one of the smallest African countries—a colonial gerrymander—but this alone should not explain the mere 135 pages of text that, together with a brief chronology and a list of acronyms, constitute most of this work. The emphasis in the entries is relentlessly modern and contemporary, as if Malawi has no discernible past. In tune with Crosby's interests, educational matters receive the greatest attention. Whatever their other failings, many of the African Historical Dictionaries have contained useful bibliographies. Here, however, only books are included, and many of these relate only tangentially to Malawi. In lieu of citing articles, there is a select list of Malawi periodicals, almost none of which will be of interest, or even available, to the volume's presumed clientele. This is supplemented by a list of general African journals that are of even less value. In the bibliography misspellings abound, capitalization is random, and currency is largely absent. Not recommended.—**David Henige**

Mauritania

101. Calderini, Simonetta, Delia Cortese, and James L. A. Webb, Jr., comps. **Mauritania.** Santa Barbara, Calif., ABC-Clio, 1992. 165p. maps. index. (World Bibliographical Series, v.141). $65.00. 016.9661. ISBN 1-85109-152-1.

This well-prepared volume in the ever-expanding World Bibliographical series is a useful compendium of materials relating to Mauritania, which persists in being one of Africa's least-known countries. Prepared by three recognized scholars of Mauritania, the work includes 405 items in several languages (predominantly French and English) that cover a variety of topics, including history, education, and religion. The annotations are ample and have numerous cross-references. The work has author, title, and subject indexes. [R: Choice, Mar 93, p. 1106]—**Dorothy C. Woodson**

Sierra Leone

102. Binns, Margaret, and Tony Binns, comps. **Sierra Leone.** Santa Barbara, Calif., ABC-Clio, 1992. 235p. maps. index. (World Bibliographical Series, v.148). $65.00. 016.9664. ISBN 1-85109-101-7.

This annotated bibliography supplies a comprehensive bibliographic list of hard-to-locate sources on Sierra Leone. A useful summary of the cultural and political history of the country is included in the introduction. The annotated entries are arranged under broad subject headings, including such topics as geography, history, traveler's accounts, women, and education. A feature relatively new to this series is a selective list of recent doctoral theses on Sierra Leone that are available in the United States and the United Kingdom. Author, title, and subject indexes are provided.—**Jane Jurgens**

South Africa

103. Limb, Peter. **The ANC and Black Workers in South Africa, 1912-1992: An Annotated Bibliography.** New Providence, N.J., Hans Zell/Reed Reference Publishing, 1993. 380p. index. $95.00. 016.32240968. LC 93-26607. ISBN 1-873836-95-3.

Since 1912 the African National Congress (ANC) has been fighting the apartheid government of South Africa. This conflict has assumed increasing importance in the last couple of decades, and the growth in the literature on this subject mirrors this fact. The book seems to be misnamed, as most of the materials listed here do not concentrate just on Black workers, but on the broader struggle, of which the contest over workers is just a part. Thus, this title is useful for finding citations to a wide range of materials on the subject.

The introduction sketches the background of the ANC, the available literature, and the scope and arrangement of this book. There are 4,016 numbered entries for books, journal articles, theses, conference papers, audiovisual materials, unpublished or archival materials, government and intergovernmental organization publications, bibliographies, and other reference works. There are an index and list of acronyms and abbreviations. Most of the entries have a line or two of annotation, but some have nothing but the bibliographical citation. The first names of the authors are not spelled out. As might be expected, a great number of the entries refer to materials from South Africa. Of real value is the list of hard-to-find materials from the ANC, which almost reside in the realm of gray literature.

Because of its scope and the large number of citations, this is now probably the best bibliography on the ANC available, with far more citations than Alfred Kagan's *The African National Congress of South Africa* (UN Centre Against Apartheid, Department of Political and Security Council Affairs, 1982). Its high price, however, will surely deter many institutions from purchasing it. The cover has the ANC logo on it, which is not widely found elsewhere. Recommended for academic, large public, and special collections interested in this subject area.—**Daniel K. Blewett**

Sudan

104. Daly, M. W., comp. **Sudan.** rev. ed. Santa Barbara, Calif., ABC-Clio, 1992. 194p. maps. index. (World Bibliographical Series, v.40). $81.00. 016.9624. ISBN 1-85109-187-4.

There are 708 numbered and briefly annotated entries for English-language items in this revised item, compared with 559 in the previous edition (previously reviewed in ARBA 84, entry 297); approximately half of these entries are for new materials. Brief annotations are included, sometimes as short as one sentence. Along with numerous cross-references, separate author/title and subject indexes are provided, and there is a general map of the country at the end. The introduction is a brief sketch of the history and current situation of that impoverished country. While there are a few citations from Sudan, most of the entries are for items from Great Britain. This reflects understandable British interest in a former colony. A few U.S. government publications are listed, and most of the periodical citations refer to *Sudan Notes and Records*, published in Khartoum since 1919. Also helpful are citations to chapters from various books. *Sudan*'s chapters cover sources for libraries and archives, history, population, peoples, politics, and other such subject areas. The statistics chapter lists only two sources, indicating the fact that Third World countries are not covered nearly as well as other parts of the globe. However, it was surprising that certain well-known titles were missing, such as *The Cambridge Encyclopedia of Africa* (see ARBA 83, entry 301) and *Encyclopedia of the Third World* (see ARBA 93, entry 137).

Daly, currently at Memphis State University, also wrote *Imperial Sudan* (Cambridge University Press, 1991), and is to be thanked for undertaking the grueling task of compiling this useful volume. However, it should be pointed out that one can also find most of the citations by searching various electronic databases, such as OCLC, RLIN, and the Social Science Citation Index. Unfortunately, as are the other volumes in this long-running series, it is vastly overpriced for the amount of material contained within its covers. Alternatively, the money spent for this book could be used to purchase some of the items listed within. The title under review is suitable for all academic institutions and large public libraries (where demand warrants it). [R: Choice, Mar 93, p. 1108]—**Daniel K. Blewett**

105. Fluehr-Lobban, Carolyn, Richard A. Lobban, Jr., and John Obert Voll. **Historical Dictionary of the Sudan.** 2d ed. Metuchen, N.J., Scarecrow, 1992. 409p. (African Historical Dictionaries, no.53). $59.50. DT155.3.V64. 962.4'003. LC 92-15858. ISBN 0-8108-2547-3.

This is an extensive update of the volume on the Sudan originally published in 1978 with Voll as editor. Building on Voll's base, Lobban and Fluehr-Lobban, both of whom teach at Rhode Island College, have created a solid and much-needed reference source. Much has changed in the huge African melting pot of the Sudan since 1978, and one of this work's major strengths is its information on those changes, along with updated access to recent scholarship on the country. The bibliography in particular deserves praise. No institution that supports African studies can afford to be without this volume. [R: Choice, June 93, p. 1600]—**James A. Casada**

ASIA

General Works

106. **Asia 1992 Yearbook.** 32d ed. Hong Kong, National Fair/Review Publishing; distr., Bristol, Pa., Taylor & Francis, 1992. 216p. illus. maps. $39.95pa. ISBN 9-627-01046-4.

Asia 1992 is a bit of a misnomer. The Asia covered by the yearbook does not include any country west of Afghanistan, nor the now-independent states of Soviet Central Asia. Instead, the volume concentrates on political and economic developments in the regions and countries from Afghanistan to Japan. The first section contains interesting and informative data for each country, such as land area (percent cultivated, percent forest, percent pasture), population (total, percent average annual growth, projected number for 2010, urban), students, workforce, prices, public expenditures, and foreign trade. Hard data are given for 1990 and estimates made for 1991. The second section contains 12 essays that report developments and analyze trends in the region. After a synopsis of events in Asia, one essay considers the results of the Gulf War and of the demise of the Soviet Union on the foreign relations of states in the region, concentrating on Japan, China, and India. Succeeding essays report and analyze population growth, sources and geographical goals of refugees, effects of aid and development banks, trade, Asian markets, commodity production, energy production and consumption, fishing, transport, and regional alignments. The third section details political and social developments, foreign relations, and economic and infrastructural changes for each country during 1991. Each country entry is accompanied by a small map and a chart with economic and business information. The final section is a page listing important events during 1991, identified by country.

This yearbook has been written by a number of experts who have packed it with interesting and important information that will be useful to international businesspeople, academics, and travelers. Published by the *Far Eastern Economic Review*, the yearbook has impeccable credentials and should be in all metropolitan and academic libraries.—**David L. White**

107. **Bibliographic Guide to East Asian Studies 1991.** New York, G. K. Hall, 1992. 570p. (Bibliographic Guides). $175.00. ISBN 0-8161-7158-0. ISSN 1046-8765.

This book is one of 23 specialized subject guides that represent materials cataloged by the New York Public Library and the Library of Congress. It is designed to ease the work of catalogers and acquisitions librarians and to provide access to hard-to-find materials for professionals in the field.

The focus of this volume is on current monographic and series titles and reprints of historical materials that have been published in Chinese, Korean, and Japanese. The materials are not esoteric or rare. Most of the entries range from the mid-1960s to the 1990s and include works published in minority languages spoken on mainland China, such as Uighur. Some English-language publications are also included. All information on a particular work has been transliterated into English script when appropriate. The entries are arranged in a dictionary list with a full catalog record that includes author, title, imprint, number of pages, subject headings, call numbers, and other appropriate cataloging information. The guide covers biographies; literature; maps; and works on economics, history, sociology, and description and travel.

This specialized guide will be useful for researchers seeking East Asian materials published in their original languages. Recommended for larger academic libraries with a focus on Asian studies.

—**Jane Jurgens**

108. Shulman, Frank Joseph, comp. and ed. **Doctoral Dissertations on Asia: An Annotated Bibliographical Journal of Current International Research. Volume 15: No. 1 & 2.** Ann Arbor, Mich., Association for Asian Studies, 1993. 202p. index. $20.00pa. ISSN 0098-4485.

The latest volume of this annual (see ARBA 89, entry 106 and ARBA 86, entry 120 for reviews of previous volumes) continues as the nearly definitive guide to doctoral research on Asia (defined as incorporating East Asia, Southeast Asia, and South Asia, including Afghanistan). It also covers dissertations on Asian communities outside of Asia. Despite the 1993 date, its 2,456 entries range from 1991 back to the early 1980s. While most of the entries can be found in the print and electronic versions of *Dissertation Abstracts International* (DAI), the volume's real value lies in identifying dissertations from Europe (Eastern and Western), Asia, and elsewhere that are not covered in DAI. With this fifteenth volume (the inclusion of numbers hearkens back to two early volumes that appeared semiannually), the absence of a cumulation of entries increasingly reduces the title's utility, because one must examine a great number of paper volumes—a task aggravated by the broad time span for the entries in each volume.

Shulman has offered some cumulations by region in the past (cited in the introduction) and indicates that a cumulation for China and Inner Asia (1976-1990) is forthcoming and that cumulations for Southeast Asia (1968-1995) and South Asia (1971-1995) are in preparation. These will be welcome tools, but the scholar of Asia who would remain current with dissertation research and the world of knowledge will still need to consult the most recent annual volumes.—**K. Mulliner**

China

109. **People's Republic of China Year Book 1991/92. Volume 11.** Edited by Editorial Department of the PRC Year Book, Beijing. Beijing, China, PRC Year Book and Hong Kong, Wah Gar Group; distr., Bristol, Pa., Taylor & Francis, c1991, 1992. 587p. illus. $130.00. ISSN 1000-9396.

This is the official yearbook of the People's Republic of China (PRC), providing an annual record of people, places, and major historical events. Published annually in both Chinese and English versions, this is the 11th edition and covers primarily the calendar year 1990 (including a month-by-month chronicle of events from January to December).

Opening with full-page cover reproductions of the national flag, emblem, and anthem of the PRC, the book continues with the constitution of the PRC and a general introduction. Next come specialized sections on the land, history, politics, legal system, economy, industry, agriculture, transportation, telecommunications, military affairs, foreign relations, science and technology, education, public health, culture and arts, sports, society, daily life, religion, provinces, autonomous regions, municipalities, special economic zones, open cities, and "burgeoning industrial centres." A beautiful full-color display of stamps issued in China in 1990 occupies four separate plates. An appendix covers copyright law, tax law, regulations governing wholly foreign-owned enterprises, and statutes encouraging overseas Chinese investment (including Hong Kong and Macao) in China. Full-page color advertisements for "outstanding enterprises" promote everything from yeast powder and canned asparagus to hard alloys and tea. Brief biographies of the most prominent political figures, celebrities, and people in the limelight are included, along with 20 obituaries. Important speeches and even important articles written by China's leaders are reproduced.

The material presented here is not altogether objective. Most of the information has been supplied by newspaper writers and drawn from *Xinhua*, China's official news agency. Additional information was provided by ministries of the state and local governments. What this yearbook offers, in fact, is the official government position, with headings claiming "remarkable successes for China's Foreign Affairs in 1990" or proclaiming that "China's Nongovernmental Diplomacy Obtains Remarkable Achievements." Everything here has been explicitly approved by the government as "reliable and authoritative."

Even so, as an almanac of information, facts, and statistics, this book contains a plentiful supply of very useful details about the PRC. While most of the material here pertains to 1990, extraordinary items and events as late as May 1991 have also been included.—**Joseph W. Dauben**

Hong Kong and Macau

110. Roberts, Elfed Vaughan, Sum Ngai Ling, and Peter Bradshaw. **Historical Dictionary of Hong Kong & Macau.** Metuchen, N.J., Scarecrow, 1992. 357p. (Asian Historical Dictionaries, no.10). $49.50. DS796.H757R64. 951.25'003. LC 92-20816. ISBN 0-8108-2574-0.

This book is meant to serve as a handy reference work for basic information on the economies, societies, and governance of both Hong Kong and Macao. It aims to document "the past and present and provide hints on the future" in the format of a historical dictionary. Because of the difficulty of deciding how to romanize Chinese words (Cantonese offers spellings quite different from those of either the now-standard mainland pinyin or the earlier widespread Wade-Giles system), the authors have chosen, when in doubt, to adopt spellings consonant with those used in official Hong Kong government documents. (Portuguese, the official language of Macao, is italicized throughout.) In addition to a map of the historical sites of Hong Kong, a brief historical and demographic introduction is followed by the dictionary itself, which runs from "Aberdeen" to "Zhou Enlai" and "Zhou Nan." Separate sections are devoted to different historical periods, Hong Kong politics and administration, the economy, society, crime, religion, law, short biographies, statistics, newspapers, and even other bibliographies about Hong Kong.

As in any dictionary, users must know in advance what they are looking for, and some entries are so vague—"Appointed Members" and "Disturbances," for example—that one must be able to second-guess how entries may have been created. Unless one is sufficiently knowledgeable to know about Po Leung Kuk or the

Godber Affair, the best way to use this volume is to consult it at random. The entries are always interesting and informative for anyone curious about Hong Kong. [R: Choice, June 93, p. 1608; LJ, Jan 93, p. 105]—**Joseph W. Dauben**

Indonesia

111. Cribb, Robert. **Historical Dictionary of Indonesia.** Metuchen, N.J., Scarecrow, 1992. 663p. (Asian Historical Dictionaries, no.9). $72.50. DS633.C75. 959.8'003. LC 92-19210. ISBN 0-8108-2542-2.

Although Indonesia is the fourth-largest nation in the world and is widely recognized for its arts (especially from Bali) and (to a lesser extent) for its regional importance in Southeast Asia, most Americans know little of its history or politics. This volume offers an excellent beginning point from which to redress such ignorance, as well as guidance for further reading. Many of the entries include references to the 1,172-title bibliography, enhancing its utility for the nonspecialist. Also, it exceeds previous volumes in the series in its coverage of flora, especially those of economic importance. In common with others in the series, the dictionary includes such useful compilations as a list of abbreviations and acronyms, a chronology, maps, and appendixes with election results and historical lists of high political officials (e.g., colonial governors, prime and other key ministers, military commanders).

While this book is a quantum improvement on a worthwhile series, it is not without shortcomings. As does much Indonesian scholarship, it tends to focus on Java at the expense of the other islands, and the inclusion of economic botany dramatizes the neglect of food—a pervasive theme in Indonesian life. A striking omission is an entry for Cut Nya Din (or Tjoet Njak Dien), the acclaimed Acehnese "national heroine" in the struggle against Dutch colonialism. However, if a library or reference collection were to have only one volume on Indonesia, this should be it.—**K. Mulliner**

112. Rowland, Ian, comp. **Timor, Including the Islands of Roti and Ndao.** Santa Barbara, Calif., ABC-Clio, 1992. 117p. maps. index. (World Bibliographical Series, v.142). $80.00. 016.95986. ISBN 1-85109-159-9.

The first question one poses when one sees this work is, "What possible thematic connection exists between Timor, Roti, and Ndao?" The physical closeness of these three islands is beyond dispute, but their historical and political connections are much slimmer. Some would argue that the only cultural thread to be pulled is the fact of past colonization, and that the differences of language and material culture are great enough to argue for separate studies.

Problems of scope and coverage plague the rest of the work as well. Early on, Rowland acknowledges his debt to Kevin Sherlock's *A Bibliography of Timor* (Canberra: Australian National University, 1980), which is widely hailed as the major work in the field; but it is hard to determine what kind of relationship Rowland envisioned between his work and Sherlock's. Overlap between the two bibliographies does exist but is not total. Sherlock did not, unfortunately, annotate his entries; Rowland, to his credit, does. As Sherlock's work is current through 1980, however, Rowland might more usefully have began his coverage with that year and have continued through the decade. Instead, this work starts its chronology with the twelfth century and ends it with the signing of the Timor Gap Treaty of 1989. The earliest published work Rowland includes, however, seems to be from 1925. Most of the pieces date from the 1960s through the 1980s. There are several pieces with the publication date 1991, but Herman C. Kemp's monumental *Annotated Bibliography of Bibliographies* (Leiden: KITLV Press, 1990) is not included. Having included material from 1991 in his work, Rowland confuses readers by not including anything about the bloody slaughter of 200 people in Dili on November 12, 1990.

The opening essay is crisp and interesting. The maps at the end are useful and the index accurate. But the work is unsatisfying.—**Ben Abel and Judith M. Brugger**

Japan

113. **The Cambridge Encyclopedia of Japan.** Richard Bowring and Peter Kornicki, eds. New York, Cambridge University Press, 1993. 400p. illus. maps. index. $49.95. ISBN 0-521-40352-9.

This encyclopedia differs from others that present information in alphabetical or chronological order. Its contents are grouped into eight categories: geography, history, language, thought and religion, arts and crafts, society, politics, and the economy. Each of these categories is further divided into 7-11 subjects that deal with numerous topics, such as the physical structure of the country, climate, education, family, judicial system, cinema, products, foreign policy, and important historical figures (including statespeople and writers). Because of the format, superb editing, and the self-contained boxed essays interspersed throughout the text, readers will get a firm impression of a well-synthesized book on the past history and present conditions of Japan, and they may be inspired to do more reading on Japan. For such readers, the list provided at the end of this encyclopedia that gives further reading in every category is helpful. Full-color and black-and-white photographs, illustrations, and maps help readers appreciate the rich tradition of Japanese culture and Japan's position in the world. The glossary is adequate; the periodization of Japanese and Chinese history is useful; and a thoughtful index is helpful. Recommended for high schools, colleges, and general libraries. [R: BR, Nov/Dec 93, pp. 57-58; LJ, 1 Nov 93, p. 72; WLB, Nov 93, p. 98]—**Seiko Mieczkowski**

114. **Directory of Japanese Technical Reports 1992-1993.** By the U.S. Department of Commerce, National Technical Information Service, Office of Business Development. Springfield, Va., National Technical Information Service, 1992. 1v. (various paging). index. (Japanese Directories Series). $40.00pa. ISBN 0-934213-33-X.

The National Technical Information Service (NTIS) is the central source for the public sale of U.S. government-sponsored research, development, and engineering reports, and for sales of foreign technical reports and other analyses prepared by national and local government agencies and their contractors or grant receivers. This directory was prepared in response to the Japanese Technical Literature Act of 1986. It consists of six main sections: reports announcements, keyword index, personal author index, corporate author index, contract grant number index, and National Technical Information Service order/report number index. Its 1,673 entries are first categorized into 38 broad subjects and then separated into 350-plus subcategories. Each entry is introduced with its subject category, report title, page count, abstract, and other reference information. For the convenience of users the directory explains the NTIS, procedure for ordering, and NTIS data on Japanese breakthrough products. This directory is useful for business and technical school libraries and for corporate research departments.—**Seiko Mieczkowski**

115. **Japan: An Illustrated Encyclopedia.** Tokyo, Kodansha; distr., New York, Macmillan, 1993. 2v. illus. maps. index. $250.00/set. DS805.J263. 952'.003. LC 93-20512. ISBN 4-06-931098-3.

This is the successor to the nine-volume *Kodansha Encyclopedia of Japan* (see ARBA 84, entry 305). Its stated purpose is to introduce Japanese history and culture to an international audience. This and more is accomplished in this impressive set. Brief, well-written, concise, and to-the-point articles are the heart of this encyclopedia. The scope is broad, covering all aspects of Japanese life, including history, geography, science, technology, folklore, business, and leisure. Although the articles are unsigned, the list of contributors includes many leading U.S., Japanese, and other international scholars and specialists. Of particular interest are the nearly 100 feature articles and pictorial studies that are interspersed throughout the set. These supplement the encyclopedia articles with essays on such topics as the place of women in Japan, bonsai trees, the Japanese view of World War II, best-sellers, food, Japanese management techniques, mixing business with pleasure, the Yakuza, life in a Japanese high school, and negotiating with the Japanese. The volumes are enhanced by more than 4,000 color photographs, illustrations, charts, and graphs. Included is a 16-page atlas, with a separate index. A 17-page illustrated chronology places Japanese history in perspective, and boldface type for topics covered in the encyclopedia section provides users with additional access to information. A 13-page subject-grouped bibliography leads readers to major English-language books on Japan. The treatment given to such topics as the attack on

Pearl Harbor and World War II are indicative of the accuracy and lack of bias found in this work. Access is excellent through a bilingual index to entry titles, as well as a classified guide that groups article titles in a broad-to-narrow arrangement.

The overall effect is a well-done, accurate, and highly readable picture of Japan in all of its aspects. Americans will be impressed with how well it answers the questions they have about this country, as well as its relation to the United States and the rest of the world. Highly recommended for most public and academic libraries. [R: Choice, Nov 93, p. 436; LJ, 1 Oct 93, pp. 86-89; RBB, 15 Dec 93, p. 778]

—**Donald E. Collins**

116. Makino, Noboru. **Total Forecast: Japan 1990s.** New York, Mansell/Cassell, 1993. 269p. $79.95. maps. ISBN 0-304-32717-4.

This book is the result of a cooperative effort by some 30 contributors in the Japanese think-tank of the Mitsubishi Research Institute. It can be read more or less in its entirety—as done by this reviewer and many Japanese readers—or used as a reference source. The original Japanese edition was published in 1992 as a continuation of a successful book published in 1989. Consequently, the most recent data are for the third quarter of 1991, while some data are only as recent as 1989.

The breadth of the coverage is imposing. The chapter topics cover economics, politics, regional issues, society, markets, industries, enterprise, and technology, each with 12-26 sections and capped by a summary viewpoint. There are figures and occasional maps. The sections concern mostly domestic Japanese issues, but some go beyond Japanese borders, such as those on the U.S. or German economies and the Pacific Rim area; and in politics on relations with Russia, the weakening United States hegemony, and the Middle Eastern political situation. Some problems discussed are universal for the developed countries, such as problems connected with international trade, the satellite cities, the health care problem, and changes in the employment structure toward knowledge-based industries. The volume traces and projects changes in the Japanese industrial structure, employment arrangements, and business practices. The chapter on technology contains some grand projections for the future—some already fulfilled and some futuristic—including biotechnology, functionalization of food, and invention of new industrial materials. The book does not contain a bibliography for further reading on particular topics. Recommended for all academic libraries and for larger public ones.—**Bogdan Mieczkowski**

Korea

117. Nahm, Andrew C. **Historical Dictionary of the Republic of Korea.** Metuchen, N.J., Scarecrow, 1993. 272p. (Asian Historical Dictionaries, no.11). $39.50. DS909.N34. 951.9'003. LC 93-3033. ISBN 0-8108-2603-8.

This historical dictionary is devoted mainly to the history and politics of the Republic of Korea, or South Korea, which emerged as a political entity in 1948. The accompanying chronology and introductory narrative, however, cover the history of all of Korea. Entries in the dictionary include historical, political, economic, social, and cultural topics; names of organizations and societies; religious sects; events; and biographical sketches of most of the important people of the era. Korean names are romanized according to the Korean Ministry of Education system, except for some names that are well known in the Western world; these have been transliterated as they appear in the Western media. A guide explains pronunciation and the Korean writing system.

An extensive bibliography of English-language publications lists bibliographies, guides, reference sources, periodicals and newspapers, and books on the history, culture, economy, politics, science, and society of Korea. Articles and dissertations are included only when no published book adequately covers the subject. Appendixes contain a government organization chart; lists of presidents, vice presidents, and prime ministers; and statistics on presidential and National Assembly elections. There is also a list of abbreviations and acronyms. Six black-and-white maps show Korea before and after partition. This will be an excellent aid for students of Korean history and politics, and useful in area studies and general reference collections. [R: Choice, Nov 93, p. 437; LJ, 15 June 93, p. 64]—**Shirley L. Hopkinson**

Malaysia

118. Kaur, Amarjit. **Historical Dictionary of Malaysia.** Metuchen, N.J., Scarecrow, 1993. 300p. maps. (Asian Historical Dictionaries, no.13). $37.50. DS596.K36. 959.5'003. LC 92-37427. ISBN 0-8108-2629-1.

The challenge of this volume is not to let its shortcomings completely obscure its redeeming features. It does provide 150 entries in 135 pages, 105 pages of bibliography, a short list of abbreviations, a chronology (providing years but not dates of events), 10 maps, several lists, and 27 tables ranging from election results to production of major products to imports and exports. Unfortunately, many of the latter provide only recent data and afford little historical comparison. Conspicuous in its absence is any guide to the Malaysian royal and honorary titles (by birth and bestowed) used throughout the volume. A strength lies in the identification of "mosquito" (minor) parties, but the book inexplicably omits the Socialist Front and its constituent Parti Rakyat and Labour Party (despite *q.v.* references to all three in other entries), which posed the most serious challenge in the 1960s. The *see also* references are useful, but blind *q.v.* and the absence of *see* references or an index compromise the volume's value. The lengthy bibliography suffers from questionable inclusions (e.g., older bibliographies and titles focusing on Singapore) and glaring omissions (e.g., the influential *Utusan Melayu* from a list of newspapers and, from a list of professional periodicals, such important titles as *Akademika, Archipel, Berita, Malay Literature*, and *Malayan Nature Journal*). However, the book's greatest failure is the limited number of dictionary entries. Probably twice as many could have been included without trivializing the text. Even the entries included tend to be pedestrian. In sum, this is a disappointing volume that may be of limited value in a reference collection for nonspecialists. [R: Choice, Dec 93, p. 587]—**K. Mulliner**

Maldives

119. Reynolds, C. H. B., comp. **Maldives.** Santa Barbara, Calif., ABC-Clio, 1993. 93p. maps. index. (World Bibliographical Series, v.158). $59.00. 016.95495. ISBN 1-85109-076-2.

This is the seventh volume on South Asia in the series. (Only Bangladesh and Sikkim remain to be covered.) The Maldives (pronounced to rhyme with "gives," not "hives") was proclaimed a republic in 1968; it only began to admit tourists and foreigners in 1972 and has a long history of isolation dating back to the twelfth century. Works cited in this fully annotated bibliography are primarily in English, although there is a smattering of French and German titles. Because the official language of the Maldives is Divehi, English-language resources on the country are necessarily incomplete. Reynolds does provide a brief sketch of indigenous language sources in the thorough and lucid introduction. The sections on politics, history, and flora and fauna account for most of the citations, which heavily represent periodical articles from the journals of British learned societies. The second biggest source of materials seems to be government publishers, both national and international. A subject-phrase search on "Maldives" in the Research Libraries Group's RLIN database produced 240 monographic hits. The present volume annotates 320 items.

At the end there is a lengthy and convenient index in a single alphabetical sequence for authors, titles, and subjects. The map provided at the end of the volume is clear and useful, despite the fact that it shows only about 10 percent of the Maldives' total island count.—**Sung Ok Kim**

Polynesia

120. Craig, Robert D. **Historical Dictionary of Polynesia.** Metuchen, N.J., Scarecrow, 1993. 298p. (Oceanian Historical Dictionaries, no.2). $37.50. DU510.C73. 996'.003. LC 93-4745. ISBN 0-8108-2706-9.

This collection of historical data covers a cultural and geographical area in the Pacific Ocean: the Polynesian Triangle, from Hawaii in the north to New Zealand in the southwest to Easter Island in the southeast. Thirteen island groups or political entities are included. The main section of the work, the dictionary, includes names of persons, places, political parties, societies, foundations, organizations,

treaties and other agreements, and terms that are relevant to the area. Most entries are one or two paragraphs in length, but those on countries or territories may be several pages long. An introduction describes the area as a whole, gives a historical summary, and discusses current conditions. A general bibliography lists bibliographies; reference works; atlases; and major publications on the histories, religions, cultural arts, economies, and social and scientific conditions in Polynesia. There are also separate bibliographies for each of the islands or island groups. Appendixes list the names of the individual Polynesian islands within the various groups and of the rulers and administrators, and give population and area statistics and the political status of each entity. The volume also contains a list of acronyms and abbreviations and a chronology. The eminently qualified Craig has brought together an immense amount of information that will be useful to students and researchers as well as to general reference collections.
—Shirley L. Hopkinson

Taiwan

121. **Republic of China Yearbook 1991-92.** Lien-sheng Ma, ed. in chief. Taipei, Taiwan, Kwang Hwa Publishing; distr., Bristol, Pa., Taylor & Francis, c1991, 1992. 663p. illus. maps. index. $45.00. ISBN 957-9227-35-7. ISSN 1013-0942.

This yearbook consists of 3 parts: events in the Republic of China, past and present, in 32 chapters; a who's who in the Republic of China; and appendixes. Preceded by national symbols and 4 biographies (the founder of the republic, the current president and vice president, and the premier), the 32 chapters deal with a variety of topics, including the year in review, geography, people, language, history, constitution and law, governments, politics, economy, culture, religion, communications, and the society. The 18 appendixes are valuable for quick reference, as they include such things as a table of Chinese dynasties, a chronology, the constitution, major documents of the year, directories, holidays, and a selected list of government statistical publications.

The nature of such a publication means it will quickly become dated. For instance, the cabinet members and elected representatives have already changed. An interim publication between editions that listed new officials and elected representatives and major events would be an invaluable supplement.

Because the yearbook is sponsored by the government, it is, to a certain extent, politically biased. The territorial map of mainland China (whose territory has been claimed as part of the Republic of China) contains old geographical names no longer used in the People's Republic of China after 1949, and includes Mongolia, an independent nation not yet recognized by the Republic of China. These may be considered ideological differences, but are clearly factual errors. Also, information relating to the People's Republic of China is far from current. For instance, the population of minorities in China is based on a 1982 Chinese census. The data are quite old as compared with the newly published *A Mosaic of Peoples' Life among China's Ethnic Minorities* (China Nationality Art Photograph Publishing House, 1992).

In general, the chapters are well written with references in English or Chinese or both. Most chapters are supplied with charts and statistical figures. This work is the best source of information about the Republic of China, although information in general therein is from 1948—basically information on the Republic of China in Taiwan.—**Tze-chung Li**

Vietnam

122. Marr, David G., with Kristine Alilunas-Rodgers, comps. **Vietnam.** Santa Barbara, Calif., ABC-Clio, 1992. 393p. index. (World Bibliographical Series, v.147). $84.00. 016.9597. ISBN 1-85109-092-4.

Over the past three decades, a good number of English-language bibliographies on Vietnam have been published, but none of them are as comprehensive, well-organized, and up-to-date as the work under review. Marr is a noted historian of Vietnamese anticolonialism and modern Vietnam. His book consists of 1,038 annotated books and articles published in English or translated from Vietnamese, French, or Russian sources into English. Entries are arranged under 32 broad subject categories, and under each category, entries are organized alphabetically by title. Although materials chosen for inclusion are appropriate, additional English-language publications written by Vietnamese should have been included, such as *Twenty Years and Twenty Days* by Nguyen Cao Ky (the former prime minister of South Vietnam), *Our Endless War* by Tran Van Don (the general who orchestrated the coup d'etat that overthrew President Ngo Dinh Diem in 1963), and articles from such scholarly journals as *The Journal of American History*.

Annotations are evaluative and brief, averaging 100 words for each item. Full bibliographical information accompanies each citation, and cross-references are provided at the end of each subject. Also included in the text are a well-written introduction surveying the history of Vietnam; a chronology; indexes of authors, titles, and subjects; and one map. Additional maps, an index of periodicals used, and a list of libraries or resource centers that hold materials on the subject would have been helpful.

This compilation will be useful to a wide variety of users, from Vietnam specialists to college students. Highly recommended for all academic and large public libraries. [R: Choice, Sept 93, p. 84]—**Binh P. Le**

AUSTRALIA

123. Albinski, Nan Bowman. **Directory of Resources for Australian Studies in North America.** Clayton, Austral., National Centre for Australian Studies and University Park, Pa., Australia-New Zealand Studies Center, Pennsylvania State University, 1992. 211p. index. $17.00pa. ISBN 0-7326-0435-4.

This sourcebook, copublished by the centers for Australian Study at Monash University and Pennsylvania State University, is designed to assist Australian scholars working in North America, and North American students of Australian history and culture, in locating materials pertinent to their studies. The directory lists 340 libraries, galleries, and museums in North America with Australiana collections. The institutions are listed according to the type of materials within the collections. Forty-six institutions, for example, are identified as housing collections of aboriginal art and artifacts; thirty-two are listed as depositories of Australian legal and government documents. For each of the 340 entries the directory provides the mailing address and telephone number of the institution, the hours and days it is open, its admission policy and fees, and a description of the size and contents of the pertinent holdings. The volume also includes a brief bibliography of Australian studies publications, an index of repositories, and an index of names. While this "what and where guide" to Australiana holdings will not have a large readership, it will be appreciated by specialists in the field of Australian studies. [R: Choice, June 93, p. 1595]

—**Terry D. Bilhartz**

124. Docherty, James C. **Historical Dictionary of Australia.** Metuchen, N.J., Scarecrow, 1992. 284p. (Oceanian Historical Dictionaries, no.1). $35.00. DU90.D63. 994'.003. LC 92-32339. ISBN 0-8108-2613-5.

The 200-plus entries in this historical dictionary include each of the capital cities, the states, population characteristics (e.g., Methodists, "New Australians," Jews), events with particular links to Australia (e.g., Rum Rebellion, Gallipoli), countries with Australian links (e.g., Great Britain, the United States, Korea), Australian institutions (e.g., dictation test, kangaroos and wallabies, overlanders, aborigines, Phar Lap, Eureka Stockade), and people (e.g., Gough Whitlam, T. W. Roberts, Patrick White, Sir John Monash, "Ned" Kelly). Averaging 100 to 150 words in length, most entries provide only basic (but clear) information; the selection of topics and the writing of each entry are clearly historical, as one would expect from the historian-author. An introduction sketches the physical environment, the historical setting, and Australian society; it serves as a good guide for the beginning reader. Four brief appendixes cover historical chronology, lists of governors-general and prime ministers, and historical statistics (14 tables plus a list of data sources). There is a 550-plus-entry bibliography of books classified by 35 topics (e.g., discovery of Australia, religion, film). Some entries are annotated. [R: Choice, July/Aug 93, p. 1748; LAR, Oct 93, p. 570; RBB, 15 Mar 93, pp. 1376-77]—**Richard A. Miller**

CANADA

125. **Corpus Almanac & Canadian Sourcebook, 1993.** 28th ed. Don Mills, Ont., Southam Information and Technology Group, 1992. 1v. (various paging). illus. maps. index. $157.50. ISBN 0-919217-59-1.

Squeezed into one volume since the previous ARBA review (see ARBA 90, entry 127), *Corpus Almanac & Canadian Sourcebook* (CACS) continues to provide users with extensive, accurate information on the world's second largest country. It includes all the information one would expect in an almanac: general (e.g., the Canadian National Anthem, star maps as seen from the Canadian skies), geography, people (e.g., demographic trends), religion, communications, transportation, and more. New to this edition are school board listings in the education chapter and government departmental mandates and pertinent legislation in the government chapters. More libraries are now listed, and more contacts have been added to the section on sources of information. Along with the subject index, there is now an index of associations.

The main competitor to CACS appears to be *Canadian Almanac & Directory* (CAD) (see ARBA 92, entry 98), although the two are less comparable than their titles imply. CAD consists largely of directory information, while CACS is about one-third directory and the rest almanac-style data. CACS provides descriptions of major agencies, associations, and governmental bodies; CAD generally just has directory data and contact people for these organizations. For the most part, the directory information in CAD is more complete than that in CACS. For example, CACS lists 11 public, academic, and special libraries (one entry does mention 10 branches) in the Yukon Territory; CAD lists 16 regular and 19 special ones. A check of a section included in both books—book publishers in Canada—reveals that CAD's list is more extensive but that CACS does contain a few not in the other book. And CAD provides information for things that CACS omits (e.g., specific types of publications, awards).

CACS's subject index is similar to that in CAD—one must search for key terms in a name rather than the name itself. However, in CACS, boldface type is used for major subject headings (e.g., energy), with bullets for elements under those headings, making its index easier to use.

Libraries in Canada should acquire both volumes. In the United States, the same is true for academic and large public libraries. For smaller U.S. libraries, CACS would be a good all-around choice, while CAD will serve those who need extensive directory information about Canada.—**D. A. Rothschild**

126. **Directory to Canadian Studies in Canada. Repertoire des Etudes Canadiennes au Canada.** 4th ed. Montreal, Association for Canadian Studies, 1993. 312p. index. price not reported. 971'.0071'171. ISBN 0-919363-29-6.

This directory focuses on agencies within Canada that promote Canadian studies. It complements the *International Directory of Canadian Studies* (see ARBA 93, entry 132) and the *Directory to Funding Sources for Canadian Studies* (Canadian Studies and Special Projects Directorate). The directory lists Canadian studies and multidisciplinary programs available in colleges and universities, research institutes, learned societies and other associations, and sources of awards and scholarships. Information is accurate and current as of 1992. Entries include descriptions, contact names, addresses, and telephone and fax numbers. Appendixes list useful reference tools and research journals.

Subject and name indexes have been added to this edition, and the table of contents has been substantially expanded. Another new feature is the emphasis on arranging subject matter according to broad categories. This edition has also been expanded to include a new section on multidisciplinary studies. This is a valuable resource for humanities and social sciences researchers both in Canada and abroad.—**Mary Hemmings**

127. Watkins, Mel, ed. **Canada.** New York, Facts on File, 1993. 701p. maps. index. (Handbooks to the Modern World). $60.00. F1008.C2. 971. LC 91-45584. ISBN 0-8160-1831-6.

This volume is a collection of informative essays and statistics on Canada. The text is divided into five parts: the provinces and territories of Canada, history, politics, economics, and social affairs. Part 1 provides basic information and recent history for each province or territory followed by a section of comparative statistics. Parts 2 to 5 contain 32 essays by distinguished Canadian scholars on relevant topics, such as "Federalism" by Donald V. Smiley; "A Global Partnership: The Canada-United States

Political Relationship in the 1990s" by John Kirton; "Natural Resources and Primary Manufacturing Industries" by Thomas I. Gunton; "Immigration and Multiculturalism" by Harold Troper; and "Canada and the United States Compared" by Seymour Martin Lipset. The emphasis in the essays is on factual information, although some do contain interpretive information by noted scholars. The statistics generally cover up to the late 1980s, while the essays stretch to 1990-1991, with some 1992 information. Each essay concludes with a short list of further reading. In-depth documentation is not provided. A detailed name, title, and subject index is supplied; it is useful in this type of reference work. This volume is an excellent reference handbook for factual information through the 1980s and for those who want more than statistical information. [R: LJ, 1 June 93, p. 102; RBB, 15 Sept 93, pp. 184-186]—**Lorna K. Rees-Potter**

EUROPE

General Works

128. Moss, Joyce, and George Wilson. **Peoples of the World: Western Europeans: The Culture, Geographical Setting, and Historical Background....** Detroit, Gale, 1993. 377p. illus. maps. index. $39.95. ISBN 0-8103-8868-5.

This is one of a series designed to briefly profile the world's various peoples in terms of their geographical environment, historical evolution, and basic cultural characteristics. Although nowhere stated, it appears to be aimed at a general library audience, or perhaps at the level of secondary education. Nine examples of old cultures (e.g., Romans, Celtics, Vikings) are followed by twenty-seven entries on cultures today. For each of these, basic data on geography and history are followed by discussions of such cultural characteristics as religion; celebrations; farming and other traditional economic activities; peculiarities of food, clothing, and shelter; and language.

Technically, the book is at best only a minimal production. The computer-generated maps that locate each group are of such poor quality as to be virtually useless, and the general map on the cover includes Turkey and much of Eastern Europe as well as the nominal subject area. Most of the photographs used as illustrations are badly outdated, and the bibliographical materials are sketchy at best. On a larger scale, the authors fail to adequately explain what is meant by a "people." In the modern world, this is an increasingly contentious issue, as countless self-identified groups struggle for political recognition of their individuality. Here, it seems inevitable to question why Faroe Islanders (about 50,000 people) have their own chapter, while Alsatians, Corsicans, Galicians, and Sardinians (to name only a few ethnically conscious groups) do not. It will be interesting to see whether other volumes in this series attempt to deal as simplistically with even more culturally complex regions of the world.—**James R. McDonald**

Armenia

129. Vassilian, Hamo B., ed. **The Armenians: A Colossal Bibliographic Guide to Books Published in the English Language.** Glendale, Calif., Armenian Reference Books, 1993. 206p. $45.00 spiralbound. Z3461.V38. 016.95662. LC 93-26487. ISBN 0-931539-03-X.

Culled from a variety of databases, including OCLC, RLIN, and the University of California catalog, this compilation contains an extensive list of works about Armenia and Armenians that have some English-language text. Arranged in alphabetical order by author and title, the bibliography contains 1,900 individual titles and almost 3,600 citations. Almost every entry includes author, title, publisher, publication date, pagination, size and frequency, and ISBN.

Vassilian calls this the first bibliography of its kind to attempt comprehensive coverage of Armenian history and culture in the English language. A survey of other bibliographies on Armenians does indeed indicate that this work has more extensive coverage than previous compilations. Nevertheless, it has some regrettable drawbacks. Unlike the excellent but extremely out-of-date bibliography *Armenia and the Armenians* (New York Public Library, 1919), this work does not have any indexes. (Vassilian does note that he will include a subject index in the next edition, making it more accessible to students of Armenian history.) Furthermore, the bibliography contains no annotations, nor does it indicate library holdings. It will be most useful for the serious scholar of Armenia.—**Donald Altschiller**

Eastern Europe

130. **The American Bibliography of Slavic and East European Studies for 1990.** Aaron Trehub with Magdalena Pietraszek, comps. and eds. Stanford, Calif., American Association for the Advancement of Slavic Studies, 1992. 407p. index. $40.00pa.; $55.00pa. (institutions). ISSN 0094-3770.

The last time the *American Bibliography of Slavic and East European Studies* was reviewed was in ARBA 87 (see entry 122). That edition covered the years 1983-1984 and was published in 1986. The present volume has a similar time gap and covers Albania, Yugoslavia, all Eastern European countries, and the former Soviet Union. Under such headings as "Emigres, Refugees, and Diasporas," "Literature," and "History," several former Soviet republics are listed separately, including such "nationalities" as Moravians. Author and subject indexes are very helpful in locating desired information. Generally speaking, this project is the most comprehensive list of books and articles published in English about Eastern Europe and will be essential to all scholars and students of this area.—**Bohdan S. Wynar**

131. Croucher, Murlin, comp. and ed. **Slavic Studies: A Guide to Bibliographies, Encyclopedias, and Handbooks.** Wilmington, Del., Scholarly Resources, 1993. 2v. $150.00/set. Z2483.S554. 016.947. LC 92-28912. ISBN 0-8420-2374-7.

In his preface Croucher states that this guide "attempts to list major reference materials for Slavic studies in English, German, French, and in any of the Slavic languages." Unfortunately, from a methodological and research-reference point of view, his objectives and the execution of this project are not satisfactory either in coverage, accuracy, or other reference features. The guide consists of two volumes containing eight sections on area studies, Eastern Europe and the Balkans, Bulgaria, Czechoslovakia, Poland, the former Soviet Union, the former Yugoslavia, and general references. There are author and title indexes. Citations for books and serials are arranged under specific subject areas and include the classification numbers for the Indiana University Library (IUL), or Library of Congress numbers in brackets if the book is not part of the IUL collection. Many entries contain brief capsule descriptive and, on rare occasions, evaluative annotations.

Croucher still uses the term *Soviet Union* "because it was the term in effect during the publication of most of the materials mentioned in the book" (p. xi). But this explanation is not justified in view of the present geopolitical realities in Eastern Europe. Croucher should have used present political state designations. Furthermore, he does not define the major concept of "Slavic Studies" (main heading), nor does he explain how many Slavic nations and states are represented in his publication. This is a weak and misleading methodological approach. For example, Lithuanians, Estonians, Latvians, Armenians, and Georgians do not belong to Slavic nations, yet he covers them. Another weak methodological point is the absence of selection criteria for included materials. If the majority of reference titles included are part of IUL holdings, then this information should be indicated on the title page. However, Croucher does not provide any statistical data pertaining to IUL Slavic holdings.

It is unfortunate that some bibliographical information is incorrect or incomplete, and many major titles are missing. For example, one finds the listing for *Bibliographic Guide to Soviet and East European Studies* that says it was canceled in 1988. In reality, this title was published in 1991 (see ARBA 92, entry 103). It is one of the major American reference tools in Slavic studies. In general the book omits some major Slavic reference sources, especially reference titles pertaining to newly established independent states in the former Soviet Union and the former Yugoslavia. *Encyclopedic Dictionary of Ethnic Organizations in the United States* (see ARBA 76, entry 394) is listed under "Emigres-Directory"; however, this publication deals in major part with American ethnic organizations, including Slavic-American institutions. There are other incorrect designations. Of *Ukraine: A Bibliographic Guide to English-Language Publications* (see ARBA 91, entry 115), it is said that "Although pro-Ukrainian prejudices dominate every annotation, this is an invaluable, unsurpassed reference aid." It seems unlikely that he checked every annotation. *Encyclopedia of Ukraine* (see ARBA 89, entry 123 and 85, entry 110) is listed under the subject heading "Ukraine-Handbook" with a "warning" that this "handbook" contains "some nationalist biases." However he does not illustrate these biases. At the same time, he lists *Ukrains'ka radians'ka entsyklopedia* under the subject heading "Ukraine-Encyclopedia," with no comment that this comprehensive work is pro-communist and thus biased. In general, this guide requires revision and major updating. [R: Choice, Dec 93, p. 590]—**Lubomyr R. Wynar**

132. Moss, Joyce, and George Wilson. **Peoples of the World: Eastern Europe and the Post-Soviet Republics.** Detroit, Gale, 1993. 415p. illus. maps. index. $39.95. ISBN 0-8103-8867-7.

This addition to Gale's Peoples of the World series appears comparable, in format and intellectual level, to companion volumes covering other geographical areas (e.g., North America, Western Europe). Text on the back cover invites the reader to "meet 34 peoples of Eastern Europe" and promises to address at least 11 miscellaneous topics, among them family structure, dress, nutrition, education, industry, and religion. The book makes a formal distinction between cultural groups and political entities. Thus, for example, Russians are treated as a cultural group with members residing in 15 countries besides Russia itself. Helpful prefatory material is followed by a brief "Ancient Cultures" section listing peoples such as Avars and Huns. A "Cultures of Today" section defines and describes 29 contemporary ethnic groups, providing information on each group's size, geographical locations, language, history, and culture, as well as a few bibliographical references. In the final major section, 22 "Country Briefs" cite facts regarding population, principal cities, topography, and current events. Also included are a small glossary and a short bibliography.

Eastern Europe's current state of flux undoubtedly presented a challenge during the compilation of this book, which is already becoming dated. For example, Czechoslovakia is still listed as a single country. In general, the work's treatment of its subject matter is very limited, sometimes superficial. The civil war raging in Yugoslavia, for instance, receives only about five paragraphs of coverage. Black-and-white maps and photographs are plentiful, but the former are not detailed, and the latter tend to be somewhat out-of-date and inadequately labeled.

Eastern Europe and the Post-Soviet Republics provides a basic overview of Eastern Europe's countries and numerous ethnic groups. It could prove useful for quick reference or as a starting point for research but could not be considered an authoritative reference tool.—**Lydia W. Wasylenko**

Great Britain

133. Gascoigne, Bamber. **Encyclopedia of Britain.** New York, Macmillan, 1993. 720p. illus. maps. $75.00. DA27.5.G37. 941'.003. LC 93-1881. ISBN 0-02-897142-6.

Great Britain and things British have long been the subject of many fine reference works, but the excellence of Gascoigne's *Encyclopedia of Britain* ensures that no apology is needed for his going over such well-trodden ground. The work is intended to be a guide to general knowledge about the past and present of Great Britain. Topics that solely concern the Republic of Ireland are excluded.

The volume contains 6,000 brief entries of 20 to several hundred words. The individual entries are well written, arranged alphabetically, and frequently illustrated with black-and-white or color pictures. Numerous cross- and *see* references allow a topic to be followed into related entries. People, places, events, and institutions from history, politics, religion, science, high culture, and popular culture form the topics of the entries. All monarchs and major cities are listed, along with the usual historical and cultural events and personages such as the Dissolution of the Monasteries, the Hundred Years War, and Alfred, Lord Tennyson. But there is more, with such unexpectedly diverse entries as *Dr. Who*, Frankie Goes to Hollywood, Gog and Magog, and scones. Although Gascoigne gave much thought to and sought multitudinous advice for his selection of entries, readers will undoubtedly miss favorite topics. It was heartening to see an entry for the novelist David Lodge but mystifying to find that Tom Sharpe was omitted. Compared to the worthy *Cambridge Illustrated Dictionary of British Heritage* (see ARBA 87, entry 506) and *Dictionary of Britain* (see ARBA 88, entry 1081), Gascoigne's volume is handsomer, larger, more eclectic, and more informative.—**Ronald H. Fritze**

Poland

134. Sanford, George, and Adriana Gozdecka-Sanford, comps. **Poland.** rev. ed. Santa Barbara, Calif., ABC-Clio, 1993. 250p. maps. index. (World Bibliographical Series, v.32). $84.00. 016.9438. ISBN 1-85109-180-7.

This is a successor to the 1984 edition by Richard Lewanski, with about 25 percent of the earlier cited works being retained. The main focus of the revised edition is on the dramatic and eventful period of the 1980s and early 1990s, from the rise of Solidarity to the first phase of post-communism. The 1984 edition should be kept for earlier historical coverage. The user will find almost 1,000 critical annotations for selected books and articles that are generally available on a wide variety of topics dealing with Poland (e.g., history, geography, economy, politics) and its people (e.g., culture, customs, religion, social organizations). The emphasis is on works written in English.

There is an excellent index in a single alphabetical sequence of authors (personal and corporate), titles of publications, and subjects. Index entries refer to both the main items and to other works mentioned in the notes to each item. Sanford is a specialist on Eastern Europe and Poland at Bristol University while Gozdecka-Sanford was a journalist and author in Poland and is now a freelance writer in England. This is an important reference source for all medium to large academic and public library collections and a must purchase for any collection emphasizing Eastern Europe.—**George S. Bobinski**

Portugal

135. Wheeler, Douglas L. **Historical Dictionary of Portugal.** Metuchen, N.J., Scarecrow, 1993. 288p. (European Historical Dictionaries, no.1). $37.50. DP535.W44. 946.9'003. LC 93-27030. ISBN 0-8108-2696-8.

The first in a new series of historical dictionaries focused on the various European countries, this book provides a detailed survey of one of Europe's more interesting, if less well known, nations. The coverage is comprehensive, considering the sweep of history from prehistoric times to the 1990s, and dealing as much with Portugal's impact on the world (e.g., explorations, colonial adventures) as with events within the national boundaries.

The work is divided into three major parts. A brief introductory section reviews Portuguese history chronologically and adds notes on the physical environment and demographics of the country. The main body of the book is in the form of an alphabetically arranged, cross-referenced dictionary that lists the people, places, dates, and events that have shaped the nation's history. Many of the entries are quite detailed: The one dealing with the late dictator Antonio de Oliveira Salazar runs some four pages. The final 100 pages of the book consist of a comprehensive bibliography, arranged in 32 sections, covering all aspects of Portugal's history, society, and economy.

Although it is possible to find fault with certain aspects of the book (e.g., the two maps are uninformative and poorly printed, some key works of historical geography seem to be missing from the bibliography), the overall result is a work of outstanding scholarship that provides both an excellent overview of Portugal and a useful starting point for future studies. It is hoped that forthcoming volumes in this series will maintain the same standards. [R: LJ, 1 Nov 93, p. 80]—**James R. McDonald**

Russia

136. Geron, Leonard, and Alex Pravda, eds. **Who's Who in Russia and the New States.** London, I. B. Tauris; distr., New York, St. Martin's Press, 1993. 1v. (unpaged). $185.00. ISBN 1-85043-487-5.

A revised, expanded edition of a 1989 publication, this directory is billed as "the most comprehensive and up-to-date guide to organizations and individuals in the political, economic, social and military life of the independent states that previously made up the Soviet Union" (dust jacket). The independent states include Armenia, Azerbaijan, Belarus, Estonia, Georgia, Kazakhstan, Kyrgyzstan, Latvia, Lithuania, Moldova, the Russian Federation, Tajikistan, Turkmenistan, Ukraine, and Uzbekistan.

The book is divided into two main parts, the first of which is relatively brief. Fifteen country entries list heads of state and key government officials, along with ministries, state committees, and other national bodies. Part 2 lists almost 7,000 significant public figures. While individuals from Russia predominate, the other states are certainly covered. As might be expected, entries for politicians, government officials, diplomats, and military officers abound, but virtually every field is represented. Among those featured are managers, historians, clergy, cosmonauts, engineers, physicists, physicians, ballet dancers, composers, writers, and at least one "worker." The fullness of biographical entries varies, depending on the prominence of and data available on individuals. Examples range from 3 lines for Arif Gadzhiev, an Azerbaijani politician, to 44 lines for Yevgeny Aleksandrovich Yevtushenko, the Russian poet, actor, and filmmaker. A typical entry may include full name and occupation; family information; education and career history; lists of publications, affiliations, and honors; address; and telephone, telex, and fax numbers.

Who's Who in Russia and the New States, a high-quality publication compiled with care, is a source of much information not yet available elsewhere. Some of the details cited may quickly become out-of-date, especially given Eastern Europe's current state of upheaval. But this fascinating work is potentially invaluable to anyone with a serious interest in contemporary Russia or the new states. [R: Choice, Nov 93, p. 440; WLB, Dec 93, p. 123]—**Lydia W. Wasylenko**

137. **Russia 1993: Political and Economic Analysis and Business Directory.** By Jonathan K. Schmidt. New York, Chamber World Network; distr., Gardena, Calif., SCB Distributors, [1993]. 328p. illus. maps. $65.00pa.

This glossy volume aims to be an overall guide to Russia for Western businesspeople. It provides a well-considered synopsis of recent events and attempts to explain the imbroglio of present politics and the ups and downs of economic reforms. In addition to being a guidebook for living in Russia, it also lists numerous contacts that could help a Westerner start a business. Although Schmidt advises that "doing business in Russia is not for the weak at heart," the tome has an optimistic tone overall. But no single volume is sufficient to fully cover entrepreneurship in Russia. Schmidt still seems to proceed from the concept of Russia as a unified empire and has not fully caught the dizzying swirl of centrifugal forces. Thus, the volume will age quickly. As long as the user considers it as a snapshot of one time and place, it may give an edge over the competition. It could also serve well as a reference work in libraries. [R: LJ, 1 May 93, p. 83; RBB, 15 Oct 93, pp. 475-76]—**Andrew Ezergailis**

Ukraine

138. **Encyclopedia of Ukraine. Volumes III, IV, V.** Danylo Husar Struk, ed. Toronto and Buffalo, N.Y., University of Toronto Press, 1993. 3v. illus. maps. $480.00/set. 947'.71'003. ISBN 0-8020-3996-0.

Encyclopedia of Ukraine, published in five volumes, serves as a complementary reference work for English-speaking people to *Entsyklopediia Ukrainoznaustva*, a multivolume Ukrainian encyclopedia initiated some 40 years ago by one of the most prominent Ukrainian scholars, Volodymyr Kubiovyc, and published by the Shevchenko Scientific Society in Europe. The publication of the Ukrainian work in the West played a significant role in the appearance of the first Soviet-Ukrainian encyclopedia, *Ukrains'ka Radians'ka Entsyklopediia*, published in 17 volumes in Kiev between 1958 and 1962. The second edition of this work was published in Ukrainian and Russian during 1977-1985 in 12 volumes.

The Ukrainian encyclopedia edited by Kubiovyc consists of two parts: a three-volume classified reference work arranged by broad disciplines or subject areas (e.g., archaeology, economy, fine arts) and a ten-volume encyclopedia in dictionary arrangement covering, in longer or briefer articles, the whole spectrum of Ukrainian historical, cultural, and political affairs. The first three-volume part of the encyclopedia was completed in 1952. With significant modifications and upgrading, this work was translated into English and published in two volumes between 1963 and 1971. George S. N. Luckyj made appropriate arrangements with the University of Toronto Press and supervised the translation of this important achievement of Ukrainian emigre scholars. It was published under the title *Ukraine: A Concise Encyclopaedia*. The present set of five volumes constitutes a revised and updated English version of the ten-volume second part of *Entsyklopediia Ukrainoznaustva*. The first volume of this work was published in 1984, the second in 1988, the remaining three in 1993. Editor-in-chief Kubiovyc (1900-1985) was an eminent geographer, demographer, and author of some 400 publications, including the monumental *Atlas of Ukraine* and *Geography of Ukraine*, both published in Ukrainian before World War II. He devoted some 40 years of his life to work on this encyclopedia, first in Ukrainian, then in English. Beginning with volume three, Professor Struk (University of Toronto) assumed the position of editor-in-chief, and the editorial board of five scholars is substantially changed, retaining only one person from previous volumes.

The first volume of *Encyclopedia of Ukraine* was reviewed in some detail in ARBA (see ARBA 85, entry 110), and at that time it was indicated that this encyclopedic work is a first-rate guide to the history and culture of Ukrainians, both in Ukraine and abroad. There is no question as to the historical significance of this set, and the high level of scholarship continues in the pages of these volumes. Among some 150 contributors there are a number of nationally or even internationally known scholars, such as O. Arkhimovych, B. R. Bociurkiw, E. Borschak, D. Chyzhevsky, E. Glowinsky, S. Hordynsky, O. Horbach, V. Holubnychy, M. Hlobenko, B. Kravtsiv, Z. Kuzelia, G. Luckyj, I. Koshelivets, V. Markus, O. Ohloblyn, Y. Pasternak, O. Pritsak, G. Shevelov, P. Odarchenko, V. Revutsky, and Yu. Starosolsky. Some articles constitute small monographs on a given subject (e.g., agriculture, Black Sea, Communist Party). More than 80 percent of the articles are short; most of them are biographies and brief descriptions of historically significant institutions, political or cultural events, economic entities, and the like. Larger articles usually contain bibliographies of related works published in several languages.

In the preface to volumes 3-5, Dr. Struk rightly indicates that scholarly excellence, which guided the editors and staff of volumes 1 and 2, has remained a goal in the writing of the last three volumes. Since the publication of volume 2, monumental changes have taken place in Ukraine, with that country becoming an independent state and undergoing many political, economic, and cultural transformations. The editorial staff provides as current information as possible (most updates of materials were prepared by early 1992) with notable changes in terminology and geographical names. New volumes also contain a number of complete and well-executed articles, such as those on landforms, the Ukrainian language, linguistics, and Lviv. Some articles are rather disappointing, such as those on labor camps by A. Frieland and C. Frieland and library science by S. Bilokin.

But, as always with a work of this magnitude, there are some shortcomings. Many articles written by scholars now deceased were translated from Ukrainian into English, apparently by staff members or members of the new editorial board, without proper consultations with appropriate scholars who are still alive and active in the scholarly community. Probably articles originally written by the late Professor O. Ohloblyn (a former member of the editorial board) are a good example of this practice. Occasionally some "updating" or adding of names was also not very appropriate (e.g., adding C. Frieland to an article on land use by Kubiovyc). Even Struk added his name to a brief article on legends originally written by internationally known scholar D. Chyzhevsky and to the article on MUR (a literary group in Germany after 1945) by equally known expert G. Shevelov. What happened to articles on literature written by George Luckyj, who is not even mentioned in the list of contributors?

These critical comments should not belittle the overall excellence of this monumental work. Indeed, as was true of the Ukrainian-language work and the first two volumes of this set, this remarkable encyclopedia can safely be recommended to all scholars interested in Eastern Europe and Ukraine as one of the best works on this subject.—**Bohdan S. Wynar**

Yugoslavia

139. Friedman, Francine, comp. and ed. **Yugoslavia: A Comprehensive English-Language Bibliography.** Wilmington, Del., Scholarly Resources, 1993. 547p. index. $120.00. Z2956.F75. 016.9497. LC 92-43079. ISBN 0-8420-2340-2.

This exhaustive bibliography, the result of a 15-year compilation project, covers publications printed in English-speaking countries from the seventeenth century to the present. It does not include works of literature, just works about Yugoslavia, and the collection should prove invaluable to any researcher delving into the history, distant or recent, of that tortured country. Not every piece of writing from the 1990s is included, for it would be almost impossible to contain the welter of recent material within a single book's covers. Most of the entries includes monographs, journal articles, chapters of books, published and unpublished theses and dissertations, papers and lectures, and unpublished working papers and manuscripts; there are also documents, pamphlets, and journals dealing primarily or exclusively with Yugoslav subjects. Generally, newspaper articles have not been included.

The volume is divided into several sections, and the material is clearly and logically organized. It can be searched either by subject (e.g., geography, history, religion) or through the alphabetized list of authors. Whenever available, the Library of Congress call number is included at the end of the entry. All in all, this bibliography should be essential for anyone researching the baffling history and ethnography of this part of the Balkan Peninsula. [R: Choice, Sept 93, p. 94; WLB, Sept 93, p. 127]

—Koraljka Lockhart

INDIAN OCEAN AREA

Seychelles

140. Bennett, George, with Pramila Ramgulam Bennett, comps. **Seychelles.** Santa Barbara, Calif., ABC-Clio, 1993. 115p. maps. index. (World Bibliographical Series, v.153). $64.00. 016.9696. ISBN 1-85109-182-3.

This is a splendid addition to the World Bibliographical Series, a series that aims to cover every country of the world in a separate volume. The range of subjects covered in each book has been wide, and the depth of coverage is impressive. Beyond the basic entries one might expect on history, geography, the economy, politics, and administration, this volume contains entries on many other subjects, such as flora and fauna, language and literature, education and the arts, the media, and the cuisine. Items in French are included in addition to those in English, for Seychelles was originally a French dependency. (The Creole spoken there is closely related to that of Haiti.) All the entries are carefully annotated, and they are extremely interesting, conveying the compilers' interest in their subject.

The introduction provides an excellent overview of Seychelles, and a series of maps appears at the end. Nothing seems to have been overlooked; even the local telephone directory is used as a sourcebook. Finally, there are indexes of authors, titles, and subjects. The scholarship is first-rate and always illuminates the subject, never becoming heavy. The compilers have admirably achieved their general aim stated as the raison d'etre of the series: "to provide ... an interpretation of each country that will express its culture, its place in the world, and the qualities and background that make it unique." [R: Choice, Dec 93, p. 580]—**John B. Beston**

LATIN AMERICA AND THE CARIBBEAN

General Works

141. **Bibliographic Guide to Latin American Studies 1991. Gui Bibliografica para los Estudios Latinoamericanos 1991.** New York, G. K. Hall, 1992. 2v. (Bibliographic Guides). $500.00/set. ISBN 0-8161-7162-9. ISSN 0162-5314.

This guide is a comprehensive annual subject bibliography of materials from throughout the world cataloged during 1990 by the University of Texas at Austin Latin American Collection (with additional entries from the Library of Congress). Complete listings for items related to the Americas are incorporated, along with works written by Latin American authors on any subject. Every country and area of the Western Hemisphere is represented. Works in all languages may be found in this guide, including indigenous dialects of the Americas.

This annual supplement to the *Catalog of the Latin American Collection of the University of Texas at Austin* (G. K. Hall, 1969) provides a valuable update to key resources. It continues to be one of the most comprehensive and reliable sources of information on materials dealing with Latin American themes and writers. However, it can be a very expensive acquisition. One hopes there will be a low-cost CD-ROM for such works. Recommended for libraries that have the *Catalog* and its other supplements and those that want the strongest possible sources of information on the Western Hemisphere.—**Roberto P. Haro**

142. **The Cambridge Encyclopedia of Latin America and the Caribbean.** 2d ed. Simon Collier, Thomas E. Skidmore, and Harold Blakemore, eds. New York, Cambridge University Press, 1992. 479p. illus. maps. index. $55.00. F1406.C36. 980'.03. LC 92-14496. ISBN 0-521-41322-2.

This encyclopedia, originally published in 1985 (see ARBA 87, entry 135), covers Mexico, Central and South America, and the Caribbean area, including the non-Latin Caribbean. It closely follows the plan of the first edition. It is divided into six broad subjects—the physical environment, the economy, the peoples, history, politics and society, and culture—which are broken down into signed articles on related topics, followed by brief bibliographies. A few contributors have been added (75, as compared to 68 in the first edition). There has been some rearrangement and updating of the text—AIDS and NAFTA are two new entries in the index. The work is noteworthy for its good illustrations, both color and black-and-white, and its variety of maps, which cover geography, history, mining, roads and railways, Amerindian language families, and many other topics.

As always, unevenness of coverage accompanies broad treatment. For example, religions with African roots are discussed only peripherally in relation to Caribbean music, and not at all in relation to Brazil, in spite of their importance. This work, with its topical approach, is in the style of many encyclopedias published in Latin American countries, and it provides good overviews of many subjects, with a thorough index giving easy access to the details therein. Nevertheless, this librarian wished for a scholarly dictionary-encyclopedia of Latin America in English, produced with entries for obscure as well as prominent figures, movements, and the like, which would expand and update Helen Delpar's *Encyclopedia of Latin America* (see ARBA 75, entry 316). This work serves well to introduce readers to many aspects of Latin America, and it is recommended for all libraries with an interest in that important region, in ethnic studies, and in related fields. [R: LAR, May 93, p. 294; RBB, 15 May 93, p. 1718; SLJ, May 93, p. 136]—**Ann Hartness**

143. Carvajal, Manuel J. **The Caribbean 1975-1980: A Bibliography of Economic and Rural Development.** Metuchen, N.J., Scarecrow, 1993. 897p. index. $89.50. Z1595.C38. 016.9729. LC 91-39695. ISBN 0-8108-2422-1.

The subtitle of Carvajal's useful bibliography is somewhat misleading: While economic and rural (and agricultural) matters are the focus, they are by no means the extent of this important compilation, which is directed toward studies having an impact on the formulation of public policy. Most related cultural subjects (literature, sociology, and even religion) are included; *Theology, Caribbean Journal of Education*, and *Ethnology*, for example, have been searched for relevant articles. The result is a book that will be needed by all except those with highly specialized interests that do not impinge on the wider political and social issues of Caribbean life.

The organization of the book enhances its use. There is a section on the Caribbean in general, followed by sections on the six major nations (Cuba is excluded because it requires a bibliography of its own, and Puerto Rico because of its special relationship to the United States) and the French, Dutch, and British territories. Many entries have key phrases, such as "Diary extracts" or "Agitation for independence," that elucidate opaque titles (especially common in university theses, it seems); more of these would improve the usefulness of the book, especially for the entry that considers "Two Caribbean Novelists." (Which ones?) Cross-references are copious and helpful, as is the 300-page index, which includes authors, journal titles, and subjects. Easily read typefaces and sturdy casing make this a convenient reference and justify the price. [R: Choice, Oct 93, p. 264]—**Marian B. McLeod**

144. **Handbook of Latin American Studies. No. 52: Humanities.** Dolores Moyano Martin, ed. Austin, Tex., University of Texas Press, 1993. 934p. index. $75.00. LC 36-32633. ISBN 0-292-75156-7. ISSN 0072-9833.

It is not surprising that this biennial edition reflects two major trends in scholarly publications for the period covered: the commemoration of the quincentennial of Columbus's arrival in the New World and the indigenous peoples of the Americas who were "discovered" by the Europeans. Indeed, the editor notes the "explosion in the writing of indigenous history" as one of the major developments in recent Latin American historical scholarship. On the other hand, this edition marks the discontinuance of the subsection on the Independence Period in Latin America, as well as special sections on Latin American folklore and film, which are now treated under other sections of the handbook according to the methodology used.

These changes aside, the handbook continues to be the standard bibliographical reference serial in its field, dating back to 1935. This edition provides more than 5,000 annotated bibliographies of articles that have appeared in some 300 journals published worldwide, covering the areas of bibliography and general works, art, history, language, literature, music, and philosophy. One of its strengths continues to be the subject and author indexes, which give even greater utility to a work that features a detailed table of contents. A longstanding weakness—the lag time between publication date and its appearance in this biennial—seems to have been addressed in this volume, but a number of older entries still appear for the first time. Given the enormity of the undertaking and the quality of the product, the price is not unreasonable. The work continues to be an indispensable reference source for the serious study of any aspect of Latin America.—**Edwin S. Gleaves**

145. Lorona, Lionel V., ed. **A Bibliography of Latin American and Caribbean Bibliographies, 1985-1989: Social Sciences and Humanities.** Metuchen, N.J., Scarecrow, 1993. 314p. index. $39.50. Z1601.A2G76. 016.01698. LC 93-14085. ISBN 0-8108-2702-6.

In 1968 Arthur E. Gropp published his *Bibliography of Latin American Bibliographies* for Scarecrow. Since that time succeeding supplements have been published by Gropp, Daniel Raposo Cordeiro, Haydee Piedracueva, and Lorona. The fourth supplement won the SALALM (Seminar on the Acquisition of Latin American Library Materials) Medina Bibliography Award. This fifth supplement thus follows a distinguished tradition. Lorona held various positions with the Research Libraries of the New York Public Library and served for 10 years as compiler and editor of SALALM's annual *Bibliography of Latin American and Caribbean Bibliographies* (see ARBA 92, entry 109) and is an acknowledged expert in this field.

The present volume covers 1985 to 1989 in the social sciences and humanities and includes items missed in earlier editions. The volume title has been expanded to include the word *Caribbean* to reflect the increasing volume of bibliographies published on that region. The 1,867 new bibliographies listed are arranged alphabetically by subjects, beginning with general works and extending from agriculture to urbanization. The longest section, on individual biography, includes 196 bibliographies alphabetically arranged by the name of the individual. The language and literature section includes 163 entries arranged by author. Other major sections include history, with 145 entries arranged by country, and libraries and archives, with 92 entries. With its detailed subject and author indexes, this volume is easy to use and serves as an important checklist for all Latin American collections and for Latin American scholars generally.—**Brian E. Coutts**

146. **South America, Central America, and the Caribbean 1993.** 4th ed. London, Europa; distr., Detroit, Gale, 1992. 718p. index. $295.00. ISBN 0-946653-86-0. ISSN 0258-0661.

This is a magnificent compilation of timely information on an area of the world about which reliable data is often in short supply. Heavy on text and tables but almost devoid of maps and illustrations, this serious and scholarly survey opens with eight substantial essays on the background of the region, covering subjects that range from economic problems to ecology and land use in Amazonian forests. Most of the book consists of country-by-country surveys of the 48 nations and dependencies that make up this vast region. While the smaller units, such as Anguilla and Montserrat, are accorded only a page or two, most countries receive the full treatment: a facts-in-brief section; essays on the nation's history and economy; a statistical survey of demographic and other data; and a major directory of the government, religion, press, publishers, radio and television, finance, trade and industry, transportation, tourism, and other aspects of national life. Both the essays and the statistical sections appear to be remarkably up-to-date, especially considering the magnitude of this project. A third section provides useful information on such regional organizations as the Andean Group and the Organization of American States.

Libraries dedicated to providing in-depth information on Latin America and the Caribbean would be hard-pressed to find a better one-volume survey on the subject. The *Handbook of Latin American Studies* (see ARBA 89, entry 126) is preferable for bibliographical information on the humanities and the social sciences, but it does not compete with the present volume in sheer volume of data and timeliness. Anyone put off by the price might keep in mind that this regional survey is little short of encyclopedic.
—Edwin S. Gleaves

Paraguay

147. Nickson, R. Andrew. **Historical Dictionary of Paraguay.** 2d ed. Metuchen, N.J., Scarecrow, 1993. 685p. maps. (Latin American Historical Dictionaries, no.24). $69.50. F2664.K64. 989.2'003. LC 92-40553. ISBN 0-8108-2643-7.

Little-known, remote, and landlocked, Paraguay has long been ignored by much of the English-speaking world. In recent years, however, it has begun to take its place among the vital, productive democracies of Latin America. This dictionary, an update of the original edition by Charles Kolinski, fills a gap in the knowledge of Paraguay by providing 1,600 well-written and authoritative entries on many aspects of Paraguayan culture, geography, history, and politics. Although an index would be helpful, the 500 cross-references facilitate the search for specific personalities, movements, events, and place-names that abound in the book. For example, the entry titled "Paraguay" not only includes a treatment on the country's name, location, topography, climate, flora and fauna, and government, but it also refers the reader to other major entries on broad periods in Paraguayan history, ranging from the conquest of Paraguay to the transition to democracy under the government of President Andres Rodriguez. Similarly, cross-references to Paraguay's various armed struggles, both internal and external, are found under the heading of "Wars." As in any such dictionary, the choice of English or Spanish can appear capricious, but, again, the cross-references serve as excellent finding aids.

A spare book almost devoid of illustrations (with no photographs whatsoever), this one-volume dictionary would be an excellent addition to any academic, public, or special library building a basic reference collection on Latin America. Among one-volume guides to Paraguay, this may well be the only choice for some of those libraries.—**Edwin S. Gleaves**

St. Vincent and Grenadine Islands

148. Potter, Robert B., comp. **St. Vincent and the Grenadines.** Santa Barbara, Calif., ABC-Clio, 1992. 212p. maps. index. (World Bibliographical Series, v.143). $70.00. 016.9729844. ISBN 1-85109-183-1.

The eastern Caribbean islands of St. Vincent and the Grenadines—with the exception of Haiti, the region's poorest country—have been independent only since 1979. This is the first major bibliography on St. Vincent and is a welcome addition to Caribbean documentation. Potter, a British geographer and cocompiler of the earlier *Barbados* (see ARBA 88, entry 142) volume in the World Bibliographical Series, has selected 631 citations on all aspects of St. Vincent and the Grenadines. The citations are consecutively numbered and arranged in 33 chapters by broad subject. Potter adheres to the series criterion of including only the more accessible English-language materials.

What sets this volume apart from many in the series is the higher quality of its annotations. A good measure of the value of a selected, annotated bibliography is in how complete and balanced an introduction to the subject can be had in a thorough reading of the annotations. Potter's bibliography succeeds well in this regard. Each citation includes a well-written, concise, informative annotation on the intellectual contents of the cited publication. Items listed (books, articles, theses, and government reports) are well chosen and include a large number of local publications. The work also has an informative introduction by Potter; two maps; and author, title, and subject indexes.—**Fred J. Hay**

Suriname and the Netherlands Antilles

149. Brown, Enid. **Suriname and the Netherlands Antilles: An Annotated English-Language Bibliography.** Metuchen, N.J., Scarecrow, 1992. 275p. index. $32.50. Z1806.B76. 016.97298'6. LC 92-10786. ISBN 0-8108-2576-7.

Suriname is one of the most underdeveloped and sparsely populated countries in South America. The Netherlands Antilles are composed of numerous islands in the Caribbean situated north of the Venezuelan coast. The populations are ethnically diverse: Amerindians, European colonists, former African slaves, and indentured workers from Asia. This bibliography contains 1,223 entries about these countries, with a focus on the humanities and the social sciences. The principal intent of the work is to provide researchers with a single comprehensive source for identifying relevant materials. All materials cited are in English or have been translated and are arranged alphabetically by author or editor. Each entry includes information on a library that holds the cited item. Numerous appendixes are useful in guiding the reader through bibliographic items not verified, lists of periodicals consulted, and addresses and telephone numbers of the libraries. There is a topical index.

This is a limited-use bibliography suitable for major research libraries with collections in Latin American history. It would have been enhanced by an essay that discussed the history of the region. [R: Choice, May 93, p. 1436]—**Dario J. Villa**

MIDDLE EAST

General Works

150. **The Encyclopaedia of Islam. Volume VII: Fascicules 125-126: Musa-Mutammim B. Nuwayra.** new ed. C. E. Bosworth and others, eds. Kinderhook, N.Y., E. J. Brill, 1992. 1v. (various paging). $37.25pa. ISBN 90-04-09591-8.

151. **The Encyclopaedia of Islam. Volume VII: MIF-NAZ.** new ed. C. E. Bosworth and others, eds. Kinderhook, N.Y., E. J. Brill, 1993. 1058p. illus. $428.75. DS37.E523. 956'.003. LC 61-4395. ISBN 90-04-09419-9.

This work was first published several decades ago. The new edition contains expanded entries with additions and corrections composed by leading scholars in the discipline. Entries are drawn from Arabic, Turkish, Persian, and Urdu and arranged according to Roman alphabetical transliteration. The entries include important individuals and families; technical terms from mathematics, literature, grammar, music, architecture, and astronomy; geographical names and terms; and titles and dynasties. Geographically, most of the entries are drawn from historically Islamic lands, but there are entries from central Europe, the Philippines, central Asia, and sub-Saharan Africa. Much information accompanies each term, along with its derivation, use, and change in meaning throughout history, and a bibliography. Important individuals are described via a short biography, an assessment of their importance, and (in the case of writers), a description of important works. Many terms are given extensive space. For instance, the entry for *Mughal* is 33 pages long and broken into subtopics, and a number of representative photographs accompany the section on Mughal architecture. Photographic plates accompany several other entries (e.g., *minbar* [pulpit], *mizwala* [sundial]). The major drawbacks of this work are the need to be somewhat familiar with Islamic/Arabic terminology to fully understand some entries and the small print.

Fascicules are issued two or three years before publication of the hardback volumes. Research libraries should take advantage of the fascicules to make the latest scholarship immediately available. *The Encyclopaedia of Islam* belongs in all academic libraries where courses on the Islamic world are taught, and in all major public libraries. [R: LJ, 15 Nov 93, p. 70]—**David L. White**

Israel

152. Reich, Bernard. **Historical Dictionary of Israel.** Metuchen, N.J., Scarecrow, 1992. 353p. (Asian Historical Dictionaries, no.8). $47.50. DS126.5.R38. 956.94'003. LC 92-5324. ISBN 0-8108-2535-X.

This work not only contains terms since 1948, the date of Israel's independence, but also includes some entries from the Biblical era and from the late nineteenth-century development of Zionism through the growing development of the Jewish community in twentieth-century Palestine up to 1948. The book begins with a chronology of events important to the development of modern Israel and follows with tables that list Israel's presidents, prime ministers, important ministers, chiefs of staff, Knesset terms, yearly immigration from 1882 to 1989, and population (broken down into communal groups). The book also includes a bibliography of books and monographs. However, no articles are included, nor do the dictionary entries include suggestions for further reading. A brief introduction describes Israel's government, society, geography, economy, and history; the reader is given an Israeli perspective on such events as the 1956 Suez War and occurrences in Lebanon after Israel's 1982 invasion. As the book was published in 1992, it does not contain an analysis of Desert Storm nor the 1992 elections in Israel.

The dictionary has entries in alphabetical order that briefly describe historical figures (e.g., Abraham); contemporary figures; important cities, towns, and villages; special commissions; political parties and groups; and entries on diamonds, El-Al, fine arts, museums, women, and the like. Entries for individuals indicate changes from their old European names to their new Hebrew ones and include brief biographies that cover major contributions.

While the book will be useful for anyone with an interest in Israel and its modern history, there are two problems. First, the explanations of religious/philosophical systems are not satisfactory. For instance, *Habad* is simply described as a variety of Hasidism, and *Hasidism* is not satisfactorily defined. The second problem is that the book is not without bias. For instance, Reich's statement that "Israel completed its withdrawal from Lebanon in 1985" is contradicted by current events. Other breaches of impartiality mar a useful book. [R: LJ, Jan 93, pp. 104-05; RBB, 1 Jan 93, pp. 825-26]—**David L. White**

4 Economics and Business

GENERAL WORKS

Bio-bibliography

153. Greaves, Bettina Bien, and Robert W. McGee, comps. **Mises: An Annotated Bibliography: A Comprehensive Listing of Books and Articles by and about Ludwig von Mises.** Irvington-on-Hudson, N.Y., Foundation for Economic Education, 1993. 391p. index. $29.95. ISBN 0-910614-79-2.

Ludwig von Mises (1881-1973) was a revolutionary in economics. He expanded upon many existing schools of thought and went on to form many new theorems. Greaves is viewed by Mises's widow as a leading scholar on Mises's works and considers this work the definitive bibliography of works by and about Mises. It is an updated and expanded version of Greaves's *The Works of Ludwig von Mises* from the same publisher (1970). Books, monographs, articles, audiocassettes, and excerpts from works by Mises are listed and annotated. Reviews of Mises's works are also included, as are books and articles about Mises. While this source is very well done, its audience is very narrow. Recommended for very large, research-oriented economics collections. [R: Choice, July/Aug 93, p. 1749]—**Bobray Bordelon**

154. Marshall, James N. **William J. Fellner: A Bio-Bibliography.** Westport, Conn., Greenwood Press, 1992. 145p. index. (Bio-bibliographies in Economics, no.1). $49.95. HB119.F45M37. 330'.092. LC 92-15462. ISBN 0-313-25856-2.

The life and writings of William J. Fellner, noted economist, teacher, and policy adviser to the U.S. government, have finally been accorded the book-length treatment that they deserve. While well-known in economic circles and academia, Fellner is best known to the public as a member of the Council of Economic Advisers, 1973-1975. Marshall, professor of economics at Muhlenberg College, has adroitly condensed the wide-ranging accomplishments of Fellner in the first half of the biography. The second half consists of an annotated bibliography of Fellner's published works as well as publications about him and his ideas. Each entry in the bibliographical section contains a concise summary, which must have been difficult to prepare in view of Fellner's output in several languages—at least a few of his writings have not (as yet) been translated into English. Fellner's distinguished career and numerous publications should be of interest to economists, students of economics, and others interested in economic policy.
—**William C. Struning**

155. Pottker, Jan. **Born to Power: Heirs to America's Leading Businesses.** Hauppauge, N.Y., Barron's Educational Series, 1992. 464p. illus. $12.95pa. HD62.25.P68. 338.6'42. LC 92-6534. ISBN 0-8120-1456-1.

Successful family businesses have flourished throughout America's history. The leaders in family businesses emphasize quality and service, maintain low risks in growth and borrowing, provide stability and long-lasting commitments, and focus on long-term goals to ensure growth and preservation for future generations. These traits are reflected in the chronicles of the founders and older leaders of major companies, but little is known about the young family successors to these businesses. Pottker's book focuses on the heirs to some of America's most influential businesses, both private and public, such as

Ronald J. Gidwitz of Helene Curtis Industries; Donna Wolf Steigerwaldt of Jockey International, Inc.; and the Cabot family of Cabot Corporation. The men and women included either work in the family business or have gone out on their own to shape their own businesses and careers.

The family companies and heirs are organized into seven sections that reflect the personality styles or roles of the heir: "Innovators," "Replicators," "Conservators," "Benchwarmers," "Stewards," "Family Feuders," and "Rebels." These categories are defined at the beginning of each section and are further illustrated by profiles of six to eight heirs and their family companies. Entries include a black-and-white photograph and a brief statistical profile of the company and its sales, earnings, employees, family history and involvement, percentage of family ownership, trading status, history, and product information. The 50 biographical profiles, based on personal interviews, include the heirs' personal and business accomplishments and failures along with future goals. There is an extensive table of contents but no index or bibliography.

This sociological approach toward the diversity of the leadership styles and qualities of the "rich kids" is significant to the future direction of American businesses. Those interested in management will find this book enlightening. It is appropriate for public and academic management collections.

—**Jennie S. Johnson**

Catalogs and Collections

156. **Harvard Business School Core Collection 1993: An Author, Title, and Subject Guide.** Mary Chatfield, comp. Boston, Harvard Business School Press; distr., New York, McGraw-Hill, 1993. 337p. index. $60.00pa.

This is a large reference book for a relatively small collection, roughly 3,500 items, that deals largely with business aspects in the United States. The entries include references to other countries and continents, but the distribution is unbalanced. Coverage of the United States fills 188 pages, compared with 17 pages considered international, 9 pages on Japan, and another 9 devoted to Europe. Africa is lucky to have four entries, which is the total for the Middle East and Islamic countries combined. (It is peculiar to put the Middle East and Islamic countries together, while Asia and the Pacific are separated from them.) The entries are alphabetical according to subject matter, beginning with accounting. However, it would have been easier had there been a classification system at the beginning of the volume. The collection is significant in that it includes a fairly large number of handbooks, and all entries include call numbers and Library of Congress reference numbers, as well as the price, although the purposes of these inclusions are not clear. Nor is it indicated whether the books in the collection are loanable. In fact, it is not clear what purpose this reference book serves outside the Harvard community; there are hardly any unique or rare items within that need to be advertised. The most peculiar feature is the 106 pages devoted to indexing by subject, author, title, and publisher. In view of these imbalances, the uneven distribution of entries, and the relatively small collection covered, one wonders whether the benefits justify the costs of this publication. [R: Choice, Nov 93, p. 432]—**Elias H. Tuma**

Dictionaries and Encyclopedias

157. Corbridge, Stuart, ed. **World Economy.** New York, Oxford University Press, 1993. 256p. illus. maps. index. (Illustrated Encyclopedia of World Geography). $45.00. HC15.W67. 330.9. LC 93-6489. ISBN 0-19-520946-X.

This volume is one of eleven in the series (others cover such phenomena as Earth's natural forces, animal life, human settlement, resources, and cultures). About 15 percent of the book gives an overview of the world economy, starting with fifteenth-century European exploration and expansion and ranging through capitalism and socialism (without defining either). Current general topics include aid and trade, international finance, international debt crisis, and health and social services. The remaining 85 percent of the work covers 22 geographical areas (e.g., Canada and the Arctic, Spain and Portugal). Within each area an essay (about 2,000-3,000 words) sketches the economy, its output and finance, raw materials, demographics and labor force, international trade, and health care, with some mention of recent changes in the economic system. These essays describe general trends with considerable skill and balance, but one should not expect great detail or deep analysis, or coverage of recent upheavals. For example, the breakup of Yugoslavia is too recent, and the deregulation and privatization in New Zealand in the eighties is too detailed for mention (although the effect of European Community changes on the New Zealand economy is mentioned). For selected countries (high-, intermediate-, and low-income economies in each area, if available), a dozen statistics are given for a recent year (e.g., merchandise exports and imports, population per physician). The graphics deserve special mention. They include life expectancy and age distribution, both by sex; pie and bar charts of exports and imports, by broad commodity and by trading partner; inflation profiles; and country maps. The 190-plus photographs are absolutely magnificent in representing important economic scenes (e.g., income disparities in Lagos, spices in Karachi, hotels on the Australian gold coast, strawberry production in Andalusia) and by themselves make this volume worth acquiring. Recommended for middle school students and up, and for general readers.—**Richard A. Miller**

158. Olson, James S., with Susan Wladaver-Morgan. **Dictionary of United States Economic History.** Westport, Conn., Greenwood Press, 1992. 667p. index. $85.00. HC102.057. 330.973'003. LC 91-32193. ISBN 0-313-26532-1.

This book is intended as a ready-reference tool and provides an excellent starting point for answering U.S. economic history questions. It deals with five centuries of U.S. economic history. More than 1,200 concise essays cover biographies, historical events, legislation, economic terms, labor unions, corporations, interest groups, elections, and economic institutions. References follow each entry and guide the user to more detailed information. *See* references and an index help link essays, and a chronology lists major events. Recommended for all business collections. [R: Choice, Mar 93, p. 1118; RBB, 15 Jan 93, pp. 936-38]—**Bobray Bordelon**

159. **The Penguin Dictionary of Economics.** 5th ed. By Graham Bannock, R. E. Baxter, and Evan Davis. New York, Penguin Books, 1992. 448p. $13.00pa. ISBN 0-14-051255-1.

This is one of many Penguin dictionaries for the general reader and for the introductory (and intermediate) student of economics (and political economy). The choice of items is wide-ranging and includes some standard tools (e.g., demand, Hicksian demand function, consumer surplus), accounting concepts (e.g., cash flow, profit, depreciation), statistics (e.g., linear relationship, heteroscedasticity), institutions (e.g., Forward market), and economists (e.g., H. George). The entries are well written, accurate, and clear. The cross-references are virtually complete and very helpful.

In no way can the entries substitute for the information derived from a textbook or a course. Also, the entries are written from a British perspective and apparently for a British audience, with illustrations drawn almost exclusively from British institutions and markets, although some United States and European entries are included (e.g., Federal Reserve System, antitrust).—**Richard A. Miller**

160. Pozin, Mikhail A., comp. **Russian-English/English-Russian Dictionary of Free Market Era Economics.** Jefferson, N.C., McFarland, 1993. 319p. $45.00. HB61.P68. 330'.03. LC 92-56681. ISBN 0-89950-876-6.

A dramatic transition from command to market economy in Russia has opened investment opportunities for numerous business and financial enterprises from English-speaking countries. Closely related to these changes is a rapidly growing flow of information between Russia and these nations, needed to sustain the research efforts by scholars and students working in business-related fields.

This comprehensive Russian-English/English-Russian commercial dictionary, containing more than 8,000 words and terms, has appeared just in time to meet the need for a bilingual dictionary of market economics. Its compiler has drawn most of his terms from Russian and American sources, such as newspapers, magazines, journals, and books, printed in the last five years. The choice of the items was based on the diverse economic and commercial requirements in such specialized fields as financial markets, trade and commerce, advertising, marketing, accounting, licensing, stock market, patents, and insurance. One also finds in the compilation some colloquial and slang items that are commonly accepted in business, as well as some terms depicting new technologies and equipment used in international trade.

Little knowledge of business terminology is required from the potential users of this book. To facilitate proper pronunciation, each Russian word has a stress mark. Each noun is identified by its gender, and all terms are identified by their function in a sentence. Whenever possible, both perfective and imperfective forms of verbs are provided. Moreover, a list of verbs indicates the cases of the nouns and the pronouns associated with them. An inquisitive reader can derive the meaning of an unknown term by referring to multiple entries, supplemented by noun and verb phrases related to the same subject. Some very specialized terms, such as *call options, futures*, or *forward contract*, are briefly defined, while the area of their usage is placed in parentheses.

This valuable dictionary is highly recommended for students of business Russian as well as for translators, economists, and entrepreneurs interested in growing market and investment opportunities in an emerging Russian free-market economy.—**Oleg Zinam**

Directories

161. **American Big Businesses Directory.** 1993 ed. Omaha, Neb., American Business Directories, 1993. 3v. index. $795.00/set. ISBN 1-56105-346-5. ISSN 1061-2173.

This directory provides basic data (name, address, telephone and fax numbers, sales volume code, employee size code, executives, corporate linkage, SIC [Standard Industrial Classification] codes, and stock identifier symbol) on all U.S. companies with 100 or more employees. The directory actually lists establishments (in most cases, with 100 or more employees each); thus, a company such as Wal-Mart may have as many as 1,000 of its retail locations included. Initially, entries are gathered from telephone directories, to which SIC codes are attached. Further data is then obtained by telephone interviews. Finally, annual sales volumes are estimated using U.S. Department of Commerce statistics. The resulting compilation is impressive. Two of the three volumes comprise an alphabetical list (including profiles) of establishments, while the third volume lists establishments by location (city within state) and SIC code; it also has a directory of key executives and directors. For reader convenience, SIC code definitions are included.

This directory can save users' time and expense in such tasks as determining market potential, managing direct mail lists, establishing sales territories, and telemarketing. The publisher can also supply the information in the directory online and on magnetic tape, diskettes, special listings, mailing labels, and CD-ROMs, and can search by such elements as brand name. In addition, the publisher can provide credit profiles.—**William C. Struning**

162. Hicks, S. David, ed. **Corporate Giving Yellow Pages 1993: Guide to Corporate Giving Contacts.** Rockville, Md., Taft Group; distr., Detroit, Gale, 1993. 343p. index. $75.00pa. ISBN 1-879784-41-6. ISSN 1058-689X.

A concise and comprehensive guide to the more than 3,900 corporate and direct philanthropic giving programs in the United States, this easy-to-use, well-organized directory provides an alphabetical list of the names, addresses, and telephone numbers of the contact people within each giving program. Three indexes allow users to more easily identify potential benefactors. Programs are indexed by the state in which a foundation or corporation is headquartered, by state list in which these sponsoring corporations maintain operations, and by the major products or industries with which these corporations are associated. The product index is arranged by a straightforward, two-digit Standard Industrial Classification (SIC) code. Because this directory provides updated information, and because it cross-references all of this information, it will be of great assistance to any number of organizations and institutions that wish to identify and contact possible benefactors.—**Timothy E. Sullivan**

163. Hicks, S. David, David Kroeger, and James De Angelis, eds. **Corporate Giving Directory 1993: Comprehensive Profiles of America's Major Corporate Foundations....** 14th ed. Rockville, Md., Taft Group; distr., Detroit, Gale, 1993. 1150p. index. $335.00pa. ISBN 1-879784-39-4. ISSN 1055-0623.

This unusual source provides detailed descriptions of 607 of the largest corporate charitable giving programs in the United States. Each company's annual contributions amount to at least $500,000, including nonmonetary donations. The total amount awarded is more than $2.7 billion, roughly half of the $6 billion projected to be given in 1993 by corporations.

The company profiles are arranged by sponsoring company name in a single alphabetical sequence. Provided in the entries are a contact name, giving levels, grant types, other types of nonmonetary support, philanthropic priorities, where given, who runs the giving program, rationale for evaluating contributions, how to approach the program, the decisionmaking process, restrictions on giving, recent giving-related statistics, and a list of awarded grants (if available). This information is based on responses to a questionnaire, telephone inquiries, research on IRS Form 990s, and examination of annual reports. Therefore, profiles vary in content. Ten different indexes provide various access points, such as by grant type, by headquarters state, and by operating location.

Similar publications include the *National Directory of Corporate Giving* (see ARBA 91, entry 144) and the *Corporate 500* (see ARBA 92, entry 823). All libraries that need information for fund-raisers need a current copy of the *Corporate Giving Directory*.—Susan C. Awe

164. **Hoover's MasterList of Major U.S. Companies 1993.** Austin, Tex., Reference Press, 1993. 607p. index. $49.95. HF3010. 338.7. ISBN 1-878753-14-2. ISSN 1066-291X.

Promoted as an affordable option to *Standard & Poor's Register of Corporations, Directors and Executives* (see ARBA 92, entry 135) or *Ward's Business Directory of U.S. Private and Public Companies* (see ARBA 93, entry 198), this volume is a basic list of 4,812 public and 1,001 private companies based in the United States and 181 foreign-based companies. This number pales in comparison to the more than 55,000 listings offered in *Standard & Poor's Register 1993*. But the text provides basic coverage across the board. Public companies include those listed on the New York Stock Exchange (NYSE), American Stock Exchange (AMEX), and NASDAQ (National Association of Security Dealers Automated Quotations) National Market. Also included are well-known companies whose trading status on an exchange was suspended, such as Continental Airlines. All the companies on *Forbes's* top 400 private companies list and most of *Inc.* magazine's 1992 list of the 500 fastest-growing companies constitute the majority of the private companies. Other sources for private firms include *Hoover's Handbook of Emerging Companies* (Reference Press, 1993) and *Hoover's Handbook of American Business* (see ARBA 93, entry 208). *Hoover's Handbook of World Business* (see ARBA 92, entry 144) served as the chief source for companies outside the United States. Special notations indicate when a company is in one of the latter two texts.

The vast majority of the listings provide basic information: name, address, telephone and fax numbers, chief executive officer, chief financial officer, most recently available annual sales figure, number of employees, stock exchange, exchange symbol, and company's major industry. Indexes by headquarters location, industry, and stock exchange symbol provide additional access points. One forward-thinking strategy on the publisher's part was to provide this information on computer disks in a variety of formats. It is unfortunate that the publisher did not use Standard Industrial Classification (SIC) codes and provide a more representative listing of each company's business interests; having a reference point common to many business texts would have made the book a more flexible addition to any business's or library's collection. Still, this work would be a useful addition to any collection needing a basic company reference. [R: Choice, Nov 93, p. 434; RBB, 1 Nov 93, p. 566; WLB, Nov 93, p. 103]
—**Susan D. Baird-Joshi**

165. **Research Services Directory: A One-Stop Guide to Commercial Research Activity.** 5th ed. Annette Piccirelli and Christopher Kasic, eds. Detroit, Gale, 1993. 930p. index. $315.00. LC 82-11898. ISBN 0-8103-7631-8. ISSN 0278-1743.

This publication is a valuable starting point for locating potential clients, collaborators, competitors, or contractors. With listings for more than 4,400 contract and proprietary research firms in the United States and Canada, this directory includes address and telephone and fax numbers plus a variety of other useful nuggets of news. The amount of information differs with each company. The company descriptions can include the firm's date of founding; former names; volume of research in U.S. dollars; annual revenues; rates; principal clients; number of staff; and professional alliances or memberships, such as the Water Pollution Board or the American Physical Society. A second section provides a more detailed account of the research and technical services provided and may include products and patents. The section on publications and information resources describes what types of publications carry the firm's research, the titles of the firm's publications, and the main subject areas of the library (if one exists). Finally, additional contact information may include telex number, electronic mail addresses, regional offices, or main personnel.

The text provides operating name, subject, geographical location, and personal name indexes. All refer the reader to the main entry via its corresponding number. The first two also include the city and state of the company. Operating name refers to the name under which a firm operates. This is not the same as the colloquial name; for example, Eastman Kodak does not have a listing under Kodak. But by including acronyms; former and alternate names; and names of affiliates, parent companies, and subsidiaries, this index provides many access points. The subject index acts as a thesaurus, pointing users to preferred and related terms. It also includes references to phrases that are commonly transposed; for example, the entry for "Analysis, spectrum" is "See: Spectrum analysis." Entries in the geographical index are grouped first by state, then alphabetically by city. Both the geographical and personal name indexes include full address; telephone, fax, and toll-free numbers; and contact person. As well as names and titles of chief executives, the personal name index covers key personnel listed in the additional contact information.

—Susan D. Baird-Joshi

166. Starer, Daniel. **Who Knows What: The Essential Business Resource Book.** New York, Henry Holt, 1992. 1239p. index. $45.00. HF54.52.U5S73. 016.65. LC 92-17132. ISBN 0-8050-1853-0.

Designed to economize the time and money spent by people seeking business information, this directory offers useful information in three formats. Entries for thousands of sources of information are arranged by subject, including one or two dozen entries per topic or industry. Each entry includes address, telephone number, and a brief description of the subject scope or services offered; some entries also include fax number and contact person. Helpful narrative advice is presented in both an appendix, which includes the pros and cons of database searching and an annotated list of major online database services, and an introduction that describes state government offices, associations, periodicals, libraries, companies, and the federal government as the author's favorite sources of information, and also delineates practical tips on getting information by telephone. Indexes offer easy access to source entries by association, periodical title, company, and detailed subject headings. The table of contents lists the approximately 500 business topics and states covered by the alphabetically arranged source entries.

Lack of information on the preparation of the directory creates some uncertainty for the user. It is not clear what the limitations of the directory's coverage are and how subject topics, industries, and directory entries were selected for inclusion. Also, specific sources used to gather the information are not identified.

Who Knows What offers, in one handy book, information that is also available from a variety of other tools, including, for example, *Small Business Sourcebook* (see ARBA 93, entry 213) and *Washington Information Directory* (see ARBA 93, entry 743). Duplication of information is most evident with the *Small Business Sourcebook*, in which coverage is more extensive, but the type and number of industries and business topics covered are about half that in *Who Knows What*. The key advantages of *Who Knows What* are its price compared to the other titles, and a reduction of the time spent searching through numerous books.

Despite the drawback that the directory's focus is not delineated, *Who Knows What* is a quick, inexpensive, and easy-to-use starting point for business information. It is recommended for any library that serves people who seek information about business topics. It is also an effective tool for managers, entrepreneurs, professionals, freelance writers, or educated consumers who frequently retrieve information themselves. [R: Choice, June 93, p. 1610-11; JAL, May 93, p. 131; RBB, 1 May 93, p. 1640; RQ, Fall 93, p. 138; WLB, April 93, p. 126]—**Danuta A. Nitecki**

167. **Who Owns Corporate America 1993: A Comprehensive Listing of More Than 75,000 Officers, Directors, and 10% Principal Stockholders....** Catherine M. Ehr, ed. Rockville, Md., Taft Group; distr., Detroit, Gale, 1993. 1716p. index. $275.00pa. ISBN 1-879784-36-X. ISSN 1061-1258.

Corporate stock ownership, according to the IRS, accounts for 36 percent of the total wealth of Americans with a net worth of at least $1 million. *Who Owns Corporate America* (WOCA) provides a complete list of officers, directors, 10 percent principal stockholders, and other so-called insiders who own, either directly or indirectly, securities registered with the U.S. Securities and Exchange Commission (SEC) and included on SEC Forms 3 and 4.

Featuring more than 75,600 entries on individuals who hold insider stock positions in nearly 4,100 public companies, WOCA will help nonprofit researchers identify wealthy prospects, target large stockholders for prospect lists, and uncover corporate affiliations of individuals (thereby facilitating biographical research). The data are presented alphabetically by the last name of the stockholder. Each entry includes full name, security or issuing company, stock exchange symbols, number of shares held, month and year of last transaction within the filing period, the class or type of security (e.g., common, preferred, class A), the individual's relationship with issuing company (e.g., officer, trustee) and with the listed security (e.g., direct, indirect, market maker), and the dollar value of the shares held. The comprehensive security name index directs users to individual insiders by the securities and issuing companies listed in the main body entries; the relationship code in parentheses indicates the individual's relationship to the issuing company. This work is an expensive but useful purchase for libraries. [R: LJ, Jan 93, p. 106; RBB, 1 Mar 93, p. 1268]—**Susan C. Awe**

Handbooks and Yearbooks

168. **Barron's Guide to Graduate Business Schools.** 8th ed. By Eugene Miller. Hauppauge, N.Y., Barron's Educational Series, 1992. 690p. index. $14.95pa. LC 89-640070. ISBN 0-8120-4863-6. ISSN 1043-190X.

This edition, as did its predecessors, aims to provide prospective graduate students at the master's level—with particular emphasis on the MBA degree (including joint degrees, such as the MBA/JD [business/law]) and more limited attention to alternative business degrees—with an overview of United States and Canadian schools. Information on the 25 or so foreign schools listed in some prior editions has been dropped; in all, nearly 650 schools are included.

The three-part arrangement of the work has been retained. First is an introductory section that offers factors to consider in choosing a school (e.g., school rankings from *Business Week*), application procedures, financial aid, and employer expectations of business master's graduates. Next, an overview of each school is presented in chart form alphabetically by state (Canadian institutions are listed by school). Data presented include accreditation/nonaccreditation by AACSB (American Assembly of Collegiate Schools of Business), degree requirements, program concentrations, enrollment, characteristics of the student body (e.g., women, minorities), faculty, admissions, and tuition. Finally, there is an expansion of the chart data with additional information (e.g., library and research facilities, computer facilities, placement services). An index to schools is provided. Besides its intended audience of prospective graduate business students, *Barron's Guide to Graduate Business Schools* will be useful in academic and public libraries with a business clientele.—**Wiley J. Williams**

169. **Business Week's Guide to the Best Executive Education Programs.** By John A. Byrne and Cynthia Greene, with *Business Week* editors. New York, McGraw-Hill, 1993. 248p. index. $24.95; $14.95pa. HD30.42.U5B97. 658.4'0071'173. LC 92-26321. ISBN 0-07-009334-2; 0-07-009335-0pa.

In this work, executive seminars and MBA programs are evaluated along the lines used in *Business Week's Guide to the Best Business Schools* (see ARBA 91, entry 139). Rankings based on survey and interview data accompany an examination of the strengths and weaknesses of each program. Introductory material explains project methodology; succeeding chapters present the top schools and programs, unranked runners-up, and the most innovative programs (e.g., managing cultural diversity). Charts that note achievements (e.g., quality of teaching) are invaluable for examining offerings of both ranked and excluded schools. Inconsistent performance is indicated in subject rankings that, for example, show Harvard as first in general management and fifth in finance. Entries offer basic information (e.g., address, costs) while tracking more unusual data in executive (e.g., years involved, growth since 1986) and graduate education (e.g., teaching methods). A varied assortment of anonymous quotations from executives and students peppers the well-written, evaluative essays. The index, with sections searchable by topic, state, and company name, continues to be somewhat superficial.

More extensive directories of courses and degree programs already have been published. What is unique in this book is the rankings, the inclusion of unusual measures (e.g., teacher performance), and the participant comments. For its depth of analysis, all libraries serving the business community should consider it. [R: RBB, 15 Feb 93, p. 1080]—**Sandra E. Belanger**

170. **The Development Report Card for the States, 1993: Economic Benchmarks for State and Corporate Decision-Makers.** 7th ed. Washington, D.C., Corporation for Enterprise Development, 1993. 215p. $70.00 spiralbound. LC 93-70699. ISBN 1-883187-00-1. ISSN 1045-4691.

This is a graphic and easy-to-use array of useful economic and social information for each of the 50 states as compiled by a nonprofit research and public policy organization. Drawing on a variety of public and private sources, the information offers not only national and regional findings but also detailed individual state summaries. Data are collected for more than 50 measures and arranged into 3 indexes and 11 subindexes. Moreover, because these data are compared with summaries since 1989, it is also possible (and most useful) to gauge the relative performance of the states over time.

Data are indexed and organized around the themes of economic performance, business vitality, and development capacity. Economic performance is gauged by such issues as employment, earnings, job quality, equity, environmental, and health conditions. Business vitality is a measure of a state's business competitiveness, entrepreneurial energy, and structural diversity, while a state's development capacity is estimated by examining human, technology, and financial resources; infrastructure; and amenities. In addition to these three indexes, other indexes examine each state's trend in human and technology resources and taxing and fiscal policies.

This guide offers a good deal of information to a variety of users. Its graphic format will make its summary statistics and indexes more accessible to users. But making quick and simple comparisons and judgments need not be the only use of this guide. Because it lists sources of data and gives some insight into its methodology, more detailed analysis can also benefit from these grades and indexes. However, as trends may be of particular interest, most users will benefit by comparing grades over time. [R: RBB, 15 Nov 93, pp. 649-50]—**Timothy E. Sullivan**

171. Frantzve, Kent R. **The Desktop Business Intelligence Sourcebook: A Comprehensive Guidebook for the Information Age.** Cincinnati, Ohio, Hyde Park Marketing Group, 1992. 188p. index. $16.95pa. LC 91-72603. ISBN 1-880186-00-4.

Marketing professional Frantzve wrote this book because, after searching for data to support a new-venture business plan, he felt there was "so little on the market to turn to for help, I decided to develop just such a sourcebook." The guide reflects both the strengths (enthusiasm and a sincere commitment to assist the reader) and weaknesses (inconsistencies, factual errors, and misleading information) of this approach. Although the work is intended as "a single-source guide to the best business data and information resources currently available" for a variety of business professionals and students, it does not provide enough guidance about these materials to function in this manner.

In essence, what the sourcebook provides is various selective lists of business-related information resources. A sampling of the chapters includes general business information guides, dictionaries and encyclopedias (with good descriptions that note the strengths of each work), business handbooks (an unannotated list of 51 apparently randomly selected works that uses a completely different bibliographical citation style than the rest of the sourcebook), industry sources (11 publications for which publishing frequency is sometimes given, sometimes not), and statistical sources (a good cross-section of resources accompanied by thorough, helpful annotations).

The section on indexes and abstracts is representative of the types of problems encountered in this work. First, although the intended audience is assumed to be unfamiliar with most information tools, the differences between indexes and abstracts are never explained, nor, for electronic databases, is the full text option identified or described. Even more problematic is the assertion in the section on electronic indexes and abstracts that "most of the major CD-ROM and online information services offer user friendly data searches that are triggered by plain English words or phrases." (Oh, would that it were so!) There is inadequate distinction made between online searches performed by the public or corporate librarian and those an individual can make via a home computer. Such phrases as "records include 150 word searchable abstracts" are used to describe a resource, but it is unlikely that a first-time business researcher would clearly understand what that means. There is no discussion of document delivery or interlibrary loan.

Although this work cannot be relied upon as a single-source reference for business research, especially for the novice intelligence gatherer, it nevertheless has its strong points and would function well as a supplement to another user-friendly but more comprehensive and thorough work: *Business Information* (see ARBA 93, entry 209). It is certainly reasonably priced for this purpose. [R: RBB, 1 Jan 93, p. 824]—**G. Kim Dority**

172. **Hoover's Handbook of Emerging Companies 1993-1994.** Patrick J. Spain, Alta Campbell, and Alan Chai, eds. Austin, Tex., Reference Press, 1993. 431p. index. $32.95. HF3010. 338.7. ISBN 1-878753-18-5. ISSN 1069-7519.

This inexpensive handbook fills a major gap in the literature. A plethora of directories cover large public companies, but information on even the most promising growth companies is scanty. The largest portion of this book consists of single-page company profiles similar to those in *Hoover's Handbook of American Business* (see ARBA 93, entry 208) and *Hoover's Handbook of World Business* (see ARBA 92, entry 144). These are well written and informative, giving company history, officers, location, products, competitors, and six years of financial data. In particular, the brief company histories and profiles present information not usually included in annual reports. The preface states that the editors wish to present "examples of exciting, rapidly growing enterprises in a wide range of industries." Companies profiled all have sales growth of 25 percent per year for 5 years or sales and net profit growth of 15 percent per year for 5 years. However, only a quarter of the firms meeting these criteria have been profiled, although others appear in lists elsewhere in the book. (The choice of firms to profile was admittedly somewhat subjective.) Another handy feature of this work is a compendium of lists of fast-growing companies, gleaned from journals such as *Inc.* and *Fortune. Hoover's* also includes various lists of its own, ranking companies by growth. Profiled companies are indexed, while those appearing only in lists are not.

Because growth companies are one of the major sources of new jobs, this book will be invaluable to job-seekers. It is also a good starting point for investors, who will want to follow up with more current and detailed financial data from other sources. This book is a bargain, as are many Reference Press titles. [R: RBB, 1 Nov 93, p. 566]—**Susan V. McKimm**

173. **How to Find Information about Companies—Vol.3.** By Washington Researchers Publishing. Washington, D.C., Washington Researchers, 1992. 759p. index. $295.00pa. ISBN 1-56365-008-8. ISSN 0278-372X.

Similar in approach to volumes 1 and 2, this latest volume offers a wealth of traditional and not-so-traditional methods for obtaining information about companies. The target audience is business intelligence gatherers, but the book has much that is appropriate for business information professionals as well. Novice and infrequent searchers will appreciate the work's common-sense, no-frills approach, with its emphasis on search strategies and tactics as well as on identifying specific information sources. The "small pond theory" and "indirect target tapping" are only two of many suggested approaches to obtaining elusive material.

Sections on private companies; divisions, subsidiaries, and products; foreign firms; service companies; and candidates for acquisition offer suggestions for locating hard-to-find information about companies of all kinds. Many of the suggested sources are free but often require some creative sleuthing. Two model studies—a privately held production company and a service company subsidiary—make fascinating reading. This volume is highly recommended to any library or information center where company information questions are received. It will be especially useful for searchers not familiar with traditional procedures and sources or for times when the traditional sources cannot provide the needed information.
—**Elisabeth Logan**

174. **The Information Please Business Almanac and Desk Reference, 1994.** Seth Godin, ed. Boston, Houghton Mifflin, 1993. 745p. maps. index. $29.95. ISBN 0-395-64384-8. ISSN 1070-4639.

This comprehensive survey and directory of the modern business world and its activities is not only a reference book that will delight, amuse, and inform a wide variety of users but also one that is well organized and easy to read. It provides an impressive array of useful and updated information covering some 762 topics drawn from more than 500 public and private sources. It is conveniently organized into sections dealing with such issues as business law and government, communications, finance, human resources, marketing, manufacturing, corporate planning and administration, office management, and personal computing. It contains facts, directories, rankings, contacts, addresses, fax and telephone numbers, online services, travel maps, amenities (e.g., lists of highly rated restaurants in larger U.S. cities), and a good deal of specific advice on how to improve the efficiency of both people and business organizations. In addition, it provides a glossary of common business terms and concepts, a list of public library reference contacts and industry newsletters, and many recommended resources to help users find more detailed information.

Whether one is searching for specific information about postal rates, looking for a telephone number, negotiating a lease, planning an international business trip, or writing a business plan, this almanac will be beneficial. It provides discernible information that can help both simplify and enrich comprehension in the business community. [R: LJ, 1 Oct 93, p. 89; RBB, 1 Dec 93, pp. 712-14]—**Timothy E. Sullivan**

175. Rega, Regina, comp. **Business & Legal CD-ROMS in Print 1993: An International Guide to CD-ROM and CD-Based Multimedia Products....** Westport, Conn., Meckler, 1993. 360p. index. $55.00pa. ISBN 0-88736-912-X. ISSN 1066-9825.

The entries in this directory have been extracted from Meckler's *CD-ROMs in Print 1993* (Meckler, 1992). This subject-based directory is the first in an annual series of reference guides to area-specific CD-ROMs. The directory is international in coverage and lists CD-ROM and CD-based multimedia products in business, economics, finance, law, and related fields, including everything from advertising and consumer information to patents and trademarks. There are 1,234 entries, and each varies in the amount of information provided. Generally included is basic information such as the number of discs, publisher, distributor, hardware requirements, frequency, price, dates of coverage, subjects covered, and a one- or two-sentence description. An index of company names and addresses lists data providers, CD-ROM publishers, software producers, and distributors. Additional indexes include Mac-compatible CDs for Macintosh workstations, multimedia CDs, Sony Electronic Book titles, and a subject index. For most general library collections, the more comprehensive *CD-ROMs in Print* will suffice, but for business and legal collections, the title is highly recommended. [R: JAL, Nov 93, p. 346]—**Byron P. Anderson**

ACCOUNTING

176. Gates, Sheldon. **101 Business Ratios: A Manager's Handbook of Definitions, Equations, and Computer Algorithms.** Scottsdale, Ariz., McLane, 1993. 261p. index. $24.95. HF5681.R25G38. 658.151'1. LC 92-90816. ISBN 1-881502-00-7.

Ratio analysis is a topic mentioned in accounting and similar types of books, but no single commonly available source lists and explains so many different ratios as does this one. Somewhat less than half this book is devoted to the individual ratios, presenting a page or two for each. The remainder consists of explanations of how ratios are useful, how to find input numbers, and how to calculate and present results; a glossary and bibliography; and other information designed to help a business set up a ratio analysis program. Should the business wish to computerize, software and computer calculations are also covered. For each ratio, Gates explains formulas as well as how to use and interpret the ratio.

Some well-known books give financial ratios by industry, such as *RMA Annual Statement Studies* (Robert Morris Associates), which annually surveys small businesses, presents ratios by SIC (Standard Industrial Classification) code, and has a lengthy preface explaining these ratios. That book has nowhere near 101 ratios but is useful for the small business owner who wants to compare operations with other businesses. Dun & Bradstreet's annual *Industry Norms and Key Business Ratios* performs a similar function, as does *Almanac of Business and Industrial Financial Ratios* (see ARBA 91, entry 233). (Gates lists these three in his bibliography as useful supplements.)

This book is a very practical tool that can be used by businesses to analyze their operations. One possible improvement would be to include ratios specific to certain types of businesses. This might, however, increase the price of this now reasonably priced book. [R: RBB, 15 April 93, p. 1537]

—Susan V. McKimm

BUSINESS SERVICES AND INVESTMENT GUIDES

Dictionaries and Encyclopedias

177. Rosenberg, Jerry M. **Dictionary of Investing.** New York, John Wiley, 1993. 368p. (Business Dictionary Series). $39.95; $14.95pa. HG4513.R67. 332.6'03. LC 92-6357. ISBN 0-471-57433-3; 0-471-57434-1pa.

As the CEO (chief executive officer) of Dreyfus recently observed when discussing the merger of Dreyfus with Mellon Bank, Americans are moving from the savings mode into the investment mode. The average American, however, is more accustomed to parking savings in banks than investing and needs some help in understanding the world of investing. This dictionary should help. It provides very short, precise definitions of more than 7,000 terms related to various financial markets. These include stocks, bonds, and mutual funds and, to a more limited extent, other areas for investment capital, such as real estate, commodities, and even antiques and collectibles. This is not an encyclopedic dictionary; it does not include essays related to the terms. It does, however, attempt to provide a basic context for each term, and helpful cross-references and *see also* references are often included. Financial terms tend to consist of phrases, which in this work are usually entered directly, word by word. In some categories, such as those related to bonds, terms are inverted. Some symbols, acronyms, and abbreviations are included. This inexpensive tool is useful for the new investor or an experienced investor looking at a new market. Gleaning from this book what the author describes as a "core definition," the investor is then able to look elsewhere with some basic understanding of the term or phrase and its market context. [R: WLB, April 93, p. 118]—**JoAnn V. Rogers**

Directories

178. **The Corporate Directory of U.S. Public Companies 1993.** San Mateo, Calif., Walker's Western Research; distr., Detroit, Gale, 1993. 1v. (various paging). index. $390.00. ISBN 1-879346-10-9.

Some 9,000 publicly owned U.S. corporations, from ABE Industrial Holdings to 999 Inc., are profiled in this directory of nearly 2,000 minutely printed pages. The entries offer general, stock, structural (e.g., subsidiaries), and financial information similar to *Walker's Manual of Western Corporations* (see ARBA 93, entry 214). While more limited in scope than *Hoover's Handbook* (see ARBA 92, entry 145), the data (but not the number of companies) far exceeds that found in a basic directory such as *Standard & Poor's Register of Corporations, Directors, and Executives* (see ARBA 92, entry 135). Seven indexes, each with a separate pagination scheme, are searchable by company name, officers and directors, major owners, subsidiaries, state, SIC (Standard Industrial Classification) code, and stock exchange. Researchers would benefit from index combinations (e.g., company, subsidiaries), a separate list of ticker symbols, and the addition of cities to the geographical index. Currently, the geographical, name, and stock exchange indexes assume a knowledge that patrons often lack. This is an excellent source for a basic corporate summary; however, the print size is a major defect given the new directives regarding access for persons with disabilities.—**Sandra E. Belanger**

179. **Directory of Registered Investment Advisors with the Securities and Exchange Commission 1993.** Charlottesville, Va., Money Market Directories, 1993. 1298p. index. $295.00pa. ISSN 1059-7433.

Based on questionnaires supplied by investment advisory organizations and individuals, the body of this directory contains a great deal of information in 34 categories. In a well-summarized, easy-to-read format, users can find information such as amounts and types of assets under management, asset allocation of different types of accounts, money managers, research, services offered, minimum account and fee schedules, and a statement on investment style and strategy. Also included is information about newsletters and publications of organizations. This year's annual directory adds categories for wrap accounts and socially screened accounts. Not all advisers provided a generous amount of detailed information, although most of the major players in the game seem to have done so.

Arranged geographically, the information can be accessed in numerous ways through alphabetical indexes of all listed advisers, plus advisers with international investments, women- and minority-owned firms, wrap account managers, advisers who suggest brokers, and advisers who provide social screening. Several useful categorized indexes are included. One provides an alphabetical list of more than 40 service specialties, such as emerging markets, hedge funds, oil and gas, and private placement. An investment style index divided by equities and fixed income, with about 15 style categories for each, provides access to advisers whose investment style for equity selection may include bottom up to sector rotation, and for fixed income may include bond substitutes to top down. The newsletter index enables the user to connect the publication with the source in the main body of the work.

As the economic and business climates change, advisers' approaches to investing may also change, making an annual compilation of this information necessary. This well-produced reference source provides excellent information for any individual or organization with money under professional management.
—**JoAnn V. Rogers**

180. Kinoshita, Sumie, ed. **Directory of Companies Offering Dividend Reinvestment Plans.** 10th ed. Laurel, Md., Evergreen Enterprises, 1993. 130p. $28.95pa. ISBN 0-933183-12-7.

181. Kinoshita, Sumie, ed. **Dividend Reinvestment Plans: 1992 Guide Almanac.** Laurel, Md., Evergreen Enterprises, 1993. 167p. $65.00pa. ISBN 0-933183-11-9.

Dividend reinvestment plans are mechanisms whereby stockholders may have dividends reinvested in a company's stock rather than paid directly in cash. The plans are growing in number and expanding in terms of features available. The *Directory of Companies Offering Dividend Reinvestment Plans* is one of three titles published by Evergreen Enterprises dealing with dividend reinvestment plans. Its purpose is to provide fundamental data useful in making decisions regarding this unique approach to stock investing. A brief introduction defines dividend reinvestment plans, discusses the various features of available plans, and describes how to use the directory of listings. Each of the 990 listings contains key data, such as name, address, telephone number, type of business, whether discounts are offered, whether fees are charged, and other special features. There is also a bibliography of books, reports, and articles related to dividend reinvestment. One appendix includes, among other items, a very useful list of companies offering discount purchases as part of their plan. A second appendix contains excerpts from Internal Revenue Service publications.

In addition to the directory, Evergreen publishes the annual *Guide Almanac*, which is a cumulation of a quarterly looseleaf service. The guide, interestingly, contains all of the basic information found in the directory plus quite a bit more. The additional information is presented in appendix A and consists of various listings, such as a record of plans that have terminated, an inventory of Canadian plans, and a series of lists organized by type of business.

Of the two publications, the guide is certainly more useful. Moreover, it would be an unnecessary duplication to purchase both.—**P. Grady Morein**

182. **Nasdaq Fact Book & Company Directory, 1993.** Gaithersburg, Md., National Association of Securities Dealers; distr., Austin, Tex., Reference Press, 1993. 231p. $19.95pa.

NASDAQ (National Association of Securities Dealers Automated Quotations) is a significant factor in U.S. security trading, well above the New York Stock Exchange (NYSE) and the American Stock Exchange (Amex) in number of companies and issues, but it lags behind NYSE in volume of shares traded.

Each year NASD publishes a combined review of NASDAQ trading and directory of NASDAQ companies. The current volume provides statistics on the performance of NASDAQ securities, individually and in aggregate, for 1992, with a historical perspective. It also offers directory information on each NASDAQ company. Numerous charts and tables indicate the performance of NASDAQ as a whole as well as salient features of trading in 1992. The major portion of the book lists members in two sections: NASDAQ national market securities and NASDAQ SmallCap securities. Data include NASDAQ symbol; SIC (Standard Industrial Classification) code; address; telephone number; name and title of contact; share volume; high, low, and closing prices; and percentage of change from 1991. The book is a useful low-cost guide for investors, analysts, and others concerned with securities trading. Some of the data are also available on computer disk.—**William C. Struning**

183. **Nelson's TechResources. Winter 1993.** Port Chester, N.Y., Nelson, 1993. 548p. index. $95.00pa. ISBN 0-922460-38-8. ISSN 1065-2396.

Primarily a buyers' guide, this resource directory complements other Nelson publications for investment advisers (see ARBA 92, entries 162, 163, 164, and 229). Organized in three sections, companies offering automated products and services (e.g., databases, simulations, software) are profiled, indicating basic information and a description of services and products. The heart of the directory resides in part 2, the product or buyers' guide. For each product or service, the producers, potential users, and key contacts are specified. Interestingly, entries for Moody's identify libraries as potential users, while those for DIALOG do not. The appearance of large type, boldface type, explanatory data (e.g., hardware specifications), and advertisements suggests that payment is required for inclusion or upgrades. There is an application index with 47 subject categories, some of which are general (e.g., statistical analysis), very detailed (e.g., back office turnkey), or basically uninformative (e.g., news). Keyword indexing would represent multiuse products better, while an alphabetical name index (e.g., companies, products) would facilitate use by a wider audience. The work's major weakness is its unexplained data collection methods. Despite its faults, this directory will prove a useful addition for business libraries with specialized investment collections.—**Sandra E. Belanger**

184. **Skinner's Directory of Security Dealer Name and Address Changes 1992-1993 (Covers 1965-1992): Including Dealers, Transfer Agents, and U.S. Public Corporations.** San Mateo, Calif., Walker's Western Research, 1992. 259p. $112.00pa. ISBN 1-879346-09-5.

This is a specialized but very useful reference work. It aptly describes itself as a "Security Dealer genealogy" and provides information on security dealer consolidations, liquidations, mergers, and absorptions between 1965 and 1992. This information is particularly of interest to trust administrators, proxy solicitors, and others who need to find the current name and address of a firm or of the successors of a firm. This work only provides information on firms with successors, but, according to the description of contents, Walker's Western Research will undertake, without cost for subscribers to this work, to find information on security dealers that have ceased operation without a successor.

The work is organized into five parts and is easy to use. The first and longest section lists security dealers alphabetically by their old name, and gives the complete old address and the complete new name and address. Action codes, indicating whether the old firm was fully or partially acquired, discontinued, liquidated, merged, or the like separate the old name and address from the "new entity/address." Other sections include an alphabetical listing with addresses of security dealers, transfer agents, transfer agents and corporations by transfer agent, and public corporations with telephone numbers and transfer agents.

This work clearly and conveniently fills a specific need. If a library needs information on the genealogy of security dealers, it should get this work.—**Richard H. Swain**

185. Wilson, Ian M., ed. **The Wilson Directory of Emerging Market Funds.** 1992-1993 ed. Saskatoon, Sask., Wilson Emerging Market Funds Research; distr., Austin, Tex., Reference Press, 1992. 236p. index. $99.95pa. ISBN 0-9696526-0-7.

This directory contains much useful data for those interested in an overview of a fast-growing area of investment for which there is not much information available in general reference sources. Two major sections provide an overview and a profile for approximately 400 existing funds investing in emerging markets in Asia, Latin America, and Europe. Using the World Bank definition of emerging market, Hong Kong, Singapore, Spain, and Austria are excluded. Taiwan and Korea are included, however. Each section arranges the funds under global, regional, and country by region.

The overview presents information such as size of the fund, date of commencement, and an asset profile. The more detailed profiles include facts on the fund's holdings, including the 10 largest assets and the geographic allocation of assets. Fund managers, investment advisers, and other key individuals and groups associated with the management of the fund are also listed. Other sections give rankings of funds by size and fund and advisers' addresses. Brief stock exchange data and contacts are included in two sections. An interesting section that precedes the index provides varying amounts of information on other sources of market research, information, and services. A lengthy description of the International Finance Corporation and its Emerging Markets Data Base, from which much of the book's contents seem to have been gathered, indicates that this rather pricey source might be useful to those in businesses associated with international investment.

The editor hopes that this annual directory will establish him as knowledgeable in this investment area and generate interest in his new bimonthly newsletter and consulting service. It should prove useful, for those with a beginning interest in foreign investment, in identifying established funds for further investigation. It is hoped that the next edition will have a better binding, a table of contents with page numbers, and running heads at the top of pages.—**JoAnn V. Rogers**

Handbooks and Yearbooks

186. Barber, Hoyt L. **Tax Havens: How to Bank, Invest, and Do Business—Offshore and Tax Free.** New York, McGraw-Hill, 1993. 243p. index. $24.95. K4464.5.B37. 343.04. LC 93-13291. ISBN 0-07-003659-4.

This thorough explanation and guide to the use of offshore arrangements for individual and business advantages (mainly the reduction of the tax burden for U.S. citizens) is intended for the nonprofessional newcomer to the topic. However, Barber assumes that the reader is somewhat informed and interested in alternative locations for the tax haven, so he provides only a very short introduction about the reasons for doing business offshore and focuses quickly on criteria for choosing a location. He lists 13 such criteria and uses them in his discussion of more than 30 locations. The chapter on how to use a tax haven deals with establishing a foreign presence by incorporating and deriving benefits from incorporation. Part 2 presents profiles of relevant information about individual locations, from Antigua to Western Samoa. These profiles include names and addresses of business contacts in government, banking, legal and accounting services, and the like. Part 3 and the appendixes contain additional contacts and resources.

If the Clinton administration tightens the tax requirements of foreign corporate entities, some of the information in this book may need to be revised fairly soon. Barber does provide a valuable current overview of the topic, however, and much of the information should continue to be useful regardless of U.S. tax law changes.—**JoAnn V. Rogers**

187. **The Business One Irwin Investor's Handbook 1993.** Phyllis S. Pierce, ed. Homewood, Ill., Irwin Professional Publishing, 1993. 196p. $20.00pa. LC 20-9300-12. ISBN 1-55623-673-5.

This handy compendium serves as a yearbook of 1992 stock, bond, and mutual fund trading and as a retrospective guide to the Dow Jones and several other market averages. Following a short reflective introduction on the state of the economy from Alfred L. Malabre, the well-informed economics news editor of the *New York Times*, the volume presents numerical tables on such items as the earnings and daily and yearly closings on the averages. The next 100 pages give 1992 trading information for the New York Stock Exchange and American Stock Exchange stocks and bonds, U.S. government bonds and notes, mutual funds, and the NASDAQ (National Association of Securities Dealers Automated Quotations). The final pages summarize basic information on foreign markets and consist mainly of the monthly high, low, and close for a three-year period. A few simple graphs also are included. Besides its function as a summary of the 1992 U.S. markets, the volume will help a beginner understand the Dow averages and what they represent.—**JoAnn V. Rogers**

188. Chalmin, Philippe, ed. **International Commodity Markets Handbook 1993.** Hertfordshire, England, Woodhead-Faulkner; distr., Englewood Cliffs, N.J., Prentice Hall Professional, Technical, and Reference, 1992. 463p. index. $39.95. ISBN 0-13-020694-6.

This book is a reference bargain in view of the amount of information provided. It is an impeccable translation from the original French, with coverage of events up to mid-1992 and with topics in several chapters ranging well beyond the narrow interpretation suggested by the title. The first two parts provide a background for the handbook, covering information on the major trends and the economic environment. Among the major trends, the reader finds excellent discussions of the results of the collapse of communism, a review of GATT (General Agreement on Tariffs and Trade) negotiations, developments in the futures markets, and regional trends. The economic environment is discussed in terms of monetary changes, currency markets (including the European Exchange Rate Mechanism and the Maastricht agreement), and stock markets. Eight central chapters focus on the commodity markets: food, agricultural nonfood, iron and steel, major metals, precious metals and diamonds, minor metals, energy, and industrial commodities. The last part briefly covers the increasingly important services.

The degree of detail is generally good and historical trends are clearly defined, but some major changes have taken place since the book was published (and will undoubtedly have taken place since the writing of this review). For up-to-date information, newspapers or individual commodity publications are necessary, but for the background it covers and for broader analysis, the present volume is indispensable. Recommended to business schools, international commodity traders, commodity exporters and importers, producers and users, and large public reference libraries.—**Bogdan Mieczkowski**

189. **The Handbook for No-Load Fund Investors, 1993.** 13th ed. By the editors of *The No-Load Fund Investor*. Homewood, Ill., Business One Irwin, 1993. 552p. $40.00pa. LC 85-645285. ISBN 1-55623-099-0. ISSN 0736-6264.

This edition follows the same outline as previous editions. It presents a very short summary of information about the no-load fund industry in 1992, followed by a cogent argument for using these funds. The third section consists of 20 chapters providing sound advice on how the individual should approach this type of investment, based on individual financial goals and objectives. While these chapters are somewhat repetitive from year to year, they do reflect upon current industry and market changes and serve to refocus the investor's attention on important matters.

Annual performance data for the 1992 calendar year are presented in tables and charts, with a comprehensive summary arranged alphabetically by fund name and data for each of 10 years plus 5- and 10-year annualized total returns. The next list of the 1,700 funds ranks the funds within investment objective categories, such as aggressive growth, income funds, and sector and industry funds. It presents the rankings in three lists that cover total return percent for 1, 5, and 10 years. A top-50 ranking for the latest year follows. A 2-year chart for each fund shows the 13-week and 39-week moving averages, and there is also a list of funds by fund family that includes total net assets of each fund. A directory includes basic information such as address, portfolio manager, details on services, and fees. A fee table enables the investor to compare the effect of various fees from one fund to another. This handbook will help both the novice and experienced fund investor and should be found in all types of libraries that serve the individual investor.—**JoAnn V. Rogers**

190. Herzfeld, Thomas J. **Herzfeld's Guide to Closed-End Funds.** New York, McGraw-Hill, 1993. 453p. index. $22.95pa. HG4930.H47. 332.63'27. LC 93-7229. ISBN 0-07-028435-0.

A closed-end fund bears some of the attributes of a mutual fund, but it is instead an entity offering a fixed amount of stock, which is then bought and sold on the open market like the shares of other companies traded on the stock exchange. These funds were hugely popular during the 1920s and have, the author says, made something of a comeback since the early 1980s. Their prices fluctuate, which means one can buy or sell shares that are at a premium or a discount to the underlying value of the holdings of the fund.

Herzfeld is something of an expert on this type of investment. Indeed, he is probably the leading authority; he has been tracking the phenomenon for many years. Here he propounds certain insights into the nature of these funds—investment vehicles that remain uncharted territory for most investors. Herzfeld emphasizes that the closed-end fund offers the chance to buy assets at a discount from net asset value, which is certainly not the case with regular mutual funds, whose shares are always offered and redeemed at net asset value.

What is impressive about this book is in its presentation. Herzfeld gives strategies for trading the funds and describes the types of closed-end funds (e.g., stock, specialty, bond, convertible bond, foreign). He discusses hedging and arbitrage, reorganizations, and takeovers and presents, in full-page format, performance data and rankings for each of 300 closed-end funds. This is important new coverage of a lesser-known opportunity to make money in the stock market, and, while closed-end funds are not without their risks, the book should be made available to the investing patron.—**Randall Rafferty**

191. Hulbert, Mark, ed. **The Hulbert Guide to Financial Newsletters.** 5th ed. Chicago, Dearborn Financial Publishing, 1993. 574p. illus. index. $27.95pa. HG4529.H86. 332.6. LC 92-35969. ISBN 0-79310-619-2.

Hulbert has made a career of evaluating the performance of newsletters that sell investment advice. He is a columnist for *Forbes* and edits the *Hulbert Financial Digest*, which monitors investment advisory newsletters. This guide is a distillation and general explanation of his methods and a straightforward rating of more than 120 investment newsletters. It starts with an introduction and six chapters that clearly and concisely explain the nature of investment newsletters and present Hulbert's views on how they should be used and judged. These initial chapters delineate the basic principle that investment newsletters should be evaluated on two points: performance and risk. In order to be evaluated, a newsletter must provide model portfolios (or clear investment recommendations that can be used to create model portfolios). Otherwise there is no concrete way to evaluate performance (i.e., return on investment). Risk is clearly tied to performance: High return involves high risk, and the guide presents a clear and objective means for stating how risk is presented and justified. Having thus established a framework for evaluation, chapter 7 then provides a clear statement of performance and risk for each newsletter, leaving it to investors to choose a newsletter based on their judgments of acceptable performance and risk.

Appendix A ranks general investment newsletters on the basis of their total returns and risk-adjusted performances for various time periods through June 30, 1992. Appendix B does the same for mutual fund newsletters. Appendix C ranks newsletters on their ability to time switches into and out of the stock, bond, and gold markets, and appendix D is a directory of newsletters giving yearly, six-month, and trial subscription rates and indicating if the newsletter provides a hot line or money management services.

This is an excellent reference work for individual investors and for libraries serving investors. It provides a wealth of information clearly and concisely, and its evaluations are based on a straightforward and well-presented vision of performance and risk. It is unfortunate that this information is contained in a perfect-bound paperback. [R: LJ, 15 Feb 93, p. 160; RBB, July 93, p. 1997; RBB, 1 Oct 93, p. 385]
—**Richard H. Swain**

192. Kinoshita, Sumie, ed. **Guide to Dividend Reinvestment Plans.** Laurel, Md., Evergreen Enterprises, 1993. 1v. (various paging). $130.00 looseleaf w/binder.

For those familiar with the *Directory of Companies Offering Dividend Reinvestment Plans* (see ARBA 90, entry 203), this looseleaf service will look familiar. The work is divided alphabetically into four sections. One section is updated each quarter, and an annual clothbound edition is also available. Listings provide directory data, exchange on which traded, Standard & Poor's Rating system, type of industry, and plan features. Appendixes provide listings grouped by categories. This is a very specialized tool and is recommended primarily for large business libraries.—**Bobray Bordelon**

193. **Market Share Reporter 1993: An Annual Compilation of Reported Market Share Data on Companies, Products, and Services.** 3d ed. Arsen J. Darnay and Marlita A. Reddy. Detroit, Gale, 1993. 689p. index. $170.00. ISBN 0-8103-8184-2. ISSN 1052-9578.

Market share is one of the most sought-after pieces of business information. One typically has to consult many sources to locate this data. This tool conveniently compiles market shares on companies, products, and services. It is filled with charts and useful explanatory notes. The arrangement is by Standard Industrial Classification (SIC) code. Indexes provide access by topic; source; place-name; products, services, and issues; company; and brands. The source index lists where the market shares were found as well as the original sources from which the data were obtained. Thus, this work can serve as a useful collection development tool. While the market shares will not always be the most current, one can use the source listing to try and locate more recent data. Highly recommended for all business collections.—**Bobray Bordelon**

194. **Morningstar Closed-End Fund Sourcebook 1993.** Wesley Kim, ed. Chicago, Morningstar, 1993. 377p. index. $95.00. ISSN 1067-6279.

The past few years have seen a marked increase in the interest given to closed-end mutual funds that operate like stocks in their issue of a fixed number of shares purchased through brokers. Because of this interest, Morningstar has added this title as an annual publication. Included in this well-constructed manual is a 36-page user's guide explaining the use of the work and its various sections. This is followed by a segment on tables and charts that supplies basic information on performance, including five- and four-star funds, funds with highest and lowest NAV (net asset value) and market price returns, and statistics on fund managers. The major part of the text follows in the review section, with a single page given to each alphabetically arranged fund. Included here is narrative as well as chapters and graphs showing investment criteria, portfolio holdings, performance summary over the years and recent quarters, and operations. The history of the fund is shown with a timeline from 1980 to 1992. Finally, there is a section of useful indexes beginning with an alphabetically arranged list of funds followed by an adviser index identifying fund advisers and their fund families. An objectives index lists funds classified by 14 different objectives, and a fund manager index identifies managers.

This manual furnishes all the technical information needed to make decisions concerning purchases in the area. However, to understand the workings and procedures of this investment, it would be necessary to consult an introductory guide.—**Ron Blazek**

195. **Morningstar Mutual Fund 500, 1993: An In-Depth Look at 500 Select Mutual Funds....** Natalia Ocokoljich, ed. Chicago, Morningstar; distr., Homewood, Ill., Business One Irwin, 1993. 500p. index. $35.00pa. ISBN 1-55623-072-9. ISSN 1067-6228.

From the universe of thousands of mutual funds followed by this research and rating service, Morningstar has selected 500 funds of exceptional merit for inclusion in this volume. Each fund is represented by a one-page numerical, statistical, and narrative description and evaluation that consists of both historical and current data. Designed to be used by the individual investor, the work does away with some industry jargon by categorizing equity funds as aggressive, core, conservative, closed-end, and hybrid, and bond funds as specialty, investment, short-term, and municipal. These categories, combined with fund objective and investment-style information, allow the investor to focus on what an individual fund is trying to do.

What Morningstar is best known for, however, is extensive performance data, particularly the risk-adjusted rating system that assigns up to 5 stars for each rated fund in an investment category for a 3-, 5-, and 10-year period. A wealth of additional performance and comparative performance data is also given. For example, for a small company fund, one can find from 1980 a yearly comparison not only with the S&P (Standard & Poor) 500 Index but also with the Wilshire 4500 Index, which is an index of U.S. equities (excluding the S&P stocks, which are large company stocks). Two narrative sections provide an overview of current investment criteria and some educational and professional history for fund managers, important and sometimes difficult information to find even in a fund prospectus.

With the ever-increasing importance of mutual fund investing to the individual investor, to the industry, and even to the U.S. economy, this inexpensive, well-designed source should be in most libraries. Its users' guide describes in some detail the methods of analysis used and gives guidance to the investor in asking questions about mutual fund investing. And the information-packed summaries of 500 funds will help investors decide which of these good funds might be appropriate for their investment objectives.—**JoAnn V. Rogers**

196. **Morningstar Mutual Fund Sourcebook 1993.** Patty Dutile, ed. Chicago, Morningstar, 1993. 2v. index. $225.00/set. ISSN 8755-4151.

This is an authoritative and comprehensive guide to mutual funds, both equity and fixed-income. All of the funds reviewed appear to be United States-based. Most of the set is composed of single-page reviews of each fund. Each review contains a broad assortment of factual information (e.g., performance summary, manager profile, basic operational data, investment criteria, portfolio composition). In addition, analytical techniques, such as style boxes and performance ratings, assist in wading through the mass of data available in order to arrive at optimal investment decisions. A readers' guide explains topics covered in the reviews and serves to increase the usefulness of the information. Because there are several thousand funds included in the texts, summary tables and charts provide perspective and points of departure for analysis, comparison, and evaluation. The funds are indexed alphabetically, by family (management), by objective, and by fund manager. Multiple indexes provide flexible access to the many entries.

The fact that Morningstar ratings are frequently quoted by practitioners reflects their standing in the investment community. *Morningstar Mutual Fund Sourcebook* provides useful guidance to investors, students of finance, and professionals in the financial community.—**William C. Struning**

197. **Morningstar Variable Annuity/Life Sourcebook 1993.** Jennifer Strickland, ed. Chicago, Morningstar, 1993. 965p. index. $195.00. ISSN 1062-3361.

Variable-annuity and variable-life policies are two forms of insurance and investment instruments; they are similar in many respects but have rather different objectives. Because of the overall complexity of these investment devices, as well as the intricate nature of their relationship, it is important that prospective buyers and investors have access to information about the increasing number of opportunities available.

This publication is designed to provide facts, figures, performance measures, and other data useful in making decisions regarding the purchase of variable-annuity and variable-life policies. The principal components of the book are the two review sections, one dealing with providers of variable-annuity policies and the other with providers of variable-life policies. The reviews consist of single-page presentations of 14 key data elements for 965 variable-annuity and variable-life policies, which are referred to as subaccounts. Information includes details such as the investment goals of the subaccount (e.g., growth, bond, international stock, specialty fund), investment criteria, multiple-year performance history, and expenses and fees. A comprehensive user's guide explains each element in detail and gives advice on how to interpret and use the data.

There are also sections of tables and charts that supply comparative performance data on the various providers. Two especially helpful chapters are "Objective Index," which lists subaccounts according to investment goals, and "Underlying Fund Index," which includes all of the subcategories within each subaccount.

This sourcebook presents a wealth of data and information useful to readers in need of assistance in selecting from the many variable-annuity and variable-life investments. Both academic and public libraries providing strong business support would find the publication worthwhile.—**P. Grady Morein**

198. Perritt, Gerald W. **The Mutual Fund Encyclopedia.** 1993-1994 ed. Chicago, Dearborn Financial Publishing, 1993. 567p. index. $35.95pa. ISBN 0-79310-617-6.

Perritt's encyclopedia aims to provide an overview and screening device for 1,300 mutual funds. Organized into a dozen categories, from money market funds to tax-exempt bond funds, it includes both load and no-load funds. The half-page entry for each fund provides directory information, the minimum amount of money necessary to begin and to add to one's investment, distribution frequency, associated fees, management company, and the name and tenure of the portfolio manager. Financial statistics for five years for total return and for investment portfolio are also given. Finally, the fund objectives and investment strategies of the managers are outlined. An index of all fund names concludes the encyclopedia.

Useful in particular for the newer investor, the lengthy introduction defines key concepts, explains characteristics of mutual funds, and sets out legal requirements. It also reviews the previous year (1992), listing name changes, mergers, liquidations, and closings. The top performing funds in each of the 12 categories/objectives are listed, and recent trends are outlined.

Perritt is also the editor and publisher of the *Mutual Fund Letter*, a monthly newsletter, and he contributes to *Forbes* magazine. In the preface he cautions that the information in the encyclopedia will be dated quickly; therefore, this work is merely a beginning. Its purpose is to help focus one's research.

Perritt's encyclopedia differs from such works as *Directory of Mutual Funds* (Investment Company Institute, annual) by providing more information about goals and strategies for fewer funds (1,300 versus 3,700). At a reasonable price and in a very readable format, Perritt's encyclopedia is useful for any public and academic library and for individuals who wish to learn about mutual funds. [R: LJ, 15 May 93, p. 64]
—**Joan B. Fiscella**

199. Sherman, Andrew J., and Donna Tozzi Cavanagh. **The Best Nonfranchise Business Opportunities.** New York, Henry Holt, 1993. 299p. index. $19.95pa. HD2346.U5S53. 658'.041. LC 92-34838. ISBN 0-8050-2208-2.

Based on a mail survey and interviews with company officials, this book lists 75 companies with nonfranchise business opportunities: dealerships, multilevel marketing, distributorships, direct sales programs, licenses, and vending machines opportunities. The book was written by a freelance business writer and a lawyer considered an expert in legal issues for small businesses. Company entries provide initial and total investment demands; company advantages; expansion history; industry focus; future outlook; and name, address, and telephone number of a contact person. Companies offer such products and services as automotive and beauty products, recreational facilities, and computer maintenance. Some well-known companies (e.g., Amway, Mary Kay Cosmetics, Avon) did not participate, raising concerns about the word "best" in the title. Part 1 includes guidelines for establishing a business of this type; part 2 is arranged by type of business opportunity, then by company. The book has a company index but no subject indexes. It is more appropriate for circulating than for reference collections.
—**Marilyn Domas White**

200. **Standard & Poor's Stock and Bond Guide.** 1993 ed. Bill Coughlin, ed. New York, McGraw-Hill, 1993. 486p. $17.95pa. LC 93-077245. ISBN 0-07-052094-1.

Data on stocks, bonds, and mutual funds are gathered in this one convenient source. For common and convertible preferred stocks there is information on trade exchange, ratings, institutional holdings, principal business, recent and 20-year price ranges, sales, dividends, financial position, capitalization, and earnings. For mutual funds, one will find similar data as well as the fund's principal objective and performance data. The corporate and convertible bonds sections also furnish important financial data and ratings. The foreign bond section supplies comparable data plus 20-year price ranges. A brief unit on selected municipals provides only ratings data. Detailed interpretation charts prior to each section help clarify data that is already carefully presented.

No single work should be used as the sole basis for investment decisions, and this work is no exception. It does not offer the in-depth information or the timeliness found in commercial advisory sources. However, its price is unbeatable, and it does provide a wealth of data in one convenient source. While not a necessity, it is recommended. [R: Choice, Nov 93, p. 439; LJ, 1 June 93, p. 110; RBB, 1 Sept 93, p. 90]—**Bobray Bordelon**

CONSUMER EDUCATION

201. Gall, Timothy L., and Susan B. Gall. **Consumers' Guide to Product Grades and Terms: From Grade A to VSOP....** Detroit, Gale, 1993. 603p. index. $69.00. ISBN 0-8103-8898-7.

Advertisers are continually trying to sell products by using such terms as "lite," "new, improved," or "satisfaction guaranteed," knowing the average consumer has no idea what those terms really mean. Developed to help the average person decipher these labels, grades, and symbols, this reference book will be valuable to any collection. The work is broken down into 21 sections that contain segments on general advertising terms, environmental concerns, automotive terminology, health and beauty terms, specific food products, and other consumer items. Providing up-to-date information on nutrition and environmental labeling, the book gives definitions and explanations for 8,000 terms, symbols, and phrases used on 630 consumer products. The information was obtained from more than 200 standards-setting organizations, industry groups, and government agencies.

The contents and comprehensive index and the clear, crisp type enhance the value of this practical, interesting reference guide. An appendix that lists standards organizations and their addresses can help people find out where and how to pursue consumer complaints. This timely, informative book will be useful in public and academic libraries. [R: Choice, Sept 93, p. 76; LJ, 15 Mar 93, p. 68; RQ, Fall 93, p. 120; WLB, June 93, p. 120]—**Diane J. Turner**

202. **The Smart Consumer's Directory.** 1993 ed. Nashville, Tenn., Thomas Nelson, 1992. 401p. $9.99pa. HC110.C63S55. 381'.33'02573. LC 92-9380. ISBN 0-8407-4503-6.

Designed to provide consumers with assistance in functioning more effectively in our complex world, *The Smart Consumer's Directory* contains a great variety of practical information. Most of part 1 consists of consumer tips on subjects such as airline travel, dangerous diets, home shopping, mail fraud, choosing a school, and buying used cars. This part also has suggestions for handling complaints and guidelines for writing a complaint letter. Part 2 contains a selection of directories for obtaining assistance. The first one, "Corporate Consumer Contact," gives contact names, toll-free numbers, and addresses for hundreds of major corporations. Other types of directories in this section include car manufacturers; Better Business Bureaus; trade associations; state, county, and city government consumer protection offices; state insurance regulators; and state utility commissions.

Recreation, travel, and leisure are the topics of part 3. Here one will find helpful hints as well as addresses and telephone numbers of tourist bureaus, parks, places of interest, and sports teams and organizations. There is also a list of toll-free numbers for major airlines, hotels, motels, and resorts. Part 4 is a list of state agencies that provide birth and death certificates and marriage and divorce records. In addition to the address for obtaining information, each entry contains data on the cost of acquiring records and further helpful remarks.

The final section of the book treats personal finance. The focus of this segment is primarily on giving advice about such subjects as using consumer credit, obtaining student loans, and securing a mortgage or home equity loan. The book concludes with 105 pages of amortization tables.

This is a useful publication for quick reference on a number of issues. While large libraries will have other sources for obtaining much of the information within, both large and small public libraries will find it worthwhile.—**P. Grady Morein**

203. **The Wholesale-by-Mail Catalog 1993.** By the Print Project. Prudence McCullough, ed. New York, HarperPerennial/HarperCollins, 1992. 626p. index. $15.00pa. ISBN 0-06-273160-2. ISSN 1049-0116.

Die-hard bargain hunters may already be familiar with the *Wholesale-by-Mail Catalog*. The uninitiated discount shopper, however, will discover in it a gold mine of U.S. and foreign mail order firms that sell goods and services at 30 percent below list or comparable retail. The catalog groups more than 500 firms into chapters by product or service type, such as food and drink and sports and recreation, with *see also* references to other listings in the catalog at the end of each chapter. In addition to address and telephone and fax information, each entry briefly tells consumers how to get information (e.g., catalog, price quote, swatches), expected savings, methods of payment accepted, products and services available, and location and hours of stores (if appropriate). The editor follows this with an in-depth look at the firm's offerings, including brand names, price comparisons to retail, guarantee and return information, and tips on particularly good buys. Some of the firms offer a *Wholesale-by-Mail* reader's discount on orders placed before February 1994. The book also includes a complete guide to buying by mail, with useful tips on ordering by telephone, ordering from foreign firms, returning merchandise, warranties, and complaints. An international size chart and indexes to company names and products round out this useful volume.

In these tough economic times, consumers are looking for bargains, and *The Wholesale-by-Mail Catalog* offers promise. The paperback cover, unfortunately, may not stand up to the usage this book could receive in a library. Recommended for public libraries.—**Kerranne G. Biley**

FINANCE AND BANKING

204. Butler, Brian, and Alan Isaacs, eds. **A Dictionary of Finance.** New York, Oxford University Press, 1993. 314p. $35.00; $10.95pa. HG151.D54. 332'.03. LC 92-42735. ISBN 0-19-215363-3; 0-19-285279-5pa.

Written for finance professionals and students and private investors, this specialized dictionary includes about 3,300 definitions of financial terms from banking, public finance, investment, and taxation; there are also entries for concepts and agencies. The book is intended as a companion to *A Concise Dictionary of Business* (see ARBA 92, entry 124). It purports to have international coverage and does include terms unique to finance in other countries and international concepts (e.g., *yen, special drawing rights*), but many definitions for common terms have a decidedly British slant. *Commercial bank*, for example, is defined by British law, and *treasury* is the U.K. government department. The British emphasis is also apparent in the relative size of the entries (e.g., the London Stock Exchange entry has 33 lines; the New York Stock Exchange, only 7). Beyond this British emphasis, however, the entries are accurate, clearly written, and free of jargon. Secondary entries for acronyms identify the agency or term and lead to the main entry under the complete term. Within definitions, an asterisk denotes any term also appearing as a main entry.

The contributors are identified, but no mention is made of their subject qualifications. Of the two editors, Butler is affiliated with Lloyds Bank, and Alan Isaacs with Market House Books. For North American libraries the book should be supplemented with similar dictionaries providing more complete coverage of North American financial institutions and concepts, such as *Dictionary of Finance* (see ARBA 89, entry 203) or *Dictionary of Finance and Investment Terms* (see ARBA 92, entry 184).
—**Marilyn Domas White**

205. Darnay, Arsen J., ed. **Finance, Insurance, & Real Estate USA: Industry Analyses, Statistics, and Leading Organizations.** Detroit, Gale, 1993. 1045p. maps. index. $169.00. ISBN 0-8103-8499-X. ISSN 1066-7350.

In the past, someone seeking analytic data on the financial services industries had to turn to many different sources. Unlike other economic sectors, the finance, insurance, and real estate (FIRE) segments are not documented by the quadrennial censuses of business. This source integrates data gathered by various regulatory and governmental agencies as well as the editor of this work. Sources used are cited throughout. The primary arrangement is by standard industrial classification (SIC). While this work is not intended to serve as a directory, it does provide some such data for industry leaders. It supplies facts for the industry as a whole as well as for specific geographic areas. Most information is from the late 1980s and includes the number of establishments, employment, pay per employee, and annual payroll. Future projections are listed in many sections. Graphics and maps help accentuate the information. This is a highly useful source for business reference collections that provide analytic information. [R: Choice, July/Aug 93, pp. 1748-49; JAL, July 93, p. 200; LJ, 15 Mar 93, p. 68; RBB, 1 May 93, pp. 1626-28]
—**Bobray Bordelon**

206. Fraser, Robert, and Christopher Long. **The World Financial System.** 2d ed. Harlow, England, Longman; distr., Detroit, Gale, 1992. 508p. index. $165.00. ISBN 0-582-09652-9.

The first edition of this work (1987) predated the 1987 equity market crash, much of Japan's economic rise, and the fall of the Soviet bloc. This work serves as both historical encyclopedia and directory. First, the historical background of international monetary relations from 1944 to 1992 is presented. Issues such as the monetary effects of war, the establishment of the IMF (International Monetary Fund), oil crises, and changes in the former Soviet bloc countries are explored in 34 chapters with subsections. While all of this information can be found elsewhere, the format simplifies the process. The remainder of the text provides directory data for international economic organizations. Detailed information, charts, and tables are provided for the organizations. Consistent format and detail make this work especially useful. A general index is provided. This examination of the sociopolitical effects of international monetary relations will make an excellent addition to academic and larger public library reference collections.—**Bobray Bordelon**

207. Klein, Gerald. **Dictionary of Banking.** Southport, England, Pitman Publishing; distr., Scarborough, Ont., Carswell, 1992. 286p. $34.25pa. ISBN 0-273-03788-9.

The author, a fellow of Britain's Chartered Institute of Bankers (a major professional organization), targets this dictionary at banking students and practitioners. The estimated 3,700 entries include generic banking terms, technical terms, institutions, and major laws, with the latter two preponderantly British. Terms relating to banking from other disciplines—economics, securities trading, retailing, shipping, insurance, estate law, and real estate—are also present. The length of entries varies widely, from one sentence to more than a page, though most are one to four sentences. Definitions often refer to British institutions and practice. Occasionally entries go beyond the definitional to procedural or legal aspects. The vocabulary is formal, and definitions are accurate.

This dictionary is recommended for collections encompassing British banking. Its treatment of U.S. institutions, laws, and practice, as well as its coverage of generic and technical banking terms, should be supplemented by two other dictionaries that similarly provide brief definitions: Jerry Rosenberg's *Dictionary of Banking* (John Wiley, 1993), with 7,500 entries, or the American Bankers Association's *Banking Terminology* (see ARBA 91, entry 210), with 5,300 entries. [R: WLB, April 93, p. 118]

—**John Lewis Campbell**

208. Munn, Glenn G., F. L. Garcia, and Charles J. Woelfel, eds. **Encyclopedia of Banking & Finance.** 9th ed. Pasadena, Calif., Salem Press, 1993. 3v. index. $235.00/set. ISBN 0-89356-496-6.

This title may seem familiar, not only because it is an excellent financial reference work but also because the 9th edition has been available since 1991 as a one-volume work. For this new "Library Edition," the publisher has made some cosmetic changes and added an index but has left the content unchanged. As the encyclopedia's content has already been described in ARBA (see ARBA 92, entry 186) and elsewhere, the differences between the two editions will be highlighted. For the "Library Edition," the work was transformed from a 1,097-page volume into three smaller volumes of about 400 pages each. The books have sturdy binding and contain acid-free paper, and the type size was increased for easier readability. The decision to finally add a comprehensive index, which is included in each volume, was an enlightened one. The encyclopedia will now be more helpful to readers who are new to banking and finance topics.

These changes may not increase the popularity of this reference tool, but they definitely increase its "reader-friendliness." Libraries that already own the one-volume edition should pass on this more expensive version unless their copies receive very high use.—**Kerranne G. Biley**

209. **Research & Development Growth Trends: Inflation Adjusted Analysis of R&D Spending.** 1992 ed. Lincolnshire, Ill., Schonfeld, 1992. 230p. $325.00 spiralbound. ISBN 1-878339-21-4.

Research and development (R&D) is an essential competitive tool. For many companies it is the key to profit, growth, and survival. This annual work presents historical and analytical data on publicly owned corporations that have R&D expenditures. Arrangement is by Standard Industrial Classification (SIC) code and alphabetically by company name within each SIC. An alphabetical summary by company names serves as both a quick reference and an index. Historical information includes R&D spending for the last five years as well as the percent share of R&D and sales expended by the company in relation to its competitors within its SIC. In addition, measures of profitability and effectiveness of the company's R&D expenditures are presented. What-if scenarios using changes in R&D expenditures are predicted, and management-by-objective values needed to raise sales for the next calendar year are included. The work provides formulas for its derivations and predictions.

This work is useful in determining industry expenditures and company comparisons and in its linking of profits to R&D investment. Because it is very specialized and its price a bit daunting, it is recommended for advanced business research collections.—**Bobray Bordelon**

210. Rosenberg, Jerry M. **Dictionary of Banking.** New York, John Wiley, 1993. 369p. (Business Dictionary Series). $14.95pa. HG151.R66. 332.1'03. LC 92-7419. ISBN 0-471-57436-8.

Rosenberg has previously authored dictionaries on business and management; investing; business acronyms, initials, and abbreviations; Wall Street acronyms; information technology; and artificial intelligence and robotics. This directory of about 7,500 entries (an impressive number) covers words, terms, and names of particular use in or applicability to banking. Many are accounting terms (e.g., *cash basis, reserve requirements*), institutions (e.g., Resolution Trust Corp.), acts (e.g., Financial Center Development Act of 1981), and particular features (e.g., telephone order). Each definition is accurate and terse. There are no definitions of financial tools (e.g., net present value, internal rate of return, Beta coefficient), although "Rule of 72" and CAPM appear. The terms are generally up-to-date. Many currencies (e.g., ruble, ringgit, kyat) appear. Some slang terms are included (e.g., *yard* [$100 bill] and *bread* [money], but not *fin* or *sawbuck*).

A similar dictionary, *Banking Terminology* (see ARBA 91, entry 210), has 406 entries that start with A, while Rosenberg's dictionary has 378 A entries; only 135 are duplicates. It is likely that neither of these dictionaries would prove adequate by itself. [R: RBB, July 93, p. 1994]—**Richard A. Miller**

211. **Who's Wealthy in America 1993: A Prospecting List and Directory of 102,000 Affluent Americans.** 3d ed. Catherine M. Ehr, ed. Rockville, Md., Taft Group; distr., Detroit, Gale, 1993. 2v. index. $365.00pa./set. ISBN 1-879784-62-9. ISSN 11048-809X.

This is an updated list of the names, addresses, lifestyle interests, educational backgrounds, and other related information about more than 100,000 wealthy Americans. Lifestyle interests are defined in this directory to include such things as the ownership of yachts, aircraft, works of art, and horses, while wealth is defined to include only those individuals with a net worth of at least $1 million. The directory is organized into two volumes. The first provides an alphabetical listing, while the second identifies those listed individuals who are so-called insiders of public companies or who own securities registered with the Securities and Exchange Commission (SEC). Insiders of public companies include not only the officers and directors of those companies but also individuals who are 10 percent principal stockholders.

The directory is not intended to be an exhaustive list of relatively affluent Americans; rather, its purpose is as a source book to help various organizations and philanthropic agencies find potential donors or interested individuals. Perhaps the most useful feature of this directory is its four well-organized indexes, which outline listed individuals by stock ownership, political contributions, state residency, and alma mater. The political contributions index lists candidates, political organizations, and political action committees (PACs). Collectively, these indexes not only provide a great deal of insight into the interests and backgrounds of these wealthy Americans but also, more significantly, will allow various organizations and agencies to more efficiently identify and contact potentially interested donors.—**Timothy E. Sullivan**

INDUSTRY AND MANUFACTURING

212. **American Manufacturers Directory.** 1993 ed. Omaha, Neb., American Business Directories, 1993. 1992p. $495.00. ISBN 1-56105-345-7. ISSN 1061-219X.

This directory includes 120,000 domestic manufacturers compiled from yellow (and business white) pages and a variety of published sources (e.g., newspapers, 10-Ks, annual reports). The main section is an alphabetical list of companies and their addresses, telephone numbers, heads, sales (11 classifications), numbers of employees (3 classifications), and Standard Industrial Classification (SIC) codes (4-digit). Minimum size for inclusion is 25 employees. Only manufacturers are listed; hence, the Bell operating companies are included because they make telephone equipment, not because they sell communications services. Also, each company is listed regardless of parentage or other financial interconnection; thus, "General Electric Co." appears 136 times. A second listing is by city, and a third is by SIC code. The database on which this publication is based is available in various forms: magnetic tape, PC diskettes, and hard copy in various formats (e.g., mailing labels, 3x5 cards). This directory is available only by lease, not by purchase; when the annual edition is superseded, the lessee must return the old edition (and pay another annual fee for continuation).—**Richard A. Miller**

213. Arpan, Jeffrey S., and David A. Ricks. **Directory of Foreign Manufacturers in the United States.** 5th ed. Atlanta, Ga., Georgia State University Business Press, 1993. 419p. index. $195.00. HD9723.A76. 338.7'67'2573. LC 79-4146. ISBN 0-88406-255-4.

This volume gives names (but no data) to complement the aggregate financial information available from the U.S. Department of Commerce. It lists about 7,000 U.S. manufacturing companies owned, directly and indirectly, by foreign firms. At the end of 1991, foreign direct investment in the United States (book value) was $408 billion, or 5 percent of U.S. net worth. The U.S. manufacturing sector is the largest recipient of foreign investment, followed by wholesale and retail trade, real estate, and finance and insurance. Ownership by firms in Japan, the United Kingdom, Germany, and Canada accounts for more than half the entries; industrial and commercial machinery, chemicals and allied products, and electrical and electronic equipment comprise about 40 percent of the entries. Each entry provides name of company (United States), address, telephone number, four-digit SIC (Standard Industrial Classification) with industry name, and parent company with address. No financial data are listed. Order is alphabetical by U.S. name. There are indexes of U.S. companies by state, parent companies, parent companies by country, and U.S. companies by four-digit product. [R: RBB, 1 Nov 93, pp. 561-62]—**Richard A. Miller**

214. **Consumer Product and Manufacturer Ratings 1961-1990: A Worldwide Directory of About 1800 Companies Rated Comparatively....** Compiled by Intrep Data Corp. Detroit, Gale, 1993. 2v. index. $395.00/set. TX335.C659. 640'.73. LC 92-33181. ISBN 0-8103-7707-1.

The 30-year period covered by this work witnessed the development of a world market for consumer products. Concomitant with this phenomenon was a heightened interest by consumers in product quality and the inevitable response by manufacturers. Meanwhile, testing organizations all over the globe were evaluating consumer products, and each one published its results. *Consumer Product and Manufacturer Ratings 1961-1990* is an attempt to quantify the results of these testing organizations by assigning ordinal numbers to their evaluations in the categories of quality, price, and value. The set permits researchers to compare a given manufacturer's consumer product with like products of other manufacturers sold during the same year on the same continent, be it Australia, Europe, Asia, or North America. The compiling organization has been successful in achieving its goal. The table of contents serves as an index, categorizing 300-plus specific product lines in 14 broad categories. The work's usefulness will be enhanced by the annual updates promised by the publisher. The compiler does acknowledge several limitations to the data. For instance, the work does not include all major brands in a particular product line because the basic data comes from product testing organizations, and they may not test all brands.

This work has substantial value for everyone, from academic researchers to consumers and from advertising agencies to marketing strategists. Academic libraries that support a business major will find the work heavily used. The work should be a must purchase for special libraries of companies in the consumer product field as well as consumer protection agencies. Large public libraries also have a ready clientele for this data. The price may be a deterrent to many other libraries. [R: LJ, 15 Feb 93, p. 156; RBB, 15 Mar 93, p. 1376]—**Dene L. Clark**

215. **Harris Manufacturers Directory, 1993.** Richard M. Fein, ed. Twinsburg, Ohio, Harris Publishing, 1993. 2v. index. $395.00/set. ISBN 1-55600-049-9. ISSN 1061-2076.

Approximately 40,000 manufacturers that employ 100 or more individuals are included in this set. The number of such manufacturers under each SIC (Standard Industrial Classification) code is listed. Most of the data is provided in an alphabetical section that details directory information, SIC codes, number of employees, estimated annual sales, and key personnel. Subsequent sections refer to this section. A feature useful to job hunters is the listing of manufacturers by state and city. Access is also provided numerically and alphabetically within SIC indexes. In addition, the 100 largest manufacturing establishments are listed nationwide and then within each state. Finally, a product section is included.

This directory serves a number of functions. It provides some of the basic data found in such directories as *Ward's Business Directory of U.S. Private and Public Companies* (see ARBA 93, entry 198) as well as product information found in *Thomas Register of American Manufacturers* (see ARBA 83, entry 785). However, it is less comprehensive than either of these sources. Its price may prove prohibitive to many libraries; thus, it is useful as an add-on service but is not essential. [R: RBB, 1 Jan 93, p. 825]—**Bobray Bordelon**

216. **Industrial Statistics Yearbook 1990.** New York, United Nations, 1992. 2v. index. $95.00/v. ISBN 92-1-061348-5(v.1); 92-1-061150-0(v.2). S/N E.92.XVII.9(v.1); E/F.92/XVII.10(v.2).

This compilation, now in its 24th edition, continues to be an important source of highly detailed data on international industry. Section 1 of volume 1, "General Industrial Statistics," provides 15 indicators of industrial activity, by industry, for each country for 1986-1990, including number of enterprises, wages and salaries, output, value of stocks, and electricity consumed. Section 2 of volume 1 covers industrial production and employment for the world, regions, and economic groups for 1978-1990. Volume 2, "Commodity Production Statistics," covers 556 commodities—from butter to razor blades—for about 200 countries and areas for 1981-1990. The volume concludes with useful indexes to commodities by ISIC (International Standard Industrial Classification) codes, in alphabetical order, and by country.

Although the reviewer of the 1983 edition (see ARBA 87, entry 241) recommended this set for small public libraries that serve high school and undergraduate students, potential buyers should be aware that this work is not particularly user-friendly. Abstruse writing and specialized terminology characterize the introductory and explanatory material, making it fairly tough going for the average user; and the level of detail provided may be far more than what most users require. While larger, more sophisticated libraries will probably want the yearbook, the smaller library seeking to reach younger patrons may want to shop around for more accessible alternatives.—**Liz Willis**

217. **RMA Annual Statement Studies 1993.** Philadelphia, Robert Morris, 1993. 890p. index. $105.00pa. ISBN 0-936742-99-2.

This publication of Robert Morris Associates (RMA), the association of bank loan and credit officers, contains composite balance sheets and income data as well as commonly used financial ratios for 406 industries, running the gamut from manufacturers and wholesalers to retailers, service industries, and contractors. The data is arranged by Standard Industrial Classification (SIC) number and is sorted by size grouping—firm assets and firm sales. For each SIC number there is also comparative historical trend data, permitting a comparison between the latest year and a five-year analysis. RMA publishes this information with some caveats. The financial statements that provide the data are not selected by any statistically reliable method; also, some industry samples are rather small in relation to the total number of firms in that industry. Another note of caution: Some companies earn much of their income from a variety of product lines, yet the data in the *Statement Studies* is presented under only one SIC number.

Almanac of Business and Industrial Financial Ratios (see ARBA 91, entry 233) and *Industry Norms and Key Business Ratios*, compiled by Dun & Bradstreet, are competing sources. The *Almanac* covers fewer businesses and uses older information, but its data comes from a greater number of companies, being based on tax returns. The Dun & Bradstreet source presents composite financial information for more than 800 different lines of business, a real strength. It is also timely, although it does not categorize companies by asset size. Most business libraries, large public libraries, and academic libraries supporting business majors will need all three titles. [R: RBB, July 93, p. 1995]—**Dene L. Clark**

218. **U.S. Industrial Outlook '93: Business Forecasts for 350 Industries.** Indianapolis, Ind., JIST Works, [1993]. 1v. (various paging). illus. index. $29.95pa. ISBN 1-56370-112-X.

This is a complete reprint of the *U.S. Industrial Outlook '93* published by the U.S. Department of Commerce. The text has been reset with larger type than the original, and it has been printed on heavier, larger paper stock. As in the original, most of the 350 industries are defined by Standard Industrial Classification (SIC) codes. The SIC system covers economic activity in nine major categories, including agriculture, mining, construction, manufacturing, and communications. The book provides easy access to information on domestic and international markets, as well as growth forecasts. This version is aimed at users who do not know how to buy from GPO.—**Susan B. Ardis**

INSURANCE

219. **Highlights of State Unemployment Compensation Laws: January 1993.** Washington, D.C., National Foundation for Unemployment Compensation & Workers' Compensation, 1993. 100p. $18.00pa. LC 82-645781. ISSN 0730-7624.

As the title suggests, this publication provides a brief overview of the most significant aspects of the unemployment compensation insurance system in the United States, a complicated system of laws, rulings, and interpretations. This edition updates previous ones by summarizing numerous changes legislated in 1992. After providing a short summary of the unemployment compensation program and its coverage requirements, the book discusses a number of areas critical to understanding the system and how it functions today. These areas include wages, contributions, benefits, extended benefits, appeals, and administration. Special attention is paid to the interface between federal and state legislation. Particularly helpful are the concise discussions of rulings and interpretations that follow the statements of federal law in each of the areas cited above. A chronology of major changes in federal unemployment compensation laws and a directory of federal officials with responsibility for administering the Federal Unemployment Tax Act are included; these constitute useful reference tools.

The issues discussed and the level at which they are presented ensure that the material can be of use to both individuals unfamiliar with this area of employment law and to more experienced practitioners. For this reason, the publication would be a useful addition to any business or law library.—**Paul F. Clark**

220. Jehle, Faustin F. **The Complete & Easy Guide to Social Security & Medicare.** 10th ed. Peterborough, N.H., Fraser-Vance Publishing; distr., Charlotte, Vt., Williamson Publishing, 1993. 174p. index. $10.95pa. LC 92-075605. ISBN 0-930045-11-4.

This guide explains social security programs and medicare in straightforward, clear terms. It describes programs, benefits, eligibility, how to apply, and how to appeal denials. In addition to the basic text it includes a directory of regional social security offices and other sources for information on both programs, and more than 80 pages of reproduced federal forms. Additional features expand its usefulness as a reference tool. It has a directory of state agencies to contact for birth and death records, including addresses, telephone numbers, and fees. The glossary of terms and the introductory chapter on the history of social security and medicare will be popular with students.

This book compares favorably with similar guides. It has the advantage of covering both social security and medicare, while many books in this vein address only one or the other.

—**Cathy Seitz Whitaker**

221. **Register of North American Insurance Companies, 1993.** South River, N.J., American Preeminent Registry, 1992. $125.00pa. ISBN 0-9633783-1-7.

This directory does satisfy some of the criteria listed in its preface and advertising material. The insurance company entries are arranged alphabetically and include the complete address and lines carried for each company. Company coverage includes businesses in the United States and Canada. The second section of the book lists, by state and province, state insurance departments, officials, and workers' compensation law highlights. According to the publisher, each entry was verified by telephone. The alternate shaded lines and the company names in boldface capital letters help define the entries. The overall appearance of the entries, however, is of crowded information and medium-quality print.

As an information professional in the insurance field and a special librarian, this reviewer found the resource to contain much less detail than is often needed by industry professionals. The professional organizations for insurers, commissioners, and the like provide extensive reference material in directory form, as well as state insurance department information. Within the industry, rating information is often needed to complete research; this type of data is not in the *Register*. Finally, from the industry perspective, workers' compensation information changes by state, by legislative session of each state, according to modifications made through code, by state-mandated standards, or by litigation. Therefore, the synopsis or overview approach to workers' compensation law presented in this work is insufficient for most industry use.

The publisher's promotional sheet for the *Register* promises that the user can "locate major insurance companies in the United States and Canada within seconds." This is impossible if the exact company name is not known. There are no indexes or cross-references by states. To locate a company geographically one must scan the entire work, one address at a time. Additionally, the criteria for inclusion in the register are not stated. Therefore, the reader does not know whether such elements as size or business volume were factors in selection or omission. Although the information in the *Register* might be sufficient for a layperson's need, similar information, with the exception of the workers' compensation overview, can be found in the "yellow pages" of the local telephone book. [R: RBB, 1 May 93, p. 1634]

—**Deborah K. Scott**

INTERNATIONAL BUSINESS

General Works

Bibliography

222. Alston, Jon P., comp. **The Social Dimensions of International Business: An Annotated Bibliography.** Westport, Conn., Greenwood Press, 1993. 312p. index. (Bibliographies and Indexes in Economics and Economic History, no.12). $65.00. Z7164.C81A46. 016.3888'8. LC 92-29466. ISBN 0-313-28029-0.

Knowledge of domestic and foreign cultural patterns will make cross-cultural business situations more comfortable and more successful. Presenting 1,326 annotated entries on material that details every aspect of the cultural and social aspects of international business, this up-to-date, comprehensive bibliography focuses on literature published between 1980 and 1991. Alston, professor of sociology at Texas A&M University, believes this field of study is becoming more mature, and the time period studied shows improvements in the quality and quantity of material on international business's cultural dimensions.

Chapters cover such subjects as "The Expatriate Experience," negotiations, and specific geographical areas (e.g., the Middle East and Africa). The selection criteria, besides the date of publication, is that the material deal with social or psychological dimensions of international issues and discuss national character. The short annotations are clear and concise. Subject and author indexes complete this work.

Because Americans are famous throughout the world for not knowing how to behave properly in other cultural settings, this excellent bibliography should prove valuable in avoiding cultural misunderstandings. Academic libraries and multinational business corporation collections will need it, and international relations students and scholars will also find this information useful. [R: Choice, June 93, pp. 1595-96]—**Susan C. Awe**

Biography

223. **Who's Who in European Business.** Compiled by Cambridge Market Intelligence. New Providence, N.J., K. G. Saur/Reed Reference Publishing, 1993. 405p. index. $165.00. HC240.W447. 338'.04'09224. LC 93-4118. ISBN 0-86291-795-6.

This new publication was prepared as a companion volume to the *Directory of European Business* (Reed Reference Publishing, 1992) and contains biographies in English for more than 5,000 executives, arranged alphabetically by surname. There are indexes by country and by company. The information was provided and the proofs read by the entrants. Each entry contains at least the biographee's address and telephone number, and most contain more information, such as career history and directorships. The entries are up-to-date as of January 1993, when the book went to press. The entry layout is very clear and easy to read, with the name in boldface type and the mailing address and telephone and fax numbers at the end of the entry. Coverage of the country index extends to the Eastern European countries of the Czech and Slovak Republics, Estonia, Latvia, Lithuania, Poland, and Russia (filed under its former name U.S.S.R.). Under each country the biographees are listed alphabetically, with the name of the company after each.

The company index gives the name of the company and its country in boldface type, with the names of the biographees and their positions in the company in alphabetical order. This work is a solid contribution to the world of European business.—**Barbara E. Brown**

224. **Who's Who in International Banking.** 6th ed. New Providence, N.J., K. G. Saur/Reed Reference Publishing, 1992. 625p. $225.00. HG3881.W475. 332.1'5'0922. LC 92-6406. ISBN 1-85739-040-7.

This newly revised sixth edition has two major parts: a biographical section and a bank directory. The biographical sketches appear in part 1. In the previous editions these sketches gave limited information, and no indication was given as to method of inclusion. For this new edition, entry is by invitation only and according to set criteria. Some 4,000 biographies with complete addresses, including fax numbers, are given for each entrant. Part 2 is a banking directory arranged alphabetically by country. This directory section lists key position titles and names for each bank. An additional feature is the biographical index at the end of each country section that gives the page entry number of the biographical sketch in part 1.

This is a very useful directory and a marked improvement over previous editions. However, the bank directory is not as comprehensive as *Polk's Bank Directory* (International Edition) (see ARBA 70, v.1, p. 174) or the *Rand McNally International Bankers Directory* (see ARBA 80, entry 816). Still, it is a worthwhile acquisition for libraries that need an international banking directory and biographical information.
—**Linda Suttle Harris**

Directories

225. **Bricker's International Directory.** 24th ed. Princeton, N.J., Peterson's Guides, 1992. 2v. index. $230.00/set. ISBN 1-56079-213-2. ISSN 1054-7835.

This directory lists "over 600 general and functional management programs that met standards of excellence for executives at relatively high levels in their organization." It provides basic, unbiased information that individuals and human resources professionals need to select university-based executive development programs at leading universities worldwide. This edition has three valuable new sections: custom programs and services offered by educational institutions, industry-specific executive education programs, and executive MBA programs.

Bricker's is organized into 11 categories, addressing executive education from its broadest perspective (the whole business environment) to its narrowest (a specific area of concern). Within the categories, programs are arranged alphabetically by institution. Some of the categories are leadership, humanities, marketing and sales, and technology management. The descriptions of each program are presented in a set, concise format for ease of comparison and evaluation. Program name and beginning date, sponsor and location, duration and 1993 dates, tuition, a program overview, participants' profile, program content, methods of instruction and schedule, faculty and facilities, special features, and official contact are given. Most descriptions are complete on one page. Established programs are reviewed, and noteworthy new programs are added annually. The information included is collected in an annual survey of providers of executive education. Criteria used to select these programs are described in detail.

In addition to the main sections, indexes provide access to the programs by institution, management level, duration, location, and subject. The two volumes are organized identically, with volume 1 (in its 24th edition) containing long-term programs and volume 2 short-term (this volume is only in its 5th edition). This well-written resource will be useful, especially in academic, business, and corporate libraries.
—**Susan C. Awe**

226. **Standard Directory of International Advertisers and Agencies 1993.** New Providence, N.J., National Register Publishing/Reed Reference Publishing, 1993. 1430p. index. $325.00pa. LC 84-62414. ISBN 0-87217-144-2.

This work is the international counterpart to the U.S. coverage in the *Standard Directory of Advertising Agencies* (1993) and the *Standard Directory of Advertisers* (1993) from the same publisher. It provides directory, key personnel, and business information for agencies and advertisers based outside the U.S. that reported billings or advertising budgets of at least $75,000.

Main access points to this massive volume are indexes to advertisers and advertising agencies; a brand name index; geographical indexes to advertisers and agencies, first by country and then by city; a listing by Standard Industrial Classification (SIC) codes; alphabetical and numerical lists of the SIC codes used; and a "who's where" of key personnel with references to companies. The principal sections (of advertisers and agencies) are both arranged by company name. In the advertisers and agencies indexes are references under subsidiaries, with parents in boldface type. Where reported (and appropriate to advertiser or agency, as the case may be), entries include address, fax and telephone numbers, major personnel, sales or billings, subsidiaries or clients, lines of business and SIC codes, and end of fiscal year. Among other features are international telephone codes and explanations of dialing procedures from North America, U.S. chambers of commerce in other countries, foreign chambers of commerce or trade delegations in the United States., a list of non-U.S. advertising associations, and foreign consulates in the United States.

Overall, this is a well-designed and professionally executed directory. It should be strongly considered by larger business collections or specialized information centers where budgets and client interest permit.
—**Nigel Tappin**

227. **World Investment Directory 1992: Foreign Direct Investment, Legal Framework and Corporate Data. Volume 1: Asia and the Pacific.** New York, United Nations, 1992. 356p. $65.00pa. ISBN 92-1-104389-1. S/N E.92.II.A.11.

This statistical source and overview from the United Nations Centre on Transnational Corporations (UNCTNC) provides a highly useful collation of information on foreign direct investment in 21 countries of the Asia Pacific region. The entire set is aimed at addressing the gap in compendia of information on the topic. The UNCTNC intends to update the work regularly (periodicity unspecified). The other five volumes in the set cover developed countries, Latin America and the Caribbean, Africa and West Asia, Central and Eastern Europe, and global trends, with data on 100 countries in all.

The main text of this volume is divided into three sections. The first provides an overview of foreign direct investment in the region during the 1980s. The second is a technical note on the scope, sources, and methodology used. The last is a section of data by country, from Bangladesh to Vietnam. Both the overview and the data section provide detailed tables on the legal environment for foreign investment (including principal relevant international and bilateral agreements and legislation); various measures of the scale of inward investment and, to a lesser extent, outward investment from these countries; indicators of the significance of transnationals for the host economy; and a good deal more. The overview includes a number of useful comparative charts and tables. Each country section indicates the sources of its information, usually various government bodies. The information is not standardized due to the wide variations in collecting methods. All information is not available for every state; for example, the Republic of Korea entry lists outward investment flows, while Singapore's does not. There are also bibliographical references to major information sources on specific countries and a selected list of UNCTNC publications.

The publication of this set represents a major step in providing access to information on this high-interest topic in today's global economy. It is a must buy for interested collections, companies, and individuals. [R: LJ, 15 April 93, p. 88]—**Nigel Tappin**

Handbooks and Yearbooks

228. **International Brands and Their Companies 1993-94: Over 97,000 International Consumer Products and Their Manufacturers, Importers and Distributors....** 3d ed. Susan L. Stetler and Allison K. McNeill, eds. Detroit, Gale, 1992. 1163p. $260.00. ISBN 0-8103-6947-8. ISSN 1050-8376.

229. **International Companies and Their Brands 1993-94: International Manufacturers, Importers and Distributors....** Susan L. Stetler and Allison K. McNeill, eds. Detroit, Gale, 1992. 848p. $260.00. ISBN 0-8103-6950-8. ISSN 1050-8384.

These comprehensive reference works cover international brands. The volume on companies lists more than 22,000 international companies. Entries are arranged alphabetically and include the addresses of the businesses and the brands they own. The companies covered include manufacturers, marketers, distributors, and importers of a variety of consumer-oriented products (e.g., food, giftware, house furnishings, office products, toys). The volume on brands lists some 75,000 brand entries, arranged alphabetically, with the names of the companies that own them.

Both volumes are highly recommended to large libraries. They are particularly helpful to international product marketers and attorneys involved in international business.—**Elie M. Dick**

230. **International Directory of Company Histories. Volume V.** Adele Hast, ed. Detroit, St. James Press, 1992. 884p. illus. index. $135.00. 338.7409. LC 89-190943. ISBN 1-55862-061-3.

231. **International Directory of Company Histories. Volume 6.** Paula Kepos, ed. Detroit, St. James Press, 1992. 748p. illus. index. $135.00. 338.7409. LC 89-190943. ISBN 1-55862-176-8.

232. **International Directory of Company Histories. Volume 7.** Paula Kepos, ed. Detroit, St. James Press, 1993. 758p. illus. index. $135.00. 338.7409. LC 89-190943. ISBN 1-55862-322-1.

Originally envisioned as a five-volume set (see ARBA 93, entry 260; ARBA 92, entry 148; ARBA 91, entry 132; and ARBA 90, entry 177 for reviews of the first four volumes), this excellent reference source continues to offer detailed, signed articles fashioned from publicly accessible information. The lengthy analyses contain basic (e.g., address, ownership) and current data (e.g., sales), along with insights on specific individuals. The percentage of foreign companies, reflecting the globalization of markets, satisfies researcher need for international coverage.

Organized initially in 38 industries, from advertising to waste services, subsequent volumes (6 and 7) have been modified in contents and structure. While the original format was retained for volume 6, the contents of volume 7 have been arranged alphabetically by company name. The last two volumes have included a new category (e.g., personal services) and approximately 200 updated (e.g., Freeport-McMoran) or new company (e.g., Gillett Holdings) entries. Indexing continues to be cumulative with each volume; however, the use of both roman and Arabic numerals in volume 7, without explanation, will be confusing for some patrons. Searching by principal industry is permitted through a new index (in volume 7), but the need for subsidiary and geographical location as access points has not been addressed. Once again, this set is recommended, particularly for libraries that serve an active business clientele.

—**Sandra E. Belanger**

233. **International Trade Statistics Yearbook, 1990. Annuaire Statistique du Commerce International.** New York, United Nations, 1992. 2v. $125.00/set. ISBN 92-1-061144-6. S/N E/F.92.XVII.2.

This French and English set shows trade statistics for 152 countries or customs areas. Each area has provided its own data, the most recent being from 1990. To supplement this historical data, the introduction lists sources of more recent monthly and quarterly data. In the first volume a preliminary section includes various notes about each country, such as valuation practices, what figures have been included and excluded, noteworthy geopolitical changes for that region, and the trade system used. Special tables in the back focus on less evident comparisons, such as fuel imports by developing economies and world exports by commodity class and region.

The primary feature of the first volume is tabular data on each reporting country. The first table covers historical annual data since 1955 for imports and exports of merchandise and gold, grouped by Standard Industrial Trade Classification (SITC). In the second table, broad economic categories, such as fuels, food, or goods for industry, display import statistics for 1984-1990; industrial origin, such as agriculture, textiles, or paper and products, groups export statistics. For 1986-1990, a third table covers imports and exports with other countries and the percentage of the world total for which that trade accounts. The two final tables list special commodity imports and exports by SITC for 1987-1990. In the latter tables, cryptic descriptive abbreviations and the SITC code are used to identify each commodity; unfortunately, the book contains no table to fully spell out what each SITC code represents. This would have been a useful tool.

The second volume includes two sections. The first part groups trade statistics by SITC commodity and lists each country's amount in U.S. dollars. The second part shows a matrix of major importers and exporters of important commodities. For example, the vertical column on one page's left side lists major importers of alcoholic beverages, while the horizontal row at the top of the page displays major exporters of the same commodity. This is an intriguing format for offering comparative information about trade between nations on specific product categories, but in order to understand which figure represents what, the reader must review the introductory explanation.—**Susan D. Baird-Joshi**

234. Johnson, Mary Elizabeth. **The International Monetary Fund 1944-1992: A Research Guide.** Hamden, Conn., Garland, 1993. 486p. index. (Research and Information Guides in Business, Industry, and Economic Institutions, v.9; Garland Reference Library of Social Science, v.770). $73.00. Z7164.F5J64. 016.3321'152. LC 93-15643. ISBN 0-8153-0230-4.

This volume is an information guide to and an annotated bibliography of materials related to the International Monetary Fund (IMF) from its founding in 1944 through 1992. The first four chapters provide an introduction to the IMF, together with entries covering the organization, function, activities, founding steps, broad history, and overviews of that body. The subsequent four chapters divide the remaining entries into roughly equal historical segments, each subdivided by topics pertinent to the time period of the particular chapter. The selection of entries appears well done. Appendixes cover IMF publications, bibliographies, facilities, committees and groups, information sources, and an organization chart. Three indexes provide access by author, title, and key word subject. Materials included were either written in English or were translated into English. Publications of a largely technical or textbook nature have been excluded, as have many of the numerous U.S. congressional hearings and reports. Many, but not all, IMF publications are included. This book could be of great use to educators, students, businesspersons, government employees, and others concerned with international economics.

—**William C. Struning**

235. **Labour Force Statistics 1970-1990. Statistiques de la Population Active.** Washington, D.C., OECD Publications & Information Center, 1992. 509p. $98.00pa. ISBN 92-64-03685-7.

This work is published yearly and includes historical time series of the evolution of the population and labor force for the 24 member countries of the Organisation for Economic Cooperation and Development (OECD). The volume begins with a useful section defining the categories for which statistics are provided. The remainder of the volume consists of three sections. Part 1 contains general tables of aggregated data and is organized by topic, with entries for each country. Among the topics for which data is provided are total population, total labor force membership, total employment, total unemployment, and employment by sector. Useful graphs reflecting the trends in each country over a 20-year period are included in this section. Part 2 presents detailed information on the manpower and employment situations on a country-by-country basis. The tables are standardized for all countries and give a general picture of the trends for the topics covered during 1970-1990. Part 3 contains times series for workforce participation rates and unemployment rates by age and sex for 16 of the member countries of the OECD during 1972-1991.

Overall, the volume is a very useful source for finding and comparing basic workforce and employment data for the countries covered. This makes the work a valuable reference tool for individuals from many fields.—**Paul F. Clark**

236. **Panorama of EC Industry 93: An Extensive Review of the Situation and Outlook of the Manufacturing and Service Industries....** Brussels, Office for Official Publications of the European Communities; distr., Lanham, Md., UNIPUB, 1993. 1v. (various paging). $175.00. ISBN 92-826-5428-1.

This massive edition of an important reference tool belongs in the library of anyone researching European Community (EC) markets. An official publication of the Commission of the European Communities, it contains enormous numbers of statistics and forecasts obtained from a broad spectrum of trade associations and from Eurostat. Although there is no index, the table of contents gives a specific breakdown by industrial sector. The latest concrete data are for 1991, and any later figures are estimates or forecasts. This is actually quite up-to-date for a monograph (especially when compared with the speed with which the United States Bureau of the Census issues its information). Efforts have been made to include production and employment statistics for all 12 member countries. The book gives a good accounting of where and how statistics have been derived.

Chapters describing the outlook and status of different industries resemble the essays in the *U.S. Industrial Outlook* (U.S. Department of Commerce, annual), or in the *Standard & Poor's Industry Surveys* (Standard & Poor's, quarterly), two publications with which most market researchers would be familiar. The *Panorama* does not have tables that rate company income and sales for specific industries as does *Standard & Poor's*, but the main companies are mentioned in the body of the essays, and there are quite a few tables ranking companies in the general introductory chapters. The use of European terminology, such as *turnover*, may necessitate keeping a dictionary handy to ascertain precise meanings. For competitive analysis, many chapters contain statistics on the United States, Japan, and other countries, depending on the product or service involved. Each chapter tells who wrote it, and gives addresses of relevant trade associations. In all, this is a basic reference tool, comparable in usefulness to a source such as the *U.S. Industrial Outlook*. [R: LJ, 15 Nov 93, p. 73]—**Susan V. McKimm**

237. **The Pulp and Paper Industry in the OECD Member Countries 1990. L'Industrie des Pates et Papiers dans les Pays Membres de l'OCDE.** Washington, D.C., OECD Publications and Information Center, 1993. 99p. $34.00pa. ISBN 92-64-03870-1. ISSN 0259-3041.

This volume covers data on production of, consumption of, capacity of, and international trade in pulp and paper products in the OECD member countries. First, annual data on production and the like for 1990 pertain to individual OECD countries for 33 products (production in tonnes). Annual data from 1983 to 1990 or 1986 to 1990 (by broad classifications of pulp and paper, wood pulp, and paper and paper making) cover rates of change of production, production versus consumption, capacity utilization, and capacity. A second section reports definitions of products. The third section gives data on international trade among OECD countries for 1990 for various breakdowns in products (e.g., total wood pulp, total wood pulp for paper and paperboard making) presented in tabular form (e.g., importing versus exporting countries). All entries are in English and French. An appendix lists the main sales outlets of OECD publications with addresses and telephone numbers.—**Richard A. Miller**

238. Terry, John V. **International Management Handbook.** Fayetteville, Ark., University of Arkansas Press, 1992. 583p. $35.00. HD62.4.T47. 658'.049. LC 91-41679. ISBN 1-55728-248-X.

As the United States becomes more a part of the one-world economy, the operation of businesses is changing dramatically and rapidly. The aim of Terry's book, stated clearly in the preface, is to build "a better understanding between peoples and a more productive economic world in which to live"; international managers are his intended audience. As he states in his introduction, the art of managing employees demands great skill, especially in a time of accelerated technological change. He is a financial consultant and former economics professor; he is also the author of the *Dictionary for Business and Finance* (see ARBA 91, entry 135). He bases his philosophy on the Golden Rule but feels this simple principle is "desperately difficult to practice."

Included in this volume to help the international manager are a world dictionary of management terminology, a list of prominent international banks, an overview of management prospects for nations from Europe to the Far East, a review of the Federal Reserve System, and biographical sketches of management specialists. Helpful appendixes also provide toll-free telephone numbers, world currencies information, world times, and weights and measures.

This information-packed volume will help to advance and disseminate management knowledge and the one-world concept of management expertise. Recommended for academic and large public libraries. [R: Choice, Mar 93, p. 1122]—**Susan C. Awe**

239. Tuller, Lawrence W. **The World Markets Desk Book: A Region-by-Region Survey of Global Trade Opportunities.** New York, McGraw-Hill, 1993. 334p. index. $29.95. HF1009.5.T85. 658.8'48. LC 92-24542. ISBN 0-07-065478-6.

A good, practical guide to world markets, this work includes sections on all regions of the world and short treatments of most countries, including the United States. Each regional and national section begins with tips for foreign traders and investors, which include the telephone numbers for foreign embassies in Washington, D.C., and specific points of advice. The advice is clear, and the analysis is to the point; for example, in the section on the Caribbean Basin, the prospective investor is told to stay away from all parts of the market in the Dominican Republic except the tourist trade until 1994. In addition to clear general discussions of political and economic conditions and prospects for trade and investment, there are "Caution Alerts" and "Red Flags" that warn of specific problems. For example, a "Red Flag" warns that the government of Germany has thus far been unwilling to offer guarantees to foreign investors against environmental liabilities and hidden property claims in the former East Germany, even though it will probably be forced to do so eventually.

Political information is up-to-date as of December 1992, including the division of Czechoslovakia and the Commonwealth of Independent States. There is no explicit treatment of the former Yugoslavia, except, at times, to mention the civil war. Thus, there is no treatment of Slovenia, which to date seems relatively free from the dangers of war. Economic data is generally current as of 1990 or 1991, and forecasts are sometimes given for 1992. The political and economic data provided will soon be superseded by standard reference works, such as the *Statesman's Year-Book* (see ARBA 92, entry 77) and the *Europa World Year Book* (see ARBA 90, entry 91), but, in all likelihood, the investment advice and analysis will be valuable for a much longer period.

The *Desk Book* presents good information and good advice in an easily comprehensible format. A practical work, it is recommended to libraries that serve people who already are or contemplate investing in or trading with other countries. [R: RBB, 1 May 93, p. 1640; WLB, April 93, p. 127]

—Richard H. Swain

240. **U.S. Sourcebook of R&D Spenders: Publicly Owned Corporations that Spend on Research & Development.** 1992 ed. Lincolnshire, Ill., Schonfeld, 1992. 131p. $325.00pa. ISBN 1-878339-18-4.

This book is a no-frills snapshot of the big spenders in research and development (R&D) around the world. Included are all 50 states, Canada, the five Scandinavian countries, many members of the European Economic Community, Chile, Hong Kong, Israel, Japan, and Zambia. In all 131 pages, only two boldface type headings break the monotony of the system font.

The heart of the text is the company listing, grouped first by state or country, then arranged within that group by ascending zip code. The stated audience is sales and marketing personnel for companies selling to R&D firms, and this arrangement supports that; grouping the companies geographically would make it easier for salespeople to cover their territory. Consistency is one saving feature. Each listing has the same information: name, address, telephone number, the names and titles of three principal executives, the stock exchange and ticker symbol, Standard Industrial Classification (SIC) code and a 28-letter description, the projected R&D budget and sales for calendar year 1992, the growth rates for these figures, and the ratio of R&D to sales. If historical data was not available for the company, the publisher used the industry model for that firm and noted its use in the listing. Unfortunately, the introduction only briefly mentions the basic figures included in each listing; sample calculations and explanations for all figures in the text would have been useful.

Hidden around the listing and the predictable alphabetical index are four index gems. Three of the indexes give the cumulative totals and averages for the same calculations stated earlier but group the information by different criteria. "Top Designated Market Areas" gives the number of companies listed for 20 U.S. cities. "Major Economic Sectors" groups the information by major SICs; "Summary," alphabetically by state and country. The final index consists of a page with the names and projected 1992 spending budgets for the top spenders.—**Susan D. Baird-Joshi**

Asia

241. **Access Nippon '93 Business Handbook: How to Succeed in Japan.** Tokyo, Access Nippon; distr., Austin, Tex., Reference Press, 1992. 423p. maps. index. $34.95pa. ISBN 1-878753-13-4. ISSN 0915-4841.

This book is packed with information indispensable for any enterprise doing or planning business in Japan. It is the fourth volume in an annual series that aims at easing access to the Japanese market, relying on intimate (if, in some contexts, rather optimistic) local knowledge. The handbook consists of two parts. The first constitutes an introduction to business in Japan, with advice on doing business there (e.g., patents, office space, taxes, the legal scene, a list of major exhibitions and conventions); information on accessing the Japanese market (with synopses of two market studies, facts on government procurement, official import promotion measures, joint research, and organizational contacts); everyday information, such as passports and visas, banking and personal finances, transportation, food, housing, communications services, and hospitals; and a survey of 28 separate Japanese industries. The second part of the handbook provides information on the 296 chief potential partners, listed by 17 industries, with addresses, chief executive officers, company outlines, capital, sales, number of employees, international concentration, and other information.

This book is helpful, informative, and potentially time-saving. It should be used by every company representative and by companies that plan to enter the Japanese market or that want to find an industrial partner. It can also be used in conjunction with *Cracking the Pacific Rim* (Probus Publishing, 1992). *Japan Trade Directory* (Gale, 1992) is more comprehensive in its business coverage but less user-friendly in terms of its bulk and price; it can supplement this volume as a more compendious reference source.

—**Bogdan Mieczkowski**

242. **China Leading Companies, 1992, Including Special Economic Zones and Coastal Cities.** Secaucus, N.J., Hualin International, 1992. 576p. $200.00. ISBN 0-9634062-0-5.

China now has one of the fastest-growing economies on Earth. The government of the People's Republic of China (PRC) is promoting foreign trade, and this directory is copublished by the China Statistical Information and Consultancy Service Center (the "commercial arm" of the PRC Statistical Bureau) and the United States-based Hualin International. The work provides statistical and directory information on more than 3,900 Chinese companies. The text is in English, but some text is repeated in Chinese (certain headlines include Chinese characters, and the names of companies and directors are given in both English and Chinese). The work is available not only in print but also on diskettes (in dBase III, Paradox, or FoxPro format) that are set up to generate mailing labels as well as to permit statistical analysis.

The work is divided into three parts: Part 1, "Company Rank," includes eight sections. Section 1 lists in rank order by gross sales the top 1,000 industrial companies nationwide, then by industrial sector, and then by region; section 2, the top 300 construction companies; section 3, the top 110 retail stores; section 4, the top 100 international economic and technical cooperation corporations; section 5, the top 500 import/export companies; section 6, the top 100 hotels; and section 7, the top 10 financial institutions. Section 8 is a full-color advertising section with full-page descriptions of more than 40 companies. Special statistical indexes are included along with the rankings in the first seven sections. Indexes include gross sales, net income, net fixed assets, export percentage, labor productivity, product development funds, and more. These indexes are explained briefly in the editorial note at the beginning of the work.

Part 2, the company index, provides directory information, including telephone numbers and postal codes, for the companies ranked in part 1. The companies are listed in alphabetical order in English. Part 3, on coastal cities, provides brief descriptions of special economic zones and cities that are officially designated and regulated to attract foreign investment.

The content of this volume is unique; much of it has never been made public before. This is clearly an official publication meant to provide information to prospective foreign investors, and as such it contains information otherwise unobtainable. Furthermore, the statistical indexes will be of interest to economists and other scholars studying the PRC as well as to potential investors. This work is indispensable to any library supporting scholarship on or business in the PRC.—**Richard H. Swain**

243. Enderlyn, Allyn, and Oliver C. Dziggel. **Cracking the Pacific Rim: Everything Marketers Must Know to Sell into the World's Newest Emerging Markets.** Chicago, Probus Publishing, 1992. 252p. maps. index. $42.50. ISBN 1-55738-254-9.

This volume demonstrates how much useful information can be put into a relatively slender reference book. The advice is knowledgeable, thoughtful, and pertinent, most of it organized systematically by country: Hong Kong, Indonesia, Japan, South Korea, Malaysia, the Philippines, Singapore, Taiwan, and Thailand. Each country coverage contains, with small individual variations, a map and nutshell data; an introductory orientation (e.g., geographic and historical background, demographics, political organization); market information (e.g., main commodities in foreign trade, hints on setting up business operations); investment climate; finance and capital markets; licensing, patents, and trademarks; visiting and locating in the country; and a list of key contacts, including local English-language publications. The amount of detail is high, comprising such facts as electric current, hotel and housing information, communications and transportation links, business hours, health care, immigration, work permits, and other government regulations. All information is well ordered and concise. The final two chapters are on information sources and on trade shows and conferences, the latter up to 1992, while most statistical data end with 1989 or 1990. A 22-table statistical appendix closes the volume. Highly recommended to all business school libraries and to all businesses, even those with only potential interest in the Pacific Rim area.—**Bogdan Mieczkowski**

244. **Japan Trade Directory 1993-94.** Tokyo, Japan External Trade Organization; distr., Detroit, Gale, 1993. 1v. (various paging). illus. maps. index. $245.00. ISBN 4-8224-0610-5.

This carefully edited, sumptuously published, and comprehensive reference guide will be quite useful for current and potential exporters to and importers from Japan. Considerably expanded in comparison with its 1985-1986 edition, it contains about 24,000 alphabetically arranged entries for products and services that are exported and imported, a guide to companies by prefectures and an alphabetical guide to trade and industrial associations, indexes of companies and their trade names, and an advertising section with helpful and attractive photographs. The volume lists about 3,000 companies and trade and industrial associations with their addresses; telephone, telex, and fax numbers; cable addresses; product names by export and import categories; and financial and other information that pertains to those business firms. Clear maps are helpful in getting oriented to industrial locations by prefecture. The directory also provides artistic photographs of regional products, traditional celebrations, striking scenery, and some stunning architecture, as well as figures that depict regional foreign trade performance. Among additional information, including advertisements, there are addresses of Japan External Trade Organization offices around the globe.

Recommended for schools of business and for business libraries. Tourists may also profit from this directory by gleaning insights into the economic life of Japan, distinctive regional products that make good souvenirs, and cultural and sports events.—**Seiko Mieczkowski**

245. **Standard Trade Index of Japan 1992-93.** 36th ed. Compiled by the Japan Chamber of Commerce and Industry. Tokyo, Japan Chamber of Commerce and Industry; distr., Bristol, Pa., Taylor & Francis, 1992. 1v. (various paging). $215.00. ISSN 0585-0444.

This index is divided into six parts, two of which are devoted to advertisements. The index of commodities and services contains more than 23,000 items, with their producers listed (divided into manufacturers and exporters and importers); those that are positively interested in trade are separately indicated. The second part lists brand names with product description and manufacturer's name, again indicating positive interest in trade. The third part contains a complete guide to the producers, with important information about each. Finally, there is an appendix on governmental agencies and foreign diplomatic and consular offices in Japan; trade and industrial organizations by area in Japan; and organizations situated overseas, tourist organizations, economic cooperation organizations, atomic agencies and institutes, government and civil inspection organizations, major exhibition centers, and the like. The two advertising sections are richly illustrated and informative.

This is an excellent source for contacts on specific commodities or services, trade, and public information. Highly recommended to firms interested in foreign trade, trade associations, governmental trade promotion organizations, and business schools.—**Bogdan Mieczkowski**

Canada

246. Brown, Barbara E., ed. **Canadian Business and Economics: A Guide to Sources of Information.** 3d ed. Ottawa, Canadian Library Association, 1992. 675p. index. $150.00. 016.330971. ISBN 0-88802-256-5.

This bibliography of Canada-related business books goes well beyond the standard reference works found in most guides to information sources. Instead, it encompasses some 7,000 titles deemed to be "of interest to business people available from bookstores or publishers or as reference material in libraries." The works cited include general business-oriented titles published in Canada, works not necessarily published in Canada but dealing with Canada-specific business topics, and publications that may be international in scope but offer separate treatment of Canadian business issues. The cutoff date for inclusion is December 1990.

The monographs, theses, government documents, periodical special issues, and more generalized business books cited are mostly English-language, although some bilingual publications and several French works with important text in English have also been included. The bibliography is not restricted to print materials; computer-based business services offered by government and private organizations are covered as well. Sadly, the note on selection criteria also states that "some subject areas, such as conservation and environment, are of only marginal interest to business people, and listings in these areas are incomplete." Although one appreciates Brown's candor, perhaps by the next edition the Canadian business community—or at least the editor—will have adopted a different view of these critical business issues.

The bibliography leads off with 38 pages of general references, then devotes the next 450 pages to subject-oriented overviews treating broad topics such as communication and transportation. Within subject sections, titles are listed by format, topic, or geographical region, whichever categorization is most useful. Entries, many of which offer descriptive annotations, note author, title, publishing data, pagination, and series information. Surprisingly, neither price nor ISBN or ISSN information is included, an odd omission given the obvious utility this work has as a collection development tool. Annotations, when included, range from several words to (occasionally) a few brief paragraphs. Although the previous edition had separate but identical English and French indexes, the decision was made to combine them in the 3d edition, resulting in a mammoth, nearly 200-page index.

With the passage of NAFTA (North American Free Trade Agreement), Canadian business issues will play an increasingly important role in the United States business environment. Consequently, although this is an expensive work, all academic or large public libraries supporting business studies or inquiries will want to consider its acquisition. It will be a mandatory purchase for all corporate libraries where North American trade is being undertaken.—**G. Kim Dority**

247. Crane, David. **The Canadian Dictionary of Business and Economics.** Toronto, Stoddart Publishing, 1993. 693p. $45.00. 330'.03. ISBN 0-7737-2691-8.

This is an updated version of Crane's *Dictionary of Canadian Economics* (Hurtig, 1979). Crane is the economics editor of the *Toronto Star* newspaper. His book is handy, well executed, current, and valuable to Canadian-focused audiences. It has extensive entries on Canadian issues, from the (nineteenth-century) National Policy through the National Energy Program of the Trudeau years to the Goods and Services Tax. Canadian information in the entries on such international terms as *Eurocurrency* is welcome.

The main section is arranged in the traditional alphabetical format. Only three pages are devoted to a preface and a selective list of abbreviations. Entries range widely in length from a sentence (e.g., "cross on the board") to a couple of double-columned pages (e.g., Charlotte Town Accord, European Community). Many entries are miniessays, not just definitions. There are extensive cross-references, with terms defined elsewhere in all capitals. There are no *see* references from most acronyms.

At least a few minor errors crop up. For example, the abbreviations (but not the main entries) give OPEC as Organization of "Oil" (actually Petroleum) Exporting Countries and the CRTC as the Canadian Radio-Television and Telecommunications "Association" (actually Commission). This book is a must buy for any Canadian-oriented collection and would be a useful addition to broader collections.

—**Nigel Tappin**

248. **The Ethical Shopper's Guide to Canadian Supermarket Products.** By Joan Helson and others. Peterborough, Ont., Broadview Press, 1992. 285p. $14.95pa. ISBN 1-55111-001-6.

This book provides information on 83 Canadian manufacturers of grocery and consumer products, ranking them from A+ to F in the following categories: candor, women's issues, charitable giving and community involvement, progressive staff policies, labor relations, environmental management, environmental performance, management practices and consumer relations, and Canadian content. A set of tables by company and another by product give these rankings. The tables are followed by a description of each company, about two or three pages long, that includes a list of the company's brand names. Remarks under each category detail the reasons for the ranking in the tables. The last three sections are designed to help consumers put the information into practice: "Options for Action," "Sources for Action," and "The Ethical Shopper's Action Report." The book concludes with indexes by company and by brand name.

This work is very useful for finding out more about each company and their brand names—information that is not readily available. The book does not tell which products to buy; that is not its purpose.

—Barbara E. Brown

249. Gagnon, Louiselle, and Charles Skeete. **Vocabulary of Public Sector Auditing. Vocabulaire de la Verification Publique.** Ottawa, Department of the Secretary of State of Canada, 1992. 291p. (Terminology Bulletin, 216). $27.25pa. (U.S.). 657.835'03. ISBN 0-660-57474-8.

The purpose of this bilingual document is to standardize the public auditing terminology used in the Canadian federal government. Included are 1,300 terms commonly used in public auditing, built upon a base list of terms from the Canadian Office of the Auditor General and supplemented with terms from well-known Canadian, British, French, and United States public auditing publications. Some terms represent unique concepts; others are merely synonyms or word variants. The major section of the work, the English-French vocabulary, has dual columns on each page, with English term entries on the left that are translated into French on the right. Arrangement of terms is alphabetical by the English form. Entries vary in detail. For 360 terms there are brief definitions. When appropriate, synonyms are given that are, in turn, cross-referenced. Some entries contain explanatory notes or references to related terms. To enable French users to locate terms in this section, a glossary has the French term in the left column and its equivalent English term on the right. There are two bilingual appendixes: one gives the text of the Canadian "Auditor's Standard Report," and the other lists official titles of Canadian and foreign government accounting agencies, professional organizations, and publications. The work also contains an introduction that details the scope and method of compilation, a user guide to symbols and abbreviations, and a bibliography of works consulted during preparation.

The work is well produced. Especially noteworthy are its thorough cross-references and bilingual indexes. Although its Canadian orientation will make it especially useful to those whose interest is Canadian government auditing, its bilingualism will appeal to translators in the field of accounting.

—John Lewis Campbell

250. **Report on Business: Canada Company Handbook 1993.** Toronto, Globe and Mail Publishing; distr., Austin, Tex., Reference Press, 1993. 1v. (various paging). $39.95pa. ISBN 0-921925-45-X. ISSN 0847-2831.

This is the 5th edition of an annual with concise, condensed information on some 1,300 Canadian companies. It is compiled by the *Globe and Mail*, Canada's leading newspaper. Companies are arranged alphabetically within industry group. Each straightforward profile includes a description of the company; an analysis of recent performance; stock price charts; five years of annual financial data and two years of quarterly data; and rankings on profits, revenues, and assets. Addresses, telephone numbers, and the name of the CEO (chief executive officer) complete the package. The price is low because this is a spin-off from the files contained on InfoGlobe, the *Globe and Mail*'s online fulltext database, and its costs have already been recouped. The front and back pages contain some advertisements. This book is extremely useful as a reliable, inexpensive guide to Canadian public companies. [R: Choice, Oct 93, p. 266; RBB, 1 Nov 93, p. 564]—**Dean Tudor**

251. Wu, Emily, and Vivian Howard. **Canadian Business in the Pacific Rim: Selected Information Sources for Canadian Business Professionals.** Halifax, N.S., School of Library and Information Studies, Dalhousie University, 1993. 78p. (Dalhousie University School of Library and Information Studies Occasional Paper, 55). $19.95 spiralbound. 016.382'097101823. ISBN 0-7703-9760-3.

This useful book contains two separate, but linked, bibliographies. Wu's "Conducting Business in the Pacific Rim" is an annotated guide of some 43 transcript pages. She indicates regional sources relevant to trade and investment in the Asia-Pacific area, including reference materials, online databases, government documents, periodicals, and organizations. Not much of this material is strictly Canadian except for the sources and contacts of the organizations. Howard's unannotated "Intercultural Dimension of Conducting Business in the Pacific Rim" covers some 24 transcript pages. Her references include etiquette, protocol, and negotiation skills from a North American (and female) perspective, highlighting recent items. Topics include nonverbal communications, women in international business, and a directory of contacts.—**Dean Tudor**

Europe

General Works

252. Blanpain, Roger. **European Employment and Industrial Relations Glossary: Belgium.** Luxembourg, Office for Official Publications of the European Communities and London, Sweet and Maxwell; distr., Lanham, Md., UNIPUB, 1992. 238p. index. $35.00pa. ISBN 0-421-44860-1.

253. Weiss, Manfred. **European Employment and Industrial Relations Glossary: Germany.** Luxembourg, Office for Official Publications of the European Communities and London, Sweet and Maxwell; distr., Lanham, Md., UNIPUB, 1992. 396p. index. $35.00pa. ISBN 0-421-44830-X.

Each of the volumes in this series is devoted to a specific European country and lists each term in the language or languages of the country, then in English. The term is then followed by a detailed explanation and references to the relevant statutes of the country and to related terms.

The entries are numbered and arranged in alphabetical order by the term in the non-English languages. Alphabetical lists of entries in the other languages and in English are found at the beginning of the volumes; these provide entry numbers. There are detailed indexes to the terms and to subordinate terms in the other languages and in English. Also included in each book are a few tables of labor statistics for the country and a bibliography. These volumes will be of most use to those researching industrial relations in Belgium or Germany.—**Barbara E. Brown**

254. **Directory of European Business.** New Providence, N.J., K. G. Saur/Reed Reference Publishing, 1992. 366p. index. $195.00. ISBN 0-86291-617-8.

With the European Common Market becoming a reality and Eastern Europe emerging as a huge new market for imports and exports, trade with the European continent is poised for growth. This new directory could be helpful to anyone seeking basic business information on the 35 European countries covered, including some former Soviet republics.

The directory is organized alphabetically by country, with each country having between 3 and 12 pages of coverage. Each country chapter has subsections on operating environment, business services, business organizations, leading companies, government agencies, and business information. The operating environment section includes general information on the business climate (e.g., the political system, economic policy, banking and business hours). The business services section contains directory listings of individual professional services firms (e.g., accountants, advertising agencies, law firms). The business organizations section includes chambers of commerce and trade/professional associations. Brief directory listings of a few of the largest (net revenues) companies in the country are given in the leading companies section. A currency table lists exchange rates for 1990 and 1991 in German marks, pounds sterling, and

United States dollars to facilitate comparisons of financial figures. An alphabetical index to organizations is helpful for locating a company or agency. The publisher does not state how often the directory will be updated.

The *Directory of European Business* does not cover as many companies as some other, more regionally specific sources, such as *Eastern European Business Directory* (see ARBA 93, entry 284). However, this directory would be a good alternative for public and academic libraries that cannot afford more expensive products. [R: Choice, Mar 93, p. 1108; RBB, 15 April 93, p. 1533]—**Kerranne G. Biley**

255. **The Economist Atlas of the New Europe.** New York, Henry Holt, 1992. 288p. illus. maps. index. $75.00. G1797.2.E2. LC 92-10565. ISBN 0-8050-1982-0.

This is not a conventional atlas. Readers expecting to find page after page of maps will be disappointed—or delighted, depending on what they need. The work's subtitle (on the cover) is close to what this publication really is: "An Illustrated Portrait." Chapter after lavishly illustrated chapter treats such topics as trade, insurance, pollution, defense, banking, political systems, the European Community, the environment, religion, languages, and much more. In the back of the book are the vital statistics for the various European countries, updated through 1990. A section of the book also gives an impressive time chart of Europe that covers roughly 2,000 years. Efforts have been made to be as up-to-date as possible on the recent changes in Czechoslovakia, Yugoslavia, and the Baltic states—a difficult task, because that part of European history is still being written. The volume is beautifully laid out and exquisitely printed and bound, with a silk ribbon marker as an added special touch. Who is this book for? Anybody who studies international relations, European economies, or demographics and politics, and any businessperson with European contacts who needs an intelligent way of getting acquainted with backgrounds of any number of European countries and topics related to them. [R: Choice, July/Aug 93, p. 1748; JAL, Sept 93, p. 274; LJ, 1 April 93, p. 90; RBB, 1 Oct 93, p. 382; RQ, Fall 93, pp. 122-23; SLJ, May 93, p. 137; WLB, May 93, p. 115]—**Koraljka Lockhart**

256. **European Business Services Directory.** Michael B. Huellmantel, ed. Detroit, Gale, 1993. 1374p. $275.00. 338.7. ISBN 0-8103-7916-3. ISSN 1063-5718.

This work contains nearly 21,000 entries that profile organizations that offer business services in more than 30 countries in Western and Eastern Europe. Among the categories included are accounting, advertising, engineering, finance, insurance, law, translation, and travel. Profiles are listed by service category, then by country and city. There are also general listings by country and by company. Each profile contains the organization's name; address; telephone, telex, and fax numbers; year founded; number of employees; financial data; services offered; geographic areas covered; languages; professional memberships; officers; variant names; branches; related companies; and SIC (Standard Industrial Classification) number. Organizations whose activities span two or more service categories are cross-referenced.

This directory should be of great interest to companies that wish to engage in business in a European country and that require the knowledge and expertise offered by the organizations listed. A major advantage of this directory over similar ones is its comprehensive coverage of business services throughout Europe, rather than coverage of only one country or region. The information within is available on magnetic tape and floppy disk, and customized arrangements of the database can be obtained as well. [R: RBB, 15 Jan 93, p. 938]—**William C. Struning**

257. Martens, Hans. **EC Direct: A Comprehensive Directory of EC Contacts.** Cambridge, Mass., Basil Blackwell, 1992. 230p. index. $34.95pa. HC241.M278. 341.24'22'025. ISBN 0-631-18796-0.

This is a practical, comprehensive, and current guide to contacting the right people in the EC (European Community) Commission. It provides an overview of the Commission and its structure. As there is a single address for all persons in the Commission, telephone and fax numbers are included to enable direct contact with them. Also included are potential contacts in other EC institutions, EC member states' permanent representatives in Brussels, private organizations that serve Europe from Brussels, and embassies of EC member states. Databases on the EC, programs receiving EC financial support, current economic data for EC countries, and practical information for visitors to Brussels are also covered. Of particular interest for those in the United Kingdom is a list of sources located there that provide EC

information. Finding specific data in the directory is aided by a table of contents, subject and name indexes, and a glossary. A few suggestions for further reading are listed. This modestly priced guide can be of great benefit for anyone seeking contacts with or information on the EC. [R: RBB, 1 Oct 93, p. 382]
—**William C. Struning**

258. Newman, Oksana, and Allan Foster. **European Business Rankings: Lists of Companies, Products, Services and Activities....** Detroit, Gale, 1992. 437p. index. $160.00. ISBN 1-873477-00-7.

Taken from more than 800 periodicals, these rankings cover major areas of business activity in Europe in 1990 and 1991. Because the compilers are from the Manchester Business School, it is not surprising that publishers in the United Kingdom were the sources for most publications. A bibliography provides standard address information, cost, and frequency of publication. Written in French, German, and English, the introduction adequately explains the primary entry format and the incomplete indexes.

A strength of this book is consistency. Every entry has a key number, a phrase to describe the rankings, the criteria through which the order was established, additional information about the listing that was in the source material, the number of listees, the top 10 items and the data by which they were ranked (e.g., the number of total staff), and the source's title, date, and page. Subject headings from *Library of Congress Subject Headings* (Library of Congress, annual) and other pertinent sources group the rankings, first by topic, then by country or region, when available. Although the subject listing is not exhaustive, it is representative of the major areas of business—advertising, tourism, energy, alcohol and tobacco, communications, law, finance, the stock exchange, manufacturing and construction, retail, wholesale, media, transportation, and services—and of the economy—wages, working hours, office rents, credit, charities, and the military. Although there are a few rankings from the former Eastern bloc and Turkey, the main geographical region covered is the former Western Europe.

A definite weakness of the text is its lack of indexes. Arranged alphabetically, the sole index lists company names, an abridged version of the ranking's title, and the key number. With regard to indexes this book is a pale shadow of its sister text, *European Market Share Reporter* (Gale, 1993). Researched by the same group, that work boasts three additional indexes.

In one tight package, Gale has bundled rankings of the largest, the highest, the biggest, and the most of anything in Europe. Advertisers, corporate strategists, and business students will find this book useful and interesting.—**Susan D. Baird-Joshi**

259. Newman, Oksana, and Allan Foster. **European Market Share Reporter: A Wide-Ranging Compilation of Statistics from Journals and Limited-Circulation Publications.** Detroit, Gale, 1993. 361p. index. $152.00. ISBN 1-873477-35-X.

A handy companion to *European Business Rankings* (Gale, 1992), this text contains market share statistics for Europe published in 1991-1992. Some statistics cover periods earlier than this. In addition to using newspapers and trade and technical periodicals, Newman and Foster (from the Manchester Business School) used Euromonitor's Market Direction database. Besides covering France, Germany, Italy, Spain, and the United Kingdom, this reference also includes tidbits from Africa, South America, and Asia. The market shares fall into one of five broad categories: corporate shares, which give the names of the companies; institutional shares; brand name shares; product, commodity, service, and facility shares; and a catch-all other category.

Arranged by two-digit Standard Industrial Classification (SIC) codes, the main entries consist of a key number, a one- or two-word description of the SIC category, and the more specific four-digit code; a title describing what market the table covers; the period covered; the actual items ranked and the method of ranking, usually in percent; and the source's name, date, page, and publisher. Some entries include graphs. An appendix provides more detailed subject access. Arranged alphabetically, the two-digit SIC codes group together the extended four-digit SICs and note the page on which each four-digit section starts. The text covers some areas, such as food, electronics, industrial machinery, and business services, more heavily than others, such as lumber, automotive dealers, hotels, or social services. Several indexes provide excellent cross-referencing. Along with the key number, the source index lists the primary source—where the market shares were found—and the original source—sources the primary one cites. The place-names index groups the reports by geopolitical region, while the company index arranges them by company name. The products, services, and issues index lists the reports alphabetically by the short SIC title. For business students and marketers, this text provides an excellent starting point for often-elusive market share information.—**Susan D. Baird-Joshi**

260. Rickson, R., comp. and ed. **European Companies: A Guide to Sources of Information. Societes Europeennes. Europaische Handelsgesellschaften.** 4th ed. Kent, England, CBD Research; distr., Austin, Tex., Reference Press, 1992. 222p. index. $89.95. ISBN 0-900246-44-8.

This useful reference source was started in 1962. It covers 35 "countries," including the Commonwealth of Independent States, Gibraltar, Andorra, and Europe as a whole. Eastern (now increasingly called Central) European coverage is good and expanding. The main part of the guide, which is alphabetical by country abbreviations, covers for each country the available official registers of companies, forms of business enterprise, published guides to company formation and administration, stock exchanges, commercial information and credit reporting services, telephone directories, company information directories, company relationship directories, directories of directors of the enterprises, finance directories, newspapers and periodicals, miscellaneous documentation, databases, and database hosts that offer access to information. The easy synoptic form of the information also includes addresses, telephone and fax numbers, and outlines of coverage by each source. Subsidiary information contained in this guide provides translations of headings into and from the main European languages, an index, dialing codes, currencies, and country letter and dialing codes. Recommended to all business schools and reference departments of large public libraries.—**Bogdan Mieczkowski**

Eastern Europe

261. Enderlyn, Allyn, and Oliver C. Dziggel. **Cracking Eastern Europe: Everything Marketers Must Know to Sell into the World's Newest Emerging Markets.** Chicago, Probus Publishing, 1992. 385p. maps. index. $42.50. ISBN 1-55738-254-9.

The efforts of the Eastern European countries to implement free-market reforms and to move toward capitalism have opened attractive economic opportunities for Western business enterprises, thanks to a huge potential consumer market, an abundant supply of skilled labor, and the availability of attractive real estate. Most of these nations have healthy aspirations to regain their prewar economic positions, and though all of them are still having hard currency problems, the forthcoming Western financial aid is slowly revitalizing their economies. The primary purpose of this volume is to help Western entrepreneurs and investors enter Eastern European markets by supplying the information needed to establish business relationships with these nations. This publication covers the territories that formerly were East Germany, Czechoslovakia, and Yugoslavia as well as Albania, Bulgaria, Hungary, and Romania. In their introduction, the authors describe, compare, and contrast the conditions in these countries and single out common themes. Major topics covered are historic and geopolitical factors, demographic aspects, politics and finance, business opportunities and policies to attract business, and data on important contacts. In a separate chapter for each country, a map, geographic data, a brief history, and a list of U.S. government and multilateral resources are provided. At the end of the volume an appendix contains much useful statistical data. This excellent source of information is highly recommended for all business executives and entrepreneurs interested in the new and expanding markets in Eastern Europe. [R: RBB, 1 April 93, p. 1454]—**Oleg Zinam**

262. Pribylovski, Vladimir, comp. **Active Figures of the Trade Union and Working Class Movement of Russia, Ukraine, Bielorussia, [and] Kazakhstan.** Moscow, Panorama of Russia; distr., Somerville, Mass., Panorama of Russia, [1992]. 72p. index. $40.00 spiralbound.

Prepared by Panorama on the initiative and with the support of the American Federation of Labor, this directory provides some 80 biographical sketches of the trade union figures in 4 countries. Sketches vary in length, usually providing personal data, education, career, and two sentences about political affiliation. There are an organization index, a "nominal" index (names), and a geographical index. No instruction exists to explain the criteria used in this compilation, and its technical execution is rather poor. It should be used with caution.—**Bohdan S. Wynar**

Great Britain

263. Alford, B. W. E., Rodney Lowe, and Neil Rollings. **Economic Planning 1943-1951: A Guide to Documents in the Public Record Office.** London, Her Majesty's Stationery Office; distr., Lanham, Md., UNIPUB, 1992. 1172p. index. $190.00pa. ISBN 0-11-440238-8.

This volume represents a monumental guide to numerous British public documents that deal with broad political and administrative measures related to economic planning between 1943 and 1951. It contains departmental and committee records most relevant to governmental attempts to control or plan the economy. Only those wartime records that specifically covered the planning of peacetime policies or their precedents are included. Despite the efforts to provide the maximum information cataloged in minimum space, the records are incomplete and cannot be used as a fully reliable guide to policy formulation of the British government during this period.

Planning proposals listed in this volume are, at their best, an amalgam of utopian ideas and practical efforts to formulate programs to reduce unemployment. One of the rationales for this survey is to throw light on the discrepancy between the ideological commitment of the Labour government to economic planning and its failure as a practical policy. Among the numerous factors that contributed to this failure were the lack of political will on the part of leadership; the administrative inertia of the Civil Service; the lukewarm response of industry; the resistance of labor unions; the lack of appeal to the general public; and a series of short-term crises that overloaded the British government and diverted its energy from long-range planning efforts.

This volume, divided into 23 chapters (including an enlightening introduction), lists a deluge of cabinet minutes and memoranda, cabinet committees, and papers of the prime minister and two departments closely identified with economic planning. The compilation is indeed a bibliographical gold mine for the researchers and general public interested in the British Labour Party's efforts to introduce central planning in Great Britain during its first postwar rule.—**Oleg Zinam**

264. **Anglo-American Trade Directory 1993.** 77th ed. Shahpari Dolatshahi, ed. London, American Chamber of Commerce (United Kingdom); distr., Bristol, Pa., Taylor & Francis, [1993]. 1v. (various paging). illus. maps. $185.00pa. ISBN 0-9520316-0-4.

This work is the most recent in a series of annual publications of the American Chamber of Commerce (United Kingdom). The directory provides a list of more than 18,000 United States and British firms that are either members of the American Chamber of Commerce (United Kingdom) or that have business links with those two countries. Entries are also given for parent companies, agents, and other firms or installations related to those listed. Most entries provide organization name, address, telephone and fax numbers, key executives, business activity, SIC (Standard Industrial Classification) code, and U.S./U.K. business connections. Listings are also given by SIC code and by U.K. regions and U.S. states. Information concerning the American Chamber of Commerce (United Kingdom) and its relationships to other American Chambers of Commerce is included, as well as general information regarding the American Embassy in London (e.g., commercial services offered; topline regulations on U.S. passports, citizenship, visas, and income taxes). The U.K. Department of Trade and Industry provides sources of data on investment in the United Kingdom. Helpful information on trade between the two countries and the relocation of personnel is included.

This directory should be of interest to those seeking trading opportunities between the United States and the United Kingdom, especially for Americans interested in doing business in Great Britain. It should also assist those who need to identify transatlantic business links.—**William C. Struning**

265. **Kelly's Business Directory 1992.** 105th ed. East Grinstead, England, Reed Information Services; distr., Bristol, Pa., Taylor & Francis, c1991, 1992. 2251p. $295.00. ISBN 0-610-00630-4. ISSN 0269-9265.

This is a classified directory to industrial, professional, and commercial organizations in the United Kingdom. The work is divided into four main parts. The first lists firms that will send literature on their products and services in response to a reader reply service card. The main classified section lists companies principally by trade or industry rather than by product. A drawback to this section is that there is no summary list of the headings used, so users have to wade through the listings to find whether the heading first thought of is included. There are some *see* references, however. Unless more is provided in accompanying advertisements, the information consists only of the address. Reference to the company listing is necessary to find the telephone or fax numbers. Next is a similar classified section aimed at the oil and gas industry and suppliers of services and products to it. Finally, there is an alphabetical list by company name. This provides directory information, including fax and telephone numbers and the heading under which the firm is placed in the classified section.

This standard U.K. business directory is, on the whole, well produced and well thought out. It deserves serious acquisitions consideration for larger business library collections or for information centers with the relevant client demand.—**Nigel Tappin**

266. **Pension Funds and Their Advisors 1992.** 15th ed. Alan Philipp, comp. and ed. London, AP Information Services; distr., Charlottesville, Va., Money Market Directories, 1992. 948p. index. $245.00. ISBN 0-906247-39-X. ISSN 0140-6647.

A useful complement to other directories published by Money Market Directories, this is a valuable source for locating pension fund investment summaries, assets controlled by managers, key country resources, and current industry trends. International companies (e.g., Nestle) and joint venture contacts can also be researched easily. The availability and performance of British pension funds and financial advisers are examined through alphabetical entries that contain standard (e.g., address), financial, and investment data. Ranked lists and location and activity indexes offer additional access points. Following the indexes are four lists devoted to pension funds and money managers in the United States, Canada, Europe, and Japan.

The organizational structure of this work is somewhat confusing, as entries for foreign funds appear between the sections on British pension funds and British advisers. Some of the information is almost inaccessible because non-British funds and advisers have been excluded from the indexes. A single index for everything would alleviate these difficulties and assist the research of patrons, particularly those with incomplete information.—**Sandra E. Belanger**

267. Riley, Sam G., ed. **Consumer Magazines of the British Isles.** Westport, Conn., Greenwood Press, 1993. 300p. index. (Historical Guides to the World's Periodicals and Newspapers). $75.00. PN5124.P4C58. 052'.09045. LC 92-19876. ISBN 0-313-28562-4.

The purpose of this title is to "provide information on a sampling of what the people of the British Isles—young or old, peer or laborer—are reading" (preface). Included are dignified, seasoned periodicals, such as *Spectator*; entertainment-oriented newcomers, such as *T.V. Time*; and digest-sized regionals, such as *Cambria*. Major international or multiedition magazines, such as *Vogue* or *Reader's Digest*, are not listed; the editor plans another title that will cover them.

An introductory essay discussing the history of British Isles magazines is followed by 50 alphabetical entries on representative magazine titles. Each entry covers the magazine's life span and ends with a list of index or abstract sources, U.S. libraries that hold files, title changes, periodicity, publishers, place or places of publication, editors, and approximate current circulation. Each entry is signed by the contributor. Appendix A is a chronological list of magazines by year founded, appendix B is a subject categorization, and appendix C is a list of other British consumer magazines. A selected bibliography and an index follow. Riley is a professor of communication studies at Virginia Polytechnic Institute and State University and has edited or coedited several major reference books on journalists and magazines. This well-written work will prove useful in academic libraries and large public libraries with an interest in the British Isles. [R: Choice, Oct 93, p. 264]—**Susan C. Awe**

Italy

268. **American Chamber of Commerce in Italy Directory 1992.** Alexandra Olgiatti, ed. Milan, Italy, American Chamber of Commerce in Italy; distr., Bristol, Pa., Taylor & Francis, 1992. 521p. $175.00pa.

This bilingual (English-Italian) directory is a guide to U.S. firms that operate in Italy and vice versa. It is divided into four sections. The first is a "white pages" section that lists member companies of the American Chamber of Commerce (AmCham) in Italy. Generally, each entry provides name; address; telephone, telex, and fax numbers; presidents, vice presidents, and other important individuals; and U.S. firms represented by the company. Section 2 is a classified list of members similar to the Standard Industrial Classification (SIC). Section 3 is a long alphabetical list of U.S. firms present in the Italian market, and section 4 does the same for Italian firms in the U.S. market. In sections 3 and 4, members of the AmCham in Italy are indicated by boldface type or italics.

Other information in the book includes AmCham aims and activities, lists of AmCham members and committees, a profile of Italy, hotels in that country, AmChams in the rest of Europe and worldwide, major trade and professional associations in the United States, and U.S. governmental and nongovernmental agencies. This book is probably unique in its coverage of United States-Italy trade and will be an essential acquisition for businesses interested in participating in such trade. Libraries that collect in international business will also want a copy.—**D. A. Rothschild**

LABOR

Bibliography

269. Lowe, Ida B., and Beth Hillman Johnson. **Collective Bargaining in Higher Education and the Professions. Bibliography No.20.** New York, National Center for the Study of Collective Bargaining in Higher Education and the Professions, Baruch College, City University of New York, 1992. 88p. index. $30.00pa. ISSN 0738-1913.

This is one of a series of unannotated bibliographies produced annually since 1973 by various scholars associated with the National Center for the Study of Collective Bargaining in Higher Education and the Professions. The 1985 volume was reviewed in ARBA 86 (see entry 308). This work contains 847 citations in the Modern Language Association format for selected monographs, serials, dissertations, conference papers, and articles in magazines, journals, and newspapers issued in 1991. Entries are arranged alphabetically under more than 45 topics ranging from academic freedom to women faculty. Most of the citations refer to collective bargaining and personnel issues involving full-time faculty at academic institutions in the United States and Canada. Some entries deal with part-time teachers, librarians, and support staff; physicians, nurses, and other health care workers; professional athletes; and members of other professions. Brief listings of relevant periodicals and organizations, indexes by author and subject, and a list of acronyms and abbreviations complete this specialized bibliography. Despite the lack of annotations, it can be very useful in identifying new research material.—**Leonard Grundt**

270. Ross, Lynn C. **Career Advancement for Women in the Federal Service: An Annotated Bibliography and Resource Book.** Hamden, Conn., Garland, 1993. 251p. index. (Public Affairs and Administration, v.28; Garland Reference Library of Social Science, v.867). $40.00. Z7164.C6R67. 016.353001'082. LC 93-19100. ISBN 0-8153-1058-7.

The scope of this book is more inclusive, and therefore the book is more useful, than the title suggests. Materials on women in the private sector and in state and local governments are included for comparison purposes. Also included are general materials on how to advance in one's career. The entries appear to have been carefully selected to be the most useful to practitioners or researchers. The annotations give a feel for the contents of the material. Popular concepts, such as the "mommy track," appear here along with more scholarly studies from academic journals.

In addition to a bibliography, the introduction gives a concise history and cites major problems related to women in the civil service. The affirmative action chapter includes the text of some relevant legal documents. So does the chapter on sexual harassment, which also gives a chronology and lists organizations to which victims can complain. Other chapters present a similar variety of information, covering training programs, associations, and other resources that women may find beneficial. The latest citation seems to be 1992, but most sources date from the 1980s.

In all, this is a well-thought-out and well-organized handbook for libraries serving human resources personnel or researchers. It would benefit from a detailed subject index, although there is an author index. To make best use of this source requires time, as the listings for organizations and other information, such as laws, are scattered throughout. Therefore, the book will be of most use to someone really involved with the subject, rather than for ready-reference.—**Susan V. McKimm**

Dictionaries and Encyclopedias

271. Briggs, Virginia L., Michael G. Kushner, and Michael J. Schinabeck. **Employee Benefits Dictionary: An Annotated Compendium of Frequently Used Terms.** Washington, D.C., BNA Books, 1992. 197p. $68.00pa. HD4928.N6B75. 331.25'5'03. LC 91-39410. ISBN 0-87179-709-7.

As in many areas of our society that are regulated, at least in part, by public policy, the area of employee benefits (e.g., pensions, annuities, insurance, profit-sharing plans, workers' compensation programs) has grown increasingly complex over time. The legislation and regulations in this area have, according to the authors, given rise to a jargon peculiar to the field of employee benefits. The purpose of this reference work is two-fold. First, it is designed to serve as a dictionary that readers can use to familiarize themselves with terminology commonly encountered in the field. Second, it is meant to serve as a "research expediter" by providing citations to allow the reader to more fully explore the terms defined.

While the book would likely be helpful in its first role, it would appear to be less useful in its second. Most of the citations given refer to laws and regulations and are given in the shorthand commonly used for these purposes. Unfortunately, the abbreviations are not defined and the format is not explained. This could well reduce the usefulness of the work to many individuals who might consult it but who will not readily understand the citations. Despite its limitations, the dictionary is a moderately useful reference tool.
—**Paul F. Clark**

272. Brzezinski, Mary Jo, ed. **Employee Benefit Plans: A Glossary of Terms.** 8th ed. Brookfield, Wis., International Foundation of Employee Benefit Plans, 1993. 202p. $25.00pa. LC 93-77756. ISBN 0-89154-465-8.

This dictionary has been updated and revised since 1975. It is a straightforward glossary, with a separate appendix spelling out acronyms and abbreviations. From a reference librarian's viewpoint, it would probably be easier to have the appendix terms interfiled in the main glossary, despite the fact that not all abbreviations are defined in the glossary. For instance, ZEBRA (Zero Balance Reimbursement Account) has a glossary definition, but YRT (Yearly Renewable Term) does not. Terms are pulled from a wide variety of related fields, such as investments and law. Libraries with access to legal sources will find the paucity of legal citations a nuisance. Although the foreword says this glossary "should not be viewed as a definitive source," and "Users should refer to standard texts and reference works," there is no bibliography or list of these standard sources. Many included terms, such as *joint venture*, can be found in general business dictionaries, so libraries probably do not need this book unless they receive many questions or have a very specialized collection. However, private personnel departments would find it useful.—**Susan V. McKimm**

Directories

273. de Vries, Andre, ed. **The Directory of Jobs & Careers Abroad.** 8th ed. Oxford, England, Vacation Work; distr., Princeton, N.J., Peterson's Guides, 1993. 408p. index. $16.95pa. ISBN 1-85458-025-6. ISSN 0143-3482.

This is a British-based handbook on finding work overseas. The book should be of considerable help in alerting potential expatriate workers to strategies and possible sources of employment. As earlier editions have been popular in the United States, the editor has included specific information for United States nationals in most chapters. Countries in Eastern Europe, the Baltics, and the United Kingdom are now included.

There are two main sections, and the first has two parts. The initial part gives advice on looking for work abroad through advertised vacancies and other formal avenues, as well as informal networks. This part also deals with such issues as language training, legal requisites, and health care. The second part provides information on 11 sectors, including journalism, teaching, and computer services, plus voluntary work, the United Nations, other international bodies, and the British government. Addresses of relevant associations, companies, and government agencies are provided. (The emphasis is on British agencies and affiliates, perhaps reducing the work's direct helpfulness for North Americans and others.)

The second main section provides information on work in Europe, the Americas, Australasia, Asia, Africa, and the Middle East. Information varies greatly: Most developed countries have quite a bit of detail, along with China and the newly industrialized states of Singapore, South Korea, and Hong Kong; Latin America, Africa, the Middle East, and Eastern Europe tend to have more generalized information and less on specific countries. Types of information include general facts, forms of work, legal issues, living standards, conditions of work, and much more in the longer entries. Many smaller, nondeveloped states have paragraph-length entries with a referral to their embassies in Great Britain and the United States. Other than the Baltic states, the former Soviet Union is not covered. This fascinating new edition should be bought by libraries, agencies, and individuals with the appropriate interests.—**Nigel Tappin**

274. **Directory of European Community Trade and Professional Associations 1992. Repertoire des Organisations Professionnelles de la Communaute Europeenne. Verzeichnis der Verbande in der Europaischen Gemeinschaft.** 5th ed. Brussels, Editions Delta; distr., Lanham, Md., UNIPUB, 1992. 515p. index. $155.00. ISBN 2-8029-0106-0. ISSN 0771-7865.

This is an official publication of the European Communities. It was compiled using information collected from questionnaires sent to European federations. Listed in the directory are those federations that are representative of European interest groups that have satisfied the following criteria: having a permanent secretariat; being a national or European association originating in a European Community (EC) country; and being a nonprofit, with a purpose relevant to the development of the EC. Three very useful indexes are incorporated in the work: an index of abbreviations and acronyms; an analytical (subject) index in French, English, and German; and an index of names, also in the three languages. The information given in the directory is usually the organization's official name, address and telephone number, including fax number; date founded; and president or chair's name. For larger organizations, additional office locations are listed. A comparison with the *Yearbook of International Organizations* (see ARBA 93, entry 75) found that many of the organizations are listed in both directories. The *Yearbook* gives additional information, including aims of the organization, structure, staff, activities, and members.

—**Linda Suttle Harris**

275. **The Linton Trainer's Resource Directory.** 2d ed. Thomas Linton, ed. Hopkins, Minn., Linton Publishing, 1992. 1v. (various paging). index. $385.00. ISBN 0-9626607-1-X. ISSN 1064-234X.

This comprehensive reference work, which first appeared as *The Linton Register* (see ARBA 91, entry 247) and is published biennially, is more than a list of training programs offered in the United States. It is composed of nine sections and a quick reference guide. The "Trainer's Resource A to Z" is the major list of companies. It is arranged by training categories for specific needs. Names and telephone numbers are given, and a notation is made if an advertisement for the company appears in the directory. A profile of the company is also given if a paid advertisement appears in the directory. The full address and a contact person's name are listed for each company in the section on suppliers, vendors, and consultants. The other sections of the directory give entries for seminars and workshops, training books, total quality management, software, training sites and conferences, and video programs.

This is an easy-to-use resource. The quick reference section is particularly helpful. Cross-referencing is evident throughout the directory, and the *see* references that appear in the main section should enable users to find correct headings for subjects. Special codes given at the end of each listing refer to training media and are especially helpful when looking for programs with films, video, software, and the like.

Similar in scope to the *Training and Development Organizations Directory* (see ARBA 93, entry 307), which is published triennially, this is a worthwhile purchase for large business collections and special libraries. It should prove invaluable to both libraries and the business community.
—**Linda Suttle Harris**

Handbooks and Yearbooks

276. **America's Top 300 Jobs.** Indianapolis, Ind., JIST Works, 1992. 473p. index. $17.95pa. ISBN 1-56370-060-3.

This directory is a reprint of *GPO Bulletin 2400: 1992-93 Occupational Outlook Handbook* (OOH) from the U.S. Department of Labor. This version is very affordable; in fact, it rivals the cost of the original publication. The print and type are similar, the pictures are the same, and there is some variation in the placement of the text, but there is no discernible difference between the content of OOH and this handbook. The book's title and format are a marketing tool to repackage public domain material and to put it into a copyrighted format. If a library has a standing order or is a depository library, it certainly does not need *America's Top 300 Jobs*. It would be better for libraries to purchase an OOH in electronic format instead of having another copy of the same information in paper format.—**Gerald D. Moran**

277. **BNA's 1993 Source Book on Collective Bargaining & Employee Relations.** Michael C. Davis, comp. Washington, D.C., BNA Books, 1993. 292p. $45.00 looseleaf w/binder. ISBN 0-87179-789-5. ISSN 1067-7356.

For decades the Bureau of National Affairs (BNA) has been publishing frequently updated looseleaf services summarizing developments in labor relations and human resources. This BNA compilation, consisting of reliable data and analyses collected from federal and private sources, is divided into five tabbed sections: collective bargaining; compensation; economics; legislative and legal; and surveys, studies, and reports. The first section covers major contracts expiring in 1993, union membership, occupational injuries, employer bargaining objectives, and anticipated bargaining issues for 1993. Employee wage and benefit costs in 1992 and prior years are in the second section. Information on the economic outlook for 1993, national economic performance in the past, productivity, employment, and unemployment is presented under the third tab. The fourth section includes analyses of labor law principles established by the courts, federal and state laws passed in 1992, OSHA (Occupational Safety and Health Administration) rulings, and the outlook for labor legislation in 1993. Under the last tab are reproduced documents on fatal work injuries, employee payments for health care, unemployment trends, and the short-term employment outlook.

This book lacks an index but has a good table of contents. Because it was compiled in 1992, some parts are no longer current. Nevertheless, because all sources are clearly labeled, it is easy to identify where the latest data can be found. Any library serving union officials, human resource managers, and others involved in contract negotiations should purchase the latest edition of this useful work (if it cannot afford to subscribe to one of the much more expensive, up-to-date BNA services). [R: RBB, 15 Sept 93, p. 184]—**Leonard Grundt**

278. **Career Guide to America's Top Industries: Business Forecasts for 350 Industries.** Indianapolis, Ind., JIST Works, [1993]. 214p. $11.95pa. ISBN 1-56370-111-1. ISSN 1069-398X.

Published for individuals such as high school seniors and their counselors or displaced workers seeking a career change, this guide to some 40 major industries found in the United States is a companion publication to the 1992-1993 edition of *America's Top 300 Jobs* (JIST Works, 1992) (the trade version of the *Occupational Outlook Handbook* from the U.S. Department of Labor). The *Career Guide* includes information on the major industries of agriculture, mining, and construction; manufacturing; transportation and communications; wholesale and retail trade; finance and insurance; and services. These categories are then broken down into specific job classifications, such as "Food Processing" in the manufacturing section and "Computer and Data Processing Services" in the services section.

Each job classification discusses the nature of the industry, employment data (including number of projected positions), working conditions, occupations found in the industry, training and advancement possibilities, earnings, outlook, and sources for additional information. Information is presented in an easy-to-read format with graphs and charts displaying statistical data derived from such sources as the Department of Commerce or Bureau of Labor Statistics. In addition, each job classification has a "significant points" section that summarizes information at the beginning of the text. In the computer and data processing services section, these points include the projection of a 90 percent growth in employment between 1990 and 2005 and the fact that one out of every four employees is a computer programmer or computer systems analyst. [R: LJ, 1 Sept 93, p. 168; RBB, 1 Dec 93, pp. 708-09]—**Dorothy M. Williams**

279. LeCompte, Michelle, ed. **Job Hunter's Sourcebook: Where to Find Employment Leads and Other Job Search Resources.** 2d ed. Detroit, Gale, 1993. 1131p. index. $57.00. ISBN 0-8103-8201-6. ISSN 1053-1874.

This edition of *Job Hunter's Sourcebook* (JHS) updates the 1991 edition (see ARBA 92, entry 222), with 25 percent more entries and a compact three-column format. Part 1 is an excellent bibliography and directory of job opportunity information for 165 high-interest professional and vocational occupations. For each occupation JHS lists publications, organizations, audiovisual, and electronic resources that give job seekers employment leads, and other useful information. Job seekers will especially appreciate the section on sources of help-wanted advertisements that is provided for each occupation. Part 2 is a clearinghouse of information that is less oriented to specific occupations. Some of the topics covered in part 2 include environmental opportunities, opportunities for older workers, and negotiating compensation packages. Most of the entries are annotated.

Although there is some duplicate coverage with its companion volumes *Professional Careers Sourcebook* (see ARBA 93, entry 411) and *Vocational Careers Sourcebook* (see ARBA 93, entry 412), JHS seems more appropriate for the person who already has the education or training required for a given occupation. Most of the resources listed in JHS could be found in other commonly owned library sources, such as *Encyclopedia of Associations* (see ARBA 91, entries 37-38) and *Directory of Executive Recruiters* (see ARBA 85, entry 159), but only after a time-consuming search. The new three-column format has allowed this edition to accommodate more entries without increasing bulk or sacrificing readability. For any library offering career resources, JHS is money well spent.—**Kerranne G. Biley**

280. Mast, Jennifer Arnold. **The Job Seeker's Guide to 1,000 Top Employers.** Detroit, Visible Ink Press/Gale, 1993. 788p. index. $22.95pa. ISBN 0-8103-9432-4.

Mast selected her 1,000 employers from lists of the largest companies and from lists of rapidly growing smaller firms. Much of her information is attributed to *Ward's Business Directory of U.S. Private and Public Companies* (see ARBA 93, entry 198), although exactly how much is not specified. Other sources used include annual reports, brochures, questionnaires, and telephone calls. Information on how to apply to companies seems to have come directly from the companies. Throughout, Mast tosses in little sidebars that give helpful hints on job-hunting and career advancement. The latest sales figures given seem to be 1990 and, for some firms, 1989. This is dated for a book with a 1993 copyright, but then the book is very inexpensive compared to similar works.

The book of this type that has been around the longest is *The Career Guide*, which is published annually by Dun & Bradstreet. Dun's covers firms with more than 2,000 employees, listing only those that are hiring. Its indexing is superior to that of *The Job Seeker's Guide* as, in addition to geographic and industry indexes, it indexes corporate branch locations and disciplines hired. *The Job Seeker's Guide to Private and Public Companies* (see ARBA 93, entry 310) also lists Mast as an editor and also acknowledges *Ward's Business Directory* (whose print version is owned by Gale). It covers 15,000-plus firms and lists almost as many firms per dollar as does the title under review. Its company profiles are, however, generally shorter. It is arranged geographically, which many users find more convenient than the alphabetical arrangement of *The Career Guide* or Mast's title. For libraries that want multiple copies or that have small career collection budgets, *The Job Seeker's Guide* is a best buy.—**Susan V. McKimm**

281. **Occupational Outlook Handbook.** 1992-93 ed. Indianapolis, Ind., JIST Works, 1992. 473p. illus. index. $21.95; $16.95pa. ISBN 1-56370-045-X; 1-56370-044-1pa. ISSN 0082-9072.

Two reprints of the U.S. Bureau of Labor Statistics's *Occupational Outlook Handbook* (OOH) are available. One is published by National Textbook; the other, reviewed here, is published by JIST Works. (Depository libraries that preselected the original [GPO] OOH received the first copy for free.)

The current edition of this basic reference work, published by GPO since 1949, describes about 250 occupations in detail, covering about 107 million jobs—87 percent of U.S. jobs. An appendix presents summary data on 80 additional occupations—about 4 percent of all jobs. (The remaining 9 percent of jobs are mainly residual categories, such as other management support workers [e.g., athletes, coaches, directors of religious activities and education], for which little meaningful information could be developed.) Prefatory material explains the organization of the handbook, where to go for additional information (organizations and publications), and a survey of forces likely to affect employment opportunities to 2005. Next come detailed descriptions of some 250 occupations arranged in 13 clusters of related jobs (e.g., executive, administrative, and managerial; professional specialty). The listing for each occupation includes the 1977 *Dictionary of Occupational Titles* (DOT) (see ARBA 79, entry 855) (and 1986 supplement) classification numbers; nature of the work; working conditions; places of employment; training, other qualifications, and advancement; employment outlook to 2005; earnings; related occupations; and sources of additional information. Photographs, tables, and graphs illustrate portions of the text. Appendixes (in addition to the previously mentioned summary data) discuss employment projection methodology, list sources of state and local job outlook information, and list DOT numbers and titles from the 1991 edition of the DOT (see ARBA 93, entry 301) published too late for inclusion in the body of this edition of the OOH. The index to occupations and industries includes numerous *see* references. Because the GPO versions of *Occupational Outlook Handbook* are not copyrighted, libraries, career counselors, and individuals considering purchase of this outstanding manual will no doubt compare the prices of the six versions (three hardcover, three softcover) available.—**Wiley J. Williams**

282. Reddy, Marlita A. **American Salaries and Wages Survey: Statistical Data Derived from More Than 300 Government, Business & News Sources.** 2d ed. Detroit, Gale, 1993. 897p. $95.00pa. ISBN 0-8103-8591-0. ISSN 1055-7628.

This directory has been compiled from salaries cited in various state and federal publications and from trade associations and journals. This data is then arranged alphabetically by job title, with geographical breakdowns under each title. A complicated system of abbreviations helps compress the information, and an abbreviations table appears on each page. There are gaps in the data reported, perhaps due to the inability to obtain permission to reprint certain data. For instance, there is no detailed breakdown of police salaries by city, although this data is available in *The Municipal Year Book 1993* (International City/County Management Association). Not even all the government data available has been included. Using just the example of Ohio, data from the Ohio Bureau of Employment Services's *Placement Wage Data for Ohio* has been included, but their *Ohio Labor Market Information* data, covering production wages, and the Ohio Department of Industrial Relations's *Prevailing Wage Rates*, covering construction contractors, have been omitted. (Of course, the lack of bibliographical control with regard to state publications makes them hard to locate in the first place.) Unfortunately, the uneven coverage leads to such discrepancies as six pages of listings under "Shipper and Receiver," data that comes from the U.S. Bureau of Labor Statistics, but about a quarter of a page of information for the position of "Sales Manager," on which the government gathers little information.

This new edition provides a section of cross-references to related job titles, something that did not appear in the first edition and that will increase the chances of finding relevant data. However, especially for professional and managerial jobs, the chance of finding the exact career or location needed becomes hit-or-miss, as these careers are tallied less often by government than are blue-collar or fairly standardized jobs. This is a fairly inexpensive reference book; more aggressive efforts to increase the completeness of coverage would be likely to increase the price. It is worth adding to any collection that serves job seekers, as there are so few reasonably priced sources of salary information available.—**Susan V. McKimm**

283. Russell, Cheryl, and Margaret Ambry. **The Official Guide to American Incomes: A Comprehensive Look at How Much Americans Have to Spend....** Ithaca, N.Y., New Strategist, 1993. 343p. index. $69.95. ISBN 0-9628092-2-5.

Providing a great deal of 1991 demographic data on incomes in the United States, this work is an extremely useful reference tool. Approximately 285 tables are organized into chapters on income trends; household, personal, and discretionary income; household income projections; spending and wealth; poverty trends; and income and geographical trends. Each chapter is prefaced by a brief introduction that notes data highlights and patterns. The tables are clear, concise, and easy to read, and specific data may be accessed through either a comprehensive table of contents or a detailed index.

The authors state in the introduction that most of the current incomes in the book are taken from the Census Bureau's 1992 Current Population Survey (data from 1991). However, two of the chapters ("Household Income Projections" and "Discretionary Income") were provided specifically for this reference work by TGE Demographics. Official discretionary income figures are not regularly collected by the government, so these statistics are particularly valuable. In addition, TGE Demographics details how the figures were estimated.

Although the tables are useful, this book seems to lack background or explanatory information. For example, Ambry's other 1993 publication, *The Official Guide to Household Spending* (New Strategist), includes a section describing how the Census Bureau's data were collected; such information is missing from this volume. In addition, the only race or ethnicity breakdowns are Black, white, and Hispanic. References on where to find income data for other groups, such as Native Americans and Asian Americans, would be useful but are not included. [R: LJ, 15 Sept 93, p. 69; RBB, 1 Dec 93, p. 716]

—**Janice M. Griggs**

284. **Working for Your Uncle: The Complete Guide to Finding a Job with the Federal Government.** By the editors of the *Federal Jobs Digest*. Ossining, N.Y., Breakthrough, 1993. 824p. illus. maps. index. $19.95pa. LC 93-070670. ISBN 0-914327-27-5.

By publishing *Working for Your Uncle*, the editors of *Federal Jobs Digest* attempt to demystify the federal hiring process. This is no small task, yet this well-written guide is packed with strategies, explanations, and examples that would-be federal employees will find helpful. The first 125 pages detail a 7-step application process that applies to anyone seeking federal employment, regardless of field or career level. The seven steps move the job seeker from identifying appropriate job titles to considering an offer. Most of the book contains extensive appendixes of more specific information, such as pay schedules, job descriptions, statistics, and contact information. Throughout the book, readers will find helpful notes set off in boxes in the outer margins, which serve as cross-references to relevant sections within *Working for Your Uncle* as well as to useful government publications. Also included are a glossary and subject index.

Several guides to federal employment have been published in recent years. All attempt to steer the reader through the same complicated process, but *Working for Your Uncle* offers more depth than others. The numerous examples of forms, schedules, vacancy announcements, and other such items give job seekers a head start on finding more specific information concerning their individual career interests. *Working for Your Uncle* is an exceptional value. Highly recommended for all libraries. [R: LJ, Aug 93, p. 92]—**Kerranne G. Biley**

Indexes

285. *International Labour Review*: **Index 1945-1991 (Vols. 51-130).** Washington, D.C., International Labor Office, 1992. 168p. $14.00pa. ISBN 92-2-108255-5.

This index to articles that appeared in *International Labour Review* (ILR) between 1945 and 1991 updates earlier, and now out-of-print, indexes published by the International Labor Office in 1930, 1935, and 1959. Articles and "reports and inquiries" published in ILR are indexed by author, subject (including country), and title. Each brief citation gives the volume and issue number, year, and page numbers.

The author and title indexes were accurate when checked against actual issues of the journal, but the subject index revealed some curiosities. For example, while there are headings for both "Agricultural Machinery" and "Agricultural Mechanization," an article titled "Agricultural Mechanization and Employment in Latin America" is indexed under agricultural machinery. Also, several appropriate conference summary articles in ILR are not listed in the index under the heading "International Labour Conference." Subheadings would be helpful for some of the more general subject headings, such as "Labour Relations" or "Unemployment." Another feature missing is cross-references. A researcher looking for articles about firing an employee would have to know that such articles are indexed under the heading "Dismissal," or that an article on job security would be listed under "Employment Security." Country-name headings reflect only the form current at publication; for example, older articles on Ceylon are listed under the current name Sri Lanka. Although inexpensive, this index is a marginal purchase because ILR is so widely indexed in other sources (e.g., *Business Periodicals Index* [see ARBA 93, entry 216]).—**Kerranne G. Biley**

MANAGEMENT

286. **Personnel Executives Contactbook: Key Hiring Contacts at 30,000 Established and Emerging U.S. Companies.** Cynthia Russell Spomer, ed. Detroit, Gale, 1993. 1901p. $149.00. ISBN 0-8103-8917-7. ISSN 1068-4751.

This new reference book was compiled in response to a need for a directory of personnel managers in various large and small companies and organizations in the United States. It is intended to help readers who are looking for employment information, especially the names of personnel executives. According to the editor, information was culled from *Ward's Business Directory of U.S. Private and Public Companies* (see ARBA 93, entry 198) and was supplemented by telephone interviews, trade journals, mass media, and business ranking lists.

In general, the directory is easy to use. The main body is divided into four parts: an alphabetical list of all companies and organizations, a geographical listing by city within each state, an industry listing according to Standard Industrial Classification (SIC) codes, and a list of executives. Each main entry contains the company name; street address; city, state, and ZIP code; telephone and fax numbers; contact person; sales figures; number of employees; and up to four SIC codes.

Even though the directory contains 30,000 entries, it represents only a fraction of possible entries. For example, under the classification "Colleges and Universities" there is a single listing (for the Houston Laser Institute). Due to its uneven coverage, this reference book is only marginally useful for job hunting. [R: RBB, 1 Dec 93, pp. 716-17; RQ, Winter 93, pp. 292-93; WLB, Oct 93, pp. 95-96]—**Hwa-Wei Lee**

MARKETING AND TRADE

287. **Advertising Ratios & Budgets: Historical and Forecasted Advertising Budgets and Ratios Covering the Period 1986-1993.** Lincolnshire, Ill., Schonfeld, 1992. 203p. $325.00pa. ISBN 1-878339-15-X.

Published annually, this title provides financial ratios based on three accounting measures: advertising expenditures, net sales, and cost of goods sold. Half of the volume provides ratios for individual companies grouped under their appropriate Standard Industrial Classification (SIC) codes. These tables include an estimate for the current year as well as ratios based on a six-year historical period for the current year and the coming year. The other half of the volume provides an additional seven arrangements, including ratios by industry, again using the SIC. The data from which the publisher calculates the financial ratios may be found in such sources as *Standard Directory of Advertisers* (Reed Reference Publishing, 1993). These sources do not manipulate the data into financial ratios, however. The *Almanac of Business and Industrial Financial Ratios* by Leo Troy (see ARBA 91, entry 233) gives comparable ratios by industry but not for individual companies. The data used to compile *Advertising Ratios & Budgets* are also more current than Troy's data. However, the work does not include data on privately owned companies. Another limitation is the fact that multi-industry companies are classified with their largest line of business, yet a substantial part of their earnings may be in other lines. The editors, The introduction cites additional reasons for exercising care in the use of the ratios.

The target market for this title is professional managers. Corporate libraries that collect material in the areas of industrial competition and advertising will need to acquire this work. If price is not a deterrent, academic libraries that support business majors and large public libraries would also find the title valuable.—**Dene L. Clark**

288. **Co-op Source Directory: The Guide to Over 6,100 Co-operative Advertising Programs. Spring 1993.** New Providence, N.J., National Register Publishing/Reed Reference Publishing, 1993. 1252p. $385.00pa. ISBN 0-87217-862-5.

Retail and wholesale owners and managers can locate assistance for advertising specific products through this extensive semiannual directory of manufacturers' cooperative programs. The programs are arranged into 52 product classifications. Information on them can be accessed through the manufacturer index, the trademark index, or the main listing under product classification. Details found in the main product classification listing include name, address, telephone number, and contact person for the company; specific products to be advertised; trademarks used for the product; eligible media that may be used for advertising; regional variations and international availability; timing for programs; eligibility requirements; advertising materials available; and type of reimbursement. The directory also contains new and deleted programs, a section on how to read a summary listing, and estimated retail sales by kind of business.

This publication provides a useful service by supplying helpful summaries of manufacturers' co-op advertising programs. Most small public and academic libraries will be unable to afford such an expensive and specific reference source, but it will be indispensable for retailers, wholesalers, manufacturers, and advertising agencies.—**O. Gene Norman**

289. **Direct Marketing Market Place [DMMP] 1993: The Networking Source of the Direct Marketing Industry.** New Providence, N.J., National Register Publishing/Reed Reference Publishing, 1993. 1061p. index. $169.99pa. LC 79-649244. ISBN 0-87217-327-5. ISSN 0192-3137.

This is by far the most comprehensive reference work for the direct marketing industry. It consists of 37 sections covering every aspect of the industry. The first 13 sections include a list of direct marketers, from associations to publishers and subscription agencies. The next 15 sections are devoted to service firms and suppliers to the industry, such as consultants, list brokers and managers, paper suppliers, and market researchers. Sections 29 to 33 cover creative services, such as advertising agencies, art services, and photographers. Sections 34 through 36 deal with direct marketing associations, courses and seminars, and a calendar of events. Section 37 is a detailed bibliography. The book concludes with an impressive, detailed index to companies and individuals, with more than 20,000 individual personnel listed.

The 1993 edition has been enlarged and significantly improved. A careful examination and checking of a few entries selected at random revealed that they were accurate and up-to-date. *Direct Marketing Market Place* is strongly recommended to all marketers, business libraries, and large public libraries.—**Elie M. Dick**

290. Hinkelman, Edward G. **Importers Manual USA: The Single Source Reference Encyclopedia for Importing to the United States.** 1993 ed. San Rafael, Calif., World Trade Press, 1992. 937p. maps. index. $87.00. HF3035.H55. 658.8'48. ISBN 0-9631864-1-8. ISSN 1065-5158.

Numerous agencies and organizations from the United States and many foreign countries contributed to this book. It is divided into sections that contain handy infolists related to importing; international law; international banking; U.S. Customs entry and clearance; and packing, shipping, and insurance. For access there are commodity, country, and general indexes. The businessperson who has a product in mind can consult the commodity index for pertinent import information. Some 135 items are listed in the contents to this index and include such categories as art, coffee, computer hardware, and jewelry. Under each commodity are sections dealing with specific aspects of importing an item, such as entry and documentation, prohibitions and restrictions, laws and regulations, and the primary countries that export the product. The country index contains useful economic, trade, banking, and product information for individuals interested in importing items from a specific country, and a list of the main U.S. imports from the country can also be found. A 17-page general index provides access to products, countries, and import information.

Only 25 books on importing are currently in print, and few of these can be compared with *Importers Manual USA*. Similar information can be found in the *World Trade Resources Guide* (see ARBA 93, entry 265), but its price is almost double that of the one being reviewed, and only 82 countries are included, compared with 100 in the *Importers Manual USA*. This publication is a useful, reasonably priced book for libraries serving clientele who need detailed information on importing. [R: Choice, July/Aug 93, pp. 1749-50; RBB, June 93, p. 1898; WLB, June 93, p. 126]—**O. Gene Norman**

291. Ibou, Paul. **Famous Animal Symbols: A Marvelous Designbook with Symbols and Trademarks.... Volume 2.** Zandhoven, Belgium, Interecho Press; distr., Carson, Calif., Books Nippon, 1992. 532p. illus. index. $59.95. ISBN 90-71614-09-3.

This book is the second in a series of three volumes that present a comprehensive selection of trademarks and logos from organizations in many countries of the world. Ibou, internationally respected designer and editor, guided the selection procedure. The second volume, as did the first, contains trademarks and symbols based on animals. Each of the more than 500 logos is presented on a full page and is in color where appropriate. The selections have been tastefully paired, with logos on facing pages that complement each other. For reader convenience, symbols are indexed by organization (owner) and by artist or designer. The emphasis is on art, with only a few pages of introductory text, which is in both English and French. The book is an artistic delight that can stimulate the imagination of a designer or provide a broad view of symbols to a manager of an organization.—**William C. Struning**

292. **International Closeout Directory '94: Comprehensive Buyers' Reference.** Cherry Hill, N.J., Closeout Network, 1993. 368p. index. $100.00pa. ISBN 0-9638369-0-0.

As the name suggests, *International Closeout Directory* provides access to more than 2,500 brokers, distributors, exporters, importers, manufacturers, and wholesalers who offer merchandise at deeply discounted prices. Merchandise offered can include production overruns, last-season models, business closings, bankruptcies, surplus inventory, closeouts, refused merchandise, and unclaimed freight. The directory is not targeted at consumers (to whom sales would be refused by most of those listed), but at such businesses as closeout and discount stores, as well as other retailers and distributors, such as variety stores, mini-marts, and chain stores. Most of the directory is a list of business firms by type of merchandise handled (e.g., automotive, food items). Each listing includes name of company, address, telephone and fax numbers, type of business, percentage of business done with discount stores, territory, cross-references to directory listings under other categories of merchandise, and names of key persons or contacts. Firms included are also indexed by type of business establishment and by product handled. A calendar of major trade shows in 1993-1994 and a list of freight companies are provided. Although there is an index to advertisers, it might be useful in future editions to refer to advertisements in the listings, because the advertisements frequently contain additional information. The *International Closeout Directory* should be of great value to any retailer or distributor who wishes to consider low-price merchandise lines. [R: LJ, Dec 93, p. 112]—**William C. Struning**

293. Klein, Barry, comp. and ed. **Marketing Made Easier: Guide to Free Product Publicity 1993-1994.** West Nyack, N.Y., Todd, 1993. 130p. index. $25.00pa. ISBN 0-915344-20-3.

This title is the first edition of a work that aims to connect the manufacturers, distributors, and marketers of new products with publications that freely publicize those new products through a new products section. The directory is divided into 2 parts: an alphabetical section that lists more than 1,000 periodicals, and a target index that contains some 120 categories under which the publications are arranged. The alphabetical section contains standard information about publications, such as publisher, address, telephone and fax numbers, and circulation. For each publication it also provides a specific statement regarding the target audience. In the target index most publications are listed under two or more categories. *Apparel Industry Magazine*, for instance, appears under the categories "Apparel," "Management," "Manufacturing," and "Textiles."

While *Gale Directory of Publications and Broadcast Media* (Gale, 1993) devotes considerable space to subject indexes to publications, it lacks the feature that makes this new work unique: the presentation of publications with a new products section. *Marketing Made Easier* was thoughtfully conceived, and while it contains an abundant number of typographical errors, they do not diminish the innate value of the work. Recommended for special libraries that serve companies engaged in new product development, academic libraries in institutions with business programs, and large public libraries with a business clientele.—**Dene L. Clark**

294. **The National Directory of Catalogs 1992.** Terry Lee Schayes, ed. New York, Oxbridge Communications; distr., Detroit, Gale, 1992. 829p. index. $225.00pa. ISBN 0-917460-40-5. ISSN 1050-5830.

This is a comprehensive directory of catalogs published in the United States. It covers more than 210 subjects, from accounting to zoology, and consists of five sections. The first represents the largest part of the book and lists catalogs by subject matter. Entries are extensive. Each starts with the catalog name, publishing house, the full address of the house (with telephone and fax numbers), and a list of key personnel and their titles. This is followed by the product line offered in the catalog, circulation, printing information, and advertising and mailing list rental information. The second and third sections list companies by state and contacts with telephone numbers. The remaining parts of the directory serve as indexes that allow the user to locate entries through the company or the catalog title. *The National Directory of Catalogs* is recommended to all individuals involved in the direct mail industry.—**Elie M. Dick**

295. **R&D Ratios & Budgets: Historical and Forecasted R&D Budgets and Ratios Covering the Period 1986-1993.** Lincolnshire, Ill., Schonfeld, 1992. 203p. $325.00pa. ISBN 1-878339-16-8.

The principal section of this work groups companies by their primary 4-digit Standard Industrial Classification (SIC) codes. Later sections include the same figures and ratios contained here. Arranged by company, R&D budget figures include historical data for 1991, an estimate for 1992, and a forecast for 1993. Two sets of ratios also provide useful information. R&D-to-sales ratios include an estimate for the current year and the high and low ratios for data for the past six years. Another ratio compares each company's ratio to that for its principal industry. To calculate the R&D-to-gross margin ratios, the cost of goods sold has been subtracted from net sales. These ratios also include the high, low, and 1992 estimates. Finally, forecasted R&D spending and sales amounts are the bases for R&D and sales growth rates. Seven other sections regroup the information using various criteria. In addition to the obligatory alphabetical listing by company name, two sections list the top 1,000 companies by R&D budget size and R&D budget growth rate. Composite industry sections provide collective figures arranged by industry name, SIC code, size of R&D budget, and R&D budget growth rate.

At first glance the information looks complete. The introduction clearly and concisely explains all calculations, the accounting measures used, construction of the composite forecast, and bias in the industry model. However, the completeness of some information is questionable. A section titled "Thoughtful Considerations" discusses all the reasons why these estimates could be wrong. Moreover, the introduction does not state how the companies listed and the SIC categories analyzed were determined. This is especially troublesome because some SIC groups list little more than company names. Out of 52 companies listed, financial information was available only for 5. This may be because the publisher relied solely on data from government filings and published financial records.

The stated audiences are people who monitor their company's competitors, budget managers, and planners for R&D companies and companies that sell to R&D firms. Libraries affiliated with R&D companies or universities with business administration programs may find this text useful.

—**Susan D. Baird-Joshi**

296. **Standard Directory of Advertisers 1993.** New Providence, N.J., National Register Publishing/Reed Reference Publishing, 1993. 2v. index. $525.00pa./set. LC 15-21147. ISBN 0-87217-232-5.

297. **Standard Directory of Advertising Agencies: January 1993.** New Providence, N.J., National Register Publishing/Reed Reference Publishing. 1242p. index. $525.00pa. LC 66-6149. ISBN 0-87217-027-6.

Advertisers features changes in organization and format from earlier editions that improve the set's use. Its first volume provides complete records for more than 25,000 companies that spend at least $75,000 on national and regional advertising. Each company is listed alphabetically by business classification, and each record contains directory information, company data (including subsidiaries and key personnel), SIC (Standard Industrial Classification) codes and business description, advertising expenditures, advertising media used, advertising agencies used, and products advertised. Now arranged alphabetically, the business classifications are composed of several categories. A list of the classifications appears in the table of contents, and a complete list of all the categories serves as an index to the classifications. The prefatory material includes suggestions for use of the directory and supplementary lists.

The second volume contains brand name, SIC, and personnel indexes. The SIC index provides both alphabetical and numerical compendiums of the codes. The listings of the 200 largest advertisers are arranged by dollar amount and by classification. Both volumes are now narrower (3-column rather than 4-column), making them easier to handle and to shelve. One further improvement in the first volume would be to move the preface to the beginning, preceding the table of contents. At present it is lost in the middle of other lists.

No organizational changes are featured in *Advertising Agencies*. The 9,700-plus agencies included have at least one national or multistate account spending more than $75,000 annually on media, are recognized non-U.S. agencies with at least one U.S. account, or belong to one of the professional associations. Alphabetical and geographical indexes precede the full listing of advertising agencies, house agencies, media buying services, sales promotion agencies, and public relations firms. The personnel indexes consist of name and agency responsibilities indexes, the latter listing personnel by 18 functional areas, such as account coordinator and media director. A services and supplies section completes the directory. [R: Choice, Sept 93, p. 90]—**Joan B. Fiscella**

298. **Trade Shows Worldwide 1993: An International Directory of Events, Facilities, and Suppliers.** 7th ed. Valerie J. Webster, ed. Detroit, Gale, 1993. 1520p. index. $195.00pa. ISBN 0-8103-7630-X. ISSN 1046-4395.

Last reviewed in its 4th edition in ARBA 91 (see entry 280), this directory contains 5,947 listings of conferences, trade shows, and other such events. Numerous conference and convention centers, visitor and convention bureaus, and a wide variety of trade show services are featured as well. Data provided for most entries includes contact information, frequency, audience, attendance, space rental, principal exhibits, registration fees, exhibition space, meeting and hotel rooms, publications, date, and location. Four rankings allow comparison with similar properties. They cover square feet of exhibition space needed, square meters of exhibition space needed, square feet of convention center space available, and number of hotel rooms and nights needed. In addition, four indexes that provide extensive accessibility include a chronological index; a geographical index; a subject index; and a master index that lists all conferences, trade shows, sponsors, and associations.

When compared with the 4th edition, the 7th edition contains 462 more pages and has 847 more entries. It is also somewhat higher in price. Two discrepancies were found: the Kentucky Library Association is listed twice (entries 3224 and 8472), and the Indiana Library Association (entry 8080) recently has been renamed the Indiana Library Federation. This expensive but comprehensive source of trade show listings will continue to be useful to libraries whose clientele depended upon earlier editions.
—**O. Gene Norman**

299. Urdang, Laurence, and Janet Braunstein. **Every Bite a Delight and Other Slogans.** Detroit, Visible Ink Press/Gale, 1992. 437p. illus. index. $15.95pa. ISBN 0-8103-9423-5.

By the early eighteenth century, the word *slogan*, originally meaning a battle cry, had been attenuated to mean a catchphrase used as a rallying cry for political and other organizations. Many of these slogans have since become part of our language and culture. Arranged somewhat like a thesaurus, this book has approximately 5,000 entries grouped alphabetically under each of 126 thematic categories, such as adhesives, health and fitness, pest control, and travel. The category headings generally contain cross-references (prefaced by *see* and *see also*). At the back of the book all slogans appear in dictionary order; those beginning with *A*, *An*, and *The* are listed both under the article and by the words following the initial article.

Cultural and technological shifts can be deduced from a careful reading of this compendium. For example, coming across a washing machine company's claim that "Millions of women have their hearts set on a new Maytag," who can fail to realize how much our society has changed? It is unfortunate that, with the exception of presidential campaign slogans, the items are not dated, although source information is given.

The editorial criteria used in compiling these selections are not clear. The banal ("The state's greatest newspaper"—*Arizona Republic*, Phoenix) lies alongside the clever ("Capitalist tool"—*Forbes*). A historic rallying cry—"Hell no, we won't go"—shares space with an advertisement for an obscure product—*Penetro*: "the salve with a base of old-fashioned mutton suet." On the whole, this book can be taken as a sort of photograph album, filled with snapshots of popular culture. Although there are many interesting and nostalgic gems in this collection, the book is not an essential reference work. [R: Choice, Jan 93, p. 776]

—**Henry J. Ricardo**

OFFICE PRACTICES

300. De Vries, Mary A. **Complete Secretary's Handbook.** 7th ed. Englewood Cliffs, N.J., Prentice Hall Career & Personal Development, 1993. 707p. index. $19.95. HF5547.5.D6. 651.3'741. LC 93-23933. ISBN 0-13-159674-8.

This is an excellent reference tool for secretaries and other office professionals. As promised in "A Word About the Seventh Edition," this volume covers basic and advanced information in a manner that is useful to both the beginning and experienced secretary, as well as other office professionals. The writing is clear and concise, and the discussions of more recent advances in office technology are expertly woven into relevant topical sections. For example, the use of computerized information storage is incorporated into the discussion on developing an effective records-management system, thus encouraging the reader to see computer systems and traditional paper files as part of an overall information management system. It should also be noted that the price for this volume is very reasonable, relative to the wealth of information provided.

The work is divided into 5 parts with 18 chapters. The first three parts cover developing records management systems, word processing, preparing and publishing reports, handling mail, telecommunications, planning meetings and travel, keeping books and records, human relations, preparation of correspondence, and word usage and grammar. Part 4 is a quick reference to facts and figures, and part 5 is a glossary of terms. The work also contains a very detailed index. Suggestions on how to actively advocate for an enhancement or expansion of one's secretarial role in the changing office environment would be a useful addition to this text. The inclusion of glossary terms pertaining to government and nonprofit entities would also be helpful.—**Kathleen Nelson Boyle**

301. **The Professional Secretary's Handbook.** rev. ed. Boston, Houghton Mifflin, 1993. 388p. illus. index. $12.95. HF5547.5.P7. 651.3'741. LC 93-5055. ISBN 0-395-66979-0.

This work is divided into 15 chapters covering basic secretarial information, including word processing, preparing correspondence and other business documents, processing mail, managing records and calendars, planning conferences and meetings, making travel arrangements, using the telephone and other telecommunications systems, English usage and style rules, accounting and data processing, formatting technical and scientific material, and business law. In addition, there is information on the secretarial profession, career planning and advancement, and job search strategies.

This work contains useful information that is not always presented in a clear and easy-to-use format and, on occasion, is not as complete as desirable. For example, form-of-address information is presented in a lengthy and comprehensive table. Review of the related chapter supplies clues as to how to use this table, but there is no explanation with the table itself. Chapter 9 addresses punctuation (among other topics) and assumes a strong knowledge of English grammar and usage—topics not addressed until chapter 10. In the section covering word usage problems, *affect* and *effect* are not discussed. In addition, the index is fairly limited. Some chapters, such as that on travel, provide very helpful information; others are less helpful. This work can be a helpful reference tool but will require some effort to use.

—**Kathleen Nelson Boyle**

TAXATION

302. **The Ernst & Young Tax Guide 1993.** By Ernst & Young. Peter W. Bernstein, ed. New York, John Wiley, 1993. 712p. index. $13.95pa. ISBN 0-471-57816-9. ISSN 1059-809X.

Filling out U.S. personal income tax forms grows increasingly complex each year. The Internal Revenue Service (IRS) provides numerous publications to guide filers through the multiplicity of forms, but they are written more from an official than a user's point of view. Thus, several comprehensive guides have been made available by nongovernmental publishers to fill the need for a user-oriented guide. One of the most readable, without sacrificing detail, is *The Ernst & Young Tax Guide*. In addition to a standard table of contents and a detailed index, the book offers a special table of contents to increase accessibility to topics of interest to particular groups of taxpayers, such as homeowners. The Ernst & Young guide reproduces the official IRS Publication 17, *Your Federal Income Tax*, and adds explanations, comments, and tips to aid taxpayers in meeting their legal obligations at the lowest cost. Also of assistance are a summary of changes in the tax laws, a list of common errors, a list of easily overlooked deductions, a tax calendar, an organizer for information and records, a glossary of relevant terms, sample forms, and tips for future planning. The most commonly used IRS forms are included, and they can be copied and used for filing returns. The book can provide assistance and insight for those who prepare their own tax forms as well as for those who would like some background to better understand their tax consultants.

—**William C. Struning**

5 Education

GENERAL WORKS

Bibliography

303. **Bibliographic Guide to Education 1991.** New York, G. K. Hall, 1992. 681p. (Bibliographic Guides). $300.00. ISBN 0-8161-7159-9. ISSN 0147-6505.

All major publications related to the field of education that have been cataloged between September 1, 1990, and August 31, 1991, by the Teachers College of Columbia University appear in this comprehensive subject bibliography. While the intent is to supplement the original *Dictionary Catalog of the Teachers College Library* (see ARBA 71, entry 686), these annual volumes also include additional selected educational materials cataloged by the Research Libraries of the New York Public Library (NYPL) and the Library of Congress.

For each entry, complete Anglo-American-style cataloging information is provided, including ISBNs, all tracings, NYPL indicator, and NYPL classmark. The guide is presented alphabetically in a dictionary arrangement, and access is possible by main entry (e.g., personal or corporate author, body, name of conference, report), added entries (e.g., coauthors, editors, compilers, translators), titles, series titles, and subject headings.

A perusal of the subject headings reveals the wide scope of subject coverage, from courses of study and department of education reports across a wide geographical area to various psychological, sociological, political, and religious aspects of education. All subjects in the curriculum and teaching methodologies related to them are represented, from preschool through higher education. All languages are included in the guide.

This supplement includes bibliographical and governmental policy information related to home schooling, homeless youth, AIDS, distance education, aging, the education of women and minorities, and other issues that reflect the 1990s. All of the G. K. Hall Bibliographic Guides (they cover 23 different fields) provide major reference assistance to librarians and scholars who wish to locate sources on an international basis.—**Lois J. Buttlar**

Catalogs and Collections

304. **The ETS Test Collection Catalog. Volume 1: Achievement Tests and Measurement Devices.** 2d ed. Compiled by Test Collection, Educational Testing Service. Phoenix, Ariz., Oryx Press, 1993. 267p. index. $55.00pa. LB3051.E79. 016.3712'6. LC 92-36992. ISBN 0-89774-743-7.

This new edition of the first volume of *The ETS Test Collection Catalog* lists nearly 2,000 achievement tests and achievement-related equivalency, screening, diagnostic, and readiness measures. Approximately 50 percent of the tests are new or updated listings from the 1986 edition (see ARBA 87, entry 314). The book's introduction has also been expanded and improved, affording greater understanding of indexing procedures, the subject content of other volumes, and the ETS Test Collection itself.

The format of this volume remains the same as others in the series: Nonevaluative descriptive entries for tests are listed in accession number order and include test title, author, descriptors and identifiers, age or grade level, an abstract, and availability information. The catalog has author, title, and subject indexes. There is no cumulative author/title/subject index for the six volumes of this catalog. Many of the indexing terms appear in more than one volume, and some tests are listed in more than one volume. A cumulative index for the series, published separately or included within the latest volume, would improve access to what is already an indispensable source of information about tests. Libraries that serve patrons in education and psychology will want to purchase this revised edition. [R: RBB, 1 Mar 93, p. 1251]

—Deborah V. Rollins

Dictionaries and Encyclopedias

305. Hirsch, E. D., Jr., Joseph F. Kett, and James Trefil. **The Dictionary of Cultural Literacy.** 2d ed. Boston, Houghton Mifflin, 1993. 619p. illus. maps. index. $24.95. E169.I.H6. 973'.03. LC 93-19568. ISBN 0-395-65597-8.

The revised version of this work presents current U.S. culture, having corrected some problems noted in the first edition (see ARBA 90, entry 304). Key additions reflect multiculturalism as well as recent events (e.g., the Gulf War). The organizational structure, employing 23 topical sections (e.g., U.S. politics, technology), has been retained. Entries continue to combine concise definitions with explanations of cultural significance, thereby clarifying ideas (e.g., equal opportunity), events (e.g., Civil War, Three Mile Island), and individuals (e.g., Thurgood Marshall). Search assistance is offered through the cross-references, pronunciation guide, topical index, and illustrations (e.g., human anatomy, political boundaries). While not replacing subject or language dictionaries, this work is essential for libraries serving patrons trying to adapt to and understand this portion of our very complex culture. Here, a diverse audience can investigate the significance of political terminology (e.g., isolationism), the meaning of common expressions (e.g., "elbow grease"), and the impact of ethnic contributions. Despite debate about what qualifies as general usage, this is a desirable acquisition for both home and library use. [R: WLB, Dec 93, pp. 76-77]

—Sandra E. Belanger

Handbooks and Yearbooks

306. Bishop, Lloyd, and Paula E. Lester. **Instrumentation in Education: An Anthology.** Hamden, Conn., Garland, 1993. 347p. index. (Source Books on Education, v.39; Garland Reference Library of Social Science, v.811). $55.00. Z7204.P88B57. 016.3'0028'7. LC 92-40361. ISBN 0-8153-0638-5.

This anthology brings together psychometric information about various instruments that have been used to measure constructs in education and the social sciences. It is designed for the researcher attempting to find available measures such as scales, questionnaires, surveys, indexes, and inventories. It includes instruments that were developed as reported in the research literature from 1950 to 1992. The main focus is on instruments dealing with the measurement of organizations and professional behavior. It does not include information on measurement dealing with topics such as personality assessment, student achievement, or related areas of research. A critique of each instrument is presented, along with comprehensive bibliographies.

Chapters represent categories containing instruments designed to analyze an organization, to evaluate the professional characteristics of an individual in the organization, to assess organizational behavior of individuals as they interact with the organization, to investigate the behavior of individuals independent of organizational affiliation, to analyze relationships between the professional and the organization, and to deal with diagnostic surveys developed for assessment and evaluation of organizations generally and schools and classrooms in particular. Three indexes have been provided to assist readers in locating appropriate instruments: an author index, a title index, and a category index with entries arranged by categories and subcategories. [R: Choice, Dec 93, p. 580]—**Edith M. Dorenfeld**

307. **The Guide to the Evaluation of Educational Experiences in the Armed Services, 1992.** Washington, D.C., American Council on Education; distr., Phoenix, Ariz., Oryx Press, 1992. 4v. index. $75.00pa./set. ISBN 0-8268-1198-0.

For 50 years the American Council on Education (ACE) has been involved in the evaluation and assessment of military education programs in order to help civilian and military communities provide credit for learning acquired by veterans and active-duty personnel in the military sector. Most of the nation's colleges and universities award such credit. This guide is the standard reference work of the evaluation system for military training in the United States. Recommendations found in the guide have assisted educational institutions in granting credit to hundreds of thousands of service people. The guide contains recommendations for hundreds of formal courses offered by the Army, the Army Military Operations Specialties (MOS), the Air Force, the Coast Guard, the Marine Corps, the Navy, and the Department of Defense. The set has information obtained from evaluations conducted through June 1992.

Courses listed are given on a full-time basis and represent 45 academic hours with qualified instructors. Evaluation teams of at least three subject-matter specialists (e.g., college professors, deans) evaluate courses on the basis of syllabi, texts, training manuals, and interviews conducted with course instructors. Each separate course entry contains the course number, location of delivery, length of course, evaluation dates, course outcomes or objectives, description of instruction, and credit-hour recommendations of the evaluation team. Each volume also contains a keyword index, an explanation of the evaluation system used by ACE, a course number index, and sample records and forms used to evaluate the learning experiences of military personnel. As the nation experiences a massive conversion of military personnel to civilian status, the usefulness of this set will no doubt take on new importance in postsecondary educational institutions.—**Jerry D. Flack**

308. **The World of Learning 1993.** 43d ed. London, Europa; distr., Detroit, Gale, 1992. 2072p. index. $330.00. LC 47-30172. ISBN 0-946653-79-8. ISSN 0084-2117.

Perennial standards in the reference world are often long established. This is true of *The World of Learning*, which is now in its 43d full-packed edition. Organizations and institutions of all kinds involved in the production, dissemination, and storage of knowledge figure here, generally arranged according to local classification practices. The foreword reflects on the recent political upheavals and realizes that stability has not yet returned. The continuing effects of the dissolution of the Soviet bloc and Yugoslavia and the "velvet divorce" of Czechoslovakia, as well as national reorganizations of education systems, mean that some entries are inevitably inaccurate. One suggestion might be to include cross-references from, or a separate index to, old names of organizations and institutions, at least where there have been changes since the previous edition. Otherwise, the only criticism might be the inclusion of international organizations in the library/information field under the misleading rubric of "Bibliography." Nevertheless, most of the information is backed by the authoritative weight of a reputable publisher and a long-established title.—**Johan Koren**

CANADA

309. Gibson, Dyanne. **Gibson's Guide to Graduate and Professional Programs at Ontario Universities.** Toronto and Buffalo, N.Y., University of Toronto Press, 1992. 205p. $19.95pa. 378.1'553'09713. ISBN 0-8020-6909-6.

A companion to Gibson's *Student's Guide to Ontario Universities* (see ARBA 92, entry 304) this handbook offers a context for graduate study with four preliminary chapters of counseling information. Chapter 5 highlights unique programs and is a selective list; missing are the University of Toronto's Master of Museum Studies and that of art conservation at McGill-Queen's University. A discursive chapter on 13 areas of professional study has details about enrollment, comparison of institutions, areas of specialization, and related programs and disciplines. University profiles complete the work. Each has an overview of the school, a note on facilities, a list of graduate degrees offered, and a summary of each professional program. Appendixes identify admission and language tests, international equivalents, and sources for funding information.

Inevitably, a guide based on survey data will be uneven in coverage and detail. Gibson's work is no exception. Part of the responsibility rests with administrators to replace all the N/A responses in the next edition. There are also anomalies; for example, the University of Guelph is listed as Guelph University. An index would be helpful. For students considering a professional program, this book provides a handy, sometimes provocative, starting point; but for graduate work in the arts and sciences, the information is cursory and scattered.—**Patricia Fleming**

310. Gibson, Dyanne. **Gibson's Student Guide to Western Canadian Universities.** Toronto and Buffalo, N.Y., University of Toronto Press, 1993. 289p. maps. $16.95pa. 378.712. ISBN 0-8020-6934-7.

This guide is addressed primarily to high school students considering attending a university in Alberta, British Columbia, Manitoba, or Saskatchewan. In the initial chapters, the author, who teaches at York University and has also written *The Student's Guide to Ontario Universities* (see ARBA 92, entry 304), offers general guidance on the nature and purpose of a university education; assessing one's interests, skills, and life direction; and investigating, choosing, and applying to a university.

The remainder of the work contains profiles of some 20 universities and degree-granting university colleges, with a lengthy chapter on interpreting this information. The profiles, averaging four to five pages in length, are based on survey questionnaires completed by the schools and are current for the 1990-1991 academic year. Each includes a capsule description of the school, admission requirements and contact information, enrollment and student body composition, scholarships, athletic and academic facilities, and detailed lists of undergraduate and professional programs offered. Residence facilities, student services, and provisions for nontraditional and international students are also covered.

The high proportion of expository content and the fact that much of the institution-specific information is available elsewhere, such as in the *Commonwealth Universities Yearbook* (see ARBA 87, entry 345), lessen this work's importance as a reference source. Its chief value is its convenient combination of information on the universities of a specific region with general advice and guidance for the prospective student.—**Gregory M. Toth**

311. Howell, Michael J. **Winning Scholarships: A Student's Guide to Entrance Awards at Ontario Universities and Colleges.** Toronto and Buffalo, N.Y., University of Toronto Press, 1992. 257p. index. $19.95pa. 378.3'4'09713. ISBN 0-8020-7720-X.

Although this guide to scholarships was written with Ontario high school students in mind, it would be useful to other Canadian students as well. In fact, the first half of the book contains advice that is relevant to anyone seeking undergraduate scholarships. There are sections on the importance of community service and extracurricular activities as well as grades; the mechanics of actually applying for awards, such as filling out applications, requesting letters of recommendation, and interviews; and the role of the parent in this process. The second half of the book lists awards from universities and community colleges in Ontario. Many of them are available to any Canadian student. There are also sections on general and employer-sponsored awards. Again, most of these are for use at any institution of higher education, not just in Ontario. Some of the awards are available to students from the United States. The book would be useful in all Canadian libraries.—**Christine E. King**

EARLY CHILDHOOD EDUCATION

312. Friedes, Harriet. **The Preschool Resource Guide: Educating and Entertaining Children Aged Two through Five.** New York, Plenum, 1993. 247p. $27.50; $17.50pa. Z7164.C5F76. 016.30523'3. LC 92-41250. ISBN 0-306-44464-X; 0-306-44473-9pa.

This work brings together a wide variety of available resources that have both educational and entertainment value for the two- to five-year-old child. A clear consideration has been made to recommend only that which is age-appropriate. The guide is prefaced by a chapter that details signs of growth and development for ages two through five. In addition, it provides examples of the kinds of activities and experiences that would suit this age range and enhance a child's life experience in a very natural way. The book is then divided into two main sections. The first covers resources available for children; the second, resources for adults who work with small children. Eleven chapters address such areas as books, computer software, toys and games, audio recordings, and professional organizations. Each begins by discussing generally, and in an age-related way, the specific topic. Both traditional and creative uses of the resources are suggested, as well as criteria for selecting materials. The chapter then lists resources available, including both descriptive and evaluative comments on each item. The book concludes with notes on kindergarten readiness and toy safety.

This guide to resources for the preschool child is of unquestionable value. While the author readily admits that no work of this kind can be truly exhaustive, this book is presented in an educationally sound manner with a very usable format. It would be of great use to any adult who works with young children. [R: BL, 1 April 93, p. 1444]—**Martha Miller Yazhari**

313. **Profiles in Childhood Education 1931-1960.** Wheaton, Md., Association for Childhood Education International, 1992. 136p. $14.00pa. LA2301.A27. 372.11'0092'2. LC 92-30308. ISBN 0-87173-127-4.

Celebrating the 100th anniversary of the Association of Childhood Education International (ACEI), this brief specialized source will appeal to libraries with comprehensive collections of early childhood education materials. Biographical sketches of 26 leaders from 1931 to 1960 are reprinted from volumes 61-69 (1985-1993) of *Childhood Education*, ACEI's professional journal. Honorees were chosen from a list of 200 names, based upon their influence on administration, government, literature, teaching, writing, speaking, or professional contributions. Included are such dignitaries as Leland B. Jacobs and Laura Zirbes. Each profile is two to five pages long. The authors of the profiles are in some respects as well known as the subjects. Unfortunately, photographs are not included. This book will appeal to those interested in the history of early childhood education in the twentieth century or in biographies of early childhood educators.—**Ilene F. Rockman**

314. Spodek, Bernard, ed. **Handbook of Research on the Education of Young Children.** New York, Macmillan, 1993. 568p. index. $65.00. LB1119.H25. 372.21'072. LC 92-21051. ISBN 0-02-897405-0.

This resource is a fine contribution to Macmillan's series of handbooks on education. Part 1, "Child Development and Early Education," includes articles on such topics as cognitive development, motor development, and peer relationships. Part 2, "Foundations of Early Childhood Educational Curriculum," offers a welcome variety of subjects: the role of play, math, social studies, science, music, multicultural education, electronic media, and so forth. Articles in part 3, "Foundations of Early Childhood Educational Policy," range from readiness screening to play environments to parental influence. One particularly welcome article is on teacher preparation. Finally, part 4 offers essays on "Research Strategies for Early Childhood Education."

The contributors, largely from the United States, are highly respected researchers and scholars. The articles are timely and usually thorough. Introductory abstracts would be useful; however, the article titles are generally accurate in their descriptions of the subjects. This excellent resource will be especially attractive to scholars, researchers, writers, teacher education students, and anyone interested in a well-organized overview of early childhood education. [R: RQ, Fall 93, pp. 128-29]—**Suzanne I. Barchers**

315. Woodill, Gary A., Judith Bernhard, and Lawrence Prochner, eds. **International Handbook of Early Childhood Education.** Hamden, Conn., Garland, 1992. 562p. index. (Garland Reference Library of Social Science, v.598). $95.00. LB1139.23.I68. 372.21. LC 92-23846. ISBN 0-8240-4939-X.

Solid in its scope, contents, and currency of information, this handbook contains original essays that compare the history, development, and growth of early childhood education (ECE) in 46 countries on 5 continents. Essays are written and signed by indigenous educators. Length is approximately 10 pages per country, with issues such as curriculum, teacher training, parental involvement, staffing, and overall funding covered. Some essays also include elements of special education and the relationship between preschool and primary education in the country.

The source brings together information not easily found in other places, as several of the countries have little English-language material written about their systems of education. Moreover, unlike the Praeger Special Series in Comparative Education of the 1980s, this source focuses on contemporary education at an early childhood level, with contributions from Africa, Asia, Europe, the Middle East, and the Americas. The work concludes with a bibliography of comparative English-language publications, contributor biographies, and a 10-page index.

This book will be useful in comparing global education practices, identifying the role of government ministries and agencies in shaping ECE policy, comparing models of education, assessing curricula, and answering such questions as "What is the global influence of Maria Montessori?" It complements *Early Childhood Education in Asia and the Pacific: A Source Book* (Garland, 1992). Recommended for students, faculty, and researchers. [R: Choice, July/Aug 93, pp. 1818-19; WLB, Mar 93, p. 111]

—Ilene F. Rockman

ELEMENTARY AND SECONDARY EDUCATION

316. **Educational Opportunity Guide, 1993: A Directory of Programs for the Gifted.** Durham, N.C., Duke University Talent Identification Program, 1993. 276p. index. $15.00pa.

At the same time that public school programs for talented students have been eliminated in many school districts for both financial and philosophical reasons, independent, state-sponsored, and other special programs for this population have flourished. School personnel, especially library media specialists and counselors, can better counsel and serve gifted and talented students if they have ready access to information about such options. The *Educational Opportunity Guide* fits this need admirably. It provides detailed descriptions of 340 summer and academic year programs for talented students. The programs are listed alphabetically by state and city. Information about international programs is also provided. Entries follow a set format. After the name and site location of each program, a descriptive overview of the program is provided. Admissions criteria, cost, age or grade level served, and a contact person are furnished.

A separate directory indexes all programs across 27 separate categories (e.g., foreign language programs; programs with scholarships for minority students). Another directory provides information about 120 different academic competitions for talented students. Directories of state department of education consultants and state associations for gifted and talented students are also included.

Most school personnel have a general awareness of special programs for gifted and talented students, but they frequently lack specific information about vital programs. This resourceful and easy-to-use guide provides a fine service in collecting and disseminating a huge amount of pertinent data for those who work with parents to guide talented students. [R: Choice, Sept 93, p. 78; RBB, 1 May 93, p. 1618]

—Jerry D. Flack

317. Haider, Thomas John, and Kathleen S. Nehmer, eds. **Educators Grade Guide to Free Teaching Aids.** 39th ed. Randolph, Wis., Educators Progress Service, 1993. 1v. (various paging). index. $44.95 looseleaf w/binder. LC 56-2444. ISBN 0-87708-253-7.

This work is a selection guide to 2,161 print educational materials that are available without charge to elementary and junior high school educators. The items listed have been evaluated for their educational appropriateness, timeliness, arrangement, style, suitability, and freedom from undesirable features. All the titles listed are available from the issuing agencies, and all the sources are listed along with their addresses.

This edition of the guide contains 167 new sources and 1,100 new titles. Some 1,062 titles listed in the 38th edition have been withdrawn. An explanation of how to use the guide contains sample letters requesting materials and directions on how best to approach issuing agencies. The materials are arranged by subject area, with a separate listing for visual and audiovisual teaching aids. Within the subject area, entries are arranged by title. Each annotation includes a brief description of the content and information necessary for accessing the item. Rarely is mention made of the number of pages in booklets or of the appropriate grade or age levels of the intended audience.

Title and subject indexes are included as well as a complete list of addresses for the sources. There is also a list of agencies that will make their materials available to Canadian educators. Of particular interest to teachers is a list of free professional growth and reference materials.

The last section of the guide details four sample units of study for use in the upper grades and junior high school. Each unit depends upon the use of free instructional materials ordered through the guide. A 40-page supplement of additional annotations is appended. This easy-to-use resource should be a useful and popular item in elementary and middle school learning centers.—**Joanne Kelly**

318. Haider, Thomas John, ed. **Elementary Teachers Guide to Free Curriculum Materials.** 50th ed. Randolph, Wis., Educators Progress Service, 1993. 384p. index. $24.95pa. LC 44-52255. ISBN 0-87708-254-5.

As with other titles in the series, this source has been completely revised since the last edition. More than 1,000 items have been added (new entries are starred for easy identification) and 978 deleted. The editor notes that industry-sponsored educational materials are included if they encourage students to inquire, discover, and develop ideas that contribute to knowledge and understanding of self, others, and the environment. These include such diverse offerings as nutrition, culture, and science experiment kits from sponsors such as the American Gas Association and the U.S. Department of Agriculture. Canadian organizations are also included. A statistical analysis reveals the majority of items to be in the area of health and physical education, closely followed by world affairs and teacher references. Although users are instructed to use official stationery when making a request from the more than 500 distributors, these guidelines can be flexibly applied, especially by homeschoolers.

Similar to previous editions, pages are color-coordinated to differentiate between the items and the separate title, subject, and source indexes. Items are alphabetically listed by title, with a brief descriptive annotation noting whether single or classroom quantities are available. Most items are free and do not have to be returned to the sponsoring organization.

This is an economical source for curriculum or education libraries. Students will appreciate the added feature of an evaluation guide from the National Association for Industry-Education Cooperation.

—**Ilene F. Rockman**

319. **Patterson's American Education. Volume LXXXIX.** 1993 ed. Mount Prospect, Ill., Educational Directories, 1993. 857p. index. $72.00. LC 4-12953. ISBN 0-910536-55-4. ISSN 0079-0230.

320. **Patterson's Elementary Education. Volume V.** 1993 ed. Mount Prospect, Ill., Educational Directories, 1993. 925p. $72.00. ISBN 0-910536-56-2. ISSN 1044-1417.

These two volumes provide a nearly complete list of schools in the United States, with the exception of private and parochial elementary schools with fewer than 100 students and special-needs elementary schools, and private secondary schools with fewer than 100 students and public special-needs secondary schools. Updated information on schools is provided in basically the same format as in past editions (see ARBA 91, entries 305-06). It is important that the user read the section at the front of each book to extract all the information available. For instance, without an explanation of the grade codes, it is doubtful that a reader would even know they are provided—a major problem with the format. In addition, the user needs to be aware that the addresses are not necessarily physical addresses but may be mailing addresses only. Still, the guides are a useful reference to the educational community as a whole and to any business needing access to the school market. —**Jo Anne H. Ricca**

HIGHER EDUCATION

Atlases

321. Fonseca, James W., and Alice C. Andrews. **The Atlas of American Higher Education.** New York, New York University Press; distr., New York, Columbia University Press, 1993. 257p. maps. index. $40.00. G1201.E68F6. 378.73'022'3. LC 93-522. ISBN 0-8147-2610-0.

Fonseca and Andrews's approach to their atlas is unique. The innovative presentation, along with a careful selection of statistical material, makes the volume an essential reference work. It is divided into 10 sections: background, enrollment, students and faculty, cultural diversity, specialized institutions, two-year colleges, outcomes of higher education, student costs and student aid, financing of higher education, and a summary. Each section contains a number of statistical elements accompanied by a map, usually of the United States, that displays the underlying demographic variables. Statistical elements within the larger sections are presented in a short paragraph or two of text that defines and explains the subject and its relevance. The maps add to the understanding of the material by showing how the statistics are spread over the United States.

While the presentation is exemplary, the type of information included is what makes the work valuable. Only the most important data have been selected from the vast amount available—data that highlight significant patterns in higher education in the United States. Dozens of maps provide information concerning total enrollment in higher education, enrollment by state, minority enrollment percentages, degrees conferred in various subjects, tuition compared by state, and the financing of higher education. Summary chapters bring much of the information together for easy comparison. A balance is achieved between public and private colleges and between four- and two-year institutions. The summary section provides as succinct a summary of trends in higher education as can be found anywhere. Within this summary is an analysis of the educational assessments conducted by institutions of higher education during the past few years, along with two informative assessment maps. *The Atlas of American Higher Education* is a valuable tool for students, college faculty and administrators, and anyone interested in obtaining information concerning the demographics of American higher education. [R: RBB, 15 Dec 93, p. 774; WLB, Dec 93, p. 75]—**Robert L. Wick**

Bibliography

322. Nordquist, Joan, comp. **The Multicultural Education Debate in the University: A Bibliography.** Santa Cruz, Calif., Reference and Research Services, 1992. 63p. (Contemporary Social Issues: A Bibliographic Series, no.25). $15.00pa. ISBN 0-937855-48-0.

This selective list of approximately 500 books, journal articles, government publications, and pamphlets focuses on various aspects of a topical issue. The material selected for inclusion is current (published in the late 1980s and early 1990s), represents different social and political viewpoints, and includes what is considered to be the authoritative work on the subject. The entries are arranged in six broad subject areas: the political correctness debate, the intellectual and political climate of the university, freedom of speech on campus, multicultural education in the university, Eurocentrism in the university curriculum, and women in the university curriculum. In each subject area, books are listed first, with reviews following the titles considered the most authoritative in two of the areas. Journal articles are then listed alphabetically by author. In addition, a section of resources covers relevant organizations. Each citation has basic bibliographic information. Brief, descriptive annotations and pagination for books would have been useful inclusions.

The book includes a brief introduction to the entire series and introductory remarks about each of the subject areas. Information about the aims, intended audience, and level of the bibliography is lacking. More information on the criteria used for selection of items is also needed. The bibliographic sources used to compile the bibliography are listed; however, the dates of searches in each source are not included. An author and title index would also have been a valuable feature.

This bibliography brings together relevant, hard-to-find material on multicultural education. It is current, timely, convenient, and manageable. The whole series is a valuable resource for academic, special, and public library users.—**Susan J. Freiband**

323. Olevnik, Peter P., with others. **American Higher Education: A Guide to Reference Sources.** Westport, Conn., Greenwood Press, 1993. 211p. index. (Bibliographies and Indexes in Education, no.12). $55.00. Z5815.U5044. 016.378'73. LC 93-25015. ISBN 0-313-27749-4.

This work is an extensive and comprehensive list of reference sources to the literature of higher education in the United States. Coverage extends from 1861 through 1992. Eight hundred titles were selected out of more than 1,600 and annotated. However, missing from the book are A. Monroe Stowe's *Studies in Collegiate Education* in the 1930-1931 *Bulletin of Lynchburg College* and Beverly A. Belson's *The Student Affairs Profession* (American College Personnel Association, 1983). The material is organized into a guide to the literature; dictionaries and encyclopedias; directories; handbooks, manuals, and other compendiums; almanacs, statistical guides, and yearbooks; abstracts, indexes, and reports; bibliographical sources; and computerized databases. The indexing is excellent—there are separate author, title, and subject indexes.

Olevnik has done a superb and creditable job in compiling this definitive bibliography to reference sources in U.S. higher education. The only shortcoming of the work is the unattractive print.
—**Gordon H. Dunkin**

324. Sparks, Linda, comp. **College Admissions: A Selected, Annotated Bibliography.** Westport, Conn., Greenwood Press, 1993. 187p. index. (Bibliographies and Indexes in Education, no.11). $47.95. Z5814.U7S685. 016.3781'056. LC 92-34759. ISBN 0-313-28483-0.

This work is a list of various sources in the area of college admissions categorized by general admission, marketing and recruitment, admission offices and officers, and foreign admissions. Although it was stated in the preface that no time limit was placed on materials, it would have been helpful had Sparks given the time span for works cited. The highlight of the work is its inclusive author index and very good subject index. This reviewer especially appreciated the entry for "gifted," which is not always available in similar works.

Missing from the book are many of the Jossey-Bass publications and *An Annotated and Extended Bibliography of Higher Education Marketing* (see ARBA 86, entry 1593). A good ERIC database search might turn up sufficient citations for far less than the cost of this book. [R: Choice, July/Aug 93, p. 1755]
—**Gordon H. Dunkin**

Directories

325. Barnett, Lynn, ed. **Beacon College Project Directory.** Washington, D.C., American Association of Community Colleges, 1992. 57p. index. $12.00pa. ISBN 0-87117-253-4.

The impetus behind the Beacon College Project was a 1988 report of the American Association of Community Colleges, which advocated creative and innovative approaches to expanding educational opportunity and enhancing the role of education in work force development. Most important, it encouraged community colleges to develop partnerships among themselves and with the communities they serve. Funded in large part by a Kellogg grant, the project is a consortium of consortia, each made up of a Beacon College and several affiliates and committed to a plan for collaborative programs or services to meet a common community need. Each revolves around a specific need, issue, or goal, such as improving retention of at-risk students, addressing issues associated with diverse communities and student bodies, enhancing academic skills for transfer students, promoting faculty development, establishing relationships with public schools and local business, encouraging student leadership, and developing innovative instructional methods and materials.

This directory, then, is a list of the 26 Beacon Colleges and their more than 200 cooperating community, junior, and technical colleges in 20 states. Each entry identifies the Beacon College or flagship campus and includes the title and a description of the initiative. A list of the associate colleges—those affiliated with the consortium—follows and includes directory information and the name of each institution's project coordinator. Some entries include Project Partners, or cooperating governmental agencies, community organizations, or corporations. There is an index by college name.

Who will find this directory useful? Certainly participants in the project itself. Most others can rely on the ERIC depository copy of this directory, available in microfiche format only as ED 349 075.
—**Pam M. Baxter**

326. Blum, Laurie. **Free Money for Athletic Scholarships.** New York, Henry Holt, 1993. 194p. index. (Free Money Series). $35.00; $14.95pa. GV583.B56. 796'.079. LC 93-4265. ISBN 0-8050-2659-2; 0-8050-2660-6pa.

327. Blum, Laurie. **Free Money for College from the Government.** New York, Henry Holt, 1993. 201p. index. (Free Money Series). $35.00; $14.95pa. LB2337.2.B573. 378.3'025'73. LC 93-13486. ISBN 0-8050-2661-4; 0-8050-2662-2pa.

328. Blum, Laurie. **Free Money from Colleges and Universities.** New York, Henry Holt, 1993. 175p. index. (Free Money Series). $35.00; $14.95pa. LB2337.2.B597. 378.3'025'73. LC 92-44655. ISBN 0-8050-2657-6; 0-8050-2658-4pa.

These books provide basic, up-to-date information on hundreds of financial aid sources for students. *Free Money for Athletic Scholarships* lists colleges and universities that give such awards to students. Important information given for each school includes a list of sports, number of scholarships, average size of scholarships, range of scholarships, and contact individuals. A list of athletic associations is also included. *Free Money for College from the Government* provides information on approximately 400 sources at both the federal and state levels. The data found in this book are mostly duplicated in other financial aid books. A description and eligibility requirements are given for the larger federal programs. *Free Money from Colleges and Universities* lists sources that are awarded by schools. These sources are listed by state and then by college and university. An index of school names and fields of study is included. This book provides only a sampling of the available aid; many schools are not even listed. Students will need to contact individual schools for further information on financial aid.

Some of the material provided in these books is found in such titles as *Scholarships, Fellowships and Loans* (see ARBA 93, entry 377). Libraries serving patrons looking for narrowly focused types of financial aid will find them useful.—**Carl Pracht**

329. Blum, Laurie. **Free Money for Graduate School.** rev. ed. New York, Henry Holt, 1993. 300p. index. (Free Money Series). $35.00; $14.95pa. LB2337.2.B58. 378.3'025'73. LC 92-44654. ISBN 0-8050-2655-X; 0-8050-2656-8pa.

This book provides a list of more than 1,000 grants and scholarships available in the United States and abroad. The information is arranged into broad subject categories that include humanities and social sciences, biological and agricultural sciences, physical sciences and mathematics, business, education, health and law, women only, ethnic only, and study and research abroad. Within these categories the granting institutions are listed alphabetically. Each entry provides address, telephone number, restrictions, application information, deadlines, and amounts available. This new edition has fully corrected listings from past issues and provides numerous additional grant sources. Appendixes contain sample applications, sample project descriptions, and a sample reference list. A four-item bibliography of other grant books is provided.

While the title implies that the work is devoted to sources of funds for graduate studies, many granting institutions listed also provide funds for undergraduate studies and even nondegree programs. *Free Money for Graduate School* does not provide as large a list or as much detail in some entries as the *Grants Register* (see ARBA 92, entry 295), which is published twice a year, or *The Directory of Research Grants* (see ARBA 93, entry 873), which is published annually, but it is a handy source of basic grant information. The work is obviously intended to be purchased by grant-seeking students and may not add substantially to basic library holdings both in print form or CD-ROM lists now available. The work is recommended for small branch public libraries or high school collections that require a quick reference work on grants, and larger library collections that wish to obtain everything available on grants and awards for their patrons.—**Robert L. Wick**

330. Bowman, J. Wilson. **America's Black Colleges.** South Pasadena, Calif., Sandcastle Publishing, 1992. 242p. maps. index. $14.95pa. LC2781.B6. 378.73. LC 92-60007. ISBN 0-9627756-1-4.

With a foreword by Marva Collins, founder and director of the famous Westside Preparatory School in Chicago, making an argument for the significance of Black colleges, this directory identifies all of the major, predominantly Black colleges in the United States. Names of institutions are arranged alphabetically within the states. Each entry includes an outline map of the United States indicating the home state of the institution and a one- or two-paragraph history of each college with a chronology of name changes, location, address, and telephone number. Also provided are a description of the college, with academic divisions, fees, and a list of distinguished alumni. Six appendixes include such things as an alphabetical list of the four-year colleges and universities, with local addresses; a list of those colleges that are supported by the United Negro College Fund; and a list of Black colleges that offer doctoral degrees. One of the most interesting sections of the appendixes is the list of firsts in Black history, in which one finds the names of Theodore Wright, first African American to receive a degree from a theological seminary in the United States; Jewel Cobb, first African-American female to head a major West Coast university; and Providence Hospital, first training hospital for African-American nurses. This directory is particularly recommended to high school students who are considering a predominantly Black college and the advantages it might offer, as well as to their parents and counselors.—**Melvin M. Bowie**

331. Cassidy, Daniel J. **Graduate Scholarship Directory: The Complete Guide to Scholarships, Fellowships, Grants and Loans....** 3d ed. Hawthorne, N.J., Career Press, 1993. 369p. index. $24.95pa. LB2337.2.C36. 378.2'025'73. LC 93-8799. ISBN 1-56414-113-6.

Over the last 10 years, Americans have spent more than $2.2 trillion on education of all kinds—a staggering figure. One wonders how it is possible to spend so much yet get so little in return. While the performance of students in school nosedives, the cost of attending skyrockets. But help may be on the way. The good news is that some $7 billion is available from nonfederal sources. The disconcerting news is that more than $6 billion went unclaimed. Where is all this money? In corporations and other private sectors of the economy. But sources to it are most easily found in the pages of this book. Subjects are listed alphabetically by field of study. A quick index and a general index aid accessibility. Under each entry is the name of the fund, its address, the amount offered, eligibility requirements, and whether the grant is renewable.

This is a must purchase for all colleges, junior colleges, and large public libraries. For students needing assistance, the only limitations they will find are those that depend on intellect.—**Mark Y. Herring**

332. Cassidy, Daniel J. **International Scholarship Directory: The Complete Guide to Financial Aid for Study Anywhere in the World.** 3d ed. Hawthorne, N.J., Career Press, 1993. 333p. index. $24.95pa. LB2337.2.C364. 378.3'025. LC 93-14516. ISBN 1-56414-112-8.

Easily accessible, well indexed, and information-crammed are modest terms to describe this outstanding reference for students seeking financial aid for study inside or outside the United States, regardless of their national origin. Selected from National Scholarship Research Service, the largest private sector financial aid research database, this guide provides 1,513 sources of financial aid for undergraduate, graduate, and even postdoctoral education.

Several indexes make the financial aid sources in the directory readily accessible. A "quick find" index includes each source's number prefaced by either a "U" for undergraduate financial aid, a "G" for graduate, or "GU" for both. A second index to fields of study records the same numbers within specific fields of study, such as earth science, and such subcategories as astronomy, energy, and geology.

Information about scholarships and awards includes a brief description of the aid offered, qualifications, application deadlines, and addresses and telephone numbers for further inquiries. Another section contains a two-page bibliography of other financial aid publications, a description of the National Scholarship Research Service and its offerings, and a sample form letter with which to request an application and program description.

The last three indexes offer a list of publications related to specific careers and occupations and to obtaining scholarships and loans for education, a numbered and alphabetical list of organizations associated with various occupations or professions, and an alphabetical list that cites the reference number for every award, book, or career association mentioned in the text. This directory should be a mandatory purchase for all high school, public, and academic libraries.—**Kathleen W. Craver**

333. Cassidy, Daniel J. **The Scholarship Book.** 4th ed. Englewood Cliffs, N.J., Prentice Hall Career & Personal Development, 1993. 400p. index. $29.95; $19.95pa. LB2337.2.C37. 378.3'4'0973. LC 93-5030. ISBN 0-13-799537-7; 0-13-799545-8pa.

One of the key directories to private sector scholarships, grants, and loans for undergraduates, this work has been compiled from the database of the world's largest private college financial aid research service. Included are brief profiles for 1,730 organizations. Each profile includes standard directory information, the amount and type of financial support offered, deadline dates for applications, fields of study covered by financial aid, and any additional notes regarding qualifications for applicants. Supplementary sections include listings of more than 100 publications that might be of additional use to applicants, as well as contact information for organizations that provide career information. A brief preface and a "Quick Find Index" (arranged by subject or career category) precede the main text. An alphabetical index by title of organization or scholarship closes the work.

This book should find its way into the collections of every counselor and library in the secondary school setting, as well as public and academic library collections. As a basic directory to further information about financial aid, it is invaluable.—**Edmund F. SantaVicca**

334. **Choose a Christian College: A Guide to Academically Challenging Colleges Committed to a Christ-Centered Campus Life.** 3d ed. Princeton, N.J., Peterson's Guides, 1992. 131p. illus. index. $12.95pa. L901.C57. 378.73. LC 92-22622. ISBN 1-56079-217-5.

This newest in the Peterson's family is not just what its subtitle suggests, but actually the official guide to member schools of the Christian College Coalition, an association of 84 small to medium-sized Protestant colleges that specialize in the liberal arts and sciences and that integrate Biblical faith with academics, emphasize a Christ-centered campus life, and require a personal Christian commitment from all full-time faculty. One can find Loma Nazarene and Wheaton College here but not Southern Methodist University, Union University (the oldest Baptist college in the United States), Notre Dame, or hundreds of others.

Similar to other Peterson's guides, the heart of this book consists of detailed profiles organized under easily scanned and compared headings. These describe enrollment, admissions procedures, denominational affiliation, faculty, library and computer resources, majors, annual costs, financial aid, and institutional mission. A majors index and a graduate programs index enable users to locate schools under areas of study, such as communications, with codes that indicate degrees offered. An athletics index lists schools under individual sports, with codes showing whether the activity is open to men or women and if scholarships are available. There are a geographical index with map and a final index that covers study-abroad opportunities. An introduction offers suggestions to help students and parents decide whether colleges such as these will suit them and how they differ from other institutions.

Keeping its limitations in mind, this guide lives up to the quality expected of anything put out by Peterson's. Moreover, it is unique, inexpensive, and sociologically interesting.—**Mary Jo Walker**

335. **Directory of Catholic Colleges & Universities, 1992.** Decatur, Ga., Kilkenny Press, [1992]. 450p. index. $19.95pa.

This directory of 200 Catholic colleges and universities in the United States provides basic higher education information in a manner similar to the Peterson's and Barron's guides: admission procedures, SAT and ACT scores, majors, tuition, financial aid, enrollment, male/female ratios, housing, student activities, and transfer requirements. It only lists Catholic or independent colleges that are historically Roman Catholic, with information about the percentage of Catholic and non-Catholic students, lay and religious faculty, and outstanding alumni. A detailed index of majors will help users identify colleges by field of interest. The listings are geographically arranged by state; however, there is no alphabetical index of the listings, a major flaw. The user's guide is extensive.

The directory provides users with a list of value-oriented institutions of higher learning, including two-year colleges. It tries to distinguish nonsectarian private and public colleges from Catholic colleges. However, the directory really is a list of institutions that are historically Catholic; they may be independent. Therefore, the half-million prospective freshmen who would like to have a Catholic college experience will have to contact the institution to determine whether or not it is suitable for them. The guide is similar in purpose to the Protestant guide called *Choose a Christian College* (Peterson's Guides, 1992), the official guide to member schools in the Christian College Coalition. That publication uses a contemporary mission statement, however.

The format of the directory leaves much to be desired. It has no title page, no fly leaf, and no half-title page. The glue is unstable in the review copy and will not take heavy usage in a high school. Typographical and other errors detract from the overall quality of the work. As college guides are heavily used in libraries, this work needs to have better binding and printing. However, good use of white space is made, and the charts are well designed.

This directory is an important addition to the reference works on colleges and universities in the United States; it is an essential purchase for all high school libraries that need religious college information. The price is exceptionally modest, therefore making it an essential investment for universities and colleges as well. [R: Choice, Mar 93, p. 1108; LJ, Jan 93, p. 94]—**Gerald D. Moran**

336. **Handbook of United Methodist-Related Schools, Colleges, Universities and Theological Schools.** Nashville, Tennessee, Division of Higher Education, General Board of Higher Education and Ministry, United Methodist Church, 1992. 311p. illus. $5.00pa.

This handbook provides a brief academic profile, number of faculty (full- and part-time), number of students (full- and part-time), and key telephone numbers (e.g., admissions, financial aid, switchboard) for all United Methodist Church-related academies, schools, two- and four-year colleges, universities, and theological schools. Moreover, the handbook contains valuable information on how to choose a college, why to consider a United Methodist institution, how to finance education, how to tap United Methodist scholarship funds, and how to use the UMC loan program for education. This is an excellent reference for people considering private education, and it may serve those thinking of public education but not yet committed to such an education.—**C. B. (Bob) Darrell**

337. Mitchell, Robert. **The Multicultural Student's Guide to Colleges: What Every African-American, Asian-American, Hispanic, and Native American Applicant Needs to Know....** New York, Farrar, Straus & Giroux, 1993. 839p. $25.00pa. L901.M58. 378.73. LC 93-21749. ISBN 0-374-52362-2.

In a descriptive style reminiscent of *The Insider's Guide to the Colleges* (see ARBA 93, entry 372), this new directory for minority students attempts to explain what life is like for such students at 200 of the country's top schools. Arranged by state, each entry starts with statistical information such as cost, nonwhite freshman admissions, percentage of nonwhite students enrolled, ethnic studies programs, and organizations for nonwhite students. It is followed by a description of what the school is like academically and socially, particularly from a minority student's perspective. Comments by actual students are interspersed throughout the text.

Although the title of the book implies that this guide is aimed at all minorities, most of the text focuses on African Americans. The author claims that the top 200 schools in the United States are profiled, but as with many selective guides, to get a geographical spread across all 50 states, many schools more academically rigorous than some of those listed here are excluded. Only five of the best-known historically Black colleges are profiled, although there is a list of all predominantly Black U.S. colleges at the end.

Minority students will still need to consult the comprehensive college directories, as many of the most racially and culturally diverse schools in the country are not profiled in this work. However, if they are considering applying to any of the colleges included, the information provided here will assist them in making informed decisions. The book will be useful in public, high school, and college libraries. [R: LJ, Aug 93, p. 94; RBB, 15 Nov 93, pp. 646-48]—**Christine E. King**

338. **The Murray Resource Directory to the Nation's Historically Black Colleges and Universities.** Washington, D.C., Logical Expression in Design/Library of Congress, 1993. 300p. illus. $59.00. LC 93-077467. ISSN 1068-1043.

This handsome volume, printed on glossy paper, is a needed and welcome updated guide to historically Black colleges and universities. Included in this state-by-state guide for each school are its address and telephone number, a history and mission statement, and general financial and admission information. The schools are listed alphabetically by state. Unfortunately, there is no index, and the directory on page 24 is not listed in the table of contents. Misleading to the casual browser, the photographs and informative commentaries interspersed throughout the directory do not coincide with the respective schools. While *Murray* is an interesting and fact-filled publication, the next edition needs better proofreading. Name changes and colleges that are now defunct should also be included.

For libraries that can afford both, *Murray* complements *The Black Student's Guide to College Success*, edited by Ruby D. Higgins (Greenwood Press, 1993). Although not restricted to historically Black colleges and universities, the *Guide* might be a better buy for restricted budgets.—**Gordon H. Dunkin**

339. **National Faculty Directory 1993: An Alphabetical List, with Addresses, of Approximately 606,000 Members of Teaching Faculties....** 23d ed. Compiled by CMG Information Services. Detroit, Gale, 1993. 3v. $605.00/set. LC 76-14404. ISBN 0-8103-7668-7. ISSN 0077-4472.

A comprehensive guide to the individuals who teach at North American colleges and universities, this directory contains the names, academic departments, schools, and addresses of more than 606,000 people at some 3,700 institutions. Volume 1 starts with an introductory note, a list of abbreviations, and a roster of colleges and universities. Volumes 2 and 3 contain the note and the abbreviations but omit the roster. After the prefatory material, the faculty members are listed in alphabetical order, and this information stretches through all three volumes. Only individuals who actually teach classes are included; those who are not teachers in specific subject areas and who are unlikely to adopt textbooks for class use (e.g., librarians with faculty status who do not teach) are not listed.

Data have been taken from academic course catalogs and faculty directories. Naturally, the directory is already out of date; for example, the deceased president of Emerson College is still listed, and his successor is noted as chief academic dean; similarly, the late Isaac Asimov still appears (he was professor of biochemistry at the Boston University School of Medicine). But on the whole the information is accurate and reliable. This set is a necessity for all college and university libraries and many public and academic libraries.—**D. A. Rothschild**

340. **Peterson's Colleges with Programs for Students with Learning Disabilities.** Charles T. Mangrum II and Stephen S. Strichart, eds. Princeton, N.J., Peterson's Guides, 1992. 660p. index. $24.95pa. L901.P48. 378.73. LC 92-20684. ISBN 1-56079-080-6.

The number of colleges offering special services to learning disabled students has dramatically increased over the last two decades. This book lists, by state, those two- and four-year colleges and universities that have special programs for these students. Information is also compiled about the schools' profiles and the particulars of the special programs offered. Practical recommendations are offered with regard to selection, advisement, study skills, and counseling support services. The "Quick-Reference Table of Colleges" provided at the beginning of the book may help to narrow the choices for prospective inquiry. It should be emphasized, and indeed is clearly listed under the specific program information, that students must qualify for the various special programs. Those who are unfamiliar with the formal designation of "learning disabled" will find the brief historical summary useful.

A great deal of thoughtfulness is reflected in the presentation and contents of this book. Recommended for educators, counselors, and anyone who has an interest in the topic.—**Jeanne Friedrichs**

341. **Peterson's Competitive Colleges 1993-1994.** 12th ed. Princeton, N.J., Peterson's Guides, 1993. 412p. index. $15.95pa. ISBN 1-56079-238-8. ISSN 0887-0152.

This work is filled with interesting facts for the prospective college student, counselor, parent, or anyone wanting to read about individual colleges. No other work includes so many facts about each college on just one page. Information for each of 359 colleges and universities covers the academic program, student body, faculty, college life, athletics, housing, how to apply, costs and financial aid, and freshman class statistics. Also included are a detailed table of contents, a majors index, and a geographical index of colleges. However, what is not clear is how the "top colleges for top students" were selected.—**Gordon H. Dunkin**

342. **Peterson's Guide to Four-Year Colleges 1994.** 24th ed. Princeton, N.J., Peterson's Guides, 1993. 2795p. illus. index. $18.95pa. ISBN 1-56079-235-3. ISSN 0894-9336.

One of the most widely consulted of the annual directories to four-year schools, *Peterson's Guide to Four-Year Colleges* contains all the basic information that prospective students and their parents require to start the search for an undergraduate school to match their needs. Most of the work is divided into two alphabetical sections. The first includes all schools and has basic information such as entrance requirements, number of undergraduates, academic program and majors offered, cost, financial aid available, and how to apply. The other section contains 2-page descriptions of more than 800 of the nearly 2,000 colleges and universities in the volume. The descriptions are based on information submitted by the schools themselves and are more inclusive than the previous entries, particularly about the history, philosophy, and location of each institution. They resemble advertising copy (which is what they are), but they do give more of a feel for what each college is like. There is also a substantial section of introductory materials, including state-by-state summary tables, financial information, entrance difficulty, ROTC programs, and what majors are offered where. This work continues to be an invaluable source of college-hunting information and should be in every reference collection, regardless of size.—**Christine E. King**

343. **Peterson's Guide to Two-Year Colleges 1994.** 24th ed. Princeton, N.J., Peterson's Guides, 1993. 746p. index. $16.95pa. ISBN 1-56079-236-1. ISSN 0894-9328.

As did the 21st edition of this standard college guide (see ARBA 91, entry 318), the 1994 volume provides detailed information, obtained directly from the schools, for more than 1,400 accredited public and private 2-year institutions in the United States. Included in the introductory section are brief discussions of two-year colleges, the process of transferring, adult students returning to school, financial assistance programs, standardized tests, and major fields of study. A comprehensive state-by-state summary table and an index of associate degree programs precede the main section, which consists of succinct, alphabetically arranged profiles of individual schools. In-depth descriptions of scores of colleges and a state-by-state index of institutions complete this authoritative, up-to-date, and easy-to-use work. It belongs in every library serving college-bound students and their families.—**Leonard Grundt**

344. **Peterson's Register of Higher Education 1993.** 6th ed. Princeton, N.J., Peterson's Guides, 1993. 1108p. index. $44.95. ISBN 1-56079-177-2. ISSN 1046-2406.

This reference guide attempts to provide up-to-date information on all accredited institutions of higher education in the United States and in the U.S. territories. The heart of the guide, the institutional profiles section, contains common data on some 3,700 American colleges, universities, and university systems offices. The profiles, which are arranged alphabetically by institution name, include such information as location, congressional district, degrees offered, date of founding, campus acreage, student enrollment, tuition and fees, library, and computer and special research resources. The volume also has six appendixes that list major agencies concerned with higher education within the U.S. Department of Education and within each of the states and territories, and the major accrediting bodies and independent nonprofit associations related to higher education. Concluding the volume is a 325-page index.

Although the compilers of the guide attempt to maintain a current database, much of the personnel information contained in this volume (or any guide of this nature) is outdated even before publication. For Sam Houston State University, 11 of the 39 administrative officers listed in the 1993 edition no longer hold the position for which they are listed. Consequently, while this guide has a great deal of interesting and hard-to-find information presented in an easy-to-read format, readers should be aware that not all of the data are fully reliable.—**Terry D. Bilhartz**

345. **Research Centers Directory 1993: A Guide to Nearly 13,000 University-Related and Other Nonprofit Research Organizations....** 17th ed. Annette Piccirelli and Camille A. Killens, eds. Detroit, Gale, 1993. 2v. index. $400.00/set. LC 60-14807. ISBN 0-8103-7617-2. ISSN 0080-1518.

This annual guide to North American university research centers and independent nonprofit research organizations has added more than 1,000 new listings since it was last reviewed (see ARBA 90, entry 326). Within its two volumes, entries are grouped into 5 broad subject areas and further divided into 17 discipline groups that are arranged alphabetically by sponsoring university and then by center. Extensive indexing has always made it easy to locate individual centers and those that perform research in specific areas. A useful geographic index lists centers alphabetically by state (or province) and then by city. This index conveniently provides each center's full name, address, telephone number, and director.

A typical entry provides complete contact information, with fax numbers appearing on about half of the entries. An organizational notes section gives a description of the staff and lists the center's parent and affiliation, year founded, sources of support, annual dollar volume of research conducted, and any branches or satellite facilities. The principal research areas are summarized along with related activities or services. Information on publications, library facilities, educational activities, and public services offered is also given. Recommended for research libraries and smaller libraries that have not updated this title in recent years.—**Diana Accurso**

346. **U.S. Student Fulbright Grants and Other Grants for Graduate Study and Research Abroad, 1994-1995.** New York, Institute of International Education, 1993. 94p. free pa.

The U.S. Congress created the Fulbright Program in 1946 to foster mutual understanding among nations through educational and cultural exchanges; it remains the premier U.S. scholarship program. During 1994-1995 the program expects to give more than 700 Americans awards to study in more than 100 nations. This booklet provides basic information concerning the Fulbright scholarship program along with information on a number of other grants and fellowships. Included are an explanation of the various grants available, a list of participating countries, eligibility requirements, application procedures, factors affecting selection, and notification procedures. The main body of the work consists of individual country summaries arranged by regions of the world. Each country listing contains the type of Fulbright or other grant available, recommended fields of study, language requirements, the dates of the academic year of the country, types of degrees offered by the host country, and general comments concerning study in the area. In some cases nonrecommended fields of study are listed.

In addition, a number of lists and tables in the back of the booklet have information on the administration of the programs, adviser workshops in the United States, a glossary of terms, responses to the most-asked questions, grants received by country of study, and other granting agencies with scholarships for study abroad. A selected bibliography is provided. There is a remarkable amount of information in this booklet. It is well organized and easy to follow, and the price is right. It should be a yearly acquisition for larger public, college, and research libraries.—**Robert L. Wick**

347. Wade, William A., ed. **Accredited Institutions of Postsecondary Education, Programs, Candidates, 1992-93: A Directory....** Washington, D.C., American Council on Education; distr., Phoenix, Ariz., Oryx Press, 1993. 716p. index. $35.00pa. L901.A48. 378.73. LC 81-641495. ISBN 0-89774-816-6. ISSN 0270-1715.

This convenient reference contains a list of accredited postsecondary educational institutions, professionally accredited programs, and candidates for accreditation from throughout the United States. A small number of U.S.-accredited institutions from outside the country is included as well. Altogether there are more than 5,000 entries arranged alphabetically by state, each including such data as the institution's name, address, telephone number, degrees, enrollment, and dates of first and most recent accreditation. In addition, there is a useful list of U.S. public systems of higher education, including addresses, telephone numbers, and names of chief executive officers. Appendixes on the accrediting process, a directory of accrediting bodies, and a general set of guidelines for the transfer and award of academic credit complete the work. Published annually for the Council on Postsecondary Accreditation by the American Council on Education, this compendium is potentially useful both within academe and to many who deal regularly with the educational establishment.—**John U. Trefny**

348. Weinstein, Miriam, ed. **Making a Difference College Guide, 1993: Education for a Better World.** San Anselmo, Calif., Sage Press, 1993. 185p. $12.95pa. L901.W45. 378.73. LC 92-20127. ISBN 0-9634618-0-X.

This is a different kind of undergraduate college guide. It identifies and profiles 71 colleges and universities that emphasize innovative programs in environmental, peace, women's and social justice studies. At least one-third of the text is devoted to the discussion and descriptions of environmental programs. These are colleges that promote community service, field studies, internships, interdisciplinary learning, and service learning overseas. Some of these colleges are little known, and some are not described in other directories. Conversely, there is a "glaring absence of big name schools in this guide" (p. iii) because they do not meet the editor's criteria of "making a difference" in their curricula.

The introductory section includes thought-provoking essays on such topics as learning about environmental studies and studying peace. Profiles of the colleges follow and make up most of the book. The colleges themselves have prepared the one- to two-page descriptions. Next come lists of "Making a Difference Studies," which are usually two pages in length. This is a truly valuable and interesting guide for today's socially aware college students. [R: Choice, Sept 93, p. 73; LJ, 1 Apr 93, p. 92]

—**Marshall E. Nunn**

Handbooks and Yearbooks

349. **Beacon: College and Career Planning on CD-ROM.** [CD-ROM]. Cambridge, Mass., Macmillan New Media, 1993. Hardware requirements: IBM-compatible PC, 286 or higher; at least 530K of conventional memory; MS-DOS 3.1 or higher; CD-ROM drive with headphone minijack; MS-DOS CD-ROM extensions 2.1 or higher; hard drive with 3MB free; VGA monitor. $495.00.

This software can be used as curriculum material or as an individual CD-ROM-based multimedia program "to help you make plans for your higher-level education and your future career." Beacon provides detailed information within 4 major databases divided into 900 civilian and military career paths; 3,200 two- and four-year colleges; 1,100 graduate schools; and 2,150 grants, scholarships, fellowships, and loan programs, and other financial aid data. All of the databases are easily accessible from the main menu. The disc also includes more than 100 audio advisory messages to assist in career decisions. Besides a four-page quick-reference guide, there are a clearly written, comprehensive user's guide; an index; and an instructor's script included with the program. Also provided are earphones that can be plugged into the CD-ROM drive; thus, a sound card is not necessary. Special features of the software include an auditory guided tour and two lists, called "Focus List" and "Your List," that allow users to individualize their search through the databases. The first is a gauge showing how many careers, schools, or financial-aid sources match the user's answers to a specific question as career or education options are explored. The second list indicates how many of these fit all of one's questions. The list of qualifying items can be viewed by simply choosing the list's icon. A user even has the option of finding out why a particular career, school, or aid source was eliminated. Profiles of user searches and personal information can be saved in the program. Other helpful features are the sample documents, such as employment resumes, the college information request letter, and the interview checklist. There is also advice on some of the subtopics.

This CD-ROM is extremely easy to install. A separate pamphlet is provided with installation instructions that are both straightforward and courteous. The program actually asked permission to change the CONFIG.SYS file if necessary, and, had it been so, it would have provided a list of changes needed. Within 10 minutes the program was up and running, and inside of 20 minutes a search had been done and printed. (The printer worked on the first try!) Searching from the four submenus is also simple. While a query in the Careers database for "Pharmacology" nets no results, because terms have to be stated as occupational titles, this is no real problem because one can search an alphabetical list of key terms and simply select the appropriate one. But this search can also be expedited by typing a short string, such as "pharma," into the new search option box. This quickly takes one to the line below "Pharmacologist" and then to the right career information. Career profiles include occupational title, education and training, salary range, employment outlook, a definition and nature of the work overview, education and training requirements, job placement data, advancement possibilities, working conditions, earnings and benefits, and a professional association to contact for more information.

Two career profiles examined in depth were "Pharmacologist" and "Librarian, School." In terms of content and accuracy, "Pharmacologist," according to a subject expert consulted, was reasonably accurate. However, "Librarian, School" had one major problem in that it lumped regular K-12 school librarians in with college and university librarians. And while coverage of both types within this profile was adequate, and it did clearly distinguish between the two, the keyword index listing should have indicated that it was covering "Librarian, Academic (School and College)." As it now stands, the career keyword index would lead one to believe that the entire category of college and university librarians has been excluded from the database—which is not true, but it *is* buried in its current index term.

Graduate school information also appears to be a little questionable at times. Some of Appalachian State University's profile data, such as the graduate school enrollment figures, did not coincide exactly with those provided by the school's own Institutional Research office. And some data, such as international enrollment, were entirely missing. Also, the school's library science program was omitted from the Teaching Education program listing, where it belongs, and instead placed incorrectly under Literature/English. Even more distressing, library science is missing entirely from the masters' programs interest list. As the source of this data was given as the College Entrance Examination Board's Annual Survey of Colleges Data Base, this is a surprising oversight.

Minor inconsistencies aside, this CD-ROM program is nonetheless recommended for those needing either a multipurpose career reference tool or an entire vocational guidance course for instructional or counseling purposes. It will be useful as a stand-alone reference database or as a major teaching method with or without assistance (a curriculum guide is available from the publisher). One should, of course, supplement it with standard printed works. But for the price, this seems to be a useful product that, given its publisher and its data source, will only improve with time.—**Carol Truett**

350. Bear, John. **Bear's Guide to Earning College Degrees Non-Traditionally.** 11th ed. Benicia, Calif., C & B Publishing, 1993. 304p. illus. index. $23.95pa. LC 91-71685. ISBN 0-9629312-0-9.

351. Bear, John. **College Degrees by Mail: 100 Good Schools That Offer Bachelor's, Master's, Doctorates and Law Degrees by Home Study.** Berkeley, Calif., Ten Speed Press, 1993. 211p. illus. index. $12.95pa. LC901.B35. 374'.473. LC 90-47097. ISBN 0-89815-589-4.

Since 1974, Bear has been writing and publishing authoritative guides for students seeking the answer to this vital question: "How can I earn a college degree without sitting in a classroom for four years?" *Bear's Guide to Earning College Degrees Non-Traditionally* has now appeared in its 11th edition, along with *College Degrees by Mail*. Together they provide the user with the best available current information on the field of alternative education.

In the opening chapters of both books, Bear offers wise words on important issues in nontraditional education, such as evaluation and accreditation of colleges, scholarships, and alternative methods of earning credit (e.g., equivalency exams, correspondence courses, credit for life experience learning). Part 3 is the first book's longest and most important section. It lists and describes accredited and nonaccredited schools offering bachelor's, master's, and doctorate programs, as well as weekend colleges. The author gives basic information on each school: cost; degrees offered and in what areas; whether the programs are residency, short residency, or nonresidency; and short descriptive notes. Following this section are interesting chapters on degree mills, a glossary, and advice for people in prison.

College Degrees by Mail generally follows a similar format in its descriptions of 113 correspondence schools. It has a valuable appendix on "Some Schools That Are Not Listed in This Book," in which Bear ties up many elusive loose ends. Bear has provided sure and reliable guides through the murky area of nontraditional education and its many mine fields.—**Marshall E. Nunn**

352. **The College Board Guide to 150 Popular College Majors.** New York, College Board, 1992. 377p. index. $16.00pa. LC 92-073632. ISBN 0-87447-400-0.

College Board has used its extensive network to provide narrative commentary on and follow-up sources for information about what they consider to be the 150 most popular college majors. The information is well packaged, providing easy access to materials about the majors, related career opportunities, and recommended high school preparation. Users will glean some important insights from the data.

There are a few weaknesses in this guide that may limit its utility. Within the College Majors Project Committee, it appears that none of the members is a Latino, and among the contributors, only one such person is listed. Moreover, the section on interdisciplinary, area, and ethnic studies lacks any information on Native American, Asian-American, and Hispanic-American studies programs. But aside from these lacunae, this is a welcome new title. It will be a valuable addition to the reference collection of most public, school, and junior college libraries. It can be used by school counselors and public librarians to help prospective college students and their parents learn about majors to consider and how to prepare for college in high school. [R: Choice, Sept 93, p. 76; VOYA, April 93, p. 65; WLB, Mar 93, p. 106]

—**Roberto P. Haro**

353. **College Costs and Financial Aid Handbook 1994.** 14th ed. New York, College Board, 1993. 316p. illus. index. $16.00pa. LC 80-648095. ISBN 0-87447-481-7.

As college costs mount, anxious parents can take advantage of several college planning books to help them with the financial package for their teenage children. One of the more respected and solid resources is *College Costs and Financial Aid Handbook* (formerly *The College Cost Book*). This reference outlines the aspects of college costs, including tuition and fees, books and supplies, room and board, and transportation. Chapters cover family income as well as family contributions and how individuals can plan to accrue enough cash for making payments. Loans are also well described, and many suggestions are given for pursuing them. Financial aid given by various federal programs is detailed along with other loan and work-study programs. This edition has information about changes in the federal student aid regulations and how they may affect students.

This is a solid book with commonsense suggestions and realistic advice geared to families. The tables are excellent; college costs and scholarships of all types, special payment plans, and tuition waivers are included. Parents and their college-bound children will do well to examine this book.—**Anne F. Roberts**

354. **The College Handbook for Transfer Students 1994.** 4th ed. New York, College Board, 1993. 536p. index. $17.00pa. LC 91-071255. ISBN 0-87447-482-5.

Do we need a separate college guide for transfer students? The answer is yes, because the standard all-purpose guides currently available contain very little (if any) information on this vital aspect of the college admissions process. This book is a gold mine of data for the 800,000-plus students who transfer to a new college each year. It details the fall 1993 admissions policies and procedures for transfer students at some 2,700 public and private, two-year and four-year colleges in the United States. The handbook is most complete in its presentation and includes profiles of the colleges, transfer out data, transfer student profiles, admission requirements and related information, special services for transfers, and annual expenses and availability of financial aid. As an added feature, there are lists of selected colleges in American Samoa, the Caroline Islands, Guam, the Mariana Islands, the Virgin Islands, Canada, France, Mexico, and Egypt. Put this valuable resource on the shelf next to the other outstanding College Board handbooks.—**Marshall E. Nunn**

355. **The College Handbook 1994.** 31st ed. New York, College Board, 1993. 1688p. index. $20.00pa. LC 41-12971. ISBN 0-87447-479-5.

In preparing its latest college guide, the College Board seems to have thought of everything. Unlike other such works, this handbook includes both two- and four-year colleges, specialized schools, traditional liberal arts colleges, senior colleges, and major universities—indeed, any school that has an undergraduate curriculum. The college descriptions, arranged alphabetically by states, can stand alone, but understanding them is greatly enhanced by reading the prefatory material, which explains the format and defines the terms used. In addition, lists of various schools grouped by different factors—religious affiliations, special programs, features, requirements, and types of settings—provide another way of selecting or evaluating schools for people who do not have a particular school in mind. Curiously, these indexes appear before the college descriptions and do not offer cross-references to those descriptions. Otherwise, *The College Handbook* is helpful, complete, and thorough, providing a balance between guidance for the inexperienced and information for the most sophisticated, without becoming bogged down in trivia, quirks, or irrelevancies. Unfortunately, it includes so much information, is printed on such thin newsprint, and uses such small type that it is somewhat awkward and unpleasant to use and probably will not withstand heavy use.

—**Rebecca Jordan**

356. **Community, Technical, and Junior Colleges Statistical Yearbook.** 1992 ed. Jim Mahoney and Edgar Jimenez, eds. Washington, D.C., American Association of Community Colleges, 1992. 78p. index. $44.00pa. ISBN 0-87117-243-7.

Each year, the American Association of Community Colleges (formerly the American Association of Community and Junior Colleges) surveys its members. This volume contains selected findings from the 1991 study. Similar to the 1990 edition (see ARBA 91, entry 328), this one is divided into two parts. In the first, data are presented for individual colleges listed alphabetically within states, territories, and foreign countries. For each institution, the yearbook furnishes its name and address; chief executive officer; type of control; full-time, part-time, and minority credit enrollment figures for fall 1990 and fall 1991; noncredit enrollment for 1990-1991; number of degrees awarded in 1990-1991; number of full-time and part-time faculty, professional staff, and administrative staff in fall 1991; and annual tuition and required fees for 1991-1992.

State-by-state summaries of selected statistics for two-year colleges are supplied in part 2. Included are the number of institutions in each state, their credit enrollment for fall 1990 and fall 1991, and minority enrollment and faculty figures for fall 1991. Public and private colleges are grouped separately. Although many data are lacking because of omissions in individual reports, this yearbook is the most complete and authoritative source for current statistical information about these schools.—**Leonard Grundt**

357. Gourman, Jack. **The Gourman Report: A Rating of Graduate and Professional Programs in American and International Universities.** 6th ed. Chicago, Dearborn Trade, 1993. 310p. $19.95pa. ISBN 0-918192-15-3. ISSN 1049-717X.

At first glance, *The Gourman Report* seems very promising. It covers more than 100 academic disciplines at a large number of institutions; it provides both a ranking and a single overall numerical score for each program. It also assesses professional programs: law, medicine, dentistry, veterinary medicine, nursing, optometry, and pharmacy, often including schools in Canada and other countries as well as the United States. Finally, it offers a rating of each accredited U.S. graduate school as a whole. Unfortunately, Gourman, a professor of political science who has been publishing his various *Reports* since 1967, gives only the vaguest indication of the sources of his information and says nothing about how recently it was obtained. Even more troubling is his reticence about the methodology employed to derive his ratings: He offers no further description than an appendix listing the number of institutions and programs evaluated, along with large numbers of undefined areas of study and faculty areas examined. This does little to explain, for example, the rank order listings of programs where, improbably, there are long runs of consecutive scores one- or two-hundredths of a point apart (on a five-point scale)—with virtually no ties—or the lengthy lists of programs in criminal justice/criminology, teacher education, and graduate education, not one of which meets with the author's approval. Previous editions of Gourman's *Report*, undergraduate as well as graduate, have been criticized for these and many other questionable features, but their reduction of institution and program assessments to seemingly precise and unequivocal scores is undoubtedly appealing to many, especially as none of the other commonly used general guides to graduate study offer such ratings. Nonetheless, until the *Gourman Report* is much more forthcoming about the sources and currentness of its information and about its methods of analysis and evaluation, it cannot be recommended as a credible guide. [R: WLB, June 93, p. 124]—**Gregory M. Toth**

358. Gourman, Jack. **The Gourman Report: A Rating of Undergraduate Programs in American and International Universities.** 8th ed. Chicago, Dearborn Trade, 1993. 365p. $19.95pa. ISBN 0-918192-14-5. ISSN 1049-7188.

This book numerically ranks undergraduate programs, preprofessional programs, administrative areas (including regents, trustees, and alumni), curricula, staff, and institutions at leading overseas and Canadian universities. In addition to scoring aspects of selected U.S. schools, the report also scores the overall academic quality of undergraduate programs throughout this country and lists those schools that do not meet its criteria in their teacher education programs and criminal justice programs. The preface and introduction indicate the criteria used in arriving at these numbers and make clear the structure and purpose of the book.

Unfortunately, although the relative strength of the numbers is indicated throughout the text (5 being the highest, 1 the lowest), at no point does the author indicate how these numbers were determined. Quite properly, he has measured criteria consistently within categories, but he does not reveal how the criteria were weighted for any one category. He provides only the numerical score, a bald reduction of a complicated opinion. Such numbers would carry more weight if we knew how they were derived; some of the evaluations are what one would expect, while others are surprising. For instance, the list of top schools in various programs is drawn almost exclusively from large, well-known institutions, leaving one to surmise that small liberal arts colleges have little to offer, despite the fact that a number of small schools rate highly in their overall academic quality. Such a discrepancy suggests that the process favors research institutions at the expense of teaching ones. On a more mundane note, proofreading has not been as careful as it should have been. [R: WLB, June 93, p. 124]—**Rebecca Jordan**

359. **The Macmillan Guide to Correspondence Study.** 5th ed. Compiled and edited by Modoc Press, Inc. New York, Macmillan, 1993. 799p. index. $100.00. ISBN 0-02-871391-5. ISSN 1068-2481.

Largely unchanged in format and scope since the 3d edition (see ARBA 90, entry 359), this work continues to be a very comprehensive guide to correspondence courses and programs at the elementary through graduate levels, including noncredit courses. It groups some 260 accredited institutions offering correspondence study in three major sections: colleges and universities; proprietary schools; and private, nonprofit, and governmental schools. Each entry begins with contact information and a description of each school, its programs, admission requirements, tuition, credit and grading systems, and accreditation. Next comes a list of its course offerings, arranged by level, including a description of each course, its credits, and any prerequisites. Further access to the entries is provided through an alphabetical list of institutions and a subject index. Although it carries a hefty price, *The Macmillan Guide* is a worthwhile resource for those who want the combination of currentness, detailed information, and comprehensiveness it offers.—**Gregory M. Toth**

360. McKee, Cynthia Ruiz, and Phillip C. McKee, Jr. **Cash for College.** New York, Hearst Books/William Morrow, 1993. 510p. index. $16.95pa. LB2337.4.M285. 378.3'0973. LC 92-42410. ISBN 0-688-12179-9.

Having managed their son's successful 1989 quest for scholarships and financial support in college, the McKees found themselves with a marketable process that this book details. The first part explains the book's structure and use and describes the stages involved in pursuing financial support for postsecondary education. The second part lists names, addresses, and information about various groups that provide scholarships, grants, and other kinds of financial assistance to students. Several appendixes provide samples of letters and resumes for students to use as well as charts to track the process so that details do not get overlooked. In short, even though much of what they say is common sense, the authors have anticipated most, if not all, of what applicants and their parents will need to know and do in seeking financial support for college.

Neither the table of contents nor the chapter listing scholarships is structured as helpfully as it might be. First, the chapters "At-a-Glance Scholarship Index" and "Scholarship Listing" both contain two subheadings, but the pages on which these subheadings begin do not appear in the table of contents. Given that "Scholarship Listing" runs to more than 300 pages, such a lapse is more than an inconvenience—it interferes with using the book. Second, within that chapter, no headings appear to indicate which subtopic appears on which page—whether one is in the section listing private foundations or the one on colleges' programs. At the very least, a chapter that is divided into subtopics should have appropriate headings on each page, and the index should not be the only means of locating specific information within a chapter. A minor point: The authors have a penchant for exclamation points. [R: RBB, 1 Dec 93, p. 709]

—**Rebecca Jordan**

361. **Minority Student Enrollments in Higher Education: A Guide to Institutions....** Garrett Park, Md., Garrett Park Press, 1993. 1v. (unpaged). index. $15.00pa. LC 87-080852. ISBN 1-880774-05-4.

This directory lists approximately 500 colleges and universities that have a significant number of minority students enrolled. What this means is that a particular ethnic minority group accounts for at least 20 percent of the student enrollment. Entries are arranged alphabetically, first by state and then by institution. Information provided comes from the U.S. Department of Education's *Directory of Post-Secondary Institutions Vol. 1* (1991-1992) and includes the name and address of the school, telephone number, enrollment, percentage of students in each major minority group, highest degree, and major programs offered. Most schools have only 1 major minority group, but approximately 30 have 2 or more, each of which constitute 20 percent or more of the total enrollment.

The reference work is divided into three sections. The brief introduction in section 1 is followed by the federal government's definitions of minority groups (Asians, Blacks, Hispanics, and Native Americans), some recent enrollment data related to them by student gender and institution type (public, private, two-year, four-year, undergraduate, graduate, and professional), and brief overviews providing historical perspectives and current status of and trends for these minorities. The second section consists of the directory data, and section 3 is a brief list of 17 additional resources to be consulted. An index by major programs concludes the work.

One inconvenience of this tool is the lack of page numbers, although the index does provide entry numbers. Still, students, guidance counselors, and other educators who wish to identify schools with large minority percentages will find this directory useful, as will scholars who are conducting research related to ethnicity or education.—**Lois J. Buttlar**

362. Phifer, Paul. **College Majors and Careers: A Resource Guide for Effective Life Planning.** rev. ed. Garrett Park, Md., Garrett Park Press, 1993. 198p. index. $15.00pa. HF5382.5.U5P445. 331.7'02'0973. LC 93-19213. ISBN 1-880774-04-6.

As did the first edition (see ARBA 88, entry 398), this work lists the interests, skills, personal attributes, and occupations that are related to 61 common college majors. Each major's two-page entry also includes published materials and organizations that can provide further information on its related careers. As before, a series of appendixes includes glossaries, a list of majors with related high school courses, and data on degrees awarded by fields of study. A bibliography of some seven pages covers additional career- and occupation-related materials.

Although this revised edition covers the same majors as the first, owners of the earlier work will want to consider purchasing this one because the individual entries have been significantly revised and updated, as has the volume's general bibliography. Moreover, this edition offers new features: a section, in question-and-answer format, with advice on choosing a major and thinking about career options; self-assessment exercises focusing on temperament, strengths and weaknesses, abilities and aptitudes, values, and interests; and indexes of majors and occupations. This new material increases an already useful work's value both as a guidance tool and as a reference work.—**Gregory M. Toth**

363. Philos, Daphne A., ed. **The A's and B's of Academic Scholarships.** Alexandria, Va., Octameron, 1993. 144p. $7.00pa. ISBN 0-945981-74-0.

This book contains descriptions of all the major merit scholarship programs—collegiate, federal, state, and private. It is addressed to students who want financial aid that is merit-based rather than need-based. Chapters 1 and 2 cover eligibility, claims of biases in standardized tests, and need versus nonneed-based awards. Chapter 3, the table of collegiate academic awards, takes up most of the book. It lists some 100,000 merit scholarships in 1,200 U.S. colleges and universities. The listing, by state and then by college, indicates award-granting program, number of awards, value range, award criteria (class standing, grade point average, SAT/ACT scores, and other factors), and other basic data. This bare-bones approach may serve a purpose in identifying and listing merit scholarships, but it does not describe them. For that vital information, such comprehensive and well-known sources as *Peterson's College Money Handbook* (see ARBA 92, entry 307) are necessary.—**Marshall E. Nunn**

364. **Rugg's Recommendations on the Colleges.** 10th ed. By Frederick E. Rugg. Compiled and edited by the College Staff of Rugg's Recommendations. Sarasota, Fla., Rugg's Recommendations, 1993. 138p. $17.95pa. LC 89-062896. ISBN 0-9608934-8-2.

Rugg's continues to be one of several choices for high school students embarking upon the college selection process. With a core list of 675 colleges, which includes all the Phi Beta Kappa institutions, general recommendations are made in 39 different fields. According to the preface, the primary method of gathering data was random student interviews. Lesser input was made by secondary school guidance personnel and college officials. The schools in which a particular program is recommended are divided into three groups (most selective, very selective, and selective). Assignment to a group is determined by the grade point average and standardized test score an institution accepts from a prospective student. Except for this basic breakdown, there is no further ranking. Additionally, a section titled "Miscellaneous Majors Pages" gives recommendations of programs in more specialized subject areas with even less detail given than for the original 39 subjects.

After much perusal through *Rugg's* and others similar to it, this reviewer has come to the conclusion that guides such as these all serve basically similar purposes. They provide some structure for students, their parents, and high school counselors as they seek a college that best suits the student's educational needs. *Rugg's* lists a wide range of schools that the contributors deem noteworthy. What they set out to do, they do well. But if one is seeking reports given in quantifiable terms, there might be more suitable sources. Recommended for high school and public libraries.—**Phillip P. Powell**

Indexes

365. **Index of Majors and Graduate Degrees 1994.** 16th ed. New York, College Board, 1993. 706p. index. $17.00pa. LC 80-648202. ISBN 0-87447-480-9.

College Board administers exams and provides services for students and faculty; it also publishes handbooks. One of the most popular of its publications is *Index of Majors and Graduate Degrees*, often kept under lock and key at reference desks in college or university libraries. This reference work includes all colleges and universities in its lists: two-year, two-year upper-division, three-year, four-year, five-year, and graduate. In addition to its usual list of majors, it has an extensive listing and description of special academic programs, a most useful section thanks to the expansion of higher education into other populations, such as the elderly, the retired, the working professional, and foreign students.

Major fields are indexed by discipline as major fields of study stipulated by the Classification of Instructional Programs, a national statistics agency. A useful glossary of special programs is also included to help the user with definitions of particular terms. This excellent reference is useful, popular, and often consulted—who could ask for more?—**Anne F. Roberts**

INTERNATIONAL EXCHANGE PROGRAMS AND OPPORTUNITIES

366. **IIE Educational Associates 1992-1993: A Guide for the Member Colleges and Universities of the Institute of International Education.** 3d ed. New York, Institute of International Education, 1992. 151p. index. $40.00pa. ISBN 0-87206-195-7.

The Institute of International Education (IIE) has been the largest and most active higher educational exchange agency in the United States for nearly 75 years. It currently manages 275 programs involving more than 10,000 individuals from 155 nations, and it administers international education, training, and research activities initiated by government and international agencies, foundations, corporations, and universities. Some 600 U.S. colleges and universities are IIE members.

This directory lists the staff members who are involved in international programs of exchange. Entries for the institutions are arranged by state, then alphabetically by name. Designee codes link the names of people with their positions or areas of responsibility. All entries give the name of the institution's president, Fulbright program advisers, IIE membership, and Open Door contacts, as well as those who are involved with policy, study abroad, and foreign nationals programs. Some entries list additional individuals who have some involvement with international exchange. All include telephone numbers. A supplement lists names in alphabetical order with telephone numbers. The list also serves as an index to the institution entry in which the name appears. An introductory section describes IIE services and publications, including the newsletter, reference books, statistical reports, research studies, conferences, outreach services available from overseas and regional U.S. offices, and contacts at IIE. Spot checking indicates accuracy in the data, which is supplied by member institutions.—**Shirley L. Hopkinson**

367. Schlachter, Gail Ann, and R. David Weber. **Financial Aid for Research and Creative Activities Abroad 1992-1994: A List of Scholarships, Fellowships, Loans, Grants, Awards, and Internships....** San Carlos, Calif., Reference Service Press, 1992. 400p. index. $40.00. ISBN 0-918276-18-7.

368. Schlachter, Gail Ann, and R. David Weber. **Financial Aid for Study and Training Abroad 1992-1994: A List of Scholarships, Fellowships, Loans, Grants, Awards, and Internships....** San Carlos, Calif., Reference Service Press, 1992. 262p. index. $30.00. ISBN 0-918276-19-5.

These two companion directories continue and replace *Financial Aid for Research, Study, Travel, and Other Activities Abroad 1990-91* (see ARBA 91, entry 346). The authors attribute the change in format to a sizable increase in the number of programs. The volume on study and training abroad has information on more than 750 funding opportunities open to Americans interested in structured or independent study. Private and public funding sources are included. Entries cover major fields of study and a broad range of countries. Study opportunities are grouped together by eligible recipients (e.g., high school students, graduate students, postdoctorates, professional/other). The research and creative activities volume lists nearly 1,200 opportunities open to Americans. Among the types of activities included are lectureships, conference attendance, writing, artistic work, work assignments, and exchange programs.

Both directories are divided into three sections: a descriptive list of financial aid programs (grouped by recipient segment), an annotated bibliography of directories, and a list of general financial aid programs. Each has a set of five indexes: program title, sponsoring organization, geographic, subject, and calendar. Each numbered entry, insofar as available data permits, provides detailed information on purpose, eligibility, financial data, duration, limitations, number awarded, and deadlines, in addition to address and telephone and fax numbers.

The directories focus specifically on opportunities open to Americans and exclude awards for which American citizens or permanent residents are ineligible. Also excluded are study awards administered by universities for their own students. Although users will find some overlap with other international study resources, the attractive format, scope, currency, and price of these titles make them worthwhile purchases for public and academic libraries. [R: Choice, Sept 93, pp. 88-90; RQ, Fall 93, pp. 125-26; WLB, April 93, p. 121]—**Ahmad Gamaluddin**

369. **Study Holidays.** 17th ed. London, Central Bureau for Educational Visits & Exchanges; distr., New York, Institute of International Education, [1992]. 192p. illus. maps. index. $22.95pa. ISBN 0-900087-90-0.

370. **Working Holidays 1993.** 41st ed. London, Central Bureau for Educational Visits & Exchanges; distr., New York, Institute of International Education, [1993]. 320p. index. $22.95pa. ISBN 0-900087-91-9.

The Central Bureau for Educational Visits & Exchanges was established by the British government in 1948 to provide information and materials on various forms of educational visits and exchanges. One of its most enduring publications is *Working Holidays*, which provides detailed descriptions of nearly 100,000 short-term, paid, or volunteer opportunities throughout the world for people ages 12 to 70. Positions fall within 12 primary categories, including archaeology, tour guides, and work camps. The work's main section lists all participating countries worldwide, together with the types of opportunities offered in each country and pertinent information, including application procedures, qualifications and costs, and working conditions (which are quite realistically described). Detailed sections of travel advice and general descriptions of the types of positions featured precede this main listing.

Another of the Central Bureau's publications is *Study Holidays*. Although its title suggests the broader scope of a source such as *Study Abroad* (see ARBA 90, entry 348), this is a guide specifically to language courses offered in schools throughout Europe. Twenty-five languages, from English and French to lesser-known tongues such as Basque, are alphabetically arranged. Under each language are the institutions where instruction is offered and relevant details, such as course scope and audience, costs, accommodations, and special features of the program. Travel advice, additional resources for language study, and profiles of the European countries offering instruction complete the work. As with *Working Holidays*, the information in this edition reveals careful updating from previous editions to ensure timeliness.

Both of these publications are current, clearly organized and written, and thorough in their treatment of their topics. They would make fine additions to academic and public library collections. However, because they are produced in England and focus on the European Community, certain sections, such as the travel tips, will not be as useful to North American travelers as to their counterparts abroad. *Work, Study, Travel Abroad, 1991-1993* (St. Martin's Press, 1992), which provides the American-oriented overview and travel advice, could be considered a supplement to these works.—**Linda Cullum**

LEARNING DISABILITIES AND DISABLED

371. Barnett, Lynn, ed. **Directory of Disability Support Services in Community Colleges 1992.** Washington, D.C., American Association of Community Colleges, 1992. 180p. $20.00pa. ISBN 0-87117-249-6.

Two years after the 1988 edition of this work was published, the Americans with Disabilities Act (ADA) was passed. The current directory contains specific information relating to accessibility, disability services, and accommodations in 619 public and private community colleges during the 1991-1992 academic year. After some introductory statistics that speak to the number of students seeking disability support services (DSS) and to the lack of data regarding outcome-related employment for these graduates, most of the directory lists the following information for each school: contact administrator, enrollment, DSS graduate numbers, DSS categories, support services and accommodations, and special features.

The spreadsheet list of support services in the second section of the directory makes comparisons between schools easy. For example, registration assistance and alternative exams are offered by the vast majority of schools. (Those few schools that lack services offered by so many others would do well to take notice.) Conversely, some services are sparsely offered, such as off-campus housing and independent-living skills. On-campus housing is not well represented, but this reflects the general nature of community colleges as commuter schools. Finally, a special features index lists colleges that identified these items in the national survey on which the directory information is based. Some features are specific, such as taped books, and some are quite general. The lack of definition for the more general features makes the information less than helpful. A footnote could be added to the preface to indicate that information about the ADA and data relevant to the directory topic are provided at the end of the book.—**Jeanne Friedrichs**

372. **The Complete Directory for People with Learning Disabilities, 1993/94: A One-Stop Sourcebook for Individuals and Professionals.** Leslie Mackenzie, ed. Lakeville, Conn., Grey House Publishing, 1993. 539p. index. $125.00pa. ISBN 0-939300-24-9.

The most positive aspects of this new annual reference book for professionals and consumers are the scope of the information and the inclusion of brief descriptions for most of the listings. While some listings do not include descriptions of the school, service, or content, the majority do, thus making judgments about follow-up investigation easier. (All entries should be required to offer at least a brief description, because providing merely a name and address is less than helpful.) The narrative format used in this directory is preferable to that in similar resources, which use abbreviation codes to condense the information in the listings. Also, the large typeface used to distinguish the listings is a helpful visual cue that makes reading easier.

The editor has provided a wide range of information, including organizations, schools, programs, media (e.g., computer-related, toys, classroom materials), periodicals, texts, resources and professional services (e.g., testing, consultants), and government agencies. In addition, the directory is available in a computerized version. This is a valuable resource for professionals and consumers because of its comprehensiveness. [R: Choice, Dec 93, p. 581; LJ, 15 Sept 93, pp. 66-68; RBB, 15 Dec 93, p. 775]
—**Jeanne Friedrichs**

373. **Directory of Facilities and Services for the Learning Disabled, 1993-94.** 15th ed. Novato, Calif., Academic Therapy, 1993. 192p. index. free pa. ($4.00 handling). ISSN 0092-3257.

This directory is a concise list, by state, of screening information that identifies appropriate private schools and services for the learning disabled. Information on the facilities includes calendar year, staffing, therapeutic services, and age or gender requirements. Information relating to other services includes a list of educational journals and magazines, special education software, publishers and networks, educational clearinghouses for information, and test publishers.

Readers should be informed that the listings are limited to private facilities and services. (The word *private* should appear in the title.) Also, in the code key, one abbreviation, "Sens," which stands for sensory integration training, is parenthetically followed by two abbreviations (OT, PT) that are not explained. To a layperson unfamiliar with rehabilitation services, these abbreviations (occupational therapy and physical therapy) may not be known. Likewise, the term *sensory integration* has been omitted from the glossary at the end. Finally, advertisements are scattered throughout the book; it would be better if they were all listed at the end.—**Jeanne Friedrichs**

NONPRINT MATERIALS AND RESOURCES

374. **Audiocassette & Compact Disc Finder: A Subject Guide to Educational and Literary Materials on Audiocassettes and Compact Discs.** 3d ed. Medford, N.J., Plexus Publishing, 1993. 1419p. index. $95.00. ISBN 0-937548-22-7.

Since 1964 the National Information Center for Educational Media (NICEM) has attempted to bring bibliographic control to the nonprint media market in education. NICEM keeps a 300,000-plus-item database of all types of educational media, out of which it produces a number of medium-specific print products, a complete online DIALOG file, and a complete CD-ROM product titled AV Online from SilverPlatter. *Audiocassette & Compact Disc Finder* is a subset of this massive database. The current edition contains some 40,000 entries that are based on information supplied by the Library of Congress and by producers and distributors of audio materials directed at the education market (materials meant for the mass market are also covered). Items from Bantam Audio Publishing and Books on Tape are listed as well as those from the Arizona Metaphysical Society.

Entries are arranged by title and contain technical descriptions plus a brief indication of content and price. Access is increased through a subject index that uses a thesaurus developed by NICEM. Subject headings are too broad; many have hundreds of titles listed. A level indication (from elementary through adult) is some help in locating useful materials. Producers and distributors are coded for subject and title indexes, and a separate producer and distributor address directory is provided.

While some errors and missing details were noted, the work serves a vital function for media centers, schools, and libraries that need to track down audio materials for purchase or preview. While the index will have to be supplemented by lists of more popular titles and with updated publishers' catalogs, the book is a must purchase for all libraries building an audio collection of moderate to large size.

—**David V. Loertscher**

375. Diffor, John C., and Elaine N. Diffor, eds. **Educators Guide to Free Filmstrips and Slides.** 45th ed. Randolph, Wis., Educators Progress Service, 1993. 169p. index. $23.95pa. LC 50-11650. ISBN 0-87708-252-9.

The latest edition of this resource guide lists 177 filmstrips, 287 sets of slides, 119 audiodiscs, 16 audiotapes, and 3 sets of transparencies, all of which are available for free loan (some may be retained permanently). This edition has been thoroughly updated, with 164 new titles and 192 deletions of materials that are no longer available. For the first time, audiodiscs have been included. Entries are listed alphabetically by title within 16 broad subject categories. The annotations are succinct and give the scope of coverage, number of items in the set, availability of teacher's guides, and the source's name. Annotations for sound items indicate whether the sound is on disc, reel tape, or cassette, and give running time in minutes. There are title, subject, and source and availability indexes; a list of 15 sources that will send their materials to Canadian schools, libraries, and industries; and a list of 23 sources that make their materials available to industries in the United States. The source and availability index gives address, terms and requirements, availability information, and page references to the listings.

While these are sponsored materials, the producers and distributors are associations, government agencies, museums and art galleries, consulates and information centers, church services, national parks, wildlife sanctuaries, and a few companies and corporations. Advertising and propaganda materials are excluded. This guide, which has been published since 1949, has proved its usefulness to schools and other institutions that seek sources of free or inexpensive items.—**Shirley L. Hopkinson**

376. **The Electronic University: A Guide to Distance Learning.** Princeton, N.J., Peterson's Guides, 1993. 193p. illus. index. $15.95pa. L901.E49. 378.1'554'02573. LC 93-28518. ISBN 1-56079-139-X.

Most of *The Electronic University* is a straightforward directory, arranged alphabetically by institution name, that lists degree programs and individual courses offered electronically. Information given includes name, address, telephone number, electronic address of institution, descriptions of programs, principal method of transmission, prerequisites, accreditation information, and name and address of a contact person. Finding aids include a subject index by academic discipline and a geographical index.

To this basic information are added a few extras. Two introductory essays written by practitioners of distance education discuss the pros and cons of this method of education; a careful reading of these essays can help prospective students decide if this method will suit their needs. A glossary of technical terms explains to the uninitiated some of the terminology used in distance education and demystifies some of its high-tech jargon. Perhaps the most useful extra in this book is the student profiles sprinkled throughout, written both by current students and by students who have already completed a program. Covering about a page each and accompanied by a picture of the student, these essays describe the student's experiences and accomplishments with distance education. The profiles put an individual face on what can be perceived as the ultimate in faceless education.

More people need frequent updating of skills or job retraining, and more are returning to education at midlife or beyond. When work and home responsibilities make full-time residential study impractical, the distance education method is an ever more popular option. This directory will fill a need for many people seeking a way to earn specific credentials without total disruption of their lives.—**Terry Ann Mood**

377. **Glossary of Educational Technology Terms. Glossar zur Bildungstechnologie.** By the Division for the Development of Education, UNESCO, for the International Bureau of Education. Lanham, Md., UNIPUB, 1992. 276p. $14.00pa. ISBN 92-3-002790-1.

This glossary is an easy-to-use, up-to-date list of terms. In the English section the German word for each term is provided, and in the German section the English equivalent is given. Definitions are succinct and demonstrate a refinement not found in many other glossaries in the field. For example, the troublesome terms *educational technology* and *instructional technology* are clearly defined here. (Nevertheless, these and other theoretical terms do not garner a wide consensus in the field and are looked upon differently by many educators in other fields.) As with similar glossaries, many general terms that add little to the work are included. Words such as *ability, adaptation, archives, credit, equipment, exhibit*, and *intensity* carry common definitions and are not unique to instructional technology. The English bibliography and much of the German bibliography are composed of a few outdated secondary resources. Dictionaries that paraphrase other dictionaries make the scholarship suspect. Nevertheless, this work fills a void and should be of value to German instructional technologists and students striving to find meaning in the terms associated with the field.—**William E. Hug**

378. Hoffman, Andrea C., and Ann M. Glannon. **Kits, Games and Manipulatives for the Elementary School Classroom: A Source Book.** Hamden, Conn., Garland, 1993. 605p. index. (Source Books on Education, v.36; Garland Reference Library of Social Science, v.892). $94.00. LB1043.H63. 372.13'3'0973. LC 92-28473. ISBN 0-8240-5342-7.

Containing 1,400 items from more than 100 U.S. producers or distributors of educational materials, this work provides a nice complement to such works as *El-Hi Textbooks & Serials in Print* (see ARBA 92, entry 285). Its emphasis is on nonprint media that are often difficult to locate, including hands-on kits, games, and other manipulatives. Kits are defined as any combination of two or more types of media, while examples of manipulatives are blocks, geoboards, and sequence cards. All items listed were thought to be available as of early 1992.

Entries are grouped into six broad sections: reading and language arts, mathematics, social studies, science and health, arts, and other subjects. Within these groupings, materials are subarranged by broad grade levels. Entries provide brief data such as title, specific grade level, a price code, format, source, descriptors (specific skills or topics that the material teaches), and a short description of the item (which normally includes number and type of pieces contained in the set). Title, descriptor, and author indexes, plus a source directory, complete this work.

Special strengths of this work include the extensive descriptor index, which runs to 100 pages, and the fact that the materials listed are not generally included in standard nonprint or educational bibliographies. However, a few criticisms can be made. Many important nonprint items were specifically excluded, including computer software; transparencies; cassettes (except those in kits); puzzles; charts; and films, filmstrips, and videos. Also, one is seldom going to look up entries through the author index. A media format index or one by grade level would have been more useful; this information could also have been included within the descriptor index as subcategories.

The cost of this work will be prohibitive for many teachers and elementary school librarians for whom the work is intended. Therefore, while both of these groups could probably benefit from having it, it is most strongly recommended for professional collections in school district media centers and large public libraries, as well as university and college libraries that support programs in education. [R: RBB, 1 Sept 93, pp.88-90]—**Carol Truett**

379. Johnson, Jenny K., ed. **Graduate Curricula in Educational Communications and Technology: A Descriptive Directory.** 4th ed. Washington, D.C., Association for Educational Communications and Technology, 1992. 394p. $36.00pa. ISBN 0-89240-065-X.

As is the case with previous editions, this directory's diverse and confusing terminology used to describe courses, programs, and degrees presents problems to readers. Even the title is misleading, because few, if any, colleges or universities use "Educational Communications and Technology" to describe courses, degrees, programs, or titles of administrative units managing programs. The directory is difficult to use when trying to locate specific programs. For example, most of the programs listed prepare school library media specialists. These programs are difficult to find, as the assumption made by the programs seems to be that the school library media specialist is part of "Educational Communications and Technology." This organization is generally known only to those professionals in direct contact with the programs listed, whether or not they agree with the arrangement. To others, even professional educators, the preparation of school library media personnel appears to be conducted elsewhere. Equally confusing is the plethora of descriptors used to identify courses.

A list of careers for which students are preparing, including enrollment data, would be useful. This would provide the reader another way to assess curricula; for example, is the program only meeting the needs of a few? The directory is, perhaps, most valuable to program chairs, coordinators, and directors who want to compare their programs with others. [R: SLMQ, Winter 93, p. 139]—**William E. Hug**

380. Maddux, Cleborne D. **Distance Education: A Selected Bibliography.** Englewood Cliffs, N.J., Educational Technology, 1992. 71p. (Educational Technology Selected Bibliography Series, v.7). $14.95pa. Z5814.D54M33. 016.3713'078. LC 92-24055. ISBN 0-87778-249-0.

With the increased emphasis on adult education, retraining, and career changes, distance education is receiving a hard look. This new bibliography brings together articles, ERIC documents, and reports gleaned from a variety of electronic and paper indexes. None of the entries is annotated, which limits the work's usefulness. Although annotating hundreds of journal articles would be a Herculean task, and probably nonproductive for brief articles, annotations for some of the major sources listed would have been helpful. Another problem is the somewhat artificial categories into which this work is divided. The first section is a list of general articles; then come sections for problems and cautions, research, descriptions of projects in the United States and abroad, and issues and trends. These can overlap; for example, some of the general articles are also about problems and cautions. Maddux does list articles in more than one section if he felt the crossover was strong. The lack of an index makes this artificial grouping even more of a problem. A reader wanting information on one aspect of distance education is forced to browse through likely sections. However, there is much material conveniently brought together into one volume. The research sections, both for the United States and for other countries, should be of interest to anyone beginning a distance education program or course. Students and practitioners of distance education will also want to consult the bibliographies compiled by Borje Holmberg, such as *Theory and Practice of Distance Education* (Routledge, Chapman & Hall, 1989), which contains a bibliography.—**Terry Ann Mood**

381. Milheim, William D. **Computer-Based Simulations in Education and Training: A Selected Bibliography.** Englewood Cliffs, N.J., Educational Technology, 1992. 58p. (Educational Technology Selected Bibliography Series, v.8). $14.95pa. Z5643.S55M54. 016.3713'97'0285. LC 92-32545. ISBN 0-87778-254-7.

Despite its title, this bibliography contains computer simulation citations from a wide variety of subject areas, including economics, engineering, manufacturing, mathematics, medicine, and psychology. Its 17 sections give full bibliographic data for each item, with citations arranged by author within the various sections. There are no annotations, which would have provided additional assistance in selecting appropriate articles. In the first two sections, a quick count of publication dates determined the following: 3 percent of the citations have no dates, 4 percent are from the 1970s, 57 percent are from the 1980s, and 36 percent are from the 1990s. No indexes are provided. However, the straightforward arrangement makes citations fairly easy to find.

This highly specialized bibliography is probably limited in usefulness to larger or specialized libraries with a strong corporate training or teacher education emphasis. Although it is relatively inexpensive, one would probably find as many useful citations, if not more, in a search of the ERIC database or on CD-ROM where one could easily narrow entries retrieved by date or specific subjects.

—**Carol Truett**

382. Osborne, C. W., ed. **International Yearbook of Educational and Training Technology 1992/93.** London, Kogan Page; distr., East Brunswick, N.J., Nichols/GP Publishing, 1992. 380p. index. $99.00. ISBN 0-89397-377-7. ISSN 0370-9732.

This yearbook is a worldwide directory of centers engaged in educational and training technologies. Centers serving international and regional clients as well as those in the United Kingdom and the United States are listed in parts 1-3; other centers throughout the world are listed alphabetically by country in part 4. Entries include center name, primary areas of interest, services, publications, contact persons, and key words describing the center's activities. An index of institutions is included; however, the keyword index has been omitted. The latter was especially useful, because it provided easy access to centers involved in diverse activities, such as adult education, computer graphics, simulations, and teleconferencing. Also, earlier editions (e.g., 1986-1987) carried an informative series of articles highlighting current developments in training technologies.—**William E. Hug**

READING

383. Hunt, Gladys, and Barbara Hampton. **Read for Your Life: Turning Teens into Readers.** Grand Rapids, Mich., Zondervan, 1992. 240p. index. $9.99pa. Z1037.A1H87. 016.809'89282. LC 92-6834. ISBN 0-310-54871-3.

Attempting to do for teenagers what her earlier book, *Honey for a Child's Heart* (Zondervan, 1989) did for children, Hunt joins forces with Hampton to provide a readers' advisory handbook that focuses on books that should be of particular interest to young adults. Aimed at teen readers rather than parents or teachers, this guide includes more than 300 entries for books that run the gamut from old classics to contemporary works. The authors have made an effort to include books that they consider to be well written as well as appealing, and ones that will not "corrupt readers or their beliefs."

Prefaced by a warning to parents and an introduction, the first half of the guide consists of nine chapters, written by Hunt, that discuss reading and books in general and include specific topics, such as "Is Imagination Going Down the Tube?" and "What Makes a Good Book?" The second part of the book is the bibliography, compiled and annotated by Hampton, and is divided into nine sections: adventure, animals, contemporary, fantasy, historical, mystery, nonfiction, science fiction, and "Tried and True." Sections are arranged alphabetically by author, with each entry including title, copyright date, suggested age level, a brief description of the story, and a commentary paragraph. The guide is concluded by a glossary and an author/title index.

Well organized, nicely presented, and highly selective, this handbook has a definite conservative Christian slant. While the books selected are excellent choices for the young adult reader and deserve places in most young adult collections, this guide will probably be most appreciated by parents, teens, and educators who share the writers' philosophical and religious views.—**Kristin Ramsdell**

VOCATIONAL AND CONTINUING EDUCATION

384. **Career Discovery Encyclopedia.** Chicago, J. G. Ferguson Publishing, 1993. 6v. illus. index. $119.95/set. HF5381.2.C37. 331.7'02'03. LC 92-32314. ISBN 0-89434-144-8.

The features that made the 1990 edition (see ARBA 91, entry 371) a useful career exploration tool for elementary through junior high school students are preserved in this new version. Occupations are arranged alphabetically in clear, concise, two-page articles that follow a consistent format: job category symbol, cross-references to articles on related occupations, description of the job and working conditions, education and training required, earnings and employment outlook, a black-and-white illustrative photograph, and sources of further information (including activities, programs, and professional associations). Each volume contains the index to the entire set and a brief glossary of career guidance terminology.

Although the publisher is promoting the encyclopedia as a completely new edition and has changed it from a four- to a six-volume format, the work still contains about 500 articles, with an unspecified number of deletions, additions, and consolidations since the 1990 edition. What is clearly new about this set is the addition to each article of symbols that represent pertinent skills (e.g., language arts, manual, people). The occupations are grouped by these skill categories in an index at the end of the set. No sources are cited for the information presented, so its authority and currentness are not readily apparent, but this work appears well suited to the needs of young users. Owners of the 1990 edition may feel that current earnings and outlook information are not crucial to this audience and decide that the other changes made do not warrant investing in this update.—**Gregory M. Toth**

385. **Cassell Careers Encyclopedia.** 13th ed. By Audrey Segal and Katherine Lea. New York, Mansell/Cassell, 1992. 768p. index. $80.00. ISBN 0-304-31675-X.

With 13 editions over the past 40 years, this title has provided an authoritative career reference resource for Great Britain. Similar to *The Encyclopedia of Careers and Vocational Guidance* (see ARBA 91, entry 374) and the *Occupational Outlook Handbook* (see ARBA 91, entry 249), it offers comprehensive information on occupations and functions as well as qualifications, skills, and training required. The book targets both adult career changers and young people exploring initial career possibilities.

A wide range of occupations is covered—about 45—as well as the armed forces and government. Many sections reflect self-employment, flexible work patterns, and nonprofit sectors. Special sections address women at work, workers with special needs, and overseas opportunities. The arrangement, restructured from earlier editions, is now by the Careers Library Classification Index and is helpful and easily understood. Information is current as of May 1992.

Formal qualifications indicated are British academic and technical diplomas, degrees, and certificates. When required, examinations are noted. Occupational sections often include typical recruitment and entry patterns, and a specific level of work can be parlayed into other careers. The index is excellent, detailed, and specific. In addition, cross-references are incorporated into the text for related information in other entries. A comprehensive list of trade and professional organizations forms an important appendix, and an extensive bibliography rounds out this thorough work.—**Barbara Conroy**

386. **The Encyclopedia of Careers and Vocational Guidance.** 9th ed. William E. Hopke, ed. Chicago, J. G. Ferguson Publishing, 1993. 4v. illus. index. $129.95/set. HF5381.E52. 331.7'02. LC 90-22141. ISBN 0-89434-149-9.

Recent major trends in the world of work are noted in this latest edition of the standard basic guide to occupational fields. It brings labor market information up-to-date and includes several articles new to this edition. As with earlier editions, volume 1 profiles various industries, such as engineering, insurance, and textiles. But the other three volumes introduce alphabetical listings of individual jobs—a distinct improvement over the previous approach of grouping jobs into 16 functional categories in volumes covering professional, technical, and special occupations. Articles are, as before, comprehensive, giving the nature of the work, requirements (training and capabilities), earnings, and employment outlook. Individuals considering a career will find helpful sections on entering the field, advancement, related occupations, and additional resources. Related articles are indicated in each entry, guiding the user to similar occupations.

Each volume contains the index to all four volumes. Two appendixes update earlier editions and cover special resources for the disabled and information on internships, apprenticeships, and training programs. However, this edition incorporates some of that information in the occupational articles. Each article provides the numbers for accessing such works as the *Standard Industrial Classification Manual* (Office of Management and Budget, 1987). Academic and high school career centers, career counselors, and libraries will make heavy use of this encyclopedia.—**Barbara Conroy**

387. Farr, J. Michael, ed. **The Complete Guide for Occupational Exploration: An Easy-to-Use Guide to Exploring Over 12,000 Job Titles....** 1993 ed. Indianapolis, Ind., JIST Works, 1993. 915p. $34.95pa. HF5382.5.U5C65. 331.7'02. LC 92-39246. ISBN 1-56370-052-2.

This work expands the newly revised version of the U.S. Department of Labor's 2d edition (1984) of the *Guide to Occupational Exploration* (GOE) and to the *Enhanced Guide to Occupational Exploration*. It employs the straightforward and comprehensive organization of the GOE, and it includes many additional features useful for students, career changers, and counselors—for about the same modest price. Most of the book is a basic arrangement of 12,000 job titles grouped into 12 major interest areas, 66 work groups, and 348 subgroups. Areas and work groups are described generally along with information about required licensure, certificates, specialized training, and relevant organizations and agencies. Subgroups are listed and coded with the *Dictionary of Occupational Titles* (see ARBA 93, entry 301) for easy reference to that volume. The source of most of this noncopyrighted information is the U.S. Department of Labor and its latest revision of the GOE.

Other helpful sections in this book that are not in the GOE include information for vocational counselors and other professionals, technical details on the setup of this volume, and an extensive list of apprenticeable occupations. A series of checklists helps users identify key factors important to a career choice and guides them to more information about specific jobs. Providing access to this resource is an alphabetical index of 30,000 job titles. [R: Choice, July/Aug 93, p. 1745; WLB, May 93, p. 114]

—**Barbara Conroy**

388. Gilbert, Sara D. **The Career Training Sourcebook: Where to Get Free, Low-Cost, and Salaried Job Training.** New York, McGraw-Hill, 1993. 268p. index. $24.95; $13.95pa. HD5715.2.G55. 331.25'92'02573. LC 92-28258. ISBN 0-07-023541-4; 0-07-023540-6pa.

This new directory of both traditional and nontraditional sources for free, low-cost, and salaried career training is as useful for those entering the work force for the first time as it is for those facing a career change. Divided into 12 chapters, the work begins by discussing the changing job market of the 1990s and the effect such changes are having on career patterns. (According to the author, the average American in the 1990s and beyond will experience an average of 6.5 careers.) It then provides a very useful formula to determine which careers an individual is best suited for and to help assess skills possessed and training needed.

Most of the book is devoted to information on a surprising variety of training sources: on-the-job learning; school-based training in colleges, universities, community colleges, and vocational schools; adult education programs; corporate training programs; government-sponsored training; union/association-sponsored training; and training for special groups. It even includes the training that can be received through franchisers, temporary agencies, and volunteering. Each of these nine chapters gives the pros and cons of the particular type of training, contact information, and sources of further data. The contact information varies in detail from program to program; telephone and fax numbers are not always given, but information about program costs is provided when applicable. The chapter organization of the book is straightforward, and there is also an index.

While more in-depth sources exist for particular types of training, such as *National Directory of Corporate Training Programs* (see ARBA 89, entry 152), this source is unusual in that it combines information on many types of inexpensive training programs and allows for easy comparison between them. This is a useful book at a reasonable price.—**Diana Accurso**

389. Greenberg, Reva M. **Education for Older Adult Learning: A Selected, Annotated Bibliography.** Westport, Conn., Greenwood Press, 1993. 219p. index. (Bibliographies and Indexes in Gerontology, no.20). $65.00. Z5814.A24G74. 016.374. LC 92-42689. ISBN 0-313-28368-0.

The basic bibliography in this compilation consists of 713 entries for books, articles, conference proceedings, government publications, dissertations, research reports, guides, and curriculum materials. These items are grouped under two broad categories. The first is concerned with general issues and key themes. It cites 242 basic readings, research study reports, and publications that give historical, philosophical, or theoretical perspectives or that describe comprehensive educational programs. The second lists 471 writings on instructional techniques and applications. A few entries are for audiovisual materials and computer programs. All entries give basic bibliographical information and well-written annotations. Because the annotations are all favorable, it appears that this is a list of recommended items, although this is not specifically stated in the introduction. A list of journals cited is provided. A section on online databases contains evaluations of ABI/Inform, AgeLine, Dissertation Abstracts, ERIC, GPO Monthly, Medline, Newspaper Abstracts, Nursing and Allied Health, and PsycINFO and shows their relevance and usefulness to the field of older adult education. There are lists of 44 aging network professional organizations and 55 selected resource organizations. There is also a list of federal statutes on the subject. None of these lists are annotated.

Greenberg is a well-known and highly qualified specialist in gerontology, especially its educational aspects. This work will be of use to all who are involved with older adult education. [R: Choice, Sept 93, p. 82]—**Shirley L. Hopkinson**

390. **The Independent Study Catalog: A Guide to Continuing Education through Correspondence Courses.** 5th ed. Princeton, N.J., Peterson's Guides, 1992. 287p. illus. index. $16.95pa. ISBN 1-56079-138-1. ISSN 0733-6020.

Published for the National University Continuing Education Association (NUCEA), this guide enables users to locate correspondence courses by subject area and by institution. All levels, from elementary to graduate study, as well as noncredit courses, are included, although most are high school and college undergraduate offerings. Entries in the main directory section are arranged by institution name and include course names, numbers and credits, level of instruction, and any supplementary instructional media, as well as institution contact information. As was the previous edition (see ARBA 90, entry 358), this one is well indexed and includes a useful introductory section on correspondence study. Because it covers 87 institutions, compared with the previous edition's 70, and has abandoned that edition's subject restrictions, it is more than twice as long. However, it includes only accredited institutions that meet NUCEA standards and does not cover proprietary schools and vocational courses. Individuals and libraries aware of this selectiveness may find this guide an acceptable alternative to the more detailed and comprehensive but more costly *Macmillan Guide to Correspondence Study* (Macmillan, 1993).

—**Gregory M. Toth**

391. Kulich, Jindra. **Adult Education in Continental Europe: An Annotated Bibliography of English-language Materials 1989-1991.** Vancouver, B.C., Centre for Continuing Education, University of British Columbia, 1993. 202p. index. (Monographs on Comparative and Area Studies in Adult Education). $22.00pa. 016.374'94. ISBN 0-88843-194-5.

This is the seventh in a series of bibliographies on comparative adult education in continental Europe. It lists 891 articles and books in the English language published between 1989 and 1991. Accessibility through libraries was a major criterion for inclusion. Typescript and photo-reproduced papers; doctoral dissertations and master's theses; and materials available only on microfilm, microfiche, or computer disks were excluded. Entries are listed under country, with general sections for Europe and Scandinavia. New sections have been created for new and emerging countries. Within each section, entries are arranged under a number of subtopics or categories. Most entries are accompanied by a descriptive annotation that is concise yet definitive. References to related works are given throughout the bibliography. Author and subject indexes, a list of periodicals searched, and a list of subject categories under which the entries are grouped supplement the bibliography. Bibliographical periodicals and journals in the fields of education, adult education, the humanities, social sciences, health science, and librarianship have been searched, apparently thoroughly.

This edition compares favorably with previous editions, both in terms of scope and of careful research. It should be of interest to students and instructors of adult or comparative education and to administrators in the field of adult education.—**Shirley L. Hopkinson**

392. Sattler, S. C., Henry A. Spille, and Lansing J. Davis, eds. **The National Guide to Educational Credit for Training Programs.** 1992-93 ed. Washington, D.C., American Council on Education and Phoenix, Ariz., Oryx Press, 1993. 1118p. $49.95pa. ISBN 0-89774-824-7. ISSN 0275-4142.

Formal educational programs and courses sponsored by noncollegiate organizations often qualify for academic credit. Thus, individuals engaging in educational offerings through business and industry, trade and professional associations, the military, and government agencies can document and submit courses for credit toward academic degrees. This volume helps those needing to determine the credit "worthiness" of specific nonacademic courses (e.g., apprenticeships, home study, corporate training) by evaluating them against standardized criteria for sound educational practice. In addition to the guidelines for the evaluation process and procedures for students to follow in obtaining credit, the listings for reviewed courses include title, dates, versions, objectives, instructional methods, and credit recommendations. This last includes vocational certificates, associate or lower division degree credits, or graduate or upper division degree credits, as well as numbers of semester hours and subjects.

Large though this volume is, it includes only a small portion of the programs offered, because a sponsor of such programs must submit courses for review. However, using the criteria and procedures can increase the likelihood of academic acceptance for parallel courses. Earlier editions of this title should be retained to ensure the widest possible coverage of reviewed sponsors. The most likely users of this volume are academic counselors and adults seeking to find whether specific educational programs can be credited to their academic plans.—**Barbara Conroy**

393. Sullivan, Eugene. **The Adult Learner's Guide to Alternative and External Degree Programs.** Phoenix, Ariz., Oryx Press, 1993. 227p. index. (American Council on Education/Oryx Series on Higher Education). $39.95pa. L901.S84. 378.73. LC 93-32154. ISBN 0-89774-815-8.

This new guide opens the door to a wide variety of undergraduate and graduate degree programs for adults unable to relocate to acquire a degree. Even with 192 alternative degree programs and 91 external degree programs included, the directory is not complete. Still, its breadth is useful for adults pursuing education for career change or skills enhancement and for career counselors and academic advisers. No other directory taps this growing roster of optional means to learn in patterns of time and locale designed to fit working lifestyles. Program information, compiled from survey forms returned by the colleges, includes description, accreditation, admission and credit requirements, completion time, student support services, enrollment, tuition and fees, and other relevant information. Each entry provides sufficient data to determine its relevance and whether further pursuit is desirable. Thus, adults can take active steps to design their study beyond on-campus academic programs.

The use of this directory for career planning depends on thorough investigation of an individual's goals as well as the programs. One appendix in particular is helpful to the decisionmaking process, providing principles of good practice for such programs to use as criteria for specific ones being considered. Another offers information on portfolio assessment instruments and guides.

—**Barbara Conroy**

6 Ethnic Studies and Anthropology

ANTHROPOLOGY AND ETHNOLOGY

394. **The Cambridge Encyclopedia of Human Evolution.** Steve Jones, Robert Martin, and David Pilbeam, eds. New York, Cambridge University Press, 1992. 506p. illus. maps. index. $95.00. GN281.C345. 579.2. LC 92-18037. ISBN 0-521-32370-3.

Within a five-year period three excellent volumes have been produced relating to human evolution. *Encyclopedia of Human Evolution and Prehistory* (see ARBA 89, entry 336) included coverage of prehistoric archaeology in some 600 illustrated articles. Two years later, *The Encyclopedia of Evolution: Humanity's Search for Its Origins* (see ARBA 92, entry 1523) provided a more general review with a strong emphasis on scientific ideas and popular culture. Now this Cambridge title offers a wide-ranging introduction to the field prepared by international experts. The arrangement is both comprehensive and usable. Ten major sections (e.g., "Patterns of Primate Evolution," "Primate Genetics and Evolution," "Human Populations, Past and Present") are followed by a concluding chapter on the evolutionary future of humankind and three appendixes (famous names in evolutionary history, a geological time scale, and a map of sites). A glossary, a reading list, and an index complete this attractively designed and illustrated publication.

As with all one-volume encyclopedias, use will disclose its many valuable facets. Among the tables are such varied examples as distinguishing features of early human species and dates of early domestication of animals. Maps are abundant and range from disease distribution (e.g., HIV infection) to prehistoric sites (e.g., rock art) to positions of crustal plates or the extent of oceans during the Paleogene. However, besides tables and maps, the volume is replete with drawings, graphs, photographs, and narrative tables. In addition, the editors have highlighted certain textual material through the use of margins and a darker background; these article and illustration inserts are itemized in the table of contents as subheadings under each of the major parts—a slightly confusing approach. For example, a section on the human brain is subsection 3.2 under part 3: "The Brain and Language." Besides several drawings of the brain found within this subsection, there are two special numbered and illustrated areas: "1. Impressions of Ancestral Brains" and "2. The Brain and Left-Handedness." The entire subsection and each of the two special inserts are individually authored.

Despite the somewhat unorthodox organization, the volume is easy to use for ready-reference because the index is extensive and comprehensive enough to separate references to text from those to illustrations or captions. Cross-references are used throughout the articles, special sections, appendixes, and index. Within the main text each article has internal *see* references and concludes with a boxed set of *see also* references that refer to related sections and page numbers.

This work is highly recommended for general and research libraries of all types because the subject areas covered are of major significance and are themselves undergoing rapid evolution. The authoritative source material is both readable and accurate within the framework of current data. [R: LJ, 1 June 93, p. 102; RBB, Aug 93, pp. 2085-86]—**Laurel Grotzinger**

395. **Encyclopedia of World Cultures. Volume IV: Europe (Central, Western, and Southeastern Europe).** Linda A. Bennett, ed. New York, G. K. Hall, 1992. 299p. maps. index. $100.00. GN307.E53. 306'.097. LC 90-49123. ISBN 0-8161-1811-6.

Timing could not be better for the publication of this volume. With European countries dividing into smaller and smaller ethnic groups and the problem of "ethnic cleansing" apparently growing, a volume that provides solid information on 116 cultures of Western, Northern, Central, Mediterranean, and Southern Europe will be useful in answering numerous questions. (The former Soviet Union countries will be profiled in volume 6.) Given that HRAF (Human Relations Area Files) is the basic source for the material, it is not surprising to find that anthropological research has played a key role in the selection process. Thus, a group or culture is listed if European anthropologists treat it as a distinct group or if there is a body of anthropological research about the group. Additional requirements were that either an anthropologist or other scholar was available to prepare the article or enough published literature existed to allow a staff researcher to write the entry. Some 77 scholars from the United States, Canada, and Europe contributed one or more of the entries. With so many groups covered, countries are broken down into various ethnic groupings. Thus, under *French* is one short paragraph with *see* references to Alsatian, Aquitaine, Auvergnats, Aveyronnais, Basques, Bretons, Burgundians, Jurassians, Occitans, Provencal, and Walloons. Also included are groups that cut across national boundaries, such as Ashkenazic Jews, Gypsies (listed under a variety of headings, such as Horahane, Roma, Romiche, Tsigani, and Zigeuner), and Saami. The basic entry format is the same as in the first three volumes of the set—basic geographic and demographic information, history and cultural relations, economy, kinship and family, sociopolitical organization, religion and expressive culture, and a short bibliography.

No other title covers the same ground as this one. A general encyclopedia would provide some of the basic cultural material along with long history sections, but for social and cultural information, this is an excellent starting point.—**G. Edward Evans**

396. **Encyclopedia of World Cultures. Volume V: East and Southeast Asia.** Paul Hockings, ed. New York, G. K. Hall, 1993. 313p. maps. index. $100.00. GN307.E53. 306'.097. LC 90-49123. ISBN 0-8161-1814-0.

The geographical coverage of this volume is vast, from Japan and Korea in the north to Timor in the south, and from Aru in the east to Myanmar (Burma) in the west. As with prior volumes in the set, the introduction provides a valuable overview of the region. It also makes the point that while a user may think there is excellent coverage of minority cultures, the volume is just a starting point for some countries. Hockings uses the example of a relatively small island (17,350 square kilometers) in eastern Indonesia that has 21 cultures, each one speaking a distinct language, to make his point.

Entries in this volume follow the same pattern as earlier volumes (see, for example, ARBA 93, entry 413). The filmography lists 172 items and has a short index to help identify film contents. Alternative names and spellings can be found in the ethnonym index, an essential tool for this culturally diverse area. Sixty-six scholars from around the world contributed one or more entries, with the volume editor contributing additional items. Those libraries that acquired the early volumes should also purchase this one.

—**G. Edward Evans**

397. **Oxford Illustrated Encyclopedia of Peoples and Cultures.** Richard Hoggart, ed. New York, Oxford University Press, 1992. 391p. illus. maps. $49.95. ISBN 0-19-869139-4.

Volume 7 of the *Oxford Illustrated Encyclopedia* deals with peoples and cultures throughout the world. As in previous volumes, which covered the natural and physical world, history, and the arts, entries are arranged in alphabetical order. They present brief and concise information on such topics as religion, education, social structures, environmental issues, popular culture, and leisure. Color photographs, maps, and many graphs enhance and expand the text. One could quarrel with the omission of certain terms, such as *birth control, polygamy,* and *infanticide,* but all in all, the book is amazingly comprehensive and up-to-date. Another useful feature of this excellent reference work is the self-contained section on the countries of the world, including the newly independent states of the former Soviet Union. Recommended for all libraries. [R: Choice, July/Aug 93, p. 1753; RBB, July 93, p. 2004]—**Natalia Sonevytsky**

ETHNIC STUDIES

General Works

398. **Resource Guide of Publications Supported by Multiculturalism Programs 1973-1992.** Ottawa, Multiculturalism and Citizenship Canada, 1993. 136p. index. free pa. 016.3058'00971. ISBN 0-662-59679-X.

The publication of this guide is important for librarians who are developing ethnic collections and for students of ethnic media. The foreword states "The purpose of this guide is two-fold: to broaden awareness of published materials dealing with themes and issues related to Canadian multiculturalism; and to promote the use of these materials by educators, researchers, and the public in general." It should be pointed out that Multiculturalism and Citizenship Canada (formerly part of the Department of the Secretary of State) has, for many years, promoted various multiculturalism programs and supported many Canadian ethnic-related research projects. The material in this guide was collected from the department's project files and in cooperation with publishers.

Entries are arranged by title in straight alphabetical order in English, French, and other languages. All entries contain full bibliographical descriptions and brief annotations. The inclusion of source material in so-called Canadian "third languages" (e.g., Polish, Ukrainian, German) is very important, because many significant materials are published in these languages. Thus, this guide is a good example for U.S. publishers of similar guides, which in many instances are limited to English-language titles. In addition to titles, this publication has indexes of names, of languages and ethnocultural groups, and of subjects. They provide easy access to listed materials. There are also lists of publishers and journals.

It is hoped that an updated edition of this guide will include additional journals published by various Canadian groups as well as a selective list of Canadian ethnic newspapers. The list of publishers also requires some updating, such as the inclusion of telephone and fax numbers for individual publishing houses. Still, this Canadian guide is a substantial addition to recent ethnic reference materials.
—**Lubomyr R. Wynar**

399. Stevens, Gregory I., with Sarah Parker Scotchmer, eds. **Videos for Understanding Diversity: A Core Selection and Evaluative Guide.** Chicago, American Library Association, 1993. 217p. $40.00pa. LC1099.3.S74. 370.19'6'0208. LC 93-2662. ISBN 0-8389-0612-5.

For too many of today's youth, "videos for understanding diversity" probably means episodes of MTV's *Beavis and Butthead*. Its medium is undoubtedly the correct one for catching and holding the attention of teenagers and college-age students, but its message can hardly be judged as sensitizing, humanizing, or uplifting. Such messages are central to the 126 videos that make up the collection described and evaluated in this review. Originally assembled as part of a project at the University of Albany, State University of New York, each of the videos deals with one or more themes, including race, ethnicity, gender, religion, culture, life stages, and stereotypes. Although some are well known (e.g., *The Autobiography of Miss Jane Pittman, Torch Song Trilogy*), most of these videos would remain unknown and unused were it not for this guide.

As a reference tool, this volume works extremely well. The introductory material is clear and to the point, and each entry contains full purchase and rental information, a summary of contents, and critical comments. The editors have allowed reviewers to express their opinions freely and to present their views in as much detail as necessary. This is especially useful for those who have to order videos without being able to view them beforehand. *Videos for Understanding Diversity* deserves to be on the shelf in almost all public and school libraries. [R: BR, Nov/Dec 93, p. 37; RBB, 1 Nov 93, p. 571; SLMQ, Summer 93, p. 266]—**Leonard J. Greenspoon**

400. Taylor, Charles A., ed. **Guide to Multicultural Resources 1993/1994.** Madison, Wis., Praxis Publications and Fort Atkinson, Wis., Highsmith Press, 1993. 474p. index. $49.00pa. ISBN 0-917846-18-4. ISSN 1050-4249.

This guide lists more than 3,000 organizations, governmental agencies, and other bodies focused on multicultural events and individuals, with an emphasis on the United States (although some selected Canadian and international organizations are included). The work is organized into five major sections: African-American, Asian-American, Hispanic-American, Native American, and multicultural resources. Each section offers a brief introductory overview of the ethnic group, followed by lists of relevant organizations and agencies grouped under such topical headings as civil rights, education, media, and social services. Each entry provides an address and telephone number, and many also include a statement of purpose and a description of services offered. Separate organization, geographical, publication, executive, and video indexes are included.

Updated from its 1989 edition, this work duplicates many of the listings in other well-known resources, such as the *Black Resource Guide* (see ARBA 93, entry 422), the *Asian-American Information Directory* (see ARBA 93, entry 421), and the *Hispanic Resource Directory* (see ARBA 93, entry 429). Its advantage lies in having pulled together so much useful information from so many diverse sources, providing users with a fairly complete overview of available resources in one easy-to-use volume. If the editor can update this work on a more regular basis, it will continue to be a useful reference tool. [R: LJ, 1 Nov 93, pp. 72-74]—**Elizabeth Patterson**

Asian-Americans

401. Gall, Susan, and Timothy L. Gall, eds. **Statistical Record of Asian Americans.** Detroit, Gale, 1993. 796p. index. $89.50. ISBN 0-8103-8918-5.

How many Chinese restaurant workers are in New York? What is the postsecondary school rate, by immigrant status and sex, of Filipino Canadians? What is the church affiliation of Korean Americans in Philadelphia? This book will answer these questions; it is packed with every conceivable kind of data concerning Asian Americans and Asian Canadians. It contains 850 tables of specific data arranged into 14 chapter categories, from attitudes and opinions to religion. Two tables of contents and an index provide access to this vast amount of self-reported data. The first table of contents lists chapter titles and subheadings. The second, expanded, lists all entry titles in the book under the appropriate chapter title and subheading. This source also contains comparative data, when reported, on Caucasians, Blacks, Hispanics, and Native Americans. Data are also broken down by sex whenever feasible. Historical data are presented in detail in the immigration and population and vital statistics sections. The bibliography is the weakest part of the book. It should be updated with more recent book entries and expanded to include more journal articles and videos. For example, the Filipino section lists only four rather outdated book references and the Korean section only five.

This work is an invaluable resource on this fast-growing segment of the North American population. It will easily establish itself as the standard and indispensable work in its field. Perhaps the publisher will also make this information available online, as it has done with some of its other reference works; electronic access, periodically updated, would enhance its value. [R: RBB, 15 Oct 93, p. 475; WLB, Nov 93, pp. 105-06]—**Marshall E. Nunn**

Blacks

402. **The African American Encyclopedia.** Michael W. Williams, ed. North Bellmore, N.Y., Marshall Cavendish, 1993. 6v. illus. maps. index. $449.95/set. E185.A253. 973'.0496073'003. LC 93-141. ISBN 1-85435-545-7.

Frederick Douglass, a great African-American scholar and statesman, once stated, "You don't know where you are going ... if you don't know where you have been." This phrase exemplifies the need for the kind of information provided in this set. The traditional framework set for African-American literature has typically identified well-known African Americans who have produced the greatest controversies or changes in their fields of expertise (e.g., business, medicine, politics, religion). Great Americans of African descent, such as Martin Luther King, Jr., Malcolm X, Bobby Seale, James Earl Jones, and Maya Angelou, are some of those who have received recognition, but these examples provide only a glimpse into how African Americans have contributed to the building of our country. More important, the set supplies a valuable first step in uncovering the contributions of thousands of less well known individuals, such as the creation of the first quilt or coverlet in America by African slaves and the achievements of African Americans during the Gulf War.

The *African American Encyclopedia* successfully achieves its goal of bringing the accomplishments of both well-known and lesser-known individuals and groups together in a well-written, concise, easy-to-read collection. It encompasses the broad history of past generations and incorporates many achievements and failures that have shaped the present. By doing so, the set provides a collage of a people and their direction in the United States. It is a valuable reference tool for any library. [R: BR, Nov/Dec 93, p. 57; Choice, Nov 93, p. 423; JAL, Sept 93, p. 274; LJ, 1 Sept 93, p. 168; RBB, July 93, pp. 1998-2000; SLJ, Nov 93, p. 147; WLB, Oct 93, p. 85]—**Kevin L. Gomez**

403. **Index to Black Periodicals 1991.** New York, G. K. Hall, 1992. 274p. $95.00. ISBN 0-8161-0479-4. ISSN 0899-6253.

This index has been published annually, with various titles and sponsors, since 1959, when G. K. Hall brought out a 1950-1959 cumulation. It remains the primary tool for locating articles published in African-American-oriented and -produced periodicals. This work is a single alphabetical arrangement of subjects, authors, and cross-references. Citations include title, author, journal title, volume, date, and pagination. It is stated that subject terms are derived from the *Library of Congress Subject Headings* (see ARBA 90, entry 602), but many deviations are included (e.g., "Black Womanism"). Book, film, and theater reviews (but not reviews for music and records, as claimed); obituaries; poems; and short stories are conveniently grouped together. Currently, the volume indexes 34 journal titles from the popular and scholarly literature; this is down from 39 in 1988. Additional titles should be indexed (e.g., *Transforming Anthropology, Social and Economic Studies*).

Improvement in the use of cross-references and consistency in the assignment of subject headings is badly needed. For instance, one citation is found for Miles Davis under his name, two under "Obituaries," and none under any of the music headings, while an article about Dizzy Gillespie is indexed both under his name and under "Musicians." Three articles are listed under "Brown, James (about)" but none under "Music," "Musicians," or "Singers." Furthermore, the work should be made more current; for years now the indexing has been running two years behind the publications indexed. In spite of these deficiencies, most public and academic libraries should subscribe to this work.—**Fred J. Hay**

404. Lee, George L. **Worldwide Interesting People: 162 History Makers of African Descent.** Jefferson, N.C., McFarland, 1992. 134p. illus. index. $17.95. CT107.L46. 920'.009296. LC 91-50939. ISBN 0-89950-670-4.

This book contains the likenesses, in black-and-white line drawings, of more than 100 Africans and African-Americans. Each drawing is accompanied by a brief sketch of the subject's accomplishments, with space on the page being almost evenly divided between drawings and text. This leaves the reader with little useful material. The premise behind the volume is that achievements of people of African descent have been neglected in textbooks, reference books, and other written materials to the extent that the Western world knows or cares very little about them. This volume is an attempt to remedy that situation by exposing the reader to a large number of names and faces of such people who have contributed to the world's cultural, economic, scientific, and religious progress.

While this premise is indeed noble, Lee fails in his goal, first by failing to give the reader something to read. The sketches are so brief that one is often left wondering just why a particular person has been designated "worldwide" or "interesting." Second, there is no indication about the significance of the contributions made by many of the subjects in the book. It would have been helpful to have put the contributions into some kind of context. Third, the reader is presented with facts about many "obscure" persons but is given no sources for further reading and investigation. Thus, Lee fails to encourage sustained interest on the part of the reader. Fourth, the book has no apparent arrangement; personalities are not presented alphabetically, chronologically, by category, or by area of work. This makes it difficult to find a particular subject without turning to the index. Lee had deemed these personalities neglected by previous writers, but he also neglects them in his own book.—**Melvin M. Bowie**

405. Nordquist, Joan, comp. **African Americans: Social and Economic Conditions: A Bibliography.** Santa Cruz, Calif., Reference and Research Services, 1992. 72p. (Contemporary Social Issues: A Bibliographic Series, no.27). $15.00pa. ISBN 0-937855-52-9.

Similar to other bibliographies in the Contemporary Social Issues series, this publication is a classified list of current (most published within the last five years) materials on a selected topic. It focuses on African-American social and economic conditions and includes 896 citations to scholarly and trade books, articles, and pamphlets arranged into 22 topics in 5 chapters. (The table of contents lists a chapter 6 but does not include a chapter 5.) Also included is a list of addresses of organizations that deal with African-American social action and research. Subject topics include standard categories such as health and housing and such salient contemporary issues as drug-addicted babies (30 citations) and Affirmative Action (62 citations). Sections on statistical sources, bibliographies, and directories are included. Minimal cross-references are provided at the end of each topic. Emphasis is on books rather than periodical literature, which was included only when an insufficient number of books on a topic had been located. Most of the citations could be easily retrieved from a university library's online catalog.

The book appears to have been based on some combination of online and print index searching without the compiler's subsequent examination of all materials. Historical works are mixed in with contemporary ones, and publications marginal to the topic are included. No indexes are provided. This bibliography's saving grace is the series' stated goal of including adequate coverage of the often-neglected small press and alternative publishers, including those specializing in progressive politics, African-American studies, multiculturalism, and feminism. [R: RBB, 15 Feb 93, p. 1707]—**Fred J. Hay**

406. Salley, Columbus. **The Black 100: A Ranking of the Most Influential African-Americans, Past and Present.** New York, Citadel Press/Carol Publishing Group, 1993. 383p. illus. index. $21.95. E185.96.S225. 973'.0496073. LC 92-39545. ISBN 0-8065-1299-7.

This is a list of 21 women, 81 men, and a social movement (Black Power) that Salley feels have been most influential in the struggle of African-Americans to achieve full equality. Each person is ranked for relative importance, with Martin Luther King, Jr., at number one and his Montgomery bus boycott associate, Rosa Parks, at one hundred. Each entry includes a photograph or other portrait, dates, and a biographical sketch. The biographies are derivative and lack sources. Moreover, although the biographical data on these individuals is covered quite well in other reference books, some errors have crept in. For example, Zora Neale Hurston's *Jonah's Gourd Vine* is classified as folklore rather than novel.

This sort of ranking is inherently subjective; there is no way to establish any validity for the hierarchy. Salley does not adequately explain why Booker T. Washington (number 3) was rated higher than W.E.B. Du Bois (number 4), or why U.S. Representative Oscar De Priest and sociologist and Fisk University president Charles S. Johnson, among others, were omitted. Two jazz musicians were included but not the very influential James Brown or any musicians from the blues genre, which has been the foundation of much of the world's popular music in the twentieth century. This reviewer also questions Clarence Thomas's fit with Salley's criteria. This book will be more appropriate for browsing than as a reference tool. [R: LJ, Jan 93, p. 105; RBB, 1 April 93, p. 1452]—**Fred J. Hay**

407. Van de Sande, Wendy S., and Ned Burels, eds. **Black Americans Information Directory 1994-95: A Guide to Approximately 53,000 Organizations, Agencies, Institutions, Programs, and Publications....** 3d ed. Detroit, Gale, 1993. 556p. index. $75.00. ISBN 0-8103-8082-X. ISSN 1045-8050.

This edition of a now-standard reference source contains 5,281 entries classified in 18 chapters. Included are associations; awards; universities; local, state, and federal governments; businesses; museums and libraries; periodicals; publishers and broadcast media; religious groups; research centers; African-American studies programs; scholarships; and videos. Most entries include name, address, telephone numbers, contact person, and a brief descriptive annotation. The video section provides name, address, and telephone number of distributor and the terms of availability. As outlined in the user's guide, most entries are derived from other Gale publications, the annual *United States Government Manual* (National

Archives and Records Administration), *Catalog of Federal Domestic Assistance* (Office of Management and Budget, 1992), and *Black Enterprise* magazine. All sections are extremely selective. For instance, the Helena, Arkansas, radio station KFFA is omitted from the listing for radio stations, yet it pioneered and still broadcasts the daily King Biscuit show, which was a major influence on the evolution of Black and white music in the United States and the world. Otherwise, the radio listings include 480 stations whose connection to Black America is not specified.

Improvements to this edition include the updating of entries; the addition of telephone numbers to many entries that previously lacked them; a new chapter on scholarships, fellowships, and loans; and an improved index. The latter, however, still lacks personal names (e.g., contact persons), geographical locations, or sufficient subject terms. Although Gale could do much to improve this directory, it remains an essential reference source for most libraries.—**Fred J. Hay**

Canadians

408. Miska, John. **Canadian Studies on Hungarians: A Bibliography. Supplement.** Victoria, B.C., Microform Biblios, 1992. 80p. index. (Canlit Bibliographic Series, no.6). $15.00 spiralbound. 016.971'00494511. ISBN 0-919279-09-0.

This current bibliography serves as a supplement to the 1987 work by the same author, *Canadian Studies on Hungarians, 1886-1986* (see ARBA 88, entry 414). The more than 700 new citations offer a much-needed update of the previously covered topics as well as add depth to the original bibliography because Miska introduces new subject areas such as music, film, and television. The entries were compiled from relevant monographs, research papers, and review articles accessible through Canadian university libraries, the National Library of Canada, and the national archives of both Canada and Hungary.

The references are arranged under two main headings: "Hungary, Hungarians" and "Hungarians in Canada." Each section is further subdivided into such topics as reference works, history, and religion. Under the subheadings, citations are listed in alphabetical order by author. Entries are short, mostly just citations with an occasional sketchy annotation. Most, but not all, sources are in Hungarian, with the English translations of the titles in brackets. Unfortunately, sometimes these translations are no more than approximate. The sections dealing with individual artists, authors, composers, and biographees contain short biographical sketches on the subjects. An author/subject index rounds off the bibliography. Despite its shortcomings, this supplement will be a helpful addition to Canadian and Hungarian studies research collections.—**Zsuzsa Koltay**

409. Strong, Lisa L., ed. **Contemporary Books Reflecting Canada's Cultural Diversity: A Selected Annotated Bibliography for Grades K-12.** Vancouver, B.C., British Columbia Teacher-Librarians' Association, 1992. 120p. illus. index. $14.40pa. 016.3058'00971. ISBN 0-921140-20-7.

Designed as an aid for selecting classroom materials that reflect Canada's multicultural mosaic, this guide separately lists appropriate fiction and information books alphabetically by author. Each entry in these lists provides bibliographical information, an annotation that describes the work and provides comments about ways to use it, a suggestion of the appropriate grade levels of the audience, and a list of topics for integrating the work into the curriculum. Separate title and subject indexes aid in locating these discussions. The guide concludes with a list of publishers and a brief, unannotated list of professional resources concerned with ethnic cultures or the teaching of works about ethnic groups.

Because the criteria for inclusion are based on principles established by the British Columbia Department of Education, the selected works are both positive about cultural differences and suitable for classroom use. Nevertheless, the book has some puzzling omissions. Brian Doyle's *Angel Square* (Groundwood, 1991), a comic investigation of ethnic and religious intolerance, and Barbara Smucker's *Amish Adventure* (Herald Press, 1983), a realistic problem novel dealing with intolerance within and without a minority group, are not annotated, although Smucker's book appears in the indexes. One could wish for a broader list of works, but the generous annotations of those included are useful, offering clear descriptions and meaningful advice or warnings about using a work in the classroom. This guide is most useful for Canadians, but United States teachers wishing to explore both other cultures and their northern neighbors may also find it helpful. [R: EL, Mar-April 93, pp. 46-47]—**Raymond E. Jones**

410. Tapper, Lawrence F. **A Biographical Dictionary of Canadian Jewry 1909-1914: From** *The Canadian Jewish Times*. Teaneck, N.J., Avotaynu, 1992. 245p. index. $35.00. F1035.J5F76. 920'.0092924071. LC 92-18521. ISBN 0-9626373-0-0.

This specialized reference work is an index of biographical data about Canadian Jews taken from the only Anglo-Jewish newspaper in Canada during 1909-1914. It consists of two parts. The first has topical entries, including bar mitzvah and confirmation announcements, biographical essays, birth announcements, deaths and obituaries, engagements and marriages, and general news items. The second and larger part includes geographical entries covering 12 cities and regions of Canada. Montreal, which contained the largest and most active Jewish community, is emphasized. The entries cover a variety of personal and family announcements, news of individual achievements, family celebrations, synagogal activities, travels, and visits. Each entry also includes the date, volume, and issue number of the *Canadian Jewish Times* from which the information was taken. An extensive name index provides quick and easy access to the people in the book. Unfortunately, except for the broad topical categories of part 1, there is no specific subject access to the data. This would have improved the usefulness of the book.

Preliminary materials include a foreword by Gerald Tulchinsky that provides an interesting historical perspective. In addition, an extensive, helpful preface by the author places the book in its historical and bibliographical context.

Tapper, a staff archivist in the National Archives of Canada, is regarded as an expert in the field of Canadian Jewish genealogy. In addition, he is contributing editor to *Avotaynu, The International Review of Jewish Genealogy*.

Advertisements from the period are interspersed throughout the text, providing needed variety and rest for the eyes. Although three columns are used to present the entries, the type is small and not easy to read. Another weak point is the short section on how to use the volume, which could have been clearer, with more detailed information about the entries, especially the cited reference to the *Canadian Jewish Times*. This would have made the book more accessible to the general Jewish reader interested in exploring family roots.

However, the book represents a unique and important contribution to Canadian Jewish genealogy and history. It is a valuable resource for reference collections in public, academic, and special libraries with an interest in these fields.—**Susan J. Freiband**

German-Americans

411. Epstein, Catherine. **A Past Renewed: A Catalog of German-Speaking Refugee Historians in the United States after 1933.** New York, Cambridge University Press, 1993. 386p. index. (Publications of the German Historical Institute). $54.95. E175.45.E67. 016.907'2022. LC 92-568. ISBN 0-521-44063-7.

This is a welcome contribution to the study of the historical profession and the contributions of refugee intellectuals in the United States. Epstein has documented the careers of 88 German-speaking refugees employed as historians in the United States, departing from earlier works on the emigres, which focused on those few who became famous. Here we find biographical and bibliographical entries on many previously forgotten or employed "in urban and small-town college communities ... without much recognition from the historical profession," as well as the stars. The result is a much fuller sense of this portion of the academic emigration, which included few of the leading historians of the 1920s (most of whom were conservative and maintained their positions under Nazi rule) and many who had to change fields to obtain jobs in the United States (often having been journalists or lawyers in Central Europe). This latter fact "challenges the common notion that American scholarship benefited from what German scholarship lost." Most of these emigres remained in the United States after the war, influencing the teaching of German history and introducing or markedly changing other specialties, such as Jewish history, Renaissance studies, the history of Roman and canon law, and the history of medicine.

Each entry offers dates and places of birth and death, dates of emigration and citizenship, a summary of educational background and professional employment, the location of the historian's archival papers, and a bibliography of the historian's works (full where no previous bibliography has been published, supplementary otherwise). Accuracy is very high. Two appendixes, one of scholars not included in the catalog, and the other a bibliography of general works on German-speaking refugee historians, are also helpful. One could only wish that the paper were of higher quality; there is no notation that it is acid-free, and it is semi-translucent.—**Louise E. Hoffman**

Hispanic-Americans

412. Kanellos, Nicolas. **Hispanic-American Almanac: A Reference Work on Hispanics in the United States.** Detroit, Gale, 1993. 780p. illus. index. $99.50. LC 92-075003. ISBN 0-8103-7944-9.

The purpose of this almanac is to be a source of information about a broad range of important characteristics of Hispanic life and culture in the United States. Whereas some such works specialize in a single segment of the Hispanic community, this almanac covers individuals with roots in all of them, from Mexican-Americans to Spanish-Americans to those from Spanish-speaking countries in Central and South America. In 25 chapters, various authors describe such aspects of the Hispanic-American existence as history, education, literature, art, sports, language, religion, and family. Under science, for example, is a series of biographies of prominent Hispanic scientists. In the section on sports there is a small error; the dates following Lefty Gomez's name are 1908-1988, but the biographical text has his death date as 1989.

As an overview of Hispanics in the United States, this work will certainly serve. Serious readers, however, will note a militant point of view in many of the chapters that may seem unnecessarily unfriendly to many would-be students of Hispanic life and culture. Despite this caveat, this is a comprehensive, albeit unbalanced, resource. [R: Choice, July/Aug 93, p. 1752; JAL, July 93, p. 201; LJ, 15 April 93, p. 86; RBB, 15 April 93, p. 1536; VOYA, Oct 93, pp. 260-61]—**Isabel Schon**

Indians of North America

413. Allen, Hayward. **The Traveler's Guide to Native America: The Great Lakes Region.** Minocqua, Wis., NorthWord Press, 1992. 192p. illus. $16.95pa. E78.G7A45. 917.704'33. LC 92-9426. ISBN 1-55971-139-6.

This book is a welcome change of pace from the usual guidebooks to Native American cultures. The introduction, foreword, and first chapter discuss the subject from the Native American perspective. For example, the author explores the sensitive issue of how museums display Native American materials. The remainder of the book consists of chapters for Ohio, Indiana, Illinois, Michigan, Wisconsin, and Minnesota. Each chapter provides a thorough background on places to visit and Native American organizations and services. Chapters are chronological in nature, with information about sites incorporated into a narrative format. Although Allen did not intend the book to be read as a novel or history book, each chapter has a natural flow that is closer to a well-written history than it is to a guidebook. This is both a strength and weakness for the book.

In the absence of an index, one must know something about the time period on which a museum or park focuses in order to locate information about it. The alternative is to skim the entire chapter until one encounters the name, which is printed in boldface type. For example, in the Minnesota chapter the section on "Ancient Times" lists the Grand Mounds and History Center in International Falls (United States-Canadian boundary), the Jeffers petroglyphs, Kathio State Park, and Mounds Park. Interwoven with information about hours, seasons of operation, and telephone numbers is a narrative about the native peoples of the area, so one has a cultural context for the sites. After dealing with precontact material, the chapters cover the French and United States impact on the cultures. Each chapter concludes with a discussion of reservations (if they exist in the state), agencies and organizations, libraries, and educational programs available. At the end of the chapter is a map of the state locating all the sites mentioned in the text. This book will probably be a high-interest item for public libraries in the region covered. [R: SLMQ, Spring 93, p. 198]—**G. Edward Evans**

414. **The American Indian: A Multimedia Encyclopedia.** [CD-ROM]. New York, Facts on File, 1993. Hardware requirements: IBM PC or compatible; DOS 3.1 or higher; VGA monitor; CD-ROM drive with MSCDEX 2.1 or higher; 640K RAM. $295.00.

This product is a fascinating introduction to the world of multimedia for the novice. Drawing principally on the collection at the Smithsonian Institution, this product includes 900 photographs, more than 1,000 biographies, sound bites of American Indian songs, 250 color illustrations, the full text for 250 documents from the eighteenth and nineteenth centuries, more than 100 legends from some 60 tribes, numerous maps, an extensive timeline, and lists of tribal locations (including historical societies and museums).

Installation of this product on the computer takes just a few minutes; then the typing of a single word brings up an attractive search screen with "What do you want to know?" buttons to push. The user can choose from copyright information, photographs, maps, drawings, sounds, documents, tribe locations, museums and societies, history, biographies, tribes, legends, or timelines. The browser soon learns how to find specific information or allow the computer to tour through topics. The user's search is tracked so that steps can be retraced if it becomes necessary to return to a point in a search. Throughout the disk are cross-reference links. For example, in the entry for Geronimo, Cochise is mentioned, and one can detour to see what he had to do with a certain treaty. Clicking on the Cochise name brings up a biographical sketch of the man from which the user can find anything else about Cochise in the encyclopedia or backtrack easily to Geronimo.

This product has been designed with full Boolean index search capabilities, local searching within a window, help screens, guided tours through specific subjects, and hyperlinked menus. Also included is a printable how-to-use guide. All text is printable to paper or disk, and all photographs can be copied to a disk in .PCX format. The product is fully networkable. Preparers of the written materials have taken great pains to make the collection "politically correct" by recognizing white exploitation of the Indians. Indian tribes of the lower United States, Canada, and Alaska are included.

It is obvious that a great deal of time has been taken not only to assemble this dazzling array of resource material but also to link it all together into a single easy-to-use multimedia product. Because this work unlocks the vast resources of the National Archives—which few have ever really probed—it becomes a treasure in itself. Of interest to everyone from children to adults, this is a fascinating and worthwhile resource that proves the worth of new technology. Recommended as a first purchase for school, public, academic, and special libraries needing information on the Indians of North America. [R: VOYA, Dec 93, pp. 328-30; WLB, Nov 93, p. 109]—**G. Kim Dority and David V. Loertscher**

415. **Bibliography of Native North Americans on Disc.** [CD-ROM]. Santa Barbara, Calif., ABC-Clio, 1992. Hardware requirements: IBM PC/XT/AT or 100% compatible; 512K memory; 20MB hard disk drive; floppy disk drive; MS-DOS or PC-DOS 3.0 or higher. $795.00. ISSN 1064-5144.

Anyone who regularly uses any of the four editions of *Ethnographic Bibliography of North America* (EBNA) (see ARBA 91, entry 380 and ARBA 77, entry 738) will welcome this product. It is more than an electronic version of the eight volumes that made up the four editions of EBNA that the Human Relations Area Files (HRAF) published between 1941 and 1990. The addition of 10,000 new entries brings the total to 60,818 citations to works about 290 native ethnic groups of North America (which means north of Mexico for EBNA). According to the user's manual, there are plans to issue annual updates, each being a cumulative disk. The current disk contains citations published between the sixteenth century (there are 106 sixteenth-century entries) and early 1992. Formats covered are books, journal articles, essays, conference papers, dissertations, and U.S. government documents; there is no coverage of popular literature, newspapers, unpublished manuscripts, maps, or audiovisual materials.

Installing the product was no problem in a Windows environment. The searching software is Dataware's CD Answer, the same software that ABC-Clio used for the Historical Abstracts and America: History and Life CD-ROMs. While there are 12 search fields (subject, descriptors, identifiers, ethnic group, region, author, title, date, entry type, journal name, publisher, and collection/series title), most people will start with the subject search. Using this field, one can search words in titles as well as descriptors, identifiers, ethnic groups, and region terms.

Because of descriptor and identifier terms, one must try several different approaches. If one keys in the term *pottery* in the subject field, the number of items called up is 230, but the same term used in the descriptor field gets a message indicating that it is not in the thesaurus. In the thesaurus is a cross-reference from pottery to ceramics; the browse feature allows for on-screen checking of thesaurus terms. So, using *ceramics* in the descriptor field yields 389 hits. Interestingly enough, using *pottery* in the subject and *ceramics* in the descriptor fields produces 224 hits. Note that the descriptors are the terms used by the

HRAF staff when they published the 1990 supplement to EBNA, which for the first time allowed subject searches. Identifiers, also developed by HRAF, are additional, more specific terms such as place-names and archaeological sites. A combined search using *pottery, ceramics, Awatovi* (an archaeological site as identifier), and *Hopi* (as ethnic group) produces one citation that combines all four terms.

The asterisk serves as the truncation symbol and is useful for those not very familiar with a subject area. *And* is the default, so any field in which one keys in multiple words can produce a large number of false drops. A novice searcher may be surprised by the number of citations found in such cases. For example, if one keys the name *Susan Peterson* in the author field, the system indicates 281 citations. Upon calling up the brief listing, one sees no "Susan Petersons" for the first entry. The full display of the first citation shows that the problem is that the item is a multiply authored work with a person named Peterson and someone else with the first name Susan. To just retrieve *Susan Peterson*, one must use *adj* (adjacent) to link words that must appear together. Boolean searches are possible, and one can use adj to specify how many words apart the terms may be (adj 4 means that up to four words may separate the search terms).

Currency is something of a problem in the database. Coverage is spotty for items published after 1987. There are 1,256 entries for 1987, 718 for 1988, 410 for 1989, 194 for 1990, 15 for 1991, and 3 for 1992. None of the journals checked had articles published after 1989 in the database. Using the browse feature with the journal field highlighted allows one to check the journals included and the number of entries from the journal. By using the sort-by-date feature, one can quickly determine the latest publication date for a journal.

A random check of entries by author's name from the 1990 supplement indicated that all those citations are in the database. In order to test the downloading capabilities, this reviewer keyed in his name and pulled up nine entries. Using the sort function, the entries were quickly reordered by date of publication (the default is by title). (One can select either an ascending or descending sort.) Downloading proved to be fairly simple, and a library can set up the system to download only to one drive. Output choices are generous—WordStar, comma delimited (fields separated by a comma), semicolon delimited, fixed field, dBase III, Lotus, Data Interchange Format (DIF), and ASCII. Uploading an ASCII file saved into WordPerfect 5.1 was simple and required very little cleanup editing. The search software is easy to use, and most students would require very little help in doing simple searches. As in many reference tools, to get the most out of the product one needs to read the user's manual. The downloading options mean that people can more quickly complete their search and free up the system for others.

This is a very useful product if the library has users who do or could use EBNA. Given the spotty coverage from 1988 to 1992, it is questionable whether one needs to buy each update. If the indexing becomes current, then it may be a worthwhile annual acquisition. [R: JAL, May 93, p. 130; RQ, Summer 93, pp. 354-57]—**G. Edward Evans**

416. Cantor, George, ed. **North American Indian Landmarks: A Traveler's Guide.** Detroit, Gale, 1993. 409p. illus. maps. index. $34.95. ISBN 0-8103-8916-9.

This is yet another guidebook to Native America. Each year seems to bring a new entry into an already crowded field. In 1992 there was *Discover Indian Reservations USA* (see ARBA 93, entry 439); in 1991 was *Native America* (see ARBA 93, entry 431); and before that was *Indian America* (see ARBA 91, entry 395). There are several other older titles. What distinguishes this book from the others? One feature is that it covers more Canadian material than is typical of other guides. Also, Cantor had the assistance of several good scholars in Native American studies in selecting materials to include. Another strength is the emphasis on historic sites, something that is generally lacking in the other guides.

The foreword by Suzan Shawn Harjo sets the tone of the volume, which is strongly pro-indigenous rights. (The entry for Dickson Mounds State Museum, Lewistown, Illinois, is an example of the overall tone.) The main text is divided into seven regions: Northeast (Quebec to Virginia), Southeast (Tennessee and North Carolina, south to Florida and west to Louisiana), Great Lakes and Ohio Valley (Ontario to Kentucky north to south, West Virginia to Wisconsin east to west), Great Plains-North (the prairie provinces of Canada to Wyoming and Minnesota to Montana), Great Plains-South (Iowa and Nebraska to Texas), Southwest and Great Basin (Idaho to Arizona and New Mexico and Colorado to Nevada), and Pacific Coast and Arctic (Alaska to California). Within a region the arrangement is by state or province and then by city. Entries range from fewer than 100 to several hundred words, and each ends with information about the site's location, hours, admission fees, and telephone number.

No guide trying to cover the whole continent can be comprehensive, and this one is no exception. Cantor places an emphasis on museums and sites with some physical remains or a monument. He includes a few reservations, but most are not listed. His coverage is good for well-known sites, and his guide will meet the needs of individuals with a general interest in and knowledge about Native Americans. [R: Choice, Oct 93, p. 264; RQ, Fall 93, p. 132; VOYA, Oct 93, p. 260; WLB, Sept 93, pp. 121-22]

—G. Edward Evans

417. Fritze, Ronald. **Legend and Lore of the Americas before 1942: An Encyclopedia of Visitors, Explorers, and Immigrants.** Santa Barbara, Calif., ABC-Clio, 1993. 319p. illus. maps. index. $65.00. E61.A72. 970.01. LC 93-13367. ISBN 0-87436-664-X.

What are the roots of Native American cultures? How did they get here? When did they arrive, or did they originate in the Americas? To answer these questions, hundreds of theories have been proposed, some the results of fanciful dreams and others developed according to archaeological evidence as that evidence has mounted. Fritze has put together an amazing array of these ideas in encyclopedia form to provide a fascinating parade of ideas. If one is interested in ancient North America, this is *the* book of 1993 to own.

Every aspect of the topic, from the sober to the outrageous, appears in some way in this book: peoples said to be precursors of, or who had pre-Columbian contact with, Native Americans (e.g., the Japanese, Hindus, Nephites, Egyptians, ancient Jews); origin theories (e.g., the Bering Land Bridge, Atlantis, Wales); and individuals who promoted various ideas (e.g., Joseph Smith, Aristotle, Thor Heyerdahl, Father Gregorio Garcia). Each entry takes its subject seriously, whether grounded in fact or fancy, and while Fritze's preferences are clear, he gives a fair hearing to all competing ideas. Other writers of skeptical literature would do well to emulate his tone, which is gently (and convincingly) persuasive rather than hostile and ridiculing, as so much debunking material can be. Each article is well written and provides links to other articles, making it easy to read all entries about a particular theory. Bibliographies are appended to most articles, and black-and-white illustrations, maps, and photographs are scattered throughout the text. This book is a must purchase for libraries and patrons interested in the topic. [R: Choice, Dec 93, p. 584; RBB, 1 Nov 93, p. 568; WLB, Nov 93, p. 105]

—David V. Loertscher and D. A. Rothschild

418. Gill, Sam D., and Irene F. Sullivan. **Dictionary of Native American Mythology.** Santa Barbara, Calif., ABC-Clio, 1992. 425p. illus. index. $65.00. E98.R3G46. 299'.7'03. LC 92-27053. ISBN 0-87436-621-6.

Gill has a long list of publications on Native American mythology, and Sullivan has also published in the field. The collaboration of these two University of Colorado professors has resulted in a very useful reference work. A short but culturally sensitive preface introduces the reader to the complex world of Native American religion, mythology, and ritual. The dictionary arrangement of entries means that material from a particular group is found throughout the book. However, a tribal index allows a user to identify all the entries pertaining to a group; it also includes a brief list of bibliographic citations about the tribe. As one would expect, groups that have been extensively studied have long lists of entries; others have only a line or two. Most of the dictionary entries range between 200 and 300 words; a few are just one sentence long. The majority of the one-line entries include a cross-reference to a longer related entry. A few, such as the entry on Hunka Lowanpi (Lakota-Sun Dance), are more than a page long. There is also an entry for Sun Dance that discusses it across tribal lines. Each term, such as the above, has a tribal and cultural area associated with it. Entries conclude with one or more references to works listed in the 47-page bibliography. In addition to entries for rituals, characters, and activities, there are more general entries that explain themes and concepts found in Native American mythology, such as Sun and Moon, Trickster(s), Tobacco, Humor, Raven, and Rain.

There is little duplication between this work and *The Encyclopedia of Native American Religions* (see ARBA 93, entry 432). The material in this volume is more detailed and scholarly in character, even for general headings such as the Sun Dance. Unlike the encyclopedia, this work contains few personal names of historic figures or references to Christianized Indian religions (e.g., Handsome Lake); one exception is the Native American Church. The two works are more complementary than they are competitive in character. Recommended for academic libraries at institutions where Native American coursework is offered and any library that serves a community with a strong interest in Native Americans. [R: Choice, May 93, p. 1441; JAL, May 93, pp. 130-31; LJ, 15 Feb 93, p. 160; LJ, 15 April 93, p. 60; RQ, Summer 93, pp. 564-65; SLJ, Nov 93, pp. 142-44; WLB, May 93, pp. 114-15]—**G. Edward Evans**

419. Klein, Barry T. **Reference Encyclopedia of the American Indian.** 6th ed. West Nyack, N.Y., Todd, 1993. 679p. index. $125.00. LC 90-070527. ISBN 0-915344-30-0.

Each new edition of this title has a different physical format. While this edition retains the one-volume approach, the pages are now larger, which allows for three columns of text on each rather than the 5th edition's two columns. The result is a more slender volume that is easier to handle. All the categories from the prior edition are present, as well as a new section, 24 pages long, on arts and crafts shops. Some of the subsections have been reordered, but the basic structure of the entries remains the same. The arts and crafts section is selective, and there is no way of knowing how the decision to include or exclude a shop was made. Both high-quality and tourist shops are equally represented. However, not all the shops in any one community are listed. The biographical section continues to exclude many activists (e.g., Dennis Banks) or merely provides an address (e.g., Russell Means) for others.

The bibliographical (roughly 4,500 in-print titles) and audiovisual (about 1,000 items) sections remain strong features, especially for general readers. Thus, the 6th edition is a good buy for libraries serving nonspecialists and having limited funds for reference works about North American Indians. [R: LJ, Jan 93, pp. 98-102; WLB, Feb 93, pp. 106-07]—**G. Edward Evans**

420. **Native Americans Information Directory: A Guide to Organizations, Agencies, Institutions, Programs, Publications, Services, and Other Resources....** Julia C. Furtaw and Kimberly Burton Faulkner, eds. Detroit, Gale, 1993. 371p. index. $75.00. ISBN 0-8103-8854-5. ISSN 1063-9632.

A new entry into the field of directories about Native Americans, this publication can claim a special marketplace niche; unlike other such directories, it has a section on native Hawaiians. Five broad headings are used to organize its material: American Indians, Alaska natives, native Hawaiians, aboriginal Canadians, and general resources on Native Americans. Within these groupings there are 15 subheadings and listings for schools, libraries, museums, research centers, print and broadcast media, publishers, videos (except for Hawaiians), and educational financial assistance. Entries for organizations provide, as a minimum, mailing address, telephone number, and a contact person. Many entries include a descriptive annotation that has information about number of members, publications, date of founding, and so on. The video entries provide a short description, release date, running time, format, and distributor/source. One major plus for this volume is its extensive master name and keyword index that makes the information easier to access.

This is a sound directory to Native American organizations. There is a good deal of overlap between it and *Reference Encyclopedia of the American Indian* (Todd, 1993). Both include information on tribal communities, national and regional organizations, federal agencies, and so forth. Although both have 1993 imprint dates, careful cross-checking reveals occasional differences in information for the same organization. Most frequently the difference is the name of the person in charge of the program or service; mailing addresses and telephone numbers are generally consistent. If a library must choose between the two directories, local needs should decide the matter. *Reference Encyclopedia's* bibliography and biographical sections are very useful and not duplicated in Gale's work, but the section on Hawaiians and the solid indexing are special to this publication. [R: Choice, Mar 93, p. 1116; LJ, Jan 93, pp. 98-102; RBB, 15 Jan 93, p. 646; VOYA, April 93, pp. 65-66]—**G. Edward Evans**

421. **Rand McNally Children's Atlas of Native Americans.** Elizabeth Fagan Adelman, ed. Skokie, Ill., Rand McNally, 1993. 77p. illus. maps. index. $14.95. E58.4.R36. 970.004'97. LC 92-6791. ISBN 0-528-83494-0.

Adelman's vigorous, balanced overview of Native Americans presents a colorful, accurate reference work at a manageable size and price. The writing style is articulate, unpedantic, factual without overpowering a child's vocabulary, and even-handed toward the divisive question of why European settlers undermined a viable culture. Colored maps in earth tones coordinate with bright photographs and drawings of people preparing food, working crafts, tending children, hunting and fishing, worshiping, and traveling. Because the text is written in the past tense and focuses on Native Americans before the 1500s, the introduction cautions the reader to think of Native Americans as still alive and deserving of respect. This statement sets a tone of appreciation for culture, achievement, and racial integrity, all of which Adelman emphasizes through nonviolent pictures, drawings, and photographs that accompany attractive topographical maps and detailed descriptions of tribal life.

Essential to the book's accessibility is its separation into geographical concentrations. Sensibly divided into five studies, each chapter delineates government, work rhythms, and daily concerns of selected tribes. Appended to each focus are additional tribes and clans as evidence of the vast pattern of Native American settlement. At the back are a slender glossary, an index, and a world map that places American migrations into the totality of human movement about the globe. As a reference tool for the parent, librarian, classroom teacher, and general reader, this atlas provides a nonjudgmental picture of a significant part of the history of the Western Hemisphere.—**Mary Ellen Snodgrass**

422. Reddy, Marlita A., ed. **Statistical Record of Native North Americans.** Detroit, Gale, 1993. 1661p. index. $89.50. ISBN 0-8103-8963-0.

Without question this is the most comprehensive single source of current statistical data on native North Americans (United States and Canada, including Eskimo/Inuit). "Current" in this work frequently means 1980 data, as detailed data on tribes from the 1990 U.S. Census are not yet available and probably will not be for several more years. The work does use what 1990 data is available. (For Canada the data comes from the 1986 Canadian Census.) Canadian material appears in a separate section. U.S. material is organized into 11 chapters: history, demographics, family, education, culture and tradition, health and health care, social and economic conditions, business and industry, water and land management, government relations, and law and law enforcement. Both historic and current data are given in most chapters, such as varying precontact population estimates, American Indian population by state 1900-1980, latchkey children, and prisoners on Death Row as of 1991. All the data came from existing sources (143 different publications); however, this work is a good example of the repackaging of data into a single useful resource and is well worth the price. A 200-page index to tribes, subjects, and places makes it easy to locate information. This work is an excellent buy for libraries serving Native Americans or those with an interest in Native American affairs. [R: Choice, Dec 93, p. 591; RBB, 15 Oct 93, p. 475; WLB, Nov 93, pp. 105-06]—**G. Edward Evans**

Japanese-Americans

423. Niiya, Brian, ed. **Japanese American History: An A-to-Z Reference from 1868 to the Present.** New York, Facts on File, 1993. 386p. illus. index. $45.00. E184.J3J3355. 973'.04956. LC 92-35753. ISBN 0-8160-2680-7.

Often referred to as America's "model minority," the Japanese-American community has been a popular topic for historians, sociologists, and other writers for at least two decades. *Japanese American History* nicely complements these writings by offering definitions and background information on many of the people, agencies, groups, and events of the Japanese-American community and its history.

The book is composed of four parts. A well-written 23-page essay relates the history of the Japanese in the United States from the beginning of immigration to the present. This is followed by a 62-page chronology that begins with the shipwreck of Japanese sailors in Hawaii in 1258 and concludes with Kristi Yamaguchi's gold medal in the 1992 Olympics. Each entry is accompanied by a paragraph describing the event and concludes with the source of the data. The heart of the book is an encyclopedic section that defines terms and provides articles of up to two pages on events, people, organizations, and groups pertinent to the Japanese-American community and its history. Each article concludes with a recommendation for further reading on the topic. Many entries are accompanied by lengthy bibliographical essays citing related studies. The final section lists 100 titles recommended as a basic library on Japanese-Americans. The volume has an excellent index, and readers are sent to pertinent articles through a good system of *see* references and the use of capital letters to indicate terms in the text that have separate entries in the encyclopedic section.

Japanese American History has much to recommend it. Despite the treatment received by this group throughout most of its history, the writers, most of whom are Asian American, have avoided bias. The articles are signed, the writing is generally good and authoritative, and there is a nice balance between the past and the present in the content. The extensive bibliographical references also provide access to the best writing on the Japanese-American experience. Highly recommended for academic libraries and for all libraries with an interest in Asian-American studies and history. [R: RBB, 1 Nov 93, pp. 567-68]—**Donald E. Collins**

Jews

424. Barnavi, Eli, ed. **A Historical Atlas of the Jewish People from the Time of the Patriarchs to the Present.** New York, Alfred A. Knopf/Random House, 1992. 299p. illus. maps. index. $50.00. DS117.J8513. 909'.04924. LC 92-53169. ISBN 0-679-40332-9.

"Too much history, not enough geography"—the words of Isaiah Berlin in reference to the Jews—perfectly captures the rationale behind this atlas, which attempts to remedy the problem by depicting the nearly constant travels of the Jews over some 3,000 years. A blend of scholarly text, evocative maps, and abundant illustrations, the atlas is arranged in rough chronological order, beginning with Old Testament history, from Abraham's world and the route he and his clan took to Egypt and the possible routes of the Exodus (effectively depicted as colored lines superimposed on a satellite photograph of the Sinai Peninsula) through the conquest of Canaan according to the Book of Joshua and, finally, the ultimate destruction of the Kingdom of Israel and the fall of its capital, Samaria, which gave rise to the mythology about the Ten Lost Tribes. Thereupon, the maps cover the many diasporas across increasingly larger areas.

But the atlas is far more than a series of maps with arrows drawn across them. Each thematic chapter goes into detail about gentile events that affected the Jews in some way, the attitudes toward Jews wherever they went, the internal struggles, the tragedies, the accomplishments—in short, the work provides a complete history, with an emphasis on how the Jews' nation-within-a-nation status shaped them. Translated from French without a trace of awkwardness, the text is evenhanded, recounting horrors without accusation. Even the chapter titled "Why Was Auschwitz Not Bombed?", an intensely emotional subject, is objective. Interspersed among the historical chapters are those on less geographically oriented subjects, such as festivals and the Talmud. Along the bottom of the pages is a timeline that encapsulates major events in Jewish history. The illustrations are stunning: Clear, sharp, and appropriate, they range from photographs of archaeological sites to paintings to fragments of parchment to a wide range of anti-Semitic caricatures, posters, and popular culture (e.g., a Nazi board game called "Jews Out! Go to Palestine!").

Only one minor complaint can be made about this book: The table of contents follows the glossary and the index, so users might not know it exists until they stumble upon it. Otherwise, this is an outstanding work that has a place in every library, even the smallest. [R: WLB, Jan 93, p. 108]—**D. A. Rothschild**

425. **The Schocken Guide to Jewish Books: Where to Start Reading about History, Literature, Culture, and Religion.** Barry W. Holtz, ed. New York, Schocken Books; distr., New York, Random House, 1992. 357p. illus. index. $17.00pa. Z6366.R4. 016.909'04924. LC 91-17760. ISBN 0-8052-1005-9.

This collection of 15 bibliographical essays serves to direct the reader to recommended books on Jewish history, philosophy, literature, and religion. Its purpose is "to offer the general reader a way to find his or her path through the maze of Jewish books that we might find in a bookstore or library." The authors are recognized experts in their fields, and Holtz is associate professor of Jewish education at the Jewish Theological Seminary of America and codirector of the Melton Research Center in New York. The presentations are oriented toward the serious lay reader rather than toward students, scholars, or researchers.

Each essay is subdivided into shorter sections, which improves readability. The bibliographical references are incorporated into the narrative (including title, author, publisher, and date) rather than presented in separate bibliographies. The essays are clear, interesting, and easy to read and understand. They identify the major issues in each field and present questions that the books explore. The editor's introduction provides a good background for the rest of the text, putting the essays in context. The design and physical appearance of the book is especially pleasing, with its use of different type styles and chapter decorations. The illustrations, mostly black-and-white photographs, serve to heighten the reader's interest in the book. This guide is a valuable compilation of information that can serve as a useful selection and reader's advisory tool for librarians, as well as a worthwhile addition to reference (and circulating) collections of temple, synagogue, Jewish community center, and public libraries. [R: LJ, 15 April 93, p. 63]
—**Susan J. Freiband**

426. Singerman, Robert, comp. **Spanish and Portuguese Jewry: A Classified Bibliography.** Westport, Conn., Greenwood Press, 1993. 720p. index. (Bibliographies and Indexes in World History, no.30). $95.00. Z6373.S7S56. 016.946'004924. LC 92-34760. ISBN 0-313-25752-3.

This scholarly compilation concludes the compiler's research, begun in the early 1970s "to bring under bibliographical control a broad range of published materials pertaining to the Jewish presence in Spain and Portugal from antiquity to the present day" (introduction). It supplements his earlier bibliography on the same topic, *The Jews in Spain and Portugal* (see ARBA 76, entry 384). It includes not only material published since 1975 but also retrospective material that escaped attention in the first bibliography. An appendix is included with errata and related notes correcting or enlarging upon earlier data.

The new work focuses on local Jewish history, Jewish-Christian polemics, and the portrayal of Spanish and Portuguese Jews in literature, with a preponderance of Spanish and Portuguese studies. It excludes areas of biblical exegesis; Talmudic commentaries; Hebrew philology, literature, and poetry; Jewish philosophy; and Cabalistic legal and rabbinical literature. In addition, the Inquisition, the Sephardic diaspora, and Ladinos are excluded.

The 5,446 bibliographical entries are arranged alphabetically by author in a broad subject classification. Material on Spain is presented first, then material on Portugal. The entries do not include the publishers of monographs or series information, which Singerman feels will be available through the OCLC or RLIN databases or in the published volumes of the *National Union Catalog*. Almost all of the entries have been personally examined by the author. Many include brief notes with relevant topics or sections and pages.

The extensive index includes cross-references. However, for the beginning or uninitiated user a brief explanation about the structure and use of the index would have been helpful. An introduction places the bibliography in context, describing its scope and limitations.

This work represents an important contribution to Sephardic Jewish scholarship and is a valuable addition to reference collections in academic and research libraries supporting Jewish studies programs. It is also an important resource for temple, synagogue, Jewish community center, and public libraries serving Sephardic Jewish communities.—**Susan J. Freiband**

427. **A Social and Religious History of the Jews: Index to Volumes IX-XVIII.** 2d ed. By Salo Wittmayer Baron. New York, Columbia University Press, 1993. 114p. $75.00. DS112.B31523B37. 909'.04924. LC 92-25418. ISBN 0-231-08856-6.

This index to 10 volumes of Baron's monumental history of the Jews facilitates access to information in this important scholarly work. It complements and follows the same format, style, and presentation as the earlier index to volumes 1 through 8. The period covered here is the late Middle Ages and the Era of European Expansion, 1200 to 1650. Because the individual volumes do not contain indexes, this book is especially important for effective use of the set. No introductory or explanatory material is included, which would have been helpful for the uninitiated user. However, a four-page chronology for the period covered by the index does appear. It lists the dates of important rules, key figures, events, and documents of the time.

The index permits easy and quick scanning of desired references. Subjects, names, and titles are presented in one alphabetical sequence. Main entries are differentiated in paragraph form from subentries, but the same typeface and size (clear and easy to read) is used for both. Subentries are logically and grammatically related to main entries. Headings are concise, and page references are clear. Entries are specific enough to permit ready access to desired material. Cross-references are included. Terms do not have noticeably large numbers of pages, but those that appear are accurate and used consistently throughout.

The physical appearance of the book is noteworthy. Permanent, acid-free paper is used. The book is Smyth sewn with a quality cloth binding and attractive gold lettering. For those libraries owning *A Social and Religious History of the Jews*, this index is an essential purchase.—**Susan J. Freiband**

7 Genealogy and Heraldry

GENEALOGY

Atlases

428. Segal, Aaron. **An Atlas of International Migration.** New Providence, N.J., Hans Zell/Reed Reference Publishing, 1993. 233p. maps. index. $100.00. G1046.E27S4. 304'.8'022'3. LC 93-19502. ISBN 1-873836-30-9.

This outstanding reference source is the first international atlas to cover the migration of humans, from their origins in eastern Africa to the flight of refugees caused by the Gulf War in 1991. Divided into four main sections on voluntary migrations, involuntary migrations, major diasporas, and global migration characteristics, this work provides an exceptional overview of human movement throughout the world. The well-written, informative introduction supplies historical background on the issue of international migration, gives the sources of the data, and provides a disclaimer about the problems of getting reliable data from some countries. Covering each region of the world, the author uses maps and texts to detail voluntary migration and global and regional involuntary migration from 1500 to 1990. The useful sources section contains a glossary, an annotated bibliography, and a regular bibliography. The index, clear illustrations, and easy-to-use format further enhance this valuable resource. Because the impacts of migrations are keys to the continued development and understanding of our multiethnic societies, this work will be important to every academic and large public library collection. [R: LJ, Dec 93, p. 116]
—**Diane J. Turner**

Bibliography

429. **Genealogies Cataloged by the Library of Congress since 1986: With a List of Established Forms of Family Names....** Washington, D.C., Cataloging Distribution Service, Library of Congress, 1992. 1349p. $70.00. Z5313.U5L53. 016.9291. LC 91-39573.

This is the most recent in a series of bibliographies that, taken as a whole, provide genealogists with a comprehensive list of the family histories available to them in the Library of Congress. This volume picks up where the discontinued series edited by Marion Kaminkow left off in 1985. It is divided into three parts. Section 1 lists 8,997 genealogies received and cataloged by the Library between January 1, 1986, and July 31, 1991. Full bibliographical information and call numbers are provided. Entries are arranged alphabetically by the surnames appearing in book titles, then by author. Despite the statement in the introduction that if a history covers more than one family, entries will also be provided under those surnames, this is frequently not the case. Many surnames mentioned as secondary or collateral families in titles are not listed in separate entries. Without a separate index, those names not treated individually will be lost to users.

Section 2 provides an alphabetical list of 10,000 authorized surnames, as well as approximately 22,000 cross-references for variant spellings. Users are instructed to find the authorized spelling in this list before attempting to find their family names in section 1. While this list is useful, users should be aware that not all variations are included and that they may not agree with the list in all instances. Researchers should still check other variations. For example, under "Yeats family," users are directed to

"USE Yates family." However, both versions are used in section 1, and the entries listed under one spelling are not duplicated under the second. This is a relatively minor problem, however, and should not greatly hinder use.

Section 3 provides a list of older genealogies that have been replaced by microfilm copies since 1983 by the Library of Congress. The arrangement is by call number, which approximates an alphabetical arrangement under country of origin and then by family. Unfortunately, no headings or subheadings of any kind are included, leaving users to laboriously seek out geographical areas and family names.

The major problem with this volume relates to the difficulty users may have in identifying surnames that are mentioned in titles but are not given individual treatment in the book. With the addition of a good surname index and perhaps a geographical index, this would be a superior work in every way. This book is part of a series that is already a standard in the field and should be purchased by all genealogical libraries and others with an interest in the subject.—**Donald E. Collins**

Chronology

430. Coldham, Peter Wilson. **The Complete Book of Emigrants 1751-1776: A Comprehensive Listing Compiled from English Public Records....** Baltimore, Md., Genealogical Publishing, 1993. 349p. index. $29.95. LC 92-75682. ISBN 0-8063-1376-5.

This fourth volume completes a magnificent work that contains virtually every reference to English emigrants of the colonial period that can be found in England. Similar to the previous volumes (see ARBA 93, entry 452; ARBA 91, entry 416; and ARBA 88, entry 429), this work is limited to English sources. Scotland, Ireland, and Wales have their own sources. This volume lists surviving records from the Plantation Apprenticeship Bindings in the Corporation of London Record Office and also includes Port Books (Public Record Office class E 190), which were registers maintained at English ports. (Unfortunately, many of these were destroyed in the last century due to an administrative decision.) Convicts and other involuntary emigrants are covered in the author's companion work, *The Complete Book of Emigrants in Bondage, 1614-1775* (Genealogical Publishing, 1988). With the exceptions of apprenticeship bindings and passenger lists, coverage is limited to those connected with mainland America (excluding Canada).

There are a very detailed name index and a ship index. The name index includes not only the emigrants but also people mentioned in the records, such as landlords. This work will be a great help to those searching for English emigrant ancestors. [R: Choice, Nov 93, p. 426; RBB, 1 Sept 93, p. 84; WLB, June 93, p. 120]—**Robert L. Turner, Jr.**

Directories

431. Bentley, Elizabeth Petty. **Directory of Family Associations.** 1993-94 ed. Baltimore, Md., Genealogical Publishing, 1993. 336p. $29.95pa. LC 93-78017. ISBN 0-8063-1383-8.

This edition of the directory is much improved from the previous one. It contains up-to-date addresses and names of contact persons for hundreds of family organizations. Arranged alphabetically by family surname, typical entries contain name, address, and telephone number; descriptive data about the family; and name of publication or newsletter, if available. Especially useful are the cross-references that include name variations or interrelated families.

The nature of this compilation makes it difficult to keep current, but Bentley has made every effort to achieve accuracy. The result is a useful tool that is necessary to all important genealogical collections.
—**Carol Willsey Bell**

432. Burgess, Michael, Mary A. Burgess, and Daryl F. Mallett. **The State and Province Vital Records Guide.** San Bernardino, Calif., Borgo Press, 1993. 96p. (Borgo Reference Guides, no.5). $20.00; $10.00pa. HA38.B87. 929'1.'02573. LC 87-6312. ISBN 0-89370-815-1; 0-89370-915-8pa.

This guide grew out of the frustration that the authors felt because they could not get current information on vital records. The book tells genealogical researchers where to order birth, death, marriage, and divorce certificates in the United States, United States insular areas and territories, and Canada. The information was compiled and verified by telephone in early 1993. For each state, insular area, territory, and province the address, telephone numbers, fees, years of coverage, and restrictions are covered in a clear, concise manner. There is no mention of whether this work will be updated on a regular basis. Except for the information about Canada, this material can be found in *Where to Write for Vital Records* (Department of Health and Human Services, 1990), although it is not as current as that in this newer work. [R: Choice, Dec 93, p. 580]—**Robert L. Turner, Jr.**

Handbooks and Yearbooks

433. Chorzempa, Rosemary A. **Polish Roots. Korzenie Polskie.** Baltimore, Md., Genealogical Publishing, 1993. 240p. illus. maps. $17.95pa. LC 93-77159. ISBN 0-8063-1378-1.

This is a work of love that can be used in several different ways: as a fascinating book to be read in its entirety; as a reference source for genealogical information; as a guide to genealogical research; and as a how-to for writing to North American and Polish institutions that can provide genealogical information, including handy Polish phrases for genealogical correspondence or document reading. The research targeted both sides of the Atlantic, including German ports and territories in the areas surrounding Poland. Many potential sources are provided, some practical for direct research, some general for getting oriented in the literature, and some that may be useful in the search for one's roots. The description of the ethnic areas of Poland includes areas outside the country where Poles are a minority, but from where some Polish emigrants originated. A brief history of Poland focuses on its human aspects. A chapter on non-Polish ethnic groups in Poland and parts of chapters on non-Polish church records, surnames, first names, languages, and genealogical societies will be of interest to ethnic groups other than Polish. (The description of non-Polish ethnic groups in Poland is indicative of the country's historical ethnic and religious tolerance.)

This book is indispensable for genealogical societies, research institutions, and government service units. Many individuals will find the book useful both for themselves and for their children, in this era of heightened interest in roots and old-country traditions. [R: LJ, 1 June 93, p. 102]—**Bogdan Mieczkowski**

434. Grenham, John. **Tracing Your Irish Ancestors: The Complete Guide.** Baltimore, Md., Genealogical Publishing, 1992. 281p. illus. $18.95pa. LC 92-74687. ISBN 0-8063-1369-2.

This book is aimed at Americans, Australians, and Canadians of Irish descent who wish to trace their ancestors in Ireland. The work covers the 32 counties of Ireland and ignores the current political divisions.

The work is divided into three parts. Part 1 lists major sources, such as census, church, civil, and land records; part 2 lists wills, registry of deeds, newspapers, directories, emigration and passenger lists, and resources that are available in the Genealogical Office in Dublin; and part 3 lists specialized reference sources under each of the 32 counties, including census returns, local history sources, local journals, gravestone inscriptions, estate records, and place-names. Family histories are provided in this section, as are lists of Church of Ireland parish records that can be found in Dublin, and reputable genealogical research services. The illustrations are very good and include Catholic parish maps for all the counties.

Tracing Your Irish Ancestors is a scholarly and clearly written reference book. It is one of the most up-to-date and thorough source books for serious researchers of Irish family history. Grenham has worked extensively for a number of years with all the sources listed and is thus able to guide readers through any peculiarities in the structures of the records.

This work is suitable for someone who is just starting out on a quest, or for someone who has begun but needs further guidance. The introductory essay gives clear guidelines on how to begin; it includes a list of United States, Canadian, and Australian sources that can be used to identify an Irish locality of origin of a family. [R: Choice, June 93, p. 1602; LJ, Jan 93, pp. 96-98]—**Linda Main**

435. Przecha, Donna, and Joan Lowrey. **Guide to Genealogy Software.** Baltimore, Md., Genealogical Publishing, 1993. 195p. index. $24.95pa. LC 93-77635. ISBN 0-8063-1382-X.

One of the most widely discussed issues in genealogical circles concerns which software to use for storing the family genealogy. This book goes a long way toward answering that question. Novices and experienced genealogists will find much of value here. The authors bring a great deal of experience to their topic, being founding members of a computer genealogy society, writers for computer genealogical publications, and authors of guides to two of the top genealogical programs on the market.

An excellent opening chapter on the basics is directed at genealogists who are unfamiliar with computers and computer software. Covered are such topics as what to expect from a genealogy program, decisions to make concerning equipment, support for software, types of programs, where to obtain programs, genealogical bulletin boards, and how programs work. The chapter concludes with sample printouts of family group sheets, pedigree charts, ahnentafel, and descendancy charts.

The heart of the book is the evaluation and analysis of individual programs. The authors provide sufficient information about each product to help prospective software purchasers make their selection, including ratings (for some titles), price, samples of actual chart printouts, availability of utility programs, availability of manuals and support for the software, and information on data entry and data management. Brief sections describing other program features, and a comments section that provides information that does not fit neatly into other categories, give the reader further evidence about possible choices of programs for acquisition. *Guide to Genealogy Software* is highly recommended to all libraries and individuals with an interest in genealogy. [R: RBB, 1 Sept 93, pp. 87-88]—**Donald E. Collins**

Indexes

436. **Biography and Genealogy Master Index.** [CD-ROM]. Detroit, Gale, 1993. Hardware requirements: IBM PC or compatible; MS-DOS or PC-DOS 3.1 or higher; MS-DOS CD-ROM Extensions 2.0 or higher; 640K of RAM; hard disk with 1MB free. $1,250.00 (1st yr.); $350.00/yr. ISBN 0-8103-4965-5.

Looking for biographical information about people has never been easier and more thorough than with the CD-ROM version of *Biography and Genealogy Master Index*. The designers of this product show the true capabilities of CD-ROM as a tool; it is far superior to the print version. If a library purchases this index each year, then finding a person by name (dates of birth and death are necessary to sort out similar entries) takes just a few moments. Sources where biographical information can be found, including whether a photograph of the person is included in the biographical source, can be printed out immediately. The publisher could have finished the tool design at this point and saved users many frustrating minutes in searching and copying down sources, but it took the next and even more valuable step. Location information can be added to this CD-ROM product so that the patron knows whether the local library or its system of branches contains the items indexed. Such information can be added to the user's hard drive on the computer that runs the disc. Any holdings symbol added to the computer's hard drive will be displayed any time the index provides sources of information, so a printout of sources comes complete with call numbers! This assumes, of course, that the library staff has added the holding symbols to the computer file. Such holding symbols can be added once and easily kept up-to-date.

The installation of the CD-ROM product onto the computer takes only a few minutes, and search screens are simple and easy to use, obviating the need to consult a manual. Patrons should be able to use the product with very little help from a professional. One piece of advice, however, is critical: One person can be listed in the index under several forms of the name. For example, E. B. White, the children's author, is listed under three forms: one without birth date, one with only a birth date, and the third with both birth and death dates. The patron will come away with incomplete information if all name forms are not searched. Gale could improve the product by having a strict name-authority policy with cross-references from variant forms. Furthermore, if the name-authority matched the Library of Congress Name Authority File, the product would take another leap in quality.

All libraries providing services directed toward biographical information should try to afford this tool as a replacement for the printed version. It is a must purchase. [R: RBB, 1 Oct 93, pp. 376-77]

—**David V. Loertscher**

437. **PERiodical Source Index 1847-1985. Volumes 9-12.** Fort Wayne, Ind., Allen County Public Library Foundation, 1992. 4v. $300.00/set.

438. **PERiodical Source Index: 1991 Annual Volume.** By the staff of the Allen County Public Library Genealogy Department. Michael B. Clegg and Curt B. Witcher, eds. Fort Wayne, Ind., Allen County Public Library Foundation, 1992. 935p. $45.00.

The genealogical collection at the Allen County Public Library in Fort Wayne, Indiana, is one of the largest collections in the country. Its genealogy periodical holdings are extensive but were unindexed, rendering the periodical collection almost useless. Now, thanks to a large grant, the library is publishing a massive 16-volume retrospective index of some 2,000 periodicals that cover 133 years. The entire project is spanning a number of years; this review covers only the families and places segment of the set and the 1991 annual volume. Other ARBA reviews have covered previously issued parts (see ARBA 92, entries 393 and 394). The set indexes biographical articles, cemetery and census records, church and court records, deeds, directories, histories, institutions, land and military records, and maps.

Volumes 9 and 10 are U.S. place-names arranged by state, then by country and record type. This will assist searchers doing exhaustive searches for individuals and families by area of the country. The index refers the reader to the periodical, volume, number, month, and year, making the search easy to conduct.

Volumes 11 and 12 constitute the family index; they index articles on individual families, cemeteries where all people buried have the same surname, a single record about an individual or between two parties, and family Bible records. Family surname journals, queries, ancestor charts, and family group sheets have been excluded. Indexing is the same as in volumes 9 and 10.

The 1991 annual indexes all periodicals received in 1991, regardless of the year published. Thus, for a complete search, the patron must search the main volumes and each of the annuals. The annual index is arranged like the main set, but all in one volume: by U.S. state, Canadian province, foreign country, research methodology, and family name.

Such an enormous project is without peer and a godsend to those doing exhaustive searching, including genealogists, historians, and reference librarians. While the Latter-day Saints church concentrates on indexing the primary sources of birth and death registers, *PERiodical Source Index* indexes secondary periodical sources. The indexing is thorough and comprehensive; these volumes are an essential tool for all libraries that have genealogical holdings of any size. The current index would be a perfect one to put on CD-ROM for even better access than it already provides. While the cost seems high, it is inexpensive considering the immense benefit. [R: RBB, 15 May 93, p. 1718]—**David V. Loertscher**

HERALDRY

439. Roberts, Gary Boyd. **The Royal Descents of 500 Immigrants to the American Colonies or the United States Who Were Themselves Notable or Left Descendants Notable in American History.** Baltimore, Md., Genealogical Publishing, 1993. 622p. index. $45.00. LC 93-79085. ISBN 0-8063-1395-1.

The author explains in his lengthy introduction that the notables treated in his work include merchants, lords mayor, clergy, bishops, lawyers, Puritan leaders, and professional soldiers who became the New England Yankees, Pennsylvania Quakers, and Tidewater planters who settled early in U.S. history. These settlers, to be included, must have been descended from royalty, and they must have left notable descendants. One standard for notability is inclusion in the *Dictionary of American Biography* (see ARBA 89, entry 25), *Who's Who in America* (Marquis Who's Who, annual), or the *National Cyclopaedia of American Biography*. Included among the present-day notables are George Herbert Walker Bush, whose ancestor was Robert II, king of Scotland; actor Peter Lawford, long-distant relative of Edward III, king of England; and Franklin Delano Roosevelt, traced to Louis IV, king of France. Roberts takes obvious pleasure in connecting more than one notable descendant to the same ancestor. Sources are cited for each chapter and are explained in the list of abbreviated sources.

Thoroughly indexed, the book is a joy to use. Recommended for libraries with serious genealogical collections.—**Carol Willsey Bell**

PERSONAL NAMES

440. **Brewer's Dictionary of Names.** By Adrian Room. New York, Mansell/Cassell, 1992. 610p. $24.95. ISBN 0-304-34077-4.

In this fascinating and informative work for the general reader, Room presents the origins of more than 8,000 names of people, places, and things, with place-names getting particular emphasis. Among the entries are those for Macgillycuddy's Reeks, Vaseline, the Davis Cup, Carnegie Hall, the Sex Pistols, Ulan Bator, and Chevy Chase (place, battle, ballad, and American actor).

The entries are arranged in double columns, with headwords (usually the best-known or most popular forms of the names) in boldface type. Following the headword is a brief descriptive phrase or sentence, the word's origin, and often some further explanatory material. Pronunciations are not provided. Cross-references are given where appropriate. The front matter includes an interesting discussion of 18 categories of names mentioned in the dictionary, a section that gives brief definitions of some of the 100 languages (from Afrikaans to Zyrian) referred to in this book, and an explanation of the form of entries. Room plays fair in warning the reader of tentative or speculative etymologies.

As the title is meant to suggest, this work is in the tradition of *Brewer's Dictionary of Phrase and Fable* (HarperCollins, 1989). It also resembles *The Penguin Dictionary of Proper Names* (see ARBA 93, entry 464), but a spot check of common entries indicates that Room's book gives more etymological details and background information. (The entries for *Sing-Sing* and *Monty Python's Flying Circus* are good examples.) No work of this scope will satisfy everyone, but the author, a prolific contributor to the world of popular reference books, has provided a bountiful feast for word lovers. [R: LAR, Dec 93, p. 693; RBB, 1 Sept 93, p. 81]—**Henry J. Ricardo**

441. Guggenheimer, Heinrich W., and Eva H. Guggenheimer. **Jewish Family Names and Their Origins: An Etymological Dictionary.** Hoboken, N.J., Ktav Publishing, 1992. 882p. $99.50. CS3010.G84. 929.4'2'089924. LC 91-46313. ISBN 0-88125-297-2.

Early biblical characters were prone to changes in name, and much was made of what a person was called. Even in today's highly mobile world, names retain their significance as social or cultural indicators; on a more personal level, they help shape our sense of identity and establish our roots. In this context, a reference tool devoted to Jewish family names might well be considered nothing less than a godsend. Unfortunately, there is little of the divine about the volume under review. Rarely has a book bearing so hefty a price presented so unattractive an appearance. The arrangement and accessibility of its contents are equally unappealing. After an informative but unfocused introduction come more than 800 pages of family names, arranged alphabetically and accompanied by a bewildering list of abbreviations and a distressingly large number of *cfs*. Nothing useful was learned about this reviewer's last name (Greenspoon), sandwiched as it was between Greenspon and Greenspun; nor was it especially helpful to find his wife's family (Morsel) essentially buried in a string of names headed by Moro. There may be a limited market for this book among some specialists. Other individuals and institutions should forego this purchase. [R: Choice, Feb 93, p. 940]—**Leonard J. Greenspoon**

442. Navarro, Yvonne. **First Name Reverse Dictionary: Given Names Listed by Meaning.** Jefferson, N.C., McFarland, 1993. 206p. index. $29.95. CS2377.N37. 929.4. LC 92-50314. ISBN 0-89950-748-4.

Although reverse dictionaries are not new, a first name reverse dictionary is. The reader simply looks up the meaning, such as *life*, and the names that mean *life* are all listed, with derivatives, diminutives, alternate spellings, and countries of origin. Female names are first, male second, and a comprehensive female-male name index comes last. The index lists only the first entry word for each given name; diminutives and derivatives are not listed. Some entries have dozens of subentries; for instance, *man* has 78 subentries, with some including over a dozen individual names.

The cross-references are sometimes confusing. For example, *Bryam* means "from the ancient cow barn." The entry is listed under *ancient* and *cow* but not *barn*. *Barn* refers one to *ancient* but not *cow*. Nor is *Bryam* in the index. Also, *truth* refers the reader to *exalted* and *fulfillment or truth*. *Fulfillment or truth* refers the reader to *exalted* and, oddly, itself. *Exalted* finally results in the name *Almira*.

Amanda means "worthy of love." When Gene Roddenberry chose that name for Spock's mother, he did so on purpose, because she had married a man incapable of showing love. When writers wish to use a name based on its meaning, this book will make their job all the easier. Also, parents wishing to choose an appropriate name for their child can easily do so.—**Kevin Perizzolo**

443. Stewart, Julia. **African Names: Names from the African Continent for Children and Adults.** New York, Citadel Press/Carol Publishing Group, 1993. 171p. $9.95pa. CS2375.A33S74. 929.4'096. LC 93-9441. ISBN 0-8065-1386-1.

Stewart has compiled more than 1,000 African names—of individuals, geographical features, cities, ethnic groups, and more—that she states are appropriate for use in naming African Americans. These names are derived from peoples and countries throughout Africa, including North Africa, and the largest concentrations are from Kenya and the Kiswahili language. Many African languages, ethnic groups, and geographical regions are not represented. Names are arranged in alphabetical order and separated into those appropriate for males and females. Each entry includes a pronunciation key and a brief gloss that usually includes ethnic, linguistic, or geographical origin and a note on the word's meaning. Stewart includes some information on changing an individual's name and the legal requirements involved; a list and map of major African languages; a list for converting an "English" name to its African equivalent (e.g., Wanda to Rwanda); and a list of "Fun, Goofy Nicknames for Your Child, a Friend, a Pet." Appendixes include a list of 175 African names used as surnames (in alphabetical order with country or region of origin); a list of recent political leaders of African countries (alphabetical by country); and a brief classified bibliography covering African writers (including novelists, nonfiction writers, and Martinique native Frantz Fanon), adventure/journey fiction (by non-Africans about Africa), academic and other works, and children's books. A separate bibliography lists works relevant to naming. There is no index. This is a convenient do-it-yourself book for those who want an African name and are not concerned with its African cultural context. [R: LJ, 15 Feb 93, p. 162; RBB, Aug 93, p. 2085]—**Fred J. Hay**

8 Geography and Travel Guides

GEOGRAPHY

General Works

Atlases

United States

444. Goetzmann, William H., and Glyndwr Williams. **The Atlas of North American Exploration: From the Norse Voyages to the Race to the Pole.** New York, Prentice Hall General Reference, 1992. 224p. illus. maps. index. $40.00. G1106.S12G6. 911.7. LC 92-8573. ISBN 0-13-297128-3.

The exploration of an entire continent can only be told in segments in a single volume. This is the case in this book on North America. It starts and ends in the far north, from the Norsemen in the tenth century to the explorers of the Arctic islands and the North Pole a millennium later, and it is restricted almost exclusively to the present United States, Canada, and Greenland. The book is divided into many short vignettes of individual excursions into specific regions: from the famous, such as the Lewis and Clark journey of 1804-1806, to the less well known, such as the exploration of Labrador during 1816-1843. Each section has a well-illustrated map of the region being discussed.

This is not a text in any sense, and continuity is to some extent sacrificed in favor of the format used. Nonetheless, the individual excerpts are more informative than anecdotal. This is the kind of volume that can serve to whet the appetite for more information on the subjects covered. It is attractive enough for any coffee table yet conveys the challenge and thrill of exploration. It is suitable for any general library and for all kinds of readers. [R: BR, Nov/Dec 93, p. 54; LJ, 15 April 93, p. 60; WLB, Feb 93, p. 101]

—**Arthur R. Upgren**

445. Harrison, James, and Eleanor Van Zandt. **The Young People's Atlas of the United States.** New York, Chambers Kingfisher Graham, 1992. 128p. illus. maps. index. $16.95. G1200.H39. 912.73. LC 92-53116. ISBN 1-85697-804-4.

This atlas—intended for the home, school, or public library—follows the general pattern of atlases for the pre-18-year-old readership by having color photographs, some color drawings, shaded relief maps that are fairly small scale, and more text than is common in most atlases. For each state, information on capital, area, population, largest cities, rivers, motto, state song, state symbols, and the like is given. The shaded relief maps show major freeways, cities, major physical features (e.g., Pike's Peak in Colorado), and national parks. While no exact intended age group is given, the size of the book is such that little hands might have some trouble with it; the text seems to be appropriate for seventh graders. [R: RBB, 15 Feb 93, p. 1086; SLJ, Feb 93, p. 122]—**Mary Larsgaard**

International

446. **Atlas of the World.** 2d ed. New York, Oxford University Press, 1993. 1v. (various paging). illus. maps. index. $65.00. G1021.A7545. 912. LC 93-676838. ISBN 0-19-521025-5.

This atlas, also published in Great Britain as *Philip's Atlas of the World*, combines the cartographic skills of George Philip, a leading map and atlas company in Great Britain, and Oxford University Press. It is comprehensive, easy to use, and up-to-date, listing recent changes in boundaries and names. The full-color maps are attractive to the eye. Three main sections are devoted to world thematic maps, city maps, and regional maps. The 47 pages of world thematic maps, charts, and diagrams constitute an appealing graphic introduction to world geography, the physical Earth, people, production, and quality of life. The city maps in 32 plates cover 68 metropolitan areas worldwide, all at a common scale of 1:200,000, which facilitates comparisons of areas and patterns of widely separated cities. (These maps recognize that in an urbanizing world, many places on which information is sought lie within metropolitan areas that require more detailed maps.) The 160 pages of regional maps include physical and political maps of the continents that are characterized by exceptional clarity, and maps of major countries and regions of the world on varying scales: 1:1,600,000 for the British Isles; 1:2,000,000 for the northeastern United States, Chicago and the Midwest, central and southern California, France, and Germany; 1:6,400,000 for most areas of Latin America and Africa; and 1:16,000,000 for parts of Russia and Central Asia not covered by more detailed maps. These regional maps successfully combine layer-colored contours and relief shading with legibility of place-names. The maps are supplemented by tables of statistical data. Two separate indexes, one to city maps and the other to regional and world maps, list about 75,000 place-names with map location and latitude and longitude.

The entire printing of the first edition of this atlas (1992) sold out within four months of publication. For this new edition the publisher updated figures for populations of countries and cities, revised boundaries (e.g., the former Yugoslavia, internal administrative divisions of Nigeria), and recorded some new place-names. However, no fundamental modifications were made. For holders of the first edition, the changes may not justify the purchase of this one. Both editions are high-quality intermediate-sized atlases with sufficient detail to be widely useful in reference collections or home libraries. They are excellent reference sources at a reasonable price. [R: LJ, Jan 93, p. 94; RBB, 15 Feb 93, pp. 1077-78; SLJ, Feb 93, p. 123 WLB, Feb 93, pp. 101-02]—**Chauncy D. Harris**

447. **The Facts on File Children's Atlas.** By David Wright and Jill Wright. New York, Facts on File, 1993. 96p. illus. maps. index. $15.95. G1021.W686. 912. LC 92-39432. ISBN 0-8160-2925-3.

This is yet another atlas for the pre-18 group—a very pleasant trend in the field of atlas publication. Similar to other atlases for this age category (e.g., Jenny Wood's *Children's Atlas of People & Places* [Millbrook Press, 1993]), the volume is replete with color photographs, cheerful text, and a *National Geographic* look. The relief maps come with scale, which is well explained in the section on enjoying maps, which also explains the convention for showing topography used in the volume. Besides an index, the atlas includes questions on every other page and a short quiz. The atlas shows a European bias in the percentage of maps devoted to Europe—21 percent of the pages; North America has 14 percent of the pages, Asia 15 percent, Africa 10 percent, South America 6 percent, and the Pacific 6 percent. This work is appropriate for home or public libraries. [R: SLJ, Nov 93, p. 147]—**Mary Larsgaard**

448. **Hammond Atlas of the World.** Maplewood, N.J., Hammond, 1992. 303p. illus. maps. index. $65.00. G1021.H2665. 912. LC 92-675635. ISBN 0-8437-1175-2.

This entirely new world reference atlas is based on a computerized geographic database, which was used to produce computer-generated maps that can be easily and rapidly modified to record changes. The creation of this computer system took five years. The maps are generally attractive and provide large-scale coverage of the major land areas of the world. Introductory material includes brief sections on the history of cartography, map projections, and use of this atlas. A thematic section of eight pages is devoted to global relationships regarding environment, population, language and religions, living standards, energy and resources, agriculture and manufacturing, climate, and vegetation. The physical world is depicted on 13 striking plates of the world and major regions that show relief of land and structures of the oceans.

The main body of the atlas consists of maps of the continents and their most important regions at increasing scales. For example, the continental political map of Europe is at 1:15,000,000, with regional maps of the United Kingdom and Ireland at 1:3,000,000; of the major parts of England, Wales, Scotland, and Ireland at 1:1,000,000; and of metropolitan London at 1:500,000. Metropolitan areas, roads, and recreational areas stand out with particular clarity. Maps of adjacent areas are identified by numbers in red triangles. Some indication of relief features is provided by inconspicuous background shading. Regional maps depict political subdivisions of countries. The background coloring and shading make the maps more attractive visually but reduce their legibility somewhat. A map index on the inside front cover, the table of contents, and an alphabetical quick reference guide simplifies the location of maps of specific areas. The 115,000-entry index records map locations of cities and other features. This is a good, all-around, mid-sized atlas, but several other atlases show regional relief features better, and other Hammond atlases depict political subdivisions of countries more clearly. [R: RBB, 15 Jan 93, pp. 940-942; RQ, Summer 93, p. 570; SLMQ, Spring 93, p. 199; WLB, Feb 93, pp. 101-02]—**Chauncy D. Harris**

449. **Hammond Atlas of the World.** concise ed. Maplewood, N.J., Hammond, 1993. 231p. illus. maps. index. $39.95; $24.95pa. G1021.H2667. 912. LC 93-6731. ISBN 0-8437-1180-9; 0-8437-1181-7pa.

With the coming of the computer into the atlas world, commercial atlas publishers at last have found an ally against the frequent changes in political names and borders. Although the initial investment is substantial (Hammond estimates the cost at more than $12 million), the firms see it as being worth it, and so will atlas users who see the result. This atlas incorporates current political information. As Hammond is based in the United States, the percentage of maps of North America is higher than would appear in atlases issued by firms based in England. Relief is shown by color in the physical map section and by shaded relief and spot heights in the rest of the atlas. The color scheme is mainly pastels (e.g., lilac, beige, grey-green). There is considerable preliminary material before the "Maps of the World" section: "Interpreting Maps," "Quick Reference Guide," "Global Relationships," "The Physical World," and "Geographical Comparisons." The atlas closes with a 60,000-entry gazetteer. This concise edition is appropriate for home, office, public, or undergraduate libraries. [R: LJ, 1 Oct 93, p. 86]—**Mary Larsgaard**

450. **Hammond Explorer Atlas of the World.** Maplewood, N.J., Hammond, 1993. 120p. maps. index. $9.95pa. G1021.H2457. 912. LC 93-1280. ISBN 0-8437-1186-8.

Hammond spent 5 years and $12 million developing a world digital database, which it is now using to put together atlases for various audiences. The *Explorer* is for precollege users and is pared down in many ways from both the *Hammond Atlas of the World* (1992) and the *Hammond Atlas of the World* concise ed. (1993). The number of pages drops considerably, from 303 in the parent to 232 in the concise to 120 in the *Explorer*; the number of maps goes from 150 to 120 to 100. The index is most noticeably lowered in size—from 115,000 names in the parent to 60,000 in the concise to a relatively puny 6,000 in the *Explorer*. The *Explorer* has almost no prefatory material (which, in this reviewer's opinion, should often be dispensed with anyway); what there is, is worthwhile—one page on map projections, two on how to use the atlas, six on world flags (for schools this is probably quite useful), and two on world statistics. Unfortunately, the physical base for the maps used in the other two books is not retained in the *Explorer*. This atlas is appropriate for use by elementary and secondary school students at school and at home. [R: LJ, 1 Oct 93, p. 86]—**Mary Larsgaard**

451. **The Kingfisher Reference Atlas: An A-Z Guide to Countries of the World.** By Brian Williams. New York, Chambers Kingfisher Graham, 1993. 215p. maps. index. $19.95. G1021.W554. ISBN 1-85697-838-9.

This colorful atlas is perfect for homes, offices, and secondary school and undergraduate libraries that have requests for page-size maps. Each country has relief, contour, and location maps; basic statistics; a brief history of the political and social background; and graphs on population, climate, and imports and exports. The work shows a Western focus by the number of pages given to such countries as France, Germany, and the United States (two or three instead of one, which is what most countries have devoted to them). The index is quite short in comparison to the number of pages of map and text and indexes only maps, not text; the list of former and alternate country names is only one page long. The maps and the text tend to be quite generalized, given the small amount of space available; but considering the constraints, they are still useful to beginning users with low-level demands. Both the maps and text are clear and easy to understand; countries are arranged in alphabetical order, so one can find them quickly. [R: RBB, 1 Sept 93, p. 88; SLJ, Nov 93, p. 147]—**Mary Larsgaard**

452. Mason, Antony. **The Children's Atlas of Exploration: Follow in the Footsteps of the Great Explorers.** Brookfield, Conn., Millbrook Press, 1993. 95p. illus. maps. index. $18.90. G1036.M3. 911. LC 92-28856. ISBN 1-56294-256-5.

Television and video games compete mightily against reading for the time and attention of children, but as long as books such as *The Children's Atlas of Exploration* keep appearing, reading has a chance. Ranging from ancient times to modern space travel, the atlas is divided into seven sections: an introduction; Europe; Asia; Africa; the Americas; the South Seas and Australia; and the "final frontiers" of polar, mountain, deep-sea, and space exploration. Unlike in many books of this nature, non-Western achievements are given their due, but without the strained appearance of political correctness and without slighting the genuine achievements of the West. In these pages the travels of Hsuan Tsang, Cheng Ho, and Ibn Battuta take their rightful place beside those of Marco Polo, Christopher Columbus, and Vasco da Gama. The text is simple without being infantile, the well-chosen illustrations appear in both black-and-white and color, and the full-color cartography is attractive and accurate. A helpful time chart and index conclude the volume. This atlas is a browser's delight for children, their parents, and their teachers; it is also a must for school and public libraries. [R: RBB, Aug 93, p. 2086]—**Ronald H. Fritze**

453. **Student Atlas of the World.** Rutland, Vt., Charles E. Tuttle, 1993. 224p. illus. maps. index. $30.00. ISBN 0-8048-1980-7.

The first part of this atlas includes 15 plates of thematic maps that provide a brief graphic summary of the main features of the globe and its structure, oceans, atmosphere, climate, landscapes, natural vegetation, population, food, minerals, and environmental problems. Following are 128 pages of regional physical (hypsometric) maps that are attractive and legible. It should be noted that this British-produced atlas (HarperCollins and Collins Longman Atlases) is strongly Europe-oriented. Maps of the main countries of Europe are at a scale of 1:2,500,000. Those of the United States and Canada are generally at only 1:7,500,000, and those of Latin America, Africa, and Asia are at still smaller (but variable) scales. The location maps on the end papers, for each continent, and on insets in each map are especially helpful. The index includes about 40,000 names with geographical coordinates and map location. The atlas is designed particularly for student use but can serve effectively as a smaller reference atlas, especially for Europe.—**Chauncy D. Harris**

454. Wood, Jenny. **The Children's Atlas of People & Places: Travel the World and Visit People in Far-Off Lands.** Brookfield, Conn., Millbrook Press, 1993. 95p. illus. maps. index. $18.90. G1021.W645. 912. LC 92-28857. ISBN 1-56294-257-3.

One of England's main exports to the United States seems to be atlases, and here is one, with 32 percent of the pages devoted to Europe and 11 percent to the United States. Color photographs, more text than one usually sees in atlases, flags, location maps, and shaded relief maps give this atlas a colorful, busy look. There is no indication of the age group for which it is intended; it appears to be appropriate for third through sixth graders. While an explanation of projection is given, there are no explanations given for scale or shaded relief, neither of which are necessarily intuitive. The text seems correct, although this reviewer would not translate *gaucho* as "mounted rancher." The maps do not show roads, just shaded relief, major rivers, and borders. The work is appropriate for home or public libraries. [R: RBB, Aug 93, p. 2086; SBF, June/July 93, pp. 150-51]—**Mary Larsgaard**

Australia

455. **The AUSMAP Atlas of Australia.** By Ken Johnson. New York, Cambridge University Press, 1993. 97p. illus. maps. index. $30.00pa. G2750.J6. 912.94. LC 91-43528. ISBN 0-521-42122-5.

This book is an unrivaled source of information (presented for the most part in pictorial form) on all aspects of Australia: physical, historical, social, political, and demographic. It is, accordingly, unusually comprehensive, authoritative, and easy to use. Although the editorial commentary advises that the contents were chosen because they suit the needs of students, they clearly suit the needs of anyone needing up-to-date, accurate information, whether on mining and mineral industries, geology and tectonics, education services, tourism, or rural activity and settlement. One section places Australia in the world scene from pre-European times to the present; another covers the characteristics of the population in both capital and small cities; and a third deals with natural resources and hazards. While the textual commentary is brief and correct, it is at times rather condescending, as in differentiating climate and weather, for example. And there are, inevitably, some minor shortcomings. Sydney is said on one occasion to have 44 local governments and on another, 39; and the Commonwealth of Nations is said to have originated "after 1945," whereas it was created by the Statute of Westminster in 1931. And describing the commercial and administrative parts of major cities as "town centres" may not please Australians. Yet such minor points are no serious matter in such a commendable work. The full-color maps, photographs, and satellite images are supplemented by line, bar, and pie graphs that aid in immediate comprehension of at times rather technical or scientific material. This is, as the publisher claims on the back cover, "more than an atlas—it is a wealth of information for anyone needing to understand Australia."

—Marian B. McLeod

Canada

456. **Canadian Oxford School Atlas.** 6th ed. Quentin H. Stanford, ed. Toronto, Oxford University Press, 1992. 216p. illus. maps. index. $18.00. ISBN 0-19-540895-0. [Also published as *Canadian Oxford World Atlas.* new ed. $29.95; $17.95pa. ISBN 0-19-540973-8; 0-19-540897-7pa.]

This full-color, very readable atlas has no introductory information and little explanatory text. Two pages cover "Understanding Topographic Maps," and before the gazetteer of Canada is a page on how to use it, with a list of map and gazetteer abbreviations.

However, the atlas is chock-full of current, detailed information and maps about Canada. Various information and maps are given for the continents, the poles, the oceans, and the rest of the world. The table of contents is thorough and very useful for locating specific maps and tables; it even includes a world map with pages indicated for information on each area. Urban land-use maps for many of the large cities of the world are fascinating and worthwhile. Near the end of the book, the section on Canadian statistics provides 74 excellent tables of information about industries, the population, the economy, climate, and the like.

The intended audience is not identified, but any student or researcher of Canada will find this work, an update of the 1985 edition, useful. Some of the maps and illustrations are easy for a high school student to understand while others may need interpretation or more study. Recommended for school and public libraries.—**Susan C. Awe**

457. **Canadian Oxford Intermediate Atlas.** 2d ed. Toronto, Oxford University Press, 1993. 96p. illus. maps. index. $22.50. 912. ISBN 0-19-540941-8.

Although the primary focus of this school atlas is on Canada's climate, economy, land, natural resources, and people, it also contains some basic information on other parts of the world. Presented in the form of graphs, charts, and maps, the information on Canada covers a wide range of topics that is supplemented by data about farming, forestry, and fishing as well as natural resource industries for each province. The abbreviated table of contents and the index, which is simply a gazetteer, are inadequate guides, so careful scanning of the contents is required to identify the information that is presented. The information on other parts of the world is provided largely to allow Canadian students to make appropriate comparisons with their own country. That information is, of course, readily available in a wide variety of other atlases.

For most United States libraries either *Philip's Atlas of Canada & the World* (see ARBA 89, entry 389) or *The Concise Atlas of Canada and the World* (see ARBA 85, entry 412) provides more comprehensive information on Canada for an adult clientele. Apart from its intended audience of Canadian students, the *Canadian Oxford Intermediate Atlas* may be of value to school and public libraries in the northern United States where students are learning about Canada.—**Norman D. Stevens**

458. Gentilcore, R. Louis, Don Measner, and Ronald H. Walder, eds. **Historical Atlas of Canada. Volume II: The Land Transformed 1800-1891.** Toronto and Buffalo, N.Y., University of Toronto Press, 1993. 184p. illus. maps. $95.00. 911'.71. ISBN 0-8020-3447-0.

The nineteenth century in Canada was an era of calamitous changes and enormous shifts in social, political, and demographic developments. As did the United States, Canada had its fair share of immigration, rebellions, economic growth, territorial expansion, and wars. This oversized book of 58 double-paged color plates (most created by computer cartography) clearly shows the evolution in Canada of international trade, manufacturing, population (e.g., language, migrations, immigration), the primary industries, and territorial growth. Along the way there are details of gold rushes, domestic architecture, the Red River settlement, and transportation byways. Both of the earlier volumes (see ARBA 91, entry 516 for volume 3 and ARBA 88, entry 529 for volume 1) were drawn by hand (the project itself began in 1979); new computer software has enabled the university to concentrate on detail and clean, high-quality plates.

Useful for those in the United States is the plate showing the movement of Canadians to that country. The atlas shows where they went and how they earned a living. But many of the plates are merely indicative, and in many cases one wishes that more plates were forthcoming. For instance, there is detail on traffic volume on toll roads in 1844. But what about 1854, 1864, or 1874? The Saint John, New Brunswick, Orange Day Parade of 1849 has its route shown because this parade led to violent religious riots. The route of D'Arcy McGee's funeral procession through Montreal in 1868 is useful, but again, merely indicative of the capability of the system. It is hoped that more of this detail will be forthcoming, if funds are available. Unfortunately, there is no index, and the table of contents, while expansive, is only in topical order.—**Dean Tudor**

Developing Countries

459. Kurian, George, ed. **Atlas of the Third World.** 2d ed. New York, Facts on File, 1992. 384p. maps. index. $125.00. G1046.G1K8. 912'.19724. LC 88-675259. ISBN 0-8160-1930-4. Countries lacking the technological wizardry of the developed countries are euphemistically referred to as Third World countries. The primary focus of this atlas is to graphically depict political divisions, population, economics, agriculture, trade, defense, and health (among others) of the 81 countries selected for this edition. Few notable improvements have been incorporated since the first edition (see ARBA 84, entry 508). Countries such as Paraguay have been omitted, and there is no explanation for this exclusion. Cartographic misrepresentations and omissions were pointed out in the previous review, but they have not been corrected in this edition. What this reviewer finds misleading to the point of disbelief is that the cartographic maps of the Sudan are identical to those of the first edition!

The intellectual and practical value of this publication for any reference collection is extremely limited, especially for academic and public libraries. Not recommended. [R: BR, May/June 93, p. 51; RBB, 1 April 93, pp. 1452-53; SLJ, Mar 93, pp. 241-42; WLB, Mar 93, p. 105]—**Dario J. Villa**

Middle East

460. Freeman-Grenville, G. S. P. **Historical Atlas of the Middle East.** New York, Simon & Schuster Academic Reference Division, 1993. 144p. maps. index. $65.00. G2206.S1F7. 911'.58. LC 93-9294. ISBN 0-13-390915-8.

This 113-map historical atlas includes maps and commentary relevant to a potpourri of cultural and political aspects of the Middle East from 2050 B.C.E. to 1993. The table of contents groups maps into broad categories, such as the Arab period, the Ottoman world, and the twentieth century. A review of specific map titles shows the book to be very diverse in coverage. Commerce, agriculture, climate, language, wars, minorities, dynasties, cities, natural resources, higher education, and religion are among the topics considered.

The work provides clear two-color maps and matching commentaries ranging from a few paragraphs to a page in length. An index to the maps provides key word access to people and place-names but does not provide access to general map topics. Students researching broad subjects such as agriculture or commerce will need to scan the table of contents. The user may also be frustrated by the absence of running section headers to provide overall section continuity. Despite these shortcomings in access, students and researchers will find this resource useful because of the comprehensive coverage, excellent maps, and easy-to-read text. [R: RBB, 1 Nov 93, pp. 565-66; WLB, Oct 93, pp. 92-93]—**Ahmad Gamaluddin**

Bibliography

461. Conzen, Michael P., Thomas A. Rumney, and Graeme Wynn. **A Scholar's Guide to Geographical Writing on the American and Canadian Past.** Chicago, University of Chicago Press, 1993. 741p. illus. maps. index. (University of Chicago Geography Research Paper, no.235). $29.95pa. Z1247.C66. 016.91173. LC 92-23520. ISBN 0-226-11569-0.

This comprehensive bibliography of United States and Canadian historical geography contains more than 10,000 citations to books, articles (including many in foreign journals), theses, and dissertations published between the mid-nineteenth century and the end of 1990. The citations are mainly to the writings of professional geographers.

The bibliography is divided into four major sections: general sources, North America, Canada, and the United States. The latter two sections are subdivided by regions, and within regions by states or provinces. There are 25 topics, such as environmental change, population, agriculture, and townscape, which subdivide each general or regional heading throughout the book. There are also two highly readable and informative bibliographical essays about the writing of historical geography in the United States and Canada, as well as author and subject indexes.

This work will supersede Douglas R. McManis's *Historical Geography of the United States: A Bibliography* (Eastern Michigan University, Division of Field Services, 1965) and Ronald E. Grim's *Historical Geography of the United States: A Guide to Information Sources* (see ARBA 84, entry 510). It includes many more journal articles than McManis and Grim's book does, and it also updates their works. Where applicable, this book uses the same regional categories for the United States as those used by McManis. While there are some mistakes in the citations, and the page counts are not given for theses and dissertations, the work will be a valuable resource to researchers. [R: Choice, Sept 93, p. 76]
—**Kathleen Farago**

462. Welton, Ann. **Explorers and Exploration: The Best Resources for Grades 5 through 9.** Phoenix, Ariz., Oryx Press, 1993. 176p. index. $29.95pa. G175.W45. 910'.9. LC 93-18190. ISBN 0-89774-799-2.

Many children dream of becoming explorers and finding places where no one else has ever been before. Alas, on this increasingly crowded Earth, the opportunity for this type of exploration has just about ended—but the dream remains. *Explorers and Exploration* harnesses that dream to aid teachers and librarians in helping students learn history, geography, and science. The work is divided into 10 chapters dealing with the Vikings, Marco Polo, Prince Henry and the circumnavigation of the Earth, Columbus's voyages, early explorers of the North American continent, Europeans in Africa, polar exploration, mountaineering, deep-sea journeys, and space exploration. Some 230 books, of which more than 200 have been published since 1986, are extensively annotated concerning their content and suitability for fifth- to ninth-grade readers. Most of the books are histories, biographies, and geographies, but some works of fiction are listed. There is an index of authors, titles, and subjects.

While the content of the introductory sections of each chapter is generally good, the chapter on Columbus veers dangerously into the realm of the politically correct in its comments on the magnitude of the so-called genocide of the native populations of North America. For the sake of the stronger eighth- and ninth-grade students, more adult books could have been listed, such as Francis Parkman's classic *LaSalle and the Discovery of the Great West* (McKay, 1990). Schoolteachers and librarians, the intended audience for this book, will find it useful for selecting books for purchase or for assignment to students. [R: RBB, 15 Dec 93, pp. 776-77; WLB, Dec 93, pp. 80-82]—**Ronald H. Fritze**

Biography

463. Baker, Daniel B., ed. **Explorers and Discoverers of the World.** Detroit, Gale, 1993. 637p. illus. maps. index. $59.95. LC 92-055094. ISBN 0-8103-5421-7.

Almost everyone has the curiosity to travel; unfortunately, money, time, and infrastructure are also required. Thus, mass tourism only began seriously in the years following World War II. For as far back as records are extant, however, the challenge of "out there" has stimulated human imagination and led those who could afford (or could persuade others to afford) the costs of an expedition to unravel the secrets of the Earth. In our time, this fascination with discovery has been extended to include the oceans and even space.

This book records the known biographical details of more than 300 "explorers," including spacecraft and submersibles as well as humans. Entries vary from half a page to seven pages, as for Columbus; each consists of a brief resume, a sketch of the explorer's life and contributions, and a bibliographical selection. Photographs and maps often illustrate the entries, which are arranged alphabetically with a geographical cross-referencing section. Of special interest is the focus on women and on non-European explorers, two groups that, although pioneers in many areas, have generally been slighted in other works.

In any compendium that involves choices, it is possible to quibble with the selections. Despite a broad-based review panel, some of the entries seem trivial, while omissions of several noted explorers of the American West (e.g., John Wesley Powell) are hard to justify. On balance, however, this is an attractive and accessible work that will provide new insights into those for whom the unknown proved an irresistible lure. [R: Choice, Oct 93, p. 265; LJ, 1 April 93, p. 90; RBB, July 93, pp. 2001-02; RQ, Winter 93, pp. 284-85; VOYA, Dec 93, pp. 332-33; WLB, Sept 93, p. 118]—**James R. McDonald**

464. Burton, Rosemary, Richard Cavendish, and Bernard Stonehouse. **Journeys of the Great Explorers.** New York, Facts on File, 1992. 224p. illus. maps. index. $34.95. G200.C38. 910.92. LC 92-9195. ISBN 0-8160-2840-0.

Explorers and exploration are perennially fascinating topics, particularly during 1992, the 500th anniversary of Columbus's voyage to America. *Journeys of the Great Explorers* attempts to satisfy that fascination by presenting the story of 30 famous travelers, from the time of Alexander the Great to the Space Age. Among the explorers featured in this volume are such figures as Christopher Columbus, James Cook, and Thor Heyerdahl; less-familiar people detailed include explorer/scholar Alexander von Humbolt and travel writer Freya Stark. Besides the biographical essays, there are nine topical essays on the explorations of Asia, North and Central America, South America, Australasia and the Pacific, Africa, the polar regions, naturalists and plant hunters, pioneer women travelers, and space. The essays are generously illustrated with black-and-white and color photographs and pictures along with detailed and well-produced maps of the routes followed by the explorers. Numerous sidebars, consisting of excerpts from primary documents, mini-essays, and chronologies, supplement the major essays. A short index of people, subjects, and places concludes the work.

Well conceived and well written, the only major problem with the book is its lack of a bibliography to serve as a guide for further reading. While it is not as comprehensive as *World Explorers and Discoverers* (see ARBA 93, entry 486), the strengths of *Journeys of the Great Explorers* are its excellent maps and lovely illustrations. Its reasonable price will make it an attractive purchase for both libraries and individuals.—**Ronald H. Fritze**

465. Larkin, Robert P., and Gary L. Peters. **Biographical Dictionary of Geography.** Westport, Conn., Greenwood Press, 1993. 361p. index. $69.50. G67.L37. 910.922. LC 92-18364. ISBN 0-313-27622-6.

Apart from a generalized appreciation that their subject involves the consideration of space and place, and an acceptance of a few basic technologies such as cartography, remote sensing, and information systems, modern geographers are an increasingly diverse group with little common ground. Given the increasing need to specialize, geography continues to witness a sort of "big bang," as individuals move steadily away from an always-minimal core of agreed knowledge to the cutting edges of various physical, cultural, and economic specialties. As a result, efforts to identify historically important contributors to the science are increasingly fraught with difficulty.

The present work, for example, offers basic biographical information on 77 geographers. Arranged in alphabetical order, the entries range chronologically from Thales of Miletus (6th century B.C.) to a dozen still-living professionals. Each entry—they range from two to seven pages—consists of a biographical sketch, a select bibliography, a personal chronology, and a few references to more detailed works. The biographies are unadorned and make little effort to place the subjects in the larger context of their times.

This book will be of interest to students of the history of geographic ideas, but it will also, based on the necessarily limited number of inclusions, be controversial in the profession despite the authors' statement that their purpose is to include representatives from as many subfields as possible. Several famous names more commonly associated with other disciplines (e.g., Charles Darwin, John Muir) seem questionable, but it is undoubtedly the composition of the still-living group that will raise the most eyebrows. [R: Choice, June 93, p. 1606; RBB, 15 April 93, p. 1532]—**James R. McDonald**

Dictionaries and Encyclopedias

466. O'Mahony, Kieran. **The Dictionary of Geographical Literacy: The Complete Geography Reference.** Seattle, Wash., EduCare Press, 1993. 374p. illus. maps. $19.95pa. ISBN 0-944638-08-2.

The promotion of geographical literacy has become something of a cause, notably in the United States. This book is one of several contributions aiming to provide concise definitions of place-names and scientific terms. It considers physical, cultural, and economic geography, as well as places, in 2,000 alphabetically arranged entries. There are some photographs (including four in color) and numerous computer-generated maps and diagrams, most of which are of such poor quality as to be virtually useless.

Apparently, although not explicitly, aimed at schoolchildren, the book is riddled with errors, banalities, and meaningless definitions. Capes and bays, for example, are defined as the long lists of geographical narrows that school-going children were forced to memorize long ago (sic), while carbon monoxide is apparently nothing more than the emission gas of automobiles (sic). Selection criteria are also questionable. Aberdeen, Scotland, population 187,000, receives half a page; Glasgow, population 1,800,000, is omitted. Darjeeling, India, with 58,000 inhabitants, is included; Madras, with 4,475,000, is not. As another typical example, six of the new nations born of the former Soviet Union are not listed.

Geographical literacy presumes an understanding of the significance of places and processes, of three-dimensional knowledge rather than the flat canvas of simple location and definition. There are currently many exciting ways by which this process is being achieved; this book adds nothing to the reference literature. [R: SLMQ, Spring 93, p. 199]—**James R. McDonald**

Handbooks and Yearbooks

467. Davis, Lee. **Man-Made Catastrophes: From the Burning of Rome to the Lockerbie Crash.** New York, Facts on File, 1993. 338p. illus. index. $40.00. D24.D38. 904. LC 91-41859. ISBN 0-8160-2035-3.

468. Davis, Lee. **Natural Disasters: From the Black Plague to the Eruption of Mt. Pinatubo.** New York, Facts on File, 1992. 321p. illus. index. $40.00. GB5014.D38. 904. LC 91-38395. ISBN 0-8160-2034-5.

469. Smith, Roger. **Catastrophes and Disasters.** New York, Chambers Kingfisher Graham, 1992. 246p. illus. index. $9.95pa. ISBN 0-550-17015-4.

These three books chronicle most of the large-scale tragedies that have occurred since the beginning of recorded language. Davis's books are companions; Smith's book is a compendium of both natural and man-made disasters. Obviously, Davis's books cover more ground. Each section in his books deals with a single type of disaster (e.g., air crashes) and contains a list of events by country, events arranged chronologically, explanatory text, an occasional glossary, and descriptions of the disasters. Each section has separate criteria for the inclusion of disasters; usually sheer numbers of people killed will result in a tragedy's appearance, but unusual events with less loss of life, such as the sinking of the *Andrea Doria*, are also described. Davis's descriptions of the tragedies are detailed, often drawing from eyewitness reports, and can be gruesome. Many times he describes both the prelude to and the aftermath of the disaster, including the social results; for example, the Triangle Shirtwaist Factory fire, which killed 145 immigrant girls, was caused by sweatshop conditions and led to the formation of the International Ladies Garment Workers Union and to the implementation of uniform fire and factory codes. In his book on man-made disasters, Davis includes riots, genocidal events, and massacres; unfortunately, he apparently did not have time to include the 1992 Los Angeles riots. Nor was Davis able to list Hurricane Andrew in the book on natural disasters.

Arranged similarly to Davis's books, Smith's book also divides the disasters by type, then lists them chronologically. He has a single chronological list of all tragedies at the beginning of the book, a useful feature. He also includes a few categories of disaster that Davis neglects: sporting disasters (e.g., the crash at Le Mans on June 12, 1955, in which a car flew into the audience) and certain types of environmental disasters (e.g., the anthrax release at Sverdlovsk in April 1979). His prose style is matter-of-fact, and in some cases this lessens the emotional impact of the disasters; however, readers will get a feel for the scope of the tragedy. Small inset boxes often enlighten users as to results of official inquiries, unique aspects of certain types of disasters (e.g., 200 rhubarb pickers were killed in an earthquake in 1202), or related events. Because of the size of the book, it is by no means complete; Smith's weakest section is probably that on windstorms, with only one major entry on U.S. tornadoes (although there is an interesting entry on British tornadoes, a subject all but ignored in North American books). His section on pandemics could be larger, as it covers only the Black Death, the Spanish flu outbreak of 1918-1920, and AIDS. As with Davis's books, Smith's work came out too early to cover Hurricane Andrew (the L.A. riots are outside his scope).

Interested libraries should acquire all three books. Davis's books are more inclusive and emotionally written, while Smith's book originated in Great Britain and describes Commonwealth tragedies that do not appear in the books by Davis. Smith also includes details that differ from Davis's; for example, in the Lockerbie bombing, Davis covers the hunt for the perpetrators, while Smith focuses more on the details of the disaster and the type of bomb used. All three are recommended. [R: Choice, July/Aug 93, p. 1745; RBB, 1 Jan 93, p. 826; WLB, May 93, p. 119]—**D. A. Rothschild**

PLACE NAMES

470. Bright, William. **Colorado Place Names.** Boulder, Colo., Johnson Books, 1993. 162p. $11.95pa. F774.B75. 917.88'003. LC 93-777. ISBN 1-55566-102-5.

If George Eichler's *Colorado Place Names* (Johnson, 1977) is in your collection, this revised and expanded edition will be a must purchase. Bright, the new author, was a professor of linguistics at the University of California, Los Angeles, before he retired and moved to Colorado. As a result of his background, this volume places greater emphasis on pronunciation and name origins than did the original publication. Because his specialty was Native American languages, place-names of Indian origin receive special attention.

Unlike that in the first edition, the arrangement is in a single dictionary format. Entries, ranging in length from two sentences to several paragraphs, start with location information and a pronunciation guide, followed by a discussion of the name's origin. Bright often indicates both the English and Spanish pronunciation for a name. He notes he does not indicate a "correct" pronunciation but lists common variations, such as four of "Colorado." All in all, this is an enjoyable book and a worthwhile addition to a western travel collection.—**G. Edward Evans**

471. **The Cambridge Dictionary of Australian Places.** By Richard Appleton and Barbara Appleton. New York, Cambridge University Press, 1992. 356p. maps. $65.00. DU90.C36. 919.4'003. LC 91-35036. ISBN 0-521-39506-2.

This is an extremely interesting and comprehensive reference work that lists nearly 5,000 entries on Australian settlements and geographical features. It provides information on historical development and present population (1986 census) and on location, altitude, and climate. (Australia has less variation in altitude and climate than any other comparable land mass.) Latitude and longitude are regularly given, and 26 maps are supplied to help in location.

About one-third of Australian place-names are Aboriginal in origin. Pronunciation guides are accordingly provided and are generally simple and clear. However, the authors have not grappled successfully with the unstressed vowel, the commonest vowel in English: the schwa. They spell it variously *a, e, i, o*, and *u*, all to indicate the same neutral grunt. Surprisingly, too, the authors record only one pronunciation for the federal capital Canberra, when there have always been two (it is sometimes stressed on the first syllable, sometimes on the second).

It should be noted that the authors have accepted the uniquely Australian terminology of city, town, and township as general usage. It is a confusing distinction that needs explanation. Normally the Australian distinction goes from "city" to "town" to "township," based on population; the word "village" is virtually nonexistent. But in looser, and common, Australian usage, "town" can reach up to mean "city" and reach down to mean "township." The five largest capital cities would certainly be called cities, but the two smallest, Hobart and Darwin, might often be called towns.

Merely from reading among the entries, one learns surprising facts about Australia: For example, the young country has its own ghost towns, such as the recently abandoned uranium mining town of Mary Kathleen in Queensland; and the capital city of Darwin has five times been destroyed by hurricanes, most recently in 1974. Sifting the historical and geographical information that is contained in this miniature encyclopedia, Americans will better understand the qualities and limitations of Australia.

—**John B. Beston**

TRAVEL GUIDES

General Works

472. **Courvoisier's Book of the Best.** By Lord Lichfield and Sue Carpenter. New York, Sterling Publishing, 1993. 256p. index. $12.95pa. ISBN 0-8069-0363-5.

This eighth edition is an extensive guide to the world's best hotels, restaurants, shops, travel, nightlife, and culture. The work is arranged by country and thereunder by each major city or "the rest of that country." Each place entry contains the best art, museums, ballet, bars and cafes, clubs, fashion designers, festivals, films, gardens, historic buildings, hotels, music, restaurants, shopping, ski resorts, theater, tours, properties, and wine to be found therein (as chosen by various celebrities and experts). Each entry has a thorough description of what is to be found in that place and lists addresses and telephone numbers. For transportation to a desired location, there is a travel directory at the back of the guide. It lists airlines, cruises, rail, tours, villas and their agents, and yacht charter. The last part of this guide is an index.

Courvoisier's Book of the Best is well organized and timely. Highly recommended for all libraries and travelers.—**Lise Rasmussen**

473. Heise, Jon O., and Julia R. Rinehart. **The Travel Book: Guide to the Travel Guides.** 2d ed. Metuchen, N.J., Scarecrow, 1993. 397p. index. $42.50. Z6011.H4. 016.9102'02. LC 93-15822. ISBN 0-8108-2697-6.

This is the 2d edition of a well-received annotated bibliography that first appeared in 1981. In addition to the acquisition of a new coauthor, this edition has been expanded by 80 pages. The book is arranged by continent and then by individual country. In the case of North American and some of the more frequently traveled European countries, this breakdown extends to states or regions and individual cities. The guide contains 385 entries for English-language travel guides covering most parts of the world, but coverage of Africa is sparse. There are only two unique entries (on Egypt) for the continent, with six other references to books in series that include other African countries. The heaviest geographical concentration is North America, with 204 travel guides represented. There are numerous *see* references to many titles from series, which would expand the number of entries considerably.

The broad range of types of travel guides included is commendable. Examples of types covered include walking guides; typical AAA-style guides that cover everything about a destination, outlet shopping directories, and guides to ghost towns in Texas. Indexing is primarily by geographical location or series title; no individual titles are given. There are some headings relating to activity or situation, such as overseas employment, types of travel (e.g., camping, rail, bicycling), and traveling for the handicapped.

A typical entry provides necessary bibliographical information plus an annotation. The breezy annotations are divided into two sections: a description of the work's contents followed by an evaluation. Sometimes the informality of the annotations can be distracting, especially in the descriptive portion. But this straightforward approach is preferable to more turgid styles. Publication dates range back to as early as 1974, with many others carrying copyright dates from the early 1980s. (The promotional pamphlet from the publisher assures that each entry is in print.) For the older guides there is some concern about the accuracy of information regarding accommodations and restaurants. Beyond that, *The Travel Book* remains a viable choice as a source for selecting travel materials. [R: Choice, Dec 93, p. 586; JAL, Nov 93, p. 347]—**Phillip P. Powell**

474. Simony, Maggie, ed. **The Traveler's Reading Guide: Ready-Made Reading Lists for the Armchair Traveler.** rev. and updated ed. New York, Facts on File, 1993. 510p. index. $50.00. Z6004.T6T73. 016.91. LC 92-8175. ISBN 0-8160-2648-3.

This volume represents the third version of a geographic area-based list of travel books and guides prepared by a retiree who is a devoted advocate of libraries and of "iterology...which I understand means the relationship between authors, travels, books and readers." She has now identified an additional public—those living full-time in their recreational vehicles—and this slant gave new spice to her third examination of the sources (see ARBA 88, entry 470 and ARBA 86, entry 419 for reviews of the previous editions).

About 5,150 monographs are included, of which about one-tenth are reprints of classics—some a century old, such as those of Robert Louis Stevenson. Authors familiar to *National Geographic Magazine* readers include Paul Theroux and Tim Severin, while *New Yorker* readers will recognize John McPhee and Jeremy Bernstein. A series of new authors' works, edited by veteran Jan Morris, is called "Destinations" (Simon & Schuster). Half of the items listed are about North America, 29 percent are on Europe, and 21 percent are scattered. The section on Asia would have been buttressed if the excellent photoessays of Martin Hurlimann's Atlantis Press (Zurich) had been mentioned. (These are widely held in liberal arts college libraries.) The subject arrangement under each country is still by format, and the greatly improved typography helps scanning. About a third of the entries are fiction; a helpful appendix contains a list of novels with English settings. The author refers elsewhere for detailed examination of the numerous series of guides (e.g., the *Insight Guides* from Prentice Hall). Recommended for all public libraries and for retiring staff members instead of gold watches! [R: LJ, 15 Feb 93, p. 162; RBB, 1 May 93, p. 1636]

—**Eugene B. Jackson**

United States

475. **Hippocrene U.S.A. Guide to Historic Black South: Historical Sites, Cultural Centers, and Musical Happenings of the African-American South.** By Jim Haskins and Joann Biondi. New York, Hippocrene Books, 1993. 206p. illus. index. $14.95pa. E185.92.H38. 975'.00496073. LC 93-18334. ISBN 0-7818-0140-0.

The history of African-Americans in the American South is a rich mixture of people, events, and places. Nowhere is Black history told as well as at historic sites—Piney Woods School in Mississippi, Dexter Avenue Church in Montgomery, and Cabbage Row in Charleston. This small reference volume is a guide to such historic places, arranged by state and then city or town. Each site is described briefly—perhaps too briefly. The information is accurate, and the indexes to cities and sites complement the text. Nevertheless, there are curious omissions—the Arthur Ashe tennis complex in Richmond; the University of South Carolina, where Blacks enrolled as early as 1873 (and from where many graduated in 1877); and

Foster Auditorium at the University of Alabama, where George Wallace stood in the school-house door. Hippocrene's *Guide to Black America* (see ARBA 93, entry 424) provides more detailed site information (e.g., admission prices, hours), but both books are clearly inferior to *Historic Landmarks of Black America* (see ARBA 92, entry 440).—**Boyd Childress**

476. Hodgson, Michael. **America's Secret Recreation Areas: Your Travel Guide to the Forgotten Wild Lands of the Bureau of Land Management.** San Francisco, Foghorn Press, 1993. 557p. illus. maps. $15.95pa. GV191.42.W47H63. 790'.02578. LC 92-21179. ISBN 0-935701-60-5.

Unlike earlier guides to the great outdoors of our western states, which are generally limited to national or state parks and speak of maintained trails, campsites, and the like, this book deals only with wilder and less frequented areas, those administered by the Bureau of Land Management (BLM). Only 12 western states (including Alaska) are covered, all of them west of or straddling the Rocky Mountains.

The work begins with a 35-page user's guide to the lands of the BLM, warning the would-be hiker or explorer that BLM lands seldom have established trails, campsites, rest rooms, or other amenities often found in state or national parks. Many "Don't do's" are listed, as well as useful hints about survival, such as waterproofing maps in rainy weather and avoiding snakes, bears, noxious insects, and other perils, as well as listing important or necessary items to pack in with you.

The regional chapters, one for each state, begin with a couple of simple maps showing locations of dozens of BLM sites or areas worth investigating. Then comes an unusual feature: 10 or so "Best of the State" hikes or outings described in detail. Following these are shorter listings describing 20 or more sites on BLM lands in each state where the adventurous can hike, boat, hunt, fish, ski, camp, cycle (foot or motor), photograph, or just plain loaf in solitude, far from the noisy and crowded parks. Information is given as to location, approach, permits (usually none), and an address from which to get maps and further information. Appendixes include lists of recreational activities, bicycling clubs, and outdoor organizations; how to order BLM maps, with charts of such maps for each state; and some data on the American Discovery Trail and on National Trails Day. This is an ideal book for the adventuresome patron in a public library.—**Raymund F. Wood**

477. Kruh, David, and Louis Kruh. **Presidential Landmarks.** New York, Hippocrene Books, 1992. 480p. illus. index. $24.95. ISBN 0-7818-0027-7.

This volume serves as a guide to sites associated with each of the presidents of the United States. The emphasis is on birth places, residences, graves, and (for recent chief executives) presidential libraries. The format makes for ease of use. Each president is treated in the order in which he served. A brief biographical sketch is followed by data on historic sites. Prospective visitors are given background information, fees, and directions to the site. Many of the sites are shown in black-and-white photographs.

Presidential Landmarks has value for those planning visits to the places described. Unfortunately, the book suffers from a number of problems. The failure to satisfactorily center chapter headings could be overlooked, if it were not for some factual errors and for a poor writing style throughout. The first page of the first chapter is indicative of these problems. The sixth word is a typographical error, and the French and Indian War ended in 1763, not 1761. Names and words are repeated with great frequency, when synonyms, pronouns, or alternative terms could have been used. Overly long sentences often cause readers to lose the meaning of what the authors are trying to say. Occasionally, words are used incorrectly, as in the reference to George Washington's gaining "notoriety" from his military exploits rather than fame.

A good editor would have helped this book a great deal. As it stands, it cannot be recommended.
—**Donald E. Collins**

478. West, Mark I. **Wellsprings of Imagination: The Homes of Children's Authors.** New York, Neal-Schuman, 1992. 145p. illus. index. $24.95pa. PS480.W47. 810.9'9282. LC 92-25753. ISBN 1-55570-097-7.

In this work West carefully examines the homes of 14 children's authors that were used as settings for one or more of their books. The settings are mostly located in the United States, with others in Canada, England, and Scotland. Only those homes open to the public are considered. The authors included range from the very well known Louisa May Alcott and Mark Twain to the more obscure Thomas Bailey Aldrich and Sarah Orne Jewett. Of the 14 authors, 6 published during the nineteenth century and 6 during the first half of the twentieth. Only two, Laura Ingalls Wilder and Thornton Burgess, published any children's books after 1950.

The lives of the authors are individually addressed, focusing on the periods when they inhabited the places described in *Wellsprings*. West has drawn insightful connections between those homes and neighborhoods and the literary settings they inspired. Streets, gardens, houses, rooms, and furnishings are vividly described, always in the context of the books in which they would later appear. One black-and-white photograph of each location is included.

Every chapter closes with detailed information on the location of the home, the hours it is open to the public, and admission fees. Related points of interest in the area are also described, and addresses for further information are listed. Written with enthusiasm and understanding, this book will be appreciated by those interested in the history of children's literature.—**Joanne Kelly**

Europe

479. Johnson, Margaret M. **Festival Europe! Fairs & Celebrations throughout Europe.** Memphis, Tenn., Mustang Publishing, 1992. 236p. maps. $10.95pa. GT4842.J64. 394.2'694. LC 90-50867. ISBN 0-914457-41-1.

Aimed at providing the European traveler with a plethora of celebrations to experience, this handy volume covers festivals and fairs in 18 countries. Included are Ireland/Northern Ireland, Great Britain (England/Scotland/Wales), Belgium, the Netherlands, Luxembourg, France, Italy, Malta, Austria, Switzerland, Germany, Spain, Portugal, Denmark, Finland, Norway, Sweden, and Greece.

The guide is arranged by country, with several countries grouped together when considered appropriate (e.g., Scandinavia includes Norway, Sweden, Denmark, and Finland). Each section includes a brief introduction, a simple map, a list of official holidays of the country being discussed, and the address and telephone number of the appropriate tourist bureau. The major part of each section consists of a chronological list of major and minor festivals and celebrations that take place from May to October. Larger countries are discussed region by region, and smaller countries are considered as a whole. Noted off-season events (e.g., the myriad winter celebrations in Austria) or items of particular interest (e.g., windmills and flowers in the Netherlands, Olympia and the Olympic games in Greece) are also included.

As its title indicates, this handbook focuses squarely on European festivals, and as such it will not substitute for the more traditional, standard guides. Nevertheless, because it contains information not always included in the more basic sources, *Festival Europe!* would be a welcome and relatively inexpensive supplement to many larger travel collections.—**Kristin Ramsdell**

Great Britain

480. **The Oxford Illustrated Literary Guide to Great Britain and Ireland.** 2d ed. Dorothy Eagle and Meic Stephens, eds. New York, Oxford University Press, 1992. 322p. illus. maps. $45.00. PR109.E18. 820.9. LC 91-20240. ISBN 0-19-212988-0.

This beautiful work could be a coffee-table book. It has numerous full-page color plates, as well as smaller illustrations, of authors, memorials to authors, manuscript pages, and places. The illustrations alone could keep a browser happy for days.

But there is also substance in this massive compilation of entries about authors' haunts and homes, their working spaces, the towns or countrysides they wrote about, and the places that memorialize them. Similar to the 1981 edition, it is arranged alphabetically by place-name, with an ample index by author. Through index and entries, one can browse through authors' lives, identifying all the places associated with them from birth through education and working lives to death and burial places, with any attendant memorial plaques. In all, some 1,300 entries are included, about 105 more than the 1981 edition.

Even this hefty work does not give full detail; for that, one would have to consult a more complete work on a particular author. For instance, under the entry for Sissinghurst, it is noted that the printing press used by Virginia Woolf for the Hogarth Press is housed there. But why? For the answer, one would have to know more completely the history of Hogarth Press and the relationship between Woolf and Sissinghurst's owners. But this book whets the appetite and makes one eager to explore.

Literary guides to the British Isles abound, but this is one of the most beautiful. Its only drawback is that it is far too heavy to tuck into a pocket and use as a guidebook on the road. It is perfect, however, for the armchair traveler or for pretravel research.—**Terry Ann Mood**

Latin America and the Caribbean

481. Kelly, Joyce. **An Archaeological Guide to Mexico's Yucatan Peninsula.** Norman, Okla., University of Oklahoma Press, 1993. 364p. illus. maps. index. $19.95pa. F1435.K45. 917.204'835. LC 92-50715. ISBN 0-8061-2499-7.

This guide provides descriptions and evaluations of 91 archaeological sites and 8 museums in Mexico's Yucatan Peninsula, covering all three states: Yucatan, Quintana Roo, and Campeche. The work is beautifully and generously illustrated with 24 color plates, more than 200 black-and-white photographs, 7 drawings, 13 maps, and 7 site plans. After an introductory section on the Yucatan Peninsula, which includes history and travel advice, the guide is organized geographically. Each entry is listed identically: site description, exploration history, and travel tips. The phonetic pronunciations and derivations of the Mayan or Spanish names, with English equivalents, are given in addition to location and map information at the beginning of each entry. All sites and museums are also rated from zero to four stars, based on the site's importance, accessibility, and overall worthwhileness. The indexes, glossary, and bibliography enhance use of the book.

Kelly has updated and expanded a previous work, *The Complete Visitor's Guide to Mesoamerican Ruins* (see ARBA 83, entry 352). Her first-hand knowledge of the archaeological sites in the Yucatan, the thoroughness of the organization and presentation of the sites and museums, the valuable travel tips found throughout the work, and the abundant illustrations—including many of the author's own drawings and maps—make this an outstanding work. Highly recommended for all libraries.—**Edward Erazo**

New Zealand

482. Jefferies, Margaret. **Adventuring in New Zealand: The Sierra Club Travel Guide to the Pearl of the Pacific.** San Francisco, Sierra Club Books; distr., New York, Random House, 1993. 424p. illus. maps. index. $15.00pa. DU405.5.J44. 919.304'37. LC 93-12366. ISBN 0-87156-571-4.

There are at least 20 recent travel guides to New Zealand in print. Some provide the basic travel information that most tourists want. Others offer advice on alternative means of visiting a country noted for its natural history, parks, and scenery. This new guide concentrates on providing, on a region-by-region basis, information about the history of New Zealand and its natural features, with only passing descriptions of major cities. It tells where to hike, where to see birds, what natural wonders to visit, what commercial guide and tour services are available, and how to see and understand Aotearoa—the land of the long white cloud. It is not an all-purpose guide; it does not provide such basic information as lists of hotels and restaurants, nor does it have advice for those who are using bicycles, motor homes, or their feet for transportation. Instead it provides more detailed historical background and a much greater depth of information on those aspects of the country most likely to be of interest to members of the Sierra Club. It fills an important and valuable niche for the ecologically correct traveler.—**Norman D. Stevens**

Ukraine

483. Zinkewych, Osyp, Volodymyr Hula, and Marta D. Olynyk, comps. and ed. **Ukraine: A Tourist Guide.** Baltimore, Md., Smoloskyp, 1993. 440p. illus. maps. $27.75pa. LC 93-84208. ISBN 0-914834-93-2.

The well-known publishing company Smoloskyp brings us this tourist guide to Ukraine. Prepared in and focused solely on Ukraine, the work is the first of its kind to be available in both English and Ukrainian editions. It will serve as an indispensable aid to the growing number of persons traveling in Ukraine, including tourists, businesspeople, diplomats, students, and journalists.

The book is organized by major geographical regions, beginning with the region of Kyiv and its capital city of the same name, and followed by the other 24 regions, arranged alphabetically. Individual chapters offer historical background information on the regions; list prominent individuals of the area; and describe the cities, towns, and villages. Points of interest, such as architectural monuments, churches, museums, and restaurants, are illustrated with some 250 black-and-white and 50 color photographs. Particularly useful to the uninitiated is the general information about Ukraine: its history, including a brief chronology of events; helpful hints on how to plan a trip; and information about exchange rates, currency, and making telephone calls. Sections of general references conclude the volume, providing lists of government officials, political parties, embassies, travel agencies, and similar elements.

All in all, this is a very useful and readable travel guide. The information offered is quite current, covering (for the most part) events and tourist information for 1992. However, some of the data should be used with caution. Because of the massive political and social upheaval in Ukraine, names of streets and institutions frequently change, as do telephone numbers, officials, and the like. However, this unavoidable inaccuracy is relatively minor, taking into consideration the overall quality of the work. The publisher promises to update the volume annually.

Competently prepared, this guide should be in the hands of all those traveling to Ukraine as well as public librarians and travel agents. For this valuable and timely publication Zinkewych and his collaborators have to be congratulated. Highly recommended.—**Bohdan S. Wynar**

9 History

ARCHAEOLOGY

484. **The Blackwell Encyclopedia of Industrial Archaeology.** Barrie Trinder, ed. Colchester, Vt., Blackwell, 1992. 964p. illus. index. $150.00. T37.E53. 609. LC 91-41700. ISBN 0-631-14216-9.

This attractive reference work is a first for the emerging discipline of industrial archaeology, and its subject matter essentially defines the field's scope. The latter is essentially the visible evidence of the conjunction of the histories of technology, industrial architecture, and regional and town planning. It is a "blue-collar" area of history that emerged from the English Midlands, where the Industrial Revolution began about 150 years ago. Research centers in this field are in the British "brick universities" rather than in "Oxbridge," where the history of science flourishes.

Although the basic arrangement of the book is by alphabetical order, with cross-references indicated by block capitals within the entries, there is also an elaborate subject outline available in an appendix. This has 18 categories such as "Transport," "Extractive Industries," and "Industrial Community," with numerous subheadings under each. "Biographies" lists 130 individuals, most of them people after whom machines or processes were named, such as Henry Bessemer.

Numerous clear illustrations include the eight-mile aerial tramway in Wuppertal, Germany; famous windmills and lighthouses; and the brick kiln at the Fraktur brick plant on the Ruple River, Boom, Antwerp province, Belgium (of personal interest to this reviewer, who passed it daily in 1945-1946 while on assignment in Boom). Certain British blast furnaces and canal boat lifts have been restored to operating condition; in other cases, only the mine tipples or tall chimneys reveal the site of former installations. It is disappointing that the Du Pont family's Elutherian Powder Mills and the Hagley Museum get bare mention. The degree and accuracy of restoration is a persistent issue—many New England textile mills have been gutted to house discount malls, while San Francisco's Ghiradelli Square has a couple of operational chocolate kettles to balance the boutiques. Recommended for academic libraries, larger municipal libraries, and even smaller public libraries located in the vicinity of present or past industrial complexes. [R: Choice, Sept 93, p. 74; LJ, 1 Feb 93, p. 70]—**Eugene B. Jackson**

485. Ehrich, Robert W., ed. **Chronologies in Old World Archaeology.** 3d ed. Chicago, University of Chicago Press, 1992. 2v. index. $150.00/set. DS54.5.C48. 930'.02'02. LC 90-11109. ISBN 0-226-19447-7.

Chronology is the foundation upon which history is built, and this work clearly demonstrates the essential role that archaeology plays in providing the labor and materials necessary for any modern reconstruction of the past. These volumes also provide ample evidence of the dramatic advances that have been made in our knowledge about the past since 1965, when the last edition of this title appeared. The approach is geographical, and, with the exception of Japan, chronologies are presented for every major region of Europe, Africa, and Asia. The chronological coverage varies for each region but generally extends from the period of the earliest settlement to somewhere between 2000 and 1500 B.C. The first volume contains 28 essays written by specialists on the archaeology of each region; each essay describes the sequences, distribution, and relationships of cultures and sites within a region. The artifacts and documentation upon which the chronologies are based are also detailed. A final summary chapter discusses interregional relationships. The second volume duplicates the geographical arrangement and provides extensive bibliographies, tables of radiocarbon dates, charts summarizing relationships between regional sequences, maps, and occasional charts illustrating types of artifacts. This set provides a comprehensive introduction to the explosion of archaeological research that the last three decades have witnessed; as such, it will prove essential in collections supporting academic programs in archaeology.

—John R. M. Lawrence

486. Flanagan, Laurence. **A Dictionary of Irish Archaeology.** Lanham, Md., Barnes & Noble Books/Rowman & Littlefield, 1992. 221p. illus. $77.50. DA920.F57. 936.1'003. LC 91-28279. ISBN 0-389-20972-4.

Described by Flanagan as a sort of personal card index for the fieldworker in archaeology, this dictionary aims to list all the major finds important in Irish archaeology. Its intent is to provide an authoritative overview of Irish archaeology for students, scholars, and general readers. Entries range from the Mesolithic period to the end of the Medieval era, but Flanagan alerts the reader to his own peculiar archaeological period labels; he refers to the Later Iron Age, where others might speak of the Early Christian or Medieval period, or to the Earlier Iron Age, where others might speak of the Iron Age. This is done in order to make "archaeological sense." Where provided, illustrations are clear and informative. Listed alphabetically and in easily readable style, some entries have multiple sections. The entry for Dundalk, Co. Louth, for instance, includes a brief overview of the history of the town of Dundalk, followed by a short description of four sets of remains in the town.

While Flanagan clearly does not consider his work to be exhaustive, he does omit reference to an important site known to this reviewer—a native of Dundalk—the souterrains found in the area in the past 25 years. According to a relatively long and presumably important entry provided in this same dictionary, souterrains are "essentially, underground passages." All in all, however, this dictionary—with its occasional references to ancient Irish saga literature and mythology—is a good and useful reference guide for those with an interest in archaeological remains from Celtic and Gaelic Ireland.—**Arthur Gribben**

487. Mignon, Molly Raymond. **Dictionary of Concepts in Archaeology.** Westport, Conn., Greenwood Press, 1993. 364p. index. (Reference Sources for the Social Sciences and Humanities, v.13). $85.00. CC70.M45. 930.1'03. LC 92-43151. ISBN 0-313-24659-9.

Although the author says this work is intended for both laypeople and students, advanced students of archaeology or anthropology will probably derive the greatest benefit from it. Seventy-four fundamental concepts in archaeology are defined and discussed at length. The arrangement is alphabetical, and each entry is divided into four parts: a list of definitions for the term, a discussion relating the historical development of the concept and the manner in which it has been applied in archaeology, a list of references cited, and a brief bibliographical essay that provides additional sources of information. Many entries are general concepts of importance in fields (e.g., culture, evolution, adaptation, migration). Others are related fields or subdisciplines of archaeology (e.g., cultural ecology, ethnoarchaeology, paleodemography, taphonomy). Still other entries define methods (e.g., sampling, quantification, survey), approaches (e.g., three-age system, central place theory, system theory), and problems (e.g., chronometric dating, pseudo-archaeology). In every case the author provides a clear definition of the term and a thorough overview of the concept's development and related research.

Unfortunately, the indexes are a disappointment. The name index lists only those persons who are mentioned in the actual text of the discussion and excludes the far more numerous citations in parenthetical references, in the lists of references, and to the bibliographical essays. The subject index is little more than a reiteration of the list of concepts with cross-references. Despite these faults, students of archaeology and anthropology will find this volume useful, and it is recommended for academic libraries supporting degree programs in those areas.—**John R. M. Lawrence**

488. Ridinger, Robert B. Marks. **African Archaeology: A Selected Bibliography.** New York, G. K. Hall, 1993. 311p. index. $45.00. Z5118.A6R5. 016.96. LC 92-7760. ISBN 0-8161-9086-0.

This new bibliography is just the thing for advanced undergraduates and master's-level students in anthropology or archaeology. Its 717 well-annotated citations give a good introduction to the basic literature that describes the discovery of ancient peoples in all parts of the African continent. The sources described are predominantly English-language monographic works; an added short section contains major serial titles whose contents are not indexed or annotated in the bibliography. There are sections on dates of the Pan-African Conferences and on national archaeological legislation as well as a general index to round out the volume.

Much of the material here will be new to nonspecialists. Knowledgeable annotations and comparative references lift this bibliography above the usual dry list of sources into a true learning tool. The organization—by modern country name and by publication date—is also particularly useful for budding scholars because it emphasizes the role of each source in the area's historiography. Thus, organization, erudition, and coverage are distinguishing qualities that make this reference book an important and necessary purchase. [R: Choice, June 93, p. 1608]—**Stephanie C. Sigala**

489. Stern, Ephraim, and Ayelet Lewinson-Gilboa, eds. **The New Encyclopedia of Archaeological Excavations in the Holy Land.** New York, Simon & Schuster Academic Reference, 1993. 4v. illus. maps. index. $355.00/set. DS111.A2N488. 933'.003. LC 92-17712. ISBN 0-13-276288-9.

The New Encyclopedia of Archaeological Excavations in the Holy Land (NEAEHL) is a revised and enlarged version of The Encyclopedia of Archaeological Excavations in the Holy Land (EAEHL) (see ARBA 80, entry 337; ARBA 79, entry 393; and ARBA 77, entry 347). In the case of each, a Hebrew version appeared first, and then the slightly updated English one. The present work is more comprehensive than EAEHL, and its binding, print quality, and photographic reproductions are also superior. Moreover, advances in the archaeological exploration of Palestine made the present revision essential. The editors are recognized authorities on the history and archaeology of Palestine, and the 365-plus articles were contributed by 205 people, including many other outstanding archaeologists. Many articles from EAEHL have been included either intact or with only a brief appendix intended to update the information.

The chronological scope of NEAEHL extends from the earliest human settlements until the Ottoman period, and geographically the work covers the territory on both sides of the Jordan River that stretches from Sinai and Elath in the south to the sources of the Jordan River in the north. The articles are arranged alphabetically and cover the important archaeological sites in the land, several general topics (e.g., churches, monasteries, marine archaeology), and various geographical regions (e.g., Galilee, Samaria). In addition, there are indexes for persons, places, and biblical texts; chronological tables; a glossary of archaeological terms; maps; color and black-and-white photographs; and numerous drawings.

While NEAEHL can indeed be recommended to academic, church, and even public libraries, there is one major issue that is troubling: the reproduction of articles from EAEHL. Although specialists familiar with the history of Palestinian archaeology will be able to distinguish between the older, reprinted articles and the newer ones, most readers will not. This is a problem, because in the last two decades not only have more sites been discovered and more research done on previously excavated sites, but critical opinion and historical reconstructions have also changed. Therefore, NEAEHL is a curious amalgamation of older articles with their attendant 1970s-era interpretations of the archaeological and historical data (e.g., K. M. Kenyon on the dubious correlation between the Bible and archaeological research regarding the destruction of Canaanite Jericho) and newer articles reflecting the most current views on the history and archaeology of Palestine. [R: Choice, Nov 93, p. 437; LJ, 1 Sept 93, pp. 172-74; RBB, 1 Dec 93, p. 707; WLB, Oct 93, pp. 92-93]—**M. Patrick Graham**

AMERICAN HISTORY

Atlases

490. **Rand McNally Atlas of American Frontiers.** By Martin Ridge. Skokie, Ill., Rand McNally, 1993. 191p. illus. maps. index. $49.95. E179.5.R53. 973. LC 92-4647. ISBN 0-528-83493-2.

The first impression one has on looking at this book is favorable. It is visually beautiful and would make a nice coffee-table book. But closer examination leaves questions. The absence of an introduction or preface leaves readers to draw their own conclusions about intended audience, purpose, and other standard concerns that a book buyer might face.

The basic format is topical. In general, two pages, including text, illustrations, and sometimes a map or two, are devoted to each topic. The brevity of text allows for no more than survey treatment. Part 5 contains reproductions of original maps dated between 1776 and 1926, and part 6 includes 15 current reference maps of the world and United States. There are a very brief subject index and an index to the current maps, but there is no index to the historical ones. Considering that this is a historical atlas, one wonders about this omission.

Many topics do not include maps, and some maps do not match the topic. For example, a map showing slave immigration from 1600 to 1808 accompanies the topic "The Civil War and the Frontier," when one showing battles in the West would be more appropriate. The subject index covers only the text and excludes the historical maps, the illustrations, and the frequently pertinent information contained in captions. For example, the index entries for outlaws Butch Cassidy and Jesse James refer only to a casual mention on page 107, while ignoring pertinent biographical data under their photographs on page 82. This exclusion policy has led to the complete absence of the Pony Express from the index, despite an illustration, a map, and a paragraph-length caption about the service on pages 82-83. Unfortunately, such omissions are numerous. And while the maps are beautiful, the printing is frequently too small, and decorative shading on letters makes them hard to read. Also, considering the title word "Frontier," one wonders why a large percentage of the maps do not relate to frontier topics. This multiplicity of problems prevents this reviewer from recommending this book. [R: WLB, Feb 93, p. 101]—**Donald E. Collins**

491. Bosse, David. **Civil War Newspaper Maps: A Historical Atlas.** Baltimore, Md., Johns Hopkins University Press, 1993. 162p. maps. index. $34.95. G1201.S5B6. 973.7'022'3. LC 92-33942. ISBN 0-8018-4553-X.

This interesting volume presents an informative study of a key chapter in the history of U.S. cartography: the timely development and distribution of maps to the general population. During the Civil War, daily newspapers quickly became the primary source for cartographic information, with many of the maps produced by the Northern press used by the military itself. Employing new technologies, newspapers responded to the public's desire for accurate and timely news from the battlefield.

Drawing on his earlier research for *Civil War Newspaper Maps: A Cartobibliography of the Northern Daily Press* (Greenwood Press, 1993), the author presents eight introductory essays on topics such as the development of journalistic mapmaking, the design and production of these maps, and the problems of accuracy and timely reporting. These are followed by 45 chronologically arranged maps that cover nearly every major theater of war. These maps illustrate design and production techniques and provide fascinating examples of the development of reporting styles. Each map is accompanied by a brief summary of the military operation depicted and a commentary on the design and accuracy of the map.

This is an interesting book indeed, but the author might have served his subject better by combining the two works into one. The essays included here would have greatly enhanced his earlier cartobibliography, and the maps would have benefited from being placed in the context of the larger bibliography. By itself, this particular work will be of value to specialized libraries focusing on cartography or Civil War history, but it may prove too focused for most general academic libraries.—**Elizabeth Patterson**

Bibliography

492. Bosse, David, comp. **Civil War Newspaper Maps: A Cartobibliography of the Northern Daily Press.** Westport, Conn., Greenwood Press, 1993. 253p. index. (Bibliographies and Indexes in Military Studies, no.5). $75.00. Z6027.U5B67. 016.9737'022'3. LC 92-43100. ISBN 0-313-28705-8.

This interesting addition to Civil War research materials makes accessible some fascinating resources frequently overlooked by scholars. Drawn from 20 Northern daily newspapers, this guide identifies more than 2,000 maps of military engagements and field positions, covering the length and breadth of the nation's battleground. Adapted from a number of sources or originally designed, these maps were often more accurate and timely than those issued by official governmental agencies. For many people they were the only way to truly visualize the events being reported.

The maps cited are grouped by the issuing newspaper and arranged chronologically. Each entry contains the title, dimensions, scale, author, engraver (when known), and notes on sources used to produce these maps. A detailed geographical, personal name, and subject index provides easy access to the maps. An appendix lists any missing issues of newspapers that could not be examined.

Although numerous Civil War atlases have been produced over the years, virtually all have overlooked newspapers as a source of contemporary reporting. This handy cartobibliography begins to fill the gap, and users can hope for a volume covering the Southern press. [R: Choice, Nov 93, p. 426]
—Elizabeth Patterson

493. Freemon, Frank R. **Microbes and Minie Balls: An Annotated Bibliography of Civil War Medicine.** Cranbury, N.J., Fairleigh Dickinson University Press/Associated University Presses, 1993. 253p. illus. index. $40.00. Z1242.F74. 016.9737'75. LC 92-52706. ISBN 0-8386-3484-2.

This book is a welcome addition to the literature of the U.S. Civil War. Although designed as a bibliography, it provides researchers and readers more than they might expect from a work of this type.

Freemon, a medical historian and professor of neurology at Vanderbilt University School of Medicine, surveys the literature of Civil War medicine. Works are grouped into primary and secondary sources. In the former category, the author claims to include all books and articles written by Civil War doctors, nurses, and hospital attendants; important contemporary medical publications; and some diaries of wounded or hospitalized soldiers. The secondary publications described in this bibliography include books and articles that deal directly with Civil War medicine, general works that discuss aspects of medical care, and descriptions of the health of political and military leaders. A good index provides access to the literature cited.

The feature that makes this book stand out is the quality of the author's writing. From the opening essay on the still-primitive nature of Civil War medicine through the exceptionally well written annotations for the books and articles cited, one seems to be reading a series of brief articles that provide an overall picture of the topic, rather than a list of mere descriptive summaries. Highly recommended for public and academic libraries and for individuals with an interest in the War between the States. [R: C&RL, Sept 93, pp. 434-35; Choice, July/Aug 93, p. 1749]—**Donald E. Collins**

494. Frewin, Anthony, comp. **The Assassination of John F. Kennedy: An Annotated Film, TV, and Videography, 1963-1992.** Westport, Conn., Greenwood Press, 1993. 170p. index. (Bibliographies and Indexes in Mass Media and Communications, no.8). $49.95. E842.9.F73. 364.1'524. LC 93-24763. ISBN 0-313-28982-4.

No subject in recent U.S. history holds as much popular fascination or remains the subject of such ongoing controversy as John F. Kennedy's assassination. This topic has already produced a cottage industry of literature, with proponents of various assassination conspiracy theories, which criticize the findings of the Warren Commission, seeming to dominate public opinion on this issue. Frewin's effort compiles film, television, and video examinations of Kennedy's assassination. Following an introduction featuring a ritualistic denunciation of the Warren Commission, this work chronicles and annotates various visual portrayals of the assassination. Chapters in this volume cover events such as the assassination in Dallas's Dealey Plaza, television broadcasts, documentaries, motion pictures, fringe motion pictures, and North American and British film and video libraries with significant assassination holdings. Entries within individual chapters feature information about producers, interviewees, date and length of broadcast, format of film or television broadcast, actors and actresses, directors, and plot summaries. An index of interviews is also included, along with a modest bibliography of secondary sources and a list of videos, documentaries, and films issued in chronological order since the assassination.

Frewin has done detailed research in compiling this effort, which will be useful for comprehensive Kennedy assassination collections. However, the scholarly quality of the book is low, as evidenced by Frewin's uncritical acceptance of conspiracy theories (which should be disproved by Gerald Posner's definitive *Case Closed* [Random House, 1993]) and its absence of reference to, and its uncritical denunciation of, governmental investigations as source material. Finally, this work is all too reflective of the romantic utopian infatuation with the Kennedy presidency and assassination, which still lingers within a large section of public opinion. It is hoped that the continuing passage of time will further diminish the often hysterical popular obsession with this event and permit more sober and pragmatic assessment of its causes and significance.—**Bert Chapman**

495. McCaslin, Richard B., comp. **Andrew Johnson: A Bibliography.** Westport, Conn., Greenwood Press, 1992. 314p. index. (Bibliographies of the Presidents of the United States, no.17). $67.50. Z8455.567.M33. 016.9735'6. LC 92-31761. ISBN 0-313-28175-0.

With the publication of this work, this series (begun by Meckler in 1988 and continued by Greenwood Press in 1992) is approximately one-quarter complete. As Arthur Schlesinger notes in the foreword, for some presidents, such as Andrew Johnson, these bibliographies are the only near-comprehensive guides available. Therefore, the series is a valuable contribution to historical scholarship. Although Johnson is not considered one of the United States's great presidents, having been the only one impeached, he did oversee issues of great import and consequence, such as the end of the Civil War and the initiation of Reconstruction. Therefore, Johnson and his times have been the subject of an avalanche of scholarly study, making the publication of this bibliography necessary and valuable.

The bibliography is arranged by type of material, such as manuscripts and archival resources, or by period in the subject's life, such as "Military Governor, 1862-1865." For those who need more than the table of contents to guide them, a good subject index and an author index are provided. Within each chapter or subdivision, entries are arranged alphabetically by author. Each entry includes a citation and a one- or two-sentence description or evaluation of the source. Academic libraries that serve schools with doctoral programs in U.S. history or libraries with a special interest in the presidency or the Civil War and Reconstruction will want this bibliography. [R: Choice, May 93, p. 1445]—**John P. Stierman**

496. O'Brien, Patrick G., comp. **Herbert Hoover: A Bibliography.** Westport, Conn., Greenwood Press, 1993. 373p. index. (Bibliographies of Presidents of the United States, no.30). $65.00. Z8414.97.025. 016.97391'6'092. LC 92-29467. ISBN 0-313-28188-2.

O'Brien, professor of history at Emporia State University, has compiled some 2,600 items, popular as well as scholarly, on all aspects of Herbert Hoover's life, with an emphasis on his presidential years. The work begins with a chronology of Hoover's life, then has chapters on manuscript and archival sources; books and articles by Hoover (95 items); general biographical items (55); early years, 1874-1895 (22); mature years, 1896-1928 (432); the 1928 election (157); his administration, 1929-1933 (779); the election of 1932 (88); administration associates, including members of the Cabinet, of Congress, and of the Supreme Court, and diplomats and journalists (360); the postpresidency years, 1933-1964 (230); Hoover's philosophy (44); personal lives of the Hoovers (70); historiographical materials (73); and iconography (15). The volume concludes with a list of periodicals covered, an author index, an index to the oral interviews, and a subject index.

Of course one is grateful to the compiler of a useful bibliography—and this one is useful—but one also wishes some things had been done differently. There is nothing in the introduction about the compiler's criteria for coverage. Why, for example, are there so few foreign publications? And why those that are listed? Why were no Quaker periodicals used? The preface notes that "dissertations and theses" (as well as books, articles, essays, and oral histories) are listed; however, many dissertations appear but no theses were found—not a serious omission, to be sure, but the claim should not have been made. Every item is annotated, but with very few exceptions the annotations consist of a short sentence, for the most important items as well as for the most trivial. (On the other hand, these brief comments are often evaluative, and that is helpful.) The subject index is far from exemplary; the cross-references are insufficient and erratic. As for format, the binding is sturdy and the typography clear. Pages 305-360, however, contain an excessive amount of white space; those 56 pages could probably be reduced by half. While it has shortcomings, the bibliography is on the whole well done and should be in most academic libraries, especially those supporting work in U.S. history.—**Evan Ira Farber**

497. Olson, James S. **The Vietnam War: Handbook of the Literature and Research.** Westport, Conn., Greenwood Press, 1993. 516p. index. $85.00. DS558.V58. 959.704. LC 92-25626. ISBN 0-313-27422-3.

Olson (professor of history, Sam Houston State University), editor of *Dictionary of the Vietnam War* (see ARBA 89, entry 457), and coauthor of the textbook *Where the Domino Fell* (St. Martin's Press, 1990), adds another to the growing and increasingly impressive body of reference books on the Vietnam War. This collection of 23 bibliographical essays treats background and primary source works, military strategy and the conduct of the war, peace negotiations, war crimes, Laos and Cambodia, women and Blacks, POW/MIAs, refugees, the antiwar movement, television and movie coverage, cartoons, and much more.

Besides Olson, who wrote approximately one-third of the essays, and two other Vietnam specialists, who each offer one essay, most of the other contributors are students, colleagues, or friends of Olson from Texas colleges. Nevertheless, almost all of the essays are quite interesting and make a contribution, at least as introductions to the bibliography on each of the topics. The lists of books at the end of each essay are extremely useful, especially for novice students. Despite its price, this volume should be alongside Marc Jason Gilbert's *The Vietnam War: Teaching Approaches and Resources* (Greenwood Press, 1991) as among the best new reference tools available on the war. Olson's volume should be in all libraries that have any Vietnam War collection at all. [R: LJ, 1 Mar 93, p. 70; RBB, Aug 93, pp. 2095-96]
—**Joe P. Dunn**

498. Parsons, Lynn H., comp. **John Quincy Adams: A Bibliography.** Westport, Conn., Greenwood Press, 1993. 217p. index. (Bibliographies of the Presidents of the United States, no.6). $55.00. Z8015.7.P37. 016.9735'5'092. LC 92-33703. ISBN 0-313-28164-5.

This is an important addition to a valuable series and will greatly facilitate the study of presidents and public policy. The compiler is a noted Adams scholar. Following a foreword by Arthur Schlesinger, Jr. (welcoming the revival of scholarly interest in politics, political leaders, and the presidency in particular), a preface by series editor Carol Bondhus Fitzgerald, an introduction to John Quincy Adams by Parsons, and a useful chronology of Adams's life, there are 12 well-organized chapters containing numbered and mostly annotated entries on a variety of sources. As Parsons notes, Adams had three careers: as diplomat and secretary of state, as president from 1825 to 1828, and as a leading congressman until his death in 1848. Therefore, this bibliography will be useful for much more than just study of the presidency. The chapters include manuscript and archival sources; Adams's writings (published and unpublished); a general biography; works on his early career as an attorney, diplomat, and senator (1788-1809); works on his mature years as a diplomat and secretary of state (1809-1825); the elections of 1824 and 1828 (contemporary and secondary sources); his presidency; administration associates (vice president, cabinet members, key members of Congress, diplomats, and Supreme Court justices); the postpresidential years; material on his childhood and personal life (with separate sections for important family members); a historiography; and an iconography. There are also a list of pertinent periodical sources, an author index, and a subject index. [R: Choice, July/Aug 93, p. 1754]—**William B. Robison**

Biography

499. Kane, Joseph Nathan. **Facts about the Presidents: A Compilation of Biographical and Historical Information.** 6th ed. Bronx, N.Y., H. W. Wilson, 1993. 433p. illus. index. $55.00. E176.1.K3. 973'.099. LC 93-9207. ISBN 0-8242-0845-5.

The U.S. presidency is a perennial subject for reference works, and one such book that is approaching the status of a classic is *Facts about the Presidents*. The 6th edition covers up to February 1993, the opening days of the Clinton administration.

As in previous editions, the work is divided into two parts: biographical data and comparative data. The biographical section is divided into entries for each president that are arranged in chronological order. Each entry supplies the usual biographical information: date and place of birth, religion, parents' name, a portrait, and similar facts. It also includes the convention ballot on which a president received his party's nomination, his appointments to the cabinet and the Supreme Court, presidential firsts, various outstanding or notorious events during each presidency, information about vice presidents and first ladies, and a bibliography.

The comparative section is a cornucopia of fascinating items about the presidents and the presidency. A list of presidential nicknames reveals that Grover Cleveland had the most (20) followed closely by Abraham Lincoln and Ulysses S. Grant (19 each). Books authored by presidents are also listed, with Teddy Roosevelt leading the field with 37. Presidential heights and weights are listed. Lincoln remains the tallest at 6'4", while Taft holds a commanding lead in weight. An index of subjects and personal names makes this information more accessible. No good library should be without this book. [R: SLMQ, Summer 93, p. 267]—**Ronald H. Fritze**

500. Purcell, L. Edward. **Who Was Who in the American Revolution.** New York, Facts on File, 1993. 548p. illus. index. $60.00. E206.P87. 973.3'092'2. LC 92-19831. ISBN 0-8160-2107-4.

Several reference books on the American Revolution have been published in recent years, including *The Blackwell Encyclopedia of the American Revolution* (see ARBA 92, entry 470), *The Encyclopedia of Colonial and Revolutionary America* (see ARBA 91, entry 504), Purcell's own *The World Almanac of the American Revolution* (St. Martin's Press, 1992), and *Women Patriots of the American Revolution* (see ARBA 92, entry 461). This new book fills a void in Revolutionary scholarship by supplying biographical information on more than 1,500 men and women who played major and supporting roles during these turbulent years. Purcell profiles American patriots, Loyalists, French allies, and British foes and highlights military commanders, foot soldiers, diplomats, politicians, and government officeholders.

The alphabetically arranged entries each include birth and death dates and a brief descriptor. The biographies range in length from a brief paragraph of about 60 or 70 words, such as the one for soldier, jurist, and teacher Nathaniel Chipman, to some 1,500 words, such as the lengthy profile of Benedict Arnold. Cross-references are included where appropriate.

Many entries include a brief bibliography for further reading, and Purcell's meticulously detailed guide to biographical sources will aid serious researchers as well as high school or college students. Regrettably, however, the bibliographies are uneven in quality. For example, renowned frontiersman and general George Rogers Clark has been the subject of several scholarly and well-received biographies, yet Purcell mentions only a brief volume that focuses on one aspect of Clark's career. [R: Choice, Dec 93, p. 589; JAL, Sept 93, p. 275; RBB, 15 Oct 93, p. 465; RQ, Winter 93, pp. 297-98; WLB, Oct 93, p. 134]
—**Jack Bales**

Chronology

501. Shrader, Charles Reginald, ed. **Reference Guide to United States Military History 1815-1865.** New York, Facts on File, 1993. 312p. illus. maps. index. $50.00. E181.R34. 973. LC 90-25673. ISBN 0-8160-1837-5.

502. Shrader, Charles Reginald, ed. **Reference Guide to United States Military History 1865-1919.** New York, Facts on File, 1993. 310p. illus. maps. index. $50.00. E181.R34. 973. LC 90-25673. ISBN 0-8160-1838-3.

These volumes are organized around three parts: the organization of U.S. armed forces and their history, biographies, and battles and events. The first part covers the chronological progression of armed forces development, defense policy, attitudes toward the military, and the conflicts of the period. The 1815-1865 volume deals with the organization of military forces during that period, national consolidation from 1815 to 1835, and the role of the military in that effort. Military reform and expansion from 1815 to 1846 are also detailed. The Mexican war and the period following are examined, and the Civil War is divided into two parts: 1862-1863 and 1864-1865. The text is handsomely supplemented by maps, illustrations, and half-tones.

The volume that examines the period from 1865 to 1919 begins with the organization of military forces, followed by Reconstruction, the Indian wars, and the Spanish-American War. The importance of the emergence of the United States as a global power, with a modern army and navy to back up that power, is dealt with in two sections. World War I is split into preparations for war and the combat operations of U.S. armed forces.

A wide spectrum of contributors from both military and civilian circles have provided excellent reference works. The organization, narrative, and illustrations of these volumes make them outstanding additions to any public, college, or university reference collection. [R: Choice, Nov 93, p. 438; LJ, 1 April 93, p. 94; RBB, 1 Nov 93, p. 569]—**Norman L. Kincaide**

Dictionaries and Encyclopedias

503. Blanco, Richard L., ed. **The American Revolution 1775-1783: An Encyclopedia.** Hamden, Conn., Garland, 1993. 2v. maps. index. (Military History of the United States, v.1; Garland Reference Library of the Humanities, v.933). $175.00/set. E208.A433. 973.3'03. LC 92-42541. ISBN 0-8240-5623-X.

The first offering in a new series, *The American Revolution 1775-1783* is a thorough and factual look at this crucial war. Essays, written by some 130 contributors, range in length from 250 to more than 25,000 words. Simplified line-drawing maps of battles and a chronology are included. The work details battles, describes people, and provides technical information on ships and armaments (e.g., naval gunnery). It is written for the military, not the social, historian. Blanco states in his introduction that space limitations eliminated many articles dealing with political, social, and cultural topics, although such information is occasionally mentioned in other articles, and a few articles on social topics do exist (e.g., war widows, desertion in the Continental Army, propaganda). The essayists have also tried to include information on the contributions of previously overlooked participants: Native Americans, women, and Blacks. Particularly useful in this context are the articles on each state's role in the war; these speak to the part played by various groups. But for the most part, this is intended as a military encyclopedia and concentrates on the specifics of the war. For an encyclopedia with more interpretative articles, see *The Blackwell Encyclopedia of the American Revolution* (see ARBA 92, entry 470).

The index is disappointing and brief, with few subheadings. Users are referred only to major articles, so they then have to scan the entire article for specific details. Future volumes in this series will be on the War of 1812, World War I, and World War II. Military historians and libraries will look forward to them all. [R: C&RL, Sept 93, pp. 433-34; Choice, Oct 93, p. 261; RBB, 15 Oct 93, p. 465; WLB, Sept 93, p. 114]—**Terry Ann Mood**

504. Carruth, Gordon. **The Encyclopedia of American Facts and Dates.** 9th ed. New York, HarperCollins, 1993. 1039p. index. $40.00. LC 92-54676. ISBN 0-06-270045-6.

From the Norse explorers of 986 to Bill Clinton's election as president in November 1992, this new edition (first published in 1956) of a now-standard reference book covers more than 1,000 years of American history. The more than 15,000 facts, events, and dates are arranged in what Carruth refers to as both concurrent and chronological order. All entries are arranged within each year in four parallel columns on two facing pages. Each column contains a number of predetermined subjects, with text continuing on the following pair of facing pages. Events are covered chronologically in related subjects by reading down the columns. By reading across the columns, users learn about significant events in all areas for any given year.

As useful an arrangement as this is, one unavoidable problem is that most users will become confused at the seemingly endless topics within the dual-page arrangement, particularly when entries at the bottom of one column are not continued at the top of the next column. Specific topics can be located through the nearly 200-page index, but users will constantly have to refer to its directions for use, as the topics are listed in five different ways.

A definite improvement over earlier editions is the summary of events that introduces each year's entries. Although users will argue about what facts and dates are and are not included, this work will be welcomed by librarians in secondary and college libraries as a first-stop, ready-reference volume in American history.—**Jack Bales**

505. **Encyclopedia of American Social History.** Mary Kupiec Cayton, Elliot J. Gorn, and Peter W. Williams, eds. New York, Scribner's, 1993. 3v. illus. maps. index. $350.00/set. HN57.E58. 301'.0973. LC 92-10577. ISBN 0-684-19246-2.

Many traditional historians have looked upon social history as peripheral and nebulous, an ill-defined field embracing topics not easily fitted into conventional studies. And this perception has been justified. Instead of pursuing the usual political and economic trends, social historians have wanted to know how and where people lived, what they ate and drank, and how they worshiped and played. To paraphrase a noted British scholar of yesteryear, social history was everything *but* economics and politics. Accordingly, the field seemingly lacked direction and focus, a criticism not altogether overcome even in this superb addition to Scribner's American Civilization series. Indeed, this new encyclopedia, whose editors are all professors of American studies at Miami University of Ohio, stretches the boundaries of social history farther than imaginable just a generation ago.

Enhanced by maps, photographs, and illustrations, this massive 2,653 page study contains 180 original essays, some by nationally prominent scholars, others by relative newcomers. The first volume traces periods of social change, adhering to a standard chronological pattern (from pre-Columbian to modern times), and includes topical essays on everything from gender, sexual orientation, and feminist social history to race, ethnicity, and class. Volume 2 examines in some depth the racial and ethnic composition of American society; regionalism from New England to Texas to California; and patterns of everyday life, featuring articles on food, clothing, housing, and work and labor. Among the issues treated in the final volume are popular culture, including sports, nightlife, and country and western music; social deviance, such as crime, alcoholism, and prostitution; and science and education, assessing the impact of technology and the research university. A bibliography accompanies each essay. Designed for easy use, each volume contains a complete table of contents; the last volume has an exhaustive index of places, people, and subjects; and every article is cross-referenced.

Any flaws in this work are minor. A separate entry on the automobile as an agent of social change would have been appropriate, and some of the authors probably attempted too much. For instance, to cover in 14 pages the full sweep of the American religious experience, from John Winthrop to Jerry Falwell, required extraordinary selectivity. Such nitpicking aside, this is a masterful achievement. It will be unaffordable to many individuals, but every high school and college library should add it to their reference collections. Students doing research on everything from history, political science, and sociology to anthropology and religion will quickly discover its value, and even scholars will find much to appreciate. [R: BR, Sept/Oct 93, p. 58; C&RL, Sept 93, p. 434; Choice, Sept 93, pp. 78-80; LJ, 1 June 93, pp. 102-04; RBB, Aug 93, p. 2082; RQ, Fall 93, pp. 123-24; SLJ, Nov 93, p. 140; WLB, May 93, p. 116]
—John W. Storey

506. **Encyclopedia of the Confederacy.** Richard N. Current, ed. New York, Simon & Schuster Academic Reference Division, 1993. 4v. $355.00. E487.55. 973.7'13. LC 93-4133. ISBN 0-13-275991-8.

In the words of the project editor, Robert M. Salkin, this encyclopedia is intended "not just to be another Civil War book, but a social, cultural and political overview of the South during the years of the Confederacy's existence." These areas of study are precisely where this work makes its greatest contribution. While recent years have witnessed considerable scholarly publishing in cultural and social approaches to history, most reference works on the Civil War period have continued to emphasize military events and personalities. The editors have succeeded in presenting a more balanced view of what life must have been like in the Confederacy. Their concerns are as much with the politicians and "plain folk" at home as with the soldiers and generals at the front. More than 1,400 topics were selected for inclusion by Current and an editorial board composed of Paul D. Escott; Lawrence N. Powell; James I. Robertson, Jr.; and Emory M. Thomas, all of whom have written widely on the history of the South and the war. So too have most of the 330 contributors, who include retired and teaching university faculty, museum curators, historical park officials, archivists, and graduate students.

The arrangement of the encyclopedia is alphabetical by topic, although overview articles and some broad subjects, such as education, health and medicine, and literature, are subdivided. The briefest entries are 250 words, but most are substantially longer. More than half of the entries are biographical; predictably, with so much of the Confederacy's energies having been expended on the conduct of the war, the largest number are devoted to military topics, particularly generals, naval officers, ships, and major battles or campaigns. Government and politics is the next largest category, with articles on each member of the Confederate cabinet and congress, state governors, government agencies, states, and major cities. The other deliberate emphases of the set are on the period of discord preceding the war, economics, culture and society, and the "Confederate legacy." Strong themes of unionism, dissent, class conflict, turbulence, and change within the Confederacy emerge. African Americans, Native American tribes, and other ethnic groups in the South receive considerable attention, as do women, children, and religious groups.

The alphabetical arrangement is supplemented by other access methods, including a list of all articles and a directory of contributors at the beginning of the first volume, plus a very useful synoptic outline of contents in the fourth volume. At the end of many nonbiographical entries are cross-references to related articles. The index is excellent for the breadth of topics covered, cross-references, and use of subtopics, but it is by no means comprehensive in terms of all citations to places and people mentioned in the text. Selectivity for citations to major figures and events is understandable, but the rationale used for the indexing of lesser-known places and people is not clear.

Each article includes a brief bibliography of 2 to 15 citations, and articles on bibliography and historiography and diaries, letters, and memoirs give students additional guidance through the enormous amount of published writings about the Confederacy. Entries on museums and archives, films and videos, and discographies identify other useful resources. Nearly 600 intelligently selected illustrations and 67 specially commissioned maps accompany the articles. The reproduction of the maps and most line drawings and engravings is exceptionally clear, but the clarity of the photographs reproduced varies with the quality of the original. The appendixes include copies of South Carolina's articles of secession, the Confederate constitution, Alexander Stephens's infamous "Cornerstone Speech," Robert E. Lee's final order to his troops, and the parole agreements of the various Confederate armies.

The closest comparable work to this is Jon L. Wakelyn's *Biographical Dictionary of the Confederacy* (see ARBA 78, entry 364). There is considerable overlap between the two works, but each includes unique entries. Wakelyn's 651 entries are generally briefer than those of the encyclopedia but tend to give more detail on the subject's personal life. By citing many lower-level bureaucrats, editors, and businesspeople not found in the new encyclopedia, Wakelyn exposes one area of weakness in the set: the lack of many biographical entries in Confederate business and economics. Also, the reader should not turn to the set expecting to find comprehensive coverage of battles and engagements; only major campaigns and battles are treated in detail. For detailed coverage of minor engagements, the researcher would be better served by *Historical Times Illustrated Encyclopedia of the Civil War* (see ARBA 88, entry 517) or the revised edition of *The Civil War Dictionary* by Mark M. Boatner III (Random House, 1988).

The intended audience for this encyclopedia is advanced undergraduate students, but both scholars and Civil War buffs can make good use of this set. Highly recommended for most academic and large public libraries. [R: LJ, Jan 94, p. 100; RBB, 1 Feb 94, p. 1021]—**John R. M. Lawrence**

507. Gale, Robert L. **Cultural Encyclopedia of the 1850s in America.** Westport, Conn., Greenwood Press, 1993. 472p. index. $95.00. E426.G147. 973.6'03. LC 93-13016. ISBN 0-313-28524-1.

Although dealing with a narrow slice of American history, this excellent encyclopedia recalls both the political tumult and cultural achievements of the 1850s. Actually, Gale extends the "decade" from 1849 to 1861, thereby allowing him to include Edgar Allan Poe and the outbreak of Civil War. This was a period in which the nation blundered toward political disaster at the same time that it reached new literary heights. The "schoolmarm poets," such as Oliver Wendell Holmes, Henry Wadsworth Longfellow, James Russell Lowell, and John Greenleaf Whittier, offered popular reading for escapists, while such major figures as Ralph Waldo Emerson, Nathaniel Hawthorne, Henry David Thoreau, Herman Melville, and Walt Whitman produced an "American Renaissance." And in deference to popular culture, such personalities as P. T. Barnum and Lola Montez and such diversions as boxing and horse racing are not overlooked. Because Gale is especially concerned about women, entries on the prominent and not-so-prominent are included, ranging from Harriet Beecher Stowe and first ladies to Fanny Fern and Adah Isaacs Menken.

A year-by-year chronology of key events and literary publications precedes the entries, which are arranged alphabetically and cross-referenced; they range in length from a paragraph to about four pages. Especially useful are the summaries of books and essays. Melville obviously is a favorite of Gale's, for virtually all his writings, such as *Moby Dick* and *Mardi*, receive extended coverage. Enhanced by an adequate (but far from exhaustive) bibliography and a thorough index of persons and publications, this work will be of interest to high school and college students as well as to many scholars. This would be a worthwhile addition to the reference collections of high school and university libraries.—**John W. Storey**

508. Nelson, Michael. **The Presidency A to Z: A Ready Reference Encyclopedia.** Washington, D.C., Congressional Quarterly, 1992. 574p. illus. index. (CQ's Encyclopedia of American Government, v.2). $100.00. JK511.P775. 353.03'13'03. LC 92-20360. ISBN 0-87187-667-1.

This volume is the second in a series of three references that make up CQ's Encyclopedia of American Government. Essays of varying lengths explore the powers of the presidency and the relationship of that office to other branches of government. Shorter entries deal with a variety of persons, things, and events that have some relevance to the office of president. Entries such as "Zoos and the Presidency" seem to have been included for the sake of having an entry for each letter of the alphabet, while those that show the floor plan of the White House and that profile some of the First Ladies (why not all of them?) are of more interest. Black-and-white portraits, photographs, and other illustrations supplement the text.

The cross-referenced topics are arranged alphabetically and are well indexed; there is also an alphabetical contents list at the front of the book, making it easy to find particular subjects. Appendixes provide a list of all presidents and vice presidents; a summary of elections, 1789-1988; each president's cabinet; a flow chart of the component parts of the U.S. government; and the text of the Constitution. A selected bibliography includes a number of titles, but, lacking annotation, it is sometimes difficult to ascertain which aspects of the presidency or which presidents a particular work might address.

With writing that is easy to follow and nontechnical, this volume should be accessible to all educational levels from high school up. According to Nelson, *The Presidency A to Z* is intended to complement, rather than replace, the more comprehensive and technical *Congressional Quarterly's Guide to the Presidency* (see ARBA 91, entry 745). [R: Choice, May 93, p. 1448; BR, May/June 93, p. 60; LJ, 1 Mar 93, p. 72; LJ, 15 April 93, p. 63; RBB, 15 Mar 93, p. 1378; WLB, Mar 93, p. 113]

—Kay O. Cornelius

509. Whisenhunt, Donald W., ed. **Encyclopedia USA: The Encyclopedia of the United States of America Past & Present. Volume 16: Cook, George Cram [to] Courts of Appeals, United States.** Gulf Breeze, Fla., Academic International Press, 1992. 247p. $36.00. ISBN 0-87569-076-9.

510. Whisenhunt, Donald W., ed. **Encyclopedia USA: The Encyclopedia of the United States of America Past & Present. Volume 17: Couse, Eanger Irving [to] Curtis, Charles.** Gulf Breeze, Fla., Academic International Press, 1992. 248p. $36.00. ISBN 0-87569-076-9.

Good things come to those who wait, and *Encyclopedia USA* is one of those good things. In 1983, Academic International Press began publishing, in alphabetical order, volumes of this work. Ten years and several editors later, they are up to volumes 16 and 17. Any topic remotely related to the United States is fair game for these two volumes. Readers are never quite sure what they will find as they thumb through the pages, seeing entries on British corn laws, cosmology, couplers, Shelby Moore Cullom, *The Crying of Lot 49*, and cults. And when they read one of these entries, they will not be disappointed. The entries are written clearly in a narrative style that is more appealing than the choppy writing found in many encyclopedias. With such a wide-open inclusion policy, however, *Encyclopedia USA* will be criticized for leaving things out. For example, if the editor includes an entry on one of Thomas Pynchon's novels, should he not then include entries on many other significant American novels?

Each entry begins with a one-sentence definition and is usually longer than a page. Some subjects, such as those on cotton or American military courts, are many pages long. All entries are signed and conclude with a bibliography, which in some cases includes critical annotations (e.g., "Creek Confederacy," "Country Music," "Cumberland, Fort"). As an index for volumes 1-10 was just published, users can expect an index covering volumes 16 and 17 later.

Although a lot of the information in *Encyclopedia USA* is accessible elsewhere, and the editor's inclusion policy is questionable, this tool puts a mountain of material in one place. For the history buff, student, or professor who patronizes the public or academic library, this set is a great find.

—John P. Stierman

Handbooks and Yearbooks

511. McCutcheon, Marc. **The Writer's Guide to Everyday Life in the 1800s.** Cincinnati, Ohio, Writer's Digest Books, 1993. 308p. illus. $18.95. E165.M5. 973.8'4. LC 92-43336. ISBN 0-89879-541-9.

In 14 thematic chapters that cover such elements of nineteenth-century life as slang, money, and the Civil War, McCutcheon provides alphabetical lists of terms and phrases, along with definitions. Many of the definitions include a quotation from a nineteenth-century source that uses the term. Some topics not addressed include religion, politics, and science (except medicine), although there is a chronology of inventions. There are also chronologies of major events, books, magazines, and popular songs, and these are some of the most useful features of the book. The section on slang usually provides at least two examples of use from various periods in the century, and the times of usage of more vulgar words are given. Each chapter is introduced by a short essay on the topic, and at the end of the book is a bibliography that lists a handful of more comprehensive sourcebooks.

Some of the entries, such as that for sex education, are lengthy enough to give the user a feel for contemporary attitudes on the subject; others, however, are scanty and all but useless. Who would learn anything, for example, from the definition for an Anne Boleyn mob—"A popular dress cap or bonnet for women in 1807"—especially when no picture has been provided? Was 1807 absolutely the only year in which women wore it? Was it worn in all the states, or would pioneer women have stared at it in fascination? McCutcheon designed the book to answer questions such as these, but often the entries are inadequate—as, indeed, they must be, stripped of context as they are. One hopes that a writer who wants to use this book is already equipped with some background knowledge of the subject. It is probably best employed as a supplement to the many primary sources that a good historical writer will use.

Although this sort of book is long overdue as a tool for writers, it is doubtful that a reference format is the best way to present this information. A similar but nonreference, and more successful, book from the same publisher is *The Writer's Guide to Creating a Science Fiction Universe* by George Ochoa and Jeffrey Osier (1993). Each chapter provides lengthy explanations of the topics within (e.g., the planets and the possibilities for terraforming them), which are ultimately more enlightening to a writer than lists of unconnected terms. [R: RBB, June 93, p. 1908]—**D. A. Rothschild**

512. Yanak, Ted, and Pam Cornelison. **The Great American History Fact-Finder.** Boston, Houghton Mifflin, 1993. 496p. illus. maps. index. $24.95; $14.95pa. E174.Y36. 973'.03. LC 92-37245. ISBN 0-395-65992-2; 0-395-61715-4pa.

Compiled by two classroom teachers whose enthusiasm for history is obvious, this volume strives to entertain as well as enlighten and inform. Surveying America's past from colonial times to the present, it contains more than 2,000 alphabetically arranged entries, each averaging approximately 50 to 75 words. While political and military events and leaders dominate, important figures and developments from the worlds of science, business, art, sports, and entertainment have also been included. And in deference to multiculturalism, attention has been paid to African Americans, women, and other minorities. Enhanced by a list of suggested readings, maps, population figures, presidents and vice presidents, Supreme Court justices, historic documents such as the Articles of Confederation and Gettysburg Address, and a thorough index, this volume will be helpful to a general audience.

While this dictionary was never intended to be exhaustive, some of the inclusions and omissions are nonetheless puzzling. Why mention so many contemporary athletes, such as Larry Bird, Joe Montana, and Michael Jordan, and exclude virtually all the major televangelists? And why omit the Cane Ridge gathering, which created the camp meeting? This work promises somewhat more than it delivers. Even so, high school and college students will find it useful. [R: BR, Nov/Dec 93, p. 56; LJ, 1 Mar 93, p. 72; WLB, June 93, p. 124]—**John W. Storey**

Indexes

513. Whisenhunt, Donald W., ed. **Encyclopedia USA: The Encyclopedia of the United States of America Past & Present. Index: Volume I.** Gulf Breeze, Fla., Academic International Press, 1992. 251p. $36.00. ISBN 0-87569-076-9.

As with most multivolume encyclopedias, *Encyclopedia USA* does not index individual volumes. Without this type of access, the goodies buried inside an encyclopedia's entries are lost. The publication of this index to volumes 1-10 (AAA to Chi) ensures that users will derive maximum use from this projected 50-volume encyclopedia.

The index uses two types of entries: primary and secondary. The former is simply the titles of the articles in the encyclopedia, but the latter identifies subjects within the articles, an obvious plus. *See* and *see also* entries are also helpful. Huge subjects, such as "Civil War, American," are subdivided, quickly guiding users to specific information. The editor could have used this convention more frequently; the entry "New York City, N.Y." has about 200 references, but no subdivisions! Librarians that already have the first 10 volumes of *Encyclopedia USA* will not want to decrease the value of their acquisition and cheat their users by skipping this helpful index.—**John P. Stierman**

ASIAN HISTORY

514. Jason, Philip K. **The Vietnam War in Literature: An Annotated Bibliography of Criticism.** Pasadena, Calif., Salem Press, 1992. 175p. index. (Magill Bibliographies). $40.00. Z1227.J37. 016.8108'0358. LC 92-12898. ISBN 0-89356-679-9.

This is a valuable addition to the ever-growing body of general and specialized Vietnam bibliographies. The author, a professor of English at the U.S. Naval Academy, previously edited a collection of essays that addressed the many genres of Vietnam War literature. In this book he provides paragraph-length annotations on works that deal with literature, including a few nonfiction narrative listings as well as a wide range of fiction, poetry, drama, and film citations. The volume is divided into background general studies (a selection of texts, bibliographic sources, readings books, oral histories, and the like; the basis of inclusion is indeterminable) and excellent lists of general and specific genre criticism. More than half the volume is devoted to the extant work on and about various major Vietnam War literature contributors. Brief descriptions of eight major specialized Vietnam War collections, including those at the William Joiner Center and at Colorado State University, and a fine index of all authors are valuable features.

The well-done annotations make this a particularly valuable source that expands on the general bibliographies by this reviewer, Marc Gilbert, Louis A. Peake, and others; and earlier literature bibliographies by Catherine Calloway, Edward K. Eckert and William J. Searle, John Newman, Sandra M. Wittman, and others. This volume should be in every undergraduate and graduate academic library. [R: Choice, May 93, p. 1444; RBB, 1 May 93, p. 1638]—**Joe P. Dunn**

515. Schwartzberg, Joseph E., ed. **A Historical Atlas of South Asia.** 2d ed. New York, Oxford University Press, 1992. 376p. illus. maps. index. (Reference Series/The Association for Asian Studies, no.2). $250.00. G2261.S1H5. 911'.54. LC 91-39119. ISBN 0-19-506869-6.

This "second impression" falls between a reprint and a new edition of the 1978 original (see ARBA 80, entry 390). It retains the same maps as the acclaimed long-out-of-print original, replacing only an accompanying overlay map of administrative divisions with one updated to 1991. Additions to the text are in the form of a 20-page "Addenda and Corrigenda," about 500 entries under "New Bibliography," a new index, and front material. The "Addenda and Corrigenda" updates research and bibliography for each of the sections but consists largely of a new essay on pre- and proto-history and of information on political developments since the original, including tables of election results and political disturbances. While appending the new text and tables is less than satisfactory (requiring that the reader be familiar with the arrangement to use the new information), it has the unquestionable virtue of holding down the cost. Similar to the original (the film for which was used to reprint much of the volume), this impression is beautifully and sturdily produced, yet, amazingly, costs only $100 more than did the original. Despite the relatively few changes, larger libraries will want to add the new impression to replace well-worn copies of the original as well as to provide the updated information and tables. Other libraries will want to consider this second chance to add an incomparable reference resource on a major world area. [R: Choice, June 93, pp. 1602-04; LJ, 15 Mar 93, p. 70]—**K. Mulliner**

AUSTRALIAN HISTORY

516. **The Oxford Illustrated Dictionary of Australian History.** By Jan Bassett. New York, Oxford University Press, 1993. 304p. illus. $49.95. 994.003. ISBN 0-19-553243-0.

This small reference book fills no clear need other than to offer some basic information on various people and events in Australian history. That convenience, however, is offset by the separation of events from their wider historical contexts, so that one ends with a sense of disjuncture and discontinuity rather than of fuller knowledge. The entries on creative artists are arbitrarily selected; one is surprised at both inclusions and omissions. For instance, there are entries for Banjo Paterson and Dorothea Mackellar, but none for Judith Wright and A. D. Hope, Australia's two major poets. One might also expect entries for the film directors Gillian Armstrong and Peter Weir in relation to that burgeoning art in Australia. Nor are the entries up-to-date, the view being perhaps that history is of the past.

Bassett records her information with complete objectivity—but also with complete lack of emotion and with no sense of what constitutes human interest. This serious defect is made worse by the flat, lifeless style of the prose. Sentences in which subject, verb, and object follow one another in unvarying sequence stifle a reader's interest. The illustrations (cartoons and photographs) that accompany the text do lighten it somewhat, but not as much as one might expect, and the photographic portraits can even reinforce the lifelessness of the text by their depiction of a constrained, withheld people. [R: Choice, Oct 93, p. 262]
—**John B. Beston**

CANADIAN HISTORY

517. Bercuson, David J., and J. L. Granatstein. **Dictionary of Canadian Military History.** Don Mills, Ont., Oxford University Press, 1992. 248p. $29.95. 355'.00971. ISBN 0-19-540847-0.

Written by two leading authorities on Canadian military and civil history, this guide fills a major reference gap. A biographical approach predominates, with places, equipment, formations, events, and concepts also being treated. The book is current through 1991. In addition to the dictionary entries, appendixes provide a variety of useful lists. Coverage is extensive, from the Angus Shops of Montreal (which made fighting vehicles) to the "zombies" (restricted duty volunteers) of World War II. The writing style is clear, direct, and forceful, with an abundant leavening of critical evaluation. Text cross-references are highlighted, and most major entries have an abbreviated further reading section (it lacks only publisher identification). The useful cross-references contain the odd inconsistency (e.g., *Naval Mutinies* is a term, but *Army Mutinies* is not).

The authors admit that space limitations prevent a comprehensive approach, so while all major topics one might expect are present, some arguably important items have been omitted. For example, there is no discussion of the Castine occupation in the War of 1812, which helped found Dalhousie University; the "Limbo" antisubmarine mortar is not mentioned; and reserve formations (e.g., the Princess Louise Fusiliers) are not covered. There are no illustrations, and weights and measures in most cases are metric only. A few errors were noted. The air-to-air missile that was canceled was the "Sparrow II," not the "Sparrow" itself; the "Mustang" fighter did not "originally" marry a U.S. airframe to a U.K. engine (that was a later development); and HMCS *Nabob* was not a converted merchant ship—it was built keel-up using a merchant hull design. A probable misprint has the same enlistment figure for the Canadian Expeditionary Force of World War I and the entire Canadian Army in World War II; the latter was nearly twice the size of the former, so this figure seems improbable. But these minor flaws do not detract from the book's substantial value.

While the work is sturdily bound with fine quality paper, the print is rather small, and annoyingly, a small capital "I" is inconsistently used instead of the numeral "1", making it difficult to determine if an "Mk. II" refers to the second or the eleventh of its type. Overall, however, this is a ready-reference tool that almost any library dealing with military history will find invaluable.—**John Howard Oxley**

EUROPEAN HISTORY

British

518. English, Barbara, and J. J. N. Palmer, eds. **Royal Historical Society Annual Bibliography of British and Irish History: Publications of 1992.** New York, Oxford University Press, 1993. 327p. index. $55.00. ISBN 0-19-820461-2.

This bibliography of scholarly publications on British and Irish history, published annually since 1975, will be useful to students and researchers in the field. It is arranged chronologically, with sections on each country for various time periods (Britain 1714-1815; Britain 1815-1914; Medieval Wales; and Scotland before the Union). Each chronological section is further subdivided by subject areas, such as religion, external affairs, visual arts, politics, and institutions. Indexes by author, personal name, place-name, and subject offer various access points. Any library whose clientele includes serious students and scholars in these areas will want to buy this publication.—**Terry Ann Mood**

519. Treasure, Geoffrey. **Who's Who in Early Hanoverian Britain (1714-1789).** Detroit, St. James Press, 1992. 450p. illus. index. (Who's Who in British History, v.6). $45.00. LC 90-64266. ISBN 1-55862-136-9.

Nearly 200 men and women who achieved leadership across a wide spectrum of society are covered in this biographical dictionary. The Early Hanoverian period for this volume begins with the accession of King George I and ends with the French Revolution. No claim is made for comprehensiveness. Some individuals were included because they were interesting and contributed to providing a "portrait of the age," one of the goals of this series. In the same vein, the biographical essays are not in alphabetical order but arranged in a loose chronological fashion, with groups composed of subjects in similar fields. There is no guide to this arrangement. The index provides direct access for readers who prefer to locate a specific subject rather than read through the volume.

The biographical sketches vary in length from one paragraph to eight pages. In addition to kings, politicians, soldiers, and clergy, there are also authors, artists, musicians, scientists, and merchants. These are rounded off with such eminent Hanoverians as Lancelot Brown, Josiah Wedgewood, Edmund Burke, and several prominent criminals. This series attempts to put each life examined into perspective rather than merely reciting basic biographical facts. This makes the biographies interesting to read, with their emphasis on character and the place of the subjects in the age. Judgments tend to be carefully balanced: Treasure provides positive elements for the three early Hanoverian kings as well as the negative elements commonly found in contemporary public opinion and history books. Another goal of this series, to provide the "latest findings of scholarship," is more difficult to judge, as the bibliographies appended to the end of the essays are limited to several standard works, very few with recent publication dates.

—**Henry E. York**

Eastern European

520. Magosci, Paul Robert. **Historical Atlas of East Central Europe.** Seattle, Wash., University of Washington Press, 1993. 218p. maps. index. (History of East Central Europe, v.1). $75.00. DJK4.S93. 911.47. LC 93-13783. ISBN 0-295-97248-3.

Some 90 maps cover all of East Central Europe from the early fifth century through 1992. The atlas encompasses Poland, the Czech Republic, Slovakia, Hungary, Romania, Slovenia, Croatia, Bosnia-Herzegovina, Yugoslavia, Macedonia, Albania, Bulgaria, and Greece. Also included are the eastern parts

of Germany, Bavaria, Austria, northeastern Italy, historical Poland-Lithuania, Belarus, Moldavia, western Turkey, and Ukraine up to the Dnieper River. Maps are arranged chronologically, with accompanying text describing the history of a particular region. Many maps show key historical events and items, including military actions, ecclesiastical structures, culture and education, demography, ethnicity, and economic factors. There is a good index covering several thousand place-names and their variant spellings. All in all, this is a well-executed atlas of interest to students of this important European region.
[R: LJ, 15 Nov 93, p. 72; RBB, 15 Dec 93, pp. 777-78]—**Bohdan S. Wynar**

French

521. Chandler, David G. **Dictionary of the Napoleonic Wars.** New York, Simon & Schuster Academic Reference Division, 1993. 570p. illus. $70.00. DC147.C47. 940.2'7. LC 93-805. ISBN 0-13-177288-0.

This scholarly work, originally published in 1979, is an outgrowth of the author's well-known military history, *The Campaigns of Napoleon* (Macmillan, 1966). It includes, in a dictionary format, a great deal of information deemed outside that work's scope or too detailed to include, or that answers questions readers sent the author. Topics covered include battles, individual biographies, contemporary political concepts, military weapons and terminology, and nonmilitary topics of interest to Napoleonic scholars (e.g., a discussion of Napoleon's reforms of civil law). Maps illustrate major battles; there are also pictures of weapons and portraits of many of the persons discussed. There is a detailed general chronological table of the life and times of Napoleon, as well as a chart pinpointing Napoleon's personal movements, day by day, during specific campaigns. There is also a substantial bibliography. Chandler's writing style is readable, if formal and old-fashioned; it is disconcerting to read his description of Toussaint L'Ouverture as the "native leader" of Haiti.

Napoleon and his times are of perennial interest to many library patrons, and this work is undoubtedly full of authoritative information on the subject. It would be of most interest to academic libraries, but could be useful to public libraries as well because of the popularity of its topic.—**Marit S. MacArthur**

German

522. Osmond, Jonathan. **German Reunification: A Reference Guide and Commentary.** Harlow, England, Longman; distr., Detroit, Gale, 1992. 311p. index. $85.00. ISBN 0-582-09650-2.

In spite of the subtitle, this volume is not a reference work in the traditional sense, because three-fourths of its pages consist of historical and topical essays. Timeliness of the subject, however, earns it at least a temporary place on the reference shelf, and its arrangement encourages such use. Part 1 includes a detailed chronology of events from 1989 to 1992 and four essays on the history and transformation of the German Democratic Republic. Part 2 contains six essays by various scholars on aspects of political, economic, and social life in eastern Germany, such as elections, trade unions, and the role of women. Part 3 is a reference section with an annotated directory of names, places, and events; relevant lists and tables; and the texts of four major treaties. Important people or concepts mentioned in part 1 are given boldface type to indicate a detailed entry in part 3.

This is an informed, readable effort by qualified scholars. Osmond, a historian at the University of Leicester, covered East Germany for the *Economist Intelligence Unit* from 1983 to 1990; his expertise is much in evidence. The linking of narrative and reference sections facilitates use, as do interspersed tables and statistics. An index and bibliography are appended, but the latter is brief; for that purpose, libraries will do better with Horst Thomsen's *Bibliography on German Unification* (Reed Reference Publishing, 1993). An unfortunate omission: the three maps listed in the table of contents are nowhere to be found.
[R: Choice, July/Aug 93, p. 1753; LJ, 15 April 93, p. 88; RBB, 15 May 93, p. 1722]—**Willa Schmidt**

Russian

523. McCauley, Martin, ed. **Directory of Russian MPs: People's Deputies of the Supreme Soviet of Russia-Russian Federation.** Harlow, England, Longman; distr., Detroit, Gale, 1992. 326p. $260.00. ISBN 0-582-09647-2.

For students of and writers covering the present political scene in Russia, this reference work is invaluable. It consists of 252 short biographies, including the voting records, of all deputies of the Russian Supreme Soviet, otherwise known as a parliament. The 252 persons described in the directory are the movers and shakers of the present Russia. McCauley has written an informative introduction, explaining the genesis and procedures of the Supreme Soviet. The major parties, factions, tendencies, and measures passed are also noted.

For those who wish well to democratic Russia, this volume makes for sad reading, because most of the deputies listed are individuals with roots in the old order. Although the Supreme Soviet was elected by majority vote, the pasts and the voting records of the members do not, on the whole, convey the sense that they are democrats. There is no substitute for this work in English, and it is recommended for all reference desks with one caveat: Should the Supreme Soviet, for whatever reason, be dissolved, the volume will instantly become one of antiquarian interest. [R: Choice, June 93, p. 1600; RBB, Aug 93, p. 2088]

—**Andrew Ezergailis**

524. Paxton, John. **Encyclopedia of Russian History: From the Christianization of Kiev to the Break-Up of the U.S.S.R.** Santa Barbara, Calif., ABC-Clio, 1993. 483p. maps. $45.00. DK36.P39. 947'.003. LC 93-29564. ISBN 0-87436-690-9.

This work contains some 2,500 entries ranging from 30 to 300 words. The coverage is very broad, including not only history but also literature, the arts, political science, geography, education, and other disciplines of the social sciences. The title of this volume is somewhat misleading, because the book covers much more than "Russian history" (unless the author, a former editor of *The Statesman's Year-Book* [see ARBA 92, entry 77] and author of several other reference books published in Great Britain, still considers everything west of Poland to be Russia). More important than this misnomer is the currency of the information, which covers the period up to the breakup of the Soviet Union and shows an uneven treatment of certain subjects. For example, the article on Latvia is half a page long and contains only two books in its bibliography—one published in 1951, the other in 1965. By contrast, there is a longer article on Lenin, with seven bibliographical entries. Many articles are simply misleading and provide false information, such as that on population. It indicates, among other things, that the 1989 population of an unspecified place, which the reader might logically assume to be Russia but is actually the Soviet Union, is 287 million. In the second part of this article, readers will find the information on the most numerous nationalities and learn that there are 44 (?) million Russians.

All in all, this is an occasionally inaccurate dictionary that has to be used with caution. There are more sophisticated reference sources on this subject. [R: LJ, Dec 93, p. 116]—**Bohdan S. Wynar**

525. Wilson, Andrew, and Nina Bachkatov. **Russia and the Commonwealth A to Z.** New York, HarperPerennial/HarperCollins, 1992. 258p. index. $30.00; $15.00pa. DK286.W5513. 947.085'4'03. LC 92-52547. ISBN 0-06-2715551-8; 0-06-273145-9pa.

Cold War terminology and attitudes are the subject of humorous anecdote and subtle satire in this delightful volume. People, places, events, ideological terms, and historical and diplomatic catchphrases are listed and detailed. Wilson and Bachkatov provide a wider view of change in the former Soviet state, with an added bonus of humor that creeps into the entries. (Perhaps the publication of this volume will encourage the authors of other reference works to lighten up a little in their entries.) The humor aside, this volume also touches on serious social, economic, and ecological problems in Russia and the Commonwealth and the challenges that face the ex-Soviet citizens. While not an in-depth reference work, this volume piques one's interest to continue the search for more information on a particular subject. In this respect it is an excellent companion to the *Dictionary of Political Parties and Organizations in Russia*

(Center for Strategic and International Studies, 1992) and is recommended for the same readership and reference collections as that volume. [R: Choice, Mar 93, pp. 1122-24; RBB, 1 Feb 93, p. 1005; WLB, Jan 93, p. 114]—**Norman L. Kincaide**

Scandinavian

526. Pulsiano, Phillip, and Kirsten Wolf, eds. **Medieval Scandinavia: An Encyclopedia.** Hamden, Conn., Garland, 1993. 768p. illus. maps. index. (Garland Encyclopedias of the Middle Ages, v.1; Garland Reference Library of the Humanities, v.934). $95.00. DL30.M43. 948'.02'03. LC 92-19300. ISBN 0-8240-4787-7.

Written for students and others who lack a command of the Scandinavian languages, this encyclopedia attempts to make current scholarship on the medieval period available in a single-volume reference. Extending in time from the age of migrations to the Reformation, it covers Denmark, Finland, Iceland, Norway, and Sweden.

More than 250 scholars contributed articles, varying from 150 words to about 5,000, on varied aspects of life and culture. The range of subjects falls largely in areas relevant to the humanities and social sciences. There are, for example, numerous articles on literature and language—sagas, annals, poetry, dialects, and others. Social life and work are covered in articles on such topics as crime and punishment, pregnancy and childbirth, calendar and time-reckoning, and ships and shipbuilding. Some knowledge of Scandinavian languages is presupposed by the alphabetical arrangement, which includes some characters found in that alphabet.

To accommodate the broad coverage, some articles are segmented geographically. For example, the article on laws is a composite of articles on Denmark, Iceland, Norway, and Sweden, each by a different scholar. While the articles are both readable and intelligible, the subject matter is often quite technical, such as that in the articles on alphabet, paleography, and place-names. The approach and content are critical, objective, and often very specialized. These features make the encyclopedia a valuable complement to the 13-volume *Dictionary of the Middle Ages* (see ARBA 90, entry 533).

Appended to each article is a list of scholarly references identifying (as appropriate) editions, translations, lexicographical aids, and the secondary literature on a given topic. These references lay out the major scholarly work on a subject and are not limited to English-language references. In addition, they are arranged chronologically, making it easier to trace the evolution of research. For the longer articles these can be quite lengthy. The references for Viking art extend to almost five full columns for an article slightly more than eight columns in length.

Numerous *see* and *see also* references guide the user to proper headings and to related articles in the text portion, and a separate index facilitates further access. Interspersed throughout the volume are black-and-white maps, photographic reproductions, and line drawings. The maps and drawings are generally excellent, but some of the photographs suffer by comparison.

Students in the field should find this a welcome tool. Although not primarily for scholars, it will prove useful as a quick reference for less-familiar topics. Large public libraries and academic libraries serving upper-level undergraduates and beginning graduate students in Scandinavian and medieval studies will want to acquire it. [R: Choice, Nov 93, p. 437]—**Bernice Bergup**

Spanish

527. Rasor, Eugene L. **The Spanish Armada of 1588: Historiography and Annotated Bibliography.** Westport, Conn., Greenwood Press, 1993. 277p. index. (Bibliographies of Battles and Leaders, no.10). $59.95. DA360.R37. 942.05'5. LC 92-31759. ISBN 0-313-28303-6.

The defeat of the Spanish Armada in 1588 has produced a multitude of scholarly and popular works. This volume, the ninth in the series and the third written by Rasor, is an extensive bibliography of primary and secondary sources. It is divided into two parts. Part 1, consisting of 5 chapters and 86 pages, is a critical, bibliographical essay describing the background of the period, the people involved, the actual event, original sources, and myths about the Armada. The works referred to in these chapters are cross-referenced to the full citations in part 2.

Part 2, 170 pages long, is an annotated bibliography of books (including some for children), journal articles, and original sources from the sixteenth century to the present. The works included are mainly in English, but primary (and some secondary) sources are also in Spanish. The 1,114 entries are arranged alphabetically by author and include full citations, together with a brief, critical annotation. The book also contains a chronology and a useful author and subject index to both parts 1 and 2. This well-researched, readable work is valuable as a reference tool not only for the scholar but also for anyone interested in the Armada and its times. [R: Choice, May 93, p. 1448]—**Kathleen Farago**

WORLD HISTORY

Atlases

528. **The Harper Atlas of World History.** rev. ed. New York, HarperCollins, 1992. 355p. illus. maps. index. $40.00. G1030.G68513. 911. LC 92-52538. ISBN 0-06-270067-7.

This is a beautifully illustrated book, a revised and updated translation from the original French version, *Histoire de l'Humanite*, which is perhaps a better title for this work than *Atlas of World History*. It is truly an atlas of human history, with diagrams, maps, illustrations, and photographs, all accompanied by extensive texts explaining everything from human evolution and the origins of humans in Africa to the Gulf War of 1990-1991. After a brief opening section devoted to the history of cartography, the basic organization is chronological. Beginning with the Paleolithic appearance of *Homo sapiens* and a discussion of the domestication of plants and animals, early chapters include "First Tools, Fire, Ritual" and the "Birth of Art." The chronological history of the world then follows, with a profusion of handsome illustrations in full color, ranging from ancient civilizations of the Mediterranean, Africa, and the Near East to Persia, India, China, and the New World. Detailed textual commentary provides much information about the art, society, economy, demography, history, politics—even the science and technology—of a given age, civilization, or culture. Detailed maps explain how the last barbarian invasions changed Europe; chart the expansion of financial and commercial capitalism; trace European migration, colonialism, and global expansion; and count world population growth. Major geopolitical changes, from the Roman Empire to the division of Europe after World War II, are explained in graphic detail. The atlas continues through time to the most recent events, ending with the reunification of Germany, the dissolution of the Soviet Union, and the birth of the Commonwealth of Independent States.

This is, indeed, an extraordinarily rich, fully illustrated, yet concise history of the world, and should be a part of every school and public library. Considering its affordability, it should be in every home library as well. [R: LJ, 15 June 93, p. 62]—**Joseph W. Dauben**

529. Myers, J. Wilson, Eleanor Emlen Myers, and Gerald Cadogan, eds. **The Aerial Atlas of Ancient Crete.** Berkeley, Calif., University of California Press, 1992. 318p. illus. maps. index. $85.00. DF261.C8A35. 914.99'8'0222. LC 91-20649. ISBN 0-520-07382-7.

This impressive volume should interest laypeople and scholars alike with its comprehensive coverage of ancient archaeological sites on Crete. Of particular interest is a brief history of aerial photography and the editors' description of how they used it and why it is so appropriate for ancient sites. Because the method is so useful—indeed, it is being used elsewhere today, such as in the Valley of the Kings in Egypt, although with manned balloons—this description is most welcome. In addition, the first part of the volume includes discussions of the island's geomorphology, climate, and vegetation, and a brief history from Neolithic times to the present day.

Most of the volume presents 44 ancient sites in alphabetical order, complete with color aerial photographs and illustrative diagrams. The author of each site description discusses the site in terms of its importance, use, situation, geomorphology, excavation history, and buildings, finishing with a bibliography (both general and specialized), a list of museums holding major finds, and the date of the aerial photography. The volume concludes not only with the expected and necessary index but also with a glossary of the terms used in the text.

As a whole, the book is both beautifully presented and informative, a necessary addition to any respectable library of works on the ancient Mediterranean world. Its lavish photographs and diagrams, informative text, and extensive bibliographies will assist any reader in locating, learning about, and researching the different sites on this important island. [R: Choice, Jan 93, p. 864]—**Susan Tower Hollis**

530. **The Times Atlas of World History.** 4th ed. Geoffrey Barraclough and Geoffrey Parker, eds. Maplewood, N.J., Hammond, 1993. 360p. illus. maps. index. $95.00. G1030.T54. 911. LC 93-23944. ISBN 0-7230-0534-6.

Opulent. Dazzling. A delight to the eyes. This new edition is all of that and more, from the handsome cover to the illustrations, graphs, maps, and typeface. The colors are of a richness that is rarely encountered. The first edition (1978) broke with the tradition of Eurocentrism; this work "aims ... to present a view of history that is world-wide in conception and presentation and which does justice, without prejudice or favour, to the achievements of all peoples, in all ages and in all quarters of the globe." However, there are certainly topics left out. For example, there is no discussion of slavery as a historical phenomenon, and while Islam and Christianity are given their due, the other religions of the world are not noticed. Still, the sections on human origins and early cultures, the first civilizations, the classical civilizations of Eurasia, the world of divided regions, the world of the emerging West, the age of European dominance, and the age of global civilization give a breathtaking panorama of the procession of humanity. A world chronology shows the parallel development of different regions of the world as well as culture and technology, and a glossary gives "supplementary information about some of the individuals, peoples, events, treaties, etc., which, because of lack of space received only brief mention." The index is easy to read, although it cannot include every possible map entry. Both the glossary and index are on handsome brown paper, separating them from the body of the work.

The written part of the work in such limited space is, perforce, thin. Any prior knowledge of a particular topic will leave the reader disappointed. If there had been recommended readings, the interested reader could use this work as the beginning of a marvelous education. Finally, this is described as an ecumenical work. Perhaps then, instead of B.C., events before Christ's birth might have been identified as occurring B.C.E. (Before the Common Era).

For whom is this work appropriate? For anyone who browses to find a delightful new fact: "I never knew that!"—**Bertram H. Rothschild**

Bibliography

531. Baxter, Colin F. **The Normandy Campaign, 1944: A Selected Bibliography.** Westport, Conn., Greenwood Press, 1992. 167p. index. (Bibliographies of Battles and Leaders, no.9). $45.00. Z6207.W8B35. 016.94054'2142. LC 91-46970. ISBN 0-313-28301-X.

The Normandy landings were, it is argued by some, the most important pitched land battles of the twentieth century. While some in the former Soviet Union might dispute this thesis, the Normandy campaign did play a decisive role in the defeat of Nazi Germany. Baxter's work starts with a narrative bibliographical essay on the various aspects of the Normandy campaign: Operation Overlord, air and naval preparations, D-Day, Operation Fortitude, and the second front. The essays are well written and informative and take up about two-thirds of the volume. What one would think of as the main portion of this work, the bibliography and sources for research, takes up the remaining third and serves mainly as footnotes to the bibliographical essays. The bibliography per se is not classed; all the entries are in alphabetical order. Baxter states in the preface that these "citations are cross-referenced from the historical narrative in Part I to the alphabetical listing in Part II and vice versa." This is not true. While there is a reference in the narrative to the assigned number of the bibliographical entry, it is useless because the bibliographical entries are arranged by the given author's name anyway. There is no cross-referencing from the bibliography to the narrative essay (referred to by the author as "vice versa"). In short, this is a select bibliography (there is no indication of selection criteria other than "my aim has been to integrate the multitude of books...into a complete tapestry"), some entries of which are annotated in a narrative essay, but one must hunt through the book for the work's location. The volume's narrative section (part 1) concludes with an essay on "Trends in Future Research" that is really a short essay on the historiography of the Normandy campaign. There is an index to the narrative portion of the volume.

Overall, this is not a bad book; it is just that the annotations are buried in the narrative essays. Baxter's annotations, when they are found, are good and well thought out. But the lack of cross-referencing from the bibliography to the essays detracts from the usefulness of what otherwise would be an excellent addition to most library shelves.—**Ralph Lee Scott**

532. Edelheit, Abraham J., and Hershel Edelheit. **Bibliography on Holocaust Literature: Supplement, Volume 2.** Boulder, Colo., Westview Press, 1993. 564p. index. $77.00. Z6374.H6E33. 016.94053'18. LC 89-70630. ISBN 0-8133-1412-7.

This volume, the second supplement to the authors' *Bibliography on Holocaust Literature* (see ARBA 87, entry 522), adds nearly 3,900 citations to those of the original publication and first supplement (see ARBA 91, entry 519) for a total of more than 18,500 items in the three volumes. In their introduction the Edelheits point out the importance of including cognate subjects (e.g., anti-Semitism, European Jewish life before Nazism, fascism, the course of World War II, the continuation of anti-Semitism after the war) in their bibliography "in order to indubitably reflect the depth of the issues involved." They stress that the organization of their bibliography emphasizes quantity over quality. Thus, this comprehensive bibliography provides annotations for selected significant works—mostly books and a few articles—in order to provide some sense of their content and methodology. The Edelheits make no effort to distinguish between more- and less-useful works except in the case of materials originating with Holocaust revisionists.

The materials listed in this work can be categorized in two ways. First, the authors differentiate between items published from 1933 to 1945 and those published after 1945. Second, there is a distinction between first-person accounts and secondary sources. Adopting a comprehensive methodology, the Edelheits have attempted to collect "all the relevant sources and make their existence known to as wide an audience as possible." Chapters of the bibliography for the period up to 1945 include European Jewry before the Holocaust, the Jewish question, fascism and totalitarianism, the Third Reich, the destruction of European Jewry, and Jewish-Gentile relations in extremes. Such chapters as those on rescue and resettlement, the legacy of the Holocaust, the post-Holocaust Gentile world, and reference and research guides cover 1945 to the present.

The bibliography includes an appendix of 33 periodical and newsletter titles that, although containing considerable data on Holocaust subjects, do not meet size or authorship criteria for inclusion in the bibliography. This is followed by a glossary of German, Hebrew, Yiddish, French, and Polish terms of Holocaust importance. It provides full names of organizations in the original language, their abbreviations or acronyms, and a brief definition. Author/title and general subject indexes are supplied.

This volume is useful for undergraduate and graduate students seeking English-language materials on the Holocaust. While it could be improved by the publication of a single subject index to all three volumes, it is recommended for all college and university libraries.—**Mark Padnos**

Chronology

533. Farina, Luciano F., and Robert W. Tolf, eds. **Columbus Documents: Summaries of Documents in Genoa.** Detroit, Omnigraphics, 1992. 166p. index. $68.00. Z6616.C73C65. 016.97001'5. LC 92-27209. ISBN 1-55888-156-5.

Christopher Columbus is one of the most familiar figures in world history, but various facts about his life have remained the subject of disputes and misconceptions by the general public. One such fact is Columbus's country of origin. For decades professional historians have accepted it as proven that he came from Genoa. During the nineteenth century, however, and continuing into the twentieth century among fringe scholars, Columbus's birthplace has been attributed to many other countries, including Switzerland, England, Spain, Germany, France, and Norway. One particularly wild theory has even suggested that Columbus was a Native American who was accidentally blown east across the Atlantic Ocean and so was simply trying to return home! But documentary evidence from Genoa shows that Columbus's grandfather moved to the vicinity of Genoa in 1429. From that point onward the Columbus family appeared in the notarial records of Genoa 179 times between 1429 and 1529.

Most of *Columbus Documents* is a list and summary of the contents of those documents. Each of the entries supplies the date of the document, the city where it was made, its archival location, the notary's name, the file location, the discoverer of the document, and a summary of the contents. There are three appendixes. One summarizes Columbus's *Book of Privileges* while another does the same for the important Monleone and Pessagno collection of Columbus documents. The third consists of lists of people from Genoa dated 1448-1470 that contain the name of Columbus family members. A large index for names, places, and entities concludes the work.

Columbus Documents is a useful calendar of significant but not readily accessible biographical information about Columbus. Although some of this information has been available in Italian, Farina and Tolf have made it available in English for the first time. [R: JAL, Mar 93, p. 56; RQ, Summer 93, pp. 562-63]—**Ronald H. Fritze**

534. **Smithsonian Timelines of the Ancient World.** By Chris Scarre. New York, Dorling Kindersley, 1993. 256p. illus. maps. index. $49.95. D54.5.S65. 930'.02'02. LC 93-1840. ISBN 1-56458-305-8.

Coffee tables worldwide should be put on notice: Many of them will probably soon be bearing another massive tome, in this case a generally first-rate production of the Smithsonian Institution. With any luck, these coffee tables will enjoy numerous respites, for this is a book that can profitably be taken up, viewed, and read by fairly young children, teenagers, and adults alike.

Visually, this timeline succeeds magnificently, with almost 2,000 illustrations, drawings, and maps. The text works well, and the prehistoric and historical movement described thereby is essentially chronological, moving from the origins of life to the European Renaissance, the establishment of the Ming dynasty, and other occurrences in the period from AD 1250 to 1500. At every point, events and developments are looked at globally and broadly.

The massive amounts of data presented here frequently lack the context that only a continuous narrative can supply, but careful users can easily compensate for that. Some readers may still find it odd that an era as late as the Renaissance is included within the designation "ancient world." More puzzling, especially for a volume with a consciously universal appeal, is the retention of the parochial time designations B.C. and A.D., which are frequently replaced in other books by the less particularistic B.C.E. (Before the Common Era) and C.E. (Common Era). But most coffee tables and their owners will overlook these deficiencies. And all libraries should do likewise and make the purchase of this reasonably priced volume a high priority. [R: LJ, 15 Nov 93, p. 73]—**Leonard J. Greenspoon**

Dictionaries and Encyclopedias

535. Hakkert, Adolf M., and others, eds. **Lexicon of the Greek and Roman Cities and Place Names in Antiquity Ca. 1500 B.C. - Ca. A. D. 500. Fascicule 1: A [...] ... - Ad Novas. 3.** Philadelphia, John Benjamins, 1992. 1v. (various paging). $35.00pa. ISBN 90-256-0985-6.

Hakkert and his collaborators have begun a truly ambitious project. To gauge the scale of their task one should compare this work to the monumental *Princeton Encyclopedia of Classical Sites* (see ARBA 77, entry 350). The latter included just 27 entries in the alphabetical sequence covered by more than 400 entries in this first fascicle. Even if the publisher's modest plans for just 40 more fascicles prove correct, the complete lexicon may include more than 26,000 entries, compared with the approximately 3,000 in the Princeton encyclopedia. Despite the title, coverage includes more than just towns and cities; forts, road stations, villas, and other sites are described. Arrangement is by the classical name of the site, and each entry indicates the ancient and modern place-names (when known), the province and country, the type of site, a brief history of the place, and a description of archaeological finds. Substantial bibliographies accompany even the briefest entries and include citations to classical and epigraphical sources as well as references in modern scholarship. The strength of the bibliographies and the breadth of coverage should make this work a valuable tool for both students and scholars.

However, improvements are needed. The modern road maps accompanying many entries are usually poorly reproduced, cluttered, confusing, and unnecessary. Clearer delineation between entries would also help. Frequent grammatical and typographical errors reflect some of the pitfalls of international projects and demonstrate the need for more careful editing. Perhaps the most significant shortcoming is the uncertainty regarding the cost and time necessary to complete the work. Subscribers face a minimum cost of $1,400 for 40 fascicles. If the 3-month wait between the first 2 fascicles defines the publication schedule, then the project may take as long as 10 years to complete. However, for libraries supporting graduate programs in ancient history and classical studies, both the time and money may be well spent.—**John R. M. Lawrence**

536. Richardson, L., Jr. **A New Topographical Dictionary of Ancient Rome.** Baltimore, Md., Johns Hopkins University Press, 1992. 458p. illus. maps. $65.00. DG68.R5. 913.7'003. LC 91-45046. ISBN 0-8018-4300-6.

This volume was conceived as an update to Samuel Platner and Thomas Ashby's *A Topographical Dictionary of Ancient Rome* (Oxford University Press, 1929), but it is no simple revision. Every entry has been entirely rewritten to reflect the enormous work of scholars during the last 60 years. In addition to many entries on recently identified sites, Richardson adds general articles on common architectural features of the ancient city (e.g., *domus, forum, thermae, via*). As did its predecessor, this dictionary describes the major monuments, buildings, sites, and regions of the ancient city of Rome, from its earliest settlement to the sixth century A.D. The geographical limits of its coverage are those of the fourteen *regiones* of the Augustan reorganization of Rome. The focus is upon pagan Rome; early Christian monuments are excluded. Entries are arranged alphabetically by the Latin name of each site or monument. For each article, the author succinctly describes what is known about the location, appearance, and use of each site and provides the reader with references to the relevant literary and epigraphical evidence and the most important secondary literature on the subject.

This volume is intended to be used in conjunction with Ernest Nash's *Pictorial Dictionary of Ancient Rome* (Praeger, 1968), so its 92 illustrations are primarily limited to site and building plans. The introduction summarizes the major literary and archaeological sources of information on the ancient city and outlines the topographical research of Renaissance and modern scholars. A chronological list of monuments and a brief glossary of architectural terms are also provided. The volume's only faults are the lack of a map to orient the reader and the lack of a general index that might connect various types of structures (e.g., libraries, statues) or people associated with the monuments (e.g., builders, architects, owners). Richardson pays tribute to Platner and Ashby for their work, which became a standard reference immediately upon publication; his volume will prove equally vital to scholars in classical studies and ancient history. [R: LJ, 1 Feb 93, p. 76; WLB, May 93, p. 121]—**John R. M. Lawrence**

Handbooks and Yearbooks

537. Frankel, Benjamin, ed. **The Cold War 1945-1991.** Detroit, Gale, 1992. 3v. illus. index. $250.00/set. LC 92-30486. ISBN 0-8103-8927-4.

This three-volume encyclopedic guide to the history of the Cold War is unquestionably one of the best references that this reviewer has encountered in any area of study. Frankel, an internationally recognized expert on U.S. national security, defense and foreign policy, and international relations theory, headed a team of researchers who assembled this extremely useful compilation. Volume 1 provides biographical essays (complete with pictures) on 149 American and Western European leaders who played key roles during the era. Volume 2 does the same for 134 figures from the Soviet Union, Eastern Europe, China, and the Third World. Volume 3 has shorter sketches on major events and themes, such as containment, glasnost, NSC-68, and the Iron Curtain speech. It also includes a detailed chronology by year, month, and day from 1939 through 1991 and an exceptional narrative history of the Cold War. Other features include a selected bibliography subdivided by the various topics of the period, where the papers of several hundred key players in Cold War policy can be located, and a full index. All essays in each volume list primary references and cross-reference other related entries.

The only disappointment is that the bibliographies have some significant glitches, and the best sources are not always cited. Two examples chosen at random illustrate. The entry for the battle of Dien Bien Phu overlooks the two best known, standard works: Bernard B. Fall's *Hell in a Very Small Place* (Da Capo Press, 1985) and Jules Roy's *The Battle of Dienbienphu* (Carroll & Graf, 1984); and the essay on Pol Pot does not note the single best work, David P. Chandler's *Brother Number One* (Westview Press, 1992). Despite this complaint, this is an extraordinarily valuable compilation that is useful for scholars, students at all levels, and the general public. Every library—public, college, and high school—should consider these volumes. [R: Choice, June 93, p. 1598; LJ, 1 Sept 93, p. 168; RBB, Aug 93, p. 2086]

—Joe P. Dunn

538. Friedman, Saul S., ed. **Holocaust Literature: A Handbook of Critical, Historical, and Literary Writings.** Westport, Conn., Greenwood Press, 1993. 677p. index. $99.50. D804.3.H35. 940.53'18. LC 92-24135. ISBN 0-313-26221-7.

Attempts to explain the Holocaust and place it in historical perspective are often overwhelmed by the enormity of the event and the evil that it represents. The current upsurge in hate crimes and ethnic nationalism make understanding this event and educating the public imperative. This handbook offers teachers, students, and researchers a wealth of material, compiled by experts, on various aspects of the Holocaust.

The book has three sections: conceptual approaches, area studies, and education and the arts. The first includes subjects such as the rise of National Socialism and the Church and the Holocaust. It also contains a great deal of information on rescuers and righteous Gentiles and their motivation as well as a chapter on Jewish women in the Holocaust Resistance. These subjects are rarely covered in the major sources. The section on area studies deals with the Holocaust in specific countries. The third section covers the Holocaust in art, literature, music, and movies. It also provides information on children's books and research centers. Each chapter is supposed to begin with an overview of the topic and continue with a critical review of the literature. Unfortunately, not all of the contributors followed this format. The essays are all interesting and of high quality, though, citing a variety of sources and including notes and bibliographies. Most of the material cited is in English.

Holocaust Literature is a valuable resource for teachers presenting this difficult subject to people unfamiliar with it, and for scholars seeking sources for further research. It is a useful addition to all library collections. [R: Choice, Dec 93, p. 586; LJ, 1 June 93, p. 104; RBB, 1 Oct 93, pp. 384-85]

—Barbara M. Bibel

539. **Great Events: The Twentieth Century.** Pasadena, Calif., Salem Press, 1992. 10v. illus. maps. index. $250.00/set. D422.G72. 909.82. LC 92-28671. ISBN 0-89356-796-5.

The upper levels of the historical profession are increasingly dominated by people who believe that events, particularly political ones, have little to do with genuine history. For them the big trends, particularly the social ones as they define them, are what really matter. For these postmodernist scholars, *Great Events: The Twentieth Century* is both a heretical and an outmoded sort of book. For the general public and students, however, this welcome set will provide convenient and reliable information about the important events of this century.

Some 472 events are highlighted in the 10 volumes. Individual entries are written by historians and teachers and follow a standard format, beginning with a descriptive title and followed by a sidebar that lists basic information (what, when, where, and who). The clearly written text supplies both the background and a narrative of the event and concludes with a discussion of its consequences. Each entry is illustrated, often dramatically, by a contemporary photograph or print. The individual events are arranged chronologically from 1900 to 1992 and range across the entire world, from political topics, such as the assassination of the Archduke Ferdinand, to social topics, such as the *Roe v. Wade* decision by the Supreme Court. There are five indexes for chronology, key words, categories, geography, and people; they allow the reader to find topics of special interest. *Great Events: The Twentieth Century* is an attractive set that belongs in any middle school, high school, or public library, and it would not be out of place in many junior college and college libraries. [R: BR, Sept/Oct 93, p. 60; WLB, April 93, p. 121]

—**Ronald H. Fritze**

540. Haythornthwaite, Philip J. **The World War One Source Book.** London, Arms and Armour Press/Cassell; distr., New York, Sterling, 1992. 412p. illus. maps. index. $42.95. ISBN 1-85409-102-6.

Modeled closely after *The Napoleonic Source Book* (see ARBA 92, entry 492), this volume will be of value to professional scholars seeking clarification of obscure facts as well as to casual readers looking for a quick summary of the Great War. Although comprehensive in scope, touching on everything from weaponry and tactics to biographical sketches of key military personalities to overviews of all the warring nations, the work is hardly exhaustive. It is aimed primarily at an English-speaking audience, so only English-language editions, with rare exceptions, have been cited, and virtually all the anecdotal material was taken from English sources contemporary with the war.

The book's design makes for easy of use. Section 1 is a chronological account listing all the major engagements of the conflict; section 2, dealing with weapons and tactics, discusses such matters as sniping, gas, and bayonet, and airplanes; section 3 accounts for the role played by each of the belligerent powers; section 4 summarizes the careers of notable military figures; and section 5, the sources, contains not only historical studies but also art, photography, literature, and recollections of the men in the trenches. Replete with an abundance of photographs, drawings, and maps, and possessed of a thorough index, this work should be added to the reference collections of high school and college libraries. [R: RBB, Aug 93, p. 2096]—**John W. Storey**

541. Weeks, John M. **Maya Civilization.** Hamden, Conn., Garland, 1993. 369p. illus. index. (Research Guides to Ancient Civilizations, v.1; Garland Reference Library of the Humanities, v.1796). $66.00. F1435.W43. 972.81'016. LC 92-22798. ISBN 0-8153-0095-6.

This bibliography on the Maya is the first in a new series intended to introduce the nonspecialist to the study of various ancient civilizations. The book begins with a bibliographical essay introducing the reader to Mayan civilization, with emphasis on the classic period, AD 300-900. The introductory material also describes resources for the further study of the Maya. Most of the book is a selective bibliography containing 1,355 entries, often annotated, to books and journal articles that are mainly in English. The bibliography is arranged by subject, with almost half of the entries devoted to regional and site reports. The book has author, place-name, and subject indexes.

When a subject is introduced, a brief narrative is provided, adding to the usefulness of the book. Broad subjects are also easy to locate through the subject index and the detailed table of contents. However, specific topics are harder to find because they are often listed under a broader heading in the index. There are also other problems with the work. The section heading "New Directions" is misleading; it implies recent research, but most of the works listed are dated before 1985. There are quite a few alphabetization errors in the index, as well as errors in entry numbers. Despite these problems, this will be a good starting place for research on Mayan civilization.—**Kathleen Farago**

Periodicals and Serials

542. Steiner, Dale R., and Casey R. Phillips. **Historical Journals: A Handbook for Writers and Reviewers.** 2d ed. Jefferson, N.C., McFarland, 1993. 274p. index. $39.95; $19.95pa. Z6205.S73. 808'.02. LC 92-51090. ISBN 0-89950-801-4; 0-89950-901-0pa.

With twice the entries of the first edition and expanded coverage to include British and Canadian and more interdisciplinary journals, this handbook should be in any library serving those with an interest in history. It will be of assistance to all historians as it lists more than 700 journals oriented toward both professional and popular audiences. For instance, the book contains information on *The American Historical Review* and *ISIS* (history of science) as well as *Backwoods Magazine* (covering muzzle-loading rifles, primitive survival, and how-to projects) and *Garden History*. The entry for each journal includes topics covered in the journal, the editor's name and address, type of readership, stylistic information for preparing the manuscript, whether refereed, acceptance rate, the time to consider the manuscript, information about reviews, and other data. The book also contains sections of advice about preparing and submitting journal articles and about book reviewing. While most of this material will be elementary for professional historians, it should be useful for neophytes, and the bibliographies concluding each section will be useful to anyone wanting further information and advice.—**David L. White**

10 Law

GENERAL WORKS

Acronyms and Abbreviations

543. **Bieber's Dictionary of Legal Abbreviations: Reference Guide for Attorneys, Legal Secretaries, Paralegals and Law Students.** 4th ed. By Mary Miles Prince. Buffalo, N.Y., William S. Hein, 1993. 791p. $45.00. KF246.B46. 349.73'0148. LC 93-13817. ISBN 0-89941-847-3.

There are approximately 30,000 entries in this compendious dictionary of legal abbreviations. According to the preface, about 3,000 have been added since the last edition. The range of coverage is wide: Law reporters, treatises, reviews, encyclopedias, dictionaries, and looseleaf services are among the many types of sources included. Entries are alphabetized as if they were one word; this is a sound choice, although it sometimes leads to anomalous results and occasionally is not followed (e.g., Texas LR and Texas Int'l L.F. are in the "Tex." entries rather than with the other "Texas" entries). In this edition, foreign-language entries have been deleted; these may be found in *World Dictionary of Legal Abbreviations* (see ARBA 93, entry 562). For researchers who have puzzled over the welter of abbreviations found in legal literature, this source will be a great boon.—**Jack Ray**

544. **Bieber's Dictionary of Legal Citations: Reference Guide for Attorneys, Legal Secretaries, Paralegals and Law Students.** 4th ed. By Mary Miles Prince. Buffalo, N.Y., William S. Hein, 1992. 372p. $29.00. KF246.P73. 340'.0148. LC 92-27176. ISBN 0-89941-824-4.

The day students enter law school, they learn that the bible of legal citation is *The Bluebook: A Uniform System of Citation*, described as a "necessary evil." (Less kindly descriptions have been used.) All types of legal papers—from law school memos to briefs before the United States Supreme Court—must follow the 300-plus pages of rules and examples set forth in *The Bluebook*. *Bieber's Dictionary of Legal Citations* is intended as a companion to the latest edition of *The Bluebook*. From "ABA" to "Zoning and Planning Law Report," *Bieber's* follows *Bluebook* rules and provides examples for citing more than 2,000 law and law-related authorities.

The 4th edition of *Bieber's* is an essential purchase for all law libraries. It should sit next to *The Bluebook* on the shelf. And next to these two books should sit two other indispensable citation aids: *Bieber's Dictionary of Legal Abbreviations* (see ARBA 90, entry 538) and the *World Dictionary of Legal Abbreviations* (see ARBA 93, entry 562).—**James S. Heller**

Bibliography

545. Hale, Terrel D., comp. **United States Sanctions and South Africa: A Selected Legal Bibliography.** Westport, Conn., Greenwood Press, 1993. 362p. index. (Bibliographies and Indexes in Law and Political Science, no.18). $65.00. KF1975.A1H35. 016.3415'82. LC 92-8787. ISBN 0-313-28521-7.

For those seeking direction in finding material related to United States sanctions and South Africa, this reference work should be among the first resources consulted. It serves as a guide through the myriad mazes that exist around the topic. It is not designed to be comprehensive; Hale's desire is to enable research to begin as well as to help direct research beyond this collection. He has been quite successful in meeting these goals. In addition, the compilation is designed to enable researchers to understand the legal activities surrounding U.S. sanctions at the national, state, and local levels.

The bibliography includes references from the turn of the century up through 1993. It is divided into 5 sections: statutes (5 entries), federal government documents (329 entries), state and municipal authorities documents (20 entries), books and dissertations (577 entries), and articles (821 entries). There are no foreign titles. The work concludes with a most useful index that includes citations by author and subject. The subject divisions are comprehensive and extremely helpful. Highly recommended for larger public libraries and university collections with substantive sources on legal aspects of sanctions and South Africa.

—Michael A. Foley

546. **International Legal Books in Print 1993-94: An Annotated Bibliography.** 2d ed. New York, K. G. Saur/Reed Reference Publishing, 1992. 2v. $375.00/set. ISBN 1-85739-001-6.

The 2d edition of this work, a companion to *Bowker's Law Books & Serials in Print* (see ARBA 93, entry 565), contains in two volumes some 29,000 author/title entries of 15,800 database records. It lists non-United States titles published in the United Kingdom, Western Europe, and all countries of the British Commonwealth. Volume 1 provides an alphabetical list of main entries. Volume 2 consists of subjects— more than 2,000 subject headings under which only titles are arranged—and a publishers directory.

Main entries ideally include author, title, state of responsibility, edition, number of volumes, imprint, place of publication, size, series title, annotation, ISBN and ISSN, binding, price, and frequency. *See* references are numerous, but no explanation of the symbol that denotes them, a right arrow, is provided.

There are quite a few discrepancies. The foreword states that the indication of audience statement has been dropped, but an illustration of the main entry in the introduction retains the indication. The entry "Christian Jr., Ernest S. Value-added tax: orthodoxy and new thinking" is provided with a *see* title reference, but its title entry lists a different author. Other entries have the same problem.

For international publications in law, a few bibliographies are available, such as *Law Books in Print* (see ARBA 93, entry 570) and the serial publication, *Law Books Published* (Glanville, biannual). *International Legal Books in Print* has distinguished itself with its comprehensive and current coverage. It would be more useful if, in the next edition, it included English-language law books published elsewhere in the world. [R: Choice, Dec 93, p. 587]—**Tze-chung Li**

547. Jorgensen, Delores A., and Barbara B. Heisinger. **A Bibliography of Indian Law Periodical Articles Published 1980-1990.** 2d ed. Buffalo, N.Y., William S. Hein, 1992. 204p. index. $45.00. LC 92-070678. ISBN 0-89941-784-4.

For anyone interested in periodical articles on Native American legal issues published between January 1980 and December 1991 (more than 2,000 articles), this may be a useful resource. The emphasis is on United States publications; only a few Canadian journal titles are included. It would be useful to know which Canadian titles the authors examined; for that matter, a list of all the journals covered would have been helpful. Lacking such information, it is impossible to get an accurate sense of how comprehensive the work is. Presumably the authors developed the bibliography based on journals held by the University of South Dakota Law School library, because that is their institutional affiliation. However, there is no statement to that effect.

Entries appear under 219 subject headings such as aboriginal rights, land use, non-Indians, and religion. Within each topic the arrangement is alphabetical by title; there are no annotations. The only other access to the material is through a table of cases. The table lists all the articles that discuss a given case; for example, under the important *Lyng v. Northwest Indian Cemetery Protective Association*, 108#S.CT.1319 (1988), one finds 23 articles briefly listed, with volume number, journal title, page number, and year of publication.

Some type of tribal indexing would have enhanced the utility of the bibliography. It is unclear why there are topical entries for some groups, such as the Creek Nation, Hawaiians, and the Mashpee Indian Tribe, and not for others, such as Jicarilla or Chippewa. In instances where the tribe is the plaintiff in the case, one will find some additional tribes listed in the table of cases. However, when the tribe is a defendant, one must scan all the cases to determine if a tribe is involved in a case. Also, even when the tribe is the plaintiff, one might not find the information, as the cases are listed under their formal title.

Thus a case involving the Chippewa is listed under Lac Courte Orielles Band of Chippewa; there are no cross-references for tribes. There are some *see* and *see also* references. All in all, this is a book of limited interest to all but the most specialized American Indian collections.—**G. Edward Evans**

548. Kavass, Igor I. **Demise of the Soviet Union: A Bibliographic Survey of English Writings on the Soviet Legal Systems 1990-1991.** Buffalo, N.Y., William S. Hein, 1992. 288p. $115.00. KL3.K38. 016.34947. LC 92-24865. ISBN 0-89941-804-X.

The book contains two parts: a bibliography by author and main title, annotated and cross-referenced, with a checklist of authors; and a subject bibliography with a checklist of subject headings. Materials covered include books, parts of books, articles, papers, and other materials published mainly in 1990 and 1991. Annotations are adequate but vary in length from two lines to two pages. A few entries are not annotated, and some include contents reproduction. Occasionally, book reviews are noted. An asterisk precedes works by Soviet authors or authors who primarily represent the official Soviet view.

There are some 600 entries with broad coverage of law, politics, economics, trade, government systems, and general studies. The book's title does not quite match its contents; many entries do not relate to the demise of the Soviet Union. The two bibliographies are preceded by a brief account of the political developments in the Soviet Union and "Legal Research in the New Age." The latter serves as a guide to resources for legal research, including information services, databases, news services, periodicals, and broadcast services.

This is a well-compiled, useful bibliography. The price, for a book of some 300 pages, will be too expensive for many libraries, however. Kavass suggests that the book may be used as a sequel to his previous works, *Soviet Law in English* (see ARBA 89, entry 492) and *Gorbachev's Law* (see ARBA 92, entry 525).—**Tze-chung Li**

549. Miller, Oscar J., and Mortimer D. Schwartz, comps. **Recommended Publications for Legal Research 1970/71.** Littleton, Colo., Fred B. Rothman, 1993. 111p. $37.50pa. ISSN 0898-266X.

This series is an anachronism in a field whose practitioners desire the latest and most current editions of books on all law-related topics. The compilers expect law librarians to use it as a selection and collection development guide, but its coverage (and that of its companion volumes) is retrospective. Thus, most of the titles included will be out of print (unless enterprising publishers use it as a guide for planning reprints).

Titles are in alphabetical order by main entry under 48 broad subject categories. A subject index includes an additional 20 headings as cross-references. There is also a main entry index. Selections were announced for publication in 1970 and 1971. Each entry receives a grade that represents the compilers' recommendation of the title for basic, intermediate, or in-depth research collections. Each citation includes author, title, place of publication, publisher, date of publication, paging, series, Library of Congress card number, ISBN, and Library of Congress class number. The list includes 686 selections. Law librarians need a guide to "opening day" collections, but a selection built around the year of publication seems artificial.—**Berniece M. Owen**

550. Walker, Samuel. **The American Civil Liberties Union: An Annotated Bibliography.** Hamden, Conn., Garland, 1992. 304p. index. (Organizations and Interest Groups, v.3; Garland Reference Library of Social Science, v.743). $50.00. KF4741.W35. 016.34273'085. LC 91-46579. ISBN 0-8153-0047-6.

This scholarly bibliography has 1454 annotations and includes all manner of publications about the American Civil Liberties Union (ACLU) since its founding three-quarters of a century ago. A brief but general introduction provides a good historical outline and current status of the ACLU. Much of the remainder of the text is broken down into six major chapters: a chapter of general works on the ACLU, such as policies, periodicals, and handbooks; a historical breakdown of publications about the ACLU from 1914 to 1979; a summary of issues dealt with between 1980 and 1991; a chapter on matters such as constitutional law, the role of the ACLU, public opinion, and international perspectives; a chapter on ACLU leaders, with a focus on ACLU founder Roger Baldwin; and a final chapter on ACLU resources, such as ACLU offices and archival material. The text is followed by thorough name and subject indexes.

This is an excellent, easy-to-read, comprehensive reference guide for anyone interested in researching the background and history of the ACLU. It belongs in reference collections of all academic law libraries as well as public libraries that can afford the fairly expensive price of a book that makes effective use of little more than 300 pages. [R: Choice, June 93, p. 1612]—**James M. Murray**

Biography

551. Cushman, Clare, ed. **The Supreme Court Justices: Illustrated Biographies, 1789-1993.** Washington, D.C., Congressional Quarterly, 1993. 576p. illus. index. $39.95. KF8744.S86. 347.73'2634. LC 93-1446. ISBN 0-87187-723-6.

This is the first single-volume illustrated reference devoted exclusively to introductory biographies of all 106 current and past U.S. Supreme Court justices. The justices are presented chronologically by appointment in essays that underscore the equal power of justices on the court regardless of historical fame or circumstance. In fact, it is the purpose of the volume to introduce the general reader to all of the justices, those fallen into obscurity as well as those better known, and to give less well known biographical information about the most famous. Because of the limitations of a single-volume biography, the appendixes and index are vital to the book. A list of the justices by chief justice and associate justice is helpful, but bibliographies that provide general and in-depth sources for each make the book an important link to information on this institution.

The biographies are too short to live up to the claim of providing full pictures of the justices, the times in which they lived, and the lives they touched. The biographies are often telegraphic in the use of unrelated facts and are by no means critical evaluations of the individuals or the periods. This leaves the reader to sort out the greater historical context of the justices. While the structure of the book implies the importance of the individual and personality in shaping history, nowhere is this view pulled together in any coherent way.

The strengths of most of the biographies are the added historical sources, views of contemporaries, and lively anecdotes. It is a useful addition to Supreme Court sources and biographies but is not a good stand-alone volume. What recommends this book most is the inclusion of comprehensive historical views of justices rarely accessible to the general reader. [R: WLB, Dec 93, p. 83-123]—**Curtis D. Holmes**

Dictionaries and Encyclopedias

552. Dahl, Henry S., with Horacio M. Marull. **Dahl's Law Dictionary. Diccionario Juridico.** Buffalo, N.Y., William S. Hein, 1992. 1v. (various paging). $55.00. K52.S6D33. 340'.03. LC 92-25881. ISBN 0-89941-807-4.

International trade, travel, and migration furnish many opportunities for legal disputes between native speakers of different languages. Spanish is a language frequently needed by Americans because of the Spanish-speaking countries in this hemisphere and the many Spanish-speaking individuals in the United States. Bilingual legal dictionaries such as this are intended to be used only for legal words or phrases, or words frequently used in legal documents; they must be used by someone with some familiarity with both languages, or with access to general dictionaries and other sources for the unfamiliar language. Nonetheless, they can be very helpful in deciphering the essential points of a legal document.

This work contains two sections: Spanish to English and English to Spanish. Many definitions consist of simple synonyms, often only one word, but an unusual and useful feature of this dictionary is the presence of more extended, authoritative definitions. These consist of direct translations of relevant parts of codes, statutes, and case law. For these authoritative definitions, an exact source is given. Spanish-language definitions are drawn from Spanish, Latin American, and Puerto Rican law, as well as the Civil Code of Louisiana, which was once a Spanish territory. Tables of abbreviations and sources are included.

Most legal or general libraries would benefit by owning this work. Recommended.
—**Marit S. MacArthur**

553. Goulet, Cyrille. **Constitutional Glossary. Lexique Constitutionnel.** Ottawa, Department of the Secretary of State of Canada, 1993. 279p. (Terminology Bulletin, 220). $23.35pa. (U.S.). 342.71'003. ISBN 0-660-58852-8.

This is one of a series of word lists designed to assist in the translation of Canadian federal government documents from one official language to the other under the auspices of Translation Services in Government Services Canada. Produced in cooperation with the Canadian Department of Justice, this book focuses on the translation of about 1,000 terms in Canadian constitutional law (which is derived from the British legal tradition) into French (and from French into English).

The first section is a 105-page alphabetical list of English terms, phrases, and alternatives and their French equivalents. Other features include references to alternative terms, indications of recommended translations, and some comments or contextual notes. The second part is a similar list (159 pages) from French to English. Words range from run-of-the-mill terms, such as *claim* and *proposal* through topical issue terms, such as *Amerind, self-government,* and *Inuit rights.* There is also an 11-page bibliography and a list of other terminology bulletins.

This work would be of use to translators of Canadian legal and political terminology between English and French. It may also be of some use to others translating non-Canadian material in these subject areas.

—**Nigel Tappin**

554. **The Oxford Companion to the Supreme Court of the United States.** Kermit L. Hall and others, eds. New York, Oxford University Press, 1992. 1032p. illus. index. $45.00. KF8742.A35O93. 347.73'26'03. LC 92-3863. ISBN 0-19-505835-6.

Although it is difficult to think of this book as being a legal reference book or a law book, it is equally difficult to imagine a law library without a copy. Indeed, all kinds of libraries, including academic, school, and public, will find this remarkable reference indispensable. It covers everything about the Supreme Court (e.g., cases, trivia, procedure, policies, biographies) and does so admirably. This is the source to find out which president appointed the most justices, what the sculptures in front of the court represent, what the court has said about pornography, or what the Dred Scott case was all about. The writing is generally crisp and interesting and, as near as can be discerned, accurate. There are a good index to the book, a table of cases, and some useful appendixes, one of which includes the text of the Constitution of the United States.

One aspect of the book that is a little difficult to fathom is its alphabetical arrangement. One would expect a book such as this to be topically arranged, with all the articles about life in the court in one place and those about certain types of cases grouped in another. However, the scope of the book is encyclopedic, so logic dictates that its arrangement is encyclopedic as well. [R: Choice, Mar 93, p. 1243; LJ, 15 April 93, pp. 62-63; SLJ, Feb 93, p. 122; WLB, Feb 93, p. 106]—**Richard A. Leiter**

555. Redden, Kenneth R., and Gerry W. Beyer. **Modern Dictionary for the Legal Profession.** Buffalo, N.Y., William S. Hein, 1993. 802p. $55.00. KF156.R42. 349.73'03. LC 92-35678. ISBN 0-89941-829-5.

Redden is the respected author of many other legal publications. Beyer is on the law faculty at St. Mary's University School of Law in San Antonio, Texas. Together they have produced a fascinating and thoroughly eclectic dictionary. While many common legal terms appear, the dictionary features modern technical jargon, medical phrases, and slang words that legal professionals may confront. (The authors hasten to point out that this dictionary is a supplement to, not a replacement for, standard legal dictionaries.) Annual updates are planned.

The authors define more than 8,000 terms, including 250 computer concepts and some 200 Spanish-language legal words. Arrangement is alphabetical. Abbreviations appear at the beginning of each section of the alphabet with references to their spelled-out forms. A few numeric phrases (e.g., "$2 Broker," "102 Monitor") precede the alphabetical list. Definitions frequently conclude with cross-references to related terms. Redden and Beyer successfully introduce legal professionals to specialty terms in the dozens of professions and careers their clients may pursue. [R: Choice, Nov 93, p. 438]—**Berniece M. Owen**

556. Witt, Elder, ed. **The Supreme Court A to Z: A Ready Reference Encyclopedia.** Washington, D.C., Congressional Quarterly, 1993. 528p. illus. index. (CQ's Encyclopedia of American Government, v.3). $110.00. KF8742.A35S8. 347.73'26'03. LC 93-2979. ISBN 0-87187-777-5.

Researchers looking for a quick reminder of the pertinent facts regarding *Baker v. Carr*, 1962; students trying to figure out what the *Knight* ruling had to do with big business; and a sociology professor seeking to make the connection between child labor and the *Dagenhart* decision will all find welcome relief here. In its usual inimitable style and source-hunting without equal, Congressional Quarterly has presented libraries with guides that will hardly stay shelved for their surfeit of use. Although *The Supreme Court A to Z* covers all legal terminology, ideas, issues, politics, and people connected with the U.S. Supreme Court, it also offers insights into sociology, political science, cultural mores, literature, and more. Landmark cases on school prayer; hot-button topics such as abortion; and essays on civil rights, freedom of religion, and the U.S. legal system will have users queuing up for more. Tables on Supreme Court nominees, seating chart of the justices, the Constitution, and an index that also includes all decisions cited make this work indispensable.

While *The Oxford Companion to the Supreme Court of the United States*, edited by Kermit L. Hall and others (Oxford University Press, 1992), is easily the more scholarly work, Congressional Quarterly's is more readable and will probably be more widely used. (Those on tight budgets should take note.) If this work is used in conjunction with *Congressional Quarterly's Guide to the U.S. Supreme Court* (see ARBA 91, entry 746), librarians will find that matters relating to this grandest court in the land will be more than adequately covered. While some libraries may not need the detail of the *Guide*, it is hard to think of a library that can afford to be without the A to Z compendium! [R: Choice, Dec 93, p. 591; LJ, 1 Sept 93, p. 177; RBB, 1 Nov 93, p. 570; SLJ, Nov 93, p. 147]—**Mark Y. Herring**

Directories

557. Bosoni, Anthony J. **Legal Resource Directory: A Guide to Free or Inexpensive Assistance for Low Income Families, with Special Sections for Prisoners.** Jefferson, N.C., McFarland, 1992. 148p. index. $28.95pa. KF336.A4. 344.73'03258'025. LC 92-50301. ISBN 0-89950-737-9.

When low-income individuals are in need of legal assistance, either as a result of criminal prosecution or in civil matters such as child custody or marriage and divorce, there are many agencies that offer free or inexpensive help. This volume lists almost 1,800 such agencies, whose services range from information and referral to hands-on representation in court. The main listing is by state, subdivided by civil law offices, criminal law offices, and special programs for prisoners. A second section covers organizations that combat death penalty sentences, nationally and by state. A third section lists state chapters of an organization called Citizens United for the Rehabilitation of Errants (CURE), which seeks to influence the political process to improve prison conditions and the correctional process. There is also an index.

Other sources for similar information are more general legal directories, such as the *Law and Legal Information Directory* (see ARBA 92, entry 543), or the National Legal Aid & Defender Association's *Directory of Legal Aid and Defender Offices* (1989-). This last source is particularly useful, especially as it lists more organizations at the city level and also organizes agencies by specialized type of assistance needed (e.g., consumer law, migrant workers). Nonetheless, this is a useful directory for any library. The author is an inmate and conducted the research for this book from prison. [R: RBB, 1 Mar 93, p. 1265]

—**Marit S. MacArthur**

558. **Butterworths Law Directory 1993: A Directory of Solicitors and Barristers....** 9th ed. New Providence, N.J., Martindale-Hubbell/Reed Reference Publishing, 1993. 1768p. $80.00. ISBN 1-85739-071-7.

This new edition offers information on a large number of legal personnel in England, Wales, and (for the first time) Scotland. There are 13 separate sections organized in ways sometimes strange to American eyes but in accordance with the organization of British law. The fullest information about firms is given in a geographical arrangement, beginning with London and then covering other towns in England and Wales. Information given for each firm sometimes includes areas of legal specialization as well as address, telephone and fax numbers, names of personnel, and other offices. There are separate indexes to more than 47,000 solicitors and more than 7,700 barristers in private practice and commerce. Information given for each individual in the indexes includes name, address, telephone and fax numbers, and date qualified. There are also indexes to English and Welsh firms, to London firms, and to firms by London postal district. An alphabetical list of organizations mixes commercial businesses, courts, and governmental entities. There is a geographical list of chambers. An international section lists British firms with offices overseas and foreign firms with branches in England and Wales. The Scottish section seems rather an afterthought; it lists firms with their personnel, but this section has no indexes. Finally, there are lists of legal executives, circuit judges, recorders, registrars, coroners, and notaries public. Although it is probably too specialized for many libraries, this directory would be useful to law libraries and to any library whose clientele includes those with international business or legal activities.

—**Marit S. MacArthur**

559. **Directory of Courthouses & Abstract and Title Companies, 1993.** 3d ed. Virginia Webster, ed. Tulsa, Okla., Harbors Publishing; distr., Tulsa, Okla., PennWell Books, 1993. 346p. index. $75.00. ISSN 0896-7830.

This directory is a straightforward list of county offices and private companies that deal with questions of land and real estate ownership throughout the United States. The editor arranges the county courthouses and companies in two separate sections, each of which is in alphabetical order by state, then by county. Most entries include the names and titles of individuals who serve as county clerks, registrars of deeds, wills and probate clerks, and tax assessors. Following the directories are indexes to counties, boroughs, and parishes; company names; and personal names. (The editor does not explain why some company names appear in boldface type in the company index.) Finally, there is a cross-reference index from the name of the county seats to the name of the counties.

The directory appears to be comprehensive; the list includes more than 3,100 counties and 2,000-plus companies. Potential users would be in banking, law, minerals, petroleum, real estate, and related industries.—**Berniece M. Owen**

560. Eis, Arlene L., comp. and ed. **Directory of Law-Related CD-ROMS 1993.** Teaneck, N.J., Infosources, 1992. 98p. index. $44.00pa. ISBN 0-939486-26-1. ISSN 1065-0334.

This is a comprehensive directory of CD-ROM titles accessible by a variety of lists and indexes. Similar to its cousins from the same publisher, *Legal Looseleafs in Print* (1993) and *Legal Newsletters in Print* (1993), it is very important both for the reference desk and for the acquisitions librarian, clerk, or office. The subject index is very helpful and fairly well laid out; one can quickly determine what has been published on CD-ROM in a particular subject area. There are also lists of titles by publisher and software. This may be helpful to the user who may prefer a certain product type. As with other titles from Infosources, once an entry is located, all of the information necessary to order the title is listed; including telephone and fax numbers, as well as pricing information and a brief description of the product.

This title suffers from two problems. First, the book became dated on the day it was printed—numerous titles are being released every day. This problem will remedy itself with annual publication and revision, something at which Infosources is very good. Second, this book contains an alarming number of advertisements. While it would be expected for the company to announce its own titles on the cover or in the end pages, it is unexpected to find advertisements for *Dialog on Disk*, Matthew Bender CD-ROM titles, and others inside the front cover and scattered throughout the first 20 pages. (One would think that the advertising revenue earned should be enough to lower the rather hefty price for a 100-page book.)

—**Richard A. Leiter**

561. **Martindale-Hubbell Bar Register of Preeminent Lawyers 1993.** 77th ed. New Providence, N.J., Martindale-Hubbell/Reed Reference Publishing, 1993. 2486p. $139.95. ISBN 1-56160-023-7.

This work "covers over 8,000 of today's most respected attorneys and law firms in the United States and Canada" (foreword). It is divided into 28 law disciplines and lists only those attorneys who have achieved the highest legal ability rating and who have demonstrated "adherence to professional standards of conduct, ethics, reliability, and diligence" (foreword). The list comprises those attorneys cited in the *Martindale-Hubbell Law Directory* (see ARBA 91, entry 581) who have received the highest ratings based on information provided in a questionnaire distributed to members of the legal profession, including members of the judiciary.

The *Register* may be a useful place to start one's search for an attorney, but it should not serve as the sole source of information for at least three reasons. First, the listed attorneys constitute approximately 1 percent of practicing attorneys in the United States and Canada. To limit one's search to this register seriously limits one's choices. Second, the majority of references focus on the larger cities in the United

States. (The two areas of exception here are the listings under "civil trial practice" and "general practice.") Third, most people never need the so-called best available legal advice; good, competent advice will serve most of them adequately.—**Michael A. Foley**

562. Naifeh, Steven, and Gregory White Smith. **The Best Lawyers in America 1993-1994.** Aiken, S.C., Woodward/White, 1993. 1017p. index. $110.00. ISSN 1067-4756.

If someone needs an attorney, this reference work is perhaps one of the first sources to consult. It is incredibly easy to use. The names of some 11,000 attorneys appear here, organized by state and listed alphabetically within each state by category (i.e., legal specialty), city, and attorney's last name. A comprehensive index of all attorneys listed concludes the work. If there is a need for a specific legal specialty, one merely need consult the category listing for the state in question.

There are, unfortunately, several difficulties with this otherwise useful directory. First, most of the "best" attorneys listed practice in large metropolitan areas. For example, more than 95 percent of the "best" attorneys in Illinois are found in Chicago. If you need recommendations in most other areas of Illinois, you are out of luck. This holds true throughout the state listings, contrary to the claim that every effort has been made to include more lawyers from outside the large commercial centers in each state. Second, recommendations from attorneys for inclusion, the voting process for inclusion, and the criteria for selection remain quite subjective. The editors acknowledge this shortcoming and note that some attorneys' names may appear more on the basis of "visibility or popularity over sheer ability." Third, many lawyers hesitate to cast negative votes for their colleagues, for a variety of reasons. It behooves anyone who consults this directory to read the brief introduction. In general, this work would begin a search for an attorney, but the search should not end here.—**Michael A. Foley**

563. Stelter, Thomas, and Jeffrey S. Stelter, eds. **Lawyers' and Creditors' Service Directory.** 1993 ed. New York, John Wiley, 1993. 2v. maps. $165.00pa./set. ISBN 0-471-59376-1. ISSN 1060-4480.

This is an annual directory for debt collectors. It provides the names, addresses, and telephone numbers of more than 30,000 agents or agencies that compile information about delinquent debts throughout the United States. The editors arrange the data in alphabetical order by state, subdivided by county. Under each county appears a list of 10 types of information providers: courthouses, sheriffs, private process servers, private investigators, repossessors, skip tracers, independent court reports, chambers of commerce, collection agencies, and litigation attorneys. A key to the types appears at the top of each county page.

At the beginning of each state section, the editors provide a map of the state with counties and major cities identified. Following is a list of state agencies that may have debtor information. Federal court names, addresses, and telephone numbers appear as well. Next is a list of every city and town within the state, with a code reference to the county in which the place is located.

The 1993 edition of this reference appears in two volumes. The organization and layout of the directory is exceptionally clear and easy to use. Instructions on how to use the guide introduce both volumes.—**Berniece M. Owen**

564. **Want's Federal-State Court Directory.** 1993 ed. Robert S. Want, ed. Washington, D.C., WANT Publishing, 1992. 218p. index. (Your Nation's Court Series). $35.00pa. ISBN 0-942008-60-X. ISSN 0742-1095.

The primary purpose of this directory is to provide convenient access to American federal and state courts. The federal section is more detailed, with listings for the Supreme Court, special courts, appellate courts, and district courts. For each type of court there is a note on jurisdiction. The current address, telephone number, and judges and other major court officials are listed for each court throughout the federal judicial system. There is an alphabetical index of all federal court judges. The state court section provides a page for each state that features a diagram depicting the basic structure of the state court systems. There are notes on the jurisdictions of the various courts and the names, addresses, and telephone numbers for important judicial personnel in each state.

In addition to these major components is much related information, including directories of major Canadian courts, of chief judges of selected countries, of the U.S. Justice Department, and of American bar associations. Also provided are an explanation of how to request information under the Freedom of

Information Act and a lengthy appendix that covers federal court statistics. Additionally, there are a list of all members of the U.S. Supreme Court, 1789-1992; a guide to how cases are litigated in the American judicial system; and a glossary of legal terms. Many of these numerous secondary segments may be as useful in general reference collections as the primary directory of courts will be.—**Henry E. York**

565. **World Law School Directory.** 1993 ed. Buffalo, N.Y., William S. Hein, 1993. 333p. $97.50. K100.A4W67. 940'.071'1. LC 93-13414. ISBN 0-89941-839-2.

Those interested in foreign law schools will find that information about them is not very readily obtained. This directory, although it has its limitations, will be of assistance. It is an updated version of an earlier directory published in 1977. For this edition, the editors sent questionnaires to schools in the earlier directory. Not all schools returned the questionnaire; those that did not are still included, with a note that the information is not updated.

Countries are listed alphabetically, with schools alphabetically within each country. One hundred and forty-one countries are listed, including the United States, although other directories would give more information about U.S. schools. Countries formerly part of the Soviet Union are also included, but very few answered the 1991 questionnaire. Information given is rather basic but should be sufficient to identify schools of interest and enable one to write for more information. Under each school are listed name, address, telephone and fax numbers, degrees offered, whether foreign students are admitted, primary languages spoken, and names of the admission officer, dean, and law librarian. There is a table of abbreviations for degrees, but there are no indexes.

Another source for similar information is the *Global Directory of Schools of Law Outside of the United States* (Graduate Group, 1992). It sometimes gives fuller information for schools but is very inconsistent, apparently printing whatever a school chose to send in response to the questionnaire. The *World Law School Directory* is a limited but carefully done work that should be useful to those seeking basic information on this topic.—**Marit S. MacArthur**

Handbooks and Yearbooks

566. Baker, Brian L., and Patrick J. Petit, eds. **Encyclopedia of Legal Information Sources: A Bibliographic Guide to Approximately 29,000 Citations for Publications, Organizations, and Other Sources of Information....** 2d ed. Detroit, Gale, 1993. 1083p. $165.00. KF1.E53. 016.34973. LC 92-18907. ISBN 0-8103-7439-0.

The editors direct this comprehensive guide to "lawyers and law-related professionals," but researchers in any field who need bibliographical and directory information on legal resources will find this encyclopedia an extremely useful tool. Under 480 topical headings, from abbreviations to zoning and planning, Baker and Petit list 29,000 citations to books, journals, online databases, organizations, and audiovisual materials. Along with an extensive outline of contents, *see* and *see also* references punctuate the topic list, so users do not have to be familiar with legal terminology to find what they want.

To assure timeliness, the editors exclude material published before 1980, although they make exceptions for classic titles. Each heading is subdivided by type of source (e.g., textbooks, directories, handbooks, associations, audiovisuals) and includes full publication information, frequency (if appropriate) and publisher or producer address. Prices are not included. Citations range from official court reports to bar association newsletters to self-help lay publications to state administrative codes.

The layout is in Gale's familiar two-column style, with wide margins, bold headings, and nicely delineated entries. The single-page user's guide is a model of its kind.—**Berniece M. Owen**

567. Eis, Arlene L., comp. and ed. **Legal Looseleafs in Print 1993.** Teaneck, N.J., Infosources, 1993. 457p. index. $90.00pa. ISBN 0-939486-28-8. ISSN 0275-4088.

This standard reference work has earned its reputation for reliability and usefulness on the basis of clear organization and accuracy. As with many of the best things in life, this one succeeds because it is so simple. At the same time, it is comprehensive.

Virtually every legal looseleaf published is listed in this book and is accessible in a variety of ways. The main portion of the book is the title section. Titles are accurately listed in clear boldface type. Each entry is packed with useful information. In addition to number of volumes and cost, the work provides cost of updates, a comparison of the costs of past updates, ISSN and LC classification numbers, alternative formats, and whether the set contains any information in another format. In addition, there is a good subject index, which does not simply refer the user to the page on which the title appears; it lists the titles and their publishers. Another helpful feature of this reference tool is the directory of publishers. This is a useful place to go to find information about publishers, such as telephone numbers and addresses. There is also a publisher index. The book contains a list of cessations and deletions that includes all publications that were listed in the last edition of the book but that have since been discontinued. Because looseleafs figure so prominently in the day-to-day research work of attorneys, this work should be found in every library's reference collection.—**Richard A. Leiter**

568. Eis, Arlene L., comp. and ed. **Legal Newsletters in Print 1993.** Teaneck, N.J., Infosources, 1993. 378p. index. $85.00pa. ISBN 0-939486-27-X. ISSN 8755-416X.

This book is detailed and useful, and it does its job with a clarity and simplicity rarely seen in the world of legal reference materials. Similar to its companion publication *Legal Looseleafs in Print* (Infosources, 1993), this work covers its subject matter in surprising detail. Its usefulness is embodied in its lack of pretension: It simply contains so much information that it begs users to come to it with any kind of question. It will virtually always have the answer.

The body of the book is the title list. Each entry contains information about cost, publisher, editor, a brief summary of the content, OCLC number, LCCN (Library of Congress Catalog-Card Number), and ISSN. The entry also lists whether the newsletter is available online and, if it is, what services carry it. There are also data about format, size, and availability of back issues.

The book also contains a number of important features in addition to the title list. There are lists of deletions from previous editions, publishers, databases, and newsletters available online. Two very important sections of the book are the lists of newsletters registered with the copyright clearance center and of newsletters that accept advertising. Extra finding tools are provided in the subject index; the thesaurus of subject headings makes this index that much more useful.—**Richard A. Leiter**

569. Leiter, Richard A., ed. **National Survey of State Laws.** Detroit, Gale, 1993. 427p. $49.95. KF386.N38. 349.73. LC 92-13519. ISBN 0-8103-8406-X.

Many legal topics, such as gun control, arouse intense public controversy on a continuing basis, and others, such as child custody, are of widespread interest because they govern the course of individual lives. This book intends to summarize and compare the laws of individual states on such topics. Forty-two of these are included here, under eight general areas. General categories are business and consumer laws, criminal laws, education laws, employment laws, family laws, general civil laws, real estate laws, and tax laws. The selection of specific topics appears somewhat arbitrary; this is attributed in part to the fact that not all topics are covered by specific statutes in many states. Under each topic is a relatively short general discussion of the issue and summary of patterns of legislation. State law provisions are laid out in tabular form, making it easy to compare points from state to state. References are given to each state's relevant statute or code section. An appendix gives abbreviations and full names of each state code.

Compilations such as this should never, of course, be considered absolutely authoritative as to a particular state's law, because they give summaries rather than specifics and may be out-of-date for a particular law. Nonetheless, this is a useful work with convenient information on many topics of interest to many people. Because it gives citations to state statutes and codes, it also could serve as a starting point for more thorough research. Serious researchers might also want to look at *Selected State Enactments* (National Conference of State Legislatures, annual), which indexes, but does not quote or summarize, provisions of state statutes.—**Marit S. MacArthur**

570. Leonard, Arthur S., ed. **Sexuality and the Law: An Encyclopedia of Major Legal Cases.** Hamden, Conn., Garland, 1993. 709p. index. (American Law and Society, v.3; Garland Reference Library of Social Science, v.1272). $95.00. KF9325.A7L46. 346.7301'3. LC 92-45133. ISBN 0-8240-3421-X.

Leonard, a leading scholar of sexuality and the law and a professor at New York Law School, has written and compiled explanations of 119 significant legal cases and decisions in the United States, at both state and national levels, up to 1992. The cases are grouped by theme: reproduction, sexual conduct, speech and association, the family, discrimination in both civilian and military sectors, educational institutions, immigration and naturalization, and estates and trusts. The great majority of cases relate to homosexuality and lesbian and gay people, and most come after the great Stonewall rebellion of 1969 in New York City (which marked the beginning of the modern lesbian and gay liberation movement). Notable exceptions are earlier cases on sterilization and the 1973 landmark abortion case, *Roe v. Wade*.

Most of the entries range from 2 to 10 pages, with greater length given to the more significant cases, such as *Roe v. Wade*; the Supreme Court decision that approved sodomy laws (*Bowers v. Hardwick*, 1986); the efforts of Perry Watkins, a "model gay soldier," to remain in the army; and the rights of a gay organization at a Catholic university (Georgetown). Leonard aims the essays at the intelligent layperson, but they can get fairly technical. To help understand the context, an introduction provides legal, historical, and sociological background.

The index provides access to specific topics, people, and organizations associated with cases. Unfortunately, many of the most important headings have no subheadings for particular aspects or specific cases. Large numbers of page numbers are simply listed without differentiation (one sure sign of an amateur index). Why, for example, do "advertising" and "custody of children" have subheadings when "American Civil Liberties Union," "homosexual conduct," "Lambda Legal Defense and Education Fund," and "Supreme Court" do not? This last heading has more than 100 undifferentiated entries! Nevertheless, this is a valuable compilation, and any library that serves people interested in sexuality and law should obtain it. [R: Choice, Oct 93, p. 268; LJ, 1 June 93, p. 106; RBB, 1 Oct 93, p. 387]—**James D. Anderson**

571. Lieberman, Jethro K. **The Evolving Constitution: How the Supreme Court Has Ruled on Issues from Abortion to Zoning.** New York, Random House, 1992. 751p. $26.00. KF4548.L54. 342.73'02. LC 92-16590. ISBN 0-679-40530-5.

This is an encyclopedia not of the Constitution per se, but of constitutional issues that have been ruled on by the Supreme Court. Most of the entries are one to four paragraphs long, although a few run for more than a page. The focus throughout is on how the Court has interpreted the Constitution as it applies to each issue. There are numerous cross-references to other entries, as well as references to an alphabetical table of cases (which indicates how the justices voted and who wrote the majority opinion). The author provides a brief overview of the Constitution and its interpretation and an essay on how the Court hears and decides cases. Supplementary features include a topical look at the Court's 1991-1992 term, the text of the Constitution, a keyword concordance to the Constitution, a "time chart" of the Court's justices (showing changes in membership since 1789), and brief biographical notes on the justices. This source will be readily understood by general readers yet could be a handy reference for any level of user. [R: JAL, July 93, p. 200; RBB, 15 April 93, p. 1534]—**Jack Ray**

572. Millman, Linda Josephson. **Legal Issues and Older Adults.** Santa Barbara, Calif., ABC-Clio, 1992. 273p. index. (Choices and Challenges: An Older Adult Reference Series). $45.00. KF390.A4M55. 346.7301'3. LC 92-31475. ISBN 0-87436-594-5.

Older adults are targets for all kinds of fraudulent schemes and thus need good legal services. A book of this size cannot answer all questions nor provide the services and advice needed to recover from (or even block) the scams and their perpetrators. Nevertheless, it goes a long way toward providing help on both counts. The objective of the book is "to identify some common legal issues and provide some basic background to seniors and their advocates." Part 1 is a narrative description of these legal issues and starts with a description of legal services: what they are, who provides them, where to find them, and how to evaluate and make the best use of them. It then deals briefly with seven issues: living wills to preserve personal autonomy; income security through employment, pensions, investments, and the like; health care; housing; consumerism; family law; and estate planning. The section ends with a lengthy bibliography of current literature on the various issues treated. Part 2 has a directory of organizations, emphasizing those concerned with the issues treated in part 1. It also contains an annotated bibliography of reference materials related to the issues. A glossary of terms and a detailed index complete the work.

This book will be of great value to older adults as well as their advisers. It achieves its objective admirably and makes a valuable contribution to the legal domain. It is recommended for any library, whether it collects the series or not, and it will be particularly useful in public libraries that serve populations of older adults and in academic or special libraries with emphases in this area. [R: LJ, 1 Mar 93, pp. 68-70; RBB, June 93, pp. 1898-1900]—**Edward P. Miller**

573. Ntumy, Michael A., ed. **South Pacific Islands Legal Systems.** Honolulu, University of Hawaii Press, 1993. 660p. $100.00. KVC117.S68. 349.95. LC 92-41464. ISBN 0-8248-1438-X.

This useful reference work describes the legal systems of 23 South Pacific islands. It is divided into three models of legal systems: the parliamentary model (e.g., the Cook Islands, Fiji, Nauru, Papua New Guinea), the presidential model (e.g., American Samoa, the Federated States of Micronesia, Guam), and the French Territories (New Caledonia, Wallis and Futuna, and French Polynesia). The delineation of these systems makes clear that legal thought in these islands reflects two fundamental principles: the rule of law, whereby constitutions are made the supreme law of the land, and common law, whereby the legal systems reflect the unique personalities and conditions of the island nations. The value of such a work cannot be gainsaid. The 13 authors, using substantive guidance from the editorial board overseeing the project, have provided the first comprehensive and coherent presentation of these legal systems.

Each chapter (one on each island nation) is written within a schema that provides a means by which to compare the various systems. For example, 20 chapters divide the legal system into 23 subsections that include the constitutional system, criminal law, torts, family law, and labor law. Rather than footnotes or endnotes, each chapter concludes with a rather comprehensive research guide that directs the reader to additional sources.

Anyone in need of information regarding the government and legal systems of the South and Central Pacific islands should turn here for their first source. The material is well organized and clearly written. Highly recommended.—**Michael A. Foley**

574. Perle, E. Gabriel, and John Taylor Williams. **The Publishing Law Handbook.** 2d ed. Englewood Cliffs, N.J., Prentice Hall Law & Business, 1992. 2v. index. $180.00 looseleaf w/binder/set. KF2750.P43. 343.73'0998. LC 92-36806. ISBN 0-13-035601-8.

Aimed at publishers of trade books and magazines and at journalists and writers, this edition of *The Publishing Law Handbook* has been extensively revised and enlarged from one volume to two. The purpose of the work is to introduce its audience to publishing and copyright law and to provide some advanced-level advice on legal cases that interpret and provide precedence in the publishing world. Numerous examples, advice, checklists, and case law provide insight into such topics as creating a contract, the right of privacy, defamation, access of the press, copyright, and trademark law.

Three new chapters have been added to this edition: magazine publishing, electronic publishing, and trademark law. Other chapters have been revised as new case law has affected the text. The chapter on electronic publishing is brief and descriptive but provides little help for the many ramifications of ownership of electronic data and imaging technology—major problems now being faced in the industry. The entire publication is bound in two oversize and difficult-to-handle looseleaf volumes for updating between editions.

For both those in business and those starting publishing operations, the volume is a good companion to *The Huenefeld Guide to Book Publishing* (Mills & Sanderson, 1992). *Huenefeld* provides a more compact and readable advice manual, whereas the *Handbook* provides a better legal perspective. For those who wish to keep abreast of the latest legal ramifications of publishing, the purchase of the 2d edition is a must, even though it may seem expensive. Because one court case without benefit of the insight provided here will cost many times the price of the volume, those who publish should have access to this volume. Those in private and professional publishing will have to take much of the advice with a grain of salt, because in a number of policies, the procedures differ from those in these segments of the market. However, the volumes do provide a good place to start seeking advice.—**David V. Loertscher**

575. Purcell, Catherine. **Guide to Law Schools in Canada.** Don Mills, Ont., ECW Press, 1992. 266p. maps. $14.95pa. 340'.071'171. ISBN 1-55022-160-4.

This well-executed, comparative directory and guide presents profiles of the 12 common and 4 civil law degree programs in Canada. It also gives a large amount of background and advice on law school and admissions. The author is a career counselor at Queens University.

Introductory sections provide information on a variety of topics, including misconceptions about law school and practice, recent trends in legal education, what to look for in a degree program, and LSAT information. Concluding sections deal with unique characteristics of particular schools, comparative statistics, and admissions addresses. The main body of the work consists of profiles of all 16 schools. Entries are based on interviews with the dean, the admissions committee chair, and at least eight students, plus a questionnaire submitted to the admissions chair and standardized statistics released by the schools. Each entry includes address and telephone number, material required for various categories of applicant (e.g., regular, mature, Native), deadlines, fees, tuition (1992-1993), admissions statistics, and a class profile. Longer sections deal with admissions, school characteristics, strengths, weaknesses, the community where the school is located, and (anonymous) student comments.

This is an excellent, low-cost handbook for those considering entering a law school in Canada. Strongly recommended as an acquisition to general Canadian libraries and to other collections where client demand warrants.—**Nigel Tappin**

576. Samuels, Jeffrey M., ed. **Patent, Trademark, and Copyright Laws.** Washington, D.C., BNA Books, 1993. 546p. index. $60.00pa. LC 84-644547. ISBN 0-87179-793-3. ISSN 0741-1219.

This volume conveniently brings together intellectual property laws from U.S. Code (USC) Titles 15, 17, and 35 and relevant sections of other statutes. It includes all statutory changes through June 1, 1991. The work is divided into six parts: U.S. Code, Title 35, Patents; U.S. Code, Title 15, chapter 22, Trademarks; U.S. Code, Title 15, chapter 63, Technology Innovation; U.S. Code, Title 17, Copyrights; other statutes; and an index. The index and the detailed table of contents that is provided for each part provide quick access to topics of specific interest. A finding list by USC section is also provided.
—**Dean H. Keller**

577. Smith, Robert Ellis, with James S. Sulanowski. **Compilation of State and Federal Privacy Laws.** Providence, R.I., Privacy Journal, 1992. 136p. $29.00pa. KF1262.A3.176. 342'.73'085. LC 76-364384. ISBN 0-930072-08-1.

This collection was last revised in 1988 and will be updated by annual supplements. The general subject of privacy is divided into 21 topics that include various types of personal records (e.g., arrest, bank, employment), credit reporting, computer crime, privileged communications, telephone solicitation, and wiretaps. Within each topic, short summaries of and citations to laws are arranged state-by-state, with federal law (if any) at the end. Appendixes feature the full texts of selected state and federal statutes and abstracts of various Canadian laws. Although continual updating will be necessary to maintain currency, and there is no information about court cases or agency regulations, this compilation is handy for quick comparisons of statutory laws on privacy.—**Jack Ray**

578. **United Nations Juridical Yearbook 1985.** New York, United Nations, 1992. 239p. $49.00pa. ISBN 92-1-133415-2. S/N E.92.V.1.

For those interested in understanding the legal elements of the United Nations (UN) and related intergovernmental organizations, this reference work is indispensable. The legislative texts, treaty provisions, and decisions of international and national tribunals cover 1984. The text is divided into four parts and eight chapters. The two chapters in part 1 cover legislative texts and treaty provisions for 1984 and 1985. Part 2 contains four chapters that provide a general review of the legal activities of the UN and related intergovernmental organizations, treaties concerning international law, decisions of administrative tribunals, and selected legal opinions of the secretariats of the United Nations and related intergovernmental organizations. Chapter 7 in part 3 is devoted to decisions and advisory opinions of international tribunals; chapter 8 notes decisions of national tribunals. Part 4 offers a comprehensive legal bibliography that is current through 1985.

The organization of the materials is clear and coherent; the bibliography is quite extensive. As this work constitutes the official annual legal report of the UN and related intergovernmental organizations, it is essential for collections that contain substantive materials on such institutions.—**Michael A. Foley**

579. Want, Robert S., ed. **Alternative Dispute Resolution Sourcebook.** 1993-94 ed. Washington, D.C., WANT Publishing, 1993. 158p. (Your Nation's Courts Series). $21.95pa. ISBN 0-942008-65-0.

WANT Publishing, best known until now for its court directories, has added a directory designed to keep readers out of court. This sourcebook covers the burgeoning field of alternative dispute resolution (ADR) in its myriad forms: arbitration, private trials, and others. As the introduction explains, the growth of ADR has been fueled by its quick, informal, and unbureaucratic nature, especially in comparison to the traditional judicial system. The network of ADR services that has come into being recently, however, is still little known to the general public and, until this directory appeared, had not been covered in such comprehensive fashion.

The originality of this sourcebook lies not in its content, as virtually all the information originates elsewhere, but in its compilation of material previously found in disparate sources. This trait turns out to be the sourcebook's greatest strength and weakness. As a directory, this work excels at bringing together agencies in various states that, despite different names and structures, perform virtually the same function. Researchers can easily find Better Business Bureaus, landlord/tenant dispute resolution services, and even attorney/client dispute resolution services. The various appendixes are equally valuable; they provide lists of publications, model forms, and reprints of various guidelines. Unfortunately, some of the reprinted material also shows the sourcebook's greatest flaw: Some of the material incorporated is dated. Some of the American Bar Association material, for example, is from 1990. This does not make the sourcebook a less valuable reference tool, but it does necessitate some caution in its use. Researchers should be advised to always check the original source of the information for any updating that may have taken place since publication.

The *Alternative Dispute Resolution Sourcebook* takes badly needed information and adds value to that information through compilation. It would be a valuable purchase for public libraries of any size that need to help clients find alternatives to the judicial system.—**David Bickford**

Indexes

580. Blaustein, Albert P., ed. **The Bicentennial Concordance: Indexes to the Constitution of the United States of America.** Littleton, Colo., Fred B. Rothman, 1992. 202p. $45.00. KF4528.5.B53. 342.73'02'02638. LC 92-9674. ISBN 0-8377-0361-1.

Perhaps because it is a relatively brief document, the United States Constitution did not have an index or table of contents. Over the years lawmakers and constitutional scholars have felt the need for such assistance, and various agencies have provided different kinds of indexes. This volume reproduces three of the best of these and adds a new computer-generated KWIC (keyword-in-context) index, a table of contents, and the full text of the Constitution. This juxtaposition of several different types of indexes provides an interesting example of the strengths and weaknesses of the several types. Two topical indexes, one by the commercial publisher West, the other provided by official sources in the *Oregon Revised Statutes*, list concepts under topics provided by the compilers, as opposed to words actually in the text of the Constitution. This can be important, as the Constitution clearly contains concepts such as *copyright* without using the actual words. The analytical index provided here, which was prepared for the U.S. House of Representatives, includes in one alphabet both assigned topics and the actual words in the Constitution's text together with the actual text of the clause in which the word or concept may be found. The KWIC index, published for the first time in this volume, provides lines containing the actual word in the Constitution in boldface type, surrounded by the words immediately next to it on either side in the original text. All three examples make it very clear that the usefulness of an index is related not only to the words or topics indexed but also, in the case of topics with multiple occurrences, the amount of information given to help distinguish which occurrence is the one desired.

Because it seems unlikely that any general library would lack a copy of the Constitution with an index, this work does not appear to be an essential purchase. But because no two indexes provide equally good access to all words and concepts, this work could prove useful to a library whose patrons include serious legal scholars.—**Marit S. MacArthur**

581. **Canada Tax Cases: Index and Citator: Consolidated from 1972 to December 1992.** John P. Renouf, ed. Scarborough, Ont., Carswell, 1993. 1v. (various paging). $140.00 looseleaf w/binder. ISBN 0-88820-148-6.

First issued as a result of the major tax reforms of 1972, this consolidated index to the *Canada Tax Cases* (CTC) (Carswell, annual) has remained consistent in its approach. Updated by looseleaf filings annually, it provides access to cases judicially noted as well as reported cases. Statutory references are detailed and easy to use. Of particular value is the correlator section. It is organized according to CTC page numbers and offers a cross-reference to cases appearing in *Dominion Tax Cases* (CCH Canadian, annual). The topical index retains the original 1972 format and is easy to use. Finally, the table of abbreviations remains reasonably consistent with standard abbreviations found in *Bieber's Dictionary of Legal Abbreviations* (see ARBA 90, entry 538) and those used by major law publishers.

—Mary Hemmings

582. **Index to Canadian Legal Literature 1992. Index a la Documentation Juridique au Canada.** library ed. Enid Lesser and Guy Cloutier, eds. Scarborough, Ont., Carswell, 1993. 823p. $450.00/yr. ISBN 0-459-54042-LE. ISSN 0832-9257.

In cooperation with Carswell, the Canadian Association of Law Libraries (CALL) has established a network of Canadian law libraries that contribute records to this index, and representatives from the association make up the editorial advisory board. The index is intended to provide comprehensive access to all secondary literature of interest to the Canadian legal community. It covers both periodical index and Canadian legal literature. Law in theory and practice, as well as related areas of criminology, taxation, and the like, are covered.

The index is bilingual. French and English topics and articles are mixed alphabetically in each section. Index entries are in the language of the original article. Sections include instructions for use, a list of periodicals indexed, subject and author indexes, tables of cases and statutes, and a book review index. Each item may appear under multiple subject headings. Subject headings are from the Library of Congress and the National Library of Canada. Every entry is a full case citation or a complete bibliographical reference.

—Berniece M. Owen

583. Teasdale, Karen H. **CLE Research Guide. Volume 2: Index to Continuing Legal Education 1991 Publications of the Law Society of Upper Canada.** Toronto, Law Society of Upper Canada, 1992. 1v. (various paging). $15.00 looseleaf w/binder. 016.34. ISBN 0-88759-969-9.

The Law Society of Upper Canada provides continuing education programs for practicing lawyers. Course materials for these programs can be purchased from the society. In 1985 the society began to offer the *CLE Research Guide*, supplying detailed access to individual presentations or articles within each course. Author, title, and subject headings provide access to the individual articles within the course titles, which are listed alphabetically at the back of the binder. Recent course titles include "Basic Securities Law," "Family Law in a Volatile Economy," and "Seniors as a Growing Client Base." The 1988-1990 supplement concluded the first volume. This second volume will be supplemented annually. This publication is of particular interest to legal practitioners in Canada.—**Mary Hemmings**

Quotation Books

584. **The Oxford Dictionary of American Legal Quotations.** By Fred R. Shapiro. New York, Oxford University Press, 1993. 582p. index. $49.95. KF159.S53. 349.73. LC 92-37829. ISBN 0-19-505859-3.

Shapiro selected quotations by Americans about law and quotations by foreigners about U.S. law for this book. His sources include popular figures, such as Will Rogers and Bob Dylan, as well as legal luminaries. Within the 3,500-plus entries, Oliver Wendell Holmes, Jr., takes honors as the most quoted, with 255 items. In general Shapiro excludes quotations about legislative and policy issues, and he does not include those having to do with the execution or investigation of crimes. The quotations range from brief phrases to long paragraphs, depending on the importance of the individual or topic.

The dictionary is alphabetical by topic. Under each topic the quotations are in chronological order and assigned sequential numbers. Cross-references to related topics appear under each heading. There is an especially useful keyword index to significant words in each passage, as well as an index by author. The full text of the United States Constitution and its amendments appears in an appendix.

Shapiro is a librarian and lecturer at the Yale Law School. In compiling the dictionary he made extensive use of LEXIS, Mead Data Central's fulltext online legal database, but he made every effort to trace quotations to their earliest known source. He includes careful citations for every quotation, and in the introductory pages he gives full instructions on how to use the book. [R: Choice, Oct 93, p. 273; LJ, 15 June 93, p. 64; RBB, 1 Oct 93, p. 569]—**Berniece M. Owen**

CRIMINOLOGY

585. Atkins, Stephen E. **Terrorism: A Reference Handbook.** Santa Barbara, Calif., ABC-Clio, 1992. 199p. index. (Contemporary World Issues). $39.50. HV6431.A87. 909.82. LC 92-28530. ISBN 0-87436-670-4.

This excellent reference handbook highlights five areas: terrorist events, people, organizations, documents, and important reference books and monographs. The author is a librarian who has been researching this topic for several years. The book is selective and current. The 164 bibliographical sources range from 1972 to 1992; however, most of the sources are from 1986 to the present. An informative introduction has 87 footnotes for 27 pages.

Atkins may, at times, overstate his case. For example, he states that terrorists try to transform the international order. It may be more correct to state that terrorists attempt to change national political issues. Atkins also claims that the biographical chapter gives an insight into the psychology of the individual terrorist. This is only partially true at best. Finally, the February 26, 1993, bombing of the World Trade Center in New York City at least partially refutes Atkins's prediction that terrorism is likely to be less intensive in the 1990s. Still, this excellent book is highly recommended for all academic and larger public libraries. [R: Choice, May 93, p. 1435; LJ, 1 April 93, p. 90; SLJ, May 93, p. 136; WLB, Mar 93, p. 115]—**Karen Y. Stabler**

586. DiCanio, Margaret. **The Encyclopedia of Violence: Origins, Attitudes, Consequences.** New York, Facts on File, 1993. 404p. index. $45.00. HM291.D484. 303.6'03. LC 92-39721. ISBN 0-8160-2332-8.

This is a fairly optimistic work. It "attempts to relate the various kinds of everyday violence, to reconceive them as a single, if complex, threat to the quality of everyday life and to life itself." It also "seeks to find the social and psychological origins ... of violent behavior, the cultural and social attitudes that sustain it ... and the consequences it has." Yet, as an encyclopedia, it provides "snapshots of the places where violence enters everyday life ... as well as a taxonomy of some of the many varieties of violence." It is the latter function that succeeds. There is no reconception of violence; the "snapshots" are useful, but there is no overarching theme.

There is much in this work that fascinates, yet because it was written by one person, biases become apparent. Rape takes up approximately 11 pages, but gangs only 4 1/2; there is no mention of religion or morality as potential influences; homelessness is in part blamed on Ronald Reagan, but no mention is made of rent control; and approximately 34 pages are devoted to women, 32 to Blacks, 7 to Hispanic Americans, and 3 to Jews. There are certain theoretical assumptions made, such as that pedophiles "act out their disorders" or that job loss "causes" low self-esteem, that are offered as if they are universally accepted constructs. Powerful arguments are presented for gun control, while the arguments against it are summarily rejected.

With the caveat that the topic is too huge for any single author or work, this is still a worthwhile endeavor, filled with a wide range of topics. In it one can learn about Vietnamese gangs and their wars with other Asian gangs, or get a good description of the Yochelson-Samenow theory of criminal thinking. The three appendixes, on "Organized Crime: Roots of America's Drug Traffic," the limitations on behavioral science in studying violence, and resources, are well written and almost worth the cost of the book by themselves.

Although its coverage is idiosyncratic, this work should be of wide interest to students, city officials, police departments, journalists, and citizens who have concerns about the epidemic of violence in our country. [R: LJ, 1 Nov 93, p. 72; RBB, 15 Dec 93, p. 776]—**Bertram H. Rothschild**

587. Dobkowski, Michael N., and Isidor Wallimann, eds. **Genocide in Our Time: An Annotated Bibliography with Analytical Introductions.** Ann Arbor, Mich., Pierian Press, 1992. 183p. index. (Resources on Contemporary Issues). $40.00pa. ISBN 0-87650-280-X.

The term "timely" may be somewhat shopworn, but it applies well to the volume under review. As the twentieth century—"the most violent and murderous in history" (p. 117)—approaches its inglorious end, the monumental tragedy of genocide has been neither fully comprehended nor resolved. A vast and ever-expanding literature continues to try to make sense of the Holocaust—the quintessential contemporary case of genocide—even while "ethnic cleansing" is taking place in Bosnia.

The excellent volume under review includes a series of eight essays on various aspects of genocide that accompany annotated bibliographies on these topics. Several of the essays and bibliographies focus on the Holocaust, including the issue of its status as a unique event and the fate of some of its survivors. Two essays contend with other incidences of genocide: the Armenian case and the Ukrainian famine. The remaining essays address more general issues, such as the nature of ethnocide, the relationship between genocide and modern war, and the possibilities of anticipating and preventing genocides. The book includes a chronology of genocides and author and title indexes.

This volume does not attempt to be comprehensive, and the annotated bibliographies are not exhaustive. There are other bibliographical guides on genocide in general and the Holocaust in particular (e.g., *The Holocaust: An Annotated Bibliography and Resource Guide* [see ARBA 86, entry 520]). But the essays in *Genocide in Our Time* are quite uniformly superior, and some of the most recent literature is covered. This reviewer found the volume immediately useful in connection with projects of his own (i.e., a chapter on state crime and a review essay on the Barbie trial). *Genocide in Our Time* can be recommended for acquisition by libraries serving many different populations, from the general public to graduate students. [R: Choice, May 93, p. 1438; WLB, June 93, pp. 124-46]]—**David O. Friedrichs**

588. Hallett, Michael A., and Dennis J. Palumbo. **U.S. Criminal Justice Interest Groups: Institutional Profiles.** Westport, Conn., Greenwood Press, 1993. 130p. index. $59.95. HV9950.H35. 364'.06'073. LC 92-45070. ISBN 0-313-28452-0.

The authors of this reference work, professors of criminal justice administration, offer as a rationale for their book the fact that criminal justice is a $71 billion industry in the United States, but hitherto no one has compiled a listing of the interest groups that attempt to influence policy in this monumental enterprise. Indeed, they note that crime and justice-focused interest groups have been surprisingly neglected in the literature. They adopt a fairly broad conception of *interest group* to include organizations operating both inside and outside the system, and groups concerned with raising consciousness about crime and justice issues as well as lobbying associations. Accordingly, the final list includes entities as diverse as Mothers Against Drunk Driving (MADD), the American Society of Criminology, and the Fraternal Order of Police.

After identifying a fairly large number of groups and associations meeting their criteria, the authors sent out a questionnaire soliciting information on such matters as organizational goals, policy positions, strategies, effectiveness, and staffing and membership attributes. Although they apparently succeeded in obtaining responses from 49 organizations and associations, they are somewhat unclear about the overall response rate for their survey.

The body of this volume is composed of an alphabetical list of identified criminal justice interest groups, with basic information on organizational history and development, specific organizational purposes, key policy activities or concerns, and publications provided for each listed entity. An appendix includes the results of the survey and a listing, topically organized, of regular publications of the various organizations. A selective bibliography and an index are also included.

This volume does not pretend to be a comprehensive listing of all organizations and associations with some interest in criminal justice policy. But the authors have made a credible case that during a period of intensified concern over crime-related public policy, their work offers a useful point of departure for identifying such organizations. Public libraries and those specifically serving criminal justice researchers could usefully add this reference work to their collections. [R: RBB, 1 Nov 93, pp. 570-71]
—**David O. Friedrichs**

589. Mickolus, Edward F. **Terrorism, 1988-1991: A Chronology of Events and a Selectively Annotated Bibliography.** Westport, Conn., Greenwood Press, 1993. 916p. (Bibliographies and Indexes in Military Studies, no.6). $125.00. HV6431.M498. 909.82'8. LC 92-46525. ISBN 0-313-28970-0.

If anyone believes that the number of terrorist acts has declined in the recent past, they only need look at Mickolus's update to his three previous books monitoring worldwide terrorism. Mickolus abstracts approximately 3,000 media accounts of terrorist acts in this latest edition, and he updates numerous 1960-1987 incidents that were abstracted in earlier editions of the chronology. He includes an extensive topical bibliography covering regional approaches to terrorism, nuclear threats, hijacking and hostage-taking, narcotics trafficking, state-supported terrorism, media coverage, counterterrorism activities, and other issues.

Mickolus relies on the definition of terrorism used in previous editions to determine what events are included in the text, but unfortunately he does not provide that definition here. The lack of an index is a more serious defect, for the text is arranged chronologically, with no access points other than date. Notwithstanding these limitations, *Terrorism, 1988-1991* will be an essential volume for those who research, study, or teach in this area. [R: Choice, Oct 93, p. 270]—**James S. Heller**

590. Palmegiano, E. M., comp. **Crime in Victorian Britain: An Annotated Bibliography from Nineteenth-Century British Magazines.** Westport, Conn., Greenwood Press, 1993. 165p. index. (Bibliographies and Indexes in World History, no.31). $59.95. Z5703.5.G7P35. 364.941'09034. LC 92-44640. ISBN 0-313-26523-2.

In recent years there has been some increase of interest in both the history of and the media coverage of crime and criminal justice. The present volume has been compiled by a professor of history at Saint Peter's College. He has systematically reviewed the contents of some 45 popular and more specialized periodicals published in Great Britain in the nineteenth century. In the introduction he summarizes his impressions of the coverage of crime and criminal justice during this era. He includes many interesting observations, although no comparative data is provided. The topics covered, decade by decade, are rates of crime, types of crime, causes of crime, law and enforcement, prosecution of criminals, sentences for crimes, classes of criminals, and crimes in the kingdom. Although sensational murders, unsurprisingly, were often highlighted by these periodicals, Palmegiano also notes considerable attention to other classes of offenses, including white-collar crime. The typeface is exceptionally small.

Most of this volume contains a checklist of 1,614 articles on crime and criminal justice in the journals reviewed, principally between the 1820s and the 1890s. Palmegiano usually summarizes the contents of the articles in a single sentence fragment.

This book should be useful to students of nineteenth-century media representations of crime and criminal justice. Libraries serving criminologists and criminal justicians are the most obvious candidates for acquiring it. [R: Choice, Sept 93, pp. 86-88]—**David O. Friedrichs**

HUMAN RIGHTS

591. **Amnesty International: The 1993 Report on Human Rights around the World.** Alameda, Calif., Hunter House, 1993. 354p. illus. maps. $26.95; $16.95pa. ISBN 0-89793-141-6; 0-89793-140-8pa. ISSN 1070-0781.

Annual reviews of human rights are produced by the U.S. government (*Country Reports on Human Rights Practices*, annual), Freedom House (*Freedom in the World* [see ARBA 92, entry 561]), and Amnesty International. Amnesty International's *Report on Human Rights around the World* has been published since 1961. The 1993 edition follows the same format used in previous years. Most of the book is a country-by-country report of human rights abuses and Amnesty International's response to them. Also included are chapters on the death penalty, refugees, and Amnesty International's cooperation with international organizations. Appendixes give factual information on Amnesty International's activities and human rights treaties and their signatories.

Amnesty International is widely recognized as an impartial observer of human rights. Unlike the other books mentioned above, its report does not attempt to promote a political agenda. Its combination of reliable information and affordable price make it a wise choice for any library.—**Cathy Seitz Whitaker**

592. Hardy, Gayle J. **American Women Civil Rights Activists: Biobibliographies of 68 Leaders, 1825-1992.** Jefferson, N.C., McFarland, 1993. 479p. index. $45.00. JC599.U5H273. 323'.092'273. LC 92-56649. ISBN 0-89950-773-5.

This work provides extensive biographical and bibliographical information on 68 women who represent a variety of ethnic backgrounds, careers, and different periods of time from the early 1800s through 1992. They have in common a profound commitment to human and civil rights. This work is unusual not only in the number and diversity of the women (for whom more than who's-who type of information is given) but also in the points of accessibility to this information. For each woman the biographical section includes a fairly detailed chronology of her life and background information on her family and other influences. The bibliographical section includes full-length and shorter works by and about the person and a section on the locations of primary source materials. The appendixes make it easy to access information on birthplaces, dates of birth, ethnicity, careers, religion, locations of civil rights activity, schools attended, and even tribal membership for the group as a whole. The comprehensive index and the table of contents also aid in quick access. The table of contents, which lists the women in alphabetical order, gives birth and death dates and a descriptive phrase such as the one for Grace Hutchins: "advocate for political rights; author; labor researcher; and economist." Some readers will be disappointed that certain women are not included; there was no attempt to include all women, and there were no strictly defined criteria for inclusion other than that the women be prominent in civil rights activities in the United States.

This work should prove especially useful in identifying women representing particular groups. Highly recommended for all libraries with women's collections.—**Lucille Whalen**

593. **Human Rights, Refugees, Migrants & Development: Directory of NGOs in OECD Countries. Droits de l'Homme, Refugies, Migrants et Developpement.** Washington, D.C., OECD Publications and Information Center, 1993. 409p. $70.00pa. ISBN 92-64-03869-8.

The Organization for Economic Cooperation and Development (OECD), a group of 24 countries working for world economic growth and development, has published a number of directories to aid the member countries in pursuing their goals. This one is a comprehensive collection of data on the work of nongovernmental organizations (NGOs) in the four interrelated fields of human rights, refugees, migrants, and development. It was carried out as a collaborative effort with the United Nations High Commissioner for Refugees, Human Rights Information and Documentation Systems International, and the International Organisation for Migration, using a detailed questionnaire sent to member countries to obtain information. Arranged by country and then by title of the organization, each entry includes a general description and the aims, publications, activities, and target groups for each NGO. Although introductory material and indexes are in both French and English, the NGO profiles are in either language, with the majority in English. Almost a third of the volume is devoted to five separate indexes on development education, development activities, human rights assistance, aid to refugees, and aid to immigrants. It is possible, for example, to find which NGOs in Canada or the United States aid refugees from Cambodia.

Although many NGOs did not respond to the questionnaire—fortunately, a list of these, with addresses, is provided—the information given is substantial and often difficult to find. For this reason, this book is highly recommended for all libraries whose clientele includes those working in the areas covered.—**Lucille Whalen**

594. Humana, Charles, comp. **World Human Rights Guide.** 3d ed. New York, Oxford University Press, 1992. 393p. maps. $35.00; $12.95pa. JC571.H788. 323'.02'.02. LC 92-9758. ISBN 0-19-507674-5; 0-19-507926-4pa.

The monitoring of human rights issues has proved to be an effective device for applying pressure on governments that continue to abuse human rights. Although several groups attempt to measure human rights throughout the world, this work is unique in that it gives information on 40 specific rights mentioned in the major U.N. human rights documents. The guide covers countries of at least one million population, but a few countries were omitted because they were in a state of turmoil, or borders were in the process of being redrawn at the time for the cutoff of gathering information—November 1991. For each country there is a general human rights rating; basic facts about the country, such as population and form of government; a boxed paragraph titled "Factors Affecting Human Rights," followed by a list of 40 freedom items with a checklist for a yes/no; and a comment. Each of the items, or rights, is given the same number throughout all countries, making it quite easy to follow one right, such as freedom of the press, through all countries. The methodology for compiling the data is fully explained in the introductory material and should be read in order to understand the ratings. Inclusion of the U.N. documents used and maps that show each country's degree of compliance with human rights is a useful added feature. The volume is valuable for anyone interested in human rights issues and should be available in academic and large public libraries. [R: RBB, 15 Feb 93, p. 1077]—**Lucille Whalen**

595. Murray, Paul T. **The Civil Rights Movement: References and Resources.** New York, G. K. Hall, 1993. 265p. index. (Reference Publications on American Social Movements). $40.00. Z1361.N39M93. 016.3231'196073. LC 92-34223. ISBN 0-8161-1837-X.

This bibliography focuses primarily on the civil rights movement between 1955 and 1968. While these dates may appear arbitrary, they represent two specific symbolic acts: the arrest of Rosa Parks in Montgomery, Alabama, which represents a new beginning in the struggle for civil rights, and the death of Martin Luther King, Jr., which represents "the symbolic end of one era and the beginning of another in the ongoing struggle for human rights and racial equality" (p. 2). Murray begins the bibliography with an incredibly usable review of the literature covering that designated period. This nine-page essay provides not only a sense of the scope of the bibliography but also some useful recommendations on where one might begin research in several different approaches to understanding that period. The bibliography is divided into nine separate but coherent sections. It is annotated, so that it is easy to determine if a particular work is relevant to one's research, and it contains works that most people can find in libraries. For example, unpublished manuscripts, dissertations, and the myriad law review articles are not cited. Also, as Murray notes, because there are extensive bibliographies that cover other aspects of the period (e.g., bibliographies on Martin Luther King, Jr.), it is not necessary to duplicate their efforts. There are very useful author and subject indexes. Not only will people be able to use this work constructively, but they might also find themselves simply reading through the annotations, which alone can awaken additional interests. Highly recommended.—**Michael A. Foley**

VICTIMS OF ABUSE

596. Nordquist, Joan, comp. **Violence against Women: A Bibliography.** Santa Cruz, Calif., Reference and Research Services, 1992. 68p. (Contemporary Social Issues: A Bibliographic Series, no.26). $15.00pa. ISBN 0-937855-50-2.

The awareness of violence against women has grown substantially in the past 15 years. This bibliography provides quick access to literature dated primarily from 1986 to 1991. (Nordquist does include some titles dating back to the 1970s based on their usefulness and availability.) Entries number approximately 600 and include books, articles in journals and books, government documents, and pamphlets. The major emphasis of this bibliography is on the social and feminist aspects of the literature instead of on the psychological aspects. The variety of topics includes the effects of violence in the media and pornography, femicide, race issues, women against violence, rape, sexual harassment, and the effects of domestic violence on children.

This work is divided into six major sections. Sections 1 through 5 contain the sources, which are divided by format and arranged alphabetically by author or title (when a corporate author is used). Some sections are further divided into subsections. Section 6 is devoted to a limited list of resources in four categories: statistics, bibliographies, directories, and organizations (some organizations are listed without telephone numbers).

The inclusion of items from academic to popular works broadens the usefulness of this bibliography. It is further enhanced by items from activist organizations and alternative, small, and feminist presses. The lack of annotations and an index are drawbacks, but for a modest cost this thin paperback will fill a need for high schools with an interest in women's issues and public and academic libraries, especially those without electronic resources. [R: RBB, 15 Feb 93, p. 1077]—**Jennie S. Johnson**

11 Library and Information Science and Publishing and Bookselling

LIBRARY AND INFORMATION SCIENCE

General Works

Acronyms and Abbreviations

597. Tayyeb, Rashid, and Krishna Chandna, comps. **Dictionary of Acronyms and Abbreviations: Library, Information & Computer Terms.** Ottawa, Canadian Library Association, 1993. 251p. $39.95pa. 020'.148. ISBN 0-88802-266-2.

Although not so designated, this volume is the 3d edition of a work first published in 1979 (see ARBA 81, entry 133), with a 2d edition in 1985 (see ARBA 87, entry 581). It includes approximately 10,000 entries. As a Canadian publication, the work also includes as many French abbreviations as possible. For each abbreviation or acronym the word equivalents are given, at times with a few additional notes to better identify the item, most often location (e.g., U.S., U.K.). The entries are arranged two columns to a page in a relatively small, but clear, typeface. Although no running heads are used, scanning entries is quite speedy. Where an abbreviation has more than one meaning, the items are listed one after another and numbered. Thus, for example, there are 10 meanings for CLA, from California Library Association to Copyright Licensing Agency. The compilers have included many general institutions if they are actively involved in library programs (e.g., IBM), and for this edition they have expanded coverage of terms related to computer science and technology (PCMCIA [Personal Computer Memory Card International Association] is still missing). The volume does not provide definitions of the terms. For CIP, only the words "Cataloging-in-Publication" are given.

For computer science subjects one can get more information from a guide such as Alan Freedman's *Computer Glossary* (Amacom, 1993), which does furnish useful annotations. Still, this dictionary will prove a helpful reference source in large libraries and information centers.—**Richard D. Johnson**

Catalogs and Collections

598. Fehrenbach, R. J., ed. **Private Libraries in Renaissance England: A Collection and Catalogue of Tudor and Early Stuart Book-Lists. Volume 1: PLRE 1-4.** Binghamton, N.Y., Medieval & Renaissance Texts & Studies, State University of New York, 1992. 321p. index. (Medieval & Renaissance Texts & Studies, v.87). $25.00. Z997.2.G7P75. 017'.1'0942. LC 91-18418. ISBN 0-86698-099-7.

599. Fehrenbach, R. J., ed. **Private Libraries in Renaissance England: A Collection and Catalogue of Tudor and Early Stuart Book-Lists. Volume 2: PLRE 5-66.** Binghamton, N.Y., Medieval & Renaissance Texts & Studies, State University of New York, 1993. 282p. index. (Medieval & Renaissance Texts & Studies, v.105). $25.00. Z997.2.G7P75. 017'.1'0942. LC 91-18418. ISBN 0-86698-151-9.

A study of books held in private libraries tells us something about the reading habits, interests, and concerns of the day. The purpose of *Private Libraries in Renaissance England* is to reconstruct lists of private library holdings from extant books and manuscripts (e.g., catalogs, inventories) from the Tudor and early Stuart periods and to merge all the lists into a computer database containing lists already published. The lists will be made available in printed form, with one or two volumes being produced each year. (Plans are under way to release the database on CD-ROM.)

Volume 1 covers Bishop Richard Cox, tutor to the young Edward VI; Sir Edward Stanhope, vicar-general of the Archbishop of Canterbury; Sir Roger Townshend, from a prominent East Anglian family; and Sir Edward Dering, a baronet from Kent. The names in volume 2 were taken from inventories of property compiled by the vice-chancellor of Oxford between 1506 and 1653 (the inventories were completed when property passed to the university). These inventories are expected to extend through volume 6, after which lists of books that belonged to people of lesser education and means will follow.

Each book list begins with a biographical essay about the owner of the books. The essays vary in length but are extremely well written and give many references to further sources. Each item in the book list is annotated to include, as far as can be identified, the title, the author and other contributors to the work, STC status (whether or not it is recorded in *Short-title Catalogue of Books Printed in England, Scotland, and Ireland and of English Books Printed Abroad, 1475-1640* [see ARBA 92, entry 61] or related works), publishing information, language, cost or appraised value, and location. Beginning with volume 2, appendixes are provided for the number of book lists edited; the names of and other information about the owners of book lists entered in the database, types of manuscripts and their dates, the Renaissance locations of the book lists, and the professions and dates of the owners. Each volume also has indexes to authors and works; editors, compilers, and illustrators; translators; stationers, including publishers, printers, and booksellers; and places and dates of publication.

These works are superb pieces of scholarship. The material is exceptionally well organized and laid out. The introduction in volume 1 explains the whole project clearly. The lists provide a fascinating glimpse into the reading interests of the period. This series is a must for any library with an interest in social or literary history, or that supports research into early libraries and reading habits.—**Linda Main**

Dictionaries and Encyclopedias

600. Ayala, Marta Stiefel, Reynaldo Ayala, and Jesus Lau. **Technical Dictionary of Library and Information Science: English/Spanish, Spanish/English. Diccionario Tecnico de Bibliotecologia y Ciencias de la Informacion.** Hamden, Conn., Garland, 1993. 662p. (Garland Reference Library of Social Science, v.815). $100.00. Z1006.T39. 020'.3. LC 92-43348. ISBN 0-8153-0655-5.

This technical dictionary is the first bilingual, comprehensive English/Spanish dictionary of library science terms. Even the preface and introduction are in both languages. The dictionary contains more than 6,400 entries. The work is divided into three sections: English entries with Spanish glosses (i.e., word equivalents) followed by English definitions; Spanish entries with English glosses followed by Spanish definitions; and "Useful Phrases/*Frases Utiles*" in eight general categories, such as signage, schedules, and facilities. The dictionary is easy to read: Entries are generously spaced, and the glosses are printed in italics. An impressive list of sources consulted is also included.

The authors state that this work is meant to describe how terms are used, not to prescribe their usage. Translating technical terms can often be tricky, but they have done a fine job. The entry for "laptop computer" serves as an example. The reader is referred to the entry under "portable computer/*computadora portatil*"—nothing about lap or top (rightfully so), but just the essence of the term. Current library and publishing computer-related terms are included, making the book perfect for the 1990s.

The *see also* notes prove useful as well. The only reservation is with the *see* notes, which sometimes seem arbitrary. For example, the entry "book publishing" provides the gloss "*publicacion de libros*," but "book preservation" provides only "*see* Preservation of Books," and then under that term provides the glosses "*conservacion de libros; preservacion de libros.*" It would have seemed just as easy to provide those terms under "book preservation" and avoid the *see* note. Two suggestions for future editions are to include more assistive/adaptive technology terminology and to add a category in the "Useful Phrases/ *Frases Utiles*" that deals specifically with library computer assistance.

The preface quotes Samuel Johnson: "Any dictionary is better than none." This dictionary seems to be far better than even the authors expected. They have done an outstanding job in producing this extremely useful and much-needed dictionary. Highly recommended for both academic and public libraries, as well as library professionals' personal libraries, in Spanish-speaking communities. [R: Choice, Sept 93, pp. 90-92; SLMQ, Summer 93, p. 264]—**Edward Erazo**

601. **Encyclopedia of Library and Information Science. Volume 44, Supplement 9.** Allen Kent, ed. New York, Marcel Dekker, 1989. 409p. illus. $115.00. LC 68-31232. ISBN 0-8247-2044-X.

602. **Encyclopedia of Library and Information Science. Volume 45, Supplement 10.** Allen Kent, ed. New York, Marcel Dekker, 1990. 420p. illus. $115.00. LC 68-31232. ISBN 0-8247-2045-8.

603. **Encyclopedia of Library and Information Science. Volume 46: Indexes to Volumes 1-45.** Allen Kent, ed. New York, Marcel Dekker, 1991. 428p. $115.00. LC 68-31232. ISBN 0-8247-2046-6.

604. **Encyclopedia of Library and Information Science. Volume 47: Indexes to Volumes 1-45 (Continued from Volume 46).** Allen Kent, ed. New York, Marcel Dekker, 1991. 1v. (various paging). $115.00. LC 68-31232. ISBN 0-8247-2047-4.

605. **Encyclopedia of Library and Information Science. Volume 48, Supplement 11.** Allen Kent, ed. New York, Marcel Dekker, 1991. 380p. illus. $115.00. LC 68-31232. ISBN 0-8247-2048-2.

606. **Encyclopedia of Library and Information Science. Volume 49, Supplement 12.** Allen Kent, ed. New York, Marcel Dekker, 1992. 361p. illus. $115.00. LC 68-31232. ISBN 0-8247-2049-0.

607. **Encyclopedia of Library and Information Science. Volume 50, Supplement 13.** Allen Kent, ed. New York, Marcel Dekker, 1992. 389p. illus. $115.00. LC 68-31232. ISBN 0-8247-2277-9.

608. **Encyclopedia of Library and Information Science. Volume 51, Supplement 14.** Allen Kent, ed. New York, Marcel Dekker, 1993. 407p. illus. $115.00. LC 68-31232. ISBN 0-8247-2051-2.

Encyclopedia of Library and Information Science (ELIS) was published in a set of 35 volumes, several volumes a year, from 1968 to 1983. Supplementary volumes have appeared annually. The set covers a diverse range of topics in the fields of library science, computers, information retrieval, and information technology. Articles have been written by scholars and are aimed at experienced and advanced readers in the field. The diversity is evident by sampling just one volume. For example, topics in volume 50 range from type font design to information management in the United Kingdom, intelligent systems, publisher billing problems, computers in the humanities, and CD-ROM databases for serials cataloging. Delving into individual articles, "Hypermedia" in the same volume was written by three British scholars but covers the international development of this technology surprisingly well. Other entries, such as Richard Krzys's coverage of the theory of encyclopedics, are brief commentaries on a single idea. In contrast, the article in volume 49 covering the automatic index of Chinese text challenges even the most sophisticated readers.

Such a diversity of coverage does fall within the scope of the publication, but individual articles tend to get lost and cannot be accessed unless some type of special in-depth indexing is done in the library owning the volumes. Volumes 46 and 47 are comprehensive indexes to the earlier volumes, but volumes 48-51 have yet to be indexed. The whole set is a good candidate for electronic access.

As a labor of love, this monumental project deserves an accolade. Recommended for research collections covering libraries, computer science, and information science. [R: JAL, Nov 93, p. 337]

—**David V. Loertscher**

609. **World Encyclopedia of Library and Information Services.** 3d ed. Robert Wedgeworth, ed. Chicago, American Library Association, 1993. 905p. illus. index. $135.00. Z1006.W67. 020'.3. LC 93-25159. ISBN 0-8389-0609-5.

This volume carries on the tradition begun with the first two editions (see ARBA 87, entry 577 and ARBA 81, entry 131), but with a minor change in title: "ALA" no longer precedes the words "World Encyclopedia." With the aim of providing current descriptive and statistical information about libraries, the encyclopedia presents an overview of the library world: library history, developments in the field, major institutions, distinguished personalities, and professional concepts and principles. This edition follows the same format as earlier editions, with alphabetically arranged articles that cover principal themes: the library and society, including history, geographical areas, and biographies; the library as an institution (emphasizing North America); theory and practice of librarianship; education and research; and international library organizations. (Unlike the second edition, the book does not include a thematic table of contents.)

There has been a 70 percent revision from the 2d edition, with many new contributors among the 437 authors. (One disquieting note: The list of authors incorrectly describes several as deceased or retired.) Articles range from 1,000 to more than 30,000 words. Page length is almost the same as in the 2d edition. An added feature is separate treatment for 5 major world libraries (Bibliotheque Nationale, British Library, Harvard University Library, Library of Congress, and New York Public Library), plus a 16-page section with color photographs of them. Additionally, black-and-white illustrations are used liberally throughout the volume. Many articles include bibliographies, and there is a lengthy index. The volume is well bound, a very clear typeface is used, and pages are handsomely arranged. ALA is to be commended on the overall appearance of this work.

Statistical information on most countries dates from the late 1980s and 1990. The new edition was being edited just as the Soviet Union was transformed into the Commonwealth of Independent States; thus, the editor decided to reprint the USSR article from the 2d edition, albeit noting that information had been received from Estonia, Lithuania, and Ukraine for separate articles. The United States article concentrates on the national library scene; the encyclopedia gives little data on individual states in the union, a job handled earlier by the now-defunct *ALA Yearbook of Library and Information Services* (see ARBA 91, entry 610). The next edition may wish to remedy this omission. Similarly, Canadian provinces may warrant separate attention.

This 3d edition fills the stated purposes of the encyclopedia well and is particularly strong for ready-reference information on libraries in other nations. It deserves a prominent place on reference shelves in larger public and academic libraries. [R: JAL, Nov 93, pp. 337-38]—**Richard D. Johnson**

Directories

610. **American Library Directory 1993-94.** 46th ed. New Providence, N.J., R. R. Bowker/Reed Reference Publishing, 1993. 2v. index. $225.00/set. LC 23-3581. ISBN 0-8352-3282-4. ISSN 0065-910X.

The *American Library Directory* is now revised annually in an attempt to maintain currency. Past reviews (see ARBA 93, entry 623) have detailed the contents of this directory. New to this edition is a section on library services and supplies. The subjects range from architecture and interior design to videocassette dealers, publishers, and wholesalers. In addition to the paid entries, there are a number of advertisements. Although there are typographical errors and the information is not as current as one would like, *American Library Directory* remains a necessary purchase for academic and public libraries.

—**Anna Grace Patterson**

611. **Washington Area Library Directory.** Compiled and edited by a Committee of Volunteers. David Shumaker, chair. Washington, D.C., District of Columbia Library Association; distr., Souderton, Pa., Data-Matic Systems, 1992. 180p. index. $90.00; price not reported pa. ISBN 0-9635577-1-8; 0-9635577-0-Xpa.

For years, librarians at all levels have had to rely upon the 11th edition of *Library and Reference Facilities in the Area of the District of Columbia* (Knowledge Industry Publications, 1983) to help them navigate through the complex maze of government libraries. With the publication of this long-awaited directory, however, their task will be much easier. Every aspect of this work is an improvement upon the previous one. Coverage has been almost doubled to include 862 government, public, law, foundation, embassy, and hospital libraries in the Washington, D.C., metropolitan area. While the majority of libraries cited are within the District of Columbia, many Maryland libraries in Montgomery, Prince George's, Howard, and Anne Arundel counties and Virginia libraries in Fairfax, Arlington, Loudoun, and Prince William counties are also included.

The information describing each library's services has also expanded significantly. In addition to listing an address, telephone number, reference librarian, and hours, each numbered library entry provides information concerning collection size, online database services, CD-ROM products, reference services information, interlibrary loan policies and procedures, fees (if any), and subject specialties. Useful personnel and subject indexes conclude the list.

The excellent information and the access to it in this directory make it an indispensable resource for any librarian who frequently requires information not only from U.S. government libraries but also from Washington, D.C.- and metropolitan area-based national associations', societies', and agencies' libraries. Acquisition librarians in all types of libraries should purchase this directory for their core reference collections. [R: LJ, 15 June 93, p. 107]—**Kathleen W. Craver**

612. **World Guide to Libraries.** 11th ed. New Providence, N.J., K. G. Saur/Reed Reference Publishing, 1993. 1179p. index. (Handbook of International Documentation and Information, v.8). $350.00. ISBN 3-598-20720-4.

Listing more than 40,000 libraries from 167 countries, this comprehensive guide is the only source available that provides international coverage of library materials and interlibrary loan programs. Included are public, academic, government, medical, and law libraries. Entries are arranged by continent and country, and then by type and city within the country. The library name is given in both English and the native language (beginning with this edition, both are also listed in the index), and typically each entry has address, telephone and fax numbers, founding date, and holdings. An entry may also note main departments and special collections, data network and interlibrary loan programs, professional organization memberships, and cross-references to the index. Completely revised and expanded, this edition is a necessity for reference collections and for all businesspeople who deal with libraries on an international basis.

—**Jo Anne H. Ricca**

Handbooks and Yearbooks

613. **ALA Survey of Librarian Salaries 1993.** By Mary Jo Lynch, Margaret Myers, and Jeniece Guy. Chicago, American Library Association, 1993. 57p. $44.00pa. ISBN 0-8389-7685-9. ISSN 0747-7201.

Each year the American Library Association (ALA) conducts a survey of salaries paid full-time professional librarians working in public, college, and university libraries. This report describes the methods and results of the 1993 survey of 946 randomly selected libraries. Also included are an annotated bibliography of other salary surveys, a copy of "ALA Policies Relating to Salary Issues," a bibliography on compensation and employee benefits, and a copy of the survey questionnaire. Salaries are given for six positions common in these libraries. Reported are salary ranges, means, and quartiles for each combination of position, geographical region, and library type. Salaries of beginning librarians are reported separately so as not to distort the results. Changes in salaries by year since 1988 are also described.

While not attempting to draw conclusions from the information, the authors offer clear suggestions to the nonstatistician for interpreting aggregate data to answer individual needs. They describe the problems they encountered in conducting the survey and explain how anomalies in the responses were resolved. The reader is left with a good understanding of both the strengths and weaknesses of the data. This document would be a useful resource for library managers in administering a salary plan or for librarians seeking employment.—**William S. Proudfoot**

614. **Annual Review of Information Science and Technology. Volume 27: 1992.** Martha E. Williams, ed. Medford, N.J., Learned Information, 1992. 429p. index. $89.00. LC 66-25096. ISBN 0-938734-66-0. ISSN 0066-4200.

Underlying the contributions to the *Annual Review of Information Science and Technology* (ARIST) is a basic framework that consists of planning information systems and services, basic techniques and technologies, applications, and the profession. In this volume, eight chapters represent these four sections. The first section has two chapters: Ruth A. Palmquist's "The Impact of Information Technology on the Individual" reviews "research or forecasts about how computer-based technologies affect the environments in which an individual functions," and Ronald D. Doctor's "Social Equity and Information Technologies" discusses information democracy in America. The technologies section is represented by a single chapter on "Parallel Information Processing" by Edie M. Rasmussen. The section on applications includes three chapters: "Data Representations for Geographic Information Systems" by Clifford A. Shaffer, "Environmental Research" by Zorana Ercegovac, and "The Information Environment of Managers" by Jeffrey Katzer and Patricia T. Fletcher. The section on the profession is given to chapters on "Education and Training for Information Science in the Soviet Union" by Pamela Spence Richards and "Ethical Considerations of Information Professionals" by Thomas J. Froelich. Chapters by Shaffer, Katzer and Fletcher, and Richards cover topics reviewed in ARIST for the first time. Shaffer introduces the field of geographic information systems (GIS) and describes "the history and state of the art for spatial data representation as it relates to GIS." Katzer and Fletcher analyze the information behaviors of managers in terms of Robert S. Taylor's model of the manager's information environment. Richards describes the status of Soviet information science education at the beginning of the 1990s in the hopes of improving the efficiency of Western cooperative and assistance projects.

Since 1966, ARIST has been on the cutting edge in offering scholarly reviews of information science and technology topics as substantiated by the published literature. This volume upholds the fine tradition of this exceptional series. [R: JAL, Nov 93, p. 333]—**Karen Markey Drabenstott**

615. **The Bowker Annual Library and Book Trade Almanac.** 38th ed. Catherine Barr, ed. New Providence, N.J., R. R. Bowker/Reed Reference Publishing, 1993. 777p. index. $149.95. LC 55-12434. ISBN 0-8352-3345-6. ISSN 0068-0540.

Current trends, research, and other data dealing with libraries over the past year are summarized in this standard work. Arranged in its usual format, the first four parts present reports from the field; an analysis of legislation, funding, and grants pertinent to libraries in 1993; education, placement, and salary information for library professionals; and research and statistical information concerning libraries and the book trade. Parts 5 and 6 contain reference information and a directory of organizations.

Beyond updating the reference material throughout the work, Bowker expanded part 4 at the request of readers who need more data in relation to budgeting concerns. It now includes a table on German academic periodicals and the average prices and price indexes for most United States publications, British and German academic books, and Latin American books. Part 2 contains a particularly useful report for all in the field: "Toward a Virtual Library: Internet and the National Research and Education Network" by Charles R. McClure, Mary McKenna, William E. Moen, and Joe Ryan discusses the concerns of librarians in dealing with the electronic future of libraries as the vision of a national electronic network connecting all libraries and users comes closer to reality. Accurate and timely as always, this is a requisite title for anyone involved with information science.—**Jo Anne H. Ricca**

616. Hannigan, Jane Anne, ed. **Library Lit. 21—The Best of 1990.** Metuchen, N.J., Scarecrow, 1992. 491p. $37.50. LC 78-154842. ISBN 0-8108-2534-1.

Citing a declining market (libraries are no longer buying collections of reprint articles), the increasing costs of reprint permissions, and the onerous chore of obtaining permissions, Scarecrow has announced that this is the final volume in the 20-year series. It may also be significant that this 1990 edition was not published until 1992, whereas previous volumes appeared in the year following the year of coverage.

As in previous volumes, the editor and a jury of respected leaders in librarianship have tried to choose the best essays produced in a year. Their goal has been to capture "a professional moment in time," to encapsulate the contemporary issues of library science. Certainly the selectors have been the creme de la creme in our line of work. In this volume they are John Berry III, Arthur Curley, Jane Anne Hannigan, Norman Horrocks, Bill Katz, and Patricia Glass Schuman.

Volume 21 includes 33 articles published in 1990. Hannigan has grouped the essays into seven sections: technology, the future, and libraries; government and libraries; school media center concerns; management approaches; children's literature; library education; and historical perspectives and collecting. The articles are thought-provoking—one might even say just plain provoking—and they really do reflect the hot topics of our time and our professional lives. [R: BL, 1 April 93, p. 1408; LAR, Oct 93, p. 573; WLB, Sept 93, p. 109]

—Berniece M. Owen

617. Kogon, Marilyn, and Lynne Lighthall. **The Canadian Library Handbook: Organizing School, Public and Professional Libraries.** rev. ed. Whitby, Ont., McGraw-Hill Ryerson, 1993. 259p. index. $49.95. 027.8. ISBN 0-07-551552-0.

Ever since it appeared in 1980, many teacher librarians have relied on *Organizing the School Library*, and gradually librarians in small public or special libraries have found that they too could use the guide. This new edition, with a new title, acknowledges the larger audience for a work of this kind. The authors focus on the "librarian" part of teacher-librarian and emphasize the commonalities among all types of library work. Their intention is to provide a manual that will help librarians handle technical services in any small library. The topics included are acquisitions, cataloging, classification, processing, collection maintenance, and circulation procedures. Appendixes cover the details of MARC formats and typing and filing catalog cards. In clear, concise language and illustrations, the authors provide practical guidance for acquiring and handling both print and audiovisual materials. A glossary and list of abbreviations, as well as an excellent, detailed index, make it easy to use the book for reference. Although the focus is Canadian, the book will be useful outside of Canada. Illustrations use the familiar card catalog format, but the information is equally appropriate for automated libraries. This useful book is recommended for anyone working in a small or medium-sized library and for library school students.—**Adele M. Fasick**

618. Olson, Stan, and Ruth Kovacs, eds. **National Guide to Funding for Libraries and Information Services.** 2d ed. New York, Foundation Center, 1993. 190p. index. $85.00pa. ISBN 0-87954-497-X.

Intended as a starting point for those seeking grants for support for libraries and information services, this guide lists 574 grantmaking foundations and 28 direct corporate giving programs that have shown a substantial interest in libraries, either in their stated purpose or through grants of $10,000 or more in the latest year of record. The information in this guide has been drawn from four other, more inclusive Foundation Center publications: *The Foundation Directory (1993); The Foundation Directory. Part 2 (1993); The National Directory of Corporate Giving (1993)*; and the Foundation Grants Index database.

All of the agencies included fall into one of five categories: independent foundation, company-sponsored foundation, direct corporate giving, operating foundation, or community foundation. Each entry in the descriptive directory (the main list) provides the address and telephone number of the grant giver, date of establishment, donors, foundation type, financial data, purpose and activities, fields of interest, types of support, limitations, publications, application information, officers and trustees, number of staff, EIN (Employer Identification Number), and recent library and information services grants. In addition to the various indexes, other useful information consists of a glossary of terms, a bibliography of funding guides, a list of Foundation Center publications, and a list of free funding information centers arranged by state. This guide is an invaluable tool for those who are seeking funds to build or renovate facilities, to increase acquisitions, to better serve special patrons, or generally to improve their library and information services. [R: LJ, 1 Oct 93, p. 131]—**Sara R. Mack**

619. Patrick, Gay D. **Building the Reference Collection: A How-To-Do-It Manual for School and Public Librarians.** New York, Neal-Schuman, 1992. 187p. index. (How-To-Do-It Manuals for School and Public Librarians, no.7). $32.50pa. Z718.1.P36. 025.5'2778'223. LC 92-31517. ISBN 1-55570-105-1.

The introductory section of this work provides the underlying rationale for general collection development with particular attention to the intended audience. Complete with guidelines, checklists, directory-type information, examples, illustrations, and bibliographical references, the introduction provides a quick overview of the practices, problems, and solutions for professionals who need help. Among the topics that receive special treatment are the rationale and procedure for surveying user needs, the strategy for systematic and aggressive weeding in several subject fields, and the use of appropriate machine aids throughout the collection development process. Appendixes provide a recommended replacement schedule and a selected list of publishers and distributors of library materials.

The core of this readable, practical text is the list of some 600 thoroughly annotated titles that represent a basic reference collection for school and public libraries. The entries are subdivided into general works, specialized subject items, and electronic materials. Annotations include an indication of appropriate grade or age level. The work concludes with subject and author/title indexes. This manual will provide a helpful beginning for school media and public librarians, as well as administrators, particularly those whose access to formal professional education is limited.—**Donald G. Davis, Jr.**

620. Wolf, Carolyn, and Richard Wolf. **Basic Library Skills.** 3d ed. Jefferson, N.C., McFarland, 1993. 177p. illus. index. $19.95pa. Z710.W64. 025.5'6. LC 92-51100. ISBN 0-89950-895-2.

This work is designed "to be a self-contained short course in the use of the library ... to provide a quick and easy way to learn to do library research ... [or] as an adjunct to a course in library usage or as part of an introductory English composition course." Then again, "it might serve as a self-paced instructional sequence for all students." The 16 chapters cover library facilities (e.g., cataloging systems), types of reference materials, CD-ROM products and online databases, subject areas (e.g., literature, governmental information, biography), nonprint materials, online computers, and "Hints for Writing Papers." Each chapter begins with learning objectives and closes with exercises, a list of important terms, and a bibliography of additional references.

It is probably impossible to design a work like this that will satisfy many—perhaps any—reference or bibliographic instruction librarians. Every reference librarian will question the inclusion or exclusion of particular titles, or the need for certain items of information, but it seems that too many of the Wolfs' choices are questionable. Why, for example, the omission of any reference works in religion except for the *Catholic Almanac* (Our Sunday Visitor, annual) and the *Catholic Encyclopedia* (see ARBA 89, entry 1339)? Why the inclusion of Besterman's *A World Bibliography of Bibliographies* (Lausanne Societas Bibliographica, 1965-66)? Although it was once basic, only the most scholarly researcher would use it today—and how many libraries have it? And why include *Historical Abstracts* (ABC-Clio, quarterly) but omit the same publisher's *America: History and Life* (quarterly), probably more relevant for this volume's audience? And there are many, many others. One crucial basic, however, has not been given enough importance, and that is the usefulness of consulting a reference librarian. It is mentioned, of course, but only at the beginning, and almost in passing, whereas it should be repeated frequently, especially for this book's audience. For this reason, *How to Look Things Up and Find Things Out* (see ARBA 89, entry 542), even though it is not as wide-ranging and is quite imperfect, might be preferred.

The main problem is that libraries are changing so rapidly that it is difficult, if not impossible, to say what will be most helpful for most libraries. Given that problem, the authors have performed a useful, if only passable, service. [R: JAL, Sept 93, pp. 266-68]—**Evan Ira Farber**

Indexes

621. **Library Literature 1992: An Index to Library and Information Science.** Cathy Rentschler, Mary M. Brereton, and Mark A. Gauthier, eds. Bronx, N.Y., H. W. Wilson, 1993. 955p. sold on service basis. LC 36-27468. ISSN 0024-2373.

Library Literature remains the outstanding index for the library and information science fields, and with *Library and Information Science Abstracts* (Plenum, 1965-) and *Information Science Abstracts* (London: Bowker-Saur, 1969-) continues to provide the most comprehensive coverage available of the professional literature. Materials derived from periodicals, articles, books, pamphlets, and library school theses from more than 200 journals and 600 monographs are indexed. Subject coverage includes automation, cataloging, government funding, CD-ROM and online searching, and publishing, among numerous others. Citations to individual book reviews follow the main body of the annual cumulation. Reviews that appear as part of a review article are also indexed by subject. A checklist of monographs completes this annual volume. Generally included in this checklist are the price, ISBN, and LC number. *Library Literature* periodically adds and deletes serials indexed. Not everyone will agree with these changes, but as a whole, most areas of interest are well covered.

H. W. Wilson has truly set the standard for others to follow in indexing. No large academic library should be without *Library Literature*, especially as it is now available on CD-ROM, on machine-readable tape, online, and on computer software.—**Anna Grace Patterson**

Periodicals and Serials

622. **Library Periodicals 1993: An Annual Guide for Subscribers, Authors, Publicists.** Molly Skeen, ed. Alameda, Calif., Periodical Guides Publishing, 1993. 55p. index. $18.00 spiralbound. Z671.L47. ISBN 0-9637676-0-7.

With its focus on library science literature, this guide features 150 journals and newsletters from Canada and the United States. Future editions, planned to be published annually, will include foreign, regional, and state materials as well. Each entry provides an overview of the newsletter or journal; publisher's name, address, and telephone and fax numbers; editor; ISSN; commencement date and frequency; size and average page count; subscription price; and where indexed. In addition, it gives information for authors and publicists, and sometimes there is a note to vendors. (Information as to whether a publication has reviews, along with applicable review information, would be particularly helpful to the latter.) Five appendixes—a bibliography, abbreviations of indexing services, a sample of author guidelines, an index of refereed journals, and a subject index—complete the spiralbound directory.

Although the information contained can be found in other sources, this work is a great time-saver because it is subject-specific. It should be helpful for its intended audience. [R: LJ, Aug 93, p. 168; RBB, 1 Oct 93, pp. 385-86]—**Jo Anne H. Ricca**

Bibliometrics

623. Sellen, Mary K. **Bibliometrics: An Annotated Bibliography, 1970-1990.** New York, G. K. Hall, 1993. 169p. index. $38.50. Z669.8.S45. 020'.72. LC 93-16426. ISBN 0-8161-1954-6.

The two existing bibliographies on this topic, *A Bibliography of Bibliometrics and Citation Analysis* by Roland Hjerppe (Royal Institute of Technology Library, 1980) and *Bibliometrics, a Bibliography and Index* by Alan Pritchard (ALLM Books, 1981), are somewhat dated, so this new work is a welcome addition to the literature. The thousands of bibliometrical studies that Sellen has included here are organized by broad Library of Congress classification, making it easy to review the bibliometrical research in a particular discipline. Annotations briefly describe the methodology of the study. There are a subject index (which includes the titles of journals analyzed in the studies listed); an author index; and a separate index of those studies that include ranked lists of journals, authors, or highly cited papers. Because such material is easily obtainable elsewhere, the huge body of work on the topic by Eugene Garfield is not included, nor are articles appearing in two major journals on bibliometrics of science publications: *Scientometrics* and *Nauchno-tekhnicheskaia Informatsiia*. Recommended for large library science collections and for other libraries where bibliometrical studies are used to aid collection development.

—**Diana Accurso**

Careers and Education

624. Sweeney, Del, and Karin Zilla, eds. **Position Descriptions in Special Libraries.** 2d ed. Washington, D.C., Special Libraries Association, 1992. 186p. $31.25pa. Z675.A2P67. 023'.2. LC 92-23534. ISBN 0-87111-402-X.

Ninety sample job descriptions contributed by 34 special librarians are included in this guide, published 10 years after the first edition. The text is divided into two broad categories: professional positions generally requiring degrees in library information science, and support positions. A notable feature is that support positions now include functions formerly considered professional, reflecting the trend toward requiring more technical training and automated skills. The positions are intended to be representative of practices rather than serving as model job descriptions. Nevertheless, the descriptions are good examples of what is required in specialized markets. And, at first glance, while the positions appear far too specialized for public or general library human resource managers, the descriptions may be used as starting or reference points for terminology used by administrators in developing new or updating old job functions in their organizations.

The position descriptions are varied and cover a wide range of jobs, including such representative areas as academic, research, business, and state library positions. The text is prefaced by a brief, excellent guide on writing descriptions and a timely article cautioning that today's librarians must be proficient in the use of automated resources in order to remain effective and productive.—**James M. Murray**

Cataloging and Classification

625. Dershem, Larry D., comp. **Library of Congress Classification Class KL-KWX: Law of Asia and Eurasia, Africa, Pacific Area and Antarctica Cumulative Schedule.** Littleton, Colo., Fred B. Rothman, 1992. 2v. (AALL Publ. Series, no.43). $130.00 looseleaf w/binder/set. Z696.U5K75. 025.4'634. LC 92-25906. ISBN 0-8377-9283-5.

This work, as are Dershem's other editions of Library of Congress classification schedules, is a physically convenient version of the LC schedule KL-KWX. The looseleaf pages provide plenty of space for adding notes, and the sturdy binders open to lie completely flat. This classification schedule, similar to other law schedules, makes heavy use of tables. To assign a number one needs to use two volumes: Volume 1 lists jurisdictions, and volume 2 has the index and the tables needed to complete the classification number. These smaller volumes, which lie flat, are more convenient to use than the original LC volumes. Although the typeface of these volumes is not quite as large or clear as LC's, it is adequate. The looseleaf format is intended to make it easy to incorporate quarterly replacement pages in the main sequence, so that the classifier does not have to consult separate lists of additions and changes. It is likely that there will be a number of changes in the area covering the jurisdictions of the former Soviet Union.

This classification covers economically and legally interesting areas in which specialized libraries may be collecting, including, among other jurisdictions, the former Soviet Union, Japan, China, and the international treaties and agreements covering Antarctica. It also covers areas of interest to legal historians, because it includes works on the ancient Egyptian, Mesopotamian, Hebrew, and Greek legal systems. It even provides a place to classify sources in cuneiform script on clay tablets. Those libraries with substantial collections in the areas covered may want to buy this edition for its convenience of use.
—**Marit S. MacArthur**

626. Moys, Elizabeth M., and others. **Moys Classification and Thesaurus for Legal Materials.** 3d ed. New Providence, N.J., K. G. Saur/Reed Reference Publishing, 1992. 386p. index. $100.00. 025.4634. ISBN 0-86291-903-7.

The assigning of call numbers to legal materials is a challenging and meticulous enterprise. If there ever was a system that could be used to make the process more accurate, consistent, and easy, the present title comes very close. The only drawback is that while this work is modeled on the Library of Congress classification system, it is really an adaptation of the K schedule. It is, therefore, of limited value to U.S. catalogers unless the schedules are heavily adapted and annotated.

On the whole, the book accomplishes all that it sets out to do with careful, systematic diligence. Its compact size and detailed index make it a truly useful tool for catalogers of the Commonwealth.
—**Richard A. Leiter**

627. Olson, Nancy B. **A Cataloger's Guide to MARC Coding and Tagging for Audiovisual Material.** De Kalb, Ill., Minnesota Scholarly Press; distr., De Kalb, Ill., Media Marketing Group, 1993. 112p. $29.50pa. ISBN 0-933474-49-0.

This work is completely devoted (except for a six-page introduction) to bibliographic records coded and tagged with the MARC used by OCLC's PRISM service. The records are also found in Olson's *Cataloging of Audiovisual Materials*, 3d edition (Minnesota Scholarly Press, 1992); thus, this publication functions as a companion volume to the latter work.

In the introductory pages there are brief notes about MARC, common 007 code patterns, lists of OCLC format documents and user groups, and how to distinguish between a MARC record that can be edited to reflect local practice and the need to create a new record. The arrangement of the bibliographic records corresponds to the chapters in the *Anglo-American Cataloguing Rules*, 2d edition, 1988 revision, with the addition of a chapter on kits and other problems. The two "other" problems show bibliographic records for a music score and a book that has nonbook materials in a pocket. A useful addition to this work is a separate chart, which can be mounted on a wall, that shows 007 fields for audiovisual materials.

This guide is highly recommended for OCLC users. It is not recommended for libraries involved with other utilities unless their staff members are very knowledgeable about the differences in the application of MARC.—**Jean Weihs**

628. Olson, Nancy B. **Cataloging Computer Files.** Lake Crystal, Minn., Soldier Creek Press, 1992. 123p. illus. (Minnesota AACR 2 Trainers Series, no.2). $25.00pa. Z695.47.047. 025.3'44. LC 92-28773. ISBN 0-936996-47-1.

Although the title page has no edition statement, the author states in the preface that this is a revision of a work that has variously appeared under the titles *A Manual of AACR 2 Examples for Microcomputer Software and Video Games* (1983) and *A Manual of AACR 2 Examples for Microcomputer Software* (1986). Because this publication is designed to be used with the *Anglo-American Cataloguing Rules*, 2d edition (AACR2), 1988 revision, the text of pertinent rules is not found here. In many instances, the rules have been summarized, Library of Congress rule interpretations have been discussed, and personal comments have been added. There is a brief discussion of subject headings and classification, and a somewhat larger description of MARC coding and tagging for OCLC input. Most of this work is devoted to 47 examples that include a picture of the chief sources of information; two catalog records, one with and one without OCLC/MARC coding and tagging; and brief comments about important points being exemplified.

This is a very useful book because the greatest changes between the AACR2 and the 1988 revision are found in the rules for computer files. It is highly recommended for those libraries involved with OCLC. However, there are some caveats. There is no index, and Macintosh and Apple software only appear in the examples. If MARC examples are an important reason for considering purchase, the staff in libraries involved with utilities other than MARC should recognize the differences in the MARC format interpretation on their local system and the examples given in this book. [R: JAL, Mar 93, pp. 33-34]

—**Jean Weihs**

629. Otchere, Freda E. **African Studies Thesaurus: Subject Headings for Library Users.** Westport, Conn., Greenwood Press, 1992. 435p. $75.00. Z695.1.A37O85. 025.4'9808'89896. LC 92-12523. ISBN 0-313-27437-1.

In order to assist students and researchers in African studies, Otchere has selected 4,000 subject terms relating to 41 countries that make up Africa south of the Sahara Desert (excluding Egypt, Libya, Tunisia, Algeria, Morocco, and Western Sahara) and the islands of Cape Verde, the Comoros, Madagascar, Mauritius, Reunion, Saint Helena, Sao Tome and Principe, and the Seychelles. Subject terms were selected from the *Library of Congress Subject Headings* (LCSH), 13th and 14th editions, through the September 18, 1991, *LC Subject Headings Weekly Lists* of the 15th edition for aspects of the culture, history, religion, geography, language, and literature of these regions. Otchere subsequently enhances these selected LCSH terms with names of 600 African peoples, nearly 600 African languages, and appropriate cross-references (broader and narrower terms) as needed to improve consistency and ease of identification and classification of language and ethnic groups. Additionally, Otchere has included the suggested Library of Congress classification numbers to assist users who browse on library shelves or who classify materials in these areas. Of special interest is the indication of both pre-1990 (DT 727-971) and post-1990 (DT 1001-3415) numbers. Two appendixes are added to complete this enhancement: the DT outline and selected free-floating subdivisions used under geographical place-names.

Otchere's enhancements have made this thesaurus an important tool for all libraries. It will assist not only students and researchers in African studies but also librarians in collection development, bibliographical instruction, reference service, genealogical research, subject analysis, and classification. [R: Choice, Feb 93, p. 943]—**Bonnie A. Dede**

630. Scott, Mona L., with Christine E. Alvey. **Conversion Tables: LC-Dewey, Dewey-LC.** Englewood, Colo., Libraries Unlimited, 1993. 365p. $60.00pa. Z696.U4S36. 025.4'31. LC 93-26938. ISBN 1-56308-017-6.

This work must be used with caution. Despite a note in the introduction that some conversions can be completed from the tables, such action may be inadvisable. The work consists of two lists, one in LC class number order, the other in Dewey order. Entries consist of two class numbers and a descriptor. There is no indication of what editions of the schedules are represented in the lists, how numbers were selected, or what pitfalls there may be in using the lists. A straightforward entry reads "027.(1-8)-Z675-Types of libraries." To construct an LC number, one must consult the Dewey schedule to determine the meaning of the actual class number, and then the LC schedule to complete the LC number appropriately. Some problems arise from the different intellectual arrangements of the two classification systems and from the extreme brevity of entries. Brevity of descriptors and the lack of hierarchical or typographical hints can also be confusing. Under Dewey, there are three entries for 027.04, each of which is termed "Europe." Each corresponds to a different LC number; AG540 concerns information bureaus, CD101-215 concerns diplomatics, and CD 1000-2000 concerns archives, but no number is given for libraries, which are encompassed by the Dewey number.

Despite its shortcomings, this work could be useful in a library that relies heavily on copy and where much copy contains only class numbers from the scheme not used. Print quality is high, and dotted lines in every fifth entry contribute to readability. Libraries that use the tables heavily might have preferred a looseleaf format, and unfortunately the gutter is too small to permit pages to be unbound and punched for binder storage.—**Janet Swan Hill**

631. **Thesaurus Guide: Analytical Directory of Selected Vocabularies for Information Retrieval, 1992.** 2d ed. By EUROBrokerS. Brussels, Office for Official Publications of the European Communities; distr., Lanham, Md., UNIPUB, 1993. 1033p. $110.00pa. ISBN 92-826-4956-3.

This guide is a list of thesauruses in use in various member countries of the European Community. The format is the same as the 1985 first edition, but the content has been substantially updated.

The thesauruses listed in the guide are divided into the following broad areas: general (which covers combination areas, such as science and technology, and which also includes libraries), information area, mathematics and physico-technical sciences, physico-chemical technology, astronomy and geosciences, agriculture and nutrition, biomedical sciences, regional and environmental sciences, social sciences, and culture and the arts. The following information is provided about each thesaurus: the title; author; organization responsible; language or languages used; available formats (e.g., paper, microform, CD-ROM); disciplines covered; number of terms, descriptors, nondescriptors, and modifiers used; display modes; relational structure; construction and maintenance guidelines; and implementation. The introduction, which explains how to use the guide, is clearly written in the three main languages of the European Community: English, French, and German.

The guide contains four indexes: an index of organizations that produced the various thesauruses and subject indexes in each of the three languages, with translations in the other two. This guide would be useful for a special library or information center that wants to use a controlled vocabulary in a particular subject discipline but that does not want to start from scratch.—**Linda Main**

632. Winaker, Lesley Richman. **EUROCOM: A Classification Schedule and Cataloging Handbook for European Community Depository Collections.** Buffalo, N.Y., William S. Hein, 1993. 139p. index. $42.50 looseleaf w/binder. Z695.1.I575W56. 025.3. LC 92-26979. ISBN 0-89941-809-0.

The author, now faculty services librarian at the University of Houston Law Libraries, began this work as an independent studies project toward her MLIS degree at the University of Texas. It is designed to classify official European Community (EC) documents, with the exception of EC statistical publications. Winaker suggests that a cataloger is able to fit the latter, as well as commercial publications dealing with the EC, into her classification. The classification has a full range of topics, from religion to plant cultivation, pharmacology to municipal engineering. A good index provides quick access to particular classification numbers.

This is a unique classification scheme; it is not an expansion of an established system. Therefore, it can only be applied to a collection that will be shelved separately from the general collection. Part of this work may have value even if the classification scheme is not used. The introduction gives an overview of the EC's historical background, institutions, publications, and databases, and ends with a two-page bibliography. A 19-page glossary adds to the introduction's information.

Those buying this work for its information rather than its classification content should be made aware in the publication itself that a purchaser will automatically be enrolled in an order for future updates unless the publisher is advised that they are unwanted. This information is now found only in the publisher's brochure. Also, the pages in the glossary and index are not full. A better use of space might decrease the size and price of the publication.—**Jean Weihs**

Comparative and International Librarianship

633. Bromley, David W., and Angela M. Allott. **British Librarianship and Information Work 1986-1990. Volume Two: Special Libraries, Materials and Processes.** London, Library Association; distr., Lanham, Md., UNIPUB, 1993. 353p. index. $105.00. 020.941. ISBN 1-85604-001-1.

Covering the years 1986-1990, this volume was published in 1993, thus providing what is essentially a historical summary and record. Eight chapters deal with various types of special libraries, four with special types of materials, and six with processes (broadly defined). A list of acronyms and abbreviations and an index are included. The chapters range in length from 6 to 21 pages of text. Lists of bibliographical references, some quite extensive, accompany each chapter in the order in which they are cited in the text.

The 59-page index is detailed, but it fails to provide the abundant access to the volume's contents that its length suggests. For example, the works cited in the chapter footnotes are not referenced in the index. Some acronyms appear in the index, but for others it is necessary to look under the spelled-out forms. There are no cross-references.—**Lawrence W. S. Auld**

634. Burnell, Richard S., ed. **The Libraries Directory 1991-93.** Cambridge, England, James Clarke; distr., Detroit, Gale, 1992. 232p. index. $115.00. 027.041. ISBN 0-227-67924-5. ISSN 0961-4575.

Since its original appearance in 1897, this directory has appeared under a variety of titles. The 1989 edition was published in the United States as *The British Library Directory* (see ARBA 90, entry 607). Similar to its American counterpart, *The American Library Directory* (see ARBA 93, entry 623), this work has served vital informational needs, and its format has been the same for many years. This edition provides basic information on 194 public libraries and 1,525 special libraries in Great Britain and Ireland. The "public libraries" are really library systems that may include dozens of regional and branch libraries. The special libraries include everything from academic and medical collections to national, museum, or association libraries.

The editor collected information by means of coded questionnaires, which are reproduced at the beginning of each section. The use of codes instead of field labels within each entry is somewhat inconvenient, but a key to the codes is printed at the top of every other page. The entries are divided first between the United Kingdom and the Republic of Ireland and then by type, public versus special. The public library entries are arranged by local authority or jurisdiction, while the special libraries are arranged by town. Entries for public libraries give more details of finances, branches, loan policies, and special services. All entries list addresses, telephone and telex numbers, key personnel, hours, main subjects collected and special collections, cooperative agreements, equipment and online services available, publications, and statistics (on holdings, staff, and finances). New in this edition are fax numbers and statistics on the number of questions handled. An index supplies additional access by subject and the names of special libraries. American libraries that support research activities on Great Britain will find this directory a useful resource.—**John R. M. Lawrence**

635. Dale, Peter, comp. **Directory of Library and Information Organizations in the United Kingdom.** London, Library Association; distr., Lanham, Md., UNIPUB, 1993. 180p. index. $60.00. 020.2541. ISBN 1-85604-092-5.

This directory focuses primarily on library and related organizations in the United Kingdom. However, Dale also includes related European groups in recognition of the growing influence of the European Community and the internationalization of the library and information professions. Even so, some groups were deliberately excluded, such as product-specific user groups, small local groups, and policy and advisory bodies whose activities are confined to a particular organization. The information in this work was obtained through searches in reference sources, direct mailings, and telephone or fax contacts. As not all efforts were fruitful, there are also some omissions resulting from lack of response.

The volume is clearly arranged in three sections: a list of acronyms of library organizations, descriptions of the organizations (the largest of the sections) represented by an acronym in the first section, and an index that includes both the acronym and the spelled-out version of the name. Institutional information includes the organization's full name, address, telephone and fax numbers, geographical scope, group activities (e.g., publications, conferences, workshops), membership criteria, and whom to contact for membership.

This is a most useful work, especially as the overlap among professional library organizations increases. The compiler indicates his desire to update the directory regularly—something that is essential, given the changes that we constantly witness. There is no doubt that an updated edition will be just as welcome as this first one.—**Marjorie E. Bloss**

636. **The Library Association Yearbook 1992.** K. A. Beecroft and R. E. Palmer, comps. London, Library Association; distr., Lanham, Md., UNIPUB, 1992. 437p. $60.00pa. ISBN 0-85365-889-7. ISSN 0075-9066.

This yearbook is divided into three parts. Part 1 contains lists of the association's various officers, committees, awards, publications, and the like. Part 2 begins with the Royal Charter and includes bylaws, regulations, rules, and the association's code of professional conduct. Part 3 is a list of members as of March 1992. The typical entry includes name, professional credentials, position, membership number, date when the individual first joined the association, and date when the individual was elected to the professional register as either a chartered member or a fellow. There is no index.—**Lawrence W. S. Auld**

Copyright

637. Strong, William S. **The Copyright Book: A Practical Guide.** 4th ed. Cambridge, Mass., MIT Press, 1993. 288p. index. $22.50. KF2994.S75. 346.7304'82. LC 92-16371. ISBN 0-262-19330-2.

Copyright used to be a topic in which the issues and probable solutions were relatively clear. However, with a major change in the law (1978) and the emergence of high technologies, users, librarians, publishers, and authors have been thrust into a new arena of cooperation and confrontation. Strong presents a readable interpretation of copyright directed toward beginners and knowledgeable readers. He has studied such issues for many years and is able to draw from and explain principles, laws, and court cases, then adds his own opinions. In doing so, he is careful to distinguish his views from those set in law. Strong covers in 11 chapters such topics as ownership, registration of copyright, rights in copyrighted works, infringement and fair use, tax treatment of copyrights, and international copyright protection. He includes electronic products as well as artistic works. The index leads easily to a topic of specific interest.

Those seeking guidance on copyright issues should consult more than one authority, because as much opinion as fact is printed, and particularly sticky problems require a variety of opinions. After reading Strong's ideas, try the larger *Publishing Law Handbook* by E. Gabriel Pearle and John Taylor Williams (Prentice Hall Law and Business, 1992). But for a readable treatise that is updated frequently, this work is a good, simple place to begin. Recommended for all parties interested in copyright.—**David V. Loertscher**

Indexing

638. Wellisch, Hans H., comp. **Indexing: A Basic Reading List.** 2d ed. Port Aransas, Tex., American Society of Indexers/Fetters Information Management, 1992. 31p. index. $15.00pa. Z695.9.W437. 016.0253. LC 91-44034. ISBN 0-936547-14-6.

Wellisch, author of the comprehensive book *Indexing from A to Z* (see ARBA 93, entry 653), has compiled a small pamphlet of works related to indexing books and periodicals. Most of the 87 entries have short descriptive or evaluative annotations. Included are articles, chapters, and books from British and North American sources. The compiler states that the work is intended specifically for newcomers to the field; excluded are works of a theoretical nature and those regarding indexing of nonbook materials. Wellisch has covered a wide range of topics, including techniques, filing, typography, and training. There is a short section on computer-aided indexing and even a section on freelancing and the business of indexing. A variety of subjects are covered as well, such as indexing medical works, technical communications, and biographies. Interestingly, the book has only an author index; the reader must dig around for works related to specific subjects. Although the work is of limited interest to librarians and the general reader, academic libraries serving institutions with library and information science schools will want to buy it.

—**Stephen Haenel**

Information Technology

639. **The FISCAL Directory of Fee-Based Research and Document Supply Services.** 4th ed. Steve Coffman and Pat Wiedensohler, comps. Los Angeles, Calif., County of Los Angeles Public Library and Chicago, American Library Association, 1993. 445p. index. $58.00pa. ISBN 0-8389-2161-2. ISSN 1067-7674.

Originally designed to facilitate communication among fee-based services, this directory is a resource tool to be used by both the operators of fee-based services and their clients. This edition has been expanded to include commercial document supply services as well as services outside North America. The 3d edition (see ARBA 92, entry 605) contained entries for 214 services, while this one has entries for 445 services. The new entries include 81 new fee-based services in U.S. libraries, 61 commercial document delivery services, and 117 fee-based information services in libraries outside the country. The format has been enlarged, allowing a full-page display for each service cited, and a uniform page layout simplifies location of specific details. The services, which are arranged alphabetically, are further accessible through seven indexes: research areas, special expertise, online services, services offered, geographical, service name, and bibliographical holdings code. The detailed instructions on how to use this book will help users, including nonlibrarians, in locating and interpreting entries and in securing the desired information or documents. The volume is perfect bound with a paper cover; the pages, perforated and drilled, can be removed and placed in a looseleaf binder if desired. [R: RBB, 1 Oct 93, p. 379]

—**Lawrence W. S. Auld**

640. **Online Inc.'s TOP 500 Library Microcomputer Software Application Programs.** Wilton, Conn., Eight Bit Books/Online, 1992. 350p. index. $44.95pa. ISBN 0-910965-09-9.

This directory of 500 "proven library-specific and general library support" computer programs provides version, release date, cost, application, producer, description, operating environment, hardware requirements, other software used, and (when available) source and a brief summary of reviews. The entries have been selected from Buyer's Guide to Micro Software (SOFT), which is available on line through BRS and DIALOG. More than 90 percent of the "general library support" programs have reviews listed, but fewer than 50 percent of the entries for library-specific programs include such citations. An introduction on how to select software for libraries includes helpful information for new users and a useful review for the more experienced. The reviews cited include ones from *Library Software Review* and *Library Technology Reports* as well as many from general computer and software magazines. This book will provide a useful first point of access for librarians and administrators looking for library-specific programs and for anyone looking for information on such general programs as database management and word processing. [R: JAL, May 93, p. 131; RBB, 1 Mar 93, pp. 1265-66]—**Betty Jo Buckingham**

Intellectual Freedom and Censorship

641. Harer, John B. **Intellectual Freedom: A Reference Handbook.** Santa Barbara, Calif., ABC-Clio, 1992. 313p. index. (Contemporary World Issues). $39.50. KF4770.Z9H3. 324.73'0853. LC 92-35565. ISBN 0-87436-669-0.

Over the years the intellectual freedom issue has given rise to a remarkable series of books, but few have encapsulated so much useful material within so small a space as this effort. Beginning with a more-or-less obligatory excursion through the history and theory of intellectual freedom—an effort as succinct as it is penetrating—the handbook progresses to a less conventional but highly useful sequence of chapters. One comprises a set of biographical sketches of prominent people involved in current intellectual freedom questions, while another chronicles important court cases, each described in summary form. A third consists of a well-detailed directory of organizations, which is followed in turn by bibliographies of print and nonprint materials, both admirably annotated. Finally, there is a glossary that focuses on the terms of art peculiar to the issue.

Throughout there is a strong emphasis on the legal side of the issues, with special efforts made to explicate technical terms for the lay reader. Such solicitude extends throughout the handbook and is one of its most attractive features. Another great strength rests in the consistently high quality of analysis. Never, for instance, does one feel burdened by data for its own sake; in Harer's hands, particulars must serve the higher goal of intelligent exposition. The result is both an introduction and an in-depth guide that will interest the novice as well as the advanced student. It especially recommends itself to those regularly exposed to intellectual freedom disputes, such as librarians, publishers, and teachers, as well as to any others who find themselves in the midst of such controversies. [R: Choice, June 93, p. 1602; JAL, Sept 93, p. 275; LJ, 1 Feb 93, p. 74; SLJ, May 93, p. 137]—**Paul L. Holmer**

642. **Intellectual Freedom Manual.** 4th ed. Compiled by the Office for Intellectual Freedom of the American Library Association. Chicago, American Library Association, 1992. 283p. index. $25.00pa. Z711.4.I57. 025.2'13. LC 92-10699. ISBN 0-8389-3412-9.

It has been only three years since the 3d edition appeared, but readers will find that this latest version of the *Intellectual Freedom Manual* has been substantially rewritten. All but two of the policies and introductions have been revised, while background articles have been reworked, and new sections have been added. A revamped organization makes the manual easier to use; each interpretation now precedes its background article, and both are linked by reference numbers. As before, the primary audience is professional librarians. For them there are suggestions in such basics as help in handling complaints and lobbying legislators, as well as the more proactive efforts of developing confidentiality reports or instituting materials selection programs. The manual will find a wider audience, however, as the challenges from an ever-widening array of groups increase and as censorship questions become the battleground in wider cultural and philosophical disputes. Anyone dealing with matters of civil liberties and intellectual freedom will want to have this volume close at hand. [R: JAL, Mar 93, pp. 27-28; SLMQ, Spring 93, p. 199]—**Paul L. Holmer**

Inter-Library Loans

643. **WLN Interlibrary Loan Policies Directory.** 2d ed. Lacey, Wash., WLN, 1993. 1v. (unpaged). index. $45.00 looseleaf w/binder.

This new edition of the *WLN Interlibrary Loan Policies Directory* is a cumulative update of the ILL (Interlibrary Loan) policies of more than 300 Pacific Northwest libraries, including Research Libraries Group (RLG) libraries, with holdings in the WLN online ILL policy file from which it is generated. Updated editions are scheduled for publication annually. Policies in the directory are arranged alphabetically by institution name followed by the National Union Catalog (NUC) symbol so they may be rearranged by NUC symbol if so desired. Each policy has a "last updated" date as well as a "printed" date so that the currency of information for a specific library can be easily determined. From the directory information submitted by the libraries and the 13 indexes, the user can find not only standard directory data but also such information as lists of libraries that lend audiovisual materials, libraries that lend unbound periodicals, and libraries that charge fees. The policy entries may also indicate whether the library accepts subject requests and what major collections and materials are represented in the holdings. Information on searching the WLN online ILL policy file is included in an appendix.

Although libraries online with WLN have ready access to this material, information on interlibrary loan policies in a quick, convenient format is always useful. This user friendly directory is printed in a very readable format; it should be of interest to libraries working with WLN institutions.

—Esther Jane Carrier

Library Automation

644. Cibbarelli, Pamela R., comp. and ed. **Directory of Library Automation Software, Systems, and Services.** Medford, N.J., Learned Information, 1993. 370p. index. $79.00pa. ISBN 0-938734-65-2.

This publication continues the biennial *Directory of Information Management Software for Libraries, Information Centers, Record Centers*. In the new edition, records management has been deemphasized, and products and services now included have been selected for relevance to the library automation marketplace. Two-thirds of the work is devoted to describing 240 software products that range in scope from card printing to bibliographic instruction to integrated library automation systems suitable for large research institutions. Only products currently commercially available and in use in North America are included. Entries are arranged alphabetically and contain skeletal information, including major functions and features, hardware requirements, cost, and address. The remainder of the work consists of directories of retrospective conversion services and products, library automation consultants, database hosts, CD-ROM distributors, conferences and meetings in 1993 and 1994, a selected bibliography, brief references to software not included (e.g., because of product discontinuation or name changes), and an index.

Entries for products and services contain only information supplied by the vendors. They are not analytical or evaluative, and some important aspects of systems may not be brought out by the uniform set of elements included. For instance, such features as authority control or in-process control are not indicated, and the yes/no presentation of data cannot indicate what sort of security or management data features may be present in a given package. Despite these shortcomings, the directory is an excellent resource and a good place to begin a comparative investigation of library automation options.

—Janet Swan Hill

645. Langlois, Jennifer. **CD-ROM 1992: An Annotated Bibliography of Resources.** Westport, Conn., Meckler, 1992. 298p. index. $45.00. Z681.3.067L36. 016.0253'0285'572. LC 93-30427. ISBN 0-88736-861-1.

This book's title is misleading. Langlois's purpose in compiling the bibliography is to identify and annotate recent books and articles on CD-ROMs as this technology relates to libraries—not the entire field, as the title implies. The "1992" is largely irrelevant because, with the exception of a few books presumably added at the last moment, there are few citations later than 1990. The 1,360 articles that appear have been arranged under 39 special interest areas, which include topics such as acquisitions, case studies, CD-I, document delivery, policy statements, and use studies. A few relevant books, computer programs, theses, and videos are separately listed after the articles. An index helps the reader locate citations that cut across topics, and Langlois has helpfully duplicated some items under more than one topic. Not quite so helpful are some problems with the index, such as subjects beginning with Mc or Mac coming at the end of the Ms. The index also could have been more detailed: for example, Microsoft might usefully have been subdivided into the company, its CD-ROM products (e.g., Microsoft Office), and the ubiquitous Microsoft CD-ROM Extensions. [R: JAL, May 93, p. 130]—**Robert Skinner**

646. Rega, Regina, comp. **OPAC Directory 1993: An Annual Guide to Online Public Access Catalogs and Databases.** Westport, Conn., Meckler, 1993. 309p. index. $60.00pa. ISBN 0-88376-883-2. ISSN 1066-1425.

Originally published (since 1990) as *Dial In*, the current edition has increased the coverage of library catalogs to approximately 280 entries and updated some 50 percent of the previous entries. Entries are arranged alphabetically by state and then city and include library's name and address, collection data (number of volumes, if serials are online), contact personnel, system data, and log on/off procedures. Some difficulty in determining the system prompts and user responses that should be used is due to the physical layout of each entry. No distinctive typeface sets this information apart. Some entries contain no instructions, the assumption being that the user will be prompted by on-screen instructions when successfully logged in. The indexes provide access by area code, institution name, system name, and collection strength.

Although the compiler states that no single directory can provide data on every possible catalog, this work falls short of providing access to even a general cross-section of libraries. Given the number of libraries with online public access catalogs (OPAC) that exist in the United States alone, this directory provides information on only a small fraction of accessible databases. Major state university systems and public or state libraries are not represented. Indiana University, Ohio State University, and the University of Illinois are a few of the academic library systems missing. The entry for the University of Cincinnati is incorrect; WLN (Western Library Network) has not been the system of use for almost two years. (All the entries, not just 50 percent of them, should have been checked for accuracy.) Users with access to the Internet and the incredible number of available gopher servers will never use this directory. Those individuals and institutions without Internet access will be disappointed in the extremely limited number of OPACs included in this volume. [R: JAL, July 93, p. 201; RBB, 15 Nov 93, p. 645]—**Vicki J. Killion**

Public Libraries

647. Arozena, Steven, ed. **Best Books for Public Libraries: The 10,000 Top Fiction and Nonfiction Titles.** New Providence, N.J., R. R. Bowker/Reed Reference Publishing, 1992. 840p. index. $75.00. Z1035.A72. 025.2'1874. LC 92-18410. ISBN 0-8352-3073-2.

This hefty work consists of a substantial list of books that the editor deems "suitable for general readers (patrons who possess a layperson's knowledge of a wide variety of subjects)." Each of the 6,000 nonfiction titles and the 4,000 works of fiction that appear is accompanied by a brief annotation and citations of reviews from among the major reviewing media. Major awards, such as the National Book Award and the Pulitzer prize, are also indicated.

A guide to books for public libraries, this book is arranged like most public libraries—using the Dewey Decimal Classification system (part 1) and fiction titles (part 2) arranged alphabetically by author. The latter section is subdivided into 15 broad genres (e.g., biographical fiction, detective and mystery fiction, fables, general fiction). This work is also generously endowed with three indexes (author, title, subject) that cover more than 250 pages.

So far, so good. But this guide to best books has a few limitations, some obvious, some not. Excluded from consideration are scholarly books, reference titles, and works for children. Fair enough. Less obvious in the title and the editor's preface is the fact that the titles chosen for inclusion in this work are, in the main, very recent ones. Although Arozena claims that this volume contains entries published from 1965 through early 1992, the great majority of the titles were published since 1985. In fact, a sample count reveals that more than 50 percent of the titles date from 1989 through 1992 and 80 percent date from 1985. Less than 7 percent are pre-1980.

Therefore, what this work gains in timeliness it loses in comprehensiveness; what it achieves in breadth of coverage it fails to provide in historical perspective. It goes without saying that the classic works of the literature of the Western world are not represented here, even when reprinted in such an excellent series as the Library of America. Nor are many of the major writers of the twentieth century included, unless they happened to have been published within a narrow window of time—essentially the late 1980s. Perhaps a more appropriate title for this guide would have been "The 10,000 Best Books of the Eighties: An Update for Public Libraries." As such, it is indeed a useful tool for collection development in public libraries. [R: EL, Mar-April 93, p. 46; RBB, 15 Feb 93, p. 1076]—**Edwin S. Gleaves**

School Libraries

648. **Your Reading: A Booklist for Junior High and Middle School.** Edited by C. Anne Webb, Paul Hirth, and the Committee on the Junior High and Middle School Booklist of the National Council of Teachers of English. Urbana, Ill., National Council of Teachers of English, 1993. 250p. index. (NCTE Bibliography Series). $16.95pa. Z1037.Y68. 011.62'5. LC 93-8652. ISBN 0-8141-5942-7.

Nearly 600 fiction and nonfiction books appropriate for middle school readers are arranged in 26 categories and annotated. Categories include animal stories, "Chills and Thrills," science fiction, and love and romance. Small in comparison to *Junior High School Library Catalog* (see ARBA 91, entry 650), the list is designed for librarians, teachers, and parents who need to recommend or purchase titles for this age group. The list covers 1991, 1992, and a few 1993 titles. A 150-title recommended list of classics published from 1940 to 1990 is included at the end. Author, title, and subject indexes are provided. Subject analyses could be more in-depth to assist in choosing books. It would have also been helpful to indicate reading level for titles of particular appeal to reluctant readers.

While this source will have to be supplemented with other bibliographies, it is a basic list of titles likely to appeal. Recommended for librarians, teachers, and parents of the younger teen set.
—**David V. Loertscher**

Special Libraries and Collections

649. **Canadian Association of Law Libraries Directory. Association Canadienne des Bibliotheques de Droit Annuaire.** Scarborough, Ont., Carswell, 1992. 101p. $25.00pa. ISBN 0-459-55168-X.

This work is the membership directory of the organization connecting major law libraries in Canada. The principal section lists the membership alphabetically, first by organization (for members not specifying a named individual) and then by surname. Full address, telephone, and fax information is provided. Many listings also give E-mail codes. Other sections allow access by province and city (or by country for non-Canadian members) and organization type (academic law libraries, private law libraries, publishers, government libraries, and courthouse or law society libraries). In addition there is a list of committee members and other officers plus the full bilingual text of the corporate charter. All sections have headings in both English and French.

This well-produced directory should be an important tool for those who need access to the Canadian legal information community. It may also be of interest to law librarians in related jurisdictions who want to network.—**Nigel Tappin**

650. **Directory of Special Libraries and Information Centers 1993: A Guide to More Than 20,800 Special Libraries, Research Libraries, Information Centers, Archives, and Data Centers....** 16th ed. Debra M. Kirby and Joanna M. Zakalik, eds. Detroit, Gale, 1992. 2v. index. $399.00/set. LC 84-640165. ISBN 0-8103-7661-X. ISSN 0731-633X.

Special libraries, defined as libraries built around a collection limited by subject matter or form, exist in colleges and universities, companies, public libraries, governmental agencies, and other types of organizations. Since its publication 30 years ago, coverage of special libraries in this well-known directory has doubled from approximately 10,000 to 20,851. Of these, 1,750 are located outside the United States and Canada.

Information given for the alphabetically arranged libraries with assigned entry numbers includes name of organization, address, telephone number, head librarian, founding date, subjects, special collections, holdings, services, automated operations, and access to computerized information services. Both volumes contain an extensive user's guide and a list of abbreviations. Seven appendixes list networks and consortia, libraries for the blind and handicapped, and depository libraries (e.g., those for the European Community). A subject index allows the user to retrieve libraries in different subject fields. Broad subject headings are used, and, for a few headings (e.g., hospital libraries), the user must browse through many entry numbers. The arrangement of entry numbers geographically by state, province, or country codes is of great help.

This reference tool continues to be of value as the standard for access to the collections of special libraries. A wealth of information is contained in these important volumes.—**Anne C. Roess**

651. Evinger, William R., ed. **Directory of Federal Libraries.** 2d ed. Phoenix, Ariz., Oryx Press, 1993. 373p. index. $97.50. Z27.5.025'73. LC 92-33458. ISBN 0-89774-674-0.

With this edition (see ARBA 88, entry 646 for a review of the earlier one), individuals seeking federal data can locate that information through federal libraries and information centers from around the world. More than 2,500 federal libraries and centers are included: The Library of Congress, the National Agricultural Library, the National Library of Medicine, the National Technical Information Service, and the Defense Technical Information Center form the nucleus of this network. Other facilities range from small libraries with only one full-time employee to very large libraries. Many of the larger libraries may be devoted to a single subject. Other libraries may have field offices, thereby forming their own networks. Included among the federal libraries are presidential, technical, engineering, hospital, penal, elementary school, and special libraries. Eighty-five new libraries have been added.

Libraries are arranged by federal agency and then alphabetically by name. Entries include the type of library; name; address; telephone and fax numbers; contact names; special collections; database services; depository status for documents from the GPO or other agencies; involvement with cooperative library organizations, E-mail, or cataloging networks; and the services of each library that are available to the public. The new edition features additional information for each entry: collection size, staff size, fax policy, contract status, CD-ROM availability; and names of publications issued. Three indexes (type of library, subject, and geographical) complete this work. Perhaps one of its most important features is that it allows potential users to determine which services are available and which are most useful to them.

—**Anna Grace Patterson**

652. French, Tom, comp. and ed. **The SCOLMA Directory of Libraries and Special Collections on Africa in the United Kingdom and in Europe.** 5th ed. New Providence, N.J., Hans Zell/Reed Reference Publishing, 1993. 355p. index. $75.00. Z3501.F75. 026.96. LC 92-45187. ISBN 0-905450-89-2.

The Standing Conference on Library Materials on Africa (SCOLMA), centered in the United Kingdom, has been in business since the 1960s, and in that time has produced several reference works and its own journal. The work under review replaces a predecessor that appeared in 1983. The scope of the survey, and the increasing interest in African studies in Europe, is demonstrated by the fact that, whereas the 1983 edition contained 275 institutions, this one provides information on no fewer than 391.

The arrangement is alphabetical by country, then by city. Details are provided on the scope and strength of holdings, number of current subscriptions, areas of strength, and the like. Mailing addresses and telephone numbers are provided, as well as—another sign of the times—fax numbers and even E-mail addresses in some cases. An extensive subject/area/institutional index completes the work.

It is interesting that 156 entries, or 40 percent of the whole, are for libraries in the United Kingdom. It is probably indeterminable whether this is a result of the survey technique or whether it accurately reflects historical interest and thereby current circumstances. Nonetheless, it is odd that none of the French departmental or chamber of commerce libraries are included, because these represent a sector with longstanding Africanist interests.—**David Henige**

653. Gallico. Alison, ed. **Directory of Special Collections in Western Europe.** New Providence, N.J., K. G. Saur/Reed Reference Publishing, 1993. 146p. index. $75.00. 026. ISBN 0-86291-616-X.

The purpose of this work is to "make known substantial collections in specific subjects which are held in large general collections" (introduction). Western Europe is defined as Belgium, Germany, Denmark, Spain, Finland, France, Italy, Netherlands, Norway, Portugal, and the United Kingdom. Compilation of the work was coordinated by the International Federation of Library Associations (IFLA) Office for International Lending. Representatives from each country were responsible for identifying candidate collections, which were then sent a common questionnaire.

Basic organization of the directory is by country and then alphabetically by institution name. Individual institutions may have several entries for different collections. Each collection entry contains subject, items added each year, oldest item, special strength, number of books, number of journals, types of materials, languages, loan region, type of copy loaned, application forms needed, restrictions on loans, whether a guide to the collection exists, existence of published catalog, and type of catalog format. Each entry is numbered with an alphanumeric code assigned to the country and collection. These code numbers are the reference keys in the indexes.

This work is a good beginning to the difficult tasks of selecting, compiling, editing, and indexing a directory of special collections in libraries. Unfortunately, it reflects all of the difficulties involved in these tasks. With only 360 entries for 12 countries it is both far from comprehensive and very uneven from one country to the next, a reflection of the difficulty of relying on volunteers to supply information. The editor could also have profited by some additional considerations about collection listing criteria. "Specific subjects in large general collections" is vague, leaving one to wonder why certain libraries were not included. The indexes, the key to a successful directory of this type, are not well constructed and need additional editing for consistency and use of cross-references. For example, postcards are not indexed as a general term in the English-language index but do appear as more specific terms under World War I postcards and topographical postcards. The indexes reflect a need for use of a multilingual controlled vocabulary (or thesaurus) of some type.

As noted earlier, however, this is a good beginning, and the editor is to be congratulated for undertaking a difficult task. Scholars in the countries represented will find it moderately helpful, and it will be particularly useful to those outside these countries, because so little has been done to assist them in their search for specialized European collections.—**Robert V. Williams**

654. Nicholson, Carol Avery, ed. **Law Library Systems Directory.** Littleton, Colo., Fred B. Rothman, 1993. 332p. (AALL Publications Series, no.44). $45.00. Z675.L2L3924. 026'.34'00973. LC 93-2893. ISBN 0-8377-0146-5.

Before purchasing a system, either hardware or software, it is useful to speak to someone who has experience with the material or equipment in order to help evaluate it. This book is the product of an extensive survey distributed nationally to members of the American Association of Law Libraries. The book lists, by library, several varieties of computer systems in use in almost 400 law libraries that responded to the survey. It is straightforward and packed full of information. Each law library is listed in alphabetical order. Each entry contains a description of the law firm, law school, or library system in statistical terms (e.g., numbers of students, lawyers, volumes). Information is then listed in brief terms by category: automation planning, library systems, local area network, bibliographical utility, retrospective conversion, tape processing, and contact person.

The information provided is nothing more than the names of the products or services used by the library. But nothing more is needed when all you want to know is who else is using what. In these terms, the book is a great success and is very useful. It does, however, suffer from two important shortcomings. First of all, there is no description of the survey that resulted in this directory, nor is there any analysis of the results. Nor is there a statement about when the surveys went out, how many were received, when they were compiled, and so forth. It would be valuable to know how many libraries responded and how many are engaged in activities or use services listed in the directory. If for no other reason than idle curiosity, it would be useful to know, for example, how many law libraries use RLIN or OCLC, or how many of those are law firms and how many are academic libraries.

The other fault that this book suffers is its format. A survey such as this may well be useless a year or two after publication, so it seems rather odd that it should be published in hardback at its cost. If this book is useful at all, it is because it contains up-to-date information. But given the absence of a statement to the contrary anywhere in the book, it is unlikely that this book will be updated any time soon.

—**Richard A. Leiter**

655. Post, Joyce A. **Gerontology and Geriatrics Libraries and Collections in the United States and Canada: A History, Description, and Directory.** Westport, Conn., Greenwood Press, 1992. 196p. index. $45.00. Z668.A58P67. 025.2'761267. LC 91-46862. ISBN 0-313-28443-1.

The literature of geriatrics and gerontology has evolved to a point where a number of specialty libraries have been developed to house the collections. Post's book documents the past, the present, and possibly the future of these libraries in a concise, easy-to-use format. The first section describes the history of geriatric and gerontology libraries in the United States and Canada. The second section summarizes, in narrative and table format, the results of an extensive 1990 survey of the libraries. The final section is a directory, arranged by state, of the libraries and librarians who responded to the survey. The usual directory information is supplemented by information on holdings, subject strengths, special collections, services provided, and automation. A five-part appendix provides the questions used in the survey, then cross-references the libraries by type (e.g., academic, geriatric resource center), selected journal holdings, collection strengths by topic area, and hardware and software available. The reference concludes with a bibliography and a general index.

The book will primarily be of interest to geriatric librarians or those considering the establishment of a geriatric specialty library. Gerontological researchers might also use the reference. It will most likely become an archival document.—**Mary Ann Thompson**

656. **Subject Collections: A Guide to Special Book Collections and Subject Emphases....** 7th ed. Lee Ash and William G. Miller, comps. New Providence, N.J., R. R. Bowker/Reed Reference Publishing, 1993. 2v. $275.00/set. ISBN 0-8352-3141-0.

One enduring legacy of the late Ash is his series of guides to libraries, *Subject Collections*. It was first published in 1958, with a total of 17,000 entries. This edition includes 65,818 entries and lists collections held by 5,882 institutions in the United States and Canada. (See ARBA 86, entry 35 and ARBA 80, entry 122 for reviews of earlier editions.) Ash reports 13,266 entries completely new to this edition, with information from 879 libraries not included in the 6th edition. He notes that because of the recent economic recession, some libraries have abandoned or sold collections previously reported. But there are increases in the number of collections on African-American culture, the environment, gays and lesbians, women, Eastern European nations, ethnic groups (especially Muslims), and music and the theater.

Entries used are Library of Congress subject headings, with some revisions for headings from the New York Public Library for the Performing Arts at Lincoln Center. (There are cross-references from headings not used.) Under each heading, institutions are arranged alphabetically, first by state and then by name. U.S. states are followed by Puerto Rico, U.S. territories, and Canada (by province). Brief directory information for the institution is given, followed by a short description of the collection. Information is based on questionnaires sent to libraries.

Several special symbols are employed. One indicates if a collection is no longer being expanded. Another means that the information has not been confirmed by the library and is either repeated from the 6th edition or based on notes made by the compilers from press releases and other sources. Since the 6th edition, this directory has been published in two reasonably sturdy volumes. Entries are arranged in three columns on each page, with running heads that aid searching. The typeface is small but clear, and there is good use of indentions to separate entries. There is no index listing the repositories included; thus, one should consult the *American Library Directory* (see ARBA 93, entry 623) for further information about the institutions. This new edition will be a valuable source in large reference collections. [R: RBB, 15 Oct 93, pp. 476-77; WLB, June 93, p. 130]—**Richard D. Johnson**

657. **Under Its Generous Dome: The Collections and Programs of the American Antiquarian Society.** 2d ed. By the Staff of the Society. Nancy H. Burkett and John B. Hench, eds. Worcester, Mass., American Antiquarian Society and Charlottesville, Va., University Press of Virginia, 1992. 190p. illus. index. $12.50pa. E172.A455. 026.973. LC 92-26828. ISBN 0-941026 38-9.

One of the major problems of historical researchers is whether a repository has the materials needed for their research. Even when repository guides are available, they are frequently poorly written and not well indexed, and cross-references to related collections are missing. Fortunately, this guide to the collections of the American Antiquarian Society (AAS) avoids all of these problems and is so reasonably priced that most researchers can afford to buy their own personal copies.

The core of the volume consists of the guide to the collections of the AAS. The sections are logically organized, beginning with general book collections and ending with manuscripts and the AAS's own archives. However, instead of the usual dull listing of individual volumes and main entries for personal collections, the discussions are both readable and informative. Each section is truly a guide, leading the reader from the general works on a topic to examples of individual books and specific collections. The essays in each section are written by AAS curators or archivists who specialize in those areas, so that collection highlights and focuses are made clear. The end results are that researchers should have a good idea of the suitability of the collections for their research—not to mention a good read. A detail index to the names and subject areas of the collections complement these essay-style entries and serve as a cross-check to similar topics covered in different sections.

The other sections in the volume, while not essential to the researcher trying to find out if the AAS has a specific book or manuscript collection, do complement the guide portion. The introductory sections on the history of the AAS and its collecting programs over 180 years provide interesting insights into how these materials came to the small town of Worcester, Massachusetts. The sections on programs, funding, and policies explain how the AAS expects to continue to be the preeminent research center on American history prior to 1876.—**Robert V. Williams**

University and College Libraries

658. Philips, Christopher Lee. **A Guide to the College Library: The Most Useful Resources for Students and Researchers.** New York, Walker, 1993. 388p. index. $49.95. Z675.U5P5. 025.5'2777'0973. LC 93-17748. ISBN 0-8027-1283-5.

This work is aimed toward college undergraduates. A short first section covers aspects of librarianship (e.g., cataloging, classification) that influence how information may be found. The second section describes major types of reference source (e.g., abstracts, CD-ROM databases, quotation books) and provides annotated citations to major examples of each type. The third section supplies bibliographies of major reference sources for "some of the most popular major areas of study," plus lists of select subject headings, breakdowns, and call numbers (i.e., classification numbers, all in LC). The final section, "Getting the Most from a College Library," explains common services of libraries, such as reference service, term-paper support, and work-study; it also covers library etiquette. The tone is almost oppressively chummy (e.g., "[t]here are a few things you need to know about the alphabet. Now, I know you all know the alphabet"), but the information contained, although brief, is good and generally up-to-date. The author is clear about the limitations of the work and enthusiastic in his support of librarians. In addition to being useful in a reference collection, this work could be a good graduation gift for a college-bound student. [R: Choice, Oct 93, pp. 271-72; JAL, Sept 93, p. 268]—**Janet Swan Hill**

PUBLISHING AND BOOKSELLING

General Works

Bibliography

659. Glazier, Loss Pequeno. **Small Press: An Annotated Guide.** Westport, Conn., Greenwood Press, 1992. 123p. index. $49.95. Z472.G58. 016.0705'0973. LC 92-15482. ISBN 0-313-28310-9.

Small Press is an annotated bibliography for the study of literary small presses and little magazines in the United States. The period covered begins in 1960 and goes up to 1992. The preface is commendable for describing exactly what the bibliography covers, and the introduction provides an excellent concise history of the small press publishing boom made possible by the mimeograph, the offset press, and the photocopier. The first section of the book lists directories, indexes, guides, and trade journals, including both standard sources and such off-the-wall publications as *Dusty Dog Reviews* and Noel Peattie's *Sipapu*. As in every section of *Small Press*, lengthy and informative annotations accompany each citation. The long second section is an annotated list of articles, dissertations, and books, most of which deal with the history or sociology of the small press movement. Glazier performs a real service here as many of the works he cites—especially the articles from older fugitive publications—would be almost impossible to track down using standard periodical indexes or computer databases. The final section is a bibliography of book-length listings of small presses. Although expensive for 138 pages, *Small Press* is worth it for libraries supporting programs in the history of the book or in avant-garde literature.—**Donald A. Barclay**

Catalogs and Collections

660. **Publishers Trade List Annual, 1992: A Buying & Reference Guide to Books & Related Products.** New Providence, N.J., R. R. Bowker/Reed Reference Publishing, 1992. 4v. illus. index. $238.00/set. LC 4-12648. ISBN 0-8352-3241-7. ISSN 0079-7855.

First published in 1873, this set contains the catalogs of North American (mostly U.S.) publishers as well as a "yellow pages" section for smaller publishers who do not have enough titles to fill four pages. Catalogs of publishers of other types of material (e.g., videos, maps) are also covered. Inclusion is contractual; companies pay to have their catalogs bound into this set. Thus, the representation of publishers is both narrow and eclectic. Giants such as Macmillan rub pages with the tiny Mollica Stained Glass Press. However, dozens of major presses, such as Random House and Simon & Schuster, do not appear. Access to the material is provided through name and subject indexes to publishers (asterisks denote bound catalogs; page numbers refer to the "yellow pages") and an index to publishers' series. The preface, indexes, and "yellow pages" are supposed to appear in the front of volume 1, but in the review copy, they are in volume 4 where they are less useful.

The set includes obscure publishers whose books might not otherwise be noted by librarians. However, the main attraction is the convenience of having these catalogs bound and indexed. Yet its price will render it a luxury, inasmuch as more up-to-date catalogs can be obtained free from the publishers. More valuable sets would either reproduce and index the catalogs of all major publishing houses or be devoted exclusively to small presses.—**D. A. Rothschild**

Directories

661. **American Book Trade Directory 1993-94.** 39th ed. New Providence, N.J., R. R. Bowker/Reed Reference Publishing, 1993. 1710p. index. $215.00. LC 15-23627. ISBN 0-8352-3317-0. ISSN 0065-759X.

This annual guide to North American book retailers and wholesalers, antiquarians, and other book trade information is more than 50 pages longer and covers some 100 more entries than the previous edition. The front matter contains some interesting graphs and statistics pertaining to such matters as independent versus chain booksellers in the United States and Canada and the number of wholesalers in these countries. Additionally, the results of retailer and wholesaler surveys are printed.

The directory chapters are arranged by state and province, and then by city; there are also short sections for the Pacific Islands, Puerto Rico, and the Virgin Islands. Firms are listed alphabetically under the cities in which they are based. Retailer entries generally include name, major type of books sold, address, date established, size, owner and manager, whether the store is a branch, nonbook items sold, and headquarters. Wholesaler entries have data pertinent to them, such as accounts. Other information includes auctioneers of literary property, appraisers of library collections, exporters and importers, rental library chains, associations, and dealers in foreign language books. The index to types of stores is a helpful feature; there is also an index to retailers and wholesalers.

Not every retailer (especially chain stores) is listed. In general, however, this book will be useful to those in the trade and to libraries in which patrons need basic information about booksellers.

—**D. A. Rothschild**

662. **Antiquarian, Specialty, and Used Book Sellers 1993: A Subject Guide and Directory.** James M. Ethridge and Karen Ethridge, eds. Detroit, Omnigraphics, 1993. 523p. index. $48.00. Z286.A55A57. 381'.45002'02573. LC 93-9133. ISBN 1-55888-766-0.

This fine directory provides up to 16 items of information on 2,961 used and specialty bookstores and bookdealers in the United States. The entries are arranged by state and, within each state, by city. Among the questionnaire-derived items of information provided for each bookseller are name, address, telephone and fax numbers, year established, name of owner, hours, size of stock, areas of specialization, and whether catalogs are issued. A huge subject index makes it easy to locate bookdealers specializing in any of some 2,000 subject areas. There are also store name and owner and manager indexes.

A check of the entries of familiar Chicago and Evanston area bookdealers revealed these entries to be accurate and up-to-date, although several used bookdealers who work out of their homes are not listed. Nevertheless, this is the most comprehensive and current directory of its type and will be of great value to bookdealers and bookscouts on their buying and bookhunting trips. It will also be of great help to book collectors and librarians seeking suppliers of out-of-print books on various topics. It is to be hoped that this excellent directory will be updated biennially and that future editions will list the major bookfairs throughout the United States (at which many of these dealers sell their wares). [R: Choice, Oct 93, p. 261; LJ, 15 June 93, p. 62; RBB, 15 Sept 93, pp. 183-84; RQ, Fall 93, pp. 118-19]—**Joseph Cataio**

663. Cabell, David W. E., ed. **Cabell's Directory of Publishing Opportunities in Education.** 3d ed. Beaumont, Tex., Cabell Publishing, 1992. 2v. index. $69.95pa./set. ISBN 0-911753-05-2.

The purpose of this directory is to help scholars in the field of education identify a source or sources that would be most likely to publish their research and other manuscripts. A broad, inclusive definition of education is employed here, as many of the journals described cover a wide variety of fields, such as library and information science, sociology, social work, anthropology, ethnic studies, psychology, computer science, physiology, foreign languages, audiology, and speech pathology.

The titles of the 444 journals that are profiled are listed at the beginning of volume 1, followed by the individual descriptions. Entries include editor's name, address, telephone and fax numbers, type of review (e.g., blind, editorial, optional), number of external and in-house reviewers, acceptance rate, time required for review, whether author can obtain a copy of reviewers' comments, whether fees are charged to review the manuscript, percentage of invited articles, sponsorship of publication, type of reader, frequency of issue, circulation, subscription price, length of manuscript and number of copies required, publishing fees, subjects emphasized by the journal, and manuscript guidelines. The prefatory material explains how authors can use the directory and the relationship between the categories of data. An alphabetically arranged title index includes circulation figures, acceptance rate, and review time (in months) as well as the page number on which the journal is described.

Unfortunately, the volumes are overpriced, as the quality of the paper binding will prevent this work from surviving the amount of use it should receive. However, scholars who publish in the field of education on a regular basis will find the extensive information in this two-volume directory extremely useful.—**Lois J. Buttlar**

664. **Directory of Poetry Publishers.** 8th ed. Len Fulton, ed. Paradise, Calif., Dustbooks, 1992. 343p. index. $16.95pa. ISBN 0-916685-34-9.

This edition of the *Directory of Poetry Publishers* features more than 2,200 book and magazine poetry publishers, from Aardvark Enterprises to *Zuzu's Petals Quarterly*. Entries range from basic mailing data to lengthy paragraphs, including details such as publication policies and preferences; names of recent contributors; number of submissions accepted; and payment amounts, if any. Listings often conclude with a candid statement on special interests; these are often irreverent and always fun to read.

Entries are international in scope, although most listings are from North America, and English is the predominant language. Poetry solicited ranges from the most experimental to more traditional forms and topics, but the emphasis rests on alternative poetry markets. The majority of repeat entries reveal some degree of revision and updating between editions, and new listings are noted as such. The alphabetical arrangement of entries is supplemented with regional and subject indexes; the latter classifies both by topic and poetic form.

This work is most directly comparable to the annual *Poet's Market* (see ARBA 90, entry 903), which offers the same kinds of information on an overlapping body of listings. Both sources are very popular with users, and differences are small but worthy of comment. Specifically, *Directory of Poetry Publishers* has a greater number of entries, a more avant-garde orientation, and superior indexing, although it lacks *Poet's Market*'s useful resources section, which contains lists of conferences, workshops, and competitions. Highly recommended for all collections, both on its own or as a companion to *Poet's Market*.

—**Linda Cullum**

665. **Directory of Publishing 1993.** Phoenix, Ariz., Oryx Press, 1992. 2v. index. $75.00pa.(v.1); $125.00pa.(v.2). ISBN 0-304-32627-5(v.1); 0-304-32628-3(v.2).

This set is an up-to-date source of data on current mainstream publishing and book trade activity in the United Kingdom, the British Commonwealth countries, other major English-language publishers (excluding the United States), and continental Europe. Each directory provides detailed coverage of name; address; telephone, fax, telex, and cable numbers; key personnel; imprints; series; and more. Volume 1 contains information on more than 1,200 publishers from 21 British Commonwealth countries. More than 600 associated organizations, such as packagers, distributors, book clubs, and translation services, are also listed. Appendixes include analyses of U.K. publishers by field of activity and indexes of ISBN prefixes, personnel names, and companies and their imprints. In contrast to the previous edition (see ARBA 90, entry 635), this one has a new index of U.K. publishers by postal code. Volume 2 covers the international publishing and book trade industries in 48 countries in Europe, both East and West. Appendixes include analyses of publishers by field of activity, publishers' international representatives, and indexes similar to those in volume 1. This set is useful for large public libraries and for academic libraries where overseas imprints are wanted or where there are questions on overseas publishing.

—**Bonnie A. Dede**

666. **European Specialist Publishers Directory.** Sarah M. Hall, ed. Detroit, Gale, 1993. 615p. index. $144.00pa. ISBN 1-873477-10-4.

This is another newcomer to the growing list of international publishers directories from which libraries may select. With more than 40 countries and nearly 2,500 publishers in Western and Eastern Europe included, the directory attempts impressive coverage. Entries are derived from the publishers' responses to Gale questionnaires. Most of the directory consists of entries arranged under main subject headings, and alphabetically by company name within subjects. Full entries list quite a bit of information, including address, telephone and fax numbers, executives, parent company, imprints, foreign distributors, discounts and return policy, and other areas of specialization. Unfortunately, a significant number of entries contain little more than address and telephone number. The subject index lists name and entry numbers for publishers who have secondary subject specializations. A geographical index lists publishers by country. Former Soviet countries are listed under the name of their state. A publisher, imprint, and distributor index lists all companies mentioned in the directory, along with an entry number.

There is a fair amount of overlap in the companies and information listed in this directory with that in R. R. Bowker's *International Literary Market Place* (ILMP) (annual). However, many cases were found in which publishers were listed in one directory but not the other. As both are comparable in price, libraries should consider the limited geographical scope of *European Specialist Publishers Directory* when making a purchase decision. This directory would be a good supplement to ILMP in libraries whose clientele heavily use this type of information.—**Kerranne G. Biley**

667. **International Literary Market Place: ILMP 1993.** New Providence, N.J., R. R. Bowker/Reed Reference Publishing, 1992. 1073p. index. $164.00pa. LC 77-70295. ISBN 0-8352-3232-8. ISSN 0074-6827.

668. **Literary Market Place: LMP 1994: The Directory of the American Book Publishing Industry....** New Providence, N.J., R. R. Bowker/Reed Reference Publishing, 1993. 1896p. index. $158.00pa. LC 41-51571. ISBN 0-8352-3346-4. ISSN 0000-1155.

Upon opening a current *Literary Market Place* (LMP) or *International Literary Market Place* (ILMP), one immediately experiences the immensity, diversity, and vitality of the book publishing industry. Everything one would want or need to know about publishing can be found in LMP or ILMP, from information about publishers, agents, trademarks, copyright, and rights of permission to lists of international organizations and a book trade calendar. In an ever-changing and expanding field, both publications have kept pace admirably, constantly adding new features and restructuring to meet user needs. (For documentation of previous changes in format to LMP refer to ARBA 92, entry 639 and ARBA 90, entry 638.) The 1994 LMP boasts more than 15,800 entries. More than 1,200 of these are first-time listings—about 30,000 names in all. The 1993 ILMP covers more than 170 countries and has more than 15,000 listings. As of 1993 an index to the book trade and allied associates has been added to LMP, and the indexes to several of its sections have been reformatted to include the states where companies providing specific services can be found. ILMP contains two new indexes: subjects and types of publications. Section numbers have been added to running and fixed heads to guide users through the material.

Given the mass and complexity of the information encompassed by these works and the diversity of markets served, the organization of these publications works remarkably well. Each book provides a gold mine of information and gives users the tools to access it. The comprehensiveness, excellent organization, and continual refinement make both publications high-performance reference tools, indispensable to librarians, writers, designers, publishers, printers, book manufacturers, booksellers, and others involved with publishing.—**Barbara Ittner**

669. **Microform Market Place 1992-1993: An International Directory of Micropublishing.** New Providence, N.J., K. G. Saur/Reed Reference Publishing, 1993. 235p. index. $75.00pa. LC 74-8411. ISBN 3-598-11094-4. ISSN 0362-0999.

This international directory, the second edition to be published by K. G. Saur, includes nearly 500 microform publishers. They are listed in alphabetical order, with numerous cross-references from variant names. For each firm, standard directory information is given: address, telephone and fax numbers, and principal staff. A brief description of the firm's publishing program follows, with microformats offered and subjects covered. Two geographical indexes list the publishers by country and subject. The directory explicitly excludes manufacturers of micrographics equipment and supplies. The volume concludes with lists of firms that have discontinued publishing or have changed names, organizations that are concerned with educational aspects of microform use or standards, and a short annotated bibliography designed to help the user of microforms and microform equipment. (For reviews of earlier editions, see ARBA 92, entry 640 and ARBA 87, entry 646.)

The directory employs the same database as *Guide to Microforms in Print* (see ARBA 93, entries 1694 and 1695) but is specially updated for this publication. Information is much fuller, and more firms are included than in the publisher index in the *Guide*. A clear sans serif typeface is used, with headings in boldface. Running heads on each page further expedite searching. The volume is compact and fits the hand nicely. Although it has a paper cover and is perfect bound, it should stand up to considerable use. As such, it will prove a useful directory in large reference collections and information centers.

—**Richard D. Johnson**

670. **Publicity and Media Resources for Book Publishers.** 1992-1993 ed. New York, Association of American University Presses and Philadelphia, Morgan-Rand, 1992. 426p. index. $150.00pa. ISBN 0-925133-22-1.

This directory, a successor to *Advertising and Publicity Resources for Scholarly Books* (see ARBA 89, entry 578), provides scholarly book publishers with easy access to more than 6,000 media outlets in which to promote their products. Included are journals, newsletters, television and radio stations, cable television stations, television and radio networks, newspapers, leading consumer magazines, and syndicated newspaper columns. The listings contain contact information as well as information on the circulation or audience of each listed media outlet.

The directory is organized into three sections: subject/topic, title/program index, and geographical index. Each section contains easy-to-locate, alphabetically arranged headings. Many entries include a one-line abstract similar to this one found under environmental sciences in the subject/topic section: "A forum for the presentation of information encompassing the entire field of hazardous waste, including high- and low-level radioactive waste, chemical waste and transuranic waste." Morgan-Rand has produced a comprehensive guide that accomplishes the goal of providing book publishers with an up-to-date, usable directory.—**Dorothy M. Williams**

671. **Publishers, Distributors & Wholesalers of the United States 1993-94.** New Providence, N.J., R. R. Bowker/Reed Reference Publishing, 1993. 2v. index. $165.00/set. ISBN 0-8352-3380-4. ISSN 0000-0671.

A more comprehensive guide to participants in the book trade than *Literary Market Place* (LMP) (Reed Reference Publishing, annual), this two-volume set lists some 70,000 active U.S. publishers, distributors, wholesalers, associations, museums, software producers and manufacturers, and audiocassette producers and distributors. Split into two volumes in 1992, the set continues to be easier to use than the single-volume version, although both volumes have grown thicker with the addition of 12,000 new entries. There seems to have been no changes in format or arrangement. The index to publishers by fields of activity breaks publishers into 10 groups: associations, Bibles, El-Hi textbooks, large-type, mass-market paperbacks, museums, on demand, remainder dealers, small presses, and software producers. Narrower categories would be useful to find specialty presses, such as those that publish comic books or foreign-language materials. This sort of information is partially available in LMP, but that annual only lists around 15,000 firms and does not supply type-of-book information for all of them. A section on Canadian publishers would also be a desirable addition. Still, for information on even the smallest publishers in the United States, this set is unmatched.—**D. A. Rothschild**

672. Sheng, Jin, and Nan Fang, eds. **Directory of Publishers in China.** Beijing, China, Foreign Languages Press; distr., San Francisco, Calif., China Books & Periodicals, 1992. 281p. $14.95pa. ISBN 7-119-01544-3.

This Chinese-English bilingual directory lists, in alphabetical order according to the Pinyin romanization system, the names of some 500 Chinese publishers registered with the Chinese Government's State Press and Publication Administration. In both the Chinese and English sections, the information provided for each publisher includes its address; telephone, cable, and fax numbers (when available); key personnel; date founded; types of books published; total titles published; and ISBN. An appendix in English includes the copyright law of the People's Republic of China and the regulations used to implement it.

The information in this directory, based on official sources, is the first complete listing of Chinese publishers. It should be a useful tool for the international book trade and for library acquisitions.

—**Hwa-Wei Lee**

673. **Small Press Center Directory.** New York, Small Press Center, 1992. 329p. index. $19.95pa. ISBN 0-9622769-4-4.

The Small Press Center was founded in 1984 as a nonprofit organization whose purpose is to promote the work of independent publishers. The Center maintains a permanent exhibit of small press books in New York City and sponsors programs to support small press publications. It is estimated that there are between 5,000 and 10,000 small press publishers in the United States who issue books with some regularity and another 30,000 who issue books occasionally. The 620 small press publishers who are members of the Center are listed in this directory, the first to be issued by the organization.

The directory consists of two main parts. The first is an alphabetical list of the presses that contains the name, address, and telephone number of the press; a brief description of its history and editorial aims; and a description of some of its most recent publications. Some of these entries are illustrated with cover art or title pages. The second section describes all 1,214 titles listed in the first section under 17 broad subject headings, some of which have been further divided. Entries are alphabetical by title under each subject and contain author's name, publisher, date, a brief annotation, pages, format, price, and ISBN. Further access to this information is provided by four indexes—subject, author, publisher, and title—all of which refer to the first section of the directory. [R: LJ, 1 April 93, p. 94]—**Dean H. Keller**

674. **Yellow Pages Industry Source Book: U.S. & Canada.** 1992-93 ed. Frederica Evan, ed. Larchmont, N.Y., SIMBA/Communications Trends, 1992. 556p. index. $295.00pa. ISBN 0-88709-052-4.

The yellow pages industry has enjoyed significant growth in recent years; revenues for 1992 were expected to approach $10 billion. Industry advocates contend that yellow pages reach 98 percent of North American households and are used by the average person twice a week. Designed for the industry, *Yellow Pages Industry Source Book* is a directory of yellow pages publishers, some 275 in all. For each publisher the work provides name, address, and telephone number; size and scope of the firm; statistics on directory circulation; largest directories; projected growth; and various other features. Although the listings are uneven for some publishers, the information for most is consistent. The directory goes on to list more than 300 advertising agencies and authorized selling representatives as well as 300 printers and suppliers. The information for these two categories is not as complete as that provided for the publishers. The volume covers firms in the United States and Canada, and geographical indexes are provided for each category. An industry who's who and a brief index conclude the volume. The result is a comprehensive guide for this growing industry. Recommended for larger libraries that support business research.—**Boyd Childress**

Handbooks and Yearbooks

675. Bringhurst, Robert. **The Elements of Typographic Style.** Point Roberts, Wash., Hartley & Marks, 1992. 254p. illus. index. $24.95; $14.95pa. Z246.B74. 686.2'24. LC 92-7746. ISBN 0-88179-110-5; 0-88179-033-8pa.

In a host of different ways, humankind throughout the ages has used typography (pictograms and letterforms) as a means of communication. Typography is an indistinct field. It covers a multitude of disciplines and attempts to endow human language with a lasting visual form. Geared toward writers, editors, designers, and desktop publishers, this pictorial dictionary provides a wide range of information that incorporates the historical, aesthetic, and philosophical aspects of typography. Bringhurst has done a good job of coverage. Chapters deal with design, rhythm and proportion, structural forms and devices, choosing and combining type, shaping the page, and alphabets selected from typesetters' specimen books and font manufacturers' catalogs. A selective biographical index of type designers whose work is featured is provided. A glossary, index, and recommended readings list conclude the text.

Margin notes lead the reader to cross-references buried within the text, provide interesting sidebars to the central themes, and expound on fascinating historical information, such as the note on page 87 regarding Pilipino, the modern version of Tagalog, the official language of the Philippines. Particularly useful for page layout is the chapter on shaping the page. Establishing the overall dimensions of a page is often a matter of limitations. Portions of this chapter discuss layouts for one- and two-page spreads, proportional type, column restrictions, balance and symmetry, page grids and modular scales, and designing pages with arithmetic; the chapter concludes with the salient point that text always takes precedence over the purity of design.

This visually oriented dictionary is a pleasant blend of terms, illustrations, typefaces, and advice in making sensitive design choices for every phase of the typographic process. Being neither a manual of editorial style nor a textbook on design, it embodies practical, hands-on advice. The sheer range of topics treated, as well as the author's knowledge of the subject, makes this a worthy purchase for most libraries. Students of letterforms will find it indispensable.—**Judy Gay Matthews**

12 Military Studies

GENERAL WORKS

Acronyms and Abbreviations

676. **Jane's Defence Glossary.** Ian Kay and Mary Walker, comps. Alexandria, Va., Jane's Information Group, 1993. 295p. $50.00pa. ISBN 0-7106-1118-8.

This is a list of acronyms and abbreviations used in military and defense circles. The items are deciphered but not defined; the glossary explains that GBCS-L stands for Ground Based Common Sensor-Light, but not what it is. Most of the terms have United States or British origins, but there are also terms from French, German, Spanish, and other languages. Abbreviations having a particular application in a specific organization or country are identified as such. A number of appendixes are used to give such information as membership of international organizations, NATO (North Atlantic Treaty Organization) names for former Soviet aircraft, and the phonetic alphabet.

Comprehensiveness, currency, clientele need, and price are four factors that help determine the selection of one acronym/abbreviation dictionary over another. In comparing *Jane's* with Bernard Pretz's *Dictionary of Military and Technological Abbreviations and Acronyms* (Routledge, Chapman & Hall, 1983) and *Acronyms, Initialisms & Abbreviations Dictionary, 1993* (AI&AD) (for a review of an earlier edition see ARBA 88, entry 1) one can see how difficult it is for a title to satisfy all criteria. Pretz is more comprehensive than *Jane's* but not as current. AI&AD is more current than *Jane's* but is not limited to military abbreviations and is more expensive. As for comprehensiveness, all three have terms that the other titles lack, suggesting that for a library serving a public concerned with military acronyms, all three would be necessary. *Jane's* high price suggests that the publisher anticipates a relatively small, specialized audience for this paperback. For most academic and public libraries, AI&AD will suffice.

—**Eric R. Nitschke**

Atlases

677. Crawford, William "Roy," L. Ann Crawford, and R. J. Crawford. **United States Military Road Atlas.** Falls Church, Va., Military Living, 1993. 144p. illus. maps. index. $16.95pa. G1201.R2C7. 355.7'0973. LC 92-38252. ISBN 0-914862-36-7.

This is a marvelous atlas. Its purpose is to depict almost 600 military bases and posts in the United States, and it is one of the best-drawn and best-produced atlases one will find anywhere. There is a map for each of the 50 states as well as for Puerto Rico, the Virgin Islands, and Guam. Scales vary to allow one map per page. The maps are wonderfully clear and uncluttered. Interstate, U.S., and selected state highways are shown in different colors. Large cities appear, of course, but the detail of the atlas is such that some very small towns are also shown. Large cities with a major concentration of military facilities are given special attention in separate maps at scales of 1:125,000 or 1:250,000. National and state parks, recreation areas, and other tourist attractions are depicted. Thus, this would be a fine atlas for anyone taking a vacation anywhere in the country.

The main feature of the atlas is its location of military installations. These are designated by symbols (e.g., a plane for Air Force) and the name in boldface type. State maps are arranged into geographical regions, and each regional section provides a number of narrative aids for the traveler. There are a section pointing out significant recreational facilities available to military personnel, directions to each of the installations, a list of important telephone numbers at each of the sites, and a mileage chart for determining distances between installations. Highly recommended for any library serving a military population and for any library interested in acquiring a fine atlas of the United States.—**Eric R. Nitschke**

Bibliography

678. Edwards, Paul M., comp. **General Matthew B. Ridgway: An Annotated Bibliography.** Westport, Conn., Greenwood Press, 1993. 110p. index. (Bibliographies of Battles and Leaders, no.8). $55.00. Z8745.25.E39. 355'.0092. LC 93-10832. ISBN 0-313-28739-2.

Many twentieth-century generals, such as Dwight Eisenhower, Norman Schwarzkopf, and Colin Powell, have influenced U.S. military practice and doctrine and have been prominent public figures. There are also military figures who have been less prominent but who exerted significant influence on U.S. military history and policy. Matthew B. Ridgway (1895-1993) is such an individual, and this annotated bibliography helps introduce readers to his career. The compilation opens with a historiographical preface and proceeds with a biographical chronology and portrait of Ridgway. The primary focus of this work consists of sections that list archives and depositories with significant documentary collections pertinent to Ridgway, and a bibliographical list of books, articles, and dissertations by and about him. Specific topics and sources covered in these annotated entries include military dictionaries, biographical information, the memoirs of civilian and military leaders, World Wars I and II, and the Korean War. The work concludes with periodical, author, and subject indexes.

This is generally a good bibliographical guide to an important but less-recognized figure in modern U.S. military history. One weakness is a major bibliographical error that misspells the name of author Patrick Glynn, incorrectly lists the title of his work as *Closing Pandora's Box* (1992) (the complete title is *Closing Pandora's Box: Arms Races, Arms Control, and the History of the Cold War*), the publisher as HarperCollins instead of Basic Books, and the book's length as 144 pages as opposed to 445 pages. Despite this editorial oversight and the excessive price for this slender volume, this is a valuable work that should stimulate additional study on this important figure in U.S. military history.—**Bert Chapman**

679. Edwards, Paul M., comp. **The Pusan Perimeter, Korea, 1950: An Annotated Bibliography.** Westport, Conn., Greenwood Press, 1993. 118p. index. (Bibliographies of Battles and Leaders, no.11). $55.00. Z3316.E39. 016.951904'2. LC 93-2586. ISBN 0-313-28740-6.

The North Korean Army invaded South Korea in June 1950. By late July the few United States, South Korean, and allied troops had been forced to withdraw to a defensive position around the city of Pusan, in the far southeast of Korea. There they repulsed attack after attack, not breaking out until mid-September. This bibliography covers the varied literature of this early period of the Korean War: the initial defeats, the withdrawals, and the stand at Pusan.

The compiler gives a good description of major archival source collections appropriate for the study of this period. There is also a very helpful section on published government documents that details sources from the United Nations, the U.S. Congress, and the departments of State and Defense. The largest part of the bibliography is devoted to secondary works dealing with either the Korean War in general or with specific actions, units, or topics. Sources include books and articles from general interest and scholarly magazines.

This work is a useful, well-organized subject bibliography. It is especially gratifying because its subject has, by and large, been neglected for many years. One hopes that Edwards's work will stimulate new interest in this "action," which strongly affected our country and its citizens. Recommended for any library whose readers are interested in military or U.S. history.—**Eric R. Nitschke**

680. Higham, Robin, and Donald J. Mrozek, eds. **A Guide to the Sources of United States Military History: Supplement III.** Hamden, Conn., Archon Books/Shoe String Press, 1993. 531p. $55.00. Z1249.M5G83. 016.355'00973. LC 92-15623. ISBN 0-208-02214-7.

The fourth volume in this series maintains the same high level of editorial excellence and first-class bookmaking exhibited in the earlier guides. The series began with the original guide in 1975 (see ARBA 76, entry 1675), followed by supplement I in 1981 (see ARBA 82, entry 1652) and supplement II in 1986 (see ARBA 87, entry 652). Each volume builds on and expands on previous publications and brings the reader up-to-date on the status of military history in each of 23 areas, from colonial forces through all the rethinking and reevaluation brought on by the end of the Cold War. The format remains the same: an overview essay in each area written by some of the most eminent experts at work in their fields of specialization. These narratives are followed by numbered bibliographic references, some of which are highlighted in the essay. The references are numbered from the original volumes; for example, the American Revolution, which had 683 citations from previous volumes, now runs up to 883. On the other hand, ordnance, introduced here for the first time, starts at 1 (what else!) and runs to 319.

It is hoped that readers can look forward to another update in five or six years. Perhaps supplement IV will add chapters on women, military in space, and interservice cooperation (and conflict?). The same high quality is a given. [R: Choice, May 93, p. 1441]—**David Eggenberger**

681. House, Jonathan M. **Military Intelligence, 1870-1991: A Research Guide.** Westport, Conn., Greenwood Press, 1993. 165p. index. (Research Guides in Military Studies, no.6). $55.00. UB250.H68. 355.3'432. LC 93-226. ISBN 0-313-27403-7.

The heart of this guide is an annotated bibliography of 881 English-language sources concerned with military intelligence from 1870 to the present. Its scope encompasses the history, organization, problems of collection and analysis, and roles in battlefield operations. Two closely related subjects are also included: electronic warfare and military deception—both processes by which an army or nation attempts to confound or mislead its opponents. An introductory essay offers a synopsis of the various problems involved in researching these subjects; this will be especially useful to the novice.

It is the nature of intelligence to be clandestine and closely guarded, and thus its narratives typically lag far behind those of actual operations. House's dual career as historian and active intelligence analyst naturally presupposes success in overcoming some of this darkness, purposeful or otherwise, and readers will find the same balanced overview that characterized his earlier study of combined arms warfare. The way intelligence matters have conflicted with U.S. constitutional liberties also recommends this guide to those concerned with wider policy issues. Author and subject indexes and a useful appendix of terms will further the helpfulness of this high-quality effort. [R: Choice, Nov 93, p. 434]—**Paul L. Holmer**

682. LaFrance, David G., and Errol D. Jones, eds. **Latin American Military History: An Annotated Bibliography.** Hamden, Conn., Garland, 1992. 734p. (Military History Bibliographies, v.12; Garland Reference Library of the Humanities, v.1024). $110.00. Z1621.L38. 016.355'0098. LC 92-12606. ISBN 0-8240-4634-X.

Because the military has played a dominant role during much of Latin America's history, and because no comparable volume currently exists, this book fills an important void. Following a brief introduction by the editors, the work is divided into 12 additional chapters arranged first chronologically (colonial, independence movements, nineteenth-century *caudillismo*) and then by country or region, from Argentina to Uruguay. The general approach in each chapter is to supply a brief introduction to the period or country, followed by a list of general works, archival sources, published documents, specialized works, periodicals, and suggestions for future research. There are also bibliographies arranged alphabetically by author.

The editors secured acknowledged experts for most sections. The colonial period is described by Mark Burkholder, a specialist on the judicial administration of the Spanish empire. One of the best chapters is that by Christon Archer, a specialist on the military in Bourbon, Mexico, who describes in great detail the military's role in the independence struggle. Other excellent chapters include Jones's discussion of Brazil and LaFrance's chapter on Mexico. Regrettably, the book lacks an index and has only one (badly printed) map. Another distraction is that page headers are misplaced in several places.

This book, which should be updated by reviews of historical indexes, is a good starting point for a student studying the role of the military in Latin America. It can be profitably used by scholars and graduate students and deserves a place in all Latin American collections. [R: Choice, June 93, p. 1606]
—**Brian E. Coutts**

683. McClean, Andrew, comp. **Security, Arms Control, and Conflict Reduction in East Asia and the Pacific: A Bibliography, 1980-1991.** Westport, Conn., Greenwood Press, 1993. 551p. index. (Bibliographies and Indexes in Law and Political Science, no.19). $95.00. Z6724.N37M37. 016.355'.03305. LC 93-18142. ISBN 0-313-27539-4.

This bibliography contains citations to more than 8,100 English-language articles, books, dissertations, and official publications. Some citations appear in more than one section of the book, resulting in a total of 12,645 entries. Most of the citations are from periodicals, ranging from scholarly journals to peace movement publications. For assistance in identifying key sources for this work, the compiler contacted 150 research institutes and publishers, many of which are located in the East Asia/Pacific area.

Entries are organized geographically, with East Asia and the Pacific divided into four broad regions that are then subdivided into chapters on countries and subregions. Surprisingly, the United States and former Soviet Union do not receive individual chapters. Instead, they are covered in a chapter labeled "The Superpowers, 1980-1991," and as subheadings within many of the chapters devoted to other countries. Access to the entries is aided greatly by an overview of the contents and a detailed table of contents, as well as author and cross-referenced subject indexes. Some of the materials cited are in-house publications that are only available from their publishers, so a listing of some 89 research institutes and academic departments, complete with addresses, is included in an appendix. In spite of this work's high price, academic libraries with a strong interest in international relations, security, or arms control in the East Asia/Pacific region should find this a useful addition to their collections.—**Melvin Marlo Brown**

684. Orgill, Andrew. **The Falklands War: Background, Conflict, Aftermath: An Annotated Bibliography.** New York, Mansell/Cassell, 1993. 132p. index. $70.00. Z1945.074. 016.997'11. LC 92-12033. ISBN 0-7201-2130-2.

On March 19, 1982, a group of Argentine scrap metal dealers raised their national flag on the tiny island of South Georgia, a British possession some 1,200 miles off the Argentine coast. This latest in a long series of diplomatic skirmishes over ownership of the Falkland Islands was followed by an Argentine military landing and British response—her largest military operation since World War II. The ultimate cost ran to 750 Argentine and 235 British deaths. It seems unbelievable, but this minor international incident produced the 822 citations found in this book. Orgill details books, document collections, and journal articles of at least 2,000 words. Although most of the entries are in English or Spanish, a few are in French, German, Russian, Italian, or Portuguese. The entries are divided into five broad subject areas: bibliographies, the sovereignty dispute, the 1982 crises, the war, and the aftermath. There are many subdivisions under each category. Although Orgill claims to have checked almost all the items, his annotations are merely descriptive and very brief. The volume's introduction serves as a bibliographical essay on the major sources; appendixes consist of indexes of journal and series titles and a subject/author listing. Although British and Argentine libraries might find this volume useful, few U.S. libraries, other than the largest research institutions, would want to pay the price for this narrow source. [R: Choice, Dec 93, p. 589]—**Joe P. Dunn**

Biography

685. Hawkins, Walter L. **African American Generals and Flag Officers: Biographies of Over 120 Blacks in the United States Military.** Jefferson, N.C., McFarland, 1993. 264p. illus. index. $25.95. E181.H38. 355'.0089'96073. LC 92-50886. ISBN 0-89950-774-3.

African Americans have played a significant role in American military history. Although the impediments were great, Black Americans have risen to the highest ranks in the military services, with Black generals as early as the Civil War. The 1- or 2-page career biographical summaries in this volume chronicle the 120 African Americans who have risen to the rank of general officer or its navy equivalent. Besides the fine summaries, the book includes a chronology of significant dates and actions in the history of Blacks and the U.S. military, a list of significant firsts by Blacks in the military, breakdowns of general officers by service and number of stars, listings by the states where they were born and the colleges and universities they attended, and a useful index.

Although far more specialized than the author's *African American Biographies* (see ARBA 93, entry 423), this volume also contains a tremendous amount of information. Its inexpensive price makes it affordable for a wide range of libraries. [R: RBB, Aug 93, p. 2085; WLB, May 93, p. 113]—**Joe P. Dunn**

Dictionaries and Encyclopedias

686. Grechko, A. A., and N. V. Ogarkov. **The Soviet Military Encyclopedia.** abridged English-language ed. Boulder, Colo., Westview Press, 1993. 4v. illus. index. $375.00/set. U24.S7213. 355'.003. LC 92-32531. ISBN 0-8133-1432-1.

The Soviet Military Encyclopedia is an eight-volume compilation published by the Soviet Ministry of Defense from 1976 to 1980. It was an unclassified, official voice of the highest level of the Soviet military, an important source for understanding Soviet military doctrine, strategy, and terminology. The U.S. editors have selected and translated the most important and useful articles for this edition. The entries are arranged in alphabetical order (in English), with transliterated Russian titles and the original Soviet authors cited. Original references for the articles are included in transliterated Russian (with English translation in brackets). A further citation shows where the article is located in the original source. Volume 4 is a two-part index that contains a list of the articles in English (with Russian in brackets) for the three-volume abridged edition and a complete index to the original source in Russian (with English translation in brackets). Despite the magnitude of this enterprise, the collapse of the Soviet Union makes these volumes of more historical than of immediate national security interest. Only the largest research libraries with specialties in military studies or the former Soviet Union will be interested in this expensive reference source.—**Joe P. Dunn**

687. **The Harper Encyclopedia of Military History: From 3500 B.C. to the Present.** 4th ed. By R. Ernest Dupuy and Trevor N. Dupuy. New York, HarperCollins, 1993. 1654p. maps. index. $65.00. D25.D86. 355'.009. LC 92-17853. ISBN 0-06-270056-1.

This massive work is the standard by which all military encyclopedias are measured. Trevor Dupuy is unquestionably the world's premier chronicler of military affairs, as testified to in this volume and its companions, *The Harper Encyclopedia of Military Biography* (see ARBA 93, entry 698) and the six-volume *International Military and Defense Encyclopedia* (Macmillan, 1993), as well as his myriad other books. This volume is a collection of chronologically and geographically organized narratives of war and warfare divided into 22 time-period chapters. Each chapter includes an introductory essay on the principal military trends, leaders, innovations, and so forth of the period; the wars of the period; and specific treatment of military affairs in each region, state, or nation. The volume also has numerous maps and pictures; a bibliography; an extensive, cross-referenced general index; and indexes of wars and of battles and sieges.

Authoritative, comprehensive, usable, readable, and relatively inexpensive for such an essential reference tool, *The Harper Encyclopedia of Military History* should be in every library. With this volume and the two sources noted above, a library will have the basic military affairs reference materials. [R: Choice, Nov 93, pp. 428-30; RBB, 1 Nov 93, pp. 564-65]—**Joe P. Dunn**

688. **International Military and Defense Encyclopedia.** Trevor N. Dupuy, ed. McLean, Va., Brassey's (U.S.), 1993. 6v. illus. index. $1,250.00/set. U24.I58. 355'.003. LC 92-33750. ISBN 0-02-881011-2.

This is a remarkable undertaking and accomplishment. The 6 volumes contain 786 alphabetically arranged articles that range from 100 to more than 10,000 words. Except for important historical treatments, the focus is on events and developments since 1945. Renowned military historian Dupuy, author of more than 60 books and editor of *The Harper Encyclopedia of Military Biography* (see ARBA 93, entry 698) and *The Harper Encyclopedia of Military History*, 4th ed. (HarperCollins, 1993), served as editor in chief for the project. The set is truly international in scope and participation; the advisory board, editorial board, and 400-plus authors represent 17 countries on 4 continents. The impressive list of contributors, most with defense and military backgrounds, includes experts from Canada, Great Britain, France, Germany, Austria, the Netherlands, Italy, Switzerland, Israel, Australia, the People's Republic of China, Japan, Egypt, India, and the United States.

The coverage, range, depth, and quality of the articles are exceptional. Sources and treatment are current. Recent events in Eastern Europe and the former Soviet Union and the 1991 Gulf War dictated the rewriting of large numbers of previously submitted entries. Excellent bibliographies and cross-references to related topics enhance the value of the entries. The auxiliary reference aids in the first and last volumes also are extremely important. These include a list of all articles and authors alphabetically and by subject area, contributors (including their positions and countries), pages of abbreviations and acronyms, and a 25,000-term comprehensive index.

A number of new military reference volumes have appeared recently, including the two noted above, *The Penguin Encyclopedia of Modern Warfare* (see ARBA 93, entry 701), *The Military History of the United States* (see ARBA 93, entry 700), and the first 2 of the projected 50 volumes of *The International Military Encyclopedia* (see ARBA 93, entry 702). Only the latter is comparable in scope, but it does not have a contributor list of the caliber of the volumes under review. It will take a mammoth effort to come anywhere close to the quality of the *International Military and Defense Encyclopedia*.

Undoubtedly, the price will significantly limit this encyclopedia's availability. This is unfortunate, because all libraries would benefit from the accessibility of this useful reference work. [R: Choice, May 93, p. 1442; JAL, July 93, p. 201; LJ, 15 Mar 93, p. 70; RBB, Aug 93, pp. 1084-85; RQ, Fall 93, pp. 129-30; WLB, April 93, pp. 121-22]—**Joe P. Dunn**

689. **The Visual Dictionary of Special Military Forces.** New York, Dorling Kindersley, 1993. 64p. illus. index. (Eyewitness Visual Dictionaries). $14.95. U262.S628. 356'.167'93. LC 92-53448. ISBN 1-56458-189-6.

Visual dictionaries (also called pictorial dictionaries) do not define, they illustrate; they do not explain, they depict. They provide images, perhaps drawings or photographs, of things (never concepts) and label the parts of those things. For example, they show that on the wheel of an automobile is a thing called a hubcap, but they do not tell what the hubcap does or why. A good visual dictionary will have clear illustrations with unambiguous labels—labels that are accurate in terminology and that are clearly connected, by lines or adjacency, to the thing to which they refer. In addition, the dictionary will have an index of terms so that one can look up a thing (e.g., a hubcap) and find out where it is illustrated.

The Visual Dictionary of Special Military Forces is a very good visual dictionary because it has all the characteristics mentioned above. Its subject is the weapons, equipment, and paraphernalia of groups such as the British SOE, SAS, and MI6; the American OSS and CIA; the Soviet KGB; and other special forces. Some of the fascinating things shown are a World War II OSS pipe pistol, a Japanese cigarette lighter camera, a German Enigma cipher machine, a UH-1 HUEY helicopter, a Humvee vehicle, and a German World War II one-man submarine. The book is organized into chapters by subjects such as snipers, parachutists, encoding/decoding, escape and survival, and concealed weapons. The color illustrations are superb, big and clear against a white background. A thin black line connects the label with the part or item indicated; there is no mistaking what is meant. An index of terms refers to the photographs.

Certainly, the book is not, nor does it claim to be, a complete catalog of special forces gear. But it could be used for enjoyment and enrichment by many in all types of libraries.—**Eric R. Nitschke**

Handbooks and Yearbooks

690. **America's Top Military Careers: The Official Guide to Occupations in the Armed Forces.** Indianapolis, Ind., JIST Works, [1993]. 473p. illus. index. $19.95pa. ISBN 1-56370-124-3.

As an employer, the U.S. military hires (or recruits) some 200,000 personnel annually, channeling them into some 100,000 training options. In a format similar to that of the annual *Occupational Outlook Handbook* (JIST Works), this extensive reference volume provides vocational information on nearly 200 military careers. The primary division of the volume is by enlisted occupations and officers' careers. Each career or assignment is briefly described, including job attributes, work environment, training, physical demands, and career opportunities. Similar civilian jobs are listed as well as an interpretative chart relating the enlisted careers to the Armed Service Vocational Aptitude Battery (ASVAB). Another useful section includes a typical career path for 38 separate assignments, indicating military career expectations for actual service people. Indexes by job title and *Dictionary of Occupational Titles* (see ARBA 93, entry 301) conclude the volume.

This invaluable book belongs in all types of reference collections, including public and high school libraries. As indicated on the volume's title page, the book is an unabridged commercial version of the Government Printing Office's *Military Careers* (1992). Considering that the JIST Works price is about half of the GPO cost, the commercial version is a true bargain. [R: LJ, Dec 93, p. 110]—**Boyd Childress**

691. Berndt, Thomas. **Standard Catalog of U.S. Military Vehicles 1940-1965.** Iola, Wis., Krause Publications, 1993. 272p. illus. $29.95. LC 92-72123. ISBN 0-87341-223-0.

Military vehicle collecting is a specialized subset of the antique car hobby that can make heavy demands in space and community appreciation. There are currently some 6,000 members of the Military Vehicle Preservation Association and a much larger audience of World War II buffs. This is basically a collector's guide to U.S. military vehicles from 1940 to 1965. It describes more than 280 models under 12 headings, from trucks through armored cars, tanks, and motorcycles. The primary intent is to provide a comprehensive identification manual and basic mechanical and technical specifications. Additionally, for most models sale values are provided for each of six collecting grades. Krause Publications is well established in the field with its *Old Cars Price Guide* magazine and is plainly ready to accommodate this growing field of interest. Large public libraries and those with an emphasis on military history will find this to be a popular item. [R: RBB, 1 Sept 93, p. 90]—**Paul L. Holmer**

692. Clodfelter, Micheal. **Warfare and Armed Conflicts: A Statistical Reference to Casualty and Other Figures, 1618-1991.** Jefferson, N.C., McFarland, 1992. 2v. index. $125.00/set. D214.C55. 904'.7. LC 91-52632. ISBN 0-89950-544-9.

This work gives statistics of military and civilian casualties suffered in wars, battles, riots, revolutions, and coup d'etats. The statistics may include those killed, wounded, missing, or captured, depending on the circumstance. Clodfelter provides a history of each situation, recounting not only the sequence of events but also the influence on casualties of such factors as the quality of leadership, arms and innovations in weaponry, medical practices, sanitary conditions, and tactics.

The conflicts covered in this work are arranged by century, then by continent, and range from the large-scale to the small. Articles on larger conflicts conclude with tables and analyses of the statistics. The Thirty Years' War, the American Civil War, both world wars, and the Napoleonic Wars appear along with the Chicago Gangster Wars of the 1920s, the Matabele War, the Chartist Uprisings, and 800-plus other wars, riots, and battles. There is an index of people, battles, and political parties.

But what are the sources of the statistics presented? Here one is left largely in the dark. The short bibliography lists only secondary works, some of which are surprisingly lightweight. The author recognizes that casualty statistics, even from so-called advanced nations, are often suspect, if not downright impossible to collect and compare. Yet it is a pity that the official documents and reports, statistical summaries from war departments and ministries, and other archival material that were used to produce this work are not cited. This is a fine compilation that belongs in the reference collection of almost every library, but one cannot help but feel that more complete documentation would have increased its authority and credibility. [R: RBB, 1 Feb 93, p. 1005; RQ, Fall 93, pp. 137-38; WLB, Mar 93, p. 115]

—**Eric R. Nitschke**

693. Goldstein, Erik. **Wars and Peace Treaties 1816-1991.** New York, Routledge, Chapman & Hall, 1992. 264p. index. $49.95. D361.G65. 904'.7. LC 91-18744. ISBN 0-415-07822-9.

This small volume covers wars and peace treaties from 1816 to 1991 in a compact, succinct style. The work names the belligerents in a conflict; explains the cause, occasion, or immediate reason for the outbreak of hostilities; describes the course of the conflict; and explains the political result.

Conflicts are divided up according to geographical area, national origin, and international event. Civil wars, such as the U.S. Civil War and the Russian Civil War, are excluded, because they were not international in nature. Some of the largest sections deal with the decline of the Ottoman empire, world wars and related conflicts, East Asian wars, and South American wars. The appendixes list the date of entry of countries into hostilities for both world wars, post-World War II peace treaties, United Nations peacekeeping operations, and major arms control agreements. This excellent work provides a great deal of historical information for lay and professional researchers and is highly recommended for public, college, university, and government reference collections. [R: RBB, 1 Sept 93, p. 91]—**Norman L. Kincaide**

694. Kennemer, Phyllis K. **Using Literature to Teach Middle Grades about War.** Phoenix, Ariz., Oryx Press, 1993. 209p. index. $29.95pa. D214.K46. 940'.7'071273. LC 92-31932. ISBN 0-89774-778-X.

While the recent Persian Gulf conflict brought war directly into the lives and homes of many of today's young people, Vietnam and the other great wars of the United States have been the topics of literature and school classwork for decades. This book contains fiction, nonfiction, and picture books, and provides thorough units for teaching six major U.S. wars. Besides the two mentioned, there are units on the Revolutionary and Civil wars and World Wars I and II. Each unit follows a set pattern: a selected chronology, recommended books (including biographies), a sample lesson plan, suggested questions and activities, and a glossary of terms. The chronology includes the first and major battles to give a sense of the scope of the war and its turning points.

While most books are aimed at grades six through eight, numerous inclusions are for the more mature or reluctant reader. And while the emphasis is on current copyright, older classics are included (e.g., *Uncle Tom's Cabin* [Random House, 1991]). Annotations cover each work's particular point of view to stimulate discussion.

A noteworthy special feature that should prove useful in teaching these units is the section on general activities for use with all units. It provides such tips as guidelines for discussion leaders, timelines, diaries or journals, "greet the greats," and webbing techniques for notetaking. One significant category omitted is audiovisual materials; however, as the emphasis is on literature and most educators are limited by local availability of such materials, this is not a serious drawback. The items found in the appendixes, which include a very thorough teacher planning guide and one for special interest groups, plus student forms for book reporting and recording and evaluation of the unit studied, should prove highly useful.

An author and title index concludes this fine work, which fills a valuable niche in the school library and curriculum areas of social studies, history, and current events and is an excellent bibliographic resource for whole language teaching. All schools and public libraries should consider it for first purchase. [R: EL, Mar-April 93, p. 47; JOYS, Fall, 93, pp. 92-93; SLMQ, Spring 93, p. 198]—**Carol Truett**

695. Perrett, Bryan. **The Battle Book: Crucial Conflicts in History from 1469 BC to the Present.** London, Arms and Armour Press; distr., New York, Sterling Publishing, 1992. 349p. index. $24.95. ISBN 1-85409-125-5.

Although several recent military encyclopedias are available, this is a handy addition to the reference literature. In a useful graphic-box form, the volume capsules 550 military engagements, from Megiddo in 1469 B.C. to the Gulf War, that have in one way or another altered the course of history. The standard citation for each battle gives date, location, war and campaign, opposing sides and commanding officers, forces engaged, casualties, and result. Most of the battles have a descriptive narrative following these basic facts. The entries are cross-referenced, and appendixes list the battles by wars, commanders, tactics, and weapons. The battles are listed in alphabetical order with number citations for easy reference to other entries.

Although it duplicates *The Penguin Encyclopedia of Modern Warfare* (see ARBA 93, entry 701) and R. Ernest Dupuy and Trevor N. Dupuy's *The Harper Encyclopedia of Military History* (HarperCollins, 1993), for quick reference this is the easiest-to-use source available. The price makes it attractive, especially for public libraries.—**Joe P. Dunn**

696. Stein, Barry Jason. **U.S. Army Heraldic Crests: A Complete Illustrated History of Authorized Distinctive Unit Insignia.** Columbia, S.C., University of South Carolina Press, 1993. 461p. illus. index. $59.95. UC533.S74. 355.1'342'0973. LC 93-3109. ISBN 0-87249-963-4.

Since 1775, the U.S. Army has been a recognized branch among the world's military services. During the years since the American Revolution, heraldic crests have identified specific Army units with colorful insignia often marked by proud mottoes of distinction. In this definitive reference volume, Stein identifies more than 3,100 such insignia. For each crest, the unit, the date adopted, a note on the crest, the motto, and a summary of unit action are included. For example, the Third Artillery unit saw action in campaigns from the War of 1812 through the Korean War. Its crest represents action in the War of 1812, the Civil War, China's Boxer Rebellion, the Seminole campaign, both world wars, the Mexican War, and the Philippine insurrection; its motto is "speed and accuracy." The insignia are illustrated in 129 color plates. While the plates make for smaller visual representation, each is clear enough to identify the features described.

The arrangement is alphabetical by the type of unit, such as artillery, aviation, engineer, military police, or transportation. Units are listed numerically under each broad classification. A glossary, a brief bibliography, and an index by motto conclude the volume. With the alphanumeric arrangement, no unit index is necessary. Other books on insignia generally do not meet the standards created by this well-prepared reference work.—**Boyd Childress**

Quotation Books

697. Tsouras, Peter G. **Warrior's Words: A Quotation Book: From Sesotris III to Schwarzkopf, 1871 BC to AD 1991.** London, Cassell; distr., New York, Sterling Publishing, 1992. 534p. index. $29.95. 828.02. ISBN 1-85409-088-7.

Books of quotations are the orators' and speech writers' bibles. This is a rather narrowly focused one, with commentaries by more than 250 military personnel who span 4,000 years of history. The author, himself a military officer, has collected quotations on almost 350 alphabetically arranged subjects (e.g., art of war, bravery, chivalry, duty, surrender, terrain, will). A good bibliography and a biographical index of commentator augment this well-done compilation. Tsouras is correct that the book should be useful for "the junior officer, the military professional, and the military enthusiast in general." It should be in the libraries of military academies, senior service schools, military research centers, and other such venues. It may have less applicability to other libraries, although its relatively low price affords the luxury of at least considering it for the more limited employment it would have in large public and university libraries. [R: Choice, Mar 93, p. 1122]—**Joe P. Dunn**

AIR FORCE

698. Bright, Charles D., ed. **Historical Dictionary of the U.S. Air Force.** Westport, Conn., Greenwood Press, 1992. 713p. index. $85.00. UG633.B75. 358.4'00973. LC 91-25461. ISBN 0-313-25928-3.

The U.S. Air Force is a major contributor to national military strength and an increasingly important factor in the promotion of U.S. foreign policy interests. *Historical Dictionary of the U.S. Air Force* serves as an introduction to the individuals, planes, strategies, organizations, events, and equipment that have contributed to the Air Force's development. The book opens with a preface explaining its organization and the abbreviations of frequently used sources. This is followed by a concise history of the U.S. Air Force. The main part of this effort contains an alphabetical list of important individuals and factors involved in shaping the development of the youngest branch of the armed forces.

The dictionary includes such figures as Giulio Duohet, Curtis LeMay, and Barry Goldwater; planes such as the F-15 Eagle, C-130 Hercules, and B-29 Superfortress; and equipment that ranges from the Norden Bombsight to Side-Looking Airborne Radar (SLAR). Other entries include the names of individual air force bases, such as Bergstrom and Carswell; important events, such as the 1945 bombing of Dresden, Operation Rolling Thunder during the Vietnam War, and the Gulf War; such operational practices as fighter escort; and important organizations, such as the North Atlantic Treaty Organization (NATO). Brief bibliographic citations are appended to these entries, and a list of contributors follows the index.

Historical Dictionary of the U.S. Air Force is a worthy addition to any library desirous of augmenting its military history holdings. Its authoritativeness is enhanced by the editor's status as a retired Air Force lieutenant colonel and by the influence of prominent military historian Robin Higham. This compilation will do much to encourage additional study of the historical and contemporary development of the U.S. Air Force. [R: LJ, 1 Apr 92, p. 112]—**Bert Chapman**

699. Kinzey, Bert. **U.S. Aircraft & Armament of Operation Desert Storm in Detail & Scale.** Shrewsbury, England, Airlife Publishing; distr., Waukesha, Wis., Kalmbach Publishing, 1993. 72p. illus. (D&S, v.40). $11.95pa. UG1243.K5. 358.4'183'097309050. LC 93-20524. ISBN 0-89024-153-8.

This book contains much more information on air combat during the Gulf War and its aftermath than the title suggests: Only one-sixth of the book is devoted to coverage of model aircraft. Both sections represent expert analysis in a compact format from a leading authority. Indeed, in several cases (particularly the excellent performance of the F-111E) Kinzey draws conclusions that are original, convincing, and at striking variance with most popular accounts. The principal content of the book is a series of two-page discussions of each of the U.S. combat (fighter, bomber, and EW [electronic warfare] support) aircraft involved. In each case operational detail, squadron assignments, and armament loadouts are highlighted. The additional detail on the armament and EW stores provides one of the best available close-ups on this material.

The strength of this work is its illustrations. The monochrome photographs are crisp and clear, the color pictures are accurately registered, and the scale drawings highlight otherwise obscure detail. In all cases, the captions are a model of concise information. The only drawback to this ready-reference volume is the lack of an index or table of contents. With fine printing on coated stock in a reasonably durable binding, this is a top-notch guide to its subject. Smaller libraries lacking access to the major reference works on aircraft and armament would find this a particularly effective substitute information source for this particular topic.—**John Howard Oxley**

700. Sullivan, George. **Military Aircraft: Modern Bombers and Attack Planes.** New York, Facts on File, 1992. 120p. illus. index. $17.95. UG1242.A28S83. 358.4'282. LC 92-6399. ISBN 0-8160-2354-9.

This volume consists of a dozen aircraft descriptions arranged in no particular order. Each is described with a short historical and operational summary and a brief data table (e.g., no weapons or fuel load breakouts). The writing style is informal and choppy, with sharp transitions from one topic to the next.

This book's inclusion criteria, nowhere stated, are the first concern. For example, despite its "F-for-fighter" designation, the F-117A is a dedicated stealth attack aircraft, yet it is not covered. Likewise, light attack and counterinsurgency aircraft are excluded. Unfortunately, data accuracy and comprehensiveness are also suspect. Some data do not match other authoritative sources (e.g., the service ceiling of the A-6 "Intruder"), while others are outright errors (e.g., the Tu-95/142 "Bear" is 100 feet too short). Major omissions are the Su-24 "Fencer" ground support aircraft and the Su-25/35 "Frogfoot" attack plane (analogous to the U.S.'s A-10, which is covered). Many attack aircraft that are still in service worldwide are also ignored, such as the Dassault/Breguet "Super Etandard," the McDonnell-Douglas A-4 "Skyhawk," the Sukhoi Su-20, and the SEPECAT "Jaguar."

Nor are these the only drawbacks. The monochrome photographs have vague captions. Some are poor-quality tone paintings, and there are no three-view or interior drawings. The lack of up-to-date information on aircraft from the former Soviet Union suggests much of the research for this part of the book is already outdated.

Thus, despite the quality printing, sturdy binding, and comprehensive index, it is difficult to determine the intended audience for this ready-reference source. Insufficiently detailed to satisfy the expert, this work's mediocre graphics and pedestrian presentation will not attract the novice. It is easy to find better sources in today's crowded military aviation field.—**John Howard Oxley**

ARMY

701. Tracey, Patrick Austin. **Military Leaders of the Civil War.** New York, Facts on File, 1993. 138p. illus. index. (American Profiles). $16.95. E467.T73. 973.7'3'0922. LC 92-34346. ISBN 0-8160-2671-8.

Long ago, Plutarch described how studying the lives of great men served and inspired him in the conduct of his own life. The editors of the American Profiles Series seem intent on inspiring young adults in the same manner. Presented in this volume are sketches of eight generals who served with distinction during this nation's bloodiest conflict. Each chapter details the entire career of its subject and includes portraits, a brief chronology, and a list of additional readings. The four Union generals included are Ulysses S. Grant, William T. Sherman, Philip H. Sheridan, and the lesser-known George Henry Thomas. Their Confederate counterparts are Robert E. Lee, Thomas "Stonewall" Jackson, "Jeb" Stuart, and James Longstreet. The portraits that emerge are indeed inspiring tales of personal sacrifice and perseverance in the face of adversity.

In books aimed at young audiences, some simplification of complex events is expected, and this is evident in the coverage of such things as Lee's first year of Confederate service, Jackson's poor performance during the Seven Days' campaign, and Pickett's charge at Gettysburg. Unfortunately, the author may occasionally mislead or confuse his young readers. Many allusions are left unexplained, and Tracey frequently refers to individuals by ranks or nicknames before they had earned these distinctions. Jackson, certainly a devout Presbyterian but never a clergyman, is described at one point as a "fire-and-brimstone Episcopalian preacher." Contradictory accounts give both Sheridan and Thomas credit for storming Missionary Ridge. Another tale of Lee and John B. Gordon at Antietam is highly suspect and bears little resemblance to Gordon's own published account of the battle. While young readers may find this volume entertaining reading despite these faults, many more comprehensive works on the Civil War and its leaders serve general reference purposes better.—**John R. M. Lawrence**

702. Tripp, F. R. **Canada's Army in World War II: Badges and Histories of the Corps and Regiments.** Toronto, Unitrade Press, 1993. 127p. illus. $10.95pa. ISBN 0-919801-98-6.

This handbook's primary purpose is to serve as a guide to the cap badges worn by Canadian Army units in World War II. A purely descriptive (rather than analytic or critical) list of the army elements in alphabetical order by their official name forms most of this book. Each of the regiments and corps has its badge illustrated by a monochrome photograph in close to full size, accompanied by the geographical origin of the formation, a sketch of its history (about 100 words), and a list of its World War II battle honors. In addition, the organization of the Canadian Army at home and overseas is outlined.

Only a couple of misprints and misspellings mar the text. However, this book has other shortcomings. The most serious relates to the fact that while the Canadian Army was based on the British "regimental" organization in World War II, how the parts were grouped into wholes (a complex undertaking) is not explained, nor is the particular formation terminology (e.g., battalions, regiments, batteries) used by the different branches of service. The result is a guide unsuitable for the novice. The absence of any index (in particular, a symbolic index to badge devices) makes it difficult to identify the provenance of a particular badge, unless it is known already. In an illustrated guide, the photographs' quality is a vital point: While most are sharply focused, a few are rather blurry. In summary, while clearly printed on good quality paper and sturdily bound, this is very much a ready-reference tool for the specialist or collector.
—**John Howard Oxley**

NAVY

703. Jones, J. Michael. **Historic Warships: A Directory of 140 Museums and Memorials Worldwide, with Histories.** Jefferson, N.C., McFarland, 1993. 245p. illus. index. $45.00. V13.A1J66. 359'.0074. LC 92-50938. ISBN 0-89950-779-4.

This compact work, written by a retired Royal Canadian Navy officer, provides the reader with a listing of 147 warships in 26 countries. The vessels listed range from the English ship *Mary Rose*, built in 1511, to the U.S. nuclear submarine *Nautilus*. Entries are arranged alphabetically by the country where each ship now resides, a format that will appeal to those who wish to visit the sites. Most entries are accompanied by a black-and-white illustration, usually a photograph. The majority of the photographs are very good, but a few are small or show only part of the ship. In addition to information such as class, tonnage, armament, propulsion plant, speed, crew complement, and date launched, each entry includes the ship's location, address, and telephone number.

The section for each country begins with a synopsis of that country's naval history, through the Gulf War. It is in the individual vessels' histories, however, that Jones takes what could have been a mere list of ships and turns it into a treat for fans of naval history. The histories vary in length and range from accounts of battles and campaigns to stories of the more recent struggles to restore or preserve the ships for posterity. The book also includes a list of abbreviations used; an index to ships, events, and people mentioned in the text; and a bibliography. While much of this information is available in other sources, this attractive, readable book should be useful for public and academic libraries with an interest in naval history. [R: RBB, 1 Nov 93, p. 565]—**Melvin Marlo Brown**

704. **The Naval Institute Guide to Combat Fleets of the World 1993: Their Ships, Aircraft, and Armament.** Bernard Prezelin, ed. Annapolis, Md., Naval Institute Press, 1993. 990p. illus. index. $140.00. LC 78-50192. ISBN 1-55750-104-1.

Published every two years as a translation and update of the French *Flottes de Combat*, this work lists and describes the ships, aircraft, and weapons systems of the world's navies. For each country, vessels are listed by type (e.g., aircraft carrier, submarine) and then by class. The work gives displacement, speed, hull dimensions, armament, propulsion plant, armor, range, and ship's company for each class in accordance with the function of the vessel. Almost all combat classes and most of the auxiliary classes are illustrated with photographs that are extraordinarily clear and well reproduced. Data is current up to July 1992.

It is natural to compare this publication with *Jane's Fighting Ships* (for previous reviews of both titles see ARBA 91, entries 694 and 695), and there are many differences. First, *Jane's* is an annual; second, the *Guide* includes brief information on weapons systems of the larger navies, which *Jane's* omits (but which are treated much more thoroughly in *Jane's Naval Weapons Systems* [Jane's Information Service, Annual]); third, while *Jane's* includes more photographs of more of the ships it lists, they are not as good as those in the *Guide*. *Jane's* includes brief information on shipborne aircraft (but very complete information on naval aircraft in *Jane's All the World's Aircraft* [see ARBA 93, entry 1780]), whereas the *Guide* includes all aircraft in a country's naval air arm, not just shipborne craft. In short, while these two publications do the same thing, they do it differently. *The Naval Institute Guide* is a very positive alternative to the more expensive *Jane's*. Librarians will consider the needs of their users and choose the publication serving those needs best, but most libraries will be well accommodated by the work under review.—**Eric R. Nitschke**

705. **The Naval Institute Guide to the Ships and Aircraft of the U.S. Fleet.** By Norman Polmar. Annapolis, Md., Naval Institute Press, 1993. 639p. illus. index. $56.95. LC 76-15840. ISBN 1-55750-675-2.

The authenticity and integrity of this reference volume cannot be questioned. It is a description, by the U.S. Navy, of the current strength of U.S. naval power in every detail. With text, pictures, charts, diagrams, and tables, it is an encyclopedic account of the navy, up-to-date through 1992 (it includes the navy's participation in Desert Storm). Here are data about the state of the fleet, defense organization, fleet organization, naval personnel, ship classifications with individual chapters on types of naval vessels, naval aviation, and naval aircraft. Also included is information on the U.S. Coast Guard and the National Oceanic and Atmospheric Administration (NOAA). Five appendixes add information on advanced technology, shipbuilding, ships transferred to foreign governments, and navy and coast guard ships preserved as memorials and museums.

Ship types are completely described with all statistical details of size, displacement, power units, armament, firepower, and equipment such as radars and sonars. Photographs of individual ships from all views add to the understanding of the various ships described. Sections on aircraft also include statistical descriptions of size, crew requirements, weights, speed, ceiling, range, armament, and other special equipment. Many books on aircraft provide top, front, and side views of the aircraft design and exploded views of construction details, interior facilities, and equipment. This one does not, but the photographs and detailed descriptions compensate (except for readers who would use the information as bases for model designs). The appendix on advanced technology gives the user descriptions of hydrofoils, water planes, and hovercraft. Every type of ship used by the navy is included in the book. A detailed index of subjects and an index of ship names and classes add to the work's usefulness. It is, perhaps, more valuable in view of the end of the Cold War and reductions being effected in the U.S. military. A coffee-table-size book, this volume will excite Navy personnel, students of ships and their sailors, and anyone interested in almost any aspect of the navy. Highly recommended for public libraries and any other library with user interest in the U.S. Navy. [R: LJ, 1 June 93, p. 108; RBB, Aug 93, p. 2094]—**Edward P. Miller**

706. **Weyers Warships of the World 1992/93. Weyers Flottentaschenbuch 1992/93.** Gerhard Albrecht, comp. Bonn, Germany, Bernard & Graefe Verlag; distr., Baltimore, Md., Nautical & Aviation Publishing, 1992. 874p. illus. $99.95. ISBN 3-7637-4506-8.

This latest edition of a respected naval annual will be welcomed by shipboard users and by naval researchers. Tremendous changes have taken place in the world in the last few years, and these changes are reflected by the world's navies. The breakup of the Soviet Union, the independence of the Baltic countries, the reunification of Germany, Operation Desert Storm, and the changes in Yugoslavia are all events that have affected NATO and the world's navies. For instance, the U.S. Navy has closed its submarine base at Holy Loch, Scotland, the Iraqi navy has been virtually destroyed, the ex-Soviet navy is not quite sure who is in charge, and the East German (GDR) navy has been disestablished. Jurgen Rhades has contributed a perceptive overview of the status of the world's navies.

There are two major parts to this book. First is a ship-by-ship list of navies arranged alphabetically by nation. The spelling of the countries is in German; hence, Agypten/Egypt is the first country listed. Second is a section of drawings and photographs of ships, also arranged by nation. A ship entry includes name, launch date, completion date, builder, displacement, length, beam, draft, crew size, armament, electronic sensors, speed, propulsion system, range, and remarks. The data are presented in abbreviated fashion using initialisms and symbols, the meanings of which are explained in the front matter. An illustrated list of GDR ships and their fate comes after the main entries, followed by several appendixes, a ship index, and an addenda of ship information that arrived too late for inclusion in the main entries. The text is in German and English.—**Frank J. Anderson**

UNIFORMS

707. Elting, John R. **Napoleonic Uniforms.** New York, Macmillan, 1993. 2v. illus. index. $250.00/set. UC485.F8E48. 355.1'4'0944. LC 93-18073. ISBN 0-02-897115-9.

The Napoleonic era was the last great age of military plumage. The bright colors used then were soon eclipsed by more practical ones that progressed from field blue and field gray to khaki and finally camouflage. These volumes illustrate the grand age of Napoleonic splendor through the uniforms worn by the French soldiers who fought to perpetrate the French revolution and the resulting empire under Bonaparte. Individual plates illustrate the uniforms of infantry, cavalry, and artillery units; historical narration is provided for each plate by Elting.

Elting divides up the eras from prerevolutionary uniforms to the Grand Armee. He also divides them geographically and by purpose or campaign; for example, one section deals with the Army of Egypt and another covers the Emigrant troops. Each part is prefaced by an index of plates and a brief description of that era or part of the French army.

Rarely does a reviewer have the opportunity to peruse such a beautiful two-volume set as this one. Elting and Macmillan should be congratulated for this fine presentation of Herbert Knotel's illustrations of the uniforms of Napoleon's Grand Armee. These volumes, with their brilliant and exact watercolor illustrations, are highly recommended for public, college, and university reference collections and for Napoleonic era enthusiasts, particularly those interested in military miniatures. The books capture the essence of the military uniform as a personal statement and a work of art. [R: LJ, 1 Sept 93, pp. 178-80]
—**Norman L. Kincaide**

708. Stanton, Shelby. **U.S. Army Uniforms of the Korean War.** Harrisburg, Pa., Stackpole Books, 1992. 243p. illus. index. $29.95. UC483.S619. 355.8'1'0973. LC 92-4007. ISBN 0-8117-1819-0.

This is one of those very satisfying books in which analyzing a part leads to a greater appreciation of the whole. In this case, Stanton's extensive discussion of uniforms recreates the grim circumstances under which the Korean War was fought, the ill-prepared condition of the armed forces, and the atmosphere of this "police action" that came so soon after everyone thought peace had finally come to the world.

The book covers all items of personal clothing, from underclothes to headgear, footwear, body armor, packs, and special items for medical personnel and others. Insignia is discussed insofar as its placement, standard and nonstandard, is concerned. This is neither an insignia album nor a book on weapons, although both are amply illustrated. Black-and-white illustrations interspersed within the text make up more than half the book. The reproductions are large and clear.

All in all, this is a well-done book on a specialized topic. It could be added to a reference collection that served a public needing such specialization. Many more libraries will want it for their general or circulating collections as a fascinating supplement to the history of this underreported war.—**Eric R. Nitschke**

WEAPONS

709. Burns, Grant. **The Nuclear Present: A Guide to Recent Books on Nuclear War, Weapons, the Peace Movement, and Related Issues....** Metuchen, N.J., Scarecrow, 1992. 633p. index. $69.50. Z6464.D6B855. 016.3271'74. LC 92-32440. ISBN 0-8108-2619-4.

This bibliography updates and extends Burns's *The Atomic Papers* (see ARBA 85, entry 611) in the same format, deleting fiction while adding a detailed nuclear chronology. This book's expanded size shows how much has been published since 1984; coverage is limited to print monographs, excluding electronic media, CD-ROMs, and video material.

Clear, interesting descriptions of the strengths and weaknesses of each item are provided. Especially good is the interrelation between different texts cited, where appropriate. The bibliographic citations use a short yet adequate form, as publisher's addresses are provided in an appendix. A selected sample of citations was checked and proved accurate.

As Burns notes, complete coverage is not possible, and a number of significant omissions were noted, such as *Space War Glossary* (see ARBA 90, entry 677), many relevant periodicals ranging from *For Your Eyes Only* to *International Defence Review*, and any reference to Wilfred G. Burchett's political bias. The occasional spelling error and missing pagination for item 2-168 were noted, but these are minor.

The book is printed on durable paper in a sturdy binding. Reading the large sans serif type is sometimes difficult, either because of imperfect impression or gaps in the forced justification. Overall, however, this is a useful research guide to the literature on nuclear war, disarmament, and radiation disasters, rendered more valuable by comprehensive indexes for both the bibliography and the chronology. [R: Choice, June 93, p. 1596; RBB, 1 May 93, pp. 1618-22]—**John Howard Oxley**

710. Graetzer, Hans G., and Larry M. Browning. **The Atomic Bomb: An Annotated Bibliography.** Pasadena, Calif., Salem Press, 1992. 168p. index. (Magill Bibliographies). $40.00. Z6724.A9G73. 016.3558'25119. LC 92-29628. ISBN 0-89356-677-2.

This 10-chapter, carefully annotated bibliography nicely spans the literature of the A-bomb. It begins with titles that treat the general background of radioactivity, fission, and fusion and ranges through those that address the lives of the atomic scientists, the tragic accounts of Hiroshima and Nagasaki, and the H-bomb and the nuclear arms race. The final chapters survey films and videocassettes and the atomic bomb in literature. An author/title index concludes the volume.

High school and college students will use this bibliography to meet their curricular needs, and adult discussion groups and general readers will find it appealing. It is clearly not intended for pursuing related topics that have a detailed history of their own, such as military strategy, the Cold War, nuclear weapons technology, or the pacifist movement. Only books are included, plus magazine articles that have been reprinted in book form. Government documents have not been surveyed. The earliest entry is 1947, the latest 1991. One complaint: The cover design is totally lacking in imagination and execution. To package a useful and well-conceived text in such an unattractive fashion serves no one well. [R: RBB, 1 May 93, pp. 1618-22]—**Charles R. Andrews**

711. Sullivan, George. **Modern Combat Helicopters.** New York, Facts on File, 1993. 120p. illus. index. (Military Aircraft). $17.95. UG1230.S85. 358.4'183. LC 92-314392. ISBN 0-8160-2353-0.

This work describes 13 modern combat helicopters, 8 of which are built in the United States and the rest in Europe, including Russia. Each 5- to 12-page chapter is devoted to one model. Each chapter includes a "Fact Sheet" identifying the manufacturer, aircraft type (e.g., armed troop transport), power plant, crew size, cruising speed, range, and dimensions. Many chapters briefly describe civilian models of the military craft. Each chapter has two to five black-and-white photographs of the aircraft on the ground and in flight. The text is written in action-adventure prose. The chapters lack three-dimensional (front, top, and side) recognition diagrams that are a standard component of more comprehensive aircraft description and recognition books. The work includes three useful appendixes and an index.

The Library of Congress CIP office has assigned one subject heading to this book—"Military helicopters - Juvenile literature"—which accurately describes the book. This should be a popular addition to juvenile libraries, but it is too trivial for adults.—**Jerome K. Miller**

13 Political Science

GENERAL WORKS

Atlases

712. Chaliand, Gerard, and Jean-Pierre Rageau. **Strategic Atlas: A Comparative Geopolitics of the World's Powers.** 3d ed. New York, HarperPerennial/HarperCollins, 1992. 223p. maps. $35.00; $18.00pa. G1046.F1C513. 327.1'01'0223. LC 91-58286. ISBN 0-06-271554-2; 0-06-273153-Xpa.

This work provides a sumptuous array of maps and accompanying data on military, economic, and other factors underlying the balance of power at both global and regional levels. The authors strive to use nonstandard (especially circular and polar) projections to convey a more accurate picture of the world and its land-sea balance. After a text introduction, the remainder of the atlas is devoted to color-coded thematic maps with accompanying statistics and brief explanatory passages. A fascinating range of views is given. Shipping routes, strategic resources, industrial centers, agricultural production, culture, history, and more are dealt with selectively. In the largest section (approximately 100 pages) the reader is treated to perspectives from the positions of major world powers, such as the United States and the former Soviet Union, and a wide variety of regional centers in Europe, Africa, the Middle East, Asia, and Latin America. It all makes for thought-provoking browsing.

There are a few weak points. The sources for data are often incompletely—or not—specified. Despite the 1992 copyright, some of the major country data comes from the mid-1980s. The military balance section emphasizes the Cold War and seems to omit arms control agreements of recent years. Despite these lapses, much of the material (particularly the maps of the former Soviet sphere) appears to be useful and up-to-date. In sum, this is an impressive work that belongs in general and specialist collections on international relations.—**Nigel Tappin**

Bibliography

713. **Guide to Political Videos. Volume 1, Number 1.** Santa Barbara, Calif., Pacifica Communications, 1993. 137p. index. $10.00pa.; $15.00pa. (institutions). ISSN 1069-5354.

Librarians and educators are being inundated with advertising blurbs for new videos. The reviewing process fir these materials is only slowly spreading in the broader professional literature (versus those titles that focus on this format), so this new title might be helpful for those looking for political videos. Each issue is scheduled to have approximately 400 entries. The entries are arranged in alphabetical order by subject category. Each includes (when available) prices for home or public rental or purchase; shipping charges; sales tax; awards won by the video; distributor; previous and series titles; producer; director; sponsor; copyright and release dates; running time; number of cassettes; a description of supplemental materials (e.g., manuals, teacher's guides); indications of closed captioning, subtitling, or dubbing; ISBN; LCCN; availability in other languages; and a short description of the video. There are separate indexes for titles, purchase prices for home use, and advertisers. The distributor/producer index of more than 60 companies is actually just an alphabetical listing of their addresses and telephone and fax numbers, with no indication of which titles they have produced. Such cross-referencing would be helpful. Also included is an order form to send to the publishers. The printing throughout is clear and easy to read.

It appears that the publisher intends to confuse matters by numbering all issues consecutively throughout the run of this title, not just within the volume year. For example, the Fall 1993 issue is volume 1, number 1, while the Spring and Fall 1994 issues will be numbered volume 2, numbers 2 and 3. One hopes that the publisher will quickly change the numbering of individual issues to the more standard format.

Pacifica Communications plans to launch a companion product in the summer of 1994 titled *Guide to Sports and Games Videos*, which might be of more use in public libraries. Librarians may feel that they have enough coverage if they already own the three-volume *Bowker's Complete Video Directory* (see ARBA 93, entry 989) or the *Video Source Book* (see ARBA 92, entry 909). *Guide to Political Videos* is a good effort that needs some fine tuning. The relatively low price does make it attractive. It is suitable for audiovisual departments, libraries, and those academic departments that have a heavy demand for videos to use in class and that do not have access to other sources.—**Daniel K. Blewett**

Biography

714. Opfell, Olga S. **Women Prime Ministers and Presidents.** Jefferson, N.C., McFarland, 1993. 237p. illus. index. $29.95. LC 92-56675. ISBN 0-89950-790-5.

This unusual volume includes articles on each of 21 women who have been prime ministers or presidents of their countries. It is not "a book of profiles," as stated on page ix, but rather a book of essays detailing both the subjects and the politics of their times. The Golda Meir and Margaret Thatcher essays are excellent. Photographs of the women and an index are included. The selected bibliography includes works on only 11 of the 21; there are no relevant books on the other 10. Some of the subjects held only the title and not the power; Domitien in the Central African Republic and Pintasilgo of Portugal held office for only six months. Eight were still in office at the time of publication (four of those only since 1990). Badly needed are maps identifying problem areas in each country and separate listings of the other main governmental and political officials and parties, especially for the longer articles. This volume will be especially useful for women's studies programs. [R: BR, Nov/Dec 93, p. 36; VOYA, Dec 93, p. 333]
—**Karen Y. Stabler**

715. **The Routledge Dictionary of Twentieth-Century Political Thinkers.** Robert Benewick and Philip Green, eds. New York, Routledge, Chapman & Hall, 1992. 244p. $59.95. ISBN 0-415-04371-9.

This volume examines political thought during the twentieth century through a biographical approach. Altogether, 159 short biographies appear, written by more than 85 contributors. Arranged in alphabetical order, the entries run from Max Adler, W. E. B. Du Bois, and Josef Stalin through Clara Zetkin. The individuals selected fall into three overlapping groups: politicians with ideas of their own, persons who have influenced political movements, and political theorists. The editors made a special effort to include individuals whose contributions have related ethnicity, gender, or the environment to political action. Each biography comes with a sketch of the person, an analysis of the person's ideas, and a brief list of references. Among other things, readers learn that Milovan Djilas "epitomizes the rise and fall of Soviet/East European communism" and that Susan Griffin's work tries "to show how scientific paradigms that assume the need to conquer nature coincide ... with patriarchal customs that depend on the oppression of women."

The biographical essays are generally well written, concise, and sophisticated, and the mini-bibliographies are helpful. The intelligent layperson will want to read this book, and even the expert will find valuable information here. Of course, some important political thinkers have been omitted. What about the ideas and actions of Mikhail Gorbachev or Lech Walesa? Why include Adolf A. Berle but not fellow New Dealer Rex Tugwell? Why Michael Harrington but not Rachel Carson, especially if the environment is a prime concern? Perhaps this extremely useful dictionary should have been longer. Recommended strongly for university, college, and public libraries. [R: Choice, Sept 93, p. 88; LAR, May 93, p. 294; RBB, 1 Nov 93, p. 569-70]—**Richard E. Holl**

716. Thackeray, Frank W., and John E. Findling, eds. **Statesmen Who Changed the World: A Bio-Bibliographical Dictionary of Diplomacy.** Westport, Conn., Greenwood Press, 1993. 669p. index. $85.00. D108.S73. 909.08'0922. LC 92-14616. ISBN 0-313-27380-4.

This volume contains 62 essays on Western statesmen, arranged in alphabetical order. The individuals selected include Dean Acheson, Konrad Adenauer, Adolf Hitler, Carlos R. Tobar, Charles-Maurice de Talleyrand, and Woodrow Wilson. Each entry comes with a brief biographical sketch and an annotated bibliography. Five useful appendixes follow. An index and a list of contributors complete the work.

The biographies are concise, balanced, and generally well written. Contributors devoted more than the usual effort to summing up their subject's significance in a final paragraph. William Earl Weeks, for example, tells us that in many ways John Quincy Adams's career paralleled the history of the American republic: "A life that had begun at the birth of independence had ended in the shadow of civil war." Prospective researchers will also find the annotated bibliographies extremely helpful, because they document both original and secondary sources and are fairly comprehensive. As is normal in a reference book of this type, selection is critically important. Editors Thackeray and Findling are to be congratulated for their choices. But reasonable users can disagree over particulars, as the editors note when they observe that other scholars might "arrive at a somewhat different lineup...." That being the case, why James G. Blaine but not John Hay? Why Mikhail Gorbachev but not Ronald Reagan? And most startling, where is Venezuelan general and statesman Simon Bolivar? Surely he and a few more Latin Americans deserve inclusion. Nevertheless, the vast majority of editorial selections were sound, making *Statesmen Who Changed the World* a valuable acquisition. Highly recommended for high school, college, university, and public libraries. [R: Choice, Oct 93, p. 273; RBB, July 93, p. 2005]—**Richard E. Holl**

Dictionaries and Encyclopedias

717. **The Oxford Companion to Politics of the World.** Joel Krieger and others, eds. New York, Oxford University Press, 1993. 1056p. maps. index. $49.95. JA61.O95. 320'.03. LC 92-25043. ISBN 0-19-505934-4.

This volume contains 650 articles from nearly 500 experts hailing from more than 40 countries. In its pages, the reader finds a mass of information on nations and individuals, along with political and diplomatic concepts, all of which serve to explicate world politics. International affairs, international law, and domestic political matters receive treatment. Arranged in alphabetical order, the entries go from (Gamal) Abdel Nasser through abortion to Zionism. Six regional maps and a comprehensive index complete the work.

The entries are generally well written and cover virtually every part of the world. The emphasis on concepts is particularly good. Interesting and enlightening discussions of modernization, environmentalism, gender, interest groups, race, the welfare state, and many more topics are included. Overlapping essays reinforce the theme that the modern world and its politics are constantly changing, with the older East-West dichotomy having given way to a new geopolitical paradigm featuring global interdependence and intense economic rivalry among the United States, Japan, and the European Community.

As in all encyclopedias, omissions are inevitable and slights do occur. For example, Bill Clinton is nowhere mentioned, and more explicit treatment of corporate liberalism is needed. Despite these flaws, *The Oxford Companion to Politics of the World* is an outstanding contribution that will be useful to scholars, politicians, diplomats—indeed, all literate people. Highly recommended for high school, college, university, and public libraries. [R: Choice, Sept 93, p. 86; LJ, 15 Mar 93, p. 72; RBB, 1 May 93, pp. 1628-30; SLJ, Aug 93, p. 208; WLB, June 93, p. 129]—**Richard E. Holl**

718. Shafritz, Jay M., Phil Williams, and Ronald S. Calinger. **The Dictionary of 20th-Century World Politics.** New York, Henry Holt, 1993. 756p. illus. $60.00. JA61.S53. 909.82. LC 93-15204. ISBN 0-8050-1976-6.

Three professors have compiled a political dictionary consisting of more than 4,000 entries on people, theories, and ideas that have affected international politics during the twentieth century. While there are similar and related compendiums, this work stands alone because of its comprehensiveness and depth of coverage.

The dictionary is arranged in continuous alphabetical order. The text is cross-referenced and includes biographical and historical references. Entries on foreign words, core concepts, theories, practices, institutions, and major international organizations are also included. Boxed-in comments are located throughout the text, providing insight and occasionally humorous comments on a number of definitions. Photographs are sparingly, but effectively, used to add meaning and expand upon definitions. The book concludes with an appendix of key concepts that are organized alphabetically by subject. There are few citations to more comprehensive sources, so interested citizens, students, and scholars must investigate further in order to complete their research. This work is especially recommended for secondary school and public libraries, as well as college and university libraries, because of its broad coverage of many little-known or little-remembered political terms. [R: LJ, 1 Sept 93, p. 177]—**James M. Murray**

Directories

719. **Political Resource Directory 1993: A Compilation of Political Professional Organizations....** national ed. Carol Hess, ed. Burlington, Vt., Political Resources, 1993. 340p. index. $95.00pa. ISBN 0-944320-05-8. ISSN 0898-4271.

The subtitle on the title page states that this is a compilation of political professional organizations providing services and products to and for the political community. According to the publicity sheet, the book contains some 7,000 listings of 3,000 organizations and 4,400 individuals, with more than 1,000 changes since the previous edition. The unnumbered, alphabetically arranged entries include address, telephone and fax numbers, geographical region served, name of principal officer, areas of specialization, percentage of total yearly work done that is political, and a brief description of what the organization does. Some organizations are very focused in the services they provide and the groups they will serve, while others are very wide ranging in their activities. Many organizations are only slightly connected to the political field and offer general services. As this volume also includes "The Official Directory of the American Association of Political Consultants" (cover), there are cross-references from brief entries in the main section to fuller entries in the yellow membership pages at the front of the book. The organizations are indexed by state, subject specialization, and principal contact person. Advertising is scattered throughout the book. Librarians will also want to examine Gale's two-volume *Consultants and Consulting Organizations Directory* (1993). This book is suitable for the reference collections of academic and public libraries.—**Daniel K. Blewett**

Handbooks and Yearbooks

720. Ameringer, Charles D., ed. **Political Parties of the Americas, 1980s to 1990s: Canada, Latin America, and the West Indies.** Westport, Conn., Greenwood Press, 1992. 697p. index. $99.50. JL195.P63. 324.27. LC 92-3032. ISBN 0-313-27418-5.

Updating and complementing *Political Parties of the Americas* (see ARBA 84, entry 465), this volume concentrates on political developments subsequent to that time, with reference to the original work as necessary and appropriate. It enlists the contributions of many of the original collaborators as well as some new authors. With change as the dominant theme in the volume, each chapter is arranged in a similar manner, with a summary background essay emphasizing recent political developments. Also included are an updated bibliography, a list and description of active political parties, and a summary historical sketch of parties that ceased to exist before 1980. For the political parties sections, a standard format is followed, with alphabetical listings by English name and cross-listings for local languages. Readers are urged to consult the earlier two volumes for more detailed party descriptions. Only one appendix is included in this volume; it contains an updated chronology for each country. Materials included in the original volumes' "genealogy" and "ideological and interest group parties" appendixes have been integrated into the chapter sections. The index is substantial, comprising more than 40 pages, and provides the reader detailed access to the volume as well as numerous *see* references to appropriate material. [R: Choice, May 93, pp. 1446-48; LJ, 1 April 93, pp. 72-74; WLB, May 93, p. 121]

—**Virginia S. Fischer**

721. **The Book of the States. Volume 29.** 1992-93 ed. Lexington, Ky., Council of State Governments, 1992. 707p. index. $79.00. ISBN 0-87292-963-9.

State government confronts many of the challenges facing the federal government and local governments. These challenges include finding sufficient funding to maintain existing programs while coping with budgetary constraints that may require spending reductions, tax increases, or both, and meeting public demand for more efficient and ethical governmental practices. *The Book of the States* is an authoritative annual providing detailed statistics and analyses of state government developments. Written by scholars and state government officials, this work contains chapters on state constitutions; state executive, legislative, and judicial branch activities; elections; finance; management and administration; selected state issues, including environmental management; intergovernmental affairs; and basic historical, geographical, and demographic data for each state. Chapters feature detailed articles on the themes covered.

This is an essential source of state government information. The entries are well documented and feature statistical tables that are arranged in a comprehensible format to enhance reader access. Although published before the 1992 general election, this volume is strongly recommended for all libraries due to its authoritative scope and high quality.—**Bert Chapman**

722. **Border and Territorial Disputes.** 3d ed. Revised and updated by John B. Allcock and others. Harlow, England, Longman; distr., Detroit, Gale, 1992. 630p. maps. index. $245.00. ISBN 0-582-20931-5.

With the daily news calling constant attention to conflicts in Eastern Europe, Africa, and throughout the world, this handbook will be a useful resource in many libraries. This edition was revised in 1992, five years after the previous edition. It is quite up-to-date concerning the recent changes in the former Soviet Union and Yugoslavia.

About 80 disputes are covered with essays that summarize the historical origins and current status of these disagreements. The essays are arranged in five sections covering broad geographical areas. Some conflicts, such as those over Palestine, Northern Ireland, and Bosnia, are discussed in considerable detail, covering about 20 pages each. These essays are ideal for those who want comprehensive, impartial overviews with substantial information but not book-length treatments. This book will also be valued as a reference source for quick identification of people and places involved in these disputes. Most sections have useful maps that show boundaries and historical changes. More maps that depict the location of ethnic and religious groups would be helpful. There is a subject index. [R: WLB, April 93, pp. 117-18]—**Henry E. York**

723. **Countries of the World and Their Leaders Yearbook 1993: A Compilation of U.S. Department of State Reports....** Frank Bair, Thomas Bowen, and Kelley Bowen, eds. Detroit, Gale, 1993. 2v. illus. maps. $155.00/set. LC 80-645249. ISBN 0-8103-7491-9.

This is a compilation of U.S. government information about all countries of the world. The major part comes from the Department of State's *Background Notes* and provides brief coverage of the historical, political, economic, and geographical backgrounds of each country. These reports are updated on an irregular basis, so that some are several years old. The report on China, for example, goes back to 1987. However, this edition does include 1992 reports on most of the USSR successor states. The *Background Notes* are useful summaries of key information, although, of necessity, they are "diplomatic" and do not always provide frank analyses of current problems.

The yearbook also includes much other information of use to world travelers: addresses of U.S. embassies and consulates and names of key officers; lists of current leadership of foreign countries; State Department advisories and warnings on health and political dangers; and the text of most of the State Department's brochures of travel tips for various parts of the world.

This is a handy compilation of useful information for international travelers. It would be useful to public and university libraries as well as to travel agencies and firms with employees who travel to many parts of the world. [R: VOYA, Aug 93, pp. 190-91]—**Frank L. Wilson**

Quotation Books

724. The Macmillan Dictionary of Political Quotations. By Lewis D. Eigen and Jonathan P. Siegel. New York, Macmillan, 1993. 785p. index. $40.00. PN6084.P6E54. 082. LC 91-40116. ISBN 0-02-610650-7.

For readers seeking an apropos quotation on a political topic, *The Macmillan Dictionary of Political Quotations* is an outstanding reference work. The volume consists of 11,000 quotations organized into 99 chapters on topics ranging from abortion to welfare and including such subjects as equality; history and historians; justice; minorities and women; power; the presidency and vice presidency; religion; and secrecy, confidentiality, and classification in between. Within individual chapters the quotations are numbered and listed alphabetically under their authors. Individual quotations supply the author's name, vital dates, and highest office, title, or profession. Citations to the source of the quotation are provided, and sometimes a note on context is supplied. Many quotations deal with more than one subject, but Eigen and Siegel have elected to list individual quotations only once. A detailed concept index, however, allows the reader to find all the quotations on a specific topic even when they are located in several different chapters. The locations of all quotations by the same author are listed in a separate author index.

Needless to say, readers will miss some of their favorite quotations, but overall the selection is judicious, wide-ranging, and up-to-date. For example, Donald Regan's 1981 statement, "I don't care. I'll be dead by then," provides a succinct summation of the spirit of the Reagan era. Then there is John Nance Garner's often-quoted quip that "The vice presidency ain't worth a pitcher of warm spit." Most libraries will want to buy this excellent compendium. [R: Choice, Nov 93, p. 430; RBB, 15 Nov 93, p. 651]

—Ronald H. Fritze

POLITICS AND GOVERNMENT

United States

Atlases

725. Martis, Kenneth C., and Gregory A. Elmes. **The Historical Atlas of State Power in Congress, 1790-1990.** Washington, D.C., Congressional Quarterly, 1993. 190p. maps. index. $56.95. G1201.F7M3. 328.73'07345'022. LC 92-46583. ISBN 0-87187-742-2.

Decennial censuses are constitutionally mandated to determine state representation in the U.S. House of Representatives. These censuses have occurred every decade since 1790 (except 1920) and have resulted in increases, decreases, or the maintenance of the status quo in state political representation and power in the House of Representatives. *The Historical Atlas of State Power in Congress, 1790-1990* documents these trends over the past two centuries. Following a historical overview of congressional apportionment, the authors examine congressional apportionment by decade and briefly discuss possible future trends in this area. The other major section of this atlas examines significant geographical trends in congressional apportionment, such as nineteenth-century differences between free and slave states, increased urbanization in the late nineteenth and early twentieth centuries, and the increased demographic and political influence of Sunbelt states in recent decades, using statistical tables and maps to document relevant developments. *Historical Atlas* ultimately sees the Sunbelt's long-term demographic and political power increasing, particularly in congressional and presidential arenas, as evidenced by such factors as recent significant gains in House seats for California, Florida, and Texas.

The authors have produced a well-written and well-researched work buttressed with comprehensible and succinct statistics and excellent maps. *Historical Atlas* is an indispensable addition to any library desirous of enhancing its political geography, American political history, or demography collections. [R: Choice, Nov 93, pp. 436-37; WLB, Oct 93, pp. 89-90]—**Bert Chapman**

Bibliography

726. **The *National Review* Politically *Incorrect* Reference Guide: Your Handbook for the *Right* Information Sources.** Russell Jenkins, John J. Virtes, and Frederick W. Campano, comps. New York, National Review Books, 1993. 308p. $19.95pa. LC 93-85244. ISBN 0-9627841-1-7.

The general purpose of the compilers is to provide an "information-source handbook covering hundreds of topics of both general interest and of particular interest to conservatives." In this they have succeeded admirably. They boast that they have included topics that "politically correct reference guides [is there such a genre?] fail or refuse to list ... such as Reaganism, Stalinism, Pornography, Gold Standard, Media Bias, Conservatism, Leftism, Welfare, Tobacco, Home Schooling, (etc.)." It is not likely that any topic has been left out. Regardless of one's political persuasion, these are important topics; they have provided a major service. This work also provides a rough guide to conservative concerns. For example, there are 4 entries under minorities, while boating has 17 and music has 29. Similarly, there are 3 articles on nuclear weapons and 60 on medieval history. One of the values of this handbook is that it provides a sense of where the conservative movement has been and, perhaps, where it is going. The foreword by Rush Limbaugh and the introduction by William F. Buckley, Jr., surely put the conservative imprimatur on this work.

The work is nicely organized. The topics are listed alphabetically and generally cross-referenced. Where available, books and articles are listed as well as organizations, with information about how to contact the latter. There are two appendixes: a list of state governors' offices and tourism bureaus, and a list of conservative publications. The topic of state/regional conservatism is in the body of the work, but it would be better placed as an appendix. Also missing is an author index. Without this index it will be a daunting task to determine how many articles or books by a particular author are listed. There is an oddity without explanation: "Included in the book are general interest topics that are non-ideological." That, of course, belies the title and leaves the reader in a quandary: how to distinguish between the ideological and nonideological entries. It would have been most helpful if some kind of marker kept them distinct.

This paperback has a solid feel to it and will stand up to considerable use. It should have broad appeal, obviously to conservatives, but also to those who have concerns about the important issues of the day. Journalists will find this a useful source of information about conservative positions, and students of political science and history will find it an invaluable resource. Educators surely will use it in making assignments to their students.—**Bertram H. Rothschild**

Biography

727. Foner, Eric. **Freedom's Lawmakers: A Directory of Black Officeholders during Reconstruction.** New York, published in cooperation with the Schomburg Center for Research in Black Culture by Oxford University Press, 1993. 290p. illus. $75.00. E185.96.F64. 920'.009296073. LC 92-31777. ISBN 0-19-507406-8.

Foner, a leading historian, has done much to revive the historical memory of the tribulations and positive accomplishments of Black Americans during Reconstruction. With *Freedom's Lawmakers*, he has supplied a biographical dictionary of 1,465 Black officials from the Reconstruction era of 1863-1877. In it he has included all individuals who served as major state officials, delegates to constitutional conventions, and legislators even if only a name and the fact that they held such an office is known. For local officials, Foner lists only those that have some additional biographical information, a decision that eliminated several hundred people for whom only their name and the fact that they held an office has survived.

Individual entries are arranged alphabetically by surname. Each begins with a head note that supplies, when known, the state where the person held office; the person's occupation; and whether the person was born in freedom or slavery, was Black or mulatto, or was literate. A biographical sketch then follows, and it concludes with a list of sources used in compiling the entry. Foner begins the directory with a detailed introduction that summarizes the collective conclusions that can be drawn about these officeholders. For example, 933 of them were literate while only 195 were known to be illiterate. This information dispels the prevalent historical myth that Black officials during Reconstruction were largely ignorant or illiterate. Several separate indexes for states, occupations, offices, birth status, and topics conclude the work.

There is some minor and necessary overlap with the coverage of existing reference works, particularly the *Dictionary of American Negro Biography* (see ARBA 84, entry 381). Still, Foner has produced a unique and scholarly work that belongs in any library interested in the Civil War and Reconstruction or African-American history. [R: Choice, Sept 93, pp. 80-82]—**Ronald H. Fritze**

Dictionaries and Encyclopedias

728. **Congress A to Z: A Ready Reference Encyclopedia.** 2d ed. Washington, D.C., Congressional Quarterly, 1993. 547p. illus. index. (CQ's Encyclopedia of American Government). $110.00. JK1067.C67. 328.73'003. LC 93-25926. ISBN 0-87187-826-7.

Congress A to Z, which was originally published in 1988 (see ARBA 89, entry 651), provides basic information on the structure and work of Congress. Most entries are no more than a page or so in length and include biographies, committee descriptions and roles, and brief definitions (e.g., *cloakrooms, debt limit, enacting clause*). A number of essays, ranging from five to seven pages in length, deal with broader topics, such as the budget process, ethics, leadership, and the Watergate scandal. Black-and-white illustrations are logically placed throughout the text. The nontechnical language will be especially welcomed by beginning students of U.S. politics, but more sophisticated users will find much to like as well.

Among the numerous appendixes are lists and diagrams outlining party leadership in Congress from 1977 to 1993; women, Black, and Hispanic members of Congress from all eras; party affiliations in Congress and the presidency since 1789; a graphic depiction of how an executive proposal becomes law; a map of major attractions in Washington, D.C.; and the text of the Constitution. A selected bibliography and an index complete the volume. While it is not inexpensive, libraries that make room for this work in their budgets will receive value for their investment.—**Gary D. Barber**

729. **Congressional Quarterly's American Congressional Dictionary.** By Walter Kravitz. Washington, D.C., Congressional Quarterly, 1993. 305p. $32.95; $22.95pa. JK9.K73. 328.73'003. LC 93-13258. ISBN 0-87187-861-5; 0-87187-864-Xpa.

Any item published by Congressional Quarterly can be assumed to be complete and accurate in its information. This assumption holds true for this excellent dictionary. A session watching C-Span with *American Congressional Dictionary* resulted in a richer understanding of the proceedings for this reviewer.

Arranged alphabetically from "Absence of a Quorum" to "Zone Whip," almost 900 terms are included, with numerous cross-references. The terms focus primarily on congressional procedures, but the author has also included some terms for organization, staff, and officers of Congress. The cross-references are of two types: *See* refers to terms directly or indirectly mentioned in the entry, and *see also* refers to related terms or terms that provide supplementary information about the entry. For example, "Budget Act" has *see* references for "Budget Process," which appears in the definition given for "Budget Act." Also under the term "Budget Act" is a *see also* reference for the Gramm-Rudman-Hollings Act of 1985, which is not mentioned in the discussion under "Budget Act" but does appear in the dictionary with its own alphabetical entry. Wherever appropriate, the explanations point out differences in procedure, practice, and terminology between the House of Representatives and the Senate, as well as, when such information is available, between the political parties in each house.

Congressional Quarterly publishes several dictionary and encyclopedic works that can complement the abundance of information found in *American Congressional Dictionary*. Any of its publications is highly recommended for persons interested in legislative and political topics. [R: RBB, 1 Dec 93, p. 709; WLB, Dec 93, p. 76]—**Christine E. Thompson**

730. Dickson, Paul, and Paul Clancy. **The Congress Dictionary: The Ways and Meanings of Capitol Hill.** New York, John Wiley, 1993. 400p. illus. $29.95. JK1067.D5. 328.73'003. LC 93-6859. ISBN 0-471-58064-3.

Words can always have political meanings, but politics can also be obscured by the use of words whose meanings are mysterious outside the field. For those outside the rarefied atmosphere of the major national and international capital of Washington, D.C., this work provides a language and reference key to understanding and participating in the system. The work is in an A to Z dictionary format and covers congressional words and terms from the beginning of the United States to the Clinton administration. From *Joe-Six-Pack* to *filibuster*, the entries include the colorful language of back-room conversations as well as the technical terms needed to understand the way Congress operates. The main dictionary text is supplemented by interesting facts and more than 100 illustrations, cartoons, and photographs. The authors provide a bibliography of some of their most important sources, which is invaluable to researchers who want to pursue individual subjects about Congress.

The book should be of interest to any age, and users will range from word hounds and browsers to professional researchers who may be stumped by particularistic vocabulary. The merging of text and illustration, along with etymologies and historical context, makes it a useful educational tool as well as a reference work. Its use of both historical and contemporary jargon will ensure a long-term utility. [R: LJ, 15 Sept 93, p. 68; RBB, 1 Dec 93, p. 709]—**Curtis D. Holmes**

731. Flanders, Stephen A., and Carl N. Flanders. **Dictionary of American Foreign Affairs.** New York, Macmillan, 1993. 833p. maps. $90.00. E183.7.F58. 327.73'003. LC 92-46618. ISBN 0-02-897146-9.

This is a historical dictionary of individuals, events, organizations, and issues involved in the conduct of U.S. foreign policy. Subject entries are followed by appendixes containing a U.S. foreign affairs time line, U.S. ambassadors to prominent countries, prominent executive branch and congressional foreign policymakers, important conferences and summits, a foreign affairs glossary, a bibliography, and selected maps. Individual entries are succinct and objective summaries of issues and personalities involved in historical and contemporary U.S. foreign policy. Examples of entries include presidents; secretaries of state, such as Henry Kissinger; treaties, such as the Panama Canal Treaty; important foreign policy events, such as the Reykjavik summit and the Iran hostage crisis; influential legislation, such as the Jackson-Vanik Amendment; and concepts influencing U.S. foreign policy, such as "domino theory," "massive retaliation," and "China Card."

Dictionary of American Foreign Affairs is a useful introduction to the study of U.S. diplomatic history and foreign policy. Its quality is strengthened by its strong historical perspective and succinct yet authoritative entries, as well as by the presence of prominent scholars, such as historian Norman Graebner, on its editorial advisory board. Particularly recommended for academic libraries despite its price. [R: Choice, Oct 93, p. 266; LJ, 1 Sept 93, p. 170; RBB, 1 Dec 93, pp. 709-10; SLJ, Nov 93, p. 142; WLB, Oct 93, pp. 86-88]—**Bert Chapman**

732. Whisker, James Biser. **A Glossary of U.S. Government Vocabulary.** Lewiston, N.Y., Edwin Mellen Press, 1992. 261p. index. $69.95. E183.W48. 320.973'0014. LC 92-41817. ISBN 0-7734-9242-9.

Operating under the principle that a person "who understands the vocabulary of any science, art, or discipline has gone a long way in commanding a particular field," Whisker focuses on U.S. politics in this glossary. Because definitions can be long and complex or short and direct, he aims at precision, realizing that any attempt to cover all ramifications only invites failure. Consequently, his definitions establish the main points in a clear, reasonable, and concise manner. With the main text of the glossary divided into sections involving diverse subject areas (e.g., ideology, the presidency, civil liberties and civil rights, political socialization), a fairly comprehensive index significantly assists in finding specific terms, acts, powers, agencies, policies, duties, taxes, and laws.

The surprise is that Whisker's glossary is more than a reference book to be consulted only when a definition of a term relevant to U.S. politics is needed. Sensible answers to many questions concerning the U.S. political scene may be quickly located with the help of this easy-to-use work. What are the major differences between Jacksonian democracy and Jeffersonian democracy? How can the ideology of anarchism embrace such extremes as "peaceful anarchism" and "terrorist anarchism"? What is the relationship, if any, between the traditional Marxist socialism and the New Left? How may amendments to the U.S. Constitution be *proposed*, and how are they *ratified*? When and why did Congress finally authorize public defenders in the public courts? And how does the Anti-Dumping Act of 1921 help to protect the jobs of U.S. workers and industry?

This work makes for fascinating general reading because of the skillful presentation of historical information. It is nearly impossible to pick it up, look for one definition, and put it down without reading further.—**Colby H. Kullman**

Directories

733. **Black Elected Officials: A National Roster.** 20th ed. Washington, D.C., Joint Center for Political and Economic Studies Press; distr., Lanham, Md., University Press of America, 1992. 534p. $65.00; $32.50pa. LC 84-51421. ISBN 0-941410-79-X; 0-941410-80-3pa.

This work provides a guide to the names and addresses of the nearly 7,500 Black elected officials serving at all levels, from local government to national politics. Each entry also provides the office held by the individual and when the term expires. The entries are organized by state; an alphabetical index is provided to assist users looking for a specific person. At the beginning of each state's section is a brief summary of the elected offices in that state, their numbers, and term lengths. In the descriptions of the U.S. congressional districts, the percentage of the Black population in each district is noted. Beyond the directory features, the *Roster* provides valuable tables summarizing the numbers of Black elected officials by category of office and over time.

This is a very useful volume for students of African-American politics and U.S. politics in general. The only problem is its timeliness: The officials listed are those sworn into office prior to February 1991. The terms of office of many of the officials listed expired in 1992 or early 1993.—**Frank L. Wilson**

734. **Congressional Staff Directory/1, 1993: Containing, in a Convenient Arrangement, Useful Information....** 39th ed. Ann L. Brownson, ed. Mount Vernon, Va., Staff Directories, 1993. 1280p. illus. maps. index. $69.00. LC 59-13987. ISBN 0-87289-102-X.

735. **Federal Staff Directory/1, 1993: Containing, in a Convenient Arrangement, Useful, Accurate and Timely Information....** 16th ed. Ann L. Brownson, ed. Mount Vernon, Va., Staff Directories, 1993. 1524p. index. $69.00. LC 59-13987. ISBN 0-87289-100-3.

736. **Judicial Staff Directory, 1993: Containing, in Convenient Arrangement, Useful, Accurate and Timely Information Concerning the Federal Justice System of the U.S. Government....** 7th ed. Ann L. Brownson, ed. Mount Vernon, Va., Staff Directories, 1992. 970p. maps. index. $69.00. LC 59-13987. ISBN 0-87289-099-6.

737. **Staff Directories on CD-ROM, 1993/1.** [CD-ROM]. Mount Vernon, Va., Staff Directories, 1993. Hardware requirements: IBM PC, XT, AT, or 100% compatible with at least 512K memory and 20 MB hard disk drive; MS-DOS 3.0 or higher. $395.00.

These annotated directories list names, federal address, telephone and fax numbers, and brief descriptions of the responsibilities of the entity. All three volumes have color-coded sections, making it easy to let your fingers do the walking. All contain biographies and an individual index. The *Congressional Staff Directory* and *Federal Staff Directory* also contain keyword subject indexes. The *Congressional Staff Directory* has photographs of congresspeople and lists basic biographical information about them and their staffs, the committees on which they sit, their staffs' responsibilities, and the zip codes of each person's district. The *Federal Staff Directory* includes the agencies of the president; the office of the president and vice president, including "Mrs. Gore's Office"; departments of the federal government; independent federal agencies, such as the Agency for International Development; and quasi-official and nongovernmental organizations, such as the Smithsonian Institution or the United Nations. This volume contains biographies of key federal executives, while the *Judicial Staff Directory* has biographies of judges. This last directory lists all judges and clerks for all federal courts and contains maps of each state and territory's federal judicial districts. It also covers the Department of Justice and lists all state courts and their associated counties and cities. The indexes in this volume are more detailed; federal judges are grouped by name, by appointing president, and by year of appointment. There are also lists of judicial nominees for the 102d Congress and the number of judges for each court.

The titles also come on CD-ROM. The user can quickly find how to format a query for a particular field by looking in the table of contents. Search operators include Boolean OR and AND, proximity operators, truncation, and range symbols. One nice feature is the hypertext links to other media (e.g., maps, photographs). Unfortunately, users must search one directory at a time. Moreover, the use of function keys would simplify many tasks, such as printing.—**Susan D. Baird-Joshi**

738. **Election Results Directory: A Complete Listing of State and Federal Legislative and Executive Branch Officials.** 1993 ed. Denver, Colo., National Conference of State Legislatures, 1993. 282p. index. $35.00pa. ISBN 1-55516-741-1.

The editors of this new directory of state and federal elected officials say it is "the earliest available directory of election results." It appears to be so, as this edition came out in January, with changes made through January 4, 1993. While the *Congressional Staff Directory* (see ARBA 91, entry 735) and its *Advance Locator* (see ARBA 88, entry 716) also contain election results, they are published every April and February, respectively. The only results missing from this new title are those for contested or undecided elections reported after December 1992.

The volume begins with "The Election in Perspective," reprinted from an issue of *State Legislatures*. Graphs and tables show the 12 states that passed term limitation initiatives in 1992, the number of women and Blacks in the various legislatures, and party control in each state legislature. Congressional information follows, showing members of the U.S. Senate and House, with asterisks denoting newly elected members. The directory section for state legislators is arranged alphabetically by state, with the District of Columbia and U.S. protectorates appended. Legislators' home mailing addresses are provided, along with district number and party affiliation. Other useful information includes statehouse addresses, bill status (with telephone numbers to call for updated information), and miscellaneous facts about each state and its government. Because it is more narrowly focused, *Election Results Directory* is a cost-effective way to update the indispensable *Congressional Staff Directory* and its supplements. [R: Choice, June 93, p. 1600; LJ, 1 May 93, p. 80; RBB, 15 May 93, p. 1722; RQ, Summer 93, pp. 565-66; WLB, May 93, pp. 115-16]—**Gary D. Barber**

739. **Federal Regional Yellow Book, Vol.I, No.1: Who's Who in the Federal Government's Departments, Agencies, Courts, Military Installations and Service Academies....** Debra J. Mayberry and others, eds. New York, Monitor Publishing, 1993. 1324p. index. $165.00pa./yr. ISSN 1061-3153.

This directory of federal regional offices and officials is designed as a companion to the *Federal Yellow Book* (see ARBA 91, entry 738). Its purpose is to supply the names, addresses, and telephone numbers of more than 20,000 people located in more than 8,000 federal government regional offices throughout the country. The directory will be updated semiannually.

Geographical, name, and subject indexes are included in the work. The geographical index is excellent for finding local offices quickly without having to page through the entire listing for a specific agency. The name index lists the telephone number for the official as well as the page location in the directory. This number can sometimes make it unnecessary to look further than the index for the required information. The subject index is primarily a list of agency names, but it does include some very broad headings (e.g., energy research). According to the editor's note, future editions will have an expanded subject index, which should make it useful for more than a listing of the agency name. Another section includes almost all of the most frequently sought agencies (e.g., Department of Defense, Federal Judicial Districts, Department of Health and Human Resources); an expansion of this section is also planned.

This directory, an excellent source, is one of Monitor's leadership directories. These sources provide directory assistance to corporate, government, and professional organizations and should be in many libraries. [R: RBB, 15 May 93, p. 1722; WLB, April 93, pp. 118-21]—**Christine E. Thompson**

740. **Government Research Directory 1993-94: A Descriptive Guide....** 7th ed. Thomas Cichonski and Charles A. Beaubien, eds. Detroit, Gale, 1992. 1252p. index. $405.00. LC 85-647549. ISBN 0-8103-7526-5. ISSN 0882-3766.

Government departments and agencies are major research centers. This research is conducted on practically every topic, and the findings derived from it are disseminated through books, journals, and government documents. Providing systematically arranged information about the government entities producing this research is the focus of *Government Research Directory*.

This publication includes the names of United States and selected Canadian government agencies. Entries are arranged by executive, judicial, and legislative branch offices, followed by alphabetical listings for executive branch departments, independent agencies, and Canadian agencies. The work concludes with subject, geographical, and master indexes. For individual organizations the entries include the name, address, telephone and fax numbers, director, organizational information (including date of origin), institutional subdivisions, staff size, areas of research, and publications and services. Some entries include library size and collection specialties for selected organizations.

This is a valuable information source for depository libraries and institutions engaged in significant levels of government-supported research. *Government Research Directory* should also help encourage library users to learn more about the multifaceted research interests and publications produced by federal agencies. Still, there is room for improvement. The Texas Sea Grant College Program is listed as being in "Brian" instead of Bryan, Texas, and the publications and services entries for individual agencies range from vague to specific, consequently giving readers an incomplete picture of agency information products and services. Finally, in this increasingly electronic era, future editions of this work should include the Internet or E-mail addresses of these agencies and the availability of their publications through file transfer protocol, Telnet, gopher, or other electronic means of access. Providing such data will augment the already significant value of this substantive information source.—**Bert Chapman**

741. Nelson, Garrison, with Clark H. Bensen. **Committees in the U.S. Congress 1947-1992. Volume 1: Committee Jurisdictions and Member Rosters.** Washington, D.C., Congressional Quarterly, 1993. 1015p. index. $225.00. JK1029.N45. 328.73'0765'025. LC 92-40252. ISBN 0-87187-729-5.

Congressional committees often determine the fate of national legislation. Many committee members have used their positions and the power derived from them to wield substantive and lasting influence on national law and policy while obtaining heightened levels of personal political power.

Nelson's compilation covers congressional committee membership and jurisdictions from 1947 to 1992. The first volume opens with a list of committees during this period, including standing, select, and joint committees. A preface contains a historical summary of the congressional committee system, with pertinent variations for the House of Representatives and Senate. The preface also emphasizes the relative decline of the seniority system in the aftermath of Watergate. The heart of this work lists the members of all congressional committees between 1947 and 1992. Entries list the statutory authorization and responsibilities of individual committees for each congressional session, membership by majority and minority parties, years of service on committees by individual members, the chair and ranking members of each committee, and pertinent notes on membership status changes for each congressional session.

As the first volume of a projected six-volume work, *Committees in the U.S. Congress* is a valuable contribution to congressional scholarship. It highlights the continuing importance of congressional committees in formulating legislation and national policymaking. It is hoped that the forthcoming volumes in this work will also contain detailed information on congressional subcommittees. *Committees in the U.S. Congress* continues the high-quality tradition of Congressional Quarterly publications and is a significant addition to libraries with large congressional studies and U.S. depository collections. [R: LJ, 1 Oct 93, p. 89; WLB, Nov 93, pp. 98-100]—**Bert Chapman**

742. Olson, Nancy L., ed. **Organizations of State Government Officials Directory 1992.** Lexington, Ky., Council of State Governments, 1992. 74p. index. $25.00pa. ISBN 0-87292-976-0.

This directory is another of the excellent publications from the Council of State Governments. It complements the *Book of the States* (see ARBA 91, entry 743) and its supplements, *State Executive Officials and the Legislatures* (see ARBA 92, entry 692) and *State Legislative Leadership, Committees and Staff* (see ARBA 92, entry 698). An earlier directory titled *National Organizations of State Government Officials Directory* (see ARBA 85, entry 651) was a narrower version of the current directory.

Olson has collected and compiled information on the functions, publications, organizational structure, and other aspects of nearly 170 national and regional organizations associated with state governments. The directory lists, in alphabetical order by name, each of the organizations being described. Each listing gives information on several major topics: general directory data; membership types and numbers; purpose of the organization; organizational structure; regular publications; recent publications, when different from the regular publications and published since 1989; and staff contacts from which further information can be obtained.

There are two tables of contents, one by official name of the organization and one by acronym. A subject index allows one to find a listing by the key word in the organization's name or the purpose of the organization. The information in this book can be found elsewhere, but libraries will find it worth the minor cost to have this information contained in one small volume. Highly recommended.
—**Christine E. Thompson**

743. **State Yellow Book: Who's Who in the Executive and Legislative Branches of the 50 State Governments. Vol. V, No. 1.** Imogene Akins, ed. Washington, D.C., Monitor Publishing, 1993. 1081p. illus. maps. index. $215.00pa. (4 issues). ISSN 0899-2207.

This valuable guide to state government offices and personnel is organized into four major sections: executive branches, legislative branches, state profiles, and national organizations to which state officials belong. Full addresses and direct telephone numbers for each department and its chief officers are listed in a user-friendly two-column format. Covered are the 50 states, American Samoa, Guam, Puerto Rico, and the Virgin Islands.

In the executive section, brief biographical information and a photograph of each governor appear. The legislative section includes photographs and short biographies of the speakers and presidents of state legislatures. All representatives and senators are listed, and standing committees are included, with chairpersons identified. State profiles provide a brief history and information on demographics, state symbols, the economy, education, statewide organizations, major military installations, and geography, as well as a brief bibliography. Counties are listed, with telephone numbers and statistics on population (1990) and income (1987). The state maps showing county boundaries vary in quality; some are not very legible (e.g., Michigan). Subject and name indexes are included; the latter should be especially useful. This work is a must for public libraries.—**Sharon Langworthy**

744. **Washington '93: A Comprehensive Directory of the Key Institutions and Leaders of the National Capital Area.** Buck J. Downs, Melissa L. Georgopolis, and Amy J. Misner, eds. Washington, D.C., Columbia Books, 1993. 1132p. index. $75.00pa. ISBN 1-880873-04-4. ISSN 0083-7393.

This annually published directory includes the names, addresses, and telephone numbers of approximately 20,000 key Washington people. It also includes the same information for approximately 4,000 local and national government agencies and institutions focusing on national and international affairs, Washington media, businesses with more than $10 million in annual revenue, large national trade and professional associations, labor unions, law firms, and many other organizations in the Washington area. Where appropriate, the editors have included a brief statement regarding the budget and focus of the organizations listed in the directory.

A thumb index is used as a quick method of finding each of the 17 chapters. The chapters are arranged according to the type of organization or person being discussed in the text (e.g., national government, local government, labor unions). There is also a general index for the entire work. It is arranged alphabetically and includes all institutions and people in the book, making it easy to find information about an institution when the reader does not know the appropriate category to search (e.g., Cato Institute is found under "Science and Policy Research").

The number of inclusions makes this directory valuable as a comprehensive list of public affairs, government, and business enterprises in the nation's capital. It should be a part of every library's reference collection.—**Christine E. Thompson**

745. **Who's Who in the Federal Executive Branch 1993.** Washington, D.C., Congressional Quarterly, 1993. 202p. $14.95 spiralbound. ISBN 0-87187-976-X.

This sourcebook contains the names, titles, and telephone numbers of important executive branch officials. Bill Clinton is named first, and thousands of others follow. Part 1 includes information on the executive office of the president, beginning with a diagram showing office assignments in the west wing of the White House. Part 2 covers the 14 cabinet departments; part 3, a host of federal agencies, boards, bureaus, commissions, and corporations. Accompanying each cabinet department and the other organizations is a headquarters address and a telephone number for information. An appendix of regional federal information sources completes this guide. Within the various parts and the appendix, material is arranged alphabetically.

Who's Who in the Federal Executive Branch 1993 provides easy access to high-ranking individuals within the executive branch and their assistants. Information on almost any subject can be gathered in a relatively efficient manner by dialing a few telephone numbers. Unfortunately, the compilers did not distinguish between civil service employees and Clinton political appointees. An asterisk used to denote the latter would have been quite helpful. Regardless, all citizens of the United States who have questions for their government, including researchers, can make valuable use of this little book; it remains a handy reference. Recommended for college, university, and public libraries.—**Richard E. Holl**

Handbooks and Yearbooks

746. **The Almanac of American Politics 1994: The Senators, the Representatives and the Governors: Their Records and Election Results, Their States and Districts.** By Michael Barone and Grant Ujifusa. Washington, D.C., National Journal, 1993. 1538p. illus. $59.95; $48.95pa. ISBN 0-89234-057-6; 0-89234-058-4pa.

Containing the usual information on congressional and administrative personnel and policies, this almanac starts with a useful quick-reference index of congresspeople by state, with references to the pages on which they are discussed. Thorough instructions on usage take the reader through the various categories for which data are provided: the U.S. population, ratings of Congress by lobbying groups, votes cast on major legislation, election results, and campaign financing. There is also a brief discussion of postwar politics and the current political situation. Each state section includes photographs of politicians and maps of the congressional districts, as well as an overview and factual data. Throughout the book the narratives are not the dry, dusty recitations of fact that might be expected; for example, the overview of Colorado is evenhanded and interestingly written. This is an important resource for public libraries whose clients wish to check on their politicians' records and performance or to find basic political statistics about the United States.—**Sharon Langworthy**

747. Batten, Donna, ed. **Encyclopedia of Governmental Advisory Organizations 1994-95: A Reference Guide....** 9th ed. Detroit, Gale, 1993. 1529p. index. $505.00. LC 73-645823. ISBN 0-8103-7460-9. ISSN 0092-8380.

This is an invaluable directory for rapid access to information on current groups that provide input about and sources of influence on the federal government. It is an extensive listing of information on national governmental advisory organizations. It includes presidential advisory, ad hoc, and White House committees; departmental, agency, and interagency committees; congressional and public advisory committees; and consultative organizations and conferences. Of the 6,500-plus entries, more than 300 are new listings. Indexes are to personnel, publications and reports, organizations by presidential administration, organizations by federal department or agency, and key words. The inclusion of fax numbers for some listings is particularly helpful.

Future editions should consider *see* references for groups that have changed names or missions, a brief section on acronyms, and E-mail numbers for groups that have them. Overall, however, this is an excellent directory and guide to groups that influence our national government. Its cost may put it out of the reach of many smaller libraries. However, it is a must purchase for most large public, academic, research, and special libraries.—**Roberto P. Haro**

748. **BNA's Directory of State Administrative Codes and Registers: A State-by-State Listing.** Compiled by Kamla J. King and Judith Springberg with the BNA Library Staff. Washington, D.C., BNA Books, 1993. 360p. $85.00pa. KF70.K56. 016.34873'025. LC 92-40198. ISBN 0-87179-765-8.

Administrative codes, rules, and regulations issued by individual state governments guide the day-to-day activities of government employees and help ensure uniform application of the laws. This new directory is designed to help legal researchers and librarians locate published compilations of administrative law for all 50 states, the District of Columbia, and U.S. territories (e.g., American Samoa, Guam). Also included are state registers, which feature notices of proposed new or amended rules and regulations.

Information for state code books includes official title, initial publication date, format, frequency, cost, publisher (address and telephone and fax numbers), finding aids, search tips, state abbreviation, Bluebook abbreviation, how to cite, and electronic availability. In addition to this is a volume-by-volume outline of each code's table of contents. The state registers are similarly described. The last few pages of the volume include a listing of state attorney general opinions.

The BNA Library staff have done an admirable job of collating all of this information, thus filling an important gap in the field of legal research. The paperback volume is sturdily bound, and its large print and uncluttered format enhance its overall utility. This should become a standard source for all law libraries.—**Gary D. Barber**

749. **Congressional Quarterly's Politics in America 1994: The 103rd Congress.** By CQ's Political Staff. Phil Duncan, ed. Washington, D.C., Congressional Quarterly, 1993. 1747p. illus. maps. index. $79.95; $49.95pa. LC 93-11559. ISBN 0-87187-774-0; 0-87187-775-9pa.

The 5th edition of *Congressional Quarterly's Politics in America* (most recently reviewed in ARBA 90, entry 691) continues to provide a thorough and detailed inside look at U.S. politics, especially the workings of Congress. The arrangement of the new edition is very similar to previous editions, and there is some expanded material provided for each district profile. The information for each state begins with a brief profile of the governor and basic state statistics (population, voting in recent presidential elections, and state legislative data). A map of the state shows the congressional districts. The main portion of each state's section is devoted to profiles of U.S. senators and slightly shorter profiles of each U.S. representative. The profile covers the member's effectiveness both in Washington and at home, listing committee assignments, key votes, voting studies (presidential support, party unity, and the conservative coalition), interest group ratings, recent election results, and campaign finance data. Additionally, there is a descriptive profile of each congressional district. Brief profiles of the five nonvoting members of the House are included. Several useful appendixes list all of the congressional committees and subcommittees with their membership, the partisan committees, joint committees, a seniority list, a pronunciation guide, and a list of the "close calls" in the 1992 election.

There are obvious comparisons to the *Almanac of American Politics* (see ARBA 91, entry 725), and libraries often have a difficult time deciding which volume to purchase. Generally, the *Almanac* provides more thorough coverage of congressional districts, including a separate full listing for the District of Columbia (which is lumped in with the nonvoting members of the House in *Politics*) and more detailed indexing. Also, the *Almanac* brings together campaign finance statistics in one convenient section; in *Politics* this data is found throughout the individual profiles. While the *Almanac* has a slight edge in superiority, both publications are highly recommended for libraries that support active political research, and old editions of both titles should be retained for historical use.—**Thomas A. Karel**

750. **CQ's State Fact Finder: Rankings across America.** By Victoria Van Son. Washington, D.C., Congressional Quarterly, 1993. 454p. index. $69.95; $39.95pa. HA214.V36. 317.3. LC 93-8929. ISBN 0-87187-916-6; 0-87187-915-8pa.

Some 325 tables appear in *CQ's State Fact Finder*, a collection of comparative data for each of the 50 states and the District of Columbia. The tables are grouped in these subject categories: agriculture, business and economy, crime and criminal justice, defense, education, energy, the environment, health, population, recreation, social services, state government, and transportation. A typical table provides total and per capita supermarket sales in an alphabetical list by state, with a corresponding list of the states in order by per capita sales. This data book can be used to easily determine which state has the most business failures, the highest revenue from lotteries, the least amount of crime, the most military installations, or the highest participation in bowling. All tables provide specific numerical data as well as the rankings. It can therefore serve as a source of information about a state when ranking is not of interest.

Additionally, *CQ's State Fact Finder* provides a state profile section that summarizes the rankings on all indicators for each state. This allows quick determination of a state's ranking in all 325 categories. Each table identifies the source of the statistics—in most cases standard U.S. government publications, although some state, nonprofit, and private sources are used. This is an interesting book for browsing as well as an efficient resource for finding comparative statistics on the states.—**Henry E. York**

751. **The Election Data Book: A Statistical Portrait of Voting in America 1992.** Compiled and edited by Kimball W. Bruce and the staff of Election Data Services, Inc. Lanham, Md., Bernan Press, 1993. 1026p. maps. $95.00. ISBN 0-89059-011-7.

This biennial publication promises to be an essential source of statistics for presidential, congressional, senatorial, and gubernatorial races in the United States. It is of interest primarily to political science researchers, whether professionals or students. The statistical information in this book is divided into individual state chapters organized around a series of 10 tables: 1990 population (including breakdowns by race and ethnic origin), 1990 voting age population, voter participation, voter registration by political party affiliation, vote for president, vote for senator, vote for governor, vote for representative in Congress, vote for president (Democratic primaries), and vote for president (Republican primaries). Each state chapter begins with a one-page abstract of information on population, electoral districts, and voting equipment in use. Other charts show voter registration and turnout trends between 1948 and 1992. Each state section includes a map depicting congressional districts and the results of the 1992 presidential, senatorial, and gubernatorial elections.

There are three additional sections in this book. A summary chapter for the United States precedes the individual state chapters. A second chapter abstracts the election data for the 70 counties with the largest populations, highlighting such information as the counties with the highest percent Hispanic population, the lowest voter turnout, and the highest percent vote for Clinton. The third chapter consists of one- and two-page color maps that illustrate election and demographic data at national, state, and county levels. An extensive introduction explains the contents and arrangement of the book and offers a detailed overview of the tables, giving definitions and sources for the statistics.

This new title invites comparison with the biennial *America Votes* (Congressional Quarterly), the venerable sourcebook of election statistics. The older title covers the same statistics, but each new volume summarizes the results of previous elections, which facilitates study over time. *The Election Data Book* has voting statistics only for the latest races, but for these it includes greater detail and various other statistics, such as race, ethnicity, and voter participation (not available in the older serial), that permit political research.—**Henry E. York**

752. Haines, Gerald K., and David A. Langbart. **Unlocking the Files of the FBI: A Guide to Its Records and Classification System.** Wilmington, Del., Scholarly Resources, 1993. 348p. index. $60.00. HV8144.F43H35. 026'.3530074. LC 92-16728. ISBN 0-8420-2338-0.

Haines, senior historian at the CIA and member of the National Archives FBI Task Force, and Langbart, an archivist, have produced a guide to the FBI's massive files now available under the Freedom of Information Act. The listing for each classification contains the number and title of the file, volume of records, dates, location, NAR disposition recommendation and access statement, and related records of both the FBI and other government agencies. Most important, a brief paragraph describes the contents of the file and the notable names that appear (e.g., Errol Flynn and Marilyn Monroe in the White Slave Traffic Act file [31]; Al Capone in Contempt of Court [69]; Lee Harvey Oswald, Abbie Hoffman, and Malcolm X under Domestic Security [100]). Specialized indexes, such as J. Edgar Hoover's confidential files, are listed. Appendixes include standard FBI abbreviations, Department of Justice and FBI Central Records Classifications systems, and FBI organizational charts. There is a general subject index. Anyone doing original research on civil rights, Communism, organized crime, terrorism, or the antiwar movement could be helped by access to the FBI files. Libraries that serve those populations should acquire this book. [R: Choice, July/Aug 93, p. 1749; WLB, June 93, p. 131]—**Deborah Hammer**

753. Hollings, Robert L. **Nonprofit Public Policy Research Organizations: A Sourcebook on Think Tanks in Government.** Hamden, Conn., Garland, 1993. 217p. index. (Organizations and Interest Groups, v.7; Garland Reference Library of Social Science, v.905). $34.00. Z7164.A2H65. 016.35309'3. LC 93-19101. ISBN 0-8153-0766-7.

This volume examines the role of think tanks in U.S. government. Think tanks are defined as nonprofit, private organizations that analyze and shape public policy. They influence government through their ideas, reports, and newspaper Op-Ed pieces, which may be conservative or liberal. Hollings looks at roughly 50 national think tanks; 30 state, local, and regional think tanks; and 300 university think tanks. He also touches on foreign think tanks. Short essays open each chapter, on subjects such as the historical development of nonprofit public policy research organizations, their activities, and influence. An annotated bibliography follows each essay, except for the last. Hollings concludes that the number of U.S. think tanks will increase in the future, spurred on by shrinking government revenues and the growing need to resort to outside scientific, technological, and societal expertise. The importance of think tanks will expand proportionally to their numbers.

Nonprofit Public Policy Research Organizations will aid researchers, especially social scientists, but will also frustrate them. The bibliographical entries are valuable; many good sources can be located. Basic information on think tanks is provided in the brief essays, although nothing very elaborate. Hollings's writing, however, is sometimes confusing. In chapter 1, for example, a topic sentence reads as follows: "The years since the end of World War II have seen an expansion of today as public policy think tanks." Typographical errors occur far too often (e.g., on page 6, a reference to Stanford "Unviersity" exists). The bibliography alone redeems this book. Recommended for college, university, and public libraries.—**Richard E. Holl**

754. McGillivray, Alice V. **Congressional and Gubernatorial Primaries 1991-1992: A Handbook of Election Statistics.** Washington, D.C., Congressional Quarterly, 1993. 265p. maps. $124.00. JK2074.M48. 324.5'4'097302. LC 93-11872. ISBN 0-87187-906-9.

The 1992 elections produced a new president and an influx of new members of congress stemming from electoral dissatisfaction with existing national affairs. Partial statistical documentation of this popular dissatisfaction is found in this volume's coverage of 1991 congressional and gubernatorial primaries. It opens with an introduction examining primary elections and unique features of individual state primaries, accompanied by a calendar listing 1992 primary and runoff dates. The principal part of this compilation lists 1991 gubernatorial and 1992 House and Senate results for each state. Entries include party registration figures for each state, congressional district maps, primary election results for House races, and statewide breakdowns by county for Senate and gubernatorial races. These statistics also include results for runoff elections.

The arrangement and scholarly quality of this work measures up to Congressional Quarterly's usual high standards, but there are weaknesses limiting its overall effectiveness. The omission of 1992 general election results gives readers only a partial picture of 1992's electoral volatility, which was characterized in numerous ways and perhaps best personified by H. Ross Perot's presidential candidacy. In addition, the high price of a volume of such limited scope will not enhance its appeal to budget-strapped libraries. Recommended primarily for libraries with comprehensive U.S. political statistics collections.

—**Bert Chapman**

755. McGillivray, Alice V. **Presidential Primaries and Caucuses 1992: A Handbook of Election Statistics.** Washington, D.C., Congressional Quarterly, 1992. 294p. maps. $124.00. JK522.M34. 324.5'4'0973. LC 92-33506. ISBN 0-87187-890-9.

Elections and voting are fascinating topics for Americans, but that interest goes beyond mere idle curiosity. Political scientists and campaign advisers have turned running for office into a veritable scientific activity. Hence students, scholars, and general readers have a need for and a persistent interest in the hard facts about how people voted. Such information for regular elections has been supplied by *America Votes* (see ARBA 92, entry 696) for a number of years. *Presidential Primaries and Caucuses* is a companion volume.

As the book's preface points out, winning the vote in presidential primaries has become crucial to gaining a presidential nomination. Thus, this new work supplies county-by-county results for the 38 state presidential-preference primaries and that of the District of Columbia. The delegate counts for the 12 states using the caucus/convention system are also summarized. Other related information in this compilation includes summaries of the primary results for 1988 and 1984 and the Republican and Democratic convention roll call votes for 1992. Outline maps of the counties are included for each state and allow readers to match voting statistics with geographical locations. Voter registration figures supply indications of voter turnout and relative party strengths. Thanks to this compilation of statistics, preliminary information about the results of primary elections is more readily available than ever before. [R: Choice, Sept 93, p. 86; RBB, 1 Oct 93, p. 386; WLB, June 93, p. 129]—**Ronald H. Fritze**

756. Scammon, Richard M., and Alice V. McGillivray, comps. and eds. **America Votes 20: A Handbook of Contemporary American Election Statistics.** Washington, D.C., Congressional Quarterly, 1993. 537p. maps. $132.00. LC 56-10132. ISBN 0-87187-784-4.

For 19 previous editions of this invaluable reference tool, Congressional Quarterly (CQ) has attempted to give pundits, would-be pundits, and spin doctors as much data on voting patterns in the United States as possible. (If only Congressional Quarterly could figure a way to get them to take time off from punditry to check their data!) This volume continues the publisher's remarkable reign by offering data on county-by-county voting patterns in every state for president and for every governor, senator, and representative, with accompanying registration figures, vote totals, percentages, and pluralities. Also included are state-by-state vote totals for presidents from Coolidge to Clinton.

Published every two years, *America Votes* continues to surmount each past performance. The uses to which this volume and its siblings can be put are limited only by the minds that use them. It is an exemplary reference choice.—**Mark Y. Herring**

757. Sweeney, Jerry K., and Margaret B. Dunning. **A Handbook of American Diplomacy.** Boulder, Colo., Westview Press, 1993. 157p. index. $35.50pa. ISBN 0-8133-1352-X.

This book was designed to serve both students and general readers interested in American diplomacy. Its six chapters cover a block of time from 1686 to 1990. Each chapter has an introductory essay, a chronology of events, a list of treaties and agreements, biographies of important figures, and an annotated bibliography of books. The bibliographies list books written by major authors who represent mainstream thinking. A glossary and an index that covers organizations, treaties, and agreements are included.

The material in this handbook is available in other sources, and one would expect a 157-page softcover to be less expensive than this. Still, the convenience of having this core collection of information on diplomatic history in an easy-to-use format will make it handy for reference work as well as popular among students. [R: Choice, Sept 93, p. 90]—**Cathy Seitz Whitaker**

758. **The Young Oxford Companion to the Congress of the United States.** By Donald A. Ritchie. New York, Oxford University Press, 1993. 239p. illus. index. $35.00. JK1067.R58. 328.73'003. LC 93-6466. ISBN 0-19-507777-6.

This encyclopedic guide, which is arranged in alphabetical order, contains more than 200 articles on the people, events, and terminology of the U.S. Congress. Some 62 articles treat prominent members of Congress, both past and present, especially Speakers of the House and Senate majority and minority leaders. Representatives include Joseph G. Cannon, Thomas S. Foley, and Sam Rayburn, and senators include George J. Mitchell, Robert F. Wagner, and Daniel Webster. Among the events covered are the Army-McCarthy hearings, the Missouri Compromise, and the Persian Gulf debate. *Bunk, hideaway offices,* and *perks* are some of the terms that receive definition.

The Young Oxford Companion to the Congress of the United States is informative, well written, and sometimes colorful. Although the book is short and the entries relatively few, this treatment of congressional history is surprisingly full. An individual biography of Abraham Lincoln is missing, but he did serve only one term in Congress. A separate entry on Harry Truman does not appear, but numerous references are made to him and the Truman Committee. There is no statement on states' rights, but one on sectionalism compensates. As in any reference of this type, selection is critically important, but it is generally good, and omissions such as those mentioned can readily be explained. All in all, Ritchie's work is admirable. Recommended for junior high, high school, and public libraries.—**Richard E. Holl**

Indexes

759. **American Foreign Policy Index. Volume 1, No. 1.** Bethesda, Md., Congressional Information Service, 1993. 2pts. $995.00/yr.

With this title, Congressional Information Service (CIS) has begun a major new series focusing on America's foreign relations. It encompasses domestic and international political, economic, and security matters that influence the conduct of U.S. foreign policy. Economic competition, terrorism, geopolitical conflicts, drug trafficking, human rights, and environmental cooperation are some of the related topics that fall within the scope of this new index. Key nonclassified documents from the U.S. government, including executive branch departments and offices, independent federal agencies, and Congress, are identified. Many nondepository titles are included, a significant asset.

This service follows the customary CIS format. Quarterly paperbound index and abstract issues cumulate into clothbound annual volumes. The indexes provide access by subject, name, issuing source, legislative bill number, and publication title and number. The abstracts summarize each document and provide full bibliographic data. The accompanying microfiche collection of the source documents is supplied in quarterly shipments.

For any researcher who requires comprehensive coverage and in-depth indexing of U.S. documents related to American foreign policy, this new title will be a valuable improvement over such titles as *Monthly Catalog of United States Government Publications* (GPO). CIS has provided a quality product in an important subject area. But improved access does not come cheaply, as can be seen by the price. [R: Choice, June 93, p. 1598; RBB, 15 Sept 93, p. 183]—**Henry E. York**

760. **Current Treaty Index: Supplement to *United States Treaty Index: 1776-1990 Consolidation*.** Igor I. Kavass, comp. Buffalo, N.Y., William S. Hein, 1992. 569p. $102.50pa. ISBN 0-89941-828-7. ISSN 0731-8189.

This is a revised and updated version of *United States Treaty Index* (see ARBA 93, entry 759). *Current Treaty Index* provides citations of slip treaties issued since June 1990, although these agreements have not yet been published by the State Department or other sources. The work opens with a conversion table for compiler-assigned treaty numbers to treaties now appearing in the State Department's official *Treaties and Other International Acts Series* (TIAS). It then proceeds with a numerical index of treaties since June 1990 that are published in TIAS and those that are not listed there. Subsequent sections include a chronological index of treaties since 1950, a country index that also includes U.S. treaties with multiple nations, and a subject index. The country index is particularly noteworthy in its inclusion of treaties reached by the United States with new nations created in the aftermath of recent and ongoing international political upheavals. Examples of these include Kazakhstan, Lithuania, and Ukraine, with treaties involving these new nations covering topics such as the establishment of diplomatic relations, investment incentives, and military education and training.

Current Treaty Index is a valuable source for accessing U.S. treaty information and will enhance the strength of Kavass's earlier efforts. More important, it will increase the ability of users to research information on treaties recently entered into by the United States before most of these pacts are formally published.—**Bert Chapman**

Periodicals and Serials

761. Peake, Hayden B. **The Reader's Guide to Intelligence Periodicals.** Washington, D.C., NIBC Press, 1992. 250p. illus. index. $39.95; $19.95pa. JF1525.I6P43. 016.32712'05. LC 91-42046. ISBN 1-878292-01-3; 1-878292-00-5pa.

Peake, a former intelligence officer, has put together a handy directory to some very interesting journals. The entries for the 137 titles are from 1 to 5 pages long and include information on the founding, history, scope, contents, and format of the title. Antiestablishment as well as more mainstream publications of the shadow world are included, and these journals focus on both current events and historical topics. Footnotes and occasional illustrations of the individual journal cover appear. Four periodic bibliographies of intelligence literature are also listed, along with four intelligence-related databases and five public database vendor systems. In addition, there are chapters for limited distribution intelligence periodicals, out-of-print titles, and scholarly or professional titles that occasionally have intelligence-related articles.

Several of the journals discussed in this title are also covered in *Military Periodicals* (see ARBA 92, entry 662), which has longer and more informative essays. While prices, address, and telephone and fax numbers for each publisher are provided, there are no ISSNs, and there is no indication of the frequency of publication, meaning that one has to look in *Ulrich's International Periodicals Directory* (see ARBA 93, entry 88) or *The Serials Directory* (see ARBA 91, entry 64) to find this information. Still, this is an informative guide, and it is recommended for academic and large public libraries as well as the appropriate specialized collections.—**Daniel K. Blewett**

African

762. Gastrow, Shelagh, ed. **Who's Who in South African Politics.** 4th ed. New Providence, N.J., Hans Zell/Reed Reference Publishing, 1993. 333p. illus. $95.00. 320.092. ISBN 1-873836-06-6.

This is the 4th edition of this work to appear since 1985. Despite the volatile nature of South African politics, this might be regarded as gilding the lily. Of the some 120 entries, 40 are entirely new, while another 36 have appeared in all 4 editions. About 70 entries are for Black or Coloured politicians, the remainder for Caucasian South Africans. The editor's principal resources have been personal interviews and newspaper articles, and each biography provides specific details of particular sources, permitting users with access to South African newspapers to build on these political biographies, which range in length from one to seven pages. Information is reasonably current; the latest sources used date from September 1992.

Each entry is introduced with a recapitulation of the subject's major offices. In addition, there are a list of acronyms and an extensive list of "office bearers" (i.e., executive members of various political parties, labor organizations, and the like). Few of these are accorded biographies, so the value of such a list in this context is dubious. The editor provides a brief preface, and there is a longer introduction summarizing the tempestuous political scene in South Africa. The book has no indexes. Given the frequently intersecting careers of the biographees, a personal name and organizational index should have been considered indispensable. It could have replaced the superfluous table of contents.

In light of the South African situation, this volume can be considered only an interim report. Already two of its more prominent subjects have died, and the fluid political situation will impel others of all stripes to enter the political arena. Under these circumstances, it would be useful to devise some kind of looseleaf arrangement, which would be less expensive and more readily updated. [R: LAR, Sept 93, p. 517]—**David Henige**

763. Jamison, Martin, comp. **Idi Amin and Uganda: An Annotated Bibliography.** Westport, Conn., Greenwood Press, 1992. 145p. index. (African Special Bibliographies, no.17). $49.95. Z3586.J36. 016.96761. LC 92-27746. ISBN 0-313-27273-5.

The specter of Idi Amin's brutal regime continues to haunt outside perceptions of Africa, as evidenced by the more than 400 entries in this bibliography, surely more than are available for any other single regime in postindependence Africa. These entries are divided into 5 broad classifications (and those in turn into 30 subcategories) and cover the period from 1967 to 1991. The stated intent is to include "scholarly research-level works" in English, but at least one-tenth of the citations are to articles in news magazines and the brief reports of the Joint Publications Research Service. The entire gamut from books to such articles is encompassed, but the constraining effects of citing only materials held in the United States are imponderable, although perhaps significant. The annotations are usually quite extensive and seem to be sound.

Aesthetically this work is unpleasing and seems to lag (surely needlessly) several years behind the potential of desktop publishing in this regard. The work is well indexed by authors, titles (even of articles), and subjects. The first of these, however, lists as authors organizations at whose meetings papers were given, as well as the editors of volumes of collected essays, both departures from accepted norms. There is also an unacceptably high incidence of typographical errors. Despite these lost opportunities to be better, this work should prove useful to those seeking information on one of the most tragic experiences of recent African history, although its price is certain to discourage all but the most profligate individuals and libraries. [R: Choice, June 93, p. 1604]—**David Henige**

764. Williams, Michael W. **Pan-Africanism: An Annotated Bibliography.** Pasadena, Calif., Salem Press, 1992. 142p. index. (Magill Bibliographies). $40.00. Z3508.P35W55. 016.3205'4'09174927. LC 92-31354. ISBN 0-89356-674-8.

This is a selected list of some 360 items that provides a good knowledge base for this subject. The relatively small number of items is countered by the lengthy evaluative annotations that accompany the citations. The introduction defines Pan-Africanism and discusses early emigration efforts and twentieth-century developments. There are sections on the origin and historical development of Pan-Africanism, organizations and movements, theoretical works, and cultural ties. There is also a large section of biographical material on 19 major and several other figures in the Pan-African movement. The important role that Americans have played in furthering this cause will probably come as a surprise to many people. Pan-Africanism is not just a concern of those in Africa, and Williams has selected many materials that discuss the political and cultural relationships of African-Americans and the movement.

Books and book chapters, as well as journal articles, are represented here, but government documents from the United States, United Kingdom, and African governments are absent, as are materials from intergovernmental organizations. Nor is there a section for reference books. The index is composed primarily of personal names. Still, Williams has prepared a useful bibliography to a topic that has received only spotty coverage in more general bibliographies on Africa. Although the price seems a little high, the work is recommended for all public and academic libraries, especially those with an interest in African studies.—**Daniel K. Blewett**

Asian

765. Lewis, D. S., and D. J. Sagar, eds. **Political Parties of Asia and the Pacific: A Reference Guide.** Harlow, England, Longman; distr., Detroit, Gale, 1992. 369p. maps. index. $145.00. ISBN 0-582-09811-4.

This work is a professionally edited, well-laid-out reference guide on a high-interest, dynamic area. It provides information on the political organizations, and the institutional context within which they operate, in the nations and territories of the Asia Pacific region. The contributors are listed as either editors with the producers of *Keesing's Record of World Events* (CIRCA, monthly) or independent British researchers. The book is divided into chapters for individual countries. Where applicable there are subsections for administratively separate dependent territories, including those of Australia, New Zealand, the United States, France, and Great Britain, in the Pacific and Antarctica. The format followed provides separate prefatory sections on the governmental system (with capital and population), the constitutional structure, the electoral system, recent electoral data, and the extent of suffrage. The length of these sections varies from a sentence to a few paragraphs. Accompanying each entry is a political map of the country concerned. There follows a listing of parties, including for each the history, address, leadership, and other available information. The parties may be grouped; for instance, under India, there are separate listings of national and regional parties, and under Australia, there are sections on major and minor parties. Guerrilla groups and defunct parties are included where relevant.

Access points include a detailed table of contents with *see* references (Burma *see* Myanma), a personal name index, and a party name index. The information is said to be current up until June 1992 wherever possible. Where collection budgets will allow, this will be a valuable acquisition. [R: Choice, May 93, p. 1446; RBB, 1 May 93, pp. 1632-34]—**Nigel Tappin**

European

General Works

766. Cook, Chris, and John Paxton. **European Political Facts 1918-90.** 3d ed. New York, Facts on File, 1992. 322p. index. $40.00. JN12.C643. 320.94'02'02. LC 91-38992. ISBN 0-8160-2766-8.

This is a fascinating compendium of data on European politics and government from World War I's close through 1990. While events since 1990 have inevitably made a newer edition necessary, this one retains considerable reference potential. In separate chapters it lays out a wide array of facts about the states of Europe. In this work Europe is broadly defined as stretching from the Atlantic to the Urals and so encompasses part of the former Soviet Union. Included are lists of heads of state and prime, foreign, and finance ministers; descriptive outlines of legislative systems and court structures; elections (usually including tables of results by party); and political parties. Most chapters are arranged alphabetically by country, from Albania to Yugoslavia. Among other features there are descriptions of present and past international organizations with European relevance, a glossary, a list of major treaties and conflicts, and a section on dependencies.

Inevitably some oddities and errors creep in. For example, the section on dependencies does not announce its partial nature, but omits some colonial territories (e.g., Libya for Italy, Rwanda and Burundi for Belgium). The current French premier, Edouard Balladur, in a former guise as finance minister in the 1986-1988 government, has his name spelled "Ballader." More seriously, John Major's tenure as U.K. prime minister is said to have started in November 1989, while in reality Margaret Thatcher left that office in the fall of 1990. Despite these irritating errors, this is a fine reference tool and deserves consideration from acquisition librarians.—**Nigel Tappin**

767. Dinan, Desmond. **Historical Dictionary of the European Community.** Metuchen, N.J., Scarecrow, 1993. 291p. maps. (International Organizations Series, no.1). $37.50pa. JN15.D56. 341.24'2. LC 93-2871. ISBN 0-8108-2666-6.

This first volume in Scarecrow's International Organizations Series provides a solid historical perspective on the European Community (EC), from its post-World War II origins to the ratification of the Maastricht Treaty in 1992. The EC's development, institutions, personalities, and policies are concisely explained in more than 150 brief entries. The entries range from Dean Acheson to Harold Wilson and from the Action Committee for a United States of Europe (1954) to the Werner Plan (1970) and the Year of Europe (1973). Many of the entries are two to three pages in length; the longest topics include common agricultural policy, Economic and Monetary Union (EMU), European Economic Community (EEC), European Parliament, and the Single Market Program. Prominent individuals who receive major attention include Charles de Gaulle, Jacques Delors, Hans-Dietrich Genscher, Roy Jenkins, Francois Mitterrand, Jean Monnet, and Margaret Thatcher. The descriptive entries are supplemented by a 27-page introductory essay on the development of the EC, and by a chronology, maps, and a list of acronyms. A comprehensive bibliography of books, reports, and official documents is also included.

The *Historical Dictionary* is an important companion volume to *The European Communities Encyclopedia and Directory* (see ARBA 92, entry 711), and it updates earlier dictionaries, such as *A Modern Companion to the European Community* (see ARBA 93, entry 767) and *The Economist Pocket Guide to the European Community* by Dick Leonard (Basil Blackwell, 1988). This volume is highly recommended for all academic libraries. [R: LJ, 1 June 93, p. 102; RBB, 1 Sept 93, p. 88]—**Thomas A. Karel**

768. **EC Information Handbook 1993/94.** Brussels, EC Committee of the American Chamber of Commerce; distr., Lanham, Md., UNIPUB, 1993. 205p. maps. index. $45.00pa.

As the editors claim in the preface, this handbook is a useful, compact guide to "the labyrinth of the European Community [EC]." Published annually, it is a timely source of information for governments, businesses, EC officials, and the general public. This edition, published in March 1993, includes new personnel appointments as of January 1993. The introductory chapter contains a number of short essays—accompanied by many charts, tables, and maps—that outline the European unification process and the structure and basic institutions of the EC.

The main segment of this guide is a detailed directory of EC institutions: the Commission, the Council of Ministers, the European Parliament, the Economic & Social Committee, and the Court of Justice. For each institution there are an organizational chart and statements on function and composition. Next comes a detailed list of subagencies with the names of officials and their addresses and telephone numbers. The 518 members of the European Parliament are identified by name, country, political group, committee assignments, and national party affiliation. There is a similar directory section on the missions of the member states to the EC. The handbook concludes with less-extensive directory information on selected European organizations, world organizations, nongovernmental organizations, and United States agencies considered of interest to businesses operating in Europe. The *Yearbook of the European Communities* (Brussels: Editions Delta, 1977-) covers much of the same information, but its style more closely resembles that of the *United States Government Manual* (National Archives and Records Administration, annual) while the *EC Information Handbook* is designed to be the "businessman's companion."

—**Henry E. York**

769. Fallik, Alain, ed. **The European Public Affairs Directory 1993.** Brussels, Landmarks; distr., Bristol, Pa., Taylor & Francis, 1992. 273p. maps. index. $130.00pa. ISBN 90-74373-02-X. ISSN 0777-5814.

This directory lists 5,000 people and organizations involved in lobbying and opinion-making in European affairs. The forming of the European Community (EC) has drawn considerable attention around the world, and Brussels is rapidly becoming the lobbying capital of Europe. Most of the entries in this directory are for individuals and organizations in Brussels. However, a few entries are included for important firms and persons outside that area.

Entries are organized into seven chapters that are listed in the table of contents. The listings are, for the most part, standardized, giving names, addresses, telephone and fax numbers, key officers in charge, and their titles. The chapter on the institutions and decisionmaking of the European Economic Community is informative and useful. It contains important protocols, maps, and access guides.

This directory will be very useful for college, university, business, and special libraries that are interested in Europe, or that closely monitor international commerce and finance and political developments that continue to shape the evolving European states. Large public libraries will also find the book useful. The publishers plan to update it annually.—**Roberto P. Haro**

770. Paxton, John, comp. **European Communities.** New Brunswick, N.J., Transaction, 1992. 182. maps. index. (International Organizations, v.1). $49.95. Z7165.E8P34. 016.34124'22. LC 91-41792. ISBN 1-56000-052-X.

The aim of this bibliography is to provide coverage of the major titles relating to the European Community (EC) since it began with the Treaty of Rome in 1958. It is intended for the general reader in search of current information, but older works of historical interest and sources specifically for business leaders have also been included. Almost all of the titles are in English. Paxton was the editor of *The Statesman's Year-Book* (see ARBA 92, entry 77) for many years and the author of the 1982 *Dictionary of the European Communities* (St. Martin's Press).

The bibliography begins with sections on the history of the European Communities and includes biographical sources and chapters on each of the member states. The major institutions of the EC and their publications are covered thoroughly. This section focuses on serials that provide continuing official documentation. Paxton notes that the EC itself issues some 3,000 publications a year. There are also extensive chapters on the social, labor, fiscal, environmental, energy, and other policies of the EC. The final chapters deal with periodicals, directories, databases, and other reference sources.

This selective, annotated bibliography effectively identifies the major works on the EC. The short annotations provide valuable comments on the contents, usefulness, and perspective of the works cited. A chronology and author, title, and subject index are also included. [R: Choice, May 93, p. 1446]

—Henry E. York

771. **Who's Who in European Institutions and Enterprises 1993: A Biographical Directory....** 3d ed. John C. Dove, ed. Zurich, Switzerland, Verlag AG; distr., Hauppauge, N.Y., Ballen Booksellers International, 1992. 2298p. illus. maps. index. (Sutter's International Red Series). $230.00. ISBN 88-85246-18-4.

Although this volume is titled *Who's Who*, it also includes considerable information of the sort found in *Statesman's Year-Book* (see ARBA 92, entry 77). One-half of the book consists of biographical entries on European politicians and government officials, while the other half is descriptive and statistical information about the European Community and the various nations of the Council of Europe. More than 4,000 people connected with the European Community, the governments of the nations of the Council of Europe, and industry and commerce form the biographical entries. They range from well-known figures, such as Lech Walesa and John Major, to obscure banking executives and members of national Olympic committees. An anonymous committee of experts has picked the biographees, who must be living to be included. The biographical information supplies the normal vital and family information as well as education, career, publications, awards, memberships, and recreational activities.

The second part of the volume begins with a section describing the various components of the government of the European Community and the Council of Europe and listing the names of the various officials. This information is followed by a country-by-country survey of the 27 nations of the Council of Europe, which includes a map, a brief history, a description of politics and government, and an economic overview. A third section provides an industry-by-industry survey of the European economy, while the fourth and fifth sections deal with cultural and social matters. A brief index allows individual companies or government agencies to be located. As a current source of European information, this title is quite useful and has been considerably expanded beyond earlier editions. [R: Choice, Oct 93, p. 274; LJ, 15 Sept 93, p. 70]—**Ronald H. Fritze**

772. **Who's Who in European Politics.** 2d ed. New Providence, N.J., K. G. Saur/Reed Reference Publishing, 1993. 1016p. index. $265.00. ISBN 1-8573-9021-0.

Three years after the first edition was published (see ARBA 92, entry 719), a substantially revised and expanded edition of this work has appeared. This edition provides short biographical sketches on more than 8,000 politicians and "political personalities" in the European nations—approximately 2,000 more entries than were contained in the first edition. The entries follow a typical who's-who format and some, for major political figures such as Boris Yeltsin, are surprisingly brief. The coverage is impressive, however. In addition to heads of state and leaders of political parties, other entries are for members of parliaments or legislative bodies, bureaucratic departments, and other political organizations. Most former heads of state, such as Margaret Thatcher or Vaclav Havel, are no longer included in the directory unless they currently hold another political position.

The second, and shorter, part of this volume is a political directory, arranged by country. This section now includes a separate listing for all of the former Soviet republics, as well as the Czech Republic, the Slovak Republic, and the various portions of Yugoslavia. A listing for the European Community is also found here. The directory lists the head of state, the governmental departments, the legislature, main political parties, trade unions, and the central bank. A biographical index lists the names of individuals who are associated with that country, the person's position, and a page number. Additional features of the volume include a glossary of terms and institutions, a detailed key to the biographical entry, and a list of abbreviations. This resource is highly recommended for most academic libraries and is an excellent companion to such standard political sources as the *Europa World Year Book* (Gale, 1992).

—**Thomas A. Karel**

773. **Yearbook of the European Communities and of the Other European Organizations. Annuaire des Communautes Europeennes. Jahrbuch der Europaischen Gemeinschaften.** 12th ed. Brussels, Editions Delta; distr., Lanham, Md., UNIPUB, 1992. 535p. illus. index. $165.00. ISBN 2-8029-0105-2. ISSN 0771-7962.

The economic unification of Western Europe is progressing steadily, with monetary union scheduled to be completed between 1997 and 1999. This process makes the European Community (EC) increasingly significant to international affairs, so that reference works such as *Yearbook of the European Communities* are also becoming more and more important.

The text appears in French, English, and German. A detailed table of contents lists sections concerning the various departments of the EC. Each section includes a descriptive introduction, lists of personnel, and addresses for organizations. Other sections include a chronology of the EC's history and a list of its official publications. An index of personal names allows specific individuals to be located.—**Ronald H. Fritze**

German

774. Stachura, Peter D. **Political Leaders in Weimar Germany: A Biographical Study.** New York, Simon & Schuster Academic Reference Division, 1993. 230p. index. $45.00. DD244.S64. 920.043. LC 92-30716. ISBN 0-13-020330-0.

Weimar Germany represents the transitional era in German history between the fall of the Wilhelmine monarchy and the rise of the Third Reich. A complicated period in German historical development, this era produced many figures who assumed or would eventually obtain prominence in Germany's modern political development. Many of these figures are profiled in *Political Leaders in Weimar Germany*.

The volume opens with an alphabetical list of individuals profiled and an introductory explanation. The principal portion of this volume consists of biographical portraits of politically prominent figures of the Weimar era and those whose rise began during this period. Individuals profiled here include personalities as diverse as Konrad Adenauer, Walther Ulbricht, Walter Rathenau, Rosa Luxemburg, Gustav Stresemann, Ernst Roehm, and others who represent the diverse ideological perspectives characteristic of the Weimarian polity. Biographical entries include sources for more substantive portrayals of these individuals and their careers. Subsequent sections include a chronology of key events in Weimar Germany, abbreviations, a glossary of important organizations and concepts, and a selective bibliography of works on Weimar Germany.

Stachura has produced a concise and substantive work that should help stimulate study on the personalities and events of this crucial period in twentieth-century German and world history. Especially recommended for academic libraries. [R: Choice, May 93, p. 1450; RBB, 1 May 93, pp. 1630-32; WLB, April 93, pp. 122-24]—**Bert Chapman**

Great Britain

775. Cornish, Rory T. **George Grenville 1712-1770: A Bibliography.** Westport, Conn., Greenwood Press, 1992. 227p. index. (Bibliographies of British Statesmen, no.3). $69.50. Z8369.253.C67. 016.94107'092. LC 91-35219. ISBN 0-313-28281-1.

This volume lists and describes a host of materials related to the life and times of George Grenville, British prime minister from 1763 to 1765. Original and secondary sources are documented. Two essays are also included: a biographical sketch of Grenville and a discussion of the Grenvillites and the press, 1763-1770. Two short indexes complete the book. Throughout, Cornish maintains that Grenville was a competent politician who emphasized efficiency and economy, and that he was not the sole author of the conflict between England and America. In many regards, his interpretation is unabashedly revisionist.

Cornish displays an extensive knowledge of Grenville's political career and parliamentary maneuverings. The bibliography is close to exhaustive, and the essays are crisp and concise. This work will be useful for scholars interested in eighteenth-century British politics and Anglo-American affairs during the 1760s.

Even so, its relatively narrow scope limits its value to experts. Of greater concern, Cornish may be too sympathetic to Grenville; one should keep this in mind when reading his assessments of manuscript collections—indeed, all sources. Recommended, with slight reservations, for university libraries. [R: Choice, May 93, p. 1438]—**Richard E. Holl**

776. Mikdadi, Faysal. **Margaret Thatcher: A Bibliography.** Westport, Conn., Greenwood Press, 1993. 269p. index. (Bibliographies of British Statesmen, no.18). $85.00. Z8869.14.M55. 016.941085'8. LC 92-38071. ISBN 0-313-28288-9.

Margaret Thatcher served as prime minister of the United Kingdom from 1979 to 1991. During her tenure she led a conservative government that rolled back many aspects of the welfare state. Some have heaped praise on her policies, while others have condemned them vigorously. But whatever one's judgments, Thatcher has proven to be one of the most significant British prime ministers of the twentieth century. Thus, Mikdadi's bibliography is a welcome first effort to provide a guide to future research on Thatcher.

The 1,455 entries are organized into 16 chapters. Some of the chapters list types of literature dealing with Thatcher (e.g., newspapers, biographies, theses). Others are topical and deal with periods of her life or types of policies (e.g., childhood and youth, foreign affairs, equal opportunities, removal from power). Many of the entries include brief descriptive annotations. Most of the items cited are from periodicals. An extended biographical essay, a detailed chronology, and separate author and subject indexes are also supplied.

Needless to say, the study of Thatcher falls under the category of contemporary history, which means that the state papers and personal manuscripts usually found in the bibliographies of politicians in this series are absent because they will remain unavailable for research for some years. Still, this work is an excellent resource for anyone beginning the study of Margaret Thatcher. [R: Choice, Oct 93, p. 270]

—**Ronald H. Fritze**

Russian

777. Gazukin, Pavel, comp., and Andrei Vasilevsky, ed. **Who Is Who in the Russian Government.** Moscow, Panorama of Russia; distr., Somerville, Mass., Panorama of Russia, 1992. 96p. illus. $25.00pa. ISBN 5-85895-001-9.

778. **Who Is Who in the Russian Government. Supplement I.** Moscow, Panorama of Russia; distr., Somerville, Mass., Panorama of Russia, 1993. 23p. $10.00pa.

Panorama calls itself an "information-expert group" and during 1992-1993 has published a number of reference sources dealing with several aspects of life in the former Soviet Union. Some of these books (or, rather, pamphlets) are briefly reviewed in this volume of ARBA. *Who Is Who in the Russian Government* offers some 30 biographical sketches in the main volume, plus 11 in the supplement. In most cases the biographical narrative is accompanied by a picture, and besides the usual personal information it includes a brief description of education and career and a list of most important positions held. All in all, it provides basic facts for the uninitiated. It must be used with caution because, in view of rapid changes in Russia, career information becomes dated quickly.—**Bohdan S. Wynar**

779. Pribylovskii, Vladimir. **Dictionary of Political Parties and Organizations in Russia.** Washington, D.C., Center for Strategic and International Studies, 1992. 129p. index. (Significant Issues Series, v.14, no.7). $14.95pa. JN6699.A795P75. 324.247'003. LC 92-14181. ISBN 0-89206-180-4.

With the recent dissolution of the Soviet Union and the disbanding of the Communist Party of the Soviet Union, it is important for the rest of the world to know what is going on politically in Russia. Therefore, a dictionary of political parties and organizations in Russia is an appropriate source for interested observers to consult. The advent of democratic-style government in Russia has resulted in the proliferation of political organizations, parties, and congresses. As a consequence, this small volume is a valuable resource for understanding Russia's political development.

The wide range of party persuasion indicates that there is still considerable political naivete in Russia. New ideas have resulted in groups that include monarchists, republicans, social democrats, Christian democrats, anarcho-syndicalists, and some leftover Marxists and communists. With such a vast spectrum of political persuasion, and for the chance to observe Russia's political evolution, this volume is essential for students, scholars, government officials, and corporate observers, and is recommended for college, university, public, government, and corporate reference collections.—**Norman L. Kincaide**

780. **Russian Government Today. Spring 1993.** Washington, D.C., Carroll Publishing, 1993. 490p. maps. index. $195.00pa.

This new directory contains listings for more than 8,500 Russian officials: 248 members of the Supreme Soviet, with brief biographical data and vote ratings; 600 members of parliamentary joint committees and commissions; 1,049 members of the Russian Congress of People's Deputies; 200 officials in the administration of the president; 450 officials in executive governmental administration; 3,150 ministry and agency officials; 1,700 republic and oblast (province) officials; 170 people in the Moscow city government; 350 members of the Russian Academy of Sciences; 60 members of the Russian Academy of the National Economy; 80 officials in the Russian Foundation of Charity and Health; 260 members and officials in commodity and stock exchanges and independent banks; 200 officials working for business associations and chambers of commerce; and officials in other organizations. The final part of the directory contains an index of names and a keyword index. A map of the Russian Federation, with the administrative-territorial division as of 1992, is provided. Four charts illustrating the administrative structures of the Supreme Soviet, the presidential administration, the Council of Ministers, and the government are interesting and helpful.

Even after the second ("parliamental") coup of October 4, 1993, this directory can be used as a reliable source of who's who in Russia nowadays, and it will possibly remain so after the December 12, 1993, election. Nevertheless, the least reliable listings are those of politicians: the members of the Supreme Soviet and the Congress of People's Deputies. In contrast, the membership of the Russian Academy of Sciences will change little. [R: Choice, Sept 93, p. 88; RQ, Winter 93, pp. 294-95]

—**Ludmila N. Ilyina**

781. Taras, Raymond C., ed. **Handbook of Political Science Research on the USSR and Eastern Europe: Trends from the 1950s to the 1990s.** Westport, Conn., Greenwood Press, 1992. 345p. index. $79.50. JN6524.H36. 321.9'2'072. LC 92-12280. ISBN 0-313-27466-5.

This book can be considered as a funeral rite, a scattering of rose petals over the coffin of Sovietology, as this research field slides into the waters of forgetfulness. Why so many learned people for so long failed to predict the demise of the Soviet Union should forever serve as an object lesson to academics the world over. The failure was most evident regarding the Soviet Union, the center of the empire; as the essays in the volume illustrate, it becomes less blatant as one goes out to the periphery, the studies of the Eastern European satellite countries. To some degree the failure of the field is illustrated by this book: It is too centralized and exclusionary, covering only the so-called "Sovietological peaks," the scholars from the large research institutions. The impact of the Soviet dissidents is not discussed, although it is well known that, since the arrival of the dissident literature, the internal polemics of the Sovietologues became less pertinent for the understanding of the Soviet Union. (After all, its dismemberment was predicted by Andrei Amalrik.) The volume also gives short shrift to the Kremlinologists, the most successful of the Sovietologists. More mention of economic analysis, such as the writings of Marshall Goldman, who, during the last phase of the Soviet Union, made numerous correct calls, could also have filled out the volume. [R: Choice, Mar 93, pp. 1112-14]—**Andrew Ezergailis**

Ukrainian

782. Mikhailovskaya, E., comp. **Ukraine: Political Parties and Organisations.** Moscow, Panorama of Russia; distr., Somerville, Mass., Panorama of Russia, 1992. 46p. $55.00pa.

Another small pamphlet produced by Panorama in 1992, it is now only of historical value. It offers brief descriptions of various political organizations with some details about leaders, goals, history, and more. Appended is a 10-page statement offering brief biographical data of some political figures, with the longest sketch on Leonid Pliushch, who resides in Paris. There is much briefer coverage of Ivan Pliushch, a chairman of the Supreme Soviet, and of Leonid Kravchuk, president of Ukraine. This directory seems to be rather unreliable even for historical information.—**Bohdan S. Wynar**

Latin American and Caribbean

783. Coggins, John, and D. S. Lewis, eds. **Political Parties of the Americas and the Caribbean: A Reference Guide.** Harlow, England, Longman; distr., Detroit, Gale, 1992. 341p. maps. index. $145.00. ISBN 0-582-09646-4.

This excellent directory of political parties in the Western Hemisphere includes entries for all countries, as well as colonies (e.g., Bermuda), overseas departments (e.g., French Guiana), and territories (e.g., U.S. Virgin Islands). Entries are arranged in alphabetical order and include capital city, population, brief history, an explanation of the constitutional structure and electoral system, a description of suffrage, results of recent elections, and an overview of all major political parties (including some minor, defunct, and illegal parties and primary guerrilla groups). Many entries also include a map. Party descriptions include English-language and native-language names, address, name of leader, orientation (e.g., conservative and aggressively free-market, centrist), and history. The editors claim that all information was correct as of March 1992. Indexes of personal names and political parties are included.

The coverage for the United States is probably the weakest. No mention is made of Jesse Jackson, the Rainbow Coalition, or the Moral Majority, and the Ku Klux Klan is listed as the single major guerrilla group. Furthermore, under the entry for the U.S. Virgin Islands, it is erroneously stated that the islands were purchased from the Dutch in 1916 rather than from the Danes in 1917. These problems, however, are the exception. For the most part, this is a carefully researched, nicely organized, and well-written reference tool that presents, in accessible form, information not available in other ready-reference sources. [R: Choice, May 93, p. 1446; LJ, 1 April 93, p. 92; RBB, 15 Oct 93, pp. 474-75; WLB, May 93, p. 121]

—**Fred J. Hay**

784. Rossi, Ernest E., and Jack C. Plano. **Latin America: A Political Dictionary.** Santa Barbara, Calif., ABC-Clio, 1992. 242p. index. (Clio Dictionaries in Political Science). $56.50. F1406.R67. 980'.003. LC 92-28946. ISBN 0-87436-608-9.

This dictionary is a revised edition of the earlier *Latin American Political Dictionary* (see ARBA 81, entry 566). Rossi and Plano have added new topics and materials, making this a useful introductory tool and guide to Latin America. Access to information is possible by three routes. First, the book is arranged by broad topics and themes, such as economic integration and historical perspective. Second, for more specific types of information, the index is useful. Finally, the extensive cross-referencing also serves as a finding device.

While this is a welcome reference tool, there are some minor problems. The map of Latin America is inadequate. Sources of additional information, even a short bibliography of general texts on Latin America, would be welcome. And there are some curious omissions. No mention is made of the Chamizal Dispute between Mexico and the United States that ended in the return to Mexico of territory in Texas. The Cuban and Haitian human exoduses (the Marielitos and the Haitian Boat People) are omitted. And no information is given about the North American Free Trade Agreement talks. Recommended for all libraries as a general guide to Latin America. [R: Choice, June 93, p. 1608; VOYA, June 93, p. 126]

—**Roberto P. Haro**

Middle Eastern

785. Rolef, Susan Hattis, ed. **Political Dictionary of the State of Israel [and] Supplement 1987-1993.** 2d ed. New York, Macmillan, 1993. 417p. maps. $65.00. DS126.5.P62. 320.95694'03. LC 93-20521. ISBN 0-02-897193-0.

In that powder keg called the Middle East, nothing may be more inscrutable than learning who the players are, what side they are on, and in whom their interests reside. This new edition of a familiar work provides much of this information for one of the Middle East's most important players: Israel. The book is meant to answer questions about the politics, personalities, political parties, laws and institutions, key terms, concepts, and events of the country. Moreover, Israel's geography and international relations are also covered. A supplement containing 150 additional entries has been added to this edition. Terms such as the Diaspora, Knesset, the Stern Gang, and Kach, and personalities such as Moshe Dayan and Yitzhak Shamir are included.

While each of the 500 entries is fully documented and carefully researched, one troubling aspect remains. When articles inevitably seep into Arab territory and concerns, some of the work's objectivity is lost to pro-Israeli interpretations of events and causation. Despite this reservation, the volume should be on the shelf of any library wishing to learn more about Israel and its people, places, and politics. [R: Choice, Nov 93, pp. 437-38]—**Mark Y. Herring**

IDEOLOGIES

786. Glenn, Robert W. **The Haymarket Affair: An Annotated Bibliography.** Westport, Conn., Greenwood Press, 1993. 363p. index. (Bibliographies and Indexes in American History, no.25). $85.00. Z7164.A52G58. 016.9773'11041. LC 92-46526. ISBN 0-313-28427-X.

The 1886 Haymarket affair, in which a labor demonstration resulted in the death of a number of police officers and demonstrators after a bomb was thrown, has tremendous importance not only for historians and union members but also for the socialist and anarchist movements. This annotated list of more than 1,500 titles will probably be the standard bibliography for at least a generation. While selective, it does include all relevant items from RLIN and America: History and Life, full indexing for 17 periodicals, and significant archive and manuscript collections, as well as art works and an extensive collection of fiction, poetry, and other literary interpretations. Generally speaking, most manuscript letters and general newspaper items, cartoons, and most memorial poems are excluded.

The materials are arranged in four sections: "Context," giving biographical and other background information; "History," including government and legal documents and the primary and secondary works analyzing events; "Argument," covering polemics; and "Imagination." The author/title/subject index provides excellent access to individual items, as do extensive cross-references within the annotations. The latter are the most notable feature of the book: Well written and well conceived, they range from simple descriptions of a short letter to page-long abstracts of important material. In fact, a reading of these could almost provide the average person an adequate knowledge of the events and their significance without further effort.

As a base for further research, as access to hard-to-get material, and as a record of an important event, this work is a model. It is unfortunate that the price will limit the market. One hopes at least some libraries are still willing to lend such reference materials to those who cannot afford them, because the information will prove valuable to the student as well as the scholar. [R: Choice, Oct 93, p. 266]
—**James H. Sweetland**

787. Wilcox, Derk Arend, Joshua Shackman, and Penelope Naas, eds. **The Right Guide: A Guide to Conservative and Right-of-Center Organizations.** Ann Arbor, Mich., Economics America, 1993. 444p. index. $74.95. LC 92-73981. ISBN 0-914169-01-7. ISSN 1064-7414.

A good directory is current, comprehensive, and easy to use. *The Right Guide* is all of these things. Although no directory can have everything, this one comes close. It contains the names, telephone numbers, and addresses of more than 500 conservative organizations worldwide; it also provides information on the organizations' publications, products, key people, and internships. Not just a directory, the guide has profiles (500 words or so) of select conservative organizations, such as the Heritage Foundation, and information on groups with "unknown status" or "no forwarding address." A periodicals section lists many regularly published conservative publications. Two indexes make access easy: the profile subject index, which outlines the main body of the source by subject, and the keyword index, which provides keyword access to all nine sections of the book. The user is further aided by descriptive section headings and useful "How to Use This Guide" pages.

The Right Guide is not without flaws and limitations, however. The table of contents has an error or two; for example, it guides the user to the International Organizations section on page 205, when in fact that section starts on page 209. Also, as comprehensive as this directory is, it cannot do it all. Reference librarians still need *The Radical Right* (see ARBA 89, entry 667) for more detailed information on many international organizations, *Guide to the American Right* (Laird Wilcox Editorial Research Service, 1992) for the few people and organizations in the United States that slipped through the cracks of the much larger source, and *Right Minds* (see ARBA 89, entry 670) for more biographical and bibliographical information on American conservatism.

The publication of this large directory is a sign of the growth of conservative thought in the United States since World War II. All public and academic libraries should make it available to the increasing number of people interested in conservative ideas. [R: Choice, May 93, p. 1448; JAL, Mar 93, p. 57; RBB, 1 April 93, pp. 1459-60]—**John P. Stierman**

INTERNATIONAL ORGANIZATIONS

788. **Books in Print of the United Nations System.** Compiled by the Advisory Committee for the Co-ordination of Information Systems (ACCIS). New York, United Nations, 1992. 721p. index. $50.00pa. ISBN 92-1-100379-2. S/N GV.E.92.0.18.

This new reference work lists more than 14,000 publications available as of June 1992 from United Nations (UN) sales offices, UN copublishers, and external publishers for the system. Publications date from 1991 or earlier and include works of specialized agencies of the UN, as well as of its principal bodies. Publications for internal or limited distribution are excluded, as are nonprint formats, posters, maps, periodicals, and verbatim records of meetings.

The main body of this work is the listing of publications. It uses terms from the *UNBIS Thesaurus* (United Nations, 1985) as broad subject categories, which are further divided by subheadings. The individual entries are listed alphabetically by title within this subject arrangement. Each entry has a sequence number that provides linkage with the various indexes and is also used in cross-references. There are a title index, a series index arranged by number within the series or alphabetically by title for unnumbered series, an organization index, and an ISBN index. Completing the work are an address listing for sales offices or agents and another for publishers outside the UN system.

There are several problems with this generally useful work. Because the bibliographical information provided by various sales offices lacks standards for content, entries are not always complete. Also, some of the subheadings cover four to five pages of triple-columned entries in tiny print. Further breakdown of these subjects would enhance access to the listings. The major problem, however, is the need for current information. ACCIS hopes that this information will eventually be included on a CD-ROM covering both in-print and out-of-print documents and publications of the UN system. That format has the potential for providing more current information. [R: LJ, 15 Mar 93, p. 68]—**Carol Wheeler**

789. **Countdown 2000. Volume II, 1993.** Brussels, EC Committee of the American Chamber of Commerce in Belgium; distr., Lanham, Md., UNIPUB, 1993. 181p. $60.00pa. ISBN 2-930073-01-2.

This work is designed for EC (European Community) specialists. Its focus is on EC proposed legislation. It is divided into 14 chapters that cover many important topics, such as consumer affairs, intellectual property, telecommunication and information technology, and transportation. Each chapter is organized into two sections. Section 1, "Worth Watching," covers the proposals to be introduced in future sessions. Section 2 lists the actual legislative initiatives that are presently being worked on by various committees within the EC. The number of entries in each chapter varies, depending on the importance of

the topic. Generally, there are between 30 and 40 entries in each chapter. The major elements of each entry are the reports on the legislative status of each initiative at various stages. The information provided is brief; users who need detailed information must consult other sources. This work should be useful as a guide to identify current and future proposed legislation, some of which will eventually become law.
—**Binh P. Le**

790. Culligan, Michael, comp., and Cynthia T. Morehouse, ed. **International Directory of Youth Internships with the United Nations, Its Related Agencies, and Non-Governmental Organizations.** 5th ed. New York, Apex Press, 1993. 52p. $7.50pa. ISBN 0-945257-47-3.

A lot of information is available in this small publication for young people looking for work-related experience in the international community. It covers internships available through the United Nations, its related specialized agencies, and various nongovernmental organizations whose work is closely affiliated with that of the United Nations. This last category includes such diverse organizations as Amnesty International, Care, the Ford Foundation, the Sierra Club, and Zero Population Growth. The introductory section provides some general orientation to prospective interns. It cautions that most internships provide no stipends and do not necessarily lead to permanent employment. These internships provide special short-term work and learning situations. Some involve independent research; "all include some tedious work."

The main segment of the publication is a directory of agencies that have internships available. Each entry provides a short description of the functions and activities of the agencies. The available internships are listed and briefly described with information needed for applying. The first appendix lists United Nations organizations and information centers. The second is an annotated bibliography of directories covering international study, careers, and internships. This is a useful list with many titles that may well be unknown to many.—**Henry E. York**

791. **The International Year Book and Statesmen's Who's Who 1992: International and National Organisations, Countries of the World, and 8000 Biographies....** 40th ed. East Grinstead, England, Reed Information Services; distr., Bristol, Pa., Taylor & Francis, 1992. 692p. $299.00. ISBN 0-611-00817-3.

This annual publication (see ARBA 80, entry 89 for a review of the 27th edition) continues its familiar format. The first section provides background information on the United Nations, its specialized and affiliated agencies, other intergovernmental organizations, and selected British and international organizations. The table of contents lists all the organizations included, except those in the last category; a separate alphabetical list of British and international organizations is provided at the beginning of that subsection.

The second section has information on countries of the world. The coverage varies widely, with some countries having 2 pages and others more than 50. A useful table of comparative statistics on 185 countries and territories precedes the alphabetically arranged narratives for each country.

The third section provides brief biographical information on approximately 8,000 individuals. This section is what makes this work unusual. Some overlap exists with *The International Who's Who* (see ARBA 92, entry 27), but there is very little overlap with *Who's Who in the World* (see ARBA 88, entry 36). Unfortunately, no criteria for inclusion are provided, other than the title page's claim that the individuals are "leading personalities in public life." While the coverage is truly international, the selections are sometimes questionable. Of nine U.S. Supreme Court justices, only David Souter and Clarence Thomas are included. Many U.S. congressional leaders are missing. A state attorney general and city mayor are included, but most state governors are not. The greatest problem, however, is the unreliability of the information. Many entries have not been updated at all or have been only partially updated, so that occupation and address do not match the current position listed.

Other shortcomings of this work include numerous typographical errors and misspellings, Roman numeral pagination on the more than 100 pages covering organizations, and a general concern about how information is updated. For example, Republic and Piedmont Airlines are still listed in the entry on the United States. Libraries already owning *The Europa World Year Book* (Gale, 1992) or *The Statesman's Year-Book* (see ARBA 92, entry 77) may not need this work unless they want the questionable biographical coverage it provides.—**Carol Wheeler**

792. Matsuura, Kumiko, Joachim W. Muller, and Karl P. Sauvant. **Chronology and Fact Book of the United Nations 1941-1991: Annual Review of the United Nations Affairs.** Dobbs Ferry, N.Y., Oceana, 1992. 598p. $75.00. ISBN 0-379-21200-5. ISSN 0066-4340.

This is the 8th edition of a detailed reprise of United Nations (UN) events. Subscribers to the same publisher's *Annual Review of United Nations Affairs* receive this work as a supplement. It is drawn primarily from the official UN journal, the *UN Chronicle*.

The volume is divided into three chapters. The first is the chronology. The second is a compendium of UN information in 14 tables, including membership with dates of admission; the 18 UN-affiliated organizations with basic information on founding, purpose, and headquarters; major office holders (including secretaries general and members of the International Court); Security Council members over time; and a list of international years, days, and decades through 1994 (Year of the Family). The last chapter gives the texts of the Charter; the International Court of Justice statute; rules of the Security Council, General Assembly, and other major bodies; and UN staff regulations.

The book seems well done, although at least one error crept in: The Universal Postal Union entry gives 1974 as its founding conference, while the rest of the entry makes it clear that 1874 must have been meant. At least some of the information is duplicated from sources to which most larger libraries subscribe, such as the *Yearbook of the United Nations* (United Nations, annual) which contains the Charter and the statute of the International Court of Justice, for example.

In sum, this is a handy reference. It should be considered for purchase where the information is not duplicated in other parts of the collection or where client demand warrants. [R: RBB, 15 May 93, p. 1721]
—**Nigel Tappin**

793. Schiavone, Giuseppe. **International Organizations: A Dictionary and Directory.** 3d ed. New York, St. Martin's Press, 1992. 337p. index. $75.00. JX1995.S325. 341.2'025. LC 92-38142. ISBN 0-312-09143-5.

This edition follows the same format as the previous one (see ARBA 88, entry 745). The main body contains alphabetically arranged entries for approximately 100 international organizations, including the United Nations, its specialized agencies, and regional or subregional groups. The entries generally range from a half page to several pages. Information about an organization's objectives, powers, and activities is provided, as well as addresses, principal officers, primary publications, and (in some cases) a short list of other sources of information. A separate section divided by field of interest provides brief information on approximately 90 organizations, including purpose, members, director, address, telephone number, and publications. Also included are an introductory essay, separate indexes by acronyms and full organization names, detailed membership charts, a list by year of organizations' founding dates, and a classified index by type of organization.

There are several shortcomings in this generally useful work. The only information about its scope or purpose appears on the dust jacket. The introductory essay, which provides valuable background, is virtually unchanged from the previous edition except for a new beginning and ending. It would benefit from textual editing and division into sections with descriptive headings to make its content more accessible. Finally, the classified index, which lists organizations without giving page numbers, includes organizations that do not appear in the index of names.

There is some overlap between this and other works. *The International Organizations and World Order Dictionary* (see ARBA 93, entry 781) contains approximately 70 of the same organizations, although not with the same level of detail. Nevertheless, its broader scope might make it more useful for some purposes. And while the *Intergovernmental Organization Directory 1984/85* (see ARBA 86, entry 710) provides more detail than Schiavone's work for 1,690 organizations, it has not been updated. All in all, Schiavone's new edition is valuable for the fairly detailed information it provides. [R: Choice, June 93, p. 1608-10; RBB, July 93, p. 2003]—**Carol Wheeler**

INTERNATIONAL RELATIONS

794. Anderson, Ewan A. **An Atlas of World Political Flashpoints: A Sourcebook of Geopolitical Crisis.** New York, Facts on File, 1993. 243p. maps. $40.00. G1046.F1A5. 327.1'01'0223. LC 92-30193. ISBN 0-8160-2885-0.

At a time when events in small, obscure points around the world often affect us, this is a very useful sourcebook on troubled areas. It provides background on 80 of the most important actual and potential trouble spots. Often, the area is very small but has strategic or economic importance. For example, Abu Musa is a island only three miles long, but its location at the opening of the Straits of Hormuz gives strategic and political importance to the dispute between Iran and the United Arab Emirates over its sovereignty.

This volume focuses especially on the link between geography and politics. Each entry features a detailed but clear map of the trouble spot with demarcations of disputed territory and key geographical features such as water bodies, passes, and marshes. The entries are concise but provide reference to other sources. With its accurate and unbiased information, this volume is an important addition to the collections of major libraries, international businesses, and newspapers. [R: Choice, May 93, p. 1435; RBB, 15 April 93, p. 1532; SLJ, 15 Sept 93, p. 66;SLMQ, Summer 93, p. 266; WLB, April 93, pp. 117-18]—**Frank L. Wilson**

795. Hill, Kenneth L. **Cold War Chronology: Soviet-American Relations 1945-1991.** Washington, D.C., Congressional Quarterly, 1993. 362p. index. $54.95. E183.8.S65H55. 327.73047. LC 93-34140. ISBN 0-87187-921-2.

The great political changes that occurred in Eastern Europe in 1989 and the breakup of the Soviet Union in 1991 have led foreign policy specialists to proclaim the end of the Cold War. Not surprisingly, retrospective studies of the Cold War are now beginning to appear, including two important new reference works: *The Cold War 1945-1991*, a three-volume set edited by Benjamin Frankel (Gale, 1993), and *Cold War Chronology*. The *Chronology*, while a useful source in its own right, can also be used as a supplement to the three-volume set. In volume 3 of *The Cold War* there is a concise 50-page chronology of important events; *Chronology* expands that material.

In addition to important political events (e.g., the U-2 incident in 1960, the Hungarian Rebellion in 1956, the Helsinki Conference of 1975, the Soviet invasion of Afghanistan in 1980), Hill includes references to major speeches (e.g., State of the Union addresses, press conferences, addresses with foreign policy implications to various organizations) and correspondence (e.g., the series of letters between Kennedy and Khrushchev, some of George Kennan's early diplomatic reports). Each event, speech, or piece of correspondence is described in a short paragraph, and its source is cited. The major sources include the *Public Papers of the Presidents of the United States* (Office of the Federal Register), the Foreign Relations of the United States series, the *Department of State Bulletin, Current Digest of the Soviet Press*, and the *New York Times*, as well as other compilations of documents. The chronology begins with President Truman's statement on V-J Day (September 1, 1945) and ends on December 25, 1991, with Gorbachev's resignation as president of the Soviet Union. Throughout the pages, clear patterns of events emerge, and a careful reader can detect major cycles of diplomacy. Although the chronological format ensures ease of use, there is also a detailed index of names and subjects. The *Chronology* is highly recommended for all academic libraries and other libraries with strong international relations collections.
—**Thomas A. Karel**

796. Minnick, Wendell L. **Spies and Provocateurs: A Worldwide Encyclopedia of Persons Conducting Espionage and Covert Action, 1946-1991.** Jefferson, N.C., McFarland, 1992. 310p. index. $45.00. JF1525.I6M56. 327.1'2'0922. LC 92-50312. ISBN 0-89950-746-8.

This work contains biographical sketches of individuals who have engaged in or have influenced intelligence operations in the four-and-a-half decades since World War II. Entries are arranged alphabetically and provide succinct portraits of the key activities of these individuals of various nationalities. Figures listed include Rudolph Abel, Peter Deriabin, Klaus Fuchs, Oleg Gordievsky, William King Harvey, Vladimir Petrov, Edwin Wilson, and Greville Wynne. The book concludes with a selective glossary of intelligence terminology, an annual summary of selected intelligence developments from 1946 to 1991, and a bibliography of pertinent works.

Minnick has produced a fairly straightforward and relatively unpolemical work on the complexities and ambiguities that affect participants in this profession. Weaknesses include the uncritical acceptance of Alger Hiss's innocence and the description of James Angleton's concern over possible Soviet penetration of the CIA as "hysterical." The bibliographic use of undocumented or conspiratorial fantasies, such as Leslie Cockburn's *Out of Control* (Atlantic Monthly, 1987) and Bob Woodward's *Veil: The Secret Wars of the CIA* (Pocket Books, 1988), diminish the generally substantive and authoritative approach of this work. Despite these flaws, *Spies and Provocateurs* is an adequate introduction to some of the prominent personalities involved in recent historical intelligence operations. [R: Choice, May 93, p. 1445; LJ, Jan 93, p. 102; RBB, 15 Feb 93, pp. 1084-85]—**Bert Chapman**

PEACE MOVEMENT

797. **Encyclopedia of Arms Control and Disarmament.** Richard Dean Burns, ed. New York, Macmillan, 1993. 3v. index. $280.00/set. JX1974.E57. 327.1'74'03. LC 92-36167. ISBN 0-684-19281-0.

Effective arms control has been a desirable but elusive goal of governments for generations. Since the end of World War II, much time and energy has been expended trying to constrain the development and use of weapons, particularly those of the atomic, chemical, biological, and radiological variety that are capable of mass destruction. The proliferation of these powerful weapons among smaller and potentially unstable nations is very dangerous. This collection of 76 lengthy essays written by experts in the field is a good source to consult for those trying to understand the concepts, difficulties, historical background, and scope of an extremely complicated and frustrating situation. Burns is chair of the department of history at California State University in Los Angeles and director of the Center for the Study of Armament and Disarmament, which has been publishing a series of short bibliographies on current international security issues. He had previously compiled the massive *Guide to American Foreign Relations Since 1700* (see ARBA 84, entry 472).

The first volume is divided into two parts that cover national and regional dimensions and themes and institutions. Regions such as Africa, Latin America, Scandinavia, and the Middle East all have chapters, while the major powers each get their own chapters. Switzerland is such an interesting case in international affairs that it rates a separate article. The 12-page introduction gives an overview of both the encyclopedia and the subject, and it has a section that matches treaties to general objectives (e.g., stabilizing the international environment). Volume 2 treats various arms control activities both before and after World War II, with 43 essays on such diverse subjects as arms control in antiquity and the disarming and rearming of Germany. The last volume contains texts of treaties, with a total of 150 formal international agreements being excerpted in this set. There are also citations to locations of the texts of the treaties. While a chronology (the twelfth century B.C. to 1992) of important treaties is included in the third volume, a chronology of all arms control efforts would also have been useful. A section on relevant sources, information about the 83 contributors with references to the essays that they wrote, and a list of acronyms are also found in these pages. The extensive index at the end of volume 3 provides good access to the contents of this set.

The scholarly articles are well written and easy to read, and are focused mainly on the post-1945 era. The subsections within each essay are clearly labeled for easy identification. *See also* cross-references are located at the beginning of each article; related research institutes and government agencies are frequently mentioned; and each article has a bibliography and conclusion at the end. However, usually only the place of publication, but not the name of the publisher, is listed, which means the reader has to do additional work to fully identify an item.

This set can be considered a companion to the three-volume *Encyclopedia of American Foreign Policy* (see ARBA 81, entry 554), which has similar long essays. The *Arms Control, Disarmament, and Military Security Dictionary* (see ARBA 90, entry 675) contained more individual entries, but they are less extensive and have no bibliographical references. For a specific reference on the recent Cold War period, see *Encyclopedia of the Cold War* by Thomas S. Arms and Eileen Riley (Facts on File, 1993). The work under consideration here is well constructed and easily recommended for the reference collections of all academic and public libraries. [R: Choice, Sept 93, p. 80; RBB, 15 Sept 93, p. 187; WLB, Sept 93, p. 116]—**Daniel K. Blewett**

798. Lacoff, Cheryl Klein, ed. **Who's Who in the Peace Corps.** 1993 ed. Greenwich, Conn., Reference Press International, 1993. 724p. index. $95.00; $75.00pa. ISBN 1-879583-03-8; 1-879583-02-Xpa. ISSN 1065-8459.

This directory provides information on about 50,000 of the 120,000 people who have served in the Peace Corps since its establishment in 1961. It is divided into six sections. The first is an alphabetical list of current and returned Peace Corps volunteers (RPCVs) with biographical data. The most complete entries list such data as country of service, birth and marriage dates, names of spouse and children, education, memberships, and business and residence addresses. However, most entries contain only a few pieces of information, usually country of service and current address. Other sections list deceased volunteers and Peace Corps staff; organizations serving RPCVs, RPCVs by state, city, or country of residence; and RPCVs by country of service.

The stated purposes of the directory are to help RPCVs locate each other and to familiarize them with organizations that serve RPCVs. The book might also be useful to educators, journalists, and social service workers seeking people with knowledge of Third World countries and their cultures and languages. Some larger libraries and businesses or agencies involved in the Third World may want to acquire it. [R: Choice, July/Aug 93, p. 1756; RBB, June 93, p. 1906; WLB, May 93, p. 122]—**Gari-Anne Patzwald**

799. Seymore, Bruce II, ed. **International Affairs Directory of Organizations: The ACCESS Resource Guide.** Santa Barbara, Calif., ABC-Clio, 1992. 326p. index. $75.00. U104.I54. 355.02'0285. LC 92-32969. ISBN 0-87436-686-0.

Publications of organizations are missing from many libraries because they are not advertised or reviewed in standard sources. Many such publications are of high quality and address important issues. In the area of international affairs, librarians now have an excellent guide to organizations, their publications, personnel, and services in this work.

ACCESS was formed in 1985 as a nonprofit clearinghouse of information on international security, peace, and world affairs. Its directory lists 865 organizations. Criteria for inclusion were substantive programs or a focus on international affairs, an intended audience at a national or international level, the organization's accessibility to that audience, and the quality of its information. Each organization has a numbered entry that is arranged alphabetically within geographic sections (the United States has the largest list, with 407 organizations). The entries contain such expected information as name, address, and publications; in addition, they have the names of specialists and their areas of expertise; internships offered; and available speakers, conferences, and even taped telephone messages. Entries are indexed by organization names, personal names, publication titles, and subjects. A 24-page "Guide to Guides" section is a list of reference books, primarily serial publications such as the *Europa World Year Book* (Gale, annual) and Amnesty International's annual report.

This work is an expanded revision of a 1988 edition (see ARBA 89, entry 681). While other directories exist, such as the *Encyclopedia of Associations* (see ARBA 90, entry 61) and *U.S. National Security Groups* (see ARBA 91, entry 784), none cover as many organizations or are as informative as the *ACCESS Guide*. One only wishes that similar directories were available in other areas of study. [R: RBB, 15 Jan 93, pp. 642-44; RQ, Summer 93, pp. 570-71]—**Cathy Seitz Whitaker**

PUBLIC POLICY AND ADMINISTRATION

800. Bianco, David P., ed. **Professional and Occupational Licensing Directory: A Descriptive Guide to State and Federal Licensing Registration, and Certification Requirements.** Detroit, Gale, 1993. 1304p. index. $89.50. ISBN 0-8103-8894-4. ISSN 1070-3322.

This is a valuable new compilation of information concerning state and federal professional licensing requirements. It covers about 1,300 job titles that require state-level or federal certification, licensing, or mandatory regulation. Because of the decentralized nature of professional and occupational licensing at the state and federal levels, this one-volume compendium is a handy guide to pertinent information in these fields. It will be useful as a ready-reference tool. For each license, it provides specific job title; full contact information on licensing agency or board, including fax number if available; educational experience and other requirements; examination information; activities authorized by the license; exemptions and reciprocity; and fees.

This work differs from the *Occupational Outlook Handbook* (JIST Works, 1993) in that it identifies those states that require licenses and whether federal credentials are necessary for each occupational category. It should be purchased by most school, public, and academic libraries and career planning and placement centers. [R: LJ, 15 Nov 93, p. 73; RBB, 15 Dec 93, p. 780]—**Roberto P. Haro**

801. **COGEL Blue Book: Campaign Finance, Ethics, Lobby Law & Judicial Conduct.** 9th ed. Joyce Bullock, ed. Lexington, Ky., Council of State Governments, 1993. 243p. $59.00pa. ISBN 0-87292-968-X.

This compilation holds 40 tables of varying descriptions. They provide information on federal agencies in the United States and Canada, as well as on states and provinces. Sections on campaign finance, ethics laws and personal financial disclosure, lobbying, and judicial conduct are included. Table 4, for example, shows agency expenditure budgets for state, federal, and provincial ethics commissions, legislative ethics committees, and other relevant bodies; table 11 lists types of candidates (by office) and organizations that must file campaign finance reports; table 25 deals with officials required to make personal financial disclosure statements; and table 35 covers education and training of lobbyists. A directory enumerating agencies and individuals who specialize in these issues completes the volume.

There is much valuable information here, but it is in raw form. Researchers interested in government ethics, especially in relation to money and lobbying, will like what they see. Some light is shed on subjects such as agency expenditures, campaign contributions, campaign spending, and financial disclosure. Addresses and telephone numbers for contact people at various levels of government can be found in the directory, and they are useful. The biggest drawback is the lack of an introductory essay or any type of connective narrative. An introductory essay designed to make sense of the tables and the great mass of undigested data in them is needed and could easily be added. Until more explanation is provided, this book will remain one better suited for insiders and experts than for the general public. Recommended for college, university, and public libraries.—**Richard E. Holl**

802. Graham, John W. **The U.S. Securities and Exchange Commission: A Research and Information Guide.** Hamden, Conn., Garland, 1993. 344p. index. (Research and Information Guides in Business, Industry, and Economic Institutions, v.8). $56.00. Z7164.S37G73. 016.35390082'58. LC 92-28409. ISBN 0-8153-0071-9.

This annotated bibliography of the Securities and Exchange Commission (SEC) comes with a brief history of the agency and a description of its configuration and purpose. Chapter 1 examines the SEC's origins, size, funding, functions, and responsibility. Chapters 2 through 12 discuss topics that fall within SEC jurisdiction (e.g., accounting, auditing, disclosure, investigation, enforcement), and titles, authors, and summations of significant books and articles are provided. Along the way, the SEC's mandate takes shape—to collect and store information on securities, to make that information available to investors, and to regulate the markets and prevent company wrongdoing. (Graham does acknowledge that the SEC sometimes allows corporations too much leeway to determine what sort of information must be reported, and that abuses can occur.)

The U.S. Securities and Exchange Commission has merit but is tarnished by sloppy editing and unimaginative prose. Error and repetition creep into the narrative. In the first paragraph of chapter 1, the word "to" is omitted from the fourth sentence. On page 6, "interfer" appears, and two pages later, "buisness." Readers variously learn that the SEC has "over 2,500 employees," "over 2,400 individuals," and "2,451 people." Fortunately, the virtues of the book outweigh its faults. The capsule summaries of books, articles, and government sources should be helpful to researchers, and commissioner biographies and instructions on accessing SEC corporate filings are convenient. Recommended for college and public libraries. [R: Choice, June 93, p. 1602]—**Richard E. Holl**

803. **Immigration Statistics 1991. Statistiques sur l'Immigration.** Hull, Que., Employment and Immigration Canada, 1992. 87p. price not reported. ISBN 0-662-59345-6.

This government document is the 1991 issue of an annual series from the Immigration Statistics Division of Employment and Immigration Canada. It provides, in tabular form, a detailed breakdown of immigration to Canada in the year treated, with some historical data.

An overview section provides immigration data for 1991 by month, top 10 countries of last permanent residence, occupation, and age and gender. The second section gives overall immigration figures from 1852 to 1991 and figures for 1991 by province or territory and port of entry. The next section, intended to provide information on issues of topical concern, has two tables on the controversial "entrepreneur" admission category and four tables on support, country of origin, age, and provincial distribution for convention refugees. The last grouping of tables is by far the largest. It contains detailed figures on new permanent residents for 1991 categorized in a variety of ways, including origin (country and region), gender, age, province (or territory) and city of intended destination, intended occupation, and labor force participation.

This document seems to be a highly useful source in its area. While it does contain a page of definitions, more explanatory material would be helpful. As is normal in this sort of publication, a few tables are less than clearly labeled. Overall, this is an important series for Canadian libraries, Canadian studies libraries, and other centers with the relevant client interests.—**Nigel Tappin**

804. McShane, Marilyn D., and Frank P. Williams III. **The Management of Correctional Institutions.** Hamden, Conn., Garland, 1993. 340p. index. (Current Issues in Criminal Justice, v.5; Garland Reference Library of Social Science, v.869). $53.00. HV9469.M37. 365'.068. LC 92-27791. ISBN 0-8153-1082-X.

The exponential increase in the prison population in the United States in recent years lends a certain urgency to the effective management of correctional institutions. The authors of this volume are prolific and well-regarded criminal justicians who received a grant to study how corrections management might be improved. They thereupon embarked on a survey of both the existing literature on the subject and of wardens of all American prisons with more than 500 inmates.

The first section of this book provides readers with an overview of the literature on corrections management, the results of McShane and Williams's survey of correctional administrators, and their proposals and recommendations for corrections management and research on such management. They characterize their views as a radical management perspective. The second part of the book consists of a selective bibliography and summaries of 100 noteworthy contributions to the literature on corrections management. In addition to basic reference information, each abstract has a list of attributes of the research methodology and the institutions studied. Name and subject indexes are included.

The Management of Correctional Institutions should be indispensable to both correctional administrators and to those doing research on corrections management. It provides a useful overview of a field characterized by considerable incoherence, and it points to fruitful new directions and initiatives. This volume is highly recommended to libraries serving correctional practitioners and researchers.

—**David O. Friedrichs**

14 Psychology

GENERAL WORKS

Bibliography

805. Baxter, Pam M. **Psychology: A Guide to Reference and Information Sources.** Englewood, Colo., Libraries Unlimited, 1993. 219p. index. (Reference Sources in the Social Sciences Series, no.6). $36.50. Z7201.B39. 016.15. LC 93-13182. ISBN 0-87287-708-6.

This volume is a useful introduction for undergraduate and graduate students to the resources in psychology. Some 600 sources are covered, emphasizing works published after 1970. The entries are grouped in four sections: general social science and reference works, specific resources in social science disciplines, general psychology reference sources, and special topics in psychology. The latter two sections will be the greatest asset for students. Within each section, works are listed alphabetically. The section on special topics in psychology is further grouped by classification headings similar to those used in *Psychological Abstracts* (American Psychological Association, monthly) and will be comfortably familiar to many advanced researchers. Each entry contains full bibliographical data and a lengthy critical abstract.

While the American Psychological Association (APA) recently issued a revised version of its own research guide (see ARBA 93, entry 804), this new volume still stands as a useful addition to the literature. Beginning students will be well served by either work, although this volume puts slightly greater emphasis on electronic resources than does the APA guide. This work breaks little new ground, but it does provide a useful tool to quickly identify valuable resources in the quiltwork of studies called psychology. [R: JAL, Nov 93, p. 347; RBB, 15 Dec 93, p. 781; WLB, Dec 93, pp. 82-83]—**Elizabeth Patterson**

806. Ress, Lisa, and William McGuire, comps. **General Bibliography of C. G. Jung's Writings.** rev. ed. Princeton, N.J., Princeton University Press, 1992. 237p. index. (Bollingen Series XX: The Collected Works of C. G. Jung, v.19). $29.50. LC 75-156. ISBN 0-691-09893-X.

Carl Gustav Jung has left students of psychology and psychoanalysis a large, complex body of literature discussing his theories, which comprise the basis for analytical psychology. From 1902 to the present, his original writings have been published primarily in German and English, including the 20-volume *The Collected Works of C. G. Jung*. This bibliography replaces the original volume 19 of the series, published in 1979.

This new bibliography alters the focus of and updates its predecessor. While the 1979 volume covered Jung's publications in 19 languages, the 1992 edition generally presents only English and German titles arranged in chronological order. The compilers include the tables of contents for some of these works but not for others, with no explanation for the omissions. A second segment of this reference tool lists the parallel contents of *The Collected Works of C. G. Jung* and the *Gesammelte Werke*, a useful feature for Jung scholars. Finally, a third section contains new bibliographical information on some of Jung's published and unpublished seminars, including the locations of these documents. The reference guide is invaluable for serious scholars of Jung; however, it has limited use for the general reader with only a passing interest in the history of psychology.—**Jonathon Erlen**

Dictionaries and Encyclopedias

807. Bruno, Frank J. **The Family Encyclopedia of Child Psychology and Development.** New York, John Wiley, 1992. 420p. index. $27.95. BF721.B7157. 155.4'03. LC 91-25322. ISBN 0-471-52793-9.

This volume explains, in lay language, the concepts, facts, and theories concerning most aspects of normal and abnormal child psychology. Meant primarily for parents, teachers, and caregivers, it contains more than 600 alphabetical entries defining key terms and concepts in developmental psychology, as well as information on the signs, symptoms, causes, and treatment options for behavioral and developmental problems, disorders, and impairments. Parents coping with a crisis will find this volume useful in understanding the specialized vocabulary often used by professionals. Brief entries describe various types of therapy and counseling. Cross-references following each entry direct the reader to relevant information elsewhere in the encyclopedia. An index of authorities is meant to guide the reader to those entries describing the ideas of thinkers and researchers in the field of child development. An appendix that listed the many national organizations and support groups that supply additional information about the various mental and behavioral disorders would have been helpful.

Although most entries appear to be current, failure to update the entries concerning intelligence scales was noted. For the Wechsler scales, the current revisions (WAIS-R, WISC-III, and WPPSI-R) are not significantly different from the descriptions given. However, the Stanford-Binet Intelligence Scale: 4th Edition (1986) is a significant revision, and the entry provided might be confusing to those attempting to interpret a current evaluation.—**Edith M. Dorenfeld**

808. Carskadon, Mary A., ed. **Encyclopedia of Sleep and Dreaming.** New York, Macmillan, 1993. 703p. index. $105.00. BF1078.E63. 154.6'03. LC 92-38048. ISBN 0-02-897085-3.

This excellent work presents 400-plus entries on the biological, medical, neurological, and psychological aspects of sleep and dreaming. Not intended as a layperson's handbook of dream images, these essays provide a scientific and scholarly summary of topics ranging from sleep disorders to biorhythms, rapid eye movement, and lucid dreaming. Brief bibliographies are provided with each entry for further study, and examples are used extensively to help clarify processes and phenomena being described. The signed entries are arranged alphabetically rather than thematically, but the extensive use of cross-references and the inclusion of scope notes—called "guideposts" by the editor—help direct readers to related topics in a clear and logical manner. An extensive index enhances this work further, making it easy to locate relevant texts quickly.

The heavy medical and scientific emphasis of most of the entries is occasionally offset by some whimsical yet informative pieces of social commentary not entirely in keeping with the overall tone of the encyclopedia. They are welcome nevertheless. Interesting pieces on everything from the history of pajamas and nightcaps to the use of pillows and lullabies in different cultures help ground the physiological phenomenon of sleep and dreaming in its very human context.

As a research work this volume proves more useful than many earlier collections, such as *The Dream* (see ARBA 88, entry 763), and more detailed than popular guides, such as M. J. Thorpy's *Encyclopedia of Sleep and Sleep Disorders* (Facts on File, 1991). In all, it is a welcome addition to the literature. [R: Choice, Sept 93, p. 80; RBB, 15 Oct 93, p. 472]—**Elizabeth Patterson**

809. **Encyclopedia of Learning and Memory.** Larry R. Squire, ed. New York, Macmillan, 1992. 678p. illus. index. $105.00. BF318.E53. 153.1'03. LC 92-15964. ISBN 0-02-897408-5.

Learning and memory studies represent one of the preeminent fields in psychology and neuroscience. They encompass an extraordinary range of investigations, from simple animal experiments to precise examinations of brain functioning to human memory investigations. The findings have had a significant impact on human experience in such disparate arenas as elementary education and clinical pathology.

The task of producing a one-volume encyclopedia to explicate the various facets of learning and memory studies must have been a daunting one, but Squire has done his job well. While no purpose for this work is stated directly, one clear goal is to provide an opportunity to understand the elegance of the thinking required to fathom the issues of learning and memory. Another is to supply current information on a variety of topics. The reader will come to understand the work of psychologists and neuroscientists in this field of endeavor. The work has 189 articles that cover the full range of current knowledge about learning and memory. Twenty-six are biographies of outstanding individuals in the field. The entries range from 500 to 2,000 words. All the contributors to the volume are active researchers in their field. The contents are alphabetically arranged, and each topic has a brief bibliography to facilitate further study. The index is extensive and easy to use.

This work is appropriate for psychologists, neuroscientists, students, and those who enjoy browsing in recondite topics. The editor's claim "The finished project provides the broadest and the richest introduction to the topic of learning and memory that is available anywhere" is correct. [R: LJ, 15 Feb 93, pp. 158-60; RBB, 15 April 93, pp. 1533-34]—**Bertram H. Rothschild**

810. Sauber, S. Richard, and others. **The Dictionary of Family Psychology and Family Therapy.** 2d ed. Newbury Park, Calif., Sage, 1993. 468p. $48.95; $23.95pa. RC488.5.D525. 616.89'156'03. LC 93-1588. ISBN 0-8039-5332-1; 0-8039-5333-Xpa.

The first edition of this dictionary was called *Family Therapy: Basic Concepts and Terms* (1985). For this edition, the title was changed to reflect the rapidly expanding field of family research and counseling. The authors produced it to bring together the many new terms coined during the past three decades. Because the field is quite new and expanding, the authors include with each definition a citation to the source that originally used the term. These are listed again in the references section and may prove as helpful to the user as will the definitions. This impressive dictionary is meant for the doctorate-level teacher, researcher, or practitioner and the graduate student in psychology, counseling, or marriage and family therapy. It will be a helpful tool, however, even to those in the same fields who have lesser degrees. Recommended.—**Nathan M. Smith**

811. Stratton, Peter, and Nicky Hayes. **A Student's Dictionary of Psychology.** 2d ed. London, Edward Arnold; distr., New York, Routledge, Chapman & Hall, 1993. 223p. illus. $15.95pa. BF31.S69. 150'.3. LC 92-30214. ISBN 0-340-56926-3.

In the preface to this edition, the authors claim to have extended the material from the first edition by adding many new entries and cross-references. However, they continue to use British spellings of words (e.g., *aetiology*) without cross-referencing the U.S. spellings (e.g., *etiology*). If this dictionary continues to be distributed in the United States, this deficiency should be corrected. Also, the authors should consistently include the founder's name with the entries for the various psychological schools. For example, under Gestalt therapy, Fritz Perls is included as its founder; however, Albert Ellis is not mentioned under Rational-Emotive Therapy (RET) as its developer. Additions such as these would make the book more informative and helpful. As it is, the dictionary is not substantive; however, it can adequately serve the introductory psychology student or layperson.—**Nathan M. Smith**

Handbooks and Yearbooks

812. Bellack, Alan S., and Michel Hersen, eds. **Psychopathology in Adulthood.** Needham Heights, Mass., Allyn and Bacon, 1993. 343p. index. $54.95. RC454.P787. 616.89. LC 93-16114. ISBN 0-205-14584-1.

Bellack and Hersen are prolific writers in the fields of psychology and therapy. In this current text they bring together contributors who present information intended to bring readers up-to-date on the latest developments concerning the study and diagnosis of adult psychopathology. The book is in two sections. The first covers, in six chapters, general issues and models of adult psychopathology. Topics discussed in section 1 include nosology, diagnosis, epidemiology, genetics, psychobiology, adult psychopathology, human development related to psychopathology, and sociological considerations with emphasis on antisocial behavior and violence. Section 1 prepares the reader to understand the material in section 2, with its chapters on major disorders: eating disorders, anxiety disorders, post-traumatic stress disorder, obsessive-compulsive disorder, depressive disorders, schizophrenia, bipolar disorders, personality disorders, substance abuse, and sexual dysfunction and deviation. Schizophrenia, because of the voluminous literature on it from the last 20 years, is allocated two chapters, in which it is defined and details of it, along with its prognostication, are presented. Although the index is not comprehensive, it is helpful.

—**Nathan M. Smith**

PARAPSYCHOLOGY

813. Clark, Jerome. **Encyclopedia of Strange and Unexplained Physical Phenomena.** Detroit, Gale, 1993. 395p. illus. index. $49.95. ISBN 0-8103-8843-X.

In the ongoing swirl of claims about anomalous events, this book will fill an interesting niche. Clark has taken on the Herculean task of researching and writing about a gamut of strange events, ranging from abductions by UFOs through *Zetetic Scholar*. Each entry is well documented, and the writing is usually clear and informative. The illustrations are interesting, but more are needed.

The book deals with "strange natural and quasi-natural phenomena, things that seem to be a part of our world but are usually disputed or ignored by conventional science." Unfortunately, in some important ways, the work falls short of its aim. In spite of the claim that conventional science (here used as a general derogation of current scientific understanding) ignores these events, there is ample evidence provided that scientists have attempted to come to grips with many of the claimed phenomena. The problem for Clark is that the findings run contrary to his apparent preferences, so he emphasizes complaints about them. For example, he characterizes all the negative conclusions by scientists about UFOs as dishonest.

Clark uses negative arguments to buttress the plausibility of an outlandish theory, but does not use them in reverse. For example, to challenge that crop circles are created by human beings, he argues that surely, by now, humans would have been caught in the act. Fair enough, but this argument must then be applied to other phenomena. Surely, by now, after so many sightings and blurry photographs, there would be some indisputable evidence of Bigfoot—a body, a habitat of some kind, an unambiguous picture. (With all seriousness, Clark argues that fuzzy pictures are apt to be valid because the photographer's hands would most likely tremble from fear engendered by the encounter.) His greatest error—and one necessary to maintain the credibility of claims of outrageous anomalies—is his misunderstanding of human perception. It is his belief that when such claims are made, only three conclusions are possible: the sighting is true, a hoax has been perpetrated, or the person making the claim is insane. Thus, he ignores the reality that humans are incompetent observers, that they easily get things wrong because of perceptual distortions. (All one needs to do is look around and notice that the Earth is flat.)

Still, this book is a pleasant browse. It is handsomely constructed, well indexed, and easy to read. While it preaches to the credulous, skeptics will also find it useful because Clark provides considerable information on claims that have been debunked and hoaxes that have been exposed. Writers will find it a useful compendium for the creation of fantastic stories, and journalists seeking background information will find it helpful, but they need to guard against its rather one-sided presentation. [R: RBB, 15 Oct 93, p. 472; RQ, Winter 93, p. 284; VOYA, Oct 93, p. 260]—**Bertram H. Rothschild**

814. Drury, Nevill. **Dictionary of Mysticism and the Esoteric Traditions.** rev. ed. Santa Barbara, Calif., ABC-Clio, 1992. 328p. illus. $49.50. BF1407.D78. 133'.03. LC 92-23484. ISBN 0-87436-699-2.

The aim of this book is to provide "concise and up-to-date information on the various symbols, esoteric technologies and personalities that [make] the world of mysticism and magic so intriguing." Its coverage goes beyond mysticism in its true definition to include the occult, aspects of parapsychology, astrology, and cultism. It is the 2d edition of the 1985 American edition titled *Dictionary of Mysticism and the Occult* (see ARBA 86, entry 741). This edition, published in Great Britain, updates the former one, particularly the biographies of persons who have died in the intervening years. There are also some corrections in details, and photographs and a bibliography have been added. The illustrations include photographs of notables in the fields covered and line drawings from various elements included. An Aubrey Beardsley drawing, several reproductions of Tarot cards, astrological charts, and occult calendars, among others, add to the definitions and usefulness of the book. The scope is unlimited by date or geography. From Australian Aborigines to Tarot, unidentified flying object (UFO), witchcraft, and Zoroastrianism, the definitions cover the field comprehensively. The "selected" bibliography gives very brief citations (only author's last name and initial) and no annotations. Still, it provides a start for further research. Where appropriate, entries include reference to basic information source books. Also, each entry identifies terms defined elsewhere in the text with boldface type.

This dictionary will be very useful in, and is recommended for, public libraries and other locations where the study of mysticism and the occult is pursued. It is somewhat expensive, but it will be helpful to librarians and patrons in any reference collection. [R: RQ, Summer 93, p. 564]—**Edward P. Miller**

815. Lacoff, Cheryl Klein, ed. **Parapsychology, New Age and the Occult: A Source Encyclopedia.** Greenwich, Conn., Reference Press International, 1993. 526p. index. $80.00; $24.95pa. ISBN 1-879583-01-1; 1-879583-00-3pa. ISSN 1065-3031.

This source encyclopedia contains 17 chapters that include associations and organizations, events, biographies of experts in their chosen fields, and distributors of products and services related to the fields of parapsychology, the new age, and the occult. It includes an alphabetically arranged bibliography of books, directories, handbooks, booklets, yearbooks, and guides. However, initial articles were not ignored in the alphabetical sequence, so a title that begins with A, An, or The is alphabetized accordingly, making the bibliography awkward to use unless the reader is aware of this flaw. There is also a list of periodicals that includes magazines, newsletters, bulletins, journals, brochures, catalogs, newspapers, and calendars; it has the same flaw in the alphabetical sequence. Otherwise, the bibliographies are excellent lists of the most important literature of parapsychology, the new age, and the occult.

Indexes to the work are extensive and excellent, including an index of publishers in new age, metaphysical, and related fields. An extensive topic index is composed of 62 topics arranged alphabetically, then subarranged to correspond to the 17 chapter headings. Once a source is located in this topic index, the reader is sent back to the corresponding chapter for the information sought. The topics are broad headings and may include several related topics within the concept. For example, the topic *acupuncture* also includes information found in the encyclopedia under acupressure. The preface includes information on how to use the topic index. [R: Choice, May 93, pp. 1445-46]—**Christine E. Thompson**

816. Murray, Elaine. **A Layman's Guide to New Age & Spiritual Terms.** Nevada City, Calif., Blue Dolphin Publishing, 1993. 199p. $12.95pa. BP605.N48M87. 133'.03. LC 92-41892. ISBN 0-931892-53-8.

When evaluating a title for reference use, one looks for contents that are substantive, authoritative, and objective. If the author has a specific viewpoint or bias toward the topic at hand, presentation should be well reasoned and supported by argument or extant literature or tenets, and alternative points of view of the issues or concepts should be discussed. A measured and well-considered approach is especially important when the subject matter is fraught with controversy and frequently regarded with skepticism and misunderstanding.

Murray's approach is hardly objective. Practically none of the more than 200 definitions she provides is substantiated. In her view, there is no doubt that gemstones enhance psychic abilities, that the effectiveness of dowsing is a scientific fact, and that gnomes exist. Users are provided no better explanation for them than that Murray believes these and other phenomena to be true. Definitions are often accompanied by her own testimonials, including contact with a spiritual guide, experiences with clairvoyance and divination, and being accompanied by an unseen personal elf named Benjie. The asides appended to entries are occasionally just plain silly.

There are several fine reference works, specifically dictionaries and encyclopedias, dedicated to spiritualism and psychic phenomena. Despite the cost, the 3d edition of *Encyclopedia of Occultism and Parapsychology* (see ARBA 92, entry 762) is a superior investment in terms of long-term value and usefulness for libraries. Better dictionary choices are *The Donning International Encyclopedic Psychic Dictionary* (see ARBA 87, entry 750) or even Norman Blunsdon's *A Popular Dictionary of Spiritualism* (London: Arco, 1962), among others. Those seeking a substantive reference work specific to New Age spiritualism cannot beat the *New Age Encyclopedia* (see ARBA 91, entry 1451).—**Pam M. Baxter**

15 Recreation and Sports

GENERAL WORKS

Acronyms and Abbreviations

817. Gendron, Celine, and others, comps. and eds. **Acrosport: Acronyms Used for Sport, Physical Education and Recreation. Acronymes en Sport, Education Physique et Loisir.** Gloucester, Ont., Sport Information Resource Centre, 1993. 231p. $34.95pa. (U.S.). 796'.0148. ISBN 0-921817-05-3.

In dealing with the tripartite world of sport, recreation, and physical education, this book attempts comprehensiveness. Listed in *Acrosport* are more than 2,500 acronyms and initialisms heard all over the world. Thus one will find national, provincial, regional, and even state groups, as well as familiar international bodies. The publishers are also the authority behind SPORT, the very large online database familiar to many library search analysts.

The unannotated entries are organized into three sections. First, all the acronyms are listed alphabetically, along with the full name and the location of their headquarters. Then there are two indexes: A reversal of the main body with the organization names followed by the acronyms, and an index of sports or activities, such as baseball, under which are grouped all the acronyms and the full names of the pertinent organizations involved (e.g., NL for National League).

The Canadian origins of this guide are evident in the list of sources. Among the works mentioned is the old warhorse *Encyclopedia of Associations*, the 25th edition of 1991 (see ARBA 91, entries 37-38) and the *Yearbook of International Organizations* (K. G. Saur, 1989). Much overlap was found with the widely used *Acronyms, Initialisms, and Abbreviations Dictionary* (see ARBA 93, entry 1).—**Randall Rafferty**

Almanacs

818. **The Information Please Sports Almanac, 1993.** Mike Meserole, ed. Boston, Houghton Mifflin, 1992. 832p. illus. $9.95pa. ISBN 0-395-63768-6. ISSN 1045-4980.

This work, now in its fourth year (see ARBA 91, entry 800), will answer a high percentage of sports questions. Virtually every sport is covered, even softball, chess, and dog showing. For example, in the section on horse racing the reader will find all past winners of the Kentucky Derby, the Preakness, and the Belmont; major stakes races of the previous year; annual money leaders (horses and jockeys) back to 1910; the winners of numerous awards; and more. In addition to presenting data, the book has very browsable stories. The book's first 50 pages cover the major sports stories of the previous year. Individual sections open with articles (up to 10 pages long) written by prominent sportswriters covering the previous year in the sport. Other facets of sports, such as sports business, media, ballparks, and arenas, are covered as well. A useful bibliography provides more than 100 sources of additional information. There is no index.—**T. McKimmie**

Atlases

819. Rooney, John F., Jr., and Richard Pillsbury. **Atlas of American Sport.** New York, Macmillan, 1992. 198p. illus. maps. index. $80.00. G1201.E63R6. 796'.0973'022. LC 91-35574. ISBN 0-02-897351-8.

The awkward size of this work, which is necessary to properly display many of its 241 color maps, makes it the kind of atlas that is difficult for libraries to house in a fashion that will preserve it while making its valuable contents readily accessible to users. The 20 striking color photographs, which portray varying aspects of sport, add little to the understanding of the subject. In fact, they detract from the significance of the atlas by making it appear to be little more than another coffee-table book. That appearance, along with the book's size and price, is likely to make some libraries think twice about purchasing it. That would be unfortunate, for this is an important reference work that provides new information of interest and value to both students of American sport and casual enthusiasts and practitioners. As Rooney and Pillsbury point out, "all mapping is a form of generalization," but the original area and dot maps that they have produced for this atlas, especially when coupled with their thoughtful commentary and analysis, shed new light on the role of sport in American society. Their emphasis on the geographical dimension of sport in America leads, for example, to a fascinating section on sports regions that divides the country into 13 areas based on the varying interests and focuses of the residents of those areas. This is one of four sections that offer commentary, maps, and statistics about the extent to which sports in general and about 75 specific sports—from football to lawn bowling—are of significance in contemporary American society. Those sections are augmented by such supplementary features as a list of sports associations, a select bibliography, a general index, and a geographical index. These reinforce this atlas's value as a significant reference work that deserves a wide audience. [R: RBB, 1 Sept 93, p. 81; SLJ, Nov 93, p. 145; WLB, June 93, p. 119]—**Norman D. Stevens**

Bibliography

820. Herron, Nancy L., ed. **The Leisure Literature: A Guide to Sources in Leisure Studies, Fitness, Sports, and Travel.** Englewood, Colo., Libraries Unlimited, 1992. 181p. index. $28.50. Z7511.L37. 016.790'01'35. LC 92-15144. ISBN 1-56308-062-1.

This guide to leisure-related sources is the first of its kind to address the growing informational needs of professionals, teachers, students, and scholars. Leisure-related activities addressed in this book are divided into four major categories: leisure studies, fitness, sports, and travel and tourism. Each section is introduced in an essay format that describes the importance of the discipline in history and its implications for society. Such areas as ethics, law, research, women, politics, education, and economics are covered. The types of sources included are guides and handbooks; standard and classic sources; noteworthy books; dissertations, bibliographies and catalogs; dictionaries and encyclopedias; directories; indexes, abstracts, and databases; core journals; conference proceedings; statistical sources; and bibliographical notes. The appendixes enhance this informational guide with a list of degree programs in U.S. colleges and universities, important publishers in each area, and a list of leisure-related associations, all with addresses and telephone numbers. Author/title and subject indexes make locating information quick and easy. Those working in the fields of sport, fitness, travel and tourism, and leisure studies will find this book valuable for familiarizing themselves with the literature in the field. This well-written and well-researched guide will be an asset to all libraries, especially those with the subject interests.

—**Jennie S. Johnson**

821. Shoebridge, Michele, ed. **Information Sources in Sport and Leisure.** New Providence, N.J., K. G. Saur/Reed Reference Publishing, 1992. 345p. index. (Guides to Information Sources). $95.00. Z7511.S48. 016.796. LC 91-21637. ISBN 0-86291-901-0.

Today's world is more conscious about recreational or free time than at any point in human history, and it is only right that the subject get careful scholarly treatment. This volume will be most welcome to students, researchers, and others in the wide-ranging field embraced by sport and leisure. Shoebridge, systems librarian at the University of Birmingham, brings together an impressive team of contributors to cover most aspects of the subject in solid detail: sports medicine, science, and sociology; the history of sport; Olympic games; fitness; coaching; and the like. Unfortunately, hunting and fishing are overlooked almost entirely, as is true in large measure for hiking, camping, canoeing, and similar activities. This would have been understandable if appropriate parameters of coverage had been delineated in detail at the outset, but such is not the case. However, for what does appear in the book, the coverage is first-rate. All libraries supporting physical education programs or sports studies should have this work. [R: Choice, Mar 93, p. 1114]—**James A. Casada**

Dictionaries and Encyclopedias

822. **The Oxford Companion to Australian Sport.** Edited by Wray Vamplew and others. New York, Oxford University Press, 1992. 430p. illus. $39.95. 796.0994. ISBN 0-19-553287-2.

Few U.S. academic or public libraries will need the kind of detailed information on Australian sports found in this guide. But for those that do, it is unrivaled. As are other Oxford companions and guides, this one has been meticulously prepared by experts under the aegis of th Australian Society for Sports History (only in Australia!), with assistance from the Australian Sports Commission. As a dominant feature of Australian society, sports truly deserves the kind of comprehensive treatment it is given here. The work concentrates on the economic, social, and political significance of sport in Australia. It is neither a treatment of the rules of the wide variety of games (e.g., vigoro) played in Australia nor of the history of sports (e.g., there is no separate entry for the Ashes) in that country. For example, U.S. sports fans who watch televised Australian Rules Football games will not understand the rules of the game any better after reading the lengthy entry on that sport—but they will better understand the basis for the game and why it is followed with such passion in Australia. The nearly 1,000 entries are arranged in straightforward alphabetical order with ample cross-references within articles. They cover not just games, people, associations and organizations, competitions, and venues but also topical issues, such as sports medicine, sport in art and literature, and violence. There are a good number of black-and-white illustrations and a brief topical bibliography. This solid treatment of sport in Australian society should serve as a model for similar volumes covering other countries.—**Norman D. Stevens**

Handbooks and Yearbooks

823. Crisfield, D. W. **Pick-Up Games: The Rules, the Players, the Equipment.** New York, Facts on File, 1993. 192p. illus. index. $27.95. GFV1201.42.C75. 790.1'922. LC 92-16296. ISBN 0-8160-2700-5.

A pick-up game is any informal game that is an offshoot of an established sport. There are no boundaries or referees, and the rules are flexible. In this book 14 main sports are organized alphabetically: badminton, baseball, basketball, croquet, field hockey, football, frisbee, golf, ice hockey, lacrosse, soccer, tennis, volleyball, and water sports. For more than 200 spinoff games Crisfield gives number of players, equipment, playing area, ages, equipment, and complete rules and instructions. The games can be played in a gymnasium, playground, sports field, back lot, or almost anywhere else; by individuals of different athletic ability; with almost any number of participants; and with easy-to-find equipment. More than 50 diagrams, 10 black-and-white photographs, an appendix of pick-up games by number of players, a glossary, suggested reading, and an index are provided. This is an excellent reference tool for children of all ages, parents, gym instructors, and camp counselors. [R: RBB, 15 Feb 93, p. 1084; SLJ, May 93, p. 136; WLB, April 93, p. 122]—**Kathleen J. Voigt**

824. **Family Fun & Games.** By the Diagram Group. New York, Sterling Publishing, 1992. 800p. illus. index. $24.95. ISBN 0-8069-8776-6.

In this age of television and electronic amusements, this reference book of games from around the world is a stimulating alternative to technological entertainment, providing more than 700 diversions for every age and ability. Each entry begins with a short introduction that states basic strategy, the country where the game originated, necessary equipment, and required number of players. Section 1 covers more than 50 board games, 34 dice games, 20 versions of dominoes, 30 versions of marbles and jacks, educational games, music games, scavenger hunts, and games from other countries. More than half of the volume, sections 2 and 3, is dedicated to card games from every country and culture and is subdivided into general card games, children's card games, gambling card games, and solitaire. The games appear alphabetically except when variations of a game are included, as in the listing for gin rummy, which appears under the parent game, rummy. All of the names are, however, listed alphabetically in the comprehensive index.

A helpful cross-reference is section 6, on finding a game. Of the six indexes, the first lists games alphabetically according to type with the following breakdown of categories: Board Games: Race Games, Strategic Games; Dice and Tile Games: Family, Gambling; Party Games and Races: Blindfold, Contests, Goal-Scoring, Musical, Observation, Parcel, Trickery; Target: Ball, Darts, Coin Throwing, Fivestones/Jacks, Marbles; Word and Picture Games: Pencil and Paper, Word Games (acting, guessing, and vocabulary games). Two indexes, "How Many Players?" and "How Many for Cards?," list the games that are suitable for one, two, three, or four players. To further aid in the search, an index is included that lists the names of game variations that are included in the book as subsections under a parent game (e.g., Black Lady [Hearts]). Alternative names are also listed when one game has two common identities (e.g., Three Naturals [Macao]). A general index with a comprehensive listing concludes the book.

A clear, concise writing makes learning a new game relatively easy and may encourage readers to turn off the television in search of a more cerebral pastime. Highly recommended for home, public, and school libraries.—**Deborah A. Taylor**

825. **The Guinness Book of Sports Records 1993.** Mark Young, ed. New York, Facts on File, 1993. 250p. illus. index. $21.95. ISBN 0-8160-2653-X. ISSN 1054-4178.

From the unconventional sport of snooker to the conventional sport of baseball, this reference book of sports records is a comprehensive source for accurate information about who excelled at what, when, and where throughout the history of organized sport. Current as of 1992, this revised and expanded edition includes more than 75 sports; gives a brief annotation of each sport's history and development in the United States; and lists (when applicable) records at the collegiate, professional, national, world, and Olympic levels. The text lists each sport alphabetically and is complimented by more than 150 black-and-white photographs, maps, and graphs. A subject index is included; the addition of a name index would be helpful.

Introduced in this edition is the "Record File"—eight full-page profiles highlighting elite performances by teams and such athletes as Wilt Chamberlain, Jackie Joyner-Kersee, and the Montreal Canadiens. True to the Guinness tradition of showcasing obscure talents, another new feature, "Timeout," illustrates more than 45 records made by normally unheralded athletes, such as who completed the greatest number of judo throws in a 10-hour period or who is the fastest snowshoer. The section on 1992 seasons in review gives a list of world champions, Olympic champions, national champions, tournament winners, and leading money winners of the 1992 sports season. The text concludes with the 1992 Olympic Games and gives a complete listing of the medalists at the 1992 winter and summer Olympic Games. This authoritative, easy-to-use reference source is an exceptional collection of sporting facts and trivia and is a must for every library and sports enthusiast. [R: RQ, Winter 93, p. 300]—**Deborah A. Taylor**

826. Kirsch, George B., ed. **Sports in North America: A Documentary History. Volume 3: The Rise of Modern Sports 1840-1860.** Gulf Breeze, Fla., Academic International Press, 1992. 390p. illus. index. $72.00. ISBN 0-87569-156-0.

The first release in a series of 10 to 12 volumes, this work presents an extensive collection of more than 150 annotated documents that pertain to the rise of organized sports in North America between 1840 and 1860. The development of sports during this era is detailed through background explanations and articles that survey the factors that contributed to the early development of American and Canadian athletics. These articles describe authentic sporting events in such intricate detail and animation that the reader is caught up in the excitement and enthusiasm of the time, the people, and the sport. Major sports covered in this collection include aquatics, baseball, boxing, cricket, equestrianism, and track and field. Each chapter introduces the sport and includes rules and regulations, constitutions and bylaws for clubs and associations, personal accounts of significant developments and events, newspaper reports of contests, and other contemporary descriptions of athletics during this period.

Scarce period resources have been compiled into one complete, well-organized reference book. Much of the material has been obtained from sporting periodicals or local newspapers of the time, because few formally organized sporting clubs and associations published records of their events. Each selection is a primary source and has been reprinted as it originally appeared except for sections deleted by the editor. A bibliography and indexes by subject, names, institutions, locations, and place-names will aid anyone wanting to learn more about the evolution of organized sports in North America.

—Deborah A. Taylor

827. Loeffelbein, Robert L. **The Recreation Handbook: 342 Games and Other Activities for Teams and Individuals.** Jefferson, N.C., McFarland, 1992. 237p. illus. $24.95pa. GV1203.L58. 793'.01922. LC 92-50310. ISBN 0-89950-744-1.

This useful book covers a range of games, from surf hockey to frisbee volleyball to billiard baseball to hopscotch rope jumping and everything in between. All 342 are "pickup games": You pick up whatever is handy and play a game on a field, a street, a vacant lot, an empty wall, a spare table, a driveway, or a patio—the games presented in this book make use of them all. Although the book provides rules, space needed, number of players, age levels, and equipment needs, the author urges readers to make up new rules or change them as desired. Most entries also provide an illustration of the playing field and descriptions of variant forms of the games. One of the advantages of these games is that they are not highly organized; no fancy uniforms, expensive, elaborate equipment, or referees are provided, and there is little adult interference—except when the adults want to join the fun! Word games and some craft and construction games are included, as well as quiet games for rainy days. All the games encourage imagination, spontaneity, and creativity and have little or no cost, as they attempt to encourage children to amuse themselves. The book has no index, so users must depend on the table of contents and browsing (the games are divided into categories and numbered). This work would be a valuable addition to most public and school libraries and would find a home in many day care centers as well. [R: RBB, 15 Jan 93, p. 947; RQ, Summer 93, pp. 375-76]—**Susan Ebershoff-Coles**

828. Throgmorton, Todd H. **Roller Coasters: An Illustrated Guide to the Rides in the United States and Canada....** Jefferson, N.C., McFarland, 1993. 154p. illus. index. $25.95. GV1860.R64T47. 791'.06'873. LC 92-50939. ISBN 0-89950-805-7.

Often considered as American as baseball and Chevrolet, the roller coaster is an integral part of amusement parks across North America. Begun as early as the late sixteenth century, the roller coaster has been the focal point of the theme park of the last 50 years. Throgmorton provides a brief history of the roller coaster; its development; and its revival in such attractions as Disneyland, Six Flags, and King's Island. Most of the text briefly documents 151 roller coasters located in 51 parks, including four Canadian parks. Arranged geographically by four regions of the nation and Canada, name, address, and telephone number are given for each park, followed by an entry for each roller coaster, with the date constructed and a brief description. Two appendixes detailing wood and steel coasters by location and an index conclude the volume.

The book is generously illustrated, and librarians will cite the need for more information and fewer pictures, such as are found in *The Amusement Park Guide* (see ARBA 92, entry 774), where admission charges, hours of operation, and fuller descriptions are included. With this recently published guide available in paperback for approximately one-half the price of *Roller Coasters*, libraries will want to select carefully. If you own *The Amusement Park Guide*, save your money. [R: RBB, June 93, p. 1904]

—**Boyd Childress**

829. Wiersma, John H., and Tina M. Wiersma, eds. **Educators Guide to Free Health, Physical Education and Recreation Materials.** 26th ed. Randolph, Wis., Educators Progress Service, 1993. 410p. index. $27.95pa. LC 68-57948. ISBN 0-87708-259-6.

Educators Guide lists some 1,700 films, filmstrips, slides, audiotapes, videotapes, and printed materials (e.g., pamphlets, rule books, maps) in the fields of health, physical education, and recreation (HPER). However, the title is misleading: 77 percent of the items pertain to health, while only 5.5 percent relate to physical education. The book is user-friendly, giving detailed instructions for ordering the materials (including the kind of paper to use). Items are indexed by both title and subject, and the pages are supposedly color-coded. However, the publisher's foreword claims to be on blue but is actually green. The editors stress that many new items are in this edition and many former ones were discontinued, yet numerous obsolete items remain. For example, few junior high school students would likely be interested in a film on former Dallas Cowboys coach Tom Landry and his 1971 team, the only football entry in the book. Thirty of the physical education films are about English riding, bowling, or shooting, while only six relate to baseball, football, or soccer. Recreation offerings include guides to wine making and flower arranging, as well as blatantly commercial films such as *Far Away Places -A Journey to Busch Gardens*. The best materials are on health. They cover a variety of topics, including home safety, first aid, and AIDS education. However, 28 percent of the health materials relate to food and nutrition. Many, such as "Tips on Picking and Using Strawberries" and "Pickle Pointers," are more appropriate for home economics than HPER. Health educators at schools lacking funds and resources may find some useful materials in this guide, as might some practitioners in public recreation. The book is virtually useless for physical educators.—**Mary Lou LeCompte**

BASEBALL

830. **The Baseball Encyclopedia: The Complete and Definitive Record of Major League Baseball.** 9th ed. New York, Macmillan, 1993. 2857p. $55.00. GV877.B27. 796.357'0973'021. LC 92-44145. ISBN 0-02-579041-2.

This edition of a venerable encyclopedia is largely an update of the 1990 8th edition. Records are now current through 1992; additionally, some data have been corrected after having been successfully challenged by intrepid researchers (e.g., Cy Young has been saddled with an additional loss in the 1890 season). There is a new section on the All-American Girls Professional League that includes yearly team standings, league champions, and a list of players. This encyclopedia does not have as much textual material or as many statistics as its rival *Total Baseball* (see ARBA 92, entry 786), but it does contain a number of features that the latter source lacks (e.g., a register of Negro Leagues players). While there is a considerable amount of overlap between the two, baseball researchers and fans will appreciate having both available. [R: Choice, Sept 93, p. 74]—**Jack Ray**

831. Dewey, Donald, and Nicholas Acocella. **Encyclopedia of Major League Baseball Teams.** New York, HarperCollins, 1993. 594p. illus. $35.00. GV875.A1A36. 796.357'64'0973. LC 92-43303. ISBN 0-06-270049-9.

There is no shortage of baseball reference books that provide more in the way of statistical information than all but the most avid fan can digest. Nor is there any shortage of histories of individual major league baseball teams. What makes this encyclopedia unique and valuable is that it provides, with only a minimum of statistical data, brief histories of the 121 teams that have comprised the 6 leagues officially recognized by major league baseball. That includes such teams as the Cincinnati Porkers as well as the better-known Cincinnati Reds, and the Federal League as well as the American League. The entries, which are arranged alphabetically by city, vary in length, with brief entries of a page or less for teams along the lines of the Porkers and approximately 25 pages for each of the long-established teams, such as the Reds. The narrative histories, which are each accompanied by a number of brief highlighted sidebars that contain amusing anecdotes, are brief and to the point, but they do not pull any punches in evaluating a team's performance, the foibles of its owners, and the reasons for its successes and failures. Each entry concludes with a brief list of a team's annual position in the final standings, win-lose record, winning percentage, games behind, and manager. There is a bibliography of just over five pages that includes most of the standard works, including individual team histories. Unfortunately, there is no index, so tracking down information about individual managers, owners, or players can only be done by skimming the text. All in all, though, this compact history of individual teams is a splendid addition to sports reference collections in all libraries. [R: LJ, 15 Oct 93, p. 58]—**Norman D. Stevens**

832. Filichia, Peter. **Professional Baseball Franchises: From the Abbeville Athletics to the Zanesville Indians.** New York, Facts on File, 1993. 290p. index. $25.95. GV875.A1F45. 796.357'64'0973. LC 92-12766. ISBN 0-8160-2647-5.

Long-forgotten baseball teams are brought back to life in this directory of North American franchises that date back to the inception of professional play in 1869. The principal arrangement is by city; within each city the arrangement is by team nickname. Name of league and years of existence are given, and if the franchise had moved from another city or later moved to a different site, that information is also provided. At the end is an alphabetical list of leagues and team nicknames. Besides the standard major and minor leagues, the Negro leagues and the All American Girls Professional Baseball League (yes, the Rockford Peaches really existed) are included. One can only marvel at the vast array of cities and towns that have hosted franchises, and be amused at some of the nicknames (e.g., the Newport, Arizona, Pear Diggers of 1908-1909; the Joliet, Illinois, Convicts of 1890-1891; the Zanesville, Ohio, Flood Sufferers of 1913; the Americus, Georgia, Pallbearers of 1906) they proudly bore. One might argue that a chronological arrangement within each city would be more desirable for a sense of historical flow, but as it stands this is a first-rate baseball reference source. [R: Choice, July/Aug 93, p. 1748; RBB, 1 Mar 93, p. 1267]—**Jack Ray**

833. Gillette, Gary. **The Great American Baseball Stat Book 1993.** New York, HarperPerennial/HarperCollins, 1993. 502p. $15.00pa. ISBN 0-06-273220-X. ISSN 1056-5116.

Baseball fans follow their favorite teams and players by comparing statistics (many cannot get enough statistics), and they are often linked to online databases that provide endless numbers for comparing and crunching. Additionally, each year sees new books and editions of baseball statistics. The Sporting News publishes the *Official Baseball Register* annually (see ARBA 92, entry 777); *Total Baseball* (see ARBA 92, entry 786), is now in its 2d edition; the *Baseball Encyclopedia* (see ARBA 90, entry 764) includes at least eight editions with updates; and the *Sports Encyclopedia* has a baseball statistical volume (see ARBA 91, entry 823). These represent some of the major sources of baseball statistics. However, *The Great American Baseball Stat Book* carries statistics to greater heights. When television and radio announcers tell the audience a player is batting .362 with two outs and runners in scoring position, they are using situational statistics, or how a player is performing in a specific situation; the *Stat Book* is replete with these numbers. Included are how a player does in day or night games, in road and home games, on grass and artificial surfaces, and much more.

The volume is divided into four major parts on regular players' situational statistics, the same for nonregular players, team and league statistics, and player career records. Another interesting part has special reports, including such categories as a page on baseball parks' effects on games and fielding records by position. The result is an inexpensive, complete record book that would do the hardiest baseball fan proud. It is a logical choice for tight library budgets. [R: RBB, June 93, p. 1898]—**Boyd Childress**

834. Lowry, Philip J. **Green Cathedrals: The Ultimate Celebration of All 273 Major League and Negro League Ballparks....** Reading, Mass., Addison-Wesley Publishing, 1992. 275p. illus. index. $24.95; $15.95pa. GV879.5.L68. 796.357'06'873. LC 91-32016. ISBN 0-201-56777-6; 0-201-62229-7pa.

This work is an oratorio for major league ballparks, especially the remaining turn-of-the-century "grande dames" (Fenway Park, Wrigley Field, Tiger Stadium, and Yankee Stadium). It is also a requiem for those parks now gone (e.g., Ebbets Field, the Polo Grounds), and it has a passage devoted to a park of fantasy—the Field of Dreams in Dyersville, Iowa. Only major league parks are listed, including those now used by minor league teams. Lowery counts the Negro Leagues among the majors, despite the paucity of their records.

Parks are arranged alphabetically by city. If more than one ballpark existed in that city, these are listed chronologically, oldest to newest. Parks are described by dimension and seating capacity, including year-by-year variances; nickname; neutral use (especially by the Negro Leagues); and phenomena, mostly structural quirks. This last category is frustratingly uneven. For instance, all season-ending tie-breaking playoffs involved the Boston Red Sox in the American League and the Brooklyn/Los Angeles Dodgers in the National League, yet this information is listed under St. Louis. More illustrations would have been nice, too. The book is printed on heavy paper that will probably last longer than the cover will.

As the titles implies, Lowery views ballparks as churches; he does not hide his contempt for the contemporary round stadia, which he refers to as "concrete ashtrays." In this way the book is different from other ballpark books that concentrate on comfort and convenience, not history or aesthetics. Overall, Lowery succeeds in his objective; *Green Cathedrals* conveys the magic of the classic parks. Highly recommended.—**R. S. Lehmann**

835. Reichler, Joseph L. **The Great All-Time Baseball Record Book.** Revised by Ken Samelson. rev. ed. New York, Macmillan, 1993. 592p. index. $25.00. GV877.R39. 796.357'021. LC 91-38197. ISBN 0-02-603101-9.

Of the making of baseball books there is no end! Baseball thrives on statistics, and baseball fans relish books of statistics—especially those that are distinctive. First published in 1981 (see ARBA 83, entry 654), this updated edition offers a wide-ranging series of comparisons that are not found, or that lie buried and not easily accessible, in the myriad of other baseball statistics books that exist. Only the wonderful electronic *Franklin Big League Encyclopedia* (Franklin Electronic, 1992) makes such comparisons quickly available, and even it lacks some of the records found here.

The information in *Great*'s four broad categories (individual batting records, individual pitching records, rookie records, and team records) is subarranged into a series of logical groupings (e.g., pinch hits), and within each subcategory, into a series of individual records (e.g., most career pinch hits). In all, records in some 475 categories are provided that cover virtually every individual and team record of interest. An excellent player index lists not only the player but also the record categories in which he is listed and highlights in boldface type the categories in which he is the record holder. What more could a baseball fan want? Libraries of all kinds are likely to find high demand for this volume. [R: Choice, Sept 93, p. 74; RBB, 15 Nov 93, pp. 650-51]—**Norman D. Stevens**

836. **The Scouting Report: 1993.** By STATS, Inc. John Dewan and Don Zminda, eds. New York, HarperPerennial/HarperCollins, 1993. 682p. illus. index. $16.00pa. ISBN 0-06-273192-0. ISSN 0743-1309.

The Scouting Report is a scaled-down version of the annual baseball abstracts, but smaller size does not equal less quality in this case. The layout is simple. The introduction explains the abbreviations and statistical information. Then there are lists of "1992 Lead Leaders" and projected 1993 "Stars, Bums, and Sleepers." Next, American League and National League teams are alphabetized by city or state (e.g., Boston Red Sox before California Angels), and in these sections, each team's players are listed alphabetically. There are two columns of text for the projected starters, the left a "Cliff Notes" of strengths and weaknesses, the right, statistics. Team chapters conclude with an overview of the organization and its top prospects. Sportswriters and STATS, Inc., compiled these reports, which are useful on many levels, from the casual fan to the statisticians and fantasy leaguers. Accessible and readable, *The Scouting Report* is highly recommended.—**R. S. Lehmann**

837. Smith, Myron J., Jr., comp. **Baseball: A Comprehensive Bibliography. Supplement 1 (1985-May 1992).** Jefferson, N.C., McFarland, 1993. 422p. index. $45.00. Z7514.B3S645. 016.796357'0973. LC 92-50892. ISBN 0-89950-799-9.

Smith has used approximately the same format as he did in his 1986 bibliography (see ARBA 87, entry 763), although some areas of more recent interest (e.g., collectibles, Rotisserie leagues) are highlighted. There are 7,771 entries in this supplement, and as before the references are culled from a remarkably wide variety of sources. Even more periodical titles are listed than were in the 1986 volume, and again a number of them do not seem likely sources of articles on baseball (e.g., *Journal of Gerontology, Mathematics Teacher*). The primary emphasis is on publications that have appeared since 1985, but Smith has also backtracked to pick up a number of earlier items that were missed. A useful resource in its own right, this supplement should be acquired, especially by libraries that own the 1986 bibliography. [R: RBB, July 93, pp. 2000-01]—**Jack Ray**

838. **The Sporting News Complete Baseball Record Book.** 1993 ed. Craig Carter, ed. St. Louis, Mo., Sporting News, 1993. 556p. $16.95pa.; $18.95 spiralbound. ISBN 0-89204-454-3pa.; 0-89204-455-1 spiralbound.

No sport has been statistically analyzed as meticulously as baseball. Consequently, there are hundreds of different statistical categories in the sport for which records are kept. *The Sporting News Complete Baseball Record Book* may not be truly complete, but it comes close. The book presents a myriad of records for batting, fielding, pitching, and miscellaneous categories that are subdivided into individual, club, and league results. There are sections for regular season, championship series, World Series, and all-star game records.

The most similar work on the market is Seymour Siwoff's *The Book of Baseball Records* (Elias Sports Bureau, annual). There is considerable overlap between the two books. Each work also offers statistics not found in the other. The Sporting News book, however, does have some distinct advantages. It provides a useful contents page, a larger typeface, and visual prompts in the margin of every page that inform users what section and category they are reading. In short, it is easier to use than Siwoff's book.

—Wayne Wilson

BASKETBALL

839. Earle, Michael V., ed. **Final Four Records 1939-1991: The History of the Division I Men's Basketball Tournament....** Chicago, Triumph Books, 1992. 174p. illus. $7.95pa. ISBN 0-9624436-7-0.

Despite the subtitle, this is not really a history. Rather, it is a detailed compilation of statistics and records of the NCAA Division I men's basketball tournament. And despite the main title, the book contains information not only on games from the Final Four but also from earlier rounds of the tournament. The statistical information presented includes an impressive range of data on teams and individual players. Among the many other categories of information are coaches' records, attendance figures, television ratings of specific games, and lists of outstanding tournament players. While this is not a complete statistical record of intercollegiate basketball, it is a comprehensive, clearly presented record of the college game's most prestigious tournament.—**Wayne Wilson**

840. Taragano, Martin. **Pro Basketball Statistics: Top Players and Teams by Game, Season and Career.** Jefferson, N.C., McFarland, 1993. 195p. illus. index. $29.95. GV885.55.T37. 796.323'64'0973021. LC 92-51094. ISBN 0-89950-804-9.

Basketball statistics continue to grow in popularity, as does the game. Compilations such as *The Sports Encyclopedia: Pro Basketball* (see ARBA 92, entry 787) and *The Basketball Abstract* (see ARBA 91, entry 829) attest to the ever-growing interest in number crunching and comparative statistics. With a slight hint of subjectivity, Taragano (also the author of *Basketball Biographies* [see ARBA 92, entry 788]) provides list after list that compare pro players statistically rather than compile data player-by-player. Divided into 8 chapters, the volume contains 169 tables of statistical information, from the top 100 players to All-Star game selection from the NBA and ABA. For example, chapter 2 lists the top centers (the top 16 and the next best 11). Fifteen tables of data follow, providing data for points and rebounds as well as other areas of comparison. The inclusion of information from the ABA years (1967-1976) is a welcome addition to basketball stats. The index, however, is a disappointment, as it is too brief and rendered practically useless for a volume of statistical tables.

Any list of the top players is subject to second-guessing. While it is difficult to justify the inclusion of many of today's stars, who are just now becoming greats of the game (e.g., Karl Malone, Kevin Johnson, John Stockton), it is hard to believe players such as Paul Silas are not included. (Known as one of the game's fiercest offensive rebounders, the intangibles Silas brought to the game are legendary.) The same holds true for ABA legend Roger Brown, as well as many other players from professional basketball's annals. While not all "greats" can be included, one wishes the scattered photographs had been deleted to make room for information on more of the game's top players. [R: RBB, 1 Dec 93, p. 717]

—**Boyd Childress**

CARD GAMES

841. Parlett, David. **A Dictionary of Card Games.** New York, Oxford University Press, 1992. 360p. illus. $11.95pa. GV1243.P315. 795.8. LC 91-42015. ISBN 0-19-869173-4.

This is a companion volume to Parlett's *A History of Card Games* (Oxford University Press, 1991). Parlett is an internationally renowned inventor, writer, and researcher in the field of games. This dictionary is a treasury of famous and interesting card games of the Western world arranged in alphabetical order for ease of reference. Parlett includes everything from the obscure to the well-known and classic, party, and family games. Obvious international favorites, as well as major national card games and several Tarot entries, can also be found. A fascinating array of solitaire games and unusual games not often encountered in books of this type are listed. Representative one-player games and a few gambling games are included, but proprietary and one-off games by known inventors and games that require special cards not widely obtainable are omitted. A list of recommendations for specific numbers of players, an appendix of terms used in cardplay, and a bibliography are supplied. This title can be used as a reference or to entertain and enlighten.—**Kathleen J. Voigt**

CHESS

842. **The Oxford Companion to Chess.** 2d ed. By David Hooper and Kenneth Whyld. New York, Oxford University Press, 1992. 483p. illus. $35.00. GV1445.H616. 794.1'092'2. LC 83-23733. ISBN 0-19-866164-9.

The first edition of this comprehensive guide to chess set a new standard for reference works on the world's most intellectual international game. This edition maintains that standard and even improves on it. For example, around 160 new biographical sketches, mainly of contemporary players, have been added, and 70 others have been deleted. In all, some 600 new entries have been added, bringing the total to about 2,600.

The same basic format of the first edition has been maintained. Once again short entries are arranged alphabetically with numerous cross-references, which are indicated by the capitalization within an entry of a term that has an entry of its own. There are also numerous board diagrams, a variety of other illustrations, and several valuable appendixes.

The Chess Encyclopedia (see ARBA 92, entry 789), which is the only other recent alternative, pales by comparison. Although now out of date, *The Encyclopedia of Chess* (see ARBA 78, entry 622) is still the only other major guide, while *Chess Personalia* (see ARBA 88, entry 799) is a useful, comprehensive guide to information about chess players and problemists. Taken together, these two titles and *The Oxford Companion to Chess* are the nucleus of a basic chess reference collection.—**Norman D. Stevens**

FITNESS

843. Karolides, Nicholas J., and Melissa Karolides. **Focus on Fitness: A Reference Handbook.** Santa Barbara, Calif., ABC-Clio, 1993. 470p. index. (Teenage Perspectives). $39.00. RA781.K27. 613.7. LC 93-21853. ISBN 0-87436-662-3.

Intended for teenagers and those who work with them, *Focus on Fitness* covers both physical and emotional fitness and includes exercise, fitness tests, injuries, eating disorders, steroid abuse, and motivation. Each chapter contains a discussion of the major aspects of the topic, followed by an annotated list of resources that includes fiction, nonfiction, nonprint materials, and information on related organizations. Prices and addresses are provided with the nonprint items. The chapters on exercise present the pros and cons of several popular types of conditioning programs, as well as charts and graphs to explain their impact. While the authors are not professionals in exercise science, they have contacted expert consultants and up-to-date sources to compile this handbook.

Although the book is comprehensive, its order and tone are questionable. Rearranging the chapters to stress positive aspects (e.g., motivation) first and beginning the chapters with positive rather than negative ideas might enhance the value of this work. The writing style is also uneven. Some sentences, even those containing big words, sound very juvenile, while others will challenge even the fitness professional. Also, a book seems an inappropriate source for learning risky activities such as riding ten-speed bicycles or swimming. This volume would be more functional if it assisted students in selecting exercise programs and instructors rather than attempting to explain how to perform those activities.

Focus on Fitness would be an appropriate text for a class on health and fitness, where activities could be learned under supervision. However, it (and especially its annotated bibliographies) will probably be used primarily as a reference for teachers. [R: LJ, 1 Sept 93, p. 170]—**Mary Lou LeCompte**

FOOTBALL

844. Fossey, Keith R. **The Football Scholarship Guide.** Kenosha, Wis., Pigskin Press, 1992. 308p. illus. maps. index. $24.95pa. LC 92-90842. ISBN 0-9633495-0-3.

By no means a typical reference book (the most significant part of it is more of a self-help book), *The Football Scholarship Guide* should still find a place in all high school libraries with football programs and in public libraries in locales with a strong high school football tradition. Its purpose, which it fulfills admirably, is to provide high school football players who are likely to be overlooked by college recruiters with information that will help them maximize their scholarship potential. Much of that information, especially that found in the first section, is not readily available elsewhere. In that section, Fossey carefully outlines the organization of college football; the National Collegiate Athletic Association (NCAA) and other rules pertaining to football scholarships; how a player can best promote himself, including the appropriate use of game videotapes; the regulations about recruitment; and the key elements of a player's support team, including his counselor, coach, athletic director, and parents. The second section, which is a region-by-region listing of all colleges with football teams, is somewhat less useful, primarily because so much of the information presented (and more) is readily available in other college guides. [R: VOYA, Feb 93, p. 383]—**Norman D. Stevens**

845. Jarrett, William S. **Timetables of Sports History: Football.** New York, Facts on File, 1993. 85p. illus. index. $17.95. GV950.J37. 796.332'0973. LC 92-34727. ISBN 0-8160-2877-X.

This is the fourth of the Facts on File timetables of sports history. Earlier volumes concentrated on baseball (see ARBA 90, entry 767), basketball (see ARBA 91, entry 830), and the Olympics (see ARBA 91, entry 812). Similar to the other books, the football volume is a chronology that covers both college and the professionals, with one page dedicated to each season after 1920. Both the regular season and bowl games and playoffs are covered, with mention of All-American college players, conference champions, and Heisman trophy winners as well as professional statistical leaders. A cursory bibliography and an index conclude the volume. The curious selection of photographs represents mostly professional players and coaches.

Reviews of earlier volumes were mixed; the accuracy of the basketball volume in particular was questioned. However, the football chronology is much more accurate. There are a few minor errors; for example, Florida's 1984 Southeastern Conference title was voided due to NCAA violations. But the volume is a good, inexpensive reference book on American football and is recommended for public libraries and smaller college libraries. [R: SLJ, May 93, p. 140]—**Boyd Childress**

846. **Official 1992 National Football League Record & Fact Book.** New York, Workman Publishing, 1992. 392p. illus. $14.95pa. ISBN 1-56305-247-4.

Authorized by the National Football League (NFL) and distributed to the media, this guide provides detailed information and statistics about current teams and players in the NFL and historical highlights of professional football. The first edition, published in 1988, was well received (see ARBA 89, entry 734). Equally valuable, this edition follows the original format. Detailed weekly schedules of the 1992 season are followed by lengthy summaries of each team's statistics and personnel. Next comes in-depth, week-by-week coverage of the 1991 season and statistics. A section on the history of the league includes a chronology that begins in 1869 and lists of the all-time records of each team against each of the other teams. Sections on records and official rules complete the coverage. A brief index at the front of the volume also functions as a table of contents.

As a comprehensive source of information on professional football, this fact book is unparalleled. Intended specifically to help those in the news media cover the sport, it is an essential reference for any sports collection.—**Barbara E. Kemp**

847. Smith, Myron J., Jr., comp. **Professional Football: The Official Pro Football Hall of Fame Bibliography.** Westport, Conn., Greenwood Press, 1993. 414p. index. (Bibliographies and Indexes on Sports History, no.1). $75.00. Z7514.F7S64. 796.332'64'0973. LC 92-42677. ISBN 0-313-28928-X.

As the popularity of professional football spreads, a corresponding body of literature has enjoyed a parallel growth. In an attempt to create a comprehensive bibliography of the sport, the Pro Football Hall of Fame has supported Smith in this handsome reference book, which documents both articles and books about pro football—its history, teams, coaches, and players. In an exhaustive list of more than 5,000 items, Smith has provided the best bibliography to date on pro football.

The volume is arranged by subject: reference works; general works; histories of teams, leagues, and games; and biographical works. The last two constitute most of the volume; the biography sections comprise more than one-half of the entries. Included are citations representing a wide range of football and sports magazines, including *Sports Illustrated, Sport Magazine, Pro Football Illustrated*, and *Football Digest*. Appropriate book titles are also listed. In general, the bibliography represents the holdings of the research library at the Pro Football Hall of Fame in Canton, Ohio. The emphasis is on American football, yet Canadian and Australian professional football are covered to a lesser degree.

While this reference book is highly recommended, minor flaws can be found throughout. For example, Gale Sayers's emotional autobiography *I Am Third* is listed under Sayers but not under Chicago Bears teammate Brian Piccolo, who was much of the inspiration for the book. On page 298, New York Jets wide receiver George Sauer's name is not inverted, nor is there any indication that Sauer was known as George Sauer, Jr. But the index, a full 70 pages, far outweighs these minor errors and makes this a standard bibliography for years to come. [R: Choice, Sept 93, p. 90; RBB, 1 Oct 93, pp. 386-87; WLB, Sept 93, p. 122]—**Boyd Childress**

848. **The Sporting News Complete Super Bowl Book.** 1993 ed. Tom Dienhart, Joe Hoppel, and Dave Sloan, eds. St. Louis, Mo., Sporting News, 1993. 480p. illus. $12.95pa. ISBN 0-89204-464-0.

The approach here is straightforward: The book provides a chapter on each Super Bowl. An 8- to 10-page essay recounts, in journalistic style, each of the 27 championships and gives game statistics. Following the descriptive chapters is a section on Super Bowl records, a roster of athletes who have played in the game, and another section on the Super Bowl career statistics of individual players in selected categories. As a bonus—not that one would know it from the title—the book also contains more than 100 pages of information on the annual postseason divisions and league championships leading up to the Super Bowl.

A simple table of contents directs readers to the appropriate sections. Hundreds of black-and-white photographs are interspersed throughout the text. This well-organized, readable, and informative annual reference is the best source for timely Super Bowl information.—**Wayne Wilson**

GOLF

849. Davies, Peter. **The Historical Dictionary of Golfing Terms: From 1500 to the Present.** New York, Michael Kesend Publishing, 1992. 188p. illus. $14.95pa. GV965.D37. 796.352'03. LC 92-27571. ISBN 0-935576-44-4.

As is evidenced by the thousands of books on the subject, golf is notable for its ability to attract followers with a serious interest in its history and lore. Now these students can extend their range of interest to include the language of golf. *The Historical Dictionary of Golfing Terms* models itself after the scholarly "dictionaries on historical principles," such as John Bartlett's *Dictionary of Americanisms* (Reprint Services, 1988), and applies their approach and format to the extraordinarily rich vocabulary that the game of golf has amassed over the last 500 years. For each word or term there are definitions, etymologies, and dated and paged quotations indicating the first recorded usage plus a representative array of later ones. Where appropriate, helpful drawings are also supplied.

Many of the terms are rather obvious (e.g., *sand, greens fee*) or technical (e.g., *stroke, drive*). These must be included for the sake of scholarly completeness but probably carry little interest for most potential users. On the other hand, a great many of the entries, representing old or colorful words, make for enjoyable reading; for example, *sclaff, hogback,* and *snake* are likely to pique curiosity. Even the illustrative quotations can often be intriguing. Because they tend to have been selected from writings by the most famous names in golfing history, they constitute almost an anthology of golfing literature.

The Historical Dictionary of Golfing Terms will be most welcome in the golf world and in larger libraries that can afford to stock highly specialized dictionaries. Recommended. [R: RBB, 15 Jan 93, p. 942]

—**Samuel Rothstein**

850. **GOLF Magazine's Encyclopedia of Golf: The Complete Reference.** 2d ed. By the editors of *GOLF Magazine.* New York, HarperCollins, 1993. 517p. illus. index. $40.00. GV965.G5455. 796.352. LC 92-16293. ISBN 0-06-270019-7.

Substantially updated since its first publication in 1979 (see ARBA 80, entry 710), this comprehensive encyclopedia contains a brief but thorough history of the sport, detailed records of all major championships and tournaments of general public interest, and biographies of major players. Information about equipment, principles, rules, and courses is also provided, and there is a reasonably detailed index.

Less lavish than *The Encyclopedia of Golf* (see ARBA 93, entry 832) and lacking that work's color illustrations, this encyclopedia contains much of the same information but covers a greater number of championships and tournaments, while *The Encyclopedia of Golf* has more data about golf courses. They are equally good in covering such items as history, equipment, rules, and terminology. Either one would be appropriate for libraries that need a single source of information about major aspects of the sport. For libraries with more extensive collections, both encyclopedias may be needed. For fans, this encyclopedia is a better choice, while *The Encyclopedia of Golf* is of greater interest to serious golfers.

—**Norman D. Stevens**

851. **Official USGA Record Book 1895-1990: USGA Championships and International Events.** Chicago, Triumph Books; distr., Detroit, Gale, 1992. 1v. (various paging). $59.95. LC 92-64444. ISBN 1-880141-39-6.

This comprehensive statistical handbook presents a wealth of data that should gladden the heart of record keepers. It provides a comprehensive list of all of the records for 95 years of the 17 championship and international events sponsored by the United States Golf Association. Divided into three sections (1895-1959, 1960-1980, and 1981-1990) for reasons that are neither clear nor explained, this book provides a brief year-by-year history of each event, a summary tabulation of the winners, and a year-by-year list of all contestants and their finish, as well as round-by-round and total scores. Both U.S. and world amateur and open championships are covered, as well as international events, such as the Curtis and Walker cup matches. There is no index, so finding information about any individual player in the 234 pages of fine print is almost impossible. In any case, most of the players and events, with a few exceptions, are of limited public interest. Information about the major name players and events can be readily found in many other golf reference books, such as *GOLF Magazine's Encyclopedia of Golf* (HarperCollins, 1993). This book will find only a very limited audience among ardent golf fans and will be of interest largely to libraries with extensive sports or golf collections. [R: LJ, Jan 93, p. 106; RBB, 15 Jan 93, p. 942; WLB, Feb 93, p. 107]—**Norman D. Stevens**

HOCKEY

852. Hollander, Zander, ed. **The Complete Encyclopedia of Hockey.** 4th ed. Detroit, Gale, 1993. 604p. illus. index. $39.95. GV847.8.N3C64. 796.962'092'2. LC 92-29950. ISBN 0-8103-8869-3.

The publication of this edition happily coincides with the 100th anniversary of the Stanley Cup, the championship trophy of the National Hockey League (NHL). First published in 1970, this work covers the World Hockey Association, collegiate and Olympic hockey, and the world championships, but its major focus remains the NHL and its teams, players, and coaches.

A history of the NHL is summarized in chapters that deal with broad, significant periods, from its beginnings in Canada through the inclusion of United States teams to the major expansion of the league in the 1960s and 1970s. Stories of the greatest players are featured in another chapter. Individual and team records, the history of the Stanley Cup, official rules, NHL coaches and officials, and other hockey facts are included in other chapters. The longest chapter, and the real heart of the book, contains the NHL player register. It gives lifetime regular season and playoff statistics of the more than 4,200 players who have appeared in an NHL game. This represents an increase of more than 1,400 names since the last edition, published in 1983.

Well researched, this comprehensive guide is enhanced by an attractive layout, a good index, numerous illustrations, and a readable text. It is an excellent addition to the personal collection of any hockey fan and to any library serving sports enthusiasts.—**Barbara E. Kemp**

853. **The National Hockey League Official Guide & Record Book 1992-93.** Compiled by NHL Communications Group and the 24 NHL Club Public Relations Directors. Chicago, Triumph Books; distr., Detroit, Gale, 1992. 424p. illus. index. $16.95pa. ISBN 1-880141-17-5.

The title page indicates that this book is produced by the National Hockey League (NHL), and the introduction states that it is the 61st edition of the game's most comprehensive statistical annual. This is almost all one needs to know before deciding on the merits or the acquisition of the guide: It is reliable, accurate, extensive, and (in view of all those previous editions) well-calculated to give its potential readers the information they want.

That information is mostly a four-part account. First, for each NHL club are listed its history, player roster, records, and statistics. Next comes the "NHL Record Book," including the Stanley Cup games; third is the "Player Register," giving detailed lifetime scoring data for all current players and highly abbreviated data on retired players; and finally, there is a special feature, the "Stanley Cup Centennial."

The skimpiness of the section on retired players—imagine giving only one line of statistical data for such hockey greats as Gordie Howe and Bobby Hull!—is one of the few deficiencies of the guide. Some other faults, of less consequence, are inconsistency in the way names are listed (e.g., *Pat* Lafontaine but *David* Ellett) and some lack of clarity and comfort in the typography (too much print is packed into the space available). Nevertheless, the guide deserves special encomiums for its numerous and excellent photographs, its reasonable price, and the novel and useful feature of supplying data on trades and draft choices.

The guide describes itself as "Hockey's Information Classic." In this case, such self-promotion is justified. [R: LJ, 1 Feb 93, p. 76; RBB, 15 Jan 93, pp. 944-46]—**Samuel Rothstein**

MARTIAL ARTS

854. **The *Aiki News* 1994 Dojo Finder: The International Guide to Aikido Schools and Instructors.** By Stanley A. Pranin and Diane Skoss. Tokyo, Aiki News; distr., Albany, N.Y., Aiki News, 1993. 118p. index. $16.95pa. GV1114.35. 796.8'154. ISBN 4-900586-15-3.

Martial arts practitioners relocating to other cities or countries often attempt to find a school teaching the same style with which they have experience. The numerous martial arts movies have also prompted interest in specific styles of martial arts. While telephone directories are often the best source for this type of information, many martial arts schools do not invest in such advertising. Thus, any directory that attempts to catalog the often tenuous existence and location of martial arts schools is welcome. This directory provides information on approximately 2,000 aikido schools in 46 countries, arranged by country, state or province, and city. Entries include addresses, telephone numbers, contact or instructor names, and rank and affiliation. Separate instructor and organization indexes are also provided.

Aikido is one of the most distinctive martial arts systems, less likely to vary from location to location than other martial arts systems. Thus, this directory will be of great value to aikido practitioners looking for new schools or colleagues. While disclaiming authority, the authors have done a remarkably good job of listing aikido schools in such diverse places as DeKalb, Illinois, or Slovenia. Even programs taught through park districts or recreation centers are listed. Public libraries in particular will welcome this effort.—**Andrew G. Torok**

855. Corcoran, John, and Emil Farkas with Stuart Sobel. **The Original Martial Arts Encyclopedia: Tradition, History, Pioneers.** Los Angeles, Calif., Pro-Action Publishing, 1993. 410p. illus. index. $24.95. LC 92-81677. ISBN 0-9615126-3-6.

As another entry in the growing number of martial arts reference books, this encyclopedia offers useful information on a subject of increasing interest for which few accurate descriptive works are available. It complements *A Dictionary of the Martial Arts* (see ARBA 93, entry 839). Because of its additional features, such as an excellent chronology, a history of martial arts in motion pictures, brief biographies of a large number of martial arts pioneers, a list of martial arts organizations and associations, and a bibliography, it is significantly more valuable than that dictionary. The text is divided into three sections: tradition, history, and pioneers. The first section includes detailed descriptions of 33 major martial arts; briefer descriptions of another 22 miscellaneous and eclectic arts; and a dictionary of the equipment, training devices, and weapons that are used. The numerous black-and-white photographs that illustrate the different arts and weapons are especially useful for the uninitiated. The additional features mentioned above, which are found in the other two sections, are also of great value, although the failure to include mailing addresses for organizations and associations is a serious oversight because that information is not readily available elsewhere.

This is probably the best single source of information on martial arts now available. Libraries should be aware, though, that it is a somewhat revised and updated version of *Martial Arts: Traditions, History, People* (Gallery Books, 1988). [R: SLJ, Oct 93, p. 168; RBB, 1 Sept 93, p. 90]—**Norman D. Stevens**

OLYMPIC GAMES

856. Lewis, Brad Alan, and Gabriella Goldstein. **Olympic Results—Barcelona 1992: A Complete Compilation of Results from the Games of the XXV Olympiad.** Hamden, Conn., Garland, 1993. 611p. (Garland Reference Library of the Humanities, v.1752). $96.00. GV7221992.049. 796.48. LC 93-15813. ISBN 0-8153-0333-5.

Lewis and Goldstein had a noble idea in this book. It includes all the results of all the competitions at the 1992 Olympic Games at Barcelona, from the qualifying rounds to the medal-deciding events. Unfortunately, it is so full of errors, omissions, and inconsistencies as to be virtually useless. One reason may be that although the International Olympic Committee (IOC) and the international federations governing the various sports maintain the official Olympic records, those were not the sources used to compile this work. Another major problem is that while the authors claim to be presenting a serious research volume, the tone is flippant and sarcastic. In answer to the question "What new sports will be added to the games?" they suggest carjacking, bungee jumping, extreme shopping, dieting, and tattooing. Worse are the errors, beginning with the misspelling of the name of the only U.S. representative to the IOC, Anita DeFrantz (spelled "DeFranz" on page viii). On page 1, Jim Spivey of the United States is listed as finishing seventh in the 1,500-meter race. On page 11, he finishes eighth in the same event (which is correct). Page 244 indicates that gymnast Henrietta Onodi is from China; page 245 correctly lists her from Hungary. The authors state that the Unified Team of athletes from the former USSR used the flags of their individual republics, when in fact it was the Olympic flag. The list of participating nations includes Bohemia (highly unlikely) and both North and South Yemen, despite the fact that the two had merged in 1990 and completed as a single nation, Yemen. Iceland and Iraq are also listed twice, with different abbreviations.

The book is inconsistent in the inclusion of times or scores, in the listing of dates and places where records were set, and in the giving or omitting of names of relay team members. Although there are two pages of abbreviations—those used for the various participating countries and "Abbreviations" (p. xxiv)—many are missing. For example, URS and GDR appear with great frequency on the lists of Olympic and world records, but nowhere in the definitions (they apply to the former Soviet Union and the former East Germany). More mysterious acronyms include YUK, MGA, KOK, IPO, SN, YUS, R, FB, FA, and FC. No explanation for these was found. The authors wanted to give a complete record of every participant and every event from beginning to end, yet they omitted the dates on which the contests occurred, a part of the record. Other omissions include the final medal totals and the number of participants. A lot of the information, including the names of the athletes, is in all capital letters. This makes it sometimes difficult to separate the athletes from their countries. Also, the headers explaining the meanings of the various columns of figures are often included only on the first page of a long series of results, making the succeeding pages difficult to interpret.

This confusing book may be of interest to a few who want to know how many contestants or how many countries participated in a particular sport at Barcelona, or how many rounds it took to determine a winner. However, as a reference work it is too inaccurate and muddled to be useful, and is certainly not worth the price! [R: LJ, Dec 93, p. 114]—**Mary Lou LeCompte**

POOL

857. **The Billiard Industry Source Book: The Directory of Billiard Supplies and Services....** 1992/1993 ed. Manteca, Calif., Que House, 1992. 448p. index. $150.00pa. ISBN 0-945071-75-2.

Pocket billiards is enjoying a renaissance. The billiard supplies and services available to tend that rebirth range from art accessories to trade show venues and advice on how to work them. In addition to names, addresses, and telephone numbers of domestic and foreign table and cue makers, this work has beverage, music, wearing apparel, video game, publisher, room fixture, sign, lesson, exhibition, darts, and travel information. The listings are extensive but would occupy only about half the space if blank pages were eliminated and the generous margins reduced. And Aragon Billiards, a table and cue maker in San Pedro, Philippines, was not listed. (Aragon supplies some members of the current world champion Filipino 9-ball team with cues.) The book encourages self-listing, so future editions will be more comprehensive. Billiard room owners will benefit from this text because it provides ready access to the supplies and services they need in their businesses.—**Marvin K. Harris**

858. **The Pool Player's National Pocket Billiard Directory: The Directory of American Billiard Information....** 1992 ed. Manteca, Calif., Que House, 1992. 268p. $150.00pa. ISBN 0-945071-51-5. ISSN 1053-7236.

Most of the text in this book is a list of addresses and telephone numbers of billiard rooms. Listings are by state and city, with each room characterized in several ways: by atmosphere and whether or not tournaments and leagues play there. The sections on etiquette, cue selection, and cue and tip care are well presented. The section of toll-free numbers for supplies and services will prove convenient and inexpensive for regular patrons. There is a wealth of additional information, including audio and video tapes, books, periodicals, and instruction. This is the best list of books compiled on the topic. Through it, the serious pocket billiards player will have ready access to playing sites and other information on the game. [R: LJ, Jan 93, p. 104; RBB, 1 Feb 93, p. 1004]—**Marvin K. Harris**

859. **The Pool Player's Road Atlas 1994.** Manteca, Calif., Que House, 1993. 218p. index. $34.95pa. GV891.P66. 794.7'3. LC 93-23609. ISBN 0-945071-80-9.

The information in this work will benefit players and spectators alike in many ways, from understanding the role of the referee to how to establish which rules will govern play. Pool etiquette, dress codes, tournament play, Calcutta, rules (general and for 8-ball and 9-ball), cue selection, a general glossary, and a hustlers' glossary are covered in the first 75 pages. Definitions included in the rules sections are not repeated in the glossary (e.g., "scoop shot"). "Shot" is nicely defined in the definitions for 9-ball in the rules section. "Completion of stroke," "settling into place," and "stopped" are examples of important details that affect play. One learns that a stroke completion ends when balls become stationary and stop spinning; that a ball that is stopped on the edge of a pocket has five seconds to fall to count for the shooter; and that if it falls too late, it was settling into place and will be replaced. Terms in the hustlers' glossary seem to apply exclusively to the game of 9-ball, but this is not stated. The lists of billiard establishments (organized by state and city) that feature league and tournament play comprise the final two-thirds of the book. Each parlor's address and telephone number are listed and facilities, food, drink, and services are also described.

Travelers looking for a pool game will find this a quick reference that duplicates much of the information in a previous offering from the same publisher, *The Pool Player's National Pocket Billiard Directory* (1992). *The Pool Player's Road Atlas* is the best of this publisher's works for the ordinary pool player and spectator; it is also useful for tournament directors.—**Marvin K. Harris**

SAILING

860. Schult, Joachim. **The Sailing Dictionary.** Revised by Jeremy Howard-Williams. 2d ed. Dobbs Ferry, N.Y., Sheridan House, 1992. 331p. illus. $29.95. GV811.S36613. 797.1'2403. LC 92-19757. ISBN 0-924486-37-6.

Originally published in German as *Segler Lexicon*, this book was translated into English, revised by Barbara Webb, and published in 1981. Now this second English-language edition has been revised by Howard-Williams to reflect changes in rules, laws, and technology. Each alphabetical segment begins with the international alphabet and code flags (e.g., alfa, bravo, charlie). Approximately 4,000 sailing terms are listed and defined. Definitions range from a few words to a half page or more. The text is fully cross-referenced and uses a double-column arrangement, with helpful diagrams and photographs strategically located in the text. The original author, the translator, and the reviser are all experienced in sailing and navigating as well as in writing and editing. The endpapers are color plates showing buoyage systems and the international code of signal flags. The typography is legible and sensible. The work is bound in illustrated calendared paper over boards that should resist staining. This is a comprehensive, up-to-date dictionary useful to both small boat sailors and blue water yachtspeople.—**Frank J. Anderson**

SWIMMING

861. **ALSA Swimmers' Guide: A Directory of Pools for Lap Swimmers.** 1993 ed. By Bill Haverland and Tom Saunders. Miami, Fla., American Lap Swimmers Association, 1993. 366p. maps. $14.95pa. ISBN 0-9635960-0-4. ISSN 1067-4535.

Business travelers who swim for fitness may welcome this directory of approximately 1,200 pools in all 50 states. Most are at least 20 yards long and open 8 or more months a year. However, not all are open to the public; many are available only to members or registered hotel guests. Descriptions include location in relation to nearby landmarks, schedules, disabled access, and locker and towel availability. The book is copyrighted by the American Lap Swimmers Association, despite the fact that the organization does not yet exist. The authors disclaim all liability caused by errors or omissions. Moreover, they warn swimmers that no attempt has been made to ascertain the pools' compliance with safety and sanitary standards. The book would be most useful if carried along by the swimmer-business traveler; otherwise it appears to have limited value.—**Mary Lou LeCompte**

WRESTLING

862. Hein, William S. **The Wrestling College and University Directory.** 2d ed. Buffalo, N.Y., Wrestling Review of Western New York, 1992. 128p. maps. $9.50 spiralbound. ISBN 0-89941-823-6.

The substance of this directory, first published in 1990, is an alphabetical listing of some 400 United States and Canadian college, university, and junior college wrestling programs. Although coaches (and sometimes programs) come and go (some of the information here is already out-of-date), this work is useful for the names, addresses, and telephone numbers of each institution's wrestling coach, athletic director, and sports information director. It also covers conference and national association affiliations, including the NCAA (National Collegiate Athletic Association), NAIA (National Association of Intercollegiate Athletics), NJCAA (National Junior College Athletic Association), NCCAA (National Christian College Athletic Association), and CACC (California Association of Community Colleges). Several indexes group the wrestling programs by conferences (e.g., Big Ten, Midwest Collegiate Athletic Conference), program levels (e.g., NCAA divisions I, II, and III) of national associations, and states and regions.

Much of the advice contained in the brief introductory essays about the dos and don'ts of the recruiting process and finding a college is aimed at high school student athletes (of less than state championship caliber) interested in participating in wrestling at the college level. For additional information, as this directory indicates, student athletes should contact the NCAA or other national associations (names, addresses, and telephone numbers are provided) and consult the several comprehensive standard guides to colleges and universities. The program listings will be most useful to high school coaches, athletic directors, or guidance counselors helping students identify institutions and programs where they can continue their academic and athletic careers. Purchase of this directory would also be appropriate for high school and local public libraries.—**James K. Bracken**

16 Sociology

GENERAL WORKS

863. Jackson, Rebecca. **The 1960s: An Annotated Bibliography of Social and Political Movements in the United States.** Westport, Conn., Greenwood Press, 1992. 237p. index. (Bibliographies and Indexes in American History, no.24). $49.95. Z7164.S66J28. 016.30348'4'0973. LC 92-24261. ISBN 0-313-27255-7.

This work focuses on the social movements of the 1960s: the protest movements, the cultural revolution, religion, music, drugs, hippies and yippies, communes, the arts, the people, the presidency, and politics. There is even a chapter on 1968, which many consider the most crucial year of the decade. The bibliography actually covers 14 years, from 1960 through the resignation of President Nixon in 1974. The reason for the overlap is that two of the most influential movements, civil rights and the anti-Vietnam War protests, began in the 1960s but carried over into the 1970s. However, there is only selective coverage of the civil rights movement as it relates to other movements covered. The chapter on the Vietnam War includes books that depict the war at home and the antiwar movement.

Only books are listed, and only editions that were personally examined by the author are included. Film documentaries and journal articles are not listed. Some of the 1,345 books included were written during the period and give first-hand, graphic accounts of the times; others were written later and contain analysis and interpretation of the events of the times. The annotations are short but adequate. There are subject, author, and title indexes. By going through this bibliography one can get a feeling for the time of turmoil that was the 1960s and early 1970s. [R: Choice, July/Aug 93, p. 1750]—**Robert L. Turner, Jr.**

864. Peters, Jacob, and Doreen L. Smith. **Organizational and Interorganizational Dynamics: An Annotated Bibliography.** Hamden, Conn., Garland, 1992. 270p. index. (Garland Library of Sociology, v.25; Garland Reference Library of Social Science, v.641). $42.00. Z7164.O7P335. 016.3023'5. LC 92-10773. ISBN 0-8240-5304-4.

Two University of Winnipeg sociologists compiled this selective bibliography using a holistic framework that treats organizational and interorganizational processes and outcomes as integrated phenomena. Included are 555 numbered entries citing journal articles, essays, collections, and monographs published in English from 1974 through 1990. Government documents, reviews, reports, dissertations, and conference papers are excluded.

After an informative introduction, the bibliography is presented in three chapters: organizational transformation, divided into organizational change, culture, and power; interorganizational relations, with sections on analysis, interlocking directorates, and joint ventures; and organizational effectiveness. Within each subdivision, entries are listed alphabetically by author. The annotations generally focus on the stated purpose of each work cited, the methodology employed, and key findings. An author index, a journal index, and a subject index complete the volume. Although the primary source for this publication—the online Sociological Abstracts database—can be easily accessed and is more up-to-date, students of organizational analysis will find this printed bibliography helpful and easy to use. [R: Choice, May 93, p. 1446]

—**Leonard Grundt**

865. Walls, David. **The Activist's Almanac: The Concerned Citizen's Guide to the Leading Advocacy Organizations in America.** New York, Fireside/Simon & Schuster, 1993. 431p. illus. index. $18.00pa. HN55.W35. 361.2. LC 92-38161. ISBN 0-671-74634-0.

Designed for concerned citizens and individuals, this book identifies and describes more than 100 nonprofit advocacy organizations in the United States, providing detailed information on each organization's purpose, background, current priorities, members, structure, resources, publications, services, tax status, number of staff, and address and telephone number. (One issue that is not addressed is how the resources are spent.) Arranged in broad subject categories (e.g., the environment, peace and foreign policy, human rights, multi-issue), the book includes 10 chapters on specific topics ranging from homelessness and animal rights to sexuality and conservatism. In each chapter the author discusses the background and history of the movement in general terms and offers a list of organizations. An overview of advocacy trends and realities is addressed in the introduction.

Walls has focused exclusively on those organizations that strive to change public policy, rather than those that simply provide services or perform research. This should be a consideration for readers who are searching for an organization to which they can contribute, financially or otherwise, because there are many charities and nonprofit organizations that are not covered within this parameter. Although this focus keeps the work at a manageable size and allows Walls to include the type of detail that is not found in other resources, readers looking for a wider spectrum from which to choose will need to search other sources, such as *National Directory of Nonprofit Organizations* (see ARBA 93, entry 195) or *Encyclopedia of Associations* (Gale, annual) for further leads and information. [R: Choice, Oct 93, p. 274; JAL, July 93, p. 100; LJ, 1 Mar 93, pp. 70-72]—**Barbara Ittner**

866. Wilson, Janet O., comp. **Intergenerational Readings/Resources 1980-1993: A Bibliography....** 2d ed. Pittsburgh, Pa., University Center for Social and Urban Research, University of Pittsburgh, 1993. 1v. (various paging). index. $15.00 spiralbound.

When the topics of children and the elderly are addressed, the focus of much of the academic and popular literature is generational inequity. This bibliography is a reminder of the many positive outcomes that derive from intergenerational programming: bringing elders, children, and youth together for mutual benefit. References are listed in small sections divided by media type, including books, journals, manuals, newsletters, databases, and videos. A directory of intergenerational programs and curricula is also included. The listings include the years 1980-1993. Where applicable, costs and addresses are provided so that researchers may easily acquire a given source. This work is concise, comprehensive, and easy to use. Highly recommended for intergenerational program planners or libraries serving students in the areas of child study or gerontology.—**Mary Ann Thompson**

AGING

867. Fradkin, Louise G., and Angela Heath. **Caregiving of Older Adults.** Santa Barbara, Calif., ABC-Clio, 1992. 250p. index. (Choices and Challenges: An Older Adult Reference Series). $45.00. HV1461.F68. 362.6. LC 92-34591. ISBN 0-87436-671-2.

The needs of our increasingly aging population for assistance and care, as well as the needs of the caregivers, are addressed in this informative reference work. It is intended primarily as a guide for caregivers, but also for professionals working with them.

Part 1 is a narrative section that provides an overview of the topic. Included are chapters on informal and formal supports; safety and welfare; housing options; nursing home placement; and financial, legal, and insurance issues. There is also information pertaining to the stress management and coping techniques of both caregivers and receivers. Each chapter ends with a list of references for further reading.

Part 2 is an annotated research section. It includes names, addresses, and descriptions of helpful national, regional, and state organizations, as well as supplementary print and nonprint resources. A glossary defines terms used by professionals in the field of aging, and a concluding index provides further access.

The book's information is organized in a convenient, easy-to-use manner. In addition, it is on a timely topic of vital interest to a growing segment of our population. [R: RBB, 15 Jan 93, p. 936]—**Anita Zutis**

868. Kapp, Marshall B., comp. **Ethical Aspects of Health Care for the Elderly: An Annotated Bibliography.** Westport, Conn., Greenwood Press, 1992. 175p. index. (Bibliographies and Indexes in Gerontology, no.17). $45.00. Z6673.35.K36. 016.174'2. LC 92-17776. ISBN 0-313-27490-8.

This is a companion volume to Kapp's 1988 annotated bibliography, *Legal Aspects of Health Care for the Elderly* (see ARBA 89, entry 491). The two provide an expansive overview of scholarly work on moral and judicial questions that pervade health care decisions for the elderly (and the nonelderly, for that matter). Kapp is correct in noting that law and ethics are not the same, but they do overlap to an important extent. The fact that legal citations are underrepresented in the later volume is a good reason why the reader should peruse both. The source material, representing 533 publications from 1980 through late 1991, is organized under 11 broad topics comprising general sources, autonomy, financing, caregiving, care for the critically ill, ethics committees, resuscitation, futile medical treatments, advance treatment directives, defining death, and research with older subjects. The annotations are clear and succinct. There are an author index and a very limited—indeed, inadequate—subject index. Although this volume provides an excellent starting point for research in the topic areas, it is not (nor does it claim to be) a comprehensive guide.—**Bruce Stuart**

869. Mockenhaupt, Robin E., and Kathleen Nelson Boyle. **Healthy Aging.** Santa Barbara, Calif., ABC-Clio, 1992. 362p. index. (Choices and Challenges: An Older Adult Reference Series). $45.00. RA777.6.M64. 613'.0428. LC 92-31474. ISBN 0-87436-642-9.

This title is a valuable addition to the series. It serves as a useful resource for older adults seeking information about such topics as preventive health care, chronic diseases, mental health, diet and nutrition, and substance abuse.

The first 12 chapters are dedicated to dispensing practical advice concerning good health maintenance. Chapter 1, for example, discusses preventive medicine from both a service and a self-care standpoint. Chapters 2 through 13 focus on the ameliorative effects of exercise; the importance of a balanced diet; the use and effects of various medications; substance abuse; injury prevention; heart disease and apoplexy; cancer prevention and treatment; chronic diseases such as diabetes, osteoporosis, and arthritis; sensory changes associated with aging, such as loss of hearing and vision; oral hygiene; and mental health.

The second part of this useful guide identifies various national organizations and associations that are dedicated to health maintenance and disease prevention. Most have local chapters in America's urban and suburban communities. Each listing contains a description of the organization's mission, accompanied by an address and telephone number. The remaining chapters furnish an annotated directory of subject-specific print and nonprint materials such as books, pamphlets, and videocassettes. A glossary of "Healthy Aging" terms and a thorough index complete the text.

Public and academic libraries that have not acquired this series should consider this title a recommended purchase. It is well organized, informative, and positive in outlook. The list of resources for further help makes this book an excellent reference tool for answering questions on the problems and concerns of older adults.—**Kathleen W. Craver**

870. Nuessel, Frank. **The Image of Older Adults in the Media: An Annotated Bibliography.** Westport, Conn., Greenwood Press, 1992. 181p. index. (Bibliographies and Indexes in Gerontology, no.18). $47.95. Z5633.A39N84. 305.26. LC 92-24259. ISBN 0-313-28018-5.

The purpose of this series is "to provide comprehensive reviews and references for the work done in various fields of gerontology." This particular work deals with the way older adults are depicted in the media. A real plus is the broadening inclusion to allow entries that concern attitudes toward older adults as recorded in journal articles, books, dissertations, and the like. The more than 550 items in the bibliography primarily cover the past 20 years, focusing on the present situation and providing information on sources of the extant research. Twenty-one chapters cover attitudes about and portrayals of older adults in such places as bibliographies, communication, cartoons, advertising, magazines, newspapers, literature, and television. The introduction provides a brief but valuable definition of aging, aging studies, and the media, and explains the format and arrangement of this work with a look at future research. Author and subject indexes give easy access to the items included. Individual annotations are complete enough to give the interested reader a good idea of what is in the cited work. The number of entries in each chapter varies from a low of 2 (advice to older adults) to a high of 164 (literature). A danger in such works can be the inclusion of only the portrayals of bad attitudes and opinions, but Nuessel has avoided that pitfall. Research topics range from studies of ancient Rome and biblical times to the contemporary era.

This book is recommended for academic and large public libraries, particularly for collections of materials focused on gerontology. It will prove valuable for anyone working with older adults. [R: Choice, July/Aug 93, p. 1753]—**Edward P. Miller**

871. Palmore, Erdman B., ed. **Developments and Research on Aging: An International Handbook.** Westport, Conn., Greenwood Press, 1993. 429p. index. $79.95. HQ1061.D48. 305.26. LC 92-25737. ISBN 0-313-27785-0.

Joining several recent reference works on gerontology and geriatrics, this is an updated edition of Palmore's *International Handbook on Aging* (Greenwood Press, 1980). Although other works discuss cross-cultural and international aspects of aging, few do so in such depth and over such a range of national experiences. Each of 25 chapters discusses a country in considerable depth and includes statistical tables and charts. The format and emphasis of each varies according to circumstances unique to that country. In general, chapters cover the demographics of the elderly population; economic and social status; living conditions, including housing and transportation; and social policy and medical programs legislated and administered by governments. As appropriate, chapters consider changes in social, economic, and legal mores and their effect on perceptions toward and services for an aging population. Some authors also discuss significant research projects supported by governments or research institutes, information clearinghouses, and gerontological publications. The length and utility of appended reference lists vary: Some are scant, whereas others are substantial and include indigenous and international literatures. An appendix identifies more than 100 international, regional, and national associations concerned with research on gerontology and geriatrics.

Sixteen country entries included here appeared in the previous edition. Of these, many were written by different authors and are substantially revised. One chapter encompasses a united Germany, whereas the chapter on the former Soviet Union tries to discuss circumstances in the new states. Several European countries were deleted, and chapters on the developing nations of Egypt, India, and China were added. Brazil, Uruguay, and Venezuela were replaced by Argentina, Brazil, and Costa Rica. In short, Palmore casts a wide net, covering countries with both high and low percentages of aged populations, developed and developing nations, those with inclusive social welfare systems for the aged and those less developed, homogeneous and ethnically diverse countries, urban and rural societies, and socialist and capitalist governments. [R: RBB, Aug 93, pp. 2086-87; RQ, Winter 93, p. 282]—**Pam M. Baxter**

872. Parham, Iris A., ed. **Gerontological Social Work: An Annotated Bibliography.** Westport, Conn., Greenwood Press, 1993. 207p. index. (Bibliographies and Indexes in Gerontology, no.19). $49.95. Z7164.04G44. 016.3626. LC 92-21543. ISBN 0-313-28538-1.

This book continues a series of gerontological bibliographies by presenting a basic guide for social work practitioners, educators, and researchers. The editor has chosen what she considers the best in books, journals, and bibliographies related to clinical practice, social work education, health services, and general social work issues. The work is organized by topical chapters and by reference type within the chapters, and it is cross-referenced by author and subject. The majority of the selected works are drawn from the 1980s and 1990s and represent the entire body of gerontological literature, not just journals or books specifically for social workers. Each reference is critically reviewed and includes its application to the field of social work. A final chapter on resources lists subscription information for gerontological journals, reviews audiovisuals, and provides directory information for agencies and organizations working with and for older adults.

This book easily meets its goal of providing an overview of the field of social work practice with the elderly and their families. An advantage that this book has over online databases, as noted in the foreword, is the discriminative process used for inclusion of a source. The reference would be helpful for professors and students in many fields, not just social work. [R: Choice, Dec 93, p. 585]

—**Mary Ann Thompson**

873. **Resources for Elders with Disabilities.** 2d ed. Lexington, Mass., Resources for Rehabilitation, 1993. 303p. index. $43.95pa. RA564.8.R47. 362.4'048'0846. LC 92-36446. ISBN 0-929718-11-9.

While recent advances in medical technology and living conditions have resulted in increased longevity for our population, they have also resulted in increased concerns about the diseases and disabling conditions associated with age. This book is an attempt to organize the consequent proliferation of services and products, in both public and private sectors, available to the elderly. It is designed as a sourcebook for the elderly, their families, other caregivers, and professional service providers. Its large-print format facilitates use by those with vision impairment.

A chapter discussing approaches to and attitudes toward aging and disabilities precedes others that deal with laws affecting elders with disabilities; specific health conditions, such as hearing and vision loss, diabetes, arthritis, Parkinson's disease, strokes, and osteoporosis; and safety recommendations for everyday living. Each chapter has an informative introductory narrative that is several pages long. This is followed by a list of references and extensive annotated lists of relevant organizations, with addresses and telephone numbers; publications and tapes; and resources for assistive devices, if appropriate. The book has an index of organizations listed in the chapters.

This guide is a timely and useful publication. Future editions that contain updated and additional information will be helpful in keeping up with growing needs in this area. [R: LJ, 15 April 93, p. 88]

—Anita Zutis

874. **Senior Citizen Services: How to Find and Contact 15,000 Providers.** Charles B. Montney and Jolen Marya Gedridge, eds. Detroit, Gale, 1993. 4v. index. $90.00/set. ISBN 0-8103-8319-5.

The dispersion of American families has led to a situation in which many older adults may be living at a distance from their primary social network. Thus many national and regional guides to services for older adults have been produced. *Senior Citizen Services* is a new addition to this type of reference guide. Four regional volumes, covering the Northeast, the South and mid-Atlantic, the Midwest, and the West, provide information on a wide range of senior services that receive funding through the Older Americans Act. Most of the listed services are free or low cost. The books do not list nursing homes, groups with political or national involvement, or services for the general public. A glossary in each volume defines terms used to describe the services, such as "case management" or "congregate meals," so that the user can be clear on what is available.

Entries are listed alphabetically by state, city or county, and agency name. The main directory section provides addresses and telephone numbers, services, hours, and eligibility. Two cross-referenced indexes are included. Key words at the top of each page, large print, and highlighted headings make the volumes easy to read and use.

These books provide a basic list of senior services in every area of the United States. The information is not comprehensive. Visibly absent, for example, is an entry for a home health agency serving each of the communities. However, a person seeking a service not listed could readily locate it by making one or two calls to the providers that are listed. Recommended for public libraries. [R: Choice, July/Aug 93, p. 1755; LJ, 1 May 93, p. 83; RBB, 15 May 93, p. 1724; RQ, Summer 93, pp. 577-78; WLB, May 93, p. 122]

—Mary Ann Thompson

875. Solomon, David H., and others. **A Consumer's Guide to Aging.** Baltimore, Md., Johns Hopkins University Press, 1992. 526p. illus. index. $45.00; $22.95pa. HQ1063.2.U6C66. 305.26'0973. LC 91-41587. ISBN 0-8018-4301-4; 0-8018-4302-2pa.

The proliferation of books on aging for the layperson reflects the increase of older adults within the baby boom cohort. Although this book is designed for adults over 50, it will provide relevant information for those persons in their thirties and forties who are facing the aging of family members. The authors, who are social workers and physicians, write a nationally syndicated column on aging, and the contents of this book reflect the interests and concerns of their readers. Individual chapters address the usual topics of fitness, physical health, insurance, finances, housing, work, and leisure. Subjects that are often excluded or superficially discussed, such as intimacy, family roles, and emotions, are also included. Each chapter provides general knowledge about the topic and ends with resources and directory information for obtaining more in-depth data.

This book is written for the layperson. It contains simple sentences, a friendly style, and large print, making it easy to read. Short vignettes are integrated throughout the chapters to ground the contents in the real experiences of older adults. The inclusion of a broad array of topics in a usable format makes this guide an excellent one-stop resource on aging. Highly recommended for public libraries or specialty libraries serving older adults.—**Mary Ann Thompson**

COMMUNITY LIFE

876. **Guide to Federal Funding for Housing and Homeless Programs.** Charles J. Edwards and Jeanne M. Williams, eds. Arlington, Va., Government Information Services, 1992. 1v. (various paging). index. $177.95 looseleaf w/binder. ISBN 0-933544-52-9.

Federal programs providing more than $26 billion are described in this guide. The 54 housing and 31 homeless program descriptions list appropriation levels, eligibility requirements, application cycles, proper uses of the funds, how to apply, and key federal contacts. The guide begins with a 25-page overview describing federal housing efforts, giving instructions for using the guide, and listing resource organizations. Section 1 covers housing programs such as preservation of low-income housing and homes for elderly and disabled people, while section 2 includes information about family support centers, emergency shelter grants, and other forms of assistance to homeless persons. A detailed table of contents and a subject index help users find relevant material.

Entries are clearly written and well presented, but it is possible to find the same information from such sources as the *Catalog of Federal Domestic Assistance* (see ARBA 84, entry 651). Further, the guide's three-ring-binder format is a distinct disadvantage in libraries, where looseleaf pages tend to disappear. While agencies seeking funds related to housing and homelessness will find the guide a convenience, libraries can live without it.—**Cheryl Knott Malone**

877. Henslin, James M. **Homelessness: An Annotated Bibliography.** Hamden, Conn., Garland, 1993. 2v. index. (Garland Reference Library of Social Science, v.534). $125.00/set. Z7164.H72H46. 016.3625. LC 92-41254. ISBN 0-8240-4115-1.

This annotated bibliography is a much-needed resource for practitioners and researchers from various fields studying the problem of homelessness, particularly in the United States. The entries, gathered from numerous sources, cover both scholarly and popular publications. Following the main bibliography of citations and annotations in volume 1, Henslin lists citations in volume 2 under 41 subtopics. The extensive collection identifies literature on homelessness from past and contemporary eras. Annotations are clear and concisely written. Topical headings provide a comprehensive picture of the multifaceted nature of the problem of homelessness.

This set makes a valuable contribution to the field of human services and to those interested in understanding this prevailing human need. It is highly recommended for educational and professional libraries. [R: Choice, Sept 93, p. 82; RBB, 1 Sept 93, p. 88; WLB, June 93, pp. 124-26]

—**Maria O'Neil McMahon**

878. **National Directory of Fire Chiefs & Emergency Departments, 1993.** 2d ed. Stevens Point, Wis., SPAN Publishing, 1993. 910p. $40.00pa. ISBN 1-880245-04-3.

This directory includes ambulance and emergency medical services as well as volunteer, public, county, and private fire or emergency departments. The largest portion of the directory is a state-by-state and then city or town listing of fire departments, fire chiefs, and emergency services available in the United States. For each the complete address and telephone and fax numbers are provided, as well as the kind of organization, such as volunteer or hospital-based. The work also lists national organizations and associations dealing with trauma and critical care, along with address and telephone and fax numbers. Another section lists state emergency service directors (EMS), again with complete addresses and telephone numbers. A products and services guide lists publications, products, and services dealing with fire fighting and emergency care. Because this guide is very specialized it would be of most value to libraries dealing with law enforcement, to fire and police departments, and to companies selling goods in this area.—**Marilyn Strong Noronha**

DEATH

879. Creighton-Zollar, Ann. **The Social Correlates of Infant and Reproductive Mortality in the United States: A Reference Guide.** Hamden, Conn., Garland, 1993. 214p. index. (Reference Books on Family Issues, v.22; Garland Reference Library of Social Science, v.766). $33.00. Z7164.D3Z64. 304.6'4'0832. LC 92-41215. ISBN 0-8153-0221-5.

This reference contains a bibliography focused on the social correlates of infant and reproductive mortality in the United States. The entries are limited to English-language publications that were identified by searching three CD-ROM databases, ERIC, PsycLIT, and Medline. In addition to 985 effectively annotated references on the social correlates of infant and reproductive mortality in the United States, this reference also includes author and subject indexes. The first 60 pages provide an introduction and background to the issue, followed by a chapter on the social factors related to these problems. Two additional chapters discuss sudden infant death syndrome and maternal and reproductive mortality. This reference guide is a useful and valuable source for those interested in gaining insight into and information on this topic or for those doing scholarly work on it. [R: Choice, Nov 93, p. 426]—**Robert L. Jones**

DISABLED

880. **Living with Low Vision: A Resource Guide for People with Sight Loss.** Lexington, Mass., Resources for Rehabilitation, 1993. 271p. index. $35.00pa. ISBN 0-929718-09-7.

In our current fast-paced, technologically oriented society, individuals who suffer from varying degrees of sight loss often find it difficult to maintain employment or even live satisfactory lives. This useful guide to organizations, publications, and devices intended for this handicapped population is an extremely valuable reference text for all public, academic, and health care libraries. It is available in both standard and large type. The work is organized into 12 chapters, each containing annotated lists of national or regional organizations; print and media materials; and, when available, devices designed for particular groups of the visually impaired. Specific chapters examine the unique needs of sight-impaired children, adolescents, veterans, and elderly individuals; other sections cover the general population of visually impaired persons. Material presented ranges from how to keep working after sight loss to improving this group's everyday lifestyle, including specifically designed recreational opportunities. Of particular value is the chapter that details the protection afforded the visually impaired by federal laws. The appendix lists the addresses and telephone numbers for major state agencies that serve those people with sight loss.

—**Jonathon Erlen**

881. **Meeting the Needs of Employees with Disabilities.** 2d ed. Lexington, Mass., Resources for Rehabilitation, 1993. 208p. index. $42.95pa. HD7256.U5M445. 658.3'045. LC 93-12504. ISBN 0-929718-13-5.

882. **Resources for People with Disabilities and Chronic Conditions.** 2d ed. Lexington, Mass., Resources for Rehabilitation, 1993. 272p. index. $44.95pa. HV1559.U6R47. 362.1'0425. LC 93-18551. ISBN 0-929718-12-7.

According to estimates, there are anywhere from 36 to 43 million people in this country with disabilities or chronic conditions. While the services for this population are growing, there are many affected individuals who are unaware of these services or their eligibility requirements. These guides are intended to help them and their family members, employers, and service providers find appropriate services that can maximize their independence and productive employment.

Meeting the Needs of Employees with Disabilities includes information aimed at keeping disabled employees at work. Chapters focus on such subjects as federal laws, environmental adaptations, assistive technology, and the school-to-work transition, as well as specific conditions such as mobility, speech, hearing, and visual impairments. Chapters include both a narrative section and an annotated guide to organizations, publications, software, and tapes. Because of the emphasis on employment-related issues, this volume does not include descriptions of the diseases, psychological concerns, or health care specialists. There are an appendix of state rehabilitation agencies and an index of organizations cited in the text.

Resources for People with Disabilities and Chronic Conditions is arranged into 11 chapters, most of which deal with specific conditions, such as communication disorders, visual impairment, epilepsy, multiple sclerosis, and diabetes. Each chapter includes an overview of the causes of the condition and, if applicable, a discussion of the needs of children and the elderly. There are also descriptions of the psychological aspects of the condition, professional service providers, the location of services, and assistive devices. This is accompanied by an annotated directory of organizations, publications, software, tapes, and guides to or providers of assistive devices. The first four chapters provide information and resources helpful in coping with all of the disabilities and chronic conditions. Similar to the other volume, this one includes an appendix of state rehabilitation agencies and an index of cited organizations.

There is some overlap of information between these two volumes, both in the narrative sections and in the annotated directories. However, the volume about employees with disabilities does include unique and useful discussions of employment-related issues. If money is not a concern, both volumes would make valuable additions to public library collections. [R: LJ, 1 Sept 93, p. 176] —**Stephen H. Aby**

883. **The National Housing Directory for People with Disabilities, 1993.** Leslie Mackenzie and others, eds. Lakeville, Conn., Grey House, 1993. 1429p. index. $150.00pa. ISBN 0-939300-13-3pa. [Hardcover version: Detroit, Gale, 1993. $180.00. ISBN 0-939300-22-2.]

Information on appropriate housing for people with physical and mental disabilities is not easy to come by. Until now, it has been scattered across a variety of sources, agencies, and organizations, making the search for answers frustrating. This directory cuts through this maze by providing social service professionals and disabled individuals with listings of approximately 20,000 public and private organizations, agencies, services, and facilities that provide or help to locate housing that meets specific needs.

The entries are arranged alphabetically by state. Within each state are listed relevant state agencies, referral agencies, intensive and intermediate care facilities, licensed group homes, and independent living facilities. Information on these facilities and services varies and may include not only the address and telephone number but also details on accessibility, funding, administration, referral agencies, disabilities served, accreditation, and ownership. Descriptions of group homes and independent living facilities may also include the number of clients or units, the age range of clients, the number and qualifications of professional staff, and (less often) the cost. The directory also has a list of federal government and national organizations, an alphabetical entry name index, and an appended one-page list of relevant associations.

This directory is projected to be updated annually. Of course, it remains to be seen if the contents change substantially enough to warrant purchasing an update every year. However, there is no mistaking the directory's value in meeting an essential need for an important, and probably inadequately served, social group. To ensure equity and good service, public libraries should update the directory regularly if their budgets allow. [R: LJ, 1 April 93, p. 92; RBB, 15 Mar 93, pp. 1377-78; RQ, Summer 93, pp. 374-75]—**Stephen H. Aby**

884. **Rehabilitation Resource Manual: Vision.** Lexington, Mass., Resources for Rehabilitation, 1993. 256p. index. $39.95pa. ISBN 0-929718-10-0.

A resource for librarians and health care service providers, this book offers nine chapters of professional organizations, publications, and referral resources concerned with the needs of people with visual impairments. For example, chapter 6, "Employment for People with Vision Loss," has a list of journals related to vocational rehabilitation and counseling. These resources follow a narrative (and in some instances a case vignette) that explains the relevance of the references to the chapter topic.

Each of the resources is indexed at the end of the book. There is a significant amount of listing duplication. In some cases the same entry is indexed four times. One benefit of this format is that the reader is provided with the most relevant resources connected with the narratives.

The narrative is not always appropriate for its intended audience of professionals. The advice and direction given is at a very basic, commonsense level. The chapter labeled "Starting a Self-Help Group" seems mislabeled, as it is not directed at vision-impaired individuals but at service providers, who are inherently disqualified from starting a self-help group (unless one of them also assumed the role of the visually impaired consumer). The case studies, which attempt to "illustrate multidisciplinary cooperation in providing services," are somewhat arbitrarily placed throughout the book, with no lead-ins or tie-ins to the rest of the chapters. Boxed advertisements are sporadically and prominently displayed along with the listings of the resources. It would have been better to group all advertisements at the end of the book. This would separate the vendor-specific sales information from the resources listings and would enhance the book's appearance.—**Jeanne Friedrichs**

FAMILY, MARRIAGE, AND DIVORCE

885. **Loving Journeys Guide to Adoption.** By Elaine L. Walker. Peterborough, N.H., Loving Journeys, 1992. 394p. maps. index. $24.95pa. HV875.55.W35. 362'.7'34'0973. LC 92-093516. ISBN 0-9633642-0-0.

This guide consists of two parts. Part 1 is an overview of adoption that explains the general requirements and procedures. It lists what kinds of children are available, how to adopt through an agency, how to adopt independently, and what it is like to adopt internationally. Part 2 is a directory listing adoption attorneys, American adoption programs, international adoption programs, public adoption agencies, adoptive parent support groups, and newspapers that accept advertisements for independent adoption. Although the book disclaims any warranty regarding specific adoption programs, agencies, or attorneys, and although it is intended only as an introduction to adoption, it appears to be a very useful guide for those seeking to adopt a child. It will serve as a useful primary adoption guide or as a companion to *The Adoption Resource Guide* (see ARBA 92, entry 882) or *The Adoption Directory* (see ARBA 90, entry 799). [R: RBB, 15 Feb 93, p. 1082]—**Nathan M. Smith**

886. Nehmer, Kathleen Suttles, ed. **Educators Guide to Free Home Economics and Consumer Education Materials.** 10th ed. Randolph, Wis., Educators Progress Service, 1993. 289p. index. $23.95. ISBN 0-87708-260-X.

One of the most frequent questions asked by library users is, "Where can I get free materials on topic X?" This unique title will be a real plus for those who need information on nutrition, family education, or consumer education. This "rainbow" edition (it has a blue title index, a yellow subject index, and a goldenrod source index) of resources includes films, videocassettes, slides, filmstrips, and pamphlet or document materials on a variety of topics. The editor gives a detailed list of significant features included in this edition and a guide for ordering materials. Each of the entries includes a brief description of the material, date, type of format, length if appropriate, and publication information. In the source index, full information is given for the source as well as such requirements as postage payment. A cross-reference is given to the pages within the sourcebook that have items from this source.

This will be a useful tool for school and public libraries that need information in these areas. It would also be useful for academic libraries supporting teacher education in home economics and consumer education. Timeliness might be the only issue if the sources become unavailable quickly.—**Mary J. Stanley**

PHILANTHROPY

Bibliography

887. Bull, C. Neil, and Nancy D. Levine, comps. **The Older Volunteer: An Annotated Bibliography.** Westport, Conn., Greenwood Press, 1993. 111p. index. (Bibliographies and Indexes in Gerontology, no.21). $49.95. Z7164.V65B85. 016.30526. LC 92-41898. ISBN 0-313-28125-4.

This new title is intended to serve as an up-to-date reference for researchers, practitioners, and planners interested in the older volunteer. Organized into 7 chapters, each with relevant topical subsections, approximately 400 entries cover a wide variety of subject areas and disciplines for the period 1980 to 1991 in North America. Citations come from a review of books, book chapters, articles, paper presentations, reports, theses, and dissertations. They cover particular programs, characteristics of older volunteers, sources of statistical information, empirical research, and special population groups. The subject and author indexes are helpful not only for locating specific topical references but also as indicators of the expanding breadth and scope of literature on the older volunteer. Where applicable, entries are cross-referenced between chapters, with the annotation in one chapter and a reference to it in another. The multiplicity of topics covered in this specific review of relevant literature highlights the emerging role in our society of the relationship between volunteering and aging. [R: Choice, Oct 93, p. 264; RQ, Winter 93, p. 292]—**Roslyn Attinson**

Directories

888. **Annual Register of Grant Support: A Directory of Funding Sources.** 26th ed. New Providence, N.J., R. R. Bowker/Reed Reference Publishing, 1992. 1231p. index. $165.00. LC 69-18307. ISBN 0-8352-3293-X. ISSN 0066-4049.

The 1993 version of the *Annual Register* retains the previous format, organizing more than 3,000 sources of funding in categories within the broad classes of humanities, international affairs and area studies, special populations, urban and regional affairs, education, sciences, social sciences, physical sciences, life sciences, and technology and industry. Indexes by subject, organization and program, geographical location, and personnel provide access points to the program descriptions. Information in the descriptions comes from the organizations listed, usually including the funding source's name, address, top personnel or board members, types of grants awarded and their purposes, eligibility requirements, and geographical restrictions. Participants in the $123 billion grants sweepstakes will appreciate the listing of the previous year's number of applicants and number of awards (when provided) for calculating the probability of success before embarking on a lengthy proposal-writing project.

If the three-inch-thick *Annual Register* gets the kind of use it should, the physical packaging may wear out before the information does. Serious researchers with money to invest in prospecting will turn to online files, such as the Foundation Center's Foundation Directory and Oryx Press's Grants, to take advantage of larger databases, Boolean search capabilities, and flexible output options. Still, the *Annual Register of Grant Support* remains a reasonably priced basic source.—**Cheryl Knott Malone**

889. **Directory of Operating Grants: An Innovative Reference Directory Pinpointing General Operating Grants Available to Nonprofit Organizations.** Loxahatchee, Fla., Research Grant Guides, 1992. 144p. index. $42.50pa. ISBN 0-945078-05-6.

This work focuses on foundations that award general operating grants to nonprofit organizations. Foundation profiles, each with an entry number, are listed alphabetically within states. A subject index cross-references 17 operating support grant areas (e.g., AIDS, education) with the entry number of foundations providing such support. Unlike the Foundation Center's *New York State Foundations* (1991), which includes some 5,000 independent, company-sponsored, and community foundations covering a broad range of program areas, this directory covers 640 foundations that provide operating grants, of which approximately 50 are in New York state. Two introductory articles on cultivating donors and proposal-writing basics are very helpful. Appendix A provides a bibliography of available local and state directories. There is also an alphabetical index of the included foundations.—**Roslyn Attinson**

890. **The Foundation Directory.** 15th ed. Compiled by the Foundation Center. Stan Olson and Margaret Mary Feczko, eds. New York, Foundation Center, 1993. 1404p. index. $185.00; $160.00pa. ISBN 0-87954-484-8; 0-87954-499-6. ISSN 0071-8092.

891. **The Foundation Directory. Part 2: A Guide to Grant Programs $50,000-$200,000.** 1993 ed. Stan Olson, Carlotta Mills, and Linda Tobiasen, eds. New York, Foundation Center, 1993. 973p. index. $160.00pa. ISBN 0-87954-489-9.

The Foundation Directory is the standard annual reference source for information about private and community grantmaking foundations in the United States. It includes descriptive entries of 6,334 foundations with assets of at least $2,000,000 or annual giving of at least $200,000. The entries represent 20 percent of all active grantmaking foundations in the United States, awarding more than 90 percent of all foundation giving in the latest year of record. Foundation information is arranged alphabetically by states, and within states by foundation name. Entries for each foundation include areas of foundation giving, types of grants and other types of support, specific limitations on foundation giving by geographical area, subject focus or types of support, and application information. Each descriptive entry is assigned a sequence number that is used as a reference in each of the indexes, which provide access to entries according to donors, officers, and trustees; geographical distribution; types of support; subject areas; foundations new to this edition; and foundation name. Fund-raisers will find carefully researched data that covers a broad range of program areas. There is also a helpful section on publications and services of the Foundation Center as well as a glossary of terms used in the grants process.

The Foundation Directory. Part 2 is a companion volume to *The Foundation Directory* that can also stand alone as a guide to smaller but significant grantmakers whose charitable giving often supports local organizations. It provides complete descriptive information on 4,327 private and community foundations in the United States that make annual grants totaling $50,000 to less than $200,000 and that hold assets of less than $2,000,000. Foundation information is arranged as in the *The Foundation Directory*. In addition, *Part 2* descriptive entries include lists of sample grants whenever available. These provide concrete indications of the foundation's fields of interest, geographical preferences, and monetary range of giving. *Part 2* has five indexes: donors, officers, and trustees; geographical distribution; types of support; subject areas; and foundation name.—**Roslyn Attinson**

892. **Guide to U.S. Foundations, Their Trustees, Officers, and Donors.** Compiled by the Foundation Center. C. Edward Murphy and Joan Seabourne, eds. New York, Foundation Center, 1993. 2v. index. $195.00pa./set. ISBN 0-87954-488-0.

This new work is a comprehensive list of some 34,000 private, community, and operating nongovernmental and nonprofit organizations that offer grants to outside applicants or that allocate their funds to their own research or to charitable programs. This directory replaces *National Data Book of Foundations* (see ARBA 93, entry 879), which was published by the Foundation Center from 1973 to 1992, and includes additional information: contact person and telephone number; geographical limitations; application information; and foundation trustees, officials, and donors. Foundations from those that grant as little as a dollar to those that provide funding in the millions of dollars are covered.

The new guide has two volumes and a supplement. Volume 1 contains five sections, the largest of which is section 1, on independent, company-sponsored, and community foundations. Section 2, on operating foundations, describes organizations that use their resources to provide services or conduct research. The first two sections are both arranged alphabetically by state; entries within each state are listed in descending order by total grant amounts paid. Section 3 consists of an appendix on foundations that have terminated, merged with other foundations, or are no longer eligible for inclusion in the guide. Section 4 is an alphabetical foundation name index, and section 5 is a community foundation name index. Because the guide does not have a subject index to identify grants by fields of interest, it is very important to use the cross-references provided.

Volume 2 contains two major parts: an alphabetical foundation trustee, officer, and donor index, and the foundation locator, which provides an alphabetical list of all of the foundations in volume 1 accompanied by the state in which they are located and codes that indicate other Foundation Center publications that might provide additional information about a particular funding organization. The supplement provides information on an additional 417 foundations identified after April 1993 that did not appear in the first edition of the guide.

This set can serve as a first step in identifying prospective funding sources in a local community or geographical area and potential connections between an organization and a grant funding source. It is the most comprehensive source of information related to sources of funding and is of utmost importance to libraries.—**Lois J. Buttlar**

893. **Major Donors 1993: A Listing of More Than 8,000 Individuals Who Have Recently Donated Major Gifts to America's Largest Nonprofit Organizations.** Mark W. Scott, ed. Rockville, Md., Taft Group; distr., Detroit, Gale, 1993. 528p. index. $175.00pa. ISBN 1-879784-35-1. ISSN 1061-1266.

This title is a compilation of more than 8,000 individual donors to charities and other nonprofit organizations. The main entries are arranged alphabetically by the donors' last names. Included within each entry are recipient organization, recipient location, donation amount, special fund within the organization to which the donation was made, and support type (which classifies the type of support provided by the donor). A list of organizations, an index to donors by organizations, and an index to donors by state of support are supplied. The latter index would be more useful if the area of interest or support given was identified, rather than just the donor's name.

This volume could be useful for coursework in philanthropic studies. Individuals looking for potential support might also find it a good tool for locating people who sponsor their intended research or need. Fund-raising organizations will find this item particularly helpful to identify donors by state or area of interest. Recommended for those libraries that have other sources in fund raising or financial support.—**Mary J. Stanley**

894. Woodworth, David, with Giles Smart, eds. **The International Directory of Voluntary Work.** 5th ed. Oxford, England, Vacation Work; distr., Princeton, N.J., Peterson's Guides, 1993. 264p. index. $15.95pa. ISBN 1-85458-085-X. ISSN 0143-3474.

This work sets out to cover the full range of voluntary work: long-term positions away from home that last for over a year, opportunities requiring only an occasional commitment, and short-term placements lasting a few weeks or months for volunteers who are able to make temporary interruptions in their normal ways of life. The first part of the directory details more than 400 organizations offering residential voluntary work throughout the world. More than 300 of these entries are for short-term placements, and they are arranged alphabetically within geographical categories (Asia/Australia, Africa, Israel, the Americas, Europe, United Kingdom, and worldwide). The rest are long-term opportunities worldwide.

The second part of the directory is devoted to the United Kingdom and covers more than 200 nonresidential volunteer opportunities, the majority of which are part-time in nature. References are arranged in alphabetical order within categories of placements: national, local, children and youth, community projects, conservation and the environment, elderly people, education, hospitals, prisons and probation, sick and disabled people, emergencies and housing, pressure groups, fund-raising and office work, and advice and counseling. Few, if any, of the voluntary opportunities described involve work formerly done by paid professionals.

Users who are exploring potential international volunteer opportunities will find this work to be a worthwhile source of information. Opportunities can be located within geographical areas; or if the user is looking for a specific organization, it can be located via the index of organizations.—**Roslyn Attinson**

Handbooks and Yearbooks

895. Chelekis, George. **The Action Guide to Government Grants, Loans, and Giveaways: The Comprehensive Guide to Getting Millions of Dollars....** New York, Perigee Books/Putnam, 1993. 510p. $24.95pa. HG177.5.U6C438. 658.15'224. LC 92-38818. ISBN 0-399-51792-8.

This work has been written primarily for the individual (e.g., businessperson, prospective homeowner, real estate investor, college student, researcher, artist) to provide a comprehensive, helpful guide through the bureaucratic maze of government funding. The introductory section covers eligibility for various grants, loans, and other financial help from federal and state government sources; it reviews the process of writing and presenting grant proposals. The extensive section on business programs includes information on funding sources, identifying the types of assistance, applicant and beneficiary eligibility, application procedure, range of approval and disapproval, regulations, guidelines and literature, and headquarters. Also listed, by state, are the field, district, and branch offices of the Small Business Administration and other useful directories for specialized federal programs and agencies as well as state grants, loans, and assistance. The section on personal benefits programs covers a variety of information on urban housing, farmers' credit assistance, veterans' affairs, guaranteed loans, state housing and real estate money, Federal Educational Assistance programs, and federal assistance for the arts and humanities. Suggested reading materials for each chapter are included in the appendix, along with a useful glossary of terms, acronyms, and abbreviations used in the loan or grant procedure. The writing style is simple and direct; the material is well organized for easy and selective access. [R: LJ, 15 Feb 93, p. 156]

—**Roslyn Attinson**

896. **Foundation Giving: Yearbook of Facts and Figures on Private, Corporate and Community Foundations.** 1993 ed. By Loren Renz and Steven Lawrence. New York, Foundation Center, 1993. 104p. $19.95pa. ISBN 0-87954-504-6.

In 1972 the Foundation Center began to develop a comprehensive database on private and community foundations, and in 1980 the Center began to consistently classify grants of the 100 largest foundations. These foundations set trends and patterns that, if reviewed over time, can give grant seekers a way of determining the needs that foundations are interested in supporting. This guide tries to give an authoritative review of the size and scope of foundations and their grants. Concentrating on the trends and developments of 1991 and the last 10 years, it gives the researcher a look at what subject areas are supported, the types of support, recipient organizations, and special beneficiaries of 33,356 grant-making foundations.

Information is broken down by region and state. The display of data in 83 tables and figures gives guidance to and perspective on the world of private foundation philanthropy. An overview of the aggregate giving of various foundations is listed, but little information on specific foundations is available, except for the largest. Trends in giving in education, health, arts, culture, humanities, human services, public benefit, environment and animal wildlife, social sciences, international affairs, and peace are all reviewed extensively. For the researcher seeking information on grant procedures and processes, the appendixes are excellent. They review regulation and classification systems for grants, list cooperating collections of special foundation resource centers in libraries throughout the United States, and provide a small bibliography of important documents and directories in foundation giving.

The price of this tool makes it affordable for even a small public library in a progressive community, and it is an excellent resource for academic, research, and public libraries. Highly recommended.
—**Gerald D. Moran**

897. **The Foundation 1000 1992/1993: In-Depth Profiles of the 1000 Largest U.S. Foundations.** Francine Jones and Georgetta Toth, eds. New York, Foundation Center, 1992. 2810p. index. $195.00pa. ISBN 0-87954-445-7.

Formerly titled *Source Book Profiles* (see ARBA 89, entry 768) and issued with quarterly updates, this newly renamed annual provides detailed information about the wealthiest foundations in the United States in an effort to help potential beneficiaries compete for top dollars. Arranged in alphabetical order by foundation name, the descriptive entries provide much in addition to the address, telephone number, contact person, and kinds of awards made. Most valuable is each entry's grants analysis section, in which well-organized tables clearly quantify a foundation's interests by subject area, type of recipient, and geographical location. The Foundation Center gathered the data from the organizations listed, news sources, and the Internal Revenue Service. Individual, family, and corporate foundations are included. Four indexes—to donors, officers, and trustees; by subject; by type of support; and geographical—enhance the volume's usability.

Although the typeface and layout are improved over the earlier versions, this single paperbound volume of more than 2,800 pages is subject to rapid wear. Libraries serving aggressive grant-seekers will want *The Foundation 1000* as will those supporting in-depth research on the giving practices of the biggest foundations in the United States.—**Cheryl Knott Malone**

898. **Funding Decision Makers 1993: Comprehensive Guide to Donor Connections.** 2d ed. S. David Hicks and Bohdan R. Romaniuk, eds. Rockville, Md., Taft Group; distr., Detroit, Gale, 1993. 1196p. index. $170.00pa. ISBN 1-879784-46-7. ISSN 1058-1235.

Keeping in mind that the vast majority of philanthropic contributions are made by individuals rather than by corporations, the Taft Group seeks to become the reference authority on the organized portion of contemporary philanthropy. Corporate and foundation officers are far more easily traceable than are individuals, and the Taft Group has made the most of compiling information from available sources.

Funding Decision Makers guides users to more than 23,000 individuals from approximately 7,800 foundations and corporate direct giving programs. Together these individuals "control more than $10 billion in grants annually, the lion's share of all corporate and foundation giving" (p. vi). Those listed include foundation chairs, trustees, directors, and administrators; direct giving executives; advisory board and grant committee members; members of public charities; and wealthy donors identified with corporate foundations and direct givers providing grants at all levels, or organizations that contribute at least $200,000 annually in cash or that have a minimum of $1.5 million in assets. Entries are arranged alphabetically by name, with numerous entries identifying place of birth; education; and funding, corporate, and nonprofit affiliations. Users can then begin to draw profiles of key individuals.

Entries about significant individuals are available, of course, in much more detail in traditional biographical sources. But this work brings them all together and enhances access through a strong indexing system. Separate indexes are devoted to place of birth and to college/university, corporate, nonprofit, and funding affiliations. The funding affiliations index provides addresses, telephone numbers, and names of key individuals. This work is far from comprehensive; one can think of philanthropic groups not covered and individuals omitted. But one can also spend an afternoon (or an entire lifetime) conducting sociological research about the decisionmakers, planning a fund-raising strategy, or designing the next capital campaign. This work is an organized compilation of paper trails, not to be missed for understanding the interests of key corporate officers.—**John Mark Tucker**

899. Hicks, S. David, ed. **Fund Raiser's Guide to Human Service Funding 1993.** 4th ed. Rockville, Md., Taft Group, 1993. 735p. index. $99.00pa. ISBN 1-879784-44-0. ISSN 1045-1951.

This work provides current contact, financial, and other important information on more than 1,100 of the leading private foundations, corporate foundations, and corporate direct givers that are active in funding nonprofit human service organizations. In the main section each organizational profile is arranged alphabetically by the name of the funding organization. Each profile gives the following information, when available: contact person (with title, address, and telephone number), financial information of the funding organization (including assets and the total amount of giving), the organization's geographical preferences for funding, grant types and recipient types, officers and directors, application procedures (a section that lists miscellaneous information that gives ideas, hints, and guidelines for getting the grants), and recent grants. This information is then sorted in indexes to headquarters location, to geographical preference, to grant type, to recipient type, to officers and directors, and to grant recipients by state and city. What is missing is an index on average grant amounts given and the organizations that give in that financial range. This index would help those who know approximately what they may need to focus on those organizations that grant in those ranges. The paperback will need to be rebound fairly quickly as it is flimsy.—**Robert L. Turner, Jr.**

900. Jones, Francine, and Georgetta Toth, eds. **Corporate Foundation Profiles.** 7th ed. New York, Foundation Center, 1992. 757p. index. $125.00pa. LC 80-69622. ISBN 0-87954-437-6.

This title provides detailed statistical information about the philanthropic pursuits of company-sponsored foundations in the United States. In other words, how many grants did the foundations make, in what fields or geographical locales were they made, and who were the lucky recipients? *Corporate Foundation Profiles* is divided into two major sections and three indexes. Part 1 constitutes most of the volume. It contains of in-depth information for 247 of the largest grantmakers. Part 2 contains 2 lists "of the 1,012 company-sponsored foundations with assets of $1 million or more or annual giving of $100,000 or more in 1989, 1990, or 1991." The first list is a statistical arrangement of annual giving by foundations in descending order from largest to smallest. The second list is an alphabetical list of the same foundations. The three indexes provide subject, type of support, and geographical access to the foundations listed in part 1.

Corporate Foundation Profiles is a companion to the other publications of the prestigious Foundation Center. Libraries desiring statistical philanthropic data may elect to purchase *Corporate 500* (see ARBA 92, entry 823). *Corporate 500* gives comparable in-depth information for the top 500 company-sponsored foundations in the United States. Academic and public libraries, as well as libraries that serve agencies seeking grants, need one or both of these titles.—**Dene L. Clark**

901. McLean, Janice W., ed. **Directory of Fund Raising and Nonprofit Management Consultants.** Rockville, Md., Taft Group; distr., Detroit, Gale, 1992. 390p. index. $49.00pa. ISBN 0-930807-25-1.

As in virtually every aspect of a highly professional and highly technical society, individuals and groups have come to recognize the need for consultants. The nonprofits, having the same needs, require guidance not only with fund-raising activity but also with the improvement of performance in management practices, in personnel development, in forecasting, and in economic matters generally.

The preface by Joanne Hayes, president of the American Association of Fund-Raising Counsel (AAFRC), discusses the work of a consultant, what the hiring nonprofits should expect in the way of consultant services, and what they should plan to do themselves. She provides tips on choosing a firm, evaluating the proposals of a firm, and the cost of counsel. She notes that, in matters of pricing, the AAFRC has adopted a Fair Practice Code and that consultants for nonprofits should proudly display their adherence to the code as well as their membership in the AAFRC.

This directory ought to become an effective tool to help nonprofit organizations identify those firms, large and small, that specialize in providing services to nonprofits. McLean has arranged entries into a section for consultants and a section for trainers. These two sections are accessed by geographical and personal name indexes and by an index arranged by types of services (e.g., human resources, marketing programs). Entries tend to resemble those in the *Encyclopedia of Associations* (Gale, annual) but with somewhat more detail in describing types of programs and recent publications.

Private and nonprofit sector bureaucracies will continue to have many of the same characteristics as for-profit institutions and will continue to need high-quality counsel. These needs will guarantee an active shelf life for this directory and subsequent editions.—**John Mark Tucker**

902. Romaniuk, Bohdan R., ed. **Foundation Reporter 1993: Comprehensive Profiles and Giving Analyses of America's Major Private Foundations.** 24th ed. Rockville, Md., Taft Group; distr., Detroit, Gale, 1993. 1179p. index. $335.00pa. ISBN 1-879784-40-8. ISSN 1055-4998.

This massive volume analyzes the 638 private foundations in the United States that are regarded as the largest and most important private philanthropies. The criterion for inclusion is either $10 million in assets or $500,000 in charitable giving.

Arranged alphabetically by name of foundation, each profile includes contact information; financial information and a summary of contributions; donor information; the foundation philosophy, an analysis of its contributions, and an indication of typical recipients; a list of officers and directors; application and review procedures; miscellaneous information; and a grants analysis and a list of recent grants awarded, providing dollar amount, name of recipient, and a brief project description. Supplementing the directory are four extensive indexes that assist the user by listing foundations by state, by location of grant recipient, by grant type, and by recipient type. Three additional indexes list officers and directors by name, by place of birth, and by alma mater. A final index of foundations concludes the volume.

Comprehensive in its treatment, this volume will prove especially useful to development officers seeking external sources of funding to support new projects and initiatives. It is a pertinent and valuable addition to both library and administrative collections.—**Edmund F. SantaVicca**

903. Terry, Max, ed. **Volunteer! The Comprehensive Guide to Voluntary Service in the U.S. and Abroad.** 1992-1993 ed. New York, Council on International Educational Exchange, 1992. 189p. illus. index. $8.95pa. ISBN 1-882036-12-3.

Now in its 4th edition, *Volunteer!* provides descriptions of more than 200 opportunities for unpaid service in the United States and abroad. Parts 1 and 2 offer useful information about what it means to serve as a volunteer on short-term assignments lasting a few days to a few months as well as in medium- to long-term commitments lasting several months to years. Part 3 describes short-term, and part 4, medium- and long-term placements arranged in alphabetical order by sponsoring organization. Each entry describes the organization and program, then lists requirements, age limitations, living arrangements, information for disabled persons wanting to serve, finances, deadline for application, and contact person. Two appendixes give information about the Council of Religious Volunteer Agencies and the Council on International Educational Exchange, cosponsors of the book. Indexes by organization name, skills needed, and program location enhance access.

Unlike the more detailed *Volunteerism* (see ARBA 92, entry 829), *Volunteer!* includes listings for international opportunities. Recommended for most libraries, this handy and inspiring little guide would also make a great gift for the person who has everything. [R: Choice, Jan 93, p. 768]—**Cheryl Knott Malone**

904. **Volunteer Work.** London, Central Bureau for Educational Visits & Exchanges; distr., New York, Institute for International Education, [1993]. 192p. illus. index. $22.95pa. ISBN 0-900087-92-7.

The Central Bureau for Educational Visits & Exchanges offers both an overview and an in-depth study of volunteers and voluntary service. The focus in this useful manual is on longer-term developmental projects located throughout the world. Information is divided into two areas: the personal aspects of volunteering and organizational contacts. For those considering voluntary work, self-analysis is advised to determine one's basic motivation. The compilers offer a checklist to aid in the process. Advice is given on evaluating the project under consideration, useful preparation and training, travel to and from the project, and the reentry impact of the volunteers' return to their former environments. Experiences of active volunteers are quoted, adding reality to the pages.

Well over 100 voluntary services and advisory boards are examined, following a consistent format that, for each, includes directory information; countries of activity; a profile of philosophy, aims, and activities; opportunities available; requirements; duration of assignments; terms and conditions, including salary or pocket money and lodging; briefing prior to and debriefing following service; applications; and publications. *Volunteer Work* is invaluable for the specialized user considering such service, and an eye-opener for others who have no comprehension of the extent and ramifications of voluntary service worldwide.—**Eleanor Ferrall**

POVERTY

905. **Poverty in Developing Countries: A Bibliography of Publications by the ILO's World Employment Programme, 1975-91.** Washington, D.C., International Labor Office, 1992. 152p. index. (International Labour Bibliography, no.12). $16.00pa. ISBN 92-2-108248-2.

The amount of poverty in developing countries is staggering, with anywhere from 50 to 70 percent of rural populations in Asia, Africa, and Latin America being poor. Over the years, the World Employment Programme of the International Labor Office (ILO) has sponsored research on the extent of and trends in poverty in developing countries, as well as on policies for its reduction. This annotated bibliography, intended for a specialized research audience, is a guide to 350 of those research reports published between 1975 and 1991.

The bibliography is divided into four sections. Section 1 is a collection of bibliographical references and abstracts arranged alphabetically by author or corporate author. Information for most entries includes not only author, title, and abstract but also date of publication, length, language of text, ISBN, cost in Swiss francs, and a Labordoc number from the ILO's Labordoc database. Most of the reports were published in Geneva or Santiago by the ILO, but a few were published commercially. Sections 2 through 4 are the author, corporate author, and subject/geographical indexes. Under each index heading there are not only relevant entry numbers but also the first line of each work's title.

While the bibliography is easy to use, it does have a few small problems. First, the abstracts are inconsistent in their organization and clarity. Some are descriptive paragraphs, while others are simply lists of keywords. Second, the readability of both types of abstracts is compromised by the use of slash marks around keywords, giving the abstracts a cluttered appearance. This is a mild distraction and is probably a consequence of the bibliography being computer-generated. On the positive side, the inclusion of the first line of a title in the indexes is often helpful. Overall, this bibliography is appropriate for academic libraries with collections on poverty or economic development in developing countries, although it is probably too specialized for more general reference collections.—**Stephen H. Aby**

SEX STUDIES

906. Clyde, Laurel A., and Marjorie Lobban. **Out of the Closet and into the Classroom: Homosexuality in Books for Young People.** Port Melbourne, Austral., D. W. Thorpe and Deakin, Austral., ALIA Press; distr., New Providence, N.J., R. R. Bowker/Reed Reference Publishing, 1992. 150p. index. $35.00pa. 016.8230080353. ISBN 1-875589-02-3.

This annotated bibliography is a work whose time has definitely come. The authors have judiciously selected 120 titles whose content depicts a homosexual main character or event in the story, a supporting homosexual character, a homosexual background character, or a mention of homosexuality or use of homosexual terms.

Works of the first designation portray a homosexual, young adult, main character or one with homosexual tendencies. A sampling of titles from this grouping includes I. Holland's *The Man Without a Face* (Lippincott, 1972) and N. Garden's *Annie on My Mind* (Farrar, Straus & Giroux, 1982). Works featuring a supporting homosexual character include books such as M. L'Engle's *A House Like a Lotus* (Farrar, Straus & Giroux, 1984) and A. Synder's and L. Pelletier's *The Truth about Alex* (New American Library, 1987). Background homosexual characters are cited in such titles as M. Kerr's *Is That You Miss Blue?* (Dell, 1975) and B. Brooks's *Midnight Hour Encores* (Harper and Row, 1986).

The last category of titles, which merely refers to homosexuality or uses homosexual terms, lists, for example, Anne Frank's *The Diary of Anne Frank* (Pan, 1954). It is this list of 10 titles whose inclusion is debatable. For example, the one-sentence reference by Anne Frank to kissing a girlfriend in bed and wanting to feel her breasts does not seem significant enough to qualify this title for inclusion in this bibliography. Also, approximately 40 percent of the works listed are British or Australian. For readers and acquisitions librarians, the dearth of U.S. titles may affect their decision to purchase the bibliography.

The annotations are well written, with appropriate references to the work's homosexual content. A useful introduction traces the changes in society's attitude toward homosexuality over the past 40 years, especially with regard to young adult books. The book's indexes cite titles within the four initial criteria. Two additional indexes list the books chronologically and alphabetically. A list of references about homosexuality in literature is also helpful.

Despite its flaws, *Out of the Closet and into the Classroom* is the first bibliography to address homosexuality in books for young adults. Public and school librarians should purchase it. [R: RBB, 1 April 93, pp. 1442-43; SLJ, Jan 93, p. 37]—**Kathleen W. Craver**

907. Garber, Linda. **Lesbian Sources: A Bibliography of Periodical Articles 1970-1990.** Hamden, Conn., Garland, 1993. 680p. (Garland Gay and Lesbian Studies, v.9; Garland Reference Library of the Humanities, v.1557). $75.00. Z5866.L44G37. 016.30548'9664. LC 92-21941. ISBN 0-8153-0782-9.

Most in-depth treatments of topics about, or of special interest to, lesbians are lost in the mainstream systems for access to periodical articles because most of the specialized journals in which they appear are not indexed by the principal indexing and abstracting services. Additionally, articles on lesbians in mainstream periodicals are usually indexed only under very general headings, forcing a searcher to sift through much unrelated material. Garber's bibliography provides a way to locate a large number of articles published between 1970 and 1990 in selected journals that specialize in feminism, women's studies, and lesbian issues (these journals are listed in the bibliography). Also included are articles, from a wide spectrum of other periodicals, that are entered under "lesbian" in major indexing and abstracting services, both print and electronic.

Articles are listed under subject headings designed especially for this bibliography. Many of these headings are quite specialized, such as "adolescent lesbians," "butch/femme," "lesbians of color," and "violence among lesbians." Each article is listed in as many subject categories as possible. Main headings are displayed at the front of the volume, along with many *see* and *see also* cross-references. In the bibliography, many main headings are subdivided by place-names or by names of individuals. Articles on individuals cannot be found directly, but only under the subject with which they are associated, such as "Southern lesbians" or "religion" (for lesbian rabbis, priests, ministers, theologians, and the like). Citations supply all the standard information with the addition of a brief descriptive annotation, when needed, to convey the sense of the article.

The only defect in this impressive compilation is a poorly designed layout. There are no scope headings at the tops of pages, and subject headings are poorly distinguished from citations, so that it is very difficult to find categories and to navigate through the bibliography. A separate index to individuals as subjects would also have been helpful. Every library that serves lesbians needs this bibliography, especially high school, public, college, and university libraries that support the needs of students and scholars investigating topics related to lesbians. [R: C&RL, Sept 93, p. 431; Choice, May 93, pp. 1440-41; RBB, 15 May 93, pp. 1722-23]—**James D. Anderson**

908. Maggiore, Dolores J. **Lesbianism: An Annotated Bibliography and Guide to the Literature 1976-1991.** Metuchen, N.J., Scarecrow, 1992. 264p. index. $32.50. Z7164.S42M33. 016.303676'63. LC 92-34699. ISBN 0-8108-2617-8.

This annotated bibliographic guide to materials on lesbians is an updated, revised edition of a guide published in 1988. The title is somewhat misleading. The book is not a comprehensive guide to materials on lesbians but a selective list of current secondary sources of particular value to the professional therapist, caregiver, or social worker who provides services to lesbian clients. The guide includes books and periodicals that provide the necessary background about lesbian history and culture. An introduction to the literature and a historical overview of the sources comprise about one-third of this bibliography. The entries are divided into general subject headings that include "The Individual Lesbian," "Minorities within a Minority," "Lesbian Families," "Oppression," "Health," and "Resources." Under the latter, very brief lists of bookstores (a total of eight), general publications, newspapers, and directories are provided. There are an excellent introduction and overview of the literature. Highly recommended for all libraries. [R: C&RL, Sept 93, p. 431]—**Jane Jurgens**

909. Richter, Alan. **Dictionary of Sexual Slang: Words, Phrases, and Idioms from AC/DC to Zig-zig.** New York, John Wiley, 1993. 250p. maps. $29.95. HQ9.R53. 306.7'03. LC 92-6316. ISBN 0-471-54057-9.

This dictionary complements Richter's previous work, *The Language of Sexuality* (see ARBA 89, entry 779), which focused on the "philosophy, sociology, and metaphor underlying sexual terminology." Expanding from 1,000-plus terms in the glossary of his 1987 book to more than 4,000 words and phrases that are the basis of this dictionary, Richter emphasizes the sexual meanings of slang words and phrases in English over the past 500 years. Alphabetically listed by headword or main entry, the words, phrases, and idioms relate to sexual actions, organs, and roles, not to aspects of reproduction. Informal taboo terms and words, such as "boy in a boat," "linguist," and "Spanish gout," form the core of the book. Richter tried to be comprehensive in his selection of terms so he could catalog the varied range of sexual terms that have evolved in the English language. When available, the etymology, nature, time of use, metaphor, and "pithy or poetic coinage" accompany the definition. Many readers may be fascinated to discover how many seemingly ordinary words (e.g., *candle, hotel, IBM, mushroom, shell, tread*) have sexual meanings.

This book can be used by scholars who are particularly interested in indications of the meaning of sexuality in culture, social change and continuity in relation to the intersection of sex and language, or all levels of the ways in which sex is articulated in the culture. Besides this scholarly use, the work will please those who hunted in vain for these words in a standard dictionary. [R: Choice, Nov 93, p. 438]
—**Suzanne G. Frayser**

SOCIAL WELFARE AND SOCIAL WORK

910. Bosoni, Anthony J. **Post-Release Assistance Programs for Prisoners: A National Directory.** Jefferson, N.C., McFarland, 1992. 164p. index. $29.95pa. HV9304.B67. 365'.66'0973. LC 91-50955. ISBN 0-89950-651-8.

Covering more than 1,400 government and private programs, this new directory should help meet the needs of the growing population of parolees and others who have been incarcerated. The primary arrangement is by state, with subarrangement by name of program. Two separate sections list programs specifically for women and veterans. Each entry includes names, address, and telephone number; an indication of who is eligible for services; and a brief description of services provided. Many also include names of contact persons, with their own telephone numbers. There is no index.

The work could be more useful. The only way for a person to find suitable agencies in a given city is to peruse all entries in all three sections. An arrangement or an index by city would have obviated this. A greater problem is the overlap among the three sections. It appears that nearly all the women's services entries also appear in the general section, and that none of the veterans' entries appear anywhere else. Users should also be aware that this directory does not include most general social service agencies. Because Bosoni (himself incarcerated) notes that he has excluded groups who refuse services to ex-prisoners, such omissions could be misleading. A quick check of one community's homeless shelters, meal centers, halfway houses, and the like confirmed that most would not discriminate. Since many ex-prisoners' needs are those of any of society's unfortunates, librarians should not rely solely on this directory in suggesting places to get help, especially for basic life-support needs.

Given the price, and the fact that most standard social service directories do not specify agencies that specialize in the needs of this population, most public libraries should consider this book. Perhaps an updated edition that corrects the difficulties of this one will come out on a regular basis. The information provided is certainly needed.—**James H. Sweetland**

911. Ginsberg, Leon. **Social Work Almanac.** Washington, D.C., National Association of Social Workers, 1992. 215p. index. $29.95pa. HV90.G53. 361.973. LC 92-31194. ISBN 0-87101-196-4.

Human services professionals welcome, value, and need scientifically verified data in support of their knowledge and skills and for effective problem solving. The *Social Work Almanac* is a collection of descriptive statistics covering a broad range of topics relating to national and international social work and social services today. The data gathered are presented in a systematic, concise manner, including the use of factual charts, tables, and diagrams. The original sources of data are clearly identified for future reference. The information offered in this text provides readers with indicators of trends, needs, and gaps in social services and social policies.

This book is a welcome addition to the field of human services. It is of particular value to social workers, social planners, policy developers, community organizers, program evaluators, social researchers, and teachers. Highly recommended for libraries in schools educating human service professionals.
—**Maria O'Neil McMahon**

912. Mendelsohn, Henry N. **An Author's Guide to Social Work Journals.** 3d ed. Washington, D.C., National Association of Social Workers, 1992. 282p. $24.95pa. HV85.M46. 016.3613'05. LC 92-20573. ISBN 0-87101-219-7.

Books that provide information on journals for prospective contributors exist in many disciplines. This edition of Mendelsohn's guide is a model for them all. It describes more than 130 core social work and social welfare journals, chosen by Mendelsohn in consultation with the National Association of Social Workers. Numerous journals have been added since the 1987 edition. Information for each title comes from a questionnaire sent to its editor, a current issue (the exact one is not noted in the description), and standard bibliographical tools. Each description gives the usual information necessary for contributors as well as subjects covered, special issues planned, and indexing sources. A list of journals arranged by subject categories makes it easy to find titles on a certain topic. Mendelsohn's thoughtful preface alerts the prospective contributor to many important caveats that can easily be overlooked. This book thus serves as an excellent source for writers as well as a good general guide to journals in social work.
—**Cathy Seitz Whitaker**

913. Weinstein, Amy J., ed. **Public Welfare Directory, 1993/94.** Washington, D.C., American Public Welfare Association, 1993. 538p. $70.00pa. LC 41-4981. ISBN 0-910106-24-X. ISSN 0163-8297.

This directory is a major guide for professional helpers needing quick access to names, addresses, and telephone and fax numbers for public human service programs in the United States, Canada, and other countries. Services are briefly identified and described. In the appendixes, information is offered on various procedures, policies, programs, and committees relating to public human services. The directory is organized in a concise format, with marginal abbreviations for each program reference. The work is a reliable, contemporary resource of particular value to human service practitioners and is an excellent reference for libraries in institutions preparing graduates for professional human services.

—Maria O'Neil McMahon

SUBSTANCE ABUSE

914. **Drug, Alcohol, and Other Addictions: A Directory of Treatment Centers and Prevention Programs Nationwide.** 2d ed. Phoenix, Ariz., Oryx Press, 1993. 646p. $68.50pa. ISBN 0-89774-623-6. ISSN 1067-814X.

This is the most comprehensive directory available that covers drug, alcohol, and behavior addiction facilities and programs. The 12,000 listed facilities are mostly those that responded to a questionnaire. (One can obtain additional information on other facilities by calling the publisher.) Included in the directory are programs supported by schools, hospitals, prisons, and state and local governments. Noticeably absent is Oregon State Hospital (which became well known in Ken Kesey's *One Flew Over the Cuckoo's Nest* [Viking Penguin, $7.95]). Entries are arranged under the 50 states and the District of Columbia; and within each state, facilities are alphabetized by city and name. Each entry includes name, address, and telephone number; addictions treated; treatment type; setting; statistics; special programs; payment method; and accommodations.

This directory has about 2,500 more entries than the 1990 U.S. Department of Health and Human Resource's *National Directory of Drug Abuse and Alcoholism Treatment and Preservation Programs*. In addition, it is easier to use and more readable. It will be valuable to health care professionals and individuals and their families seeking help. Recommended for public and academic libraries. [R: RBB, 1 Sept 93, pp. 84-86]—**Karen Y. Stabler**

915. Gilbert, M. Jean, Beatriz Solis, and Juana Mora, comps. **Alcohol-Related Issues in the Latino Population 1980-1990: An Annotated Bibliography.** Berkeley, Calif., Chicano Studies Library Publications, University of California, 1992. 129p. index. (Chicano Studies Library Publications Series, no.17). $25.00pa. Z7721.G54. 016.36229'22'08968073. LC 92-17367. ISBN 0-918520-20-7.

Adding to the growing literature of ethnic studies is this well-designed illumination of the epidemiology, prevention, and treatment of alcohol use among Latino youth and adults. Studies focus on the population of Mexican Americans, Puerto Ricans, Cubans, and Central Americans living in the United States.

Nearly 250 citations representing articles, bibliographies, books, book chapters, dissertations, and government publications published from 1980 to 1990 are descriptively annotated based upon computer searches of several databases and research centers. Surprisingly, ERIC, the Monthly Catalog of U.S. Government Publications, and Ethnic Newswatch were not searched.

Arrangement is alphabetical by author, with the citation noting the source and the number of references cited in the original work. Author and title indexes are provided, but entries are not numbered. Annotations span several hundred words and are often modifications of the original author's abstract.

This is a welcome contribution to the field and should be of assistance to researchers and policymakers. The price will necessitate careful consideration before purchasing, but should not prevent academic libraries with strong Hispanic populations on social science collections from acquiring it.

—**Ilene F. Rockman**

916. MacDonald, Scott B., and Bruce Zagaris, eds. **International Handbook on Drug Control.** Westport, Conn., Greenwood Press, 1992. 454p. index. $85.00. HV5801.I575. 363.4'5. LC 91-35118. ISBN 0-313-27375-8.

This excellent volume has no rival in its subject area. It is manifestly not intended to persuade one of the obviously negative nature of the drug trade, and it does not present maudlin case studies. It does present facts and figures in essay format for 21 different countries or areas: the United States, Canada, Bolivia, Brazil, Caribbean offshore, Colombia, Mexico, Panama, Peru, the Southern Cone, Western

Europe, the Netherlands, Sweden, the United Kingdom, the former Soviet Union, Afghanistan, Iran, Pakistan, Turkey and India, the Golden Triangle (Burma, Laos, and Thailand), and Singapore. The authors have published widely on international law and economics.

The country essays, while focused on the narcotics trade, marshal their evidence in the context of general historical conditions. Documentation is regularly provided. For example, the statement that "Most of Southwest Asian heroin is refined or shipped through Pakistan" is buttressed by a U.S. House Committee on Foreign Affairs publication, *U.S. Narcotics Control Programs Overseas*. As might be expected, national and international governments provide many of the statistics; however, the results of individuals' research is also included. Framing essays on general problems, such as a fascinating one on money laundering and an informative one on the undertakings of the United Nations, complete this highly useful compilation.—**Judith M. Brugger**

917. Porterfield, Kay Marie. **Focus on Addictions: A Reference Handbook.** Santa Barbara, Calif., ABC-Clio, 1992. 242p. index. (Teenage Perspectives). $39.50. RC564.3.P67. 616.86. LC 92-26623. ISBN 0-87436-674-7.

This is the kind of book guidance counselors or classroom teachers will want to use to plan antidrug use campaigns in their schools. *Focus on Addictions* is a reference monograph that does three things. First, it provides essays on such general themes as alcoholism, drug addiction, tobacco, eating disorders, impulse control disorders, and codependency. Second, each section references other monographs (including fiction), a variety of nonprint works, and even the more ephemeral kinds of materials issued by the National Clearinghouse for Alcohol and Drug Information or the American Cancer Society. Third, it provides addresses for organizations, such as Cocaine Anonymous, and telephone numbers for hotlines, such as the Food Addiction Hotline.

Despite the fact that this book fits the reference book profile, in that its source lists overpower its essays and that some of the essays bulge with data on percentages, dollar amounts, and age ranges, the majority of the essays are not overly reference-like. They are easy to read, and they lend themselves to oral presentation. [R: LJ, Jan 93, p. 104; RBB, 1 Mar 93, p. 1263; SLJ, Feb 93, p. 123; VOYA, June 93, p. 126]—**Judith M. Brugger**

YOUTH AND CHILD DEVELOPMENT

918. **Caring for Kids with Special Needs: Residential Treatment Programs for Children and Adolescents.** Princeton, N.J., Peterson's Guides, 1993. 481p. illus. index. $89.95. HV863.C35. 362.7'32'0973. LC 92-36346. ISBN 1-56079-168-3.

This new guide is intended to help both parents and professionals find suitable treatment facilities for children and adolescents with a wide array of emotional problems, including addictive disorders, learning disabilities, and eating disorders. (Many of the institutions accommodate adults as well as young people, but none of the entries states what percentage of the patients are in each category.) The guide includes some 817 institutions that responded to a questionnaire distributed during the spring and summer of 1992. A reference chart that lists the facilities by state with a checklist of their important characteristics serves as a guide to locating those institutions that have the services the user seeks.

The entries are arranged in alphabetical order. The following headings appear under each entry: general information, participants, program, staff, facilities, education, costs, and contacts. Because the data is based on the institutions' responses to the questionnaire, there is considerable unevenness in coverage. The format contains two columns per page, and the space devoted to the descriptions ranges from half a column to one and one-half columns. There is no indication that a more complete entry necessarily correlates to a superior institution. In fact, one of the drawbacks of this compendium is the lack of ratings of the facilities.

A section entitled "Expanded Descriptions" contains detailed information about some 35 institutions. At first glance it appears that these institutions were specifically chosen for special treatment. However, the introduction states that these institutions simply responded more completely to the questionnaire. [R: Choice, June 93, p. 1598; RBB, June 93, pp. 1892-94]—**Carol R. Glatt**

919. Cochran, Moncrieff, ed. **International Handbook of Child Care Policies and Programs.** Westport, Conn., Greenwood Press, 1993. 688p. index. $115.00. HQ778.5.I58. 362.7. LC 92-25746. ISBN 0-313-26866-5.

　　This book offers a comprehensive overview of child care practices, programs, and policies in 29 countries. It is written with sensitivity to the impact of a country's history, culture, and ideology on its development of child care services. Research-based cross-national comparisons of related demographics and child care programs and policies are provided. Schematic frameworks are offered for easy reference and comparison of different countries according to type of care, age range, duration of service, number of children, and other data. The similarities in child care practices among countries of physical proximity with common history and language are highlighted. The book concludes with a general, contemporary bibliography for future reference.

　　Child care practices are being transformed throughout the world due to major changes in social roles and circumstances. This reference provides readers with a global picture of similarities and differences in trends and developments in a variety of countries. It is a timely contribution to the field of child welfare, and highly recommended for students and practitioners concerned with child and family policies and services.—**Maria O'Neil McMahon**

920. Franck, Irene, and David Brownstone. **What's New for Parents.** New York, Prentice Hall General Reference, 1993. 232p. illus. index. $12.00pa. HQ769.F718. 649'.1. LC 92-39944. ISBN 0-671-85036-9.

　　What's New for Parents provides an overview of contemporary approaches, resources, and references relating to a variety of topics of interest to parents with children of different ages. Articles are arranged to reflect what is new in fun and games, family health and safety, learning and education, and parenting resources. Information presented is brief and limited. Nevertheless, suggestions and references may help awaken parental interest and lead to further study for greater detail and understanding. The book will need continued updating as new references, products, and approaches are introduced. It may serve as a support and guide for parents, particularly those with limited time to seek out references or for those with little experience in child-rearing. It may also be a reference for those who work with parents in a support-giving capacity.—**Maria O'Neil McMahon**

921. Gillis, Jack, and Mary Ellen R. Fise. **The Childwise Catalog: A Consumer Guide to Buying the Safest and Best Products for Your Children.** 3d ed. New York, HarperPerennial/HarperCollins, 1993. 472p. illus. index. $14.00pa. RJ61.G418. 649'.122'0296. LC 92-54682. ISBN 0-06-273182-3.

　　This outstanding resource of consumer guidelines and products for newborns through age five should be a mandatory purchase for parents, preschools, and public libraries. At its present low cost it also makes an excellent gift for first-time parents. The previous edition was published in 1990 (see ARBA 91, entry 191). All products have been updated since then and include the most current model numbers and price ranges.

　　Part 1 addresses children's products by listing such things as all the items a parent needs before the baby arrives, followed by other goods, such as bicycle helmets and scooters for two- to five-year-olds. Almost every product features an excellent set of purchasing criteria together with the best manufacturers and prices. More important, recalled products and their brand names and model numbers are listed. Part 2 evaluates services for children, such as dental and pediatric care. A separate chapter is devoted to travel by car, bus, and air. Part 3 furnishes information about protecting children not only from environmental dangers but also from fireworks, decks, stairs, balconies, and swimming pools, to name a few hazards. Another chapter contains a very useful section on childproofing a home. The last chapter is a melange of information about child abuse, health care organizations, children's catalogs, government agencies, and parenting and safety associations. A detailed index enables users to access information by product or safety issues.

　　Between them the authors have six children and numerous nieces and nephews. Perhaps all this parenting is what brings a welcome air of intimacy and warmth to this indispensable guide. While much of the product advice, especially concerning safety, is accompanied by sobering statistics of children's injuries and deaths, users will find that this catalog is designed to truly assist them and relieve their anxiety.—**Kathleen W. Craver**

922. Merkel-Holguin, Lisa A., with Audrey J. Sobel. **The Child Welfare Stat Book 1993.** Washington, D.C., Child Welfare League of America, 1993. 156p. $32.95 spiralbound. ISBN 0-87868-531-6.

The Child Welfare Stat Book 1993 is a comprehensive source of statistical information regarding children and families in the United States. The data, compiled mainly from 1987 to 1993, appears accurate and is well presented, with multiple graphs and tables employed. Several statistical comparisons are offered according to time intervals, states, ages, or race/ethnicity. Sources used to obtain data are clearly referenced throughout the text. Information is organized according to alphabetized subject areas for easy reference. This valuable guide on child welfare needs and services will be particularly useful to educators, human service practitioners, and child and family program and policy developers. It is highly recommended for libraries in human service agencies and educational institutions preparing students to work with children and families.—**Maria O'Neil McMahon**

923. Reeves, Diane Lindsey. **Child Care Crisis: A Reference Handbook.** Santa Barbara, Calif., ABC-Clio, 1992. 173p. index. (Contemporary World Issues). $39.50. HQ778.7.U6R44. 362.7'12. LC 92-38144. ISBN 0-87436-645-3.

There is no question that good, affordable child care is of paramount interest and importance. The subject is timely and controversial. This source brings together disparate information to assist in understanding the issue and in providing a quick overview of the salient points. Unfortunately, the source is neither comprehensive, logical in its selectivity, nor particularly unique. Moreover, with a focus on the United States, the series title "Contemporary World Issues" may be misleading.

Arranged in seven chapters, the source contains a brief 8-page chronology of events from 1828 to 1991; 18 biographical sketches of "activists, experts, and policymakers" that include pediatrician T. Berry Brazelton and Representative Patricia Schroeder; a 36-page section of facts and data culled from standard statistical sources; an 18-page directory of "major national child care support organizations," which can also be found in such sources as the *Encyclopedia of Associations* (Gale, annual); a 13-page annotated bibliography; and an alphabetical list of state regulatory agencies, referral networks, and child care and family regulations. A 12-page index rounds out the work.

The author notes that this book serves as a one-stop resource and guide to further research. This is an oversimplification. The work can serve as a starting point for undergraduates or interested laypeople, but it is too elementary for scholars or serious researchers. [R: Choice, July/Aug 93, p. 1754; RBB, 15 Jan 93, p. 936; VOYA, June 93, p. 126; WLB, April 93, p. 117]—**Ilene F. Rockman**

924. Sutherland, Neil, Jean Barman, and Linda L. Hale, comps. **Contemporary Canadian Childhood and Youth: A Bibliography.** Westport, Conn., Greenwood Press, 1992. 492p. index. (Bibliographies and Indexes in World History, no.29). $69.50. Z7164.C5S94. 016.30523'0971. LC 92-27766. ISBN 0-313-28586-1.

This work is a comprehensive bibliography of contemporary writings in English about children and youth in Canada. It is based on an extensive search and review of books, monographs, reports, scholarly and professional articles, and magisterial and doctoral theses and dissertations. References are identified geographically according to Central, Atlantic, and Northern Canada; the Prairies; British Columbia; and general. Subject and author indexes are provided.

This collection of references serves as a major source of information for researchers conducting studies relating to Canadian children or youth. It and its companion, *History of Canadian Childhood and Youth* (Greenwood Press, 1992), provide an inclusive reference guide to recognized, serious English-language writings about the topics. It is strongly recommended for libraries in schools that offer programs to prepare human service providers for work with Canadian children and youth. [R: Choice, June 93, p. 1611]

—**Maria O'Neil McMahon**

925. Sutherland, Neil, Jean Barman, and Linda L. Hale, comps. **History of Canadian Childhood and Youth: A Bibliography.** Westport, Conn., Greenwood Press, 1992. 486p. index. (Bibliographies and Indexes in World History, no.28). $69.50. Z7164.C5S94. 016.30523'0971. LC 92-27767. ISBN 0-313-28585-3.

This is an ambitious bibliography of all English-language works on the history of Canadian childhood and youth. It seems to have no subject limitations, although (not surprisingly) its primary areas of coverage are health, education, and welfare. The 7,998 citations, which span the twentieth and late nineteenth centuries, include books, articles, government reports, dissertations, and monographs, with the most recent sources dating from 1989.

The entries are arranged alphabetically by author under six geographical chapter headings (e.g., British Columbia, northern Canada). Each citation includes, wherever possible, the author, title, and imprint. An introduction addresses the methodological aspects of the bibliography's compilation, including the journals searched for citations. Subject and author indexes provide additional access to the entries.

The broad subject coverage of this bibliography is a strength. Also, even though the entries are ostensibly about Canadian childhood and youth, much of the cited research is relevant for and applicable to non-Canadian populations. On the other hand, users may be disappointed by the lack of annotations. Preferring comprehensive coverage over annotations, although a legitimate choice by the compilers, nonetheless limits one's ability to evaluate the citations. Similarly, the geographical organization of the entries, also useful and legitimate, does not aid subject access. Consequently, the only means of subject searching is through the subject index, which is deficient due to a lack of subheadings. Many of the headings have dozens, sometimes hundreds of entry numbers after them. Still, the bibliography may be useful to university collections on childhood and youth and Canadian studies. [R: Choice, June 93, p. 1611]—**Stephen H. Aby**

926. Zvirin, Stephanie. **The Best Years of Their Lives: A Resource Guide for Teenagers in Crisis.** Chicago, American Library Association, 1992. 122p. index. $18.00pa. Z7164.Y8Z95. 016.30523'5. LC 92-5575. ISBN 0-8389-0586-2.

Using subject matter, format, depth of treatment, and writing style as criteria for selection, Zvirin has collected fiction and nonfiction books, as well as approximately 50 videos, and placed them under 9 broad themes or chapter headings that include "Family Matters"; "School Daze"; "Me, Myself and I"; and "Sex Stuff." More focused, talk show-type topics, such as self-esteem, marriage, peer pressure, and health and wellness, are treated within each theme. Entries are separated into fiction and nonfiction and then arranged alphabetically by authors' last names. Each entry gives complete bibliographical information and a recommendation for the age-appropriate audience. A 150- to 200-word summary and evaluation accompanies each nonfiction entry. The author makes clear a title's strong and weak points in each of the evaluations. Fiction titles are treated only to a one- or two-sentence annotation.

The resources in this collection were written or produced for teens rather than for adults. They were selected as examples of the increasing number of self-help resources aimed at young adults who are facing difficult decisions. As an added boost to the self-help focus, Zvirin has included essays or interviews with writers of popular materials for teens. A lengthy essay by writer and photojournalist Jill Krementz talks about how her series, "How It Feels," was born, and an interview with Eda LeShan discusses her work as a psychotherapist and how she used her own experiences in writing self-help books for teenagers. At the end of the book is a filmography of currently available videos with short annotations. This book could serve as a valuable selection aid for collections in middle and high schools and public libraries. [R: EL, Mar-April 93, p. 43; SLJ, Jan 93, p. 37]—**Melvin M. Bowie**

17 Statistics, Demography, and Urban Studies

DEMOGRAPHY

927. Ambry, Margaret. **The Official Guide to Household Spending: The Number One Guide to Who Spends How Much on What.** 2d ed. Ithaca, N.Y., New Strategist, 1993. 428p. index. $69.95. ISBN 0-9628092-3-3.

A solid source of marketing information, this reference work provides tables detailing how much household consumers spend for approximately 1,000 products and services, everything from homes and cars to pies, tarts, and turnovers. The book is based on the 1992 Consumer Expenditure Survey conducted by the Bureau of the Census and analyzed and published by the Bureau of Labor Statistics (data are for 1991). It is organized into 10 chapters of broad spending categories (e.g., shelter and utilities, entertainment), and each chapter includes sections on spending trends and spending by age, income, household type, and household size. Chapter 11 offers a summary and supplemental tables, and the appendix includes information on the survey used to compile the data, a glossary of expenditure items and terms used, and a detailed index to specific items. A well-written and well-organized introduction clearly describes how to use and interpret the tables and how to project changes in market shares to the year 2000. The tables are easy to read; headings are straightforward; and the data are well spaced. In addition, respective categories and divisions (e.g., food and age) are noted at the top of each right-hand page for handy reference.

This edition covers a greater number of products and services than did the first (entitled *Consumer Power* [see ARBA 92, entry 171]). Other additions include tables by household size and market share and a chapter on gifts. The supplemental tables now offer information on spending levels in selected metropolitan areas in the United States. Strongly recommended for public, business, and academic libraries.
—**Janice M. Griggs**

928. **Census Snapshot for All U.S. Places, 1990.** Compiled by the research staff of Toucan Valley Publications. Milpitas, Calif., Toucan Valley, 1992. 582p. $48.00pa. HA201. 317.94. ISBN 0-9634017-0-X.

This publication is a convenient gathering of limited 1990 Census data on 23,435 places in the United States. "Place" in this publication is defined as a borough, city, town, village, or census designated place. Statistics are provided for the total population of a place, as well as ethnic breakdowns by white, Black, American Indian, Asian/Pacific Islanders, and "other." A separate column is provided for Hispanics. However, Hispanics are factored into the total figures for white percentages and may also be represented in the "other" category. Other data provided include percentages of the population in 4 categories: 5 and under, 6-17, 18-64, and 65 and older. Land area, median household income, and median home value are also provided for each place.

Many libraries and information centers may find this statistical compilation useful as a form of ready reference and easy access to Census data. However, given the undercounts during the 1990 Census and rapid changes in the population of places, especially when military bases are closed or industry folds its tents and moves elsewhere, the data included may not be completely accurate. Nonetheless, this work may be a good purchase for many smaller and specialized libraries that require a quick source of limited types of Census data and that do not have an overriding concern about exactness. [R: RBB, 1 May 93, p. 1624]—**Roberto P. Haro**

929. **The First Demographic Portraits of Russia 1951-1990.** Shady Side, Md., New World Demographics, 1993. 129p. maps. $149.00pa. LC 93-083755. ISBN 0-9632883-4-2.

New World Demographics is in the business of packaging statistical data in a snapshot, or "portrait," format that highlights categories of interest to social scientists and businesspeople. This new publication on the Russian Republic provides a wealth of information about the republic as a whole, its 12 regions, and (most importantly) its 79 administrative units (oblasts). There is an alphabetical list of the oblasts and their administrative centers (usually the principal city), with helpful maps. The demographic portrait of each oblast fills an entire page and includes data on location, population and population change, urban migration, a working age profile, family size, nationalities, vital statistics, housing space (square meters per capita), industrial employment, educational attainment, car ownership, television sets, and private telephones. A full-page explanation of each portrait category is given, with definitions, graphs, and maps. The result is a most interesting sociological look at the Russian people.

While considerable specialized data is collected in this book, its title is misleading. Most of the statistics are from 1989, with only the population figures stretching back to 1951 (in 10-year intervals). Vital statistics are provided for 1970, 1980, 1985, and 1989; industrial employment is given only for 1985; and housing space shows a comparison between 1985 and 1989 only. It is, obviously, difficult to gather accurate current statistics while the nations of the former Soviet Union are in a state of flux, and this book represents a noble effort to organize the available data. Although it is quite expensive, this work is highly recommended as a companion to other recent statistical compilations, *Soviet Statistics since 1950* (see ARBA 93, entry 142) and *The USSR Facts & Figures Annual* (see ARBA 82, entry 364), both of which provide much more detailed data, but only on a national level.—**Thomas A. Karel**

930. **The FirstBook of Demographics for the Republics of the Former Soviet Union 1951-1990.** Shady Side, Md., New World Demographics, 1992. 1v. (various paging). maps. $89.00pa. LC 92-64068. ISBN 0-9632883-0-X.

This first book of the demographics of the 15 republics of the post-Soviet Union contains much of interest to sociologists with an interest in that region of the world. Data of demographic interest and those bearing on population are given for each of the republics and for oblasts (the generally state-sized political and administrative subdivisions of the larger republics that are not of sufficient political independence to create a federal system of government). Most population information derives from the most recent census, which occurred on January 12, 1989, and thus is not very obsolete. The book is accompanied by a map that shows the boundaries of the republics and their capitals, as of the date of the last census, as well as the boundaries of the oblasts and the locations of the cities that constitute the oblast administrative centers. Alone among the republics, Russia and Ukraine are divided into regions that are intermediate in scale between the oblast and the republic. These are indicated on the map and in the book as separate entries.

Some of the information consists of changes in population and other variables over the period of time beginning in 1951. The tables seem easy to use, and the book is likely to remain the most useful source of data on the Soviet and post-Soviet world for some time to come.—**Arthur R. Upgren**

931. Mattson, Mark T. **Atlas of the 1990 Census.** New York, Macmillan, 1992. 168p. maps. $90.00. G1201.E2M3. 304.6'0973'09049. LC 92-24006. ISBN 0-02-897302-X.

Every 10 years, the U.S. Bureau of the Census collects and presents to the world an impressive amount of information concerning the characteristics of the U.S. population. Professionals in countless fields make use of this data, but to the public at large it remains largely inaccessible, primarily because it is rarely offered in a simplified and intelligible format. This specialized atlas attempts to remedy the problem by summarizing the 1990 census in a series of regional and national maps on which various statistics are shown, and in a further group of more detailed plates that provide information at the county level.

The atlas is divided into six major sections: population, households, housing, race and ethnicity, economy, and education; a brief introduction to each part and useful comparisons to 1980 are provided. The county maps are divided into six regions, which keeps the dimensions of the book manageable; there are also county identification maps, a table of metropolitan area characteristics, and a glossary. The use of color is good, and the atlas is generally well produced and attractively presented, although several of the maps are printed slightly off-register.

A number of unfortunate errors detract from the credibility of the data presentation. For example, Sandy, with a population of about 75,000, mysteriously and consistently replaces Salt Lake City as Utah's major city; and on at least one plate the Northwest region is called the Northeast. These mistakes probably reflect a certain haste to rush this data into print, a probability reinforced by the fact that much of the work is based on preliminary census findings rather than the later, more refined numbers. Nonetheless, this is a useful and accessible reference that should prove a valuable addition to any library. [R: BR, May/June 93, p. 56; Choice, May 93, p. 1445; LJ, 1 April 93, p. 92; LJ, 15 April 93, p. 61; RBB, 15 Mar 93, p. 1376; WLB, Mar 93, p. 105]—**James R. McDonald**

932. Person, James E., Jr., and Sean R. Pollock, eds. **Statistical Forecasts of the United States.** Detroit, Gale, 1993. 804p. index. $89.50. ISBN 0-8103-8922-3.

The intent of *Statistical Forecasts of the United States* (SFUS) is to provide a broad range of subject-specific forecasts that can be used by anyone needing to figure out what the United States will look like in the coming decades. It is arranged into 14 topical chapters: agriculture; business, banking, finance, and economics; construction and housing; crime, law enforcement, and prisons; education; environmental issues and natural resources; health, medical care, and human services; income, prices, and spending; labor, employment, occupations, and earnings; military affairs; population, the family, and vital statistics; recreation; science, energy, and technology; and transportation. Each chapter is further divided into subtopics, within which are presented more than 800 tables, charts, graphs, and short narratives. The titles of all tables, graphs, and the like are included in the table of contents, an approach that somewhat mitigates the frustrations found in the work's inconsistent subject index. All entries cite the source document, as well as the original source of the data if it is not the cited document. In addition to the subject index, there is also a very useful index of projections by year.

Coverage is strong or weak depending on which subject area one examines. Crime has only 10 entries, while education offers more than 100. Because they are drawn from diverse, unrelated sources, the statistics included cannot be compared with one another and are often of varying degrees of reliability (and credibility). Individuals or organizations that need hard, targeted data in any given area will probably need to search further than the numbers provided in SFUS; however, this publication would be quite handy for pulling together a broad overview of what the future might look like or for providing forecast snapshots to incorporate in scenario-building strategies. [R: LJ, 15 Nov 93, pp. 73-74; RBB, 1 Oct 93, p. 387; WLB, Dec 93, p. 83]—**G. Kim Dority**

933. **The Sourcebook of County Demographics.** census ed. Washington, D.C., CACI Marketing Systems; distr., Detroit, Gale, 1992. 2v. maps. $295.00/v. ISBN 0-918417-11-2.

This two-volume edition provides the latest demographic information gleaned from the 1990 census. Volume 1 offers population, housing, and household data from the census Summary Tape File 1 (STF 1). Volume 2 contains sample data from STF 3, providing income, education, labor force, and detailed housing information.

The work is arranged alphabetically by state. Each state entry is separated into five profile sections and then subdivided into smaller data units. Headers in large, readable type note each state and profile section. Some of the tabular subheadings are rather tiny but should be legible to most users. Particularly helpful are summaries at the bottom of each page that allow users to compare county data with state and U.S. averages.

Data are presented in a format that is easy to read and understand. Brief explanations of variables are provided in a separate prefatory section. Users should note that volume 1 was published separately, before STF 3 became available, so its income reports are updates to the 1980 census. Actual 1990 census incomes are contained in volume 2. The set includes useful appendixes, such as those on 1980-1990 population change by county and county maps for each state; however, these are replicated in both volumes, from pages 89 through 288. The set therefore contains 200 pages of duplication.

Other sources, such as *County and City Data Book* (see ARBA 80, entry 771) and its annual update *County and City Extra* (see ARBA 93, entry 980), contain the same information, which is also drawn from the census as well as from other federal agencies. In addition to demographics, these works provide statistics on manufacturing, agriculture, retail, and the like and include data for metropolitan areas and cities of 25,000 or more. Although the information in *The Sourcebook of County Demographics* has been repackaged and is thus a bit easier to access and understand, a library considering its purchase must weigh its benefits against the fact that this government information is available elsewhere, as noted above, and for much less money.—**Janice M. Griggs**

STATISTICS

934. Balachandran, M., and S. Balachandran, eds. **State and Local Statistics Sources: A Subject Guide to Statistical Data on States, Cities, and Locales....** 2d ed. Detroit, Gale, 1993. 1912p. $135.00. ISBN 0-8103-5468-3. ISSN 1047-3394.

This guide aims to supply standard and specialized statistical sources of state and local data (see ARBA 91, entry 897 for a review of the first edition). For this edition the editors list an additional 3,600 sources, many of which are devoted to a particular city or county. This coverage expansion is that which has been most requested by users. The new sources nearly triple the number of publications listed and bring the total of citations to 60,000-plus. A third appendix has been added; it identifies those publications that provide data on all 50 states.—**Nathan M. Smith**

935. **Europe in Figures.** 3d ed. Brussels, Eurostat; distr., Lanham, Md., UNIPUB, 1992. 255p. illus. maps. index. $25.00pa. ISBN 92-826-3372-1.

This almanac-type reference tool is designed by Eurostat, the Statistical Office of the European Communities, for educational purposes. One of Eurostat's tasks is to provide the European Community (EC) (Belgium, Denmark, Germany, Greece, Spain, France, Ireland, Italy, Luxembourg, the Netherlands, Portugal, and the United Kingdom) with information about EC policies and developments. The book's 18 sections are subsumed in a variety of broad areas: general statistics, economy and finance, population and social conditions, energy and industry, agriculture, forestry and fisheries, external trade and balance of payments, services and transport, and environment. The book concludes with a brief index, an explanation of abbreviations, and a bibliography. This ready-reference tool, which is rich with colored pictures and statistical charts and tables, will be valuable to all who are seeking information about the EC.

—**Nathan M. Smith**

936. Mitchell, B. R. **International Historical Statistics: The Americas, 1750-1988.** 2d ed. New York, Stockton Press, 1993. 817p. $250.00. ISBN 1-56159-062-2.

This volume contains a plethora of statistical data compiled for 15 North American and 12 South American countries and covering the years from 1750 to 1988. The majority of the data has been collected from official publications that vary in quality and reliability. (According to Mitchell, nations carved out of the former British empire generally have fewer gaps in their records than nations that were formerly Spanish colonies.) The volume contains useful comparative data about a wide range of subjects, including population statistics broken down by sex, age, and major administrative units of the various nations; national birth, death, and marriage rates; complex indicators of national wealth (e.g., gross domestic product, net national product, gross [private fixed] capital formation); employment and unemployment figures and percentages; measurements of agricultural and industrial productivity; transportation, communication, and educational statistics; wholesale and consumer price indexes; and national financial data, such as currency in circulation and commercial bank deposits. Unfortunately, the layout of the tables and footnotes is not particularly user-friendly, and the volume does not include an index.

While the volume provides readers with an abundance of useful and hard-to-find information, extracting the data will be a tedious and time-consuming task. Recommended for research libraries. [R: Choice, Oct 93, p. 270; RBB, 15 Nov 93, p. 651]—**Terry D. Bilhartz**

937. Slater, Courtenay M., and George E. Hall, eds. **Places, Towns and Townships.** Lanham, Md., Bernan Press, 1993. 706p. $69.95. ISBN 0-89059-014-1.

Using data from the 1990 Census of Population and Housing, the 1987 Census of Retail Trade, the 1987 Census of Service Industries, and the 1987 Census of Manufactures, the editors of the *County and City Extra* (see ARBA 93, entry 908) have produced this statistical compilation. It covers all 23,435 incorporated and census-designated places in the United States, as well as almost 12,000 minor civil divisions (MCDs) in 12 states where MCDs serve as general-purpose local governments.

This volume consists primarily of two tables, the first for places with a 1990 population of 10,000 or more and the second for places with a population below 10,000. Within each table, data are presented alphabetically by state, with place-names listed alphabetically within each state. In states with MCD information reported, MCDs follow place-names. Subjects covered in the first table include area, population, race, age, households, income, poverty, housing, education, employment, disability, retail trade, service industries, and manufacturing. Only population, race, age, and housing statistics are in the second table.

Places, Towns and Townships contains very reliable information, and its coverage of small hamlets is unique. Helpful introductory material, explanations of geographical concepts, and source notes in the appendixes contribute to its usefulness. On the other hand, the lack of a place-names index makes finding a specific locality a bit difficult. Nevertheless, this companion to the *County and City Extra* is highly recommended for most libraries. [R: LJ, 1 Oct 93, p. 84]—**Leonard Grundt**

938. **Statistical Abstract of the United States 1992: The National Data Book.** 112th ed. Springfield, Va., National Technical Information Service, 1992. 979p. maps. index. $34.00; $29.00pa. LC 4-18089. ISBN 0-16-038081-2; 0-16-038080-4pa.

This compendium, compiled and published annually by the Census Bureau of the U.S. Department of Commerce, should be considered a basic reference. It consists of substantial and comprehensive data about the United States, mostly of a socioeconomic and demographic character with a bit of geographical and climatological information as well. This edition is testimony to the durability of the document. From participation in sports activities to average Scholastic Aptitude Test scores to comparisons in expenditures arranged by state or city, there is something to interest almost everyone conducting research or studies on any feature on American society.

Current problems such as crime and pollution are documented in a number of ways, some of which have not yet been fully explored or studied for the information they provide. These, along with such standard data as vital statistics, make this annual publication a major reference for readers at all levels.
—**Arthur R. Upgren**

939. **Statistical Yearbook for Asia and the Pacific 1991. Annuaire Statistique pour l'Asie et le Pacifique.** New York, United Nations, 1992. 467p. $65.00pa. ISBN 92-1-119597-7. ISSN 0252-3655. S/N E/F.92.II.F.1.

This is an updated compilation of useful and specific social, economic, and political statistics for countries throughout Asia and the Pacific. Data are arranged alphabetically by country from Afghanistan through Vietnam, and include developing economies as well as the developed ones of Australia, Japan, and New Zealand. These statistics are logically arranged in an easy-to-use and consistent format. Data are included for such wide-ranging topics as population and public health, labor, national income accounts, agriculture, industry, energy, transportation, external trade, wages and prices, finance, education, medical facilities, and housing. The yearbook provides summary tables, or "Regional Statistical Indicators," which help provide a regional context for these economic and social statistics. These tables will allow users to more easily make interregional and intraregional comparisons.

The obvious advantage of this volume is that it collects and collates data from a number of sources, thereby making this information much more accessible to a variety of users. In order to facilitate further and more detailed research, principal sources and publications for these data are outlined by country in an appendix. Another appendix provides conversion coefficients and factors in order to compare various systems of weights and measures. Whenever available, data are included up through 1990, but as the tables also provide data for the preceding 10 years, users will be able to construct insightful measures of how these statistics have varied since 1980.—**Timothy E. Sullivan**

940. **World Statistics in Brief: United Nations Statistical Pocketbook.** 14th ed. New York, United Nations, 1992. 117p. (Department of Economics and Social Development Statistical Office. Statistical Papers, Series V., no.14). $7.50pa. ISBN 92-1-161344-2. S/N E.92.XVII.5.

This small book contains basic statistics for 168 countries or areas around the world. The data in this edition generally cover the years 1980, 1985, and 1989. The purpose of the volume, which was compiled by the Statistical Office of the United Nations Secretariat, is to supply the world community with up-to-date, standardized national data so that the international public will become more aware of countries' development efforts. Among the data included in the volume are population statistics with the percentages of men, women, children, elderly, and urban dwellers within each world area; facts on national economic activity, such as gross domestic product, size of labor force, and volume of imports and exports; and education, health, and nutrition statistics, including illiteracy rates, government education expenditures, life expectancy, and infant mortality rates. A brief bibliography of other UN publications is provided for readers who desire more detailed statistics and technical descriptions of the methods used in the compilation of the data. This compact, inexpensive volume is a useful ready-reference guide for basic facts on the social and economic development of the various areas of the world.—**Terry D. Bilhartz**

URBAN STUDIES

941. **American Small City Profiles.** Compiled by the research staff of Toucan Valley Publications. Milpitas, Calif., Toucan Valley, 1993. 339p. maps. $35.00pa. ISBN 0-9634017-6-9.

This book covers 324 intermediate-sized cities of the United States, with at least one located in each of the 50 states. Two criteria must be met for inclusion: the 1990 population of each incorporated city must exceed 25,000, and the city must be located outside a Metropolitan Statistical Area (MSA) as defined by the U.S. Office of Management and Budget (OMB), or inside one that contains no city with more than 100,000 people. For each entry the population distributions by age and race are given, along with household income, home value, unemployment and crime rates, climate and elevation, and various services.

The volume is usable as a comparison study between cities, within limits. One weakness in this approach derives from the OMB definition of an MSA. The MSA must follow county lines—except in New England, where town lines suffice—and county sizes vary greatly. Corporate limits are also extremely unrepresentative of a total metropolitan area. Core cities that have not annexed many suburbs reflect inner-city conditions much more than those that have. The wide variations in both cities and counties allow enormous differences in the actual sizes of the communities included. For example, Harrisburg and West Palm Beach, with populations larger than half a million, are included, as are Grand Island and Mason City, which are less than one-tenth as large. On the other hand, Sioux Falls and Cedar Rapids, which fall right in between, are excluded only because the core city is larger than 100,000. Whenever corporate limits or MSAs define the data, gross inequities inevitably follow. [R: Choice, Dec 93, p. 579; LJ, 1 Oct 93, p. 84; RBB, 15 Dec 93, p. 773]—**Arthur R. Upgren**

942. Crampton, Norman. **The 100 Best Small Towns in America.** New York, Prentice Hall General Reference, 1993. 392p. $12.00pa. HT123.C68. 307.76'0973. LC 92-8214. ISBN 0-671-84671-X.

In the spirit of *Places Rated Almanac* (see ARBA 91, entry 908), *50 Fabulous Places to Raise Your Family* (Career Press, 1993), and other periodic surveys, there is now this genial guide to the best of small-town life in the United States. Defining a small town as a place with between 5,000 and 15,000 inhabitants, Crampton further restricted his pool to communities with their own economic bases (as opposed to those that function primarily as "bedroom towns" for metropolitan areas). Suburbs within MSAs (Metropolitan Statistical Areas) were thus excluded, which makes for a somewhat limited—although highly traditional—view of a small town. Crampton also concentrated on those places that are growing, according to 1990 census figures.

Inclusion in the top 100 depends chiefly on 7 main criteria: per capita income, racial diversity (proportion of minority population), the size of the 25- to 34-year-old age group, number of physicians, rate of serious crime, college-educated population, and amount of local spending for public education. Other measures that were considered include whether a town is a county seat, if it has its own newspaper, if it is the home of an institution of higher education (e.g., Williamstown, Massachusetts; Lewisburg, Pennsylvania), whether the scenery is nice, and the town's proximity to an MSA. Factors such as recreational facilities and cultural institutions, which play a large role in other ranking schemes, tend to be downplayed in this book.

The profiles of the 100 towns are listed alphabetically, with several ranked listings appended in the back of the book. Each profile is three pages long and provides brief information on location, population, growth rate, per capita income, geography, climate, economic base, newspaper, television and radio, health care facilities, schools, educational level of the population, library, recreation, cost of housing, cost of electricity, cost of natural gas, sales tax, state income tax, and churches. Additionally, there are a short general description of the town and assorted comments from a sampling of residents. While this book is hardly essential for any library, it is recommended as a complement to *Places Rated Almanac* for those libraries with a proven need for this kind of material. [R: WLB, May 93, p. 117]—**Thomas A. Karel**

943. Garoogian, Rhoda, Andrew Garoogian, and Jacqueline Diaz, eds. **America's Top Rated Cities: A Statistical Handbook.** 1992 ed. Boca Raton, Fla., Universal Reference, 1992. 5v. $129.95pa./set. LC 92-80903. ISBN 1-881220-00-1.

This set of books gives a substantial amount of data about the large cities of the United States. Despite its name, most of the metropolitan areas of half a million to a million inhabitants or more are included, along with a few smaller ones. The division of the cities into the five volumes is geographical but not along customary lines. For example, Philadelphia and Pittsburgh fall into two different books, whereas Cleveland and Charleston are found in the same one. The information given is appropriate for business purposes. State and municipal finances and family income distributions are followed by demographics, employment data, taxes and commercial real estate, utilities, and convention facilities. The final section for each city covers housing, education, health, crime, climate, and air and water quality.

This publication makes the same error found in most similar surveys: All facts apply only to corporate limits, not to metropolitan regions. Cities such as Boston and Hartford contain only about 15 percent of their regions, whereas San Diego and Jacksonville include almost all of theirs. Direct comparisons will be flawed if the data are taken at face value. This can be seen from the appendixes to each volume, which contain tables comparing the cities in a number of areas. For example, the western cities appear to have much higher crime and air pollution rates than their eastern counterparts. [R: Choice, Feb 93, p. 935; LJ, 1 Feb 93, p. 70]—**Arthur R. Upgren**

944. Rosenberg, Lee, and Saralee Rosenberg. **50 Fabulous Places to Raise Your Family.** Hawthorne, N.J., Career Press, 1993. 320p. maps. index. $17.95pa. HN60.R65. 306'.0973. LC 92-39518. ISBN 1-56414-034-2.

The authors of *50 Fabulous Places to Retire in America* (see ARBA 93, entry 921) have now compiled a guide to the most desirable places to live, if family life is a high priority. This book does not provide rankings of the 50 communities; rather, a number of criteria have determined the best places. Profiles of the 50 towns are arranged alphabetically by state and range from Vestavia Hills, Alabama (near Birmingham) to Spokane, Washington, with a varied listing in between. Major cities on the list include Sacramento, California; Indianapolis, Indiana; and Austin, Texas. However, smaller, less familiar locales dominate the list, such as Eden Prairie, Minnesota; Henderson, Nevada; and Mount Lebanon, Pennsylvania. Each profile is five pages long and follows a standard format, which includes "fabulous features" (and possible drawbacks), the real estate situation, cost of living (with emphasis on utilities and child care costs), taxes, climate, economic outlook, the public education system, medical care, crime and safety, community life, recreation, environmental conditions, transportation, and a select list of publications and organizations. Data are quite current and provide a solid means of evaluating the community. Introductory chapters discuss such practical matters as developing a financial strategy for relocating, evaluating schools, conducting an out-of-town job search, and moving efficiently and sanely. Libraries that own similar titles, such as *Livable Cities Almanac* (see ARBA 93, entry 920) or *Places Rated Almanac* (see ARBA 91, entry 908), should consider adding this title to their reference collections. [R: RBB, 15 April 93, p. 1534; WLB, May 93, p. 117]—**Thomas A. Karel**

945. Thomas, G. Scott. **Where to Make Money: A Rating Guide to Opportunities in America's Metro Areas.** Buffalo, N.Y., Prometheus Books, 1993. 327p. $34.95; $17.95pa. HT123.T45. 307.76'0973. LC 92-37008. ISBN 0-87975-762-0; 0-87975-795-7pa.

This book ranks the 73 metropolitan areas in this country with more than half a million in population in different categories with emphasis on business, economic, and employment opportunities. Thomas makes the best of the fatally flawed data available to him. The flaw lies in the census definition of a metropolitan area, which must adhere to county lines in some states and not others. Thus, the raw data is not homogeneous, because counties vary widely in size from one state to another.

The ratings of the regions seem to be predicated on the concept that the past is the guide to the future. However, they do not reflect the changing unemployment rates since 1990, the last year for which data are given. Furthermore, the frailty of this approach can be shown by a single example, such as the widely predicted drying up of the Colorado River in this decade, which would greatly lower the ratings of the entire Southwest. Any difference in the weighting of each factor in surveys of cities is also likely to change their rankings greatly. This is the main reason why lists of this kind differ considerably from one to another.

Despite the inherent and unavoidable weaknesses in any prediction of the future, this book contains much information about present metropolitan life that is worth attention. Most of it is readily available in standard references, such as the *World Almanac and Book of Facts* (see ARBA 90, entry 3), but some of the comments may be of interest to readers. [R: LJ, 1 Feb 93, p. 76]—**Arthur R. Upgren**

946. Willis, Alan. **American Suburbs: Rating Guide and Fact Book.** Milpitas, Calif., Toucan Valley, 1993. 846p. maps. $74.00pa. HA214.W55. 307.74'0973. LC 93-4750. ISBN 0-9634017-5-0.

This is a compilation that ranks 1,770 suburbs in the largest 50 metropolitan areas (roughly those having almost or more than one million inhabitants). The criteria include an overall composite rank and, in some cases, the median (or other value) household income and home value, crime rate, education of the inhabitants, commute times, and percent and length of home ownership. The suburbs included are limited to the ones with a 1990 population of more than 10,000 people. Thus, they are limited for the most part to those that are close to the core city or cities and tend to be reasonably fully developed as a result. A few more distant outlying places appear if their populations exceed the minimum of 10,000. (Census designated places are densely settled concentrations of population that are identified by name. They are not necessarily incorporated.) Explanatory notes in the introduction describe the listings and the methods used to derive the information and include a commendable description of U.S. suburbs and their evolution over the last two centuries. This volume achieves its goals; its only significant limitations are those inherent in any demographic compilation: The data may become out of date fairly quickly as suburbs change their characteristics in our mobile society. [R: Choice, Dec 93, p. 592; LJ, 15 Sept 93, p. 70; RBB, 15 Dec 93, p. 773]—**Arthur R. Upgren**

18 Women's Studies

ALMANACS

947. Snyder, Paula, ed. **The European Women's Almanac.** New York, Columbia University Press, 1992. 399p. maps. $35.00. HQ1587.S69. 305.4'094. LC 92-13451. ISBN 0-231-08064-6.

This compilation claims to be the first sourcebook on women in Europe. A statistical and anecdotal view of European women, it is presented in a readable, uncluttered format. Twenty-six countries are discussed, with some gaps due to political and size considerations. Especially noteworthy is the fact that Russia and its recently independent European republics are not included.

At the beginning of each entry is a brief general statistical overview. On the following pages the information almost exclusively covers women's issues in their widest sense. Areas discussed include equal rights, gay rights, health care (including abortion information), child care, maternity and paternity benefits, and employment. In addition, each country entry has several tables that provide statistics on general population characteristics, birth and death rates, labor characteristics, and major indicators for women's health.

At the end of several country entries is a section titled "Letters from...." These letters (or excerpts from speeches and other writings) lend a certain amount of humanity to the presentation. The reader is often given a clearer idea of a woman's status in a country in spite of what appear to be farsighted and far-reaching laws in that land, especially when compared to laws in the United States.

At the end of each country's chapter is a list of addresses of organizations that support feminist causes in that country. Also in this list is the address of that country's embassy in London. (There is no mention of Washington, D.C.) The almanac was compiled and initially published in Great Britain. For Americans there will be some adjustment because monetary comparisons are primarily made in pounds rather than dollars.

Considering the usefulness of this book and Europe's rapidly changing face, it is hoped that there will be timely updates of this almanac. A similar current publication that covered the United States would be helpful, as the only apparent such effort is the *Women's Rights Almanac* (see ARBA 75, entry 848). Recommended for both public and academic collections. [R: Choice, July/Aug 93, p. 1755; LJ, 1 Mar 93, p. 68; RBB, 1 April 93, p. 1454; WLB, Mar 93, p. 111]—**Phillip P. Powell**

BIBLIOGRAPHY

948. Bindocci, Cynthia Gay. **Women and Technology: An Annotated Bibliography.** Hamden, Conn., Garland, 1993. 229p. illus. index. (Women's History and Culture, v.7; Garland Reference Library of Social Science, v.517). $39.00. Z7963.T43B55. 016.30543'6. LC 92-34400. ISBN 0-8240-5789-9.

The extensive subject of women and technology covers a number of topics, and this selective bibliography touches on many of them. It is "an initial attempt to briefly summarize research efforts on the area of women and technology" (p. xi), focusing on English-language articles, books, dissertations, and conference proceedings published between 1979 and 1991. Most entries have short, informative annotations, except for collections, for which content notes are given.

The entries are arranged by broad categories, such as clerical, engineers/inventors, home work, household technology, industrial work, reproductive technology, women in development, and work. The categories are not well-defined; for example, industrial work and work both cover factory, mill, and mining labor, and women in development refers to women in developing countries. There is also an unfortunate lack of cross-references in both the text and the subject index, and the index is overly literal. For example, there are separate headings for gendering of jobs, gendering of work, occupational segregation, and sexual division of labor, with no *see also* references.

Despite its limitations, this is a valuable source in a burgeoning field served by few other bibliographies. As such, it is a worthwhile purchase for academic and research libraries. [R: Choice, Sept 93, p. 74; LJ, 1 June 93, p. 100]—**Susan Davis Herring**

949. Goetsch, Lori, and Sarah B. Watstein, eds. **On Account of Sex: An Annotated Bibliography on the Status of Women in Librarianship 1987-1992.** Metuchen, N.J., Scarecrow, 1993. 244p. index. $32.50. Z682.4.W65O53. 016.02'082. LC 93-8164. ISBN 0-8108-2701-8.

This volume is the third in a series of bibliographies on the status of women in librarianship. Intended to be comprehensive, it includes materials published between 1987 and 1992 that relate to the status of women in librarianship and that contribute to an understanding of women's evolving status and position in the library and information science professions. Included are books, articles, essays, conference reports, and pamphlets. Nearly all entries are annotated.

The bibliography is arranged chronologically by publication date, with author and subject indexes keyed to the citation number following the bibliography. Produced for the Committee on the Status of Women in Librarianship of the American Library Association, the bibliography is the collective work of a dozen women from different types of libraries and regions around the country, representing a broad range of professional and personal strengths. The aim of the annotations is to provide enough information to enable a user to determine whether the citation is worth retrieving. Citation identification and tracking is the result of both systematic and serendipitous approaches. The major indexing and abstracting sources are reviewed. Many citations, however, can only be located by an issue-by-issue analysis of periodicals and journals. Still others were identified by browsing the contents tables and indexes of books published in library science and related fields. This comprehensive bibliography belongs in any library that has the earlier volumes or wants a record on women in librarianship for the period covered. [R: JAL, Nov 93, p. 337; LJ, 15 Nov 93, p. 107]—**Janet Mongan**

950. Holt, Constance Wall. **Welsh Women: An Annotated Bibliography of Women in Wales and Women of Welsh Descent in America.** Metuchen, N.J., Scarecrow, 1993. 834p. index. $69.50. Z7964.G72W345. 016.30548'89166073. LC 93-22208. ISBN 0-8108-2610-0.

This is a welcome addition to the fast-growing literature of women's studies. The title seems restrictive until the contents are examined, revealing a wide and comprehensive treatment of the topic. Holt visited libraries in Wales, England, and the United States in order to locate materials about women in Wales and women of Welsh descent in the United States. The result is a list of more than 2,100 books, articles, dissertations, and manuscripts on the topic, covering all periods of history. For the most part, the works cited are in English, although a separate chapter is devoted to materials in Welsh.

The book shows evidence of being prepared by a good reference librarian. The contents are divided into broad subject areas, including medicine, biography, literature, religion, sociology, education, art, and history. Each chapter presents materials related to Wales first, followed by those concerned with the United States. Entry format is similar to what might be found in an annotated library catalog. Full bibliographical information is followed by an annotation, the library in which the item is located, the call number in that library, and a list of subject headings pertinent to that entry. Most items were personally examined by the author. If the item was not seen, this is noted. The book is well indexed by authors, titles, subjects, periodical titles, and library locations.

This book is impressive. Historians, researchers in women's studies, genealogists, librarians, and others will find it of value. Recommended for college and university libraries and others with an interest in the subject. [R: Choice, Oct 93, p. 267]—**Donald E. Collins**

951. Huls, Mary Ellen. **United States Government Documents on Women, 1800-1990: A Comprehensive Bibliography.** Westport, Conn., Greenwood Press, 1993. 2v. index. (Bibliographies and Indexes in Women's Studies, no.17). $79.50/v. Z7964.U49H85. 016.3054. LC 92-38990. ISBN 0-313-29016-4.

Public documents, speeches, and hearings can provide a wealth of information to anyone with the time and resources to sift through all the material. For nearly 200 years various government agencies, commissions, and congressional committees have been producing many such documents. While some of these documents have received attention, many others have unfortunately remained relatively obscure. These two volumes will be of immense benefit to researchers by improving the efficiency of a detailed search of government documents concerned with women's issues. They are logically organized and easy to use, and they provide an insightful and thorough view of not only the historical and contemporary conditions that have affected women's health and welfare but also, quite significantly, the government's perception of those conditions.

Collectively these two volumes contain nearly 7,000 annotated entries on a wide variety of issues relating to the economic, social, and political status of women. These annotations are concise and yet detailed enough to allow users to easily determine the potential usefulness of particular documents for further research. Entries also include documentation numbers to ease retrieval of a document from any depository library. Documents have been grouped by subject and then listed chronologically and by issuing agency. Volume 1 deals with more general works and social issues, including such topics as women's organizations, discrimination, suffrage and political participation, education, health, fertility and maternity, birth control, divorce and child support, poverty, violence against women, and female offenders. Volume 2 deals with women in the labor force and covers such topics as employment, wages and pay equity, health and safety, statistical reports and industry studies, women and the military, household employment, women entrepreneurs, vocational education, child care, and the elderly, as well as a section on the Women's Bureau.

The volume of public documents is as impressive as it is intimidating in its breadth and depth. These two comprehensive volumes will be an invaluable guide to those attempting to find and understand the actual and perceived role of women throughout the course of U.S. history and into the future. [R: Choice, Dec 93, p. 586; JAL, Nov 93, p. 347; RBB, 15 Dec 93, p. 781]—**Timothy E. Sullivan**

952. Nordquist, Joan, comp. **Feminist Theory: A Bibliography.** Santa Cruz, Calif., Reference and Research Services, 1992. 76p. (Social Theory: A Bibliographic Series, no.28). $15.00pa. ISBN 0-937855-55-3.

This bibliography provides a rich guide to 15 years of relevant materials on feminist theory from English-speaking countries. It is divided into three general categories: feminist theory in general, feminist theory in the social science disciplines in the academic setting, and feminist literary criticism. Each category begins with a subdivision titled "General" that lists works of general interest within that broader category. Thereafter, subdivisions are made in terms of specific categories.

Feminist theory in general includes material on women of color and lesbian feminist theory as well as works by African-American, Hispanic-American, Asian-American, and Native American women. Another subdivision in this section covers feminist theory and postmodern social theory and includes references to such thinkers as Michel Foucault, as well as to poststructuralist theories as they relate to feminist theory. The second category, after the general subdivision, is divided into feminist concepts of knowledge, sociology, political science, anthropology, and history. The third category is structured along lines similar to the first category.

Many of the works cited are not currently included in online computer searches, so there is no easy way to identify many of these references. This series should be in all college and university libraries and in public libraries serving a general intellectual community.—**Michael A. Foley**

953. Vyas, Anju, and Sunita Singh, comps. **Women's Studies in India: Information Sources, Services and Programmes.** Newbury Park, Calif., Sage, 1993. 257p. index. $28.95. HQ1181.I4V93. 305.4'0954. LC 92-16714. ISBN 0-8039-9438-9.

This compact book is not a comprehensive list of all published works about women of India but a work listing source materials published in India and Southeast Asia. In addition to literature published before 1990, this book also covers organizations that could provide primary literature or important contacts for interviews. The compilers have been original and inclusive in the types of materials they examined. About half of the book covers standard source materials: bibliographies and indexes; directories and handbooks for institutions; collective biographies; statistical sources, many of which are published by the national government; scholarly journals; dissertations; government publications, policies, and programs; funding sources for research; and conferences and seminars. The other half consists of information critical to women's lives and their societal and familial roles: women's organizations and agencies; popular press and special issues devoted to women; popular media events, such as exhibitions, a women's museum, and street theater; women's studies courses; women's information centers and libraries; networks that dispense information related to women, such as the Women's Information Network for Asia and the Pacific (WINAP); and publishers with series devoted to women. Each section includes an introduction explaining what impact this type of literature has on women's lives and why it is important for researchers. In addition to this logical grouping, indexes for authors, geographical location, and keywords provide additional access points.

Several features make this book particularly useful. Many of the sections have annotations explaining the contents of the publications or the purposes of the organizations. Probably due to the many languages in India, the compilers also note what a publication's primary language is. For many organizations and journals, the compilers give the address and sometimes a contact person.

This scholarly compilation contains a great deal of information for people at all levels and stages of research. Collections at an organization or research center concerned with India, a women's studies program, or a collegiate library with a focus on Southeast Asia or women's studies would benefit greatly from this work.—**Susan D. Baird-Joshi**

954. **WAVE: Women's Audio-Visuals in English: A Guide to Nonprint Resources in Women's Studies.** Madison, Wis., University of Wisconsin System Women's Studies Librarian, [1993]. 88p. illus. $2.00pa.

This guide lists 800-plus films, videos, filmstrips, slide shows, and audiocassettes pertaining to women produced between 1985 and 1990. Titles were culled from distributors' and producers' catalogs, filmographies, and reviews from a variety of library and feminist periodicals, such as *Choice, Media Report to Women, Off Our Backs,* and *Signs.* Arranged by some 20 subject categories, each entry provides the title, type (documentary, narrative, experimental, or other), date, formats, length, distributor, rental and sale prices, source, and a short description. A brief introduction explains the guide and includes suggested resources for more detailed information on the listed titles. Subject and title indexes enhance access. An appendix provides distributors' addresses and telephone and fax numbers.

The guide updates such sources as *Audiovisuals for Women* (see ARBA 81, entry 805), Margaret Hohenstein's *Films and Videotapes about Women* (University of Wisconsin System Women's Studies Librarian, 1984), *Films for, by, and about Women* (see ARBA 81, entry 1096), and *Films for, by, and about Women, Series II* (see ARBA 86, entry 1339). *Powerful Images* (Isis International, 1986) lists multilingual materials and has an international focus.

Produced to fill the gap left when the semiannual bibliography *New Books on Women & Feminism* (also compiled by the University of Wisconsin System Women's Studies Librarian) stopped including audiovisual resources, WAVE serves a valuable purpose and is recommended for academic and large public libraries. Future issues are promised. [R: Choice, Sept 93, p. 92; RBB, 1 May 93, p. 1618]

—**Linda A. Krikos**

955. Weber, Lynn, and others, eds. **Women of Color and Southern Women: A Bibliography of Social Science Research, 1975 to 1988. Annual Supplement, 1991/92.** Memphis, Tenn., Center for Research on Women, Memphis State University, 1992. 180p. index. $10.00pa. LC 90-656447. ISBN 0-9621327-3-X. ISSN 1054-1969.

This third supplement adds approximately 900 references to the original bibliography that covered the literature from 1975 to 1988 and its two subsequent annual supplements. The Research Clearinghouse on Women of Color and Southern Women, an online database now totaling more than 6,000 bibliographical citations to the latest research on these groups of women, provided these references. Included are books, book chapters, articles, dissertations, working papers, conference papers, and selected nonprint media. A succinct introduction explains the background of the project, its methodology, and definitions of terms. A complete list of racial and ethnic descriptors, several sample citations, and a partial list of sources follow the introduction.

The bibliography retains the format of the previous ones. It divides chronologically numbered citations into six major categories: culture, education, employment, family, health, and activism and social movements. These, in turn, subdivide by six racial or ethnic groups: African American, Asian American, Latina, Native American, Southern, and women of color. Materials listed under women of color cover more than one of the particular groups or focus on race generally. Citations are complete, include 3 to 12 subject descriptors, and may repeat under more than one category. Author and keyword indexes refer the user to citation numbers and enhance access.

This title provides a valuable service to researchers. It includes sources not covered by women's studies or traditional social science indexes. It eases access to subjects difficult to find (or nonexistent) in library catalogs and other bibliographies and indexes, covers all the social sciences plus history and health, and uses current terminology and preferred designations by group members (based partially on *A Women's Thesaurus* [see ARBA 88, entry 905]). Future supplements may want to include the terms *videos, slides, films,* and *filmstrips* in the keyword index to aid in finding nonprint media. Although *Women, Race, and Ethnicity* (see ARBA 93, entry 931) includes the humanities, sciences, and literature as well as the social sciences, its coverage of the literature begins in the mid-1980s, and there are no plans for more editions. This supplement also updates *Women of Color in the U.S.* (see ARBA 90, entry 862) to a certain extent. Highly recommended for academic collections.—**Linda A. Krikos**

BIOGRAPHY

956. Bataille, Gretchen M., ed. **Native American Women: A Biographical Dictionary.** Hamden, Conn., Garland, 1993. 333p. index. (Biographical Dictionaries of Minority Women, v.1; Garland Reference Library of Social Science, v.649). $40.00. E98.W8B38. 920.72'08997. LC 92-19990. ISBN 0-8240-5267-6.

At last there is a solid source for biographical information about Native American women. Some 231 women born between 1595 and 1960 appear in this well-written volume. More than 60 contributors prepared the entries, and each entry has at least one reference to further information about the biographee. Some of the entries are a pleasure to read, most uncommon in a reference work (e.g., Kenneth Lincoln's pieces on Mary TallMountain and Luci Tapahonso). There is a fair representation of Canadian and arctic women (31). The women one expects to find—Pocahontas, Sacagawea, Sarah Winnemucca Hopkins, Maria Montoya Martinez, and Nampeyo—are here. In addition, there is a strong representation of contemporary women, with 65 entries for women born between 1941 and 1960 (e.g., Wilma Mankiller, Leslie Marmon Silko, Gail Tremblay). Most entries are between 400 and 600 words long and provide basic biographical information and some sense of the person's life and contributions. Another section has background information about the contributors.

Several appendixes enhance the utility of this work. One is a list of entries by specialization of the biographees, such as activism, law, social work, and storytelling. Other appendixes provide breakdowns of the entries by decades of birth, by state or province of birth, and by tribal affiliation. A detailed index completes the volume. This is an excellent resource for any library serving individuals with strong interests in Native Americans. [R: Choice, Sept 93, p. 86; LJ, 15 April 93, pp. 86-88; RQ, Fall 93, p. 131; WLB, June 93, pp. 126-29]—**G. Edward Evans**

957. Campbell, Karlyn Kohrs, ed. **Women Public Speakers in the United States, 1800-1925: A Bio-Critical Sourcebook.** Westport, Conn., Greenwood Press, 1993. 509p. index. $75.00. HQ1412.W67. 305.42'092'2. LC 92-14615. ISBN 0-313-27533-5.

Although recent years have seen a growing number of reference books devoted to women as writers, less attention has been paid to women as orators and rhetoricians. This new biocritical sourcebook devoted to women as public speakers is thus very welcome as it chronicles the struggles of women "to be heard and to be heeded in the face of the hostility of the church, the courts, the professions, and the press" (introduction).

The sourcebook describes the lives and accomplishments of 37 women, including social reformer Jane Addams; educator Emma Willard; Clara Barton, founder of the American Red Cross; abolitionist Sojourner Truth; radical Emma Goldman; and many of the famous women who devoted their lives to women's rights and women's suffrage. The contributors are experts in their field; their entries are well written and well researched. Campbell has evidently allowed them a good deal of freedom in their choice of material: some devote space to their subject's career and achievements, while others emphasize the rhetorical strategies the women employed as speakers. However, each entry does contain background material, a critical discussion of the subject's speeches, and a conclusion summarizing the importance of her work. The bibliography that follows includes library collections, biographies, critical sources, and a chronology of major speeches and writing. There is an index as well. This excellent book should be useful to libraries with collections on both women's studies and public speaking. [R: Choice, June 93, p. 1612; RBB, 1 Sept 93, p. 92]—**Lynn F. Williams**

958. **International Who's Who of Professional and Business Women.** 2d ed. Ernest Kay, ed. Cambridge, England, International Biographical Centre; distr., Bristol, Pa., IPS/Taylor & Francis, 1992. 702p. index. $155.00. ISBN 0-948875-85-2.

In the foreword of this work, the editor makes a special point of asserting that there is no charge or fee for inclusion in the volume, but he does not state what criteria were used. Paging through the book likewise offers no clue as to criteria. Instead, the names seem to be a rather haphazard collection—some of which are appropriate to the book's title and purpose. The reader will find such names as Corazon Aquino, Angela Lansbury, and Sandra Day O'Connor, but where are Isabel Allende, Winnie Mandela, Jeane Kirkpatrick, Agnes Varda, Gloria Steinem, and thousands of other women who have made achievements in business and professional fields? At the same time, others included are lauded for such dubious accomplishments as designing their own swimming pools.

It is interesting to note that most of the well-known names in this collection are those of women who are well past the point in their careers when they are making contributions in their given fields. In addition, the people chosen for this supposedly international directory are generally Western English speakers, a fact that is supported by examining the geographical index, where the most names occur in the sections for Australia, Canada, England, and the United States. Of the seven women selected for dedications, all are U.S. citizens, and only one was born outside of the United States. A subject index reveals further imbalances in fields represented, with educators, for instance, claiming more than a page of listings while athletes and doctors have a mere fraction of the space.

Biographical descriptions in this work are limited to flat portraits that make even someone such as the late Marian Anderson, whose extraordinary career was sheer inspiration, sound tedious. Because of these deficiencies, one can only speculate about the intent and usefulness of this volume.—**Barbara Ittner**

959. Olsen, Kirsten. **Remember the Ladies: A Women's Book of Days.** Norman, Okla., University of Oklahoma Press, 1993. 222p. illus. index. $17.95pa. CT3202.045. 920.72. LC 93-16868. ISBN 0-8061-2558-6.

This selective collection of 380 biographical sketches is diverse and lively. From Hypatia to Grace Hopper, Joan of Arc, and Janis Joplin, Olsen supplies an engaging collection of notable women in a format ideal for browsing. The "book of days" calendar approach is not strictly followed; although most sketches are listed under either birth or death date, so many dates are undocumented that a good proportion of the biographies are entered on arbitrary days not otherwise assigned. The sketches are short—most around 300 words—and interesting, although details such as marriages and birth or death dates are sometimes omitted. The calendar arrangement is augmented by a name index for those needing more traditional access. A highly selective bibliography is included, but there are no references at the individual entries.

Remember the Ladies is neither as comprehensive nor as scholarly as *The International Dictionary of Women's Biography* (see ARBA 84, entry 673), although it includes a few entries not listed there. However, it does offer a distinctive flavor, some additional details, and more than 100 portraits. The engaging style and low price make it a good choice for any library. It is especially appropriate for public and school libraries.—**Susan Davis Herring**

960. Salem, Dorothy C., ed. **African American Women: A Biographical Dictionary.** Hamden, Conn., Garland, 1993. 622p. illus. index. (Biographical Dictionaries of Minority Women, v.2; Garland Reference Library of Social Science, v.706). $75.00. E185.96A45. 920.72'089'96073. LC 92-45727. ISBN 0-8240-9782-3.

This dictionary is dedicated to writers, librarians, archivists, and others who admire African-American women for their ability to achieve and excel in spite of often difficult circumstances. Thus, the positive tone of this volume picks up where many of the other recent works on African-American women have left off. The volume is a successful attempt to "render accessible fundamental information and research sources for this significant group of American women" (preface). It contains information on mostly historical achievements of 300 women, although there is some inclusion of contemporary ones. The women range in birth dates from Lucy Terry (b.1730) to Gail Devers (b.1966). Not as comprehensive as the two-volume *Black Women in America* (Carlson, 1993), or the single-volume *Notable Black Women* (Gale, 1992), this volume offers a less ambitious but still useful tool on the lives of important achievers among Black women. Arranged in dictionary style with a center insert of almost 60 black-and-white photographs, the main entries are in boldface capitals with maiden names, pseudonyms, or a.k.a. names in bracketed capitals. Discussions in the articles do a very good job of placing the individual within the historical context in which she was born, lived, and worked. Articles are signed, and there are a list of contributors, a list of entries by career category, and a very good general index.

What is probably one of the book's most attractive features is its size, the style and size of the typeface, and the quality of the paper. The photographs are also of very good quality, so it is truly a nice-looking volume. While some libraries and individuals can afford more expensive volumes on the subject of African-American women, few of them will find a more readable and attractive source than this.
—**Melvin M. Bowie**

961. Sova, Dawn B. **The Encyclopedia of Mistresses.** Stamford, Conn., Longmeadow Press, 1993. 289p. illus. $12.98. HQ806.S68. 306.73'6. LC 92-13774. ISBN 0-681-41382-4.

It is difficult to write a dispassionate review of a book whose premise is so offensive. Why laud the "woman behind the man" in this day and age? The fact that these women had sexual relationships with famous men is a poor focal point for a reference work. In the author's own words, "few of the mistresses have attracted interest for their own stories, aside from those born into powerful families or those who have achieved fame or notoriety on their own." Why are we being asked to read about the former, if only the men they knew made them notable? Those who have achieved fame or notoriety on their own can be found in a variety of other biographical sources, so why would a reader look for them here, where their primary "role" is as a man's mistress?

Sova asserts that she went through numerous texts and references about the men in order to find information about many of these women. Looking at the bibliography, it is obvious that her texts are primarily secondary sources. Of 154 books cited, only 9 are autobiographical works by the subjects of this book. Current scholarship in women's studies emphasizes searching out the facts in as many primary sources as possible because women have received short shrift in secondary sources for so long. There is little evidence of scholarship here; it is just a cut and paste of other biographers' work. Not recommended.
—**Sharon Langworthy**

962. Telgen, Diane, and Jim Kamp, eds. **Notable Hispanic American Women.** Detroit, Gale, 1993. 448p. illus. index. $59.95. E184.S75N68. 920.72'089'68073. LC 92-42483. ISBN 0-8103-7578-8.

As part of a new series of books from Gale, which includes *Who's Who Among Hispanic Americans* (see ARBA 92, entry 357), *Hispanic Americans Information Directory* (see ARBA 93, entry 428), and *The Hispanic-American Almanac* (1993), this attractively designed work contains 300 biographical sketches of prominent women. Represented are women of Mexican, Puerto Rican, Cuban, Spanish, Central American, and South American heritage; they were selected by an eight-person advisory board.

The work begins with an alphabetical list of entrants, followed by an occupation index and an ethnicity index. Biographical sketches range from 500 to 2,500 words, often accompanied by photographs. The sketches, written and signed by contributing authors, drew their data from telephone interviews or previously published information. They focus on personal, career, and family influences that have contributed to the success of these women. From politician Polly Baca to entertainer Raquel Welch, the work includes women from all walks of life who have not abandoned their Hispanic roots. Personal information is not glossed over, and biographees are often candid in the obstacles that they had to overcome to achieve their goals. A 19-page subject index concludes the book.

The work is easy to use and well conceived, and it will inspire young women to achieve excellence in their chosen professions. It deserves a place on the shelves of all libraries. [R: Choice, July/Aug 93, p. 1753; LJ, Aug 93, p. 96; RBB, 15 Oct 93, p. 474; RQ, Fall 93, pp. 132-33; WLB, June 93, p. 126-29]
—**Ilene F. Rockman**

963. **The World Who's Who of Women.** 11th ed. Ernest Kay, ed. Cambridge, England, International Biographical Centre; distr., Bristol, Pa., IPS/Taylor & Francis, 1992. 1108p. $195.00. ISBN 0-948875-80-1.

The main differences between this volume and the publishers' *International Who's Who of Professional and Business Women*, 2d edition (1992), are its larger size (nearly 7,500 entries in this book as opposed to 4,500 in the other), its wider scope, and the absence of geographical and occupational indexes. The lack of a geographical index makes it difficult to check which countries are represented, but this volume does seem to include a larger number of women from non-English-speaking countries. The dedications include women from such places as the West Indies, the Philippines, Bangladesh, and Finland. Many names occur in both volumes, but the editor does not explain the difference between the two books or how candidates were chosen for inclusion in either one. This book does seem to include more notables, such as Margaret Thatcher, Nancy Reagan, and Winnie Mandela, although they are buried among the names of personnel assistants, administrative secretaries, and accountants.

With the exception of comments regarding geographical representation, the criticisms of *International Who's Who of Professional and Business Women* all apply to this book. There is no apparent logic to the work, and the same stiff writing style plagues both volumes. With its indiscriminate coverage and uninteresting copy, it is difficult to think of a reason to purchase this guide.—**Barbara Ittner**

CATALOGS AND COLLECTIONS

964. Holland, Patricia G., and Ann D. Gordon, eds. **The Papers of Elizabeth Cady Stanton and Susan B. Anthony: Guide and Index to the Microfilm Edition.** Wilmington, Del., Scholarly Resources, 1992. 203p. $50.00. Z6616.S689P37. 016.3054'2. LC 92-22829. ISBN 0-8420-4077-3.

The papers of Elizabeth Cady Stanton and Susan B. Anthony represent the efforts of these pioneers in the U.S. women's movement to redefine gender politics. The two were founders of the National Woman Suffrage Association and the weekly newspaper *Revolution*. Prodigious writers, they coauthored the *History of Woman Suffrage* (Fowler & Wells, 1881-1886) and produced autobiographies.

Holland and Gordon have collected material found in 202 libraries and government agencies and 671 periodicals. The 45 reels have been organized in three series. The first series (reels 1-3) is the complete, refilmed *Revolution*. The second series (reels 4-5) consists of the archival collection of the National Woman Suffrage Association. The third series (reels 6-45) is a chronological collection of correspondence, speeches, articles and other written works, interviews, financial records, legal papers, and diaries. Holland and Gordon outline the history and progress of this project and provide guidelines for citations, dating of documents, abbreviations used within the documents, and their organization. They also supply a list of missing supplementary documents and provide biographical and genealogical information for researchers, as well as several pages of portraits.

The index is clearly organized and designed to supplement the largely chronological organization of the third series of microfilm. Even without the microfilm set, this guide and index will serve as a useful tool for women's studies researchers preparing independent projects.—**Mary Hemmings**

DICTIONARIES AND ENCYCLOPEDIAS

965. Hine, Darlene Clark, Elsa Barkley Brown, and Rosalyn Terborg-Penn, eds. **Black Women in America: An Historical Encyclopedia.** Brooklyn, N.Y., Carlson Publishing, 1993. 2v. illus. index. $195.00/set. E185.86.B542. 920.72'08996073. LC 92-39947. ISBN 0-926019-61-9.

When *Notable Black American Women* (see ARBA 93, entry 52) appeared, students of history and women's studies and reference librarians across the country were pleased. At last there was a reference work of authority, breadth, and depth on the lives and contributions of African-American women. Now comes a work of even greater magnitude. This ambitious set could conceivably become the definitive work on the history and contributions of African-American women. It comes at a time of heightened awareness of the worth of all women in the world, and when Black women are being listened to as significant contributors to global and cultural understanding.

As implied by its subtitle, this work is as much encyclopedic as it is biographical. Not only are the lives of Black women presented in signed articles, but there are also 164 topics treated throughout the work. From the abolitionist movement to Zeta Phi Beta sorority, the topics represent some of the major contexts in which Black women have worked, struggled, and achieved. Noticeably absent from the topics list, however, are literature and art. While they are not discussed under these two topics, women from literature and art are included in individual biographies and under such topics as the Harlem Renaissance. Surprising inclusions are radio, rap music, and vaudeville and musical theater. There is a very detailed discussion of Black women's contributions to nursing and the nursing profession, no doubt because of one of the editors' earlier work and interest in that area. However, taken as a whole, the discussions lend depth and breadth to understanding the lives of the women chronicled. One of the most fascinating and provocative discussions is that on feminism in the twentieth century. Black feminism is compared to the women's movement, and the writer states that "Black feminism has not striven solely to secure equal rights for women with men, because gaining equal rights with Black men would not necessarily lead to liberation for African-American women."

Volume 2 contains a chronology of Black women in the United States, from 1619, when three African women were put ashore at Jamestown, Virginia, to 1992, when Virginia Fuller was named athletic director at Northeastern Illinois University (becoming the first Black woman to hold that position at a Division I school). Volume 2 also contains an extensive bibliography of basic resources that includes an alphabetical list of the names of major research collections of primary materials and their addresses. A classified list of biographical entries categorizes the subjects by field of endeavor, and a very detailed subject index to both volumes is supplied. The set is generously illustrated with black-and-white photographs of biographees and relevant historical artifacts. All articles are signed and include a bibliography of sources used. There are cross-references throughout the work that lead the user to related topics or biographies. The editorial advisory board consists of 21 women who represent some of the most prestigious universities in the country. (Information on all editors and contributors is included at the end of volume 2.)

When comparing this set to *Notable Black American Women*, the conclusion is that each work contributes in a unique way to understanding and appreciating the lives and work of African-American women. Each offers material that is absent from the other. For example, Kathleen Battle, the Metropolitan Opera singer, was not included in the earlier book but is briefly discussed in the current set. On the other hand, Willie B. Barrow, an important organizer with Jesse Jackson's Operation Push in the 1960s, appears in the earlier work but not in the current one. Because the two works complement and supplement each other, librarians and other users should consider purchasing both. However, *Black Women in America* is by far the more comprehensive. Highly recommended for all types of libraries. [R: BR, Sept/Oct 93, p. 64; Choice, June 93, p. 1596; JAL, July 93, p. 200; LJ, 15 Feb 93, p. 156; RBB, 1 May 93, pp. 1614-16; RQ, Summer 93, p. 561; SLJ, May 93, pp. 137-38; WLB, May 93, p. 113]—**Melvin M. Bowie**

DIRECTORIES

966. Fulford, Margaret, ed. **The Canadian Women's Movement, 1960-1990: A Guide to Archival Resources. Le Mouvement Canadien des Femmes, 1960-1990.** Toronto, ECW Press, 1992. 380p. illus. index. $70.00. 305.42. ISBN 1-55022-156-6.

This is a useful bilingual guide to the resources on the women's movement in Canada from 1960 to 1990. It covers a wide variety of material on many organizations and associations that were influential in the movement during this period. Some of the available material is scattered in many archival depositories across Canada, but much of it remains with an individual association or organization.

Two distinct lists of individual organizations are grouped alphabetically under related Canadian provinces. One concerns those organizations whose records have been turned over to an archive; the other is a list of organizations that still hold their records. The individual citations usually include the organization's name; the location of the records; the collection's official record group or name (where appropriate), a summary of its contents, the amount of material in it, and its condition; access policy; and finding aids (if they exist). Most, but not all, of the entries are in English. All but one of the entries for Quebec are only in French.

Locating primary source materials is always difficult, and this kind of guide is always welcome. It will prove valuable to academic research institutions with strong collections in women's studies.

—Jane Jurgens

967. Henry, Dawn, comp., and Susan A. Hallgarth, ed. **DWM: A Directory of Women's Media.** 16th ed. New York, National Council for Research on Women, 1992. 268p. index. $30.00pa. ISBN 1-880547-11-2.

This edition is the first to be published by the National Council for Research on Women. It is thicker and sleeker than its predecessors, which were published by the Women's Institute for Freedom of the Press. (For reviews of earlier editions see ARBA 89, entry 821 and ARBA 83, entry 701.) Intended as an update to those earlier editions, this one includes some new entries and new descriptions of publications, especially newsletters. The publishers' goal is to improve access to the woman-owned and generated organizations and works that the book lists, elements described as essential to publicizing and preserving the truth of women's lives. It is international in scope, with primarily nonmainstream resources. Entries range from *American Baptist Woman* to *Sappho's Isle* (a tri-state lesbian newspaper). It also defines media broadly, listing bookstores, writers' groups, speakers' bureaus, libraries, archives, museums, and music organizations among its main categories.

The directory is arranged by category, the largest of which is periodicals, followed by 12 smaller sections. Entries were updated and compiled from questionnaires and are cross-referenced in three indexes according to publication or organization name (including parent organization, where appropriate), names of individuals, and geographic location. Most entries have descriptions, and some include subscription or membership information. Following the main directory is an extensive list of additional resources. This section begs all sorts of questions, and these entries should be incorporated into the main directory in future editions.

Although it overlaps such works as the *Women's Information Directory* (Gale, 1992) the strength of this volume is its specialization in publications and media. It continues to be more thorough with each edition and a valuable reference for public and academic libraries. [R: LJ, Jan 93, pp. 94-96]

—Glynys R. Thomas

968. **Women's Information Directory: A Guide to Organizations, Agencies, Institutions, Programs, Publications, Services, and Other Resources....** Shawn Brennan, ed. Detroit, Gale, 1993. 795p. index. $75.00. ISBN 0-8103-8422-1. ISSN 1063-0554.

This work contains more than 10,800 listings of resources relevant to U.S. women and women's issues. An advisory board of prominent women's information specialists aided Brennan in the selection and arrangement of the work. Included in the guide are descriptive listings, which are arranged into 26 chapters according to type of information provided, and a complete master name and subject index. Most of the entries contain contact data and descriptive information about the association or product, such as the date of its founding and the purpose or service it performs. Many women will appreciate the information contained in the chapters that describe 1,194 national women's organizations, 2,061 state and local women's organizations, 1,715 organizations to assist battered women, 1,218 displaced homemaker programs, and 351 federal and state agencies and domestic assistance programs. Students and researchers of both genders will also be interested in the lists and descriptions of libraries, museums, and galleries with special collections of interest to women; women's colleges, research centers, and women's studies programs; publications, publishers, and booksellers that focus on topics for, by, and about women; and scholarships, fellowships, loans, awards, and prizes that are available to women. This guide is highly recommended for public and school libraries that attempt to provide up-to-date directories of human service organizations in their reference collections. [R: Choice, June 93, p. 1612; JAL, May 93, p. 131; LJ, 1 April 93, p. 94; RBB, 15 Mar 93, p.1379; RQ, Summer 93, p 580; WLB, April 93, pp. 126-27]

—Terry D. Bilhartz

HANDBOOKS AND YEARBOOKS

969. Barrett, Jacqueline K., and Jane A. Malonis, eds. **Encyclopedia of Women's Associations Worldwide: A Guide to Over 3,400 National and Multinational Nonprofit Women's and Women-Related Organizations.** Detroit, Gale, 1993. 471p. index. $80.00. LC 93-13702. ISBN 1-873477-25-2.

In addition to Gale's other encyclopedias of associations, it has now launched the first edition of *Encyclopedia of Women's Associations Worldwide* (EWAW). The main body of the work contains more than 3,400 listings for nonprofit, national, and multinational women's or women-related organizations. It is broken down by region into eight chapters and then alphabetically by country within each chapter. Two indexes are included: an alphabetical list by name of organization and a subject index.

While the subject index is interesting, it is also disappointing. Many of the subjects listed are *see* references, so that several subjects are lumped together under one category. Business and management, for example, brings together 11 *see* references to create a list of more than 150 organizations. While the list is helpful, it will be cumbersome to have to read through each listing to find an organization that deals with computers or advertising. The same is done for the sciences and the social sciences, except that when one looks up philology and is told to *see* social sciences, one finds no philology organization under that category. (A philology organization is found under the humanities category, where it actually belongs.)

While interesting categories such as aviation and prostitution list a fair number of organizations, categories such as rape and sexual abuse seem underrepresented, and several small U.S. organizations devoted to these subjects and known to this reviewer are not included. Organizations with as few members as five and as recently formed as 1992 have made it in, such as the China Association for Women's Journals and Periodicals, but the Daughters of the American Revolution was somehow overlooked.

This encyclopedia, however, remains an invaluable resource for anyone needing information about women's organizations around the world. It is hoped that this invaluable resource will be updated on a regular basis and be available in every public and academic library.—**Patricia A. Sarles**

970. Read, Phyllis J., and Bernard L. Witlieb. **The Book of Women's Firsts: Breakthrough Achievements of Almost 1,000 American Women.** New York, Random House, 1992. 511p. illus. index. $24.00; $16.00pa. CT3260.R428. 920.72'0973. LC 92-16872. ISBN 0-679-40975-0; 0-679-74280-8pa.

Putting a new twist on an old idea, this handy compendium documents the breakthrough achievements of nearly 1,000 American women from the seventeenth century to the present. Diversity is the watchword, and this eclectic, multicultural listing includes notable feminine firsts in a wide variety of endeavors, from the scholarly, serious, and noble to the daring, offbeat, and whimsical. Athletes, reformers, and criminals are all represented, and entries include everything from the first woman chosen as principal chieftain of a major Native American tribe to the first woman to go over Niagara Falls in a barrel. Alphabetically arranged by person, each entry features the reason for inclusion, a biographical sketch, and (in some cases) a photograph. Entries vary in length from several sentences to a page or more, and a relatively brief index provides some subject access.

Attractive and highly readable, this biographical handbook supplements the existing "firsts" literature. It provides information not easily found elsewhere and should be a useful addition to the general reference collections of most public and some academic libraries. [R: BR, Nov/Dec 93, p. 36; SLJ, Feb 93, p. 124; WLB, Feb 93, p. 103]—**Kristin Ramsdell**

INDEXES

971. Castillo-Speed, Lillian, comp. and ed. **The Chicana Studies Index: Twenty Years of Gender Research 1971-1991.** Berkeley, Calif., Chicano Studies Library Publications, University of California, 1992. 426p. index. $90.00. Z1361.M4C457. 305.48'86872073. LC 92-10870. ISBN 0-918520-21-5.

This reference tool provides access to gender research on all aspects of the Chicana experience in the United States. It includes 6,792 numbered entries (representing approximately 1,150 citations) arranged by subject, then alphabetically by author. Each citation entry, in addition to the full bibliographical description, includes language and a list of index terms with major descriptor terms noted. On the average, each citation is indexed under three terms. Subject headings from the 4th edition of the *Chicano Thesaurus for Indexing Chicano Materials* (University of California, Office of the Librarian) are used. The book includes separate author and title indexes, as well as cross-references. Journal and book articles, books, dissertations, and reports are covered. Biographical articles were generally excluded, while critical articles on Chicana authors are included. Creative writing, poetry, short stories, and novels are also excluded. The index expands and updates the author's earlier bibliography, *Chicana Studies: A Selected List of Materials since 1980* (1990). All materials were selected for inclusion on the basis of their usefulness for research. The introduction provides a useful orientation for the reader. There is also a section on how to use the index, with sample citations and a brief but clear description of each part. A list of the periodicals indexed is included.

A complete bibliographical citation for each periodical, rather than simply a title, place, and publisher, would have been more useful. Although the book is designed in two columns, which makes reading easier, using different sizes and styles of type for subject headings and author's names would have improved the book's attractiveness and readability. However, it is an important, useful tool for students, scholars, and researchers interested in women's studies, particularly Chicana studies. It brings together in a single, easy-to-use volume much valuable bibliographical information for use in the reference collections of academic and research libraries, as well as urban public libraries serving Hispanic communities.—**Susan J. Freiband**

QUOTATION BOOKS

972. Maggio, Rosalie, comp. **The Beacon Book of Quotations by Women.** Boston, Beacon Press, 1992. 390p. index. $25.00. PN6081.5.B43. 082'.082. LC 92-4697. ISBN 0-8070-6764-4.

973. Partnow, Elaine, comp. and ed. **The New Quotable Woman.** rev. ed. New York, Facts on File, 1992. 714p. index. $40.00. PN6081.5.N49. 082'.082. LC 91-25960. ISBN 0-8160-2134-1.

As Partnow points out in the preface to her compilation *The New Quotable Woman*, only one-half of one percent of the quotations in the new edition of John Bartlett's *Familiar Quotations* (see ARBA 93, entry 89) were made by women. This imbalance alone makes timely the simultaneous appearance of two collections of quotations by women. Partnow's book is a revision of two earlier volumes and, as they were, is arranged chronologically by author, starting with Eve and going to women who flourished in the 1970s and 1980s. The more than 15,000 quotations are printed in double columns. Four indexes cover biography, subject, career and occupation, and ethnicity and nationality. Maggio's *The Beacon Book of Quotations by Women* is also in a two-column format, but its 5,000 quotations are arranged by subject, and authors are listed in an index. There is also a subject index, which is not very useful, as it duplicates the main listing.

The two books have many similarities. Both compilers discuss the problem of sexist language in their introductions and reveal a feminist slant in their choices. Many of the same authors appear in both volumes, ranging from the literary (e.g., Jane Austen, Maya Angelou) to the political (e.g., Clare Booth Luce, Bess Truman) to the notorious (e.g., Mae West). But the passages chosen rarely duplicate each other, even for authors such as Julia Ward Howe, who produced only one memorable work.

The researcher focusing on the work of distinguished women through the centuries will prefer the Partnow volume, with its larger number of entries and its detailed biographical and subject indexes. But the browser or writer seeking a quotation for a specific occasion will find the Maggio compilation easier to use as well as more attractively bound and printed. Either would be a worthwhile purchase to place beside Bartlett's. [R: BR, Nov/Dec 93, p. 36; JAL, May 93, p. 130; SLJ, Jan 93, p. 145; SLJ, Mar 93, p. 242]
—**Lynn F. Williams**

Part III
HUMANITIES

19 Humanities in General

GENERAL WORKS

Bibliography

974. Erlich, Richard D., and Thomas P. Dunn, comps. **Clockworks: A Multimedia Bibliography of Works Useful for the Study of the Human/Machine Interface in SF.** Westport, Conn., Greenwood Press, 1993. 324p. index. (Bibliographies and Indexes in World Literature, no.37). $75.00. Z5935.5.E74. 016.7. LC 93-1069. ISBN 0-313-27305-7.

Erlich and Dunn, editors of two useful anthologies of articles on mechanized environments—*The Mechanical God* (Greenwood Press, 1982) and *Clockwork Worlds* (Greenwood Press, 1983)—have at last produced an annotated bibliography to accompany these works. *Clockworks* covers a wide range, from fiction (in both anthologies and complete works) to scholarly endeavors (reference and literary criticism) to other media, including stage, screen, and television; the visual arts; and music. The annotations, although brief, are informative and accurate. The bibliography covers a vast amount of material, although it is far from complete. There are substantial omissions in fiction and in scholarship, although the wide range of the subject probably makes these inevitable. This will be a useful reference book for libraries and scholars with collections of or an interest in science fiction or utopian and dystopian literature. Recommended. [R: Choice, Dec 93, p. 584]—**Lynn F. Williams**

975. McCormick, Frank. **Sir John Vanbrugh: A Reference Guide.** New York, G. K. Hall, 1992. 228p. index. (Reference Guide to Literature). $40.00. Z8925.15.M38. 016.72. LC 92-13099. ISBN 0-8161-8990-0.

Sir John Vanbrugh is an uncommonly interesting figure in British cultural history because he was a leading playwright and enjoyed even greater success as an architect who held the high position of Comptroller of the Office of Works. His brilliant Restoration comedies were warmly received in his own time, and his work on two English baroque architectural masterpieces, Blenheim Palace and Castle Howard, made him a figure of immense distinction.

McCormick, professor of English at Eastern Illinois University, has compiled an annotated bibliography of more than 700 entries on the literature covering Vanbrugh's life and career. Arranged chronologically and spanning 1694 to 1990 (with one additional entry for 1991 for a book by McCormick), this is a highly detailed and complete account of the published materials on Vanbrugh. McCormick offers caveats that there may be brief reviews of plays and personal diary and notebook accounts of visits to Vanbrugh houses that he has not covered, but all substantial writings have been searched out and described. There are two indexes. The first is a list of authors or titles (when no author exists), and the second is an index to topics and allusions with multiple references to Vanbrugh's plays, buildings, Whig associates, and eventful life. As academic circles on both sides of the Atlantic have witnessed increased interest in the baroque era since the 1920s, researchers and librarians will find this publication of value not only for the life of the man who has been called "the Shakespeare of architects" but also for the eighteenth century in Great Britain and the manners and customs of an extended historical period.—**William J. Dane**

Biography

976. Harmon, Justin, and others. **American Cultural Leaders from Colonial Times to the Present.** Santa Barbara, Calif., ABC-Clio, 1993. 550p. index. (Biographies of American Leaders). $65.00. NX503.A49. 700'.92'273. LC 93-36284. ISBN 0-87436-673-9.

This third volume in a series that presents brief biographical information about leaders of the United States includes 360 individuals—men and women, living and dead, foreign and native-born—who have made significant contributions to American culture. Specific fields encompassed are art, dance, film, literature, music, and theater. Omitted are television, radio, other forms of entertainment, journalism, and criticism.

Arranged in alphabetical order, the entries contain a brief identification of the individual and the area of significant achievement or contribution. This is followed by short biographical profiles (750-1,500 words) that highlight specific achievements. Cross-references are given as appropriate. Concluding each entry is a one- to four-item bibliography for further reading. A list of entries, a preface, and a user guide to entry format prove useful not only to clarify the nature of the information supplied but also to elucidate why certain key contributors to American culture have been omitted from the work.

Given the brevity of information, this volume likely will prove most useful to secondary school students and college freshmen and sophomores. Public libraries with limited budgets might also avail themselves of it, especially for those whose collections are weak in biography. The work will function well in the general reference setting, complemented as necessary by more advanced and specialized biographical tools.—**Edmund F. SantaVicca**

977. Law, Jonathan, ed. **European Culture: A Contemporary Companion.** New York, Mansell/Cassell, 1993. 403p. $70.00; $24.95pa. ISBN 0-304-32718-2; 0-304-32720-4pa.

This guide identifies and provides an intellectual context for more than 1,000 people who are important contributors to both Eastern and Western culture since 1945. Although most entries are brief assessments of important people, also included are key institutions, cultural movements, and artistic genres and schools. Culture is understood in the humanistic rather than the anthropological sense, so that major emphasis is given to painting, sculpture, architecture, music, literature, theater, and film. However, some significant figures and themes from the sciences, philosophy, theology, and the social sciences have been included if the editor felt they had an important impact on thought. High culture is given preference over popular culture, although one might argue that Monty Python (not included) was as important to contemporary culture as the Boulting Brothers (twins who directed many British satirical comedies in the 1950s and 1960s, who are included). On the other hand, this exclusion may be due to the fact that preference is given to creators of cultural works rather than to performers.

Entries are concise, but not so brief as only to identify a subject: The entry on the British novelist Iris Murdoch, for example, not only names the most important of her 23 novels but also describes why she is a significant cultural figure. Readers should also remember that this book's focus is on European figures, even if, as with the British poet Thom Gunn, they have spent most of their creative lives in the United States.

Two biographical companions that somewhat resemble this guide are *The Penguin Companion to the Arts in the Twentieth Century* (see ARBA 87, entry 868) and Justin White's *Makers of Modern Culture* (Facts on File, 1981), but these books focus on all of the twentieth century, rather than just the post-World War II period. Although readers needing more detailed information will need to consult other sources, *European Culture* is a welcome addition to the ready-reference collection.—**David Isaacson**

Catalogs and Collections

978. Kristeller, Paul Oskar, comp. **Iter Italicum:.... Volume VI:.... Supplement to Italy (G-V), Supplement to Vatican and Austria to Spain.** Kinderhook, N.Y., E. J. Brill, 1992. 595p. $228.57. Z6611.H8K7PA57. 001.3. LC 64-3533. ISBN 90-04-09455-5.

This is the final volume of Kristeller's monumental finding guide to the manuscripts of Renaissance humanism. Called *Iter* ("Journey") in the tradition of earlier reports on voyages of discovery into manuscript repositories, and *Italicum* because Italy, the point of origin of the intellectual movement in question, was

Kristeller's initial focus, this enormously valuable survey has been in gestation since the 1930s and under way in print since 1963. A great part of Kristeller's own life work (he was honored in 1992 for volumes 4 and 5 with the Charles Homer Haskins Medal of the Mediaeval Academy of America), the *Iter* has become something of a collaborative effort, with librarians, archivists, and teaching scholars contributing corrections and additions as the work progressed. The present volume, covering much of Italy, the Vatican, and various other countries, including Poland and Japan, is of this sort, bringing up-to-date earlier reports on the pertinent holdings in the areas reviewed. As was the rest of the set, it is richly detailed and will be essential for many decades to come. It follows the usual order of country, city or town, library, collection, shelf-mark, and reports on humanistic manuscripts, chiefly Latin or Italian, from 1350 to 1600.

No academic library supporting original research into any aspect of European culture during this period can afford to be without the entire *Iter*. The same is, of course, true for major public libraries with research emphases that include Western Europe in the later Middle Ages and the early modern period. A good index is still needed for this volume; one has recently been provided for volume 5, and presumably one for volume 6 is already in preparation.—**John B. Dillon**

Dictionaries and Encyclopedias

979. Biedermann, Hans. **Dictionary of Symbolism.** New York, Facts on File, 1992. 465p. illus. index. $45.00. AZ108.B5313. 302.23. LC 91-44933. ISBN 0-8160-2593-2.

The rather provocative subtitle on the cover of this translation, by James Hulbert, of Biedermann's *Knaurs Lexikon der Symbole* (Munich: Droemer Knaur, 1989) suggests that its entries might trace the myths of Orpheus and Aphrodite through Elvis and Marilyn. At the same time, Biedermann claims to draw from sources that transcend "Eurocentric concerns" to offer the first one-volume overview of symbolism in Asia, Africa, and the New World as well. In fact, the closest the collection comes to interpreting what might be regarded as modern cultural icons are prefatory references to Sherlock Holmes, Tarzan, and E.T. (one might perhaps also include the entry for "U.F.O."). Instead of these, Biedermann claims to focus on symbolic figures that have left "deeper impressions in our cultural life." The multicultural coverage and interpretation of symbols, in the meantime, gives way by and large to the likes of Moses, Munchhausen, and the muses, whose Western significations are presented without other cultural parallels.

Beneath this sort of hype is, in fact, a very convenient and solidly scholarly dictionary that identifies and defines a selection of approximately 2,000 fairly traditional symbols and figures of the world's cultures, with an irresistible emphasis on Western culture and Germanic culture in particular (e.g., the entries for Flying Dutchman and William Tell). Although significant attention is given to symbolic personalities (deities, prophets, and heroes), Biedermann's most useful contributions are for things. Entries for different animals, colors, flowers, and numbers, as well as for such things as hands, mountains, stars, and wheels, give both specific and culturally diverse information. The entry for "ax," for example, cites different symbolic uses in cultures ranging from Minoan to Afro-Brazilian. This is just the sort of information students and scholars frequently need to help explicate literary passages. Indexes for topics and for some 600 black-and-white illustrations provide quick access.

Biedermann's dictionary does not supersede, either in scope of coverage or in interpretive diversity, more comprehensive standard works, such as James Hastings's *Encyclopedia of Religion and Ethics* (Scribner's, 1908-1927) and Mircea Eliade's *Encyclopedia of Religion* (see ARBA 88, entry 1392). Similarly, other equally selective dictionaries, such as *Symbolism: A Comprehensive Dictionary* (see ARBA 87, entry 866), cover topics (e.g., leopards, leprechauns) that Biedermann omits. As a convenient one-volume handbook that gives specific details about many of the world's traditional symbols, Biedermann's dictionary finds a niche somewhere between these other comprehensive and selective sources and will be quite useful. [R: Choice, May 93, p. 1435; BR, May/June 93, p. 54; RBB, 1 Feb 93, p. 1001]

—**James K. Bracken**

980. **The Cassell Dictionary of Literary and Language Terms.** By Christina Ruse and Marilyn Hopton. London, Cassell; distr., New York, Sterling Publishing, 1992. 313p. $17.95. 403. ISBN 0-304-31927-9.

Justifying the publication of yet another literary dictionary, the authors state that this one is written for beginning students and English-as-a-second-language students, and that it includes terms from many disciplines. The definitions are often extremely short, sometimes only a line or two. Considering that brief does not always mean clear, do beginning students really need such a simplified approach, or would they be better served by more thorough discussions of particular terms?

As for the selection of terms, this dictionary does have terms from fields other than literature and language, including theater, journalism, and advertising. However, the broad subject matter means that no one area is covered exhaustively. Words about the theater include stage terms such as *apron stage* and *proscenium*, but not *upstage* or *downstage*. Complete dictionaries in the relevant fields would give users more chances of finding all the definitions sought. Another category of terms included are those that the authors describe as "vocabulary items that may not be readily identifiable as literary terms but are common in course work and essays." However, this does not make this dictionary unique, as many of those words, such as *essay* and *thesis*, are also defined in the older literary dictionaries. Supplementary material in this book is limited to a three-page time line of literary history. Again, such a time line appears in at least one older work, and more substantially.

This work would be an acceptable addition to a large collection with multiple literary and language dictionaries. But if the library needs only a single dictionary of these terms, this probably should not be the one. [R: RBB, 1 Mar 93, p. 1250]—**Terry Ann Mood**

981. Cevasco, G. A., ed. **The 1890s: An Encyclopedia of British Literature, Art, and Culture.** Hamden, Conn., Garland, 1993. 714p. index. (Garland Reference Library of the Humanities, v.1237). $95.00. DA560.A18. 941.081'03. LC 92-42341. ISBN 0-8240-2585-7.

In this work almost 300 scholars have contributed articles on some 800 topics concerning the 1890s in Great Britain. This decade's art, literature, and culture—so vibrant, experimental, stimulating, frivolous, serious, self-conscious, contradictory, and frustrating—are covered thoroughly and accessibly in an easy-to-use, well-designed, and well-written encyclopedia. Most articles are on individuals (e.g., authors, artists, scientists, journalists, actors, politicians), but other topics include political and aesthetic doctrines, periodicals, individual books (more than 100 entries), philosophical and theological movements, and cultural "institutions" (e.g., the Cafe Royal, the Rhymers' Club). Although the work aims to delineate British culture during that period, several Continental influences are included. Each entry has a short bibliography and cross-references where appropriate, and there is a useful index. The tone is direct and almost colloquial, while the level of detail and analysis strikes a happy balance between the scholarly and the popular (tending toward the latter). This remarkable reference work belongs in most academic and large public libraries. [R: Choice, Dec 93, p. 579; LJ, Aug 93, p. 92; RBB, 1 Oct 93, pp. 382-83]

—**Jeffrey R. Luttrell**

982. McConkey, Wilfred J. **Klee as in Clay: A Pronunciation Guide.** 3d ed. Lanham, Md., Madison Books; distr., Lanham, Md., National Book Network, 1992. 61p. index. $6.95pa. NX163.M3. 700'.92'2. LC 91-26863. ISBN 0-8191-8247-8.

This is a small paperback guide to the most frequently mispronounced names of major contributors to Western culture. Although limited to approximately 400 names (in sections on architecture, literature and drama, music and dance, painting, and sculpture), it is a good guide to "foreign" name pronunciation in the arts from the fourteenth century to the present. An alphabetical index leads back to entries by page number. Entries include names in alphabetical order within sections, birth and death dates, and simple pronunciations. Examples of artists with difficult names are Horst Antes, German architect; Isabel Allende, Chilean novelist; Giovanni Boccaccio, Italian novelist; Edvard Munch, Norwegian painter; Saki, pen name for Hector Hugh Munro, British satirist and humorist; Vladimir Nabokov, Russian-born novelist; V. S. Naipaul, Trinidad-born novelist of Indian parentage; and Stefan Zweig, Austrian writer.

This edition eliminates some names found in earlier editions because reputations have grown enough that the names are pronounced correctly now. Other names have been added. The standard for pronunciations is that of knowledgeable Americans related to the arts, from art curators and gallery staffs to cultural attaches and faculty members of universities. For some names the original-language publications have been dropped in favor of more "naturalized" pronunciations that eschew sounds that Americans are not used to producing. This useful and easy-to-carry guide will prove most valuable to media personalities in radio and television.—**Maureen Pastine**

Directories

983. Gullong, Jane M., and Noreen Tomassi, eds. **Money for International Exchange in the Arts.** New York, ACA Books/American Council for the Arts, 1992. 122p. index. $14.95pa. NX398.G85. 700'.79'73. LC 92-35492. ISBN 1-879903-01-6.

The purpose and use of this short guide are expressed in the introduction, which says that support for international exchange in the arts "must be pieced together from a variety of sources, idiosyncratic in their goals and interests." This section goes on to detail possibilities and strategies for obtaining funds.

The body of the work is divided into five parts: service organizations, foundations, corporations, international contacts, and government agencies. Included in the typical entry are organization name and address, contact person, profile (a sentence or two of history or a few facts about scope and emphases), eligibility (whose grant applications are more likely to be rewarded), application procedure, and deadlines. Indexes by name of organization, by geographical area (region), by discipline (six headings), and by type of support given (e.g., technical, fellowships, research, travel) make the data easily accessible. The work is compact, the format, good. Recommended for specialized collections. [R: Choice, July/Aug 93, p. 1752; RBB, 15 May 93, p. 1718]—**Robert N. Broadus**

Handbooks and Yearbooks

984. Magill, Frank N., ed. **Great Events from History II: Arts and Culture Series.** Pasadena, Calif., Salem Press, 1993. 5v. index. $375.00. NX456.G72. 700'.9'04. LC 93-28381. ISBN 0-89356-807-4.

This is the third set in Magill's *Great Events from History Series*, following the *Science and Technology Series* (see ARBA 92, entry 1465) and the *Human Rights Series* (see ARBA 93, entry 617). It joins the original 12-volume series, which surveyed historical events from 4,000 B.C. to 1979. This new set focuses on the twentieth century, covering 493 topics in artistic and cultural life from 1897 to 1992. Topics range from the traditional fine arts to popular developments such as radio, television, and rock music.

The chronologically arranged articles follow the customary Magill format. They begin with a ready-reference listing that indicates the category of event, time, and locale. Next comes a two- or three-line summary of the event. Principal personages involved are then listed, and finally the essay on the topic appears, which is divided into four sections: a summary of the event, the impact of the event, a brief bibliography, and cross-references to related articles in the series. The set concludes with a very useful index that allows access by broad categories, subject and key words, individuals, and places.

Typical of Magill reference works, this set is aimed at an undergraduate audience. The style is simple and factual, and the tone is that of an introductory college course for students with no prior knowledge of the subject. One has the sense that some of the topics, while arguably important, are not exactly "events" and have been forced into that mold by the editor (e.g., "Radio broadcasting dominates home leisure," "Beat Movement rejects mainstream values"). Also, many of the articles seem trivial (e.g., "Brooks Brothers introduces button-down shirts"), particularly because they share equal space with truly significant events. Nevertheless, the set serves as a good, readable starting point for further study. [R: LJ, Jan 93, p. 96; RBB, 15 April 93, pp. 1534-35; WLB, Feb 93, p. 104]—**Jeffrey R. Luttrell**

985. Ward, Charles A. **Moscow and Leningrad: A Topographical Guide to Russian Cultural History. Volume 2: Writers, Painters, Musicians and Their Gathering Places.** New Providence, N.J., K. G. Saur/Reed Reference Publishing, 1992. 309p. index. $90.00. ISBN 3-598-10834-6.

This three-volume series strives to present an exhaustive topographical index to Russian cultural history associated with St. Petersburg and Moscow. While volume 1 concentrates on architecture by presenting and briefly describing 700 buildings, the second volume covers the addresses of influential writers, painters, and musicians. The book is more than a registry of places, however; it also offers an introduction to the lives, works, and backgrounds of these cultural figures. Chapter 1, "Writers Before the 1840's," starts with Russia's earliest secular writer, Tsar Ivan IV the Terrible; chapter 2, "Writers 1840's-1920's," ends with Vladimir Mayakovsky's suicide in 1930. Chapter 3 discusses painters from Andrey Rublev to Nikolay Konstantinovich Rerikh. Chapter 4 covers musicians such as Mikhail Glinka and Peter Ilich Tchaikovsky. The next two chapters focus on the streets of Moscow and St. Petersburg. This section lists significant addresses arranged by street. The work is made complete by the addition of maps, an appendix of changed street names, a bibliography, an index of names, and an index of topics.

This well-researched book will help both cultural historians and committed visitors to Russia who want to move beyond the standard tourist sights to enhance their understanding of Russian culture and history. Thus, not only Slavic and historical research libraries but also serious travel collections will benefit from this work.—**Zsuzsa Koltay**

Periodicals and Serials

986. Barlow, Richard G. **The Fifth Directory of Periodicals Publishing Articles on American and English Language and Literature, Criticism and Theory, Film, American Studies, Poetry and Fiction.** Athens, Ohio, Swallow Press/Ohio University Press, 1992. 349p. index. $49.95; $19.95pa. LC 65-9218. ISBN 0-8040-0958-9; 0-8040-0962-7pa. ISSN 0070-6094.

This directory is designed to help authors of scholarly articles and creative pieces identify periodicals to which they can submit their manuscripts. It is a much-needed update of the out-of-print version published in 1974. Fortunately, the past 19 years saw the birth of a large number of new periodicals in the humanities, especially in fields such as film, women's studies, interdisciplinary approaches to literature, and comparative literature. The introduction gives a number of practical suggestions to authors, such as avoiding humorous and cute statements, focusing on research, and providing precise citations. The main body of the book is broken down into the general categories of literature journals, criticism and theory, film journals, language and linguistic journals, American studies journals, and fiction and poetry journals. A typical entry for a periodical title is introduced by general publication information, including institutional affiliation, address, subscription rate, founding year, sponsorship, and frequency. Next, major fields of interest, manuscript information, and payment information are given. Major indexing services covering the publication and copyright information round out each entry. A subject index provides more detailed access to periodical titles. This well-researched and clearly structured directory will be a much-appreciated, valuable, and affordable tool for authors in the humanities. [R: Choice, Mar 93, p. 1104; RBB, 1 Feb 93, p. 1002]—**Zsuzsa Koltay**

987. **MLA Directory of Periodicals: A Guide to Journals and Series in Languages and Literatures 1993-95. Periodicals Published in the Americas.** 7th ed. Kathleen L. Kent, comp. New York, Modern Language Association of America, 1993. 357p. index. $130.00pa. ISBN 0-87352-651-1.

This successful spin-off from the complete *MLA Directory of Periodicals* (see ARBA 89, entry 69) has, since its first appearance in 1984, provided libraries and scholars with a useful list of United States and Canadian periodicals indexed in the *MLA International Bibliography* (see ARBA 86, entry 1077). More than 3,200 periodicals are indexed in that bibliography; this directory lists the 1,344 titles in that larger work that are published in the Americas. Each alphabetical entry provides extensive data on the scope and editorial and submission requirements of each publication, as well as details on location, staff, and sponsoring organization, if any. Approximately 80 percent of the entries have been verified directly by MLA editors; those titles that have not been verified are clearly marked. Several additional indexes provide information on the journal title abbreviations used by the MLA, subjects covered by these periodicals, names of editorial staff, sponsoring organizations, languages published, and periodicals that list an author-anonymous policy. As with earlier issues of this directory, smaller libraries should continue to find that this more focused—and less expensive—volume amply meets their needs for bibliographical and document verification purposes.—**Elizabeth Patterson**

20 Communication and Mass Media

GENERAL WORKS

988. **Gale Directory of Publications and Broadcast Media 1993: An Annual Guide to Publications and Broadcasting Stations....** Julie Winklepleck, Eric J. Restum, and Scott Stange, eds. Detroit, Gale, 1993. 3v. with update. maps. index. $280.00/set. ISBN 0-8103-7528-1. ISSN 1048-7972.

This directory provides detailed information about radio, television, and cable stations and systems as well as newspapers, magazines, journals, and periodicals. Publication entries encompass 19 different kinds of data that include all of the expected information, such as name and address, plus such items as printing method, trim size, advertising rates, and circulation statistics. The same is true for broadcast entries. Collectively, the volumes yield an enormous amount of information.

To help locate broadcasting facilities and print material, the directory has ample keys and indexes. For example, a key to entries is printed at the bottom of each page, eliminating the need to flip back and forth over a single key. The master index is arranged alphabetically, disregarding media type; subject indexes are organized geographically (maps are included) and by subject. Detailed statistics are provided (e.g., the number of newspapers published in each state arranged by type). The number of AM, FM, television, and cable stations and systems is also listed by state. The directory contains explicit information for making comparisons as well as finding key personnel, such as newspaper feature editors.

The directory should be of value to a wide audience, from those needing circulation information or advertising costs for a local newspaper to those seeking undeveloped markets. Special interest groups can locate ethnic publications; college fraternities and religious groups will also find publications of interest. In conclusion, the directory has numerous uses and should be considered for reference collections in medium-size libraries and as a standard resource in large public, academic, and special libraries.
—**William E. Hug**

989. **Guide to Worldwide Postal-Code and Address Formats, 1993: Practical Tips for Standardizing Foreign Addresses.** Nelson, Marian, ed. New York, Nelson Associates, 1993. 137p. index. $99.50 spiralbound.

This guide is updated and published coincidental with world and postal changes. Still a unique work (according to its publisher), it is invaluable for anyone who deals with foreign correspondence. Containing information on address systems throughout the world in the same format as its predecessors, it is divided into five sections, with an index concluding the book. New material since the first edition includes recent changes that have affected international addresses, tips on reading foreign handwriting, U.K. county names and abbreviations, and the new format for military mail. In addition, there is information on the format for EURODIP, interruptions in mail service, foreign-language terms for returned mail, and key contacts for selected information sources throughout the world.

When initially reviewed in ARBA 91 (see entry 941), the guide was praised for its content, but the physical quality was criticized in comparison to the price. Well, the price has gone up, but the quality has soared. Now printed on both sides of the page in easy-to-read print, there is even more information, as well as labeled dividers to ease the process of finding it and a much sturdier cover. Overall, this product is a worthwhile purchase.—**Jo Anne H. Ricca**

990. Lent, John A., comp. **Bibliographic Guide to Caribbean Mass Communication.** Westport, Conn., Greenwood Press, 1992. 301p. index. (Bibliographies and Indexes in Mass Media and Communications, no.5). $59.95. Z5634.C37L45. 016.30223'09729. LC 92-19373. ISBN 0-313-28210-2.

991. Lent, John A., comp. **Bibliography of Cuban Mass Communications.** Westport, Conn., Greenwood Press, 1992. 357p. index. (Bibliographies and Indexes in Mass Media and Communications, no.6). $65.00. Z5634.C9L46. 016.30223'097291. LC 92-24462. ISBN 0-313-28455-5.

These two works are a compendium of literature on mass communication. The extensive amount of pertinent materials on Cuba required a separate book to do justice to the resources. Both books contain listings for sources that reflect contemporary and historical perspectives; they are drawn from books, periodicals, conference papers, dissertations, and theses. Quite a few of the resources mentioned are in documents that are difficult to locate and access. Most of the citations for the Caribbean work are in English, while the one on Cuba includes many in Spanish. The latter has a valuable introduction to Cuban mass media, while the former provides sections on major regions in the Caribbean. Both have author and subject indexes.

These are highly specialized, expensive bibliographic guides that may not be suitable for purchase by public and smaller libraries. Academic and specialized libraries with a focus on Cuba and the Caribbean may want to add them to their collections. Unfortunately, these types of bibliographic guides tend to become dated quickly. Consequently, unless they are updated regularly, they will serve mainly as sources of historical information. [R: Choice, June 93, pp. 1606-1607]—**Roberto P. Haro**

992. **The World Media Handbook 1992-94.** New York, United Nations, 1992. 504p. $65.00pa. ISBN 92-1-100488-8. S/N E.92.I.21.

This 2d edition is more comprehensive than its predecessor; more than 160 countries are listed instead of the original 68. However, the price has doubled. Again, indicators (population size, income, life expectancy, media availability, official languages, literacy, and telephone and telex availability) are provided as background for a list of newspapers, magazines, news agencies, broadcast and television stations, and communications education sources. In general, this factual and statistical material is quite valuable and accurate; however, there are numerous glaring errors. For example, readers are asked to assume that there are no telephones in Belize (although an international code is given) and that no tertiary education is provided; that illiteracy in Cuba is as high as 6 percent and that it is nonexistent in the United States; that in India the only official languages are Hindi and English (only 14 papers are listed for this country, when 16 are provided for other countries); that in New Zealand, Maori is not an official language, and all Maoris are literate; that Canada has no illiterates; that Cyprus is in western Asia; that the Louisville *Courier-Journal* deserves inclusion while the New York *Post, New York Daily News*, and *Newsday* do not; and that the *Christian Science Monitor* has a circulation of 1,135,000 daily (it is currently about 100,000). There could be more consistency in editing; some papers have *The*, while in others the article is omitted. Notwithstanding the shortcomings and errors, this is a most valuable reference work for those in the field. [R: 15 May 93, p. 64]—**Marian B. McLeod**

AUTHORSHIP

General Works

993. **The AWP Official Guide to Writing Programs.** 6th ed. D. W. Fenza and Beth Jarock, eds. Norfolk, Va., Associated Writing Programs and Paradise, Calif., Dustbooks, 1992. 243p. index. $15.95pa. ISBN 0-916685-30-6.

More than 300 graduate and undergraduate writing programs in the United States and Canada are profiled in this indispensable and inexpensive resource for writers-to-be seeking practical and timely information on creative writing education. There also is a large section describing conferences, colonies, and centers, which offers details on programs ranging from the two-week Aspen Writers' Conference to the "Hawk, I'm Your Sister" program in Santa Fe, New Mexico (an eight-day writing retreat and canoe trip for women). Depending on the institution, creative writing programs may include poetry, playwriting, scriptwriting, translation, fiction, and other forms of writing. The directory is arranged alphabetically by educational institution and lists telephone number, degrees offered, required course of study, other requirements (e.g., foreign language, written examinations), scholarships and fellowships, length of residency, and current faculty listings. Programs are indexed by state and by degrees offered.

Compiled by the Associated Writing Programs, a national nonprofit organization located at Old Dominion University in Norfolk, Virginia, this comprehensive, single-volume source focuses on creative writing education. It is not a source on creative writing careers. A gentle warning is issued in the preface: "Please keep in mind that—although academe has never been more hospitable to living authors—the competition for full-time, tenure-track academic jobs remains extremely fierce."—**Jo A. Cates**

994. Collingwood, Donna, with Robin Gee, eds. **Mystery Writer's Marketplace and Sourcebook.** Cincinnati, Ohio, Writer's Digest Books, 1993. 312p. index. $17.95. ISBN 0-89879-612-1. ISSN 1068-8528.

For many years *Writer's Market* (see ARBA 91, entry 945) has been the leading market guide for writers working in a variety of genres. Apparently the producers of that volume decided that the mystery genre has enough established and aspiring writers to merit the publication of a separate market guide dealing only with that field. *Mystery Writer's Marketplace and Sourcebook* seeks to be a one-stop volume for those who write, or who would like to write, mystery, suspense, and crime short stories, articles, and novels. In addition to a thorough market guide, other topics include trends in crime fiction and writing the mystery. Other sections deal with literary agents who handle the genre; mystery writers' organizations, conventions, contests, and awards; references, including a glossary; and book stores specializing in mystery. In addition to the general index, another index provides a list of 20 categories of mysteries sought, ranging from "Amateur Sleuth," "Cozy," "Hard-Boiled Detective," and "Malice Domestic" to "Urban Horror" and young adult.

What this volume aims to do, it does well and thoroughly, but other books and magazines contain the same information. Mystery writers will no doubt be quite willing to pay the price to have personal copies of this volume, but the wider *Writer's Market* will probably continue to be the volume of choice for libraries that can afford only one such market guide. [R: RBB, 15 Dec 93, pp. 778-79]
—**Kay O. Cornelius**

995. **Directory of Publications Resources, 1993-94: Selected Books, Software, Periodicals, Organizations, Courses, Contests, Grammar Hotlines, and Tools.** Linda Jorgensen and Paula Moore, eds. Alexandria, Va., EEI, 1993. 121p. index. $14.00pa. ISBN 0-935012-15-X.

This biennial publication from EEI (formerly Editorial Experts, Inc.) provides an excellent overview of an eclectic field. It is geared to a variety of publication professionals: publishers; editors; authors; desktop publishers; and designers in book, magazine, and newsletter publishing. Although it is a compilation of selected works, it contains an impressive amount of information. The goal is to present a broad range of professional tools to help users "acquire and maintain professional excellence."

EEI has listed more than 100 books, 73 software packages, 25 periodicals, and numerous organizations (from the United States, Canada, and abroad), as well as training programs, contests, and grammar hotlines. The annotations are generally descriptive and, in the publisher's term, "neutral." One can assume sources are recommended by their inclusion. The books listed include word guides; style guides; writing, editing, and usage references; and computer and desktop publishing books. A comprehensive range of software types is listed, such as word processing, editing, and indexing programs; desktop publishing, graphics, and spreadsheet software; and even optical character recognition and virus protection programs. In such a small space, an exhaustive listing is impossible. To overcome this shortcoming, the editors have provided some guidance to sources of more detailed information in the short introductions to each section.

In all, there are few surprises here. Many of the standard, well-loved works are included. The strength of the book lies in the wide range and variety of sources. Libraries that provide reference works in the field of publishing will want to buy it, as it is an excellent reference to tools for publishers.
—**Stephen Haenel**

996. Mogilner, Alijandra. **Children's Writer's Word Book.** Cincinnati, Ohio, Writer's Digest Books, 1992. 354p. $19.95. PE1691.M57. 428.1. LC 92-17778. ISBN 0-89879-511-7.

Writer's Digest Books has established a tradition of producing valuable reference works for writers. This book is a fine addition to their line for children's writers. Mogilner has compiled graded word lists for kindergarten through sixth grade readers. Most of the work consists of an alphabetical list, lists of words by grade, and a thesaurus of synonyms for different grade levels. The alphabetical list contains all words used in the graded word lists (more than 6,000 words). The lists were compiled from basic word lists, then checked by reading specialists and panels of children. The trickiness of selecting and using words for different grade levels is not ignored by the author; she admits that word lists are not exact. Indeed, such lists will vary from school district to school district and from publisher to publisher. This book was created to fill a need for overall general guidance to word choice.

This work, though, is not simply a list of words but a detailed guide to using age-appropriate words. Each grade-level list begins with an introduction covering social changes, "In the Classroom" (what topics are introduced and the general nature of the curriculum), publishing (specifics of the market for that age level, such as type of popular stories and appropriate sentence lengths), and writing samples.

This book will help take the guesswork out of word choice and should enable authors to write more accurately to specific age levels. Educational writers, classroom educators, and those creating children's and young adult literature will find the book particularly useful. The author's insights on the children's publishing market will also prove helpful. Libraries that offer works of interest to writers should buy this book.
—**Stephen Haenel**

997. Speck, Bruce W., comp. **Publication Peer Review: An Annotated Bibliography.** Westport, Conn., Greenwood Press, 1993. 277p. index. (Bibliographies and Indexes in Mass Media and Communications, no.7). $65.00. Z5165.P3. 016.0704'1. LC 92-42695. ISBN 0-313-28892-5.

The controversial practice of peer review, in which a manuscript or system is subjected to a critical evaluation by other experts in the same field, has been hotly contested for decades. Despite the fact that peer reviewing is frequently used as a criterion for foundation grants and tenure, very little empirical research has been done on the benefits and pitfalls of this practice. Speck attempts to fill this void with the second of his projected four-volume series dealing with editing. The first volume was *Editing* (see ARBA 92, entry 897). *Publication Peer Review* is an annotated bibliography covering 780 books and journal articles published between 1960 and 1991. The citations are arranged in alphabetical order by the author's last name. The annotations vary in length and scope, ranging from 15 to 250 words. The OCLC number has been included with each citation to simplify the location of the individual items. There are a fairly detailed subject index and a separate author index that picks up secondary authors. [R: Choice, Oct 93, p. 272]—**Steven J. Schmidt**

998. **Who's Who in the Writers' Union of Canada: A Directory of Members.** 4th ed. Toronto, Writers' Union of Canada; distr., Toronto, Playwrights Union of Canada, 1993. 382p. illus. $25.00pa. 810.9'0054. ISBN 0-9690796-3-X.

This book provides access to living Canadian writers. Librarians in the United States will recognize many of the names in this directory, such as Margaret Atwood, Robertson Davies, Mordecai Richler, and Farley Mowat. There are many more; the book has 731 full entries and a list of the other members of the Writers' Union of Canada, to total 920. Each entry has a brief biography provided by the subject and, in most cases, a picture. Also, each entry has a list of selected publications, awards, readings, lectures, and workshops, and a mailing address. (For those wishing to preserve their privacy, the mailing address is that of the Writers' Union, but one can at least send a letter to each writer.) A valuable feature of the book is found in the brief chronological picture of "The Writers' Union—How We Started." The Union was formed in 1970 in the face of "the encroachment of American culture and the takeover of major Canadian publishing houses by U.S. firms," with the establishment of the Royal Commission on Book Publishing. The Union was formed to include writers in the whole process of maintaining Canadian culture and publishing. Membership is restricted to those who have had books published in the previous five years or who have prior publications still in print.

This directory will be very useful to anyone interested in Canadian writers. Heartily recommended for large public and academic libraries, especially those with collections of Canadiana.—**Edward P. Miller**

999. **The Writer's Handbook.** 1993 ed. Sylvia K. Burack, ed. Boston, The Writer, 1993. 873p. index. $29.95. LC 36-28596. ISBN 0-87116-167-2.

Less flashy than its competitor, *Writer's Market* (see ARBA 91, entry 945), Burack's revised and expanded edition of *The Writer's Handbook* is still one of the standard reference sources for budding authors. The 1993 edition contains more than 100 articles that offer advice and inspiration to budding authors from some of the best-known writers in the business. The first 60 pages feature inspirational pieces on the writing process from Ursula K. Le Guin, Mary Higgins Clark, and a dozen others. The articles deal with such common problems as writer's block, education for writers, and dealing with criticism and rejection. The next section delves into the nuts and bolts of writing technique. This section, which runs for more than 500 pages, features an interview with Dick Francis and a piece by Anne Perry on creating a series character. The final portion of this hefty volume consists of nearly 300 pages of freelance markets for books, articles, greeting cards, and fillers. There is a title index to the listing in this section. Finally, *The Writer's Handbook* offers an up-to-date list of literary prizes, writers' conferences, and literary agents.—**Steven J. Schmidt**

Style Manuals

1000. Butcher, Judith. **Copy-Editing: The Cambridge Handbook for Editors, Authors and Publishers.** 3d ed. New York, Cambridge University Press, 1992. 471p. illus. index. $44.95. PN162.B86. 808'.02. LC 90-47567. ISBN 0-521-40074-0.

The two standard references in the field of copyediting are Karen Judd's *Copyediting: A Practical Guide* (see ARBA 91, entry 949) and this work, first published in 1975. Although Butcher's guide has British editors as its primary audience, it is a useful and authoritative source of information for United States publishing professionals as well.

The text is organized into three general areas. The first group of chapters addresses the basic steps involved in turning a manuscript into a book, including an overview of the copyeditor's function, how to estimate and spec pages, how to prepare the manuscript for typesetting, and how to handle illustrations and proofs. The next several chapters treat specific parts of the book (e.g., front matter, indexes, glossaries, bibliographies) with practical, detailed instructions as to how each of these items should be handled. The remaining chapters cover various types of manuscripts—literary material; multiauthor and multivolume works; science and math; classical, law, and music books; and reprints and new editions—and their special editing circumstances. Among this wealth of information, the chapter devoted to house style will be especially helpful to fledgling editors struggling to define and document their own house style.

Reflecting the increasingly global nature of all our economies as well as the electronic tools now available to writers and publishers, this edition has added guidelines for dealing with manuscripts submitted on computer disk or as camera-ready copy; updated information on copyright law (although a British emphasis is present, there is also coverage of United States copyright issues); suggestions for avoiding sexist, racist, or "parochial" (country-specific) language and imagery; and reference guides on Hebrew, Arabic, and non-Western calendars and characters.

Smaller libraries needing a basic guide to copyediting will probably find that Judd's *Copyediting* is sufficient to their needs; however, for professional editors, authors, publishers, and larger libraries, *The Cambridge Handbook* will be an important supplementary reference to have on hand. Although the writing style is dry, the work offers practical, prescriptive guidelines organized in an easily accessed format.
—**G. Kim Dority**

1001. **The Chicago Manual of Style.** 14th ed. Chicago, University of Chicago Press, 1993. 921p. $40.00. Z253.U69. 808'.027'0973. LC 92-37475. ISBN 0-226-10389-7.

A lot of adjectives apply to this new edition of a style manual published since 1906: long-awaited, definitive, authoritative, well known, classic. Some 200 pages longer than its predecessor (see ARBA 83, entry 85), *Chicago* (as it is fondly known) has been revamped in almost every chapter to reflect current usage. It continues to be divided into three main sections—bookmaking, style, and production and printing—but now has 19 chapters rather than 20, because material on documentation, which stretched over three chapters in the 13th edition, has been combined into "Documentation 1: Notes and Bibliographies" and "Documentation 2:

Author-Date Citations and Reference Lists." In fact, the single most significant change in the book is that all the material on documentation has been rewritten, updated, and reorganized for greater ease in finding examples and increased unification of topics. There is better coverage of the citation of nonprint forms, medieval references, and electronic documents.

Other major changes include the addition of many more examples of usage and form (e.g., the spelling guide for compound words and words with prefixes and suffixes); a more thorough discussion of the role of computers in publishing; the inclusion of material on the exterior of a book (e.g., the jacket, the artwork); the complete revision of the chapter on copyrights and permissions; increased coverage of speech, quotations, and indirect and interior discourse (e.g., stream of consciousness); and, most thoroughly, the revision of the entire section on documentation. The lesser changes are legion and cannot all be listed; examples are the revision of the bibliography and glossary, the new section on Hebrew in the foreign languages chapter, and updated terms for various ethnic groups. The index is notably larger than before, and the typeface is more widely spaced and easier to read.

Not everything has changed, of course. The format, which has been alternately helpful to and annoying to users, has been retained. But who can quibble with a work that has basically shaped editorial policy in the United States? Every library, even the smallest, should replace their earlier editions with this one. Individuals and institutions connected with publishing, particularly scholarly and book publishing, will want to do the same. Those who do not have it are strongly urged to obtain it if they wish to be in tune with the way this country edits. [R: LJ, 15 Oct 93, p. 58; RBB, 1 Oct 93, p. 381]—**D. A. Rothschild**

1002. Li, Xia, and Nancy B. Crane. **Electronic Style: A Guide to Citing Electronic Information.** Westport, Conn., Meckler, 1993. 65p. index. $15.00pa. PN171.D37L5. 808'.02. LC 93-24523. ISBN 0-88736-909-X.

As we delve deeper into the electronic age of communication and information storage, it becomes necessary to rethink our old and sometimes outdated ways of citation. This work gives librarians, students, and others new and updated versions of how to cite the vast warehouse of information stored in more than 6,800 databases, 3,000 networked discussion groups, and 200 electronic journals. Using the American Psychological Association as a guide, Li and Crane have taken this standard reference work and added new dimensions to include electronic information. In addition to the standard citation, they have added type of medium (e.g., CD-ROM, Telenet) and an availability statement (e.g., directory and address of the file). Place of publication and publisher have been dropped. However, the two new additions will help anyone find the original electronic information given as a source. The remainder of the book addresses the new issues of citation of personal electronic mail, bulletin board conferences and discussion groups, and computer programs.

The beginning chapters of the guide start with the basic formats of sources. Type of information is broken down further, with variations used based on information source (e.g., type of medium, availability). The variations may seem minor but should be watched closely, or future researchers may find themselves lost in a vast electronic maze of information. What is lacking is an explanation for some of the variations in the citations. For instance, when an author is not listed, the type of medium is placed before the date instead of after it.—**Kevin W. Perizzolo**

NEWSPAPERS AND MAGAZINES

1003. **Bacon's Media Calendar Directory 1993.** 11th ed. Edited by Bacon's Information Inc. Chicago, Bacon's Information, 1993. 839p. index. $230.00 looseleaf w/binder. ISSN 0736-4644.

Editorial calendars for major North American magazines and professional journals form the core of this work. The journals are listed alphabetically under such subject headings as "Home Center Operations," "Epicurean," and "Nursing." Each entry includes the name of the publication, its editorial address, frequency of publication, issuance, circulation, telephone and fax numbers, editorial and advertising contacts, lead time required, editorial profile, advertising rates, and editorial focus and special issues. A selected group of major daily newspapers, arranged alphabetically by state, is featured in a separate section with similar information provided. There are indexes to subjects and products, trade shows and conventions, convention sites, and publications.

One-time users may have difficulty navigating the subject categories, which, unfortunately, are not included in the table of contents. The list of journals is extensive but not complete (e.g., there are no entries for *Chocolatier, Emergency Librarian, Parabola,* or *Utne Reader*), and some of the journals do not publish their editorial calendars. Finally, it would be nice to have a complete list of staff writers and editors in such a publication. In spite of these minor criticisms, this work will be extremely helpful to public relations and advertising professionals and freelance writers, who, through constant use, will become well acquainted with the book's format.—**Barbara Ittner**

1004. **Bacon's Newspaper/Magazine Directory 1993.** 41st ed. Bacon's Information, ed. Chicago, Bacon's Information, 1992. 2v. index. $250.00pa./set. ISSN 0162-3125.

The stated goal of Bacon's directories is to provide contacts in the United States and Canada to whom those in public relations can send news releases for publication. For this edition, the name has been changed from *Bacon's Publicity Checker* (see ARBA 92, entry 899), the page size has been enlarged, and a paperbound format has replaced the comb-binding.

The first of the 2 volumes of this set identifies more than 9,200 business, trade, professional, farm, hobby, enthusiast, and consumer magazines and newsletters. The second volume does the same for 1,700 daily and 8,300 weekly, semiweekly, and triweekly newspapers and news services. The magazine volume codes its entries by subject areas ("market classifications"), which are grouped alphabetically by subject areas. It is necessary to consult the cross-reference of subjects at the beginning to get the code number, then check the code number list for the page. Each number-coded entry includes address information, circulation, frequency, publisher, types of news releases sought, advertising rate, and key staff, but no price for a subscription, year the magazine started, or source of indexing. Many of the entries in this edition contain a short description of the scope and reader focus of the magazine. There are an index of all titles and an index of publishers of four or more titles with the names of those magazines. No index of publications by city or state is provided for the magazine volume.

The newspaper volume is arranged geographically under daily and nondaily newspapers, and a third listing provides special indexes (e.g., news services and syndicates, syndicated columnists). The newspaper entries include comprehensive lists of the names of management and news executives and of section editors and columnists. Circulation (daily and Sunday) and advertisement rates are noted. For the weekly section, nondaily and independent papers have similar information, adding days of issue. Those papers that are published as a chain or group refer to the main entry under "multiple publishers" at the end of each state listing. These papers often share a news release through different editions. In the third section, the "daily newspapers locator" provides city and entry number for those newspapers that have no specific city as part of the title.

Bacon's directories are attractive to the eye and well organized. Although they are complex due to their myriad of diverse information, they are carefully designed for relative ease of use. Because there is no subscription price or indexing service data, Bacon's serves a different purpose than the standard library periodical directories. With this limitation in mind, the set can still be helpful for collection development, and the average library user may prefer the format and limited geographical scope to the more comprehensive directories. Recommended for mid-size and larger public libraries and academic or special libraries where there would be an interest.—**Gary R. Cocozzoli**

1005. Bjorner, Susanne, comp. and ed. **Newspapers Online: A Guide to Searching Daily Newspapers Whose Articles Are Online in Full Text.** 2d ed. Needham Heights, Mass., BiblioData, 1993. 1v. (various paging). index. $120.00 looseleaf w/binder. ISBN 1-879258-07-2.

Newspapers Online is a looseleaf directory of more than 150 daily newspapers throughout the world that make their contents available electronically through one of several vendors (Data-Star, DataTimes, DIALOG, Dow Jones News, Retrieval, InfoGlobe, Infomart, or Mead) or that publish fulltext versions on CD-ROM. The 1992 edition, which covered 125 United States and Canadian newspapers, has been expanded to include 18 European, Middle Eastern, Asian, and Australian newspapers. Newspapers are grouped regionally into four areas: Asia and Australia, Europe and the Middle East, Canada, and the United States. A typical entry covers two pages and includes name, address, telephone number, and editor; a paragraph describing the region served; a list of the major newsmakers in the area; a description of the paper and its contents and circulation; electronic availability online and on CD-ROM; and search tips. For example, the entry for the *Louisville Courier Journal* notes that it is available online from DataTimes and

Dow Jones News from March 19, 1988, onward, and that a CD-ROM version is published by Newsbank. Database assistance telephone numbers are available for the paper and vendors. Especially useful is a section titled "Tips for Searching Online Vendor Systems," which discusses the peculiarities of each vendor.

This is an exciting new source and one likely to be in heavy demand as more and more libraries migrate to electronic and CD-ROM access to newspapers in lieu of keeping large backfiles on microform. Published annually, a subscription includes two updates to keep one's directory current.—**Brian E. Coutts**

1006. **The Cover Story Index 1960-1991.** Robert Skapura, ed. Fort Atkinson, Wis., Highsmith Press, 1992. 531p. $42.00. ISBN 0-917846-08-7. ISSN 1054-433X.

1007. **The Cover Story Index: 1992 Supplement.** Robert Skapura, ed. Fort Atkinson, Wis., Highsmith Press, 1993. 33p. $33.00pa/3 yrs. ISBN 0-917846-23-0. ISSN 1054-433X.

The *Cover Story Index 1960-1991* is an updated and expanded version of the 1960-1989 volume (see ARBA 91, entry 964). The coverage now includes nine additional magazines: *Business Week, Congressional Digest, Discover, Life, Ms., National Geographic, Omni, Psychology Today,* and *USA Today*. The indexing of these magazines (except *Life*) date back to 1981, despite the title. *Newsweek, Time,* and *Life* are covered from 1960, while coverage of *US News and World Report* is from 1974 onward; equal emphasis was given to several stories in *US News* prior to 1974, with no cover stories as such. Some examples of new topics covered in the 1960-1991 volume and the 1992 supplement are interactive video, multiculturalism, Rodney King, and H. Ross Perot. The chronology section still includes only *Time, Newsweek,* and *U.S. News and World Report*. The arrangement of the cover stories is the same—in reverse chronological order, with the most recent citations appearing first. The subject index and subject headings list continue to be valuable.

There will be annual supplements in 1993 and 1994, with a cumulative volume to cover 1990-1995. The main index and the supplement represent some unique indexing to valuable information and are highly recommended for school, public, and academic libraries.—**R. Errol Lam**

1008. Griffiths, Dennis, ed. **The Encyclopedia of the British Press 1422-1992.** New York, St. Martin's Press, 1992. 694p. $79.95. PN5114.E53. 072'.09. LC 92-29118. ISBN 0-312-08633-4.

Covering William Caxton through Robert Maxwell, this encyclopedia is an excellent reference tool for information about specific journalists and their national and regional newspapers as well as for a historical perspective on the British press. The encyclopedia begins with six essays that chronologically cover the British press. Most of the work consists of 3,000 alphabetical entries that describe people (e.g., editors, cartoonists, typographers), specific newspapers (listed under latest title with cross-references from earlier titles), and subjects or terms relevant to press history (e.g., Fleet Street, D-notice, telegraphed news). The entries include references to works by or about the person or newspaper; terms within the descriptions that appear as separate entries are noted. The editor's scope note states that entries were selected for balanced and representative works and that only living journalists over the age of 30 who are editors or whose works are opinion-forming have been profiled. Additional information includes a press chronology, national and regional circulations, a list of women editors, and a list of Fleet Street editors. There are 25 brief articles about topics related to journalism—professional associations and organizations, newspaper libraries, circulation audits, women in British journalism, and the like. Griffiths has included an adequate thematic bibliography.

This encyclopedia is highly recommended for large public libraries and all academic libraries. It will be useful to political scientists and historians in fields that rely on newspapers for contemporary reporting and analysis. Librarians and bibliographers also will find this a good ready-reference tool for identifying and verifying newspaper titles. [R: Choice, May 93, p. 1440; RBB, Aug 93, p. 2088; WLB, June 93, p. 123]—**Linda A. Naru**

1009. Potter, Vilma Raskin. **A Reference Guide to Afro-American Publications and Editors 1827-1946.** Ames, Iowa, Iowa State University Press, 1993. 104p. $18.95. Z6944.N39P63. 015.73034'08996073. LC 91-17167. ISBN 0-8138-0677-1.

In 1946, the Lincoln University School of Journalism published a small pamphlet, *Checklist of Negro Newspapers in the United States (1827-1946)*, which had been prepared by Warren H. Brown, then Director of Negro Relations for the Council for Democracy. The book under review contains the listings in that pamphlet along with additional material. Brown had listed 467 daily and weekly newspapers with information about dates of publication, institutions holding early issues, and names of editors and publishers. All this information has been reproduced, with some corrections. Potter, a professor emerita of English at California State University, Los Angeles, has added several indexes (place of publication, year of publication, and editor) as well as some supplementary lists of newspapers. She has also included material on doing research using this and similar works on the topic, information on African-American women journalists before 1890, and some background material on Brown.

Brown's listing was incomplete, not only because some materials were unavailable to him but also because he intentionally omitted some editors he did not care for, such as Marcus Garvey and Adam Clayton Powell. Usefulness of this volume, then, is more limited than its title implies. Even if that were not the case, it would still be of interest mainly to libraries supporting advanced graduate work in African-American studies. [R: Choice, Sept 93, p. 88; RBB, June 93, pp. 1902-04]—**Evan Ira Farber**

1010. Wachsberger, Ken, ed. **Voices from the Underground.** Tempe, Ariz., Mica Press, 1993. 2v. $74.50pa. LC 92-082780. ISBN 1-8794610-3-X.

The social upheaval of the late 1960s and early 1970s is almost inexplicable to those who experienced it, let alone to those who came after. Few sources better capture the energy, zeal, wisdom, idealism, naivete, nihilism, arrogance, and ignorance of the era than the thousands of underground newspapers that emerged and disappeared during that time. This mammoth two-volume undertaking resurrects that ethos.

Volume 1, subtitled "Insider Histories of the Vietnam Era Underground Press," is a collection of 26 essays on underground papers from the era written by their editors, founders, or other key activists. They are very interesting social histories, but the retrospectives—products of greater age, maturity, and historical insight—do not quite reflect the reality of much of this alternative press. As one commentator remarks, the time all seems like a dream now, a period when one could not tell what was real and what was not. Much of the underground press was more a drivel of profanity, drugs, sex, and youthful rebellion than meaningful and lasting social commentary. Nonetheless, this is a fascinating collection.

The much slimmer volume 2, subtitled "A Directory of Resources and Sources on the Vietnam Era Underground Press," is more important; indeed, it is a vital reference tool. It includes an annotated bibliography of the underground press, dictionaries of special collections on social movements from the era, and a report on efforts to preserve underground press resources on microfilm. There are appendixes that list where one can find extant copies of these sources. An invaluable tool for anyone contemplating research about, or relying upon, these materials, this volume is essential for any research library.

This set far surpasses earlier works on underground sources, such as *Famous Long Ago* by Raymond Mungo (Beacon Press, 1970), David Armstrong's *A Trumpet to Arms* (Sound End Press, 1981), and Abe Peck's *Uncovering the Sixties* (Pantheon, 1985). It should be a standard reference source in every library where research is conducted on the 1960s and 1970s.—**Joe P. Dunn**

RADIO, TELEVISION, AUDIO, AND VIDEOS

Bibliography

1011. Gopen, Stuart. **Gopen's Guide to Closed Captioned Video.** Framingham, Mass., Caption Database, 1993. 547p. index. $29.95pa. LC 93-90366. ISBN 0-9635726-0-1.

Most television sets manufactured for sale in the United States after July 1993 will have built-in closed-caption decoders. Gopen, a former video store owner and the father of a deaf child, has compiled this guide to closed-caption videos primarily as a service to the 26 million hearing-impaired persons in the United States, but also to assist other potential users, such as adults and children learning to read and those learning English as a second language. The guide lists more than 5,000 videos arranged into 23 categories. Closed-caption status has been confirmed by actual viewing, because Gopen has found that some videos on the market are mislabeled. For each video are provided running time, rating, source, price, and a synopsis. Hollywood movies in such categories as adventure, comedy, horror, romance, and war represent most of the listings, and for these Gopen also identifies director, stars, and captioning agency. In addition to Hollywood movies, the guide lists a substantial number of children's, business-oriented, and documentary videos as well as a smaller number of videos in such broad categories as instructional, exercise, sports, music, and religion.

Bowker's Complete Video Directory (see ARBA 93, entry 989) has a closed-caption index, but it lists only those videos captioned by the National Captioning Institute. Gopen lists videos captioned by this and at least five other sources. *The Video Source book* (see ARBA 92, entry 909) has a closed-caption index too, but comparison with Gopen's title index shows Gopen to be more comprehensive. Unfortunately, Gopen's book has no subject index. This is the one significant deficiency of this otherwise well-made reference tool, because the only way to determine if there are captioned videos on a particular subject (e.g., libraries, mathematics) is to scan the title index for likely candidates or to turn the pages one by one.

—Joseph W. Palmer

1012. Kraeuter, David W. **British Radio and Television Pioneers: A Patent Bibliography.** Metuchen, N.J., Scarecrow, 1993. 206p. index. $27.50. Z7224.G7K72. 016.621384'027241. LC 93-24643. ISBN 0-8108-2716-6.

This volume, a counterpart to the author's previous bibliography of U.S. patents for radio and television, covers British technical patents. Entries are arranged by inventor and include patent title, patent number, year granted, and any co-grantees. The 29 inventors, including well-known names such as Guglielmo Marconi, were taken from Orrin E. Dunlap's *Radio's 100 Men of Science* (Harper and Brothers, 1944) and Sidney Gernsback's *Radio Encyclopedia* (Gernsback, 1927). Patent information was obtained primarily from the British Patent Office. A patent title index is included in each entry for inventors with more than 10 patents to their credit. At the end of the volume, a personal name index cross-references those patents with more than one grantee. The cumulated title index permits subject access to the patents listed.

The years covered by the volume are unclear. A chronological index would be helpful for researchers concerned only with a given period of British broadcasting history. Lack of numbering on the page beginning each entry may frustrate the user. This is a serviceable volume for a limited subject area.

—Glynys R. Thomas

1013. MacDonald, Barrie. **Broadcasting in the United Kingdom: A Guide to Information Sources.** 2d ed. New York, Mansell/Cassell, 1993. 316p. index. $100.00. Z7224.G7M33. 384.54'0941. LC 92-30097. ISBN 0-7201-2086-1.

This thorough, well-organized volume will justify its steep purchase price. While retaining the best features of the first edition, including a broadcasting chronology and critical background information on the structure of the industry, this edition adds relevant sources since the passage of the Broadcasting Act of 1990. Accessible to the layperson and professional researcher alike, this guide is informative and useful. With the exception of technical materials, such as patents, it not only lists resources but also provides excellent background information and detail. It describes the general principles of research in this evolving field, the various types of media research one encounters, and primary and secondary sources of information. Further reading sections at the ends of most chapters direct the user to sources of current information where the text treats an evolving or quickly outdated topic. Chapter 2 provides essential detail on the relationship of government to the media in the United Kingdom and explains differences between the United States and British systems.

Works mentioned in the text are included in the index, although putting a separate bibliography of printed works at the end of chapter 4 in future editions may better facilitate ready-reference. This work is an essential purchase for comprehensive broadcasting and communications collections and a good single source on this topic for larger general libraries.—**Glynys R. Thomas**

Directories

1014. **Bacon's Radio/TV Directory 1993.** 7th ed. Edited by Bacon's Information, Inc. Chicago, Bacon's Information, 1992. 1025p. maps. index. $250.00pa. ISSN 0891-0103.

Bacon's Radio/TV Directory provides complete programming and format information for all the radio and television stations on the air at the time of publication. Some 10,000 commercial and public broadcast stations in the United States are listed. Additional sections provide information on cable networks, television and radio networks, and syndications. Key station personnel are listed by name, with around 70,000 people included. Typical entries contain the call letters of the station, frequency modulation type (AM or FM), frequency in hertz, telephone and fax numbers, mailing address, major network affiliation, studio address location (if different from station transmitter), profile of format (e.g., urban contemporary, golden oldies), target audience (often shown by age), station power in watts, news and talk show data, percentage of locally produced programming, major sports programming, specially produced syndicated programming, and specific staff assignments (e.g., sports, sales). The volume is arranged by state and studio location. Indexes are provided to the main listings by station call letter. There is also an index of networked and syndicated programs. An appendix consists of maps of the major markets covered by specific stations.

This volume is without equal and contains much information on broadcasting stations in the United States. It is a more comprehensive marketing tool than the standard reference work on the subject, *Broadcasting and Cable Market Place* (see ARBA 93, entry 992). Considering the information provided, the cost is modest.—**Ralph Lee Scott**

Handbooks and Yearbooks

1015. **The ARRL Handbook for Radio Amateurs 1993.** 70th ed. Robert Schetgen and others, eds. Newington, Conn., American Radio Relay League, 1992. 1214p. illus. index. $25.00. LC 41-3345. ISBN 0-87259-170-0.

From the first scratchy, intermittent lines of interrupted speech that sounded as if they came from another planet, to the nearly crystal clear voice modulation that did, in fact, come from outer space, amateur radio has come a long way in more than seventy years. For the electrostatic field aficionado wanting to lay down the law (Coulomb's, that is) across the airways, no better guide exists than the ARRL's vade mecum. This radio buff's bible contains the chapter and verse for every transmission. Highlighted in this edition are power supplies, image-mode coverage, antennas and propagation, and instructions on building a low-cost HF frequency transmitter. In addition to these useful and informative discussions are the usual fare on electrical fundamentals, how to become an amateur radio ham, principles of radio transmission and receiving, and on-the-air broadcasting, all amply indexed.

Generously illustrated with pictures, diagrams, formulas, and much more, the ARRL guide is an excellent tool. The volume would be useful for everyone from the effusive novice who heads to the public library for basic information to the knitted-brow professor who teaches an introductory course in communications. All of this for such a low price places this volume not only in the best-buy category but also in the top quarter of all reference books.—**Mark Y. Herring**

1016. Rodriguez, Paul Anthony, ed. **Total TV Book.** Los Angeles, Calif., Homily Press; distr., Gardena, Calif., SCB Distributors, 1993. 1v. (unpaged). $39.00pa. ISBN 0-9637522-0-0.

This easy-to-read reference book for individuals who need information about production companies and distribution outlets delves into the creation, implementation, and financing of television production in the United States. Readers can track company or distributor names easily because of the alphabetical arrangement. Entries are printed in larger than average type, making the search for specific companies pleasant to the eye. This text provides complete mailing and telephone information for all listings, along with credits for some of the production companies.—**Dorothy M. Williams**

1017. Swartz, Jon D., and Robert C. Reinehr. **Handbook of Old-Time Radio: A Comprehensive Guide to Golden Age Radio Listening and Collecting.** Metuchen, N.J., Scarecrow, 1993. 806p. index. $92.50. PN1991.3.U6S93. 791.44'75'0973. LC 92-42120. ISBN 0-8108-2590-2.

Included in this handbook is a descriptive log of more than 2,000 different old-time radio programs, with information about casts, announcers, networks, lengths of program, durations of appearances, and the numbers of episodes available. When appropriate, story lines are included. The work is more comprehensive than an earlier one, *Radio's Golden Years* (see ARBA 82, entry 1242), which contains 1,500 programs with descriptive information as well as photographs. An appendix provides information about collecting these programs but not specific buying information. However, dealers are noted, along with fan clubs. A list of public collections of these materials includes addresses but no telephone numbers. There are also a useful selected annotated bibliography of book-length sources used in the preparation of this handbook and performer and program name indexes. Indexing appears to be very thorough. Recommended for interested readers, from the hobbyist to the researcher. [R: RBB, 1 Nov 93, p. 564; WLB, Nov 93, pp. 102-03]—**Helen M. Gothberg**

1018. **The Traveler's Country Music Radio Atlas 1993.** Port Hueneme, Calif., Hanalei Publishing, 1992. 80p. maps. $4.95pa.

This is a handy booklet that lists all country music stations state by state and locates the most powerful ones (5,000+ watts for AM, 10,000+ watts for FM) on maps of the states. The maps are not intended for lost drivers but for lost listeners, showing just enough information to find the nearest station. AM stations are represented by an oval, and FM by a rectangle. Only the most powerful stations are shown on the maps—to save constant channel changing while driving—but all stations are listed, divided by AM and FM and by high and low power. Not surprisingly, Texas has the most stations, and Alaska, the fewest. Smaller states are grouped together (e.g., all of New England), and the provinces of Canada appear at the end. In the middle is a map of the United States showing "Nite Rider": 50,000-watt "clear channel" stations that can be heard across many states, especially at night when many stations sign off the air.

With the growing popularity of country music as a format, the promise to update this atlas annually is a good idea, and so is the solicitation of help from readers. Perfect for anyone to use with other maps and atlases in planning a long car trip, this work is highly recommended.—**R. S. Lehmann**

1019. *Variety* and *Daily Variety* **Television Reviews. Volume 16: 1989-1990.** Hamden, Conn., Garland, 1992. 1v. (various paging). $165.00. PN1992.3.U5V36. 791.45'75'0973. LC 89-17088. ISBN 0-8240-3795-2.

This volume is a comprehensive and extensive supplement to the 15-volume *Variety Television Reviews, 1923-1988*. It is arranged chronologically and reproduces hundreds of television reviews that were published in both the Hollywood-based *Daily Variety* and the weekly New York *Variety* during 1989 and 1990. If a review of a program appeared in both *Daily Variety* and *Variety*, only the full review from the longer *Daily Variety* entry is represented. A reference to the *Daily Variety* is given from the corresponding *Variety* listing of any doubly reviewed program. The types of programs represented are from network, cable, syndicated, public, and international television. Home videos and videocassettes are also reviewed. A title index includes not only specific names of programs but also specials and documentary series. The selected name index is useful, but no criteria are evident for inclusion in this index.

This series continues to be a unique historical record of the popular medium of television. It will be of significant reference value to the patrons of mid-sized and large public libraries and academic libraries. Highly recommended.—**R. Errol Lam**

1020. **The Video Source Book 1993: A Guide to Approximately 126,000 Programs Currently Available on Video....** Julia C. Furtaw, Beth A. Fhaner, and Christine Tomassini, eds. Detroit, Gale, 1993. 2v. index. $240.00/set. ISBN 0-8103-7606-7. ISSN 0748-0881.

Given the ease with which videotapes can be made and duplicated, the number of potential sources of videos is unlimited. No single publication can hope to assemble an exhaustive list of videotapes available from commercial, educational, and private agencies. Published annually since 1979, *Video Source Book* provided, for a decade, the single most complete listing. In 1990, a formidable rival, *Bowker's Complete Video Directory* (see ARBA 93, entry 989), appeared. In response, Gale has made successful efforts to expand and improve its publication, more than doubling its listings in the past four years and introducing valuable enhancements, such as price information for most entertainment videos and for newer educational titles. Typical entries include good annotations, credits, and source information. For entertainment features, star ratings (one to four stars) are given, reflecting evaluations culled from unspecified review sources. There are indexes for subject, credits, and special format (closed caption, videodisc, and 8mm). All videos are listed in a single alphabetical sequence, and there is a single set of indexes. The format has been changed in this edition; entries are extremely easy to read and browse. In contrast, *Bowker's* divides its entertainment and education listings into separate volumes, each with its own indexes, which sometimes makes it cumbersome to use, and its closely spaced entries are difficult to browse. On the other hand, *Bowker's* appears to have the edge in terms of current listings, and it has some additional indexes (e.g., Spanish-language films). The 1993 edition of *Source Book* lists 84,300 videos (representing 126,000 programs), and the 1993 supplement adds 3,900 programs. This is close to the 89,000 found in the 1993 edition of *Bowker's*. However, raw numbers are misleading. The Gale database is much older than *Bowker's*; it contains a substantial number of older videos, some of which may be out of print. When this reviewer investigated the availability of 10 videos on genealogy listed in the 1993 edition of the *Video Source Book*, only 3 were found to be obtainable. Five others had been withdrawn, and the distributors of the remaining two did not answer inquiries. Most of these videos dated from the 1970s. It is noteworthy, however, that the 1993 supplement lists four excellent new videos on genealogy, none of which could be found in the 1993 *Bowker's*. Spot checks confirmed that both *Video Source Book* and *Bowker's* contain numerous current videos not found in the other publication. Even when a video is found in both publications, each source often gives useful information about the video that is not found in the other. Thus, the two publications complement each other. *Video Source Book* is available on magnetic tape, but, unlike *Bowker's*, it is not (as of this writing) obtainable on CD-ROM.

—**Joseph W. Palmer**

Indexes

1021. **Transcript/Video Index, 1992: A Comprehensive Guide to Television and Radio News and Public Affairs Programming. Volume 5: Number 13.** Denver, Colo., Journal Graphics, 1993. 2v. $49.95pa./set. ISBN 1-879-762-06-4.

The current edition of this index (first reviewed in ARBA 93, entry 1001) notes the steady growth in cable and network television public affairs programs by its expansion into two volumes. Similar to its one-volume predecessor covering 1991, the 1992 volumes continue to be arranged by broad subject headings, with only a few personal name headings offered for newsworthy individuals (e.g., "Bill Clinton"). While only 84 television shows (covering the intellectual spectrum from *Geraldo* to *Nova*) were formerly indexed, the new edition covers 125 shows, including some radio programs. Features unique to the present edition also include sections on transcript sets available on a particular topic (e.g., music censorship) and videocassettes available for purchase.

While online fulltext databases such as LEXIS/NEXIS have (for many libraries) eclipsed the need for an index to Journal Graphics transcriptions, this source offers access to scores of transcripts from news and "tabloid television" shows not currently available electronically. Basic information (e.g., the show's title, a brief abstract, cost for a transcript) is clearly presented, and ordering transcripts from Journal Graphics is easy, although the current edition does not list prices for shows. Recommended for public and academic libraries.—**David K. Frasier**

21 Decorative Arts

GENERAL WORKS

1022. Ehresmann, Donald L. **Applied and Decorative Arts: A Bibliographic Guide.** 2d ed. Englewood, Colo., Libraries Unlimited, 1993. 629p. index. $75.00. Z5956.A68E47. 016.745. LC 92-28156. ISBN 0-87287-906-2.

The previous edition was reviewed in ARBA 78 (see entry 827); the current edition updates and expands on it. Some 927 entries dated between 1975 and 1991 have been added, and 349 new titles appear in the pre-1975 entry list as well. A new chapter on wallpaper is included, and there is more in-depth coverage of regional American applied and decorative arts. Exhibition and museum catalogs are now included; they were not in the first edition.

The work is arranged alphabetically by media types. A representative selection of media covered includes arms and armor, ceramics, clocks, costumes, enamels, furniture, glass, ivory, jewelry, lacquer, leather, medals and seals, metalwork, textiles, and toys and dolls. Within each media category, entries are listed alphabetically by author and title. Each entry has the pertinent bibliographic information needed to locate the item and a brief evaluative abstract of about 75-100 words. Many entries have cross-references to other works for additional information. An author/title index and a subject index complete the volume.

This book is a timely update to a growing field of research and collecting. Many other bibliographies discuss specific topics, but few try and cover as wide-ranging a list of media types as this one does; and it does it well at a reasonable price. This is an important addition to any library fielding questions on the topic. [R: RBB, 15 Oct 93, pp. 465-66]—**Gregory Curtis**

COLLECTING

Antiques

1023. **The David & Charles Encyclopedia of Everyday Antiques.** By Ronald Pearsall. North Pomfret, Vt., David & Charles/Trafalgar Square, 1992. 256p. illus. index. $34.95. 745.103. ISBN 0-7153-9868-7.

The word "everyday" in the title refers to commonly found antiques (dating up to the early twentieth century) that can be purchased for less than 500 pounds. Because this encyclopedia is published in Great Britain and leans toward European collectibles, its U.S. readers might have a difficult time finding or affording some of the goods. The alphabetical list contains entries that describe items (e.g., Dutch furniture, funerary wares, Mogul carpets), materials (e.g., copper, jet, earthenware), processes (e.g., die-stamping, silvering), factories (e.g., Minton), and design features (e.g., mihrab, famille rose). Some are so broad that many books have been written about them (e.g., Victoriana, tables); others are very specific (e.g., patch stand, egg cup). Entries range in length from a sentence to several paragraphs that give production dates, cultural history, and tips for collectors.

Short chapters touch on major style periods, cleaning and refurbishing antiques, and repair; brief biographies of 12 famous personalities in the field, a list of important pottery and porcelain factories (mostly British), and a bibliography round out the volume. The index covers items mentioned in entries but does not include headings for main entries. Thus, the only way to find articles on dining-room silver and tea-time silver is by browsing, because the index does not list "silver," nor does the text in the entry for silver provide cross-references. The book is copiously illustrated with catalog and advertising art and attractive color and black-and-white photographs, many of which show objects in their original settings in the home.

Libraries on a budget should acquire encyclopedias that are either more comprehensive or more narrowly focused on a particular style or type of object, depending upon collection needs. Those with large reference or circulating collections on antiques may want to add this readable title.

—Deborah V. Rollins

1024. **Tuttle Dictionary of Antiques & Collectibles Terms.** By Don Bingham and Joan Bingham. Rutland, Vt., Charles E. Tuttle, 1992. 243p. $19.95pa. NK30.B54. 745'.03. LC 91-67337. ISBN 0-8048-1756-1.

This useful and comprehensive dictionary furnishes definitions of approximately 4,000 terms. Words are arranged alphabetically followed by the type of category (e.g., furniture) in parentheses. Definitions are brief but informative. The work begins with an introduction that provides much data along with suggestions and strategies. Especially noteworthy are the segments covering auctions and the detection of reproductions and fakes. Attention is paid to armor and arms, cast iron, ceramics, clocks and watches, furniture, glass, jewelry, oriental rugs, pewter, silver, and gold. Initially, treatment is given to the definitions of antiques as compared to collectibles. The Binghams generally think of antiques as "belonging to an earlier period ... generally prior to World War II," rather than applying the 100-year rule. Items with variant names, such as *pram* and *perambulator*, are defined under each term, with cross-references given to the others. A table of patent numbers with corresponding dates should prove useful in dating manufactured objects. This work concludes with a bibliography of sources useful to collectors and dealers.—**Ron Blazek**

Books

1025. **Bookman's Price Index: A Guide to the Values of Rare and Other Out-of-Print Books. Volume 46.** Daniel F. McGrath, ed. Detroit, Gale, 1993. 910p. $218.00. LC 64-8723. ISBN 0-8103-8215-6. ISSN 0068-0141.

Each volume of *Bookman's Price Index* (BPI) (which began in 1964) brings together in one alphabetical sequence the catalogs of a large number of high-quality antiquarian bookdealers. The aim of the series is to help collectors, dealers, and librarians determine the current market value of the listed books. This latest volume of BPI gives the values of some 20,000 titles (some titles have several listings) listed in the catalogs of 135 dealers, mostly Americans. The majority of the books listed are either first editions of American and British novels or out-of-print books on various facets of American and European history. Because the prices listed in BPI are dealer asking prices rather than the prices for which the books were actually sold, it is usually wise to consult *American Book Prices Current*, a series that supplies prices of collectible books sold at auction. And as the focus of BPI is on literature and history, those trying to determine the current market value of out-of-print books in the areas of science, technology, medicine, art, photography, music, and the social sciences will be better served by the catalogs of specialty dealers. Still, BPI continues to be the most comprehensive and up-to-date one-volume source of prices for collectible English literature and collectible American and European history.—**Joseph Cataio**

1026. Carter, John. **ABC for Book Collectors.** Corrections and additions by Nicolas Barker. 6th ed. New Castle, Del., Oak Knoll Books, c1980, 1992. 219p. $25.00. 002'.075. LC 91-30020. ISBN 0-938768-30-1.

This was the first, and continues to be the best, dictionary of words, phrases, and abbreviations of the antiquarian and used book trade in the United States and Great Britain. Its approximately 450 alphabetically arranged entries are clear, detailed, and informative and reflect Carter's great erudition and dry wit. Because the focus of the work is on the terms used in the catalogs of United States and British used and rare book dealers, entries that deal with printers, presses, publishers, and foreign-language terms have been kept to a minimum. Those seeking such terms or definitions of terms in the broader realms of book publishing and printing should consult *Glaister's Glossary of the Book* (see ARBA 81, entry 35) or

The Bookman's Glossary by Jean Peters (R. R. Bowker, 1983). But novice book collectors and librarians puzzled by the terms and descriptions found in the catalogs of used and rare book dealers or in book auction catalogs need only consult this fine work.—**Joseph Cataio**

1027. Siegel, David S., and Susan Siegel. **The Used Book Lover's Guide to New England.** Yorktown Heights, N.Y., Book Hunter Press, 1993. 337p. maps. index. $14.95pa. LC 92-097220. ISBN 0-9634112-0-9.

This excellent directory of used book dealers in New England will quickly become outdated as new dealers set up shop and old dealers go out of business or change location or hours. Still, this is an extremely useful guide to more than 600 such dealers, and for many of them the information is likely to be accurate for a while. The text is arranged alphabetically by state, within each state by type of shop, and within each type by town. The alphabet is not necessarily the best arrangement for a travel guide; it is especially problematic for a small area such as New England where distances are shorter and where one is more likely to look for the states to be arranged geographically (e.g., Maine, New Hampshire, Vermont). That problem is overcome in part by a series of good area maps that show the shops' locations in the states. It would still be more useful to have area maps that in several cases cross state boundaries.

At the beginning of the listings for each state are alphabetical lists by dealer and by location; there is also an index by the subject specialties of the dealers. If one knows only the name of a dealer in New England and not the state, it may be necessary to consult each of the six state dealer listings. For each dealer, clear and concise information is given about mailing and street address, telephone and fax numbers, size of stock, topical specialties, hours, services, area map for further directions, acceptance of credit cards, owner, year established, and (in many cases) brief comments based on visits by the Siegels.
—**Norman D. Stevens**

1028. Siegel, David S., and Susan Siegel. **The Used Book Lover's Guide to the Mid-Atlantic States: New York, New Jersey, Pennsylvania & Delaware.** Yorktown Heights, N.Y., Book Hunter Press, 1993. 367p. maps. index. $15.95pa. LC 93-91597. ISBN 0-9634112-1-7.

This is an excellent tool for locating more than 900 used book dealers in New York, New Jersey, Pennsylvania, and Delaware. It follows the same arrangement and format as its recent companion, *The Used Book Lover's Guide to New England* (1993). The alphabetical arrangement by city or town within three broad categories (open shops, open by appointment, or mail order) for each state is, unfortunately, even more problematic here, given the distances involved, than it was for the New England volume. Reliance on the handy area maps for each state is even more necessary and valuable. Fortunately those maps, a brief state-by-state list of shop names, the general arrangement, and the thorough index make this guide relatively easy to use. The same clear and concise information for each dealer that is found in the New England guide is found here. This, plus the charming annotations, makes this book an extremely useful tool for librarians and users. Again, however, caution is suggested in using it as a shopping guide for travelers, because shops come and go and change their hours with some regularity. (Call first!) Presumably other volumes will follow; it is hoped that all will be revised regularly.—**Norman D. Stevens**

Coins

1029. **Official Whitman Coin Dealer Directory.** 6th ed. Racine, Wis., Western Publishing, 1993. 219p. $4.95pa.

Anyone who has ever put Lincoln cents into those blue folders or looked up a coin in the red *Guide Book of United States Coins* (Western Publishing, annual) is familiar with the Whitman name. Numismatic supplies have been associated with the Whitman label for more than 50 years. This directory provides information related to more than 800 coin dealers and suppliers. Each entry gives address, telephone numbers, primary specialty areas, services available (e.g., mail orders, supplies, bullion market, investment services), and professional memberships. The book is organized by specialties, including ancient and medieval coins, foreign coins, paper money, and U.S. coins. Within each category, dealers are listed alphabetically by state or country. Additional chapters on mints and official agents, auction and mail bidding, and numismatic literature are included. There is an alphabetical index to all dealer entries.

CRAFTS

1030. Graubner, Wolfram. **Encyclopedia of Wood Joints.** Newtown, Conn., Taunton Press, 1992. 151p. illus. index. $21.95pa. TT185.G76613. 684'.08. LC 91-38456. ISBN 1-56158-004-X.

For amateur and professional woodworkers, knowledge of the 600 or so joints used where supporting and supported elements meet in the construction of buildings and the making of furniture are a key to success. Of course, the wide range of reference works and handbooks on woodworking all cover some aspects of joinery. The true value of this outstanding text is that it includes more joints than any other work and brings a variety of information together in one place so as to foster an understanding of the differences in joints and the selection of an appropriate joining technique for a particular project.

The text is arranged into the four major standard American classifications (splicing joints, oblique joints, corner and cross joints, and edge joints), but an appendix lists standard European and Japanese classifications. Within each classification, three to nine types of joints are discussed in detail. The succinct but carefully worded text for each technique is accompanied by both black-and-white photographs and line drawings so that there is little opportunity for misunderstanding a technique or botching its application. This basic handbook promises to become a standard tool that will find (and deserve) widespread, continuing use.—**Norman D. Stevens**

1031. **Quilt Groups Today: Who They Are, Where They Meet, What They Do, and How to Contact Them.** Paducah, Ky., American Quilter's Society, 1992. 336p. illus. $14.95pa. TT835.052. 746.46'026. LC 92-13726. ISBN 0-89145-999-5.

Quilting has seen an increase in popularity in the last several years. The diversity of groups in existence throughout the world is the primary focus of this directory. More than 1,000 groups were surveyed by the American Quilter's Society and included in this volume. The Society plans to publish updates and has included a survey at the end of this directory for those groups wishing to be listed. The groups range in size from those as small as five members to those with several hundred.

This directory is divided by state followed by an international listing by country. In each state and country the quilt groups are listed by their group name. Unfortunately, the absence of a geographical index makes looking for groups difficult and should be considered in future updates. Entries include the group name, address, area served, date of establishment, number of members, skill level of the members, and meeting time and place. A self-description written by each group describes its focus in the community and its accomplishments, activities, programs, projects, publications, and donations. Some black-and-white photographs are included; color photographs would enhance the quilting handiwork illustrated.

Quilters at any level will find this book ideal for contacting other quilters, sharing new quilting and fund-raising ideas, and promoting the international love of quilting. Public libraries and special collections whose users include quilters should consider this volume. [R: Choice, Feb 93, p. 944]—**Jennie S. Johnson**

1032. Sellen, Betty-Carol, with Cynthia J. Johanson. **20th Century American Folk, Self Taught, and Outsider Art.** New York, Neal-Schuman, 1993. 462p. illus. index. $90.00. NK805.S46. 745'.025'73. LC 93-3146. ISBN 1-55570-142-6.

This reference appears closely on the heels of *Museum of American Folk Art Encyclopedia of Twentieth-Century American Folk Art and Artists* (see ARBA 92, entry 982), to which it is related. Both make claims for a separate study of contemporary artists whose works fall between coverage of academic art considered by art historians and the traditional art given attention by folklorists. The area between this coverage is vague, however, and the label of "contemporary nontraditional folk art" or "twentieth-century American folk, self-taught, and outsider art" (as given by Sellen and Johanson in this volume) does not add clarity. It is also questionable whether the coverage is as lacking as the authors of this volume claim; it is unclear whether the absence of academic studies in the volume owes to the authors' intent or ignorance.

The authors carve out a niche by concentrating on galleries and museums that have defined a kind of art outside the academy for themselves. Certainly the use of the term "folk art," by the authors' own admission, is problematic and may confuse users of the volume, for it is not compatible with folkloristic scholarship, which has a large and established reference literature of its own. While the Museum of American Folk Art's volume gave priority to artists' biographies, this volume devotes much more room to listings of galleries, art centers, museums, and organizations promoting this vague type of art. In addition, Sellen and Johanson's volume includes more bibliographical references and adds annotations that the Museum of American Folk Art book did not have. Rather than being a major bibliographical reference, however, the volume resembles a finder's aid for galleries and collectors in the business of promoting "naive" or "primitive" art (to cite yet two more labels used by the authors). From the academic point of view, however, the very premises of this volume may be suspect, and unfortunately the resulting effort may mislead rather than guide researchers.—**Simon J. Bronner**

1033. Whisker, James Biser. **Pennsylvania Potters 1660-1900.** Lewiston, N.Y., Edwin Mellen Press, 1993. 330p. $79.95. ISBN 0-7734-9262-3.

1034. Whisker, James Biser. **Pennsylvania Silversmiths, Goldsmiths and Pewterers 1684-1900.** Lewiston, N.Y., Edwin Mellen Press, 1993. 323p. $79.95. NK7112.W55. 739.2'092'2748. LC 93-2691. ISBN 0-7734-9260-7.

1035. Whisker, James Biser. **Pennsylvania Workers in Brass, Copper and Tin 1681-1900.** Lewiston, N.Y., Edwin Mellen Press, 1993. 228p. $69.95. HD8039.M52U688. 331.7'669'09748. LC 93-16080. ISBN 0-7734-9258-5.

Part of a series focusing on early practitioners of various trades in Pennsylvania, these titles provide checklists of potters and metalworkers. The books contain a general introduction, biographical entries for the artisans, and a bibliography. The introduction in each volume gives a brief overview of the apprenticeship tradition and indentured servitude in the early United States. These practices, as well as traditional father-son partnerships, provided the means by which most skills in the cottage industries were learned. Examples appropriate to the trade covered in each book are inserted into what is essentially the same essay. This section is poorly organized and edited, containing errors in punctuation, grammar, and spelling.

Biographical entries vary greatly in length, depending upon the amount of information available. They are arranged in alphabetical order by name and note occupation and type of work if known, dates, town, county, and the bibliographical sources. Other details may include names of partners, apprentices, and relatives; street address; financial data; number of employees; production figures; types and amounts of raw materials used; and interesting quotations (often excerpted from newspaper advertisements). Marked pieces that have been attributed to a maker are mentioned.

A variety of source materials were consulted. They include U.S. censuses of population and industry; city, regional, and state directories; newspapers; tax and land conveyance records; county histories; and apprenticeship or indenture records. Most of these sources, as well as books, articles, dissertations, and document collections, are listed in the bibliographies. There are no entries in either volume's bibliography for U.S. censuses, although Whisker relies heavily on data provided therein.

There can be no doubt that Whisker has done an enormous amount of research in literally hundreds of original and secondary sources. However, a typical source note at the end of a biographical entry that reads [tax; U.S. Census] makes it difficult to determine where specific pieces of information are located. Fortunately, newspaper dates and book page numbers are provided. There are no indexes of persons by county and town—something that might have been useful to local history researchers. Libraries that collect in the areas of Pennsylvania history or the history of industry and technology may want to consider these specialized titles.—**Deborah V. Rollins**

PHOTOGRAPHY

1036. **The Focal Encyclopedia of Photography.** 3d ed. Leslie Stroebel and Richard Zakia, eds. Stoneham, Mass., Butterworths, 1993. 914p. illus. $125.00. TR9.F6. 770'.3. LC 92-44267. ISBN 0-240-80059-1.

Those already familiar with earlier versions of this encyclopedia will be pleased with the 3d edition, the first since 1969. Although still-relevant material has been retained and updated, technical changes and vocabulary shifts since then have been so extensive that only about 25 percent of the previous entries remain. At the same time, the scope of attention, which before was primarily scientific, has been extended to a far-wider range of subjects. The result is a substantially new product that includes, for example, aesthetics, education, law, and commerce while preserving a command of technical matters. Only three areas have been excluded: cinematography, video, and electronic still photography. Readers will be happy to see that the excellent drawings of prior editions have been retained and augmented with new graphics and photographs. Larger format and type are further improvements, and the slightly increased size is still convenient. This is a substantial work for serious students and professionals and should be one of the cornerstones of any photographic reference collection. [R: Choice, Dec 93, p. 584; WLB, Nov 93, p. 102]
—**Paul L. Holmer**

1037. **McBroom's Camera Bluebook: A Complete, Up-to-Date Price and Buyers Guide to Cameras, Lenses & Accessories.** 1994 ed. Amherst, N.Y., Amherst Media, 1993. 239p. illus. index. $24.95pa. LC 93-71386. ISBN 0-936262-21-4.

Camera buffs who have made use of *McBroom's Price Guide to Modern Cameras* (see ARBA 92, entry 958) will welcome this edition under a new title, "Bluebook" better emphasizing the particular focus on used as well as new cameras, lenses, and accessories. The edition updates past material and adds a section on large-format cameras, although, as before, the emphasis is on more popular models rather than rare or specialized items. The system of valuation is that popularized by *Shutterbug* magazine, which divides price ranges into new, mint, excellent, and used. Overall organization also is familiar, with material arranged under 35 millimeter, medium format, and large format. In addition, an index and glossary ease the way for the user, especially for the beginner. This concern for the novice is perhaps the best feature of the book: The discussion of the relative merits of each model is uniformly instructive without descending into either technical jargon or brand-name partisanship. McBroom's effort deserves praise. [R: LJ, 1 Sept 93, pp. 170-72; RBB, 1 Dec 93, p. 716]—**Paul L. Holmer**

1038. O'Connor, Diane Vogt. **Guide to Photographic Collections at the Smithsonian Institution. Volume III.** Washington, D.C., Smithsonian Institution Press, 1992. 342p. illus. index. $49.95pa. Q11.S79. 026'.779'074753. LC 89-600116. ISBN 1-56098-188-1.

This work continues the documentation of the photographic collections held by the Smithsonian Institution. Where volume 2 (see ARBA 92, entry 1467) dealt with scientific research bureaus, this one covers seven art bureaus and one office: the Cooper-Hewitt Museum, the Freer Gallery of Art, the Hirshhorn Museum and Sculpture Garden, the National Museum of African Art, the National Museum of American Art, the National Portrait Gallery, the Sackler Gallery of Art, and the Office of Horticulture. Some 180 photographic collections with 3.5 million photographs are recorded.

Following a brief introduction and an essay titled "The Mechanical Eye: Photographs and the Arts," each agency is discussed. A brief outline and history of the bureau or office gives some background on the collections. The collection entries, arranged alphabetically within the framework of the owning bureau or office, include collection code, name of the collection, dates of photographs, origins, physical description, subjects, arrangement, captions, finding aids, and restrictions. Most collection descriptions range from one-half to one page in length. A creator index, a forms and processes index, and a subject index complete the work. An added bonus is the reproduction of several of the images found in the various collections.

As noted in the review of volume 2, this work represents a valuable resource for researchers of photographs in the areas covered by the volume. Ease of use and a well-thought-out page format contribute to the attractiveness of the work. Recommended for all libraries with interests in art, anthropology, photography, or American culture.—**Gregory Curtis**

22 Fine Arts

GENERAL WORKS

Bibliography

1039. Gray, John, comp. **Action Art: A Bibliography of Artists' Performance from Futurism to Fluxus and Beyond.** Westport, Conn., Greenwood Press, 1993. 343p. index. (Art Reference Collection, no.16). $75.00. Z5936.P47G73. 016.7'009'04. LC 92-46415. ISBN 0-313-28916-6.

This bibliography is international in scope and focuses on action art, or the development of live performance art (as opposed to painting and sculpture). It covers such movements as futurism, dadaism, Russian constructivism, destruction in art, New York avant-garde festivals, guerrilla art, and the Bauhaus during the period from about 1909 to 1975 (with emphasis on the 1950s and 1960s), with a few key items from 1975 to 1992. (There is little on the 1970s and later, as that time period is well covered in books, journals, videos, and exhibition catalogs.)

The work is divided into three major sections, with the first covering action art from 1909 to 1952 and the second from the 1950s through the 1970s. The third and most important section contains biographical and critical studies of the artists and artist groups. The approximate 3,700 entries for 115 artists and artist groups are numbered and provide birth and death dates of the artist and country of origin. The five appendixes (e.g., reference works, libraries and archives searched) and four indexes (artist, subject, title, and author) make this a usable and comprehensive source for documentation of a field largely ignored until the 1970s. [R: Choice, Nov 93, p. 432]—**Maureen Pastine**

Biography

1040. Kelly, Bernice M., comp., and Janet L. Stanley, ed. **Nigerian Artists: A Who's Who & Bibliography.** New Providence, N.J., published for the National Museum of African Art Branch, Smithsonian Institution Libraries, Hans Zell/Reed Reference Publishing, 1993. 600p. index. $175.00. N7399.N5K46. 709'.2'2669. LC 92-40052. ISBN 0-905450-82-5.

Works by prolific bibliographer Stanley have radically transformed the information landscape of African art in the last decade. Here she collaborates with Kelly to produce the continent's first artist biography. Some 350 twentieth-century Nigerian artists are covered in great detail, including directory information, career summary, education, exhibition history, commissions, awards, publications, and a personal bibliography. While a few individuals (e.g., Sokari Douglas Camp) have exhibited in English-speaking countries, others are less well known to Westerners; Kelly's diligent research on them is particularly useful.

The volume is exemplary in many ways. Although the artist biographies make up the core of the volume, they are not its only valuable component. For students, the introduction to and chronology of Nigerian art give clear and useful summaries of modern movements in that country. End matter includes a four-part annotated bibliography of modern Nigerian art, listing books, theses, and magazines; exhibition materials and reviews;

audiovisuals; and archival collections. A subject index, an index of artists by name, and an index of artists by media conclude what will be the standard work on Nigerian art at least until the end of the decade. [R: Choice, Dec 93, p. 587]—**Stephanie C. Sigala**

1041. Kerr, Joan, ed. **The Dictionary of Australian Artists: Painters, Sketchers, Photographers and Engravers to 1870.** New York, Oxford University Press, 1992. 889p. illus. $195.00. 709.94. ISBN 0-19-553290-2.

The early art history of Australia has many things in common with the early art history of the U.S. Midwest. Both are characterized by embryonic activity and ill-documented itinerant artists until permanent art galleries and schools began to be established in the 1860s. Just as in the U.S. Midwest, it has been hard to find information about the pioneers of culture in the antipodes until relatively recently.

Containing information about 2,500 painters, sketchers, photographers, and engravers, this hefty volume is a landmark of cooperative research. It appears that anyone who claimed artistic credentials is included, from the humble daguerreotypist to the artist formally trained in the latest British techniques. Each is documented in a readable essay written by one of 195 contributors. Many essays include bibliographical references and photographs of the artists or their work. In addition, a useful summary of art historical trends in Australia to 1870 is contained in Kerr's introduction, while a list of major art exhibitions of the period completes the volume.

This book has all the components of a great reference work: It is thorough, well edited, attractively designed, and full of hard-to-find information. A comparable treatment of U.S. pioneer artists would be welcome. [R: Choice, Nov 93, p. 428]—**Stephanie C. Sigala**

1042. Sharylen, Maria. **Artists of the Pacific Northwest: A Biographical Dictionary, 1600s-1970.** Jefferson, N.C., McFarland, 1993. 252p. index. $45.00. N6528.S52. 709'.2'2795. LC 92-56693. ISBN 0-89950-797-2.

Drawing on published materials and general biographical dictionaries for artists, Sharylen has produced the first biographical guide to artists in Oregon, Washington, Idaho, Alaska, and British Columbia. Following scattered pioneering efforts in the northwest in the seventeenth and eighteenth centuries, organized artistic activity began in this area in the 1890s; the 4,000 artists documented were thus mostly active in the early and mid-twentieth century.

Despite the quantity of artists included, the quality of information about each one is disappointing. Readers often must be satisfied with a frustratingly sketchy career chronology. This is understandable for elusive local artists, but less so for some nationally recognized names. There is no evidence that Sharylen consulted periodicals, newspapers, or city directories (usually considered to be gold mines of artistic data). Although an appendix provides addresses of art museums, schools, and organizations in the northwest, nowhere does Sharylen cite information from any art or local history collection. In fact, there is no indication, either in the entry or in the *very* selected biography, where information on an individual artist came from or where more information can be found. Students and researchers will want to know more than this amateur effort provides. Not recommended.—**Stephanie C. Sigala**

Dictionaries and Encyclopedias

1043. Walker, John A. **Glossary of Art, Architecture, & Design since 1945.** 3d ed. New York, G. K. Hall, 1992. 1v. (unpaged). illus. $95.00. N34.W34. 709'.04. LC 91-44265. ISBN 0-8161-0556-1.

Last revised in 1977 (see ARBA 78, entry 789), the current edition of this work revises and enlarges upon the previous one. Arranged alphabetically by topic, each entry includes a definition, cross-references to other related topics, and a bibliography for further study. Many of the entries are on recent concepts. For example, there are 33 entries under the general heading of *postmodern*, a term that came into existence shortly after the last edition. Entries range from a quarter of a page to a page in length. Numerous illustrations accompany the text and make a significant contribution to the explanation of some of the more obtuse entries. The work also contains an extensive bibliography divided into art, architecture, design, and general works. It is arranged in chronological order, with the most recent entry from 1991.

A lengthy subject index provides multiple entry points for many of the concepts. This edition will complement similar dictionaries, such as *The Oxford Companion to Twentieth-Century Art* (see ARBA 83, entry 815), because it discusses many less well known concepts and terms.

It is good to see the revision of this standard art reference source. It is a worthy addition to the shelves of any library fielding questions on art, architecture, design, or modern culture. Highly recommended.

—**Gregory Curtis**

Handbooks and Yearbooks

1044. **The Art World Directory: Arts Review Yearbook 1993.** Sue Holding, ed. London, Arts Review; distr., Atlantic Highlands, N.J., Humanities Press, 1993. 130p. illus. $29.95pa. ISBN 0-85331-633-3.

This 2,000-entry directory is a British source for the art world. It is published by *Arts Review*, Britain's leading monthly art magazine, and is the magazine's 1993 yearbook. Included are galleries and museums—London, regional, Scottish, and Welsh. Location, founding date, hours, director, types of exhibits, and artists represented are included for each entry. Concluding the directory section are country houses, art consultants, art societies, fairs, friends, art tour companies, artists' materials, packers and restorers, sculpture parks, print publishers and dealers, art facilities, audiovisual materials, art book publishers and fine art magazines, art book shops and antiquarian art book dealers, crafts workshops and art schools, an advertiser's index, and competitions. There are also nine articles on the current British art situation and British galleries; they were written by well-known artists, curators, directors, and consultants and are informative and easy to read. The volume concludes with an advance diary of exhibitions and competitions. A useful directory for all Britishers in the art field and for those artists traveling to Britain, this work is a must for special art library collections.—**Kathleen J. Voigt**

1045. Franklin-Smith, Constance, ed. **Art Marketing Sourcebook for the Fine Artist: Where to Sell Your Artwork.** Renaissance, Calif., ArtNetwork, 1992. 330p. index. $21.95pa. HF5415.122.F3. 659.197. ISBN 0-940899-19-1.

Art Marketing Sourcebook (AMS) is in direct competition with *Artist's Market* (AM) (see ARBA 91, entry 1017), published annually by Writer's Digest Books. AM lists 2,500 markets; AMS 2,000-plus art world professionals. AM incorporates much more advisory text and offers close-up profiles of working artists and a few illustrations; these features are not found in AMS. Finally, of the four sections in AMS—dealers, galleries, organizations, and publishers—AM is superior for galleries and publishers. But that takes the artist who wants to sell only halfway. AMS stresses networking as the means to success. Because one must get to know dealers and join organizations, AMS devotes ample space to listing networking possibilities. It also includes a sample contract and gallery, exhibition, and royalty agreements (with the caveat to prepare before negotiating a deal). Each entry contains a complete address and other pertinent information, such as the all-important "commission taken" statement and grant availability notice. The arrangement of the listings is alphabetical by state, then by city. A name index at the end provides further access.

The difference between the two titles is apparent, but neither book overshadows the other. They do share some information but are more complementary than repetitious. In certain ways AMS, with its uncluttered listings, is easier to use and more exact. However, AM covers the field better for commercial outlets. Both guides are an excellent starting point and should be read together. Recommended for all art reference, marketing, and job placement collections.—**Bill Bailey**

1046. Henkes, Robert. **The Art of Black American Women: Works of Twenty-Four Artists of the Twentieth Century.** Jefferson, N.C., McFarland, 1993. 274p. illus. index. $35.00. N6538.N5H45. 704'.042'09730904. LC 92-50955. ISBN 0-89950-818-9.

This aptly titled volume is a critical interpretation of selected works of art by two dozen African-American women rather than a source of biographical information on the artists. Entries vary in their depth of evaluation, ranging in length from 6 to 22 pages. Each chapter considers one artist, describing and critiquing her major works, many of which are illustrated in quarter-, half-, or full-page plates. The chapters conclude with a section headed "Career Highlights," consisting of information on dates of birth and education; awards; exhibitions; and bibliographies for books, articles, and catalogs of works.

The inclusion of 13 color plates only serves to emphasize the injustice done to the artists' works in the black-and-white reproductions used liberally throughout the book. This is a source in which to read about these works, not view them to advantage. The index is extremely poor. The subject of "Women" (a recurring motif in these works) is not indexed, but if one thinks to look under "Female," a series of anonymous page numbers is found that do not even identify which artist is being cited. The author makes frequently insightful and occasionally obvious critical statements, heavily weighted to laudatory and positive observations. Because of its highly focused subject matter and its status as one of the few books in print strictly pertaining to female Black artists, this would be a useful inclusion in general and art reference collections. It should be viewed as a point of departure for further investigation into the emotionally rich cultural area of African-American art. [R: RBB, 1 Oct 93, pp. 377-78; VOYA, Dec 93, p. 333]

—**James Moffet**

1047. Sproccati, Sandro, ed. **A Guide to Art.** New York, Harry N. Abrams, 1992. 287p. illus. index. $29.95. LC 91-77141. ISBN 0-8109-3366-7.

The worth of this reference book is found in the subtitle on the cover: "A Handy Reference to Artists, Their Works, and Artistic Movements from the Fourteenth Century to the Present Day." The main focus is on artistic movements, which makes the guide different from seemingly related works. Dictionaries of artists and their works abound; they have some mention of movements. Dictionaries of artists and their works associated with certain movements are also available. But to concentrate on movements entirely is usually the aim of survey works in one thick volume or in multivolumes. Sproccati's guide is not a dictionary. Rather, it is a concentrated survey in narrative form. The comparison with standard art dictionaries is made because this guide is of their class and most likely will be used as a quick reference. Sproccati has, however, done such a fine job of distilling 700 years of art movements that any student of art will want to read the guide from cover to cover.

Twenty-six movements or trends are covered, with brief artist biographies lining the lower third of many pages. One to three color illustrations appear per page, and even in reduced size the fidelity to the original is excellent. The first appendix names the world's great art museums and notes the great artists represented in each. The second appendix, and the only flaw in the guide, is a glossary of fewer than 30 art terms; it should either have been left out or expanded. (Preferably left out, as the main text serves as a glossary of movements and other artistic preoccupations.)

Artistic movements have not been handled so deftly before in such an attractive primer. Sproccati charts art history effortlessly to demonstrate that artists do indeed follow the same muse as long as it pleases them. Highly recommended. [R: RBB, 15 Jan 93, pp. 938-40]—**Bill Bailey**

1048. Webber, F. R. **Church Symbolism: An Explanation of the More Important Symbols of the Old and New Testament, the Primitive, the Mediaeval and the Modern Church.** 2d ed. Cleveland, Ohio, J. H. Jansen, 1938; repr., Detroit, Omnigraphics, 1992. 413p. illus. index. $62.00. BV150.W4. 704.9'482. LC 92-42460. ISBN 1-55888-941-8.

This classic from the late 1930s has now been reprinted on acid-free paper for continued survival. A picture is worth a thousand words, and the skeuomorphs, so to speak, presented here from the Old and New Testaments and from the primitive, medieval, and modern church are all explained. The opening chapters on the language of symbolism and its purpose serve as a stable foundation upon which to build. Then follow explanations of symbols of the Holy Spirit, Jesus Christ, his passion, sacred monograms, the four evangelists, the Greek and Latin church fathers, and much more.

Blake once said that the Bible was the great code of all Western art. Examination of this volume proves once again the validity of his thought-provoking contention. Almost nothing written, drawn, sculpted, engraved, or sung since A.D. 300 can be understood without a guide such as this.

—**Mark Y. Herring**

Indexes

1049. **Art Price Index International '94: 1992-1993 Auction Season.** Peter Hastings Falk and others, eds. Madison, Conn., Sound View Press, 1993. 2v. $165.00/set. ISBN 0-932087-24-8.

Art Price Index International (APII) is the first international price guide published in North America. The volume for the auction year 1992-1993 (July 1992 through June 1993) lists more than 142,000 entries and 50,000-plus artists in alphabetical order, and covers 362 auction houses in 27 countries. The artists are from all eras, and the entries under each artist are subdivided into four basic fine art categories: paintings, works on paper, sculpture, and prints. The essential fields of information the editors sought include artist's name, price result, title, medium, date of the work, signature (or stamping) information, and dimensions. Prices are provided in three currencies: United States dollars, British pounds, and German deutsche marks.

APII is the only international guide that shows all the works that failed to sell, or the BIs, as they are called in the auction business. These are represented by the low figure of their estimate range, followed by BI. The editors also wanted to serve the massive grass-roots art market; therefore, they lowered the starting price for a work's inclusion to $100 rather than $600-$1,500, as in the old guides.

The volumes are easy to read and have durable reinforced bindings. This set is the most affordable guide of its kind on the market. A comprehensive reference tool, it is practical for dealers, appraisers, collectors, and curators.—**Kathleen J. Voigt**

1050. **Illustration Index VII: 1987-1991.** By Marsha C. Appel. Metuchen, N.J., Scarecrow, 1993. 492p. $59.50. N7525.A67. 011'.37. LC 93-5153. ISBN 0-8108-2659-3.

Continuing in the tradition of the previous volumes of this series (see ARBA 90, entry 964), the current work provides access to more than 19,000 subjects encompassing 28,000 individual entries. As in previous editions, the illustrations appear in standard periodicals that most public or academic libraries carry, such as *American Heritage, Gourmet, National Geographic, Smithsonian, Sports Illustrated,* and *Travel/Holiday*. Abundant cross-references throughout the volume direct the user to additional illustrations on the chosen topic. Each entry gives the title of the magazine, the date, page number or numbers, whether the picture is color or black-and-white, and its relative size (e.g., full page, half page). A useful inclusion is the addresses for the periodicals indexed, which allow the researcher to contact the publisher for copyright permission if reproduction of the image is planned.

As visuals grow in importance in society, locating relevant illustrations becomes crucial to the researcher. The continued publication of this series contributes significantly to our ability to access the visual environment. Highly recommended for all academic, public, and special libraries where there is a need to locate illustrations in easily found periodicals.—**Gregory Curtis**

ARCHITECTURE

1051. Harris, Cyril M., ed. **Dictionary of Architecture & Construction.** 2d ed. New York, McGraw-Hill, 1993. 924p. illus. $59.50. LC 92-43562. ISBN 0-07-026888-6.

The first edition of Harris's dictionary was published in 1975 and received much acclaim (see ARBA 76, entry 445). Over the past 18 years, hundreds of new terms, especially from the associated fields of architecture and construction, have been added or revised by a working group of 52 experts in nearly 80 areas. The new edition now features some 22,500 definitions along with 2,000 illustrations. The format of each page has been enhanced by two to four illustrations per page within the text, rather than in the margins, as in the earlier edition. The terms are in boldface type, followed by clear and concise definitions. For some terms there are several definitions when they are used in a variety of related fields, as well as cross-references within a field. Reliance is heavy on terminology, symbols, and abbreviations used by the American Institute of Architects, ASTM, and ANSI standards.

As in all compilations of this type, some users may find their favorite work term missing or interpreted differently than in their own daily use. Frequently there might be questions about the derivation of a term, which this volume does not attempt to give. All in all, however, the book will continue to stand as the authoritative single-volume dictionary in the field. [R: Choice, Sept 93, p. 78; RBB, 1 Oct 93, p. 380]—**Robert J. Havlik**

1052. **Index to Italian Architecture: A Guide to Key Monuments and Reproduction Sources.** Edward H. Teague, comp. Westport, Conn., Greenwood Press, 1992. 278p. index. (Art Reference Collection, no.13). $55.00. NA111.T4. 016.72'0945. LC 92-5350. ISBN 0-313-28436-9.

This traditional illustration index facilitates access to pictures of many landmarks of Italian architectural history. It provides citations to illustrations of approximately 1,800 works reproduced from 89 titles that form a representative survey of the major periods of Italian architectural history. The majority of titles are standard monographic series that are likely to be available in academic, public, and special libraries with art and architectural collections.

The index is organized into five parts. Part 1, the site index, is the principal index; it lists works alphabetically by specific geographical location. For each work, the following information is provided: name and alternative name of work; date of work; architect; and citation information organized according to exterior view, interior view, plan, section, or elevation. Part 2, the architect index, alphabetically lists architects and others responsible for works cited in the site index. Part 3, the chronological index, groups the works according to centuries and sites. Part 4, the type index, organizes the works by building or structure types. Part 5, the work index, lists names and alternative names of works and parts of works. While column headings would be of help in the site index, this classic example of a manual database will be useful to specialized collections, not only for access to pictures but also as a reference to the textual information that normally accompanies them.—**Jay Schafer**

1053. Jackson, Kathryn A., with Peter Di Maso. **Canadian Architecture Collection: A Guide to the Archives. Collection d'Architecture Canadienne.** Montreal, Blackader-Lauderman Library of Architecture and Art, McGill University, 1993. 226p. index. $25.00pa. 016.72'0971. ISBN 0-7717-0275-2.

When the city of Montreal and the word "architecture" are mentioned, the first thing to come to mind is the Habitat project of Moshe Safdie for Expo '67. In truth, however, Montreal has had a long and outstanding reputation for fine architecture and architects. The center of this excellence has been the McGill School of Architecture. With the help of the Blackader-Lauderman Library of Architecture and Art of McGill University, a series of scholarly guides have been published about their Canadian Architecture Collection (CAC), which is an archival unit of the library. This particular volume is an overall guide to the archives. It consists of 95 entries for architects and architectural firms that have deposited materials in the archives. Almost all have contributed to the architecture of Montreal or graduated from or taught at McGill. Information such as their biographies, the origin of the collections, and the number of items and their description by type is given. Because many of the contributions are from architectural firms, there are appropriate *see* references to individual architects. In addition to the works of Safdie, who has made the CAC the primary repository of his works, other well-known architects, such as Arthur Erickson, Percy Erskine Nobbs, Edward and W. S. Maxwell, Ramsay Traquair, and John Bland, are represented. The work is in both French and English.—**Robert J. Havlik**

1054. Kleinbauer, W. Eugene. **Early Christian and Byzantine Architecture: An Annotated Bibliography and Historiography.** New York, G. K. Hall, 1992. 779p. index. (Reference Publication in Art History). $125.00. Z594.3.C56K55. 016.723'1. LC 92-9801. ISBN 0-8161-8316-3.

In this contribution, Kleinbauer maintains high standards of art historical scholarship and of reference publishing. His experience as president of the International Center of Medieval Art and as a professor at UCLA and at Indiana University (where he is associate director of the School of Fine Arts) indicates a lifetime of scholarly commitments.

As are many enumerative bibliographies, this work seeks to be comprehensive but not exhaustive. Kleinbauer has examined standard sources in the field, including *Literature on Byzantine Art, 1892-1967* (see ARBA 77, entry 860) and *Art and Architecture in the Balkans* (see ARBA 85, entry 870), as well as various annual guides to the literature. The final product consists of more than 2,600 entries. Some annotations are as brief as three lines in length, while many others are three times longer.

What overwhelms the reader is the narrative, an introduction of approximately 100 pages: "Prolegomena to a Historiography of Early Christian and Byzantine Architecture." It is a masterpiece of historical scholarship on major subjects, scholars, and schools of thought, and it contains numerous references to key entries. The section of annotated entries is followed by a brief addendum, a bibliographical essay on nineteenth-century photography of early Christian and Byzantine architecture, and author and subject indexes. This is a fine bibliographical resource that represents a thorough knowledge of history, art, architecture, and religion in a wide range of cultural, artistic, and linguistic traditions.

—**John Mark Tucker**

1055. Van Vynckt, Randall J., ed. **International Dictionary of Architects and Architecture.** Detroit, St. James Press/Gale, 1993. 2v. illus. index. $250.00/set. NA40.I48. 720'.9. LC 93-13431. ISBN 1-55862-089-3.

If weight were the only criterion, the combined 15.5 pounds of these two volumes would make them very important. But weight is only one impressive statistic about this important set. Featured in these volumes are essays by some 220 experts that cover 523 architects and 467 buildings and sites that have figured prominently in Western architectural history. Volume 1 is devoted to architects, and volume 2 covers buildings and sites. The architect volume gives a short biographical outline of the architect, followed by a concise chronology of the architect's major built works. Then there is a chronological list of books and articles by and about the person and the works, followed by a signed critical essay averaging about 1,000 words. Architects are listed alphabetically by name. The architecture volume features dates of construction, architect (if known), and a selected list of books and articles about the building or site, followed by a critical essay. The buildings and sites are listed by country, then town, and then name, under three major groups: classical sites and monuments, Europe, and the Americas. Both of the volumes are well illustrated with some 1,133 photographs and floor plans. Indexing and cross-referencing are important in a set such as this, so there is a building index in volume 1 and an architect index in volume 2. There are also extensive notes on the contributors of the essays.

Comparison can be made of these volumes with the five-volume *Encyclopedia of Architecture*, which began publication in 1988. (See ARBA 91, entry 1026 for a review of volume 5.) These two volumes are more limited in scope, but the entries are more detailed and informative because of the emphasis on chronological and bibliographical references. [R: JAL, Nov 93, pp. 346-47; LJ, 15 Sept 93, p. 68; WLB, Nov 93, p. 103-05]—**Robert J. Havlik**

DRAWING

1056. Jacobson, Ronald L. **Television-Related Cartoons in *The New Yorker* Magazine: Over 1250 Cartoon Descriptions (1950 through 1990) Indexed by Cartoonist and Subject.** Jefferson, N.C., McFarland, 1993. 165p. index. $42.50. NC1428.N47. 741.5'973. LC 92-56653. ISBN 0-89950-777-8.

Combining humor with social commentary is the aim of the cartoons that appear in the *New Yorker*. Collected albums illustrating some of the magazine's cartoons have appeared in the past. Until now, however, anyone interested in researching these cartoons, rather than merely viewing them, needed to search through the weekly issues of the *New Yorker* in hopes of discovering appropriate works. With this bibliography, that difficulty has ended for those interested in cartoons related to television. After an introduction highlighting some of the cartoons found in the bibliography, the entries are arranged chronologically by date of publication. Each entry includes the page on which it appeared, subject of the cartoon, cartoonist, and a brief description of the cartoon. Cartoonist and subject indexes add alternative means of access.

With comics increasingly becoming accepted as a field of academic study, those interested in cartoons, popular art, social commentary, or television criticism will profit from this work. Others may want to pass because of the limited scope of the subject matter. Other subject-specific bibliographies based on these cartoons would be welcome.—**Gregory Curtis**

GRAPHIC ARTS

1057. **British Printmakers 1855-1955: A Century of Printmaking from the Etching Revival to St. Ives.** Brookfield, Vt., Garton in association with Scolar Press/Ashgate Publishing, 1992. 326p. illus. $129.95. ISBN 0-85967-968-3.

This book is an illustrative look at British artists/printmakers during printmaking's revival from the nineteenth century to the mid-twentieth century, when new methods, materials, and equipment provided extraordinary opportunities to perfect the art and increase productivity. The work concentrates on printmakers who specialized in the field (as opposed to oil color and artists in other media who also made prints) and includes essays on the progression and development of printmaking, its different forms (e.g., etching, wood cut, lithograph), and influential artists and exhibitors/exhibitions (e.g., Francis Seymour Haden and James Abbott McNeill Whistler; the Senefelder Club, 1908-1934; the London Society of Painters-Printers, 1948).

With 585 illustrations separated primarily by method (e.g., linocut print), this oversized book is a rare and exciting find. Because the book's coverage is confined to three specific areas (time [1855 to 1955], origin [Great Britain], and classification [artists/printmakers]), the work is a concise, well-detailed reference. Well cross-referenced and heartily appendicized, the book also provides a brief biography of the artists presented and additional materials and sources on the subject. However, one element is missing in its chapters: process descriptions. For example, although a vague understanding of what a lithograph is can be acquired through the essays, a short paragraph defining the process and materials used would have enhanced the offering and made it more accessible to the nonartist. A brief explanation of what makes a wood engraving different from a woodcut does appear in chapter 1, and had this treatment been executed throughout, the book would have been perfect. Nevertheless, this exquisite art book belongs in every serious art and reference library. It could also easily decorate a coffee table for the casual but appreciative browser.—**Joan Garner**

1058. Paradis, Line. **Graphic Arts Vocabulary. Vocabulaire des Industries Graphiques.** Ottawa, Department of the Secretary of State of Canada, 1993. 573p. illus. (Terminology Bulletin, 210). $48.05pa. (U.S.). 686.2'03. ISBN 0-660-58025-4.

It is welcome news that Canada's Department of the Secretary of State has joined forces with a specialized Communication Group to publish a bilingual (English and French) dictionary of about 1,600 words and concepts. Graphic arts production has undergone phenomenal changes in almost all areas, and this updated and highly specialized vocabulary is aimed at those working directly in the field, including translators and writers. A list of the briefest selection of terms highlights the complexities of an evolving language: *Ben Day process, layboy, computer-aided design* (CAD), *printer control language, laser diode image setter, dorure sur tranche*, and *generation de points*. The principal content of the book consists of an English-to-French vocabulary, with concise definitions in each language. This is followed by a straightforward French-to-English glossary; appendixes relating to type classification schemes, paper sizes, typographical units, and the parts of a book; and an 11-page bilingual bibliography.

In summary, this is an up-to-the-minute dictionary of the graphic arts for production staff and allied fields. It has been compiled with maximum care for the myriad details found in any sphere of developing technology of increasing complexity. This publication has the added merit of listings in two international languages and should greatly assist those directly involved in the hands-on field of graphic arts.

—**William J. Dane**

1059. Thomson, Ellen Mazur, comp. **American Graphic Design: A Guide to the Literature.** Westport, Conn., Greenwood Press, 1992. 282p. index. (Art Reference Collection, no.15). $55.00. Z5956.D5T46. 016.7416'0973. LC 92-23786. ISBN 0-313-28728-7.

Another information gap has been filled. Graphic design sources usually are appended to comprehensive art or design bibliographies. When that occurs the selective listings do not represent the field adequately. Thomson, a printmaker, graphic designer, and librarian, has rectified this lack of focus with a thorough guide. She includes the art (e.g., color, theory, history) and the applied art (e.g., advertising, posters, illustration photography) of graphic design. Under 20 chapter headings she lists the best dictionaries and encyclopedias, bibliographies, biographical references, creative and talent directories, directories of collections, auction catalogs and sales records, indexes, online databases and CD-ROMs, and special subject monographs on the topic. Her emphasis is on current publications and materials, although some historical entries are mixed in (e.g., an 1860 and 1883 treatise on chromolithography). Each source cited is briefly annotated, but enough is said to make a selection. Thomson does not cover literature on fine prints and book art, cartography and stamp design, or commercial printing unless it relates directly to the design process. The last chapter on periodicals contains mostly in-print listings, with a few defunct publications. Professional organizations and associations by state fill the appendix.

Thomson's main intention—to collect the essential sources, the ones most often used and referred to by practitioners and students—has been fully realized. No longer will graphic design seem a lesser appendage to American art; its vitality is now more evident. Recommended for all art collections.
—**Bill Bailey**

1060. Winnan, Audur H. **Wanda Gag: A Catalogue Raisonne of the Prints.** Washington, D.C., Smithsonian Institution Press, 1993. 315p. illus. index. $75.00. NE539.G34A4. 769.92. LC 92-20937. ISBN 1-56098-221-7.

This ambitious volume is more than a catalog of prints. The author begins his work on this intriguing, romantic artist with a biographical overview assembled from a vast collection of diaries and notebooks housed in the Van Pelt Library at the University of Pennsylvania. He sprinkles his discussion with photographs, diary entries, and reviews. The second section, the catalog of prints, is organized with attention to arrangement and chronology, providing a fascinating glimpse of Gag's development. Children's literature specialists will especially appreciate seeing the drawings from the dummy of *ABC Bunny*. The final section is devoted to selected diary entries and letters, complete with a guide to her abbreviations and vernacular. This section is not only for the reader intrigued with the intimate details of Gag's life but also for anyone interested in the art or society of the early 1900s. Readers will be grateful to Winnan, who has created a triumphant volume that provides a rare glimpse of a passionate, gifted artist.
—**Suzanne I. Barchers**

PAINTING

1061. Carr, Dawson W., and Mark Leonard. **Looking at Paintings: A Guide to Technical Terms.** Malibu, Calif., with British Museum Press, J. Paul Getty Museum, 1992. 84p. illus. $10.95pa. ND31.C37. 750'.3. LC 91-24329. ISBN 0-89236-213-8.

As the authors note in the foreword, "This book is intended as a guide for the museum visitor who wishes to know more about the materials and techniques of paintings, as well as the terminology used to describe their visual effects." With more than 120 terms defined and 65 black-and-white and color illustrations used, the work will assist in understanding the information presented in catalogs or on wall labels.

Carr and Leonard have created a noble guide with clearly written terms and paintings chosen to illustrate techniques, materials, and the effects on artwork from time, abuse, and the elements (e.g., *craquelure*, a pattern of cracks that develops on a painting as a result of drying and aging). Nicely cross-referenced, the book will certainly aid the novice museum-goer. However, as the authors have "necessarily omitted" schools, styles, eras, and materials and techniques that have been introduced since 1900 (presumably to condense the book enough to carry easily), so have they created the need to obtain a second or even a third guide that provides the information left out here. Thus, their well-intentioned brevity has been defeated and the use of the book has been limited. Still, it is a nice little work that will help anyone wanting to gain the total art experience.—**Joan Garner**

1062. Cummins, Julie, ed. **Children's Book Illustration and Design.** Glen Cove, N.Y., PBC International; distr., New York, Rizzoli, 1992. 240p. illus. index. $60.00. NC965.C43. 741.6'42'09048. LC 91-31457. ISBN 0-86636-147-2.

This resource is an oversize, full-color collection of representative illustrations from 80 highly respected children's book illustrators. Brief biographical notes, quotations from the artist, and awards received are included within the one to four pages devoted to each illustrator.

Designing a book that adequately portrays this vast and varying collection of illustrators is a formidable undertaking. Cummins explains the collaborative process that involved artists and editor in selecting illustrations that provide a range of mediums and styles. Although at first glance there appears to be a dizzying assortment of images, when one approaches each illustrator's pages as a unit, the care taken with each section is apparent.

As any good book should do, it left this reviewer wanting more, such as 100 artists to encompass some curious omissions (e.g., Chris Van Allsburg, Maurice Sendak). The reader is provided with only a slice of the illustrator's career and philosophy; serious researchers will need to consult other resources for additional biographical information. However, this outstanding resource will be a joy to anyone studying or simply enjoying children's book illustration. [R: BL, 1 Jan 93 p. 812]—**Suzanne I. Barchers**

1063. Gealt, Adelheid M. **Painting of the Golden Age: A Biographical Dictionary of Seventeenth-Century European Painters.** Westport, Conn., Greenwood Press, 1993. 770p. index. $125.00. ND456.G43. 759.04'6. LC 92-40223. ISBN 0-313-24310-7.

Upper-division students in most art history curricula are required to take a course in Baroque art that focuses on "old Master" painters such as Peter Paul Rubens, Michelangelo Merisi da Caravaggio, and Pieter Brueghel. They will welcome this handy new English-language addition to a reference shelf dominated by works in French, German, and Italian. Gealt has done a fine job of covering some 300 major painters from all over Europe. The most famous artists receive a multipage entry with intelligent synopses of career highlights and significant works. In addition, each entry is augmented with an additional list of paintings not covered in the text and an abbreviated bibliography. Multiple concluding appendixes list painters by geographical area, provide an exhaustive bibliography, and give a detailed index to the text of the book.

There is an urgent need for biographical information in English on Baroque artists. Art librarians ultimately need a volume that covers architects and sculptors as well as painters. A biographical dictionary covering the entire Baroque period, rather than just its first century, is also needed. In the meantime, this excellent work will be heavily used and may inspire other useful reference books. [R: LJ, 1 Sept 93, p. 180]
—**Stephanie C. Sigala**

1064. Henkes, Robert. **Themes in American Painting: A Reference Work to Common Styles and Genres.** Jefferson, N.C., McFarland, 1993. 260p. illus. index. $39.95. ND205.H42. 759.13. LC 92-53599. ISBN 0-89950-734-4.

Many art historians would consider history painting, landscape, and portraiture to be the major American contributions to art. However, "Modes of Transportation," "The Clown," "The Crucifixion," and "Natural Disasters" are among the 13 topics covered. Each essay proceeds leisurely from one painting to another in a manner reminiscent of a classroom slide lecture. This is a fine methodology when Henkes illustrates the works he discusses or covers well-known artists, but this does not happen consistently. Often the reader is left in the dark for significant stretches of text without illustrations or cross-references for guidance.

Despite the promise of coverage of America's finest paintings in this volume, one looks in vain for a scholarly, well-documented discussion of American art history. There are no footnotes; the bibliography depends heavily on general art appreciation texts; and the narrative is in the first person. Thus, it is a stretch to call this volume a reference book: what it resembles is a collection of old art appreciation lecture notes discussing some random themes in American art of the 1930s and 1940s. [R: RBB, 1 May 93, pp. 1636-38]—**Stephanie C. Sigala**

1065. Wingfield, Mary Ann. **A Dictionary of Sporting Artists 1650-1990.** Wappingers Falls, N.Y., Antique Collectors' Club, 1992. 354p. index. $89.50. ISBN 1-85149-140-6.

The Antique Collectors' Club operates to provide prices for and information about a wide range of collecting pursuits and hobbies. Formed in 1966, the Club is British and, in addition to monographs, publishes the well-known monthly *Antique Collecting*. The dictionary listings in this work are mostly for British artists who painted "at least one good sports painting" during their careers. When that is the case—one painting up to a handful—only the title, date, and size are given for each. Otherwise, the entry is longer and establishes the artist as a certain kind of genre painter.

The introduction makes clear there never was a British school of sporting painters. Rather, the artists painted sports scenes as the whim struck them, not as a singular pursuit. The sports index reflects predominantly British interests: angling, coursing, cricket, croquet, curling, dogfighting, donkey racing, dressage, equestrian, fencing, ferreting, fox hunting, lawn bowls, lawn tennis, the National Hunt, rugby, and shooting. Some unusual entries are for the Eton Wall Game, jousting, pigsticking, ratting, and tent-pegging. To appeal to an American audience, American football and what the Club calls "real" tennis are included. The artists lived from around 1650 to the present and may have painted many sports scenes. But, as noted, the Club's criterion for inclusion in this work is that the artist painted at least one good sports painting. Knowing monetary value as it does, the Club bases its decision on sales records and ownership. Recommended for either sports or art collections with strong British holdings.—**Bill Bailey**

SCULPTURE

1066. Kleiner, Diane E. E. **Roman Sculpture.** New Haven, Conn., Yale University Press, 1992. 477p. illus. index. (Yale Publications in the History of Art). $55.00. NB115.K57. 733'.5. LC 91-46265. ISBN 0-300-04631-6.

There are few books that focus solely on Roman sculpture. The only recent one cited by the author is Donald Strong's *Roman Art* (Harmondsworth, 1976), and even that work includes such techniques as painting and mosaics. Hence the impetus for this volume. Kleiner's book examines Roman sculpture by concentrating on both commissioned works and the art of freedmen and slaves, and on major monuments as well as less well publicized works. In addition, the author seeks to examine Roman sculpture in its cultural, political, and social contexts. This work, therefore, is organized chronologically and describes historical events and the influences of the people (most notably the ruling class) upon each other as well as on the sculpture created. Minimal mention is made of Roman sculpture outside of Rome, however.

This work is well written. There are many photographs, and although they are all in black-and-white (under the circumstances, color is unnecessary), they are of excellent quality. Each chapter concludes with a bibliography, and a glossary of Greek and Latin terms precedes the index. All in all, this volume is highly recommended to art libraries and libraries with strong art collections. It will more than amply fill the glaring hole in their Roman sculpture collections.—**Marjorie E. Bloss**

1067. Penny, Nicholas. **Catalogue of European Sculpture in the Ashmolean Museum 1540 to the Present Day.** New York, Clarendon Press/Oxford University Press, 1992. 3v. illus. index. $575.00/set. NB454.P46. 735'.074'42574. LC 92-21820. ISBN 0-19-951329-5.

The 12 cartloads of rarities presented by Elias Ashmole to Oxford University in 1683 have grown and metamorphosed into one of Britain's most important general art collections, the Ashmolean Museum, under the guidance of such well-known art historians as Arthur Evans and Kenneth Clarke. Penny, Keeper of Western Art at the Ashmolean in the 1980s, provides the first thorough look at the Ashmolean European sculpture collections in this three-volume publication. Volume 1 covers Italian sculpture (primarily

Renaissance and Baroque bronzes *all' antica*); volume 2 treats French and other continental sculpture (with many significant late nineteenth-century works); and volume 3 includes British representational works through the present day. Because of the long history of and various collecting patterns at the Ashmolean, each volume has at least one relevant essay on a significant collector or period in the museum's history.

Penny's basic organization in each volume is twofold: Known artists' works are treated alphabetically, while unnamed works are treated chronologically. This dichotomy makes it somewhat difficult to get a clear view of strengths in any one area, but a multitude of indexes provide admirable cross-referencing. Each entry contains comprehensive information about the provenance of the work, black-and-white illustrations, and a half-page discussion. The volumes are dignified in appearance, well bound, and scholastic landmarks of intellectual value—not flashy, but worth a high price in academic art libraries.

—**Stephanie C. Sigala**

23 Language and Linguistics

GENERAL WORKS

1068. **Annotated Bibliography of the Official Languages of Canada. Bibliographie Analytique des Langues Officielles au Canada.** Ottawa, Office of the Commissioner of Official Languages, n.d. 53p. price not reported.

Bilingualism, twin streams of language where both are official and neither dominates, never caught on in the United States, and probably never will. In Canada, however, parallelism in language is not just (generally) accepted—it is the law. And, as do laws everywhere, bilingualism engenders its own cumbersome bureaucracy and a daunting mountain of paperwork and documentation to implement it and keep it running. This slender booklet (printed in French and English in side-by-side columns) begins with an introduction that sketches the advent and development of bilingualism and quickly moves to the rationale for a classified bibliography of the problems attendant upon its implementation.

The bibliography is arranged by topic (e.g., attitudes of Canadians towards official bilingualism, federal-provincial collaboration, costs, linguistic demography). Subject and author indexes round out the coverage. The overall impression most readers will come away with is likely to be stunned astonishment at what is *involved* in setting up a bilingual program for a huge nation such as Canada. Just mounting such a law must have been staggering, and implementing and monitoring its provisions seem expensive and time-consuming. Still, the government-sponsored bilingualism of Canada is in its 33d year, and, unless the francophones secede from the union and set up their own nation, it will go on and on.

For all types of Canadian libraries, this work would seem a must-acquisition. Collections in the United States are unlikely to need this title, and calls for it will probably vary inversely with distance from the international border.—**Bruce A. Shuman**

1069. **Ethnologue Index.** 12th ed. Barbara F. Grimes, ed. Dallas, Tex., Summer Institute of Linguistics, 1992. 312p. $15.00pa. LC 73-646678. ISBN 0-88312-819-5.

1070. **Ethnologue: Languages of the World.** 12th ed. Barbara F. Grimes, ed. Dallas, Tex., Summer Institute of Linguistics, 1992. 938p. maps. index. $35.00pa. LC 73-646678. ISBN 0-88312-815-2.

Ethnologue is a compilation of information on 6,528 languages worldwide, an increase of 360 languages over the previous edition. It represents data from the Ethnologue Language Archive, a computerized sociolinguistic database at the Summer Institute of Linguistics in Dallas. It is organized by world region: the Americas, Africa, Europe, and Asia and the Pacific, with each section listing individual countries. This edition incorporates the new geography of the former Soviet Union, changes in Yugoslavia, and some geographic name changes. Included for each country are estimates of the literacy rate and of the data accuracy, names of major religions, population statistics, and estimates of blind and deaf populations. Languages and dialects for each country are listed along with their typology and brief geographic and socioeconomic information. Because the data were collected through survey questionnaires, some entries are more complete than others. Much of the information represents estimates rather than rigorous scientific data. Interspersed throughout the text are linguistic maps of continents and countries. The volume is supplemented with 21 pages of bibliography; a table that lists languages of special interest, including gypsy, Jewish, Creole and Pidgin, and sign languages; and copies of the survey questionnaires.

The companion volume is a computer-produced index that contains some 37,000 entries for the language and dialect names detailed in the main volume. Each entry identifies the language, dialect or alternate names, a three-letter language identification code, and the country or countries with which it is most closely identified. For example, Komba, a language of Papua, New Guinea, is coded as KPF.

This is a specialized study primarily meant for linguistic translators, anthropologists, and missionaries. It should be considered by large research libraries and subject collections.—**Bernice Bergup**

1071. Fitzmyer, Joseph A., and Stephen A. Kaufman. **An Aramaic Bibliography. Part I: Old, Official, and Biblical Aramaic.** Baltimore, Md., Johns Hopkins University Press, 1992. 349p. $56.00. Z7053.F57. 016.492'29. LC 91-21491. ISBN 0-8018-4312-X.

Funded in part by the National Endowment for the Humanities, this work is the kind of rare scholarly achievement that must depend on external funding if it is ever to see the light of day. This is the first volume in the Comprehensive Aramaic Lexicon Project, scheduled to appear in an unspecified number of parts depending, perhaps, on the availability of additional grant support.

The work grew out of efforts to identify the *editio princeps* of Aramaic texts, writings, or inscriptions from the emergence of the language down to the Syriac period. Part 1 covers Old Aramaic and Standard or Official Aramaic, categories that encompass the period 900 B.C.E. to 613 B.C.E. (the fall of Nineveh) and the period to about 200 B.C.E. A brief section is devoted to biblical Aramaic with references to appropriate passages in Ezra and Daniel. Part 2, not yet published, is scheduled to cover the middle period of Aramaic (200 B.C.E. to 300 C.E.).

Fitzmyer and Kaufman have arranged the volume into two sections, the second of which provides complete bibliographical data. Part 1 identifies general studies, including standard collected works. Entries for the texts, with references to the secondary literature discussing those texts, make up most of the volume and are arranged geographically, then by type of document (e.g., literature, letters, contracts, fragments), then chronologically by date of publication.

The entire work is carefully crafted and thoughtfully arranged. It should become a standard source, unsurpassed for decades. Seminarians and other scholars who would find this work useful will need a working knowledge of French, German, English, and Italian (not to mention ancient languages).
—**John Mark Tucker**

1072. Jung, Heidrun, and Udo O. H. Jung. **The Dictionary of Acronyms and Abbreviations in Applied Linguistics and Language Learning.** 2d ed. New York, Peter Lang, c1991, 1992. 2v. (Bayreuth Contributions to Glottodidactics, v.1). $124.80pa./set. ISBN 3-631-43867-2.

Together with other kinds of clippings, acronyms have become an indispensable part of the professional jargons in many languages. As useful and important as they are, they also present a major problem for millions of foreign-language learners and their instructors all over the world. This new dictionary offers substantial help in overcoming this obstacle. It is a dignified and, in many respects, greatly enhanced successor to a 1985 edition with a different title and publisher (*Elsevier's Foreign-Language Teacher's Dictionary of Acronyms and Abbreviations* [see ARBA 87, entry 1034]).

The two-volume dictionary now contains more than 13,000 entries, with acronyms and abbreviations of thousands of international, national, and regional associations, societies, centers, and the like. International car identification signs, country codes, names of airlines, and many general and common acronyms are also listed. English is the most heavily represented language, followed by acronyms and abbreviations in French, German, Spanish, and a sprinkling of other languages. The authors acknowledge that one of their major problems has been the establishing of criteria concerning inclusions and exclusions. In this respect, many of their acronyms are now "historical," bearing witness to the recent political and social changes that swept away, among others, numerous institutions of the former Soviet Union and the German Democratic Republic (East Germany). On the other hand, their entries for abbreviations of United States and Canadian universities are quite spotty and do not seem to indicate a systematic pattern.

Volume 1 alphabetically lists all acronyms and otherwise clipped forms that comprise the authors' database. Numerous entries in volume 1 contain additional information, such as addresses and telephone and fax numbers of given institutions. Sometimes even references to articles or books on a subject are provided. Volume 2 is an inverted index that lists all the full forms of words or word combinations together with their abbreviated forms. This welcome feature facilitates two-way searching: beginning with an acronym and using volume 1, or starting from a full name in volume 2, finding the respective abbreviation there, and then going to volume 1 for further relevant information.

The high cost of this dictionary makes it even less accessible to individuals than its predecessor. Language learners, teachers, translators, researchers in applied linguistics, and reference librarians should hope that their libraries will order this useful and versatile reference work.—**Lev I. Soudek**

1073. Kabdebo, Thomas. **Dictionary of Dictionaries.** New Providence, N.J., K. G. Saur/Reed Reference Publishing, 1992. 253p. index. $100.00. 016.423. ISBN 0-86291-775-1.

This reference guide to dictionaries takes the widest possible definition of *dictionary*. Although many of the entries are traditional mono- and bilingual language dictionaries, virtually any sort of alphabetically arranged reference volume is eligible for inclusion, from *The Encyclopedia of American Scandal* (see ARBA 90, entry 492) to the *Dictionary of Mental Handicap* (see ARBA 91, entry 854). The work differs from such standard works as *Guide to Reference Books* (see ARBA 93, entry 670), and *Walford's Guide to Reference Materials* (see ARBA 93, entries 21 and 98) in two respects. For one, it is much smaller—about 6,000 titles contained in about 1,000 subject headings, versus more than 20,000 titles for the standard reference guides. For another, it is alphabetically arranged by subject categories, which are sometimes idiosyncratic (e.g., "Do It Yourself," "Social Security," "Table Alphabetical"). Each article entry describes and evaluates relevant titles. This is in contrast to the more exhaustive guides that arrange their contents by standard categories and subcategories. The articles are cross-referenced, and there is a good index.

The virtues of this work are brevity and ease of use. The down sides are more numerous. In some cases the books chosen are far from the best choices. Note, for example, the omission of the outstanding *Handbook of Russian Literature* (see ARBA 86, entry 1221) in favor of the short, out-of-date *Dictionary of Russian Literature* (see ARBA 73, entry 1358). In general, the citations, which are basically limited to English-language works, lean toward British works that are less accessible to the American user. While handy for personal libraries or less sophisticated users, this work cannot be recommended for research institutions. [R: Choice, July/Aug 93, pp. 1750-52; WLB, June 93, p. 123]—**D. Barton Johnson**

1074. Vancil, David E., comp. **Catalog of Dictionaries, Word Books, and Philological Texts, 1440-1900: Inventory of the Cordell Collection, Indiana State University.** Westport, Conn., Greenwood Press, 1993. 397p. index. (Bibliographies and Indexes in Library and Information Science, no.7). $75.00. Z2015.D6V36. 016.423. LC 92-30883. ISBN 0-313-28700-7.

This work catalogs the pre-1901 portion of the Cordell Collection of Dictionaries, reportedly the world's largest. The collection's aim is to gather dictionaries that aid in tracing the development of English and to collect works that pertain to the history of Western lexicography. Both English- and foreign-language titles are included. The catalog, current through 1991, describes 5,046 titles. It complements *English-Language Dictionaries, 1604-1900* (see ARBA 89, entry 936), which provides fuller descriptions of its 2,328 separate entries but does not include the Cordell Collection's substantial foreign-language holdings.

The new catalog has still other advantages. In addition to the usual alphabetical listing (by author, compiler, or title), it has three supplementary indexes. The date index provides a year-by-year list of the first printings of each title, supplying an overview of the history of lexicography. The language index ranges from African to Wendish, showing that the collection and its catalog are of interest to a much wider audience than just historians of English. If the date and language indexes are of interest primarily to philologists, the subject guide is a treasure trove for historians of all human knowledge, as it ranges from anecdotes to zoology. (The history of humankind and its world lies in our dictionaries.)

Vancil's preface and section on use of the catalog are clear and concise. No less welcome is his inclusion of Warren N. Cordell's remarks, in which the bookman gracefully sketches the story of his collecting odyssey. [R: WLB, May 93, p. 113]—**D. Barton Johnson**

ENGLISH-LANGUAGE DICTIONARIES

Abridged

1075. **The American Heritage College Dictionary.** 3d ed. Boston, Houghton Mifflin, 1993. 1630p. illus. maps. $18.95; $19.95 (thumb index); $21.95 (deluxe). PE1628.A6227. 423. LC 92-42124. ISBN 0-395-66917-0; 0-395-44638-4 (thumb index); 0-395-66918-9 (deluxe).

1076. **Merriam-Webster's Collegiate Dictionary.** 10th ed. Springfield, Mass., Merriam-Webster, 1993. 1559p. illus. index. $20.95; $21.95 (indexed). PE1628.M36. 423. LC 93-20206. ISBN 0-87779-708-0; 0-87779-709-9 (indexed).

While both of these popular and respected volumes perform the same function, they are less similar than one might think. Each, of course, has the basics: a list of words and terms, information on abbreviations used and how to use the dictionary, an essay on the English language, biographical and geographical names, and small pronunciation guides on every right-hand page. And, on the whole, the definitions in each book are similar; however, each occasionally stresses details that the other does not. For example, in the definition of *geisha, American Heritage* mentions "A woman in Japan trained from girlhood in conversation, dancing, and singing...," while *Merriam-Webster's* merely states, "A Japanese girl or woman who is trained to provide entertainment and lighthearted company...." While the two dictionaries generally define the same words, each contains terms that the other omits. For example, in the Z section, the last five words in *American Heritage* are *zymolysis, zymometer, zymosis, zymurgy,* and *zyzzyva*, whereas in *Merriam-Webster's* they are *zymase, -zyme, zymogen, zymogram,* and *zymosan.* For new words and terms, *American Heritage* alone contains *virtual reality, generation X,* and *mountain bike,* while *Merriam-Webster's* alone contains *focaccia, radwaste,* and *-gate* as a suffix (e.g., "nannygate"). Neither book defines *graphic novel*, although the term is almost 20 years old. Also, the choices of biographical names differ, with *American Heritage* including many figures from popular culture that *Merriam-Webster's* omits (e.g., the members of the Beatles). One disappointing deletion from *Merriam-Webster's* is the section that provided names and addresses for colleges and universities.

Perhaps the major difference between the two dictionaries in the treatment of words is with proper nouns and their preferable spellings. For example, *Merriam-Webster's* prefers *Athabascan* over *Athabaskan*, while *American Heritage* reverses that order. Capitalization preferences can also differ. Finally, *American Heritage* interfiles abbreviations and biographical and geographical names with the main listing; *Merriam-Webster's* has a separate section for each.

The two dictionaries are physically different in several ways, the most obvious one being the number of illustrations used: *American Heritage* usually has at least one per page, more often two, sometimes as many as four. Moreover, many of its illustrations are photographs. In *Merriam-Webster's*, there appears to be one picture for every two pages, and these are line drawings. Both books average about 58 terms per page. *American Heritage* has more white space in the margins (where pictures appear), and the typeface used makes it seem as if there is more space between entries.

Both dictionaries are excellent, accurate, and useful. For personal use, the dictionary chosen will probably be the most attractive one, in which case *American Heritage* has the edge, with its abundant photographs. For those needing authority, especially on capitalization, *Merriam-Webster's* has the reputation. But it would be best to shelve both, because of the unique words and information in each and because two similar-but-different definitions can often complement each other. [R: Choice, Oct 93, p. 270; LJ, 1 Sept 93, p. 172; RBB, 1 Sept 93, p. 80; SLJ, Nov 93, p. 145; WLB, Sept 93, p. 121]

—D. A. Rothschild

1077. **Funk & Wagnalls Standard Dictionary.** 2d ed. New York, HarperCollins, 1993. 954p. $4.99pa. ISBN 0-06-100708-0.

To define itself as one of the elite U.S. dictionary publishers, HarperCollins has to compete against four of the best: Houghton Mifflin, Simon and Schuster, Merriam-Webster, and Random House. To affect the pocket dictionary market in particular, as opposed to the markets for unabridged and desk dictionaries, HarperCollins has to grapple with questions about scope and purpose. Why do people carry and use small dictionaries? Shouldn't small, easily republishable dictionaries excel in currentness?

This dictionary's best feature is its 75,000 properly spelled words. A unique and helpful feature is that collateral terms are supplied. When, for example, the adjectival form in common use is not etymologically related to its noun, such as *canine* and *dog*, the dictionary provides this form in the entry for the noun. It also provides entries for irregular inflected forms, such as *went* and *genera*, referring the user back to the present indicative or nominative singular form, as appropriate. The pronunciation system is simple and easy to use, and pages are not wasted on the so-called bonus sections (e.g., grammatical rules, lists of the presidents).

Although the pages are felicitously composed, with ample white space and a pleasing serif font, it is hard to imagine a situation in which this dictionary could offer regular intellectual satisfaction. It claims to have many new entries, but a handful of current, stable, unremarkable "new" words, such as *database, neonate, condo,* and *pre-teen,* pulled from the newspaper are not included. Its coverage of slang is uneven. For example, the affectionate use of *baby* between loving adults is not admitted; *wetback* makes it in with the label "Offensive"; and *bitch,* meaning "a malicious or promiscuous person, esp. a woman," is only "Slang." Despite the claim on the back cover that "authoritative etymologies" are provided, the etymologies are very brief. Often they consist of no more than "[ME]" or "[<F]" and should be excised from future editions. Historical context is not provided: the definition for tavern does not state that the second meaning, "inn," is now obsolete. Within each entry, related meanings are grouped together, but "[t]here is, otherwise, no significance to their order; the first definition is not necessarily for the earliest use, nor is it the most frequently used." Nor will this dictionary help one choose between exacerbate and exasperate.—**Judith M. Brugger**

1078. **The Pocket Oxford Dictionary of Current English.** 8th ed. Della Thompson, ed. New York, Clarendon Press/Oxford University Press, 1992. 1074p. $14.95. ISBN 0-19-861256-7.

This new edition is on the large side for an abridged dictionary but too small to rate the term *unabridged.* It boasts more than 65,000 entries and 75,000 definitions. The front cover notes that this is the best-selling pocket dictionary. (Including "Current English" in its name seems an attempt to absolve itself of providing etymology.) Amid the front matter is the notation that this edition owes much in its content and style to the eighth edition (1992) of the *Concise Oxford Dictionary,* and is now following the practice of "denesting," the listing of words in a single alphabetical sequence of main entries, with fewer items "nested" at the end of entries. Admittedly, this practice makes for a user-friendlier term-arrangement. Another pleasing feature is that this edition, for the first time, lists separately entries and definitions for words that begin with such familiar prefixes as "over-," "re-," and "un-."

When an already condensed dictionary is further condensed to pocket size, some information is necessarily lost. The user may thus find definitions a bit scant, and, at times, not all that helpful. *Football,* for example, is dismissed generically as "an outdoor team game ... played with a large inflated ball." Look up *lothario* and the work says that the term refers to "a character in a play," then refers to *libertine,* which, in turn, leads to *licentious,* defined only as "sexually promiscuous."

The book's accent is decidedly British, but that is to be expected from a work that bears the time-honored name of Oxford. Still, it would be nice for the multiple definitions of *lift* to include one for "elevator." (*Elevator* is just an airplane part or a "hoisting machine.") *Postbox, letter-box,* and *pillar-box* are present, but *mailbox* is dismissed as a U.S. term for *letter-box.* Refreshingly international are the entries for profanity (noted as "vulgar" or "coarse slang"). Usage notes are ubiquitous and do an admirable job of explaining the uses of idiom. All in all, seekers of downsized, inexpensive dictionaries cannot expect to do better than this one, especially at its price.—**Bruce A. Shuman**

Etymology

1079. Danner, Horace Gerald, and Roger Noel. **A Thesaurus of Word Roots of the English Language.** Lanham, Md., University Press of America, 1992. 773p. $75.00. PE1580.D36. 422'.03. LC 92-9743. ISBN 0-8191-8666-X.

Designed for students of English etymology, this text is not a thesaurus in the usual sense. Rather, it serves to group words by their elements, assigned such technical names as "Simple Root" and "Leading Root Compound." The purpose is to show how parts combine to form different words.

Unlike the usual alphabetical dictionary arrangement, the thesaurus lists individual word parts alphabetically. Thus, for example, the element "klept"—from the Greek word *kleptein*, meaning "to steal"—combines with other roots to form words such as *kleptomaniac*, which refers to a person who steals from impulse rather than need, and *biblioklept*, which refers to a person who steals books.

The authors have constructed an elaborate outline for categorizing and analyzing each element. The serious student will appreciate the complexity of the analysis and the many examples provided as illustrations. Especially helpful are the definitions and notes supplied for many words. Users may consult the appendixes for an index identifying the roots of English words and for a list of root frequencies. In addition to its use as a textbook, the thesaurus will complement research collections in linguistics.

—**Bernice Bergup**

1080. Garrison, Webb. **Why You Say It.** Nashville, Tenn., Rutledge Hill Press, 1992. 356p. index. $16.95; $10.95pa. PE1580.G37. 422'.03. LC 92-26951. ISBN 1-55853-147-5; 1-55853-128-9pa.

Thoroughly revised since its first hardcover appearance in 1955, this inexpensive, attractively designed paperback will delight and inform. Alphabetically arranged in 19 cleverly titled sections, such as "Why Don't Folks Say Precisely What They Mean?" "Stories to Be Taken with a Grain of Salt," and "Sports Talk Often Follows the Ball," most of these more than 600 terms and phrases are drawn from everyday conversation. In many instances, even the widely read user may be surprised—and amused—at the derivations (e.g., "read the riot act," "lynching," "pull one's leg"). Occasionally, however, one's response may be "pretty obvious!" (e.g., "bush league," "roll with the punches"). Garrison will also explain whether "diddly-squat" can be used in polite conversation and whether V. M. Molotov really had anything to do with his explosive cocktail. A good index and a well-balanced bibliography conclude the work.

How many etymologies and phrase books does a collection need? If three examples from three recent popular titles are any measure, all three titles would be required to locate these terms: "different strokes for different folks" (*Have a Nice Day—No Problem* [E. P. Dutton, 1992]), "the cat is out of the bag" (*Loose Cannons and Red Herrings* [see ARBA 90, entry 1007]) and "takes two to tango" (*Why You Say It*).

—**Charles R. Andrews**

1081. Holloway, Joseph E., and Winifred K. Vass. **The African Heritage of American English.** Bloomington, Ind., Indiana University Press, 1993. 193p. illus. maps. index. $24.95. PE3102.N4H65. 427'.973'08996. LC 92-18270. ISBN 0-253-32838-1.

This examination of African influences on English vocabulary and grammar is an unfortunate example of raw material not yet ready for public consumption. Arranged in what appears to be good order, the material lacks adequate presentation, adaptation, and commentary to make it fully accessible to most readers and researchers. Nuggets of information lie buried in the drift of material, such as a chart of male and female given names that reflect African words for days of the week. A study of this information, particularly "Beneba" for "Tuesday," suggests where the character Beneatha Younger in Lorraine Hansberry's *A Raisin in the Sun* received her unusual first name. However, Holloway and Vass fail to make such connections with their research.

The volume opens with an acknowledgment, a dedication to researcher Lorenzo Dow Turner, and a list of abbreviations. Woven into this prefatory matter are drawings, maps, and photographs that require more commentary to justify their existence in an introduction. Similar to the beginning, the text itself, preceded by a rather frail statement of purpose, is a blend of lists, maps, and sparse explanation. To comprehend what Holloway and Vass have in mind for application of text to research and what they conclude from their study, the reader must rely on surmise. Offsetting a timid index is a vast and impressive list of bibliographical source materials. Perhaps Holloway and Vass need to return to the sources and delineate more clearly the merger of African vocabulary with American English rather than provide readers with lists and leave them to form their own hypotheses.—**Mary Ellen Snodgrass**

1082. Moore, Bob, and Maxine Moore. **Up from the Roots: Growing a Vocabulary.** Ferndale, Calif., New Chapter Press; distr., Chicago, Independent Publishers Group, 1993. 198p. illus. index. $13.95pa. LC 92-060937. ISBN 0-942257-20-0.

This book, designed to help students develop a rich and varied English vocabulary, consists of essays on more than 200 basic Latin and Greek word roots. Each essay shows connections among numerous words deriving from the root word. Besides defining the word, essays provide sample sentences; synonyms; antonyms; literary and historical quotations; occasional puns (for comic relief and to enhance comprehension); words that are often mistakenly assumed to be related to the root; and various combining word forms, such as prefixes and suffixes commonly associated with the root. Molly Ivins, the popular syndicated columnist, provides a warm introduction to this text, testifying that Bob Moore was one of the best teachers she ever had.

Unlike a conventional etymological dictionary, which typically provides a brief history of a word's origin and possibly a few related words, this book concentrates, as a good textbook should, on teaching users a way of thinking about words. Bob Moore is justifiably proud of the approach to teaching vocabulary exemplified by this book. *Up from the Roots* is the culmination of two decades of teaching vocabulary at the Chinquapin School, which Bob Moore founded in Houston to teach inner-city Houston children skills they would need to succeed in college. He asserts that the average SAT verbal score for his students is from 52 to 80 points above the national average, and that these students are regularly admitted to the very best colleges. Because this is a book primarily intended as a classroom text, it seems more useful for prolonged use, and thus should be in the circulating rather than the reference collection.
—**David Isaacson**

1083. Thurner, Dick. **Portmanteau Dictionary: Blend Words in the English Language, Including Trademarks and Brand Names.** Jefferson, N.C., McFarland, 1993. 174p. $27.50. PE1175.T54. 423'.1. LC 92-51011. ISBN 0-89950-687-9.

The term *portmanteau word* was coined by Lewis Carroll in *Through the Looking Glass*. Humpty Dumpty tells Alice that the language of the poem "Jabberwocky" includes a number of words, such as "slithy," that combine two words (in this case *lithe* and *slimy*), much like the two compartments of the Victorian suitcase called a portmanteau. Thurner has collected thousands of these blended words in English, which date from very early times to the present, to form this specialized dictionary. He combed numerous general and specialized dictionaries for these words. A list of abbreviations of the titles of these sources appears at the beginning of the dictionary. Besides unabridged dictionaries such as the *Oxford English Dictionary* (OED) (see ARBA 90, entry 1006), dictionaries of new words, slang, regionalisms, euphemisms, technical terms, unusual words, and trade names have been used as sources. One puzzling omission in what otherwise seems to be a comprehensive list of sources is *The Random House Dictionary of the English Language* (see ARBA 88, entry 1095).

A typical entry is very concise (for some users, it may be too concise), consisting of an abbreviation noting the part of speech, the two or more words that form the blend noted in parentheses, a brief definition, and the abbreviation of the dictionary used as a source for the entry. An example is "agreemony n. (agree + acrimony) Agreeableness, the opposite of acrimony. OED." Although the sources Thurner uses may present more detailed definitions of many of these words, some users may find it useful to have them gathered together in one dictionary. [R: Choice, Dec 93, pp. 591-92]—**David Isaacson**

General Usage

1084. Bollard, John K., Frank R. Abate, and Katherine M. Isaacs, eds. **Pronouncing Dictionary of Proper Names: Pronunciations for More Than 23,000 Proper Names....** Detroit, Omnigraphics, 1993. 894p. $68.00. PE1137.P82. 423'.1. LC 93-608. ISBN 1-55888-311-8.

Imagine that a newscaster is required to read the following story on the air: "Today *Lech Walesa* and *Boutros Boutros-Ghali* attended a United Nations benefit art exhibit, viewing masterpieces by *Van Gogh* and *Klee* while sipping *Pouilly Fuisse*. During lunch they were heard discussing the situations in *Tbilisi* and *Bosnia-Herzegovina*; the Hanging Gardens of *Nebuchadnezzar*; the differences between *Cairo*, Egypt, and *Cairo*, Illinois; and the plight of the *Xhosa*."

Faced with this situation, the newscaster would certainly be more confident if this reference work was at hand. The names in this new dictionary were selected for currency, frequency, or difficulty of pronunciation and include a wide range of people, places, and things, both historical and contemporary. Each page is arranged in three columns, the first column containing keywords in boldface type and brief descriptions of the words. A simplified phonetic respelling (e.g., "*HAW-sah*" for *Xhosa*) appears in the second column, while the International Phonetic Alphabet (IPA) transcription is given in the last column. Variants are given, often the original language pronunciation followed by acceptable U.S. versions. Cross-references for alternative names are given in square brackets following the headword. A very thorough and helpful introduction includes the selection criteria, a description of the two pronunciation systems, and a list of abbreviations. Brief pronunciation guides are given on each page, with full versions given on the insides of the covers.

The editors have performed a valuable service in compiling this useful, user-friendly dictionary. The book will be an essential resource for journalists, broadcasters, public speakers, academics, and anyone interested in the correct pronunciation of troublesome names. [R: JAL, Nov 93, p. 347; LJ, 1 Nov 93, p. 80; WLB, Dec 93, p. 82]—**Henry J. Ricardo**

1085. **The Columbia Guide to Standard American English.** By Kenneth G. Wilson. New York, Columbia University Press, 1993. 482p. $24.95. PE2835.W55. 428'.00973. LC 92-37887. ISBN 0-231-06988-X.

With about 6,500 alphabetically arranged entries covering many aspects of word choice, pronunciation, grammar, and idiomatic usage, this new guide emphasizes contemporary *American* usage rather than British usage. Capitalized entry words denote those that define and explain general grammatical and linguistic terms used in the guide, while lowercase print is used for the usage items themselves. Alternative pronunciations and spellings are given where appropriate. There is considerable cross-referencing. In his useful introduction, Wilson describes the five levels of Standard American speech (intimate, casual, impromptu, planned, and oratorical) and the three levels of Standard American writing (informal, semiformal, and formal) referred to throughout the book. The guide ends with a bibliography.

This reference work is both prescriptive and descriptive, although the author's frequent use of the phrase "it depends" makes it clear that the level and context of the usage are important. Throughout, Wilson is careful to discuss differences between the spoken and the written language. In addition to the expected discussions of *hopefully, which/that, bring/take*, and *like/as*, there are treatments of such topics as the regional pronunciations of *merry/Mary/marry*, British English, sexist language, and politically correct (PC) language.

A person consulting this book about a usage problem will usually find a clear, concise, and authoritative answer, complete with examples. The book is more current and comprehensive than the *Harper Dictionary of Contemporary Usage* (see ARBA 86, entry 1047). Those looking for a more scholarly treatment of problematical usage might turn to *Webster's Dictionary of English Usage* (see ARBA 90, entry 1005). Overall, this handbook is recommended for library and individual purchase as a valuable tool for students, writers, and editors—indeed, for anyone looking for well-written, no-nonsense guidance to clear communication. [R: Choice, Nov 93, pp. 440-42; LJ, 1 May 93, p. 83; RBB, 1 Sept 93, pp. 82-84; RQ, Winter 93, pp. 280-81; WLB, Sept 93, p. 121]—**Henry J. Ricardo**

Homonyms and Homographs

1086. Hobbs, James B., comp. **Homophones and Homographs: An American Dictionary.** 2d ed. Jefferson, N.C., McFarland, 1993. 302p. $29.95. PE2833.H63. 423'.1. LC 92-56651. ISBN 0-89950-776-X.

Hobbs, professor emeritus from Lehigh University, has compiled an entertaining and useful reference work. This edition contains 7,149 homophones—words that sound the same but have different spellings and meanings (e.g., *earn* and *urn*), and 1,469 homographs—words that are spelled the same but have different pronunciations and meanings (e.g., *Junker*, a member of the Prussian aristocracy, and *junker*, an automobile ready for scrapping). In the case of both homophones and homographs, this edition supplies twice as many entries as appeared in the well-received 1986 version. Hobbs introduces his compilation with an informative overview of homophones and homographs in which he briefly explains his system for selection and organization. He excludes colloquialisms, obsolete, archaic, and rarely used words as well as those associated with regional dialects but includes names of countries, cities, and races. Included, for example, are *chili, chilly,* and *Chile.* The body of the book is made up of the words themselves, followed by short definitions. The book concludes with a brief annotated bibliography.

This carefully constructed work can be used by librarians and teachers as a traditional reference source or can simply be enjoyed by those who delight in the twists and turns of the English language. It is a treasure chest for the punster. (Did he *eek* out a living [by continually expressing surprise] or *eke* it out [by living day-to-day with difficulty]?) Highly recommended for all academic, public, and secondary school libraries. [R: RBB, 15 Dec 93, p. 778]—**Donald C. Dickinson**

1087. Linfield, Jordan L., and Joseph Krevisky. **Word Traps: A Dictionary of the 5,000 Most Confusing Sound-Alike and Look-Alike Words.** New York, Macmillan, 1993. 374p. $12.00pa. PE1595.L56. 423'.1. LC 92-25760. ISBN 0-02-052751-9.

Secretaries, journalists, students, professors, and others whose primary mode of communication places great emphasis on the correctness of the written word will celebrate this handy dictionary of confusing homonyms and look-alike words. Arrangement is alphabetical, with each entry consisting of two or more words that are (or might be) confused in their spelling. Examples include such similar words as "farther, father, further," and "lager, laggard, larger, logger, laager." Under each entry the authors have included subentries for each of the similar items. On one line, the correct spelling, pronunciation, indication of part of speech, and a simple definition are presented. If one looks under any of the terms that follow the first term, one is cross-referenced back to the main entry.

Simple in concept and arrangement, this work is likely to find itself on many a writer's desk, next to dictionaries of synonyms, antonyms, and the like. With growing literacy problems evidenced among the populations that libraries serve, virtually any reference collection can benefit from having such a volume included among its dictionaries and manuals of style. It is useful for audiences ranging from adolescents to adult scholars.—**Edmund F. SantaVicca**

Idioms, Colloquialisms, and Special Usage

1088. Blevins, Winfred. **Dictionary of the American West.** New York, Facts on File, 1993. 400p. illus. maps. $35.00. PE2970.W4B5. 427'.978'03. LC 92-4336. ISBN 0-8160-2031-0.

Although the last couple of decades have brought a spate of "western word" books, there is still room for Blevins's book, mainly because it contains more words than most others (about one-and-a-half times as many as *Dictionary of the Old West* [see ARBA 78, entry 350]), but also because it includes words that, Blevins claims in the introduction, have been omitted in other works. These include Pidgin Indian words; French-trapper words; Mormon words; and even a few modern words, such as *National Park Service, relocation center,* and *bolo tie.*

Most of the entries are for words and expressions peculiar to the West—*bog rider, boggy-top* (an open-face apple pie), *carcajou* (a wolverine), *Eighty-niner* (from Oklahoma's land rush of that year), *gancho* (a shepherd's crook), *palo alto* (a slouch hat), *shakey* (an irrigation ditch), and so on. But there are also many entries of an explanatory nature, such as those for each of the major tribes of the Great Plains, as well as entries for such topics as Mormons, plural marriage, the Ghost Dance, homestead, keelboat, and Stetson (the latter contains photographs of nine different kinds of cowboy hats).

For most Hispanic terms Blevins gives pronunciation; and when appropriate, derivations are also supplied, although these are sometimes inaccurate (e.g., *manga* means *sleeve* in Spanish, not *cloak*) or simply lacking (e.g., there is no connection made between bolo tie and the word *bola*, meaning originally a pair of small balls on the end of a line). The entry for *Mariachi* states that it is borrowed from Spanish. Actually, it is a Mexican corruption of the English *marriage*, because such bands were customarily called in to play at wealthy marriages. A further reading section at the end has some suggestions as to journals, biographies, and fiction that give the spirit of the West. [R: Choice, July/Aug 93, p. 1744; LJ, Jan 93, p. 94; RBB, 1 April 93, pp. 1454-55; SLJ, Oct 93, p. 171]—**Raymund F. Wood**

1089. Hendrickson, Robert. **Whistlin' Dixie: A Dictionary of Southern Expressions.** New York, Facts on File, 1993. 251p. (Facts on File Dictionary of American Regional English, v.1). $24.95. PE2926.H46. 427'.975'03. LC 91-47861. ISBN 0-8160-2110-4.

Hendrickson's introduction is so engaging and instructive that turning this dictionary into a history might not have been a bad idea. He explains that southern dialect derives mainly from Cajun, Creole, Gumbo, Gullah, and Conch sources. Each culture gave birth to a distinctive mode of expression, which mixed together results in today's colorful southern language. This dictionary is rich in descriptive terms, exclamations, folk wisdom, and name-calling. Flipping through the pages is like listening to every southerner ever encountered in life or in a book. The contents leap out at you, unlike more scholarly works. One criticism is that Hendrickson did not attribute every definition. It would have added authority to know this word came from Cajun roots, that word from Creole. For some entries Hendrickson does cite the literary source, such as Margaret Mitchell's *Gone with the Wind* and the novels of William Faulkner, Marjorie Kinnan Rawlings, and Erskine Caldwell. He also consulted standard scholarly works. Offensive words were retained because they are historically correct (if not politically correct). However, profanity was left out. One type of inclusion seems overemphasized: the many unique southern pronunciations, such as "sody" for soda. Such pronunciations are not defined, just cleared up for comprehension. Recommended for all libraries. [R: Choice, May 93, p. 1442; SLJ, Oct 93, p. 170; SLMQ, Summer 93, p. 267; WLB, April 93, pp. 124-26]—**Bill Bailey**

1090. **An Index by Region, Usage, and Etymology to the *Dictionary of American Regional English*, Volumes I and II.** Tuscaloosa, Ala., for American Dialect Society by University of Alabama Press, 1993. 178p. (Publication of the American Dialect Society, no.77). $16.00pa. PE1702.A5. 427'.973. LC 93-14627. ISBN 0-8173-0694-3.

This index to the *Dictionary of American Regional English* (DARE), volumes 1 and 2 (see ARBA 86, entry 1050 and ARBA 93, entry 1062), contains virtually all regional, social, and usage labels in the first two volumes of DARE; terms for linguistic processes that contributed to the formation of headwords; and references to other varieties of English and to foreign languages from which the headwords derive. Index terms have been taken from the head sections of the DARE entries, which include pronunciations; lists of variant forms; etymologies; regional, social, and usage labels; and editorial notes. In format, the index is arranged with headwords followed by a short quotation showing the immediate context of the item as it appears in the entry, retaining the DARE abbreviations. The main labels are "Regional," "Social," "Usage," "Etymological Processes," "Languages," "Other Sources," and "MAP," indicating entries or senses that include maps. Not all entries in the DARE are included in the index, as some are not indexable or do not fit any of the categories well enough to have been flagged by the computer for inclusion.

It is presumed that those using the index will have access to the complete DARE. However, the index can be quite useful on its own. For example, a writer who wishes to use authentic terms from Scots will find four pages of Scots terms and phrases, A through H. While most words are not defined as such, their presence provides valuable information unavailable in any other single volume. All users of DARE should welcome this index. [R: WLB, Oct 93, p. 90]—**Kay O. Cornelius**

1091. **Prentice Hall Encyclopedic Dictionary of English Usage.** 2d ed. By N. H. Mager and S. K. Mager. Englewood Cliffs, N.J., Prentice Hall Professional, Technical, and Reference, 1993. 427p. $27.95. PE1628.M23. 428'.003. LC 92-22944. ISBN 0-13-276858-5.

The Magers state in the preface that this guide is intended for educated professionals who write. It is a dictionary and, to a limited degree, a style manual and grammar guide. It also includes some abbreviations. Other useful examples are forms of address and salutations for army, air force, and naval officers. Pronunciation is given for difficult words, and there are some newer words included. There are almost two pages on the use of possessives, and there are many examples of when to use capital letters for words such as *army*.

In spite of these qualities, this volume does not rate high as a usage manual. Very few usage examples are noted, and a number of common words are defined. A few words are included with no commentary, such as *dressing room*. The *Encyclopedic Dictionary* does not compare favorably with other recent usage books, such as *Webster's Dictionary of English Usage* (see ARBA 90, entry 1005) or the less comprehensive, but more prescriptive, *Plain English* (see ARBA 89, entry 957). This work may be helpful in the home or office, but its usefulness in reference work is limited. [R: Choice, Oct 93, p. 268]—**Helen M. Gothberg**

Juvenile

1092. Root, Betty. **My First Dictionary.** New York, Dorling Kindersley, 1993. 96p. illus. index. $16.95. ISBN 1-56458-277-9.

This 1,000-term word book with colorful photographs and drawings and brief definitions is not a dictionary in the usual sense. It shows no parts of speech, etymologies, or variant meanings or word forms. Instead, its purpose is to help young children equate objects or concepts with the English words used to describe them. The definitions without the illustrations would not be too meaningful (e.g., "your lungs are inside your chest. You have two lungs for breathing"). Indeed, the accurate, colorful illustrations convey the meaning of most terms much more clearly than do the written definitions. The work is designed to be used by an adult with a child as the child learns the letters of the alphabet, alphabetical order, and the association of things and actions with the words used to name or describe them. The book would also be a useful way to increase reading vocabulary and to get older early readers used to the idea of using a dictionary to learn about words on their own.

But in spite of its overall visual and intellectual quality and usefulness, it is not without its faults. Some of the definitions are vague, inaccurate, and inconsistent. For instance, the definitions of *alligator* and *crocodile*, two similar but different creatures, make no meaningful distinctions between the two and do not describe them similarly: "An alligator is a reptile with thick, scaly skin and lots of sharp teeth," but a "crocodile is an animal with large jaws and a powerful tail that helps it swim." Even the illustrations do not help; one is a drawing, the other a photograph. The definition of a "daisy" fits dozens of other flowers and not even all daisies: "A daisy is a flower with white petals and a yellow center." And strangely, "a cliff is a high, steep rock near the sea," ignoring thousands of similar earth, rock, and ice structures inland and being possibly confusing to children who live near them. Despite these problems, given its intended purposes and audience, this word book will be a highly useful addition to children's library collections and home libraries. [R: RBB, 1 Dec 93, p. 716]—**Blaine H. Hall**

1093. Root, Betty. **300 First Words.** Hauppauge, N.Y., Barron's Educational Series, 1993. 155p. illus. index. $9.95. PE1449.D277. 428.1. LC 92-44750. ISBN 0-8120-6356-2.

Another English import from Root designed to help children develop their language skills, this one shows, in clear, colorful photographs, common objects most children would find around the house or in the world outside, albeit some of them only on a farm, in the zoo, or on television. Its purpose is to help young children identify familiar objects to an adult and talk about them. With only four related objects on facing pages, the child can easily identify and make distinctions among different things—animals, foods, items of clothing, toys, tools, musical instruments, utensils, furniture, linens, sewing materials, and many more. To younger children, the word under each picture may mean little, but as they begin to develop reading skills, the words can help to increase their vocabulary. The index will also help them identify words and objects beginning with the same sound or letter.

Only a few minor problems mar the book's overall usefulness and excellence. Occasionally, the picture and the object seem to be based on British usage. The picture for *dresser*, for instance, is clearly a U.S. chest of drawers, and the *cupboard* on the same page looks more like what we would consider a dresser. Also, the numerous animals and insects are all represented by molded sculptures, not actual animals, probably a compromise to facilitate the photography. And most U.S. kids would find a recorder, the wooden flute-like instrument, rather esoteric. A piano would probably be a better choice. Nonetheless, given its intended purposes and audience, this word book will be a useful addition to children's library collections and home libraries.—**Blaine H. Hall**

1094. **Webster's New World Dictionary for Young Adults.** Jonathan L. Goldman and Andrew N. Sparks, eds. New York, Prentice Hall General Reference, 1992. 1040p. illus. $18.00. PE1628.5.W38797. 423. LC 92-3061. ISBN 0-13-945734-8.

Although the publisher calls this a brand new illustrated dictionary, it maintains some of the content of its predecessor, *Webster's New World Dictionary for Young Readers* (see ARBA 80, entry 1119), while incorporating some significant changes and updates. Approximately 47,500 entries cover words and phrases in this dictionary, which is designed for middle schoolers aged 11-14. Of these, 2,700 represent new entries. There are, as well, approximately 2,150 idioms; 430 biographical entries; 1,200 geographical names of countries, cities, rivers, and mountains (e.g., Kampala, Kampuchea, Kanchenjunga); and 1,350 etymologies.

This edition is about 175 pages longer than its predecessor, even though some supplemental charts and maps have been omitted. It retains the two-column format but more effectively combines a clear typeface with white space for greater contrast and ease in scanning. A pronunciation key highlighted on a colored background is repeated on each two-page spread. Word histories and synonyms are highlighted in similar fashion and are interspersed throughout; small black-and-white drawings and photographs illustrate selected words.

Definitions are clearly written and easy to understand. Among the new terms are words such as *dork, Commonwealth of Independent States,* and *Yeltsin,* emphasizing the book's focus on contemporary language as well as on geographical and biographical currency. Multiculturalism is the overall focus, from the photograph of multiethnic youngsters decorating the cover through the choice and text of the word histories. The word *Eskimo,* for example, is selected in this edition for a word history and given much fuller treatment. With its many practical features, this dictionary is an excellent choice for the middle school student and will prove useful for collections serving that population. [R: RBB, 1 Mar 93, p. 1268; SLMQ, Spring 93, p. 200; SLJ, Nov 93, p. 144; WLB, Mar 93, p. 115]—**Bernice Bergup**

New Words

1095. **Trash Cash, Fizzbos, and Flatliners: A Dictionary of Today's Words.** By Sid Lerner, Gary S. Belkin, and the editors of the American Heritage Dictionaries. Boston, Houghton Mifflin, 1993. 221p. index. $19.95; $8.95pa. PE1630.L44. 423'.1. LC 92-33849. ISBN 0-395-64021-0; 0-395-64020-2pa.

Do you know the meanings of the three "today's words" in the title? This reviewer knew only one—*flatliners*—primarily from the 1990 film of the same name. *Trash cash* refers to advertising leaflets designed to look like U.S. currency to catch the attention of passersby, and *fizzbo* (For Sale by Owner) is someone who sells a property without the services of a real estate agent. But unfamiliarity with those and other terms in no way diminishes the value and pleasure of this modest, reasonably priced volume.

A brief introduction stresses the transitory nature of the language, the task of keeping up-to-date as one that never ends, and the difficult choices of inclusion and exclusion of new words. The text is alphabetically arranged. Each entry for the 1,200-plus new words, phrases, and terms includes the part of speech; a concise definition; and an occasional cross-reference, usage level note, and quoted example of its use. As with any dictionary of new words, some will be familiar to many readers (e.g., Scud and Patriot missiles, wake-up call); some are less familiar (e.g., valspeak, boogie board); and there are those whose inclusion is odd (e.g., Ozurgeti, Tver, and Vyatka [all formerly USSR cities]). Perhaps best identified as a *dictionary of the moment* by its compilers, this thoroughly informative and enjoyable guide should certainly find a place on the shelves of most reference departments, along with recent current-word dictionaries and handbooks such as *The New New Words Dictionary* (see ARBA 90, entry 1004), *The Third Barnhart Dictionary of New English* (see ARBA 91, entry 1059), and *The Oxford Dictionary of New Words* (see ARBA 93, entry 1065). [R: RBB, 15 Feb 93, p. 1077]—**Charles R. Andrews**

Other English-Speaking Countries

1096. **The Australian Concise Oxford Dictionary.** 2d ed. J. M. Hughes, P. A. Mitchell, and W. S. Ramson, eds. New York, Oxford University Press, 1992. 1375p. $35.00. 423. ISBN 0-19-553442-5.

The *Australian Concise Oxford Dictionary* (ACOD) is essentially a watered-down derivative of the *Concise Oxford Dictionary of Current English* (see ARBA 91, entry 1048). In spite of the various introductions, which are made to sound scientifically detached, its viewpoint is colonial. The standard of measurement is always that of England, the chief concession to Australian usage being to record actual Australian additions to the English lexicon. Australian changes in the meanings of already existing terms and Australian differences in pronunciation are not adequately represented. Modifications in meaning from those understood in Great Britain are often missed by the editors, probably because these modifications are less obvious than terms that are new. *Callow,* for instance, has a very negative connotation in Australia akin to *uncouth,* while *dumpy* can have the positive connotation of cuteness. Such differences are important but are not recognized in the ACOD.

The International Phonetic Alphabet is no doubt the best way to indicate pronunciation, but the transcriptions of Australian speech are inaccurate and misleading. According to this dictionary, an educated Australian sounds more like Kenneth Branagh or Raymond Burr than Paul Hogan! Of the cardinal vowels of Italian (*a, e, i, o,* and *u*), which are often cited as standard, only *a* (as in *father*) exists in Australian speech. And the diphthong in Australian *now* sounds like that in Texan speech, not British, while the diphthong in *my* sounds like the version in Ireland and New York City (rather like "moy"). For specifically Australian English, one would do better to turn to the *Dictionary of Australian Colloquialisms* (see ARBA 92, entry 1052). [R: Choice, Oct 93, p. 261]—**John B. Beston**

1097. Berg, Donna Lee. **A Guide to the Oxford English Dictionary.** New York, Oxford University Press, 1993. 206p. $18.95. PE1617.049B47. 423. LC 91-41383. ISBN 0-19-869179-3.

The *Oxford English Dictionary* (OED) (see ARBA 90, entry 1006) has been called the greatest dictionary in any language and the most extensive reference work ever written. It is indeed a monumental cumulative result of the painstaking work of generations of brilliant English lexicographers. The project, whose foundations were laid in 1858, culminated in 1989 with the publication of the 20-volume 2d edition of the OED (which, among many other additions, includes huge numbers of lexical units coined in the United States). With almost 300,000 entries, more than 600,000 word units, millions of quotations, and only very brief introductory instructions, the OED can frequently overwhelm its users and diminish their ability to make full use of its many resources. This is where the guide under review offers welcome help. Its first part provides a systematic set of instructions, with examples taken from the OED, that explain the various facets of information that can be gleaned from typical entries. Many complex bits of information are exemplified in this section: pronunciation (both British and American), parts of speech, variant forms, different social meanings, etymologies, and more. The second part is a language student's delight. It contains an "A-Z Companion," an alphabetical encyclopedic collection of entries describing and exemplifying lexicographic concepts, linguistic terminology, and other topics related to the OED. "Facts and Figures" provides a quantitative survey of salient statistical data that characterize the OED. A chronology of events surveys those (from 1755) relevant to the history of this marvelous dictionary. This is a fine tool that will help scholars, students, and general users to make better use of the OED. [R: Choice, Dec 93, p. 580; JAL, Nov 93, p. 346; RBB, 1 Sept 93, p. 82; WLB, Nov 93, p. 102]—**Lev I. Soudek**

1098. **The Cassell Concise English Dictionary.** new ed. Betty Kirkpatrick, ed. London, Cassell; distr., New York, Sterling Publishing, 1992. 1577p. $19.95. ISBN 0-304-34067-7.

This is issued as a new, not a revised, edition of the 1989 *Cassell Concise English Dictionary* (see ARBA 90, entry 995), and it does in fact have an appendix that registers new words that have become more widely used since 1989. Nevertheless, it is not difficult to note the absence of recent words one would expect to be recorded, such as *carjack, break dancing,* and *phone mail.* But within the wider range of more established words, the dictionary is comprehensive and very clearly arranged.

There is no statement of policy on what is to be understood by "English," whether the English of Great Britain, of the United States, or both. The dictionary was published in Great Britain, however, and records essentially British English, with some concessions to American English as it has affected British English. Where there are differences between British and American English in pronunciation (e.g., *sloth, leisure*), meanings of words (e.g., tan, mahogany), or grammatical forms (e.g., a number of verb forms, both strong and weak), only the British forms are recorded. Thus, the audience for the dictionary is one oriented toward British usage.—**John B. Beston**

1099. **The New Shorter Oxford English Dictionary on Historical Principles.** Lesley Brown, ed. New York, Oxford University Press, 1993. 2v. $99.50/set. ISBN 0-19-861271-0.

These two volumes constitute an authorized abridgment of the 2d edition of the *Oxford English Dictionary* (OED) (see ARBA 90, entry 1006). The last edition of this abridgment (see ARBA 75, entry 1252) was based on the first edition of the OED. While the 2d edition of the OED includes words used in English since the Middle Ages, most of the words in the *New Shorter* have been in use since 1700. The 163,000-plus words and phrases constitute almost two-thirds of the original definitions. The typical entry is a condensed version of the entry in the parent volumes. Most space is saved not by shortening the definitions but by significantly limiting the number of quotations. The OED includes chronologically arranged quotations to establish earliest recorded use of a word, with generous subsequent quotations documenting different senses of the word through the following centuries. Quotations in the *New Shorter* are far fewer and meant to illustrate major meanings rather than to document word histories.

It is important to recognize that some of the *New Shorter* entries differ in definition from those in the 2d edition of the OED. For example, the OED defines *armadilla* as "a small fleet of ships of war" or "a small war vessel." The *New Shorter*, however, defines this word as "a small (Spanish) fighting ship. Also, a small naval squadron." Users familiar with the OED will recognize the intricate system of abbreviations and order of information presented in the entries in the *New Shorter*: 22 pages of small print in the prefatory guide to the use of the dictionary are devoted to explaining how to interpret entries.

Potential buyers of the *New Shorter* who cannot afford the 20 volumes of the OED may want to consider the compact edition of that massive work, which requires a magnifying glass to read and contains the full text of the 2d edition but is obviously inconvenient for prolonged use. On the other hand, as the *New Shorter* includes some words not found in the 2d edition, as well as some different definitions, libraries catering to discriminating users should acquire it as a supplement to the OED, not as a condensation of it.—**David Isaacson**

1100. **The Oxford Modern English Dictionary.** Julia Swannell, ed. New York, Clarendon Press/Oxford University Press, 1992. 1287p. $19.95. ISBN 0-19-861267-2.

Dictionaries offer far more information than just word definitions, although that is what most people think of as their major value. Probably fewer users in this age of computers need to check their spelling (although *spellcheck* is not a term defined in this volume), but usage remains a problem for many writers of letters, term papers, or books. *The Oxford Modern English Dictionary* is designed to emphasize "the language of every day but also including the essential vocabulary of science and technology, especially computers and matters environmental." Definitions are up-to-date, with *latchkey child* and *nerd* appearing, and *bug* and *network* defined in computer terms as well as their more general meanings. The editor's claim that computer and environmental terms are emphasized is upheld by the inclusion of *ASCII, computer virus, ecosystem*, and *greenhouse effect*, but neither *LAN* nor *Internet* has made the book.

Trying to keep a dictionary current is an endless task, and this edition manages reasonably well. One problem for American readers is that major entries are placed under the British spellings of words such as *colour*, although a cross-reference is listed under *color*. Other Briticisms are the definitions of *biscuit* and the spelling of *honour*. Brief notes on usage are a helpful feature of the book. The difference between *effect* and *affect* and *credible* and *credulous* are noted briefly. The clear, legible typeface is also a plus. Altogether, this dictionary will be welcomed by students and the general public as a practical reference aid. It deserves a place in school and public libraries.—**Adele M. Fasick**

Slang

1101. Beard, Henry, and Christopher Cerf. **The Official Politically Correct Dictionary and Handbook.** New York, Villard Books/Random House, 1993. 194p. $10.00pa. PN6162.B372. 818'.5402. LC 93-29964. ISBN 0-679-74944-6.

This four-part "processed tree carcass" consists of a dictionary of PC terms (to find meanings, but also to find out how we are oppressed), a thesaurus (to find inoffensive alternatives to offensive terms), a discussion of other suspect words and concepts (to explore the core thoughts, customs, and beliefs that underlie our "belief systems," itself a suspect concept), and a glossary of bureaucratically suitable (BS) language (to help us succeed in today's corporate, military, and political worlds). Because language is "*the* major force in 'constructing' what we perceive as reality," Beard and Cerf aim to help us update our language, for, according to Betsy Warland, "Change language, we change everything."

Sure, we all need to be sensitive to others' feelings, particularly the feelings of the "significant others," and even the "insignificant others," in our lives. But as a bald male, being described as "hair disadvantaged" offends my sensitivity to language stupidity far more than it offends my sensitivity about my physical appearance. And what schnauzer, boa, pig, or tarantula will strike back when called a "pet" rather than a "nonhuman animal companion"? Or will calling an egg or a glass of milk "stolen nonhuman animal products" make them taste any different, or will we merely gag at the verbal pomposity? As Terry Eagleton, the British critic, observed: "It is silly to call fat people 'gravitationally challenged'—a self-righteous fetishism of language which is no more than a symptom of political frustration."

As does all satiric humor, this dictionary and handbook gathers for our delight and ridicule the misguided linguistic excesses of the proponents of political correctness. But just to show they are playing it straight with their terminology, each term is traced to a specific source document. The work is a good buy for a humor collection—and it is all politically correct.—**Blaine H. Hall**

Spelling

1102. Moseley, David. **Canadian Spelling Dictionary.** 7th ed. Toronto, Stoddart Publishing, 1993. 332p. illus. index. $14.95pa. 423'.1. ISBN 0-7737-5559-4.

More a general English-language spelling dictionary for Canadians than a dictionary of Canadian spellings of English words, this volume is a derivative of a similar volume published in Great Britain by the same author. Designed for users of all ages, it contains cartoons and drawings to illustrate and simplify some of the concepts presented. Using a phonetical approach to vowel sounds, Moseley identifies 15 basic Canadian-English vowel classifications. Identifying basic visual and linguistic patterns becomes the basis for his approach to solving spelling difficulties.

The dictionary is divided into three main parts that encompasses five sections, with groupings by vowel sounds. Each main section is color-coded with short vowels on white paper, long vowels on blue, and the final section (which includes vowels preceding the letter R, double vowel sounds, and diphthongs) again on white. For each section, groupings are by initial letter in alphabetical order. Sound symbols are included at the top right corner of each page, with brief descriptive and graphic reminders at the bottom. Prefatory material includes a substantial "to the user" section that details how the dictionary is organized and should be used and that highlights special features. This is really the only place in the volume that acknowledges the unique features of Canadian pronunciation; it indicates that there are some regional distinctions noted elsewhere in the volume and designated by a dot beside the word.

While a usable reference tool for a wide range of general users, this dictionary will be most useful for Canadian schoolchildren. Its format and illustrative material are most appropriate for young readers, and the content, while including some scientific and mathematical vocabulary, is not likely to appeal to more sophisticated users.—**Virginia S. Fischer**

1103. **The Paragon House Spelling Dictionary.** New York, Paragon House, c1990, 1993. 582p. $12.95pa. PE1146.P26. 423'.1. LC 92-32326. ISBN 1-55778-597-X.

Spelling dictionaries are difficult to acknowledge as useful. It is always more profitable to look in a standard dictionary for correct spelling, and at the same time review the various definitions, alternate spellings, parts of speech, etymology, and other inclusions. Previous spelling dictionaries have appeared with unusual slants. *Webster's Spell It Right Dictionary* (see ARBA 89, entry 968) juxtaposed a column of wrong with right spellings. The result proved disappointing, because the wrong spellings were far off even for simple words. *Word Finder* (see ARBA 88, entry 1079) was more eccentric. The user locates the sound symbol BLN and scans its listings: abalone, balloon, baloney, beeline, bland, blind, blown, bologna, bowline, and by-line. Of course, other BLN words exist, and with no definitions, the listing is a grab bag.

The Paragon House dictionary does not juxtapose spellings, nor does it employ phonetics. It lists more than 70,000 words with what it calls a capsule definition for unfamiliar and confusing words. Certainly, this is an improvement over no definitions, but the added feature is less than a capsule. For example, *dharma* is tagged a "Hindu custom." Actually *dharma* means "the ultimate law of all things," which is a Hindu and Buddhist philosophical/religious concept of the greatest importance, not a mere custom. Moreover, after promising to define unfamiliar and confusing words, the dictionary lets some slip through undefined, such as *desquamate, kerfuffle,* and *trug.* [R: Choice, July/Aug 93, p. 1754]

—**Bill Bailey**

1104. Proctor, William. **The Terrible Speller: A Quick-and-Easy Guide to Enhancing Your Spelling Ability.** New York, William Morrow, 1993. 174p. $15.00. PE1145.2.P76. 428.1. LC 93-21946. ISBN 0-688-09981-5.

Proctor, a freelance writer, has compiled this book to "help the terrible speller become a competent speller." In the longest section of the book he supplies a list of "the toughest 228" and explains how to master them; for example, *shenanigan* has no double letters, and *nicotine* includes *tin* and *e.* Proctor does not expect readers to remember all these rules but hopes some of his suggestions will be helpful. Following "the toughest 228" he supplies short chapters on the difficulties of double letters (e.g., *disapear* or *disappear*), word endings (e.g., *readable* or *redible*), silent assassins (e.g., *potato* or *potatoe*) and a summary called "Latin in 20 Minutes." All of the tips in this book are useful and should help strengthen the skills of the feeble speller. The tone is light and the text eminently readable. This is not a reference book in the formal sense, but one that many library selectors will wish to add to their general self-help section. Recommended for school, public, and academic libraries. [R: BL, 15 Oct 93, p. 401]

—**Donald C. Dickinson**

Synonyms and Antonyms

1105. **Random House Word Menu.** By Stephen Glazier. New York, Random House, 1992. 977p. index. $22.00. PE1680.G58. LC 92-13539. ISBN 0-679-40030-3.

This fascinating book had its genesis in lists of specialized words that the author compiled for use in his historical novels. Roughly 75,000 entries are divided into 7 major classes (nature, science and technology, domestic life, institutions, arts and leisure, language, and the human condition), which in turn branch into nearly 800 subdivisions. One difference between this work and a thesaurus is that here words are related by *subject* and not grouped according to the usual synonym-antonym relation, except for a section giving nearly 4,000 adjectives describing human personality and behavior. Also, clear and concise definitions of most words are provided. Fundamentally, this is a collection of glossaries that has the features of a reverse dictionary. For example, readers who have forgotten the word for an ornamental metal holder for a coffee cup could start their search in the domestic life section, browsing down through chapter 7 ("The Home"), the subheading "Ornamental and Functional Articles," and finally to "Functional Household Articles and Appliances," where they will find the desired word, *zarf*. The book also provides some features of an almanac—basic information on nations of the world, states of the United States, and major world cities. The last part of the book is a useful alphabetical index of every word whose definition is given in the text.

Overall, the *Word Menu* is broader in its coverage and more detailed than either *Descriptionary* (see ARBA 93, entry 1072) or the *Illustrated Reverse Dictionary* (Reader's Digest Books, 1990). This significant reference work is heartily recommended for individual and library purchase because of its inspired classification system and encyclopedic range. [R: Choice, Feb 93, p. 939; RBB, 1 Jan 93, pp. 826-27; WLB, Jan 93, pp. 113-14]—**Henry J. Ricardo**

Terms and Phrases

1106. Collings, Rex. **A Crash of Rhinoceroses: A Dictionary of Collective Nouns.** Wakefield, R.I., Moyer Bell, 1993. 186p. illus. $16.95. PE1689.C69. 423'.1. LC 93-1053. ISBN 1-55921-096-6.

This is a diverting book as well as a work of considerable scholarship, a treat for those who are attuned to the endless possibilities for creativity offered by words. It is concerned with the names that have been created to describe collections of animals, people, and things. Among European languages, English is unique in the wealth of its collective terms—consider, for instance, the dearth of them in German. This book is the most complete reference work that records and also explains the use of collective terms from medieval times to the present. Many of the terms listed here are obsolete (e.g., "a blush of boys"), but new ones are constantly being created (e.g., the "crash of rhinoceroses" of the title). The creation has in all periods proceeded from various reasons: sometimes for specificity, sometimes for amusement, sometimes even for derision.

The book is quintessentially English. It would especially appeal to an audience fascinated by English place-names and English surnames. Collins presents his material with a characteristically English sense of humor, in mock-serious style and with a deliberate opiniatedness. He reveals his English orientation when, for instance, he illustrates the collective "batch" only by "a batch of bread," evidently unaware of the common U.S. expression, "a batch of cookies." The collective nouns are listed alphabetically. A cross-index of subjects is also provided. Finally, the selected bibliography is helpfully and at times amusingly annotated.—**John B. Beston**

Thesauri

1107. **The Oxford Thesaurus.** American ed. By Laurence Urdang. New York, Oxford University Press, 1992. 1005p. index. $19.95. PE2832.U7. 423'.1. LC 91-3938. ISBN 0-19-507354-1.

Compiled by American lexicographer Urdang, the American edition of *The Oxford Thesaurus* joins other distinguished reference works from Oxford University Press. More than 275,000 words are arranged in 2 parts: an alphabetical list of headwords and synonyms proper, and an index that includes additional words not located in the dictionary. Following each headword in the first part are sets of synonyms grouped together by meaning, each grouping numbered in sequence. For example, the word *muddy* lists synonyms for three different meanings as an adjective (1 fouled, 2 confused, 3 drab) and two meanings as a verb (4 obscure, 5 dirty). Although no definitions are provided, each variant meaning is illustrated with a sample sentence. Synonyms that appear as separate headwords in the dictionary list are identified by a degree sign. Depending on use, words are labeled as colloquial, slang, taboo, archaic, old-fashioned, technical, or literary. Geographical usage is identified as United States, British, Australian, Canadian, or New Zealand.

The index proper is a more extensive wordlist composed both of headwords marked with a degree sign and other words for which synonyms are likely to be wanted. Each entry in the index is followed by headwords from the dictionary section, the particular sense identified by the number assigned in the main list.

While the main function of a thesaurus is to supply synonyms or alternate expressions, the grouping of terms provides clues to meaning. Thus, the headword section serves as something of a dictionary, while the index is quite useful for its listing of idioms and idiomatic expressions (e.g., "big cheese," "haul [someone] over the coals").

Although the work is an American edition, it follows the British practice of alphabetizing letter-by-letter rather than word-by-word, as is the more usual American practice. American spellings are used, although less-common British spellings may also be found for some words. An especially glaring mistake appears on page ix: the word *dress* in one of the examples appears in place of *drama*.

Persons wanting precise definitions and distinctions in meaning spelled out will need to look elsewhere. However, this thesaurus has its merits, among which are an attractive and easy-to-read format and a convenient size for personal handling. Many will find it useful, as will most libraries. [R: Choice, Feb 93, p. 946; SLJ, Feb 93, p. 130]—**Bernice Bergup**

NON-ENGLISH-LANGUAGE DICTIONARIES

General Works

1108. Goursau, Henri, and Monique Goursau. **European Dictionary: French-English-German-Spanish-Italian-Portuguese. [Euro Dictionary].** Hampshire, England, Mosaik Books; distr., Cincinnati, Ohio, Seven Hills Book, c1989, 1992. 768p. $17.95. ISBN 3-576-80000-X.

When this book arrived in the mail, this reviewer browsed through it, wondering who would have need for such a publication. Now, several weeks later, and after a more thorough perusal, the question remains. Radio announcers in need of a quick, superficial answer to a question? Library employees who answer general reference questions by telephone? Passengers on cruise ships as an assist in dinner conversations? Regardless, the book is carefully prepared. It features 8,000 common words (and a few phrases) translated from French into English, German, Spanish, Italian, and Portuguese. The dictionary repeats in that order—the second section starts with English words, then German, and so on. Each page consists of six columns of words, with their translations given horizontally. For instance, the English word *leather* is followed (across the page) by the French *cuir*; then the German *Leder*; Spanish *cuero*; Italian *cuoio, pelle*; and Portuguese *couro*. The words' meanings are not included. Only German entries include gender abbreviations, while the Romance languages are provided with an ending that one has to attach to the word after substituting the last vowel (e.g., the Italian "*bugiardo, a*" means a male liar is a *bugiardo*, a female one a *bugiarda*). This is not explained anywhere in the dictionary. Otherwise, it is an attractive volume, beautifully printed and bound, with no typographical errors.—**Koraljka Lockhart**

Albanian

1109. Hysa, Ramazan. **Albanian-English Dictionary.** New York, Hippocrene Books, 1993. 510p. $14.95pa. ISBN 0-87052-077-6.

This is a dictionary principally for Albanian users: Nearly all the front matter is in Albanian only. However, Anglophone readers will be able to use it as well, although they will have to realize that there are digraphs, such as *dh, gj, sh, xh,* and *zh,* that have their own place in the alphabet. For example, *nj* is considered one grapheme with a position of its own in the alphabetical sequence, whereas *ng* is considered as two (the information is given, but in a somewhat cryptic way). Also, users will have to get accustomed to such abbreviations as *f.k.=folje kalimtare* 'transitive verb'; these translations are clearly given in the list. As the dictionary is intended for Albanians, there are few grammatical indications beyond the normal word classes.

Strangely enough, despite its audience, the dictionary does not give English pronunciations. However, it offers a rich selection of English synonyms. Naturally, Albanian speakers could have trouble because of the lack of discrimination in an entry such as *leftëtár* 'warrior, combatant, fighter.' But many, perhaps most, entries do discriminate the meaning by glosses in both languages. Collocations and standing expressions are well developed. Users are not expected to lose much time with repeated searches; many standing collocations, such as *shpall luftë* 'to declare war,' can be found under both entry words. It should be mentioned that the selection of (standing) collocations is quite inclusive, or broad. On the whole, this is one of the best dictionaries of the Hippocrene series.—**L. Zgusta**

Chinese

1110. Chen, Janey, with Ena G. Simms. **A Practical English-Chinese Pronouncing Dictionary.** Rutland, Vt., Charles E. Tuttle, c1970, 1992. 601p. $19.95pa. LC 78-77122. ISBN 0-8048-1877-0.

This dictionary of more than 15,000 words contains many useful features not normally found in other such works. A paperback reprint of a 1970 volume (see ARBA 71, entry 1392), it is intended for Westerners, especially missionary workers, who wish to learn Mandarin or Cantonese pronunciations of the Chinese language. The body of the dictionary is arranged alphabetically by English words. Following each English word are the corresponding Chinese characters and pronunciations in both Mandarin and Cantonese. Pronunciation is recorded in three systems: Chinese phonetics, the Yale system of romanization for Mandarin with tone signs, and the modified Yale system of romanization for Cantonese with tone signs. Even though there is a conversion table for the Yale, Wade-Giles, and Pinyin systems of romanization and Chinese phonetics that is placed immediately following the introduction and before the dictionary proper, failure to incorporate the Pinyin system in the main dictionary is a serious shortcoming. The appendixes offer many unusual features, including names of books in the Old and New Testaments, names of the Christian churches and organizations in Hong Kong, British military service terms, simplified and original Chinese characters, names of the months, the 24 solar terms, a summary of Chinese dynasties, the 100 family names, Chinese family trees and relationships, the 12 branches or horary characters, and a numerical list of radicals.

Similar to Chinese chop suey, this dictionary has a little bit of everything—except it forgot to include the term "chop suey." A good number of misspelled words can also be found throughout the dictionary. For example, a frontispiece table of archaic and modern provincial names and capitals is identified on the second page as "Archajc Names and Cpitals." The spelling and typographical errors have been reprinted from the 1970 original (and were noted in the original ARBA review).—**Hwa-Wei Lee**

Dakota

1111. Riggs, Stephen Return. **A Dakota-English Dictionary.** St. Paul, Minn., Minnesota Historical Society Press, c1890, 1992. 665p. $24.95pa. PM1023.R55. 497'.5. LC 92-28736. ISBN 0-87351-282-0.

1112. Williamson, John P. **An English-Dakota Dictionary.** St. Paul, Minn., Minnesota Historical Society Press, c1902, 1992. 264p. $12.95pa. PM1023.W62. 423'.975. LC 92-28737. ISBN 0-87351-283-9.

The Dakota language, a member of the Siouan family, is spoken in Minnesota, North and South Dakota, Montana, and adjacent areas of Canada (Lakota, also spelled Lakhota, is part of the same dialect group). In 1834 a group of Protestant missionaries, operating in Minnesota and including Riggs, created a written form of Dakota and began translation of the Bible. A grammar and a Dakota-English dictionary by Riggs were published at the Smithsonian Institution in 1852, followed in 1890 by the expanded dictionary, which has now been reprinted. *An English-Dakota Dictionary* is a companion volume by a son of one of Riggs's coworkers; the younger Williamson grew up as a bilingual in a Dakota community, where he followed his father into missionary work.

The two books use similar spelling systems, but both neglect the contrast of aspirated stops (*ch kh ph th*) versus unaspirated stops (*c k p t*). The volumes share a foreword by Carolynn I. Schommer that, unfortunately, is naive from a linguistic standpoint. It is claimed that Riggs's spelling system "works quite well in Dakota language courses, provided the instructor insists that the students acquire a speaking knowledge of Dakota expressions before they refer to the written form." In other words, the system can be used properly only by those who already speak the language, not by those who are learning it. Nevertheless, these reprints are welcome, making classic works newly available to the Dakota language community as well as to linguistic scholars.—**William Bright**

French

1113. **Collins-Robert French-English, English-French Dictionary. Dictionnaire Français-Anglais, Anglais-Français.** 2d ed. By Beryl T. Atkins and others. New York, HarperCollins, 1993. 570p. $20.00. PC2640.C688. 443'.21. LC 92-40825. ISBN 0-06-275513-7.

Although the publisher calls it the new standard edition, this is actually a new edition of the *Collins-Robert Concise French-English/English-French Dictionary*. The authors have emphasized ease of use. Generous usage notes are a special strength, and subtle variations in meaning are carefully illustrated by sample phrases. Mild colloquialisms, very slangy words, and old-fashioned terms are consistently identified; variant forms and meanings are clearly marked; and the introductory matter and appendixes (French verbs, and French and English abbreviations) are useful.

The authors claim particular attention to proper names, especially for geographical areas. However, while country and important city names are here, a European slant is evident in the scarcity of U.S. state and city names, bodies of water, and so on (e.g., the Alps are here, but not the Smoky Mountains; the Thames, but not the Mississippi). In fact, Americanisms are given short shrift throughout: "Hello" refers the reader to "hallo" for an entry, and skeletons are in the cupboard, but not in the closet. This is not an essential purchase, but it will be adequate for libraries needing an up-to-date, concise bilingual dictionary.
—**Emily L. Werrell**

1114. **The Stoddart Colour Visual Dictionary: French-English.** By Jean-Claude Corbeil and Ariane Archambault. Toronto, Stoddart Publishing, 1992. 896p. illus. index. $55.00. 443'.21. ISBN 0-7737-2642-X.

This is one of those reference works that is both very useful and highly entertaining to browse through. It provides attractive, detailed color illustrations of the objects of everyday life and of technical terminology and gives the nouns for them in both English and French. A table of contents lists 28 general areas (e.g., farming, human being, measuring devices) and the specific illustrations under each (e.g., structure of a plant, carpentry tools, fabric care symbols), and there is an index of all terms listed in each language. One can use this work to find the name of a familiar object or the meaning of an unfamiliar word. Terms included are intended to be those of everyday life and the more general technical terms for each field. The book also explains an amazing amount of specialized terminology that may not be known in one's own language.

The computer-generated color illustrations are extremely clear, detailed, attractive, and precisely labeled, and a definite improvement on the same authors' previous work, the *Facts on File English/French Visual Dictionary* (see ARBA 87, entry 1033), which has black-and-white illustrations. One limitation of the book is that for most objects only one (or at most, two) names are given in each language, but there may be several in use. The authors do attempt to give geographical variants in both languages (American and British, Parisian and Quebecois French). The index (and coverage) can be eclectic; *pipe wrench* is listed but not *wrench*, and the word *worm* will lead to specific objects used in weaving and gun cleaning, but not to the animal. These limitations are minor; this very interesting and useful book would be a welcome addition to most libraries.—**Marit S. MacArthur**

German

1115. **Collins German-English, English-German Dictionary Unabridged. Pons Collins Deutsch-Englisch, Englisch-Deutsch.** 2d ed. By Peter Terrell and others. New York, HarperCollins, 1993. 902p. $50.00. PF3640.C68. 433'.21. LC 90-4093. ISBN 0-06-017801-9.

Despite the press release announcing this volume as part of a "new series of top-of-the-line, unabridged bilingual dictionaries," and the imprint date of June 30, 1993, in the advertisement, this dictionary is merely a reprint of the 2d edition, which appeared in 1991. (It was simultaneously published in Germany as *Pons Collins Deutsch-Englisch, Englisch-Deutsch*.) Aside from its clear and easy-to-read type, this work has little to recommend it over the *Oxford Duden German Dictionary* (see ARBA 91, entry 1085). It must be said that *Collins* can certainly serve the student of German in many ways. Each entry provides clear definitions and idiomatic expressions and indicates part of speech, gender, and stressed syllables. However, while German pronunciation is extremely regular, some users might be uneasy at the absence of phonetic spellings. (*Oxford Duden* does provide pronunciation.) A general review of *Collins* quickly reveals its weaknesses and even a few mistakes: The commonly used word *Abitur*, for example, is designated as "rare"—although thousands of young Germans are involved in the process culminating in "das Abitur" every year (graduation exams in high school) and often talk of nothing else. In general, however, the Collins dictionary offers reliable definitions and numerous examples of usage. But given the acceptance of the *Oxford Duden* as the new standard single-volume German dictionary, not to mention its cost—half of what HarperCollins demands for this reprint—libraries should acquire the *Oxford Duden* work before or instead of *Collins*. [R: Choice, Dec 93, p. 581]—**Valerie R. Hotchkiss**

Hebrew

1116. **Renyi Picture Dictionary: Hebrew and English.** Toronto, Editions Renyi; distr., Toronto, McClelland & Stewart, 1992. 1v. (unpaged). illus. index. $19.95. ISBN 0-921606-38-9.

This work is designed to help young children acquire language and dictionary skills in English or Hebrew. The publisher claims that, given the large number of terms (3,336), the dictionary can also be used to teach Hebrew to older children and adults, or for teaching English as a second language. The primary sequence is English, although the title indicates otherwise, as does the layout: Each page contains 20 frames, with a Hebrew word on top of the frame, a centered illustration, a sequential number at the lower left, and the English term on the bottom. The large numerical headlines give the impression that there is a classified rather than an alphabetical arrangement. Some English terms are followed by variants with an asterisk, apparently Briticisms. This feature is unexplained in the introduction, and there are no cross-references from the variants.

The Hebrew index refers to frame number, not to the English term; it is claimed that use of this index will expand children's numeracy skills. The index is incomplete (e.g., the Hebrew equivalent of *iron mask* is not found under either component). Hebrew infinitives are sometimes entered under the particle meaning *to*, other times under the base form. Similar variation is found in the dictionary proper: Verbs may be translated by the Hebrew infinitive, the masculine past tense, the feminine past, or even nouns. There is no grammatical information.

The most serious problem is that the dictionary is riddled with errors in Hebrew spelling and vocalization. A mixture of classic *defective* orthography and of modern *plene* orthography is used, without explanation. The Hebrew introduction features numerous errors in Hebrew vowel points. There seem to have been problems with the Hebrew computerized typesetting, resulting in variation in the fonts for headwords. The vowel points are barely legible in the boldface font. Also, the illustrations are unattractive and often unclear. The one for *jewel* looks like a circus tent, and the word *steel* is illustrated by a picture of four knives.

Although part of the Editions Renyi Heritage Series, this Hebrew dictionary includes no terms from Jewish culture, because the publisher uses a basic English picture dictionary to which foreign-language equivalents are added. It is thus defective in lexicon, grammar, orthography, design, illustration, and indexing. Sarah Peless's *Miloni = My Dictionary: Hebrew-English Illustrated Dictionary for Children* (Ramat Aviv, Israel: Centre for Educational Technology, 1981), although containing fewer terms, is a far superior work.—**Bella Hass Weinberg**

Indonesian

1117. **Tuttle's Concise Indonesian Dictionary: English-Indonesian, Indonesian-English.** By A. L. N. Kramer, Sr., and Willie Koen. Rutland, Vt., Charles E. Tuttle, 1993. 519p. $14.95pa. LC 92-63347. ISBN 0-8048-1864-9.

This book contains nearly 18,000 entries—about three-fifths English-Indonesian and two-fifths Indonesian-English—and is described as a major revision of *Van Goor's Concise Indonesian Dictionary* from the same publisher (1966). It is small, but not small enough for most pockets, and sturdy, with a plastic cover and an easy-to-read typeface. It is probably as large a volume as a traveler would like to carry, but an English-speaker would likely prefer that the Indonesian-English section comprised three-fifths of the volume. The publisher contends that the book is unusual in reflecting the 1972 spelling reforms even though Indonesian-published dictionaries have used the revised spelling in later editions. Such an assertion also ignores the standard *An Indonesian-English Dictionary* (see ARBA 90, entry 1046). But that book (with 618 pages) is hardly a compact dictionary.

One must consider the purpose of a compact dictionary. For a traveler it should reflect the current language, both spoken and written. This volume moves in that direction, but it omits colloquialisms and has a tendency to opt for words of Dutch origin rather than English, a pattern that might be followed by older Indonesians but reversed by younger ones. Indonesian is a dynamic language, both spoken and in print, with a proclivity for acronyms. Indeed, occasional reading of the popular press is extremely difficult, as so many new words are incorporated.

This volume is fine as a beginning but hardly adequate for the serious student. The same may be said of its value in a reference collection. While it is certainly better than nothing, it is best when accompanied by *An Indonesian-English Dictionary* and the Indonesian-only *Kamus Besar Bahasa Indonesia* [Indonesian Language Big Dictionary] (Jakarta: Department Pendidikan dan Kebudayaan, Republic of Indonesia, 1988) and *Kamus Bahasa Indonesia Kontemporer* [Contemporary Indonesian Language Dictionary] by Peter and Yenny Salim (Jakarta: Modern English Press, 1991).—**K. Mulliner**

Japanese

1118. **Collins Shubun English-Japanese Dictionary.** New York, HarperCollins, 1993. 635p. $10.00pa. ISBN 0-00-433405-1.

With its more than 27,000 entries, this work seems to have been prepared for the general user. Each entry is given with phonetic signs of the International Phonetic Alphabet, the guiding chart of which is provided. The Japanese equivalent of each entry is provided first in Japanese orthography, then in romanized Japanese. More space, with example sentences and phrases, is given to such words as *any, be, get, off,* and *this* than is given to other entries. In the supplement, information and explanations are provided for Japanese numbers, counters, particles, and sentence construction. There are also sentences to be used in conversation for various occasions, such as visiting, dining, shopping, and moving around, and they should be of practical utility for users of the dictionary. A small point of criticism is that there are no Japanese equivalents for a number of entries, only the phonetically Japanized English in roman letters and *katakana*. The result is that Japanese users will not understand the meaning of the words and will be able to only approximately pronounce it. A less expensive and less bulky alternative is *The Practical English-Japanese Dictionary* (see ARBA 92, entry 1082).—**Seiko Mieczkowski**

1119. **Kodansha's Romanized Japanese-English Dictionary.** By Timothy J. Vance. New York, Kodansha America, 1993. 666p. $25.00pa. PL679.V36. 495.6'321. LC 92-45652. ISBN 4-7700-1603-4.

This dictionary is a completely rewritten version of *The New World Japanese-English Dictionary for Juniors* (Kodansha America, 1990). Vance has succeeded in meeting the demands of English-speaking students of Japanese who are at different levels, which has made the dictionary more flexible. Some of the desirable features of the volume are its 16,000 entries, which are many more than found in similar dictionaries; useful sample sentences in both romanized and Japanese script, followed by English translations; brief yet comprehensive explanations about particles (expressions called "pseudo-suffixes" that are used for making compound words); labels to particular speech levels, such as formal or colloquial and honorific or humble; and cross-references to synonyms and antonyms and to other locations in the dictionary. The section on the organization of the entries is a good guide to the dictionary and to its two appendixes, which cover inflections of verbs and adjectives, and Japanese numerals, counters, and numbers.

Kodansha's manages to provide, in fewer than 700 pages, considerably more information than *Basic Japanese-English Dictionary* (see ARBA 90, entry 1049), with its 3,000 entries designed for beginners (it is quite good on that level). *Kodansha's* is highly recommended for the study of Japanese on all levels. [R: LJ, 15 June 93, p. 64]—**Seiko Mieczkowski**

1120. **Merriam-Webster's Japanese-English Learner's Dictionary.** Springfield, Mass., Merriam-Webster, 1993. 1121p. illus. index. $27.95. PL679.K38213. 495.6'321. LC 93-27294. ISBN 0-87779-164-3.

This dictionary is designed for use by students at all levels and by business professionals who intend to master practical modern Japanese. Each Japanese entry, which as accent marks, is shown in roman letters, then by the standard writing in *hiragana* or *katakana*; this is followed, where appropriate, by another writing in parentheses that contains *kanji*, and then the English equivalent is given. Model sentences and phrases are provided for most entries, with the given word highlighted in the example sentence or phrase for easier recognition. These examples are also shown in a consistent order: first in romanized Japanese, then in normal Japanese orthography, and finally in the corresponding English translation. Explanations of particles, prefixes, and suffixes are helpful. Special usage boxes at selected entries help the user understand such words as *omou* (think) and *kooshuudenwa* (public telephone) and get further acquainted with the culture of Japan. The appendix contains a clear guide to Japanese pronunciation and an outline of Japanese grammar.

In 1989, Bonjinsha and Oxford University Press published *Basic Japanese-English Dictionary* (see ARBA 90, entry 1049), with 2,873 entries useful for introductory-level users. The present dictionary has around 9,000 entries, and it has achieved its aim of making the Japanese language more accessible to its users. Highly recommended for business and academic users.—**Seiko Mieczkowski**

1121. **NTC's New Japanese-English Character Dictionary.** Jack Halpern, ed. Lincolnwood, Ill., National Textbook, 1993. 1992p. index. $49.95. ISBN 0-8442-8434-3.

This extremely comprehensive dictionary, with 4,421 *kanji* (Chinese character) entries, 834 cross-referenced entries, and 60,000 meanings for 42,000 words and word elements, is designed to let the user gain an in-depth understanding of *kanji*. The entries in this dictionary offer two distinctive features: a central or core meaning that defines the most dominant meaning of each *kanji*, and SKIP (the System of Kanji Indexing by Patterns). The entries are listed according to the four patterns under the SKIP: the left-right pattern, which has the greatest number of entries and to which *kanji* such as *ki-ru* (cut) and *kawa* (river) belong; the up-down, such as *ni* (two) and *bun* (sentence); the enclosure, such as *hi* (sun) and *yama* (mountain); and the solid, such as *hi* (fire) and *ame* (rain). Each entry is presented with the core meaning, number of strokes, stroke order, grade (meaning whether the entry is used as one of the Jooyoo *kanji*), frequency of usage, the element of the radical, *on-kun* readings in roman writing, compounds, synonyms, and the *kanji* form and pronunciation of the entry in China today. Compound formations, homophones, and example sentences and phrases are shown where appropriate. The first 200 pages are devoted to explanations for using the dictionary. The 11 appendixes contain helpful information on SKIP rules, counting the strokes, writing *kanji*, core meanings arranged by frequency, and the Jooyoo *kanji* list. At the end of the dictionary are indexes of radicals, patterns, and *on-kun*, which make finding any needed *kanji* simple and easy. The compilation of the dictionary is thorough and represents an immense achievement. Highly recommended to all students, professionals, and libraries.—**Seiko Mieczkowski**

Korean

1122. Eccardt, Thomas, with Oh Wonchul, comps. **Korean.** New York, Hippocrene Books, 1993. 178p. (Hippocrene Handy Dictionaries). $8.95pa. ISBN 0-7818-0082-X.

This dictionary is of the same type as the other small volumes in the Hippocrene Handy Dictionaries series, but it has a higher standard than the others, partly because the compilers have given much thought to the needs of the traveler in Korea. They realized that because Korean is not written in Roman script, the probability is minimal that a foreigner would try to locate items in a Korean-English list; therefore, this part of the dictionary is only 10 pages long. There are a few most-frequent Korean words listed on these pages, in transcription with the original script following and with simple English equivalents. There follow some 20 more pages of topically organized Korean words, phrases, and short sentences that could be useful to a traveler. It is good to have a topical survey of the names of days, months, and the like, and the selection of the topics is usually good, but pragmatic considerations are largely lacking; for instance, the section on going through customs contains a score of expressions, but not the most useful one—"Nothing!"

Some 120 pages are given to the English-Korean part of the dictionary. The entries are well selected and well constructed. The main thing is that polysemy is discriminated (e.g., *court [of law]...; tennis court...*). The editors have the reasonable policy of discriminating even if the other sense is not given (e.g., *crown [dental]* to warn users not to use the equivalent offered should they want to talk about royal crowns). However, the sequence of senses within the entries could be improved. The Korean equivalents are given in the original script and in a clear, broad transcription.

The front matter offers an outline of Korean grammar. When one reads the introductory sentence warning users that they "may wonder how Koreans can communicate in such a strange medium [as the Korean language]," one mobilizes all the reserves of one's internal fortitude before the onslaught of what one expects to follow. But one is pleasantly surprised, because what follows is a reasonable, no-nonsense nucleus of Korean grammar of the descriptivist type, with the basic structural patterns clearly presented and explained, and with their equivalence to English patterns well illustrated. There can be no doubt that this is the best member so far of the Hippocrene Handy Dictionaries.—**L. Zgusta**

Latvian

1123. Sosare, M., and I. Borzvalka. **Latvian-English, English-Latvian Dictionary.** New York, Hippocrene Books, 1993. 286p. $14.95pa. ISBN 0-7818-0059-5.

All English-Latvian dictionaries to date, including this one, have been the work of Latvian linguists, who, although competent, lack full fluency in the nuances of English. Their bias is also toward British rather than U.S. usage. For example, in this book the word *shipment* is given two meanings, which, while not wrong in the narrow sense, miss general usage. The first, *shipment* as a noun, is translated as *iekraušana* (*kuģī*) which means loading in a ship. Second, (*kuģa*) *krava* means the load of a ship. Both translations are possible meanings of the word, but the authors err in only connecting the word with ships. Considering the lack of good English-Latvian dictionaries, this reprint from the Soviet era will have to do while we wait for a better one. Although there are lengthier dictionaries, this one is as good as any for quick reference when the highest precision is not desired.—**Andrew Ezergailis**

Ojibway

1124. Baraga, Frederic. **A Dictionary of the Ojibway Language.** St. Paul, Minn., Minnesota Historical Society Press, c1880, 1992. 1v. (various paging). $24.95pa. PM853.B28. 497'.3. LC 92-28915. ISBN 0-87351-281-2.

Ojibway is an Algonquian language spoken in an area centering on the Great Lakes, from Saskatchewan to Quebec and from North Dakota to Michigan. Its regional variants are known by such alternative names and spellings as Ojibwa, Ojibwe, Otchipwe, Chippewa, Ottawa, Odawa, Algonkin, and Saulteaux; the people call themselves Anishinaabe and their language Anishinaabemowin. Baraga (1797-1868), a

Catholic priest from Slovenia, was sent in 1835 to serve as a missionary in the Lake Superior region, and his Ojibway grammar was first published in 1850 (posthumously revised, 1878). An Ojibway-English and English-Ojibway dictionary appeared in 1853; its 2d edition (revised by Albert Lacombe, not always for the better, in 1887-1880) is here reprinted for use both by scholars and by the Native American community.

The useful foreword to this edition by John D. Nichols (with an up-to-date bibliography) points out that Baraga's spelling system for Ojibway was impressionistic and failed to record vowel length consistently. Thus "nibing" can represent either *niibing* "during the summer" or *nibiing* "in water." In addition, Baraga inconsistently wrote "p, t, k" for some occurrences of Ojibway initial *b, d, g*. Nevertheless, his work remains a model of missionary linguistics: the largest Ojibway dictionary, the most useful guide to dialectal differences, and an invaluable tool for retrieving ancient words from the memories of living speakers.—**William Bright**

Persian

1125. Haim, S. **English-Persian Dictionary.** New York, Hippocrene Books, 1987, 1993. 700p. $16.95pa. ISBN 0-7818-0056-0.

1126. Haim, S. **Persian-English Dictionary.** New York, Hippocrene Books, 1989, 1993. 1v. (various paging). $16.95pa. ISBN 0-7818-0055-2.

This two-volume work is the newly released U.S. printing of a bilingual dictionary revised and published in this form in 1989 in Tehran, Iran. The Persian-English volume defines some 30,000 words and idioms, while the English-Persian volume includes more than 40,000 entries. These dictionaries are aimed at the native speaker of Persian. Therefore, transliteration from the Persian alphabet is only included for those words for which the pronunciation might be ambiguous. An effort has been made to include some scientific and technical vocabulary.

Haim completed and published his first English-Persian/Persian-English dictionaries in 1936. Since that time, Haim dictionaries in both their more voluminous and abbreviated forms have been considered the standard reference books for native speakers of Persian who study English. With the numbers of Persian speakers and students of the language increasing in this country, it is very timely that such an affordable set of dictionaries should become available through a U.S. publisher.
—**Martha Miller Yazhari**

Portuguese

1127. **The Oxford-Duden Pictorial Portuguese-English Dictionary.** New York, Clarendon Press/Oxford University Press, 1992. 384p. illus. index. $49.95; $19.95pa. ISBN 0-19-864172-9; 0-19-864182-6pa.

This pictorial dictionary is designed to convey information visually rather than by abstract descriptions or explanations. It is divided into broad categories of knowledge and activity: the physical and social environments; agriculture and forestry; trades, crafts, and industry; transportation, communications, and information technology; offices, banks, and stock exchanges; the community; recreation and sports; entertainment, culture, and art; and animals and plants. Each double page contains a plate illustrating the objects associated with a subject (e.g., infant care and layette, bridges, or ball games) together with their names in English and Portuguese. Detailed tables of contents and alphabetical indexes in both languages facilitate access. (The repetition of a major heading in the Portuguese table of contents at the beginning and in the middle of the category—*Negocios, Profissoes e Industria*—and an inappropriately boldfaced heading in the English index—"Printing," create confusion.)

This work, with its technical terms and specialized words, serves as a useful supplement to general bilingual dictionaries. It will be welcome in all libraries needing Portuguese language coverage. [R: Choice, July/Aug 93, pp. 1753-54]—**Ann Hartness**

Russian

1128. Andreyeva, Victoria. **1000 Russian Verbs.** New York, Hippocrene Books, 1992. 362p. $9.95pa. ISBN 0-87052-107-1.

Verbs, especially under their imperfective and perfective aspects, represent the chief area of difficulty in Russian grammar. Andreyeva's manual, which lists 1,000 frequently used Russian verbs and emphasizes a comparison of them in their aspects, is therefore a very useful supplement to the barer entries in a dictionary.

The Russian verbs are arranged alphabetically, with separate entries for their imperfective and perfective forms. The chief parts of both aspects are provided (present, past, simple or compound future depending on aspect, and principles). A perfective infinitive is listed under the entry for an imperfective infinitive, but there is an occasional mistake, such as the failure to list *lech'* under *lozhit'sya* (to lie down) as its perfective form.

English equivalents for the Russian verbs are generously and intelligently provided, a respect in which this U.S. printed manual is superior to most Russian printed dictionaries. The use of verbs is often illustrated by quotations from classic Russian writers, but not always consistently or even compellingly— witness the otiose quotation from Blok to illustrate *lovit* (to catch): *I, brosaya, krichala: Lovi!* (And as she threw it, she called out, "Catch!"). The lack of stress marks on the Russian verbs is a surprising omission, one that will inevitably send the student back to a dictionary to check the stress. If the book is revised, the addition of stress marks would be helpful.—**John B. Beston**

1129. Benson, Morton, and Evelyn Benson. **Russian-English Dictionary of Verbal Collocations (REDVC).** Philadelphia, John Benjamins, 1993. 269p. $45.00; $22.95pa. PG2271.B46. 491.73'21. LC 92-34482. ISBN 1-55619-483-8; 1-55619-484-6pa.

Idioms, or collocations, are the smallest units of meaning consisting of more than one word. Knowledge of idioms in one language does not facilitate a learner's ability to form collocations in a second language, because these combinations can neither be predicted nor logically derived by a student. Most ordinary bilingual dictionaries do not provide adequate information on the idioms and collocations needed by translators and students of the language. Especially indispensable are verbal collocations. This unique, innovative bilingual dictionary contains about 4,600 main entries of verbs and more than 20,000 verbal collocations, combinations, and phrases derived from them. It is an excellent reference source, greatly needed by English-speaking students of Russian, Russian-speaking students of English, and translators who work with both languages. It provides thousands of collocational differences between Russian and English, which are of vital importance for both language learners and translators. This dictionary also contains grammatical collocations (verb plus preposition, verb plus specific case), lexical collocations (verb plus adverb), and numerous verbal phrases, including idioms and figurative expressions. The Bensons strove to cover the usages in modern Russian; a large number of examples were taken from the contemporary Russian press. However, some now obsolete political expressions from a bygone Soviet era have been retained to provide a broader linguistic base for translators and language students. This contribution is highly recommended for all Russian-English and English-Russian translators as well as for all intermediate and advanced students of these two languages.—**Oleg Zinam**

1130. **Hippocrene Standard Dictionary: Russian-English, English-Russian.** By Oleg Beniukh and Ksana Beniukh. New York, Hippocrene Books, 1993. 1v. (various paging). $16.95pa. ISBN 0-7818-0083-8.

This bilingual dictionary, a combination of two earlier Russian-English and English-Russian volumes originally designed for native Russian speakers, contains about 12,000 Russian and a like number of English words, each with mostly single-word definition-equivalents. Its asserted advantage is that each word is accompanied by a stress-marked phonetic transcription in the Latin or Cyrillic alphabet. Also included are a list of place-names and a Russian restaurant menu prefaced by a short essay on Russian cuisine. The editors state that their work is intended for use by students, tourists, and businesspeople.

The dictionary's aims are modest, but it cannot be recommended to English speakers. While the user can look up single words, there is little or no indication of how they are used in common contexts, nor any significant information on grammatical usage. Nor is the transliteration system well designed for rendering pronunciation, so language students will find the dictionary of little use. Definitions are sometimes inadequate, and the choice of words for inclusion seems eccentric. In some cases, it is impossible to tell which of several meanings is relevant. For example, *korshun* is simply defined as "kite." But is it the bird or the toy? Are English-speaking tourists or businesspeople likely to encounter this work? Or do they need to know that "Iberian" translates into Russian as *iazyk drevnikh iberov*, "the language of the ancient Iberians"? The essay on Russian cuisine has some useful information but is marred by its marginal English, such as "The traditional Russian cooking has come to us through the depths of history."

Apart from a few recent additions to the Russian vocabulary, this dictionary is inferior to several already on the market. Although obviously intended for use "on the run," it is too bulky for pocket or purse. Those in need of an inexpensive, handy, bilingual dictionary would do better with *Romanov's Pocket Russian-English and English-Russian Dictionary* (see ARBA 72, entry 1295), the Langenscheidt pocket dictionaries, or those in the Collins Gem series.—**D. Barton Johnson**

1131. **Renyi Picture Dictionary: Russian and English.** Toronto, Editions Renyi; distr., Toronto, McClelland & Stewart, 1992. 1v. (unpaged). illus. index. $19.95. ISBN 0-921606-34-6.

This Russian-English picture dictionary for young children contains 3,336 terms, almost all colorfully illustrated. Abstract words are covered by short model sentences. Although designed for English-speaking children learning Russian, the volume could also be used by Russian speakers, thanks to a Russian-language index.

The English user (who must know the Russian alphabet) looks up a word to find a numbered picture with the English word at the bottom and its Russian equivalent at the top. The pictures are obviously the book's greatest attraction, but it is difficult to see how they can, in many cases, substantially enhance vocabulary acquisition. It is conceivable that the presence of a picture would serve as a mnemonic link between the English and Russian words. Another possibility is that the child may spend more time browsing because the illustrations are designed to appeal to a child's level of interest.

The pictures, while sometimes charming, are occasionally misleading. For example, *legend* is illustrated by a picture of a cyclops, and *hopeless* portrays a puzzled jockey sitting backwards on his horse. One can also question the selection of words. Does a child learning Russian need to know the word for *kiln, microwave oven*, or *maggot*? Another limitation is the lack of stress marks on the Russian words. Nor is elementary grammatical information included, such as noun gender or verb aspect. In short, while this dictionary, with its attractive, large format, may engage a child's attention, it can be effectively used only under the immediate supervision of an instructor or in a bilingual home.—**D. Barton Johnson**

Spanish

1132. **Collins Spanish-English, English-Spanish Dictionary. Collins Diccionario Español-Inglés, Inglés-Español.** By Teresa Alvarez Garcia and others. New York, HarperCollins, 1993. 1v. (various paging). $20.00. PC4640.C53. 463'.21. LC 92-39311. ISBN 0-06-275514-5.

1133. **Collins Spanish-English, English-Spanish Dictionary Unabridged. Collins Diccionario Español-Inglés, Inglés-Español.** 3d ed. By Colin Smith with others. New York, HarperCollins, 1993. 1v. (various paging). $50.00. PC4640.S595. 463'.21. LC 91-36013. ISBN 0-06-275504-8.

The unabridged edition of these dictionaries lists more than 230,000 entries and 440,000 translations, while the smaller edition has more than 135,000 entries and 220,000 translations. Both indicate usage level and have up-to-date coverage of business, political, and technical terms. The compilers are careful in trying to indicate Spanish-American usage. It might have been helpful to the Spanish-speaking person if it were indicated where differences exist between British and United States vocabulary usage.

The bilingual dictionary field is becoming a slightly crowded one. However, the unabridged edition has much to recommend it for its currency and its attention to lexicographical detail. It contains an almost 80-page section on language in use, with "thousands of phrases and expressions grouped according to the function that is being performed when they are used in communication." This is a useful addition to the type of information that a dictionary can and should provide.

Libraries interested in purchasing current bilingual Spanish-English dictionaries would do well to consider the unabridged edition. Individuals might find the standard edition more suitable.

—Hensley C. Woodbridge

Tongan

1134. Tu'inukuafe, Edgar. **A Simplified Dictionary of Modern Tongan.** Auckland, N.Z., Polynesian Press; distr., Honolulu, University of Hawaii Press, 1992. 278p. $26.95pa. ISBN 0-908597-09-6.

Tongan is a Polynesian language of some 100,000 speakers—quite a considerable number, considering the number of speakers of other related languages of this family and area. This dictionary contains both English-Tongan and Tongan-English parts, plus appendixes containing topically organized phrases and sentences and a sketch of grammar. For its size, and for the state of Polynesian lexicography, the book is quite good.

The dictionary is said to be "simplified," which apparently means "short," or "containing basic information only." For instance, there is no indication of the pronunciation of the English items in either section, nor are there any grammatical or syntactic indications. But the vocabulary selected is good; it is modern and consists of frequently occurring words. There is some discrimination of polysemous meaning; also, some lexicalized expressions, nominal and verbal, are listed. The Tongan-English part follows the same policy. It is only natural that one part of the dictionary is a reversal of the other; however, in the process of reversing, some discrepancies (luckily only minor ones), have crept into the text. For example, the English-Tongan part has the entry **gasp** (for breath) *tau'aki*, whereas the Tongan-English part has **tau'aki** *to gasp while dying*. There also is the problem of semantic parallelism, or lack of it: a "young girl" will be younger than a "girl," but a "young man" will not be younger than a "boy"; hence, how does one refer to "young boy"? Perhaps *kei talavou*? That is, however, glossed as "young people." These are minor things, but more rigorous control could have eliminated them.

Sometimes the reversal is unnecessary and wastes space; for example, the English-Tongan part gives **steeple** as *taua 'o ha falelotu 'oku fasi'i ki 'olunga*, which means "tower of any church building narrow in the upper part." This is good, because Tongan users will meet the English word and get the Tongan explanation of it, but English users do not get the translation concocted above and must rely on their wits if they wish to talk about steeples. However, to give in the Tongan-English part the entry **taua** *tower* (~ 'o ha falelotu 'oku fasi'i ki 'olunga) *steeple* is probably unnecessary because the phrase contained in the parentheses will hardly occur in a Tongan text. Anybody who knows the impact of missionaries on Polynesian languages and societies will agree that the presence of the pertinent vocabulary in the dictionary is useful. Since borrowed words and transplanted names show strong phonological adaptation to Tongan, it is good that even the latter are listed; sometimes there are interesting variants, such as English-Tongan **Jesus** *Sisu; Sesu. Sesu* is the Roman Catholic version of the name; *Sisu* is based on the English pronunciation of the name.

The grammatical appendix is too short for any serious purpose; it should be radically expanded. Some information offered there should be transferred into the entries. Examples are the English-Tongan entries **brother** (of a man) *tokoua*, (of a woman) *tuonga'ane*; **sister** (of a man) *tuofafine*, (of a woman) *tokoua*. The exemplification of this comes only in the appendix, where both the question "How many brothers and sisters do you have?" and its answer are given twice, once when addressed to, and answered by, a boy and then a girl.

The series of "simplified dictionaries" promises to publish similar dictionaries of Modern Fijian, Niuean, and Cook Islands Maori. These will be quite useful, particularly if some improvements, such as exemplified above, are made.—**L. Zgusta**

Turkish

1135. **The Oxford Turkish Dictionary.** By Fahir Iz, H. C. Hony, and A. D. Alderson. New York, Oxford University Press, 1992. 1v. (various paging). $75.00. ISBN 0-19-864190-7.

The original edition of the *Oxford Turkish-English Dictionary* was authored by Hony and Iz; its 3d edition (see ARBA 86, entry 1074) was prepared by Alderson and Iz. The authorship of the *Oxford English-Turkish Dictionary* is identical, and its 2d edition, published in 1978 (see ARBA 79, entry 1153), was also prepared by Alderson and Iz. Oxford University Press has now prepared this combined edition of the two dictionaries. The owner of the two separate dictionaries will find no reason to buy this edition, because there is no change whatsoever. Many pages were compared, and in each case the older editions and the present printing are identical to the letter. This is a pity, for two reasons. First, this dictionary allows a type of nesting of the entries that is considered admissible only in very small dictionaries. For instance, the entry *know* (noun) has the subentries *be in the ~, ~able, ~-all, ~-how, ~ing, a ~smile, and ~ly*. The first two subentries are not really good; something like *a ~~smile, ~~ly*, or a new entry for *knowing* would be much better.

The other thing that makes one somewhat uneasy is sentences in the cover blurb such as "English-Turkish coverage includes new English words and senses." This information pertains to the 1978 edition! This will probably mislead potential buyers into thinking the vocabulary is up-to-date, when it is 15 years old. Many a dictionary blurb contains statements of this type, and *caveat emptor* is the general rule, but they are unworthy of a publisher such as Oxford University Press. In any case, this is a reprint of the best English and Turkish bidirectional, bilingual dictionary in existence. [R: Choice, Nov 93, p. 434]

—L. Zgusta

Welsh

1136. Evans, H. Meurig. **Welsh-English, English-Welsh Dictionary.** New York, Hippocrene Books, 1992. 611p. $19.95pa. ISBN 0-7818-0136-2.

The particularly valuable feature of this dictionary is its modern vocabulary. It is not overburdened with expressions relating to fairies, hobgoblins, wizards, and similar words from folk tales, but instead contains lexical items from contemporary registers of life. As in most languages that have been modernized only relatively recently, Welsh frequently has competing synonyms for modern lexical items, such as borrowings on the one hand and loan translations and other coinages on the other. Laudably, the dictionary neglects neither set, without giving too many competitors. There is no need to disambiguate such pairs, or groups, of synonyms because the situation is quite clear. Other constellations might have required more information.

The dictionary seems to be primarily intended for a speaker of English who tries to handle Welsh. This is quite clear from the way information about lenition is given and from such entries in the Welsh-English section as *asewyllys*—will, desire, testament. English speakers know the difference between the English equivalents' meaning and select one of them according to the context read or intended. So far so good; but English speakers will be lost in the English-Welsh section where they read entries such as *whip*—chwip, fflangell, ysgogiad. There being no discrimination of meaning, they probably will reason that, in the same way as above, *chwip* is a borrowing from English, *fflangell* from Latin (*flagellum*), so they might settle for the native *ysgogiad*. This, however, has a transferred meaning, something like "impulse, incitement." Discrimination of meaning will be the chief task for any future edition.

The front matter and back matter contain various valuable bits of information beyond the usual sketch of the history and present spread of Welsh and indications concerning orthography, alphabet, and pronunciation. There is a succinct, understandable treatment of the phenomena of lenition (called "mutations")—something like sandhi, with good advice on how to seek a mutated form under the headword, which is always in the absolute form. A survey of Welsh word-formational prefixes and suffixes increases the power of the word list, and a table of Welsh endings makes orientation in a text easier for the beginner. Very valuable also are lists of the vastly diverging English and Welsh personal

Yiddish

1137. **Harduf's Transliterated Yiddish-English Dictionary. Fourth Volume: A-Z.** Willowdale, Ont., Harduf Books, 1992. 270p. $85.50. ISBN 0-920243-20-7.

D. M. Harduf, working independently in Toronto, has been issuing dictionaries on the Yiddish language with impressive frequency. Most Yiddishists are familiar with his handy *English-Yiddish, Yiddish-English Dictionary* published in 1983. Using this reference as a base, Harduf added transliterations to a larger-size version in 1991 called *Transliterated English-Yiddish Yiddish-English Dictionary* (see ARBA 93, entry 1106). Although these dictionaries were not the most scholarly or comprehensive available, they were clearly printed and easy to use, and included many contemporary words.

Answering an increasing demand for transliterated guides, Harduf's latest contribution is a dictionary that, unlike his previous references, is alphabetized by the English transliteration. Once again he has remained true to his principles of an easy-to-use, well printed, and up-to-date reference. While giving a new alphabetization by transliterated word, he fortunately has not eliminated versions of the Yiddish words that use Hebrew letters. However, he has stuck by his nonstandard use of "ei" (instead of "ey") and "ai" (instead of "ay"), which may confuse some users. Detracting from the work also is the fact that his designations of the words as parts of speech are written in by hand and are not given for all words. However, some users will appreciate the fact that the dimensions of the book are an eye-saving letter size and that it is printed on white, wood-free paper. Harduf has included some 8,000 words, including contemporary words such as *relief map* (*relyef-mape*), *relativity* (*relativitet*), and *countersign* (*kegenchasmenen*). This is more than double the number of transliterated words in another popular dictionary alphabetized by transliterated letters—*The Yiddish Dictionary Sourcebook* (see ARBA 87, entry 1057). But the moderately priced *Sourcebook* also gains favor by including an English-Yiddish dictionary and notes on pronunciation, grammar, and history. Harduf's new transliterated reference can be used best in conjunction with his previous volumes on transliterated English to Yiddish and Yiddish to English. The volumes have relevance for college libraries and collections in German, Hebrew, linguistics, and Jewish studies.

—**Simon J. Bronner**

24 Literature

GENERAL WORKS

Bibliography

1138. Gerry, Thomas M. F. **Contemporary Canadian and U.S. Women of Letters: An Annotated Bibliography.** Hamden, Conn., Garland, 1993. 287p. index. (Garland Bibliographies of Modern Critics and Critical Schools, v.21; Garland Reference Library of the Humanities, v.1354). $45.00. Z1376.W65G46. 016.81'08'09287. LC 92-35184. ISBN 0-8240-6989-7.

The purpose of this bibliography is to provide access to the writings of a "group of [United States and Canadian] women writers who ... have written both poetry and/or fiction, and literary criticism and/or theory" (p. xi). The selection of writers is based on Gerry's knowledge of United States and Canadian literature. Each of the first 16 chapters consists of a list of the writings of an author, with critical and theoretical works annotated. Generally, works unavailable in either the Library of Congress or the National Library of Canada are excluded, except for some items sent to Gerry by the authors listed. A section of related bibliographies selectively lists bibliographies and critical works on women of letters on whom substantial work has already been done (e.g., Maya Angelou, Margaret Atwood). A subject index and a rather self-serving, apologetic introduction are included.

The highly subjective nature of this expensive work renders it of little value to most serious students and researchers. Some larger literature and women's collections may find it of some use as many of the writers included are not widely known (although almost all appear in *Contemporary Authors* [see ARBA 93, entries 1108-09] and related works), but generally it is not recommended.—**Gari-Anne Patzwald**

1139. Harner, James L. **Literary Research Guide: A Guide to Reference Sources for the Study of Literatures in English and Related Topics.** 2d ed. New York, Modern Language Association of America, 1993. 766p. index. $37.00; $19.50pa. Z2011.H34. 016.8209. LC 92-36922. ISBN 0-87352-558-2; 0-87352-559-0pa.

With his first edition (see ARBA 91, entry 1097), Harner replaced an earlier literary guide (see ARBA 84, entry 1099). For this new edition Harner estimates that approximately half the entries from his first edition have been revised. This new edition includes 1,194 entries; 1,248 other works and 745 reviews are cited in the annotations and headnotes. New reference works that appeared after February 1989 and before April 1992 have been added, and forthcoming works are noted, as are significant works in progress. Materials deemed no longer important have been deleted.

Organization is retained from the first edition, with some minor changes to accommodate the additions and deletions. Harner has used a system for numbering entries with spaces left for adding items in future editions. Most items from the first edition have the same entry number in the second, although occasionally a number from the first is replaced with an addition in the second. This convention allows for easy comparison between editions to see where there are changes.

Harner uses four criteria in selecting materials: thoroughness, accuracy, good organization, and adequate indexing. Judged by his own criteria, Harner's work exemplifies all these characteristics. Annotations are detailed, supplying full descriptions of sources and publishing histories, and evaluating both merits and deficiencies. Harner arranges works within a given category in descending order of importance.

The subtitle belies the wide range encompassed by the phrase "related topics." Among these are art and literature; book trade and publishing history; book collecting; children's literature; computers and the humanities; and literature in combination with film, folklore, medicine, music, philosophy, religion, science, history, political science, and psychology.

Harner is not shy in his pronouncements, noting, for example, in entry 90 that "annotations ... while full, lack proportion and are frequently inaccurate or untrustworthy in their evaluations," or that a work is "more useful for its treatment of background, than for critical insights." Yet he is fair as well as judicious, commenting, for example, in entry 2315: "The clear summaries of major theories, ideas, and works make Sambrook the best guide to the backgrounds necessary for an understanding of eighteenth-century literature."

For the serious undergraduate as well as the seasoned scholar, this work is a gold mine of information and a model of its kind. This edition is an essential purchase for libraries that own the earlier edition and for those academic libraries or large collections that have failed to acquire it. [R: Choice, Sept 93, p. 82; JAL, July 93, pp. 200-01]—**Bernice Bergup**

1140. Marshall, Donald G. **Contemporary Critical Theory: A Selective Bibliography.** New York, Modern Language Association of America, 1993. 201p. index. $32.00; $15.50pa. Z6514.C97M37. 016.801'95. LC 92-33515. ISBN 0-87352-963-4; 0-87352-964-2pa.

This is a bibliography of 1,690 books devoted to contemporary critical theory. A brief historical introduction is followed by a chapter on general critical theory and 14 chapters on types of critical theory (e.g., structuralism, psychoanalytic, Marxist, feminist). Each chapter lists books by and about individual theorists as well as critical surveys and anthologies. Many of the listings have brief descriptive annotations, and a few have evaluative annotations.

Contemporary Critical Theory does a good job of indicating the present state of literary theory. The introductory "Guide for the User" defines the scope of the bibliography well. While the annotations for the works cited are sometimes too brief to be illuminating, the descriptive paragraphs are usually helpful in describing the basic tenets of the critical schools or the individual critics. A similar work is *Research in Critical Theory since 1965* (see ARBA 90, entry 1067), which lists 5,000 works but is limited to works published from 1965 to 1987. *Critical Survey of Literary Theory* (see ARBA 89, entry 993) also contains useful bibliographies. But *Contemporary Critical Theory* is a compact, well-arranged, relatively inexpensive guide to the current schools of literary theory; it should be a priority purchase for academic libraries supporting courses in critical theory.—**Jonathan F. Husband**

1141. Nordquist, Joan, comp. **Deconstructionism: A Bibliography.** Santa Cruz, Calif., Reference and Research Services, 1992. 68p. index. (Social Theory: A Bibliographic Series, no.26). $15.00pa. ISBN 0-937855-51-0.

Deconstructionism has insinuated itself into a surprising number of academic disciplines, and studies of it and its effects are legion. This latest entry in the Social Theory series attempts to provide quick and easy access to books and articles in books dealing with this hottest of intellectual topics. Its chief virtue is that it emphasizes the major authoritative contributions to the philosophical and literary aspects of deconstructionism and gives access to important articles in books, a resource too often overlooked in standard bibliographies and online computer databases. It is also handy, cleverly organized, and current. There are sections devoted to books by and about the major theorists, books about deconstructionism, articles about deconstructionism in other books (very useful), and bibliographies on the subject. The citations are clear and fully indexed. Users must beware, however, of the work's limitations: periodical literature is not covered, and only English-language material is included. Also, few readers are likely to be enlightened by John M. Rosen's turbid and choppily edited introduction. By virtue of its currency, ease of use, and concentration on major English-language sources, this bibliography should be a useful addition to academic as well as public libraries.—**Jeffrey R. Luttrell**

1142. Strouf, Judie L. H. **The Literature Teacher's Book of Lists.** West Nyack, N.Y., Center for Applied Research in Education; distr., Englewood Cliffs, N.J., Prentice Hall Professional, Technical, and Reference, 1993. 405p. illus. $29.95 spiralbound. PN59.S87. 809. LC 92-40675. ISBN 0-87628-548-5.

For creative school and public librarians and English instructors, this companion volume to the *New Reading Teacher's Book of Lists* (Prentice Hall, 1985) should be a mandatory purchase. It provides a great deal of interesting, literary information that can be easily incorporated into applicable lesson plans or used for stimulating bulletin board or book displays. Subject areas range from best-selling children's books to onomatopoeic examples. All of the lists supply enough items so that modifications, by either adding or eliminating titles, can be made. Although such topics as nursery rhymes are included, the majority of lists emphasize materials that are suitable for secondary and college levels.

The author correctly recommends perusing the table of contents as a means of access. Because the information offered is so varied and somewhat serendipitous, the table of contents is divided into nine sections: literature, books, genres, poetry, drama, themes, literary periods, potpourri, and endings. (The latter two sections feature such lists as euphemisms, oxymora, and young adult periodicals.) Within these divisions, alphabetical, chronological, and logical arrangements are imposed. Simply browsing the contents of each section, however, is probably the most efficacious means to become familiar with the interesting lists of literary allusions, common traits of gifted children, Pulitzer prize winners, figures of speech, elements of drama, allegories, multicultural works, and authors by ethnic group.

The sole flaw in this useful compendium is the potpourri-like quality of the lists. An index might have added an extra dimension of access that would characterize this book as an excellent reference title in addition to being an outstanding literary activities source.—**Kathleen W. Craver**

1143. Welch, Jeffrey Egan. **Literature and Film: An Annotated Bibliography 1978-1988.** Hamden, Conn., Garland, 1993. 341p. index. (Garland Reference Library of the Humanities, v.1114). $53.00. Z5784.M9W375. 016.8088'0048. LC 92-18074. ISBN 0-8240-5843-7.

Welch's earlier bibliography of literature and film covered material published from 1909 to 1977. This volume covers the next 10 years. The items appear alphabetically by author within the year published. Following is an author/editor index, a title index that includes a code for the type of literature and the film adaptation's release date, an index of subject names, and a subject idea index.

Welch did not try to produce a comprehensive bibliography; rather, he selected items in three categories. First he includes books and articles that discuss the process of adapting a literary work (e.g., play, novel, short story, poem) to the screen. Second are discussions of the similarities and differences between film and literature and the influence one may have on the other. Third are references to literature and film study classes in schools and colleges. Welch omits film reviews unless they have a lengthy discussion of the literary source. He also omits general articles on adaptations and articles in standard reference works. He does not include dissertations, theses, or novels based on screenplays.

Welch provides brief annotations for most of the citations, and he quotes directly from the original to give readers a better sense of the article's focus. This is a welcome resource for film studies researchers.
—**Berniece M. Owen**

Biography

1144. Chevalier, Tracy, ed. **Contemporary World Writers.** 2d ed. Detroit, St. James Press, 1993. 686p. $135.00. PN51.C6235. 809'.04. LC 93-5352. ISBN 1-55862-200-4.

Anyone comparing this work with the first edition, published in 1984 as *Contemporary Foreign-Language Writers* (St. Martin's Press), will be struck by the significant increase in the number of writers included: approximately 340 living authors representing more than 60 countries, some 200 more than the previous edition. The key criterion for inclusion remains: living writers whose work has been translated, in whole or in part, into English. Among the diversity of nationalities represented are Cameroonian, Faroese, Ivorian, Macedonian, and Sudanese.

For each entry a biographical sketch concludes with a current address of the writer or the person's literary agent. This is followed by a bibliography listing verse, fiction, plays, and other works, the titles arranged chronologically within each category. The bibliographies are composed mostly of books but may include for some, especially Japanese, Russian, and *samizdat* writers from Central and Eastern Europe, works initially published in journals. Original editions are cited in the original language along with the first British and United States editions of English translations. For works not translated into English, a literal English translation of the title is supplied in brackets.

The primary bibliography is supplemented by a roster of secondary sources that may include published bibliographies and critical studies in English if available. Signed essays critique the writer's work. In some entries, writers comment on their own work, although this is not a significant feature. Pseudonyms are cross-referenced to the author's main entry.

An important new feature of this edition is a nationality index listing writers under current as well as past nationality. The title index includes only those from the fiction, play, and verse sections and may exclude titles that fall into the category of other works. Collections in comparative literature as well as large public libraries will want to acquire this up-to-date survey of contemporary writers, both for the bio-bibliographical information and as a tool for collection development in modern literatures.

—**Bernice Bergup**

1145. Combs, Richard E., and Nancy R. Owen. **Authors: Critical & Biographical References.** 2d ed. Metuchen, N.J., Scarecrow, 1993. 478p. index. $49.50. PN524.C57. 016.809. LC 93-774. ISBN 0-8108-2679-8.

Combs refers to this volume as a finding tool for critical references and biographical materials about authors ("author" is defined as any writer of prose, poetry, fiction, or nonfiction about whom something has been written). This edition more than doubles the coverage of English-language critical and biographical commentaries found in the first edition (see ARBA 71, entry 1340). Reference works about a single author are not included, and passages are listed only if the entry cited is at least six pages long.

The book consists of three parts. First, the 3,317 authors about whom critical and biographical material was found are listed alphabetically. All references found for each author are listed by title and include pagination for the cited passages. References that contain biographical material (as opposed to literary criticism) are denoted with the symbol "(b)." The reader follows the alphabetical code to part 2 of the text, which lists all 1,158 books analyzed and contains bibliographical information (author/editor, publisher, and place and date of publication) for all books. Part 3 is an alphabetical list of all authors and editors whose works are cited. This reference work is easy to use and should lead literary scholars from high school through graduate school to vital criticism and biographical materials about authors. [R: Choice, Dec 93, p. 581; RBB, 1 Dec 93, p. 708]—**Jerry D. Flack**

1146. **DISCovering Authors: Biographies & Criticism on 300 Most-Studied Writers.** [CD-ROM]. Detroit, Gale, 1993. Hardware requirements: IBM XT, AT, PS/2, or compatible; MS-DOS or PC-DOS 3.1 or higher; MSCDEX version 2.0 or higher; 640K of RAM; hard disk drive with 1M free space or floppy diskette. $500.00. ISBN 0-8103-5057-2.

From Aristophanes and Maya Angelou to Paul Zindel and Emile Zola, *DISCovering Authors* is an excellent resource for almost any library. This CD-ROM version of selections from the Gale series includes a wide range of authors from a variety of cultures, genres, and time periods selected by a committee of librarians, teachers, and editors. Each entry generally includes four to seven excerpted essays from other Gale series. The search menus are very easy to use, and the commands are standard mnemonics or very intuitive. The full citation can be printed, or any portion of the text may be selected to be printed or saved to disk.

One of the particularly nice features of this CD-ROM, in addition to the fact that it is extremely user-friendly, is the ability to search the personal data on authors in any field contained in the record, including dates, nationality, politics, religion, avocational interests, genre, and even media adaptations (thus identifying writers for students to contrast or compare). When searching the "Personal Data on Authors," a function key will display a list of words or phrases that may be searched, allowing any number of these to be selected and linked by Boolean operators, even using truncation and proximity operators. There is also an advanced search mode that allows the critical material to be searched by keywords and Boolean operators.

First-time users like the clear screens, easy scrolling and selection, abundant function keys, main menu toggle, and on-screen help. The disc is accompanied by a concise reference guide with easy-to-follow directions for installation and configuration, full search directions, a complete index, and a laminated help card. Of particular value in instructional planning is the appendix, which lists all the subject terms and cross-references used, such as "African-American Life and Thought," "Class Structure," "Fatalism," "Individual and Society," "Materialism," "Rebellion," and "War." Users want more authors included and ask when other authors would be available.

Gale has addressed the only criticism of the reference guide by shipping all new products with a printed list of authors covered on the disc. The toll-free technical support number is either staffed or a call is returned promptly. The disc is reasonably priced for a stand-alone station, and there is a sliding price scale for network versions for up to eight simultaneous users. All Gale products are available for a 30- or 60-day trial period. The release of a Macintosh version has been announced. [R: Choice, Nov 93, p. 442; LAR, Sept 93, p. 517; RBB, 1 May 93, pp. 1616-18; RQ, Summer 93, pp. 557-58; SLJ, May 93, p. 46]—**Betty Bankhead**

1147. **The International Authors and Writers Who's Who.** 13th ed. Ernest Kay, ed. Cambridge, England, International Biographical Center; distr., Bristol, Pa., IPS/Taylor & Francis, 1993. 1004p. $175.00. ISBN 0-948875-51-8.

This book poses a quandary for those who need biographical and address data for modern authors. It includes more than 8,000 entries for authors from all over the world. The majority are from North America and Europe because, according to consultant editor M. J. Shields's foreword, the less-than-cherished role held by writers in many repressive regimes has resulted in little information on these individuals. Most of the writers listed will indeed be of interest to an international audience, although some have less widespread appeal.

The trouble with this book lies in the criteria for inclusion, or lack thereof. Shields states that entrants are "those who produce as a main activity books, plays, articles, or journalistic contributions, whether literary, commercial, technical, or scientific." It is also pointed out that the book cannot possibly list everyone, and that some who had been listed in previous editions have been dropped. There are no other criteria for inclusion listed, leaving one to wonder who chose the names and why some individuals were omitted. Important authors who do not appear include Toni Morrison, Clive Barker, and William F. Buckley, Jr. Other entries are out-of-date, such as that for Orson Scott Card, which ends in 1985. Another problem is that entry length is not synonymous with importance or fame, just how much information was provided. (It would help to know whether the listed individuals supplied the data or whether entries were compiled from outside sources.) The appendixes vary in their usefulness. Appendix A lists eight pages of literary agents, most from the United States; this information is available elsewhere in greater quantity. More helpful is the international list of literary organizations in appendix B, although it is by no means complete. In appendix C are past and present winners of various literary awards; this is a useful section. Overall, this book is cautiously recommended for public libraries in which there is a lot of interest in authors and for academic libraries that support programs in literature.—**D. A. Rothschild**

1148. Lindfors, Bernth, and Reinhard Sander, eds. **Twentieth-Century Caribbean and Black African Writers. Second Series.** Detroit, Gale, 1993. 443p. illus. index. (Dictionary of Literary Biography, v.125). $120.00. LC 92-41196. ISBN 0-8103-5384-9.

The present volume, together with volume 117 of the *Dictionary of Literary Biography* (see ARBA 93, entry 1110), is a bio-bibliography of 34 major Anglophone writers, almost all of whom are bilingual or multilingual, from Africa and the Caribbean. This second series concentrates on writers from Kenya, Uganda, Sudan, Somalia, Barbados, and Trinidad and Tobago. The first series dealt with writers from Gambia, Ghana, Guyana, St. Lucia, and Dominica. Both series include figures from Nigeria and Jamaica and Black writers from South Africa. Another volume is planned for Caucasian South African writers.

The writers, selected on the basis of influence and reputation, represent a wide spectrum of literature—novelists, dramatists, and poets—dealing with the colonial past as well as contemporary social and political issues. V. S. Naipaul (Trinidad) and Wole Soyinka (Nigeria) may be more familiar to users; less so are such writers as Nuruddin Farah (Somalia) and Richard Rive (South Africa). Preceded by bibliographies of the writer's work, essays focus on critical aspects and are interspersed with black-and-white photographs and illustrations, mostly dust jackets and reproductions of drafts and manuscripts. Critical analysis varies.

The entry for Andrew Salkey gives capsule summaries for most of his works; by contrast, Es'kia (Ezekiel) Mphahlele's work is discussed in greater detail and depth. Such unevenness is often a hazard in composite works such as this. However, this volume, along with its companion in the series, highlights what is called in the introduction "The internationalization of English." They can usefully serve collections focusing on expanding world literatures.—**Bernice Bergup**

Dictionaries and Encyclopedias

1149. Jeffrey, David Lyle, ed. **A Dictionary of Biblical Tradition in English Literature.** Grand Rapids, Mich., William B. Eerdmans, 1992. 960p. $79.99. PR149.B5D53. 820.9'382'03. LC 92-30648. ISBN 0-8028-3634-8.

Reflecting the significant role that the Bible has played in English literature from the Middle Ages to the present, this impressive compilation identifies and elucidates biblical terms, parables, phrases, motifs, concepts, quotations, people, and places that are frequently alluded to in the secular works of English-language writers. Its nearly 900 entries treat such topics as blindness, "handwriting on the wall," Jacob's ladder, "light under a bushel," "out of the mouths of babes," Ruth, and the unicorn. The alphabetically arranged articles were contributed by an international team of more than 150 scholars and by Jeffrey, a professor of English literature at the University of Ottawa. Although some entries provide only a brief identifying statement, most are more substantial, ranging in length from a paragraph to 10 pages and often including bibliographical references. The major articles identify the biblical context of the allusion, provide a synthesis of interpretations by theologians and other biblical commentators, and cite references to the passage in the works of English and U.S. authors. As one might expect, earlier writers such as Chaucer, Shakespeare, Milton, and Spenser figure prominently in the allusions, but the entries also refer to a wide range of nineteenth- and twentieth-century authors, among them Mark Twain, Emily Dickinson, James Joyce, J. R. R. Tolkien, and Flannery O'Connor. Following the dictionary portion is a 100-page section of annotated bibliographies that cover general biblical studies, the history of biblical interpretation, and biblical tradition in English-language literatures. The latter includes a valuable list of studies of biblical references in the works of specific English and U.S. authors.

This work is considerably more extensive and comprehensive than Walter B. Fulghum's *A Dictionary of Biblical Allusions in English Literature* (Holt, Rinehart and Winston, 1965), but it does not replace the earlier work. Its usefulness could have been greatly enhanced by the provision of an index to the authors whose allusions are quoted and an index to keywords in entry headers. Although the lack of indexes diminishes its effectiveness, this dictionary is a major scholarly achievement that will be a valuable resource for general readers, students, and literary and biblical scholars. [R: Choice, July/Aug 93, p. 1748; JAL, July 93, p. 200; RBB, 1 Mar 93, pp. 1251-52; RQ, Summer 93, pp. 563-64; WLB, Mar 93, p. 108]
—**Marie Ellis**

1150. Makaryk, Irena R., comp. and ed. **Encyclopedia of Contemporary Literary Theory: Approaches, Scholars, Terms.** Toronto and Buffalo, N.Y., University of Toronto Press, 1993. 656p. index. $150.00; $39.95pa. 801'.95. ISBN 0-8020-5914-7; 0-8020-6860-Xpa.

Literary criticism has burgeoned recently. To the traditional critical theories are now added the Chicago School, feminist criticism, Marxist criticism, deconstruction, formalism, structuralism, post-structuralism—the list is long. Critics now address not only the older literary theories but also the works of scholars in psychology and philosophy. It is an increasingly chaotic tangle—but the *Encyclopedia of Contemporary Literary Theory* imposes some order on it.

Part 1 contains articles on the newer theories of criticism, all written by notable scholars and filled with references to other articles in the encyclopedia. Each article is several pages long and presents the history of the critical school, details its leading proponents and major themes, and gives a bibliography of further references. Part 2 gives biographical sketches—again with bibliographies—of leading critics and influential thinkers; and part 3 offers definitions of some of the newer critical terms.

All in all, the book offers a complete look at the criticism contemporaneous with and newer than New Criticism. It fills an almost empty niche. While there are many books that discuss and explain a particular literary theory, books that cover them all are few. Some of the old stalwarts of literary criticism, such as *Handbook to Literature* (see ARBA 87, entry 1076), define some of the traditional schools of criticism, and a fairly new effort, *A Dictionary of Critical Theory* (see ARBA 93, entry 1114), contains articles on a number of new theories of criticism. But there is definitely room for the *Encyclopedia of Contemporary Literary Theory*. More than a ready-reference book, it will be used by both new students of literature and those whose studies were concentrated in a time when the New Criticism was indeed new. [R: Choice, Nov 93, p. 430]—**Terry Ann Mood**

1151. Milward, Peter. **An Encyclopedia of Flora and Fauna in English and American Literature.** Lewiston, N.Y., Edwin Mellen Press, 1992. 224p. $69.95. PR149.A7M55. 820.9'36. LC 92-14298. ISBN 0-7734-9539-8.

References to plants and animals, both literal and metaphorical, are found in virtually all literatures; the English-language literatures seem to be especially rich in such allusions. Milward (Sophia University, Tokyo) has not attempted to compile an exhaustive catalog of every plant and animal mentioned by English and American literary authors. Rather, he has written a guide to the more frequently occurring fauna and flora in the works of a selected list of major (almost all English) writers.

Plants and animals are listed separately, the entries in both lists being arranged alphabetically. The articles range in length from half a page to three pages; the average is about a page. They usually include an introductory paragraph that describes the natural history of the plant or animal, followed by a more extensive discussion of its appearances in literature; there is liberal use of direct quotation. Because the works treated are almost invariably classics that will be available in multiple editions in all but the smallest libraries, no specific bibliographic citations are provided. The author's biology is occasionally sketchy, but his linguistic and literary analyses are perceptive and informative. Because the work is limited in scope to a relatively small list of authors, it cannot be regarded as a comprehensive reference on the subject, but it should be useful in most libraries that support undergraduate English programs.—**Paul B. Cors**

1152. Serafin, Steven R., and Walter D. Glanze, eds. **Encyclopedia of World Literature in the 20th Century. Volume 5: Supplement and Index.** New York, Crossroad/Continuum Publishing, 1993. 732p. illus. index. (Frederick Ungar Book). $150.00. PN771.E5. 803. LC 81-3357. ISBN 0-8264-0571-1.

It is not necessary to say much about a book that is a supplement to a classic. Anyone who has the *Encyclopedia of World Literature in the 20th Century* (see ARBA 86, entry 1083; ARBA 85, entry 992; and ARBA 84, entry 1103), which is itself an update of an earlier four-volume set with the same title, will naturally want it. Volume 5 provides a number of articles on national literatures, authors, critics, and literary movements and trends. Its main focus is on little-researched literatures, genres, and authors. The survey articles it contains—on about 35 national literatures—for the most part treat those literatures that are receiving new and increased attention after the political and social upheavals of the last few years, among them Iranian, Lithuanian, Hungarian, Mexican, Palestinian, and Egyptian. Author articles are sometimes completely new, sometimes an update of an article in an earlier volume. Such newly acclaimed authors as Larry McMurtry, August Wilson, and Isabel Allende are included. In the area of literary criticism, the supplement contains articles on Jacques Derrida, Michel Foucault, and Jacques Lacan, and on such topics as feminist criticism and postmodernism.

Bibliographies for each article contain up-to-date references, and the index in the volume refers to all four previous volumes as well as to articles in this one. Libraries that own the basic set will naturally want to purchase this volume. [R: RBB, 1 Nov 93, p. 564; WLB, Nov 93, p. 101]—**Terry Ann Mood**

Handbooks and Yearbooks

1153. Bear, John. **The #1 *New York Times* Bestseller: Intriguing Facts about the 484 Books That Have Been #1 *New York Times* Bestsellers....** Berkeley, Calif., Ten Speed Press, 1992. 262p. illus. index. $16.95pa. Z1033.B3B43. 016.381'45002'0973. LC 92-9706. ISBN 0-89815-484-7.

This is a chronological list of all the books, fiction and nonfiction, that were number-one best-sellers according to the *New York Times Book Review* from 1942 through 1992. For each of the 484 books listed, a brief 100- to 200-word plot or subject summary is provided, along with tidbits of interesting information about the book and its author. There are numerous reproductions of the dust jackets and pages of these best-sellers as well as the magazine advertisements used to sell them. There are also reprints of magazine articles about best-sellers and a variety of original charts and graphs pertaining to these best-sellers, such as the best-selling books of all time and authors who wrote a number-one best-seller before the age of 35. Although not as detailed or wide-ranging as *The Popular Book* by James Hart (University of California Press, 1950) or similar older works, this is nevertheless a useful overview of the books and subjects that have most interested the people of the United States over the past half-century. It is to be hoped that future editions will include a bibliography of books and articles about best-sellers as well as pictures of the authors. [R: LJ, 1 Mar 93, p. 68]—**Joseph Cataio**

1154. Bishop, Edward L., ed. **Dictionary of Literary Biography Documentary Series: An Illustrated Chronicle. Vol. Ten: The Bloomsbury Group.** Detroit, Gale, 1992. 369p. illus. index. $113.00. LC 82-1105. ISBN 0-8103-7581-8.

Continuing the format of the preceding titles in the *Dictionary of Literary Biography* [DLB] *Documentary Series*, this volume on the Bloomsbury Group comprises an eclectic collection of photographs, facsimiles of manuscripts, paintings, letters, diaries, reviews, and miscellaneous archival documents. Covered are the nine principal members of that varied group of talented, eccentric, independent, and creative intellectuals who met in the Bloomsbury section of London from roughly 1905 to 1940 and whose influence was so powerful in the world of literature, art, politics, and economics. These include three figures who have had previous entries in the DLB (E. M. Forster, Leonard Woolf, and Virginia Woolf) and six who have not (Clive Bell, Vanessa Bell, Roger Fry, Duncan Grant, John Maynard Keynes, and Lytton Strachey). A typical entry is that for Virginia Woolf's *To the Lighthouse*, which includes two letters, a diary entry, a book review, a manuscript facsimile, and a reproduction of the dust jacket. In all there are 60 entries, followed by checklists for each person, which include a bibliography of the person's writings, a list of biographies, and the location of the person's archives. There is also a bibliography of works about the Bloomsbury Group.

Due to the vast range of intellectual and artistic achievement of the Bloomsbury Group, this is a somewhat less cohesive book than previous volumes in this series, but there is much that is new, interesting, or difficult to find here. Taken as a whole, it is a valuable addition to Bloomsbury literature. The only disappointing feature is the often-mediocre quality of the reproductions, difficult to excuse in a book this expensive.—**Jeffrey R. Luttrell**

1155. Brunel, Pierre, ed. **Companion to Literary Myths, Heroes and Archetypes.** New York, Routledge, Chapman & Hall, 1992. 1223p. index. $99.95. ISBN 0-415-06460-0.

This work, the English translation of the French *Dictionnaire des Myths Litteraires* (1988), takes a unique approach to mythology and literary myths. Containing 125 entries arranged alphabetically, it is not an encyclopedia of mythological terms, characters, and events, but rather deals with literary myth, which "consists of the story implied by the myth ... and of the new meanings that are added to it." Because of these new meanings, the literary myths are regenerated for each subsequent generation and speak in new ways to the problems of a different age. Also, because this work treats literary myths, rather than traditional myths, the focus is not on a single text but on the way the myth is treated in many texts over its "linguistic evolution." For example, the chapter on Antigone goes much further than evaluating Sophocles' original Thebian tragedies; it discusses the ways in which the myth was retold in subsequent ages to address the issues of that age.

This in-depth treatment of a single literary myth limits the number of myths that can be treated, but the editor covers a broad range of subjects. While the majority of the entries are on Western myths, there are sections on African, Latin American, Hindu, and Chinese myths and legends. Classical mythological figures, such as Cain, Black Tezcatlipoca, Medusa, and Satan are included, as well as more modern figures who have come to be seen in mythological terms, such as Don Juan, Carmen, Louis XIV, and Napoleon. There are entries on specific mythical beasts such as the phoenix, and entries on themes that recur in mythology, such as the flood. One slightly odd choice is the inclusion as parallel entries of very general concepts that need to be addressed, such as literary and mythological narratives. These concepts infuse the other entries to such an extent that finding them listed alphabetically was a little surprising.

This work is a wonderful discussion of the effects and place of mythology in literature, giving a new dimension to the subject and providing the reader with a true sense of the impact of myth on culture. The individual entries are well written and scholarly and treat their topics in great detail. The editor suggests in the preface that this is only the first of several editions on literary myths. This reviewer looks forward to more volumes. This book will be a valuable reference for students of mythology and literature and is recommended for academic and humanities libraries. [R: WLB, May 93, pp. 113-14]—**Tama J. Serfoss**

1156. **Dictionary of Literary Biography Yearbook: 1991.** James W. Hipp, ed. Detroit, Gale, 1992. 389p. illus. index. $113.00. LC 82-645187. ISBN 0-8103-7601-6. ISSN 0731-7867.

In order to ensure that the Dictionary of Literary Biography (DLB) series remains current, the *Dictionary of Literary Biography Yearbook: 1991* (DLB *Yearbook*) covers the literary events of the featured year. The DLB *Yearbook* is divided into two sections. The first section covers topics such as the 1991 Nobel prize in literature (won by Nadine Gordimer); surveys of the year's work in novels, short stories, poetry, drama, and literary biographies; interviews with George Greenfield, James Ellroy, and David Rabe; and various essays, including "New Literary Periodicals" and "Book Reviewing in America: V." The second section commemorates literary figures who died during 1991: Fredson Thayer Bowers, Theodor Seuss Geisel, Graham Greene, Fletcher Markle, Vera Nabokov, Isaac Bashevis Singer, and Alden Whitman. Also included in the DLB *Yearbook* are a list of literary prizes and awards, a necrology, and a checklist of contributions to literary history and biography. A cumulative index to the entire DLB, including the DLB *Documentary Series* and the DLB *Yearbook*, completes the volume. Consistent with the high standards of quality displayed in the DLB, this work is recommended for libraries already receiving the series.—**Lori L. Oling**

1157. Howes, Kelly King. **Characters in 19th Century Literature.** Detroit, Gale, 1993. 597p. index. $49.95. ISBN 0-8103-8398-5.

In addition to identifying some 2,200 characters in the works of 100 major writers, this volume provides excellent summaries of approximately 200 key works by novelists, dramatists, and short story writers. Moreover, the characters are placed within their literary contexts. A panel of librarians and teachers chose writers based on their inclusion in school curricula. While this might suggest a limited secondary school emphasis, undergraduates and graduate students would also find this work extremely helpful as an introduction and as a reviewing tool.

"Nineteenth century" is interpreted as the time period when most of the literary works were produced; some authors published in the late eighteenth century, and others extended into the twentieth century. Although the majority of writers included are English, American, and French, the work seeks to be as representative as possible. Well-known authors are treated more extensively; for example, Charles Dickens is allotted 26 pages and Jane Austen, 20, while the Spanish dramatist Manuel Tamayo y Baus is given 2.

For the works of each author, plot summaries are followed by a detailed analysis of the characters, generally with a critical evaluation of their literary significance and the historical context of the work in which they appear. The summaries are clear, and the discussion of characters is generally lucid and perceptive, presenting an excellent overview of critical interpretation.

Each section concludes with a selected bibliography for further reading, among which are listings for other series published by Gale. Aside from these references, which may cite newer criticism, the other bibliographic references seem to be rather dated for some authors (e.g., the most recent edition cited for Fyodor Dostoyevsky is 1983). This work should find a wide and appreciative audience among the general public and high school, college, and other advanced students. [R: Choice, June 93, p. 1604; RBB, 1 Mar 93, pp. 1250-51; SLJ, Nov 93, p. 144; VOYA, Aug 93, p. 190]—**Bernice Bergup**

1158. Magill, Frank N., ed. **Magill's Survey of World Literature.** North Bellmore, N.Y., Marshall Cavendish, 1993. 6v. illus. index. $389.95/set. PN523.M29. 809. LC 92-11198. ISBN 1-85435-482-5.

Although many educators and librarians compare Magill's various series of literary surveys with Cliffs Notes and other questionable study aids, the volumes are useful to researchers of all ages. Just as students often consult (with the approval of librarians!) standard subject encyclopedias to acquire basic information about a variety of topics, so do they similarly acquire introductory knowledge about authors and their works by reading Magill's volumes. The key, of course, in both cases is for students not to let their research end here, but to consult other sources, particularly secondary ones that emphasize insight rather than information.

This six-volume ready-reference set summarizes and analyzes more than 740 works by 215 significant world writers. These authors, from antiquity to the late twentieth century, include Homer, Sophocles, Dante Alighieri, Miguel de Cervantes, Daniel Defoe, Jane Austen, George Eliot, Virginia Woolf, Salman Rushdie, and P. D. James, and represent virtually all genres and 30-plus nationalities. American writers are excluded because they are covered in *Magill's Survey of American Literature* (see ARBA 92, entry 1157).

The set is arranged alphabetically by author. Each signed essay includes a one-sentence note about the author's literary significance; a biography; general analyses that discusses such characteristics as the writer's plot, theme, style, and setting; specific analyses of principal works, organized by genre, then chronologically within each genre; a 1- or 2-paragraph summation of the author's literary achievements and place in world literature; and an unannotated bibliography of some 6 to 12 secondary sources. Also included are author and title indexes; a glossary of literary terms appears in each volume.

Although this set is, contrary to its title, more of a survey of world authors than of world literature, few students will mind. The standardization of the entries (a tradition of Magill's works) and each essay's readability will make this a popular item in high school, public, and academic libraries. [R: BR, May/June 93, p. 55]—**Jack Bales**

1159. Rintoul, M. C. **Dictionary of Real People and Places in Fiction.** New York, Routledge, Chapman & Hall, 1993. 1184p. $99.95. ISBN 0-415-05999-2.

For those who have wondered if E. M. Forster's *Howards End* was inspired by a real house or if any fictional characters have been based on F. Scott Fitzgerald, this work is a treasure trove of such information. Covering approximately 1,000 English-language novels and short stories, the dictionary consists of 4 sections. The heart of the work is an alphabetical list of more than 4,000 real people, places, publications, groups, and other entities that have served as the basis for fictional counterparts. Entries in this section provide brief biographical or other descriptive information and note the name of the fictional counterpart and the author, title, and publication date of the work in which it appeared. In addition, the compiler provides a reference to, and generally a quotation from, the biography, critical work, letter, or other source that substantiates the identification.

The other major section is arranged first by author and then by titles of works from which characters are identified. Under each title, fictional names are paired with their real counterparts. Additional sections provide access by fictional names and titles of works. As the title index provides only the author's name rather than the pages on which the work is mentioned, the user must move from it to the author section rather than directly to the main section.

This volume includes approximately 1,000 more entries than *The Originals* (see ARBA 87, entry 1113) and more than 6 times the number in *Who Was Really Who in Fiction* (see ARBA 88, entry 1138). Yet the amount of duplication among these three sources is surprisingly low. Each of the earlier titles has special strengths, and both include characters from foreign-language works. However, this dictionary not only has the advantage of including significantly more entries but also is the only one of the three that provides verification for the identifications noted.—**Marie Ellis**

1160. **The Scribner Writers Series on CD-ROM.** [CD-ROM]. New York, Scribner's, 1993. Hardware requirements: IBM PC or compatible with a 386 or higher processor; at least 2MB of RAM; hard disk drive with 2MB free; CD-ROM drive that supports ISO 9660 CD-ROM discs; VGA monitor; MS-DOS 3.3 or later; Microsoft Windows 3.1. $695.00.

The Scribner Writers Series on CD-ROM contains 510 of the "most popular" entries from 9 of Scribner's literary criticism collections. Selection was based on the recommendations of high school librarians and college English professors. The essays and their bibliographies are provided exactly as they appear in the print versions, with no abridgment or condensing. In fact, each essay includes a citation to the print volume whence it came; thus the heading for Albert Camus's entry notes not only his birth and death dates, the number of pages in the essay, and the essay's author, but also "European Writers, 1990, Vol. 13, p. 3049-3078."

The essays reflect the high standards librarians have always found in the Scribner print references. However, in this CD-ROM version the publisher has made excellent use of the Windows graphic interface to produce a resource that is also easy to navigate and search; that is supportive of an intuitive intellectual exploration process; and that is easily customized in terms of output, whether one wants to print 10 pages, reorganize a paragraph for personal use, or download an entire 40-page essay. Installation is simple and quick, because the set-up program is contained on the CD-ROM instead of on a separate floppy disk, as with many CDs. Once installed, the program becomes a regular icon within the Windows program manager.

The four basic search avenues, presented as buttons to choose from as the program opens, are name of writer, genre, time period, and nationality. In addition, there is a quick start option that, if selected, presents an explanation of the various ways to search for information. Alternatively, the user may access any of the options offered in the menu bar at the top of the window: File, Edit, Bookmark, and Help. Other choices are provided in a separate set of buttons located beneath the menu bar, including, Contents, Go Back, History, Index, and Search. Although a laminated quick-reference card and an easy-to-understand 42-page manual accompany the disk (technical support is also available from Macmillan via a toll-free telephone number), they will rarely be referred to because it is so easy to wander through the menus and options buttons to figure out how to perform any given task.

In addition to searching on one of the four main avenues, one can use Boolean operators to search for, say, postmodernism and France, or use the Categories function to search by genre, language, nationality, race, sex, time period, or birth date (or any combination thereof). The program prompts the user throughout the search process, assisting with either the development of a simple search strategy or a more complex Boolean search. The search words are always highlighted within the articles found, so users can clearly see the results of their inquiries. In addition to the intuitiveness of the search process, there is also an online help menu organized into six topics that aid the novice searcher: navigating in Scribner Writers, finding information, printing and copying, bookmarks and annotation, buttons and menus, and keyboard techniques. Even the most inexperienced researchers will easily find their way to the desired information in this well-designed program.

Within the essays, writers for whom there are separate entries are highlighted, indicating that they can immediately be "jumped to" using Windows' hypertext hotlinks connection. If one wants to append a personal comment to an especially useful passage, this is easily done using the Annotate function; the Bookmark function, on the other hand, enables users to flag a location to return to after exploring in other areas. Should one be interested only in the bibliography provided for each essay, however, simply clicking on the word *bibliography* at the beginning of each essay will bring it forward in its own window.

It is hard to imagine how this product could be improved. The publisher has done a fine job of combining excellent content with a simple, easy-to-use interface, resulting in a resource that will be useful for every high school and college literature student. [R: RBB, 15 Dec 93, p. 779]—**G. Kim Dority**

Indexes

1161. **Gale's Literary Index.** [CD-ROM]. Detroit, Gale, 1993. Hardware requirements: IBM PC or compatible; MS-DOS or PC-DOS 3.1 or higher; MS-DOS CD-ROM Extensions 2.0 or higher; 640K RAM; hard disk with 1MB free. $149.00/yr. ISBN 0-8103-4961-2.

Updated every six months, Gale's Literary Index on CD-ROM is a master index to the hundreds of volumes in the 32 literary series published by Gale. It covers more than 110,000 authors and 120,000-plus titles. Anyone who has ever tried to track down all series references to a single story will appreciate this handy tool.

There are two types of records: author and title. The author record lists dates; variant names; Gale series titles that contain biographies of the author (including volume numbers); and a title list of works by the author with the Gale series titles, volumes, and page numbers where they appear. Authors with pseudonyms may have more than one entry. Thus, two of the three Gale titles listed for Charles Lutwidge Dodgson are not among the five for Lewis Carroll. Fortunately, the user can easily toggle between the variant name entries. The title record notes the author's name and provides the series titles, volumes, and page numbers in which a particular literary work may be found. Foreign titles are listed in both the original language and English.

Search options include author, title, and extended search. Author and title searches are very easy to perform without any reference to help screens or documentation. Extended searches allow single-item or Boolean searching for any of the following fields: author words, title words, author birth or death year or year ranges, and nationality. Word lists are available for author, title, and nationality fields. The resulting display will depend upon the strategy implemented. For instance, a search for the title word *coeur* will bring up a list of all literary works covered by Gale titles that contain the word. A search for

Russian and birth year range 1750-1850 will bring up a list of 24 authors. The searcher may then select a title or author and go to the corresponding record containing the Gale series title information. Search results may be displayed, printed, or copied to disk. Some print and download options may be adjusted during installation. There is no way to display or print only those titles owned by the library, nor can the user mark portions of a record (such as the tagged titles) for printing.

It is not easy to determine which volumes of the various Gale series are covered by the index. A quick check of table of contents entries from *Children's Literature Review* (see ARBA 93, entry 1141) found that the 1992 disk covers volumes 1-26. Volume 26 was the first of three volumes published in 1992. Because users will want to know which print indexes must also be searched, the title list in the documentation should be revised to indicate volume number ranges for each series.

Single-user and network installation procedures are easy to follow, and Gale provides toll-free technical assistance. Titles owned by the library may be tagged with a default or customized message (e.g., call number). The supporting documentation also uses examples of typical research scenarios to demonstrate the search options. A help card for point-of-use searching is included. On-screen help is available at any time by pressing a function key, although this option is omitted from the command menu at the bottom of the screen. Despite minor flaws, this time-saving index will be useful to any library that subscribes to some or all of the major literary series published by Gale.—**Deborah V. Rollins**

Periodicals and Serials

1162. **Directory of Literary Magazines 1993-94.** Wakefield, R.I., Moyer Bell, 1993. 262p. index. $10.95pa. Z6513.C37. LC 85-648720. ISBN 1-55921-065-6. ISSN 0884-6006.

The Council of Literary Magazines and Presses has produced a workmanlike directory of some 500 literary magazines, published either in North America or abroad. It contains all the relevant information about each publication: title, address, and telephone number; editor; editorial statement; payment (often in copies of the magazine); copyright; and subscription price. Of this, the editorial statements, quoted directly from the editor, are the most interesting and revealing, being sometimes quirky and always individualistic. Each entry is clearly arranged, set off from the next one with ample white space to make it stand out.

For all this, it is doubtful that the *Directory of Literary Magazines* will be a necessary purchase for many libraries, not while the doyen of such publications, *International Directory of Little Magazines and Small Presses* (see ARBA 92, entry 636) is available. The *International Directory* includes the same information about each entry but has 10 times the number of entries, and it includes little magazines in all subject areas, from crime and criticism to labor and law. That work also has a subject index that enables the user to sift out the literary magazines from the political or ecological, and a regional index for both U.S. states and foreign countries. Unless a library specializes only in things literary, why not spend the extra money (about $15) for the larger volume?—**Terry Ann Mood**

CHILDREN'S LITERATURE

Bibliography

1163. **American Library Association Best of the Best for Children.** Denise Perry Donavin, ed. Chicago, American Library Association, 1992. 366p. illus. index. $30.00; $20.00pa. Z1037.A496. 011.62. LC 92-24234. ISBN 0-679-40450-3; 0-679-74250-6pa.

"Success grows from the passion to know, a passion stimulated and satisfied by the special content of quality media" (p. xiii). Supported by this belief, the editor of and contributors, advisers, and consultants to this book have labored to compile a list of about 1,500 books, magazines, videos, audiotapes, computer software programs, toys, and travel experiences recommended for adults to share with children. Each type of media has a separate chapter with an introduction, and the annotated entries are arranged alphabetically by title within age levels that range from infancy through the teenage years. An author-title index is included, and supplemental bibliographies for adults are found at the end of each chapter.

The intent of this book is to identify and recommend quality materials to share with children in a nonschool setting. And the items included here are truly quality materials that both children and adults can enjoy. Furthermore, there is a continuing emphasis on leading the child from audiovisual materials back to books, partially accomplished through sections called "Connections," included in the entries (where relevant) and listing specific books related to the main entry. Throughout the book, materials on a specific theme, such as "Fractured Fairy Tales," "Multicultural Fare," or sex education, are gathered together and highlighted. This is a nice idea, and it works well intellectually. Unfortunately, the physical layout does not support these sections, and they often interrupt a regular entry mid-sentence for two or three pages. Extensive cross-referencing within and between entries broadens the utility of this bibliography, but more page numbers in the body of the text would have facilitated use. Page numbers are given only for titles in the same chapter as the reference or in thematic sections. Most of the time, users must look up the title in the index in order to locate it. The sections on materials for younger users and for media are especially current and useful, but the section on teenage reading lists more older classics, such as Robert Cormier's *The Chocolate War* (1974) and Betsy Byars's *Summer of the Swans* (1971). More recent titles could have been included here.

Overall, this title does identify and promote the use of quality materials for children, and it is especially valuable because it includes nonbook items. It will be most useful in public libraries in communities with involved parents or in private homes. It could also be used in collection development. Recommended.
—**Carol A. Doll**

1164. Bodart, Joni Richards. **100 World-Class Thin Books, or What to Read When Your Book Report Is Due Tomorrow!.** Englewood, Colo., Libraries Unlimited, 1993. 204p. index. $27.50. Z1037.B66. 028.1'62. LC 92-2351. ISBN 0-87287-986-0.

What school (not to mention many a public) librarian has not sought in vain for such a book as this when asked the inevitable, "My book report is due in the morning. Do you have a thin book...?" Aptly subtitled, this long-awaited gem from well-known booktalk expert Bodart has its titles conveniently arranged into thin, thinner, and thinnest categories. All books included are 200 pages in length or less, suitable for middle and high school students, and "good reads."

The book is particularly geared to the needs of students. The book entries include, besides basic bibliographical data, such items as grade level, related subject areas, readability (e.g., quick read, average, thoughtful), genre, and paperback availability. Then six major areas follow with more than enough ideas to launch even the most reluctant reader successfully into a book report, whether oral or written. Areas included are subjects of the book, characters, an actual brief booktalk, major ideas or themes, book report ideas, and booktalk ideas. Needless to say, all of these features should prove useful to librarians and teachers as well.

A special bonus is the appendixes, which offer tips for effective book reports and booktalks. The indexing is especially well done. Besides an author, a title, and a curriculum-area index, there are indexes by genre, readability, and specific subjects. Subjects included appear to be those popular with young adults (e.g., child abuse, crime and delinquency), and there are 13 different genre categories represented.

The choice of titles is varied and balanced, including books for both sexes and those by classic and contemporary authors, from John Steinbeck to Jerry Spinelli. This is a definite first-purchase choice for school and public librarians and for teachers who wish to encourage and motivate their students to read. [R: SLMQ, Summer 93, p. 264; VOYA, Aug 93, p. 187]—**Carol Truett**

1165. **Books for You: A Booklist for Senior High Students.** Shirley Wurth, ed., and the Committee on the Senior High School Booklist of the National Council of Teachers of English. Urbana, Ill., National Council of Teachers of English, 1992. 259p. index. (NCTE Bibliography Series). $16.95pa. Z1037.B724. 011.62'5. LC 92-26206. ISBN 0-8141-0365-0.

This is the 11th edition of a list of books recommended to high school students and their teachers. Nearly 800 fiction and nonfiction titles published between 1988 and 1991 are divided into 33 subject areas that range from adventure and survival to science and the environment, careers and jobs, and sports.

A directory of publishers and indexes of authors, titles, and subjects are included. In general, a wide variety of topics, genres, and reading levels are listed. The 60 entries under biography and autobiography include both famous and ordinary people (e.g., women, scientists, rock stars, sports figures, and minorities). The annotations, written for young adults, adequately represent the books and could appeal to young readers. One major strength of this bibliography is the mixture of fiction and nonfiction titles under most subject headings.

As with all books of this nature, one can approve of or quarrel with specific authors or titles included or omitted. Still, some sections could be stronger. While such authors as Isaac Asimov, A. C. Crispin, and Anne McCaffrey are represented in the science fiction section, David Brin, Lois McMaster Bujold, Larry Niven, and Charles Sheffield are not. Also, only five titles are identified as Westerns. Is it that there are not more Westerns of sufficient quality, or is it that the compilers would rather have young adults read biography? And given the nature of young adult preferences, it would be nice if there were an indication of which titles are available in paperback. While not the definitive bibliography of trade publications, this is a very useful list for high school teachers, library media specialists, and young adult librarians. [R: EL, Mar-April 93, p. 47; RBB, 15 Feb 93, p. 1080; SLMQ, Spring 93, p. 198; VOYA, June 93, p. 123]—**Carol A. Doll**

1166. Criscoe, Betty, and Philip J. Lanasa, III. **Award-Winning Books for Children and Young Adults 1990-1991.** Metuchen, N.J., Scarecrow, 1993. 702p. illus. index. $79.50.

This volume complements the initial volume (see ARBA 91, entry 1110), which contained the 1989 winners in literature for children and young adults. Listed are 234 awards from around the world, an increase of 32 awards over those in the previous volume. Awards are listed alphabetically, and many have annotations and biographical and bibliographical information about the author. The covers of some titles are also shown in black-and-white. Following the text are appendixes that list books in various categories: "Hall of Fame," age/grade level, genre, and subject (the latter added since the prior volume). Alphabetically indexed are articles, authors, awards, books, films, illustrators, people receiving special awards, and translators.

The book is intended as a reference tool for librarians, teachers, parents, bookstore owners, scholars, children, and young adults. It seems unlikely that it would be accessible to very many children and young adults, but writers and editors of children's and young adult literature could also use the information in a variety of ways. Knowing what kinds of books have received awards and the companies that published them would be quite useful to authors seeking ideas and markets for their own work.

Because the information in this volume could be valuable to many people, it would see much use if made available to the general public. The print is easy to read and the book opens nearly flat for easy access, but copies receiving heavy use might need reinforcement to keep the spine from separating. The latest awards are not listed, of course, due to the long lead time required for publication, but what this volume does, it does very well. It should be a welcome addition to any reference collection. [R: BR, Nov/Dec 93, p. 38; EL, Sept-Oct 93, pp. 43-44; RBB, 1 Sept 93, p. 82; SLMQ, Summer 93, p. 265]

—**Kay O. Cornelius**

1167. Cucheran, Ruby, and others. **A Palette of Possibilities: Integrating the Visual and Literary Arts through Picture Books.** Vancouver, B.C., Vancouver School Board, 1992. 225p. illus. $25.40pa. 011.62. ISBN 1-55031-352-5.

This volume selects picture books for use across the curriculum in such subjects as science, math, and social studies. The first of its three major sections consists of unannotated lists of titles in which major artistic techniques, such as line, pattern, or color, are prominent. The second section, arranged by author, is an annotated bibliography that lists artistic elements and techniques and briefly suggests cross-curricular activities. The final section of seven appendixes includes a list of illustrators, a title index, and an annotated bibliography of alphabet books.

Although its introduction claims that this volume "is not simply another bibliography to support selection of curriculum resources," it does not establish "useful connections between picture book resources and the artistic elements and principles of design that are the basis of visual arts education." For one thing, it never explains how the artistic elements it lists have any bearing on other matters. How does accepting that line is the main artistic element in *Where the Wild Things Are* help a teacher to present that title or to connect it to other curricular pursuits? The book needs far more than four detailed examples to aid the puzzled teacher. The suggested uses for titles are conventional, but sensitive educators will cringe at the lack of grammatical understanding in the directive to "Find command, active, and passive verb tenses in the book." A few activities have children applying their understanding of a work's major artistic technique, but these are too few to make this a recommendable title.—**Raymond E. Jones**

1168. Estes, Sally, ed. **Popular Reading for Children III: A Collection of *Booklist* Columns.** Chicago, American Library Association, 1992. 64p. index. $4.95pa. ISBN 0-8389-7599-2.

The third in a series of compilations of *Booklist*'s "Popular Reading" columns, this annotated list covers the seven years since the 1986 edition (see ARBA 87, entry 1086). Each bibliographic article is devoted to a single subject. Included are animal fantasy, historical fiction, humor for various ages, boys' favorites, eerie reading, and teen romance. The list concludes with a discussion of series titles and recommendations for other good reading for upper primary and middle school children. While some of the titles are older, they are standards or classics found in many school and most public library collections.

Although a portion of the articles appear exactly as they did in *Booklist*, some earlier lists have been updated to include more recent titles. Each entry includes author, title, publisher, date, price, ISBN, an annotation, and grade level. The work is indexed by both author and title. Librarians will find this handy, inexpensive tool useful for advising children in their book selection. [R: SLMQ, Spring 93, p. 197]
—**Joann H. Lee**

1169. Fakih, Kimberly Olson. **The Literature of Delight: A Critical Guide to Humorous Books for Children.** New Providence, N.J., R. R. Bowker/Reed Reference Publishing, 1993. 269p. index. $39.95. Z6514.W5F35. 016.827008'09282. LC 93-20159. ISBN 0-8352-3027-9.

Including 784 annotations of fiction and nonfiction works written by North American, British, and Australian authors, this source includes such diverse listings as fables, jokes, poems, and short stories targeted to ages 3-14. Some surprises pop up, such as *Little Women* and *Hansel and Gretel*, which some might not classify as humorous. Yet of the 17 categories established by the author, these works appear to fit within the guidelines of "laughter together" and "gothic humor." Brief critical annotations also include the book's format, price, availability, and target level. Rounding out the work are indexes for authors, illustrators, titles, subjects, and characters. Some 70 percent of the entries have been published within the last 10 years.

Unlike *Robert Quakenbush's Treasury of Humor* (Doubleday, 1990), which is a picture book for children, this source is written for adults to guide children's reading. The range of formats included is impressive, even covering picture books, board books, anthologies, and short riddles. Likewise, it is encouraging to see such subject headings as "Self-esteem" and "Tolerance" as a means for children to learn through humor.

This work should prove to be popular with children's librarians, teachers, parents, and educators. It will be useful for public, school, and academic collections. [R: WLB, Sept 93, p. 118]—**Ilene F. Rockman**

1170. Hayden, Carla D., ed. **Venture into Cultures: A Resource Book of Multicultural Materials and Programs.** Chicago, American Library Association, 1992. 165p. illus. index. $25.00pa. Z1037.9.V46. 011.62. LC 91-43373. ISBN 0-8389-0579-X.

In seven chapters, each authored by different librarians, educators, or members of the American Library Association, this book offers resources that cover the African-American, Arab-American, Asian-American, Hispanic-American, Jewish, Native American, and Persian-American cultures. Following an introduction, each section includes a bibliography of recommended titles, some programming ideas, and a list of resources for adults. To be included, a cultural or ethnic group has to reside in the United States in significant numbers, and items recommended have to be deemed accurate in terms of cultural representation. The bibliographies for each chapter include sections for fiction, nonfiction, picture books, and folklore. An effort was made to include alternative and small press titles. A selected bibliography of materials for adults is appended, and an index to the volume is subdivided by culture.

The range of cultures included in this title is quite broad, which is an advantage. The programming suggestions given are practical and creative and probably would be successful in a library or media center setting. However, except for those for the Arab-American and Native American cultures, they tend to stress holidays or festivals. (One activity suggests making greeting cards for Martin Luther King Day.)

The bibliographies of recommended titles for each chapter do contain a good variety of authors and titles, but they are sometimes rather brief and may be too limited. For example, of 39 titles listed in the nonfiction section for the Native American chapter (which emphasizes the tribes of the Great Plains), there are 12 titles about the Aztec, Mayan, and Incan cultures, but no titles about the Native Americans of the Pacific Northwest. There are other bibliographies that are more comprehensive that librarians and media specialists could consult for multicultural books, such as *Our Family, Our Friends, Our World* (see ARBA 93, entry 1127). Although there is a list of contributors in the book, little information is given about the experience or education that would qualify them to compile the materials in each chapter. Finally, the preface states, "The annotated lists within each chapter include ... media." This would have been an important contribution to multicultural materials. Unfortunately, very few media have been included. The Hispanic-American chapter is the only one with a section in the bibliography identified as media audiovisual materials. A few films, sound recordings, filmstrips, and book and cassette sets are scattered throughout the other chapters, and some catalogs are given as sources for audiovisual items. Such materials are available, as shown by *School Library Journal*'s six-part series on cultural diversity videos (published between January 1992 and September 1993). This title could be useful for its programming ideas, but other titles provide more depth in the bibliographies and appropriate audiovisual materials. [R: BL, 1 Jan 93, p. 813; EL, Mar-April 93, pp. 45-46; SLJ, May 93, p. 36]—**Carol A. Doll**

1171. Helbig, Alethea K., and Agnes Perkins. **Dictionary of American Children's Fiction, 1985-1989: Books of Recognized Merit.** Westport, Conn., Greenwood Press, 1993. 368p. index. $55.00. PS374.C454H45. 813'.54099282'03. LC 92-19613. ISBN 0-313-27719-2.

This work brings together in one volume the award-winning children's and young adult fiction for the five-year period between 1985 and 1989. It is the first in a planned series of five-year updates and does not include children's picture books. The authors, both professors of children's literature, claim to have read every title cited and have written lengthy plot summaries and their own critical analyses for each one. Included with each title entry is the award or awards the work has received. Author entries include a brief biography and mention of the person's previous works and awards, and character entries describe that character's importance to the story. Asterisks next to an entry indicate that there are additional entries for that title in the dictionary. Although there can be as many as five entries for each title, the entries do not duplicate each other.

The intended audience is primarily children's librarians and teachers, although Helbig and Perkins include literary scholars, parents, and booksellers as potential users as well. Regardless of the awards given to a particular work, they offer commentary for each title and provide their own opinions about the work's literary merit based on depth of characterization, believability of plot, and the handling of sensitive subjects (e.g., sexual abuse, domestic violence). A list of awards given to children's books is provided in the back of the book. This list lumps together all the titles receiving any given award over a five-year period, but, unfortunately, the exact year in which each title received its award is not mentioned. The authors also do not state whether the awards list is exhaustive or whether only certain awards were chosen for inclusion in this book. Such information would have been valuable for the layperson interested in definitions for each award and the awards' criteria. Nonetheless, children's librarians and teachers will be able to refer to this comprehensive work for its detailed plot summaries, authors' biographies, character analyses, and awards received. [R: LJ, Jan 93, p. 98; RBB, June 93, p. 1880]—**Patricia A. Sarles**

1172. Helbig, Alethea K., and Agnes Regan Perkins. **Dictionary of Children's Fiction from Australia, Canada, India, New Zealand, and Selected African Countries: Books of Recognized Merit.** Westport, Conn., Greenwood Press, 1992. 583p. index. $85.00. PR9084.H45. 823.009'9282'09171241. LC 91-35234. ISBN 0-313-26126-1.

Information about English-language children's books written in countries other than the United States and Great Britain is difficult to locate. This dictionary lists such literature from Canada, Australia, New Zealand, India, Nigeria, and South Africa. Australia and Canada are the best represented, with 76 and 53 authors, respectively. Picture books are excluded, but 263 fiction titles, most of which have won literary or library awards, are listed. Annotations are long enough to describe the plot and the important characters in each book; they give a good sense of the tone and quality of the story. Entries are also given for authors and main characters. Appendixes list the authors and titles by country and the books by awards. A detailed index provides subject access.

This carefully researched and sound critical work not only introduces U.S. teachers and librarians to many books unknown to them but also evaluates the works and gives an overview of the literary production of the various countries. Works of this kind are useful in increasing children's understanding and appreciation of other countries and cultures. This book deserves a place in most libraries and professional education collections, and publishers could use it to select titles for publication in the United States. [R: Choice, May 93, p. 1442; RBB, Aug 92, p. 2035]—**Adele M. Fasick**

1173. Jensen, Julie M., and Nancy L. Roser, eds. **Adventuring with Books: A Booklist for Pre-K - Grade 6.** 10th ed. Urbana, Ill., National Council of Teachers of English, 1993. 603p. index. (NCTE Bibliography Series). $19.95pa. Z1037.N346. 011.62. LC 93-30112. ISBN 0-8141-0079-1.

This edition, as did its predecessors, brings together an annotated list of recommended books for the elementary years. A product of the College of Education at the University of Texas, Austin, the guide includes 2,000 annotated titles published between 1988 and 1992, making it smaller than *Children's Catalog* (see ARBA 92, entry 610) and much smaller than *A to Zoo* (R. R. Bowker, 1993). The titles continue to be grouped under 13 headings, such as biography, celebrations, classics, and fantasy. The brief annotations are mostly descriptive, with a dash of evaluation. All included titles are recommended for libraries and the home. Author and title indexes are adequate, but the subject index, while extensive, could be coordinated with its competitors for a more in-depth analysis. Although relatively small considering the huge number of children's books available, *Adventuring* is recommended for all libraries, teachers, and parents interested in children's literature and in building quality collections for the younger set.—**David V. Loertscher**

1174. **Kids' Favorite Books: Children's Choices 1989-1991.** New York, Children's Book Council and Newark, Del., International Reading Association, 1992. 96p. illus. index. $8.00pa. ISBN 0-87207-370-X.

1175. **Teens' Favorite Books: Young Adults' Choices 1987-1992.** Newark, Del., International Reading Association, 1992. 78p. illus. index. $8.00pa. ISBN 0-87207-378-5.

A joint committee of the Children's Book Council and the International Reading Association cooperated in producing these two books. They include titles chosen by young people for the years specified in the titles. Each includes standard bibliographical information (usually for hardcover editions) and a brief annotation. The focus of the annotations is on the appeal of each title to young readers. Because these are selective lists, all of the annotations are positive. No comparisons are made to indicate whether the books differ in literary or artistic merit, although they range from critically acclaimed works by authors of the stature of Cynthia Voigt and Rosemary Sutcliffe to ephemeral high school romances. *Kids' Favorite Books* lists titles under the age groups of the intended readers; *Teens' Favorite Books* lists them under broad subject headings. Indexes by author and title (and illustrator for the children's books) make access to individual works easier. These bibliographies will be useful to teachers and parents. Librarians may want to use them to supplement more standard selection aids.—**Adele M. Fasick**

1176. Lima, Carolyn W., and John A. Lima. **A to Zoo: Subject Access to Children's Picture Books.** 4th ed. New Providence, N.J., R. R. Bowker/Reed Reference Publishing, 1993. 1158p. illus. index. $49.95. Z1037.L715. 011.62. LC 93-6224. ISBN 0-8352-3201-8.

It grows and grows. *A to Zoo* began as a way to find picture books by very specific subjects because the *Sears List of Subject Headings* and the LC/AC list were so poor. Both the scope and function of the tool now expands in the 4th edition to embrace a major collection-building tool. There is no more comprehensive (but selective) source of information about picture books. *A to Zoo*'s size speaks of the rapid proliferation of picture books in the past 10 years. This edition lists 14,000 picture books with complete bibliographical descriptions arranged by author (but not annotations, as *Children's Catalog* [see ARBA 92, entry 610] has). A second section lists each title under several of 800 subject headings. Title and illustrator indexes are also provided.

The subject heading method deserves mention. Rather than adopt standard library subject heading practice, *A to Zoo* uses indirect entry. Thus, individual animal names are arranged under animals (e.g., Animals - Mice; Animals - Oxen). This indirect approach actually makes the list more useful for collection development because there are fewer places to look for building collections that emphasize particular topics. However, users cannot take these subject headings and transfer them into automated systems without conversion.

As a collection-building tool or as a place to find "that certain book" on a specific topic, this tool is without peer. Its price is very reasonable considering its scope. It is essential for elementary school and children's libraries and research collections dealing with children's literature. [R: SLMQ, Fall 93, p. 56]—**David V. Loertscher**

1177. Montanaro, Ann R. **Pop-Up and Movable Books: A Bibliography.** Metuchen, N.J., Scarecrow, 1993. 559p. index. $59.50. Z1033.T68M65. 016.7416'42. LC 92-39374. ISBN 0-8108-2650-X.

Books in which actions by the reader cause motion in the illustrations are the subject of this extensive bibliography. More than 1,600 such books published in English between the 1850s and 1991 are listed and described. An introduction gives the interesting history of these books with movable parts, from centuries-old scholarly works to the complex, sophisticated publications for children produced today. The preface explains the various types of movable illustrations and the terminology used to describe them.

Entries are arranged alphabetically by title, and each entry contains standard bibliographical data as well as a brief description that includes the number and type of movable illustrations. Considerable attention has been given to providing complete descriptions, even where paging and other publication information was not readily available. A verification statement indicates the source of the information about the book.

Many books of this type appear in series; thus, there is a series index containing as many titles as could be verified. A names index includes not only the usual author and illustrator but also such various contributors as paper engineers and designers. The date index categorizes the titles by publication date as closely as possible.

Titles intended for adult readers as well as children are included, and it is occasionally difficult to determine from the description the intended audience of the books. Even a broad indication would have been helpful. Users are limited to author and title searches of the books; the omission of a subject index is a hindrance.

Pop-up and movable books have been addressed only marginally in professional literature, and they are seldom listed in reviews or bibliographies. The comprehensive and unique nature of this book makes it a useful tool that will be welcomed by librarians, historians, and collectors.—**Joanne Kelly**

1178. Roberts, Patricia L., and Nancy Lee Cecil. **Developing Multicultural Awareness through Children's Literature: A Guide for Teachers and Librarians, Grades K-8.** Jefferson, N.C., McFarland, 1993. 216p. index. $24.95pa. Z1361.E4R63. 305.8'00973. LC 93-15144. ISBN 0-89950-879-0.

This bibliography provides almost 240 listings of multicultural fiction, folk literature, and biography appropriate for elementary through junior high school students. (Some listings are duplicated in the different grade level sections, and all are duplicated in the extended activities sections, so it is not possible to determine the exact number of works included.) The authors feel these works will aid teachers and librarians in modifying cultural stereotypes. There are five major subsections: African-American, Asian-American, European-American, Latino-American, and Native American. The book is further subdivided by grade levels K-3 and 4-8. Each listing, besides giving complete bibliographical data and a thorough annotation, provides a target activity aimed at helping "children internalize ways to modify cultural stereotypes." For example, Ai-Ling Louie's *Yeh-Shen: A Cinderella Story from China* (Putnam, 1988) has as its target activity or theme "The Cinderella Story Is Found in Different Cultures" and even lists eight other versions for comparison. Some titles also include optional activities, such as related books to read or role-playing scenarios. The most unusual feature of the book is provided by the two concluding sections, which contain about 20 extended activity units. These contain a full teaching unit with theme, overview, new vocabulary words, activity materials, motivating activities, purpose for reading and listening, discussion questions, retelling, additional extended activities, interdisciplinary ideas, and recreational reading.

Besides increasing the number of these extended units and correcting a few editing glitches, there is little to criticize in this work, which seems fairly straightforward and easy to use. Most titles have current publication dates or are well known enough to be available. The book's price is reasonable enough to fit into many school and most public library budgets; it is also affordable for individuals.
—**Carol Truett**

1179. Roberts, Patricia L., Nancy L. Cecil, and Sharon Alexander. **Gender Positive! A Teachers' and Librarians' Guide to Nonstereotyped Children's Literature, K-8.** Jefferson, N.C., McFarland, 1993. 192p. index. $24.95pa. LB1575.R63. 372.64. LC 92-56686. ISBN 0-89950-816-2.

More than 200 fiction and nonfiction books from the nineteenth and twentieth centuries (1884-1992) are contained in this selective K-8 bibliography and teaching guide. Coverage includes biographies, folk literature, and various forms of fiction (historical, realistic, and fanciful). Although no specific criteria for inclusion are noted, the introductory essay does mention gender balance, occupational variety, reversal of traditional roles, variety in character types, and contributions of both females and males. The authors indicate that books have been included "whose main characters have one or more of the valued attributes noted earlier." Annotations are descriptive and approximately a paragraph in length. They are followed by several paragraphs of follow-up discussion, research, or writing activities to be used by the teacher. Extended activity units for grades K-3 and 4-8 conclude the work. The biographical section omits titles about Billie Jean King, Amelia Earhart, and Eleanor Roosevelt, and there is no bibliography of further references.

This source continues the tradition of *Girls Are People Too!* (see ARBA 83, entry 139) and *A Guide to Non-Sexist Children's Books* (see ARBA 77, entry 1142) but also includes instructional strategies. It can be useful as long as teachers and librarians recognize its limitations. [R: BR, Nov/Dec 93, p. 38; LAR, Dec 93, p. 698]—**Ilene F. Rockman**

1180. Schon, Isabel. **Books in Spanish for Children and Young Adults: An Annotated Guide. Series VI. Libros Infantiles y Juveniles en Espanol.** Metuchen, N.J., Scarecrow, 1993. 291p. index. $35.00. Z1037.7.S384. 016.8609'9282. LC 92-33302. ISBN 0-8108-2622-4.

This book is a guide to bilingual books, as well as books in Spanish, for preschool to high school readers. The books are on subjects such as lifestyles, literature, biography, and history. This volume covers books from 15 countries published since 1989, although, as in previous volumes, books are mainly from Spain, Argentina, Mexico, and the United States.

Books are first listed by country of origin and then by subject. Information for each includes availability, price, and recommended grade levels. Schon uses four descriptors to rate the books: outstanding, marginal, not recommended, and "caveat emptor" (little literary or artistic quality). Entries that fall under the first three ratings usually include short annotations that summarize and evaluate the books. The appendix includes a list of book dealers in Spanish-speaking countries and a list of U.S. book dealers specializing in books in Spanish. Schon tries to make it as easy as possible to obtain these books. Also included are title and author indexes. This book will be primarily useful to libraries wishing to build or expand Spanish-language collections for children. [R: RBB, 15 May 93, p. 1718]—**Carl Pracht**

1181. Shapiro, Lillian L., and Barbara L. Stein. **Fiction for Youth: A Guide to Recommended Books.** 3d ed. New York, Neal-Schuman, 1992. 263p. index. $35.00pa. Z1037.F44. 016.80883'083. LC 92-33190. ISBN 1-55570-113-2.

Based on the premise that there are many good twentieth-century fiction titles available, this annotated bibliography recommends a wide variety of specific titles to young adults. While the work primarily lists adult titles, some young adult books are also included. The intent of this bibliography is to motivate capable readers to read more or higher-quality books. It is arranged alphabetically by author, and there are title and subject indexes.

Overall, the authors were successful in compiling a fine list of books. Many genres are represented here, from classics, science fiction, and suspense and mystery to historical fiction and contemporary realism. This indicates a willingness to recognize fine writing independent of its category. Many of the good young adult authors are represented here, such as Sue Ellen Bridgers, Robert Cormier, and Walter Dean Myers. Furthermore, the bibliography includes titles that reflect a wide variety of ethnic and cultural backgrounds, including Japanese, African, Latin American, French, British, Indian, Native American, Black American, Jewish, and Chinese. A thorough subject index allows access by topic, genre, or geographical location.

While somewhat uneven in quality, the annotations do generally convey the tone of each book, explore its character development, and convey a sense of its strengths. At the same time, it would be helpful if copyright dates were given for each title. For example, no date is given for Geoffrey Household's *Rogue Male* (1937), and the only date given for Elliott Arnold's *Blood Brother* is 1979 (it was first published in 1947).

Generally, this is a good list of books for young adults and some adult readers. It will be of most interest to high school library media centers, public libraries, and community colleges. [R: BR, Nov/Dec 93, p. 38; VOYA, Aug 93, p. 189]—**Carol A. Doll**

1182. Sherman, Gale W., and Bette D. Ammon. **Rip-Roaring Reads for Reluctant Teen Readers.** Englewood, Colo., Libraries Unlimited, 1993. 164p. illus. index. $22.50pa. Z1037.S524. 028.5'35. LC 93-6439. ISBN 1-56308-094-X.

Unfortunately, the world is divided into readers and nonreaders. And somewhere between the love affair that kindergartners and first graders have with books and reading, and fifth or sixth grade, many students lose this enthusiasm. This book is specifically aimed at this broad group of youngsters, commonly called reluctant readers, that frustrates teachers, media specialists, and often their parents.

The authors have pulled together the basic booktalking scoop on 40 carefully selected "contemporary, spellbinding books" evenly divided between middle and junior high and high school, and all written by outstanding authors. Criteria for selection were recent publication date, short length, appealing format, eye-catching cover, high interest, meaningful subject matter, appropriate reading level, notable authors, and excellent writing. Each three-page book entry consists of complete ordering information, genre, themes, reading and interest levels, review sources, author and plot information, how to introduce the book, and two versions of mini-booktalks (in the aisle and in the author's own words). There are also literature and curriculum extensions for each as well as alternative book report activities and three reproducible bookmarks that promote further reading by the same author, genre, theme, or topic area. The latter features also foster curriculum integration and team teaching activities between librarian and teacher, as do the five indexes (e.g., genre, curricular activities). The layout and format of the book are excellent, facilitating both "on the fly" booktalking as well as in-depth planning with faculty.

The only complaints are that the authors did not include more books, especially more mysteries, including one by Lois Duncan. However, she is included on a bookmark, and the authors achieved their own purposes with the work, which was not to be comprehensive but selective and to build bridges to other, similar works. A superb tool for today's overworked librarian or teacher, this book should not be overlooked. It appears to have been very carefully edited and to include what were very difficult but discriminating choices by the authors; thus, it is highly recommended for all schools with grades 6-12. It should also be in public libraries for parent and librarian use as a reader's advisory.—**Carol Truett**

1183. Storey, Dee. **Twins in Children's and Adolescent Literature: An Annotated Bibliography.** Metuchen, N.J., Scarecrow, 1993. 399p. index. $42.50. Z1037.A1S82. 016.8109'9282. LC 92-40560. ISBN 0-8108-2641-0.

Books of fiction that have twins as characters are described here. The 366 stories analyzed were published between 1904 and 1992 and include in- and out-of-print titles the author was able to locate. There are individual titles as well as books in series, books in which twins are the central characters, books in which twins are secondary or even minor characters, books with twin animal characters, and books about characters that seem to be twins but are not.

The numbered entries are organized by author. Each entry includes bibliographical data, a grade level recommendation, an annotation, information about the twin's family, information about the twins, and a list of related subject headings (both to the story in general and to the twins in particular). Many entries also have interesting notes about the fictional twins from their authors.

Four indexes should markedly increase the usefulness of the book. A twin index identifies the books according to the place of the twins in the stories—as main, secondary, or minor characters. Each of these categories is further subdivided into identical twins, fraternal twins, or those not identified as either.

Author, title, and subject indexes are also appended. Unfortunately, errors mar the accuracy of the indexes. For example, the main characters in *Jacob Have I Loved* are listed as female/male twins. There are occasional blind references from subjects listed in the entries to those in the index. Most regrettably, numbers listed in the indexes are sometimes given inaccurately and lead to incorrect entries.

The topic of twins as a subject for bibliographies has been addressed only marginally in professional literature. The comprehensive nature of this book makes it a unique and useful tool in spite of its shortcomings. [R: BR, Nov/Dec 93, p. 57; LAR, Oct 93, p. 568; RBB, 15 May 93, p. 1725; SLMQ, Summer 93, p. 266]—**Joanne Kelly**

1184. Thomas, James L. **Play, Learn, and Grow: An Annotated Guide to the Best Books and Materials for Very Young Children.** New Providence, N.J., R. R. Bowker/Reed Reference Publishing, 1992. 439p. index. $27.00. Z1037.T46. 028.1'62. LC 92-15458. ISBN 0-8352-3019-8.

This work is intended as a selection guide to print and nonprint resources for use with preschool children. The thrust of *Play, Learn, and Grow* is the literacy development of very young children, and opening articles discuss current theory and practice in the field along with practical suggestions for implementation. Especially useful is "Matching Books to Young Children," a detailed chart of characteristic growth patterns and their implications for selection and use of books at each stage of development, along with examples of suitable titles.

The materials included in the book have been selected using criteria that address literary quality, appropriateness of material, and educational value. Some 1,074 titles have met those criteria. In addition to books and magazines, there are entries for selected audiocassettes, compact discs, filmstrips, records, computer software, and videocassettes. While many classics for children are included, the majority of the works have been published within the last 15 years.

Entries are arranged alphabetically by title, and each entry contains a brief annotation as well as bibliographical data, age recommendation, subject headings, and genre type. In addition, purchase priority, other published review sources, and awards are given. An additional annotated list of 97 selected professional print resources provides practical and useful background information for parents, educators, and librarians. Another list gives information about organizations that provide assistance to those who work with preschoolers. The book closes with name, subject, age/category, age/purchase priority, and format indexes. *Play, Learn, and Grow* is a well-organized and useful resource and an invaluable collection development tool for those involved with early childhood education. [R: EL, May-June 93, pp. 46-47; RBB, 15 Feb 93, p. 1084; SLMQ, Spring 93, p. 198; WLB, Mar 93, p. 113]—**Joanne Kelly**

1185. Walter, Virginia A. **War and Peace Literature for Children and Young Adults: A Resource Guide to Significant Issues.** Phoenix, Ariz., Oryx Press, 1993. 171p. index. $27.50pa. U21.2.W3445. 303.6'6. LC 92-29729. ISBN 0-89774-725-9.

Anyone considering this work should also examine the very similar work by Phyllis K. Kennemer, *Using Literature to Teach Middle Grades about War* (Oryx Press, 1993). However, there are several major differences in the two titles. For example, *War and Peace* is broader in scope, not limited to only six major U.S. wars; it includes material on other wars as well as on the problems involved in creating peace. It also lists works for children of all ages, not just grades 6 through 8.

Another major difference is that Walter devotes almost a third of her bibliography to children's developmental needs and related issues, tying these to the use of this type of material. She includes such problems as the difficulty a young child has in comprehending certain events or situations, such as concentration camps, the Holocaust, or the bombing of Hiroshima, and children's lack of a historical perspective. Especially good advice on guidelines and cautions in selecting and using books on war with young children is presented, and the author relates this to Jean Piaget's stages of cognitive development.

There is also a very fine overview of the major themes and issues involved in learning about war, such as the tension between the futility and the nobility of war, heroism, survival, the child's perspective, and ideology or propaganda and how it generally fails to achieve its purpose. This discussion, which comprises the first three chapters, is punctuated with references to books that illustrate Walter's major points. Also noteworthy are the work's sections on peace and conflict resolution, timeless truths from folk and fairy tales, and poems that show the ridiculousness of anger and war.

Concise annotations are provided for each of the 480 items in the bibliography, plus complete citations and suggested grade levels. Both well-known and lesser-known titles are included. Other special features are a final annotated section of resources for adults, a literature web for teaching Katherine Paterson's *Park's Quest*, and an activity web for Eleanor Coerr's *Sadako and the Thousand Paper Cranes*. Four indexes, including one of broad subjects, enhance the book's usefulness, particularly for curriculum development purposes.

Given the current world situation, a library or individual that has the funds should probably purchase both of these works. If one must make a choice, consider *Using Literature* first if a narrower focus is desired and *War and Peace* if the developmental issues involved in teaching these sensitive topics are of more concern, as this is Walter's strong point. [R: SLJ, July 93, p. 34]—**Carol Truett**

Biography

1186. Gallo, Donald R., comp. and ed. **Speaking for Ourselves, Too: More Autobiographical Sketches by Notable Authors of Books for Young Adults.** Urbana, Ill., National Council of Teachers of English, 1993. 235p. illus. $14.95pa. PS129.S644. 813'.54099283. LC 92-44193. ISBN 0-8141-4623-6.

This companion volume to *Speaking for Ourselves* (see ARBA 91, entry 1118) profiles 89 additional writers for young adults. Adhering to a format similar to that of the first volume, selected authors disclose interesting details about their lives and writing careers. Their comments are personal and engaging. Students will discover, for example, that Brock Cole had an almost parent-free childhood, moved from school to school, and enjoyed it all; and Sonia Levitan decided at the age of twelve to become a writer, loves it still but hates rejection. Each sketch averages one to two pages in length and is accompanied by a photograph and a bibliography of the author's works.

Throughout the book, in profile after profile, two patterns emerge. First, the majority of the authors express a love of reading. Second, they encourage perseverance when embarking on a writing career. Potential young authors could not receive more valuable advice for this profession or many other related ones.

For students needing comprehensive biographical information about contemporary authors, these brief profiles will not satisfy them. They will need to consult the *Sixth Book of Junior Authors & Illustrators* (see ARBA 90, entry 30). Librarians who regularly booktalk these authors, however, will find it a treasure. It offers just the right amount of chatty, intimate detail about a writers' lives that sheds light upon their writing themes, styles, and characters. It is also very helpful for preparing public relations posters, brochures, and handouts prior to an author's visit. School and public libraries should definitely acquire copies of both volumes. Their costs make them reference bargains. [R: SLMQ, Fall 93, p. 58]—**Kathleen W. Craver**

1187. **Major Authors and Illustrators for Children and Young Adults: A Selection of Sketches from *Something about the Author*.** By Laurie Collier and Joyce Nakamura. Detroit, Gale, 1993. 6v. illus. index. $265.00/set. LC 92-073849. ISBN 0-8103-7702-0.

In an attempt to provide a more affordable biographical source on children's authors, Gale has pulled together sketches from its *Something about the Author* (see ARBA 91, entry 1119) set, on more than 800 of the most popular authors and illustrators, into a single set of six volumes. Multiple entries for the same person were edited for this set, and 60 percent of the sketches were recorrected by the biographees themselves. A board of school and public librarians selected the people to be included by mail ballot, and emphasis is upon United States, Canadian, and United Kingdom coverage. As expected, entries are identical in format to the parent volumes and include a biographical sketch, a picture of the author (if available), a bibliography of writings by and about the author, sidelight anecdotes and sample illustrations from the author's works if appropriate, and a list of sources consulted. As with the original volumes, the user can expect accuracy and authority in the sketches.

The problem for librarians is, of course, whether they should purchase this set. For those that have complete holdings of *Something about the Author*, the answer is probably no. New collections could substitute this set in place of older volumes and begin their subscription to *Something about the Author* with the 1993 volumes. Libraries that hold incomplete runs should consult the set or its advertising, which lists the authors covered, before making a decision. At current prices, this set is a little more expensive than a single-year subscription to the main volumes—another factor that will help one weigh value versus coverage. For all libraries including children's literature, one of the two sets is a basic purchase. [R: Choice, May 93, p. 1444; RBB, 1 Jan 93, p. 826; SLJ, May 93, p. 136; VOYA, June 93, pp. 125-26; WLB, Mar 93, p. 112]—**David V. Loertscher**

1188. McElmeel, Sharron L. **An Author a Month (for Dimes).** Englewood, Colo., Teacher Ideas Press/Libraries Unlimited, 1993. 185p. illus. index. $23.50pa. Z718.1.M368. 027.62'5. LC 92-21381. ISBN 0-87287-952-6.

This third volume in the *Author a Month* group is a resource for teachers following the whole-language philosophy of connecting books to achieve broad curriculum goals. Similar to its 1988 and 1990 predecessors, it focuses on nine authors or illustrators (Martha Alexander, Caroline Arnold, Graeme Base, Byrd Baylor, Jan Brett, Anthony Browne, Joanna Cole, Eric Kimmel, and Janet Stevens) and provides abbreviated capsule units on three more (Demi, Keiko Kasza, and Patricia Polacco). Each chapter includes a reproducible author poster and large-type biography; an overview for the teacher; suggested introductory strategies; and an "Idea Cupboard," an annotated alphabetical bibliography that contains suggested activities. A cumulative index of McElmeel's *Author a Month* and *Bookpeople* (see ARBA 93, entry 1142) collections and a full index complete the book.

The summaries are useful selection guides, but the suggested activities vary markedly in quality. McElmeel notes that teachers must implement her basic ideas themselves, but more examples, such as a story map for a cumulative tale, would have made this work vastly more useful. Furthermore, too often, as with Anthony Browne's *Gorilla*, the emphasis on factual research ignores central thematic and literary elements. In addition, because of the alphabetical arrangement of the Idea Cupboard, teachers will have to devise programs to make the author units workable. These units, however, are the least significant element of this book, which is more useful for suggesting connections between the annotated titles and books by other authors. Teachers looking for a "canned" program will be disappointed; those willing to explore will find some useful suggestions for thematically connecting a wide variety of books. [R: SLMQ, Summer 93, p. 265]—**Raymond E. Jones**

Dictionaries and Encyclopedias

1189. Carruth, Gorton. **The Young Reader's Companion.** New Providence, N.J., R. R. Bowker/Reed Reference Publishing, 1993. 681p. illus. index. $39.95. PN1008.5.C373. 809'.89282'03. LC 93-6662. ISBN 0-8352-2765-0.

This illustrated encyclopedia aims at the promotion of reading among young people from the fifth grade onward. Some 800 of the more than 2000 brief, alphabetically arranged entries are on individual books recommended as good reads. Supplementing these title entries are approximately 750 on authors, 280 on historical personages, and 200 on myth, legend, imaginary places, and symbols. In addition to describing a book and indicating its reading level, entries frequently suggest related titles. A cross-referenced subject index makes research easy.

Although the clear, informative entries succeed in another stated objective—avoiding dry, intimidating prose—they are not without flaws. Author entries are inconsistent: Ostensibly including only material that illuminates an author's subjects, some contain traditional biographical data, whereas others do not even mention nationality. Content is also occasionally puzzling. For example, Esther Hautzig receives an entry, but the prolific Leon Garfield does not; all Chinua Achebe's novels, except the one called his most famous, are described; and winners of the American Newbery Award are cited, but not those of the British Carnegie Medal. Some entries also are dated; the one for Peter Dickinson mentions none of his award-winning books of the last 20 years. In spite of such flaws, some bland subject entries, and inclusion of too many adult books, this useful resource is a necessary purchase for any library that values young readers. [R: Choice, Dec 93, p. 581; RBB, 1 Nov 93, p. 571; VOYA, Oct 93, p. 260; WLB, Dec 93, p. 123]
—**Raymond E. Jones**

1190. Tuten-Puckett, Katharyn E. **My Name in Books: A Guide to Character Names in Children's Literature.** Englewood, Colo., Libraries Unlimited, 1993. 242p. index. $24.00pa. PN1008.5.T87. 809'.927'03. LC 93-2660. ISBN 0-87287-979-8.

This dictionary of names is a must for anyone who works with children's literature. Arranged alphabetically by name with full bibliographical citations, including ISBN, a brief annotation, and award designation, it is an excellent resource for the teacher, teacher's aide, librarian, researcher, and child. Young readers should delight in finding and recognizing real and fictionalized names. What a wonderful way to spark an interest in reading! The book is also a tool for helping the young child learn to use and appreciate a good reference source. An excellent author/title index and a title index are also included. Hopefully, more editions will follow. [R: WLB, Oct 93, p. 90]—**Gordon H. Dunkin**

Handbooks and Yearbooks

1191. **Children's Books: Awards & Prizes: Including Prizes and Awards for Young Adult Books.** 1992 ed. Compiled and edited by the Children's Book Council. New York, Children's Book Council, 1992. 404p. index. $85.00; $57.50pa. ISBN 0-933633-01-7; 0-933633-02-5pa. ISSN 0069-3472.

First published in 1969, this edition is the first in six years. The work is divided into four important parts: United States awards selected by adults; United States awards selected by young readers; Australian, Canadian, New Zealand, and United Kingdom awards; and international awards. Each section is arranged by the name of the award, and bibliographical information is given for award winners arranged by year from the award's inception to those announced by the end of 1992. A new section lists periodicals that publish best-book lists and individual bibliographies of the best (a good checklist for the collection builder).

This work invites comparison with similar sources. Dolores Blythe Jones has authored a more comprehensive list: *Children's Literature Awards and Winners* (see ARBA 89, entry 1022), which is done in main volumes and supplements. Formerly an annual, *Award-Winning Books for Children and Young Adults* by Betty Criscoe and Philip J. Lanasa III (Scarecrow, 1992) has become a biannual and includes annotations and pictures of the book covers, making it more of a current selection guide for librarians and teachers. The most comprehensive source is Laura Smith's *Children's Book Awards International* (McFarland, 1992), which lists winners from the inception of the award through 1990.

For quick reference, *Awards & Prizes* is probably the volume of choice because of its size and portability. For librarians wanting more comprehensive coverage, the Gale volumes are preferable (assuming they are kept current), and for in-depth information aiding in selection of individual titles, the Criscoe and Lanasa volume is the first choice. All libraries that stock children's literature should have at least one of these sources. [R: RBB, 1 Sept 93, p. 82; SLJ, Oct 93, p. 52; SLMQ, Summer 93, pp. 264-65]—**David V. Loertscher**

1192. Gillespie, John T., and Corinne J. Naden. **Juniorplots 4: A Book Talk Guide for Use with Readers Ages 12-16.** New Providence, N.J., R. R. Bowker/Reed Reference Publishing, 1993. 450p. index. $34.00. Z1037.G514. 028.5'5'0973. LC 92-35670. ISBN 0-8352-3167-4.

Eighty-one books recommended for use with middle school and high school students are analyzed here. The authors' primary goal is to provide information to help teachers, media specialists, and librarians with booktalks. For each title there are a lengthy plot summary, a brief discussion of theme, several specific incidents that could be highlighted during the booktalk, a list of additional related titles, and citations to reviews of the book and to biographical information about the author. Two sets of author, title, and subject indexes are included; one set is for this volume only, and one set is cumulative.

The plot summaries capture the important incidents and mood of each title and would help professionals review titles already read. The additional selections are valuable both for the specific titles suggested and for their potential to prompt professionals to consider other suitable titles. The general subject and genre arrangement of the books into chapters works well. The author/title/subject indexes allow quick access to this and the preceding three volumes of the series. Unfortunately, only titles fully discussed are so indexed. Access to books listed as related titles in the indexes is limited to this volume only. Entries tend to be descriptive, not critical. But this suits the primary purpose of the volume, and, because each title included was recommended in several standard bibliographies and reviewing sources, the books are of recognized quality. It would be helpful, however, if the copyright dates were given for each title (e.g., Virginia Hamilton's *The House of Dies Drear* was not first published in 1984).

Overall, this is a useful volume that does promote booktalking but is not extraordinary in content or scope. It will be most useful to those professionals in school media centers or public libraries who want to be booktalkers. [R: BR, Nov/Dec 93, p. 38; SLJ, July 93, p. 34; SLMQ, Summer 93, p. 265]

—Carol A. Doll

1193. Kovacs, Deborah, and James Preller. **Meet the Authors and Illustrators: 60 Creators of Favorite Children's Books Talk about Their Work.** Ontario, Scholastic Canada, c1991, 1992. 142p. illus. $9.95pa. 810.9'9282. ISBN 0-590-74291-4.

This book differs from other author-and-illustrator biographical sources in that the focus here is on the process each person goes through in creating a book or illustration. The 60 subjects are well known and well loved and represent broad cultural diversity.

The book is divided into two parts: the creators of picture books and the creators of intermediate books. Only brief biographical information is provided within each two-page author or illustrator profile, the thrust of the material being the description of the creative process, the discipline techniques, and the struggles experienced by each subject. Most of this information was gathered through direct interviews. Details of childhoods and adult lives are described only as they have influenced that creative process. An activity to extend children's learning is included with each profile; often these activities have been suggested by the author or illustrator. The profile is completed with a photograph of the subject and a list of selected titles. A series of creative literary extension activities is appended along with an extensive bibliography of source material.

This work complements standard biographical sources, such as *Something about the Author* (see ARBA 91, entry 1119). For teachers and librarians engaged in whole language activities and for those who want to encourage children's creative efforts, this will provide grist for the mill.—**Joanne Kelly**

1194. Simpson, Martha Seif. **Summer Reading Clubs: Complete Plans for 50 Theme-Based Library Programs.** Jefferson, N.C., McFarland, 1992. 204p. index. $18.95pa. Z718.1.S57. 027.62'5. LC 91-51231. ISBN 0-89950-721-2.

This useful volume contains blueprints for 50 different library reading programs. Some of the themes are familiar favorites (e.g., outer space, robots, dinosaurs), but others are more imaginative (e.g., the theater, occupations, medieval times), and with 50 themes to choose from there is sure to be something of interest here. For each theme Simpson provides a catchy introduction that she says may be used by libraries in program promotions, as well as fun ideas for corresponding materials, such as membership cards, bookmarks, and certificates of participation. There is a long list of suggested activities that goes along with each unit and, of course, theme-related books for both younger (K-3) and older (4-7) readers. Appropriate nonfiction titles are also included as well as suggestions for films and videos (film and video ordering information is provided). The numerous recommended titles are fully indexed by author and title.

There are so many ideas here that even veteran children's librarians will find the book useful as a starting point or as a way to freshen up proven programs of their own. All librarians will want to augment the suggested titles with local favorites and newly published works, as only pre-1992 imprints are included. This helpful work would be even better if it included some paper patterns or sketches to help librarians give life to the many creative ideas. Nonetheless, it is highly recommended. [R: BL 1 Jan 93, p. 813]—**Diana Accurso**

1195. Smith, Laura. **Children's Book Awards International: A Directory of Awards and Winners, from Inception through 1990.** Jefferson, N.C., McFarland, 1992. 649p. index. $75.00. Z1037.A2S45. 028.1'62'079. LC 91-50940. ISBN 0-89950-686-0.

More than 40 countries are represented in this tool, which lists some 11,000 examples of international children's literature awards. Here users can find the full gamut of awards, from the Premio Argentina de Escritores (Argentina Writers Prize) to the Levstikova Nagrade (Fran Levstik Prize) from the former Yugoslavia. Arrangement is first by country, then by title of award. Entries provide the name of the award, sponsoring organization, name and address of contact person, date established, criteria and purpose of the award, and winners through 1990 (but not runners-up). Extensive indexes provide access by book title, author, illustrator, and sponsor. Unlike *Children's Books: Awards and Prizes* (Children's Book Council, 1992) there is no subject access by type of award (e.g., books selected by children, regional history awards). Yet the magnitude and scope of the source clearly overshadow *Children's Literature Awards and Winners* (see ARBA 89, entry 1022) and *Award-Winning Books for Children and Young Adults* by Betty Criscoe and Philip J. Lanasa III (Scarecrow, 1992). To her credit, Smith has included awards that have ceased, making the ready-reference process much simpler because only this one source needs to be consulted. Although the price may be high, the content is solid. The book is appropriate for comprehensive children's literature collections and those interested in comparative literature. [R: Choice, May 93, p. 1449; SLJ, Oct 93, p. 52; WLB, Mar 93, p. 106]—**Ilene F. Rockman**

Indexes

1196. Anderson, Vicki. **Fiction Index for Readers 10 to 16: Subject Access to Over 8200 Books (1960-1990).** Jefferson, N.C., McFarland, 1992. 477p. $35.00. Z1037.A52. 016.80883'0835. LC 91-50954. ISBN 0-89950-703-4.

This work provides subject access to more than 8,200 fiction books. Publication dates of indexed books range from 1960 to 1991 with earlier Newbery winners, some classics, and some basic library collection books. Some books are not in print, but no indication is given of in-print status because the list is not intended as a buyer's guide but as a source for identification, organization, and broader use of the books on the shelves. The core of the work is an annotated bibliography of titles arranged alphabetically by author and including publisher and publishing data. Anderson provides a one- or two-sentence plot description for each book, but no evaluation. A subject index of some 225 headings lists each work alphabetically by author under up to 4 subjects. Subjects are topical words that were chosen for ease of use by readers, but they appear to be arbitrary. Books featuring countries other than the United States are given the single topic "Countries other than United States," with a locational designation in parentheses following the title. While the author states that the country name is given, at times a city or even a continent appears. *See* and *see also* references are given.

The resource includes lists of books with fewer than 100 pages, books with more than 300 pages, and books that have been translated into English from other languages. The title index includes authors' names.

The strength of this resource is the comprehensive nature of the lists. The selection of books and authors is wide, and easy access to them is provided.—**Patricia Tipton Sharp**

1197. Green, Marybeth, and Beverly Williams. **Literature Activity Books: An Index to Materials for Whole Language and Shared Literature.** Englewood, Colo., Libraries Unlimited, 1993. 203p. $27.00pa. Z1037.G8. 011'.62. LC 92-40996. ISBN 1-56308-011-7.

This book is intended as a time-saving guide to whole language literature activity books. Each entry in its alphabetical indexes of subjects, authors, and titles of literary works contains recommended grade levels and codes keyed to items in the literature materials guide. This guide, arranged by publisher, briefly describes an individual activity book or series; lists the children's titles it treats; and rates the series with stars to indicate its success in stimulating critical thinking, integrating activities into language arts and interdisciplinary studies, and extending a children's book.

Although it addresses a genuine need, *Literature Activity Books* has serious deficiencies. Annotations in the excessively brief materials guide are so generalized and repetitive that they do not clearly describe the exact contents of an activity book or indicate how it differs from other books. Furthermore, the annotations, which provide abstract descriptions and positive evaluations rather than concrete and analytical assessments, do not support the star ratings. Why, for example, does *Creative Encounters*, described as "Full of creative activities" that enable "the student to appreciate various author's [sic] styles and develop comprehension/problem solving skills," merit no stars at all? Another weakness is that annotations do not assess the quality of individual titles in a publisher's series. Finally, the selection of publishers is not complete: It ignores, for example, excellent guides from Book Wise that admirably fulfill the goals stated in the preface. For these reasons, this work is not an adequate guide for selecting activity books.—**Raymond E. Jones**

CLASSICAL LITERATURE

1198. **The Concise Oxford Companion to Classical Literature.** M. C. Howatson and Ian Chilvers, eds. New York, Oxford University Press, 1993. 575p. $14.95pa. PA31.H69. 880.9'001'03. LC 92-18585. ISBN 0-19-282708-1.

This is a shortened and slightly revised version of *The Oxford Companion to Classical Literature*, 2d ed. (see ARBA 90, entry 1099). The abridgment has been accomplished by omitting the background articles on general cultural topics and condensing most of the historical, geographical, and political articles of the earlier work; a few minor entries on mythology and all the appendixes have also been dropped. However, the real meat of the work—the entries on literary genres and techniques, authors, and individual literary works—has been retained essentially unaltered. It is not apparent that much new material has been added, although there are a few new entries for topics and persons formerly treated as part of a larger subject.

Libraries owning *The Oxford Companion...* will not find this work an essential reference acquisition (although it may have a place in the circulating collection where interest in classical literature is strong). It will be worth considering by smaller libraries and by individuals who need an inexpensive but authoritative and readable handbook of Greek and Roman literature.—**Paul B. Cors**

1199. Farrier, Susan E. **The Medieval Charlemagne Legend: An Annotated Bibliography.** Hamden, Conn., Garland, 1993. 646p. index. $83.00. (Garland Medieval Bibliographies, v.15; Garland Reference Library of the Humanities, v.984). $83.00. Z6521.C43F37. 016.8088'0351. LC 92-24797. ISBN 0-8240-0949-5.

This impressive scholarly bibliography includes more than 2,700 citations to the medieval tradition of the vast Charlemagne legend. Although literary studies form most of the work, studies of Charlemagne as a historical and political figure are included. The latter, however, have been chosen for their value to literary scholars. Generally, texts in the major European languages, as well as Irish, Welsh, Latin, and Occitan, are cited. In areas that have been well studied, the focus is on the scholarship of the last 20 years. In sections dealing with lesser-known texts, Farrier has attempted to include older works. She has also made an effort to include those articles published in festschriften, which are often difficult to find. Unpublished dissertations have been included only if they treat some neglected aspect of the tradition.

The bibliography is divided into three parts covering the historical Charlemagne, medieval biographies and chronicles, and Charlemagne literature; this last part is by far the largest. Each of the parts is further divided into more specific topics. In general, these sections are organized around major characters. There are two appendixes, one listing Charlemagne's obscure relatives and the other organizing the Charlemagne texts by language. Two principal indexes provide access by authors, editors, translators, subjects, and works. Two smaller indexes lead to entries of modern translations and the names of honorees of the festschrift. The indexes are well constructed and provide good access to the material.

The value of the bibliography is increased by the summaries and annotations. Farrier has included a brief plot summary before the section for each text, in which she names the principal characters and describes the action of the story. Each entry includes an annotation intended to help scholars decide whether to locate a copy of the material. Even items that were not seen have bracketed annotations compiled from other sources. This bibliography is intended for serious scholars and researchers in French and medieval studies, and libraries serving programs and researchers in these academic areas should have this title in their collections. [R: Choice, June 93, p. 1600]—**Barbara E. Kemp**

1200. Hall, Clifton D. **A Complete Concordance to Gottfried Von Strassburg's *Tristan*.** Lewiston, N.Y., Edwin Mellen Press, 1992. 616p. $109.95. PT1526.Z5H35. 831'.6. LC 92-42222. ISBN 0-7734-9203-8.

A successor to Melvin Valk's *Word-Index to Gottfried's Tristan* (University of Wisconsin Press, 1958), this is the first computer-produced concordance to this Middle High German epic poem. It is divided into five separate lists. The KWIC (keyword in context) concordance follows the now-customary format with the headword highlighted in the center of a line containing five to seven words on either side. Within each headword section, the lines are in ascending order by line number. Line endings are indicated, and the total number of times the headword is used is also noted. To conserve space, some 324 function words and high-frequency words are listed separately in the verse concordance, where only the line in which they appear is printed. To make this section more useful, the headwords are sorted by the adjacent word to the right, possibly revealing "patterns which would otherwise remain undisclosed because of sheer numbers." This is followed by the frequency list, ranking all words in descending order of frequency and showing the number of times the word is used and its percentage of the whole. A reverse index of forms lists all words in reverse alphabetical order, followed by a list of proper names, showing the total number of occurrences for each.

The organizing principles of the work are set out in the preface, where Hall notes that editing decisions are predicated on the assumption that users will be conversant enough with Middle High German to be able to locate variant forms of the words they are seeking. Within reasonable limits, no effort has been spared to make this concordance as useful as possible to scholars.—**Jeffrey R. Luttrell**

DRAMA

1201. Trudeau, Lawrence J., and Linda M. Ross, eds. **Drama Criticism: Criticism of the Most Significant and Widely Studied Dramatic Works from All the World's Literatures. Volume 1.** Detroit, Gale, 1991. 576p. illus. index. $75.00. ISBN 0-8103-7911-2. ISSN 1056-4349.

1202. Trudeau, Lawrence J., and others, eds. **Drama Criticism: Criticism of the Most Significant and Widely Studied Dramatic Works from All the World's Literatures. Volume 2.** Detroit, Gale, 1992. 552p. illus. index. $75.00. ISBN 0-8103-7958-9. ISSN 1056-4349.

1203. Trudeau, Lawrence J., and others, eds. **Drama Criticism: Criticism of the Most Significant and Widely Studied Dramatic Works from All the World's Literatures. Volume 3.** Detroit, Gale, 1993. 574p. illus. index. $75.00. ISBN 0-8103-7959-7. ISSN 1056-4349.

How did Sigmund Freud demonstrate the way in which Sophocles' *Oedipus Rex* supports his assumptions regarding the Oedipus complex? In the plays of Richard Brinsley Sheridan, what is the difference between the language of humor and the language of wit? What are the difficulties faced by actors who take on the role of Elwood P. Dowd in Mary Chase's *Harvey?* Why did James Baldwin shift in 1955 from writing novels to composing dramas, a decision he would later call "a desperate and even irresponsible act"? In what ways is Ntozake Shange's *For Colored Girls Who Have Committed Suicide / When the Rainbow Is Enuf* a "choreopoem" that is so rich that it lends itself to multiple interpretations? How does August Wilson portray the conflict between African Americans who have come to terms with the hard realities of their lives and those who have not? The answers to such questions as these and thousands more are easily found in this incredibly useful series on world-famous dramatists and their plays.

Designed principally for beginning students of literature and theater and for the average playgoer, *Drama Criticism* introduces its readers to the most frequently studied playwrights and presents discerning commentary on dramatic works of enduring popular appeal. This series is unlike other sources of information about playwrights (e.g., *Contemporary Literary Criticism* [see ARBA 92, entry 1104]) because it directs more concentrated attention to individual dramatists than is possible in the broader, survey-oriented approach.

James Baldwin, William Wells Brown, Karel Capek, Mary Chase, Alexandre Dumas (*fils*), Charles Fuller, Nikolai Gogol, Lillian Hellman, Christopher Marlowe, Arthur Miller, Yukio Mishima, Richard Brinsley Sheridan, Sophocles, and Thornton Wilder are highlighted in volume 1; Aristophanes, Albert Camus, William Congreve, *Everyman*, Federico Garcia Lorca, Lorraine Hansberry, Henrik Ibsen, Wole Soyinka, John Millington Synge, John Webster, and August Wilson, in volume 2; and Bertolt Brecht, Pedro Calderon de la Barca, John Dryden, Athol Fugard, Langston Hughes, Thomas Kyd, Menander, Joe Orton, Jean-Paul Sartre, and Ntozake Shange, in volume 3. Author entries consist of an author heading (playwright's most common name, birth and death dates, name variations, and pseudonyms), a portrait of the author (when available), a biographical and critical introduction, a list of principal works, author commentary, overviews and general studies of the dramatist's entire literary career, criticism of individual plays, explanatory annotations, bibliographical citations, and a further reading list. When movie adaptations exist, they are included.

A strength of *Drama Criticism*'s design is that it does not assume that readers possess a wide background in literary studies and, consequently, gently leads them through the diverse and often bewildering body of commentary that exists, giving reviews of important productions as well as heightening awareness of drama as a dynamic art form that is only fully recognized in performance. Concluding cumulative author, nationality, and title indexes help significantly in finding specific information about authors, plays, and productions.—**Colby H. Kullman**

FICTION

General Works

1204. Mendes, Peter. **Clandestine Erotic Fiction in English 1800-1930: A Bibliographical Study.** Brookfield, Vt., Scolar Press/Ashgate Publishing, 1993. 479p. illus. index. $124.95. 016.823009. ISBN 0-85967-919-5.

This descriptive bibliography focuses on works of erotic fact and fantasy that were published from 1885 to 1930 clandestinely—that is, by publishers and printers who attempted to hide their identities with title pages of misleading information. Most of the volumes originated in London, Brussels, Amsterdam, Rotterdam, and Paris, and Mendes provides a retrospective survey of European pornography production back to 1800, including sketches of the principal publishers and printers. Besides supplying detailed bibliographical information for all printings of all titles for the 45-year period, Mendes has tried to ascertain who wrote the works; when and where they were printed; who published them; and how they were advertised, distributed, and sold. He has reproduced title and textual pages in attempts to classify distinguishing characteristics of the various printers. He also includes a checklist of erotic fiction published from 1800 to 1884, eight appendixes, and several indexes.

Although European pornography has been studied by previous bibliographers, Mendes's research appears to be more thorough and complete than that of his predecessors. Recommended for university libraries.—**Jack Bales**

1205. Taylor, Desmond, with Philip E. Hager. **The Novels of World War II: An Annotated Bibliography.** Hamden, Conn., Garland, 1993. 2v. index. (Garland Reference Library of the Humanities, v.1130). $135.00/set. Z5917.W33T39. 016.8083'9358. LC 92-35187. ISBN 0-8240-5684-1.

This two-volume bibliography is a companion to Taylor and Hager's earlier compilation, *The Novels of World War I* (see ARBA 82, entry 1262). This set covers 3,371 novels published from 1938 through 1990, arranged chronologically by the year of publication and then alphabetically by author within each year. Most of the entries are generously annotated, up to 200 words in length. The compilers attempted to include all English-language novels as well as novels that have been translated into English, so that the major European novels on the war are covered. However, many obscure British and Australian novels were not seen. Juvenile works are not included here, nor are short story collections. This latter criterion eliminates a few important works, most notably James Michener's *Tales of the South Pacific* (instead, Michener is represented only by a rather odd choice, his 1983 novel *Poland*).

The range of books included in the bibliography runs from pulp adventure novels to elegant dramas (e.g., Aharon Appelfeld's *Badenheim 1939*, Jerzy Kosinski's *The Painted Bird*). The bibliography also provides a renewed acquaintance with the classic World War II books—*The Naked and the Dead, From Here to Eternity, The Young Lions, The Caine Mutiny, Mister Roberts, Catch-22, The Cruel Sea, The Bridge on the River Kwai*—as well as a revelation of hundreds of lesser-known or deservedly forgotten titles. Many unlikely authors turn up in this compilation, among them Sax Rohmer, James Roosevelt, Vladimir Pozner, Arthur C. Clarke, Kay Boyle, Victoria Sackville-West, Erskine Caldwell, and even Barbara Cartland. Among the most recent novels covered are Thomas Fleming's *Time and Tide* (1987), Marge Piercy's *Gone to Soldiers* (1987), Horst Bienek's *Earth and Fire* (translation published 1988),

Rick DeMarinis's *The Year of the Zinc Penny* (1989), and Jack Higgins's *Cold Harbour* (1990). There is a useful introduction to the bibliography, plus author and title indexes that are keyed to the entry numbers. This bibliography is recommended for academic and large public library collections. [R: Choice, Nov 93, pp. 439-40]—**Thomas A. Karel**

Crime and Mystery

1206. Breen, Jon L. **What about Murder? 1981-1991: A Guide to Books about Mystery and Detective Fiction.** Metuchen, N.J., Scarecrow, 1993. 376p. index. $39.50. Z5917.D5B73. 016.813'087209. LC 92-34547. ISBN 0-8108-2609-7.

Breen has won Edgar Allan Poe awards for his scholarship in mystery literature. He is also the author of six mystery novels. Thus, he brings authority to the task of assembling and critiquing the best books that have been written about mystery literature in the past decade. This work is a sequel to the parent volume of the same name published in 1981 (Scarecrow). The current volume consists of annotations of 565 works arranged across several broad categories of scholarship and writing related to the mystery genre. Those include histories, reference books, special subjects (e.g., mystery novels with Christmas backgrounds), collected essays and reviews about mystery literature, technical manuals (e.g., books on how to write mystery stories), works on individual authors (e.g., Agatha Christie), and anthologies of mystery stories. Breen's comprehensive index greatly eases the task of finding desired information quickly. The annotations are long and provide abundant information and criticism.

Breen writes with the sureness of a person possessing an encyclopedic knowledge of the field. His writing style is reader-friendly, being conversational in tone and never pedantic. If there is a fault with the writing, it lies in Breen's tendency to scold authors and editors who do not measure up to his high expectations. Despite this caution, the book remains a fine resource for anyone who loves to read, write, and study mystery literature. [R: LAR, Dec 93, p. 694; LJ, 1 June 93, p. 100; RQ, Fall 93, pp. 136-37]—**Jerry D. Flack**

1207. Cassiday, Bruce, comp. and ed. **Modern Mystery, Fantasy and Science Fiction Writers.** New York, Continuum Publishing, 1993. 673p. index. (Library of Literary Criticism). $75.00. PN3503.M526. 809.3'87. LC 92-33859. ISBN 0-8264-0573-8.

This volume is a much-needed addition to the highly respected Library of Literary Criticism series. Until now there has been no single source in which to locate criticism in mystery, fantasy, and science fiction. Such critiques have been generally disregarded in reference works of modern criticism even though they have regularly appeared in both popular and scholarly journals. Consequently, this volume will be welcomed by librarians, students, journalists, and scholars.

Eighty-eight authors are represented in the more than 800 entries, which are excerpted from approximately 112 publications. The majority of the authors in this volume are twentieth-century writers, but in order to adequately reflect the beginnings of a genre, certain nineteenth-century authors have been included. For example, Edgar Allan Poe is considered the originator of the modern mystery story, while science fiction dates back to Jules Verne; therefore, both men are included, along with several others whose works contributed to the development of the genre.

The authors are arranged alphabetically; most of the excerpts dealing with them appear chronologically. Cassiday deviated from this pattern only when he felt that a more recent excerpt would serve as a better introduction than an earlier one. His superb editorial skills have produced a very readable and useful work that also contains a list of works mentioned and an index to critics.—**Sara R. Mack**

1208. DellaCava, Frances A., and Madeline H. Engel. **Female Detectives in American Novels: A Bibliography and Analysis of Serialized Female Sleuths.** Hamden, Conn., Garland, 1993. 157p. index. (Garland Reference Library of the Humanities, v.1685). $26.00. Z1231.D47D45. 016.813'087209352042. LC 93-30644. ISBN 0-8153-1264-4.

Female detectives have become increasingly popular over the past years—witness Sara Paretsky's V. I. Warshawski and Sue Grafton's Kinsey Milhone. The emphasis in this reference work is on adult U.S. female sleuths, focusing on those who are main characters, not secretarial assistants or part of a team effort. (Nancy Drew, the Dana Girls, and other teenagers are not included.) There are a few twists to this presentation. Rather than just listing works that feature these characters, the authors have attempted to explore the attitudes toward, characterizations of, and developments of female sleuths over the past 100 years as well as focusing on social issues dealt with in the novels, such as sexism, racism, gay and lesbian concerns, and substance abuse. The bibliographical portion profiles some 160 female investigators in 636 books. Entries are arranged by time period, then alphabetically by author, with novels listed chronologically. Profiles of individual sleuths are succinct and informative, and a table in the introduction identifies them by occupation. There are author, book title, and sleuth name indexes. This well-thought-out reference is interesting to read. Fans, researchers, and libraries with substantial mystery collections will want this title.—**Joy Hastings**

1209. Niebuhr, Gary Warren. **A Reader's Guide to the Private Eye Novel.** New York, G. K. Hall, 1993. 323p. (Reader's Guides to Mystery Novels). $45.00. PN3448.D4N54. 809.3'872. LC 93-22212. ISBN 0-8161-1802-7.

The private eye novel is one of the significant U.S. contributions to the mystery literature genre. Niebuhr, a Wisconsin library director and a devoted mystery lover, traces the evolution of this popular type of mystery fiction from the seminal works of legendary private eye creators, such as Dashiell Hammett and Raymond Chandler, to contemporary authors of note, such as Sue Grafton, Sara Paretsky, and Bill Pronzini.

Most of the text is devoted to plot summaries of more than 1,000 novels by 90 authors, alphabetically arranged by author. The individual entries are informative and succinct. Additionally, the author provides lists of pseudonyms, creators, and series characters as well as a decade-by-decade listing of private eye fiction from 1920 through 1992. One interesting chapter reveals locations of private eye mysteries set within the United States through a state-by-state listing. Worldwide locations are also noted. A catalog of unique background settings for private eye novels, including libraries, beauty pageants, dude ranches, and trains, forms another chapter. Topics as diverse as alcoholism, archaeology, basketball, the White House, and mining are used to cross-reference works in a chapter labeled as miscellaneous information. The final chapter consists of Niebuhr's candidates for the top 100 mystery novels featuring private eyes.

If there is a fault with this volume, it is Niebuhr's omission of any biographical data about the authors. Regardless, mystery lovers and librarians who serve mystery devotees should find this book both highly informative and fun to read.—**Jerry D. Flack**

1210. Slide, Anthony. **Gay and Lesbian Characters and Themes in Mystery Novels: A Critical Guide to Over 500 Works in English.** Jefferson, N.C., McFarland, 1993. 199p. index. $35.00. PR1309.D4S55. 823'.0872093520664. LC 92-56695. ISBN 0-89950-798-0.

Gay and lesbian characters abound in works of fiction—and, as this book illustrates, in mystery fiction in particular. Slide, author of more than 20 books on the cinema, makes the point that while the genre of the gay mystery novel is not new, its inclusion into mainstream mystery fiction is. Gay and lesbian characters have often been negatively depicted; however, over the years, reflecting real life, the stereotypes have diminished in fiction, with today's characters often portrayed sensitively. This book traces these characters through more than 500 works in English from the 1930s to the present; it includes characters created by both famous and lesser-known mystery writers. The entries are alphabetically arranged, mostly by author, although some also appear by theme. Most author entries begin with a brief biographical sketch and are followed by an annotation that describes the characters in the author's works; the entries on themes refer the reader to author entries.

Mystery aficionados will love this excellent reference work. An index to more than 350 characters, an additional title index, and a bibliography (mostly of bibliographies) make it a valuable research tool for the genre. Highly recommended for mystery lovers in both public and academic libraries. [R: LJ, Aug 93, p. 98; RBB, 1 Nov 93, pp. 562-64]—**Edward Erazo**

Science Fiction, Fantasy, and Horror

1211. Clute, John, and Peter Nicholls, eds. **The Encyclopedia of Science Fiction.** New York, St. Martin's Press, 1993. 1370p. $75.00. PN3433.4.E53. 809.3'8762'03. LC 92-47048. ISBN 0-312-09618-6.

When the first edition of this volume, *The Science Fiction Encyclopedia* (see ARBA 80, entry 1212), was published in 1979, it gained Nicholls a Pilgrim Award for scholarship from the Science Fiction Research Association and was widely recognized as the most useful single reference to this popular genre. But in the 14 years that have passed since then, the field has grown vastly, and the need for a new edition has been obvious. Thus, librarians and readers with more than a casual interest in science fiction (SF) will welcome this work's appearance.

The new edition has been expanded to almost double its original size, with a concomitant growth in coverage. Original entries have been updated, expanded, and rewritten, with many new writers and subjects added. Despite the editors' disclaimer, most entries are up-to-date well into 1992. New thematic entries, such as those on cyberpunk, steampunk, poetry, virtual reality, and technothriller, demonstrate current trends; new entries on feminism, women as portrayed in science fiction, and women SF writers illustrate the growing importance of these topics.

The lively and often opinionated language of the first edition has in some cases been toned down. For example, a 1979 reference to C. S. Lewis's use of "slightly cheap linguistic tricks" (in *Out of the Silent Planet*) has been changed to "rather facile linguistic tricks." This is a loss, as is the removal of the black-and-white illustrations of authors and magazine covers, which were muddy but often wonderfully campy. This edition nevertheless remains a pleasure for the browser and an essential tool for the researcher. It should be in the reference section of community libraries as well as large research institutions. [R: Choice, Oct 93, p. 265; JAL, Sept 93, p. 274; RBB, 1 Nov 93, p. 562; VOYA, Dec 93, p. 332]—**Lynn F. Williams**

1212. Cox, Greg. **The Transylvanian Library: A Consumer's Guide to Vampire Fiction.** San Bernardino, Calif., Borgo Press, 1993. 264p. index. (Borgo Literary Guides, no.8). $30.00; $20.00pa. Z5983.V36C69. 016.808'8'0375. LC 88-36553. ISBN 0-89370-335-4; 0-89370-435-0pa.

An editor and author of short fiction has compiled an extensive chronological bibliography of all the vampire fiction he has read. Tracing the evolution of the literary form from 1819 to 1992 and from straight horror stories to multilayered tales often featuring the vampire as hero, Cox offers synopses and personal ratings (1 to 4 bats) of 250-plus short stories and novels written by an international group of some 200 authors. Each annotation also lists author, title, original publisher and date, number of pages, and television or movie adaptations of the work. Separate author, title, and character indexes and a select bibliography follow. *Vampires Unearthed* (see ARBA 84, entry 1137) is broader in scope but unannotated. Cox's bibliography is the only one that annotates and evaluates fiction. Easy to use and a pleasure to read, this work should be widely available. [R: RBB, 1 Oct 93, p. 387]—**Deborah Hammer**

1213. Hall, Hal W., ed. **Science Fiction and Fantasy Reference Index 1985-1991: An International Author and Subject Index to History and Criticism.** Englewood, Colo., Libraries Unlimited, 1993. 677p. $90.00. Z5917.S36S297. 016.8093'8762. LC 92-43531. ISBN 1-56308-113-X.

Since the mid-1960s, Hall has been indexing all the secondary works available in books, magazines, and newspapers on science fiction, fantasy, and horror literature and film. This effort culminated in the publication in 1987 of *Science Fiction and Fantasy Reference Index 1878-1985* (see ARBA 88, entry 1152). Although the editor estimated that it included only about 50 or 60 percent of what actually exists, this massive 2-volume compilation was by far the most extensive and thorough bibliography of material in the field, the first place for a researcher to start. However, the exponential growth of critical writing on science fiction has already made a continuation necessary, and the present volume, which covers the 6 years from 1985 to 1991, contains more than 16,250 new citations, including a number of items overlooked by the earlier bibliography.

This work follows the same general arrangement as the previous one: a list of books and magazines indexed, and then two general listings by subject and author. The alphabetization is done by computer and so has some peculiarities. Each citation is complete in itself, without cross-references. This results in a great deal of often unnecessary repetition, as when two slightly differing versions of a single author's name are treated separately, or when an article on the Strugatsky Brothers serialized in *Quarber Merkur* receives eight separate citations. Most items are in English, with spotty coverage of other languages. Some reviews of films but not of books are included (Hall also publishes a series of book review indexes). Most of the items were seen by Hall himself and come not only from obvious sources, such as *Locus* and *Extrapolation*, but also from such unlikely venues as the *Wall Street Journal* and the *Western Ohio Journal*.

As was its predecessor, this updated index is an invaluable tool for the researcher, made even more essential by the retirement of Marshall Tymn and the loss of Tom Clareson, compilers of earlier bibliographies. Any library with a research collection in science fiction and fantasy will need it. [R: Choice, Dec 93, p. 590]—**Lynn F. Williams**

1214. Reginald, Robert. **Science Fiction and Fantasy Literature 1975-1991: A Bibliography of Science Fiction, Fantasy, and Horror Fiction Books and Nonfiction Monographs.** Detroit, Gale, 1992. 1512p. index. $199.00. Z5917.S36R4212. 016.80883'876. LC 92-28219. ISBN 0-8103-1825-3.

This bibliography is a continuation of the author's *Science Fiction and Fantasy: A Checklist, 1700-1974* (see ARBA 80, entry 1214) and is intended to be used in conjunction with the original, as the numbering continues from that volume. According to Reginald the 22,000 entries in this edition comprise 98 percent of the science fiction (SF), fantasy, and horror books published in the English language over the past 17 years. Full bibliographical information is given for each entry. Also noted are pseudonyms and significant variations in content, title, or byline. The alphabetical author index comprises the major portion of the book, with title and series indexes following. In addition, there is a list of book doubles and major award winners.

As the genre has grown and branched, so has this bibliography. Horror fiction, shared-world fiction, Christian world fantasy, important nonfiction, and criticism have been included. Omitted are biographical sketches, stage plays, poetry, songs, graphic novels, and comic books. The introductory sections are informative and explain the work's purpose, stating what is and is not included and the sources used in the compilation. The comprehensive volume constitutes a major resource for and contribution to the SF/fantasy/horror field. Those that have the first work will want this. It is a definite purchase for core collections and those with an avid SF clientele. [R: Choice, May 93, p. 1448; LJ, 1 June 93, p. 108-10; RBB, 15 April 93, p. 1538; WLB, April 93, p. 124]—**Joy Hastings**

Short Stories

1215. Magill, Frank N., ed. **Critical Survey of Short Fiction.** rev. ed. Pasadena, Calif., Salem Press, 1993. 7v. index. $425.00/set. PN3321.C7. 809.3'1'03. LC 92-41950. ISBN 0-89356-843-0.

This work consists mainly of two sections. The article section, which is arranged alphabetically by author, contains biographical information about the author, a bibliography of works about that person, and a list of the individual's principal short fiction and other literary forms and major works. Also included in each article is a well-written analysis, usually between four and six pages in length, of the author's works. The second section is a collection of 12 essays that discuss the development of the short story from antiquity to modern times. Although the essays are generally interesting, the real value of the work lies in the first section. The work also includes an annotated bibliography of short story criticism, a short fiction chronology, brief definitions of terms and techniques, and an author/title index.

In comparison to the 1981 edition of *Critical Survey of Short Fiction* (see ARBA 83, entry 1131), the revised edition has been updated and expanded. Of the 363 articles on individual authors, 65 are completely new, and 227 of the existing entries have been substantially revised. In the essay section, five of the essays are new; the others have been revised and updated. Despite these changes, many libraries that own the 1981 edition will not find enough new material to justify the purchasing of the revised edition. However, the work remains an extremely useful tool and is recommended for libraries where students may need to locate information on a particular short story or author. [R: Choice, Dec 93, p. 582; LJ, Aug 93, pp. 90-92; RBB, 1 Oct 93, pp. 378-79; RQ, Winter 93, pp. 298-99]—**Lori L. Oling**

1216. **Short Story Criticism: Excerpts from Criticism of the Works of Short Fiction Writers. Volume 11.** David Segal and others, eds. Detroit, Gale, 1992. 528p. illus. index. $85.00. LC 88-641014. ISBN 0-8103-7953-8. ISSN 0895-9439.

1217. **Short Story Criticism: Excerpts from Criticism of the Works of Short Fiction Writers. Volume 12.** David Segal and others, eds. Detroit, Gale, 1993. 527p. illus. index. $85.00. LC 88-641014. ISBN 0-8103-7955-4. ISSN 0895-9439.

One of the newer components of Gale's successful Literary Criticism Series is *Short Story Criticism*. Similar to their predecessors, these latest volumes present excerpts from English-language criticism of the works of short story writers of all eras and nationalities. Each entry features a variety of critical passages pertaining to a particular short story collection, novella, or novella collection. Excerpts are arranged chronologically and prefaced with explanatory notes about the critic being quoted; a complete citation follows each excerpt to aid further research. Additional details provided for each author include a list of principal works, biographical and bibliographical information, photographs, and the author's own comments (when available). A separate bibliography of general sources on short fiction is updated with each volume. Another feature, sure to please reference librarians and English instructors, is an explanation of the proper way to cite this source.

Coverage is thorough and varied. Volumes 11 and 12 devote an average of 50 pages apiece to 17 authors—including Ann Beattie, Arthur Conan Doyle, Miguel de Unamuno, Ursula K. Le Guin, Saki, and Robert Louis Stevenson. Representation by female and minority authors is weak at present, an omission that should be addressed in future volumes. There is also some overlap of critical material within various parts of the Literary Criticism Series as a whole, although never more than a 20 percent duplication.

Comparisons may be drawn between *Short Story Criticism* and another standard reference source on the short story, *Critical Survey of Short Fiction*, edited by Frank N. Magill (Salem Press, 1993). Budget permitting, purchase of one need not preclude the other. While the *Critical Survey* offers excellent overviews of a large number of British and American authors, *Short Story Criticism* provides broader and evolving coverage (with a projected three new volumes per year), an unusual introduction to literary criticism for students, and a valuable departure point for researchers. This graphically pleasing tool is recommended for academic libraries, many of which will want to place it on standing order.

—**Linda Cullum**

1218. **Twentieth-Century Short Story Explication: New Series. Volume I: 1989-1990.** By Warren S. Walker. Hamden, Conn., Shoe String Press, 1993. 366p. index. $49.50. Z5917.S5W35. 016.8093'1. LC 92-22790. ISBN 0-208-02340-2.

This popular and useful guide to short story explication begins a new series with this volume. The new series is not a replacement but a continuation that follows the same format: an alphabetical arrangement by author's name or pseudonym, subarranged by title of the short story (in English translation if a foreign title). The arrangement is somewhat confusing, particularly with the non-Western authors, because names are not inverted to put surnames first.

The volume includes more than 5,650 entries for 815 authors. According to Walker, 343 of the authors are new to this volume, with a total of 2,647 writers represented in the entire body of work. Representative of the increased international coverage are 133 Hispanic and 73 Chinese writers who appear for the first time in this work. The explications are limited to those written in the major languages of Western Europe. Entries are abbreviated as in the previous series, but the preface has an explanation of the shortened citations. A list of the 536 books analyzed and the 321 journals cited also identifies the abbreviations used in the entries. Most of the entries are for publications from 1989 through the end of 1990, but some earlier ones that were not available or were overlooked in previous editions are also included. A few entries are repeated from the earlier works; these are marked with a plus sign.

For the uninitiated, one weakness of this volume and its predecessors is the lack of cross-referencing for pseudonyms or double names. Such cross-referencing could easily be accommodated in the index, which is a redundant list of the authors' names. These minor irritations are overcome by the uniqueness of the work, which provides a checklist of criticism pertaining to one genre for use by faculty and students at all levels. [R: Choice, July/Aug 93, p. 1756; JAL, July 93, p. 201]—**Margo B. Mead**

NATIONAL LITERATURE

American Literature

General Works

1219. Carter, Susanne, comp. **Mothers and Daughters in American Short Fiction: An Annotated Bibliography of Twentieth-Century Women's Literature.** Westport, Conn., Greenwood Press, 1993. 132p. index. (Bibliographies and Indexes in Women's Studies, no.19). $49.95. Z1229.W8C37. 016.813'01083520431. LC 93-10822. ISBN 0-313-28511-X.

This is a collection of 242 titles related to the theme of mothers and daughters in U.S. short fiction. They are grouped into seven thematic categories presented in alphabetical order: abuse and neglect, aging, alienation, death, expectations, nurturance, and portraits. The collection is introduced by a short essay on mother-daughter relationships, and each category is prefaced by a short introduction. Entries, numbered sequentially, are accompanied by brief summaries of the work. Author, title, and subject indexes are provided.

Carter neglects to make any clear statement of purpose explaining why this compilation was attempted or what void is being filled by its creation. The scope of the bibliography is never defined, and the methodology is never presented, and readers are left wondering how and why Carter chose the books she did. They also have no idea of how current the bibliography is, and its thematic organization is left unexplained. Annotations are mere summaries filled with quotations from the original works. (The bibliographical format of the records is clearly explained, however, and conforms to MLA Handbook standards.)

Researchers in women's literature will be better off avoiding this bibliography. It generates far more questions than it answers.—**Daphne Fallieros Potter**

1220. Cook, Ralph T. **City Lights Books: A Descriptive Bibliography.** Metuchen, N.J., Scarecrow, 1992. 313p. illus. index. $39.50. Z473.C58C66. 015.974'61. LC 92-36462. ISBN 0-8108-2621-6.

Since its founding in 1955 by poet Lawrence Ferlinghetti, City Lights Books in San Francisco has published more than 230 works that include the writings of more than 1,500 authors, many of whom have been the subjects of popular and scholarly studies. Many of the press's authors (including Ferlinghetti) are associated with the Beat Movement of the 1950s and 1960s—a philosophy that bespoke a rejection of middle-class values and lifestyles. Among the more prominent of these Beat writers are Jack Kerouac, Allen Ginsberg, Gregory Corso, William S. Burroughs, and Richard Brautigan.

Cook, who has studied the Beat Generation writers for the past 20 years, has compiled a descriptive bibliography of all City Lights books, pamphlets, and broadsides published from 1955 through 1990. He provides detailed descriptions of title pages, collation, contents, paper and bindings, and publication histories. Unlike many bibliographers, he meticulously defines his terms and explains his methodology, thereby making his volume useful even for the nonspecialist who is unfamiliar with the arcane jargon of descriptive bibliography. A chronological table of contents, author and title indexes, and 16 photographs all nicely complement the book. Cook's bibliography will prove to be invaluable not only to researchers but also to librarians, rare book dealers, and book collectors. [R: WLB, Mar 93, p. 106]—**Jack Bales**

1221. Drew, Bernard A. **Western Series and Sequels.** 2d ed. Hamden, Conn., Garland, 1993. 304p. illus. (Garland Reference Library of the Humanities, v.1399). $44.00. Z1251.W5D74. 016.813'0874. LC 92-22569. ISBN 0-8240-9648-7.

Western Series and Sequels might more rightly be called "Frontier Series and Sequels," as it includes some series set on non-Western frontiers. The included series range across the literary spectrum from children's books to bodice rippers, romances, pornography, family sagas, and graphic novels. There are also examples of quality literature, such as Edward Abbey's two-novel Western series featuring the legendary eco-warrior George Hayduke. For each series entry there is a list of the books in the series with dates of publication and publisher. The authors of each series are given (if known), and most entries include a brief description of the nature of the series along with plot summaries of a representative novel or two. Coverage includes both U.S. and foreign series and is generally limited to twentieth-century series. Series are listed alphabetically by either the title of the series or the name of the series's main character. There are an author index and a general index.

This edition of *Western Series and Sequels* expands the first one by including entries for more than 350 additional series. The introduction is little changed, but Drew has added a list of secondary sources. This edition is sturdily bound and printed on acid-free paper, but the typography is often sloppy. *Western Series and Sequels* will be useful as a collection-management and reference tool in public libraries serving readers with tastes for Westerns. Among academic libraries, only those supporting strong programs in popular culture or western American literature will want to purchase this book. [R: Choice, Sept 93, p. 78]—**Donald A. Barclay**

1222. Flora, Joseph M., and Robert Bain. **Contemporary Fiction Writers of the South: A Bio-Bibliographical Sourcebook.** Westport, Conn., Greenwood Press, 1993. 571p. index. $75.00. PS261.C565. 813'.5409'03. LC 92-36515. ISBN 0-313-28764-3.

Explore the world of Pat Conroy's "Lowcountry," discover the "boomerang" return motion that is built into Barry Hannah's fiction, view the Southern racial situation as it is found in Ellen Douglas's stories of the South in the early and mid-twentieth century, study Larry Brown's ability to fuse Vietnam fiction and a Southern novel in *Dirty Work*, watch Ellen Gilchrist's female protagonists struggle for self-knowledge and self-recognition, and find out why John Kennedy Toole was a Southern Catholic writer for whom the loss of faith was critical. Reporting on the many good books Southerners have written within the last thirty years, *Contemporary Fiction Writers of the South* presents a flowering of talent comparable to the Southern Renascence in the first four decades of this century. Maintaining that none of the authors discussed has yet earned the reputation of a William Faulkner, a Eudora Welty, a Flannery O'Connor, or a Robert Penn Warren, but that many have already achieved international reputations, Flora and Bain highlight 49 Southern writers of fiction who have either stayed at home to write or who rank among those expatriates who live outside the South but still draw on their heritage for their fiction. Influenced by World War II, the Vietnam War, the civil rights movement, new understandings of race and cultures, changing roles for women, and sexual freedoms afforded by the age of the pill, this new generation of Southern writers record their responses to "such radical changes in the South as the decline of rural living and the rise of cities and towns, the influence of television and shopping malls, Southerners' obsession with sports and cars, the preoccupation with getting rich, and the social mobility that comes with wealth" (p. xii). The powerful voices of all classes of society, as well as the formidable talents of Blacks and women, are more significant to this second Renascence than they were to the first.

To be included in this valuable study of contemporary Southern fiction, each author needs to have written at least four books (one exception is Alex Haley), to have been reviewed widely, and to have achieved critical recognition outside of the South. Written by knowledgeable scholars, each essay contains five parts: a biographical sketch, a discussion of the author's major themes, an assessment of reviews and scholarship, a chronological list of the author's works, and a bibliography of selected criticism. Love and honor and courage and sacrifice, a sense of place, the importance of religion, a celebration of the gothic and the grotesque, the respect for art and letters, the complexity of family relationships, the influence of the past on the present, and a sense of being different from the rest of the nation—all are to be discovered in this book. [R: RBB, 15 Nov 93, p. 649]—**Colby H. Kullman**

1223. Jordan, Casper LeRoy, comp. **A Bibliographical Guide to African-American Women Writers.** Westport, Conn., Greenwood Press, 1993. 387p. index. $65.00. Z1229.N39J67. 016.8108'09287'08996. LC 93-6561. ISBN 0-313-27633-1.

Compiled by a former librarian and library school educator, this bibliography lists writings by and about African-American women writers through 1991. The approximately 900 creative writers, biographers, essayists, and critics included range chronologically from the eighteenth-century poet Lucy Terry to Lorene Cary, whose first novel appeared in 1991. In addition to such major writers as Maya Angelou, Gwendolyn Brooks, and Alice Walker, the bibliography covers numerous lesser-known and obscure figures, many of whom are not generally included in standard sources.

Arranged alphabetically by author, the entries identify primary works first, followed by a section for secondary sources. References to critical and other secondary works include books, articles in popular magazines and scholarly journals, chapters in books, and dissertations. Book reviews are excluded. Due to an extension of the cut-off date for the bibliography, publications from 1988-1991 appear in separate sections at the end of an author's entry. A separate supplementary section near the end of the volume covers writers whose first publications appeared between 1988 and 1991. Additional chapters list anthologies of Black writings and general biographical and critical works. The index includes not only the authors treated but also the authors, editors, translators, and compilers of secondary works cited.

Substantial portions of this bibliography overlap the coverage of previous bibliographies, such as *Black American Women in Literature* (see ARBA 90, entry 858) and *The Pen Is Ours* (see ARBA 92, entry 1150). Unfortunately, comparison with both of those works and with *Toni Morrison: An Annotated Bibliography* (see ARBA 89, entry 1080) and *Zora Neale Hurston: A Reference Guide* (see ARBA 88, entry 1177) reveals that Jordan has omitted a significant number of titles. However, due to its breadth of coverage, it can serve as a starting point for research on Afro-American women writers, particularly for minor and previously neglected figures. [R: Choice, Nov 93, p. 423; RBB, 15 Dec 93, p. 774; WLB, Nov 93, p. 98]—**Marie Ellis**

1224. Nelson, Emmanuel S., ed. **Contemporary Gay American Novelists: A Bio-Bibliographical Critical Sourcebook.** Westport, Conn., Greenwood Press, 1993. 421p. index. $69.50. PS374.N63C66. 813'.54099206642. LC 92-25762. ISBN 0-313-28019-3.

A remarkable compilation of bio-bibliographical information on 50-plus novelists, this work is likely to be used over and over by students, researchers, and others looking for information on the authors included. Each writer is treated by a different essayist who provides basic biographical information and discussions of major works and themes, critical reactions, and primary and selected secondary bibliographical information. Essays average 4 to 20 pages, and each is a solid treatise on its particular author. The work is prefaced by an introduction that explains the parameters and tenets of gay literature and the perception of gay literature over time. An appendix provides a list of small presses and selected journals that regularly publish gay fiction. A separate index and biographical profiles of essayists are included.

There is no current work with which this title can be compared. For the present it stands alone as a comprehensive sourcebook to gay authors. One hopes that it will serve as a model for other editors and publishers. Any public or academic collection with strengths in American literature and the literary tradition would benefit from this work. [R: Choice, July/Aug 93, p. 1745; LJ, Jan 93, p. 94; RBB, 1 April 93, p. 1454; RQ, Fall 93, pp. 120-21]—**Edmund F. SantaVicca**

1225. Peck, David R. **American Ethnic Literatures: Native American, African American, Chicano/Latino, and Asian American Writers and Their Backgrounds: An Annotated Bibliography.** Pasadena, Calif., Salem Press, 1992. 218p. index. (Magill Bibliographies). $40.00. Z1229.E87P43. 016.8109'920693. LC 92-12897. ISBN 0-89356-684-5.

This bibliography is composed of eight chapters: general works on ethnic America; historical background; the teaching of ethnic literature; works on and collections of American ethnic literature; and Native American, African-American, Hispanic-American, and Asian-American literatures. Briefly annotated (for nonfiction and collections) citations are arranged within overlapping categories. An author/title index appears.

Inevitably, in a work so inclusive, mistakes appear. There are typographical and editorial errors (e.g., "Bureau of American Anthropology" rather than Ethnology), errors of judgment (e.g., the inclusion of the pseudonymous Indian, Least Heat-Moon, in the Native American lists), errors of omission, and errors of fact (e.g., the statement that 1920-1930 was the decade that "saw the major writings" of Zora Neale Hurston, who published her first book in the 1930s). Other problems include the inclusion of too many Black neoconservative analysts to the exclusion of Black progressive thinkers and the assertion that the degrading stereotypes of Asian-Americans are more "insidious" and "durable" than those associated with other ethnic groups. Peck is absolutely correct in his statement that the diverse ethnic groups included by the term *Asian-American* tend to get homogenized by the media, yet in his overly brief treatment of

Asian-American literature he fails to convey its diversity and richness. This bibliography should, however, be a useful reference for teachers, especially new instructors of American ethnic literature. [R: Choice, June 93, p. 1608; RBB, 15 April 93, p. 1534]—**Fred J. Hay**

1226. Pollack, Sandra, and Denise D. Knight, eds. **Contemporary Lesbian Writers of the United States: A Bio-Bibliographical Critical Sourcebook.** Westport, Conn., Greenwood Press, 1993. 640p. index. $99.50. PS153.L46C65. 810.9'9206643. LC 92-39468. ISBN 0-313-28215-3.

Contemporary Lesbian Writers is a welcome addition to a growing body of resource tools documenting the gay and lesbian experience. This collection of 100 biographical sketches of contemporary "women-identified" writers focuses upon known and less well known U.S. writers of poetry, fiction, and drama. The emphasis is upon those writers whose lesbianism has had a profound impact on their writing. Although lesbian writers have been included in general references about women literary figures, such as the multivolume *American Women Writers* (see ARBA 84, entry 1152 and ARBA 80, entry 1239), this is one of the first ready-reference tools devoted exclusively to lesbian writers of the twentieth century. It complements *Contemporary Gay American Novelists*, edited by Emmanuel S. Nelson (Greenwood Press, 1993), and similar works.

Contemporary Lesbian Authors includes such familiar names as Marilyn Hacker, Adrienne Rich, Jane Chambers, May Sarton, and Audre Lorde, as well as the more unfamiliar Kitty Tsui, Mary Wings, Sara Schulman, Ruthann Robson, and Sapphire. Each entry contains a brief biography, a summary of the author's major works and themes, and how the author was critically received in the media. A complete bibliography of the author's works is provided, as well as a list of selected secondary readings in difficult-to-locate sources. An excellent introduction titled "Deconstructing the Absolute—Reality and Difference" traces the history of the genre and the difficulties and struggles in bringing a unique, often-challenged perspective into print. The volume also contains a list of publishers of lesbian works, a list of selected periodicals and journals pertaining to lesbian writers, and a bibliography of selected nonfiction on lesbian issues.

This volume is a welcome addition to any public or academic library. [R: LJ, 15 Sept 93, p. 68; RBB, 1 Nov 93, p. 561]—**Jane Jurgens**

Drama

1227. Furtado, Ken, and Nancy Hellner. **Gay and Lesbian American Plays: An Annotated Bibliography.** Metuchen, N.J., Scarecrow, 1993. 217p. index. $27.50. Z1229.G25F87. 016.8108'0920664. LC 93-17078. ISBN 0-8108-2689-5.

A welcome addition to the growing repertoire of reference works treating primary sources of gay and lesbian literature, this work functions as both bibliography and directory. Included are more than 700 dramatic works that have at least one gay character or theme. Not since 1979, when Terry Helbing's *Gay Theatre Alliance Directory of Gay Plays* (JH Press) was published, has any extensive list of gay and lesbian plays been published. This present volume includes titles that have been in existence for many years but that have never been brought together in any sort of comprehensive catalog or compilation.

After a brief introduction explaining the scope of the work, Furtado and Hellner present an alphabetical list of playwrights. Under each author, individual works are arranged alphabetically by title and include the following information: type of play, plot synopsis or description (approximately 100 words), number of acts, number of male characters, number of female characters, indication of doubling, number of interiors and exteriors, production information, and indications of how to obtain the script. Following the main text are an index of plays by title; a list of incomplete plays; and directory lists of agents, playwrights, and theaters. A 29-item bibliography of related books completes the work. Already planning for the next edition, the authors have also provided a blank submission form for future inclusion.

Students, scholars, actors, directors, playwrights, and other researchers and practitioners with interest in American gay and lesbian plays will find this work a necessary part of their information resources collections. Collections of modern and contemporary drama should not be without it. [R: JAL, Nov 93, p. 346; RBB, 1 Nov 93, pp. 562-64]—**Edmund F. SantaVicca**

1228. Gavin, Christy. **American Women Playwrights 1964-1989: A Research Guide and Annotated Bibliography.** Hamden, Conn., Garland, 1993. 493p. index. (Garland Reference Library of the Humanities, v.879). $75.00. Z1231.D7G38. 016.812'54099287. LC 92-42768. ISBN 0-8240-3046-X.

Limited to works by and about women playwrights active during the 25-year period from 1964 to 1989, Gavin's bibliography is thorough and well researched. The tone of the introduction and some of the annotations, however, betray her aversion to traditional theater, which she views as dominated by Caucasian males. For example, her claim that plays by women, such as Marsha Norman's *'night Mother* and Wendy Wasserstein's *The Heidi Chronicles*, have been ignored by the theatrical community, academia, and the general public is unfounded, because both plays won Pulitzer Prizes (as Gavin admits) and had very successful runs in New York City. Elsewhere, Gavin further distinguishes among female playwrights by singling out "multicultural" playwrights for special attention.

Despite the lapses into subjectivity, Gavin has produced a well-organized work, dividing it into three sections: an introductory bibliographical essay; an annotated list of general works on the topic; and, by far the largest section, an annotated bibliography of works by individual playwrights and secondary literature about the women and their plays. The author index is useful, but a list of multicultural playwrights without page references serves no obvious purpose. Recommended for theater collections. [R: Choice, Oct 93, p. 266; RBB, 1 Oct 93, p. 377]—**Valerie R. Hotchkiss**

Fiction

1229. **Facts on File Bibliography of American Fiction 1866-1918.** James Nagel and Gwen L. Nagel with Judith S. Baughman, eds. New York, Facts on File, 1993. 412p. index. $95.00. Z1231.F4B46. 016.813'4. LC 92-32466. ISBN 0-8160-2116-3.

This is the second installment of Facts on File's bibliography of American fiction writers. The first covered the period 1919-1988 (see ARBA 92, entry 1162); a future compilation will survey the years 1588-1865. Volumes devoted to drama, poetry, and nonfiction are also planned. The present work treats 149 authors whose important writings were published between the Civil War and World War I. Selection was determined by an advisory board for the series; according to an editors' note, scores of writers not found in earlier standard bibliographies were added. A check against Gale's mammoth Dictionary of Literary Biography series yielded 40 names not covered there, and other sources in the field showed even less overlap. Predictable stalwarts—Willa Cather, Mark Twain, and Edith Wharton, for example—are included, but so are virtual unknowns, such as Mary Hallock Foote, Edward Noyes Westcott, and William McFee. Humorists, children's and genre writers, and regionalists make up many of the unique names.

Entries are from 2 to 10 pages in length and are signed by a variety of contributing scholars. Each contains a biographical headnote followed by lists of bibliographies, primary works, correspondence, biographies, archives, and selected critical studies (e.g., books, special journals, book sections, articles). Arrangement of the latter is alphabetical by critic instead of chronological or by work covered, which hinders ease of use. The cutoff date for all listings is December 31, 1988, unfortunately making them somewhat dated.

With similar bibliographies already available, many libraries will find this work redundant. Still, Facts on File has provided a concise, serviceable guide useful primarily to undergraduates or scholars dealing with previously neglected peripheral writers. [R: Choice, May 93, p. 1440; LJ, 1 May 93, pp. 80-82]—**Willa Schmidt**

1230. **Index to American Short Story Award Collections 1970-90.** By Thomas E. Kennedy. New York, G. K. Hall, 1993. 116p. $40.00. Z1231.F4K46. 016.813'0108054. LC 92-38295. ISBN 0-8161-1819-1.

Many thousands of short stories are published annually, most of them in literary magazines with small circulations. A few are selected for "best" short story anthologies, but the vast majority remain unindexed and unlauded. This work provides information on seven of the most important short story awards series in the United States: the Pushcart Prize, the American Fiction Series, the AWP Short Fiction

Award, the Drue Heinz Literature Prize, the Flannery O'Connor Award, the University of Illinois Short Fiction Series, and the Iowa School of Letters Award. Each honors outstanding stories and collections of stories that, in most cases, originally appeared in U.S. literary quarterlies and small magazines.

By listing winners of longstanding short story awards in one place, this work enables those interested in short stories to find individual authors and titles. Although the index spans only 20 years, the stories may go back as far as 50 years. The choices of the editors may also be studied as representative of the best of the small press, generally considered to be the guardians of noncommercial, literate short stories. Thus, this book might be valuable for a collection that emphasizes short stories. The general public will probably not find much of interest in it.—**Kay O. Cornelius**

1231. Lachman, Marvin. **A Reader's Guide to the American Novel of Detection.** New York, G. K. Hall, 1993. 435p. (Reader's Guides to Mystery Novels). $45.00. PS374.D4L28. 813'.08720924. LC 92-25726. ISBN 0-8161-1803-5.

Mysteries are a popular form of recreational literature. *A Reader's Guide to the American Novel of Detection* is a new guide to this genre. The author covers novels by authors from the United States and Canada published between 1878 and 1991. The detectives in these books are, for the most part, amateurs who do not earn a living solving crimes. Subsequent volumes in the series will cover professional detectives and police officers.

The main body of the book is an alphabetical list of authors with brief summaries of their major works. This constitutes a virtual who's who of amateur detective fiction with a few notable exceptions: Sarah Shankman's Samantha Adams series, Susan Dunlap's Vejay Haskell, and Faye Kellerman's Rina Lazarus. No plots are revealed, and entries with incomplete bibliographies are indicated with an asterisk. If the American and British editions of a work have different titles, both are listed. Unlike *Critical Survey of Mystery and Detective Fiction* (see ARBA 90, entry 1106), no analysis is provided.

This source also has a number of features that will be useful for mystery readers. Lists of authors' pseudonyms, series characters and their creators, occupations of series characters, locations (geographical), settings, and historical periods of stories will help people looking for specific types of mysteries. A list of stories taking place during holidays provides access to other special themes. A section of miscellaneous information offers a list of novels that go beyond the expected in telling the reader about a subject (e.g., Elizabeth Peters on archaeology, Amanda Cross on feminism, Elliott Roosevelt on Franklin Roosevelt's presidency). Overall, *A Reader's Guide to the American Novel of Detection* is a good addition to literature collections. [R: Choice, Oct 93, p. 268; RBB, Aug 93, p. 2095]—**Barbara M. Bibel**

Individual Authors

S. N. Behrman

1232. Gross, Robert F. **S. N. Behrman: A Research and Production Sourcebook.** Westport, Conn., Greenwood Press, 1992. 197p. index. (Modern Dramatists Research and Production Sourcebooks, no.3). $55.00. PS3503.E37Z68. 813'.52. LC 92-26481. ISBN 0-313-27852-0.

Written for those unfamiliar with S. N. Behrman, those interested in the technical aspects of the theater, or those curious about the people with whom Behrman worked, this text provides both background and bibliographies for a playwright, author, and social critic whose best-known work is *Fanny*. Because Behrman wrote prolifically, Gross limits himself to Behrman's work as dramatist and screenwriter, including and annotating only those other pieces that illuminate his dramatic output.

Although each chapter has its own purpose, the codes and numbers used for cross-referencing and indexing are somewhat unhelpful. For instance, the letter *A* is used for Behrman's fiction (the second section of the primary bibliography), a designation that stems neither from the bibliography's subject nor from its position in the book. Also, the chapter "Plays: Summaries, Productions, and Critical Overviews," which discusses the plays chronologically, is followed by the first primary bibliography, which lists them alphabetically. Of course, these two lists serve different purposes—one emphasizes production history, the other publications—but given that the chronology at the beginning of the book already indicates the order of productions, perhaps combining all the information about each play in one entry would simplify matters. Curiously, each secondary bibliography is arranged not by type of item or by author but by chronology. In general, though, the appreciation of Behrman, the production notes, and the bibliographic annotations are helpful and well written.—**Rebecca Jordan**

Emily Dickinson

1233. Duchac, Joseph. **The Poems of Emily Dickinson: An Annotated Guide to Commentary Published in English, 1978-1989.** New York, G. K. Hall, 1993. 525p. (Reference Publication in Literature). $55.00. Z8230.5.D83. 016.811'54. LC 92-32694. ISBN 0-8161-7352-4.

With its companion volume (*The Poems of Emily Dickinson: An Annotated Guide to Commentary Published in English, 1890-1977* by Duchac [G. K. Hall, 1979]), this edition brings Dickinson criticism to the close of its first 100 years. Duchac points out that during the last decade, two new trends in Dickinson criticism have emerged. First, a politically correct one: The chief emphasis over the last 10 years has been that Dickinson is a *woman* poet, whereas before she had been viewed as simply an especially American one. Second, a more technical concern deals with the position of the poems in the discovered fascicles. A number of critics have made much of the placement of the poems therein and what patterns may be ascertained with respect to poems preceding and following the one under scrutiny. Both trends are covered amply here.

The volume aims at thoroughness and will allow students, faculty, and Dickinson aficionados access to all the major and minor criticism of her poems. Even very brief (e.g., a paragraph) explications are covered. Explications of her poems published in Japan are also included, although Duchac points out how elusive these materials are.

Poems are arranged by first lines followed by the date of the criticism (earliest first) and citation. In most cases a line or two of the explication is included. With both these volumes, librarians should be able to supply everyone with some explication of just about any poem by Dickinson. [R: RQ, Winter 93, pp. 293-94]—**Mark Y. Herring**

Hilda Doolittle (H. D.)

1234. Boughn, Michael. **H.D.: A Bibliography 1905-1990.** Charlottesville, Va., for the Bibliographical Society of the University of Virginia by University Press of Virginia, 1993. 229p. index. $39.50. Z8237.4.B68. 016.811'52. LC 92-28953. ISBN 0-8139-1412-4.

Because this is the only bibliography of H.D. (Hilda Doolittle, 1886-1961), it will probably be added to the shelves of most larger academic and public libraries. It is divided into two parts—work by H.D. and work on H.D. The five sections of part 1 include H.D.'s books, pamphlets, and broadsides; her contributions to books and pamphlets; her contributions to periodicals; her translations; and miscellanea (e.g., musical settings and recordings). Each entry in the first section provides such standard information as title, edition, type design, pagination, paper quality and size, the contents, and the institutions where the edition can be found. The entries in each of the other four sections are also bibliographically complete.

The five sections of part 2 list reviews of her books by title (grouped chronologically); chronologically arranged articles about her in periodicals; books and parts of books about H.D.; dissertations and theses; and miscellaneous publications, such as published letters, catalogs, photographs, and obituaries. The study concludes with an index of titles by H.D. and a general name and title index. The book is well bound and reasonably priced, with a particularly handsome dust jacket. [R: Choice, Oct 93, p. 262]
—**Charles R. Andrews**

Chester Himes

1235. Fabre, Michael, Robert E. Skinner, and Lester Sullivan, comps. **Chester Himes: An Annotated Primary and Secondary Bibliography.** Westport, Conn., Greenwood Press, 1992. 216p. index. (Bibliographies and Indexes in Afro-American and African Studies, no.30). $55.00. Z8406.8.F33. 016.813'54. LC 92-18316. ISBN 0-313-28396-6.

Chester Himes (1909-1984) was an influential Afro-American writer best known for his early novel *If He Hollers Let Him Go* (1945) and his detective novels (most notably *Cotton Comes to Harlem* [1965], which was made into a successful film in 1970). He achieved his greatest fame in France, where he lived for much of his creative life, and one of the strengths of this new bibliography is that a significant amount of French material is included. There has been renewed bibliographical interest in Himes after a flurry of brief items appeared in the 1970s. A major critical study, *Chester Himes* by Gilbert Muller (Twayne, 1989), contains a substantial bibliography, and Himes is prominently featured in Joseph Weixlmann's long bibliographical essay "African American Autobiography in the Twentieth Century" (*Black American Literature Forum* 24 [Summer 1990]: 375-415).

This annotated bibliography offers a complete listing of Himes's works, arranged by type of writing: all United States, French, and British editions of his books (both fiction and nonfiction); first periodical appearances of his writings; collected short fiction; manuscripts; and a filmography. Solid annotations are provided for Himes's nonfiction pieces but not for his short fiction. The secondary bibliography is arranged by decades, from 1945 through 1990, and most of these entries are also well annotated. The items are listed alphabetically by author for each year of publication. Book-length studies, book chapters, periodical articles, reviews, dramatic works, and even broadcast interviews are included. However, the compilers missed Muller's 1989 study. A useful introductory essay surveys Himes's career and evaluates his critical reception. The bibliographical challenge of working on Himes is detailed, and brief consideration is given to his influence on other writers. A chronology of Himes's life is also a helpful feature, as are author and title indexes.

In spite of occasional gaps in the critical literature, this work will stand as the definitive bibliography on Himes for some time to come. It is highly recommended for all academic libraries and other libraries with strong African-American collections.—**Thomas A. Karel**

Dorothy Parker

1236. Calhoun, Randall. **Dorothy Parker: A Bio-Bibliography.** Westport, Conn., Greenwood Press, 1993. 174p. index. (Bio-bibliographies in American Literature, no.4). $45.00. PS3531.A5855Z6. 818'.5209. LC 92-30882. ISBN 0-313-26507-0.

This volume will introduce many younger readers to, and reacquaint others with, the varied literary contributions of a writer who could, by turns, be "America's wittiest woman" or a "catty, heartless" witch. The study begins with an informative preface, followed by a 39-page biographical sketch. The major part of this nicely balanced work consists of primary and secondary bibliographies. The former is divided into six sections: books, short stories, screenplays, published interviews, miscellaneous work, and individual pieces; the arrangements within are essentially chronological. The secondary bibliography, preceded by Calhoun's critical analysis, is chronologically arranged (1922-1992), with annotated entries in each year listed alphabetically. Following the two bibliographies is an appendix of three biographical sketches by Richard E. Lauterbach (1944), Wyatt Cooper (1968), and Joseph Bryan III (1985); Cooper and Bryan had known Parker as a friend over the years. With its combination of scholarly and personal elements, this sprightly bio-bibliography will be a welcome addition to academic, public, and school libraries.

—**Charles R. Andrews**

Ann Petry

1237. Ervin, Hazel Arnett. **Ann Petry: A Bio-Bibliography.** New York, Macmillan, 1993. 115p. index. $45.00. Z8676.9.E78. 016.813'54. LC 92-36575. ISBN 0-8161-7278-1.

This bio-bibliography includes a chronology, an introduction, two bibliographies, several interviews, and an index. The bibliographies are divided by primary and secondary works, and the first is subdivided by genre (e.g., fiction, prose, poetry). Both are arranged alphabetically and numbered; the index refers to these numbers rather than to page numbers. Although this is the first compilation of such sources in one text, the secondary bibliography includes only those sources Ervin has seen. Thus, more material on Petry may be available than this bibliography suggests. Oddly enough, the chronology serves as the primary biographical source; it precedes the introduction, and both are relegated to prefatory materials. If the book began with an essay that provides a more formal appreciation or an overview of Petry's life and importance, this approach would help those who know little or nothing about this writer. Certainly, it would fit naturally into the main text, and truly prefatory material, such as acknowledgments, methods, and scope, could remain where it is. The bibliographical entries are generally thorough, including information on original publication and on reprints and using cross-references as necessary. The annotations, however, vary in scope and purpose. Some provide only plot summaries; others are evaluative. Perhaps more consistency would strengthen them—at least the thesis of each secondary article, in addition to its relative importance. Most helpful are the interviews with which the volume concludes. In several of these a genuine sense of Petry's values, personality, aesthetic, and life emerges.—**Rebecca Jordan**

Robert Reginald

1238. Burgess, Michael. **The Work of Robert Reginald: An Annotated Bibliography & Guide.** 2d ed. San Bernadino, Calif., Borgo Press, 1992. 176p. index. (Bibliographies of Modern Authors, no.5). $27.00; $17.00pa. Z8736.47.R43. 016.8093'876. LC 87-6306. ISBN 0-8095-0505-3; 0-8095-1505-9pa.

Robert Reginald is one of Burgess's many pseudonyms, and this volume—published by the press he founded in 1975—is an exhaustive annotated bibliography of a prodigious writer, bibliographer, scholar, librarian, and publisher. Burgess is particularly well known in science fiction circles and has written, edited, or published dozens of works in this field.

While this bibliography is a useful list of Burgess's many publications (although some of the items cited are merely one-page, in-house flyers and order forms), the work is, regrettably, padded with paeans to the author's scholarship and intelligence. An introduction, preface, and afterword all gush with cloying tributes, as does the lengthy chronology of his life that he wrote (e.g., following 1965, he states that he "scores in the 99-1/2th percentile on SAT test"). Parts of the volume are devoted to listing his public appearances, works for which he was a consultant, and even books that were dedicated to him (with dedications printed). In one section Burgess lists the different Library of Congress class numbers for himself as an author, bibliographer, and publisher. It is unfortunate that Burgess did not heed his own words, published in volume 6 of *Contemporary Authors, New Revision Series* (Gale, 1982): "It's difficult to say much about oneself without seeming pompous or just plain silly."—**Jack Bales**

Lionel Trilling

1239. Leitch, Thomas M. **Lionel Trilling: An Annotated Bibliography.** Hamden, Conn., Garland, 1993. 626p. index. (Garland Bibliographies of Modern Critics and Critical Schools, v.19; Garland Reference Library of the Humanities, v.1303). $99.00. Z8885.48.L43. 016.818'5209. LC 92-23192. ISBN 0-8240-7128-X.

Although he is not as often read today as he was in his lifetime, Lionel Trilling is one of the most important literary and cultural critics of the twentieth century. And while he was primarily read by other scholars, Trilling hoped that at least some of his criticism and fiction would be appreciated by a general audience. Accordingly, as Leitch points out in his preface, this primary and secondary bibliography, while directed to scholars, is also intended for a general audience.

The book is divided into three parts: primary works, secondary works, and background works. Primary works include separate sections on books and essay collections; prefaces and books edited; essays, stories, poems, and review articles; reviews; and symposia, interviews, and miscellanea. Secondary works are similarly divided into separate bibliographical forms, including books, essays, and review articles about Trilling; reviews of books by him and about his writings; and dissertations. There are separate author and title indexes.

Leitch has clearly performed a labor of love. Each citation is carefully annotated, and major works, such as Trilling's books, receive long, thoughtful, objective summaries. The extensive introductory essay is only partly an overview of Trilling's career; it is also an assessment of Trilling's major contributions, both as a critic and writer of fiction, and is a model of the intense moral, psychological, and literary attention Trilling applied to everything he observed.

Leitch notes that while numerous critical studies have been written of Trilling, as yet no biography has been written. If Leitch himself is not intending to write such a book, he has certainly made some other writer's work much easier. [R: Choice, June 93, p. 1606; LJ, 1 June 93, p. 106]—**David Isaacson**

Mark Twain

1240. LeMaster, J. R., and James D. Wilson, eds. **The Mark Twain Encyclopedia.** Hamden, Conn., Garland, 1993. 848p. index. (Garland Reference Library of the Humanities, v.1249). $95.00. PS1330.M37. 818'.409. LC 92-45662. ISBN 0-8240-7212-X.

Addressed primarily to the general reader, this book covers all significant aspects of Twain's life and career. Some 180 scholars, most of them associated with U.S. universities and colleges, have contributed more than 700 articles to it. Coverage of Twain's life is extensive, with biography primarily used to provide insight into his works. Each entry concludes with a selective bibliography, and many entries include cross-references to related encyclopedia entries. Separate entries are devoted to Twain's novels; travel writings; and most of the short stories, sketches, and essays. These articles introduce major themes and outline important critical perspectives. The long entry on *The Adventures of Huckleberry Finn*, for instance, not only provides a brief plot summary but also discusses the extensive controversy about whether Twain diluted the moral force of the novel in his concluding chapters, as well as the book's alleged racial stereotyping. Other articles are devoted to large themes, such as Twain's humor; use of imagery; and attitudes toward sex, war, and religion. Some articles focus on specific characters, such as Huckleberry Finn. The book includes a detailed chronology of Twain's life, a genealogy of Twain and his wife, and an extensive index.

The entries read corroborate the editors' description of the book as reflecting a wide variety of scholarly judgments about Twain. This reviewer is also pleased to note that two scholars he knows, one an authority on Twain's illustrators, the other an expert on Twain's creation of the Angel Fish Club, have contributed entries on these subjects for the encyclopedia. While this book is primarily directed to the general reader, its synthesis of much disparate information will be welcomed by scholars. [R: Choice, Sept 93, p. 84; LJ, 1 May 93, p. 83; RBB, 15 Oct 93, p. 474; WLB, May 93, p. 119]—**David Isaacson**

Walt Whitman

1241. Myerson, Joel. **Walt Whitman: A Descriptive Bibliography.** Pittsburgh, University of Pittsburgh Press; distr, Ithaca, N.Y., CUP Services, 1993. 1097p. index. (Pittsburgh Series in Bibliography). $250.00. Z8971.5.M93. 016.811'3. LC 92-25927. ISBN 0-8229-3739-5.

Myerson's introduction thoroughly describes his purpose, scope, and methodology in compiling this bibliography. Nine sections and an appendix cover all books and pamphlets written by Walt Whitman, including all editions and reprintings through 1991 (in English and other languages); all collected editions of Whitman's writings through 1991; miscellaneous collections of the poet's work through 1991; all titles in which material by the poet appears for the first time in a book or a pamphlet (including prose, poetry, and letters); all first U.S. or English publications in newspapers and magazines of Whitman's materials through 1991; proof copies, circulars, and broadsides of his poetry and prose through 1892; prose and poetry reprinted in books and pamphlets through 1892; separate publications of individual poems and prose works through 1991; references to possible publications by the poet that are not covered in the bibliography; and principal works about Whitman. There are an index to the poems in *Leaves of Grass* and an index to the whole volume. Where applicable, entries include exhaustive detail about the material examined by the bibliographer, sometimes including fascimiles of the title and copyright pages, notes, articles, advertisements, and the like. Where required, meticulous physical descriptions of the work are provided, and location information is given in order to track down the work. Chronological arrangement makes the bibliography easy to use and the path of Myerson's research simple to follow.

Methodical research, well-thought-out presentation, and valuable information make this descriptive bibliography an excellent sourcebook on the works of Whitman. It is a must have for any serious Whitman collection, a valuable tool for the Whitman scholar, and a model for other bibliographies of this type.
—**Daphne Fallieros Potter**

Thornton Wilder

1242. Walsh, Claudette. **Thornton Wilder: A Reference Guide 1926-1990.** New York, G. K. Hall, 1993. 449p. index. (Reference Guide to Literature). $50.00. Z8975.7.W34. 016.818'5209. LC 91-13287. ISBN 0-8161-8790-8.

This well-conceived, scholarly, and attractively formatted volume about the first U.S. author to win the Pulitzer Prize in two genres should find a place on the reference shelves of almost all public and academic libraries. The text is chronologically arranged, beginning in 1926 with reviews of *The Cabala* and ending in 1990 with reviews of the fortieth anniversary revival of *Our Town*.

Within each "annual" section, the annotated entries are alphabetically arranged by author or by the first word of the title of the work when the author is unknown. Of considerable help in using the text is the inclusion at the top of each page of the year being covered. In attempting to consolidate all the criticism about Wilder's works written in English over this 64-year span, Walsh cites three criteria governing the compilation—accuracy, completeness, and neutrality. Her insistence on citing journal titles in full in the reviews is commendable and helpful; the only abbreviations are of Wilder's works, and those are listed in the prefatory material. Her method of citing references in both the author and the subject indexes (e.g., 1932.4—year and numbered entry) lends itself well to the textual arrangement and greatly facilitates index use. A useful chronology and an informative introduction begin the volume. [R: Choice, Sept 93, p. 92]
—**Charles R. Andrews**

British Literature

General Works

1243. Greenfield, John R., and David Brailow, with Arlyn Bruccoli, eds. **Dictionary of British Literary Characters: 18th- and 19th-Century Novels.** New York, Facts on File, 1993. 655p. index. $65.00. PR830.C47D5. 823'.80927'03. LC 90-3998. ISBN 0-8160-2179-1.

Taking *The Pilgrim's Progress* as its starting point and ending with authors who published most of their novels before 1890, this dictionary, the first half of a proposed two-volume series, provides brief descriptions of major and minor characters. It is exhaustive in its selection of novels by established authors and representative in its choice of novels by writers who were popular in their day or who have received some critical attention in ours. It includes more than 11,000 characters found in nearly 500 novels. The preface explains the editors' criteria for selecting these secondary novels and for choosing which characters to include.

The text is divided into two parts. The first, the dictionary proper, provides thumbnail sketches of these characters, beginning with Lord A— and ending with Apollonia Zulmer. The second, the index, arranges these characters by author and novel. Thus, if one knows the name of a particular character, one can use the first part; if one remembers only the novel, one can use the index to find the character's name. The dictionary entries describe the characters, specify their roles in whatever novels they inhabit, and indicate their functions and importance in those novels. For those characters that appear in more than one novel, the entries provide an overview of their careers. Of course, the importance of a character determines the length of its entry. [R: Choice, Oct 93, p. 265; RBB, 1 Oct 93, pp. 380-81; RQ, Winter 93, pp. 282-83; WLB, Sept 93, p. 115]—**Rebecca Jordan**

1244. Howard-Hill, T. H. **British Literary Bibliography, 1970-1979: A Bibliography.** New York, Clarendon Press/Oxford University Press, 1992. 912p. index. (Index to British Literary Biography, v.7). $180.00. Z2011.A1H68. 016.01682. LC 91-2557. ISBN 0-19-818183-3.

This volume continues coverage in a series that lists bibliographical works about British textual and bibliographical history, whether published as monographs or as articles. Although the primary focus is on works published in the 1970s, items published between 1890 and 1969 that were missed in other volumes of this index have been included under appropriate subject headings. Arrangement is chronological under subject and then alphabetical by author. Types of works include checklists, catalogs, guides, and bibliographies. Most of the material listed has been examined by the compiler, is in English or other European languages, and is available at major research libraries. Many entries include brief objective annotations, and some include citations to reviews.

Major divisions of this volume include general bibliographies of English literature; bibliography and textual criticism; general and period bibliography (with chronological subdivisions); regional bibliography (of the British Isles); book production and distribution; forms, genres, and subjects; and authors (almost half of the book is devoted to an alphabetical list of British authors, both well known and minor). There is an index of authors, editors, compilers, and publishers, and one of subjects. Some subject headings are duplicates of those in the bibliography itself, while others provide access to terms not in the book.

Although the price of this book reflects the considerable disadvantage (from a United States point of view) in the exchange rate with Great Britain, this volume is an indispensable work of meticulous scholarship. It is especially necessary for libraries owning previous volumes in the series. [R: Choice, Mar 93, p. 1114]—**David Isaacson**

1245. **Index of English Literary Manuscripts. Volume II: 1625-1700. Part 2: Lee-Wycherley.** Peter Beal, comp. New York, Mansell/Cassell, 1993. 656p. $500.00. 016.8208. ISBN 0-7201-1997-9.

This index of all known surviving manuscripts by literary authors from the period 1625-1700 with surnames beginning with L to Z completes the earlier volume published in 1987 of those with names A to K. Of the 24 writers included in part 2, some, such as Nathaniel Lee and George Sandys, are minor literary figures who left almost no examples of their handwriting; others are major writers, such as Samuel Pepys, John Milton, the Cavalier poets, and Izaak Walton. Repositories of the manuscripts are listed alphabetically under both institutions and private owners, followed by an alphabetical list of names and addresses of auction houses and book sellers. There are 24 pages of manuscript facsimiles never previously reproduced. Some display a full page of poetry or part of a letter; others are simple autographs.

Each author is introduced by information on modern scholarly and standard editions of the author's work and an essay that discusses provenance, the writer's working methods, and sources. Each work is then given a code symbol and number. The alphabetically arranged titles are divided into such topics as verse, prose, dramatic works, and miscellaneous. Surviving correspondence is numbered and described. When books from authors' libraries are known, especially if signed or annotated, they too are given. Even annotations by later authors, such as those in Herman Melville's or Thomas Hardy's copies of Milton, are mentioned along with their whereabouts. Because this expensive volume contains information difficult (if not impossible) to find elsewhere, at least in such an organized, professionally annotated form, it is an invaluable research tool for scholars of seventeenth-century literature.—**Charlotte Lindgren**

1246. **Index of English Literary Manuscripts. Volume III: 1700-1800. Part 3: Alexander Pope—Sir Richard Steele....** Margaret M. Smith and Alexander Lindsay, comps. New York, Mansell/Cassell, 1992. 460p. index. $350.00. 016.8208. ISBN 0-7201-2038-1.

Volume 3 is intended as a comprehensive survey of eighteenth-century manuscripts divided alphabetically into four books. Part 3 deals with 11 of the authors: Alexander Pope, Matthew Prior, Ann Radcliffe, Allan Ramsay, Samuel Richardson, the Earl of Shaftesbury, William Shenstone, Richard Brinsley Sheridan,

Christopher Smart, Tobias Smollett, and Richard Steele. It begins with the addresses of the repositories of the manuscripts and of auction houses and booksellers. Following a list of regularly used abbreviations are 11 full-page facsimiles of a letter or page handwritten by each author.

Informational essays about the manuscripts range from 17 pages, in the case of Pope, to a single page for Radcliffe, for whom only one letter and some surviving entries in a commonplace book are still extant. In addition to principal works and locations of papers, frequent topics of discussion are recent attributions and misattributions, drawings and sketches, editors and biographers, correspondence, and annotations. A list of specific abbreviations precedes bibliographical information on verse, prose, dramatic works, diaries and notebooks, and marginalia in printed books and manuscripts. Titles are in boldface type followed by description, first publication, numbered siglum, transcriber if known, and the present owner and location of the manuscript and any microfilm copies. The book concludes with an index of first lines from author entry sections of the first three parts of volume 3. The organization and layout of this quarto-size volume, with its broad margins, indentations, and wide spacing, facilitate the use of this expensive, but invaluable, research book.—**Charlotte Lindgren**

Individual Authors

Patrick Branwell Bronte

1247. Neufeldt, Victor A., ed. **A Bibliography of the Manuscripts of Patrick Branwell Bronte.** Hamden, Conn., Garland, 1993. 156p. index. $46.00. Z6616.B8287B53. 016.828'809. LC 93-8646. ISBN 0-8153-1563-5.

Unlike that of his three sisters, the literary achievements of Patrick Branwell Bronte have gone relatively unnoticed. Moreover, as Bronte scholar Neufeldt points out in the introduction, barriers to the serious study of Branwell Bronte's works remain. A good deal of his writing—particularly the prose—is unpublished; much of what is in print appears in fragmented or inaccurate form; and the manuscripts are scattered among at least a dozen different collections in England and the United States.

This ambitious compilation serves as a starting point for an accurate assessment of the quality of Branwell Bronte's writings by providing, to the extent possible, complete and accurate descriptions of all of his manuscripts, excluding letters. The work's 289 entries, which include questionable and variant texts, are arranged alphabetically in four sections: prose manuscripts, poetry manuscripts, translations, and miscellaneous manuscripts. Extensive information is provided for each manuscript, including a brief description of its contents, often with cross-references to other entries; details about the physical characteristics, such as type of script, format, size, and length; the manuscript's location; and where the first complete publication appears, if at all. A chronological index, designed to give a brief overview of the sequence of the works, concludes the bibliography. This source is certain to be indispensable to Branwell Bronte scholars and is recommended for large research libraries and those with comprehensive Victorian literature collections.—**Linda Cullum**

Elizabeth Barrett Browning

1248. Donaldson, Sandra. **Elizabeth Barrett Browning: An Annotated Bibliography of the Commentary and Criticism, 1826-1990.** New York, Macmillan, 1993. 642p. index. $55.00. Z8124.4.D66. 016.821'8. LC 92-24448. ISBN 0-8161-8910-2.

This comprehensive bibliography of commentary and criticism on the Victorian poet Elizabeth Barrett Browning is a major research tool for students, scholars, and others interested in her life and work. The entries are arranged chronologically by year and alphabetically by author within each year, except for reviews of works during her lifetime, which are placed at the beginning of the year in which they appeared. French and Italian critical works are included, but German and Japanese ones are not. The index is in two parts. The first provides location of entries on Browning's works, and the second is a general index of persons, places, other publications, and biographical references. Various subjects and events are indexed as well.

This volume was built upon two base bibliographies: Leslie Nathan Broughton, Clark Sutherland Northup, and Robert Pearsall's *Robert Browning: A Bibliography, 1830-1950* (Cornell University Press, 1954) and *Bibliographies of Twelve Victorian Authors* by Theodore G. Ehrsam and Robert H. Deily (Octagon House, 1968). Other published bibliographical books and articles are included and annotated throughout the chronological sequence of entries, along with biographical works, dissertations, and collections of Browning materials. There are also entries related to libraries holding crucial resources. The annotations and commentary are very well done. Other important facets of this bibliography are the suggestions from critics and Donaldson for further research and study.

This is a crucial work for the study of Elizabeth Barrett Browning. The range of criticism and commentary covers scholarly journals, theological publications, journals of political commentary, women's magazines, books, and collections of her works. This publication is easy to use and the most complete of the many bibliographical works available on the poet. [R: Choice, Nov 93, p. 428]

—Maureen Pastine

Leslie Charteris

1249. Barer, Burl. **The Saint: A Complete History in Print, Radio, Film and Television of Leslie Charteris' Robin Hood of Modern Crime, Simon Templar, 1928-1992.** Jefferson, N.C., McFarland, 1993. 419p. illus. index. $55.00. PR6005.H348Z59. 823'.912. LC 92-53509. ISBN 0-89950-723-9.

Leslie Charteris's creation, Simon Templar, a.k.a. the Saint, has survived to become a quasi-immortal after nearly 75 years of incarnations in various media. This book provides a detailed and lively look at both the character and the creator, solidly based on extensive research in the Charteris Collection at Boston University. The last 160 pages, approximately two-fifths of the text, consist of appendixes that give plot synopses of radio programs with air dates and production credits; descriptions of the films and their credits, illustrated with movie stills, many featuring Roger Moore (who later starred as another hero, James Bond); additional script synopses; a bibliography; and a general index with title references. This is a good, although overpriced, reference for popular culture buffs and libraries. [R: Choice, Sept 93, p. 74]

—Mary Jo Walker

Geoffrey Chaucer

1250. Benson, Larry D. **A Glossarial Concordance to the Riverside Chaucer.** Hamden, Conn., Garland, 1993. 2v. (Garland Reference Library of the Humanities, v.1699). $200.00/set. PR1941.B46. 821'.1. LC 93-8477. ISBN 0-8153-1290-3.

This two-volume glossarial concordance to Larry Benson's *Riverside Chaucer* (Houghton Mifflin, 1986) (a widely respected edition of the complete works) supersedes John Strong Perry Tatlock and Arthur G. Kennedy's *Concordance to the Complete Works of Geoffrey Chaucer* (P. Smith, 1963) and is the sole concordance to include brief definitions. All words are concorded except titles, glosses, implicits, and explicits. Spellings are listed under words they represent rather than in alphabetical order by each variant spelling (i.e., the work is not primarily a spelling concordance). Entries also contain references to that word in the *Oxford English Dictionary* (see ARBA 90, entry 1006) and the *Middle English Dictionary* (see ARBA 92, entry 1037) so that readers may examine easily how other writers, particularly later writers, may have employed the words. Volume 1 contains information on the organization of entries, how the concordance works, and the concordance. Volume 2 contains a supplementary concordance that includes the B and C fragments of the *Romaunt of the Rose*, the *Supplementary Propositions to the Astrolabe*, "Complaynt d'Amours," and "A Balade of Complaint." This volume also contains an index of spellings in the main concordance, an index of spellings in the supplementary concordance, an index of Modern English Equivalents, a ranked list of high-frequency spellings, a ranked list of high-frequency words, and frequency lists of spellings and words in the supplementary concordance. For a concordance of spellings, Akio Oizumi's 10-volume *A Complete Concordance to the Works of Chaucer* (Hy Cohen, 1991) is superior. But for searching for meanings, Benson's work is superior. This concordance is indispensable for libraries housing Chaucer's works, Middle English literature, and Middle English linguistic studies.

—C. B. (Bob) Darrell

Charles Dickens

1251. Glancy, Ruth F. *A Tale of Two Cities*: **An Annotated Bibliography.** Hamden, Conn., Garland, 1993. 236p. index. (Garland Dickens Bibliographies, v.12; Garland Reference Library of the Humanities, v.1339). $40.00. Z8230.G58. 016.823'8. LC 92-40546. ISBN 0-8240-7091-7.

Students facing the task of writing a critical paper on Dickens's *A Tale of Two Cities* can use this thorough bibliography to transform the potentially worst of times into the best of times. Regardless from which angle they approach the novel, this three-part bibliography, complete with a detailed subject and name index, will help them identify and evaluate relevant published works. Its 672 annotated entries are arranged in three sections. The first lists materials relating to the novel's genesis and publication history, including all important editions published during the author's lifetime; later editions containing new prefatory or critical material; adaptations in other media (film, musicals, radio, voice recordings, and abridgments); and criticism of these adaptations. The second section lists critical studies alphabetically by author in six broad topical categories (e.g., contemporary reviews, literary influences, parallels). The final section lists omnibus Dickens and Victorian novel bibliographies. Lengthy annotations summarize the arguments made in the criticism, ranging from the novel's reception by its Victorian contemporaries through scholarly considerations published during 1991. The annotations refer by entry number to other items that treat a similar theme or that argue against an earlier interpretation. Citations to reviews appear at the conclusion of annotations of books, a helpful feature for researchers who want to augment Glancy's descriptive annotations with critical opinions. Undergraduates will appreciate the overview of major themes and the critical consensus (or contradictions) regarding those themes presented in Glancy's introduction. They and more advanced students of Dickens and his famous, much-studied novel with its problematic conclusion will likewise appreciate the timesaving work Glancy has done for them in identifying these primary and secondary works and in describing the scope of each.—**James Rettig**

Richard Jefferies

1252. Miller, George, and Hugoe Matthews. **Richard Jefferies: A Bibliographical Study.** Brookfield, Vt., Scolar Press/Ashgate Publishing, 1993. 787p. illus. index. $129.95. ISBN 0-85967-918-7.

It is hard to imagine a more comprehensive bibliography than this one of the works of rural British writer Richard Jefferies (1848-1887). Miller and Matthews have spent the past 20 years collecting and researching Jefferies's works in order to produce this exhaustive record of more than 1,500 individual items by or about their subject. Jefferies's known periodical contributions, books, and pamphlets are listed and carefully described, as are all works that have been anthologized or collected. Information about his extant manuscripts, letters, and associated documents is also provided. A list of relevant biographical and critical studies through 1987 completes the study, and attractive illustrations enrich the work throughout.

The book's most extensive section, and its most fascinating, is the one in which each of the 42 published editions of Jefferies's books and pamphlets is described. Every title is prefaced by an in-depth introduction explaining the circumstances surrounding the composition and first publication of the text or, in the case of posthumous publications, their relationship to the canon of his works. These discussions are based on surviving correspondence, publishers' records, and entries in Jefferies's notebooks, providing a unique and authoritative perspective on both the man and his writing.

With its unfailing thoroughness, stylistic clarity, and meticulous attention to detail, this work is certain to be an indispensable source for the study of Jefferies's works and will set a standard for future bibliographical studies. Despite its cost, it is highly recommended for large research libraries.
—**Linda Cullum**

William Langland

1253. Alford, John A. **Piers Plowman: A Guide to the Quotations.** Binghamton, N.Y., Medieval & Renaissance Texts & Studies, State University of New York at Binghamton, 1992. 153p. index. (Medieval & Renaissance Texts & Studies, v.77). $15.00. PR2017.Q67A44. 821'1. LC 91-31220. ISBN 0-86698-088-1.

This work by the author of *Piers Plowman: A Glossary of Legal Diction* (Boydell & Brewer, 1987) and numerous articles published in *Speculum, Medium Aevum,* and *Chaucer Review* consolidates what is known about nearly 600 different quotations in Latin and French (counting repeated instances, nearly 1,200 in all) in William Langland's poem. With the translations and commentary, the quotations account for nearly half the poem's substance and, perhaps, much of its form. The volume begins with an introductory essay and analyzes the various lines of transmission of the quotations. The quotations are then presented in three ways. Index 1 lists them in text order and provides extensive information on sources and analogies. Index 2 arranges the biblical quotations in biblical order. Index 3 arranges all the quotations in alphabetical order.

Alford's work is the first comprehensive guide to the Latin and French quotations in all three versions (Athlone edition), and it facilitates access to Langland's quotations and their sources. It will also serve as an invaluable research tool and as a foundation for further study of their artistic function. This guide is recommended for English collections in large academic libraries.—**Mark Padnos**

C. S. Lewis

1254. Lowenberg, Susan. **C. S. Lewis: A Reference Guide 1972-1988.** New York, G. K. Hall, 1993. 304p. index. (Reference Guide to Literature). $55.00. Z8504.37.L68. 016.823'912. LC 92-42316. ISBN 0-8161-1846-9.

Those who found *C. S. Lewis: An Annotated Checklist of Writings about Him and His Works* (see ARBA 75, entry 1390) valuable for research will heartily welcome this sequel to that bibliography. Too bad it leaves the last five years uncovered—but one can hope a third compilation is in the works. Lowenberg collects in one list all the books and chapters in books, essays, periodical articles, and doctoral dissertations published between July 1972 and December 1988. These items each contain biographical, bibliographical, or critical information about Lewis and his works. Book reviews, master's theses, audio and visual materials, games and software, and reports of meetings of C. S. Lewis societies are excluded. Reprints are also left out unless significant revisions were made. And, as is expected, the book contains a bibliography of Lewis's writings.

The introduction is a well-written summary of Lewis's life that explores a number of controversies that arose in the 1980s surrounding Lewis's works. Lowenberg approaches these issues with delicacy, but her annotations provide more information for the reader. For example, the summary of *The C. S. Lewis Hoax* by Kathryn Lindskoog (Multnomah, 1988) clearly states Lindskoog's main arguments. Lowenberg's annotations are all excellent in this way. The citations are arranged in chronological order by year of publication, then in alphabetical order by author name. (The previous checklist was in subject order.) The year of publication appears at the top of every page, a helpful feature for locating the citations. The chronological arrangement makes the author-subject index invaluable. A small number of the works cited were not examined by Lowenberg; these are noted with asterisks. In these cases either the source of the citation or the summary from *Dissertation Abstracts International* is provided. This checklist is invaluable for both scholars and lay readers of Lewis.—**Patricia M. Leach**

Christopher Marlowe

1255. Brandt, Bruce E. **Christopher Marlowe in the Eighties: An Annotated Bibliography of Marlowe Criticism from 1978 through 1989.** West Cornwall, Conn., Locust Hill Press, 1992. 215p. index. $30.00. Z8550.4.B7. 822'.3. LC 91-32885. ISBN 0-933951-45-0.

Beginning where *Christopher Marlowe: An Annotated Bibliography of Criticism since 1950* (see ARBA 81, entry 1321) ends (through 1977), Brandt's annotated bibliography essentially covers 1978-1989, although it does include a few titles missing from the former collection. This work has 542 items traditionally arranged according to editions, bibliographies, and concordances; general critical and biographical studies; separate chapters for each of the plays; and a chapter devoted to poetry and translations. Brandt also includes a chapter on novels based on Marlowe's life and on non-English Marlowe translations. The study also has an author and a subject index. The annotations (more than 400 entries are annotated) are objective, full, and concisely and clearly written. Inclusion of articles in foreign languages—grouped by the language—is especially useful because of the growing body of Marlowe criticism in languages other than English. Strongly recommended for graduate and undergraduate libraries housing collections on drama, the English Renaissance, Shakespeare, and English intellectual history.

—C. B. (Bob) Darrell

William Shakespeare

1256. Champion, Larry S. **The Essential Shakespeare: An Annotated Bibliography of Major Modern Studies.** 2d ed. New York, G. K. Hall, 1993. 568p. index. $70.00. Z8811.C53. 016.8223'3. LC 92-39078. ISBN 0-8161-7332-X.

This collection of more than 1,800 (including more than 600 new ones) of the most significant articles, books, and monographs of twentieth-century Shakespearean scholarship includes not only the classical studies but also ranges through structuralist, poststructuralist, deconstructionist, feminist, and cultural-materialist criticism since 1984. Moreover, Champion includes major studies from throughout the world, including influential studies from Japan. This book organizes the entries into chapters devoted to general studies, poems and sonnets, English history plays, comedies, tragedies, and romances. The annotations are detailed, generally accurate, clear, and objective in tone. There is a detailed index. *The Essential Shakespeare* remains an indispensable tool for efficient research for undergraduate students, graduate students, and busy teachers, and will prove valuable even to veteran Shakespearean scholars. [R: Choice, Nov 93, p. 424]—**C. B. (Bob) Darrell**

1257. Griffiths, Trevor R., and Trevor A. Joscelyn. **Shakespeare's Quotations.** Studio City, Calif., Players Press, 1992. 667p. index. $39.95. PR2892.G68. 822.3'3. LC 92-54180. ISBN 0-88734-620-0.

Originally published in the United Kingdom in 1985, this first United States edition marshals some 2,000 quotations, each presented in context, from all of Shakespeare's poems and plays (including the recently attributed *Two Noble Kinsmen*). All works are represented fairly, with selections from the lesser-known comedies and histories taking their place beside everyone's favorite lines; for example, there are as many quotations listed from *As You Like It* and *Henry IV Part I* as from *King Lear*. Because of the work's emphasis on context, quotations are arranged sequentially by play or poem, rather than the more common topical grouping. Following each quotation is an explanation that establishes the context and offers any other relevant information. An extensive keyword index, providing subject access to the quotations, concludes the work.

The issue, of course, is whether this compilation contributes anything new to an already crowded field: There are, after all, more than a dozen collections currently in print, including Charles DeLoach's comprehensive *The Quotable Shakespeare* (see ARBA 89, entry 1117) with more than 6,000 entries, and almost 2,000 Shakespeare quotations in that library staple, Bartlett's *Familiar Quotations* (see ARBA 93, entry 89). This work's uniqueness resides in the wealth of explanatory information provided, which ranges from glosses on problematic words and phrases to explications of extended passages. Explanations are thorough and unbiased, indicating where controversy surrounds a passage and noting significant intertextual allusions and critical studies. The result is a compelling mix of quotations and analysis, making this an appealing source for both casual readers and Shakespeare devotees alike. Recommended for large academic and public libraries.—**Linda Cullum**

1258. McLeish, Kenneth. **Shakespeare's Characters: A Players Press Guide.** Studio City, Calif., Players Press, 1992. 252p. $39.95. PR2989.M36. 822.3'3. LC 90-53234. ISBN 0-88734-608-1.

This guide lists in alphabetical order every character in Shakespeare's plays (but not his other poetry) and gives a capsule sketch of each, ranging from half a line for walk-ons to about a page for major figures. The listing also includes summaries of each play. The book seems to be aimed at readers only slightly familiar with the Bard, perhaps a high school student struggling with an assigned paper or an inexperienced actor asked to take a part in an amateur production.

McLeish is an actor and BBC commentator rather than a scholar: His character sketches are reasonably accurate but unsophisticated and old-fashioned. His approach is reminiscent more of Victorian critics such as A. C. Bradley than of anyone writing in the past 50 years. On the other hand, his obvious love of Shakespeare and his commonsense suggestions on acting will probably be more helpful to the novice than the esoteric readings of many recent academic critics. But most readers would probably get more out of simply reading the plays themselves in well-annotated editions. Recommended for a limited audience. [R: RBB, 1 April 93, p. 1460]—**Lynn F. Williams**

1259. **Shakespearean Criticism. Volume 19: Yearbook 1991: A Selection of the Year's Most Noteworthy Studies of William Shakespeare's Plays and Poetry.** Detroit, Gale, 1993. 459p. index. $114.00. LC 86-645085. ISBN 0-8103-7968-6. ISSN 0883-9123.

Originally planned to be 10 volumes long, *Shakespearean Criticism* has now progressed to 19. Building on the historical base of the first 10, the succeeding volumes have focused on 2 topics: the performance history of Shakespeare's plays and annual yearbooks of notable, innovative criticism published during that year. Volume 19, the 1991 yearbook, includes the complete texts of 43 articles and chapters covering 25 plays. The collection is eclectic, with no apparent bias. Gender and social issues are major topics, but linguistics, misrepresentation, and the themes of change, division, and violence are also covered. The vast majority of the essays deal with the plays as written literature, but two focus on the plays as films. One of the particular strengths of this series is its inclusion of chapters from monographs, which frequently are not cited in the popular indexing sources available to high school and undergraduate students.

Similar to the rest of the series, this yearbook is an important, easily accessible source for some of the best critical studies on Shakespeare. Any library serving students at the high school or undergraduate college level should seriously consider its purchase.—**Susan Davis Herring**

1260. Tardiff, Joseph C., and others, eds. **Shakespearean Criticism: Excerpts from the Criticism of William Shakespeare's Plays and Poetry.... Volume 18.** Detroit, Gale, 1992. 491p. illus. index. $114.00. LC 86-645085. ISBN 0-8103-7967-8. ISSN 0883-9123.

This work follows a tradition that started with volume 11, the first of the Performance Series. This series builds on the historical base of original volumes, which covered the critical history of the plays and poems up to 1988, to trace the performance and staging history of Shakespeare's plays. The current volume deals with *The Merry Wives of Windsor, Much Ado about Nothing*, and *Troilus and Cressida*. For each play the editors have supplied a brief introduction and history, followed by lengthy excerpts from critical reviews, commentaries, and essays on staging issues. The selections are arranged chronologically, starting with the first known production of each play. The reviews and commentaries are carefully chosen to illustrate a wide variety of opinions and interpretations and are arranged to show the frequently conflicting views of different critics. The essays on staging issues offer practical considerations of problems and their solutions, often from the producers themselves. A lengthy annotated bibliography completes each section.

The volumes in this series offer important commentary and criticism on the performances of Shakespeare's plays. Any library serving high school or college students interested in literature or theater will find them well worth the cost.—**Susan Davis Herring**

Leslie Stephen

1261. Fenwick, Gillian. **Leslie Stephen's Life in Letters: A Bibliographical Study.** Brookfield, Vt., Scolar Press/Ashgate Publishing, 1993. 436p. index. $79.95. ISBN 0-85967-912-8.

This bio-bibliographical study is more than a chronology and bibliography of Victorian critic and biographer Leslie Stephen. It is the first really comprehensive guide to his life, writing, and publishing, with emphasis on the *Dictionary of National Biography* (see ARBA 91, entry 13). Following a chronology of his life and writing from his birth in 1832 to his death in 1904, Fenwick discusses his life and the purpose of her research in the introduction. The book is divided into nine sections: books, pamphlets, translations, contributions to periodicals, the *Dictionary of National Biography* (which includes a lengthy essay on his role as founding editor and an alphabetical listing of all his identified contributions), works by others that he edited, posthumous publications, miscellaneous items (e.g., his memorial for his friend Henry Fawcett), and published letters (including quoted extracts). Each section has an alphabetical list of titles followed by a cogent essay discussing composition and publication; analytic descriptions of first English and U.S. editions, reissues, and reprints; and references cited.

Supplementary materials include eight pages of illustrations, such as drawings and annotations found in his books, and five appendixes that list his income from 1855 to 1903, the locations of manuscripts and resource materials, inscriptions and annotations by Stephen in books from the Leonard and Virginia Woolf Collection at Washington State University, excerpts from his writings in *The Library of Literary Criticism of English and American Writers* (Reprint Service, 1992), and books and articles about him. This book, indispensable for scholars of Stephen, is also entertaining reading for anyone interested in the history of nineteenth-century publishing.—**Charlotte Lindgren**

Oscar Wilde

1262. Mikolyzk, Thomas A., comp. **Oscar Wilde: An Annotated Bibliography.** Westport, Conn., Greenwood Press, 1993. 489p. index. (Bibliographies and Indexes in World Literature, no.38). $69.50. Z8975.M56. 016.828'809. LC 93-14052. ISBN 0-313-27597-1.

Since his death in 1900, Oscar Wilde's reputation as a wit and writer has been steadily increasing. Today he is widely adulated as a leading dramatist, novelist, and critic. That editors, scholars, and general readers appreciate the depth and appeal of Wilde's works can be supported by the existence of some 15,000 articles and books devoted to his life and writings. As with virtually all bibliographies, this one is incomplete, having in all about 4,000 entries. For a variety of reasons, a great deal of material has been passed by, but the most significant has been duly listed.

In his *Oscar Wilde Revalued* (1993) Ian Small gives an excellent overview of Wildean scholarship that got seriously under way in the 1960s; and when analyzed, he maintains, research done over the past 30 years portrays a figure quite different from the tragic egoist found in Richard Ellmann's *Oscar Wilde* (1987). Mikolyzk's bibliography allows Wilde enthusiasts to search out such materials and arrive at their own conclusions. Unfortunately, while Mikolyzk's annotations are basically sound and reflective of the quality and usefulness of the sources he has compiled, all too often he resorts to such negatives as "simple," "small," "trite," and "inadequate" or such hyperboles as "important," "unique," "solid," and "thoroughly documented." Not being a Wilde scholar himself, Mikolyzk would have been wise to limit such terms. Frequently, his oversimplifications border on falsifications. To his credit, however, he has provided scholars and devotees of Wilde with a volume that will aid in their research, stimulate critical thinking, and add to their appreciation and knowledge of an important literary figure whose reputation seems destined to grow geometrically.—**G. A. Cevasco**

Poetry

1263. Hasenfratz, Robert J. **Beowulf Scholarship: An Annotated Bibliography, 1979-1990.** Hamden, Conn., Garland, 1993. 424p. index. (Garland Medieval Bibliographies, v.14; Garland Reference Library of the Humanities, v.1422). $66.00. Z2012.H23. 016.829'3. LC 93-17683. ISBN 0-8153-0084-0.

One might think that by now everything possible has been said about the great Old English epic *Beowulf*, but the flood of scholarship goes on. Japanese scholars have added notably to the body of commentary on this poem, and new work comes from many other countries. *Beowulf Scholarship* continues the annotated bibliography by Douglas Short, which covered the period from 1705 through 1978. Entries are arranged chronologically by year and alphabetically by authors' names. The annotations are substantial and informative, some running to several pages. New translations are characterized by quoting their versions of lines 4-11 of the poem. There are a number of indexes arranged by author, subject, word, and line, so that scholars looking for new insights may easily find what they are searching for. All in all, this is a valuable addition to *Beowulf* scholarship. Recommended for large research libraries with collections in medieval literature.—**Lynn F. Williams**

1264. Hester, M. Thomas, ed. **Seventeenth-Century British Nondramatic Poets. First Series.** Detroit, Gale, 1992. 414p. illus. index. (Dictionary of Literary Biography, v.121). $112.00. LC 92-17232. ISBN 0-8103-7598-2.

This volume of the well-known Dictionary of Literary Biography (DLB) series focuses on British poets who wrote during the reign of James I (1603-1625). Sandwiched between the glory and security of the Elizabethan age and the upheaval of the Restoration, these writers were caught in a period of radical change in religion, social life, and politics, which is reflected in their work.

The 27 poets featured in this volume include some, such as Ben Jonson, John Donne, and Lady Mary Wroth, who are widely recognized, and others who are less well known. An appendix gives brief entries on eight additional minor poets who, curiously, are not listed in the cumulative index. The entries follow the usual DLB pattern, containing a list of works by the writer, a biocritical essay, and bibliographies that give biographical and critical references and locations of manuscripts. Each essay is illustrated with portraits, title pages, and manuscript pages. A separate bibliography of further readings lists general monographic studies on the period.

Although the essays offer little new information for the serious scholar, they do provide solid background knowledge and sources for further study for the student or interested reader. This volume is a worthwhile addition to the DLB series, but it can also stand alone as a valuable introductory reference on the major poets of the early seventeenth century. [R: Choice, May 93, p. 1449]—**Susan Davis Herring**

1265. Martinez, Nancy C., and Joseph G. R. Martinez. **Guide to British Poetry Explication. Volume 2: Renaissance.** New York, G. K. Hall, 1992. 540p. (Reference Publication in Literature). $45.00. Z2014.P7M34. 016.821009. LC 90-49129. ISBN 0-8161-8920-X.

This work attempts to fill a known void left by *Poetry Explication: A Checklist of Interpretation*, 3d ed. (see ARBA 82, entry 1299). It covers explications for poems of all lengths and is not restricted to poems of 500 lines or fewer. Covering what the authors call the Renaissance, the work includes authors in alphabetical order, followed by references to explications. This work truly is a guide, because it contains no actual explications. Some care must be taken to ensure that the reader is not led astray with assumptions about explication. *Explication* is defined here in the same way as it was defined in the *Checklist*: "an examination of a work of literature for a knowledge of each part, for the relations of these parts to each other, and for their relations to the whole" (p. viii). Other definitions are possible.

The book suffers from a major flaw: it has no index. It is true that the arrangement allows easy access, but only if the reader knows the name of the author or the poem. This work is recommended for research collections in academic libraries. Although it will not be a major reference tool, it is better than anything else on the market.—**C. D. Hurt**

1266. Martinez, Nancy C., Joseph G. R. Martinez, and Erland Anderson. **Guide to British Poetry Explication. Volume 3: Restoration-Romantic.** New York, G. K. Hall, 1993. 576p. (Reference Publication in Literature). $50.00. Z2014.P7M34. 016.821009. LC 90-49129. ISBN 0-8161-1997-X.

The present work is the third of a four-part set that already includes Old English-medieval (see ARBA 92, entry 1221) and Renaissance (G. K. Hall, 1992) volumes and that will conclude with the Victorian through contemporary periods. Greatly expanded from its immediate predecessor *Poetry Explication: A Checklist of Interpretation since 1925* (see ARBA 82, entry 1299), this volume adds a number of poets previously excluded, such as Thomas Lovell Beddoes and Samuel Rogers, and significantly increases listings for the better-known names. Some 69 Samuel Taylor Coleridge works are listed, for example, compared to 29 in the older edition, while William Wordsworth entries jump from 71 to 233! Citations to explications are gleaned from 100-plus periodicals plus a healthy selection of book-length criticism; coverage is from 1925 through early 1992. Only English-language criticism is included, although the addition of foreign-language commentary is planned for future editions. Poets are listed alphabetically, as are the poems under each name and criticism under each poem by author.

This is an easy-to-use, information-packed reference gem. Although the MLA Bibliography on CD-ROM has somewhat replaced it, particularly for the most recent decade, any library with users seeking information on British poetry will still find it well worth the money.—**Willa Schmidt**

1267. Ringler, William A., Jr. **Bibliography and Index of English Verse in Manuscript 1501-1558.** New York, Mansell/Cassell, 1992. 315p. $190.00. Z2014.P7R55. 016.821'208. LC 92-18051. ISBN 0-7201-2099-3.

This highly specialized, expensive volume that indexes early Tudor verse manuscripts is a companion to Ringler's previously published *Bibliography and Index of English Verse, 1476-1558* (see ARBA 90, entry 1166). The manuscript verses were found in almost 400 extant documents primarily located in libraries and museums in the United Kingdom and the United States. Ringler has had to make informed judgments on whether verses are alternate variations of a single poem or altogether separate works. Exact dating is difficult, as is attribution of authors, because such information appears less often in manuscripts than in printed works.

The guide to the use of the index explains the organization. The bibliography is arranged alphabetically by the location sigla followed by shelfmark, description of manuscript contents, citations of printings, number of poems from the appropriate dates in the manuscript, and a sequential list of poems by TM (early Tudor Manuscript Transcription) number. An alphabetized index of first lines includes the poem's TM number and siglum, verse form, date of transcription, rhymed refrain, and genre and subject category. A final index lists verses under such headings as subjects, refrains (alphabetized by last words), verse forms and rhyme schemes, numbers of lines, English poets, composers and translators, historical people, and foreign languages. Three appendixes provide concordances that cross-reference Tudor manuscript poems, Tudor print poems, and the *Index of Middle English Verse* (MLA of America, 1943). For specialists in early Tudor verse, this volume is an indispensable research tool.—**Charlotte Lindgren**

African Literature

1268. Moser, Gerald, and Manual Ferreira. **A New Bibliography of the Lusophone Literatures of Africa. Nova Bibliografia das Literaturas Africanas de Expressao Portuguesa.** 2d ed. New Providence, N.J., Hans Zell/Reed Reference Publishing, 1993. 432p. index. (Bibliographical Research in African Literatures, no.2). $80.00. Z3874.L5M595. 016.89608'096. LC 93-19931. ISBN 1-873836-85-6.

For students of Lusophone African literature, this work will be a godsend. It replaces an edition published in 1981 and includes materials published as late as 1991. More than 3,200 entries, most briefly annotated, range from Cape Verde to Guinea-Bissau to Sao Tome and Principe to Mozambique to Angola, with nearly half relating to the last. Broad arrangement is by country, each subdivided into oral literature (virtually nil), creative writing (much the largest category), and historical and literary criticism. Well over 1,000 authors are covered in an appendix of "biographical notes," and there are author and subject indexes. The introduction is too brief to be useful.

In terms of coverage and access, *New Bibliography* is almost exemplary. But a serious handicap obtrudes: Only books and chapters are included. Excluding matter on the basis of format can never be intellectually justified or satisfying. As it is, the task of identifying journal literature remains, a problem that might have been at least alleviated had the authors included a section on reference works in the field. A far less serious problem is that the accents for capital letters occupy their own spaces rather than appear above the letter, leaving a most peculiar aspect.

Unlike many reference works of late, this work aids rather than frustrates users with its technical aspects. It is unfortunate that the limits of interested parties are never likely to be quite the same as those imposed by the authors.—**David Henige**

Australian Literature

1269. Clancy, Laurie. **A Reader's Guide to Australian Fiction.** New York, Oxford University Press, 1992. 372p. index. $25.00pa. ISBN 0-19-554620-2.

A Reader's Guide to Australian Fiction is different from a history of Australian fiction in that the author entries are more even in length, and nearly all of an author's works are listed. In a preface Clancy gives an account of the book's origins—but not of its aims, which have not been sufficiently thought through. There is only a very general concept of what the contents of the author entries should be. Many of the novels here simply have their plot summarized, while others are evaluated, and some are impatiently or even glibly dismissed (e.g., Thomas Keneally's *A Dutiful Daughter*). Mostly Clancy defers to prevailing literary opinion, but occasionally he shows a discerning appreciation of a neglected work, such as Jessica Anderson's *An Ordinary Lunacy*. Biographical information is scanty and uneven: we are told of an author's birthplace and a little of the early years but almost nothing of the mature life.

The main weakness of the book, however, is that it shows a disregard of scholarship: there are no bibliographical references or recommendations. Indeed, Clancy appears to have only a passing acquaintance with Australian literary scholarship. The book is useful for basic information on writers and their works, but for anything beyond that data, one will quickly have to turn elsewhere—and without any guidance from Clancy.—**John B. Beston**

Canadian Literature

1270. Bennett, Joy, comp. **A Catalogue of the Letters, Tapes & Photographs in the Irving Layton Collection.** Calgary, Alta., University of Calgary Press, 1993. 204p. index. $17.95pa. 016.811'54. ISBN 1-895176-02-6.

This is a companion volume to *A Catalogue of the Manuscripts in the Irving Layton Collection* (University of Calgary Press, 1988). Materials about Layton have been collected at Concordia University in Montreal since 1969. Layton is an acknowledged "personality" in Canadian letters as well as a professional poet. He has authored more than 45 books, has been widely translated, and has been nominated for the Nobel prize in literature several times. This catalog gives some organization to several thousand pages of letters as well as to other materials: 5 scrapbooks, loosely covering 1943 through 1966; 6 videocassettes; a film; 69 sets of audio tapes beginning with 1960; and 91 photographs and slides. These audiovisual materials are composed of interviews, readings, and radio and television shows. The many indexes include one dealing with authors and titles, referring to correspondents, photographers, and producers as well as to the works cited. The entries in the subject index refer to persons or topics mentioned in the correspondence, discussed in the tapes, or pictured in the photographs. Descriptions of the contents themselves do not delve into subject matter.—**Dean Tudor**

1271. **Canadian Writers and Their Works: Cumulated Index, Fiction Series.** Donald W. McLeod, ed. Toronto, ECW Press, 1993. 102p. $20.00pa. 016.813'009. ISBN 1-55022-142-6.

1272. **Canadian Writers and Their Works: Cumulated Index, Poetry Series.** Donald W. McLeod, ed. Toronto, ECW Press, 1993. 137p. $20.00pa. 016.811'009. ISBN 1-55022-143-4.

The cumulated index volumes to *Canadian Writers and Their Works* are revised and edited compilations of the indexes that appeared in each volume of both titles. Contained in the poetry series index are all titles of poems discussed in the texts, as well as titles of critical works of importance and periodicals. The fiction index contains similar references for works in that series. In both, critics named or quoted are included in addition to proper names (excluding places, academic institutions, characters, and minor relatives). Arrangement is alphabetical by word and then chronological for various editions of a work. Author's last name is also listed if titles are similar. At the front of each index is a contents listing for each of the 10 volumes of the poetry or fiction series, with authors included.

For those libraries having few of either series, neither book will be an essential purchase, as the individual volumes contain complete indexes. However, for others with all volumes in each series or with research interest in Canadian literature, these volumes would greatly enhance access to the series and are well worth purchase.—**Virginia S. Fischer**

1273. **ECW's Biographical Guide to Canadian Novelists.** Toronto, ECW Press, 1993. 252p. illus. $25.00pa. ISBN 1-55022-151-5.

1274. **ECW's Biographical Guide to Canadian Poets.** Toronto, ECW Press, 1993. 282p. illus. $25.00pa. ISBN 1-55022-152-3.

These books are ideal reference tools for the small but growing reference collection on Canadian studies. They are based on the material created for ECW Press's Canadian Writers and Their Works series, but they are geared to high school students (and, by extension, to any non-Canadian undergraduates studying Canadiana).

In the book on novelists, 49 individuals (e.g., W. O. Mitchell, Hugh MacLennan, Margaret Atwood, Marian Engel, Mavis Gallant) are identified in short essays; in that on poets, 48 people (e.g., Archibald Lampman, A. M. Klein, Miriam Waddington, Milton Acorn) are covered. Each essay contains birth date and place, career highlights, awards, and important works. The arrangement is chronological by period of literary endeavor, and each essay concludes with useful footnotes.

There are few critiques, no overall index, and no general bibliography for further reading and study. The accompanying drawings of each author tend to be dark and do not reveal anything about character. Nevertheless, these works are good introductions to Canadian literary figures.—**Dean Tudor**

1275. **An Index to the Contents of the Periodical *Canadian Literature* Nos. 1-102.** Glenn Clever, comp. Ottawa, Tecumseh Press, 1992. 217p. $7.95pa. 809'.8971. ISBN 0-919662-25-0.

This is a paperback edition of the 1984 author and subject index to the first 102 volumes of the journal *Canadian Literature*, an important resource in its field. Articles are indexed by authors and subjects. Articles about individual literary works are indexed under the names of authors of the works. Subject headings tend to be very broad (e.g., drama and theater, names of specific countries). A list of subject headings is included.

As this volume covers the early years of *Canadian Literature*, when it was less widely indexed and cited than it later became, it will be useful where there is interest in Canadian literature and culture. Supplements covering *Canadian Literature* through volume 131 are available.—**Gari-Anne Patzwald**

1276. Moore, Jean M., Apollonia Steele, and Jean F. Tener, comp. and eds. **The Alden Nowlan Papers: An Inventory of the Archive at the University of Calgary Libraries.** Calgary, Alta., University of Calgary Press, 1992. 585p. index. (Canadian Archival Inventory Series, no.10). $34.95pa. (U.S.). 016.811'54. ISBN 1-895176-15-8.

Tenth in the Canadian archival inventory series program established through the Social Science and Humanities Research Council of Canada at the University of Calgary, this inventory presents the work of Maritime writer Alden Nowlan and integrates the three accessions acquired by the university between 1981 and 1985. A writer who produced in many literary genres, Nowlan's work—as poet, novelist, dramatist, short story writer, and journalist—is all the more impressive in light of the fact that he never completed elementary school.

To accommodate the diversity of materials, archival arrangement is within a number of interrelated series. Correspondence series are arranged alphabetically by correspondent (whenever identified) with the first file containing unidentified pieces. Manuscripts have been divided into four series—drama, fiction, poetry, and prose—with arrangement alphabetical by titles and then chronological within each (with the exception of the prose series, which is just chronological). Undated manuscripts have been assigned dates based on Nowlan's known period of residence in various parts of New Brunswick. The published work series has a wide variety of materials arranged chronologically. The audiovisual series lists diverse materials, such as audiotapes, photographs, and posters. A miscellaneous series is divided into three sections: notes and materials, research, and financial records. The final series contains works on Nowlan arranged alphabetically by author. Completing the inventory are four brief appendixes of material acquired from other people. Two indexes—one of Nowlan's titles and a general index—complete the volume and provide research documentation. As with other works in the series, this volume is a premier research tool.—**Virginia S. Fischer**

1277. Panofsky, Ruth. **Adele Wiseman: An Annotated Bibliography.** Don Mills, Ont., ECW Press, 1992. 130p. index. $30.00. 016.813'54. ISBN 1-55022-103-5.

Adele Wiseman, who died in 1992, was the author of two books: *The Sacrifice* and *Crackpot*. The former won a Governor General's award in Canada in the mid-1950s. Wiseman also wrote two plays (neither of which has been produced professionally), a children's book, some poetry, nonfiction, and arts contributions. This annotated bibliography describes the various editions of her works and manuscripts.

In addition, it descriptively accounts for works about Wiseman (mainly reviews and critiques) published in North America. Thus this book is a first place to look for anything by or about Wiseman. It comes complete with an index of her critics.—**Dean Tudor**

1278. Pollock, Zailig, Usher Caplan, and Linda Rozmovits. **A. M. Klein: An Annotated Bibliography.** Toronto, ECW Press, 1993. 390p. index. $65.00. 016.811'52. ISBN 1-55022-095-0.

A. M. Klein (1909-1972) was a poet, fiction writer, essayist, journalist, Zionist, lawyer, and socialist politician who is regarded as one of the finest Canadian writers, and perhaps the finest Canadian poet, of his generation. His collected works are being published by the University of Toronto Press, and he is now represented by this bibliography. It is divided into two parts. Part 1 lists material that can be identified as having been written by Klein: books, articles, manuscript collections, and some 3,500 briefly annotated journalistic pieces. Part 2 lists and abstracts all major Canadian writings on Klein, material on him found in Jewish books and periodicals, and a selection of reviews of his books. A subject index to Klein's journalistic contributions and an index to critical writing about Klein are included.

This bibliography is thorough, accurate, and well annotated. It gathers together material that has hitherto been scattered or buried in dissertations or issues of periodicals. Academic and large public libraries in Canada will certainly want this volume, but Klein's lack of recognition outside Canada will limit purchase in the United States to collections specializing in Canadian literature.

—**Jonathan F. Husband**

Chinese Literature

1279. Martin, Helmut, and Jeffrey Kinkley, eds. **Modern Chinese Writers: Self-Portrayals.** Armonk, N.Y., M. E. Sharpe, 1992. 380p. illus. index. (Studies on Modern China). $55.00; $22.00pa. PL2277.M65. 895.109'0052. LC 91-31578. ISBN 0-87332-816-7; 0-87332-817-5pa.

This volume contains extraordinary autobiographies of 43 modern Chinese writers. They are meant to convey the "hopes, fears, and everyday problems of China's writers." Those published here were selected from a longer list of more than 100 writers, part of a Chinese-German joint venture that came to an abrupt halt in 1986-1987 due to what the editors describe as a deteriorating political climate in China. A Chinese version, however, appeared in 1989 but omitted Bei Dao, Cong Weixi, Liu Binyan, Wang Ruowang, and Wu Zuguang, among others. The volume reviewed here includes not only these controversial figures but also authors from Taiwan and one from Hong Kong. The emphasis is on serious rather than popular authors, but some space is devoted to tensions between literary and mass-market writers. The original titles of all autobiographies are given in both Chinese and English, along with the bibliographical references to where they first appeared. Some have been abridged for the purposes of this anthology, and minor errors have been corrected.

The German version of this book carries a more expressive title: *Bittere Traume*—"Bitter Dreams," although a loose translation of the Chinese title, *Chuangzuotan*, "Casual remarks on the creative process," describes what each of the authors provides in the self-portraits they have written of their lives and thoughts as writers. Each self-portrait is accompanied by a brief introduction about the author, along with a photograph. A glossary of Chinese terms, names, major political events, and literary landmarks will help readers unfamiliar with China's history and contemporary literature to orient themselves to the most important names, dates, places, and events referred to in the book. Martin offers a thoughtful retrospective introduction on the subject of "enforced silence or emigre uncertainties," in which he considers the fate of Chinese writers in the aftermath of the Tiananmen Square massacre of June 4, 1989.

As Kinkley says in his introduction, this book shows "how Chinese society and its creative writing have supported, competed, and fought with each other for the past forty years and more, on both sides of the Taiwan Strait." Most of the selections translated here, he stresses, were meant "for Chinese eyes; they reveal political treachery and social cowardice with a directness that is by turns hair-raising and humorous."—**Joseph W. Dauben**

European Literature

1280. **European Writers: Selected Authors.** George Stade, ed. New York, Scribner's, 1992. 3v. index. $250.00/set. PN501.E9. 809'.894. ISBN 0-684-19583-6.

Aimed at high school students and undergraduates, this compilation includes 68 of the 261 essays that appeared in the 14-volume *European Writers* (see ARBA 92, entry 1231). Selected on the basis of a survey of school and college librarians regarding the authors most frequently studied, the alphabetically arranged articles are unabridged, averaging 20 pages in length. Six articles treat genres or themes (e.g., "Arthurian Legend," "Medieval Drama"); two cover the poems *Beowulf* and *Romance of the Rose*; and the remainder are devoted to major writers, ranging chronologically from St. Augustine to Gunter Grass. In addition to prominent literary figures such as Miguel de Cervantes and Victor Hugo, the compilation also features significant writers in history, philosophy, religion, and other disciplines (e.g., Rene Descartes, Martin Luther). The well-written essays focus on the authors' lives and works within the context of their times and provide critical analyses of major works and discussion of principal themes. Bibliographies of selected primary and secondary works follow each article. As the bibliographies on earlier figures were compiled more than 10 years ago, it would have been useful if they had been updated for this edition.

Each volume includes a table of contents for the set, and volume 3 contains a detailed index to authors, titles of works, themes, genres, and topics. Index references note page number and column but unfortunately do not include the volume number. Because inclusive pagination is not indicated on the spines of the volumes, this omission hampers efficient access to the set. Volume 3 also includes sections that categorize the writers chronologically and by language as well as a complete list of essays in the parent set. For libraries that need greater depth than that provided by Stanley J. Kunitz and Vineta Colby's *European Authors, 1000-1900* (H. W. Wilson, 1967) but cannot afford the 14-volume edition of *European Writers*, this abridged version offers a welcome alternative. [R: Choice, June 93, p. 1600; LJ, 1 June 93, p. 104; SLJ, Nov 93, p. 145]—**Marie Ellis**

1281. Pynsent, Robert B., with S. I. Kanikova, eds. **Reader's Encyclopedia of Eastern European Literature.** New York, HarperCollins, 1993. 605p. index. $50.00. PN849.E9R38. 809'.8947'03. LC 93-2953. ISBN 0-06-270007-3.

Originally published in Great Britain by Dent under the title *The Everyman Guide to East European Literature*, this U.S. edition is identical to the original. It is a handy biographical dictionary of well-known as well as lesser-known literary figures from several Eastern European countries, including Georgia and Armenia but omitting Russia. Pynsent is a professor of Czech and Slovak literature at the School of Slavonic and East European Studies, University of London, and Kanikova is currently a lecturer in Bulgarian literature at the same institution. Twenty-four contributors wrote longer and shorter articles on several hundred writers, and there are also a number of articles (e.g., Georgian folk poetry) discussing types of literature and (briefly) literature of all nationalities covered in this volume. This biographical source will appeal to the uninitiated. [R: Choice, Oct 93, p. 272; RBB, 15 Oct 93, p. 475; WLB, Sept 93, p. 122]—**Bohdan S. Wynar**

French Literature

1282. Arden, Heather M. **The Roman de la Rose: An Annotated Bibliography.** Hamden, Conn., Garland, 1993. 385p. index. (Garland Medieval Bibliographies, v.8; Garland Reference Library of the Humanities, v.1358). $59.00. Z8374.6478.A73. 841'.1. LC 93-15492. ISBN 0-8240-5799-6.

Students of medieval literature will welcome this learned and helpful bibliography of modern scholarship (1850-1992) on *The Roman de la Rose*. Widely read in its own and succeeding centuries, this poem has become a key text for the study of many aspects of the later Middle Ages; consequently, it now possesses a significant and varied critical literature of its own. Arden controls this literature very well, and her detailed, informative annotations of close to 800 individual contributions will make this a valuable aid for undergraduates and advanced students alike.

However, the book could be better organized. Most sections, including the very large ones on critical studies and on (reception and) influence, are arranged alphabetically by author rather than chronologically, while the initially misleading index omits author references for writings entered in these alphabetical sequences (the essential note on "The Index," now buried on p. xxx, should have appeared as a headnote to the index itself). Such a scheme assists those wishing to find out more about citations already garnered elsewhere, but unnecessarily impedes other approaches, such as the ready identification of contributions produced in or after a given decade or by a given critic or historian. That said, the coverage is still excellent, the annotations are of exceptionally high quality, and the book (although cumbersome) is still a needed one.—**John B. Dillon**

1283. Brosman, Catharine Savage, ed. **Nineteenth-Century French Fiction Writers: Romanticism and Realism, 1800-1860.** Detroit, Gale, 1992. 415p. illus. index. (Dictionary of Literary Biography, v.119). $112.00. LC 92-17232. ISBN 0-8103-7596-6.

This volume discusses 19 major French writers whose work appeared in the first half of the nineteenth century. The essays, ranging in length from 8 to 30 pages, are detailed enough to provide an understanding of the political, social, cultural, and creative influences on each writer's work. They also succinctly describe and characterize that work while generally eschewing the jargon of literary criticism. They will thus serve as solid background reading for undergraduates and other general users.

Preceding the text of each essay is a bibliography of primary works, including collections. Following the essays are references to published correspondence, bibliographies, biographies, and other secondary materials. The locations of the writers' papers—diaries, letters, manuscripts, and the like—are also provided. Brosman's 17-page introduction contributes a useful overview of the period, the evolution of the novel in France, romanticism and realism, and critical responses to and interest in nineteenth-century French fiction.

Completing the volumes are a bibliography of books for further reading and a cumulative index to all the Dictionary of Literary Biography (DLB) volumes. Volume 119 will be a valuable addition to the reliable and respectable DLB series. [R: Choice, May 93, p. 1445]—**Emily L. Werrell**

1284. Coleman, Kathleen. **Guide to French Poetry Explication.** New York, G. K. Hall, 1993. 594p. index. (Reference Publication in Literature). $55.00. PQ401.C65. 841.009. LC 92-22129. ISBN 0-8161-9075-5.

The first of the publisher's poetry explication series to cover a language other than English, this volume will be of great use to graduate and undergraduate students, as well as reference librarians. Its main purpose is to guide the user to explications or interpretations of poetry by major authors writing in French. Poetry from the Middle Ages to contemporary times is included, but the author's selection criteria are what make the book so useful in academic situations. She has emphasized poets generally included in the French literary canon and explications found in materials listed in standard bibliographies and likely to be found in U.S. academic libraries. All of the sources have been published between 1960 and 1990, either in English or French. The language of the explication is indicated, which increases the usefulness of this volume for undergraduate students. Another selection criterion of value to many students is the exclusion of short explications.

The arrangement also facilitates use. The poets are listed alphabetically, with individual poems and the cited explications listed alphabetically under each poet. An index of critics and brief bibliographies of French poetry manuals and major sources consulted provide some additional information and access, but in general do not add significantly to the work.

The volume is easy to use, and the checklist of interpretations will certainly help many students. This title should be available in any library serving students of French poetry. [R: Choice, Nov 93, p. 426; RQ, Winter 93, pp. 286-87]—**Barbara E. Kemp**

1285. Norell, Donna M., comp. **Colette: An Annotated Primary and Secondary Bibliography.** Hamden, Conn., Garland, 1993. 552p. index. (Garland Reference Library of the Humanities, v.805). $87.00. Z8182.3.N66. 016.848'91209. LC 92-26827. ISBN 0-8240-6620-0.

Somewhat surprisingly, until now there has been no book-length primary or secondary bibliography of the French literary writer Colette (1873-1954), despite the important place she has come to assume in the canon of twentieth-century literature. This book attempts, provisionally but with great success, to fill both needs. An annotated bibliography of more than 2,000 numbered items (plus unnumbered others in several appendixes), it is comprehensive, although not exhaustive, for both French- and English-language texts and criticism. Items 1 through 1,055 cover Colette's French writings and their English translations (both American and British), while items 1,056 through 2,271 cover criticism, biography, and the like in English and other major Western languages. Appendixes list special journal issues devoted to Colette; German, Italian, and Spanish translations of her works; and indexes of French and English book titles (keyed to numbers in the primary bibliography) and of Colette's editors, English translators, illustrators, and so forth.

The chief drawback of this work is that the secondary bibliography is arranged alphabetically by author rather than chronologically (with secondary authors indexed alphabetically), thus preventing the application by individual users of date cutoffs fitting their own research needs. That said, the book is, on the whole, very useful and a must for virtually all academic libraries. [R: Choice, July/Aug 93, p. 1753; LJ, 1 April 93, p. 92]—**John B. Dillon**

German Literature

1286. Elfe, Wolfgang D., and James Hardin, eds. **Twentieth-Century German Dramatists, 1889-1918.** Detroit, Gale, 1992. 388p. illus. index. (Dictionary of Literary Biography, v.118). $112.00. LC 92-19190. ISBN 0-8103-7595-8.

Each entry in this volume begins with the rubric "PLAY PRODUCTIONS," listing the first performances of each drama. This is followed by a primary bibliography of the author's works, the most important section of which is a chronological list of all of the author's book publications. The text of the entry is a thorough account of the dramatist's life that attempts to place the person in proper perspective within the history of German drama and theater. A secondary bibliography and a statement about the author's literary estate end the entry.

The volume covers dramatists from Hermann Bahr (1863-1934) through Stefan Zweig (1881-1942), with essays on such significant authors as Gerhart Hauptmann, Hugo von Hofmannsthal, Arno Holz, Karl Kraus, Heinrich Mann, Arthur Schnitzler, Fritz von Unruh, and Frank Wedekind. The contributors to the volume, chiefly Germanists from the United States, Canada, and Great Britain, are experts on their respective authors. The appendix contains an essay by Roy C. Cowen on the development of German drama and theater from the advent of naturalism in 1889 to the Nazi takeover of Germany in 1933. Cinematic productions by the dramatists are touched on in the entries, as are the contributions of many dramatists as drama critics. A list of books for further reading appears at the end of the volume.

This volume is recommended for undergraduate and graduate German collections. Small college libraries may find its price prohibitive.—**Mark Padnos**

1287. Elfe, Wolfgang D., and James Hardin, eds. **Twentieth-Century German Dramatists, 1919-1992.** Detroit, Gale, 1992. 567p. illus. index. (Dictionary of Literary Biography, v.124). $113.00. LC 92-26833. ISBN 0-8103-5383-0.

Companion to *Twentieth-Century German Dramatists, 1889-1918* (Gale, 1992), the present volume spans a significantly greater time period and covers almost twice as many writers. The 50 German, Austrian, and Swiss-German playwrights highlighted include representatives of 1920s expressionism, such as Ernst Toller and Franz Werfel; a selection of *Neue Sachlichkeit* authors; and an array of National Socialist, exile, and postwar dramatists that includes Hanns Johst, Bertolt Brecht, Heiner Muller, Gunter Grass, Friederich Duerrenmatt, and Peter Weiss. Eight of the 50 were born after 1940. Some, such as Else Lasker-Schuler or Hermann Broch, are better known for other genres and have also appeared in earlier series volumes.

The usual DLB entry format of primary bibliography, illustrated bio-bibliographical essay, and secondary bibliography is followed here with one helpful addition: A list of first performances of the author's dramas opens each entry, preceding the list of published works. An introduction by the editors divides years and persons covered chronologically, and an essay on the German radio play and a brief bibliography of related works conclude the volume. Undergraduates and English speakers looking for an introduction to recent German drama will find this an excellent resource.—**Willa Schmidt**

1288. Klett, Dwight A. **Ludwig Tieck: An Annotated Guide to Research.** Hamden, Conn., Garland, 1993. 201p. index. (Garland Reference Library of the Humanities, v.902). $33.00. Z8879.63.K55. 016.838'609. LC 93-624. ISBN 0-8240-5622-1.

Tieck's is a name familiar to every student of German literature. An undisputed leader of the German Romantic Movement at the turn of the nineteenth century, known particularly for his novellas and plays, he also achieved renown as a philologist, editor, critic, and international scholar. His translations of literary giants such as William Shakespeare, Miguel de Cervantes, and Dante Alighieri significantly enriched his compatriots' understanding of European culture. It is all the more astounding, therefore, that Klett's is the first book-length bibliography of secondary sources dealing with his life and work.

A detailed table of contents lists sections and subsections covering biography, criticism, letters (the only primary source material included), comments on Tieck as translator and critic, reception and comparative studies, and writings on his numerous connections with other writers and countries. The 727 entries are given brief, often evaluative annotations and range from the early nineteenth century to 1990. Excluded are articles from literary histories, reference volumes, popular magazines, newspapers, reviews, and most dissertations. An index of authors and editors is appended, but subject access is provided only by the table of contents. This is a well-done, useful contribution to the world of literary scholarship. [R: Choice, Nov 93, p. 436]—**Willa Schmidt**

Iberian Literature

1289. Bleiberg, Germán, Maureen Ihrie, and Janet Pérez, eds. **Dictionary of the Literature of the Iberian Peninsula.** Westport, Conn., Greenwood Press, 1993. 2v. index. $195.00/set. PN849.S6D54. 860'.03. LC 90-2755. ISBN 0-313-21302-X.

According to the publishers, this set has been compiled by more than 90 experts and includes representatives from all major peninsular literatures: Catalan, Galician, Portuguese, and Spanish. Data are also provided on Basque authors, literary genres, and period. After a biographical-critical sketch of the author there follows a bibliography of primary texts, works translated into English, and critical studies.

This set should be the first consulted for the literatures of this area, especially with regard to Catalan, Galician, and Portuguese material. The work is of such high quality and so valuable that adverse comments seem like so much quibbling. However, there are a few typographical errors. For example, "Whitson" (1,320) should be Whitston. *Galdós and His Critics* by Anthony Percival (University of Toronto Press, 1985) is superior to, and more up-to-date than, the two Galdós bibliographies listed. No volume numbers are given for the Márquez Villanueva (926) and the Artigas (958) articles. In the López Estrada reference (1,081), *a* should be *à*. In at least two places the journal title was omitted, thus rendering the citation almost useless. Occasional references are made to Rudder's bibliography of English translations of Spanish literature, yet those who deal with Catalan authors seem not to know of the Dagenais-Woodbridge bibliographical article, the first (and only) bibliography of Catalan literature in English translation.

It would have been nice to see the major bibliography for each author or genre included. Numerous important, fairly recent author bibliographies do not appear. Still, this is a work of great scholarship and should be in all reference collections. [R: Choice, Nov 93, p. 428; RBB, 15 Dec 93, pp. 775-76]

—**Hensley C. Woodbridge**

Indic Literature

1290. Nelson, Emmanuel S., ed. **Writers of the Indian Diaspora: A Bio-Bibliographical Critical Sourcebook.** Westport, Conn., Greenwood Press, 1993. 468p. index. $85.00. PR9485.45.W75. 820.9'891411. LC 92-27898. ISBN 0-313-27904-7.

Biographical dictionaries are very useful source books for researchers and information seekers. There are many such dictionaries on authors available, but this is the first time that a biographical dictionary deals with authors of Indian descent. A total of 58 entries are arranged alphabetically by the last name of the author. Many individuals included are major international figures, such as Kamia Markandaya, Ved Mehta, V. S. Naipaul, Raja Rao, Santha Rama Rau, and Salman Rushdie. A majority of the writers are from India, but a few are from Bangladesh, Canada, Pakistan, Sri Lanka, the West Indies, and other parts of the world. Each chapter has been divided into various subject headings, such as biography, major works and themes, critical reception, and works by and about the author (in a chronological order that includes both primary and secondary works). Biographical information on all writers is up-to-date, reliable, and detailed. It includes their education, major life achievements, and a summary of their major works. Writers who write and publish in non-English languages are not included. All 58 biographies have been written by well-known authors. An appendix lists writers with their place of birth and places of domicile.

This is an excellent book that fills a major gap in the literature. Its price is very high, but it is recommended for all reference collections.—**Ravindra Nath Sharma**

Irish Literature

1291. Cahalan, James M. **Modern Irish Literature and Culture: A Chronology.** New York, G. K. Hall, 1993. 374p. index. $45.00. PR8718.C35. 820.9'9415. LC 92-15105. ISBN 0-8161-7264-1.

Close to 400 years (1601-1992) of Irish literary and political events are chronicled and interwoven in this slim volume, which is arranged by year. To provide a context for the literary information, Cahalan begins each year's entry with a digest of the year's political climate and events. He organizes the literary information that follows by category; most years have such headings as drama, poetry, and fiction. Some years also include other categories, such as architecture and cultural institutions. Among the events mentioned are publications of major literary works, first appearances of periodicals, publications of important writings in these periodicals, and debuts of plays. The result is a fact-packed but readable narrative of Irish literature. Read straight through, it gives a thorough look at Irish literature; read in pieces, it can highlight particular years or illuminate the development of a particular literary form.

Because the names of literary and political figures necessarily appear in many entries, whenever their accomplishments warranted, Cahalan supplies brief, single-paragraph biographies of about 30 figures. One can thus get an immediate grounding in the importance of a particular figure without consulting all the relevant years. Cahalan also provides a bibliography of secondary works from which he garnered much of his information.

In his introduction, Cahalan suggests that his book is best used in conjunction with *A Chronology of Irish History since 1500* by J. E. Doherty and D. J. Hickey (B&N Imports, 1989), and *Dictionary of Irish History* (1987), also by Doherty and Hickey. These works, concentrating on history and politics, provide a more solid structure on which to hang an understanding of the literature than do Cahalan's brief overviews of each year's politics and add to the usefulness of Cahalan's book. However, Cahalan's work can stand alone, giving any reader a clear look at the sweep of Irish literature and its intermingling with the life of politics. [R: Choice, May 93, p. 1436; RBB, June 93, p. 1900; WLB, April 93, p. 122]
—**Terry Ann Mood**

1292. Joshi, S. T., and Darrell Schweitzer. **Lord Dunsany: A Bibliography.** Metuchen, N.J., Scarecrow, 1993. 365p. index. (Scarecrow Author Bibliographies, no.90). $42.50. Z8248.42.J67. 016.828'91209. LC 93-8453. ISBN 0-8108-2714-X.

This work, the only bibliography of the Irish author Edward John Moreton Drax Plunkett, 18th Baron Dunsany (1878-1957), offers a meticulously compiled record of the plethora of publications by this prolific novelist, dramatist, poet, and essayist. Regarded during his lifetime as one of the premier Irish writers, Dunsany has now emerged as perhaps the leading figure in modern fantasy literature. In fact, his stories have had a significant influence on J. R. R. Tolkien, Ursula Le Guin, and other fantasists. Joshi, a senior editor of the literary criticism division of Chelsea House Publishers and a Lovecraft scholar, and Schweitzer, a Dunsany scholar and active fantasist, insist that their bibliography must be considered preliminary. They admit that they did not have access to a very detailed ledger of his publications kept by Dunsany from 1906 to his death. (The ledger, presumably still in the possession of the Dunsany estate, records dates of writing and magazine and book publications of each of Dunsany's works and would be an invaluable reference tool for the bibliographer should it become available.)

The authors have arranged their work in three sections. The first one lists works by Dunsany in English, including books and contributions to books and periodicals. The genres presented are fiction, essays, poetry, plays, book reviews, and correspondence. The entries for individual book titles, for example, provide place, publisher, and publication date, in addition to the titles of all pieces included. All significant items here, as in the rest of the bibliography, have been annotated. This section is followed by a list of works by Dunsany in translation, covering fiction, essays, and plays. The final section lists secondary literature in dictionaries, encyclopedias, bibliographies, books about Dunsany, criticism in books and periodicals, Dunsany theses and dissertations, and reviews. Three indexes provide access to the contents of the bibliography: a name index, an index to works by Dunsany, and an index of periodical titles in which Dunsany works or secondary Dunsany literature have appeared.

This remarkable work will be a principal source for Dunsany scholars for years to come. Highly recommended as an addition to all graduate English collections.—**Mark Padnos**

1293. Ricigliano, Lorraine. **Austin Clarke: A Reference Guide.** New York, G. K. Hall, 1993. 180p. index. (Reference Publication in Literature). $45.00. Z8174.7.R53. 016.821'921. LC 92-42514. ISBN 0-8161-7384-2.

This is a worthy addition to G. K. Hall's respected Reference Publication in Literature series. It is well arranged, well indexed, easy to use, and seemingly thorough. Clarke has been a subject of critical writing since a year after the publication of his first major work, *The Vengeance of Fionn*, written in 1917. Despite this interest, there has been no bibliography of criticism until now. Ricigliano's book thus fills a gap. It covers criticism from 1918 through the fall of 1992. Entries are arranged chronologically by year, with the entries in each year arranged alphabetically by title. Each entry is annotated. Ricigliano includes all 500 critical writings that have been written in English about Clarke. In addition, she lists some selected articles in French and German to give an idea of the international influence that Clarke had. The bibliography encompasses books, articles, book chapters, dissertations, reviews, and media. Not included are books that contain only brief mentions of Clarke, general encyclopedia articles, or what Ricigliano considers works of marginal value.

The appendix and the index add to the book's value. In the former, Ricigliano lists individual poems and plays by Clarke, with a notation of where they might be found in his collected works. The index offers a variety of entry points to specific critical works: by particular poems or plays by Clarke mentioned in the criticism; by the title of works compared with Clarke's; or by other literary authors compared with Clarke, such as William Butler Yeats, Wallace Stevens, or James Joyce. All authors of the works cited are also indexed, as are subjects such as genre, theme, or term. Most libraries with a clientele doing research in English or Irish literature will want this book.—**Terry Ann Mood**

Japanese Literature

1294. Lewell, John. **Modern Japanese Novelists: A Biographical Dictionary.** New York, Kodansha America, 1993. 497p. illus. $50.00. PL747.55.L48. 895.6'3409. LC 92-11324. ISBN 4-7700-1649-2.

Lewell provides annotated bibliographies of 57 well-known modern Japanese writers, 47 of whom are men and 10 women. His chronological coverage extends from S. Tsubouchi (1859-1935) to Y. Tsushima (1948-). The ideological backgrounds of these writers represent a spectrum from naturalism, socialism, proletarianism, and existentialism to new school and the like. Lewell produced this dictionary using exclusively English translations and describes the process by which he produced it. The dictionary thus can guide English-speaking readers in their approach to and appreciation of Japanese novels and stories, although it is useful to readers with knowledge of Japanese as well. Coverage of writers varies in length from 3 to 20 pages. Lewell provides a biography of each writer and evaluates the main works. His evaluations are thoughtful and sensitive and show creative insights. At the end of each entry, Lewell provides a list of works translated into English and references to critical studies about each writer. Sources listed under general reading discuss modern Japanese novelists and offer a good introduction to Japanese literature; the glossary is also useful. The volume is recommended for all public, college, and university libraries, and it may also be helpful to instructors of Japanese studies. [R: Choice, Nov 93, p. 436; RBB, 1 Nov 93, p. 568]—**Seiko Mieczkowski**

1295. Mamola, Claire Zebrowski. **Japanese Women Writers in English Translation: An Annotated Bibliography. Volume 2.** Hamden, Conn., Garland, 1992. 452p. index. (Garland Reference Library of the Humanities, v.1317). $72.00. Z3308.L5M34. 016.8956'08'09287. LC 89-1319. ISBN 0-8240-7077-1.

Volume 1 of this book was published by the same author under the same title in 1989. The present volume has 1,337 entries and consists of four parts: fiction writings (87 entries), nonfiction writings (832), specialized works (418), and dissertations (48). Mamola has annotated the entries in the first two parts. Her annotations appear to be merely synopses of the works cited. She does not make any value judgments on the quality of the original, in effect encouraging readers to make up their own minds and also placing on them the burden of selection. The section on nonfiction covers biographies, religion, education, topics on women, anthropological works, problems of the society, problems caused by World War II, and other problems as they affected the lives of women. The entries in specialized listings vary; they are connected with linguistics and technical research reports in various fields, such as sociology, economics, politics, and art. Dissertation listings are from *Doctoral Dissertations on Asia* (University Microfilms for the Association for Asian Studies, 1989-1990). The index is comprehensive. In researching the work, Mamola used bibliographies available in the United States, Canada, Japan, and Europe, thus ensuring comprehensive coverage. This book can serve not only as a guide to the study of Japanese women but also as a source of information on life in Japan and on some of the problems faced by its population. [R: Choice, June 93, p. 1607]—**Seiko Mieczkowski**

Latin American and Caribbean Literature

1296. Cortes, Eladio, ed. **Dictionary of Mexican Literature.** Westport, Conn., Greenwood Press, 1992. 768p. index. $85.00. PQ7106.D53. 860.9'972'03. LC 91-10529. ISBN 0-313-26271-3.

Forty-one scholars cover the most significant writers, literary schools, and cultural movements in Mexican literary history, emphasizing twentieth-century figures. The individual sketches include a biography, critical comments, a bibliography of the author's works (usually just the books), and a bibliography of important biographical and critical studies. These vary in length from 17 pages on Emilio Carballido to less than a half page for Javier Penalosa. It seems that everything ever written by Carballido was listed, whereas for most other authors only their books are given. The various sections on literary genres in Mexico are quite useful. English translations are given for the works of many of the authors when such exist; however, omitted are translations of the works of Rosario Castellanos, and translations of Mariano Azuela's works are listed with no indication of the translator or the fact that they are translations. Juan de la Cueva lived in New Spain from 1574 to 1577; surely this does not qualify him to be considered as a Mexican author. Luis Cernuda appears to have lived in Mexico for less than a decade and yet is given much more space than Manuel Gutierrez whose *Escritos ineditos de Sabor satirico "Plato del dia,"* edited by Boyd G. Carter and Mary Ellen Carter (University of Missouri Press, 1972) is missing and who is one of the great *modernistas* of Mexico.

The section on journals, periodicals, and supplements translates *anuario* as, variously, "yearly journal," "yearly publication," or "journal"; "annual" or "yearbook" would be more consistent. In many places there is no indication as to when a journal ceased publication. *Tiempo* is not a "weekly journal of humanities," but a newsweekly similar to *Time* and *Newsweek* (its title in the United States is *Hispanoamericano*).

Nevertheless, this is the finest reference work of its kind in English. It is hoped that a revised and corrected edition will soon appear. [R: Choice, May 93, p. 1438; LJ, 15 April 93, p. 58; RBB, 1 April 93, pp. 1455-56; WLB, April 93, p. 124]—**Hensley C. Woodbridge**

1297. Flores, Angel. **Spanish American Authors: The Twentieth Century.** Bronx, N.Y., H. W. Wilson, 1992. 915p. $100.00. PQ7081.3F57. 860.9'868. LC 92-7591. ISBN 0-8242-0806-4.

This is an extraordinarily useful bio-bibliographical dictionary of twentieth-century Spanish American authors. Following a biography, often compiled from data in letters to Flores, are critical comments on the author. The bibliography is divided between a list of the author's books (sometimes with their English translations) and a list of books and articles about the author. There was an editorial board of 6 scholars and an advisory committee of 17 scholars; 66 scholars wrote the biographies and critiques. However, the scholar responsible for the entry is usually not identified, and while many of the entries have been translated from Spanish, the names of the translators often do not appear.

Better editing would have resulted in greater consistency. The Pablo Neruda bibliography by Woodbridge and Zubatsky is duplicated (588-589). Only one reference appears in the "About" section for Paco Ignacio Taibo II. The reference to the *Diccionario de escritores mexicanos* (1967) should be replaced by *Diccionario de escritores mexicanos: siglo xx* (Mexico: UNAM, 1988), 333-343 (189). In the Rulfo entry, UNED does not appear in the list of abbreviations.

Yet these are microscopic blemishes on a work that will be of inestimable value to librarians and students of Spanish American literature, for nothing like it now exists in a single volume. (It would be nice if a companion volume on Brazilian authors could be produced that used this volume as a model.) The sketches run from the nine on Neruda to two pages for Taibo II. Every effort has been made to provide accurate biographical data; for example, the correct date of Rulfo's birth is given. The data on English translations should be useful to those who either do not have access to the original Spanish or who cannot read this language. The bibliographies are a tribute to Flores's vast knowledge of the field; many 1990, 1991, and 1992 publications are listed. Although now dead, Flores lives on through the reference books, critical studies, and translations that he compiled, edited, wrote, and produced during his lifetime. Hispanists owe him a debt of gratitude for his contributions to their field. [R: Choice, May 93, p. 1443; JAL, Mar 93, p. 57; RBB, 1 April 93, p. 1460; RQ, Summer 93, p. 578; SLJ, Nov 93, p. 142; WLB, April 93, p. 124]—**Hensley C. Woodbridge**

1298. Foster, David William, ed. **Handbook of Latin American Literature.** 2d ed. Hamden, Conn., Garland, 1992. 799p. index. (Garland Reference Library of the Humanities, v.1459). $95.00; $18.95pa. PQ7081.A1H36. 809'.898. LC 92-16452. ISBN 0-8153-0343-2; 0-8153-1143-5pa.

This is the 2d edition of a work that was published in 1987 (see ARBA 88, entry 1251). Except for those on the Dominican Republic, Haiti, and Paraguay, the original essays have been updated, and there is a new chapter on Peru. Sections on Latino writing in the United States, paraliterature, and film are completely new.

This handbook is unique in that no other volume deals with Latin American literature through a country-by-country discussion. It is the work of 23 scholars; some studies have been written first in Spanish and then translated. Both the data in the articles and the bibliographies are extremely up-to-date. The contributors have dealt with such topics as women writers, gay and lesbian writers, ethnic minority writers, texts that challenge traditional genre distinctions, and the like. An occasional item in the annotated bibliographies could be updated. There exists a 1987 edition of the *Diccionario general de la literatura venezolana (autores)*, (Merida: Editorial Venezolano); the handbook refers only to the 1974 edition.

There is no reason that this volume should not receive the outstanding reviews that the 1987 volume got. The essays read well without too much critical jargon. They are accurate and fulfill Foster's goal of providing a source of information for general readers and non-Hispanists as well as meeting the needs of students and researchers.

The three added sections will probably be the most valuable to those individuals or libraries that already own the earlier edition. Foster and the contributors should be congratulated for producing such a valuable and useful discussion of Latin American literature, film, and paraliterature.

—**Hensley C. Woodbridge**

1299. Isbister, Rob, and Peter Standish, comps. **A Concordance to the Works of Jorge Luis Borges (1899-1986), Argentine Author.** Lewiston, N.Y., Edwin Mellen Press, c1991, 1992. 7v. $79.95/v. PQ7797.B635Z459. 868. LC 91-45038. ISBN 0-7734-9628-9.

This set is a welcome addition to reference works on the great Argentine author. The title may be a little misleading; "A Concordance to Four Prose Works by ..." might be more accurate. Still, this set will be extremely useful to Borges scholars. It is unfortunate that in these days of limited library budgets, its price may be prohibitive for many.

The body of the work covers the four main prose volumes: *Ficciones, El aleph, El informe de Brodie*, and *El libro de arena*. The editions used for analysis were those published by Alianza/Emece (Madrid, 1971). The compilers note that the total item count is 125,671, which represents a vocabulary of 18,053 different items. These four volumes include 58 prose pieces; it is not always easy to classify Borges's writings according to literary genre. Perhaps at a later date, someone will produce a concordance to his poetry.—**Hensley C. Woodbridge**

1300. Loewenstein, C. Jared. **A Descriptive Catalogue of the Jorge Luis Borges Collection at the University of Virginia Library.** Charlottesville, Va., University Press of Virginia, 1993. 254p. index. $35.00. Z8109.36.L63. 016.868. LC 91-35120. ISBN 0-8139-1333-0.

The University of Virginia boasts the world's finest and most complete collection of works by and about Jorge Luis Borges, the Argentine poet and writer who is considered to be one of the twentieth century's best literary artists and is hailed as the primary Latin American writer. This work is a catalog of that collection, which contains many rare and otherwise unavailable items. The advantage of access to this collection is that scholars will be able to examine and analyze Borges's works, which were often altered in later printings from their first appearance. The aim is to provide researchers with Borges's earliest works in scarce original versions and to trace changes in his writings throughout his career. Included are 979 entries identifying items in the collection. They are arranged alphabetically by author under 13 generic headings: works (collected and selected), poetry, essays, short stories, anthologies, collaborations, prologues and edited works, translations by Borges, manuscripts, miscellany, criticism and biographies, interviews, and bibliographies. Author and title indexes add to accessibility. Each entry contains author, full title, edition, imprint statement, pagination statement, size and format, and series statement. A large number of citations are annotated to provide further data, such as full edition or printing statement, provenance or association, transcriptions, and analysis of contents. The introduction and preface provide added insights into Borges's life and works as well as into this collection and its value. Loewenstein is Ibero-American bibliographer at the University of Virginia.

Although many more Borges items exist than those listed here, this is the most comprehensive single collection. Therefore, the work will be of great value to scholars who focus on Borges or Latin American letters. Recommended for large academic libraries and special collections dealing with world literature.
—**Edward P. Miller**

1301. Paravisini-Gebert, Lizabeth, and Olga Torres-Seda, comps. **Caribbean Women Novelists: An Annotated Critical Bibliography.** Westport, Conn., Greenwood Press, 1993. 427p. index. (Bibliographies and Indexes in World Literature, no.36). $69.95. Z1595.C364. 809'.89287'09729. LC 92-37915. ISBN 0-313-28342-7.

This is an extraordinary bibliographical study of Caribbean women novelists. The compilers note that the bibliography focuses specifically on works by and about Caribbean women who have published at least one novel since 1950. This volume deals with women novelists from 21 geographical areas who have written in Creole, French, English, Spanish, Dutch, and Papiamento.

For example, pages 121-135 provide material by and about Rosario Ferre and are divided into novels, excerpts, short stories, poetry, essay and other nonfiction, interviews conducted by, translations, criticism, reviews, interviews, and miscellaneous. The novels and critical studies are provided with extremely useful annotations. There are a list of authors by country and indexes of novels, critics, and themes and key words. An appendix covers literature in the Netherlands Antilles.

A few errors exist. It is amazing to see the British Library still referred to as the British Museum Library. The city of publication is usually given, yet only Venezuela is given for Monte Avila (this publisher is in Caracas). On page 330 the compilers note their inability to locate poetry by Mireya Robles in *Papeles de Son Armadans*, probably the finest Spanish literary journal of the Franco period.

Because this volume is extremely comprehensive and accurate and covers so many geographical areas, cultures, and languages, it should be an excellent starting point for the study of women novelists of the Caribbean. The compilers are to be congratulated for this volume and for the data that it contains. [R: Choice, Sept 93, p. 88; RBB, 15 May 93, p. 1720]—**Hensley C. Woodbridge**

POETRY

1302. **The New Princeton Encyclopedia of Poetry and Poetics.** Alex Preminger and T. V. F. Brogan, eds. Princeton, N.J., Princeton University Press, 1993. 1383p. $125.00; $29.95pa. PN1021.P75. 808.1'03. LC 92-41887. ISBN 0-691-03271-8; 0-691-02123-6pa.

As stated in the preface, this work is intended to be a comprehensive, comparative reference source for anyone "interested in the history of any poetry in any national literature of the world, or in any aspect of the technique or criticism of poetry." As such, it has entries, organized alphabetically, that range in scope from a survey of English poetry (there are separate entries for Cornish, Scottish, and Welsh poetries) to essays on meter and on structuralism, to definitions of anaphora, consonance, and renga. The cross-referenced contents list is helpful.

This volume is a major revision and expansion of the 1974 *Princeton Encyclopedia of Poetry and Poetics* (see ARBA 76, entry 1213). Some topics (e.g., "Rock Lyric") have been deleted, others (e.g., "Blues," "Politics and Poetry") added; all entries that have been retained have been revised. Besides the very significant revisions, the editors identify as major changes the increased attention given to non-Western and emergent poetries, the inclusion of all recent critical and theoretical movements relevant to poetry, the expanded bibliographies accompanying individual entries, and the increased use of cross-referencing.

The revised entry on American Indian poetry illustrates these changes. In 1974 the section of the essay on North America was limited to song from the oral tradition and hence indicated that American Indian poetry had no ongoing living tradition. The bibliography indicated that ancient Mexican poetry was included in the essay's scope, although the essay included only a passing reference to Aztec lyrics. The 1993 essay assumes that Native American poetry is "rich, diverse and persistent," thus recognizing an ongoing tradition. While making some of the same descriptive observations as the earlier essay, this one is attentive to the important scholarly work of the past 30 years, particularly in the field of ethnopoetics. Several paragraphs are devoted to contemporary poetry by Native Americans, emphasizing both the continuities between present and past and the thematic and stylistic diversity among the contemporaries. Mexican poetry is now included in the essay's section on Central America. There are two cross-references (none appeared in 1974), and the bibliography has been expanded and updated. Both the 1974 and the 1993 essays are well written; the more recent one will be much more useful to academics, and much more reflective of the whole field for general readers. Similar changes are evident in the 1993 entry on "Persona": It elaborates on uses of the term in recent psychological and sociological studies (treated only briefly in 1974) and adds discussion of modern critics' and theorists' treatments of voice and questioning of the idea of self. There are eight cross-references (only two in 1974), and the bibliography has more than doubled.

Probably inevitably, in a project involving so many contributors (approximately 375) and such a wide range of topics, some of the entries do not fully meet their own or the volume's goals. The entry on music and poetry, for example, should have been called "Music and Poetry in the European Tradition," for apart from one brief reference to an ancient Egyptian hymn and the inclusion of Edgar Allan Poe in a list, it never steps beyond Europe. Similarly, the entry on feminist poetics might better have been divided into one surveying poetry by women and one on feminist theory and criticism. As it is, the essay is weighted toward the former, although the bibliography cites numerous works on feminist poetics that would have yielded material for a more clearly focused entry. Such occasional weaknesses notwithstanding, the entries are generally clearly focused, well written, and sufficiently detailed to be of use, as the editors intended, to readers of varying degrees of expertise. Highly recommended for all academic and general libraries. [R: Choice, Oct 93, p. 271; JAL, Sept 93, p. 275; LJ, 1 Sept 93, p. 174; RBB, 15 Dec 93, p. 779; WLB, Oct 93, pp. 93-95]—**Robin Riley Fast**

1303. Young, Robyn V., ed. **Poetry Criticism: Excerpts from Criticism of the Works of the Most Significant and Widely Studied Poets.... Volume 5.** Detroit, Gale, 1992. 527p. index. $75.00. LC 91-118494. ISBN 0-8103-8333-0. ISSN 1052-4851.

References collections that have already obtained the first four volumes of this latest undertaking from Gale will of course wish to order this addition to the series. Similar to Gale's genre-oriented *Short Story Criticism* (see ARBA 91, entry 1143), *Poetry Criticism* (PC) was set up in response to librarians who serve high school, college, and public libraries and who noted an increasing number of requests for critical material on poets and poetry.

Volume 5 features nine poets, from Matthew Arnold and e. e. cummings to Johann Wolfgang von Goethe and Sappho. Each author section contains an appropriate biographical and critical introduction, as well as a portrait of the poet (when available) and assorted illustrations pertinent to the author's career. Then there are a dozen or more generous excerpts with the kind of information useful in doing a paper on a poet's prominent themes, individual poems, poetic techniques, or the critical reception of poets and their works. Early reviews written by the poet's contemporaries are often included to indicate initial reactions, while current analyses provide a modern view. Appended to each section are primary and secondary bibliographies. A detailed cumulative title index lists all individual poems and titles contained in the PC series. Smaller reference collections that do not have many of the books and journals from which the critical excerpts have been taken will find PC to be of special value.—**G. A. Cevasco**

WIT AND HUMOR

1304. Nilsen, Don L. F. **Humor Scholarship: A Research Bibliography.** Westport, Conn., Greenwood Press, 1993. 382p. index. (Bibliographies and Indexes in Popular Culture, no.1). $65.00. Z6514.W5N54. 016.128'3. LC 92-38989. ISBN 0-313-28441-5.

The aim of this bibliography is to document a veritable explosion in humor studies. That the study of humor is one of the most rapidly expanding academic fields is borne out by the fact that the overwhelming majority of the publications listed appeared within the last 20 years. The book is organized into 10 broad categories, most of which are further subdivided, resulting in a total of 45 separate subgenres of humor studies. Chapters are devoted to such topics as humor and the individual, language play and rhetorical devices, humor and the media, and humor and ethnicity. Each section begins with a short essay that introduces the topic of the bibliography to follow, along with a few relevant specimens of humor. The bibliographies range in length from 1 or 2 pages to 40, with a discernible emphasis on U.S. humor. There is a helpful appendix on humor resources that lists humor journals, newsletters, publishers, organizations, and scholars. There is also an index of authors and subjects.

The author clearly intends this to be more than just a list of publications in the field. The essays are meant to serve both as a guide to research and as an introduction to humor studies for the neophyte. The dichotomy between serious scholarship and just plain fun is pointed up both by the somewhat unscholarly tone of the essays and by the wide range of sources from which the bibliographies have been compiled. These sources run the gamut from scholarly publications to dime-store literature, with titles ranging from *Fantasy, Nonsense, Parody, and the Status of the Real* to *The Official Irish Joke Book*. [R: Choice, Sept 93, p. 86]—**Jeffrey R. Luttrell**

25 Music

GENERAL WORKS

Bibliography

1305. Arnold, Ben. **Music and War: A Research and Information Guide.** Hamden, Conn., Garland, 1993. 431p. index. (Music Research and Information Guides, v.17; Garland Reference Library of the Humanities, v.1581). $70.00. ML128.W2A75. 016.7815'99. LC 93-24938. ISBN 0-8153-0826-4.

The scope of this work is music within the tradition of Western art music that refers to war. The work is organized historically in eight chapters, four dealing with twentieth-century music, the remainder with earlier style periods. Separate chapters are devoted to World Wars I and II and to the Vietnam conflict. Particular attention is paid to such specific issues as the Holocaust, the atomic bomb, and protest.

Each chapter has an essay, one or more annotated lists of selected works, and supplementary lists of works not annotated. The annotated lists are arranged first by country, then by composer. Works are listed by title, with medium of performance, publication data for the score, recording information, and Library of Congress call number. In back are four excerpts from scores; an illustrated title page; a bibliography; and title, composer, and subject indexes.

Arnold has done a thorough job in selecting appropriate works for inclusion and in bringing many lesser-known works to attention. In some cases the war reference is specific, as in various pieces depicting battles. Many works touching on the aspect of human suffering through warfare are included. Drawing from secondary sources, he provides detailed descriptions of such works as "A Survivor from Warsaw." The work's title does not reflect the restriction in scope to Western art music, so users looking for military band music and the like will be disappointed. Also, the annotation to "Child of Our Time" should mention that it documents the events of Kristallnacht (not listed in the subject index).

This book provides a useful starting point for upper-level undergraduate and beginning graduate students, as well as for casual inquirers. It belongs in all libraries that support the study of music as a humanistic discipline. Above all, it is a thought-provoking work on a subject that, in the juxtaposition of two intrinsically incongruous elements, is a sad commentary on the human condition.—**Ian Fairclough**

1306. Baron, John H. **Baroque Music: A Research and Information Guide.** Hamden, Conn., Garland, 1993. 587p. index. (Music Research and Information Guides, v.16; Garland Reference Library of the Humanities, v.871). $90.00. ML116.B37. 016.78'09'032. LC 92-19620. ISBN 0-8240-4436-3.

Although admittedly selective, Baron's annotated bibliography will be of great help to those attempting to find their way in the extensive literature on baroque music. In addition to general books and articles, the guide lists specific references that deal with prominent types of vocal and instrumental music; important composers; specific countries; aspects of music theory and aesthetics; music patronage, pedagogy, printing and iconography; and modern revivals of baroque music. The 1,400-plus items include books, dissertations, collections of essays, and single essays drawn primarily from collections rather than journals. In addition to the expected publication information, each entry relays number of pages, ISBN and LC (or, when necessary, Dewey) number, citations in RILM (Repertoire International de la Litterature Musicale) and Dissertation Abstracts, and UM (University Microfilms) order numbers (for dissertations). Some items that Baron has not examined personally are listed with publication information only; others are annotated from information supplied in abstracts or reviews. Most annotations, however, are by Baron and reflect his broad knowledge of the material. Cross-references appear throughout the book, and indexes of authors, subjects, and names are supplied at the end.

Baron's comments present clear, often detailed summaries of the information available in his sources. They also evaluate the usefulness of the material, a great help to students making their first forays into the world of baroque music. Yet one is occasionally surprised to find Baron accepting uncritically some dubious assertions about major points or composers (e.g., Manfred F. Bukofzer's erroneous evaluation of the importance of instrumental music in the baroque). Also, while Baron has selected his sources with a keen eye to their helpfulness in getting into the larger mass of literature, there is next to nothing on prominent women (e.g., Barbara Strozzi, Isabella Leonarda), and the helpful research guide *G. F. Handel: A Guide to Research* (see ARBA 90, entry 1250) is strangely absent. Because Baron's format is the same for anthologies, journals, and books in series, the locations of some items might escape the neophyte researcher. These problems aside, Baron's work is well done and very welcome. It will be used with pleasure by the students, scholars, performers, and music lovers for whom he wrote it. [R: Choice, June 93, p. 1596]—**Karin Pendle**

1307. Krummel, D. W. **The Literature of Music Bibliography: An Account of the Writings on the History of Music Printing & Publishing.** Berkeley, Calif., Fallen Leaf Press, 1992. 447p. index. (Fallen Leaf Reference Books in Music, no.21). $75.00. ML112.K765. 016.0705'794. LC 92-10492. ISBN 0-914913-21-2.

The main title of this work leads one immediately to think of the standard guide to music reference, Vincent Duckles's *Music Reference and Research Materials*, now in its 4th edition (see ARBA 90, entry 1213). However, while Duckles and his successor, Michael A. Keller, had as their goal to provide a selective guide to reference sources and research tools in music, Krummel's goal is at once narrower and much broader. Narrower, because the scope is limited to writings about music printing and publishing; broader, because the author goes beyond reference works to cover historical surveys; technological treatises; printed music as graphic art; the business of music publishing; national literatures of selected countries and regions; and the institutional setting, including music libraries, antiquarians, collectors, and bibliophiles.

Krummel defines music bibliography in his chapter on theory as the study of the printed documents of music. A broader definition to include all aspects of the dissemination of texts (librarians may prefer the term "information" here) was earlier dismissed as being beyond the author's human limitations. Nevertheless, Krummel has amassed an impressive array of writings from the earliest days of music publishing to the 1990s, each with its own annotation, intermixed with narrative and ending with some artful arguments on music publishing and its effect on Western music. Some errors, such as the misnumbering of the few figures, differences in the title of chapter 7 from the table of contents to the actual chapter, and the absence of Krummel's name from the author index despite the large number of his own writings that are listed in the text, mar this otherwise excellent and interesting work. [R: Choice, Sept 93, p. 84]—**Johan Koren**

1308. Lowenberg, Carlton. **Musicians Wrestle Everywhere: Emily Dickinson & Music.** Berkeley, Calif., Fallen Leaf Press, 1992. 210p. illus. index. (Fallen Leaf Reference Books in Music, no.19). $39.50. ML134.5.D5L7. LC 92-9923. ISBN 0-914913-20-4.

The merging of two disparate components of the arts, the first created independently of the other, always has intriguing possibilities. Such is the case with some 276 individual composers' settings of Emily Dickinson's poetry to music over the last century. This volume identifies these compositions in a detailed list of more than 1,600 musical settings of 654 of Dickinson's poems and letters. The works range from operas to rock music, from songs for solo voice and piano to large works for orchestra and chorus. Among the important composers who have incorporated the texts of Dickinson's poetry in their music are Aaron Copeland, Elliott Carter, Roy Harris, John Adams, Gloria Coates, Samuel Barber, Ernst Bacon, Ned Rorem, and Max Morath. Quite simply, this book is excellent, not only for the treatment and scope of its subject but also from the point of organization and clarity of information. The author has access to a considerable amount of primary material; he owns what is considered to be the most comprehensive private collection of books by and about Emily Dickinson outside of Massachusetts.

The major portion of the volume is an alphabetical-by-composer list of the musical settings of Dickinson's words. These are subarranged chronologically and then by title of composition. Each entry includes such information as the date of the composition, performance medium, when the first performance occurred, and recordings. A number of miniessays describe the reasons why the composers selected Dickinson's works.

Following the main body of the work are a concordance, four appendixes, a bibliography, sources, and five indexes. The latter are essential to the volume. They include a general index and indexes to the first lines of the poems, music settings by Johnson number, composers and titles, and performance mediums. The volume also includes an informative foreword, a preface, and an introduction. All aspects of this work have been researched in great detail and organized most effectively for all levels of scholarship.—**Marjorie E. Bloss**

Catalogs and Collections

1309. Benjamin, Ruth, and Arthur Rosenblatt. **Movie Song Catalog: Performers and Supporting Crew for the Songs Sung in 1460 Musical and Nonmusical Films, 1928-1988.** Jefferson, N.C., McFarland, 1993. 352p. index. $45.00. ML128.M7B46. 016.78242'1542. LC 92-56630. ISBN 0-89950-764-6.

Combining entries for the titles of 60 years of movie songs along with other essential facts about the movies in which the songs appeared—year of release, country of origin, running time, director, and producing studio—has resulted in an information-packed sourcebook. The uniqueness of this work is enhanced by the inclusion of the names of music directors (e.g., the name of the director of that peppy orchestra backing Jeanette Macdonald and Maurice Chevalier in *One Hour with You*), writers of the musical scores, and orchestras. When musical backup was provided, such as a vocal group behind the solo performers, the name of that group is given. Names of dubbers who sang on soundtracks for on-screen performers are also listed. (According to this reference, Ava Gardner really did sing "Bill" in the 1951 version of *Show Boat*.) The point is that this reference has many purposes. Many of the entries are followed by a sampling of what reviewers in the *New York Times* or *Variety* had to say about the movie when it first opened. The three indexes are alphabetical by performer, songwriter, and song title.

This is an impressive and exhaustive reference volume. Considering the importance of movies in contemporary society, and with their reappearance in videocassette form, this book will find many uses in library and individual collections. [R: Choice, Dec 93, p. 580; RBB, 15 Dec 93, pp. 778]
—**Louis G. Zelenka**

1310. Rumbold, Valerie, and Iain Fenlon, eds. **A Short-title Catalogue of Music Printed Before 1825 in the Fitzwilliam Museum, Cambridge.** New York, Cambridge University Press, 1992. 168p. illus. $90.00. ML136.C212F58. 016.78'026'3. LC 91-29977. ISBN 0-521-41535-7.

This thin but very useful volume provides much basic information on the pre-1825 printed scores in Cambridge, England's Fitzwilliam Museum. This library, one of Great Britain's most important, has been built around the collection of seventeenth- and eighteenth-century music amassed by Viscount Richard Fitzwilliam. The formerly available catalog of this library, published in 1893, can be difficult to locate, and it cannot provide information on materials acquired for the collection during the past century; hence the need for the new catalog.

Rumbold—who did the lion's share of the work for the present bibliography—and Fenlon present their materials in a clear, accessible form. After an introduction telling of the life and musical activities of Fitzwilliam comes a preface dealing with the catalog. The body of the volume is taken up with an alphabetical list, by composer or—when the composer is unknown—by title of the work, of all music in the collection published before 1825. This varied group of works includes music for solo voices (e.g., songs, cantatas, operas), choruses, or small vocal ensembles (e.g., the many volumes of catches and glees). Among these scores the most prominent places are given to works of Handel and to French operas of the seventeenth and eighteenth centuries. Also important in the collection are volumes of works for keyboard instruments (primarily harpsichord) and pieces for instrumental ensembles (e.g., sonatas, concerti grossi). Despite the fact that Fitzwilliam's life spanned the active careers of Haydn, Mozart, and Beethoven, hardly any works by these composers appear in his library.

Entries for all works provide basic information only: short title, publication information, some brief annotations (e.g., dates or authors of texts not given in the source), and cross-references as needed. The alphabetical catalog is followed by some reproductions of interesting title pages or musical excerpts from the collection and a list by shelf number of the works indexed. A final, unexpectedly fascinating section provides a chronological list of Fitzwilliam's acquisition of the volumes in his music library, from 1763, when he purchased a volume of Bononcini's cantatas, to 1815, when he added Porter's *Cathedral Music* to his collection. While the lists do not provide detailed information on the items cataloged, they are an excellent place for scholars to begin their acquaintance with the music in the Fitzwilliam Museum.

—**Karin Pendle**

Chronology

1311. Weaver, Robert Lamar, and Norma Wright Weaver. **A Chronology of Music in the Florentine Theater 1751-1800: Operas, Prologues, Farces, Intermezzos, Concerts, and Plays with Incidental Music.** Warren, Mich., Harmonie Park Press, 1993. 996p. illus. index. (Detroit Studies in Music Bibliography, no.70). $60.00. ML1733.8.F6W45. 782.1'0945'51. LC 93-7492. ISBN 0-89990-064-X.

The music scholar will find ample value in this well-organized volume, which continues the authors' research that started in the 1970s. (Volume 1, *A Chronology of Music in the Florentine Theater, 1590-1750*, was introduced by the same publisher in 1978.) It starts with an exhaustive historical survey of the period covered and includes biographical sketches of the various dukes and regents, their family trees, descriptions of theaters where performances were taking place, and overviews of the theater scene divided into such categories as opera and ballet. The chronology itself follows, with works presented in the order in which they occurred, with generous notations. In the back of the book are indexes by category (e.g., librettists, choreographers and directors, publishers and vendors) and title (of operas, intermezzi, and the like), a bibliography, and a general index.

This book is strictly for music students and musicologists, but it also offers ample rewards to the musically curious, who can discover here, for instance, that Mozart did not mean much in Florence during the period covered, but that Paisiello reigned supreme, followed closely by Ferdinando Rutini, Michele Neri Bondi, Giuseppe Moneta, and Domenico Cimarosa. One can also find surprises, such as detailed records of numerous opera performances, made at the time they took place, with everything meticulously documented but for one thing: the composer. Owners of the first volume in this series should note that volume 2 includes 25 pages of addenda and corrigenda to volume 1. No typographical errors were found!—**Koraljka Lockhart**

Dictionaries and Encyclopedias

1312. **Encyclopedia of Music in Canada.** 2d ed. Helmut Kallmann and others, eds. Toronto and Buffalo, N.Y., University of Toronto Press, 1992. 1524p. illus. index. $95.00. 780'.971. ISBN 0-8020-2881-0.

The first edition of the *Encyclopedia of Music in Canada* (EMC) appeared in 1981. This version is about 448 pages longer, an increase of almost 50 percent, and there have been many other changes. About 800 new entries have been created, while 200 or so have been dropped (some of them inexplicably, such as the entry for John Norris, the founder of *Coda*, Canada's main jazz periodical). Most of the increase has come from entries on pop music, followed closely by jazz. New classical musicians have been added if they arose during the 1980s, but otherwise it is business as usual for the EMC.

The index has been rejiggered to allow for more cross-references, and items in the text that have their own separate entries have been asterisked. Many thematic articles have been added, such as ones that deal with funding and patronage, volunteerism, feminist music, native Canadian music, and music as a social phenomenon. These sprawling essays are, of course, counterbalanced by long lists of medals and prizes (either separately or within each biographical entry). Lots of facts, names, and dates appear, which is perfect for a secondary source that tries to nail down the who, what, where, and when of music in Canada. There are details about non-Canadians who worked in Canada, as well as details about Canadians who worked outside of Canada.

If anything is missing, it is criticism: why and how things happen, how a group or orchestra sounds, and so forth. But that is all opinion in many cases, and this is not the book for that sort of data. Included, where appropriate in each entry, are up-to-date bibliographies, lists of compositions, discographies, and filmographies. The physical product has three columns across each page with an extremely small typeface. Because the pages are oversized to start with, the book is a real bargain at its price.—**Dean Tudor**

1313. Marco, Guy A., ed. **Encyclopedia of Recorded Sound in the United States.** Hamden, Conn., Garland, 1993. 910p. index. (Garland Reference Library of the Humanities, v.936). $125.00. ML102.S67E5. 780.26'6'03. LC 93-18166. ISBN 0-8240-4782-6.

While a large number of books on recordings have been published, almost all of these are discographies or collectors' guides. Fortunately, to the scattering of existing biographies and histories can now be added this excellent encyclopedia. All types of music are covered, from the invention of the phonograph in 1877 to today's compact disc. The title notwithstanding, the nature of the recording industry, particularly the early years, means that a substantial amount of coverage relates to the other side of the Atlantic. The majority of the entries are written by Marco, with a few by the 30 contributors. Coverage includes terms, biographies, and topics. Most entries are under 50 lines, but there are a number of longer ones on a variety of topics, such as piano recordings, sonic restoration of historical recordings, Canada, pseudonyms, country and western music recordings, and loudspeakers. Two special features are a list of articles at the beginning and a bibliography and key to citations in the back.

A few editorial inconsistencies need to be corrected (e.g., there is no entry for James C. Petrillo in spite of what the entry under "AFM" and the list of articles say). A less trivial problem is that some of the artist biographies seem only to mention recordings in passing (e.g., the entry for Claudio Abbado). While there is a very brief entry for composer recordings, the reader will look in vain for entries under Igor Stravinsky, Aaron Copeland, or other composers who made significant numbers of recordings. A suggestion for the next edition: While a strength of this encyclopedia is its numerous cross-references, it would be helpful to have an entry for the history of recordings that referred the reader to major articles (e.g., those on cylinder and disk) that are scattered throughout the work. [R: Choice, Nov 93, pp. 430-32]
—**Robert Skinner**

Discography

1314. Erlewine, Michael, Scott Bultman, and Stephen Thomas Erlewine, eds. **All Music Guide: The Best CDs, Albums & Tapes.** San Francisco, Miller Freeman, 1992. 1176p. index. $19.95pa. LC 92-60948. ISBN 0-87930-264-X.

At first glance, this guide may appear to be yet another catalog a la *Schwann* (e.g., *Schwann Artist Issue* [see ARBA 90, entry 1236]), but further examination reveals a work that has more in common with the video guides of Leonard Maltin and his cronies than the sober listings of *Schwann*. For this source sets itself no less a goal than providing a signpost to the 23,000 "best" recordings in all formats—cassette, vinyl, and compact disc, from a database of 100,000—reviewed by music writers or others with expertise in the field, whether as retailers, collectors, disc jockeys, or performers.

Arrangement is by music genre, beginning with rock, pop, and soul and ending with jazz. Other genres include, not surprisingly, rap, blues, country, classical, Christmas, and children's; more surprisingly, women's music and gay music are listed as separate genres. Each genre is provided with an introduction defining its scope; boxes describing subgenres, terms, or important composers interspersed throughout the text; and, in some cases, "music maps" charting the evolution of the genre. Ultimately, however, each entry is arranged by artist or composer, each of whom is given a short biography, followed by a listing of the best recordings with the date of release and a short comment on each. Symbols by selected album titles indicate either a landmark recording, an essential collection, or a recommendation that this be a first purchase of a particular artist. The full database of this impressive guide is slated to become available in 1993 on CD-ROM and online in record stores. [R: Choice, July/Aug 93, p. 1743; RBB, 1 Feb 93, p. 1000]—**Johan Koren**

Handbooks and Yearbooks

1315. Graham, Ronnie. **The World of African Music.** London, Pluto Press; distr., Boulder, Colo., Westview Press, 1992. 235p. maps. index. (Stern's Guide to Contemporary African Music, v.2). $59.95. ML3502.5.G73. 780'.967'09048. LC 92-9308. ISBN 0-7453-0552-0.

This valuable reference is not a superficial review of the African pop scene but rather is a serious continuation of the author's first volume from 1988 (which provided coverage from 1955 to 1985) and an intensification of his valuable *Da Capo Guide to Contemporary African Music* (see ARBA 89, entry 1233). Each sub-Saharan country is individually treated, along with the islands of the Indian and Atlantic oceans and the regions of northeast Africa, with a historical perspective and discussion of the regional musical idioms. Under each of the latter is an updated discussion on the contributions of the major figures (adding those who have emerged since 1985), with discographies. The idioms include pop genres such as juju, gospel, kikuyu, reggae, and new wave makossa, as well as traditional music, musical theater, dance, and "art" music. Graham's subjective comments are welcome and conveniently appended. The bibliography is rich with important citations, particularly distinguished by reference to British and African research. The curious will find many stimuli, while the informed will appreciate the new information. This is a major informational resource on its subject by an important scholar.—**Dominique-Rene de Lerma**

1316. **The Pro/Am Book of Music and Mythology.** Thomas P. Lewis, comp. and ed. White Plains, N.Y., Pro/Am Music Resources, 1992. 2v. illus. index. $59.95(v.1); $49.95(v.2). ISBN 0-912483-51-2(v.1); 0-912483-82-2(v.2).

This highly specialized source provides a wealth of information and fascinating reading for those interested in the relationship between music and mythology, religion, and folklore. A projected three-volume set, *The Pro/Am Book of Music and Mythology* is divided into two parts. *Music in Mythology* is contained in volumes 1 and 2; *Essay on Myth and Reality* will comprise the third volume, scheduled for publication in April 1993. (Part 2 was not available for this review). Volume 1 of part 1 includes acknowledgments and a foreword, an extensive introductory essay, and the main body of the work. Volume 2 consists of two supplementary sections and a list of sources for text readings and a general index for part 1. Somewhat unusual in concept, this alphabetically arranged guide consists largely of entries, often of article length, that draw from more than 260 sources to document and discuss the role of music in the world's mythologies. Articles cover topics from Aboriginal (Australian) practices and beliefs to Zoroaster; footnotes and references abound; and many musically related stories and tales are included in their entirety. While the incorporation of the two supplements into the main body of the text would make access easier, this work is still an invaluable resource for writers and researchers of music and myth. It deserves a place in the libraries of individual scholars and in the reference collections of most academic and public libraries.—**Kristin Ramsdell**

1317. Sutton, Alan, comp. **A Guide to Pseudonyms on American Records, 1892-1942.** Westport, Conn., Greenwood Press, 1993. 148p. index. $49.95. ML158.S9. 780'.92'2. LC 93-4768. ISBN 0-313-29060-1.

Discographers and cultural historians with an interest in the title's half-century will welcome this handy resource that documents its approach up to the 1942 recording ban. Various factors, not all contractual, made it necessary for some recording artists to use pseudonyms as they moved from label to label, or even when they remained faithful to one. This publication is based on quite extensive searches (even some auditions) and cross-references to reconcile name variants of recording artists—vaudevillians (e.g., Butterbeans and Susie, Will Rogers, Al Jolson), concert artists (e.g., Reinald Werrenrath, Carlos Salzedo, Leopold Stokowski), pop singers (e.g., Sophie Tucker, Judy Garland), and jazz and blues figures (e.g., Fletcher Henderson, Alberta Hunter). En route one finds memberships specified for some ensembles (e.g., the Haydn Quartet, Invincible Four). Entries in the main body of the book register three groups of pseudonyms: vocalists by both domestic and foreign issues (when based on U.S. masters), and instrumentalists. The first appendix cites legal names; the second identifies record labels and their related affiliations. Two indexes distinguish vocalists from instrumentalists and provide references from professional names to the alternatives and to ensemble memberships. The front matter is a related history and specification of methodology.—**Dominique-Rene de Lerma**

Indexes

1318. Bonin, Jean M. **Piano-Beds & Music by Steam: An Index with Abstracts to Music-Related United States Patent Records, 1790-1874.** Berkeley, Calif., Fallen Leaf Press, 1993. 236p. index. (Fallen Leaf Reference Books in Music, 24). $69.50. ML3790.B67. 780'.27273. LC 92-93191. ISBN 0-914913-17-4.

Among the approximately 156,000 U.S. patents issued from 1790 to 1874 are more than 1,000 records related in one way or another to music. Many of them were mechanical inventions intended to improve or change the sound or action of existing musical instruments. Bonin has diligently identified and transcribed these musical listings, supplementing them with useful indexes for names, geographical distribution, and subjects. The bizarre and whimsical (e.g., no. 714, "Bed and Musical-instrument Board Combined") stand alongside the more substantial (e.g., no. 23, "Piano-forte," describing a metal frame for piano strings developed by the pioneer instrument maker Alpheus Babcock) in this unique chronology, giving evidence of the proverbial Yankee ingenuity within an evolving and lively musical culture of an expanding country. Researchers in U.S. music should not overlook this valuable tool.
—**John E. Druesedow, Jr.**

1319. Murray, Sterling E. **Anthologies of Music: An Annotated Index.** 2d ed. Warren, Mich., Harmonie Park Press, 1992. 215p. (Detroit Studies in Music Bibliography, no.68). $35.00. ML128.A7M87. 016.78'026'3. LC 92-34086. ISBN 0-89990-061-5.

This is the 2d edition of an index of music score anthologies designed mainly for survey courses in music history. Including citations for 4,670 items by more than 60 composers in 66 volumes, this edition is about one-third larger than the first. Arnold Schering's *Geschichte der Musik in Beispielen* (Leipzig: Breitkopf & Hartel, 1931), an old standard, is the earliest anthology indexed, and K [sic] Marie Stolba's *The Development of Western Music* (Wm. C. Brown, 1991) appears to be the latest. In several cases, anthologies that have gone through more than one edition are indexed in their entirety, edition by edition. Citations are arranged alphabetically by composer (subdivided by title) and contain useful information about notation, texts (if any), and commentary in the source publications. The concluding genre locator index of nearly 400 terms and cross-references provides further access to the indexed material. The cross-referencing structure is not extensive or elaborate but may be adequate for most needs. Given the relative paucity of recently published indexes for the more general historical anthologies of scores, college teachers and students alike will find Murray's work a welcome and practical guide to the newer publications as well as to some from past decades.—**John E. Druesedow, Jr.**

COMPOSERS

1320. Baytelman, Pola. **Isaac Albeniz: Chronological List and Thematic Catalog of His Piano Works.** Warren, Mich., Harmonie Park Press, 1993. 124p. index. (Detroit Studies in Music Bibliography, no.72). $35.00. ML134.A45A12. 016.786'092. LC 93-35580. ISBN 0-89990-067-4.

Baytelman's catalog of Albeniz's piano works is an updated list that includes a thematic index and historical commentaries on individual works. The author has also suggested a chronological order. This was no simple task, because a clear chronological sequence of Albeniz's works has always been hindered by complications of loss and erratic publishing practices. This title also contains an introduction that focuses on keyboard music in Spain before Albeniz, a biography of Albeniz, and his three stylistic periods. There are five very useful appendixes. Overall, libraries with large music collections will find this title useful. Also, this work should support any curriculum that offers a piano major.—**C. Michael Phillips**

1321. Bortin, Virginia. **Elinor Remick Warren: A Bio-Bibliography.** Westport, Conn., Greenwood Press, 1993. 285p. index. (Bio-bibliographies in Music, no.46). $65.00. ML134.W32B7. 780'.92. LC 93-20008. ISBN 0-313-25879-1.

Most students of American music will know the name of Elinor Remick Warren, although the youngest among them may not realize the extent and success of her career. Bortin has been working to remedy this problem, first with a full biography and now with this bio-bibliography. The image of Warren that emerges is impressive. A pianist as well as a composer, she accompanied many of the first-rank singers who programmed and recorded her songs. Practical as well as artistic, she did not shrink from providing arrangements of her works for various, sometimes strikingly different groups of performers. Bortin sorts out these potential confusions over Warren's oeuvre in a clear and user-friendly manner.

In the catalog Warren's 150 extant works are listed in alphabetical order by title. Each entry includes basic bibliographical information plus a selected list of performances given during Warren's lifetime. The next section of the book, a discography, includes both commercial and noncommercial recordings and is keyed to the works list. There follows an excellent annotated bibliography of reviews, general articles, theses, and books dealing with Warren. Bortin includes quotations from many newspaper articles that would otherwise be difficult to locate. Three appendixes (lists of Warren's works chronologically and by category, and information on the texts used in her vocal music) and an index close the volume.

The biography of Warren that opens the book is compact and to the point. It is followed by 70 pages of transcribed conversations between Bortin and Warren that should have been edited and organized with more rigor. Warren is clearly a composer whose work must stand for her, as she provides few insights into her music or her compositional process in these interviews. (Nor do Bortin's questions succeed in drawing her out.) A final note: Buyers should check the appendixes to see that all pages are printed and in order. The review copy contained several that were blank or misplaced.—**Karin Pendle**

1322. Craggs, Stewart R. **Alun Hoddinott: A Bio-Bibliography.** Westport, Conn., Greenwood Press, 1993. 237p. index. (Bio-bibliographies in Music, no.44). $55.00. ML134.H54C7. 016.78'092. LC 92-38456. ISBN 0-313-27321-9.

Hoddinott, the prolific contemporary Welsh composer, is president of the Cardiff Festival of 20th Century Music. An overview of his total output reveals works such as 17 concerti for various instruments, 4 string quartets, 10 sonatas for piano, 7 symphonies, 5 operas, and various songs and choral works. Many of his works have been performed by world-renowned performers and orchestras.

Craggs presents a comprehensive survey of the composer's life and works; the latter is especially well done. Having researched Hoddinott for 12 years, Craggs provides a great deal of data regarding each composition, even the names of the cast for the premiere of each opera. Compositions are given detailed examination, which will help the reader quickly become familiar with the dimensions and importance of each work. This work is divided into seven sections: a biography, a list of works and performances, a discography, a bibliography, an alphabetical list of compositions, a chronological list of main compositions, and the general index. The annotated bibliography includes 444 entries, and the discography has 57 entries. The volume is cross-referenced throughout, with each unit keyed mnemonically to the other units.

The volume will assist composers, musicologists, musicians, and those interested in the creative process of the contemporary composer. Highly recommended for music library reference divisions.

—**Robert Palmieri**

1323. Craggs, Stewart, comp. **William Walton: A Source Book.** Brookfield, Vt., Scolar Press/Ashgate Publishing, 1993. 333p. index. $69.95. ISBN 0-85967-934-9.

This is Craggs's third bibliographical publication on Walton. The revised edition of his *William Walton: A Catalogue* (see ARBA 91, entry 1269) appeared in 1990. The *Source Book* inevitably contains some duplication of information but is nevertheless a distinct work, addressing researchers intent on a more thorough investigation of Walton's life and works.

The body of the book is in two sections. The chronology presents events in Walton's life, his works, and first performances in tabular form. The section on manuscripts and first editions expands the catalog into a descriptive bibliography. The data in this section include for each manuscript the size, binding, transcription of the title page, pagination, and so forth, with comments on the type of information on each page (e.g., music, blank) and analogous details for the first edition (including print run where available). Works are presented in order by title, with references by number to the *Catalogue*. Also included are a separate list of collections of letters and a list of Walton's recordings (as conductor and spoken). A comprehensive bibliography appears to be arranged by work and includes record sleeve notes (note that English usage customarily reserves the term "programme note" for one distributed at a performance, and these are not included). However, other material is included in this A-Z sequence, under "General." The general index lists personal and other names, works, and events.

The *Source Book* is a companion to the *Catalogue* but does not substitute for it. The *Catalogue* provides easier access to information and is more suited to collection development, whereas the *Source Book*'s chronology provides a dimension and a means of access that are not available in the earlier work. Only the most serious scholars will find the extent of descriptive detail necessary; however, Craggs has served such people well. His book is a must for collections supporting doctoral programs in the history of twentieth-century music.—**Ian Fairclough**

1324. Demsey, David, and Ronald Prather, with Judith Bell. **Alec Wilder: A Bio-Bibliography.** Westport, Conn., Greenwood Press, 1993. 274p. index. (Bio-bibliographies in Music, no.45). $55.00. ML134.W638D4. 016.78'092. LC 92-38455. ISBN 0-313-27820-2.

Alec Wilder (1907-1980) was an American musical composer whose works represent a broad spectrum of distinctive music styles from popular to jazz; they even extend to chamber, orchestral, and opera compositions. Wilder was also a writer of books, notably *American Popular Song* (Oxford University Press, 1972). To prepare this work, numerous archives and institutional collections were researched. The biographical segment is concise—fewer than 30 pages—but adequate. Wilder frequently wrote for solo instruments—indeed, often for instruments not usually scored extensively for solo parts. The authors have considered this, and under the section on works and performances, the listings are arranged alphabetically by instrument. Dates and locations of premiere performances and special selected performances are also given. Both here and in the discography section, the listings are carefully arranged by categories, such as chamber music, keyboard music, popular songs, musical theater, art songs, operas, ballet music, and music for children.

The bibliography is extensive and includes books, articles, dissertations, reviews of books, and works by and about Wilder. Ancillary materials include annotated lists of unpublished writings as well as unpublished music manuscripts that now reside in the Alec Wilder Archive at the Eastman School of Music in Rochester, New York. Also listed here are 38 radio programs, *American Popular Song*, that Wilder hosted over National Public Radio from 1976 to 1980. This scholarly work is highly recommended for the music library collection.—**Louis G. Zelenka**

1325. Grattan, Virginia L. **American Women Songwriters: A Biographical Dictionary.** Westport, Conn., Greenwood Press, 1993. 279p. illus. index. $39.95. ML106.U3G73. 782.42'092'273. LC 92-32211. ISBN 0-313-28510-1.

Grattan has compiled a useful tool for anyone wishing to study the role of women as creators of American popular song during the last two centuries. Neither a history nor a critical evaluation of the literature—nor even a particularly scholarly work—this book provides biographies, ranging in length from a half page to five pages, of women composers and lyricists, the majority active since 1920. For convenience the author groups the entries under several categories: pop/rock, motion pictures, musicals, blues, jazz, folk, country, hymns, and gospel, and adds a section on women writers of nineteenth- and early twentieth-century parlor songs. After a stripped-down history of each type of song, each section presents, in alphabetical order, biographies of up to 30 women. At the end of each biography is a list of materials to be consulted for further information. Although Grattan's writing is at best journalistic and often colloquial, her manner is well suited to her subjects and her potential readers.

Comparison of Grattan's biographies with those in *The New Grove Dictionary of American Music* (NGA) (see ARBA 88, entry 1277) illuminates several areas where she has something of an edge over that most scholarly source. First, she includes many women whom the editors of NGA considered too unimportant to mention. Moreover, Grattan is more likely than NGA to provide material of a personal or anecdotal nature, which the general reader will enjoy, and to list more items in her bibliographies. Yet Grattan and NGA give conflicting information on many women listed in both sources (e.g., NGA disagrees with Grattan on the year of Madonna's birth, and Peggy Lee may have written more than 200 songs [Grattan] or more than 500 songs [NGA]). This is not to say that NGA is invariably correct, but simply to point out that such conflicts can only be resolved by consulting additional sources of information.

More disturbing is Grattan's lack of clarity in stating exactly what her subjects have contributed to American popular song. Some were composers, others were lyricists, while still others wrote both tunes and lyrics; but it is difficult to determine which women belong in which category. One also cannot be sure whether a composer actually wrote the music down or whether she simply sang her tunes to someone capable of notating them and adding harmony and orchestration. Some women also collaborated with other poet-composers on specific songs, but the nature of the collaboration is seldom described. Grattan has provided a good starting-point in the search for materials on women songwriters, but her book is inadequate as a sole source of information. [R: Choice, Nov 93, p. 432; LJ, 15 Mar 93, p. 68; RBB, July 93, p. 2000; RQ, Winter 93, p. 279; SLMQ, Fall 93, p. 58]—**Karin Pendle**

1326. Guttmann, Hadassah. **The Music of Paul Ben-Haim: A Performance Guide.** Metuchen, N.J., Scarecrow, 1992. 255p. index. $32.50. ML410.B44909. 784.092. LC 92-5279. ISBN 0-8108-2551-1.

Paul Ben-Haim (1897-1984) has been criticized as a conservative composer, but despite this all-too-easy-to-use label, his music continues to be performed. The success of a composer should be measured by the life of the composer's works, and Ben-Haim's music lives on to this day. In her work Guttmann presents a detailed description and analysis of selected compositions. She employs the La Rue system of analysis in her descriptions, which charts out the style and structure of a composition. Guttmann analyzes 10 works by Ben-Haim, including several works for a piano; a trio for violin, cello, and piano; a quintet (clarinet and string quartet); a violin sonata; a work for flute and string trio; a work for violin and piano; and a work for solo voice or instrument and piano. A unit following the formal analysis offers suggestions for performance of the previously examined compositions. As with any performance guide, these suggestions are to be taken lightly, as the ultimate performance standard is set by the performer. However, Guttmann's suggestions are rather basic and pose no problem of forcing a performance standard.

Other chapters in *The Music of Paul Ben-Haim* deal with the life of the composer; a bibliography (40 items); a list of Ben-Haim's works; a discography (25 items); and copies of letters from Leopold Stokowski, Leonard Bernstein, and Jascha Heifetz (all supposedly reflecting Ben-Haim's stature as a composer). A general index completes the volume. (For a more detailed view of Ben-Haim's complex life and his struggle in becoming a "Jewish composer," see *Paul Ben-Haim: His Life and Works* by Jehoash Hirshberg [Jerusalem: Israeli Music, 1990].)

Guttmann's book is a welcome introduction to the works of Ben-Haim. It should help musicians understand the music of one of Israel's foremost composers. Recommended for music library reference divisions.—**Robert Palmieri**

1327. Kent, Christopher. **Edward Elgar: A Guide to Research.** Hamden, Conn., Garland, 1993. 523p. index. (Composer Resource Manuals, v.37; Garland Reference Library of the Humanities, v.1017). $81.00. ML134.E613K46. 016.78'092. LC 92-32217. ISBN 0-8240-8445-4.

One could hardly wish for a more thorough presentation of material than that found in Kent's research guide to Elgar. Although, as Kent admits, his subject is among the best documented of our recent composers, the material available emphasizes the factual side of knowledge and research rather than the analytical side. Hence, about two-thirds of this volume is taken up with a chronological catalog of Elgar's compositions, completed or just in fragments, from 1866 through 1933. For each entry Kent lists (wherever applicable) the locations of manuscript sources (including sketches) and proofs, sources of texts or music (the latter in cases where Elgar has arranged the music of another composer), names of dedicatees, published editions, arrangements by Elgar or others of any given piece, cross-references to other titles in the catalog, and locations of information on the specific piece in question. Just reading through this catalog can give one an idea of the growth in Elgar's popularity and marketability, as well as how long he waited for it. Not until the mid-1880s do his works begin to appear with any regularity, and he had to wait until the premiere of his *Enigma Variations* in 1899, when he was over 40 years old, for a success that would prove to be the beginning of international fame.

After the catalog of works begins an annotated list of writings by and about Elgar and his music. This bibliography is divided into 12 subcategories according to literary classifications or musical genres and is to some extent selective. The volume ends with lists of the contents of several Elgar archives, largely in British libraries and museums, and with several helpful indexes. Included in the archives are materials Elgar owned, letters to or by him or members of his family, clipping files, and scrapbooks. For most, Kent has provided helpful annotations.

Garland's guides to research have provided much important and reliable information in the past. Kent's contribution takes its not-unworthy place among this excellent company.—**Karin Pendle**

1328. Klemme, Paul T. **Henk Badings, 1907-87: Catalog of Works.** Warren, Mich., Harmonie Park Press, 1993. 201p. index. (Detroit Studies in Music Bibliography, no.71). $35.00. ML134.B157A2. 016.78'092. LC 93-31384. ISBN 0-89990-065-8.

The Dutch composer Henk Badings wrote more than 600 compositions, both for electronic and computer as well as more traditional resources. This is the first comprehensive catalog of Badings's music and was compiled with the assistance of the composer's wife. The catalog is arranged by genre and includes a finding list of commercial recordings, bibliographies of articles by Badings and writings about him, and a short biography. Four appendixes and an index provide access by title, by chronology, and to his didactic works. A typical entry includes date of composition, publisher, duration, date of premiere, and similar information. The almost 100-item discography is largely limited to commercial recordings on LP and compact disc. This catalog has been well researched and makes a fine addition to the long-running series.—**Robert Skinner**

1329. Millington, Barry, ed. **The Wagner Compendium: A Guide to Wagner's Life and Music.** New York, Schirmer Books/Macmillan, 1992. 431p. illus. index. $35.00. ML410.W13W122. 782.1'092. LC 92-32214. ISBN 0-02-871359-1.

Hard on the heels of the extremely successful *Mozart Compendium*, edited by H. C. Landon (Schirmer Books, 1990), comes another definitive volume, this one devoted to one of the most written-about personages in the history of the civilized world. So, who needs another book on Wagner? Probably everyone who either dabbles in, deals with, or is deeply involved in music. If a person wants just one book on this composer, this should be it. If one has many Wagner books, this one will still be essential for quick fact-finding and handy reference. The editor, a noted Wagner authority, has put together a collection of writings (many are his own) that covers every aspect of Wagneriana. An exhaustive chronology of the composer's life starts the book; in the back is a glossary that covers terms from *Abgesang* to *Zukunftsmusik*. The main body of the book includes essays on Wagner's operas, staging, the Wagnerian singing style, conducting, and the like, all updated through the present. The excellence of the writing, the intelligence of the editing, and the total absence of typographical errors make this volume a rare example of a perfectly thought-out and put-together reference book.—**Koraljka Lockhart**

1330. Perone, James E. **Howard Hanson: A Bio-Bibliography.** Westport, Conn., Greenwood Press, 1993. 327p. index. (Bio-bibliographies in Music, no.47). $65.00. ML134.H173P47. 780'.92. LC 93-2589. ISBN 0-313-28644-2.

Howard Hanson was a staunch advocate of U.S. music, continually supporting young composers. His 40 years as director of the Eastman School of Music were marked by the excellence of that school. Unfortunately, his own music has largely been neglected except for his "Romantic" Symphony. At the present there is a revival of his music, with important CD recordings made with conductors Leonard Slatkin and Gerard Schwarz.

Perone's work presents a broad introduction to Hanson and his music. The volume's structure follows the usual series format: A concise biography of Hanson is followed by the main corpus of the book, which contains a cataloging system for Hanson's compositions. Each work is listed by genre (e.g., theater, opera, ballet, orchestra), with information as to date of composition, publisher, contents, commission, dedication, manuscript location, and premiere and other performances; there is also a bibliography for each work. Also arranged by genre is a discography of Hanson's works usefully accompanied by reviews of the recordings. The unit containing the general bibliography (which is annotated) is arranged chronologically and contains a catalog of written works dealing with biographical references, articles about Hanson, and Hanson's own writings (books and newspaper and journal articles). The volume is cross-referenced throughout. There are appendixes of his awards and honorary degrees (36 U.S. degrees), a chronological list of compositions, and an alphabetical list of compositions. The general index includes all names (e.g., people, compositions, organizations).

It is hoped that Perone will follow this excellent work with an extensive in-depth biography of Hanson. This bio-bibliography is highly recommended for all music library reference divisions and should be of special interest to composers, musicologists, and music educators.—**Robert Palmieri**

1331. Reeder, Ray. **The Bach English-Title Index.** Berkeley, Calif., Fallen Leaf Press, 1993. 184p. (Fallen Leaf Reference Books in Music, no.20). $33.00. ML134.B1R43. 016.7822'2'0268. LC 92-37177. ISBN 0-914913-23-9.

One is hard-pressed to think of another composer whose sheer virtuosic talent exceeds Bach's. To have written the Brandenburg Concertos is one thing, but to have added to it a host of heavenly others (e.g., the Mass in B minor) places him in a class whose roll takes only seconds to call.

Reeder's book provides music majors of all levels with a practical way of locating Bach's works that are cited only by English-language titles. The book lists phrases and words used as translations, paraphrases, scores, librettos, and original text, covering more than 14,000 entries and more than 16,000 titles and textual incipits. Moreover, the title and first-line listing includes not only separate titles and movements of Bach's vocal works but also choral preludes and chorales that bear titles of hymn tunes. Any library supporting a music program will want to purchase this excellent volume. [R: Choice, Oct 93, p. 272; WLB, Sept 93, p. 114]—**Mark Y. Herring**

1332. Sherman, Charles H., and T. Donley Thomas. **Johann Michael Haydn (1737-1806): A Chronological Thematic Catalogue of His Works.** Stuyvesant, N.Y., Pendragon Press, 1993. 385p. illus. index. (Thematic Catalogues, no.17). $64.00. ML134.H28A33. 016.78'092. LC 93-8282. ISBN 0-918728-56-8.

This is one of the most comprehensive volumes in a low-keyed series embracing a diverse group of composers including Giovanni Pergolesi, John Coprario, Alessandro Stradella, and Virgil Thomson. They are mostly minor composers, some indeed all but forgotten; Michael Haydn and Pergolesi are the most illustrious in the series. One therefore approaches this catalog with more than the usual interest, and one's expectations are met and surpassed.

The catalog has been decades in the compilation, dating back to the late 1950s. The proofreading of Latin and German titles is accordingly nearly perfect, but the classification system has become so refined that it seems complex rather than clear. Because Haydn characteristically dated his scores, this catalog is primarily organized chronologically; within that framework, the compositions are recorded thematically (e.g., vocal or instrumental, sacred or secular). There is a supplementary index by titles or first lines.

The authors survey and evaluate previous Haydn catalogs, notably those by Nikolaus Lang, Werigand Rettensteiner, and Lothar Perger, and acknowledge their debt to their predecessors. Their own catalog, however, supersedes all previous ones, recording new data that has come to light during their research.—**John B. Beston**

1333. **The Twentieth-Century Composer Speaks: An Index of Interviews.** By Mari Nishimura. Berkeley, Calif., Fallen Leaf Press, 1993. 189p. (Fallen Leaf Reference Books in Music, no.28). $39.50. ML118.N57. 780'.92'2. LC 93-29548. ISBN 0-914913-29-8.

This is a source book of an unusual kind. It lists more than 1,000 published interviews with classical music composers who are or have been active in the latter half of the twentieth century. For most of the composers listed, one or two interviews are cited, although a few (e.g., Stravinsky) are represented by more than a dozen. Each entry includes the name and birth date of the composer and the date and place of the interview. These entries are followed by the name of the interviewer or interviewers and the major topics discussed. Mention is made of any of the interviewee's compositions that were discussed and whether biographical information or a list of works is included in the published interview. A full reference is given to the publication and language in which the interview appears in print, and notes may follow for a few cases.

It is clear that this is a source for musical scholars and others with an interest in one or more contemporary composers. It will be very useful for obtaining information that may be otherwise inaccessible about composers and their opinions, lives, and works. It belongs in personal or other libraries serving anyone engaged in the study of individual or collective influences upon recent trends in classical music.—**Arthur R. Upgren**

1334. Vidali, Carole F. **Alessandro and Domenico Scarlatti: A Guide to Research.** Hamden, Conn., Garland, 1993. 1v. (various paging). index. (Composer Resource Manuals, v.34; Garland Reference Library of the Humanities, v.1125). $62.00. ML134.S218V5. 016.78'092'2. LC 93-16636. ISBN 0-8240-5942-5.

This guide is of great importance to students and performers seeking material on these composers. The biographical and critical material in English about their lives and works is out-of-date or buried in scholarly articles and dissertations, and the editions of their works are often also out-of-date. Edward J. Dent's book on Alessandro is nearly 90 years old, and Ralph Kirkpatrick's book on Domenico is 50 years old (and becomes more and more controversial in light of more recent scholarship). These are the books most readily available and the ones most musicians will use, but they must be supplemented by less accessible materials. Vidali's guide leads the user to them.

The book considers each composer separately. A contents page for the whole book would have been useful, as one must hunt to find the contents for the Domenico section after the last page of the Alessandro section. General material considers lives, documents, cultural milieu, and relationships to other composers. Studies of the music consider vocal and instrumental music separately. Performance practice, editions of the works, and sources are covered in separate sections. Discographies are also included. Excellent annotations accompany the entries. It would be of benefit to many if this guide were to spur book and music publishers to recognize the need for current studies in English of these great composers, and for new publications of their scores based on contemporary scholarship. Until such publications are available, this work will be an indispensable guide through the maze of scattered sources.—**George Louis Mayer**

INSTRUMENTS

1335. Bedford, Frances. **Harpsichord and Clavichord Music of the Twentieth Century.** Berkeley, Calif., Fallen Leaf Press, 1993. 608p. index. (Fallen Leaf Reference Books in Music, no.22). $69.50. ML128.H35B39. 016.7864. LC 93-27827. ISBN 0-914913-19-0.

Bedford offers a useful compilation of harpsichord and clavichord literature written in the twentieth century. She catalogs some 5,600 compositions by 2,700 composers and hopes to stimulate interest in the study and performance of these works, saying that harpsichordists should program the best of them alongside the best of the baroque literature. In researching this volume, she investigated numerous music centers and libraries (including private collections) and also contacted publishers, harpsichordists, and composers. For international readers, the foreword and introduction are given in English, German, and French.

The book is divided into two parts. The first deals with harpsichord music and the second with clavichord music. Most of the material lies in the harpsichord section, which is subdivided into works for harpsichord solo, multiple harpsichords, harpsichord and other instruments, ensembles with harpsichord, orchestra with harpsichord, voice and harpsichord, and more. The short clavichord section is not subdivided. Back material includes two appendixes (composers' addresses and a list of publishers, music centers, and libraries) and eight indexes.

Bedford's contribution to the field of keyboard literature is vital; her work reveals the brisk activity maintained by the revival of these two venerable keyboard instruments, and it proves that contemporary composers are interested in writing works for them. Her excellent volume will be an invaluable resource for music library reference divisions and especially useful to keyboard performers, teachers, and students.
—**Robert Palmieri**

1336. Heier, Uli, and Rainer E. Lotz, eds. **The Banjo on Record: A Bio-Discography.** Westport, Conn., Greenwood Press, 1993. 597p. index. (Discographies, no.52). $75.00. ML156.4.B36B3. 016.7878'80266. LC 92-38459. ISBN 0-313-28492-X.

Heier and Lotz attempt to list in this discography all banjo recordings issued on cylinders or 78 rpm discs from 1889 up to the introduction of long-playing records in the mid-1950s. Both Heier and Lotz are specialists in banjo history; Heier is an active banjoist in the group Doctor Jazz Ambulance, and Lotz has edited and written frequently in the gramophone field. The work is organized by performer or group. Recordings are listed chronologically by matrix number and take digit. Also provided are name of the piece, location, date, manufacturer, catalog number, and a brief biography of the performer. The editors have provided additional short essays on the history of the banjo, banjo recordings, types of banjos, a bibliography, and an addenda and corrigenda. Major essays have been provided by Lowell Schreyer and Robert Lloyd Webb. There is a title index to works listed in the discography section, and there are 23 unnumbered pages of photographic reproductions of banjo disc labels (illustrating some 92 labels).

The work is very well done and is an excellent example of the discography genre. Music libraries and most reference collections will find the work useful. Record collectors will also want to purchase this volume. Anyone with an interest in the history of the banjo will find this book to be their bible for years to come.—**Ralph Lee Scott**

1337. Maxwell, Grant L. **Music for Three or More Pianists: A Historical Survey and Catalogue.** Metuchen, N.J., Scarecrow, 1993. 467p. illus. index. $42.50. ML700.M39. 785.62. LC 92-37842. ISBN 0-8108-2631-3.

Literature for piano duet and duo-piano has been the focus of many catalogs and surveys. However, literature for three or more pianists has not had a similar profile. Maxwell's work, a historical survey and catalog of this literature, lists a great number and variety of compositions. Maxwell traces the multiple-pianist genre from J. S. Bach through the late twentieth century.

The catalog is divided into 10 different categories that include transcriptions and arrangements, graded pieces for class piano, and anthologies. Each entry is analyzed and includes important information, such as the number of pianos and pianists required, publisher, duration, number of pages, and location of score (when held by a library). This title also includes a discography and a practical index based on number of pianos and hands required.

This work will be of interest to large music libraries. Also, libraries that support a music curriculum that includes class piano and facilities for multiple piano performance should find this title useful. [R: Choice, Dec 93, p. 588]—**C. Michael Phillips**

1338. **The Oxford Companion to Musical Instruments.** By Anthony Baines. New York, Oxford University Press, 1992. 404p. illus. $35.00. ML102.I5B34. 784.19'03. LC 92-8635. ISBN 0-19-311334-1.

In the introduction Baines (who is the dean of British writers on musical instruments) describes this work as an "offspring" of the *New Oxford Companion to Music* (see ARBA 84, entry 889) and, as such, not to be compared with the three-volume *New Grove Dictionary of Musical Instruments* (see ARBA 86, entry 1252) or the longer and more technical *Musical Instruments* by Sibyl Marcuse (W. W. Norton, 1975). In fact, however, this work contains information not included in these longer works, such as a separate illustrated article on the Irish Uilleann (or union) bagpipes.

This work is intended for the general reader and consists of short articles arranged in dictionary order. There are articles for individual concepts, techniques, and instruments (e.g., trumpet); families of instruments (e.g., brass); and characteristic groupings of instruments (e.g., brass band). The emphasis is on the instruments of Europe, but instruments of non-Western cultures are included. The longest article, on the organ, is more than 12 pages long; the shortest articles are only a sentence or two. The work is heavily illustrated with drawings and photographs, and musical examples are given illustrating characteristic passages and the range of the instrument.

This superb work is highly recommended to any library needing a one-volume general dictionary of musical instruments. It would not be a necessary purchase for a library already owning the *New Grove Dictionary of Musical Instruments*, but it does include information omitted from this more "prestigious" source. [R: RBB, 15 Mar 93, p. 1378; SLJ, Nov 93, p. 140; WLB, Mar 93, p. 112]—**Richard H. Swain**

1339. Schleuter, Stanley L., comp. **Saxophone Recital Music: A Discography.** Westport, Conn., Greenwood Press, 1993. 287p. (Discographies, no.53). $65.00. ML156.4.S3S34. 016.7887'0266. LC 93-2588. ISBN 0-313-29001-6.

This is the first significant addition to saxophone discography since the publication of *Saxophone Soloists and Their Music 1844-1985* (see ARBA 87, entry 1246). The compiler has facilitated access by arranging his entries in several sequences: first by composer, next by performer, then by label (with solo recordings differentiated from ensemble). Albums, compact discs, and commercial audio recordings of classical saxophone music are included. The volume concludes with a list of record companies (addresses only, no telephone or fax numbers).

Works such as this, while valuable, are more properly classified as finding lists. For example, there is no indication of important discographical information such as place or date of recording, whether an item is out-of-print (and if so, when), or (in most cases) any indication of the original piece on which an arrangement has been based. In spite of this, the book's publication will be welcomed by all those interested in saxophone recital and concert music.—**Robert Skinner**

MUSICAL FORMS

Church

1340. **Sacred Choral Music in Print: 1992 Supplement.** By F. Mark Daugherty and Susan H. Simon. Philadelphia, Pa., Musicdata, 1992. 304p. index. (Music-In-Print Series, v.1t). $95.00. ML128.V7E78. 016.7825'22'0263. LC 92-27658. ISBN 0-88478-029-5.

1341. **Sacred Choral Music in Print: Master Index 1992.** Philadelphia, Pa., Musicdata, 1992. 413p. (Music-In-Print Series, v.1X). $95.00. ML128.V7S2. 016.7825'22. LC 92-43440. ISBN 0-88478-030-9.

1342. **Secular Choral Music in Print: 1993 Supplement.** F. Mark Daugherty and Susan H. Simon, eds. Philadelphia, Musicdata, 1993. 223p. index. (Music-In-Print Series, v.2t). $95.00. ML128.V7D3. 016.7825'4'0263. LC 93-28494. ISBN 0-88478-031-7.

Musicdata publishes a number of in-print music lists that range from choral to orchestral. *Sacred Choral Music in Print* is a subset of the more general *Choral Music in Print Master Index 1991* (see ARBA 92, entry 1285), which tries to distinguish sacred from secular choral works. The supplement contains sacred music published between 1988 and 1992. Prepared for the church choral director, it lists composers, individual titles, and collection titles, complete with numerous cross-references in a single alphabet. A separate arranger and publisher index is included. Each main entry (under composer) contains details such as instrumentation, contents (if a collection), voicing, and such usage as "Xmas" or "Epiphany." Unlike in previous editions, one cannot find a listing under topics such as *Good Friday*. The listings, similar to those in *Books in Print* (Reed Reference Publishing, annual), rely on the catalogs of publishers for their information, with publishers making corrections as various editions are issued.

For libraries owning all three of the volumes of *Sacred Choral Music in Print* (see ARBA 89, entry 1223 and ARBA 87, entry 1251 for reviews of the first two), the publisher has also prepared the *Sacred Choral Music in Print: Master Index*, a single index to composers and titles. It cuts the search from a three-step process to a two-step one. It also provides a quick bibliography of a composer's entire in-print works.

Choral directors in schools, colleges, and communities will benefit from Musicdata's in-print list for secular music that includes U.S. and European publishers of choral music. This 1993 supplement to *Secular Choral Music in Print* (see ARBA 89, entry 1219) is the second update to be published since the main volume appeared. This list is arranged by composer and title in one sequence, with a separate arranger index and a directory of publishers.

For churches and choral directors, these tools are essential purchases. Libraries will want to sort through the various in-print music titles published by Musicdata to decide which editions of the total in-print music database should be acquired and with what frequency.—**David V. Loertscher**

1343. Walker, Diane Parr, and Paul Walker. **German Sacred Polyphonic Vocal Music between Schutz and Bach: Sources and Critical Editions.** Warren, Mich., Harmonie Park Press, 1992. 434p. index. (Detroit Studies in Music Bibliography, no.67). $45.00. ML128.S2W34. 016.7825'22026. LC 92-18215. ISBN 0-89990-054-2.

The authors have compiled an extensive bibliography of extant German sacred vocal music for three or more voices from approximately the last half of the seventeenth century—from the end of the Thirty Years War in 1648 to the beginning of the careers of Bach and Handel around 1700. The book opens with an introduction valuable for both the historical background it provides and for its clear instructions for interpreting the bibliography. The main part of the work includes a considerable amount of useful information. First, the voice parts for which the music is intended are listed, as well as the instrumental performing forces. When a liturgical occasion is designated, that is also included. Three different types of source locations are noted: manuscripts, published collections by individual composers, and published commemorative pamphlets that contain music for a special occasion. RISM (Repertoire International des Sources Musicale) and Reich numbers are included where appropriate. Format—score, parts, or choirbook—is indicated, as is availability on microfilm. Finally, modern scholarly editions are noted. Although the body of the work is arranged alphabetically by author, indexes to titles, performing forces, and liturgical occasions are included. The volume is easy to use and to read. At its relatively modest cost, it is a must for academic music libraries.—**Allie Wise Goudy**

Classical

1344. **Best Rated CDs: Classical 1992.** Voorheesville, N.Y., Peri Press, 1993. 562p. index. $19.95pa. ISBN 1-879796-07-4.

The basic idea behind this guide is very good: to publish a guide to the best-rated CDs, with excerpts of reviews from 38 music magazines, encompassing both mainstream and specialized publications. There are a few problems in execution, though. First of all, works have been grouped into eight categories, making it necessary to do a lot of riffling when searching for works of a particular composer or works that might fit into two categories (e.g., Maurice Ravel's *Daphnis et Chloe*). The book's editor asks for suggestions in his preface, so here is one: arrange the book by composers and let the compositions fall where they may. Excerpted reviews make for fascinating reading, but one occasionally raises an eyebrow at statements such as "A hands-down loser!" (p. 89) or "... the barely adequate recording is second-rate by today's best standards" (p. 420), particularly when one considers the publication's title. Another peculiarity: Several esoteric operas appear, such as Schoeck's *Massimilla Doni* or Hasse's *Cleofide*, but the list of Verdi works includes neither *Otello* nor *Don Carlos*, both masterpieces with a number of available award-winning CD recordings. No doubt subsequent editions of this guide will correct these and other oversights. In the meantime, this is still a valuable resource for anyone looking for record ratings and critical assessments of selected musical works. [R: SLMQ, Summer 93, p. 264]—**Koraljka Lockhart**

1345. Gray, Anne. **The Popular Guide to Classical Music.** New York, Birch Lane Press/Carol Publishing Group, 1993. 353p. illus. index. $24.95. MT6.G74P6. 781.6'8. LC 92-21111. ISBN 1-55972-165-0.

This is a book that will be either loved or hated, depending on the reader. It is written as an attempt to get away from the dry handbook style and to present the subject matter with some flair. In this, it succeeds up to a point, but the author often gets carried away in chapter headings such as "They Carry a Little Stick" (conductors) or "Mystique Immortelle" (an afterword on music in general). In the appendix there is a short list of the world's most popular symphonies, which includes some of what one would expect, but also items such as Kalinnikov's Symphony No. 1, Rimsky-Korsakov's (*not* Koraskov ...) "Antar" Symphony, and the Goldmark "Rustic Wedding" Symphony, which may be personal favorites but are hardly tops in the world. Mahler is included with his Symphony No. 1 and just the adagietto movement from his Symphony No. 5. The brief composer sketches include the following amazing detail on Rachmaninoff: "escaped Communism by moving to Dresden in 1906." An extended chapter deals with women composers, conductors, and performers, which may be the volume's strongest point. The chapter with biographies of today's most active conductors is just as informative. On the other hand, when discussing contemporary composers, the author mentions Sofia Gubaidulina but omits Alfred Schnittke and Arvo Part altogether, making for a somewhat lopsided view of Eastern European composers active today.

To sum it up, this is a fascinating but often frustrating book. People with heightened sensitivities but not too much knowledge of music might find it of great value.—**Koraljka Lockhart**

1346. **International Who's Who in Music and Musicians' Directory (in the Classical and Light Classical Fields).** 13th ed. David M. Cummings, ed. Cambridge, England, International Biographical Centre; distr., Bristol, Pa., IPS/Taylor & Francis, 1992. 1357p. $165.00. ISBN 0-948875-11-9.

Although this title was first published in 1935, it was only with the 5th edition in 1969 that new editions began appearing every couple of years. The latest editions have become significantly more rigorous in their criteria for inclusion, unlike some of the earlier ones, in which the piano teacher down the road was more likely to be included than an internationally recognized concert pianist. All of the 8,000 persons covered are practitioners of Western art music, and 2,000 of these are new to this edition. Format of entries is typical of who's-who-type resources, with heavy emphasis on significant career dates. As in the previous editions, seven appendixes cover such areas as names and addresses of orchestras, major competitions, and musical organizations. These are largely superfluous, as similar lists are available in a variety of other publications, and one has to wonder what the purpose is of the U.S. portion of the libraries appendix, which is restricted entirely to public libraries. Regardless, this series remains an essential purchase for larger music collections.—**Robert Skinner**

1347. Koshgarian, Richard. **American Orchestral Music: A Performance Catalog.** Metuchen, N.J., Scarecrow, 1992. 762p. $72.50. ML128.O5K67. 016.784'0973. LC 92-35275. ISBN 0-8108-2632-1.

American Orchestral Music is an ambitious project that offers information on approximately 7,000 published and manuscript works by 900 U.S. composers born in the last 100 years. Orchestral music in this case is defined as works for orchestra, concertos, orchestral works with chorus, orchestral works with vocal solos, and works for chamber orchestra. Arranged alphabetically by composer, entries include the information necessary for programming the composition: title, date of composition, duration, instrumentation, and publisher (if the work is published). A variety of useful appendixes provide additional access by duration, vocal soloists, solo instruments, and type of chorus. Publishers' and composers' addresses are also supplied.

The stated purpose of this book is to assist conductors, orchestra managers, and others in selecting their repertoire by U.S. composers. This it accomplishes quite well. It will, however, also prove valuable for its listing of composers' published and unpublished orchestral output. [R: Choice, May 93, p. 1444; RQ, Summer 93, pp. 560-61]—**Allie Wise Goudy**

1348. Rabson, Carolyn. **Orchestral Excerpts: A Comprehensive Index.** Berkeley, Calif., Fallen Leaf Press, 1993. 221p. (Fallen Leaf Reference Books in Music, no.25). $35.00. ML128.O5R2. 016.7842. LC 92-46475. ISBN 0-914913-26-3.

Collections of orchestral excerpts are published for specific instruments and consist of the parts of works that the instrumentalist would want to practice. Usually the selections consist of difficult, tricky, and short solo passages of well-known works for orchestra. Players preparing for auditions and for performances in orchestras want these for practice because complete parts for their instruments are usually unavailable for loan or purchase. Students also want them as part of their studies. This index provides, by composer and work, a list of the collections, arranged by instrument, that contain the excerpts. Thus, a horn player looking under the entry for Mahler's Symphony No. 4 will find that five different publications of excerpts for horn contain passages from this specific work. The index has been thoughtfully and skillfully prepared. Because type and layout can make or break an index, it is pleasant to report that the presentation of the information in well-spaced double columns makes it effortless to use.

This work is specialized but of great value and importance to those in need of this information, which has not been available in this format. It will be useful to students and players and to those that serve them in libraries. [R: RBB, 15 Dec 93, p. 780]—**George Louis Mayer**

1349. Rangel-Ribeiro, Victor, and Robert Markel. **Chamber Music: An International Guide to Works and Their Instrumentation.** New York, Facts on File, 1993. 271p. index. $45.00. ML128.C4R3. 016.785'0026. LC 92-43442. ISBN 0-8160-2296-8.

This resource book is one of the best, most practical, and most up-to-date guides to the chamber music repertory yet to appear. Every effort has been made to create an easy-to-use list of about 8,000 citations of musical works for 3 to 20 performers in every possible combination. Those looking under composers will find what they have composed, and those looking for works for a specific combination of instruments will learn who composed works for the grouping.

The book is in three parts: composers up to the time of Haydn and Mozart, composers from Beethoven to the present, and a quick-reference index to indicate combinations for which each composer wrote. Under the composer entries in the main parts of the book, information about the year of composition (or publication), the key and duration of the work, and publishers is provided as well as the works and the instrumentation for each. Works for voice and instruments are also included; information about alternate scoring is provided; and the use of unusual instruments is singled out for special note. This information is provided in a grid format. The presentation could not be more concise and is easily understandable at a glance.

No such listing could be complete, but Rangel-Ribeiro and Markel have done an admirable job of including the important works of the past that are apt to be performed. They have also included broad coverage of recent composers of note.

Librarians and other professionals who work with musicians looking for repertory for small (and often unusual) combinations of instruments know how often such information is desired. This book will undoubtedly be the sourcebook of choice for many because of its ease of use and usefulness. [R: Choice, Oct 93, p. 272; LJ, 15 June 93, p. 64; RBB, 15 Sept 93, pp. 186-87; RQ, Winter 93, pp. 279-80]—**George Louis Mayer**

1350. Scott, William, comp. **A Conductor's Repertory of Chamber Music: Compositions for Nine to Fifteen Solo Instruments.** Westport, Conn., Greenwood Press, 1993. 164p. index. (Music Reference Collection, no.39). $49.95. ML128.C4S37. 016.785'00264. LC 93-18458. ISBN 0-313-28979-4.

Scott's compilation is a list of more than 1,000 compositions for 9 to 15 instruments. This list is an important source for training conductors when a full orchestra is not available. Scott's compilation may also serve to expand a conductor's repertoire. The title begins with a list of instrumental abbreviations, a list of music publishers, and a historical survey of conducting chamber music. The body of the work is an alphabetical list by composer. A classification of this list follows. Among the classifications are compositions for strings, woodwinds, brass, harp, keyboard, saxophone, and percussion. Following the body and classification is a helpful title index. Libraries with large music collections will find this title useful. Also, this work should support any curriculum that offers orchestral conducting. [R: Choice, Dec 93, p. 590]—**C. Michael Phillips**

Operatic

1351. Almquist, Sharon G., comp. **Opera Mediagraphy: Video Recordings and Motion Pictures.** Westport, Conn., Greenwood Press, 1993. 269p. index. (Music Reference Collection, no.40). $55.00. ML158.6.O6064. 016.7821'0267. LC 93-28491. ISBN 0-313-28490-3.

The compilation of such a mediagraphy is full of pitfalls. Does the compiler set limitations, and, if so, what are they? Almquist does not make her guidelines very clear, so entries exist for commercial products, for some items that could only be obtained with difficulty or through rental, and for a few titles available from small, specialized distributors. Qualifying standards aside, this compilation only represents a fraction of what has been filmed or videotaped and what the customer can find on the shelves of large video departments in large stores or can readily obtain by mail. Thus, the book is of limited usefulness to the opera buff who wants to purchase such material. The sad truth of this genre is that the best recent filmings and tapings have been done of artists who cannot begin to match some of the performances given by artists of a generation or two ago, despite the much more primitive picture quality, and distribution of some of the best documents is limited. Still, many major filmed and videotaped productions are omitted here.

The virtue of the book is the splendid coverage of the items it does include. Full credits of the filmed or videotaped product are given, including casts (citing actors when singers sing and actors take their place on the screen and when the singers lip-synch to prerecorded sound tracks—both practices that produce nearly unwatchable products), timings, color, sound (mono or stereo), and short bibliographies of articles and reviews. The one quibble is that while those involved in the filming are given credit, those responsible for directing the stage work that was filmed are sometimes not. Even if packaging omits this information, it can readily be found in other sources (e.g., see the entry for the Metropolitan's 1991 "Un Ballo in Maschera," where the opera director's name does not appear). The performer index reinforces the idea that, to many, opera is only about singers and conductors. Some people do want information about designers, directors, choreographers, dancers, and others, especially in an index that covers a visual team effort. This information is given in the entries, but not having it indexed robs this work of much of its potential usefulness.

A list of distributors is included. Those really interested in this subject are urged to use it to get the catalogs that really cover this field. A great book on this subject is badly needed; this one does not fill the gap.—**George Louis Mayer**

1352. Cowden, Robert H., ed. **Opera Companies of the World: Selected Profiles.** Westport, Conn., Greenwood Press, 1992. 336p. index. $75.00. ML12.063. 782.5'02'95. LC 91-24186. ISBN 0-313-26220-9.

Some 139 opera companies around the world are described in this comprehensive directory. Coverage is limited to professional companies with regular seasons, plus a few of the longer-running summer opera festivals. The entries, arranged alphabetically by country and city, include the name of the organization, a narrative account of both the history of the company and its current operations, a bibliography of important publications about the company (when they exist—not every entry includes a bibliography), mailing address, telephone and fax numbers, and principal administrator. Most entries also provide some background information on the operatic history of the city in which the company is located. All entries are either signed by the author or based on material furnished by the company; a list of contributors and their professional affiliations is provided. An appendix gives brief directory information (name, address, and telephone and fax numbers) and, in most cases, a few lines of descriptive text for an additional 28 smaller companies.

Robert Turnbull's *The Opera Gazetteer* (Rizzoli, 1988) is a similar work, although somewhat less comprehensive in coverage, (with 114 companies); its entries tend to be briefer but do include information on ticket prices and box office hours not found in *Opera Companies of the World*. The work under review is an authoritative, up-to-date, and genuinely international directory that provides a wealth of information on the world's opera houses.—**Paul B. Cors**

1353. DeVenney, David P., and Craig R. Johnson. **The Chorus in Opera: A Guide to the Repertory.** Metuchen, N.J., Scarecrow, 1993. 203p. index. $29.50. ML128.C48D47. 782.1. LC 92-33252. ISBN 0-8108-2620-8.

This guide is sure to be useful to many choral conductors wishing to program a different repertoire. Its organization is straightforward, and the authors sum up a lot of information in a short space. Operas are surveyed in alphabetical order by composer, and each entry cites the location of the chorus within the work, its vocal requirements, its length, and a judgment of its relative difficulty, plus a short summary of its dramatic context. The catalog is followed by several indexes organized by opera titles, first lines and titles of scenes, names of librettists, choral performing forces, difficulty levels, and duration of the excerpts.

Unfortunately, this guide is not without its problems. Of necessity selective, it takes as its basis the excellent *Definitive Kobbe's Complete Opera Book* (see ARBA 89, entry 1226), a British publication that tends, as might be expected, to be oriented toward the tastes and repertoires of European opera houses. Hence, while we find information in the present guide on choruses by Julius Benedict, Rutland Boughton, and Vincent Wallace, we are given no information on choruses in the works of such prominent U.S. opera composers as Douglas Stuart Moore, Carlisle Floyd, Philip Glass, or even Scotland-born U.S. resident Thea Musgrave. Moreover, although there are many excellent choruses in the works of composers who are included (e.g., Francois-Adrien Boieldieu), the guide contains information on a very small percentage of them. Another limitation that seems quite arbitrarily defined is that of what is and is not an opera. According to DeVenney and Johnson, Claudio Monteverdi's *Arianna* and Francis Poulenc's *La Voix Humaine* are not operas, even though their composers would have disagreed. The fact that there are no choruses in these examples does not justify the mistaken categorization. On the other hand, the guide lists several choruses from Louis Hector Berlioz's *La Damnation de Faust*, which is definitely not an opera, nor did its composer intend it to be.

DeVenney and Johnson also trip on their own inconsistencies regarding languages and versions of the operas. Choruses from the unmistakably French works of Giacomo Meyerbeer are cited in Italian, as are those from Gaspare Spontini's *La Vestale* and Verdi's *Les Vepres Siciliennes*, both French operas. On the other hand, choruses from Christoph Willibald von Gluck's originally Italian opera *Alceste* appear with French titles from the 1776 version (libretto by du Roullet), while the title, date, and librettist listed in the main heading refer to the 1762 (Italian) version. Nor are these the only problems the authors have with languages. Misprints occur in opera titles (e.g., *The Saint of Blee[c]ker Street*), composers' names, and titles of the choruses (e.g., "O figlie a mabili di Don Magnifico"). In fact, at times neither the location of the chorus nor its context are represented accurately. The chorus "De Carthage les Cieux" (with the last word misspelled) begins Act III, not Act I, of Berlioz's *Les Troyens*, where it celebrates not the end of a period of captivity but the culmination of a period of prosperity. And one does wonder how a "blind woman" in the crowd of *Le Prophete's* fourth act would have any way of identifying the Prophet (or anyone else) as her son. In short, although this guide is helpful and the effort will surely be appreciated, it should not be used without reference to more reliable information from such sources as *The New Grove Dictionary of Opera* (Stockton Press/Grove's Dictionaries of Music, 1992) or the scores themselves.

—**Karin Pendle**

1354. Henrysson, Harald. **A Jussi Bjorling Phonography.** 2d ed. Stockholm, Svenskt Musikhistoriskt Arkiv; distr., Portland, Oreg., Amadeus Press/Timber Press, 1993. 382p. index. illus. index. $32.95pa. ISBN 91-85172-10-3.

Originally published in 1982 under the joint authorship of Jack Porter and Henrysson, this discography (or phonography, as Henrysson prefers to call it) is a first-rate piece of work that far surpasses the first edition in content, usefulness, and even physical appearance. Containing nearly 200 additional pages, this edition devotes nearly 40 of them to an extensive chronological table of Jussi Bjorling's (hereafter, JB) life and career, which merges information on his studies, performances, and other major events in his life with dates, locations, and materials recorded in studio sessions. Henrysson corrects a few errors from the first edition (e.g., JB's first solo recordings were made on September 4, not on September 18, 1929) and demonstrates the care and clarity that characterize the rest of his catalog. Indeed, even persons with no particular interest in JB's recordings will find this chronology of his life invaluable. Henrysson's list of JB's opera, operetta, and oratorio roles is similarly detailed, including the total number of times JB sang each role and the locations of the performances.

The main catalogs of recordings are introduced by a prose summary of JB's surprisingly extensive career as a recording artist (dead at the age of 49, JB made his first recordings when he was 9). The volume's central catalogs cover studio recordings, recordings resulting from live or broadcast performances, and even "performances rumored but not proved to be preserved." All are arranged chronologically and provided with information on the original issue and subsequent reissues of each item. These listings are cross-referenced and indexed in as many ways as one could desire: by record label, format (e.g., tape, LP, DC), composer, title, and collaborating artists (e.g., conductors, accompanists, other singers). Because many of JB's recordings were released under more than one label, Henrysson does librarians and record collectors a great service by indicating which recordings, despite their contradictory appearances, preserve the same performance. All in all, this discography deserves high praise and can serve as a model for future scholars.—**Karin Pendle**

1355. Larue, C. Steven, ed. **International Dictionary of Opera.** Detroit, St. James Press/Gale, 1993. 2v. illus. index. $250.00/set. ML102.O6I6. 782.1'03. LC 92-44271. ISBN 1-55862-081-8.

Part of the introduction to this splendid two-volume dictionary sums it up best: "[It] provides students, teachers, researchers, and opera enthusiasts with a comprehensive source of biographical, bibliographical, and musicological information on people and works important to the history and development of opera." Some entries usually found in dictionaries of this kind are not included here (e.g., items on individual cities, opera houses, and companies), but the ones selected have been presented in a wonderful new way. Performing artists past and present all start with a brief biographical sketch, followed by signed essays on their artistry, strong points, and even weak points—the latter often presented with total (and hard-to-find) honesty and objectivity. Composer entries are followed by a thorough list of compositions, with librettist and premiere information attached.

An opera lover will find this dictionary extremely hard to lay aside, because it brims with intelligent, readable, and fair assessments in every category it covers. The publication is backed by an impressive advisory board, and the 200 contributors/writers come from academia, music writing, newspapers, and magazines. Printed on heavy coated stock, the reproductions are of a quality rarely found nowadays. In addition, most of the selected illustrations are striking, often rare and unusual, although contemporary productions shots seems to lean heavily on the British side (e.g., Covent Garden, Glyndebourne), which is somewhat understandable in view of the British provenance of the dictionary. This reviewer, an editor with a peculiar knack for spotting typographical errors, has not been able to find a single such mistake in several extended periods of browsing through this excellent set of volumes. If one cannot afford *The New*

Grove Dictionary of Opera (Stockton Press/Grove's Dictionaries of Music, 1992) (and even if one can) and wants a bit more than *The Oxford Dictionary of Opera* (Oxford University Press, 1992) can provide, this publication will provide the perfect answer. Highest possible recommendation. [R: Choice, Oct 93, p. 267; LJ, 1 May 93, pp. 82-83; RBB, Aug 93, p. 2092; RQ, Winter 93, pp. 288-89]—**Koraljka Lockhart**

1356. **The New Grove Dictionary of Opera.** Stanley Sadie, ed. New York, Grove's Dictionaries of Music, 1992. 4v. illus. $850.00/set. ML102.O6N5. 782.1'03. LC 92-36276. ISBN 0-935859-92-6.

In the preface, the editor is firm in making the point that this work bears very little relationship to the coverage of opera that appeared in *The New Grove Dictionary of Music and Musicians* (see ARBA 81, entry 1016), which is now more than a decade old. He claims that close to 90 percent of this set is new or newly written by the best available author for each entry. The scope is vast, covering singers, conductors, directors, authors, and composers and a huge number of subjects, such as translation, libretti, recordings, opera glasses, and supertitles. Performers and composers receive coverage of their operatic activities, not their careers as a whole. Operas have entries with some historical information and excellent plot summaries that vary in length and detail according to importance. Non-Western musical stage works with a different kind of history and performing tradition are excluded.

A book with approximately 1,300 authors cannot be expected to have one standard, one viewpoint, or one level of quality. No editor, not even the skillful Sadie, could achieve that, but a high quality and a prevailing consistency are almost always in evidence. The long articles on composers and subjects always command respect. Certainly, most of the big names of the distant and recent past are here, and the entries are usually written by well-known specialists. General assessment, usually right on target, is given along with the career facts. The shorter entries on singers and others raise, as always in a book of this kind, the question of why some are included and others excluded. Recently established singers, such as Cecilia Bartoli, Ben Heppner, and Thomas Hampson, are included, but Renee Fleming and Sharon Sweet, perhaps too new, are not. Usually, it is possible to justify choices to one's own satisfaction, but some seem downright capricious. Why, among prominent American-based opera directors, did Tito Capobianco get in and Frank Corsaro stay out? And why, of the two Russian baritones now having great international careers, is Sergey Leiferkus in and Vladimir Chernov out? Among writers and editors some major American figures, such as Irving Kolodin and Robert Jacobson, would seem to qualify for inclusion as others of less importance are to be found in these pages. Some decisions for entries of cities and places also seem arbitrary. The major Wagner festival of the 1920s and 1930s in Zoppot (then Germany, now Poland) gets a brief entry with no bibliography, whereas Santa Cruz, Wilmington, and many other cities with limited operatic histories get good coverage. Why some entries are unsigned (e.g., those on Teresa Stratas, Charles Kullman, and Marcella Sembrich) is a mystery.

Errors are inevitable (but few in number). For example, Mirella Freni never sang Suzel at the Metropolitan. Marie Powers, who made a specialty of the role of Madame Flora in Menotti's *The Medium*, is credited as having sung the New York premiere, but she did not; she sang the revised version on Broadway a year after it was first produced. Yet Claramae Turner is correctly given credit for creating the role in her entry. (Both articles are written by the same author.) The entry for the conductor Maurice Abravanel states that "he conducted Weill's *Knickerbocker Holiday* (1938) with Marian Anderson as soloist." It appears that a line or two of type disappeared to combine two events into this fictitious one.

The one real weakness of the work is in the inconsistencies and omissions in the bibliographies for the performer entries. Some, such as the one for Kathleen Ferrier, are models that list all important and up-to-date book sources; some have poor lists; some have none; and some omit major books while listing sources of lesser importance. For example, autobiographies of Rita Hunter and Rosa Ponselle and a major biography of Grace Moore are not listed. This is the only element of this work that exhibits no sense of quality control. Major subject entries, on the other hand, have superb bibliographies.

The illustrations deserve special praise. Although not too well reproduced, the choices are excellent; unfamiliar prints, paintings, engravings, and photographs abound. Appendixes cover role names, first-line and title entries for arias and ensembles, a list of contributors, and illustration acknowledgments.

This is a major reference work with a serious and scholarly approach to a subject often considered frivolous and treated accordingly. It can generally be consulted with confidence and read with pleasure. [R: Choice, July/Aug 93, pp. 1752-53; LJ, 15 Feb 93, pp. 160-62; LJ, 15 April 93, pp. 61-62; RBB,1 April 93, p. 1452]—**George Louis Mayer**

1357. **The Oxford Dictionary of Opera.** By John Warrack and Ewan West. New York, Oxford University Press, 1992. 782p. $40.00. ML102.O6W37. 782.1'03. LC 92-6730. ISBN 0-19-869164-5.

For years, opera enthusiasts and professionals have used the Rosenthal-Warrack *Concise Oxford Dictionary of Opera* (Oxford University Press, 1986) as a kind of an opera Bible. The present volume is an outgrowth of the same, but it is considerably expanded, containing 4,500 entries, which include 750 composer sketches; 600 opera entries with all relevant cast, premiere, synopsis, and performance details; 900 singer biographies; and more. The opera synopses are no longer thumbnail summations of the plot; for example, *La Forza del Destino* was previously told in 49 words, and now it takes up 250. (The reader who finds value in short opera plots should keep the old volume by the side of the new one.) Being a British publication, the book includes some spelling peculiarities common to Great Britain (e.g., "Rakhmaninov," "Shalyapin"). The dictionary is extremely detailed in its listings of operas based on works by famous writers; its Shakespeare section alone covers an exhaustive array of works written between 1692 and 1991.

A few mistakes have crept in. Hans Hotter is listed as retired, although he continues to perform, and vital statistics for Tiana Lemnitz say (*b.* Metz, 26 Oct. 1897; *d?*) although the legendary singer celebrated her 95th birthday with great fanfare in 1992. In preparing the new edition, Warrack and West discarded a number of entries that pertained to relatively obscure singers of yesteryear (e.g., Claire Dux, Leopold Sachse, Albert Saleza), a somewhat questionable decision in a reference book of this kind. Among the singers of the younger generation, one can find Cecilia Bartoli but not Dolora Zajick, Cecilia Gasdia, Sharon Sweet, or Neil Shicoff, all artists of considerable international repute. Still, this dictionary is going to prove of immense value to anyone who deals with opera. [R: RBB, 15 Feb 93, pp. 1082-84; SLJ, May 93, pp. 139-40]—**Koraljka Lockhart**

1358. Stroff, Stephen M. **Opera: An Informal Guide.** Chicago, A Cappella Books; distr., Chicago, Independent Publishers Group, 1992. 205p. index. $11.95pa. ML1700.S94. 782.1. LC 92-33208. ISBN 1-55652-170-7.

This is a small paperback that makes no pretension of being a seminal work on the topic, and Stroff readily admits that discussions on opera can be highly subjective. Keeping these points in mind, a newcomer to opera can profit from this book. Stroff takes operatic history, from Monteverdi and Purcell to the present, and divides it into eight eras, generally an era per chapter. Representative operas from each era (totaling 50) are listed. Within each operatic entry there is a synopsis, often providing background information. In addition, a paragraph titled "Keynotes" covers musical highlights, including noteworthy arias. Stroff concludes the entry with a recommended recording of the opera and follow-up choices of other operas by the same composer.

The book requires relatively close attention to discern that Stroff does know his topic (he has credentials as a music journalist and editor). In his writing he displays an appreciation of Bel Canto singing with its elegant legato lines. Also, it is gratifying to note that Stroff does not take the attitude that the most recent performance, recording, or artist is necessarily the best. A good many of the recommendations are recordings from the 1940s through the 1960s that have been reissued on CD. He also discusses videos of famous singers of the past. One chapter, although rather oddly placed in the book, is devoted to singers who were born in the second half of the nineteenth century and who sang and recorded before World War II. Here the reader is offered recommendations of recordings of these who were part of the golden age of singing.

For musical purists, more comprehensive works are available. This book is recommended to anyone who wishes to be wittily, knowledgeably, and gently introduced to opera.—**Phillip P. Powell**

Popular

General Works

1359. **The Billboard Book of American Singing Groups: A History, 1940-1990.** By Jay Warner. New York, Billboard Books/Watson-Guptill, 1992. 542p. illus. $21.95pa. ML106.U3W2. 782.42164'0973. LC 92-18328. ISBN 0-8230-8264-4.

Warner defines the vocal group as "three or more vocalists singing in harmony" or a musical group in which vocals are the most prominent feature. His book strives to offer a general foundation on the key players of this style and presents the information in an easy-to-read, entertaining fashion. The very obscure or different groups generally do not appear here (although one or two do crop up)—this is really a book about the big guns of American vocal music. Considerable attention is given to groups of the 1940s and 1950s, with only a brief nod to groups of the 1970s and 1980s. The somewhat uneven coverage does not detract too much from the book; as one of the only references devoted entirely to modern American popular vocal music, *American Singing Groups* fills a gap in the subject literature with a lot of good information. It is divided into 10-year sections, from the 1940s to the 1990s. Each section begins with a historical overview of the decade that mentions major events, trends, and stars who affected the sound of that period. Within each section, notable acts are listed alphabetically and thumb-indexed for easy access. Short biographies, liberally sprinkled with anecdotes and interesting facts, accompany every entry, and detailed discographies are provided in many cases. Numerous references are made throughout the book to various Billboard charts, giving helpful indications of a group or song's popularity. The few photographs included show the looks of the times.

This work does not attempt to be comprehensive, but it does fulfill its goal as an entertaining and trivia-packed guide to the history of vocal music in America. It is a useful addition to any popular-music reference collection.—**Daphne Fallieros Potter**

1360. **The Billboard Book of Number One Hits.** 3d ed. By Fred Bronson. New York, Billboard Books/Watson-Guptill, 1992. 822p. illus. index. $21.95pa. ML156.4.P6B76. 016.78164'0973'0266. LC 92-20318. ISBN 0-8230-8298-9.

This book provides the stories behind the songs for all the number one pop and rock hits on the *Billboard* charts, starting with July 9, 1955 (Bill Haley's "Rock around the Clock"), and ranging all the way to Vanessa Williams's performance of "Save the Best for Last" (number one on March 21, 1992). The major change in this edition since the previous one (see ARBA 90, entry 1292) is the addition of 106 songs that reached number one since June 18, 1988 (the ending date of the 2d edition). The various lists in the back of the book (e.g., most number one songs by writer) have also been updated. New to this edition are lists of most weeks at number one by artist (Elvis Presley, 79) and by song ("Don't Be Cruel/Hound Dog," 11), and lists of the biggest jumps to number one (the Beatles' "Can't Buy Me Love," from 27 to 1) and falls from that position (Billy Preston's "Nothing from Nothing," from 1 to 15). Bronson's introduction is a bit longer but is essentially unchanged. A few of the older entries have been updated, such as that for "Runaway" and its performer, Del Shannon, who committed suicide in 1990.

Although the price has risen by about a third, the amount of new information in the 3d edition justifies the increase (and the book is still inexpensive). All but the most budget-strapped owners will want to update their editions. For those who own none of the editions, it is one of the best books on rock and pop music available, with excellently written entries and a considerable amount of information on the most popular songs and performers of the last 40 years.—**D. A. Rothschild**

1361. Downey, Pat. **The Golden Age of Top 40 Music (1955-1973) on Compact Disc.** Boulder, Colo., Pat Downey, 1992. 453p. $39.95pa. LC 92-90455. ISBN 0-9633718-1-9.

This work contains the Top 40 singles from 1955-1973 and identifies those compact discs that include these singles. It is divided into two sections: artists and song titles. Alphabetically arranged by artist, the first section lists singles under each artist chronologically. Each entry consists of the year of peak popularity; highest position on the Cash Box charts; a designator of monophonic, stereophonic, or electronic recording; actual song length; recording label; title of CD; and pertinent comments by Downey. The song title section is alphabetical by title and includes the artist name, year of peak popularity, highest position on the charts, and a symbol denoting availability on CD. Also in this section, identical songs by different artists are shaded together. In general, access to information is easy.

A work similar in content is Bill Shapiro's *Rock & Roll Review* (Andrews & McMeel, 1991). Although Shapiro's book is less expensive, it should not supplant Downey's in the library collection. Whereas Shapiro's book covers 1955-1990, it only contains entries from approximately 220 different artists. Downey's work, on the other hand, while covering only 18 years, surveys more than 1,000 artists, and the listings under each artist are more complete. Additionally, the system that Downey has devised to rank the quality of each CD is more objective than the system used by Shapiro.

This work would be appropriate for both academic and public libraries. Downey has provided an especially helpful guide for anyone trying to replace an LP collection with a higher-quality CD collection and for baby boomers searching for music from their generation.—**Lori L. Oling**

1362. Gambacinni, Paul, Jonathan Rice, and Tim Rice. **British Hit Albums.** 5th ed. Enfield, England, Guinness Publishing; distr., New York, Billboard Books/Watson-Guptill, 1992. 416p. illus. $21.95pa. ISBN 0-8230-7851-5.

Gathering its information primarily from the Record and Tape Retailer charts, this work lists the top-selling albums in Great Britain from 1958 to 1991. As is pointed out in the introduction, this work covers hits albums on the British charts—although American artists appear in the work, it does not reflect the American charts in any way.

The book consists mainly of two sections: "The Artists" and "Facts and Feats." In "The Artists," artists (both individuals and groups) appear alphabetically, with albums listed chronologically under each entry. Also contained in each entry are the date the album first appeared on the chart, title, label and catalog number, highest position ever attained on the chart, and total weeks on the chart. In typical Guinness style, the "Facts and Feats" section compiles the data in a multitude of ways, displaying facts such as who had the most number-one albums in a calendar year or who had the most albums on the chart at one time. Besides these two major sections, there is also a short year-by-year overview that highlights important events in the music industry, such as debuts or deaths of influential musicians and the technological innovations made in that year.

The work would be more useful to reference librarians if it contained a table of contents. Also, the explanations for the lists in the "Facts and Feats" section often take some studying and comparison with other lists to determine exactly what information is being presented. This work is not recommended for the ready-reference collection, but it does contain a plethora of information that would be useful to anyone interested in the modern British music scene.—**Lori L. Oling**

1363. **The Guinness Encyclopedia of Popular Music.** Colin Larkin, ed. Chester, Conn., New England Publishing, 1992. 4v. index. $295.00/set. ISBN 1-882267-00-1.

More than 80 contributors and consultants have assisted in this massive and amiable compilation. Larkin has written an excellent introduction that discusses in some depth what is meant, or can be meant, by the not-very-definite term *popular music*. He clearly points out that popular music has shaped and been shaped by the many changes in civilization throughout this century. Noteworthy is the section that begins, "And then came rock 'n' roll."

Entries are largely biographical discussions of popular artists, their styles, and their works. A musical artist may be a composer, a performer, a bandleader, or a combination of the three. Groups (e.g., Alabama) are also listed. Bands of the big band era, including the "sweet music" bands, swing and some hotel orchestras, their leaders, some members, and arrangers are usually listed under the leader's name. Some examples include Cab Calloway, the Dorsey brothers, Duke Ellington, Johnny Mercer, and Glenn Miller. There are also entries for musical terminology, music publishing houses, and recording companies. Other categories receive an entry in their own right. For example, certain musical shows that affected popular music are listed by title. Such an entry includes author, composer, major songs, and a brief history of the major productions and film versions. Some examples are *Brigadoon, Call Me Madam*, and *Hair*.

Entries cover nearly everything included in popular music, but, as one would expect with the media dominance of Western civilization, the emphasis is on the music of Great Britain, the United States, and Canada. However, Central and South American and African pop artists and styles are represented, including Jamaican reggae. Larkin acknowledges that considerable weight has been given to contemporary, living, and still-developing artists.

Major artists have been given more space than newer ones. However, the length of an entry is not indicative of the item's relative importance. To some extent, chart positions, record labels, and record sales are given. Gold, silver, and platinum discs are usually listed. A limited discography follows each entry. The discographies are purposefully incomplete, as the aim is to allow the reader to further investigate the work of a particular artist.

An extensive bibliography is alphabetical by artist and genre. As an aid in locating nonspecific titles, Larkin has added categories, such as country and jazz and pop. Additionally, highly recommended books are listed at the end of particular entries in the main text, rather than in the bibliography. The index is alphabetical and appears to be thorough and accurate, with main entries listed in boldface type. Others whose names appear in the text are also included.

The contributors seemed to have enjoyed writing their entries and are quite willing to share this pleasure with readers. Several quotations will illustrate this. About Brenda Lee it is said, "Even in early adolescence, she had an adult husk of a voice that could slip from anguished intimacy through sleepy insinuation to raucous lust even during 'Let's Jump the Broomstick'... and other jaunty classics." Ted Lewis's "best-known routine was to the song 'Me and My Shadow,' while his singing of the phrase, 'Is everybody happy?', was used whenever appropriate—and frequently when it was not. For all his schmaltzy performing style, over the years Lewis was admired by almost as many jazz musicians as criticized him." This mammoth study of popular music of the past 100 years is an essential work. [R: Choice, Mar 93, p. 1112; LJ, Jan 93, p. 98; LJ, 15 April 93, pp. 60-61; RBB, 15 Feb 93, pp. 1080-82; SLJ, Feb 93, pp. 122-23; WLB, Jan 93, p. 108]—**Louis G. Zelenka**

1364. **Joel Whitburn Presents Daily #1 Hits 1940-1992.** Menomonee Falls, Wis., Record Research, 1993. 379p. index. $30.00 spiralbound. ISBN 0-89820-095-4.

This list of number one hits has been compiled from more than 50 years of Billboard's top pop singles charts. The first edition, from the same publisher, appeared in 1989, and this is the first follow-up edition. Be sure to read the one-page introduction carefully, as it clarifies a few simple rules followed in the listings.

Arrangement is chronological, similar to the familiar planning calendar—one page for each day of the year—and each page is arranged in descending order by year. Entries are from January 1, 1940, through May 1, 1993. An entire song entry consists of the year, the number of days in the number one position, and the title and artist for the hit single. An alphabetical title section at the back of the book serves as a quick index.

This handy spiralbound work is a must for school libraries and media centers from middle school on up. College libraries will want to add it to their collection for quick research answers. Retrospective radio station programmers certainly will want it, and public librarians will need a copy handy for those seeking answers to trivia questions.—**Louis G. Zelenka**

1365. Kiner, Larry F., and Philip R. Evans. **Al Jolson: A Bio-Discography.** Metuchen, N.J., Scarecrow, 1992. 808p. illus. index. $79.50. ML156.7.J64K4. 016.78242164'092. LC 92-40029. ISBN 0-8108-2633-X.

Remember the story of the little girl who said that a book told her rather more about penguins than she really wanted to know? So it is with this weighty tome about one (not very nice) entertainer of a bygone era. But surprisingly, after all these years, there are three Al Jolson societies still in existence, two in the United States and one in England, attesting to the enduring popularity of this controversial star of the first talkie. Ironically, given today's climate of political correctness, many of Jolson's performances (in blackface and sporting an exaggerated cornpone/molasses accent) would be banned, panned, or picketed if he were to appear onstage today.

This bio-discography is a lot more discography than biography, but it is an impressive feat of gathering recorded information about its subject. The work begins with a curious biographical sketch, which is in no way biography as it fails to offer even the performer's place and date of birth, and it seems to prefer to bring him into existence with his first known performance, in 1907. He was then listed in *Billboard* as "Al Jolson, Blackfaced comedian with the operatic voice. Never idle." (He must have done something right, because his subsequent performing career spanned 43 years.) There follows a chronological arrangement by specific date, consisting of recording sessions, movie dates, and vaudeville appearances, running all the way to April 1950, when he cut his last record. As for Jolson the man, it seems people either loved him or hated him. Considerable insight into the less-agreeable aspects of Jolson's personality comes through, as we learn that he would belch audibly during the singing of songs he did not like, so that record producers would be unable to use the cuts.

Evans and Kiner's large book supplies an exhaustive musicography and filmography for Jolson's prolific career, with a number of thematic indexes. It is thus possible to find out exactly how many times, precisely when, and with whom Jolson recorded songs such as "Mammy" or "Rockabye Your Baby with a Dixie Melody." Most libraries will not need so vast a compendium of facts about one performer. For libraries collecting entertainment memorabilia, however, this book provides a great deal of painstakingly gathered information, presented with attention to small details.—**Bruce A. Shuman**

1366. Paymer, Marvin E., ed. **Facts behind the Songs: A Handbook of American Popular Music from the Nineties to the '90s.** Hamden, Conn., Garland, 1993. 564p. illus. index. (Garland Reference Library of the Humanities, v.1300). $95.00. ML102.P66F2. 781.64'0973. LC 93-24342. ISBN 0-8240-5240-4.

It would not be an exaggeration to say that this book may have a thousand uses for a million readers. From the tunes that our great-grandparents sang around the piano in the 1890s to the hits of the 1990s, Paymer has produced a delightful and useful compilation. Some, such as "A Bicycle Built for Two" (1892), are still being sung.

The work is divided into two parts: the articles, which contain summaries of song histories about a given subject or key word, and the catalog of songs, which is an alphabetical list of the 4,400 songs mentioned in the articles. If a song is searched by the title entry, the user is provided with the date of the earliest copyright or publication of that song, the names of the composer and lyricist, and a cross-reference to the article containing more information about the song. For example, under "Anatomy" can be found songs about the parts of the body. Then, if one looks under, say, "Heart Songs," more than 30 titles can be found that mention the heart in the title, such as "My Heart Belongs to Daddy" (1938).

The articles include definitions of terms, such as scat singing, and also some information about recording companies and music publishers. A limited number of illustrations of sheet music covers, composers, and performers aid in the user's overall understanding of popular song over the past century. This reference source is a must for all public and academic libraries.—**Louis G. Zelenka**

1367. **The Rolling Stone Album Guide.** Anthony DeCurtis and James Henke with Holly George-Warren, eds. New York, Random House, 1992. 835p. $20.00pa. ML156.4.P6R62. 781.66'026'6. LC 92-50156. ISBN 0-679-73729-4.

One of the most well known of the guides to popular music, this book is now in its 3d edition. According to the cover, it deals with rock, pop, rap, jazz, blues, country, soul, folk, and gospel; however, some comedy recordings and world beat groups (e.g., 3 Mustaphas 3) are also reviewed. With such a wide range, none of the categories are comprehensive. Thus, treatments are limited to the best-known or recently popular groups; however, there are unexpected inclusions, such as the Chipmunks and the short-lived Bonzo Dog Band. Previous volumes cover some groups that are no longer listed, so they have not necessarily been superseded by this book.

The reviews have been produced by four individuals, but there is not much variation in either style or preferences. Performers are listed alphabetically and provided with a capsule history and a discography in which each available album is rated (from one-half to five stars). Opinions tend to agree with the majority; thus, those hoping, for example, for a description of Bruce Springsteen as "overrated" will not find it here. Some cross-references from individuals to their related groups (e.g., from Bob Dylan to The Traveling Wilburys) would have been helpful. The section on music collections is quite short, although it does seem to contain the most important ones.

The trouble with books such as this is that the opinions are subjective, and groups or albums that one likes may come in for an undeserved (and unfair) roasting. Ultimately, finding music one likes depends on what one hears, not what one reads. Also, this book has a "hipper-than-thou" attitude that may annoy more people than it enlightens. Still, as far as any book of this nature can be authoritative, this one is, and it will certainly be popular. [R: BR, Mar/April 93, p. 34; Choice, July/Aug 93, p. 1743; VOYA, April 93, p. 66]—**D. A. Rothschild**

1368. Sayers, Scott P., Jr., and Ed O'Brien. **Sinatra: The Man and His Music: The Recording Artistry of Francis Albert Sinatra—1939-1992.** Austin, Tex., TSD Press, 1992. 303p. illus. $39.95; $24.95pa. ISBN 0-934367-24-8.

This well-prepared and comprehensive Sinatra discography covers his recordings from 1939 to 1992. The recordings are divided into four major categories: the early years, the Columbia years, the Capitol years, and the Reprise years. The latter three are under the labels mentioned, while the early years are an assortment of labels, including Victor, RCA, and Brunswick. Orchestras and arrangers are documented. This is followed by "Sinatra: From A to Z," which lists all issued and unissued recordings with the recording date and by label.

Notable new research for this discography includes listings of more than 100 studio film recordings. Most were made for a specific film and are not otherwise commercially available. By consulting studio archives and session sheets, the authors have provided the running times, arranger, and number of takes. Their research also supplies information on recordings conducted by Sinatra, his V-Discs (United States Government Overseas Victory Disc Program recordings from 1943 to 1949), CDs, and Grammy nominations and awards. Billboard chart ratings for singles and LPs from 1940 through 1991 require only eight pages of text to list but provide the general popular music historian with an excellent overview of the Sinatra era.

A liberal sprinkling of photographs adds to the work's appeal and even encourages browsing. Most of these have captions, although several interesting photographs provide no identification of persons alongside Sinatra—the only disappointment of the work. As a quick-reference discography, this Sinatra study is highly recommended.—**Louis G. Zelenka**

Jazz and Blues

1369. Bregman, Robert, Leonard Bukowski, and Norman Saks. **The Charlie Parker Discography.** Redwood, N.Y., Cadence Jazz Books; distr., Redwood, N.Y., North Country Distributors, 1993. 88p. index. $14.00pa. ISBN 1-881993-25-6.

Charlie "Bird" Parker, one of the foremost exponents of the alto saxophone, composer of hundreds of songs, and still a model after which many aspiring young musicians pattern themselves, gave the musical world a unique sound and phrasing that many knowledgeable jazz musicians swear have not been equaled, before or since. This work lists all of "Bird's" known surviving musical recordings in an extensive discography, ranging from 1940 to 1954 and numbering 219 sessions. There is no biographical information about the subject anywhere between its covers; the focus is purely on Parker's recordings. On the plus side, Bregman, Bukowski, and Saks have endeavored to be as accurate as possible in the listing of dates, locations, personnel sitting in on the session, and tunes. Verification, while difficult in some cases, was provided by contemporaries of Parker, who either played with him or were present at the recording sessions, and who thus can authenticate information (as best as their memories serve).

The acknowledgments in the front of the book include such heavy hitters as Leonard Feather, Dizzy Gillespie, and Max Roach. Special attention is given to chronological order, so that the serious student of Parker's music can follow his career from its formative years to its abrupt, tragic end. In his stellar, too-short, career, Parker played solo; with various combos; with big bands and performing stars of the era (e.g., Gillespie, Sarah Vaughan, Miles Davis, Stan Kenton); with strings; as leader of his own quartet, quintet, all-stars, and orchestra; and in countless (but here meticulously counted) jam sessions. The back of the book provides two good indexes of artists and tunes, and there is also a loose-leaf page *updating* those indexes, showing, if nothing else, a strong desire to be thorough and up-to-date.

For fans of "Bird," or jazz in general, this slender volume will provide much valuable information about what Parker played, with whom, where, and when. One cannot help wishing, however, for some reference information within the dated entries, telling, for instance, who wrote the songs, anything distinctive about the session, and other circumstances of the gig. Still, for its limited audience, it is solid!—**Bruce A. Shuman**

1370. Herzhaft, Gerard. **Encyclopedia of the Blues.** Fayetteville, Ark., University of Arkansas Press, 1992. 513p. illus. index. $32.00; $16.95pa. ML102.B6H4313. 781.643'03. LC 92-7386. ISBN 1-55728-252-8; 1-55728-253-6pa.

Just about everybody can name a few blues musicians, present or past (do the names Ray Charles and B. B. King ring a bell?), but there is so much fusion and crossover in American musical forms that it is possible to locate blues musicians equally in rock, gospel, popular, or other genres. This title, originally a French-language work known as *Nouvelle Encyclopedie du Blues* and recently translated into English, contains a single alphabetical arrangement of people, places, and instruments, all connected with the blues, a uniquely American musical form that grew out of the appalling conditions of life among rural African-Americans in the early decades of this century. There is virtually no front matter, just a rudimentary preface in which Herzhaft (an obvious aficionado) thanks and acknowledges those who furnished assistance to his project. He then launches into his alphabet, without so much as a definition of the musical form he is discussing (but maybe that is just as well, as nobody has ever defined the blues to everyone else's satisfaction).

Among the performer entries are discussions of common blues instruments (e.g., harmonica [aka "blues harp"]), guitar, and piano, and geographical locations noted for having spawned a type of blues or a number of exponents (e.g., Louisiana, Mississippi, Memphis, St. Louis, Chicago). An interesting entry for "White blues" launches into a serious debate (without conclusion) over whether Caucasians deserve to be considered blues singers or merely imitators. The uninitiated will be struck by some of the nicknames blues musicians have chosen for themselves (e.g., Gatemouth, Cripple, Scrapper, Howlin' Wolf, Homesick, Leadbelly, Smokey Hogg). Then there are repetitive descriptive or evocative nicknames (e.g., lots of people named Little, Big, Sonny, Slim, or Blind).

The work is sprinkled with half-page, black-and-white photographs and concludes with some valuable reference material, including a bibliography, a selected discography, an index by instrument, and a general index. Music collections will probably want this title, but one cannot help wishing that some general discussion of the "birth of the blues" had been provided. [R: Choice, May 93, p. 1442; RBB, 1 Jan 93, p. 825]—**Bruce A. Shuman**

1371. Hilbert, Robert, with David Niven. **Pee Wee Speaks: A Discography of Pee Wee Russell.** Metuchen, N.J., Scarecrow, 1992. 377p. illus. index. (Studies in Jazz, no.13). $45.00. ML156.7.R88H5. 788.7'165'092. LC 92-37522. ISBN 0-8108-2634-8.

Clarinetist Charles Ellsworth "Pee Wee" Russell (1906-1969) was a true jazz original. From his earliest affiliations with legendary pioneers such as Jack Teagarden and Bix Beiderbecke, through his long association with various Dixieland and mainstream groups, to the final years that included collaborations with such modernists as Jimmy Giuffre and Thelonious Monk, Russell was revered (and at times vilified) for a unique approach to his instrument that rendered his work instantly identifiable. Never pretty in the conventional sense, his tone was nonetheless starkly expressive. And although less than that of an orthodox virtuoso, his technical facility was still sufficient to support a quirky, angular rhythmic/melodic style that never failed to fascinate.

Russell's recording career spanned 46 years, from 1922 to 1968. This discography includes all his known recorded performances, including film soundtracks, television and radio broadcasts, concerts, and private noncommercial recordings. The recording sessions are listed chronologically and contain the normal discographical information, which includes date and location, complete personnel listings, and song titles. Hilbert, a professional discographer who plays the clarinet and has also written a biography of Pee Wee Russell, is well-qualified to produce this discography.—**A. David Franklin**

1372. Lees, Gene. **Jazz Lives: 100 Portraits in Jazz.** Willowdale, Ont., Firefly Books, 1992. 216p. illus. index. $39.95. 781.65'092. ISBN 1-895565-12-X.

While the typical biographical guide to jazz musicians provides the requisite basic information, this one goes a step farther. It adds valuable insights acquired through Lees's personal acquaintance with his subjects throughout a long and varied career in jazz that has included editing *Down Beat* magazine, publishing his own highly respected *Jazzletter*, and setting lyrics to music composed by the likes of Antonio Carlos Jobim. Lees's commentary accompanies 100 candid duotone photographs of musicians in their private moments taken over a four-year period by award-winning Canadian photographer John Reeves. The musicians profiled have participated in and, in some cases, made major contributions to the history of jazz from the early 1920s to the present. Several outstanding Canadians are included. Although well-known figures such as Benny Carter, Artie Shaw, the Modern Jazz Quartet, Dave Brubeck, and Dizzy Gillespie are present, such lesser-known major talents as Bill Challis—Paul Whiteman's chief arranger in his glory days—and Bill Holman—who served in a similar capacity for Stan Kenton in the 1950s—are

also included. All are treated warmly and respectfully both by the photographer and by the author, so their brief profiles assume a human dimension frequently lacking in standard reference works.
—A. David Franklin

1373. Lord, Tom. **The Jazz Discography. Volume 5.** Redwood, N.Y., Cadence Jazz Books; distr., Redwood, N.Y., North Country Distributors, 1993. 608p. $45.00pa. ISBN 1-881993-04-3.

1374. Lord, Tom. **The Jazz Discography. Volume 6.** Redwood, N.Y., Cadence Jazz Books; distr., Redwood, N.Y., North Country Distributors, 1993. 1v. (various paging). $45.00pa. ISBN 1-881993-05-1.

Together, the latest two volumes in a series first reviewed in ARBA 93 (see entries 1287-89) cover "Dahlander" through "Axel Fischbaker." As noted in the earlier review, the discographer's intent is to provide pertinent information on every known jazz recording, regardless of style, made between 1898 and the publication of the latest volume. This is in contrast to traditional discographies, which normally deal with a single jazz style or a limited time period. Although it is not likely that all inadvertent omissions can be avoided, so far the work, which is generated by a specially designed computer database, is unsurpassed in comprehensiveness. The completed set is expected to contain approximately 20 volumes. Although a four-year timetable was originally planned, production is now ahead of schedule.—**A. David Franklin**

Rap

1375. McCoy, Judy. **Rap Music in the 1980s: A Reference Guide.** Metuchen, N.J., Scarecrow, 1992. 261p. index. $32.50. ML128.R28M3. 782.42164. LC 92-39684. ISBN 0-8108-2649-6.

This is a bibliography that had to be compiled, and now that the phenomenon of this literary idiom has secured international acculturation, its classical period may be over. The fragile musical relationship of rap might eventually become a counterpart to opera's recitative or *Sprechstimme*, but, as it stands, its connection to the purely musical is far less important than to Black oral-tradition improvisation or to the sociological factors of the text, usually offered from the perspective of the American ghetto or of youthful angst and protest. The annotated entries start with 1980 and end, as the date index quickly reveals, 11 years later. More than 1,000 entries on the literature appear, supplemented by annotations on 76 recordings. The compiler's well-disciplined librarian orientation is manifest in the indexes by artist and personality (including critically important name variants), album titles, and subject—the last unexpected but most valuable. This work is most worthy of consideration for collections of popular culture and Black studies. [R: Choice, Dec 93, p. 588; JAL, Sept 93, p. 275; RBB, 15 Oct 93, p. 475; RQ, Fall 93, pp. 133-34; VOYA, Oct 93, p. 261]—**Dominique-Rene de Lerma**

Rock

1376. Edwards, John W. **Rock 'n' Roll through 1969: Discographies of All Performers Who Hit the Charts, Beginning in 1955.** Jefferson, N.C., McFarland, 1992. 475p. illus. index. $35.00. ML156.4.R6E33. 016.7842166'026'6. LC 91-50945. ISBN 0-89950-655-0.

The title claims inclusion of all performers who hit the charts, but the introduction specifies that the majority of performers "who have achieved a charting single on the Billboard Hot 100 or an album on the Top 200 Albums, that fall into the classification of popular or rock music" are included. This is typical of the rather haphazard focus of this reference work. Each entry lists the personnel and instruments played (if a group), hit singles and albums (with highest chart position), category, geographical location, and assorted tidbits. The choice of facts revealed and the degree of detail are perplexing and inconsistent. For instance, readers learn that Sam Cooke was shot to death on December 11, 1964, at the age of 29, but information on Ritchie Valens's demise does not give the date, only that he "died in the plane crash that also killed Buddy Holly and the Big Bopper." There is an interesting reminder that Judy Collins was the inspiration for the Crosby, Stills, and Nash song "Suite: Judy Blue Eyes," but few are likely to care that Peppy Thielheim (of the Blues Magoos) changed his last name to Castro in the 1970s. Grainy, poor-quality black-and-white publicity stills appear throughout.

Some very minor groups absent from most other compilations, such as the Flirtations ("Nothing But a Heartache"), are included in this one, which is valuable. Overall, however, the directory of choice for this period is still *Rock On*, volume 1 (see ARBA 76, entry 1029) and volume 2 (see ARBA 85, entry 1218).—**Richard W. Grefrath**

1377. Hale, Mark. **HeadBangers: The Worldwide MegaBook of Heavy Metal Bands.** Ann Arbor, Mich., Popular Culture, Ink., 1993. 542p. illus. index. (Rock & Roll References Series, no.37). $65.00. LC 92-81112. ISBN 1-56075-029-4.

Opening with a foreword by Ted Nugent, one of the leading celebrities in heavy metal music, this encyclopedic work is as international as its title implies. Directory information is included for 3,458 international heavy metal bands. The term *heavy metal* is interpreted liberally to cover bands from the 1960s through the 1980s (and sparse coverage into the 1990s) with biographical and discographical information.

Well-known groups listed include Black Sabbath, Motorhead, Guns 'N' Roses, Anthrax, and Slayer. At the heart of the book is coverage of less well known, even obscure bands. Entries follow a basic format: home town, date founded, date disbanded, personnel, and recordings in chronological order by title and label number. The degree of comprehensiveness with which a band is treated depends upon which of three categories it falls into: non- or peripherally metal bands, metal bands, or major/important metal bands.

The information was gathered through extensive research into fan magazines, album liner notes, books, and interviews with subject specialists and record companies. Some 75 full-page portraits are provided. Appendixes (including a bibliography) take up eight pages, while the seven indexes (including the unusual index of band styles and influences) run for approximately 100 pages.

Although generally well produced, *HeadBangers* uses some awful abbreviations and uses them frequently. For instance, "bn." is used for the date groups started, while "d." is used for the date they broke up. Each entry includes a great deal of information in a small space, thus testing the limits of legibility. Using sequential numbers in addition to album titles makes the discussion of band histories easier to follow. Biographical information is rather brief, but the discographical materials are quite detailed. While most useful to public libraries that serve teenagers and young adults, *HeadBangers*, which contains material not found elsewhere, has applications in the academic library too. [R: RBB, Aug 93, p. 2090; WLB, May 93, p. 119]—**Megan S. Farrell**

1378. **The Harmony Illustrated Encyclopedia of Rock.** 7th ed. New York, Harmony Books/Crown, 1992. 208p. illus. $19.00pa. ML102.R6H37. 781.66'03. LC 92-13813. ISBN 0-517-59078-6.

From ABBA to ZZ Top, this encyclopedia has been the standard source for profiles of rock groups for almost 20 years. (For recent reviews, see ARBA 90, entry 1295 and ARBA 87, entry 1268.) This perennial young adult favorite retains its alphabetical, four-column format while offering fully revised text, illustrations, and discographies. Profiles of individual groups identify original members, list the date the band formed, and summarize the band's history in approximately 4 to 10 paragraphs. An appendix contains two-sentence profiles of less important or peripheral artists. Artists were selected for inclusion based on their contributions to rock music and the projected longevity of their importance.

Written in a tight, journalistic style, the encyclopedia is easy to use and attractive, featuring color photographs of both performers and album cover art. Many rock "family trees" by noted chronicler Peter Frame are included, helping readers visualize the often confusing lineage of and relationships between seminal bands and artists. The simple but helpful discographies list albums issued and singles that achieved positions on either the U.S. or U.K. charts. Record industry terms and awards for both the United States and United Kingdom are defined in the introduction. Now that the CD format is the standard, the encyclopedia no longer designates certain releases as available on CD.

Although a slight British bias has been present in all previous editions and continues in this one, it is not detrimental to the overall usefulness of the volume. The encyclopedia remains a basic reference source for college, public, and high school libraries. [R: VOYA, Feb 93, pp. 382-83]—**Megan S. Farrell**

1379. McKeen, William. **Bob Dylan: A Bio-Bibliography.** Westport, Conn., Greenwood Press, 1993. 307p. index. (Popular Culture Bio-bibliographies). $49.95. ML420.D98M25. 782.42162'0092. LC 92-32212. ISBN 0-313-27998-5.

As one of the most influential musicians of our times, Bob Dylan has been the subject of numerous books. Most meet their aims better than this one. Five major parts cover this multifaceted artist: a biography, his work and influence, a song catalog and bibliography of work by and about him, his performances (e.g., discography, concert itineraries, film work), and a chronology. In a work of this type an exhaustive, not selective, bibliography is expected; here, the bibliography section is a mere eight pages long. It is weighted in older material (1960s and 1970s) and omits many more recent substantive pieces, even those by major critics such as Greil Marcus. Although the section documenting performances appears good, the volume contains many proofreading errors. The most glaring of these oversights appears in the first sentence of the first page (Highway "51" in the Mississippi Delta instead of Highway 61—amazing because it is also the title of one of Dylan's most famous songs and albums) and is indicative of things to come. Valuable information is presented, but McKeen's volume does not meet the level of quality established by previous books in the series. [R: Choice, Oct 93, p. 270]—**Megan S. Farrell**

1380. Wiener, Allen J. **The Beatles: The Ultimate Recording Guide.** New York, Facts on File, 1992. 291p. illus. index. $35.00. ML156.7.B4W53. 016.78242166'092'2. LC 91-40635. ISBN 0-8160-2511-8.

Written with Beatles audio- and videophiles in mind, this guide documents all group and solo Beatles recordings, from the earliest years through 1991. It contains an introduction, a general and a recording chronology, a discography, and a chapter on bootlegs and unreleased recordings. In addition, there are two appendixes, a list of references and recommended periodicals, and an index. Throughout the book are black-and-white photographs of picture sleeves for both commercial and bootleg singles and albums.

The general chronology chapter presents a great deal of information about the day-to-day lives of the Beatles. Fans will enjoy reliving the famous moments, such as the Beatles' 1964 arrival in the United States and the premiere of *A Hard Day's Night*. Even more entertaining are the lesser-known facts, such as John Lennon's rendition of "Hava Nagila" for a 1969 interview on Israeli radio. Fans will also be delighted by the information provided in appendix A, "The Beatles as Supporting Players." This appendix contains a chronological list of all the songs that the Beatles wrote but other artists recorded. The author also notes if any of the Beatles ever sang or played on any of these "giveaway songs."

There is some confusion as to why Wiener divided the book the way he did. To find information about a single event, readers must locate that event in all three chapters and then piece the story together for themselves. Further, information presented in one chapter is sometimes repeated in another. There is also one glaring (probably typographical) error on the first page of the book, which states that George Harrison was born in "Waretree," Liverpool; he was born in Wavertree. This was, however, the only error found. All in all, this work presents an impressive amount of material and should be added to the collection of any serious Beatles fan. [R: BR, Mar/April 93, pp. 52-53; Choice, Feb 93, p. 947]—**Lisha E. Goldberg**

Salsa

1381. Figueroa, Rafael, comp. **Salsa and Related Genres: A Bibliographical Guide.** Westport, Conn., Greenwood Press, 1992. 109p. index. (Music Reference Collection, no.38). $45.00. ML128.S24F5. 016.78162'969729. LC 92-23778. ISBN 0-313-27883-0.

For those who enjoy the lively rhythms of the hot and saucy Latin music called salsa, this bibliographical guide may be their passport to learning more about its roots and its influence on popular American musical culture. Figueroa has gleaned written material from books, articles, dissertations, encyclopedias, videos, and liner notes from recordings. Primarily English-language sources are cited to make this work appeal to the non-Latin world. The citations are divided into four major groups: general topics treating the different countries of Latin America, works about styles and rhythms of the genre, biographies of performers and composers, and discussions of the instruments particular to the genre. Citations are cross-referenced, and anomalies in filing Spanish names are explained.

Figueroa indicates that entries have self-explanatory titles or are general profiles; otherwise, they have brief annotations. This seems to be an excuse for providing disappointingly few annotations. If this work hopes to be a true guide to the literature rather than a simple bibliography, it must provide more guidance to the reader. Some articles are not self-explanatory and convey only broad subject information, such as "Salsa and Latin Jazz." There is no indication whether the article is informative and detailed or simplistic and informal. Many articles appeared in such easily accessible sources as *Time, New York Times Magazine*, and *People Weekly*, so Figueroa likely had access to them. He also states that he had access to the resources of the CONCLAVE program, which maintains databases of Hispanic music material and that CONCLAVE made available most of the titles reviewed in the book. Yet, in the same paragraph, he explains that much of the material cited is difficult to find. It is not clear which materials he was or was not able to review. These problems notwithstanding, there is useful material here, and this work will be a time-saver to those researching this area of Latin music.—**Gregg S. Geary**

Steel Band

1382. Thomas, Jeffrey, comp. **Forty Years of Steel: An Annotated Discography of Steel Band and Pan Recordings, 1951-1991.** Westport, Conn., Greenwood Press, 1992. 307p. index. (Discographies, no.49). $55.00. ML156.4.S8T5. 016.785'68. LC 92-23777. ISBN 0-313-27952-7.

Steel bands did not originally result from wartime littering of oil drums, although that practice did subsequently provide the Trinbagonians (natives of Trinidad and Tobago) with readily available materials, as this excellent discography documents. The practice is evidence of what T. J. Anderson, exploring distinctions in Black musical cultures, has termed "inspired intensity." The results in this instance are certainly remarkable and have spread throughout the Caribbean, particularly to the United States and England. The book's preface provides the first comprehensive history of this miscegenated Black phenomenon, while the main body of the work is dedicated to alphabetical and disciplined citation of the issues by recording ensemble. Among the titles and composers specified for each recording are not infrequent typographical errors (e.g., "Jrving" Berlin, "Mayerbeer") and inconsistencies (Mozart's *Eine kleine Nachtmusik* seems ubiquitous here also, but the format of including the composer's name is not always honored). The appendixes provide addresses for the record manufacturers and distributors (some of which, as could be expected, are small operations), an index of the names of calypsonians, and sources that provided the data. The indexes cover performers, arrangers and conductors, titles of record albums, years of issue, and titles of recorded works. The concluding bibliographies present material not available elsewhere. Despite its shortcomings, this guide will prove more valuable than a mere discography (the repertoire list is important by itself), and this study should be welcomed by all people in Caribbean studies. **Dominique-Rene de Lerma**

26 Mythology, Folklore, and Popular Culture

FOLKLORE

1383. Bennett, Gillian, and Paul Smith. **Contemporary Legend: A Folklore Bibliography.** Hamden, Conn., Garland, 1993. 340p. index. (Garland Folklore Bibliographies, v.18; Garland Reference Library of the Humanities, v.1307). $56.00. Z5981.B46. 016.398'09173'2. LC 93-15549. ISBN 0-8240-6103-9.

Bennett and Smith's bibliography introduces to the folklore canon the first one-volume compendium of material about urban legends. Culled from academia, popular journals, conference papers, "migratory anecdotes," beast fables, UFO sightings, mass panics, and books, the work focuses on 1,000 primary and secondary case studies, queries, articles, and notes. Using the research of editors from Germany, France, Poland, Russia, Scandinavia, and Australia, the authors have completed serious scholarship akin to other works in the Garland Folklore series in scope, tone, and refinement.

The compendium begins with a series preface; acknowledgments; and a precise introduction delineating purpose, parameters, exceptions, organization of entries, and order. Concluding with a call for corrections and suggestions, the authors demonstrate a candor and pragmatism appropriate to the immediacy and impermanence of so current and ephemeral a body of lore. The text, which is divided into four chapters, is organized alphabetically by author and provides title, source, and date. Brief summaries capture the gist of the rumor, legend, quip, essay, tale, or core legend. Significant to entries are connections to cults; old saws; and such arcane and bizarre happenings as the missing hitchhiker, the Kentucky fried rat, the cat in the microwave, and playing disc recordings backwards to detect hidden messages touting Satanism. The inclusion of last-minute entries, an appendix of bulletins and newsletters of interest to folklorists, and author and general indexes rounds out a useful reference tool.—**Mary Ellen Snodgrass**

1384. Ettlinger, John, and Ruby Day. **Old English Proverbs Collected by Nathan Bailey, 1736, Edited from His *Dictionarium Britannicum*....** Metuchen, N.J., Scarecrow, 1992. 163p. $22.50. PN6420.B3. 398.9'21. LC 92-25185. ISBN 0-8208-2593-7.

The 1,200 proverbs in this collection were originally included in Nathan Bailey's enlarged 1736 edition of the *Universal Etymological English Dictionary*, where they were located under key words. According to Ettlinger and Day, most studies of proverbs missed Bailey's contribution because it was not a separately published book. Bailey's contributions to lexicography are similarly not well known today, as they have been eclipsed by his much more famous successor, Samuel Johnson, whose dictionary was published in 1755.

This collection not only revives the work of a largely forgotten scholar but also adds to our knowledge of proverbs. A typical entry includes a statement of the proverb, its derivation from another language (if known), an explanation of its figurative meaning (if Bailey thought it was necessary), and (when Bailey thought it was appropriate) a didactic illustration.

While other proverb collections are more extensive (e.g., the classic *Oxford Dictionary of English Proverbs* [see ARBA 72, entry 1330]), and while some more general quotation books contain proverbs among other kinds of quotations (e.g., *The Macmillan Book of Proverbs, Maxims, and Famous Phrases* [see ARBA 89, entry 1245]), this book will also be useful to readers in search of proverbs they may not be able to find in other sources. It also has a somewhat quaint historical value.—**David Isaacson**

1385. Glinert, Lewis. **The Joys of Hebrew.** New York, Oxford University Press, 1992. 292p. $22.00. PN6414.G58. 398.9'924. LC 92-28624. ISBN 0-19-507424-6.

Glinert's compendium of some 850 common Hebrew terms is a rare blend of scholarship, practicality, wisdom, and a glint of wit. Arranged alphabetically, the entries list Hebrew terms of varying degrees of specificity (e.g., *Kabala, Bar Mitzvah*) alongside clear translations and definitions. Short commentaries include citations from the Bible, Talmud, and Midrash and works by Elie Wiesel, Sholem Aleichem, Martin Buber, and other worthy philosophers, novelists, and poets. Glinert's versatility and sensitivity to scholarly needs puts him in touch with basic reference questions raised by non-Jews: holy days and other calendar terms, mundane idioms, liturgical questions, prayers, place names, foods, and common nouns (e.g., *peot*, the sidecurls that adorn the pious). His humanistic bent inclines him to a melange of expressions, from deeply spiritual litanies to folk exclamations and jingles. Essential to the book's accessibility are a lively introduction to Hebrew; a guide to transliteration; the respelling of entries in Hebrew lettering; and a brief list of Hebrew given names, such as David, Miriam, and Esther, alongside the Sephardic and Ashkenazi pronunciations.

The value of this book as a reference tool should be obvious. Glinert's "little something extra" is the generous dollop of humanism, the warmth and beauty of Hebrew expressions that date back to early Jewish communities who found their release from religious oppression in the honing of sharp tongues. The cover, a brilliant sapphire blue surrounding a blazing menorah, sets the tone of this "celebration of Hebrew."—**Mary Ellen Snodgrass**

1386. Gribben, Arthur. **Holy Wells and Sacred Water Sources in Britain and Ireland: An Annotated Bibliography.** Hamden, Conn., Garland, 1992. 179p. index. (Garland Folklore Bibliographies, v.17; Garland Reference Library of the Humanities, v.1594). $29.00. Z5983.W36G75. 016.39826. LC 92-23000. ISBN 0-8153-0831-0.

While modern science can deal adequately with the technical aspects of water, it can hardly deal with its meaning in human society and its role in human expression. Concepts of fertility, nurturing, relief, and regeneration within a rich store of religious poetic language have had a profound influence on modern expressions of hydromythology, particularly in relation to holy wells, wishing wells, spas, and bottled water. The task of listing every published reference to such matters in all portions of the globe is Sisyphean in its implication. This volume, accordingly, limits itself to one delimited geopolitical area: Great Britain and Ireland.

A brief preface by the noted folklorist Barre Toelken ranges over the chief reasons water has remained central not only to human survival but also to human wonderment and expression. Then follows an informative 30-page introduction by Gribben that discusses such topics as traditional water beliefs, water in religious scriptures, and hydromythologies to demonstrate that water is far more than the sum of its hydrogen and oxygen parts. Almost 600 annotated entries of books, articles, and other written materials that focus on holy wells and sacred springs in England, Scotland, Wales, and Ireland are listed. Individual entries include respected scholarly sources and nineteenth-century antiquarian writings. A comprehensive subject index completes this latest addition to the excellent Garland Folklore Bibliographies series.

—**G. A. Cevasco**

1387. Haboucha, Reginetta. **Types and Motifs of the Judeo-Spanish Folktales.** Hamden, Conn., Garland, 1992. 965p. index. (Garland Folklore Library, v.6; Garland Reference Library of the Humanities, v.1397). $135.00. GR98.H225. 398.2'0467. LC 92-8897. ISBN 0-8240-9727-0.

Compiling tale-type and motif indexes is an immense task, meant to aid historic-geographic analyses by folklorists, literary scholars, and anthropologists. Use of these indexes today is not as widespread as it was before the 1960s, when the historic-geographic was the primary form of analysis in folktale research. Nonetheless, the recent appearance of a bibliography of tale-type and motif indexes (*Tale-Type and Motif-Indexes* [see ARBA 88, entry 1323]) and articles in scholarly journals on renewing the historical-geographic approach offers an opportunity to place a tale-type index in a contemporary perspective.

Based on Haboucha's doctoral dissertation completed in 1973, the reference book comprehensively indexes available sources for international folktale types, thus offering a classification for comparative work. Haboucha mostly follows the organization of the standard Aarne-Thompson classification system, and checks with others such as Andrejev, Ashliman, and Boggs for additional types. She also contributes several new types of her own for consideration. Under each type, Haboucha offers an abstract of the plot, motifs represented, commentary, and references to published Judeo-Spanish variants as well as parallels in other global sources. This attention to detail has resulted in an enormous, meticulous reference. Renowned folklore scholars Alan Dundes and Samuel Armistead offer prefaces that consider the impact of this reference on folklore and Judeo-Spanish scholarship.

This book will be particularly welcomed by Jewish scholars who are concerned with comparative narrative research that addresses questions of origin and diffusion. In addition, scholars working in folktale studies, especially in Europe and the Middle East, will have to consult this work for the possibilities it raises of cultural lending and borrowing.—**Simon J. Bronner**

1388. Mieder, Wolfgang. **International Proverb Scholarship: An Annotated Bibliography. Supplement II (1982-1991).** Hamden, Conn., Garland, 1993. 927p. index. (Garland Folklore Bibliographies, v.20; Garland Reference Library of the Humanities, v.1655). $95.00. Z7191.M543. 016.3989. LC 90-3049. ISBN 0-8153-1133-8.

Mieder's compendium of proverb scholarship adds 1,500 entries to his original volume (see ARBA 84, entry 53), which contains 3,000 items. The purpose of his work is to list analytic discussions of world proverbs. It covers African, Akkadian, Anglo-American, Arabic, Aramaic, Burmese, Czech, Dutch, Estonian, French, German, Greek, Haitian, Hebrew, Hungarian, Irish, Italian, Latin, Latvian, Native American, Persian, Polish, Rumanian, Russian, Slovakian, Somali, Spanish, Sumerian, Swedish, Tongan, and Yiddish. Although this list appears to cover much of the world, the preponderance of the work is Anglo-American, with 11 languages contributing only a single proverb to the 30-page list.

The compendium begins with a preface and introduction. The text is organized alphabetically by author and names title, source, and date. Brief summaries capture the gist of the study or commentary. There are exhaustive name and subject indexes and a listing by language of individual proverbs that received scholarly study. Many of the proverbs appear in the target language. Although the focus of this work remains Euro-based, the intensity of the scholarship reflects the bibliographer's belief that the study of simple truths warrants scholarly attention.—**Mary Ellen Snodgrass**

1389. Neugaard, Edward J. **Motif-Index of Medieval Catalan Folktales.** Binghamton, N.Y., Medieval & Renaissance Texts & Studies, State University of New York, 1993. 129p. (Medieval & Renaissance Texts & Studies, v.96). $18.00. GR237.C3N48. 025.4'63982'09467. LC 92-16905. ISBN 0-86698-110-1.

This small volume fills a gap in Stith Thompson's *Motif-Index of Folk Literature* (Indiana University Press, 1955-1958) by providing a catalog of the motifs found in the short prose narratives of medieval Catalan literature, a much-neglected corpus of materials. Commonly called *exempla* due to the large number that include explicit moral messages, the greatest number of these narratives originated in the traditional literature of India, arriving on the Hispanic peninsula via Persia and through translation from the Latin into the vernacular. Related to medieval Spanish tales, the 1,324 tales indexed in this volume show a greater number of motifs than are present in the larger medieval Spanish collection of approximately 1,500 folktales.

Along with the index, whose format follows that of Thompson's *Motif-Index*, Neugaard provides, among other things, a short discussion of medieval Hispanic literature as well as descriptions of each of the works used in the index. A bibliography of these works along with other collections consulted but lacking in motifs follows, it in turn being followed by the "Additional Bibliography." The latter includes a selection of those works consulted while constructing the present index in addition to other works dealing with medieval Hispanic literature.

This volume deserves a place in any library serving those working in comparative literature. It makes a major contribution to the increasing corpus of materials that complements and supplements Thompson's work, and it will facilitate research in medieval Hispanic literature, thus leading to a greater understanding of the development of not only Spanish prose fiction but also of prose fiction in Western Europe.

—**Susan Tower Hollis**

1390. **The Oxford Companion to Australian Folklore.** Gwenda Beed Davey and Graham Seal, eds. New York, Oxford University Press, 1993. 381p. illus. $49.95. 398.20994. ISBN 0-19-553057-8.

The Oxford Companion to Australian Folklore is a good basis for further work in the field rather than an established authority. Until the 1950s, the term *folklore* was hardly known in Australia. Ironically, this work is the first in the world—occasioned, as its editors point out, by the scarcity of material, not by the abundance. The preface and introduction explain the genesis and scope of the work. The editors distinguish folklore from high culture and popular culture while acknowledging that it influences both and is influenced by them. Among the forms of folklore they list are language and literature, music and dance, myths and legends, customs, and crafts. The format of the book is encyclopedic, with entries by a number of experts alphabetically arranged. But there is no index, hence no way of knowing the nature of the entries other than by educated guessing and by skimming. The lack of an index is the book's main deficiency.

Although a nation's folklore necessarily provides clues to the nature of its culture, the editors refrain from interpreting Australian culture. They appear to be governed less by objectivity than by defensiveness: This reviewer can detect in them evidence of chauvinism and also an unwillingness to acknowledge the deeply negative nature of Australian culture (see the entries on the Australian legend and wartime folklore.) Interpretation is an inescapable part of folklore scholarship.

On the whole, the volume has admirably advanced knowledge of its field, which is still only partly researched. The entries are well written, well researched, and always interesting. [R: Choice, Nov 93, p. 437]

—John B. Beston

MYTHOLOGY

1391. **Brewer's Book of Myth and Legend.** J. C. Cooper, ed. London, Cassell; distr., New York, Sterling Publishing, 1992. 309p. $21.95. ISBN 0-304-34084-7.

This book derives largely from the *Dictionary of Phrase and Fable* compiled by Ebenezer Brewer at the end of the nineteenth century. The present work preserves Brewer's dictionary form and his often anecdotal entries. According to Cooper, the aim of the update has been to add entries about Oceania, Africa, and Native Americans, as Brewer's preoccupation was with classical Greek, Roman, Celtic, and Norse mythology.

This is not the first contemporary volume to mine Brewer's folkloristic compilations. A much fatter, if more diffuse, volume appeared in 1992 as *Brewer's Dictionary of 20th-Century Phrase and Fable* (see ARBA 93, entry 1294). The present volume has the advantage of focus for the modern reader, although users will notice that entries include beliefs, sayings, and folktales as well as the myths and legends mentioned in the title. The compilation has popular, rather than scholarly, appeal. At best the approximately 4,000 entries give explanations of one half of one column in length and only provide a sample of international mythological and legendary terms and figures known today. No bibliography is given, and literary references are to the world of letters rather than to the voices of the folk. The volume has historical interest and is easily accessible, but its research use is limited. [R: RBB, June 93, p. 1892]

—Simon J. Bronner

1392. Conway, D. J. **The Ancient & Shining Ones: World Myth, Magick & Religion.** St. Paul, Minn., Llewellyn, 1993. 437p. illus. maps. index. $17.95pa. BF1623.G63C66. 291.2'11. LC 93-29628. ISBN 0-87542-170-9.

The author believes that neo-Pagan rituals enable us to gain access to "the vast pools of energy" available from the "Ultimate Source," the reality behind the world's multitude of gods and goddesses. The book does not proselytize, but seeks to enlighten those who are enamored with the religions of antiquity. The myths and rituals of a wide variety of world religions of antiquity are briefly described in serial order. Each description is followed by a catalog of the deities and a bibliography for that religion. The author feels that Judaism, Christianity, and Islam should be the subject of a separate book, so they are not described. Extensive treatment of the Qabala and other more esoteric subjects is particularly interesting and helpful. There are an index and a section called "cross-reference" where topics such as fertility, prosperity, and weapons are cross-referenced with the various deities associated with each. The descriptions of myth and ritual and lists of deities are potentially very helpful and are adequate for an abbreviated treatment of a complex and often obscure phenomenon.

Characteristics or actions of a deity are sometimes described in the discussion of myth and not repeated in the catalog listing of deities, which can make the latter seem incomplete. Also, the bibliographies are puzzling. It is not surprising to see many books that describe, or are produced from within, occult movements as well as works of acknowledged scholars (e.g., Samuel N. Kramer for Mesopotamia, Carl Jung for Greece). But why is Thorkild Jacobsen, for example, not also there for Mesopotamia, or Robert Graves for Greece?—**Robert T. Anderson**

1393. Grant, Michael, and John Hazel. **Who's Who in Classical Mythology.** New York, Oxford University Press, 1993. 367p. $14.95pa. BL715.G68. 292.1'3'03. ISBN 0-19-521030-1.

1394. Sykes, Egerton. **Who's Who in Non-Classical Mythology.** Revised by Alan Kendall. New York, Oxford University Press, 1993. 235p. $14.95pa. BL303.S9. 291.1'3. ISBN 0-460-86136-0.

Both of these volumes are intended to provide succinct biographical information about mythological characters throughout the world's traditions. Grant and Hazel's work is a reprint of their 1973 volume, published in England under the same title and in the United States as *Gods and Mortals in Classical Mythology* (see ARBA 74, entry 1205). It provides well-written descriptions of the major characters of Greek and Roman mythology. Major figures receive entries of up to a few pages in length, although most entries are a paragraph long. No illustrations are included, unlike the original edition, but a set of family trees and a brief bibliography are appended. The book will serve popular and ready-reference usage, but it lacks scholarly apparatus, such as references to the classical texts.

Sykes's dictionary, originally published in 1952 as *Everyman's Dictionary of Non-Classical Mythology*, has been minimally revised in this edition with the addition of some entries, some minor textual changes, and some unexplained deletions of entries. Unlike Grant's work, this volume's entries are quite short—usually one or two sentences long. Most of the text is helpful, but some entries do not indicate the nationality or cultural origin of the topic. The title is somewhat misleading, as there are entries not only for names of personal figures but also for places, customs, and creation legends. The range of mythologies covered is quite wide, although European and Near Eastern myths receive the largest amount of space. A good bibliography of narrative sources is provided.

Both dictionaries do a good job of briefly describing the story behind mythological figures and are easy to use, unlike some topically oriented sources such as *Larousse World Mythology* (Hamlyn, 1965). However, libraries already owning more substantial books, such as *Crowell's Handbook of Classical Mythology* (see ARBA 71, entry 1351) or Pierre Grimal's *Dictionary of Classical Mythology* (see ARBA 87, entry 1275), will find little new in Grant and Hazel's work. *Crowell's* and Grimal's dictionary additionally contain more detail, exact references to the classical literature, maps, and pronunciation guides. Sykes's volume exists in a subject having fewer good sources of this type and might be more useful, although other good works include *Dictionary of World Mythology* (see ARBA 81, entry 1132, for review of an earlier edition) and the eclectic but uneven *Facts on File Encyclopedia of World Mythology and Legend* (see ARBA 89, entry 1250).—**Christopher W. Nolan**

1395. Jordan, Michael. **Encyclopedia of Gods: Over 2,500 Deities of the World.** New York, Facts on File, 1993. 337p. index. $40.00. BL473.J67. 291.2'11. LC 92-46762. ISBN 0-8160-2909-1.

Encyclopedia of Gods contains more than 2,500 entries on deities from both ancient and contemporary cultures. It does not include figures considered by Jordan—a broadcaster and writer—to be demigods, demons, or mythical heroes. A chart depicting the chronology of the principal religions and cultures covered in the book includes Akkadian-Babylonian, Aztec, Buddhist, Celtic, Christian, Egyptian, Greek, Hurrian, Inca, Islamic, Judaism, Mayan, Nordic-Icelandic, Roman, and Sumerian. In the introduction, historical background is provided for the (presumably) less familiar cultures, such as the Sumerian, Celtic, Hindu, and Mayan. Entries are in alphabetical order, without breakdown into ethnic or cultural groups, and each entry is listed under the name by which the deity is most commonly known. The modern geographical region of the world in which the deity is recognized is given in square brackets. The encyclopedia employs two types of entries. Entries for deities who may be regarded as being of major significance within their cultural area are headed by boldface capitals and are covered more thoroughly, while the rest are treated in less detail. However, in all cases the information includes the original cultural source. Also included is the role of the deity in the pantheon; the immediate genealogy is listed, and when mythology plays a significant part in the understanding or makeup of the personality, its outlines may be included and the literary source identified. A distinction is drawn between sky and astral personalities, and where cross-references to other deities have seemed appropriate to Jordan, they are included. When a name originates in a script form other than Roman (e.g., Sanskrit), phonetic equivalents are provided in the spelling.

The dust jacket for *Encyclopedia of Gods* indicates that the volume will be an invaluable resource for students and researchers as well as the general reader in mythology and legend. This is generally true, although it is hoped that the reader will not take the introduction—or at least parts thereof—too seriously, such as the section in which Jordan seems to subscribe to the long-discredited solar mythology propounded by such individuals as nineteenth-century German scholar Friedrich Max Muller (1823-1900). [R: Choice, Dec 93, p. 587; RBB, 15 Oct 93, pp. 470-72]—**Arthur Gribben**

1396.   Macrone, Michael. **By Jove! Brush Up Your Mythology.** New York, Cader Books/HarperCollins, 1992. 237p. illus. index. $17.00. BL722.M318. 292'.13. LC 92-52541. ISBN 0-06-270023-5.

Macrone uses humor in this small volume to retell the classic tales of the gods, demigods, heroes, antiheroes, monsters, and charmed objects that populate Greek and Roman mythology. *By Jove!* is designed to be read for pure entertainment, but while one is being entertained, one also learns the story behind many of the common words and phrases found in today's language. Words such as *terminal, lethal, cypress,* and *Aphrodite*; phrases such as "Herculean task" and "a panacea"; and the signs of the zodiac all have their roots in classical mythology.

By Jove! follows closely in the footsteps of the author's first two works: *Brush Up Your Shakespeare!* (see ARBA 91, entry 1213) and *It's Greek to Me!* (see ARBA 92, entry 1026), bringing with it Macrone's lighthearted touch. While his wit is occasionally sophomoric, overall *By Jove!* serves as a good introduction to classical mythology. The book is divided into six sections, each dealing with a different category of mythical being. Within the biographical sections, the entries are in chronological order, allowing the reader to trace the bloodlines of the gods. Tom Lulevitch's 40 pen-and-ink illustrations, including a family tree of the Titans, exactly capture the lighthearted nature of this volume.—**Steven J. Schmidt**

1397.   **The Oxford Guide to Classical Mythology in the Arts, 1300-1990s.** By Jane Davidson Reid with Chris Rohmann. New York, Oxford University Press, 1993. 2v. index. $195.00/set. NX650.M9R45. 700. LC 92-35374. ISBN 0-19-504998-5.

This work brings together in one place an amazing wealth of art resources, not just paintings, sculptures, and drawings but also poetry, drama, and literature, all of which in some way incorporate aspects of classical mythology. While the book makes no claim to be complete—and one hopes it will be the first edition of many—it nevertheless lists more than 30,000 works of art relating to deities, heroes, events, and places from classical mythology. Its organization by subject (e.g., Achilles, Arcade, Bacchanalia) allows the reader to see the ebbs and flows of interest in the different subjects over time. For example, no fewer than 50 pages are devoted to Aphrodite (Venus), from a Latin poem dating from 1160-1170 to a 1990 English poem.

Without question, the guide is user-friendly. Headnotes on the subject, listed under its Greek name with cross-references to the Roman, introduce it and are followed by a list of the appropriate classical sources. Occasional references to further sources also appear (e.g., Erich Neumann's *Amor and Psyche* under "Psyche"). The listings of artworks follow, arranged in chronological order. At the end of the last entry is a list of sources followed by an index of artists, including all the entries relevant to each individual.

One cannot underestimate the value of this set to scholars and interested laypersons from many disciplines. Its interdisciplinary nature, its chronological and subject ordering, and its invaluable cross-references provide the raw material for many studies on cultural history, arts, and artists of the Western world from the thirteenth century on. No respectable research or college library can afford to be without the guide, and many writers and scholars will also choose to invest in it for their personal libraries. [R: Choice, Dec 93, pp. 589-90; LJ, 1 Sept 93, p. 176; RBB, 15 Nov 93, pp. 652; WLB, Oct 93, p. 95]—**Susan Tower Hollis**

1398. Willis, Roy. **World Mythology.** New York, Henry Holt, 1993. 311p. illus. maps. index. $45.00. BL311.W66. 291.1'3. LC 93-3045. ISBN 0-8050-2701-7.

More than 500 color photographs, charts, and maps and a handsomely formatted, informative text make this volume a pleasure for general readers as well as scholars. The foreword is by Robert Walter, director of the Joseph Campbell Foundation. Myths are organized by such themes as creation, cosmic disasters, supernatural beings, heroes, and tricksters in the first section, and by geographical areas of origin in the larger second section.

Nineteen parts of the world, from Egypt, the Middle East, Greece, and Rome to the Orient, Europe, the Americas, Africa, Australia, and Oceania, are covered. For each there is a time chart, a map marking sacred sites and the spread of influence, ruled areas, ornaments appropriate to the country, and important information, such as the life of Buddha, a comparative list of the Greek and Roman pantheons, or the meaning of El Dorado. Each major section is divided thematically under headings such as "Creation," "Gods and Goddesses," or "The Underworld."

The volume concludes with an extensive list of books for further reading both under general works and by geographical area. The index is well cross-referenced, making it easy to compare myths by looking under such words as cosmic egg, fire deities, or animal myths or to locate items by country of origin or name. Although far from exhaustive in its treatment, *World Mythology* would be a welcome addition to any library for either quick reference or enjoyable reading.—**Charlotte Lindgren**

POPULAR CULTURE

1399. Bettelheim, Judith, ed. **Cuban Festivals: An Illustrated Anthology.** Hamden, Conn., Garland, 1993. 261p. illus. index. (Studies in Ethnic Art, v.3; Garland Reference Library of the Humanities, v.1444). $40.00. GT4825.A2C83. 394.2'697291. LC 93-18140. ISBN 0-8153-0310-6.

Bettelheim and contributor David Brown are proteges of the renowned chronicler and champion of the African-Atlantic world, Robert Farris Thompson. This work is a valuable contribution to that scholarship. It includes the first English translation of Cuban anthropologist Fernando Ortiz's "The Afro-Cuban Festival 'Day of the Kings.'" This 45-page essay, translated and annotated by British historian Jean Stubbs, is supplemented by a 49-page glossary by Brown. While Ortiz's essay is an analysis of historical accounts of the festival in Havana, he, Stubbs, and Brown offer considerable comparable data from other locations in Cuba and the African Diaspora. Cuban scholars Rafael Brea and Jose Millet contributed the useful "Glossary of Popular Festivals," which includes many terms that originated with the Haitian migration to eastern Cuba at the end of the eighteenth century. Bettelheim contributes two pieces, one on the Carnival in Cuba's most African city, Santiago de Cuba, and the other on the Haitian-derived carnival groups of the Tumba Francesa and Tajona. The book ends with Cuban poet Pedro Perez Sarduy's "Flashback on Carnival, a Personal Memoir." The work includes 36 illustrations (from Ortiz's essay and other publications, and photographs by Bettelheim of Carnival in Santiago de Cuba) and an index. The high quality and interdisciplinary nature of the scholarship, the focus on the varieties of Afro-Cuban festivals, and the pan-Diaspora orientation of its contributors make this an essential reference book for African-American and Latin American collections.—**Fred J. Hay**

1400. Dewey, Patrick R. **Fan Club Directory: 2000 Fan Clubs and Fan Mail Addresses in the United States and Abroad.** Jefferson, N.C., McFarland, 1993. 104p. index. $19.95pa. LC 92-51012. ISBN 0-89950-767-0.

Whether the subject is a television show, movie, sports team, comic strip, movie star, musician, or literary figure, there is generally an associated fan club. Because there is no national or international clearinghouse for fan clubs, and many clubs are quite obscure, getting in touch with them can often be tricky. However, Dewey has made this task much easier with his *Fan Club Directory*. Besides the more established fan clubs, such as those for Abbott and Costello, Elvis Presley, and James Dean, the directory includes up-to-date listings for newer clubs, such as those for Boyz II Men, Paul Reiser, and Jason Priestly.

Although the work consists mainly of an easy-to-read alphabetical list of the fan clubs and their addresses, the strength of the book is in the index, which provides several cross-reference points to supplement the alphabetical listing. Without it, who would think to look in the alphabetical listing under

"Happy Humpers" if one were interested in joining a fan club for Engelbert Humperdinck? Unfortunately, the index, while invaluable, could have benefited from more proofreading; there are several examples of missed cross-referencing (e.g., Touch of Days fan club is not listed under *Days of Our Lives*). All in all, the directory is a recommended source for addresses of a wide variety of fan clubs. [R: VOYA, Dec 93, p. 332; WLB, Dec 93, p. 78]—**Lori L. Oling**

1401. **The Guinness Book of Records 1993.** Peter Matthews and others, eds. New York, Facts on File, 1992. 319p. illus. index. $22.95. ISBN 0-8160-2644-0. ISSN 0300-1679.

Quick! When was the first recorded lumberjack sport competition? (1572 in the Basque region of Spain.) What canary broke the world's record for longevity? (Joey, who lived 34 years with the Ross household of Hull, Great Britain.) What were those crazy kids in the woodworking class at Shakamak High School in Jasonville, Indiana, doing on March 29, 1990? (Launching the world's largest yo-yo, which measured 6 feet in diameter and weighed 820 lbs. It was launched from a 160-foot crane and "yo-yoed" 12 times.)

The Guinness Book of World Records is a standard work for all libraries regardless of size. It continues to inform and delight on a vast range of topics. General categories include Earth and space, the living world, human beings, science and technology, buildings and structures, transportation, the business world, arts and entertainment, the human world, human achievements, and sports and games. Now in its third year of being published in the United States by Facts on File, this work has 300 new color photographs and more than 2,000 updated records. Access to this extravaganza of facts is provided by a detailed subject index and a name index. A must purchase for public libraries and a great purchase for home libraries.—**G. Kim Dority**

1402. Johnson, Lois S. **Happy Birthdays Round the World.** New York, Rand McNally, 1963; repr., Detroit, Omnigraphics, 1993. 128p. illus. index. $28.00. GT2430.J64. 394.2. LC 93-24339. ISBN 1-55888-174-3.

The reference collections of elementary schools will be enriched by the addition of this small work, which presents a 3- to 5-page commentary about birthday customs in 24 nations on all continents, including pronunciation guides to words in other languages included in the essays. The author chose countries in which birthday customs usually differ from those in the United States. Simple black-and-white illustrations show festival costumes common in each land represented. Part 1, "Birthday Customs and How They Grew," briefly discusses the common traditions of birthday parties, presents, cakes, candles, games, songs, and birthday trees.

This indexed reprint will be a useful addition to collections with a multicultural emphasis and will support thematic units in geography and international culture. The reading level is appropriate for grades 3-6. Birthday books for younger elementary students include Elizabeth Laird's *Happy Birthday! A Book of Birthday Celebrations* (Philomel, 1988), a brief discussion of customs in other countries that gives many ideas for how to celebrate this special day, and Gail Gibbons's *Happy Birthday* (Holiday House, 1986), a colorful and festive examination of the historical beliefs, traditions, and celebrations of birthdays.—**Vandelia L. VanMeter**

1403. *The People's Almanac* **Presents the Book of Lists: The '90s Edition.** By David Wallechinsky and Amy Wallace. Boston, Little, Brown, 1993. 491p. illus. index. $17.95. AG106.P487. 031. LC 93-17197. ISBN 0-316-92079-7.

It has been 10 years since this work last appeared, and happily, it has not lost any of its youthful exuberance with age. It continues to be a source of bizarre, amusing, and even occasionally enlightening facts and figures. Although its use as a ready-reference source is questionable due to the highly eclectic mix of information included, *The Book of Lists* is a delightful (if addictive) resource for browsing and serendipitous finds. Its 320 lists are arranged within 16 categories: people, movies and television, the arts, health and food, animals, work, family and relationships, crime, politics and world affairs, America, travel, literature, words, advice, sports, and miscellany. Among these categories, sample lists include "15 People Buried 2 or More Times," "18 Celebrities Who Were Cheerleaders," "General Colin Powell's 13 Rules to Live By," "11 Olympic Medalists Who Acted in Movies," "16 Memorable Responses to Critics,"

"15 Politically Incorrect Terms and Their Alternatives," and "Odd Jobs of 35 Celebrities." Although certainly not a necessary purchase, *The Book of Lists* provides good value for the price and would be a welcome addition to all public libraries.—**G. Kim Dority**

1404. **The *Rolling Stone* Index: Twenty-Five Years of Popular Culture 1967-1991.** Jeffrey N. Gatten, comp. Ann Arbor, Mich., Popular Culture, Ink., 1993. 1096p. $85.00. LC 92-81114. ISBN 1-56075-030-8.

Libraries whose users are interested in rock music and popular culture will find this to be an important index to their *Rolling Stone* issues. A bit of effort is required to use this index, as its 73,000 entries (to late 1991) are divided, first, into focused indexes: articles and columns (title and subject); book reviews (author and reviewer); concert reviews (reviewer and title); cover appearances; letters to the editor; movie reviews (movie and reviewer); poetry (author and title); random notes; and record reviews (artist, reviewer, and title). Those are followed by two master indexes, one to author and reviewer names and one to titles. Thin paper—which one fears will tear readily—has been used, probably to keep this work from becoming a two-volume set; the typeface is small but readable (it gets smaller for the two master indexes). The first articles and columns index and the book reviews index need a modifier—in both cases, "by title"—and there is no indication as to which subject heading thesaurus was used. The publisher plans to follow this work with annual indexes. [R: Choice, Sept 93, p. 82; LJ, 1 May 93, p. 83; RBB, 15 May 93, p. 1723; WLB, May 93, pp. 121-22]—**Mary Larsgaard**

1405. Scott, Randall W., comp. **The Comic Art Collection Catalog: An Author, Artist, Title, and Subject Catalog of the Comic Art Collection, Special Collections Division, Michigan State University Libraries.** Westport, Conn., Greenwood Press, 1993. 1435p. $199.95. PN6725.M53. 741.5'074'77427. LC 93-7599. ISBN 0-313-28325-7.

An unannotated catalog of the largest collection of comic art-related material in the United States, this work does a service for those interested in the genre by listing some 70,000 works, many for the first time. Included are comic books, graphic novels, magazines, scrapbooks, fanzines, strips, promotional material, history and criticism, fotonovelas, works on animation, comic book scripts, Big Little Books, and other related items acquired as of mid-1991. The material is listed in a single alphabetical sequence that includes authors, artists, titles, subjects, and series titles. Although the library does not own every relevant work ever produced, this is as close to an exhaustive book on the subject as exists anywhere, even cataloging such ephemera as the Jack T. Chick religious tracts.

While the information in this book is tremendously valuable and probably unique, the format is problematic. The typeface is workmanlike, and while subject headings are in all capital letters, they are not bolded, indented, or otherwise set off from the regular entries, making them harder than necessary to distinguish. There seems to be no logic as to which series entries list the individuals who worked on them; for example, that for *Deadshot* provides both writers and the artist, but that for *Zooniverse* lists no one. Entries are repeated under the title and every person listed; for example, the same entry for *Deadshot* is listed under the title, John Ostrander, Luke McDonnell, and Kim Yale. Cross-references (e.g., Yale, Kim, *see* Deadshot) or an index would cut down dramatically on this space-wasting practice. Another redundancy is the constant repetition of subject headings and authors; one at the beginning of each section of material (and another if the section stretches over a page) would be more economical.

This work, flaws notwithstanding, will be a necessity for all libraries that support popular culture research. Other libraries, even those with substantial collections of graphic novels or comic books, will have to carefully judge their need for this kind of information before purchasing this expensive title.
—**D. A. Rothschild**

1406. Spicer, Dorothy Gladys. **Yearbook of English Festivals.** New York, H. W. Wilson, 1954; repr., Detroit, Omnigraphics, 1993. 298p. $38.00. GT4843.S6. 394.2'6'0942. LC 93-8916. ISBN 0-7808-0002-8.

In view of the many examples of travel literature, it is not surprising to see a reprinting of Spicer's volume after "only" 40 years. The main arrangement of the text is chronological, and background on local customs and traditions is sufficient to merit the volume a place in folklore collections. One is a bit taken aback by the section titled "England's 'Two' Calendars," which states that the local observances of many festivals listed are held on the "Old Style" date rather than on the "New Style" date, even though the calendar change was official in September 1752.

It is good that the research conducted so carefully on site so many years ago has reappeared in a bright, plastic-impregnated board cover. Recommended for serious travel and folklore collections if the original volume is missing or has been worn out by use.—**Eugene B. Jackson**

1407. Thompson, Don, and Maggie Thompson, eds. **Comic-Book Superstars.** Iola, Wis., Krause Publications, 1993. 255p. illus. $16.95. LC 93-77544. ISBN 0-87341-256-7.

Few reference books on the individuals who create comics have focused on the modern scene. Most cover historical figures, with a few current figures thrown in almost as an afterthought. Others deal primarily with the writers and artists of strips, neglecting the body of people whose work is confined to comic books. On the surface, *Comic-Book Superstars* fills this reference need by including "creators ... whose work has appeared in what we could determine were comic books which received wide potential distribution throughout the comic book direct market" (introduction). Entries, which are based on questionnaires and are thus not always complete, try to provide the person's name, address (personal, office, or agent), birth date and place, college or other advanced training, comics-related education, biggest creative influences, 1993 comics projects, past projects, favorite comics from other people, and dream project. While most of the individuals did answer all the questions, the amount of information they provided varies widely. The inclusion of photographs and self-portraits from some of the entrants is a nice touch, although they too vary in quality, some being sharp, others blurry. The book concludes with 12 birthday lists of people born in each month.

This work has two problems, one minor, one major. The minor problem is that the questions asked are not overly informative. While it is nice to know about the dream projects of cartoonists, such knowledge provides few insights into what makes these people tick. Users would find biographical questions more interesting and revealing (e.g., why did they become involved with comic books? Do they do anything else to support themselves? Have they encountered any difficulties in their work?). The book's major problem is its omission of a host of important figures in the genre, such as art spiegelman and Francoise Mouly, Rob Liefeld, and Alan Moore. The Thompsons acknowledge this problem—which, after all, is a hazard of questionnaire-based directories—in the introduction, but one wonders if they could have provided some basic information on significant individuals, as is done in the Marquis Who's Who books.

Overall, this book is not perfect, but it is the only work that provides data on many of these people. Its price is attractive for a hardcover and helps recommend it to public and college libraries, as well as fans and comic book store owners. It is hoped that a subsequent edition will address the problems mentioned.—**D. A. Rothschild**

27   Performing Arts

GENERAL WORKS

Bio-bibliography

1408. Billman, Larry. **Betty Grable: A Bio-Bibliography.** Westport, Conn., Greenwood Press, 1993. 306p. index. (Bio-bibliographies in the Performing Arts, no.40). $45.00. PN2287.G66B55. 791.43'028'092. LC 93-17579. ISBN 0-313-28156-4.

Although somewhat out of favor today with film historians, who dismiss her work as "fluff," Betty Grable, the "girl with the great gams," was a true movie star in every sense of the term. In a multifaceted career spanning 35 years, Grable distinguished herself as box-office gold in a series of musicals well represented by the 1943 release *Sweet Rosie O'Grady*. In that same year she posed for the immortal "Peek-a-Boo" swimsuit photograph, which not only proved to be the most popular pin-up of World War II but also became a popular culture icon.

Scriptwriter Billman has painstakingly compiled and annotated a comprehensive bio-bibliography on all facets of Grable's life and career, which amounts to a respectful tribute to an enduring star. A brief but illuminating biographical section is followed by a chronology of significant dates and occurrences in Grable's life. The filmography lists her 83 shorts and feature films and provides cast, credits, songs, synopsis, reviews, and comments on each of them. More significantly, Billman notes all of Grable's television, radio, stage, and nightclub appearances. For collectors of Grable memorabilia, he supplies invaluable chapters on the star's discography and collectibles. Also sure to be of interest to diehard Grable fans is a chapter on miscellanea that collects information on the star as diverse as her vital statistics and the location of her star on the Hollywood Walk of Fame. A concluding 218-item bibliography focuses on unique material about Grable. Sparsely illustrated, the volume contains an adequate index. Recommended for academic libraries supporting film collections or any institution owning other titles in the series.
—**David K. Frasier**

1409. Buehrer, Beverley Bare. **Boris Karloff: A Bio-Bibliography.** Westport, Conn., Greenwood Press, 1993. 283p. index. (Bio-bibliographies in the Performing Arts, no.39). $49.95. PN2287.K25B84. 791.43'028'092. LC 93-9587. ISBN 0-313-27715-X.

This book provides a comprehensive guide to the work of Boris Karloff and will contribute to an understanding of the actor beyond the enduring image of Frankenstein's monster. The extensive filmography and the lists of broadcast and recorded appearances point out that Karloff's thespian talents were successfully applied to nonmonster roles (in film and on stage) and to the interpretive reading of children's stories. In the casual biographical narrative, the author describes Karloff's birth in England as William Henry Pratt, his struggles to become an actor, his transformation into Boris Karloff, and his famous roles in Hollywood horror films. Factual sources about Karloff's personal life and early career are somewhat scarce, although Buehrer reports available information and anecdotes. The filmography describes 170 movies in which Karloff appeared or played the leading role. Each entry includes film credits, a plot synopsis, Buehrer's comments on the film's significance in cinematic history or to Karloff's career, and citations to reviews. The sections on stage appearances, radio and television broadcasts, and the discography contain citations to the works and brief annotations. The book includes a bibliography of books and periodical articles about Karloff. The index is adequate. A few publicity photographs illustrate Karloff's famous roles. This book should be selected for collections supporting research in the history of film and popular culture.—**Linda A. Naru**

1410. Horn, Barbara Lee. **Ellen Stewart and La Mama: A Bio-Bibliography.** Westport, Conn., Greenwood Press, 1993. 301p. index. (Bio-bibliographies in the Performing Arts, no.41). $59.95. PN2287.S6793H67. 792'.0232'092. LC 93-24755. ISBN 0-313-28734-1.

This volume deals with Ellen Stewart and the theater she founded. It contains a chronology of Stewart's life and association with her La Mama theater; a short biography of Stewart; a chronological list of 1,439 La Mama productions from 1962 to 1993 that gives their titles, opening dates, and authors; an annotated listing of book, newspaper, and periodical items that deal with Stewart and the theater; and a year-by-year list of awards given to Stewart and La Mama theater productions.

Stewart is indeed an important figure in the history of off-off-Broadway and experimental theater in the United States because of her nurturing and presentation of new plays and playwrights. Horn has provided an important service for historians by gathering together biographical citations where they can be used as a starting point for research.—**Charles Neuringer**

1411. Horn, Barbara Lee. **Colleen Dewhurst: A Bio-Bibliography.** Westport, Conn., Greenwood Press, 1993. 151p. index. (Bio-bibliographies in the Performing Arts, no.37). $39.95. PN2287.D462H6. 792'.028'092. LC 92-31652. ISBN 0-313-28733-3.

This volume includes a brief sketch of the life and career of one of America's foremost stage and film actresses; a comprehensive, annotated list of the productions in which she appeared or that she directed; and a bibliography of articles about her life and work. The entries about productions are arranged chronologically. Each entry for a film, television, or stage production contains a date of distribution or performance runs, cast, credits, citations to reviews, and (for the nonclassics) a plot synopsis. The section that lists writings about Dewhurst is also arranged chronologically, and each entry contains an annotation on the cited article. There is an index to titles of productions and people as well as a chronology of Dewhurst's life.

The biographical material is a bit choppy; the information on productions and citations to interviews and reviews are the most important resources in this bio-bibliography. The books, magazines, and newspapers cited will be found in most public libraries. This work is recommended for public libraries with popular film collections and for collections that support research in popular culture.—**Linda A. Naru**

1412. Jackson, Kathy Merlock. **Walt Disney: A Bio-Bibliography.** Westport, Conn., Greenwood Press, 1993. 347p. index. (Popular Culture Bio-bibliographies). $49.95. NC1766.U52D5437. 791.43'092. LC 92-19842. ISBN 0-313-25898-8.

One of the most important figures in American popular culture, Walt Disney has, curiously, never been well served by biographers, who usually have been either worshipful or gleefully accusatory. Nor has there been much bibliographical control or quality guidance over the body of material about him and his achievements. This work attempts to fill these gaps. Jackson's biography tends toward the friendly but is accurate as far as it goes, although it covers no new ground and is rather bland. Jackson emphasizes what Disney did over who he was, so that the biography, especially the latter part, reads like a history of Disney Studio's film and television releases; there is little about the man that might explain why he had such an impact. However, a series of interviews and articles by and about Disney offer a few insights into the public side of his personality.

More useful are the reference-oriented sections. The first of these, sandwiched between the biography and the interviews, is a series of paragraphs on Disney's impact on mass media and popular culture. Casual readers who vaguely associate him with animation and theme parks will be surprised to see just how many innovations he pioneered in these areas, not to mention his influence on television, children's literature, music, marketing, and even city planning (thanks to Disney World). The bibliographical essay will guide users to a variety of the best books and articles, both positive and negative, on the man and his achievements. The bibliographical checklist that follows the essay provides publication information for those works mentioned in the essay. Appendixes contain a chronology of the key events in the life of Disney and his company; a filmography that covers all of Disney's output, from the pre-Mickey Mouse series to the films produced after Disney died (1967) through 1992 (although recent cinematic shorts, such as *Tummy Trouble*, are not listed); television credits through 1992; awards through 1991; and Disney theme parks, including the proposed Port Disney. The index that concludes the book combines authors, titles, and subjects but is not comprehensive enough; for example, one cannot look under "strike, animator's" to be taken to that subject—one must know to look under the names of the two unions involved or under "wildcat strike at studio" in the entry on Disney. It would help if subentries under large topics were arranged alphabetically rather than in page/chronological order.

Valuable for its bibliography, this book has a place in libraries that support the study of popular culture, animation, mass media, comic art, or children's literature. Public libraries can consider it, although they will probably find that a full biography will get more use from their patrons. [R: Choice, Oct 93, p. 267]—**D. A. Rothschild**

1413. Kear, Lynn. **Agnes Moorehead: A Bio-Bibliography.** Westport, Conn., Greenwood Press, 1992. 276p. illus. (Bio-bibliographies in the Performing Arts, no.36). $45.00. PN2287.M698K4. 791.43'028'092. LC 92-28064. ISBN 0-313-28155-6.

This overview of the life and career of Agnes Moorehead serves as a comprehensive reference work for both researchers and her fans. The volume is illustrated by several black-and-white photographs. A brief biography, a chronology of her life events, and a list of awards and nominations precede chapters that document a notable career that spanned more than four decades. These chapters include an extensive filmography, which constitutes most of the book, and television, radio, and stage appearances, with accompanying media reviews. An annotated bibliography that covers information about Moorehead (other than reviews) in magazines, books, and newspapers is followed by an index that provides additional subject access to other sections of the volume. This work is a helpful and informative reference for its intended audience and supplements the history of the performing arts in the United States.—**Anita Zutis**

1414. McCready, Sam. **Lucille Lortel: A Bio-Bibliography.** Westport, Conn., Greenwood Press, 1993. 278p. index. (Bio-bibliographies in the Performing Arts, no.42). $59.95. PN2287.L653M37. 792'.0232'092. LC 93-23892. ISBN 0-313-27605-6.

Some theatergoers may enter the Lucille Lortel Theatre, one of New York's Greenwich Village off-Broadway houses, wondering who Lortel is. Knowledgeable members of the theater community will readily acknowledge that the "Queen of Off-Broadway," as she has been called, has been a positive force in the theater for many decades. She had a short but promising career as an actress in the 1920s but gave it up when she married. In the 1940s she turned a barn on her Westport, Connecticut, estate into the White Barn Theatre (which continues to operate). In the mid-1950s, her husband gave her the Theatre de Lys as a gift (it was renamed for her in 1981). She also produced plays on Broadway and was the artistic director of the ANTA (American National Theatre and Academy) Matinee Series, which operated in her theater for about twenty years. She has promoted risky new plays and revived worthy old ones, and has given roles to many young performers who have gone on to successful careers. Also, she never seemed to fear controversial subjects (e.g., AIDS) when others did. In short, she has been a vital force in the theater for many decades.

This book contains a brief biography of Lortel and sections related to her accomplishments. Those for her Broadway and off-Broadway productions have extensive entries for each work with credits, casts, review excerpts, and commentary. Those for the ANTA Matinee Series and the White Barn Theatre are shorter but contain appropriate information. Appendixes list her many awards and honors, an article about her matinee series, and a list of her sporadic productions at the Library of Congress. The illustrations in the book show her as a fetching young actress and as a distinguished personage more than 60 years later. The index covers everything. The excellent book deals not only with the life and career of a woman dedicated to the best that the world of the theater can offer but also with an important piece of theater history.

—**George Louis Mayer**

1415. Molt, Cynthia Marylee. **Vivien Leigh: A Bio-Bibliography.** Westport, Conn., Greenwood Press, 1993. 303p. index. (Bio-bibliographies in the Performing Arts, no.35). $45.00. PN2598.L46M65. 792'.028'092. LC 92-23785. ISBN 0-313-27578-5.

Vivien Leigh was a popular and skilled English stage and film actress for more than 30 years. She left her mark on our collective memories through her portrayal of Scarlett O'Hara in the film *Gone with the Wind*. This volume in the excellent Bio-bibliographies in the Performing Arts series is something of a disappointment. It consists of a preface, a biographical essay that takes up more than a third of the book, a chronology, stage appearance data, a filmography, a list of unrealized projects, awards and nominations, a videography, a list of radio and television appearances, a discography, a list of collectibles, a bibliography, archival resources, posthumous tributes, and a general index.

The biographical essay is somewhat flaccid and uncritical and too often bogs down with trivia. There is little effort made to illuminate the essence of Leigh's skills and accomplishments as an actress. Her documented bouts of mental illness, which seemed to have had profound effects on her life and work, are completely ignored. The reader would be better off to consult the various biographies cited in this work's biographical section. The resource information sections are extensive but sometimes loaded with irrelevant citations.

It is difficult to recommend this volume to the serious theater or film history scholar. Its main appeal may be to fans who want to know more about the actress.—**Charles Neuringer**

1416. Murphy, Donn B., and Stephen Moore. **Helen Hayes: A Bio-Bibliography.** Westport, Conn., Greenwood Press, 1993. 354p. illus. index. (Bio-bibliographies in the Performing Arts, no.38). $49.95. PN2287.H35M87. 792'.028'092. LC 93-83. ISBN 0-313-27793-1.

Helen Hayes was known as "the First Lady of American Theater," and this interesting bio-bibliography does justice to her long and successful career. The work opens with an insightful biography of the actress's life, which is followed by photographic highlights from her performances and a detailed chronology. Separate chapters are devoted to chronologically arranged stage, film, television, and radio performances. Where applicable, cast lists, synopses of productions, and reviews of Hayes's performances are included. The extensive annotated bibliography, arranged alphabetically, would have better served users if it had also been placed in chronological order. The bibliography has an unusual feature: the inclusion of photographs as separate entries. Because the list is extensive it could have been assigned to its own section or an appendix.

The work concludes with appendixes of awards and honors and tape and video recordings. There is a detailed index. Obviously a labor of love, this extensive work will be extremely useful to theatrical researchers and interesting to theater buffs. [R: Choice, Dec 93, p. 588]—**Christine E. King**

1417. Roberts, Jerry. **Robert Mitchum: A Bio-Bibliography.** Westport, Conn., Greenwood Press, 1992. 415p. index. (Bio-bibliographies in the Performing Arts, no.32). $47.95. PN2287.M648R63. 791.43'028'092. LC 92-23784. ISBN 0-313-27547-5.

Robert Mitchum made his film debut in 1943 playing a bit part in a Hopalong Cassidy western. Fifty years and more than 100 films later, Mitchum is recognized as one of Hollywood's great natural actors and also as one of its perennial bad boys. His busts, brawls, and controversies are legendary. Roberts has exhaustively researched Mitchum's career for this bio-bibliography. The massive annotated bibliography cites 1,311 books and articles from sources as diverse as the *Daily Mail, Variety, Women's Wear Daily*, and the *National Enquirer*. Roberts also conducted a lengthy interview with the usually taciturn Mitchum.

The volume begins with a short, discreet biography and a chronological filmography that provides, for each of Mitchum's films, credits, cast, a synopsis, review quotations, and interesting anecdotes. It is unfortunate that the review citations are so incomplete (e.g., "Archer Winston, *New York Post*"—no date, issue, or page number is listed); researchers could find them difficult to track down. A television credits section describes Mitchum's television roles and appearances, while other sections summarize his stage, recording, and writing credits; radio appearances; and awards (not all of them flattering). Brief film credits are also given for Mitchum family members (his brother and sister and several of his children and grandchildren had acting careers).

Roberts has collected an enormous amount of information. Cinema research collections will want to acquire this book.—**Joseph W. Palmer**

1418. Woods, Jeannie M. **Maureen Stapleton: A Bio-Bibliography.** Westport, Conn., Greenwood Press, 1992. 158p. index. (Bio-bibliographies in the Performing Arts, no.34). $42.95. PN2287.S675W66. 792'.028'092. LC 92-23787. ISBN 0-313-27761-3.

As the first bio-bibliography of Maureen Stapleton, a well-known and highly respected stage actress and film/television star, this is a long-awaited work. Stapleton has won many awards, including Oscar, Emmy, and Tony awards. Her artistic growth and development is reviewed in the biographical section of this book. A chronology highlights important moments in her career and private life. The major part of the volume lists her stage, television, and film performances in three separate sections. A selective bibliography is divided into two sections: citations to interviews, archival sources, photographic essays, and biographical and general references from her career; and selected reviews of individual film, television, and stage productions. There is an index of her performances and cross-references to the volume as a whole, and an appendix lists nominations, awards, and honors.

The bibliographical citations frequently do not include page numbers but seem to cover most of Stapleton's performances, from her first Broadway appearance in 1946 (in *The Playboy of the Western World*) through one of her last performances in 1992 (*Last Wish*, a television performance on the right-to-die issue). The sections on film and television performances note whether video productions are available and the companies that produced them. Citations included in the major sections of stage, television, and film performances include dates, length of production, credits, cast, synopsis, a summary of reviews, and commentary.—**Maureen Pastine**

Dictionaries and Encyclopedias

1419. Ogden, Tom. **Two Hundred Years of the American Circus: From Aba-Daba to the Zoppe-Zavatta Troupe.** New York, Facts on File, 1993. 402p. illus. index. $50.00. GV1815.O33. 791.3'03. LC 92-31880. ISBN 0-8160-2611-4.

This handbook and guide to 200 years of the American circus, as distinguished from British or Continental, covers just about everything one might want to know. Entries vary in length from a few lines to several pages, with many cross-references in the text and many *see also* references at the end of important articles. About one-third of the entries are biographical, such as those for P. T. Barnum, Joseph Gatti, Annie Oakley, Jenny Lind, and other lesser-known personalities that either organized or performed under the big top from about 1793 to 1993. Another portion contains subject entries on such topics as clowns, cyclists, circuses, the flying trapeze, horses, midgets, passing leap, push pole, and other terms known to the public. Interspersed with them are items of circus jargon, such as dukey run (a two-day engagement with only a box lunch, a dukey, on the second day), gennie (a portable generator), giraffe (an extra-high unicycle), and kinker. Also, there are historical articles on all of the great circus companies whose names have become synonymous with circus life in the United States, such as Ringling Brothers, Buffalo Bill's Wild West, and Sells-Floto Circus.

This book does not give much space to magical tricks or escape artists, although some have appeared in circuses. Harry Houdini is not listed. But famous elephants, such as King Tusk (50 years old in 1992 but still on the road), are given as much space as their trainers or fellow performers. An especially valuable article deals with some 75 movies that portray, in whole or in part, some aspects of circus life. Besides cross-references, whenever a main-entry word or name is mentioned in the articles, the text is printed in boldface type to indicate further information. There are many black-and-white illustrations throughout. In addition, there are a good bibliography and a full index. This is an excellent reference work on a little-known topic. [R: LJ, Aug 93, p. 96; RBB, 1 Dec 93, p. 717]—**Raymund F. Wood**

Directories

1420. **Handel's National Directory for the Performing Arts.** 5th ed. New Providence, N.J., R. R. Bowker/Reed Reference Publishing, 1992. 2v. index. $250.00/set. LC 73-646635. ISBN 0-8352-3250-6.

This edition of the resource directory for the performing arts is an update of the 1988 version. The first volume deals with dance, instrumental and vocal music, theater, and performing arts organizations and facilities. The second volume concerns itself with educational institution programs in the performing arts. The data were gathered through mail and telephone surveys and literature searches. The citations are presented alphabetically by state and territory. Within each state, separate citations for dance, music, theater, and the like are given for each alphabetically arranged community.

Each citation in volume 1 ideally contains name, address, telephone number, name of artistic and administrative personnel, board members, number of staff, budget and attendance statistics, founding date, and performance facilities. The citations for volume 2 carry much of the same information but also include courses, degrees, number of faculty and students, technical training, and financial assistance. The completeness of each citation varies. Besides a general index there are indexes to special dance, instrumental music, vocal music, theater, performing series, and facilities.

This directory provides valuable information about thousands of performing arts programs. But, as can be expected in a work of such scope, incomplete and out-of-date citations and omissions do occur. The reader should use this reference work in conjunction with other directories. [R: LJ, 1 May 93, p. 82; RBB, Aug 93, p. 2090]—**Charles Neuringer**

Handbooks and Yearbooks

1421. Smith, Leon. **Famous Hollywood Locations: Descriptions and Photographs of 382 Sites....** Jefferson, N.C., McFarland, 1993. 354p. illus. index. $45.00. PN1995.67.L67S64. 791.43'025'79494. LC 92-56697. ISBN 0-89950-886-3.

For devotees of Hollywood movies and television shows shot on location, this text provides both history and locale. It describes and locates various sites used in such shows, arranging its material geographically. Smith has as his primary audience those people interested in such shows and wishing to visit the sites used in filming sequences. Each entry includes a synopsis of the significant movie or television show filmed at the site, mentions other shows and films that employed the same site, provides information on the particular scenes in which the site figured, and includes bits of California, movie, or television history. The text includes numerous photographs, most taken since 1980, and indicates the changes that have occurred at the site between its initial appearance in the film and the present. Having verified the accuracy of his information through research and field trips, Smith also includes keys to finding these places on the Thomas Brothers map of Los Angeles, both old and revised versions, to aid the would-be visitor. The book certainly meets its intended purpose, although its tone is somewhat starstruck and its purpose seems slight for library binding.—**Rebecca Jordan**

DANCE

1422. **Bibliographic Guide to Dance 1991: Seventeenth Supplement [to]** *Dictionary Catalog of the Dance Collection.* New York, G. K. Hall, 1992. 3v. (Bibliographic Guides). $450.00/set. ISBN 0-8161-7157-2. ISSN 0360-2737.

This annual supplement is an extensive subject bibliography and list of materials cataloged by the New York Public Library's Dance Collection from September 1990 through August 1991. The collection is believed to be the most comprehensive one of its kind, including nonbook and printed materials in various languages and periodical indexing on all aspects and forms of dance.

The format is similar to that in previous supplements. Access is by main entry, added entries, subject headings, titles, series titles, and geographical names. An alphabetical sequence provides full bibliographical information for each nonbook entry and for main entries of book materials. Secondary entries for these materials contain condensed citations. Up to five subdivisions (e.g., "works about," "audio materials") may be used under a heading to ensure that diverse materials related to a subject are grouped together.

The liberal use of cross-references and scope and history notes enhances the usefulness of this guide. It is invaluable to collections and to researchers involved with any aspect of dance.—**Anita Zutis**

1423. Bremser, Martha, and Larraine Nicholas, eds. **International Dictionary of Ballet.** Detroit, St. James Press, 1993. 2v. illus. index. $230.00/set. GV1585.I57. 792.8'03. LC 93-25051. ISBN 1-55862-084-2.

This comprehensive reference resource on ballet has thorough coverage of international performances, stressing North America, Europe, and Russia; there is a minor amount of data on modern dance. Covered are biographies of dancers, choreographers, companies, designers, composers, librettists, and teachers. Along with performances, the editors review dancers, ballet roles, and choreographers' works. Designed to provide access for students, performers, scholars, researchers, and general readers, the compendium lists entries in alphabetical order and includes a generous sprinkling of photographs and drawings, such as a drawing of Carolina Rosati's 1847 London portrayal of Thea.

An unusually clear and accessible listing, this book opens with a succinct editors' note followed by a note on sources and a list of advisers and contributors. Signed entries follow a clear pattern, as with the entry for Twyla Tharp, which gives a highly compressed overview of her biography, including training and career highlights. A time line of her works follows, naming for each the date, program, and performance place and city. An appended list of other works gives her videos and television presentations. The entry concludes with a bibliography of works by and about Tharp, a full-page photograph of her at work with Mikhail Baryshnikov, and a lengthy discussion of her art. At the end of volume 2 the editors list entries by country and by professions and institutions and conclude with brief notes on contributors. The writing, which is informative, straightforward, and concise, is suited to this substantive dictionary.
—**Mary Ellen Snodgrass**

1424. **Index to Dance Periodicals: 1991.** New York, G. K. Hall, 1993. 546p. $125.00. ISBN 0-8161-0574-X. ISSN 1058-6350.

G. K. Hall's annual guide to periodical literature on dance and dance-related topics is a lengthy bibliography drawn from a larger body of data on the same subject. Covered in this indexing are biographies, obituaries, performances, features, interviews, news articles, and reviews of books, videos, television programs, and movies. Designed to provide access for students, performers, scholars, researchers, and general readers, the compendium lists in alphabetical order and describes articles from 86 American and international journals and periodicals published in the calendar year, such as *Arabesque, Folk Music Journal* (England); *India: Magazine of Her People and Culture* (India); *Monsalvat* (Spain); *New York Woman; Parabola*; and the *UCLA Journal of Dance Ethnology* (United States).

An unusually clear and accessible listing, this book opens with a succinct preface and precise notes on how to use the index, including criteria for inclusion, arrangement, title styles, references, reviews, and a brief citation format illustrated by a 10-item sample entry, which is labeled and explained. Preceding the body of the index are an overview of periodicals and a separate list of addresses for each. The text is well organized with guide words, clear (if terribly small) typefaces, a balance of boldface type to set off citations, and cross-references in all capital letters. Subject entries cover a variety of related materials (e.g., Germany [East], statistics, women choreographers). Although this index is highly specialized and quite expensive for the average library, it is valuable to arts critics, teachers, librarians, dance professionals, historians, and appreciators of the world of dance.—**Mary Ellen Snodgrass**

1425. Schonberg, Bent, and others, eds. **World Ballet and Dance 1992-93: An International Yearbook.** London, Dance Books; distr., Pennington, N.J., Princeton Book, 1993. 329p. illus. $29.95pa. ISBN 1-85273-042-0.

Schonberg's annual review of dance contains useful, if limited, overviews of the key performances of most nations of the world. Researchers, professional dancers, and interested parties are provided with brief glimpses of programs and critical commentary on the direction taken by companies and choreographers, as demonstrated by the mixed results of performances by the National Ballet of Canada in the 1992-1993 season. These critiques, which tend to be crisp, succinct, and incisive, are not without compassion for the world market, as demonstrated by the entry on Cuba's troubled economy and the need for pointe shoes. Likewise, *World Ballet and Dance* places within the political milieu the efforts of Pace Dance and other troupes attempting to serve the creative tastes and needs of South Africa, where the struggle for reform enlivens and inspires the art scene. A generous, dignified historical note appears in part I with the obituaries of Kenneth MacMillan and Rudolf Nureyev.

Essential to this annual's accessibility are an appealing color cover (which goes uncredited in the text); attractive typography and layout; 38 black-and-white photographs; and addresses, telephone and fax numbers, various directors (general, lighting, and music), choreographers, guest teachers, set designers, administrators, principals and guest dancers, size of the corps de ballet, number of performances, tours, and premieres for major companies (which are alphabetized by country). This book has value, both as critique and reference tool, for the arts critic, teacher, librarian, dance professional, historian, and appreciator of the world of dance.—**Mary Ellen Snodgrass**

FILM

Bibliography

1426. Cella, Catherine. **Great Videos for Kids: A Parent's Guide to Choosing the Best.** New York, Citadel Press/Carol Publishing Group, 1992. 157p. index. $7.95pa. PN1992.945.C45. 016.79143'75'083. LC 92-31006. ISBN 0-8065-1377-2.

This really should be called "Great Non-Movie Videos for Kids" because, except for animated films, no movies are included in this delightful guide. This work contains reviews of videos arranged in several categories: animation, book-based, educational, family topics (including sections on dramas and documentaries, drugs, the environment, and sex education), folk and fairy tales, holidays, instruction (including arts, dance and exercise, sports, and miscellaneous), and music. Each entry lists the company that produced the video, the approximate running time, a recommended viewing age (which may differ from what is on the video box), and a fun-to-read annotation. No price information is included. The videos selected for this guide had to meet professional standards of video and audio production and also had to have little or no violence, racial stereotyping, or gender bias. Those videos that are particularly outstanding are preceded by a star. A video suppliers list provides names, addresses, and telephone numbers; a title index is also included. Cella has also put together a baker's dozen of best lists, such as best birthday party video, best first video for toddlers, best bedtime videos, best dinosaur videos, and best detective videos. Most of these videos are listed in other source books; however, this work has style. Public libraries will want a copy or two.—**Robert L. Turner, Jr.**

1427. Hecht, Hermann. **Pre-Cinema History: An Encyclopaedia and Annotated Bibliography of the Moving Image before 1896.** New Providence, N.J., published in association with the British Film Institute by Bowker-Saur/Reed Reference Publishing, 1993. 476p. illus. index. $155.00. ISBN 1-85739-056-3.

Prior to his death in 1985, Hecht had devoted more than 30 years to compiling and meticulously annotating the history of pre-cinema to 1896 as it was chronicled in nearly 400 international publications and numerous other works. His wife's decision to edit and publish this monumental 3,700-entry volume in association with the British Film Institute constitutes one of the major events in cinema studies reference publishing. Chronologically arranged entries spanning the period between 1321 and 1985 trace the development of pre-cinema, from the camera obscura to more sophisticated forms of optical entertainment, such as the Victorian era's Dowcra Triple Lantern. Hecht's annotations, more accurately miniessays, simplify complex technical ideas, place the various devices into historical context, and unerringly refer the researcher to related material. In essence, they constitute a tireless scholar's personal notes on the material he compiled and assimilated for future publication. As such, many entries contain long passages lifted directly from the original source but footnoted by the author. Name and subject indexes are detailed and provide adequate access to the annotations. An eight-page illustration section reproduces original engravings from historical sources and charts the evolution of pre-optical devices, from their earliest astronomical and technical applications to their exploitation in the area of popular entertainment (which, by making motion picture projection possible, gave birth to an entire industry).

While the scope of this work primarily limits it to film centers and large research libraries supporting film studies programs, it also offers interesting insights into the social and economic history of a nascent industry that have dramatic implications for other areas of social science. Highly recommended. [R: Choice, Nov 93, pp. 432-434; LAR, Aug 93, p. 461]—**David K. Frasier**

1428. Rocks, David T. **W. C. Fields—An Annotated Guide: Chronology, Bibliographies, Discography, Filmographies, Press Books, Cigarette Cards, Film Clips and Impersonators.** Jefferson, N.C., McFarland, 1993. 131p. illus. index. $27.50. PN2287.F45R6. 016.79143'028'092. LC 92-56688. ISBN 0-89950-794-8.

This reviewer is skeptical of works whose authors tell you how comprehensive they are compared to similar works. But despite Rocks's self-promotion in the introduction, this book is an impressive collection of Fieldsiana. Although the subtitle is somewhat misleading (it contains one bibliography and one filmography and, frankly, who needs more?), the book as a whole is an extensive collection of literature and ephemera. The chronology follows Fields's career from birth through his various occupations as vaudevillian, juggler, actor, and radio personality, primarily by listing shows with which Fields was involved. Interjections by the author provide missing personal information or elucidate entries. The bibliography lists press books and typescripts in addition to books, periodicals, and pamphlets. The filmography entries for Fields's films list producer, director, cast, part played by Fields, availability, and playing time (in a bothersome inconsistency, Rocks occasionally lists a film's number of reels rather than time length). Rocks notes advertisement tie-ins and mentions which scripts Fields authored. In the section on music and recordings, sheet music entries name study books, not scores. "Miscellaneous" includes cigarette cards and Fields impersonators. Rocks also notes pertinent impersonator scenes in films. A few interesting illustrations, such as copies of a handbill, a radio script, and cartoons, break up the text. Entries are numbered continuously and referenced in the index. Recommended for comprehensive film and Fields collections.—**Glynys R. Thomas**

1429. Rovin, Jeff. **The Laserdisc Film Guide: Complete Ratings for the Best and Worst Movies Available on Disc.** 1993-1994 ed. New York, St. Martin's Press, 1993. 320p. $15.95pa. PN1992.95.R68. 016.79143'75. LC 92-33340. ISBN 0-312-08703-9.

This is a timely first book in a proposed series that takes advantage of the resurgence of laser discs (also called videodiscs) as a form of home entertainment. In a twist on the usual movie guide format, this guide not only reviews films on videodisc but also critiques the technical quality of the discs. Approximately 300 laser discs (of some 7,000) available in the United States are included. Selections represent each genre and include films of better-known directors. An enthusiast, the author describes the laser disc's evolution, provides information on reputable suppliers and recommends two periodicals devoted to laser discs: *LaserScene Monthly* and *Laser Disc Newsletter*.

Alphabetized by film title, each entry includes a movie rating, director, and running time, followed by two reviews. The first reviews the film; the second covers technical aspects of the laser disc version, including audio and video quality, the presence or absence of chapters (a term that is not explained) and letterboxing, and format. The distributor is also listed. Film reviews average 500 words; technical reviews are shorter. A helpful (but incomplete) glossary is included at the end of the book.

Laser disc collectors, public libraries, and libraries that collect laser discs will want to own a copy. Libraries with volumes of *The Laser Video File* (New Visions, 1991-) will probably not need to purchase this book. [R: RBB, 15 Mar 93, p. 1377]—**Glynys R. Thomas**

Biography

1430. Cook, Samantha, ed. **International Dictionary of Films and Filmmakers. [Volume] 4: Writers and Production Artists.** 2d ed. Detroit, St. James Press, 1993. 836p. illus. $115.00. ISBN 1-55862-040-0.

The making of a feature film entails the collaborative efforts of hundreds, sometimes thousands, of people. While some people can name who starred in a film, and the *cognoscenti* can supply the director's name, how many know the name of the person who made all those neat horror masks in the last fright flick or wrote the pounding score that made the chase scenes seem even scarier? This fourth volume of a revised five-volume set honors those unsung heroes of the film industry: production artists. The term is intentionally vague, encompassing many specialized fields, including (but not limited to) art directors, animators, cinematographers, costume designers, composers, arrangers, lyricists, editors, choreographers, stunt coordinators, special effects personnel, and sound technicians. This large tome contains 530 entries, each supplied with a brief biographical reference, a complete filmography, a selected bibliography of articles about the person, and a dissertative critical essay by a specialist in the field. There are 62 new entrants in the work, and all the other information has been updated and revised since the publication of the first edition. One definitional change: Animators, once classed, curiously, with directors, are now included as production artists, which seems only right and fitting.

For non-English film titles (of which there are many in this book), translations (or alternate translations, where there is discrepancy) and transliterations are furnished. Throughout the tiny-print glossy pages are scattered frequent black-and-white photographs of persons discussed or stills and lobby cards of the actors in their movies. Not surprisingly, few of these names are household words, or ever were, but that is the special value of this volume. A cross-reference index from personal names to film titles would have made it ever better. The whole set is recommended as essential for both the serious film scholar and for the settling of bar bets about who gave the Creature from the Black Lagoon that mangy costume and such a silly grin.—**Bruce A. Shuman**

1431. Karney, Robyn, ed. **The Hollywood Who's Who: The Actors and Directors in Today's Hollywood.** New York, Continuum; distr., Detroit, Gale, 1993. 499p. $42.50. PN1988.2.W46. 791.43'028092'273. LC 93-18636. ISBN 0-8264-0632-7.[Also available in paperback from Continuum. $18.95pa. ISBN 0-8264-0588-6.]

Profiling approximately 600 contemporary actors, actresses, and directors, this compilation covers an eclectic assortment of individuals, ranging from young actresses, such as Winona Ryder, to screen veterans, such as Gregory Peck, to figures outside the mainstream, such as Divine. Although a few deceased performers are featured, the emphasis is on individuals who are currently acting or directing in Hollywood. Presumably, lack of the Hollywood connection is what excluded Emma Thompson and Kenneth Branagh, but other notable omissions, such as Richard Attenborough, Ben Kingsley, and Bridget Fonda, are difficult to justify.

The alphabetically arranged entries were written by the editor and 10 additional contributors, most of whom are British film critics and journalists. Ranging in length from 500 to 1,500 words, entries include basic biographical information, but their primary strength lies in their film commentary, which is almost always entertaining, provocative, and opinionated. For instance, Kim Basinger is described as having "limited talent" and Jami Gertz as an "actress with no apparent qualifications for the job." The chronologically arranged filmography at the end of each profile unfortunately excludes made-for-television films, thus depriving the user of a complete picture of a performer's or director's career. Also, filmographies are not always reliable; for example, *Little Miss Marker* is omitted from Julie Andrews's list of films. Although some 1993 releases (e.g., *The Remains of the Day, The Age of Innocence*) are included, other films released earlier in the year (e.g., *The Fugitive, Sleepless in Seattle*) are not.

This volume covers more of today's American actors and directors in greater depth than any other single source. However, it is flawed by numerous typographical errors, sloppy research (e.g., Julia Roberts was born in Symrna, not Atlanta, and her parents conducted theater workshops in Atlanta, not Atlantic City), and inconsistency in currency between entries (e.g., *Jurassic Park* is omitted from Sam Neill's filmography, but it appears in Laura Dern's and Jeff Goldblum's).—**Marie Ellis**

1432. Parish, James Robert, and Don Stanke. **Hollywood Baby Boomers.** Hamden, Conn., Garland, 1992. 670p. illus. index. (Garland Reference Library of the Humanities, v.1295). $75.00. PN2285.P333. 791.43'028'092273. LC 91-38768. ISBN 0-8240-6104-7.

Hollywood baby boomers are defined in this biographical dictionary as actors and actresses born between 1946 and 1964. Because of space limitations, only a few members of the baby boomer generation—50 men and 30 women—are portrayed. The names range from Glenn Close and Mel Gibson to Gregory Harrison and Mandy Patinkin.

Every biography begins with a quotation from the featured individual that gives the reader a glimpse into that person's mindset (e.g., "I would never take a part irresponsibly, knowing that the media so strongly affects our society" [Lindsay Wagner]). The biographies continue to define their subjects by relaying aspects of their lives that have given them their direction, such as childhood incidents, personal interests, and acting accomplishments. Each biography is accurate as of March 1991. The entries conclude with complete filmographies and lists of television series, albums, and future releases. A complete index concludes the text and includes a listing of actors and actresses who are not featured but who are mentioned throughout.

The use of footnotes would have given validity to the text. Most quotations are cited with a resource, but some are unsubstantiated, making the accuracy of the statement debatable (e.g., "One bio revealed that his mood swings ranged from aloofness, when he chose to be remote, to friendliness and conviviality" [Tom Berenger]). Included with each biography is a movie still of the personality. While most are characteristic of the individuals, a few do not give fair representations of the celebrities. The photograph of Cybill Shepherd, for example, is from the movie *The Heartbreak Kid* and displays a profile view of her, with most of the picture consisting of her co-stars. With their extensive background in the writing of Hollywood biographies, the authors have delivered well-researched and thought-provoking biographies that are informative as well as entertaining.—**Deborah A. Taylor**

Dictionaries and Encyclopedias

1433. McAlister, Micheal J. **The Language of Visual Effects.** Los Angeles, Calif., Lone Eagle, 1993. 160p. illus. index. $18.95pa. TR858.M325. 778.5'345'03. LC 92-16846. ISBN 0-943728-47-9.

McAlister, who worked on the visual effects in such films as *E.T.* and *Die Hard 2* and who won an Oscar for *Indiana Jones and the Temple of Doom*, knows from experience the difficulty many in the film industry have understanding the jargon used by visual effects people. Thus he has compiled this concise, up-to-date glossary of commonly used terms. These include such highly specialized expressions as "garbage matte," "glow pass," "rod puppet," and "rough composite" as well as more general filmmaking and computer terms that are important to the field. Definitions are brief and specific and should be understandable to the layperson who is familiar with the basics of film technology. When words used in a definition are themselves defined elsewhere, they are written in capitals. This creates an effective and extensive network of cross-references. The volume is especially useful for its thorough coverage of computer-based effects. It includes dozens of clear illustrations and color plates. The volume concludes with three useful indexes that list terms relating to computer graphics, to blue screen and optics, and to plates and illustrations. This is a handy and authoritative publication.—**Joseph W. Palmer**

1434. Moston, Doug. **Coming to Terms with Acting: An Instructive Glossary.** New York, Drama Book, 1993. 202p. $16.95pa. PN2061.M67. 792'.03. LC 93-4440. ISBN 0-89676-121-5.

Moston attempts to define a set of terms used in actor training and acting theory. While most of the defined terms come primarily from the method approach to acting, some technical terms (e.g., "stage right," "stage left," "arena stage") are discussed. Each entry starts with a one-line definition followed by an extended discussion. The quality and quantity of the discussions vary from perfunctory to historically and anecdotally rich. Moston sometimes supplies exercises to illustrate his definitional discussions. The writing is lively and humorous, so the book is a pleasure to read. The volume will be of great use to those who are bewildered by the often arcane language used in discussions of acting technique (especially those terms used by the adherents of method acting). While other acting theorists will probably not endorse all of Moston's definitions, this volume is an excellent start toward developing a common language for theater workers. [R: LJ, 15 Sept 93, p. 69]—**Charles Neuringer**

Directories

1435. Rodriguez, Paul Anthony, ed. **Big Screen Book.** Los Angeles, Calif., Homily Press; distr., Gardena, Calif., SCB Distributors, 1993. 1v. (unpaged). $39.00pa. ISBN 0-9637522-1-9.

This is a strange book. In the introduction it says that this work is divided into sections that correspond to the different aspects of production and distribution and that these are listed in the table of contents. But there is no table of contents, and the work is divided into two sections that are divided neither by aspects of production nor distribution. One section is called "The Companies," and the other is "The Players." In the first section, companies are listed in alphabetical order, with address and telephone and fax numbers. (Nowhere are criteria for inclusion given.) Some key people and their titles are also listed. Next for each company is a small section that lists some of the movies that it produced. In "The Players," the names of the key people in "The Companies" are arranged in alphabetical order along with their company name and telephone number.

If one knows a company or an executive, one can find them in the book, but if one is looking for a guide to production companies and the types of materials they produce, this book is inadequate. Not recommended.—**Robert L. Turner, Jr.**

1436. Shiri, Keith, comp. and ed. **Directory of African Film-Makers and Films.** Westport, Conn., Greenwood Press, 1993. 194p. index. $79.50. PN1993.5.A35S48. 016.79143'0233'09226. LC 92-22105. ISBN 0-313-28756-2.

Most movie-going Americans can name very few African films and may find it startling to learn just how many have been made in the past 65 years. *African*, in the context of this book, refers to every nation on the continent, not (as is often intended by the term) Africa south of the Sahara. In all, directors from 29 nations are represented, from Algeria to Zimbabwe. Thus, in addition to significant filmmakers from the "Black" African countries, there are numerous contributors from the Arabic-speaking world. English and French are the principal languages of African film, but other languages represented include Afrikaans; Arabic; Portuguese; Italian; and native tongues such as Amharic, Bambara, Dyula, Hausa, Malagasy, and Swahili.

The principal arrangement of the entries is alphabetical by director's surname, with brief biographical sketches provided from returned questionnaires and supplemented, where available, by other sources. Each named person has a filmography that gives titles and years. It would be nice if some descriptive information were provided about the films, but all that is given is title, title translated into English (where necessary), alternative titles (where extant), and year. The biographical information is uneven, depending on what was supplied, and emphasizes the film-related aspects of the director's life. Annoyingly, some titles vary considerably; it is not unusual for a film to have three or four different names. The second part of the work consists of several cross-indexes, in which film titles, educational institutions, film organizations, and mentioned people are separately listed. To the film-literate, but nonspecialist, Westerner, there will be few familiar names or titles (except, perhaps, for the celebrated *The Gods Must Be Crazy* and its sequel), but Shiri, who works at the African Centre in London, has done a good job of organizing the filmic output of an entire continent over 65 years. Because this book covers such an esoteric subject and is priced so high, libraries and special collections will want to evaluate it for purchase based on need. [R: Choice, Mar 93, p. 1120]—**Bruce A. Shuman**

Filmography

1437. Del Vecchio, Deborah, and Tom Johnson. **Peter Cushing: The Gentle Man of Horror and His 91 Films.** Jefferson, N.C., McFarland, 1992. 465p. illus. index. $45.00. PN2598.C94D4. 791.43'028'092. LC 92-50302. ISBN 0-89950-654-2.

Del Vecchio, former president, and Johnson, an early member, of the American Peter Cushing Club, have put together a fascinating filmography on their idol. All his 91 films are here, including some that have never been released and those in which his part was completely edited out. There are full credits and a cast listing for each endeavor. The dates used are by year of production and therefore are generally earlier than those given in other sources. The titles used are the U.S. release titles, which may lead to some confusion because several of Cushing's films had different titles in different countries. A synopsis, which sometimes is not clear, is given for each film. This is then followed by a section of commentary that contains excerpts from reviews and some of Cushing's comments about the work. The authors have tried to include all known television, stage, and radio appearances of Cushing during his film career. There is also a detailed index.

Cushing comes across in this book as a wonderful human being, an actor's actor who never gave a bad performance but whose choice of films was sometimes detrimental to his career. It is a shame that such great talent was spent in so many forgettable films. This work will be of great interest to those who enjoy Peter Cushing and horror pictures. Large film collections will want a copy.—**Robert L. Turner, Jr.**

1438. Enser's Filmed Books and Plays: A List of Books and Plays from Which Films Have Been Made, 1928-1991. Ellen Baskin and Mandy Hicken, comps. Brookfield, Vt., Ashgate Publishing, 1993. 970p. index. $69.95. ISBN 1-85742-026-8.

For those of us who want to see if the book was better than the movie, this is the source to use. It has more than 6,000 entries covering sound films and is divided into 3 main sections. The film title index is the heart of the volume. Films are listed in alphabetical order, giving the title; studio name and country of origin; date of release; director; author and title of book (if the book title differs from that of the film); an indication if the film was adapted from a play; an indication of whether it is an animated film, a children's film, a television movie, or a television miniseries; and whether it is available on video. The second section is the author index, which lists the authors of the books and plays and refers to the films made from the literary works. The third section is the "Change of Original Title" index, which lists new titles given to films. There are three additional indexes for musicals, made-for-television movies, and animated films. In these indexes, only the names are given; one must go back to the film title index to get the rest of the information. There are also lists of country abbreviations and of production and distribution companies. This work will be used in the reference collection as well as in the circulating collection. Highly recommended. [R: Choice, Nov 93, p. 423; LAR, Aug 93, p. 461; RBB, 1 Nov 93, p. 562]

—**Robert L. Turner, Jr.**

1439. Film Superlist: Motion Pictures in the U.S. Public Domain, 1940-1949. updated ed. By Walter E. Hurst. D. Richard Baer, ed. Hollywood, Calif., Hollywood Film Archive, 1992. 662p. index. $345.00. PN1998.H85. 016.79143'75'097309044. LC 92-9041. ISBN 0-913616-27-3.

This book is a value-added copy of the *Catalog of Copyright Entries, Cumulative Series, Motion Pictures 1940-1949* published by the Library of Congress in 1953 and available in many depository libraries. (Volumes 1 and 3, also available from Hollywood Film Archive, cover the years 1894-1939 and 1950-1959.) Alphabetically arranged entries of film titles in the original catalog show original copyright owner, registration date and number, production credits, distribution company, story content, and play or novel (if any) from which the film was adapted. An index lists persons and organizations associated with each motion picture. *Film Superlist* bullets those films for which copyright has been renewed and adds a handwritten renewal registration number and renewal date. Slightly more than half of the copyrights in this volume were renewed; copyrights that were not renewed during the twenty-eighth year after original registration are probably lost, and the films go into the public domain. One caveat: The introduction states "the lack of a renewal is no guarantee that a film has lost all copyright protection," and not all renewals are valid. Readers are advised to obtain a copyright search report from the Copyright Office and to consult an attorney if necessary.

The writers have aided the entrepreneur—who might wish to track down a film print and reproduce it for video distribution—by starring approximately 400 significant titles for which no copyright renewal was found. These are gathered in an appendix that quotes exact text from Copyright Office search reports for each title. Key actors and characters, such as Paul Muni, Claude Rains, and Anne Baxter in *Angel on My Shoulder* or the Academy Award-winning Three Little Pigs cartoon *Pigs in a Polka*, are highlighted in each entry. Copyright renewal information was transcribed from the *Catalog of Copyright Entries*. Libraries that wish to assist patrons in performing their own searches should own *Researching Copyright Renewal* (Rothman, 1989). Those that have extensive film collections or receive many questions on copyright may find *Film Superlist* well worth the price. [R: LJ, 1 Feb 93, p. 72]—**Deborah V. Rollins**

1440. Hayes, R. M. **The Republic Chapterplays: A Complete Filmography of the Serials Released by Republic Pictures Corporation, 1934-1955.** Jefferson, N.C. McFarland, 1992. 165p. illus. index. $32.50. PN1995.9.S3H38. 016.79143'75'0973. LC 92-50305. ISBN 0-89950-665-8.

The term *chapterplay* may not win instant recognition in the minds of today's adults, but between 1934 and 1955 chapterplays were eagerly sought, avidly watched, and generally acclaimed. A form of serial (not to be confused with shorts, which were self-contained with tidy denouements), chapterplays were stories told in series, each installment having a terrifying and seemingly hopeless ending (from which the expression "cliffhanger" came) that impelled viewers to visit the theater the following week to see how the hero or heroine would get out of the predicament.

Author and filmmaker Hayes bills this work as a complete filmography, rather than a narrative discussion, and provides complete documentation for each of nearly 70 serialized adventure films. The work begins with a long and informative introduction, but that is all the narrative or prose that appears. Whereas Tom Weaver, in his *Poverty Row Horrors!* (McFarland, 1992) provided gossip about his film subjects, Hayes just chronologically lists the serialized films he has selected (all from Republic or a satellite company), with complete casts, episode names, figures, and dates.

This work, while displaying meticulous and impressive scholarship, is not for all film collections. Those seeking titillation or the previously unrevealed indiscretions of marginal old-time actors and moviemakers are advised to look elsewhere. If, on the other hand, one wants to know the name of the man who played "sailor/bushwacker[sic]/Rama/Fezal/guard/lobby henchman" in Republic's *Secret Service in Darkest Africa* (1943-44, 15 episodes), this is the book to consult.—**Bruce A. Shuman**

1441. Helt, Richard C., and Marie E. Helt. **West German Cinema 1985-1990: A Reference Handbook.** Metuchen, N.J., Scarecrow, 1993. 259p. index. $32.50. PN1993.5.G3H426. 791.43'0943. LC 92-39433. ISBN 0-8108-2647-X.

The reunification of Germany in 1990 signaled the end of the West German film industry as a separate entity. For this reason, the Helts considered it appropriate to prepare this supplement to their *West German Cinema since 1945* (see ARBA 88, entry 1360). Together these volumes claim to list every West German theatrical feature film released between 1945 and 1990, including numerous international coproductions. Excluded are most television films, educational films, and documentaries. Films are listed alphabetically by German title with date, English title, and a one- or two-sentence plot summary. Also given are the names of directors, screenplay authors, camera persons, composers, producers, and principal performers. Indexes provide access by director, performer, and English title. There is also a section that offers a few lines of biographical information on directors not profiled in the previous volume. An interview with Munich film critic Hans Gunther Pflaum, concerning changes in the West German cinema and the accomplishments of the East German cinema, is interesting but exceedingly brief. Cinema researchers will find this a useful update to the original volume. [R: JAL, July 93, p. 201]

—**Joseph W. Palmer**

1442. Karsten, Eileen, with Dorothy-Ellen Gross. **From Real Life to Reel Life: A Filmography of Biographical Films.** Metuchen, N.J., Scarecrow, 1993. 475p. index. $52.50. PN1995.9.B55K37. 016.79143'651. LC 93-9160. ISBN 0-8108-2591-0.

Filling an overlooked reference niche is *From Real Life to Reel Life*, a filmography of commercially produced English-language biopics. This comprehensive volume (listing more than 1,000 entries) also includes foreign features and documentaries available with English subtitles or dubbing. Each entry provides filmographic details and may be accessed through the many indexes. Although *From Real Life* is an excellent first outing that breaks new ground, many elements of it could be improved. Karsten recognizes the importance of made-for-television films in the development of the biopic but does not differentiate them in the filmography. Works of fiction are included and treated as fact (e.g., *Badlands* does *not* depict Charles Starkweather's life). Entries for couples are listed under only one name, but there is no consistency as to which partner gets the entry (e.g., for Clyde Barrow *see* Bonnie Parker; for Nancy Spungen *see* Sid Vicious). Strong on historical figures, weak on contemporary ones, and probably offering unique coverage of television true-crime movies, this volume will serve the needs of public libraries. [R: Choice, Dec 93, p. 587; JAL, Sept 93, p. 274; RBB, 15 Sept 93, p. 187; WLB, Oct 93, pp. 88-89]
—**Megan S. Farrell**

1443. Langman, Larry. **A Guide to Silent Westerns.** Westport, Conn., Greenwood Press, 1992. 577p. illus. index. (Bibliographies and Indexes in the Performing Arts, no.13). $75.00. PN1995.9.W4L33. 016.79143'6278. LC 92-23783. ISBN 0-313-27858-X.

Delightfully opinionated annotations are the highlight of this well-researched, definitive guide to silent Westerns. The entries for the silent versions of *Riders of the Purple Sage*, for instance, include an analysis of the disappointing performance by Tom Mix in the context of his happy-go-lucky screen personality and the appeal of horseback riding stunts. The discussion of William S. Hart's classic *Hell's Hinges* describes the eventual audience rejection of his realistic portrayal of the West. The author is a film historian whose mastery of silent film scholarship is evident throughout.

More than 5,400 silent Western feature films, documentaries, shorts, and serials from the 1890s through 1930 are included, alphabetically by title, with basic cast and credits. Most have annotations that provide plot summary and evaluation; for some, all that is known is the title, date, and movie company, as early films (especially one-reelers) omitted credits, and records have often not been kept. There is also a directory of the film companies whose Westerns are listed—from prominent ventures, such as Broncho Billy Anderson's Essanay Company, to obscure outfits, such as Oil Field Amusements. An index of actors, directors, and screenwriters rounds out the volume.

The excellent introduction deserves special mention for its articulate summary of the silent Western film era. Important issues are examined, including the historical development of the Western hero and the degree to which Westerns portrayed the West realistically or as a mythical, idealized setting. [R: Choice, June 93, p. 1606; WLB, Feb 93, pp. 104-05]—**Richard W. Grefrath**

1444. Lopez, Daniel. **Films by Genre: 775 Categories, Styles, Trends, and Movements Defined....** Jefferson, N.C., McFarland, 1993. 495p. index. $45.00. PN1998.L63. 791.43'75. LC 92-56661. ISBN 0-89950-780-8.

Few feature films are unique; with resemblances and sequels so common that it is frequently hard to tell some of them apart by name. For this reason, movie buffs seek to classify films so they may be readily identified by genre. Classification, however, is an idiosyncratic process, with room for disagreement. Lopez assigns about 2,500 genre feature films (with a few television films "included for the sake of completeness") into 775 genres. He strives to categorize genre films (from "abstract" to "zombie"), and includes such intriguing classes as "adventure," "coming-of-age," "kidnap," "road," "truck," and even "schlock!" (no accolade, surely). Trying to pigeonhole things, Lopez even subdivides "erotic," breaking that group down into "gay," "cross-dressing," "hard core," "R-rated," and other such classes. There are fine lines of distinction (one supposes) between terms used by most of us interchangeably (e.g., "horror," "gorefest," "monster," "terror," "*grand guignol*"). But such terms cry out for definition, and Lopez, an Australian film writer, does not provide much of that. Where is the line of demarcation between horror and terror, or comedy-drama and seriocomedy? Help in these distinctions comes via *see* and *see also* references, but do not depend on them (or Lopez's witty commentary) to sort it all out.

There is an index of titles, but Lopez obviously believes that it is important to list each film in as many places as he thinks fits its content or style, so overlap of categories is common—*Breaking Away* and *Dr. Strangelove*, for example, each show up on five separate lists. Each genre includes a brief description; subgenres or related types of films; and a listing of movies that best exemplify the class, giving original title (or titles; some have multiple names, others are translated), nationality, year, and director or filmmaker. For information on the films themselves one needs to consult other sources. Despite this criticism, this book has practical (selection) value and is an entertaining attempt to find common thematic threads in movies, but using it for reference purposes may be problematical due to ambiguity over what goes where. [R: LJ, 1 Nov 93, p. 76]—**Bruce A. Shuman**

1445. Martin, Len D. **The Allied Artists Checklist: The Feature Films and Short Subjects....** Jefferson, N.C., McFarland, 1993. 222p. illus. index. $45.00. PN1999.A4M37. 016.79143'75'0973. LC 92-56665. ISBN 0-89950-782-4.

Formed in the 1940s and ultimately sold to Lorimar Productions in 1980, the Allied Artists Pictures Corporation produced and distributed a variety of films ranging in quality from B movies to *Cabaret* and *Friendly Persuasion*. Film historian Martin has produced a comprehensive filmography of the studio's output, including the independent and foreign films released through Allied Artists when domestic production was focused on television. The format is similar to the author's *The Columbia Checklist* (see ARBA 92, entry 1350). Each numbered entry is arranged alphabetically by film title and gives basic information such as the release date, running time, genre, production and cast credits, and a brief plot synopsis. Helpful appendixes include a list of titles by release date, films in several series, and Western stars and their Allied Artists films. There is a brief bibliography and an extensive index of names. The latter is especially helpful in that the name is linked to a specific entry rather than simply a page number. Students, researchers, and film buffs will find this book both useful and interesting.—**Barbara E. Kemp**

1446. Parish, James Robert. **Gays and Lesbians in Mainstream Cinema: Plots, Critiques, Casts and Credits....** Jefferson, N.C., McFarland, 1993. 496p. illus. index. $49.95. PN1995.9.H55P37. 791.43'653. LC 92-56678. ISBN 0-89950-791-3.

This filmography covers 272 mainstream films produced from 1914 to 1992 (mostly 1960s to 1990s) and how they depict gay and lesbian characters. Parish has written more than 75 books on Hollywood and the entertainment industry. Each 400- to 1200-word essay analyzes the film and its characters and includes much information about the cast, credits, and production; excerpts from reviews; and miscellaneous film trivia. Dozens of black-and-white photographs and movie posters appreciably enhance the work. Unlike similar works, such as Steve Stewart's *Gay Hollywood Film & Video Guide* (Companion, 1993), it includes less often portrayed lesbian characters. The name-title index is 71 three-column pages long. A chronology lists films produced by year.

This comprehensive work is more than a detailed reference book about homosexuals in films, for Parish implies that it provides a social history of the twentieth-century United States as seen through the depiction of one of its minorities. He attributes the increase in films with gay and lesbian characters to a change in the regulatory codes of the U.S. film industry, especially since the 1960s.

This book reflects our changing national interest in accepting diversity in both U.S. society and the films that mirror it. Well written and well researched, it belongs in every large public and academic library. [R: LJ, 1 Nov 93, p. 78]—**Edward Erazo**

1447. Parish, James Robert. **Prostitution in Hollywood Films: Plots, Critiques, Casts and Credits for 389 Theatrical and Made-for-Television Releases.** Jefferson, N.C., McFarland, 1992. 593p. illus. index. $49.95. PN1995.9.P76P37. 791.43'653. LC 91-51213. ISBN 0-89950-677-1.

With Parish (author of over 75 books on the entertainment industry) publishing about 3 books a year in the field, it was bound to happen: the "world's oldest profession" has finally met the "world's most prolific" writer on film. In this extensive filmography of prostitution in mainstream American-made feature films and made-for-television movies, Parish has chosen one of Hollywood's most exploitable and durable film genres. Beginning with the 1913 silent, *The Inside of the White Slave Traffic*, and concluding with *Whore* (1991), Parish's workmanlike study discusses some 389 films in which prostitution is portrayed in every conceivable fashion. As noted in a brief introduction, the dramatic elements inherent in the world of sex-for-sale has provided some of America's best-known performers (e.g., Elizabeth Taylor [*Butterfield 8*], Jane Fonda [*Klute*]) with an opportunity to turn in award-winning performances.

In this volume Parish follows the well-worn format of his earlier studies in film genres, such as *The Great Detective Pictures* (see ARBA 91, entry 1381) and *Prison Pictures from Hollywood* (see ARBA 92, entry 1364). Films are arranged alphabetically by title, with studio, running time, and a fairly complete list of cast and credits provided. Each entry also contains a miniessay that synopsizes the film, offers a thoughtful analysis, and includes an overview of critical opinion culled from mainstream sources (e.g., the *New York Times, Variety*). Keeping with the spirit of his oft-censored subject matter, Parish also offers a brief but useful history of the regulatory codes in the American film industry. An appendix presents a chronology (1913-1991) of the films discussed in the text. The work is well indexed and has numerous photographs. Recommended for all film collections.—**David K. Frasier**

1448. Richard, Alfred Charles, Jr. **Censorship and Hollywood's Hispanic Image: An Interpretive Filmography, 1936-1955.** Westport, Conn., Greenwood Press, 1993. 588p. index. (Bibliographies and Indexes in the Performing Arts, no.14). $75.00. PN1995.9.L37R53. 791.43'6520397. LC 92-40161. ISBN 0-313-28842-9.

Compiled by a professor of Latin American history, this source covers some 4,000 films over a 19-year period. The author selected these years because the Production Code Administration influenced how Hispanics were portrayed and required filmmakers to eliminate stereotypes. Between 1936 and 1955 Hollywood did indeed change how it presented the image of Hispanics.

Entries are numbered, arranged by year, then subdivided alphabetically by film title. Production information is presented along with an annotation describing the film's Hispanic significance. Several indexes (title, actor and actress, place, song, and subject) conclude the work. Surprises include the appearance of Woody Woodpecker (as the star of "Hollywood Matador" in 1942), the misspelling of Grauman's Chinese Theatre, and the mention of contemporary actor Richard Dreyfus in the entry for the 1937 film *Life of Emile Zola* (he starred in a 1991 television remake).

The book joins a growing number of titles that include *Hispanic Hollywood* (Carol Publishing Group, 1990), *Latinos in Hollywood* (Floricanto Press, 1991), and the author's earlier publication, *The Hispanic Image on the Silver Screen* (see ARBA 93, entry 1363). Recommended for ethnic studies and film collections. [R: Choice, Oct 93, p. 272]—**Ilene F. Rockman**

1449. Senn, Bryan, and John Johnson. **Fantastic Cinema Subject Guide: A Topical Index to 2500 Horror, Science Fiction, and Fantasy Films.** Jefferson, N.C., McFarland, 1992. 682p. illus. index. $45.00. PN1995.9.F36S46. 016.79143'615. LC 91-51230. ISBN 0-89950-681-X.

While there is no dearth of film reference catalogs devoted to the individual subgenres that comprise fantastic cinema, Senn and Johnson's imaginative subject guide to the overlapping genres of horror, science fiction, and fantasy provides a pleasant and informative alternative to the usual straightforward list of films. The book's arrangement owes much to *The Movie List Book* (see ARBA 91, entry 1387), which initiated the practice of grouping theme-related films under topical headings. The 2,500 feature-length fantastic films identified are grouped under 81 subject headings that range from the Abominable Snowman to zombies.

A brief introduction to each topical heading defines the subject and notes any significant historical trends in the genre. Films are alphabetically arranged under the heading, and basic data, such as year of release, distributor, country of origin, alternate titles, production/cast credits, and a brief synopsis, are supplied for each title. Inexplicably, running times and video availability are not included. Many entries have a quotation (often hilarious) from the film as well as interesting pieces of information gleaned from legitimate reference sources and fan publications. (A caveat from the authors: the genre is rife with misinformation, and popular publications are often more notable for their enthusiasm than their accuracy.) Appendixes are included for blaxploitation, 3-D, and Western films in the genre. Extensively cross-referenced and well illustrated, the work contains an adequate title index. Highly recommended for fans and any type of library supporting patron interest in such films.—**David K. Frasier**

1450. Sloan, Jane E. **Alfred Hitchcock: A Guide to References and Resources.** New York, G. K. Hall, 1993. 602p. index. (Reference Publication in Film). $60.00. PN1998.3.H58S57. 791.43'0233'092. LC 92-15103. ISBN 0-8161-9057-7.

Documenting the work of Alfred Hitchcock and his critical reception is no small feat. His 57 films range from the era of silent black-and-white productions to latter-day technicolor talkies. While his reputation for suspense is well known, critics have also examined Hitchcock's work for Marxist, feminist, and psychoanalytical themes, among many others. Sloan takes on the formidable task of describing each of Hitchcock's feature films scene-by-scene, assessing the critical reception, and describing the secondary literature from 1919 to 1990. For good measure she throws in a biographical essay, film credits, and archival sources. Sloan comes well prepared; in 1983 she compiled a similar guide to the work of Robert Bresson.

The largest section of this work is the 300 pages devoted to the Hitchcock filmography. Sloan goes beyond a simple synopsis by providing thorough descriptions of each scene, including occasional camera angles and direct quotations. The plot summaries average about five pages for each movie. She cleverly highlights the director's cameo in each film with a superscript H. Not everything in Hitchcock's films lends itself to objective description, but Sloan acquits herself well with the Dali-like dream sequence of *Spellbound* and the falling nightmare effect of *Vertigo*.

The annotated bibliography and its supplement contain more than 900 citations and abstracts to English and foreign-language books and articles, plus citations to newspaper articles, dissertations, and film reviews. While some tend to the ephemeral, others, such as the movie reviews by Graham Greene, have considerable interest. Sloan's book concludes with separate indexes for the filmography and the bibliography. This comprehensive account of the primary and secondary works on Hitchcock is an essential guide to the director's long career and enduring influence. [R: Choice, July/Aug 93, p. 1755]—**John P. Schmitt**

1451. Wetta, Frank J., and Stephen J. Curley. **Celluloid Wars: A Guide to Film and the American Experience of War.** Westport, Conn., Greenwood Press, 1992. 296p. index. (Research Guides in Military Studies, no.5). $45.00. PN1995.9.W3W48. 791.43'658. LC 92-8210. ISBN 0-313-26099-0.

Appealing to those who wish to understand war films for what they are, Wetta and Curley see Americans as "a warlike people, their nation born, sustained, and expanded in conflict." Consequently, war films are unique historical documents with much to say about the American character and are as valuable in their own way as the more traditional sources historians use to reconstruct the past. *Celluloid Wars* addresses the complex historical, aesthetic, social, and cultural issues involving films about American wars. Chapters 1 and 2 define war films as a genre; discuss in detail four critical approaches to war, each emphasizing a different aspect of war films (subject, audience, filmmakers, and technique); and explore the interrelationship between fictional war films and actual combat experience. Chapters 3 through 14 contain lists of war films arranged alphabetically by the individual American wars they depict: early American wars (colonial wars, Revolutionary War, War of 1812); wars with Mexico (Texas Revolution, Mexican War); the American Civil War; the Indian wars (1622-1890); new imperial wars (Spanish-American War, Philippine and Moro insurrections); World War I; World War II wartime films; World War II postwar films; the Korean War; the Vietnam War; banana wars and interventions (military actions in Third World countries); and nuclear warfare (actual and imagined).

Each chapter opens with a chronology that includes references to films that relate to specific historical events, then provides a brief commentary emphasizing themes and key films in their historical contexts. Filmographies follow, with each film listed alphabetically by title. The film's director, producer, screenwriter, principal actors, distributing company, year of release, and running time are given. Very helpful is the use of one to four asterisks to highlight the historical or aesthetic importance of each film. Films that receive four asterisks are annotated.

Two invaluable bibliographies bring *Celluloid Wars* to a close. The war film bibliography lists about 100 of the most important books and articles written about war films; and "General Reference to Film" cites works chosen for their usefulness in doing film research. *Celluloid Wars* will attract a broad audience: war historians, popular culture enthusiasts, film buffs, and literature professors. [R: Choice, Jan 93, p. 778]—**Colby H. Kullman**

Handbooks and Yearbooks

1452. Bartel, Pauline. **The Complete *Gone with the Wind* Sourcebook.** Dallas, Tex., Taylor Publishing, 1993. 166p. illus. $14.95pa. PN1997.G59B365. 791.43. LC 92-35649. ISBN 0-87833-817-9.

This handbook is intended for people wishing to collect materials related to the film *Gone with the Wind* (GWTW). The needlepoint, ceramics, dolls, face fans, advertising, jewelry, linens, stationery, and so forth that are of interest to these collectors picture the characters and sets from the film, not those described in the book. For example, dolls are painted to look like Hattie McDaniel, and their clothing resembles costumes used in the film. Bartel gives practical advice on starting a collection and discusses collectibles of today and yesterday. Much space is devoted to listing business concerns engaged in selling GWTW items.

Libraries with complete American film or Americana collections may wish to purchase this guide. All other collections are better served by *Gone with the Wind on Film* (see ARBA 91, entry 1390).

—Milton H. Crouch

1453. Bushnell, Brooks. **Directors and Their Films: A Comprehensive Reference, 1895-1990.** Jefferson, N.C., McFarland, 1993. 1035p. $125.00. PN1998.B85. 791.43'0233'0922. LC 92-56633. ISBN 0-89950-766-2.

This is an extremely comprehensive reference work for access to films and their directors. The coverage, as the title implies, is historical, for the book lists films (and not just feature films, either) produced since 1895, deemed to be the wellspring year of motion pictures. Part 1 is an alphabetical listing by director (when appropriate, the director's pseudonyms are given) and the person's films listed in chronological order, with year of release and alternate titles. Part 2 is a very thorough list of more than 108,000 films, from *A* to *Zyte*. Each film is provided with only the name of the director and the year of release. Made-for-television films are not included unless they received a theatrical release, which seems an arbitrary distinction, but one supposes that Bushnell (a computer programmer and independent filmmaker) had to draw the line somewhere. The 1990 cut-off date for inclusion suggests that regular updates will be forthcoming.

This is not a browser's book: There are no tidbits of extraneous information, no illustrations, and no attempt to be anything beyond a vast, comprehensive listing of films and their directors. One nice feature is that any film issued under multiple names is listed under each name, including translations and transliterations of names that originally were in non-roman alphabets. The reader will probably note with surprise just how many films have been released under two or more titles in the same language, and even more when foreign titles are added. All major film collections will welcome this reference work, but for smaller collections and libraries catering to the amateur film buff, there are other ways to get much the same information—not nearly as comprehensive, perhaps, but much cheaper and more fun to read. [R: LJ, 1 Nov 93, p. 72]—**Bruce A. Shuman**

1454. Baur, Tassilo, comp. and ed. **Special Effects and Stunts Guide.** 2d ed. Los Angeles, Calif., Lone Eagle, 1993. 232p. index. $39.95pa. ISBN 0-943728-54-1. ISSN 1045-0750.

Lone Eagle directories are important reference tools for those in the film and video industries. Primarily intended as aids for locating and selecting talent, there are a total of nine directories, including ones that list film directors, television directors, film actors, film writers, television writers, cinematographers, agents and casting directors, film composers, and various other specialties. The present volume lists special effects and stunts professionals. As in all Lone Eagle directories, the emphasis is on well-established, currently active artists and technicians. To be included, listees must have done significant work in major feature films released in theaters since 1976. The volume opens with a name index followed by listings arranged in five sections: physical effects, optical effects, makeup effects, digital effects, and stunts coordinators. The digital effects coverage is new and represents an important enhancement over the 1989 edition (see ARBA 90, entry 1331). Persons are listed in each section with their most important and most recent films. Academy Award-nominated work is identified. Usually (but not always) there is a contact address and telephone number. Many entries include professional title and guild affiliation, and some provide birth date and birthplace. The extensive film title index that concludes the volume enables the searcher to identify the people responsible for the special effects in a particular film. Libraries that target service to the film industry will want to acquire this volume.—**Joseph W. Palmer**

1455. **BFI Film and Television Handbook 1993.** David Leafe, ed. London, British Film Institute; distr., Bloomington, Ind., Indiana University Press, 1992. 328p. illus. index. $28.95pa. 348'.8'0941. ISBN 0-85170-344-5.

Although it first appeared in 1983, the *BFI Film and Television Handbook 1993* is a major improvement over the previous annual editions. Besides the customary directory information, the 1993 edition now provides some 50 pages of statistics and commentary on the film, television, and video industries in the United Kingdom. The year covered by this annual is 1991, but a number of the statistics presented go back as far as 1980. It is interesting to learn that all top 20 films at the U.K. box office were from the United States. For those who think British television is all *Masterpiece Theater*, it will come as a surprise that three of the top five most-watched shows were episodes of the soap opera *Coronation Street*.

Besides such statistics, the handbook has a directory of addresses and telephone numbers for archives and libraries, bookstores, cinemas, film studies programs, distributors, film societies, laboratories, and other related organizations or entities. The directory also lists new publications on films as well as production starts for films and the releases of new films in the United Kingdom between April 1991 and March 1992. These lists provide the title, producers, directors, and casts for such diverse films as *The Crying Game* and *Terminator 2*. There is an index for titles and subjects. Besides being a compendium of useful and handy information, the handbook is an attractive publication with many color photographs and excellent graphics and design.—**Ronald H. Fritze**

1456. **Halliwell's Filmgoer's and Video Viewer's Companion.** 10th ed. John Walker, ed. New York, HarperCollins, 1993. 834p. $60.00; $25.00pa. ISBN 0-06-271570-4; 0-06-273239-0pa. ISSN 1066-2912.

Halliwell established a niche for himself with his two film reference handbooks, *Halliwell's Film Guide* (see ARBA 90, entry 1332) and this *Companion*. The objectives are the same, but the approach differs: The *Guide* covers films, while the *Companion* deals primarily with people. The 10th edition mentions "video" in the title, although this aspect does not seem to have made an impact on the contents of the *Companion*; it is still the massive, brief-entry, ready-reference source we have turned to since 1965 hoping to find the name of everyone who ever played James Bond.

The thousands of entries mostly include the personal names of actors, directors, writers, and cinematographers, plus a few screen characters. These are brief entries, rarely straying beyond a laconic "American leading actor" and a fairly complete list of film appearances. The annotator waxes more eloquent about historical figures, reflecting his bias for the films of the 1930s and 1940s. The entry for the Marx Brothers run to a page and a half, including some of their best quotations. Also present are entries for film themes (e.g., social conscience), film styles (e.g., horror, 3-D, parody), film conventions (e.g., mirrors, soft focus), and film subjects (e.g., sex, politics).

The 10th edition of the *Companion* is current through 1992 and corrects many of the shortcomings of the last edition (see ARBA 90, entry 1347). It is better for short-fact reference than a deeper understanding of the medium, but no similar work includes quite so much.—**John P. Schmitt**

1457. **The Motion Picture Guide: 1993 Annual (The Films of 1992).** John Miller-Monzon and David Straussman, eds. New York, BASELINE; distr., New Providence, N.J., Reed Reference Publishing, 1993. 635p. index. $148.00. ISBN 0-918432-95-2.

The original *Motion Picture Guide* was a 12-volume set that provided reviews and credits for most of the significant feature films released in the United States up through 1984. The first 9 volumes covered 1927-1984, with volume 10 the silent era; the final 2 volumes were indexes. Annual supplements update this basic set, each providing reviews of films released during the previous year. In 1992, a CD-ROM edition of the guide was published that contained reviews of sound films from the original edition plus most of the annuals. Because of copyright complications, the silent era had to be excluded.

The present volume is the eighth annual supplement to the original edition. It is so full of valuable information that even libraries that do not own previous volumes may wish to consider beginning a subscription. The 1993 volume offers lengthy, intelligent, staff-written reviews of 529 feature films released during 1992. Included are very detailed credits, substantial plot descriptions, evaluations, and star ratings. While ratings are usually well argued, they do represent one person's point of view, which may not match the overall critical consensus. It would greatly enhance the reference value of this publication if citations to other reviews were provided, ideally with quotations, so a reader might gain an insight into the actual critical reception the film received.

Excellent indexes list films by country of origin, genre, star rating, and MPAA (Motion Picture Association of America) rating. The name index is outstanding. It exhaustively indexes credits in 18 categories, including such diverse specialties as actors, animators, costumes, directors, music composers, set directors, screenwriters, source authors, and stunts. A master index lists all films reviewed in previous annuals with year of release. There is also a list of 1992 Academy Award nominees and winners. Finally, there is an excellent, well-annotated obituaries section.—**Joseph W. Palmer**

1458. **The *New York Times* Film Reviews 1989-1990.** Hamden, Conn., Garland, 1992. 564p. illus. index. $165.00. LC 70-112777. ISBN 0-8240-7591-9. ISSN 0362-3688.

Since the publication of its five-volume set of film reviews covering 1913-1968 (see ARBA 72, entry 1168a), the *New York Times* has issued biennial supplements of its motion picture reviews reproduced exactly as they originally appeared. Through the years, this set (now at 17 volumes and current through 1990) has become a standard reference source for film studies. It not only provides reviews and capsule filmographies for hundreds of movies that played New York, but it also reproduces thought-provoking review articles on film genres/trends (e.g., "Feminist Heroines: Endangered Species") and movie personalities (e.g., "Bette Davis: The Epitome of Hollywood") written by such well-known *Times* critics as Vincent Canby, Janet Maslin, and Caryn James. Each article concludes with the bibliographic citation from its original newspaper publication.

Articles are chronologically arranged by the date in which they first appeared in the *Times* and include all photographs that originally accompanied the text. Articles that comment on the best and award-winning films (e.g., Academy Awards, New York Film Critics) appear at the end of each year's reviews. Three indexes (title, personal name, and corporate name) provide excellent access to the volume. This work is an essential purchase for all academic and large public libraries.—**David K. Frasier**

1459. Nowlan, Robert Anthony, and Gwendolyn Wright Nowlan. **The Name Is Familiar: Who Played Who in the Movies? A Directory of Title Characters.** New York, Neal-Schuman, 1993. 1014p. $75.00pa. PN1995.9.C36N696. 791.43'028'0922. LC 92-42877. ISBN 1-55570-054-3.

A logical adjunct to the research they began in 1990 with the publication of *Movie Characters of Leading Performers of the Sound Era* (see ARBA 91, entry 1362), the Nowlans have compiled an impressive directory of English-language feature films (1918 through the first half of 1992) whose titles refer to a particular character or characters. Divided into three complementary cross-referenced sections, the volume's format facilitates effective use. In section 1, approximately 4,500 actors are alphabetically listed with their film title roles. Each entry includes the film's date of release and studio. Section 2, reminiscent of *Memorable Film Characters* (see ARBA 86, entry 1324), offers an alphabetical list of almost 9,000 title characters as well as a capsule description of the role, the actor portraying it, and the film's release date and production company. Section 3 is particularly imaginative and useful. In it the Nowlans have identified approximately 9,000 films whose titles refer to particular characters. In addition to obvious "name" selections, such as *Dr. Zhivago*, they also include descriptive titles that identify a character (e.g., *The Unholy Wife*) or titles with pronouns that suggest a character (e.g., *I Was a Teenage Werewolf*). Entries include the name of the title character and its performer, other leading cast members and director, and (yet again) the film's year of release and studio affiliation. While some academic and public libraries may balk at paying this much for an oversized paperback with a fragile binding, this comprehensive directory is recommended for those collections supporting strong patron interest in film. [R: Choice, Oct 93, p. 271; JAL, Sept 93, p. 275; LJ, 1 Mar 93, p. 70; RBB, Aug 93, p. 2094; WLB, Oct 93, pp. 90-92]—**David K. Frasier**

1460. Stewart, Steve. **Gay Hollywood Film & Video Guide: Over 75 Years of Male Homosexuality in the Movies.** Laguna Hills, Calif., Companion, 1993. 297p. illus. index. $15.95pa. LC 93-71831. ISBN 0-9625277-3-4.

This guide to more than 400 gay films provides complete descriptions with one- to five-star ratings. Genres for the films, which span the 1910s to the 1990s, include just about everything: action, adventure, animation, comedy, documentary, drama, fantasy, foreign, horror, musical, science fiction, and thriller. For each entry the description contains director, cast, genre, plot, quotations, MPAA (Motion Picture Association of America) rating, and companion films (films with similar themes). For purposes of this work, "gay film" is broadly defined as a film that depicts, in theme or in character, male homosexuality, male androgyny, asexuality, bisexuality, transvestitism, and transsexuality. The book does not include either lesbian-themed or pornographic films.

The author states that the book is meant as a companion work to the many film books on homosexuality already published, and specifically mentions film historian Vito Russo's *The Celluloid Closet* (HarperCollins, 1987), which is credited as the inspiration for this book in the acknowledgments. The guide has an easy-to-read format and almost 40 pages of indexes. More than 50 black-and-white film shots also enhance the book. This guide, an effective one-volume reference source, is recommended for both public and academic libraries.—**Edward Erazo**

1461. Weaver, Tom. **Poverty Row Horrors! Monogram, PRC and Republic Horror Films of the Forties.** Jefferson, N.C., McFarland, 1992. 376p. illus. index. $36.50. PN1995.9.H6W38. 791.43'616. LC 92-50324. ISBN 0-89950-756-5.

The "Poverty Row" of this title refers to those American movie studios that made films on the cheap (and on the quick) during 1940-1946. Some of those films are now cult classics, while others serve mainly as fodder for those individuals who overdub facetious dialogue on the Comedy Channel's Science Fiction Theatre. More than 100 such films were made during the early 1940s, with little attention to production values and direction ranging (in Weaver's words) "from insipid to atrocious." Yet some of these films featured stars with names already legendary in the horror genre, such as Boris Karloff and Bela Lugosi.

Weaver, about whom no biographical information is furnished, writes in an informed, entertaining style, as he discusses each of the 1940s horror movies (31), illustrated with black-and-white photographs. He provides for each selection a narrative essay, snatches of dialogue, ruminations on plot devices, and even tidbits of gossip about the on- and off-camera antics of the principals. The overall result is an extremely readable series of insights into a genre of moviemaking now 50 years gone. In addition to this work's considerable reference value, browsing this book will send readers of a certain age back to those dim, dark days (was it always Saturday afternoon, or does it just seem that way in memory?) when they nervously chewed oversalted popcorn and squirmed in tacky, sticky seats while permitting Hollywood's second-rank filmmakers to scare them, and never mind the tinny music, poor lighting, inaudible dialogue, or inconsistent plots. This work is appropriate for all larger movie book collections.—**Bruce A. Shuman**

Indexes

1462. *Film News* **Index, 1939-1981.** Rohama Lee, ed. Fort Atkinson, Wis., Highsmith Press, 1992. 173p. $59.00pa. ISBN 0-917846-10-9.

For more than 40 years, *Film News* chronicled the world of nontheatrical films. In *Film News Index, 1939-1981*, Lee provides a brief history of that industry and the journal she edited for 34 years as well as access to its contents. The text is divided into four sections: articles, reviews, a name index, and a subject index. The first two sections, arranged alphabetically by title, annotate each article and review, providing both cinematic and bibliographical information as well as cross-references between articles and reviews. The annotations range from objective one-sentence summaries to lengthier, more subjective evaluations. The name and subject indexes provide access to film titles.

The prefatory sections, prepared by Lee, are both well written and informative. The indexes, however, were prepared by a class and are less effective. Among other things, the quality of the prose varies, pagination is not continuous (a fact that makes the table of contents somewhat odd), and proofreading is less accurate than it might be—typographical and punctuation errors appear. The order of sections suggested by the prefatory material is not followed by the index. A firmer editorial hand might have provided a unity that the book lacks. Nonetheless, the work provides an entry into an aspect of the film industry that is often ignored.—**Rebecca Jordan**

1463. Slattery, William J., Claire Dorton, and Rosemary Enright. **The Kael Index: A Guide to a Movie Critic's Work, 1954-1991.** Englewood, Colo., Libraries Unlimited, 1993. 287p. $38.00pa. PN1998.3.K34S63. 016.79143'75. LC 93-11821. ISBN 1-56308-119-9.

During her 24-year tenure (1968-1991) as the film critic in residence at the *New Yorker*, Pauline Kael published hundreds of reviews on the way to establishing herself as one of the most respected and widely read film critics in the United States, if not the world. In addition to movie reviews appearing in other serial sources, such as *Film Quarterly*, the *New Republic, Vogue*, and *Life*, Kael also produced 10 books of highly regarded film criticism, all characterized by her special brand of insight, humor, and enthusiasm. This alphabetically arranged index provides access to her reviews by movie titles; names of actors, directors, and screenwriters; and corporate entities (e.g., Paramount Pictures) that are discussed in Kael's monographic work. Cross-references are adequate, with foreign film titles often cited under their English-language titles. Entries for directors include lists of their films and references to Kael's discussion of them within her indexed works. A 123-item selected bibliography of articles about this premier film reviewer culled from film journals, newspapers, and the popular press is also offered. Recommended for film libraries and those academic institutions supporting a large film studies program.
—**David K. Frasier**

THEATER

Bibliography

1464. Marill, Alvin H. **More Theatre: Stage to Screen to Television.** Metuchen, N.J., Scarecrow, 1993. 2v. $149.50/set. PN2189.M32. 792.9'5. LC 93-4687. ISBN 0-8108-2717-4.

This two-volume work supplements and updates *Theatre: Stage to Screen to Television* (see ARBA 82, entry 1096). The author traces the production history of 150 pieces of literature (most often plays) through their multiple adaptations and reincarnations as staged plays, movies, and television productions. Each entry provides a plot synopsis; historical and critical comments; and a detailed list of stage, screen, and television productions. Venues, opening dates, and production and cast lists are given. A special section of additions and corrections to the 1981 volume is also supplied.

The author gives no criteria for inclusion in this reference work except to say that Greek classics, Shakespeare, Gilbert and Sullivan, and traditional fairy tales are excluded. However, exceptions are made if a modern adaptation of one of the excluded pieces of literature was recently produced. While each citation is highly detailed, the reader is handicapped by the lack of a table of contents or any type of index. A cross-referenced index of original and adapted titles would be very useful. This work is an interesting and useful reference work for general readers and theater historians if the plays they are interested in are among the works included.—**Charles Neuringer**

1465. Miletich, Leo N. **Broadway's Prize-Winning Musicals: An Annotated Guide for Libraries and Audio Collectors.** Binghamton, N.Y., Harrington Park Press/Haworth Press, 1993. 255p. index. $29.95; $14.95pa. ML156.4.M8M54. 016.7821'4'0266. LC 92-4125. ISBN 1-56024-288-4; 1-56023-018-5pa.

This is an indispensable guide, a "starter kit" to the world of the American musical theater's audio recordings. It provides a list of the best and most readily available shows that spans the genre's entire history and includes original, revival, studio, and film casts. Four chapters, "Act One" through "Act Four," are based on objective criteria and list musicals that have won the Antoinette Perry (Tony), the New York Drama Critics Circle Award, the Pulitzer prize, and the Grammy. Each chapter begins with an introduction of the award and follows with a chronological listing of winners since its inception. Each entry notes title, composer, opening date, and cast members. A synopsis of the play follows with reviews (both favorable and unfavorable) of the opening night's performance. Awards the play won in other categories, film information, and record labels of the various published scores complete the annotation. "Act Five" provides an alphabetical list of shows that did not win major awards, although their creators and performers often did. The more than 70 titles cited were chosen for their historical and artistic importance, their entertainment value, the quality of their performances, and their availability. This is not a comprehensive listing, but it does give a good representation of the variety of Broadway's musical styles. The "Overture" presents a historical background on the musical and its composers and on technological developments in the industry. Appendixes include tips on searching for old recordings; histories, biographies, and books on recordings; recorded anthologies of musicals; and updated information through the 1992-1993 season. General and song indexes conclude the book.

A valuable, informative reference work, this book covers a full spectrum of information in a condensed and readable form. Highly recommended for librarians and audio collectors. [R: RBB, 15 Oct 93, pp. 466-68]—**Deborah A. Taylor**

1466. Ortolani, Benito, ed. **International Bibliography of Theatre: 1988-1989.** Brooklyn, N.Y., Theatre Research Data Center, Brooklyn College, City University of New York, 1993. 951p. index. $270.00. ISBN 0-945419-03-1.

International coverage of books and articles on the theater is provided in this work, as well as those on the relationship between the theater and current trends in politics, education, philosophy, and the like. More than 6,000 classified entries and some 18,000 subject references cover books, articles, dissertations, and other theater documents published primarily in English during 1988 and 1989. Generally excluded are reprints, texts of plays, purely literary scholarship, and book and performance reviews.

Entries are divided into 9 categories (e.g., dance, media), which are subdivided into subsidiary components (e.g., ballet, film), then further divided into 13 possible aspects (e.g., administration, design-technology). Each entry contains complete bibliographical information, language of document, time and place to which it pertains, type of document (e.g., historical study), and a brief abstract of its contents. The subject index, which provides primary access to the classified section, is composed of geographical and personal names and subject terms, such as economics or Jewish theater. Entries include the heading, aspect, description of item, and classed entry number. This section also has *see* and *see also* references. A geographical-chronological index enables access by country, and a document authors index, by name. Other helpful features include lists of indexed periodicals by full title and acronym.

This volume is the first of three designed to provide a timely listing of scholarship worldwide. After publication of the third volume, annual books will index the previous year's publications. If timeliness is also achieved, this comprehensive bibliography will be doubly welcomed.—**Anita Zutis**

Biography

1467. Berney, K. A., ed. **Contemporary Dramatists.** 5th ed. Detroit, St. James Press, 1993. 843p. index. $130.00. ISBN 1-55862-185-7.

Containing more than 300 entries for individuals writing in English, this edition of *Contemporary Dramatists* lists playwrights from previous editions who are not included in this volume by citing within the text the most recent edition of *Contemporary Dramatists* that contains an entry on them. This makes it extremely important to have all five editions on the reference shelf. Information for each writer consists of a biography, a complete list of produced or published plays and all other separately published books, and a signed essay. In addition, the entrants were invited to comment on their work. Rick Cluchey, for example, tells how he became involved with the theater for the first time while serving time at San Quentin.

Original British and United States editions of all books are listed, as are other first editions. The very first production, first productions in both Great Britain and the United States, and first productions in London and New York are also presented. Cited in the critical studies section are all books written about the playwright as well as reviews and essays that have been recommended by the entrant.

Why are Jerome Lawrence and Robert E. Lee, of *Inherit the Wind* fame, so often referred to as "the thinking man's playwrights"? In what ways is Robert Anderson's *Tea and Sympathy* a subtle indictment of the witch-hunt as well as a perceptive commentary on the failure of compassion in a society that demands conformity as the price for acceptance? In his third play and first professionally produced drama,

Dutchman, how did Amiri Baraka achieve the cultural revolution of the Black man in white America? In what ways does death hold a unique place in Wole Soyinka's dramatic world? Before his skyrocketing journey into prominence with his two-part, roughly seven-hour production of *Angels in America*, what previous plays had Tony Kushner written and had produced? The answers to thousands of significant questions such as these are just a few moments away with *Contemporary Dramatists* at hand. Celebrating contemporary playwrights who work in English, this outstanding reference tool awaits the pleasure of all persons interested in the theater. It will be helpful to the casual browser as well as to the serious scholar.
—Colby H. Kullman

Chronology

1468. Greene, John C., and Gladys L. H. Clark. **The Dublin Stage, 1720-1745: A Calendar of Plays, Entertainments, and Afterpieces.** Cranbury, N. J., Lehigh University Press/Associated University Presses, 1993. 473p. index. $65.00. PN2602.D8G7. 792'.09418'3509033. LC 91-58886. ISBN 0-934223-22-X.

The authors are interested in the activities occurring on Dublin stages during a 25-year span sandwiched between what are considered as two "golden ages." They use the encyclopedic *The London Stage, 1660-1800* (Southern Illinois University Press, 1960-1968) as a model for their presentation. They supply the reader with a day-to-day chronology of plays, performance venues, cast lists, and any special miscellaneous information about the performances from 1720 to 1745. These raw data are the heart of the volume. However, as the authors admit, the basic information about the performances is scanty; they had to gather their data exclusively from Dublin newspaper advertisements. Often theaters did not advertise, and so there is little representative information to be gathered from that source. The information that appears in this volume is unavoidably riddled with enough gaps to raise serious questions about its utility as a useful secondary source to the theater historian. The authors acknowledge this problem and have done the best that can be done with the materials they had to use. Ultimately, what the reader will get from this volume is an improvement over what is currently available and certainly better than no information at all.

The authors open their volume with an excellent essay on the Dublin stage as it existed during that 25-year span. They deal with playhouses, the nature of the theatrical season, types of performances, theater personnel, production policies, costumes, stage practices, scenery, machinery, music, dancing, the nature of the repertory, and more. Much of their essay is fascinating, but many of their conclusions are tentative because of the skimpiness of basic information. They are often forced to make hypotheses on the basis of (not unreasonable) guesses and extrapolations from what occurred on the London stage during that period.

The authors provide a bibliography, an index of Dublin stage workers and personnel, an author and play index, a performance index, and a general name and subject index. All of these indexes are useful for recreating (as best as can be done) a very interesting stage in the development of Irish theater. [R: Choice, Nov 93, p. 432]—**Charles Neuringer**

1469. Wearing, J. P. **The London Stage 1950-1959: A Calendar of Plays and Players.** Metuchen, N.J., Scarecrow, 1993. 2v. index. $129.50/set. PN2596.L6W3847. 792'.0942109045. LC 93-17179. ISBN 0-8108-2690-9.

This is the seventh in a series of day-by-day calendars of productions at major London theaters. Fifty-two theaters are included, encompassing 3,117 productions of entire works performed for the fee-paying public from 1950 to 1959. Among those excluded are variety, cinematographic, and magic programs. Chronologically arranged entries list title; genre, such as opera or play; author; theater; date and length of run; number of performances; cast; and other production information. A short bibliography refers to a representative sample of first-night reviews, with the occasional inclusion of additional reviews. A brief comment relating to the production in question concludes the entry. The main section is followed by an appendix that lists titles and authors of plays performed at selected theaters not included in the calendar. Title and general indexes contain cross-references to the main productions. In addition, the latter index also provides supplementary information on individuals (e.g., birth and death dates, other occupations).

The series is intended to cover London stage productions from 1890 to the present. Future editions will help round out the picture of this phase of the performing arts.—**Anita Zutis**

Dictionaries and Encyclopedias

1470. Boulanger, Norman C., and Warren C. Lounsbury. **Theatre Lighting from A to Z.** Seattle, Wash., University of Washington Press, 1992. 197p. illus. $24.95 spiralbound. PN2091.E4B59. 792'.023'03. LC 92-14620. ISBN 0-295-97214-9.

This volume has been prepared by two professionals from the theater academic world. They write about what they know of lighting equipment, techniques, and concepts, and their book is first-rate. The alphabetical arrangement by subjects, specific equipment, and lighting effects works very well. The pages are large, the layout is spacious, and the illustrations are plentiful and excellent. Cross-references are there when needed. Some topics, such as lighting practice and design for lighting, are the equivalent of short chapters. Descriptions are precise all directions are clear; advice is always practical. The best piece of advice in the book occurs under "apparition." Costly and complicated ways of achieving this effect are outlined, but the suggestion is also made: "If no equipment is available, the simplest solution is for the actor to pretend to see the apparition in the wings or at the rear of the auditorium." It is easy to imagine the relief of a technician learning the ropes in a community theater at getting such good technical advice from the masters. This book will be useful in any school or organization that serves inexperienced theater technicians.—**George Louis Mayer**

1471. **The Cambridge Guide to Theatre.** updated ed. Martin Banham, ed. New York, Cambridge University Press, 1992. 1104p. illus. $24.95pa. PN2035.C27. 792'.0321. LC 88-25804. ISBN 0-521-42903-X.

Starting with the Abbey Theatre and ending 1,101 closely printed pages later with Carl Zuckmayer, this reference work is a panoramic compilation of the history and present practices in theater in all parts of the world. The volume cites actors, playwrights, directors, producers, technical innovations and practices, famous theaters and troupes, dramatic theories, types of performances, histories of various national theater movements, and more. The entries range from the obscure and long forgotten to the contemporary and well-known aspects of theater. Each entry is signed by its contributor, and many of them offer further suggested readings and short bibliographies. A list of contributors and a short list for general further readings are provided. The volume is profusely illustrated.

This scholarly reference work is an updated version of the 1988 edition and has incorporated much new material. However, the reader may be occasionally surprised by some omissions (e.g., Laurence Olivier's 1989 death is not mentioned in his entry). But aside from these minor cavils, this work is an extraordinary achievement and rivals already existing encyclopedias of the theater. Because of its modest price it can, and should, be on every theater lover's bookshelf.—**Charles Neuringer**

1472. **The Concise Oxford Companion to the Theatre.** Phyllis Hartnoll and Peter Found, eds. New York, Oxford University Press, 1992. 568p. $35.00. PN2035.C63. 792'.03. LC 91-23749. ISBN 0-19-866136-3.

Aiming once again for worldwide coverage, although discernibly biased toward British and United States theater, this edition of *The Concise Oxford Companion to the Theatre* is most welcome. The first edition appeared in 1972 at a time when the Fringe was a comparatively recent phenomenon and the opening of Britain's National Theatre building was still four years away. Since then, a whole new generation of playwrights, directors, producers, actors, scene designers, and technicians have come into their own, many of them now famous throughout the world.

In order to update and augment the material of the first edition yet not greatly exceed the original length, some of the less important citations have been deleted. More information has been provided in the entries for playwrights by elaborating on the subjects about which they wrote. Survey essays give greater detail about the careers of many playwrights, actors, directors, producers and other important people associated with the theater. Duplication of information under different headings has been skillfully avoided. For example, the entry on Tovstonogov ends with his move to the Gorky Theater, and his biography continues in that entry. Asterisks within the text and small capitals in signpost entries enable the reader to search widely for further information. Important people who are mentioned in an article but do not have an entry of their own appear in boldface type with dates. Dates that follow play titles are those of first performance or revivals, depending on the context.

While generally mainstream in its approach, *The Concise Oxford Companion to the Theatre* considers the Fringe, the off-Broadway, and the avant-garde. The user can quickly locate authoritative information on a wide variety of subjects, such as the difference between "down stage" and "up stage," the changing duties of the stage manager throughout history, the dates of Katharine Hepburn's famous portrayals of Rosalind in *As You Like It* and Beatrice in *Much Ado about Nothing*, and the story of a Red Army deserter who hid in a pigsty for 41 years (Athol Fugard's *A Place with the Pigs*). *The Concise Oxford Companion to the Theatre* maintains its place of prominence as a treasured desktop reference tool for anyone interested in the theater. [R: RBB, 1 Mar 93, p. 1251]—**Colby H. Kullman**

1473. Hischak, Thomas S. **Stage It with Music: An Encyclopedic Guide to the American Musical Theatre.** Westport, Conn., Greenwood Press, 1993. 341p. index. $45.00. ML102.M88H6. 792.6'0973. LC 92-35321. ISBN 0-313-28708-2.

This encyclopedic guide provides access to information about highlights of the American musical theater from the nineteenth century to 1992. Covering such a broad subject in a single volume necessitates both short entries and selective criteria for inclusion. There are approximately 300 entries for individual musicals, as well as entries for performers and other creative artists such as directors, technical designers, choreographers, producers, librettists, lyricists, and composers. The preface gives some indication of the criteria for selection, but in general the entries seem to be based on personal preferences. Users will often question why an individual who has appeared in only one or two musicals or had one show-stopping number is given an entry, while another with similar credentials has not. Similarly, any fan of the musical theater may be disappointed not to find entries for a favorite show, song, or artist.

Hischak has provided an extensive index to proper names and show and song titles, which helps to find many mentioned in the entries but not granted individual entries. There also are a few entries for musical series, such as the Ziegfeld Follies, and for broad subjects and genres, such as concept musicals, flop musicals, and British imports. In relation to the latter category, the author has emphasized American musicals and artists, but British authors, productions, and artists who have impacted the Broadway theater are included. Again, there are no specified criteria given as to how such impact is determined or measured.

In addition to vague selection criteria, the work is hampered by a rather annoying page layout. The decision not to invert proper names used as entries makes scanning a page rather difficult, because the eye cannot simply move down a left-justified margin. In spite of these deficiencies, the dictionary approach does provide different access from that of the more comprehensive *American Musical Theatre* (see ARBA 93, entry 1385). Students of the musical will probably find little new in this work, but it is an interesting, easily browsed potpourri of facts and opinions about a beloved American art form. [R: Choice, Dec 93, p. 586; RBB, Aug 93, p. 2095]—**Barbara E. Kemp**

1474. Leiter, Samuel L. **The Encyclopedia of the New York Stage, 1940-1950.** Westport, Conn., Greenwood Press, 1992. 946p. index. $195.00. PN2277.N5L365. 792'.097471. LC 92-7397. ISBN 0-313-27510-6.

This is the third volume of a series devoted to the New York stage in the twentieth century. Its predecessors dealt with the periods 1920-1930 (see ARBA 86, entry 1355) and 1930-1940 (see ARBA 90, entry 1367). This volume covers nearly 1,150 alphabetically listed productions, including plays, musicals, revues, revivals, and return engagements from 1940 to 1950. Only Broadway and off-Broadway theaters are included.

An extensive introductory essay provides an overview of issues and developments on the New York stage during the 1940s. Most of the work is devoted to an alphabetical list of productions. Multiple productions of the same work are in chronological order. Each entry includes production notes and a substantial, frequently entertaining, annotation that describes the plot and the critical reviews the play received. The 10 appendixes draw together additional information about the legitimate theater in this period. They include a chronology; a list of productions by type; awards, novels, and plays that provided sources for plays and musicals; institutional theaters and foreign companies and their offerings; the longest-running shows; a seasonal breakdown of production totals; and a list of all the theaters where the productions were staged. An extensive bibliography of books follows. Finally, there are name and title indexes.

This encyclopedia is an important reference source on theater in the 1940s. Unfortunately, it is also very expensive, but libraries that have the earlier works will probably want to purchase this volume. [R: Choice, May 93, p. 1444]—**Christine E. King**

1475. Reid, Francis. **The ABC of Stage Lighting.** New York, Drama Book, 1992. 129p. illus. $16.95pa. ISBN 0-89676-119-3.

This book is a list of definitions for words and terms used in stage lighting (e.g., ellipsoidal, flash box, light spread). It includes illustrations of equipment and materials used and provides a cross-reference of international terms applied to the same piece of equipment or application.

As noted in the prolog, "Even experienced lighting people can find some of the [stage lighting] terminology obscure. This is perhaps inevitable with a visual art form so dependent upon complex technology: not only are visual experiences notoriously difficult to describe in words, but the pace of technological advance is such that much of the equipment becomes obsolescent before it is fully established." However true that statement is, because of the cost of stage lighting equipment, theaters with a modest (if not nonexistent) budget for lighting hold on to and use what they have until it dies—whether outdated or not. It appears that Reid is well aware of this phenomenon and other such concerns as he has compiled a well-thought-out, enlightening reference with which any professional designer, stagehand, or theater volunteer can work.

As Reid also mentions in the prolog, "All entries represent the author's own understanding of what the words mean and reflect his own use of them." He goes on to almost apologize for this. However, he need not have. This work is exactly what every serious lighting person needs as a companion piece to the scores of scholastic books on the subject—a genuine "real world" reference from someone who has been in the business for 30-plus years! *The ABC of Stage Lighting* belongs in every academic and public library, and on every theater lighting shelf next to the lamp catalog and gel/color filter sampler. [R: Choice, Feb 93, p. 944]—**Joan Garner**

Directories

1476. McCallum, Heather, and Ruth Pincoe, comps. **Directory of Canadian Theatre Archives.** Halifax, N.S., School of Library and Information Studies, Dalhousie University, 1992. 217p. index. (Occasional Papers Series, no.53). $24.95 spiralbound. 026'.792'0971. ISBN 0-7703-9709-3.

This work is a revision of *Theatre Resources in Canadian Collections* (1973) and reflects the increased interest in Canadian theater history since then. The guide describes materials on live theater and broadcast performance in more than 300 collections held by public and university archives, libraries, university drama departments, theater schools, theater companies, organizations, museums, and individuals. Entries are arranged by province, then city, then repository. Each entry includes the name, address, and telephone number of the repository and a brief (but adequate) description of each collection. Resources covered include publicity materials, programs, scrapbooks, designs, scripts, correspondence, diaries, and audio and video recordings. A name and title index is included. An appendix describes materials relating to the Canadian Broadcasting Corporation. There is also an excellent bibliography of publications concerned with Canadian theater. This reasonably priced guide will bring Canada's rich theatrical heritage to the attention of scholars and students and will be a useful resource for journalists, theater personnel, and the general public.—**Gari-Anne Patzwald**

1477. **TCG Theatre Directory 1993-94.** New York, Theatre Communications Group, 1993. 90p. $5.95pa. ISBN 1-55936-075-5.

The Theatre Communications Group's (TCG's) annual guide to nonprofit professional theaters across the United States lists the 243 constituent and 70 associate theaters that together comprise the TCG. It serves not only as a reference source but also as a communications tool for the theaters, organizations, and artists of America's national theater community. The first main section, on TCG's theaters, provides basic contact information, such as the address, telephone numbers, performance season, and names of staff. Information on each theater's Actor's Equity Association contract is included. The second section, on organizations and associations, contains the names of 50 organizations offering services to both individuals and institutions of the nonprofit professional theater. Contact information is provided, as well as a brief statement as to the organization's purpose, functions, and programs. An index to theaters by state allows for geographical access to this handy directory.—**Anita Zutis**

1478. **Want's Theater Directory.** 1993 ed. Robert S. Want, ed. Washington, D.C., WANT Publishing, 1993. 122p. index. (American Theatre Series). $12.95pa. ISBN 0-942008-66-9. ISSN 1064-1300.

This slim volume contains within its covers an odd concatenation of information. It supplies a list of Broadway shows that are on tour, their destinations and dates, and booking agents. This is followed by a list of current Broadway shows with one- or two-line capsule reviews. The third section (the largest) is a directory listing, with addresses and telephone numbers, of theaters within the United States and Canada. The next section is reserved for state-by-state information about entertainment venues for children and young adults. A list of current productions on the London stage and a select listing of plays at various Paris and Berlin theaters are supplied. After that is to be found a list of Tony award and Pulitzer prize winners. A set of seating charts for some Broadway theaters concludes the information in this volume. The index deals only with the theater directory.

The main problem with this reference work is that it attempts to deal with too wide a variety of topics. The information it supplies is skimpy and incomplete, and no attempt seems to have been made to be exhaustive or comprehensive. The seating charts are useful if one intends to attend one of the selected theaters. This reference work may be useful if it happens to have the information sought, but because of its skimpiness and the short life span of the Broadway productions it lists, it will be of little use to the knowledgeable theater enthusiast. [R: RBB, 1 Oct 93, p. 388]—**Charles Neuringer**

Handbooks and Yearbooks

1479. **Cambridge Guide to American Theatre.** Don B. Wilmeth and Tice L. Miller, eds. New York, Cambridge University Press, 1993. 547p. illus. index. $49.95. PN2220.C35. 792'.0973. LC 92-35030. ISBN 0-521-40134-8.

Continuing the time-honored tradition of earlier Cambridge guides, this latest addition to the series concisely, yet comprehensively, covers the U.S. theatrical scene from its inception to the present (early 1992). Although the book includes a number of revised and updated entries gleaned from the *Cambridge Guide to World Theatre* (see ARBA 90, entry 1362), it also contains a host of new entries, reflecting an intentional bias in the direction of *current* U.S. theater. It also provides two additional resources: a selected bibliography of recommended readings and a biographical index for people who do not have entries of their own in the guide.

In a format similar to that used by other guides in the series, the entries are alphabetically arranged by author, title, and subject in a single dictionary-style list. A preface, an introductory essay chronicling the history of the U.S. stage, a list of contributors, and a list of topics introduce the guide. The signed entries vary in length from several sentences to several pages and, in some cases, include brief bibliographies and photographs. Cross-references are shown in boldface type.

Current, well researched, and highly accessible, this handbook shows all the signs of becoming a basic reference source on U.S. theater. It should find a welcome place in the collections of most public and academic libraries *and* on the desks of theater arts faculty, students, and participants. [R: Choice, June 93, pp. 1596-98; LJ, 15 Feb 93, p. 156; RBB, 15 Oct 93, p. 468; WLB, Dec 93, pp. 75-76]

—**Kristin Ramsdell**

1480. **The Oxford Companion to American Theatre.** 2d ed. By Gerald Bordman. New York, Oxford University Press, 1992. 735p. $49.95. PN2220.B6. 792'.0973. LC 91-16720. ISBN 0-19-507246-4.

This thorough revision of the first edition (see ARBA 85, entry 1269) presents an up-to-date guide to the American stage from its beginnings to the present. More than 3,000 entries provide significant information about playwrights, plays, actors, directors, producers, songwriters, dramatic movements, theatrical concepts, famous playhouses, and celebrated companies. Unlike *The Oxford Companion to the Theatre* (see ARBA 84, entry 932) this volume includes entries for several hundred American plays either of recognized commercial success or of enduring aesthetic or historical importance. A number of foreign plays that had great success on the American stage or that influenced American theater significantly are also to be found in this volume. In addition to the giants among American authors, actors, directors, producers, and other theatrical notables, Bordman presents more than a representative cross-section that covers not only all aspects of the theater but also all years and, wherever possible, all important theatrical centers.

Readers will discover summaries of plays as varied as *The Contrast, The Octoroon, Of Mice and Men, Ma Rainey's Black Bottom, The Heidi Chronicles,* and *A Lie of the Mind*. Entries new to this edition include plays (e.g., *Fences, M. Butterfly, Burn This*) as well as biographies (e.g., Dustin Hoffman, Raul Julia, August Wilson). Particularly strong are the entries covering workshops and companies, such as the Actor's Workshop, the Alley Theatre Company, the Actors Theatre of Louisville, and the Dallas Theater Center. In addition to traditional forms of theater, entries occur for minstrelsy, vaudeville, Wild West shows, tent shows, and other instances of live theater. Omitted are a number of figures and plays recognized by off-Broadway or by more venturesome regional critics and audiences. Most rising young talents will have to wait for a later edition. Off-Broadway is considered important enough for inclusion, but off-off-Broadway is not. August Wilson and his major plays may be found, but Jose Rivera and his work are not represented. Overall, *The Oxford Companion to American Theatre* is an epic undertaking that deserves high praise for its usefulness as a companion ever available to assist reference librarians, theater scholars, and theater lovers the world over.—**Colby H. Kullman**

Indexes

1481. **Play Index 1988-1992: An Index to 4,397 Plays.** Juliette Yaakov and John Greenfieldt, eds. Bronx, N.Y., H. W. Wilson, 1993. 542p. $80.00. LC 64-1054. ISSN 0554-3037.

How could the theater community and those who serve it manage without this superb reference tool? It lists plays published more or less within the years listed in the title (some older publications that did not get in the previous edition are included) as well as collections of plays. It has very specific subject entries that range from adolescence to aging, from nuns to prostitutes, from poverty to wealth, and from birthdays to funeral rites and ceremonies. Puppet plays, television plays, musicals, and monologues are included. The main entry for a play (under author) also has a brief but informative annotation about the play's subject, locale, period, number of scenes, and set and cast requirements. Choice of layout, typefaces and type sizes make everything sought stand out on the page in user-friendly fashion. The other parts of the book are devoted to cast analysis (size and type of cast), a list of collections indexed, and a directory of publishers and distributors. This is a perfect reference tool.—**George Louis Mayer**

28 Philosophy and Religion

PHILOSOPHY

Bibliography

1482. Burr, John R. **World Philosophy: A Contemporary Bibliography.** Westport, Conn., Greenwood Press, 1993. 380p. index. (Bibliographies and Indexes in Philosophy, no.3). $79.95. Z7125.W87. 016.1'09'047. LC 93-18031. ISBN 0-313-24032-9.

The purpose of this reference work is to provide a representative sample of books and monographs that have been published between 1976 and 1992, although the majority of the citations focus on 1976-1986. The book essentially constitutes a supplement to the author's previous bibliography, *Handbook of World Philosophy*. The two works complement one another, with the earlier work covering 1945-1976. No articles are cited.

The bibliography begins with a list of 32 works categorized under the heading "World Philosophy." Many of these citations are annotated. Most of the work divides into regions: Africa, the Middle East, Asia, Eastern Europe, Western Europe, Australia and New Zealand, Latin America, and North America. Each region is further subdivided by country. The author does not consider the works cited to be exhaustive. In addition to 3,919 entries, one finds invaluable author and subject indexes. The subject index provides not only general categories (e.g., epistemology) but also divisions within categories (e.g., references to specific works as well as references to specific concepts or content).

"World Philosophy" designates "a distinct class of philosophical works emphasizing 'relevant philosophical developments everywhere in the world.'" While that definition hardly satisfies, the book itself is quite useful. Anyone pursuing philosophical inquiry will find it essential. Highly recommended.
—**Michael A. Foley**

1483. Cassel, Jeris F., and Robert J. Congleton. **Critical Thinking: An Annotated Bibliography.** Metuchen, N.J., Scarecrow, 1993. 403p. index. $47.50. Z5814.C88C37. 016.16. LC 92-35306. ISBN 0-8108-2635-6.

Critical thinking: What is it? Can it be taught, and if so, how? Such questions are hardly much newer than the recorded history of human thought. In recent decades, however, they have been invested with new life and significance as "Critical Thinking" became the label for an identifiable movement, and something of a buzzword, in U.S. education from the elementary to the graduate and professional levels. Cassel and Congleton have documented, selectively yet in depth, a bit more than a decade's worth of literature from and about that movement: 1980 through 1991. This literature examines or advocates critical thinking from a wide range of theoretical, empirical, and applied perspectives. Chapters cover, for example, definitions and concepts; research; professional development and teacher training; testing and evaluation; and teaching in specific subject areas such as reading and writing, library instruction, humanities, and social and natural sciences. It includes a useful subject index and an author index.

Each of the 930 entries is very helpfully annotated, and chapters on theoretical matters include cross-references so that one can trace who is responding to whom. This feature does point up the fact that the Critical Thinking movement is not characterized by unanimity about its concepts, goals, and methods—all the more reason why anyone who shares its concerns is well advised to consult this bibliography. [R: Choice, Sept 93, pp. 74-76; RBB, 1 Oct 93, pp. 379-80]—**Hans E. Bynagle**

1484. Dreisbach, Christopher. **R. G. Collingwood: A Bibliographical Checklist.** Bowling Green, Ohio, Philosophy Documentation Center, Bowling Green State University, 1993. 139p. index. $29.00. ISBN 0-912632-93-3.

Collingwood continues to be a philosopher and historian of considerable interest to the academic community, as shown by the large number of secondary entries in Dreisbach's bibliography. This work attempts to give a comprehensive list of all works and manuscripts by Collingwood, as well as nearly all articles, essays, books, and reviews of the philosopher's work. Dreisbach differs from earlier bibliographers by organizing the entries alphabetically according to type of material, instead of chronologically or by location of manuscripts. The arrangement is straightforward and easy to use.

Although this is a checklist, Dreisbach has added some features that enhance the work's utility. Secondary works that have vague or nondescriptive titles receive brief annotations to indicate their relevance to Collingwood's thought. Books about Collingwood that have themselves been reviewed receive notes listing the reviews. Also, the author and subject indexes are supplemented by a periodical index, based on the proper assumption that critical works appearing in certain periodicals frequently are written from a particular perspective or school of thought.

This work includes few additional primary works not found in the best previous bibliography, Donald S. Taylor's *R. G. Collingwood: A Bibliography* (see ARBA 89, entry 1305). Its major contribution is the inclusion of more than twice as many critical works on Collingwood as found in Taylor's work, which focuses mainly on the philosopher's views of history and art. Taylor, however, provides superior annotations and remains very useful.—**Christopher W. Nolan**

1485. Easton, Patricia, Thomas M. Lennon, and Gregor Sebba. **Bibliographia Malebranchiana: A Critical Guide to the Malebranche Literature into 1989.** Carbondale, Ill., Southern Illinois University Press, 1992. 189p. index. $24.95. Z8544.7.E37. 016.194. LC 90-20698. ISBN 0-8093-1603-X.

Since the publication of the definitive edition of Nicholas Malebranche's *Ouevres Completes* (1958-1984), scholars have shown renewed interest in this seventeenth-century philosopher-priest. Increased attention has produced an abundance of scholarship, making necessary this book. Sebba privately printed and circulated a preliminary bibliography of work by and about Malebranche is 1959. Lennon updated Sebba's annotated list through 1976, and he and Easton extended coverage into 1989.

The bibliography is divided into two parts: works by Malebranche and works on Malebranche. Part 1 consists of 28 pages. Part 2 has three sections on bibliography, biography, and studies, the latter comprising three-fourths of the book. Research published on the philosopher in English, French, Italian, German, Spanish, Dutch, Polish, Japanese, Latin, and Russian is included, although most is in English or French. Critical annotations in English accompany a majority of the citations. An index provides access to subjects and names mentioned in citations or annotations. Authors of material listed in part 2 are not included in the index because they are easily found in alphabetical order in each section. The *Bibliographia Malebranchiana* will be useful to students and scholars needing an exhaustive guide to Malebranche literature or to academic libraries collecting heavily in the history of philosophy.—**John P. Stierman**

1486. Evans, Calvin D., comp. **Soren Kierkegaard Bibliographies: Remnants, 1944-1980 and Multi-Media, 1925-1991.** Montreal, McGill University Libraries, 1993. 185p. illus. (Fontanus Monograph Series, 2). $25.00. ISBN 0-7717-0272-8.

As a supplement to the *International Kierkegaard Bibliographic Database* (IKBD) by Stephane Hogue, the present volume adds "remnants" (leavings by authors about the subject matter) from 1944 to 1980 and multimedia presentations of Kierkegaard from 1925 to 1991. Each monographic entry contains a full bibliographical citation with further citations of book reviews. Some entries have descriptive subject matter; others merely cite the material.

The volume is a welcome addition to IKBD, containing as it does material not found in that source. It contains photographs, sketches, and scenes from plays involving Kierkegaard, making its usefulness extend beyond the merely bibliographical. Evans contends that the Danish Don has been misinterpreted by modern existentialists who ignore or discount Kierkegaard's Christian commitment. This understanding informs and enriches his bibliography. The lack, however, of any indexes detracts and distracts from the work's helpfulness.

Scholars and laypeople alike will consult this resource often. Understanding of Kierkegaard has been profoundly enhanced by this addition to an important corpus of literature.—**Mark Y. Herring**

1487. Kaylor, Noel Harold, Jr. **The Medieval *Consolation of Philosophy*: An Annotated Bibliography.** Hamden, Conn., Garland, 1992. 262p. (Garland Medieval Bibliographies, v.7; Garland Reference Library of the Humanities, v.1215). $41.00. Z8106.3.K38. 016.189. LC 92-459. ISBN 0-8240-5548-9.

Kaylor's bibliography focuses on the reception of Boethius's *De Consolatione Philosophiae* in the medieval vernacular traditions. It would not be an exaggeration to claim that no other text except the Bible played such a formative role in the intellectual life of the Middle Ages. A primary school text throughout Europe from at least the time of Alcuin (ca. 800), the work also found its way into the vernacular through translations by no lesser figures than King Alfred, Notker, Chaucer, and Queen Elizabeth. In four chapters on Old English, Medieval German, Medieval French, and Middle English traditions, Kaylor offers a brief overview of trends in scholarship and an annotated list of relevant titles from the nineteenth century to 1992.

The introductions and descriptions are rather basic and at times so general as to be of little value (e.g., "This book is useful for the general information it gives on Alfred and his work as a translator"). Moreover, despite the universality of Latin in the Middle Ages and the importance of the original as a school text, the influence of the Latin text is not a topic (although some works that address broader themes of intellectual influence are cited in the introduction). A bibliography at the end of the work lists many—but not all—of the works included in each chapter. For example, one finds articles on King Alfred's translation in the concluding bibliography that do not appear in the annotated bibliography on Old English versions. This confusing arrangement lessens the book's usefulness. [R: Choice, July/August 93, p. 1752]—**Valerie R. Hotchkiss**

1488. Navia, Luis E. **The Presocratic Philosophers: An Annotated Bibliography.** Hamden, Conn., Garland, 1993. 722p. index. (Garland Reference Library of Social Science, v.704). $110.00. Z7128.P83N38. 016.182. LC 93-16207. ISBN 0-8240-9776-9.

The Presocratics laid the groundwork for Western philosophy by raising questions, both philosophical and scientific, that formed the basis for subsequent inquiry. Navia's aim in producing this bibliography was to annotate a substantial body of works representing varied points of view, selected from what he calls a "wide spectrum of literature." As he illustrates, the Presocratics have been the subject not only of scholarly and professional investigation but also of fictional works, poetry, and musical compositions. For example, the philosopher Empedocles is the subject of Friedrich Holderlin's dramatic poem "Der Tod des Empedokles" and of Matthew Arnold's "Empedocles on Etna."

The present work lists and describes almost 2,700 items from the scholarly literature, beginning with bibliographical works, source collections, and general studies, followed by single chapters devoted to each of the 11 major philosophers in this group. The chapter on Pythagoras, as Navia notes, is an addendum and update to his earlier work *Pythagoras: An Annotated Bibliography* (see ARBA 91, entry 1401). Foreign titles are given in their original language with the English translation in brackets, some modern Greek, Russian, and Turkish titles excepted.

Annotations are descriptive; they are not meant to summarize but to emphasize what Navia deemed distinctive. Judged from this focus, he has been successful. What is less clear, however, with the exception of the chapter on Pythagoras, is the methodology of selecting the nearly 450 journals included and the time frame of the literature reviewed. Someone searching the bibliography for a particular philosopher, such as Heraclitus, would have little idea of the sources and the time period Navia searched in making his selections. This is, nonetheless, an immensely helpful bibliography introducing serious students to the literature of the Presocratics. Scholarly collections will want to acquire it despite the high cost. [R: Choice, Dec 93, pp. 588-89]—**Bernice Bergup**

1489. Nordquist, Joan, comp. **Jean Paul Sartre: A Bibliography.** Santa Cruz, Calif., Reference and Research Services, 1993. 76p. index. (Social Theory: A Bibliographic Series, no.29). $15.00pa. ISBN 0-937855-57-X.

Similar to the other titles in the series, this work lists English-language works and translations of writings by and about Jean-Paul Sartre. Most of the articles about Sartre appear in readily available periodicals found in most research collections. Arranged in four sections (books by Sartre, essays and interviews with Sartre, books about Sartre, and articles about Sartre), the bibliography lists multiple entries for many works. The reason for this editorial decision is, "If one title is not in a library, either because it is not owned or because it is checked out, perhaps the other will be." Two keyword indexes assist the researcher in locating books and articles. One might question why Nordquist did not combine the indexes.

The introduction to the series implies that these volumes are geared to undergraduates, especially introductory classes. The works seem better suited to advanced undergraduates or introductory graduate students wishing to begin research on the given individual. The volume appears to be produced through desktop publishing, with a softcover format that may not withstand heavy usage. Also, due to the continual addition of new material, updates will be a necessity. Recommended for any college or university library supporting research programs in the humanities, social sciences, or cross-disciplinary studies.—**Gregory Curtis**

1490. Perrin, Robert G. **Herbert Spencer: A Primary and Secondary Bibliography.** Hamden, Conn., Garland, 1993. 1005p. index. (Garland Reference Library of the Humanities, v.1061). $145.00. Z8830.35.P47. 016.192. LC 93-12108. ISBN 0-8240-4597-1.

In the latter half of the nineteenth century, Herbert Spencer enjoyed a popular reputation and wide readership seldom achieved by any philosopher or social theorist, but in the first half of the twentieth century, he sank into relative obscurity. Serious engagement with his thought, at least, became rare, although students of intellectual history remained generally familiar with Spencer as the philosopher of universal evolution (he, not Darwin, coined the phrase "survival of the fittest") and apostle of social Darwinism (although not in as brutal a version as is sometimes attributed to him). The past few decades, however, have seen Spencer's work come in for renewed attention. Perrin's ambitious primary and secondary bibliography reflects this increased interest and may well stimulate a good deal more.

Perrin has not merely recorded (as exhaustively as seems humanly possible) writings by and about Spencer in English, from the latter's first publication in 1839 (a letter to a magazine) through 1992; he has also managed to annotate virtually every item, often at considerable length. Of his 2,082 entries, 322 represent Spencer's own prolific output, ranging from letters to the 10-volume *System of Synthetic Philosophy*. Books and pamphlets are listed alphabetically, articles and letters chronologically. The secondary literature is divided over 13 broad subject chapters, such as biographical and general studies, ethics, biology, psychology, sociology, and social thought. This arrangement compensates in part for the absence of a detailed subject index. An index of names lists the expected names of authors, but also includes, on a mysteriously selective basis, some titles of publications in which cited literature appeared.

Preceding the bibliography proper is an excellent 98-page introduction surveying Spencer's life, career, and thought. The picture it presents is generally balanced and certainly not uncritical, although Perrin's sympathy for Spencer's social and political outlook is almost as transparent, here and in some of the annotations, as his concern to combat certain misconceptions and durable misrepresentations of Spencer's ideas.—**Hans E. Bynagle**

1491. Schultz, William R., and Lewis L. B. Fried. **Jacques Derrida: An Annotated Primary and Secondary Bibliography.** Hamden, Conn., Garland, 1992. 882p. index. (Garland Bibliographies of Modern Critics and Critical Schools, v.18; Garland Reference Library of the Humanities, v.1319). $140.00. Z8226.85.S38. 016.194. LC 92-12592. ISBN 0-8240-4872-5.

Insofar as a bibliography can be exhaustive while the author still lives, Schultz and Fried have succeeded. Books, parts of books, books in other languages, chapters or other contributions to books, articles, interviews, reviews, and translations by Derrida fill out the primary sources, some one-fifth of the book. The remaining portion contains the same general headings about Derrida. Mirabile dictu, the volume also has an author and name index but no title index (one wishes publishers would make all three mandatory to facilitate ease of access by laypeople and scholars alike).

One useful, commendable aspect of the book is a section on the controversy over Derrida's intellectual contributions. This is especially important in light of the recent, sussultatory revelations about Jean-Paul Sartre, Simone de Beauvoir, and other philosophical eminences. The usual proofreading faux pas appear throughout. Those wishing something on the order of completeness about Derrida will want to buy this volume. [R: Choice, May 93, pp. 1448-49]—**Mark Y. Herring**

Dictionaries and Encyclopedias

1492. Cooper, David E., ed. **A Companion to Aesthetics.** Cambridge, Mass., Basil Blackwell, 1992. 466p. index. $74.95. ISBN 0-631-17801-5.

Bringing together the many and varied aspects of aesthetics into a single volume is no easy task. Cooper has done a commendable job in this respect. With 130 articles that range from 1,200 to 4,000 words (a few longer ones are included), most of the topics and concepts a reader in aesthetics is likely to encounter are dealt with in this volume. Arranged alphabetically by topic, each well-written article contains a brief bibliography and cross-references to other related articles. All articles are signed. Authors and theoreticians are discussed within the context of the subject, but a lengthy discussion of them is also included under their names as well. This editorial decision requires the reader to check two or more entries for complete coverage. This arrangement is not too difficult, however, due to the useful subject index with subtopics. Any library with interests in aesthetics, philosophy, art, literature, languages, music, or the humanities in general will find this a useful purchase. [R: Choice, July/Aug 93, p. 1745]

—**Gregory Curtis**

1493. Cottingham, John. **A Descartes Dictionary.** Cambridge, Mass., Basil Blackwell, 1993. 187p. index. (Blackwell Philosopher Dictionaries). $39.95; $17.95pa. B1831.C67. 194. LC 92-39483. ISBN 0-631-17683-7; 0-631-18538-0pa.

Some of the reference sources in philosophy give too much information, providing confusion rather than clarity. To reach the population not ready for the advanced philosophy reference tools, Blackwell has introduced the Blackwell Philosopher Dictionaries, a series of philosopher-specific dictionaries aimed at the student or general reader. Cottingham's work, a recent addition to the series, is clearly aimed at the novice, and successfully reaches its audience.

The author, head of the philosophy department at the University of Reading, knows his subject well; his credits include translations of Descartes, a biography, and *The Cambridge Companion to Descartes* (Cambridge University Press, 1992), not a reference book. *A Descartes Dictionary* is more a reader's companion than a dictionary. Most entries are more than a page long and focus on a word or theme running through Descartes's philosophy, such as "faith" or "God." In each entry, the author provides his own analysis and cites the locations of the item in the French philosopher's treatises. Cottingham displays great skill in placing the concept within the history of philosophy before discussing its Cartesian usage (e.g., see "idea"). Advanced philosophy students will find this book useful, but they have other choices in the reference collection. *A Descartes Dictionary*, similar to *World Philosophy* (see ARBA 84, entry 1012), will give beginners the insight they need to understand Descartes's philosophy.

A Descartes Dictionary is a great improvement over the *Descartes Dictionary* (see ARBA 72, entry 1206), which is little more than a collection of quotations from Descartes's writings. Any college or university library with an active philosophy department will want to acquire this dictionary and, if the other titles in the series are as good as this one, the rest of the set.—**John P. Stierman**

1494. Dunlop, Charles E. M., and James H. Fetzer. **Glossary of Cognitive Science.** New York, Paragon House, 1993. 146p. (Paragon House Glossary for Research, Reading, and Writing). $17.95; $8.95pa. BF311.D84. 153.4'03. LC 92-27750. ISBN 1-55778-566-X; 1-55778-567-8pa.

Cognitive science refers to an interdisciplinary field that investigates the nature and processes of cognition—in human beings, of course, but also, as the preface to this little dictionary puts it, in "other animals, and machines (if such a thing is possible)." It inclines toward treating cognition as a set of processes that can at least in theory be carried out by a computer—although that assumption is not without challengers. The field straddles the disciplines of computer science, psychology, linguistics, and philosophy, contributions from all of which are covered here. A fifth contributing area, neuroscience, is intentionally not addressed. The rationale offered for this omission—to the effect that mentality may not ultimately be limited to biological systems—seems less than compelling, but one suspects there are pragmatic justifications for it as well.

As it is, this glossary offers, within its compact format, a helpful, wide-ranging compilation of definitions and explanations of terminology, names, and other references prevalent in the literature of the field. It is aimed not at specialists but at students and teachers, and will also be valued by researchers in other domains whose interests intersect with those of cognitive science. Explanations are kept minimally technical. Cross-references abound so that the user can usually fill in, by pursuing the linkages, any gaps in understanding left by a given explanation. Often it is even possible, with a little persistence, to construct from linked entries a succinct overview of some significant aspect of the field. [R: Choice, Sept 93, p. 78]

—**Hans E. Bynagle**

1495. Fetzer, James H., and Robert F. Almeder. **Glossary of Epistemology/Philosophy of Science.** New York, Paragon House, 1993. 149p. (Paragon House Glossary for Research, Reading, and Writing). $17.95; $8.95pa. BD150.F47. 121'.03. LC 92-22762. ISBN 1-55778-558-9; 1-55778-559-7pa.

This book is an alphabetically arranged glossary of terms, personal names, concepts, and the like related to epistemology and the philosophy of science. The authors are both professors of philosophy and authors of texts in the fields they cover. Although the two disciplines seem disparate, they relate closely when considered in the context of understanding and seeking knowledge. Entries consist of concepts and the most influential and best-known scholars in the fields through the ages (Plato and Aristotle are both included). Where terms and modifications of terms can be included under more generic labels, *see* and *see also* references are provided. The language used in the definitions is generally scholarly rather than popular or laical, in spite of the preface's description of it as "down to earth." The authors were selective rather than exhaustive in what they included. Nevertheless, they have included some concepts, notably probability theory, that may seem out of place in these fields, but were included as "not widely understood, even among professional philosophers" and important in context.

The price of this book will make it attractive for any library, although a small book such as this is probably better for the shelf of a student, scholar, or writer. It will find good use in a specialized philosophy of science collection. In addition, it is recommended for large public and academic libraries, where it will serve as a companion to other, more elaborate books in the subject areas. Many of these other works are cited in the selective, annotated bibliography provided in the final pages of the book.—**Edward P. Miller**

1496. **The HarperCollins Dictionary of Philosophy.** 2d ed. By Peter A. Angeles. New York, Harper-Perennial/HarperCollins, 1992. 342p. $25.00; $13.00pa. ISBN 0-06-271564-X; 0-06-461026-8pa.

This one-volume dictionary is intended to be an at-hand reference for beginning students of philosophy. It contains more than 3,000 brief definitions of major philosophical concepts, and it was expanded in this edition by some 100 biographical notes. There are no references to sources or collaborators consulted, implying that all entries were written by the author alone. This may account for the work's relatively simple and uniform style of presentation.

The dictionary is not a substitute for, nor a supplement to, the current edition of D. D. Runes's *Dictionary of Philosophy* (see ARBA 84, entry 1010). Although it contains very few entries not directly listed in Runes's compilation (e.g., *dikalosyne, square of opposition*), it lacks references to many philosophical views considered too advanced for an introductory course in philosophy (e.g., *Scotism, Surrealism*). The focus of the compilation is primarily on Western philosophy, excluding overviews of such philosophies as Chinese, Islamic, and Jewish. Many important modern contributors to philosophy, including Friedrich Engels and Sigmund Freud, are not directly mentioned.

Libraries that already own the original edition of this dictionary may wish to update it; others with more extensive reference collections in philosophy will probably consider it a low priority. The dictionary ought to sell well in book stores serving undergraduate students and the public.—**Joseph Z. Nitecki**

1497. McLeish, Kenneth, ed. **Key Ideas in Human Thought.** New York, Facts on File, 1993. 789p. $45.00. B41.K48. 031. LC 93-24150. ISBN 0-8160-2707-2.

A successor to the *Dictionary of Cultural Literacy* (Houghton Mifflin, 1993), this compilation of 2,500 terms provides a simple and clearly written description of various concepts and their origins, meanings, and significances. Most entries include additional reading lists and cross-references to related concepts. Entries were selected by a panel of experts in major academic and applied disciplines. The subjects range from extensive descriptions (e.g., three and a half pages on concepts related to Marxism) to brief notes (e.g., a seven-line entry on mixed economy), and from highly complex or technical concepts to euphemistic ones, such as Godel's theorem and jingoism.

The viewpoint is predominantly English. Of the 36 contributors, all but 4 hold degrees from English universities. The spelling is British, and some concepts popular in England have no United States counterparts (e.g., there is an entry for "Angry Young Men" but not for "yippie" or "baby-boomer"). The compilation is reasonably, but not completely, current (e.g., it covers fractals and fiber optics but not entrepreneurship or virtual reality). Yet some terms listed in the compilation, such as indigenous metaphysics, cannot be easily found even in specialized dictionaries.

A major limitation of the compilation is its unknown scope. The editor defines it metaphorically in his introduction as primarily "the river of ideas," placing less emphasis on its "tributaries." However, the balance within and between the two notions is sometimes lacking; for example, there are entries for "Africanism (Pan-Africanism)" and "Arabism (Pan-Arabism)" but not for "Pan-Americanism" or "Pan-Slavism." Computer-related terms are extensively covered, but there is no reference to librarianship, the organization and classification of recorded knowledge, bibliography, or censorship.

Obviously, to satisfy the subject ignorance of all its potential users, the compilation would have to be much larger than this compact, single-volume publication. Overall, the book will be of value to people looking for the concepts listed in it. Recommended for general reference collections. [R: LJ, 15 Oct 93, p. 60]—**Joseph Z. Nitecki**

Directories

1498. **Directory of American Philosophers 1992-1993.** 16th ed. Archie J. Bahm and Richard H. Lineback, eds. Bowling Green, Ohio, Philosophy Documentation Center, Bowling Green State University, 1992. 476p. index. $59.00; $99.00 (Institutions). ISBN 0-91263290-9.

This well-established biennial directory has been in continuous publication since 1963, and its organization has changed little over the years (see ARBA 91, entry 1406). Philosophy departments in the United States and Canada are arranged by state or province. Each entry lists the department's address, type of university it is affiliated with, enrollment, highest degree offered, and telephone number. Next, the faculty are listed with degrees, rank, and specialties. Professors emeriti are the final element in the department's listing. This is followed by sections on assistantships, centers and institutions, societies, journals, and publishers. Names and addresses of philosophers are in separate listings, divided into those with and without institutional affiliation. There is also a brief statistical table that summarizes the data in the volume. Each section is thoroughly indexed. This directory remains a useful, well-organized, attractively presented, and up-to-date reference source.—**Jeffrey R. Luttrell**

Quotation Books

1499. Ayer, A. J., and Jane O'Grady, eds. **A Dictionary of Philosophical Quotations.** Cambridge, Mass., Basil Blackwell, 1992. 528p. index. $29.95. ISBN 0-631-17015-4.

Attempting to give the essence of philosophical ideas put forth by approximately 340 philosophers is no easy task. The editors of this work do an admirable job. It contains neither lengthy passages nor quick witticisms that invoke remembrances of longer statements. What the editors try to present is a brief but thorough quotation of the topic analyzed by the philosopher. Sometimes this is accomplished in one sentence, sometimes in a page; however, most entries run to a short paragraph. A large percentage of individuals included are modern philosophers from the late nineteenth and twentieth centuries. This editorial decision makes sense because it may be difficult to find references to some modern philosophers, while references to well-established figures appear in many other sources. The selection contains only those within the Western European tradition. No attempt is made to include Eastern Europeans, although some who influenced modern East European thought have entries. A glossary and subject index conclude the volume.

Any library should include this volume on its shelves. It will be used by a wide-ranging audience, and it is reasonably priced. Especially attractive is the arrangement of the subject index, which allows users to analyze various authors' thoughts on the same topic, and the inclusion of modern philosophers for a view of contemporary philosophical thought. Highly recommended. [R: Choice, July/Aug 93, p. 1748]
—Gregory Curtis

RELIGION

General Works

Bibliography

1500. Davis, Lenwood G., comp. **Daddy Grace: An Annotated Bibliography.** Westport, Conn., Greenwood Press, 1992. 130p. index. (Bibliographies and Indexes in Afro-American and African Studies, no.28). $45.00. Z8364.D3. 016.2899. LC 91-42599. ISBN 0-313-26504-6.

This work illuminates the career of Bishop Charles "Sweet Daddy" Grace. Born about 1882 in the Cape Verde Islands, Grace came to New Bedford, Massachusetts, around 1901. Over the next two decades he busied himself as a railroad short-order cook, salesman of sewing machines and patent medicine, cranberry picker, and grocery store owner. In 1923 or 1924 he started the United House of Prayer for All People, Church of the Apostolic Faith, in Charlotte, North Carolina. With headquarters in Washington, D.C., his church was incorporated by 1927. At the time of his death in Los Angeles on January 12, 1960, Grace's church, with congregations in major cities from Florida to California, claimed more than 4,000,000 members, had an estimated worth of $25 million, and owned an assortment of businesses.

Although not as well known as Father Divine, Grace encountered similar skepticism. Outsiders frequently dismissed both men as fraudulent con artists. This bibliography will enable students of American religion, especially those interested in cults and the African-American experience, to more easily locate the necessary materials to assess Grace for themselves. It has 261 annotated entries on books, encyclopedias, articles, theses and dissertations, and unpublished manuscripts, as well as appendixes on everything from Grace's quotations to current addresses for House of Prayer churches. This fine work should be in all college and university libraries.—**John W. Storey**

1501. Flake, Chad J., and Larry W. Draper, comps. **A Mormon Bibliography 1830-1930: Indexes to** *A Mormon Bibliography* **and** *Ten Year Supplement.* Salt Lake City, Utah, University of Utah Press, 1992. 208p. $25.00. Z7845.M8F55. 016.2893. LC 92-4569. ISBN 0-87480-400-0.

The exhaustive bibliographies that list materials by and about Mormons for the first century of Mormon history appeared in 1979 (*A Mormon Bibliography 1830-1930* [University of Utah Press]) and in 1989 (*A Mormon Bibliography 1830-1930: Ten Year Supplement* [see ARBA 91, entry 1435]). The authors have now prepared an exhaustive title, chronological, and language index to the set, providing further access to the documents listed. There is still no subject approach to the documents either in the original volumes or in this index. Recommended for libraries that own the original volumes.
—**David V. Loertscher**

1502. Hartley, Loyde H. **Cities and Churches: An International Bibliography.** Metuchen, N.J., American Theological Library Association and Scarecrow, 1992. 3v. index. (ATLA Bibliography Series, no.31). $195.00/set. Z7782.H37. 016.27'009173'2. LC 92-18819. ISBN 0-8108-2583-X.

Hartley has compiled an ambitious annotated bibliography of more than 19,200 sources that deal with church-city relationships. The citations are listed chronologically by year of publication, and within each year, alphabetically by author's name. Volume 1 includes 7,745 sources published between 1800 and 1959; volume 2 encompasses 7,585 items published between 1960 and 1979; and volume 3 cites 3,917 materials that appeared between 1980 and 1991, a brief addendum of items collected after identifying numbers were assigned to the preceding citations, a large author index, and a larger subject index. Also included in the set is a foreword by Martin Marty; an introductory essay that describes the purposes, structure, and uses of the bibliography; and eight chapter introductions that provide historical overviews and timelines of the periods covered in each chapter.

No bibliography attempting to encompass such a large and hard-to-define subject can be exhaustive. This set focuses primarily on the encounter between religion and the modern (post-1800) city, and is more heavily weighted toward the experiences of Christian churches in England and the United States than the experiences of non-Christian groups in other parts of the world. But despite these limitations, Hartley has amassed an impressive listing of often hard-to-find items. As the first comprehensive bibliography on urban religion, this set will be greatly appreciated by historians, sociologists, clerics, city planners, and others who are interested in exploring the sometimes peaceful, sometimes inimical relationship between the church and the modern city. Recommended for research libraries. [R: Choice, Mar 93, p. 1114]

—**Terry D. Bilhartz**

1503. Korsch, Boris. **Religion in the Soviet Union: A Bibliography, 1980-1989.** Hamden, Conn., Garland, 1992. 639p. index. (Garland Reference Library of Social Science, v.659). $100.00. Z7757.S65K67. 016.2'00947. LC 92-10129. ISBN 0-8240-7096-8.

This massive bibliography provides a list of nearly 6,000 Soviet publications that deal with the broad scope of religious activity in the former Soviet Union during the critical period of transition between Leonid Brezhnev and Mikhail Gorbachev. A variety of materials are covered: books, pamphlets, journal articles, reviews, dissertations, authorized religious works, and *samizdat* (unofficial) publications. Each item is numbered consecutively, and the publications are arranged alphabetically by author within each major section of the bibliography. All languages of the Soviet republics are included, with an English translation of the titles.

The central purpose of the bibliography, as stated by Korsch, is "to present Soviet religious policies as illustrated by propaganda in a sociopolitical and ideological context, framed in accordance with the CPSU and Soviet government objectives of the moment." His lengthy historiographic essay provides background to this compilation and discusses its multidisciplinary scope. Sociopolitical and economic aspects of religion are stressed, but there is also much information on other aspects of Soviet life: atheistic education, art, medicine, philosophy, law, psychology, the natural sciences, and the military.

The bibliography is divided into several major sections: bibliographies and reference works, Marxism-Leninism on religion and atheism, Soviet publications on religion and atheism (1980-1989), reviews, dissertations, censored religious publications, uncensored religious publications, and an addendum. Each item contains full bibliographical information, with occasional explanatory notes. A detailed subject index is keyed to the item numbers. This specialized resource is highly recommended for major research libraries and comprehensive theological collections. [R: C&RL, Sept 93, p. 428; Choice, May 93, p. 1444]

—**Thomas A. Karel**

1504. Tomasi, Silvano M., and Edward C. Stibili. **Italian Americans and Religion: An Annotated Bibliography.** 2d ed. Staten Island, N.Y., Center for Migration Studies, 1992. 365p. index. $19.50. Z7757.U5T65. 016.282'73'08951. LC 92-20267. ISBN 0-934733-52-X.

This new edition of a work first published in 1978 (see ARBA 80, entry 1051) expands the original by some 600 entries, representing primarily (but not exclusively) new sources that have appeared in the interim. Other revisions include the updating of entries on archival repositories, the rearrangement of the section on parish histories by state and locality, the improvement of some annotations for previously cited books and articles, the addition of locations for parish histories and hard-to-find books, and a new index.

As a bibliography providing detailed coverage of a special aspect of religious history, this work remains exemplary. And while it presents the Italian-American religious experience as overwhelmingly a chapter in the history of Catholicism, it does not ignore other dimensions, as signaled, a bit ironically, by the very first entry, which is on the American Baptist Historical Society.—**Hans E. Bynagle**

1505. Turner, Harold W. **Bibliography of New Religious Movements in Primal Societies. Volume 6: The Caribbean.** New York, G. K. Hall, 1992. 303p. index. $45.00. Z7835.C86T87. 016.291'046. LC 77-4732. ISBN 0-8161-9089-5.

The sixth and last volume of this bibliographical series covers the non-Western religious movements among the Amerindian, Asian, and especially African-derived populations of the Caribbean Islands, the countries of the Spanish Main (French Guiana, Suriname, Guyana, and Venezuela), the Bahamas, and Bermuda. (African-American religious movements of other Central and South American countries are included in volume 5 on Latin America.) Separate sections are included for the transnational phenomena of Rastafarians and Black Caribs. Citations—consecutively numbered, divided by country, and arranged alphabetically by author's name—include standard bibliographical information, and many also contain brief annotations. Each chapter is prefaced by a short but useful introduction. Entries (1,926 total) are duplicated when appropriate but with the addition of unique annotations. Annotations for general works include page numbers relevant to area or topic. Subject and author indexes are provided.

Most of the citations are from scholarly publications (including doctoral and master's theses), but substantial pieces from the popular press and even some novels are included. Turner has attempted to be comprehensive and—while there are omissions (e.g., citations on the obscure Mandingues of northern Haiti)—the coverage is excellent, especially of English-language sources. A thorough reading reveals only a few typographical errors (e.g., Minty rather than Mintz, a missing date of publication). This volume, and the series of which it is a part, will be the standard by which future efforts in documentation of new religious movements in non-Western societies will be judged. [R: Choice, June 93, p. 1611]—**Fred J. Hay**

1506. Whitney, Barry L. **Theodicy: An Annotated Bibliography on the Problem of Evil 1960-1990.** Hamden, Conn., Garland, 1993. 650p. index. (Garland Reference Library of the Humanities, v.1111). $98.00. Z7850.W48. 016.214. LC 92-42769. ISBN 0-8240-7638-9.

For more than a millennium, theologians and philosophers have followed Augustine in arguing that all moral evil is the result of the misuse of human free will. In the past 30 years, however, hundreds of scholars have readdressed the ancient problem of reconciling an omnipotent and omniscient God with the reality of human suffering and have questioned God's power over evil. This volume, written to complement Barry Whitney's 1989 Paulist Press publication *What Are They Saying about God and Evil*, attempts to list and annotate the most relevant and important books and articles on theodicy that have appeared since 1960.

The work lists approximately 2,600 items that have been published in (or translated into) English. Of these items, Whitney provides brief summaries of the main arguments and conclusions on about 1,500 publications he deems most pertinent to the contemporary debate. The annotated entries are arranged into thematic chapters that treat such topics as free will theodicy, best possible world theodicy, natural evil theodicy, Hick's Irenaean theodicy, and process theodicy. Chapter introductions present an overview of the central areas of debate and their leading spokespersons. The chapter introductions, although only three to six pages in length, are insightful and enhance the book's usefulness. The volume also includes an alphabetical index of the authors whose publications are cited. Recommended for seminaries and research libraries. [R: Choice, Sept 93, p. 92]—**Terry D. Bilhartz**

1507. Young, Arthur P., and E. Jens Holley with Annette Blum, comps. **Religion and the American Experience, 1620-1900: A Bibliography of Doctoral Dissertations.** Westport, Conn., Greenwood Press, 1992. 479p. index. (Bibliographies and Indexes in Religious Studies, no.24). $75.00. Z7757.U5Y68. 016.2'00973. LC 92-28450. ISBN 0-313-27747-8.

The underlying premise of this useful bibliography is that American history cannot be fully appreciated without some understanding of religion. Accordingly, the compilers, who are all librarians, have carefully examined *Dissertation Abstracts International* (University Microfilms International, monthly) through June 1991 to find doctoral dissertations that deal with this country's religious experience from 1620 to 1900. The resulting 4,240 entries in this book are grouped into two categories: those that deal with specific denominations and movements, and those of a thematic nature that embrace several church bodies. Among the denominations with the most citations are Catholic, 410; Congregational, 368; Baptist, 220; and Judaism, 116. There are also 175 entries on Transcendentalism, indicative of the compilers' broad, inclusive approach. The topical studies touch on everything from art and architecture to ethnic groups to science and religion to women.

Organized for easy use, all citations, which are subsumed alphabetically under either a denomination or a topic, are indexed by author and subject. Unfortunately, the subject index is not altogether reliable. One study that clearly deals with racial attitudes, for instance, is not listed under that subject. Despite this minor problem, however, this work should be in all university libraries. It will be of considerable help to students and scholars researching the impact of religion on American life. [R: C&RL, Sept 93, pp. 429-30; Choice, June 93, p. 1612]—**John W. Storey**

1508. Young, Josiah U., III. **African Theology: A Critical Analysis and Annotated Bibliography.** Westport, Conn., Greenwood Press, 1993. 257p. index. (Bibliographies and Indexes in Religious Studies, no.26). $55.00. BT30.A438Y68. 230'.0967. LC 92-38979. ISBN 0-313-26487-2.

Theology scholar Young has written a concise overview of African theology that comprises the first five chapters of this book. The remaining four chapters make up a bibliography containing 609 numbered citations to published materials. Young has classified the theology of Africa into three groups: the Old Guard, who are concerned with the Christianization of African culture ("inculturation"); the New Guard, who focus on the Africanization of Christianity ("acculturation") in the neocolonial context; and the Black theology of South Africa, a theology born of the struggle against apartheid and closely associated with the Black theology of North America, especially as it has been developed by James Cone.

Young states that the bibliography consists primarily of English- and some French-language writings published between 1955 and 1992. In reality, it also contains older imprints and reprints of pre-1955 publications. The bibliography is not intended to be comprehensive but to be selective and representative of the breadth of the topic. Bibliographical data in citations is generally accurate and complete, although it lacks original publication dates for reprints. Annotations are in-depth, well written, and scholarly and include extensive cross-references. Publications from Young's three classes of theology are included in two chapters; there are also chapters of citations on historical and social analysis and traditional religions. Bibliography chapters are arranged alphabetically by author. Author, title, and subject indexes are included. This book is an outstanding introduction to the growing discipline of African theology. [R: Choice, July/Aug 93, p. 1757; RQ, Winter 93, p. 278]—**Fred J. Hay**

Biography

1509. Bowden, Henry Warner. **Dictionary of American Religious Biography.** 2d ed. Westport, Conn., Greenwood Press, 1993. 686p. index. $75.00. BL72.B68. 209'.2'2. LC 92-35524. ISBN 0-313-27825-3.

The first edition of this dictionary (see ARBA 78, entry 999) contained biographies of 425 significant American religious figures who had died prior to July 1, 1976. In this revision Bowden has added 125 biographies and extended the *terminus ad quem* for inclusion to July 1, 1992. Among the new names are William F. Albright, Edgar Cayce, Fanny Crosby, L. Ron Hubbard, and Alan Watts. All of the original articles were retained, and 350 of them were at least slightly revised in content or in the bibliographies following each article. Two other changes were made: the addition of a selected general bibliography at the end of the volume, and the separation of the alphabetical sections of the dictionary.

As with the first edition, the articles are well written, and they are just long enough to summarize the interesting and important facets of the biographees' lives and to whet the reader's appetite for more. The biographical references listed at the end of each article direct the reader to additional (usually fuller) sources, when these are available. In some cases there are few, if any, sources listed because a particular person is not included in the standard reference sources chosen by Bowden. This scarcity of information on some of the individuals makes one wish that the author had increased his pool of standard sources. This, however, is not a major complaint and in no way detracts from the overall value and utility of the dictionary. Recommended. [R: Choice, Nov 93, pp. 423-24; RBB, 15 Oct 93, p. 470]—**Craig W. Beard**

1510. **Who's Who in Religion 1992-1993.** 4th ed. New Providence, N.J., Marquis Who's Who/Reed Reference Publishing, 1992. 580p. $129.00. LC 76-25357. ISBN 0-8379-1604-6.

This edition of a standard directory profiles living religious leaders—church officials, clergy, religious educators, and lay leaders—throughout the world. There are 15,600 sketches (more than double the number in the 3d edition), more than 8,800 of which are first-time entries. Individuals chosen for *Who's Who in Religion* are selected by the Marquis editorial staff, who examine "literature, communications media, and other available data sources" (preface) and solicit nominations from a 41-member board of advisers. Then the staff determines whether a person's religious work or achievement merits inclusion.

The following information is presented for each person when available and applicable: name, occupation, vital statistics, parents, marriage, children, education, professional certification, career, writings and creative works, civic and political activities, military service, awards and fellowships, professional and association memberships, clubs and lodges, political affiliation, home address, office address, and thoughts on life. Most of this information is supplied by the biographees. When they did not provide the information, it was researched and compiled by the editorial staff. These entries are identified by an asterisk.

When a work has proved to be as beneficial in meeting an information need as this one has, it almost seems petty to criticize it. However, one observation might be allowed. Although it would be impossible to include *all* current religious leaders, and some names will inevitably be left out, it is unclear why a number of "outstanding individuals" (preface) were not included (e.g., Robert Alter, Kurt Aland, Walter Brueggemann, Elizabeth Achtemeier). It is all the more baffling in light of the appearance of many relatively unknown names. That aside, *Who's Who in Religion* is still a recommended purchase for libraries with religion or extensive biographical collections.—**Craig W. Beard**

Dictionaries and Encyclopedias

1511. Erickson, Hal. **Religious Radio and Television in the United States, 1921-1991: The Programs and Personalities.** Jefferson, N.C., McFarland, 1992. 228p. index. $39.95. BV656.E75. 261.5'2'0973. LC 92-50304. ISBN 0-89950-658-5.

This dictionary serves as a history of American (mainly United States) religious radio and television broadcasting during 1921-1991. Alphabetically arranged entries cover program titles, program categories (e.g., children's programs), personalities, networks, and organizations. Broadcasters and programs heard or seen in a single community are generally excluded. The narrative for each entry ranges from a few lines to several pages. In the entries for such personalities as Jim Bakker, Jerry Falwell, and Aimee Semple McPherson, the text provides lively and colorful background while attempting to portray these individuals objectively.

Several features of this work enhance its reference value. The introduction provides informative background on the history of religious broadcasting and ties together the content of the individual entries. A bibliography of scholarly and popular books and articles gives researchers suggested sources for further reading. An index enhances access to information about the people, places, programs, stations, and other elements cited within the entries, and cross-references link related entries.

While the content is well presented and the narrative engaging, this book is not without errors. For example, Princeton (New Jersey) Theological Seminary has been misplaced in Missouri, and the somewhat convoluted formation of the National Broadcasting Company (NBC) has been mistakenly attributed to AT&T. In addition, there are numerous typographical errors. In spite of these problems, this work by a media historian fills a void and will be a welcome addition to reference collections serving researchers in media history and religion. [R: Choice, May 93, p. 1440; RBB, 15 Feb 93, p. 1084; RQ, Summer 93, pp. 576-77]—**Carol Wheeler**

1512. Hexham, Irving. **Concise Dictionary of Religion.** Downers Grove, Ill., InterVarsity Press, 1993. 245p. $15.99pa. ISBN 0-8308-1404-3.

Containing more than 2,000 entries of varying lengths, this succinct dictionary of religion features world religions, new religions, worldviews, religious leaders, cults, beliefs and practices, doctrines and ideas, and scriptures and sacred texts. Hexham's motivation was to produce a "book of practical value to the struggling student." The result is a book recognizing that most of its readers will share an essentially Christian orientation but that they need access to information on the world's religions, information that is often difficult to find. This recognition has led to the inclusion of materials on African and other neglected religious traditions as well as New Age religions and cults. For example, Hexham includes more information on Joseph Smith (founder of Mormonism) than on the father of modern theology, Friedrich Schleiermacher, and he devotes more space to Abraham Kuyper than to Thomas Aquinas. This book not only will assist Hexham's "struggling student" but also will be valuable to various religious education enterprises, such as church libraries, religious education classes, and various media and press rooms.
—C. B. (Bob) Darrell

1513. Mather, George A., and Larry A. Nichols. **Dictionary of Cults, Sects, Religions and the Occult.** Grand Rapids, Mich., Zondervan, 1993. 384p. $24.99. BL31.M295. 200'.3. LC 92-36212. ISBN 0-310-53100-4.

The primary purpose of this volume seems to be to inform its readers about cults, sects, and other alternative religions and religious movements that "are among the most interesting, popular, and influential in the American religious experience" (p. ix). The authors approach their work from an unapologetically evangelical Christian perspective, which is especially evident in their presentation of the teachings of the included groups and individuals. Religious groups and movements are treated in longer articles usually divided into three sections: history, teachings, and a summarizing conclusion. Related topics such as doctrines, holy books, and terminology receive briefer treatment. The entries are alphabetically arranged. Numerous cross-references tie associated entries together so that readers can get a more complete picture on any topic of interest. There are also four appendixes and a bibliography that is classified according to the major groups and movements.

Although there is some useful information contained here, more attention to editorial details could have eliminated several unnecessary weaknesses. A few terms are consistently misspelled (e.g., "Anglo-Israeliism" for Anglo-Israelism). The authors should have provided either more blind entries or a subject index; for example, readers must know to look first under "World Community of Ali Islam in the West" (how many of them would?), because they cannot look under "Black Muslims" or "Nation of Islam" and be referred there. The bibliography contains a section titled "Gay Theology," but there is no such entry in the dictionary; rather, this section corresponds to the entry for "Universal Fellowship of Metropolitan Community Churches." There are also places where the writing and organization of material could be cleaned up. Because Mather and Nichols foresee future editions of this work, perhaps these weaknesses can be addressed.

Because of the slant of this work, it would be appropriate for comprehensive collections and those focusing on evangelical titles. Other collections will be well served by *Encyclopedic Handbook of Cults in America* (see ARBA 93, entry 1410), *Encyclopedia of American Religions* (see ARBA 91, entry 1415), *New Age Encyclopedia* (see ARBA 91, entry 1451), and *Encyclopedia of Occultism and Parapsychology* (see ARBA 92, entry 762). [R: Choice, Sept 93, p. 84; LJ, 1 June 93, pp. 106-08; RBB, July 93, p. 2001]
—Craig W. Beard

1514. Murphy, Larry G., J. Gordon Melton, and Gary L. Ward, eds. **Encyclopedia of African American Religions.** Hamden, Conn., Garland, 1993. 926p. index. (Religious Information Systems, v.9; Garland Reference Library of Social Science, v.721). $125.00. BR563.N4E53. 200'.89'96073. LC 93-7224. ISBN 0-8153-0500-1.

This encyclopedia includes approximately 1,200 entries written by the editors or one of 32 contributors. Entries vary in length from a paragraph to essays exceeding 12 large, double-column pages, and each includes a bibliography. Contributed pieces are signed. Individuals (more than 800), denominations, churches, organizations, schools, and movements of relevance to African-American religious life are included. The encyclopedia also includes excellent prefatory essays on African-American religion, Martin Luther King, Jr., and Black feminist theology; a chronology; an alphabetical list of entries; a selected, classified bibliography; a directory of African-American churches and religious organizations; a biographical cross-reference index by religious tradition; and an index.

Typographical errors have crept in (e.g., Rolling Fork, not "Fort," Mississippi; Jesse Jackson was born in South Carolina, not North Carolina), as well as errors of fact (e.g., John Coltrane did not "author" *My Favorite Things*). The book's greatest deficiency is what is omitted: preachers (e.g., C. L. Franklin), visionary artists (e.g., James Hampton), gospel musicians (e.g., Blind Willie Johnson), scholars (e.g., Sterling Stuckey), religious communities (e.g., Adat Beyt Moshe), and imported Afro-Caribbean religions (e.g., Santeria). Conjure/Hoodoo is not included, nor is Cornel West, Afrocentrism, or John Work. The bibliography lacks a section on music, and the index does not include proper names that occur in the text. In spite of these omissions, this is a monumental achievement and one that is essential to a core reference collection in African-American religion. [R: WLB, Dec 93, p. 77-78]—**Fred J. Hay**

Directories

1515. Melton, J. Gordon. **Directory of Religious Organizations in the United States.** 3d ed. Detroit, Gale, 1993. 728p. index. $125.00. ISBN 0-8103-9890-7. ISSN 1062-8851.

This work provides contact and descriptive information on 2,489 for-profit and nonprofit organizations headquartered in the United States and engaged in activities for religious purposes. This new edition contains 861 more entries than the second edition of 1982 and 920 more than the first edition. The book is divided into five sections. The first supplies, in a standard format, name and address of the organization, chief contact person, telephone and fax (but not E-mail) numbers, religious affiliation, founding date, size of staff, and membership. The mission, goals, purposes, and activities of the organization are detailed. And, where appropriate, publications, audio/video, radio and television programs, remarks, and alternate contacts may also be supplied.

The other four sections of the work are indexes. The personnel index identifies directors or alternate contact persons. The function index classifies the organizations according to 18 chief functions or types of services provided (e.g., academic and theological, foreign missions, social justice). Some organizations are listed under as many as three functions. The religious affiliation index classifies the tradition or family with which the organization is associated or from which it draws its influence. Fifty-two categories, from Adventist to Zoroastrian, are employed here. Finally, the master name and keyword index functions as an all-inclusive, one-stop listing of all organizations, products, and services in the directory.

This edition differs from its predecessors to the extent that many more for-profit organizations, such as religious publishers and consultants, and an enlarged listing of serial publications issued by the organizations are included. It also differs in that certain types of organizations once included are now eliminated: offices of Christian denominational bodies (except archives and historical offices) covered in the *Encyclopedia of American Religions* (Gale, 1993); Roman Catholic religious orders covered in the *Catholic Directory*; and social service organizations primarily serving one community.

While the directory complements the *Encyclopedia of American Religions* (another Melton work), it is best compared with another Gale publication, the *Encyclopedia of Associations* (Gale, annual) (particularly section 11: Religious Organizations). The directory is larger in number of pages as well as number of entries, and while there is a high degree of overlap between the two works (nearly 40 percent of the directory entries are unique, whereas only 20 percent of the encyclopedia entries are), the two sources still fail to cover everything (e.g., American Center for Law and Justice, Burgon Society, Coalition on Revival, Institute for Christian Economics, and Laymen for Religious Liberty are not included in either source). And unfortunately, as is the case in all such compilations, changes occur prior to or just shortly after publication (e.g., the National Jewish Information Service and Wolgemuth & Hyatt Publishers are now defunct).

This is an increasingly important work. This edition is well edited (relatively free of errors) and well produced, with good use of boldface type and white space, a sturdy binding, and an attractive cover. It should be acquired by all but the smallest academic and public libraries.—**Glenn R. Wittig**

Handbooks and Yearbooks

1516. Harris, Ian, and others. **Contemporary Religions: A World Guide.** Harlow, England, Longman; distr., Detroit, Gale, 1992. 511p. index. $175.00. ISBN 0-582-08695-7.

Any misapprehension that the agglomerations of cults, sects, and religions is a purely American phenomenon may be dispelled by this volume. After all, it should not be forgotten that the tragic Branch Davidian stand-off involved members from Australia and Great Britain. The Branch Davidians have not found a place in this book, however, reflecting the limitations of a source that claims to cover all beliefs, all significant branches of faiths, and every country. Selection was based (according to the preface) on the size of a group or its influence, or the continuance of a particular tradition.

The work is divided into three sections, the first of which contains essay overviews of major religious traditions, including the new movements of the twentieth century. Part 2 is the most extensive of the three, providing an alphabetical list of movements and groups, from Adventists to Zoroastrians, in entries that range from a paragraph to three columns in length. Perhaps the most valuable section is the geographical part 3, which provides a survey of the religious situation for every country of the world. Again, length varies, from a few lines for such small countries as Denmark or the Central African Republic to more than two pages for Malaysia. In general, only major movements are discussed, although the return of the old Norse religion to Iceland is mentioned in passing. This guide to contemporary religions is recommended as an alternative, geographical approach to the study of world religion. It will be useful for public and academic libraries. [R: LAR, May 93, p. 292; RBB, June 93, p. 1894]—**Johan Koren**

1517. Kelly, Aidan, Peter Dresser, and Linda M. Ross. **Religious Holidays and Calendars: An Encyclopedic Handbook.** Detroit, Omnigraphics, 1993. 163p. index. $60.00. CE6.K45. 529'.3. LC 92-41189. ISBN 1-55888-348-7.

This volume is organized into two main sections. The first is an introduction to the history of religious calendars that comprises almost the first third of the book (more than any other comparable reference work). The second is an alphabetical list of nearly 300 religious holidays. Each entry gives the name of the holiday, dates of observance, and a brief discussion. Following these sections are a bibliography; a monthly index of holidays; an index of holidays classified by religion; and a master index of holidays, names, organizations, and events.

There are several reference works that list national and international holidays, both religious and civil, and there are those that list only religious holidays. Among the former are two standard guides, *Anniversaries and Holidays* (see ARBA 85, entry 1230) and *Holidays and Anniversaries of the World* (see ARBA 91, entry 1341). The well-known holidays of the major religions, such as Christmas, Passover, and Ramadan, are included in both guides and in *This Day in Religion* (see ARBA 92, entry 1413), which focuses somewhat on Judaism and Eastern religions but emphasizes Christian holidays. Another recent volume, *An Almanac of the Christian Church* (see ARBA 89, entry 1328), is obviously devoted to a particular tradition. In comparison to these titles, one of the most useful contributions of *Religious Holidays and Calendars* is the inclusion of holidays celebrated by newer, and sometimes smaller, groups (e.g., Christian Science, the Theosophical Society).

While this work has its strengths—the introductory essays and the inclusion of otherwise overlooked holidays—it is not a replacement for the other guides mentioned. One limitation is that it consciously omits all but a few Roman Catholic and Orthodox saints' days, most of which are included in *Holidays and Anniversaries of the World*. For libraries without comprehensive religion collections, this will likely be a supplementary rather than a primary purchase. However, libraries with such collections and some larger public libraries will find it useful for the gaps it fills. [R: BR, Nov/Dec 93, p. 58; JAL, May 93, p. 131; RBB, July 93, pp. 2004-05; SLJ, Nov 93, p. 145; WLB, June 93, p. 130]—**Craig W. Beard**

1518. Melton, J. Gordon. **Encyclopedia of American Religions.** 4th ed. Detroit, Gale, 1993. 1217p. index. $175.00. ISBN 0-8103-6904-4. ISSN 1066-1212.

This is the latest of Melton's numerous publications on religion in America and includes both historical and current information on religious and spiritual groups—both extant and defunct—in the United States and Canada. It is a complete revision of the 3d edition (see ARBA 91, entry 1415) and has 140 additional entries.

The author's criteria for inclusion are clear, and the entire volume is executed with precision. The body of the work consists of three parts: 2 essays that trace the course of religion in the United States and Canada; 22 essays on the 20 families of religious/spiritual groups treated; and a directory listing of 1,730 groups, arranged in the families described in section 2, with a variety of information on each (e.g., name, address, description, membership, educational facilities, periodicals). Several pertinent bibliographical citations are usually included, and sometimes Melton appends a few additional remarks. Articles vary in length from a brief paragraph to about four pages, and a user's guide and three indexes (geographical, subject, and name and keyword) round out the volume.

The work is compact (double columns and narrow margins), clearly printed, and a delight to use, and its availability in electronic form (tape or diskette) provides an attractive alternative. This book is a sine qua non for the reference collections of public, academic, and theological libraries.

—M. Patrick Graham

Buddhism

1519. Prebish, Charles S. **Historical Dictionary of Buddhism.** Metuchen, N.J., Scarecrow, 1993. 387p. (Historical Dictionaries of Religions, Philosophies, and Movements, no.1). $42.50. BQ130.P74. 294.3'03. LC 93-4247. ISBN 0-8108-2698-4.

This work auspiciously inaugurates a new series of historical dictionaries from Scarecrow. It begins with a brief, but graceful, preface in which Prebish acknowledges the difficulty of his undertaking. There is a guide to pronunciation that unfortunately (but understandably) finesses the problems of Tibetan transcription and pronunciation. Next comes a list of scriptures in three canonical languages of Buddhism (Pali, Chinese, and Tibetan), a chronology of major events in Buddhism, a map showing important Buddhist sites, and an excellent 34-page introduction sketching the history of Buddhism and the problems inherent in its study. The dictionary covers 288 pages, and there is a 98-page classified bibliography.

The definitions are concise, yet complete enough to give the sense of the diversity of doctrines and cultures comprising Buddhism. Prebish manages not to favor any particular doctrine or culture, and he also includes major historical figures not only from the history of Buddhism but also from the history of Western Buddhist scholarship. The classified bibliography is well organized along the lines of *Guide to Buddhist Religion* (see ARBA 82, entry 1125), and it includes works as recent as 1991.

There are more than 60 pages of prefatory and explanatory material in addition to the dictionary, and, although there are numerous cross-references, it would be helpful to have a means (i.e., an index) to trace the doctrines of each of the various Buddhist schools and to follow up events in the history of Buddhism within the dictionary. An index would also make it much easier to move between entries in the dictionary and the information covered in the prefatory material. For example, there are no cross-references between the entries for "Councils-Rangoon" and "Pali Canon," and there is no easy way for a reader to move between the entries in the dictionary and the discussions of councils in the introduction.

It is always possible to criticize such a work for omitting one or another term, but Prebish has done a remarkable job in covering the important events and doctrines in the diverse cultures that have embraced Buddhism. The addition of an index and the correction of a few minor typographical errors would move this work from the realm of the merely fine to the truly remarkable. All in all, this is a good work that belongs in the collection of any library interested in presenting the world's religions to its patrons. [R: Choice, Dec 93, p. 589; LJ, 15 Oct 93, p. 62; RBB, 1 Nov 93, p. 566]—**Richard H. Swain**

Christianity

General Works

Bibliography

1520. Benedetto, Robert. **P. T. Forsyth Bibliography and Index.** Westport, Conn., Greenwood Press, 1993. 162p. index. (Bibliographies and Indexes in Religious Studies, no.27). $59.95. Z8309.4.B46. 016.230'58'092. LC 92-46527. ISBN 0-313-28753-8.

Sometimes described as the (Karl) Barth before Barth, Peter Taylor Forsyth is a significant but little-known theological thinker of the late nineteenth and early twentieth centuries. A prolific writer, Forsyth produced 25 books, at least 260 articles, more than 50 pamphlets, and an unknown number of reviews. Unfortunately, his work, until now, has never been readily accessible. His prose, characterized by freshly minted terms known only to him, was often obscure, and his books usually lacked indexes and footnotes. Hence, this bibliography by Benedetto, an associate librarian at Union Theological Seminary in Virginia, will be enormously helpful to scholars. Of particular note, Benedetto has painstakingly indexed all of Forsyth's major books. The bibliography consists of three parts: publications by Forsyth, literature about him, and Benedetto's indexes of Forsyth's works (which make up almost 60 percent of this volume). Materials in the first two parts are grouped according to type, such as books, anthologies, essays, and dissertations. This bibliography should be added to the reference collections of seminaries and universities offering religious studies. [R: Choice, Oct 93, p. 262]—**John W. Storey**

1521. Caldwell, Sandra M., and Ronald J. Caldwell. **The History of the Episcopal Church in America, 1607-1991: A Bibliography.** Hamden, Conn., Garland, 1993. 528p. index. (Religious Information Systems, v.13; Garland Reference Library of the Humanities, v.1635). $82.00. Z7845.A5C34. 016.283'73. LC 92-45272. ISBN 0-8153-0936-8.

This is a partially annotated bibliography of 3,868 items that deal with the history of the Episcopal Church in the United States found either as dissertations or published separately as books, pamphlets, or articles. Its six main divisions are reference works, general histories, period histories, topical works, biographies, and local histories. The two fullest sections are those devoted to biographies and local history. The local histories are arranged either by state or by county or city. Biographical references are included for nonchurchpeople when these refer to the individual and the relationship to the Episcopal Church. For example, of the entries under Robert E. Lee, two are titled "Robert E. Lee: Churchman" and another is "God and General Lee." The biographical section should be of the greatest use to those seeking material about clergy not discussed in the more standard biographical dictionaries, such as the *Dictionary of American Biography* (see ARBA 89, entry 25). There is an extensive index.

This bibliography is the fullest yet compiled on its subject. Its annotations, where critical, are quite useful and show an excellent knowledge of the field. The volume is well organized and well indexed and should be in every library with an interest in U.S. religious history. [R: Choice, Nov 93, p. 424]
—**Hensley C. Woodbridge**

1522. Crumb, Lawrence N. **The Oxford Movement and Its Leaders: A Bibliography of Secondary and Lesser Primary Sources. Supplement.** Metuchen, N.J., Scarecrow, 1993. 303p. index. (ATLA Bibliography Series, no.24). $37.50. Z7845.O83C78. 016.283'42. LC 93-16025. ISBN 0-8108-2700-X.

This is a supplement to the earlier edition, published in 1988 (see ARBA 89, entry 1331). Reasons for issuing the supplement include the presence of an unusually large number of items that have been published since the original edition; a year-long study in England by Crumb; and an increased use of computer technology, which made it possible to find many more items. The supplement contains 1,836 entries, bringing the total number in the set to 7,524. This supplement also corrects errors in citations made in the earlier work. Included are publications in English and translations from several foreign languages: French, Finnish, Italian, Japanese, Polish, Serbo-Croatian, and Spanish. The bibliography is arranged chronologically, beginning with 1810, the date usually considered as the starting date for the

Oxford Movement, and concluding with 1990. The index provides complete subject access. John Henry, Cardinal Newman was the principal player in this movement; hence most entries relate to him and his *Apologia Pro Vita Sua* (Oxford University Press, 1991).

Crumb is both a librarian and a student of Church history, particularly the Oxford Movement. Students and scholars in the field will find many sources for research in this book, which will be useful to theological libraries, particularly Anglican (Episcopal) seminaries.—**Edward P. Miller**

1523. Davidson, Linda Kay, and Maryjane Dunn-Wood. **Pilgrimage in the Middle Ages: A Research Guide.** Hamden, Conn., Garland, 1993. 480p. (Garland Medieval Bibliographies, v.16; Garland Reference Library of the Humanities, v.1379). $74.00. BV5067.D38. 248.4'63'0902. LC 92-27624. ISBN 0-8240-7221-9.

Would that all reference sources were as well executed as this one. This is a treasure trove of primary and secondary sources on the medieval conception of pilgrimages and their appearance in art, music, literature, architecture, and political and religious history. The first two chapters provide an overview of the subject and describe where the study of medieval pilgrimages must begin. The next four chapters focus on specific sites, such as Jerusalem and Santiago de Compostela (a trip the authors themselves undertook from Southern France). The next chapter traces the treatment of pilgrimages in the fine arts. The second part of the book is devoted to an annotated bibliography of sources on the pilgrimages.

The appendix closes out the volume with general sources on the medieval period. It is a pity that this last section did not include either of C. S. Lewis's very fine studies, *Allegory of Love* (Clarendon Press, 1936) and *The Discarded Image* (Cambridge University Press, 1964). Both are still considered the *loci classici* for their areas. Despite these omissions and the absence of a subject index, the volume is excellent for beginning work in the area, and for reminding us, with William Langland, that "Pilgrimes are we alle." [R: Choice, June 93, p. 1600]—**Mark Y. Herring**

1524. Fahey, Michael A., comp. **Ecumenism: A Bibliographical Overview.** Westport, Conn., Greenwood Press, 1992. 384p. index. (Bibliographies and Indexes in Religious Studies, no.23). $69.50. Z7845.1.F34. 016.2708'2. LC 92-28449. ISBN 0-313-25102-9.

Ecumenical activities among Christian denominations, rather than non-Christian, are the focus of this well-done annotated bibliography. About 1,300 items are listed in 7 groups: reference materials, historical accounts, confessional views, dialogs, regions, three documents (*The Augsburg Confession, The Leuenberg Agreement*, and *A Plan of Union*), and doctrinal issues. Publications are principally those issued between 1950 and 1992. They cover most languages except Russian and Greek and exclude purely devotional works. Articles are not listed, but 84 ecumenical journal titles are included. The annotations are well written and balanced and reflect the opinion of the compiler. Author, title, and subject indexes are supplied. There has not been a comprehensive bibliography on this topic for some time. [R: Choice, May 93, p. 1440]—**James P. McCabe**

Biography

1525. Carey, Patrick W. **The Roman Catholics.** Westport, Conn., Greenwood Press, 1993. 375p. index. (Denominations in America, no.6). $55.00. BX1406.2.C346. 282'.73. LC 93-20125. ISBN 0-313-25439-7.

This work presents a history of Catholicism in the United States and about 145 biographical sketches of the major figures who shaped the religion in this country. Each of the eight chapters of the narrative history is followed by extensive bibliographical notes, and a bibliographical essay is included at the end of the work. The biographies are about a page in length and include bibliographies of works by and about each person. A large number of the subjects are women. Both the narrative history and the biographical sketches are clearly written and do not avoid controversial aspects of U.S. Catholicism. A chronology of U.S. Catholic history and an index are also included.—**James P. McCabe**

1526. Jones, Alison. **Saints.** New York, Chambers Kingfisher Graham, 1992. 243p. illus. index. $9.95pa. ISBN 0-550-17014-6.

That individuals whose lives of faith and virtue are worthy of commendation is obvious from the number of books written about them. This latest addition to an ever-increasing bibliography is a useful one-volume guide to men and women of exemplary holiness, immovable morality, and extraordinary ability. Among them are monarchs, monks, lawyers, teachers, martyrs, and common folk. A few have been virtually forgotten; others have become legendary and inspired poets and painters.

The 200 or so saints profiled in this volume have been drawn from all levels of society and varied national groups. They range from the earliest days of the church up to contemporary times. Their entries run about 500 words, state the essential facts (distinguishing between pious fictions and historical records), list the feast-days, and indicate the relative importance of each biographee.

Other hagiographical volumes may be better researched, more complete, better illustrated, and more specialized in one way or another. But any library that does not shelve *The Who's Who of Heaven* (see ARBA 89, entry 1337), *The Oxford Dictionary of Saints* (see ARBA 88, entry 1424), or *A Calendar of Saints* (see ARBA 88, entry 1423) should obtain this handy reference tool. The moderate price makes it a worthwhile addition to all reference collections.—**G. A. Cevasco**

1527. **The Oxford Dictionary of Saints.** 3d ed. David Hugh Farmer, ed. New York, Oxford University Press, 1992. 530p. $13.95pa. BR1710.F34. 270'.092'2. LC 92-6722. ISBN 0-19-283069-4.

This edition of a useful work has been revised and expanded to include approximately 1,500 saints. Entries are brief—about half a page in length—and include bibliographical references. The selection of saints includes all English saints, most well-known saints from other countries, and recently canonized saints. Appendixes include a list of patronages (i.e., the patron saint of ...), a list of principal iconographical emblems, an index of place-names, and a calendar of feast days. This work should be in most reference collections, but it cannot substitute for more comprehensive works.—**James P. McCabe**

Dictionaries and Encyclopedias

1528. Balz, Horst, and Gerhard Schneider, eds. **Exegetical Dictionary of the New Testament. Volume 3.** Grand Rapids, Mich., William B. Eerdmans Publishing, 1993. 566p. index. $49.99. BS2312.E913. 225.4'8'03. LC 90-35682. ISBN 0-8028-2411-0.

This is the third and final volume of *Exegetical Dictionary of the New Testament* (EDNT); for reviews of earlier volumes, see ARBA 93, entry 1426 and ARBA 91, entry 1423. In biblical studies, *exegesis* typically refers to the researcher's effort to uncover the meaning of a text for its first audience. Consequently, the EDNT aims to discuss the meanings of all the words in the Greek New Testament (NT), guiding the reader toward an accurate exegesis of the biblical text. Each entry includes the Greek term, its English transliteration, information about its linguistic form, a definition, a discussion of most of its occurrences in the NT, and a bibliography. The major articles in the present volume are those on the Greek terms for *virgin, parousia, father, Paul, faith, fulfill, perfect, end, spirit, conscience, savior*, and *salvation*.

Although the German original of this volume appeared a decade earlier, the translators have enhanced its value for English readers by correcting errors in the text, and when there are English translations of works cited in the bibliographies of the German original, those versions are cited. While a few errors remain (e.g., the transliteration of *paraphronia* is omitted), the work is generally well edited.

The EDNT mediates the vast literature on NT interpretation for students, pastors, and teachers and is essential for all libraries that support the study of the Christian Bible. The work is convenient to use, concise, and readable; Eerdmans has produced another winner by making this important reference tool widely available to English-speaking audiences.—**M. Patrick Graham**

1529. Beit-Hallahmi, Benjamin. **The Illustrated Encyclopedia of Active New Religions, Sects, and Cults.** New York, Rosen Publishing, 1993. 341p. illus. index. $49.95. BL80.2.B385. 291.9'03. LC 93-18928. ISBN 0-8239-1505-0.

Containing more than 2,200 alphabetically arranged and cross-referenced entries, this is a useful guide to the mysterious world of contemporary cults, sects, and new religions. To be included in this encyclopedia, a group had to satisfy three primary criteria. It could be no older than 200 years; it must present some new claim to divine truth; and its members had to believe in a supernatural domain populated by deities, souls of the dead, and, perhaps, angels and devils. Scholarly literature usually defines a sect as a group that has arisen from a schism and so has had an earlier tie to another religious organization. A cult, by contrast, is usually a more deviant group, one that has had no connection to previous religious traditions. Popularly, both terms today are used to describe movements outside the mainstream, usually small bodies lacking in social standing because of size and deviation from the "norm." Accordingly, this volume includes such diverse groups as Second Adventists, Mormons, Branch Davidians, "Moonies," Hare Krishnas, the Church of Scientology, Campbellites, and the Father Divine Movement. Many of the entries are very brief, consisting of only a sentence or two. Others, such as the one on the Ghost Dance of 1890, are 400 to 600 words long. Replete with photographs, bibliographical references for many of the entries, and a synoptic index, this work will be of considerable interest to students, teachers, and others searching for information on new religious movements. It would be a worthwhile addition to the reference collections of high school and college libraries. [R: RBB, 1 Nov 93, pp. 566-67]—**John W. Storey**

1530. Clifton, Chas S. **Encyclopedia of Heresies and Heretics.** Santa Barbara, Calif., ABC-Clio, 1992. 156p. illus. maps. index. $50.00. BT1315.2.C55. 273'.03. LC 92-29996. ISBN 0-87436-600-3.

The author of this work, a freelance writer specializing in Western spiritual traditions, offers a few long but mostly brief entries, alphabetically arranged, on 128 "controversial people, sects, movements, and other historical events." The emphasis, based on a review of entry key words, is on heretics (individuals and groups) more than heresies. Historical events, while mentioned in the jacket blurb, have not been included. Also lacking from this work are entries for heresy and heretics; these ideas are discussed only briefly in the book's introduction. Again, the introduction has to be read almost in its entirety to discern the time period covered; coverage ceases with the sixteenth century.

Clifton correctly recognizes that there are not many reference books available on this theme, and that the available few are not comprehensive in scope. But he has failed to correct the situation in this publication, which is neither comprehensive in coverage (an encyclopedia) nor balanced in what is included. Besides lacking entries for heretics and heresy, entries are also missing for Apollinarius and Apollinarianism, Macedonianism or Pneumatomachism, Monothelitism, Priscillianism, and Semi-Arianism or Eusebianism, as well as for individuals and groups, such as Basil of Ancyna, John Cassian, Encratites, Priscilla and Maximilla, Sergius, or Severus. With regard to balance, the work offers uneven coverage of subjects. Gnosticism and witchcraft might merit six to eight pages of discussion, but the seven pages devoted to the Albigenses and Albigensians is out of proportion to that offered for Arianism (one page), Donatism (three-fourths page), Inquisition (two and a half pages), Pelagius (three-fourths page), and Waldensians (one and a half pages). While many cross-references are employed (e.g., Arius to Arianism, Huss to Hus, Templars to Knights Templars), others are lacking (e.g., Heloise to Abelard, Donatus to Donatism, Praxeas to Modalism). Some entries focus on the heresy rather than the person (e.g., Arianism), whereas others focus on the person rather than the heresy (e.g., Pelagius). Entries appear for Joan of Arc but not for Savonarola and for Servetus but not for Socinus. The few illustrations included in the work do not contribute anything significant; a line drawing of Simon de Monfort appears with the Albigenses entry, yet there is neither an entry nor cross-reference for the same under "S." The multivolume *New Catholic Encyclopedia* (J. Heraty Associates, 1989) is far superior, and the *Oxford Dictionary of the Christian Church* (see ARBA 75, entry 1220) and the *New International Dictionary of the Christian Church*, edited by J. D. Douglas and Earle E. Cairns (Zondervan, 1988), are more than adequate to address general questions about these subjects. [R: BR, Sept/Oct 93, p. 65; Choice, May 93, p. 1436; RBB, 1 Feb 93, pp. 1001-02; WLB, May 93, pp. 116-17]—**Glenn R. Wittig**

1531. ***Our Sunday Visitor*'s Catholic Dictionary.** Peter M. J. Stravinskas, ed. Huntington, Ind., Our Sunday Visitor, 1993. 496p. $26.95. LC 93-83237. ISBN 0-87973-507-4.

The more than 3,000 terms in this lexicon are well chosen and distinctly defined. All have special definitions not found in common dictionaries. Diverse entries range from biblical times to the present day and are meant to allow a better and broader understanding of Catholicism's heritage and practice. Defined are terms dealing with doctrine, liturgy, religious orders, vestments, hagiography, papal encyclicals, and canon law. Most definitions run several sentences and provide clear, detailed explanations of significant terms, from *Abba, abiogenesis,* and *abulia* to *Zelanti, zucchetto,* and *Zwinglianism.* Even such better-known entries as *baptism, canonization,* and *Easter* supply interesting bits of information for the well-informed Catholic and the curious non-Catholic. And to get at the core meaning of various terms, etymologies are included. Each entry is also respelled to look the way it sounds, allowing proper pronunciation of troublesome polysyllabic Greek and Latin derivatives. Where applicable, definitions are cross-referenced with appropriate biblical verses.

This trove makes a good read and is a delight to browse, as one would expect, being edited by a well-known scholar of and writer on catechesis, whose one-volume *Catholic Encyclopedia* (Our Sunday Visitor, 1991) was well received. If a good reference book is to be judged by the editorial skills of its editor and its thoroughness, accuracy, and usefulness, then this one deserves a place on most reference shelves, especially in light of its moderate price.—**G. A. Cevasco**

Directories

1532. **The Official Catholic Directory ... 1993: Containing Ecclesiastical Statistics of the United States, Puerto Rico, the Virgin Islands....** New Providence, N.J., P. J. Kenedy/Reed Reference Publishing, 1993. 1886p. illus. maps. index. $199.00. LC 81-30961. ISBN 0-8352-3297-2. ISSN 0078-3854.

This 176th edition of *The Official Catholic Directory* includes the latest up-to-date information on the Catholic clergy, diocesan offices, officials, parishes, schools, hospitals, charities, and all other such organizations in the United States, Puerto Rico, Guam, the Virgin Islands, and the Caroline and Marshall islands. In addition, it covers the Vatican, foreign missions, and missionary activities. Enhancing this edition are such new features as a fold-out map designating some 200 jurisdictions, the latest Catholic population figures, a 40-plus-page section of products and services, several glossaries, and separate alphabetical listings for all sorts of affiliated agencies of the Roman Catholic Church in the United States. The completeness and accuracy of the volume is beyond question, because all statistical information has been confirmed and approved by each diocese. Even the Internal Revenue Service relies on this directory to identify the tax-exempt status of Catholic organizations (the first 40 copies of this prodigious work go to that agency). As the directory is a unique composite of an important segment of the population of the United States, most large reference libraries will probably want to shelve this plethora of ecclesiastical information, especially those collections whose edition of the directory may be several years old.
—**G. A. Cevasco**

Handbooks and Yearbooks

1533. Balmer, Randall, and John R. Fitzmier. **The Presbyterians.** Westport, Conn., Greenwood Press, 1993. 274p. index. (Denominations in America, no.5). $49.95. BX8935.B355. 285'.1. LC 92-17840. ISBN 0-313-26084-2.

A recent addition to the publisher's Denominations in America series, this volume follows the now familiar Greenwood Press formula. The authors begin with a very readable, narrative essay that historically surveys the Presbyterian tradition in the United States. This essay is remarkably well balanced, carefully documented, and thoughtfully succinct as it is, especially in the early and middle periods; however, the final section of the essay seems to tilt toward the ecumenical interests and trendy concerns of, and to neglect the contributions of, evangelicals within and without the principal denomination.

The biographical dictionary of Presbyterian leaders includes entries for 96 mostly deceased figures of varying importance to the denomination, such as Jane Addams and John Witherspoon. Ironically, the dissident Carl McIntire is the only living person to merit inclusion. Following the essential historical facts for each entry, the authors present a brief essay assessing the person's achievements and significance and conclude with references to the figure's major works and biographical references. A short denominational chronology, a helpful bibliographical essay, and an index conclude the volume.

This volume and series will be useful in collections serving collegiate religious and American studies programs, as well as the general public where regional and local interests warrant. Research and theological libraries may well find these efforts convenient syntheses for review purposes. [R: Choice, Sept 93, p. 73]—**Donald G. Davis, Jr.**

Bible Studies

Bibliography

1534. Mills, Watson E. **A Bibliography of the Nature and Role of the Holy Spirit in Twentieth-Century Writings.** Lewiston, N.Y., Edwin Mellen Press, 1993. 344p. index. $79.95. ISBN 0-7734-2366-4.

Mills is an accomplished editor and bibliographer in the field of biblical studies and brings to the present task a wealth of experience and knowledge. This bibliography includes 3,998 entries arranged alphabetically by author, a general index, and a Scripture index. The print is clear, and the text has been edited carefully (cf., though, "Ritschls" for *Ritschl* [p. 329], "dis-sertation" for *dissertation* [p. 105], and "Sweeden" for *Sweden* [p. 340]).

Although the bibliography will undoubtedly prove useful for some students and scholars, it could have been improved by increased attention to three areas. First, although the preface explains the genesis of the book in the author's career, it does not adequately define its topic and scope, nor does it elaborate the principles of selection that guided its compilation. The title notes that it is limited to works produced in the twentieth century, and the preface states that the author intended to gather the major works on the topic. The reader, though, is left to wonder why unpublished conference papers, popular publications, and works on peripheral areas (e.g., archaeology and the Bible) were included and what cutoff date Mills used for the inclusion of publications (the most recent works appear to date from 1991). Moreover, a quick check of the RLIN database reveals a number of significant works with the subject heading "Holy Spirit" that were omitted from the bibliography (e.g., John K. Mackett's "Eusebius of Caesarea's Theology of the Holy Spirit" [Marquette University Ph.D. thesis, 1990]; John R. W. Stott's, *The Baptism and Fullness of the Holy Spirit* [InterVarsity Press, 1964]).

Second, the bibliographical citations are less than complete. Mills has omitted such useful information as the names of the series in which books appeared, their places of publication, and the degree for which the dissertation or thesis was granted. Finally, the indexing is inadequate and seriously limits the usefulness of the volume. The general index omits some references to key personalities and religious traditions, and it sometimes neglects to cite entries relevant to the topics listed. Therefore, in light of the bibliography's limitations and substantial price, few libraries may find it a worthwhile acquisition.

—**M. Patrick Graham**

1535. Stone, Jon R. **A Guide to the End of the World: Popular Eschatology in America.** Hamden, Conn., Garland, 1993. 329p. index. (Religious Information Systems, v.12; Garland Reference Library of the Humanities, v.1713). $51.00. BR517.S76. 236'.9. LC 92-35100. ISBN 0-8153-1312-8.

The author's doctoral dissertation ("The Boundary Dynamics of Religious Communities: The Case of American Evangelicalism, 1940-1965") was the precursor to the present bibliography. Bracketed by a brief introductory chapter and a summary/conclusion, the body of this volume consists of three parts, each of which includes explanatory essays and bibliographical citations of books and pamphlets produced since 1798. The first is devoted to the general discussion of popular eschatology in America and the secondary literature that discusses it. The second part is titled "The Literature of American Millennialism" and treats the material in 10 chronological segments, to which are appended two sections: selected amillennial, postmillennial, and antipremillennial works and a list of journals and periodicals. The final part of the book is a series of brief biographical sketches of and bibliographies for the leading figures in American millennialism (e.g., Dwight L. Moody, Oral Roberts, Hal Lindsey).

The author has undertaken a monumental task, and the disclaimers that he makes along the way attest to his awareness of the terminological and methodological problems that plague such a project. His prose is usually clear, his citations accurate (although occasionally bits of bibliographical information have been omitted; see entries 1229, 1261, and 1271), and his selection of material reasonable. Although this volume will not dispense with the researcher's need to gather bibliography when exploring the intricacies of American millennialism—periodical literature, for example, has been omitted here—the task has been eased considerably. The book is recommended for academic libraries supporting the study of American religion. [R: Choice, Nov 93, p. 439]—**M. Patrick Graham**

1536. Thompson, Henry O. **The Book of Daniel: An Annotated Bibliography.** Hamden, Conn., Garland, 1993. 547p. index. (Books of the Bible, v.1; Garland Reference Library of the Humanities, v.1310). $84.00. Z7772.J1T48. 016.224'5. LC 92-9349. ISBN 0-8240-4873-3.

This is the inaugural volume of a projected series of annotated bibliographies on the books of the Bible, including the Apocrypha. In the introduction Thompson summarizes the content of Daniel—including the apocryphal portions, Susanna and Bel and the Dragon—and the controversial matters surrounding the book. The bibliography contains more than 1,800 entries for books, periodical articles, and dissertations. Emphasis is on materials in English, although other languages are included. Most of the non-English titles are translated into English and placed in parentheses following the original titles. The coverage is comprehensive for the past 50 years and selective for previous years. The majority of the items in the bibliography are arranged by author in a single alphabetical listing. There is a separate list of dissertations, some of which also appear in the main section. Scripture and subject indexes provide access to items dealing with specific passages or topics.

The strength of this work is its comprehensiveness. Within the guidelines established for the series, Thompson has compiled a thorough guide to the literature on Daniel, the person and the book. The abstracts often are helpful for getting the gist of the items, even though not all entries include abstracts, and Thompson's style is uneven and sometimes choppy. The major weakness of the bibliography is the poor subject access. The subject index appears to be a keyword index (possibly computer-generated) rather than a well-organized subject index. For this reason, there are redundant headings: "New Testament" and "NT," "Old Testament" and "OT," "Jehovah" and "Yahweh," "Eschatology" and "Eschatological," and "Apocalypse" and "Revelation" (both referring, in most cases, to the NT Revelation/Apocalypse of John). Words from periodical titles are indexed as subjects. In addition, there are no headings for authorship, date, compositional unity, or Daniel as prophecy, even though the bibliography includes sources that deal with these topics. Because of its comprehensiveness, theological libraries will want to add this title, but public and general academic collections can do without it. [R: Choice, Oct 93, p. 273]—**Craig W. Beard**

Biography

1537. Brownrigg, Ronald. **Who's Who in the New Testament.** New York, Oxford University Press, 1993. 286p. $13.95pa. BS2430.B67. 225.9'22. ISBN 0-19-521031-X.

Similar to Joan Comay's *Who's Who in the Old Testament* (Oxford University Press, 1993), to which this is a companion volume, Brownrigg's book is a reprint of the original 1971 publication (see ARBA 72, entry 1194). The extensive illustrations of the first printing have been eliminated, but otherwise the entries are unchanged. Libraries with standard biblical dictionaries and encyclopedias or those with a serviceable copy of the 1971 edition will have no need for this softcover version. Serious students and scholars will turn to the major biblical dictionaries, especially the recently published *Anchor Bible Dictionary* (Doubleday, 1992), for a more serious and occasionally more extensive treatment of these names, rather than rely on this volume, which is based on thin and now very much dated scholarship.

—**Harold O. Forshey**

1538. Comay, Joan. **Who's Who in the Old Testament Together with the Apocrypha.** New York, Oxford University Press, 1993. 398p. $15.95pa. BS570.C64. 221.9'2. ISBN 0-19-521029-8.

This is a softcover printing of a 1971 publication (see ARBA 72, entry 1198) without the extensive illustrations that appeared in the older work. Save for the deletion of the illustrations and acknowledgments related to them, the book is unchanged. Hence, the limited scholarship on which this work is based is now more than 20 years out-of-date. Particularly noticeable is the inconsistency and unreliability of the frequent translations of the names into English (e.g., the name "Abital," although borne by a woman, is translated as "father of dew"). Only libraries lacking some of the standard biblical dictionaries and a serviceable copy of the original printing would find this a useful addition. The recently published six-volume *Anchor Bible Dictionary* (Doubleday, 1992) is one of several more reliable and comprehensive alternatives. The companion volume by Ronald Brownrigg, *Who's Who in the New Testament* (see ARBA 72, entry 1194), has simultaneously been republished in a softcover edition.—**Harold O. Forshey**

Catalogs and Collections

1539. Klein, Michael L. **Targumic Manuscripts in the Cambridge Genizah Collections.** New York, Cambridge University Press, 1992. 136p. illus. index. (Cambridge University Library Genizah Series, no.8). $99.95. ISBN 0-521-42076-8.

This addition to the Cambridge University Library Genizah Series complements Malcolm C. Davis's four-volume catalog, *Hebrew Bible Manuscripts in the Cambridge Genizah Collections* (Cambridge University Press, 1978-), because the fragments Klein includes were not treated by Davis unless they had been placed by mistake in binders labeled "Bible." Klein has provided a brief description of 1,580 fragments of Targum in the Cambridge Genizah Collections following the order established by the editor for the catalogs of the Cambridge Collections.

Each entry has a canonical reference, an indication of the language of the text with an identification of the particular Aramaic Targum, and a physical description. The latter includes identification of material (paper or vellum), number of leaves, state of preservation, script, vocalization (Tiberian, Babylonian, Palestinian, or unpointed) and idiosyncratic additional information, including the form of representation of the divine name. At the end of appropriate entries there are references to texts actually published, although the author has correctly eschewed including a full bibliography on the grounds of redundancy. Decorations are noted and collected in three pages of drawings. Twenty-four fragments are reproduced in facsimile in black-and-white plates that are of reasonable (although not exceptional) quality. These were selected, Klein indicates, as representative of most of the major text types and scribal variations. This bibliography will be an important resource for specialists.—**Harold O. Forshey**

1540. Roberts, Helene E., and Rachel Hall. **Iconographic Index to New Testament Subjects Represented in Photographs and Slides of Paintings in the Visual Collections, Fine Arts Library, Harvard University. Volume I: Narrative Paintings of the Italian School.** Hamden, Conn., Garland, 1992. 254p. illus. (Garland Reference Library of the Humanities, v.1154). $55.00. ND1430.R6. 755'.4. LC 91-36350. ISBN 0-8240-4385-5.

Because it identifies paintings by artist and title and gives their locations, this work should prove useful whether or not the reader has access to the collections at Harvard's Fine Arts Library. Using a complex classification system called ICONOCLASS, the paintings are listed hierarchically in seven major categories that are based on the events described in the New Testament and apocryphal literature. Within each category or event, paintings are listed in subcategories according to what or who else is depicted in the painting (e.g., angels, devils, saints). An index of concepts, terms, and proper names directs the reader to a list of paintings that contain the objects, actions, or persons indexed, whether or not the painting is about them.

This work is preceded by the author's *Iconographic Index to Old Testament Subjects...* (see ARBA 88, entry 1049). A volume that lists devotional rather than narrative paintings is promised.

—**James P. McCabe**

Dictionaries and Encyclopedias

1541. **Nelson's Quick Reference Bible Dictionary.** By William Smith. Nashville, Tenn., Thomas Nelson, 1993. 770p. illus. $7.99pa. BS440.S6. 220.3. LC 92-47031. ISBN 0-8407-6906-7.

This dictionary represents both an abridgment and a minor revision of the multivolume work edited by William Smith in the late nineteenth century. The current work, apparently revised in the early twentieth century, is meant to serve an audience of Sunday school teachers and laity, rather than scholars. Brief entries give succinct information on people, places, flora, fauna, and concepts found in the Bible. Occasional theological issues are treated at slightly longer length. Many black-and-white drawings illustrate the text.

Unfortunately, the work readily reveals its dated nature and shows omissions. The article on women contains both text and a picture that may be considered derogatory to modern Near Eastern cultures; additionally, it lacks any mention of women as portrayed in the New Testament. Jews during the period of Jesus are almost always described negatively, such as in the misleading article on the Pharisees. Information on the authors and contexts of the various books of the Bible indicates nothing of the various theories proposed over the last hundred years. Topics related to sexuality are conspicuously absent.

Other than historical interest, there is little reason for reference collections to contain this work. More current and evenhanded scholarship can be found in single-volume dictionaries, such as *Harper's Bible Dictionary* (see ARBA 86, entry 1382), or in multivolume sets, such as the *Anchor Bible Dictionary* (Doubleday, 1992).—**Christopher W. Nolan**

1542. **Roget's Thesaurus of the Bible.** By A. Colin Day. San Francisco, Calif., HarperSanFrancisco, 1992. 927p. index. $28.00; $30.00 (indexed). LC 92-53896. ISBN 0-06-061773-X; 0-06-061772-1 (indexed).

A traditional way of investigating biblical themes is locating occurrences of related terms in the Bible with the aid of a concordance. One drawback to this approach is that themes such as baptism, faith, and justification are sometimes present in the text even though the actual words do not appear. This is further complicated by the fact that a concordance is based upon a particular version or translation of the Bible. Thus, what is needed is a thematic or topical guide that is tied neither to the exact words in the text nor to a specific version or translation. For decades the most widely used tool answering this description has been *Nave's Topical Bible* by Orville Nave (Hendrickson, 1988), which lists Bible verses, passages, and references under alphabetically arranged topical headings. Related headings are linked together by cross-references. Although based upon the King James Version, *Nave's* is not dependent upon it for its usefulness.

Day has taken the "topical Bible" concept and given it an interesting twist. Instead of using an alphabetical arrangement, he chose the classified arrangement of *Roget's Thesaurus* (Longman's 1982 revision) as his organizational scheme. Then, for clarity, he modified some of the category names, which are indicated in the outline list of categories that precedes the thesaurus proper. In this way, Day was able to group similar themes such as evidence, testimony, and witness, which are presented as separate entries in *Nave's*. Also in contrast with *Nave's*, Day does not include actual Bible text with the references. Rather, for brevity, he provides concise paraphrases. Alphabetical access to topics is provided in the subject index. There is also an index of Bible references.

Diehard *Nave's* users may have no use for *Roget's*, but there will be, no doubt, those that greatly prefer the latter. Also, some may disagree with Day's placement within his scheme of a particular verse or passage. But the same can be said of *Nave's*. At the end of the day, it will come down to personal preference. Because of this, and because *Roget's* is a well-executed work, it deserves a place alongside *Nave's* in school, public, and academic libraries. [R: Choice, May 93, p. 1438; WLB, Mar 93, pp. 113-15]—**Craig W. Beard**

1543. Trenchard, Warren C. **The Student's Complete Vocabulary Guide to the Greek New Testament: Complete Frequency Lists, Cognate Groupings & Principal Parts.** Grand Rapids, Mich., Zondervan, 1992. 340p. index. $10.95pa. PA863.T74. 487'.4. LC 92-33255. ISBN 0-310-53341-4.

There is no shortage of handbooks to help students of New Testament Greek with the task of acquiring a working vocabulary. In 1990 three were published: *Mastering Greek Vocabulary* by Thomas A. Robinson (see ARBA 92, entry 1073), *Building Your New Testament Greek Vocabulary* by Robert E. Van Voorst (William B. Eerdmans), and a new edition of *Lexical Aids for Students of New Testament Greek* by Bruce M. Metzger (Edinburgh: T&T Clark). Now Trenchard has placed his work into the arena as a more complete vocabulary guide than its predecessors.

This volume is organized into five sections: cognate groups (common words sharing a basic root), word frequency (arranged in descending order according to occurrence), principal parts of verbs (including only those forms that appear in the New Testament), proper words (e.g., personal names), and miscellaneous lists (e.g., proclitics, enclitics, feminine nouns of the second declension). In addition, there is an index of all the Greek words appearing in the volume.

What most distinguishes this work from those of Metzger, Robinson, and Van Voorst is the extent of the vocabulary presented here. The other guides include words based on frequency—those that occur 10 times or more. Trenchard includes all the words in the Greek New Testament—all of them in the word frequency list and most of them in the cognate groups—a choice deemed unnecessary by the former but that students may welcome. Another feature students will appreciate is the exhaustive list of verbs with their principal parts.

Like snowflakes, no two vocabulary guides are exactly alike. Each has features that distinguish it from the others and make it more or less useful to students. However, because of its reasonable cost and expanded coverage, even libraries that have any or all of the other guides should add this one to the collection.

—Craig W. Beard

Handbooks and Yearbooks

1544. **Nelson's Quick Reference Bible Handbook.** Nashville, Tenn., Thomas Nelson, 1993. 383p. $7.99pa. BS417.N45. 220.6'1. LC 92-47032. ISBN 0-8407-6904-0.

This little book is a revised and enlarged edition of *A Layman's Overview of the Bible*, published in 1987. Arranged in the order of the Bible, there are four parts: the Old Testament, the New Testament, the Apocrypha, and "Exploring the Bible." The preface identifies the book's purpose as a kind of tour director, providing "enough background information,... cues and clues" so that the Bible reader will not "overlook the most important features" of individual books. The introduction gives a brief but excellent account of how the Bible came to be what it is and its contemporary form and meaning.

Each part is divided into chapters composed of books with similar intent or importance. For example, part 1 has chapters for books of the law, books of history, major prophets, and minor prophets. Each chapter begins with a brief introduction identifying the books, their basic purposes, and the date line. Each section deals with a separate book, giving the reader keys to understanding, accounts of scholarly research on authorship, historicity, theological importance, an outline of contents, and the like. One useful feature is a summary chart for the book that reflects its focus, key references divisions, topics, locales, and time periods. Scripture quotations are from the New King James Version of the Bible and the New Revised Standard Version (1989). Part 3, the Apocrypha, has much shorter versions of the sections on canonical books of the Old and New Testaments. As this part of the Bible is perhaps less well understood than the rest, this shortening is unfortunate. Nevertheless, a bibliography of works for further reading reduces this shortcoming. Part 4 will be a help to those wishing to arrange a scheduled study of the Bible. The suggestion is made that this book would serve as a supplement or guide for members of a Bible study group, and this reviewer agrees wholeheartedly. The paperback binding reduces its shelf life as a library reference work; still, it is highly recommended for public libraries, church and synagogue congregational library collections, and any Bible student wanting a quick handheld reference guide.—**Edward P. Miller**

1545. **The Oxford Companion to the Bible.** Bruce M. Metzger and Michael D. Coogan, eds. New York, Oxford University Press, 1993. 874p. maps. index. $45.00. BS440.M434. 220.3. LC 93-19315. ISBN 0-19-504645-5.

In this well-written volume of biblical scholarship, some 250 contributors offer biblical criticism and historical background on more than 700 topics, from Aaron to Zion. Introductory material, lists of abbreviations, an index, maps, and a bibliography make this an easily used volume. Its orientation leans toward mainstream Protestant theology, although it includes information about Judaism, Islam, Roman Catholicism, orthodoxy, and fundamentalism.

The volume is at its best when it speaks about the interaction of different academic disciplines, cultures, and individuals with the Bible. Articles such as "African American Traditions and the Bible," "Freud and the Bible," and "Science and the Bible" are highly readable and interesting. However, information concerning biblical material and theology appears uneven. Different approaches to the Bible by major branches of Christianity and Judaism are not explored. Equal treatment is given to the book of Nahum (a minor prophet) and to Mary, the mother of Christ. *Rabbi, bishop, deacon,* and *elder* are covered, while other clergy are not, such as *pastor, pope,* and *vicar.* Less-familiar Bible characters, such as Joab, David's commander-in-chief, are not listed in the body of the text nor in the index. Some theological terms, such as *millennium,* are also overlooked.

Overall, *The Oxford Companion to the Bible* will be an excellent addition to the library of every church, religious school, and Bible scholar. It will also be of interest to the well-informed layperson, but it will need to be supplemented by a standard Bible dictionary or encyclopedia. [R: LJ, 15 Sept 93, p. 69; RBB, 15 Dec 93, p. 780]—**Darlene H. Franklin**

1546. Rogerson, John. **The Bible: Cultural Atlas for Young People.** New York, Facts on File, 1993. 96p. illus. maps. index. $17.95. BS621.R65. 220.9. LC 92-34670. ISBN 0-8160-2908-3.

Producing historical atlases for children is no easy matter, but this work is part of a series of essentially historical atlases originally published in Great Britain under the auspices of Lionheart Books, a publisher known for its excellent resources for young people. All follow a similar structure that has become standard for historical atlases: the combination of text with maps and illustrations, rather than the simple reproduction of incomprehensible geographical charts of the countryside at different points in history.

A table of dates precedes sections on the history and the geography of the Bible lands, each of which consists of two-page spreads as chapters, with titles such as "Moses and the Exodus," "David's Empire," "The Passion of Jesus," "Galilee." Stunning color photographs of the landscape or reproductions of art pieces accompany the maps and text, in some cases with drawings that reproduce reconstructions of scenes or buildings. The reader is treated to credible depictions of what David's Jerusalem or Solomon's or Herod's temples may have looked like. Throughout, a text intelligible to a junior high student or perhaps an advanced sixth grader provides essential and interesting information. The religious content is confined to a few muted statements where the existence of God is clearly assumed, but with no dogmatic affirmations of faith. This unusual reference source is highly recommended for public and school libraries.

—**Johan Koren**

Indexes

1547. **Nelson's Quick Reference Bible Concordance.** By Ronald F. Youngblood. Nashville, Tenn., Thomas Nelson, 1993. 408p. $7.99pa. BS425.Y749. 220.5'208. LC 92-47033. ISBN 0-8407-6907-5.

This is an abridged edition of the author's *New Compact Key-Reference Concordance* (Thomas Nelson, 1992). It is based on the New King James Version but is intended to be helpful to users of other translations in the Authorized Version tradition. In his preface Youngblood tells the reader his choice of references has "focused on key doctrines, familiar verses, and passages that the average Bible reader is most likely to want to look up." Otherwise, he provides no criteria for inclusion or exclusion. A dagger following an entry heading is used to inform the reader that every occurrence of a word is listed. Each word is accompanied by what the author deems to be the most important Scripture references in which it is found. He also includes the context.

The reader is given no clue as to whether a given word translates more than one Hebrew or Greek word or whether it is one of multiple translations of the same word. For frequently occurring expressions there may be only one occurrence cited, obscuring patterns of usage for the reader. For example, the author cites only one instance of the recurring reference to possession of the land in Deuteronomy. Consequently, this concordance is of very limited utility and of interest only to lay readers of the Bible who eschew modern critical translations and serious scholarly interpretation. It will not, therefore, be of interest to most libraries.—**Harold O. Forshey**

1548. **NKJV Exhaustive Concordance: New King James Version.** Nashville, Tenn., Thomas Nelson, 1992. 1251p. $29.99. BS425.N55. 220.5'2033. LC 92-28532. ISBN 0-8407-4261-4.

This is an exhaustive concordance to the New King James Version of the Bible. Similar to the recently published *NRSV Concordance Unabridged* and *NRSV Exhaustive Concordance* (see ARBA 92, entries 1442 and 1443), it contains every word in the translation, including articles, prepositions, and possessives. The latter lists are in a large appendix at the back of the book. Unlike the previous two concordances, this book does not have charts, explanatory articles, lists of such items as biblical flora and fauna, or outlines and references for biblical topics of study. Coinciding with *NRSV Exhaustive Concordance*, this concordance contains 32 key phrases (against more than 600 in *Unabridged*). Other features of this concordance are words cross-referenced with the King James Version (KJV) and a thumb index that offers a highly visible indication of the alphabetical sections of the book. *NRSV Exhaustive Concordance*, also published by Thomas Nelson, contained fewer cross-references to the original KJV than *Unabridged* and certainly fewer than the present work.—**Robert T. Anderson**

Periodicals and Serials

1549. **An Index to English Periodical Literature on the Old Testament and Ancient Near Eastern Studies. Volume V.** William G. Hupper, comp. and ed. Metuchen, N.J., American Theological Library Association and Scarecrow, 1992. 708p. (ATLA Bibliography Series, no.21). $72.50. Z7772.A1H86. 016.221. LC 86-31448. ISBN 0-8108-2618-6.

The fifth volume of this work, containing approximately 10,000 entries—close to a third of which are cross-references—continues where the previous volume left off on the subtopic of literary criticism of the Old Testament. The volume opens with a major section on the *Religionsgeschichte* of the Old Testament, including materials on priests and priesthoods; altars, high places, and the like; sacrifices and offerings; temples; holy days and fests; worship and sects; cults; and ideas about philosophy, Hokhmah, the apocalypse, and Messianic expectations. It then moves to mythology in general, including folklore, legends, and so forth, with a special section on Lilith. Following this material is a bibliography on comparative religions of the ancient world. The concluding sections focus on philological and epigraphic studies, including the alphabet, onomatology and teknonymy, the different language groupings—making use of more than 22 different fonts (including cuneiform and Egyptian hieroglyphics)—and references on the Bible as literature, encompassing studies in poetry; narrative devices such as rhyme, repetition, and patterns; form criticism; and literary style.

This volume is a bit more user-friendly than the previous volumes in that it provides a brief explanation of the sigla used, previously available only in volume 1; however, as did its predecessors, it neglects to remind the user that despite the more than 600 journals used, there are no references that post-date the 1969-1970 journal year. One trusts that somewhere these references are being compiled for use, perhaps on computer disk. None of this comment is meant to minimize the importance of this multivolume work, and scholars and laypeople alike should look forward to the speedy appearance of the final volumes.—**Susan Tower Hollis**

1550. Mills, Watson E. **An Index to Periodical Literature on the Apostle Paul.** Kinderhook, N.Y., E. J. Brill, 1993. 345p. index. (New Testament Tools and Studies, v.16). $71.50. Z8665.45.M55. 016.2259'2. LC 93-7974. ISBN 90-04-09674-4.

Mills is a New Testament scholar and editor who is well known for his earlier publications. The present work updates an earlier bibliography under the same title by Bruce M. Metzger (1st ed., 1960; 2d ed., 1970). As Metzger's book has certainly proven to be a useful tool (especially for the periodical literature before 1950), the decision to update is reasonable. Mills arranges the bibliographical entries under Metzger's original subject headings, to which he has added three others: homosexuality, archaeology, and soteriology. Under each heading Metzger's entries are followed by Mills's additional citations. Numbers for the latter are distinguished from the former by boldface type and a decimal extension.

The bibliography is open to important criticisms in three areas: instructions for users, subject access, and presentation. Although the first edition of Metzger's work gave the reader important information about the scope, chronological coverage, arrangement, and method of compilation, the present edition does not. Moreover, the relation of this bibliography to the two earlier editions by Metzger is confused by misleading references (e.g., the first edition [1960] is cited twice as the "1966 edition").

Subject access in the two earlier editions by Metzger was difficult (even with the occasional cross-references) because each entry was printed under only one subject heading, and there was no subject index. The present edition of the work adds no new cross-references, and, consequently, a bad situation has become worse. A work on Calvin and Luther's interpretations of Paul's letter to the Galatians (entry 1607.2), for example, is listed among works on Galatians but omitted in the "History of Interpretation" section, which includes other works on Luther's understanding of Paul (cf. entry 2950). Thus, the user can never be confident that the entries listed under a subject heading are the only relevant ones.

The presentation of material in the bibliography could have been improved by two modest changes. First, subject headings at the top of each page—even to the limited extent of those in the 1960 edition—would have saved the reader much effort. Furthermore, the "Exegesis of Individual Passages" sections under each of Paul's writings could have included a marginal reference to the chapter of the writing, so that the reader's eye could more quickly find the relevant entries. Although the present work does indeed make a contribution to scholarship, many libraries may find that it offers little that is not already available in a combination of the earlier editions by Metzger and the current CD-ROM version of the ATLA Religion Database.—**M. Patrick Graham**

Quotation Books

1551. Draper, Edythe. **Draper's Book of Quotations for the Christian World.** Wheaton, Ill., Tyndale House, 1992. 1406p. index. $19.95. PN6081.D7. 082. LC 91-35165. ISBN 0-8423-5109-4.

Intended as a comprehensive collection of classic and contemporary quotations of importance for the Christian world, this new offering provides more than 12,000 quotations from ancient times to the present. A large number of proverbs and unattributed quotations are included; quotations from sacred texts are not. As is often the case with specialized collections of quotations, the choices for inclusion reflect the compiler's worldview and experience. This collection provides extensive coverage of some nineteenth- and twentieth-century figures rarely quoted in other sources (e.g., A. W. Tozer, Oswald Chambers, Charles R. Swindoll, Erwin C. Lutzer). Unfortunately, many important theologians and writers do not receive comparable coverage. The inclusion of quotations that have no particularly Christian or even spiritual content calls into question the title of the collection.

The main body of the work is arranged under approximately 500 topics. The numbered entries are indexed in separate keyword and author indexes. The author index omits authors for whom more than 200 quotations appear. Because it provides entry numbers without any additional information, researching for other authors with large numbers of quotations is rather daunting.

This work is intended for students, teachers, public speakers, business leaders, pastors, and families. The lack of specific source citations limits its usefulness for scholarly purposes, as does the uneven coverage of Christian and spiritual thinkers. However, its reasonable price and large number of quotations may make it worth considering for collections with other books of religious quotations.—**Carol Wheeler**

Islam

1552. Koszegi, Michael A., and J. Gordon Melton, eds. **Islam in North America: A Sourcebook.** Hamden, Conn., Garland, 1992. 414p. index. (Religious Information Systems Series, v.8; Garland Reference Library of Social Science, v.852). $59.00. BP67.A1I82. 297'.0973. LC 92-17794. ISBN 0-8153-0918-X.

Three major manifestations of Islam in North America—that brought by African slaves, that brought by immigrants from the Middle East, and Afro-American Islam—are the focus of this book. Other subjects examined include the Islamic Sectarian Movement in America, Sufism (Islamic mysticism), and the relationship between Islam and Christianity as organized religions. Beginning with a general overview of the subject, the text proceeds with chapters on specific topics. Each chapter contains pertinent essays or reports and a bibliography of related sources. Nearly 1,300 citations are included for books, articles, lectures, dissertations, and reprints. In addition, the editors have compiled a directory of North American Islamic organizations and centers.

Although this book does not pretend to be all-inclusive or encyclopedic, it would have greatly benefited from a little more commentary and historical background. The most regrettable flaw of the work is its incomplete index, which makes navigating the information difficult, especially for the novice. Only authors and titles of periodicals that appear in the bibliographies are indexed, excluding material from the articles or directory listings. Coupled with a decidedly establishment orientation, this factor makes for an interesting but insufficient resource. Still, it remains a valuable sourcebook and overview of the growing phenomenon of Islam in North America. The editors should be congratulated for publishing the first of its kind in this area of study. Useful to scholars with some background in the subject, the book will also be of interest to students of religion, members of the Islamic community, and general readers. [R: RBB, 15 April 93, p. 1536]—**Barbara Ittner**

1553. Shaikh, Farzana, ed. **Islam and Islamic Groups: A Worldwide Reference Guide.** Harlow, England, Longman; distr., Detroit, Gale, 1992. 316p. index. $155.00. ISBN 0-582-09146-2.

Not the religious dimension of Islam but the political is the focus of this guide. Country-by-country, it surveys Islam as a political presence in more than 100 countries, considering origins and development, current demographic representation, relationship with the state, and noteworthy political activity in modern times. Each country included has a significant, but not necessarily large, Islamic presence. Austria and Korea, for instance, are omitted, while Belgium and South Africa, each with a 2 percent Muslim population, get four-page articles. Traditionally and predominantly Islamic nations—Egypt, Iraq, Indonesia, and the like—tend, of course, to get lengthier treatment. Some surprises may await the nonexpert, such as the South American country of Suriname, whose Muslim population is estimated to be between 20 and 30 percent. Following the narrative sections for most countries are lists of politically active Islamic organizations (e.g., political parties, popular fronts and movements, government bodies, associations). Information provided usually includes names in the original language and English; founding date; leadership; structure and aims; and sometimes membership, publications, or affiliate organizations.

Contributors and their credentials are identified, but sources of information are not cited, and there is only a 10-item general bibliography. Information on clandestine or semiclandestine organizations, as the introduction notes, often comes from unconventional sources; some of it must be "regarded as tentative rather than authoritative," although few clues are supplied as to which is more and which is less reliable. Used with this caution in mind, the work is a useful compilation of information otherwise not readily available (or available at all). [R: Choice, June 93, p. 1604; LJ, 15 May 93, pp. 62-63; RBB, July 93, p. 2003]

—**Hans E. Bynagle**

Judaism

1554. **The Blackwell Dictionary of Judaica.** By Dan Cohn-Sherbok. Cambridge, Mass., Basil Blackwell, 1992. 597p. $74.95; $24.95pa. 296. ISBN 0-631-16615-7; 0-631-18728-6pa.

This work is designed to fill a need for "a single-volume comprehensive dictionary which contains basic information about Judaism and the Jewish people" (p. ix). Cohn-Sherbok does not view it as a replacement for multivolume Judaica reference works. In the preface, he demonstrates thorough knowledge of other one-volume dictionaries and encyclopedias of Judaism but claims that this one has a broader scope—"all aspects of Jewish civilization." His primary audience is "students of Jewish life and thought."

The dictionary contains 7,000 entries in a single A-Z sequence, arranged letter by letter. There are a table (a two-page chronology of Jewish history) and two maps (the Ancient Near East and Ancient Israel). Terms included derive from many fields of Jewish experience; the work is especially rich in entries for prominent figures and organizations in recent Jewish history. The amount of information given is sometimes inconsistent. For example, while three books are cited in Uriel Weinreich's entry, none are listed in the entry for his father, Max, author of the classic *History of the Yiddish Language* (University of Chicago Press, 1980). The entries for Jewish political parties are praiseworthy, but surely "Ladino" (Judeo-Spanish language, 3 lines) deserves as much space as "Yevsektzia" (Jewish branch of the Russian Communist Party, 11 lines). An anti-Orthodox tone seems to permeate some of the entries for Jewish observance; for example, under "Purity, ritual," the author lists practices that "persist."

A hyperscholarly Romanization is employed for Hebrew terms, and most users will not read the prefatory note on transliteration. After unsuccessfully seeking an entry for *Sefer Mitsvot Gadol* (Library of Congress Romanization), this reviewer assumed that there was none, but then serendipitously encountered eight entries beginning with the word *Sepher* (book). In contrast, a nonsystematic Romanization is used for Yiddish. *Yontif*, the Yiddish term for *holiday*, is not linked to its Hebrew etymon, *Yom Tov*. The choice of Yiddish entries is poor, primarily slang.

The dictionary has an attractive two-column format, with headwords in large boldface type. The text has been carefully edited, and cross-references are well controlled. This reference work is handier to use than the 16-volume, large-format *Encyclopaedia Judaica* (see ARBA 73, entry 274), which requires a double lookup via the index for many Judaic terms that are not headwords. The paperback edition of this dictionary has a generous gutter margin; buy this format and bind it to avoid the price of the hardcover. [R: Choice, May 93, p. 1436; RBB, 1 Mar 93, p. 1250]—**Bella Hass Weinberg**

1555. Breslauer, S. Daniel. **Judaism and Human Rights in Contemporary Thought: A Bibliographical Survey.** Westport, Conn., Greenwood Press, 1993. 195p. index. (Bibliographies and Indexes in Religious Studies, no.25). $49.95. BM645.H85B74. 296.3'877. LC 92-38996. ISBN 0-313-27994-2.

Breslauer continues his bibliographical studies on Judaism and ethics in this work, his third in the series. This volume covers the relationship of Jews and human rights—including such topics as the Holocaust and emigration from the former Soviet Union—and Jewish writings about human rights in a broader perspective. More than 800 entries have been drawn from books and articles written mostly in English. The bibliography is clearly intended for serious scholars, but theses and dissertations are inexplicably excluded.

Breslauer provides a very useful bibliographical essay covering the history and development of Jewish thought on human rights. Subsequent chapters offer annotated citations for topics such as the classical sources of Jewish ethics, theoretical works on human rights, and practical issues (e.g., women's rights). A section on Jews as victims and as violators of human rights contains relevant material on the current Palestinian issue. The annotations are the strongest feature of the book; they are always succinctly descriptive and occasionally evaluative, revealing an excellent knowledge of each item being cited and providing substantial assistance to researchers. Three indexes supplement the bibliography, but the subject index is much too brief (only 35 headings for 800 items). Fortunately, the classified arrangement of the work compensates for this shortcoming.

The current volume overlaps only slightly with Breslauer's earlier works (*Contemporary Jewish Ethics* and *Modern Jewish Morality* [see ARBA 87, entries 402 and 403]). The focus is quite specialized, but the inclusion of Jewish serials not indexed in major periodical indexes makes this a useful addition to many research collections. [R: Choice, Nov 93, p. 424]—**Christopher W. Nolan**

1556. Nulman, Macy. **The Encyclopedia of Jewish Prayer: Ashkenazic and Sephardic Rites.** Northvale, N.J., Jason Aronson, 1993. 429p. index. $50.00. BM660.N85. 296.4'03. LC 92-33637. ISBN 0-87668-370-7.

Jewish prayer books are a rich source of theological, historical, and cultural information. Firmly set within a traditional framework, Nulman's encyclopedia is an insightful but limited guide to this wealth of knowledge. The insight comes from Nulman's very full and well-documented discussions of more than 1,000 prayers as they have developed in both Ashkenazic and Sephardic communities. He has mined the commentaries to good effect and succeeded in bringing together relevant material from an impressively wide variety of traditional sources. In general, the prayers are arranged in alphabetical order, according to their initial wording.

Although this exclusive principle of organization, supported by several indexes, is altogether appropriate for those who already know something about Jewish liturgy, it effectively rules out just about everyone else. Lacking as it does any full-scale introduction, synthetic articles, or subject index, this volume is inaccessible to the many individuals who would otherwise be interested in consulting it, for example, for references to women or the concept of repentance contained in Jewish prayers. For these reasons, it can only be recommended for purchase to specialized libraries and educational institutions.
—**Leonard J. Greenspoon**

1557. Olitzky, Kerry M., Lance J. Sussman, and Malcolm H. Stern, eds. **Reform Judaism in America: A Biographical Dictionary and Sourcebook.** Westport, Conn., Greenwood Press, 1993. 347p. index. (Jewish Denominations in America). $75.00. BM750.R39. 296.8'346'0973. LC 92-25794. ISBN 0-313-24628-9.

This biographical dictionary is the second in a set of three covering the major branches of American Judaism. Unlike the earlier volume, *Conservative Judaism in America* (see ARBA 89, entry 1343), which was authored by one writer, this volume contains entries by a variety of scholars and rabbis. Approximately 170 important American Reform leaders from the period 1824-1976 are profiled in this work. Several essays on the history of Reform Judaism and its major institutions are also included, as well as historical lists of the major officers of Reform organizations.

The core of the dictionary is the alphabetically arranged entries of one to two pages on each of the figures, covering their religious contributions and basic life events, such as birthplace and children. The tone of the pieces is consistently objective, avoiding obvious bias in descriptions of theological or political controversies. Primary and secondary bibliographies are appended to all of the entries. The secondary sources are especially useful, as they frequently list newspaper articles, obituaries, theses, and other references less accessible to the average researcher. A bibliography on Reform Judaism is appended to the dictionary; it lists a large number of synagogue histories, memoirs, and unpublished sources in addition to the standard monographic and journal literature.

This work provides useful and comprehensive biographies of leaders in an important American religious tradition. Many of these leaders are difficult to find in other religious biographical sources, so this work fills a useful niche. Additionally, the lengthy bibliography on Reform Judaism provides access to a large realm of unpublished materials. [R: Choice, Nov 93, p. 438]—**Christopher W. Nolan**

Part IV
SCIENCE AND TECHNOLOGY

29 Science and Technology in General

BIBLIOGRAPHY

1558. Gottlieb, Jean S. **A Checklist of the Newberry Library's Printed Books in Science, Medicine, Technology, and the Pseudosciences ca. 1460-1750.** Hamden, Conn., Garland, 1992. 312p. (Garland Reference Library of the Humanities, v.1195). $67.00. Z7405.H6G67. 001.3. LC 92-17941. ISBN 0-8240-5171-8.

The motivation for this book is to provide a list of early books held in the Newberry Library of Chicago, best known for its humanities collections, that deal with science broadly interpreted. It accomplishes the task in some respects but has major drawbacks for the researcher. The coverage appears to be thorough, with some 2,700 titles listed for the period 1460-1750. The listing is purely alphabetical by author; there are no listings by subject, date, or place and no index. Authors included in compilations are not cross-listed. Thus the volume yields its treasures only to the assiduous browser. There is another oddity: No assistance is provided to the scholar interested in obtaining access to the works listed—not even the address of the Newberry Library.—**Harold Goldwhite**

1559. Iatridis, Mary D. **Teaching Science to Children.** 2d ed. Hamden, Conn., Garland, 1993. 199p. index. (Source Books on Education, v.35; Garland Reference Library of Social Science, v.747). $30.00. Z5818.S3I24. 016.3723'5044. LC 92-28047. ISBN 0-8153-0090-5.

Teachers, curricular specialists, parents, and children's writers could all put this guide to good use. For example, any parent with a hazy understanding of constructivist theory would be enlightened by the first chapter, as well as by several of the texts identified. Moreover, anyone who lacked a feeling for the transformation from ordered pedagogy to hands-on and integrated science could acquire it by reading the summaries of texts and noting their publication dates.

Sections on texts and science activity books (drawn from the 1960s to the present) are satisfactory, but the portion on how to maneuver in the nonfiction literature for children (from the late 1980s to the present, and compiled by Miriam Maracek) is superb. The index (author and subject) makes a good entryway to topical issues in science education and subdiscipline-based activities. Science activity books cited range from sublime encounters (e.g., *Bubbles, Rainbows and Worms*) to sensational ones (e.g., *The Amazing Dirt Book*). An add-on chapter regarding science and the special-needs student serves as a reminder of how much more we need to do to reach all learners. The many-faceted, multidisciplinary nature of science comes through on every page. This volume would meet the needs of a wide audience in school and public libraries. [R: RBB, June 93, p. 1880]—**Diane M. Calabrese**

1560. Rothenberg, Marc. **The History of Science and Technology in the United States: A Critical and Selective Bibliography. Volume II.** Hamden, Conn., Garland, 1993. 197p. index. (Bibliographies on the History of Science and Technology, v.17; Garland Reference Library of the Humanities, v.815). $32.00. Z7405.H6R67. 016.50973. LC 81-43355. ISBN 0-8240-8349-0.

This volume continues and supplements Rothenberg's 1982 bibliography of the same title (see ARBA 84, entry 1228), bringing the listing up to 1987. The need for a second volume is clear: More than 650 items have been selected from this 8-year period, reflecting the increased interest in the history of science and technology and the related exponential growth in the literature. The entries represent articles, monographs, chapters or sections of books, and dissertations. Almost all entries include brief, evaluative, informative annotations.

As was the first volume, this is a selective bibliography that provides solid coverage of major secondary sources dealing with the history of science and technology in the United States. An intelligent subject arrangement is supplemented by author and subject indexes. An engaging and useful appendix discusses access to manuscript collections.

Any library holding Rothenberg's 1982 bibliography should add the current one. Libraries that serve patrons interested in the history of science and technology and that do not already have the first volume should seriously consider acquiring both. [R: Choice, Nov 93, p. 438]—**Susan Davis Herring**

1561. *Science Books & Films'* **Best Books for Children 1988-91.** Maria Sosa and Shirley M. Malcom, eds. Washington, D.C., American Association for the Advancement of Science, 1992. 300p. index. $40.00. Z7401.S362. 016.5. LC 92-27208. ISBN 0-87168-505-1.

This excellent bibliography is a must for teachers developing science curricula and for academic libraries with teacher education programs. This resource, along with others in the series (see ARBA 89, entry 1345 and ARBA 85, entry 1327), can help one plan a quality science education course that will stir interest among both children and teachers. The annotated bibliography quickly enables one to make knowledgeable book choices for library collections or to develop reading lists for science teachers and students in elementary and secondary education.

The books cited in this volume are alphabetically arranged in broad subject areas, contain bibliographical information supplied by the publisher, and have the original review from the journal *Science Books & Films*. The table of contents, the author and subject indexes, and the reading level indicators in each entry can help tailor selections to an audience ranging from kindergarten through 9th grade. Listing only the books that received a "recommended" or "highly recommended" rating in the journal, this easy-to-use bibliography is a first-rate acquisitions tool for librarians in school, public, and academic libraries. [R: BL, 1 April 93, p. 1445]—**Diane J. Turner**

1562. **Walford's Guide to Reference Material. Volume 1: Science and Technology.** 6th ed. Marilyn Mullay and Priscilla Schlicke, eds. London, Library Association; distr., Lanham, Md., UNIPUB, 1993. 943p. index. $195.00. ISBN 1-85604-015-1.

With two new editors, the work on this edition was completed in early 1993. The number of entries has increased by more than 1,000, with some sections substantially expanded (e.g., conservation, solar heating, artificial intelligence, microcomputers). As in previous editions, a number of academic, special, and public libraries were consulted, and each entry includes a full bibliographical citation with ISBN or ISSN but no cost listed, as in previous editions. As was true in previous editions, *Walford* is more comprehensive in comparison to *Guide to Reference Books* (see ARBA 93, entry 12) and is much stronger in international coverage. Highly recommended to all academic, special and larger public libraries.

—**Bohdan S. Wynar**

BIOGRAPHY

1563. Eason, Ron, and Sarah Rookledge. **Rookledge's International Handbook of Type Designers: A Biographical Directory.** Carshalton Beeches, England, Sarema Press; distr., Wakefield, R.I., Moyer Bell, c1991, 1993. 209p. illus. $19.95. 686.220922. ISBN 1-55921-092-3.

Typography is a broad term that can mean different things to different people. All typography is creative; no design problem can be resolved without thoughtful and imaginative treatment of typeforms. Interpreting the meaning of words through the manipulation of typefaces is the work of type designers. The lives and careers of more than 175 of these individuals are profiled here in an alphabetical arrangement, from Adobe Systems to Gundrun Zapf-von Hesse. Some 700 text typefaces are discussed, beginning with Gutenberg and proceeding to present-day designs. Sparsely illustrated with photographs of designers, typefaces, and alphabet samples, this book offers relatively obscure and narrowly focused information.

While this volume does not attempt fresh research, it does bring together, in a convenient format, information from a range of sources to stimulate interest in type and in those who have made it their life's work. There may be some debate on the merit of the designers selected for inclusion, but the brief entries will clear the shroud of anonymity surrounding most type designers. A subject index and typeface list provide invaluable access for scholars, designers, typographers, and graphic artists.

Other brief biographies of type designers do exist, generally buried within works such as *Twentieth Century Type Designers* (Taplinger, 1987) and *Modern Encyclopedia of Typefaces 1960-90* (Van Nostrand Reinhold, 1990), but this entertainingly presented biography is unique. It may strengthen one's sensitivity to letterforms and their creators and help dispel the mystery that surrounds this intriguing subject.

—**Judy Gay Matthews**

1564. **Who's Who in Science and Engineering 1992-1993.** New Providence, N.J., Marquis Who's Who/Reed Reference Publishing, 1992. 1084p. $199.00. LC 92-80582. ISBN 0-8379-5751-6.

The premier edition of this new member of the Marquis Who's Who family follows the familiar format of the well-respected series of reference works. Included are biographies of nearly 22,000 scientists, doctors, and engineers from around the world (although the majority are from the United States). Entries, which generally are approved by the biographee, include up to 20 types of information, such as personal data, address, career information, affiliations, and professional achievements and awards. In cases in which persons selected for inclusion did not respond, biographies were researched by staff members. (Those entries are identified as such.) Inclusion is based on Marquis's standard of "reference interest," and the stated editorial policy is to facilitate communication within the scientific community. To fulfill this aim, selected biographies from the "soft" sciences and support professions, such as education and administration, are also included. This diversity significantly heightens the work's value to users exploring rapidly changing or loosely defined areas of study. Specific descriptions of achievements assist the user in identifying the exact area of the biographee's work.

The value of this work as a networking tool is greatly enhanced by the professional area index, which divides individuals into more than 100 specialties and then is further subdivided geographically. Also included is a list of recipients of some 150 awards, arranged by field, and a geographical index.

—**William S. Proudfoot**

DICTIONARIES AND ENCYCLOPEDIAS

1565. **The Dorling Kindersley Science Encyclopedia.** New York, Dorling Kindersley, 1993. 448p. illus. maps. index. $39.95. ISBN 1-56458-328-7.

The poor state of science education in the United States and its effects on the competitiveness of U.S. technology are well known. Perhaps more damaging, insufficient understanding of the forces that drive the universe has led to distrust of the scientific "establishment" and widespread belief in pseudosciences. Efforts to increase the scientific literacy of the population must start with children; a fascination with the physical world instilled at an early age will, it is hoped, last a lifetime. *The Dorling Kindersley Science Encyclopedia* has been designed with this goal in mind. From its glittering cover to the sharp, brilliant photographs that are the publisher's trademark, this work is designed to grab and hold a child's attention.

The front matter consists of a guide to the book's use, time charts of scientific discoveries, "How Scientists Work," and depictions of safety codes (e.g., dust hazard, flammable liquid). The main body of the book consists of chapters on matter, reactions, materials, forces and energy, electricity and magnetism, sound and light, Earth, weather, space, living things, how living things work, and ecology. After an introduction, these broad subjects are broken into dozens of more specific subsections; for example, weather begins with sections on sunshine, seasons, and climates. Although none of this material is arranged alphabetically, the index makes it easy to find topics. Each page is about half text and half illustrative pictures and photographs (there are no irrelevant images). Illustrations can be anything from a tornado to the internal construction of a hearing aid (there are a lot of cutaways) to a hermit crab with an anemone on its shell. Their clarity and appropriateness will fascinate readers, as they give life to formerly unfathomable processes. The text is appropriate for older children and young adults; it is simple without being condescending and explains things very clearly. Many subsections contain a capsule biography of an important researcher in the area (complete with picture), and all have a small box of cross-references to related topics. The information is as current as possible. A section of "Fact Finders" after the main chapter contains maps, charts, tables, laws, and other ready-reference material (e.g., endings and prefixes of chemical names, temperature scales, frequency ranges of musical instruments). A glossary and the index complete the book.

Sometimes text is printed on top of a graphic, rendering both less legible. Temperatures are given in Celsius rather than Fahrenheit. Some of the photographs are too small to be very meaningful. There are some really spectacular tornado pictures available, but the ones used in the book are unimpressive. But these are minor criticisms of a work that does exactly what its creators intended it to do and does it well. Highly recommended for school and public libraries and for individuals. [R: RBB, 1 Dec 93, p. 710; SLJ, Nov 93, p. 140]—**D. A. Rothschild**

1566. **Encyclopedia of Physical Science and Technology.** 2d ed. Robert A. Meyers, ed. San Diego, Calif., Academic Press, 1992. 18v. illus. index. $2,500.00/set. Q123.E4974. 503. LC 92-6959. ISBN 0-12-226930-6.

Most scientists and engineers do not normally read encyclopedias. They are more apt to seek out information in the primary literature, even when exploring a new or unfamiliar subject. However, in the process of reviewing this particular work, this reviewer has come to appreciate the value of such resources for introductions to new topics, for review, or as a prelude to more extensive studies.

This is the 2d edition of a work first published in 1987. It is approximately 20 percent longer than the first edition, with 705 articles in several volumes spanning approximately 14,000 pages. An eighteenth volume is devoted solely to indexes: a list of contributors, a relational index listing for each entry several other articles that may contain related information, and a standard subject index with more than 70,000 entries! This particular feature represents a considerable improvement over the earlier edition. The editor and the executive advisory board have been retained from the first edition. One new member has been added to the latter group, bringing its total to eight. All are exceptionally distinguished in their respective fields of physical science or technology. The 49-member editorial advisory board is largely the same as that in 1987 and is similarly well qualified. The authors of individual articles appear to have been carefully selected for their expertise and ability to provide balanced overviews of their assigned topics.

The encyclopedia is intended for use by the scientific and engineering community: undergraduates, graduate students, research personnel, academic staff, industrial and institute scientists and engineers, and even individuals working in such fields as the media, law, or management. Many of the entries assume basic mathematical skills through undergraduate calculus and differential equations, but most of the work is descriptive prose accessible even to nontechnical readers. Each entry starts with a table of contents, a glossary, and a brief introductory definition of the subject. The latter is a nice feature, as it quickly informs the reader about what the article is likely to cover and what it will not. The articles average 20 pages in length, and most can be characterized as major, authoritative expositions of their respective subjects. The volumes are well illustrated, with an average of one figure, photograph, or table every two pages.

Several examples will indicate the level of expertise that has been brought to this undertaking. The article on fractals has been written by Benoit B. Mandlebrot, universally recognized as the most important developer of this field for the past 20 years. Similarly, for the discussion of explosive fusion devices, it is difficult to imagine a more qualified author than Edward Teller. Several entries have been written by Nobel laureates.

As pointed out above, there are a number of contributions that did not appear in the 1987 edition. A cursory examination of volume 10 alone turned up microcomputer buses and links, micromechanical devices, microprocessors and microprocessor-based systems, modulation, and several others. Of the entries that appear in both editions, the vast majority have been updated and bear 1992 copyrights, although a few have been carried over intact from the earlier set. There are some examples of topics appearing in both editions, but with entirely separate treatments by different authors. In a handful of cases, a 1992 copyright has been given to a 1987 entry with virtually no revision except perhaps for the addition of a reference or two. In general, however, the editor and authors appear to have made every effort to update and improve upon the earlier work.

Among the more unusual entries are articles on scientific information services, nuclear energy, risk analysis, railway engineering, and severe thunderstorms. There are two delightful chapters on elementary and modern topics in number theory. (The sections on Fermat's Last Theorem will have to be revised in the next edition.) Recent developments in physics or materials science such as proton decay, quasicrystals, and nanostructured materials are well represented here. It is difficult to describe the breadth of the entire work without actually listing the entries. In general, an enormous and surprisingly diverse range of subjects is covered and easily accessed through the superb index.

There are two other works to which this one might be compared. The first is the *McGraw-Hill Encyclopedia of Science and Technology* (see ARBA 93, entry 1446). As suggested by the title, its scope is considerably broader than that of the Academic Press publication. Moreover, its entries are typically shorter and more qualitative, on the technical level of an ordinary encyclopedia. The second comparison is to the *Encyclopedia of Applied Physics* (see ARBA 93, entries 1733-34), which is a work-in-progress begun in 1991, with only a few volumes published to date. This set is similar in scope and technicality to the *Encyclopedia of Physical Science and Technology*, with editorial consultants and authors of comparable reputation. However, an examination of the available volumes shows a different selection of topics that in many ways complements those reviewed here. For example, the *Encyclopedia of Applied Physics* has articles on accelerators and aerodynamics but not on acetylene. Even subjects in common, such as artificial intelligence, aluminum, or atmospheric acoustics, are sufficiently different to make both sets of encyclopedias worth consulting.

In summary, this is a magnificent work of enormous potential value to those who will use it. It would be easy to find fault with specific aspects of such a vast undertaking—favorite subjects omitted or others given too much emphasis, isolated deficiencies, entire articles that appear weaker than others, or even the occasional typographical error—but such pettiness would serve little purpose. The work, on balance, is exceptionally well done and of unquestionable quality. It should be part of the technical collections of libraries everywhere, for the general public as well as for academicians, government researchers, and their counterparts in the private sector. [R: LJ, 15 April 93, p. 84]—**John U. Trefny**

1567. Gibilisco, Stan. **The Concise Illustrated Dictionary of Science and Technology.** Blue Ridge Summit, Pa., TAB Books, 1993. 520p. illus. maps. $36.95; $24.95pa. Q123.G54. 503. LC 92-22545. ISBN 0-8306-4152-1; 0-8306-4153-Xpa.

Without trepidation, Gibilisco ventures out to provide a concise introduction to terms in science and technology for middle and secondary grade students. His effort is a very good start, probably as good as anyone could do. Even so, readers will start to notice omissions (e.g., virtual reality, prokaryote [although it appears in a table], eukaryote), conversions (e.g., menopause at age 40), obfuscations (e.g., equinox, solstice), oversimplifications (e.g., the animal classification tree), and errors (e.g., the abdomen is the third of three major insect body parts, not the "central" body part). The most noticeable problems lie in Gibilisco's selective inclusion of "some famous scientists." Charles Darwin is in; Alfred Russel Wallace is not. Sally Ride also merited inclusion. Because the author is open to suggestions, the next edition will probably have many fewer entries that provoke readers. In the meantime, the book is modestly priced, and it has much in its favor. By turning to one volume, the user can confirm that a willy-nilly is a hurricane in Australia and that pyridoxine is vitamin B-6. There are real precision and strength to the definitions of words from the spheres of engineering and space technology. And, the end-tables on a variety of topics (e.g., Beaufort scale, constants, solar system, space probes) make a very strong supplement. [R: RBB, 15 April 93, pp. 1532-33]—**Diane M. Calabrese**

1568. **The Kingfisher Science Encyclopedia.** Catherine Headlam, ed. New York, Chambers Kingfisher Graham, c1991, 1993. 768p. illus. index. $39.95. Q121.K55. 503. LC 92-43209. ISBN 1-85697-842-7.

This voluminous resource includes many unusual features, such as "milestones," which provides chronologies of events in each area of science; fact boxes describing statistics for the biggest, highest, and longest physical features; cross-references; biographies on leading scientists; and projects and experiments, ranging from observing simple chemical reactions to growing plants. The work is intended for use by children from ages 8 to 14. Easy-to-understand subject symbols are used throughout the text, which includes nearly 1,000 entries on every scientific topic. The book has many colorful pictures, illustrations, and drawings, as well as numerous cross-references. It concludes with a comprehensive three-part index of more than 3,000 entries: a main index, a subject index, and a special feature index. The primary beneficiaries of this excellent encyclopedia are public and elementary school libraries. [R: RBB, 1 Dec 93, p. 710; SBF, Dec 93, p. 371; SLJ, Nov 93, p. 140]—**James M. Murray**

1569. **The Raintree Illustrated Science Encyclopedia.** Austin, Tex., Raintree/Steck-Vaughn, c1991, 1992. 18v. illus. maps. index. $329.00/set. Q121.R34. 503. LC 90-40559. ISBN 0-8172-3800-X.

This outstanding set is the 3d edition of a science encyclopedia aimed at elementary and middle school children (approximately ages 8-14). Unlike most other encyclopedias for this age group, which have a thematic approach, this is a true ready-reference source, with short to medium-length articles on an exhaustive array of topics. While thematically arranged encyclopedias are perhaps easier for children to use when preparing school reports, the Raintree approach allows for much greater detail. Furthermore, once a child has learned to follow up on all the *see* and *see also* references (as many as 10 in a typical one-page article), a wealth of material can be assembled on almost any topic, and research skills honed at the same time.

The volumes of this set contain entries ranging from one paragraph to five or more pages, on topics as specific as individual chemical compounds or as broad-ranging as the solar system. Most fields of science, technology, science history, and mathematics are covered. The length of articles is determined as much by children's interest in a subject as by a subject's importance to science (e.g., "Dinosaurs" gets six pages, "Evolution" four), but most subjects are given at least adequate treatment. All entries are written in language accessible to the target audience. In fact, the writers and subject area consultants, many of whom are university researchers and educators, have done a masterful job of making difficult subjects (e.g., particle physics, chemical reactions, radio astronomy) understandable, while never straying far from about a fifth-grade reading level. Whenever there is controversy about what is known or the interpretation of results, such is indicated (e.g., quasars, the greenhouse effect).

Another remarkable aspect of this work is that in contrast to most ready-reference sources, sight is not lost of the fact that science is primarily process, not dogma—something we do, not something we memorize. Most longer entries start out with the history and experimentation that have led to the discovery of a particular fact. Many of the illustrations show scientists at work or are diagrams of experiments. Volume 18, which contains directions for 34 science projects, further underlines this attitude of science as an activity. The projects, designed to be performed with little adult help, give students practice in setting up experiments, making observations, drawing conclusions, and presenting the results. Symbols in the text of the other volumes indicate when there is a project related to a particular entry.

Volume 18 also contains several pages of bibliographies on broad topics in science, with grade levels given for each book. Then there is a very thorough 72-page index, further augmenting the set's cross-referencing. Illustrations, both photographs and color diagrams, are clear and appropriate throughout but do not overwhelm the text, as is the case with many other reference sources for children. Public and school libraries, as well as parents, will find this a valuable resource for its practical usefulness and the air of excitement it lends to the subject.—**Carol L. Noll**

1570. **Systems & Control Encyclopedia: Supplementary Volume 2.** Madan G. Singh, ed. Tarrytown, N.Y., Pergamon Press, 1992. 1087p. index. $390.00. ISBN 0-08-040601-7.

As is any good encyclopedia supplement, this one is stuffed with interesting tidbits. For example, hypertext is not a product of the 1980s; its origin can be traced to 1945 and a never-made product: Memex. Vannevar Bush, President Roosevelt's war research leader, gets credit for the theoretical framework. Although only 6 of the 71 articles were written specifically for this book—65 were culled from the *Concise Encyclopedia* series—the editor has selected them for breadth and depth. Consequently, the volume can stand alone as an introduction to developments in systems and control at the end of the last decade (cited references include few from the 1990s). The reader learns that models can be simplified (by aggregation); that biotelemetry still holds promises, but they are largely unmet; that learning environments such as Intermedia at Brown University point the future of education; that virtual computer environments are here; and that expert systems are everywhere. The reader can maneuver easily through this encapsulation of the sphere where the technological and biological worlds meet, thanks to alphabetical arrangement of articles by topic, ample cross-referencing in the index, and the liberal use of subheadings and bullets. Useful diagrams are fully integrated and not oversized.—**Diane M. Calabrese**

1571. Tung, Louise Watanabe. **Japanese/English, English/Japanese Glossary of Scientific and Technical Terms.** New York, John Wiley, 1993. 1146p. $79.95. Q123.T844. 503. LC 92-28867. ISBN 0-471-57463-5.

Tung is an accredited member of the American Translators Association and is an experienced translator of technical papers and patents. Her project consists of 120 subject areas with terms from several fields of science: 3,000 from chemistry, 1,600 from mathematics, 3,700 from physics, 900 from computer and logic, 3,000 from engineering, and 3,700 from biology. Some uncommon terms from biology, botany, chemistry, and zoology are listed.

The glossary has two sections, Japanese into English and English into Japanese. In both sections the Japanese terms are shown in roman letters for reading and in Chinese characters, *hiragana*, or *katakana* script (or all three) for writing or the Japanese equivalent to English. Every entry, categorized by subject area in parentheses next to the English term, is listed in a single line. Thus, for example, the term *haichi*, which is used in four categories, occupies four lines. As much as possible, Tung tried to use native Japanese equivalents (instead of terms adopted or adapted from English that constitute the so-called "Japlish") for the English terms and vice versa, and her effort is praiseworthy. The glossary does not seem to contain an adequate number of computer terms (e.g., *software, laser printing, disk*), but it does contain the term *document* (*bunsho*), which is indicated as a computer term. This book is useful for all university and research-oriented college libraries. [R: Choice, Sept 93, p. 92]—**Seiko Mieczkowski**

DIRECTORIES

1572. **Directory, 1992: AAAS Consortium of Affiliates for International Programs.** Washington, D.C., American Association for the Advancement of Science, [1992]. 250p. index. free pa.

The AAAS Consortium of Affiliates for International Programs (CAIP) was formed by 14 professional societies at the 1976 AAAS annual meeting in Boston. The CAIP is a broad-based multidisciplinary network of scientific and engineering societies with interest in the international dimension of their disciplines. It currently constitutes a network of more than 240 scientific and engineering societies in more than 53 countries. This directory will help familiarize users with the services offered by AAAS. The contents include a guide for users; an introduction; CAIP representatives, staff liaisons, and international committees; descriptions of CAIP member organizations; and services, privileges, and special awards accorded to foreign members and foreign scientists and engineers. The section on CAIP representatives is a directory of CAIP regular and foreign corresponding member societies. Regular member societies are from the United States, Canada, and Puerto Rico. Foreign corresponding members are listed by country in alphabetical order. The section on CAIP member organizations describes the history, goals, and activities of these bodies. The CAIP charter, publications of CAIP members, and a list of the terms of representatives can be found in the appendixes. There is an index of names, representatives, and staff liaisons. Recommended as a reference tool for foreign students at the undergraduate, graduate, and postdoctorate levels.—**Marilynn Green**

1573. **Directory of AAAS Science and Engineering Fellows 1973-1992.** Washington, D.C., American Association for the Advancement of Science, 1992. 257p. index. free pa.

Science and Engineering Fellows provide perspective and expertise to various branches of the U.S. Congress and a number of other federal agencies, such as the State Department and the Environmental Protection Agency. The program, begun in 1973, filled a void that had developed as the issues confronting the Congress became increasingly technical. This directory provides a look at where fellows served and what they are doing now. Being jolly good fellows, all 760 fellows to date participated in the request for information. Entries include telephone number, years served as a fellow and assignment, current position, and policy and technical expertise. The volume is well indexed.

The intent of the directory is to keep fellows in touch with each other and the AAAS in touch with former fellows. While it is not made known whether the fellows consult in their fields, the volume is a useful tool for identifying experts in various scientific and technical fields. Certainly the price is right.
—**Andrew G. Torok**

1574. **European Research Centres: A Directory of Scientific, Industrial, Agricultural, and Biomedical Laboratories.** 9th ed. Harlow, England, Longman; distr., Detroit, Gale, 1993. 2v. index. $630.00/set. ISBN 0-582-09625-1.

1575. **Pacific Research Centres: A Directory of Scientific, Industrial, Agricultural, and Biomedical Laboratories.** 4th ed. Harlow, England, Longman, 1993. 392p. $375.00. ISBN 0-582-21669-9.

Identical in format, these reference works offer updated directory information to 12,000-plus research and technology institutes in Europe and more than 3,500 such institutes in Pacific countries, both excluding the former Soviet Union. University laboratories as well as industrial companies are listed, covering a wide variety of scientific areas of research, including aerospace, chemical and material sciences, electronics, engineering, and environmental sciences. Entries are arranged alphabetically by country in the language of origin and include address, telephone, telex, and fax information as well as the name of a contact and a description of activities and publications. Individual departments and laboratories are listed as subsidiaries within the entries of their parent organizations. Indexes provide detailed access to these subsidiaries, as well as cross-references for English translations and for acronyms. *European Research Centres* (ERC) includes titles of establishments and subject indexes. *Pacific Research Centres* (PRC) offers these two indexes plus an index of establishments by subject, which is essentially a mailing list organized alphabetically by subject, then by country, and then by organization. Although such an index and address list for ERC would be very useful, it is not included but instead is priced separately. Considering that the two-volume set is already very expensive, the extra index should have been included.

The number of sources included in both ERC and PRC is impressive (note that the United Kingdom represents one-fourth of the European entries), although individual entries vary depending on the information that each research institute provided in a written questionnaire. Recommendations for improvement stated in previous reviews (see ARBA 90, entry 1431 and ARBA 87, entries 1391-92) still apply: Ease of use could be improved if parent institutions were added to running heads, because entries for parents and subsidiaries may be listed pages apart. Also, additional indexes, such as a city index and a title index by subject, should be added without an increase in price. These reference sources are complemented by *International Research Centers Directory* (see ARBA 93, entry 68) and *European Sources of Scientific and Technical Information* (see ARBA 92, entry 1460). [R: Choice, Sept 93, p. 80]
—**Janice M. Griggs**

1576. **European Sources of Scientific and Technical Information.** 10th ed. Harlow, England, Longman; distr., Detroit, Gale, 1993. 412p. index. $300.00. ISBN 0-582-10103-4.

This directory lists government offices, libraries, private institutions, and other European sources of information in 26 categories related to science and technology. The coverage ranges from general resources, such as information centers and patent offices, to specific disciplines, such as agriculture, medicine, or the timber industry. Twenty-nine countries are represented, although not all are included in every category. Two indexes list the individual establishments and subjects. A typical entry includes the name, address, and contact person of the office; a description of its library and consulting services; and representative publications. A key descriptor for each institution in each category is "subject coverage." This does not seem to be uniformly treated. For example, several centers have described their subject expertise in detailed subcategories such as serums, sugar, or superconductors, while others simply use such general phrases as "physics and related fields." As a result, the subject index can be misleading because listings are referenced only to those establishments that specifically mention them. While relatively expensive, the book contains much useful information and will appeal to institutions and individuals that need to frequently consult European sources. [R: Choice, Sept 93, p. 80]—**John U. Trefny**

1577. **Financial Aid for Minorities in Engineering and Science.** Garrett Park, Md., Garrett Park Press, 1992. 1v. (unpaged). index. $4.95pa. LC 87-82105. ISBN 0-912048-98-0.

This pamphlet is an attempt to bring together sources of financial aid for minority students and is specifically directed toward those who will study in engineering or science programs. The minorities mentioned most often in the text are African-Americans, Hispanic-Americans, and Native Americans; a few entries are noted as designated for female students, presumably of any background. The main section is a list of 327 scholarships, fellowships, and loans primarily from national or regional organizations. Each entry includes address information and a description of who may qualify, what benefits will be provided, and other details as may be required (e.g., application deadlines). Surprisingly, only about 50 percent of the entries seem to be specifically designated for minorities in the entry's description, but all are science- or technology-related. While it is possible that these other organizations have an interest in serving minorities, it appears that anyone may apply for their funding.

The short introductory section has charts that cover minority enrollment data and degrees granted in science and technology. End matter includes a short list of associations in science and technical areas and a limited bibliography of career information. There is an index of majors that is keyed to the entries in the main section.

Although not as comprehensive as standard sources, this work's convenience and accessibility will ensure its use in libraries. It is unfortunate that the quality of the typeface and its reproduction look unprofessional and that the criteria for inclusion of some entries is not carefully defined, but neither issue seriously detracts from the usefulness of the work.—**Gary R. Cocozzoli**

1578. **International Directory of Testing Laboratories.** 1993 ed. Compiled by ASTM. Philadelphia, Pa., ASTM, 1992. 369p. index. $69.00pa. ISBN 0-8031-1770-1. ISSN 0895-7866.

This annual publication of the American Society for Testing and Materials lists more than 1,400 commercial materials testing laboratories throughout the world and provides access to the information both geographically and by laboratory capabilities. Information is supplied by the laboratories, which pay a fee to be listed. Entries are arranged geographically and describe laboratories in terms of 16 fields of testing, 58 categories of materials and products, and 7 classifications of laboratory services. Descriptions include location, telephone and fax numbers, contact names, number and type of staff, and type of tests performed and materials analyzed. Narrative descriptions of specialties and capabilities are provided by each laboratory.

A particular strength of the directory is its indexing. In addition to the name index is a subject index that includes all fields of testing, laboratory services, and subcategories of materials and products referred to in the main entries. It is then subdivided geographically. An additional convenience for the user is a pullout card of the coding system, so it is not necessary to refer to the front matter when using the laboratory listings.—**William S. Proudfoot**

HANDBOOKS AND YEARBOOKS

1579. **AAAS Handbook 1993/1994: Officers, Organization, Activities.** Washington, D.C., American Association for the Advancement of Science, 1993. 158p. index. $10.95pa. ISBN 0-87168-542-6.

This handbook provides an excellent overview of the organization, activities, and history of the American Association for the Advancement of Science (AAAS). It provides names and postal addresses of officers and representatives for each of the committees, sections, and divisions in the organization, but does not include their telephone numbers or E-mail addresses. It lists telephone numbers only for AAAS staff. The activities section briefly describes each publication, program, and meeting, and provides an address for further information. Descriptions of awards and grants include guidelines, procedures for nomination, and deadlines.

An extensive history of AAAS, founded in 1848, is included. It contains a timeline of significant events and a complete list of past officers and meetings. Copies of significant policy statements and the AAAS constitution, bylaws, and articles of incorporation are provided.

The 292 affiliated organizations are listed, but no index to their participation in committees and sections is provided. In fact, the book's weakest point is the indexing. The only index is a slightly expanded version of the table of contents in alphabetical order, with no significant subject access (e.g., no entry for "Microbiology").—**William S. Proudfoot**

1580. Barhydt, Frances Bartlett, and Paul W. Morgan. **The Science Teacher's Book of Lists.** Englewood Cliffs, N.J., Prentice Hall Career & Professional Development, 1993. 500p. illus. $29.95 spiralbound. LB1585.B286. 507'.1'2. LC 92-26920. ISBN 0-13-793381-9.

Everybody seems to love lists, and "books of lists" have become a publishing phenomenon. This new addition to the genre will delight science teachers in grades K-12. It consists of 290 lists in most subjects areas taught in science and health classrooms. Topics covered range from the mundane (e.g., an alphabetical list, with physical and chemical data, of the elements) to the practical (e.g., a nutritional comparison of various candy bars) to the eclectic (e.g., a three-page list of superstitions). There are fairly complete glossaries for a number of subjects, including botany, physics, chemistry, and the earth sciences. Unfortunately, there is no index, so one must depend on the subject-area arrangement and detailed table of contents to find specific information.

A good science program is based on experiments and hands-on learning, but an informational approach as presented here has its role also. Many children are just plain fascinated by odd facts and statistics. (Witness the familiarity of many young sports fans with current and past baseball statistics.) Although most of these lists consist of facts, they are not dry facts, but ones combined and presented in intriguing and fascinating ways. The purpose of these lists is to provide ideas for class discussion, student projects, or lesson plans. The spiral format makes the lists easy to photocopy, and creative teachers will find many uses for them.—**Carol L. Noll**

1581. Giscard d'Estaing, Valerie-Ann, and Mark Young, eds. **Inventions and Discoveries 1993: What's Happened, What's Coming, What's That?** New York, Facts on File, 1993. 248p. illus. index. $24.95. ISBN 0-8160-2865-6. ISSN 1064-7600.

This work is an updated and Americanized version of Giscard d'Estaing's initial work, *The Book of Inventions*, published in France in 1980. Her classic one-volume encyclopedia on invention and discovery was first published in the United States as *The World Almanac of Inventions* (see ARBA 86, entry 7). The American Young coedited this new edition. Inventions and discoveries are classified in categories that include weapons and warfare, agriculture and gardening, the arts, information technology, science, and everyday life. The 12 broad topic areas serve as chapter headings. Each broad field or classification is further subdivided, and the history and evolution of each specialty area are described. For example, in a chapter on transportation, the chronological development of shipping, railroads, public transportation, bicycles, motorcycles, airplanes, and helicopters is presented. The organization of the material may be especially valuable for teachers and media specialists working with students in the construction of time lines.

The text is free of technical jargon and easy to read. Illustrations and photographs enhance virtually every page. Because thousands of inventions and discoveries are chronicled, individual entries do not have great depth, but they do provide readers with enough background information so that further research into specific topic areas should not be difficult. The contents reveal the origins of fields such as geometry and geophysics as well as the history of less spectacular inventions and discoveries, such as mustard, beer, and Cabbage Patch dolls. One positive feature of this new edition is the set of profiles of notable people, such as Albert Einstein and Rachel Carson, found in every chapter. Human-interest stories also are well placed throughout the book. Readers meet the man who invented Coca-Cola (John S. Pemberton) and the woman who gave the world the chocolate chip cookie (Ruth Wakefield).

Each chapter ends with two special features. "What on Earth?" explores unusual inventions in each field. Eccentric projects, such as a top hat that doubles as a bee hive, the "Kitty Sitter" (an automobile seat belt for cats), and trombones made of crystal by Japanese master glass artist Sasaki Garasu, are featured. "Tomorrow's World" highlights works in progress and projects future developments in each topic area. These profiles explore new ideas and products that promise to change the way people live. One example is the ovionic battery, developed in 1992, which may lead the way to electric vehicles. The book includes an appendix listing the names of Nobel prize winners (1901-1992) in chemistry, physics, and medicine/physiology. Both name and subject indexes are provided.

This reference work is versatile enough to serve both casual readers, who are likely to enjoy the human-interest stories, and students engaged in tracing the evolution of jet aircraft or automobiles. It is a worthy addition to the existing body of literature about invention and discovery. [R: Choice, Nov 93, p. 434; RBB, Aug 93, p. 2092]—**Jerry D. Flack**

1582. Lennon, Mary Beth, and Barbara Walthall, comps. and eds. **Sourcebook for Science, Mathematics, & Technology Education 1992.** Washington, D.C., American Association for the Advancement of Science, 1992. 218p. index. $12.95pa. ISBN 0-87168-429-2.

The AAAS (American Association for the Advancement of Science) has collected many educational programs in science, mathematics, and technology into a useful sourcebook. The programs are arranged within broad types of organizations, such as scientific organizations and societies, state and federal organizations and agencies, private foundations, museums, and science-technology centers. A resource section provides information on resources related to curriculum development; activities for teachers, students, and parents; and assistance to underrepresented groups, such as minorities and people with disabilities. This section also includes a list of science and mathematics education journals. Brief descriptions of activities or programs for many of the entries are provided as well as addresses, contact persons, and telephone numbers.

To get at this information, users can refer to the indexes of names, organizations and programs, geographical regions, and publications. However, they would have to know the name of the organization or specific program. The table of contents is helpful in listing a few organizations, but users will still need to browse through the different listings. In spite of this, the sourcebook is a helpful reference tool for directing the public to educational programs in science, technology, and mathematics. The AAAS, in its active role in this area, keeps aware of activities and expands each edition of the sourcebook.—**Anne C. Roess**

1583. Magill, Frank N., ed. **Magill's Survey of Science: Applied Science Series.** Pasadena, Calif., Salem Press, 1993. 6v. index. $475.00/set. TA145.M298. 620. LC 92-35688. ISBN 0-89356-705-1.

The fifth in a series of six overviews of science, this set's 382 articles cover the applied sciences, from aerospace to zone refining. The largest number of articles deal with engineering and materials science. The articles are written to provide the general reader with basic insights into these scientific topics; thus, they uniformly attempt to avoid excessive jargon and do not assume any previous knowledge of the subjects. Authors are typically U.S. university faculty or industry professionals.

The average article contains an introductory apparatus with key definitions and a brief statement of the topic's importance. The text then proceeds in three parts: overview, uses of the technology, and context (usually the historical or social environment of the technology). Cross-references and a brief annotated bibliography are appended to each article. An extensive subject index is included in the last volume. The general quality of the essays is quite good, as most authors succeed in interpreting technical topics for the general reader. Several essays, such as those on bridge design and wood, give poor treatment to their historical contexts. Still, most authors write clearly about the uses of the technologies. Many of these topics would have been greatly augmented by the use of illustrations.

There seem to be no exact competitors to this Magill series. The current set's articles are lengthier than those in most general encyclopedias, as well as those in *Van Nostrand's Scientific Encyclopedia* (see ARBA 90, entry 1430). The *McGraw-Hill Encyclopedia of Science & Technology* (see ARBA 93, entry 1446), which often requires more from its readers, has superior coverage and fine illustrations; its presence in an academic collection probably makes Magill an optional addition. Magill is best suited for those collections needing good coverage from a more general source. [R: LJ, Dec 93, p. 114; WLB, June 93, p. 126]—**Christopher W. Nolan**

1584. **Science and Technology Desk Reference: 1,500 Answers to Frequently-Asked or Difficult-to-Answer Questions.** Edited by the Carnegie Library of Pittsburgh Science and Technology Department. Detroit, Gale, 1993. 741p. index. $39.95. LC 92-075423. ISBN 0-8103-8884-7.

This interesting and fun reference book contains many nuggets of scientific information. Some of them are trivia that would be of interest to those who collect obscure facts, but some of them are the sort of information hard to come by in a general reference. Such facts as a list of women who won the Nobel Prize can be found by a search of many sources or many parts of one source. Each entry contains a reference to the source of the information, making it possible to verify it or to obtain more data. The topics are quite varied, from chemistry to technology and space. The book is organized in sections that lead the reader to specific topics within those areas. An extensive index provides access to the topics. This is essential, since the order within each area does not follow any particular arrangement.

This book would be of great use to children and to science teachers looking for topics for investigation or discussion. It is also an interesting evening read for scientists or general readers who want their interest piqued in a new area. [R: Choice, June 93, p. 1610; LJ, 15 Mar 93, p. 74; RBB, 1 May 93, pp. 1634-36; RQ, Fall 93, pp. 134-35; WLB, May 93, p. 122]—**Margretta Reed Seashore**

1585. Shroyer, Jo Ann. **Quarks, Critters, and Chaos: What Science Terms Really Mean.** New York, Prentice Hall General Reference, 1993. 245p. index. $25.00; $15.00pa. Q123.S519. 501.4. LC 92-22614. ISBN 0-671-84744-9; 0-671-84745-7pa.

The catchy title of this book reflects the background of the author as a writer and a reporter for Minnesota Public Radio. As one might expect, the book is an engagingly written account of various scientific and technological topics, especially those in the news in recent years. Topics are organized into four general sections covering chemistry and physics, biology, earth science, and technology. Within each section, discussions of topics proceed in a way that builds on previous discussions. But each topic is self-contained, so one need not have read previous discussions in order to understand any particular topic. There are also cross-references to other topics.

Overall, the information presented is not bad, although there are occasional errors in spelling and some factual errors (e.g., Pluto is not half the size of Earth). The index is adequate but could have been more useful if it were more detailed. This book is primarily for the layperson wanting to come up to speed on current topics in science and technology. It does have reference value in libraries; however, other, more pedestrian, but alphabetically arranged works, such as *Dictionary of Scientific Literacy* (see ARBA 93, entry 1445), are probably more useful in this regard. [R: LJ, 1 April 93, p. 94]—**Joseph Hannibal**

1586. Stanley, Autumn. **Mothers and Daughters of Invention: Notes for a Revised History of Technology.** Metuchen, N.J., Scarecrow, 1993. 1116p. index. $97.50. T36.S73. 305.43'6. LC 92-42054. ISBN 0-8108-2586-4.

The neglect of women inventors in historical research is widespread and pernicious; only recently has any real attempt been made to recognize their many contributions. Stanley has spent many years gathering the information on women inventors that is presented in this massive work. Divided into general subjects—agriculture, health and medicine, sex and fertility, tools and machines, and computers—the book presents a wide but detailed view of women's inventions from prehistory through the twentieth century, emphasizing the diversity and importance of women's inventions, whether officially recognized (i.e., patented) or not. Inventions are described, and brief profiles are given for women inventors when biographical information is available. The book closes with an impressive 125-page bibliography.

Some weaknesses are apparent. Stanley's research is extensive but has been superseded in places. For example, it is amusing to read that the ubiquitous portable hair dryer is "a minor but possibly commercially interesting invention" (560). Although she names nearly 2,000 women inventors, she also misses several notable ones, such as Stephanie Kwolek, inventor of Kevlar. The bibliography, while extensive, excludes some important sources, including the U.S. Patent Office's *Buttons to Biotech*. Her definition of technology is broad, ranging from agricultural implements to computer languages; however, the inclusion of fields such as exercise programs (e.g., Jazzercise) is somewhat questionable. The focus on U.S. women, although enhanced by some British, French, and Russian examples, is limiting, and the failure to include patent numbers is a real detriment to the serious researcher.

However, despite its drawbacks, this is a unique and invaluable source that belongs in any library. No other book covers the subject as thoroughly or in as much detail.—**Susan Davis Herring**

1587. **World Technology Policies.** Harlow, England, Longman; distr., Detroit, Gale, 1992. 940p. $220.00. ISBN 0-582-05730-2.

In an age that pits ASCII against ISO, one longs for a guide to science and technology policy worldwide. Living in the West, it is easy to forget that what burns as smoldering coals or outright conflagration in this country may not have even been lit in another. Thus, this volume provides a one-stop shop for science and technology policies worldwide.

The volume opens with a discussion of internationalization of standards and the progress of its major perpetrators. The WHO (World Health Organization), FAO (Food and Agriculture Organization of the United Nations), and the Third World Academy of Sciences are discussed along with many others. Arranged by regions, the book includes Africa, the Middle East, the Americas, Asia, Australasia, the Antarctic, and Europe. Under each major heading, countries are listed as subheads. The first section of the volume is devoted to a discussion of defense issues, environmental policies, information policies, and new issues. Educational bodies, organizations, governmental flow charts, budget statements, and more are crammed into this impressive single volume.

For libraries owning the original Longman guides to science and technology (which provided the basis for this work), this one-volume tome may be unnecessary. But for small libraries unable to afford the originals, or for larger ones that want a ready-reference tool, this work is desirable.—**Mark Y. Herring**

30 Agricultural Sciences

GENERAL WORKS

Bibliography

1588. Goreham, Gary A., David L. Watt, and Roy M. Jacobsen. **The Socioeconomics of Sustainable Agriculture: An Annotated Bibliography.** Hamden, Conn., Garland, 1992. 334p. index. (Garland Reference Library of the Humanities, v.1332). $53.00. Z5074.E3G69. 016.3381. LC 92-16285. ISBN 0-8240-7127-1.

A few individuals have culled their personal and institutional libraries for works in sustainable agriculture, have asked a larger circle of scholars to add to the focused collection, and have written synopses of their finds. The happy ending is this eclectic but enormously useful annotated bibliography. Most entries fall between the years 1975 and 1991; a few important works published earlier than 1975 are included. From extractivism to theology, the reader discovers many varied and unexpected links to sustainable agriculture. Five themes emerged as the authors prepared the volume (e.g., which criteria might be used to declare a farm sustainable), and those themes are attended to in an introduction. Topical and author indexes provide easy access to the 495 books and book chapters, 447 articles, and 110 other (mostly federal and state) publications. The problems—some topical indexes are too broad, a book chapter is listed with no date or location known, departments but no institutions are listed for several individuals in the acknowledgments—are inconsequential. One work cited asks whether sustainability has "the aura of a Holy Grail." This compilation indicates that there is nothing mystical about sustainable agriculture. There is, however, a great deal of wonder in its multifarious connections. [R: Choice, May 93, p. 1441]—**Diane M. Calabrese**

1589. Norton, Judith A., comp. **New England Planters in the Maritime Provinces of Canada 1759-1800: Bibliography of Primary Sources.** Toronto and Buffalo, N.Y., University of Toronto Press, 1993. 403p. index. $125.00. 016.630'9715. ISBN 0-8020-2840-3.

During the period from 1759 to 1800, more than 8,000 farmers migrated from eastern New England to the Maritime Provinces of Canada. The history of this migration and settlement is covered in documents in New England and Canada. Historians researching this event can use this bibliography to locate the more than 3,000 primary documents listed here. An excellent introduction outlines the migration, describes how the bibliography is put together, and describes the types of documents covered: government documents, personal papers, business records, society documents, and newspapers. An entry for each document includes its source, the format, relevant dates, number of items contained in it, number of pages, and a descriptive annotation. The Canadian documents are organized according to province, country, town, and document type. The New England documents are arranged by state and document type. There are indexes to planters, nonplanters, New England town and church records, Nova Scotia and New Brunswick places, and subjects. A map of Nova Scotia as of 1767 is provided for reference.

This bibliography is a well-organized, excellent reference source, and it will be of great assistance to New England and Canadian historians in locating the documents listed. It should be in the reference collections of the appropriate major academic libraries.—**John Laurence Kelland**

Handbooks and Yearbooks

1590. **FAO Yearbook: Fertilizer. Vol. 41: 1991. FAO Annuaire: Engrais. FAO Anuario: Fertilizantes.** Rome, FAO of the United Nations; distr., Lanham, Md., UNIPUB, 1992. 147p. (FAO Statistics Series, no.106). $40.00pa. ISBN 92-5-003197-1. ISSN 0251-1525.

This work contains tabular data on the annual worldwide production, imports and exports, consumption, and prices of fertilizers. Depending upon the category, data from 1980 to 1990 or 1991 are listed. The book is printed in English, Spanish, and French, although there is little textual content, and no graphs or other illustrations are presented. More than 200 countries are treated depending upon availability of data. Fertilizer categories are nitrogenous, phosphate, potash, mixed and complex, and miscellaneous.

The purpose of the publication is simply to supply data, so no conclusions or additional discussion is presented. For instance, there is no information on application methods or major crops. Preliminary text explains the fertilizer products covered, the pricing (including subsidies), and the classification of countries as developed or developing. Because prices are shown in local currency, a table of exchange rates to U.S. dollars is included.

This yearbook appears to be the most comprehensive compilation of fertilizer data on a worldwide basis. Due to its breadth of coverage, detail is limited, so other publications will have to be consulted for specific information for any particular country. However, this does not limit its usefulness; the book should be a part of every reference library's collection.—**Michael G. Messina**

1591. **FAO Yearbook: Production. Vol. 45: 1991. FAO Annuaire: Production. FAO Anuario: Produccion.** Rome, FAO of the United Nations; distr., Lanham, Md., UNIPUB, 1992. 265p. (FAO Statistics Series, no.104). $50.00pa. ISBN 92-5-003194-7. ISSN 0071-7118.

The Food and Agriculture Organization (FAO) of the United Nations annually compiles statistics pertinent to agriculture and reports them in French, Spanish, and English. This publication provides the most comprehensive and current source of such data available on the countries and commodities of the world. Data were gathered by each country or estimated by the FAO, and use is made of information gathered since 1961 on some 600 commodities and processed products from 200 countries. Pesticide data are currently undergoing a system revision and are thus not provided. The material is organized by country, and commodity and prefatory notes are provided to clarify abbreviations and the like in the tables. General categories of information include land, population, agricultural production (animal and plant) by commodity, a statistical summary of crops by regions, and a list of crop statistics by country, with data for the past six years typically reported. However, production indexes are for 12 years, and land use and population are at 5-year intervals since 1975.—**Marvin K. Harris**

1592. **FAO Yearbook: Trade. Volume 45: 1991. FAO Annuaire: Commerce. FAO Anuario: Comercio.** Rome, FAO of the United Nations; distr., Lanham, Md., UNIPUB, 1992. 383p. (FAO Statistics Series, no.109). $45.00pa. ISBN 92-5-003215-3.

Bruce Chatwin created a stir in the 1970s when he wrote *In Patagonia* and proved that a telephone directory could be a route to a country's history and natural history. The revelations of this directory are no less delicious. In the basic and fortuitous information category, the precipitous decline of the U.S. dollar in the 1980s is recorded in the exchange rate table, and the steep increase in the U.S. appetite for agricultural imports (about 50 percent over the decade of the 1980s) is also documented. From raisins to rubber, it is easy to find out who is buying and who is selling. There are also clues as to which countries favor which commodities. For example, in 1989-1991, Saudi Arabia imported the most sheep and goats, with Libya and Italy also taking in great numbers. Surprises are everywhere: In 1991, the U.S. imported one-sixth of the amount of wheat it exported. Clever investors might find tips in export gains (e.g., soybeans). The tabular presentations are of two sorts: item focus, with comparisons by country, and country focus, with comparisons for general categories of commodities. Text is in English, French, and Spanish. The layout appeals visually and technically (e.g., same-line reporting of exports and imports). Explanatory symbols denote the reliability of all amounts recorded.—**Diane M. Calabrese**

1593. **The International Markets for Meat 1992/93.** Geneva, General Agreement on Tariffs and Trade; distr., Lanham, Md., UNIPUB, 1993. 116p. $20.00pa. ISBN 92-870-1080-3. ISSN 0259-8213.

This is the 13th annual report covering world markets for meat. It analyzes the market for beef animals and meat in 1992 and provides forecasts for 1993. It includes cattle numbers, slaughter levels, production, prices, imports, consumption, and exports of beef animals and meat. The signatories to the General Agreement on Tariffs and Trade (GATT) include Argentina, Australia, Austria, Belize, Brazil, Bulgaria, Canada, Colombia, Egypt, the European Community, Finland, Guatemala, Hungary, Japan, New Zealand, Nigeria, Norway, Paraguay, Poland, Romania, South Africa, Sweden, Switzerland, Tunisia, the United States, Uruguay, and Yugoslavia. The purpose of the agreement is to diminish obstacles to and restrictions on world trade in beef animals and meat and to improve the international framework for world trade in these products. The manuscript is divided into an overview; bovine meat markets of Western Europe, Eastern Europe, Africa, South America, Oceania, and Asia; and pig meat, poultry, and sheep meat. It also contains statistical tables. The book is well written and easy to read and contains many tables, figures, and graphics.

Even though the sources of the data vary, this is the best information available on the subject. It is essential for anyone interested in international trade and meat products.—**Herbert W. Ockerman**

1594. Iversen, Edwin S., and Kay K. Hale. **Aquaculture Sourcebook: A Guide to North American Species.** New York, AVI/Van Nostrand Reinhold, 1992. 308p. illus. index. $49.95. SH33.I94. 639.8'097. LC 92-12536. ISBN 0-442-00992-5.

The aquaculture industry, one that farms fish, shellfish, and other fresh-, brackish-, and saltwater animals, has become big business, and the need for information on these species has boomed. This sourcebook provides data on the many fish, crabs, shrimp, lobsters, turtles, snails, and even alligators grown for food and profit in North America.

The book first discusses the present state of aquaculture in the United States, Canada, and Mexico, then progresses to chapters on more than 100 individual animal species grown for human food and nonfood purposes. Each species description is usually a page or two long and includes the scientific and common names, a physical description and a black-and-white drawing, the geographical range where the species is found, reproduction, age, growth, food, diseases and parasites, predators, and its potential for successful rearing and marketing. The descriptions end with a short list of references for further reading.

The book has nine appendixes that include a glossary of terms used in the book, a list of the major aquacultural groups, common and scientific names of species discussed in the book, a list of what species are farmed commercially in each state and region, black-and-white pictures of parasites and of important predators on aquacultural species, a list of national aquaculture associations, and a measurement conversion table. The work does not have information on business aspects such as facilities; finances; legal issues; or transporting, processing, or marketing aquacultural products.

This sourcebook contains excellent information on more than 100 animal species with potential for food or profit. Its nontechnical language makes it of use to the novice seeking information on growing a species for profit, as well as for the expert wanting information on a species. Recommended for public and academic libraries; it may also be a useful text for aquaculture courses.—**Diane B. Rhodes**

1595. McGee, Denis C. **Soybean Diseases: A Reference Source for Seed Technologists.** St. Paul, Minn., APS Press, 1992. 151p. illus. index. $28.00pa. LC 92-72079. ISBN 0-89054-141-8.

The soybean is one of the most important commercially grown plants in the world, with uses that range well beyond the edible ones. Thus, diseases in the crop can be disastrous. This book has information on all soybean diseases caused by fungi, bacteria, mycoplasmas, and viruses. It is divided into three parts: seedborne and seed-transmitted diseases, seedborne-only diseases, and diseases that are transmitted in other ways. In each part, the diseases are further subdivided into those caused by fungi, by bacteria, and by viruses (and by mycoplasmas in the third part). Every entry covers disease name, pathogen, symptoms, economic importance (how much damage it does), distribution, other hosts, variability, control, seedborne aspect, effect on seed quality, pathogen transmission, seed treatments, seed health tests, and key references. The latter range in number from 1 to nearly 100, depending on how common the disease is and how much it has been studied. Black-and-white photographs depict the effects of the diseases on the plants. The typeface is easy to read, and there is good use of white space. No typographical errors were detected in a random check of entries. This reference will be useful to those in botany, biology, and agriculture.—**D. A. Rothschild**

1596. **Quality Declared Seed: Technical Guidelines for Standards and Procedures.** Rome, FAO of the United Nations; distr., Lanham, Md., UNIPUB, 1993. 186p. (FAO Plant Production and Protection Paper, 117). $20.00pa. ISBN 92-5-103278-5.

This manual is provided as a service to countries that lack a seed certification program. It is designed to provide quality control during seed production that is less demanding on government resources than seed certification but that is adequate to provide good-quality seed within countries and in international trade. Within this system, eligible cultivars (varieties) are designated, seed producers are registered, and national authorities are established for monitoring purposes. Seed production practices, including growing, inspecting, testing, and labeling, are defined. More than 60 species are treated, including cereals, legumes, oil crops, grasses, and vegetables. Some crops have separate treatment for hybrids and open-pollinated cultivars. The requirements for designation as quality declared seed are given for each crop. Each entry contains the requirements for seed cleaning, sorting, and storing; field standards (e.g., isolation, weeds); inspection techniques; seed purity; and germination testing. While these standards are not applicable to countries or states with formal seed certification programs, the work may be useful to libraries serving agricultural students.—**T. McKimmie**

1597. Rao, D. S. Prasada. **Intercountry Comparisons of Agricultural Output and Productivity.** Rome, FAO of the United Nations; distr., Lanham, Md., UNIPUB, 1993. 154p. (FAO Economic and Social Development Paper, 112). $17.00pa. ISBN 92-5-103239-4.

Across the five-year intervals from 1970 to 1990, New Zealand ranked first in the world in per capita agricultural output, although China has been the world's biggest agricultural producer since 1985. The United States, China, and the former Soviet Union each claim more than a 10 percent share of world agricultural production; India is close behind the 3 countries. For readers fascinated by such comparative statistics, this volume offers immense satisfaction. It is easy to use; for example, there is ample explanation of methods for converting to international currency units and making comparisons using a parity (in purchasing power) approach. Rao offers some analyses of tabular material (from the database) but also includes data so readers can draw inferences of their own. Some of the data has been massaged; for example, no distinctions are made with regard to quality or variety of commodities. But on the whole, the volume permits comparisons among the 103 countries of the world that account for 99 percent of the world's agricultural output and 98 percent of the world's population. References are provided. A detailed table of contents substitutes for an index.—**Diane M. Calabrese**

1598. **World Statistical Compendium for Raw Hides and Skins, Leather, and Leather Footwear 1972-1990.** 5th ed. Rome, FAO of the United Nations; distr., Lanham, Md., UNIPUB, 1992. 131p. $35.00pa. ISBN 92-5-103190-8.

Marketing and economic researchers usually turn to this source when they seek current estimates showing international variations in statistical data pertaining to the hides, skins, and derived products of animals; income; retail business; import and export values; and production of leather footwear. This compendium is arranged into four sections: livestock population, raw hides and skins, leather, and footwear. Section 1 gives population numbers for each type of livestock by geographical area. Sections 2-4 cover production and trade information. Statistical data for about 180 countries are included, organized by country. Summary tables and analytical notes are provided.

The present edition includes figures up to 1990. Revisions of previous country series have been undertaken in cases where new information has become available. The integrated approach used in the previous compendiums has been adopted.—**Marilynn Green**

FOOD SCIENCES AND TECHNOLOGY

Bibliography

1599. Newman, Jacqueline M. **Melting Pot: An Annotated Bibliography and Guide to Food and Nutrition Information for Ethnic Groups in America.** Hamden, Conn., Garland, 1993. 240p. (Garland Reference Library of Social Science, v.708). $38.00. Z7914.F63N48. 016.641. LC 92-46351. ISBN 0-8240-7756-3.

Similar to the first edition (see ARBA 87, entry 391), this unique volume continues to provide an understanding of the food habits and dietary and nutrition practices of America's many ethnic groups. This edition has been thoroughly revised and expanded, with hundreds of new entries. More than 50 percent of the entries from the earlier edition have been dropped. Repeating the format of the previous edition, each chapter begins with a discussion of food behavior, eating patterns, religious practices and their influences on diet, and health problems relating to dietary habits. Following this are a bibliography of references from scholarly books and journals and a bibliography of cookbooks. The annotated entries are succinct and useful.

The print is larger and the typeface darker, making this edition easier to read. Also, the term "Black-Americans" has been replaced with the currently favored "African Americans," while the more appropriate term "Native Americans" replaces the confusing "Indian Americans." Asian Indians are included this time; however, Eastern European, Russian, and Slavic groups are still omitted, as is Europe as a whole. As before, there are no indexes. Individuals and libraries in the food, health, nutrition, and social service fields who did not purchase the first edition should consider buying this new one. There are enough new entries that those who did purchase the previous edition might want this one.—**Joy Hastings**

Dictionaries and Encyclopedias

1600. **Encyclopaedia of Food Science, Food Technology, and Nutrition.** R. Macrae, R. K. Robinson, and M. J. Sadler, eds. San Diego, Calif., Academic Press, 1993. 8v. illus. index. $2,100.00/set. TX349.E47. 664'.003. ISBN 0-12-226850-4.

The crowded field of nutrition and food science has another entrant in this encyclopedia, but this work distinguishes itself in a number of ways. A thorough search of OCLC indicates that there has not been anything of this significance in food science published in the last four decades. And, of course, this set contains the most recent information. The international view of the work is evident in the lists of editors, advisory board members, and article contributors. The editorial and advisory board members are largely from the United Kingdom, but the 1,000-plus contributors are from 50 nations, working in academia, independent institutes, and corporations.

The set consists of seven volumes of encyclopedia and an index volume. The volumes are sewn and casebound and will wear well. The text volumes are made up of more than 500 broad subject entries. Each subject entry includes at least one article. Each article is signed by its author and has a list of further readings on the topic. Articles are often richly illustrated with graphs, tables, photographs, and line drawings and can be up to 3,000 words long for a major topic.

The chief editors lay out the thrust of the work very nicely when they say, "This encyclopedia has been designed to provide the most comprehensive coverage of all aspects of the science of food, at all stages along the food chain." Food production, such as agriculture and horticulture, has not been included, but the end of the chain, consumers and nutrition, has been included. That makes this set unique in the field of food science reference materials. Among the broad topics covered are chemicals (e.g., alcohol, acesulphame), human needs (e.g., the elderly, adolescents), foods (e.g., buckwheat, melons, fish), nutritional diseases (e.g., anemia), diets (e.g., macrobiotic, vegan), food treatments (e.g., high heat, irradiation, homogenization), quality control and legislation (e.g., Codex), and nutrients (e.g., iron, the various vitamins).

The index volume is made up of three sections. The first is a list of the contents of the other seven volumes, which is convenient because it saves one from pulling all of the other volumes to see which broad topics they contain. The second section is a list of the contributors and their addresses. The third section is the index, which is lengthy and professionally done. The typeface is very readable; there are not a cumbersome number of page references per topic; the subject subdivisions are well set in for easy reading; and boldface and italic typefaces are used to differentiate the pages for individual articles or graphs. Readers will be able to find very precise topics, such as cot death or low alcohol cider, but double postings (e.g., "elevators, grain" and "grain elevators") seem absent, which is disappointing. However, *see* and *see also* references are abundant.

This set was really designed for students, faculty, and researchers in the food sciences, but the writing in it is so good that almost any layperson with some education can use it. The set will be equally useful for food technologists as well as nutritionists and dietitians. Because of its price it will probably be limited to academic and special libraries, but it is also recommended to larger research-oriented public libraries and two-year colleges. [R: Choice, Dec 93, p. 584; RBB, 15 Nov 93, p. 650; WLB, Nov 93, p. 101]

—**Lillian R. Mesner**

1601. Lipinski, Robert A., and Kathleen A. Lipinski. **The Complete Beverage Dictionary.** New York, Van Nostrand Reinhold, 1992. 425p. $34.95. TP503.L56. 663'.03. LC 91-41315. ISBN 0-442-23987-4.

Written by qualified authors in the food, beverage, and health fields, this international dictionary contains more than 6,100 technical, foreign, slang, and everyday terms related to all aspects of the beverage industry, including alcoholic and nonalcoholic beverages. Terms defined in the book range from *absolute alcohol, ale*, and *cold duck* to *decaffeinated, cola*, and *bottled water*. Wine label terms are also defined in the work, and a list of bottle sizes can be found. The language of origin is indicated for selected terms.

Another comprehensive beverage dictionary does not appear to be readily available. Neither the *Subject Guide to Books in Print 1992/93* (R. R. Bowker, 1992) nor *Forthcoming Books* lists a beverage dictionary. The only dictionary limited to beverages found on OCLC's FirstSearch is *Beverage Dictionary* by Harold J. Grossman (J. O. Dahl, 1938). This 62-page book was limited to alcoholic beverages and now is out of print. Thus, the Lipinskis' dictionary fills a void. They could have enhanced their work by including pronunciation of terms, a selected bibliography of sources, and illustrations. Nevertheless, this dictionary will be a welcome addition to libraries that have academic programs or that field questions related to foods and beverages.—**O. Gene Norman**

1602. **The Wellness Encyclopedia of Food and Nutrition: How to Buy, Store, and Prepare Every Variety of Fresh Food.** By Sheldon Margen and the editors of the University of California at Berkeley *Wellness Letter*. New York, Rebus; distr., New York, Random House, 1992. 512p. illus. index. $29.95. TX353.M344. 613.2. LC 92-13017. ISBN 0-929661-03-6.

Information about every type of whole, fresh food available in supermarkets, specialty food shops, and health food stores can be found in this comprehensive work. Organized in nine chapters, it includes a nutrition directory and separate sections on vegetables; fruits; exotic fruits and vegetables; grains and grain products; legumes, nuts, and seeds; meats and poultry; fish and shellfish; and dairy and eggs. Each chapter offers basic information about the topic in an introduction. Listings for specific food items follow, describing the item in general terms, delineating specific varieties, discussing availability, offering shopping and storage tips, and giving preparation guidelines and serving suggestions. Nutritional tables accompany each description, detailing calorie, protein, carbohydrate, dietary fiber, fat, saturated fat, cholesterol, and sodium content for the food, as well as noting the key nutrients it contains. A glossary of cooking terms, information on fats and oils, and definitions of herbs and spices are contained in three separate (but somewhat sketchy) appendixes.

With a large typeface, a clean layout, numerous color photographs, and clear, straightforward descriptions, this volume is a pleasure to use. The information is reliable and complete. Valuable as a guide to food and nutrition, it will make buying, storing, and preparing fresh food easier for the general consumer. [R: LJ, 1 Feb 93, pp. 74-76; WLB, Jan 93, p. 114]—**Barbara Ittner**

1603. Zak, Victoria, and Peter Vash. **The Dieter's Dictionary and Problem Solver: An A to Z Guide to Nutrition, Health, and Fitness.** Nashville, Tenn., Rutledge Hill Press, 1992. 394p. index. $19.95. RM222.2.Z348. 613.2'5. LC 92-11242. ISBN 1-55853-172-6.

This is another dieter's guide, but with a difference. Instead of promoting a gimmick-ridden diet plan, this book approaches both dieting and fitness from the basis of the best current knowledge in the two fields. (Some people who need a hard-boiled-eggs-and-grapefruit diet routine probably will not even be able to relate to this guide—it is too sensible.) The authors have cowritten another book on basically the same subject. Zak is a writer in the field of health and fitness and has national publications to her credit. Vash is an endocrinologist, teaching internist, and author on the treatment of obesity and eating disorders.

The title states that this book is a dictionary, but it is much more. The introduction stresses the fact that patterns of food and exercise behavior will determine the pounds that we shed. Part 1 of the book discusses 20 problems of weight gain and how they can be managed effectively. Part 2 is a diet program that relies directly on the new food pyramid produced by the U.S. government. The chapter goes over each section of the pyramid very carefully. Then some meals and menus are demonstrated, and a calendar for a four-week period is offered as a guide to learning the process of changing patterns.

The third part of the book is the dictionary, which runs for nearly 250 pages. It covers diets, exercise, behavior modification, nutrition education, food cue control, lifestyle training, physiology, biochemistry, and psychology. Some entries are quite extensive. For instance, the entry on cholesterol is 13 pages long and includes diagrams, charts of foods, types of medications, and a basic explanation of what kinds of cholesterol there are. Many of the entries give information that dispels myths that have sprung up thanks to fad dieting.

This is a well-written book with an easy, user-friendly style. It would fit well in both general and private collections.—**Lillian R. Mesner**

Directories

1604. Frank, Robyn C., and Holly Berry Irving, eds. **The Directory of Food and Nutrition Information for Professionals & Consumers.** 2d ed. Phoenix, Ariz., Oryx Press, 1992. 332p. index. $55.00pa. TX353.D56. 641'.02573. LC 92-23680. ISBN 0-89774-689-9.

The purpose of this directory is to bring together the various sources of available information on food and nutrition for both the consumer and the professional. The editors, with their specialized knowledge of these subjects (both work in the National Agricultural Library), have done just that, taking a diverse amount of information and putting it into a centralized, easy-to-read and -use reference. This edition is virtually all-new, greatly expanded and updated, not just a recap of the first edition. There are hundreds of new entries, and the chapters devoted to print sources emphasize materials published since the 1984 edition (see ARBA 85, entry 1353).

The 2 major sections contain 14 chapters covering a wide variety of resources. Part 1 consists of organizations, academic programs offering degrees in all areas of food and nutrition, more than 150 software programs, and 70-plus worldwide databases. Each entry contains considerable information. The resources in part 2 emphasize print sources (e.g., books, journals, newsletters); book, A-V, and software producers; health-conscious cookbooks; consumer magazines; reading lists; hot lines; help lines and clearinghouses; and local, state, and regional contacts for national organizations. Virtually every entry is annotated and full bibliographical information provided. Each chapter is prefaced with an introduction explaining the scope, how it was compiled (usually by questionnaires), and further sources of data. There are two subject indexes, one for each of the main sections. Both should be consulted for best retrieval results. This edition also includes the newly issued USDA Food Guide Pyramid and the revised 1989 Recommended Daily Allowances. The price on this edition is lower, making it more affordable. The editors have created an authoritative reference that will be helpful not only to food, health, and nutrition professionals and librarians but also to the general public. [R: RBB, 1 Feb 93, p. 1001]—**Joy Hastings**

Handbooks and Yearbooks

1605. Blue, Anthony Dias. **Buyer's Guide to American Wines: The Right Wine for the Right Price.** 2d ed. New York, HarperPerennial/HarperCollins, 1992. 230p. $13.50pa. ISBN 0-06-273158-0.

Blue manages to cover some 5,000 wines in this book; all are arranged alphabetically by winery and then by date. He covers the usual introductory material on what wine and tasting are all about in 16 pages, and he concludes with a list of all the good value wines (taking price into consideration) and all the wines that scored 90 and above. In between is the directory: Each wine is given a ranking out of 100, its vineyard designation, its suggested retail price, and about seven words of description (e.g., "Celery and other vegetables dominate," "Pineapple and tropical fruit flavors"). Not everybody is listed; Blue seems to be a little short on the Pacific Northwest (neither Hoodsport nor Quilceda Creek are here).

Since the last edition, there have been some changes. Blue has changed to a 100-point rating system instead of stars, and he has left in far too many older wines (some of them are not current enough for the retail shelves [particularly the whites], while only a handful can be found on restaurant lists). While on the title page it says "currently available wines," Blue has very few 1990 and 1991 wines listed, although with the 1992 copyright date one assumes that many 1990 white wines could have been tasted and evaluated. Some 1990 reds are included, but few 1990 whites are, although the whites are generally in the bottle and available for sale before the reds.—**Dean Tudor**

1606. **Codex Alimentarius. Volume 6: Fruit Juices and Related Products.** 2d ed. Rome, FAO of the United Nations; distr., Lanham, Md., UNIPUB, 1992. 124p. $15.00pa. ISBN 92-5-103221-1.

The FAO/WHO (Food and Agriculture Organization of the United Nations/World Health Organization) commission responsible for this publication currently represents 141 different member countries. The commission's purpose is to establish standards to protect the health of consumers, to ensure fair practices in the food trade, and to publish this information in the *Codex Alimentarius* as regional and worldwide standards. This publication covers fruit juices, concentrated fruit juices and fruit nectars preserved exclusively by physical means, concentrated fruit juices with preservatives for manufacturing, and vegetable juices. There is also a section on methods of analysis and sampling. This is followed by guidelines for mixing fruit juices and nectars. Twenty-seven fruit juices and nectars and vegetable juices and twenty-one methods of analysis, including fermentability and determination of contaminants, are outlined.

This book, compiled by experts in the field, is essentially the only source of this type of information. It is necessary for anyone interested in the manufacturing of fruit juices who is attempting to keep up with the newest in regulations and specifications.—**Herbert W. Ockerman**

1607. **Codex Alimentarius. Volume Eight: Fats, Oils and Related Products.** Rome, FAO of the United Nations and World Health Organization; distr., Lanham, Md., UNIPUB, 1993. 133p. $15.00pa. ISBN 92-5-103268-8.

This manuscript is designed to aid in the execution of the food standards program. It is aimed at protecting the health of consumers and facilitating international trade in food. It covers edible fats, oils, and related products: edible soya bean oil, arachis oil, cottonseed oil, sunflower seed oil, rapeseed oil, maize oil, sesame seed oil, safflower seed oil, olive oil, mustard seed oil, low erucic acid rapeseed oil, coconut oil, palm oil, palm kernel oil, grape seed oil, babassu oil, lard, rendered pork fat, premier jus, tallow, margarine, specified vegetable fat products, and specified animal or mixed animal and vegetable fat products. Each section includes scope, description, essential composition and quality factors, food additives (e.g., colors, flavors, antioxidants), contaminants, hygiene, labeling, nomenclature for names, labeling of nonretail containers, and methods of analysis. A code of practice for storage and transport and an appendix are also included. As are all FAO books, this is an authority in its field and would be essential for anyone interested in edible fats and oils, particularly those interested in international trade.—**Herbert W. Ockerman**

1608. **Compendium of Food Additive Specifications: Addendum 1.** Rome, FAO of the United Nations; distr., Lanham, Md., UNIPUB, 1992. 141p. (FAO Food and Nutrition Paper, 52). $15.00pa. ISBN 92-5-103214-9.

This compendium is authored by the joint FAO/WHO (Food and Agriculture Organization of the United Nations/World Health Organization) expert committee on food additives, which makes it the world's leading authority in this area. The manuscript includes past and current information up through February 1992. It lists details on 41 individual food additives. Eight of these are new listings, and all but nine have full specifications that are designated as "tentative" to indicate that additional information is needed before "full status" is granted. Individual entries contain information on additives, such as synonyms, definitions, chemical names, CAS (Chemical Abstract Service) number, chemical formula, structural formula, molecular weight, assay, description, functional uses, and characteristics such as identification test and purity test (including the procedure, the limits, and the methods of assay). A table of contents is included, but no references are listed. This well-organized book is absolutely essential for those in the food area who are trying to keep track of the latest information on food additives.—**Herbert W. Ockerman**

1609. **The Guide to Cooking School, 1993.** 5th ed. Coral Gables, Fla., ShawGuides, 1992. 310p. $16.95pa. LC 88-92516. ISBN 0-945834-16-0. ISSN 1040-2616.

This edition contains detailed descriptions of 345 cooking schools in 39 states and 22 countries with vital statistics for an additional 192 vocational-technical and community college programs. The guide has been completely updated, and 81 new listings have been added. Entries for the cooking schools, arranged alphabetically by states and countries, include year founded, specialties, location and facilities, student-to-teacher ratio, faculty description with credentials, costs, refund policies, and contact information. For community colleges, information included is abbreviated and more difficult to discern. More than 150 of the schools that offer career training report a job placement rate of 90 to 100 percent for graduates. Also listed here are 128 U.S. Department of Labor-registered cooking apprenticeships and 13 culinary and accrediting organizations.

To help users find the information they want, 5 indexes give access by 17 categories of specialties, professional programs, travel and vacation programs, children's courses, and restaurants with cooking school affiliations. There is also an alphabetical master index. Two new sections are school rankings by tuition costs and school rankings by percentage of applicants accepted. This inexpensive, easy-to-use reference source is a worthwhile addition to any public or academic library.—**Susan C. Awe**

1610. Newstrom, Harvey. **Nutrients Catalog: Vitamins, Minerals, Amino Acids, Macronutrients....** Jefferson, N.C., McFarland, 1993. 538p. index. $55.00. QP141.N48. 613.2'8. LC 92-56671. ISBN 0-89950-784-0.

Descriptions of essential nutrients are presented in this reference book. Each entry lists the various names by which the nutrient is known, the common classification, the chemical forms, symptoms associated with a dietary deficiency, side effects from an excessive amount of the nutrient, toxicity, inhibitors, helpers or cofactors, food sources, possible application, recommended daily doses, and warnings of specific problems associated with the nutrient. This is followed by appendixes that list essential nutritional elements that could be used for the treatments of various symptoms, the vitamin B complex designations, nutrient ratios, nutrient unit conversions, a rather extensive biographical section, and an extremely extensive cross-reference index. A major portion of the book is in table format. The work is easy to use and should be valuable to people interested in the nutritional, biochemical, and health aspects of essential nutrients.—**Herbert W. Ockerman**

1611. **Pesticide Residues in Food 1992. Evaluations. Part I: Residues.** Rome, FAO of the United Nations; distr., Lanham, Md., UNIPUB, 1993. 886p. (FAO Plant Production and Protection Paper, 118). $90.00. ISBN 92-5-103341-2.

This is part 1 of a two-volume evaluation of pesticides (the other volume covers toxicology) by joint FAO (Food and Agriculture Organization) and WHO (World Health Organization) committees. Updated yearly, it is an expanded and detailed analysis of selected pesticide residues, a summary of which appears in the annual volume of reports (see ARBA 92, entry 1498). Some of the listed compounds have been previously evaluated and reported on in earlier publications. In this instance, new information is summarized and reference made to these publications. Other, older compounds are reevaluated as part of an ongoing periodic review, and a comprehensive discussion is presented. New compounds are also noted. Most of the entries offer complete information on identity, chemical and physical properties, and formulations. Where available, registered and proposed uses and trial results are given. The methods of analysis and straightforward appraisal of the compounds are quite helpful, as are the MRLs (maximum residue limits) for reporting countries. The comprehensive information provided and the fact that much of the data is not easily found elsewhere offset the high price. This volume will be helpful to academics, governments, and organizations that need complete and current information on pesticides.—**Joy Hastings**

1612. Smith, Judith Scharman, and Scott D. Smith. **The Low-Fat Supermarket.** Lancaster, Pa., Starburst, 1993. 299p. $10.95pa. LC 92-81392. ISBN 0-914984-44-6.

This book is about fats, particularly fats in the foods we eat, whether processed or fresh. It is essentially a guide to the amounts of fat in various products. Chapter 3 is a series of charts of various foods given in serving sizes, number of calories per serving, grams of fat per serving, milligrams of sodium per serving, milligrams of cholesterol per serving, and percent of fat per serving. The chapter arranges foods by classes (e.g., bakery, dairy, frozen, meats, pudding) and then by brand names. Most major brands are listed. Other chapters give valuable information on fat in the diet. Chapter 1 discusses fats themselves: what is a saturated fat, where fats are hidden, cholesterol, and how much fat is necessary in the diet, among other things. Chapter 2 is an excellent discussion of what the new labeling laws are going to mean and how they are different from the current labels, with their vague and misleading terms. Chapter 4 gives good instructions on how to cook without fats (but not recipes), and chapter 5 is a very unsettling overview of fats in fast foods. Just about all of the major fast-food chains are mentioned.

A recent study found that nearly 60 percent of people in the general population do not know their cholesterol levels (even though they have been tested) or how to manage their diets to get away from fats. Some of these people had also been told by their doctors that they had heart conditions and some clogging of the arteries. This book would truly be a boon to these individuals. It is written very simply and clearly. The publisher gives a disclaimer at the beginning of the book that the information in the tables comes from the food manufacturers, the government, or food labels. These sources were probably the best the Smiths, a medical doctor and a registered dietitian, could use, given the food industry's frequent hesitation at revealing ingredients in its foods. Even if some of the information is not completely accurate, the book will still give people a means of designing their food habits so that they can cut their fat intake. This book would not be appropriate for a research collection, but it would be a good buy anywhere else, particularly for health counselors and individuals. [R: RBB, 1 April 93, p. 1457]—**Lillian R. Mesner**

1613. Whitman, Joan, and Dolores Simon. **Recipes into Type: A Handbook for Cookbook Writers and Editors.** New York, HarperCollins, 1993. 258p. index. $25.00. TX644.W47. 808'.066641. LC 89-46129. ISBN 0-06-270034-0.

Students and writers have a wide variety of style manuals to help them format their research papers and articles, but what helps one lay out a recipe? Works such as *The Chicago Manual of Style* (University of Chicago Press, 1993) are useless when one is trying to lay out a recipe for Ham Roulade with Mustard-Sour Cream Sauce. *Recipes into Type* fills that important gap for would-be cookbook writers from Craig Claiborne to your Aunt Edith. It is a delightful blend composed of one part style manual and one part quick-fact reference book, with a pinch of dictionary thrown in for added zest. The authors bring a simple and logical style to the way recipes are formulated and presented based upon 54 combined years experience as food and family and style editors. In addition to the style manual, this slim volume contains a list of nearly 1,500 food-related words, most of which do not appear in standard dictionaries. There are also descriptions of basic foodstuffs, a list of substitutions, average serving sizes, common weights and measures with metric conversion, and an index.—**Steven J. Schmidt**

FORESTRY

1614. **Compendium of Pulp and Paper Training and Research Institutions.** Rome, FAO of the United Nations; distr., Lanham, Md., UNIPUB, 1992. 65p. (FAO Forestry Paper, 105). $10.00pa. ISBN 92-5-103231-9.

1615. **Forest Products Prices 1971-1990. Prix des Produits Forestiers. Precios de Productos Forestales.** By Forestry Policy and Planning Division, FAO Forestry Department. Rome, FAO of the United Nations; distr., Lanham, Md., UNIPUB, 1992. 254p. index. (FAO Forestry Paper, 104). $30.00pa. ISBN 92-5-003224-2.

These works contain mostly tabular data on worldwide forest products prices from 1971 to 1990 and pulp and paper training and research institutions. Paper number 104 is the ninth issue of its kind. Its stated principal objective is to provide price data useful for medium- and long-term policy formulation and the evaluation of investment projects. However, the difficulty of accumulating such data makes this publication not particularly useful for evaluating short-term projects. Supplementary information for specific areas and products will be necessary for such evaluations. The paper is divided into two major parts. Part 1 contains products group tables for each of 17 major types of forest products. Within each table, data are compiled by country, with comments about specific pricing details. The details are mostly in English, but they are in French or Spanish where these are the languages of origin. Graphs are included at the beginning of each of the major products groups to emphasize overall development of prices. Part 2 contains country tables organized by major product.

Paper number 105 lists institutions that specialize in professional training in the pulp and paper industry sector and organizations involved in research and development programs worldwide. It is a simple-to-use document arranged alphabetically by country. Each institution is described by its name and address; director; telephone, telex, and fax numbers; and a short description of the program, when available. Each of these Forestry Papers provides data not contained in any other single source. They should be available in a reference library.—**Michael G. Messina**

1616. **Directory of the Wood Products Industry, 1993.** Pamela G. Malpas, ed. San Francisco, Calif., Wood Technology Books/Miller Freeman, 1992. 1047p. index. $227.00.

This directory provides complete coverage of basic information on primary and secondary wood manufacturing corporations in North America. A continuation of the biennially published *Directory of the Forest Products Industry*, the directory will be published annually beginning with the 1993 edition. Its title has been changed to reflect broader coverage of the wood products manufacturing industry. Prior editions covered mostly high-tech primary manufacturing, but this and future editions will include engineered wood products and intermediate stages of secondary manufacturing as well.

The directory is divided into 10 sections, most of which represent different methods of categorizing the information. Section 1 contains six essays by industry experts on economics and technology. Section 2 lists contact information for head and division offices by state or province and city. Information organized by major type of processing facility, state or province, and city is presented in section 3. A plethora of details on products, species, equipment, and the like is included in each entry. Sections 4, 5, and 6 are similarly organized but deal with wood treating, wholesalers, and secondary wood products manufactures. Section 7, likely the most valuable, cross-references corporations by type of product or species used. Entries are simply company name and location with a notation denoting primary or secondary facility, but the user can refer to previous sections for further information. Section 8 is a directory of government agencies and universities important to the wood products industry. Section 9 is a buyers' guide to products and services, and section 10 contains a general index listing companies alphabetically, with page numbers referring the user back to sections 2 through 6.

It would be difficult, if not impossible, to rival this directory as a more complete source of information on the wood products industry. It should be contained in every reference library, as it is indispensable to anyone seeking information on the North American wood products industry.—**Michael G. Messina**

HORTICULTURE

Dictionaries and Encyclopedias

1617. **The American Horticultural Society Encyclopedia of Gardening.** Christopher Brickell and Elvin McDonald, eds. New York, Dorling Kindersley, 1993. 648p. illus. index. $59.95. SB450.95.A45. 635. LC 93-3042. ISBN 1-56458-291-4.

This stunning how-to gardening guide covers all the steps and techniques of creating and maintaining a healthy and beautiful garden. Nearly 600 pages of sound and practical information on subjects ranging from propagation and pests to fences and tools are organized around basic gardening processes and procedures. The work is lavishly illustrated in typical Dorling Kindersley style, with more than 3,000 color photographs and drawings.

The book is arranged in two parts: creating the garden and maintaining the garden. Within each section, chapters address specific topics such as the lawn, greenhouses and frames, and plant problems. Many types of gardens, from rock and container to perennial, are covered. The text is studded with feature boxes (on specific plant groups or interest areas, such as topiary), plant lists, and cross-references. Specific plants, such as tomatoes, are discussed within their appropriate chapters, but no centralized directory of plants is given.

The breadth of the subject covered and the diversity of contributors, while impressive, are probably also the biggest obstacles to the book's practicality. Generalities can lead to misunderstandings and even misinformation. For example, a section on climate discusses its effect on gardening in different regions, but these important regional differences are not integrated into the text. So when an author recommends varieties of tomatoes or squash, no mention is made that their success varies greatly from region to region. In spite of this minor shortcoming, the book will serve as a comprehensive and practical reference to novice and seasoned gardeners. More than that, it will be a joy to anyone interested in gardening. [R: LJ, 15 Nov 93, p. 68]—**Barbara Ittner**

1618. Bagust, Harold, comp. **The Gardener's Dictionary of Horticultural Terms.** London, Cassell; distr., New York, Sterling Publishing, 1992. 377p. illus. $29.95. 635.0321. ISBN 0-304-34106-1.

This dictionary is intended for gardeners, students, writers, and horticulturalists. Included are definitions for gardening tools, growing media, propagation methods, plant organs, soil types, landscaping, and diseases. Definitions are brief but generally adequate. Wisely, neither common nor scientific plant names are included. This work will be particularly useful to students of botany for its definitions of hundreds of botanical terms, such as *cyme, glaucous, pinnate,* and *terete*. A few of the definitions are inadequate, such as that for *potting soil*. In this instance the reader is directed to "John Innes Composts," where there are in fact four recipes for potting soils. While this terminology works well in the British Isles, readers in the United States may experience minor problems. Hundreds of excellent line drawings add to the information and to the aesthetics of the book. In all, the work is quite valuable and appropriate for any academic or public library. [R: LJ, 15 May 93, p. 62; RBB, July 93, p. 2002]—**T. McKimmie**

1619. **Rodale's All-New Encyclopedia of Organic Gardening: The Indispensable Resource for Every Gardener.** Fern Marshall Bradley and Barbara W. Ellis, eds. Emmaus, Pa., Rodale Press, 1992. 690p. illus. index. $29.95; $17.95pa. SB453.5.R633. 635.0484. LC 91-32088. ISBN 0-87857-999-0; 0-87596-599-7pa.

This book (the companion volume to the PBS show *Your Organic Garden*) is the source for those who think gardening organically means watching helplessly while a legion of pests consumes everything in sight, as well as for experienced organic gardeners. The successor to a 30-year-old classic (*The Encyclopedia of Organic Gardening*, edited by J. I. Rodale), this thick volume covers the myriad ways a gardener can prevent and defend against pests and diseases of all kinds. Many of the preventive measures are time-honored and were covered in the earlier volume, but many of the nontoxic pesticides listed are relatively new developments.

The encyclopedia consists of around 700 medium-length entries on everything from abelia (a type of flowering shrub) to zucchini. Interspersed are 26 longer core articles—extensive treatments of important topics, such as garden design, composting, and pruning and training—which, taken together, form a handbook of organic gardening theory and practice. It should be noted that the encyclopedia does not just deal with vegetable gardens; ornamentals, fruit trees, and even houseplants are discussed. Techniques discussed include recognizing and promoting beneficial insects and animals, arranging and planning a garden to prevent disease and pest problems, and choosing appropriate cultivars.

Throughout the book black-and-white line drawings augment the text. Many articles include a glossary of key words, and there are numerous useful charts and tables and an extensive index. This should become the new indispensable classic for the home gardener.—**Carol L. Noll**

1620. **Rodale's Illustrated Encyclopedia of Perennials.** By Ellen Phillips and C. Colson Burrell. Emmaus, Pa., Rodale Press, 1993. 533p. illus. index. $27.95. SB434.P48. 635.9'32. LC 92-30109. ISBN 0-87596-570-9.

The encyclopedia part takes up only the final third of this three-part book. Part 1 deals with design and includes a long chapter that highlights seven sample perennial garden designs. Part 2 is all about growing perennials: gardening basics, climate, controlling pests and diseases, propagation, and a quick-reference culture table for the approximately 160 genera covered in the encyclopedia section. There is even a chapter on fresh and dried flower arrangements. Part 3, the encyclopedia, contains more than 200 pages. Perennials are arranged alphabetically by botanical (genus) name. Entries follow a standard format, beginning with a description that includes mention of notable species and cultivars within the genus. One very helpful feature is the use of pronunciation aids for genus and species names. Besides the description, each entry also has brief sections on how to grow the plant and its landscape uses. At least one photograph accompanies the entry. The photographs are all in full color and show both flowers and foliage. A comprehensive index includes cross-references from common plant names to their botanical names.

Phillips and Burrell are experienced writers with backgrounds in horticulture and garden design. As with other Rodale publications, this book is loaded with practical information and how-to advice. It also offers encouragement and inspiration, due in part to the many appealing color photographs throughout the book. The encyclopedia entries in this volume are similar to those of the recent *Encyclopedia of Perennials* (see ARBA 93, entry 1508), although listing less than half the genera presented in that work. Considering its reasonable price and high quality, this is an excellent choice for novice gardeners looking for a starter book that is complete in one handy volume, for public libraries, and for college libraries supporting courses in landscape design and horticulture. [R: RBB, 1 May 93, p. 1634]—**William H. Wiese**

1621. Steele, Joelle. **Interior Landscape Dictionary.** New York, Van Nostrand Reinhold, 1992. 151p. illus. $39.95. SB419.25.S74. 747'.98. LC 92-19932. ISBN 0-442-01121-0.

Aimed at the interior horticulturist, this capable lexicon defines approximately 700 botanical terms in the increasingly popular field of interior landscaping. The definitions are short (one or two sentences) and understandable to the layperson, technical jargon having been conscientiously minimized. The terminology covered ranges from the fairly obvious, such as *transplanting* and *overwatering*, to the genuinely useful, such as *tropism* (a directional growth movement of a plant that occurs in response to an external stimulus). The text is enhanced by a generous supply of black-and-white illustrations (both photographs and line drawings), at least one per page. Concluding the volume are helpful guides to pronunciation of Latin names, binomial nomenclature, and a good bibliography.

Although valuable as a basic lexicon, this is not a how-to book for gardeners. Pests such as mealy bugs and whiteflies are defined, but no indication is given on how to control them. The same is true of fungus diseases, such as the common problem of indoor seed starting; *damping off* is correctly defined, but the key word *fungicide* is not mentioned. This is not to fault the book for failing to achieve what it did not intend, but its appeal could have been considerably broadened by adding this sort of information.
—**Richard W. Grefrath**

1622. Taylor, Patrick. **The 500 Best Garden Plants.** Portland, Oreg., Timber Press, 1993. 320p. illus. index. $19.95pa. ISBN 0-88192-257-9.

The bulbs, herbaceous perennials, shrubs, climbers and wall plants, and trees described in this collection are, in the author's opinion, the best of their kind for a small or moderate-sized garden. Main entries give the genus of a plant with a brief note, and then appropriate species are described, with their special qualities detailed. Material in the descriptions varies from plant to plant but usually includes use, cultivation, hardiness, propagation, and place of origin. In addition, each entry notes hardiness zones for both Europe and the United States and the mature size of a plant "as expected in a protected southern garden in England." Although written from a working knowledge of English gardens, the author has done a superb job of identifying species that are also available in the United States. Most are easy-to-find varieties, but those that require a little more searching are well worth the effort.

Taylor concludes the work with a particularly helpful list of plants for different sites, hardiness zone maps for the United States and Europe, and an index of the botanical and common names of the plants. With more than 300 clear photographs, this book is wonderful for identifying mystery plants in the garden, and the accompanying chatty text makes it not only extremely informative but a great read. Anyone who loves plants will love this book!—**Jo Anne H. Ricca**

Handbooks and Yearbooks

1623. Armitage, Allan M. **Specialty Cut Flowers: The Production of Annuals, Perennials, Bulbs and Woody Plants for Fresh and Dried Cut Flowers.** Portland, Oreg., Varsity Press/Timber Press, 1993. 372p. illus. maps. index. $39.95. SB405.A68. 635.9'66. LC 92-34463. ISBN 0-88192-225-0.

This horticulture reference book deals with specialty cut flowers, which the author defines as all flowers except roses, carnations, and chrysanthemums. The flowers are grouped into annuals, perennials, bulbs, and woody plants (which are used not only for their flowers but also for their fruit and foliage). The more than 200 plant entries include both Latin and common names, height and spread in feet, color of blooms, plant hardiness, and origin by both country or region and plant family. Each entry also provides detailed information on propagation, handling, environmental factors, greenhouse or field performance, and pests and diseases. Some 50 line drawings and 99 color plates handsomely illustrate the flowers in bloom. Of special note is the section on drying and preserving cut flowers in the introduction. Indexes and references also enhance the work, as do the helpful tables throughout the book.

The bibliography seems particularly thorough; it includes books, seed guides, proceedings, newsletters, and periodicals. The indexes to botanical and common names make finding any species easy. This one-volume reference is packed with information, not surprising because the author is a professor of horticulture at the University of Georgia and author of several other books on the subject. His knowledge and love of cut flowers come through on every page. This excellent book is recommended for all public and academic libraries.—**Edward Erazo**

1624. **Ball Pest & Disease Manual.** By Charles C. Powell and Richard K. Lindquist. Geneva, Ill., Ball Publishing, 1992. 332p. illus. index. $56.00. SB608.07P69. 635.9'2. LC 91-35855. ISBN 0-9626796-4-X.

A plant in ill health probably suffers from chronic problems, so think of it in holistic terms and identify the interplay of suboptimal environmental parameters and nuisance organisms that diminish its health. In diagnosing, observe carefully. Water deeply and not often, follow sanitary practices, and adhere to instructions on chemicals. And, in tackling diseases and pests, prevention is often better than a cure. Time-tested procedures for confronting plant-threatening insects, fungi, bacteria, and viruses give this volume its core. The prosaic style stems partly from the amount of information packed into the text.

Plant propagation and protection require planning; sample programs for poinsettias, geraniums, and Easter lilies illustrate how to do it. An extensive appendix (with names, addresses, and telephone numbers) includes suppliers, consultants on ornamental plants and harmful insects, analytical laboratories, extension specialists, and software companies that offer materials in environmental control. The poor contrast in many of the black-and-white photographs renders them useless; however, the color plates that follow chapter 3 are so good that they enable even a novice to distinguish a rust from a Botrytis and an aphid from a whitefly. Introductions to common insect pests and disease-causing agents are succinct and accurate. Expansion of the tantalizing throw-away lines (e.g., "plant disease contributed to the defeats of Alexander the Great and the fall of the Roman Empire") would have been nice.—**Diane M. Calabrese**

1625. **The Bernard E. Harkness Seedlist Handbook.** 2d ed. Mabel G. Harkness, comp. Portland, Oreg., Timber Press, 1993. 506p. index. $29.95pa. SB408.H36. 635.9'42'0216. LC 92-21121. ISBN 0-88192-226-9.

This is really the 5th edition of a work begun by Bernard E. Harkness in 1974, but it is the 2d edition in which his widow, Mabel G. Harkness, has continued to compile and update the handbook (see ARBA 88, entry 1479 for a review of the 1986 edition). This edition has 25 percent more entries and has removed many errors and duplications found in the previous edition. Also, a few more references were added. Other than this, the handbook is unchanged in its format and scope. It remains a handy, quick, compact guide for rock and alpine gardeners to plants from the seeds offered by the Scottish Rock Garden Club, the Alpine Garden Society (England), and the American Rock Garden Society. The present edition includes information from the previous four versions with additional updating to include the seedlist information through 1990.—**Nathan M. Smith**

1626. Bloom, Alan, and Adrian Bloom. **Blooms of Bressingham Garden Plants: Choosing the Best Hardy Plants for Your Garden.** New York, HarperCollins, 1992. 320p. illus. index. $35.00. ISBN 0-00-412329-8.

As stated in the subtitle, the purpose of this book is to help gardeners select the best plants for their gardens. By best, the authors also mean the easiest—thus, the focus on long-lasting plants. A directory of permanent garden plants and cultivars comprises the body of the work. More than 5,000 species are grouped into 6 sections: perennials, grasses and hardy ferns, alpines, conifers, heaths and heathers, and shrubs. The largest sections are those on perennials and shrubs. Each section is color-coded (along page edges) for easy reference and includes general guidelines for selection, use, and maintenance; planting plans; and suggested groupings of plants. More than 750 color photographs and illustrations grace the text. In addition, lists of plants suited to particular growing conditions (e.g., acid soils) or possessing certain qualities (e.g., fragrance) are given. Within sections, the plants are listed alphabetically by their scientific names, followed by their common names. (Plants are indexed by both names.) A brief description follows, including specifics on approximate height, width, months in flower, and relative hardiness zones, as well as special features of the plant, considerations and tips for cultivation, and lists of varieties when appropriate.

Although the book has a decidedly English bias (e.g., the section on heaths and heathers), the authors have taken pains to make it accessible to North Americans. Measurements are given in both metric and standard terms, and zones cover a wide range of North American climates. The wealth of information offered and practical guidelines given make this a worthwhile volume for both novice and experienced gardeners.—**Barbara Ittner**

1627. Dean, Jan. **The Gardener's Reading Guide.** New York, Facts on File, 1993. 250p. illus. index. $23.95. Z5996.A1D43. 016.635. LC 92-24321. ISBN 0-8160-2754-4.

This delightful book will have great appeal to all types of gardeners: the professional, the amateur, and the armchair. Books that range from the practical to the esoteric and from the garden in fiction to gifts and crafts from the garden are all covered in this comprehensive bibliography. Each entry includes a very brief description. Personal comments are interspersed sporadically, giving the book a unique character. As Dean frankly states in his criteria, the annotations reflect his opinions and preferences. But this is what gives the book its charm. Other unusual features include a section devoted to gardening for the disabled and the elderly, gardening for profit, and garden videos. In all, there are more than 3,000 entries. The categories are so inclusive, encompassing container gardens, gardens around the world, foliage, and watering methods, that one would be hard-pressed to find a topic that is overlooked. Dean has concentrated on books published in the past 15 years but does include older books that he particularly favors. A most useful feature is the chapter on where to find books, plus a list of publishers.

Although some avid gardeners may quibble over omissions of their favorite books, Dean clearly states that the choices are his, limited by space constraints and his own predilections. He has chosen well. [R: Choice, Oct 93, p. 265; LJ, 15 April 93, p. 82; RBB, July 93, pp. 2002-03; RQ, Winter 93, pp. 285-86]—**Carol R. Glatt**

1628. Dickerson, Brent C. **The Old Rose Advisor.** Portland, Oreg., Timber Press, 1992. 400p. illus. index. $65.00. SB411.65.O55D53. 635.9'33372. LC 91-29686. ISBN 0-88192-216-1.

Everyone will enjoy this book, from the rose enthusiast to the individual who appreciates fine flora art work. This extensive guide to "old" roses will get the most uninspired gardener out to look at some of those flowering shrubs that have been there "forever" with a different eye. Once one learns that they may be varieties that were originally seen only in gardens in Europe, it is easy to appreciate the place that these roses have in modern culture.

This volume contains 274 color plates; historical information on roses from the United States, Great Britain, and France; full descriptions of roses, including physical description, original name, date of introduction, and breeder/introducer; listings on more than 2,300 different varieties; and even some extinct, or possibly extinct, varieties. There is also an extensive discussion on rose groups and the varieties within these groups. A complete index and 10 appendixes aid in finding roses, whether it be by year of introduction, color, breeder/introducer, or group.

It is rare to find a book that is both a complete reference and a pleasure to just pick up and enjoy. This is such a book.—**Linda Sue Smith**

1629. Halliwell, Brian. **The Propagation of Alpine Plants and Dwarf Bulbs.** Portland, Oreg., Timber Press, 1992. 193p. illus. index. $24.95. ISBN 0-88192-254-4.

Halliwell offers this book as an update and expansion of the previous standard, Lawrence Hill's *The Propagation of Alpines* (Faber and Faber, 1950). A retired curator of alpine plants at Kew, he addresses rock gardeners on both sides of the Atlantic. Garden enthusiasts and collectors who cannot locate plants through commercial sources may choose to grow them from seed or cuttings. Because plants vary widely in their responses to propagation techniques, Halliwell offers specific guidance for 2,000 genera, as well as in-depth information on the techniques. He reviews the pros and cons of sexual propagation through seeds versus vegetative propagation through cuttings, rootings, grafts, sectioning of bulbs and tubers, and other methods. Throughout this section he mentions products that can be used to facilitate the process of propagation. This book is addressed to rock gardeners, but the selection of bulbs, ferns, and woody and herbaceous plants includes many of the most familiar garden plants. A must for large horticultural collections, this book is also well worth consideration by smaller libraries needing up-to-date information on propagation techniques.—**Beth Clewis**

1630. Johnson, Eric A., and Scott Millard. **The Low-Water Flower Gardener.** Tucson, Ariz., Ironwood Press; distr., Boulder, Colo., Johnson Books, 1993. 144p. illus. index. $14.95pa. LC 92-73645. ISBN 0-9628236-1-9.

In the western and southwestern United States, water is at a premium and anything gardeners can do to reduce its use is beneficial to the ecology (as well as to their wallets). This book contains information on more than 280 different species of low-water-usage flowers. The thorough section on soils and soil improvement will help any gardener make better use of water. There are also some helpful suggestions for companion plantings. Most of the information given in this book appears to be directed at gardeners in California, even though the book's cover indicates that it is meant for all of the southwestern and Rocky Mountain states. Much of the information provided is basic common sense for all but the novice.—**Linda Sue Smith**

1631. Salley, Homer E., and Harold E. Greer. **Rhododendron Hybrids: Includes Selected, Named Forms of Rhododendron Species.** 2d ed. Portland, Oreg., Timber Press, 1992. 344p. illus. $59.95. SB413.R47S25. 635.9'3362. LC 91-44638. ISBN 0-88192-184-X.

Although they might know that rhododendrons come in a number of colors, users will be amazed when looking through this volume to learn that there are more than 5,000 hybrids listed. Needless to say, this is the book for any rhododendron fancier to have. In its new edition, *Rhododendron Hybrids* has been revised to include all new registered hybrids from 1985 to 1991. (However, vireyas are not included this time.) There is also greater inclusion of unregistered hybrids, as well as Weldon Delp's creations. The major change between editions, however, is organizational. Hybrids are now arranged by grex (a group of sister seedlings of the same parentage, but with variations in traits). This saves a great deal of space by reducing the duplication of parentage diagrams. Along with parentage, a description of the hybrid includes size at maturity, habit, flowers and foliage, hardiness, and awards received. Also included are 592 color photographs of hybrids that have not appeared in either the *Rhododendron Yearbook* of the Royal Horticultural Society or the *Journal of the American Rhododendron Society*. Landscapers will appreciate this aid to choosing the right hybrid for each situation, but breeders will find the most joy in this volume.—**Angela Marie Thor**

1632. Thomas, Graham Stuart. **Ornamental Shrubs, Climbers and Bamboos, Excluding Roses and Rhododendrons.** Portland, Oreg., Sagapress/Timber Press, 1992. 583p. illus. index. $49.95. ISBN 0-88192-250-1.

This is a companion work to the author's delightful *Perennial Garden Plants* (see ARBA 92, entry 614). As was the first book, it is individualistic, informative, and eminently sensible, but in this case it focuses on ornamental shrubs (loosely defined and including small trees), climbers, and bamboos, excluding roses and rhododendrons. The work begins with seven short chapters, each a brief introduction and personal perspective on aspects of shrub cultivation, including its history, the use of shrub form and color in the garden, classification, and horticulture (including mechanics). The last chapter is a guide to the use of the book.

Most of the work is given to an alphabetical list (by genus and then by species and variety) of shrubs and, in separate sections, vines and bamboos. Each description is a model of brevity, with coded information on height, breadth, foliage, hardiness, flower color, season of flower, and mode of propagation. This is followed by a short discussion of the points of interest of the species, often including place of origin, particular beauty, cultivational specialties, and other such data. Several are illustrated by photographs, unfortunately not all in color. The work concludes with a useful list of shrubs and climbers for special purposes, allowing the gardener to find species suitable for particular sites or possessing particular features of shape or flower color—or even those that are "rabbit-proof"!

As in the previous volume, the author writes from immense experience developed in cultivating these plants in Surrey, England, and often speaks of their success in that country. While effort has been made to include data on North American climatic zones, users must be aware that North America presents a vast and complicated array of soils, moistures, and temperatures that are not matched in England. Nonetheless, this book is packed with information and is a pleasure to read as well as a reference of value to North American gardeners.—**Bruce H. Tiffney**

VETERINARY SCIENCE

1633. Dictionary of Animal Health Terminology in English, French, Spanish, German and Latin. Compiled by Office International des Epizooties. Roy Mack, ed. New York, Elsevier Science Publishing, 1992. 426p. $157.00. SF609.D55. 636.089'03. LC 92-9212. ISBN 0-444-88085-2.

This book was formerly a part of the *Dictionary of Animal Production Terminology* published in 1985 by the European Association for Animal Production. Increased specialization in animal production has warranted dividing the original dictionary into two volumes. One volume focuses on animal husbandry terms; this one lists veterinary terms. Subject coverage includes all aspects of veterinary medicine, including anatomy, physiology, and diseases. The dictionary gives equivalents for words and phrases in English, French, Spanish, German, and Latin. It does not provide definitions as the book is meant to be a reference tool for those people working in the field of animal health who need to understand the foreign-language terms and phrases they encounter. The dictionary is easy to use. It is divided into five sections to correspond with each language. Terms and phrases in the English section have their translations listed in each entry. The terms and words in the remaining sections always refer back to the English section for equivalents.—**Patricia S. Wilson**

31 Biological Sciences

BIOLOGY

1634. Barron, Sarah, Matthew Witten, and Gongxian Liu. **A Bibliography on Computational Molecular Biology.** Upland, Pa., DIANE Publishing, [1992]. 115p. $40.00 spiralbound. ISBN 0-941375-91-9.

This work lists 2,230 references to journal articles, technical reports, and conference papers on computational and mathematical aspects of DNA mapping and sequence analysis. Coverage includes the mid-1970s through 1991. Arrangement of the entries is alphabetical by author. The list includes references from the literature of mathematics, computer science, and biology, clearly illustrating the interdisciplinarity of the topic. The reprography of the work is poor, and the book lacks an index, so access by key words, title, or source is restricted, limiting the usefulness of this work.—**Christine M. Sheetz**

1635. Hollar, David W. **The Origin and Evolution of Life on Earth: An Annotated Bibliography.** Pasadena, Calif., Salem Press, 1992. 235p. index. (Magill Bibliographies). $40.00. Z5322.E9H65. 575. LC 92-12899. ISBN 0-89356-683-7.

This book is entering a field that is fairly well populated with bibliographies. An OCLC search turned up quite a number of records of books on the subjects that are covered in this one. However, it is not known whether those other books also include journal articles. Hollar's work does not list such articles; it covers 800-plus books on evolution that date from the 1800s to the present.

The introduction is an overview of the history of evolution and genetics and an explanation of the contents of the chapters. The rest of the book is a straightforward bibliography that is arranged by topics and subtopics and then by author. What makes this a useful work is that each entry contains a substantial annotation. There is an author index, but the real entry to the information in the book is through the table of contents. There is no indication of Hollar's background or authority on the subject. He states in the introduction that many of the listed books are for laypeople as well as professionals. Therefore, the bibliography would be a good addition to almost any kind of collection. [R: Choice, June 93, p. 1604]
—**Lillian R. Mesner**

1636. Lederberg, Joshua, ed. **Encyclopedia of Microbiology.** San Diego, Calif., Academic Press, 1992. 4v. illus. index. $695.00/set. QR9E53. 576'.03. LC 92-4429. ISBN 0-12-226890-3.

This encyclopedia is a collection of about 200 essays written by 300-plus authors on topics relating to microbiology, including both basic and applied areas. Topics cover food and medical microbiology, biotechnology, taxonomy, genetics, culture of microorganisms, the archaebacteria, and much more. Most subjects that one would expect to find are covered, although not every topic is included. While the preface claims that the intended audience includes high school and college students as well as teachers and researchers, the level of vocabulary and background knowledge required make it a dubious choice for most high school students. However, the essays are a good introduction to or overview of microbiology for more advanced readers. The amount of detail in the essays varies, and some articles, such as those on foods (e.g., bread, beer, wine) or wastewater treatment, may be of interest to the general public.

For the most part the articles (even on the most esoteric subjects) are accurate and reasonably understandable, although some authors' styles are rather dense. There are many figures and tables, most of them clear and helpful. A brief bibliography is included with each essay for further information. Unfortunately, there is no master glossary, although each essay includes definitions of important terms. The encyclopedia includes both a subject index and an index that cross-references related essays.

While the arrangement and coverage of the encyclopedia will not satisfy everyone, and the price will put it out of the reach of many libraries, it is well worth the money for academic and special libraries. It is useful for applied areas such as medicine, biotechnology, and agriculture as well as for more basic fields. There really is nothing else comparable in either coverage or currency on the market, and the encyclopedia is a valuable tool for both faculty and graduate students.—**Diane Schmidt**

BOTANY

General Works

Bibliography

1637. Gentry, Alwyn H. **Bignoniaceae—Part II (Tribe Tecomeae).** Bronx, N.Y., New York Botanical Garden, 1992. 370p. illus. index. (Flora Neotropica, v.25, pt.2). $69.00pa. QK205.F58. 581.98'012. LC 85-647083. ISBN 0-89327-368-6.

Gentry (senior curator of the Missouri Botanical Garden Herbarium) continues his 1980 studies with this work, which includes 19 native genera, 203 native species, 11 additional subspecies, and 7 varieties. The presentation of 49 species of *Jacaranda*, coauthored with Wilfried Morawetz (who completed his doctoral dissertation on that genus), includes 13 species and 1 subspecies described as new. A key to genera precedes an alphabetical list of 23 genera. For example, the genus *Jacaranda* includes the original citation, type species, synonyms, a description of the plants, and their distribution, followed by a key to species. The first described, *Jacaranda acutifolia*, includes citation, type, description, distribution, representative specimens examined, common names, and a paragraph describing how this species differs from others in the genus. Distribution maps include overlap symbols for two or more species.

Three bibliographical errors discovered include quotation marks surrounding the year in the *Jacaranda duckei* citation; a blind citation to *Tabebuia* hybridization as "Gentry, 1989a," which is missing from the Gentry entries in "Literature Cited," and the omission of the first initial, "L." in "Bureau, E. & K. Schumann. 1896-1897. Bignoniaceae." Gracielza Dos Santos and Regis B. Miller provided a detailed study of *Tecomeae* wood anatomy to form an appendix to this helpful monograph. Recommended for research scholars, graduate students, and curators for herbaria collecting neotropica specimens.
—**Helen M. Barber**

1638. Kirkbride, Joseph H., Jr. **Biosystematic Monograph of the Genus *Cucumis* (Cucurbitaceae): Botanical Identification of Cucumbers and Melons.** Boone, N.C., Parkway, 1993. 159p. illus. index. $47.50. (with disk). QK495.C96K57. 583'.46. LC 92-82126. ISBN 0-9635752-0-1.

The purpose of this compact monograph is to provide a precise taxonomic guide to the identification and scientific naming of cucumbers and melons. The book is written in an easy-to-follow, logical manner. The author builds the framework for identification and naming of specimens within the genus *Cucumis* by giving its taxonomic history, morphologic characteristics important to classification, and biosystematic data, including biochemistry, cytology, and crossability. An additional section devoted to materials and methods is included. Database construction of information on *Cucumis* specimens is addressed in this section, with information on how to use the MS-DOS disk accompanying the book. The disk is the electronic format of the printed information in the book, thus allowing multiple points of access.

The major portion of the book is devoted to the author's approach to the taxonomy of *Cucumis* and begins with a summary of the characteristics of *Cucumis cucumis* and *C. melo* devoted to key-ranked systems to classification in a step-by-step manner. The book is well referenced throughout and includes four pages of illustrations. It is enhanced by appendixes covering *C. melo* and *C. sativus*, a DELTA

Character List, and a numerical list of taxa. In addition, two indexes cover the exsiccatae and scientific names. The experienced botanist should find this book a valuable source in the study of *Cucumis*, but it is not for neophytes unless they are well versed in botanical terms.—**Patricia S. Wilson**

Dictionaries and Encyclopedias

1639. Harborne, Jeffrey B., and Herbert Baxter, eds. **Phytochemical Dictionary: A Handbook of Bioactive Compounds from Plants.** Bristol, Pa., Taylor & Francis, 1993. 791p. index. $325.00. ISBN 0-85066-736-4.

There are thousands of natural organic compounds in plants. A pharmacist, nutritionist, chemist, biologist, or phytochemist may have the common or systematic name but may want to know more about the compound. This work provides that data on 2,793 compounds. Information is given on the chemical structure of the compound, the class to which it belongs, in what plant genus and species it is found, biological activity, commercial use, the molecular formula, and molecular weight. For example, Taxol B, recently in the news as a treatment for cancer, is listed in this dictionary under its trivial or systematic name of Cephalomannine. The chemical structure, formula, and weight are given as well as the information that it is "found in all parts of the yew tree, *Taxus baccata* (Taxaceae)," that it has "antileukaemic and antitumour activities," and that it "is cytotoxic in cell culture experiments."

The work is arranged under the major groups of compounds: carbohydrates and lipids, nitrogen-containing compounds (excluding alkaloids), alkaloids, phenolics, and terpenoids. Within these groups a general introduction is given, followed by chapters on subgroups, such as amino acids, amines, glucosinolates, and proteins and peptides under the nitrogen-containing compounds. References to the literature are provided for the introduction to the group but not for the individual compounds. The reader is referred to other publications for these references.

The index contains only the names of the compounds, with *see* references from their synonyms and *see under* references from similar compounds. It does not index the information in the text, such as a heading for "antileukaemic activity" or "sedative"; nor does it have headings for the various plant species from which these compounds are derived. Other publications will need to be consulted for this information. The *Dictionary of Plants Containing Secondary Metabolites* by J. S. Glasby (Taylor & Francis, 1991) can be used to find a plant species name and its organic compounds; then the *Phytochemical Dictionary* can be consulted for further information on the compounds.

This is a valuable source for information on higher plant compounds from primary and secondary metabolisms. The only other up-to-date work on this topic is the 10-volume German set *Chemotaxonomie der Pflanzen* by Robert Hegnauer (Birkhauser, 1962-1992), which is arranged by plant family. *Phytochemical Dictionary* is recommended for academic, special, and large public libraries.—**Diane B. Rhodes**

1640. Neal, Bill. **Gardener's Latin: A Lexicon.** New York, Algonquin Books/Workman Publishing, 1992. 136p. illus. $14.95. QK9.N42. 581'.014. LC 92-2652. ISBN 0-945575-94-7.

This slim little book lists common Latin species names (but not generic names) for a number of garden plants, along with their English translations. This information can be useful, because sometimes the species name provides information about the appearance, hardiness, or growth patterns of the plant. One such example is the word *palustris*, which means marsh-loving. In other cases the names are simply quaint or charming. The author also provides a number of marginal notes about particularly interesting herbal uses, stories, and poetry about garden plants. The note about the name *isabellinus* (meaning dirty yellow) is a good example: The term comes from the story that the Archduchess Isabella did not change or wash her underwear for three years! As well as the notes, there are also a number of attractive woodcuts of various plants.

The book is really designed for the curious gardening enthusiast, not for the serious student of botany. It is attractive and informative, although not an essential reference. Libraries with large populations of gardeners might find it useful, because it does provide information that is otherwise difficult for the general public to obtain.—**Diane Schmidt**

1641. Stearn, William T. **Botanical Latin: History, Grammar, Syntax, Terminology and Vocabulary.** 4th ed. North Pomfret, Vt., David & Charles/Trafalgar Square, 1992. 546p. illus. index. $45.00. ISBN 0-7153-0052-2.

Botanical Latin is the standard guide to the vocabulary and grammatical conventions used in describing plants in the botanical literature. Botanists and other scientists use this form of Latin to compose and read the Latin portions of their literature, but horticulturists and gardeners must also grapple with the Latin (and Greek) derivations of the official names of plants. The latter group will find the vocabulary portion of *Botanical Latin* most useful, although other books exist to target their needs (e.g., Bill Neal's *Gardener's Latin* [Workman Publishing, 1992]).

The format of this edition has not changed greatly from the previous one (1983) except in "minor emendations" to the text and bibliographies, a larger format, and the addition of 400 entries to the vocabulary. Major sections cover grammar, specialized terminology, Greek words, symbols, and examples of full botanical descriptions with English translations. Stearns writes in a wonderfully clear and erudite style, but due to its technical approach, this book is best suited to specialized and large comprehensive collections. [R: LJ, 15 Mar 93, p. 74]—**Beth Clewis**

1642. Stearn, William T. **Stearn's Dictionary of Plant Names for Gardeners: A Handbook on the Origin and Meaning of the Botanical Names of Some Cultivated Plants.** London, Cassell; distr., New York, Sterling Publishing, 1993. 363p. $29.95. ISBN 0-304-34149-5.

To many gardeners, the scientific names of plants may as well be written in Greek (of course, many are, or are written in Latin). This welcome volume (a revision of the author's earlier *Gardener's Dictionary of Plant Names* [1972]) lists some 6,000 Greek and Latin words commonly encountered as generic and specific names of cultivated plants. Each entry includes indications for pronunciation and a short summary of the meaning of the name in English. In the case of generic names, their affinity to plant family is also indicated. In truth, the volume covers far more than 6,000 plants, as the same specific name, or close variants, may recur in association with different generic names.

The work is a distinct improvement over a Latin-Greek dictionary, as it also includes generic and specific names derived from the names of historical figures, together with thumbnail biographies. The author is perhaps the world authority on the subject of botanical names, and the work has a resulting scholarly air, but this is leavened by tidbits of humorous natural and human history. As a result, the volume is almost readable by itself and not just a reference book.

The basic nature of the work is complemented by an introduction to the logic behind plant naming, a brief bibliography, and a dictionary of vernacular names that provides English and scientific names for some 3,000 plants. The latter is introduced by a wonderful (and all-too-brief) discussion of the origin of some English common names of interest. Recommended for almost any collection used by enthusiastic gardeners and plant lovers. [R: LJ, 1 Sept 93, p. 177]—**Bruce H. Tiffney**

Handbooks and Yearbooks

1643. **Flora of North America North of Mexico.** Edited by Flora of North America Editorial Committee. New York, Oxford University Press, 1993. 2v. illus. maps. index. $75.00/v. QK110.F55. 581.97. LC 92-30459. ISBN 0-19-505713-9(v.1); 0-19-508242-7(v.2).

These are the first 2 volumes of a projected 14-volume set detailing the species of pteridophytes, gymnosperms, and angiosperms of North America from the Mexican border to the Canadian Arctic and Greenland. As befits such a massive undertaking, it is a team effort, with individual experts treating each of the families and genera. The work is introduced by 15 essays in the first volume that cover the physical environment of North America, the evolution of its recent flora, modern vegetation types and phytogeography, and the statistics and premises of the taxonomic treatment. While of varying quality and comprehensiveness, all of these essays are authoritative and will probably become standard references.

The second volume is the first of the systematic series and covers the pteridophytes and gymnosperms. Keys lead one to families within each group. Each family is introduced by a brief summary followed by a key to genera. Genera are similarly introduced, followed by a key to species. Species descriptions are complete, with references to important characters, phenological data, habitat, pertinent literature, important and unresolved problems, and possible rare or endangered status, among other information. Species descriptions are accompanied by a distribution map. Illustrations are provided to genera and some species. The use of experts on each group means that the treatments are current and, therefore, often different from those found in all but the most recent literature (although as policy, no new names will be introduced in this series). For this reason, as well as their comprehensive nature, these volumes will be a basic reference from which much of the next century's investigation of the North American flora will take its departure.

—**Bruce H. Tiffney**

1644. **The Jepson Manual: Higher Plants of California.** James C. Hickman, ed. Berkeley, Calif., University of California Press, 1993. 1400p. illus. maps. index. $65.00. QK149.J56. 581.9794. LC 92-21365. ISBN 0-520-08255-9.

With 173 families, 1,222 genera, and 5,862 species (including more than 1,000 species of naturalized aliens), California offers one of the richest vascular plant floras in North America—not surprising, given its environmental diversity. *The Jepson Manual* is the most recent (supplanting P. A. Munz's *A California Flora* [University of California Press, 1959]) field guide to this flora, although at 1,400 pages one will quickly develop new muscles carrying it in the field. The *Manual* is a cooperative venture, authored by 200 specialists, each treating the families or genera with which they are most familiar. It is also based on a different premise than is Munz's work, as the *Manual* seeks to provide scientifically accurate keys to and descriptions of the flora in a manner accessible to the interested layperson. Thus, the *Manual* features a range of clear, nested keys to families, genera, and species, backed up by an excellent illustrated glossary and making extensive use of vegetative (not just floral) characters. Further, the volume contains numerous illustrations of individual species, including vegetative, floral, and fruiting characters. One mild but surmountable drawback is that, in order to conserve space, abbreviations are used extensively in the descriptions of characters. Similarly, distribution maps are absent, and distributions are conveyed by a series of key letters, tied to a detailed map. Almost 60 pages of introductory material provide historical background on the *Manual*, its use, the evolution of the California flora and its climates, and phytogeography. The families are presented in alphabetical order, perhaps offending purists, but greatly facilitating the *Manual*'s practical use. Individual species descriptions include both data of scientific interest (e.g., chromosome numbers, nomenclatural synonymy) and more general interest (e.g., toxicity, weediness, horticultural value). This is a grand work in several senses. Accurate, comprehensive, and useful, it stands to be *the* California flora for years to come, and to bring pleasure to generations of those fond of California's plants. [R: Choice, Oct 93, p. 316]—**Bruce H. Tiffney**

1645. Leake, Dorothy VanDyke, John Benjamin Leake, and Marcelotte Leake Roeder. **Desert and Mountain Plants of the Southwest.** Norman, Okla., University of Oklahoma Press, 1993. 239p. illus. maps. index. $18.95pa. QK142.L43. 581.979. LC 92-50716. ISBN 0-8061-2489-X.

This book is a compilation of line drawings and descriptions of some of the plants of the mountains and deserts of the southwestern United States, especially in the Sonoran Desert of Arizona. The list of plants covered is incomplete, but the authors acknowledge this in their introductory statements and suggest alternative sources for more complete coverage. Although the work is useful for plant identification, this is not the authors' sole intent. Rather, they planned the book for readers with a love of plants who enjoy learning not only the names and physical characteristics of plants but also folklore and other items of general interest.

The book treats a range of plant life, from club mosses and ferns to trees. One exception is the large grass family. Text and drawings are organized by 65 plant families, each referenced in the table of contents. The book begins with a guide to plant families that arranges the families into 15 groups generally based upon reproductive morphology. Families are then represented by one to several species, with text consisting of common and scientific names, a line drawing of all or part of the plant, and a description containing clues to identification and general information. A glossary of technical terms and a section of illustrated plant characteristics are included, thereby increasing the usefulness of the book for a lay audience. A bibliography contains suggested sources for further reading. Finally, an index of families and species with both common and scientific names assists quick reference. The book is recommended to those wishing to learn more about U.S. southwestern plant life, provided they do not expect a complete, detailed guide to identification.—**Michael G. Messina**

1646. Rohwer, Jens G. **Lauraceae: Nectandra.** New York, New York Botanical Garden, 1993. 332p. illus. maps. index. (Flora Neotropica, 60). $43.50pa. QK205.F58. 581.98'012. LC 85-647083. ISBN 0-89327-373-2.

This is a professional botanical monograph in the ongoing series describing the flora of the New World tropics (between the tropics of Cancer and Capricorn). This particular volume concerns the genus Nectandra in the family Lauraceae. The introduction provides data on various aspects of the genus, including overall morphology, anatomy, ecology, and biogeography. This is followed by a key to the 114 species recognized in this treatment. Each species description includes a detailed diagnosis and a description of its distribution, ecology, local names, and local uses. Each description is terminated by a discussion of how this species may be distinguished from others in the genus. Several descriptions are accompanied by line drawings of salient characters or distribution maps. The work ends with a brief bibliography and indexes to dried specimens and local and scientific names. This highly technical work will be of greatest interest to collections focused on systematic botany.—**Bruce H. Tiffney**

1647. Whistler, W. Arthur. **Flowers of the Pacific Island Seashore: A Guide to the Littoral Plants....** Honolulu, Isle Botanica; distr., Honolulu, University of Hawaii Press, 1992. 154p. illus. $18.95. ISBN 0-8248-1528-9.

This beautifully illustrated little book is a guide to the common flowering plants of the Polynesian seashore, although a large number of the species also occur in Micronesia and Melanesia. The introduction describes the different types of islands and their seashore habitats, and includes a geographical checklist of the species covered. The heart of the book is given to single-page descriptions of 120 species. These are alphabetically listed within five habit groups: trees, shrubs, herbs, vines, and grasses and sedges. Each description includes the genus, species and family names, a summary of native vernacular names, a brief technical description, and a brief summary of distribution and economic and cultural importance. Each species is illustrated with a superb close-up photograph of foliage, flowers, and often fruit. The book ends with a glossary, a brief bibliography, and indexes to common and scientific names.

There are no keys, but the excellent photographs and small number of species in each habit category make "picture-matching" identification relatively easy, although pictures of the overall plant (not just close-ups) would be useful in many cases. The hardcover weight may discourage casual users from carrying it to the field, but the printed scale on the cover is welcome. While the book is excellent for amateurs, professional botanists might have wished for more detailed treatment of each species. Perhaps a second edition could be larger.—**Bruce H. Tiffney**

Indexes

1648. **Australian Plant Name Index.** By Arthur D. Chapman. Canberra, Austral., AGPS Press; distr., Portland, Oreg., ISBS, c1991, 1992. 4v. $195.00pa./set. 016.581994. ISBN 0-685-53180-5.

What's in a name? One of the most important concerns of the professional botanist is to make certain that one name is applied to one, and only one, group of biological organisms, such as a species. However, while species are unique, human endeavor is often imprecise, and several names may be applied by different workers to one species, or further study may reveal that what a worker has called one species is really two or more. The possibilities for confusion are immense, and thus it is no surprise that plant systematists have tried to establish standardized rules by which names are applied and changed, and to publish standardized compendiums of names. Of these, the most important and famous is the ongoing, multivolume *Index Kewensis Plantarum Phanerogamarum* (Oxford University Press, 1895-).

The *Australian Plant Name Index* is, in a sense, a subset of the *Index Kewensis* concerned specifically with the names of plants of Australia and its offshore islands. The work provides an alphabetical list of all published names of taxa at and below the generic level of angiosperms, gymnosperms, ferns, and lycopods found in Australia. Each entry provides the name of the author of the taxon, the place it was published, and the family to which it belongs. Individual entries may have additional information, including the location of the type specimen, secondary literature references of import, base names, and comments. Much to the credit of Chapman, the introduction indicates that original references, rather than secondary sources, were consulted in assembling these volumes, eliminating the perpetuation of older errors.

This reference will be indispensable to any research library concerned with Australian flora. It will, however, enthrall only the professional plant systematist!—**Bruce H. Tiffney**

Flowering Plants

1649. Arends, J. C. **Studies in Begoniaceae IV: Biosystematics of *Begonia Squamulosa*| Hook.f. and Affiliated Species in Section *Tetraphila* A.DC.** Wageningen, the Netherlands, Wageningen Agricultural University; distr., Lanham, Md., UNIPUB, 1992. 222p. illus. index. (Wageningen Agricultural University Papers, 91-6). $63.00. ISBN 90-6754-211-3.

There are more than 900 species (and 10,000 horticultural varieties) in the genus *Begonia* of common houseplant fame. This book is concerned with six related species within the genus and is a testament to the level of detail necessary to develop a reasonable understanding of living plants. Three chapters introduce the species in question and the materials used. These are followed by six chapters on the morphological and cytological characters of the species and a summary of the findings. A short tenth chapter presents a key to the species and technical descriptions. References and an index to infraspecific names conclude the book. The illustrations include both photographs and line drawings to show morphological and cytological features.

This botanical monograph is of excellent quality. However, it will likely have limited appeal beyond professional botanists in light of its technical (although clearly written) presentation and its limited scope.
—**Bruce H. Tiffney**

1650. Clough, Katherine. **Wildflowers of Prince Edward Island.** Charlottetown, P.E.I., Ragweed Press, 1992. 150p. illus. index. (Island Pathways). $12.95 spiralbound. 582.13'09717. ISBN 0-921556-27-6.

Prince Edward Island, off the eastern coast of Canada, is the smallest and most densely populated Canadian province. This new wildflower guide is meant for the tourist or resident hiker. It is a simple-to-use, concise guide to 90 (out of approximately 1,000) of the most common, showiest wildflowers likely to be encountered on the island. Entries are arranged by color and accompanied by small color photographs of uneven quality. The book is a convenient pocket size. All descriptions are readable and nontechnical and include information on flowering season and habitat. Most of Prince Edward Island has been cultivated at one time or another, so many of the most common species are introduced aliens; few unique species remain. All species pictured in this book also occur on the mainland.—**Carol L. Noll**

1651. Coffey, Timothy. **The History and Folklore of North American Wildflowers.** New York, Facts on File, 1993. 356p. illus. index. $40.00. QK110.C56. 582.13'097. LC 92-18392. ISBN 0-8160-2624-6.

The history and folklore of the uses (medical, nutritional, and cosmetic) of more than 700 familiar wildflowers, mainly from English-speaking North America, are treated in this compilation. Entries have been chosen from several popular guides to North American wildflowers and are arranged in familial order. Each entry contains the common, scientific, and vernacular names of the wildflower, with a paragraph or two describing the history and folklore connected with the plant. The text consists largely of quotations from older medical, nature, and travel writers. Emphasis is on historical uses of the plants rather than modern pharmacological or commercial derivatives. Approximately half of the entries are illustrated by line drawings taken from old engravings. A 285-item bibliography and indexes of the names of persons mentioned and of plant names are included.

This is a unique compilation, as claimed in the foreword, but it is an eclectic work, at the crossroads of folklore, ethnography, economic botany, and history, that needs to be used in conjunction with titles such as *Dictionary of Useful Plants* (see ARBA 76, entry 1373). The bibliography is not as extensive as *A Bibliography on Herbs, Herbal Medicine, "Natural" Foods, and Unconventional Medical Treatment* (see ARBA 83, entry 1463). There are a few minor errors in the text (e.g., the Battle of Culloden Moor was fought in 1746, not 1726). While not of major reference value, this book is enjoyable to browse, full of interesting historical and folkloric tidbits, and worthy of library purchase on those accounts. [R: Choice, Dec 93, pp. 629-30; LJ, Aug 93, p. 90; RBB, 1 Nov 93, p. 566; RQ, Winter 93, p. 287]

—Jonathan F. Husband

1652. Cullen, J., ed. **The Orchid Book: A Guide to the Identification of Cultivated Orchid Species.** New York, Cambridge University Press, 1992. 529p. illus. index. $39.95. SB409.065. 635.9'3415. LC 91-39794. ISBN 0-521-41856-9.

This work is intended to provide a botanically correct, convenient aid to identifying orchid species in general cultivation. The main part of the text is an updated revision and rearrangement of the section on the family Orchidaceae in the second volume of *The European Garden Flora* (Cambridge University Press, 1984). It does not claim to provide a complete description of the structure and biology of the family as a whole, but it does supply a bibliography for further research. An introductory section has a key to genera and a description of the parts of the plant structure important for classification. The main section gives information about individual genera and species; about 900 species are covered. Entries are arranged in systematic order rather than alphabetically by genus and species, but an index provides alphabetical access. General information on each genus includes some cultivation information and bibliographical references.

This is not a book for those who seek beautiful orchid illustrations. Color photographs are given for only 16 species; there are black-and-white drawings of particular parts of flowers to aid in identification of some species. The text does give bibliographical citations to sources in which published illustrations of certain species may be found.

A library with a limited botanical collection might prefer a more comprehensive, lavishly illustrated volume, such as *The Manual of Cultivated Orchid Species* (MIT Press, 1981). This is nonetheless a well-done and useful book for any library serving hobbyists or those interested in botany. [R: Choice, July/Aug 93, p. 1795]—**Marit S. MacArthur**

1653. Davies, Dilys. **Alliums: The Ornamental Onions.** Portland, Oreg., Timber Press, 1992. 168p. illus. maps. index. $29.95; $22.95pa. ISBN 0-88192-224-2; 0-88192-241-2pa.

This slim volume is a horticultural appreciation of the genus *Allium*, familiar to most as the source of onion, garlic, chives, leeks, and several other flavorful herbs central to culinary satisfaction. However, the genus stretches far beyond these commonly known pot herbs to embrace some 700 species, many of which please the gardener's eye rather than the palate.

The book commences with an account of *Allium* in history and passes to chapters on recipes, the classification of *Allium*, its geographical distribution, and its cultivation (covering propagation, pests, and siting of various species in the garden). Most of the book is given to an alphabetical listing of some 150 species. Each entry usually includes a description of the flowering and vegetative aspects, the distribution, some ecological or phenological data, and brief hints as to horticulture. Many entries are accompanied by a drawing or photograph. Indexes to common and scientific names, a glossary, hardiness maps, and a tiny bibliography complete the work.

The book is very much for horticulturists; it has some shortcomings for professional botanists. For example, each species entry is accompanied by a list of further references, but nowhere in the book are these references properly cited in full detail. Also, coverage is not complete, and one can detect a European focus in the taxa covered and the methods of their cultivation, although species throughout the world are described. These nitpicking observations aside, this work is delightfully written and quite informative.

—**Bruce H. Tiffney**

1654. Fell, Derek. **The Encyclopedia of Flowers.** New York, Smithmark, 1992. 208p. illus. index. $19.98. ISBN 0-8317-2816-7.

This book of plants, divided into annuals, perennials, bulbs, shrubs, and small trees, is selective, Fell having chosen those plants that he feels make the most impact in a garden. Criteria for inclusion included plant availability and flowering effect, with hardy, easy-to-care-for varieties given priority over more challenging and tender ones. Listed by botanical name, each entry provides common name, flower characteristics, leaves, habit, culture, season of bloom, hardiness, and uses. Following this information is a short commentary of varying information about each plant. A map of hardiness zones in the United States is given at the back of the book, along with an index.

The author, a renowned photographer of flowers, has included a photograph of each specimen with its description. The pictures are lovely, but some are taken at such a distance that the detail of the flower is lost. Perhaps Fell felt that showing how these plants looked en masse was more important. Other than this minor complaint, the book should help gardeners feel more secure in their selection of plants. [R: BL, 1 Mar 93, p. 1146]—**Jo Anne H. Ricca**

1655. Kirkpatrick, Zoe Merriman. **Wildflowers of the Western Plains: A Field Guide.** Austin, Tex., University of Texas Press, 1992. 240p. illus. index. $29.95; $14.95pa. QK135.K57. 582.13'0978. LC 91-3232. ISBN 0-292-79061-9; 0-292-79062-7pa.

This is not really a wildflower guide in the sense of a book that easily enables the identification of unknown flowers. Rather, it is a compendium of excellent photographs of wild flowers (far better than the norm in standard wildflower guides), coupled with occasionally interesting facts about their ecology and history, forming a creation of beauty and some insight. Coverage includes plants with attractive flowers that grow on the High Plains to the east of the Rocky Mountains, from the western Dakotas and Nebraska south to the panhandle of Texas and eastern Colorado and New Mexico. Entries are alphabetical by family, then by genus and species within family. Each species description includes a detailed explanation of the morphology of the plant, its distribution, and a section of remarks on its natural and human history. The latter occasionally includes interesting information on Native American use of the plant. Each entry is accompanied by at least one color photograph.

There is no real guide or key to identification. While there is a short description of the characters of important families, this will not help the uninitiated identify an unknown flower. The book may be used for identification only by laborious "picture-matching." Fortunately, the quality of the photographs makes this an easier job than in many "field guides," but even an excellent picture cannot show all the characters needed in all cases for identification.—**Bruce H. Tiffney**

1656. McQueen, Jim, and Barbara McQueen. **Miniature Orchids.** Portland, Oreg., Timber Press, 1992. 192p. illus. index. $24.95pa. ISBN 0-88192-265-X.

Miniature versions of everyday things fascinate many people. A book on miniature versions of exquisite, living, flowering plants should be even more intriguing. This work can be used as a catalog of beautiful flowers, a botanical guide to miniature orchid species, or a manual on how to cultivate these plants, many of which can be successfully grown in an apartment.

Approximately 300 species are described, each with a small but attractive color photograph of its flowers. The McQueens' writing style is informal and not excessively technical but still conveys a good deal of information. Under each species are given the person who first described it, its natural geographical range and habitat, a detailed description of plant and flowers, and advice on how best to cultivate it. There are also chapters on the characteristics of the orchid family, orchids in cultivation, and plant names and botanical Latin, as well as a glossary of botanical terms and an index.

As the book points out, miniature orchid species are not always easy to obtain. It would have been helpful if the McQueens had included names and addresses of orchid nurseries so the reader would at least have a place to start. That problem aside, this is an attractive little book on an area of botany not well covered elsewhere. Recommended for any library that includes books on botany or gardening.
—**Marit S. MacArthur**

1657. **Plants and Flowers of Great Britain and [Northern] Europe.** Hampshire, England, Mosaik Books; distr., Cincinnati, Ohio, Seven Hills Book, 1993. 264p. illus. index. $29.95. ISBN 3-576-80003-4.

This book is similar in structure and content to field guides such as *New Generation Guide to the Wild Flowers of Britain and Northern Europe* (see ARBA 88, entry 1518), but it differs in the quality and quantity of its color photographs. Introductory chapters review plant structure, emphasizing features used in identification; vegetation zones; and keys to the plants depicted in the descriptive sections, which are arranged by flower color. Each page contains entries for six plants, including for each a photograph, botanical and common names, appearance of leaves, inflorescence, flowers, fruits, habitat, and time of bloom. Facing pages provide close-up photographs of flowers and leaves against a black background for clarity. A more compact format would enhance the value of this book as a field guide, but it remains a useful tool for those wishing to familiarize themselves with the wildflowers of Great Britain and Northern Europe.—**Beth Clewis**

1658. Pridgeon, Alec, ed. **The Illustrated Encyclopedia of Orchids.** Portland, Oreg., Timber Press, 1992. 304p. illus. index. $39.95. ISBN 0-88192-267-6.

This large, beautiful book lists and provides color illustrations for more than 1,100 species of orchids. The entries in its alphabetical listing are intended to appeal to both the knowledgeable enthusiast and the beginner; thus, although it provides brief but reasonably detailed technical information, such as taxonomic authority, geographical distribution, description, and cultivation requirements, it also explains pronunciation and gives interesting etymological explanations for the Greek and Latin botanical names. There are a glossary of botanical terms, an index, and a bibliography for further reading. A readable prefatory section describes the orchid family and the interesting stratagems its members have developed to grow and achieve pollination in sometimes inhospitable conditions. There are also a section on hybridization, general cultural information, and an explanation of why many orchid species are endangered and what the reader can do to help.

This work is a successful compromise between the technical and the popular. Libraries wanting a more detailed guide to species identification might prefer the *Manual of Cultivated Orchid Species* by Helmut Bechtel, Phillip Cribb, and Edmund Launert (MIT Press, 1981). That work, however, does not provide illustrations for all species described and is perhaps too technical for many readers. This book is highly recommended for its beautiful photographs and readable, accessible information; it should be a popular addition to any general or botanical collection. [R: BL, June 93, p. 1759; Choice, July/Aug 93, p. 1794]—**Marit S. MacArthur**

1659. Roland, Albert E., and A. Randall Olson. **Spring Wildflowers.** Halifax, N.S., Nimbus Publishing and Nova Scotia Museum; distr., Post Mills, Vt., Chelsea Green, 1993. 138p. illus. index. (Field Guide Series). $9.95pa. 582.13'09716. ISBN 1-55109-050-3.

Spring in Atlantic Canada and Upper New England is a most bountiful and welcome season. This pocket-sized guide to herbaceous wildflowers, shrubs, and trees of Nova Scotia is a simple and easy-to-use handbook for the beginning wildflower enthusiast. Entries are arranged by flowering time (early, mid-, or late spring), then by plant type (woody or nonwoody). The approximately 250 entries are short, nontechnical, and accompanied by pen-and-ink drawings. The text, although brief, contains interesting details of plant ecology and history. There is an adequate index and very good introductory material, including a glossary of botanical terms.—**Carol L. Noll**

1660. Taylor, Ronald J. **Sagebrush Country: A Wildflower Sanctuary.** Missoula, Mont., Mountain Press, 1992. 211p. illus. index. $12.00pa. QK141.T39. 582.13'0979. LC 92-13520. ISBN 0-87842-280-3.

The cold deserts of North America often appear desolate, but in the right season the "sagebrush country," extending from eastern Washington and northeastern California to western Wyoming and northwestern Colorado, can be as beautiful as any garden. Several wildflower books on western North America include coverage of this area, but this volume offers an ecologically based guide specifically to the herbaceous and shrubby wildflowers of this underappreciated portion of North America. Those seeking more professional coverage of this area would have to consult state floras where available, or the incomplete but growing *Intermountain Flora* (New York Botanical Garden, 3 volumes published).

The introduction summarizes the basics of sagebrush community ecology. Much of the work is devoted to descriptions of individual wildflowers, organized alphabetically by family and accompanied by excellent color photographs that often illustrate both flower morphology and plant habit. The coverage is not exhaustive but does touch on the most frequently observed species. Individual descriptions include interesting and informative bits of natural history. Users can identify unknowns either by picture-matching or by using the dichotomous key to plant families at the end of the work. This requires some familiarity with flower morphology, but a good glossary and accompanying illustrations make this relatively simple. Indexes to scientific and common names and a list of plants common in various ecological zones round out the work. The sole fault of the work is that the pictures lack a scale and that the accompanying descriptions cite plant size in the most vague terms (e.g., "small," "large"). This excellent, simple guide belongs in the field, not on the library shelf, but it would be a particularly fine addition to libraries in the northern Great Basin.—**Bruce H. Tiffney**

1661. Tiner, Ralph W. **Field Guide to Coastal Wetland Plants of the Southeastern United States.** Amherst, Mass., University of Massachusetts Press, 1993. 328p. illus. maps. index. $50.00; $17.95pa. QK125.T55. 582.0975. LC 92-36526. ISBN 0-87023-832-9; 0-87023-833-7pa.

Describing and illustrating more than 250 species of southeastern coastal wetland plants, with references to 200 more, this is an easy-to-use, authoritative field guide for amateurs and specialists. It is a companion volume to the author's well-received *A Field Guide to Coastal Wetland Plants of the Northeastern United States* (see ARBA 88, entry 1515), which covers wetland plants from Maine to Maryland. This new guide covers Virginia through Florida and west through Texas. It is arranged in four sections: an overview of the present state of coastal wetland ecology, keys to the identification of coastal wetland and aquatic plants, descriptions and black-and-white illustrations of the plants, and maps and lists of coastal wetlands found in each state. Seven easy-to-use keys identify the aquatic plants, emergent plants, shrubs, trees, and vines; there is also an illustrated key to flowering herbs. The keys refer to page numbers in the text where a full description of that plant or group of plants may be found.

The majority of the book includes the plant descriptions and illustrations. They are arranged under plants of tidal fresh coastal waters, plants of salt and brackish coastal wetlands, and plants of tidal fresh coastal wetlands. Two plant descriptions are found on each page, with corresponding black-and-white illustrations on the facing page. Each entry includes the common and scientific names, family, a description, flowering period, fruiting period, habitat, range and list of similar species, and wetland indicator status. The final section lists and shows on a map the coastal wetlands of each state in the southeast. A list of references to consult for further reading, a glossary of terms used in the keys and descriptions, and an index to common and scientific names complete this thorough work.

For those libraries that already own Tiner's guide to wetland plants of the northeast, this guide is essential to complete the coverage for the entire east coast. (For those who may want a more general guide in one volume, *The Smithsonian Guide to Seaside Plants of the Gulf and Atlantic Coasts* [see ARBA 88, entry 1513] is a good choice that includes full-color photographs of the plants.) Highly recommended for academic, large public, and botanical libraries.—**Diane B. Rhodes**

Fungi

1662. Horn, Bruce, Richard Kay, and Dean Abel. **A Guide to Kansas Mushrooms.** Lawrence, Kans., University Press of Kansas, 1993. 297p. illus. index. (Kansas Nature Guides). $29.95; $19.95pa. QK617.H67. 589.2'22'09781. LC 92-30996. ISBN 0-7006-0570-3; 0-7006-0571-1pa.

This is a gem of a mushroom guide for a state that many might think of as a mycological desert. In actuality, Kansas is home to at least 750 species of mushrooms. They are particularly abundant in the wetter northeastern corner of the state. Because of Kansas's central location, the ranges of northern, southern, eastern, and western North American species overlap there. Although this guide pictures and describes only a portion (150 species) of this mushroom bounty, all of the most common, showiest, or most edible species are here.

The introductory material in this guidebook is the best yet in a regional guide. In addition to the usual material on mushroom habitat, nomenclature, life cycles, and field identification, all written in enjoyable and even humorous nontechnical language, there is an outstanding section on mushroom photography. The guide uses straightforward, simple keys; clear, representative color photographs; and nontechnical descriptive text. As the authors admit, to be sure of identifying an unknown specimen, it is advisable to have access to four or five mushroom guides, but for residents of Kansas and surrounding states, this book will surely be a good first source. [R: Choice, Nov 93, p. 482]—**Carol L. Noll**

Grasses and Weeds

1663. Davis, Linda W. **Weed Seeds of the Great Plains: A Handbook for Identification.** Lawrence, Kans., University Press of Kansas, 1993. 145p. illus. index. ([Kansas] Agricultural Experiment Station Contribution, no.92-125). $25.00. SB612.G73D38. 632'.58'0978. LC 93-15615. ISBN 0-7006-0651-3.

This illustrated handbook provides silhouettes and color photographs of 280 species of weedy plants growing in crops, rangelands, and lawns, and along roadsides of the Great Plains. From the opening map of the geographical region covered, the cited references, and finding lists spread over 22 groups, all data is made readily accessible to county agents, farmers, and interested amateurs. The heart of the book includes seed descriptions: species number (according to Cronquist's sequence of families), scientific names and authority, common name, and the unit of dispersal (i.e., true seed or fruit). The first paragraph of the description concerns shape and structure, such as outline shape, cross-section shape, and three-dimensional form. The second paragraph covers surface texture, sheen, and color. The third describes size. Lastly comes distribution. The middle of the book includes 280 superb color plates of 3 to 8 seeds per plate. Both a glossary and an illustrated glossary precede the index, which includes common and scientific names.

Only one typographical error was discovered. However, an important oversight concerns the failure to include the warning "poisonous," unless that word is part of the common name. Referring back to the *Flora of the Great Plains* (see ARBA 88, entry 1519) reveals ample warnings (e.g., *Solanum carolinense* Carolina horse-nettle: "There is one report of a child having died from eating the berries"). Despite this omission, this beautiful book is recommended to undergraduate, graduate, and public libraries.

—Helen M. Barber

1664. Hatch, Stephen L., and Jennifer Pluhar. **Texas Range Plants.** College Station, Tex., Texas A&M University Press, 1993. 326p. illus. maps. index. (W.L. Moody, Jr., Natural History Series, no.13). $35.00; $14.95pa. QK188.H38. 581.6'09764'09153. LC 92-5073. ISBN 0-89096-538-2; 0-89096-521-8pa.

This very functional book describes 140 grasses, forbs, shrubs, and trees of economic importance on Texas rangelands. Although this is one of a plethora of plant identification books, it fills a unique niche because it offers statewide coverage of a particular ecosystem. The book has been written to be "reader-friendly," as the authors have not assumed a complete botanical background, but instead have provided introductory material on forb, grass, and woody plant morphology and physiology. Line drawings illustrating botanical terms are numerous in this section and will provide any reader with the background needed to use the book. An excellent glossary is included, and the index lists scientific names as well as common names (sometimes several) for each species. A list of useful references is included for readers seeking related or additional information.

Two pages are devoted to each species, including a full-page line drawing of whole plants and plant parts important for field identification. The species narratives contain common and scientific names for species and family; longevity (annual, biennial, or perennial); season of growth (warm or cool); origin (native or introduced); economic value; description of floral, vegetative, and growth characteristics; and habitat. Additional information on livestock losses and distinguishing characteristics is included where available. Finally, several sentences describe the species in common terms and provide interesting folklore. The book should be useful for readers working in a variety of disciplines and with a range of educational backgrounds, from high school student to research scientist. [R: Choice, Oct 93, p. 316]

—Michael G. Messina

1665. Lonard, Robert I. **Guide to Grasses of the Lower Rio Grande Valley, Texas.** Edinburg, Tex., University of Texas-Pan American Press, 1993. 240p. illus. index. $18.95pa. QK495.G74L6. ISBN 0-938738-08-9.

This is a specialized guide to the more than 183 species of native and introduced grasses found in the Lower Rio Grande Valley, Texas. This geographical area also includes the adjoining northeastern section of Mexico. Keys to identification and illustrated descriptions of each species are included. Although keying out grasses may often be difficult, the dichotomous keys included here are clear and lead the researcher through successive choices until the plant is identified. The author includes introductory information on grass plant identification as well as a glossary of terms used in the keys to make the keying out process more successful. Once the plant has been tentatively identified in the key, a page number to the description is provided where more positive identification can be made. The description is usually a page in length and includes the scientific name, the author of the name, the common name in English or Spanish, and a description of the vegetative and reproductive structures of the plant. A general flowering period is provided as well as the geographical area where the plant is usually found and an indication of whether it is native to the area or introduced. Each description includes a small, numbered, black-and-white illustration of the plant. The number refers the reader to a more detailed, artistic drawing found at the end of the text.

Lonard has published other books on plants of this region, including *Woody Plants of the Lower Rio Grande Valley, Texas* (Texas Memorial Museum, University of Texas, Austin, 1991). His knowledge of plants and grasses of this area is evident in this work, which is primarily for students, specialists, and professionals in botany, although a dedicated amateur may also be able to use the book successfully. Recommended for botanical libraries as well as libraries in colleges or universities with specialties in the botanical sciences.—**Diane B. Rhodes**

Medicinal and Edible Plants

1666. Ody, Penelope. **The Complete Medicinal Herbal.** New York, Dorling Kindersley, 1993. 192p. illus. index. $29.95. RM666.H33038. 615'.321. LC 92-53451. ISBN 1-56458-187-X.

"More misinformation regarding the efficacy of herbs is currently being placed before consumers than at any previous time, including the turn-of-the-century heyday of patent medicines." This is a quotation from *The New Honest Herbal* by Varro E. Tyler (George F. Strickland, 1987). Once again, a beautifully photographed and illustrated book guaranteed to entice many readers is perpetuating information based upon the writings of authors who are no longer considered authorities or whose opinions are without benefit of modern research.

A brief introduction to the origins of Western herbalism challenges readers to look at these alternative systems as solutions to health care that are just as valid now as they were thousands of years ago. Approximately half of the book is a representative selection of more than 120 herbs with medicinal properties; each is described in detail as to parts used, actions, active ingredients, and "character" (e.g., hot, cold, dry, sweet, sour), based on traditional Western, Ayurvedic (classical Indian), or Chinese classifications. A section on herbal remedies includes instructions on preparing medications that Ody claims can be safely used at home as alternatives to over-the-counter drugs. Grouped according to body systems, life stages, or actions, the section on home remedies lists a selected number of ailments or complaints, the appropriate herb, its action, use and dosage, and precautions.

The author, a practitioner of herbal medicine, has written a how-to manual with specific recipes and recommended therapeutics but offers little or no evidence to substantiate her claims. Everything is good for practically anything! The bibliography is brief and very selective. In today's litigious society, the numerous warnings, precautions, and disclaimers found throughout the text are required, but readers should be warned that some information in the text contradicts known scientific research (e.g., poke root, Qi energy), and other information is simply based on folklore. Unfortunately, this book will reach its intended audience of herbal enthusiasts and proponents of self-prescription, but one hopes it will do so only through private sales, not library loans. [R: WLB, June 93, p. 120]—**Vicki J. Killion**

1667. Ratsch, Christian. **The Dictionary of Sacred and Magical Plants.** Santa Barbara, Calif., ABC-Clio, 1992. 223p. index. $49.50. ISBN 0-87436-716-6.

Ratsch, a German cultural anthropologist, covers approximately 200 plants (arranged alphabetically by common name) used for magical or psychotropic purposes in cultures around the world (ancient or modern). Additional entries cover the use of plants in making beer, incense, snuff, wine, and witch's ointments. This is an enlarged English-language edition of the *Lexikon der Zauberplanzen aus Ethnologischer Sicht* (1988); references in the text and bibliography cite many European sources.

The translator notes that English lacks an accurate synonym for the German word *Rausch*, which "represents a door, or a vehicle, or a bridge to a realm filled with unknowns—and hence with potential knowledge" (p. 12). The word *inebriation* does not capture this sense of searching for altered states, which the author emphasizes in discussing how each plant has been prepared and used. Each entry also provides the pharmacological components and effects of each plant, if known. Additional features of the book include an introduction to the magical uses of plants, a glossary, and a botanical name index, but no subject index.

Much of this information will be of interest to students of anthropology. This is a difficult book to recommend for public libraries, however, given the perennial search for new experiences by young people. In this reviewer's opinion, the occasional notes on plant toxicity do not offset the constant references to the sexual and mind-altering effects of these plants. Public librarians should therefore be warned of the concerns this book might raise in the minds of parents and other community members. [R: BR, Sept/Oct 93, p. 62; Choice, July/Aug 93, p. 1754; RBB, 1 Feb 93, p. 1001; RQ, Summer 93, p. 565; SLJ, Feb 93, pp. 123-24]—**Beth Clewis**

Mosses and Lichens

1668. **Indices to the Species of Mosses and Lichens Described by William Mitten.** Bronx, N.Y., New York Botanical Garden, 1992. 113p. (Memoirs of the New York Botanical Garden, v.68). $20.25pa. QK1.N525. 581. LC 92-20789. ISBN 0-89327-378-3.

Barbara M. Thiers (Cryptogamic Herbarium, New York Botanical Garden) has coordinated these helpful indexes of 1,000-plus species of bryophytes described by William Mitten between 1851 and 1903. This pharmaceutical chemist, who lived in Hurstpierpoint, near Brighton, in Sussex, England, taught himself bryology so successfully that specimens sent to Kew were forwarded to Mitten for sorting and naming. By looking beyond political boundaries to observe the same taxa occurring throughout broad ranges, Mitten's species have not been set aside as synonyms, and his publications remain useful to modern Himalayan and northern and central Andean bryologists. This volume was prepared as a curatorial tool for the New York Botanical Garden staff (the Garden owns Mitten's herbarium) and to assist bryologists consulting Mitten types.

A 72-item section of literature in which new species of mosses were described by Mitten forms the bibliographic key to which each plant in the six broad indexes refers. Each index to mosses from Africa, Asia, Australasia, the tropics and south temperate America, Europe and North America, and to lichens has been prepared by different specialists. Each entry includes the plant name and citation, locality data, location of specimens, typification, and notes. The six moss and lichen indexes are combined into a final index to bryophyte and lichen names. This meticulously prepared publication will assist taxonomists and researchers working with the William Mitten collection. Highly recommended. **Helen M. Barber**

Trees and Shrubs

1669. Coombes, Allen J. **Trees.** New York, Dorling Kindersley, 1992. 320p. illus. index. (Eyewitness Handbooks). $29.95; $17.95pa. LC 92-52782. ISBN 1-56458-075-X; 1-56458-072-5pa.

Trees is a photograph-based identification guide to more than 500 trees from around the world. The hundreds of photographs are of exceptional quality. Unlike other identification guides, the photographs include not only mature summertime foliage but also flowers, fruit, bark, immature leaves, and autumn colors. The book begins with about 30 pages of information useful for identifying, understanding, and appreciating trees. Included are material taxonomists use for classifying trees, tips on observing and measuring trees, a guide for using this book, and discussion of the various parts of a tree and their functions. A complete and well-illustrated comparison of the leaves, flowers, and fruits of conifers and broadleaves is contained in this section. The book's introductory identification guide is extremely easy to use and is based on leaf type and margin. The guide refers to pages in the remainder of the book so the reader can locate the tree in question. Very technical jargon, which can discourage casual users of other identification guides, is avoided. Readers with little or no previous botanical training can use this handbook after spending only a short time reading the introductory section.

The only shortcoming of this book is its coverage of a limited number of species. Naturally, any book that sets out to include the world's trees but contains descriptions of only about 500 has to exclude all but the most prominent species. However, this does not diminish the book's usefulness to those who appreciate the value of trees. This book should be part of every reference library's collection.

—Michael G. Messina

1670. Godet, Jean-Denis. **Mosaik's Photographic Key to the Trees and Shrubs of Great Britain and Northern Europe: A New System for Identifying Trees by Their Leaves and Needles. [Trees and Shrubs of Great Britain and Northern Europe].** Hampshire, England, Mosaik Books; distr., Cincinnati, Ohio, Seven Hills Book, 1993. 215p. illus. index. $29.95. ISBN 3-576-80004-2.

Some 260 species of trees and shrubs are described and illustrated in this work. All illustrations are color photographs. An introductory chapter provides the botanical terms for leaf shapes. Twenty of the more common trees are given special treatment: For each species the entire tree, leaves, flowers, bark, buds, and wood are shown, and the species is described and discussed, including characteristics of the wood and natural history. A one-page guide describes how the key summaries to the species work. Five illustrated key summaries follow; these are the botanical keys to species, as they allow one to track down a species based on characteristics. The five "keys" that follow are species descriptions with very detailed photographs of leaves and branches. There are a glossary of botanical terms and indexes to common and scientific names.

One of the strong points of this guide is the color photographs, which are excellent. Those of the leaves are so sharp that every vein is shown. The full-page discussions of common trees are also good. In the key summaries, the lettered characteristics by which one tracks down a species should be emphasized with larger type, and smaller type should be used for the species shown, so the nature of the key system would be clearer for the inexperienced reader. Otherwise, this is an excellent tree and shrub guide for Great Britain and Europe.—**John Laurence Kelland**

1671. Jones, David L. **Cycads of the World.** Washington, D.C., Smithsonian Institution Press, 1993. 312p. illus. maps. index. $45.00. LC 93-83068. ISBN 1-56098-220-9.

Cycads are among the most interesting, if unfamiliar, plants in the world. Their origin predates that of the dinosaurs, but today they are relicts, 185 species of living fossils, known to paleontologists and to a limited audience of horticulturalists who appreciate their history and distinctive shapes. In part this is because of the absence of any general introduction to the systematics and horticulture of the group: The last comprehensive treatment was first published in 1919, although there have been some more recent regional summaries. The present volume remedies that situation.

The first 100 pages cover a range of topics, including cycad history, ecology, biogeography, human use, and an extensive section on cultivation that deals with such things as propagation and pests. The remaining 200 pages are given to species descriptions, which are arranged alphabetically by genus, then species. Keys are provided to the genera and to the species in smaller genera but are lacking for large genera. This is unfortunate, and while the descriptions of species are clear, horticulturalists may find it difficult to identify some unknowns. The descriptions are often accompanied by outstanding color photographs that offset the absence of keys to some degree but that are not always diagnostic. The descriptions include much botanical, geographical, and horticultural information.

The photographs and graphics make the book of coffee-table quality, and the text is eminently readable in its own right, inviting the interest of amateurs. However, professional botanists will also find the book of value, as it pulls together a diverse literature and provides information otherwise difficult to obtain. This is not the ultimate cycad book, but it is a welcome delight until the ultimate book is written.

—**Bruce H. Tiffney**

1672. Jorgenson, Lisa. **Grand Trees of America: Our State and Champion Trees.** Niwot, Colo., Roberts Rinehart, 1992. 120p. illus. $8.95pa. LC 91-66677. ISBN 1-879373-15-7.

This book lists the largest individual trees (champion trees) of many species, as well as the official tree species of each of the 50 states. An introduction discusses the history of forests in the United States, with maps of virgin forest coverage of this country at different periods. A chart shows when each of 25 tree species appeared in the fossil record. For each state, the official state tree is named (both common and scientific name are given), described, and illustrated. Facts such as average height and circumference are supplied. Also, the national champion tree (or trees) residing in that state is listed, with circumference, height, and spread data provided. (The tree receives a point score based on these measurements.) An appendix lists species that have no champions and provides a form so readers can nominate champion trees. Instructions are given on how to measure a large tree and nominate it. The book is written for children, but it would also be of interest to adults.

This excellent book fills an unusual niche and fulfills an educational mission for children. It would be a worthy addition to school and public library collections. [R: SBF, Jan-Feb 93, p. 19]

—**John Laurence Kelland**

1673. Martin, Laura C. **The Folklore of Trees and Shrubs.** Chester, Conn., Globe Pequot Press, 1992. 221p. illus. index. $24.95. GR785.M37. 398'.368216. LC 91-42213. ISBN 1-56440-018-2.

This alphabetical compendium, the third of a trilogy from Globe Pequot Press that includes *Wildflower Folklore* (1993) and *Garden Flower Folklore* (1987), describes 100 trees and shrubs, providing the common name, botanical name, and family of each plant. It also gives information on the origin and cultivation of the trees and shrubs. There is a detailed description of the identifying characteristics of the trees, and each listing is accompanied by beautiful and botanically accurate illustrations of the structure of the plant and drawings of the leaves, flowers, and fruit or seed pods.

The remainder of each entry is devoted to the history, symbolism, and medicinal uses of the trees. The information ranges from the etymological roots of the names of the trees to the use of the Kentucky Coffee tree by Native Americans to treat insanity to the fact that the Franklinia, named after Benjamin Franklin, was saved from extinction through cultivation. In some of the entries there are references to the mythical symbolism and superstitions associated with the trees and shrubs. For example, junipers were once planted at home entrances to keep witches away because it was believed that a witch could only pass a juniper after she had counted each of its needles. But greater emphasis is placed on the practical uses and history of the wood and other products of the trees. For instance, tamarack lumber was used for railroad cross-ties, the sap of the sweet gum tree is used to scent gloves in France, and willow bark has been used for centuries as a painkiller. The index lists only scientific names and the most widely used common names; lesser-known names are not included in the index, although they are provided in the full entry.

Overall, this is an interesting, informative work. While it does not go into great depth on the folklore, it is a thorough introduction to the material covered. This is a good reference for general audiences and could be very useful to amateur botanists and students of folklore.—**Tama J. Serfoss**

1674. **Peterson First Guide to Trees.** By George A. Petrides. Boston, Houghton Mifflin, 1993. 128p. illus. index. $4.95pa. QK110.P45. 582.16097. LC 92-36586. ISBN 0-395-65972-8.

Although the Peterson Guide series is the best-known field guide series intended for the amateur naturalist, even these nontechnical, popular books may be difficult for the beginner (or the young student) to use, because they try to be comprehensive and include all species or types in a given area. This new series is designed to meet the need for a simpler introductory series of guides. Its primary focus is on the most common species—in the case of this book, 243 of the many kinds of trees existing in North America.

The entries are arranged in six groups by leaf type and arrangement (e.g., trees having needles and cones, trees having opposite compound leaves). All are accompanied by excellent color drawings of leaves, bark, and fruit or flowers. Descriptions are brief and nontechnical. Even true novices should have no problem using this guide to identify trees in their yards, in parks, and while hiking.—**Carol L. Noll**

NATURAL HISTORY

1675. Dance, S. Peter. **Shells.** New York, Dorling Kindersley, 1992. 256p. illus. index. (Eyewitness Handbooks). $29.95; $17.95pa. QL404.D37. 594'.0471. LC 91-58223. ISBN 1-56458-032-6; 1-56458-060-1pa.

This very attractive and well-designed guide to seashells was written by a shell expert who is the author of several other books about shells. The work serves as an identification guide to more than 500 species of seashells worldwide, with a heavy emphasis on gastropods (e.g., snails, limpets, conchs, cowries, tritons, whelks, cones) and bivalves (e.g., clams, oysters, scallops, cockles). A few representatives of the tusk shells, chitons, and cephalopods are also included.

A useful introduction provides some general information about shells, terminology, identification, and starting a collection. An identification key (by shape) is included for the species covered. The entry for each species includes a color photograph (usually more than one view and with the distinguishing features pointed out), scientific and common names, a brief description, size, habitat and range, region of the world where found, and frequency of occurrence.

Although this volume is by no means comprehensive, most of the shells shown are not rare and are therefore very collectible. Collectors interested only in shells that can be found along U.S. shores will be better served by guides designed for that purpose, such as *The Audubon Society Field Guide to North American Seashells* (see ARBA 82, entry 1499) or *Peterson First Guide to Shells of North America* (see ARBA 91, entry 1549), which is a simplified guide for beginners. Many shell enthusiasts, however, will want this handbook, as it manages to convey the beauty of shells and, at the same time, to serve as a practical identification guide for hundreds of species. Recommended for public libraries. [R: BR, Mar/April 93, pp. 53-54; SBF, Dec 93, p. 273]—**William H. Wiese**

1676. **Endangered Wildlife of the World.** North Bellmore, N.Y., Marshall Cavendish, 1993. 11v. illus. maps. index. $399.95/set. QL83.E55. 591.52'9. LC 92-14974. ISBN 1-85435-489-2.

A few years ago media attention focused on snail darters; now (at least in April 1993) the television and newspapers are full of stories about old-growth forests and northern spotted owls. In addition to these species, hundreds of others worldwide are on the verge of or tending toward extinction. The cast includes vertebrates, invertebrates, and plants. Which animals are in jeopardy, where, and why is the theme of this work.

Each volume of this encyclopedia provides the nonprofessional reader the first worldwide coverage, at the species level, of the disaster facing the animal kingdom. In excess of 1,200 species and subspecies drawn from lists of the U.S. Fish and Wildlife Service and International Union for the Conservation of Nature and Natural Resources are discussed. Species may be found alphabetically by common name, although some are located under their group name (e.g., boas, salmon) and also are cross-referenced. Each species is assigned one of five categories, most falling into "threatened" or "endangered." Species accounts begin with a classification (e.g., class, order, family) followed by a description of the animal and its natural history, including reproductive biology, habitat, diet, and more. A range map shows present and (often) former range. Each article contains information on factors producing the at-risk status and efforts being made to preserve the species. Articles bear their authors' names, but a surprisingly limited number of individuals contributed entries, considering the number of species covered. While most of the encyclopedia is devoted to vertebrates, for which the largest amount of information is available, many species of invertebrates are described, including snails, clams, and butterflies.

At the end of volume 10, characteristics of several biomes, including deserts, grasslands, forests, and polar regions, are briefly presented. In this volume, too, are short sections on what must be done to save endangered wildlife, encompassing questions of management of natural resources and captive breeding programs. One chapter covers the problem of the vanishing numbers of amphibians. Volume 11 includes several types of indexes, a list of national and state wildlife organizations and wildlife refuges, and a bibliography divided by vertebrate group.

How useful and problem-free is this encyclopedia? Simply because of the encyclopedia format, many of the articles are repetitive, especially in regard to the human-related factors leading to the contraction of a species' range and population size. Obviously, each article is designed to be read independently, but as a result, many common biological features are repeated in each separate alphabetical entry. Closely related species are grouped, and these sections are preceded by a color-enhanced box with general information about the group. At least one section has such a box with no species described following that box. Pages are divided into three columns, with each succeeding alphabetical entry beginning wherever the last ends. Thus, the pages look like those of a poorly laid-out newspaper. The 10-point typeface and widely spaced lines quickly fill each page, giving the volumes the appearance of children's books. Text material is divided by subheads that often read like those in a newspaper story, and the text includes modifiers (e.g., "mighty" river) inappropriate to an ostensibly objective work.

Almost all the entries are accompanied by excellent photographs; some occupy a full page. But for some species, drawings are used, and most of these convey no useful image of the animal; some are merely a few ink lines. To use poor line drawings of mollies (a group of fishes) suggests that an intensive effort to find photographs was not made. Some photographs do not identify the species, and in several cases where good photographs are easily available, none are provided (e.g., echidna, elephant shrew). In still other cases, photographs of species are offered without accompanying descriptions.

Errors in the text are numerous. For example, babirusa teeth are referred to as "horns"; elsewhere, paddlefish are erroneously said to have bones only in their jaws. At one point, squawfish length is given as up to three feet; at another it is said to reach six feet. In the section on vanishing amphibians, the reader is told that "present" amphibians still form a connecting link between fish and reptiles. The discussion on coelacanths contains several errors, including the statement that the notochord is a "predecessor of the bony spinal column and spinal cord." Common names are used for most alphabetical listings. In most cases this is fine because these names are widely used in English. But "cod" applies to a very different kind of fish in Australia than in North America, and more than a few readers could be misled. There are also spelling and proofreading errors. In a phylogeny (vol. 11), the word *phylums* is used rather than *phyla*. Elsewhere is *subgenuses* (should be *subgenera*). Weights and lengths are given in English and metric units. In at least one place the K is left out, and 2.5 lbs. is given as 1.2 g.

Some of the species accounts include bits of mythology and superstitions about an animal. While interesting, they usually do not contribute to understanding the demise of the species. With regard to teeth, it is said that seven sets are developed in elephants. Elsewhere, rodent teeth are said to regenerate throughout life. The choices of words—"sets" and "regenerate"—is inappropriate and misleading for characterizing dental development in these mammals. Strangely, some species are not included (e.g., giant clams), and some included species are not generally considered threatened or endangered (e.g., bobcats). Overall, these errors suggest inadequate checking for accuracy.

For whom is this encyclopedia designed? Not for professionals in biology, conservation, or wildlife management; the descriptions are too basic. Not for collegiate and university libraries, because the original sources are usually available. Probably the volumes will be useful in general public libraries and some school libraries, although the encyclopedia's cost could be high for one subject. Other works on endangered species include *Atlas of Endangered Species* by John Burton (Macmillan, 1991), *Endangered Vertebrates* (see ARBA 91, entry 1553), and the *Audubon Wildlife Report* (Academic Press, annual). None is as comprehensive at the species level or contains as many pictures as this encyclopedia. However, some of these books present a more ecologically focused view on the dangers of habitat destruction, which is the core of the problem of species endangerment. How valuable and useful a contribution is this set? Overall, it should be useful as a reference for the general reader, and many people could learn more about a specific group than is available in a short newspaper article. [R: LJ, 1 May 93, p. 80; RBB, 1 May 93, pp. 1624-26; SLJ, Nov 93, p. 142; WLB, Nov 93, pp. 101-02]—**David Bardack**

1677. Evers, David C. **A Guide to Michigan's Endangered Wildlife.** Ann Arbor, Mich., University of Michigan Press, 1992. 103p. illus. maps. $12.95pa. QL84.22.M5E94. 333.95'4137'09774. LC 91-36785. ISBN 0-472-08159-4.

Michigan can be added to the list of states (including California and Minnesota) that have published books on their endangered wildlife. Each of Michigan's 84 endangered and threatened vertebrates and invertebrates are profiled in 2-page accounts that include sections on identification, range, habitat and habits, limiting factors, and how to help. Most of the species accounts are accompanied by a color photograph of the animal described and an outline map of its distribution within Michigan. Appendixes include a list of extinct and extirpated species in Michigan and a bibliography of 28 items.

This popularly written (and priced) account will be useful for conservationists within Michigan and adjacent states. Libraries outside of the area covered will want it only if they are striving for complete ecology or natural history collections. The species accounts are, for the most part, available in standard field guides and handbooks, and no attempt is made in this volume to write a general account of Michigan's ecology. [R: Choice, Jan 93, p. 822]—**Jonathan F. Husband**

1678. Foreman, Dave, and Howie Wolke. **The Big Outside: A Descriptive Inventory of the Big Wilderness Areas of the United States.** rev. ed. New York, Harmony Books/Crown, 1992. 499p. maps. index. $16.00pa. QH76.F67. 333.78'2'0973. LC 92-2272. ISBN 0-517-58737-8.

Foreman and Wolke have cataloged a wealth of data on the major wild areas in the United States. In doing so they present a detailed overview of the major problems facing wilderness areas today, such as fragmentation, resource extraction, and off-road vehicle use. *Wilderness* is defined here as roadless areas of more than 100,000 acres in the West or 50,000 acres in the East, regardless of ownership or management, roadlessness being a better indicator of "real" wilderness than statutory designation. (By thus disregarding ownership boundaries, the authors have created an unusual document.) Consequently, some designated wilderness areas may not be included. Strong arguments for the defense of wilderness and prescriptions for preservation, restoration, and reconnecting wild areas are presented without concern for any groups that may be offended.

The book contains an analysis of wilderness issues at both the regional and state levels. The inventory contains descriptions of 385 wilderness areas, including the current status and ownership of the land, political realities that may affect the land status in the future, corridors to other wild areas, comments on floral and faunal diversity, and the history of land use in the area. Much of this information can be found nowhere else. This kind of inventory is essential for an understanding of the status of wilderness areas and ecosystems in the United States and will be a valuable tool for those focusing on wilderness problems and solutions. The book includes bibliographical references. It is excellent for reference collections and invaluable for wilderness seekers.—**T. McKimmie**

1679. Gress, Bob, and George Potts. **Watching Kansas Wildlife: A Guide to 101 Sites.** Lawrence, Kans., University Press of Kansas, 1993. 104p. illus. maps. $9.95pa. QL177.G73. 508'.09781. LC 92-41094. ISBN 0-7006-0594-0.

Kansas offers a remarkable diversity of habitats for those wishing to enjoy the outdoors, with its exceptional scenery and wildlife. From the Cheyenne Bottomlands to the Flint Hills, this guidebook helps visitors and residents alike to find the choice natural areas across the state. For each of the 101 selected sites, there is an account with general description of the area's flora and fauna, as well as special attractions (e.g., wildflower fields, prairie dog colonies, bison herds, nesting bald eagles, prairie chicken leks). The authors are careful to include a wide selection of natural features, emphasizing vertebrates but also including insects, vegetation, and even geological formations. The brief accounts (up to a page each) have roadway directions and a list of facilities at the sites. There are regional maps; local maps would have been quite helpful. Spectacular color photographs of nature are scattered throughout the text. The authors, a park director and a biology professor, have made this an information-packed directory for wildlife watching in the Sunflower State.—**Charles Leck**

1680. **The Grolier World Encyclopedia of Endangered Species.** Danbury, Conn., Grolier, 1993. 10v. illus. maps. index. $319.00/set. QL82.S4513. 591.52'9'03. LC 92-54833. ISBN 0-7172-7192-7.

For many years *The Red Data Book*, compiled by the International Union for Conservation of Nature and Natural Resources (IUCN), has been the authoritative list of endangered species. But those long lists can in no way compare to the impact when looking through *The Grolier World Encyclopedia of Endangered Species*. Here, in nine volumes plus index, one will find all those species listed as "rare," "vulnerable," "endangered," or "extinct" in *The Red Data Book*. Most species are accompanied by a recent color photograph—more than 700 in all, each commissioned for this series.

The encyclopedia is arranged by geographical region: Africa, Asia, North America, South America, Oceania, and Europe. Some areas, such as Africa, require two volumes to cover all the species. Within each region the animals are arranged according to family, order, and class. There are no insects or fish, but marine mammals are included. Each entry lists the status, whether endangered, and the like, along with a map showing current distribution. A description of the species includes physical characteristics; patterns of feeding, mating, and migration; natural habitat; and the factors threatening the species. If any action has been taken to preserve the species, this information is also included.

The first volume contains a brief description of the planet Earth. Each region is then introduced by a general description, and within the region there is a discussion of the mammals, birds, and reptiles and amphibians that occur there. The index volume has descriptions of the national parks of the world as well as a brief directory of the larger environmental organizations. The index is in two parts: One covers animal names, and one lists animal types. Unfortunately, the index by animal name does not contain scientific names. These could have easily been incorporated, as they are included in the entries, and thus made the index that much more useful. The index by animal type is a type of KWOC (keyword-out-of-context) index, which leads to little quirks such as finding Alice Springs mouse only under *mouse* but not under *rodent*, because rodent is not part of the term. However, the index of common names should satisfy most patrons, and the omission does not detract from the overall usefulness of this set. [R: RBB, 1 Sept 93, pp. 86-88; SLJ, Nov 93, p. 144]—**Angela Marie Thor**

1681. Kricher, John C. **A Field Guide to the Ecology of Western Forests.** Boston, Houghton Mifflin, 1993. 554p. illus. index. (Peterson Field Guide Series). $24.95; $16.95pa. QH104.5.W4K74. 574.5'2642'0978. LC 92-35792. ISBN 0-395-46725-X; 0-395-46724-1pa.

Kricher and illustrator Gordon Morrison have followed their *Field Guide to Eastern Forests* (see ARBA 89, entry 1386) with a lucid guide to the ecology of western forests. Using the Peterson system of "indicator species" of plants and animals living together in biotic communities, Kricher divides the western forests into eight large groups. Brief chapters on forest ecology, life zones, and widespread western mammals prepare enthusiasts who are going birding, botanizing, fishing, or hunting to interpret what they find.

Each forest is divided into two or more types interspersed with fascinating essays, such as "Bird Guilds." Geographical location led this reviewer to focus on the Chihuahua Desert, one of the few not illustrated among the 48 colored plates. Lists of indicator plants (trees, shrubs, and herbaceous species) and indicator animals (birds, mammals, reptiles, and amphibians), a description (including similar communities and range), remarks (about its flora and fauna), and where to visit all form an excellent overview. Regrettably, the section on references omits the Audubon Society Nature Guides' *Deserts* by James MacMahon (Alfred A. Knopf, 1985) with its Chihuahua Desert essay identifying precise plants and animals. The omission of a map may be explained by the greater complexity of western forests.

The book brims with definitions (e.g., of an ecotone), warnings (e.g., against grizzlies), and philosophical considerations (e.g., controlling forest fires). This introduction may lead to consulting the Sierra Club Naturalist's Guides for geological and climatic information on smaller geographical regions, such as *The Southern Rockies* (see ARBA 92, entry 444). This handy guide will assist young scholars working on nature badges, vacationers seeking understanding, and biology and ecology undergraduates.
—**Helen M. Barber**

1682. Pearson, Steve, and Alison Pearson. **Rainforest Plants of Eastern Australia.** Kenthurst, Austral., Kangaroo Press; distr., Cincinnati, Ohio, Seven Hills Book, 1992. 224p. illus. index. $45.00. 582.090952. ISBN 0-86417-474-8.

Stumbling across the patch of ground a bower bird had decorated, which deftly incorporated the light blue discards of modern civilization (a straw, a pen, and a plastic strip), was a pleasurable serendipity in this reviewer's trip to northeast Queensland. For anyone who has visited Australia's rainforest remnant, here is a chance to reminisce. To open this book is to hold a piece of the rainforest in one's hands. Reexamine the rainforest, or get a high-fidelity armchair feeling of its texture and diversity. Check the keys to plants, which are built on flower structure and color (cued for the color-blind), to take the short route to assigning names. Read the descriptions of plants and learn a great deal about the uses Aborigines made of them, from food to fish poison. Or use the index of common names to ferret out scientific name counterparts. Simplicity is the rule. Yet a glossary, an index to scientific names, and illustrations make the book robust. The photographs of more than 550 plants are superb. In this case, one can identify a plant by its picture. Among the profusion of plant photographs, a few birds (e.g., cuckoo, halcyon [kingfisher]) appear as well.—**Diane M. Calabrese**

1683. Riley, Laura, and William Riley. **Guide to the National Wildlife Refuges.** rev. ed. New York, Collier Books/Macmillan, 1992. 684p. maps. index. $16.00pa. QH76.R54. 333.95'0973. LC 92-15459. ISBN 0-02-063660-1.

National Wildlife Refuges exist in every state; there are nearly 500 of them. This work, a revision of the 1979 edition (see ARBA 80, entry 590), provides descriptions of more than 200 of these sanctuaries. It is well researched and filled with information on the natural history of the refuge, including its plants, mammals, insects, and especially birds. Entries average about two pages. A general description of the biological importance of the refuge is followed by lists of the specialty species occurring in the area. The Rileys' enthusiasm for these areas is apparent and contagious. Details on how to get there, what to look for and how best to see the refuge, places to stay, times to visit, local history, and other nearby attractions make this work a must for the traveler. The book includes addresses and telephone numbers and is indexed by animal and place-name. Recommended for all libraries. [R: RBB, 15 April 93, p. 1535]—**T. McKimmie**

1684. **The Way Nature Works.** Robin Rees, ed. New York, Macmillan, 1992. 359p. illus. maps. index. $35.00. QH13.W38. 508. LC 92-12283. ISBN 0-02-508110-1.

Presented as a family reference, this book answers thousands of questions about the natural world, from how birds fly to the causes of lightning. Thematic subjects cover global geology, weather, evolution, reproduction, animal behavior, and ecosystems. Within each section are a series of double-page spreads, each dealing with a key subject; sections have from 13 to 31 spreads, yielding a large single-volume reference. The earth sciences section, for example, has spreads on volcanoes, plate tectonics, ice ages, rock formation, tides, and 15 other inclusive subjects. Each spread has an introductory overview, text, and intricate color illustrations (the book has more than 1,000 paintings and photographs). These scientific illustrations have detailed captions that carefully explain the portrayed processes. In general, the college-level text is well written and informative. There is an extensive system of cross-references, as well as a glossary and a general index. Students and others curious about the natural sciences will find this an accurate and visually stimulating reference. [R: LJ, Jan 93, p. 106; RBB, 15 Feb 93, p. 1085]—**Charles Leck**

ZOOLOGY

General Works

1685. **Animal Life.** New York, Prentice Hall General Reference, c1991, 1992. 160p. illus. (Prentice Hall Illustrated Dictionary). $19.00. QL9.A55. 591'.03. LC 92-19466. ISBN 0-13-681719-X.

With an eye toward middle and junior high school students, Prentice Hall has produced a series of illustrated dictionaries, of which *Animal Life* is one. The back cover proclaims "the full range of species from hamsters to hyraxes," but as with any dictionary, these claims should be taken with a grain of salt. The volume contains more than 800 entries, yet there is no indication as to how a species was chosen or excluded. Using the dictionary, it is hard to come up with a pattern. For example, why include finches but not sparrows? Farm animals are seemingly avoided. When one looks up goats, only the wild species are mentioned, yet there is no separate entry for sheep, which also have wild counterparts. Sheep are only mentioned under the heading "Domesticated Animals."

Entry information is not very consistent. Under goats the family name is given, yet other species, such as gophers, are merely "small mammals." Information is sometimes scattered. The three parts of an insect are listed under the entry "abdomen" (as well as under the other two parts, head and thorax), yet no mention of the three parts is listed under the entry for insects.

Each entry includes the part of speech along with an example of use in a sentence. Cross-references are printed in boldface type. For the most part, entries are alphabetical, although when a large entry takes up more than one page, it may not appear precisely in alphabetical order. The entries are concise and easily understood, and the illustrations are adequate. For brief explanations, this dictionary would probably be sufficient, but it should only be considered as a supplement to more in-depth volumes. [R: BL, 1 Jan 93, pp. 822-24; SLJ, Feb 93, p. 123]—**Angela Marie Thor**

1686. **The Atlas of Endangered Animals.** By Steve Pollock. New York, Facts on File, 1993. 64p. illus. maps. index. $16.95. QL83.P65. 591.52'9. ISBN 0-8160-2856-7.

Children have become keenly aware of endangered animals, and their curiosity about these species is catered to in this highly illustrated atlas. Sections are arranged geographically, with presentations of noteworthy threatened animals from each region. The selected species include many well-known ones (e.g., giant panda, whooping crane) and a variety of lesser-known organisms. Numerous mammals, birds, reptiles, some fishes, and a few invertebrates are listed.

Species accounts are appropriate for juvenile literature, with an illustration of each animal and several short paragraphs of text on the animal's natural history and conservation. Symbols are used to summarize status (e.g., threatened, rare, extinct) and reasons for their endangered condition (e.g., habitat destruction, hunting, pollution). Throughout, distribution of the animals is shown on colorful regional maps.

Because of space limitations, only a small portion of the world's endangered fauna are included. For example, the four pages devoted to the United States present just eight species. The book's introduction is informative about people's interactions with animals and is also attractively illustrated. Young students will appreciate the glossary and the section on further information about wildlife conservation groups. [R: RBB, 15 May 93, pp. 1717-20; SBF, Nov 93, p. 238; SLJ, May 93, p. 139]—**Charles Leck**

1687. **The Kingfisher Illustrated Encyclopedia of Animals: From Aardvark to Zorille....** New York, Chambers Kingfisher Graham, 1992. 379p. illus. index. $19.95. QL7.K56. 591'.03. LC 92-53113. ISBN 1-85697-801-X.

This is the revised, enlarged edition of the *Dictionary of Animals* (see ARBA 86, entry 1507). It provides simple descriptions of more than 2,000 animals from around the world. After brief introductory material on animal classification, the book is arranged in alphabetical order from aardvark to zorille (an animal that resembles a skunk and is found in Africa). Each brief description is from a paragraph to a column in length and includes information on the size, habitat, and behavior of the animal. At the end of each description, the names of the order, family, genus, and species of the animal are provided. Short articles on selected topics, such as animal language and parental care, are also included. Full-color photographs and drawings of selected animals are featured on every page. A glossary of terms used in the book and indexes to subjects and to common and scientific names complete the book.

A comparable, more advanced encyclopedia (although it does not cover the invertebrates) is the *Macmillan Illustrated Animal Encyclopedia* (see ARBA 85, entry 1430). But for those wanting a more elementary work, the *Kingfisher Illustrated Encyclopedia of Animals* is a colorful and easy-to-use work at a nominal cost. For junior high through high school level, it would also be useful in public, school, and home libraries. [R: SLJ, Feb 93, p. 121]—**Diane B. Rhodes**

1688. O'Brien, Tim. **Where the Animals Are: A Guide to the Best Zoos, Aquariums, and Wildlife Attractions in North America.** Old Saybrook, Conn., Globe Pequot Press, 1992. 301p. illus. index. $12.95pa. QL76.5.N7027. 590'.74'473. LC 92-20081. ISBN 1-56440-077-8.

This guidebook is a very useful introduction to more than 250 of the best zoos, aquaria, wildlife sanctuaries, and other animal exhibits in the United States and Canada. All 50 states plus the District of Columbia are included, but Canada is represented by only 16 attractions. While most of the places listed are fairly typical animal exhibits, O'Brien does include some unusual attractions, such as the Educated Animal Zoo in Hot Springs, Arkansas, and the Anheuser-Busch Clydesdales in Merrimack, New Hampshire. The information provided for each attraction includes its address and telephone number, general background and history, hours and time of year open, cost, highlights of the exhibits and entertainment, extras (e.g., trains, children's zoos), food service, amount of time to allow, directions to the attraction, and other nearby attractions. The attractions are not ranked, but the acknowledged best places, such as the San Diego Zoo, do receive an extra-enthusiastic introduction. A spot check of a number of attractions did not uncover any major errors, and certainly the types of information provided are just what the potential visitor would most like to know. The book is a wonderful guide for both libraries and individuals.—**Diane Schmidt**

Birds

1689. Andrews, Robert, and Robert Righter. **Colorado Birds: A Reference to Their Distribution and Habitat.** Denver, Colo., Denver Museum of Natural History, 1992. 442p. illus. maps. index. $24.95pa. QL684.C6A53. 598.29788. LC 92-5872. ISBN 0-916278-68-9.

This reference provides an enormous synthesis of distributional records for the 443 species of Colorado birds. It is the first major review of the state's avifauna in 27 years, and as such it incorporates the latest information from a wide variety of field studies (including the Colorado breeding bird atlas project and the state's Latilong distribution study). The authors are prominent field ornithologists, and they have carefully documented the birds' abundance from thousands of field observations. They also used the expert assistance of more than 50 sectional reviewers. For each species there are one or more seasonal distribution maps, a bar graph of seasonal occurrence, and several paragraphs about status. The discussion focuses on current conditions, but historical changes in distribution are also reviewed. Each species account has a shorter section on habitat preferences, and often there is a list of noteworthy records. The book's introductory section provides an overview of the state's avian habitats. The specialized information in this volume will be useful for amateur birders, ornithologists, and environmental resource managers. [R: Choice, Jan 93, p. 760]—**Charles Leck**

1690. Arndt, Thomas. **Atlas of Conures: Aratingas and Pyrrhuras.** Neptune, N.J., T. F. H. Publications, 1993. 352p. illus. maps. index. $39.95. ISBN 0-86622-542-0.

Conures are a diverse and attractive group of parakeets popular in the pet trade. As treated here the group includes about 40 species, equally divided between two genera (*Aratinga* and *Pyrrhura*. This work provides a comprehensive guidebook for the aviculturist or prospective owner of these birds. The book was originally published in German (1981); this English translation adopts recent nomenclature for the parakeet species names. (Unfortunately, there appear to have been no bibliographical additions since the first publication.)

Introductory chapters review the acquisition of healthy birds, nutrition, housing (from cage to aviary), sexing, and breeding. In the detailed discussions, particular emphasis is given to the needs and care of each type of conure. The author incorporates his own extensive experiences and those of other aviculturists from the literature. Species accounts include distribution and description of subspecies, notes on behavior, and captivity suggestions. Each species and race is well illustrated by full-color paintings. The text also has many photographs (e.g., of natural habitats), and there is a rich assortment of domesticated varieties in photographic supplements. (All of the art material is printed by a lamination process that gives striking glossy illustrations.) This book is a valuable reference for aviculturists and bird hobbyists interested in these birds and their rearing.—**Charles Leck**

1691. Beavers, Randell A. **The Birds of Tikal: An Annotated Checklist for Tikal National Park and Peten, Guatemala.** College Station, Tex., Texas A&M University Press, 1992. 153p. illus. maps. index. (W. L. Moody, Jr., Natural History Series, no.12). $29.50; $12.95pa. QL687.G9B43. 598.2972812. LC 92-2919. ISBN 0-89096-525-0; 0-89096-518-8pa.

The 403 species of birds contained within this volume represent the avian population of Tikal National Park, which is located in the north-central part of the Department of Peten, Guatemala. The species within the checklist are arranged under their respective families, which are arranged phylogenetically. Given for each of the species listed are the common and scientific names, when last reported, habitat, nesting and behavioral information, relative abundance, and occurrence throughout the year. This information, for the most part, is presented in codes, which are explained fully before the checklist. In addition to the checklist, a total of 114 accounts of Peten species not previously treated in books on the region are presented. For each of the species considered within the accounts the common and scientific names, status (e.g., visitor, very rare transient), and sighting information are provided. A brief introduction to the checklist contains information on bird identification, travel to and accommodations in Peten, and the ornithological history of and geographical information on Peten (including a number of black-and-white photographs of the region). The appendixes provide a list of Peten species by status (e.g., residents, summer residents), a list of species based on specimen records from Peten, and a list of Peten species based on sight records only.

A six-page bibliography and a combined index to scientific and common names complete the checklist. Because this work is extremely specific, only college and university libraries with strong programs in ornithology and libraries in and around Guatemala should consider purchasing it.—**George H. Bell**

1692. Bhushan, Bharat, and others. **A Field Guide to the Waterbirds of Asia.** New York, Kodansha America, 1993. 224p. illus. maps. index. $25.00pa. QL691.A1F54. 598.295. LC 93-18482. ISBN 4-7700-1740-5.

This is a compact, unique, excellent field guide. No other book treats all of Asia's waterbirds. The area covered is vast: Pakistan, India, central Asia, most of Russia east of the Urals, Japan, the Philippines, China, and all of Southeast Asia, including Indonesia and Malaysia. Not covered here are sea or pelagic birds, of which there are few in most of Asia anyway. It is refreshing to see a thoroughly modern, state-of-the-art guide written and illustrated by Asians (most bird books on remote parts of the world have been done by Americans or Europeans).

The majority of this book is devoted to species accounts. These are concise, authoritative write-ups with brief sections on general commentary; the appearance of breeding, nonbreeding, and juvenile birds; voice; similar species; habitat; and distribution. In the current style of modern field guides, the beautifully rendered color plates (paintings) are on pages facing the species accounts for convenient reference. Attractive and accurate, the paintings do a fine job of depicting variation: birds of both sexes, juveniles, at rest and in flight, and breeding and nonbreeding plumages. Appended is a systematic list (table) showing the status of these waterbirds in 24 Asian countries. The index and bibliography are good. There is also a glossary, and three pages show bird topography (names for the parts of birds' plumage, legs, and bills). Lacking are range maps, which are much less essential for water than for land birds. Waterbirds' ranges are often difficult to map because of their restriction to narrow shorelines, small islands, or widely dispersed marshes and lakes. However, the textual description of the ranges is adequate.

This is a superb field guide. Because many of these waterbirds are found outside of Asia—many occur in North America—it has good application beyond Asian areas. Most highly recommended.
—**Henry T. Armistead**

1693. Bond, James. **A Field Guide to Birds of the West Indies.** 5th ed. Boston, Houghton Mifflin, 1993. 256p. illus. index. (Peterson Field Guide Series, 18). $24.95; $19.95pa. ISBN 0-395-67701-7; 0-395-67669-Xpa.

More than 400 species of birds are found in the West Indies, and all are included in this identification guide. In earlier editions this book has been a classic, the standard reference for birders and field ornithologists in the region. Bond was a noted scientist and curator of birds at the Academy of Natural Sciences, Philadelphia. He specialized in and had extensive experience with the Caribbean avifauna. The text is devoted to species accounts that include the following information for each bird: a plumage description, the habitats, calls and songs, nesting habits, and range (with dates for those species that are migratory). Identifications are facilitated by excellent artwork—155 species are portrayed in color plates (by Don Eckelberry), and 186 are shown in line drawings. Bond also has been careful to include local names for each species, whether they are in English, Spanish, or French.

This edition contains some new information, particularly distributional records and references to recent reports. It will continue as the basic field guide for visitors and residents interested in West Indian bird life.—**Charles Leck**

1694. Brauning, Daniel W., ed. **Atlas of Breeding Birds in Pennsylvania.** Pittsburgh, Pa., University of Pittsburgh Press; distr., Ithaca, N.Y., CUP Services, 1992. 484p. illus. maps. index. $34.95. QL684.P4A85. 598.29748. LC 91-24998. ISBN 0-8229-3692-5.

State bird atlases are vital and important documents for regional planners, administrators, biologists, and land use specialists. This one is among the very best. It displays 318,600 records, the results of work in the 4,928 atlas blocks of Pennsylvania by more than 2,000 volunteers during the 7-year period from 1983 to 1989—a massive, highly successful undertaking. Complex yet easily interpreted maps chart, with a system of colored squares, the ranges and relative abundance of the 190 species found breeding in this state. Opposed to the maps are detailed analyses of each species by authoritative writers. High-quality drawings depict each species. Also valuable are the graphs showing the birds' abundance as determined by the North American Breeding Bird Survey from 1965 to 1990 in Pennsylvania, a body of data separate from (but obviously closely related to) the purpose of the atlas work. Various plastic overlays can be placed on top of the maps to discern the birds' distribution according to physiographic areas, forest types, elevation, precipitation, river drainage systems, areas of glaciation, and similar elements. This is a treasure trove of valuable information that should be useful and interesting for decades, and a thoroughly professional production that cannot be too highly recommended.—**Henry T. Armistead**

1695. Collar, N. J., and others. **Threatened Birds of the Americas: The ICBP/IUCN Red Data Book. Part 2.** 3d ed. Washington, D.C., Smithsonian Institution Press, 1992. 1150p. illus. maps. index. $75.00. ISBN 1-56098-267-5.

The International Council for Bird Preservation (ICBP) and World Conservation Union (IUCN) regularly issue authoritative reviews of endangered species of birds through the Red Data Book series. This volume includes all threatened species (about 300) of Central America, South America, and the Caribbean. There are also shorter summary accounts for 25 such species from North America and the Neotropical Pacific. The work collates the efforts of 7 authors and more than 100 international contributors. The account for each of the endangered birds includes a short abstract, a detailed description of the species distribution, population changes and threats, ecology (especially habitat requirements and foods), and conservation measures proposed or taken. Often there are further remarks on the species taxonomy.

There are several valuable appendixes, including a list of all the threatened birds by severity of their situation (the most critical need urgent action) and a list of these species by country (Brazil has the most, almost a third of the total). There is also a list of 325 additional bird species of the Americas that are currently of near-threatened status. A comprehensive bibliography has 2,000 references through 1992. This is an essential reference book for conservationists concerned with threatened birds of the world.
—**Charles Leck**

1696. **Handbook of the Birds of Europe, the Middle East, and North Africa: The Birds of the Western Palearctic. Volume VI: Warblers.** New York, Oxford University Press, 1992. 728p. illus. maps. index. $150.00. ISBN 0-19-857509-2.

1697. **Handbook of the Birds of Europe, the Middle East, and North Africa: The Birds of the Western Palearctic. Volume VII: Flycatchers to Shrikes.** New York, Oxford University Press, 1993. 577p. illus. maps. index. $150.00. ISBN 0-19-857510-6.

These two volumes maintain the same superb, monumental standards of excellence and thoroughness of the previous five. (Volume 8 will complete this magnificent compendium.) The geographical area covered is immense, about 1,000 miles south into North Africa, northern Saudi Arabia and east to the Persian Gulf, the Iranian border, the Caspian Sea, and Russia to just east of the Urals, Iceland, and the Arctic Islands north of Scandinavia and Russia. These two volumes describe 108 species of land birds: warblers (unrelated to the New World birds of the same name), flycatchers, shrikes, tits, nuthatches, and more. Only six of these species regularly occur in North America, in contrast to the first four volumes on waterbirds, many of which also occur in the New World. Every species is exhaustively covered by the highly referenced text. Graphics for each species include colored maps showing Western Palearctic and world distribution; sonograms (but vocalizations are also well described); beautiful, accurate color plates (paintings); and additional line drawings for many species. The massive but well-organized text, an average of 20 pages per species, has sections for every bird on subspecies, field characters, habitat, distribution, population, movements, food, social pattern and behavior, voice, breeding, plumages, bare parts, molts, measurements, weights, structure, geographical variation, and recognition. There are also color photographs of about four differently marked eggs for every species.

Considering the encyclopedic, well-illustrated contents, this set is certainly not overpriced. The best regional handbook, in the classical *Handbuch* sense, ever done for any area of the world, it has set the standard for all other such efforts, such as the excellent *Handbook of Australian, New Zealand & Antarctic Birds* (see ARBA 92, entry 1563), still in production. This is a complete reference set that will endure a lifetime. It cannot be too highly recommended. [R: Choice, Nov 93, pp. 482-84]—**Henry T. Armistead**

1698. Johnsgard, Paul A. **Cormorants, Darters, and Pelicans of the World.** Washington, D.C., Smithsonian Institution Press, 1993. 445p. illus. maps. index. $49.00. QL696.P4745J64. 598.4'3. LC 92-31997. ISBN 1-56098-216-0.

This volume covers three of the six living families of the pelecaniform birds: the cormorants, darters, and pelicans. Its format is the same as Johnsgard's recent Smithsonian publication *Hawks, Eagles, & Falcons of North America* (1990). One seven-chapter section describes the biology, ecology, and evolutionary relationships of the three families. The second section treats each of the 43 living (and one extinct) species individually, in 2 to 10 pages, including physical description, reproduction, food, social behavior, ecology, population status, and evolutionary relationships. Distribution maps and color photographs of each species are included, as well as a bibliography of more than 900 items. The index is limited to avian taxa (genus and species).

This is the only monograph or reference work covering the world's cormorants, darters, and pelicans. The nine North American species have been treated previously as a group, most recently in volume 1 of the now defunct *Handbook of North American Birds*, edited by Ralph Palmer (Yale University Press, 1962), but the three families have never been treated on a worldwide basis. The accounts are succinct but inclusive and thorough, clearly written in technical language, well documented, and up-to-date as of 1991. The volume is well produced, a model of what a biological monograph should be. It is a necessary item for ornithological libraries or large life science collections. [R: Choice, Dec 93, p. 631]

—**Jonathan F. Husband**

1699. Johnsgard, Paul A. **Ducks in the Wild: Conserving Waterfowl and Their Habitats.** New York, Prentice Hall General Reference, 1993. 160p. illus. maps. index. $30.00. LC 92-21999. ISBN 0-671-85007-5.

The world does not really need another duck book. There are already dozens, many excellent, including several other waterfowl titles by Johnsgard. What does this one add to existing duck literature? Not much. It is basically a collection of short species accounts for all the world's ducks (105), with a color photograph and a tiny map showing each species' world breeding distribution. The accounts are good as far as they go, with an emphasis on behavior and nesting. Appended to these are brief chapters on the magic of waterfowl, extinct and endangered ducks, watching waterfowl, an identification key, a glossary, references, waterfowl conservation and habitat preservation groups, and an index. So little of the text concerns conservation that the subtitle is somewhat of a misnomer.

Johnsgard has probably published more books (25, with several more in the works) on birds than any other American, many of them well received. To be sure, he is a ranking ornithologist (a biology professor at the University of Nebraska), and all of the material here is of good quality. However, it adds little to what is already available. This is a nice coffee-table book, but otherwise it is rather superfluous.

—**Henry T. Armistead**

1700. Paulson, Dennis. **Shorebirds of the Pacific Northwest.** Seattle, Wash., University of Washington Press, 1993. 406p. illus. maps. index. $40.00. AL683.P36P38. 598.3'3'09795. LC 92-19050. ISBN 0-295-97233-5.

This excellent reference will be of interest and application far beyond its United States and Canadian Pacific Northwest domain, because many shorebirds (familiarly known as sandpipers) are widespread not only in North America but also throughout the world. Paulson is director of the Slater Museum of Natural History in Tacoma, Washington. He and artist Jim Erckmann both have doctorates in zoology. The detailed, authoritative text is enhanced by fine graphic materials: 98 color photographs, 52 figures (e.g., maps, drawings), 10 distribution maps, 36 tables, and 5 appendixes (including weights and measurements). There are more than 80 pages of general, introductory commentary covering plumages, identification, geography, and conservation. Most of the book is composed of species accounts for each of the 78 species.

There are sections on distribution, Northwest status, habitat and behavior, structure, plumage, subspecies, identification, flight, voice, further questions, notes, photographs, and references for each bird. The photographs section is especially interesting because it comments on age, sex, plumage, molt stage, and other such features of birds in photographs from other standard reference books where such information was not included in the original text. For each species there are also bar graphs showing plumage stage, occurrence, and abundance throughout the year. In addition to all these virtues *Shorebirds of the Pacific Northwest* is a sturdy and attractively designed monograph.

A high-quality production that should set a new standard for regional treatment of animal groups, this work will be useful for biologists, naturalists, ecologists, and birders. Most highly recommended.

—**Henry T. Armistead**

1701. Peterson, Roger Tory, Guy Mountfort, and P. A. D. Hollom. **A Field Guide to Birds of Britain and Europe.** 5th ed. Boston, Houghton Mifflin, 1993. 261p. illus. maps. index. (Peterson Field Guide Series, 8). $24.95; $19.95pa. ISBN 0-395-66931-6; 0-395-66922-7pa.

The 5th edition of this classic Peterson title is the most important yet. (See *A Field Guide to the Birds of Britain and Europe* [see ARBA 76, entry 1429] for a review of the 3d edition). In the present work, all of the 548 species accounts have either been rewritten or added, the accidentals section has been expanded to 171 species to include recent vagrants on the British and European list, and the range maps of species distribution have been redrawn or updated. Peterson has painted 19 new color plates, and the others have been redrawn. As well as his high standard of illustration, the basic layout has been retained. The introductory section covers the basics of bird identification and is followed by the species accounts, which form the backbone of the guide. The color plates are located as one unit in the middle of the book, with the range maps and index located at the end of the text.

This guide suffers from the need for extensive cross-referencing, as the species accounts and range maps are not found on the pages facing the color plates. If one is not used to this method it may seem awkward. However, there are short species annotations alongside every plate description. Unfortunately, the authors have indicated no authority for their order of species classification. This discussion would be useful, because there have been many changes in taxonomic treatment in the ornithological literature since the last edition. This is a required reference for any science collection or for any library currently holding previous editions. [R: LJ, 1 Nov 93, pp. 74-76]—**Katherine Margaret Thomas**

1702. Taylor, Barbara. **The Bird Atlas.** New York, Dorling Kindersley, 1993. 64p. illus. maps. index. $19.95. ISBN 1-56458-327-9.

This outsized book by two leading British naturalists consists of just 64 pages, most of them highly illustrated and with thumbnail annotations about the birds shown. It is for the most part arranged by habitats within continent or country and provides a brief, general overview of 270 of the world's 9,000-plus bird species. It is not really a reference book but a work best suited for idle public or school library use, especially browsing. As such it is an adequate source with lively, mediocre to good paintings, plus photographs of birds in situ and an interesting and authoritative (if patchy and hit-or-miss) text. Full of energy and color, it could spark an interest in birds and their habitats in the casual reader. [R: RBB, 1 Dec 93, p. 708; SLJ, Nov 93, pp. 120-21; WLB, Dec 93, p. 75]—**Henry T. Armistead**

Butterflies

1703. Glassberg, Jeffrey. **Butterflies through Binoculars: A Field Guide to Butterflies in the Boston, New York, Washington Region.** New York, Oxford University Press, 1993. 160p. illus. index. $49.95. QL551.N65G58. 595.78'9'0974. LC 92-33087. ISBN 0-19-507982-5.

This book might be the East Coast butterfly watcher's best friend. While it only covers butterflies of the Boston-New York-Washington, D.C., corridor, it contains almost everything butterfly watchers for that area might want. There are descriptions of over 150 species of butterflies, including size (given as larger or smaller than a common species such as the Cabbage White—a nice touch), identification hints, habitat, range, season, food, and comments. There is a separate section of photographic plates for each species, often with more than one picture per species. In addition, there are several appendixes, including information on the best butterfly watching sites, seasonality and abundance of butterflies in New York, a butterfly checklist, and butterfly societies and clubs. The price is perhaps a little high for the casual butterfly watcher, but for a public or academic East Coast library, the guide is well worth the money. Standard field guides, such as *Field Guide to Eastern Butterflies* (see ARBA 93, entry 1549), cover many more butterflies in a wider region at a lower price, but Glassberg's descriptions are excellent, and the guide is well designed and useful. [R: Choice, Dec 93, p. 628]—**Diane Schmidt**

Domestic Animals

1704. Alderton, David. **Cats.** New York, Dorling Kindersley, 1993. 256p. illus. index. (Eyewitness Handbooks). $29.95; $17.95pa. SF442.A44. 636.8. LC 92-7611. ISBN 1-56458-073-3; 1-56458-070-9pa.

Packed with 700 small, full-color photographs of more than 250 types of cats, this hand-sized book provides a systematic approach to cat identification. Text, never separated from the photographs, traces the evolution of the domestic cat, looks at how cats are classified, and examines feline anatomy in detail. Tips are provided on choosing the right cat, sexing kittens, grooming, and handling and showing.

Visual identification keys help one recognize the different types of cats. Each entry combines a precise description with annotated photographs to highlight the main characteristics and distinguishing features. Color-edged head and foot bands provide country of origin, ancestry, date of origin, and temperament. Fur swatch photographs show the precise type and color of the fur, while a glossary provides understanding of breeders' terms.

A straightforward section on how the book works takes one through an annotated example of how an entry is organized. Senses and instincts cover "cat napping," rearing cats together, hunting skills, climbing and balancing, scent marking, and why cat's eyes glow in the dark. Many of the photographs provide both the adult and kitten stages in playful poses that give a feel for the body structure and strength of these agile animals. A section on nonpedigreed cats is thoughtfully provided so that one can find the family pet illustrated and described. Artists, students, and librarians will welcome this clever, readable guide.—**Judy Gay Matthews**

1705. Alderton, David. **Dogs.** New York, Dorling Kindersley, 1993. 304p. illus. index. (Eyewitness Handbooks). $29.95; $17.95pa. SF426.A434. 636.7. LC 92-53450. ISBN 1-56458-179-9; 1-56458-176-4pa.

This descriptive and pictorial guide to more than 300 breeds of dogs, from the most recognizable to the lesser known, is not limited to those breeds affiliated with the American Kennel Club (AKC) as listed in their *Complete Dog Book* (see ARBA 93, entry 1552). Instead, it includes breeds from around the world but does not list the registry affiliations of the breeds, as does *Atlas of Dog Breeds of the World* (see ARBA 91, entry 1580). Following a history of the domestic dog, the introduction includes a guide to the use of the book and sections on choosing and caring for a dog and showing dogs competitively. A well-arranged pictorial identification chart helps to identify a breed by size and other key characteristics, such as shape of head and hair type. The entries are arranged in six categories: companion dogs, gun dogs, herding dogs, hounds, terriers, and working dogs.

Each entry is a half page to two pages in length, with full-color photographs of the mature dog and a close-up of the head, with identifying features noted and other varieties of the breed pictured. Swatches show typical colors of hair, and the short narrative includes a history of the breed and pertinent remarks. Bars at the top and bottom of the entry give the country and date of origin, purpose of the breed, typical height and weight, and a note about temperament. A graphic depicts the size of the mature animal in relation to a six-foot human. A list of addresses of dog-related organizations, a glossary, and an index with cross-references to alternate names for breeds complete this guide, which would serve as a good supplement to the AKC publication for references to non-U.S. breeds.—**Margo B. Mead**

1706. De Prisco, Andrew, and James B. Johnson. **Canine Lexicon.** Neptune City, N.J., T. F. H. Publications, 1993. 896p. illus. $79.95. ISBN 0-86622-198-0.

Dog fanciers will spend hours with this informative and entertaining dictionary of more than 3,500 terms from all topics relating to the dog, both domestic and wild. The terms are arranged alphabetically from AAD (advanced agility dog) to zygomatic arch (the bony ridge of the skull under the eye). Each term is discussed in at least a paragraph. Many terms are illustrated with outstanding color photographs, which are found on every page of this fascinating book.

Almost any term or subject that has to do with dogs is included here. The work pictures and describes more than 500 dog breeds from around the world as well as wild species, such as the coyote, wolf, and fox. In addition to descriptions of the more common dog breeds, rare and extinct breeds also appear, as do descriptions of the various groups of dogs, such as terriers and draft dogs. There are articles on dog care, such as dental care and grooming, as well as some veterinary articles on diseases. Show terminology is also found, with information on standards, obedience, dog trials, and events. Some large topics, such as canine behavior and choosing a dog, are covered in four to six pages.

The format is eye-catching and appealing. At the top of each page and enclosed in a color banner are the terms covered at the beginning and end of that page. Extensive cross-references lead the reader to similar or related topics. Color banners run down the outside of each page and contain captions for the photographs on those pages. The photographs, primarily by Isabelle Francais, are amazing for their color and for capturing the essence of each breed and its behavior.

This up-to-date book is unusual in its broad coverage. The *Atlas of Dog Breeds of the World* (see ARBA 91, entry 1580) is similar but primarily contains information on the dog breeds. *Canine Lexicon* will be enjoyed in all public and school libraries. [R: LJ, 15 April 93, pp. 82-84; RBB, 1 May 93, pp. 1622-24; WLB, June 93, pp. 119-20]—**Diane B. Rhodes**

1707. Edwards, Elwyn Hartley. **Horses.** New York, Dorling Kindersley, 1993. 256p. illus. index. (Eyewitness Handbooks). $29.95; $17.95pa. SF285.E353. 636.1. LC 92-53469. ISBN 1-56458-180-2; 1-56458-177-2pa.

Horses is a compact, handy, easy-to-use guide with excellent illustrations. Short chapters describe the development of the horse family, conformation, colors, markings, life cycle, uses, and equipment. The major part of the text devotes a single page or double-page spread to a brief description of 100-plus horse breeds arranged by size of horse, from ponies to large (draft) horses. In each of these divisions the descriptions are arranged by geographical area, then alphabetically by breed. Each entry includes the origin of the horse, the "history, breeding and characteristics in word and illustration." The next section is a chart on types of horses that traces the various breeds, from the earliest to the most recent. The many color photographs will aid in the identification of little-known breeds.

The glossary is spotty and of limited value, as the definitions relate to minor aspects of the development of the horse. Several definitions ("on the bit," "above the bit," and "tied in below the knee") are inaccurate or confusing. The index has two errors in pagination: the Bavarian Warmblood and the Belgian Warmblood. But despite these limitations, this is a well-organized, carefully crafted, ready-reference book. Well worth the modest paperback price just for the historical development and photographs. It will be useful in all types of reference departments.—**Joann H. Lee**

1708. **Project BREED Directory: A Nationwide Source Book for Rescue of All Breeds of Dogs and Other Species.** Germantown, Md., Project BREED, 1993. 168p. index. $25.00pa. LC 90-660072. ISBN 0-938073-03-5. ISSN 1045-2044.

Arranged by 32 dog breeds as well as by other animals (bat, domestic ferret, and domestic rabbit), this work provides general information on people in the United States who rescue these animals. Each entry supplies the name of the organization, a contact person (with address and telephone number), the type of service provided for the animal, and the conditions that must be met in order to adopt the animal. General information, such as behavior, size, color, and life span on each of the breeds of dogs is listed. Some general information about bats, ferrets, and rabbits is also provided. A list of Project BREED area coordinators, arranged by state, is given in the opening pages. It would have been useful if all listings throughout the book were arranged by state as well as by type of animal. Indexes to dog breeds, bats, ferrets, and rabbits are included, as well as an index to topics and organizations.

Highly recommended for public libraries. College and university libraries should consider it, as well as people who are involved in this type of activity.—**George H. Bell**

1709. Wear, Terri A. **The Horse's Name Was ...: A Dictionary of Famous Horses....** Metuchen, N.J., Scarecrow, 1993. 211p. index. $27.50. SF278.W43. 636.1. LC 92-37724. ISBN 0-8108-2599-6.

The Horse's Name Was ... attempts to identify horses of history, film, literature, television, and mythology. Its range is broad, although Wear does not claim to be comprehensive. The book is divided into three sections. The major portion is a list of horse's names arranged in dictionary form, with many cross-references from authors, owners, historically prominent individuals, mythological characters, and similar people. The main entry, by horse's name, describes and gives the significance of each name. The brief index is made up of general headings, such as mythological, literary, race, and movie horses. A list of additional readings follows.

Some of the research is rather casual. For instance, one entry identifies a horse as belonging to Princess Anne, with no further data given, and the cross-references to Elizabeth I and Elizabeth, Queen Mother, imply that the two are the same. The bibliography includes very few recent titles.

Wear recommends this book for use by crossword puzzle enthusiasts, trivia collectors, and historians, as well as horse lovers. It is certainly not an essential purchase, but it is a fairly thorough exploration of a very specific subject. If a high school or public library fields many questions about horses, this will answer some of them. [R: BR, Nov/Dec 93, p. 58; RBB, 1 May 93, p. 1628]—**Joann H. Lee**

1710. Wilcox, Bonnie, and Chris Walkowicz. **Atlas of Dog Breeds of the World.** Neptune, N.J., T. F. H. Publications, 1993. 2v. illus. index. $129.95/set. ISBN 0-86622-855-1.

This new edition is divided into two volumes, which makes the book easier to handle. There is little change in the content of the work from earlier editions, but it continues to be an outstanding reference work. The many illustrations of the 400-plus breeds listed are in full color and very well done. The standard information on size, color, weight, coat, and registries that accept the breed is supplemented by good descriptions of the dogs. An extensive breed name cross-reference is useful because dogs have different names in different countries. For example, the Great Pyrenees is known as the Pyrenean Mountain Dog in Great Britain and in France, its country of origin, it is called the Chien de Montagne de Pyrenees. Many of the breeds are not well known even in their own homelands, so dog lovers will enjoy just browsing through this book.—**Susan Ebershoff-Coles**

Fishes

1711. Axelrod, Herbert R. **The Most Complete Colored Lexicon of Cichlids: Every Known Cichlid Illustrated in Color.** Neptune, N.J., T. F. H. Publications, 1993. 864p. illus. index. $100.00. ISBN 0-86622-422-X.

1712. Conkel, Donald. **Cichlids of North & Central America.** Neptune, N.J., T. F. H. Publications, 1993. 191p. illus. maps. index. $49.95. ISBN 0-86622-444-0.

Abounding with color photographs, the *Lexicon* provides general information on all species of fish in the family Cichlidae. Approximately 1,200 species are included. The genera and species are presented under geographical sections, including Lake Tanganyika, Lake Malawi, Lake Victoria, Southern and Eastern Africa, Western Africa, the Middle East and Asia, Madagascar, Central America, and South America.

Information provided for each genera variably includes the person who first described it and the year of description, reproduction, behavior, number of species, external anatomical characteristics, and coloration. In like manner, the descriptive account of each species varies, ranging from one to several paragraphs and usually containing the person who first described the species and year of description, size, nesting, behavioral patterns, coloration, and taxonomic variations. General information on cichlids is provided in the introductory section, and a scientific name index completes the work.

Also filled with colorful photographs, *Cichlids of North & Central America* (CNCA) covers 126 species of cichlid found throughout North and Central America. The fish are arranged under their subgenus; a general description of the subgenus is included, as well as the person who first described the group and when, size, basic external anatomical characteristics, behavior, reproduction, nesting, coloration, and feeding habits. Each species has its scientific, alternative scientific, and common names; namer and date of naming; geographical distribution; habitat; diet; size; coloration; and anatomical features listed. Large range maps and photographs of the area can be found in the introductory section, along with classification; ecology; anatomy; feeding habits; reproduction; aquarium management; and holding, shipping, and acclimatization techniques. A short bibliography and a common/scientific name index conclude this work.

CNCA is far more narrowly focused than *Lexicon*, and a number of differences exist as well, including the amount of information provided in the descriptive accounts of genera and species. For example, CNCA gives proper pH and temperature range for the species; *Lexicon* does not. The length of the descriptive accounts also varies. In CNCA, one-and-a-half columns describe the pastel cichlid, while in *Lexicon* a paragraph is devoted to that fish. Taxonomy and genera differ; CNCA considers the scientific name of a species to be *Cichlasoma lyonsi*, while *Lexicon* names it *Herichthys lyonsi*. Cross-references to alternate species names are not provided in CNCA; *Lexicon* has them in its index. The two works do share some photographs.

Both works are recommended for colleges and universities with strong programs in zoology, especially in ichthyology. Large public libraries and fish enthusiasts may want one or both.—**George H. Bell**

1713. Bohlke, James E., and Charles C. G. Chaplin. **Fishes of the Bahamas and Adjacent Tropical Waters.** 2d ed. Austin, Tex., University of Texas Press, 1993. 771p. illus. index. $100.00. QL631.B2B64. 597.097296. LC 92-20389. ISBN 0-292-70792-4.

Containing nomenclatural changes and additions since the 1968 edition, this volume considers 507 species of fish from that edition as well as an additional 58 species. The species are arranged under their respective families. Scientific and common names of the families are given along with a brief description that includes the number of species in the family group. For each of the fish included are given the scientific name, the person who first named it, its common name, size, basic external anatomy, coloration, habits and habitats, and geographical distribution. Each entry is a page long. A black-and-white line drawing of the fish accompanies the descriptive matter. Keys to the genera and species are also present. Colored plates of selected fish can be found near the beginning of the volume.

The introductory material contains general information on the Bahamas, information on nomenclatural changes and additions, and basic line drawings depicting the shapes of the fish within families (pictorial key). A brief glossary, a bibliography containing 349 entries, and a common/scientific name index conclude the source.

Recommended for those college and university libraries with strong programs in zoology, especially ichthyology. Large public libraries collecting in this area may also want a copy.—**George H. Bell**

1714. Boschung, Herbert T. **Catalogue of Freshwater and Marine Fishes of Alabama.** Tuscaloosa, Ala., University of Alabama Press, 1992. 266p. maps. index. (Alabama Museum of Natural History Bulletin, no.14). $40.00pa. ISSN 0196-1039.

This scientific checklist of Alabama's fishes is a highly technical museum publication. The text reviews the distributions of almost 300 freshwater species and more than 650 marine species. Each species account succinctly gives nomenclature (scientific and common names and published synonyms). Distributional information is detailed for Alabama, and there are often statements for regional records outside the state boundaries. With marine fishes there also are brief summaries of the species' entire international range. (Distributional maps would have been useful for some of the freshwater species with restricted ranges.)

Introductory material includes a zoogeographical overview of Alabama's fish life. The comprehensive literature cited lists more than 1,000 references to 1992 publications, including thesis material. There are complete indexes for common and scientific names. Illustrations would have been a welcome addition, particularly for some of the local or endangered species. This catalog will be useful for professional ichthyologists and other vertebrate biologists interested in this southern fish fauna.—**Charles Leck**

1715. **FAO Yearbook: Fishery Statistics: Catches and Landings. Vol. 72: 1991. FAO Annuaire: Statistiques des Peches. FAO Anuario: Estadisticas de Pesca.** Rome, FAO of the United Nations; distr., Lanham, Md., UNIPUB, 1993. 653p. maps. (FAO Fisheries Series, no.40; FAO Statistics Series, no.111). $65.00. ISBN 92-5-003328-1.

This trilingual (English, Spanish, and French) compilation contains information on catches and landings of all types of marine stocks, including fishes, marine mammals and reptiles, crustaceans, pearls, sponges, and aquatic plants. The data include recreational fishing and aquaculture as well as commercial fishing. Numerous tables break down the data by species or group of species, by major fishing areas (both inland and ocean), and by continents or countries. The most recent data are from 1992, and statistics from some previous years are also included. There are also numerous graphs and, important in these days of rapid changes in the status of political units, notes on individual countries.

The information found in this yearbook is useful for anyone interested in fisheries or aquatic biology, although of course the accuracy of the data depends on the reporting unit. The tables and graphs are well organized and readable, and the notes are informative. While this mass of data is not for every library, it is highly useful for ecologists interested in marine populations, for economists, and even for some nonspecialists (e.g., the marine mammal catches and landings may be of interest to many). The FAO also provides the data from the yearbook in machine-readable form.—**Diane Schmidt**

1716. Gilbert, Carter R., ed. **Rare and Endangered Biota of Florida. Volume II: Fishes.** Gainesville, Fla., University Press of Florida, 1992. 247p. illus. maps. index. $54.95; $24.95pa. QL617.73.U6R37. 333.95'6137'09759. LC 91-31922. ISBN 0-8130-1121-3; 0-8130-1122-1pa.

This work considers rare and endangered species of fish found in Floridian waters. For each of the fish listed, the common and scientific names, family, order, and status (e.g., threatened, rare) are given. In addition, the entries consider general external anatomical features, size, relationship to similar species, coloration, geographical distribution, habitat, life history and ecology, the basis upon which the status classification was given, and recommendations to preserve the species. A black-and-white drawing of the fish, a geographical range map of Florida, and a brief bibliography accompany the descriptive accounts. A total of 39 species descriptions comprise encompass the main portion of the work.

Introductory information consists of a brief history of the FCREPA (Florida Committee on Rare and Endangered Plants and Animals), definitions of the status categories, an outline of Florida's aquatic ecosystem, a description of aquatic habitats, and a checklist of the Florida fish species included in present and previous (1978) FCREPA lists. Official federal and state classifications and unofficial FCREPA designations are tabulated in the FCREPA list. The species contained within the list are arranged under their respective families. A list of contributors and a subject/common/scientific name index conclude the source. Recommended for college and university libraries having strong programs in zoology, as well as for college, university, and public libraries in Florida. Large public libraries throughout the nation may also have some use for it.—**George H. Bell**

1717. **The Macmillan Book of the Marine Aquarium: A Definitive Reference to More Than 300 Marine Fish and Invertebrate Species....** By Nick Dakin. New York, Macmillan, 1992. 400p. illus. index. $75.00. SF457.1.D35. 639.3'42. LC 92-45126. ISBN 0-02-897108-6.

This book is for those who plan to set up a marine aquarium. It provides essential information on setting up, choosing fish or invertebrates, and what food and maintenance each species needs. Written for the general public, it is divided into six sections: the marine environment, setting up the aquarium, marine fish and invertebrate care, tropical marine fishes, tropical marine invertebrates, and the cold-water aquarium. For each fish species are provided an illustration, common and scientific names, distribution, size, diet, aquarium behavior, and invertebrate compatibilities. For each invertebrate the common and scientific names are listed, along with a description and picture. All species are illustrated with large, vivid, excellent color photographs. The appendix on marine algae explains how to add algae and keep them under control. The appendix on species to avoid gives the reason for doing so (e.g., difficult maintenance, pest species, incompatibility with other species). There are a glossary, a general index, and a species index.

If one wants a marine aquarium, this is an essential book. The appendix on species to avoid is an excellent idea. There is an error that should be corrected in the next edition: the horseshoe crabs and the crustacea are listed as being in separate phyla, but they both belong to the phylum Arthropoda. However, this will not affect the aquarium builder, and the book is recommended for home use. [R: Choice, Nov 93, p. 428; LJ, Aug 93, p. 92; RBB, 1 Dec 93, pp. 710-12; SBF, Dec 93, p. 270]—**John Laurence Kelland**

1718. Michael, Scott W. **Reef Sharks and Rays of the World: A Guide to Their Identification, Behavior and Ecology.** Monterey, Calif., Sea Challengers, 1993. 107p. illus. index. $24.95pa. QL638.9.M525. 597.3. LC 92-46402. ISBN 0-930118-18-9.

Perhaps the group most divers and snorkelers want to see—or fear most to see—is the sharks and their relatives the rays. Michael's slender work should be useful to all but the dedicated elasmobranch aficionado. A third of the text provides introductory material on feeding, hunting strategies, development, social behavior, and interaction between sharks and divers. There are a brief glossary and a pictorial key to families. An attentive diver who has carefully studied the pictorial key should be able to recognize and identify the more common sharks and rays. The remainder of the book provides capsule descriptions of more than 160 species, including identifying characteristics; size; geographical range; features of reproductive biology; and a potpourri of ecological, feeding, and activity comments under the general rubric of biology. Photographs accompanying each description are mostly excellent; they show entire individuals, and many are seen as they might appear to a swimmer.—**David Bardack**

1719. Nakamura, I., and N. V. Parin. **FAO Species Catalogue. Vol. 15: Snake Mackerels and Cutlassfishes of the World (Families Gempylidae and Trichiuridae): An Annotated and Illustrated Catalogue....** Rome, FAO of the United Nations; distr., Lanham, Md., UNIPUB, 1993. 136p. illus. maps. index. (FAO Fisheries Synopsis, no.125, v.15). $25.00pa. ISBN 92-5-103124-X.

This is the first global review of the classification, biology, and commercial catch of these oceanic predators, which are mainly tropical but do range into temperate seas. Not as commercially important as the related mackerels and tunas, cutlassfish are the best-known members of the trichiurid family in Pacific commercial fisheries. After a general discussion of related families, each of the 23 species of gempylids and 32 species of trichiurids are depicted in illustrated keys and individual drawings that show the full body and significant body details. Each entry includes diagnostic features, habitat, prey, distribution, interest to fisheries, and references to the literature. This latest volume of the *FAO Species Catalogue* is recommended to all levels of academic libraries with collections in marine biology or fisheries.
—**Roger Steeb**

1720. Nelson, Joseph S., and Martin J. Paetz. **The Fishes of Alberta.** 2d ed. Edmonton, Alta., University of Alberta Press, 1992. 437p. illus. maps. index. $34.95; $24.95pa. 597.092'97123. ISBN 0-88864-235-0; 0-88864-236-9pa.

This work provides descriptive information on 59 species of fish inhabiting the Canadian province of Alberta. The fish are arranged under their respective families. General information regarding each of the families is presented, as well as keys to the species in many cases. Given for each of the species listed are the common and scientific names, the person who named it, and the derivation of the scientific name. In addition, coloration, basic identifying external anatomy, size, geographical distribution, egg production, life span, and other interesting facts (including historical notes) are considered. A picture of the fish (most are in black-and-white) and a geographical range map accompany the descriptive accounts. The amount of information and length of the description vary from species to species. Appearing in the first seven chapters is information on fishing, fish management, the fish ecology of Alberta, postglacial origins of the fish, taxonomic information, a checklist of Alberta fish, evolution of Alberta fish, maps, the use of keys, and definitions of fish characteristics. In addition, pictorial keys to the 15 families of Alberta fishes precede the descriptive accounts.

A number of appendixes provide additional information on such topics as species introduced or collected in Alberta, features of some Alberta lakes, and discharge of major Alberta rivers. A glossary, a bibliography, and a combined common/scientific name index conclude the work.

Recommended for colleges and universities with strong academic programs in zoology, especially ichthyology. Libraries in Canada, especially Alberta, will also wish to consider it. [R: Choice, Oct 93, p. 317]

—George H. Bell

1721. Wischnath, Lothar. **Atlas of Livebearers of the World.** Neptune City, N.J., T. F. H. Publications, 1993. 336p. illus. index. $79.95. ISBN 0-86622-368-1.

Most people have peered into aquarium tanks at pet stores to admire the fish with startlingly bright colors. This book's 980 full-color photographs can give readers an armchair view of the hundreds of common livebearing aquarium fish, such as mollies, guppies, swordtails, and platys, as well as the uncommon wild species found in fresh to brackish water. After introductory chapters on the biology, origin, and habitat of livebearers, the book is arranged systematically, covering the main families and genera and providing brief species descriptions and taxonomy. Information on the natural habitats of these fish and guidelines on caring for and breeding them are also provided. Every page of this large work is filled with striking color photographs of the individual species and the places where many species were collected. A bibliography of sources for further reading and an index to common and scientific names are included at the end.

This is a thorough and beautiful work for the serious aquarist and for the amateur who never knew there were so many varieties of guppies. It serves as the most comprehensive source on freshwater livebearing aquarium fish, surpassing the classic *Atlas of Freshwater Aquarium Fishes* by Herbert Axelrod (T. F. H. Publications, 1989). Recommended primarily for public libraries; it will also be useful in academic libraries with holdings in ichthyology.—**Diane B. Rhodes**

Insects

1722. Bright, Donald E. **The Weevils of Canada and Alaska. Volume 1: Coleoptera: Curculionoidea, excluding Scolytidae and Curculionidae.** Ottawa, Agriculture Canada, 1993. 217p. illus. maps. index. (Insects and Arachnids of Canada, pt.21). $34.95pa.; $45.45pa. (U.S.). 595.7'68'0971. ISBN 0-660-14433-6.

1723. Foottit, Robert G., and William R. Richards. **The Genera of the Aphids of Canada. Homoptera: Aphidoidea and Phylloxeroidea.** Ottawa, Agriculture Canada, 1993. 766p. illus. index. (Insects and Arachnids of Canada, pt.22). $54.95pa.; $71.45pa. (U.S.). 595.7'52. ISBN 0-660-14669-X.

These two titles continue this superb series on the insects and arachnids of Canada. (See ARBA 93, entries 1563-64 for reviews of previous volumes.) Part 21 on the weevils describes only 90 of the estimated 600 species. (The remaining descriptions will be treated in two forthcoming volumes.) Part 22 contains comprehensive, comparative descriptions of the Canadian genera of aphids.

The two volumes are arranged in a similar manner. Each has an introductory section with explanatory information on the insect's life history and biology, classification keys (to genus and species), and a several-page-long biological description of the genera with plenty of references to figures, maps, and drawings. Both volumes include extensive bibliographies, a glossary of anatomical and biological terms, and an index of genus names. Particular credit should be given to the illustrators for the excellent quality of the line drawings and figures. They are detailed, well presented, easy to read, and a good size (not all crammed on one page).

Unfortunately, most of the text in these titles is English-only except for the classification keys, which are in both English and French. This is surprising for a federal government publication of such high caliber and will make the effective use of these books more difficult for some French speakers. Although well made, the books do not lie flat very easily unless propped open, which might be awkward if one's hands are busy handling specimens in the field or lab.

These works are intended, as noted in the introduction to part 21, for nonspecialists, but they will appeal to professionals as well. And, fortunately, the introductory segments and glossaries are helpful sources should nonspecialists or students become overwhelmed by the biological terms.

—**Katherine Margaret Thomas**

1724. Cooper, Bruce E., and Jeffrey M. Cumming. **Diptera Types in the Canadian National Collection of Insects. Part 2: Brachycera (Exclusive of Schizophora). Types de Dipteres de la Collection Nationale des Insectes du Canada. Deuxieme Partie.** Ottawa, Agriculture Canada, 1993. 105p. index. (Publication, 1896/B). $24.95pa.; $32.45pa. (U.S.). 595.77'1'07471. ISBN 0-660-57979-0.

Material cataloged in part 2 of this practical series describes a suborder of Diptera, the Brachycera. Brachycera are medium to large flies, the more familiar of which are the annoying horse and deer flies of summer, with five or fewer antennal segments. A short introduction and abstract provide the reader with sufficient information to use the book effectively. As in the first part, *Nematocera* (see ARBA 92, entry 1579), the arrangement of entries is alphabetical by family, genus, and species. This second volume includes all primary types in the CNC (Canadian National Collection) as of December 31, 1991. Literature references to the original type description, the CNC catalog number, and full label data are provided with every entry. The final pages include an addendum to Nematocera types that were overlooked in part 1, a comprehensive bibliography, and an index to genera.

A drawback for French-speaking users is that although the title, introduction, and abstract are bilingual, most of the text—the type descriptions—is not. Also, the presence of the addendum (albeit short) makes one wonder what may have been overlooked in this volume. The material cataloged in this book is a small percentage of what is available in the CNC, and for entomology specialists it is invaluable.—**Katherine Margaret Thomas**

1725. Foote, Richard H., F. L. Blanc, and Allen L. Norrbom. **Handbook of the Fruit Flies (Diptera: Tephritidae) of America North of Mexico.** Ithaca, N.Y., Cornell University Press, 1993. 571p. illus. maps. index. $95.00. QL537.T42F66. 595.77'4. LC 92-52844. ISBN 0-8014-2623-5.

This handbook, 39 years in the making, is a guide to the identification of 300 species of adult fruit flies found in North America. It is written by recognized authorities and should prove to be a standard identification guide for years to come. Introductory chapters cover adult morphology, biology, classification of the group, care and handling of specimens, and the use of the handbook. An illustrated key to the Canadian and United States genera leads to descriptions of each genus arranged in alphabetical order, from *Acidogona* to *Zonosemata*. Keys to the identification of species in each genus are also provided.

Each genus and species description begins with a significant literature review. References to the original description and to taxonomy, hosts, type data, and biology are included as well as to names under which the taxon has also been known. References are arranged in chronological order. Only author, year, and page number are provided in these references; a full citation is included in the bibliography at the end of the text. A paragraph of recognition characters, the geographical distribution, and hosts of each taxon follow the literature review. Because this is primarily an identification guide, full descriptions of each taxon are not included, only the information necessary for identification. Several black-and-white drawings and photographs illustrate many of the recognition characters, especially wing patterns, for species identification. Black-and-white distribution maps are also found throughout the text. An impressive 51-page bibliography and indexes to insect names (common and scientific) and host plant names complete the work.

This group of flies is one of the most economically important group of insects in the world, as many are very destructive to fruit and vegetable crops. This thorough guide should prove useful to horticulturalists, biologists, conservationists, students, and specialists for identifying these insects. Highly recommended for university and agricultural libraries.—**Diane B. Rhodes**

1726. Goulet, Henry, and John T. Huber, eds. **Hymenoptera of the World: An Identification Guide to Families.** Ottawa, Agriculture Canada, 1993. 668p. illus. index. (Publication, 1894/E). $48.75pa.; $63.35pa. (U.S.). 595.79. ISBN 0-660-14933-8.

This book was written out of a need for a comprehensive and recent identification guide to the families of Hymenoptera of the world, a ubiquitous order of insects that includes wasps, ants, bees, and sawflies. The guide's aim is to enable users to identify families. It is assumed that more specialized texts will be used to identify genus and species. The intended audience includes both specialists and students new to the field of hymenopteran taxonomy. In total, 99 families and 20 superfamilies are treated, and all living (extant) families are keyed.

The first four chapters provide an excellent introduction to the study of Hymenoptera. Essential topics such as hymenopteran classification and basic insect morphology are dealt with in considerable detail. Importantly, the editors have attempted to use the simplest terminology for structures. The instructions on how to use insect keys are clear, as is a glossary replete with well-labeled diagrams. The beginning student will find the section listing newsletters for hymenopterists and literature on hymenoptera invaluable. The remaining 12 chapters are devoted to identification keys to the superfamilies. Each chapter includes prefatory notes, literature references, series, family or subfamily key, and full-page habitus drawings of a typical member of each superfamily.

The diagrams, habitus drawings, and figures, although exceptionally clear and detailed, suffer from a lack of scale. No indication is given as to the relative size of the depicted structures. A word of warning: This rather bulky paperback is unlikely to withstand heavy use. Overall, it is a significant addition to the international literature and an essential reference for the specialized collection.

—**Katherine Margaret Thomas**

1727. Hogue, Charles L. **Latin American Insects and Entomology.** Berkeley, Calif., University of California Press, 1993. 536p. illus. index. $85.00. QL476.5.H64. 595.7098. LC 91-48184. ISBN 0-520-07849-7.

Maria Sibylla Merian, European artist and naturalist, left a Labadist colony in 1688 and lived the next 11 years in Amsterdam. In 1699, Merian and a daughter traveled to Suriname. They spent less than two years there, but the opus they produced (*Metamorphosis Insectorum Surinamensium*) built a foundation for taxonomic work by Carolus Linnaeus and others. Hogue incorrectly places Merian in Suriname for 10 years; diminishes her formidable efforts at drawing, engraving, and describing by citing minor errors; and spells Sibylla wrong. Thus, the tone is set for a selectively—and not always rigorously—constructed volume. Introductions to insects and related groups and their habits are standard fare. References used stall in the 1970s. North American species (e.g., *Gerris remigis*) are often illustrated instead of Latin American ones. Eight pages of color plates are tempting but only make the sparse pen-and-ink drawings seem less adequate. However, some things are done very well. Related references follow corresponding sections of text, and anecdotes (e.g., Ma'kech beetle as Mayan prince, katydids and forlorn love) engagingly break up descriptive prose. Spanish and Portuguese equivalents are provided for many English and Latin names. Also, historical connections are nicely threaded; for example, verruga (a rickettsial disease vectored by sand flies) menaced the soldiers of Francisco Pizarro, although not enough to stop their takeover of Peru. The index is comprehensive. But the list of included taxa will not be of much use except to specialists, because of its arrangement.—**Diane M. Calabrese**

1728. McNamara, Jean. **A Catalog of Types of Coleoptera in the Canadian National Collection of Insects. Supplement III. Catalogue des Types de Coleopteres de la Collection Nationale des Insectes du Canada.** Ottawa, Agriculture Canada, 1993. 65p. index. $24.95pa.; $32.45pa. (U.S.). 595.7'6'074. ISBN 0-660-57939-1.

This catalog is the third supplement to the original 1970 catalog written by R. de Ruette (refer to the *Memoirs of the Entomological Society of Canada* [72]). Previous supplements have appeared in the *Canadian Entomologist* in 1977 and 1984. The third supplement includes all type material that was cataloged and added to the Coleoptera (beetles) section of the CNC (Canadian National Collection) between January 1981 and December 1989. Although this catalog is not thick, McNamara has put a huge effort into organizing, researching, and updating the information. The catalog has a simple layout. The introductory section, written in English and French, includes brief notes on the history of the collection and a table listing the number of specimens represented by various types. Also included is a list of corrections to and omissions in the previous supplements and original work.

Each descriptive entry (English text only) includes the reference to the original description for each species cited, collection dates, data on type material for each species, and the CNC catalog number. The descriptions are arranged alphabetically by family, genus, and species name. What the entries lack are some comments on specimen quality, a useful resource for researchers not familiar with the collection. A useful cumulative index to species-group names for supplements 1, 2, and 3 completes the catalog. This work is written by an entomologist for Coleoptera specialists and would be a valuable reference in a collection with an entomology focus.—**Katherine Margaret Thomas**

1729. Metcalf, Robert L., and Robert A. Metcalf. **Destructive and Useful Insects: Their Habits and Control.** 5th ed. New York, McGraw-Hill, 1993. 1v. (various paging). illus. index. $85.00. SB931.M47. 632'.7. LC 92-18374. ISBN 0-07-041692-3.

The legacy of a standard reference for entomologists and lay readers is intact. This edition retains the tone and flavor of the earlier versions: dense, not turgid; rich, not overdone. There are important additions among the topics: integrated pest management, the Mediterranean fruit fly, and soybean pests. But the original and extremely useful chapters on morphology and classification remain; they are as good as any such introductions get. Trying to balance human interactions with insects is not easy; and it is nice to see the authors hark back to Rachel Carson's *Silent Spring* as a reminder of the difficulties in maximizing the best and minimizing the worst.

Quibblers can point to opportunities to update drawings (e.g., sawfly wing venation) that were missed, or places where recent references were overlooked. But they would be nitpicking. The omission of discussion of why mosquitoes are not suspected as HIV carriers is the most serious, and the inclusion of the section on pests of tobacco might perplex general readers. Overall, however, this old friend has become more interesting and valuable with age. It is a rare book, one that is genuinely worth its price and merits wide adoption.—**Diane M. Calabrese**

1730. **Peterson First Guide to Caterpillars of North America.** By Amy Bartlett Wright. Boston, Houghton Mifflin, 1993. 128p. illus. index. $4.95pa. QL548.W75. 595.78'04332'097. LC 92-36585. ISBN 0-395-56499-9.

Serendipity has its way: This no-nonsense guide to 125 species of caterpillars also makes a good guide to the same number of butterflies and moths. Identifications require only simple decisions about morphology, such as whether a caterpillar is smooth or hairy and worm- or slug-shaped, and close attention to color patterns (markings) and protrusions. Excellent illustrations mean that just comparing live insects and drawings will take the aspiring lepidopterist a long way. The short descriptions of each species provide information on host plant associations and distribution—the absence of distribution maps is the only quibble one can mount with the guide. And while matching caterpillars and their names, the novice taxonomist will learn many fascinating things about butterflies and moths. For example, some caterpillars resemble bird droppings (for camouflage); some adults and caterpillars show a superficial resemblance in coloration and markings (e.g., white underwing); the monarch caterpillar, with its black, yellow, and white stripes, is unmistakable; and false "faces" on caterpillars are enough to frighten away some bird predators. Finally, no one should tangle with utriculating hairs that certain caterpillars use to ward off enemies. This book is an inexpensive gem.—**Diane M. Calabrese**

Mammals

1731. **Asdell's Patterns of Mammalian Reproduction: A Compendium of Species-Specific Data.** By Virginia Hayssen, Ari van Tienhoven, and Ans van Tienhoven. Ithaca, N.Y., Comstock Publishing/Cornell University Press, 1993. 1023p. index. $75.00. QP251.H33. 599'.016. LC 92-56775. ISBN 0-8014-1753-8.

This important new reference work represents a major effort by three zoologists to continue and update Sydney A. Asdell's famous work, *Patterns of Mammalian Reproduction* (Comstock, 1946, revised 1964). The scope of the new work differs from Asdell's in two ways. First, emphasis is on empirical analysis of mammalian reproduction instead of physiological interpretations; second, data on domestic and laboratory species are not included. The work is organized taxonomically by order and family, the primary entry point for information. Two excellent indexes help users locate material within the body of the work: An index of mammalian species provides entry into the appropriate family, and an index of common names of more than 300 well-known mammals includes scientific names and family references.

The authors examined 150 core journals; these are listed and will serve some librarians as a collection development aid and help others identify publication opportunities for research faculty. A few field guides are included, another good selection aid for users. Bibliographical citations are complete. An outstanding feature of the work for many users will be the care taken to review and update taxonomic information.

This work complements several important reference works; indeed, one measure of its importance is the company it keeps: J. P. Vaissaire's *Sexualite et Reproduction des Mammiferes Domestiques et de Laboratoire* (Paris, Maloine, 1987), *Walker's Mammals of the World* (see ARBA 93, entry 1572), and *Grzimek's Encyclopedia of Mammals* (see ARBA 91, entry 1593). It is an essential purchase for academic libraries.—**Milton H. Crouch**

1732. **Audiovisual Resources in Primatology, Wisconsin Regional Primate Research Center.** Madison, Wis., Wisconsin Regional Primate Research Center, 1993. 152p. index. $10.00 spiralbound.

This is an annotated list of audiovisual items held in the library collection of the Wisconsin Regional Primate Research Center (WRPRC). The WRPRC is a part of the University of Wisconsin at Madison and is involved in studies of captive and wild primates and biomedical research. The stated intent of the WRPRC collection is to preserve the audiovisual record of nonhuman primates, many of which are now threatened or endangered. Topics covered include behaviors of numerous primate species, ecology, conservation, animal husbandry, laboratory animals, facilities, and research. Items are grouped under videotapes, audiotapes, slides, films, and records. Videotapes constitute a major portion of the collection. There are nearly 400 entries in total. Each entry includes title, producer's name and address, date, and other applicable information for that item, such as running time, number of slides in a set, and whether it is in color or black-and-white. The annotation immediately following the item listing usually consists of one or two short descriptive paragraphs, with taxonomic names of the primates covered shown in boldface type. Taxonomic and common name indexes are provided, as well as a title index. This book can serve as a useful reference source for researchers and handlers of primates, because nearly all of the items listed can be borrowed directly from the WRPRC.—**William H. Wiese**

1733. Brown, Gary. **The Great Bear Almanac.** New York, Lyons & Burford, 1993. 325p. illus. maps. index. $30.00. QL737.C27B765. 599.74'446. LC 93-7686. ISBN 1-55821-210-8.

This popular book is packed with facts and lore on bears of the world. The easy-to-read text and the many illustrations, photographs, color plates, maps, and charts will entertain and inform readers for hours. Part 1, "Bears in Their World," covers the evolution of bears and briefly describes the eight species of bears found in the world, their anatomy and physiology, and bear behavior. Part 2, "Bears in the Human World," covers the interactions of bears and humans. In this part, the author shows the many ways bears have influenced humans in their daily lives, including the more whimsical ways, such as the use of the word *bear* for athletic teams, bears in religion (e.g., references to them in the Bible), bear festivals (e.g., the Ainu Bear Festival in Japan), bears in astronomy, bear myths, and bears in art and literature, as well as information on bear attacks and the use of bears and bear parts for medicinal purposes. Part 2 concludes with chapters on the conservation status of bears. The appendixes cover evolution, bears included in CITES (Convention on International Trade in Endangered Species of Wild Fauna and Flora), and a list of organizations involved in bear studies or concerns. A bibliography and index complete the work.

Written by a man with 31 years in the National Park Service who has served as bear management specialist at Yellowstone National Park, this work reflects his first-hand knowledge and dedication to bears gained during these years. Another book on bears by Terry Domico, *Bears of the World* (Facts on File, 1988) is also a good choice, as it has more information on individual bear species and features 160 color photographs of bears. Recommended for public and school libraries from junior high on up, as well as academic libraries. It is primarily a popular work for the amateur naturalist, but it will also be useful for park rangers, conservationists, and students. [R: LJ, Aug 93, p. 90; RBB, 1 Oct 93, p. 384]

—**Diane B. Rhodes**

1734. Corbet, G. B., and J. E. Hill. **Mammals of the Indomalayan Region: A Systematic Review.** New York, Oxford University Press, 1992. 488p. illus. maps. index. $110.00. QL729.A785C67. 599.0954. LC 92-299. ISBN 0-19-854693-9.

This is the first manual of the mammals of the Indomalayan region to be produced in many years. The authors provide basic information on more than 1,000 species of mammals in the region, which stretches from India in the east to the islands of the western Pacific Ocean. The species accounts include taxonomic information, accepted scientific and common names, synonyms, range, and remarks (including rarity) for all species. Most species also have information on subspecies and ecology. There are black-and-white line drawings and range maps for selected mammals, as well as a number of tables identifying species of a particular genus. The appendixes include a checklist of recent species in the region, a gazetteer, and biographical notes on the collectors and describers of the regional fauna. This last is particularly useful for taxonomists and science historians. There are also a 3,000-item bibliography and an index. The information included in this manual cannot be found in any other single volume, so it is very useful for mammalogists and others interested in the fauna of this region. The manual is not designed for casual readers, but experts will find it valuable.—**Diane Schmidt**

1735. Humphrey, Stephen R., ed. **Rare and Endangered Biota of Florida. Volume I: Mammals.** Gainesville, Fla., University Press of Florida, 1992. 392p. illus. maps. index. $59.95. QL706.83.U6R37. 599'.0042'09759. LC 91-36368. ISBN 0-8130-1127-2.

Serving as a testament to the steady increase in numbers of extinct, endangered, and threatened mammal species, this 2d edition of a work published originally in 1978 lists more species in every category. The first edition was a 52-page work; the new edition is nearly 8 times longer. It follows the same format but includes more information. The first edition was part of a highly acclaimed six-volume work on Florida's endangered plants and animals, and this is one of the revised volumes from that set.

The work lists and describes the Florida mammal species that are close to extinction, why they got there, and how to improve their lot. It is introduced by discussions on the major habitats where these animals live. The following chapters are devoted to each of the 43 mammal species determined by the Florida Committee on Rare and Endangered Plants and Animals to be recently extinct, recently extirpated (disappeared from Florida but possibly still alive in another area), endangered, threatened, a species of special concern, rare, or status undetermined. Each species is thoroughly described by individual authors who provide taxonomy, description, population size, distribution and history of distribution, geographical range, habitat requirements, cause of threat, habitat modification responses, key behaviors, conservation measures taken, and conservation measures proposed. Each species chapter ends with a list of literature cited. Range maps and black-and-white photographs of most species illustrate the species descriptions.

This new edition continues the work of the first in alerting people to the declining status of Florida species and providing vital information on species biology and habitat that may be used by conservationists, legislators, wildlife managers, and the general public to try to halt the devastating decline in our wildlife populations. Highly recommended for all libraries.—**Diane B. Rhodes**

1736. **International Directory of Primatology.** Madison, Wis., Wisconsin Regional Primate Research Center, University of Wisconsin, 1992. 1v. (unpaged). index. $10.00 spiralbound.

This directory brings together material on a wide variety of primate information sources and programs that otherwise would take many hours of searching to find. Compiled by the Wisconsin Regional Primate Research Center staff, it is intended as a means to aid primate research and communication between the various researchers and organizations around the world.

The directory is organized into five sections: organizations arranged geographically, field studies, population management groups, primate societies, and information resources. To help direct one to information in these sections, there are indexes to organizations, species, programs, and personal names. Beside each entry in the index is a section and page number where that information can easily be found in the text.

In this handy work one can find the address, mission, key personnel (with telephone numbers), and species supported for 183 primate research centers, such as the Red Howler Project in Guarico, Venezuela; find the address, mission, clientele, services, and collections of information agencies, such as the British Library of Wildlife Sounds; find out who has a database on the *Lemur catta* (the Indianapolis Zoo does); and find a bibliography on the behavior of captive gorillas. The cost is a bargain for a work that would benefit all academic and large public libraries, and especially all primate research labs.—**Diane B. Rhodes**

1737. Katona, Steven K., Valerie Rough, and David T. Richardson. **A Field Guide to Whales, Porpoises, and Seals from Cape Cod to Newfoundland.** 4th ed. Washington, D.C., Smithsonian Institution Press, 1993. 316p. illus. index. $15.95pa. LC 93-84473. ISBN 1-56098-333-7.

This comprehensive field guide was first published in 1975. It documents all species of cetaceans (whales, dolphins, and porpoises) and pinnipeds (seals, sea lions, and walruses) that inhabit the waters from Cape Cod to Newfoundland. The text gives accounts of 22 species of toothed and baleen whales and 7 species of seals. Also, because they are common and frequently sighted in the study area, the authors have included descriptions of basking sharks, leatherback turtles, and ocean sunfish. The text of the accounts is anecdotal and descriptive, providing relevant breeding, feeding, and behavior characteristics. It is accompanied by detailed line drawings and black-and-white photographs, which provide an indispensable aid to identification. Emphasis is put on identifying these mammals from a distance, because this is the most frequent form of observation.

The introductory pages give a useful background to the study of whales at sea, including certain guidelines and federal regulations one should be aware of when approaching and watching whales. Likewise, the appendixes provide a wealth of information on whale and seal watching trips in Canada and the United States, and current references to journal, book, video, and film sources. Teachers and parents will find these references particularly useful, as titles suitable for younger and amateur readers have been delineated. This highly readable guide is appropriate for the novice and expert alike and should be in any library with a basic marine mammal collection.—**Katherine Margaret Thomas**

1738. Maynard, Thane. **Saving Endangered Mammals: A Field Guide to Some of the Earth's Rarest Animals.** New York, Franklin Watts, 1992. 57p. illus. maps. index. (Cincinnati Zoo Book). $15.90; $22.71 (library binding). QL706.8.M38. 599'.0042. LC 92-14439. ISBN 0-531-15253-7; 0-531-11076-1 (library binding).

Youngsters interested in the plights and conservation of some rare animals will find this book a good introduction. The author has selected 25 species of disappearing mammals for a global overview of our threatened ark. The author is director of conservation at the Cincinnati Zoo, an institution renowned for its programs with endangered wildlife.

Each species is presented in a profile that includes a page of text and a full-page color photograph. The text summarizes the animal's range (with map), diet, behavior, habitat, and other important aspects of its natural history. There is considerable emphasis on the ecological threats to these mammals (e.g., pollution, overhunting, habitat loss) and their current endangered status. There is also a somewhat optimistic discussion of conservation efforts for these creatures, from captive breeding programs to the protection of wild populations. This book is one of an educational series designed to involve young people in global conservation, and it meets the challenge of being both appealing and informative. It has a short glossary, a list of conservation organizations, and suggestions for further readings. [R: SLJ, Mar 93, pp. 214-15]—**Charles Leck**

1739. **The Multimedia Encyclopedia of Mammalian Biology: Incorporating** *Grzimek's Encyclopedia of Mammals.* [CD-ROM]. New York, McGraw-Hill, 1992. Hardware requirements: IBM PC or compatible, 386 or better; SVGA monitor; hard disk with 2MB of space; 2MB of RAM; MS-DOS 3.3 or higher; Microsoft Windows 3.0 set up for 256 colors; Microsoft-compatible mouse. $995.00. ISBN 0-07-707-7008.

The classic, well-regarded, five-volume *Grzimek's Encyclopedia of Mammals* (see ARBA 91, entry 1593) has been augmented with more than 3,000 color images (e.g., maps, charts, motion pictures) from the BBC Natural History Unit archives. Although the producers would have us believe that this tool is extremely easy to use, straightforward, and congenial, it is actually a highly sophisticated, authoritative reference work. As with the printed encyclopedia, both biological and behavioral information about mammals can be retrieved. The Windows software facilitates searching of primary text, supplementary articles from specialists, and additional material (e.g., glossary, bibliography, graphics). Access is provided through three searching modes (e.g., browse, search, trail), with the user choosing the approach (e.g., text, data) and level of difficulty. The controlled lists (e.g., taxonomy, biogeographical, thematic, vocabulary) scanned in the browsing mode are not reproduced in the user's guide, a feature that would greatly assist beginners. The search modes support single- or combined-term searching, with the ability to create trails for others to follow. The Firstlines option, the equivalent of title lists, is a useful option.

Familiarity with Windows is essential. The software's flexibility is both an asset and a detriment. Individual windows, which are supplemented with command lines, icons, and search mode indicators, can be enlarged to full-screen size. Unfortunately, reproduction quality is reduced, and the Windows environment is harder to adapt to requirements mandated for ADA compliance. Search assistance is offered through a suggested guided tour (which would function better as a tutorial), help screens, and printed documentation (a very small looseleaf user's manual). While the tour instructions seem clear, the screen, upon initial viewing, appears complicated. The manual, with no index, must be consulted to verify step sequences and command structures. While this is not unusual when dealing with a new software package, an index would help.

As would a game, the flexibility and multimedia approach will entice the user, but extensive practice is necessary to search it well without better user documentation. Some custom features (e.g., cut and paste documents, printing, saving strategies) will not function as designed in institutions anticipating heavy use by undergraduates. An area requiring further clarification is the frequency of updates incorporating information on newly discovered mammals.—**Sandra E. Belanger**

1740. Porter, Valerie. **Pigs: A Handbook to the Breeds of the World.** Ithaca, N.Y., Comstock Publishing/Cornell University Press, 1993. 256p. illus. index. $35.00. LC 92-56193. ISBN 0-8014-2920-X.

This book describes all known pig breeds from around the world, covering feral and domestic pigs, commercial hybrid breeds, and even extinct and endangered breeds. More than 200 color drawings are included. Porter wrote a similar successful work on cattle breeds, titled *Cattle* (see ARBA 93, entry 1491).

Beginning with chapters on feral pigs and pig breeding, the book is arranged by geographical area where the pigs are raised. The history and cultural influences on pig breeding and the types of breeds commonly raised in that geographical area are discussed. The book concludes with appendixes on pig-breeding companies of the United Kingdom, some of the extinct breeds of the world, some synonyms, a bibliography of sources (although no footnotes are provided in the text that refer to these sources), and an index. Highlighting the text is a section of 24 black-and-white labeled outline drawings with corresponding full-color plates (all drawn by Jake Tebbit) illustrating the various breeds.

The information is interesting, even for the general reader. For example, Christopher Columbus was said to have brought the first domestic pigs to Cuba, whence feral populations were transported to the colonies, where they quickly adapted and became so abundant in some areas they began helping themselves to the colonists' new plantings. The pig breed descriptions are also delightful. The Irish Greyhound pig is described as "tall and bony, with a very long head and snout, and so long-legged that it was apparently an adept high-jumper."

Almost all the information one will need about any pig breed, living or extinct, is covered here. The mix of historical, cultural, and factual material makes for a surprisingly interesting text that can be enjoyed by a wide audience. Highly recommended for public, academic, and agricultural libraries.
—**Diane B. Rhodes**

1741. Wassink, Jan L. **Mammals of the Central Rockies.** Missoula, Mont., Mountain Press, 1993. 161p. illus. maps. index. $12.00pa. QL719.R63W37. 599.09787. LC 92-46268. ISBN 0-87842-237-4.

Wassink is a student of wildlife management whose reputation is based on field guides of regional interest, such as *Birds of the Central Rockies* (see ARBA 92, entry 1572) and several well-produced titles in media format. His purpose here is to provide an easy-to-use field guide to all the large mammals of the central Rockies and the most common small ones, including rodents, rabbits, bats, shrews, and opossums. He introduces users to the importance of scientific classification and promotes interest in his discussion of individual species by providing good, brief accounts of life cycles, identifying characteristics, and habitats. Care is taken to emphasize distinctive behavior patterns and descriptions of other species that may superficially resemble the mammal under discussion. His descriptions are short but quite good, the best one being a discussion of the moose, "who looks like it was designed by a committee." The photographs are the key to identification, and the face-front, full-bodied views promote understanding and interest. The 50 photographs show animals in their environment; those taken to illustrate details, such as bull elk or mule deer horns in velvet, add to the reference value of the guide. There are a helpful glossary; an index; and, for those who might wish to know more, a carefully selected bibliography of scientific monographs. [R: Choice, Nov 93, p. 484]—**Milton H. Crouch**

1742. Whitehead, G. Kenneth. **The Whitehead Encyclopedia of Deer.** Stillwater, Minn., Voyageur Press, 1993. 597p. illus. $140.00. ISBN 1-85310-362-4.

Whitehead is one of the world's authorities on managing small deer populations. Among his many publications are *Deer of the World* (Viking, 1972) and at least two important monographs on their history, distribution, and management in Great Britain and Ireland. The purpose of this subject encyclopedia is to provide a source of information about all the world's deer species. A major portion of the work is devoted to their biology, including sections on taxonomy, diseases, parasites, hybridization, and distribution. Management concerns and questions associated with stalking and hunting receive careful attention. Hundreds of tables, photographs, and charts increase user understanding and the encyclopedia's reference value for serious students. Unique features are the well-illustrated sections on deer trophies and deer iconography. A carefully organized 57-page bibliography, citing both scholarly and popular publications, is an outstanding feature.

The encyclopedia is decidedly English in flavor, but coverage is international. The book's seven-sectional arrangement might confuse users who associate encyclopedias with a cover-to-cover alphabetical arrangement instead of a multisectional one. No matter—any problems with language or arrangement are quickly resolved. The encyclopedia is intended for laypeople but will complement academic collections as well. [R: LJ, 1 June 93, p. 110; RBB, 1 Sept 93, pp. 91-92]—**Milton H. Crouch**

1743. Wilson, Don E., and DeeAnn M. Reeder, eds. **Mammal Species of the World: A Taxonomic and Geographic Reference.** 2d ed. Washington, D.C., Smithsonian Institution Press, 1993. 1206p. index. $75.00. QL708.M35. 599'.0012. LC 92-22703. ISBN 1-56098-217-9.

This is the new edition of a checklist that has become the standard for mammalian taxonomy. It lists 4,629 (up from 4,170 in the first edition) existing or recently extinct species from around the world. The most up-to-date list, it provides, for each species, the publication where it was first named and described, the type locality, geographical distribution, conservation status, synonyms, and additional taxonomic notes. A lengthy bibliography of references cited in the work attests to the comprehensive research done to produce this checklist and also provides suggestions for further reading.

The major difference between this edition and the first is the way it was compiled and edited. The first edition was the result of the reviews of approximately 160 specialists who contributed their individual views of valid names and references. It was decided that this approach was too free with dissenting opinions on taxonomic names; therefore, this edition was authored by 20 specialists, who adopted the taxonomic arrangement that they thought best synthesized the current literature for their area. The information for this edition is in an electronic database, which will make it easier to update future editions. Another difference is that the ISIS (International Species Inventory System) numbers used in the first edition were left out of this one. A table contained in the introduction summarizes the differences between the first and second editions in number of genera and species listed for each order and family (86 new names in the order Rodentia). It also shows rearrangements of taxons, especially the substitution of seven new orders for the old order Marsupialia.

A comparable checklist is *A World List of Mammalian Species* (see ARBA 92, entry 1581). That work does not contain taxonomic references and is not as complete or up-to-date, but it does contain and index the common names of each mammal, something *Mammal Species of the World* does not do. For its comprehensive, current, and authoritative contents, *Mammal Species of the World* should be an essential purchase for all academic and large public libraries and those special libraries with holdings in mammalian studies. [R: Choice, Sept 93, p. 84]—**Diane B. Rhodes**

Marine Animals

1744. Baretta-Bekker, J. G., E. K. Duursma, and B. R. Kuipers, eds. **Encyclopedia of Marine Sciences.** New York, Springer-Verlag, 1992. 311p. illus. maps. $39.00pa. GC9.E56. 551.46. LC 92-2877. ISBN 0-387-54501-8.

The recent growth in interest in the marine sciences makes this a good time for a new encyclopedia. This one is a small paperback with 1,850 terms from the disciplines making up marine science: marine biology, chemistry, geology, and physical oceanography. For each term a definition is provided, as well as a brief explanatory paragraph. Cross-references to other terms in the encyclopedia are marked with an arrow. Where needed, basic mathematical formulas are included. Some of the terms are accompanied by line illustrations.

This encyclopedia is very well written. It will be useful to undergraduate students. In contrast to *The Facts on File Dictionary of Marine Science* (see ARBA 89, entry 1670), the illustrations in this encyclopedia are credited to their source publications, full references for which appear in a list on the last pages; also, this encyclopedia is written at a higher level. The coverage of the different component disciplines within marine science appears to be balanced, although some readers will want to consult reference sources in these disciplines for more information. The book is appropriate for reference collections in academic libraries. [R: Choice, Feb 93, p. 938]—**John Laurence Kelland**

1745. The Great Book of the Sea: A Complete Guide to Marine Life. Philadelphia, Courage Books/Running Press, 1993. 275p. illus. maps. index. $29.98. LC 92-54935. ISBN 1-56138-270-1.

This guide covers marine invertebrates, fish, reptiles, birds, and mammals. A major introductory chapter deals with the ocean environment and many general characteristics of marine animals, as well as marine ecosystems. A brief look at fishing is also included. In the invertebrate and vertebrate chapters that follow, descriptive text covers the habits and general biology of each group (family, order, or class), and a color painting of each species is provided. There is an index of common and scientific names.

This large guide can serve as a kind of encyclopedia of marine animal life. It provides the reader with clear, excellent illustrations of many species and a wealth of fascinating facts about them. The book is clearly aimed at the general public, yet the text is written at quite a high level that is better suited to readers with a good vocabulary in general biology. An appendix covering the classification of marine animals and a good glossary would be helpful. (By comparison, *The Encyclopedia of Aquatic Life* [see ARBA 86, entry 1508] has an excellent glossary.) One problem is that some of the fish illustrations are labeled only with scientific names, while common and scientific names are used in the text. Still, the guide will be useful for the general public and in high school and college libraries. [R: RBB, Aug 93, p. 2090]
—**John Laurence Kelland**

1746. Halstead, Bruce W. **Dangerous Aquatic Animals of the World: A Color Atlas.** Princeton, N.J., Darwin Press, 1992. 264p. illus. maps. $60.00. QL100.H297. 591.6'5'0916. LC 91-13746. ISBN 0-87850-045-6.

This work divides dangerous aquatic organisms into invertebrates and vertebrates and further separates those groups of animals that sting from those that are poisonous. In addition, wound-producing and electric aquatic animals and human parasitic catfish are considered.

The particular animal groups listed are usually discussed in some depth. Such details as habitat, size, external anatomy, behavioral patterns, and coloration are provided. Information on the species includes common and scientific name, size, coloration, habitat, geographical distribution, and mode of attack. An emphasis, as one would imagine, is placed on information about the mechanics of how the animal injures as well as its stinging apparatus or venom produced. Cross-references to the plates accompany the species accounts. More than 470 colored photographs, a number of lack-and-white photographs, and labeled line drawings illustrate the book. Pictures showing the animals' effects on humans are also provided. A list of geographical range maps; a section on prevention, first aid, and emergency treatment procedures; a glossary; and a short bibliography conclude the handbook. Although the volume lacks an index, the table of contents helps one find major common animal groups. Recommended for high school, public, college, and university library collections.—**George H. Bell**

1747. Veron, J. E. N. **Corals of Australia and the Indo-Pacific.** Honolulu, University of Hawaii Press, c1986, 1993. 644p. illus. maps. index. $90.00. QL377.C5V43. 593.6. LC 92-24064. ISBN 0-8248-1504-1.

Scuba divers, snorkelers, and many others intrigued by denizens of the sea are drawn to coral reefs (even pictures of reefs), a dominant tropical and subtropical feature of the Earth. The coral reefs of the Indo-Pacific are a taxonomically rich assemblage of these animals, most of which live in complex colonies clustered on top of or adjacent to one another. In particular, the Great Barrier Reef of Australia, extending along the northeast coast of the country, is exceptional for its geographical extent and richness of species in a largely ecologically undisturbed area. Caribbean reefs are impoverished by comparison.

This book has hundreds of excellent photographs of corals showing their characteristic shapes, their colors (due to symbiotic algae), some of their individual polyps, and broader views of the reef (from above and underwater) and the islands some reefs surround. The photographs alone are worth the price of the book. About 10 percent of the volume is a concise introduction to the structure of reefs, the physical and biological factors affecting coral occurrence and growth, the distribution of coral communities across a reef, the life history of corals, the evolution of reefs, and a brief explanation of coral classification. The rest of the tome is a systematic account of Australian reef-building corals, with spectacular photographs of many species. Worldwide distribution maps for many groups are shown. Species and their identifying characters, color, abundance, and potential for confusion with similar species are briefly described.

Veron offers a first-class coffee-table book on the major calcium carbonate producers of the sea. A diver could identify many corals (but by no means all) through comparing the pictures in this work with the real animal and without damaging the reef in order to bring samples to the surface—which no longer have a life-like look when taken out of water anyway. [R: Choice, Dec 93, p. 629]—**David Bardack**

Reptiles and Amphibians

1748. Cogger, Harold G., and Richard G. Zweifel. **Reptiles & Amphibians.** New York, Smithmark, 1992. 240p. illus. maps. index. $24.98. ISBN 0-8317-2786-1.

Cogger and Zweifel, recognized herpetologists, assembled and edited the contributions of 16 noted scholars in producing this extraordinary book on amphibians and reptiles. Artist-biologist David Kirshner produced the many fine color illustrations that add vitality to and provide examples for every discussion. The numerous superb color photographs are the products of some of the world's best naturalist-photographers.

The narrative is organized into three parts. The first six chapters deal with world amphibians and reptiles in general. Higher taxa are introduced; then, classification, origins and historical topics, habitats and adaptations, behavior, and endangered species are sequentially covered. Part 2 has three chapters devoted to caecilians, salamanders and newts, and frogs and toads. Part 3 has chapters on turtles and tortoises, lizards, snakes, amphisbaenians, the tuatara, and crocodiles and alligators. Notes on contributors and an index are appended.

This is a book almost anyone can read, comprehend, and enjoy. It is accurate in detail, highly informative, lavishly and colorfully illustrated, and written with exceptional clarity for a general audience. Technical vocabulary is present but minimal. Recommended highly for general purchase by public, secondary school, and college libraries. [R: SLJ, Feb 93, p. 121]—**Edmund D. Keiser, Jr.**

1749. Collins, Joseph T. **Amphibians and Reptiles in Kansas.** 3d ed. Lawrence, Kans., University Press of Kansas, 1993. 397p. illus. maps. index. (Public Education Series University of Kansas, Museum of Natural History, no.13). $29.95; $19.95pa. QL653.K3C64. 597.6'09781. LC 93-18564. ISBN 0-89338-044-X; 0-89338-043-1pa.

This is the third edition of Collins's exemplary reference work on the amphibians and reptiles of Kansas. Earlier editions appeared in 1974 and 1982. Included among the improvements to this edition are addenda to county and state distribution records, updated range maps and size maxima, revisions of many species accounts, and the addition of 96 superb color plates. Nomenclature is current, and the bibliography now extends into 1992.

The preface has 3d edition modifications and acknowledgments. The introduction contains historical perspectives, briefings on state physiography and observing Kansas herpetozoans, species account explanations, and comments on endangered, threatened, and alien species. The taxonomic accounts are grouped by vernacular names of higher taxa (e.g., amphibians, then salamanders). Each group has introductory comments. Families within a group and their included genera and species are ordered alphabetically. Each of the 97 Kansas species has its own concise account. A monochrome photograph and headings consisting of common and scientific names and a color plate reference introduce each species account. Successive paragraphs covering descriptions, size, range, habits and habitat, breeding, food, subspecies in Kansas, and remarks follow. Distribution records are indicated by centered county spots on Kansas maps.

Taxonomically ordered dichotomous keys to identification of adults are illustrated by excellent line drawings. The glossary is superficial, but the bibliography, particularly the Kansas section, is extensive. An index to common and scientific names ends the book.

This is a superb regional work that should be in high school, university, and public libraries of Kansas and neighboring states. Anyone interested in the Kansas herpetofauna will find this book invaluable.
—**Edmund D. Keiser, Jr.**

1750. Culotta, Wendy A., and George V. Pickwell. **The Venomous Sea Snakes: A Comprehensive Bibliography.** Malabar, Fla., Krieger Publishing, 1993. 504p. index. $79.50. Z7996.S64C84. 016.59796'09162. LC 90-42244. ISBN 0-89464-469-6.

This collection of subject bibliographies primarily covers the scientific literature of the world's sea snakes to 1990. Sea snake taxa are those included in Malcolm Smith's 1926 *Monograph of the Sea-snakes (Hydrophiidae)* (London: British Museum). Casual and anecdotal publications are included if they add valuable information to extant literature. Approximately 2,500 references are arranged in 24 subject chapters and several indexes. Culotta and Pickwell are competent biologists who have authored technical papers on sea snakes. Prefaced sections include comments on the bibliography from the perspectives of a marine biologist and a science librarian. A 48-page list of cited journals and their abbreviations precedes chapter 1.

Each chapter is a subject-focused bibliography on a specific topic of sea snake biology. Chapter 1 lists pre-Linnaean and other pre-nineteenth-century references. Chapters 2 and 3 include broad-spectrum technical and natural history references. Subsequent chapters deal with taxonomy, distribution, reproduction and growth, evolution and genetics, ecology, parasites, predators, morphology, biochemistry, husbandry, and uses by humans. Sea snake physiology takes up two chapters, and five are devoted to venoms and bites. Nontechnical references are included in chapter 23. The final chapter is on additional bibliographical sources. Each chapter ends with a genus-species index. Citations conform to the *CBE Style Manual*, 5th ed. (Council of Biology Editors, 1983). Entries are numbered according to the chapter and listing sequence. Illustrations are limited to 10 color photographs of sea snakes on the inside covers. An author index is appended.

The bibliography is thorough and useful, but the subject is narrow and will appeal only to a limited audience. Recommended for purchase primarily by libraries supporting marine biology or graduate-level herpetology programs.—**Edmund D. Keiser, Jr.**

1751. Rossi, John. **Snakes of the United States and Canada: Keeping Them Healthy in Captivity. Volume I: Eastern Area.** Malabar, Fla., Krieger Publishing, 1992. 209p. illus. maps. index. $49.50. SF515.5.S64R67. 639.3'96. LC 91-2199. ISBN 0-89464-590-0.

Veterinarian Rossi combined his hobby and profession to produce this work on the maintenance of selected species of North American snakes in captivity. Volume 1 emphasizes species of the eastern United States. The narrative includes a brief introduction and four parts. Part 1 discusses general care of serpents. Topics include capture, housing, cleaning, temperature, humidity and lighting, substrates, feeding, psychological factors, hibernation, sexing, breeding, eggs and young, size, ecdysis, parasites, and treatment of infections and parasites. Tables, line drawings, and monochrome photographs support this unit.

Part 2, on individual species care, has 43 accounts of harmless snake species. Two species of water snakes are combined into one account, and separate accounts are allocated for two subspecies of *Lampropeltis triangulum*. Each account includes a captive maintenance section and a box containing a range map and condensed comments on maintenance difficulty, sizes, food, cage size, substrate, ventral heat, ultraviolet light, temperature range, and special considerations.

Part 3, on venomous snakes, discusses maintenance and transportation of dangerous reptiles and includes seven species accounts. Part 4, "Disasters," has seven captive snake anecdotes. Brief lists of herpetological societies and references are appended. Indexes of common names and subjects complete the book. One hundred annotated color photographs, six or seven to a page, are bound within parts 1 and 2.

Information content is good but focuses on the experiences of the author and his associates. Much that is conjectural is dispersed within the factual. This lends interest and uniqueness to the text, but less disciplined readers may infer unwarranted conclusions. The narrative is easy to read but verbose and occasionally awkward. The book's binding fell away after limited handling. Despite these shortcomings, this is an entertaining and informative work that should appeal to anyone who keeps snakes in captivity. Recommended for general purchase by public and college libraries.—**Edmund D. Keiser, Jr.**

1752. Smith, Hobart M., and Rozella B. Smith. **Synopsis of the Herpetofauna of Mexico. Volume VII: Bibliographic Addendum IV and Index, Bibliographic Addenda II-IV 1979-1991.** Niwot, Colo., University Press of Colorado, 1993. 1082p. $60.00. Z7996.R4S645. 016.5976'0972. LC 92-36642. ISBN 0-87081-284-X.

Distinguished author-herpetologists Hobart M. Smith and the late Rozella B. Smith have again combined their productive talents to complete their seventh and final volume on the amphibians and reptiles of Mexico. These seven volumes will be an important reference series for generations to come. Volume 7 focuses on the literature and nomenclature and includes bibliographical addendum 4 and taxonomic indexes for bibliographical addenda 2, 3, and 4. Addendum 4 indexes 6,606 titles that appeared from 1979 through May 1991. Addendum 2 appeared in 1977 (volume 5) and addendum 3 in 1980 (volume 6).

A brief introduction explains the format and procedures used in volume 7 and notes differences from previous volumes. The taxonomic indexes that follow include those on salamanders (Caudata), frogs and toads (Anura), caecilians (Gymnophiona), turtles (Testudines), lizards (Sauria), amphisbaenians (Amphisbaenia), snakes (Serpentes), and crocodilians (Crocodylia). Each taxonomic index is divided into subunits that consist of an introduction, a primary index, and a synonym list. The introductions provide numerical information on included citations and comments of historical and taxonomic interest. Each primary index is an alphabetical list of junior and senior synonyms of genera, species, and subspecies. Junior synonyms are followed by names in present usage in parentheses. One or more abbreviated citations follow each name. These uniformly include the last name of the author, the synopsis volume in which the complete citation is referenced, the citation index number, and the page or pages on which the taxon appears. The synonym lists are alphabetically arranged by taxa in present-day use. Each senior taxon is followed by an indented list of junior synonyms.

Although the print is small and illustrations (other than a single graph) are absent, this volume is massive. Anyone working on the vertebrate fauna of Mexico will find this book and its predecessors to be indispensable. Recommended for general reference purchase by college and university libraries.

—**Edmund D. Keiser, Jr.**

32 Engineering

GENERAL WORKS

1753. **Ei Thesaurus.** Jessica L. Milstead, ed. Hoboken, N.J., Engineering Information, 1992. 790p. $130.00. ISBN 0-87394-119-5.

To make the use of its abstracting services more effective, Engineering Information (EI) has published this thesaurus in different editions over the years. However, on January 1, 1993, EI began using a different vocabulary to index its products, bringing unity to the print *Engineering Index* and the electronic Compendex indexes. This new vocabulary does not just update past lists but "reflects a complete re-thinking" of how to approach engineering topics. Inverted terms are replaced with natural language style, and the complex heading/subheading arrangement is adapted to more direct terminology. The cross-references to broader, narrower, similar, or preferred terms are very effective in pinpointing the proper nomenclature. Many formerly used terms have been dropped, and these are noted with an asterisk and a *see* reference. The date of first use is noted for all holdover terms, but the majority of terms are new or redefined for this edition. For example, there are 27 subdivisions under the entry "cars," but none are still being used (e.g., "Cars—Passenger"..."USE: Passenger cars"). The date on the former use tag is important for searching versions indexed before the changeover date, as the user will benefit from knowing the terminology employed at that time. An additional feature in this book is the listing of the hierarchical classification codes, newly expanded beyond three digits, which systematizes the subject fields of engineering and areas covered in the thesaurus. In the front matter is a full explanation of how to consult the thesaurus. Any library that uses the print or electronic versions of the *Engineering Index* will find this work to be an essential acquisition.—**Gary R. Cocozzoli**

AGRICULTURAL ENGINEERING

1754. Hall, Carl W., and Wallace C. Olsen, eds. **The Literature of Agricultural Engineering.** Ithaca, N.Y., Cornell University Press, 1992. 416p. index. (Literature of the Agricultural Sciences). $59.50. S674.3.L58. 630. LC 92-24516. ISBN 0-8014-2812-2.

Unevenness describes this book. It is more than the literature of the profession; it is a nice compendium of a discipline, including advances and directions of the profession, with the literature presented in bibliographical essays. Some of the chapters (e.g., those on developing countries and food engineering) are excellent: They integrate the background of a specific area of agricultural engineering with its literature so that anyone interested in that area can easily read the chapter and go to those comprehensive sources. Unfortunately, to get to these chapters one must wade through a preface that does not state the intent of the work and then three chapters that are not focused. The last half of the book presents the core literature as derived from citation analysis with rankings from scientists from developed and developing countries. Organizationally, this work is lacking, but the content has merit; however, it takes a lot of energy and digging to find that merit. [R: Choice, Sept 93, p. 84]—**Patricia S. Wilson**

ASTRONAUTICAL ENGINEERING

1755. Cassutt, Michael. **Who's Who in Space: The International Space Year Edition.** New York, Macmillan, 1993. 439p. illus. index. $75.00. TL788.5.C37. 629.45'0092. LC 92-19275. ISBN 0-02-897092-6.

This book, a revised edition of the author's first work, *Who's Who in Space: The First 25 Years* (see ARBA 88, entry 1587), is a classified biographical dictionary of the first 31 years of space exploration. Data are provided for individuals from the U.S. space program, the Soviet space program, and the 23 other countries that have sent people into space. Entries include the astronaut's name, birth date and place, childhood, education, service record, contribution to space program, and current status. Most entries are illustrated by photographs. While a few of the Soviet photographs are rather crude, they are most likely the best available. Additional useful tables include space acronyms and abbreviations; manned space flights, 1961-1992; X-15 flights; a chronological log of space flights; manned time-in-space log; U.S. and Soviet mission flight crews; teacher-in-space candidates; and journalist-in-space candidates. There is an index to the biography section, but it does not reference the tables. Also included is a center photograph section that illustrates NASA mission crew patches, group photographs of U.S. astronauts the author feels are pioneers, and a much smaller section of Soviet pioneers. The volume is hardbound and is attractive in design and layout.

This volume compares favorably with Douglas Hawthorne's *Men and Women of Space* (Univelt, 1992). However, the entries in Hawthorne contain more information and are better and more accurate. For example, Cassutt gives Yuriy Sheffer's birth date as June 3, 1947, when it is in fact June 30, 1947; and he fails to record the death of Alexandr Shchukin in a plane crash on August 18th, 1988. While the Cassutt volume is better illustrated, and hence more appealing, Hawthorne's work is better edited and more comprehensive in scope. Libraries not wanting to purchase both would do better to stick with *Men and Women of Space*. [R: Choice, Nov 93, p. 424; LJ, Aug 93, p. 90; RBB, 1 Nov 93, p. 571; RQ, Winter 93, p. 298; SLJ, Nov 93, p. 140; WLB, Sept 93, pp. 124-27]—**Ralph Lee Scott**

1756. Davies, J. K. **Space Exploration.** New York, Chambers Kingfisher Graham, 1992. 275p. illus. index. $9.95pa. ISBN 0-550-17013-8.

This little volume, the fifteenth in the Chambers Compact Reference Series, covers 100 topics in space exploration. Each topic receives a brief explanation of its origin, developments in its field, its potential for future research and use, and any troubles encountered. Most entries also have one or more shaded sidebars giving information on people involved or specific examples of events or activities significant in the item's importance to the overall topic. Illustrations contribute markedly to the entries by adding pictures of people, equipment, events, and exploration sites. The entries are not as complete as those in encyclopedia or journal articles, but they are useful for getting quick, brief information or as a first step in literary research or more comprehensive information retrieval. Davies has provided an introduction that gives a short history of the 35 years of space exploration and its future and potential. Although the book is arranged alphabetically by topic, there is also a complete subject index that gives access to specific items, names, and subjects within individual entries. Technological terms are expressed in language understandable to the layperson, and the writing style is intelligent, interesting, and readable.

Davies's intention "to present the essential facts" and leave it to the reader "to follow up the minutiae with more detail if he or she pleases" has been accomplished. He has summarized information on the various topics admirably, supplying essays that do indeed present "the essential facts." The book is highly recommended for public and school libraries of all sizes. Any library can afford it, and it will be a valuable addition to the reference shelves.—**Edward P. Miller**

1757. Hawthorne, Douglas B. **Men and Women of Space.** San Diego, Calif., Univelt, 1992. 904p. $90.00. ISBN 0-912183-08-X.

Men and Women of Space is a complete and comprehensive biographical dictionary of individuals who have traveled in space. Russian cosmonauts, United States test pilots, and people from "all space-faring nations of the world" are listed. Biographical information is comprehensive, including the date and circumstances of the individual's death (e.g., "On a railroad bridge at Ippolitovka ... while undergoing 'a serious spiritual crisis' and in a state of intoxication, [Grigoriy Nelyubov] threw himself under a train").

Typical entries include current status in space program, nickname, date and place of birth, military and marital status, children, education, publications, memberships, decorations and awards, physical description, recreational interests, life experience, space experience, spaceflight assignments, place and manner of death (if deceased), and an extensive bibliography on the person. The volume is well written. The layout, typeface, and binding are attractive. There are, alas, only two illustrations (the cover and the frontispiece); more photographs would have helped break up the long text entries. But the work contains some 650 biographies, which may account for the lack of illustrations. Most reference collections will find this work useful. Highly recommended for young adults.—**Ralph Lee Scott**

1758. Long, Mark. **The World Satellite Annual, 1993/1994: The Official Supplement to** *The World Satellite Almanac.* Ft. Lauderdale, Fla., Mark Long Enterprises, 1992. 438p. illus. maps. index. $59.95pa. ISBN 0-929548-09-4.

This is a major reference work on communications satellites. It contains a wide variety of up-to-date information on satellite technology. Although anything written about this fast-changing technology is sure to be out-of-date when published, this work contains a wide range of useful information on current satellites and their operational systems. The typeface and layout are very attractive. There are chapters on direct broadcast systems (DBS), compressed digital video (CDV), satellite digital audio, INTELSAT, how to align a satellite dish mount, high density television (HDTV), and transponder technical data (called the transponder loading reports). For each ITU (International Telecommunication Union) transmission region, extensive information is given on new and in-service communications satellites that have been placed in orbit. Appendixes are devoted to "Margin Above Receiver Threshold" charts, future satellite launch manifests, and the names and addresses of national satellite television services providers.

The publisher quotes Vice President Albert Gore, Jr., as saying that this book is "*The* essential reference for anyone attempting to understand ... telecommunications developments." It would be hard to get a better endorsement! The work is a good place to start for reference questions on operational communications satellites. Most libraries will want to own this comprehensive volume.—**Ralph Lee Scott**

CHEMICAL ENGINEERING

1759. **Encyclopedia of Chemical Processing and Design. [Volume] 36: Phosphorus to Pipeline Failure, Subsidence Strains.** John J. McKetta and William A. Cunningham, eds. New York, Marcel Dekker, 1991. 548p. $195.00. TP9.E66. 660.2'8'003. LC 75-40646. ISBN 0-8247-2480-1.

1760. **Encyclopedia of Chemical Processing and Design. [Volume] 37: Pipeline Flow, Basics to Piping Design.** John J. McKetta and William A. Cunningham, eds. New York, Marcel Dekker, 1991. 563p. illus. $195.00. TP9.E66. 660.2'8'003. LC 75-40646. ISBN 0-8247-2480-1.

1761. **Encyclopedia of Chemical Processing and Design. [Volume] 38: Piping Design, Economic Diameter to Pollution Abatement Equipment, Alloy Selection.** John J. McKetta and William A. Cunningham, eds. New York, Marcel Dekker, 1991. 520p. illus. $195.00. TP9.E66. 660.2'8'003. LC 75-40646. ISBN 0-8247-2480-1.

1762. **Encyclopedia of Chemical Processing and Design. [Volume] 39: Pollution, Air, Costs: Parameters for Sizing Systems to Polymers, Polyamides, Aliphatic.** John J. McKetta and William A. Cunningham, eds. New York, Marcel Dekker, 1992. 461p. illus. $195.00. TP9.E66. 660.2'8'003. LC 75-40646. ISBN 0-8247-2480-1.

1763. **Encyclopedia of Chemical Processing and Design. [Volume] 40: Polymers, Polyamides, Aromatic, to Polymers, Polyvinylchloride.** John J. McKetta and William A. Cunningham, eds. New York, Marcel Dekker, 1992. 492p. illus. $195.00. TP9.E66. 660.2'8'003. LC 75-40646. ISBN 0-8247-2490-9.

1764. **Encyclopedia of Chemical Processing and Design. [Volume] 41: Polymers, Rubber Modified to Pressure-Relieving Devices, Rupture Disks, Low Burst Pressures.** John J. McKetta and William A. Cunningham, eds. New York, Marcel Dekker, 1992. 512p. illus. $195.00. TP9.E66. 660.2'8'003. LC 75-40646. ISBN 0-8247-2480-1.

1765. **Encyclopedia of Chemical Processing and Design. [Volume] 42: Pressure-Relieving Devices, Rupture Disks, Selection of to Process Control and Dynamics, Savings from Upgrading.** John J. McKetta and William A. Cunningham, eds. New York, Marcel Dekker, 1993. 504p. illus. $195.00. TP9.E66. 660.2'8'003. LC 75-40646. ISBN 0-8247-2492-5.

1766. **Encyclopedia of Chemical Processing and Design. [Volume] 43: Process Control, Feedback Simulation to Process Optimization.** John J. McKetta and William A. Cunningham, eds. New York, Marcel Dekker, 1993. 531p. illus. $195.00. TP9.E66. 660.2'8'003. LC 75-40646. ISBN 0-8247-2493-3.

This review covers volumes 36 to 43 of this continuing saga. A flashback to a 1988 review of volume 28 (see ARBA 89, entry 1478) reveals that some 15 volumes have been added since then. However, progress has only been from lactic acid to "pro," which does not augur well for completing the set in the projected 45 volumes. Indeed, the last 11 volumes have been concerned with the letter "p," and the letter still has not been completed!

While it is tempting to compare this set to the venerable *Kirk-Othmer Encyclopedia of Chemical Technology* (K-O) (John Wiley, 1993), such comparison is not particularly fruitful, because the editors have defined *chemical technology* (K-O) and *chemical processing and design* (*Encyclopedia of Chemical Processing and Design*) (ECPD) quite differently. For example, the set under consideration devotes some 122 pages to physical properties, and there is not even such an entry in Kirk-Othmer (physical properties, however, are frequently given in articles on particular substances). ECPD includes such topics as pipeline failure—again, no corresponding entry exists in Kirk-Othmer. On the other hand, powder metallurgy is covered in K-O but not mentioned in ECPD. One is tempted to draw the conclusion that both works are necessary to remedy each other's deficiencies.

Specific substances have been Kirk-Othmer's strength. Again, the great disparities in subject headings preclude direct comparison with ECPD. Scanning the K-O index, however, does seem to indicate a great many more entries for specific substances, as opposed to procedures and the like. A number of entries are puzzling; ECPD, for instance, includes a section on problem solving, a topic ignored by K-O. To illustrate the different emphases, K-O devotes only 12 pages to process research and development, and *process* is not mentioned again except in the index. ECPD, however, devotes 691 pages to a series of headings beginning with *process*, from process analysis through process optimization (and they are not through with *process* yet!). Kirk-Othmer seems to provide more bibliographical references for many topics, and the references are usually up-to-date. ECPD contains many more illustrations, which may be due to the emphasis on manufacturing processes. Also, ECPD appears to have a greater emphasis on the economics of the various processes. Indeed, beginning with volume 28, the editors of ECPD began putting some overall cost tables in the front of each volume, presumably to allow patrons to extrapolate the figures given in the text. Examining the credentials of contributors is not particularly helpful. In the present case, ECPD is superior to K-O in that its editors provide the titles of the contributors, while K-O merely lists their names.

One thing is certain: Both the present work and Kirk-Othmer will need to proceed with subsequent editions (should they ever complete the present ones), and it is hoped that succeeding editions have the important rubrics attached at all alphabetical stations, instead of proceeding glacier-like from A to Z. Overall, the *Encyclopedia of Chemical Processing and Design* is most likely to be useful to academic libraries supporting chemical engineering education and to larger public libraries.—**Edwin D. Posey**

1767. Forsberg, Krister, and S. Z. Mansdorf. **Quick Selection Guide to Chemical Protective Clothing.** 2d ed. New York, Van Nostrand Reinhold, 1993. 99p. $14.95 spiralbound. TP149.F67. 604.7'028'9. LC 93-11308. ISBN 0-442-01215-2.

This guidebook contains information on hazardous chemicals and suggests recommendations for the selection of chemical protective clothing. Now in a new edition, this compilation was derived from more than 12,000 test records taken from almost 100 sources. It gives information on 500-plus chemicals and 15 materials used in some 300 different types of protective clothing. The guide contains five major sections: an introduction, the selection and use of chemical protective clothing, a chemical index, selection recommendations, and a glossary. The CAS (Chemical Abstracts Service) registry number; the chemical names and synonyms; the risk codes that designate toxicity, harmfulness, corrosiveness, and irritability; and the color code recommendations, which designate barriers of resistance to breakthroughs from less than one hour to greater than eight hours, are all quite helpful in understanding the data. The glossary in the final section equips the reader to use this guide more effectively. Recommended for a library whose users are in disciplines within safety engineering or industrial hygiene.—**John H. Hunter**

1768. **Kirk-Othmer Encyclopedia of Chemical Technology. Volume 7: Composite Materials to Detergency.** 4th ed. Mary Howe-Grant, ed. New York, John Wiley, 1993. 1117p. illus. $275.00. TP9.E685. 660'.03. LC 91-16789. ISBN 0-471-52675-4.

Kirk-Othmer has been the quintessential tool for the provision of information on all aspects of chemical engineering for many years. This latest edition continues this tradition, and the revisions attempt to cover the rapid advances of the last 14 years. Comparison of the same alphabetical coverage between the 3d and 4th editions of this volume reveals that four items were dropped from the 3d edition, and five new ones were added. A cursory scan of the bibliographical references indicates that most recurring articles have been updated. Entries tend to be quite broad, such as "Cyanides," and the usual entry point for the completed set is through the index. Where publication is prolonged over several years, as in the present case, the lack of such an index is a serious handicap. Owners of the 3d edition will do well to keep it available to patrons, because it will serve somewhat as an index to the newer, incomplete edition.

Because of its inherent value, as well as its reputation, this new edition will be a required purchase for most academic and technical libraries, as well as larger public libraries. Highly recommended.

—**Edwin D. Posey**

1769. Lydersen, Aksel L., and Ingrid Dahlo. **Dictionary of Chemical Engineering: English/French/German/Spanish.** New York, John Wiley, 1992. 250p. illus. index. $54.95pa. TP9.L83. 660'.03. LC 92-12716. ISBN 0-471-93392-9.

This is an expanded revision of a book first published in Norwegian in 1988. The entire text was translated into English, and corresponding vocabulary in Spanish, French, and German was added. Terminology consists of both words and symbols used in chemical engineering, chemical manufacturing, and the related skilled trades. The terms are presented first in English, followed by the corresponding terms in French, German, and Spanish. Then the term is defined in English.

What sets this book apart is the inclusion of definitions, which are rarely included in multilanguage dictionaries. Even more rare is the inclusion of figures and illustrations. Nearly one-third of the entries have an illustration, most of which were taken from Lydersen's textbooks *Fluid Flow and Heat Transfer* (John Wiley, 1979) and *Mass Transfer in Engineering Practice* (John Wiley, 1985). The appendixes consist of lists of vocabulary by language, with references to the English definition. All in all, this is a very nice dictionary.—**Susan B. Ardis**

1770. **Riegel's Handbook of Industrial Chemistry.** 9th ed. James A. Kent, ed. New York, Van Nostrand Reinhold, 1992. 1288p. illus. index. $114.95. TP145.R54. 660. LC 92-22660. ISBN 0-442-00175-4.

This veteran reporter of the "scene" in the U.S. chemical process industry appears about every eight years. (The 8th edition of this work was reviewed in ARBA 84, entry 1493.) This industry has been followed carefully because it traditionally is the largest user of U.S. scientific and technological resources, is the major expender of U.S. commercial research and development funds, and has been a source of a favorable balance-of-trade position for decades. In fact, on a worldwide basis, DuPont and Dow rank fifth and sixth, with Exxon in the eighth position.

The preface highlights the new chapters that cover waste minimization, safety considerations in plant design and operation, emergency response planning, and statistical applications in quality control and experimental planning. There are a total of 50 contributors, including former executives at the Environmental Protection Agency. While old processes were commonly used for production in the past, waste disposal considerations mean that companies are looking to more treatable final products, so very new processes are no longer exceptional.—**Eugene B. Jackson**

1771. Rosato, Dominick V. **Rosato's Plastics Encyclopedia and Dictionary.** 2d ed. Munich, Carl Hanser; distr., New York, Oxford University Press, 1993. 818p. illus. $154.00. ISBN 3-446-16490-1.

Rosato's joins a growing number of handbooks and encyclopedias specifically on plastics, polymers, reinforced plastics, and composites and resins. Some recent examples include the multivolume and expensive *Encyclopedia of Polymer Science and Engineering* (see ARBA 91, entries 1769-71), the tabular properties presentation of *D.A.T.A. IPS Plastics Materials Digest*, and the compilation of articles and advertisements found in the *Modern Plastics Encyclopedia*. Obviously there is wide variation in the way each covers this diverse field; however, there is still a place for a multicoverage, one-volume, easy-to-read reference book that concentrates on engineering and chemical technologies, including the behavior, handling, and processing of plastic materials, along with the chemistry, properties, and composition of existing plastics. *Rosato's* does all of this as well as covering the usual chemical compositions, trade names, and process terms. However, there are some surprises. For example, who would ever think one could look up "catsup bottle" and find out so much about the Heinz plastic bottle, or find a very informative illustration of two-color injection molding?

This is a fascinating handbook—it has personality, as the definition of metals aptly demonstrates: "Metals are generally superior to plastics in strength and heat resistance. However, most products only have to endure what the human body can endure, thus most plastics can take the heat." This handbook should be on almost any reference shelf where users or librarians need basic, clearly written, and illustrated information on all aspects of chemistry, engineering, and manufacturing of plastics. And it should be examined by those who appreciate a reference book with a personality and a soupcon of the just plain interesting. [R: Choice, Sept 93, p. 88]—**Susan B. Ardis**

CIVIL ENGINEERING

1772. Eckstein, Richard M. **Directory of Building and Equipment Grants: An Innovative Reference Directory....** 2d ed. Loxahatchee, Fla., Research Grant Guides, 1992. 216p. index. $49.50pa. ISBN 0-945078-04-8.

The intent of this volume is to help nonprofit organizations obtain equipment or even structures through grants from nonprofit or for-profit foundations or from the federal government. Its several sections provide directory-type information on the many foundations extant, the procedures and requirements for eligibility for federal programs, and three brief sections on all facets of grantsmanship.

Just as no one book of quotations is sufficient, no one list of foundations is sufficient. For example, entries for Texas were checked, and no listing for the Welch Foundation, Houston, was found, yet it supports senior university faculty members in chemistry and biochemistry with specific emphasis on sophisticated research equipment.

The four special libraries maintained by the Foundation Center have good reputations for their telephone and mail services but are obviously geographically limited for visits. As there is a high correlation between library patron usage and interest in "volunteerism," there is bound to emerge a supply of new people interested in grantsmanship. This present tool would merit consideration by a range of public libraries.—**Eugene B. Jackson**

1773. Stein, J. Stewart. **Construction Glossary: An Encyclopedia Reference and Manual.** 2d ed. New York, John Wiley, 1993. 1137p. index. $95.00. TH9.S78. 690'.03. LC 92-443. ISBN 0-471-56933-X.

Anybody interested in the construction business will find this new edition of a classic in the field to be of inestimable value. More than 30,000 entries are arranged according to the Construction Specification Institute's (CSI) MASTERFORMAT. This arrangement includes 16 divisions: general requirements, site work, concrete, masonry, metals, wood and plastics, thermal and moisture protection, doors and windows, finishes, specialties, equipment, furnishings, special construction, conveying systems, mechanical, and electrical. Added are three more sections on professional services, construction categories, and technical-scientific and related data; a directory of reference data sources; three appendixes for abbreviations for scientific, engineering, and construction terms; weights and measures; and carpentry abbreviations. Finally, a complete alphabetical index and a detailed table of contents provide ample access by individual term or by special detailed subject area. Each term is defined in detail and related to its use within the subject area. When used in several subject areas or CSI divisions, terms are repeated and definitions refined for each area or division.

Stein is an architect and engineer with many years of experience in the field and several other publications under his belt. His expertise is unquestioned. This reference tool should find use in any large reference collection, whether academic, special, or public—any library serving the information needs of the groups of professionals at which it is targeted: architects and engineers, contractors, real estate brokers, attorneys, government agencies, lending institutions and appraisers, and students. Highly recommended. [R: Choice, June 93, p. 1611]—**Edward P. Miller**

COMPUTING ENGINEERING

1774. Chen, C. H., ed. **Computer Engineering Handbook.** New York, McGraw-Hill, 1992. 1v. (various paging). illus. index. (Computer Engineering Series). $79.50. TK7888.3.C652. 621.395. LC 92-6203. ISBN 0-07-010924-9.

The intent of this book is to provide comprehensive coverage of the fundamentals of computer engineering. It stands out from its predecessors in many ways. First, it is dedicated only to topics concerning computer engineering. Because of this limited scope, more details are included. Second, the book is current and up-to-date, with coverage of many technological advances. Third, it is organized into major areas that are covered in depth by respected authorities. Fourth, instead of dividing the materials into a great number of subject topics, it takes a more tutorial approach, covering major areas together in context. These areas include digital logic and design, computer architecture and arithmetic, computer graphics, computer vision, parallel computing, and computer networks. A detailed index is useful for locating specific areas of interest to the reader.

The material in this book will serve well as an introduction to computer engineering. It can be used as a refresher and update for experts in the field. Highly recommended for public and professional libraries.
—**John Y. Cheung**

1775. Morris, Derrick, and Boris Tamm, eds. **Concise Encyclopedia of Software Engineering.** Tarrytown, N.Y., Pergamon Press, 1993. 400p. index. Advances in Systems, Control, and Information Engineering). $280.00. QA76.758.C68. 005'.03. LC 92-27942. ISBN 0-08-036214-1.

In accordance with its aim to provide concise but comprehensive information about software engineering, this encyclopedia ranges from abstract data types to virtual machines. The editors warn that those readers requiring extended study of specific topics will have to look elsewhere, and to this end they include a bibliography with each entry. Entries cover both theory and practical applications. One of the strong points of this work is the perspective one gets from its international contributors. For example, members of the Estonian Academy of Sciences wrote a number of the articles. (A co-editor is also a member of the academy.) On the other hand, this work suffers from the same problem as many computer science books: Much of the information is dated before it reaches print. In addition, far too many of the references for further study were published 5, 10, or more years ago. In the fast-changing computer industry, this is ancient history. Thus, this work will be useful to those who require an overview of software engineering, but researchers in need of more current information will do better with conference proceedings and journals in the field.—**Renee B. Horowitz**

ELECTRIC ENGINEERING AND ELECTRONICS

1776. Doyon, Yves. **Glossary [of] Security Equipment. Materiel de Securite.** Ottawa, Department of the Secretary of State of Canada, 1993. 183p. $22.05pa. (U.S.). 621.389'28'03. ISBN 0-660-56483-1.

This glossary is a French-English, English-French word equivalence list for security terms that have been officially accepted by the Terminology and Linguistic Services Directorate in Canada. "Security" as used here has a broad scope, including terms for card readers, cameras, motion detectors, and other antiintrusion devices, but excluding most fire protection and intelligence equipment.

The words are presented in two columns. The first column is a straight alphabetical list of both French (black ink) and English (blue ink) terms intermixed, with the corresponding term of the other language in the second column. In some cases, several words of exact meaning are clustered within an entry and separated by semicolons. The entire entry is then repeated under each word within the group. There is no index, but an index is not needed with this easy-to-use structure. Although there are no definitions, the French term does include the gender of the word. A bibliography reflects the wide range of English and French sources used to verify the words in the list.

The paperback binding is sturdy and should hold up to reference use. Although the audience for this work is limited, the book is an appropriate acquisition for those serving police and other governmental officials, technical writers, and business and industry in French-English language situations.—**Gary R. Cocozzoli**

1777. Fink, Donald G., and H. Wayne Beaty, eds. **Standard Handbook for Electrical Engineers.** 13th ed. New York, McGraw-Hill, 1993. 1v. (various paging). illus. index. $110.50. TK151.S8. LC 56-6964. ISBN 0-07-020975-8.

The new edition of this classic work has rewritten or expanded chapters and some new material covering computer technologies in electrical engineering for power management; system planning; plant monitoring; environmental considerations; and advances in residential, commercial, and industrial applications of electrical power. The scope of engineering is extensive within the 28 chapters, and the book will answer a broad range of questions, from information on circuits, wiring, motors, power transmission, and illumination to the unexpected, such as properties of Douglas fir wood. Each chapter is written by one or more experts and includes an outline of specific contents (with references to paragraph numbers, not pages) and bibliographical and general references for further investigation for each subsection of the chapter. The final chapter covers standards in electrotechnology, including national and international standards groups and an overview that includes standards terminology. The text is well illustrated with charts, tables, diagrams, and a few photographs.

The index (which refers to page numbers, not paragraph numbers) is very general and cites, for the most part, just the major subsections. It is a disappointment, because a more extensive index is necessary to fully use the contents of the text.

This sophisticated text is geared to those with engineering background. Still, this work has general information on a variety of subjects that can be useful in many reference situations. Recommended for all technical libraries and for any academic or public library that could use a basic source of technical data. However, those owning the previous edition will want to consider carefully before adding this update, as the changes from the previous edition are not extensive.—**Gary R. Cocozzoli**

1778. Graf, Rudolf F., and William Sheets. **Encyclopedia of Electronic Circuits. Volume 4.** Blue Ridge Summit, Pa., TAB Books, 1992. 729p. index. $60.00; $29.95pa. TK7867.G66. 621.3815'.3 LC 84-26772. ISBN 0-8306-3896-2; 0-8306-3895-4pa.

This volume contains many circuits and circuit designs, a number of which were not covered in the preceding volumes. The circuits have all been previously published elsewhere and are therefore publicly available. (However, notation is made that some elements may be covered by letters patents either held or applied for, and the user is cautioned on use of such circuits.) Overall, this is a standard, very useful work. Its major portion is, of course, the circuits, which are produced in very readable format. The scope of the work is very broad, ranging from model and hobby circuits to standard and specialized receivers. Now the world will know how to build an electronic wheel of fortune as well as a Wein-Bridge-based oscillator. The scale of the circuits is large enough to make them usable in the laboratory and small enough to keep the size of the volume manageable.

The work is organized into 104 chapters. The chapter delineation is probably too fine for most general use but does allow direct entry into the work. The index is excellent and matches the specificity of the chapter headings. Graf and Sheets chose not to put the sources of the circuits with the actual figures but to put them in a separate section, which may be bothersome to some, but it fits with the overall intent of the work.

This is an excellent continuation of a series of circuitry handbooks. The book can stand alone, but is best used in conjunction with the prior three volumes. Highly recommended for a variety of information centers.—**C. D. Hurt**

1779. Graf, Rudolf F. **The Modern Measuring Circuit Encyclopedia.** Blue Ridge Summit, Pa., TAB Books, 1993. 229p. illus. index. $12.95pa. TK7867.G67. 621.381'5. LC 92-9564. ISBN 0-8306-4156-4.

This unpretentious volume could well find a place on the workbench of electronic hobbyists, technicians, students, or beginning designers. Right away, it is evident that the common failing of circuit books—having transcription errors—is avoided, because more than 200 circuits have been reproduced from the original sources, accompanied by the citation to that source, and a couple of paragraphs of comments by Graf, who is a senior member of the Institute of Electrical & Electronics Engineers—the leading professional society in the field. To illustrate the scope, 13 subfields of circuits are covered, of which the most obvious handle voltage, display, oscilloscopes, temperature, and probes. Most references are to late 1980s sources, but some 1970s classics are noted. Besides periodicals, industrial sources are well represented. Each entry averages three-quarters of a page.—**Eugene B. Jackson**

1780. Graf, Rudolf F. **The Modern Power Supply and Battery Charger Circuit Encyclopedia.** Blue Ridge Summit, Pa., TAB Books, 1992. 133p. index. $10.95pa. TK2943.G73. 621.31'242. LC 91-33708. ISBN 0-8306-3923-3.

Graf is the author of many popular compendiums of circuit information. His new book deals with two topics—power supplies and batteries—that are currently very popular with hobbyists, engineers, and students. He brings together information originally found in such diverse places as company databooks; NASA Tech Briefs; and journals such as *EDN, Popular Electronics*, and *Electronics Today*.

Users will find a wealth of practical, ready-to-use information packed into a small, inexpensive book. The text consists of schematic drawings arranged by application, along with a brief description of how each circuit works and a reference to the circuit's original source. The applications include fixed, variable, and flexible power supplies; battery chargers; and battery zappers. This book fills a real niche, one that will become more important as power supplies and batteries are used more frequently by electronic designers to meet the public's demands for more powerful wireless electronic devices and gadgets.
—**Susan B. Ardis**

1781. Harper, Charles A., and Martin B. Miller. **Electronic Packaging, Microelectronics, and Interconnection Dictionary.** New York, McGraw-Hill, 1993. 235p. illus. (Electronic Packaging and Interconnection Series). $39.50. TK7804.H34. 621.381'046'3. LC 92-40712. ISBN 0-07-026688-3.

This slim volume is at the interface between the subjects of electronics and solid-state manufacturing. Cooperation in its compilation was provided through JEDEC (Joint Electronic Devices Engineering Council), the relevant technical group on terms, definitions, and symbols. To illustrate the book's emphasis on the manufacturing side, a random sample of 37 entries was searched in 2 recently reviewed pocket books of electronic engineering: *Newnes Electronics Engineer's Pocket Book* (Butterworths, 1993) and *HarperCollins Dictionary of Electronics* (see ARBA 92, entry 1595); there were only five full duplications among the three books. Although many industrial and manufacturing engineers would need their own copies, libraries serving or near semiconductor manufacturing and assembly operations or equivalent trade schools would be the major purchasers.
—**Eugene B. Jackson**

1782. Lenk, John D. **Lenk's Digital Handbook: Design and Troubleshooting.** New York, McGraw-Hill, 1993. 305p. index. $39.95. TK7868.D5L43. 621.381. LC 92-12064. ISBN 0-07-037516-X.

Designed for programmers, technicians, and hobbyists, this handbook addresses the repair of digital circuits and equipment. The testing and troubleshooting approaches to integrated circuits and microprocessors are applicable to any system. However, to fully use this manual, a basic grasp of analog electronics is required. Including a glossary would help beginners and the forgetful understand the field's numerous acronyms and buzzwords.

The first five chapters review logic, circuits, test equipment, and the like. The remaining five focus on techniques, procedures, and troubleshooting examples (e.g., VCRs, CD-ROMs). Diagrams illustrate functions (e.g., microprocessors) as well as procedures (e.g., checking paths). The excellent index affords easy access to all discussions of problems and equipment. Missing is a bibliography of the publications (often by Lenk) to which readers are referred.

This guide is not for the neophyte. Although well organized, clearly written, and very practical, it is more a refresher for the technically semiliterate and a guidebook for the knowledgeable. Lenk, an authority on consumer electronics, has created an excellent companion to electronics encyclopedias and sourcebooks. Libraries will find this, the essential repair guide, a welcome addition to their collections.—**Sandra E. Belanger**

1783. Lewin, Paul, comp. **European Electric Utility Directory, 1993.** Tulsa, Okla., PennWell Books, 1993. 510p. index. $210.00pa. ISSN 1069-2363.

This is a good, but not outstanding, directory. Part of the reason the directory is not better is the typography. It appears that the work was produced from camera-ready copy and that little page design was employed. The results are some interesting widows and orphans and a text that is readable but not pleasing. However, the content of the work is good. The listings include standard directory information (name, address, and telephone, telex, and fax numbers), offices in other areas, major personnel (including members of the board), shareholders, other holdings of the unit, fuel used, and output. In some cases there are narrative descriptions of major units or organizations. The material is all descriptive, with no comparisons.

Overall, this is a reasonable work that is priced beyond the reach of most libraries. For the information contained, it can be recommended to major collections and those with a specific interest in electrical engineering and electrical utilities. Because of the price, libraries must carefully consider whether the data within is worth the expense.—**C. D. Hurt**

1784. **McGraw-Hill Circuit Encyclopedia and Troubleshooting Guide. Vol. 1.** By John D. Lenk. New York, McGraw-Hill, 1993. 630p. illus. index. $59.50. TK7867.T463. 621.3815. LC 92-333275. ISBN 0-07-037603-4.

This volume provides practical information for the diagnosis and repair of many currently used electronic circuits. Twenty major categories are discussed, plus a generous selection of special-purpose circuits. Each group of circuits is preceded by a succinct exposition of correct procedures for troubleshooting that type of circuit; next, numerous diagrams with descriptive material are provided for each group. More than 700 circuits are included. The diagrams are credited to manufacturers' catalogs or data sheets, pointing the user to more detailed information if required. A useful substitution and cross-reference table adds to the work's value. This series will be of greatest utility to colleges, universities, and vocational schools with programs in electronics. Larger public libraries will also find it to be useful to patrons, and it is definitely recommended for individual purchase by electronics technicians and experimenters.—**Edwin D. Posey**

1785. **McGraw-Hill Encyclopedia of Engineering.** 2d ed. Sybil P. Parker, ed. New York, McGraw-Hill, 1993. 1414p. illus. index. $95.50. TA9.M36. 620'.003. LC 92-43106. ISBN 0-07-051392-9.

With the skyrocketing costs of engineering and reference books, the price for this encyclopedia is a good one for the number of pages, abundance of articles, and value to specific engineering target groups and small technical libraries. However, a word of caution is in order for larger, comprehensive technical libraries. Most science librarians are familiar with the *McGraw-Hill Encyclopedia of Science & Technology* (MEST) (see ARBA 93, entry 1446), which is now in its 7th edition and contains several thousand excellent and comprehensive articles on science and technology. Because the scope of MEST is so broad, and the set is so expensive, McGraw-Hill regathers and reprints articles on specific subjects, at lesser cost, for those who do not wish to purchase the entire 20 volumes. *McGraw-Hill Encyclopedia of Engineering* was compiled from the 7th edition of MEST. (The first edition of this work was assembled from the 5th edition of MEST in 1982.) It includes selections on the following engineering fields: civil, design, electrical, industrial, mechanical, metallurgical, mining, nuclear, petroleum, power, and production, plus several articles on physical and thermodynamic principles that are applicable to engineering. The volume does not cover chemical engineering but does touch on architectural and building engineering. The articles are clearly written by experts and are well illustrated. The bibliographies are fairly up-to-date but often include older landmark titles. Articles are cross-referenced by title, and there is an extensive index. Large libraries with the latest edition of the *McGraw-Hill Encyclopedia of Science & Technology* and the yearbooks that update it need to decide if they can afford both works. [R: Choice, Oct 93, p. 268; JAL, Sept 93, p. 275; RQ, Winter 93, pp. 290-91; WLB, Sept 93, pp. 119-21]—**Robert J. Havlik**

1786. **McGraw-Hill's National Electrical Code Handbook.** 21st ed. By J. F. McPartland and Brian J. McPartland. New York, McGraw-Hill, 1993. 1262p. illus. index. $54.50. TK260.N2. 621.319'24'0218. LC 81-642618. ISBN 0-07-045901-0. ISSN 0277-6758.

Since 1897, the National Electrical Code (NEC) has attempted to codify the necessary precautions to be observed in harnessing electrical power for industrial, commercial, and residential use. Its provisions are incorporated into many building codes and laws. The 1993 version contains hundreds of major and minor revisions, thus necessitating a new edition of this explanatory handbook. The NEC itself is somewhat terse, creating a need for explanation and amplification, which this volume supplies.

This latest edition of the publisher's NEC handbooks (published since 1932) is probably the most useful of several competing publications. The other major contender is the National Fire Protection Association's *NEC Handbook* (1993), which prints the entire code plus explanatory material. The McPartlands, however, cover the vast majority of sections, "especially all sections that have proved troublesome or controversial" (preface). The book provides lengthy and clear explanations of many sections of the NEC, and is amply illustrated by clear diagrams and photographs where needed. After the 1990 edition, the publisher filled the three-year gap between major code revisions with two annual supplements dealing with problems, revisions, and errata; it is hoped that these useful supplements will be continued for the next triennium.

In view of the large number of changes in the new edition of the NEC, all major technical libraries, many special libraries, and most public libraries will need to acquire this useful volume, especially if they maintain a current codes and standards collection. Highly recommended.—**Edwin D. Posey**

1787. Wedgwood, C. G., ed. **European Electronics Directory 1993: Components and Sub-Assemblies.** Oxford, England, Elsevier Advanced Technology; distr., Tarrytown, N.Y., Pergamon Press, 1993. 573p. index. $360.00. ISBN 1-85617-175-2.

This is a computer-compiled directory of responses to surveys of 10,300 European manufacturers and representatives in the electronics industry. More than one-third of the book is taken up with a classified advertisement section for 1,600 products. There are three directories: manufacturers, agents and representatives, and sales subsidiaries, all listed by country. For each business a listing includes name; address; telephone, telex, and fax numbers; managers; subsidiary status; number of employees; and amount of sales. Because each company contributed information, the listings are not consistent in the amount of data presented. The codes used in the directory are very complicated and are only listed in the preface. More code legends would make the directory more useful. (The directory is too complex for so little guidance to have been provided.) There are an index of all companies and a glossary of German and French product names.

Because the directory is dominated by the commercial classified advertisements, has poorly developed usage directions, and is expensive, it would be more useful to companies in the electronics business world than to libraries. It would also be more useful in an electronic format rather than in paper, because its information will become dated very rapidly. Not recommended.—**Gerald D. Moran**

ENVIRONMENTAL ENGINEERING

1788. **Current Environmental Engineering Summaries.** 1993 ed. Rockville, Md., Government Institutes, 1993. 1110p. $89.00. LC 93-078621. ISBN 0-86587-346-1.

This reference work contains many environmental engineering summaries. The work has been compiled from *Engineering Index Monthly* (EIM). More than 6,000 items are included. The summaries include an abstract number, title (translated if the title is in a non-English language), an abstract, and the bibliographical citation. With the exception of the abstract number, the information in this work is the same information that is contained in the 1992 EIM, which raises issues of currency.

The arrangement of the work is by subject. The subjects are defined by the authority list of EIM, although there are some variations in the subheadings, which are formed using the EIM term followed by a more specific term, if required. The work is descriptive, not critical, which can present a problem. A large part of the information is somewhat elusive in the sense that some is foreign, some is proceedings publications, and some is technical reports. Knowing that this information exists but not being able to obtain it is frustrating. (However, knowledge that such information exists is sometimes critical.)

The material here can all be obtained, with some minor effort, through EIM. This work pulls together material for those who either do not have access to EIM or who need a compilation of materials in one place. For these needs, this work will be extremely useful. Annual editions appear to be promised, and this will assist in currency. Overall, this is a good compilation. It retains the excellent indexing and abstracting of EIM and will find good use in specialized collections.—**C. D. Hurt**

1789. Lee, C. C. **Environmental Engineering Dictionary.** 2d ed. Rockville, Md., Government Institutes, 1992. 462p. $88.00; $68.00pa. LC 92-71561. ISBN 0-86587-298-8; 0-86587-328-3pa.

Dictionaries usually make surprisingly good reading. This one is no exception. Make no mistake about *cooking liquor* and *yellow cake*. Familiar enough in a kitchen, they take on very different meanings in the world of environmental engineering. Cooking liquor, for example, is a mixture used to dissolve lignin in woodchips. *Airport* and *litter* might seem like unnecessary inclusions, yet in the spirit of completeness—which the volumes achieves—they do fit. For most of the more than 12,000 terms defined, a reference is given. Environmental Protection Agency acronyms are included in definitions and in a tidy alphabetical appendix. The cross-referencing is excellent.

The switches between colon and sentence-driven formats might have been avoided to give the volume a more consistent flow. However, from *A-scale sound level* to *noble gas* to *zooxanthella*, technical and lay users will find this volume a lucid and comprehensive access point to the words that build the language of environmental scientists. Even *Superfund operation* is explained succinctly. [R: Choice, May 93, p. 1440]—**Diane M. Calabrese**

GENETIC ENGINEERING

1790. Bains, William. **Biotechnology from A to Z.** New York, Oxford University Press, 1993. 358p. illus. index. $19.95pa. ISBN 0-19-963334-7.

This extended glossary of 280 entries is intended for the nonexpert. It makes very few assumptions, other than that readers have some basic information on modern biology. The introduction was written by G. Kirk Raab, CEO of Genentech, a well-known company in the biotechnology field. His essay is basically a call to the public to be better informed about the impact and desirability of biotechnology.

Each entry is written in clear prose, as the first two sentences in the entry for *chirality* demonstrate: "Chirality is the chemical version of 'handedness'. Some molecules have distinct left- and right-hand forms...." Too often, specialized glossaries and dictionaries are aimed at the user population most likely to already know, or to be able to infer, what a term means. Many of the entries are related, so, in order to cut down on repetition, the author has included cross-references and an index. In a book of this type it is important to have a good index—and this one is more than adequate. This would be a good book for public libraries and other general science libraries with a need for short, clear definitions of biotechnology terminology.—**Susan B. Ardis**

HUMAN ENGINEERING

1791. Stramler, James J., Jr. **The Dictionary for Human Factors/Ergonomics.** Boca Raton, Fla., CRC Press, 1993. 413p. $55.00. TA166.S77. 620.8'2'03. LC 92-2348. ISBN 0-8493-4236-8.

Human factors, or ergonomics, is generally concerned with the systematic study of human-machine, human-computer interaction. It is also concerned with improving working conditions, operations, or individual well-being as it relates to production, the work place, and similar elements. Consequently, this multidisciplinary field touches on many areas of engineering, product design, workplace safety, and industrial medicine. The breadth of this field has meant that definitions and terminology often vary from subfield to subfield.

Stramler began this dictionary both to collect and define the terminology already in use and to "serve as a terminological base or definitional standard" for human factors vocabulary. As a first step toward his goals, he has defined 6,500-plus words, of which approximately 15 percent include a commentary. Generally these commentaries provide information on how anthropometric measurements are made (e.g., how human reach is measured). While seemingly highly specialized, this dictionary would be at home in any reference collection that deals with management, industrial engineering, or product design.—**Susan B. Ardis**

MATERIALS SCIENCE

1792. **ASM Handbook. Volume 3: Alloy Phase Diagrams.** Hugh Baker, ed. Materials Park, Ohio, ASM International, 1992. 1v. (various paging). index. $135.00. TA459.M43. 620.1'6. LC 90-115. ISBN 0-87170-381-5.

ASM International (formerly the Society of Steel Treating) joined with the National Institute of Standards of Technology (NIST) (formerly the National Bureau of Standards) to evaluate and compile all known alloy phase diagrams. The resulting 2,965 phase diagrams were published in 3 volumes by ASM in 1991. From these, 1,100 binary and 313 ternary diagrams were selected for the present book, which also contains an index to all known alloy phase diagrams. (Another volume to follow will contain only ternary diagrams.) The first chapter is a very cogent introduction to thermodynamics as it applies to phase diagrams and the science and terminology of the diagrams themselves. A number of credible examples of the practical engineering use of phase diagrams are included. Properties of elements in the appendixes include melting and boiling points, allotropic transformations, magnetic phase transitions, and crystal lattice parameters. In all, this is a very impressive work.—**Robert B. McKee**

1793. **ASM Materials Engineering Dictionary.** J. R. Davis, ed. Materials Park, Ohio, ASM International, 1992. 555p. illus. $85.00. LC 92-73858. ISBN 0-87170-447-1.

This comprehensive compilation of terms was culled from previously published collections, primarily various editions of *Metals Handbook* (see ARBA 92, entries 1618-19). Following a guide to the dictionary, a list of figures, tables, and technical briefs, the reader will find alphabetical lists of terms, from *A* (the symbol for a repeating unit in a polymer chain) to *zone sintering* (highly localized progressive heating during sintering to produce a desired grain structure). All the definitions cover materials science, physical metallurgy, electrometallurgy, heat treatment, foraging, fractography, failure analysis, and many more specialized areas. This collection contains approximately 7,500 terms, 700 illustrations, and 250 tables with 64 technical briefs. These last provide concise overviews of the properties, compositions, and applications of selected materials and direct the reader to more detailed information in a recommended reading list. Eight appendixes cover such things as conversion factors, the Greek alphabet, the periodic table, and abbreviations and symbols. The price is very reasonable for the information provided. This dictionary is highly recommended to libraries serving engineering disciplines. [R: Choice, Sept 93, p. 73]
—**John H. Hunter**

1794. Bever, Michael B., ed. **Concise Encyclopedia of Materials Economics, Policy & Management.** Tarrytown, N.Y., Pergamon Press, 1993. 460p. illus. index. (Advances in Materials Science and Engineering). $240.00. TA402.C6593. 620.1'1'03. LC 91-37830. ISBN 0-08-037056-X.

This is a collection of articles, by some 70 authors, whose only commonality is that they deal in some way with materials. Some seem to be motivated solely by the need to discuss a word starting with a letter of the alphabet, such as A (availability), or P (process). (The latter begins with "The concept of a process ... is Primordial.") On the other hand, there are useful and cogently written sections, including a good short treatment of input-output analysis, the history of mineral prices since 1950, a survey of product liability law and practice both here and abroad, the status of critical mineral stockpiling in the United States, and a survey of the recycling of paper and plastics. In addition to the bibliography that accompanies each article, there is a bibliography of information sources.—**Robert B. McKee**

1795. Cahn, Robert W., and Eric Lifshin, eds. **Concise Encyclopedia of Materials Characterization.** Tarrytown, N.Y., Pergamon Press, 1993. 641p. illus. index. (Advances in Materials Science and Engineering). $300.00. TA402.C659. 620.1'1'03. LC 92-10673. ISBN 0-08-040603-3.

This title is an addendum of sorts to the original *Encyclopedia of Materials Science and Engineering* (see ARBA 87, entry 1570). There are 11 of these concise encyclopedias in addition to supplements to the original encyclopedia. "Concise" is a relative term—while a length of 641 pages may not fit some individuals' definitions of concise, given the subject breadth of the title, this is a concise work. This is an encyclopedia in one of the original senses of the term: It is a collection of directed essays written by experts, and arranged alphabetically by topic. The overwhelming majority of the contributors are North American or European. Each of the essays is an in-depth, signed article that normally contains a short introduction and then expands on the area with specific information. The essays average three to four pages in length and are complemented by a bibliography. The text is accompanied by good line drawings and some black-and-white graphics. For those unfamiliar with specific topics or unsure of the proper terminology, there is a well-developed subject index.

The quality of the essays is generally high. The writing style is clean and straightforward. The currency of the material is a decided plus, as is the fact that the volume is planned to be consistently updated. Overall, this is a work that deserves serious consideration from collections in science and engineering. It will be best used in collections where the *Encyclopedia of Materials Science and Engineering* and its supplements are owned. However, it can stand alone and will suffice in college collections very nicely. Highly recommended for special, academic, and larger public collections.—**C. D. Hurt**

1796. **Worldwide Guide to Equivalent Irons and Steels.** 3d ed. Materials Park, Ohio, ASM International, 1993. 1v. (various paging). $159.00. LC 92-76023. ISBN 0-87170-454-4.

This large work contains listings of equivalent irons and steels across the world. Equivalent, as it is used in this work, means essentially similar but rarely identical. The work consists of eight major categories of materials: cast iron, cast stainless steel, steel casting, alloy steel, carbon steel, high strength and structural steel, wrought stainless steel, and tool steel. The arrangement of the material is oriented to the U.S. grades of materials, with appropriate references to other materials.

The entries for items are in tabular format. This format is not especially attractive, but it is consistent throughout the volume. The information for each entry consists of a specification, designation of the alloy, description, chemical composition, and tensile properties. Some entries do not have all five categories of information. There is also some variance in the information contained in the categories labeled *specification, designation,* and *standard*. The editors acknowledge this problem. A greater problem, also acknowledged, is the geopolitical changes that have taken place since the work went to press. It is hoped that these changes will result in greater consistency in the information received in the future.

The book includes designation and specification indexes. Beyond this, the arrangement of the material is straightforward within the tables that make up the volume. An interesting addition is a section on standards organizations. A glance at it will help the user appreciate the effort that compiling the volume took.

This work will not find use anywhere but in a very specialized collection. The work is overdetailed if the purpose it will be put to is as a handbook for U.S. specifications and descriptions of iron and steel. But where there is a need to determine cross-references and equivalences (as defined by the editors) or to correlate various irons and steels, this is an excellent volume. Highly recommended for specialized collections or some research collections in metallurgy, materials science, or engineering.—**C. D. Hurt**

MECHANICAL ENGINEERING

1797. **Handbook of Power, Utility and Boiler Terms and Phrases.** 6th ed. Tulsa, Okla., PennWell Books, 1992. 153p. $49.95pa. TJ164.H28. 621.042'03. LC 92-25349. ISBN 0-87814-385-8.

This glossary covers the terminology of boilers and related equipment. It is divided into 13 subject areas that parallel the general order of the heating process, starting with fuel, moving through the combustion process, and finishing with emissions control. The goal is for clear identification of terms and expressions rather than for extensive definition. With numerous sections of alphabetically arranged words, the work would be impossible to use without the master index of terms at the front that notes the page where the word is defined. This is not a keyword index: Some of the words have alternate entries or cross-references, while others inexplicably do not. Even though this inconsistency will not seriously hamper use of the text for many users, it makes the work less accessible.

Most of the words and expressions gathered for this volume will not be readily found or defined as carefully in other reference works. Some of the words are quite colorful (e.g., "Black Liquor," "Coke Breeze," "French Coupling"), but even seemingly standard terms (e.g., "Draft") have very specialized meanings in this field. The appendix is a convenient list of abbreviations and acronyms found in government and agency publications. The work is suitable for technical libraries and for large public libraries with sophisticated reference needs.—**Gary R. Cocozzoli**

1798. **I.B.I. International Bearing Interchange Guide: World's Most Complete History of Bearing Number Alternatives.** 12th ed. St. Louis Park, Minn., Interchange, 1993. 2v. illus. index. $225.00/set. ISBN 0-916966-34-8. ISSN 1053-7198.

Interchangeability of parts of complex mechanical devices has been an issue since the days of the cotton gin and the frontier revolver. By World War II the efforts of the Army on parts replacement resulted in various standardized parts catalogs. (Even so, some armored battalions were equipped with Jeeps all made by Willys Motors and others with Jeeps all made by Ford "so as to be sure.") Around this time Si H. Friedman was working for a bearing supply contractor and thought more interchange of bearings and other similar parts was possible and could be expedited by lists of all machine elements and dimensions. His work on the listings resulted, in 1966, in the *International Bearing Interchange* (IBI).

The twelfth edition of *Bearings*, compiled by 13 people, consists of 2 thick volumes. Volume 1 has more than 1,000 suppliers and manufacturers listed on its first pages; then the parts numbers are given in order, including prefixes and suffixes. The parts listings show the "IBI Group" to which they have been assigned in volume 2. The 461 pink pages list smaller ball bearings, clutch bearings, waterpump bearings, and medium bearings; the 354 green pages list tapered cones and cups, subarranged by size; and the 216 yellow pages list needle and roller bearings that lack dimensions and curved rollers from .125" to 37" bore. For example, choosing "Spicer-Dana" from the list of manufacturers and suppliers in volume 1 and selecting its part number 550106-1, one notes it has been assigned to interchange category number IBI Group 50882. This is found, fully dimensioned, on page 11 of volume 2's yellow pages, and it interchanges with parts from Kenilworth and White, among others. (Note that the part chosen has a suffix of "1"; it will also be found in *P.S.I. Guide: Prefix/Suffix Identification Guide for Bearings* [Interchange, 1992].)

While this example sounds complicated, it was followed immediately by the staff of an auto supply store patronized by this reviewer; the staff were very interested in this tool. It should appeal to libraries that cater to vocational and junior colleges with programs in automotive and mechanical shops and to special libraries that serve complex industrial installations.—**Eugene B. Jackson**

1799. **P.S.I. Guide: Prefix/Suffix Identification Guide for Bearings.** St. Louis Park, Minn., Interchange, 1992. 411p. $95.00pa. ISBN 0-916966-33-X.

This work's extra subtitle tells all: "World's Most Complete History of Prefix/Suffix Designations. A Computer Generated Identification Guide for Various Types of Anti-Friction Ball and Roller Bearings." As there is frequently the need to replace more than one type of part, other guides published by Interchange cover oil seals, drive belts, drive line and transmission parts, filters, brake drums and rotors, and hoses.

An example of the information in this book is the use of S1 as a prefix. This means it was manufactured by the international firm SKF, and "The meaning is specific to the particular cone and cup. Identifies a change in an external non-fitting dimension." On the other hand, S1 as a suffix might mean the bearing is a product of INA Bearing Company from its plants in Fort Mill, South Carolina; Bensalem, Pennsylvania; Cheraw, South Carolina; Spartanburg, South Carolina; or the home plant in Sutton Coldfield, West Midlands, United Kingdom. Each of the several sections has glossary, lubricants, and address list sections.

Science and technology departments of libraries in industrial towns will need to consider these parts identification books. The main users would be hobbyists who repair their own automobiles and such industrial combustion-powered aids as lawn mowers, snow blowers, and mulchers.—**Eugene B. Jackson**

MINING ENGINEERING

1800. **Elsevier's Dictionary of Mining and Mineralogy in English, French, German and Italian.** A. F. Dorian, comp. New York, Elsevier Science Publishing, 1993. 300p. $187.50. TN10.D67. 622'.03. LC 92-35138. ISBN 0-444-89039-4.

The vocabulary of mining owes as much to the colorful language of miners as it does to the technical language of engineering and geology. Terms such as *gophering* (haphazard mining in irregular holes), *fossicking* (searching for gold by prospecting abandoned workings), and *point of the horse* (the point at which a lode ramifies in various directions) are examples of terms that have become part of this very old and richly described human activity. This dictionary provides brief definitions of a wide range of technical (and not so technical) mining terms covering mining equipment, processes, and structures both natural and constructed, as well as mineralogy terms, such as definitions of rocks, minerals, and geologic eras. It is divided into two sections. Section 1, the basic table, alphabetically lists 3,585 terms in English. Nearly all terms are followed by brief nontechnical definitions, usually in 20 words or fewer. For each term, the French, German, and Italian equivalents are given. Section 2 consists of three alphabetical listings, in French, German, and Italian, that refer the user to the terms in section 1.

This work provides a quick reference to mining and mining-related terms and would be particularly useful in the field or to individuals reading the literature related to mining and seeking definitions of terms. Those seeking more complete information are directed by the compiler to look elsewhere.—**Ann E. Prentice**

NUCLEAR ENGINEERING

1801. Dresser, Peter D., ed. **Nuclear Power Plants Worldwide.** Detroit, Gale, 1993. 556p. index. $129.00. ISBN 0-8103-8880-4. ISSN 1067-9979.

This new reference book is a nontechnical guide to the history and present status of each of 741 commercial nuclear power plants in the world. Each plant profile, arranged by country, presents standard information, such as plant name, location, owning utility, and manager, and basic facts, such as status, reactor type, electric power generated, reactor and generator suppliers, designer, constructor, key dates of milestones, and operating costs. The plant report, the main part of each profile, covers construction and operating performance and such issues as safety, environment, social, health, finances, and regulation. Each plant is numbered and coded by symbols to indicate its current operational status, and each profile is signed.

This work was compiled using information from plant managers and published sources, such as association, industry, and antinuclear groups publications; government documents; and media coverage in newspapers, magazines, and books. The sources, listed at the end of each profile, are in chronological order, beginning with the oldest source, not with the most recent (as stated in the detailed user's guide). Each plant report reads as a narrative history and varies in length depending on each plant's problems. In some instances, words conveying an emotional context, such as "China Syndrome" instead of "meltdown," appear in the text.

This book serves as an introduction to the nuclear power industry for the general user. A broad spectrum of views of the industry is presented. A description of how a nuclear power plant works, along with U.S. Nuclear Regulatory Commission plant assessments, maps, a glossary, a technical problems index, and a general index provide the user with access to a great deal of information. [R: RBB, 1 Nov 93, p. 568]—**Anne C. Roess**

33 Health Sciences

GENERAL WORKS

Atlases

1802. Shannon, Gary W., and Gerald F. Pyle. **Disease and Medical Care in the United States: A Medical Atlas of the Twentieth Century.** New York, Macmillan, 1993. 150p. maps. index. $95.00. RA804.S54. 614.4'273. LC 93-18364. ISBN 0-02-897371-2.

This book combines geography, medicine, and epidemiology to provide a historical perspective on selected health problems in the United States throughout the twentieth century. Using color-indexed maps, the book allows the reader to easily visualize the changes across individual states, regions, and the United States as a whole in incidence and prevalence rates of heart disease, stroke, cancer, tuberculosis, infant mortality, AIDS, influenza, and motor vehicle crashes. Individual chapters give a brief narrative history of each of the health problems, including associated risk factors and surrounding controversies. The second major section of the reference documents, in a similar format, the numbers and distribution of physicians, dentists, and hospital beds.

The book accomplishes its purpose in a way that is most appropriate for the general reader. The absence of bibliographical references limits its use among academic readers, except as a general encyclopedia-type reference. The major deterrent is the cost, which is prohibitive considering the size and content of the book.—**Mary Ann Thompson**

Dictionaries and Encyclopedias

1803. **Macmillan Health Encyclopedia.** Richard Bohlander and others, eds. New York, Macmillan, 1993. 9v. illus. index. $360.00/set. RA776.M174. 610'.3. LC 92-28939. ISBN 0-02-897439-5.

Health information is always in demand. Middle and high school students often do research on organ systems, diseases, and related topics for biology and health classes. This encyclopedia is designed to support school curricula and provide an up-to-date overview of these subjects.

The nine volumes cover broad subject areas: body systems; communicable diseases; noncommunicable diseases and disorders; nutrition and fitness; emotional and mental health; sexuality and reproduction; drugs, alcohol, and tobacco; safety and environmental health; and health care systems. Within each volume, subjects are arranged alphabetically. Entries range in length from one paragraph to several pages. Color illustrations, diagrams, and charts enhance the text. In addition to the master index in volume 9, each volume has its own index and glossary. An elaborate system of ross-references refers users to related entries and terms used. A brief bibliography of sources and a list of organizations providing information on the topics covered appear at the end of each volume. Most references cited are from the 1980s.

The information in the articles is current and easy to understand, but the organization of volumes by subject makes it somewhat cumbersome to find specific topics without using the master index. Acupuncture, for example, appears in the volume on noncommunicable diseases and disorders, with *see also* references to the articles on alternative health care in the health care systems volume and endorphins in the body systems volume. The volume on health care systems contains articles on the various health professions, which will be useful for students doing career research. It also covers such issues as health insurance and medical ethics. The safety and environmental health volume deals with first aid and safety during natural disasters as well as home and job safety and general problems (e.g., the ozone layer, oil spills, population growth). The drugs, alcohol, and tobacco volume covers over-the-counter, prescription, and recreational drugs.

Macmillan Health Encyclopedia is a good starting point for students doing research. It is similar in scope to the *Marshall Cavendish Encyclopedia of Family Health* (see ARBA 93, entry 1617), which costs $100 more. Although the latter covers organ systems and diseases in more detail, it has a British focus and does not provide the information on health care systems and professions and environmental health and safety that the Macmillan set offers. *Macmillan Health Encyclopedia* is an excellent source for school and public libraries. [R: BR, Sept/Oct 93, pp. 56-57; RBB, 15 Sept 93, pp. 188-89; SBF, Aug/Sept 93, pp. 175-76; SBF, Oct 93, p. 203; SLJ, Nov 93, p. 145]—**Barbara M. Bibel**

1804. Slee, Vergil N., and Debora A. Slee. **Health Care Reform Terms: A Glossary of Words, Phrases, & Acronyms....** advance ed. St. Paul, Minn., Tringa Press, 1993. 90p. $9.95pa. ISBN 0-9615255-4-1.

This title is a valuable tool for those involved in health care reform efforts or for the average citizen wanting clarification of terms employed in the national debate. The glossary is arranged alphabetically and contains clear, understandable definitions and descriptions of words, phrases, acronyms, organizations, committees, and governmental programs relevant to the health care reform discussion. In addition, the book is well cross-referenced. The terms range from very basic ones that are likely to be familiar to many (e.g., insurance) to the more specialized ones primarily used by industry insiders (e.g., Blue Indigo Corporation). Examples of organizations and programs described include the American Hospital Association, the Pepper Commission, and the Veterans Administration.

One caveat worth mentioning is also noted by the authors in their preface: The terms can mean different things to different people, and the terminology used by health care reformers can change. When reading specific reports, laws, and the like, terms in the material may vary somewhat from those in this text. Perhaps such a volume as this can help standardize the discussion. Also, addresses and telephone numbers are given for some, but not all, organizations and government agencies and program offices. The authors are encouraged to add this information for all such listings. Caveats aside, this is a very helpful and easy-to-use ready-reference tool. [R: RBB, 15 Nov 93, p. 645]—**Kathleen Nelson Boyle**

1805. **Women's Encyclopedia of Health & Emotional Healing: Top Women Doctors Share Their Unique Self-Help Advice....** By Denise Foley, Eileen Nechas, and the editors of *Prevention* magazine. Emmaus, Pa., Rodale Press, 1993. 517p. illus. index. $27.95. RA778.F66. 613.0424. LC 92-23361. ISBN 0-87596-151-7.

Accurate, objective information about women's health can be difficult to find, because subjects such as hormone replacement therapy, cancer treatment options, and contraception are controversial. *Women's Encyclopedia of Health & Emotional Healing* offers self-help advice about a variety of female health problems. The alphabetical entries are two to four pages long. Many subjects are needlessly divided, such as birth control pills and contraception, and breast care, breast surgery, and fibrocystic breast. There are also entries for subjects of minor importance, such as blemishes, cellulite, and wrinkles. All of the information is at a superficial level. There are no bibliographies, anatomical diagrams, or referral lists.

While the book contains useful practical advice on discussing condom use with sexual partners and preventing cystitis, the general level of information and the lack of references make it useless as a research tool. *The New Our Bodies Ourselves* (Simon & Schuster, 1992) is a superior source, offering detailed, illustrated information with references and referral sources. *Women's Encyclopedia of Health & Emotional Healing* could be part of a circulating collection, but it is not a necessary purchase. [R: LJ, 1 Feb 93, pp. 70-72]—**Barbara M. Bibel**

Directories

1806. Axelrod, Natalie, Michelle Hill, and Michelle Leonard, eds. **Register of North American Hospitals, 1993.** South River, N.J., American Preeminent Registry, 1992. 746p. maps. index. $97.95pa. ISBN 0-9633783-0-9. ISSN 1062-7340.

This work provides information on almost 9,500 hospitals in the United States and Canada. Unfortunately, much of this information is already outdated. The register is presented alphabetically by state (including Puerto Rico and the U.S. Virgin Islands), followed by Canada. The directory entries are arranged alphabetically by city within a particular state. On the beginning page of each state listing is a map; names of the governor and U.S. senators; and basic information about area codes, zip codes, and number of hospitals and beds. This source includes indexes to chief administrative officers, chief medical officers, and hospitals. Many of the names provided are no longer accurate, which may or may not be a problem, depending on how the information will be used. Nonprofit organizations and others conducting a direct-mail campaign may order computer-generated mailing lists of hospitals from the publisher. This reviewer suggests first double-checking with the publisher to verify the currency of the information.

The *Register of North American Hospitals* expands such works as the *1993 Hospital Phone Book* (U.S. Directory Service, 1993), as it provides the names of more hospitals and is more comprehensive than the *Phone Book*. It is hoped that a revised edition will be forthcoming with more current data. Recommended for college, university, and medical libraries. [R: RBB, 1 Mar 93, pp. 1267-68]—**Marilynn Green**

1807. Backus, Karen, ed. **Medical and Health Information Directory 1992-93: A Guide....** Detroit, Gale, 1993. 3v. index. $485.00/set. LC 85-645724. ISBN 0-8103-7524-9. ISSN 0749-9973.

The 6th edition of this work provides comprehensive access to organizations, institutions, agencies, and information sources in the medical and health fields. Each volume covers a separate area and has its own master name and keyword index, so it can be used independently. Volume 1 lists some 16,400 agencies, institutions, and organizations, including government agencies, research centers, professional organizations, foundations, and schools. Volume 2 covers more than 9,700 libraries, audiovisual producers and services, publishers and publications, and databases. Volume 3 provides access to 23,000-plus clinics, treatment centers, care programs, and other health services. There are scope notes in each volume explaining the criteria for inclusion. The entries include name, address, and telephone number of the organization or institution. Journal, directory, and newsletter entries contain frequency, and institutional entries list the director's name. The directory is easy to use; the entries are grouped by subject and arranged geographically by state and city, then alphabetically by name.

This directory is very useful because of its broad scope, but it is quite expensive and contains some information available in standard sources, such as the *Encyclopedia of Associations* (Gale, annual). Smaller libraries may not want to purchase all three volumes, but health science collections will enjoy the convenience of having everything in one source. This set is also available on disk and magnetic tape for electronic access.—**Barbara M. Bibel**

1808. **Holistic Health Directory, 1992-1993.** Brighton, Mass., New Age Journal, [1993]. 128p. illus. index. $5.95pa.

This directory provides names, addresses, and telephone numbers for practitioners of alternative healing therapies throughout the United States and Canada. The directory is divided into four sections: natural and holistic health, bodywork and energy healing, counseling, and resources. Each of the first three sections begins with a glossary that defines the treatment modalities included in the section. This is followed by lists of practitioners arranged alphabetically by state under the modality headings. Practitioners are listed only under headings under which they paid to be listed; therefore, practitioners of several modalities may not appear under all of them.

The compilers admit that the directory is not comprehensive, but given the much-publicized interest in alternative health care among American consumers and the difficulty in locating practitioners, this inexpensive publication will at least give patrons a place to start. The directory is in a magazine format (which includes a substantial amount of product advertising), and library shelving and control may be somewhat problematic. Nevertheless, it is recommended for public libraries where interest warrants.—**Gari-Anne Patzwald**

1809. Lesko, Matthew, with Mary Ann Artello and Andrew Naprawa. **What to Do When You Can't Afford Health Care: An "A-to-Z" Sourcebook for the Entire Family.** Kensington, Md., Information USA, 1993. 769p. index. $24.95pa. ISBN 1-878346-16-4.

This work contains information on free and low-cost health care and other health care-related services, primarily those available from state and federal agencies. The work is divided into three main sections. The first addresses how to obtain free and low-cost medical treatment, including information on how to obtain such care from hospitals or through clinical trials, a list of state public health hotlines, and information on services for the handicapped and disabled. The second (and largest) section, arranged alphabetically by disease and health-related topic, covers Abetalipoproteinemia to Zoonoses, and everything in between. Under each topic, information is provided on clearinghouses and hotlines to contact and publications and videos to order; addresses and telephone numbers are given. The third section lists consumer resources for free and low-cost legal help to resolve health-related legal issues, such as the right to quality treatment or billing disputes. The section is organized by topic, covering such areas as aging-related issues, health clubs, and medical bills.

The book also includes "The Art of Getting a Bureaucrat to Help You"; sample success stories; and three useful appendixes covering clinical studies, free medications, and state health statistics. The table of contents and the index, with its extensive cross-referencing, are excellent tools for quickly locating information. The work does not generally list private nonprofit organizations, which also offer free and low-cost services. However, this work is a comprehensive and useful resource for federal and state services and would be a valuable addition to any reference collection. [R: LJ, 1 May 93, p. 83; RBB, 15 Oct 93, p. 477]—**Kathleen Nelson Boyle**

1810. **Medical Utilization Review Directory: A Comprehensive Ranking and Listing of Providers and Users....** Susan Namovicz and Spencer Vibbert, eds. Washington, D.C., Faulkner & Gray, 1993. 517p. index. $295.00pa. ISBN 1-881393-04-6.

The medical utilization review (UR) industry exists to provide an objective review of medical services for clients, ensuring that such services are medically reasonable, warranted, and provided in the most appropriate setting. According to the introduction of this work, clients of medical UR services include insurers, manufacturers, government agencies, and health care providers. The directory provides information on U.S. medical UR companies, insurance companies providing or subcontracting UR services, and users of UR services. About half of the directory is devoted to medical review companies. Each one-page listing gives the company's address, telephone and fax numbers, and date founded. In most cases, a company's status (public, private, or nonprofit) is given. Other entry information includes gross revenues, key executives, services reviewed, fee structure, techniques, medical criteria and appeals, clients, and licensing. Insurance company listings are much shorter, giving address, telephone and fax numbers, key executives, UR techniques, staff, and subcontractors. The section of the directory on users of UR services also has shorter entries containing address, telephone and fax numbers, contact person, type of organization, parent company, and UR vendor. A series of interviews with UR industry leaders, a discussion of state laws regulating UR, the text of National Utilization Review Standards, a ranking of the top 50 UR companies, and a glossary round out the directory. Indexes list companies alphabetically and on a state-by-state basis. Recommended for medical libraries and appropriate corporate libraries.

—**Kerranne G. Biley**

Handbooks and Yearbooks

1811. **ACCIS Guide to United Nations Information Sources on Health.** New York, United Nations, 1992. 227p. index. $36.00pa. ISBN 92-1-100363-6. S/N GV.E.91.0.11.

Most people think that United Nations health activities are the exclusive domain of the World Health Organization (WHO). Although WHO has primary responsibility in this area, there are at least 27 other UN system organizations that touch upon various aspects of personal and environmental health, disease prevention and control, and health care delivery around the globe. Similar to other ACCIS (Advisory Committee for the Coordination of Information Systems) guides, this one begins with a brief description of relevant organizations, including addresses, telephone numbers, a capsule history, a description of general functions, and an indexed key to health information resources by subject matter and the organizational subunit that produces them. The remainder of the book describes these information resources under 11 broad subject headings. Individual entries describe each subunit's history and purpose, list relevant databases and representative health-related publications, and explain how the information may be obtained. End material includes a comprehensive index and an international list of libraries that offer public reference facilities for WHO publications. The byzantine structure of the UN is reflected in the organization of this guide—not for beginners or casual users, but an invaluable resource for serious scholars of international health.—**Bruce Stuart**

1812. **Dial 800 for Health.** Compiled by the People's Medical Society. Allentown, Pa., People's Medical Society, 1993. 95p. index. $5.95pa. ISBN 0-9627334-9-0.

1813. **The National Family Healthcare Handbook: The Complete Directory of Associations, Services, and Support Groups.** Montvale, N.J., Medical Economics Data, 1993. 112p. illus. free pa.

The empowered health care consumer, seeking and acting on health information from a variety of sources, is more the norm than the exception in the 1990s. These two small books list many health care resources for the consumer and the health professional. The People's Medical Society adds to its series of consumer health care guides with its directory of 300 health-related organizations with toll-free telephone numbers. The organizations are listed alphabetically by topic area. Each citation includes the usual directory information, hours of operation, and a brief description of services. A cross-index by title and subject is provided.

The National Family Healthcare Handbook lists more than 1,700 health care associations, support groups, and professional organizations, including the 300 referenced by the People's Medical Society book. The comprehensive directory provides address and telephone numbers (mostly toll calls) arranged alphabetically by topic. Occasional short notations describe the purpose or services of the agencies. No table of contents or index is given. The book appears to be produced for home use; it includes sections on first aid and CPR and spaces to record personal health data. As constructed, the book would not withstand repeated use in a general library. [R: LJ, 1 May 93, p. 80]—**Mary Ann Thompson**

1814. **Guide to Federal Funding for Hospitals and Health Centers.** Amy McAuliffe, ed. Arlington, Va., Government Information Services, 1993. 1v. (various paging). $297.00 looseleaf w/binder. ISBN 0-933544-55-3.

Many hospitals and health centers are looking for additional funding for their projects in these days of concern over rising health care costs and diverse reform proposals. This new guide provides information on 187 federal funding opportunities (exclusive of Medicare-Medicaid and biomedical research assistance) currently available, with general descriptions and directions for the application process. (Seven billion dollars is said to be targeted to help fund health service programs!) Having determined the purpose or function and the recipients of the proposed service project, the grant seeker uses the subject index to locate relevant programs, which might appear under several of the 10 major categories into which the book is divided. Each program entry discusses its purpose, eligibility, use of funds, restrictions, matching requirements, how to apply, selection criteria, funds available in fiscal year 1993, contact person, recent legislation, and so forth. A quick-check box indicates the flow of the money, who can ultimately get it, who administers the program, the type of aid (e.g., grant, loan, cooperative agreement), and general requirements. Government jargon is generally avoided. A special index cross-references the programs described to corresponding entries in the government's *Catalog of Federal Domestic Assistance* (Office of Management and Budget, 1992). Appendixes list regional offices of the Department of Education and the Department of Health and Human Services, as well as state agencies to contact about surplus personal property.

Trustees, development officers, and grant writers of health service institutions should find this meticulously compiled guide a good starting point in the lengthy and complicated search for federal funds. A subscription to the update service will be necessary for effective use.—**Harriette M. Cluxton**

1815. **HMO/PPO Directory 1993: U.S. Managed Healthcare Organizations in Detail Plus Key Decision Makers.** Montvale, N.J., Medical Economics Data, 1992. 1v. (various paging). $175.00. ISBN 1-56363-043-5. ISSN 0887-4484.

This directory of health maintenance organizations (HMOs) and preferred provider organizations (PPOs) is organized into sections that contain data about the organizations. There are alphabetical listings of HMOs, PPOs, and personnel. The personnel listing contains addresses and telephone numbers. The listings of the HMOs and PPOs are arranged by state. Each organization has an entry that includes address, telephone number, number of subscribers, for-profit status, director and other key personnel, qualifications for physician and hospital members, and some information about level of service. Most entries are fairly complete, although few list whether or not a second surgical opinion is required. A few entries contain only address and telephone number.

This directory may be of use to the business staff of hospitals and medical practices. If available in a public library, it might be useful for an individual trying to select such an organization. But it gives no information as to quality of service and so cannot be used as a sole reference.—**Margretta Reed Seashore**

1816. Morgan, Kathleen O'Leary, Scott Morgan, and Neal Quitno, eds. **Health Care State Rankings 1993: Health Care in the 50 United States.** Lawrence, Kans., Morgan Quitno, 1993. 456p. index. $43.95pa. ISBN 0-9625531-4-X. ISSN 1065-1403.

This book is a useful source of health statistics as well as a list of state rankings. Some of the subjects covered are births, deaths, health care professionals, cancer, alcohol consumption, hospitals and health care facilities, personnel, finances, smokers, seat belt users, and some communicable diseases. All of the information is in tabular form, and the source is listed at the bottom of each table. The 17 sources of information are all reliable agencies and include the American Cancer Society, the American Hospital Association, the American Medical Association, divisions of the U.S. Department of Health and Human Services, and the U.S. Bureau of the Census. If a library cannot afford all the documents from these agencies, this is a good, inexpensive alternative. [R: Choice, May 93, pp. 1441-42; LJ, 15 Mar 93, pp. 68-70; RBB, Aug 93, p. 2091]—**Betsy J. Kraus**

MEDICINE

General Works

Acronyms and Abbreviations

1817. Davis, Neil M. **Medical Abbreviations: 8600 Conveniences at the Expense of Communications and Safety.** 6th ed. Huntington Valley, Pa., Neil M. Davis, 1993. 204p. $11.95pa. LC 92-90412. ISBN 0-931431-06-9.

The subtitle of this pocket manual clearly expresses the viewpoint that distinguishes it from other lists of medical abbreviations. Davis, head of pharmacy activities at Temple University, editor of *Hospital Pharmacy*, and CEO of the Institute for Safe Medication Practices, points out the dangers lurking in misreading or misinterpretation of medical abbreviations; he actually marks some items "this is a dangerous abbreviation," and asserts that drug names and certain common words, such as unit, should never be abbreviated.

Items are listed in capital letter form only, with two columns of small type per page. Symbols and normal laboratory values are listed at the end of the book. Extensive coverage, biennial revision and expansion, small size, and low cost make this a first-choice compilation for health care students and workers at all levels, as well as medical records personnel.—**Harriette M. Cluxton**

1818. Jablonski, Stanley, comp. and ed. **Dictionary of Medical Acronyms & Abbreviations.** 2d ed. Philadelphia, Hanley & Belfus, 1993. 330p. $15.95pa. LC 92-71427. ISBN 1-56053-052-9.

Medical acronyms and abbreviations are abundant and increasing rapidly because they are useful and because they provide for an economy of effort, facilitate communication, and decrease space needed for written words. This dictionary is an easy-to-use source for understanding the words behind the acronym or abbreviation. The abbreviations and acronyms listed in this dictionary are those most frequently found in a systematic scanning of books and periodicals at the National Library of Medicine. This edition has some 2,000 more entries than the first one. Sections on symbols and the Greek alphabet are included to assist the reader. This handy and valuable reference would be more useful if brief explanations followed selected acronyms and abbreviations.—**Robert L. Jones**

Atlases

1819. Parker, Steve. **The Body Atlas.** New York, Dorling Kindersley, 1993. 63p. illus. index. $19.95. QM27.P266. 611. LC 92-54307. ISBN 1-56458-224-8.

This is a new offering in a series of large-format atlases from the publisher. It is a magnificent paean to the human body, bearing very little resemblance to drab, technical anatomy atlases such as *Gray's Anatomy*. The illustrations, all in glowing color, are detailed yet understandable. Both the illustrations and the text explain the function as well as the form of each part of the body, from head to toe.

The Body Atlas first illustrates each of the systems of the body, such as the skeletal and nervous systems. Then specific body parts and organs are described, accompanied by detailed drawings and illustrations of the part in action. Interesting historical and physiological facts are included. While the text is written to be readable by older elementary students, there is enough information in the text and pictures to satisfy anyone short of a medical professional. [R: WLB, Oct 93, p. 86]—**Carol L. Noll**

Bibliography

1820. Mizel, Mark S., and Glenn B. Pfeffer, eds. **Selected Bibliography of the Foot and Ankle with Commentary.** Park Ridge, Ill., American Academy of Orthopaedic Surgeons, 1992. 321p. $20.00pa. ISBN 0-89203-061-5.

This is a selective, annotated bibliography on topics related to the foot and ankle. The subjects covered include anatomy; biomechanics; and fractures and disorders associated with the foot and ankle, such as neuromuscular disorders, reflex sympathetic dystrophy, hallus valgus, and compartment syndromes. Virtually all the citations are from the journal literature, with a few references to book chapters. The brief annotations are descriptive, with no attempt to evaluate the article or compare it to similar articles on the topic—other than an occasional note about a classic study.

The preface states that the selections are a representative sampling of the literature but gives no criteria for selection. The most recent publication date is 1991. While anatomy and biomechanics are reasonably static fields, treatment modalities for diseases and fractures change, sometimes quite rapidly. A primary consideration in the medical literature is currency. As this type of compilation becomes dated even prior to publication, it is difficult to determine its purpose or usefulness.

The target audience is practitioners, students, and medical researchers. Each of these groups would be better served by securing a computer search of the topic that interests them from MEDLINE, the National Library of Medicine database. The database indexes articles, including abstracts, as they are published in the medical literature, so that one can easily find a completely current bibliography on any desired subject.—**Carol R. Glatt**

1821. Rogal, Samuel J., comp. **Medicine in Great Britain from the Restoration to the Nineteenth Century, 1660-1800.** Westport, Conn., Greenwood Press, 1992. 258p. index. (Bibliographies and Indexes in Medical Studies, no.8). $65.00. Z6661.G7R63. 016.61'0941'09033. LC 91-39004. ISBN 0-313-28115-7.

From 1600 to 1800, British medicine saw a significant number of individuals lead the advance of medical science. Along with these influential medical writers, lesser-known physicians, various types of alternative healers, and blatant quacks published scores of medical treatises. This bibliography claims to cover the monographic and other medical works published in England, Wales, Scotland, and Ireland during those two centuries. Unfortunately a combination of poor organization, lack of knowledge about appropriate resources, and low-level scholarship undercut this volume's promise and usefulness.

Rogal, whose vita demonstrates no background in British history of medicine, lists 2,057 entries divided into 24 topical chapters, varying from anatomy to specific diseases to professional groups. No selection criteria are stated in the preface. Rogal chose the entries for this volume by merely consulting a number of standard bibliographies that are readily available in most research libraries rather than actually examining the cited items. A significant omission in this questionable selection process is the failure to use the main catalog of 1600-1800 medical publications produced by the Wellcome Institute for the History of Medicine, the main bibliographic tool for this material. Many of the cited items are not annotated, and those that are provide little assistance to the user, for almost all of the annotations are biographical sketches of the publications' authors rather than critical comments about the publications. The author index is both confusing and misleading in its organization and is more likely to frustrate than assist the reader. This volume will be of very limited use, if any, to librarians and scholars, who will be better served by relying on the standard bibliographic reference sources on seventeenth- and eighteenth-century British medical publications. [R: Choice, July/Aug 92,p. 1660]—**Jonathon Erlen**

1822. Rutkow, Ira M. **The History of Surgery in the United States 1775-1900. Volume 2: Periodicals and Pamphlets.** San Francisco, Norman Publishing, 1992. 434p. illus. index. (Norman Surgery Series, no. 2, 4; Norman Bibliography Series, no.2, 5). $175.00. Z6666.R87. 016.617'0973. LC 87-62662. ISBN 0-930405-48-X.

During the past decade there has been a renewed interest in the history of various medical specialties, including surgery. This bibliographic study completes a two-volume series that claims to thoroughly examine the evolution of surgical literature in the United States between 1775 and 1900. While praiseworthy in what they accomplish, these volumes fail to completely fulfill this promise.

In this volume Rutkow describes, and in many cases analyzes, 1,413 journal articles and pamphlets written by Americans on a wide variety of surgical topics during this 125-year period. These annotations range from one sentence to more than one page in length. This bibliography is organized chronologically around the following surgical specialties: general surgical practice, urology, anesthesia, plastic surgery, gynecology, thoracic surgery, ophthalmology, otorhinolaryngology, and neurological surgery. Of particular value is the inclusion of 117 illustrations reproduced from the cited works. A major contribution of this volume is the biographical information provided for most of the cited authors. Another item of significant value is its discussion of surgical firsts and eponyms that are difficult to locate in other histories of surgery. Rutkow does the history of medicine community an important favor by pointing out the errors and poor scholarship present in many standard history of surgery texts and the need for scholars to rely on primary rather than secondary materials in their research efforts.

The one glaring flaw in this otherwise totally impressive work is Rutkow's failure to acknowledge late eighteenth- and nineteenth-century American surgeons' debt to European surgical advances. Thus, the book jacket's claim that "this book documents all significant developments in American surgery up to 1900" is far from accurate. To complete this valuable survey, Rutkow needs a third volume that examines the strong impact of European surgery and the work of such dominant, influential figures as Dominique Jean Larrey, Astley Cooper, and Antonio Scarpa on their American counterparts.—**Jonathon Erlen**

1823. Schmitz, Cecilia M., and Richard A. Gray. **The Gift of Life: Organ and Tissue Transplantation: An Introduction to Issues and Information Sources.** Ann Arbor, Mich., Pierian Press, 1993. 108p. index. $12.95pa. ISBN 0-87560-309-1.

The major objective of this work is to provide a clear understanding of the topic of tissue and organ transplants. The aim is to encourage people to become tissue and organ donors by answering the questions they may have about the process. The work provides brief synopses of each of the key topics. Following the introduction, summaries of 85 key articles are provided. There is a thorough discussion of the legal, medical, and philosophical issues involved in organ and tissue transplants. A full range of topics related to organ transplants is covered, including donor death, success rates of various types of tissue transplants, and the marketing of organs. Historical background is provided in discussing the issues. After extensive research, the authors selected the best of the case studies (e.g., the Karen Ann Quinlan case) to illustrate the complexity of the decisions that face the patient's family and physicians. The section headings are clear, and the sequence of the presentation of ideas is orderly and logical.

Information is presented in straightforward language. The summaries by medical experts are critiqued at the end of each discussion, and vital statistics are provided (e.g., survival rates from living kidneys is 9,690; from cadavers it is 9,190).

The book does not go into depth on any one issue; however, it does provide additional reading lists. There is no attempt to integrate moral, legal, and medical issues, but this may have been intentional. A strength of this work is that both sides of controversial issues receive equal coverage. One weakness is the omission of the Uniform Determination of Death Act (UDDA) adopted by 27 states and the District of Columbia. A thorough understanding of, or experience with, organ transplants is needed by the layperson in order to use the information presented in this book. However, *The Gift of Life* would serve as an excellent reference for a medical practitioner or as an educational tool for potential donors, their families, medical students, doctors, and nurses.—**Marilynn Green**

Catalogs and Collections

1824. **Catalogue of Films and Videos in the British Medical Association Library.** London, Library Association; distr., Lanham, Md., UNIPUB, 1993. 335p. index. $60.00. 016.61. ISBN 1-85604-082-8.

This is the first comprehensive list of the 2,000 films and videos in the Library of the British Medical Association. Most items are current through September 1992, but the archival collection includes health and medicine titles even back to the 1920s, plus some special donated collections. The list serves as an index to the library's holdings and as an authoritative guide to high-quality films and videos useful for medical and health education. Peer review was provided by the British Medical Association's Board of Science and Education. Entries, arranged alphabetically by title, include full physical description, target audience, producer, and a synopsis. Titles are also listed in a simple subject index following the main section.

It is claimed that the collection is intensively used by individual and institutional (library) members of the association; this listing should materially aid such usage. Entrants in the annual film and video competition should also consult it, as well as persons with special interests in the historical and current usage of audiovisual materials in medical and health education in England. However, despite its excellence, few North American libraries will have much practical use for this catalog.—**Harriette M. Cluxton**

Dictionaries and Encyclopedias

1825. Bodiwala, G. G., A. W. McCaskie, and M. M. Thompson. **International Translation Guide for Emergency Medicine: An Aid to History-Taking and Patient Evaluation.** Stoneham, Mass., Butterworths, 1993. 227p. $59.95pa. RC.3.B63. 616.02'5'03. LC 91-47857. ISBN 0-7506-1259-2.

This is a novel and potentially invaluable new resource for hospital emergency room personnel. It lists thousands of phrases and questions in English, French, German, Hindi, Italian, Russian, and Spanish. Each question or phrase is numbered so that physicians can find the appropriate question in their language, then find the translation in the patient's language. All questions are given in a form requiring only a yes or no answer. Because the Russian and Hindi translations are given in those scripts (and pronunciation might be difficult in some of the other languages), this system works best if the patient (or someone accompanying the patient) can read.

This book will be of obvious use to hospital emergency rooms and first aid squads likely to encounter tourists or immigrants. It also could be of interest to travelers with chronic health problems, who might consider carrying a copy.—**Carol L. Noll**

1826. Cameron, Myra. **Lifetime Encyclopedia of Natural Remedies.** West Nyack, N.Y., Parker Publishing; distr., Englewood Cliffs, N.J., Prentice Hall Career & Personal Development, 1993. 426p. index. $27.95. RM666.H33C36. 615.8'82. LC 93-1957. ISBN 0-13-535220-7.

The author of this volume does not have a degree in the healing arts but has done extensive research in alternative methods of treatment that may prevent or alleviate many common ailments. Her findings are presented here for 100 common maladies such as acne, food allergies, motion sickness, and varicose veins. For each condition, information is provided about the nature of the condition, dietary recommendations, vitamin and mineral supplements that may aid healing, suggested homeopathic remedies, exercise (if the condition warrants it), folk remedies, and specific body areas to stimulate with acupressure. There are also references to sources in the bibliography where the particular ailment is discussed. The length of advice for each condition varies depending upon its cure.

The information presented is clear, concise, and easily understood by the layperson. It is wisely recommended that readers consult a trained physician before making drastic changes in their health regimen and that they follow these recommendations at their own risk. All the ingredients suggested can be obtained from supermarkets and health food stores. The folk remedies do not call for dangerous substances, and precise amounts and directions are given for every treatment and remedy. A table of contents and index make the information very easy to find. The special quality of this book is that it concisely presents a variety of treatments for each malady all in one place.—**Marilyn Strong Noronha**

1827. **Encyclopedia of Health Information Sources: A Bibliographic Guide to Over 13,000 Citations for Publications, Organizations, and Databases on Health-Related Subjects.** 2d ed. Alan M. Rees, ed. Detroit, Gale, 1993. 521p. $165.00. Z6658.E54. 016.61. LC 93-22416. ISBN 0-8103-6909-5.

First published in 1986, this work is a guide to publications, databases, and organizations dealing with health-related subjects. The 2d edition contains more than 13,000 citations from 6,715 unique sources covering the medical specialties, allied health professions, alternative health disciplines, health care administration, and education. This edition includes CD-ROM as well as online databases, telephone and fax numbers for sources, and 27 new topics. Material from the first edition (see ARBA 88, entry 1641) has been extensively revised. It is also available on diskette and magnetic tape for electronic access.

An outline of contents lists the subject headings. Extensive cross-references in the outline and the text facilitate access. The text is arranged alphabetically by subject. Within each subject the citations are grouped alphabetically by type, such as abstracting, indexing, and current awareness; associations; and journals. Each citation includes the title, name and address of publisher, telephone and fax numbers, and frequency of issuance or publication date. Most of the sources included have been published in 1988 or later. Both technical and lay resources are listed. There are no evaluations of the sources, but the editor chose them from the *Brandon Core Lists, The Library for Internists VII*, Alfred M. Brandon's *The Core Collection of Medical Books and Journals* (Chichester, England: Medical Information Working Party, n.d.), and favorable reviews.

While not exhaustive, the *Encyclopedia of Health Information Sources* is an excellent starting point for students doing research and a fine resource for collection development. Because it covers both the popular and scientific literature and includes alternative health and socioeconomic information, it is useful for both public and academic libraries.—**Barbara M. Bibel**

1828. **Encyclopedia of Immunology.** Ivan M. Roitt, ed. San Diego, Calif., Academic Press, 1992. 3v. illus. $450.00/set. ISBN 0-12-226760-5.

This encyclopedia contains a wealth of information. The set consists of entries about a variety of topics relating to immunology. These entries are written by experts in the field, and each contains a short reference list of works as recent as 1990. The entries, while brief, attempt to provide an overview of the topic as well as its author's insights into the important issues in the area. The topics vary from basic areas, such as lymphokines, to clinical subjects, such as chronic granulomatous disease and the immunologic response to infection. As with many multiauthored texts, there is variability among entries. While some are relatively long and provide considerable detail, others are shorter and more general. None is more than three or four pages long. A few provide simple diagrams, and tables summarize data in others.

This set would be useful to clinicians in a variety of medical specialties, particularly pediatrics, internal medicine, and genetics. Immunologists will have access to this material in other ways. Although many of the references would be available through a MEDLINE search, this set makes the information handy, and a quick reading of an entry provides a useful overview of the topic and access to the relevant literature.

—**Margretta Reed Seashore**

1829. **Melloni's Illustrated Medical Dictionary.** 3d ed. By Ida G. Dox, B. John Melloni, and Gilbert M. Eisner. Pearl River, N.Y., Parthenon Publishing, 1993. 533p. illus. $28.95. R121.D76. 610'.3. LC 92-48306. ISBN 1-85070-479-1. [This is also available in paperback from HarperCollins as *The HarperCollins Illustrated Medical Dictionary*, 1993. $19.00pa. LC 92-53299. ISBN 0-06-273142-4.]

Health-conscious lay readers struggling to keep up with the rapid expansion of medical terminology have available an outstanding resource in the new edition of this dictionary, which has been a useful source of health sciences information for more than a decade. This edition maintains the structure and perspective of the original book but has incorporated many useful suggestions from readers. It is a compilation of more than 26,000 common terms for all the health sciences. Approximately 2,500 simple, specific illustrations help readers better understand the textual definitions, which are clear and precise. Sections on abbreviations and symbols, prefixes, suffixes, combining forms, and pronunciation at the beginning of the book are very helpful and contribute to the ready-reference nature of the dictionary (although pronunciations should also appear in the main part of the book for effective use). To facilitate location of a desired term, the first and last terms on a page are printed in color at the outside of the bottom margin of each page. Also, commonly used chemical compounds and drugs are included as defined terms, and synonyms of words are noted at the ends of the definitions. New to this edition is the use of illustrated tables of the major anatomical groupings. Overall, this book is clearly an improvement over previous volumes.—**Robert L. Jones**

1830. **The Random House Health and Medicine Dictionary.** New York, Random House, 1992. 387p. $7.00pa. R121.R214. 610'.3. LC 92-25714. ISBN 0-679-41590-4.

Although designed as a portable reference to help the layperson understand the "terms the experts use when talking about your health" (preface), this pocket dictionary has few features beyond mere definitions to assist that process. Considering the audience, is it sufficient just to write out the acronym (e.g., CFS-chronic fatigue syndrome) or state the French form (e.g., fixed idea-idee fixe)? Many chemical terms remain equally obtuse. The terms included (about 8,000) are selected from the publisher's Living Dictionary database, which is constantly updated, so the claim for exceptional currency may be justified—but *tamoxifen* does not appear.

The desire to produce a compact, inexpensive dictionary has caused two serious problems for this book: the use of a typeface so small that many will find it impossible to read with any degree of comfort, and an imprinted flexible slipcover from which the text can be readily removed. While useful for allied health personnel, this product hardly fulfills its announced purpose. A better choice is *Dictionary of Medical Terms for the Nonmedical Person* (see ARBA 90, entry 1655).—**Harriette M. Cluxton**

1831. Rothman, Barbara Katz, ed. **Encyclopedia of Childbearing: Critical Perspectives.** Phoenix, Ariz., Oryx Press, 1993. 446p. illus. index. $74.50. RG525.E52. 618.2'003. LC 92-14975. ISBN 0-89774-648-1.

Although a few of the 257 articles in this one-volume encyclopedia cover medical topics, it should be understood that this is not a medical or nursing text. The emphasis is on the sociology, anthropology, history, and politics of childbirth, fertility, and adoption. It is a rather eclectic alphabetical arrangement of individual articles by experts and practitioners in many fields, even including theology and art history. Many are fascinating, particularly articles on birth imagery in art and the history of various aspects of childbirth in the United States. However, there is an inherent problem in the entire concept of this text: Many of the topics treated are controversial, and in each case only one point of view is represented. All the contributors have been chosen from a fairly narrow range of the political and academic spectrum, and on many topics (e.g., abortion, many aspects of the childbirth process) the articles read more like political tracts than informational entries. Still, this is an unusual work and could be useful for many arcane topics related to childbearing. Where else could one quickly find an article (with bibliography) on shoes for babies or dreams during pregnancy? [R: RBB, June 93, p. 1896; RQ, Summer 93, pp. 366-67]—**Carol L. Noll**

1832. Segen, J. C., comp. and ed. **The Dictionary of Modern Medicine.** Park Ridge, N.J., Parthenon Publishing, 1992. 800p. illus. $75.00. R121.S429. 610'.3. LC 91-39484. ISBN 1-85070-321-3.

Medicine is changing rapidly. Increasing specialization and interdisciplinary collaboration have created new terminologies that do not appear in traditional medical dictionaries. *The Dictionary of Modern Medicine* is designed to complement these sources. It focuses on the jargon, acronyms, and neologisms of the new medical disciplines rather than the anatomical and biochemical terms found in the classic dictionaries.

This source contains terms from law, ethics, computer science, and current affairs that relate to medicine. Entries range in length from a few sentences to more than a page and provide summaries of current information. A sampling of entries includes *Roe v. Wade* and Nancy Beth Cruzon, with brief synopses of the legal decisions; Club Med dermatitis and Seder syncope, food-related ailments; authorship and author inflation, issues in academic medicine; gork, derogatory medical student slang for comatose patients; and WYSIWYG (what you see is what you get), referring to computer displays. The book also contains information on diseases and treatments, (e.g., Lyme disease).

The Dictionary of Modern Medicine is informative, entertaining, and accessible. Lay readers can understand the definitions, but they are not too simple for professionals. The dictionary fills a gap in biomedical reference collections by supplementing and updating standard medical dictionaries.—**Barbara M. Bibel**

1833. **Taber's Cyclopedic Medical Dictionary.** 17th ed. Clayton L. Thomas, ed. Philadelphia, F. A. Davis, 1993. 2590p. illus. index. $27.50; $29.95 (indexed). R121.T144. 610'.3'21. LC 62-8364. ISBN 0-8036-8313-8; 0-8036-8312-X (indexed).

First published in 1940, this dictionary serves nursing and allied health professionals as well as laypeople. Its encyclopedic approach provides comprehensive explanations not only of medical terms but also of disease entities and biological and social concepts. New terms in this edition cover such topics as burnout, mass sociogenic illness, and surrogate parenting. Some 2,200 terms have been added for this edition, for a total of 56,600 entries. Other features include new appendixes for universal precautions and nursing organizations (United States and Canada), and a nursing theory appendix that is an abstract of Jacqueline Fawcett's *Analysis and Evaluation of Conceptual Models of Nursing*, 2d ed. (Davis, 1989).

This edition includes 75 tables, few of which have been revised. "Methods of Disinfection" has not been updated since 1970, nor "Weight Tables" since 1983. The fibromyalgia classifications have been updated to the 1990 guidelines. Most of the appendixes have been revised, notably poisons, drug abuse, and medical emergencies.

Efforts were made to modernize vocabulary and eliminate hyphenation, yet older terms such as "catarrh" are not ignored and receive attention from a historical perspective. This edition retains the classic features of previous editions, such as translations for Spanish, Italian, French, and German health-related questions used in the treatment of patients, and some 200 detailed 2-color illustrations. At the same time, this edition provides much-needed updating to current information on the diagnosis and treatment of a number of diseases, such as AIDS. Printed on durable, lightweight paper, the volume is portable and easy to handle, especially with thumb indexes. Recommended for nursing and health care collections.—**Mary Hemmings**

Directories

1834. Detwiler, Susan M., ed. **The Detwiler Directory of Medical Market Sources.** Warsaw, Ind., S. M. Detwiler, 1993. 1v. (various paging). index. $195.00pa. ISSN 1058-2797.

Access to medical information and services has become more difficult to manage with the proliferation of resources. Researchers have to consult a myriad of different reference tools, depending on the type of information they are seeking. *The Detwiler Directory* is an attempt to provide this information in one easy-to-use volume. The first section is an alphabetical profile list of about 1,000 of the major associations, commercial research firms, government agencies, and publishers in the health care field. The following information is provided, when applicable, for each entry: name, address, telephone and fax numbers, year established, membership, stated purposes, and subject entries in this text. A subject index provides access to the first section through more than 550 terms. The publication index cross-references some 2,500 medically related works to the profile section. Finally, the acronym index links the main medically related acronyms with their organizations' complete titles.

Certainly the 1,000 or so main entries in this new volume do not exhaust all frequently requested medical information queries, so large libraries can continue to rely on such basic reference guides as *Books in Print* (Reed Reference Publishing, 1993). However, for quick, basic medical reference service, and for the needs of most hospital libraries, *The Detwiler Directory* will prove an invaluable reference tool.—**Jonathon Erlen**

1835. Nolen, Anita L., and Mary Carrington Coutts, eds. **International Directory of Bioethics Organizations.** Washington, D.C., Kennedy Institute of Ethics, Georgetown University, 1993. 371p. index. $35.00pa. ISBN 1-883913-11-X.

The past two decades have witnessed the worldwide proliferation of biomedical ethics programming created by a wide variety of societies, organizations, and institutions. This annotated guide, describing 278 such programming centers, is arranged alphabetically by the 42 countries and the 40 U.S. states where major bioethics programs are located. When available, the following information is provided for each entry: address, telephone and fax numbers, director and key faculty names, publications, and educational programming. Inclusion in this directory is limited to groups working in the broad field of biomedical ethics, thus eliminating those focusing on specific areas, such as genetics and euthanasia, and individual hospital ethics committees (unless their activities have community-wide relevance). Three useful indexes list entries that are international in focus, that grant academic degrees, or that provide consulting services. This reference guide is a valuable addition to the biomedical ethics literature and will prove extremely useful in large public, academic, and health science libraries.—**Jonathon Erlen**

1836. **Product Development Directory 1993: An Historical Index to FDA 510(k) Filings by Product Category.** Montvale, N.J., Medical Economics Data, 1992. 1v. (various paging). $190.00. ISBN 1-56363-040-0.

1837. **Product SOS 1993: The Official Directory of FDA Problem Reports.** Montvale, N.J., Medical Economics Data, 1992. 1v. (various paging). $325.00. ISBN 1-56363-041-9.

Both books concern requirements for the development of medical products since enactment of the Medical Devices Amendments in April 1976. Each contains a summary of the FDA (Food and Drug Administration) regulations for the aspect covered, plus explicit directions for effective use of the directory. The *Product Development Directory* lists the 510(k) filings for approval to market medical products. After checking the keyword index for the FDA standard product category name, the user can consult the directory of products section to find all previous filings for similar products, by company, with a history of the approval process and a unique number for use in requesting detailed product information from the FDA. A separate index lists all the companies who have filed, with contact information and all the filings they have made. All filings since 1976 are included, hence "historical" is truthfully applied.

Manufacturers or importers of medical devices are required to report to the FDA any claims that their products have caused death or injury, or have malfunctioned and hence could cause certain effects if the malfunction were to recur. In the directory of products section in *Product SOS 1993*, under medical device names, companies with their summarized incident reports are listed, with results of FDA review, if any, for the period from August 1991 to June 1992. Identification of problem elements can be made, as well as comparison of similar products. Such data are valuable to manufacturers and potential purchasers. Also, legal and medical researchers may find the abstracted reports, under a device heading such as "Prosthesis, Breast, Non-inflatable, Internal," important when pursuing a subject such as silicone breast implants. The suppliers profiles section provides a contact directory by company, with the number and category of problems during the report period. Another small section gives the suppliers' disclaimers as presented to the FDA.

Because a medical device or product can be anything from tongue depressors to wheelchairs to a triglyceride reagent, the breadth and amount of data accumulated in these books are truly staggering. While they are primarily valuable for manufacturers, distributors and healthcare purchasing agents may profit by consulting them to supplement information in *Medical Device Register* (see ARBA 89, entry 1525).—**Harriette M. Cluxton**

Handbooks and Yearbooks

1838. Brace, Edward R., and John P. Pacanowski. **Childhood Symptoms: Every Parent's Guide to Childhood Illnesses.** Revised by Ed Weiner. New York, HarperPerennial/HarperCollins, 1992. 338p. index. $30.00; $15.00pa. LC 91-55391. ISBN 0-06-271532-1; 0-06-273078-9pa.

This is a revised edition of a 1985 publication (see ARBA 86, entry 1647). Although much of the text is unchanged, with some updating (and a few additions, such as entries for AIDS and Lyme disease), the work has been completely rearranged into two sections instead of one. The first section alphabetically lists diseases, disorders, and conditions. Each of these entries describes a medical condition, then gives possible courses of treatment, either by the parent or a physician. The second section, covering complaints, concerns, and problems, lists and discusses more general health concerns a parent might have about a child. The idea seems to be that if the parent already knows the medical nature of the problem, it can be found most easily in the first section, but if the concern is more vague it can be found in the second section. Many ailments are discussed in both (e.g., "Ear Infections" in the first section, "Earache" in the second). There are cross-references leading to related entries within and between the sections.

Several useful appendixes have also been added since the first edition: a glossary, a dictionary of the various medical specialties, and a section on physiological and developmental norms. There is also an index, correcting a conspicuous problem with the first edition. The book still suffers from a lack of illustration and is no substitute for a complete family medical guide. It is, however, a quick, easy reference for most childhood medical concerns and useful in answering that age-old question, "Should I call the doctor?"—Carol L. Noll

1839. Griffith, H. Winter. **Complete Guide to Symptoms, Illness & Surgery for People over 50.** New York, Body Press/Putnam, 1992. 868p. illus. index. $18.95pa. RA777.6.G75. 618.97. LC 91-44129. ISBN 0-399-51749-9.

Health care professionals attempt to consistently provide patients and clients with comprehensive information about symptoms, illnesses, surgeries, and medications, so that these people can make valid, informed choices about their health. The reality of patient/provider communication, however, is less than ideal. Thus, references such as this are helpful supplements for patients who want to know more about their health and medical situations. Individual sections discuss common symptoms, illnesses, surgeries, and general information about categories of medications. Each of the alphabetically arranged topics outlines special considerations for older adults, home care and self treatment, and situations when physician consultation is needed. An appendix offers beneficial information on a variety of issues important to older adults, ranging from health promotion and disease prevention to abuse and driving abilities. Finally, the book offers a list of references and organizations that can provide additional data on selected health issues. An index is provided.

The book is thorough, accurate, and practical for use by the consumer. Its sole negative is that it is not printed in large type—but doing so would have resulted in an unwieldy text. Highly recommended.
—Mary Ann Thompson

1840. Hood, Howard A., ed. **Abortion in the United States: A Compilation of State Legislation. 1992 Supplement.** Buffalo, N.Y., William S. Hein, 1993. 284p. $65.00. KF9315.Z95A26. 344.73'04192. LC 90-86246. ISBN 0-89941-753-1.

The release of *Abortion in the United States* in 1991 (see ARBA 92, entry 1669) was most timely as a useful reference to a rapidly developing area of the law. The original two-volume work provides an easy and convenient way to examine abortion statutes state-by-state or by subject. However, readers had to update their findings by checking the latest supplements to the various state codes, such electronic databases as LEXIS, and the different volumes of *Shephard's Citations* (McGraw-Hill). The 1992 supplement serves to update and expand the original work. The original set contains the texts of state statutes on abortion issues and notes on related legislation up to approximately the end of 1989. The supplement has these texts from 1990, 1991, and the first half of 1992. It also includes some pre-1990 statutory provisions that were not available when the main volumes were compiled, as well as several state constitutional provisions dealing with abortion. Following the practice of the main work, the supplement includes notes on the important judicial cases of this period and, in a special appendix, reproduces the full text of all opinions presented by the Supreme Court in the important case of *Planned Parenthood of Southeastern Pennsylvania v. Casey.*

In one respect the supplement is more selective than the main work, which contains all summaries of cases pertaining to abortion that were decided after 1973. The supplement is limited to texts of laws that focus on abortion and that deal with it in a substantial way. The 1992 supplement to *Abortion in the United States* will have wide appeal for legal scholars, political interest groups, hospitals, members of the medical and legal professions, students, and legislators who want to keep pace with recent developments in abortion issues. It is an important source for academic, college, law, and public libraries.—**Marilynn Green**

1841. **Professional Guide to Diseases.** 4th ed. Springhouse, Pa., Springhouse Publishing, 1992. 1311p. illus. index. $32.95. RT65.P69. 616. LC 91-5213. ISBN 0-87434-388-7.

This reference guide for nurses and allied health professionals provides basic information on more than 600 diseases in an easily accessible format. First published in 1982, it was revised in 1987 and 1989. The 4th edition has been completely updated to reflect the rapid changes in medicine. It contains the latest information on AIDS, the newly recognized hepatitis variants, and chronic fatigue and immune dysfunction.

The book is organized by broad subject areas. The first six chapters cover conditions affecting the whole body (e.g., genetic disorders, infection, trauma), while the remaining chapters deal with specific organs and symptoms (e.g., endocrine disorders, respiratory disorders). Each section has an introduction that gives an overview of the normal anatomy and physiology of the organ system, followed by a brief definition of the disease and its causes, incidence, and prognosis; signs and symptoms; diagnosis; and treatment. Appropriate material for patient education and self-care are included. Charts, illustrations, and black-and-white photographs supplement the text. These are clear, but the photographs of skin conditions and stained slides would be more effective in color. There is a selected bibliography at the end of each section and a list of referral agencies inside the back cover. An appendix contains brief information on rare diseases.

Professional Guide to Diseases is easy to use and presents information clearly. Lay readers will be more comfortable with this work than with *The Merck Manual* (Merck, 1987) because of the illustrations and the simpler language. It is a good ready-reference tool for health science, patient education, and public library collections.—**Barbara M. Bibel**

1842. Rose, Barry. **The Family Health Guide to Homeopathy.** Berkeley, Calif., Celestial Arts/Ten Speed Press, 1992. 320p. illus. index. $32.95pa. RX76.R75. 615.5'32. LC 93-3586. ISBN 0-89087-695-9.

This colorful and attractive guide to homeopathic remedies is arranged like many similar works. The first of its two sections describes categories of diseases or conditions (e.g., burns, heart attacks, infectious diseases) and gives homeopathic remedies for each. The second section, a *materia medica*, lists homeopathic medicines and describes their uses. There are attractive black-and-white illustrations of body systems and color illustrations of plants from which homeopathic remedies are derived. An introduction gives a brief history of homeopathy and compares it to orthodox medicine. There is a useful index.

The author is a British physician who practices both homeopathic and conventional medicine. While the work is from Great Britain, where homeopathy is much more accepted and employed than it is in North America, terminology has been adjusted to serve North American audiences. This book is not unlike other similar and equally useful homeopathy books. Its strength is a very readable format; its drawback is a paperback format that libraries may find needs rebinding. Recommended where demand indicates.
—**Gari-Anne Patzwald**

1843. Sinclair, Brett Jason. **Alternative Health Care Resources: A Directory and Guide.** West Nyack, N.Y., Parker Publishing; distr., Englewood Cliffs, N.J., Prentice Hall Professional, Technical, and Reference, 1992. 498p. index. $24.95; $12.95pa. R733.S56. 362.1'025'73. LC 92-28096. ISBN 0-13-030073-X; 0-13-156522-2pa.

This directory contains almost 400 entries for self-help groups, professional organizations, institutions, foundations, and periodicals that provide information and services relating to alternative therapies, disease prevention through lifestyle change, and related health issues. It is arranged alphabetically by health condition or therapy. Each entry includes name, address, fax and telephone numbers, services and publications offered, and dues or charges (if any).

Sinclair claims to include all major organizations in each category. However, information on many others (as well as on the vast majority of those listed in the directory) is available in such resources as the *Encyclopedia of Associations* (Gale, annual). In general, this book's usefulness is very limited. Sinclair never clearly defines *alternative*, but his definition is obviously narrow enough to exclude listings for many national organizations that provide information on both conventional and unconventional therapies. The descriptions of the organizations are very general, poorly written, and often not very helpful. The index, which lists organizations by name and not by keyword, is inadequate. The limited number of listings that may be unique to this book do not compensate for the directory's deficiencies. Not recommended.—**Gari-Anne Patzwald**

1844. Winter, Arthur, and Ruth Winter. **Consumer's Guide to Free Medical Information by Phone and by Mail.** Englewood Cliffs, N.J., Prentice Hall Professional, Technical, and Reference, 1993. 328p. index. $24.95; $14.95pa. R118.4.U6W56. 610. LC 92-24402. ISBN 0-13-096199-X; 0-13-333535-6pa.

Health care information is widely available on almost every health-related concern, but accessing this information can often be difficult and frustrating. This work is a useful source for locating accurate, current information on more than 300 health-related issues, from sports injuries to the latest cancer treatments. The authors are experts on and have experience writing about medical and health topics. Each topic is introduced by a descriptive paragraph followed by information on relevant public and private organizations and institutions that offer free medical information or assistance by phone or by mail. Many of the identified organizations will, upon request, make referrals to local medical experts and support groups. A helpful section on how to use this book is included. This guide is a very easy-to-use source of valuable health information.—**Robert L. Jones**

Psychiatry

1845. Ammerman, Robert T., Cynthia G. Last, and Michel Hersen, eds. **Handbook of Prescriptive Treatments for Children and Adolescents.** Needham Heights, Mass., Allyn and Bacon, 1993. 438p. index. $66.95. RJ499.3.H366. 618.92'689. LC 92-49080. ISBN 0-205-14825-5.

This work cites much current research concerning the diagnostic and treatment issues about child and adolescent disorders. Its contributions present the most efficacious treatment and strategies gleaned from contemporary research efforts. Unfortunately, current research still has many shortcomings and is not yet definitive enough to identify the best treatments. Thus, the treatments described are often eclectic or "multimodal." The handbook's chapter organization is a great strength. Each chapter has an identical format, with identical subject headings and subheadings. There is a description of the disorder, followed by clinical features, associated features, epidemiology, and etiology. A case illustration and summary are included in each chapter.

The editors and contributors are university-affiliated, which is both a strength and a weakness. Because of their academic orientation, the authors are highly research oriented, and most support their contentions about treatment with empirical data. However, most of the case illustrations in the handbook come from clinic settings or private practitioners, and their treatment strategies do not transfer well to applied settings. In addition, some of the case illustrations used by the contributors are hypothetical in nature or are composites of several cases. Such material does not demonstrate treatment efficacy.

The chapters are usually clear and well written and present assessment and treatment strategies supported at least in part by empirical evidence. But chapter 14, concerning gender identity disorders, does not maintain such clarity or the prescriptive spirit and does not include much evidence to support the contentions made. Also, the handbook does not have a chapter about, or any serious consideration of, childhood psychosis or childhood onset of schizophrenia. The latter is discussed briefly in the chapter on autistic disorders, largely to differentiate it from autism. Why the editors chose to omit this disorder is unclear. Perhaps it is because of the editors' strict adherence to the classifications in the DSM-III-R manual that subsumes childhood schizophrenia and autism (as a subtype) under the classification of pervasive developmental disorders. Whatever the reason, the omission is regrettable.

In the chapter about autistic disorders, the contributors indicate that "the majority" of children with autism are "in fact retarded." They conclude this from studies that stated that most such children had IQs in the moderate to severe range of retardation. The contributors also found moderate retardation in the case they presented for illustration. There are problems with the findings and their conclusion. For one thing, it is questionable whether standard intelligence tests should be used for evaluating autistic children. The test, even its nonverbal sections, relies heavily on verbal functioning, and autistic children generally suffer from severe expressive and receptive language impairments. In addition, because of these impairments, the children often score at significantly different levels on each portion of the test, invalidating the Fuss Scale scores (a composite) as indicators of overall intellectual ability.

The handbook has much to offer professionals and graduate students who are involved in the study and practice of psychotherapy with children and adolescents. It would be a welcome addition to university, medical, and professional libraries, as well as to personal libraries of clinical and school psychologists, psychiatrists, and other practitioners.—**Marilyn Rothschild**

1846. **The Columbia University College of Physicians and Surgeons Complete Home Guide to Mental Health.** Frederic I. Kass, John M. Oldham, and Herbert Pardes, eds. New York, Henry Holt, 1992. 476p. index. $35.00. RC460.C59. 616.89. LC 92-1534. ISBN 0-8050-0724-5.

This guide to mental health is comprehensive, informative, and useful for a general readership. It is a book readers can consult to better understand their own attitudes and behaviors as well as those of their friends and family. The information is up-to-date and practical and is written by a distinguished group of mental health professionals and researchers.

The guide is organized into four sections: mental illness assessment and treatment; common problems and disorders among adults; common problems and disorders among children and adolescents; and special issues and problems covering a wide range of topics, from suicide and women's issues to stress, legal and ethical relationships, and the outlook for mental health technologies and approaches. A glossary of psychiatric terms is included, and many chapters include case histories that illustrate mental disorders and their treatment. This readable, well-organized text is a useful mental health guide for any home library. [R: WLB, Mar 93, pp. 106-108]—**Robert L. Jones**

1847. Meyer, Robert G. **The Clinician's Handbook: Integrated Diagnostics, Assessment, and Intervention in Adult and Adolescent Psychopathology.** 3d ed. Needham Heights, Mass., Allyn and Bacon, 1993. 518p. index. price not reported. RC469.M457. 616.89. LC 92-21932. ISBN 0-205-14230-3.

This book provides general diagnostic perceptions, ties these concepts to assessment and test data for diagnostic categories, and then coordinates the concepts to make viable intervention procedures for varying mental illnesses. Meyer shared his information with up to 25 practicing clinical psychologists (unnamed) and used their feedback to develop his final draft. He does not describe his theoretical orientation nor how it might influence his choice of intervention suggestions. He also does not differentiate the orientation of the five leading psychologist-reviewers of his manuscript. In this reviewer's experience, one's psychological viewpoint can make a difference in how one diagnoses, how one interprets test data, and how one integrates information to engineer courses of treatment. Meyer does cite many research studies as verification for test interpretations and treatment options. He does not, however, report the nature of the subjects or conditions of these studies. This knowledge could affect the reader's use of the treatment recommendations.

The author does incorporate the latest personality tests, which are useful to practicing clinicians. He also tackles difficult diagnostic questions (e.g., malingering, suicide potential). He offers insight into psychopharmacology for nonmedical practitioners and case presentation for legal questions. All of these offerings add up to a useful, practical diagnostic handbook for the modern clinician as an aid to clinical judgments. However, several typographical errors mar the text.—**Karen Berland**

1848. Van Hasselt, Vincent B., and Michel Hersen, eds. **Handbook of Behavior Therapy and Pharmacotherapy for Children: A Comparative Analysis.** Needham Heights, Mass., Allyn and Bacon, 1993. 383p. index. $55.95. RJ505.B4H34. 618.92'89142. LC 92-49851. ISBN 0-205-13949-3.

The editors of this handbook provide a dual perspective, both behavioral and pharmacological therapies, on eight selected childhood disorders. These conditions range from anxiety and depression to autism and psychophysiological disorders. This is one of the few texts to examine both approaches in tandem, which provides the opportunity to assess how these different therapeutic approaches can be complementary. The editors are both faculty members in the psychology department at Nova University and have extensive scholarly and clinical experience. There is a list of chapter contributors and the institutions they represent.

Part 1 of the book contains separate overviews of behavioral and pharmacological strategies. The remaining 16 chapters describe the behavioral and pharmacological treatments for 8 disorders. This type of presentation allows one to identify biases inherent in each approach. Each chapter contains a useful reference section. Each section of the book describing a childhood condition provides both a theoretical perspective and the etiology of the problem, as well as the dual treatment strategies. Case studies and a summary section that includes insight about future issues within the therapies described are also presented for each condition.

—**Robert L. Jones**

1849. Westley, David. **Mental Health and Psychiatry in Africa: An Annotated Bibliography.** New Providence, N.J., Hans Zell/Reed Reference Publishing, 1993. 205p. index. $75.00. RC451.A4W47. 616.89'0098. LC 93-20491. ISBN 1-873836-90-2.

During the 1970s, while teaching in Nigeria, the author became interested in mental illness in Africa. This annotated bibliography, an outgrowth of his fascination with this subject, covers the period from the 1950s (when Western psychiatry was introduced in Africa) to the present. Journal articles, monographs, and anthologies in the fields of education, anthropology, psychology, and psychiatry are included. The concise annotations vary in length from a sentence to a paragraph. The book contains an introduction that defines some trends in transcultural psychiatry as applied to Africa and how traditional healing methods are used. Westley briefly explains some differences between the definitions of mental illness from the perspective of the trained psychiatrist and that of the native healer. The materials cited are limited to only a few countries, among them Nigeria, Uganda, Ghana, and Senegal. The author does not claim that these countries are typical of the African continent, so the reader obtains only a narrow view. The annotations are arranged alphabetically by author. While there are both geographical and subject indexes, a categorical arrangement of the material would have added considerably to the usefulness of this volume.

The topic is unusual and, with the growing interest in alternative medicine, should have considerable appeal. However, the price will preclude widespread availability and undoubtedly limit purchase to comprehensive African studies collections. [R: Choice, Dec 93, p. 592]—**Carol R. Glatt**

Specific Diseases

AIDS

1850. **The AIDS Directory: An Essential Guide to the 1500 Leaders in Research, Services, Policy, Advocacy, and Funding.** Katherine E. Jankowski, ed. Washington, D.C., Buraff/Millin, 1993. 814p. index. $250.00pa. ISBN 1-882594-00-2. ISSN 1065-6162.

The primary purpose of this impressive directory is to assist health care professionals, the general public, local government, and community leaders in accessing human and organizational resources for potential collaboration. In achieving that purpose, the main body of text presents alphabetically arranged (by organization) profiles of pertinent agencies and the like. Each entry contains basic directory information and includes the mission statement, organization type, services provided, focus areas, officers, publications, memberships, and miscellaneous notes about the agency or organization. Also of value are separate lists of congressional contacts, federal programs that fund AIDS-related research and services, periodical and other serial resources, and national and state hotlines. A thesaurus, keyed to indexes that supplement the main text, also appears in the introductory section of the work. This is useful in navigating through the indexes by location; by type of organization; by type of support; by services provided; by focus areas; by officers, directors, and staff; to grantmaking organizations and organizations supported; and to organizations with publications. A master index to organizations by name concludes the work. Although costly for the average library, this directory is a superb addition to agency and organization information collections. [R: Choice, July/Aug 93, p. 1743; LJ, 15 April 93, p. 82; RBB, 15 May 93, p. 1717; RQ, Fall 93, pp. 115-16; WLB, June 93, p. 119]—**Edmund F. SantaVicca**

1851. **AIDS: 1,000 Full-Text Statistical Abstracts from the *A Matter of Fact* Database, 1984-1992.** Compiled by the staff of *A Matter of Fact*. Ann Arbor, Mich., Pierian Press, 1993. 106p. (Statistical Perspectives Series, no.1). $15.00pa. ISBN 0-87650-329-6.

For individuals and libraries that do not have access to *A Matter of Fact* (see ARBA 93, entry 910) in any of its accessible formats (tape, CD-ROM, online, print), this volume should prove useful as a resource guide to statistical information on AIDS. The volume is a simple compilation of 1,082 citations and abstracts yielded by searching the database using the terms AIDS, HIV, and *Kaposi's sarcoma*. One of the values of this work is that approximately 25 percent of the abstracts come from congressional hearings, while another 15 percent come from the *Congressional Record*. The remaining entries come from selected and varied periodical and newspaper sources.

Arranged in reverse chronological order from 1992 to 1984, the abstracts do not include raw numbers in the form of charts or tables. Instead, the data represent statistically supported arguments presented in a writer's or speaker's own words, thereby providing a documentary path for the analysis of pro and con arguments regarding AIDS, the formulation of public policy, and other issues pertinent to research and funding initiatives relative to the syndrome. Complete citations are presented for each entry, along with cross-references to other terms and abstracts that average 100-200 words in length.

Individuals researching this topic, whether for course work or administrative, or personal reasons, will find this thin volume useful as an annotated pathfinder to statistical information, both recent and historical. Health and public policy collections will also be enhanced by this information.—**Edmund F. SantaVicca**

1852. Hombs, Mary Ellen. **AIDS Crisis in America: A Reference Handbook.** Santa Barbara, Calif., ABC-Clio, 1992. 268p. index. (Contemporary World Issues). $39.50. RA644.A25H655. 362.1'969792'00973. LC 92-48841. ISBN 0-87436-648-8.

Of the many new introductory works, guides, and overviews on the AIDS crisis, this new volume ranks near the top. Hombs has managed to summarize, abstract, and extract key information on the syndrome, placing it in a cohesive and logical format throughout. An introductory chapter presents basic definitions, demographics, and policy issues related to AIDS. This is followed by a selective chronology and some biographical sketches. In another chapter, facts and statistics pertaining to AIDS—for the nation, the world, states, and specific populations—are presented along with summaries of public opinion polls.

Key government and agency reports fill another chapter, along with firsthand accounts and societal responses. Legal aspects of AIDS are treated in a following chapter, which also presents a selective chronology of federal legislation since 1982. The remaining two chapters of the work function as minireference tools. One chapter lists organizations, hotlines, and government agencies, all in a directory format; the other presents a bibliography of print and nonprint materials useful for the average reader. There are a glossary and an index. With its pleasant, logical format and readability by a variety of audiences, this work should find its way into reference collections in school, public, and academic libraries. [R: Choice, May 93, p. 1442; JAL, May 93, p. 130; LJ, Jan 93, p. 98; RBB, 15 Mar 93, pp. 1374-76: VOYA, June 93, pp. 124-25; WLB, April 93, p. 117]—**Edmund F. SantaVicca**

1853. Huber, Jeffrey T. **A Dictionary of AIDS-Related Terminology.** New York, Neal-Schuman, 1993. 165p. $39.95. RC607.A26H895. 616.97'92'003. LC 92-31265. ISBN 1-55570-117-5.

As the general and specialized literature on AIDS continues to increase, this dictionary will aid most readers in the clarification of terms and concepts mentioned in that literature. Although aimed at a broad audience, the definitions in this book are clearly more appropriate for the generalist and nonspecialist. For example, or chemical formulas nor medical or diagnostic definitions are included. However, abbreviations, acronyms, initialisms, historical terms, pertinent medical and psychological terms, prominent physicians, researchers, organizations, and information sources are included and defined or identified. This alone makes the work a valuable addition to most reference collections.

Entries range from 1-20 lines on average, clarifying and distinguishing the importance of the entry to the field of AIDS. In the case of individuals and organizations, addresses/telephone numbers are supplied.

For the novice to AIDS literature and for the average student—high school or undergraduate—this dictionary will be of great benefit. The advanced researcher will need to consult more appropriately detailed sources. [R: BR, Sept/Oct 93, p. 56; Choice, July/Aug 93, pp. 1745-46; JAL, May 93, p. 130; LJ, 15 Feb 93, p. 158; RBB, 15 Mar 93, pp. 1374-76; SLJ, Nov 93, p. 144; WLB, May 93, p. 114]—**Edmund F. SantaVicca**

1854. **London International Atlas of AIDS.** By Matthew Smallman-Raynor, Andrew Cliff, and Peter Haggett. Cambridge, Mass., Basil Blackwell, 1992. 430p. illus. maps. index. $125.00. G1046.E51S6. 614.5'993. LC 92-19737. ISBN 0-631-17812-0.

Although this work was completed in early 1992—with consequent limitations on the currency of information—it will nonetheless serve as a key information source on the history of AIDS and HIV. With 10 chapters arranged in 4 major sections, this prose atlas examines the virological character of AIDS and the information sources upon which knowledge about HIV is based. Also examined in no small manner are the origins and global spread of AIDS, with both international and regional coverage—this with a focus on the contrasting geographical spread of HIV and AIDS. Detailed economic analyses, coupled with economic and other projections, conclude the work.

As a chronicle of AIDS and HIV, especially for the decade of the 1980s (and before), there is no other single source so replete with explanations, analyses, tables, charts, graphs, and the like. The authors have produced a visually stimulating and coherent review of information and sources that will likely be used by a variety of audiences. A comprehensive list of references and sources (1,207 items), with full bibliographical descriptions, supplements the text. Sources of information are further keyed to the visual aids.

This work will prove indispensable for any medical or nursing collection. Large public and academic collections will also be enhanced by its inclusion. [R: WLB, Sept 93, p. 118]—**Edmund F. SantaVicca**

1855. Nordquist, Joan, comp. **Women and AIDS: A Bibliography.** Santa Cruz, Calif., Reference and Research Services, 1993. 76p. (Contemporary Social Issues: A Bibliographic Series, no.29). $15.00pa. ISBN 0-937855-56-1.

The number of women who have AIDS is steadily increasing, but the medical establishment has, until recently, ignored the differences in the way that this disease affects them. This bibliography provides an overview of AIDS in women. It includes books, pamphlets, and articles published within the last five years from the medical, psychological, political, and sociological literature. It contains sections covering different subject areas, such as pregnancy and AIDS, drugs and AIDS, and women of color and AIDS. Entries for books, pamphlets, and documents are separated from those for articles. Items are listed alphabetically by author or title. The section on resources includes directories and bibliographies as well as a list of AIDS organizations with addresses (but no telephone or fax numbers).

This small bibliography is important because it covers a largely neglected aspect of the AIDS epidemic. The material on underserved populations, such as people of color, prisoners, prostitutes, and lesbians, is especially valuable. Annotations would have been helpful, but the currency of the information and its relative inaccessibility elsewhere make this bibliography an essential addition to all collections.

—**Barbara M. Bibel**

1856. Young, Ian. **The AIDS Dissidents: An Annotated Bibliography.** Metuchen, N.J., Scarecrow, 1993. 264p. $32.50. Z6664.A27Y68. 362.1'969792. LC 93-23958. ISBN 0-8108-2675-5.

A welcome addition to the growing body of literature on AIDS, this volume brings together more than 700 English-language items that focus on alternative or dissident perspectives on a variety of issues pertinent to the syndrome. Among the topics included are the HIV hypothesis, experimental therapies, AZT, blood testing and screening, cultural issues, activism, mental and spiritual aspects, policies and politics, race, vitamin therapies, safe sex, holistic therapies, and intravenous and recreational drugs. Young is careful to define the great scope of the writers included: radical dissidents, political dissidents, proponents of holistic and alternative therapies, proponents of mental and spiritual approaches, alarmists, and survivors.

Arranged by format, the work is especially strong in its coverage of books, pamphlets, and monographs, along with extensive coverage of dissident articles. Shorter sections include lists of audiotapes and of periodicals. A final section includes four brief documents considered to be of interest. Full bibliographical descriptions are presented, with annotations selectively including an extract from the particular item. An introduction, title index, and postscript enhance the volume. This volume should prove of value to AIDS organizations and clinics and medical and public health collections, as well as those in the social sciences. [R: LJ, Dec 93, p. 116]—**Edmund F. SantaVicca**

Birth Related Conditions

1857. Partridge-Brown, Mary. **In Vitro Fertilization Clinics: A North American Directory of Programs and Services.** Jefferson, N.C., McFarland, 1993. 234p. index. $28.50pa. RG133.5.P37. 362.1'981'7800257. LC 92-56679. ISBN 0-89950-817-0.

Since 1978, when the first child was born with the aid of assisted reproductive technology (ART), more than 250 ART programs have been created in the United States and Canada. This reference guide was created to help the millions of women and men who suffer from fertility problems and can use these ART services. The first chapter describes, in lay terminology, the basic causes of infertility and the differences between the three main approaches to ART: in vitro fertilization (IVF), gamete intrafallopian transfer (GIFT), and zygote intrafallopian transfer (ZIFT), as well as several lesser-known ART methods.

Partridge-Brown mailed questionnaires to all the ART programs in Canada and the United States and requested the following information: program services, costs, requirements and restrictions, program staff, and success figures. Because many of these facilities either did not return these forms or included only partial answers, this directory does not provide comprehensive coverage of all ART programs. However, it does contain telephone numbers and addresses for all ART facilities, including those that did not participate in this survey. A concluding section presents an annotated list of eight organizations that interested parties can contact for more information on ART. While far from a complete survey, this work will help the general reader understand some of the basic elements of ART and where to locate ART programs. [R: Choice, Dec 93, p. 589; LJ, 1 Sept 93, p. 174; RBB, 15 Nov 93, p. 645]—**Jonathon Erlen**

Cancer

1858. Altman, Roberta, and Michael J. Sarg. **The Cancer Dictionary.** New York, Facts on File, 1992. 334p. index. $35.00. RC262.A39. 616.99'4'003. LC 91-46941. ISBN 0-8160-2608-4.

Although arranged as a dictionary to include almost every word used in connection with cancer—some 2,500 terms—this text is virtually encyclopedic in coverage, far more than a series of definitions. Entries range from cross-references through succinct one-paragraph explanations to lengthy discussions, particularly for the most common types of cancer. Intended to help patients and their caretakers confront cancer by understanding the facts about it, the articles are painstakingly written and cover all aspects of the subject (e.g., symptoms, diagnostic tests, risk factors, staging, conventional and even alternative treatments, prevention). Many articles contain the statement, "For specific information on the latest state-of-the-art treatment, call —." Pronunciation of medical terms is given and photographs and "Facts on File" diagrams appear occasionally. Useful appendixes include lists of support organizations for cancer and AIDS; comprehensive cancer centers by state; clinical trials groups; and drugs used in treating cancer and AIDS, arranged by clinical and brand names. A brief bibliography precedes a categorized subject index.

This book makes readily accessible a phenomenal amount of current cancer information and is a natural for the library reference desk. Both professional workers and the lay audience to whom it is addressed should find it useful. Highly recommended! [R: BR, May/June 93, pp. 51-52; Choice, May 93, p. 1435; SBF, May 93, pp. 103-04; WLB, Mar 93, pp. 105-06]—**Harriette M. Cluxton**

1859. Fink, John M. **Third Opinion: An International Directory to Alternative Therapy Centers for the Treatment and Prevention of Cancer and Other Degenerative Diseases.** 2d ed. Garden City Park, N.Y., Avery Publishing, 1992. 312p. index. $14.95pa. RC271.A62F56. 362.1'96994. LC 91-41082. ISBN 0-89529-503-2.

This directory resulted from the author's search for alternative treatments for his young daughter, who was ill with cancer. It provides a list of clinics, doctors, health practitioners, educators, support groups, and practitioners of alternative medicine and treatments. Every person and institute listed was contacted by the author and responded to specific questions. The information is basic, consisting of telephone number, address, personnel, travel directions, illnesses treated, length of stay, and costs. Coverage includes the United States and foreign countries.

The directory is divided into four major sections: treatment centers, educational centers, support groups, and information services. A substantial index makes it easy to locate specific information. The appendixes list available services alphabetically by country and region. A bibliography of books, providing supportive evidence for alternate therapies, is also included. The information collected by Fink is difficult to find; this directory will save interested persons much research time. It is a valuable addition to the field of alternative medicine.—**Marilyn Strong Noronha**

1860. Moss, Ralph W. **Cancer Therapy: The Independent Consumer's Guide to Non-Toxic Treatment & Prevention.** New York, Equinox Press/Movable Type, 1992. 523p. index. $19.95pa. RC263.M643. 616.99'406. LC 92-4076. ISBN 1-881025-06-3.

The intent of this guide is to counter the argument that the use of nontoxic or less-toxic cancer treatments is not supported by research reported in peer-reviewed medical and scientific journals. The guide is divided into nine sections according to the type of treatment (e.g., vitamin, herbal, electromagnetic). Each section begins with a general discussion that is followed by subsections that describe specific treatment agents. A special symbol identifies those agents that may be used to augment conventional treatments. A list of references to articles in reputable scientific journals follows all subsections. At the end of each section is a list of treatment centers that employ the particular modality being discussed. The concluding section of the guide describes a small sample of treatments that have not been researched but that show promise. A table guides the user to treatments for specific cancers and also indicates which of the agents described in the book may have uses in the treatment of AIDS. A subject index and a glossary are included. Although the text is somewhat polemical in tone and most of the journal articles cited are too technical for laypeople, this guide is a relatively inexpensive source from which to begin gathering information on many of the alternative cancer treatments that have come to public attention. [R: LJ, 1 Sept 92, p. 170]—**Gari-Anne Patzwald**

Chemically Related Conditions

1861. Wilson, Cynthia. **Chemical Exposure and Human Health: A Reference to 314 Chemicals with a Guide to Symptoms and a Directory of Organizations.** Jefferson, N.C., McFarland, 1993. 339p. index. $45.00. RB152.W49. 615.9'02. LC 92-51010. ISBN 0-89950-810-3.

Chemicals of all kinds are playing more and more of a role in our society. They are everywhere, and for better or for worse, we are all exposed to them. However, besides general ignorance and misunderstanding, there is reluctance among the public at large and in industry, business, and the health care community to deal with the health-related problems of chemicals. This reference to more than 300 chemicals is a guide to the problems that can be produced by these substances and the products in which they can be found. Wilson is executive director of the Chemical Injury Information Network, and she has effectively organized this guide for practical use. The introduction and the first chapter provide an overview of chemical-related health concerns and society's delayed response to the significance of this matter. Subsequent chapters cover specific health problems and the chemicals that can induce them, common products and their chemical components, the primary biological target areas affected by specific chemicals, and sources of chemical exposure. There is also a useful chemical directory, as well as a bibliography and information on environmentally concerned health and public interest organizations and publications.—**Robert L. Jones**

Neurological Disorders

1862. Bair, Frank E., ed. **Alzheimer's, Stroke, and 29 Other Neurological Disorders Sourcebook: Basic Information for the Layperson....** Detroit, Omnigraphics, 1993. 579p. illus. index. (Health Reference Series, v.2). $80.00. ISBN 1-55888-748-2.

This new reference text examines 30 common neurological disorders. Based on material from the National Institute of Neurological and Communicative Disorders and Stroke, this volume provides patients and their families appropriate information so they can cope with these illnesses. The neurological conditions discussed range from the familiar (e.g., stroke, epilepsy, cerebral palsy) to the more unusual (e.g., Joseph disease, Friedereich's ataxia). Each neurological disorder is covered in a separate chapter. The following types of material are presented for these diseases: symptoms, general descriptions, diagnostic methods, statistics of occurrence, treatment options, and organizations that provide information or support for those suffering from these conditions. Three additional chapters describe basic neuroanatomy and neurophysiology, how aging affects the brain, and the value of the PET (positron emission tomography) scanner.

While this book is primarily intended for the public, the occasional use of highly technical terminology may confuse the general reader. However, the use of diagrams and illustrations and the comprehensive index add to the effectiveness of this volume, which should be included in any library's patient education section. [R: LJ, 1 June 93, p. 100; RBB, 1 Sept 93, pp. 80-81; RQ, Fall 93, p. 118]—**Jonathon Erlen**

Rare Diseases

1863. Thoene, Jess G., ed. **Physicians' Guide to Rare Diseases.** Montvale, N.J., Dowden Publishing, 1992. 1080p. illus. index. $69.50. LC 92-71122. ISBN 0-9628716-0-5. ISSN 1053-9727.

Thoene defines a rare disease as any illness with fewer than 200,000 reported cases in the United States. Primary care physicians may have trouble diagnosing or finding information to share with patients who suffer from these unusual disorders. This volume is intended for these doctors rather than for rare disease specialists.

To assist primary care physicians, Thoene, working with the National Organization for Rare Disorders, has created this guide, which provides coverage for nearly 400 rare diseases organized into 13 broad categories. For each disorder the following information is presented: general description, etiology, symptomatology, standard and experimental therapies, national organizations and support groups, and an unannotated bibliography of current medical literature. A separate section lists the addresses and telephone numbers for all the resource groups found in the preceding chapters. The concluding segment contains a directory of orphan drugs arranged by diseases. Charts and a color atlas of visual diagnosis, along with a comprehensive index, are helpful. The technical language found throughout this book will limit its usefulness to lay audience, but it will prove very valuable to primary care physicians and should be included in the collection of all health science libraries.

—**Jonathon Erlen**

NURSING

1864. Stinson, Shirley M., Joy L. Johnson, and Glennis Zilm. **History of Nursing Beginning Bibliography: A Proemial List with Special Reference to Canadian Sources.** Calgary, Alta., Faculty of Nursing, University of Alberta, 1992. 97p. index. $12.00pa. 016.61073'09. ISBN 0-88864-772-7.

Some 1,000 entries constitute this first published list of references pertaining to the history and politics of nursing in Canada. Selected international sources, in particular from the United Kingdom and the United States, are included for their influence on nursing developments.

Originally developed for a graduate nursing course at the University of Alberta, the list includes more than just references to the history of nursing. The purpose of Stinson's course was to enable students to obtain a firm grasp of the origins of the profession of nursing by understanding the social and professional contexts of the time. The bibliography is divided into five categories offering selected references in such areas as social and health policy, economics, history of medicine, social and political development of nursing, and functional foci of nursing (i.e., practice, administration, education, and research).

Arranged alphabetically by author within each category, the majority of the entries are secondary sources. Each entry is brief: author, title, publisher, and date. While many entries could be placed in more than one of the subject categories, the source is classified only according to a major topic. The author index includes all authors listed in the bibliography. The subject index is based on a special classification system developed with the assistance of University of Alberta librarians. While the classification system and the subject arrangement are useful in determining the content of the source, they are no substitute for annotations.

The broad spectrum of works related to the history and politics of nursing will be most useful to faculty in Canadian schools, but there are a number of valuable resources enumerated that an English-speaking instructor or historiographer could use. As the authors state, the major limitation of the bibliography is its introductory nature. Inclusions and suggestions are solicited, as are comments on its utility, for future editions.—**Vicki J. Killion**

1865. **Who's Who in American Nursing 1993-1994.** 5th ed. New Providence, N.J., Marquis Who's Who/Reed Reference Publishing, 1993. 893p. index. $139.00. LC 84-650523. ISBN 0-8379-1002-1.

The Society of Nursing Professionals, in recognition of service and commitment to the nursing profession, has compiled more than 27,000 biographical entries in this edition of *Who's Who in American Nursing 1993-1994*. Concentration on formal education, progressive career track, and organizational involvement enabled the society to target those individuals active in the field. Information comes from the biographees. Selection is judged on either the position of responsibility held or the level of attainment achieved by the individual. Admissions based on position include heads of colleges, nursing directors of major hospitals, officials of state departments of public health, or heads of major associations. Admission for individual achievement is based on qualitative criteria, including education, career advancement, contributions to the nursing literature, awards and fellowships, civic activities, and organizational leadership roles. Information contained within each entry is similar to all other *Who's Who* publications. The professional area index categorizes the nursing professionals by state and city within their specialties, including administration, community health, consultation, critical care, education, gerontology, maternal and women's health, medical and surgical, midwifery, occupational health, oncology, pediatrics, psychiatry, rehabilitation, and research.

While not comprehensive, the directory does provide access to a group of professionals who have been ignored in the past, but who may well become one of the most important participants in health care reform. Health sciences libraries, in particular those that serve schools of nursing and large medical centers, should add this to their collections.—**Vicki J. Killion**

OPTOMETRY

1866. Hendrickson, Homer. **Eponyms of Behavioral Optometry.** Santa Ana, Calif., Optometric Extension Program Foundation, 1993. 133p. $15.00pa. RE960.H46. 617.7'5'03. LC 92-16340. ISBN 0-943599-24-5.

Behavioral optometry includes conventional optometry (the diagnosis, measurement, and treatment of vision problems, often with corrective lenses) plus the fields of developmental vision and of visual training, with multiple activities related to each of them. This small volume is a source book and partial dictionary of eponyms applied to tests, theories, procedures, equipment, instruments, and apparatus that have become known to optometry in the last 60 years. (Because the author died before completing this project, and it is known that many more such eponyms exist, the publishers ask for readers to contribute more of them—hence the description "partial dictionary.") Because most terms are specific to this discipline, very few can be found in ophthalmic or medical dictionaries. After indicating whether it is a test, procedure, or other item to which a person's name has become attached, entries concisely describe its development, how it is performed, and its purpose, and give references and sources when applicable. The book is valuable for persons interested in optometry and its history.—**Harriette M. Cluxton**

PHARMACY AND PHARMACEUTICAL SCIENCES

Dictionaries and Encyclopedias

1867. **Encyclopedia of Pharmaceutical Technology. Volume 4: Design of Drugs to Drying and Driers.** James Swarbrick and James C. Boylan, eds. New York, Marcel Dekker, 1991. 515p. illus. index. $188.00. RS192.E53. 615'.1'0321. LC 88-25664. ISBN 0-8247-2803-3.

1868. **Encyclopedia of Pharmaceutical Technology. Volume 5: Economic Characteristics of the R&D-Intensive Pharmaceutical Industry to Fermentation Processes.** James Swarbrick and James C. Boylan, eds. New York, Marcel Dekker, 1992. 565p. illus. index. $188.00. RS192.E53. 615'.1'0321. LC 88-25664. ISBN 0-8247-2804-1.

1869. **Encyclopedia of Pharmaceutical Technology. Volume 6: Film Coatings and Film-Forming Materials: Evaluation to Generic Drugs and Generic Equivalency.** James Swarbrick and James C. Boylan, eds. New York, Marcel Dekker, 1992. 489p. illus. index. $188.00. RS192.E53. 615'.1'0321. LC 88-25664. ISBN 0-8247-2805-X.

1870. **Encyclopedia of Pharmaceutical Technology. Volume 7: Genetic Engineering to Hydrogels.** James Swarbrick and James C. Boylan, eds. New York, Marcel Dekker, 1993. 484p. illus. index. $188.00. RS192.E53. 615'.1'0321. LC 88-25664. ISBN 0-8247-2806-8.

The first volume of the *Encyclopedia of Pharmaceutical Technology* appeared in 1988. Marcel Dekker has been publishing one or two volumes per year since then. The encyclopedia focuses on the scientific, technical, economic, legal, and ethical aspects of the pharmaceutical industry. Similar to the *Kirk-Othmer Encyclopedia of Chemical Technology* (John Wiley, 1991-), this source covers scientific concepts and industrial processes in detail. All articles are signed and written by experts who are active in pharmaceutical research at universities or industrial facilities. Graphs, charts, and illustrations enhance the text. All articles have bibliographies.

The volumes are arranged alphabetically. Each volume has a list of contributors and their affiliations, a table of contents, and an index. Volumes 5, 6, and 7 also list the contents of the previous volumes in the set. Entries are lengthy—most are 20 to 25 pages—and cover their subjects thoroughly. The subjects range from pure and applied science, such as enzymes and fermentation processes, to techniques, such as gas chromatography and electron beam sterilization; industrial processes and products, such as direct compression tableting and drug delivery and therapeutic systems; management issues, such as heating, ventilation, and air conditioning; and legal and ethical concerns, such as the ethics of drug making. The depth and breadth of coverage offered by the *Encyclopedia of Pharmaceutical Technology* make it an excellent source for academic and special libraries supporting research programs in the health sciences, pharmacology, and chemical engineering.—**Barbara M. Bibel**

1871. Glasby, John S. **Encyclopedia of Antibiotics.** 3d ed. New York, John Wiley, 1992. 515p. $225.00. RM267.G56. 615'.329'03. LC 92-93. ISBN 0-471-92922-0.

From *aabomycin* to *zygosporin g*, this work presents general information on those antibiotics known to exist at present. The amount of information given for each of these antibiotic entries varies. In most cases the molecular formula, structural formula, melting point, specific rotation, cultivation, tolerance levels in animals (a few in humans), and medicinal activity are given, as well as a few references to the journal and patent literature. The length of the description varies from a few sentences to several paragraphs. For example, *aureomycin*, which has been known for quite some time, has a page devoted to it, while *histidomycin a* is discussed in a small paragraph. Cross-references from one antibiotic name to another are contained within the listings. There is no index to the work.

General introductory information to this dictionary/encyclopedia describing the type of material included in entries, and a brief explanation regarding length of entries, would have proved useful; Glasby alludes only that entries include chemical/medical data. In essence, an introduction discussing the philosophy of this compilation, or at the least prefaces and introductions to the first and second editions, should have been included. One has to assume that entry length is proportional to the amount of current knowledge about the antibiotics. Even with this shortcoming, this book is highly recommended for college, university, and specialized libraries. All pharmaceutical libraries should have a copy, and large public libraries should consider purchasing one.—**George H. Bell**

1872. **Multilingual Dictionary of Narcotic Drugs and Psychotropic Substances under International Control.** New York, United Nations, 1993. 509p. $42.00. ISBN 92-1-048056-2. S/N E/F/S.93.XI.2.

This work was developed to provide international drug control authorities with complete and accurate information on the variety of names under which narcotic drugs and psychotropic substances appear. The original 1983 charge of producing a reference manual to include substances under international control by virtue of the United Nations Single Convention on Narcotic Drugs, 1961; of the Convention as amended by the 1972 Protocol; and of the Convention on Psychotropic Substances, 1971, continues in the present revised edition. The 1988 addendum, substances recently placed under control, and pertinent data extracted from the literature are also incorporated into this edition.

Part 1 is the alphabetically arranged monograph section. The International Nonproprietary Name (INN) is used for the majority of the entries. If an INN is not established, the names used in the international drug control treaties or the name most commonly applied to the drug is used. In general, slang and colloquialisms have not been included. Each monograph also includes the nature of the substance, molecular formula, molecular weight, structural formula, systematic chemical name, and the law of control that applies to the drug. Generic and trade names, code designations, and illicit trafficking names are also given.

Part 2 is an alphabetical cross-index of names, excluding Arabic, Chinese, and Russian names. Separate cross-indexes from the English name to each of these languages occurs at the end of the book.

Other than the extensive lists of synonyms for many of the drugs, most of the physical and chemical information is available in greater detail in other references. The value of the dictionary is its original purpose: a complete list of drugs currently under international control.—**Vicki J. Killion**

1873. Tousignaut, Dwight R., ed. **IPA Thesaurus and Frequency List.** 6th ed. Bethesda, Md., American Society of Hospital Pharmacists, 1992. 279p. $45.00pa. ISBN 1-879907-25-9.

Consisting of approximately 70,000 terms used from 1970 to 1992, this work allows the user to select controlled vocabulary terminology for use in searching the International Pharmaceutical Abstracts (IPA) database. Of the 70,000 terms listed, a total of 20,000 are cross-references. Terms are listed alphabetically; with no hierarchical arrangement. For each term listed, the number of times the term has been used in indexing during the period is given. Frequencies are given for the current preferred term as well as the nonpreferred (nonpreferred terms were terms of choice at one time). Current preferred terms are indicated by a large boldface type period, and terms used during the past two years are printed in boldface type. *See* and *see also* references are provided, and tips in making use of the thesaurus for the searching of IPA are given. Recommended for those institutions that search IPA either through a vendor or on compact disc.—**George H. Bell**

1874. Yentis, S. M., N. P. Hirsch, and G. B. Smith. **Anaesthesia A-Z: An Encyclopaedia of Principles and Practice.** Stoneham, Mass., Butterworths, 1993. 473p. $79.95. 617.9. ISBN 0-7506-0174-4.

Compiled to be a concise overview of medical and related information, this work is aimed at examination candidates for the Fellowship of the Royal College of Anaesthetists. Specifically, it is aimed at Part 3 fellowship candidates. Subject areas covered within this encyclopedic dictionary are physiology, pharmacology, anatomy, physics, statistics, history, clinical anesthesia, equipment, intensive care, medicine, and surgery. Length of articles varies from a paragraph to a page. The majority of entries are defined to enhance reader's basic medical technique. Such information as half-life, metabolism, uses, and effect on the body's system is given for anesthetic agents. Line drawings (many labeled), diagrams, graphs, tables, and structural organic formulas enhance many articles. Cross-references to the proper entry occur within alphabetical sequence of the text. No index is present.

Although this work is aimed at a specific and narrow audience, any interested person could make use of the information within its pages. Recommended for all college, university, and large public libraries. Highly recommended for medical and pharmacological schools.—**George H. Bell**

Directories

1875. **Linscott's Directory of Immunological and Biological Reagents.** 7th ed. Santa Rosa, Calif., Linscott's Directory, 1993. 239p. index. $70.00pa. ISBN 0-9604920-6-2.

This is a directory of companies that supply biological reagents used in laboratory research, particularly in the fields of immunology, developmental biology, oncology, and cell biology. Approximately 35,000 entries list sources for reagents or custom reagent-producing services. Entries are arranged in six broad classes: monoclonal antibodies and hybridomas; polyclonal antibodies; tissues, blood products, biochemicals, enzymes, cytokines, lectins, and venoms; living organisms and their derivatives and cell cultures; immunoassay and other kit systems; and custom services. For each reagent or service specified, a source abbreviation is given. A section at the back of the book lists addresses and fax and telephone numbers for about 1,400 suppliers. There are separate indexes for antibodies and nonantibody materials.

This book is for ordering only—no information is given about use, purity, or other details of reagents listed. It will be updated with supplements through summer 1993; new edition will be produced every two years.—**Carol L. Noll**

Handbooks and Yearbooks

1876. **British Pharmacopoeia 1993.** London, HMSO; distr., Lanham, Md., UNIPUB, 1993. 2v. index. $345.00/set. ISBN 0-11-321543-6.

The *British Pharmacopoeia 1993* provides guidelines and standards for the quality of substances, preparations, and articles used in medicine and pharmacy and is a legally enforceable document throughout the United Kingdom, most of the Commonwealth, and many other countries. This new edition, which supersedes the *British Pharmacopoeia 1988*, also consolidates and extends the 1988 edition with its 1989, 1990, 1991, and 1992 addenda and incorporates the monographs of the *European Pharmacopoeia*.

Volume 1 contains monographs for medicinal/auxiliary substances and infrared spectra. Each monograph includes such information as definition, preparation methods, physical/chemical characteristics, storage, labeling, and use. Volume 2 comprises the sections on formulated preparations, blood products, immunological products, radiopharmaceutical preparations, and surgical materials. The appendixes describe the details of procedures for testing compliance with the standards, and a comprehensive index are also located in this volume.

A pharmacopoeia contributes to quality control in the manufacturing process and provides a publicly available statement about the quality of a product or a component of a product is expected to meet at any time during its use. Its greatest value, then, is to the pharmacist or pharmaceutical manufacturer. Librarians who have clients with requests for information on British drugs should not rely upon this work to answer the requests. Thus, this resource should be included in libraries with collections in pharmacy and pharmaceutical sciences, but it is not necessary for libraries providing drug information to the consumer or layperson.—**Vicki J. Killion**

1877. Griffith, H. Winter. **Complete Guide to Prescription & Non-Prescription Drugs.** New York, Body Press/Putnam, 1993. 1076p. index. $15.95pa. RM301.15.G75. 615'.1. LC 92-21993. ISBN 0-399-51766-9.

Questions about drugs are among the most common reference desk inquiries. *Complete Guide to Prescription & Non-Prescription Drugs* is one of several available to answer questions. Organized in chart format, it contains information on more than 5,000 brand-name and 700 generic drugs. Charts are arranged alphabetically by generic name or drug class (e.g., analgesics, ephedrine). Each chart contains brief information about brand names, uses, dosages, adverse reactions or side effects, overdose symptoms and treatment, and precautions on use with other drugs or foods. The beginning of the book has detailed instructions for use. A brand- and generic-name directory, charts of additional drug interactions, a glossary, and an index complete the work.

This book is written in nontechnical language for consumers. While it is relatively easy to use, it has some disadvantages. A person taking a common drug who is unsure of its name or type may have a problem locating it. The charts for acetaminophen, estrogen, and other frequently prescribed drugs refer the user to the brand-name directory to find the identity of the medication. There is no color drug-identification chart. Charts for drugs with long lists of possible interactions refer readers to the chart of additional interactions, and people who fail to check it may miss important information.

The Complete Drug Reference (see ARBA 93, entry 1662) contains more information in a layout that is easier to read and is a better choice for reference collections. *Complete Guide to Prescription & Non-Prescription Drugs* is an appropriate choice for circulating collections or for libraries with extreme budget constraints. [R: RBB, 15 Jan 93, p. 936]—**Barbara M. Bibel**

1878. **Handbook of Psychotropic Drugs.** Springhouse, Pa., Springhouse Publishing, 1992. 308p. index. $24.95pa. RM315.H347. 615'.78. LC 91-5206. ISBN 0-87434-391-7.

Psychotropic drugs are widely used to treat seizure disorders, depression, hyperactivity, anxiety, Parkinson's disease, and psychoses. They are also used as sedatives. Health care professionals managing patients who take these medications often need information about the drugs. The *Handbook of Psychotropic Drugs* is a good ready-reference source of this information.

The book is divided into two major sections: therapeutic classes and generic drugs, and pharmacologic classes. The first section covers all the drugs used to treat specific conditions (e.g., antidepressants, anticonvulsants, antipsychotics). Each chapter contains an overview of the condition, a list of all the drugs by generic name, an explanation of the drugs' effects and mechanisms of action, adverse reactions, and clinical considerations. Brief entries with specific information for each drug follow. The section on pharmacologic classes (e.g., amphetamines, benzodiazepines) allows readers to view a whole drug class and compare drugs within it by referring back to the generic entries in the first section. Appendixes contain DSM-III-R and ICD-9-CM codes for diagnosis and numeric lists, recommended laboratory tests, drug reactions, trade names and manufacturers, management of acute substance abuse, and a schedule of controlled substances. An index facilitates access.

This book will be useful in hospital wards, emergency rooms, and clinics, and in health science reference collections, because it contains important facts about pregnancy risks, effects of drugs on laboratory tests, and information for patients. It is easy to use, reasonably priced, practical, and current.—**Barbara M. Bibel**

1879. **The PDR Family Guide to Prescription Drugs.** Montvale, N.J., Medical Economics Data, 1993. 930p. illus. index. $24.95pa. ISBN 1-56363-020-6.

The *Physicians' Desk Reference* (PDR) (Medical Economics Data, annual) is one of the standard sources for information about prescription drugs. Now the publisher of the PDR has produced *The PDR Family Guide to Prescription Drugs*, which contains some of the same information in lay language. The book has more than 360 entries covering approximately 1,000 of the most frequently prescribed medications. The entries are arranged alphabetically by brand name and contain information about the condition for which the drug is prescribed, how to take the drug, side effects, contraindications, warnings, interactions with other drugs and foods, recommended dosage, overdosage, and pregnancy and breast-feeding considerations. *See* references direct users to the brand-name entries from the generic names. Both brand and generic names appear in the master index.

In addition to drug profiles, the PDR contains a series of disease overviews that provide brief information about common conditions (e.g., heart disease, cancer, high blood pressure), and their treatments. The work also has a drug identification chart with color pictures, information on safe use of medication, lists of sugar- and alcohol-free products, products that may cause photosensitivity, and a list of poison control centers.

This source is best suited to the home library because the information provided is so brief. *The Complete Drug Reference* (see ARBA 93, entry 1662) provides objective information about more drugs (more than 6,000 prescription and over-the-counter drugs) in greater detail. It is a better choice for libraries.—**Barbara M. Bibel**

1880. **Physicians' Desk Reference, 1993.** 47th ed. Montvale, N.J., Medical Economics Data, 1993. 2687p. illus. index. $57.95. ISBN 1-56363-015-X.

Physicians' Desk Reference (PDR) provides essential information on prescription and OTC (over the counter) drugs and diagnostic products. The main section contains full product information, provided by the manufacturers (with FDA [Food and Drug Administration] approval), on 2,500-plus pharmaceuticals, covering their use, dosage, clinical pharmacology, adverse reactions, and more. In this edition, generic names have been added to the brand names in the product-name index. The manufacturers' index, product-category index, and generic- and chemical-name index follow their customary formats. A significant addition to the colored pictures of capsules and pills in the product-identification section is the page number of the item's description.

Once virtually restricted to doctors and pharmacists, PDR should be available in all medical and most public libraries. Although its information is technical, many health care consumers consult it; no one in this reviewer's household takes any medicine without doing so. The addition of new drugs and discontinuance of old ones, changes in FDA regulations, and new research necessitate keeping each edition up-to-date. The foreword explains how to obtain the two supplements between annual editions and describes other PDR formats and related products.—**Harriette M. Cluxton**

1881. **Physician's Drug Handbook.** 5th ed. Springhouse, Pa., Springhouse Publishing, 1993. 1190p. index. $26.95pa. ISBN 0-87434-534-0. ISSN 1043-3953.

Covering all aspects of drug information, from pharmacology to toxicity or overdose management, this handbook includes virtually all drugs in current clinical use in the United States. Written and reviewed by clinical pharmacists, the information is presented for the physician, nurse, or pharmacist, not for the layperson. Sections on pharmacodynamics (the mechanism and effects of the drug's action) and pharmacokinetics (absorption, distribution, metabolism, and excretion of the drug), while informative, will require additional definition for the casual user. Other sections on adverse reactions, overdose and treatment, and especially "information for the patient" are written as instructions that the physician should give patients.

Arranged alphabetically by generic name, each entry includes, besides the aforementioned sections, the pharmacologic and therapeutic classification, controlled substance schedule, pregnancy risk, dosage forms and strengths, contraindications, interactions, and special considerations. The appendix includes a charted summary of recommended chemotherapy protocols and of antibiotic effectiveness against pathogens. The index lists trade names, generic names, and drug classes. One minor point: The user is directed to the appropriate page number for the generic drug entry if a trade name is used, but the generic name is not given as a *see* reference.

Although the handbook is written for the physician (one can almost see it protruding from the coat pocket of a harried medical resident), it could be used to clarify the manufacturer's package inserts reprinted in the *Physicians' Desk Reference* (Medical Economics Data, 1993). Health sciences libraries, larger public libraries, or libraries with consumer health information collections may want to consider purchasing it.—**Vicki J. Killion**

1882. **Physicians' Generix 1992.** New York, Physicians' Generix/Data Pharmaceutica, 1992. 1v. (various paging). index. $68.00. ISBN 1-880891-02-6.

This comprehensive compendium, now in its 2d edition, contains a wealth of information on prescription drugs. In this era of HMOs (health maintenance organizations), Medicare, and the increased emphasis on managed medicine, a publication of this type fills a very important void in the arena of medicine and health care. The volume is divided into three major sections. Section 1 contains the comprehensive keyword index. Section 2 has product and information material, and also includes listings for 1,835 separate prescription drugs. Section 3 provides supplier profiles. All of the sections contain in-depth information, such as pharmacological and therapeutic category indexing, cross-referencing for multiple ingredients in combination, equivalency ratings (therapeutic and pharmacological equivalents), and benchmark price (average wholesale price). The helpful keyword section enhances access to specific information by the use of both brand and generic names of drugs and page numbers to the product-information section. The readable typeface and organized table of contents add to the usefulness of this publication. This title is highly recommended to most libraries because of its useful content, readability, and reasonable price.—**John H. Hunter**

1883. **Red Book, 1993.** Montvale, N.J., Medical Economics Data, 1993. 660p. illus. index. $44.00pa. ISBN 1-56363-022-2.

This hefty paperback serves as a prime desk reference for pharmacists, regardless of the venue of their practice. It identifies drugs and related products by brand and generic names, manufacturers, and drug numbers; gives information on format, packaging, and prices; and provides drug class, evaluation status (from the FDA's "Orange Book"), or other description as appropriate. Much of the data is coded, so familiarity with the various symbols, abbreviations, and lists is necessary for efficient use.

Separate sections furnish answers to questions that may be asked by consumers, such as addresses of manufacturers, poison control centers, drug-food interactions, and sources of home health care products. There are illustrated pages for product identification similar to those appearing in *Physicians'*

Desk Reference (Medical Economics Data, 1993); however, clinical pharmacology and indications for use of the various drugs are not included. (*Drug Facts and Comparisons*, a monthly looseleaf service, is widely used by pharmacists for this purpose.)

Red Book has been providing business-related information on drug, health, and beauty products to the pharmacy community for 97 years and is well regarded in its specialized field. Update and computerized services are available.—**Harriette M. Cluxton**

1884. Stern, Edward L. **Prescription Drugs and Their Side Effects. Compiled and edited by H. Winter Griffith.** New York, Body Press/Putnam, 1993. 224p. index. $9.95pa. RM302.5.S75. 615'.7042. LC 92-48219. ISBN 0-399-51805-3.

People are often concerned about the possible side effects of and adverse reactions to their prescription drugs. Because doctors and pharmacists are usually too busy to explain, they turn to the library for information. To this end, *Prescription Drugs and Their Side Effects* provides data on more than 400 of the National Prescription Audit's most frequently prescribed drugs.

The entries are arranged alphabetically by brand or generic drug name. Entries by generic name do not contain lists of brand names, which will make it difficult for users who know only the brand name of their medication, as there are neither illustrations nor cross-references. There are also some duplicate entries (e.g., acetaminophen with codeine, Tylenol with codeine). The entries include generic name, dosage form and strength, route of administration, therapeutic indications, precautions, side effects, and adverse reactions. The information is very brief and written in simple lay language. Drug category and drug name indexes complete the text.

This book provides only rudimentary information, so it is inadequate for reference collections. *The Complete Drug Reference* (see ARBA 93, entry 1662) contains comprehensive, up-to-date information, color pictures for identification, pictograms explaining proper administration of drugs, and outstanding general information about drugs. It is a much better choice for reference purposes.—**Barbara M. Bibel**

1885. Trissel, Lawrence A. **Handbook on Injectable Drugs.** 7th ed. Bethesda, Md., American Society of Hospital Pharmacists, 1992. 1023p. index. $119.00. ISBN 1-879907-20-8.

This new edition covers 262 commercially available injectable drugs, including 20 new ones since the last edition and 10 that are only available outside the United States. The entries are arranged alphabetically by chemical names. General information is listed first for each entry, with the most common product names, sizes and strengths, pH, adult and pediatric dosages, and drug stability. The product names are then listed in a table that includes the manufacturers, concentrations available, remarks, numbers for the cited references, and the drugs' compatibility or incompatibility. Also presented are 16 pages on investigational drugs; 10 pages on intravenous infusion solutions; 7 pages on parenteral nutrition solution formulas; 1,521 references cited in the main text; and an index with nonproprietary drugs in boldface type, trade names in regular type, and investigational drugs in italics. This excellent source of information is recommended for hospital and medical libraries.—**Betsy J. Kraus**

1886. Zimmerman, David R. **Zimmerman's Complete Guide to Nonprescription Drugs.** 2d ed. Detroit, Gale, 1993. 1125p. index. $39.95. RM671.A10Z55. 615'.1. ISBN 0-8103-8874-X.

This book is a useful guide for determining which over-the-counter (OTC) drug could be used to relieve a symptom or an ailment. All the information on the drugs or their active ingredients has been taken from the FDA's Over-the-Counter Drug Review. The volume starts with a symptom index and concludes with a general index that includes broad topics, specific diseases, and generic or brand drug names. Each entry is a broad topic with descriptions of the symptoms, what causes them, what active ingredients or drugs are approved by the FDA or conditionally approved for use, and any drugs that are disapproved. Detailed information on each drug usually gives action; side effects; effectiveness; and a table that lists either an active ingredient or brand name, dosages for adults and children, and a rating for the OTC drug or comments on the drug not found elsewhere. One of the most comprehensive books on OTC drugs, the work is recommended for libraries that collect drug information. [R: LJ, 15 Feb 93, p. 162; RBB, 15 Feb 93, p. 1086]—**Betsy J. Kraus**

34 High Technology

GENERAL WORKS

1887. **The Directory of Video, Computer and Audio-Visual Products 1993.** 38th ed. Fairfax, Va., International Communications Industries Association, 1993. 656p. illus. $70.00pa. LC 53-35264. ISBN 0-939718-14-6. ISSN 0884-2124.

This directory has been compiled by ICIA (International Communications Industries Association), the trade association for organizations involved in the manufacture, sale, and use of communications products. The main part of this book consists of a list of suppliers of video, audiovisual, and computer support equipment such as monitors, CD players, and computer furniture. The listings are provided by the manufacturers of the products. Models in each category are listed alphabetically by company name. The information supplied varies according to the type of equipment, but generally includes a picture of the item, model number, price, interfaces, functions and features, power needed, weight, dimensions, other models, and accessories. After the equipment listing are sections dealing with software, services, related equipment and accessories, and trade names.

The directory also contains a useful glossary and a contributor index. The index would be more useful if it included product names. Scattered throughout the book is information about ICIA, including a discussion of its role in the communications industry. A directory of ICIA members is divided into three parts: dealers, consultants, and video and film distributors. There are also lists of manufacturers and producers and of international members and associate members.

The directory does not evaluate or compare features of the equipment listed. However, for any organization that needs to purchase video or audiovisual equipment or computer-related products, this directory will be invaluable.—**Linda Main**

ARTIFICIAL INTELLIGENCE

1888. **Artificial Intelligence Abstracts Annual 1991. Volume 8.** New Providence, N.J., R. R. Bowker/Reed Reference Publishing, 1992. 396p. index. $250.00. ISBN 0-8352-3151-8. ISSN 0000-1244.

In this, the age of information, abstracts are crucial. This work abstracts publications in artificial intelligence, an emerging area in computer science. Applications of artificial intelligence, however, are interdisciplinary and reach out to almost every aspect of human life. This volume has a detailed list of all abbreviations and information sources related to the abstracts. In addition, in the year-in-review section there is an article on the legal aspects of expert systems. A detailed record of all 1991 conferences related to artificial intelligence is also provided.

The abstracts are organized according to how they would be used. There are four major categories: economics and issues, applications, research, and markets. This categorization allows a finer division of the types of articles and abstracts sought by the user. There are six different indexes: subject, geographical, patents, industry, author, and source. The source list is quite impressive, covering many magazines, journals, transactions, proceedings, and symposiums. Patents issued related to artificial intelligence are also included. This annual is highly recommended for both professional and public libraries because it is a very helpful and useful index for those interested in artificial intelligence.—**John Y. Cheung**

1889. Vollnhals, Otto. **A Multilingual Dictionary of Artificial Intelligence: English, German, French, Spanish, Italian.** New York, Routledge, Chapman & Hall, 1992. 423p. index. $135.00. Q334.2.V65. 006.3'03. LC 91-36370. ISBN 0-415-07465-7.

This glossary joins two other translation tools published in the last few years in the burgeoning field of artificial intelligence: the English and French *Artificial Intelligence Vocabulary* (see ARBA 90, entry 1706) and the English and German *Dictionary of Artificial Intelligence and Neuronal Networks* (see ARBA 93, entry 1671). Terms were chosen after an extensive survey of the current artificial intelligence literature. They represent theoretical concepts common or basic to the whole field; specialized terms from such subfields as expert systems (which receives the most emphasis), neural networks, natural language processing, image processing, speech recognition, and robotics; and terms relevant to artificial intelligence from other fields, such as logic, mathematics, computer programming, and linguistics.

The work is effectively and efficiently organized. The main section is an alphabetical, numbered list of about 3,000 English base terms and 600 cross-references from their synonyms and abbreviations. Entries for base terms contain, as appropriate, the part of speech, when there is ambiguity; the subfield of artificial intelligence in which it occurs; abbreviations, synonyms, and antonyms; related terms; and German, French, Spanish, and Italian equivalents, with gender notations. There are no definitions. The non-English equivalents are alphabetically arranged in their individual language indexes and keyed to the numbered entries in the main list.

Comparison of the terms with those in the subject index of a recent general text indicates that the author included a large percentage of representative terms. Comparison of Vollnhals's translations with those in the two works mentioned above shows substantial agreement. Typography and layout are pleasing. This glossary should prove quite useful. [R: LAR, Jan 93, p. 46]—**John Lewis Campbell**

COMPUTING

General Works

Acronyms and Abbreviations

1890. Albala, Elie, comp. **Computer Acronyms & Abbreviations.** Chambly, Que., Alpel Publishing, 1992. 96p. $12.95pa. 004'.03. ISBN 0-921993-06-4.

This book provides the fulltext form for more than 4,000 acronyms and abbreviations used in computing. No definitions of the terms are provided, and neither abbreviations incorporating numbers nor those that use non-Latin alphabetical characters are covered. The emphasis in this work appears to be on mainframe computer operations, because many important microcomputer terms are missing. A quick check against an article in a major personal computing magazine uncovered nearly two dozen missing acronyms. These ranged from those that are manufacturer-specific (e.g., QEMM, XT) to some that are obscure yet highly generic (e.g., adpcm) to some that are in everyday use in the PC world (e.g., CGA, IRQ). In addition, some abbreviations that are explained fail to include all major alternatives. For example, MPC is defined as "Multi-Processor Controller" but not as "Multimedia Personal Computer," certainly the more common current usage. While the work is clearly printed on good-quality paper with a durable perfect binding, such serious omissions disqualify it as a definitive quick-reference tool, especially in the microcomputing environment.—**John Howard Oxley**

1891. **The OSI Dictionary of Acronyms and Related Abbreviations.** By Wendy E. Brown and Colin MacLeod Simpson. New York, McGraw-Hill, 1993. 193p. $29.95; $19.95pa. TK510.5.B77. 004.6'0148. LC 92-110216. ISBN 0-07-057600-9; 0-07-057601-7pa.

Do not be mislead by the seemingly esoteric nature of this title. Open Systems Interconnection (OSI) protocols overlap such a wide area of computer and telecommunications technology that this dictionary will be of value to anyone needing to keep current with networks and interconnectivity of computer systems. Definitions are short, often no more than the acronyms exploded, but this is usually sufficient for those knowledgeable enough to read the literature. Where applicable, relevant national and international standards are referenced. Two small sections after the dictionary proper are devoted to application definitions (this is "application," as in the top layer of the OSI Reference Model) and OSI standards. Highly recommended.—**Robert Skinner**

Bibliography

1892. Best, Reba A., and D. Cheryn Picquet, comps. **Computer Law and Software Protection: A Bibliography of Crime, Liability, Abuse and Security, 1984 through 1992.** Jefferson, N.C., McFarland, 1993. 239p. index. $42.50pa. K564.C6A154. 016.343099'9. LC 92-56631. ISBN 0-89950-840-5.

Prosecuting creators of computer viruses, defending the "look and feel" of software products, protecting the privacy of electronic mail, and debating the government's right to regulate data encryption: These are just a few of the legal issues that play an increasingly integral part in the lives of computer software producers and users. Potential abuses of computers are nothing new, of course: The first edition of this guide (*Computer Crime, Abuse, Liability and Security* [see ARBA 86, entry 1678]) was published in 1985 and already contained 1,704 entries (although some of these were more ephemeral news reports rather than scholarly analyses). The 3,304 nonannotated entries in this edition are divided into two sections—books and articles—and are indexed by coauthor and subject. Perhaps when the next edition appears, there will be a third section: items in electronic formats. At that point presumably there will be references to resources such as the Electronic Frontier Foundation and the Computer Underground Digest. Even without these, *Computer Law and Software Protection* remains the most comprehensive bibliography on this subject in existence.—**Robert Skinner**

1893. **Bibliographic Guide to Computer Science 1991.** New York, G. K. Hall, 1992. 225p. (Bibliographic Guides). $175.00. ISBN 0-8161-7155-6. ISSN 0896-8098.

Partly serving as a supplement to MIT's printed catalog, this work is more comprehensive than its predecessor (see ARBA 90, entry 1709). Materials from the Stanford Libraries, particularly in expert systems and simulation, have been added for better coverage of the theoretical and mathematical aspects of computer science. A single dictionary arrangement offers access by author, title, series, and subject. The full bibliographical information that appears in main entries includes both East and West Coast holdings—a real plus for researchers. The identification of all relevant research material is hampered by the lack of subject headings for the most unusual items (e.g., institutional reports, theses, dissertations), the confusing similarity in type size of subject headings and holdings, and the exclusion of cross-references from buzzwords to appropriate headings.

The proliferation of databases and expanding Internet access to library catalogs continues to reduce the importance of annual subject bibliographies, particularly in such rapidly changing technological fields where key word searching and more frequent updating are a necessity. However, as a historical record of major works in the field, this bibliography is outstanding in the tradition of other G. K. Hall printed catalogs and will be an attractive addition for libraries with related collections.—**Sandra E. Belanger**

1894. Carande, Robert J. **Information Sources for Virtual Reality: A Research Guide.** Westport, Conn., Greenwood Press, 1993. 157p. index. $49.95. Z5643.I57C37. 016.006. LC 92-45083. ISBN 0-313-28804-6.

This guide to information resources and research strategies in virtual reality (VR) begins with a short introduction that outlines major achievements and research agendas of the past 30 years. Although VR is not really defined, the author concludes that a defining characteristic of VR is a computer environment in which at least one part of the user's physical presence is isomorphically represented in that environment. Following the introduction, 15 chapters each deal with a separate bibliographical form: periodical indexes, reports, proceedings, monographs, biographies, patents, and so on. Each chapter begins with an introduction to the bibliographical form as it relates to VR. It then lists and describes the sources, how to find them, and how to use them. The instructions usually include index entries and look-up strategies specific to VR, although some of the material is rather generic. Some of the chapters include electronic sources, and there is a separate chapter on electronic conferences. A final chapter is organized by research objectives, telling how to find information that may cut across bibliographical formats—items such as financial data on VR companies, hardware and software evaluations, and product descriptions. There is a good index of about 200 leads with modified subheads.

It must be kept in mind that this is a research guide, not a bibliography. No journal articles are listed, and the monograph chapter lists only 13 "significant books." Some of the chapters include short lists of recent publications but nothing like a complete bibliography. A more complete bibliography would have enhanced the book, although it would have dated it sooner. As a research guide, it will serve not only as an introduction to the bibliographical tools of a rapidly growing field but also as a reference source to help locate those tools. [R: Choice, Dec 93, p. 581]—**A. Neil Yerkey**

Dictionaries and Encyclopedias

1895. Chiri, Alfredo U. **Spanish-English, English-Spanish Dictionary of Computer Terms.** New York, Hippocrene Books, 1993. 212p. $16.95. ISBN 0-7818-0148-6.

With computer terminology so rapidly proliferating in English and Spanish, this dictionary provides a much-needed, up-to-date reference source of equivalent terms. More than 5,700 terms from computer technology in the two languages are included in this ambitious work. The terms cover programming languages, graphics, video, telecommunications, artificial intelligence, and hardware related to both mainframe and personal computers. The terms, selected as the most likely to cause "translative differences" (introduction), are listed alphabetically, first Spanish to English, then the reverse. Parts of speech are also given.

This reviewer found only one fault with the dictionary: The phonetic pronunciations are odd in both languages. For example, the pronunciation for Spanish *de* is wrongly given as *day* in English. Pronunciations for Spanish speakers of English words included with incorrect, additional syllables: For the term *base de conocimientos* the three-syllable term "knowledge base" becomes a five-syllable "NO-LED'-YE-BE-IS."

Otherwise the dictionary is fine, covering the terminology thoroughly. It contains, for example, 15 entries beginning with the Spanish word *tecla* ("*key*," as in keyboard). Although a poor guide for pronunciation, for its wealth of computer terminology this inexpensive book is recommended as a reference source for both academic and public libraries in English-Spanish bilingual communities.—**Edward Erazo**

1896. **Encyclopedia of Microcomputers. Volume 7: Evolution of Computerized Maintenance Management to Generation of Random Numbers.** Allen Kent and James G. Williams, eds. New York, Marcel Dekker, 1991. 445p. illus. $188.00. LC 74-29436. ISBN 0-8247-2706-1.

1897. **Encyclopedia of Microcomputers. Volume 8: Geographic Information System to Hypertext.** Allen Kent and James G. Williams, eds. New York, Marcel Dekker, 1991. 432p. illus. $188.00. LC 74-29436. ISBN 0-8247-2707-X.

1898. **Encyclopedia of Microcomputers. Volume 9: Icon Programming Language to Knowledge-Based Systems: APL Techniques.** Allen Kent and James G. Williams, eds. New York, Marcel Dekker, 1992. 380p. illus. $188.00. LC 74-29436. ISBN 0-8247-2708-8.

1899. **Encyclopedia of Microcomputers. Volume 10: Knowledge Representation and Reasoning to the Management of Replicated Data.** Allen Kent and James G. Williams, eds. New York, Marcel Dekker, 1992. 371p. illus. $188.00. QA76.15.E52. 004.16'03'21. LC 87-15428. ISBN 0-8247-2279-5.

The entire area of microcomputers and the phenomena that surround them is one in rampant expansion. This is the reason why a reference work on the subject is so important. It is also the reason why such a reference work is so difficult to realize. This field changes so quickly that any article published runs the risk of being soon outdated, and entire topics may be overlooked in the rush to get the volumes published. Even so, the arrival of volumes 7, 8, 9, and 10 of the *Encyclopedia of Microcomputers* (EVO to MAN inclusive) is an event to mark. The publisher has gone to a lot of expense and effort to get these handsome books to market.

There are several major problems with this set, however, and they have to do with the difficulties cited earlier: timeliness and choice of material. The space available has been divided into a small number of relatively long articles rather than a larger number of smaller articles. Many of the long individual entries are quite complete, but the price paid is that a large number of topics are not represented at all. Indeed, this is the most vexing problem with the entire series. There are articles on Intel Corp. and Honeywell Bull, Inc. (*sic*) but nothing on IBM. Lexisoft appears but not Logitech. There is an entry on interpreters for high-level languages but nothing on the Internet, and graph coloring is described, but groupware is not.

The title of the set would lead the user to think that there might be a focus on *microcomputers* rather than on computing in general. However, the volumes include an article on information malpractice—a well-written and thoroughly interesting entry, but why does it appear in the *Encyclopedia of Microcomputers*? Similarly, there are articles on hashing, holography, Huffman coding, and intelligent systems. These are all well written and interesting, but their relationship to the subject of microcomputers is tenuous.

A third problem, perhaps not so serious in itself but annoying to the user, is the relaxed approach the editors have taken toward the titles and the indexing of the articles. The article on computer viruses is called "Hardware/Software: Computer Viruses," requiring users to look in an unexpected place for the topic of computer viruses. In another section, both the Icon and FORTRAN computer languages are represented. However, Icon appears in the article "Icon Programming Language," while FORTRAN is found under "Computer Languages: FORTRAN." The articles themselves, once they have been found, prove to be well written. Some have been drafted by recognized experts in that field, although other articles are not so fortunate. There does not seem to be a central glossary of terms or entries, although this may appear in the last volume.

The books are richly bound in heavy covers with gold embossing. They look imposing on the bookshelf. With some tighter editorial control, they might be as useful to a prospective buyer as their appearance suggests.—**George M. White**

1900. Longley, Dennis, Michael Shain, and William Caelli. **Information Security: Dictionary of Concepts, Standards and Terms.** New York, Stockton Press, 1992. 620p. index. $130.00. ISBN 1-56159-069-X.

While computer and database security has always been a concern, particularly to the military, outbreaks of computer viruses, worms, data sabotage, and computer crackers (a more appropriate term than hackers) have considerably broadened the potential audience for this tool. *Information Security* is the best dictionary devoted to this complicated subject and replaces Longley's earlier *Data & Computer Security* (see ARBA 89, entry 1628). While most definitions are under 100 words, important topics, such as information technology security evaluation criteria and virus, are given multiple pages. The authors have done a good job in making the some 4,000 definitions as accessible as possible. The only obvious improvement would be to add more citations to the literature beyond the two-page bibliography and scattered citations throughout the volume. [R: Choice, July/Aug 93, p. 1752]—**Robert Skinner**

1901. **McGraw-Hill Data Communications Dictionary: Definitions and Descriptions....** By William F. Potts. New York, McGraw-Hill, 1993. 268p. index. $34.95. TK5105.P675. 004.6'03. LC 91-48333. ISBN 0-07-003154-1.

With terms ranging from "bit stuffing" to "LU-LU session," this is a well-organized and comprehensive dictionary of data transmission systems and computer networks. Potts promises to provide comprehensive but concise definitions; in this he succeeds. The preface offers introductory material in a terse few pages, and users do not have to wade through peripheral material. The book is aimed at data communications professionals, and there are sections on general, SNA (Systems Network Architecture), and vendor terms; recommendations and standards (including standards arranged by number and a very useful list, by country, of international and national standards organizations, with telephone number and address); IBM communications products and information display systems; interchange codes; and Systeme International units of measure. Numerous cross-references also make this a handy ready-reference tool. When looking up the term *server*, for example, the user is led on a journey to ECF (Enhanced Connectivity Facility), which leads to an explanation of SRPI (Server/Requester Program Interface), with *see also* references to logical unit (an end user in an SNA network) and ECF. The informed novice will most likely consult the general terms section, but both the computer literate and illiterate will be able to use this dictionary with relative ease. [R: SBF, June/July 93, p. 132]—**Jo A. Cates**

1902. **Prentice Hall's Illustrated Dictionary of Computing.** By Jonar C. Nader. Englewood Cliffs, N.J., Prentice Hall Professional, Technical, and Reference, 1992. 526p. illus. $30.00pa. QA76.15.N33. 004'.03. LC 92-19637. ISBN 0-13-719998-8.

This book is a competitive entry into the list of modestly priced computing dictionaries, and it has several features that may make it the preferred reference for many users. Probably most important is the effort to encourage the use of terminology that meets international standards. Many definitions in this book have been approved by the International Organization for Standardization (ISO), the International

Electrotechnical Commission, and other important standard-setting organizations. These definitions, clearly designated by the use of square brackets, will be especially valuable to those readers who wish to use terms accurately and in accordance with international practice. In addition, the author includes a style manual especially focused on situations that commonly occur in writing about computing. This section provides both the preferred format for using many common abbreviations and acronyms as well as examples of incorrect usage. Those who write about computing may find these tips useful.

In other respects, the number of terms, clarity of the definitions, and general layout in this book are comparable with competing dictionaries. Cross-references are furnished, correct pronunciation is indicated in some cases, and illustrations are included. This book has a number of significant advantages and no apparent liabilities; it will be a valuable tool for many readers.—**Harry E. Pence**

1903. Ralston, Anthony, and Edwin D. Reilly, eds. **Encyclopedia of Computer Science.** 3d ed. New York, Van Nostrand Reinhold, 1993. 1558p. illus. index. $125.00. QA76.15.E48. 004'.03. LC 92-14553. ISBN 0-442-27679-6.

In 605 articles contributed by 370 experts, this new reference book provides the reader with lucid and comprehensive treatments of the standard hardware and software topics, including theory, history, and applications. In particular, there are authoritative discussions of virtually all the major computer science developments in the 10 years since the 2d edition of this work (see ARBA 84, entry 1247).

The articles, ranging from short one- or two-paragraph explanations of terms to multipage treatments of topics, are arranged in double columns, with titles in boldface type capital letters. Cross-references abound beneath article titles and within entries. Most articles end with references to further reading in the professional literature. The uniformly well-written articles are complemented by many helpful diagrams, black-and-white photographs of people and machines of historical importance, and an impressive 12-page color inset showcasing advanced computer applications and computer graphics. Six appendixes provide useful information on such ancillary topics as acronyms and doctorate-granting university departments. There is also an informative and amusing timeline of significant events in the history of computing. The name index and the general index will greatly assist a reader in seeking information on specific topics.

Although the intellectually curious general reader can profit from many of the articles, including those on computers in society and women in computing, this reference work will be most useful to students and professionals in technological areas. The recent two-volume *Macmillan Encyclopedia of Computers* (see ARBA 93, entry 1678), not as authoritative as the work under review, may be more suitable for the nonprofessional. The prestige of the *Encyclopedia of Computer Science*'s editors and contributors, the depth and breadth of its entries, and the overall utility of this new edition make this the standard one-volume reference in the field of computer science. [R: Choice, May 93, p. 1438]—**Henry J. Ricardo**

1904. Spencer, Donald D. **Computer Dictionary.** 4th ed. Ormond Beach, Fla., Camelot Publishing, 1993. 459p. illus. $24.95pa. QA76.15.S64. 004'.03. LC 92-34432. ISBN 0-89218-239-3.

A spot check reveals no significant changes from the 3d edition (see ARBA 93, entry 1681), published a year earlier. The wide coverage of hardware and software topics and the concise, easy-to-understand definitions make this a useful reference for students, teachers, businesspeople, and computer professionals. With the addition of An Wang, Kenneth Olsen, Fernando Corbata, and Paul Allen, the number of calculating/computing pioneers whose portraits appear at the end of the book has been increased to 74. Contrary to stated policy, a biographical entry for Olsen does not appear in the dictionary proper, although his name (misspelled) appears, appropriately, in the Digital Equipment Corporation entry. The inaccuracies and omissions of the 3d edition persist here, augmented by a bothersome mix-up in the sequence of pages from 392 through 435.

There seems to be no need for an individual or library owning the 3d edition of Spencer's dictionary to purchase this latest one. Wait for the next edition and hope that more care is taken. [R: Choice, July/Aug 93, p. 1756; RBB, 15 April 93, p. 1532]—**Henry J. Ricardo**

1905. Williams, Robin, with Steve Cummings. **Jargon: An Informal Dictionary of Computer Terms.** Berkeley, Calif., Peachpit Press, 1993. 676p. illus. index. $22.00pa. ISBN 0-938151-84-3.

This book must have been a lot of fun to write, and it meets the author's objective of providing "definitions that simple people like me and my mother could understand" (p. viii). Starting with numerical terms such as *020, 030,* and *040* (nicknames for Macintosh chips) and proceeding alphabetically after that,

Williams defines and discusses roughly 2,000 terms. A term that is used in a definition and that has an entry of its own is italicized. Icons distinguish paragraphs specific to Macintosh computers from those specific to PCs (IBM-compatible computers). Illustrations and cartoons are sprinkled throughout. The end matter includes a useful appendix on reading a computer advertisement and a very helpful index of all words and names, including those that do not have separate entries but that appear within some definition.

Sure, the writing is "cute" in places, with references to friends and relatives of Williams; and yes, the attempts at humor are sometimes sophomoric. While specific products such as *WordStar* and Microsoft's *Word* are given entries, the popular software package *WordPerfect* is ignored except for a passing mention under *online help*. The term *service bureau* appears italicized in several places but is nowhere defined. Yet there are discussions of words and phrases such as *learning curve, Comdex, electronic sex, Pink operating system*, and *baudy language* (symbols and abbreviations used in E-mail messages), which are not found in most other computer dictionaries. The treatments of graphics, font technology, and desktop publishing are particularly good. The book provides a great deal of useful information in a very user-friendly way and is recommended for personal and library purchase as a valuable tool for the beginning to average computer user. [R: JAL, Nov 93, p. 346]—**Henry J. Ricardo**

Directories

1906. Bennett, Stephen J., and Richard Freirman, eds. **Microcomputer Market Place 1993.** New York, Random House, 1992. 795p. index. $30.00pa. ISBN 0-679-73928-9. ISSN 1066-1824.

The microcomputer marketplace is arguably the most volatile one currently existing. Companies come and go. Average growth factors are well above those of other economic sectors, while at the other end of the scale companies go bankrupt at an alarming rate. This book claims to be "The Complete Guide to PC Software and Hardware Vendors, Service Providers and Information Sources," and it has largely succeeded. Nine chapters provide the names, addresses, telephone and fax numbers, and main products of huge numbers of companies involved in the small computer business. Hardware and software companies are listed, of course, but also included are advertising agencies, trade show sponsors, international distributors, venture capital firms, leasing companies, and executive recruiters. In addition, there are listings of radio and television talk shows, syndicated computer columnists and electronic bulletin boards, lists of universities with accredited computer curricula, and recreational camps with computer programs. In short, if the phenomena of microcomputers interests you at any level, you will find a company that satisfies your needs somewhere in these pages.

There are a few flaws, one of which is unavoidable—most of the information was collected during the period January 1, 1991, to mid-January 1992. In an industry where 15 percent of the players may close their doors during the year, a two-year delay means that the information is unavoidably dated. The other flaw is more serious. The depth of coverage of the industry has been paid for at the price of tunnel vision: There is a dearth of non-U.S. information. Looking for information about the ATI Graphics Ultra Pro, a *PC Magazine* "Editors' Choice" product? You will not find it here—it is Canadian. How about the transputer, built by INMOS? No, it is British. The book is not exclusively about U.S. products, but there is a lot missing that U.S. readers would want to know about. Even so, the book has much to recommend it, and at the price, it is a bargain. It should find a welcome place on the shelves of any serious computer reference desk. [R: LJ, 15 May 93, p. 64]—**George M. White**

1907. **Gale Directory of Databases.** Kathleen Young Marcaccio, Kathleen Lopez Nolan, and Gwen E. Turecki, eds. Detroit, Gale, 1993. 2v. index. $119.00pa./set. ISBN 0-8103-5746-1.

This directory strives to be the most comprehensive guide available to commercially produced electronic databases. Formed by the merger of Gale's *Computer-Readable Databases* and Cuadra/Gale's *Directory of Online Databases* and *Directory of Portable Databases*, this new directory covers the international electronic database industry completely and includes more than 8,100 databases, 3,100 database producers, 800 online services, and 760 vendors or distributors of database products. Updated every six months, the directory is available in book form, diskette or magnetic tape, and online. A CD-ROM version is planned for the near future, and an online version through DIALOG will replace Computer-Readable Databases (File 230).

The directory is introduced with an essay by Martha E. Williams titled "The State of Databases Today: 1993." The essay offers an informative statistical breakdown of the electronic database industry, using data from this guide and other compilations. The rest of the directory is arranged into three sections: online databases and product descriptions (for CD-ROMs, diskettes, magnetic tape, handheld, and batch access database products), database producers, and online services. It includes three indexes per volume: an excellent subject index, a geographical index, and a master index that lists all the organization and product information in sequence. All indexes and categories are clearly labeled, thumb-indexed, and easy to follow. Catchwords at the top of each page facilitate finding particular entries.

Up-to-date and reliable product descriptions have been provided by the database producers. Records include such valuable information as product names, contact information, type of database (e.g., fulltext, bibliographical, image), a contents note, subject coverage, main language of database, geographical coverage, time span, updating schedule, online availability or vendor information, system and software requirements, and alternative electronic formats. Pricing information is sometimes given.

Gale's directory makes easy work of finding reliable database information that could otherwise be obtained only by scouring numerous other references. It will be a useful tool for libraries and research centers that require a complete guide to the world's commercial electronic databases. [R: Choice, July/Aug 93, p. 1749; RBB, June 93, pp. 1896-98; RQ, Fall 93, p. 127]—**Daphne Fallieros Potter**

1908.   Hildebrandt, Darlene Myers, comp. and ed. **Computing Information Directory: A Comprehensive Guide to the Computing Literature.** 10th ed. Colville, Wash., Hildebrandt, 1993. 487p. index. $229.95pa. QA76.M942. ISBN 0-933113-03-X. ISSN 0887-1175.

In 16 information-packed chapters covering a wide range of computing topics, Hildebrandt attempts to provide a "road map through the computer literature." This directory seems aimed primarily at librarians, especially those responsible for computer science collections, but it should be useful to educators, end users, researchers, and computing consultants as well. It complements such works as the latest edition of the *ACM Guide to Computing Literature* (see ARBA 91, entry 1720 for a review of an earlier edition). In addition to listing periodicals, bibliographies, and sources of reviews (of books, hardware and software products, and the like), the directory also points the reader to indexing and abstracting services, tutorials, analyses of career and salary trends, and information on publishers. Each chapter has an introduction, sometimes rather subjective and didactic, by Hildebrandt. There are Key Word In Context (KWIC) indexes in each chapter and a very useful master subject index that forms chapter 16.

In general, this comprehensive directory is an excellent source of information on computer resources, but it has some problems. Too many of the periodicals listed in chapter 1 are labeled "CEASED" or "SUSPENDED," thereby limiting their usefulness. Computing center newsletters, while discussed thoroughly and interestingly, are not likely to be as useful as Hildebrandt believes, because many of these have limited distribution, and no comprehensive index of articles is available. Chapter 12 describes "how to" articles in various periodicals, but leaves out the important professional tutorial publications of IEEE (Institute of Electrical and Electronic Engineers). Overall, despite these cavils, this directory can be recommended as a valuable resource for public, academic, and research libraries.—**Henry J. Ricardo**

Handbooks and Yearbooks

1909.   Juliussen, Karen Petska, and Egil Juliussen. **The Computer Industry 1993 Almanac.** 6th ed. Austin, Tex., Reference Press, 1993. 801p. illus. index. $45.00. ISBN 0-942107-04-7.

While it seems that every computer industry magazine one picks up has some sort of statistical chart or listing, such as the "Top 50 General Purpose Computing Systems" or "Byte: Readers Choice Awards 1992," finding these when they are needed can be quite a problem. *Computer Industry Almanac* has been making this task considerably easier since its first edition was published in 1987. Lists are taken from about 100 publications and organizations, with an effective cutoff date of spring 1993. The almanac begins with an overview of the computer industry, followed by chapters on companies, people, products and technologies, advertising, conferences, education, employment, financial data, forecasts, important events between January 1991 and May 1993, the international marketplace, associations, publications, and research and electronic information.

This last category includes some library-related lists, such as an online and E-mail service directory. There are some interesting general statistics mixed in with the lists of companies, products, and services; for example, 64 percent of all computer companies are located in California, Massachusetts, Texas, New York, and New Jersey. And while the United States at the end of 1992 had 45.3 percent of the world's computers, it had 51.4 percent of the computing power. The almanac should be a valuable tool for most libraries.—**Robert Skinner**

1910. **The Macintosh Bible: Thousands of Basic and Advanced Tips, Tricks and Shortcuts....** 4th ed. By Arthur Naiman and others. Berkeley, Calif., Peachpit Press, 1992. 1241p. illus. index. $32.00pa. QA76.8.M3M325. 004.165. LC 92-16851. ISBN 1-56609-009-1.

The first edition of this work, published in 1987, became a popular reference guide for the Macintosh. A 2d edition appeared in 1989 (see ARBA 89, entry 1624) and a 3d in 1991. This edition, published in fall 1992 and three times the length of the first, is up-to-date as of summer 1992. It thus provides a preview of the Performas and the Newton. Because of continuing rapid changes, the publisher promises three free updates to this edition.

Naiman and his associates cram much information into 20 chapters. Each is devoted to one subject (e.g., hardware, storage and memory, fonts, word processing, graphics). The first chapter gives a series of tips and advice for the novice. The style is breezy and informal, with little symbols (icons) in the margins that call attention to a "very good feature," "gossip/trivia," "very hot tip," "important warning," and so forth. Numerous screen displays and examples of fonts and graphics are given, but there are no photographs. A short bibliographical essay, other sources for information, a good glossary, a helpful directory of companies and products, and an index conclude the volume.

This volume has something for everyone, both beginner and advanced user. Because of its thickness and paper binding, it will not stand up to heavy use. For an added sum three disks (described in the volume) filled with freeware and shareware programs and utilities can be purchased. This volume is one of two Macintosh books (the other is Cary Lu's *The Apple Macintosh Book*, 4th ed. [Microsoft Press, 1992]) that should be in every library's collection of books on personal computers.—**Richard D. Johnson**

1911. Nehmer, Kathleen Suttles, ed. **Guide to Free Computer Materials.** 11th ed. Randolph, Wis., Educators Progress Service, 1993. 444p. index. $37.95pa. ISBN 0-87708-249-9.

This handbook provides educators with a comprehensive source survey of free subject-classified computer-related materials. Besides indicating what is available and from whom, the guide covers acquisition methodology and devotes a quarter of its pages to a glossary. A wide range of no-cost items is listed. Thorough title, subject, and source indexes and extensive coverage of resources for the older Commodore and Apple machines (which are widely distributed in North American schools) enhance the book's utility. Most of the free materials (about 55 percent of which are new to this edition) are demonstration disks or catalogs, but there are also helpful guides to solving practical problems, such as virus infections and computer security.

The major defect of this book is its unnecessary bulk: It is printed in monospace typescript on single-sided pages, and the rather old-fashioned computer glossary is superfluous. Worse, the method of referring entries (which are themselves somewhat repetitive) to a separate order address section is both clumsy and wasteful, because fewer than one-fourth of the companies listed have more than one entry. Clearly printed on color-coded paper for each guide section, this catalog is intended for one year's use only, and the lay-flat binding will not last longer under the heavy use it will surely receive from its intended audience.—**John Howard Oxley**

Computer Graphics

1912. Spencer, Donald D. **Illustrated Computer Graphics Dictionary.** Ormond Beach, Fla., Camelot Publishing, 1993. 305p. illus. $24.95pa. T385.S66. 006.6'03. LC 91-9433. ISBN 0-89218-117-6.

This work provides a nonspecialist reference for words and terms relating to the broad spectrum of producing images with a computer. While concentrating on computer graphics (e.g., painting, drawing), the book also covers terminology pertaining to desktop publishing, fractal geometry, computer science, graphic design, data communications, scientific visualization, computer-aided design, computer programming, and business graphics. Hardware, software, peripherals, magazines, brand names, computer graphics-related organizations, exhibits, and conferences are included as well.

Despite the fact that hardware equipment and software programs change virtually overnight in the computer graphics field (making it difficult for the common computer user to keep up), Spencer has compiled a remarkably up-to-date, highly informative, and complete dictionary of terms and illustrations. Color illustrations are even included in the definitions of a few of the more pertinent and important terms dealing with color and its use in computer graphics. (Books of this kind too often exclude color, one of the most important applications with which graphic artists must concern themselves.)

Computer graphics students, instructors, and professionals will find *Illustrated Computer Graphics Dictionary* an invaluable reference tool. It is also recommended for the reference shelf of any library. [R: Choice, July/Aug 93, p. 1756; RBB, 15 April 93, p. 1532]—**Joan Garner**

Software

1913. Brant, Bob. **Bob Brant's Best of Macintosh Shareware.** New York, Windcrest Books/McGraw-Hill, 1993. 350p. illus. index. $29.95pa. (with disk). QA76.8.M3B72. 005.365. LC 92-14427. ISBN 0-8306-4203-X.

It does not take most users long to discover that in addition to widely advertised and promoted commercial software available for their computers, there is a large category of programs from what might be called the equivalent of print's small presses. Variously known as shareware (usually distributed on a "try it for free and if you like it, then send money to the author" basis) or freeware (public domain software that is given away), this software can rival commercial products in terms of quality and functionality, or offer enhancements that would not be profitable to market. For IBM PCs there are both books and shareware magazines. For the Macintosh there are no magazines, but several books exist. Brant's is not the most comprehensive, but he covers only software that he highly recommends, and his descriptions of the software are more complete than other sources. In addition to discussing some 200 products, he provides several introductory chapters that, while not necessarily pertinent to shareware, will nevertheless be valuable to all but the Macintosh expert. A bonus with this book is a disk containing some 20 pieces of shareware. Brant writes entertainingly and informatively, and while everyone will have favorites that he omits, his recommendations overall seem well thought out. Especially helpful is his advice on acquiring shareware, although academic users on the Internet who want to get these programs might like a list of the major repositories (e.g., Stanford's InfoMac Archive) where shareware resides.—**Robert Skinner**

1914. **Directory of U.S. Government Software for Mainframes and Microcomputers.** By the Technology Administration, U.S. Department of Commerce. Springfield, Va., National Technical Information Service, 1993. 1v. (various paging). index. $65.00pa. ISBN 0-934213-37-2.

The mission of the National Technical Information Service (NTIS) Federal Computer Products Center is to improve public access to government-produced computer products. This directory is part of that effort. It contains descriptions of 550 mainframe and microcomputer programs from 100 federal agencies. The programs, of which about 40 percent are micro-based, are available from NTIS at prices ranging from $15 to $2,000. The main entries give the program's title, originating agency, an abstract, keyword descriptors, date written, and specifications (e.g., how supplied, language used, required hardware and software). The main arrangement is by discipline, with indexes by subject and agency.

These programs will be of most interest to the business and scientific communities, although anyone with a specialized need might find it worthwhile to browse through the subject index. Needless to say, some of the programs are more useful than others. For example, such programs as management of battlefield supplies have limited applicability. Others, such as employee attendance systems, cashflow analysis, or histogram generators, may have wide applicability. Many are useful but specialized, such as public housing management, dike stability, and fire hazard assessment.—**A. Neil Yerkey**

1915. **The Software Encyclopedia 1993: A Guide for Personal, Professional and Business Users.** New Providence, N.J., R. R. Bowker/Reed Reference Publishing, 1993. 2v. index. $222.00pa./set. ISBN 0-8352-3329-4.

In a world where change comes normally, an encyclopedia of computer-related material would be something like a large photograph of an extended family. By the time the prints came back from the photographer, the family members could still recognize themselves. But in a world of computers such as ours, many of the older relatives have died, the younger members have grown up, and new children have been born before the negatives have even hit the developer.

So it is with *The Software Encyclopedia 1993*, which contains many different software packages, programs, operating systems, games, compilers, and interpreters, among other things. Some are old familiar friends. Some are no longer useful. Some are missing. The only category of software that the publishers have deliberately omitted is that of educational programs aimed at the scholastic market. Educational programs for home use are included.

Books of this type are catalogs, and the single most important feature of a catalog is the method of indexing the entries. There are five indexes used here: a title index, a publisher index, a guide to systems, a guide to applications, and a system compatibility index. Thus, if the title of a program or its publisher is known, suitable entries can be located quickly. If the area of application or the platform is known, entries can also be located (except, perhaps, not so quickly). This is a very positive feature and adds greatly to the value of the publication.

There is a dearth of freeware and shareware entries. Some very well known programs, such as the PKzip programs for compression and the F-Prot programs for virus detection, are not represented, nor is the SUIT user interface implementor. This is the greatest weakness in the volumes. Also, small software publishers and individual creators are greatly underrepresented.

Overall, the encyclopedia is an extremely useful aid for finding the availability and source of computer software for a multitude of platforms. It is not perfect, but it is a good place to look.—**George M. White**

OPTICAL STORAGE DEVICES

CAD/CAM

1916. Laine, Claude. **Combinatory Vocabulary of CAD/CAM in Mechanical Engineering. Vocabulaire Combinatoire de la CFAO Mecanique.** Ottawa, Department of the Secretary of State of Canada, 1993. 145p. (Terminology Bulletin, 219). $20.75pa. (U.S.). 620.0042'02'85. ISBN 0-660-58029-2.

Designed for francophones, this text is for persons concerned about the exact word or phrase to express an idea—translators, students, technicians, technical writers, and so forth. The focus is primarily on French idioms used in CAD/CAM engineering; most of the information was taken from standards and monographs for computer-integrated manufacturing. The book covers concepts related to this field, such as graphics, modeling, robotics, and production. The stated purpose is to allow "language professionals ... to express themselves in the same register as French-speaking CAD/CAM specialists" (p. viii). The text's main body is in French, but an English-French glossary provides additional access.

A main entry consists of the English word or phrase, the equivalent French words or phrases, a brief definition, notes about usage, and idiomatic expressions associated with the phrases. One nice feature of the definitions is that highlights set off words found elsewhere in the book. The idiomatic expressions are grouped by the grammatically correct way to use a word or phrase; in some instances, words may precede or follow a verb, noun, adjective, or preposition. However, the lists of idiomatic expressions and their grammatical usages do not include precise meanings. One improvement would be to subdivide each group by definition and include examples of correct use.

Translated into both French and English, the user's guide adequately explains the symbols used to group phrases and gives examples of editorial notes, abbreviations, and synonyms. A bibliography in French and a list of other publications by the Translation Bureau complete the features.

In addition to French- and English-language professionals, libraries and research institutions catering to the international community would find this book useful.—**Susan D. Baird-Joshi**

CD-ROM

1917. Nicholls, Paul T. **CD-ROM Buyer's Guide & Handbook: The Definitive Reference for CD-ROM Users.** 3d ed. Wilton, Conn., Eight Bit Books, 1993. 699p. illus. index. $44.95pa. ISBN 0-910965-08-0.

In less than 10 years, the number of CD-ROM products available commercially has gone from 2 titles to more than 3,000. With low-cost drives and a wide variety of CD-ROMs now on the market, libraries, businesses, and even individuals are embracing CD-ROM technology in increasing numbers. Intended to assist anyone involved with CD-ROMs, this medium-priced paperback contains 3 main categories of material: extensive background information on CD-ROM technology and the industry, bibliographical citations for hundreds of articles on all aspects of CD-ROM, and reviews of a core of nearly 200 CD-ROM titles. The CD-ROM reviews are arranged by subject and cover a wide range of products, from children's games to sophisticated periodical indexes. A well-organized index rounds out the book.

Intended for beginners as well as experienced buyers and users, the book is relatively free of jargon. The excellent bibliography is organized by subject, and the included citations are quite recent, many from the past two years. The majority of the CD-ROM reviews are very good, with ratings for ease of installation and use, quality of data, documentation, and "search power." Although diverse, the collection of reviews seems to favor libraries and corporate buyers, as many of the titles are quite expensive.

Billed as "the definitive reference for CD-ROM buyers," this attractively presented, well-organized book lives up to its ambitious claim by offering a large amount of fascinating and useful information on all aspects of the CD-ROM world. Highly recommended for any academic, public, school, or special library dealing with CD-ROMs.—**Melvin Marlo Brown**

1918. **CD-ROM Finder: The World of CD-ROM Products for Information Seekers.** 1993 ed. Medford, N.J., Learned Information, 1993. 585p. $69.50pa. ISBN 0-938734-70-9.

Carrying on the tradition of its predecessor, *Optical Publishing Directory* (see ARBA 92, entry 1720), but with the same subtitle, this work claims to have doubled the number of entries to more than 1,400 listings of CD-ROM products in virtually all areas. Criteria for inclusion are the same as in the previous edition (i.e., "viability in the general marketplace"). The introduction to this edition states that it is intended for a professional audience of library and information scientists, doctors and other health care professionals, attorneys, bankers, businesspersons, and the like. However, virtually anyone with a CD-ROM player and an interest in bibliographical research could benefit from this work. For example, Microsoft Bookshelf is a compilation of 10 standard reference works (e.g., dictionary, thesaurus, spelling checker) that would be of use to anyone. Generally speaking, works included are those most likely to be purchased by organizations or institutions, if for no other reason than price.

Product profiles are alphabetically arranged by disc title, and details are outlined within the four major categories of description, content summary, system requirements, and market data. The applications (subject) index is greatly expanded from the previous edition, now up to 85 categories (from 13). There is also a company/product index and a company index that provides complete order data.

Cross-references to more commonly known names of products would be a helpful feature, as would the addition of page numbers in the applications index (although the latter is not a necessity as the entries are in alphabetical order anyway). One might quibble with a few of the categories (e.g., Microsoft Bookshelf is in language rather than general reference), and to accommodate the increased number of listings, this edition has much smaller type, a real loss from the previous edition. Still, this new directory seems well worth the cost for all who must keep up with the CD-ROM market.—**Carol Truett**

1919. **CD-ROMs in Print 1993: An International Guide to CD-ROM, CD-I, CDTV, Multimedia & Electronic Book Products.** Regina Rega, comp. Westport, Conn., Meckler, 1993. 736p. index. $95.00pa. ISBN 0-88736-881-6. ISSN 0891-8198.

This guide is another collection of data on the state of the current optical disc market, specifically for those products commercially offered on CD-ROM. CD-ROM, CD-I, CDTV, multimedia, and electronic book products from all over the world are included.

The guide begins with an introduction that lists the structure of the guide and gives information about the makeup of the sections. There are close to 500 pages worth of data on 3,502 CD-ROM titles, including information on the number of discs in a set, data available, publisher name, U.S. and non-U.S. distributors, compatible drives, formats and software, system requirements, frequency of updates, pricing, dates of coverage, language of data, subjects covered, and descriptions. Data are provided by the publishers. Twelve indexes at the end of the guide offer breakdowns on such things as data providers, software providers, Macintosh CD-ROMs, information level, and subject. Interspersed throughout the guide are numerous advertisements for CD-ROMs and related products.

CD-ROMs in Print offers an impressive array of information to the reader. Unfortunately, there are some problems. The advertisements make the table of contents difficult to locate (it is hidden between two full-page ads). And without access to the table of contents, the indexes are difficult to find and use. A lack of introductory material for the indexes makes them hard to follow. Additionally, the indexes would be more useful if they included page numbers of CD-ROM titles mentioned.

While there is repeated mention of the guide's international coverage, the emphasis is clearly on materials emanating from Japan. In keeping with the Japanese theme is the introductory essay "CD-ROM Opportunities in Japan for Overseas Publishers." Apparently a holdover from a report on CD-ROM distribution in Japan from *CD-ROMs in Print 1992*, the presence of the piece is awkward. Other than an interesting look at the state of optical publishing in Japan, the report does not appear to serve any purpose for the reader.

Although the guide covers many titles, there are problems with thoroughness and accuracy. There is no mention of one of SilverPlatter's major offices (the one in Arlington, Virginia) in the U.S. distributor index; and a CD-ROM product that has been available for two years (Perseus, from Yale University Press) is listed as "in preparation." Additionally, there are discrepancies between advertisements in the guide and their entries (e.g., for Countries of the World the ad lists the price as $395; the record within the guide lists the price as $495). Finally, while the guide's introduction states that it is the "most comprehensive international listing of commercially available CD-ROMs," it fails to cover at least two titles mentioned in one of its own ads, and lists several titles that are not commercially available.

CD-ROMs in Print 1993 is a large guide. It offers good coverage of Japanese optical disc products and lists a wide variety of domestic and foreign titles, from the expected (e.g., *New York Times* on Disc) to the unexpected (e.g., Lettuce Cooking Dish of the Day "365"). If a wide variety of titles is the need rather than complete accuracy, this guide will serve as a useful supplement to a CD-ROM reference shelf.—**Daphne Fallieros Potter**

1920. Sorrow, Barbara Head, and Betty S. Lumpkin. **CD-ROM for Librarians and Educators: A Resource Guide to Over 300 Instructional Programs.** Jefferson, N.C., McFarland, 1993. 155p. index. $24.95pa. LB1028.7.S67. 371.3'34'0216. LC 92-56700. ISBN 0-89950-800-6.

Any teacher or librarian who might have doubts about the availability of appropriate CD-ROM databases for teaching purposes should benefit from this directory, whose purpose is "to present a dependable and useful annotated collection of CD-ROM resources." Titles were chosen for their value in the classroom or for independent study and include materials for kindergarten through college, with particular emphasis on curriculum-related CDs. The concise entries are alphabetically arranged under 27 subjects and categories, including reference, art, AIDS, science, music, English, foreign languages, consumer information, travel, and current affairs. There are also specific documentary forms, such as citations found in indexes. Interestingly, while five CD-ROM encyclopedias are included, the work does not list World Book's Information Finder.

The standard format followed for each CD-ROM entry includes title, producer, format, subject, price, grade level, hardware, special software needed, distributor to contact for purchase, and a descriptive review of the program. While critical evaluations are not included for individual titles, each entry was presumably chosen after careful review by the authors for objectivity, appeal to students, educational content, timeliness, format, factual credibility, and inclusion of information "pertinent to students' growth." The authors also include almost five pages of software and hardware evaluation criteria for use by teachers and librarians in making their own selections of appropriate CD-ROM databases for classroom or library use. Special features of the work are a concise discussion of CD-ROM basics, including CD-ROM networks; a sample lesson plan; search strategies and tips; and examples of common menu commands. There are also a list of CD-ROM drive manufacturers and a set of questions to ask in selecting a CD-ROM distributor.

This useful and reasonably priced work concludes with a helpful glossary, suggested readings that include both general library and specific CD-ROM journals, plus a separate, brief bibliography and an index. Highly recommended for individuals and for all sizes and types of libraries. [R: BR, Nov/Dec 93, pp. 56-57; SLJ, Oct 93, p. 52]—**Carol Truett**

Microforms

1921. **Bibliographic Guide to Microform Publications 1991.** New York, G. K. Hall, 1992. 391p. (Bibliographic Guides). $260.00. ISBN 0-8161-7165-3. ISSN 0891-3749.

Librarians and researchers involved with microforms collection may be interested in this printed guide. Microformed books and nonserial materials cataloged by the New York Public Library (NYPL) and Library of Congress between September 1, 1990, and August 31, 1991, are clearly laid out and explained, making this a useful resource for those who do not have access to the more frequently updated electronic bibliographical resources. The introduction lists the types of materials covered in the guide: monographs, government publications, pamphlets, ephemeral material, dissertations, technical reports, and manuscript collections from the United States and foreign countries. Serial publications are not included.

Important usage information for this and all G. K. Hall Bibliographic Guides is provided in the preface, where access information is discussed and a sample record is parsed and annotated. Access to records is offered via main entry, added entries, titles, series titles, and subject headings, all integrated into one alphabetical sequence. Full bibliographical information (following the Anglo-American Cataloguing Rules) is offered in the main entry, with abbreviated information given for the other entries. NYPL or LC call numbers are given for all records.

The principal drawback to this guide is its obsolescence—the fact that it is but a snapshot of an ever-growing collection, and taken over two years ago at that. Shorter turnaround time from collection to publication would improve the guide's utility. For librarians (especially catalogers and acquisitions and reference librarians) and researchers without access to electronic bibliographical utilities, this work will be a useful addition to their collections.—**Daphne Fallieros Potter**

TELECOMMUNICATION

1922. **Telecommunications Directory 1994-95: An International Guide to Organizations, Systems, and Services....** 6th ed. John Krol and Gwen E. Turecki, eds. Detroit, Gale, 1993. 1060p. index. $325.00. LC 83-646142. ISBN 0-8103-7748-9. ISSN 1055-8454.

In the not too distant past, a telecommunications directory appealed to a fairly specialized audience. Today, with every week bringing new mergers and joint projects of the telephone companies, cable television providers, cellular corporations, and media conglomerates, a book such as this becomes almost a necessity in keeping track of the players who will be exerting significant influence over our lives. More than 2,400 companies, organizations, services, and consultants are covered that relate to cellular radio, electronic mail, facsimile, local area networks, microwave networks, satellite services, teleconferencing, videotex, and various aspects of voice and data communications. Entries, which are alphabetically arranged, consist of company name, address, head, year of founding, type of business, number of staff, general description, examples of specific applications, geographical areas served, publications, and rate structure (if applicable). Access is facilitated through four indexes: function, geographical, personal name, and master name and keyword. A number of entries relate to the Internet, including some of the mid-level Internet providers, but libraries will still require Internet-specific directories for full coverage of this burgeoning field.—**Robert Skinner**

35 Physical Sciences and Mathematics

GENERAL WORKS

1923. Grinstein, Louise S., Rose K. Rose, and Miriam H. Rafailovich, eds. **Women in Chemistry and Physics: A Biobibliographic Sourcebook.** Westport, Conn., Greenwood Press, 1993. 721p. index. $99.50. QD21.W62. 540'.92'2. LC 92-40224. ISBN 0-313-27382-0.

This work profiles 75 women who achieved prominence in the fields of chemistry or physics. Covering nearly three centuries, it is limited in scope to those who were born prior to 1933 or who are deceased. The foreword emphasizes the struggle that women have had in obtaining scientific educations and careers. Those profiled achieved success in various ways, including publications, editing, teaching, professional leadership, or overcoming societal or familial obstacles in gaining an advanced degree. The chapters average about eight pages, and each is divided into three sections. A biographical section details family background, education, career development, and important influences upon career direction. This section tends to be quite personal. The work section covers significant contributions to the chosen field, such as research, problems solved, service, and honors. The bibliography section denotes works by or about the person profiled. This section ranges in length from a few references to more than 100. Appendixes provide entry by places and years of birth, fields of interest, and countries of work. Short biographies of contributors are included, and the index is by subject and name. This work is very consistent in quality despite the fact that nearly all the biographies are written by different authors. Highly recommended for academic libraries.—**T. McKimmie**

ASTRONOMY

1924. Dibon-Smith, Richard. **StarList 2000: A Quick Reference Star Catalog for Astronomers.** New York, John Wiley, 1992. 400p. $29.95pa. QB65.D53. 523.8'022'3. LC 92-2907. ISBN 0-471-55895-8.

This comprehensive handbook is divided into three parts: a star catalog (StarList) and sections on binary and variable stars. The core of the book is the StarList, a compendium of more than 2,400 stars with apparent magnitude greater than 5.5, along with selected others of interest. Arranged by constellation, the StarList includes a wide variety of data for each sun, such as right ascension, declination, apparent and absolute magnitudes, spectral type, distance, radial velocity, and proper motion. The sections on binaries and variable stars include additional data relevant to those types of stars (e.g., orbital period and separation for binaries, range of magnitude and periods for variables).

In addition to this information, the author provides a wealth of additional features, including diagrams of the orbits of 35 binaries with periods of 300 years or more, a list of variable stars by type, bar charts of magnitude differences for prominent variables, and most favorable viewing dates for variables. An unusual but welcome item is a group of computer programs written in BASIC for amateur astronomers to find the Julian date, to determine a star's position, to calculate right ascension, and so on. More than 60 pages of indexes round out this well-written and well-organized handbook.

Aimed primarily at intermediate and advanced amateur astronomers, the work could also be used by a professional in certain situations. Likewise, it would be useful to reference librarians in both public and academic libraries. In addition to the book's high-quality content, two other features make it worth a second look. First, unlike many books of its type, it is reasonably priced and therefore within reach of most readers. Second, although a paperback, it lies open flat for easy use at the desk or telescope.—**Robert A. Seal**

1925. **The Facts on File Atlas of Stars and Planets.** By Ian Ridpath. New York, Facts on File, 1993. 80p. illus. maps. index. $16.95. OB45.R53. 520. LC 92-32463. ISBN 0-8160-2926-1.

An astronomy atlas has a formidable goal. It has to explain, in essence, the universe, from atoms to galaxies. It should address the history of human discovery of the universe as well as the evolution of the universe. Illustrations are required, and they should be informative, accurate, and up-to-date. A liberal use of color is desirable. This book has attained these goals and more. The author, an established astronomer, has put together facts and data in a delightful way. He presents a mixture of text, data boxes, and illustrations that are easily read and a pleasure to the eye. The book is packed with spectacular photographs from the Voyager space probes, the Hubble Space Telescope, and surface observatories.

The atlas describes the Earth, Moon, Sun, other solar system members, stars, star charts, galaxies, and the origin of the universe. Additional chapters cover telescopes and binoculars and the electromagnetic spectrum; there is even a quiz. The author has included a philatelic illustration and a descriptive note related to the subject of each chapter. This very nice feature could spark some specialized stamp collecting. This book is recommended for public, school, and college reference collections. [R: RBB, 15 Oct 93, p. 472; RQ, Winter 93, p. 285; SBF, Oct 93, p. 201]—**Margaret F. Dominy**

1926. Hetherington, Norriss S., ed. **Encyclopedia of Cosmology: Historical, Philosophical, and Scientific Foundations of Modern Cosmology.** Hamden, Conn., Garland, 1993. 686p. illus. index. (Garland Reference Library of the Humanities, v.1250). $125.00. QB980.5.E53. 523.1'03. LC 92-43456. ISBN 0-8240-7213-8.

Aimed at the highly educated person, this compendium covers the structure and evolution of the universe from a variety of angles: cultural, historical, philosophical, and scientific. An emphasis is placed on the cosmologies of different peoples (e.g., Ancient Egyptian, Islamic, Chinese) as well as on astronomers and other scientists who played key roles in the development of cosmological theory (e.g., Johannes Kepler, Tycho Brahe, Ptolemy, Nicolaus Copernicus). Arranged alphabetically, the work includes entries of varying lengths (one paragraph to many pages) on all aspects of the subject. There are a few black-and-white illustrations, and most entries include short bibliographies. Cross-references and an index add to the utility of the book.

But despite its wealth of information about a relatively narrow field in the area of astronomy, the book is not highly readable, nor is it very useful for general science reference work. The text is rather dull and at times a bit difficult to plow through. In addition, many entries are highly mathematical, far beyond most college-educated readers. It is sort of three books in one: a history of cosmology, a philosophical work, and a very advanced treatise on the physics of our universe. Each might stand well alone, but together the marriage is somewhat uneasy. Large research libraries and specialists may consider purchasing this volume, but the average library and most readers are urged to seek information elsewhere, such as in the *Encyclopedia of Astronomy and Astrophysics* (see ARBA 90, entry 1744) or *The Astronomy and Astrophysics Encyclopedia* (see ARBA 93, entry 1704). [R: Choice, Nov 93, p. 430]—**Robert A. Seal**

1927. **McGraw-Hill Encyclopedia of Astronomy.** 2d ed. Sybil P. Parker and Jay M. Pasachoff, eds. New York, McGraw-Hill, 1993. 531p. illus. index. $75.50. QB14.M3725. 520'.3. LC 92-40523. ISBN 0-07-045314-4.

A subset of the multivolume *McGraw-Hill Encyclopedia of Science & Technology* (see ARBA 93, entry 1446), this work consists of 225 articles written by prominent astronomers and other specialists from around the world. Emphasizing the physical rather than the descriptive aspects of astronomy, its underlying theme is the study of the heavens through electromagnetic radiation: visible light, ultraviolet, infrared, x-ray, radio, and so forth. The text is clearly written but rather advanced, with a fair amount of mathematics, and therefore is most appropriate for nonastronomer scientists, advanced college students, and educated laypeople.

This edition, published a decade after the first, includes 21 new and 20 revised articles covering recent discoveries and new theories of the universe. Profusely illustrated with both color and black-and-white photographs, the book also contains a variety of diagrams, charts, and tables of data. Arranged alphabetically by topic, entries range from a few paragraphs to several pages in length and include short bibliographies and cross-references. The alphabetical arrangement results in the spread of similar topics throughout the book, a somewhat awkward situation overcome for the most part by an excellent index of some 3,000 entries. [R: Choice, Oct 93, p. 268; JAL, Sept 93, p. 275; WLB, Sept 93, pp. 119-21]—**Robert A. Seal**

1928. Pasachoff, Jay M. **A Field Guide to the Stars and Planets.** 3d ed. Boston, Houghton Mifflin, 1992. 502p. illus. maps. index. (Peterson Field Guides). $24.95; $15.95pa. QB64.P37. 523. LC 92-17556. ISBN 0-395-53764-9; 0-395-53759-2pa.

The 3d edition of this familiar field guide is better than ever, with more color celestial photographs, revised numerical data, and an updated text. While most Peterson's Guides are limited in scope geographically, this handy book can be used from any point on the Earth's surface. Further, although it is aimed at amateurs, it would be useful to a professional as well. Its features are too numerous to be covered in a short review; however, its strongest point is its illustrations, especially the star maps and sky atlas, both black on white for ease of use in stargazing.

The book's 15 chapters provide a broad overview of the heavens, taking the reader on a whirlwind tour of the constellations, planets, stars, moons, galaxies, nebulas, and more. Charts, tables, and graphs provide a wide variety of information in different formats for easy retrieval and interpretation. Appendixes cover the constellations, the brightest and nearest stars, double and variable stars, planetary positions and moons, and much more. A glossary and bibliography round out this fine field guide, which is up to the usual high quality of Peterson's Guides: The text is excellent, the color photographs stunning, and the format eminently easy to use. Recommended for all types of libraries, including personal collections.—**Robert A. Seal**

1929. Terrell, Dirk, Jaydeep Mukherjee, and R. E. Wilson. **Binary Stars: A Pictorial Atlas.** Malabar, Fla., Krieger Publishing, 1992. 383p. index. $57.50; $42.50pa. QB821.T47. 523.8'41. LC 91-27786. ISBN 0-89464-041-0; 0-89464-698-2pa.

A casual observation of a clear night sky reveals several thousand stars. These appear to be single objects scattered about us, but this appearance is deceptive. Virtually all stars are part of multiple star systems; a single star, such as our Sun, is rare. Most stars are part of a binary, or double-star system—two stars gravitationally bound together. Observations of these star systems have provided astronomers with data on stellar masses, sizes, and temperatures. This atlas provides data for more than 300 binary systems. The data are presented in both graphical and tabular form. The graphical display is the primary purpose of this atlas. Each system is shown in different phases of its orbital revolution accompanied by the corresponding light curve. The atlas is arranged in sections by relative orbital size. A glossary of terms and an index arranged by constellation are included. There is also a chapter with suggestions on using the atlas in the classroom.

The authors have provided a useful teaching tool by showing the great variety of binary systems, light curves, and system dynamics. Recommended for astronomy collections and for the interested amateur.
—**Margaret F. Dominy**

1930. **The Visual Dictionary of the Universe.** New York, Dorling Kindersley, 1993. 64p. illus. index. (Eyewitness Visual Dictionaries). $15.95. QB68.E94. 520'.3. LC 93-22419. ISBN 1-56458-336-8.

The goal of this work is to provide the reader "instant access to the specialized vocabulary of astronomy and cosmology in a way that is clear, informative, and easy to understand." In addition to meeting this goal, the dictionary also does an excellent job of explaining the systems of the universe and how the nearly 3,000 specialized terms identified fit into the larger context of these interrelated systems.

Following the format of other works in this series, *Universe* is arranged in 2-page topical sections that present an array of 200 stunning graphics, including photographs, models, and illustrations. Coverage in the 26 sections includes broad system overviews (e.g., the universe, galaxies, the Milky Way, the solar system), specifics (e.g., stars, the Sun, the Earth, Uranus, asteroids and meteoroids), and related topics (e.g., observing space, manned space exploration, lunar exploration). A separate section is devoted to such astronomical data as specifications for the sun and all the planets, a list of famous comets and solar and lunar eclipses, lists of the brightest stars and the nearest stars, and a table describing the local group of galaxies. A roughly 60-term glossary and an index to the 3,000 terms identified in the dictionary conclude this excellent work. Given its reasonable price, it is heartily recommended for all public libraries and for both elementary and secondary school libraries.—**G. Kim Dority**

CHEMISTRY

Bibliography

1931. Bottle, R. T., and J. F. B. Rowland, eds. **Information Sources in Chemistry.** 4th ed. New Providence, N.J., K. G. Saur/Reed Reference Publishing, 1993. 341p. index. (Guides to Information Sources). $75.00. QD8.5.147. 540'.72. LC 92-17946. ISBN 1-85739-016-4.

This is an invaluable tool for the information specialist or researcher in the field of chemistry who is seeking information sources. The book is organized into three major areas: general sources, pure chemistry, and industrial chemistry. General sources include the primary literature, abstracting and indexing services, dictionaries and other references, online searching, and dealing with chemical structures on the computer. Specifics within the fields of pure chemistry and industrial chemistry are addressed (e.g., standard tables of physico-chemical data, patents, government publications, gray literature). A wide range of subjects is covered, from inorganic chemistry to agrochemicals.

Written in a straightforward style, the publication is easy to read and use, either from the chapter overview approach or by using the index. Ample references indicate well-researched topics. Cross-indexing within the text is excellent, and an index-glossary of acronyms and databases is included.

The primarily British contributors have a rich background in research, information science, or both. An area of potential weakness in the book is that in some chapters the information is slanted toward British sources. This compact volume should be of interest to all people seeking information sources in chemistry.
—**Patricia S. Wilson**

Dictionaries and Encyclopedias

1932. Ash, Michael, and Irene Ash, comps. **Chemical Tradename Dictionary: The Comprehensive Sourcebook for Locating and Identifying Chemical Tradename Product Lines....** New York, VCH, 1993. 529p. $85.00. TP9.A73. 660'.03. LC 92-35154. ISBN 1-56081-625-2.

This book provides a link between about 10,000 trade names of chemical products, which are arranged alphabetically with their manufacturers and general descriptions of their industrial applications. There is also a list of manufacturers' addresses. While of limited utility to academic chemists, this compilation could save industrial chemists a lot of time. [R: Choice, July/Aug 93, pp. 1743-44]
—**Harold Goldwhite**

1933. **Hawley's Condensed Chemical Dictionary.** 12th ed. By Richard J. Lewis, Sr. New York, Van Nostrand Reinhold, 1993. 1275p. $69.95. QD5.C5. 540'.3. LC 92-18951. ISBN 0-442-01131-8.

Hawley's has long been recognized as one of the standard chemical dictionaries, and this new edition continues the features that made the previous editions so useful (see ARBA 88, entry 1739 and references therein). More than 1,000 new terms have been added, and many citations have been updated by the addition of data on hazardous properties. This makes it especially surprising that the entry on superconductivity remains unchanged since the previous edition and still lists 25K as the maximum transition temperature. While there are other examples of this problem, these cases are fortunately rare. Not only are the definitions clear and understandable, but—equally important—the clean layout, readable typeface, and extensive use of cross-referencing make it a pleasure to use this book. Although this work contains fewer citations than some of its competitors, the discussion is more extensive, which will often be more useful to the reader than a short definition.

Other valuable features included are Chemical Abstract Service numbers; properties of, preparation, uses, and hazards for the chemical compounds; and brief biographical sketches of Nobel prize-winning chemists. Three helpful appendixes are provided, covering the origins of some chemical terms, highlights in the history of chemistry, and an alphabetical list of the manufacturers of trademarked products. This is an excellent reference; it should be seriously considered by libraries planning to update their collection of chemical dictionaries.—**Harry E. Pence**

1934. Howard, Philip H., and Michael Neal. **Dictionary of Chemical Names and Synonyms.** Chelsea, Mich., Lewis, 1992. 1v. (various paging). $149.95. TP9.H65. 660'.03. LC 92-9160. ISBN 0-87371-396-6.

This massive dictionary contains chemical names, manufacturers' names, Chemical Abstracts Service (CAS) Registry Numbers, and molecular formulas for some 20,000 significant compounds chosen from major industrial products and compounds of concern in the environment. They are arranged in three lists: by CAS Registry Number; alphabetically, including synonyms; and by formula. The volume is useful for determining the chemical identity and CAS Registry Number (for further online searching) of a compound for which only a manufacturer's name is available. It is well produced and clearly arranged. Because of its size and weight it would be nice if its contents were made available in CD-ROM format. [R: Choice, Feb 93, p. 940]—**Harold Goldwhite**

1935. **McGraw-Hill Encyclopedia of Chemistry.** 2d ed. Sybil P. Parker, ed. New York, McGraw-Hill, 1993. 1236p. illus. index. $95.50. QD5.M36. 540. LC 92-41482. ISBN 0-07-045455-8.

This is a comprehensive encyclopedia of current chemistry that covers, in hundreds of articles, all areas of the subject plus some topics in physics needed to understand modern chemistry. There is generous use of diagrams and structural formulas, as well as a comprehensive index. Each article has a selective list of references. The authoritatively written articles are mainly drawn from the *McGraw-Hill Encyclopedia of Science and Technology* (see ARBA 93, entry 1446), with some updating. The resulting book is a kind of super-textbook, useful for readers with a background in chemistry, but to be used with discretion. For example, the article on fullerenes is current, with a 1991 reference; that on computational chemistry has a 1982 citation as its most recent. [R: Choice, Oct 93, p. 268; JAL, Sept 93, p. 275; RQ, Winter 93, p. 290; WLB, Sept 93, pp. 119-21]—**Harold Goldwhite**

1936. Noether, Dorit, and Herman Noether. **Encyclopedic Dictionary of Chemical Technology.** New York, VCH, 1993. 297p. $59.50. ISBN 1-56081-329-3.

This is a concise reference tool designed for nontechnical and specialized chemical practitioners. It serves as a bridge between general and specialized dictionaries as well as between dictionaries and encyclopedias. It does not generally include physical properties; however, many illustrations and brief paragraphs are provided throughout the volume. Other features include tables of acronyms used for chemicals, processes, and institutions, along with a proliferation of abbreviations. Cross-references are used as necessary.

Librarians and others with limited budgets will find this a valuable and useful tool to have available for patrons and ready-reference. Highly recommended for individuals who need brief descriptions of technical terms.—**Estelle A. Davis**

1937. Patterson, Austin M. **Patterson's German-English Dictionary for Chemists.** Revised by James C. Cox. 4th ed. New York, John Wiley, 1992. 890p. $64.95. QD5.P3. 540'.3. LC 90-45365. ISBN 0-471-66991-1.

This German-to-English dictionary is excellent for translation purposes. Even though it was written for chemists, scientists in other areas will find it invaluable. The well-documented introduction gives the format, rules, variations, and arrangement of the entries. Reading it is essential to the use of the dictionary. Features include verbs listed not only in present tense but also with past tense and past participle in parentheses. In the appropriate alphabetical listings the past tense and past participle are separately defined for the convenience of the translator. Nouns, adjectives, and adverbs are listed in appropriate detail. Gender and plural forms for nouns are included. Parts of speech for other words, such as adjectives and adverbs, are also listed, making this a very user-friendly dictionary. Three tables are provided: old-style German letters, the Greek alphabet, and abbreviations. This dictionary is recommended for those who need to translate German scientific information into English.—**Patricia S. Wilson**

1938. Wittfoht, A. M. **Plastics Technical Dictionary: English-German, German-English.** Munich, Carl Hanser Verlag; distr., New York, Oxford University Press, 1992. 1v. (various paging). illus. index. $85.00. ISBN 0-19-520952-4.

This book is an unchanged but handy one-volume version of the original three-volume dictionary published in 1981. It is an excellent technical dictionary of great value to those seeking equivalents of English or German terms related to plastics technology. Each of its 3 sections contains some 500 pages and is paginated separately. The third section is the key to the work. It has 26 parts, each devoted to an important topic in plastics technology (e.g., blow molding, coating, foams, mills, mixers, presses, spinning, welding). Parts average 20 pages in length and contain many illustrations, with clear indications of how the terms in the 2 languages are applied to machines and processes. This third section has subject indexes in each language. The first and second sections are English-German and German-English plastics technical dictionaries; they include all the terms shown in the third section, and are also well illustrated.—**Harold Goldwhite**

Directories

1939. Warr, Wendy, Peter Willett, and Geoff Downs, eds. **Directory of Chemistry Software 1992.** Oxford, England, Cherwell Scientific Publishing and Washington, D.C., American Chemical Society, 1992. 204p. index. $34.95pa. ISBN 0-9518236-0-4.

The purpose of this directory is to provide comprehensive coverage of scientific software for chemists. Detailed information helps the user select software for either personal or laboratory use. A variety of hardware platforms, prices, a description of the capabilities of the program, and a summary description are provided for each entry. Several packages are associated with molecular modeling and computational chemistry. Most are designed to perform particular functions, usually with limited facilities for transferring information to and from packages. A majority of the programs are PC-based due to the standardization and ease of programming graphics for the IBM PC and the Macintosh.

The directory does not generally provide information on freeware, shareware, or noncommercial packages. Statistics and mathematics packages are also not included, and chemical databases are not covered (with the exception of the Protein Structure Databank). This directory is highly recommended to those in academic settings, research-oriented institutions, and industry.—**Estelle A. Davis**

Handbooks and Yearbooks

1940. Groom, Nigel. **The Perfume Handbook.** New York, Routledge, Chapman & Hall, 1992. 323p. illus. $29.95. ISBN 0-412-46320-2.

Reminiscent of Neiman-Marcus and the famous $250 chocolate chip cookie recipe, many couture designers have preferred to keep the multiple ingredients of modern perfumes a secret. *The Perfume Handbook* is not the place to find such formulas. In the preface Groom states that the intended purpose of the book is "reasserting the importance of the trained perfumer and reaffirming them as artists." Presented in dictionary style, the book contains entries for hundreds of plants used in perfumery, names of perfumes and the houses that create them, and artists and craftspeople who design and manufacture the flacons in which perfumes are contained. There are longer entries for several topics, including perfume, perfume burner, care of perfume, choice of perfume, classification of fragrances, perfume containers, perfume creation, perfume families, and perfume making at home. Modern concerns, such as the use of animal perfume materials, are addressed.

For scientific identification, botanical names are provided. Where more than one botanical name exists, all are listed. A bibliography of sources appears at the back of the book. Appendix A contains a list of fragrances, most of which are still being marketed. Appendix B contains recipes and formulas to make potpourri and perfume at home (which cannot hope to simulate the quality fragrances produced by commercial perfumeries). This book will be of value to people who wish to try making fragrances themselves or who have a general interest in perfume. [R: LJ, 15 April 93, p. 60]—**Marilynn Green**

Indexes

1941. Lee, C. C. **Environmental Law Index to Chemicals.** Rockville, Md., Government Institutes, 1993. 324p. $55.00pa. ISBN 0-86587-338-0.

This is a useful guide to more than 3,000 chemical compounds that are subject to regulation under major environmental laws, including the Clean Air Act, the Clean Water Act, the Occupational Safety and Health Act, the Toxic Substances Control Act, and the Superfund Act. The compounds are listed alphabetically by name, together with their Chemical Abstracts Service (CAS) registry numbers and a notation of the acts under which each is regulated. There is also a separate numerically ordered list of the CAS registry numbers and the corresponding chemical name. One minor annoyance is that the definitions of abbreviations in the main alphabetical listing follow rather than precede the listing.—**Harold Goldwhite**

Thesauri

1942. Ash, Michael, and Irene Ash, comps. **Industrial Chemical Thesaurus.** 2d ed. New York, VCH, 1992. 2v. $295.00/set. Z695.1.C5I52. 025.4'954. LC 92-22095. ISBN 1-56081-615-5.

This set contains approximately 40,000 up-to-date, international trade names by which more than 6,000 generic chemicals are known and marketed worldwide. The chemical products that are included find application in the surfactant, paint, agriculture, cosmetic, food, plastic, elastomer, and specialty chemical industries, as well as numerous other areas. Volume 1 contains alphabetical entries of industrial chemicals, including synonyms, CAS (Chemical Abstract Service) registry number, definition, classification, formula, properties, precautions, toxicity data, and applications. This is followed by the entry's trade name equivalents and then by trade names that contain that chemical. Volume 2 lists all trade name products alphabetically followed by their manufacturers and the chemical entries under which the trade name is grouped in the first volume. This makes it possible to find chemical alternatives for a product from only one trade name. This volume also contains a directory of 1,200 chemical producers including corporate offices, divisions, and international branches. This edition provides data about generic chemicals and includes a separate list of trade name products containing the chemical entry as a major constituent. A variety of indexes make the volume easy to use. There is no indication that a computer software version is also available, as was true with the first edition (see ARBA 87, entry 228).

While nowhere near as comprehensive (or as expensive) as Beilstein's *Handbuch der Organischen Chemie* (Springer-Verlag, 1918-), this book will be a useful tool for the chemical technologist, formulator, and market researcher; purchasing departments; and other professionals involved with chemical products and their applications. [R: Choice, July/Aug 93, p. 1750]—**Andrew G. Torok**

EARTH AND PLANETARY SCIENCES

General Works

1943. Cormier, Chantal. **Canadian Quaternary Vocabulary. Vocabulaire Canadien du Quaternaire.** Ottawa, Department of the Secretary of State of Canada, 1992. 154p. (Terminology Bulletin, 209). $25.95pa. (U.S.). 551.7'9'0971. ISBN 0-660-57486-1.

The specialized vocabulary of Quaternary geology, especially as used in North America, is treated in this English-French/French-English dictionary. The main part of the dictionary, an English-French vocabulary, includes about 900 main entries. This section also includes selected definitions, taken from the *Glossary of Geology* (see ARBA 89, entry 1660), in both English and French. A French-English glossary follows.

Roughly half of the terms found in this book are also directly translated in the 2d edition of J.-P. Michel and R. W. Fairbridge's *Dictionary of Earth Sciences: English-French, French-English* (Wiley, 1992). Individual elements of terms consisting of two or more parts in the *Canadian Quaternary Vocabulary*, but not directly translated in the Michel and Fairbridge book, can sometimes be found as separate entries in the dictionary, so there is even more overlap between the two books. When translations differ, however, those in the *Canadian Quaternary Vocabulary* seem to be better for North Americans.

Most people needing only an occasional translation of a term related to Quaternary geology can get by using Michel and Fairbridge's dictionary. Specialists dealing with the North American Quaternary, however, will find this new book helpful.—**Joseph Hannibal**

1944. **Oxford Illustrated Encyclopedia of the Universe.** Archie Roy, ed. New York, Oxford University Press, 1992. 199p. illus. $45.00. ISBN 0-19-869140-8.

This is another in the useful series of Oxford encyclopedias; it parallels those on the physical world and the natural world. In excess of 1,100 entries cover stellar structure and evolution, astronomical instruments and measurements, characteristics of planets and their satellites, the solar system, and cosmological matters of black holes and pulsars. Because descriptions and definitions in a scientific encyclopedia depend on use of multiple technical terms, such words are marked with asterisks to indicate cross-references to related subjects. (There are probably a couple of thousand asterisks.) Brief biographies of important astronomers and their contributions are included. There are more than 100 high-quality drawings and photographs illustrating astronomical laws, depicting planetary surfaces, or showing stellar distribution in the northern and southern hemispheres. These illustrations effectively enhance the text. Tables of astronomical data and physical constants are included. For readers of *Scientific American* or the weekly science section of the *New York Times*, and others who need a concise definition or explanation of a technical term, this is a useful book. [R: Choice, Oct 93, p. 271; LAR, Aug 93, p. 462; RBB, 1 Dec 93, p. 716]—**David Bardack**

1945. Rivard, Denis. **Ozone Layer Dictionary. Dictionnaire de la Couche d'Ozone.** Ottawa, Department of the Secretary of State of Canada, 1993. 493p. (Terminology Bulletin, 218). $48.05pa. (U.S.). 363.73'84. ISBN 0-660-58897-8.

This new edition has been revised to include some 3,000 terms. The original French-language work (*Dictionnaire de la Protection de la Couche d'Ozone* [Terminology and Linguistic Services Directorate, 1989]) has been improved by the addition of English definitions that parallel the existing French definitions. All equivalences have been reviewed according to the most up-to-date sources, resulting in the addition of new technical terminology. Entries are composed of brief definitions presented in a simple glossary format without punctuation marks, word derivations, or parts of speech indicated. The terms are in alphabetical order according to the English key words; there is also a French-English vocabulary.

Among the compounds commonly known as halogens, chlorofluorocarbons (CFCs) are strongly suspected of contributing to ozone depletion. The list of CFCs in this dictionary provides the full systematic name of the chemical products for all the halogenated compounds. Readers will also find terms relating to remote sensing instruments that are carried on board satellites, balloons, and rockets and that are used to measure these chemical substances. Recommended for undergraduate college and university libraries and for those using terminology related to the protection of the ozone layer.—**Marilynn Green**

1946. **The Visual Dictionary of the Earth.** New York, Dorling Kindersley, 1993. 64p. illus. index. (Eyewitness Visual Dictionaries). $15.95. QE7.E94. 550.'3. LC 93-18571. ISBN 1-56458-335-X.

This recent addition to the Eyewitness Visual Dictionaries series offers a fascinating, graphically stunning geological overview of the Earth and all its systems. Included among its 25 two-page topical sections are coverage of geological time; the rock cycle; mineral resources; and processes such as faulting and folding, mountain building, and weathering and erosion. In addition, the Earth's waters (rivers, lakes and groundwater, coastlines, oceans, and seas) are addressed, as well as the atmosphere and weather. Similar to other volumes in this series, *Earth* features exquisitely reproduced photographs, models, and illustrations presented in two-page topical spreads. Concise explanatory narratives introduce each topic, placing the graphics and their identifying terms within the broader context of the planet's geological system. A text section listing Earth data (e.g., highest, longest, largest, deepest), a one-page glossary that defines some 60 terms, and a 3,000-word index round out the dictionary.

Although the book's purpose is identification (rather than definition) of terms, the concise, well-written explanatory material that introduces each two-page layout makes this an excellent guide for anyone seeking to understand the Earth and how it works. It would be a worthwhile addition to the science collections of public, elementary, and secondary school libraries.—**G. Kim Dority**

Climatology

1947. Bair, Frank E., ed. **Weather of U.S. Cities: A Guide to the Weather Histories of 270 Key Cities and Weather Observation Stations in the United States and Its Island Territories....** 4th ed. Detroit, Gale, 1992. 1080p. $200.00. ISBN 0-8103-4827-6.

This updated edition includes data through 1990 for cities in all 50 states; Washington, D.C.; Puerto Rico; and 9 Pacific islands. Libraries that already have the 6th edition of *The Weather Almanac* from the same publisher (see ARBA 93, entry 1722) may not need this book. *The Weather Almanac* has some great maps and explanations that are not included here. However, this volume does include data for nearly three times more U.S. cities. The normal data is based on the years 1951-1980 and the extremes are given through 1985; a second grouping for each station has data through 1990. The normal and extreme data should have been brought up-to-date; nevertheless, in the book's present format it does give a little extra information to readers alert to these differences. This compilation or *The Weather Almanac* should be available for the general reader in all libraries. (Perhaps this information could be made available on a computer network, so that each library would not need to have such a book.)—**Allen E. Staver**

1948. **Climatological Atlas of Snowfall and Snow Depth for the Northeastern United States and Southeastern Canada.** By Richard P. Cember and Daniel S. Wilks. Ithaca, N.Y., Northeast Regional Climate Center, Cornell University, 1993. 1v. (unpaged). maps. (Northeast Regional Climate Center Research Series, no.RR 93-1). $30.00 spiralbound.

This volume is a record of snowfall derived from hundreds of stations in the eastern United States and Canada. It presents, in statistically useful percentile format, monthly and annual snowfall, snow depths on a weekly basis throughout the winter, and length and depth of snow cover. The records cover more than a century for many stations. An introduction explains the data and their statistical treatment, and the maps present the information in contour form throughout the region covered.

Because of the widespread interest in snowfall and snow cover, the book is also useful as a teaching resource in science classes: It demonstrates that the measurement of snowfall can be and has been standardized. Meteorologists are aware that almost any failure to properly account for drifting, melting, and other processes spuriously decreases the measured snowfall. Careless estimates are always on the low side, which may partly account for probably the most widely and firmly held mistaken climatological belief: that snowfalls have decreased greatly over recent decades. One of the purposes of science is to dispel erroneous conclusions, and a well-taught science course should include that as one of its goals. Thus, compilations of data such as this one are also useful as teaching aids in science. Partly for this reason, the atlas is recommended for many libraries, especially those serving schools at all levels.—**Arthur R. Upgren**

1949. Maunder, W. John, comp. **Dictionary of Global Climate Change.** New York, Routledge, Chapman & Hall, 1992. 240p. $45.00. QC981.8.C5M38. 551.6. LC 92-19059. ISBN 0-412-03901-X.

This book is more than a dictionary; it is a condensed encyclopedia covering such diverse topics as volcanic eruptions and their effects, chlorofluorocarbons, ozone, methane, the carbon cycle, sunspots, the pH scale, and the "slow climate system: oceans & glaciers" with their slower response time. An "informed perspective on environmental matters of profound importance to us all" summarizes its purpose. It has explanations of scientific terms and concepts; meanings of acronyms; and the history, tasks, and findings of many international organizations, such as the World Meteorological Organization's Commission on Climatology (presided over by Maunder). The origins and roles of many other projects involved in monitoring climatic change are also summarized. Results from several international conferences include the most recent one in Rio de Janeiro in June 1992. The Intergovernmental Panel on Climate Change's assessment reports are particularly noteworthy even though it is stated that "confidence in (their) regional estimates is low."

Maunder wrote a classic—*The Value of the Weather* (Methuen, 1970)—and now provides this volume. It will be valuable to both the casual reader looking for a definition and to researchers interested in the findings and ongoing work of international groups working on climatic change, its effects, and possible control. [R: Choice, May 93, p. 1445]—**Allen E. Staver**

Geology

1950. **GeoRef: References and Selected Abstracts to the World's Literature in Geology.** [CD-ROM]. Norwood, Mass., SilverPlatter, 1990-1993. 3 discs. Hardware requirements: IBM PC or compatible; 640K of RAM with 500K free; hard disk drive with 3.2MB free; MS-DOS or PC-DOS 3.1 or higher; MS-DOS CD-ROM Extensions 2.0 or higher. $3,100.00/set.

GeoRef, the CD-ROM version of the American Geological Institute's geoscience database, is a set containing more than 1.5 million records covering North America since 1785 and other areas of the world since 1933. GeoRef corresponds to four major geoscience publications: *Bibliography of North American Geology* (U.S. Geological Survey, various dates), *Bibliography and Index of Geology Exclusive of North America* (Geological Society of America, 1933-1968), *Geophysical Abstracts* (U.S. Geological Survey, 1929-1971), and *Bibliography and Index of Geology* (see ARBA 90, entries 1763-64). Due to the manner in which the American Geological Institute stores information, the records are not divided strictly by year. Disc 3 primarily holds the most current data, 1988 to the present, but does contain some records with publication years prior to 1988. Similarly, disc 2 has the highest concentration of records with publication years 1980-1987 but also contains records prior to 1980 and after 1987. Disc 1 contains mainly records with the earliest publication years. Therefore, for complete retrieval, especially when searching for publication dates, searches should be performed on all three discs. SilverPlatter is one of the major CD-ROM publishers, and all SilverPlatter CD-ROMs have similar interfaces, so users with other products from them will be able to get up and running on this database quickly and easily. Each SilverPlatter database has an online guide that outlines its unique features, describing the database fields and listing special terminology. A single keystroke brings up the guide at any point in the search, with a menu of guide topics, each of which will provide several screens of information.—**Janet Mongan**

Hydrology

1951. Demayo, Adrian, and Evan Watt. **Glossary of Water Terms: English-French. Glossaire de l'Eau: Francais-Anglais.** Cambridge, Ont., Canadian Water Resources Association, 1993. 1v. (various paging). $17.50pa. 553'.703. ISBN 0-9694535-3-1.

This bilingual glossary contains more than 500 entries emanating from France as well as from the French-Canadian provinces. The term *water* has been interpreted in its widest sense to include soil science, geology, aquatic engineering, food science, weeds, and horticulture. The emphasis is on ecology and the environment. The simple dictionary style is clear and easy to use. Entries follow one another in alphabetical order letter-by-letter (e.g., *PH shock* follows *photosynthesis*). Parts of speech, gender, and number are given for the French as applicable. Next, the synonyms (if any) and the definition are given. Closely related terms appear in parentheses following a *see also* notation. A sentence or phrase using the entry word appears in parentheses at the end of most entries. Recommended for reference collections in public, academic, or agricultural libraries and for those with an interest in oceanography, offshore technology, geology, or shoreline and waterway management.—**Marilynn Green**

1952. **International Glossary of Hydrology.** Paris, Unesco and Geneva, World Meteorological Organization; distr., Lanham, Md., UNIPUB, 1992. 413p. $45.00pa. ISBN 92-3-002745-6.

In 1960, at the first session of the World Meteorological Organization (WMO) Commission for Hydrometeorology, the need for a comprehensive and accurate glossary of hydrological terminology was recognized. Unesco, as part of its International Hydrological Decade beginning in 1964, had a similar goal. The two groups combined forces and in 1974 jointly published the first edition of this glossary (see ARBA 76, entry 1472). Since that date, numerous joint panels have met to improve the work and update it, in light of new technology and terminology. This edition has been completely revised and now contains approximately 1,800 terms, versus the 1,600 in the old edition. (Actually, there are 400-plus new terms due to the elimination of obsolete ones.)

This edition is in three main parts: equivalent terms in English, French, Russian, and Spanish, with their definitions; alphabetical indexes in the same languages; and the Universal Decimal Classification (UDC) for hydrology. Each English term has a serial number that is the key to the index. Synonymous terms are cross-referenced, as are variations between U.S. and British spelling and usage. The quality of the publication is a reflection of the long, hard work that took place between the two editions. With the number of critical hydrology-related problems in the world, as well as the large amount of work and money going into solving them, this glossary will be much used.—**Robert J. Havlik**

1953. Maidment, David R., ed. **Handbook of Hydrology.** New York, McGraw-Hill, 1993. 1v. (various paging). illus. maps. index. $110.50. GB662.5.M35. 551.48. LC 92-18193. ISBN 0-07-039732-5.

Hydrology is the science of the transport of water and its constituents on or near the land surface via precipitation, evaporation, infiltration, groundwater flow, runoff, and streamflow. Since the International Hydrological Decade (1965-1974), so much new information has accumulated that a new handbook on the subject has been necessary. The task fell on Maidment of the University of Texas at Austin, who is also editor of the *Journal of Hydrology*. More than 50 experts have contributed to the 29 chapters of this exhaustive volume. The chapters are grouped into four sections: the hydrologic cycle, covering the flow of water through the phases of the hydrologic cycle; hydrologic transport, treating the motion of constituents and contaminants carried with the flow; hydrologic statistics, dealing with the analysis of hydrologic data and quantification of uncertainty; and hydrologic technology, describing computer programs, advanced data collection and forecasting methods, and procedures for hydrologic design. Photographs, illustrations, maps, tables, charts, formulas, and extensive, up-to-date bibliographies abound; there are also an appendix of hydrologic unit conversions and a 48-page index. Anyone who has to deal with the Earth's water resources in any capacity will find this handbook a necessity.—**Robert J. Havlik**

1954. Miller, E. Willard, and Ruby M. Miller. **Water Quality and Availability: A Reference Handbook.** Santa Barbara, Calif., ABC-Clio, 1992. 430p. maps. index. (Contemporary World Issues). $39.50. TD223.M53. 333.91'0973. LC 92-33057. ISBN 0-87436-647-X.

This volume begins with an introductory chapter on the background of water sources, water supply, the means for increasing water supply, and the distribution and variability of precipitation. Another section gives a short synopsis of the laws and regulations governing water supply, irrigation, water quality, flood control, and oil and water pollution. Most of this book is made up of sections 5 and 6. Section 5 is an annotated bibliography of reference books, books, journal articles, and governmental reports on water-related topics. While coverage in this section is acceptable, a wonderful reference and source of data, *The Water Encyclopedia* (see ARBA 91, entry 1785), is not included. However, bibliographies from Vance Publications are well represented; they make up more than a third of the reference book section. Most of the items in this section are from the 1980s, although a couple of classics from the 1950s are listed. Section 6 consists of a bibliographical list of films, filmstrips, and videocassettes. Topics covered include groundwater, conservation, oil spills, irrigation, and acid precipitation. Each entry includes viewing time, a one-sentence description, and the address and telephone number of the vendor or supplier.

It is unclear what group might best benefit from this book. Any academic library with a strong water quality collection would have the data books, journals, and indexes needed to find this and more up-to-date information, and individuals probably do not need something this limited in time coverage. This is possibly for public policy and general collections. [R: Choice, May 93, p. 1445; RBB, 1 April 93, p. 1460; VOYA, Aug 93, p. 191]—**Susan B. Ardis**

Mineralogy

1955. Keller, Peter C. **Gemstones of East Africa.** Phoenix, Ariz., Geoscience Press, 1992. 144p. index. $50.00. QE392.5.A3K4. 553.8. ISBN 0-945005-08-3.

East Africa is one of the world's richest but least-known sources of gems. Similar to Brazil and Sri Lanka in its geological structure, it too has deposits of nearly all known families of important gems. It is an area just coming into importance, with little information predating 1970, and until now there has been no comprehensive survey of the region. Keller, a noted geologist, natural history museum director, and author, has assembled this overview of East African gems. He begins with an introductory chapter that describes the geological history of the region and the resulting major type of gem in each formation: diamonds in the granite Tanzanian Shield; nearly every gem other than diamonds in the schist, gneiss, crystalline limestone Mozambique Belt; and sapphires in the Rift Valley. Descriptions of these regions include maps, illustrations, and numerous references.

Remaining chapters provide in-depth information on each of the gem families. For each gem the following information is provided: a map showing distribution and major deposits and locations, the mining history of the gem, properties of the gem, and important gems mined at each site. Each chapter also includes photographs of the gem and provides references for further study. The result is a well-written, well-presented introduction to an area of increasing importance to geologists and mineralogists.—**Ann E. Prentice**

1956. O'Donoghue, Michael. **An Illustrated Guide to Rocks & Minerals.** New York, Smithmark, 1992. 192p. illus. index. $24.98. ISBN 0-8317-6389-2.

The author's intent is to create an interest in rocks and minerals that will motivate the reader to seek out additional sources of information. The initial sections of the book provide coverage of such topics as how rocks and minerals are formed, mineral chemistry, and how to identify minerals. For most of these subjects there is too little information to provide a useful overview. The main section of the book contains illustrations and descriptions of approximately 100 minerals arranged according to the London Natural History Museum's *Chemical Index of Minerals*, with elements followed by compounds and classes. Chemical compound, form, habit, hardness, specific gravity, and major location are given for each mineral. Minerals included range from the well known to the less well known. Given that only 3 percent of the known minerals are included, it would be useful to know on what basis these minerals were selected.

The final section provides information on major mineral deposits. Of the 38 listed, two-thirds are in Europe and the United States. Asia and Africa, which have many of the world's richest deposits, are represented by a combined total of six sites. Of the 35 museum collections listed, a third are in Russia. Here again, a rationale for inclusion of sites would be helpful. Although the photography makes this a pleasing book, the content is not as useful as that which is available in other introductions to rocks and minerals. [R: RBB, 1 Feb 93, p. 1002; SLJ, Jan 93, p. 146]—**Ann E. Prentice**

1957. Schumann, Walter. **Handbook of Rocks, Minerals, and Gemstones.** Boston, Houghton Mifflin, 1993. 380p. illus. index. $35.00; $18.95pa. QE433.8.S3813. 552. LC 92-28505. ISBN 0-395-51138-0; 0-395-51137-2pa.

This is just what the rock collector has been looking for: a well-illustrated, easily carried guide to the most common rocks and minerals. For this handbook the author has selected 600 of the most commonly found minerals from the approximately 3,000 that have been identified. General information is provided on such topics as the origin of minerals, with emphasis placed on those properties most useful for identification. Brief, clearly written information is given on various ways to identify minerals, such as by color, hardness, or specific gravity.

The handbook is divided into three sections—minerals, rocks, and meteorites—with each section further subdivided by major category. Within the mineral section are three categories: rock formers, which include minerals such as quartz, feldspar, and mica; constituents of ores, such as copper and silver; and precious stones. Minerals and rocks are grouped by similar type within their subdivisions, making identification easier. To locate a specific rock or mineral, one must use the index. Information for each mineral includes several criteria for identification plus localities where it is commonly found. On the facing page is an excellent illustration of the mineral. Illustrations of precious stones are of both cut and uncut gems. The section on rocks provides useful introductory information on rock formation and classification. This section is subdivided into igneous and sedimentary rocks and follows a format similar to that of the section on minerals. A very brief section on meteorites and their formation and identification completes the handbook.—**Ann E. Prentice**

1958. Sinkankas, John. **Gemology: An Annotated Bibliography.** Metuchen, N.J., Scarecrow, 1993. 2v. index. $179.50/set. Z5998.S55. 016.5538. LC 92-42847. ISBN 0-8108-2652-6.

Sinkankas, perhaps the most outstanding gemologist of the twentieth century, has created an impressive bibliography on his subject. Arranged by author, some 7,500 treatises on gemology, gems, and the jewelry trade appear in this work. Entries begin with a brief biographical sketch of the author and continue with the title, collation, notes, contents, and annotation. The annotations are extremely well written and are successful in conveying the essence of the work in hand; they are excellent examples of the best in contemporary modern bibliography. The volumes are illustrated throughout with pictures of major works in the field. There is a brief, lively sketch of Sinkankas at the end of the set that chronicles his role in twentieth-century gemology. An index is provided at the end of volume 2. It appears to be of the same high quality as the rest of the work.

Most reference libraries will find this set useful. Leads for many reference questions will be found through this, the most comprehensive work on the subject. Public interest in gems and gemology will be heightened through browsing of this work. [R: Choice, Oct 93, p. 273; RBB, Aug 93, pp. 2088-90; RQ, Winter 93, p. 286]—**Ralph Lee Scott**

Paleontology

1959. Benton, Michael. **Dinosaur and Other Prehistoric Animal Factfinder.** New York, Chambers Kingfisher Graham, 1992. 256p. illus. maps. index. $12.95pa. QE862.D5B45. 560. LC 92-53119. ISBN 1-85697-802-8.

More than 200 of the best-known dinosaurs and other prehistoric animals are arranged alphabetically within their scientifically recognized orders in this fact finder. Information boxes at the top of each page provide the name of the animal and an explanation of its meaning, a pronunciation guide, the individual who named the animal, and the year in which it was discovered. Geographical sites are indicated on an outline map of the continents. True dinosaurs are treated slightly differently from other prehistoric animals. A map shows the period—Triassic, Jurassic, or Cretaceous—during which the dinosaur lived and the approximate position of the continents during that period. Black dots on the maps identify where dinosaur fossils have been discovered. The geological age of the animal is shown on a "time ribbon," offering a quick way to compare the ages of different species. A silhouette shows the animal's size relative to an adult human, with the height and length given. The color of the silhouette indicates which suborder the dinosaur belongs to.

The descriptions are thoroughly up-to-date, encapsulating the latest information about the appearance, lifestyle, and relationships of the dinosaurs and other prehistoric creatures. Opening chapters summarize theories of their origins, fossil hunting in the 1800s, major recent finds, how the Earth's strata are dated and analyzed, how fossils are formed and classified, and how the various groups of prehistoric animals are related. Supporting and enriching this text, and evoking the world of the past with amazing vividness, are hundreds of highly detailed paintings and drawings. Line drawings of representative skeletons abound; special charts illustrate how major groups of animals are related to those living today. Curiously, a two-page spread explains the evolution of modern-day humans and Neanderthal man (under *E*), but Neanderthal man (as a fossil) is presented under *N*. Both are indexed, however, under *humans*.

The guide under review compares favorably with *Macmillan Children's Guide to Dinosaurs and Other Prehistoric Animals* (see ARBA 93, entry 1732) and *The New Illustrated Dinosaur Dictionary* by Helen Roney Sattler (Lothrop, Lee & Shepard, 1990). The Macmillan guide brings dinosaurs and other prehistoric animals to life with handsome, detailed, full-color illustrations; it also addresses current controversies that surround the study of dinosaurs: How did they evolve? Were they warm-blooded? Are they related to birds? How did they become extinct? *The New Illustrated Dinosaur Dictionary* offers more than 250 black-and-white line drawings and synthesizes current research for nonscientists.

Dinosaur and Other Prehistoric Animal Fact Finder seems certain to capture dinosaur fans' attention in a big way. For the wonderful illustrations and the lucidity of its text, it will establish itself as a major storehouse of current information on some of the largest and most extraordinary animals that ever existed on Earth. [R: SLJ, Feb 93, p. 120]—**Judy Gay Matthews**

1960. Lambert, David. **The Ultimate Dinosaur Book.** New York, Dorling Kindersley, 1993. 192p. illus. maps. index. $29.95. QE862.D5L4246. 567.9'1. LC 93-21885. ISBN 1-56458-304-X.

Dinosaurs were successful for a very long time—about 160 million years. During that time they adapted to a wide range of conditions and environments. This adaptation contributed to the success of the dinosaurs and to their incredible diversification. Despite variations, all dinosaurs shared a basic body plan. Some were as large as a whale, and others were no bigger than a chicken. There were two-legged, four-legged, clawed, hoofed, fanged, and toothless forms.

Beginning with theories of how dinosaurs evolved, the introductory section examines how dinosaurs lived and may have died and the consequences of fossilization, excavation, and reconstruction that have resulted in lifelike museum displays. At the core of *The Ultimate Dinosaur Book* (produced in association with the National History Museum, London) are 55 detailed dinosaur profiles. Every major group is represented: theropods, sauropodomorphs, thyreophorans, ornithopods, and marginocephalians. Photographs of fossilized remains are annotated. A fact box for each group includes global location, diet, classification, placement in the Mesozoic era, size compared to a human, and time in which the dinosaur flourished. More than 500 superb color illustrations reveal anatomic details, such as skull formation, internal organs, limb structure, and ambulatory methods. No detail of anatomy has been overlooked: Feet bones, cervical vertebrae, knee joints, spinal columns, and skin texture are all shown in stunningly rendered drawings. Detailed scenarios show how dinosaurs fed and fought and interacted as groups or herds.

A dictionary provides names of all dinosaur genera. Each genus name is followed by a pronunciation guide. Informal or unofficial names appear in quotation marks. A glossary and index complete the book. More visually lavish than *Dinosaur and Other Prehistoric Animal Factfinder* (Chambers Kingfisher Graham, 1992), which offers 200 alphabetically arranged profiles of the best-known dinosaurs and other prehistoric animals, *The Ultimate Dinosaur Book* is highly recommended as a fascinating exploration of the past and an authoritative guide to these extraordinary creatures. [R: BL, 15 Oct 93, p. 402]—**Judy Gay Matthews**

1961. Levi-Setti, Riccardo. **Trilobites.** 2d ed. Chicago, University of Chicago, 1993. 342p. illus. index. $45.00. QE821.L46. 565'.393. LC 92-38716. ISBN 0-226-47451-8.

For most fossil animals the essential "character" of an individual is usually best conveyed through reconstructed skeletons, sometimes with flesh and color added. But for trilobites, primarily early to mid-Paleozoic arthropods whose rather complex structures are visible on their external surfaces, good photographs often convey more character than the specimen itself. The trilobites Levi-Setti shows in this book, all in black-and-white photographs (in excess of 225 plates), offer sharp, clear views of these fossils with their features and faults shown in a style suggestive of the cold, detailed faces of humans typical of Richard Avedon's photographs. In this edition there are many more plates and new information based on studies since 1975, the date of the first edition. Among these are several X-rays of specimens. While the first edition showed trilobites in a taxonomic arrangement, the majority of photographs in this edition are grouped by the geological period in which they occurred.

After placing trilobites in their systematic setting among the arthropoda, the author describes the essential morphology of these animals, with an extensive section on the mechanisms of vision. Delving into the complex compound eyes of modern and extinct arthropods, he moves on to a brief but adequate discussion of the physics of vision a la Descartes and Huygens. This is a stimulating section more focused on raising questions than providing simple adaptational just-so stories. The whole book successfully transforms these extinct "butterflies of the sea" from pictures to magnificent, functional animals. It would make a fine coffee-table addition but is also a first-class professional treatise.—**David Bardack**

1962. **Rand McNally Picture Atlas of Prehistoric Life.** By Robert Muir Wood. Skokie, Ill., Rand McNally, 1992. 64p. illus. maps. index. $16.95. QE765.H39. 560. LC 92-5761. ISBN 0-528-83525-4.

Rand McNally presents this attractive prehistoric view of life for the young reader. Illustrated by Tim Hayward, the book is divided into five sections that cover the young Earth, conquering the land, the age of the giants, the dawn of the mammals, and the age of the humans. There are a glossary and an index, both basic and oriented toward juvenile readers.

This book contains much information for beginning readers on a popular topic. The illustrations are well done and present important concepts clearly. Some material is advanced and will be of interest to young adult readers writing papers on prehistoric topics. Highly recommended for collections serving young readers. [R: RBB, 1 Feb 93, p. 1004]—**Ralph Lee Scott**

1963. **The Visual Dictionary of Dinosaurs.** New York, Dorling Kindersley, 1993. 64p. illus. maps. index. (Eyewitness Visual Dictionaries). $14.95. QE862.D5D5173. 567.9'1'03. LC 92-53446. ISBN 1-56458-188-8.

The 3,000 items identified in this visual dictionary are drawn from more than 200 detailed photographs and graphic illustrations depicting a broad range of dinosaurs and related topics. As is usual with the volumes in this series, the materials are arranged in two-page topical spreads that include a brief explanatory narrative and then the items and their accompanying labels. The work leads off with an overview of dinosaurs, then addresses the relevant geological ages (Triassic, Jurassic, and Cretaceous) and moves on to the various types of dinosaurs, dinosaur parts (e.g., hands, claws, feet), and dinosaur relatives (modern birds and crocodiles). A concluding section focuses on dinosaur classification. An index of approximately 3,000 terms provides access for the reader who knows the term in question and seeks the visual representation.

The strength of this dictionary is its graphical renderings. Lifelike models, fossilized skeletons, exquisitely detailed drawings, and clear photographs bring a feeling of immediacy to the pages that is rarely encountered in print works dealing with this popular subject. Although the work's vocabulary level is beyond the comprehension of most youngsters, they will nevertheless be riveted by the pictures. Thus, this work can be highly recommended for the science collections of school libraries from elementary through high school as well as for all public libraries. [R: RBB, 1 Dec 93, p. 717]—**G. Kim Dority**

PHYSICS

1964. McDonald, P. C., comp. **Directory of Low Temperature Research and Development in Europe.** 7th ed. Philadelphia, Institute of Physics Publishing, 1992. 333p. index. $95.00. ISBN 0-7503-0176-7.

This edition, published by the Low Temperature Group of the Institute of Physics, is the first to combine listings from the United Kingdom with those from continental Europe. More than 300 institutions involving nearly 1,500 individual researchers are described. Each institutional entry includes its location; telephone, fax, and E-mail information (if available); a list of staff members with their personal expertise; and an inventory of specialized facilities. Among the topics included are theory, cryogenic techniques, low-temperature physical property measurements, and the processing of bulk and thin-film materials. Separate indexes are given for the institutions, staff members, specialty areas, and facilities. A minor flaw is that staff members are indexed by last name only, combining seven individuals named Williams, for example, under a single heading. The book is nicely organized and should prove especially useful as a reference for companies involved in products or services related to low-temperature research and development.—**John U. Trefny**

1965. **McGraw-Hill Encyclopedia of Physics.** 2d ed. Sybil P. Parker, ed. New York, McGraw-Hill, 1993. 1624p. illus. index. $95.50. QC5.425. 530'.03. LC 92-43215. ISBN 0-07-051400-3.

One of five new editions of encyclopedias of selected fields in science and engineering, this volume on physics follows its first-edition antecedent by approximately 10 years. It includes 828 entries spread over 1,563 pages, with additional indexes and an appendix on scientific notation. The articles have been selected from the 7th edition of the *McGraw-Hill Encyclopedia of Science & Technology* (see ARBA 93, entry 1446). The scope and format are similar to those of the *Encyclopedia of Physics* (see ARBA 92, entry 1747) but with more (and generally briefer) entries. Typical contributions are written in a descriptive narrative style with a minimum of mathematical detail. Technically, the text seems to have been set at an advanced undergraduate or beginning graduate student level. Handsomely illustrated and carefully edited, this is an outstanding value at a relatively modest price. [R: Choice, Oct 93, p. 268; JAL, Sept 93, p. 275; WLB, Sept 93, pp. 119-20]—**John U. Trefny**

MATHEMATICS

1966. James, Robert C., and Glenn James. **Mathematics Dictionary.** 5th ed. New York, Van Nostrand Reinhold, 1992. 548p. index. $42.95; $29.95pa. QA5.J33. 510'.3. LC 92-6757. ISBN 0-442-00741-8; 0-442-01241-1pa.

Throughout the preparation of each edition of this dictionary, the objective has been to make it useful for students, scientists, engineers, and others interested in the meaning of mathematical terms and concepts. It is intended to be essentially complete in the coverage of topics that occur in precollege or undergraduate college mathematics courses, as well as covering many topics from beginning graduate-level courses.

This is by no means a mere word dictionary; neither is it an encyclopedia. It is a correlated condensation of mathematical concepts, designed for time-saving reference work. Nevertheless, the general reader can come to an understanding of a new concept by looking up unfamiliar terms in the definition and following this procedure down to familiar concepts.

When preparing this edition, the Jameses emphasized revising and updating topics included in previous editions and introducing many new topics, so as to reflect recent developments in mathematics. An important feature, continued and extended in this edition, is the multilingual index in French, German, Russian, and Spanish. The English equivalents of mathematical terms in these languages enable the reader not only to learn the English meaning of a foreign term but also to find its definition in the body of this book.—**Janet Mongan**

1967. **Mathematical Sciences Professional Directory 1993.** Providence, R.I., American Mathematical Society, 1993. 227p. index. $40.00pa. ISBN 0-8218-0179-1. ISSN 0737-4356.

This professional directory begins with a list of American Mathematical Society staff and includes their electronic mail addresses, as well as nonuser-specific electronic Internet addresses for the Society and *Mathematical Reviews* staff. The next section lists the officers and committee members of the society; it has its own index. These pages are followed by a directory that includes 37 related professional organizations, 7 government agencies, and a 4-page list of worldwide organizations that have reciprocity agreements with the society. The final major section lists U.S. departments in the mathematical sciences and other facilities in academic institutions, indicating the highest degree offered in the mathematical sciences. There are also lists of institutions in Canada, Central America, and the Caribbean. Six pages list nonacademic organizations. The final 10 pages contain an index of colleges and universities.

—**Janet Mongan**

1968. Thiessen, Diane, and Margaret Matthias, eds. **The Wonderful World of Mathematics: A Critically Annotated List of Children's Books in Mathematics.** Reston, Va., National Council of Teachers of Mathematics, 1992. 241p. illus. index. $17.00pa. Z6651.W85. 016.51. LC 92-36493. ISBN 0-87353-353-4.

The major objective of *The Wonderful World of Mathematics* is to provide a critically annotated list of good children's books in mathematics. (Children's books in mathematics are dominated in number and quality by counting books.) The books reviewed were chosen for their ease of use—by teachers in the classroom, on a one-to-one basis between parent and child, or for individual enjoyment. Reviews cover nearly 500 trade books for children from preschool to grade six, describing for each the content, accuracy, appropriateness of illustrations, writing style, and presence of reader activities. Each book is rated for its usefulness in teaching mathematical concepts. The following four classifications are used: early number concepts, number extensions and connections, measurement, and geometry and spatial sense. An overview for each of the four main categories can be found at the beginning of every section. More detailed descriptions of the types of books appear before each subsection, and some books are cross-referenced under more than one category. Vignettes give an idea of how some of the books have been successfully used. Situations from elementary, junior high, and college classrooms illustrate how students of different ages can enjoy and use the books. As the authors state, by exploring appropriate books in the college classroom, teachers can extend their knowledge about resources, teaching activities, and children's thinking all at the same time.—**Janet Mongan**

36 Resource Sciences

ENERGY RESOURCES

Bibliography

1969. Sarfoh, Joseph A., comp. **Energy in the Development of West Africa: A Selected Annotated Bibliography.** Westport, Conn., Greenwood Press, 1992. 114p. index. (African Special Bibliographic Series, no.16). $45.00. Z5853.P83S27. 016.33379'0966. LC 91-32542. ISBN 0-313-26416-3.

The present work does a poor job of living up to its title. Of the 802 entries, the first 141 deal with the developing world in general and the next 186 are concerned with Africa as a whole, so that only about one-half of the citations refer to West Africa itself. Even there the coverage is uneven. Nigeria has 210 entries, for instance, whereas the 8 Francophone West African countries manage only 80 among them. In all cases, even that of Nigeria, the coverage is little more than an idiosyncratic potpourri of references, with little success in achieving representativeness—selected perhaps, but hardly selective.

There are author and title indexes, but the latter is of little benefit to readers. For example, Burkina Faso is so listed in the listing of entries, but it is indexed only under its former name, Upper Volta. The term *dams* has only two index entries, but there are many more entries than this simply for the Akosombo Dam across the Volta River—none of which is indexed. There are separate index entries for "Cote d'Ivoire" and "Ivory Coast," two names for the same country. There are other errors. Not recommended. [R: Choice, July/Aug 93, p. 1755]—**David Henige**

Biography

1970. ***Financial Times* Who's Who in World Oil & Gas 1993.** 11th ed. Harlow, England, Longman; distr., Detroit, Gale, 1992. 529p. index. $190.00. ISBN 0-582-09271-X.

This reference book contains biographical information on 3,701 executive personnel working in companies, consulting firms, government agencies or departments, and universities and research organizations involved in the oil and gas industries. This includes CEOs, presidents, vice presidents, directors, managers, partners, and ministers. The biographical data includes current and previous appointments, business address and telephone number, personal details (e.g., birth date, nationality), qualifications, professional memberships, honors and awards, and publications. Company and geographical indexes list all personnel under each company or country.

What is the editorial policy for the selection of names? Most of the key companies listed in the companion publication *Financial Times Oil and Gas International Year Book* (see ARBA 93, entry 1748) are included, but the number of names varies for the same companies. For example, Enron Corporation has only 3 names listed in *Who's Who*, while in the *Oil and Gas International Year Book* there are more than 20 names listed, some of which would fit into the categories for the former publication. The majority of the listings are for personnel in companies, and biographical information varies greatly among the entries.

This reference book has been used by the oil and gas industries for a long time. Its information is certainly useful, but it would be much more useful if it included the names of many personnel now excluded.—**Anne C. Roess**

Directories

1971. **Asia-Pacific/Africa-Middle East Petroleum Directory, 1993.** 9th ed. Tulsa, Okla., PennWell Books, 1992. 495p. index. $135.00pa. ISSN 0748-4089.

1972. **European Petroleum Directory, 1993.** 13th ed. Tulsa, Okla., PennWell Books, 1992. 518p. index. $135.00pa. ISSN 0275-3871.

Again, PennWell has used its extensive worldwide oil and gas company database to produce new editions of these two directories. All companies are listed alphabetically within countries. Europe includes Eastern European countries, some of which are still undergoing name changes. The interests of the companies include drilling, exploration, production, refining, marketing, transportation, petrochemicals, pipelines, engineering and construction, and equipment and service. Standard information is given: addresses; personnel names and titles; telephone, fax, telex, and cable numbers; and a company description. There are company and geographical indexes. These directories continue to be good sources for names of personnel at the many branch offices and subsidiaries of companies located around the world.—**Anne C. Roess**

1973. **Natural Gas Industry Directory, 1993.** 3d ed. Tulsa, Okla., PennWell Books, 1993. 295p. index. $140.00pa. ISSN 1051-3973.

This reviewer, who reviewed the first edition, *Worldwide Natural Gas Industry Directory* (see ARBA 92, entry 1758), is still unsatisfied with the work's format and content. Again there are two separate sections for distribution companies and gas utilities. They could be combined into gas distribution utilities. More use of *see* references referring to companies in different sections is necessary. In the sections, subsidiary companies are listed in smaller type under the principal company. But there are some errors. For example, Peoples Gas, Light & Coke Company is listed as a distribution company, but its holding company, Peoples Energy Corporation, does not appear as an entry or in the company or geographical indexes. (It is mentioned in the descriptive text.) International coverage continues to be very limited, as is mention of associations, organizations, and regulatory agencies.

The intent of the directory to cover the natural gas industry is well meant but does not give users the complete picture. A better understanding of the natural gas industry is needed as it relates to PennWell's extensive oil and gas companies database. Readers should continue to use this directory with caution.—**Anne C. Roess**

1974. **Petroleum Software Directory, 1994.** 10th ed. Tulsa, Okla., PennWell Books, 1993. 305p. index. $180.00pa. ISSN 0743-6750.

This work consists of descriptions of computer software programs used in the petroleum industry. The programs are arranged by software company within 21 different applications. A new application, "ecological/environment," has been added since the 1990 edition (see ARBA 90, entry 1785). The 21 application terms, briefly described by subterms on the first page of the software programs section, continue to range from accounting and statistics to well completion, logging, servicing, and workover. All pertain to the petroleum industry. The software entries include program name and description, language, memory requirements, operating system, special accessories, compatibles, and price. A software company section lists company names, addresses, telephone numbers, contact personnel, and software package names. Programs by application, programs by title, and company indexes allow the user to retrieve specific information. This annual directory serves the petroleum industry's need for access to the many software packages applicable to it.—**Anne C. Roess**

1975. **U.S.A. Oil Industry Directory, 1993.** 32d ed. Tulsa, Okla., PennWell Books, 1993. 566p. index. $150.00pa. ISSN 0082-8599.

This annual directory provides a complete listing of principal oil companies in the United States. The six main sections cover integrated oil companies, independent producers, fund companies, marketing firms, associations, and government agencies. Taking a suggestion from a previous review (see ARBA 88, entry 1494) the publishers have restored the personnel index. This index, along with a government agencies index, a company index, and domestic and international geographical indexes, provides the user a variety of ways to find information quickly. Entries for companies, associations, and government agencies are arranged alphabetically within each section, which enhances use. Information included in the entries ranges from sketchy listings containing organization name, address, and telephone number to detailed entries that supply informative company histories and comprehensive personnel and subsidiaries lists.

An introductory article (reprinted from *Oil & Gas Journal*, September 28, 1992) contains an overview of and reflects the constant changes in the petroleum industry. An obvious change, caused by a slump in prices for petroleum products, is that now the top 300 oil and gas companies in the United States are listed instead of the 400 companies that were listed when this directory was previously reviewed. With a format that is easy to use and up-to-date information on an ever-changing industry, this annual directory continues to be of value to any academic, special, or public library that provides patrons with information on the petroleum industry.—**Diane J. Turner**

1976. **U.S.A. Oilfield Service, Supply & Manufacturers Directory, 1993.** 10th ed. Tulsa, Okla., PennWell Books, 1993. 582p. index. $135.00pa. ISSN 0736-038X.

This directory provides a thorough listing of U.S.-based companies involved in providing diverse oil field services. The oil field supply section lists those companies engaged in wholesale or retail sales of products used in every phase of the petroleum industry. The service section covers those companies that provide everything from drilling services to catering services, and the manufacturers section deals with companies that specialize in the engineering, design, and construction of a wide range of oil field equipment.

Entries consist of a brief company history, contact personnel and addresses, subsidiaries, and branch or district offices (if applicable). An alphabetical company index and a domestic and international geographical index are included; they help with finding specific locations and companies. As noted in a previous review (see ARBA 90, entry 1786), a general subject index would make it easier to find particular services or equipment, thus enhancing retrieval of information and adding value to this source. By keeping up with the ever-changing oil industry, PennWell Books continues to provide a quality product.—**Diane J. Turner**

1977. Wilson, A., and others, eds. **Major Energy Companies of Europe 1993.** London, Graham & Trotman; distr., Detroit, Gale, 1992. 261p. index. $323.00. ISBN 1-85333-876-1. ISSN 0268-2311.

This title covers 17 European countries but includes no Eastern European companies. Individual company entries are fairly long, giving not only address and telecommunications information but also officers, principal lines of business, parents and subsidiaries, financial data, bank, number of employees, and other tidbits (e.g., trade names). Nonenergy-related products and services are listed in the company entries: For instance, Grazer Stadtwerke of Austria provides funeral services. Some facts, such as directors' names or principal shareholders, would be hard to find elsewhere. Because not all entries are parent companies, financials are sometimes limited to sales, although most contain earnings as well. Most figures are updated through 1990, although a few companies have 1991 data, and some only have 1989. There is no preface or introduction to explain scope, selection criteria, target audience, or format. Alphabetical indexes by company and country are provided, but as the book is alphabetical by country, the latter seems redundant. There is no subject index, even though activities of companies included range from fuel distribution to construction of turnkey plants to nuclear safety consulting.

Whole World Oil Directory (see ARBA 84, entry 1509) covers a broader geographic area, is cheaper, and has subject indexing, but it tells less about the companies, and it covers only petroleum energy. Unfortunately, the price of *Major Energy Companies of Europe* will limit its market to large business collections or those with a special need for this information.—**Susan V. McKimm**

Handbooks and Yearbooks

1978. Crowson, Phillip. **Minerals Handbook 1992-93: Statistics and Analyses of the World's Minerals Industry.** New York, Stockton Press, 1992. 319p. $140.00. TN151.M49. 333.8'5. LC 85-645605. ISBN 1-56159-054-1.

This work, now in its 6th edition, continues the practice of the earlier editions of deriving data from a variety of primary and secondary sources. It pulls together, in tabular form, revised and updated annual figures for 1989 to 1990. The handbook contains a table of contents and two pages of sources and notes.

Within the body of the work are eight topical summary tables that cover areas dealing with production and reserves by main geopolitical groupings: the United Kingdom, the European Community, Japan, and the United States. Following these tables are separate sections on each of the 48 minerals covered in this edition. These sections contain, in fuller detail, world reserves and reserve bases, world production, productive capacity, secondary production or recycled materials, adequacy of reserves, consumption, end use pattern, value of contained metal in annual production substitutes and technical possibilities, prices, marketing arrangements, and supply and demand by main marketing arrangements and areas. The author cautions readers that much of the data has been condensed from their original formats, and that there may be some margins of error in the reporting of some of the material. Although somewhat expensive, this work would be a worthwhile purchase for facilities serving the minerals and metals industries.—**John H. Hunter**

1979. **Energy Information Abstracts Annual 1991. Volume 16.** New Providence, N.J., R. R. Bowker/Reed Reference Publishing, 1992. 720p. index. $475.00. ISBN 0-8352-3152-6. ISSN 0739-3679.

This edition of a basic source of energy information focuses on research and development, resources and consumption, economics, and the industrial application of energy and technologies. Part 1, contains the preface, a description of Bowker A&I databases, a user's guide, standard abbreviations, and a source list. The second part of the book includes graphic and tabulated data on 1991 energy trends, a list of conferences and events, and other materials. The list of conferences could be larger; it omits the GENI (Global Energy Network International) meeting on July 11-13, 1991, in Winnipeg, Canada. The third and main part of the reviewed volume contains a section on abstracts and an index section. The first of these presents 22 review categories, an abstracted title list by review category, and the review section. The review categories and abstracted title list help readers find necessary sources according to broad areas of interest. The information has been taken directly from scientific, technical, and business publications; conference and symposia proceedings; and academic, government, and corporate reports. The index section contains numerous indexes, such as a general subject key-term list, a geographic key-term list, an author index, and a source index.

This annual publication can be recommended to libraries, research and educational institutions, business agencies and corporations, and common associations. It would also be helpful to individual scientists who are interested in getting current, detailed, and multidisciplinary information on energy.

—**Ludmila N. Ilyina**

1980. **Energy Statistics Sourcebook.** 7th ed. Tulsa, Okla., PennWell Books, 1992. 476p. index. $165.00pa. ISSN 0889-5260.

This sourcebook is a compendium of selected basic key statistics useful for oil and gas industry analysis over a period of 10 years through 1991; some tables contain 15 to 50 years of data. Annual and monthly data are presented. The key series for each industry sector—exploration and drilling, production, reserves, refining, stocks, imports and exports, demand and consumption, natural gas, price, revenues and expenditures, offshore, transportation, and energy—are taken from the 65,000 time series contained in the *Oil & Gas Journal* Energy Database.

This edition contains two new categories: U.S. finding costs and active rigs by type (oil and gas wells). Table footnotes also give the original source of data, such as the Energy Information Administration. The appendixes contain a chronology of major events in the oil and gas industry, a glossary, member nations of key energy organizations such as OPEC, conversion factors, and a subject index. Some of the key statistics are graphed to show trends. The tables are also available on diskettes for IBM-compatible personal computers in Lotus 1-2-3 worksheets.

The economics staff of the *Oil & Gas Journal* have produced a very useful analytical tool of industry data in one handy volume. It cannot be as detailed as the database, but it presents a balanced statistical picture of the oil and gas industry.—**Anne C. Roess**

1981. **Energy Statistics Yearbook, 1990. Annuaire des Statistiques de l'Energie.** New York, United Nations, 1992. 482p. $80.00. ISBN 92-1-061148-9. S/N E./F.92.XVII.3.

The introduction succinctly summarizes the purpose of this work: It is a comprehensive collection of international energy statistics prepared by the United Nations Statistical Office. It is 34th in a series of annual compilations and updates the statistics shown in the previous volume. The objective of the yearbook is to provide comparative data on trends in commercial and secondary forms of energy for countries around the world. Data for each type of fuel and aggregate data for the total mix of commercial fuels are shown for individual countries and areas and are summarized into regional and world totals. Information is compiled primarily from annual questionnaires distributed by the United Nations Statistical Office.

Following the format of the other United Nations publications, information is in both English and French. A table of contents in the front of the volume enables the user to locate the specific energy statistic needed. This is an essential source in libraries where there is demand for this type of information.

—Marilyn Strong Noronha

1982. *Financial Times* **Mining International Year Book 1993.** Kay Larkin, ed. Detroit, Gale, 1992. 521p. maps. index. $215.00. ISBN 0-582-09273-6.

This directory provides information about 675 companies around the world that are in the business of mining, producing, and distributing metals, minerals, and precious stones. Entries contain short company histories and descriptions of the businesses, properties owned, and mineral interests. Contact information includes office addresses and names of the officers and directors. Financial information consists of the type of ownership and a capital and financial statement that usually covers the previous three years. An introductory section has useful current information about the industry, such as the effects of the breakup of the Soviet Union on the industry. A currency conversion table (rates as of December 1991) and a weights and length conversion table are given along with a short glossary of financial terms used in the company profiles. Also supplied is a directory of 94 mining-related associations that will prove useful for gathering industry information.

There are three indexes: geographic, product (metal or mineral), and company/association name. The geographic index is divided by country, except for Canada, Australia, and the United States, which include province, territory, and state listings. Handy maps appear here. Finally, there are tables of the world production of eight metals. A small amount of advertising is present but does not detract from the usefulness of this work.—**T. McKimmie**

1983. Golob, Richard, and Eric Brus. **The Almanac of Renewable Energy.** New York, Henry Holt, 1993. 348p. illus. index. $50.00. TJ808.3.G65. 333.79'4. LC 92-13963. ISBN 0-8050-1948-0.

The authors, with their experience at Information Systems, a consulting firm concerned with scientific, environmental, and energy issues, present a broad overview of renewable energy sources—alternatives to traditional energy sources (natural gas, petroleum, coal, and nuclear fission). The main part of the almanac consists of chapters covering hydroelectricity; biomass; geothermal; solar thermal; photovoltaic energy conversion; wind; and tidal, ocean thermal, and wave energy. Each chapter describes the scope and distribution of each energy source, different approaches for using each source, environmental considerations, and future prospects for their contribution to the energy supply.

In addition to these seven chapters, the authors have included three other chapters to help place the role of renewable energy in the context of the overall energy picture. A chapter on the traditional mix of fuels discusses the environmental impacts and social costs of relying on these sources. An energy storage chapter describes how storage technologies can be used with renewable energy sources. The last chapter covers energy efficiency. Two appendixes—statistical tables and information sources (e.g., books, organizations)—and an index complete the almanac. This is a useful reference tool for the general reader who wants an overview of these energy resources. [R: Choice, Sept 93, p. 161; SBF, June/July 93, p. 142]—**Anne C. Roess**

1984. **International Energy Statistics Sourcebook.** 2d ed. Tulsa, Okla., PennWell Books, 1992. 668p. $165.00pa. ISSN 1058-2487.

The sourcebook consists of data from *Oil and Gas Journal*'s Energy Database. Data from this database can be purchased in book form or on diskette. The paper sourcebook is a compilation of printed copies of spreadsheets that are grouped into three major sections. The first consists of a series of statistical tables describing a specific industry segment, such as exploration and drilling, for all countries of the world. Each spreadsheet covers a different period of time, but all end with 1990. For example, the spreadsheet covering crude oil reserves begins with 1952, while the one on natural gas liquid production begins with 1987. The second and largest section contains country statistical tables. These are arranged by hemisphere and then individual country. Each country's statistics are prefaced by a map showing the geographical location and a chart giving population, GNP (gross national product), and the consumer price index from 1969 to 1990. Many of the data compilations are annual summaries, but some, such as crude oil production, are given both monthly and annually so that users can study seasonal and cyclical patterns. The third section covers OPEC (Organization of Petroleum Exporting Countries) and the OPEC countries.

It should be noted that all of the data is highly aggregated; as a result, no data is provided at the oil field, state, or province level. For this type of information other sources must be used, such as *International Petroleum Encyclopedia* (see ARBA 90, entry 1783).

While it is easy to find a chart needed, the spreadsheet approach, with alternating shaded and white grids, makes each one a bit hard to read. However, this book will meet many users' needs for basic oil and gas information by country.—**Susan B. Ardis**

1985. Johansson, Thomas B., and others, eds. **Renewable Energy: Sources for Fuels and Electricity.** Washington, D.C., Island Press, 1993. 1160p. illus. maps. index. $85.00; $45.00pa. 621.042. LC 92-14194. ISBN 1-55963-139-2; 1-55963-138-4pa.

If the world is ever to achieve the goal of using its resources on a sustainable basis, it becomes increasingly clear that the place to start is with energy. Shrinking reserves of oil and gas, the environmental negatives involved in burning coal, and the psychological taboos against conventional nuclear energy mean that substantial quantities of "new wave" energy resources will be required if world living standards are to be enhanced (or even simply maintained) in the face of rapid population growth. The United States faces a particularly acute long-term problem, because although it has only about 5 percent of the world's people, it consumes some 30 percent of the world's total energy.

Inevitably, energy will become more expensive as pricing begins to reflect the true costs of acquisition. But what technologies are the most promising, given the constraints of cost, availability, technological feasibility, and environmental concern? This detailed volume gathers state-of-the-art thinking by experts from numerous countries on a dozen alternative energy options, ranging from wind power, biomass, and ethanol to ocean energy, geothermal, solar, and photovoltaic systems.

An input document for the 1992 United Nations Conference on Environment and Development in Rio de Janeiro, the book features excellent technical writing, useful tables and diagrams, bibliographies for each of the 23 chapters, interesting and current statistical data, and an overall index. As the timetable for investment decisions on twenty-first-century energy options becomes more pressing, this book, with its even-handed scientific approach, should prove an invaluable reference.—**James R. McDonald**

ENVIRONMENTAL SCIENCE

Almanacs

1986. **The Information Please Environmental Almanac, 1993.** Compiled by World Resources Institute. Boston, Houghton Mifflin, 1993. 656p. maps. index. $21.95; $10.95pa. ISBN 0-395-63767-8; 0-395-63766-Xpa. ISSN 1057-8293.

This almanac is compiled by the World Resources Institute, an international nonprofit research and policy organization. Now in its second year, the work presents a plethora of data on all timely environmental issues. Its stated purpose is to provide "facts to guide your daily actions," an environmentalist's handbook of statistics on a variety of topics of local, national, and global importance.

The almanac is divided into four major sections. The first, "State of the Planet," discusses the 1992 Earth Summit and presents a calendar of highlights of the year, although oddly the year extends from October 1991 to July 16, 1992. The second section, "Close to Home," includes chapters on water, wastes, energy, transportation, air pollution, and grassroots activities. Section 3, "A National View," presents chapters on items of national importance, including cold war cleanup, ecotourism, wildlife, wetlands and forests, and industry. State and provincial profiles are included on such environmentally important facts as energy use and production, wastes, transportation, water, pollution, and environmental expenditures. Section 4, "A Global View," discusses ozone depletion, the greenhouse effect, and land degradation. Also included are tabular country comparisons including such concerns as population density, life expectancy, and commercial energy use. Finally, characteristics of environmental importance are discussed in 143 country profiles.

The essays are well written and target a lay audience. Numerous text boxes on ancillary issues add to the readability of the almanac. Graphs and figures are abundant, legible, and pertinent. Coverage seems a bit pro-environment and one-sided in places but is never inflammatory. The almanac is recommended to anyone seeking a single reference source containing environmental data and analysis of all of the current issues.—**Michael G. Messina**

Atlases

1987. **The Atlas of Endangered Places.** By Steve Pollock. New York, Facts on File, 1993. 64p. illus. maps. index. $16.95. GF75.P65. 304.2'8. LC 92-20388. ISBN 0-8160-2857-5.

Geography, in a broad sense, is a study of places and their people, but there are various ways to look at the geography of an area. *The Atlas of Endangered Places* looks at the world with the eye of an environmentalist: What is happening to a particular area that is endangering that place and, in turn, its people? This thin atlas breaks the world up into 18 geographical units (e.g., Central and Southern Africa, the Pacific islands). Each area has a map that provides a basic illustration of the topography, along with major cities, waterways, parks, and other important landmarks. Symbols are used to depict the changes taking place in the environment. These can be found both on the maps and at the beginning of the accompanying text. Definitions for the symbols are given at the beginning of the text, along with the page on which a detailed explanation occurs. This makes for a lot of flipping back and forth, which some might find a nuisance. Facing the map, the text details the major changes affecting the area, along with some photographs. As this atlas is intended for school-age children, the explanations are brief and broad. They do, however, provide good food for thought and will hopefully get students interested in finding out more.

The subject index is minimal and is in need of expansion. The map index appears to include only those locations and features that appear in boldface print on the maps, but no explanation is given. Most terms are explained within the text, but about a dozen broad terms were put into a glossary. The flaws are few, and this atlas should provide a good jumping-off place for further study. [R: RBB, 15 May 93, pp. 1717-20; SBF, Nov 93, p. 238; SLJ, May 93, p. 139]—**Angela Marie Thor**

Bibliography

1988. **Bibliographic Guide to the Environment 1991.** New York, G. K. Hall, 1992. 328p. (Bibliographic Guides). $165.00. ISBN 0-8161-7222-6. ISSN 1063-6153.

This work, the first of a planned series of annual volumes, indexes more than 3,200 publications in environmental studies. It is similar in format to the other Bibliographic Guides (more than 20 of these cover various subjects) published by G. K. Hall, many of which began in the 1970s. The work is arranged alphabetically, and access is by subject, author, and title. Included are the materials cataloged by the Library of Congress and the New York Public Library from September 1, 1990, to August 31, 1991. Because the Library of Congress catalogs documents, many state and federal government documents are included. Entries provide standard bibliographical information, assigned subject headings, and call numbers. The choice for listing some of the subject headings is questionable. For example, "Horses - breeding" and "Food Storage Pests - Control" are included, but "Solar Energy" is not. Considering today's proliferation of electronic indexes, this serial will be useful to only a limited number of libraries.—**T. McKimmie**

1989. **Environmental Accounting: Current Issues, Abstracts and Bibliography.** New York, United Nations, 1992. 86p. $15.00pa. ISBN 92-1-104400-6. S/N E.92.II.A.23.

This literature review was prepared for the Intergovernmental Working Group of Experts on International Standards of Accounting and Reporting (ISAR). It addresses the concern that many transnational corporations need guidance for reporting environmental liabilities and expenditures consistent with the ISAR recommendations for environmental accounting. It is intended to be a helpful guide to the issues and literature of corporate environmental accounting.

The survey consists of three sections. A review article first summarizes the literatures coverage of the environmental issues: corporate reaction to environmental issues, current corporate accounting practices for environmental impact, and the relationship of environmental auditing to environmental accounting. Canadian, British, and United States sources are emphasized, because most of the environmental accounting developments appear in those sources.

The bibliography, consisting of 304 citations covering 1980-1992 (with more emphasis on the later years), is arranged by author under numbered subject categories within general heading issues (e.g., general, accounting, auditing, and sustainable development in the second section). Descriptive abstracts of 75 of the more important citations, as indicated by asterisks in the bibliography section, appear in a separate abstract section.

This review provides a comprehensive survey of recent literature on environmental accounting. It is a first attempt, and a very good one at that. The bibliography will likely be expanded to include literature from other countries if this guide generates a large amount of interest.—**Anne C. Roess**

1990. **The Island Press Bibliography of Environmental Literature.** Joseph A. Miller and others, comps. Washington, D.C., Island Press, 1993. 396p. index. $48.00. Z5322.E2I85. 333.7. LC 92-14099. ISBN 1-55963-189-9.

This annotated bibliography lists major literature sources treating 156 general environmental topics. The book is not an exhaustive treatise on the literature available on all topics. As only 3,084 sources are listed, there is an average of fewer than 20 sources per topic. However, the compilers' goal is to serve many users with a ready-reference source functioning as a primer for research, rather than a final, encyclopedic coverage of all topics.

The bibliography is organized into two parts of seven sections each. Part 1, on the natural environment, emphasizes components of the biosphere or natural resources, such as air, water, land, plants, trees, and animals. Part 2, on the human environment, treats elements such as society, ethics and philosophy, the arts, education, law and politics, economics, health, technology and engineering, and the methods of science. Within each of the 14 sections, items are subdivided into groups, within which 10 to 40 references are listed alphabetically by title. The introduction to each section lists the groupings of references, describes their subject content, and refers to related sections in the bibliography. All items in the bibliography are numbered consecutively. A quick reference index in the beginning of the book directs users to general topics. An author-title index and a very detailed subject index are also included.

The compilers purposely selected publications that are mostly from the 1980s while including only several important older works and classics. They focused on books and journals but included other guides to additional literature, such as encyclopedias and abstract publications. Their annotations are descriptive rather than analytical. Although incomplete in its coverage, this bibliography should be contained in reference libraries for those initiating a search of almost every major environmental topic. [R: Choice, Nov 93, p. 434; LJ, 15 Sept 93, p. 68; RBB, 1 Dec 93, pp. 714-15; WLB, Nov 93, pp. 100-01]—**Michael G. Messina**

1991. Jansma, Pamela E. **Reading about the Environment: An Introductory Guide.** Englewood, Colo., Libraries Unlimited, 1993. 252p. index. $27.50. Z5861.J36. 016.3637. LC 92-12976. ISBN 0-87287-985-2.

Environmental issues are playing a more prominent role in business, government, social, and personal decisionmaking today. Simultaneously, information about the environment, both in the scientific and policy areas, is growing at an overwhelming rate. The purpose of this annotated bibliography is to allow a layperson quick access to relevant information from reliable sources. It is an effective research tool for the nonspecialist and has more than 750 entries that are either in books or popular magazines found in most public libraries. Each reference lists the author, publisher, and date of publication. The scope, organization, and bias of each entry are discussed briefly, as is the overall scientific level of the reference.

The text has 16 chapters. Each begins with a summary essay that describes important elements within the chapter's topic. Symbols also identify the nature of the presentation. They highlight sources that are good overviews of the chapter topic, scholarly treatments of the subject, or excellent factual sources. This annotated bibliography is an easy-to-use, well-organized source of helpful information for laypeople and policymakers to gain access to information on environmental issues. [R: LJ, 15 Sept 93, pp. 68-69; RBB, 1 Dec 93, pp. 714-15; WLB, Nov 93, pp. 100-01]—**Robert L. Jones**

1992. Meridith, Robert. **The Environmentalist's Bookshelf: A Guide to the Best Books.** New York, G. K. Hall, 1993. 272p. index. $40.00. Z5861.M45. 016.3637. LC 92-18613. ISBN 0-8161-7359-1.

The history of the environmental movement is perhaps best defined in the books written by its leaders, for many of the most influential proponents of the movement have been convincing and compelling writers. Thus, Meridith has made a worthwhile contribution by surveying more than 200 prominent environmentalists and compiling the books considered to be their most significant. Based on the number of times a title was mentioned, the resultant list is divided into 3 categories: a core list of the 100 most recommended books; a second list of 250 books that were mentioned several times; and a third list of titles that seemed significant, although they were only mentioned once. The books represent a broad spectrum of environmental opinions and were written from the mid-nineteenth century to the present. Because most of the individuals polled are from the United States, works published in North America are emphasized. Otherwise, these recommendations represent an excellent cross-section of the development of environmental ideas. Recommended as an especially useful resource. [R: Choice, July/Aug 93, p. 1752; RBB, 1 Oct 93, pp. 383-84; SBF, Aug/Sept 93, p. 173]—**Harry E. Pence**

Biography

1993. Axelrod, Alan, and Charles Phillips. **The Environmentalists: A Biographical Dictionary from the 17th Century to the Present.** New York, Facts on File, 1993. 258p. illus. index. $45.00. S926.A2A94. 363.7'0092'2. LC 92-38773. ISBN 0-8160-2715-3.

Although talked about as a new trend, environmentalism is a thing of not only our present but also our past. How far past is a debatable issue, but for the authors of The Environmentalists, the seventeenth century is past enough. More than 600 individuals are included in this biographical dictionary, along with key organizations and agencies that have affected the environment, both negatively and positively. The emphasis is placed on U.S. figures, but the coverage is international. The criterion for inclusion is that an individual's contributions are generally acknowledged as landmarks in the development of ecology. This allows for both Charles Darwin and Ronald Reagan to be included. Organizations must have proved themselves as crucial to the field of ecology, as well as representative of its various facets, such as the National Rifle Association or the International Whaling Commission. Entries for people include brief biographical backgrounds, along with their contributions to the ecology movement. An individual's important publications are sprinkled throughout the text, and, when available, a bibliography of further reading about a person is given. Some black-and-white photographs are included. The volume is served by a very good index. All in all, this dictionary will provide a good jumping-off point for those interested in the people and organizations behind the Green movement. [R: RBB, 15 Dec 93, p. 776]—**Angela Marie Thor**

Dictionaries and Encyclopedias

1994. Art, Henry, ed. **The Dictionary of Ecology and Environmental Science.** New York, Henry Holt, 1993. 632p. illus. $60.00. GE10.D53. 363.7'003. LC 92-38526. ISBN 0-8050-2079-9.

The key word in the title of this work is "science": Most of the 8,000-plus terms defined come from biology, earth and atmospheric science, chemistry, and physics. It does not deal extensively with the socioeconomic aspects of environmental issues, although there are some entries for environmental organizations, public agencies, legislative acts, and political and legal terms. (The editor is a botanist, and most of the contributors are also scientists.) The alphabetically arranged entries are concise, mostly one or two sentences long, and clear; some include line drawings, but most do not. Among the appendixes are a measurement conversion table, periodic and alphabetical tables of the elements, a geological time scale, a taxonomic chart for living organisms, and the Beaufort wind scale. There is no index, but there are numerous cross-references in the text.

Overall, this is a comprehensive and accurate reference source. While it is aimed at professionals, researchers, and advanced students, and is thus most suitable for academic and research libraries, the work should not be too difficult for anyone with a serious interest in ecology and a basic grounding in science. [R: Choice, Dec 93, p. 582; JAL, Sept 93, p. 274; RBB, 1 Oct 93, p. 381; WLB, Nov 93, p. 100-01]—**Paul B. Cors**

1995. Crump, Andy. **Dictionary of Environment and Development.** Cambridge, Mass., MIT Press, 1993. 272p. $40.00; $16.95pa. GE10.C78. 363.7'003. LC 92-36484. ISBN 0-262-03207-4; 0-262-53117-8pa.

Maintaining a reasonable balance between environmental protection and economic development is perhaps the most crucial issue of our time, so a reference work combining the topics is potentially quite useful. The alphabetically arranged articles emphasize the economic, political, and social aspects of environmental issues, with little coverage of strictly scientific or technological subjects; they include topics (mostly broad), organizations, people (mostly politicians, not environmentalists), and a few specific places and events. Entries vary in length from a paragraph to two pages; they are clearly written and understandable to nonspecialists.

Originally published in the United Kingdom, the work employs British spellings and metric measures; this should not be a problem for most readers. What may be problematic can be summarized by two quotations from the foreword. "[The book] remains unbiased; it lets the reader decide" is followed by "it offers many examples of the misuse of resources from the wealthy, industrialized, 'developed' nations ... the wealthy are destroying the planet." There is nothing wrong with having a viewpoint, and this viewpoint is by no means uncommon or unfounded, but is it fair to claim objectivity when the book is clearly presenting value judgments? The reader must indeed decide.

There is considerable overlap with Irene Franck and David Brownstone's *The Green Encyclopedia* (Prentice-Hall General Reference, 1992). Franck and Brownstone provide much more coverage of scientific concepts, environmentally significant locations, and individual species of plants and animals and are generally more balanced in presenting all sides of controversial issues. Crump includes especially good coverage of the environmental aspects of crops and diseases not found in Franck and Brownstone. The works are as much complementary as competitive.—**Paul B. Cors**

1996. Franck, Irene, and David Brownstone. **The Green Encyclopedia.** New York, Prentice Hall General Reference, 1992. 486p. illus. $35.00; $20.00pa. TD9.F73. 363.7'003. LC 92-12240. ISBN 0-13-365685-3; 0-13-365677-2pa.

"An A-to-Z sourcebook of environmental concerns—and solutions" (cover), this book provides a convenient and up-to-date source of information on virtually every current environmental issue. While focusing on the United States, it gives good coverage of international problems and programs as well. The articles include not only topics (e.g., endangered species, toxic chemicals, giant panda, DDT) but also events (e.g., the Earth Summit, the Exxon *Valdez* oil spill), organizations, United States and United Nations governmental agencies, places (worldwide coverage of national parks is quite thorough), and people (mostly living or recently deceased environmental activists but also a few major historical figures). Written for nonspecialists, the articles are clear, precise, and nonjudgmental in tone; all sides of controversial issues are fairly presented.

The information and action guides, which give a quick overview of major organizations, governmental agencies, and information sources concerned with special areas, are a useful feature. Most of them are less than a page in length and are found in the alphabetical section, but a few longer ones appear separately in a special information section following the alphabetical listings. Other useful features of this section are lists of endangered species, wetlands of international importance, Superfund sites, tabular data on toxic chemicals, and detailed instructions on radon reduction methods. There is a well-selected bibliography of currently available titles. While there is no index, the extensive cross-references in the text effectively take its place. [R: BR, May/June 93, p. 51; Choice, June 93, p. 1602; JAL, May 93, p. 131; RQ, Summer 93, pp. 568-69; SLJ, May 93, p. 137]—**Paul B. Cors**

1997. Jacob, Helene. **Vocabulary of Hazardous Materials in the Workplace. Vocabulaire des Matieres Dangereuses Utilisees au Travail.** Ottawa, Department of the Secretary of State of Canada, 1993. 1039p. illus. (Terminology Bulletin, 215). $51.95pa. (U.S.). 363.17. ISBN 0-660-57958-8.

The growing attention being given to hazardous materials in the workplace has created a need for precise definitions and terminology. This book, based on official Canadian sources, is a bilingual (French and English) compilation of some 3,200 concepts covered in 10,000 entries about such topics as chemical analysis, handling, emergency measures, and occupational health and medicine. Its utility is limited to those who are bilingual in French and English, because many entries have definitions in only one language accompanied by a note or example in the other. The 600 pages of vocabulary are followed by a 300-page French-English glossary and 8 short appendixes that cover labeling and ingredient-disclosure requirements of Canadian law.—**Harold Goldwhite**

1998. King, James J., comp. **The Environmental Dictionary.** 2d ed. New York, Executive Enterprises; distr., Tulsa, Okla., PennWell Books, 1993. 977p. $89.95. LC 92-070350. ISBN 0-7816-0171-1.

This new edition contains 300 more pages than the first edition, with more than 5,000 updated Environmental Protection Agency definitions of terms. Two sources of definitions were used for this publication: 40 CFR (the Code of Federal Regulations), revised as of July 1, 1987, and the Federal Register for the period covering July 1, 1987, through June 30, 1992. Each definition is worded exactly as it appears in 40 CFR, so there is no confusion over words with unclear or overlapping meanings. The guide to usage contains definition source, definition entry format, sequence of definitions, cross-referencing format, and finding aids. The introduction helps one use the dictionary correctly; for example, definitions from this book should not be quoted or cited—for this purpose one is advised to refer to 40 CFR and the Federal Register.

The main part of this volume is the environmental dictionary, which presents definitions of environmental terms. The next part is the appendix, which contains the index to 40 CFR. A special guide explains the construction and interrelationship of the CFR and the Federal Register, and how to use this appendix. The third part of the dictionary provides acronyms and abbreviations for the most frequently mentioned organizations, programs, documents, and terms connecting technical and technological approaches to environmental problems. This dictionary is highly recommended for specialists dealing with concrete human impacts on the environment.—**Ludmila N. Ilyina**

1999. **McGraw-Hill Encyclopedia of Environmental Science & Engineering.** 3d ed. Sybil P. Parker and Robert Corbitt, eds. New York, McGraw-Hill, 1993. 749p. illus. maps. index. $85.50. GE10.M38. 628'.03. LC 92-42118. ISBN 0-07-051396-1.

This newly revised work provides articles on environmental topics arranged in alphabetical order from acid rain to zooplankton. Most of the articles are derived from the 7th edition of the 20-volume *McGraw-Hill Encyclopedia of Science & Technology* (see ARBA 93, entry 1446), with additional articles prepared especially for this volume.

This edition has been revised and updated from the previous one. In addition, it has an added focus on environmental engineering, hence the title change from the previous edition of the *McGraw-Hill Encyclopedia of Environmental Science* (see ARBA 81, entry 1504) to the *McGraw-Hill Encyclopedia of Environmental Science & Engineering*. It is shorter than the previous edition, which had more than 250 articles in 858 pages; this one includes 217 articles in 740 pages. The beginning section of feature articles on broad environmental topics was eliminated, and the book concentrates instead on the alphabetically arranged articles dealing with specific topics. Some of the articles taken from the parent set have been enhanced and updated in this work. For example, the article on groundwater hydrology includes the original article, plus a new two-page section with two additional figures (written by a new author) and an updated bibliography.

This new edition will be of most use to those who do not own the parent work. Those libraries that do own this set, however, will find the updated articles to be of use. It is also convenient to have environmental articles available in just one volume. Recommended for school, academic, and public libraries. [R: Choice, Oct 93, p. 268; JAL, Sept 93, p. 275; RQ, Winter 93, pp. 290-91; WLB, Sept 93, pp. 119-21]—**Diane B. Rhodes**

2000. Porteous, Andrew. **Dictionary of Environmental Science and Technology.** rev. ed. New York, John Wiley, 1993. 439p. illus. $29.95pa. TD169.3.P67. 628'.03. LC 92-8937. ISBN 0-471-93544-1.

This dictionary is a revised edition of an earlier work by this author and a colleague (*The Environment: A Dictionary of the World Around Us*) published in 1976. This edition focuses on the science and technology of environmental protection and resource management. The author's purpose is to encourage environmental literacy by providing basic definitions and data on a plethora of topics. This goal is largely attained, as almost every conceivable topic related to the environment is covered.

The dictionary is arranged by topic words or phrases that are treated with anything from a short sentence up to several pages. Topics within discussions that are addressed elsewhere are printed in capital letters, signaling to the reader that further related information is available. Eighty figures and numerous tables add significantly to the work's value. Appendixes include the periodic table, conversion factors for common units, and environmental agencies and organizations from around the world.

Although the dictionary will be useful to readers from many disciplines, the author has interjected his biases on certain topics. For instance, the coverage on herbicides includes phrases such as "herbicides have enormous ecological implications by destroying food sources, habitats, etc."; "The use of defoliants ... can permanently destroy tropical forests"; and "Once the tree cover is removed, the soil is subjected to erosion and precious nutrients are rapidly leached away." No mention is made of such facts as that some herbicides are less lethal than table salt and aspirin. This sort of one-sided coverage, which is somewhat preachy in places, detracts from an otherwise useful reference source.—**Michael G. Messina**

2001. Rivard, Denis. **Vocabulary of Global Warming. Volume I: Contributors to the Greenhouse Effect. Vocabulaire du Rechauffement Climatique.** Ottawa, Department of the Secretary of State of Canada, 1992. 597p. (Terminology Bulletin, 214). $48.05pa. (U.S.). 551.51. ISBN 0-660-57945-6.

The foreword notes that the purpose of this publication is to address the needs of language professionals and knowledge workers in environmental fields. The introduction outlines the scope of the series, which deals with the various environmental problems at the end of the twentieth century. The user's guide explains the format of entries and is followed by the two main parts of the book—the English-French vocabulary and the French-English one. The bibliography includes 110 main published sources and other Translation Bureau publications, such as Terminology Bulletins and those in the Glossary series.

The quality of individual explanatory entries, as well as that of the translations, is excellent. However, differences in the translations of numerous entries are puzzling. Sometimes the English entries are richer in explanatory content than the French ones; sometimes the reverse is true. Occasionally the English and French versions differ significantly (e.g., *Peru Current*). Nevertheless, the vocabulary constitutes an interesting and valuable contribution to the environmental literature. It will be helpful for all bilingual scientific workers dealing with global warming. [R: Choice, Oct 93, pp. 272-73]—**Ludmila N. Ilyina**

2002. Sullivan, Thomas F. P. **Environmental Regulatory Glossary.** 6th ed. Rockville, Md., Government Institutes, 1993. 623p. $65.00. LC 92-43330. ISBN 0-86587-353-4.

For those who work extensively with federal environmental regulations, the various government agencies sometimes seem to resemble the character in Lewis Carroll's *Through the Looking Glass* who says, "When I use a word, it means just what I choose it to mean—neither more nor less." For regulatory purposes, the definitions of scientific terms are determined from statutes and from the codes developed by the various regulatory agencies. These definitions may not correspond to the latest scientific knowledge, and in some cases terms that appear to be similar may not be defined in exactly the same way by different agencies. Determining the appropriate definition to use is important, however, as an incorrect interpretation may expose a company to fines or other legal action for noncompliance.

Sullivan and his editorial team have put together a compendium of more than 4,000 environmental terms, acronyms, and definitions used by the major regulatory agencies. Each listing is identified according to sources, which is necessary, because, as already noted, different agencies do not always use the same definition. This new edition is significantly expanded and includes terms from the amendments to the Clean Air Act. The potential purchaser should be aware of the author's clear warning that this is not intended to be a scientific dictionary; however, those who interpret or teach environmental law and regulations will find this book to be a very useful resource.—**Harry E. Pence**

Directories

2003. Deziron, Mireille, and Leigh Bailey, eds. **A Directory of European Environmental Organizations.** Cambridge, Mass., Basil Blackwell, c1991, 1992. 177p. index. $59.95. TD171.5.E85D49. 363.7'0025'4. ISBN 0-631-18386-8.

This directory covers the major governmental and nongovernmental environmental groups of Western European countries as well as some international institutions that influence environmental policy in Europe. The objectives of this directory are outlined in the foreword and preface: to provide all interested readers with information that can be easily accessed. The arrangement of the contents is very simple. Part 1, on governmental organizations, includes information about five international organizations: the European Community, Council of Europe, Organization for Economic Cooperation and Development, United Nations Environmental Programme, and World Health Organization in chapter 1; and chapter 2 describes environmental institutions in 12 Western European countries. Part 2, on nongovernmental organizations, includes two chapters, one pertaining to international organizations and the second to national. Appended are alphabetical and country indexes and a list of abbreviations. At the end of the book the editors have provided a form for new groups that wish to be included in future editions or for those already listed to provide updated information.

It would be desirable if future editions of this valuable directory included not only Western but also Eastern European organizations. Still, it is a helpful source of reliable environmental information for all categories of users. [R: Choice, Feb 93, pp. 936-38]—**Ludmila N. Ilyina**

2004. Katz, Linda Sobel, Sarah Orrick, and Robert Honig. **Environmental Profiles: A Global Guide to Projects and People.** Hamden, Conn., Garland, 1993. 1083p. index. (Garland Reference Library of Social Science, v.736). $125.00. GE1.K38. 363.7'0601. LC 92-41800. ISBN 0-8153-0063-8.

Environmental Profiles describes projects, programs, organizations, agencies, and individuals concerned with almost any environmental issue. More than 7,000 projects, 3,000 individuals, and 115 countries are covered. The entries originated from two extensive surveys, so inclusion was partly voluntary. The scope is very broad and includes issues not normally associated with traditional conservation, such as health, education, population, and family planning. The book differs from similar ones (e.g., *World Directory of Environmental Organizations* [see ARBA 93, entry 1773]) in that it does more than simply list each organization; it also includes information on scope, size, and resources.

Arranged alphabetically by country, profiles are then grouped under government, nongovernmental organization, private organizations, and universities. Coverage within each of these headings is classified by organization, projects and people, and resources. A global/regional section lists those projects that are international in scope. An appendix shows organizations in alphabetical order, with country included, under several important issues: air quality/emission control, biodiversity/species preservation, deforestation, energy, global warming, health, population planning, recycling/waste management, sustainable development, transportation, and water quality. Finally, a very extensive index allows readers to locate projects dealing with specific species, countries, and the like.

Useful as an environmentalist's handbook, *Environmental Profiles* supplies information readers can use to communicate with others sharing similar interests. Users can range from those in environmental organizations to researchers to educators. The book is recommended to anyone seeking information on a global scale about current efforts aimed at a plethora of environmental issues. [R: Choice, Sept 93, p. 82; RBB, 1 Oct 93, p. 383; WLB, Sept 93, p. 116]—**Michael G. Messina**

2005. **The Lead Detection & Abatement Directory 1993-1994: Everything You Need to Know, Everyone You Want to Reach.** Bethesda, Md., IAQ Publications, 1993. 333p. index. $75.00pa. ISBN 0-9633003-2-6.

The first edition of this trade directory contains diverse information on an industry concerned with one of the greatest environmental hazards, lead poisoning. Divided into 12 sections, the source includes thousands of lead testing firms, abatement firms, training firms, and products. Also listed are federal and state government agencies and environmental, building, and health organizations concerned with issues involved in lead poisoning. All sections include brief annotated descriptions detailing content, criteria for listing, and arrangement. The alphabetical entries within each section include information (when available) such as address, telephone number, key personnel, activities, and qualifications. Also provided are a brief, informative overview of the lead contamination problem; two major alphabetical indexes; and a format with clear boldface type that enhances its use.

Anyone looking for information on lead poisoning will find this book useful. It would be a worthwhile addition to large academic and public libraries. [R: Choice, Nov 93, p. 436]—**Diane J. Turner**

2006. **State Lead Poisoning Prevention Directory 1992.** Denver, Colo., National Conference of State Legislatures, 1992. 92p. $12.00pa. ISBN 1-55516-492-7.

Lead continues to be a significant cause of environmental disease, especially among small children. The states play an important role in the identification of groups who are threatened by lead pollution, so it is helpful to have this comprehensive directory of the individuals in each state who are in charge of various aspects of the problem. Listings are by state, and in each case at least two individuals are identified who are responsible for the health, environmental, or occupational safety aspects of lead pollution. Because the names were obtained through a telephone survey in early 1992, the information is still relatively current. In addition to providing the names and addresses of contact persons, some state listings also include brief comments on the lead abatement program. The topic is rather specialized, but groups that are concerned with lead pollution should find this directory extremely useful.—**Harry E. Pence**

2007. Trzyna, Thaddeus C., Jennifer Trzyna Caughman, and Roberta Childers. **California Environmental Directory: A Guide to Organizations and Resources.** 5th ed. Sacramento, Calif., California Institute of Public Affairs, 1993. 128p. maps. index. $40.00pa. HC107.C23E556. 301.31'09794. LC 77-642158. ISBN 0-912102-98-5.

This newly revised and expanded edition of the *California Environmental Directory* continues to be the most inclusive guide to local, regional, and federal environment-related agencies, university programs, and major associations in California. Arranged in the same easy-to-use format as the 4th edition (see ARBA 89, entry 1401), this updated directory provides new material and also includes many lesser-known but important groups. The user's guide at the beginning is an excellent source for background information on the various organizations and provides a broad overview of those concerned with safeguarding the environment and managing natural resources. The appendix lists useful reference books and can help researchers focus on their topic of concern and reach beyond the state to resources available throughout the world. One excellent reference source not listed in the appendix is *Gale's Environmental Sourcebook* (see ARBA 93, entry 1768), which is very useful in the field of environmental research. The *California Environmental Directory* is an excellent tool for libraries, businesses, institutions, and anyone interested in targeting California's environment-related organizations.—**Diane J. Turner**

2008. **World Energy and Nuclear Directory: Organizations and Research Activities in Atomic and Non-Atomic Energy.** 2d ed. Harlow, England, Longman; distr., Detroit, Gale, 1993. 480p. index. $450.00. ISBN 0-582-22965-0.

This is the 2d edition of an extremely valuable reference for any person or group concerned with nearly any aspect of energy. The book consists of more than 3,000 listings of government agencies, university departments, and private companies involved worldwide with coal, gas, nuclear, or water power technology; electricity production; radiation problems and waste handling; and renewable energy and solar power.

The arrangement of entries is alphabetical by country. For each entry there is a variable amount of information (the compilers have clearly run up against a number of situations in which they were thwarted by political or commercial secrecy: North Korea, for example, with its highly suspect nuclear program, has no listings). Typically, the more complete entries include addresses and electronic contacts, responsible individuals, scope and pertinent interests, staff numbers and budget, activities, publications, and representative clients. There are indexes to the various establishments listed (by name) and also to subject matter.

The major (and deliberate) omission here is oil. No doubt the editorial view has been that including agencies dealing with petroleum research would result in an absolutely unwieldly volume, but the result is nonetheless something of a letdown. Even at its hefty price, this work is an important reference for anyone interested in networking on energy. Planners, researchers, and environmentalists can all find some useful contacts.—**James R. McDonald**

Handbooks and Yearbooks

2009. **Basic Guide to Pesticides: Their Characteristics and Hazards.** By Shirley A. Briggs and the staff of Rachel Carson Council. Bristol, Pa., IPS/Taylor & Francis, 1992. 283p. illus. $39.50. RA1270.P4B73. 363.17'92. LC 92-7024. ISBN 1-56032-253-5.

A major product of the environmental movement is information on pesticides. Material Safety Data Sheets (MSDS) must accompany shipments and be posted in work places for inspection by workers. The Rachel Carson Council argues that this book is unbiased and the product of extensive work in gathering (often using the Freedom of Information Act), organizing, verifying, and compiling the information presented. (The council notes, however, that they too are at the mercy of some of their sources.) Chapter 2 explains on how to use this guide, followed by chapters on indexing of pesticide names (common, trade, chemical, and CAS [Chemical Abstracts Service]), characteristics, chemical classes, and references. There are six appendixes.

Rachel Carson awakened us to pesticide dangers, but this is an uncontroversial, rehashed treatment of primarily old material. Previous compendiums, such as *Pestline* (see ARBA 91, entry 1785), mined similar territory with equal somnolence. There are repeated cautions regarding data reliability, but how aldicarb pesticide characteristics become combined with lindane under the trade names Sentry and Temik was news to this reviewer. Phosalone was withdrawn from the market by the manufacturer but was not noted as being unavailable in the United States. The parenthetical numbers in the charts must refer to the common references, but this was not made clear. The Rachel Carson name may attract new readers to this material, but how it will result in cleaner air, soil, and water is not clear. This legacy deserves better presentation.—**Marvin K. Harris**

2010. **Book of Lists for Regulated Hazardous Substances 1993.** Rockville, Md., Government Institutes, 1993. 427p. $67.00pa. ISBN 0-86587-337-2.

There seems to be no end to the regulations with which businesses must comply. These, of course, can be found in the Code of Federal Regulations (CFR), but at times a business needs a fast reference to a particular list within the regulations. The *Book of Lists for Regulated Hazardous Substances* provides this service for 72 lists that a group of environmental attorneys, engineers, and consultants have deemed most sought. These lists are from eight major acts (dated July 1, 1992, in the CFR), including the Occupational Safety and Health Act and the Clean Water Act. In the book the term *list* can also mean a table (e.g., "Table Z-1-A: Limits for Air Contaminants") or a set of standards (e.g., "Treatments Standards Expressed as Waste Concentrations"). These lists are identical to those found in the CFR; no editorial commentary is provided. The exact source and title are listed, so users can go back to the CFR for further information. Access is only through the table of contents, which includes the name of the act, the name of the list, and the source. For most users, this is probably sufficient access, as they will have been referred to a particular list. With this volume, they will readily find the lists most desired.—**Angela Marie Thor**

2011. Davis, Daniel J., Julie A. Davis, and Grant T. Christianson. **Firefighter's Hazardous Materials Reference Book and Index.** 2d ed. New York, Van Nostrand Reinhold, 1993. 1333p. index. $139.95. TH9446.H38D39. 628.9'2. LC 92-33266. ISBN 0-442-01346-9.

Intended for first responders, *The Firefighter's Hazardous Material Reference Book and Index* presents 913 hazardous materials in a clear, easy-to-reference format. Each substance gets its own page, and boldface headings make it simple to quickly locate information on such subjects as health hazards, fire hazards, and recommended protective gear. This edition covers 36 more compounds than did the first edition (see ARBA 92, entry 1781) and features a category of information, "Container Hazards," not included in the first edition. Also, many bits of information that were marked "not available" in the previous edition have been added to this one. The biggest improvement over the first edition is the addition of a 400-page hazardous materials reference book index. For each of its approximately 800 entries, this index provides page references to 8 important hazardous substance reference books, including *Sax's Dangerous Properties of Industrial Materials* (Van Nostrand Reinhold, 1992) and *Hazardous Chemicals Desk Reference* (PennWell, 1993). This feature makes the work useful not only for first responders but also for library researchers who wish to compare hazardous materials information from a variety of sources. As with the first edition, there are a chemical names index and a DOT (Department of Transportation) number index but no trade-name index.

Overall, the 2d edition greatly improves on its predecessor. Libraries supporting programs in hazardous waste management or environmental engineering should purchase this book, even if they already own the first edition.—**Donald A. Barclay**

2012. **Education for the Earth: A Guide to Top Environmental Studies Programs.** Princeton, N.J., Peterson's Guides, 1993. 175p. index. $10.95pa. GE80.E33. 363.7'071'173. LC 92-33025. ISBN 1-56079-164-0.

This useful, timely, and well-arranged guide provides detailed information on 100-plus undergraduate environmental studies programs at colleges and universities in the U.S. The programs have been chosen for evaluation using strict criteria that were developed by members of the Alliance for Environmental Education.

The guide is divided into three sections. The first includes a description of the setup of the program profiles and the criteria used to evaluate the programs. A second section, "Career Watch 2000," is a compilation of five informative essays written by prominent environmental leaders. These essays provide a realistic perspective on the trends and training needed within a certain career field.

The third section, and the largest part of the book, consists of one-page program profiles. Each profile details basic "Fast Facts" about the program and the school. More in-depth information is given on the mission of the program, campus facilities, and the career opportunities available to students upon graduation. This setup enables the reader to easily compare each of the programs. The profiles are organized into chapters by these career areas: environmental engineering and design, environmental health, environmental science, environmental studies, and natural resources management.

To remain current, this guide will need to be updated on a regular basis, as contact persons, addresses, tuition fee amounts, and the like change. Also, being a paperback, it will not last long with regular use. However, it is a much-needed resource for the growing number of people interested in pursuing careers in the environmentally conscious 1990s. [R: LJ, 1 Feb 93, p. 72; RBB, 1 Mar 93, p. 1263; SLJ, Nov 93, p. 142; WLB, Mar 93, pp. 108-11]—**Katherine Margaret Thomas**

2013. Kimball, Debi. **Recycling in America: A Reference Handbook.** Santa Barbara, Calif., ABC-Clio, 1992. 254p. index. (Contemporary World Issues). $39.50. TD794.5.K55. 363.72'82'0973. LC 92-29984. ISBN 0-87436-663-1.

After being discussed for some time, recycling is finally becoming a major focus of environmental attention. Factors responsible for this heightened interest include the high cost of solid-waste disposal, stricter environmental regulations, and the discovery that some so-called biodegradable materials can survive in modern landfills for decades without decomposing. As more communities establish mandatory recycling programs, there is an increasing demand for information about the process. This book offers an excellent introduction, readily accessible to those with little previous background.

Two especially useful sections discuss specific materials that are often recycled and summarize state laws and regulations. Other worthwhile material includes a brief history of the recycling movement; names and addresses of local, state, and national organizations concerned with recycling; and a reference list. In addition there are a glossary of terms, a list of acronyms (especially useful in a field where acronyms are so common), and a good index.

This is a well-written book about a topic of considerable interest to the public. Recommended. [R: Choice, June 93, pp. 1604-06; LJ, 15 April 93, p. 61; RBB, 1 Feb 93, pp. 1004-05; SLJ, Feb 93, p. 122; VOYA, June 93, p. 125]—**Harry E. Pence**

2014. Newton, David E. **Global Warming: A Reference Handbook.** Santa Barbara, Calif., ABC-Clio, 1993. 183p. index. (Contemporary World Issues). $39.50. QC981.8.G56N48. 363.73'87. LC 93-24821. ISBN 0-87436-711-5.

The possibility of global warming, having been of concern to scientists for about 20 years, became of interest to the general public in the 1980s, when 6 out of 10 years were the warmest in recorded history. This work chronicles the complexities of a debate that leaves policymakers unsure of what actions to take. Written for the concerned citizen at the undergraduate level, there is a wealth of information here. Discussion of how human activities are changing the atmosphere and how these changes may affect our climate is supplemented by physical and historical material on weather and climate. Statistical data and tables include emissions and atmospheric levels of gases that could contribute to global warming, including carbon dioxide, methane, nitrous oxide, and CFCs. A directory lists organizations with an interest in environmental or climate research and their publications. The annotated bibliography of books and reports will be very useful. There are an index, a glossary, and an acronyms list. The work, however, seems not to have been particularly well thought through. For example, the listing of organizations, such as the Sierra Club, or of biographies, such as that of George Herbert Walker Bush, merely detracts from the focus of the book. The work is timely, however, and will be a useful reference for academic and public libraries.—**T. McKimmie**

2015. Patnaik, Pradyot. **A Comprehensive Guide to the Hazardous Properties of Chemical Substances.** New York, Van Nostrand Reinhold, 1992. 763p. index. $124.95. RA1211.P38. 615.9'02. LC 91-42694. ISBN 0-442-00191-6.

The increasing concern about chemical hazards in the scientific community makes this book particularly valuable. The 46 chapters of its main section treat chemical compounds in groups arranged either by functional group type (e.g., carboxylic acids, azo dyes) or by function (e.g., herbicides, oxidizers). Each chapter discusses many individual compounds, giving CAS (Chemical Abstract Service) Registry number, physical properties, uses, health hazards, fire and explosion hazards, and (in many cases) suggestions about storage and disposal and comments about hazardous reaction products derived from the compound. Each chapter has references to recent literature about the compounds discussed. This compendium of information is particularly helpful because it can suggest to a chemist possible hazards of analogous compounds, even if they are not listed. There is a useful brief introduction about hazards in general and federal regulations. The full indexes include CAS Registry numbers, CAS Chemical Substance listings, and a general index.—**Harold Goldwhite**

2016. Pohanish, Richard P., and Stanley A. Greene, eds. **Hazardous Substances Resource Guide.** Detroit, Gale, 1993. 510p. index. $175.00. ISBN 0-8103-8494-6.

The environment continues to be the preferred cause of our time, and environmental consciousness is awakening in all sections of the population. However, as concern about the impacts of hazardous materials at every level, from worldwide to local, has grown, it has become apparent that most of the relevant reference works either have been prepared by and for specialized technical and scientific users, or have been so popularized as to make them scientifically unreliable. This book attempts to bridge the gap by combining scientific rigor with a clear writing style and an emphasis on the concerns of ordinary people.

The major focus of the work is a section in which 1,047 alphabetically listed hazardous substances are discussed in terms of their alternative names, "danger profile," uses, appearance, effects of long- and short-term exposure, and storage recommendations. Making the book even more valuable is a lengthy section (with contact information) of resource listings, including hot lines and information clearinghouses; poison control centers (by state); relevant state, federal, and international organizations; publications; and databases. A user's guide and a detailed layperson's introduction to understanding hazardous substances also add to the book's value, as do a glossary and complete indexes arranged by chemical names, Chemical Abstract Service (CAS) numbers, and resources.

This is a state-of-the-art publication for any individual or agency professionally concerned with hazardous materials. It should also find a place in many general collections as public interest in and concern about these substances continues to expand. [R: Choice, June 93, p. 1602; LJ, 1 May 93, p. 82; RBB, 15 April 93, pp. 1535-36]—**James R. McDonald**

2017. **Recycling Sourcebook: A Guide to Recyclable Materials.** Thomas J. Cichonski and Karen Hill, eds. Detroit, Gale, 1993. 563p. index. $75.00. ISBN 0-8103-8855-3. ISSN 1064-4938.

The editors state in the introduction that this book is intended to be a "comprehensive and convenient guide to the recycling of household, office, and other consumer-generated waste." They have done an excellent job of fulfilling this objective. The first part of the book consists of two major sections. First, concise essays discuss materials that are currently recycled. These articles deal with the production of the original material, possible problems with isolating the material, current recycling technology, and potential markets for the recycled product. Second, specific projects are reviewed that can serve as models for developing local recycling initiatives. The articles in this section span a broad spectrum of situations—rural and urban, industrial and home—providing practical advice that can be very useful. The second part of the book consists of an extensive list of recycling organizations, agencies, and publications; an appendix; a glossary; and an excellent index.

This is an unusually complete and accessible treatment of recycling and should be valuable for anyone planning to become involved in these efforts. Highly recommended. [R: JAL, July 93, p. 201; LJ, 15 May 93, p. 64; RBB, 1 Feb 93, pp. 1004-05; RQ, Summer 93, p. 576; VOYA, April 93, p. 66]—**Harry E. Pence**

2018. Waldo, Andrew B., and Richard deC. Hinds. **Chemical Hazard Communication Guidebook: OSHA, EPA and DOT Requirements.** 2d ed. New York, McGraw-Hill, 1993. 583p. $69.95. ISBN 0-07-967755-7.

Few workplaces can boast of being chemical free. If nothing else, the photocopier needs some chemicals to run. Of course, not all chemicals are considered hazardous, but for those that are, various U.S. agencies have regulations to protect both those in the workplace and the public at large. Trying to wade through these regulations is no easy task, but the authors of this book, one a consultant on health, safety, and environmental issues, the other a lawyer specializing in environmental regulations and litigation, have updated this extremely useful guide.

Each chapter deals with a specific act or series of legislation, providing first a general introduction, then specifics such as material covered, requirements, and enforcement. Included are OSHA's (Occupational Safety and Health Administration's) Hazardous Communication Standard (HCS), which requires employers to provide information to employees concerning the hazards of the chemicals they work with; EPA's (Environmental Protection Agency's) Superfund Amendment and Reauthorization Act (SARA), which requires employers to provide the community with information about the identity and amount of hazardous chemicals at their facility, as well as releases of hazardous chemicals into the environment; and the DOT's (Department of Transportation's) regulations concerning the shipment of hazardous materials.

To assist employers, a model hazard communication program and an outline for an employee training course that complies with OSHA's requirements are included. The reference guide provides an outline of the principal requirements of the OSHA, EPA, and DOT regulations covered, giving a summary as well as a reference to the regulation. This section takes up approximately one-third of the book. The glossary is a great aid to clarifying those terms that have a different definition within each agency. There are also listings, both alphabetical and by CAS (Chemical Abstracts Service) number, of hazardous and extremely hazardous substances. This work should prove handy for both library and laboratory.—**Angela Marie Thor**

2019. Weiskel, Timothy C., and Richard A. Gray. **Environmental Decline and Public Policy: Pattern, Trend and Prospect.** Ann Arbor, Mich., Pierian Press, 1992. 224p. index. (Knowledge Windows Series, no.1). $25.00pa. ISBN 0-87650-289-3.

Weiskel is a social anthropologist and historian with an interest in environmental issues; Gray is senior editor for Pierian Press. The five chapters that make up this volume are adaptations of Weiskel's testimony to the U.S. Senate during hearings on the Global Environmental Protection Act of 1988. Gray has added annotated bibliographies to four of the chapters. Much of what appears here was originally published in 1990 as a multipart article, "The Anthropology of Environmental Decline," in RSR (*Reference Services Review*). The book, however, adds new materials and expands the contents of the RSR articles. As the title suggests, the emphasis is on environmental policy: devising such policy; the relationship between development (especially agricultural) and environmental decline in Third World countries, with a separate case study of Africa; and past, present, and future aspects of the global environment and humankind's relationship with it.

Weiskel applauds modern efforts to unite natural history and human history, rather than to treat them as separate and unrelated disciplines. He emphasizes that as humans, we are inextricably part of the environment whether we recognize it or not; we cannot be at war with the natural world without being at war with ourselves. Although there are many reasons for pessimism, Weiskel is an optimist in the sense that he feels there is still time for policymakers, with the support of a well-informed citizenry, to halt and reverse environmental decline at all levels, from local to global.

This volume can be considered a reference source because of its detailed and lengthy annotated bibliographies that cover numerous and varied environmental books and articles. *Environmental Decline and Public Policy* is written for teachers, students (both high school and college), and the general public and is recommended for libraries serving these categories of readers.—**William H. Wiese**

37 Transportation

AIR

2020. **The Visual Dictionary of Flight.** New York, Dorling Kindersley, 1992. 64p. illus. index. (Eyewitness Visual Dictionaries). $14.95. TL547.E85. 629.133'014. LC 92-7670. ISBN 1-56458-101-2.

Covering every form of atmospheric flight (space flight is not included), from the Montgolfier balloon of 1783 to the SST and Airbus of today, this work provides access to the meaning of nearly 2,000 aeronautical terms by means of fully labeled, richly detailed color paintings and photographs. Each double-page spread covers one major topic and includes a short summary text as well as the illustrations. Thorough indexing allows the reader to find every illustration of a term (e.g., under *rudder*, 20 different aircraft are listed); it is also possible, although probably less easy, to start with the airplane itself and, by searching through the illustrations, determine the names and functions of its components. Auxiliary equipment, not all of it limited to aeronautical uses (e.g., *flashlight*), is also included.

Although the publisher lists the book's age level as "10 up" and the Library of Congress has cataloged it as "juvenile literature," it is difficult to believe that many 10-year-olds would be able to deal with either the concepts or the vocabulary presented. It seems more likely that the book's audience will be serious aviation fans and students or amateur pilots of high school age or above. This is an unusual book of strong visual appeal that will be a useful complement to the standard aeronautical dictionaries; it will not, however, replace them. [R: RBB, 15 Mar 93, pp. 1378-79]—**Paul B. Cors**

GROUND

Dictionaries and Encyclopedias

2021. Edwards, John. **Auto Dictionary.** Los Angeles, Calif., HPBooks/Price Stern Sloan, 1993. 194p. illus. $24.95; $16.95pa. TL9.E33. 629.2'03. LC 92-23954. ISBN 1-55788-067-0; 1-55788-056-5pa.

Defining the surprising variety of terms and phrases associated with automobiles is the *Auto Dictionary*. This A-to-Z listing covers engineering terms, automotive components, equipment, technology, racing jargon, and hot-rod slang, along with brief histories of major automotive manufacturers. Although easily comprehensible by laypeople, the definitions are never simplistic. Nearly every page features good-quality illustrations, including photographs and diagrams. Written and edited by automotive professionals, the dictionary presents a lot of information in a mid-sized book and will be a boon to consumers and technicians alike. The combination of usefulness, reliability, and low price make it a particularly good value. [R: RBB, 15 Nov 93, pp. 645-46]—**Megan S. Farrell**

2022. Jackson, Alan A. **The Railway Dictionary: An A-Z of Railway Terminology.** Dover, N.H., Alan Sutton, 1992. 339p. illus. $34.00. TF9.J33. 625.1'03. LC 92-8999. ISBN 0-7509-0038-5.

As do all ancient and arcane crafts, railroads have an extensive and distinctive vocabulary. To railroad workers, rail historians, and railfans, much of this vocabulary is almost second nature, but to the rest of the world it can be amazingly obscure. This well-constructed book includes definitions for some 6,000 railroad terms, ranging from strictly technical vocabulary to railroad workers' slang and the names of railroad companies and famous trains. It also includes explanations of hundreds of initials and abbreviations. Individual definitions range from a few words to about 200 words long. All appear to be clear, accurate, and carefully constructed. From the point of view of U.S. libraries, the greatest strength of this volume is its international scope. The book was originally published in England, and its focus is primarily British, but it is also strong on U.S. terminology, as well as words associated with railroads on the Continent and the rest of the world.

One potential problem in a work of this type lies in distinguishing between U.S. and British vocabularies, which can be very different for technical subjects. When it comes to words that have different meanings in different countries, *The Railway Dictionary* does very well; an assiduous search for words famous for causing international confusion turned up fewer than half a dozen for which the dictionary failed to make the differences in usage very clear. Many other railroad words, however, are used in one nation but not the other, and the book frequently fails to note that a given English word is not used in the United States.

Because of its international scope, this volume should be a convenient first place to look, especially where British railroads, railroad company initials, or the names of railroads or famous trains are involved. It will not eliminate the need for a dictionary of purely U.S. terminology, but it will answer many technical and historical railroad questions, and it will provide reasonably priced, English-language coverage of the world of railroads.—**Frederick A. Schlipf**

Directories

2023. **Motor Carrier Professional Services Directory 1993.** Catherine M. Mahe, comp. Linda S. Rothbart, ed. Alexandria, Va., American Trucking Associations, 1993. 273p. index. $35.00pa. ISBN 0-88711-168-8.

This guide for trucking businesses is practical, compact, and easy to use. Its intent is to enable motor carriers to find relevant outside help with ease and to point to alternatives for price and quality comparisons. The guidebook's tripartite division helps in finding information in four different ways. In section 1 the user finds information about outside expert assistance in 63 different areas, from accident analysis to workers' compensation. Even though this part is not subdivided by geographical regions, it is easy to find the nearest specialist in a given category of expertise by checking the few pages of each category. Cross-references direct the user to section 2, where the expert service providers are described in more detail. It contains basic information on each expert business, giving addresses, telephone numbers, names of chief executive officers, types of services provided, representative clients of each business, and categories of services provided. Section 3 contains geographical and name indexes. Advertising matter in this very serviceable guidebook gives additional information.—**Bogdan Mieczkowski**

Handbooks and Yearbooks

2024. Drury, George H., comp. **The Train-Watcher's Guide to North American Railroads.** 2d ed. Waukesha, Wis., Kalmbach Publishing, 1993. 288p. illus. maps. index. (Railroad Reference Series, no.11). $14.95pa. TF23.D75. 385'.025'7. LC 92-35627. ISBN 0-89024-131-7.

Since the first edition of this popular handbook appeared in 1984 (see ARBA 85, entry 1722), the railroads of the United States have undergone extensive reorganization. Many of the lines active in 1984 have disappeared through merger, sale, or abandonment, but there have been even more new regional and local railroads created as the major companies rid themselves of secondary lines to concentrate on a few high-traffic routes. This edition has been completely rewritten: Virtually nothing in the 1984 version remains valid.

Covering the United States, Canada, and Mexico (changes in the latter two countries have been much less dramatic, although both have considerably reduced passenger service), the book includes all railroads more than 200 miles long or with more than 1,000 freight cars in interchange service, as well as all the commuter operating authorities and a few other lines that the compiler finds interesting. The alphabetically arranged entries include name, a short narrative description, a simplified route map, address, mileage, reporting marks (the initials used on freight cars), number of locomotives and cars owned, principal freight commodities handled, location of repair shops, junctions with other lines, radio frequencies, and passenger routes (if any are still operated). Details vary; not all categories of information apply to all railroads. Many entries also include bibliographical references. Written for hobbyists, the book does not attempt to provide the managerial or fiscal data found in business references. Supplemental matter includes a list of rail transit systems, a key to reporting marks, a short guide to good train-watching spots, and a glossary of railroad terms. Libraries of all types will find this a convenient and inexpensive source of information on the railroad industry.—**Paul B. Cors**

2025. McDonald, Charles W. **Diesel Locomotive Rosters: U.S., Canada, Mexico.** 3d ed. Waukesha, Wis., Kalmbach Publishing, 1992. 239p. illus. $12.95pa. TJ619.2.M33. 625.2'66'0973. LC 92-17907. ISBN 0-89024-112-0.

This work is almost 50 percent larger than the 2d edition (see ARBA 87, entry 1742), reflecting both an increase in the number of railroads (from 400 to 540) as new regional and shortline carriers come into existence, and the addition of a new section covering industrial locomotives. Its goal remains the same: to list and briefly describe all diesel, gasoline, and electric locomotives on the companies' current rosters, based on data supplied by the operators. The main section covering common carriers is arranged alphabetically by company name and subarranged numerically by the locomotives' road numbers; data on model, builder, date built, and (when relevant) previous owner are presented in tabular format. Technical descriptions of locomotive models are again summarized in an introductory section. Photographs of the more commonly used locomotive models are included, although it has not been possible to illustrate every kind of locomotive still in use.

The list of industrial locomotives (i.e., those used by manufacturing, mining, lumber, and agricultural firms to move cars on switching tracks within their properties) is the first such listing ever attempted. While the author acknowledges that it is incomplete and may contain some errors, it is nevertheless a surprisingly extensive compilation. Arrangement is alphabetical by state or province (Mexico is not covered in this section), city, and company; the information on individual locomotives is the same as in the main section, although sometimes less full, depending on what the operators have provided.

This edition is both bigger and better than its predecessors. Serious rail enthusiasts will want their own copy, but it will also be useful to public and special libraries.—**Paul B. Cors**

2026. Morlan, Michael. **American Automobile Collections and Museums: A Guide to U.S. Exhibits.** Shawnee, Kans., Bon A Tirer Publishing, 1992. 252p. illus. index. $15.95pa. LC 92-70150. ISBN 1-878446-10-X.

Morlan's work is the most recent guide to U.S. exhibits of automobiles. It lists 140 in the United States, none in Canada. (The introduction notes that some collections are not included, sometimes at the request of the owners.) Entries contain brief descriptions of each collection, usually with comments on notable specimens; directions to the museums; admission charges; hours of operation; notes on availability of restaurants, gift shops, and film; and sometimes an illustration. For comparison, *Automobile Quarterly's Directory of North American Automobile Museums* (Automobile Quarterly, 1992) lists 220 in the United States and 18 in Canada. Most of that book's entries are somewhat shorter but contain similar basic information and more illustrations. But the big difference lies in Morlan's inclusion of lists of holdings for most collections; these are absent from the *Automobile Quarterly* volume. This factor may well be of more importance to most travelers than sheer numbers.—**Walter C. Allen**

2027. **Statistical Report on Road Accidents in 1990. Rapport Statistique sur les Accidents de la Route en 1990.** Paris, European Conference of Ministers of Transportation; distr., Washington, D.C., OECD Publications & Information Center, 1992. 77p. $27.00pa. ISBN 92-821-0174-6.

This annual publication of road accident trends in ECMT (European Conference of Ministers of Transport) member countries, associate nations (Australia, Canada, Japan, and the United States), and observer nations (Morocco) provides 14 statistical tables ranging from number of people killed and casualties to road vehicle population. Some of the same data may be found in *Statistics of Road Traffic Accidents in Europe* (see ARBA 93, entry 1785), issued annually by the United Nations Economic Commission for Europe, but each title has features not found in the other. The United Nations publication is purely statistical, but it is useful in that it includes the following kinds of tables: nature of the accidents and surroundings, number of accidents due to the influence of alcohol, and number of persons killed or injured by age group. While the *Statistical Report on Road Accidents in 1990* omits those data, it does provide interpretive comments for and an analysis of the data. It also describes road safety measures taken by each of the ECMT countries in 1989 and 1990. The tables are easy to read, and the analyses provide the appropriate insight needed to interpret the figures. One disconcerting feature is that the statistical tables identify the ECMT countries by letters that are not obvious to a U.S. audience. (The publisher could eliminate this confusion by including a legend.) This title is highly recommended for libraries that collect materials in the areas of transportation, international trade, and European studies.—**Dene L. Clark**

2028. Sturm, Gary L., and Mark J. Landgraf. **The Compendium of American Railroad Radio Frequencies.** 12th ed. Waukesha, Ill., Kalmbach Books, 1993. 197p. maps. (Railroad Reference Series, no.12). $16.95pa. 385. ISBN 0-89024-161-9.

Railroading was the first major North American industry to rely on electric communications (the telegraph) and began experimenting with radio as long ago as 1910. Today, virtually every North American railroad relies upon radio not only to direct the operation of its trains but also in such support activities as maintenance of way and security forces. Railroad enthusiasts are well aware of all this broadcasting, and many enjoy eavesdropping on it via scanner, hence the compilation of this directory.

This is the title's first commercial edition (the previous editions were privately published by the authors and, judging by the paucity of OCLC records, were not acquired by libraries). Following an explanatory introduction (which includes a list of nonradio railroads and a short bibliography), listings for United States and Canadian railroads are given in four sections: common carriers, industrial railroads, transit systems, and museums and tourist lines. In each section the arrangement is alphabetical by company name; under the companies, frequencies used system-wide are given first, followed by those used in specific localities. Maps are provided for a few large systems to clarify regional usage. A short international section provides information on selected railroads of Australia, Germany, Great Britain, Ireland, Mexico, New Zealand, and Sweden. A supplemental listing by major metropolitan areas and an update giving last-minute changes are appended.

Railroad enthusiasts will want their own copy to carry with them, but many libraries will also find this a useful addition to their transportation and telecommunication collections. There is no other comparable work available.—**Paul B. Cors**

WATER

2029. Heden, Karl E. **The Great Lakes Guide to Sunken Ships.** Brookline Village, Mass., Branden Publishing, 1993. 304p. illus. index. $19.95pa. G525.H37. 977. LC 92-43727. ISBN 0-8283-1973-1.

An updated and enlarged edition of *Directory of Shipwrecks of the Great Lakes*, published in 1966, the present volume includes almost twice as many entries as the previous edition. The work starts with a brief geographical essay on the Great Lakes and a list of U.S. Life Saving Service stations in the late 1800s. The directory follows. Entries are arranged alphabetically by the name of the vessels and may include type of vessel, tonnage, date lost, approximate location, cargo, shipmaster, value of cargo and vessel, and lives lost. The most complete entries are for newer losses. Many of the entries are not as thorough, however, due to the limited information about the vessel and the date of the sinking. The entry for the *China* serves as an example of the many entries from the late nineteenth century: "China—vessel of 314 tons, 20 November 1883, stranded Cape Hurd, Lake Huron." Following the directory are several photographs of the vessels listed in the directory. A list of vessel sinkings, both recreational and commercial, concludes the volume. The recreational listings cover the years from 1969 to 1989, while the commercial lists cover 1969 to 1980. This is a useful guide for those interested in salvage, diving, ships, shipwrecks, or the Great Lakes area.—**Gregory Curtis**

2030. Parker, Mark, and Ed McKnew. **PowerBoat Guide.** 3d ed. Camden, Me., International Marine; distr., Blue Ridge Summit, Pa., TAB Books, 1992. 1v. (unpaged). illus. $29.95. ISBN 0-8774236-0-1.

This yacht brokers' and boat buyers' "bible" lists some 850 inboard power boats. It includes convertibles, sportfishermen, motor yachts, family cruisers, trawlers, and express cruisers. The 42 chapters are arranged alphabetically by manufacturer's name, beginning with Albin and ending with

Wellcraft. Following this is a 125-page section on notable designs. The manufacturer's initial page gives a brief history of the company, a list of models, and the address and telephone number of the main office. A typical entry page has an underway photograph of the boat at the top, a 200-word review of the boat, a list of specifications, and a deck plan. Front matter includes a table of contents, a cross-reference index, an introduction, a glossary of terms, a yacht broker and dealer index, and a marine surveyor index. The authors live in Florida and are themselves yacht brokers.—**Frank J. Anderson**

2031. Ritchie, L. A., ed. **The Shipbuilding Industry: A Guide to Historical Records.** New York, Manchester University Press/St. Martin's Press, 1992. 206p. index. (Studies in British Business Archives). $59.95. Z6834.S5S54. 016.62382'0941. LC 92-9472. ISBN 0-7190-3805-7.

This volume will be welcomed by naval and maritime researchers. It features brief histories of about 200 British shipbuilding firms, along with lists of their surviving records and their location. The book starts out with an essay, "Modern British Shipbuilding, 1800-1990" by Anthony Slaven (professor of business history at the University of Glasgow), which traces the ups and downs of the industry over almost 200 years. Next is a survey of the records of the shipbuilding industry by Michael S. Moss (archivist at the University of Glasgow), which lists the types of records the researcher will find and their potential uses. A short user's guide leads into the primary section of the book—"Shipbuilders: Lists of Records"— where the information is arranged alphabetically by name of company. A history of each company precedes the listing and location of its records. "Trade Organisations: Lists of Records" follows, along with three brief appendixes. The book is separately indexed by name, place, and subject. The design, layout, and printing are nicely done. [R: Choice, Mar 93, p. 1120]—**Frank J. Anderson**

Author/Title Index

Reference is to entry number.

A. M. Klein: an annot bibliog, 1278
A Matter of Fact, staff of, 1851
A to Zoo, 4th ed, 1176
AAAS hndbk 1993/94, 1579
Abate, Frank R., 1084
ABC for bk collectors, 1026
ABC of stage lighting, 1475
Abel, Dean, 1662
Abortion in the US, 1992 suppl, 1840
Access Nippon '92 business hndbk, 241
ACCIS gd to UN info sources on health, 1811
Accredited insts of postsecondary educ, programs, candidates, 1992-93, 347
Acocella, Nicholas, 831
Acrosport, 817
Action art, 1039
Action gd to govt grants, loans, & giveaways, 895
Active figures of the trade union & working class movement of Russia, Ukraine, Bielorussia, & Kazakhstan, 262
Activist's almanac, 865
Adele Wiseman: an annot bibliog, 1277
Adelman, Elizabeth Fagan, 421
Adult educ in continental Europe, 391
Adult learner's gd to alternative & external degree programs, 393
Adventuring in New Zealand, 482
Adventuring with bks, 10th ed, 1173
Advertising ratios & budgets, 287
Advisory Committee for the Coordination of Information Systems (ACCIS), 788
Aerial atlas of ancient Crete, 529
Africa: a gd to ref material, 94
Africa south of the Sahara 1993, 91
African American ency, 402
African American generals, 685
African American: social & economic conditions, 405
African American women, 960
African archaeology, 488
African heritage of American English, 1081
African names, 443
African socio-economic indicators 1989, 92
African studies thesaurus, 629
African theology, 1508
Agnes Moorehead: a bio-bibliog, 1413
AIDS: 1,000 full-text statistical abstracts from the A Matter of Fact database, 1984-92, 1851
AIDS crisis in America, 1852
AIDS dir, 1850
AIDS dissidents, 1856
Aiki News 1994 dojo finder, 854
Akins, Imogene, 743
Al Jolson: a bio-discography, 1365
ALA survey of librarian salaries 1993, 613
Albala, Elie, 1890
Albanian-English dict, 1109
Albinski, Nan Bowman, 123
Albrecht, Gerhard, 706
Alcohol-related issues in the Latino population 1980-90, 915
Alden Nowlan papers, 1276

Alderson, A. D., 1135
Alderton, David, 1704, 1705
Alec Wilder: a bio-bibliog, 1324
Alessandro & Domenico Scarlatti: a gd to research, 1334
Alexander, Sharon, 1179
Alford, B. W. E., 263
Alford, John A., 1253
Alfred Hitchcock: a gd to refs & resources, 1450
Alilunas-Rodgers, Kristine, 122
All music gd, 1314
Allcock, John B., 722
Allen County Public Library Genealogy Department, staff of, 438
Allen, Hayward, 413
Allied Artists checklist, 1445
Alliums, 1653
Allott, Angela M., 633
Almanac of American pols 1994, 746
Almanac of renewable energy, 1983
Almeder, Robert F., 1495
Almquist, Sharon G., 1351
ALSA swimmer's gd, 1993 ed, 861
Alston, Jon P., 222
Alternative dispute resolution sourcebk, 1993-94 ed, 579
Alternative health care resources, 1843
Altman, Roberta, 1858
Alun Hoddinott: a bio-bibliog, 1322
Alvey, Christine E., 630
Alzheimer's, stroke, & 29 other neurological disorders sourcebk, 1862
Ambry, Margaret, 283, 927
America votes 20, 756
American Antiquarian Society, staff of, 657
American automobile collections & museums, 2026
American bibliog of Slavic & E European studies for 1990, 130
American big businesses dir, 1993 ed, 161
American bk trade dir 1993-94, 661
American Chamber of Commerce in Italy dir 1992, 268
American Civil Liberties Union: an annot bibliog, 550
American cultural leaders from colonial times to the present, 976
American ethnic lits, 1225
American foreign policy index, v.1, no.1, 759
American graphic design, 1059
American Heritage college dict, 3d ed, 1075
American Heritage Dictionaries, editors of, 1095
American higher educ, 323
American Horticultural Society ency of gardening, 1617
American Indian: a multimedia ency, 414
American Lib Assn best of the best for children, 1163
American lib dir 1993-94, 610
American Library Association Reference Books Bulletin Editorial Board, 3
American manufacturers dir, 1993 ed, 212
American orchestral music, 1347
American Revolution 1775-1783: an ency, 503
American salaries & wages survey, 2d ed, 282
American small city profiles, 941
American social leaders, 78

American suburbs, 946
American women civil rights activists, 592
American women playwrights 1964-89, 1228
American women songwriters, 1325
America's black colleges, 330
America's secret recreation areas, 476
America's top military careers, 690
America's top rated cities, 1992 ed, 943
America's top 300 jobs, 276
Ameringer, Charles D., 720
Ammerman, Robert T., 1845
Ammon, Bette D., 1182
Amnesty Intl: the 1993 report on human rights around the world, 591
Amphibians & reptiles in Kans., 3d ed, 1749
Anaesthesia A-Z, 1874
ANC & black workers in S Africa, 1912-92, 103
Ancient & shining ones, 1392
Anderson, Erland, 1266
Anderson, Ewan A., 794
Anderson, Vicki, 1196
Andrew Johnson: a bibliog, 495
Andrews, Alice C., 321
Andrews, Robert, 1689
Andreyeva, Victoria, 1128
Andriot, Donna, 55
Angeles, Peter A., 1496
Anglo-American trade dir 1993, 264
Angola, 96
Animal life, 1685
Ann Petry: a bio-bibliog, 1237
Annotated bibliog of the official langs of Canada, 1068
Annual register of grant support, 26th ed, 888
Annual review of info sci & tech, v.27, 614
Anthologies of music, 2d ed, 1319
Antiquarian, specialty, & used bk sellers 1993, 662
Appel, Marsha C., 1050
Appleton, Barbara, 471
Appleton, Richard, 471
Applied & decorative arts, 2d ed, 1022
Aquaculture sourcebk, 1594
Aramaic bibliog, pt.1, 1071
Archaeological gd to Mexico's Yucatan peninsula, 481
Archambault, Ariane, 1114
Arden, Heather M., 1282
Arends, J. C., 1649
Armenians: a colossal bibliographic gd to bks published in the English lang, 129
Armitage, Allan M., 1623
Arndt, Thomas, 1690
Arnold, Ben, 1305
Arozena, Steven, 647
Arpan, Jeffrey S., 213
ARRL hndbk for radio amateurs 1993, 1015
Art, Henry, 1994
Art mktg sourcebk, 1045
Art of black American women, 1046
Art price index intl '94, 1049
Art world dir: arts review yrbk 1993, 1044
Artello, Mary Ann, 1809
Artificial intelligence abstracts annual 1991, 1888
Artists of the Pacific Northwest, 1042
A's & B's of academic scholarships, 16th ed, 363
Asdell's patterns of mammalian reproduction, 1731
Ash, Irene, 1932, 1942
Ash, Lee, 656

Ash, Michael, 1932, 1942
Asia 1992 yrbk, 106
Asia-Pacific/Africa-Middle East petroleum dir, 1993, 1971
ASM hndbk, v.3, 1792
ASM materials engineering dict, 1793
Assassination of John F. Kennedy, 494
ASTM, 1578
Atkins, Beryl T., 1113
Atkins, Stephen E., 585
Atlas of ...
   American higher educ, 321
   American sport, 819
   breeding birds in Pa., 1694
   conures, 1690
   dog breeds of the world, 1710
   endangered animals, 1686
   endangered places, 1987
   intl migration, 428
   livebearers of the world, 1721
   N American exploration, 444
   the 1990 census, 931
   the Third World, 2d ed, 459
   the world, 2d ed, 446
   world pol flashpoints, 794
Atomic bomb, 710
Audiocassette & CD finder, 3d ed, 374
Audiovisual resources in primatology, Wis Regional Primate Research Center, 1732
AUSMAP atlas of Austral., 455
Austin Clarke: a ref gd, 1293
Australian concise Oxford dict, 1096
Australian plant name index, 1648
Author a month (for dimes), 1188
Authors: critical & biographical refs, 2d ed, 1145
Author's gd to social work jls, 3d ed, 912
Auto dict, 2021
Award-winning bks for children & young adults 1990-91, 1166
Awesome almanac—Ill., 84
Awesome almanac—Ind., 86
Awesome almanac—Mich., 87
Awesome almanac—Minn., 85
Awesome almanac—Wis., 83
AWP official gd to writing programs, 6th ed, 993
Axelrod, Alan, 1993
Axelrod, Herbert R., 1711
Axelrod, Natalie, 1806
Ayala, Marta Stiefel, 600
Ayala, Reynaldo, 600
Ayer, A. J., 1499

Bach English-title index, 1331
Bachkatov, Nina, 525
Backus, Karen, 1807
Bacon's Information, Inc., 1003, 1004, 1014
Bacon's media calendar dir 1993, 1003
Bacon's newspaper/mag dir 1993, 1004
Bacon's radio/TV dir 1993, 1014
Baer, Beverly, 59
Baer, D. Richard, 1439
Bagust, Harold, 1618
Bahm, Archie J., 1498
Bailey, Leigh, 2003
Bain, Robert, 1222
Baines, Anthony, 1338
Bains, William, 1790

Bair, Frank, 723
Bair, Frank E., 1862, 1947
Baker, Brian L., 566
Baker, Daniel B., 463
Baker, Hugh, 1792
Balachandran, M., 934
Balachandran, S., 934
Ball pest & disease manual, 1624
Balmer, Randall, 1533
Balz, Horst, 1528
Banham, Martin, 1471
Banjo on record, 1336
Bannock, Graham, 159
Baraga, Frederic, 1124
Barer, Burl, 1249
Baretta-Bekker, J. G., 1744
Barhydt, Frances Bartlett, 1580
Barker, Nicolas, 1026
Barlow, Richard G., 986
Barman, Jean, 924, 925
Barnavi, Eli, 424
Barnett, Lynn, 325, 371
Baron, John H., 1306
Baron, Salo Wittmayer, 427
Barone, Michael, 746
Baroque music: a research & info gd, 1306
Barr, Catherine, 615
Barraclough, Geoffrey, 530
Barrett, Jacqueline K., 48, 969
Barron, Sarah, 1634
Barron's Educational Series, Inc., editors of, 32
Barron's gd to graduate bus schools, 8th ed, 168
Barron's new student's concise ency, 2d ed, 32
Bartel, Pauline, 1452
Baseball: a comp bibliog, suppl.1, 837
Baseball ency, 9th ed, 830
Basic gd to pesticides, 2009
Basic lib skills, 3d ed, 620
Baskin, Ellen, 1438
Bassett, Jan, 516
Basta, Margo McLoone, 2
Bataille, Gretchen M., 956
Batten, Donna, 747
Battle bk, 695
Baughman, Judith S., 1229
Baur, Tassilo, 1454
Baxter, Colin F., 531
Baxter, Herbert, 1639
Baxter, Pam M., 805
Baxter, R. E., 159
Baytelman, Pola, 1320
Beacon bk of quotations by women, 972
Beacon: college & career planning on CD-ROM, 349
Beacon college project dir, 325
Beal, Peter, 1245
Bear, John, 350, 351, 1153
Beard, Henry, 1101
Bear's gd to earning college degrees non-traditionally, 350
Beatles: the ultimate recording gd, 1380
Beaty, H. Wayne, 1777
Beaubien, Charles A., 740
Beavers, Randell A., 1691
Bedford, Frances, 1335
Beecroft, K. A., 636
Beit-Hallahmi, Benjamin, 1529
Belkin, Gary S., 1095

Bell, Judith, 1324
Bellack, Alan S., 812
Benedetto, Robert, 1520
Benewick, Robert, 715
Beniukh, Ksana, 1130
Beniukh, Oleg, 1130
Benjamin, Ruth, 1309
Bennett, George, 140
Bennett, Gillian, 1383
Bennett, Joy, 1270
Bennett, Linda A., 395
Bennett, Pramila Ramgulam, 140
Bennett, Stephen J., 1906
Bensen, Clark H., 741
Benson, Evelyn, 1129
Benson, Larry D., 1250
Benson, Margie, 83
Benson, Morton, 1129
Bentley, Elizabeth Petty, 431
Benton, Michael, 1959
Beowulf scholarship, 1263
Bercuson, David J., 517
Berg, Donna Lee, 1097
Bernard E. Harkness seedlist hndbk, 2d ed, 1625
Berndt, Thomas, 691
Berney, K. A., 1467
Bernhard, Judith, 315
Bernstein, Peter W., 302
Best bks for public libs, 647
Best lawyers in America 1993-94, 562
Best nonfranchise bus opportunities, 199
Best rated CDs: classical 1992, 1344
Best, Reba A., 1892
Best yrs of their lives, 926
Bettelheim, Judith, 1399
Betty Grable: a bio-bibliog, 1408
Bever, Michael B., 1794
Beyer, Gerry W., 555
BFI film & TV hndbk 1993, 1455
Bhushan, Bharat, 1692
Bianco, David P., 800
Bible: cultural atlas for young people, 1546
Bibliographia Malebranchiana, 1485
Bibliographic gd to ...
    Caribbean mass comm, 990
    computer sci 1991, 1893
    dance 1991, 1422
    E Asian studies 1991, 107
    educ 1991, 303
    Latin American studies 1991, 141
    microform pubns 1991, 1921
    the environment 1991, 1988
Bibliographical gd to African-American women writers, 1223
Bibliography & index of English verse in ms 1501-58, 1267
Bibliography of ...
    Cuban mass communications, 991
    Indian law per articles published 1980-90, 2d ed, 547
    Latin American & Caribbean bibliogs, 1985-89: social scis & humanities, 145
    native N Americans on disc, 415
    new religious movements in primal societies, v.6, 1505
    the mss of Patrick Branwell Bronte, 1247
    the nature & role of the holy spirit in 20th-century writings, 1534

Bibliography on computational molecular biology, 1634
Bibliography on Holocaust lit, suppl. v.2, 532
Bibliometrics: an annot bibliog, 1970-90, 623
Bicentennial concordance, 580
Bieber's dict of legal abbrevs, 4th ed, 543
Bieber's dict of legal citations, 4th ed, 544
Biedermann, Hans, 979
Big outside, rev ed, 1678
Big screen bk, 1435
Bignoniaceae—pt.2 (tribe tecomeae), 1637
Billboard bk of American singing groups, 1359
Billboard bk of no.1 hits, 3d ed, 1360
Billiard industry source bk, 1992/1993 ed, 857
Billman, Larry, 1408
Binary stars, 1929
Bindocci, Cynthia Gay, 948
Bingham, Don, 1024
Bingham, Joan, 1024
Binns, Margaret, 102
Binns, Tony, 102
Biographical dict of Canadian Jewry 1909-14, 410
Biographical dict of geography, 465
Biography: an annot bibliog, 16
Biography & genealogy master index [CD-ROM], 436
Biography today, 1992 annual cum, 11
Biondi, Joann, 475
Biosystematic monograph of the genus Cucumis (Cucurbitaceae), 1638
Biotechnology from A to Z, 1790
Bird atlas, 1702
Birds of Tikal, 1691
Bishop, Edward L., 1154
Bishop, Lloyd, 306
Bjorner, Susanne, 1005
Black Americans info dir 1994-95, 407
Black elected officials, 20th ed, 733
Black 100, 406
Black, Richard, 96
Black women in America, 965
Blackwell dict of ...
    Judaica, 1554
    20th-century social thought, 73
Blackwell ency of industrial archaeology, 484
Blakemore, Harold, 142
Blanc, F. L., 1725
Blanco, Richard L., 503
Blank, Denise, 3
Blanpain, Roger, 252
Blashfield, Jean F., 84, 85
Blaustein, Albert P., 580
Bleiberg, German, 1289
Blevins, Winfred, 1088
Bloom, Adrian, 1626
Bloom, Alan, 1626
Blooms of Bressingham garden plants, 1626
Blue, Anthony Dias, 1605
Blum, Annette, 1507
Blum, Laurie, 326, 327, 328, 329
BNA Library Staff, 748
BNA's dir of state administrative codes & registers, 748
BNA's 1993 source bk on collective bargaining & employee relations, 277
Bob Brant's best of Macintosh shareware, 1913
Bob Dylan: a bio-bibliog, 1379
Bodart, Joni Richards, 1164
Bodiwala, G. G., 1825

Body atlas, 1819
Bohlander, Richard, 1803
Bohlke, James E., 1713
Bollard, John K., 1084
Bond, James, 1693
Bonin, Jean M., 1318
Book of ...
    Daniel: an annot bibliog, 1536
    lists for regulated hazardous substances 1993, 2010
    the states, v.29, 721
    women's firsts, 970
Book review index, 1991 cum, 59
Bookman's price index, v.46, 1025
Books & pers online, 44
Books for you, 11th ed, 1165
Books in print 1993-94, 7
Books in print of the UN system, 788
Books in print plus, 8
Books in Spanish for children & young adults, 1180
Border & territorial disputes, 3d ed, 722
Bordman, Gerald, 1480
Boris Karloff: a bio-bibliog, 1409
Born to power, 155
Bortin, Virginia, 1321
Borzvalka, I., 1123
Boschung, Herbert T., 1714
Bosoni, Anthony J., 557, 910
Bosse, David, 491, 492
Bosworth, C. E., 150, 151
Botanical Latin, 4th ed, 1641
Botswana, 99
Bottle, R. T., 1931
Bottomore, Tom, 73
Boughn, Michael, 1234
Boulanger, Norman C., 1470
Bowden, Henry Warner, 1509
Bowen, Kelley, 723
Bowen, Thomas, 723
Bowker annual lib & bk trade almanac, 38th ed, 615
Bowman, J. Wilson, 330
Bowring, Richard, 113
Boylan, James C., 1867, 1868, 1869, 1870
Boyle, Kathleen Nelson, 869
Brace, Edward R., 1838
Bradley, Fern Marshall, 1619
Bradshaw, Peter, 110
Brailow, David, 1243
Brandt, Bruce E., 1255
Brant, Bob, 1913
Brauning, Daniel W., 1694
Braunstein, Janet, 299
Breen, Jon L., 1206
Bregman, Robert, 1369
Bremser, Martha, 1423
Brennan, Shawn, 968
Brereton, Mary M., 621
Breslauer, S. Daniel, 1555
Brewer's bk of myth & legend, 1391
Brewer's dict of names, 440
Brickell, Christopher, 1617
Bricker's intl dir, 24th ed, 225
Briggs, Shirley A., 2009
Briggs, Virginia L., 271
Bright, Charles D., 698
Bright, Donald E., 1722
Bright, William, 470

Bringhurst, Robert, 675
British hit albums, 5th ed, 1362
British librarianship & info work 1986-90, v.2, 633
British literary bibliog, 1970-79, 1244
British pharmacopoeia 1993, 1876
British printmakers 1855-1955, 1057
British radio & TV pioneers, 1012
Broadcasting in the UK, 2d ed, 1013
Broadway's prize-winning musicals, 1465
Brockway, Sandi, 74
Brogan, T. V. F., 1302
Bromley, David W., 633
Bronson, Fred, 1360
Brosman, Catharine Savage, 1283
Brown, Barbara E., 246
Brown, Catherine, 19
Brown, Elsa Barkley, 965
Brown, Enid, 149
Brown, Gary, 1733
Brown, Lesley, 1099
Brown, Wendy E., 1891
Browning, James A., 88
Browning, Larry M., 710
Brownrigg, Ronald, 1537
Brownson, Ann L., 734, 735, 736
Brownstone, David, 920, 1996
Bruccoli, Arlyn, 1243
Bruce, Kimball W., 751
Brunel, Pierre, 1155
Bruno, Frank J., 807
Bruntjen, Scott, 10
Brus, Eric, 1983
Brzezinski, Mary Jo, 272
Buehrer, Beverley Bare, 1409
Building the ref collection, 619
Bukowski, Leonard, 1369
Bull, C. Neil, 887
Bullock, Joyce, 801
Bultman, Scott, 1314
Burack, Sylvia K., 999
Burels, Ned, 407
Burgess, Mary A., 432
Burgess, Michael, 432, 1238
Burkett, Nancy H., 657
Burnell, Richard S., 634
Burns, Grant, 709
Burns, Richard Dean, 797
Burr, John R., 1482
Burrell, C. Colson, 1620
Burton, Rosemary, 464
Bushnell, Brooks, 1453
Business & legal CD-ROMS in print 1993, 175
Business One Irwin investor's hndbk 1993, 187
Business Week, editors of, 169
Business Week's gd to the best executive educ programs, 169
Butcher, Judith, 1000
Butler, Brian, 204
Butterflies through binoculars, 1703
Butterworths law dir 1993, 558
Buyer's gd to American wines, 2d ed, 1605
By Jove!, 1396
Byrne, John A., 169

C. S. Lewis: a ref gd 1972-88, 1254
Cabell, David W. E., 663

Cabell's dir of publ opportunities in educ, 3d ed, 663
Cadogan, Gerald, 529
Caelli, William, 1900
Cahalan, James M., 1291
Cahn, Robert W., 1795
Calderini, Simonetta, 101
Caldwell, Ronald J., 1521
Caldwell, Sandra M., 1521
Calhoun, Randall, 1236
California environmental dir, 5th ed, 2007
Calinger, Ronald S., 718
Cambridge dict of Australian places, 471
Cambridge ency, 33
Cambridge ency of ...
    human evolution, 394
    Japan, 113
    Latin America & the Caribbean, 142
Cambridge gd to American theatre, 1479
Cambridge gd to theatre, updated ed, 1471
Cambridge Market Intelligence, 223
Cameron, Myra, 1826
Camp, Roderic Ai, 12
Campano, Frederick W., 726
Campbell, Alta, 172
Campbell, Karlyn Kohrs, 957
Canada, 127
Canada tax cases: index & citator, 581
Canada's army in WW II, 702
Canadian architecture collection, 1053
Canadian Assn of Law Libs dir, 649
Canadian bus & economics, 3d ed, 246
Canadian bus in the Pacific Rim, 251
Canadian dict of bus & economics, 247
Canadian global almanac 1993, 1
Canadian lib hndbk, 617
Canadian obituary record 1991, 18
Canadian Oxford intermediate atlas, 457
Canadian Oxford school atlas, 6th ed, 456
Canadian quaternary vocabulary, 1943
Canadian spelling dict, 7th ed, 1102
Canadian studies on Hungarians: a bibliog. Suppl., 408
Canadian women's movement, 1960-90, 966
Canadian writers & their works: cum index, fiction series, 1271
Canadian writers & their works: cum index, poetry series, 1272
Cancer dict, 1858
Cancer therapy, 1860
Canine lexicon, 1706
Cantor, George, 416
Caplan, Usher, 1278
Carande, Robert J., 1894
Career advancement for women in the fed serv, 270
Career discovery ency, 384
Career gd to America's top industries, 278
Career training sourcebk, 388
Caregiving of older adults, 867
Carey, Patrick W., 1525
Caribbean 1975-80, 143
Caribbean women novelists, 1301
Caring for kids with special needs, 918
Carnegie Library of Pittsburgh Science and Technology Department, 1584
Carpenter, Sue, 472
Carr, Dawson W., 1061
Carruth, Gordon, 504

Carruth, Gorton, 1189
Carskadon, Mary A., 808
Carter, Craig, 838
Carter, John, 1026
Carter, Susanne, 1219
Carvajal, Manuel J., 143
Cash for college, 360
Cassel, Jeris F., 1483
Cassell careers ency, 13th ed, 385
Cassell concise English dict, new ed, 1098
Cassell dict of literary & lang terms, 980
Cassiday, Bruce, 1207
Cassidy, Daniel J., 331, 332, 333
Cassutt, Michael, 1755
Castillo-Speed, Lillian, 971
Catalog of dicts, word bks, & philological texts, 1440-1900, 1074
Catalog of types of Coleoptera in the Canadian Natl Collection of Insects, suppl.3, 1728
Cataloger's gd to MARC coding & tagging for AV material, 627
Cataloging computer files, 628
Catalogue of ...
   European sculpture in the Ashmolean Museum 1540 to the present day, 1067
   films & videos in the British Medical Assn lib, 1824
   freshwater & marine fishes of Ala., 1714
   medieval & renaissance mss in the Beinecke Rare Bk & Mss Lib, Yale Univ, v.3, 30
   the 15th-century printed bks in the Harvard Univ Lib, v.2, 31
   the letters, tapes & photographs in the Irving Layton collection, 1270
Catastrophes & disasters, 469
Cats, 1704
Caughman, Jennifer Trzyna, 2007
Cavanagh, Donna Tozzi, 199
Cavendish, Richard, 464
Cayton, Mary Kupiec, 505
CD-ROM buyer's gd & hndbk, 3d ed, 1917
CD-ROM finder, 1993 ed, 1918
CD-ROM for librarians & educators, 1920
CD-ROM 1992, 645
CD-ROMs in print 1993, 1919
Cecil, Nancy L., 1179
Cecil, Nancy Lee, 1178
Cella, Catherine, 1426
Celluloid wars, 1451
Cember, Richard P., 1948
Censorship & Hollywood's Hispanic image, 1448
Census snapshot for all US places, 1990, 928
Central African Republic, 97
Cerf, Christopher, 1101
Cevasco, G. A., 981
Chai, Alan, 172
Chalian, Gerard, 712
Chalmin, Philippe, 188
Chamber music: an intl gd to works & their instrumentation, 1349
Champion, Larry S., 1256
Chandler, David G., 521
Chandna, Krishna, 597
Chaplin, Charles C. G., 1713
Chapman, Arthur D., 1648
Characters in 19th century lit, 1157
Charlie Parker discography, 1369

Chatfield, Mary, 156
Checklist of American imprints for 1843, 10
Checklist of the Newberry Lib's printed bks in sci, medicine, tech, & the pseudosciences ca. 1460-1750, 1558
Chelekis, George, 895
Chemical exposure & human health, 1861
Chemical hazard communication gdbk, 2d ed, 2018
Chemical tradename dict, 1932
Chen, C. H., 1774
Chen, Janey, 1110
Chester Himes: an annot primary & secondary bibliog, 1235
Chevalier, Tracy, 1144
Chicago manual of style, 14th ed, 1001
Chicana studies index, 971
Child care crisis, 923
Child welfare stat bk 1993, 922
Childers, Roberta, 2007
Childhood symptoms, 1838
Children's atlas of exploration, 452
Children's atlas of people & places, 454
Children's bk awards intl, 1195
Children's Book Council, 1191
Children's bk illus & design, 1062
Children's bks: awards & prizes, 1992 ed, 1191
Children's bks in print 1992, 9
Children's writer's word bk, 996
Childwise cat, 3d ed, 921
Chilvers, Ian, 1198
China leading cos, 242
Chiri, Alfredo U., 1895
Choose a Christian college, 3d ed, 334
Chorus in opera, 1353
Chorzempa, Rosemary A., 433
Christianson, Grant T., 2011
Christopher Marlowe in the 80s, 1255
Chronologies in old world archaeology, 3d ed, 485
Chronology & fact bk of the UN 1941-91, 792
Chronology of music in the Florentine theater 1751-1800, 1311
Church symbolism, 2d ed, 1048
Cibbarelli, Pamela R., 644
Cichlids of North & Central America, 1712
Cichonski, Thomas, 740
Cichonski, Thomas J., 2017
Cities & churches, 1502
City Lights bks, 1220
Civil rights movement, 595
Civil War newspaper maps: a cartobibliography of the N daily pr, 492
Civil War newspaper maps: a histl atlas, 491
Clancy, Laurie, 1269
Clancy, Paul, 730
Clandestine erotic fiction in English 1800-1930, 1204
Clark, Gladys L. H., 1468
Clark, Jerome, 813
Clarkson, Christopher, 29
CLE research gd, v.2, 583
Clegg, Michael B., 438
Clever, Glenn, 1275
Cliff, Andrew, 1854
Clifton, Chas S., 1530
Climatological atlas of snowfall & snow depth for the NE US and SE Canada, 1948
Clinician's hndbk, 3d ed, 1847

Clockworks, 974
Clodfelter, Micheal, 692
Clough, Katherine, 1650
Cloutier, Guy, 582
Clute, John, 1211
Clyde, Laurel A., 906
CMG Information Services, 339
Cochran, Moncrieff, 919
Codex alimentarius, 2d ed, v.6, 1606
Codex alimentarius, v.8, 1607
Coffey, Timothy, 1651
Coffman, Steve, 639
COGEL blue bk, 9th ed, 801
Cogger, Harold G., 1748
Coggins, John, 783
Cohn-Sherbok, Dan, 1554
Cold war 1945-91, 537
Cold war chronology, 795
Coldham, Peter Wilson, 430
Coleman, Edwin J., 45
Coleman, Kathleen, 1284
Colette: an annot primary & secondary bibliog, 1285
Collar, N. J., 1695
Collective bargaining in higher educ & the professions, bibliog no.20, 269
Colleen Dewhurst: a bio-bibliog, 1411
College admissions, 324
College Board gd to 150 popular college majors, 352
College costs & financial aid hndbk 1994, 353
College degrees by mail, 351
College hndbk for transfer students 1994, 354
College hndbk 1994, 355
College majors & careers, rev ed, 362
College Staff of Rugg's Recommendations, 364
Collier, Laurie, 1187
Collier, Simon, 142
Collings, Rex, 1106
Collingwood, Donna, 994
Collins German-English, English-German dict unabridged, 2d ed, 1115
Collins, Joseph T., 1749
Collins Shubun English-Japanese dict, 1118
Collins Spanish-English, English-Spanish dict, 1132
Collins Spanish-English, English-Spanish dict unabridged, 3d ed, 1133
Collins-Robert French-English, English-French dict, 2d ed, 1113
Colombo, John Robert, 1
Colorado birds, 1689
Colorado place names, 470
Columbia gd to standard American English, 1085
Columbia Univ College of Physicians & Surgeons complete home gd to mental health, 1846
Columbus docs, 533
Comay, Joan, 1538
Combinatory vocab of CAD/CAM in mechanical engineering, 1916
Combs, Richard E., 1145
Comic art collection cat, 1405
Comic-bk superstars, 1407
Coming to terms with acting, 1434
Committee of Volunteers, 611
Committee on the Junior High and Middle School Booklist of the National Council of Teachers of English, 648
Committee on the Senior High School Booklist of the National Council of Teachers of English, 1165
Committees in the US Congress 1947-92, v.1, 741
Community, technical, & jr colleges statistical yrbk, 1992 ed, 356
Companion to aesthetics, 1492
Companion to literary myths, heroes & archetypes, 1155
Compendium of ...
    American railroad radio frequencies, 12th ed, 2028
    food additive specifications, addendum 1, 1608
    pulp & paper training & research insts, 1614
Compilation of state & fed privacy laws, 1992 ed, 577
Complete & easy gd to social security & medicare, 10th ed, 220
Complete beverage dict, 1601
Complete bk of emigrants 1751-76, 430
Complete concordance to Gottfried Von Strassburg's Tristan, 1200
Complete dir for people with learning disabilities, 1993/94, 372
Complete ency of hockey, 4th ed, 852
Complete gd for occupational exploration, 1993 ed, 387
Complete gd to prescription & non-prescription drugs, 1877
Complete gd to symptoms, illness & surgery for people over 50, 1839
Complete Gone with the Wind sourcebk, 1452
Complete medicinal herbal, 1666
Complete secretary's hndbk, 7th ed, 300
Comprehensive gd to the hazardous properties of chemical substances, 2015
Compton's ency & fact-index, 34
Computer acronyms & abbrevs, 1890
Computer dict, 4th ed, 1904
Computer engineering hndbk, 1774
Computer industry 1993 almanac, 1909
Computer law & sftwr protection, 1892
Computer-based simulations in educ & training, 381
Computing info dir, 10th ed, 1908
Concise dict of natl bibliog, 13
Concise dict of religion, 1512
Concise ency of ...
    materials characterizations, 1795
    materials economics, policy & mgmt, 1794
    sftwr engineering, 1775
Concise illus dict of sci & tech, 1567
Concise Oxford companion to classical lit, 1198
Concise Oxford companion to the theatre, 1472
Concordance to the works of Jorge Luis Borges (1899-1986), Argentine author, 1299
Conductor's repertory of chamber music, 1350
Congleton, Robert J., 1483
Congress A to Z, 2d ed, 728
Congress dict, 730
Congressional & gubernatorial primaries 1991-92, 754
Congressional Quarterly's American congressional dict, 729
Congressional Quarterly's pols in America 1994, 749
Congressional staff dir/1, 1993, 734
Conkel, Donald, 1712
Constitutional glossary, 553
Construction glossary, 2d ed, 1773
Consumer mags of the British Isles, 267
Consumer product & manufacturer ratings 1961-90, 214
Consumer's gd to aging, 875

Consumer's gd to free medical info by phone & by mail, 1844
Consumer's gd to product grades & terms, 201
Contemporary bks reflecting Canada's cultural diversity, 409
Contemporary Canadian & US women of letters, 1138
Contemporary Canadian childhood & youth, 924
Contemporary critical theory, 1140
Contemporary dramatists, 5th ed, 1467
Contemporary fiction writers of the South, 1222
Contemporary gay American novelists, 1224
Contemporary legend, 1383
Contemporary lesbian writers of the US, 1226
Contemporary religions: a world gd, 1516
Contemporary world writers, 2d ed, 1144
Conversion tables: LC-Dewey, Dewey-LC, 630
Conway, D. J., 1392
Conzen, Michael P., 461
Coogan, Michael D., 1545
Cook, Chris, 766
Cook, Ralph T., 1220
Cook, Samantha, 1430
Cooke, Jean, 39
Coombes, Allen J., 1669
Co-op source dir: spring 1993, 288
Cooper, Bruce E., 1724
Cooper, David E., 1492
Cooper, J. C., 1391
Copy-editing, 3d ed, 1000
Copyright bk, 4th ed, 637
Corals of Austral. & the Indo-Pacific, 1747
Corbeil, Jean-Claude, 1114
Corbet, G. B., 1734
Corbitt, Robert, 1999
Corbridge, Stuart, 157
Corcoran, John, 855
Cormier, Chantal, 1943
Cormorants, darters, & pelicans of the world, 1698
Cornelison, Pam, 512
Cornish, Rory T., 775
Corporate dir of US public cos 1993, 178
Corporate fndn profiles, 7th ed, 900
Corporate giving dir 1993, 163
Corporate giving yellow pages 1993, 162
Corpus almanac & Canadian sourcebk, 1993, 125
Cortes, Eladio, 1296
Cortese, Delia, 101
Cottingham, John, 1493
Coughlin, Bill, 200
Countdown 2000, v.2, 789
Countries of the world & their leaders yrbk 1993, 723
Courvoisier's bk of the best, 472
Coutts, Mary Carrington, 1835
Cover story index 1960-1991, 1006
Cover story index: 1992 suppl, 1007
Covert culture sourcebk, 76
Cowden, Robert H., 1352
Cox, Greg, 1212
Cox, James C., 1937
CQ's Political Staff, 749
CQ's state fact finder, 750
Cracking Eastern Europe, 261
Cracking the Pacific Rim, 243
Craggs, Stewart, 1323
Craggs, Stewart R., 1322
Craig, Robert D., 120
Crampton, Norman, 942

Crane, David, 247
Crane, Nancy B., 1002
Crash of rhinoceroses, 1106
Crawford, L. Ann, 677
Crawford, R. J., 677
Crawford, William "Roy", 677
Creighton-Zollar, Ann, 879
Cribb, Robert, 111
Crime in Victorian Britain, 590
Criscoe, Betty, 1166
Crisfield, D. W., 823
Critical survey of short fiction, rev ed, 1215
Critical thinking, 1483
Crosby, Cynthia A., 100
Crossing barriers, 17
Croteau, Maureen, 57
Croucher, Murlin, 131
Crowson, Phillip, 1978
Crumb, Lawrence N., 1522
Crump, Andy, 1995
Crystal, David, 33
Cuban festivals, 1399
Cucheran, Ruby, 1167
Cullen, J., 1652
Culligan, Michael, 790
Culotta, Wendy A., 1750
Cultural ency of the 1850s in America, 507
Cumming, Jeffrey M., 1724
Cummings, David M., 1346
Cummings, Steve, 1905
Cummins, Julie, 1062
Cunningham, William A., 1759, 1760, 1761, 1762, 1763, 1764, 1765, 1766
Curley, Stephen J., 1451
Current environmental engineering summaries, 1993 ed, 1788
Current, Richard N., 506
Current treaty index, 11th ed, 760
Cushman, Clare, 551
Cycads of the world, 1671

Daddy Grace: an annot bibliog, 1500
Dahl, Henry S., 552
Dahlo, Ingrid, 1769
Dahl's law dict, 552
Dakin, Nick, 1717
Dakota-English dict, 1111
Dale, Peter, 635
Daly, M. W., 104
Dameron, J. Lasley, 61
Dance, S. Peter, 1675
Dangerous aquatic animals of the world, 1746
Daniels, Peggy Kneffel, 49, 50
Danner, Horace Gerald, 1079
Darnay, Arsen J., 193, 205
Data: where it is & how to get it, 45
Daugherty, F. Mark, 1340, 1342
Davey, Gwenda Beed, 1390
David & Charles ency of everyday antiques, 1023
Davidson, Linda Kay, 1523
Davies, Dilys, 1653
Davies, J. K., 1756
Davies, Peter, 849
Davis, Daniel J., 2011
Davis, Evan, 159
Davis, J. R., 1793

Davis, Julie A., 2011
Davis, Lansing J., 392
Davis, Lee, 467, 468
Davis, Lenwood G., 1500
Davis, Linda W., 1663
Davis, Michael C., 277
Davis, Neil M., 1817
Day, A. Colin, 1542
Day, Ruby, 1384
De Angelis, James, 163
De Prisco, Andrew, 1706
de Vries, Andre, 273
De Vries, Mary A., 300
Dean, Jan, 1627
Dean, Love, 90
Deconstructionism: a bibliog, 1141
DeCurtis, Anthony, 1367
Del Vecchio, Deborah, 1437
DellaCava, Frances A., 1208
Demayo, Adrian, 1951
Demise of the Soviet Union, 548
Demsey, David, 1324
Dershem, Larry D., 625
Descartes dict, 1493
Descriptive cat of the Jorge Luis Borges collection at the Univ of Va. lib, 1300
Desert & mountain plants of the southwest, 1645
Desktop bus intelligence sourcebk, 171
Destructive & useful insects, 5th ed, 1729
Detwiler dir of medical market sources, 1834
Detwiler, Susan M., 1834
Developing multicultural awareness through children's lit, 1178
Development report card for the states, 1993, 170
Developments & research on aging, 871
DeVenney, David P., 1353
Dewan, John, 836
Dewey, Donald, 831
Dewey, Patrick R., 1400
Deziron, Mireille, 2003
Di Maso, Peter, 1053
Diagram Group, 824
Dial 800 for health, 1812
Diaz, Jacqueline, 943
Dibon-Smith, Richard, 1924
DiCanio, Margaret, 586
Dickerson, Brent C., 1628
Dickson, Paul, 730
Dictionary for human factors/ergonomics, 1791
Dictionary of ...
   acronyms & abbrevs, 597
   acronyms & abbrevs in applied linguistics & lang learning, 1072
   AIDS-related terminology, 1853
   American children's fiction, 1985-89, 1171
   American foreign affairs, 731
   American religious biog, 2d ed, 1509
   animal health terminology, 1633
   architecture & construction, 2d ed, 1051
   Australian artists, 1041
   banking, 207, 210
   biblical tradition in English lit, 1149
   British literary characters: 18th- & 19th-century novels, 1243
   Canadian military hist, 517
   card games, 841
   chemical engineering, 1769
   chemical names & synonyms, 1934
   children's fiction from Austral., Canada, India, New Zealand, & selected African countries, 1172
   concepts in archaeology, 487
   cults, sects, religions & the occult, 1513
   cultural literacy, 2d ed, 305
   dicts, 1073
   ecology & environmental sci, 1994
   environment & dvlpmt, 1995
   environmental sci & tech, rev ed, 2000
   family psychology & family therapy, 2d ed, 810
   finance, 204
   geographical literacy, 466
   global climate change, 1949
   investing, 177
   Irish archaeology, 486
   literary biog documentary series, v.10, 1154
   literary biog yrbk: 1991, 1156
   medical acronyms & abbrevs, 2d ed, 1818
   Mexican lit, 1296
   modern medicine, 1832
   mysticism & the esoteric traditions, rev ed, 814
   natl biog: missing persons, 15
   Native American mythology, 418
   philosophical quotations, 1499
   pol parties & orgs in Russia, 779
   real people & places in fiction, 1159
   sacred & magical plants, 1667
   sexual slang, 909
   sporting artists 1650-1990, 1065
   stats & methodology, 79
   symbolism, 979
   the American west, 1088
   the lit of the Iberian Peninsula, 1289
   the Napoleonic wars, 521
   the Ojibway lang, 1124
   20th-century world pols, 718
   US economic hist, 158
Dienhart, Tom, 848
Diesel locomotive rosters, 3d ed, 2025
Dieter's dict & problem solver, 1603
Diffor, Elaine N., 375
Diffor, John C., 375
Dilbert, Sheila, 35
Dinan, Desmond, 767
Dinosaur & other prehistoric animal factfinder, 1959
Diptera types in the Canadian Natl Collection of Insects, pt.2, 1724
Direct mktg market place [DMMP] 1993, 289
Directories in print 1993, 46
Directors & their films, 1453
Directory, 1992: AAAS consortium of affiliates for intl programs, 1572
Directory of ...
   AAAS sci & engineering fellows 1973-92, 1573
   African film-makers & films, 1436
   American philosophers 1992-93, 1498
   building & equipment grants, 2d ed, 1772
   Canadian theatre archives, 1476
   Catholic colleges & univs, 1992, 335
   chemistry sftwr 1992, 1939
   cos offering dividend reinvestment plans, 10th ed, 180
   courthouses & abstract & title cos, 1993, 559
   dvlpmt research & training insts in Africa, 93
   disability support servs in community colleges 1992, 371

Directory of ... *(Continued)*
  European bus, 254
  European community trade & professional assns 1992, 274
  European environmental orgs, 2003
  facilities & servs for the learning disabled, 1993-94, 373
  family assns, 1993-94 ed, 431
  fed libs, 2d ed, 651
  food & nutrition info for professionals & consumers, 2d ed, 1604
  foreign manufacturers in the US, 5th ed, 213
  fund raising & nonprofit mgmt consultants, 901
  Japanese technical reports 1992-93, 114
  jobs & careers abroad, 8th ed, 273
  law-related CD-ROMS 1993, 560
  lib & info orgs in the UK, 635
  lib automation sftwr, systems, & servs, 1993 ed, 644
  literary mags 1993-94, 1162
  low temperature research & dvlpmt in Europe, 7th ed, 1964
  natl helplines 1993, 47
  operating grants, 889
  poetry pubs, 8th ed, 664
  publication resources, 1993-94, 995
  publishers in China, 672
  publ 1993, 665
  registered investment advisors with the SEC 1993, 179
  religious orgs in the US, 3d ed, 1515
  resources for Australian studies in N America, 123
  Russian MPs, 523
  special collections in W Europe, 653
  special libs & info centers 1993, 650
  the wood products industry, 1993, 1616
  US govt sftwr for mainframes & microcomputers, 1914
  video, computer & audio-visual products 1993, 1887
Directory to Canadian studies in Canada, 4th ed, 126
DISCovering authors [CD-ROM], 1146
Disease & medical care in the US, 1802
Distance educ: a selected bibliog, 380
Dividend reinvestment plans, 1992 gd almanac, 181
Division for the Development of Education, UNESCO, for the International Bureau of Education, 377
Dobkowski, Michael N., 587
Docherty, James C., 124
Doctoral dissertations on Asia, v.15, nos.1 & 2, 108
Dogs, 1705
Dolatshahi, Shahpari, 264
Donadio, Stephen, 71
Donaldson, Sandra, 1248
Donavin, Denise Perry, 1163
Dorian, A. F., 1800
Dorling Kindersley sci ency, 1565
Dorothy Parker: a bio-bibliog, 1236
Dorton, Claire, 1463
Dove, John C., 20, 21, 771
Downey, Pat, 1361
Downs, Buck J., 54, 744
Downs, Geoff, 1939
Dox, Ida G., 1829
Doyon, Yves, 1776
Drama criticism, v.1, 1201
Drama criticism, v.2, 1202
Drama criticism, v.3, 1203
Draper, Edythe, 1551

Draper, Larry W., 1501
Draper's bk of quotations for the Christian world, 1551
Dreisbach, Christopher, 1484
Dresser, Peter, 1517
Dresser, Peter D., 1801
Drew, Bernard A., 1221
Drug, alcohol, & other addictions, 2d ed, 914
Drury, George H., 2024
Drury, Nevill, 814
Dublin stage, 1720-45, 1468
Duchac, Joseph, 1233
Ducks in the wild, 1699
Duncan, Phil, 749
Dundas, Pamela, 46
Dunlop, Charles E. M., 1494
Dunn, Thomas P., 974
Dunning, Margaret B., 757
Dunn-Wood, Maryjane, 1523
Dupuy, R. Ernest, 687
Dupuy, Trevor N., 687, 688
Dutile, Patty, 196
Duursma, E. K., 1744
DWM: a dir of women's media, 16th ed, 967
Dziggel, Oliver C., 243, 261

Eagle, Dorothy, 480
Earle, Michael V., 839
Early Christian & Byzantine architecture, 1054
Eason, Ron, 1563
Easton, Patricia, 1485
EC direct, 257
EC info hndbk 1993/94, 768
Eccardt, Thomas, 1122
Eckstein, Richard M., 1772
Economic planning 1943-51, 263
Economist atlas of the New Europe, 255
Ecumenism: a bibliographical overview, 1524
ECW's biographical gd to Canadian novelists, 1273
ECW's biographical gd to Canadian poets, 1274
Edelheit, Abraham J., 532
Edelheit, Hershel, 532
Education for older adult learning, 389
Education for the Earth, 2012
Educational opportunity gd, 1993, 316
Educators gd to ...
  free filmstrips & slides, 45th ed, 375
  free health, physical educ & recreation materials, 26th ed, 829
  free home economics & consumer educ materials, 10th ed, 886
  free social studies materials, 33d ed, 81
Educators grade gd to free teaching aids, 39th ed, 317
Edward Elgar: a gd to research, 1327
Edwards, Charles J., 876
Edwards, Elwyn Hartley, 1707
Edwards, John, 2021
Edwards, John W., 1376
Edwards, Paul M., 678, 679
Ehr, Catherine M., 167, 211
Ehresmann, Donald L., 1022
Ehrich, Robert W., 485
Ei thesaurus, 1753
Eigen, Lewis D., 724
1890s: an ency of British lit, art, & culture, 981
Eis, Arlene L., 560, 567, 568
Eisner, Gilbert M., 1829

Eldridge, Grant J., 52
Election data bk, 751
Election Data Services, staff of, 751
Election results dir, 1993 ed, 738
Electronic packaging, microelectronics, & interconnection dict, 1781
Electronic style, 1002
Electronic univ, 376
Elementary teachers gd to free curriculum materials, 50th ed, 318
Elements of typographic style, 675
Elfe, Wolfgang D., 1286, 1287
Elinor Remick Warren: a bio-bibliog, 1321
Elizabeth Barrett Browning: an annot bibliog of the commentary & criticism, 1826-1990, 1248
Ellen Stewart & La Mama: a bio-bibliog, 1410
Elliott, Stephen P., 42
Ellis, Barbara W., 1619
Elmes, Gregory A., 725
Elsevier's dict of mining & mineralogy, 1800
Elting, John R., 707
Employee benefit plans, 8th ed, 272
Employee benefits dict, 271
Encyclopaedia of ...
    food sci, food tech, & nutrition, 1600
    Islam, new ed, v.7, 151
    Islam, new ed, v.7, fascicules 125-26, 150
Encyclopedia of ...
    African American religions, 1514
    American facts & dates, 9th ed, 504
    American religions, 4th ed, 1518
    American social hist, 505
    antibiotics, 3d ed, 1871
    arms control & disarmament, 797
    assns CD-ROM, 51
    assns intl orgs 1993, 48
    assns 1994, v.1, 49
    assns 1994, v.2, 50
    assns: regional, state, & local orgs 1992-93, 52
    banking & finance, 9th ed, 208
    Britain, 133
    careers & vocational guidance, 9th ed, 386
    chemical processing & design, v.36, 1759
    chemical processing & design, v.37, 1760
    chemical processing & design, v.38, 1761
    chemical processing & design, v.39, 1762
    chemical processing & design, v.40, 1763
    chemical processing & design, v.41, 1764
    chemical processing & design, v.42, 1765
    chemical processing & design, v.43, 1766
    childbearing, 1831
    computer sci, 3d ed, 1903
    contemporary literary theory, 1150
    cosmology, 1926
    electronic circuits, v.4, 1778
    flora & fauna in English & American lit, 1151
    flowers, 1654
    gods, 1395
    governmental advisory orgs 1994-95, 747
    health info sources, 2d ed, 1827
    heresies & heretics, 1530
    Jewish prayer, 1556
    learning & memory, 809
    legal info sources, 2d ed, 566
    lib & info sci, v.44, 601
    lib & info sci, v.45, 602
    lib & info sci, v.46, 603
    lib & info sci, v.47, 604
    lib & info sci, v.48, 605
    lib & info sci, v.49, 606
    lib & info sci, v.50, 607
    lib & info sci, v.51, 608
    major league baseball teams, 831
    marine scis, 1744
    microbiology, 1636
    microcomputers, v.7, 1896
    microcomputers, v.8, 1897
    microcomputers, v.9, 1898
    microcomputers, v.10, 1899
    mistresses, 961
    music in Canada, 2d ed, 1312
    pharmaceutical tech, v.4, 1867
    pharmaceutical tech, v.5, 1868
    pharmaceutical tech, v.6, 1869
    pharmaceutical tech, v.7, 1870
    physical sci & tech, 2d ed, 1566
    recorded sound in the US, 1313
    Russian hist, 524
    sci fiction, 1211
    sleep & dreaming, 808
    strange & unexplained physical phenomena, 813
    the blues, 1370
    the British pr 1422-1992, 1008
    the Confederacy, 506
    the N.Y. stage, 1940-50, 1474
    Ukraine, vs. 3-5, 138
    violence, 586
    women's assns, 969
    wood joints, 1030
    world cultures, v.4, 395
    world cultures, v.5, 396
    world lit in the 20th century, v.5, 1152
Encyclopedia USA, v.16, 509
Encyclopedia USA, v.17, 510
Encyclopedia USA index v.1, 513
Encyclopedic dict of chemical tech, 1936
Endangered wildlife of the world, 1676
Enderlyn, Allyn, 243, 261
Energy in the dvlpmt of W Africa, 1969
Energy info abstracts annual 1991, 1979
Energy stats sourcebk, 7th ed, 1980
Energy stats yrbk, 1990, 1981
Engel, Madeline H., 1208
English, Barbara, 518
English-Dakota dict, 1112
English-Persian dict, 1125
Enright, Rosemary, 1463
Enser's filmed bks & plays, 1438
Environmental accounting, 1989
Environmental decline & public policy, 2019
Environmental dict, 2d ed, 1998
Environmental engineering dict, 2d ed, 1789
Environmental law index to chemicals, 1941
Environmental profiles, 2004
Environmental regulatory glossary, 6th ed, 2002
Environmentalists: a biographical dict, 1993
Environmentalist's bkshelf, 1992
Eponyms of behavioral optometry, 1866
Epstein, Catherine, 411
Erickson, Hal, 1511
Erlewine, Michael, 1314
Erlewine, Stephen Thomas, 1314

Erlich, Richard D., 974
Ernst & Young, 302
Ernst & Young tax gd 1993, 302
Ervin, Hazel Arnett, 1237
Essential researcher, 57
Essential Shakespeare, 2d ed, 1256
Estes, Sally, 1168
Ethical aspects of health care for the elderly, 868
Ethical shopper's gd to Canadian supermarket products, 248
Ethnologue, 1070
Ethnologue index, 12th ed, 1069
Ethridge, James M., 662
Ethridge, Karen, 662
ETS test collection cat, v.1, 2d ed, 304
Ettlinger, John, 1384
Euro dict, 1108
EUROBrokerS, 631
EUROCOM, 632
Europa world yr bk 1992, 82
Europe in figures, 3d ed, 935
European business rankings, 258
European business servs dir, 256
European communities, 770
European cos, 4th ed, 260
European culture, 977
European dict, 1108
European electric utility dir, 1993, 1783
European electronics dir 1993, 1787
European employment & industrial relations glossary: Belgium, 252
European employment & industrial relations glossary: Germany, 253
European market share reporter, 259
European petroleum dir, 1993, 1972
European pol facts 1918-90, 766
European public affair dir 1993, 769
European research centres, 9th ed, 1574
European sources of scientific & technical info, 10th ed, 1576
European specialist publishers dir, 666
European women's almanac, 947
European writers: selected authors, 1280
Evan, Frederica, 674
Evans, Calvin D., 1486
Evans, H. Meurig, 1136
Evans, Philip R., 1365
Evers, David C., 1677
Every bite a delight & other slogans, 299
Evinger, William, 651
Evolving constitution, 571
Exegetical dict of the N.T., v.3, 1528
Explorers & discoverers of the world, 463
Explorers & exploration, 462

Fabre, Michael, 1235
Factfinder, 39
Facts about the presidents, 6th ed, 499
Facts behind the songs, 1366
Facts on File atlas of stars & planets, 1925
Facts on File bibliog of American fiction 1866-1918, 1229
Facts on File children's atlas, 447
Fahey, Michael A., 1524
Fakih, Kimberly Olson, 1169
Falk, Peter Hastings, 1049
Falklands War: background, conflict, aftermath, 684

Fallik, Alain, 769
Family ency of child psychology & dvlpmt, 807
Family fun & games, 824
Family health gd to homeopathy, 1842
Famous animal symbols, v.2, 291
Famous Hollywood locations, 1421
Fan club dir, 1400
Fang, Nan, 672
Fantastic cinema subject gd, 1449
FAO species cat, v.15, 1719
FAO yrbk: fertilizer, v.41, 1590
FAO yrbk: fishery stats, 1715
FAO yrbk: production, v.45, 1591
FAO yrbk: trade, v.45, 1592
Farina, Luciano F., 533
Farkas, Emil, 855
Farmer, David Hugh, 1527
Farr, J. Michael, 387
Farrier, Susan E., 1199
Faulkner, Kimberly Burton, 420
Feczko, Margaret Mary, 890
Federal Jobs Digest, editors of, 284
Federal regional yellow bk, v.1, no.1, 739
Federal staff dir/1, 1993, 735
Fehrenbach, R. J., 598, 599
Fein, Richard M., 215
Fell, Derek, 1654
Female detectives in American novels, 1208
Feminist theory, 952
Fenlon, Iain, 1310
Fenwick, Gillian, 1261
Fenza, D. W., 993
Ferreira, Manual, 1268
Festival Europe, 479
Fetzer, James H., 1494, 1495
Fhaner, Beth A., 1020
Fiction for youth, 3d ed, 1181
Fiction index for readers 10 to 16, 1196
Field gd to ...
    birds of Britain & Europe, 5th ed, 1701
    birds of the W Indies, 5th ed, 1693
    coastal wetland plants of the SE US, 1661
    the ecology of W forests, 1681
    the stars & planets, 3d ed, 1928
    the waterbirds of Asia, 1692
    whales, porpoises, & seals from Cape Cod to Nfld., 4th ed, 1737
Fifth dir of pers, 986
50 fabulous places to raise your family, 944
Figueroa, Rafael, 1381
Filichia, Peter, 832
Film news index, 1939-81, 1462
Film superlist, updated ed, 1439
Films by genre, 1444
Final 4 records 1939-91, 839
Finance, insurance, & real estate USA, 205
Financial aid for ...
    minorities in engineering & sci, 1577
    research & creative activities abroad 1992-94, 367
    study & training abroad 1992-94, 368
Financial Times mining intl yr bk 1993, 1982
Financial Times who's who in world oil & gas 1993, 1970
Findling, John E., 716
Fink, Donald G., 1777
Fink, John M., 1859

Firefighter's hazardous materials ref bk & index, 2d ed, 2011
First demographic portraits of Russia 1951-90, 929
First name reverse dict, 442
FirstBook of demographics for the republics of the former Soviet Union, 930
FISCAL dir of fee-based research & document supply servs, 4th ed, 639
Fise, Mary Ellen R., 921
Fishes of Alta., 2d ed, 1720
Fishes of the Bahamas & adjacent tropical waters, 2d ed, 1713
Fitzhenry, Robert I., 68
Fitzmier, John R., 1533
Fitzmyer, Joseph A., 1071
500 best garden plants, 1622
Flake, Chad J., 1501
Flanagan, Laurence, 486
Flanders, Carl N., 731
Flanders, Stephen A., 731
Flora, Joseph M., 1222
Flora of North America Editorial Committee, 1643
Flora of N America north of Mexico, 1643
Flores, Angel, 1297
Flowers of the Pacific Island seashore, 1647
Fluehr-Lobban, Carolyn, 105
Focal ency of photography, 3d ed, 1036
Focus on addictions, 917
Focus on fitness, 843
Foley, Denise, 1805
Folklore of trees & shrubs, 1673
Foner, Eric, 727
Fonseca, James W., 321
Football scholarship gd, 844
Foote, Richard H., 1725
Foottit, Robert G., 1723
Foreman, Dave, 1678
Forest product prices 1971-90, 1615
Forestry Policy and Planning Division, FAO Forestry Department, 1615
Forsberg, Krister, 1767
Forty yrs of steel, 1382
Fossey, Keith R., 844
Foster, Allan, 258, 259
Foster, David William, 1298
Found, Peter, 1472
Foundation Center, 890, 892
Foundation dir, 15th ed, 890
Foundation dir pt.2, 1993 ed, 891
Foundation giving, 1993 ed, 896
Foundation 1000 1992/93, 897
Foundation reporter 1993, 902
Fradkin, Louise G., 867
Franck, Irene, 920, 1996
Frank, Robyn C., 1604
Frankel, Benjamin, 537
Franklin-Smith, Constance, 1045
Frantzve, Kent R., 171
Fraser, Robert, 206
Free money for ...
    athletic scholarships, 326
    college from the govt, 327
    graduate school, rev ed, 329
Free money from colleges & univs, 328
Freedom's lawmakers, 727
Freeman-Grenville, G. S. P., 460

Freemon, Frank R., 493
Freirman, Richard, 1906
French colonial Africa, 95
French, Tom, 652
Frewin, Anthony, 494
Fried, Lewis L. B., 1491
Friedes, Harriet, 312
Friedman, Francine, 139
Friedman, Saul S., 538
Fritze, Ronald, 417
From real life to reel life, 1442
Fulford, Margaret, 966
Fulton, Len, 664
Fund raiser's gd to human serv funding 1993, 899
Funding decision makers 1993, 898
Funk & Wagnalls standard dict, 2d ed, 1077
Furtado, Ken, 1227
Furtaw, Julia C., 420, 1020

Gabon, 98
Gagnon, Louiselle, 249
Gale dir of databases, 1907
Gale dir of publications & broadcast media 1993, 988
Gale, Robert L., 507
Gale's literary index [CD-ROM], 1161
Gall, Susan, 401
Gall, Susan B., 201
Gall, Timothy L., 201, 401
Gallico, Alison, 653
Gallo, Donald R., 1186
Gambacinni, Paul, 1362
Garber, Linda, 907
Garcia, F. L., 208
Garcia, Teresa Alvarez, 1132
Gardener's dict of horticultural terms, 1618
Gardener's Latin, 1640
Gardener's reading gd, 1627
Gardinier, David E., 98
Garoogian, Andrew, 943
Garoogian, Rhoda, 943
Garrison, Webb, 1080
Gascoigne, Bamber, 133
Gastrow, Shelagh, 762
Gates, Sheldon, 176
Gatten, Jeffrey N., 1404
Gauthier, Mark A., 621
Gavin, Christy, 1228
Gay & lesbian American plays, 1227
Gay & lesbian characters & themes in mystery novels, 1210
Gay Hollywood film & video gd, 1460
Gays & lesbians in mainstream cinema, 1446
Gazukin, Pavel, 777
Gealt, Adelheid M., 1063
Gedridge, Jolen Marya, 874
Gee, Robin, 994
Gemology, 1958
Gemstones of E Africa, 1955
Gender positive!, 1179
Gendron, Celine, 817
Genealogies catalogued by the Lib of Congress since 1986, 429
Genera of the aphids of Canada, 1723
General bibliog of C. G. Jung's writings, rev ed, 806
General Matthew B. Ridgway: an annot bibliog, 678
Genocide in our time, 587

Gentilcore, R. Louis, 458
Gentry, Alwyn H., 1637
GeoRef [CD-ROM], 1950
George Grenville 1712-1770: a bibliog, 775
George-Warren, Holly, 1367
Georgopolis, Melissa L., 54, 744
German reunification, 522
German sacred polyphonic vocal music between Schutz & Bach, 1343
Geron, Leonard, 136
Gerontological social work, 872
Gerontology & geriatrics libs & collections in the US & Canada, 655
Gerry, Thomas M. F., 1138
Gibilisco, Stan, 1567
Gibson, Dyanne, 310
Gibson's student gd to W Canadian univs, 310
Gift of life, 1823
Gilbert, Carter R., 1716
Gilbert, M. Jean, 915
Gilbert, Sara D., 388
Gill, Sam D., 418
Gillespie, John T., 1192
Gillette, Gary, 833
Gillis, Jack, 921
Ginsberg, Leon, 911
Giscard d'Estaing, Valerie-Ann, 1581
Glancy, Ruth F., 1251
Glannon, Ann M., 378
Glanze, Walter D., 1152
Glasby, John S., 1871
Glassberg, Jeffrey, 1703
Glazier, Loss Pequeno, 659
Glazier, Stephen, 1105
Glenn, Robert W., 786
Glinert, Lewis, 1385
Global warming, 2014
Glossarial concordance to the Riverside Chaucer, 1250
Glossary of ...
    art, architecture, & design since 1945, 3d ed, 1043
    cognitive sci, 1494
    educl tech terms, 377
    epistemology/philosophy of sci, 1495
    security equipment, 1776
    US govt vocabulary, 732
    water terms, 1951
Godet, Jean-Denis, 1670
Godin, Seth, 174
Goetsch, Lori, 949
Goetzmann, William H., 444
Golden age of top 40 music (1955-1973) on CD, 1361
Goldman, Jonathan L., 1094
Goldstein, Erik, 693
Goldstein, Gabriella, 856
Goldstein, Martha, 42
GOLF Magazine, editors of, 850
GOLF Magazine's ency of golf, 2d ed, 850
Golob, Richard, 1983
Gopen, Stuart, 1011
Gopen's gd to closed captioned video, 1011
Gordon, Ann D., 964
Goreham, Gary A., 1588
Gorn, Elliot J., 505
Gottlieb, Jean S., 1558
Goulet, Cyrille, 553
Goulet, Henry, 1726

Gourman, Jack, 357, 358
Gourman report: a rating of graduate & professional programs in American & intl univs, 6th ed, 357
Gourman report: a rating of undergraduate programs in American & intl univs, 8th ed, 358
Goursau, Henri, 1108
Goursau, Monique, 1108
Government research dir 1993-94, 740
Gozdecka-Sanford, Adriana, 134
Graduate curricula in educl communications & tech, 4th ed, 379
Graduate scholarship dir, 3d ed, 331
Graetzer, Hans G., 710
Graf, Rudolf F., 1778, 1779, 1780
Graham, John W., 802
Graham, Ronnie, 1315
Granatstein, J. L., 517
Grand trees of America, 1672
Grant, Michael, 1393
Graphic arts vocab, 1058
Grattan, Virginia L., 1325
Graubner, Wolfram, 1030
Gray, Anne, 1345
Gray, John, 1039
Gray, Richard A., 1823, 2019
Great all-time baseball record bk, rev ed, 835
Great American baseball stat bk 1993, 833
Great American hist fact-finder, 512
Great bear almanac, 1733
Great bk of the sea, 1745
Great events from hist 2: arts & culture series, 984
Great events: the 20th century, 539
Great Lakes gd to sunken ships, 2029
Great videos for kids, 1426
Greaves, Bettina Bien, 153
Grechko, A. A., 686
Green cathedrals, 834
Green ency, 1996
Green, Marybeth, 1197
Green, Philip, 715
Greenberg, Reva M., 389
Greene, Cynthia, 169
Greene, John C., 1468
Greene, Stanley A., 2016
Greenfield, John R., 1243
Greenfieldt, John, 1481
Greer, Harold E., 1631
Grenham, John, 434
Gress, Bob, 1679
Gribben, Arthur, 1386
Griffith, H. Winter, 1839, 1877, 1884
Griffiths, Dennis, 1008
Griffiths, Trevor R., 1257
Grimes, Barbara F., 1069, 1070
Grinstein, Louise S., 1923
Grolier world ency of endangered species, 1680
Groom, Nigel, 1940
Gross, Dorothy-Ellen, 1442
Gross, Robert F., 1232
Guggenheimer, Eva H., 441
Guggenheimer, Heinrich W., 441
Guide to ...
    art, 1047
    British poetry explication, v.2, 1265
    British poetry explication, v.3, 1266
    cooking schools, 1993, 1609

dividend reinvestment plans, 192
fed funding for hospitals & health centers, 1814
fed funding for housing & homeless programs, 876
free computer materials, 11th ed, 1911
French poetry explication, 1284
genealogical sftwr, 435
grasses of the lower Rio Grande valley, Tex., 1665
Kans. mushrooms, 1662
law schools in Canada, 575
Michigan's endangered wildlife, 1677
multicultural resources 1993/94, 400
photographic collections at the Smithsonian Inst, v.3, 1038
pol videos, v.1, no.1, 713
pseudonyms on American records, 1892-1942, 1317
silent Westerns, 1443
the college lib, 658
the end of the world, 1535
the evaluation of educl experiences in the armed servs, 1992, 307
the ms collections in the rare bk & ms lib of Columbia Univ, 28
the natl wildlife refuges, rev ed, 1683
the Oxford English Dict, 1097
the sources of US military hist, suppl.3, 680
US fndns, their trustees, officers, & donors, 1993 ed, 892
US govt pubns, 1993 ed, 55
worldwide postal-code & address formats, 1993, 989
Guinness bk of records 1993, 1401
Guinness bk of sports records 1993, 825
Guinness ency of popular music, 1363
Gullong, Jane M., 983
Guttmann, Hadassah, 1326
Guy, Jeniece, 613

Haboucha, Reginetta, 1387
Hager, Philip E., 1205
Haggett, Peter, 1854
Haider, Thomas John, 317, 318
Haim, S., 1125, 1126
Haines, Gerald K., 752
Hakkert, Adolf M., 535
Hale, Kay K., 1594
Hale, Linda L., 924, 925
Hale, Mark, 1377
Hale, Terrel D., 545
Hall, Carl W., 1754
Hall, Clifton D., 1200
Hall, George E., 937
Hall, Hal W., 1213
Hall, Kermit L., 554
Hall, Rachel, 1540
Hall, Sarah M., 666
Hallett, Michael A., 588
Hallgarth, Susan A., 967
Halliwell, Brian, 1629
Halliwell's filmgoer's & video viewer's companion, 10th ed, 1456
Halpern, Jack, 1121
Halstead, Bruce W., 1746
Hammond atlas of the world, 448
Hammond atlas of the world, concise ed, 449
Hammond explorer atlas of the world, 450
Hampton, Barbara, 383
Handbook for no-load fund investors, 1993, 189

Handbook of ...
  American diplomacy, 757
  behavior therapy & pharmacotherapy for children, 1848
  hydrology, 1953
  Latin American lit, 2d ed, 1298
  Latin American studies, no.52, 144
  old-time radio, 1017
  pol sci research on the USSR & E Europe, 781
  power, utility & boiler terms & phrases, 6th ed, 1797
  prescriptive treatments for children & adolescents, 1845
  psychotropic drugs, 1878
  research on the educ of young children, 314
  rocks, minerals, & gemstones, 1957
  the birds of Europe, the Middle East, & N Africa, v.6, 1696
  the birds of Europe, the Middle East, & N Africa, v.7, 1697
  the fruit flies (Diptera: Tephritidae) of America north of Mexico, 1725
  United Methodist-related schools, colleges, univs & theological schools, 336
Handbook on injectable drugs, 7th ed, 1885
Handel's natl dir for the performing arts, 5th ed, 1420
Hannigan, Jane Anne, 616
Happy birthdays round the world, 1402
Harborne, Jeffrey B., 1639
Hardin, James, 1286, 1287
Harduf's transliterated Yiddish-English dict, 4th v., 1137
Hardy, Gayle J., 592
Harer, John B., 641
Harkness, Mabel G., 1625
Harmon, Justin, 976
Harmony illus ency of rock, 7th ed, 1378
Harner, James L., 1139
Harper atlas of world hist, rev ed, 528
Harper bk of quotations, 3d ed, 68
Harper, Charles A., 1781
Harper ency of military hist, 4th ed, 687
HarperCollins dict of philosophy, 2d ed, 1496
Harpsichord & clavichord music of the 20th century, 1335
Harris, Cyril M., 1051
Harris, Ian, 1516
Harris, Laurie Lanzen, 11
Harris manufacturers dir, 1993, 215
Harrison, James, 445
Hartley, Loyde H., 1502
Hartnoll, Phyllis, 1472
Harvard Bus School core collection 1993, 156
Hasenfratz, Robert J., 1263
Haskins, Jim, 475
Hast, Adele, 230
Hastings, Elizabeth Hann, 75
Hastings, Philip K., 75
Hatch, Stephen L., 1664
Haverland, Bill, 861
Hawai'i, 90
Hawkins, Walter L., 685
Hawley's condensed chemical dict, 12th ed, 1933
Hawthorne, Douglas B., 1757
Hayden, Carla D., 1170
Hayes, Nicky, 811
Hayes, R. M., 1440
Haymarket affair, 786
Hayssen, Virginia, 1731

Haythornthwaite, Philip J., 540
Hazardous substances resource gd, 2016
Hazel, John, 1393
H.D.: a bibliog 1905-90, 1234
HeadBangers, 1377
Headlam, Catherine, 1568
Health care reform terms, advance ed, 1804
Health care state rankings 1993, 1816
Healthy aging, 869
Heath, Angela, 867
Hecht, Hermann, 1427
Heden, Karel E., 2029
Heier, Uli, 1336
Hein, William S., 862
Heise, Jon O., 473
Heisinger, Barbara B., 547
Helbig, Alethea K., 1171, 1172
Helen Hayes: a bio-bibliog, 1416
Hellner, Nancy, 1227
Helson, Joan, 248
Helt, Marie E., 1441
Helt, Richard C., 1441
Hench, John B., 657
Hendrickson, Homer, 1866
Hendrickson, Robert, 1089
Henk Badings, 1907-87: cat of works, 1328
Henke, James, 1367
Henkes, Robert, 1046, 1064
Henry, Dawn, 967
Henrysson, Harald, 1354
Henslin, James M., 877
Herbert Hoover: a bibliog, 496
Herbert Spencer: a primary & secondary bibliog, 1490
Herron, Nancy L., 820
Hersen, Michel, 812, 1845, 1848
Herzfeld, Thomas J., 190
Herzfeld's gd to closed-end funds, 190
Herzhaft, Gerard, 1370
Hess, Carol, 719
Hester, M. Thomas, 1264
Hetherington, Norriss S., 1926
Hexham, Irving, 1512
Hicken, Mandy, 1438
Hickman, James C., 1644
Hicks, S. David, 162, 163, 898, 899
Higham, Robin, 680
Highlights of state unemployment compensation laws, 219
Hilbert, Robert, 1371
Hildebrandt, Darlene Myers, 1908
Hill, J. E., 1734
Hill, Karen, 2017
Hill, Kenneth L., 795
Hill, Michelle, 1806
Hinds, Richard deC., 2018
Hine, Darlene Clark, 965
Hinkelman, Edward G., 290
Hipp, James W., 1156
Hippocrene standard dict: Russian-English, English-Russian, 1130
Hippocrene USA gd to historic black south, 475
Hirsch, E. D., Jr., 305
Hirsch, N. P., 1874
Hirth, Paul, 648
Hischak, Thomas S., 1473
Hispanic-American almanac, 412
Historic warships, 703

Historical atlas of ...
   Canada, v.2, 458
   E central Europe, 520
   S Asia, 2d ed, 515
   state power in congress, 1790-1990, 725
   the Jewish people from the time of the patriarchs to the present, 424
   the Middle East, 460
Historical dict of ...
   Austral., 124
   Buddhism, 1519
   golfing terms, 849
   Hong Kong & Macau, 110
   Indonesia, 111
   Israel, 152
   Malawi, 2d ed, 100
   Malaysia, 118
   Paraguay, 2d ed, 147
   Polynesia, 120
   Portugal, 135
   the European Community, 767
   the Republic of Korea, 117
   the Sudan, 2d ed, 105
   the US air force, 698
Historical jls, 2d ed, 542
History & folklore of N American wildflowers, 1651
History of ...
   Canadian childhood & youth, 925
   nursing beginning bibliog, 1864
   sci & tech in the US, v.2, 1560
   surgery in the US 1775-1900, v.2, 1822
   the Episcopal church in America, 1607-1991, 1521
HMO/PPO dir 1993, 1815
Hobbs, James B., 1086
Hockings, Paul, 396
Hodgson, Michael, 476
Hoffman, Andrea C., 378
Hoggart, Richard, 397
Hogue, Charles L., 1727
Holding, Sue, 1044
Holistic health dir, 1992-93, 1808
Holland, Patricia G., 964
Hollander, Zander, 852
Hollar, David W., 1635
Holley, E. Jens, 1507
Hollings, Robert L., 753
Hollom, P. A. D., 1701
Holloway, Joseph E., 1081
Hollywood baby boomers, 1432
Hollywood who's who, 1431
Holocaust lit, 538
Holt, Constance Wall, 950
Holtz, Barry W., 425
Holy wells & sacred water sources in Britain & Ireland, 1386
Hombs, Mary Ellen, 1852
Homelessness: an annot bibliog, 877
Homophones & homographs, 2d ed, 1086
Honig, Robert, 2004
Hony, H. C., 1135
Hood, Howard A., 1840
Hooper, David, 842
Hoover's hndbk of emerging cos 1993-94, 172
Hoover's masterlist of major US cos 1993, 164
Hopke, William E., 386
Hoppel, Joe, 848

Hopton, Marilyn, 980
Horn, Barbara Lee, 1410, 1411
Horn, Bruce, 1662
Horses, 1707
Horse's name was..., 1709
House, Jonathan M., 681
How to find info about cos, v.3, 173
Howard Hanson: a bio-bibliog, 1330
Howard, Philip H., 1934
Howard, Vivian, 251
Howard-Hill, T. H., 1244
Howard-Williams, Jeremy, 860
Howatson, M. C., 1198
Howe-Grant, Mary, 1768
Howell, Michael J., 311
Howes, Kelly King, 1157
Huber, Jeffrey T., 1853
Huber, John T., 1726
Huellmantel, Michael B., 256
Hughes, J. M., 1096
Hula, Volodymyr, 483
Hulbert gd to financial newsletters, 5th ed, 191
Hulbert, Mark, 191
Huls, Mary Ellen, 951
Human rights, refugees, migrants & dvlpmt, 593
Humana, Charles, 594
Humor scholarship, 1304
Humphrey, Stephen R., 1735
Hunt, Gladys, 383
Hupper, William G., 1549
Hurst, Walter E., 1439
Hymenoptera of the world, 1726
Hysa, Ramazan, 1109

Iatridis, Mary D., 1559
I.B.I. intl bearing interchange gd, 12th ed, 1798
Ibou, Paul, 291
Iconographic index to N.T. subjects represented in photographs & slides of paintings in the visual collections, Fine Arts Lib, Harvard Univ, v.1, 1540
Idi Amin & Uganda, 763
Ihrie, Maureen, 1289
IIE educl assocs 1992-93, 366
Illustrated computer graphics dict, 1912
Illustrated ency of active new religions, sects, & cults, 1529
Illustrated ency of orchids, 1658
Illustrated gd to rocks & minerals, 1956
Illustration index 7, 1050
Image of older adults in the media, 870
Immigration stats 1991, 803
Importers manual USA, 1993 ed, 290
In vitro fertilization clinics, 1857
Independent study cat, 5th ed, 390
Index by region, usage, & etymology to the Dict of American Regional English, v.1 & 2, 1090
Index of ...
   English literary mss, v.2, pt.2, 1245
   English literary mss, v.3, pt.3, 1246
   majors & graduate degrees 1994, 365
Index to ...
   American short story award collections 1970-90, 1230
   black pers, 403
   Canadian legal lit 1992, 582
   dance pers: 1991, 1424
   English per lit on the O.T. & ancient Near Eastern studies, v.5, 1549
   intl public opinion, 1991-92, 75
   Italian architecture, 1052
   per lit on the apostle Paul, 1550
   the contents of the per Canadian Lit nos.1-102, 1275
   the critical vocabulary of Blackwood's Edinburgh Mag, 1830-40, 61
   who's who bks 1992, 14
Indexing: a basic reading list, 638
Indices to the species of mosses & lichens described by William Mitten, 1668
Industrial chemical thesaurus, 2d ed, 1942
Industrial stats yrbk 1990, 216
Information please bus almanac & desk ref, 1994, 174
Information please environmental almanac, 1993, 1986
Information please kids' almanac, 2
Information please sports almanac, 1993, 818
Information security: dict of concepts, standards & terms, 1900
Information sources for virtual reality, 1894
Information sources in chemistry, 4th ed, 1931
Information sources in sport & leisure, 821
Instrumentation in educ, 306
Intellectual freedom: a ref hndbk, 641
Intellectual freedom manual, 4th ed, 642
Intercountry comparisons of agricultural output & productivity, 1597
Intergenerational readings/resources 1980-93, 866
Interior landscape dict, 1621
International affairs dir of orgs, 799
International authors & writers who's who, 13th ed, 1147
International bibliog of theatre: 1988-89, 1466
International brands & their cos 1993-94, 228
International closeout dir '94, 292
International commodity markets hndbk 1993, 188
International cos & their brands 1993-94, 229
International dict of ...
   architects & architecture, 1055
   ballet, 1423
   films & filmmakers, 2d ed, v.4, 1430
   opera, 1355
International dir of ...
   bioethics orgs, 1835
   co hists, v.5, 230
   co hists, v.6, 231
   co hists, v.7, 232
   primatology, 1736
   testing labs, 1993 ed, 1578
   voluntary work, 5th ed, 894
   youth internships with the UN, its related agencies, & non-governmental orgs, 5th ed, 790
International ency of learned societies & academies, 36
International energy stats sourcebk, 2d ed, 1984
International glossary of hydrology, 2d ed, 1952
International histl stats: the Americas, 1750-1988, 2d ed, 936
International hndbk of child care policies & programs, 919
International hndbk of early childhood educ, 315
International hndbk on drug control, 916
International Labour Review: index 1945-91, 285
International legal bks in print 1993-94, 546
International literary market place 1993, 667
International markets for meat 1992/93, 1593
International mgmt hndbk, 238

International military & defense ency, 688
International monetary fund 1944-92, 234
International orgs: a dict & dir, 3d ed, 793
International proverb scholarship, suppl.2, 1388
International scholarship dir, 3d ed, 332
International trade stats yrbk, 1990, 233
International translation gd for emergency medicine, 1825
International who's who in music & musicians' dir, 13th ed, 1346
International who's who of professional & bus women, 2d ed, 958
International writings of Bohdan S. Wynar, 1949-92, 80
International yr bk & statesmen's who's who 1992, 791
International yrbk of educl & training tech 1992/93, 382
Intrep Data Corp., 214
Inventions & discoveries 1993, 1581
IPA thesaurus & frequency list, 6th ed, 1873
Ireland's index to inspiration, 69
Irvin, Linda, 48
Irving, Holly Berry, 1604
Isaac Albeniz: chronological list & thematic cat of his piano works, 1320
Isaacs, Alan, 204
Isaacs, Katherine M., 1084
Isbister, Rob, 1299
Islam & Islamic groups, 1553
Islam in N America, 1552
Island Pr bibliog of environmental lit, 1990
Italian Americans & religion, 2d ed, 1504
Iter Italicum, v.6, 978
Iversen, Edwin S., 1594
Iz, Fahir, 1135

Jablonski, Stanley, 1818
Jackson, Alan A., 2022
Jackson, Kathryn A., 1053
Jackson, Kathy Merlock, 1412
Jackson, Rebecca, 863
Jacob, Helene, 1997
Jacobsen, Roy M., 1588
Jacobson, Nancy, 83, 86
Jacobson, Ronald L., 1056
Jacques Derrida: an annot primary & secondary bibliog, 1491
Jakubiak, Joyce, 58
James, Glenn, 1966
James, Robert C., 1966
Jamison, Martin, 763
Jane's defence glossary, 676
Jankowski, Katherine E., 1850
Jansma, Pamela E., 1991
Japan: an illus ency, 115
Japan Chamber of Commerce and Industry, 245
Japan trade dir 1993-94, 244
Japanese American hist, 423
Japanese women writers in English translation, v.2, 1295
Japanese/English, English/Japanese glossary of scientific & technical terms, 1571
Jargon: an informal dict of computer terms, 1905
Jarock, Beth, 993
Jarrett, William S., 845
Jason, Philip K., 514
Jazz discography, v.5, 1373
Jazz discography, v.6, 1374
Jazz lives, 1372
Jean Paul Sartre: a bibliog, 1489

Jefferies, Margaret, 482
Jeffrey, David Lyle, 1149
Jehle, Faustin F., 220
Jenkins, Russell, 726
Jensen, Julie M., 1173
Jepson manual, 1644
Jewish family names & their origins, 441
Jimenez, Edgar, 356
Job hunter's sourcebk, 2d ed, 279
Job seeker's gd to 1,000 top employers, 280
Joel Whitburn presents daily #1 hits 1940-92, 1364
Johann Michael Haydn (1737-1806): a chronological thematic cat of his works, 1332
Johanson, Cynthia J., 1032
Johansson, Thomas B., 1985
John Quincy Adams: a bibliog, 498
Johnsgard, Paul A., 1698, 1699
Johnson, Beth Hillman, 269
Johnson, Craig R., 1353
Johnson, Eric A., 1630
Johnson, James B., 1706
Johnson, Jenny K., 379
Johnson, John, 1449
Johnson, Joy L., 1864
Johnson, Ken, 455
Johnson, Lois S., 1402
Johnson, Margaret M., 479
Johnson, Mary Elizabeth, 234
Johnson, Tom, 1437
Jones, Alison, 1526
Jones, David L., 1671
Jones, Errol D., 682
Jones, Francine, 897, 900
Jones, J. Michael, 703
Jones, Steve, 394
Jordan, Casper LeRoy, 1223
Jordan, Michael, 1395
Jorgensen, Delores A., 547
Jorgensen, Linda, 995
Jorgenson, Lisa, 1672
Joscelyn, Trevor A., 1257
Joshi, S. T., 1292
Journeys of the great explorers, 464
Joys of Hebrew, 1385
Judaism & human rights in contemporary thought, 1555
Judicial staff dir, 1993, 736
Juliussen, Egil, 1909
Juliussen, Karen Petska, 1909
Jung, Heidrun, 1072
Jung, Udo O. H., 1072
Juniorplots 4, 1192
Jussi Bjorling phonography, 2d ed, 1354

Kabdebo, Thomas, 1073
Kadrey, Richard, 76
Kael index, 1463
Kalck, Pierre, 97
Kallmann, Helmut, 1312
Kamp, Jim, 962
Kane, Joseph Nathan, 499
Kanellos, Nicolas, 412
Kanikova, S. I., 1281
Kapp, Marshall B., 868
Karney, Robyn, 1431
Karolides, Melissa, 843
Karolides, Nicholas J., 843

Karsten, Eileen, 1442
Kasic, Christopher, 165
Kass, Frederic I., 1846
Katona, Steven K., 1737
Katz, Linda Sobel, 2004
Kaufman, Stephen A., 1071
Kaur, Amarjit, 118
Kavass, Igor I., 548, 760
Kay, Ernest, 958, 963, 1147
Kay, Ian, 676
Kay, Richard, 1662
Kaylor, Noel Harold, 1487
Kear, Lynn, 1413
Keller, Peter C., 1955
Kelly, Aidan, 1517
Kelly, Bernice M., 1040
Kelly, Joyce, 481
Kelly's business dir 1992, 265
Kendall, Alan, 1394
Kennedy, Thomas E., 1230
Kennemer, Phyllis K., 694
Kent, Allen, 601, 602, 603, 604, 605, 606, 607, 608, 1896, 1897, 1898, 1899
Kent, Christopher, 1327
Kent, James A., 1770
Kent, Kathleen L., 987
Kepos, Paula, 231, 232
Kerr, Joan, 1041
Kett, Joseph F., 305
Key ideas in human thought, 1497
Kid's address bk, 53
Kids' favorite bks, 1174
Kiger, Joseph C., 36
Killens, Camille A., 345
Kim, Wesley, 194
Kimball, Debi, 2013
Kiner, Larry F., 1365
King, James J., 1998
King, Kamla J., 748
Kingfisher children's ency, 37
Kingfisher illus ency of animals, 1687
Kingfisher ref atlas, 451
Kingfisher sci ency, 1568
Kinkley, Jeffrey, 1279
Kinoshita, Sumie, 180, 181, 192
Kinzey, Bert, 699
Kirby, Debra M., 650
Kirkbride, Joseph H., Jr., 1638
Kirk-Othmer ency of chemical tech, 4th ed, v.7, 1768
Kirkpatrick, Betty, 1098
Kirkpatrick, Zoe Merriman, 1655
Kirsch, George B., 826
Kits, games & manipulatives for the elementary school classroom, 378
Klee as in clay, 982
Klein, Barry, 293
Klein, Barry T., 419
Klein, Gerald, 207
Klein, Michael L., 1539
Kleinbauer, W. Eugene, 1054
Kleiner, Diane E. E., 1066
Klemme, Paul T., 1328
Klett, Dwight A., 1288
Knight, Denise D., 1226
Kodansha's romanized Japanese-English dict, 1119
Koen, Willie, 1117

Kogon, Marilyn, 617
Korean, 1122
Kornicki, Peter, 113
Korsch, Boris, 1503
Koshgarian, Richard, 1347
Koszegi, Michael A., 1552
Kovacs, Deborah, 1193
Kovacs, Ruth, 618
Kraeuter, David W., 1012
Kramer, A. L. N., Sr., 1117
Kravitz, Walter, 729
Krevisky, Joseph, 1087
Kricher, John C., 1681
Krieger, Joel, 717
Kristeller, Paul Oskar, 978
Krochalis, Jeanne, 29
Kroeger, David, 163
Krol, John, 1922
Kruh, David, 477
Kruh, Louis, 477
Krummel, D. W., 1307
Kuipers, B. R., 1744
Kulich, Jindra, 391
Kurian, George, 459
Kushner, Michael G., 271

Labour force stats 1970-90, 235
Lachman, Marvin, 1231
Lacoff, Cheryl Klein, 798, 815
LaFrance, David G., 682
Laine, Claude, 1916
Lambert, David, 1960
Lanasa, Philip J., III, 1166
Landgraf, Mark J., 2028
Langbart, David A., 752
Langlois, Jennifer, 645
Langman, Larry, 1443
Language of visual effects, 1433
Larkin, Colin, 1363
Larkin, Kay, 1982
Larkin, Robert P., 465
Larue, C. Steven, 1355
Laserdisc film gd, 1993-1994 ed, 1429
Last, Cynthia G., 1845
Latin America: a pol dict, 784
Latin American insects & entomology, 1727
Latin American military hist, 682
Latvian-English, English-Latvian dict, 1123
Lau, Jesus, 600
Lauraceae: nectandra, 1646
Law, Jonathan, 977
Law lib systems dir, 654
Lawrence, Steven, 896
Lawyers' & creditors' serv dir, 1993 ed, 563
Layman's gd to new age & spiritual terms, 816
Lea, Katherine, 385
Lead detection & abatement dir 1993-94, 2005
Leafe, David, 1455
Leake, Dorothy VanDyke, 1645
Leake, John Benjamin, 1645
LeCompte, Michelle, 279
Lederberg, Joshua, 1636
Lee, C. C., 1789, 1941
Lee, George L., 404
Lee, Rohama, 1462
Lees, Gene, 1372

Legal issues & older adults, 572
Legal looseleafs in print 1993, 567
Legal newsletters in print 1993, 568
Legal resource dir, 557
Legend & lore of the Americas before 1492, 417
Leisure lit, 820
Leitch, Thomas M., 1239
Leiter, Richard A., 569
Leiter, Samuel L., 1474
LeMaster, J. R., 1240
Lenk, John D., 1782, 1784
Lenk's digital hndbk, 1782
Lennon, Mary Beth, 1582
Lennon, Thomas M., 1485
Lent, John A., 990, 991
Leonard, Arthur S., 570
Leonard, Mark, 1061
Leonard, Michelle, 1806
Lerner, Sid, 1095
Lesbian sources, 907
Lesbianism: an annot bibliog & gd to the lit 1976-91, 908
Lesko, Matthew, 1809
Leslie Stephen's life in letters, 1261
Lesser, Enid, 582
Lester, Paula E., 306
Levine, Michael, 53
Levine, Nancy D., 887
Levi-Setti, Riccardo, 1961
Lewell, John, 1294
Lewin, Paul, 1783
Lewinson-Gilboa, Ayelet, 489
Lewis, Brad Alan, 856
Lewis, D. S., 765, 783
Lewis, Richard J., Sr., 1933
Lewis, Thomas P., 1316
Lexicon of the Greek & Roman cities & place names in antiquity ca. 1500 B.C. - ca. A.D. 500, fascicule 1, 535
Li, Xia, 1002
Libraries dir 1991-93, 634
Library Assn yrbk 1992, 636
Library lit 1992, 621
Library lit. 21, 616
Library of Congress classification class KL-KWX, 625
Library pers 1993, 622
Lieberman, Jethro K., 571
Lifetime ency of natural remedies, 1826
Lifshin, Eric, 1795
Lighthall, Lynne, 617
Lima, Carolyn W., 1176
Lima, John A., 1176
Limb, Peter, 103
Lindfors, Bernth, 1148
Lindquist, Richard K., 1624
Lindsay, Alexander, 1246
Lineback, Richard H., 1498
Linfield, Jordan L., 1087
Ling, Sum Ngai, 110
Linscott's dir of immunological & biological reagents, 7th ed, 1875
Linton, Thomas, 275
Linton trainer's resource dir, 2d ed, 275
Lionel Trilling: an annot bibliog, 1239
Lipinski, Kathleen A., 1601
Lipinski, Robert A., 1601

Literary market place 1994, 668
Literary research gd, 2d ed, 1139
Literature & film: an annot bibliog 1978-88, 1143
Literature activity bks, 1197
Literature of ...
 agricultural engineering, 1754
 delight, 1169
 music bibliog, 1307
Literature teacher's bk of lists, 1142
Liu, Gongxian, 1634
Living with low vision, 880
Lobban, Marjorie, 906
Lobban, Richard A., Jr., 105
Loeffelbein, Robert L., 827
Loewenstein, C. Jared, 1300
Lonard, Robert I., 1665
London intl atlas of AIDS, 1854
London stage 1950-59, 1469
Long, Christopher, 206
Long, Mark, 1758
Longley, Dennis, 1900
Looking at paintings, 1061
Lopez, Daniel, 1444
Lord Dunsany: a bibliog, 1292
Lord Lichfield, 472
Lord, Tom, 1373, 1374
Lorona, Lionel V., 145
Lotz, Rainer E., 1336
Lounsbury, Warren C., 1470
Loving Journeys gd to adoption, 885
Lowe, Ida B., 269
Lowe, Rodney, 263
Lowenberg, Carlton, 1308
Lowenberg, Susan, 1254
Low-fat supermarket, 1612
Lowrey, Joan, 435
Lowry, Philip J., 834
Low-water flower gardener, 1630
Lucille Lortel: a bio-bibliog, 1414
Ludwig Tieck: an annot gd to research, 1288
Lumpkin, Betty S., 1920
Lund, Kimberley, 19
Lydersen, Aksel L., 1769
Lynch, Mary Jo, 613

Ma, Lien-sheng, 121
MacDonald, Barrie, 1013
MacDonald, Scott B., 916
Macintosh bible, 4th ed, 1910
Mack, Roy, 1633
Mackenzie, Leslie, 372, 883
Macmillan bk of the marine aquarium, 1717
Macmillan dict of pol quotations, 724
Macmillan gd to correspondence study, 5th ed, 359
Macmillan health ency, 1803
Macrae, R., 1600
Macrocosm USA, 74
Macrone, Michael, 1396
Maddux, Cleborne D., 380
Mager, N. H., 1091
Mager, S. K., 1091
Maggio, Rosalie, 972
Maggiore, Dolores J., 908
Magill, Frank N., 984, 1158, 1215, 1583
Magill's survey of sci: applied sci series, 1583
Magill's survey of world lit, 1158

Magosci, Paul Robert, 520
Mahe, Catherine M., 2023
Mahoney, Jim, 356
Maidment, David R., 1953
Major authors & illustrators for children & young adults, 1187
Major donors 1993, 893
Major energy cos of Europe 1993, 1977
Makaryk, Irena R., 1150
Making a difference college gd, 1993, 348
Makino, Noboru, 116
Malcom, Shirley M., 1561
Maldives, 119
Mallett, Daryl F., 432
Malonis, Jane A., 969
Malpas, Pamela G., 1616
Mammal species of the world, 2d ed, 1743
Mammals of the central Rockies, 1741
Mammals of the Indomalayan region, 1734
Mamola, Claire Zebrowski, 1295
Management of correctional insts, 804
Mangrum, Charles T., II, 340
Man-made catastrophes, 467
Mansdorf, S. Z., 1767
Marcaccio, Kathleen Young, 1907
Marco, Guy A., 1313
Margaret Thatcher: a bibliog, 776
Margen, Sheldon, 1602
Marill, Alvin H., 1464
Mark Twain ency, 1240
Markel, Robert, 1349
Market share reporter 1993, 193
Marketing made easier, 293
Marr, David G., 122
Marshall, Donald G., 1140
Marshall, James N., 154
Marten, James, 89
Martens, Hans, 257
Martin, Dolores Moyano, 144
Martin, Helmut, 1279
Martin, Laura C., 1673
Martin, Len D., 1445
Martin, Robert, 394
Martindale-Hubbell bar register of preeminent lawyers 1993, 561
Martinez, Joseph G. R., 1265, 1266
Martinez, Nancy C., 1265, 1266
Martis, Kenneth C., 725
Marull, Horacio M., 552
Mason, Antony, 452
Mason, Eileen, 70
Mast, Jennifer Arnold, 280
Mathematical scis professional dir 1993, 1967
Mathematics dict, 5th ed, 1966
Mather, George A., 1513
Matsuura, Kumiko, 792
Matthews, Hugoe, 1252
Matthews, Peter, 1401
Matthias, Margaret, 1968
Mattson, Mark T., 931
Maunder, W. John, 1949
Maureen Stapleton: a bio-bibliog, 1418
Mauritania, 101
Maxwell, Grant L., 1337
Maya civilization, 541
Mayberry, Debra J., 739

Maynard, Thane, 1738
Mayne, Alan J., 77
McAlister, Micheal J., 1433
McAuliffe, Amy, 1814
McBroom's camera bluebk, 1994 ed, 1037
McCallum, Heather, 1476
McCaskie, A. W., 1825
McCaslin, Richard B., 495
McCauley, Martin, 523
McClean, Andrew, 683
McConkey, Wilfred J., 982
McCormick, Frank, 975
McCoy, Judy, 1375
McCready, Sam, 1414
McCullough, Prudence, 203
McCutcheon, Marc, 511
McDonald, Charles W., 2025
McDonald, Elvin, 1617
McDonald, P. C., 1964
McElmeel, Sharron L., 1188
McGee, Denis C., 1595
McGee, Robert W., 153
McGillivray, Alice V., 754, 755, 756
McGrath, Daniel F., 1025
McGraw-Hill circuit ency & troubleshooting gd, v.1, 1784
McGraw-Hill data communications dict, 1901
McGraw-Hill ency of ...
    astronomy, 2d ed, 1927
    chemistry, 2d ed, 1935
    engineering, 2d ed, 1785
    environmental sci & engineering, 3d ed, 1999
    physics, 2d ed, 1965
McGraw-Hill's natl electrical code hndbk, 21st ed, 1786
McGuire, William, 78, 806
McIlwaine, John, 94
McKee, Cynthia Ruiz, 360
McKee, Phillip C., Jr., 360
McKeen, William, 1379
McKetta, John J., 1759, 1760, 1761, 1762, 1763, 1764, 1765, 1766
McKnew, Ed, 2030
McLean, Janice W., 901
McLeish, Kenneth, 1258, 1497
McLeod, Donald W., 1271, 1272
McNamara, Jean, 1728
McNeill, Allison K., 228, 229
McPartland, Brian J., 1786
McPartland, J. F., 1786
McQueen, Barbara, 1656
McQueen, Jim, 1656
McShane, Marilyn D., 804
Measner, Don, 458
Medical abbrevs, 6th ed, 1817
Medical & health info dir 1992-93, 1807
Medical utilization review dir, 1993 ed, 1810
Medicine in Great Britain from the Restoration to the 19th century, 1660-1800, 1821
Medieval & renaissance mss in the Walters Art Gallery, v.2, 29
Medieval Charlemagne legend, 1199
Medieval Consolation of Philosophy: an annot bibliog, 1487
Medieval Scandinavia, 526
Meet the authors & illustrators, 1193
Meeting the needs of employees with disabilities, 2d ed, 881

Melloni, B. John, 1829
Melloni's illus medical dict, 3d ed, 1829
Melting pot: an annot bibliog & gd to food & nutrition info for ethnic groups in America, 1599
Melton, J. Gordon, 1514, 1515, 1518, 1552
Men & women of space, 1757
Mendelsohn, Henry N., 912
Mendes, Peter, 1204
Mental health & psychiatry in Africa, 1849
Meridith, Robert, 1992
Merkel-Holguin, Lisa A., 922
Merriam-Webster's collegiate dict, 10th ed, 1076
Merriam-Webster's Japanese-English learner's dict, 1120
Meserole, Mike, 818
Metcalf, Robert A., 1729
Metcalf, Robert L., 1729
Metzger, Bruce M., 1545
Meyer, Robert G., 1847
Meyers, Robert A., 1566
Michael, Scott W., 1718
Mickolus, Edward F., 589
Microbes & minie balls, 493
Microcomputer market place 1993, 1906
Microform market place 1992-93, 669
Mieder, Wolfgang, 1388
Mignon, Molly Raymond, 487
Mikdadi, Faysal, 776
Mikhailovskaya, E., 782
Mikolyzk, Thomas A., 1262
Miletich, Leo N., 1465
Milheim, William D., 381
Military aircraft: modern bombers & attack planes, 700
Military intelligence, 1870-1991, 681
Military leaders of the Civil War, 701
Millard, Scott, 1630
Miller, E. Willard, 1954
Miller, Eugene, 168
Miller, George, 1252
Miller, Joseph A., 1990
Miller, Martin B., 1781
Miller, Oscar J., 549
Miller, Ruby M., 1954
Miller, Tice L., 1479
Miller, William G., 656
Miller-Monzon, John, 1457
Millington, Barry, 1329
Millman, Linda Josephson, 572
Mills, Carlotta, 891
Mills, Watson E., 1534, 1550
Milstead, Jessica L., 1753
Milward, Peter, 1151
Minerals hndbk 1992-93, 1978
Miniature orchids, 1656
Minnick, Wendell L., 796
Minority student enrollments in higher educ, 361
Mises: an annot bibliog, 153
Miska, John, 408
Misner, Amy J., 54, 744
Mitchell, B. R., 936
Mitchell, P. A., 1096
Mitchell, Robert, 337
Mizel, Mark S., 1820
MLA dir of pers 1993-95, 987
Mockenhaupt, Robin E., 869
Modern Chinese writers, 1279
Modern combat helicopters, 711

Modern dict for the legal profession, 555
Modern Irish lit & culture, 1291
Modern Japanese novelists, 1294
Modern measuring circuit ency, 1779
Modern mystery, fantasy & sci fiction writers, 1207
Modern power supply & battery charger circuit ency, 1780
Modoc Press, Inc., 359
Mogilner, Alijandra, 996
Molt, Cynthia Marylee, 1415
Money for intl exchange in the arts, 983
Montanaro, Ann R., 1177
Montney, Charles B., 46, 874
Moore, Bob, 1082
Moore, Jean M., 1276
Moore, Maxine, 1082
Moore, Paula, 995
Moore, Stephen, 1416
Mora, Juana, 915
More theatre, 1464
Morehouse, Cynthia T., 790
Morgan, Kathleen O'Leary, 1816
Morgan, Paul W., 1580
Morgan, Scott, 1816
Morlan, Michael, 2026
Mormon bibliog 1830-1930: indexes to A Mormon Bibliog and 10 yr suppl, 1501
Morningstar closed-end fund sourcebk 1993, 194
Morningstar mutual fund 500, 1993, 195
Morningstar mutual fund sourcebk 1993, 196
Morningstar variable annuity/life sourcebk 1993, 197
Morris, Derrick, 1775
Morris, Nancy J., 90
Morse, Ronald A., 45
Mosaik's photographic key to the trees & shrubs of Great Britain & N Europe, 1670
Moscow & Leningrad: a topographical gd to Russian cultural hist, v.2, 985
Moseley, David, 1102
Moser, Gerald, 1268
Moss, Joyce, 128, 132
Moss, Ralph W., 1860
Most complete colored lexicon of cichlids, 1711
Moston, Doug, 1434
Mothers & daughters in American short fiction, 1219
Mothers & daughters of invention, 1586
Motif-index of medieval Catalan folktales, 1389
Motion picture gd, 1993 annual, 1457
Motor carrier professional serv dir 1993, 2023
Mountfort, Guy, 1701
Movie song cat, 1309
Moys classification & thesaurus for legal materials, 3d ed, 626
Moys, Elizabeth M., 626
Mrozek, Donald J., 680
Mukherjee, Jaydeep, 1929
Mullay, Marilyn, 1562
Muller, Joachim W., 792
Multicultural educ debate, 322
Multicultural student's gd to colleges, 337
Multilingual dict of artificial intelligence, 1889
Multilingual dict of narcotic drugs & psychotropic substances under intl control, 1872
Multimedia ency of mammalian biology [CD-ROM], 1739
Munn, Glenn G., 208

Murphy, C. Edward, 892
Murphy, Donn B., 1416
Murphy, Larry G., 1514
Murray, Elaine, 816
Murray, Paul T., 595
Murray resource dir to the nation's historically black colleges & univs, 338
Murray, Sterling E., 1319
Museums of the world, 4th ed, 60
Music & war, 1305
Music for 3 or more pianists, 1337
Music of Paul Ben-Haim, 1326
Musicians wrestle everywhere, 1308
Mutual fund ency, 1993-1994 ed, 198
My 1st dict, 1092
My 1st ency, 41
My name in bks, 1190
My soul looks back, 'less I forget, 72
Myers, Eleanor Emlen, 529
Myers, J. Wilson, 529
Myers, Margaret, 613
Myerson, Joel, 1241
Mystery writer's marketplace & sourcebk, 994

Naas, Penelope, 787
Naden, Corinne J., 1192
Nader, Jonar C., 1902
Nagel, Gwen L., 1229
Nagel, James, 1229
Nahm, Andrew C., 117
Naifeh, Steven, 562
Naiman, Arthur, 1910
Nakamura, I., 1719
Nakamura, Joyce, 1187
Name is familiar, 1459
Namovicz, Susan, 1810
Napoleonic uniforms, 707
Naprawa, Andrew, 1809
Nasdaq fact bk & co dir, 1993, 182
National dir of ...
    catalogs 1992, 294
    fire chiefs & emergency depts, 1993, 878
    mags 1994, 62
National faculty dir 1993, 339
National family healthcare hndbk, 1813
National gd to educl credit for training programs, 1992-93 ed, 392
National gd to funding for libs & info servs, 2d ed, 618
National Hockey League official gd & record bk 1992-93, 853
National housing dir for people with disabilities, 1993, 883
National Review politically incorrect ref gd, 726
National survey of state laws, 569
National trade & professional assn of the US 1993, 54
Native American women, 956
Native Americans info dir, 420
Natural disasters, 468
Natural gas industry dir, 1993, 1973
Naval Institute gd to combat fleets of the world 1993, 704
Naval Institute gd to the ships & aircraft of the US fleet, 15th ed, 705
Navarro, Yvonne, 442
Navia, Luis E., 1488
Neal, Bill, 1640
Neal, Michael, 1934

Nechas, Eileen, 1805
Nehmer, Kathleen S., 317
Nehmer, Kathleen Suttles, 886, 1911
Nelson, Emmanuel S., 1224, 1290
Nelson, Garrison, 741
Nelson, Joseph S., 1720
Nelson, Marian, 989
Nelson, Michael, 508
Nelson's quick ref Bible concordance, 1547
Nelson's quick ref Bible dict, 1541
Nelson's quick ref Bible hndbk, 1544
Nelson's techresources, winter 1993, 183
Neufeldt, Victor A., 1247
Neugaard, Edward J., 1389
New bibliog of the Lusophone lits of Africa, 2d ed, 1268
New ency of archaeological excavations in the Holy Land, 489
New England planters in the Maritime provinces of Canada 1759-1800, 1589
New Grove dict of opera, 1356
New Princeton ency of poetry & poetics, 1302
New quotable woman, rev. ed, 973
New shorter Oxford English Dict on historical principles, 1099
New topographical dict of ancient Rome, 536
New York Public Lib bk of 20th-century American quotations, 71
New York Times film reviews 1989-90, 1458
New Zealand bks in print 1993, 5
Newcomb, Annette, 87
Newman, Jacqueline M., 1599
Newman, Oksana, 258, 259
Newspapers online, 2d ed, 1005
Newstrom, Harvey, 1610
Newton, David E., 2014
NHL Club Public Relations Directors, 853
NHL Communications Group, 853
Nicholas, Larraine, 1423
Nicholls, C. S., 15
Nicholls, Paul T., 1917
Nicholls, Peter, 1211
Nichols, Larry A., 1513
Nicholson, Carol Avery, 654
Nickson, R. Andrew, 147
Niebuhr, Gary Warren, 1209
Nigerian artists, 1040
Niiya, Brian, 423
Nilsen, Don L. F., 1304
1960s: an annot bibliog of social & pol movements in the US, 863
Nineteenth-century French fiction writers, 1283
Nishimura, Mari, 1333
Niven, David, 1371
NKJV exhaustive concordance, 1548
Nobari, Nuchine, 44
Noel, Roger, 1079
Noether, Dorit, 1936
Noether, Herman, 1936
Nolan, Kathleen Lopez, 1907
Nolen, Anita L., 1835
No-Load Fund Investor, editors of, 189
Nonprofit public policy research orgs, 753
Nordquist, Joan, 322, 405, 596, 952, 1141, 1489, 1855
Norell, Donna M., 1285
Normandy campaign, 1944, 531
Norrbom, Allen L., 1725

North American Indian landmarks, 416
Norton, Judith A., 1589
Notable Hispanic American women, 962
Novallo, Annette, 58
Novels of WW II, 1205
Nowlan, Gwendolyn Wright, 1459
Nowlan, Robert Anthony, 1459
NTC's new Japanese-English character dict, 1121
Ntumy, Michael, 573
Nuclear power plants worldwide, 1801
Nuclear present, 709
Nuessel, Frank, 870
Nulman, Macy, 1556
#1 New York Times bestseller, 1153
Nutrients cat, 1610

O'Brien, Ed, 1368
O'Brien, Patrick G., 496
O'Brien, Tim, 1688
Occupational outlook hndbk, 1992-93 ed, 281
Ocokoljich, Natalia, 195
O'Connor, Diane Vogt, 1038
O'Donoghue, Michael, 1956
Ody, Penelope, 1666
Office for Intellectual Freedom, American Library Assn, 642
Office International des Epizooties, 1633
Official Catholic dir 1993, 1532
Official gd to American incomes, 283
Official gd to household spending, 2d ed, 927
Official 1992 NFL record & fact bk, 846
Official politically correct dict & hndbk, 1101
Official USGA record bk, 1895-1990, 851
Official Whitman coin dealer dir, 6th ed, 1029
Ogarkov, N. V., 686
Ogden, Tom, 1419
O'Grady, Jane, 1499
Old English proverbs collected by Nathan Bailey, 1736, 1384
Old rose advisor, 1628
Older volunteer, 887
Oldham, John M., 1846
Olevnik, Peter P., 323
Olgiatti, Alexandra, 268
Olitzky, Kerry M., 1557
Olsen, Kirsten, 959
Olsen, Wallace C., 1754
Olson, A. Randall, 1659
Olson, James S., 158, 497
Olson, Nancy B., 627, 628
Olson, Nancy L., 742
Olson, Stan, 618, 890, 891
Olympic results—Barcelona 1992, 856
Olynyk, Marta D., 483
O'Mahony, Kieran, 466
On account of sex, 949
100 best small towns in America, 942
101 business ratios, 176
100 world-class thin bks, 1164
1000 Russian verbs, 1128
Online Inc.'s top 500 lib microcomputer sftwr application programs, 640
OPAC dir 1993, 646
Opera: an informal gd, 1358
Opera cos of the world, 1352
Opera mediagraphy, 1351

Opfell, Olga S., 714
Orchestral excerpts, 1348
Orchid bk, 1652
Organizational & interorganizational dynamics, 864
Organizations of state govt officials dir 1992, 742
Orgill, Andrew, 684
Origin & evolution of life on Earth, 1635
Original martial arts ency, 855
Ornamental shrubs, climbers & bamboos, 1632
Orrick, Sarah, 2004
Ortolani, Benito, 1466
Osborne, C. W., 382
Oscar Wilde: an annot bibliog, 1262
OSI dict of acronyms & related abbrevs, 1891
Osmond, Jonathan, 522
Otchere, Freda E., 629
Our Sunday Visitor's Catholic dict, 1531
Out of the closet & into the classroom, 906
Outhwaite, William, 73
Owen, Nancy R., 1145
Oxford companion to ...
    American theatre, 2d ed, 1480
    Australian folklore, 1390
    Australian sport, 822
    chess, 2d ed, 842
    musical instruments, 1338
    pols of the world, 717
    the Bible, 1545
    the Supreme Court of the US, 554
Oxford dict of ...
    American legal quotations, 584
    opera, 1357
    saints, 3d ed, 1527
Oxford gd to classical mythology in the arts, 1300-1990s, 1397
Oxford illus dict of Australian hist, 516
Oxford illus ency of peoples & cultures, 397
Oxford illus ency of the universe, 1944
Oxford illus literary gd to Great Britain & Ireland, 2d ed, 480
Oxford modern English dict, 1100
Oxford movement & its leaders, suppl, 1522
Oxford thesaurus, American ed, 1107
Oxford Turkish dict, 1135
Oxford-Duden pictorial Portuguese-English dict, 1127
Ozone layer dict, 1945

P. T. Forsyth bibliog & index, 1520
Pacanowski, John P., 1838
Pacific research centres, 4th ed, 1575
Paetz, Martin J., 1720
Painting of the golden age, 1063
Palette of possibilities, 1167
Palmegiano, E. M., 590
Palmer, J. J. N., 518
Palmer, Pamela, 61
Palmer, R. E., 636
Palmisano, Joseph M., 58
Palmore, Erdman B., 871
Palumbo, Dennis J., 588
Pan-Africanism: an annot bibliog, 764
Panofsky, Ruth, 1277
Panorama of EC industry 93, 236
Papers of Elizabeth Cady Stanton and Susan B. Anthony, 964
Paradis, Line, 1058

Paragon House spelling dict, 1103
Parapsychology, new age & the occult, 815
Paravisini-Gebert, Lizabeth, 1301
Pardes, Herbert, 1846
Parham, Iris A., 872
Parin, N. V., 1719
Parish, James Robert, 1432, 1446, 1447
Parker, Geoffrey, 530
Parker, Mark, 2030
Parker, Steve, 1819
Parker, Sybil P., 1785, 1927, 1935, 1965, 1999
Parlett, David, 841
Parsons, Lynn H., 498
Partnow, Elaine, 973
Partridge-Brown, Mary, 1857
Pasachoff, Jay M., 1927, 1928
Past renewed, 411
Patent, trademark, & copyright laws, 576
Patnaik, Pradyot, 2015
Paton, John, 37
Patrick, Gay D., 619
Patterson, Anna Grace, 4
Patterson, Austin M., 1937
Patterson's American educ, v.89, 319
Patterson's elementary educ, v.5, 320
Patterson's German-English dict for chemists, 4th ed, 1937
Paulson, Dennis, 1700
Paxton, John, 524, 766, 770
Paymer, Marvin E., 1366
PDR family gd to prescription drugs, 1879
Peake, Hayden B., 761
Pearsall, Ronald, 1023
Pearson, Alison, 1682
Pearson, Steve, 1682
Peck, David R., 1225
Pee Wee speaks, 1371
Penguin dict of economics, 5th ed, 159
Pennsylvania potters 1660-1900, 1033
Pennsylvania silversmiths, goldsmiths & pewterers 1684-1900, 1034
Pennsylvania workers in brass, copper & tin 1681-1900, 1035
Penny, Nicholas, 1067
Pension funds & their advisors 1992, 266
People's Almanac presents the bk of lists: the '90s ed, 1403
People's Medical Society, 1812
Peoples of the world: Eastern Europe & the post-Soviet republics, 132
Peoples of the world: W Europeans, 128
People's Republic of China yr bk 1991/92, 109
Perez, Janet, 1289
Perfume hndbk, 1940
PERiodical source index 1847-1985, v.9-12, 437
PERiodical source index 1991 annual v., 438
Perkins, Agnes, 1171
Perkins, Agnes Regan, 1172
Perle, E. Gabriel, 574
Perone, James E., 1330
Perrett, Bryan, 695
Perrin, Robert G., 1490
Perritt, Gerald W., 198
Persian-English dict, 1126
Person, James E., Jr., 932
Personnel executives contactbk, 286

Pesticide residues in food 1992, evaluations pt.1, 1611
Peter Cushing: the gentle man of horror & his 91 films, 1437
Peters, Gary L., 465
Peters, Jacob, 864
Peterson 1st gd to caterpillars of N America, 1730
Peterson 1st gd to trees, 1674
Peterson, Roger Tory, 1701
Peterson's colleges with programs for students with learning disabilities, 340
Peterson's competitive colleges 1993-94, 341
Peterson's gd to 4-yr colleges 1994, 342
Peterson's gd to 2-yr colleges 1994, 343
Peterson's register of higher educ 1993, 344
Petit, Patrick J., 566
Petrides, George A., 1674
Petroleum sftwr dir, 1994, 1974
Pfeffer, Glenn B., 1820
Phifer, Paul, 362
Philipp, Alan, 266
Philips, Christopher Lee, 658
Phillips, Casey R., 542
Phillips, Charles, 1993
Phillips, Ellen, 1620
Philos, Daphne A., 363
Physicians' desk ref, 1993, 1880
Physician's drug hndbk, 5th ed, 1881
Physicians' gd to rare diseases, 1863
Physicians' generix 1992, 1882
Phytochemical dict, 1639
Piano-beds & music by steam, 1318
Piccirelli, Annette, 165, 345
Pick-up games, 823
Pickwell, George V., 1750
Picquet, D. Cheryn, 1892
Pierce, Phyllis S., 187
Piers Plowman: a gd to the quotations, 1253
Pietraszek, Magdalena, 130
Pigs: a hndbk to the breeds of the world, 1740
Pilbeam, David, 394
Pilgrimage in the middle ages, 1523
Pillsbury, Richard, 819
Pincoe, Ruth, 1476
Places, towns & townships, 937
Plano, Jack C., 784
Plants & flowers of Great Britain & N Europe, 1657
Plastics technical dict, 1938
Play index 1988-92, 1481
Play, learn, & grow, 1184
Pluhar, Jennifer, 1664
Pocket Oxford dict of current English, 8th ed, 1078
Poems of Emily Dickinson: an annot gd to commentary published in English, 1233
Poetry criticism, v.5, 1303
Pohanish, Richard P., 2016
Poland, rev ed, 134
Polish roots, 433
Political dict of the state of Israel, suppl. 1987-93, 2d ed, 785
Political leaders in Weimar Germany, 774
Political parties of ...
  Asia & the Pacific, 765
  the Americas and the Caribbean, 783
  the Americas, 1980s to 1990s, 720
Political resource dir 1993, 719
Pollack, Sandra, 1226

Pollock, Sean R., 932
Pollock, Steve, 1686, 1987
Pollock, Zailig, 1278
Polmar, Norman, 705
Pool player's natl pocket billiard dir, 1992 ed, 858
Pool player's road atlas 1994, 859
Popular gd to classical music, 1345
Popular reading for children 3, 1168
Pop-up & movable bks, 1177
Porteous, Andrew, 2000
Porter, Valerie, 1740
Porterfield, Kay Marie, 917
Portmanteau dict, 1083
Position descriptions in special libs, 2d ed, 624
Post, Joyce A., 655
Post-release assistance programs for prisoners, 910
Potter, Robert B., 148
Potter, Vilma Raskin, 1009
Pottker, Jan, 155
Potts, George, 1679
Potts, William F., 1901
Poverty in developing countries, 905
Poverty row horrors, 1461
Powell, Charles C., 1624
PowerBoat gd, 3d ed, 2030
Pozin, Mikhail A., 160
Practical English-Chinese pronouncing dir, 1110
Pranin, Stanley A., 854
Prather, Ronald, 1324
Pravda, Alex, 136
PRC Year Book, Beijing, Editorial Department, 109
Prebish, Charles S., 1519
Pre-cinema hist, 1427
Preller, James, 1193
Preminger, Alex, 1302
Prentice Hall encyclopedic dict of English usage, 2d ed, 1091
Prentice Hall's illus dict of computing, 1902
Presbyterians, 1533
Preschool resource gd, 312
Prescription drugs & their side effects, 1884
Presidency A to Z, 508
Presidential landmarks, 477
Presidential primaries & caucuses 1992, 755
Presocratic philosophers, 1488
Prevention magazine, editors of, 1805
Prezelin, Bernard, 704
Pribylovski, Vladimir, 262
Pribylovskii, Vladimir, 779
Pridgeon, Alec, 1658
Prince, Mary Miles, 543, 544
Print Project, 203
Private libs in renaissance England, v.1, 598
Private libs in renaissance England, v.2, 599
Pro basketball stats, 840
Pro/Am bk of music & mythology, 1316
Prochner, Lawrence, 315
Proctor, William, 1104
Product dvlpmt dir 1993, 1836
Product SOS 1993, 1837
Professional & occupational licensing dir, 800
Professional baseball franchises, 832
Professional football, 847
Professional gd to diseases, 4th ed, 1841
Professional secretary's hndbk, rev ed, 301
Profiles in childhood educ 1931-60, 313

Project BREED dir, 1708
Pronouncing dict of proper names, 1084
Propagation of alpine plant & dwarf bulbs, 1629
Prostitution in Hollywood films, 1447
Przecha, Donna, 435
P.S.I. gd, 1799
Psychology: a gd to ref & info sources, 805
Psychopathology in adulthood, 812
Public welfare dir, 1993/94, 913
Publication peer review, 997
Publicity & media resources for bk pubs, 1992-1993 ed, 670
Publishers, distrs & wholesalers of the US 1993-94, 671
Publishers trade list annual, 1992, 660
Publishing law hndbk, 2d ed, 574
Pulp & paper industry in the OECD member countries 1990, 237
Pulsiano, Phillip, 526
Purcell, Catherine, 575
Purcell, L. Edward, 500
Purchasing an ency, 4th ed, 38
Pusan perimeter, Korea, 1950, 679
Pyle, Gerald F., 1802
Pynsent, Robert B., 1281

Quality declared seed, 1596
Quarks, critters, & chaos, 1585
Quick selection gd to chemical protective clothing, 2d ed, 1767
Quilt groups today, 1031
Quitno, Neal, 1816

R. G. Collingwood: a bibliographical checklist, 1484
R&D ratios & budgets, 295
Rabson, Carolyn, 1348
Rachel Carson Council, staff of, 2009
Rafailovich, Miriam H., 1923
Rageau, Jean-Pierre, 712
Railway dict, 2022
Rainforest plants of E Austral., 1682
Raintree illus sci ency, 1569
Ralson, Anthony, 1903
Ramson, W. S., 1096
Rand McNally atlas of American frontiers, 490
Rand McNally children's atlas of Native Americans, 421
Rand McNally picture atlas of prehistoric life, 1962
Randall, Lilian M. C., 29
Random House health & medicine dict, 1830
Random House word menu, 1105
Rangel-Ribeiro, Victor, 1349
Rao, D. S. Prasada, 1597
Rap music in the 1980s, 1375
Rare & endangered biota of Fla., v.1, 1735
Rare & endangered biota of Fla., v.2, 1716
Rasor, Eugene L., 527
Ratsch, Christian, 1667
Read for your life, 383
Read, Phyllis J., 970
Reader's ency of E European lit, 1281
Reader's gd to ...
    Australian fiction, 1269
    intelligence pers, 761
    the American novel of detection, 1231
    the private eye novel, 1209
Reading about the environment, 1991
Recipes into type, 1613

Recommended publications for legal research 1970/71, 549
Recommended ref bks 1993, 4
Recreation hndbk, 827
Recycling in America, 2013
Recycling sourcebk, 2017
Red bk, 1993, 1883
Redden, Kenneth R., 555
Reddy, Marlita A., 193, 282, 422
Reeder, DeeAnn M., 1743
Reeder, Ray, 1331
Reef sharks & rays of the world, 1718
Rees, Alan M., 1827
Rees, Robin, 1684
Reeves, Diane Lindsey, 923
Reference bks bulletin 1991-92, 3
Reference ency of the American Indian, 6th ed, 419
Reference gd to ...
   Afro-American publications & eds 1827-1946, 1009
   US military hist 1815-65, 501
   US military hist 1865-1919, 502
Reform Judaism in America, 1557
Rega, Regina, 175, 646, 1919
Reginald, Robert, 1214
Register of N American hospitals, 1993, 1806
Register of N American insurance cos, 1993, 221
Rehabilitation resource manual: vision, 884
Reich, Bernard, 152
Reichler, Joseph L., 835
Reid, Francis, 1475
Reid, Jane Davidson, 1397
Reilly, Edwin D., 1903
Reinehr, Robert C., 1017
Religion & the American experience, 1620-1900, 1507
Religion in the Soviet Union, 1503
Religious holidays & calendars, 1517
Religious radio & TV in the US, 1921-91, 1511
Remember the ladies, 959
Renewable energy, 1985
Renouf, John P., 581
Rentschler, Cathy, 621
Renyi picture dict: Hebrew & English, 1116
Renyi picture dict: Russian & English, 1131
Renz, Loren, 896
Report on bus: Canada co hndbk 1993, 250
Reptiles & amphibians, 1748
Republic chapterplays, 1440
Republic of China yrbk 1991-92, 121
Research & dvlpmt growth trends, 1992 ed, 209
Research centers dir 1993, 345
Research servs dir, 5th ed, 165
Resource gd of pubns supported by multiculturalism programs, 398
Resources for ...
   elders with disabilities, 2d ed, 873
   people with disabilities & chronic conditions, 2d ed, 882
   the future, 77
Ress, Lisa, 806
Restum, Eric J., 988
Reynolds, C. H. B., 119
Rhododendron hybrids, 2d ed, 1631
Rice, Jonathan, 1362
Rice, Tim, 1362
Richard, Alfred Charles, Jr., 1448
Richard Jefferies: a bibliographical study, 1252

Richards, William R., 1723
Richardson, David T., 1737
Richardson, L., Jr., 536
Richter, Alan, 909
Ricigliano, Lorraine, 1293
Ricks, David A., 213
Rickson, R., 260
Ridge, Martin, 490
Ridinger, Robert B. Marks, 488
Ridpath, Ian, 1925
Riegel's hndbk of industrial chemistry, 9th ed, 1770
Riggs, Stephen Return, 1111
Right gd, 787
Righter, Robert, 1689
Riley, Dorothy Winbush, 72
Riley, Laura, 1683
Riley, Sam G., 267
Riley, William, 1683
Rinderknecht, Carol, 10
Rinehart, Julia R., 473
Ringler, William A., Jr., 1267
Rintoul, M. C., 1159
Rip-roaring reads for reluctant teen readers, 1182
Ritchie, Donald A., 758
Ritchie, L. A., 2031
Rivard, Denis, 1945, 2001
RMA annual statement studies 1993, 217
Robert Mitchum: a bio-bibliog, 1417
Roberts, Elfed Vaughan, 110
Roberts, Gary Boyd, 439
Roberts, Helene E., 1540
Roberts, Jerry, 1417
Roberts, Patricia L., 1178, 1179
Robinson, Judith Schiek, 56
Robinson, R. K., 1600
Rock 'n' roll through 1969, 1376
Rocks, David T., 1428
Rodale's all-new ency of organic gardening, 1619
Rodale's illus ency of perennials, 1620
Rodriguez, Paul Anthony, 1016, 1435
Roeder, Marcelotte Leake, 1645
Rogal, Samuel J., 1821
Rogerson, John, 1546
Roget's thesaurus of the Bible, 1542
Rohmann, Chris, 1397
Rohwer, Jens G., 1646
Roland, Albert E., 1659
Rolef, Susan Hattis, 785
Roller coasters, 828
Rolling Stone album gd, 1367
Rolling Stone index, 1404
Rollings, Neil, 263
Rollyson, Carl, 16
Roman Catholics, 1525
Roman de la rose: an annot bibliog, 1282
Roman sculpture, 1066
Romaniuk, Bohdan R., 898, 902
Rookledge, Sarah, 1563
Rookledge's intl hndbk of type designers, 1563
Room, Adrian, 440
Rooney, John F., Jr., 819
Root, Betty, 1092, 1093
Rosato, Dominick V., 1771
Rosato's plastics ency & dict, 1771
Rose, Barry, 1842
Rose, Rose K., 1923

Rosenberg, Jerry M., 177, 210
Rosenberg, Lee, 944
Rosenberg, Saralee, 944
Rosenblatt, Arthur, 1309
Roser, Nancy L., 1173
Ross, Linda M., 1201, 1517
Ross, Lynn C., 270
Rossi, Ernest E., 784
Rossi, John, 1751
Rothbart, Linda S., 2023
Rothenberg, Marc, 1560
Rothman, Barbara Katz, 1831
Rough, Valerie, 1737
Routledge dict of 20th-century pol thinkers, 715
Rovin, Jeff, 1429
Rowland, Ian, 112
Rowland, J. F. B., 1931
Rowland-Entwhistle, Theodore, 39
Roy, Archie, 1944
Royal descents of 500 immigrants to the American colonies or the US, 439
Royal Histl Society annual bibliog of British & Irish hist: publications of 1992, 518
Rozmovits, Linda, 1278
Rugg, Frederick E., 364
Rugg's recommendations on the colleges, 10th ed, 364
Rumbold, Valerie, 1310
Rumney, Thomas A., 461
Running Pr cyclopedia, 40
Ruse, Christina, 980
Russell, Cheryl, 283
Russia & the Commonwealth A to Z, 525
Russia 1993: pol & economic analysis & bus dir, 137
Russian govt today, spring 1993, 780
Russian-English dict of verbal collocations (REDVC), 1129
Russian-English/English-Russian dict of free market era economics, 160
Rutkow, Ira M., 1822

S. N. Behrman: a research & production sourcebk, 1232
Sacred choral music in print: master index 1992, 1341
Sacred choral music in print: 1992 suppl, 1340
Sadie, Stanley, 1356
Sadler, M. J., 1600
Sagar, D. J., 765
Sagebrush country, 1660
Sailing dir, 860
Saint: a complete hist in print, radio, film & TV, 1249
Saints, 1526
Saks, Norman, 1369
Salem, Dorothy C., 960
Salley, Columbus, 406
Salley, Homer E., 1631
Salsa & related genres, 1381
Samuels, Jeffrey M., 576
Sander, Reinhard, 1148
Sanford, George, 134
Sarfoh, Joseph A., 1969
Sarg, Michael J., 1858
Sattler, S. C., 392
Sauber, S. Richard, 810
Saunders, Tom, 861
Sauvant, Karl P., 792
Saving endangered mammals, 1738
Saxophone recital music, 1339

Sayers, Scott P., Jr., 1368
Scammon, Richard M., 756
Scarre, Chris, 534
Schayes, Terry Lee, 294
Schetgen, Robert, 1015
Schiavone, Giuseppe, 793
Schinabeck, Michael J., 271
Schlachter, Gail Ann, 367, 368
Schleuter, Stanley L., 1339
Schlicke, Priscilla, 1562
Schmidt, Jonathan K., 137
Schmitz, Cecilia M., 1823
Schneider, Gerhard, 1528
Schocken gd to Jewish bks, 425
Scholar's gd to geographical writing on the American & Canadian past, 461
Scholarship bk, 4th ed, 333
Schon, Isabel, 1180
Schonberg, Bent, 1425
Schult, Joachim, 860
Schultz, William R., 1491
Schumann, Walter, 1957
Schwartz, Carol A., 49
Schwartz, Mortimer D., 549
Schwartzberg, Joseph E., 515
Schweitzer, Darrell, 1292
Science & tech desk ref, 1584
Science Bks & Films best bks for children 1988-91, 1561
Science fiction & fantasy lit 1975-91, 1214
Science fiction & fantasy ref index 1985-91, 1213
Science teacher's bk of lists, 1580
SCOLMA dir of libs & special collections on Africa in the UK & in Europe, 5th ed, 652
Scotchmer, Sarah Parker, 399
Scott, Mark W., 893
Scott, Mona L., 630
Scott, Randall W., 1405
Scott, William, 1350
Scouting report: 1993, 836
Scribner writers series on CD-ROM, 1160
Seabourne, Joan, 892
Seal, Graham, 1390
Sebba, Gregor, 1485
Secular choral music in print: 1993 suppl, 1342
Security, arms control, & conflict reduction in E Asia & the Pacific, 683
Segal, Aaron, 428
Segal, Audrey, 385
Segal, David, 1216, 1217
Segen, J. C., 1832
Selected bibliog of the foot & ankle with commentary, 1820
Sellen, Betty-Carol, 1032
Sellen, Mary K., 623
Senior citizen servs, 874
Senn, Bryan, 1449
Serafin, Steven R., 1152
Serials dir, 7th ed, 63
Serials dir: EBSCO CD-ROM, summer 1993, 64
Seventeenth-century British nondramatic poets, 1264
Sexuality & the law, 570
Seychelles, 140
Seymore, Bruce II, 799
Shackman, Joshua, 787
Shafritz, Jay M., 718
Shaikh, Farzana, 1553

Shailor, Barbara A., 30
Shain, Michael, 1900
Shakespearean criticism, v.18, 1260
Shakespearean criticism, v.19, yrbk 1991, 1259
Shakespeare's characters, 1258
Shakespeare's quotations, 1257
Shannon, Gary W., 1802
Shapiro, Fred R., 584
Shapiro, Lillian L., 1181
Sharylen, Maria, 1042
Sheets, William, 1778
Shells, 1675
Sheng, Jin, 672
Sherman, Andrew J., 199
Sherman, Charles H., 1332
Sherman, Gale W., 1182
Shipbuilding industry, 2031
Shiri, Keith, 1436
Shoebridge, Michele, 821
Shorebirds of the Pacific Northwest, 1700
Short story criticism, v.11, 1216
Short story criticism, v.12, 1217
Short-title cat of music printed before 1825 in the Fitzwilliam Museum, Cambride, 1310
Shrader, Charles Reginald, 501, 502
Shroyer, Jo Ann, 1585
Shulman, Frank Joseph, 108
Shumaker, David, 611
Siegel, Alice, 2
Siegel, David S., 1027, 1028
Siegel, Jonathan P., 724
Siegel, Susan, 1027, 1028
Sierra Leone, 102
Simms, Ena G., 1110
Simon, Dolores, 1613
Simon, Susan H., 1340, 1342
Simony, Maggie, 474
Simplified dict of modern Tongan, 1134
Simpson, Colin MacLeod, 1891
Simpson, Martha Seif, 1194
Sinatra: the man & his music, 1368
Sinclair, Brett Jason, 1843
Singerman, Robert, 426
Singh, Madan G., 1570
Singh, Sunita, 953
Sinkankas, John, 1958
Sir John Vanbrugh: a ref gd, 975
Skapura, Robert, 1006, 1007
Skeen, Molly, 622
Skeete, Charles, 249
Skidmore, Thomas E., 142
Skinner, Robert E., 1235
Skinner's dir of security dealer name & address changes 1992, 184
Skoss, Diane, 854
Slater, Courtenay M., 937
Slattery, William J., 1463
Slavic studies, 131
Slee, Debora A., 1804
Slee, Vergil N., 1804
Slide, Anthony, 1210
Sloan, Dave, 848
Sloan, Jane E., 1450
Small pr: an annot gd, 659
Small pr center dir, 673
Smallman-Raynor, Matthew, 1854
Smart consumer's dir, 1993 ed, 202
Smart, Giles, 894
Smith, Colin, 1133
Smith, Doreen L., 864
Smith, G. B., 1874
Smith, Gregory White, 562
Smith, Hobart M., 1752
Smith, Judith Scharman, 1612
Smith, Laura, 1195
Smith, Leon, 1421
Smith, Margaret M., 1246
Smith, Myron J., Jr., 837, 847
Smith, Paul, 1383
Smith, Robert Ellis, 577
Smith, Roger, 469
Smith, Rozella B., 1752
Smith, Scott D., 1612
Smith, William, 1541
Smithsonian timelines of the ancient world, 534
Snakes of the US & Canada, v.1, 1751
Snodgrass, Mary Ellen, 17
Snyder, Paula, 947
Sobel, Audrey J., 922
Sobel, Stuart, 855
Social & religious hist of the Jews, 2d ed: index to vs.9-18, 427
Social correlates of infant & reproductive mortality in the US, 879
Social dimensions of intl bus, 222
Social work almanac, 911
Socioeconomics of sustainable agriculture, 1588
Software ency 1993, 1915
Solis, Beatriz, 915
Solomon, David H., 875
Soren Kierkegaard bibliogs, 1486
Sorrow, Barbara Head, 1920
Sosa, Maria, 1561
Sosare, M., 1123
Sourcebook for sci, math, & tech educ 1992, 1582
Sourcebook of county demographics, census ed, 933
South America, Central America, & the Caribbean 1993, 146
South Pacific islands legal systems, 573
Sova, Dawn B., 961
Soviet military ency, abridged English-lang ed, 686
Soybean diseases, 1595
Space exploration, 1756
Spain, Patrick J., 172
Spanish American authors, 1297
Spanish & Portuguese Jewry, 426
Spanish Armada of 1588, 527
Spanish-English, English-Spanish dict of computer terms, 1895
Sparks, Andrew N., 1094
Sparks, Linda, 324
Speaking for ourselves, too, 1186
Special effects & stunts gd, 2d ed, 1454
Specialty cut flowers, 1623
Speck, Bruce W., 997
Spencer, Donald D., 1904, 1912
Spicer, Dorothy Gladys, 1406
Spies & provocateurs, 796
Spille, Henry A., 392
Spodek, Bernard, 314
Spomer, Cynthia Russell, 286
Sporting News complete baseball record bk, 1993 ed, 838

Sporting News complete Super Bowl bk, 1993 ed, 848
Sports in N America, v.3, 826
Spring wildflowers, 1659
Springberg, Judith, 748
Sproccati, Sandro, 1047
Sprug, Joseph W., 69
Squire, Larry R., 809
St. Vincent & the Grenadines, 148
Stachura, Peter D., 774
Stade, George, 1280
Staff dirs on CD-ROM, 1993/1, 737
Stage it with music, 1473
Stamp, Robert M., 18
Standard & Poor's stock & bond gd, 1993 3d, 200
Standard cat of US military vehicles 1940-1965, 691
Standard dir of ...
    advertisers 1993, 296
    advertising agencies, Jan 1993, 297
    intl advertisers & agencies 1993, 226
Standard hndbk for electrical engineers, 13th ed, 1777
Standard per dir 1993, 67
Standard trade index of Japan 1992-93, 245
Standish, Peter, 1299
Stanford, Quentin H., 456
Stange, Scott, 988
Stanke, Don, 1432
Stanley, Autumn, 1586
Stanley, Janet L., 1040
Stanton, Shelby, 708
Starer, Daniel, 166
StarList 2000, 1924
State & local stats sources, 2d ed, 934
State & province vital records gd, 432
State lead poisoning prevention dir 1992, 2006
State yellow bk, v.5, no.1, 743
Statesmen who changed the world, 716
Statistical abstract of the US 1992, 938
Statistical forecasts of the US, 932
Statistical record of Asian Americans, 401
Statistical record of native N Americans, 422
Statistical report on road accidents in 1990, 2027
Statistical yrbk for Asia & the Pacific 1991, 939
STATS, Inc., 836
Stearn, William T., 1641, 1642
Stearn's dict of plant names for gardeners, 1642
Steele, Apollonia, 1276
Steele, Joelle, 1621
Stein, Barbara L., 1181
Stein, Barry Jason, 696
Stein, J. Stewart, 1773
Steiner, Dale R., 542
Stelter, Jeffrey S., 563
Stelter, Thomas, 563
Stephens, Meic, 480
Stern, Edward L., 1884
Stern, Ephraim, 489
Stern, Malcolm H., 1557
Stetler, Susan L., 228, 229
Stevens, Gregory I., 399
Stewart, Julia, 443
Stewart, Steve, 1460
Stibili, Edward C., 1504
Stinson, Shirley M., 1864
Stoddart colour visual dict: French-English, 1114
Stone, Jon R., 1535
Stonehouse, Bernard, 464

Storey, Dee, 1183
Stramler, James H., Jr., 1791
Strategic atlas, 3d ed, 712
Stratton, Peter, 811
Straussman, David, 1457
Stravinskas, Peter M. J., 1531
Strichart, Stephen S., 340
Strickland, Jennifer, 197
Stroebel, Leslie, 1036
Stroff, Stephen M., 1358
Strong, Lisa L., 409
Strong, William S., 637
Strouf, Judie L. H., 1142
Struk, Danylo Husar, 138
Student atlas of the world, 453
Student contact bk, 58
Student's complete vocabulary gd to the Greek N.T., 1543
Student's dict of psychology, 2d ed, 811
Studies in begoniaceae 4, 1649
Study holidays, 17th ed, 369
Sturm, Gary L., 2028
Subject collections, 7th ed, 656
Subject index to feature articles & special reports in ency yrbks 1975-91, 35
Sudan, rev ed, 104
Sulanowski, James S., 577
Sullivan, Eugene, 393
Sullivan, George, 700, 711
Sullivan, Irene F., 418
Sullivan, Lester, 1235
Sullivan, Thomas F. P., 2002
Summer reading clubs, 1194
Supreme Court A to Z, 556
Supreme Court justices, 551
Suriname & the Netherlands Antilles, 149
Survey Research Consultants International, 75
Sussman, Lance J., 1557
Sutherland, Neil, 924, 925
Suttles, Sharon F., 81
Suttles, Steven A., 81
Sutton, Alan, 1317
Swannell, Julia, 1100
Swarbrick, James, 1867, 1868, 1869, 1870
Swartz, Jon D., 1017
Sweeney, Del, 624
Sweeney, Jerry K., 757
Sykes, Egerton, 1394
Synopsis of the herpetofauna of Mexico, v.7, 1752
Systems & control ency, suppl. v.2, 1570

Taber's cyclopedic medical dict, 17th ed, 1833
Tale of two cities: an annot bibliog, 1251
Tamm, Boris, 1775
Tapper, Lawrence F., 410
Tapping the govt grapevine, 2d ed, 56
Taragano, Martin, 840
Taras, Raymond C., 781
Tardiff, Joseph C., 1260
Targumic mss in the Cambridge Genizah collections, 1539
Tax havens, 186
Taylor, Barbara, 1702
Taylor, Charles A., 400
Taylor, Desmond, 1205
Taylor, Patrick, 1622
Taylor, Ronald J., 1660
Tayyeb, Rashid, 597

TCG theatre dir 1993-94, 1477
Teaching sci to children, 2d ed, 1559
Teague, Edward H., 1052
Teasdale, Karen H., 583
Technical dict of lib & info sci, 600
Teens' favorite bks, 1175
Telecommunications dir 1994-95, 1922
Television-related cartoons in the New Yorker, 1056
Telgen, Diane, 962
Tener, Jean F., 1276
Terborg-Penn, Rosalyn, 965
Terrell, Dirk, 1929
Terrell, Peter, 1115
Terrible speller, 1104
Terrorism: a ref hndbk, 585
Terrorism, 1988-91, 589
Terry, John V., 238
Terry, Max, 903
Test Collection, Educational Testing Service, 304
Texas, 89
Texas range plants, 1664
Thackeray, Frank W., 716
Theatre lighting from A to Z, 1470
Themes in American painting, 1064
Theodicy: an annot bibliog, 1506
Thesaurus gd, 1992, 631
Thesaurus of word roots of the English lang, 1079
Thiessen, Diane, 1968
Third opinion, 2d ed, 1859
Thoene, Jess G., 1863
Thomas, Clayton L., 1833
Thomas, G. Scott, 945
Thomas, Graham Stuart, 1632
Thomas, James L., 1184
Thomas, Jeffrey, 1382
Thomas, T. Donley, 1332
Thompson, Della, 1078
Thompson, Don, 1407
Thompson, Henry O., 1536
Thompson, M. M., 1825
Thompson, Maggie, 1407
Thomson, Ellen Mazur, 1059
Thornton Wilder: a ref gd 1926-90, 1242
Threatened birds of the Americas, pt.2, 3d ed, 1695
300 1st words, 1093
Throgmorton, Todd H., 828
Thurner, Dick, 1083
Times atlas of world hist, 4th ed, 530
Timetables of sports hist: football, 845
Timor, 112
Tiner, Ralph W., 1661
Tobiasen, Linda, 891
Tolf, Robert W., 533
Tomasi, Silvano M., 1504
Tomassi, Noreen, 983
Tomassini, Christine, 1020
Torres-Seda, Olga, 1301
Total forecast: Japan 1990s, 116
Total TV bk, 1016
Toth, Georgetta, 897, 900
Toucan Valley Publications, research staff of, 928, 941
Tousignaut, Dwight R., 1873
Tracey, Patrick Austin, 701
Tracing your Irish ancestors, 434
Trade shows worldwide 1993, 298
Train-watcher's gd to N American railroads, 2d ed, 2024

Transcript/video index, 1992, 1021
Transylvanian lib, 1212
Trash cash, fizzbos, & flatliners, 1095
Travel bk, 2d ed, 473
Traveler's country music radio atlas 1993, 1018
Traveler's gd to native America: the Great Lakes region, 413
Traveler's reading gd, rev & updated ed, 474
Treasure, Geoffrey, 519
Trees, 1669
Trees & shrubs of Great Britain & N Europe, 1670
Trefil, James, 305
Trehub, Aaron, 130
Trenchard, Warren C., 1543
Trilobites, 2d ed, 1961
Trinder, Barrie, 484
Tripp, F. R., 702
Trissel, Lawrence A., 1885
Trudeau, Lawrence J., 1201, 1202, 1203
Trzyna, Thaddeus C., 2007
Tsouras, Peter G., 697
Tu'inukuafe, Edgar, 1134
Tuller, Lawrence W., 239
Tung, Louise Watanbe, 1571
Turecki, Gwen E., 1907, 1922
Turner, Harold W., 1505
Tuten-Puckett, Katharyn E., 1190
Tuttle dict of antiques & collectibles terms, 1024
Tuttle's concise Indonesian dict, 1117
20th century American folk, self taught, & outsider art, 1032
Twentieth-century Caribbean & black African writers, 2d series, 1148
Twentieth-century composer speaks, 1333
Twentieth-century German dramatists, 1889-1918, 1286
Twentieth-century German dramatists, 1919-92, 1287
Twentieth-century short story explication: new series, v.1, 1218
Twins in children's & adolescent lit, 1183
Two hundred yrs of the American circus, 1419
Types & motifs of the Judeo-Spanish folktales, 1387

U.S. Department of Commerce, NTIS, Office of Business Development, 114
Ujifusa, Grant, 746
Ukraine: a tourist gd, 483
Ukraine: pol parties & orgs, 782
Ulrich's intl pers dir 1993-94, 65
Ulrich's plus [CD-ROM], 66
Ultimate dinosaur bk, 1960
Under its generous dome, 2d ed, 657
United Nations juridical yrbk 1985, 578
United States govt docs on women, 1800-1990, 951
United States military road atlas, 677
United States sanctions & S Africa, 545
University of California at Berkeley Wellness Letter, editors of, 1602
Unlocking the files of the FBI, 752
Up from the roots: growing a vocab, 1082
Upshall, Michael, 42
Urdang, Laurence, 299, 1107
U.S. aircraft & armament of Operation Desert Storm in detail & scale, 699
U.S. army heraldic crests, 696
U.S. army uniforms of the Korean war, 708
U.S. criminal justice interest groups, 588

U.S. Department of Commerce, Technology Administration, 1914
U.S. industrial outlook '93, 218
U.S. Securities & Exchange Commission, 802
U.S. sourcebk of R&D spenders, 1992 ed, 240
U.S. student Fulbright grants & other grants for graduate study & research abroad, 346
U.S.A. oil industry dir, 1993, 1975
U.S.A. oilfield serv, supply & manufacturers dir, 1993, 1976
Used bk lover's gd to New England, 1027
Used bk lover's gd to the mid-Atlantic states, 1028
Using lit to teach middle grades about war, 694

Vamplew, Wray, 822
Van de Sande, Wendy S., 407
Van Hasselt, Vincent B., 1848
Van Son, Victoria, 750
van Tienhoven, Ans, 1731
van Tienhoven, Ari, 1731
Van Vynckt, Randall J., 1055
Van Zandt, Eleanor, 445
Vance, Timothy J., 1119
Vancil, David E., 1074
Variety & Daily Variety TV reviews, v.16, 1019
Vash, Peter, 1603
Vasilevsky, Andrei, 777
Vass, Winifred K., 1081
Vassilian, Hamo B., 129
Venomous sea snakes, 1750
Venture into cultures, 1170
Veron, J. E. N., 1747
Vibbert, Spencer, 1810
Vidali, Carole F., 1334
Video source bk 1993, 1020
Videos for understanding diversity, 399
Vietnam, 122
Vietnam war: hndbk of the lit & research, 497
Vietnam war in lit, 514
Violence against women, 596
Virtes, John J., 726
Visual dict of ...
 dinosaurs, 1963
 flight, 2020
 special military forces, 689
 the Earth, 1946
 the universe, 1930
Vivien Leigh: a bio-bibliog, 1415
Vocabulary of ...
 global warming, v.1, 2001
 hazardous materials in the workplace, 1997
 public sector auditing, 249
Vogt, W. Paul, 79
Voices from the underground, 1010
Voll, John Obert, 105
Vollnhals, Otto, 1889
Volunteer! 1992-1993 ed, 903
Volunteer work, 904
Vyas, Anju, 953

W. C. Fields—an annot gd, 1428
Wachsberger, Ken, 1010
Wade, William A., 347
Wagner compendium, 1329
Waithe, Deborah, 67
Walder, Ronald H., 458

Waldo, Andrew B., 2018
Walford's gd to ref material, v.1: sci & tech, 6th ed, 1562
Walker, Diane Parr, 1343
Walker, Elaine L., 885
Walker, John, 1456
Walker, John A., 1043
Walker, Mary, 676
Walker, Neil E., 59
Walker, Paul, 1343
Walker, Samuel, 550
Walker, Warren S., 1218
Walkowicz, Chris, 1710
Wallace, Amy, 1403
Wallechinsky, David, 1403
Walliman, Isidor, 587
Walls, David, 865
Walsh, Claudette, 1242
Walsh, James E., 31
Walt Disney: a bio-bibliog, 1412
Walt Whitman: a descriptive bibliog, 1241
Walter, Virginia A., 1185
Walthall, Barbara, 1582
Wanda Gag: a cat raisonne of the prints, 1060
Want, Robert S., 564, 579, 1478
Want's fed-state court dir, 1993 ed, 564
Want's theater dir, 1993 ed, 1478
War & peace lit for children & young adults, 1185
Ward, Charles A., 985
Ward, Gary L., 1514
Warfare & armed conflicts, 692
Warner, Jay, 1359
Warr, Wendy, 1939
Warrack, John, 1357
Warrior's words, 697
Wars & peace treaties 1816-1991, 693
Washington area lib dir, 611
Washington '93, 744
Washington Researchers Publishing, 173
Wassink, Jan L., 1741
Watching Kans. wildlife, 1679
Water quality & availability, 1954
Watkins, Mel, 127
Watson, Carol, 41
Watstein, Sarah B., 949
Watt, David L., 1588
Watt, Evan, 1951
WAVE: women's audio-visuals in English, 954
Way nature works, 1684
Wear, Terri A., 1709
Wearing, J. P., 1469
Weather of US cities, 4th ed, 1947
Weaver, Norma Wright, 1311
Weaver, Robert Lamar, 1311
Weaver, Tom, 1461
Webb, C. Anne, 648
Webb, James L. A., Jr., 101
Webber, F. R., 1048
Weber, Lynn, 955
Weber, R. David, 367, 368
Webster, Valerie J., 298
Webster, Virginia, 559
Webster's new world dict for young adults, 1094
Webster's new world ency, college ed, 42
Webster's new world ency, pocket ed, 43
Wedgeworth, Robert, 609
Wedgwood, C. G., 1787

Weed seeds of the Great Plains, 1663
Weeks, John M., 541
Weevils of Canada & Alaska, v.1, 1722
Weiner, Ed, 1838
Weinstein, Amy J., 913
Weinstein, Miriam, 348
Weiskel, Timothy C., 2019
Weiss, Manfred, 253
Welch, Jeffrey Egan, 1143
Wellisch, Hans H., 638
Wellness ency of food & nutrition, 1602
Wellsprings of imagination, 478
Welsh women, 950
Welsh-English, English-Welsh dict, 1136
Welton, Ann, 462
West, Ewan, 1357
West German cinema 1985-90, 1441
West, Mark I., 478
Western reader's gd, 88
Western series & sequels, 2d ed, 1221
Westfall, Gloria D., 95
Westley, David, 1849
Wetta, Frank J., 1451
Weyers warships of the world 1992/93, 706
What about murder? 1981-91, 1206
What to do when you can't afford health care, 1809
What's new for parents, 920
Wheeler, Douglas L., 135
Wheeler, Leslie, 78
Where the animals are, 1688
Where to make money, 945
Whisenhunt, Donald W., 509, 510, 513
Whisker, James Biser, 732, 1033, 1034, 1035
Whistler, W. Arthur, 1647
Whistlin' Dixie: a dict of S expressions, 1089
Whitaker's bks in print 1993, 6
Whitehead ency of deer, 1742
Whitehead, G. Kenneth, 1742
Whiteley, Sandy, 3
Whitman, Joan, 1613
Whitney, Barry L., 1506
Who is who in the Russian govt, 777
Who is who in the Russian govt, suppl.1, 778
Who knows what, 166
Who owns corporate America 1993, 167
Who was who in America with world notables, index 1993, 23
Who was who in the American Revolution, 500
Wholesale-by-mail cat 1993, 203
Who's wealthy in America 1993, 211
Who's who in ...
    America 1992-93, 24
    American nursing 1993-94, 1865
    Canada, 1992, 19
    classical mythology, 1393
    early Hanoverian Britain (1714-1789), 519
    European bus, 223
    European insts & enterprises 1993, 771
    European pols, 2d ed, 772
    intl banking, 6th ed, 224
    Italy 1992, 20
    Mexico today, 2d ed, 12
    non-classical mythology, 1394
    religion 1992-93, 1510
    Russian & the new states, 136
    sci & engineering 1992-93, 1564
    S African pols, 4th ed, 762
    space: the intl space yr ed, 1755
    Spain 1992, 21
    the east 1993-94, 25
    the fed executive branch 1993, 745
    the N.T., 1537
    the O.T., together with the Apocrypha, 1538
    the Peace Corps, 1993 ed, 798
    the south & southwest, 23d ed, 26
    the world 1993-94, 22
    the Writers' Union of Canada, 4th ed, 998
Who's who of emerging leaders in America 1993-94, 27
Why you say it, 1080
Whyld, Kenneth, 842
Wiedensohler, Pat, 639
Wiener, Allen J., 1380
Wiersma, John H., 829
Wiersma, Tina M., 829
Wilcox, Bonnie, 1710
Wilcox, Derk Arend, 787
Wildflowers of Prince Edward Island, 1650
Wildflowers of the W plains, 1655
Wilks, Daniel S., 1948
Willett, Peter, 1939
William J. Fellner: a bio-bibliog, 154
William Walton: a source bk, 1323
Williams, Beverly, 1197
Williams, Brian, 451
Williams, Frank P., III, 804
Williams, Glyndwr, 444
Williams, James G., 1896, 1897, 1898, 1899
Williams, Jeanne M., 876
Williams, John Taylor, 574
Williams, Martha E., 614
Williams, Michael W., 402, 764
Williams, Peter W., 505
Williams, Phil, 718
Williams, Robin, 1905
Williamson, John P., 1112
Willis, Alan, 946
Willis, Roy, 1398
Wilmeth, Don B., 1479
Wilson, A., 1977
Wilson, Andrew, 525
Wilson, Cynthia, 1861
Wilson dir of emerging market funds, 1992-1993 ed, 185
Wilson, Don E., 1743
Wilson, George, 128, 132
Wilson, Ian M., 185
Wilson, James D., 1240
Wilson, Janet O., 866
Wilson, Kenneth G., 1085
Wilson, R. E., 1929
Winaker, Lesley Richman, 632
Wingfield, Mary Ann, 1065
Winklepleck, Julie, 988
Winnan, Audur H., 1060
Winning scholarships, 311
Winter, Arthur, 1844
Winter, Ruth, 1844
Wischnath, Lothar, 1721
Wiseman, John A., 99
Witcher, Curt B., 438
Witlieb, Bernard L., 970
Witt, Elder, 556
Witten, Matthew, 1634

Wittfoht, A. M., 1938
Witty words, 70
Wladaver-Morgan, Susan, 158
WLN interlib loan policies dir, 2d ed, 643
Woelfel, Charles J., 208
Wolf, Carolyn, 620
Wolf, Kirsten, 526
Wolf, Richard, 620
Wolke, Howie, 1678
Women & AIDS, 1855
Women & tech, 948
Women in chemistry & physics, 1923
Women of color & S women annual suppl, 1991/92, 955
Women prime ministers & presidents, 714
Women public speakers in the US, 1800-1925, 957
Women's ency of health & emotional healing, 1805
Women's info dir, 968
Women's studies in India, 953
Wonchul, Oh, 1122
Wonderful world of mathematics, 1968
Wood, Jenny, 454
Wood, Robert Muir, 1962
Woodill, Gary A., 315
Woods, Jeannie M., 1418
Woodworth, David, 894
Worcester, Wayne, 57
Word traps, 1087
Work of Robert Reginald, 2d ed, 1238
Working for your uncle, 284
Working holidays 1993, 370
World ballet & dance 1992-93, 1425
World economy, 157
World ency of lib & info servs, 3d ed, 609
World energy & nuclear dir, 2d ed, 2008
World financial system, 2d ed, 206
World gd to libs, 11th ed, 612
World human rights gd, 3d ed, 594
World investment dir 1992, v.1, 227
World law school dir, 1993 ed, 565
World markets desk bk, 239
World media hndbk 1992-94, 992
World mythology, 1398
World of African music, 1315
World of learning 1993, 308
World philosophy, 1482
World Resources Institute, 1986
World satellite annual, 1993/94, 1758
World statistical compendium for raw hides & skins, leather, & leather footwear 1972-90, 5th ed, 1598
World stats in brief, 14th ed, 940

World tech policies, 1587
World War I source bk, 540
World who's who of women, 11th ed, 963
Worldwide gd to equivalent irons & steels, 3d ed, 1796
Worldwide interesting people, 404
Wrestling college & univ dir, 2d ed, 862
Wright, Amy Bartlett, 1730
Wright, David, 447
Wright, Jill, 447
Writer's gd to everyday life in the 1800s, 511
Writer's hndbk, 1993 ed, 999
Writers of the Indian diaspora, 1290
Wu, Emily, 251
Wurth, Shirley, 1165
Wynar, Bohdan S., 4, 80
Wynn, Graeme, 461

Yaakov, Juliette, 1481
Yanak, Ted, 512
Yearbook of English festivals, 1406
Yearbook of the European Communities & of the other European orgs, 12th ed, 773
Yellow pages industry source bk, 1992-93 ed, 674
Yentis, S. M., 1874
Young, Arthur P., 1507
Young, Ian, 1856
Young, Josiah U., III, 1508
Young, Mark, 825, 1581
Young Oxford companion to the congress of the US, 758
Young people's atlas of the US, 445
Young reader's companion, 1189
Young, Robyn V., 1303
Youngblood, Ronald F., 1547
Your reading, 9th ed, 648
Yugoslavia: a comprehensive English-lang bibliog, 139

Zagaris, Bruce, 916
Zak, Victoria, 1603
Zakalik, Joanna M., 650
Zakia, Richard, 1036
Zilla, Karin, 624
Zilm, Glennis, 1864
Zimmerman, David R., 1886
Zimmerman's complete gd to nonprescription drugs, 2d ed, 1886
Zinkewych, Osyp, 483
Zminda, Don, 836
Zvirin, Stephanie, 926
Zweifel, Richard G., 1748

Subject Index

Reference is to entry number.

Abbreviations
Dictionary of acronyms & abbrevs, 597
Dictionary of acronyms & abbrevs in applied linguistics & lang learning, 1072
Dictionary of medical acronyms & abbrevs, 2d ed, 1818
OSI dict of acronyms & related abbrevs, 1891

Abortion
Abortion in the US, 1992 suppl, 1840

Academic Libraries. *See* **Libraries, University & College**

Accounting
Environmental accounting, 1989

Acquired Immune Deficiency. *See* **AIDS**

Acronyms. *See also* **Abbreviations**
Dictionary of acronyms & abbrevs, 597
Dictionary of acronyms & abbrevs in applied linguistics & lang learning, 1072
OSI dict of acronyms & related abbrevs, 1891

Acting
Coming to terms with acting, 1434

Activity Programs in Education
Literature activity bks, 1197

Actors
Agnes Moorehead: a bio-bibliog, 1413
Boris Karloff: a bio-bibliog, 1409
Colleen Dewhurst: a bio-bibliog, 1411
Helen Hayes: a bio-bibliog, 1416
Maureen Stapleton: a bio-bibliog, 1418
Vivien Leigh: a bio-bibliog, 1415

Adams, John Quincy
John Quincy Adams: a bibliog, 498

Administrative Agencies
Federal regional yellow bk, v.1, no.1, 739
Federal staff dir/1, 1993, 735
Staff dirs on CD-ROM, 1993/1, 737
State yellow bk, v.5, no.1, 743
Who's who in the fed executive branch 1993, 745

Adoption
Loving Journeys gd to adoption, 885

Adult Children
Caregiving of older adults, 867

Adult Education
Adult educ in continental Europe, 391
Adult learner's gd to alternative & external degree programs, 393
Education for older adult learning, 389

Adventure Stories. *See* **Detective & Mystery Stories**

Advertising
Advertising ratios & budgets, 287
Co-op source dir: spring 1993, 288
Standard dir of intl advertisers & agencies 1993, 226
Standard dir of advertisers 1993, 296
Standard dir of advertising agencies, Jan 1993, 297

Aeronautics
Visual dict of flight, 2020

Aesthetics
Companion to aesthetics, 1492

Africa
Africa: a gd to ref material, 94
Africa south of the Sahara 1993, 91
African archaeology, 488
African names, 443
African socio-economic indicators 1989, 92
African studies thesaurus, 629
African theology, 1508
Directory of African film-makers & films, 1436
Directory of dvlpmt research & training insts in Africa, 93
Energy in the dvlpmt of W Africa, 1969
French colonial Africa, 95
Gemstones of E Africa, 1955
Handbook of the birds of Europe, the Middle East, & N Africa, v.6, 1696
Handbook of the birds of Europe, the Middle East, & N Africa, v.7, 1697
Mental health & psychiatry in Africa, 1849
Pan-Africanism: an annot bibliog, 764
SCOLMA dir of libs & special collections on Africa in the UK & in Europe, 5th ed, 652
World of African music, 1315

African Americans. *See* **Afro-Americans**

African Languages
African heritage of American English, 1081

African Literature (Portuguese)
New bibliog of the Lusophone lits of Africa, 2d ed, 1268

African National Congress
ANC & black workers in S Africa, 1912-92, 103

Africans
Worldwide interesting people, 404

Afro-American Women
African American women, 960
Ann Petry: a bio-bibliog, 1237
Art of black American women, 1046
Bibliographical gd to African-American women writers, 1223
Black women in America, 965
Women of color & S women annual suppl, 1991/92, 955

Afro-Americans
African American ency, 402
African American: social & economic conditions, 405
African heritage of American English, 1081
American ethnic lits, 1225
Black Americans info dir 1994-95, 407
Black 100, 406

Chester Himes: an annot primary & secondary bibliog, 1235
Civil rights movement, 595
Encyclopedia of African American religions, 1514
Freedom's lawmakers, 727
Hippocrene USA gd to historic black south, 475
My soul looks back, 'less I forget, 72
Worldwide interesting people, 404

Aged
Caregiving of older adults, 867
Complete gd to symptoms, illness & surgery for people over 50, 1839
Consumer's gd to aging, 875
Education for older adult learning, 389
Ethical aspects of health care for the elderly, 868
Gerontological social work, 872
Gerontology & geriatrics libs & collections in the US & Canada, 655
Healthy aging, 869
Image of older adults in the media, 870
Legal issues & older adults, 572
Resources for elders with disabilities, 2d ed, 873
Senior citizen servs, 874

Aged Volunteers
Older volunteer, 887

Agents Provocateurs
Spies & provocateurs, 796

Agricultural Engineering
Literature of agricultural engineering, 1754

Agricultural Productivity
FAO yrbk: production, v.45, 1591
Intercountry comparisons of agricultural output & productivity, 1597

AIDS (Disease)
AIDS crisis in America, 1852
AIDS dir, 1850
AIDS dissidents, 1856
AIDS: 1,000 full-text statistical abstracts from the A Matter of Fact database, 1984-92, 1851
Dictionary of AIDS-related terminology, 1853
Women & AIDS, 1855

Aikido
Aiki News 1994 dojo finder, 854

Air Travel
United States military road atlas, 677

Aircraft Carriers
Naval Institute gd to combat fleets of the world 1993, 704

Airplanes
U.S. aircraft & armament of Operation Desert Storm in detail & scale, 699
Visual dict of flight, 2020

Alaska
Weevils of Canada & Alaska, v.1, 1722

Albanian Language—Dictionaries—English
Albanian-English dict, 1109

Albeniz, Isaac
Isaac Albeniz: chronological list & thematic cat of his piano works, 1320

Alberta
Fishes of Alta., 2d ed, 1720

Alcoholic Beverages
Complete beverage dict, 1601

Allied Artists Picture Corporation
Allied Artists checklist, 1445

Alliums
Alliums, 1653

Almanacs
Canadian global almanac 1993, 1
Information please kids' almanac, 2
Information please sports almanac, 1993, 818

Alpine Flora
Desert & mountain plants of the southwest, 1645
Propagation of alpine plant & dwarf bulbs, 1629

Alternative Medicine
Alternative health care resources, 1843
Third opinion, 2d ed, 1859

Alternative Press
Voices from the underground, 1010

American Antiquarian Society
Under its generous dome, 2d ed, 657

American Civil Liberties Union
American Civil Liberties Union: an annot bibliog, 550

American Fiction
Contemporary fiction writers of the South, 1222
Facts on File bibliog of American fiction 1866-1918, 1229

American Literature. *See also names of individual authors*
American ethnic lits, 1225
Bibliographical gd to African-American women writers, 1223
Characters in 19th century lit, 1157
Contemporary Canadian & US women of letters, 1138
Contemporary gay American novelists, 1224
Contemporary lesbian writers of the US, 1226
Encyclopedia of flora & fauna in English & American lit, 1151
Vietnam war in lit, 514

American Periodicals
Directory of literary mags 1993-94, 1162

American Wit & Humor
Official politically correct dict & hndbk, 1101
Television-related cartoons in the New Yorker, 1056

Americanisms
American Heritage college dict, 3d ed, 1075
Columbia gd to standard American English, 1085
Dictionary of the American west, 1088
Homophones & homographs, 2d ed, 1086
Index by region, usage, & etymology to the Dict of American Regional English, v.1 & 2, 1090

Oxford thesaurus, American ed, 1107
Trash cash, fizzbos, & flatliners, 1095
Whistlin' Dixie: a dict of S expressions, 1089

Amin, Idi
Idi Amin & Uganda, 763

Amino Acids In Human Nutrition
Nutrients cat, 1610

Amphibians
Amphibians & reptiles in Kans., 3d ed, 1749
Reptiles & amphibians, 1748

Amusement Parks
Roller coasters, 828

Anesthesia
Anaesthesia A-Z, 1874

Anglo-American Cataloging Rules
Cataloging computer files, 628

Angola
Angola, 96

Animals
Dictionary of animal health terminology, 1633
Encyclopedia of flora & fauna in English & American lit, 1151
Kingfisher illus ency of animals, 1687

Animals, Fossil. *See* **Paleontology**

Ankle
Selected bibliog of the foot & ankle with commentary, 1820

Anonyms & Pseudonyms
Guide to pseudonyms on American records, 1892-1942, 1317

Anthologies
Ireland's index to inspiration, 69

Anthony, Susan B.
Papers of Elizabeth Cady Stanton and Susan B. Anthony, 964

Anthropo-Geography
AUSMAP atlas of Austral., 455
Economist atlas of the New Europe, 255

Antibiotics
Encyclopedia of antibiotics, 3d ed, 1871

Antiquarian Booksellers
Antiquarian, specialty, & used bk sellers 1993, 662

Antiques
David & Charles ency of everyday antiques, 1023

Antiquities
Chronologies in old world archaeology, 3d ed, 485

Aphididae
Genera of the aphids of Canada, 1723

Applied Linguistics
Dictionary of acronyms & abbrevs in applied linguistics & lang learning, 1072

Aquaculture
Aquaculture sourcebk, 1594

Aquarium Fishes
Atlas of livebearers of the world, 1721

Aquariums
Where the animals are, 1688

Aquatic Animals
Dangerous aquatic animals of the world, 1746

Aramaic Philology
Aramaic bibliog, pt.1, 1071

Archaeology
African archaeology, 488
Dictionary of concepts in archaeology, 487
Dictionary of Irish archaeology, 486
New ency of archaeological excavations in the Holy Land, 489

Architecture
Canadian architecture collection, 1053
Dictionary of architecture & construction, 2d ed, 1051
Early Christian & Byzantine architecture, 1054
Index to Italian architecture, 1052
International dict of architects & architecture, 1055

Armenia
Armenians: a colossal bibliographic gd to bks published in the English lang, 129

Arms Control
Encyclopedia of arms control & disarmament, 797
Security, arms control, & conflict reduction in E Asia & the Pacific, 683

Art
Art mktg sourcebk, 1045
Art of black American women, 1046
Art price index intl '94, 1049
1890s: an ency of British lit, art, & culture, 981
Glossary of art, architecture, & design since 1945, 3d ed, 1043
Guide to art, 1047
Nigerian artists, 1040

Art Patronage
Money for intl exchange in the arts, 983

Artificial Intelligence
Artificial intelligence abstracts annual 1991, 1888
Multilingual dict of artificial intelligence, 1889

Artificial Satellites
World satellite annual, 1993/94, 1758

Artists
American cultural leaders from colonial times to the present, 976
Artists of the Pacific Northwest, 1042
Dictionary of Australian artists, 1041
Klee as in clay, 982
Moscow & Leningrad: a topographical gd to Russian cultural hist, v.2, 985
Nigerian artists, 1040

Arts
Action art, 1039
American cultural leaders from colonial times to the present, 976
Art world dir: arts review yrbk 1993, 1044
Clockworks, 974
Great events from hist 2: arts & culture series, 984
Money for intl exchange in the arts, 983
Oxford gd to classical mythology in the arts, 1300-1990s, 1397

Ashmolean Museum
Catalogue of European sculpture in the Ashmolean Museum 1540 to the present day, 1067

Asia. *See also names of countries*
Asia 1992 yrbk, 106
Bibliographic gd to E Asian studies 1991, 107
Doctoral dissertations on Asia, v.15, nos.1 & 2, 108
Political parties of Asia & the Pacific, 765
Statistical yrbk for Asia & the Pacific 1991, 939
World investment dir 1992, v.1, 227

Asia, Southeastern
Mammals of the Indomalayan region, 1734

Asian-Americans
American ethnic lits, 1225
Statistical record of Asian Americans, 401
Women of color & S women annual suppl, 1991/92, 955

Astronauts
Men & women of space, 1757

Astronomy
Facts on File atlas of stars & planets, 1925
Field gd to the stars & planets, 3d ed, 1928
McGraw-Hill ency of astronomy, 2d ed, 1927
Visual dict of the universe, 1930

Atheism
Religion in the Soviet Union, 1503

Athletes
Oxford companion to Australian sport, 822

Atlases
Atlas of the world, 2d ed, 446
Canadian Oxford school atlas, 6th ed, 456
Canadian Oxford intermediate atlas, 457
Children's atlas of people & places, 454
Facts on File children's atlas, 447
Hammond atlas of the world, 448
Hammond atlas of the world, concise ed, 449
Hammond explorer atlas of the world, 450
Student atlas of the world, 453
Young people's atlas of the US, 445

Atomic Energy. *See* Nuclear Energy

Atomic Bomb
Atomic bomb, 710

Attack & Defense (Military Science)
Jane's defence glossary, 676

Attack Planes
Military aircraft: modern bombers & attack planes, 700

Audiocassettes in Education
Audiocassette & CD finder, 3d ed, 374

Audio-Visual Equipment
Directory of video, computer & audio-visual products 1993, 1887

Audio-Visual Materials
American Lib Assn best of the best for children, 1163
Play, learn, & grow, 1184
WAVE: women's audio-visuals in English, 954

Australia
AUSMAP atlas of Austral., 455
Australian plant name index, 1648
Cambridge dict of Australian places, 471
Corals of Austral. & the Indo-Pacific, 1747
Dictionary of Australian artists, 1041
Directory of resources for Australian studies in N America, 123
Historical dict of Austral., 124
Oxford companion to Australian folklore, 1390
Oxford companion to Australian sport, 822
Oxford illus dict of Australian hist, 516
Rainforest plants of E Austral., 1682

Australian Literature
Reader's gd to Australian fiction, 1269

Authors. *See also* Children's Literature; *names of individual authors*
Authors: critical & biographical refs, 2d ed, 1145
Canadian writers & their works: cum index, fiction series, 1271
Contemporary fiction writers of the South, 1222
Contemporary world writers, 2d ed, 1144
DISCovering authors [CD-ROM], 1146
Dorothy Parker: a bio-bibliog, 1236
Gale's literary index [CD-ROM], 1161
International authors & writers who's who, 13th ed, 1147
Lord Dunsany: a bibliog, 1292
Ludwig Tieck: an annot gd to research, 1288
Magill's survey of world lit, 1158
Mark Twain ency, 1240
Modern Chinese writers, 1279
Moscow & Leningrad: a topographical gd to Russian cultural hist, v.2, 985
New bibliog of the Lusophone lits of Africa, 2d ed, 1268
Oxford illus literary gd to Great Britain & Ireland, 2d ed, 480
Scribner writers series on CD-ROM, 1160
Spanish American authors, 1297
Speaking for ourselves, too, 1186
Twentieth-century Caribbean & black African writers, 2d series, 1148
Wellsprings of imagination, 478
Who's who in the Writers' Union of Canada, 4th ed, 998
Writers of the Indian diaspora, 1290

Authors & Publishers
Publishing law hndbk, 2d ed, 574

Authorship. *See also* Publishers & Publishing
Directory of publication resources, 1993-94, 995
Ireland's index to inspiration, 69
Mystery writer's marketplace & sourcebk, 994
Writer's hndbk, 1993 ed, 999

Authorship—Style Manuals
Chicago manual of style, 14th ed, 1001

Automobiles
American automobile collections & museums, 2026
Auto dict, 2021

Aviation. *See* **Aeronautics**

Bach, Johann Sebastian
Bach English-title index, 1331

Badings, Henk
Henk Badings, 1907-87: cat of works, 1328

Bahamas
Fishes of the Bahamas & adjacent tropical waters, 2d ed, 1713

Ballet
International dict of ballet, 1423
World ballet & dance 1992-93, 1425

Bamboo
Ornamental shrubs, climbers & bamboos, 1632

Banjo Music
Banjo on record, 1336

Banks & Banking
Dictionary of banking, 207
Dictionary of banking, 210
Encyclopedia of banking & finance, 9th ed, 208
Who's who in intl banking, 6th ed, 224

Baseball
Baseball: a comp bibliog, suppl.1, 837
Baseball ency, 9th ed, 830
Encyclopedia of major league baseball teams, 831
Great American baseball stat bk 1993, 833
Great all-time baseball record bk, rev ed, 835
Green cathedrals, 834
Professional baseball franchises, 832
Scouting report: 1993, 836
Sporting News complete baseball record bk, 1993 ed, 838

Basketball
Final 4 records 1939-91, 839
Pro basketball stats, 840

Battery Chargers
Modern power supply & battery charger circuit ency, 1780

Battles
Battle bk, 695

Beacon College Project
Beacon college project dir, 325

Bearings (Machinery)
I.B.I. intl bearing interchange gd, 12th ed, 1798
P.S.I. gd, 1799

Bears
Great bear almanac, 1733

Beatles
Beatles: the ultimate recording gd, 1380

Beetles
Catalog of types of Coleoptera in the Canadian Natl Collection of Insects, suppl.3, 1728
Weevils of Canada & Alaska, v.1, 1722

Begoniaceae
Studies in begoniaceae 4, 1649

Behavior Therapy
Handbook of behavior therapy & pharmacotherapy for children, 1848
Handbook of prescriptive treatments for children & adolescents, 1845

Behavioral Optometry
Eponyms of behavioral optometry, 1866

Behrman, S. N.
S. N. Behrman: a research & production sourcebk, 1232

Beinecke Rare Book & Manuscript Library
Catalogue of medieval & renaissance mss in the Beinecke Rare Bk & Mss Lib, Yale Univ, v.3, 30

Belgium
European employment & industrial relations glossary: Belgium, 252

Beneficial Insects
Destructive & useful insects, 5th ed, 1729

Ben-Haim, Paul
Music of Paul Ben-Haim, 1326

Beowulf
Beowulf scholarship, 1263

Best Sellers
#1 New York Times bestseller, 1153

Beverages
Complete beverage dict, 1601

Bible
Bible: cultural atlas for young people, 1546
Book of Daniel: an annot bibliog, 1536
Dictionary of biblical tradition in English lit, 1149
Exegetical dict of the N.T., v.3, 1528
Iconographic index to N.T. subjects represented in photographs & slides of paintings in the visual collections, Fine Arts Lib, Harvard Univ, v.1, 1540
Index to per lit on the apostle Paul, 1550
Index to English per lit on the O.T. & ancient Near Eastern studies, v.5, 1549
Nelson's quick ref Bible concordance, 1547
Nelson's quick ref Bible dict, 1541
Nelson's quick ref Bible hndbk, 1544
New ency of archaeological excavations in the Holy Land, 489
NKJV exhaustive concordance, 1548
Oxford companion to the Bible, 1545
Roget's thesaurus of the Bible, 1542
Student's complete vocabulary gd to the Greek N.T., 1543
Targumic mss in the Cambridge Genizah collections, 1539
Who's who in the N.T., 1537
Who's who in the O.T., together with the Apocrypha, 1538

Bibliographical Citation
Electronic style, 1002

Bibliography
ABC for bk collectors, 1026
Books in print 1993-94, 7
Books in print plus, 8
British literary bibliog, 1970-79, 1244
Whitaker's bks in print 1993, 6

Bibliography—Best Books
Adventuring with bks, 10th ed, 1173
American Lib Assn best of the best for children, 1163
Best bks for public libs, 647
Books for you, 11th ed, 1165
Dictionary of American children's fiction, 1985-89, 1171
Dictionary of children's fiction from Austral., Canada, India, New Zealand, & selected African countries, 1172
Literature teacher's bk of lists, 1142
100 world-class thin bks, 1164
Play, learn, & grow, 1184
Science Bks & Films best bks for children 1988-91, 1561
Your reading, 9th ed, 648

Bibliometrics
Bibliometrics: an annot bibliog, 1970-90, 623

Bielorussia
Active figures of the trade union & working class movement of Russia, Ukraine, Bielorussia, & Kazakhstan, 262

Biographical Films
From real life to reel life, 1442

Biography
Biography: an annot bibliog, 16
Biography & genealogy master index [CD-ROM], 436
Biography today, 1992 annual cum, 11
Concise dict of natl bibliog, 13
Crossing barriers, 17
Index to who's who bks 1992, 14
International authors & writers who's who, 13th ed, 1147
Who was who in America with world notables, index 1993, 23
Who's who in America 1992-93, 24
Who's who in American nursing 1993-94, 1865
Who's who in European insts & enterprises 1993, 771
Who's who in Italy 1992, 20
Who's who in Mexico today, 2d ed, 12
Who's who in the east 1993-94, 25
Who's who in the south & southwest, 23d ed, 26
Who's who in the world 1993-94, 22
Who's who of emerging leaders in America 1993-94, 27
World who's who of women, 11th ed, 963

Biological Reagents
Linscott's dir of immunological & biological reagents, 7th ed, 1875

Biology
Bibliography on computational molecular biology, 1634
Multimedia ency of mammalian biology [CD-ROM], 1739

Biotechnology
Biotechnology from A to Z, 1790

Birds
Atlas of breeding birds in Pa., 1694
Bird atlas, 1702
Birds of Tikal, 1691
Colorado birds, 1689
Field gd to birds of Britain & Europe, 5th ed, 1701
Field gd to birds of the W Indies, 5th ed, 1693
Handbook of the birds of Europe, the Middle East, & N Africa, v.6, 1696
Handbook of the birds of Europe, the Middle East, & N Africa, v.7, 1697
Shorebirds of the Pacific Northwest, 1700
Threatened birds of the Americas, pt.2, 3d ed, 1695

Birthdays
Happy birthdays round the world, 1402

Bjorling, Jussi
Jussi Bjorling phonography, 2d ed, 1354

Black English
African heritage of American English, 1081

Blacks
Black elected officials, 20th ed, 733
My soul looks back, 'less I forget, 72
Worldwide interesting people, 404

Blackwood's Edinburgh Magazine
Index to the critical vocabulary of Blackwood's Edinburgh Mag, 1830-40, 61

Blues (Music)
Encyclopedia of the blues, 1370

Boards of Trade
American Chamber of Commerce in Italy dir 1992, 268
Anglo-American trade dir 1993, 264

Boats & Boating
PowerBoat gd, 3d ed, 2030

Boethius
Medieval Consolation of Philosophy: an annot bibliog, 1487

Boilers
Handbook of power, utility & boiler terms & phrases, 6th ed, 1797

Bombers
Military aircraft: modern bombers & attack planes, 700

Bonds
Standard & Poor's stock & bond gd, 1993 3d, 200

Book Collecting
ABC for bk collectors, 1026

Book Industries & Trade
Award-winning bks for children & young adults 1990-91, 1166
Children's bk awards intl, 1195

Book Reviewing
Historical jls, 2d ed, 542

Book Talks
Juniorplots 4, 1192

Booklist
Popular reading for children 3, 1168

Books
Book review index, 1991 cum, 59
Books & pers online, 44
#1 New York Times bestseller, 1153

Booksellers & Bookselling
American bk trade dir 1993-94, 661
Antiquarian, specialty, & used bk sellers 1993, 662
Bowker annual lib & bk trade almanac, 38th ed, 615
International literary market place 1993, 667
Literary market place 1994, 668
Publishers trade list annual, 1992, 660
Used bk lover's gd to New England, 1027
Used bk lover's gd to the mid-Atlantic states, 1028

Borges, Jorge Luis
Concordance to the works of Jorge Luis Borges (1899-1986), Argentine author, 1299
Descriptive cat of the Jorge Luis Borges collection at the Univ of Va. lib, 1300

Botanical Chemistry
Phytochemical dict, 1639

Botany
Australian plant name index, 1648
Bignoniaceae—pt.2 (tribe tecomeae), 1637
Botanical Latin, 4th ed, 1641
Desert & mountain plants of the southwest, 1645
Flora of N America north of Mexico, 1643
Gardener's Latin, 1640
Jepson manual, 1644
Lauraceae: nectandra, 1646

Botswana
Botswana, 99

Boundary Disputes
Atlas of world pol flashpoints, 794
Border & territorial disputes, 3d ed, 722

Broadcasting
Broadcasting in the UK, 2d ed, 1013
Gale dir of publications & broadcast media 1993, 988

Bronte, Patrick Bramwell
Bibliography of the mss of Patrick Branwell Bronte, 1247

Browning, Elizabeth Barrett
Elizabeth Barrett Browning: an annot bibliog of the commentary & criticism, 1826-1990, 1248

Buddhism
Historical dict of Buddhism, 1519

Budget in Business
R&D ratios & budgets, 295

Building
Construction glossary, 2d ed, 1773
Dictionary of architecture & construction, 2d ed, 1051

Buildings
Directory of building & equipment grants, 2d ed, 1772

Bulbs
Propagation of alpine plant & dwarf bulbs, 1629

Business. *See also* **Corporations**
Harvard Bus School core collection 1993, 156

Business Enterprises
Born to power, 155
Business & legal CD-ROMS in print 1993, 175
Canadian bus in the Pacific Rim, 251
Hoover's hndbk of emerging cos 1993-94, 172
Hoover's masterlist of major US cos 1993, 164
Kelly's business dir 1992, 265

Business—Information Services
Data: where it is & how to get it, 45
Information please bus almanac & desk ref, 1994, 174
Who knows what, 166

Business—Information Sources
Desktop bus intelligence sourcebk, 171

Business Names
International brands & their cos 1993-94, 228
International cos & their brands 1993-94, 229

Business Schools
Barron's gd to graduate bus schools, 8th ed, 168
Business Week's gd to the best executive educ programs, 169

Businessmen
Who's who in European bus, 223

Butterflies
Butterflies through binoculars, 1703

Buyer's Guides. *See* **Consumer Education**

CAD/CAM Systems
Combinatory vocab of CAD/CAM in mechanical engineering, 1916

Calendars
Religious holidays & calendars, 1517

California
California environmental dir, 5th ed, 2007
Famous Hollywood locations, 1421
Jepson manual, 1644

Cameras
McBroom's camera bluebk, 1994 ed, 1037

Canada
American lib dir 1993-94, 610
Annotated bibliog of the official langs of Canada, 1068
Aquaculture sourcebk, 1594
Baseball: a comp bibliog, suppl.1, 837
Biographical dict of Canadian Jewry 1909-14, 410
Canada, 127
Canada tax cases: index & citator, 581
Canada's army in WW II, 702
Canadian architecture collection, 1053
Canadian Assn of Law Libs dir, 649
Canadian bus & economics, 3d ed, 246
Canadian bus in the Pacific Rim, 251
Canadian dict of bus & economics, 247
Canadian global almanac 1993, 1

Canadian lib hndbk, 617
Canadian obituary record 1991, 18
Canadian Oxford intermediate atlas, 457
Canadian Oxford school atlas, 6th ed, 456
Canadian quaternary vocabulary, 1943
Canadian women's movement, 1960-90, 966
Catalog of types of Coleoptera in the Canadian Natl Collection of Insects, suppl.3, 1728
CLE research gd, v.2, 583
Climatological atlas of snowfall & snow depth for the NE US and SE Canada, 1948
COGEL blue bk, 9th ed, 801
Constitutional glossary, 553
Contemporary bks reflecting Canada's cultural diversity, 409
Contemporary Canadian childhood & youth, 924
Corpus almanac & Canadian sourcebk, 1993, 125
Dictionary of Canadian military hist, 517
Diesel locomotive rosters, 3d ed, 2025
Diptera types in the Canadian Natl Collection of Insects, pt.2, 1724
Directory of Canadian theatre archives, 1476
Directory to Canadian studies in Canada, 4th ed, 126
Electronic univ, 376
Encyclopedia of music in Canada, 2d ed, 1312
Ethical shopper's gd to Canadian supermarket products, 248
Flora of N America north of Mexico, 1643
Genera of the aphids of Canada, 1723
Gerontology & geriatrics libs & collections in the US & Canada, 655
Gibson's gd to graduate & professional programs at Ont. univs, 309
Gibson's student gd to W Canadian univs, 310
Glossary of security equipment, 1776
Guide to law schools in Canada, 575
Guide to the college lib, 658
Historical atlas of Canada, v.2, 458
History of Canadian childhood & youth, 925
History of nursing beginning bibliog, 1864
Hymenoptera of the world, 1726
Immigration stats 1991, 803
Index to Canadian legal lit 1992, 582
Meet the authors & illustrators, 1193
New England planters in the Maritime provinces of Canada 1759-1800, 1589
Political parties of the Americas, 1980s to 1990s, 720
Report on bus: Canada co hndbk 1993, 250
Resource gd of pubns supported by multiculturalism programs, 398
Roller coasters, 828
Scholar's gd to geographical writing on the American & Canadian past, 461
State & province vital records gd, 432
Train-watcher's gd to N American railroads, 2d ed, 2024
Vocabulary of global warming, v.1, 2001
Weevils of Canada & Alaska, v.1, 1722
Who's who in Canada, 1992, 19
Winning scholarships, 311

Canadian Fiction
Canadian writers & their works: cum index, fiction series, 1271
ECW's biographical gd to Canadian novelists, 1273

Canadian Literature
Contemporary Canadian & US women of letters, 1138
Index to the contents of the per Canadian Lit nos.1-102, 1275

Canadian National Collection of Insects
Catalog of types of Coleoptera in the Canadian Natl Collection of Insects, suppl.3, 1728
Diptera types in the Canadian Natl Collection of Insects, pt.2, 1724

Canadian Poetry
Canadian writers & their works: cum index, poetry series, 1272
ECW's biographical gd to Canadian poets, 1274

Cancer
Cancer dict, 1858
Cancer therapy, 1860
Third opinion, 2d ed, 1859

Cards
Dictionary of card games, 841

Career Development
Career advancement for women in the fed serv, 270

Career Education
Career training sourcebk, 388

Caregiving
Caregiving of older adults, 867

Caribbean Area
Bibliographic gd to Caribbean mass comm, 990
Bibliography of Latin American & Caribbean bibliogs, 1985-89: social scis & humanities, 145
Cambridge ency of Latin America & the Caribbean, 142
Caribbean 1975-80, 143
Caribbean women novelists, 1301
Political parties of the Americas and the Caribbean, 783
South America, Central America, & the Caribbean 1993, 146
St. Vincent & the Grenadines, 148

Cars (Automobiles). *See* **Automobiles**

Cartography
Civil War newspaper maps: a cartobibliography of the N daily pr, 492
Civil War newspaper maps: a histl atlas, 491

Cataloging
Cataloger's gd to MARC coding & tagging for AV material, 627
Cataloging computer files, 628
EUROCOM, 632

Catalogs, Commercial
National dir of catalogs 1992, 294

Catalogs, On-Line
OPAC dir 1993, 646

Catalogs, Subject
Subject collections, 7th ed, 656

Catholic Church
Directory of Catholic colleges & univs, 1992, 335

Official Catholic dir 1993, 1532
Our Sunday Visitor's Catholic dict, 1531
Roman Catholics, 1525

CD-I Technology
CD-ROMs in print 1993, 1919

CD-ROM
Audiocassette & CD finder, 3d ed, 374
Biography & genealogy master index [CD-ROM], 436
CD-ROM 1992, 645
CD-ROM buyer's gd & hndbk, 3d ed, 1917
CD-ROM finder, 1993 ed, 1918
CD-ROM for librarians & educators, 1920
CD-ROMs in print 1993, 1919
Directory of law-related CD-ROMS 1993, 560

CD-ROMs
Beacon: college & career planning on CD-ROM, 349
Books in print plus, 8
DISCovering authors [CD-ROM], 1146
Encyclopedia of assns CD-ROM, 51
Gale's literary index [CD-ROM], 1161
GeoRef [CD-ROM], 1950
Multimedia ency of mammalian biology [CD-ROM], 1739
Scribner writers series on CD-ROM, 1160
Serials dir: EBSCO CD-ROM, summer 1993, 64
Ulrich's plus [CD-ROM], 66

Celebrities
Kid's address bk, 53

Censorship
Intellectual freedom: a ref hndbk, 641

Central African Republic
Central African Republic, 97

Central America
South American, Central America, & the Caribbean 1993, 146

Chamber Music
Chamber music: an intl gd to works & their instrumentation, 1349
Conductor's repertory of chamber music, 1350
Saxophone recital music, 1339

Characters & Characteristics in Literature
Characters in 19th century lit, 1157
Companion to literary myths, heroes & archetypes, 1155
Dictionary of British literary characters: 18th- & 19th-century novels, 1243
My name in bks, 1190
Shakespeare's characters, 1258

Characters & Characteristics in Motion Pictures
Name is familiar, 1459

Charitable Uses, Trusts, & Foundations
Corporate fndn profiles, 7th ed, 900
Foundation reporter 1993, 902

Charlemagne, Emperor, 742-814—Romances
Medieval Charlemagne legend, 1199

Charteris, Leslie
Saint: a complete hist in print, radio, film & TV, 1249

Chaucer, Geoffrey
Glossarial concordance to the Riverside Chaucer, 1250

Chemical Engineering
Dictionary of chemical engineering, 1769
Encyclopedia of chemical processing & design, v.36, 1759
Encyclopedia of chemical processing & design, v.37, 1760
Encyclopedia of chemical processing & design, v.38, 1761
Encyclopedia of chemical processing & design, v.39, 1762
Encyclopedia of chemical processing & design, v.40, 1763
Encyclopedia of chemical processing & design, v.41, 1764
Encyclopedia of chemical processing & design, v.42, 1765
Encyclopedia of chemical processing & design, v.43, 1766
Industrial chemical thesaurus, 2d ed, 1942
Quick selection gd to chemical protective clothing, 2d ed, 1767

Chemicals
Chemical exposure & human health, 1861
Chemical tradename dict, 1932
Comprehensive gd to the hazardous properties of chemical substances, 2015
Dictionary of chemical names & synonyms, 1934

Chemistry
Directory of chemistry sftwr 1992, 1939
Encyclopedia of chemical processing & design, v.36, 1759
Encyclopedia of chemical processing & design, v.37, 1760
Encyclopedia of chemical processing & design, v.38, 1761
Encyclopedia of chemical processing & design, v.39, 1762
Encyclopedia of chemical processing & design, v.40, 1763
Encyclopedia of chemical processing & design, v.41, 1764
Encyclopedia of chemical processing & design, v.42, 1765
Encyclopedia of chemical processing & design, v.43, 1766
Encyclopedic dict of chemical tech, 1936
Hawley's condensed chemical dict, 12th ed, 1933
Industrial chemical thesaurus, 2d ed, 1942
Information sources in chemistry, 4th ed, 1931
Kirk-Othmer ency of chemical tech, 4th ed, v.7, 1768
McGraw-Hill ency of chemistry, 2d ed, 1935
Patterson's German-English dict for chemists, 4th ed, 1937
Riegel's hndbk of industrial chemistry, 9th ed, 1770

Chess
Oxford companion to chess, 2d ed, 842

Child Care
Child care crisis, 923
Child welfare stat bk 1993, 922
Childwise cat, 3d ed, 921
International hndbk of child care policies & programs, 919

Child Development
Family ency of child psychology & dvlpmt, 807
Handbook of research on the educ of young children, 314
Preschool resource gd, 312
What's new for parents, 920

Childbirth
Encyclopedia of childbearing, 1831

Children
Author a month (for dimes), 1188
Contemporary Canadian childhood & youth, 924
History of Canadian childhood & youth, 925
Literature of delight, 1169

Children—Diseases
Childhood symptoms, 1838

Children—Institutional Care
Caring for kids with special needs, 918

Children's Atlases
Kingfisher ref atlas, 451

Children's Encyclopedias & Dictionaries
Compton's ency & fact-index, 34
Factfinder, 39
Kingfisher children's ency, 37
Kingfisher sci ency, 1568
My 1st dict, 1092
My 1st ency, 41

Children's Films
Best yrs of their lives, 926

Children's Literature. *See also* **Children's Stories**
A to Zoo, 4th ed, 1176
Adventuring with bks, 10th ed, 1173
American Lib Assn best of the best for children, 1163
Award-winning bks for children & young adults 1990-91, 1166
Books in Spanish for children & young adults, 1180
Children's bk awards intl, 1195
Children's bks: awards & prizes, 1992 ed, 1191
Children's bks in print 1992, 9
Children's writer's word bk, 996
Fiction for youth, 3d ed, 1181
Gender positive!, 1179
Kids' favorite bks, 1174
Literature activity bks, 1197
Major authors & illustrators for children & young adults, 1187
Meet the authors & illustrators, 1193
My name in bks, 1190
Palette of possibilities, 1167
Play, learn, & grow, 1184
Popular reading for children 3, 1168
Pop-up & movable bks, 1177
Summer reading clubs, 1194
Using lit to teach middle grades about war, 694
Venture into cultures, 1170
War & peace lit for children & young adults, 1185
Wellsprings of imagination, 478
Young reader's companion, 1189
Your reading, 9th ed, 648

Children's Stories
Best yrs of their lives, 926
Dictionary of American children's fiction, 1985-89, 1171
Dictionary of children's fiction from Austral., Canada, India, New Zealand, & selected African countries, 1172
Fiction index for readers 10 to 16, 1196
Twins in children's & adolescent lit, 1183

China
China leading cos, 242
Directory of publishers in China, 672
People's Republic of China yr bk 1991/92, 109

Choral Music
Chorus in opera, 1353
Sacred choral music in print: master index 1992, 1341
Sacred choral music in print: 1992 suppl, 1340
Secular choral music in print: 1993 suppl, 1342

Christian Art & Symbolism
Church symbolism, 2d ed, 1048

Christianity—Middle Ages, 600-1500
Pilgrimage in the middle ages, 1523

Chronically Ill
Resources for people with disabilities & chronic conditions, 2d ed, 882

Church Colleges
Choose a Christian college, 3d ed, 334
Directory of Catholic colleges & univs, 1992, 335
Handbook of United Methodist-related schools, colleges, univs & theological schools, 336

Church of England
Oxford movement & its leaders, suppl, 1522

Cinematography
Language of visual effects, 1433
Special effects & stunts gd, 2d ed, 1454

Circus
Two hundred yrs of the American circus, 1419

Citation of Legal Authorities
Bieber's dict of legal abbrevs, 4th ed, 543
Bieber's dict of legal citations, 4th ed, 544

Cities & Towns
American small city profiles, 941
American suburbs, 946
America's top rated cities, 1992 ed, 943
Cities & churches, 1502
100 best small towns in America, 942
Where to make money, 945

City Lights Books
City Lights bks, 1220

Civil Rights
Civil rights movement, 595
World human rights gd, 3d ed, 594

Civilization
Blackwell dict of 20th-century social thought, 73
Covert culture sourcebk, 76
Dictionary of cultural literacy, 2d ed, 305
Harper atlas of world hist, rev ed, 528

Clarke, Austin
Austin Clarke: a ref gd, 1293

Classical Literature
Concise Oxford companion to classical lit, 1198

Classification
Conversion tables: LC-Dewey, Dewey-LC, 630
EUROCOM, 632
Library of Congress classification class KL-KWX, 625

Clavichord Music
Harpsichord & clavichord music of the 20th century, 1335

Climatology
Climatological atlas of snowfall & snow depth for the NE US and SE Canada, 1948
Dictionary of global climate change, 1949

Closed Captioned Television
Gopen's gd to closed captioned video, 1011

Closed-End Funds. *See* **Mutual Funds**

Clothing, Protective
Quick selection gd to chemical protective clothing, 2d ed, 1767

Coastal Flora
Field gd to coastal wetland plants of the SE US, 1661

Coin Dealers
Official Whitman coin dealer dir, 6th ed, 1029

Cold War
Cold war 1945-91, 537
Cold war chronology, 795

Colette
Colette: an annot primary & secondary bibliog, 1285

Collectibles
Tuttle dict of antiques & collectibles terms, 1024

Collection Development (Libraries)
Subject collections, 7th ed, 656

Collective Bargaining
BNA's 1993 source bk on collective bargaining & employee relations, 277
Collective bargaining in higher educ & the professions, bibliog no.20, 269

College Costs
College costs & financial aid hndbk 1994, 353

College Majors
College majors & careers, rev ed, 362

College Sports
Wrestling college & univ dir, 2d ed, 862

Collingwood, R. G.
R. G. Collingwood: a bibliographical checklist, 1484

Colorado
Colorado place names, 470

Columbus, Christopher
Columbus docs, 533

Comic Books, Strips, Etc.
Comic art collection cat, 1405
Comic-bk superstars, 1407

Commercial Art
American graphic design, 1059

Commercial Products
Consumer product & manufacturer ratings 1961-90, 214

Commodity Futures
International commodity markets hndbk 1993, 188

Commonwealth of Independent States
Russia & the Commonwealth A to Z, 525

Communism
Handbook of pol sci research on the USSR & E Europe, 781

Community Colleges
Beacon college project dir, 325
Community, technical, & jr colleges statistical yrbk, 1992 ed, 356
Peterson's gd to 2-yr colleges 1994, 343

Compact Disc Read-Only Memory. *See* **CD-ROM**

Composers
Alec Wilder: a bio-bibliog, 1324
Alessandro & Domenico Scarlatti: a gd to research, 1334
Alun Hoddinott: a bio-bibliog, 1322
Edward Elgar: a gd to research, 1327
Elinor Remick Warren: a bio-bibliog, 1321
Henk Badings, 1907-87: cat of works, 1328
Howard Hanson: a bio-bibliog, 1330
Johann Michael Haydn (1737-1806): a chronological thematic cat of his works, 1332
Music of Paul Ben-Haim, 1326
Twentieth-century composer speaks, 1333
Wagner compendium, 1329
William Walton: a source bk, 1323

Compulsive Behavior
Focus on addictions, 917

Computer Crimes
Computer law & sftwr protection, 1892

Computer Engineering
Computer engineering hndbk, 1774

Computer Graphics
Illustrated computer graphics dict, 1912

Computer Industry
Computer industry 1993 almanac, 1909

Computer Networks
McGraw-Hill data communications dict, 1901
OSI dict of acronyms & related abbrevs, 1891

Computer Science
Bibliographic gd to computer sci 1991, 1893
Computing info dir, 10th ed, 1908
Dictionary of acronyms & abbrevs, 597
Encyclopedia of computer sci, 3d ed, 1903
Jargon: an informal dict of computer terms, 1905

Computer Software
Directory of chemistry sftwr 1992, 1939
Directory of US govt sftwr for mainframes & microcomputers, 1914
Guide to free computer materials, 11th ed, 1911
Guide to genealogical sftwr, 435
Online Inc.'s top 500 lib microcomputer sftwr application programs, 640
Petroleum sftwr dir, 1994, 1974
Software ency 1993, 1915

Computer-Assisted Instruction
CD-ROM for librarians & educators, 1920
Computer-based simulations in educ & training, 381

Computers. *See also* **Microcomputers**
Computer acronyms & abbrevs, 1890
Computer dict, 4th ed, 1904
Computer law & sftwr protection, 1892
Directory of video, computer & audio-visual products 1993, 1887
Prentice Hall's illus dict of computing, 1902
Spanish-English, English-Spanish dict of computer terms, 1895

Concordia University. Libraries. Special Collections
Catalogue of the letters, tapes & photographs in the Irving Layton collection, 1270

Confederate States of America
Encyclopedia of the Confederacy, 506
Military leaders of the Civil War, 701

Conservation of Natural Resources
Environmentalists: a biographical dict, 1993

Conservatism
Right gd, 787

Conservative Literature
National Review politically incorrect ref gd, 726

Construction Industry
Construction glossary, 2d ed, 1773

Consultants
Directory of fund raising & nonprofit mgmt consultants, 901

Consumer Education
Childwise cat, 3d ed, 921
Consumer's gd to free medical info by phone & by mail, 1844
Consumer's gd to product grades & terms, 201
Educators gd to free home economics & consumer educ materials, 10th ed, 886
Ethical shopper's gd to Canadian supermarket products, 248
Smart consumer's dir, 1993 ed, 202
Wholesale-by-mail cat 1993, 203

Continuing Education
Adult learner's gd to alternative & external degree programs, 393
Independent study cat, 5th ed, 390
Macmillan gd to correspondence study, 5th ed, 359
National gd to educl credit for training programs, 1992-93 ed, 392

Cookery
Recipes into type, 1613

Cooking Schools
Guide to cooking schools, 1993, 1609

Copy-Reading
Copy-editing, 3d ed, 1000

Copyright
Copyright bk, 4th ed, 637
Patent, trademark, & copyright laws, 576
Publishing law hndbk, 2d ed, 574

Corals
Corals of Austral. & the Indo-Pacific, 1747
Reef sharks & rays of the world, 1718

Cormorants
Cormorants, darters, & pelicans of the world, 1698

Corporations
American big businesses dir, 1993 ed, 161
Corporate dir of US public cos 1993, 178
Corporate giving dir 1993, 163
Corporate giving yellow pages 1993, 162
Directory of foreign manufacturers in the US, 5th ed, 213
Ethical shopper's gd to Canadian supermarket products, 248
Foundation dir, 15th ed, 890
Foundation dir pt.2, 1993 ed, 891
Foundation giving, 1993 ed, 896
Guide to US fndns, their trustees, officers, & donors, 1993 ed, 892
Hoover's hndbk of emerging cos 1993-94, 172
Hoover's masterlist of major US cos 1993, 164
How to find info about cos, v.3, 173
Nelson's techresources, winter 1993, 183
Vocabulary of public sector auditing, 249
Who owns corporate America 1993, 167

Correctional Institutions
Management of correctional insts, 804

Correspondence Schools & Courses
Bear's gd to earning college degrees non-traditionally, 350
College degrees by mail, 351
Electronic univ, 376
Independent study cat, 5th ed, 390
Macmillan gd to correspondence study, 5th ed, 359

Cosmology
Encyclopedia of cosmology, 1926

Counter Culture
Voices from the underground, 1010

Country Music
Traveler's country music radio atlas 1993, 1018

Courtesans
Encyclopedia of mistresses, 961

Courts
Want's fed-state court dir, 1993 ed, 564

Creative Writing
AWP official gd to writing programs, 6th ed, 993

Crete (Greece)
Aerial atlas of ancient Crete, 529

Crime & Criminals
Crime in Victorian Britain, 590

Criminal Justice, Administration of
U.S. criminal justice interest groups, 588

Criminology. *See* **Crime & Criminals**

Critical Thinking
Critical thinking, 1483

Criticism
Contemporary Canadian & US women of letters, 1138
Contemporary critical theory, 1140
Deconstructionism: a bibliog, 1141
Encyclopedia of contemporary literary theory, 1150
Short story criticism, v.11, 1216
Short story criticism, v.12, 1217

Cuba
Bibliography of Cuban mass communications, 991
Cuban festivals, 1399

Cucumis
Biosystematic monograph of the genus Cucumis (Cucurbitaceae), 1638

Cults
Dictionary of cults, sects, religions & the occult, 1513
Illustrated ency of active new religions, sects, & cults, 1529

Culture
European culture, 977
Oxford illus ency of peoples & cultures, 397

Cushing, Peter
Peter Cushing: the gentle man of horror & his 91 films, 1437

Cut Flowers
Specialty cut flowers, 1623

Cycadaceae
Cycads of the world, 1671

Dakota Language—Dictionaries—English
Dakota-English dict, 1111
English-Dakota dict, 1112

Dancing
Bibliographic gd to dance 1991, 1422
Index to dance pers: 1991, 1424
World ballet & dance 1992-93, 1425

Data Bases
CD-ROM for librarians & educators, 1920
Electronic style, 1002
Gale dir of databases, 1907
OPAC dir 1993, 646

Data Protection
Computer law & sftwr protection, 1892

Data Transmission Systems
McGraw-Hill data communications dict, 1901
OSI dict of acronyms & related abbrevs, 1891

Debtor & Creditor
Lawyers' & creditors' serv dir, 1993 ed, 563

Deconstruction
Deconstructionism: a bibliog, 1141

Decorative Arts
Applied & decorative arts, 2d ed, 1022
Tuttle dict of antiques & collectibles terms, 1024

Deer
Whitehead ency of deer, 1742

Degrees, Academic
Bear's gd to earning college degrees non-traditionally, 350
College degrees by mail, 351

Delegated Legislation
BNA's dir of state administrative codes & registers, 748

Demography
First demographic portraits of Russia 1951-90, 929
Social work almanac, 911
Sourcebook of county demographics, census ed, 933
Statistical forecasts of the US, 932

Derrida, Jacques
Jacques Derrida: an annot primary & secondary bibliog, 1491

Descartes, Rene
Descartes dict, 1493

Descriptive Cataloging
Cataloging computer files, 628

Desert Gardening
Low-water flower gardener, 1630

Desert Plants
Desert & mountain plants of the southwest, 1645

Design
American graphic design, 1059

Detective & Mystery Films
Mystery writer's marketplace & sourcebk, 994
Saint: a complete hist in print, radio, film & TV, 1249

Detective & Mystery Stories
Female detectives in American novels, 1208
Gay & lesbian characters ... in mystery novels, 1210
Modern mystery, fantasy & sci fiction writers, 1207
Reader's gd to the American novel of detection, 1231
Reader's gd to the private eye novel, 1209
Saint: a complete hist in print, radio, film & TV, 1249
What about murder? 1981-91, 1206

Developing Countries
Atlas of the Third World, 2d ed, 459
Directory of dvlpmt research & training insts in Africa, 93
Poverty in developing countries, 905

Dewhurst, Colleen
Colleen Dewhurst: a bio-bibliog, 1411

Dickens, Charles
Tale of two cities: an annot bibliog, 1251

Dickinson, Emily
Musicians wrestle everywhere, 1308
Poems of Emily Dickinson: an annot gd to commentary published in English, 1233

Dictionaries. *See* **Encyclopedias & Dictionaries**

Dictionaries, Polyglot
Dictionary of animal health terminology, 1633
Euro dict, 1108
European dict, 1108

Dictionary of American Regional English
Index by region, usage, & etymology to the Dict of American Regional English, v.1 & 2, 1090

Diet
Melting pot: an annot bibliog & gd to food & nutrition info for ethnic groups in America, 1599
Nutrients cat, 1610

Digital Electronics
Lenk's digital hndbk, 1782

Dinosaurs
Dinosaur & other prehistoric animal factfinder, 1959
Rand McNally picture atlas of prehistoric life, 1962
Ultimate dinosaur bk, 1960
Visual dict of dinosaurs, 1963

Diplomats
Statesmen who changed the world, 716

Diptera
Diptera types in the Canadian Natl Collection of Insects, pt.2, 1724

Direct Marketing
Direct mktg market place [DMMP] 1993, 289

Directories
Directories in print 1993, 46

Disabled. *See* **Handicapped**

Disarmament
Encyclopedia of arms control & disarmament, 797

Disasters
Catastrophes & disasters, 469
Man-made catastrophes, 467
Natural disasters, 468

Discoveries in Geography
Children's atlas of exploration, 452
Explorers & exploration, 462

Diseases
Physicians' gd to rare diseases, 1863
Professional gd to diseases, 4th ed, 1841

Disney, Walt
Walt Disney: a bio-bibliog, 1412

Dispute Resolution (Law)
Alternative dispute resolution sourcebk, 1993-94 ed, 579

Dissertations, Academic
Religion & the American experience, 1620-1900, 1507

Distance Education
Distance educ: a selected bibliog, 380
Electronic univ, 376

Dividend Reinvestment
Guide to dividend reinvestment plans, 192

Dogs
Atlas of dog breeds of the world, 1710
Canine lexicon, 1706
Dogs, 1705
Project BREED dir, 1708

Drama
American women playwrights 1964-89, 1228
Drama criticism, v.1, 1201
Drama criticism, v.2, 1202
Drama criticism, v.3, 1203
Gay & lesbian American plays, 1227
More theatre, 1464
Play index 1988-92, 1481
Twentieth-century German dramatists, 1919-92, 1287

Dramatic Music
Chronology of music in the Florentine theater 1751-1800, 1311

Dramatists
Contemporary dramatists, 5th ed, 1467
Twentieth-century German dramatists, 1889-1918, 1286

Dreams
Encyclopedia of sleep & dreaming, 808

Drug Abuse. *See* **Substance Abuse**

Drugs
British pharmacopoeia 1993, 1876
Complete gd to prescription & non-prescription drugs, 1877
Handbook of psychotropic drugs, 1878
Handbook on injectable drugs, 7th ed, 1885
International hndbk on drug control, 916
Multilingual dict of narcotic drugs & psychotropic substances under intl control, 1872
PDR family gd to prescription drugs, 1879
Physicians' desk ref, 1993, 1880
Physician's drug hndbk, 5th ed, 1881
Physicians' generix 1992, 1882
Prescription drugs & their side effects, 1884
Red bk, 1993, 1883
Zimmerman's complete gd to nonprescription drugs, 2d ed, 1886

Ducks
Ducks in the wild, 1699

Dunsany, Edward John Moreton Drax Plunkett, Baron
Lord Dunsany: a bibliog, 1292

Dylan, Bob
Bob Dylan: a bio-bibliog, 1379

Early Childhood Education
Handbook of research on the educ of young children, 314
International hndbk of early childhood educ, 315
Profiles in childhood educ 1931-60, 313

Earth Satellites. *See* **Artificial Satellites**

Earth Sciences. *See also* **Geography; Geology**
Oxford illus ency of the universe, 1944
Visual dict of the Earth, 1946

East Asia
Security, arms control, & conflict reduction in E Asia & the Pacific, 683

East Europeans
Peoples of the world: Eastern Europe & the post-Soviet republics, 132
Reader's ency of E European lit, 1281

Eating Disorders
Focus on addictions, 917

Ecology
Dictionary of ecology & environmental sci, 1994
Island Pr bibliog of environmental lit, 1990

Economics
Business & legal CD-ROMS in print 1993, 175
Canadian dict of bus & economics, 247
Development report card for the states, 1993, 170
Dictionary of environment & dvlpmt, 1995
Economic planning 1943-51, 263
International writings of Bohdan S. Wynar, 1949-92, 80
Penguin dict of economics, 5th ed, 159
Russian-English/English-Russian dict of free market era economics, 160
United States sanctions & S Africa, 545
William J. Fellner: a bio-bibliog, 154
World economy, 157

Ecumenical Movement
Ecumenism: a bibliographical overview, 1524

Editing
Directory of publication resources, 1993-94, 995
Publication peer review, 997

Education
Bibliographic gd to educ 1991, 303
Guide to the evaluation of educl experiences in the armed servs, 1992, 307
World of learning 1993, 308

Education, Elementary
Elementary teachers gd to free curriculum materials, 50th ed, 318
Kits, games & manipulatives for the elementary school classroom, 378
Patterson's elementary educ, v.5, 320

Education, Higher
Accredited insts of postsecondary educ, programs, candidates, 1992-93, 347
American higher educ, 323
Atlas of American higher educ, 321
Cabell's dir of publ opportunities in educ, 3d ed, 663
Collective bargaining in higher educ & the professions, bibliog no.20, 269
Peterson's register of higher educ 1993, 344

Education of Adults. *See* **Adult Education**

Education, Secondary
Patterson's American educ, v.89, 319

Educational Media Centers. *See* **Instructional Materials Centers**

Educational Technology
Glossary of educl tech terms, 377
Graduate curricula in educl communications & tech, 4th ed, 379
International yrbk of educl & training tech 1992/93, 382

Educational Tests & Measurements
ETS test collection cat, v.1, 2d ed, 304
Instrumentation in educ, 306

Elections
America votes 20, 756
Congressional & gubernatorial primaries 1991-92, 754
Congressional Quarterly's pols in America 1994, 749
Election data bk, 751
Election results dir, 1993 ed, 738
Historical atlas of state power in congress, 1790-1990, 725
Presidential primaries & caucuses 1992, 755

Electric Engineering
McGraw-Hill's natl electrical code hndbk, 21st ed, 1786
Standard hndbk for electrical engineers, 13th ed, 1777

Electric Utilities
European electric utility dir, 1993, 1783

Electronics
Electronic packaging, microelectronics, & interconnection dict, 1781
Encyclopedia of electronic circuits, v.4, 1778
European electronics dir 1993, 1787
McGraw-Hill circuit ency & troubleshooting gd, v.1, 1784
Modern measuring circuit ency, 1779

Elgar, Edward
Edward Elgar: a gd to research, 1327

Emergency Medicine
International translation gd for emergency medicine, 1825
National dir of fire chiefs & emergency depts, 1993, 878

Emigration & Immigration
Atlas of intl migration, 428
Complete bk of emigrants 1751-76, 430
Immigration stats 1991, 803

Employee Fringe Benefits
Employee benefit plans, 8th ed, 272
Employee benefits dict, 271

Employees, Training of
Linton trainer's resource dir, 2d ed, 275
National gd to educl credit for training programs, 1992-93 ed, 392

Encyclopedias & Dictionaries. *See also* **Children's Encyclopedias & Dictionaries**
Barron's new student's concise ency, 2d ed, 32
Cambridge ency, 33
Compton's ency & fact-index, 34
Dictionary of dicts, 1073
People's Almanac presents the bk of lists: the '90s ed, 1403
Purchasing an ency, 4th ed, 38
Running Pr cyclopedia, 40
Subject index to feature articles & special reports in ency yrbks 1975-91, 35
Webster's new world ency, college ed, 42
Webster's new world ency, pocket ed, 43

Endangered Species
Atlas of endangered animals, 1686
Endangered wildlife of the world, 1676
Grolier world ency of endangered species, 1680
Guide to Michigan's endangered wildlife, 1677
Threatened birds of the Americas, pt.2, 3d ed, 1695

Endowments
Annual register of grant support, 26th ed, 888
Corporate fndn profiles, 7th ed, 900
Foundation dir, 15th ed, 890
Foundation dir pt.2, 1993 ed, 891
Foundation giving, 1993 ed, 896
Foundation 1000 1992/93, 897
Foundation reporter 1993, 902
Guide to US fndns, their trustees, officers, & donors, 1993 ed, 892
Major donors 1993, 893
National gd to funding for libs & info servs, 2d ed, 618

Energy. *See* **Force & Energy**

Engineering
Directory, 1992: AAAS consortium of affiliates for intl programs, 1572
Directory of AAAS sci & engineering fellows 1973-92, 1573
Ei thesaurus, 1753
Japanese/English, English/Japanese glossary of scientific & technical terms, 1571
Magill's survey of sci: applied sci series, 1583
McGraw-Hill ency of engineering, 2d ed, 1785

England
Butterworths law dir 1993, 558
Dictionary of banking, 207
London stage 1950-59, 1469
Private libs in renaissance England, v.1, 598
Private libs in renaissance England, v.2, 599
Yearbook of English festivals, 1406

English Drama
Sir John Vanbrugh: a ref gd, 975

English Fiction
Dictionary of British literary characters: 18th- & 19th-century novels, 1243
Out of the closet & into the classroom, 906

English Language
American Heritage college dict, 3d ed, 1075
Canadian spelling dict, 7th ed, 1102
Cassell dict of literary & lang terms, 980
Catalog of dicts, word bks, & philological texts, 1440-1900, 1074
Children's writer's word bk, 996
Columbia gd to standard American English, 1085
Crash of rhinoceroses, 1106
Dictionary of cultural literacy, 2d ed, 305
Dictionary of the American west, 1088
Fifth dir of pers, 986
Funk & Wagnalls standard dict, 2d ed, 1077
Glossarial concordance to the Riverside Chaucer, 1250
Guide to the Oxford English Dict, 1097
Homophones & homographs, 2d ed, 1086
Index by region, usage, & etymology to the Dict of American Regional English, v.1 & 2, 1090
Merriam-Webster's collegiate dict, 10th ed, 1076
New shorter Oxford English Dict on historical principles, 1099
Oxford modern English dict, 1100
Oxford thesaurus, American ed, 1107
Paragon House spelling dict, 1103
Pocket Oxford dict of current English, 8th ed, 1078

Portmanteau dict, 1083
Prentice Hall encyclopedic dict of English usage, 2d ed, 1091
Pronouncing dict of proper names, 1084
Random House word menu, 1105
Terrible speller, 1104
Thesaurus of word roots of the English lang, 1079
Trash cash, fizzbos, & flatliners, 1095
Up from the roots: growing a vocab, 1082
Webster's new world dict for young adults, 1094
Whistlin' Dixie: a dict of S expressions, 1089
Why you say it, 1080
Word traps, 1087

English Language—Acronyms. *See* **Acronyms**

English LanguAge—Australia—Dictionaries
Australian concise Oxford dict, 1096

English Language—Dictionaries—Albanian
Albanian-English dict, 1109

English Language—Dictionaries—Chinese
Practical English-Chinese pronouncing dir, 1110

English Language—Dictionaries—Dakota
Dakota-English dict, 1111
English-Dakota dict, 1112

English Language—Dictionaries—French
Canadian quaternary vocabulary, 1943
Collins-Robert French-English, English-French dict, 2d ed, 1113
Combinatory vocab of CAD/CAM in mechanical engineering, 1916
Constitutional glossary, 553
Glossary of security equipment, 1776
Glossary of water terms, 1951
Graphic arts vocab, 1058
Ozone layer dict, 1945
Stoddart colour visual dict: French-English, 1114
Vocabulary of hazardous materials in the workplace, 1997
Vocabulary of public sector auditing, 249

English Language—Dictionaries—German
Collins German-English, English-German dict unabridged, 2d ed, 1115

English Language—Dictionaries—Hebrew
Renyi picture dict: Hebrew & English, 1116

English Language—Dictionaries—Indonesian
Tuttle's concise Indonesian dict, 1117

English Language—Dictionaries—Japanese
Collins Shubun English-Japanese dict, 1118
Japanese/English, English/Japanese glossary of scientific & technical terms, 1571

English Language—Dictionaries—Korean
Korean, 1122

English Language—Dictionaries—Latvian
Latvian-English, English-Latvian dict, 1123

English Language—Dictionaries—Ojibwa
Dictionary of the Ojibway lang, 1124

English Language—Dictionaries—Persian
English-Persian dict, 1125

English Language—Dictionaries—Polyglot
Elsevier's dict of mining & mineralogy, 1800

English Language—Dictionaries—Portuguese
Oxford-Duden pictorial Portuguese-English dict, 1127

English Language—Dictionaries—Russian
Hippocrene standard dict: Russian-English, English-Russian, 1130
Renyi picture dict: Russian & English, 1131
Russian-English/English-Russian dict of free market era economics, 160

English Language—Dictionaries—Spanish
Collins Spanish-English, English-Spanish dict, 1132
Collins Spanish-English, English-Spanish dict unabridged, 3d ed, 1133
Dahl's law dict, 552
Spanish-English, English-Spanish dict of computer terms, 1895

English Language—Dictionaries—Tongan
Simplified dict of modern Tongan, 1134

English Language—Dictionaries—Turkish
Oxford Turkish dict, 1135

English Language—Dictionaries—Welsh
Welsh-English, English-Welsh dict, 1136

English Language—Dictionaries—Yiddish
Harduf's transliterated Yiddish-English dict, 4th v., 1137

English Language—Great Britain—Dictionaries
Cassell concise English dict, new ed, 1098

English Literature
British literary bibliog, 1970-79, 1244
Characters in 19th century lit, 1157
Dictionary of biblical tradition in English lit, 1149
1890s: an ency of British lit, art, & culture, 981
Encyclopedia of flora & fauna in English & American lit, 1151
Fifth dir of pers, 986
Index of English literary mss, v.2, pt.2, 1245
Index of English literary mss, v.3, pt.3, 1246
Literary research gd, 2d ed, 1139
Modern Irish lit & culture, 1291

English Philology
Catalog of dicts, word bks, & philological texts, 1440-1900, 1074

English Poetry
Bibliography & index of English verse in ms 1501-58, 1267
Guide to British poetry explication, v.2, 1265
Guide to British poetry explication, v.3, 1266

Environmental Chemistry
Chemical exposure & human health, 1861
Environmental law index to chemicals, 1941

Environmental Engineering
Current environmental engineering summaries, 1993 ed, 1788
Dictionary of environmental sci & tech, rev ed, 2000
Environmental engineering dict, 2d ed, 1789

Environmental Health
Chemical exposure & human health, 1861

Environmental Law
Green ency, 1996

Environmental Literature
Island Pr bibliog of environmental lit, 1990

Environmental Policy
Bibliographic gd to the environment 1991, 1988
California environmental dir, 5th ed, 2007
Dictionary of ecology & environmental sci, 1994
Dictionary of environment & dvlpmt, 1995
Education for the Earth, 2012
Environmental accounting, 1989
Environmental decline & public policy, 2019
Environmental dict, 2d ed, 1998
Environmental law index to chemicals, 1941
Environmental profiles, 2004
Environmental regulatory glossary, 6th ed, 2002
Environmentalists: a biographical dict, 1993
Environmentalist's bkshelf, 1992
Information please environmental almanac, 1993, 1986
McGraw-Hill ency of environmental sci & engineering, 3d ed, 1999
Reading about the environment, 1991

Environmental Protection
Data: where it is & how to get it, 45
Dictionary of environmental sci & tech, rev ed, 2000
Directory of European environmental orgs, 2003
Environmentalist's bkshelf, 1992
Green ency, 1996

Epic Poetry
Beowulf scholarship, 1263

Epidemiology
Disease & medical care in the US, 1802

Episcopal Church
History of the Episcopal church in America, 1607-1991, 1521

Eponyms
Eponyms of behavioral optometry, 1866

Erotic Literature
Clandestine erotic fiction in English 1800-1930, 1204

Ethnic Groups
American ethnic lits, 1225
Melting pot: an annot bibliog & gd to food & nutrition info for ethnic groups in America, 1599
Venture into cultures, 1170

Ethnic Relations
International writings of Bohdan S. Wynar, 1949-92, 80

Ethnology
Encyclopedia of world cultures, v.4, 395
Encyclopedia of world cultures, v.5, 396

Euphemisms
Official politically correct dict & hndbk, 1101

Europe
Adult educ in continental Europe, 391
Catalogue of European sculpture in the Ashmolean Museum 1540 to the present day, 1067
Dictionary of the Napoleonic wars, 521
Directory of European bus, 254
Directory of European community trade & professional assns 1992, 274
Directory of European environmental orgs, 2003
Directory of special collections in W Europe, 653
Economist atlas of the New Europe, 255
Europe in figures, 3d ed, 935
European business rankings, 258
European cos, 4th ed, 260
European culture, 977
European electric utility dir, 1993, 1783
European electronics dir 1993, 1787
European market share reporter, 259
European pol facts 1918-90, 766
European research centres, 9th ed, 1574
European sources of scientific & technical info, 10th ed, 1576
European specialist publishers dir, 666
European women's almanac, 947
Festival Europe, 479
Handbook of the birds of Europe, the Middle East, & N Africa, v.6, 1696
Handbook of the birds of Europe, the Middle East, & N Africa, v.7, 1697
Mosaik's photographic key to the trees & shrubs of Great Britain & N Europe, 1670
Painting of the golden age, 1063
Panorama of EC industry 93, 236
Peoples of the world: W Europeans, 128
Plants & flowers of Great Britain & N Europe, 1657
Slavic studies, 131
Trees & shrubs of Great Britain & N Europe, 1670
Who's who in European bus, 223
Who's who in European insts & enterprises 1993, 771
Who's who in European pols, 2d ed, 772

Europe, Eastern
American bibliog of Slavic & E European studies for 1990, 130
Cracking E Europe, 261
Handbook of pol sci research on the USSR & E Europe, 781
Historical atlas of E central Europe, 520
Slavic studies, 131
Who's who in Russian & the new states, 136

European Communities
Countdown 2000, v.2, 789
EC info hndbk 1993/94, 768
EUROCOM, 632
European public affair dir 1993, 769
Historical dict of the European Community, 767
Panorama of EC industry 93, 236

European Economic Community
EC direct, 257
European communities, 770
Yearbook of the European Communities & of the other European orgs, 12th ed, 773

European Literature
European writers: selected authors, 1280

Evolution (Biology)
Origin & evolution of life on Earth, 1635

Exchange of Persons Programs
Money for intl exchange in the arts, 983

Ex-Convicts
Post-release assistance programs for prisoners, 910

Executive Agencies. *See* **Administrative Agencies**

Exercise
Focus on fitness, 843

Exhibitions
Trade shows worldwide 1993, 298

Explorers
Atlas of N American exploration, 444
Children's atlas of exploration, 452
Explorers & discoverers of the world, 463
Journeys of the great explorers, 464

Export Marketing
International trade stats yrbk, 1990, 233
World markets desk bk, 239

Falklands Islands War, 1982
Falklands War: background, conflict, aftermath, 684

Family
Dictionary of family psychology & family therapy, 2d ed, 810
50 fabulous places to raise your family, 944

Fans—Societies & Clubs
Fan club dir, 1400

Fantastic Fiction
Modern mystery, fantasy & sci fiction writers, 1207
Science fiction & fantasy lit 1975-91, 1214
Science fiction & fantasy ref index 1985-91, 1213

Fantasy—Film Catalogs
Fantastic cinema subject gd, 1449

Farmers
New England planters in the Maritime provinces of Canada 1759-1800, 1589

Fasts & Feasts
Religious holidays & calendars, 1517

Federal Aid to Education
Free money for college from the govt, 327
U.S. student Fulbright grants & other grants for graduate study & research abroad, 346

Federal Grants. *See* **Grants-In-Aid**

Fellner, William John
William J. Fellner: a bio-bibliog, 154

Feminism
Canadian women's movement, 1960-90, 966
Feminist theory, 952

Papers of Elizabeth Cady Stanton and Susan B. Anthony, 964
Women public speakers in the US, 1800-1925, 957

Fertility Clinics
In vitro fertilization clinics, 1857

Fertilizers
FAO yrbk: fertilizer, v.41, 1590

Festivals
Cuban festivals, 1399
Festival Europe, 479
Yearbook of English festivals, 1406

Fiction. *See also* **Detective & Mystery Stories; Science Fiction**
Fiction for youth, 3d ed, 1181
Novels of WW II, 1205

Field Crops
Quality declared seed, 1596

Fields, W. C.
W. C. Fields—an annot gd, 1428

Filmstrips
Educators gd to free filmstrips & slides, 45th ed, 375

Finance. *See also* **Investments**
Business & legal CD-ROMS in print 1993, 175
Dictionary of finance, 204
Finance, insurance, & real estate USA, 205
Vocabulary of public sector auditing, 249
World financial system, 2d ed, 206

Fine Arts. *See* **Art**

Fire Fighters
Firefighter's hazardous materials ref bk & index, 2d ed, 2011
National dir of fire chiefs & emergency depts, 1993, 878

Fisheries
FAO yrbk: fishery stats, 1715

Fishes
Catalogue of freshwater & marine fishes of Ala., 1714
Cichlids of North & Central America, 1712
Fishes of Alta., 2d ed, 1720
Most complete colored lexicon of cichlids, 1711

Fitzwilliam Museum
Short-title cat of music printed before 1825 in the Fitzwilliam Museum, Cambride, 1310

Flies. *See* **Diptera**

Flora. *See* **Botany**

Florida
Rare & endangered biota of Fla., v.1, 1735
Rare & endangered biota of Fla., v.2, 1716

Flowers. *See also* **Wild Flowers**
Encyclopedia of flowers, 1654
Plants & flowers of Great Britain & N Europe, 1657

Folk Art
20th century American folk, self taught, & outsider art, 1032

Folk Literature
Motif-index of medieval Catalan folktales, 1389
Types & motifs of the Judeo-Spanish folktales, 1387

Folk Music
World of African music, 1315

Folklore
Oxford companion to Australian folklore, 1390

Food. *See also* **Nutrition**
Compendium of food additive specifications, addendum 1, 1608
Directory of food & nutrition info for professionals & consumers, 2d ed, 1604
Encyclopaedia of food sci, food tech, & nutrition, 1600
Melting pot: an annot bibliog & gd to food & nutrition info for ethnic groups in America, 1599
Wellness ency of food & nutrition, 1602

Foot
Selected bibliog of the foot & ankle with commentary, 1820

Football
Football scholarship gd, 844
Official 1992 NFL record & fact bk, 846
Professional football, 847
Sporting News complete Super Bowl bk, 1993 ed, 848
Timetables of sports hist: football, 845

Force & Energy
Data: where it is & how to get it, 45
Energy info abstracts annual 1991, 1979
Energy stats sourcebk, 7th ed, 1980
Energy stats yrbk, 1990, 1981
International energy stats sourcebk, 2d ed, 1984

Forecasting
Resources for the future, 77

Foreign Study
Financial aid for research & creative activities abroad 1992-94, 367
Financial aid for study & training abroad 1992-94, 368
International scholarship dir, 3d ed, 332
Study holidays, 17th ed, 369
Working holidays 1993, 370

Forest Ecology
Field gd to the ecology of W forests, 1681

Forest Products
Directory of the wood products industry, 1993, 1616
Forest product prices 1971-90, 1615

Forsyth, Peter Taylor
P. T. Forsyth bibliog & index, 1520

Fossils. *See* **Paleontology**

France
Dictionary of the Napoleonic wars, 521
French colonial Africa, 95

Medieval & renaissance mss in the Walters Art Gallery, v.2, 29
Napoleonic uniforms, 707
Tale of two cities: an annot bibliog, 1251

Free Material
Educators grade gd to free teaching aids, 39th ed, 317
Educators gd to free filmstrips & slides, 45th ed, 375
Educators gd to free health, physical educ & recreation materials, 26th ed, 829
Educators gd to free home economics & consumer educ materials, 10th ed, 886
Educators gd to free social studies materials, 33d ed, 81
Elementary teachers gd to free curriculum materials, 50th ed, 318
Guide to free computer materials, 11th ed, 1911

Freedom of Information
Intellectual freedom manual, 4th ed, 642

French Language—Dictionaries—English
Canadian quaternary vocabulary, 1943
Collins-Robert French-English, English-French dict, 2d ed, 1113
Combinatory vocab of CAD/CAM in mechanical engineering, 1916
Constitutional glossary, 553
Glossary of security equipment, 1776
Glossary of water terms, 1951
Graphic arts vocab, 1058
Ozone layer dict, 1945
Stoddart colour visual dict: French-English, 1114
Vocabulary of hazardous materials in the workplace, 1997
Vocabulary of public sector auditing, 249

French Literature
Guide to French poetry explication, 1284
Medieval Charlemagne legend, 1199
Nineteenth-century French fiction writers, 1283

French-Canadian Literature
Contemporary Canadian & US women of letters, 1138

Frontier & Pioneer Life
Rand McNally atlas of American frontiers, 490

Fruit Juices
Codex alimentarius, 2d ed, v.6, 1606

Fruit-Flies
Handbook of the fruit flies (Diptera: Tephritidae) of America North of Mexico, 1725

Fund Raising
Annual register of grant support, 26th ed, 888
Directory of fund raising & nonprofit mgmt consultants, 901
Fund raiser's gd to human serv funding 1993, 899
Funding decision makers 1993, 898

Futures Market
U.S. industrial outlook '93, 218

Gabon
Gabon, 98

Gag, Wanda
Wanda Gag: a cat raisonne of the prints, 1060

Games
Family fun & games, 824
Pick-up games, 823
Recreation hndbk, 827

Gardening
American Horticultural Society ency of gardening, 1617
Gardener's reading gd, 1627

Gay Men
Contemporary gay American novelists, 1224
Gay & lesbian American plays, 1227
Gay & lesbian characters ... in mystery novels, 1210
Gay Hollywood film & video gd, 1460
Out of the closet & into the classroom, 906
Sexuality & the law, 570

Gempylidae
FAO species cat, v.15, 1719

Gems
Gemology, 1958

Genealogy
Biography & genealogy master index [CD-ROM], 436
Directory of family assns, 1993-94 ed, 431
Genealogies catalogued by the Lib of Congress since 1986, 429
Guide to genealogical sftwr, 435
PERiodical source index 1847-1985, v.9-12, 437
PERiodical source index 1991 annual v., 438
Polish Roots, 433
Royal descents of 500 immigrants to the American colonies or the US, 439
State & province vital records gd, 432
Tracing your Irish ancestors, 434

Generals
Military leaders of the Civil War, 701

Genocide
Genocide in our time, 587

Geographers
Biographical dict of geography, 465

Geographical Names. *See* **Names, Geographical**

Geography. *See also under names of places*
Dictionary of geographical literacy, 466
Children's atlas of exploration, 452

Geography, Historical
Harper atlas of world hist, rev ed, 528
Times atlas of world hist, 4th ed, 530

Geology
Canadian quaternary vocabulary, 1943
GeoRef [CD-ROM], 1950

Geopolitics
Atlas of world pol flashpoints, 794
Strategic atlas, 3d ed, 712

German Language
Collins German-English, English-German dict unabridged, 2d ed, 1115
Glossary of educl tech terms, 377
Patterson's German-English dict for chemists, 4th ed, 1937

German-Americans
Past renewed, 411

Germany
European employment & industrial relations glossary: Germany, 253
German reunification, 522
Political leaders in Weimar Germany, 774
Twentieth-century German dramatists, 1889-1918, 1286
Twentieth-century German dramatists, 1919-92, 1287

Gerontology
Developments & research on aging, 871
Gerontology & geriatrics libs & collections in the US & Canada, 655

Gifted Children
Educational opportunity gd, 1993, 316

Global Warming
Global warming, 2014
Vocabulary of global warming, v.1, 2001

Gods
Ancient & shining ones, 1392
Encyclopedia of gods, 1395

Goldsmiths
Pennsylvania silversmiths, goldsmiths & pewterers 1684-1900, 1034

Golf
GOLF Magazine's ency of golf, 2d ed, 850
Historical dict of golfing terms, 849
Official USGA record bk, 1895-1990, 851

Gone with the Wind (Motion Picture)
Complete Gone with the Wind sourcebk, 1452

Gottfried Von Strassburg
Complete concordance to Gottfried Von Strassburg's Tristan, 1200

Government Agencies. See Administrative Agencies

Government Consultants
Nonprofit public policy research orgs, 753

Government Departments. See Administrative Agencies

Government Publications. See also under name of country
Canadian bus & economics, 3d ed, 246
French colonial Africa, 95
Guide to US govt pubns, 1993 ed, 55
Tapping the govt grapevine, 2d ed, 56

Grable, Betty
Betty Grable: a bio-bibliog, 1408

Grace, Daddy
Daddy Grace: an annot bibliog, 1500

Graduate Students
Free money for graduate school, rev ed, 329
Graduate scholarship dir, 3d ed, 331

Graduate Work. See Universities & Colleges—Graduate Work

Grants-In-Aid
Action gd to govt grants, loans, & giveaways, 895
Directory of operating grants, 889
Guide to fed funding for hospitals & health centers, 1814

Graphic Arts
American graphic design, 1059

Grasses
Guide to grasses of the lower Rio Grande valley, Tex., 1665

Great Basin
Sagebrush country, 1660

Great Britain
Art world dir: arts review yrbk 1993, 1044
BFI film & TV hndbk 1993, 1455
British hit albums, 5th ed, 1362
British librarianship & info work 1986-90, v.2, 633
British pharmacopoeia 1993, 1876
British printmakers 1855-1955, 1057
British radio & TV pioneers, 1012
Broadcasting in the UK, 2d ed, 1013
Cassell concise English dict, new ed, 1098
Concise dict of natl bibliog, 13
Consumer mags of the British Isles, 267
Crime in Victorian Britain, 590
Dictionary of natl biog: missing persons, 15
Directory of lib & info orgs in the UK, 635
Economic planning 1943-51, 263
1890s: an ency of British lit, art, & culture, 981
Encyclopedia of Britain, 133
Encyclopedia of the British pr 1422-1992, 1008
George Grenville 1712-1770: a bibliog, 775
Kelly's business dir 1992, 265
Libraries dir 1991-93, 634
Margaret Thatcher: a bibliog, 776
Medicine in Great Britain from the Restoration to the 19th century, 1660-1800, 1821
Mosaik's photographic key to the trees & shrubs of Great Britain & N Europe, 1670
Oxford dict of saints, 3d ed, 1527
Oxford illus literary gd to Great Britain & Ireland, 2d ed, 480
Pension funds & their advisors 1992, 266
Plants & flowers of Great Britain & N Europe, 1657
Royal Histl Society annual bibliog of British & Irish hist: publications of 1992, 518
Shipbuilding industry, 2031
Spanish Armada of 1588, 527
Trees & shrubs of Great Britain & N Europe, 1670
Vivien Leigh: a bio-bibliog, 1415
Whitaker's bks in print 1993, 6
Who's who in early Hanoverian Britain (1714-1789), 519

Great Lakes
Great Lakes gd to sunken ships, 2029
Traveler's gd to native America: the Great Lakes region, 413

Great Plains
Weed seeds of the Great Plains, 1663
Wildflowers of the W plains, 1655

Greek Language, Biblical
Exegetical dict of the N.T., v.3, 1528
Student's complete vocabulary gd to the Greek N.T., 1543

Greenhouse Effect, Atmospheric
Vocabulary of global warming, v.1, 2001

Grenville, George
George Grenville 1712-1770: a bibliog, 775

Group Homes
Caring for kids with special needs, 918

Guiana
Caribbean 1975-80, 143

Guillaume de Lorris
Roman de la rose: an annot bibliog, 1282

Handbooks, Vade-Mecums, Etc.
Courvoisier's bk of the best, 472
Essential researcher, 57

Handicapped
Meeting the needs of employees with disabilities, 2d ed, 881
National housing dir for people with disabilities, 1993, 883
Resources for people with disabilities & chronic conditions, 2d ed, 882
Teaching sci to children, 2d ed, 1559

Hanson, Howard
Howard Hanson: a bio-bibliog, 1330

Happiness
Medieval Consolation of Philosophy: an annot bibliog, 1487

Harpsichord Music
Harpsichord & clavichord music of the 20th century, 1335

Harvard Business School. Baker Library
Harvard Bus School core collection 1993, 156

Harvard University
Catalogue of the 15th-century printed bks in the Harvard Univ Lib, v.2, 31
Iconographic index to N.T. subjects represented in photographs & slides of paintings in the visual collections, Fine Arts Lib, Harvard Univ, v.1, 1540

Hawaii
Hawai'i, 90

Haydn, Michael
Johann Michael Haydn (1737-1806): a chronological thematic cat of his works, 1332

Hayes, Helen
Helen Hayes: a bio-bibliog, 1416

Haymarket Square Riot, Chicago, Ill, 1886
Haymarket affair, 786

Hazardous Substances
Book of lists for regulated hazardous substances 1993, 2010
Firefighter's hazardous materials ref bk & index, 2d ed, 2011
Hazardous substances resource gd, 2016
Vocabulary of hazardous materials in the workplace, 1997

H.D. (Hilda Doolittle)
H.D.: a bibliog 1905-90, 1234

Health
Dieter's dict & problem solver, 1603
Educators gd to free health, physical educ & recreation materials, 26th ed, 829
Focus on fitness, 843
HMO/PPO dir 1993, 1815
Macmillan health ency, 1803
Random House health & medicine dict, 1830

Health Care. *See* **Medical Care**

Health Risk Assessment
Chemical hazard communication gdbk, 2d ed, 2018

Hebrew Language—Dictionaries—English
Renyi picture dict: Hebrew & English, 1116

Herbs
Complete medicinal herbal, 1666
Lifetime ency of natural remedies, 1826

Heresies, Christian
Encyclopedia of heresies & heretics, 1530

Herpetology
Synopsis of the herpetofauna of Mexico, v.7, 1752

High Altitude Gardening
Low-water flower gardener, 1630

High School Libraries—Book Lists
Books for you, 11th ed, 1165

Higher Education. *See* **Education, Higher**

Himes, Chester B.
Chester Himes: an annot primary & secondary bibliog, 1235

Hispanic-Americans
Alcohol-related issues in the Latino population 1980-90, 915
American ethnic lits, 1225
Hispanic-American almanac, 412
Notable Hispanic American women, 962
Women of color & S women annual suppl, 1991/92, 955

Hispanola
Caribbean 1975-80, 143

Historians
Past renewed, 411

Historic Ships
Historic warships, 703

Historic Sites
Hippocrene USA gd to historic black south, 475

Historical Geography. *See* **Geography, Historical**

History
Chronologies in old world archaeology, 3d ed, 485
Great events: the 20th century, 539
Historical jls, 2d ed, 542
Lexicon of the Greek & Roman cities & place names in antiquity ca. 1500 B.C.—ca. A.D. 500, fascicule 1, 535
Smithsonian timelines of the ancient world, 534

Hitchcock, Alfred
Alfred Hitchcock: a gd to refs & resources, 1450

Hockey
Complete ency of hockey, 4th ed, 852
National Hockey League official gd & record bk 1992-93, 853

Hoddinott, Alun
Alun Hoddinott: a bio-bibliog, 1322

Holistic Medicine
Holistic health dir, 1992-93, 1808

Holocaust, Jewish (1939-1945)
Bibliography on Holocaust lit, suppl. v.2, 532
Holocaust lit, 538

Holy Spirit
Bibliography of the nature & role of the holy spirit in 20th-century writings, 1534

Holy Wells
Holy wells & sacred water sources in Britain & Ireland, 1386

Home Economics
Educators gd to free home economics & consumer educ materials, 10th ed, 886

Homelessness
Guide to fed funding for housing & homeless programs, 876
Homelessness: an annot bibliog, 877

Homeopathy
Family health gd to homeopathy, 1842

Homosexuality
Contemporary gay American novelists, 1224
Gay & lesbian American plays, 1227
Gay & lesbian characters ... in mystery novels, 1210
Gays & lesbians in mainstream cinema, 1446
Out of the closet & into the classroom, 906

Hong Kong
Historical dict of Hong Kong & Macau, 110

Hoover, Herbert, 1874-1964
Herbert Hoover: a bibliog, 496

Horror Films
Fantastic cinema subject gd, 1449
Peter Cushing: the gentle man of horror & his 91 films, 1437
Poverty row horrors, 1461

Horror Tales
Science fiction & fantasy lit 1975-91, 1214
Transylvanian lib, 1212

Horses
Horses, 1707
Horse's name was..., 1709

Horticulture
Gardener's dict of horticultural terms, 1618

Hospitals
Register of N American hospitals, 1993, 1806

Hotlines (Counseling)
Directory of natl helplines 1993, 47

Household Surveys
Official gd to household spending, 2d ed, 927

Housing
Guide to fed funding for housing & homeless programs, 876

Human Anatomy
Body atlas, 1819

Human Ecology
Environmentalist's bkshelf, 1992
Island Pr bibliog of environmental lit, 1990
Reading about the environment, 1991

Human Engineering
Dictionary for human factors/ergonomics, 1791

Human Evolution
Cambridge ency of human evolution, 394

Human Geography. *See* **Anthropo-Geography**

Human Reproduction
Encyclopedia of childbearing, 1831
In vitro fertilization clinics, 1857

Human Rights
Amnesty Intl: the 1993 report on human rights around the world, 591
Human rights, refugees, migrants & dvlpmt, 593
Judaism & human rights in contemporary thought, 1555
World human rights gd, 3d ed, 594

Human Services
Fund raiser's gd to human serv funding 1993, 899

Human-Computer Interaction
Information sources for virtual reality, 1894

Humanism—Manuscripts
Iter Italicum, v.6, 978

Humanities
Key ideas in human thought, 1497

Hungarian-Canadians
Canadian studies on Hungarians: a bibliog. Suppl., 408

Hydrology
Handbook of hydrology, 1953
International glossary of hydrology, 2d ed, 1952

Hymenoptera
Hymenoptera of the world, 1726

Iberian Literature
Dictionary of the lit of the Iberian Peninsula, 1289

Illinois
Awesome almanac—Ill., 84

Illustrators
Children's bk illus & design, 1062
Major authors & illustrators for children & young adults, 1187
Meet the authors & illustrators, 1193

Immigrants
Resource gd of pubns supported by multiculturalism programs, 398

Immunology
Encyclopedia of immunology, 1828
Linscott's dir of immunological & biological reagents, 7th ed, 1875

Imports
Importers manual USA, 1993 ed, 290

Income
Official gd to American incomes, 283

Incunabula
Catalogue of the 15th-century printed bks in the Harvard Univ Lib, v.2, 31

Indexing
Indexing: a basic reading list, 638

India
Women's studies in India, 953

Indiana
Awesome almanac—Ind., 86

Indiana State University. Cordell Collection
Catalog of dicts, word bks, & philological texts, 1440-1900, 1074

Indians of North America
American ethnic lits, 1225
Bibliography of Indian law per articles published 1980-90, 2d ed, 547
Bibliography of native N Americans on disc, 415
Dictionary of Native American mythology, 418
Legend & lore of the Americas before 1492, 417
Native American women, 956
Native Americans info dir, 420
North American Indian landmarks, 416
Rand McNally children's atlas of Native Americans, 421
Reference ency of the American Indian, 6th ed, 419
Statistical record of native N Americans, 422
Traveler's gd to native America: the Great Lakes region, 413
Women of color & S women annual suppl, 1991/92, 955

Indic Literature
Writers of the Indian diaspora, 1290

Indonesia
Historical dict of Indonesia, 111
Tuttle's concise Indonesian dict, 1117

Indo-Pacific Region
Corals of Austral. & the Indo-Pacific, 1747

Industrial Archaeology
Blackwell ency of industrial archaeology, 484

Industrial Equipment
Directory of building & equipment grants, 2d ed, 1772

Industrial Productivity
Industrial stats yrbk 1990, 216

Industrial Relations
BNA's 1993 source bk on collective bargaining & employee relations, 277
European employment & industrial relations glossary: Belgium, 252
European employment & industrial relations glossary: Germany, 253

Industrial Statistics
RMA annual statement studies 1993, 217

Industry
U.S. industrial outlook '93, 218

Infants
Social correlates of infant & reproductive mortality in the US, 879

Infants' Supplies
Childwise cat, 3d ed, 921

Information Science
Annual review of info sci & tech, v.27, 614
British librarianship & info work 1986-90, v.2, 633
Dictionary of acronyms & abbrevs, 597
Encyclopedia of lib & info sci, v.44, 601
Encyclopedia of lib & info sci, v.45, 602
Encyclopedia of lib & info sci, v.46, 603
Encyclopedia of lib & info sci, v.47, 604
Encyclopedia of lib & info sci, v.48, 605
Encyclopedia of lib & info sci, v.49, 606
Encyclopedia of lib & info sci, v.50, 607
Encyclopedia of lib & info sci, v.51, 608
Encyclopedia of computer sci, 3d ed, 1903
Library lit 1992, 621
Library lit. 21, 616
Library pers 1993, 622
National gd to funding for libs & info servs, 2d ed, 618
Thesaurus gd, 1992, 631
World ency of lib & info servs, 3d ed, 609

Information Services
Data: where it is & how to get it, 45
Directory of natl helplines 1993, 47
FISCAL dir of fee-based research & document supply servs, 4th ed, 639
Information security: dict of concepts, standards & terms, 1900
Position descriptions in special libs, 2d ed, 624

Insects
Destructive & useful insects, 5th ed, 1729
Genera of the aphids of Canada, 1723
Latin American insects & entomology, 1727

In-Service Training. *See* **Employees, Training of**

Instructional Materials Centers
Recommended ref bks 1993, 4

Insurance
Finance, insurance, & real estate USA, 205
Highlights of state unemployment compensation laws, 219
Medical utilization review dir, 1993 ed, 1810
Morningstar variable annuity/life sourcebk 1993, 197
Register of N American insurance cos, 1993, 221

Intelligence Officers
Spies & provocateurs, 796

Intelligence Service
Reader's gd to intelligence pers, 761

Intercultural Education
Developing multicultural awareness through children's lit, 1178
Videos for understanding diversity, 399

Interdisciplinary Approach in Education
Using lit to teach middle grades about war, 694

Intergenerational Relations
Intergenerational readings/resources 1980-93, 866

Interior Landscaping
Interior landscape dict, 1621

Inter-Library Loans
WLN interlib loan policies dir, 2d ed, 643

International Agencies
Books in print of the UN system, 788
European pol facts 1918-90, 766
International orgs: a dict & dir, 3d ed, 793
International yr bk & statesmen's who's who 1992, 791

International Business Enterprises
Access Nippon '92 business hndbk, 241
Bricker's intl dir, 24th ed, 225
China leading cos, 242
Cracking E Europe, 261
Cracking the Pacific Rim, 243
Directory of European bus, 254
Economic planning 1943-51, 263
European business rankings, 258
European business servs dir, 256
European cos, 4th ed, 260
European market share reporter, 259
International dir of co hists, v.5, 230
International dir of co hists, v.6, 231
International dir of co hists, v.7, 232
International mgmt hndbk, 238
International monetary fund 1944-92, 234
International trade stats yrbk, 1990, 233
Japan trade dir 1993-94, 244
Major energy cos of Europe 1993, 1977
Panorama of EC industry 93, 236
Report on bus: Canada co hndbk 1993, 250
Social dimensions of intl bus, 222
Standard dir of intl advertisers & agencies 1993, 226
World markets desk bk, 239

International Education
IIE educl assocs 1992-93, 366

International Labour Review
International Labour Review: index 1945-91, 285

International Monetary Fund
International monetary fund 1944-92, 234

International Organizations. *See also* **International Agencies**
Europa world yr bk 1992, 82

Internship Programs
International dir of youth internships with the UN, its related agencies, & non-governmental orgs, 5th ed, 790

Inventions
British radio & TV pioneers, 1012
Inventions & discoveries 1993, 1581

Investments
Business One Irwin investor's hndbk 1993, 187
Dictionary of investing, 177
Directory of cos offering dividend reinvestment plans, 10th ed, 180
Directory of registered investment advisors with the SEC 1993, 179
Dividend reinvestment plans, 1992 gd almanac, 181
Handbook for no-load fund investors, 1993, 189
Hulbert gd to financial newsletters, 5th ed, 191
Market share reporter 1993, 193
Morningstar closed-end fund sourcebk 1993, 194
Morningstar mutual fund sourcebk 1993, 196
Morningstar variable annuity/life sourcebk 1993, 197
Pension funds & their advisors 1992, 266
Wilson dir of emerging market funds, 1992-1993 ed, 185
World investment dir 1992, v.1, 227

Ireland
Dictionary of Irish archaeology, 486
Dublin stage, 1720-45, 1468
Modern Irish lit & culture, 1291
Oxford dict of saints, 3d ed, 1527
Royal Histl Society annual bibliog of British & Irish hist: publications of 1992, 518

Irish
Modern Irish lit & culture, 1291
Tracing your Irish ancestors, 434

Iron
Worldwide gd to equivalent irons & steels, 3d ed, 1796

Islam
Encyclopaedia of Islam, new ed, v.7, 151
Encyclopaedia of Islam, new ed, v.7, fascicules 125-26, 150
Islam & Islamic groups, 1553
Islam in N America, 1552

Israel
Historical dict of Israel, 152
Political dict of the state of Israel, suppl. 1987-93, 2d ed, 785

Italian-Americans
Italian Americans & religion, 2d ed, 1504

Italy
American Chamber of Commerce in Italy dir 1992, 268
Index to Italian architecture, 1052
Who's who in Italy 1992, 20

Japan
Access Nippon '92 business hndbk, 241
Cambridge ency of Japan, 113
Directory of Japanese technical reports 1992-93, 114
Japan: an illus ency, 115

Standard trade index of Japan 1992-93, 245
Total forecast: Japan 1990s, 116

Japanese Language—Dictionaries—English
Japanese/English, English/Japanese glossary of scientific & technical terms, 1571
Kodansha's romanized Japanese-English dict, 1119
Merriam-Webster's Japanese-English learner's dict, 1120
NTC's new Japanese-English character dict, 1121

Japanese Literature
Japanese women writers in English translation, v.2, 1295
Modern Japanese novelists, 1294

Japanese-Americans
Japanese American hist, 423

Jazz Music
Charlie Parker discography, 1369
Jazz discography, v.5, 1373
Jazz discography, v.6, 1374
Jazz lives, 1372
Pee Wee speaks, 1371

Jean de Meun
Roman de la rose: an annot bibliog, 1282

Jefferies, Richard
Richard Jefferies: a bibliographical study, 1252

Jews
Biographical dict of Canadian Jewry 1909-14, 410
Historical atlas of the Jewish people from the time of the patriarchs to the present, 424
Reform Judaism in America, 1557
Schocken gd to Jewish bks, 425
Social & religious hist of the Jews, 2d ed: index to vs.9-18, 427
Spanish & Portuguese Jewry, 426

Job Descriptions
America's top 300 jobs, 276
Career gd to America's top industries, 278
Complete gd for occupational exploration, 1993 ed, 387
Directory of jobs & careers abroad, 8th ed, 273
Occupational outlook hndbk, 1992-93 ed, 281

Job Hunting
Job hunter's sourcebk, 2d ed, 279
Job seeker's gd to 1,000 top employers, 280

Johnson, Andrew
Andrew Johnson: a bibliog, 495

Jolson, Al
Al Jolson: a bio-discography, 1365

Journalism
Encyclopedia of the British pr 1422-1992, 1008
Publication peer review, 997

Judaism
Blackwell dict of Judaica, 1554
Encyclopedia of Jewish prayer, 1556
Judaism & human rights in contemporary thought, 1555
Reform Judaism in America, 1557
Schocken gd to Jewish bks, 425
Social & religious hist of the Jews, 2d ed: index to vs.9-18, 427

Judges
Supreme Court justices, 551

Judicial Districts
Judicial staff dir, 1993, 736
Staff dirs on CD-ROM, 1993/1, 737

Jung, Carl Gustav
General bibliog of C. G. Jung's writings, rev ed, 806

Junior Colleges
Community, technical, & jr colleges statistical yrbk, 1992 ed, 356
Peterson's gd to 2-yr colleges 1994, 343

Junior High School Libraries—Book Lists
Your reading, 9th ed, 648

Kael, Pauline
Kael index, 1463

Kansas
Amphibians & reptiles in Kans., 3d ed, 1749
Guide to Kans. mushrooms, 1662
Watching Kans. wildlife, 1679

Karloff, Boris
Boris Karloff: a bio-bibliog, 1409

Kazakhstan
Active figures of the trade union & working class movement of Russia, Ukraine, Bielorussia, & Kazakhstan, 262

Kennedy, John F. (John Fitzgerald)
Assassination of John F. Kennedy, 494

Kierkegaard, Soren
Soren Kierkegaard bibliogs, 1486

Kings & Rulers
Encyclopedia of mistresses, 961
Statesmen who changed the world, 716

Klein, Abraham Moses
A. M. Klein: an annot bibliog, 1278

Knowledge, Theory of
Glossary of cognitive sci, 1494
Glossary of epistemology/philosophy of sci, 1495

Korea
Historical dict of the Republic of Korea, 117

Korean War, 1950-1953
Pusan perimeter, Korea, 1950, 679
U.S. army uniforms of the Korean war, 708

Labor & Laboring Classes
International Labour Review: index 1945-91, 285
Labour force stats 1970-90, 235

Labor Movement
Cities & churches, 1502

Ladino (Spanish Jews)
Types & motifs of the Judeo-Spanish folktales, 1387

Langland, William
Piers Plowman: a gd to the quotations, 1253

Language & Languages
Annotated bibliog of the official langs of Canada, 1068
Dictionary of dicts, 1073
Study holidays, 17th ed, 369

Language, Universal
Ethnologue, 1070
Ethnologue index, 12th ed, 1069

Latin (Medieval & Modern)
Iter Italicum, v.6, 978

Latin America
Bibliographic gd to Latin American studies 1991, 141
Bibliography of Latin American & Caribbean bibliogs, 1985-89: social scis & humanities, 145
Bignoniaceae—pt.2 (tribe tecomeae), 1637
Cambridge ency of Latin America & the Caribbean, 142
Censorship & Hollywood's Hispanic image, 1448
Handbook of Latin American lit, 2d ed, 1298
Handbook of Latin American studies, no.52, 144
Latin America: a pol dict, 784
Latin American insects & entomology, 1727
Latin American military hist, 682
Lauraceae: nectandra, 1646
Political parties of the Americas and the Caribbean, 783
Political parties of the Americas, 1980s to 1990s, 720

Latvian Language—Dictionaries—English
Latvian-English, English-Latvian dict, 1123

Law
Best lawyers in America 1993-94, 562
Bibliography of Indian law per articles published 1980-90, 2d ed, 547
Bieber's dict of legal abbrevs, 4th ed, 543
Bieber's dict of legal citations, 4th ed, 544
Business & legal CD-ROMS in print 1993, 175
Butterworths law dir 1993, 558
Canada tax cases: index & citator, 581
Canadian Assn of Law Libs dir, 649
CLE research gd, v.2, 583
Dahl's law dict, 552
Demise of the Soviet Union, 548
Directory of law-related CD-ROMS 1993, 560
Encyclopedia of legal info sources, 2d ed, 566
Guide to law schools in Canada, 575
International legal bks in print 1993-94, 546
Law lib systems dir, 654
Lawyers' & creditors' serv dir, 1993 ed, 563
Legal looseleafs in print 1993, 567
Legal newsletters in print 1993, 568
Martindale-Hubbell bar register of preeminent lawyers 1993, 561
Modern dict for the legal profession, 555
Moys classification & thesaurus for legal materials, 3d ed, 626
National survey of state laws, 569
Oxford dict of American legal quotations, 584
Recommended publications for legal research 1970/71, 549
South Pacific islands legal systems, 573
Unlocking the files of the FBI, 752
World law school dir, 1993 ed, 565

Layton, Irving
Catalogue of the letters, tapes & photographs in the Irving Layton collection, 1270

Lead—Toxicology
Lead detection & abatement dir 1993-94, 2005
State lead poisoning prevention dir 1992, 2006

Learned Institutions & Societies
International ency of learned societies & academies, 36

Learning
Encyclopedia of learning & memory, 809
World of learning 1993, 308

Learning Disabilities
Complete dir for people with learning disabilities, 1993/94, 372
Directory of facilities & servs for the learning disabled, 1993-94, 373

Learning Disabled
Peterson's colleges with programs for students with learning disabilities, 340

Leather Goods
World statistical compendium for raw hides & skins, leather, & leather footwear 1972-90, 5th ed, 1598

Legal Aid
Legal resource dir, 557

Legal Literature
Index to Canadian legal lit 1992, 582

Legends
Brewer's bk of myth & legend, 1391
Contemporary legend, 1383
Medieval Charlemagne legend, 1199

Legislation
Congressional Quarterly's American congressional dict, 729

Leigh, Vivian
Vivien Leigh: a bio-bibliog, 1415

Leisure
Information sources in sport & leisure, 821
Leisure lit, 820

Lesbians
Contemporary lesbian writers of the US, 1226
Gay & lesbian American plays, 1227
Gay & lesbian characters ... in mystery novels, 1210
Lesbian sources, 907
Lesbianism: an annot bibliog & gd to the lit 1976-91, 908

Lewis, C. S.
C. S. Lewis: a ref gd 1972-88, 1254

Lexicography
Catalog of dicts, word bks, & philological texts, 1440-1900, 1074

Libraries
American lib dir 1993-94, 610
Basic lib skills, 3d ed, 620
Building the ref collection, 619
Libraries dir 1991-93, 634
Washington area lib dir, 611
World gd to libs, 11th ed, 612

Libraries—Automation
CD-ROM 1992, 645
Directory of lib automation sftwr, systems, & servs, 1993 ed, 644

Libraries—Censorship
Intellectual freedom manual, 4th ed, 642

Libraries, Children's
Author a month (for dimes), 1188
Building the ref collection, 619
Summer reading clubs, 1194

Libraries—Governmental, Administrative, Etc.
Directory of fed libs, 2d ed, 651

Libraries, Private
Private libs in renaissance England, v.1, 598
Private libs in renaissance England, v.2, 599

Libraries, Special
Directory of special libs & info centers 1993, 650
Position descriptions in special libs, 2d ed, 624

Libraries—Special Collections
Directory of special collections in W Europe, 653
Gerontology & geriatrics libs & collections in the US & Canada, 655
Voices from the underground, 1010

Libraries, University & College
Guide to the college lib, 658

Library Association
Library Assn yrbk 1992, 636

Library Personnel Management
Position descriptions in special libs, 2d ed, 624

Library Resources
SCOLMA dir of libs & special collections on Africa in the UK & in Europe, 5th ed, 652

Library Science
Basic lib skills, 3d ed, 620
Bowker annual lib & bk trade almanac, 38th ed, 615
British librarianship & info work 1986-90, v.2, 633
Dictionary of acronyms & abbrevs, 597
Directory of lib & info orgs in the UK, 635
Encyclopedia of lib & info sci, v.44, 601
Encyclopedia of lib & info sci, v.45, 602
Encyclopedia of lib & info sci, v.46, 603
Encyclopedia of lib & info sci, v.47, 604
Encyclopedia of lib & info sci, v.48, 605
Encyclopedia of lib & info sci, v.49, 606
Encyclopedia of lib & info sci, v.50, 607
Encyclopedia of lib & info sci, v.51, 608
International writings of Bohdan S. Wynar, 1949-92, 80
Library lit 1992, 621
Library lit. 21, 616
National gd to funding for libs & info servs, 2d ed, 618
Technical dict of lib & info sci, 600
World ency of lib & info servs, 3d ed, 609

Licenses
Professional & occupational licensing dir, 800

Lichens
Indices to the species of mosses & lichens described by William Mitten, 1668

Life
Origin & evolution of life on Earth, 1635

Literary Characters. *See* **Characters & Characteristics in Literature**

Literary Landmarks
Oxford illus literary gd to Great Britain & Ireland, 2d ed, 480
Wellsprings of imagination, 478

Literary Prizes
Index to American short story award collections 1970-90, 1230

Literature
Author a month (for dimes), 1188
Authors: critical & biographical refs, 2d ed, 1145
Cassell dict of literary & lang terms, 980
City Lights bks, 1220
Contemporary world writers, 2d ed, 1144
Dictionary of literary biog documentary series, v.10, 1154
Dictionary of literary biog yrbk: 1991, 1156
Encyclopedia of contemporary literary theory, 1150
Encyclopedia of world lit in the 20th century, v.5, 1152
Gale's literary index [CD-ROM], 1161
Literature teacher's bk of lists, 1142
Magill's survey of world lit, 1158
Medieval Charlemagne legend, 1199

Little Presses
Directory of literary mags 1993-94, 1162
Small pr: an annot gd, 659
Small pr center dir, 673

Lobbying
COGEL blue bk, 9th ed, 801

Lobbyists
Activist's almanac, 865

Lortel, Lucille
Lucille Lortel: a bio-bibliog, 1414

Love Poetry
Roman de la rose: an annot bibliog, 1282

Low Temperature Research
Directory of low temperature research & dvlpmt in Europe, 7th ed, 1964

Lower Rio Grande Valley (Tex.)
Guide to grasses of the lower Rio Grande valley, Tex., 1665

Low-Fat Diet
Low-fat supermarket, 1612

Macao
Historical dict of Hong Kong & Macau, 110

Macintosh (Computer)
Bob Brant's best of Macintosh shareware, 1913
Macintosh bible, 4th ed, 1910

Magic
Ancient & shining ones, 1392

Mail-Order Business
Wholesale-by-mail cat 1993, 203

Malawi
Historical dict of Malawi, 2d ed, 100

Malaysia
Historical dict of Malaysia, 118

Maldives
Maldives, 119

Malebranche, Nicolas
Bibliographia Malebranchiana, 1485

Mammals
Asdell's patterns of mammalian reproduction, 1731
Mammal species of the world, 2d ed, 1743
Mammals of the central Rockies, 1741
Mammals of the Indomalayan region, 1734
Multimedia ency of mammalian biology [CD-ROM], 1739
Saving endangered mammals, 1738

Man
African archaeology, 488
Atlas of endangered places, 1987
Chronologies in old world archaeology, 3d ed, 485

Management
Business Week's gd to the best executive educ programs, 169

Managerial Accounting
101 business ratios, 176

Manned Space Flight
Who's who in space: the intl space yr ed, 1755

Manufactures
American manufacturers dir, 1993 ed, 212
Consumer product & manufacturer ratings 1961-90, 214
Harris manufacturers dir, 1993, 215
RMA annual statement studies 1993, 217

Manuscript Preparation (Authorship)
Directory of publication resources, 1993-94, 995
Publication peer review, 997

Manuscripts
Bibliography & index of English verse in ms 1501-58, 1267
Bibliography of the mss of Patrick Branwell Bronte, 1247
Catalogue of medieval & renaissance mss in the Beinecke Rare Bk & Mss Lib, Yale Univ, v.3, 30
Columbus docs, 533
George Grenville 1712-1770: a bibliog, 775
Guide to the ms collections in the rare bk & ms lib of Columbia Univ, 28
Index of English literary mss, v.2, pt.2, 1245
Index of English literary mss, v.3, pt.3, 1246
Iter Italicum, v.6, 978
Medieval & renaissance mss in the Walters Art Gallery, v.2, 29
Papers of Elizabeth Cady Stanton and Susan B. Anthony, 964

Marc System
Cataloger's gd to MARC coding & tagging for AV material, 627

Marine Aquariums
Macmillan bk of the marine aquarium, 1717

Marine Biology
Great bk of the sea, 1745

Marine Fishes
Fishes of the Bahamas & adjacent tropical waters, 2d ed, 1713

Marine Sciences
Encyclopedia of marine scis, 1744

Marketing
Art mktg sourcebk, 1045
FAO yrbk: trade, v.45, 1592
International closeout dir '94, 292
Marketing made easier, 293

Marlowe, Christopher
Christopher Marlowe in the 80s, 1255

Martial Arts
Original martial arts ency, 855

Mass Media
Bibliographic gd to Caribbean mass comm, 990
Bibliography of Cuban mass communications, 991
DWM: a dir of women's media, 16th ed, 967
Gale dir of publications & broadcast media 1993, 988
World media hndbk 1992-94, 992

Materials
ASM materials engineering dict, 1793
Concise ency of materials characterizations, 1795
Concise ency of materials economics, policy & mgmt, 1794

Mathematics
Mathematical scis professional dir 1993, 1967
Mathematics dict, 5th ed, 1966
Sourcebook for sci, math, & tech educ 1992, 1582
Wonderful world of mathematics, 1968

Mauritania
Mauritania, 101

Mayas
Archaeological gd to Mexico's Yucatan peninsula, 481
Maya civilization, 541

Meat
International markets for meat 1992/93, 1593

Mechanical Engineering
Combinatory vocab of CAD/CAM in mechanical engineering, 1916

Medical Care
Dial 800 for health, 1812
Disease & medical care in the US, 1802
Encyclopedia of health info sources, 2d ed, 1827
Guide to fed funding for hospitals & health centers, 1814
Health care reform terms, advance ed, 1804
Health care state rankings 1993, 1816

Medical utilization review dir, 1993 ed, 1810
National family healthcare hndbk, 1813
What to do when you can't afford health care, 1809

Medical Ethics
International dir of bioethics orgs, 1835

Medical Supplies
Product dvlpmt dir 1993, 1836
Product SOS 1993, 1837

Medicare
Complete & easy gd to social security & medicare, 10th ed, 220

Medicinal Plants
History & folklore of N American wildflowers, 1651

Medicine
Checklist of the Newberry Lib's printed bks in sci, medicine, tech, & the pseudosciences ca. 1460-1750, 1558
Consumer's gd to free medical info by phone & by mail, 1844
Detwiler dir of medical market sources, 1834
Dictionary of medical acronyms & abbrevs, 2d ed, 1818
Dictionary of modern medicine, 1832
Dictionary of sacred & magical plants, 1667
Encyclopedia of health info sources, 2d ed, 1827
Lifetime ency of natural remedies, 1826
Macmillan health ency, 1803
Medical abbrevs, 6th ed, 1817
Medicine in Great Britain from the Restoration to the 19th century, 1660-1800, 1821
Melloni's illus medical dict, 3d ed, 1829
Microbes & minie balls, 493
Professional gd to diseases, 4th ed, 1841
Random House health & medicine dict, 1830
Taber's cyclopedic medical dict, 17th ed, 1833

Memory
Encyclopedia of learning & memory, 809

Mental Illness
Clinician's hndbk, 3d ed, 1847
Columbia Univ College of Physicians & Surgeons complete home gd to mental health, 1846
Mental health & psychiatry in Africa, 1849

Metal Trade
Pennsylvania workers in brass, copper & tin 1681-1900, 1035

Metals
ASM hndbk, v.3, 1792

Mexican Literature
Dictionary of Mexican lit, 1296

Mexican-American Women
Chicana studies index, 971

Mexico
Aquaculture sourcebk, 1594
Archaeological gd to Mexico's Yucatan peninsula, 481
Diesel locomotive rosters, 3d ed, 2025
Synopsis of the herpetofauna of Mexico, v.7, 1752
Train-watcher's gd to N American railroads, 2d ed, 2024
Who's who in Mexico today, 2d ed, 12

Michigan
Awesome almanac—Mich., 87
Guide to Michigan's endangered wildlife, 1677

Michigan State University. Libraries
Comic art collection cat, 1405

Microbiology
Encyclopedia of microbiology, 1636

Microcomputers
Encyclopedia of microcomputers, v.7, 1896
Encyclopedia of microcomputers, v.8, 1897
Encyclopedia of microcomputers, v.9, 1898
Encyclopedia of microcomputers, v.10, 1899
Microcomputer market place 1993, 1906

Microelectric Packaging
Electronic packaging, microelectronics, & interconnection dict, 1781

Microforms
Bibliographic gd to microform pubns 1991, 1921
Microform market place 1992-93, 669

Micronesia (Federated States)
Flowers of the Pacific Island seashore, 1647

Middle Ages
Smithsonian timelines of the ancient world, 534

Middle Atlantic States
Used bk lover's gd to the mid-Atlantic states, 1028

Middle East
Handbook of the birds of Europe, the Middle East, & N Africa, v.6, 1696
Handbook of the birds of Europe, the Middle East, & N Africa, v.7, 1697
Historical atlas of the Middle East, 460
Index to English per lit on the O.T. & ancient Near Eastern studies, v.5, 1549

Middle School Libraries—Book Lists
Your reading, 9th ed, 648

Migrant Labor
Human rights, refugees, migrants & dvlpmt, 593

Military Art & Science
Harper ency of military hist, 4th ed, 687
International military & defense ency, 688
Military intelligence, 1870-1991, 681
Modern combat helicopters, 711
Soviet military ency, abridged English-lang ed, 686
United States military road atlas, 677

Military History
Harper ency of military hist, 4th ed, 687
Using lit to teach middle grades about war, 694
Warfare & armed conflicts, 692
Wars & peace treaties 1816-1991, 693

Military Uniforms. *See* **Uniforms, Military**

Millennialism
Guide to the end of the world, 1535

Mineralogy
Elsevier's dict of mining & mineralogy, 1800
Gemstones of E Africa, 1955
Handbook of rocks, minerals, & gemstones, 1957
Illustrated gd to rocks & minerals, 1956

Minerals in the Body
Nutrients cat, 1610

Mines & Mineral Resources
Financial Times mining intl yr bk 1993, 1982
Minerals hndbk 1992-93, 1978

Mining Engineering
Elsevier's dict of mining & mineralogy, 1800

Minnesota
Awesome almanac—Minn., 85

Minorities
Cities & churches, 1502
Contemporary bks reflecting Canada's cultural diversity, 409
Developing multicultural awareness through children's lit, 1178
Financial aid for minorities in engineering & sci, 1577
Minority student enrollments in higher educ, 361
Multicultural educ debate, 322
Multicultural student's gd to colleges, 337
Resource gd of pubns supported by multiculturalism programs, 398
Venture into cultures, 1170

Mises, Ludwig Von
Mises: an annot bibliog, 153

Mistresses
Encyclopedia of mistresses, 961

Mitchum, Robert
Robert Mitchum: a bio-bibliog, 1417

Monsters
Encyclopedia of strange & unexplained physical phenomena, 813

Moorehead, Agnes
Agnes Moorehead: a bio-bibliog, 1413

Mormon Bibliography, 1830-1930
Mormon bibliog 1830-1930: indexes to A Mormon Bibliog and 10 yr suppl, 1501

Mosses
Indices to the species of mosses & lichens described by William Mitten, 1668

Mothers
Mothers & daughters in American short fiction, 1219
Social correlates of infant & reproductive mortality in the US, 879

Motion Picture Actors & Actresses
Betty Grable: a bio-bibliog, 1408
Hollywood baby boomers, 1432
Hollywood who's who, 1431
Name is familiar, 1459
Robert Mitchum: a bio-bibliog, 1417

Motion Picture Producers & Directors
Big screen bk, 1435
Directors & their films, 1453
Directory of African film-makers & films, 1436
Hollywood who's who, 1431
International dict of films & filmmakers, 2d ed, v.4, 1430

Motion Pictures
Allied Artists checklist, 1445
BFI film & TV hndbk 1993, 1455
Catalogue of films & videos in the British Medical Assn lib, 1824
Complete Gone with the Wind sourcebk, 1452
Enser's filmed bks & plays, 1438
Famous Hollywood locations, 1421
Film news index, 1939-81, 1462
Film superlist, updated ed, 1439
Films by genre, 1444
Gays & lesbians in mainstream cinema, 1446
Halliwell's filmgoer's & video viewer's companion, 10th ed, 1456
Kael index, 1463
Laserdisc film gd, 1993-1994 ed, 1429
Literature & film: an annot bibliog 1978-88, 1143
More theatre, 1464
Motion picture gd, 1993 annual, 1457
Movie song cat, 1309
New York Times film reviews 1989-90, 1458
Prostitution in Hollywood films, 1447
Republic chapterplays, 1440
West German cinema 1985-90, 1441

Multiculturalism. *See* **Pluralism (Social Sciences)**

Museums
Museums of the world, 4th ed, 60

Mushrooms
Guide to Kans. mushrooms, 1662

Music
All music gd, 1314
American orchestral music, 1347
Anthologies of music, 2d ed, 1319
Baroque music: a research & info gd, 1306
Best rated CDs: classical 1992, 1344
Encyclopedia of music in Canada, 2d ed, 1312
German sacred polyphonic vocal music between Schutz & Bach, 1343
Harpsichord & clavichord music of the 20th century, 1335
Literature of music bibliog, 1307
Music & war, 1305
Piano-beds & music by steam, 1318
Popular gd to classical music, 1345
Pro/Am bk of music & mythology, 1316
Short-title cat of music printed before 1825 in the Fitzwilliam Museum, Cambridge, 1310
Twentieth-century composer speaks, 1333

Musical Instruments
Oxford companion to musical instruments, 1338

Musical Revues, Comedies, Etc.
Broadway's prize-winning musicals, 1465
Stage it with music, 1473

Musicians
Billboard bk of no.1 hits, 3d ed, 1360
International who's who in music & musicians' dir, 13th ed, 1346
Moscow & Leningrad: a topographical gd to Russian cultural hist, v.2, 985
World of African music, 1315

Mutual Funds
Herzfeld's gd to closed-end funds, 190
Morningstar mutual fund 500, 1993, 195
Mutual fund ency, 1993-1994 ed, 198

Mysticism
Dictionary of mysticism & the esoteric traditions, rev ed, 814

Mythology
Ancient & shining ones, 1392
Brewer's bk of myth & legend, 1391
By Jove!, 1396
Oxford gd to classical mythology in the arts, 1300-1990s, 1397
Pro/Am bk of music & mythology, 1316
Who's who in classical mythology, 1393
Who's who in non-classical mythology, 1394

Names
Brewer's dict of names, 440
Dictionary of real people & places in fiction, 1159
Klee as in clay, 982
Pronouncing dict of proper names, 1084

Names, Geographical
Colorado place names, 470
Lexicon of the Greek & Roman cities & place names in antiquity ca. 1500 B.C.—ca. A.D. 500, fascicule 1, 535

Names, Personal
African names, 443
First name reverse dict, 442
Jewish family names & their origins, 441
My name in bks, 1190

Narcotics, Control of
International hndbk on drug control, 916

National Museum of American History (U.S.)
Guide to photographic collections at the Smithsonian Inst, v.3, 1038

National Parks & Reserves
Guide to the natl wildlife refuges, rev ed, 1683

National Security
Security, arms control, & conflict reduction in E Asia & the Pacific, 683

Natural History
Way nature works, 1684

Natural Resources
Atlas of the Third World, 2d ed, 459
Dictionary of environmental sci & tech, rev ed, 2000

Naturalists
Environmentalists: a biographical dict, 1993

Nature Conservation
Green ency, 1996

Naval Museums
Historic warships, 703

Netherlands Antilles
Suriname & the Netherlands Antilles, 149

Neurologic Manifestations Of General Diseases
Alzheimer's, stroke, & 29 other neurological disorders sourcebk, 1862

New Age Movement
Layman's gd to new age & spiritual terms, 816
Parapsychology, new age & the occult, 815

New England
Used bk lover's gd to New England, 1027

New Yorker
Television-related cartoons in the New Yorker, 1056

New Zealand
Adventuring in New Zealand, 482
New Zealand bks in print 1993, 5

Newberry Library
Checklist of the Newberry Lib's printed bks in sci, medicine, tech, & the pseudosciences ca. 1460-1750, 1558

Newspapers
Bacon's media calendar dir 1993, 1003
Bacon's newspaper/mag dir 1993, 1004
Gale dir of publications & broadcast media 1993, 988
Newspapers online, 2d ed, 1005

Nigeria
Nigerian artists, 1040

Normandy (France)
Normandy campaign, 1944, 531

North America
Atlas of N American exploration, 444
History & folklore of N American wildflowers, 1651

Northeastern States
Butterflies through binoculars, 1703
Climatological atlas of snowfall & snow depth for the NE US and SE Canada, 1948

Northern Ireland
Dictionary of Irish archaeology, 486
Modern Irish lit & culture, 1291

Northmen
Medieval Scandinavia, 526

Nova Scotia
Spring wildflowers, 1659

Novelists
Contemporary gay American novelists, 1224
Critical survey of short fiction, rev ed, 1215
ECW's biographical gd to Canadian novelists, 1273
Reader's gd to Australian fiction, 1269

Nowlan, Alden
Alden Nowlan papers, 1276

Nuclear Arms Control
Nuclear present, 709

Nuclear Energy
Nuclear power plants worldwide, 1801
World energy & nuclear dir, 2d ed, 2008

Nursing
History of nursing beginning bibliog, 1864
Professional gd to diseases, 4th ed, 1841

Nutrition
Dieter's dict & problem solver, 1603
Directory of food & nutrition info for professionals & consumers, 2d ed, 1604
Encyclopaedia of food sci, food tech, & nutrition, 1600
Melting pot: an annot bibliog & gd to food & nutrition info for ethnic groups in America, 1599
Nutrients cat, 1610
Wellness ency of food & nutrition, 1602

Occultism
Checklist of the Newberry Lib's printed bks in sci, medicine, tech, & the pseudosciences ca. 1460-1750, 1558
Dictionary of cults, sects, religions & the occult, 1513
Dictionary of mysticism & the esoteric traditions, rev ed, 814
Parapsychology, new age & the occult, 815

Occupations
Career training sourcebk, 388
Complete gd for occupational exploration, 1993 ed, 387
Encyclopedia of careers & vocational guidance, 9th ed, 386
Occupational outlook hndbk, 1992-93 ed, 281

Oceania
South Pacific islands legal systems, 573

Office Practice
Complete secretary's hndbk, 7th ed, 300
Professional secretary's hndbk, rev ed, 301

Oils & Fats
Codex alimentarius, v.8, 1607

Ojibwa Langauge—Dictionaries—English
Dictionary of the Ojibway lang, 1124

Olympic Games (25th: 1992: Barcelona, Spain)
Olympic results—Barcelona 1992, 856

On-Line Bibliographic Searching
Books & pers online, 44
Newspapers online, 2d ed, 1005

Opera
Chorus in opera, 1353
International dict of opera, 1355
New Grove dict of opera, 1356
Opera: an informal gd, 1358
Opera cos of the world, 1352
Opera mediagraphy, 1351
Oxford dict of opera, 1357
Wagner compendium, 1329

Orchestral Music
American orchestral music, 1347
Orchestral excerpts, 1348

Orchids
Illustrated ency of orchids, 1658
Miniature orchids, 1656
Orchid bk, 1652

Organic Gardening
Rodale's all-new ency of organic gardening, 1619

Organizational Sociology
Organizational & interorganizational dynamics, 864

Ornithology. *See* **Birds**

Outer Space
Space exploration, 1756

Oxford English Dictionary
Guide to the Oxford English Dict, 1097

Oxford Movement
Oxford movement & its leaders, suppl, 1522

Ozone Layer
Ozone layer dict, 1945

Pacific Area
Canadian bus in the Pacific Rim, 251
Cracking the Pacific Rim, 243
Flowers of the Pacific Island seashore, 1647
Political parties of Asia & the Pacific, 765
Security, arms control, & conflict reduction in E Asia & the Pacific, 683
Statistical yrbk for Asia & the Pacific 1991, 939
World investment dir 1992, v.1, 227

Pacific Northwest
Artists of the Pacific Northwest, 1042

Painting
Iconographic index to N.T. subjects represented in photographs & slides of paintings in the visual collections, Fine Arts Lib, Harvard Univ, v.1, 1540
Looking at paintings, 1061
Painting of the golden age, 1063
Themes in American painting, 1064

Paleontology
Dinosaur & other prehistoric animal factfinder, 1959
Rand McNally picture atlas of prehistoric life, 1962

Palestine
New ency of archaeological excavations in the Holy Land, 489

Pan-Africanism
Pan-Africanism: an annot bibliog, 764

Paper Industry
Pulp & paper industry in the OECD member countries 1990, 237

Paraguay
Historical dict of Paraguay, 2d ed, 147

Parapsychology. *See* **Psychical Research**

Parenting
What's new for parents, 920

Parker, Dorothy
Dorothy Parker: a bio-bibliog, 1236

Parrots
Atlas of conures, 1690

Patent Laws & Legislation
Patent, trademark, & copyright laws, 576

Paul the Apostle, Saint
Index to per lit on the apostle Paul, 1550

Peace
Amnesty Intl: the 1993 report on human rights around the world, 591
International affairs dir of orgs, 799
War & peace lit for children & young adults, 1185
Who's who in the Peace Corps, 1993 ed, 798

Peer Review
Publication peer review, 997

Pelicans
Cormorants, darters, & pelicans of the world, 1698

Pennsylvania
Pennsylvania potters 1660-1900, 1033
Pennsylvania silversmiths, goldsmiths & pewterers 1684-1900, 1034
Pennsylvania workers in brass, copper & tin 1681-1900, 1035

Perennials
Rodale's illus ency of perennials, 1620

Performance Art
Action art, 1039

Performing Arts
Handel's natl dir for the performing arts, 5th ed, 1420

Perfumes
Perfume hndbk, 1940

Periodicals
Bacon's media calendar dir 1993, 1003
Bacon's newspaper/mag dir 1993, 1004
Books & pers online, 44
Consumer mags of the British Isles, 267
Cover story index 1960-1991, 1006
Cover story index: 1992 suppl, 1007
Index to black pers, 403
MLA dir of pers 1993-95, 987
National dir of mags 1994, 62
Reference gd to Afro-American publications & eds 1827-1946, 1009
Serials dir, 7th ed, 63
Serials dir: EBSCO CD-ROM, summer 1993, 64
Standard per dir 1993, 67
Ulrich's intl pers dir 1993-94, 65
Ulrich's plus [CD-ROM], 66

Persian Gulf War, 1991
U.S. aircraft & armament of Operation Desert Storm in detail & scale, 699

Persian Language—Dictionaries—English
Persian-English dict, 1126

Personal Computers. *See* **Microcomputers**

Personal Names. *See* **Names, Personal**

Personnel Management
Personnel executives contactbk, 286

Pesticides
Ball pest & disease manual, 1624
Basic gd to pesticides, 2009
Pesticide residues in food 1992, evaluations pt.1, 1611

Petroleum Industry & Trade
Asia-Pacific/Africa-Middle East petroleum dir, 1993, 1971
European petroleum dir, 1993, 1972
Financial Times who's who in world oil & gas 1993, 1970
Natural gas industry dir, 1993, 1973
Petroleum sftwr dir, 1994, 1974
U.S.A. oil industry dir, 1993, 1975
U.S.A. oilfield serv, supply & manufacturers dir, 1993, 1976

Petry, Ann
Ann Petry: a bio-bibliog, 1237

Pharmaceutical Technology
Encyclopedia of pharmaceutical tech, v.4, 1867
Encyclopedia of pharmaceutical tech, v.5, 1868
Encyclopedia of pharmaceutical tech, v.6, 1869
Encyclopedia of pharmaceutical tech, v.7, 1870
IPA thesaurus & frequency list, 6th ed, 1873

Philanthropists
Major donors 1993, 893

Philosophers
Descartes dict, 1493
Directory of American philosophers 1992-93, 1498
Jean Paul Sartre: a bibliog, 1489
Presocratic philosophers, 1488
Soren Kierkegaard bibliogs, 1486

Philosophy
Blackwell dict of 20th-century social thought, 73
Dictionary of philosophical quotations, 1499
Glossary of cognitive sci, 1494
HarperCollins dict of philosophy, 2d ed, 1496
Key ideas in human thought, 1497
Medieval Consolation of Philosophy: an annot bibliog, 1487
World philosophy, 1482

Photography
Dictionary of Australian artists, 1041
Focal ency of photography, 3d ed, 1036
McBroom's camera bluebk, 1994 ed, 1037

Phylloxeridae
Genera of the aphids of Canada, 1723

Physical Education & Training
Acrosport, 817
Educators gd to free health, physical educ & recreation materials, 26th ed, 829

Physical Fitness
Dieter's dict & problem solver, 1603
Focus on fitness, 843
Leisure lit, 820

Physical Sciences
Encyclopedia of physical sci & tech, 2d ed, 1566

Physically Handicapped
Directory of disability support servs in community colleges 1992, 371

Physics
McGraw-Hill ency of physics, 2d ed, 1965

Piano Music
Isaac Albeniz: chronological list & thematic cat of his piano works, 1320
Music for 3 or more pianists, 1337

Picture Books for Children
A to Zoo, 4th ed, 1176
Palette of possibilities, 1167

Picture Dictionaries
My 1st dict, 1092
Oxford-Duden pictorial Portuguese-English dict, 1127
Renyi picture dict: Hebrew & English, 1116
Renyi picture dict: Russian & English, 1131
Running Pr cyclopedia, 40
Stoddart colour visual dict: French-English, 1114
Visual dict of dinosaurs, 1963
Visual dict of flight, 2020
Visual dict of the Earth, 1946
Visual dict of the Universe, 1930

Pictures
Illustration index 7, 1050

Piers the Plowman
Piers Plowman: a gd to the quotations, 1253

Planets
Field gd to the stars & planets, 3d ed, 1928
Oxford illus ency of the universe, 1944

Plants. *See also* **Wild Flowers**
Ball pest & disease manual, 1624
Bernard E. Harkness seedlist hndbk, 2d ed, 1625
Blooms of Bressingham garden plants, 1626
Cycads of the world, 1671
Encyclopedia of flora & fauna in English & American lit, 1151
500 best garden plants, 1622
Gardener's Latin, 1640
Jepson manual, 1644
Ornamental shrubs, climbers & bamboos, 1632
Stearn's dict of plant names for gardeners, 1642

Plastics
Plastics technical dict, 1938
Rosato's plastics ency & dict, 1771

Pluralism (Social Sciences)
Contemporary bks reflecting Canada's cultural diversity, 409
Guide to multicultural resources 1993/94, 400
Venture into cultures, 1170
Videos for understanding diversity, 399

Poetics
New Princeton ency of poetry & poetics, 1302

Poetry
A. M. Klein: an annot bibliog, 1278
Austin Clarke: a ref gd, 1293
Canadian writers & their works: cum index, poetry series, 1272
Directory of poetry pubs, 8th ed, 664
ECW's biographical gd to Canadian poets, 1274
New Princeton ency of poetry & poetics, 1302
Poetry criticism, v.5, 1303
Seventeenth-century British nondramatic poets, 1264

Poland
Poland, rev ed, 134
Polish roots, 433

Policy Scientists
Nonprofit public policy research orgs, 753

Political Consultants
Political resource dir 1993, 719

Political Parties
Dictionary of pol parties & orgs in Russia, 779
Political parties of Asia & the Pacific, 765
Political parties of the Americas and the Caribbean, 783
Political parties of the Americas, 1980s to 1990s, 720

Political Science
COGEL blue bk, 9th ed, 801
Dictionary of 20th-century world pols, 718
Guide to pol videos, v.1, no.1, 713
Macmillan dict of pol quotations, 724
Oxford companion to pols of the world, 717
Political leaders in Weimar Germany, 774
Routledge dict of 20th-century pol thinkers, 715

Pollution
Atlas of endangered places, 1987

Polynesia
Flowers of the Pacific Island seashore, 1647
Historical dict of Polynesia, 120

Pool (Game)
Billiard industry source bk, 1992/1993 ed, 857
Pool player's natl pocket billiard dir, 1992 ed, 858
Pool player's road atlas 1994, 859

Popular Culture
Fan club dir, 1400

Popular Literature
#1 New York Times bestseller, 1153

Popular Music
Banjo on record, 1336
Billboard bk of American singing groups, 1359
Billboard bk of no.1 hits, 3d ed, 1360
British hit albums, 5th ed, 1362
Facts behind the songs, 1366
Golden age of top 40 music (1955-1973) on CD, 1361
Guinness ency of popular music, 1363
Joel Whitburn presents daily #1 hits 1940-92, 1364
Movie song cat, 1309
Rolling Stone album gd, 1367
World of African music, 1315

Porpoises
Field gd to whales, porpoises, & seals from Cape Cod to Nfld., 4th ed, 1737

Portugal
Dictionary of the lit of the Iberian Peninsula, 1289
Historical dict of Portugal, 135

Portuguese Language—Dictionaries—English
Oxford-Duden pictorial Portuguese-English dict, 1127

Portuguese Literature—African Authors. *See* **African Literature (Portuguese)**

Postal Addresses. *See* **Street Addresses**

Potters
Pennsylvania potters 1660-1900, 1033

Poverty
Poverty in developing countries, 905

Power Resources
Energy in the dvlpmt of W Africa, 1969

Power-Plants
Handbook of power, utility & boiler terms & phrases, 6th ed, 1797

Prayer
Encyclopedia of Jewish prayer, 1556

Precious Stones
Gemology, 1958
Gemstones of E Africa, 1955
Handbook of rocks, minerals, & gemstones, 1957

Preferred Provider Organizations (Medical Care)
HMO/PPO dir 1993, 1815

Pregnancy
Encyclopedia of childbearing, 1831

Presbyterian Church
Presbyterians, 1533

Preschool Children
Play, learn, & grow, 1184
Preschool resource gd, 312

Presidents
Encyclopedia of mistresses, 961
Facts about the presidents, 6th ed, 499
Presidency A to Z, 508
Presidential landmarks, 477
Presidential primaries & caucuses 1992, 755

Press
Encyclopedia of the British pr 1422-1992, 1008

Press Law
Publishing law hndbk, 2d ed, 574

Pressure Groups
U.S. criminal justice interest groups, 588

Primates
Audiovisual resources in primatology, Wis Regional Primate Research Center, 1732
International dir of primatology, 1736

Prince Edward Island
Wildflowers of Prince Edward Island, 1650

Printing
Elements of typographic style, 675
Graphic arts vocab, 1058
Yellow pages industry source bk, 1992-93 ed, 674

Printmakers
British printmakers 1855-1955, 1057

Privacy, Right of
Compilation of state & fed privacy laws, 1992 ed, 577

Produce Trade
FAO yrbk: trade, v.45, 1592

Product Safety
Product SOS 1993, 1837

Professional Education
Gibson's gd to graduate & professional programs at Ont. univs, 309

Projectors
Pre-cinema hist, 1427

Proofreading
Copy-editing, 3d ed, 1000

Proposal Writing for Grants
Action gd to govt grants, loans, & giveaways, 895

Prostitution
Prostitution in Hollywood films, 1447

Protective Clothing. *See* **Clothing, Protective**

Proverbs
International proverb scholarship, suppl.2, 1388
Joys of Hebrew, 1385
Old English proverbs collected by Nathan Bailey, 1736, 1384
Witty words, 70

Psychiatry
Columbia Univ College of Physicians & Surgeons complete home gd to mental health, 1846
Handbook of behavior therapy & pharmacotherapy for children, 1848
Handbook of prescriptive treatments for children & adolescents, 1845
Mental health & psychiatry in Africa, 1849

Psychical Research
Parapsychology, new age & the occult, 815

Psychological Tests
Instrumentation in educ, 306

Psychology
Best yrs of their lives, 926
Clinician's hndbk, 3d ed, 1847
Family ency of child psychology & dvlpmt, 807
General bibliog of C. G. Jung's writings, rev ed, 806
Psychology: a gd to ref & info sources, 805
Psychopathology in adulthood, 812
Student's dict of psychology, 2d ed, 811

Public Library—Book Lists
Best bks for public libs, 647

Public Opinion
Index to intl public opinion, 1991-92, 75

Public Relations
Publicity & media resources for bk pubs, 1992-1993 ed, 670

Public Welfare
Public welfare dir, 1993/94, 913

Publicity
Marketing made easier, 293

Publishers & Publishing
Books in print of the UN system, 788
Directory of poetry pubs, 8th ed, 664
Directory of publishers in China, 672
Directory of publ 1993, 665
European specialist publishers dir, 666
New Zealand bks in print 1993, 5
Publicity & media resources for bk pubs, 1992-1993 ed, 670
Publishers, distrs & wholesalers of the US 1993-94, 671
Publishers trade list annual, 1992, 660
Small pr: an annot gd, 659
Yellow pages industry source bk, 1992-93 ed, 674

Pulpwood Industry
Compendium of pulp & paper training & research insts, 1614

Quality of Life
50 fabulous places to raise your family, 944
100 best small towns in America, 942

Quilting
Quilt groups today, 1031

Quotations
Beacon bk of quotations by women, 972
Dictionary of philosophical quotations, 1499
Draper's bk of quotations for the Christian world, 1551
Harper bk of quotations, 3d ed, 68
Joys of Hebrew, 1385
Macmillan dict of pol quotations, 724
My soul looks back, 'less I forget, 72
New quotable woman, rev. ed, 973
New York Public Lib bk of 20th-century American quotations, 71
Oxford dict of American legal quotations, 584
Shakespeare's quotations, 1257
Witty words, 70

Radio
ARRL hndbk for radio amateurs 1993, 1015
Bacon's radio/TV dir 1993, 1014
British radio & TV pioneers, 1012
Handbook of old-time radio, 1017
Religious radio & TV in the US, 1921-91, 1511
Traveler's country music radio atlas 1993, 1018

Railroads
Compendium of American railroad radio frequencies, 12th ed, 2028
Diesel locomotive rosters, 3d ed, 2025

Railway dict, 2022
Train-watcher's gd to N American railroads, 2d ed, 2024

Rain Forest Plants
Rainforest plants of E Austral., 1682

Range Plants
Texas range plants, 1664

Rap (Music)
Rap music in the 1980s, 1375

Rare Books
Bookman's price index, v.46, 1025

Rare Fishes
Rare & endangered biota of Fla., v.2, 1716

Rare Mammals
Rare & endangered biota of Fla., v.1, 1735

Ratio Analysis
101 business ratios, 176

Raw Materials
World statistical compendium for raw hides & skins, leather, & leather footwear 1972-90, 5th ed, 1598

Rays (Fishes)
Reef sharks & rays of the world, 1718

Reading
Literature activity bks, 1197
Read for your life, 383

Real Property
Finance, insurance, & real estate USA, 205

Reconstruction
Freedom's lawmakers, 727

Recreation
Acrosport, 817
Educators gd to free health, physical educ & recreation materials, 26th ed, 829
Information sources in sport & leisure, 821

Recreation Areas
America's secret recreation areas, 476
United States military road atlas, 677

Recycling (Waste, Etc.)
Recycling in America, 2013
Recycling sourcebk, 2017

Reference Books
Canadian bus & economics, 3d ed, 246
Guide to the college lib, 658
Literary research gd, 2d ed, 1139
Recommended ref bks 1993, 4
Reference bks bulletin 1991-92, 3
Slavic studies, 131
Student contact bk, 58
Walford's gd to ref material, v.1: sci & tech, 6th ed, 1562

Reference Services (Libraries)
Recommended ref bks 1993, 4

Refugees
Human rights, refugees, migrants & dvlpmt, 593

Reginald, R.
Work of Robert Reginald, 2d ed, 1238

Register of Births, Etc.
State & province vital records gd, 432

Regulatory Agencies. *See* **Administrative Agencies**

Religion
Bibliography of new religious movements in primal societies, v.6, 1505
Concise dict of religion, 1512
Dictionary of American religious biog, 2d ed, 1509
Dictionary of biblical tradition in English lit, 1149
Dictionary of Native American mythology, 418
Directory of religious orgs in the US, 3d ed, 1515
Encyclopedia of American religions, 4th ed, 1518
Illustrated ency of active new religions, sects, & cults, 1529
Italian Americans & religion, 2d ed, 1504
Religion in the Soviet Union, 1503
Who's who in religion 1992-93, 1510

Religions
Ancient & shining ones, 1392
Contemporary religions: a world gd, 1516
Dictionary of cults, sects, religions & the occult, 1513

Renewable Energy Sources
Almanac of renewable energy, 1983
Renewable energy, 1985

Report Writing
100 world-class thin bks, 1164

Reptiles
Amphibians & reptiles in Kans., 3d ed, 1749
Reptiles & amphibians, 1748

Republic Picture Corporation
Republic chapterplays, 1440

Research
Action gd to govt grants, loans, & giveaways, 895
Directory of dvlpmt research & training insts in Africa, 93
European research centres, 9th ed, 1574
Government research dir 1993-94, 740
International ency of learned societies & academies, 36
Nonprofit public policy research orgs, 753
Research centers dir 1993, 345
Research servs dir, 5th ed, 165
Student contact bk, 58

Research & Development Contracts
R&D ratios & budgets, 295
Research & dvlpmt growth trends, 1992 ed, 209
U.S. sourcebk of R&D spenders, 1992 ed, 240

Retirement
Consumer's gd to aging, 875

Rewards (Prizes, Etc.)
Children's bks: awards & prizes, 1992 ed, 1191

Rhododendron
Rhododendron hybrids, 2d ed, 1631

Ridgway, Matthew Bunker
General Matthew B. Ridgway: an annot bibliog, 678

Rock Music
Billboard bk of no.1 hits, 3d ed, 1360
Bob Dylan: a bio-bibliog, 1379
Harmony illus ency of rock, 7th ed, 1378
HeadBangers, 1377
Rock 'n' roll through 1969, 1376

Rocks
Handbook of rocks, minerals, & gemstones, 1957
Illustrated gd to rocks & minerals, 1956

Rocky Mountains
Mammals of the central Rockies, 1741

Roller Coasters
Roller coasters, 828

Rolling Stone
Rolling Stone index, 1404

Roman de la Rose
Roman de la rose: an annot bibliog, 1282

Rome (Italy)
New topographical dict of ancient Rome, 536

Roses
Old rose advisor, 1628

Roti (Indonesia)
Timor, 112

Royal Descent, Families of
Royal descents of 500 immigrants to the American colonies or the US, 439

Russell, Pee Wee
Pee Wee speaks, 1371

Russia
Active figures of the trade union & working class movement of Russia, Ukraine, Bielorussia, & Kazakhstan, 262
Dictionary of pol parties & orgs in Russia, 779
Directory of Russian MPs, 523
Encyclopedia of Russian hist, 524
First demographic portraits of Russia 1951-90, 929
Moscow & Leningrad: a topographical gd to Russian cultural hist, v.2, 985
Russia & the Commonwealth A to Z, 525
Russia 1993: pol & economic analysis & bus dir, 137
Russian govt today, spring 1993, 780
Who is who in the Russian govt, 777
Who is who in the Russian govt, suppl.1, 778
Who's who in Russian & the new states, 136

Russian Language—Dictionaries—English
Hippocrene standard dict: Russian-English, English-Russian, 1130
1000 Russian verbs, 1128
Renyi picture dict: Russian & English, 1131
Russian-English dict of verbal collocations (REDVC), 1129
Russian-English/English-Russian dict of free market era economics, 160

Sailing
Sailing dir, 860

Saint (Fictitious Character)
Saint: a complete hist in print, radio, film & TV, 1249

Saints
Oxford dict of saints, 3d ed, 1527
Saints, 1526

Salsa
Salsa & related genres, 1381

Saxophone Music
Saxophone recital music, 1339

Saxophonists
Charlie Parker discography, 1369

Scandinavia
Medieval Scandinavia, 526

Scarlatti, Alessandro
Alessandro & Domenico Scarlatti: a gd to research, 1334

Scarlatti, Domenico
Alessandro & Domenico Scarlatti: a gd to research, 1334

Scholarships
A's & B's of academic scholarships, 16th ed, 363
Cash for college, 360
Financial aid for research & creative activities abroad 1992-94, 367
Financial aid for study & training abroad 1992-94, 368
Football scholarship gd, 844
Free money for athletic scholarships, 326
Free money for graduate school, rev ed, 329
Free money from colleges & univs, 328
International scholarship dir, 3d ed, 332
Money for intl exchange in the arts, 983
Scholarship bk, 4th ed, 333
U.S. student Fulbright grants & other grants for graduate study & research abroad, 346
Winning scholarships, 311

School Libraries
Author a month (for dimes), 1188
Building the ref collection, 619
Canadian lib hndbk, 617
Science Bks & Films best bks for children 1988-91, 1561

School Media Centers. *See* Instructional Materials Centers

Science
AAAS hndbk 1993/94, 1579
Checklist of the Newberry Lib's printed bks in sci, medicine, tech, & the pseudosciences ca. 1460-1750, 1558
Concise illus dict of sci & tech, 1567
Directory of AAAS sci & engineering fellows 1973-92, 1573
Directory, 1992: AAAS consortium of affiliates for intl programs, 1572
Dorling Kindersley sci ency, 1565
European research centres, 9th ed, 1574
European sources of scientific & technical info, 10th ed, 1576
Glossary of epistemology/philosophy of sci, 1495
History of sci & tech in the US, v.2, 1560
Japanese/English, English/Japanese glossary of scientific & technical terms, 1571
Key ideas in human thought, 1497
Kingfisher sci ency, 1568
Magill's survey of sci: applied sci series, 1583
Quarks, critters, & chaos, 1585
Raintree illus sci ency, 1569
Science & tech desk ref, 1584
Science Bks & Films best bks for children 1988-91, 1561
Science teacher's bk of lists, 1580
Sourcebook for sci, math, & tech educ 1992, 1582
Systems & control ency, suppl. v.2, 1570
Teaching sci to children, 2d ed, 1559
Walford's gd to ref material, v.1: sci & tech, 6th ed, 1562
Way nature works, 1684
Who's who in sci & engineering 1992-93, 1564

Science Fiction
Clockworks, 974
Encyclopedia of sci fiction, 1211
Modern mystery, fantasy & sci fiction writers, 1207
Science fiction & fantasy lit 1975-91, 1214
Science fiction & fantasy ref index 1985-91, 1213

Science Fiction Films
Fantastic cinema subject gd, 1449

Scotland
Butterworths law dir 1993, 558

Screenwriters
International dict of films & filmmakers, 2d ed, v.4, 1430

Sculpture
Catalogue of European sculpture in the Ashmolean Museum 1540 to the present day, 1067
Roman sculpture, 1066

Sea Life. *See* Marine Biology

Sea Snakes
Venomous sea snakes, 1750

Seals (Animals)
Field gd to whales, porpoises, & seals from Cape Cod to Nfld., 4th ed, 1737

Seashore Area
Flowers of the Pacific Island seashore, 1647

Secretarial Practice. *See* Office Practice

Sects
Dictionary of cults, sects, religions & the occult, 1513
Illustrated ency of active new religions, sects, & cults, 1529

Security, International
International affairs dir of orgs, 799

Security Systems
Glossary of security equipment, 1776

Self-Help for the Disabled
Meeting the needs of employees with disabilities, 2d ed, 881

Senior Citizens. *See* Aged

Sequels (Literature)
Western series & sequels, 2d ed, 1221

Serial Publications
National dir of mags 1994, 62
Serials dir, 7th ed, 63
Serials dir: EBSCO CD-ROM, summer 1993, 64
Standard per dir 1993, 67
Ulrich's intl pers dir 1993-94, 65
Ulrich's plus [CD-ROM], 66

Services Industries
Best nonfranchise bus opportunities, 199

Sex
Dictionary of sexual slang, 909
Gender positive!, 1179
On account of sex, 949
Sexuality & the law, 570

Seychelles
Seychelles, 140

Shakespeare, William
Essential Shakespeare, 2d ed, 1256
Shakespearean criticism, v.18, 1260
Shakespearean criticism, v.19, yrbk 1991, 1259
Shakespeare's characters, 1258
Shakespeare's quotations, 1257

Shareware (Computer Software)
Bob Brant's best of Macintosh shareware, 1913

Sharks
Reef sharks & rays of the world, 1718

Shells
Shells, 1675

Ships
Great Lakes gd to sunken ships, 2029
Naval Institute gd to combat fleets of the world 1993, 704
Naval Institute gd to the ships & aircraft of the US fleet, 15th ed, 705
Shipbuilding industry, 2031

Shopping
Ethical shopper's gd to Canadian supermarket products, 248

Shore Birds
Shorebirds of the Pacific Northwest, 1700

Short Stories
Critical survey of short fiction, rev ed, 1215
Index to American short story award collections 1970-90, 1230
Mothers & daughters in American short fiction, 1219
Twentieth-century short story explication: new series, v.1, 1218

Short Story
Critical survey of short fiction, rev ed, 1215
Short story criticism, v.11, 1216
Short story criticism, v.12, 1217

Shrubs
Folklore of trees & shrubs, 1673
Mosaik's photographic key to the trees & shrubs of Great Britain & N Europe, 1670
Trees & shrubs of Great Britain & N Europe, 1670

Sierra Leone
Sierra Leone, 102

Signs & Symbols
Dictionary of symbolism, 979
Famous animal symbols, v.2, 291

Silent Films
Guide to silent Westerns, 1443

Silversmiths
Pennsylvania silversmiths, goldsmiths & pewterers 1684-1900, 1034

Sinatra, Frank
Sinatra: the man & his music, 1368

Slavic Countries
American bibliog of Slavic & E European studies for 1990, 130
Slavic studies, 131

Sleep
Encyclopedia of sleep & dreaming, 808

Slides (Photography)
Educators gd to free filmstrips & slides, 45th ed, 375

Slogans
Every bite a delight & other slogans, 299

Small Business
Action gd to govt grants, loans, & giveaways, 895
Best nonfranchise bus opportunities, 199

Snakes
Snakes of the US & Canada, v.1, 1751

Snow
Climatological atlas of snowfall & snow depth for the NE US and SE Canada, 1948

Social Action
Activist's almanac, 865

Social History
Covert culture sourcebk, 76
Encyclopedia of American social hist, 505

Social Indicators
50 fabulous places to raise your family, 944
100 best small towns in America, 942

Social Movements
1960s: an annot bibliog of social & pol movements in the US, 863

Social Reformers
Activist's almanac, 865
American social leaders, 78

Social Sciences
Blackwell dict of 20th-century social thought, 73
Dictionary of stats & methodology, 79
Educators gd to free social studies materials, 33d ed, 81

Key ideas in human thought, 1497
Macrocosm USA, 74

Social Security
Complete & easy gd to social security & medicare, 10th ed, 220

Social Service
Author's gd to social work jls, 3d ed, 912
Social work almanac, 911

Software Engineering
Concise ency of sftwr engineering, 1775

Software Protection
Computer law & sftwr protection, 1892

Soldiers
Warrior's words, 697

Songs
American women songwriters, 1325

Sound Recordings
Encyclopedia of recorded sound in the US, 1313
Guide to pseudonyms on American records, 1892-1942, 1317
Jussi Bjorling phonography, 2d ed, 1354
Rolling Stone album gd, 1367

South Africa
ANC & black workers in S Africa, 1912-92, 103
Who's who in S African pols, 4th ed, 762

South Africa—Foreign Economic Relations—United States
United States sanctions & S Africa, 545

South America
South American, Central American, & the Caribbean 1993, 146

South Asia
Historical atlas of S Asia, 2d ed, 515
Mammals of the Indomalayan region, 1734

Southern States
Contemporary fiction writers of the South, 1222
Hippocrene USA gd to historic black south, 475
Whistlin' Dixie: a dict of S expressions, 1089

Southwestern States
Desert & mountain plants of the southwest, 1645

Soviet Union
Demise of the Soviet Union, 548
Dictionary of pol parties & orgs in Russia, 779
Encyclopedia of Russian hist, 524
Handbook of pol sci research on the USSR & E Europe, 781
International writings of Bohdan S. Wynar, 1949-92, 80
Religion in the Soviet Union, 1503
Russia & the Commonwealth A to Z, 525
Soviet military ency, abridged English-lang ed, 686

Soviet Union—Foreign Relations—United States
Cold war chronology, 795

Soybean—Diseases & Pests
Soybean diseases, 1595

Space Flight
Men & women of space, 1757

Spain
Dictionary of the lit of the Iberian Peninsula, 1289
Motif-index of medieval Catalan folktales, 1389
Spanish Armada of 1588, 527
Who's who in Spain 1992, 21

Spanish Language—Dictionaries—English
Collins Spanish-English, English-Spanish dict, 1132
Collins Spanish-English, English-Spanish dict unabridged, 3d ed, 1133
Dahl's law dict, 552
Spanish-English, English-Spanish dict of computer terms, 1895

Special Forces (Military Science)
Visual dict of special military forces, 689

Special Libraries. *See* **Libraries, Special**

Spellers
Canadian spelling dict, 7th ed, 1102
Paragon House spelling dict, 1103

Spencer, Herbert
Herbert Spencer: a primary & secondary bibliog, 1490

Spies
Spies & provocateurs, 796

Sports
Acrosport, 817
Atlas of American sport, 819
Free money for athletic scholarships, 326
Guinness bk of sports records 1993, 825
Information please sports almanac, 1993, 818
Information sources in sport & leisure, 821
Leisure lit, 820
Oxford companion to Australian sport, 822
Pick-up games, 823
Recreation hndbk, 827
Sports in N America, v.3, 826

Sports Art
Dictionary of sporting artists 1650-1990, 1065

Springs
Holy wells & sacred water sources in Britain & Ireland, 1386

Stage Lighting
ABC of stage lighting, 1475
Theatre lighting from A to Z, 1470

Stanton, Elizabeth Cady
Papers of Elizabeth Cady Stanton and Susan B. Anthony, 964

Stapleton, Maureen
Maureen Stapleton: a bio-bibliog, 1418

Stars
Binary stars, 1929
Facts on File atlas of stars & planets, 1925
Field gd to the stars & planets, 3d ed, 1928
StarList 2000, 1924

State Aid to Education
Free money for college from the govt, 327

State Governments
Almanac of American pols 1994, 746
Book of the states, v.29, 721
CQ's state fact finder, 750
Election results dir, 1993 ed, 738
Organizations of state govt officials dir 1992, 742
State yellow bk, v.5, no.1, 743

Statesmen
Statesmen who changed the world, 716

Statistics
Europe in figures, 3d ed, 935
International histl stats: the Americas, 1750-1988, 2d ed, 936
Places, towns & townships, 937
State & local stats sources, 2d ed, 934
Statistical abstract of the US 1992, 938
Statistical yrbk for Asia & the Pacific 1991, 939
World stats in brief, 14th ed, 940

Steel
Worldwide gd to equivalent irons & steels, 3d ed, 1796

Steel Band Music
Forty yrs of steel, 1382

Stephen, Leslie
Leslie Stephen's life in letters, 1261

Stewart, Ellen
Ellen Stewart & La Mama: a bio-bibliog, 1410

Stock Companies
Nasdaq fact bk & co dir, 1993, 182

Stockbrokers
Skinner's dir of security dealer name & address changes 1992, 184

Stocks. *See also* **Investments**
Business One Irwin investor's hndbk 1993, 187
Standard & Poor's stock & bond gd, 1993 3d, 200

Street Addresses
Guide to worldwide postal-code & address formats, 1993, 989

Student Aid
A's & B's of academic scholarships, 16th ed, 363
Cash for college, 360
College costs & financial aid hndbk 1994, 353
Financial aid for minorities in engineering & sci, 1577
Financial aid for research & creative activities abroad 1992-94, 367
Financial aid for study & training abroad 1992-94, 368
Free money for college from the govt, 327
Free money from colleges & univs, 328
Graduate scholarship dir, 3d ed, 331
International scholarship dir, 3d ed, 332
Scholarship bk, 4th ed, 333

Subculture
Covert culture sourcebk, 76

Subject Headings
African studies thesaurus, 629
Ei thesaurus, 1753
Industrial chemical thesaurus, 2d ed, 1942

Substance Abuse
Drug, alcohol, & other addictions, 2d ed, 914
Focus on addictions, 917

Success
Book of women's firsts, 970

Sudan
Historical dict of the Sudan, 2d ed, 105
Sudan, rev ed, 104

Sudden Infant Death Syndrome
Social correlates of infant & reproductive mortality in the US, 879

Surgery
History of surgery in the US 1775-1900, v.2, 1822

Suriname
Suriname & the Netherlands Antilles, 149

Sustainable Agriculture
Socioeconomics of sustainable agriculture, 1588

Swimming Pools
ALSA swimmer's gd, 1993 ed, 861

Swine
Pigs: a hndbk to the breeds of the world, 1740

Taiwan
Republic of China yrbk 1991-92, 121

Tale of Two Cities
Tale of two cities: an annot bibliog, 1251

Tax Havens
Tax havens, 186

Tax Returns
Ernst & Young tax gd 1993, 302

Teaching—Aids & Devices
Educators grade gd to free teaching aids, 39th ed, 317
Educators gd to free filmstrips & slides, 45th ed, 375
Educators gd to free health, physical educ & recreation materials, 26th ed, 829
Educators gd to free home economics & consumer educ materials, 10th ed, 886
Educators gd to free social studies materials, 33d ed, 81
Elementary teachers gd to free curriculum materials, 50th ed, 318
Guide to free computer materials, 11th ed, 1911

Technology
Checklist of the Newberry Lib's printed bks in sci, medicine, tech, & the pseudosciences ca. 1460-1750, 1558
Concise illus dict of sci & tech, 1567
Encyclopedia of physical sci & tech, 2d ed, 1566
European research centres, 9th ed, 1574
European sources of scientific & technical info, 10th ed, 1576
History of sci & tech in the US, v.2, 1560

Science & tech desk ref, 1584
Sourcebook for sci, math, & tech educ 1992, 1582
Systems & control ency, suppl. v.2, 1570
Walford's gd to ref material, v.1: sci & tech, 6th ed, 1562
Who's who in sci & engineering 1992-93, 1564
World tech policies, 1587

Teenagers
Best yrs of their lives, 926
Juniorplots 4, 1192
Rip-roaring reads for reluctant teen readers, 1182

Telecommunication
Telecommunications dir 1994-95, 1922

Television
BFI film & TV hndbk 1993, 1455
Bacon's radio/TV dir 1993, 1014
British radio & TV pioneers, 1012
Famous Hollywood locations, 1421
More theatre, 1464
Religious radio & TV in the US, 1921-91, 1511
Television-related cartoons in the New Yorker, 1056
Total TV bk, 1016
Variety & Daily Variety TV reviews, v.16, 1019

Terrorism
Terrorism: a ref hndbk, 585
Terrorism, 1988-91, 589

Testing Laboratories
International dir of testing labs, 1993 ed, 1578

Texas
Texas, 89

Thatcher, Margaret
Margaret Thatcher: a bibliog, 776

Theater. *See also* **Drama**
Cambridge gd to American theatre, 1479
Cambridge gd to theatre, updated ed, 1471
Concise Oxford companion to the theatre, 1472
Directory of Canadian theatre archives, 1476
Dublin stage, 1720-45, 1468
Ellen Stewart & La Mama: a bio-bibliog, 1410
Encyclopedia of the N.Y. stage, 1940-50, 1474
International bibliog of theatre: 1988-89, 1466
London stage 1950-59, 1469
Lucille Lortel: a bio-bibliog, 1414
More theatre, 1464
Oxford companion to American theatre, 2d ed, 1480
TCG theatre dir 1993-94, 1477
Want's theater dir, 1993 ed, 1478

Theodicy
Theodicy: an annot bibliog, 1506

Theology
African theology, 1508
Draper's bk of quotations for the Christian world, 1551

Therapeutics
Lifetime ency of natural remedies, 1826

Tieck, Ludwig
Ludwig Tieck: an annot gd to research, 1288

Timor
Timor, 112

Title Companies
Directory of courthouses & abstract & title cos, 1993, 559

Tongan Language—Dictionaries—English
Simplified dict of modern Tongan, 1134

Toxicology
Chemical exposure & human health, 1861
Comprehensive gd to the hazardous properties of chemical substances, 2015

Toy & Movable Books
Pop-up & movable bks, 1177

Trade & Professional Associations
Directory of European community trade & professional assns 1992, 274
National trade & professional assn of the US 1993, 54

Trade Catalogs. *See* **Catalogs, Commercial**

Trade Names. *See* **Business Names**

Trade-Unions
Active figures of the trade union & working class movement of Russia, Ukraine, Bielorussia, & Kazakhstan, 262

Trademarks
Patent, trademark, & copyright laws, 576

Traffic Accidents
Statistical report on road accidents in 1990, 2027

Transfer Students
College hndbk for transfer students 1994, 354

Transplantation of Organs, Tissues, Etc.
Gift of life, 1823

Travel
Leisure lit, 820
Travel bk, 2d ed, 473
Traveler's reading gd, rev & updated ed, 474

Treaties
Current treaty index, 11th ed, 760

Trees
Folklore of trees & shrubs, 1673
Grand trees of America, 1672
Mosaik's photographic key to the trees & shrubs of Great Britain & N Europe, 1670
Trees, 1669
Trees & shrubs of Great Britain & N Europe, 1670

Trials
Haymarket affair, 786

Trichiuridae
FAO species cat, v.15, 1719

Trilling, Lionel
Lionel Trilling: an annot bibliog, 1239

Trilobites
Trilobites, 2d ed, 1961

Tristan
Complete concordance to Gottfried Von Strassburg's Tristan, 1200

Tropics
Bignoniaceae—pt.2 (tribe tecomeae), 1637

Trucking
Motor carrier professional serv dir 1993, 2023

Turkish Language—Dictionaries—English
Oxford Turkish dict, 1135

Twain, Mark
Mark Twain ency, 1240

Twins
Twins in children's & adolescent lit, 1183

Type & Type-Founding
Elements of typographic style, 675

Type Designers
Rookledge's intl hndbk of type designers, 1563

Uganda
Idi Amin & Uganda, 763

Ukraine
Active figures of the trade union & working class movement of Russia, Ukraine, Bielorussia, & Kazakhstan, 262
Encyclopedia of Ukraine, vs. 3-5, 138
International writings of Bohdan S. Wynar, 1949-92, 80
Ukraine: a tourist gd, 483
Ukraine: pol parties & orgs, 782

Underdeveloped Areas. *See* **Developing Countries**

Unidentified Flying Objects
Encyclopedia of strange & unexplained physical phenomena, 813

Uniforms, Military
Napoleonic uniforms, 707

United Nations
Chronology & fact bk of the UN 1941-91, 792
International yr bk & statesmen's who's who 1992, 791
United Nations juridical yrbk 1985, 578

United States. Air Force
Historical dict of the US air force, 698

United States—Armed Forces
African American generals, 685
America's top military careers, 690
Guide to the evaluation of educl experiences in the armed servs, 1992, 307

United States. Army
Military leaders of the Civil War, 701
U.S. army heraldic crests, 696
U.S. army uniforms of the Korean war, 708

United States—Census
Atlas of the 1990 census, 931
Census snapshot for all US places, 1990, 928
Historical atlas of state power in congress, 1790-1990, 725

United States—Church History
Guide to the end of the world, 1535
Roman Catholics, 1525

United States. Congress
Committees in the US Congress 1947-92, v.1, 741
Congress A to Z, 2d ed, 728
Congress dict, 730
Congressional Quarterly's American congressional dict, 729
Congressional Quarterly's pols in America 1994, 749
Congressional staff dir/1, 1993, 734
Staff dirs on CD-ROM, 1993/1, 737
Young Oxford companion to the congress of the US, 758

United States—Constitution
Bicentennial concordance, 580
Evolving constitution, 571

United States—Economic Conditions
Development report card for the states, 1993, 170
Dictionary of US economic hist, 158

United States. Federal Bureau of Investigation
Unlocking the files of the FBI, 752

United States—Foreign Economic Relations— South Africa
United States sanctions & S Africa, 545

United States—Foreign Relations
American foreign policy index, v.1, no.1, 759
Cold war chronology, 795
Dictionary of American foreign affairs, 731
Handbook of American diplomacy, 757

United States—Historical Geography
Rand McNally atlas of American frontiers, 490
Scholar's gd to geographical writing on the American & Canadian past, 461

United States—History
Cultural ency of the 1850s in America, 507
Encyclopedia of American facts & dates, 9th ed, 504
Encyclopedia USA, v.16, 509
Encyclopedia USA, v.17, 510
Encyclopedia USA index v.1, 513
Great American hist fact-finder, 512

United States—History—Civil War, 1861-1865
Civil War newspaper maps: a cartobibliography of the N daily pr, 492
Civil War newspaper maps: a histl atlas, 491
Microbes & minie balls, 493
Military leaders of the Civil War, 701

United States—History—Revolution, 1775-1783
American Revolution 1775-1783: an ency, 503
Who was who in the American Revolution, 500

United States—History, Military
Guide to the sources of US military hist, suppl.3, 680
Reference gd to US military hist 1815-65, 501
Reference gd to US military hist 1865-1919, 502

United States—Imprints
Checklist of American imprints for 1843, 10

United States in Motion Pictures
Celluloid wars, 1451

United States. Navy
Naval Institute gd to the ships & aircraft of the US fleet, 15th ed, 705

United States—Officials & Employees
Freedom's lawmakers, 727
Washington '93, 744
Working for your uncle, 284

United States—Politics & Government
Almanac of American pols 1994, 746
Congressional Quarterly's American congressional dict, 729
Glossary of US govt vocabulary, 732
National Review politically incorrect ref gd, 726
1960s: an annot bibliog of social & pol movements in the US, 863

United States—Population
Atlas of the 1990 census, 931

United States—Race Relations
Civil rights movement, 595

United States—Religion
Religion & the American experience, 1620-1900, 1507

United States. Securities & Exchange Commission
U.S. Securities & Exchange Commission, 802

United States—Social Conditions
Encyclopedia of American social hist, 505
1960s: an annot bibliog of social & pol movements in the US, 863
Writer's gd to everyday life in the 1800s, 511

United States—Statistics
CQ's state fact finder, 750

United States. Supreme Court
Evolving constitution, 571
Oxford companion to the Supreme Court of the US, 554
Supreme Court A to Z, 556
Supreme Court justices, 551

Universities & Colleges
Adult learner's gd to alternative & external degree programs, 393
America's black colleges, 330
Beacon: college & career planning on CD-ROM, 349
Cash for college, 360
College hndbk 1994, 355
College hndbk for transfer students 1994, 354
Directory of Catholic colleges & univs, 1992, 335
Electronic univ, 376
Gibson's student gd to W Canadian univs, 310
Gourman report: a rating of undergraduate programs in American & intl univs, 8th ed, 358
Handbook of United Methodist-related schools, colleges, univs & theological schools, 336
Making a difference college gd, 1993, 348
Multicultural student's gd to colleges, 337
Murray resource dir to the nation's historically black colleges & univs, 338
Peterson's gd to 4-yr colleges 1994, 342
Peterson's register of higher educ 1993, 344

Universities & Colleges—Admissions
College admissions, 324
Peterson's competitive colleges 1993-94, 341

Universities & Colleges—Curricula
College Board gd to 150 popular college majors, 352
Index of majors & graduate degrees 1994, 365
Peterson's colleges with programs for students with learning disabilities, 340
Rugg's recommendations on the colleges, 10th ed, 364

Universities & Colleges—Faculty
National faculty dir 1993, 339

Universities & Colleges—Graduate Work
Barron's gd to graduate bus schools, 8th ed, 168
Gibson's gd to graduate & professional programs at Ont. univs, 309
Gourman report: a rating of graduate & professional programs in American & intl univs, 6th ed, 357

University of Calgary. Libraries. Special Collections Division
Alden Nowlan papers, 1276

University of Virginia Library
Descriptive cat of the Jorge Luis Borges collection at the Univ of Va. lib, 1300

Urban Folklore
Contemporary legend, 1383

Urban Studies. *See* **Cities & Towns**

Vampires
Transylvanian lib, 1212

Vanbrugh, John
Sir John Vanbrugh: a ref gd, 975

Vehicles, Military
Standard cat of US military vehicles 1940-1965, 691

Veterinary Medicine
Dictionary of animal health terminology, 1633

Video Discs
Laserdisc film gd, 1993-1994 ed, 1429

Video Recordings
Catalogue of films & videos in the British Medical Assn lib, 1824
Great videos for kids, 1426
Guide to pol videos, v.1, no.1, 713
Halliwell's filmgoer's & video viewer's companion, 10th ed, 1456
Transcript/video index, 1992, 1021
Video source bk 1993, 1020
Videos for understanding diversity, 399

Vietnam
Vietnam, 122

Vietnamese Conflict, 1961-1975
Vietnam war: hndbk of the lit & research, 497
Vietnam war in lit, 514
Voices from the underground, 1010

Violence
Encyclopedia of violence, 586

Virtual Reality
Information sources for virtual reality, 1894

Visually Handicapped
Living with low vision, 880
Rehabilitation resource manual: vision, 884

Vitamins in Human Nutrition
Nutrients cat, 1610

Vocabulary
Children's writer's word bk, 996
300 1st words, 1093

Vocational Guidance
America's top military careers, 690
Beacon: college & career planning on CD-ROM, 349
Career discovery ency, 384
Cassell careers ency, 13th ed, 385
College majors & careers, rev ed, 362
Complete gd for occupational exploration, 1993 ed, 387
Encyclopedia of careers & vocational guidance, 9th ed, 386

Vocational Rehabilitation
Meeting the needs of employees with disabilities, 2d ed, 881

Voluntarism
International dir of voluntary work, 5th ed, 894
Volunteer! 1992-1993 ed, 903
Volunteer work, 904

Wages
American salaries & wages survey, 2d ed, 282

Wagner, Richard
Wagner compendium, 1329

Wales
Butterworths law dir 1993, 558
Welsh women, 950

Walton, William
William Walton: a source bk, 1323

War
Celluloid wars, 1451
International affairs dir of orgs, 799
Novels of WW II, 1205
Using lit to teach middle grades about war, 694
Vietnam war in lit, 514
War & peace lit for children & young adults, 1185

Warren, Elinor Remick
Elinor Remick Warren: a bio-bibliog, 1321

Warships
Weyers warships of the world 1992/93, 706

Washington (D.C.)
Washington area lib dir, 611
Washington '93, 744

Water
Glossary of water terms, 1951

Water Animals. *See* **Aquatic Animals**

Water Birds—Asia
Field gd to the waterbirds of Asia, 1692

Water Quality
Water quality & availability, 1954

Wealth
Who's wealthy in America 1993, 211

Weather
Weather of US cities, 4th ed, 1947

Weeds
Weed seeds of the Great Plains, 1663

Welsh Americans
Welsh women, 950

Welsh Language—Dictionaries—English
Welsh-English, English-Welsh dict, 1136

West (U.S.)
Dictionary of the American west, 1088
Field gd to the ecology of W forests, 1681
Western reader's gd, 88
Western series & sequels, 2d ed, 1221

West Indies
Caribbean 1975-80, 143
Political parties of the Americas, 1980s to 1990s, 720

Western Films
Guide to silent Westerns, 1443

Wetland Flora
Field gd to coastal wetland plants of the SE US, 1661

Whales
Field gd to whales, porpoises, & seals from Cape Cod to Nfld., 4th ed, 1737

Whitman, Walt
Walt Whitman: a descriptive bibliog, 1241

Wild Flowers
History & folklore of N American wildflowers, 1651
Sagebrush country, 1660
Spring wildflowers, 1659
Wildflowers of Prince Edward Island, 1650
Wildflowers of the W plains, 1655

Wilde, Oscar
Oscar Wilde: an annot bibliog, 1262

Wilder, Alec
Alec Wilder: a bio-bibliog, 1324

Wilder, Thornton
Thornton Wilder: a ref gd 1926-90, 1242

Wilderness Areas
America's secret recreation areas, 476
Big outside, rev ed, 1678

Wildlife Conservation
Atlas of endangered animals, 1686
Endangered wildlife of the world, 1676
Grolier world ency of endangered species, 1680
Guide to Michigan's endangered wildlife, 1677
Guide to the natl wildlife refuges, rev ed, 1683

Saving endangered mammals, 1738
Where the animals are, 1688

Wildlife Watching
Mammals of the central Rockies, 1741
Watching Kans. wildlife, 1679

Wine & Wine Making
Buyer's gd to American wines, 2d ed, 1605

Wisconsin
Awesome almanac—Wis., 83

Wiseman, Adele
Adele Wiseman: an annot bibliog, 1277

Wit & Humor
Humor scholarship, 1304
Literature of delight, 1169
Witty words, 70

Women
American women civil rights activists, 592
American women playwrights 1964-89, 1228
American women songwriters, 1325
Beacon bk of quotations by women, 972
Bibliographical gd to African-American women writers, 1223
Book of women's firsts, 970
Career advancement for women in the fed serv, 270
European women's almanac, 947
Female detectives in American novels, 1208
International who's who of professional & bus women, 2d ed, 958
Mothers & daughters in American short fiction, 1219
Mothers & daughters of invention, 1586
Native American women, 956
New quotable woman, rev. ed, 973
On account of sex, 949
Remember the ladies, 959
United States govt docs on women, 1800-1990, 951
Violence against women, 596
Welsh women, 950
Women & AIDS, 1855
Women & tech, 948
Women in chemistry & physics, 1923
Women prime ministers & presidents, 714
Women public speakers in the US, 1800-1925, 957
Women's ency of health & emotional healing, 1805
Women's info dir, 968
World who's who of women, 11th ed, 963

Women, Afro-American. *See* **Afro-American Women**

Women's Studies
Canadian women's movement, 1960-90, 966
WAVE: women's audio-visuals in English, 954
Women of color & S women annual suppl, 1991/92, 955
Women's studies in India, 953

Wood Products
Directory of the wood products industry, 1993, 1616

Woodwork
Encyclopedia of wood joints, 1030

World Health
ACCIS gd to UN info sources on health, 1811

World History
Times atlas of world hist, 4th ed, 530

World Politics
Atlas of world pol flashpoints, 794
Countries of the world & their leaders yrbk 1993, 723
Europa world yr bk 1992, 82
Oxford companion to pols of the world, 717
Statesmen who changed the world, 716
Strategic atlas, 3d ed, 712
World tech policies, 1587

World Records
Book of women's firsts, 970
Guinness bk of records 1993, 1401

World War, 1914-1918
World War I source bk, 540

World War, 1939-1945
Canada's army in WW II, 702
Normandy campaign, 1944, 531
Novels of WW II, 1205

Wrestling
Wrestling college & univ dir, 2d ed, 862

Writers' Union of Canada
Who's who in the Writers' Union of Canada, 4th ed, 998

Writing Centers
AWP official gd to writing programs, 6th ed, 993

Yiddish Language—Dictionaries—English
Harduf's transliterated Yiddish-English dict, 4th v., 1137

Young Adult Literature. *See also* **Children's Literature**
Award-winning bks for children & young adults 1990-91, 1166
Books for you, 11th ed, 1165
Books in Spanish for children & young adults, 1180
Children's bk awards intl, 1195
Fiction index for readers 10 to 16, 1196
Juniorplots 4, 1192
100 world-class thin bks, 1164
Read for your life, 383
Rip-roaring reads for reluctant teen readers, 1182
Speaking for ourselves, too, 1186
Teens' favorite bks, 1175
Twins in children's & adolescent lit, 1183
War & peace lit for children & young adults, 1185
Young reader's companion, 1189

Youth
Contemporary Canadian childhood & youth, 924
History of Canadian childhood & youth, 925

Yucatan Peninsula
Archaeological gd to Mexico's Yucatan peninsula, 481

Yugoslavia
Yugoslavia: a comprehensive English-lang bibliog, 139

Zoology
Animal life, 1685

Zoos
Where the animals are, 1688